FULL PRONUNCIATION KEY

Each symbol, or letter, below stands for a sound, a sound you can recognize in the short, common words following it. With these symbols, the pronunciation of each entry word is shown just after the word, in brackets, like this: **moth·er** [muth′ər].

Parentheses around a symbol, as in **set·tle** [set′(ə)l], mean that you are free either to say the sound or to leave it out.

The heavy mark, ′, shows that the syllable it follows is given the strongest, or primary, stress, as in **sis·ter** [sis′tər]. A lighter mark, ′, shows that the syllable it follows is given stress but a secondary, lighter stress, as in **tax·i·cab** [tak′sē·kab′].

a	add, map	m	move, seem	u	up, done
ā	ace, rate	n	nice, tin	û(r)	urn, term
â(r)	care, air	ng	ring, song	yo͞o	use, few
ä	palm, father	o	odd, hot	v	vain, eve
b	bat, rub	ō	open, so	w	win, away
ch	check, catch	ô	order, jaw	y	yet, yearn
d	dog, rod	oi	oil, boy	z	zest, muse
e	end, pet	ou	out, now	zh	vision, pleasure
ē	even, tree	o͞o	pool, food	ə	the schwa,
f	fit, half	o͝o	took, full		an unstressed
g	go, log	p	pit, stop		vowel representing
h	hope, hate	r	run, poor		the sound spelled
i	it, give	s	see, pass		a in above
ī	ice, write	sh	sure, rush		e in sicken
j	joy, ledge	t	talk, sit		i in possible
k	cool, take	th	thin, both		o in melon
l	look, rule	th	this, bathe		u in circus

THE
HARCOURT BRACE
SCHOOL
DICTIONARY

THE
HARCOURT BRACE
SCHOOL
DICTIONARY

HARCOURT BRACE JOVANOVICH, INC.

New York   Chicago   San Francisco   Atlanta   Dallas

Illustrations: Diamond Art Studio

Maps: Harbrace

CONTENTS

	HOW TO PAGES
TO TEACHERS AND PARENTS	11
HOW TO USE YOUR DICTIONARY	
by Dimmes McDowell	15
Finding a Word	19
Finding the Right Meaning	27
Pronouncing a Word	36
Pronunciation Key	37
Spelling and Your Dictionary	41
The Spelling Chart	46
Abbreviations	48
HOW TO GET THE MOST FROM YOUR DICTIONARY	
by Dimmes McDowell	53
The Right Meaning	53
Reading the Figures	54
Word Parts and Meanings	55
Mix-ups and Confusions	57
The Right Synonym	58
Usage Notes	58
Parts of Speech	59
Word Histories	60
More than the Most	61
REGIONAL PRONUNCIATION	
by James B. McMillan	62
BRITISH AND AMERICAN SPELLINGS	
by James B. McMillan	64
THE HARCOURT BRACE SCHOOL DICTIONARY	**pages 1—864**

ADVISORY BOARD

TO TEACHERS AND PARENTS

An elementary school dictionary should be both a useful reference book to help children with questions they have about words they encounter in their reading and study, and a textbook with ample material for the study of words and usage in connection with the language arts. *The Harcourt Brace School Dictionary* has been designed to play both roles.

It has been freshly constructed, from word list to pictures, maps, and diagrams, and it is up to date. Its most immediately noticeable feature is the use throughout of a second color. In recent years, color has come into use in practically all textbooks and has proved both useful and attractive. Now color has been extended to the dictionary, where it is especially helpful in maps and diagrams.

The most important feature is the word list. In building the word list, two steps were taken to correlate more closely the vocabulary covered in the dictionary and the vocabulary of modern textbooks.

First, each member of the Board of Curriculum Specialists prepared and recommended a list of words now in common use in his subject in the elementary grades. Many of the words are by no means new words, but some are new to the elementary grades, brought into use by the educational trend that created the new mathematics and science courses, among others.

Second, our staff read scores of textbooks published within the last five or six years and other scores of juvenile books widely used today for supplementary or enrichment reading.

We have attached more weight to these studies as guides to currency than we have to the excellent but aging word lists, such as *The Semantic Count*, which were also consulted.

The offering of words in each of the subjects of the elementary curriculum is as large as space permits, and is especially large in mathematics and science. Some of these words even as late as ten years ago would very likely have been thought too advanced for the elementary school. Now they are in daily use in textbooks and classroom discussion.

As in science and mathematics, new materials and methods are being introduced into language arts courses, whether in the area of traditional grammar, transformational grammar, or some other type based on linguistic study. In line with this trend, we have included features and materials once thought too advanced for the elementary level. They have been very carefully adapted to the understanding of the elementary student, both in the presentation of facts and in the wording. They make up an unusual body of material readily available for various sorts of word studies.

Take etymology as an example. The etymologies in a typical college dictionary, showing unknown source words from languages scarcely heard of by the average elementary student, would of course be meaningless at the elementary level. But we have put such basic information in simple words, with no technical terms, no abbreviations, and no unglossed source words from other languages. *The Harcourt Brace School Dictionary* has over 500 etymologies systematically chosen to show English words borrowed from more than fifteen other languages and to illustrate some twenty of the important processes of word formation, change, and development.

With the same sort of simple treatment, additional notes distinguish between the meanings of synonyms and point out differences in force or color. Other notes clearly differentiate unrelated words likely to be confused because of a similarity of sound or appearance. Still further notes give guidance on English usage and levels of language. The usefulness of these materials, either for individual reference or for classroom discussion, scarcely needs to be pointed out.

Because this dictionary is intended for use across the rather broad span of five grades (4–8), there will be a considerable difference in the maturity of students at opposite ends of this span. To accommodate both groups, the section on how to use the dictionary is divided into two parts. The first part, for use by beginners in the fourth and fifth grades, explains the basic dictionary skills. The second part, for students in the sixth, seventh, and eighth grades, explains more advanced dictionary uses. This arrangement of teaching material makes it easy to use both in class instruction and for individual study. The front matter also explains additional features of the dictionary omitted here because of lack of space.

The Harcourt Brace School Dictionary
is up to date, but it is orthodox rather than radical in its arrangement and presentation of the usual, expected information. Most of the other good elementary dictionaries are substantially similar in these respects, though without a few of the refinements put to use here. *The Harcourt Brace School Dictionary* has its entries arranged in a single, convenient alphabetical list. Its system of showing pronunciations uses only a few easily distinguished diacritical marks and is simple to learn and use. Inflectional forms that are irregular or easily confused are shown early in the entry where they cannot be mistaken for idioms or run-on derivatives. Definitions are followed by illustrative phrases or sentences whenever these are helpful. The pictures, maps, and diagrams have been drawn especially for this book.

Many people have been helpful to us in the preparation of this dictionary. We have long since given our thanks directly to them, but we wish to thank publicly a few of them.

First, we want to thank Maria Cimino, Librarian-in-charge, Central Children's Room, the New York Public Library, whose knowledge and experience proved invaluable in helping to shape and balance the large list of juvenile books we read for vocabulary.

Second, we want to thank all of the members of our three boards for their untiring interest, their help, and their patience during the long months in which this dictionary was being built. They have contributed much, and they have our sincere gratitude.

HOW TO USE
YOUR DICTIONARY

HOW TO USE
YOUR DICTIONARY

by Dimmes McDowell

In consultation with Albert H. Marckwardt and Phil C. Lange

This book has been made to help you learn many things about English words—for example, how they are spelled, what they mean, how you pronounce them and use them in sentences.

The only way to get this much information into one book is to use a system that has a special short way of saying things. This system is like a code that makes it easy for you to find whatever you want. The code has nine very important parts. Each part is used over and over again in the dictionary. So first of all, you will need to know the names of the parts and how they work in the code system.

Here are the names of the nine parts of the code system:

1. Main Entry
2. Main Entry Word
3. Pronunciation
4. Part of Speech
5. Inflectional Form
6. Definition
7. Illustrative Example
8. Syllable Dot
9. Run-on Entry Word

All of these nine parts will be taken up, beginning on the next page, and explained, so that you can see what each one looks like and how it helps you use your dictionary.

The dictionary explains some words in only one or two lines. It can tell you all that you need to know about such words by using only a few parts of the code. To explain some other words, however, it often needs all nine.

To show you all nine parts in use, the dictionary's explanation of one such word, the word **lucky**, is printed at the top of the next page. As you will see, the names of the parts are printed around it, and each part is connected to its name by a red line.

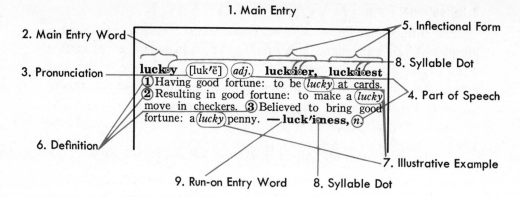

1. Main Entry
2. Main Entry Word
3. Pronunciation
5. Inflectional Form
8. Syllable Dot
4. Part of Speech
6. Definition
7. Illustrative Example
9. Run-on Entry Word
8. Syllable Dot

The explanation of **lucky** just above shows you all nine parts of the dictionary code. When you read about each part below, it is a good idea to look up here at **lucky** again to remind yourself how that particular part fits in.

1. Main Entry

A **main entry** is the particular part of the dictionary that explains a certain word. In the sample, the word being explained is **lucky.**

2. Main Entry Word

Each **main entry word,** the word to be explained, like **lucky,** is the first word of its main entry. It is printed in heavy type and begins a little to the left of the other lines of the main entry. Sometimes two words (or even more) that go together in a combination, like **ice cream,** are explained together. Such a combination is a main entry word, too.

3. Pronunciation

The way to say, or **pronounce,** the main entry word is shown just after the word itself. The **pronunciation** has its own kind of code, which you will learn about later. Here you can see how it looks for **lucky:**

[luk′ē]

4. Part of Speech

The **parts of speech** are the names of the different ways that words can be used in sentences: noun, verb, adjective, adverb, and so on. In the dictionary code, these names are abbreviated this way: *n.* (for *noun*), *v.* (for *verb*), *adj.* (for *adjective*), *adv.* (for *adverb*), and so on. So the *adj.* in the sample entry above means that **lucky** is used as an adjective, and the *n.* after **luckiness** means it is used as a noun.

5. Inflectional Form

The **inflectional forms** of a word are forms changed by adding a **morpheme.** A morpheme is a small unit of meaning, sometimes a whole word, sometimes only part of a word. For instance, the first inflectional form of **lucky** is **luckier.** The sound spelled **-er** and meaning *more* has been added to **lucky,** so **luckier** means *more lucky.* The second inflectional form is **luckiest.** This is **lucky** with the morpheme written **-est,** which means *most,* added, so **luckiest** means *most lucky.* The morpheme which means *more than one,* or *plural,* usually written **-s** or **-es,** is added to a great many nouns. For instance, **cars** is an inflectional form of **car,** and the morpheme *plural* makes **cars** mean *more than one car.*

But inflectional forms are printed in your dictionary only when you might have trouble with them because they do not, or might not, follow the spelling rules you already know. Notice that **cars** is not shown because it is made in the ordinary way, just by adding **-s** to **car.** But **luckier** and **luckiest** are shown because the **y** of **lucky** changes to **i** when a morpheme is added.

6. Definition

The **definitions** tell you what a word means. When a word has more than one meaning, the definitions are numbered to show the different ways the word can be used. Some words have a great many—twenty or twenty-five. The meaning that is used most often comes first, then the next most used, and finally the one that is least often used. Later you will discover how to select the definition that fits your need.

7. Illustrative Example

To make a definition easier to understand or to show you exactly how a word is used, an *illustrative example* often follows a definition. The entry for **lucky** has one following each definition. Notice how they bring out differences in meaning.

8. Syllable Dot

The **dots** in many words printed in heavy type show how the written words are divided into **syllables.** Knowing the syllables helps you to pronounce a word or to spell it without getting mixed up. The dot also shows you where you can break a word if you come to the end of a line and have room to write only part of the word. For example, you write **lucki-** at the end of one line and **ness** on the next line. You can see other examples of syllable dots in the inflectional forms **luckier** and **luckiest. Lucky** also has two syllables, but you never divide a word so as to leave a single letter on a line.

The entry for **lucky** is printed again here so that you will not need to turn back two pages to look at it. Below the **lucky** entry, the last of the nine parts of the dictionary code is explained.

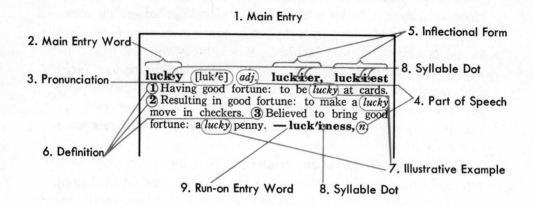

1. Main Entry
2. Main Entry Word
3. Pronunciation
5. Inflectional Form
8. Syllable Dot
4. Part of Speech
6. Definition
7. Illustrative Example
9. Run-on Entry Word
8. Syllable Dot

9. Run-on Entry Word

A **run-on entry word** is a new word made by putting together the main entry word and another piece of meaning, or morpheme. **Luckiness** at the end of the **lucky** entry is **lucky** (with the **y** changed to **i**) and the morpheme **-ness**. It does not need to have its own main entry, because its meaning is simply the meaning of **lucky** plus the meaning of **-ness**. So **luckiness** is put after the definitions of **lucky** and is called a run-on entry because it tags along at the end. (Note that its part of speech is given, too.)

If you ever find a run-on entry word that you cannot understand, you can read the main entry definitions and look up **-ness** or **-ly** or whatever the added morpheme is that is giving you trouble. When you put the definition of the main entry word and the definition of the morpheme together, you know what the run-on entry word means.

Now you have studied the nine most important parts of the dictionary code system:

1. Main Entry
2. Main Entry Word
3. Pronunciation
4. Part of Speech
5. Inflectional Form
6. Definition
7. Illustrative Example
8. Syllable Dot
9. Run-on Entry Word

You will learn more about all these parts of your dictionary in the following pages. But first be sure that you can name and describe the nine most important parts of the dictionary code system.

Finding a Word

With the hundreds of pages in this book and the thousands of main entries, how do you find the word you want? You have three guides:

1. The alphabet
2. The letter tabs
3. The guide words

ALPHABETICAL ORDER

All the main entries in this book are arranged in one list in the order of the alphabet from **A** to **Z.** It doesn't matter whether the word begins with a small letter or a capital letter, because there is only one list. All the words starting with **A** or **a** come first; those starting with **B** or **b** next; then those starting with **C** or **c**, and so on. To find an entry that will tell you about a particular word, you must know the letters of the alphabet in their regular order:

A B C D E F G H I J K L M N O P Q R S T U V W X Y Z
a b c d e f g h i j k l m n o p q r s t u v w x y z
a b c d e f g h i j k l m n o p q r s t u v w x y z

Suppose that you wanted to find the entry for **ship.** The word **ship** starts with **s.** If you know the alphabet, you know that words starting with **s** come after the words starting with **r** and before the words beginning with **t.**

But the first letter of a word is not enough to tell you whether a word comes before or after another word that begins with the same letter. It would not help you with **sand, ship, small,** and **sun** because all four begin with **s.** So you must go past the first letter to the second letter. The second letters of these words are **a, h, m,** and **u,** and they are in alphabetical order.

Now try the second letters in another group of words. Here are **base, beam, bite, bond,** and **bunt.** When you look at the second letters of these words, you see that they are **a, e, i, o,** and **u.** Are they in alphabetical order? There is an alphabetical list of these words in the box at the right. With these words, the second letters tell you the order.

base
beam
bite
bond
bunt

You may have to go farther than the second letter. In the box at the right, the first and second letters are the same in all four words. So you must go past them to the third letter. You can see that the four words are in alphabetical order.

brave breath bridge brother

Even three may not be enough. In the second box on the right, all four words start with the same three letters. Go past them all to the fourth letter. Are they in alphabetical order? If you wanted to add a fifth word, **worry**, to the four in the list, you would put it after **worm** and before **worth.** Then the list would look like the third box at the right. You can see that **d, k, m, r,** and **t** are in alphabetical order.

word work worm worth

You may have to pass the first four letters, or even more, to decide the right alphabetical order of a word. Look at **mechanic, mechanical, mechanical advantage, mechanical drawing, mechanics, mechanism,** and **mechanize.** You will see that the first seven letters are the same in all of them. You just

word work worm worry worth

go past the letters that are the same until you come to one that is different, as you did with the second and the third letters when you were looking for the fourth.

The dictionary has two special ways of helping you with alphabetical order. **Letter tabs** and **guide words** both show you quickly where you are.

USING LETTER TABS AND GUIDE WORDS

If you open your dictionary and look at the outside margin of the right-hand page, you will see a single letter in a red box. This is the **letter tab,** and it tells you in one quick look what letter of the alphabet will be the first letter of the entry words on that page.

Try turning over several pages near the middle of this book and use just the letter tab to discover what part of the alphabet you are in. Then suppose you are looking up **witch.** If you open to a page with an S tab, you know you will find the word you want nearer the back of the book, because **W** comes after **S.** If you open to a **Y** tab, you must turn back toward the front of the book, because **W** comes before **Y.**

The **guide words** at the top of each page will help you find words quickly, too. They look like this:

acolyte 7 activate

ac·o·lyte [ak′ə·līt] *n.* A helper or assistant, especially an altar boy who assists at Mass.

ac·ro·bat [ak′rə·bat] *n.* A person skilled in tumbling, stunts on a

ac·ri·mo·ny [ak′rə·mō′nē] *n.* Bitterness or hard feeling, especially in speech or manner.

ac·ti·vate [ak′tə·vāt] *v.* **ac·ti·vat·ed, ac·ti·vat·ing** To make active. — **ac′ti·va′tion** *n.*

add, āce, câre, pälm; end, ēqual; it, īce; odd, ōpen, ôrder; to͝ok, po͞ol; up, bûrn; ə = a in *above*, e in *sicken*, i in *possible*, o in *melon*, u in *circus*; yo͞o = u in *fuse*; oil; pout; ch**eck**; ri**ng**; **th**in; **th**is; **zh** in *vision*. For ¶ reference, see page 64 · HOW TO

When you look at this sample page (with the middle torn out to save space), you see that **acolyte** is the first main entry word at the top of the left-hand column and **activate** is the last main entry word at the bottom of the right-hand column. The guide words at the top tell you that all the words on this page are in alphabetical order between **acolyte** and **activate**. You know right away that you can find **across** on this page, but you cannot find **abbey** or **ace** or **add** because alphabetically they do not come between **acolyte** and **activate**.

Here is another example:

flourish 282 flush

making bread, cake, etc. **2** *v.* To cover or sprinkle with flour. — **flour′y** *adj.*
flour·ish [flûr′ish] **1** *v.* To grow or fare well or

flu·id [flo͞o′id] **1** *n.* Any substance able to flow easily; a liquid or gas. Water, air, and steam are fluids. **2** *adj.* Able to flow or pour easily; not

fluffy. **2** Covered or filled with fluff: *fluffy* kittens; *fluffy* blankets. — **fluff′i·ly** *adv.* — **fluff′i·ness** *n.*

flurried the players.
flush[1] [flush] **1** *v.* To become or cause to become red in the face; redden: He *flushed* with embar-

At the left is the first main entry word that begins on page 282— **flourish.** You may notice that in the example, **floury** is above **flourish** and is printed in heavy type. But **floury** is a run-on entry word, not a main entry word. The first main entry word is **flourish.** On the right is the last main entry word to begin on that page—**flush.**

Notice that page 282 has no letter tab, as page 7, part of which is shown above, does have. This is because 282 is a left-hand page. But every page has guide words, and these are the best and quickest way of finding what words are on the page.

Chief can be found on the page with these guide words at the top:

chicory   122   chinchilla

And **afternoon** is on the page that begins like this:

aforementioned   14   agency

Can you fit each of the words in the left-hand column below between the right pair of guide words at the right? For example, **mount** fits between **motto** and **move** because **mou-** fits between **mot-** and **mov-** in alphabetical order.

mount	
mirror	
monkey	
match	

masterful	material
motto	move
minute	miser
Monday	monopoly

Mirror must be on the page where **minute** and **miser** are the guide words because **mir-** comes between **min-** and **mis-**. You should fit **monkey** between **Monday** and **monopoly,** and **match** between **masterful** and **material.**

You can see in these examples that sometimes you need to think about more than the first two letters of the guide word. You might have to go to the fourth or fifth letter. But you can save yourself time and trouble by learning to look at the guide words at the top of the page.

When you have learned to use the letter tabs and the guide words, you will find that they are very helpful. They show you how to get to the right page very quickly, and getting to the right page is very important. These useful guides will keep you from having to read down both columns, page after page, before you get to the right spot. So when you are looking for a word, remember these three things:

1. The order of the alphabet
2. The letter tabs
3. The guide words

SPOTTING THE TROUBLEMAKERS

You have already learned that all the main entries in this book are arranged in one list in the order of the alphabet from A to Z. If you will remember this rule, you will not have any trouble with some words that might seem to be a little unusual.

When you look carefully at the list on the right, you can see that all these words are in alphabetical order, letter by letter. Then notice these two things:

> all
> all-American
> all-around
> allay
> Alleghenies

1. The capital letters in **all-American** and **Alleghenies** do not change the usual order.

2. The hyphens in **all-American** and **all-around** do not change the usual order.

Now look at two other samples:

> donkey
> don't
> door
> dot

> obtain
> occasion
> o'clock
> odd

3. The apostrophes in **don't** and **o'clock** do not change the usual order.

The last list, with the **ice** words in it, follows the rule, too:

> ice
> Ice Age
> iceboat
> icecap
> ice cream

4. The fact that **Ice Age** and **ice cream** are both main entries made by putting together two other main entry words does not change the usual order.

Alphabetical order is not changed at all by a capital letter or a hyphen or an apostrophe or by a combination of main entry words taken together, like **ice cream.** You move in exactly the same way from the first letter to the second to the third and so on in the usual order.

Combinations

It is very important to remember about this single alphabetical order when you are hunting for something like **ice cream.** As you can see, looking up **cream** under **C** would not help you find either the meaning or the spelling of **ice cream.**

Imagine for a minute that you do not know what a **post office** is. Now try looking up **office.** You won't learn much, because **post office** is another combination and so is listed with the **P** words.

Of course, you know both **ice cream** and **post office.** But suppose the combination was **breast stroke** or **sting ray,** which you had never seen before. Would you get lost when **stroke** and **ray** didn't help you? Or would you try the **B** words and the **S** words?

Look at the combinations in these sentences:

The plane was late because of bad weather and a strong **head wind.**

Today our teacher brought an old violin and a **French horn** to class.

America is rich in **raw materials** and **natural resources.**

The family has a **nest egg** ready for its vacation trip.

Remember that a main entry may be explaining a combination made up of two words, or even more. Think about **New Year's Day** or **Fourth of July** or **United States of America.** Each one is in your dictionary. But if you are looking at the middle instead of the beginning of a combination, your dictionary cannot help you until you discover the first letter of the first word of the combination.

Capitalized Words

Capitalized words are easy to find in sentences and in the dictionary. **Iceland** and **Alleghenies** always begin with a capital letter, and you have already seen how they fit into the usual alphabetical order. Sometimes, though, you could easily overlook a capitalized word that you are looking for. For example, look at these two main entries:

> **at·las** [at′ləs] *n.* A book of maps.
> **At·las** [at′ləs] *n.* In Greek myths, a giant who supported the heavens on his shoulders.

You can see that if you just looked at **atlas,** you could easily miss the entry for **Atlas.** You might mix up a book and a giant if you forgot about the capital letter **A.**

In the next example, you will miss a president of the United States unless you look past the entry that begins with a small **g** and find the right one beginning with a capital letter:

> **grant** [grant] **1** *v.* To give; bestow: We *grant* him pardon; The king *granted* permission. **2** *v.* To accept as true; concede: I *grant* it will be hard. **3** *n.* Something that is granted, as a sum of money, a piece of land, etc. **4** *n.* The act of granting. — **take for granted** To accept . . .
> **Grant** [grant], **Ulysses Simpson,** 1822–1885, U.S. general in the Civil War and 18th president of the U.S., 1869–1877.

Would you think of looking twice for **brown** and **Brown** or **mark** and **Mark** or **concord** and **Concord?**

Make sure you have checked carefully for both capital letters and small letters. If you haven't checked them, you may be looking at the wrong entry even when the rest of the spelling is the same.

Look-alike Words

If two words (or three words or four words) have *exactly* the same spelling but are different words with different meanings, your dictionary helps you by numbering them like this:

> **meal**[1] [mēl] *n.* **1** The edible seeds of any grain, coarsely ground: a sack of *meal.* **2** Any powdery material produced by grinding.
> **meal**[2] [mēl] *n.* **1** The food served or eaten at certain times during the day. **2** The time or occasion of eating.

When you see a word marked [1], be sure to remember that after it there is another marked [2] and sometimes one marked [3] and so on. Unless you check all the numbered words, you can find yourself getting mixed up.

For example, suppose you were reading an adventure story in which the hero was diving for buried treasure off a Florida key. What is this "key"? You know that the author of the story can't possibly mean that he is diving off "a small metal instrument for moving the bolt or tumblers of a lock." This is what you would find in the main entry for **key**[1]. Keep looking and you will find the main entry word numbered [2]:

> **key**[2] [kē] *n., pl.* **keys** A low island, especially one of coral, along a coast: the Florida *Keys.*

Now the story begins to make sense. No one could dive off a door key, but hunting for buried treasure near a low island is certainly possible.

Would you be able to find **China** and **china?** Or **drill**[1], **drill**[2], **drill**[3], and **drill**[4]? You won't have any problem with these look-alike words if you remember two things:

1. Look for a separate main entry for a capitalized word.
2. Look at all the numbered entries until you find the one you need.

Sound-alike Words

Sound-alike words are the real troublemakers to find in your dictionary. These are the words that sound exactly alike but are spelled differently. Look at these common examples:

to	rain
too	reign
two	rein
threw	fair
through	fare

Here the sound-alikes at least begin with the same letter of the alphabet. But listen to the **n** sound when you say these:

knight   know

night   no

When you find a word like **knight** or **know** while you are reading, looking it up in the dictionary is easy because you can see the correct spelling in your book or magazine. But if you are writing a composition about King Arthur's court and can't remember how to spell the word for the men who fought on horseback and rescued beautiful ladies, what do you do? Your dictionary can help you when you can use the pronunciation code and the spelling chart. You will learn about them later, and you will be able to find sound-alike troublemakers easily.

Unnecessary Problems

Some people do not find a word that they want to know about and think that it is not in the dictionary because they forget that some words are not main entries. In the following very short main entry, there are four words that you might be looking for:

> **clas·si·fy** [klas′ə·fī] *v.* **clas·si·fied, clas·si·fy·ing** To put or divide into classes or groups: to *classify* books. — **clas′si·fi′er** *n.*

Be sure that you look at all the words in heavy type, not just the main entry word: **classify, classified, classifying,** and **classifier.**

Here is another short entry. This one has five words in heavy type:

> **lust·y** [lus′tē] *adj.* **lust·i·er, lust·i·est** Full of health and vigor; robust: a *lusty* infant. — **lust′i·ly** *adv.* — **lust′i·ness** *n.*

Would you have missed **lustier, lustiest, lustily,** and **lustiness** because you stopped looking after **lusty?**

If you are having trouble finding a word, remember these three things:

1. A word beginning with a capital letter may have an entry of its own, like **atlas** and **Atlas.**
2. Two or more words that have the same spelling will be numbered, and each one will have an entry of its own, like **key**[1] and **key**[2].
3. Some words are not main entry words, but any word that you are looking for will be in heavy type, like **lustily** and **lustiness.**

There are thousands of words in your dictionary. It is almost certain that the one you want is here. Don't give up too soon.

Finding the Right Meaning

One of the most important things your dictionary does is to tell you what words mean.

When is **noon?**

> **noon** [nōon] *n.* Twelve o'clock in the daytime.

How much is a **gallon?**

> **gal·lon** [gal′ən] *n.* A liquid measure equal to 4 quarts or 8 pints.

What is a **marionette?**

> **mar·i·o·nette** [mar′ē·ə·net′] *n.* A jointed figure or doll made to move by pulling strings, used in shows on small stages; puppet.

Each one of these words has just one meaning, so each main entry has only one definition. That definition answers the question right away.

But many words have several meanings, and each meaning has its own numbered definition. Here is an example of an entry with two definitions:

> **com·fort·er** [kum′fər·tər] *n.* **1** A person who comforts. **2** A thick, quilted cover for a bed.

Now think which definition of **comforter** fits with this sentence:

Mother stored the comforter in the closet during the summer.

Did you pick definition **2** to fit the sentence? No one would put a *person* in a closet for the summer. But many mothers put away heavy blankets and other winter bedding that is not needed during the warm weather.

What did Mary and Susan use for music when they danced?

> **al·bum** [al′bəm] *n.* **1** A book or booklike container, used for keeping stamps, pictures, autographs, etc. **2** A long-playing record or records.

Only definition **2** answers the question because a record makes music and a book does not.

Now look at a word that has three meanings:

> **a·pri·cot** [ā′pri·kot *or* ap′ri·kot] **1** *n.* A juicy, orange-colored fruit similar to a small peach. **2** *n.* The tree bearing this small fruit. **3** *n., adj.* Yellowish orange.

Can you answer these three questions from the three definitions?

1. What did James have in his lunch bag?
2. What did Mr. Clark chop down last week?
3. What shade is Barbara's new dress?

You can see that definition **1** answers question 1 this way: "James had a juicy, orange-colored fruit in his lunch bag." He could not have a tree in a bag, and he would not have a color for lunch.

Definition **2** and question 2 must go together, because a tree can be chopped down but a fruit or a color cannot. And Barbara cannot wear a fruit or a tree, so her dress must be a yellowish orange color.

When a word has only two or three meanings, the one that is used most often comes first in the dictionary, then the next most often used, and finally the one that is least used.

When a word has a great many meanings, a number of them usually have the same general idea and make a group. Others all have another general idea and make another group. And so on.

Look at this longer entry for a word you already know:

> **ice** [īs] *n.*, *v.* **iced, ic·ing 1** *n.* Frozen water; water in solid form. **2** *v.* To chill by adding ice: to *ice* juice. **3** *v.* To cover or become covered with ice: The windshield *iced* up. **4** *v.* To turn to ice; freeze: The pond *iced* over. **5** *n.* The frozen surface of a body of water. **6** *n.* A substance resembling ice in form. **7** *n.* A frozen dessert made of fruit juice, sugar, and water. **8** *n.* Frosting. **9** *v.* To spread icing over (a cake, etc.).

The first meaning is: Frozen water; water in solid form. This is the general idea in all the first seven definitions. They come one after another in a group. But definitions **8** and **9** have a different general idea, frosting on a cake. These two make a second group.

You are not likely to get mixed up about the frozen water that cools your fruit juice and the frosting that goes on your birthday cake. Why not? Because you use what is called the **context** to give you clues about the right meaning.

USING THE CONTEXT

The **context** is the rest of the sentence or paragraph in which a particular word is found and which suggests or influences the word's meaning. Look at **ice** in this context:

Mary, please put more ice in the ginger ale.

As soon as you see "ginger ale," you know that here **ice** means frozen water. But if the sentence mentioned baking or cakes, you could tell that frosting was being talked about, not frozen water.

In the same way, the context gives you the clue about the meaning of **apricot** in each of these sentences:

James had an apricot in his lunch bag.

Here "lunch bag" is the clue to something to eat, a fruit.

> Mr. Clark chopped down his apricot last week.

Here "chopped down" is the clue to the tree.

> Barbara's apricot dress is bright and becoming.

Here "dress" is the clue to a color, not a fruit or tree.

If you forget to think about the context, you may pick the wrong meaning. It would not make sense to say this:

> Mary, please put more frosting in the ginger ale.

Ice is a word that you know, and you would not make this mistake. But remember that with a new word, you must think about whether the definition makes sense in the context in which the word is used.

USING SUBSTITUTION

When you are looking for the right meaning, there is a very useful way to help yourself find it and to make sure that you really understand the new word. This is called **substitution,** which just means putting a definition in place of a new word.

See what you get when you use substitution for **contusion.**

1. You read this sentence:

> Jack had a bad contusion from falling off his bicycle.

2. You find **contusion** in your dictionary.

> **con·tu·sion** [kən·tōō′zhən] *n.* A bruise.

3. You substitute the definition of **contusion** for the word **contusion** and get this sentence:

> Jack had a bad bruise from falling off his bicycle.

You have substituted a word you know—**bruise**—for a harder word—**contusion.** This makes it very clear what happened to Jack.

When a word has more than one meaning, you can try substituting until you find the correct definition for your sentence. Here is an example.

1. You read this sentence:

> At the party, Mr. Jackson met many luminaries.

2. You find **luminaries** in your dictionary.

> **lu·mi·nar·y** [lōō′mə·ner′ē] *n., pl.* **lu·mi·nar·ies 1** A body that gives out light, especially the sun or moon. **2** A person who has achieved great fame.

3. You try substituting definition **1** in your sentence and get:

> At the party, Mr. Jackson met many **bodies that give out light, especially the sun or moon.**

Does it make sense? Certainly not!

4. You try definition **2:**

> At the party, Mr. Jackson met many **persons who have achieved great fame.**

Now you have the right meaning for your sentence.

Notice that when you substituted definition **2,** you had to make a change. "Many luminaries" means more than one, so "a person" needs to be changed to "persons," which also means more than one.

Sometimes when you are substituting, you will have to change even more of your sentence to make it sound natural.

> The **lonesome** dog howled all night.

> **lone·some** [lōn′səm] *adj.* **1** Feeling lonely.
> **2** Causing or expressing loneliness.

If you substitute without thinking, your new sentence is poor. You would never say this:

> The **feeling lonely** dog howled all night.

But you could say either of these:

> The dog **that was feeling lonely** howled all night.
> The dog, **feeling lonely,** howled all night.

Substitution can be very helpful, but only if you make sure that your new sentence sounds right. If you remember this, you now have two important guides to finding the correct meaning:

1. The hints and suggestions given by the **context** that make you know which definition fits.
2. The **substitution** of each definition of a word for the word itself until you are sure which definition makes the best sense.

USING ILLUSTRATIVE EXAMPLES

In your search for the right meaning, you can find helpful clues in the illustrative examples which your dictionary gives for hard words. They are added to the definitions to show you the word in action. When you looked at the main entry for **ice,** you saw this definition with an example:

> **2** *v.* To chill by adding ice: to *ice* juice.

Do you see how the example of juice helps you right away? You cannot confuse ice and juice with frosting and cake. Here is another example with a less familiar word:

> **aq·ui·line** [ak′wə·līn *or* ak′wə·lin] *adj.* **1** Of or like an eagle. **2** Curving or hooked, like an eagle's beak: an *aquiline* nose.

Without the example in definition **2** you might wonder what kind of curving thing could be described as **aquiline.** But with the example, you have a picture in your mind, perhaps of someone you know who has a nose like this or perhaps of a painting of George Washington, where his **aquiline nose** shows up clearly.

In the main entry for **apt,** each of the definitions has an illustrative example to help you tell the difference among them:

> **apt** [apt] *adj.* **1** Having a natural tendency; likely: Fish are *apt* to be biting then. **2** Quick to learn: an *apt* pupil. **3** To the point; fitting: an *apt* suggestion. — **apt′ly** *adv.* — **apt′ness** *n.*

If you try substituting the other definitions in the examples, you can soon see that they do not work:

> Fish are **quick to learn** to be biting then.
> Fish are **fitting** to be biting then.

Try the others, and then think about the way the illustrative examples give you clues to the meaning of **apt** in a particular way.

USING THE LABELS AND OTHER EXPLANATIONS

Sometimes in a main entry you will find a definition that has what is called a **label.** These labels tell you some special thing about that meaning of the word—when it is used, perhaps, or where you might hear it. Labels can help you use a new word as well as help you find the correct definition.

Suppose you heard someone say this:

> "Jack's new dog is a real **circus.**"

Because you know that one dog can't be a whole circus, with elephants and acrobats and clowns, you look at the main entry:

> **cir·cus** [sûr′kəs] *n.* **1** A traveling show of acrobats, clowns, trained animals, etc. **2** *informal* A funny, entertaining person or thing. **3** In ancient Rome, a stadium for sports, etc.

Definition **2** is the one you want. See how it is labeled: *informal.* This means that you can call Jack's dog a **circus** in everyday talk with your friends, but you will not be likely to use it when you are writing a composition or giving a speech.

Another useful label is *slang*. It tells you that a word or one meaning of a word is not standard English. Everyone uses **slang** words and meanings sometimes, but there are times when it is best not to use slang. If you want to use slang, try to be sure that the time and place are right for it. Look at this example:

> **lid** [lid] *n.* **1** A hinged or removable cover for a box, pot, etc. **2** An eyelid. **3** *slang* A hat.

When you come on a word that is new to you, it may sometimes be helpful to know in what country or what part of the United States it is commonly used. The label will tell you. Here is an example:

> **pet·rol** [pet′rəl] *n. British* Gasoline.

Now you know that what we call gasoline in the United States is called petrol in Great Britain. This British word **petrol** is also used in many other places, but in all of them it is thought of as British.

Now and then a meaning needs more explanation than just a label. This explanation is given at the end of the definition, set off by a colon, as in this example:

> **fie** [fī] *interj.* Shame! For shame!: rarely used today except humorously.

The addition to the definition tells you that when you say, "Fie!" most people will think you are being funny. If you want to be taken seriously, say something else, like "Shame on you!"

A label or special explanation can help you when you are talking or writing, as well as explaining something that you may find when you are reading. It is important if you are to understand the word and use it correctly.

FINDING THE IDIOMS

An **idiom** is a group of words, or an expression, that has a special meaning of its own when these words are used together. It doesn't make sense when the ordinary definitions of the words are substituted. For example, when you say, "You took the words out of my mouth," what are you really saying? You are really saying, "I was just going to say the same thing," but your sentence would sound foolish to someone who did not know the idiom.

Suppose you were told not to **borrow trouble.** You surely would not do it willingly. But if you know the idiom, you know you were told not to worry when nothing is wrong.

Very often idioms are so familiar that you don't have to think twice about them. But some of them will be new to you, and your dictionary code has a way of showing you their meanings.

Because they do not fit with any of the ordinary definitions, they are put after all the definitions. They are printed in heavy type to make them stand out clearly. Here is an example:

> **log·ger·head** [lôg′ər·hed′ or log′ər·hed′] *n.* **1** A large sea turtle found in tropical Atlantic waters. **2** A stupid person; blockhead. — **at loggerheads** Quarreling.

If you read that two men were **at loggerheads,** would definitions **1** and **2** tell you what they were doing? If you try substitution, what do you get?

> Two men were at large sea turtles found
> in tropical Atlantic waters.
> Two men were at stupid persons.

You are no better off than you were before. But the words **at loggerheads** are an expression that has a special meaning of its own, so you find the idiom given at the end of the entry. Now you can substitute and make sense:

> Two men were quarreling.

Look at the entry for **cockle** and try substituting definitions **1, 2,** and **3** in the sentence that follows.

> **cock·le**[1] [kok′əl] *n.* **1** An edible shellfish with ridged shells. **2** A cockleshell. **3** A wrinkle; pucker. — **warm the cockles of one's heart** To give heartfelt joy or pleasure.

The coach's praise **warmed the cockles of** Tom's **heart.**

Not one of the three ordinary definitions makes sense in the sentence. You know that there is no clear connection between Tom's heart and a shellfish or a shell or a wrinkle. You have found another idiom.

In the entry below, can you see how **make allowances for** does not fit the numbered definitions and why it must be treated as an idiom?

> **al·low·ance** [ə·lou′əns] *n.* **1** An amount or portion of something given at more or less regular intervals: a weekly *allowance* of money; a daily *allowance* of food. **2** An amount added or subtracted for some reason: We'll give an *allowance* of $200.00 for your old car. — **make allowances for** To take into account; allow for: We had to *make allowances for* his youth.

When you are having trouble finding the right meaning, remember to check after the regular definitions for an idiom in heavy type. That may be your answer when none of the definitions seems to fit.

Sometimes a picture can be more helpful than just words, and so a figure is added to the definition.

bur·ro [bûr′ō] *n., pl.* **bur·ros** A small donkey, used for riding or for carrying packs in the SW U.S.

Here the drawing shows you how tall the **burro** is compared to the man, how long its ears are, and how it can carry heavy loads and make itself a very useful animal.

Burro

Another time you might be looking up `Adriatic Sea.` The definition tells you the basic facts, that it extends from the Mediterranean mostly between Italy and Yugoslavia. The map beside the definition shows you exactly where it is and what its shape is, and shows all the countries bordering it or near it.

A·dri·at·ic Sea [ā′drē·at′ik] A sea extending from the Mediterranean, mostly between Italy and Yugoslavia.

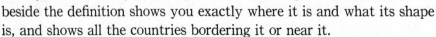

The figures fill out meanings and add many facts. There are pictures and diagrams of many different kinds of things in your dictionary: tools and instruments, clothes, boats, wild animals, even bones. Some are familiar; some are very strange and foreign. All of them give a better idea of the thing or process explained in the entry. Here are some that you will find:

Carpenters and builders use an instrument called a **level** to make sure that something is exactly level, or horizontal. It has a glass tube filled with a liquid in which an air bubble floats. The figure shows two views of this instrument. One shows it with the air bubble exactly in the middle. In this position it shows that the surface being tested is level, or horizontal. In the other view, the **level** is tilted up at one end, and the air bubble has floated over to the raised end, showing that it is not horizontal.

Level

Now take a look at the **orbit** of a satellite going around the earth. Here are the entry and the figure, which is a diagram:

or·bit [ôr′bit] **1** *n.* The path taken by a planet, comet, satellite, space vehicle, etc., as it moves around its center of attraction. Orbits are usually in the form of ellipses. **2** *n.* The probable position of an electron in relation to its atomic nucleus. **3** *v.* To move or cause to move in or as if in an orbit.

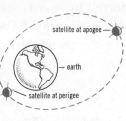

Orbit of a satellite

Notice that the path of the satellite is not a round ring always the same distance from the earth. The point on the actual path closest to the earth, called **perigee**, and the point farthest away from it, called **apogee**, are marked on the diagram.

Next take a look at some human bones. Here are the entry and figure for **scapula**:

scap·u·la [skap′yə·lə] *n.*, *pl.* **scap·u·las** or **scap·u·lae** [skap′yə·lē] The shoulder blade.

Scapulas

The figure shows the two **scapulas** in color and also the other main bones of the upper part of the body in black, so that you can see how they all fit together.

Remember to look at each figure just as carefully as you look at each definition when you need to know the meaning of a word.

REVIEW LIST OF THE GUIDES TO THE RIGHT MEANING

You have now learned about six different guides that help you pick out the definition that you need. They also help you understand new words and how they are used. These are the guides:

1. Context
2. Substitution
3. Illustrative examples
4. Labels
5. Idioms
6. Figures

Pronouncing a Word

You have been learning how to find and understand the meanings of words in the dictionary. Another way the dictionary helps you is to tell you how to say the words correctly.

Because this book can't make the sounds that you make when you say a word, it has a special printed code for these sounds. Each sound you need for talking has a special code symbol, and only one.

When you say **cool** quietly to yourself, can't you hear why the code symbol for the first sound in this word is **k**? Now look at the pronunciation from the main entry for **cool**:

[ko͞ol]

How do you learn what sound to make for the o͞o symbol that comes after the **k**? In the Pronunciation Key you can find this symbol and two familiar words that have this sound—**pool** and **food**. When you say these sample words, you hear the same o͞o sound that you make when you say **cool**.

Can you think of other words whose pronunciation code might look something like **kool**? You might think of this one:

fool [fo͞ol]

Now check the Pronunciation Key on the opposite page and find out what sound is coded by each symbol. When you put these sounds together quickly, you will say the word correctly.

Notice that the Pronunciation Key gives the symbol for each of the sounds and one or more familiar words that have that sound in them. Because the first symbol in **fo͞ol** is **f**, look in the Key to find that symbol and the familiar words that have the **f** sound. It is the same sound that you use when you begin to say **fit**. Now look at the o͞o symbol and find the words **pool** and **food**, which have the o͞o sound. If you make the sound at the beginning of **fit** and add the o͞o sound from **pool**, you only need to look up the **l** symbol to be able to say **fool**. Look up **l** in the Key and then make the three sounds one after another, quickly and without stopping after each one: **f o͞o l**. Did you say **fool**?

Try to decode this pronunciation by looking at the Key for each of the symbols:

[chās]

The symbol **ch** is used for the sound at the beginning of **check**. The **ā** is the sound at the beginning of **ace**. And **s** is the sound at the beginning of **see**. Can you put these three sounds together as one word sound and say the word **chase**?

a	add, map	o͞o	pool, food
ā	ace, rate	o͝o	took, full
â(r)	care, air	p	pit, stop
ä	palm, father	r	run, poor
b	bat, rub	s̲	see, pass
ch	check, catch	sh	sure, rush
d	dog, rod	t	talk, sit
e	end, pet	th	thin, both
ē	even, tree	t̶h̶	this, bathe
f	fit, half	u	up, done
g	go, log	û(r)	urn, term
h	hope, hate	yo͞o	use, few
i	it, give	v	vain, eve
ī	ice, write	w	win, away
j	joy, ledge	y	yet, yearn
k	cool, take	z	zest, muse
l	look, rule	zh	vision, pleasure
m	move, seem	ə	the schwa,
n	nice, tin		an unstressed
ng	ring, song		vowel representing
o	odd, hot		the sound spelled
ō	open, so		a in above
ô	order, jaw		e in sicken
oi	oil, boy		i in possible
ou	out, now		o in melon
			u in circus

fo͞ol

If you look at the entry for **pie,** you see that it begins like this:

pie [pī] *n.* A baked dish of fruit, custard, meat,
etc., in, on, or covered by a pastry crust.

When you check the Key for the **p** sound and the **i** sound, you say the word properly. But notice that the **e** in the main entry does not appear in the pronunciation. Sometimes the sound **i** is spelled **ie,** as it is here in **pie.** The pronunciation tells you only about sounds. Do not confuse the spelling with the sound symbols. You say the sounds for **pi,** but you write **pie.** You say the sounds for **ko͞ol,** but you write **cool.**

In the list of coded symbols, you may have noticed one that looks like an **e** printed upside down: ə. It is a real pronunciation symbol, not a mistake. The ə is called a **schwa,** pronounced **shwä** (the **sh** sound from **sure,** plus the **w** from **win,** plus the **ä** from **father**). It represents a sound that we make very frequently when we speak English. You may find it in words spelled with different letters, but the sound is the same. Try out the sample words in the Pronunciation Key, and listen carefully: **a** in **above, e** in **sicken, i** in **possible, o** in **melon, u** in **circus.** In each of these words the sound of what was spelled **a, e, i, o,** and **u** was just about the same. Look at these other everyday words that have the schwa sound in them:

EVERYDAY WORDS	SPELLED WITH	BUT SOUNDED AS
around, wom**a**n	a	ə
nick**e**l, soft**e**n	e	ə
terr**i**ble, penc**i**l	i	ə
conditi**o**n, lem**o**n	o	ə
foc**u**s, loc**u**st	u	ə

Learning the sound represented by the ə symbol is very important, for you will find the schwa sound in a great number of words. Also, remembering this different-looking symbol will remind you that pronunciation symbols are not the same as the letters of the alphabet. For example, **tacks** and **tax** are spelled differently, but both have exactly the same sounds: [taks]. Don't mix up sound symbols and the letters you use to spell words. They are not the same.

When you need to look up a pronunciation symbol to remind yourself of the sound it represents, you can always look at the Pronunciation Key that you have just been using. It is also printed inside the front cover of your dictionary. You will probably prefer to look back there, because it is very easy to turn to when you need it. But when you have learned to use the full Pronunciation Key, there is another, even quicker way of checking your memory of the code.

THE SHORT KEY

Look at the bottom of any of the right-hand pages of the alphabetical part of your dictionary. This is what you see:

add, āce, câre, pälm;   end, ēqual;   it, īce;   odd, ōpen, ôrder;   to͝ok, po͞ol;   up, bûrn;
ə = a in *above*, e in *sicken*, i in *possible*, o in *melon*, u in *circus*;   yo͞o = u in *fuse*;   oil;   pout;
check;   ring;   thin;   this;   zh in *vision*.   For ¶ reference, see page 64 · HOW TO

As you can see, only one sample word is given, and usually the code symbol is printed right in the word instead of being in a separate column.

Notice also that some of the symbols are not in the Short Key. When you have learned to use the full Pronunciation Key, you can recognize the **f** in **fool,** the **p** in **pie,** and the **l** in **rule** without any trouble. But the o͞o symbol or the i symbol or the ə symbol may take longer to learn, so they are printed for you throughout the book.

Can you find the o͞o from **tool** in the Short Key above? Can you find the i in **pie?** The Short Key words are po͞ol and īce.

Remember that when the Short Key does not help you, you turn to the full Pronunciation Key inside the front cover of your book.

THE STRESS MARKS

The pronunciation code tells you more than the sounds of the letters. To say words correctly, you have to make the right sounds, of course. But in many words, some of the sounds are stressed more than others. This means that one part of the word is said more strongly and with greater emphasis than the rest. This difference is shown by a stress mark, which comes just after a syllable that is to sound louder.

The dictionary uses two marks to show stress. The one you will see most often is called the **primary stress mark** and looks like this: ′ This is how it works in the pronunciation code:

If you will say **sister** quietly to yourself, you will hear that the **sis** part is stressed more than the **ter** part. Now look at the coded form:

[sis′tər]

The primary stress mark points out the syllable that you make more emphatic by the way you say it. The **tər,** which has no stress mark, is called an **unstressed syllable.**

If you try out other members of the family, you will find that they are examples of words where the stress falls on the first syllable:

muth′ər   fä′thər   bruth′ər   bā′bē

Longer words sometimes have to be stressed more than once, but one syllable usually has a stronger stress than another stressed syllable. The syllable with the weaker stress is marked with the second stress mark, called a **secondary stress mark.** It looks like this: ´ Both marks are used in the pronunciation of **grandmother.** Can you see the difference between them?

[gran(d)′muth′ər]

The primary stress mark ′ shows you that **grand** gets the most stress. The secondary stress mark ′ shows you that **muth** gets some stress, but not so much as **grand.** And the **ər** is not stressed at all, so it is an unstressed syllable. If you wonder about the **d** in parentheses above, some people pronounce it, while others do not.

If you will say **grandfather** quietly to yourself, you will find that this is another word that has both a primary stress and a secondary stress, and it also has an unstressed syllable.

[gran(d)′fä′thər]

When you are looking at the syllables in the coded pronunciations, remember that these are the syllables that you *say.* They are not always the same as the syllables that you use to divide a word at the end of a line of writing or printing.

syl·la·ble [sil′ə·bəl]

To divide the word **syllable** correctly when you write it, you can write **syl-** on one line and **lable** on the next line. But see how in the pronunciation the **la** becomes just **ə.** Do not confuse the spelling syllables that you see in the main entry words with the speaking syllables in the pronunciations.

VARIANT PRONUNCIATIONS

Sometimes there is more than one correct way to pronounce a word. These are called **variant pronunciations**, which means that they vary or are different from each other. Your dictionary shows them to you in either of two ways. The more common way looks like this:

to·ma·to [tə·mā′tō *or* tə·mä′tō]
ei·ther [ē′thər *or* ī′thər]

The one that comes first is the one most often used in the United States today. You will probably want to use this first pronunciation, but if you live in a part of the country where you hear the second form more often, remember that both are correct.

The second way of showing variant pronunciations looks like this:

due [d(y)o͞o]

Some people pronounce the word **due** as [do͞o], but others pronounce it as [dyo͞o]. Either is correct. Notice that **y** is put between parentheses. They mean that the sound indicated between them may be pronounced or left out, whichever is more common where you live. Remember that whenever you see a symbol for a sound between parentheses in a pronunciation you may make the sound or leave it out, whichever is natural for you.

THE GUIDES TO CORRECT PRONUNCIATION

When you read a new word and want to know how to say it correctly, remember that the pronunciation code provides you with these guides:

1. A symbol for every sound
2. Pronunciation Key (inside cover)
3. Short Key (right-hand pages)
4. Stress marks
5. Variant pronunciations

Spelling and Your Dictionary

While you were learning how to find words in your dictionary, you were also beginning to learn some of the ways this book can help you with spelling problems. For example, look again at the list of entries beginning with **all.**

How many words do you see that are spelled with a capital letter?

all
all-American
all-around
allay
Alleghenies

Two: **all-American** and **Alleghenies.**

How many are spelled with a hyphen?

Two: **all-American** and **all-around.**

In order to spell correctly, you must know where the capitals and the hyphens belong.

See what these other lists show you about words spelled with apostrophes. The main entry words show you where to put the apostrophes in **don't** and **o'clock.**

donkey	obtain
don't	occasion
door	o'clock
dot	odd

Now, when you turn the page, look at a longer list beginning with **ice** and see what it can tell you about spelling.

How many main entry words shown on the list are spelled starting with capital letters?

Two: **Ice Age** and **Iceland.**

How many are spelled as two words with a space between?

Two again: **Ice Age** and **ice cream.**

Now see how many are spelled as one word.

Seven: **ice, iceberg, iceboat, icebox, ice-breaker, icecap, Iceland.**

It seems strange that **iceboat** is spelled as one word when **ice cream** is two. But English words are not very orderly about this, and there is no rule for you to follow. To spell them correctly, though, you can always look them up and know that the dictionary entry is right.

ice
Ice Age
ice·berg
ice·boat
ice·box
ice·break·er
ice·cap
ice cream
Ice·land

Notice something else in this **ice** list. These main entry words show you where you can divide them when you come to the end of a line of writing or printing. The places are shown by the syllable dots.

When the word has just one syllable and no dot, you cannot divide the word. **Ice** is the only entry in this list with just one syllable. Of course, **Ice** and **Age** and **ice** and **cream** have no dots either, but the dividing place in combinations like these is already shown by the space between **Ice** and **Age** and between **ice** and **cream.**

How many of the words in the **ice** list have just one dot, which shows you that they can be divided in just one place? There are five: **iceberg, iceboat, icebox, icecap,** and **Iceland.** These are called two-syllable words. How many three-syllable words are there? They will have two dots. Did you find that there is just one? **ice·break·er.**

VARIANT SPELLINGS

Once in a while, but not very often, there is more than one correct way to spell a word. These are called **variant spellings,** which just means that they vary or are different from each other. Your dictionary shows them to you this way:

> **fledg·ling** or **fledge·ling** [flej′ling] *n.* **1** A young bird just learning to fly. **2** A young, inexperienced person; beginner.

In this entry, the second spelling, right after the main entry word, has an extra **e** after the first **g.** Either spelling is correct, but the one most often used is put first. This is the one that you will want to use yourself, but you may find the other in a book someday and wonder why the extra **e** is there unless you remember about variant spellings.

SPELLING INFLECTIONAL FORMS

Inflectional forms are most often made by adding a small piece of meaning, or **morpheme,** at the end of a word. When you add **s** to **mother,** you make the inflectional form **mothers.**

Mother is called the **root word,** because it is the word from which other words grow. The commonest morphemes added to make inflectional forms are **s, es, ed, ing, er, est.** You add them to root words every day when you talk or write. Think about these examples:

To make a word that means more than one of something, you usually add **s.**

book, books	teacher, teachers
chair, chairs	game, games

But when the root word already has an **s** at the end or when it ends in **ch, sh, x,** or **z,** you add **es.**

	glass, glasses
hunch, hunches	tax, taxes
dish, dishes	buzz, buzzes

To show that something has already happened, you add **ed.**

They play**ed** a very good game yesterday.

To show that something is or was going on, you add **ing.**

The team is play**ing** very well today.

To describe something as more than some other thing, you add **er.**

An elephant is tall**er** than a horse.

To show that something is the most of several things, you add **est.**

Hawaii is our new**est** state.

In all these examples, **s, es, ed, ing, er,** or **est** is added right at the end of the root word, with no change in the root word. These forms are not given in your dictionary. You look up the main entry of the root word and add the endings yourself.

If the word you are looking up has one of these endings, you may discover that you need to find the root word. For example, to find the meaning of **newest,** you look up **new.** For **taller,** you look up **tall.** For **played,** you look up **play.**

Remember that whenever you do not find inflectional forms in your dictionary, they are made in the usual way—by adding the common endings to the root word.

Whenever the inflectional forms are *not* made in the usual way, they will be in this book. Look at these examples where there is a change in the root word before the ending is added:

sky, skies   army, armies
The **y** changes to **ie** before the **s**.

hire, hired, hiring   cage, caged, caging
The **e** is dropped before **ed** and **ing**.

bat, batted, batting   jam, jammed, jamming
The last letter doubles before **ed** and **ing**.

pretty, prettier, prettiest   jolly, jollier, jolliest
The **y** changes to **i** before **er** and **est**.

All these inflectional forms are in your dictionary because of these changes in the root word. Other inflectional forms are given because they may not fit the **s** and **es** rule:

potato, potatoes   *but*   **rodeo, rodeos**
halo, halos *or* **haloes**

Other English words have even greater spelling differences between the root word and the inflectional forms:

child, children   bring, brought
mouse, mice   scarf, scarves
ring, rang   teach, taught

And look at these very unusual forms:

good, better, best   much, more, most   bad, worse, worst

Usually when the words are alphabetically far apart this way, each word has its own entry. For example, you will find **mice** as the inflectional form in the main entry for **mouse,** and you will also find **mice** as a main entry in proper **mi-** alphabetical order. This helps you find the root word even though you begin by looking up another form of it.

If you are not sure that an inflectional form is made in the usual way, it is wise to check. For instance, without checking, could you have formed these plurals correctly?

genus, *plural* **genera   deer,** *plural* **deer**
crisis, *plural* **crises   mother-in-law,** *plural* **mothers-in-law**

When you are not sure about spelling an inflectional form, remember these three things:

1. When your dictionary does *not* give the spelling of inflectional forms, you add **s, es, ed, ing, er, est** to the root word in the regular way.

2. When the root word changes spelling before an ending, the inflectional form is spelled out (**jam, jammed**).

3. When the inflectional form is very unusual, it is spelled out (**genus, genera**).

USING THE SPELLING CHART

The Spelling Chart is made to help you with words that you have heard but may never have seen. Could you, for example, spell **know** if you had only heard it? It sounds just like **no,** but you could not find it in your dictionary if you looked for it under **N.**

Different words may show the same sound by several spellings. The **n** sound that you hear in **no** and **know** can have all these spellings:

gn   kn   mn   nn   pn

In the Spelling Chart, the **n** sound is explained like this:

SOUND   SPELLING

n as in *n*ice   *gn*ome, *kn*ow, *mn*emonic, *n*ote, ba*nn*er, *pn*eumatic

When you have heard a word that sounds like **nat,** you may not be able to find it under **N.** But if you turn to the Spelling Chart, you see that the beginning sound could be spelled six different ways. The first would be **gnat.** Look for this word **gnat** under **G,** and you find the correct spelling for the word you have heard.

If you heard the sound **haf,** could you find any such word in your dictionary? No, but when you check the Spelling Chart, you find that the **f** sound can have these spellings:

f as in *f*it   *f*ake, co*ff*in, cou*gh*, ha*lf*, *ph*ase

You have already tried to find **haf** as a correct spelling, so **fake** does not give you the clue. Now you try each of the other possible spellings:

haff, hagh, half, haph

The next two are just as useless as **haf.** But the fourth spelling in the list of five is correct. The word you want is spelled **half.**

Look at the Spelling Chart and count how many spellings the **a** sound in **āce** can have. Did you find nine?

a   ai   ao   au   ay   ea   ei   eig   ey

Notice that the spellings are given in alphabetical order. Sometimes, when you see the possibilities, you will remember the word you want. Or you may be able to guess right about which spelling to try first.

You will find the Spelling Chart very helpful for finding words that you have heard but never seen.

THE SPELLING CHART

SOUND	AS IN	POSSIBLE SPELLING
a	add	c*a*t, pl*ai*d, c*a*lf, l*au*gh
ā	ace	m*a*te, b*ai*t, g*ao*l, g*au*ge, p*ay*, st*ea*k, sk*ei*n, w*ei*gh, pr*ey*
â(r)	care	d*a*re, f*ai*r, pr*ay*er, wh*e*re, b*ea*r, th*ei*r
ä	palm	d*a*rt, *ah*, s*e*rgeant, h*ea*rt
b	bat	*b*oy, ru*bb*er
ch	check	*ch*ip, bat*ch*, righ*t*eous, bas*ti*on, struc*tur*e
d	dog	*d*ay, la*dd*er, call*ed*
e	end	m*a*ny, *ae*sthete, s*ai*d, s*ay*s, b*e*t, st*ea*dy, h*ei*fer, l*eo*pard, fr*ie*nd, *Oe*dipus
ē	even	C*ae*sar, qu*ay*, sc*e*ne, m*ea*t, s*ee*, s*ei*ze, p*eo*ple, k*ey*, rav*i*ne, gr*ie*f, ph*oe*be, cit*y*
f	fit	*f*ake, co*ff*in, cou*gh*, hal*f*, *ph*ase
g	go	*g*ate, be*gg*ar, *gh*oul, *gu*ard, va*gue*
h	hope	*h*ot, *wh*om
hw	where	*wh*ale
i	it	pr*e*tty, b*ee*n, t*i*n, s*ie*ve, w*o*men, b*u*sy, gu*i*lt, l*y*nch
ī	ice	*ai*sle, *ay*e, sl*ei*ght, *ey*e, d*i*me, p*ie*, s*igh*, gu*i*le, b*uy*, tr*y*, l*y*e
j	joy	e*dg*e, sol*di*er, mo*du*late, ra*g*e, exa*gg*erate, *j*am
k	cool	*c*an, a*cc*ost, sa*cch*arine, *ch*ord, ta*ck*, a*cq*uit, *k*ing, tal*k*, li*qu*or
l	look	*l*et, ga*ll*
m	move	drach*m*, phleg*m*, pal*m*, *m*ake, li*m*b, gram*m*ar, conde*mn*
n	nice	g*n*ome, *kn*ow, *mn*emonic, *n*ote, ba*nn*er, *pn*eumatic
ng	ring	si*n*k, so*ng*, meri*ngue*
o	odd	w*a*tch, p*o*t

SOUND	AS IN	POSSIBLE SPELLING
ō	open	b*eau*, y*eo*man, s*ew*, *o*ver, s*oa*p, r*oe*, *oh*, br*oo*ch, s*ou*l, th*ough*, gr*ow*
ô	order	b*a*ll, b*a*lk, f*au*lt, d*aw*n, c*o*rd, br*oa*d, *ough*t
oi	oil	p*oi*son, t*oy*
ou	out	*ou*nce, b*ough*, c*ow*
o͞o	pool	rh*eu*m, dr*ew*, m*o*ve, can*oe*, m*oo*d, gr*ou*p, thr*ough*, fl*u*ke, s*ue*, fr*ui*t
o͝o	took	w*o*lf, f*oo*t, c*ou*ld, p*u*ll
p	pit	ma*p*, ha*pp*en
r	run	*r*ose, *rh*ubarb, ma*rr*y, dia*rrh*ea, *wr*iggle
s	see	*c*ite, di*c*e, *ps*yche, *s*aw, *sc*ene, *sch*ism, ma*ss*
sh	rush	o*c*ean, *ch*ivalry, vi*ci*ous, *ps*haw, *s*ure, *sch*ist, pre*sci*ence, nau*se*ous, *sh*all, pen*si*on, tis*su*e, fis*si*on, po*ti*on
t	talk	walk*ed*, though*t*, *p*tarmigan, *t*one, *Th*omas, bu*tt*er
th	thin	*th*ick
~~th~~	mother	*th*is, ba*the*
u	up	s*o*me, d*oe*s, bl*oo*d, y*ou*ng, s*u*n
yo͞o	fuse	b*eau*ty, *eu*logy, qu*eue*, p*ew*, *ewe*, ad*ieu*, v*iew*, f*u*se. c*ue*, *you*th, *yu*le
û(r)	burn	y*ear*n, f*er*n, *err*, g*ir*l, w*or*m, j*our*nal, b*ur*n, Gu*er*nsey, m*yr*tle
v	eve	o*f*, Ste*ph*en, *v*ise, fli*vv*er
w	win	ch*oi*r, q*u*ilt, *w*ill
y	yet	on*i*on, hallelu*j*ah, *y*earn
z	zoo	wa*s*, s*c*issors, *x*ylophone, *z*est, mu*zz*le
zh	vision	rou*ge*, plea*s*ure, inci*si*on, sei*z*ure, gla*zi*er
ə		*a*bove, fount*ai*n, dark*e*n, clar*i*ty, parl*ia*ment, cann*o*n, porp*oi*se, vici*ou*s, loc*u*st

Abbreviations

In your dictionary, you will find the shortened forms of words that we call **abbreviations**, just as you find the words themselves. **U.S.** for **United States, hr.** for **hour,** and **yd.** for **yard** are examples of ones that you already know.

Abbreviations are alphabetized in exactly the same way words are. Look at these lists of main entry words and main entry abbreviations:

us
U.S.
U.S.A.
usable

nitwit
N.J.
N. Mex.
no

Notice that when you are looking for an abbreviation in your dictionary, you go past the first letter of an abbreviation to the second letter and so on, just as you do when you are looking for an alphabetized word: **us, U.S., U.S.A.**

Sometimes you may not be sure whether you should look something up under its abbreviated form or its full form. Suppose you want to find the capital of Minnesota. Do you go to **Saint Paul** in alphabetical order? If you do, you find no entry for **Saint Paul.** But at the end of the entry for **saint,** you will find this note:

> ◆ In this dictionary, individual saints are listed under their given names. Place names beginning with **Saint** are listed under **St.**

So you turn to the words beginning with **St.** and, in its usual alphabetical order, you find this:

St. Paul [sānt pôl] The capital of Minnesota.

You know that an abbreviation is a shortened form of a full word or of a phrase. Its meaning, then, is the full form it stands for. For example, **TV** stands for **television,** and **television** is its meaning. If the full form is familiar to you, as **television** is, you will not need to go any farther.

But suppose the abbreviation is **DNA.** This stands for a chemical substance, **deoxyribonucleic acid,** found in all living things. Very likely you may not know what this is. If you want to know, you can turn to the main entry for the full form, in its alphabetical place, and find out.

You should remember one other part of the dictionary code when you are looking at the main entry for an abbreviation. For many entries no pronunciation is needed. There is nothing hard about saying **TV** or **U.S.** correctly. And for **ft.** in 10 *ft.* you just say the word it stands for, **feet.** But sometimes an abbreviation is used as the usual name of something and is pronounced as if it were a word. The entry for **NATO** shows you how the pronunciation of an abbreviation might look:

> **NATO** [nā′tō] The North Atlantic Treaty Organization, a military alliance of Belgium, Canada, Denmark, France, Great Britain, Greece, Iceland, Italy, Luxemburg. the Netherlands, Norway, Portugal, Turkey, the U.S. and West Germany.

Now you see that you do not just name the letters. Instead, you say:

[nā′tō]

These entries can tell you other things besides the meanings of abbreviations, and you will want to look at each part carefully.

YOUR DICTIONARY'S ABBREVIATIONS

To save space, your dictionary uses some abbreviations in its code system and in its definitions. Many of them you already know. But when you find an unfamiliar one, you can easily discover its meaning either by looking it up in alphabetical order or by checking back with the list given here:

n. noun
pron. pronoun
v. verb
adj. adjective, adjectival
adv. adverb, adverbial
prep. preposition
conj. conjunction
interj. interjection
pl. plural
sing. singular
def. definition
defs. definitions

in. inch or inches
ft. foot or feet
U.S. United States
A.D. indicating dates after the birth of Christ
B.C. indicating dates before the birth of Christ
NE northeast
NW northwest
SE southeast
SW southwest

HOW TO GET
THE MOST FROM YOUR
DICTIONARY

HOW TO GET THE MOST FROM YOUR DICTIONARY

by Dimmes McDowell

In consultation with Albert H. Marckwardt and Phil C. Lange

The first section, "How to Use Your Dictionary," explained many things about this book: how to find a word; how to use the code system in the main entry; how to get information from the entry about spelling, pronunciation, inflectional forms, meanings, and so on. With these skills, you can use your dictionary. You can look up a word and learn enough about it so that you can understand it and use it. But you may not be learning everything about the word that the dictionary has to offer. Often there is more. To make full use of your dictionary, you will want this additional information, too.

This section explains what the additional information is and how you can find it and make use of it. The section has nine main topics. Here is the list:

1. The Right Meaning
2. Reading the Figures
3. Word Parts and Meanings
4. Mix-ups in Meanings
5. The Right Synonym
6. Usage Notes
7. Parts of Speech
8. Word Histories
9. More than the Most

The Right Meaning

As you know, many words in the dictionary have more than one meaning. Usually, when they do not have more than four or five definitions, it is not hard to find the one you want, either by using the context or by substituting the suitable definition for the new word.

For example, look at the two sentences below and the main entry under them:

I have an appointment in the principal's office at ten o'clock tomorrow morning.
The appointments of the ballroom will be blue and gold.

ap·point·ment [ə·point′mənt] *n*. **1** Selection for, or a placing in, an office or position not filled by election. **2** Such an office or position. **3** The person chosen. **4** An agreement to meet someone at a certain place and time. **5** (*usually pl.*) Furniture or equipment.

You know at once that **appointment** in the first sentence is explained by definition **4** because of the place and time mentioned right in the sentence. You also know that only definition **5** fits **appointments** in the second sentence because nothing in the other definitions can be described as having those colors.

Suppose, however, that you need to find exactly the right meaning in a very long main entry, one with fifteen, twenty, or even more definitions. This is harder. It takes more careful attention to context and more thinking than are needed to get the right meaning for **appointment**.

Would you expect a common word like **good** to make one of these long entries? It does. It has eighteen numbered definitions and ten definitions of idioms—twenty-eight altogether. Here are all of them:

good [good] *adj.* **bet·ter, best,** *n*. **1** *adj.* Having the proper qualities; admirable. **2** *adj.* Skillful: a *good* pianist. **3** *adj.* Kind: a *good* turn. **4** *adj.* Well-behaved; polite: a *good* child. **5** *adj.* Proper; desirable: *good* manners. **6** *adj.* Favorable: a *good* opinion. **7** *adj.* Pleasant; agreeable: *good* company. **8** *adj.* Beneficial; helpful: *good* advice. **9** *n*. Benefit; advantage: for the *good* of mankind. **10** *adj.* Genuine; valid: a *good* excuse. **11** *adj.* Above the average in quality, degree, or kind: *good* food; a really *good* fur coat. **12** *adj.* Unspoiled; fresh: *good* meat. **13** *adj.* In a sound or satisfactory condition: *good* eyesight; a *good* chair. **14** *adj.* Satisfactory or appropriate, as for a particular purpose: *good* weather for flying. **15** *adj.* Great or fairly great in amount, extent, etc.: a *good* share. **16** *adj.* Thorough; sufficient: a *good* spanking. **17** *adj.* Full: a *good* mile away. **18** *n*. A thing that is good. — **as good as** Almost; nearly; practically. — **for good** For the last time; permanently. — **good and** *informal* Very; extremely: This chilli is *good and* hot. — **good for 1** Capable of lasting or remaining valid or in operation (for a certain period of time). **2** *informal* Able or willing to pay, give, or produce (something). — **make good 1** To be successful. **2** To replace; repay. **3** To fulfill (a promise, threat, etc.). **4** To prove. — **to the good** To the credit, profit, or advantage of someone or something.

When you read through all the definitions, you find three or four with very broad and general meanings. These would fit in many contexts, but they don't tell you anything exact—desirable, favorable or pleasant, above average, and proper. Most of the other definitions show certain ways of being desirable, favorable, or proper on a particular occasion or in some set of special circumstances. **Good** weather for flying will not seem **good** to the farmer who wants rain; he would rather have a **good** rain.

Now suppose you want to know what **good** means in this sentence:

These lamb chops are good.

Certainly lamb chops are not kind, skillful, or polite. They may be above average, desirable, or pleasant, or all three, but you need to know in what way. Most of the definitions in the main entry for **good** either do not fit at all or do not fit very well. Only two do fit and have something to say that is clearly related to lamb chops—definitions **11** and **12**. As a matter of fact, the illustrative phrases let you know that you have something in these two: *good* food and *good* meat. The next thing to do is to choose between them. To do this, you have to think carefully about the context.

Who is speaking? When? In what circumstances? If it was your mother when she was planning to serve the chops for dinner or when she was taking them out of the refrigerator, she was probably thinking of **good** in the sense it has in definition 12—"Unspoiled; fresh: *good* meat"—and therefore healthful and desirable for the family to eat. If it was a little later, and you yourself made the remark after you had had a few bites, you probably meant that the chops struck you as being "Above the average in quality, degree, or kind: *good* food," as definition 11 puts it. You were finding them pleasant to eat because of their taste.

The sentence taken by itself makes sense when **good** is used in either of these two meanings. But the broader context, including *who* said it and *when*, decides which meaning was intended.

Before we leave the entry for **good**, let us look at one more sentence:

These chops are good and tough.

You can go through all the numbered definitions without finding what **good** means in that sentence. If you go on past them, though, you will find the idiom—**good and.** It is labeled *informal* and looks like this:

— **good and** *informal* Very; extremely.

By substituting, you know that the sentence above means this:

These chops are extremely tough.

Many long entries with many definitions need the same kind of care we just gave to the entry for **good.** It is not hard to get a general idea of what one of these words means. It is hard to choose the exact meaning you want out of a large number. Think about all the circumstances that make up the context. They will tell you the right definition to choose.

Remember these two points. Don't stop at the first definition that might possibly fit but does not exactly. The one that fits exactly may come later in the entry. It may even be down among the idioms. Second, think hard about what is really being said and what the circumstances really are. Otherwise, you may miss the point—and the right definition—entirely.

Reading the Figures

Whenever a figure (a picture, diagram, or map) appears with a main entry, you are certain to find clearer and fuller information than you could get from just a definition. Be sure to look at the figures carefully.

an·gle[1] [ang′gəl] *n., v.* **an·gled, an·gling 1** *n.* A geometric figure formed by two rays that have the same end point. **2** *n.* The space between such rays or surfaces, measured in degrees. **3** *v.* To move or turn at an angle: The halfback *angled* down the field. **4** *n.* A point of view; standpoint: The problem was discussed from all *angles*.

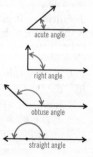

acute angle

right angle

obtuse angle

straight angle

With the entry for **angle** there is a figure that has four parts. Under each part is a **caption,** a group of words that help you to understand the figure.

Read the entry for **angle** and then look at the figures and captions carefully. This entry shows you several ways in which reading the figures can be useful.

Notice that the main entry gives you two general definitions of an angle in definitions 1 and 2. Notice, too, that the figure shows you four special kinds of angles. Each one is named under a part of the figure: ACUTE ANGLE, OBTUSE ANGLE, RIGHT ANGLE, and STRAIGHT ANGLE. To find exactly what you want to know, you may have to look up one or more of these combinations, which you will find in their alphabetical places. For example:

right angle One of the angles formed when two lines intersect so as to form four angles that have the same measure; an angle of 90°.

By studying the figure and looking up the special types of angle shown, you gathered many facts not in the definitions.

Of course, the dictionary does not tell you as much about angles as your mathematics book does. It has to include words from all your schoolbooks—mathematics, social studies, science, and so on—as well as words you will find in stories, magazines, and newspapers. There is not space enough to explain all the details, but sometimes, as with **angle,** the definitions and a figure can be quick reminders of what you have already studied in other books.

How else can figures and their captions help you? For example, how do you use an abacus? The definition tells you what an abacus is and what its purpose is. Look at the figure and read the caption. They tell you much more about how it works than the definition can.

ab·a·cus [ab′ə·kəs] *n.* A device using beads that slide on rods for adding, subtracting, etc.

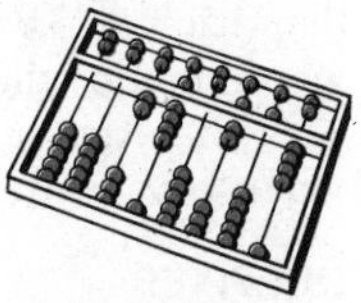

Chinese abacus set at 290,754. Upper beads count 5 each when lowered; lower beads count 1 each when raised.

How big are violins and cellos? The pictures at **cello** and **violin** show people play-ing each one. Because you know about how big a person is, you can compare the instruments with the players and get information about their sizes.

Other figures give you some clue to the usual or average size of an object right in the caption. Look at these examples:

Albatross, about 10 ft. across wings
Alpaca, 42 inches high at shoulder

But under some figures no sizes are given. For example, no size is given for **ray,** the fish. The reason is that one variety of ray is as much as 20 feet across, another is only 4 or 5, and still another is quite small. There is no single, usual size for rays. When no size is given, you can expect that two individuals may be as different in size as the largest and smallest rays. This is in itself a piece of information. Remember this when you are using the figures and the captions to add to what the definitions tell you.

Word Parts and Meanings

Many of our words are made up of two or three or even more parts. Probably the easiest to recognize and understand are those in which common words have been put together like building blocks to form a new word with a new meaning. Here are some familiar samples:

schoolgirl   basketball
teammate   fruitcake
dinnertime   breakwater

When you really stop to think about these words, you realize how handy they are. For instance, one word—**schoolgirl**—takes four to say another way—*girl attending a school* —or maybe even five—*girl going to a school.* Notice, too, that when you say what **schoolgirl** means in four or five words, you not only add words. You also change the order, and **girl** comes before **school.**

Sometimes, the order can stay the same, but to make the meaning clear, you must explain one of the word parts. A **breakwater** is a barrier like a wall or dam to **break** the force of waves, or **water,** coming in. You have added "the force of" and you have explained that in the new word, **water** means "waves."

It is not safe always to believe that the meanings of the parts add up to the usual, modern meaning of the longer word, even though you do add and explain. In some words the original meaning of the parts has disappeared entirely. **Blackball** shows you how this can happen. Formerly, each member of a club voted on whether to take someone in as a new member by dropping a little ball like a marble into a box. A white one meant a vote for the candidate; a black one was a vote against. Today, there is no ball in the meaning of this word and no color. Now **blackball** means any kind of vote against a person. It can also mean deciding to keep someone out of a group even when there is no formal vote taken. **Schoolgirl** and **dinnertime** you know, but would you have understood the meaning of **blackball** without looking it up?

SUFFIXES

Word parts may be whole words like **school** and **girl** or small parts like **-ed** or **-est**. Both are small units of meaning, called **morphemes**. Morphemes added at the end of a word, like **-ing**, are also called **suffixes**.

For years, whether you realize it or not, you have been using suffixes to be sure that other people understand what you mean. When a baby first begins to make the sound that means moving legs and feet in a particular way, he may say nothing but "Walk." Then, before long, he learns about **-ed** and **-ing** and can hear the difference between "Daddy **is walking** home" and "Daddy **walked** home." Here the **-ed** sound means that the walk is finished and over, and the **-ing** sound means that it is going on.

There are many other suffixes that you use every day. Here are two more: **-er** and **-est**. Barbara, Susan, and Debby are all **short**. But when you add **-er** and **-est** to the root word, you do something to **short** and show the differences among the three girls:

Barbara is **short**.
But Susan is **shorter**.
And Debby is **shortest** of all.

The suffixes that make inflectional forms like **walked, walking, shorter,** and **shortest** are usually so common and so familiar that we don't think much about them. Although we use them almost automatically, they are good examples of the way in which a small word part can change the meaning of what is being said or read or written.

Other suffixes are added to root words not to make inflectional forms but to make other words. Many of these are almost as common as **-ed** and **-ing**. To make an adverb, you add **-ly** to an adjective, as with **swift** and **swiftly**. Or you add **-al** to a noun to make an adjective, as with **nation** and **national**. You also tack on **-ment** or **-tion** (or just **-ion**) to mean a state, condition, or process of (something), as **agreement** made from **agree** or **tension** made from **tense**.

Here are some other familiar examples:

-**able**, as in readable
-**er**, as in walker
-**ical**, as in astronomical
-**ist**, as in artist
-**ive**, as in automotive
-**ness**, as in richness

You will very often find that words made with suffixes like **-al, -ment,** and **-ly** appear in your dictionary as run-on entries. Don't forget that all these suffixes are in the dictionary in their alphabetical places, so that you can look them up there to find either their spelling or their meaning.

Whenever the addition of a suffix changes the meaning of a word in some special way, you will have to look that word up as a main entry. Can you see why you might have to look up these two words?

as·tron·o·mer [ə·stron′ə·mər] *n.* A person who is an expert in astronomy.
as·tro·nom·i·cal [as′trə·nom′i·kəl] *adj.* **1** Of or having to do with astronomy. **2** Almost too large to imagine, like the numbers in astronomy; enormous: *astronomical* expenses.

If you think about it for a minute, you will realize that **astronomer** is different from **walker,** a person who walks. You can't say: one who *astronomes*. So **astronomer** is a word that you might have to look up to get the right meaning.

You know many other **-ical** words, like **economical** and **alphabetical**, so why should you look up **astronomical?** Because it has that special second definition, which might be the one you need: "almost too large to imagine." You could figure out definition **1** for yourself, but you might not know about definition **2**. It is a good idea to look up new words made with suffixes unless you are very sure that the simple and obvious meaning is what you need.

PREFIXES

Morphemes that are added ahead of roots are called **prefixes**. The **pre-** in their name is a good example. It means before in time or order, and you have seen it used in many other words: **prepare, predict, precede, prepay.**

You already know a great number of prefixes and use them all the time. One of the most familiar is **un-,** which means not or the opposite of. It can be added to hundreds of words; some are **unkind, uncomfortable, unusual, uneasy.** Just about as common is **re-,** meaning over again or back again, as in **renew,** to make new over again, or **repay,** to pay back again.

Do you recognize **post-,** which means after or coming after, in **postscript,** something written after the rest of a letter? **Anti-,** opposed to or against, as in **antiaircraft? Sub-,** under, as in **submarine?**

If you know all the parts of a word, usually you have a good idea of what the word as a whole means. For example, **re-** plus **pay** plus **-ment** equals **repayment.** And **un-** plus **alter** plus **-able** equals **unalterable.**

Sometimes, though, one of the word parts can fool you. Here is one that you know, but can you see how someone might be tricked by it?

un·armed [un·ärmd'] *adj.* **1** Not armed; without arms or weapons, especially a gun. **2** Without sharp prickles or points, as the spines, plates, etc., of some animals or plants.

In **unarmed,** the **arm** part means weapon, not a part of the body. This makes an important difference in the meaning of the word.

Learn all you can about prefixes and suffixes and other word parts. They are very handy to know. But remember too that you will often have to look up entries for words that have very common word parts in order to be absolutely sure of their correct meanings.

Mix-ups and Confusions

Unfortunately, our language sometimes makes it hard for us to keep some words sorted out from some other words either because they look so much alike or because they sound so much alike. Your dictionary has several ways of helping you with these problems.

HOMOGRAPHS

When you were learning to find entries in your dictionary, you discovered words that might seem to be difficult to find because two (and sometimes more) completely different words are spelled exactly the same. These are called **homographs,** and there are a good many of them.

Just turning over the pages of entries beginning with **F,** for example, you would find thirty-four of this particular kind of word. You could make a list beginning with **fair**[1] and **fair**[2]. It would include **fell,** which has four numbered entries, **fine,** which has three, **forte,** two, and **fry,** two. Other letters of the alphabet would show you many more.

Many times, these homographs are pronounced alike as well as spelled alike, but not always. For example, one's **forte**[1], or strong point, is pronounced [fôrt], but when you use **forte**[2] to describe loud music, you say either [fôr'tā] or [fôr'tē]. If you discover homographs that are new to you, don't look just at the meaning. Check the pronunciations too, and learn them. Otherwise, you will sound as though you are using the wrong word even though you know the correct definition.

Here are some familiar homographs that are pronounced differently. Do you recognize them?

minute[1]	minute[2]
wind[1]	wind[2]
sewer[1]	sewer[2]
wound[1]	wound[2]

HOMOPHONES

Different words that are pronounced exactly the same way are called **homophones.** Some of them are homographs as well as homophones, but only some; many sound the same and are spelled differently. Look at these three words, for example:

fair[1] [fâr]
fair[2] [fâr]
fare [fâr]

All three have the same pronunciation and so are homophones. But only **fair**[1] and **fair**[2] are homographs.

Some homophones may look something alike even when the spelling is not exactly the same. Very often, though, there is not much resemblance between them. Notice the spelling differences in the words in this list:

rain, reign, rein	[rān]
brake, break	[brāk]
peal, peel	[pēl]
flour, flower	[flour]
no, know	[nō]
nice, gneiss	[nīs]

Remember that homophones may have the same spellings, or similar spellings, or completely different-looking spellings. It is the pronunciation that matters.

CONFUSIONS OF MEANING

There are some words that are neither homographs nor homophones but that do look and sound pretty much alike. Often it is very easy to get them mixed up and to say or write the wrong one.

Your dictionary has a special way of straightening them out for you. At the end of a main entry, the confusing group of words is sorted out in a special note. Here is a sample, which you would find with the main entry for **decent**:

◆ *Decent, descent,* and *dissent* look and sound rather alike but are not related. *Decent* [dē′sənt] is from a Latin word meaning *fitting* and still means *fitting* or *proper. Descent* [di·sent′] comes from a Latin verb meaning *to climb down,* and it still means *a coming down. Dissent* [di·sent′] is from a Latin verb meaning *to feel opposed* or *apart.* It is now either a noun meaning *disagreement* or a verb meaning *to disagree.*

Do you see how the note makes clear the differences in spelling, pronunciation, and meaning?

Notice that it is introduced by a special sign ◆. (You will find that this book uses ◆ to point out several kinds of extra information that add to what the usual parts of the entry tell you. The other kinds will be explained later.)

Now suppose that you had looked up the main entry for **descent**. How would you know about the special information that is given under **decent**? At the end of the **descent** entry there is this note:

◆ See DECENT.

And with the **dissent** entry there is the same note:

◆ See DECENT.

Both of them send you to the right place to get the full explanation. Notes like this are called **cross-references,** and they are well worth following up if you wish to get the most from your dictionary.

The Right Synonym

Another kind of note marked ◆ helps you with the differences between **synonyms.** Synonyms are words with meanings that are very much the same but not exactly so. The words themselves do not necessarily look or sound at all alike.

When it is important for you to recognize these differences in meaning, a synonym note is printed at the end of one entry and cross-references are printed at the end of the others. In the following example, the note appears with the entry for **reason** and the cross-references with **purpose** and **motive.**

◆ *Reason, purpose,* and *motive* explain why people behave in certain ways. When your teacher asks why you did not do your homework, he wants a *reason,* such as "I was sick," or "I lost the assignment." The *purpose* of homework is to give you practice in learning by yourself, but your *motive* in doing it may simply be to get good grades.

If you have read this synonym note carefully, you should be able to explain the differences between the **reason** for looking up cross-references, the **purpose** of cross-references, and your **motive** for paying attention to them. Can you do it?

Usage Notes

There is more to writing and speaking English than knowing what the separate words mean and how they are spelled and pronounced. Words must be put together correctly to make proper sentences, and the words that are used must be suitable to the time and place at which they are used.

You have already seen how this dictionary labels certain main entries and definitions *informal* or *slang.* These labels warn you against putting something unsuitable into a dignified, formal composition or speech. When such a label is not enough to explain exactly how a word can be used, a ◆ note will tell you what you need to know. For example, is it ever correct to use **ain't?** Here is the dictionary's explanation:

ain't [ānt] A contraction of: Am not: I *ain't* going. *Ain't* is also used for *are not, is not, has not,* and *have not.* ◆ *Ain't* is not considered acceptable English today, although speakers and writers sometimes use it for humorous effect.

This note explains why you may see **ain't** in books when the author is trying to be funny or when a character is supposed to be speaking nonstandard English. But most people, including your teacher, usually classify a person who uses **ain't** seriously as untaught and handicapped by poor background. When you know the difference, it is wise to use acceptable English only.

Other ◆ notes help you with still more complicated problems of correct usage. To see how this works, look first at the main entry printed here:

as·tro·nau·tics [as′trə·nô′tiks] *n.* The science and art of flight in space. ◆ See -ICS.

Now imagine that you have looked up the cross-reference, and read the main entry for the suffix **-ics:**

-ics A suffix meaning: **1** An art, science, or field of study, as in *mathematics*. **2** Methods, systems, or activities, as in *acrobatics, athletics*. ◆ Nouns ending in *-ics* that refer to arts, sciences, or fields of activity were originally plural, meaning things relating to a field. Later they came to mean all such things relating to a field, taken as a single collection, and they became singular: *Politics* is exciting; *Physics* is his favorite subject. Such words seldom take *a, an,* or *the*. Nouns in *-ics* that refer to specific details, qualities, or methods within a field are plural and often take articles: The *acoustics* in this hall are bad; These *statistics* are from the last census.

The entry for **astronautics** gives you the basic dictionary information: spelling, pronunciation, and meaning. But to get the most possible information, you follow up the cross-reference and learn about the correct use of words ending in **-ics.** Do you see the two points this ◆ note is making? First, it tells when to use a singular verb and when to use a plural verb. And, second, you learn that ordinarily you do not use *a, an,* or *the* with these words when the singular verb is the correct one.

Every time a word ending in **-ics** appears in your dictionary, it is followed by the cross-reference "See -ICS." Usage notes like this give you another reason to look up cross-references whenever you find them.

Parts of Speech

The dictionary abbreviations that show parts of speech can help you in more ways than one. Perhaps the most common is something you have never given any special thought to: Take a noun that you know, like **cart.** Can you use it as a verb, too?

You know that many small children have carts, and you know that you can say, "She will take Junior to the playground in his **cart.**"

Can you also say, "She will **cart** Junior to the playground"?

cart [kärt] **1** *n.* A heavy, two-wheeled vehicle for carrying heavy loads, usually pulled by a horse. **2** *n.* A light, usually two-wheeled vehicle for small loads or for riding: a pony *cart*; a grocery *cart*. **3** *v.* To carry in a cart.

Cart may be the name of the thing—the noun—that Junior is conveyed or carried in, as in definition **2.** And it may also be the conveying or carrying of Junior from one place to another—the verb—as in definition **3.** You can use **cart** both as a noun and as a verb.

But think about **car:** "The **car** is headed for the main road." **Car** is most certainly a thing named, a noun. But try using it as a verb: "They will **car** him to the station." Or "They **carred** to Mexico last summer." It can't be done, and the main entry for **car** tells you so:

car [kär] *n.* **1** Any vehicle used to carry people or goods, especially an automobile. **2** A vehicle for use on rails, as a railroad car or a streetcar. **3** The enclosed platform on which people or things are carried in an elevator.

All these definitions are noun definitions. You see that **car** is not used as a verb.

Although you would not be likely to be confused about cars, suppose you came across a new word and had to use it properly. First you hear a friend say, "My little brother's **prattle** kept me from finishing my homework." In this sentence, **prattle** is the name of the special noise that the small boy is making, so it is a noun. But can you use **prattle** as a verb? Can you say to another friend, "Junior **prattled** away and kept Archie from finishing his homework"? You must find out whether it is like **car** and can be used only as a noun or whether it is like **cart** and can be both a noun and a verb.

prat·tle [prat′(ə)l] *v.* **prat·tled, prat·tling,** *n.* **1** *v.* To talk foolishly or like a child. **2** *n.* Foolish or childish talk. **3** *n.* The sound of childish speech, or a sound like it. — **prat′tler** *n.*

The entry tells you that **prattle** can be used both ways.

ADJ. USE AND N. USE

After you begin to look at the parts of speech labels in your dictionary entries, you will find even more answers to "Can I use it?" For example, how many ways can you use the word **mail?**

I will **mail** your letter. (Used as a verb.)
The postman brought the **mail** early. (Used as a noun.)
He drove the new **mail** truck. (Used as an adjective.)

In the third sentence you can see **mail** being used in a special way—adjectivally. Your dictionary tells you about using a word this way by putting *adj. use* right after the definition number. Here is how it looks in the main entry for **mail:**

mail[1] [māl] **1** *n.* Letters or parcels sent or received through a governmental postal system. **2** *n.* The postal system itself. **3** *n.* Postal matter collected or delivered at a certain time: the morning *mail.* **4** *adj. use:* a *mail* truck. **5** *v.* To send by mail; put into the mail.

Definition **4** lets you know that what may look like the noun defined in definition **3** can be used adjectivally. Usually, as here, no definition is needed. An illustrative phrase shows you the use and meaning.

In very much the same way, what looks like an adjective can sometimes be used as a noun. You can see this happening in the first two definitions of **rich:**

rich [rich] *adj.* **1** Having a lot of money, goods, or property; wealthy. **2** *n. use:* Rich people: *The rich* are sometimes generous.

Rich, which is usually used adjectivally, can have a noun use. You don't have to say "rich people" every time. You can quite properly say "the rich" and mean the same thing.

ADJECTIVES RELATED BY MEANING

In some entries you will find a definition labeled *n.* (for noun) with a ◆ sign right in the definition. These are entries for nouns that have especially related adjectives. These adjectives are often very different in looks and in sound from the nouns that they relate to. Without a hint, you might not have any idea where to look to find one of them. Your dictionary gives you the clue in this way:

dog [dôg] *n., v.* **dogged, dog·ging** **1** *n.* A tame, flesh-eating animal kept as a pet or used to guard, guide, hunt, herd, etc. ◆ Adj., *canine.* **2** *v.* To follow like a hunting dog; hound: Misfortune *dogged* his steps. **3** *n.* A device for gripping or holding logs, etc.

You can see that if you were on the subject of dogs and could not think of **canine,** you would not know where to look for it without a hint. The note sends you straight to **canine,** and when you turn to it, you find it means of or like a dog, or like a dog's.

Another example is the noun **moon** and its related adjective **lunar,** which you know from your science books. And do you recognize **feline** as the adjective relating to **cat?** Watch for these helpful hints.

PRONUNCIATION AND PARTS OF SPEECH

Usually all the parts of speech for a certain word sound alike. For example, **cart** is pronounced [kärt] whether it is used as a noun or as a verb.

But sometimes there are differences. Here is the pronunciation of a familiar word that illustrates the point:

[*n.* hous; *v.* houz]

When you use **house** as a noun, you say [hous]. When you use it as a verb, you say [houz].

Can you come to my [hous] today?
The camp can [houz] eighty boys.

Your dictionary puts parts of speech labels into the pronunciation as well as into the definitions to give you all the information that you need.

Try saying these two sentences to hear the differences between the parts of speech:

The dentist had to [ik·strakt′] my aching tooth.
Vanilla [eks′trakt] is often used in cakes.

Do you hear why the pronunciation for **extract** looks like this?

ex·tract [*v.* ik·strakt′, *n.* eks′trakt]

Remember to check pronunciation and parts of speech to be sure you are making the sound that is correct in your sentence.

Word Histories

Our language has been growing and changing for many centuries. When people have a new idea to explain or something that they need to name, they may add a new word to the vocabulary. Not too long ago, for example, a new and different mealtime became common and popular enough so that it needed a description of its own. Now we have this word:

brunch [brunch] *n.* A meal, usually in the late morning, combining breakfast and lunch. ◆ This word is a blend of *br(eakfast)* and *(l)unch.*

The ◆ note of this entry tells you what the word was made from and how it was made. Word histories like this are called **etymologies.** Whenever they might be interesting and useful to you, they follow the definitions in an entry and are introduced by the ◆ sign.

You are well acquainted with the two English words that **brunch** comes from. Usually, though, the etymology of a word must be traced back through many years, long before there was any English as we know it. Therefore, you will often find an explanation like this one, which goes back to the language of the ancient Greeks:

as·tron·o·my [ə·stron′ə·mē] *n.* The study of the stars, planets, and other heavenly bodies, their make-up, positions, motions, etc. ◆ *Astronomy* comes from two Greek words meaning *arrangement* or *distribution of the stars*, the early study having been mainly the mapping of stars.

This etymology not only tells you where our word **astronomy** came from. It also shows you how astronomy has changed over the centuries, for now men can study the make-up and motion of heavenly bodies as well as map their positions.

Now look at a main entry that comes just a little before **astronomy** in alphabetical order:

as·tro·naut [as′trə·nôt] *n.* A person who travels in space. ◆ *Astronaut* is parallel to *aeronaut,* a balloon pilot, and is formed from the Greek roots *nautes,* meaning *sailor,* and *astro-,* meaning (*between or among*) *stars.*

This ◆ note takes you through two stages of history. Like **brunch, astronaut** is a new word in the world's vocabulary, but its two parts have been around for a long time. Again they both come to us from the ancient Greeks, who may have dreamed of sailing in the air and reaching the stars, but could not do either one.

Therefore, before the 1700's, there was no need to borrow **aero-** (air) and **nautes** (sailor) and put them together to describe the balloon pilots who were just then beginning their experiments. And now, today, we have borrowed this idea from the 1700's and another Greek word to make a still newer word appropriate to modern scientific developments—sailors among the stars.

Etymologies can give you much useful information about our words. They can tell you interesting stories from times past. And sometimes they can be fascinating just for themselves, as they show you how people build and change their language.

More than the Most

When you have learned how to use your dictionary and how to get the most from it, have you finished? In one sense, yes. In another sense, no.

Your dictionary is a **reference book.** This means that now and then, as you need to, you *refer to* it for a special piece of information—perhaps for the spelling of **pneumonia** or the pronunciation of **audacity** or the meaning of **nuthatch.** It is not meant to be a book that you read straight through, beginning with page 1 and going on to the end. When you have found a particular spelling, you may have finished.

But you will find that the dictionary can also *refer* you *from* the entry you have looked up *to* sources of information outside this book. It doesn't do this in so many words, but if you truly know how to use it and can think about what you actually need to know, you will find that you and the dictionary together bring you to the proper answers.

After you have read the entry for **angle,** should you look up the entry for **right angle?** And then should you go to your math book to review all you have studied about angles?

When you find that **lunar** is the adjective related to **moon,** should you go to your science book to review, say, lunar eclipses?

Your dictionary can give you the necessary clues. What you do with them depends on you. Here is an example of the way you can pick up the trail by noting all the clues. Suppose that "Paul Revere" is a new name to you. He might be a character in a story or someone living today or an important person from the past or an imaginary figure like Jack Frost.

Re·vere [ri·vir′], **Paul,** 1735–1818, American patriot and silversmith famous for his midnight ride to Lexington, Mass., to warn the colonists that the British troops were coming.

You realize right away that he was a real person because the dates of his birth and death are given at the beginning of the entry. Since he rode to give warning to *colonists,* he must have done it before the Americans won the Revolutionary War. Now you know that he was important in American history about that time, so there will be more information about him in a social studies or history book or in an encyclopedia. Or the library may have a book about him in the biography section.

If you look up **Aegean,** the trail leads to an atlas.

If you look up **boron,** you head for a chemistry book.

If you look up **mousse,** you may find you need a cookbook.

Learn to use your dictionary as a reference book in two directions. Then you will really get the most from it.

REGIONAL PRONUNCIATION

by James B. McMillan

A correct pronunciation is one commonly used by educated people. This dictionary shows at least one correct pronunciation for each word listed. It does not show pronunciations typical of uneducated people.

If educated people all sounded alike, there would be only one correct pronunciation for each word. They don't, as you can discover by listening to them carefully on television. A person brought up in one region usually sounds a little different from those brought up in other regions. Though we can usually understand people from England, Scotland, Ireland, or Australia, they sound rather strange to us. And even one educated person will probably pronounce a word one way if he says it slowly by itself and another if he says it rapidly as part of a sentence. *Let him see her* as a rapid sentence may sound like /let-im-sē-ûr/ or /let-əm-sē-ər/, but the four words spoken slowly and separately are pronounced /let/, /him/, /sē/, /hûr/. All these pronunciations are correct, though this dictionary does not show many rapid forms.

How does a dictionary arrive at correct pronunciations? Its editors listen to and record the speech of educated people everywhere in the English-speaking world. They choose and put in the dictionary the most common pronunciation they hear.

The dictionary does not make a pronunciation. No law makes it. No school makes it. Educated people talking make it. The dictionary simply shows the way they commonly talk.

This dictionary shows sounds by a system of simple symbols made up of plain letters, letters with special marks over them, and stress marks, a system much more regular and accurate than ordinary spellings. There is a full key to these symbols in the front of the book, and at the bottom of every right-hand page there is a short key showing the symbols not already familiar to you. For each symbol a short, common key word shows the sound in use. These key words let the system adjust itself so as to cover many differences in pronunciation, especially those that are geographical. For example, the dictionary shows [âr'ē] as the pronunciation of *airy*. If you look up the symbol /â/ in the key, you find the key word *care*, showing that *airy* has the same vowel sound as *care*. Now some people have the *a* of *marry* in *care*; some have the *e* of *merry*; and some have a third sound. No matter how *care* is pronounced by educated people in your region, the vowel sound of *airy* is the same as that of *care*. Though people in other regions may differ, the vowel sound of *airy* is the vowel sound of *care* for them, too. This is how the key adjusts itself to educated speech in different regions. There is no single correct way to pronounce *care* and other words with the same vowel.

Sometimes more than one pronunciation has to be given. In some places *blouse* is pronounced [blous]; in others [blouz]. Both are shown in this dictionary. In some places *dew* and *due* are pronounced like *do* as [dōō]. In other places they are sounded [dyōō]. This dictionary shows these by a single set of symbols, [d(y)ōō], the parentheses indicating the (y) can either be sounded or be left out, whichever is customary where you come from. Any symbol in parentheses in a pronunciation may be sounded or omitted as seems comfortable to you.

Now let us take some classes of sounds which are replaced by variants in some parts of the country. Though these variants are acceptable, for reasons of space they are not shown in the dictionary proper.

1. /ä/ as in *pälm* is the same sound as *o* in *odd* in most of the United States but not in New England nor in Britain.

2. /â/ as in *câre* has in some places the same sound as *e* in *merry*, and in other places it has the sound of *a* in *marry*.

3. /ô/ as in *ôrder* is the usual vowel sound for all words like *call*, *hall*, *awful*, and *law*, but many educated people use /ä/, as in *pälm*, for all these words.

4. /i/ as in *it* is the vowel sound for words like *here*, *near*, *mere*, and *bier*, but many speakers use a sound closer to /ē/ in *ēven*.

5. /ē/ as in *ēven* is the vowel sound at the end of words like *city*, *happy*, and *candy*, but many speakers use a sound closer to /i/ in *it*.

6. /ûr/ as in *bûrn* in various parts of the country has too many different sounds for a

dictionary to list. You can sometimes tell where a person grew up from the way he says words like *bird, herd, curd, yearn,* and *word*.

7. /r/ before a consonant or at the end of a word, as in *barn, hard, poor,* and *sir,* has many accepted pronunciations and in parts of New England and the South may have no sound at all. This dictionary might properly have shown this /r/ in parentheses, though it does not.

Other variants are not geographical, happen anywhere, and seem to be a matter of personal choice. The word *economics* is a good example. Some well-known people pronounce it as [ek′ə·nom′iks], and others as well known pronounce it as [ē′kə·nom′iks]. Some people pronounce the state of *Nevada* as [nə·vad′ə] and others call it [nə·vä′də]. In such instances this dictionary gives both pronunciations, and of course either is correct.

BRITISH AND AMERICAN SPELLINGS

by James B. McMillan

The British and the Americans not only pronounce some words differently but also spell a good many differently. For instance a *tire* here is usually a *tyre* in England.

This dictionary does not enter many special British spellings. In reading books or papers written in Great Britain you are likely to come on five or six groups of words spelled in the British manner. Because some Americans like and use British spellings and some British people like and use ours, there are frequent exceptions. But in the main you will find the following groups of words spelled differently in the U.S. and Great Britain.

1. Words ending in -*or* in the U.S. such as *color, honor, humor, harbor,* and *neighbor* commonly end in -*our* in England, as *colour, honour, humour, harbour,* and *neighbour.* But when -*or* indicates the doer of some action, as *donor, operator,* or *governor* the British spelling is the same as ours.

2. Words ending in -*er* such as *center* and *meter* in the U.S. are likely to end in -*re* in England, as *centre* and *metre.* But in this country *theatre* is about as common as *theater.* And in England -*er* meaning *more,* as in *greener,* or meaning the doer of an action, as in *speaker,* are written -*er,* not -*re.*

3. Many verbs always ending in -*ize* in the U.S., such as *patronize,* have two spellings among the British, -*ise* or -*ize.* The ending -*ise,* as in *patronise,* seems a little more common.

In the main part of the dictionary, words shown or described in one of the three numbered paragraphs just above will carry the number of that paragraph. Of course they will have the usual U.S. spelling. But the number will let you know that the British have a different way of spelling them. If you turn back here you can find the difference. For instance, **rumor** carries the number **1.** If you turn to paragraph 1 you will see that the British spell it *rumour.*

The two groups that follow below are not numbered. The dictionary usually shows both U.S. and British spellings for words in the first group. The second talks about the British habit of putting in hyphens. You will not need to turn here to understand every hyphen you see in a British book.

Words with a single *l* at the end of a final, unaccented syllable, such as *channel, travel,* and *ravel* usually double the *l* in England before -*ed,* -*er,* or -*ing,* as in *channelled, traveller,* and *ravelling,* but do not double it in the U.S., as in *channeled, traveler,* and *raveling.*

Given a choice between a hyphenated word and a solid block, we tend to prefer the block, as in *nonpartisan, photoelectric, nonskid;* but the British choose the hyphen, as in *non-partisan, photo-electric, non-skid.*

A

a or **A** [ā] *n.*, *pl.* **a's** or **A's** **1** The first letter of the English alphabet. **2** *U.S.* The highest or best grade for school work.

a [ə *or* ā] An indefinite article used before nouns or noun phrases. It means: **1** One; one particular kind of: *Rice is a food.* **2** Any: Did you see *a man?* **3** Each; in each; for each; per: ten cents *a dozen.* ◆ See AN.

Aar·on [âr′ən *or* ar′ən] *n.* In the Bible, the first Hebrew high priest, the brother of Moses.

A.B. Abbreviation of BACHELOR OF ARTS.

a·back [ə·bak′] *adv.* Backward; behind. — **taken aback** Surprised; suddenly confused; upset.

ab·a·cus [ab′ə·kəs] *n.* A device using beads that slide on rods for adding, subtracting, etc.

a·baft [ə·baft′] **1** *adv.* Toward the stern; aft. **2** *prep.* Farther aft than: *abaft* the mainmast.

a·ba·lone [ab′ə·lō′nē] *n.* An edible shellfish having a flat shell lined with mother-of-pearl.

Chinese abacus set at 290,754. Upper beads count 5 each when lowered; lower beads count 1 each when raised.

a·ban·don [ə·ban′dən] **1** *v.* To give up wholly; forfeit: *abandon* all hope. **2** *v.* To leave; desert; forsake. **3** *n.* A giving up of self-control: to dance with *abandon.* **4** *v.* To yield (oneself) to feeling or impulse. — **a·ban′don·ment** *n.*

a·ban·doned [ə·ban′dənd] *adj.* **1** Deserted; left behind; forsaken. **2** Evil; shameless: an *abandoned* rascal.

a·base [ə·bās′] *v.* **a·based, a·bas·ing** To lower in rank or position; humble: His cowardly act *abased* him. — **a·base′ment** *n.*

a·bash [ə·bash′] *v.* To confuse or embarrass; shame: She was *abashed* by the applause.

a·bate [ə·bāt′] *v.* **a·bat·ed, a·bat·ing** To make or become less in value, force, or intensity: The wind *abated;* to *abate* noise. — **a·bate′ment** *n.*

ab·bess [ab′is] *n.* A woman who heads a group of nuns connected with an abbey.

ab·bey [ab′ē] *n.*, *pl.* **ab·beys** **1** A community of monks or nuns ruled by an abbot or an abbess; monastery or convent. **2** A church or building connected with a monastery or convent.

ab·bot [ab′ət] *n.* A man who heads a group of monks connected with an abbey.

ab·bre·vi·ate [ə·brē′vē·āt] *v.* **ab·bre·vi·at·ed, ab·bre·vi·at·ing** **1** To reduce (a word or phrase) to a short form standing for the whole: *New York* is *abbreviated* to *N.Y.* **2** To cut short or condense: He *abbreviated* his answer.

ab·bre·vi·a·tion [ə·brē′vē·ā′shən] *n.* **1** The act or process of abbreviating. **2** A shortened form of a word or phrase. ◆ *Abbreviation* and *contraction* both mean a shortened form, as of a word or phrase. An *abbreviation* is any shortened form, as *U.S.* for *United States.* A *contraction* is formed by leaving out something in the middle and closing up what is left, as *can't* for *cannot.*

ABC [ā′bē′sē′] *n.*, *pl.* **ABC's** **1** (*usually pl.*) The alphabet. **2** The basic or elementary part, as of a subject: the *ABC* of arithmetic.

ab·di·cate [ab′də·kāt] *v.* **ab·di·cat·ed, ab·di·cat·ing** **1** To resign from (the throne or other high position). **2** To give up a high position. — **ab′di·ca′tion** *n.*

ab·do·men [ab′də·mən *or* ab·dō′mən] *n.* **1** In animals with backbones, the part of the body that contains the digestive tract, in mammals below the chest and above the pelvis; belly. **2** In insects, the hindmost section of the body.

ab·dom·i·nal [ab·dom′ə·nəl] *adj.* Of, in, or having to do with the abdomen.

ab·duct [ab·dukt′] *v.* To carry off or lead away (a person) unlawfully; kidnap: She was *abducted* and held for ransom. — **ab·duc′tion** *n.* — **ab·duc′tor** *n.*

Abdomen of an ant

a·beam [ə·bēm′] *adv.* **1** Across a ship at right angles. **2** At one side about even with a ship: The tugboat came *abeam* of the freighter.

a·bed [ə·bed′] *adv.* In bed.

---

add, āce, câre, pälm;   end, ēqual;   it, īce;   odd, ōpen, ôrder;   tŏŏk, pōōl;   up, bûrn;
ə = a in *above*, e in *sicken*, i in *possible*, o in *melon*, u in *circus*;   y**ōō** = u in *fuse*;   oil;   pout;
check; ring; thin; this; zh in *vision*.   For ¶ reference, see page 64 · HOW TO

A·bel [ā′bəl] *n.* In the Bible, the second son of Adam, killed by his older brother Cain.

ab·er·ra·tion [ab′ə·rā′shən] *n.* **1** A departure from what is right, correct, or natural. **2** A mild mental disorder. **3** The failure of a lens or mirror to bring all light rays to a single focus.

a·bet [ə·bet′] *v.* **a·bet·ted, a·bet·ting** To encourage and help, especially in doing wrong: to *abet* a bank robber.

a·bey·ance [ə·bā′əns] *n.* A state of being held up or put aside for future action: The question was held in *abeyance* until a study was made.

ab·hor [ab·hôr′] *v.* **ab·horred, ab·hor·ring** To feel hatred or disgust for; loathe. ◆ See HATE.

ab·hor·rence [ab·hôr′əns] *n.* **1** A feeling of disgust, repulsion, or loathing. **2** Something that causes this feeling: Filth is an *abhorrence*.

ab·hor·rent [ab·hôr′ənt] *adj.* Causing abhorrence; repulsive; disgusting: *abhorrent* crimes.

a·bide [ə·bīd′] *v.* **a·bode** [ə·bōd′] or **a·bid·ed, a·bid·ing 1** To continue in a place; remain: to *abide* at home. **2** To last a long time: Evil shall not *abide*. **3** To wait for: He is *abiding* the coming of a better world. **4** To put up with; endure: I can't *abide* noise. **— abide by 1** To submit to and follow. **2** To fulfill: to *abide by* an agreement.

a·bid·ing [ə·bī′ding] *adj.* Continuing without changing or growing less: *abiding* love.

a·bil·i·ty [ə·bil′ə·tē] *n., pl.* **a·bil·i·ties 1** The quality or state of being able; power to do or perform. **2** (*pl.*) Talents. **3** Skill; craft: natural *ability* developed by coaching.

ab·ject [ab′jekt *or* ab·jekt′] *adj.* **1** Contemptible; low: an *abject* coward. **2** Hopelessly bad; crushing: *abject* poverty. **— ab′ject·ly** *adv.*

ab·jure [ab·jŏŏr′] *v.* **ab·jured, ab·jur·ing** To take an oath publicly to give up (a religion, belief, etc.).

a·blaze [ə·blāz′] *adj.* **1** In flames; blazing. **2** Very bright; brilliant: The lights were *ablaze*. **3** Excited; ardent: His anger was *ablaze*.

a·ble [ā′bəl] *adj.* **a·bler, a·blest 1** Having the power or whatever is needed to do something: He is *able* to run fast. **2** Skillful; competent: an *able* surgeon; an *able* performance.

-able A suffix meaning: **1** Capable of being, as in *adjustable*, capable of being adjusted. **2** Inclined or likely to, as in *changeable*, likely to change. **3** Fit to be, as in *lovable*, fit to be loved.

a·ble-bod·ied [ā′bəl·bod′ēd] *adj.* Strong and healthy; physically fit.

able-bodied seaman An experienced and skilled sailor.

ab·lu·tion [ə·blōō′shən] *n.* (*often pl.*) A washing or cleaning of the body, as in a religious ceremony.

a·bly [ā′blē] *adv.* With ability; skillfully.

ab·ne·ga·tion [ab′nə·gā′shən] *n.* Self-denial.

ab·nor·mal [ab·nôr′məl] *adj.* Not normal or average; unusual; irregular: Cats with six toes are *abnormal*. **— ab·nor′mal·ly** *adv.*

ab·nor·mal·i·ty [ab′nôr·mal′ə·tē] *n., pl.* **ab·nor·mal·i·ties** An abnormal thing or condition.

a·board [ə·bôrd′] **1** *adv.* On, in, or into a train, ship, etc.: Get *aboard*. **2** *prep.* On, in, or into: The boys played checkers while *aboard* the bus.

a·bode [ə·bōd′] **1** Past tense and past participle of ABIDE. **2** *n.* The place where one lives or stays; home; dwelling; residence.

a·bol·ish [ə·bol′ish] *v.* To do away with; put an end to; nullify: Bad laws should be *abolished*.

ab·o·li·tion [ab′ə·lish′ən] *n.* **1** The act of abolishing. **2** The state of being abolished. **3** The ending of slavery in the U.S.

ab·o·li·tion·ist [ab′ə·lish′ə·nist] *n.* **1** (*sometimes written* **Abolitionist**) One of the people who wanted to end slavery in the U.S. **2** A person who wants to abolish something.

A-bomb [ā′bom′] *n.* An atomic bomb.

a·bom·i·na·ble [ə·bom′in·ə·bəl] *adj.* **1** Very bad or disgusting. **2** Hateful. **— a·bom′i·na·bly** *adv.*

a·bom·i·nate [ə·bom′ə·nāt] *v.* **a·bom·i·nat·ed, a·bom·i·nat·ing** To think of with hate, loathing, or strong dislike.

a·bom·i·na·tion [ə·bom′ə·nā′shən] *n.* **1** Something abominable. **2** Strong loathing.

ab·o·rig·i·nal [ab′ə·rij′ə·nəl] *adj.* Of or having to do with aborigines; primitive.

ab·o·rig·i·ne [ab′ə·rij′ə·nē] *n.* (*often pl.*) One of the earliest people, plants, or animals known to have lived in a particular area.

a·bor·tion [ə·bôr′shən] *n.* **1** Birth before the offspring has developed enough to live. **2** A failure of anything before it develops.

a·bor·tive [ə·bôr′tiv] *adj.* **1** Coming to nothing; failing; futile: an *abortive* revolt. **2** Born while too undeveloped to live.

a·bound [ə·bound′] *v.* **1** To be abundant or in plentiful supply: Pigeons *abound* in some cities. **2** To teem or be filled: The world *abounds* with trees. **3** To be rich: Alaska *abounded* in gold.

a·bout [ə·bout′] **1** *prep.* Having to do with: a book *about* dogs. **2** *adv.* Close to; almost; approximately: *about* five dollars. **3** *adv.* Here and there: to wander *about*. **4** *prep.* Here and there in or on: to move *about* the room. **5** *prep.* Around; encircling: to spin *about* an axis; a wall *about* the city. **6** *adv.* Halfway around: Turn *about*. **7** *prep.* Just ready; on the point of: I was *about* to say that.

a·bout-face [*n.* ə·bout′fās′, *v.* ə·bout′fās′] *n., v.* **a·bout-faced, a·bout-fac·ing 1** *n.* A turn halfway around, to the rear. **2** *v.* To face or go in the opposite direction.

a·bove [ə·buv′] **1** *adv.* In a higher place; farther up: the sky *above*. **2** *prep.* Higher than; over: a shelf *above* the stove; Her grades are *above* average. **3** *prep.* Beyond; past: Turn left *above* the church. **4** *adv.* Earlier in a book, article, etc.: mentioned *above*. **5** *adj.* Already mentioned: the *above* instructions. **6** *prep.* Too good to stoop to; superior to: He's *above* lying. **— above all** Most important; first of all.

a·bove·board [ə·buv′bôrd′] *adv., adj.* Without deceit, fraud, or trickery; in open sight.

a·brade [ə·brād′] *v.* **a·brad·ed, a·brad·ing** To rub off; wear away: to *abrade* shoe soles.

A·bra·ham [ā'brə·ham] *n.* In the Bible, the ancestor and founder of the Hebrew people.

a·bra·sion [ə·brā'zhən] *n.* **1** A scraped area, as a skinned place. **2** The process of wearing or rubbing something away.

a·bra·sive [ə·brā'siv] **1** *adj.* Causing or tending to cause abrasion. **2** *n.* A hard material, as sand, used to rub or wear softer materials away.

a·breast [ə·brest'] *adv., adj.* Side by side: to walk three *abreast*. **— abreast of** or **abreast with** Even with; not behind: *abreast of* events.

a·bridge [ə·brij'] *v.* **a·bridged, a·bridg·ing** **1** To put into fewer words, as a book or speech. **2** To shorten, as in time: to *abridge* a lesson. **3** To deprive of or lessen: to *abridge* a right.

a·bridg·ment [ə·brij'mənt] *n.* **1** A reduction in length; an abridging. **2** A shortened or condensed version of a book, play, etc.

a·broad [ə·brôd'] *adv.* **1** Out of one's country; in or into foreign lands: to live *abroad*. **2** Out of one's home; outdoors: to stroll *abroad*. **3** At large; all around: Rumors are *abroad*.

ab·ro·gate [ab'rə·gāt] *v.* **ab·ro·gat·ed, ab·ro·gat·ing** To put an end to; annul; repeal: to *abrogate* a treaty. **— ab'ro·ga'tion** *n.*

a·brupt [ə·brupt'] *adj.* **1** Sudden: an *abrupt* turn. **2** Steep: an *abrupt* cliff. **3** Sudden; hasty: an *abrupt* departure. **4** Rude or curt, as in speech; brusque: He gave an *abrupt* answer. **— a·brupt'ly** *adv.* **— a·brupt'ness** *n.*

ab·scess [ab'ses] *n.* A collection of pus in some part of the body, resulting from an infection.

ab·scessed [ab'sest] *adj.* Having an abscess.

ab·scis·sa [ab·sis'ə] *n., pl.* **ab·scis·sas** or **ab·scis·sae** [ab·sis'ē] On a graph, the distance of a point from the vertical axis.

ab·scond [ab·skond'] *v.* To go away suddenly and hide: Fearing arrest, the racketeer *absconded*.

ab·sence [ab'səns] *n.* **1** The state of being away or not present: *absence* from home. **2** A period of being away: a week's *absence*. **3** Lack: an *absence* of vitamins in the diet.

The abscissa of *p* is 3.
The abscissa of *q* is −5.

ab·sent [*adj.* ab'sənt, *v.* ab·sent'] **1** *adj.* Not present; away: He was *absent* from work. **2** *v.* To take or keep (oneself) away: He *absented* himself from the meeting. **3** *adj.* Lacking; missing: If vitamin C is *absent*, scurvy is likely. **4** *adj.* Showing a lack of attention; preoccupied: an *absent* stare. **— ab'sent·ly** *adv.*

ab·sen·tee [ab'sən·tē'] *n.* A person who is absent, as from a job.

ab·sent-mind·ed [ab'sənt·mīn'did] *adj.* Not paying attention to what is happening around one; forgetful. **— ab'sent-mind'ed·ly** *adv.* **— ab'sent-mind'ed·ness** *n.*

ab·so·lute [ab'sə·lōōt] *adj.* **1** Having no restrictions; unlimited; unconditional: an *absolute* monarch. **2** Complete; perfect: *absolute* order. **3** Pure; unmixed: *absolute* alcohol. **4** Not relative to anything else: *absolute* temperature. **5** Positive; sure: *absolute* certainty.

ab·so·lute·ly [ab'sə·lōōt'lē *or* ab'sə·lōōt'lē] *adv.* **1** Completely. **2** Positively.

absolute zero In theory, the temperature at which molecular motion stops and all heat disappears, − 459.7° F. or − 273° C.

ab·so·lu·tion [ab'sə·lōō'shən] *n.* A release from guilt or punishment for sin; forgiveness.

ab·solve [ab·zolv'] *v.* **ab·solved, ab·solv·ing** **1** To declare (a sinner) free from sin, guilt, or penalty: The priest *absolved* him. **2** To release, as from a promise, obligation, or debt.

ab·sorb [ab·sôrb' *or* ab·zôrb'] *v.* **1** To take in and hold; suck in: Towels *absorb* water. **2** To take the full attention of; occupy fully: Music *absorbs* him. **3** To take in without reflecting back: Felt *absorbs* sound. **4** To take in and make part of itself: The city *absorbs* the suburbs.

ab·sor·bent [ab·sôr'bənt *or* ab·zôr'bənt] *adj.* Able to or tending to absorb.

ab·sorp·tion [ab·sôrp'shən *or* ab·zôrp'shən] *n.* **1** An absorbing. **2** Complete attention.

ab·stain [ab·stān'] *v.* **1** To keep oneself back; refrain by choice: He *abstains* from smoking. **2** To keep oneself back from voting: Six delegates *abstained*. **— ab·stain'er** *n.*

ab·ste·mi·ous [ab·stē'mē·əs] *adj.* Eating and drinking sparingly; temperate.

ab·sten·tion [ab·sten'shən] *n.* An abstaining or refraining, especially from voting.

ab·sti·nence [ab'stə·nəns] *n.* The doing without, fully or partly, of certain foods, drinks, habits, or pleasures.

ab·stract [*adj., n.* ab'strakt, *v.* ab·strakt'] **1** *adj.* Not dealing with anything specific or particular; general: an *abstract* idea of truth. **2** *adj.* Expressing a quality thought of as separated from any object possessing the quality: "Redness" is an *abstract* word. **3** *adj.* Made to offer a form or pattern rather than to represent real objects: *abstract* art. **4** *adj.* Hard to understand: Nuclear physics is very *abstract*. **5** *n.* A summary or outline covering the main points of a book, article, speech, etc. **6** *v.* [*sometimes* ab'strakt]

An abstract painting

---

add, āce, câre, pälm;   end, ēqual;   it, īce;   odd, ōpen, ôrder;   tŏŏk, pōōl;   up, bûrn;

ə = a in *above*, e in *sicken*, i in *possible*, o in *melon*, u in *circus*;   yōō = u in *fuse*;   oil;   pout;

check; ring; thin; this; zh in *vision*.   For ¶ reference, see page 64 · HOW TO

To make an abstract of, as a book, etc. **7** *v.* To remove or take away, especially in secret. **— in the abstract** In theory; without consideration of particular factors. **— ab·stract′ly** *adv.*

ab·stract·ed [ab·strak′tid] *adj.* Not paying attention; absent-minded. **— ab·stract′ed·ly** *adv.*

ab·strac·tion [ab·strak′shən] *n.* **1** An abstract idea, word, etc.: Mathematics deals with *abstractions.* **2** Absent-mindedness. **3** An abstract drawing, painting, sculpture, etc.

ab·struse [ab·stroos′] *adj.* Hard to understand.

ab·surd [ab·sûrd′ *or* ab·zûrd′] *adj.* Unreasonable; ridiculous: What an *absurd* tale!; The hat looks *absurd.* **— ab·surd′ly** *adv.*

ab·surd·i·ty [ab·sûr′də·tē *or* ab·zûr′də·tē] *n.*, *pl.* **ab·surd·i·ties 1** Foolishness; stupidity; nonsense: the *absurdity* of war. **2** An absurd statement, action, etc.

a·bun·dance [ə·bun′dəns] *n.* A full or plentiful supply; more than enough.

a·bun·dant [ə·bun′dənt] *adj.* **1** Existing in plentiful supply; ample. **2** Rich; abounding: Marshes *abundant* in wildfowl. **— a·bun′dant·ly** *adv.*

a·buse [*v.* ə·byooz′, *n.* ə·byoos′] *v.* **a·bused, a·bus·ing,** *n.* **1** *v.* To make wrong or improper use of: to *abuse* a privilege. **2** *n.* A wrong or improper use. **3** *v.* To treat harshly or cruelly. **4** *v.* To talk to or of harshly or scornfully. **5** *n.* Harsh or cruel treatment or words. **6** *n.* An improper or harmful practice, habit, etc.

a·bu·sive [ə·byoo′siv] *adj.* **1** Cruel or harsh: *abusive* treatment. **2** Harsh or insulting; scolding: *abusive* words. **— a·bu′sive·ly** *adv.*

a·but [ə·but′] *v.* **a·but·ted, a·but·ting** To end or border: Our lot *abuts* on the park.

a·but·ment [ə·but′mənt] *n.* A supporting structure for an arch or the end of a bridge, wall, etc.

a·bys·mal [ə·biz′məl] *adj.* Too deep to measure; bottomless; immeasurable: *abysmal* stupidity. **— a·bys′mal·ly** *adv.*

a·byss [ə·bis′] *n.* **1** A bottomless space, as a crack in the earth; chasm. **2** The lowest depth, too deep to measure: an *abyss* of shame.

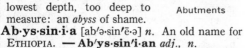

Abutments

Ab·ys·sin·i·a [ab′ə·sin′ē·ə] *n.* An old name for ETHIOPIA. **— Ab′ys·sin′i·an** *adj., n.*

a.c. *or* **A.C.** Abbreviation of ALTERNATING CURRENT.

a·ca·cia [ə·kā′shə] *n.* **1** A tree or shrub found in warm regions, having feathery leaves and small, usually yellow flowers. **2** The locust tree.

ac·a·dem·ic [ak′ə·dem′ik] *adj.* **1** Of or having to do with schools, colleges, or studies; scholarly. **2** *U.S.* Having to do with general or liberal rather than technical education. **3** Having little or no practical use; theoretical: It is *academic* to discuss the distant future. **— ac′a·dem′i·cal·ly** *adv.*

a·cad·e·my [ə·kad′ə·mē] *n., pl.* **a·cad·e·mies 1** A private high school or preparatory school. **2** A school for a particular field of study: a military *academy.* **3** An association of learned men working to promote the arts or sciences.

a cap·pel·la [ä′kə·pel′ə] Sung without instrumental accompaniment.

ac·cede [ak·sēd′] *v.* **ac·ced·ed, ac·ced·ing 1** To give consent or agreement; say yes: to *accede* to a plea. **2** To come or enter, as to a high office: to *accede* to the throne.

ac·cel·er·ate [ak·sel′ə·rāt] *v.* **ac·cel·er·at·ed, ac·cel·er·at·ing 1** To increase speed or the speed of: The car *accelerated*; to *accelerate* the motor. **2** To cause to happen sooner: Zip codes *accelerate* delivery.

ac·cel·er·a·tion [ak·sel′ə·rā′shən] *n.* **1** An increase in speed or velocity. **2** Any change in velocity. **3** The rate of such change at any instant.

ac·cel·er·a·tor [ak·sel′ə·rā′tər] *n.* **1** Something that accelerates, especially a machine that gives very high speeds to atomic particles. **2** The pedal controlling the speed of an automobile engine.

ac·cent [*n.* ak′sent, *v.* ak′sent *or* ak·sent′] **1** *n.* The additional force given to some words or syllables in speech; stress. **2** *v.* To pronounce with force: *Accent* the first syllable of "every." **3** *n.* A mark showing where the stress is located in a word, often (′) for a strong stress and (′) for a weaker one. **4** *v.* To provide with marks showing stressed syllables. **5** *n.* In some languages, a mark placed over or under a letter to show a special pronunciation. **6** *n.* A manner of speaking characteristic of a region or foreign country: a French *accent.* **7** *n.* In music, the stress given to a tone or chord by position, loudness, etc. **8** *n.* Emphasis. **9** *v.* To emphasize: to *accent* the horror of war.

ac·cen·tu·ate [ak·sen′choo·āt] *v.* **ac·cen·tu·at·ed, ac·cen·tu·at·ing 1** To strengthen the effect of; emphasize; stress: Her dress *accentuates* her height. **2** To mark or pronounce with an accent. **— ac·cen′tu·a′tion** *n.*

ac·cept [ak·sept′] *v.* **1** To take (something offered or given): to *accept* a gift. **2** To agree to; answer with a yes: to *accept* an offer. **3** To receive with warmth, as a person; approve. **4** To take as truth: to *accept* a theory. **5** To adjust to; submit to: to *accept* reality. **6** To agree to an offer, invitation, etc.: He invited me and I *accepted.* ✦ See EXCEPT.

ac·cept·a·ble [ak·sep′tə·bəl] *adj.* Good enough to be accepted; pleasing; welcome. **— ac·cept′a·bly** *adv.* **— ac·cept′a·bil′i·ty** *n.*

ac·cep·tance [ak·sep′təns] *n.* **1** The act of accepting: The union's *acceptance* of the wage offer ended the strike. **2** The condition of being accepted. **3** Recognition or approval: the *acceptance* of an idea.

ac·cess [ak′ses] *n.* **1** The opportunity to approach, get, or enter: *access* to court records. **2** A means of entrance; passage; path.

ac·ces·si·ble [ak·ses′ə·bəl] *adj.* **1** Possible to reach; obtainable. **2** Easily reached or got at. — **ac·ces′si·bil′i·ty** *n.*

ac·ces·sion [ak·sesh′ən] *n.* **1** An attaining of an office, dignity, or right: *accession* to power. **2** An increase by something added: an *accession* of land. **3** An addition, as a book to a library.

ac·ces·so·ry [ak·ses′ə·rē] *n.*, *pl.* **ac·ces·so·ries,** *adj.* **1** *n.* Something added for looks, comfort, or convenience, as a belt, gloves, and purse to go with a dress. **2** *adj.* Added to a main thing; helping: an *accessory* benefit. **3** *n.* A person who knowingly helps or encourages another to commit a crime, or who helps or hides the criminal after the crime.

ac·ci·dent [ak′sə·dənt] *n.* **1** Something that happens unexpectedly or without plan or design. **2** An unlucky event that causes damage or harm, such as a collision, fall, etc. **3** Chance; luck: It happened by *accident*.

An automobile accident

ac·ci·den·tal [ak′sə·den′təl] **1** *adj.* Occurring unexpectedly and without plan; chance. **2** *n.* In music, a sharp, flat, or natural that applies in only one measure. — **ac′ci·den′tal·ly** *adv.*

ac·claim [ə·klām′] **1** *v.* To hail and declare by acclamation: They *acclaimed* him king. **2** *v.* To show approval of; applaud: They *acclaimed* the plan. **3** *n.* Praise; applause; approval.

ac·cla·ma·tion [ak′lə·mā′shən] *n.* **1** A shout or some other indication of general approval or welcome: to vote by *acclamation*. **2** Acclaim or the act of acclaiming.

ac·cli·mate [ə·klī′mit *or* ak′lə·māt] *v.* **ac·cli·mat·ed, ac·cli·mat·ing** To adapt or become adapted to new surroundings or a new climate: The plant *acclimated* to cold weather.

ac·cli·ma·tize [ə·klī′mə·tīz] *v.* **ac·cli·ma·tized, ac·cli·ma·tiz·ing** Another word for ACCLIMATE. ¶3

ac·co·lade [ak′ə·lād] *n.* **1** A light blow with the flat side of a sword, given to a man when he is made a knight. **2** Any great honor or praise.

ac·com·mo·date [ə·kom′ə·dāt] *v.* **ac·com·mo·dat·ed, ac·com·mo·dat·ing** **1** To hold comfortably; be suitable for: The cage *accommodates* two birds. **2** To provide for; lodge: to *accommodate* a guest. **3** To do a favor for; help. **4** To change so as to be fit; acclimate; adjust: to *accommodate* oneself to a new climate.

ac·com·mo·dat·ing [ə·kom′ə·dā′ting] *adj.* Helpful and eager to please; obliging; willing.

ac·com·mo·da·tion [ə·kom′ə·dā′shən] *n.* **1** An adjustment. **2** Anything that supplies a need; convenience. **3** (*usually pl.*) *U.S.* Room and board; lodgings. **4** A compromise or agreement:

The two sides made an *accommodation*. **5** A favor; good turn. **6** Willingness to help or oblige.

ac·com·pa·ni·ment [ə·kum′pə·ni·mənt] *n.* **1** Something going along with something else: corned beef with cabbage as an *accompaniment*. **2** Music played or sung along with the main part to enrich and support it.

ac·com·pa·nist [ə·kum′pə·nist] *n.* A person, usually a pianist, who plays accompaniments.

ac·com·pa·ny [ə·kum′pə·nē] *v.* **ac·com·pa·nied, ac·com·pa·ny·ing** **1** To come or go along with; escort: *Accompany* me home. **2** To happen or occur with: Flies *accompany* filth. **3** To play a musical accompaniment to or for.

ac·com·plice [ə·kom′plis] *n.* A helper or partner in committing a crime.

ac·com·plish [ə·kom′plish] *v.* **1** To carry out; effect: to *accomplish* a change. **2** To finish.

ac·com·plished [ə·kom′plisht] *adj.* **1** Finished; completed: The job is *accomplished*. **2** Skillful, as in an art or in social graces; well-trained.

ac·com·plish·ment [ə·kom′plish·mənt] *n.* **1** The act of accomplishing; completion. **2** Something done or completed; achievement. **3** A skill or ability, especially a social grace.

ac·cord [ə·kôrd′] **1** *v.* To give as due or earned; grant: *Accord* honor to the winner. **2** *v.* To be or cause to be in agreement: to *accord* with the facts. **3** *n.* A state of agreement or concord; harmony: After discussion they reached an *accord*. — **of one's own accord** By one's own choice; voluntarily.

ac·cord·ance [ə·kôr′dəns] *n.* Agreement, especially in the expression **in accordance with.**

ac·cord·ing [ə·kôr′ding] *adj.* In accord or agreement; harmonizing. — **according to 1** As told by or in: *according to* the book. **2** In agreement with; by: *according to* the law. **3** In proportion to; in harmony with: to dress *according to* how cold it is.

ac·cord·ing·ly [ə·kôr′ding·lē] *adv.* **1** In a fitting manner: Seeing danger, he acted *accordingly*. **2** Therefore; thus; so.

ac·cor·di·on [ə·kôr′dē·ən] **1** *n.* A portable musical instrument in which wind from a bellows, controlled by keys or buttons, causes metal reeds to sound. **2** *adj.* Looking like the folds in the bellows of an accordion: *accordion* pleats.

ac·cost [ə·kôst′ *or* ə·kost′] *v.* To stop and speak to; speak to first: A stranger *accosted* him.

Accordion

ac·count [ə·kount′] **1** *v.* To hold to be; consider: I *account* that a lie. **2** *n.* A statement, narrative, or explanation. **3** *n.* A record of money paid out, received, or owing. **4** *n.* Worth; importance: That boy is of no

---

add, āce, câre, pälm; end, ēqual; it, īce; odd, ōpen, ôrder; to͞ok, po͞ol; up, bûrn;
ə = a in *above*, e in *sicken*, i in *possible*, o in *melon*, u in *circus*; yo͞o = u in *fuse*; oil; pout;
check; ring; thin; this; zh in *vision*. For ¶ reference, see page 64 · HOW TO

account. **— account for 1** To give an explanation of: Shooting stars are easy to *account for.* **2** To be responsible for; answer for: to *account for* a decision. **— call to account** To insist on an explanation from: He was *called to account* for his errors. **— on account of** Because of; for the sake of: The airport was closed *on account of* fog. **— on no account** Under no conditions; never. **— turn to account** To use to get profit or advantage.

ac·count·a·ble [ə·kount′ə·bəl] *adj.* **1** Liable to be called to account; responsible: to be *accountable* for damage. **2** Capable of being explained.

ac·count·ant [ə·koun′tənt] *n.* A person whose work is to keep or go over records of money received or paid out: My *accountant* figures my income tax.

ac·count·ing [ə·koun′ting] *n.* **1** The practice or methods of recording financial dealings. **2** A statement or examination, as of finances, etc.

ac·cou·ter [ə·kōō′tər] *v.* To provide with clothing or equipment; outfit.

ac·cou·ter·ments [ə·kōō′tər·mənts] *n.pl.* **1** The equipment of a soldier except for weapons and uniforms. **2** Trappings; outfit.

ac·cou·tre [ə·kōō′tər] *v.* **ac·cou·tred, ac·cou·tring** Another spelling of ACCOUTER.

ac·cou·tre·ments [ə·kōō′trə·mənts] *n.pl.* Another spelling of ACCOUTERMENTS.

ac·cred·it [ə·kred′it] *v.* **1** To give official authority or credentials to: to *accredit* an ambassador. **2** To take as true; believe in: to *accredit* a report. **3** To accept as meeting official standards, as a college, school, or hospital.

ac·cre·tion [ə·krē′shən] *n.* **1** Growth or increase, especially by external addition or accumulation. **2** An increase or addition; something additional.

ac·crue [ə·krōō′] *v.* **ac·crued, ac·cru·ing** To come about as a natural growth, addition, or result; accumulate: Unpaid taxes *accrue* rapidly.

ac·cu·mu·late [ə·kyōōm′yə·lāt] *v.* **ac·cu·mu·lat·ed, ac·cu·mu·lat·ing** To heap or pile up; gather together; collect: He *accumulated* a fortune; Dirt *accumulates* quickly.

ac·cu·mu·la·tion [ə·kyōōm′yə·lā′shən] *n.* **1** Material gathered together: an *accumulation* of snow six feet deep. **2** A collecting or gathering together: Blowers prevent *accumulation* of gas.

ac·cu·ra·cy [ak′yər·ə·sē] *n.* Freedom from all errors or mistakes; exactness; precision.

ac·cu·rate [ak′yər·it] *adj.* Having or making no error; exact; true: *accurate* work; an *accurate* barometer. **— ac′cu·rate·ly** *adv.*

ac·curs·ed [ə·kûr′sid *or* ə·kûrst′] *adj.* **1** Deserving a curse; damnable. **2** Cursed; doomed.

ac·cu·sa·tion [ak′yōō·zā′shən] *n.* **1** A charge of having done something wrong or illegal or of being something bad. **2** The offense charged.

ac·cu·sa·tive [ə·kyōō′zə·tiv] **1** *adj.* In grammar, showing a direct object or a word agreeing with one. *Him, them,* and *whom* are in the accusative, or objective, case. **2** *n.* The accusative case. **3** *n.* A word in this case.

ac·cuse [ə·kyōōz′] *v.* **ac·cused, ac·cus·ing** To charge with having done something wrong or illegal or with being bad. **— ac·cus′er** *n.*

ac·cus·tom [ə·kus′təm] *v.* To make familiar or adapted by habit: to *accustom* oneself to noise.

ac·cus·tomed [ə·kus′təmd] *adj.* Habitual; usual: at the *accustomed* hour. **— accustomed to** In the habit of; used to.

ace [ās] *n.* **1** A single spot, as on a playing card, domino, etc. **2** A playing card, etc., marked with a single spot. **3** A person who is an expert at something. **4** *adj. use:* an *ace* repairman. **5** In tennis, etc., a point won by a single stroke. **— within an ace of** Very close to; to the brink of: He was *within an ace of* winning when his car broke down.

ac·e·tate [as′ə·tāt] *n.* **1** A chemical compound made from acetic acid, as one of its salts. **2** Cellulose acetate, a compound made from acetic acid and cellulose, used in making rayon.

a·ce·tic acid [ə·sē′tik] A weak, sharp-smelling acid that is found in vinegar.

a·cet·y·lene [ə·set′ə·lēn] *n.* A colorless gas, burned in air to make light, and with oxygen to produce heat for welding, etc.

ache [āk] *v.* **ached, ach·ing,** *n.* **1** *v.* To hurt with a dull, steady pain: My eyes *ache.* **2** *n.* A dull, steady pain. **3** *v.* To want very much: I'm *aching* to go.

a·chieve [ə·chēv′] *v.* **a·chieved, a·chiev·ing** **1** To accomplish; do well: Flight was *achieved* in 1903. **2** To get or reach by effort: to *achieve* a goal.

a·chieve·ment [ə·chēv′mənt] *n.* **1** Something accomplished; a feat. **2** The act of achieving.

A·chil·les [ə·kil′ēz] *n.* In Greek myths, the greatest Greek hero of the Trojan war, killed by an arrow shot into his right heel, the only place where he could be wounded.

ac·id [as′id] **1** *n.* A chemical compound having a sour taste and the ability to react with a base, forming water and a salt. Acids corrode most metals and some destroy living tissue. **2** *adj.* Of, like, producing, or containing an acid. **3** *adj.* Biting; sharp; bad-tempered: an *acid* remark. **— ac′id·ly** *adv.*

a·cid·i·ty [ə·sid′ə·tē] *n.* The state, degree, or quality of being acid: high *acidity.*

ac·knowl·edge [ak·nol′ij] *v.* **ac·knowl·edged, ac·knowl·edg·ing** **1** To admit the truth or reality of: He *acknowledged* his failure. **2** To recognize as; state to be: They *acknowledged* him their leader. **3** To show that one has received or is thankful for: to *acknowledge* a letter or gift.

ac·knowl·edg·ment [ak·nol′ij·mənt] *n.* **1** The act of acknowledging; recognition; acceptance. **2** Something done or given to show that one has received something or is thankful for something.

ac·me [ak′mē] *n.* The highest point; peak; summit: the *acme* of conceit.

ac·ne [ak′nē] *n.* A skin disease due to clogged oil glands and causing pimples on the face and upper body.

ac·o·lyte [ak′ə·līt] *n.* A helper or assistant, especially an altar boy who assists at Mass.

ac·o·nite [ak′ə·nīt] *n.* **1** The monkshood or any of several related plants, some poisonous. **2** A sedative drug obtained from these plants.

a·corn [ā′kôrn] *n.* The fruit of the oak tree, a nut containing a single seed.

a·cous·tic [ə·kōōs′tik] *adj.* Of or having to do with sound or hearing. **— a·cous′ti·cal· ly** *adv.*

a·cous·tics [ə·kōōs′tiks] *n.* **1** The science that deals with sound. **2** The qualities of a room that affect sounds. ◆ See -ICS.

Acorn

ac·quaint [ə·kwānt′] *v.* **1** To make familiar; inform: I *acquainted* him with what went on in his absence. **2** *adj. use:* I'm *acquainted* with her.

ac·quain·tance [ə·kwān′təns] *n.* **1** Personal knowledge of a person or thing. **2** A person with whom one is slightly familiar. **— make someone's acquaintance** To get to know someone.

ac·qui·esce [ak′wē·es′] *v.* **ac·qui·esced, ac·qui·esc·ing** To give in or consent quietly: to *acquiesce* to a demand; to *acquiesce* in a plan.

ac·qui·es·cent [ak′wē·es′ənt] *adj.* Giving in or consenting quietly. **— ac′qui·es′cence** *n.*

ac·quire [ə·kwīr′] *v.* **ac·quired, ac·quir·ing 1** To come to own; get; obtain: to *acquire* wealth. **2** *adj. use:* an *acquired* trait.

ac·quire·ment [ə·kwīr′mənt] *n.* **1** The act of acquiring. **2** Something acquired, especially a skill or ability gained after much effort.

ac·qui·si·tion [ak′wə·zish′ən] *n.* **1** The act of acquiring. **2** Something that is acquired: His new *acquisitions* are rare French stamps.

ac·quis·i·tive [ə·kwiz′ə·tiv] *adj.* Anxious to acquire things. **— ac·quis′i·tive·ness** *n.*

ac·quit [ə·kwit′] *v.* **ac·quit·ted, ac·quit·ting 1** To free from blame; declare not guilty: to be *acquitted* of a crime. **2** To conduct (oneself); do one's part: He *acquitted* himself like a hero.

ac·quit·tal [ə·kwit′(ə)l] *n.* A setting free from a criminal charge by a verdict of not guilty.

a·cre [ā′kər] *n.* **1** A measure of area equal to 43,560 square feet. **2** (*pl.*) Lands; estate: *acres* of tall corn. ◆ This word comes from an Old English word meaning *field.*

a·cre·age [ā′kər·ij] *n.* **1** The number of acres in an area: The campus has an *acreage* of 400. **2** Land sold by the acre.

ac·rid [ak′rid] *adj.* **1** Burning; bitter; irritating, as a taste or odor. **2** Sharp; biting; acid, as a remark.

ac·ri·mo·ni·ous [ak′rə·mō′nē·əs] *adj.* Full of bitterness and hard feelings; sharp; caustic: an *acrimonious* argument.

ac·ri·mo·ny [ak′rə·mō′nē] *n.* Bitterness or hard feeling, especially in speech or manner.

ac·ro·bat [ak′rə·bat] *n.* A person skilled in tumbling, stunts on a trapeze, rings, etc.

ac·ro·bat·ic [ak′rə·bat′ik] *n.* Of or like an acrobat: an *acrobatic* stunt.

ac·ro·bat·ics [ak′rə·bat′iks] *n.pl.* Stunts performed by or as if by an acrobat; gymnastics. ◆ See -ICS.

Acrobats

a·crop·o·lis [ə·krop′ə·lis] *n.* **1** A high part of an ancient Greek city, fortified in case of attack. **2** (*written* **Acropolis**) The high, fortified part of ancient Athens.

a·cross [ə·krôs′ *or* ə·kros′] **1** *adv.* From one side to the other: five feet *across*. **2** *adv.* On or at the other side: We soon will be *across*. **3** *prep.* On the other side of; beyond. **4** *prep.* From one side or part of to the other: to ride *across* a field. **5** *prep.* So as to meet or happen on: to come *across* a lost glove.

act [akt] **1** *n.* Something done; deed; action. **2** *n.* A process; activity: in the *act* of eating. **3** *v.* To do something; function; perform: to *act* in an emergency. **4** *v.* To behave; acquit oneself: to *act* bravely. **5** *n.* A pretense; sham: Her shyness was an *act*. **6** *v.* To pretend; make believe: She's only *acting*. **7** *v.* To imitate; behave like: Don't *act* the fool. **8** *v.* To perform, as in a drama or play: to *act* Hamlet. **9** *n.* A large division of a play or opera. **10** *n.* One of a number of performances on a program: a comedy *act*. **11** *v.* To have an effect: Sunlight *acts* on plants. **12** *n.* A law; statute: an *act* of the legislature. **— act as** To function in a particular way: to *act as* a control. **— act for** To substitute for; work on behalf of. **— act on** To do something because of: to *act on* someone's advice. **— act up** *informal* To behave mischievously or playfully.

ACTH A hormone from the pituitary gland that causes the adrenal glands to produce cortisone. ACTH from hogs makes human beings produce cortisone.

act·ing [ak′ting] *adj.* Holding office temporarily or in someone's place: the *acting* mayor.

ac·tion [ak′shən] *n.* **1** The process of acting, doing, or working. **2** A deed; act. **3** (*pl.*) Habitual behavior; conduct: the *actions* of an idiot. **4** Vigor; energy; initiative: a man of *action*. **5** Influence: the *action* of sunlight on colors. **6** The way a mechanism moves or works: The spring's *action* is fast. **7** A battle; combat: killed in *action*. **8** A lawsuit. **— take action 1** To start to do something; begin to operate. **2** To start a lawsuit.

ac·ti·vate [ak′tə·vāt] *v.* **ac·ti·vat·ed, ac·ti·vat·ing** To make active. **— ac′ti·va′tion** *n.*

ac·tive [ak'tiv] **1** *adj.* Showing action; busy: an *active* man. **2** *adj.* Working; in action: an *active* volcano. **3** *adj.* Indicating a verb whose subject performs its action. In the sentence "Mary kicked her sister" *kicked* is active. **4** *n.* The form of a verb that is active; active voice. — **ac'tive·ly** *adv.*

ac·tiv·i·ty [ak·tiv'ə·tē] *n., pl.* **ac·tiv·i·ties** **1** The state of being active; action; movement. **2** An action: the *activities* of bandits in the hills. **3** An occupation or pastime: to keep busy with many *activities*.

ac·tor [ak'tər] *n.* **1** A person who performs in plays, motion pictures, etc. **2** A person who acts; doer.

ac·tress [ak'tris] *n.* A female actor.

Acts of the Apostles The fifth book of the New Testament, relating the beginnings of the Christian church.

ac·tu·al [ak'chōō·əl] *adj.* Existing in fact; real.

ac·tu·al·i·ty [ak'chōō·al'ə·tē] *n.* The condition of being actual; reality.

ac·tu·al·ly [ak'chōō·əl·ē] *adv.* As a matter of fact; really: The cripple *actually* walked.

ac·tu·ate [ak'chōō·āt] *v.* **ac·tu·at·ed, ac·tu·at·ing** **1** To put into action: valves *actuated* by cams. **2** To impel to act: He was *actuated* by fear.

a·cu·men [ə·kyōō'mən] *n.* Quickness and sharpness of mind; shrewdness: business *acumen*.

a·cute [ə·kyōōt'] *adj.* **1** Coming to a sharp point. **2** Reaching a crisis quickly; severe, as a disease. **3** Sharp; intense: *acute* pain. **4** Extremely important; critical; grave: *acute* problems. **5** Very perceptive or sensitive; keen: an *acute* ear. **6** High in pitch; shrill. — **a·cute'·ly** *adv.* — **a·cute'ness** *n.*

acute accent A mark (') used in some languages over a vowel to show its length or quality or to show stress.

acute angle An angle of less than 90 degrees.

ad [ad] *n. informal* An advertisement.

A.D. Abbreviation of Anno Domini, a Latin phrase meaning "in the year of the Lord." It indicates dates after the birth of Christ: A.D. 43.

right angle   acute angle

ad·age [ad'ij] *n.* An old, much-used saying generally thought to be true; proverb: "Out of sight, out of mind" is an *adage*.

a·da·gio [ə·dä'jō *or* e·dä'zhē·ō] *n., pl.* **a·da·gios** **1** *adj.* In music, slow. **2** *adv.* Slowly. **3** *n.* A section of music which is slow.

Ad·am [ad'əm] *n.* In the Bible, the first man.

ad·a·mant [ad'ə·mənt] **1** *n.* A stone or material too hard to be broken. **2** *adj.* Unyielding; stubborn.

Ad·ams [ad'əmz], **John,** 1735–1826, U.S. statesman and second president of the U.S., 1797–1801.

Ad·ams [ad'əmz], **John Quincy,** 1767–1848, U.S. statesman and sixth president of the U.S., 1825–1829. He was the son of John Adams.

Ad·ams [ad'əmz], **Samuel,** 1722–1803, American patriot, signer of the Declaration of Independence.

Ad·am's apple [ad'əmz] A lump at the front of the throat, formed by the thyroid cartilage, often prominent in men.

Adam's apple

a·dapt [ə·dapt'] *v.* **1** To change and make suitable for a new use: to *adapt* a play for television. **2** To adjust to new conditions: The polar bear has *adapted* itself to the Arctic.

a·dapt·a·ble [ə·dap'tə·bəl] *adj.* Changed or changing easily to fit conditions. — **a·dapt'a·bil'i·ty** *n.*

ad·ap·ta·tion [ad'əp·tā'shən] *n.* **1** A change made or the process of changing, so as to fit or meet new conditions, uses, or surroundings. **2** Something made by adapting: The play is an *adaptation* of the book.

add [ad] *v.* **1** To find a number equal to (two or more other numbers taken together). **2** To increase by; put together with: to *add* a room to a house. **3** To say or write as an extra thought or idea; include: Let me *add* that this is tiring. — **add to** To increase; make larger. — **add up to 1** To make a total of: Five and five *add up to* ten. **2** To combine to signify; mean: Those actions *add up to* a crime.

ad·dend [ad'ənd *or* ə·dend'] *n.* A number or quantity that is added or to be added.

ad·der [ad'ər] *n.* **1** A small, poisonous, European snake; viper. **2** A small, nonpoisonous North American snake. ◆ This word was originally *nadder*, but people saying *a nadder* began to attach the *n* to the article, not the noun, which became *an adder*.

ad·dict [*v.* ə·dikt', *n.* ad'ikt] **1** *v.* To yield (oneself) by habit: He was *addicted* to alcohol. **2** *n.* A slave to a habit, especially the taking of narcotic drugs. — **ad·dic'tion** *n.*

adding machine A machine, having a keyboard, that can perform addition and sometimes subtraction, multiplication, and division.

ad·di·tion [ə·dish'ən] *n.* **1** The act or process of adding: The *addition* of several numbers. **2** Something that is added; an annex. — **in addition** or **in addition to** Besides; also. ◆ *Addition*, something added, and *edition*, something published, are sometimes confused. *Addition* is from the Latin word *addere*, meaning *to give to*, while *edition* is from Latin *edere*, meaning *to give out*.

ad·di·tion·al [ə·dish'ən·əl] *adj.* Added or to be added; extra. — **ad·di'tion·al·ly** *adv.*

ad·di·tive [ad'ə·tiv] *n.* A substance added in small quantities to improve a product in some way: *Additives* make gasoline burn better.

ad·dle [ad'(ə)l] *v.* **ad·dled, ad·dling 1** To become or cause to become confused or muddled. **2** *adj. use: addled* brains. **3** To spoil, as eggs.

ad·dress [ə·dres′] **1** *v.* To speak to or deliver a speech to: He *addressed* the audience. **2** *n.* A speech. **3** *n.* [*also* ad′res] The writing on an envelope or package telling where it is to go, or the place thus indicated. **4** *v.* To write on (a letter, package, etc.) where it is to go. **5** *v.* To direct or send: to *address* a plea. **6** *v.* To direct the force or attention of (oneself): Let us *address* ourselves to the problem.

ad·dress·ee [ad′res·ē′] *n.* The person to whom mail, a package, etc., is addressed.

ad·duce [ə·d(y)ōōs′] *v.* **ad·duced, ad·duc·ing** To offer as proof or as an example.

ad·e·noids [ad′ə·noidz] *n.pl.* Growths of glandular tissue in the passage from the nose to the throat. When swollen they make breathing and speaking difficult.

a·dept [ə·dept′] **1** *adj.* Skillful; adroit: *adept* at tennis. **2** [*also* ad′ept] *n.* A person highly skilled or expert. **— a·dept′ly** *adv.*

ad·e·qua·cy [ad′ə·kwə·sē] *n.* The state or quality of being sufficient or good enough.

ad·e·quate [ad′ə·kwit] *adj.* Equal to what is needed; good enough or sufficient: *adequate* food for the dinner. **— ad′e·quate·ly** *adv.*

ad·here [ad·hir′] *v.* **ad·hered, ad·her·ing** **1** To stick fast or stick together: Gum makes a stamp *adhere*. **2** To hold or remain devoted: to *adhere* to one's principles. **3** To follow closely: to *adhere* to a plan.

ad·her·ence [ad·hir′əns] *n.* The act or state of adhering; attachment; faithfulness.

ad·her·ent [ad·hir′ənt] **1** *n.* A loyal supporter; faithful follower. **2** *adj.* Sticking tightly; attached.

ad·he·sion [ad·hē′zhən] *n.* **1** A sticking together. **2** Firm attachment, as to a cause.

ad·he·sive [ad·hē′siv] **1** *adj.* Designed or tending to stick fast; sticky: *adhesive* tape. **2** *n.* An adhesive substance, as glue.

a·dieu [ə·d(y)ōō′] *interj., n., pl.* **a·dieus** or **a·dieux** [ə·d(y)ōōz′] Good-by.

ad in·fi·ni·tum [ad in′fə·nī′təm] A Latin phrase meaning: To infinity; without stopping; endlessly: He talked *ad infinitum*.

a·di·os [ä′dē·ōs′ *or* ad′ē·ōs′] *interj.* Good-by.

ad·i·pose [ad′ə·pōs] *adj.* Of or having to do with animal fat; fatty.

Ad·i·ron·dacks [ad′ə·ron′daks] *n.pl.* A mountain range in NE New York. Also **Adirondack Mountains.**

adj. Abbreviation of: **1** ADJECTIVE. **2** ADJECTIVAL.

ad·ja·cent [ə·jā′sənt] *adj.* Lying near or close by; adjoining: *adjacent* countries.

adjacent angle Either of two angles that have the same vertex, a side in common, and their second rays on opposite sides of the common ray.

Adjacent angles

ad·jec·ti·val [aj′ik·tī′vəl] *adj.* Having to do with or used as an adjective. **— ad′·jec·ti′val·ly** *adv.*

ad·jec·tive [aj′ik·tiv] *n.* A word that is used to limit or tell something about a noun, as *purple* in "She held a purple flower," or *hot* in "The water was hot."

ad·join [ə·join′] *v.* **1** To be next to; border on: Our yard *adjoins* his lawn. **2** To be close together or in contact: The two houses *adjoin*.

ad·journ [ə·jûrn′] *v.* **1** To stop with the intention of beginning again later, as a meeting: The court was *adjourned*. **2** To reach the end of a session or time of meeting: The legislature *adjourned* for the year. **— ad·journ′ment** *n.*

ad·judge [ə·juj′] *v.* **ad·judged, ad·judg·ing** **1** To determine or declare, especially legally or formally: The man was *adjudged* insane. **2** To award by law: The accident victim was *adjudged* $50,000.

ad·junct [aj′ungkt] *n.* Something added to a main thing, less important and not needed, but helpful.

ad·jure [ə·jŏŏr′] *v.* **ad·jured, ad·jur·ing** **1** To ask earnestly; entreat: She *adjured* the Indians to spare her son. **2** To command or charge solemnly. **— ad′ju·ra′tion** *n.*

ad·just [ə·just′] *v.* **1** To arrange so as to fit or match: to *adjust* stirrups for a tall rider. **2** To regulate for a desired result: to *adjust* a thermostat. **3** To arrange in a satisfactory way; settle: to *adjust* a claim for insurance. **4** To adapt oneself; get accustomed: to *adjust* to the climate.

ad·just·a·ble [ə·jus′tə·bəl] *adj.* Capable of being changed or regulated: an *adjustable* focus.

ad·just·er [ə·jus′tər] *n.* A person who adjusts, especially one who adjusts insurance claims.

An adjustable hospital bed

ad·just·ment [ə·just′mənt] *n.* **1** The act or process of adjusting or the state of being adjusted; regulation; arrangement. **2** A means of adjusting; a control. **3** A settlement or reconciling, as of a disagreement, claim, debt, etc.

ad·ju·tant [aj′ōō·tənt] *n.* An officer who helps a commanding officer by preparing orders, writing letters, keeping records, etc.

ad·lib [ad′lib′] *v.* **ad·libbed, ad·lib·bing** *informal* To invent or make up (a speech, musical passage, etc.) on the spot.

ad·min·is·ter [ad·min′is·tər] *v.* **1** To be in charge of; manage: He *administers* the hospital. **2** To give, as a medicine: to *administer* aspirin for a headache. **3** To give out, as a punishment: to *administer* the death penalty. **4** To give, as an oath or sacrament: to *administer* baptism. **5** To be of service: to *administer* to the poor.

ad·min·is·tra·tion [ad·min′is·trā′shən] *n.* **1** The managing of a business, bureau, office, etc. **2** (*sometimes written* **Administration**) A group of people in charge of a government, especially, in the U.S., the President and his Cabinet. **3** The term of office of a government official: The Civil War began during Lincoln's *administration*. **4** A group of people who manage something: the school *administration*.

ad·min·is·tra·tive [ad·min′is·trā′tiv] *adj.* Having to do with administration; executive: the *administrative* department. — **ad·min′is·tra′tive·ly** *adv.*

ad·min·is·tra·tor [ad·min′is·trā′tər] *n.* **1** A person who administers something; executive; manager. **2** A person selected by a court to manage the estate of a dead person.

ad·mi·ra·ble [ad′mər·ə·bəl] *adj.* Worthy of being admired; excellent. — **ad′mi·ra·bly** *adv.*

ad·mi·ral [ad′mər·əl] *n.* **1** A person who commands a navy or a fleet of ships. **2** A naval rank. In the U.S. Navy, an admiral is an officer of the second highest rank.

Admiral of the Fleet In the U.S. Navy, the highest ranking officer.

ad·mi·ral·ty [ad′mər·əl·tē] *n., pl.* **ad·mi·ral·ties** **1** (*written* **Admiralty**) The branch of the British government that deals with the navy and naval affairs. **2** A branch of law dealing with matters related to the sea and ships.

ad·mi·ra·tion [ad′mə·rā′shən] *n.* **1** A feeling of wonder, approval, and satisfaction for someone or something good, beautiful, rare, etc.: We had great *admiration* for his courage. **2** A person or thing that causes this feeling.

ad·mire [ad·mīr′] *v.* **ad·mired, ad·mir·ing** To regard or look upon with wonder, pleasure, and approval: I *admire* her. — **ad·mir′er** *n.*

ad·mis·si·ble [ad·mis′ə·bəl] *adj.* Capable or worthy of being allowed, considered, or admitted: an *admissible* theory; no dogs *admissible*.

ad·mis·sion [ad·mish′ən] *n.* **1** The act of admitting or the condition of being admitted: A locked door prevented his *admission* to the house. **2** Permission to enter: to deny someone *admission*. **3** The price charged for being admitted: *Admission* is 50 cents. **4** A confession or acknowledgment that something is true: an *admission* of defeat.

ad·mit [ad·mit′] *v.* **ad·mit·ted, ad·mit·ting** **1** To allow to enter or join: This key will *admit* you; He was *admitted* to the fraternity. **2** To have room for; contain: This theater *admits* only 400 people. **3** To confess or acknowledge: He *admitted* his guilt. **4** To permit or give a chance: This problem *admits* of several answers.

ad·mit·tance [ad·mit′(ə)ns] *n.* The right or permission to enter: *Admittance* was denied him.

ad·mit·ted·ly [ad·mit′id·lē] *adv.* By admission or agreement: *Admittedly*, it is hard work.

ad·mix·ture [ad·miks′chər] *n.* **1** A mixture. **2** Anything added to something else to make a mixture.

ad·mon·ish [ad·mon′ish] *v.* **1** To criticize mildly or tell of a fault: He *admonished* us about our spelling. **2** To warn: The minister *admonished* his flock to avoid evil. — **ad·mon′ish·ment** *n.*

ad·mo·ni·tion [ad′mə·nish′ən] *n.* A mild criticism, warning, or reminder: an *admonition* to be on time.

ad·mon·i·to·ry [ad·mon′ə·tôr′ē] *adj.* Serving to admonish or give warning: The teacher raised an *admonitory* finger for silence.

a·do [ə·dōō′] *n.* Activity; fuss; bustle: Much *ado* was made over John's leaving for camp.

a·do·be [ə·dō′bē] *n.* **1** A brick that is dried in the sun instead of in an oven or kiln. **2** The earth or clay of which such brick is made. **3** *adj. use:* an *adobe* house.

Adobe house

ad·o·les·cence [ad′ə·les′əns] *n.* The period of life during which a person grows from a child to an adult, roughly from about 12 to 21.

ad·o·les·cent [ad′ə·les′ənt] **1** *adj.* Growing up from a child to an adult. **2** *adj.* Having to do with or characteristic of adolescence. **3** *n.* A person between the ages of 12 or 13 and 21.

A·don·is [ə·don′is] *n.* **1** In Greek myths, a young man loved by Aphrodite because he was extremely handsome. **2** Any very handsome man.

a·dopt [ə·dopt′] *v.* **1** To take (a child of other parents) by legal means into one's family to be raised as one's own child. **2** *adj. use:* an *adopted* son. **3** To take and have or use as one's own: to *adopt* a new hair style. **4** To choose or vote to accept: to *adopt* a new law. — **a·dop′tion** *n.*

a·dor·a·ble [ə·dôr′ə·bəl] *adj.* **1** Worthy of love or adoration. **2** *informal* Charming; lovable: an *adorable* child.

ad·o·ra·tion [ad′ə·rā′shən] *n.* **1** The act of adoring. **2** A feeling of great love or admiration.

a·dore [ə·dôr′] *v.* **a·dored, a·dor·ing** **1** To worship. **2** To love and honor with great devotion: to *adore* one's parents. **3** *informal* To like very much: She *adored* riding and hunting. — **a·dor′er** *n.*

a·dorn [ə·dôrn′] *v.* To decorate or increase the beauty of: She *adorned* the table with flowers.

a·dorn·ment [ə·dôrn′mənt] *n.* **1** The act of adorning something. **2** Something, as a decoration, that adorns: rings, bracelets, and other *adornments*.

ad·re·nal [ə·drē′nəl] **1** *adj.* On or near the kidney. **2** *adj.* Of or from the adrenal glands. **3** *n.* An adrenal gland.

adrenal gland One of a pair of small glands

resting on top of the kidneys. They secrete many substances needed by the body, especially adrenaline.

Ad·ren·a·lin [ə·dren′ə·lin] *n.* A brand of adrenaline, or epinephrine: a trademark.

ad·ren·a·line or **ad·ren·a·lin** [ə·dren′ə·lin] *n.* A powerful hormone produced by the adrenal glands that raises blood pressure, quickens breathing, and otherwise prepares the body for activity or defense. Fear or anger stimulates its secretion.

A·dri·at·ic Sea [ā′drē·at′ik] A sea extending from the Mediterra-nean, mostly between Italy and Yugoslavia.

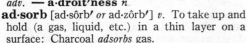

a·drift [ə·drift′] *adj., adv.* Loose and moving with wind or current, as a boat.

a·droit [ə·droit′] *adj.* Skillful; clever; expert: *adroit* in acrobatics. **— a·droit′ly** *adv.* **— a·droit′ness** *n.*

ad·sorb [ad·sôrb′ or ad·zôrb′] *v.* To take up and hold (a gas, liquid, etc.) in a thin layer on a surface: Charcoal *adsorbs* gas.

ad·sorp·tion [ad·sôrp′shən or ad·zôrp′shən] *n.* The process of adsorbing or being adsorbed.

ad·u·la·tion [aj′o͞o·lā′shən] *n.* Too great or hypocritical praise; flattery: teen-age *adulation* of a singer.

a·dult [ə·dult′ or ad′ult] **1** *n.* A person, animal, or plant that is fully grown. **2** *adj.* Grown-up; mature. **3** *n.* A person who has come of age, usually one 21 or more. **4** *adj.* Of or for adults.

a·dul·ter·ate [ə·dul′tə·rāt] *v.* **a·dul·ter·at·ed, a·dul·ter·at·ing** To make less good by adding cheap or impure materials: to *adulterate* hamburger with horse meat. **— a·dul·ter·a′tion** *n.*

a·dul·ter·ous [ə·dul′tər·əs] *adj.* Having to do with or committing adultery.

a·dul·ter·y [ə·dul′tər·ē] *n., pl.* **a·dul·ter·ies** Unfaithfulness to one's husband or wife.

adv. Abbreviation of ADVERB.

ad·vance [ad·vans′] *v.* **ad·vanced, ad·vanc·ing,** *n., adj.* **1** *v.* To move forward or upward: The army *advanced.* **2** *v.* To help onward; further; promote: to *advance* the progress of science. **3** *n.* The act of going forward; progress: to stop an army's *advance.* **4** *adj.* Located in front; going before: an *advance* guard. **5** *v.* To offer or put forward: to *advance* a suggestion. **6** *v.* To put in a better or higher rank, position, or situation: We *advanced* him to the fifth grade. **7** *n.* An improvement or promotion: He was given an *advance* in his job. **8** *v.* To make happen earlier: to *advance* the date of a party. **9** *v.* To lend: They *advanced* us money. **10** *n.* A loan. **11** *n.* Payment of money before it is due: an *advance*

on one's salary. **12** *adj.* Made or done ahead of time: an *advance* payment. **13** *v.* To increase in value or cost: The cost of living *advanced* a great deal. **14** *n.* An increase or rise: an *advance* in price. **15** *n.* (*pl.*) Attempts to gain someone's friendship or favor. **—in advance 1** In front: We drove *in advance* of the truck. **2** Before due; beforehand.

ad·vanced [ad·vanst′] *adj.* **1** Ahead of or more difficult than others, as in progress or thought: an *advanced* class; an *advanced* book. **2** At a late stage of life or time: He was *advanced* in years. **3** Located in front or ahead.

ad·vance·ment [ad·vans′mənt] *n.* **1** The act of advancing. **2** Progress: the *advancement* of science. **3** A promotion.

ad·van·tage [ad·van′tij] *n.* **1** Any circumstance or condition that benefits someone or helps toward success: The heavier wrestler had the *advantage* over his opponent. **2** Benefit or gain; profit: It is to your *advantage* to be there. **—take advantage of 1** To use for one's own benefit or gain: *Take advantage of* our good library. **2** To use selfishly or unfairly: By not behaving, we *took advantage of* her good nature. **—to advantage** For benefit or profit; to good effect.

ad·van·ta·geous [ad′vən·tā′jəs] *adj.* Giving an advantage; favorable; profitable: an *advantageous* offer. **— ad′van·ta′geous·ly** *adv.*

ad·vent [ad′vent] *n.* **1** The coming or arrival of a person or thing: the *advent* of winter. **2** (*written* **Advent**) The birth of Christ. **3** (*written* **Advent**) A season including the four Sundays before Christmas.

ad·ven·ti·tious [ad′ven·tish′əs] *adj.* Accidentally acquired or added: His famous wife gave his career an *adventitious* interest.

ad·ven·ture [ad·ven′chər] *n., v.* **ad·ven·tured, ad·ven·tur·ing 1** *n.* An unusual or thrilling experience: a day full of *adventures.* **2** *n.* A dangerous or difficult undertaking: the *adventure* of climbing mountains. **3** *v.* To do difficult, dangerous, or exciting things: to *adventure* on the moon. **4** *v.* To risk: to *adventure* one's life. ◆ This word comes through French from Latin *adventura,* meaning (an event) *about to happen.*

ad·ven·tur·er [ad·ven′chər·ər] *n.* **1** A person who looks for or takes part in adventures. **2** A person who tries to advance himself or become rich by dishonest or shady methods.

ad·ven·ture·some [ad·ven′chər·səm] *adj.* Adventurous; daring.

ad·ven·tur·ous [ad·ven′chər·əs] *adj.* **1** Liking or seeking adventure; fond of taking risks: an *adventurous* man. **2** Full of risk: an *adventurous* climb. **— ad·ven′tur·ous·ly** *adv.*

ad·verb [ad′vûrb] *n.* A word that usually tells when, where, why, how, or how much and modi-

add, āce, câre, pälm;   end, ēqual;   it, īce;   odd, ōpen, ôrder;   to͝ok, po͞ol;   up, bûrn;
ə = a in *above,* e in *sicken,* i in *possible,* o in *melon,* u in *circus;*   yo͞o = u in *fuse;*   oil;   pout;
check; ring; thin; this; zh in *vision.*   For ¶ reference, see page 64 · HOW TO

fies a verb, an adjective, or another adverb, as *quickly* in "She walked quickly," *very* in "a very red nose," and *too* in "We arrived too late." ◆ See -LY¹.

ad·ver·bi·al [ad·vûr′bē·əl] *adj.* **1** Of or having to do with an adverb: an *adverbial* use. **2** Used like an adverb: an *adverbial* phrase.

ad·ver·sar·y [ad′vər·ser′ē] *n., pl.* **ad·ver·sar·ies** An opponent, as in a contest; enemy.

ad·verse [ad·vûrs′ *or* ad′vûrs] *adj.* **1** Acting against; opposing: *adverse* winds. **2** Unfavorable: *adverse* reviews of a book. **3** Harmful: an *adverse* effect. — **ad·verse′ly** *adv.*

ad·ver·si·ty [ad·vûr′sə·tē] *n., pl.* **ad·ver·si·ties** Great hardship, misfortune, or trouble.

ad·ver·tise [ad′vər·tīz] *v.* **ad·ver·tised, ad·ver·tis·ing** **1** To make known or praise publicly, usually in order to sell: to *advertise* cars on TV. **2** To ask for or about something, as in a newspaper: to *advertise* for a lost dog. — **ad′·ver·tis′er** *n.* ◆ This word comes from a Latin word meaning *to turn toward,* and now has the sense of turning the public's attention to something in order to sell it.

ad·ver·tise·ment [ad′vər·tīz′mənt *or* ad·vûr′tis·mənt] *n.* A public notice that advertises something, as in a newspaper or on television.

ad·vice [ad·vīs′] *n.* A suggestion or opinion on what one ought to do or how to do it: He gave us *advice* on how to build a bookcase.

ad·vis·a·ble [ad·vī′zə·bəl] *adj.* Worth advising; sensible; wise.

ad·vise [ad·vīz′] *v.* **ad·vised, ad·vis·ing** **1** To give advice to. **2** To recommend. **3** To tell or inform: *Advise* him of the new plan.

ad·vis·ed·ly [ad·vī′zid·lē] *adv.* After careful thought; deliberately: to use a word *advisedly.*

ad·vise·ment [ad·vīz′mənt] *n.* Careful and deliberate thought or consideration: He said he would take the matter under *advisement.*

ad·vis·er or **ad·vis·or** [ad·vī′zər] *n.* **1** A person who advises. **2** A teacher in a school who advises students about studies, careers, etc.

ad·vi·so·ry [ad·vī′zər·ē] *adj.* **1** Having the right or ability to advise: an *advisory* council. **2** Containing advice: an *advisory* report.

ad·vo·ca·cy [ad′və·kə·sē] *n.* The act of defending or supporting a person, an idea, or a cause: His *advocacy* of the new law was a great help.

ad·vo·cate [*v.* ad′və·kāt, *n.* ad′və·kit] *v.* **ad·vo·cat·ed, ad·vo·cat·ing,** *n.* **1** *v.* To speak or write in favor of; defend; support: He *advocates* plenty of exercise. **2** *n.* A person who argues for or favors publicly: an *advocate* of physical fitness. **3** *n.* A lawyer who pleads another's case before a court.

adz or **adze** [adz] *n.* A tool like a broad chisel on an ax handle, its edge set crosswise.

Adz

Ae·ge·an [i·jē′ən] **1** *n.* A sea between Greece and Asia Minor. It is an arm

of the Mediterranean Sea. **2** *adj.* Of or in this sea or the lands around it: an *Aegean* civilization.

Mediterranean Sea

ae·gis [ē′jis] *n.* **1** In Greek mythology, a breastplate or shield used by Zeus and by Athena. **2** Protection, support, or sponsorship: a lifesaving course under the *aegis* of the Red Cross.

Ae·ne·as [i·nē′əs] *n.* In Greek and Roman legend, the Trojan warrior who wandered for seven years after the destruction of Troy. He is the hero of the Aeneid.

Ae·ne·id [i·nē′id] *n.* A Latin epic poem by Vergil, telling of the adventures of Aeneas.

ae·on [ē′ən] *n.* Another spelling of EON.

aer·ate [âr′āt] *v.* **aer·at·ed, aer·at·ing** **1** To put air or gas into. **2** To make fresh by passing air through: to *aerate* water. — **aer·a′·tion** *n.*

aer·i·al [âr′ē·əl] **1** *adj.* Of or in the air. **2** *adj.* Light as air; airy. **3** *adj.* Of, by, or for aircraft or flying: an *aerial* attack. **4** *n.* An antenna, as for a radio or television set.

aer·i·al·ist [âr′ē·əl·ist] *n.* A person who performs acrobatic stunts on a tightrope, trapeze, etc.

aer·ie [âr′ē] *n.* **1** The nest of a bird of prey, as an eagle, built on a crag or other high place. **2** The brood or young of such a bird. **3** A house or fortress built on a high place.

aer·o·bic [âr·ō′bik] *adj.* Living or occurring only in the presence of oxygen, as certain microorganisms: *aerobic* bacteria.

aer·o·dy·nam·ics [âr′ō·dī·nam′iks] *n.* The study of the motions of air and other gases when acted upon by various forces, especially forces produced by moving objects. ◆ See -ICS.

aer·o·naut [âr′ə·nôt] *n.* A person who flies an aircraft, especially a balloon.

aer·o·nau·ti·cal [âr′ə·nô′ti·kəl] *adj.* Of or having to do with aeronautics: an *aeronautical* chart.

aer·o·nau·tics [âr′ə·nô′tiks] *n.* The science and art of designing, making, and flying aircraft. ◆ See -ICS.

aer·o·plane [âr′ə·plān] *n. British* A spelling of AIRPLANE.

aer·o·sol [âr′ə·sôl] *n.* A mass of extremely small liquid or solid particles suspended in a gas, as fog, an insecticide, etc.

aer·o·space [âr′ō·spās] *n.* The earth's atmosphere and outer space, considered as a single region.

Aes·chy·lus [es′kə·ləs] *n.,* 525–456 B.C., Greek writer of tragic plays.

Ae·sop [ē′səp *or* ē′sop] *n.,* ?620–?560 B.C., Greek writer whose collection of fables has been popular for over two thousand years.

aes·thet·ic [es·thet′ik] *adj.* **1** Of or having to do with beauty in art, nature, etc.: an *aesthetic* view. **2** Very fond of or sensitive to beauty: an *aesthetic* person. **3** Of or relating to aesthetics. — **aes·thet′i·cal·ly** *adv.*

aes·thet·ics [es·thet′iks] *n.* A branch of philosophy that attempts to explain the nature of beauty or of beautiful things. ◆ See -ICS.

a·far [ə·fär′] *adv.* At, from, or to a distance. — **from afar** From a long distance: We saw the mountain *from afar.*

af·fa·ble [af′ə·bəl] *adj.* Very pleasant, friendly, and courteous. — **af′fa·bil′i·ty** *n.* — **af′fa·bly** *adv.*

af·fair [ə·fâr′] *n.* **1** An action or occasion: The dance was quite an *affair.* **2** Concern: What he does is his own *affair.* **3** (*pl.*) Important matters or concerns: *affairs* of state. **4** An object or thing: The raft was a crude *affair.*

af·fect[1] [ə·fekt′] *v.* **1** To act on; have an effect on: Fear *affects* the mind just as disease *affects* the body. **2** *adj. use: affected* parts of the body. **3** To have an emotional effect on; make sad, thoughtful, etc.: The play *affected* us a great deal. **4** *adj. use:* an *affecting* scene. ◆ See EFFECT.

af·fect[2] [ə·fekt′] *v.* **1** To like to have, wear, use, etc.; prefer: She *affects* large hats. **2** To imitate or pretend to have in order to create an effect: He *affects* a British accent.

af·fec·ta·tion [af′ek·tā′shən] *n.* An artificial way of acting or talking meant to create an effect: Her interest in sports is an *affectation.*

af·fect·ed [ə·fek′tid] *adj.* Not natural; artificial: an *affected* voice. — **af·fect′ed·ly** *adv.*

af·fec·tion [ə·fek′shən] *n.* **1** A feeling of kindness, fondness, or love for someone or something. **2** A diseased or unhealthy condition: an *affection* of the eye.

af·fec·tion·ate [ə·fek′shən·it] *adj.* Having or expressing affection; loving; fond. — **af·fec′tion·ate·ly** *adv.*

af·fer·ent [af′ər·ənt] *adj.* Leading inward or toward the center: an *afferent* nerve.

af·fi·ance [ə·fī′əns] *v.* **af·fi·anced, af·fi·anc·ing** **1** To promise in marriage. **2** *adj. use:* The *affianced* couple was very happy.

af·fi·da·vit [af′ə·dā′vit] *n.* A written statement sworn to be true.

af·fil·i·ate [ə·fil′ē·āt] *v.* **af·fil·i·at·ed, af·fil·i·at·ing** To join or unite, as with a larger body: Our club is *affiliated* with a national club. — **af·fil′i·a′tion** *n.* ◆ This word comes from a Latin word meaning *to adopt,* related to the Latin word *filius,* meaning *son.*

af·fin·i·ty [ə·fin′ə·tē] *n., pl.* **af·fin·i·ties** **1** A natural attraction or liking: She has an *affinity* for children. **2** A person to whom one is strongly drawn. **3** A close relationship or similarity: Red and orange have an *affinity* with each other.

af·firm [ə·fûrm′] *v.* To insist or maintain to be true; say positively: He *affirmed* that he had made a careful check.

af·fir·ma·tion [af′ər·mā′shən] *n.* **1** The act of declaring something to be true. **2** Something declared or held to be true.

af·firm·a·tive [ə·fûr′mə·tiv] **1** *adj.* Saying that something is true; saying yes: an *affirmative* reply. **2** *n.* A word or gesture that shows agreement or approval: To answer yes is to answer in the *affirmative.* **3** *n.* In a debate, the side in favor of the proposition being debated: The *affirmative* will speak before the negative.

af·fix [*v.* ə·fiks′, *n.* af′iks] **1** *v.* To attach or fasten to something: to *affix* a label to a box. **2** *v.* To add at the end: to *affix* one's signature. **3** *n.* Something added or attached, as a prefix or suffix to a word.

af·flict [ə·flikt′] *v.* To give pain or trouble to: He is *afflicted* with an aching back.

af·flic·tion [ə·flik′shən] *n.* **1** Any suffering or distress of body or mind. **2** The cause of such suffering: Deafness is an *affliction.*

af·flu·ent [af′lōō·ənt] *adj.* **1** Wealthy. **2** In plentiful supply; abundant. — **af′flu·ence** *n.*

af·ford [ə·fôrd′] *v.* **1** To be able to pay for: Can you *afford* the trip? **2** To be able to do or be, without risk or harm: He can *afford* to be kind. **3** To give; provide: Good books *afford* knowledge.

af·fray [ə·frā′] *n.* A public brawl or fight.

af·front [ə·frunt′] **1** *v.* To insult or offend openly: He *affronted* his teacher by laughing. **2** *n.* An insult or a rude act done in public: His laughter was an *affront* to us all.

Af·ghan [af′gən *or* af′gan] **1** *n.* A person born in or a citizen of Afghanistan. **2** *adj.* Of or from Afghanistan. **3** *n.* (*written* **afghan**) A wool blanket or shawl, knitted or crocheted in colorful patterns.

Af·ghan·i·stan [af·gan′ə·stan] *n.* A small, independent kingdom in south central Asia.

a·field [ə·fēld′] *adv.* **1** Off the regular or usual route or track: to stray far *afield.* **2** Away from home; abroad. **3** In, on, or to the field.

a·fire [ə·fīr′] *adj., adv.* On fire.

a·flame [ə·flām′] *adj.* **1** Flaming; on fire. **2** Colored like flames: with cheeks *aflame.*

AFL–CIO An organization of labor unions, formed when the American Federation of Labor and the Congress of Industrial Organizations merged in 1955.

a·float [ə·flōt′] *adj., adv.* **1** Floating, as on water or air. **2** At sea: We were *afloat* over a month. **3** In circulation; rumored: Stories were *afloat.* **4** Flooded: The leak left the floor *afloat.*

a·flut·ter [ə·flut′ər] *adj.* **1** Fluttering. **2** Disturbed; excited: Her heart was *aflutter.*

a·foot [ə·fŏŏt′] *adv., adj.* **1** On foot: to travel *afoot.* **2** In progress; about: dirty work *afoot.*

---

add, āce, câre, pälm; 　 end, ēqual; 　 it, īce; 　 odd, ōpen, ôrder; 　 tŏŏk, pōōl; 　 up, bûrn;
ə = a in *above,* e in *sicken,* i in *possible,* o in *melon,* u in *circus;* 　 yōō = u in *fuse;* 　 oil; 　 pout;
check; ring; thin; this; zh in *vision.* 　 For ¶ reference, see page 64 · HOW TO

a·fore·men·tioned [ə·fôr'men'shənd] *adj*. Mentioned before: the *aforementioned* papers.

a·fore·said [ə·fôr'sed'] *adj*. Said before.

a·fore·thought [ə·fôr'thôt'] *adj*. Thought of or planned beforehand, especially in the phrase **malice aforethought**: There was no *malice aforethought* in his actions.

a·foul [ə·foul'] *adj*. In a tangle; entangled. — **run afoul of** To get into difficulties with: to *run afoul of* the law.

a·fraid [ə·frād'] *adj*. **1** Full of fear or dread: to be *afraid* of heights. **2** Mildly concerned or distressed: I am *afraid* we're late.

a·fresh [ə·fresh'] *adv*. Once more; again: He must do all his work *afresh*.

Af·ri·ca [af'ri·kə] *n*. The second largest continent, located in the Eastern Hemisphere south of Europe.

Af·ri·can [af'ri·kən] **1** *adj*. Of or from Africa. **2** *n*. A person born or living in Africa. **3** *n*. An African Negro.

aft [aft] *adv*. At, near, or toward the stern or rear part of a ship.

af·ter [af'tər] **1** *prep*. In the rear of; further back than; following: He marched *after* me. **2** *adv*. In the rear; behind: to follow *after*. **3** *prep*. In search of: Strive *after* wisdom. **4** *prep*. In relation to; concerning; about: He asked *after* your aunt. **5** *prep*. At a later time than: It is *after* five o'clock. **6** *adv*. Afterward; later: They arrived shortly *after*. **7** *adj*. Later: In *after* years they lived as friends. **8** *prep*. Following repeatedly: day *after* day. **9** *prep*. Next below in rank or importance: He is *after* the king in power. **10** *prep*. According to the nature, wishes, or customs of: a man *after* my own heart. **11** *prep*. In imitation of; in the manner of: a painting *after* Rembrant. **12** *prep*. In honor or remembrance of: He is named *after* his father. **13** *conj*. Following the time that: I went to bed *after* I got home.

af·ter·ef·fect [af'tər·ə·fekt'] *n*. An effect that follows or results from a main effect: This medicine often has an unpleasant *aftereffect*.

af·ter·math [af'tər·math] *n*. **1** A result or consequence, especially if it is bad or injurious: the *aftermath* of the storm. **2** The second crop or mowing of grass to come from the original planting.

af·ter·noon [af'tər·nōon'] *n*. The part of the day between noon and sunset.

af·ter·thought [af'tər·thôt'] *n*. A thought that comes after rather than before an action, decision, etc., and is thus too late to be useful.

af·ter·ward [af'tər·wərd] *adv*. At a later time: This is what happened *afterward*.

af·ter·wards [af'tər·wərdz] *adv*. Afterward.

Ag The symbol for the element SILVER. ◆ The Latin word for silver is *argentum*.

a·gain [ə·gen'] *adv*. **1** Another time; once more: The ball bounced *again*. **2** To, at, or in the same place or condition as before: Here we go *again*. **3** In addition: half as much *again*. **4** On the other hand: I may go, and *again* I may not.

a·gainst [ə·genst'] *prep*. **1** In the opposite direction to; opposing: We sailed *against* the wind. **2** In contact with; upon: The boat was dashed *against* the rocks. **3** In opposition to; contrary to: The class acted *against* her wishes. **4** In contrast to: The trees were seen *against* the sky. **5** In preparation for.

Ag·a·mem·non [ag'ə·mem'non] *n*. In Greek myths, the leader of the Greek armies in the Trojan War.

a·gape [ə·gāp'] *adv.*, *adj*. **1** Wide open; gaping: His mouth was *agape*. **2** In a condition of wonder, surprise, or excitement: We were *agape* at the news.

a·gar-a·gar [ä'gär·ä'gär *or* ä'gär·ä'gär] *n*. A jellylike substance obtained from certain kinds of seaweeds, and used in the artificial cultivation of bacteria.

Mouth agape

Ag·as·siz [ag'ə·sē], **Louis,** 1807–1873, U.S. naturalist born in Switzerland.

ag·ate [ag'it] *n*. **1** A type of quartz that is streaked with colored bands. **2** A playing marble that looks like this.

a·ga·ve [ə·gä'vē *or* ə·gā'vē] *n*. A plant of tropical America, Mexico, and the sw U.S., having stiff, thick leaves and a tall stalk that bears flowers. Some kinds yield a fiber used for making rope.

age [āj] *n.*, *v*. **aged, ag·ing** or **age·ing 1** *n*. The length of time any person or thing has been in existence: the *age* of six. **2** *n*. The last part of one's life: *Age* had bent his back. **3** *n*. A stage or period of life: middle *age*. **4** *v*. To make or become old or mature: The French *age* wine very carefully; My grandfather *aged* a lot last year. **5** *n*. A particular period in the history of man or of the earth: the Middle *Ages*; the *age* of the dinosaur. **6** *n*. (*usually pl.*) A generation: He will be appreciated by future *ages*. **7** *n*. (*usually pl.*) *informal* A long time: He's been gone for *ages*. — **of age** 21 or more years old and with the full legal rights of an adult.

-age A suffix meaning: **1** The act or condition of, as in *marriage*, the act of marrying or the condition of being married. **2** A collection or group of, as in *fruitage*, a collection or group of fruit. **3** The cost of, as in *postage*, the cost of mailing something by post. **4** The amount of, as in *dosage*, the amount of a dose. **5** The home of, as in *orphanage*, the home of orphans.

a·ged *adj*. **1** [ā'jid] Old: His mother is quite *aged*. **2** [ājd] Of the age of: a child *aged* six. ◆ See OLD.

age·less [āj'lis] *adj*. **1** Seeming never to grow old: an *ageless* person. **2** Eternal; timeless.

a·gen·cy [ā'jən·sē] *n.*, *pl.*, **a·gen·cies 1** The power or means by which something is done: Through the *agency* of water we ground our grain. **2** A firm or establishment where business is carried on for others: an employment *agency*.

a·gen·da [ə·jen′də] *n.* A list of things to be done or discussed: Here is the *agenda* for today's meeting. ◆ *Agenda* was originally the plural form of the Latin word *agendum.* It is now often taken as a singular noun and has a regularly formed plural, *agendas.*

a·gent [ā·jənt] *n.* **1** A person or organization that has the authority to act for someone else: He is her business *agent.* **2** A person or thing that produces a certain effect or result: Oxygen is the *agent* that causes rust.

ag·gran·dize [ə·gran′dīz *or* ag′rən·dīz] *v.* **ag·gran·dized, ag·gran·diz·ing 1** To increase the power, rank, wealth, etc., of: The party *aggrandized* itself by taking in reform groups. **2** To make great or greater, as in size. **— ag·gran·dize·ment** [ə·gran′diz·ment] *n.* ¶3

ag·gra·vate [ag′rə·vāt] *v.* **ag·gra·vat·ed, ag·gra·vat·ing 1** To make worse, more serious, or more unpleasant: The smart of iodine *aggravated* the pain of the cut. **2** *informal* To make angry; provoke: to *aggravate* someone. **3** *adj. use:* a very *aggravating* person.

ag·gra·va·tion [ag′rə·vā′shən] *n.* **1** A making worse. **2** *informal* Anger; irritation.

ag·gre·gate [*v.* ag′rə·gāt, *adj., n.* ag′rə·git] *v.* **ag·gre·gat·ed, ag·gre·gat·ing,** *adj., n.* **1** *v.* To gather together; collect: The wet sand was *aggregated* into one hard lump. **2** *adj.* Gathered into a whole; total: The *aggregate* number of his fans was tremendous. **3** *v.* To amount to; add up to: The tickets sold will *aggregate* above 10,000. **4** *n.* The entire amount; total. **— in the aggregate** Collectively; as a whole.

ag·gre·ga·tion [ag′rə·gā′shən] *n.* A gathering of separate things: a huge *aggregation* of people.

ag·gres·sion [ə·gresh′ən] *n.* **1** An attack, especially an unprovoked attack: That country was accused of *aggression.* **2** A tendency to attack or fight.

ag·gres·sive [ə·gres′iv] *adj.* **1** Quick to attack or start a fight: an *aggressive* country. **2** Very active; vigorous; energetic: an *aggressive* player.

ag·gres·sor [ə·gres′ər] *n.* A person or nation that attacks first or starts a quarrel.

ag·grieved [ə·grēvd′] *adj.* Having cause for complaint; ill-treated; wronged: The *aggrieved* tenants complained to their landlord.

a·ghast [ə·gast′] *adj.* Shocked or horrified: We were *aghast* at her rude behavior.

ag·ile [aj′əl] *adj.* Able to move or do something quickly and easily: *agile* fingers; an *agile* mind. **— ag′ile·ly** *adv.*

a·gil·i·ty [ə·jil′ə·tē] *n.* Quickness and easiness in the use of body or mind: Most sports test both physical and mental *agility.*

ag·i·tate [aj′ə·tāt] *v.* **ag·i·tat·ed, ag·i·tat·ing 1** To disturb or move: The wind *agitates* the lake. **2** To excite or stir up: News of the crash *agitated* him. **3** To try to arouse interest in changing something by speaking, writing, etc.: Women *agitated* a long time for the vote.

ag·i·ta·tion [aj′ə·tā′shən] *n.* **1** The act of moving or shaking. **2** Excitement or nervousness: His *agitation* at the bad news was seen by all. **3** The arousing of public interest in order to change something: *agitation* for equal rights.

ag·i·ta·tor [aj′ə·tā′tər] *n.* **1** A person who stirs up discontent in order to change things. **2** A thing that agitates: the *agitator* of a machine.

a·glow [ə·glō′] *adj.* In a glow; glowing.

ag·nos·tic [ag·nos′tik] *n.* A person who believes that we can never know for certain whether God does or does not exist.

a·go [ə·gō′] **1** *adj.* Gone by; past: a year *ago.* **2** *adv.* In the past: It happened long *ago.*

a·gog [ə·gog′] *adj.* Full of eager curiosity; excited: to be all *agog* about something.

ag·o·nize [ag′ə·nīz] *v.* **ag·o·nized, ag·o·niz·ing 1** To suffer or cause to suffer terrible physical or mental pain. **2** *adj. use:* an *agonizing* moment. ¶3

ag·o·ny [ag′ə·nē] *n., pl.* **ag·o·nies 1** Terrible suffering of body or mind; anguish. **2** The struggle that often comes just before death.

a·grar·i·an [ə·grâr′ē·ən] *adj.* Having to do with land, especially farm land, and how it is owned, distributed, and used: a plan for *agrarian* reform.

a·gree [ə·grē′] *v.* **a·greed, a·gree·ing 1** To consent: John *agreed* to go. **2** To admit the truth of; grant: He *agreed* that we had not worked hard enough. **3** To have the same opinions, ideas, etc.; concur: I can't *agree* with him. **4** To come to terms: They *agreed* on a settlement. **5** *adj. use:* The *agreed* amount was five dollars. **6** In grammar, to correspond in person, number, case, or gender. **— agree with** To be good for; suit: Spices do not *agree with* me.

a·gree·a·ble [ə·grē′ə·bəl] *adj.* **1** Giving pleasure; pleasing: an *agreeable* companion. **2** Ready or willing to agree: I am *agreeable* to your plan. **3** Suitable; conforming: clothes *agreeable* to the weather. **— a·gree′a·bly** *adv.*

a·gree·ment [ə·grē′mənt] *n.* **1** A sameness or harmony of opinion: We were in *agreement* on many questions. **2** A contract, treaty, or understanding between people, nations, etc.: a trade *agreement* between England and Canada. **3** Correspondence between words as to person, number, case, or gender.

ag·ri·cul·tur·al [ag′rə·kul′chər·əl] *adj.* Of, having to do with, or used in agriculture.

ag·ri·cul·ture [ag′rə·kul′chər] *n.* The art or science of cultivating the soil; the raising of crops, livestock, or both; farming.

a·ground [ə·ground′] *adj., adv.* On or onto a shoal, or bottom; stranded.

a·gue [ā′gyōō] *n.* **1** A fever, as malaria, marked by alternating periods of chills, fever, and sweating. **2** A chill accompanied by shivering.

ah [ä] *interj.* An exclamation expressing by the way it is said emotions such as surprise, disgust, satisfaction, joy, etc.

a·ha [ä·hä′] *interj.* An exclamation expressing surprise, joy, triumph, etc.

a·head [ə·hed′] **1** *adv.* In front; to the front; before: March *ahead* of us. **2** *adv.* In advance: They telegraphed *ahead* for rooms. **3** *adv.* Onward; forward: Go *ahead* with your plans. **4** *adj.* Better or more advanced in some respect: This car is *ahead* of that one in looks.

a·hoy [ə·hoi′] *interj.* A sailor's call, used to hail a person or ship.

aid [ād] **1** *v.* To help or assist. **2** *n.* Help or assistance: *Aid* came just in time. **3** *n.* A person or thing that helps: a visual *aid* used in teaching.

aide [ād] *n.* An assistant, as an aide-de-camp or an executive who helps to run a business.

aide-de-camp [ād′də·kamp′] *n., pl.* **aides-de-camp** An officer who serves as a personal assistant to a high military or naval officer.

ai·grette [ā′gret *or* ā·gret′] *n.* **1** A tuft of feathers, as from the tail of an egret. **2** A headdress of jewels in the shape of a plume.

ail [āl] *v.* **1** To cause pain or discomfort to; trouble: His back was *ailing* him. **2** To be ill.

ai·le·ron [ā′lə·ron] *n.* A movable surface hinged to the back edge of each wing of an airplane. The pilot tilts the ailerons to bank the plane.

ail·ment [āl′mənt] *n.* An illness, usually not too severe but often chronic.

When the right aileron is up and the left down, the airplane banks to the right.

aim [ām] **1** *v.* To direct (a weapon, remark, etc.) at some object or person: He *aimed* the gun at us; I *aimed* my remarks at the whole class. **2** *n.* The act of aiming: He had a deadly *aim*. **3** *v.* To have as a purpose or goal; try: He *aimed* to make the team this year. **4** *n.* A purpose or goal: John's *aim* was to become a doctor. **— take aim** To point a gun at some target.

aim·less [ām′lis] *adj.* Having no aim or purpose: an *aimless* life. **— aim′less·ly** *adv.*

ain't [ānt] A contraction of: Am not: I *ain't* going. *Ain't* is also used for *are not, is not, has not,* and *have not.* ◆ *Ain't* is not considered acceptable English today, although speakers and writers sometimes use it for humorous effect.

air [âr] **1** *n.* The mixture of invisible gases that forms the atmosphere of the earth, consisting chiefly of the gases oxygen, nitrogen, carbon dioxide, and hydrogen. **2** *n.* The open space around and above the earth; sky: The *air* was full of birds flying. **3** *adj.* Admitting or regulating air: an *air* filter. **4** *adj.* Operated by air: an *air* drill. **5** *adj.* Of, by, or for aircraft: an *air* attack. **6** *n.* A slight wind or breeze. **7** *v.* To expose to the air so as to ventilate, dry, or make fresh: *Air* the blankets. **8** *n.* The general look or manner of a person or thing: He had an honest *air* about him. **9** *n.* (*pl.*) An affected, unnatural, or haughty way of acting: Don't put on *airs*. **10** *v.* To make known or make public: The people *aired* their troubles to the mayor. **11** *n.* A melody or tune: an old Irish *air*. **— in the air** **1** Going around; abroad: Something is *in the air*. **2** Unsettled. **— on the air** Broadcasting or being broadcast, as by radio.

air base A base for military aircraft.

air brake A brake operated by compressed air.

air-con·di·tion [âr′kən·dish′ən] **1** *v.* To equip with or ventilate by air conditioning. **2** *adj. use:* an *air-conditioned* theater.

air conditioning A system for treating the air in buildings, rooms, and other enclosed places in order to keep the air clean, dry, and at a comfortable temperature. **— air conditioner**

air·craft [âr′kraft′] *n., pl.* **air·craft** Any machine or vehicle designed to travel from place to place through the air, as airplanes, balloons, and helicopters.

Aircraft carrier

aircraft carrier A warship that serves as a base for aircraft which take off from and land on its long, level, open deck.

Aire·dale [âr′dāl] *n.* A large terrier with a short, wiry tan coat and black markings.

air·field [âr′fēld′] *n.* A field equipped for the landing and take-off of aircraft.

air force The branch of a country's armed forces equipped to wage war in or from the air.

air gun A gun that uses compressed air to propel its bullet or projectile.

Airedale

air·i·ly [âr′ə·lē] *adv.* In a light, high-spirited manner; jauntily; gaily: He waved *airily* to us.

air·ing [âr′ing] *n.* **1** An exposure to air in order to dry, freshen, etc. **2** Exercise in the air: to take a brief *airing*.

air·less [âr′lis] *adj.* Lacking air, especially fresh air; stuffy: an *airless* room.

air·lift [âr′lift′] **1** *n.* The carrying of passengers and cargo by air, especially when other means of access are closed off. **2** *v.* To carry or transport by this method: to *airlift* supplies.

air·line [âr′līn′] *n.* or **air line** **1** A system for transporting people and freight by air. **2** A company operating such a system. **3** A regular route flown by aircraft.

air mail **1** Mail carried by airplanes. **2** A system for carrying such mail.

air·man [âr′mən] *n., pl.* **air·men** [âr′mən] An enlisted man in the U.S. Air Force.

air mass A large body of air having a generally uniform temperature and humidity: A cold *air mass* is moving down from the Arctic.

air·plane [âr′plān′] *n.* A vehicle that flies through the air. It is able to remain aloft by means of the lift produced when air moves over its wings as it is driven forward by the action of propellers or by jet propulsion.

air pocket A strong downward current of air that sometimes causes an airplane to drop sharply from a level course.

air·port [âr′pôrt′] *n.* A large area equipped for aircraft to land and take off and for the loading and unloading of passengers, freight, etc.

air pressure 1 The pressure of air in a confined space. The pressure increases as the space grows less. **2** Atmospheric pressure.

air raid An attack or raid by aircraft.

air·ship [âr′ship′] *n.* A balloon that can be driven and steered; dirigible.

air·sick [âr′sik′] *adj.* Sick at one's stomach from riding in an aircraft. **— air′sick′ness** *n.*

air speed The speed of an aircraft relative to the air through which it travels rather than its speed in relation to the ground below.

air·strip [âr′strip′] *n.* A flat, smooth surface on land, snow, or ice that can be used for the take-off or landing of aircraft.

air·tight [âr′tīt′] *adj.* **1** Able to hold air or gas in or out: an *airtight* cover. **2** Having no weak spots; flawless: an *airtight* argument.

air·way [âr′wā′] *n.* A route traveled by aircraft.

air·y [âr′ē] *adj.* **air·i·er, air·i·est 1** Of, having to do with, or in the air. **2** Open to the air: an *airy* porch. **3** Thin or light as air; delicate: *airy* curtains. **4** Lighthearted or gay in manner: *airy* music. **5** Not real or practical; fanciful.

aisle [īl] *n.* **1** A passageway, as in a theater or church, that separates one section of seats from another section: the center *aisle*. **2** A passageway along the inside wall of a church, separated from the main section by pillars.

a·jar [ə·jär′] *adj., adv.* Partly open, as a door.

A·jax [ā′jaks] *n.* In Greek myths, a Greek hero of the Trojan War, second in bravery only to Achilles.

a·kim·bo [ə·kim′bō] *adj., adv.* With hands on the hips and elbows outward: to stand *akimbo*.

a·kin [ə·kin′] *adj.* **1** Having the same family; related. **2** Similar or alike in certain ways: Our feelings were more *akin* to joy than sorrow.

Ak·ron [ak′rən] *n.* A city in NE Ohio, world's largest rubber manufacturing center.

Arms akimbo

-al A suffix meaning: **1** Of or having to do with something, as in *musical*, of or having to do with music. **2** The act or process of doing something, as in *refusal*, the act of refusing.

Al The symbol for the element ALUMINUM.

Ala. Abbreviation of ALABAMA.

Al·a·bam·a [al′ə·bam′ə] *n.* A state in the SE U.S.

al·a·bas·ter [al′ə·bas′tər] **1** *n.* A smooth white or tinted stone, often carved into vases or small statues. **2** *adj. use:* an *alabaster* vase.

a·lack [ə·lak′] *interj.* An exclamation expressing regret or sorrow: seldom used today.

a·lac·ri·ty [ə·lak′rə·tē] *n.* A willingness and promptness: to help someone with *alacrity*.

A·lad·din [ə·lad′(ə)n] *n.* In the Arabian Nights, a boy who was able to summon a genie by rubbing a magic lamp or a magic ring.

Al·a·mo [al′ə·mō] *n.* A vacant mission building made into a fort in San Antonio, Texas, that was attacked and taken by Mexicans in 1836.

à la mode or **a la mode** [ä′ lə mōd′] **1** With ice cream: I like pie *à la mode.* **2** Stylish; fashionable.

a·larm [ə·lärm′] **1** *n.* A sudden feeling of fear: We were filled with *alarm* at the noise. **2** *v.* To fill with fear; frighten: The noise *alarmed* us. **3** *adj. use:* an *alarming* fact. **4** *n.* Any signal or sound used to warn others of danger. **5** *n.* A device, as a bell or siren, used to give such a signal. **6** *n.* A call to arms or to be ready to fight a flood, fire, etc.

alarm clock A clock that can be set in advance to ring or buzz at a particular time.

a·larm·ist [ə·lär′mist] *n.* A person too ready to be alarmed or to alarm others.

a·las [ə·las′] *interj.* An exclamation expressing sorrow, regret, disappointment, etc.

A·las·ka [ə·las′kə] *n.* A state of the U.S. in NW North America. **— A·las′kan** *adj., n.*

alb [alb] *n.* A long, white linen vestment, or robe, worn by a priest while celebrating Mass.

Al·ba·ni·a [al·bā′nē·ə] *n.* A country in the Balkans, south of Yugoslavia. **— Al·ba′ni·an** *adj., n.*

Al·ba·ny [ôl′bə·nē] *n.* The capital of New York.

al·ba·tross [al′bə·trôs] *n.* A large, web-footed sea bird with a hooked beak. It is capable of flying for long distances over the sea.

al·be·it [ôl·bē′it] *conj.* Even though; although: a strong, *albeit* slender, support.

Al·ber·ta [al·bûr′tə] *n.* A province in western Canada.

al·bi·no [al·bī′nō] *n., pl.* **al·bi·nos** A person or animal having very pale or white skin and hair and often pink or light blue eyes, due to a lack of normal coloring matter.

Al·bi·on [al′bē·ən] *n.* Another name for ENGLAND: used mostly in poems.

Albatross, about 10 ft. across wings

---

add, āce, câre, pälm; end, ēqual; it, īce; odd, ōpen, ôrder; tŏŏk, pōōl; up, bûrn;
ə = a in *above*, e in *sicken*, i in *possible*, o in *melon*, u in *circus*; yōō = u in *fuse*; oil; pout;
check; ring; thin; this; zh in *vision*. For ¶ reference, see page 64 · HOW TO

al·bum [al′bəm] *n.* **1** A book or booklike container, used for keeping stamps, pictures, autographs, etc. **2** A long-playing record or records.

al·bu·men [al·byōō′mən] *n.* **1** The white of an egg. **2** Albumin.

al·bu·min [al·byōō′mən] *n.* A protein found in many plant and animal juices and tissues, as in egg white, blood, muscle, milk, etc.

al·che·mist [al′kə·mist] *n.* A person who practiced alchemy in the Middle Ages.

al·che·my [al′kə·mē] *n.* **1** An early form of chemistry practiced in the Middle Ages that tried to find a way to change common metals into gold and to discover a substance that could keep a person forever young. **2** Any power that changes or transforms.

al·co·hol [al′kə·hôl] *n.* **1** A clear, colorless, flammable liquid with a pungent taste, formed from fermented sugars in grain, grapes, etc. It is the intoxicating agent in wine, gin, etc., and is used in medicine and as a fuel. **2** Any liquor containing alcohol. **3** A chemically related but poisonous liquid distilled from wood. **4** Any similar chemical compound. ◆ This word comes originally from an Arabic word for a fine powder used to paint the eyelids.

al·co·hol·ic [al′kə·hôl′ik] **1** *adj.* Of, containing, or caused by alcohol: an *alcoholic* drink. **2** *n.* A person who suffers from alcoholism.

al·co·hol·ism [al′kə·hôl′iz·əm] *n.* A chronic disease, perhaps mental, causing an irresistible urge to drink too much alcoholic liquor.

Al·cott [ôl′kət], **Louisa May,** 1832–1888, U.S. author.

al·cove [al′kōv] *n.* **1** A recess or small section of a room opening out from the main section: a dining *alcove*. **2** A small, often arched hollow place, as in a wall: Put the vase in the *alcove*.

Alcove

Al·deb·a·ran [al·deb′ə·rən] *n.* A red star, one of the brightest in the sky, in the constellation Taurus.

al·der [ôl′dər] *n.* A shrub or small tree that resembles the birch and grows best in wet soil.

al·der·man [ôl′dər·mən] *n., pl.* **al·der·men** [ôl′dər·mən]. In some cities and towns, a member of the local government or city council.

ale [āl] *n.* An alcoholic drink that is similar in taste to beer, made from malt and hops.

a·lee [ə·lē′] *adj., adv.* At, on, or to the side of a ship that faces away from the wind.

a·lert [ə·lûrt′] **1** *adj.* Very watchful and ready, as for sudden action: an *alert* little dog. **2** *adj.* Mentally quick and intelligent. **3** *n.* A warning or signal against attack or danger. **4** *n.* The time during which such a warning is in effect. **5** *v.* To warn or prepare, as for danger or attack: They *alerted* us early about the storm. **— on the alert** Very watchful and ready: Keep *on the alert* for trouble. **— a·lert′ness** *n.*

A·leu·tian Islands [ə·lōō′shən] A chain of volcanic islands sw of Alaska, belonging to the U.S.

Al·ex·an·der the Great [al′ig·zan′dər], 356–323 B.C., king of Macedonia and conqueror of a large empire that consisted of most of the known world from the Mediterranean Sea to India.

Al·ex·an·dri·a [al′ig·zan′drē·ə] *n.* A city in the United Arab Republic. It was an ancient capital of Egypt, founded by Alexander the Great.

al·fal·fa [al·fal′fə] *n.* A cloverlike plant having deep roots and purple flowers. It is grown as a food for horses and cattle. ◆ This word comes directly from Spanish. The origin of it was an Arabic word meaning *the best kind of fodder*.

al·gae [al′jē] *n.pl.* A large group of simple plants growing in water or damp places and lacking true roots, stems, or leaves. Many algae are seaweeds. ◆ This word comes from the Latin word *algae*, which is the plural of *alga*, meaning *seaweed*.

al·ge·bra [al′jə·brə] *n.* A branch of mathematics that deals with the relations between numbers. Actual numbers are often replaced by letters so that these relations may be determined; for instance, if $2a + b = 10$, and $b = 4$, then $a = 3$. ◆ This word comes from an Arabic word meaning *the reunion of broken parts*, such as broken bones. It came to have the meaning of setting up and solving an equation.

al·ge·bra·ic [al′jə·brā′ik] *adj.* **1** Of or having to do with algebra. **2** Used in algebra.

Al·ge·ri·a [al·jir′ē·ə] *n.* A country in NW Africa. **— Al·ge′ri·an** *adj., n.*

Al·giers [al·jirz′] *n.* The capital city and chief port of Algeria.

Al·gon·qui·an [al·gong′kwē·ən *or* al·gong′kē·ən] **1** *n.* A family of languages spoken by many tribes of North American Indians. **2** *adj.* Of or having to do with this family of languages.

Al·gon·quin [al·gong′kwin *or* al·gong′kin] *n.* A North American Indian who belongs to any of certain tribes that speak an Algonquian language.

a·li·as [ā′lē·əs] **1** *n.* A false name taken so as to hide one's real name: Criminals often have many *aliases*. **2** *conj.* Otherwise called or known as: Jones *alias* Smith.

al·i·bi [al′ə·bī] *n., pl.* **al·i·bis,** *v.* **al·i·bied, al·i·bi·ing 1** *n.* The fact or the defense that a person suspected of a crime was in another place when it was committed. **2** *n. informal* An excuse for any fault or failure. **3** *v. informal* To offer excuses.

al·ien [āl′yən *or* ā′lē·ən] **1** *adj.* Of or belonging to another country; foreign. **2** *adj.* Not natural; strange: Such an outburst of anger was *alien* to his nature. **3** *n.* A person who is not a citizen of the country in which he is living; a foreigner.

al·ien·ate [āl′yən·āt *or* ā′lē·ən·āt] *v.* **al·ien·at·ed, al·ien·at·ing** To make unfriendly; lose the friendship of: to *alienate* an old friend. — **al′·ien·a′tion** *n.*

a·light¹ [ə·līt′] *v.* **a·light·ed** or **a·lit, a·light·ing** **1** To descend and come to rest; settle: The bird *alighted* on the branch. **2** To get off or dismount: to *alight* from a horse. **3** To come upon by accident: to *alight* upon an answer.

a·light² [ə·līt′] *adj.* Lighted; on fire: The sky was all *alight* with the blaze.

a·lign [ə·līn′] *v.* **1** To arrange or form into or as if into a line: Please *align* the glasses on the shelf. **2** To join with others for or against something: Several nations *aligned* themselves against the use of force.

a·lign·ment [ə·līn′mənt] *n.* **1** Position, place, or arrangement in a line: to be out of *alignment*. **2** An adjustment of views to match those of others.

a·like [ə·līk′] **1** *adj.* Like or similar to one another: The pattern on these plates is not *alike*. **2** *adv.* In the same way or manner: The twins even talk *alike* now.

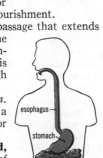

The black arrow is out of alignment.

al·i·men·ta·ry [al′ə·men′trē *or* al′ə·men′tə·rē] *adj.* Of or having to do with food or nourishment.

alimentary canal The passage that extends from the mouth through the esophagus, stomach, and intestines to the anus. Food is digested as it passes through this canal.

al·i·mo·ny [al′ə·mō′nē] *n.* Money that a court orders a man to pay to his divorced or separated wife.

a·line [ə·līn′] *v.* **a·lined, a·lin·ing** Another spelling of ALIGN.

a·line·ment [ə·līn′mənt] *n.* Another spelling of ALIGN-MENT.

a·lit [ə·lit′] Alternative past tense and past participle of ALIGHT¹: They *alit* from the bus.

a·live [ə·līv′] *adj.* **1** Living; possessing life. **2** In existence or operation; active: to keep hope *alive*. **3** Lively; brisk; alert: very much *alive*. — **alive to** Sensitive to; aware of: *alive to* the needs of the poor. — **alive with** Full of living things or signs of life.

esophagus

stomach

small intestine
large intestine
Alimentary canal

al·ka·li [al′kə·lī] *n., pl.* **al·ka·lis** or **al·ka·lies** A substance, as potash, soda, or ammonia, that neutralizes acids by combining with them to form salts. Alkalis turn pink litmus paper blue, and many of them are used to make soap.

al·ka·line [al′kə·līn *or* al′kə·lin] *adj.* Of, like, or containing an alkali. — **al·ka·lin·i·ty** [al′kə·lin′ə·tē] *n.*

al·ka·loid [al′kə·loid] *n.* Any of a large number of bitter, often poisonous substances found chiefly in plants. Many of them, like quinine and morphine, are used in medicine.

all [ôl] **1** *adj.* The entire quantity or whole of: *All* Europe was at war. **2** *adj.* The entire number of; every one of: *All* men are mortal. **3** *adv.* Wholly; entirely: The toys fell *all* apart. **4** *n.* Everything that one has; the whole: to give one's *all*. **5** *pron.* Everything: *All* is lost; *All* is over. **6** *pron.* Everyone: *All* were condemned. **7** *adv.* For each; on each side: a score of three *all*. **8** *adj.* The greatest possible: in *all* haste. **9** *adj.* Any whatever: The situation was beyond *all* help. **10** *adj.* Nothing except; only: He was *all* skin and bones. — **above all** Most important: *Above all* don't miss the train. — **after all** In spite of everything; neverthe-less. — **all at once** Suddenly. — **all in** *informal* Tired; exhausted. — **all in all** Everything considered; on the whole. — **at all** **1** In any way: I can't do it *at all*. **2** To any degree, amount, or extent: We had no luck *at all*. — **in all** Altogether: ten books *in all*.

Al·lah [al′ə *or* ä′lə] *n.* In the Moslem religion, the name for God.

all-a·round [ôl′ə·round′] *adj.* **1** Able to do many things; versatile: an *all-around* athlete. **2** Having many uses: an *all-around* knife. **3** Broad; complete: an *all-around* education.

al·lay [ə·lā′] *v.* **al·layed, al·lay·ing** To quiet, soothe, or reduce: to *allay* hunger and fear.

al·le·ga·tion [al′ə·gā′shən] *n.* **1** Something declared to be true but without any proof: Who could take such *allegations* seriously? **2** The act of alleging.

al·lege [ə·lej′] *v.* **al·leged, al·leg·ing** **1** To declare to be true but without proving it: It was *alleged* that he was not the real heir. **2** To give as an argument or reason: He *alleged* illness in order to leave early.

al·leged [ə·lejd′ *or* ə·lej′id] *adj.* Declared to be true but without proof; supposed: an *alleged* ability to see into the future. — **al·leg·ed·ly** [ə·lej′id·lē] *adv.*

Al·le·ghe·ny [al′ə·gā′nē] *n.* **1** A mountain range extending from Pennsylvania to Virginia. **2** A river in western New York and Pennsylvania.

al·le·giance [ə·lē′jəns] *n.* **1** Loyalty to a government or ruler. **2** Devotion or loyalty, as to a person or cause.

add, āce, câre, pälm; end, ēqual; it, īce; odd, ōpen, ôrder; tʊʊk, pʊʊl; up, bûrn;
ə = a in *above*, e in *sicken*, i in *possible*, o in *melon*, u in *circus*; yʊʊ = u in *fuse*; oil; pout;
check; ring; thin; this; zh in *vision*. For ¶ reference, see page 64 · HOW TO

al·le·gor·i·cal [al′ə·gôr′ə·kəl] *adj.* Having to do with or using allegory.

al·le·go·ry [al′ə·gôr′ē] *n.*, *pl.* **al·le·go·ries** A story that uses the surface meaning figuratively to teach a lesson or explain something about life.

al·le·gro [ə·lā′grō *or* ə·leg′rō] *adj.*, *adv.*, *n.*, *pl.* **al·le·gros 1** *adj.*, *adv.* In music, fast and lively in tempo. **2** *n.* A musical composition or a section of one in a fast tempo.

al·le·lu·ia [al′ə·lōō′yə] *n.*, *interj.* Another spelling of HALLELUJAH.

al·ler·gic [ə·lûr′jik] *adj.* **1** Resulting from or having to do with an allergy. **2** Having an allergy.

al·ler·gy [al′ər·jē] *n.*, *pl.* **al·ler·gies** A condition of abnormal sensitiveness to certain foods, pollens, dust, etc. Hives and hay fever are commonly caused by allergies.

al·le·vi·ate [ə·lē′vē·āt] *v.* **al·le·vi·at·ed, al·le·vi·at·ing** To make lighter or easier to bear; relieve: to *alleviate* pain. — **al·le′vi·a′tion** *n.*

al·ley[1] [al′ē] *n.*, *pl.* **al·leys 1** A narrow street or passageway between or behind buildings. **2** A bowling alley.

al·ley[2] [al′ē] *n.*, *pl.* **al·leys** A large marble used to shoot at other marbles in a game.

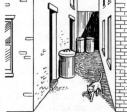

An alley

All·hal·lows [ôl·hal′ōz] *n.* Another name for ALL SAINTS' DAY.

al·li·ance [ə·lī′əns] *n.* **1** A formal agreement or union made between nations, states, or individuals: A treaty is an *alliance* between nations just as a marriage is an *alliance* between families. **2** The people or nations who make such an agreement.

al·lied [ə·līd′ *or* al′īd] *adj.* **1** United, joined, or combined: *allied* armies. **2** Closely related: *allied* subjects.

Al·lies [al′īz *or* ə·līz′] *n.pl.* All of the nations, as England, Russia, France, the U.S., etc., who fought against the Axis powers of Germany, Italy, and Japan in World War II.

al·li·ga·tor [al′ə·gā′tər] *n.* A large reptile found mainly along rivers of the SE U.S., much like a crocodile but with a broader snout. Leather is made from its skin.

alligator pear Another name for AVOCADO.

al·lit·er·a·tion [ə·lit′ə·rā′shən] *n.* The use of the same sound at the beginnings in a group or line of verse, as the f's in the phrase "A fair field full of folk."

Alligator, about 12 ft. long

al·lo·cate [al′ə·kāt] *v.* **al·lo·cat·ed, al·lo·cat·ing 1** To set apart for a special purpose: to *allocate* money for a birthday gift. **2** To distribute or divide: to *allocate* one's energy among several jobs. — **al′lo·ca′tion** *n.*

al·lot [ə·lot′] *v.* **al·lot·ted, al·lot·ting** To give out or assign as a share or portion: to *allot* chores; to *allot* ten minutes to each speaker.

al·lot·ment [ə·lot′mənt] *n.* **1** The act of allotting. **2** A share or portion.

all-out [ôl′out′] *adj.* Complete and entire; total: *all-out* war.

al·low [ə·lou′] *v.* **1** To permit: Talking is not *allowed* here; *Allow* me to go. **2** To give or assign; allot: He *allowed* us five dollars for our expenses. **3** To admit or concede: to *allow* a point in an argument. **4** To count on, as an addition or deduction: *Allow* more space on this page for your signature. — **allow for** To consider or take into account: In flying to Europe, *allow for* the difference in time.

al·low·a·ble [ə·lou′ə·bəl] *adj.* That can be allowed; permitted; admissible.

al·low·ance [ə·lou′əns] *n.* **1** An amount or portion of something given at more or less regular intervals: a weekly *allowance* of money; a daily *allowance* of food. **2** An amount added or subtracted for some reason: We'll give an *allowance* of $200.00 for your old car. — **make allowances for** To take into account; allow for: We had to *make allowances for* his youth.

al·loy [*n.* al′oi *or* ə·loi′, *v.* ə·loi′] **1** *n.* A mixture of two or more metals or of a metal and some other substance: Brass is an *alloy* of copper and zinc. **2** *n.* A cheaper metal mixed with a valuable metal. **3** *v.* To mix so as to form an alloy. **4** *v.* To lessen or decrease; mar: The fun of our trip was *alloyed* by many little mishaps.

all right 1 Correct or satisfactory: Your answers are *all right*. **2** Well or well enough: The fan is working *all right*. **3** Healthy; not hurt: His arm is *all right*. **4** Yes. **5** Certainly: I'll be there *all right!* ◆ *Alright* is a spelling of *all right* which is not yet acceptable.

all-round [ôl′round′] *adj.* All-around.

All Saints' Day November 1, a Christian feast in memory of all saints and martyrs.

all·spice [ôl′spīs′] *n.* **1** The dried, aromatic berry of the pimento, a West Indian tree. **2** A spice made from this berry, having a flavor like that of many spices mixed together.

all-star [ôl′stär′] *adj.* Made up of the best players: an *all-star* baseball team.

al·lude [ə·lōōd′] *v.* **al·lud·ed, al·lud·ing** To refer to something indirectly; just mention: He only *alluded* to last summer's trip.

al·lure [ə·lōōr′] *v.* **al·lured, al·luring**, *n.* **1** *v.* To draw or entice by something tempting. **2** *v.* To fascinate: India *allured* him. **3** *adj. use:* an *alluring* woman. **4** *n.* Fascination.

al·lure·ment [ə·lōōr′mənt] *n.* **1** The act of alluring. **2** An attractive or fascinating quality or thing: the *allurement* of her voice.

al·lu·sion [ə·lōō′zhən] *n.* A slight or casual mention or suggestion of something: He made a hasty *allusion* to our defeat.

al·lu·vi·al [ə·lōō′vē·əl] *adj.* Composed of earth or sand left or deposited by running water.

al·ly [ə·lī′ *or* al′ī] *v.* **al·lied, al·ly·ing,** *n., pl.* **al·lies 1** *v.* To join or unite for a particular purpose, as for defense: England *allied* herself with France. **2** *n.* A person or country joined with another for a particular purpose. **3** *n.* (*usually written* **Ally**) One of the Allies. ◆ See ALLIES. **4** *n.* A close friend or helper.

al·ma ma·ter [al′mə mā′tər *or* äl′mə mä′tər] The school or college where one is being or has been educated. ◆ *Alma mater* comes from a Latin phrase meaning *fostering mother.*

al·ma·nac [ôl′mə·nak] *n.* A yearly calendar giving the days, weeks, and months of the year with facts about the weather, sun, moon, etc.

al·might·y [ôl·mīt′ē] *adj.* Able to do all things. — **the Almighty** God, the Supreme Being.

al·mond [ä′mənd *or* am′ənd] *n.* **1** A small tree that grows in warm temperate regions. **2** The oval-shaped, edible nut of this tree.

al·most [ôl′mōst *or* ôl·mōst′] *adv.* Very nearly; all but: We are *almost* finished.

alms [ämz] *n.* (*used with a singular or plural verb*) A gift or gifts, usually money, for the poor.

alms·house [ämz′hous′] *n.* A house in which poor persons are taken care of; poorhouse.

al·oe [al′ō] *n., pl.* **al·oes 1** A South African plant with thick, fleshy leaves and showy red or yellow flowers. **2** (*pl.*) (*used with a singular verb*) A bitter-tasting medicine made from the leaves of this plant, used as a laxative.

a·loft [ə·lôft′] *adv.* **1** In or to a high or higher place; on high; high up. **2** At, to, or toward the masthead of a ship.

a·lo·ha [ə·lō′ə *or* ä·lō′hä] *n., interj.* Love: Hawaiian word used as a greeting and a farewell.

a·lone [ə·lōn′] *adv., adj.* **1** Without anyone or anything near, about, etc.: The horse was *alone* in the meadow; to live *alone.* **2** With nothing more: The pictures *alone* are worth the price. **3** Only: He *alone* understood. **4** Without equal: As an artist, he stands *alone.* — **let alone 1** Not to disturb or tamper with. **2** And certainly not; not to say: He can't even float, *let alone* swim.

a·long [ə·lông′] **1** *prep.* Through or over the length of; by the side of: to walk *along* the shore. **2** *adv.* Onward; forward: The years roll *along.* **3** *adv.* By the side; near: a brook running *along* by the hedge. **4** *adv.* With one: Bring a friend *along.* **5** *adv.* Advanced: The afternoon is well *along.* — **all along** From the beginning: I expected trouble *all along.* — **along with 1** Together with. **2** As well as: There are some poor players *along with* some good ones.

a·long·side [ə·long′sīd′] **1** *adv.* Close to or along the side. **2** *prep.* Side by side with; at the side of: The truck pulled in *alongside* my car.

a·loof [ə·lōōf′] **1** *adj.* Cool or distant in manner or action; unsympathetic. **2** *adv.* At a distance; apart: to stay *aloof* from the crowd.

a·loud [ə·loud′] *adv.* **1** Loud enough to be heard. **2** With the voice: Read it *aloud.*

al·pac·a [al·pak′ə] *n.* **1** An animal of South America resembling a sheep and related to the llama. **2** Its long, silky wool, or a kind of cloth made from it. **3** A glossy fabric made of cotton and sheep's wool.

al·pen·stock [al′pən·stok′] *n.* A long iron-pointed staff used by mountain climbers.

al·pha [al′fə] *n.* **1** The first letter in the Greek alphabet. **2** The beginning or first of anything.

Alpaca, 42 inches high at shoulder

alpha and omega Both the first and the last; beginning and end; sum total.

al·pha·bet [al′fə·bet] *n.* **1** The letters that form the separate parts or elements of a written language, arranged in a fixed order. **2** Any system of characters or symbols representing the sounds of speech.

al·pha·bet·ic [al′fə·bet′ik] *adj.* Alphabetical.

al·pha·bet·i·cal [al′fə·bet′i·kəl] *adj.* **1** Arranged in the order of the alphabet. **2** Of or having to do with an alphabet. — **al′pha·bet′·i·cal·ly** *adv.*

al·pha·bet·ize [al′fə·bə·tīz′] *v.* **al·pha·bet·ized, al·pha·bet·iz·ing** To put in alphabetical order. ¶3

alpha particle A positively charged particle consisting of two protons and two neutrons, the same as the nucleus of a helium atom, emitted by a radioactive substance.

al·pine [al′pīn] *adj.* **1** Of or like a mountain. **2** (*written* **Alpine**) Of or having to do with the Alps or the people living there.

Alps [alps] *n.pl.* A mountain system of Europe, curving from SE France through Italy, Switzerland, and Austria into Yugoslavia.

al·read·y [ôl·red′ē] *adv.* Before or by this time or a time previously mentioned: We have *already* seen the show. ◆ *Already* should not be confused with *all ready,* which means *completely ready.*

Al·sace-Lor·raine [al′säs·lə·rān′] *n.* A disputed border region between NE France and SW Germany, surrendered to Germany in 1871, regained by France in 1919, annexed by Germany in 1940, and regained by France in 1945.

al·so [ôl′sō] *adv.* Besides; too; in addition: She sings and *also* dances.

---

add, āce, câre, pälm; end, ēqual; it, īce; odd, ōpen, ôrder; toŏk, pōol; up, bûrn;
ə = a in *above*, e in *sicken*, i in *possible*, o in *melon*, u in *circus*; yōō = u in *fuse*; oil; pout;
check; ring; thin; this; zh in *vision.* For ¶ reference, see page 64 · HOW TO

al·tar [ôl′tər] *n.* **1** A raised table used in most Christian churches in celebrating Mass or Communion. **2** Any raised place or structure on which sacrifices may be offered to a god.

altar boy A boy who assists at the altar; an acolyte.

al·ter [ôl′tər] *v.* To make or become different; change: The dress will have to be *altered*.

al·ter·a·tion [ôl′tə·rā′shən] *n.* **1** The act of changing something. **2** A change made.

al·ter·ca·tion [ôl′tər·kā′shən] *n.* An angry, noisy dispute or quarrel.

al·ter·nate [*v.* ôl′tər·nāt, *adj., n.* ôl′tər·nit] *v.* **al·ter·nat·ed, al·ter·nat·ing,** *adj., n.* **1** *v.* To follow or cause to follow one after another by turns: Day *alternates* with night; *Alternate* the two colors. **2** *v.* To take turns: We *alternated* in mowing the lawn. **3** *adj.* Existing, happening, or following by turns: *alternate* periods of work and study. **4** *adj.* Every other or every second: The dances took place on *alternate* nights. **5** *n.* A substitute, especially a person chosen to take over for another if needed. — **al′ter·nate·ly** *adv.* — **al′ter·na′tion** *n.*

Red and black beads alternate in the necklace.

alternating current An electric current that reverses its direction of flow regularly and rapidly.

al·ter·na·tive [ôl·tûr′nə·tiv] **1** *n.* A choice between two or sometimes more things. **2** *n.* Either of the two or more things to be chosen. **3** *adj.* Offering a choice of two or more things: *alternative* plans. — **al·ter′na·tive·ly** *adv.*

al·tho [ôl·thō′] *conj.* Another spelling of ALTHOUGH.

al·though [ôl·thō′] *conj.* In spite of the fact that; even if; though.

al·tim·e·ter [al·tim′ə·tər *or* al′tə·mē′tər] *n.* An instrument for measuring height, used in aviation to determine how high a plane is flying.

al·ti·tude [al′tə·t(y)ood] *n.* **1** The height above any given point, especially above sea level: a balloon at an *altitude* of 1,500 feet. **2** A high place or rank.

al·to [al′tō] *n., pl.* **al·tos 1** The lowest female voice; contralto. **2** A very high male voice. **3** A person with such a voice. **4** The part or range sung by such a voice. **5** *adj. use: alto* saxophone.

al·to·geth·er [ôl′tə·geth′ər] *adv.* **1** Completely; wholly; entirely: He was not *altogether* happy. **2** With everything considered or included; in all: *Altogether*, the bill comes to $20.

al·tru·ism [al′troo·iz′əm] *n.* Unselfish regard for the welfare of others. — **al′tru·ist** *n.*

al·tru·is·tic [al′troo·is′tik] *adj.* Concerned with the welfare of others; unselfish.

al·um [al′əm] *n.* A compound of mineral salts, used in medicine, in baking powder, to stop bleeding from small cuts, etc.

a·lu·min·i·um [al′yə·min′ē·əm] *n.* The British and Canadian spelling of ALUMINUM.

a·lu·mi·num [ə·loo′mə·nəm] *n.* **1** A lightweight, bluish white metallic element that does not tarnish easily. It has a wide range of uses. **2** *adj. use: aluminum* pots and pans.

a·lum·na [ə·lum′nə] *n., pl.* **a·lum·nae** [ə·lum′nē] A female graduate or former student of a college or school.

a·lum·nus [ə·lum′nəs] *n., pl.* **a·lum·ni** [ə·lum′nī] A male graduate or former student of a school or college. ◆ The plural form *alumni* often refers to persons of both sexes.

al·ways [ôl′wāz *or* ôl′wiz] *adv.* **1** For all time; forever: We will *always* be friends. **2** Every time; on all occasions: You *always* say that.

am [am] The first person singular form of the verb BE in the present tense: I *am* here.

AM or **A.M.** Abbreviation for AMPLITUDE MODULATION, a form of radio transmission.

A.M. or **a.m. 1** The morning. **2** The period from midnight to noon. ◆ *A.M.* is an abbreviation of *ante meridiem*, a Latin phrase meaning *before noon.*

a·mal·gam [ə·mal′gəm] *n.* **1** An alloy of mercury and another metal or metals. **2** Any mixture or combination of things.

a·mal·ga·mate [ə·mal′gə·māt] *v.* **a·mal·ga·mat·ed, a·mal·ga·mat·ing 1** To form an amalgam. **2** To unite or combine: The two companies voted to *amalgamate*. — **a·mal′ga·ma′tion** *n.*

am·a·ryl·lis [am′ə·ril′is] *n.* A plant having large flowers that look something like lilies.

a·mass [ə·mas′] *v.* To heap up; accumulate, especially as wealth or possessions for oneself.

am·a·teur [am′ə·choor *or* am′ə·t(y)oor] *n.* **1** A person who practices any art, study, or sport for enjoyment but not for money. **2** A person who does something without sound training or skill. **3** *adj. use:* an *amateur* cast. ◆ *Amateur* and *connoisseur* both come from the French and have Latin roots, *amateur* from a word meaning *to love, connoisseur* from a word meaning *to know.* Thus an *amateur* literally means "one who loves," and a *connoisseur* "one who knows," although in actual everyday use this distinction is not always maintained. An *amateur* may have a great deal of knowledge to go along with his enthusiasm, and a *connoisseur*, who knows enough to make sharp critical judgments in his field, would be odd indeed if he didn't love his subject.

am·a·teur·ish [am′ə·choor′ish *or* am′ə·t(y)oor′·ish] *adj.* Done as by an amateur; not expert. — **am′a·teur′ish·ly** *adv.*

a·maze [ə·māz′] *v.* **a·mazed, a·maz·ing** To bewilder with wonder or surprise; astonish; perplex: His knowledge *amazed* his teachers.

a·maze·ment [ə·māz′mənt] *n.* Bewilderment resulting from surprise; astonishment.

a·maz·ing [ə·mā′zing] *adj.* Causing amazement; astonishing; wonderful. — **a·maz′·ing·ly** *adv.*

Am·a·zon [am′ə·zon] *n.* **1** A very large river of South America, flowing from the Andes of Peru eastward across Brazil to the Atlantic. **2** In Greek mythology, one of a race of female warriors. **3** (*usually written* **amazon**) Any large, strong, or athletic woman.

am·bas·sa·dor [am·bas′ə·dər *or* am·bas′ə·dôr] *n.* **1** An official of the highest rank sent to represent his government in another country. **2** Any representative or messenger.

am·ber [am′bər] **1** *n.* A hard, brittle, brownish yellow or reddish yellow fossil resin found in the earth, used for jewelry, varnish, etc. **2** *n., adj.* Dark yellowish orange.

am·ber·gris [am′bər·grēs *or* am′bər·gris] *n.* A grayish, waxy substance from the intestines of the sperm whale, used in making perfume.

am·bi·dex·trous [am′bə·dek′strəs] *adj.* Able to use both hands equally well: Being *ambidextrous*, he could draw with either hand.

am·bi·ent [am′bē·ənt] *adj.* Surrounding; encompassing: in the *ambient* spaces of the sky.

am·bi·gu·i·ty [am′bə·gyōō′ə·tē] *n., pl.* **am·bi·gu·i·ties** **1** A possibility of more than one meaning. **2** An ambiguous expression, situation, etc.

am·big·u·ous [am·big′yōō·əs] *adj.* **1** Capable of being understood in more senses than one; having more than one possible meaning: an *ambiguous* reply. **2** Doubtful or uncertain: an *ambiguous* position. — **am·big′u·ous·ly** *adv.*

am·bi·tion [am·bish′ən] *n.* **1** An eager desire to succeed or to achieve something, as wealth or power. **2** The object of such a desire: His *ambition* was to be a great surgeon.

am·bi·tious [am·bish′əs] *adj.* **1** Moved by or possessing ambition; eager to succeed. **2** Requiring great skill or much effort for success; challenging; difficult: an *ambitious* undertaking. — **am·bi′tious·ly** *adv.*

am·ble [am′bəl] *v.* **am·bled, am·bling,** *n.* **1** *v.* To move at an easy, leisurely pace: to *amble* down a country lane. **2** *v.* To move, as a horse, by lifting and putting down first the two legs on one side and then the two legs on the other side. **3** *n.* The gait of a horse when ambling. **4** *n.* Any leisurely movement or pace.

am·bro·sia [am·brō′zhə *or* am·brō′zhē·ə] *n.* **1** The food of the old Greek and Roman gods, supposed to give eternal life. **2** Any delicious food or drink.

am·bu·lance [am′byə·ləns] *n.* A specially equipped vehicle for carrying the sick and wounded.

am·bus·cade [am′bəs·kād′] *n., v.* **am·bus·**

cad·ed, am·bus·cad·ing 1 *n.* An ambush. **2** *v.* To ambush.

am·bush [am′bŏŏsh] **1** *n.* A concealed place where troops, or others, lie hidden waiting to attack. **2** *n.* Those who are waiting to attack. **3** *v.* To hide in order to attack. **4** *v.* To attack from a concealed place; waylay.

a·me·ba [ə·mē′bə] *n., pl.* **a·me·bas** or **a·me·bae** [ə·mē′bē] A very small, simple form of animal life, consisting of a single cell and visible only through a microscope.

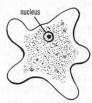

Ameba

a·mel·io·rate [ə·mēl′yə·rāt] *v.* **a·mel·io·rat·ed, a·mel·io·rat·ing** To make or become better; improve: to *ameliorate* slum conditions. — **a·mel′io·ra′tion** *n.*

a·men [ā′men *or* ä′men] **1** *interj.* So it is; so be it: a word used at the end of a prayer. **2** *n. informal* Any expression of hearty agreement or conviction: *Amen* to that!

a·me·na·ble [ə·mē′nə·bəl *or* ə·men′ə·bəl] *adj.* **1** Willing to yield or submit; responsive: The boys proved *amenable* to discipline. **2** Answerable: All citizens are *amenable* to the law. — **a·men′a·bly** *adv.*

a·mend [ə·mend′] *v.* **1** To change for the better; correct; reform: You must *amend* your ways. **2** To change or alter: To *amend* the rules.

a·mend·ment [ə·mend′mənt] *n.* **1** A change for the better. **2** A removal of faults; correction. **3** A change, as of a law, bill, etc.

a·mends [ə·mendz′] *n.pl.* Something done or given to make up for a wrong, a loss, injury, etc.: to make *amends* for one's bad manners.

a·men·i·ty [ə·men′ə·tē] *n., pl.* **a·men·i·ties** **1** The quality of being pleasant or agreeable: the *amenity* of a warm tropical night. **2** (*pl.*) Things, such as good manners, that make life pleasant and comfortable: to practice the *amenities.*

A·mer·i·ca [ə·mer′ə·kə] *n.* **1** The United States. **2** The lands in the Western Hemisphere, especially either of the two continents, North America or South America.

A·mer·i·can [ə·mer′ə·kən] **1** *adj.* Of, from, or in the U.S. **2** *n.* A person born in or a citizen of the U.S. **3** *adj.* Of, from, or in the Western Hemisphere. **4** *n.* A person born or living in the Western Hemisphere.

American Indian An Indian (def. 1).

A·mer·i·can·ism [ə·mer′ə·kən·iz′əm] *n.* **1** A trait, custom, or tradition of the people of the U.S. **2** A word, phrase, or usage peculiar to or originating in the U.S.: The word "carpetbagger" is an example of an *Americanism.* **3** Devotion to the U.S., its institutions, and traditions.

A·mer·i·can·ize [ə·mer′ə·kən·iz′] *v.* **A·mer·i·**

can·ized, A·mer·i·can·iz·ing To make or become American, as in ideals, customs, speech, etc. — **A·mer′i·can·i·za′tion** *n.* ¶3

American Revolution The war for independence carried on by the thirteen American Colonies against Great Britain, 1775–1783. It is also called the Revolutionary War.

am·e·thyst [am′ə·thist] **1** *n.* A variety of quartz having a purple or violet color, used as a gem. **2** *n., adj.* Purplish violet.

a·mi·a·ble [ā′mē·ə·bəl] *adj.* Pleasing in disposition; agreeable; friendly. — **a′mi·a·bil′i·ty** *n.* — **a′mi·a·bly** *adv.*

am·i·ca·ble [am′i·kə·bəl] *adj.* Showing or promoting good will; friendly; peaceable: an *amicable* settlement. — **am′i·ca·bly** *adv.*

a·mid [ə·mid′] *prep.* In the midst of; among.

a·mid·ships [ə·mid′ships] *adv.* In or at the middle of a ship: The torpedo struck *amidships.*

a·midst [ə·midst′] *prep.* Amid.

a·mi·go [ə·mē′gō] *n., pl.* **a·mi·gos** A friend; comrade: a Spanish word.

a·mi·no acid [ə·mē′nō *or* am′ə·nō] Any of a group of organic chemical compounds containing carbon, hydrogen, nitrogen, and oxygen. When proteins are digested they are broken down into amino acids.

a·miss [ə·mis′] **1** *adv.* In a wrong or defective way; improperly; erroneously: Have I spoken *amiss?* **2** *adj.* Out of order; wrong; imperfect: Something is *amiss.*

am·i·ty [am′ə·tē] *n., pl.* **am·i·ties** Peaceful relations, as between governments; friendship.

am·me·ter [am′mē′tər] *n.* An instrument for measuring the strength of an electrical current.

am·mo·nia [ə·mōn′yə] *n.* **1** A colorless, suffocating gas formed from nitrogen and hydrogen. **2** Ammonia gas dissolved in water, used for cleaning, etc.

am·mu·ni·tion [am′yə·nish′ən] *n.* **1** Any missiles fired from guns or launched as rockets, or explosive weapons such as bombs, mines, or grenades. **2** Anything used for attack or defense: Medical facts were his *ammunition* against smoking.

am·ne·sia [am·nē′zhə *or* am·nē′zhē·ə] *n.* A partial or complete loss of memory caused by injury, sickness, or severe shock.

am·nes·ty [am′nəs·tē] *n., pl.* **am·nes·ties** An official pardon for offenses committed against a government.

a·moe·ba [ə·mē′bə] *n., pl.* **a·moe·bas** or **a·moe·bae** [ə·mē′bē] Another spelling of AMEBA.

a·mok [ə·muk′ *or* ə·mok′] *adv.* Another spelling of AMUCK.

a·mong [ə·mung′] *prep.* **1** In or into the midst of: He lived *among* the Eskimos; a small hut *among* the trees. **2** By the combined efforts of: *Among* us, we ought to finish the work. **3** In the class, group, or number of: to be *among* the living. **4** In portions for each of: The food was divided *among* them. **5** Mutually between: to have quarrels *among* friends. ◆ See BETWEEN.

a·mongst [ə·mungst′] *prep.* Among.

am·o·rous [am′ər·əs] *adj.* **1** Inclined to fall in love: an *amorous* nature. **2** Of or arising from love: an *amorous* sigh. — **am′o·rous·ly** *adv.*

a·mor·phous [ə·môr′fəs] *adj.* **1** Not crystallized, though solid: Glass is *amorphous.* **2** Without definite form or shape: *amorphous* clouds.

A·mos [ā′məs] *n.* **1** In the Bible, a Hebrew prophet who lived during the eighth century B.C. **2** A book of the Old Testament.

a·mount [ə·mount′] **1** *v.* To reach or add up in number or quantity: Your bill *amounts* to ten dollars. **2** *n.* A sum total: The *amount* due is ten dollars. **3** *n.* Quantity: a small *amount* of flour. **4** *v.* To be equal in effect or importance: Not taking the test *amounts* to failing it.

a·mour [ə·mŏŏr′] *n.* A love affair, especially a secret or unlawful one.

am·pere [am′pir *or* am·pir′] *n.* The unit for measuring the strength of an electric current. It is equal to the current that flows through a resistance of one ohm under an electromotive force of one volt.

am·per·sand [am′pər·sand *or* am′pər·sand′] *n.* The character (&) meaning *and:* Jones & Company.

am·phib·i·an [am·fib′ē·ən] **1** *adj.* Of or having to do with a class of cold-blooded animals adapted for life both on land and in water. **2** *n.* Any amphibian animal, such as frogs and salamanders, whose young have gills and develop through a larval or tadpole stage into animals that breathe with lungs. **3** *n.* Any animal, as a seal or sea lion, that breeds and raises young on land but lives and hunts largely in the water. **4** *adj.* Amphibious. **5** *n.* An airplane that can take off from or alight on land or water. **6** *n.* A vehicle that can be driven on land or on water.

am·phib·i·ous [am·fib′ē·əs] *adj.* **1** Living or adapted to life on land or in water. **2** Capable of operating or landing on either land or water.

am·phi·the·a·ter or **am·phi·the·a·tre** [am′fə·thē′ə·tər] *n.* **1** An oval or circular building with seats in tiers rising from a central open space. **2** Anything resembling this, as a hollow surrounded by sloping hills.

Amphitheater

am·ple [am′pəl] *adj.* **am·pler, am·plest 1** Large; spacious; roomy: an *ample* clothes closet. **2** More than enough; abundant; liberal. **3** Sufficient; adequate: an *ample* allowance.

am·pli·fi·ca·tion [am′plə·fi·kā′shən] *n.* **1** An extending or enlarging by adding or increasing something. **2** The creation of a strong electric current that is an enlarged copy of a weaker one, in effect making a weak one strong.

am·pli·fi·er [am′plə·fī′ər] *n.* **1** A person or thing that amplifies. **2** Any of various electronic devices that produce amplification, as in a radio.

am·pli·fy [am′plə·fī] *v.* **am·pli·fied, am·pli·fy·ing 1** To enlarge or increase in power, capacity, etc. **2** To make more full or complete: *Amplify* your essay by giving more details. **3** To produce amplification of: to *amplify* an electric current.

am·pli·tude [am′plə·t(y)ood] *n.* **1** The quality of being ample; fullness; abundance. **2** The amount of swing to either side of a middle position made by a wave, as of water, sound, light, etc., or by an object, as a pendulum.

amplitude modulation The changing of the amplitude of a radio wave in a way that corresponds with the sound or other signal to be broadcast.

am·ply [am′plē] *adv.* In an ample manner; liberally; sufficiently: She was *amply* repaid.

am·pu·tate [am′pyoo·tāt] *v.* **am·pu·tat·ed, am·pu·tat·ing** To cut off (a limb, etc.) by using surgery. — **am′pu·ta′tion** *n.*

Am·ster·dam [am′stər·dam] *n.* A seaport, the largest city and officially, though not actually, the capital of the Netherlands.

a·muck [ə·muk′] *adv.* In a murderous or violent state or manner, especially in the phrase **run amuck,** to become murderous or violent.

am·u·let [am′yə·lit] *n.* An object worn as a charm to keep off evil or bad luck.

A·mund·sen [ä′moon·sən], **Roald,** 1872–1928, Norwegian explorer who discovered the South Pole in 1911.

a·muse [ə·myooz′] *v.* **a·mused, a·mus·ing 1** To occupy pleasingly; entertain: to *amuse* a child with a toy. **2** To cause to laugh or smile: I *amused* him with a joke. ◆ See ENTERTAIN.

a·muse·ment [ə·myooz′mənt] *n.* **1** The condition of being amused. **2** Something that amuses; pastime.

a·mus·ing [ə·myoo′zing] *adj.* Causing amusement, fun, laughter, etc. — **a·mus′ing·ly** *adv.*

an [ən *or* an] An indefinite article that is used instead of the article *a* before words beginning with a vowel sound, as *an* owl but *a* dog, *an* honor but *a* house, *an* automobile but *a* universe.

-an A suffix meaning: **1** Of or having to do with, as in *Elizabethen,* having to do with Queen Elizabeth I or her reign. **2** A person born or living in or having to do with, as in *Italian,* a person born or living in Italy, or in *librarian,* a person connected with a library.

a·nach·ro·nism [ə·nak′rə·niz′əm] *n.* **1** An error that places, shows, or mentions something in a time when it was not known or did not exist. **2** A person or thing existing or occurring out of its proper time.

An anachronism

an·a·con·da [an′ə·kon′də] *n.* A very large, nonpoisonous snake of South America that crushes its victims in its coils.

an·aer·o·bic [an′âr·ō′bik] *adj.* Living or flourishing where there is no free oxygen: *Anaerobic* bacteria cause gangrene.

an·aes·the·sia [an′is·thē′zhə] *n.* Another spelling of ANESTHESIA.

an·aes·thet·ic [an′is·thet′ik] *n., adj.* Another spelling of ANESTHETIC.

an·a·gram [an′ə·gram] *n.* **1** A word or phrase formed by changing the order of the letters of another word or phrase: "Rate" is an *anagram* of "tear." **2** (*pl.*) A game in which the players make words by changing or adding letters.

an·al·ge·sic [an′əl·jē′zik *or* an′əl·jē′sik] **1** *n.* A drug or medicine that relieves pain: Aspirin is an *analgesic.* **2** *adj.* Relieving or lessening pain.

a·nal·o·gous [ə·nal′ə·gəs] *adj.* Alike or similar in certain respects: The flow of electricity is *analogous* to the flow of water.

a·nal·o·gy [ə·nal′ə·jē] *n., pl.* **a·nal·o·gies** A likeness that exists between two objects that are in other respects not the same: There is a certain *analogy* between the wings of a bird and the wings of an insect.

a·nal·y·sis [ə·nal′ə·sis] *n., pl.* **a·nal·y·ses** [ə·nal′ə·sēz] **1** The separation or breaking up of something into its smaller parts or elements so as to be able to examine or describe the thing more closely: *Analysis* of air shows more than six gases. **2** A written statement of such an analysis. **3** Psychoanalysis.

an·a·lyst [an′ə·list] *n.* A person who analyzes.

an·a·lyt·ic [an′ə·lit′ik] *adj.* Analytical.

an·a·lyt·i·cal [an′ə·lit′ə·kəl] *adj.* **1** Having to do with or using analysis: *analytical* chemistry. **2** Inclined to examine critically or closely: an *analytical* mind. — **an′a·lyt′i·cal·ly** *adv.*

an·a·lyze [an′ə·līz] *v.* **an·a·lyzed, an·a·lyz·ing 1** To make an analysis of: to *analyze* the results of an election. **2** To examine critically or closely: to *analyze* behavior. ¶3

an·ar·chist [an′ər·kist] *n.* **1** A person who believes all governments should be abolished. **2** A person who rebels against authority and encourages the breaking of all laws or rules.

an·ar·chy [an′ər·kē] *n., pl.* **an·ar·chies 1** The total absence of government. **2** A condition of lawless confusion and disorder.

a·nath·e·ma [ə·nath′ə·mə] *n.* **1** A very serious ban or curse, especially one placed by a church upon a person, book, doctrine, etc. **2** A person or thing that is banned or cursed. **3** A person or thing that is extremely disliked.

a·nath·e·ma·tize [ə·nath′ə·mə·tīz] *v.* **a·nath·e·ma·tized, a·nath·e·ma·tiz·ing** To pronounce an anathema against; curse.

an·a·tom·i·cal [an′ə·tom′i·kəl] *adj.* Of or having to do with anatomy or dissection.

add, āce, câre, pälm; end, ēqual; it, īce; odd, ōpen, ôrder; took, pool; up, bûrn;
ə = a in *above*, e in *sicken*, i in *possible*, o in *melon*, u in *circus*; yoo = u in *fuse*; oil; pout;
check; ring; thin; this; zh in *vision*. For ¶ reference, see page 64 · HOW TO

a·nat·o·mize [ə·nat′ə·mīz] *v.* **a·nat·o·mized,
a·nat·o·miz·ing 1** To dissect (an animal or
plant). **2** To examine critically; analyze. ¶3
a·nat·o·my [ə·nat′ə·mē] *n.*, *pl.* **a·nat·o·mies
1** The structure of a person, plant, or animal.
2 The human body or skeleton. **3** The study of
the structure of the body. **4** The cutting apart
of a body in order to study its separate parts and
how they are put together. **— a·nat′o·mist** *n.*
-ance A suffix meaning: **1** The act or fact of, as
in *resistance*, the act or fact of resisting. **2** The
quality or condition of being, as in *tolerance*, the
quality or condition of being tolerant. **3** A thing
that, as in *insurance*, a thing that insures.
an·ces·tor [an′ses·tər] *n.* **1** A person from
whom one is descended, generally a person
further back than a grandfather; forefather.
2 An animal of an earlier type from which later
animals have developed: The wolf is an *ancestor*
of the dog.
an·ces·tral [an·ses′trəl] *adj.* Of, having to do
with, or inherited from ancestors: an *ancestral*
estate; *ancestral* traits.
an·ces·try [an′ses·trē] *n.*, *pl.* **an·ces·tries
1** All of one's ancestors. **2** Line of descent;
birth: He is of noble *ancestry*.
an·chor [ang′kər] **1** *n.* A metal implement with
hooks that grip the bottom,
lowered into the water by a
chain or rope to keep a ship
from drifting. **2** *v.* To keep
(a ship or boat) secure or held
in place by means of an
anchor. **3** *v.* To lower the
anchor; stay, held by an
anchor. **4** *n.* Something that
gives security or support:
Reading was often an *anchor*
for him in times of trouble. **5** *v.* To fix firmly;
make secure: to *anchor* the table to the floor.
an·chor·age [ang′kər·ij] *n.* **1** A place for
anchoring. **2** The act of anchoring. **3** The
condition of being anchored. **4** Something that
gives support, security, or steadiness: an
anchorage for the tent.
an·cho·rite [ang′kə·rīt] *n.* **1** A person who has
withdrawn from the world for religious reasons.
2 A hermit.
an·cho·vy [an′chō·vē *or* an·chō′vē] *n.*, *pl.* **an·
cho·vies** A very small salt-water fish resembling
the herring, eaten as an appetizer.
an·cient [ān′shənt] **1** *adj.* Existing or occurring
in times long past, especially in times before the
fall of the western Roman Empire in 476.
2 *adj.* Of great age; very old. **3** *n.* (*often pl.*)
The people who lived in ancient times.
and [and] *conj.* **1** As well as; added to; also:
eggs *and* butter *and* cheese. **2** As a result: He
got his feet wet *and* caught a cold. **3** *informal*
To: He'll come *and* get me at six.
an·dan·te [än·dän′tā *or* an·dan′tē] **1** *adj.*, *adv.*
In music, moderately slow in tempo. **2** *n.* A
musical composition or a section of one in an
andante tempo.

Anchor

An·der·sen [an′dər·sən], **Hans Christian,**
1805–1875, Danish writer of fairy tales.
An·des [an′dēz] *n.pl.* A lofty mountain system
in western South America.
and·i·ron [and′ī′ərn] *n.* One of a pair of metal
supports for holding
wood in an open fire-
place.
An·drom·e·da [an·
drom′ə·də] *n.* **1** In
Greek myths, a maid-
en rescued from a sea
monster by Perseus,
who then married her.
2 A northern constel-
lation.

Andirons

an·ec·dote [an′ik·
dōt] *n.* A brief account or story, usually of an
interesting or entertaining nature: an *anecdote*
about Jefferson.
a·ne·mi·a [ə·nē′mē·ə] *n.* A condition in which
the blood has too few red corpuscles or too little
hemoglobin, resulting in a loss of energy, a pale
appearance, and other symptoms.
a·ne·mic [ə·nē′mik] *adj.* Of or having anemia.
an·e·mom·e·ter [an′ə·mom′ə·tər] *n.* An instrument for measuring the speed of the wind.
a·nem·o·ne [ə·nem′ə·nē] *n.* **1** A perennial plant
having flowers with no petals but sepals in
various colors. **2** The sea anemone.
an·er·oid barometer [an′ə·roid] An instrument for measuring atmospheric pressure. The
flexible top of a box with all air removed bends in
or flattens as pressure changes, moving a pointer.
an·es·the·sia [an′is·thē′zhə *or* an′is·thē′zhē·ə]
n. A local or general loss of sensation, especially
of pain, produced by various drugs, ether, etc.
an·es·thet·ic [an′is·thet′ik] **1** *n.* A drug, gas,
etc., that causes unconsciousness or deadens
sensation, as ether. **2** *adj.* Having to do with or
producing anesthesia.
an·es·the·tist [ə·nes′thə·tist] *n.* A person
trained to administer anesthetics.
an·es·the·tize [ə·nes′thə·tīz] *v.* **an·es·the·
tized, an·es·the·tiz·ing** To cause to be
insensible, especially to pain, by means of an
anesthetic.
a·new [ə·n(y)ōo′] *adv.* **1** Again: Begin *anew.*
2 Over again in a different way: Write the play
anew.
an·gel [ān′jəl] *n.* **1** A heavenly being who
serves God as a messenger or attendant. **2** A
person thought of as like an angel in goodness,
purity, or beauty. **3** Any spirit, especially one
that guards or protects. **4** *informal* A person who
backs a venture such as a new play with money.
◆ This word comes from the Latin word *angelus*,
which in turn came from a Greek word meaning
messenger (of God).
an·gel·fish [ān′jəl·fish] *n.*, *pl.* **an·gel·fish** *or*
an·gel·fish·es 1 A type of shark having winglike fins. **2** A brightly colored tropical fish.
angel food cake A delicate, spongy cake
made without shortening or egg yolks.

an·gel·ic [an·jel′ik] *adj.* **1** Of or having to do with angels. **2** Like an angel; pure; beautiful.

An·ge·lus [an′jə·ləs] *n.* **1** A prayer celebrating the Annunciation. **2** A bell rung morning, noon, and evening as a call to recite this prayer.

an·ger [ang′gər] **1** *n.* The feeling aroused against a person or thing that annoys, offends, opposes, or injures one. **2** *v.* To make or become angry: He *angered* us all; She *angers* easily.

an·gle¹ [ang′gəl] *n., v.* **an·gled, an·gling** **1** *n.* A geometric figure formed by two rays that have the same end point. **2** *n.* The space between such rays or surfaces, measured in degrees. **3** *v.* To move or turn at an angle: The halfback *angled* down the field. **4** *n.* A point of view; standpoint: The problem was discussed from all *angles*.

acute angle

right angle

obtuse angle

an·gle² [ang′gəl] *v.* **an·gled, an·gling** **1** To fish with a hook and line. **2** To try to gain something by using schemes or tricks.

straight angle

an·gler [ang′glər] *n.* **1** A person who angles for fish. **2** A large-mouthed salt-water fish having long flexible filaments attached to its head with which it attracts smaller fish.

an·gle·worm [ang′gəl·wûrm′] *n.* An earthworm.

An·gli·can [ang′glə·kən] **1** *adj.* Of or having to do with the Church of England. **2** *n.* A member of the Church of England. **—An′gli·can·ism** *n.*

An·gli·cize [ang′glə·sīz] *v.* **An·gli·cized, An·gli·ciz·ing** To give to or take on an English form, character, pronunciation, etc.: to *Anglicize* the pronunciation of a foreign word. ¶3

an·gling [ang′gling] *n.* Fishing with a hook and line.

Anglo- A combining form meaning: English, as in *Anglo-American*, English and American.

An·glo-Sax·on [ang′glō-sak′sən] **1** *n.* A member of the Germanic people living in England who were conquered by the Normans in 1066. **2** *n.* Their language; Old English. **3** *adj.* Of or having to do with these people or their language.

An·go·ra [ang·gôr′ə] *n.* **1** The former name of ANKARA. **2** A kind of cat, originally from Ankara, with long silky hair. **3** A kind of goat, originally from Ankara, with long silky hair. **4** The hair of this goat, also called **Angora wool,** used in making mohair. **5** An imitation of Angora wool made from rabbit hair.

an·gry [ang′grē] *adj.* **an·gri·er, an·gri·est** **1** Feeling or showing anger: an *angry* man; an *angry* tone of voice. **2** Stormy: an *angry* sky or sea. **3** Badly inflamed: an *angry* sore. **— an′· gri·ly** *adv.*

ang·strom [ang′strəm] *n.* A unit for measuring extremely small lengths or sizes, especially wavelengths of light. It is often called an **angstrom unit.** In one inch there are 254 million angstroms.

an·guish [ang′gwish] *n.* Great suffering of mind or body; agony: the *anguish* of Jesus on the Cross.

an·guished [ang′gwisht] *adj.* Feeling, showing, or caused by anguish: an *anguished* cry.

an·gu·lar [ang′gyə·lər] *adj.* **1** Having or describing an angle or angles; sharp-cornered: an *angular* outline. **2** Measured by an angle: *angular* distance. **3** Bony; gaunt: an *angular* jaw.

an·gu·lar·i·ty [ang′gyə·lar′ə·tē] *n., pl.* **an·gu·lar·i·ties** **1** The condition of being angular. **2** An angle or sharp corner.

an·i·line [an′ə·lin] *n.* An oily, poisonous compound derived from benzene and much used for making dyes, plastics, etc.

an·i·mal [an′ə·məl] **1** *n.* A living being that is not a plant. Unlike plants, most animals can move and feel but cannot make their own food. **2** *n.* Any such creature other than man. **3** *adj.* Of or having to do with animals: *animal* life. **4** *n.* A man who acts like a beast or brute. **5** *adj.* Like a beast or a beast's: *animal* desires. ◆ This word comes directly from Latin, where it meant a *living being.*

an·i·mal·cule [an′ə·mal′kyool] *n.* Any very small or microscopic animal, as an ameba.

animal kingdom One of the three great divisions of nature, including all animals.

an·i·mate [*v.* an′ə·māt, *adj.* an′ə·mit] *v.* **an·i·mat·ed, an·i·mat·ing,** *adj.* **1** *v.* To give life to. **2** *adj.* Living. Animate nature includes both animals and plants. **3** *v.* To fill with zest and spirit: Gay tunes *animated* the marchers. **4** *v.* To inspire: to be *animated* by love.

an·i·mat·ed [an′ə·mā′tid] *adj.* Having spirit or zest; lively. **— an′i·mat·ed·ly** *adv.*

animated cartoon A series of drawings shown as a motion picture with moving figures. Each drawing is slightly changed from the one before to make the movement.

an·i·ma·tion [an′ə·mā′shən] *n.* **1** Life. **2** Liveliness; spirit.

an·i·mos·i·ty [an′ə·mos′ə·tē] *n., pl.* **an·i·mos· i·ties** Strong dislike or hatred; enmity.

an·i·mus [an′ə·məs] *n.* **1** Animosity. **2** The animating spirit or purpose; guiding force.

an·ise [an′is] *n.* **1** A small plant, related to the carrot, grown for its seed. **2** This seed, used as a flavoring and in medicine.

An·ka·ra [ang′kə·rə] *n.* The capital of Turkey.

an·kle [ang′kəl] *n.* The joint connecting the foot and the leg.

an·klet [ang′klit] *n.* **1** A band worn around the ankle as an ornament or fetter. **2** A short sock worn especially by women and girls.

---

add, āce, câre, pälm; end, ēqual; it, īce; odd, ōpen, ôrder; took, pool; up, bûrn; ə = a in *above*, e in *sicken*, i in *possible*, o in *melon*, u in *circus*; yoo = u in *fuse*; oil; pout; check, ring; thin; this; zh in *vision.* For ¶ reference, see page 64 · HOW TO

an·nals [an′əlz] *n.pl.* **1** A record of events year by year. **2** History or records: the *annals* of exploration.

An·nap·o·lis [ə·nap′ə·lis] *n.* The capital of Maryland. The U.S. Naval Academy is there.

an·neal [ə·nēl′] *v.* To make (glass or metal) tougher and less brittle by heating and then slowly cooling.

an·ne·lid [an′ə·lid] *n.* A worm whose body is made up of segments like rings, as the earthworm and leech.

an·nex [*v.* ə·neks′, *n.* an′eks] **1** *v.* To add as an additional part: The U.S. *annexed* Texas in 1845. **2** *n.* Something annexed. **3** *n.* An addition to a building, or another building used along with the main one. **— an′nex·a′tion** *n.*

an·ni·hi·late [ə·nī′ə·lāt] *v.* **an·ni·hi·lat·ed, an·ni·hi·lat·ing** To destroy completely. **— an·ni′hi·la′tion** *n.*

an·ni·ver·sa·ry [an′ə·vûr′sə·rē] *n.,* *pl.* **an·ni·ver·sa·ries** **1** The day of the year on which an event took place in some preceding year: the *anniversary* of the founding of the U.N. **2** A celebration on such a day. **3** *adj. use:* an *anniversary* celebration. ◆ This word comes from two Latin words meaning *to turn the year.*

an·no Dom·i·ni [an′ō dom′ə·nē] In the year of our Lord: a Latin phrase. ◆ See A.D.

an·no·tate [an′ō·tāt] *v.* **an·no·tat·ed, an·no·tat·ing** To furnish with notes explaining or commenting on: Homer's epics have been fully *annotated.*

an·no·ta·tion [an′ō·tā′shən] *n.* **1** The act of annotating. **2** An explanatory note or comment.

an·nounce [ə·nouns′] *v.* **an·nounced, an·nounc·ing** **1** To give public notice of; proclaim. **2** To declare the arrival of: to *announce* guests. **3** To make known to the senses: A whistle *announced* the arrival of the ferry.

an·nounce·ment [ə·nouns′mənt] *n.* **1** The act of announcing. **2** Something announced. **3** An often formal public or private notice of an event: a wedding *announcement.*

an·nounc·er [ə·noun′sər] *n.* A person who announces, especially one who gives the news or introduces performers, etc., on radio or TV.

an·noy [ə·noi′] *v.* To bother; irritate: His loud talking *annoys* me.

an·noy·ance [ə·noi′əns] *n.* **1** An annoying or being annoyed. **2** The angry feeling caused by being annoyed: His *annoyance* made him answer sharply. **3** Something that annoys.

an·nu·al [an′yōō·əl] **1** *adj.* Coming or happening once each year, especially at or around the same time: *annual* elections. **2** *adj.* Taking a year: the *annual* cycle of the seasons. **3** *adj.* For a year: *annual* income. **4** *adj.* Of a plant, living or lasting only a year or a season. **5** *n.* An annual plant. **6** *n.* A book or magazine published once a year. **— an′nu·al·ly** *adv.*

an·nu·i·ty [ə·n(y)ōō′ə·tē] *n.* **1** A sum of money paid each year: Mrs. Lucas gets an *annuity* from her father's estate. **2** The right to receive such yearly payments.

an·nul [ə·nul′] *v.* **an·nulled, an·nul·ling** To do away with; declare to be void and canceled: to *annul* a law or marriage. **— an·nul′ment** *n.*

an·nu·lar eclipse [an′yə·lər] An eclipse of the sun in which a narrow ring of the sun is visible around the dark circle of the moon.

Annular eclipse

an·num [an′əm] *n.* The Latin word for *year,* often used in the phrase *per annum.*

An·nun·ci·a·tion [ə·nun′sē·ā′shən] *n.* **1** The angel Gabriel's announcement to Mary that she was to be the mother of Jesus. **2** The Christian festival on March 25 commemorating this event.

an·ode [an′ōd] *n.* The positive pole or electrode of a battery, electron tube, etc., that attracts negatively charged particles.

a·noint [ə·noint′] *v.* To apply oil or ointment to, often as part of a religious ceremony: The new queen was *anointed* by the bishop. **— a·noint′ment** *n.*

a·nom·a·lous [ə·nom′ə·ləs] *adj.* Different from the usual; irregular or abnormal.

a·nom·a·ly [ə·nom′ə·lē] *n.,* *pl.* **a·nom·a·lies** **1** A deviation from the common rule; irregularity. **2** Something anomalous: A wingless bird is an *anomaly.*

a·non [ə·non′] *adv.* **1** In a little while; soon. **2** At another time.

anon. Abbreviation of ANONYMOUS.

an·o·nym·i·ty [an′ə·nim′ə·tē] *n.* A being anonymous.

a·non·y·mous [ə·non′ə·məs] *adj.* **1** By or from a person not named or not identified: an *anonymous* gift or poem. **2** Whose name is unknown: *anonymous* victims of war. **— a·non′y·mous·ly** *adv.*

a·noph·e·les [ə·nof′ə·lēz] *n.* A kind of mosquito that can transmit the malaria parasite.

an·oth·er [ə·nuth′ər] **1** *adj., pron.* One more: *another* day; Let me have *another.* **2** *adj.* Not the same; different: *another* man. **3** *pron.* A different one: I would prefer *another.* **4** *adj.* Of the same kind as: *another* Einstein.

ans. Abbreviation of ANSWER.

an·swer [an′sər] **1** *n.* A reply or response by word or action, as to a letter, question, etc. **2** *v.* To reply or respond to: to *answer* a question; to *answer* the telephone. **3** *n.* A solution to a problem. **4** *v.* To be sufficient; serve: The soft earth *answered* for a bed. **5** *v.* To be responsible or accountable: to *answer* for someone's safety or honesty. **6** *v.* To correspond; match: to *answer* to a description. **— answer back** To reply rudely or defiantly: The boy *answered back.*

an·swer·a·ble [an′sər·ə·bəl] *adj.* **1** Responsible: He is *answerable* to the company for all receipts. **2** That can be answered or refuted.

ant [ant] *n.* A small crawling insect belonging to an order that includes bees and wasps. Ants live in tunnels in wood or in the ground in well-organized colonies.

-ant A suffix meaning: **1** In the act of doing, as in *defiant*, in the act of defying. **2** A person or thing that does something, as in *servant*, a person who serves.

an·tag·o·nism [an·tag′ə·niz′əm] *n.* Mutual opposition, especially with hostile feelings.

an·tag·o·nist [an·tag′ə·nist] *n.* A person who fights or contends with another; adversary.

an·tag·o·nis·tic [an·tag′ə·nis′tik] *adj.* Opposed; hostile. — **an·tag·o·nis′ti·cal·ly** *adv.*

an·tag·o·nize [an·tag′ə·nīz] *v.* **an·tag·o·nized, an·tag·o·niz·ing** To make an enemy of: The speaker *antagonized* the crowd. ¶3

Ant·arc·tic [ant·ärk′tik] **1** *n.* (**the Antarctic**) The south polar region. **2** *adj.* (*sometimes written* **antarctic**) Of or having to do with the Antarctic.

Ant·arc·ti·ca [ant·ärk′tə·kə] *n.* A continent including the South Pole and mostly within the Antarctic Circle, largely covered with ice.

Antarctic Circle A circle at about 66° 33′ south latitude, beyond which the sun cannot be seen in the depth of winter, taken as the boundary of the south frigid zone.

ante- A prefix meaning: Before, in time or space, as in *antediluvian*, before the Flood, or *anteroom*, a room in front of a main room.

ant·eat·er [ant′ē′tər] *n.* Any of several mammals that have long, sticky tongues and feed mainly on ants and termites.

an·te·ce·dent [an′tə·sēd′(ə)nt] **1** *adj.* Coming earlier; happening before; previous. **2** *n.* A person, thing, or event that comes or happens earlier. **3** *n.* The word, phrase, or clause to which a pronoun refers. In "The song which he sang is very old," *song* is the antecedent of *which*. **4** *n.* (*pl.*) A person's past life or ancestry.

an·te·cham·ber [an′ti·chām′bər] *n.* An anteroom.

an·te·date [an′ti·dāt′] *v.* **an·te·dat·ed, an·te·dat·ing** **1** To come or happen before: The bow *antedates* the crossbow. **2** To give a date to earlier than the actual date: The document was signed on June 5 but was *antedated* to June 1.

an·te·di·lu·vi·an [an′ti·di·lōō′vē·ən] **1** *adj.* Before the Flood. **2** *n.* A person, animal, or plant that lived before the Flood. **3** *adj.* Very old or old-fashioned. **4** *n.* A very old or old-fashioned person.

an·te·lope [an′tə·lōp] *n., pl.* **an·te·lope** or **an·te·lopes** **1** A small, graceful animal with spiral horns, like a deer but related to the goat. **2** The pronghorn of the U.S. and Canada.

an·ten·na [an·ten′ə] *n.* **1** *pl.* **an·ten·nae** [an·ten′ē] One of a pair of jointed, sensitive feelers on the head of various insects, crabs, lobsters, etc. **2** *pl.* **an·ten·nas** A system of wires, rods, or reflecting surfaces for transmitting or receiving radio waves.

Butterfly antennae

an·te·ri·or [an·tir′ē·ər] *adj.* **1** At, near, or toward the front; fore. **2** Earlier in time.

an·te·room [an′ti·rōōm′] *n.* A room leading to a more important or main room; waiting room.

an·them [an′thəm] *n.* **1** A song or hymn of praise, patriotism, or devotion: a national *anthem*. **2** A piece of sacred music, often with words taken from the Bible.

an·ther [an′thər] *n.* A slender stem at the center of a flower that bears the pollen.

ant·hill [ant′hil′] *n.* or **ant hill** A mound of earth piled up by ants in building their underground nest.

an·thol·o·gy [an·thol′ə·jē] *n., pl.* **an·thol·o·gies** A collection of selected poems or other writings by various authors.

Anthers

an·thra·cite [an′thrə·sīt] *n.* Coal that burns slowly and with little flame; hard coal.

an·thrax [an′thraks] *n.* An infectious and often fatal bacterial disease, chiefly of cattle, sheep, and goats, and sometimes transmitted to man.

an·thro·poid [an′thrə·poid] **1** *adj.* Like a human being; manlike, said of certain apes. **2** *n.* A manlike ape, such as the gorilla.

an·thro·pol·o·gy [an′thrə·pol′ə·jē] *n.* The science that st..dies the development of man, physical, social, and cultural, including his customs and beliefs. — **an′thro·pol′o·gist** *n.*

anti- A prefix meaning: **1** Opposed to; against, as in *antislavery*, opposed to slavery. **2** An opposite of, as in *anticlimax*, the opposite of a climax. **3** Working against or counteracting, as in *antiseptic*, working against a septic condition.

an·ti·air·craft [an′tē·âr′kraft] *adj.* Used or directed against enemy aircraft.

an·ti·bi·ot·ic [an′ti·bī·ot′ik] *n.* A substance such as penicillin, produced by a microorganism or fungus, that kills or weakens microorganisms harmful to man.

an·ti·bod·y [an′ti·bod′ē] *n., pl.* **an·ti·bod·ies** A substance formed in the body that immunizes it against a specific invading agent, as a particular virus or poison.

an·tic [an′tik] **1** *n.* (*usually pl.*) A prank or funny act: We laughed at the dog's *antics*. **2** *adj.* Odd; ludicrous: *antic* behavior.

An·ti·christ [an'ti·krīst'] *n.* The great enemy or adversary of Christ.

an·tic·i·pate [an·tis'ə·pāt] *v.* **an·tic·i·pat·ed, an·tic·i·pat·ing 1** To look forward to; expect: to *anticipate* a happy time. **2** To foresee and act on beforehand: to *anticipate* someone's wishes. **3** To invent, discover, or do in advance of: Leonardo *anticipated* the flying machine. **4** To be ahead of in doing: Russia *anticipated* the United States in orbiting a satellite.

an·tic·i·pa·tion [an·tis'ə·pā'shən] *n.* **1** The act of anticipating. **2** Expectation: People fled in *anticipation* of a flood.

an·ti·cli·max [an'ti·klī'maks] *n.* A sudden descent from the important to the unimportant or silly. Example: The disaster destroyed a great ship, its cargo, 917 people, and a kitten.

an·ti·dote [an'ti·dōt] *n.* Anything that will counteract or remove the effects of a poison, disease, or any evil.

An·tie·tam [an·tē'təm] *n.* A village in western Maryland, the site of a Civil War battle.

an·ti·freeze [an'ti·frēz'] *n.* A substance put into a liquid to keep it from freezing, as in an automobile radiator.

an·ti·gen [an'tə·jən] *n.* A substance that, when introduced into the body, helps it produce antibodies.

an·ti·his·ta·mine [an'ti·his'tə·mēn] *n.* Any of several drugs used to treat colds and allergic conditions, as asthma and hay fever.

An·til·les [an·til'ēz] *n.pl.* A chain of islands that separate the Caribbean from the Atlantic and the Gulf of Mexico. Cuba and Puerto Rico are two of the larger islands of the Antilles.

an·ti·mo·ny [an'tə·mō'nē] *n.* A brittle silver-white metallic element, used in making alloys and in medicine.

an·tip·a·thy [an·tip'ə·thē] *n.*, *pl.* **an·tip·a·thies 1** A strong feeling of dislike or aversion. **2** A person or thing so disliked.

an·tip·o·des [an·tip'ə·dēz] *n.* (*used with a singular or plural verb*) A place or region at the other end of a line through the center of the earth.

an·ti·quar·i·an [an'ti·kwâr'ē·ən] **1** *adj.* Of or having to do with antiques or antiquities. **2** *n.* A person who studies, collects, or deals in relics from old times.

an·ti·quat·ed [an'ti·kwā'tid] *adj.* Old-fashioned; out-of-date.

an·tique [an·tēk'] **1** *adj.* Of or from early times; very old: an *antique* car over 50 years old. **2** *n.* Something made long ago, as furniture, china, silver, etc. **3** *adj.* Old-fashioned; out-of-date: an *antique* vacuum cleaner.

an·tiq·ui·ty [an·tik'wə·tē] *n.*, *pl.* **an·tiq·ui·ties 1** The quality of being very old. **2** Ancient times, especially before the Middle Ages. **3** The people of ancient times. **4** (*usually pl.*) Relics of ancient times.

an·ti-Sem·i·tism [an'ti·sem'ə·tiz'əm] *n.* Feeling, discrimination, or action against Jews.

an·ti·sep·tic [an'ti·sep'tik] **1** *adj.* Preventing infection by killing or stopping the growth of germs. **2** *n.* A substance, such as iodine or alcohol, that does this.

an·ti·slav·er·y [an'ti·slā'vər·ē] *adj.* Against slavery.

an·ti·so·cial [an'ti·sō'shəl] *adj.* **1** Not sociable; aloof. **2** Harmful to society, as is crime.

an·tith·e·sis [an·tith'ə·sis] *n.*, *pl.* **an·tith·e·ses** [an·tith'ə·sēz] **1** A direct opposite: Love is the *antithesis* of hate. **2** A contrasting of two opposite words, ideas, or phrases. Example: My hopes soar; my feet stay on the ground. **3** Opposition; contrast: the *antithesis* of war and peace.

an·ti·tox·in [an'ti·tok'sin] *n.* **1** A substance produced in the body to counteract a specific bacterial poison. **2** A serum containing this substance, injected to prevent a disease such as tetanus.

an·ti·trust [an'ti·trust'] *adj.* Opposed to corporations or groups that form monopolies: an *antitrust* law.

ant·ler [ant'lər] *n.* **1** A horn, usually branched, grown and shed each year by a deer or related animal. **2** Any branch of such a horn.

ant·lered [ant'lərd] *adj.* Having antlers.

an·to·nym [an'tə·nim] *n.* A word opposite to another in meaning. "Good" and "bad" are antonyms.

Ant·werp [ant'wûrp] *n.* A seaport in northern Belgium.

a·nus [ā'nəs] *n.* The opening at the extreme lower end of the alimentary canal through which solid waste matter leaves the body.

Antlers

an·vil [an'vil] *n.* **1** A heavy block of iron or steel on which heated metal is hammered into shape. **2** A bone of the inner ear.

anx·i·e·ty [ang·zī'ə·tē] *n.*, *pl.* **anx·i·e·ties 1** An uneasy, worried feeling about what may happen; concern. **2** A great or too great desire: his *anxiety* to be popular.

anx·ious [angk'shəs] *adj.* **1** Worried; uneasy. **2** Causing or marked by anxiety; worrying: an *anxious* matter; *anxious* days. **3** Very eager: *anxious* to please. **— anx'ious·ly** *adv.*

Anvil

an·y [en'ē] **1** *adj.* One of a group, no matter which: Take *any* piece. **2** *pron.* One or more or a part: Will *any* of the girls go? **3** *adj.* Some, however much or little: Did Linda eat *any* supper? **4** *adj.* Every: *Any* fool knows that! **5** *adv.* At all; to any extent: Are they *any* nearer? **6** *adj.* Enough to count: hardly *any* noise. ◆ Both *any* and *one* come from the Old English word *ān*, meaning *one*. ◆ *Any*, meaning "*at all*," is sometimes used informally to end a question or a negative statement: Did you hurt yourself *any*? I didn't mind it *any*.

an·y·bod·y [en′i·bod′ē *or* en′i·bud′ē] *pron.* Any person; anyone.

an·y·how [en′i·hou′] *adv.* **1** In any way whatever; by any means: *anyhow* you look at it; Plan it *anyhow* you choose. **2** In any event: He's the smartest, *anyhow*. **3** Carelessly; haphazardly.

an·y·one [en′i·wun′] *pron.* Any person; anybody. ◆*Anyone* and *any one* may mean any single person. *Anyone* means any person at all: Can *anyone* identify the criminal? *Any one* means any individual from a group or class: *Any one* of these men may be guilty.

any one 1 Any single: *Any one* person can do it by himself. **2** Any single person or thing of a group or class: *Any one* of these wires may be live. ◆ See ANYONE.

an·y·thing [en′i·thing′] **1** *pron.* Any thing, event, or matter whatever: Did *anything* happen? Was *anything* lost? **2** *n.* A thing of any kind: She grabbed *anything* and everything she could lay her hands on. **3** *adv.* In the least; at all: Your hat isn't *anything* like mine.

an·y·way [en′i·wā′] *adv.* Anyhow.

an·y·where [en′i·(h)wâr′] *adv.* In, at, or to any place.

a·or·ta [ā·ôr′tə] *n., pl.* **a·or·tas** or **a·or·tae** [ā·ôr′tē] The great artery rising from the left side of the heart, through which blood passes to all parts of the body except the lungs.

heart
aorta

a·pace [ə·pās′] *adv.* Swiftly: We hurried on *apace*.

A·pach·e [ə·pach′ē] *n., pl.* **A·pach·es** or **A·pach·e** A member of a group of nomadic Indians of the sw U.S., noted as warriors.

a·part [ə·pärt′] **1** *adv.* In pieces or to pieces: to take something *apart*; The ship broke *apart*. **2** *adv.* Separated away from each other: Keep them *apart*. **3** *adv.* Aside: She stood *apart* from the crowd. **4** *adj.* Separate; distinct: a breed *apart*. **5** *adv.* One from another: No one can tell the twins *apart*. **— apart from** Except for: *Apart from* us, nobody's going.

a·part·ment [ə·pärt′mənt] *n.* A suite of rooms, or a single room, to live in.

apartment house A building with apartments.

ap·a·thet·ic [ap′ə·thet′ik] *adj.* Lacking feeling, interest, or concern; indifferent. **— ap′a·thet′i·cal·ly** *adv.*

ap·a·thy [ap′ə·thē] *n.* **1** Lack of feeling. **2** Lack of interest or concern; indifference.

ape [āp] *n., v.* **aped, ap·ing 1** *n.* A large monkey with no tail, that can stand and walk almost erect. The chimpanzee, gorilla, and gibbon are apes. **2** *n.* Any monkey. **3** *n.* A mimic. **4** *v.* To mimic or imitate.

Ap·en·nines [ap′ə·nīnz] *n.* A mountain range in central Italy.

ap·er·ture [ap′ər·chər] *n.* An opening or hole.

a·pex [ā′peks] *n., pl.* **a·pex·es** or **ap·i·ces** [ap′ə·sēz] **1** The highest point; tip; top. **2** A climax.

a·phe·li·on [ə·fē′lē·ən] *n.* The point farthest from the sun in the orbit of a planet or other body moving around the sun. ◆ The words *aphelion, perihelion, apogee,* and *perigee* come from four Greek words: *apo,* meaning *from; peri,* meaning *around* or *near to; hēlios,* meaning *sun;* and *gē,* meaning *earth.* Thus *aphelion* literally means *away from the sun; apogee, away from the earth; perihelion, near to the sun;* and *perigee, near to the earth.*

a·phid [ā′fid *or* af′id] *n.* A tiny insect that sucks the juices of plants.

aph·o·rism [af′ə·riz′əm] *n.* A brief statement of a general truth; maxim. "Cowards don't win battles" is an aphorism.

Aph·ro·di·te [af′rə·dī′tē] *n.* In Greek myths, the goddess of love and beauty.

a·pi·ar·y [ā′pē·er′ē] *n., pl.* **a·pi·ar·ies** A place where bees are kept.

a·piece [ə·pēs′] *adv.* For or to each one; each: Give them a dime *apiece*.

a·plomb [ə·plom′] *n.* Poise or self-possession; self-confidence.

a·poc·a·lypse [ə·pok′ə·lips] *n.* **1** A prophecy or revelation. **2** (*written* **Apocalypse**) The book of Revelation, the last book in the Bible.

A·poc·ry·pha [ə·pok′rə·fə] *n.pl.* Books included in some versions of the Old Testament but not accepted by all as fully genuine or inspired.

a·poc·ry·phal [ə·pok′rə·fəl] *adj.* Having little or no authenticity; probably untrue.

ap·o·gee [ap′ə·jē] *n.* The point farthest from the earth in the orbit of the moon or other satellite of the earth. ◆ See APHELION.

A·pol·lo [ə·pol′ō] *n.* In Greek and Roman myths, the god of the sun, music, poetry, prophecy, and medicine.

orbit of satellite
satellite at apogee
earth
satellite at perigee

a·pol·o·get·ic [ə·pol′ə·jet′ik] *adj.* Having to do with or expressing apology; showing regret for something; admitting a fault or failure. **— a·pol′o·get′i·cal·ly** *adv.*

a·pol·o·gist [ə·pol′ə·jist] *n.* A person who speaks or writes in defense of a faith, idea, cause, etc.

a·pol·o·gize [ə·pol′ə·jīz] *v.* **a·pol·o·gized, a·pol·o·giz·ing 1** To make an apology; ask pardon or express regret for something: to *apologize* for an insult. **2** To defend something in writing or speech. ¶3

---

add, āce, câre, pälm;　　end, ēqual;　　it, īce;　　odd, ōpen, ôrder;　　to͝ok, po͞ol;　　up, bûrn;

ə = a in *above*, e in *sicken*, i in *possible*, o in *melon*, u in *circus*;　　yo͞o = u in *fuse*;　　oil;　　pout;

check; ring; thin; this; zh in *vision*.　　For ¶ reference, see page 64 · HOW TO

a·pol·o·gy [ə·pol′ə·jē] *n.*, *pl.* **a·pol·o·gies**
1 Words saying that one is sorry or asking
pardon for a fault, offense, or mistake. **2** A
defense or justification in writing or speech. **3** A
bad substitute: a poor *apology* for an omelet.

ap·o·plec·tic [ap′ə·plek′tik] **1** *adj.* Of, having,
or tending toward apoplexy: an *apoplectic* fit.
2 *n.* A person subject to apoplexy.

ap·o·plex·y [ap′ə·plek′sē] *n.* Sudden loss of the
ability to feel, think, or move. It is caused by the
bursting or blocking of a blood vessel in the
brain.

a·pos·ta·sy [ə·pos′tə·sē] *n.* Desertion of a
previous loyalty, as to one's religion, country,
party, etc.

a·pos·tate [ə·pos′tāt] *n.* A person who deserts
his faith, country, party, etc.

a·pos·tle [ə·pos′əl] *n.* **1** (*often written* **Apostle**)
One of the twelve disciples of Christ sent out to
preach the gospel. **2** A missionary or preacher in
the early Christian Church. **3** A missionary who
first brings Christianity to a nation or region:
The *apostle* to Ireland was St. Patrick. **4** A
leader of any reform or belief: an *apostle* of
civil rights.

ap·os·tol·ic [ap′ə·stol′ik] *adj.* **1** Of or having to
do with the Apostles or apostles: *apostolic*
writings; *apostolic* faith. **2** (*often written*
Apostolic) Papal: an *Apostolic* letter.

a·pos·tro·phe¹ [ə·pos′trə·fē] *n.* A symbol (')
used: **1** To mark the omission of a letter or
letters, as *I'm* for *I am* or *can't* for *cannot*. **2** To
show the possessive case: *Jane's* dog; the *girls'*
hats. **3** To form certain plurals: three *5's*;
crossed *t's*.

a·pos·tro·phe² [ə·pos′trə·fē] *n.* A speech
addressed to someone absent or dead, or to a
thing: an *apostrophe* to Lincoln.

a·poth·e·car·y [ə·poth′ə·ker′ē] *n.*, *pl.* **a·poth·**
e·car·ies A druggist or pharmacist.

a·poth·e·o·sis [ə·poth′ē·ō′sis *or* ap′ə·thē′ə·sis]
n., *pl.* **a·poth·e·o·ses** [ə·poth′ē·ō′sēz *or* ap′ə·
thē′ə·sēz] **1** The raising of a person to the level of
a god; deification: the *apotheosis* of an emperor.
2 Glorification.

Ap·pa·la·chi·an Mountains [ap′ə·lā′chē·ən
or ap′ə·lāch′ən] A mountain system of eastern
North America extending from Quebec to
Alabama. Also **Appalachians.**

ap·pall or **ap·pal** [ə·pôl′] *v.* **ap·palled,**
ap·pall·ing To fill with dismay or horror: He
was *appalled* by the sight of such poverty.

ap·pall·ing [ə·pôl′ing] *adj.* Causing horror or
dismay; frightful. **— ap·pall′ing·ly** *adv.*

ap·pa·ra·tus [ap′ə·rā′təs *or* ap′ə·rat′əs] *n.*, *pl.*
ap·pa·ra·tus or **ap·pa·ra·tus·es 1** A device
or machine for a particular purpose: an X-ray
apparatus. **2** All of the devices, tools, equipment,
etc., for a particular use.

ap·par·el [ə·par′əl] *n.*, *v.* **ap·par·eled** or
ap·par·elled, ap·par·el·ing or **ap·par·el·**
ling 1 *n.* Clothing. **2** *v.* To clothe, dress, or
dress up: a band *appareled* in red.

ap·par·ent [ə·par′ənt] *adj.* **1** Obvious: It's

apparent he is not well. **2** That only appears to
be; seeming: His *apparent* courage is only a
bluff. **— ap·par′ent·ly** *adv.*

ap·pa·ri·tion [ap′ə·rish′ən] *n.* **1** A ghost;
spirit; phantom. **2** Anything remarkable that
appears.

ap·peal [ə·pēl′] **1** *v.* To ask earnestly for something: to *appeal* for help. **2** *n.* An earnest
request. **3** *v.* To call on someone for a decision
in one's favor: Denied the car by his father, he
appealed to his mother. **4** *n.* Such a call. **5** *v.* To
be attractive or interesting: Does this *appeal* to
you? **6** *adj. use:* an *appealing* smile. **7** *n.*
Power to attract or interest: Chess has lost its
appeal. **8** *v.* To ask to have (a case) tried again
by a higher court. **9** *n.* Such a request.

ap·pear [ə·pir′] *v.* **1** To come into sight;
become visible: Juliet *appeared* on the balcony.
2 To seem or seem likely: The report *appears* to
be true. **3** To come before the public: to *appear*
on television. **4** To come formally into court.
5 To be published.

ap·pear·ance [ə·pir′əns] *n.* **1** The act of
appearing. **2** A coming before a court or an
audience. **3** The outward look of a person or
thing: a well-kept *appearance*. **4** A pretense: an
appearance of working hard. **5** An apparition.

ap·pease [ə·pēz′] *v.* **ap·peased, ap·peas·ing**
1 To satisfy: to *appease* hunger. **2** To calm or
soothe, especially by giving in to demands.

ap·pease·ment [ə·pēz′mənt] *n.* **1** The act of
appeasing. **2** The policy of making concessions
in order to maintain peace.

ap·pel·late court [ə·pel′it] A court having the
power to change the judgment of a lower court.

ap·pel·la·tion [ap′ə·lā′shən] *n.* An added name
or title. William the Conqueror's *appellation* was
"the Conqueror."

ap·pend [ə·pend′] *v.* To add or attach: to
append a footnote.

ap·pend·age [ə·pen′dij] *n.* Something attached to a larger or main part. Legs, tails,
fins, wings, etc., are appendages.

ap·pen·dec·to·my [ap′ən·dek′tə·mē] *n.*, *pl.*
ap·pen·dec·to·mies The removal of a person's
appendix by surgery.

ap·pen·di·ci·tis [ə·pen′di·sī′tis] *n.* Inflammation of the appendix.

ap·pen·dix [ə·pen′diks] *n.*, *pl.* **ap·pen·dix·es**
or **ap·pen·di·ces** [ə·pen′də·sēz] **1** An addition
or appendage, as of supplementary matter at
the end of a book. **2** A narrow, closed tube
extending out from the large intestine, in the
lower right side of the abdomen. It has no
known use.

ap·per·tain [ap′ər·tān′] *v.* To have to do with;
belong; relate: problems *appertaining* to fair
taxation.

ap·pe·tite [ap′ə·tīt] *n.* **1** A desire for food.
2 Any strong desire or liking: an *appetite* for
sports.

ap·pe·tiz·er [ap′ə·tīz′ər] *n.* Anything that
makes one hungry before a meal. Olives, celery,
clams, etc., are often used as appetizers. ¶3

ap·pe·tiz·ing [ap′ə·tī′zing] *adj.* Stimulating the appetite: an *appetizing* meal. ¶3

ap·plaud [ə·plôd′] *v.* **1** To show approval by clapping the hands, shouting, cheering, etc.: The audience *applauded*. **2** To commend; praise.

ap·plause [ə·plôz′] *n.* A show of approval by clapping the hands, shouting, cheering, etc.

ap·ple [ap′əl] *n.* **1** A round, fleshy, edible fruit having a thin skin of a green, red, or yellow color and a hard core enclosing seeds. **2** Any of the trees bearing this fruit.

ap·ple·sauce [ap′əl·sôs′] *n.* Apples cut up, sweetened, and stewed to a soft pulp.

ap·pli·ance [ə·plī′əns] *n.* A machine for doing a task in home or office, as an air conditioner, washer, or toaster.

ap·pli·ca·ble [ap′li·kə·bəl] *adj.* That can be applied; suitable: a dye not *applicable* to leather. **— ap′pli·ca·bil′i·ty** *n.*

ap·pli·cant [ap′li·kənt] *n.* A person who applies for something, such as a job.

ap·pli·ca·tion [ap′li·kā′shən] *n.* **1** The act of applying. **2** Something applied: an *application* to relieve sunburn. **3** A particular way of being applied or used: A single word may have many different *applications*. **4** A request, especially a formal written request, as for a job. **5** Close attention and real work: *application* to one's studies.

ap·plied [ə·plīd′] *adj.* Put to practical use. An applied science's aim is to put scientific facts and theories to practical use.

ap·pli·qué [ap′li·kā′] *n., adj., v.* **ap·pli·quéd, ap·pli·qué·ing 1** *n.* Ornaments made by sewing or fastening one material on another. **2** *adj.* Trimmed or decorated with appliqué. **3** *v.* To trim or decorate with appliqué.

ap·ply [ə·plī′] *v.* **ap·plied, ap·ply·ing 1** To put on: to *apply* paint to a wall, cream to the face, etc. **2** To put to a particular use: to *apply* pressure to fruit to squeeze out the juice. **3** To devote (oneself) with effort: He *applied* himself to his studies. **4** To make a formal request or petition: to *apply* for a job. **5** To be suitable or appropriate; relate: This rule *applies* to you.

ap·point [ə·point′] *v.* **1** To select for a position, office, or duty; designate. **2** To decide on (a time or place); fix or set: The session opened at the hour *appointed*. **3** To equip; furnish: a well-*appointed* cabin.

ap·point·ee [ə·poin′tē′] *n.* A person appointed to some office or position.

ap·poin·tive [ə·poin′tiv] *adj.* Filled by appointment, not by election: an *appointive* office.

ap·point·ment [ə·point′mənt] *n.* **1** Selection for, or a placing in, an office or position not filled by election. **2** Such an office or position. **3** The person chosen. **4** An agreement to meet someone at a certain place and time. **5** (*usually pl.*) Furniture or equipment.

Ap·po·mat·tox [ap′ə·mat′əks] *n.* A village in central Virginia. Lee surrendered to Grant there in 1865, ending the Civil War.

ap·por·tion [ə·pôr′shən] *v.* To divide and give out in fair proportional shares or according to some rule. **— ap·por′tion·ment** *n.*

ap·po·site [ap′ə·zit] *adj.* Appropriate; to the point: an *opposite* remark.

ap·po·si·tion [ap′ə·zish′ən] *n.* **1** The placing of a noun or its equivalent after another to explain it, both having the same grammatical form. **2** The relation existing between such a pair. In "Mars, the god of war, was worshiped in Rome," *Mars* and *the god of war* are in apposition.

ap·pos·i·tive [ə·poz′ə·tiv] **1** *adj.* Having to do with or in apposition. **2** *n.* A noun or its equivalent placed after another in apposition.

ap·prais·al [ə·prā′z(ə)l] *n.* **1** The act of appraising. **2** The estimate of value, quality, quantity, etc., reached by appraising.

ap·praise [ə·prāz′] *v.* **ap·praised, ap·prais·ing 1** To decide the value of; set a price on: to *appraise* a house. **2** To estimate the amount, quality, or worth of. **— ap·prais′er** *n.*

ap·pre·ci·a·ble [ə·prē′shē·ə·bəl *or* ə·prē′shə·bəl] *adj.* Enough to be noticed or estimated: an *appreciable* angle. **— ap·pre′ci·a·bly** *adv.*

ap·pre·ci·ate [ə·prē′shē·āt] *v.* **ap·pre·ci·at·ed, ap·pre·ci·at·ing 1** To recognize the merit of; understand and value or enjoy: to *appreciate* good literature. **2** To be aware of or sensitive to: to *appreciate* someone else's problems. **3** To be grateful for: We *appreciate* your help. **4** To make or become more valuable: Fine homes *appreciate* a neighborhood.

ap·pre·ci·a·tion [ə·prē′shē·ā′shən] *n.* **1** Recognition of value or excellence, especially a favorable criticism. **2** Awareness or sensitivity. **3** Gratitude. **4** Increase in value or amount.

ap·pre·ci·a·tive [ə·prē′shē·ā′tiv *or* ə·prē′shə·tiv] *adj.* Having or showing appreciation. **— ap·pre′ci·a′tive·ly** *adv.*

ap·pre·hend [ap′rə·hend′] *v.* **1** To capture; arrest: to *apprehend* a criminal. **2** To grasp mentally; understand: to *apprehend* a problem. **3** To dread: to *apprehend* a conflict.

ap·pre·hen·sion [ap′rə·hen′shən] *n.* **1** A worried expectation of something bad; dread or fear. **2** An arrest or capture. **3** Understanding; mental grasp.

ap·pre·hen·sive [ap′rə·hen′siv] *adj.* Fearful; worried: The strange noises in the forest made us *apprehensive*. **— ap′pre·hen′sive·ly** *adv.*

ap·pren·tice [ə·pren′tis] *n., v.* **ap·pren·ticed, ap·pren·tic·ing 1** *n.* A person who works for another in order to learn a trade or business. Formerly he had to work for several years without pay. **2** *v.* To bind by legal agreement as an apprentice. **3** *n.* Any learner or beginner. **— ap·pren′tice·ship** *n.*

---

add, āce, câre, pälm;   end, ēqual;   it, īce;   odd, ōpen, ôrder;   tŏŏk, pōōl;   up, bûrn;
ə = a in *above*, e in *sicken*, i in *possible*, o in *melon*, u in *circus*;   yōō = u in *fuse*;   oil;   pout;
check;   ring;   thin;   this;   zh in *vision*.   For ¶ reference, see page 64 · HOW TO

ap·prise [ə·prīz′] *v.* **ap·prised, ap·pris·ing**
To notify; inform: to be *apprised* of a coming
event.

ap·proach [ə·prōch′] **1** *v.* To come nearer in
space or time: Christmas is *approaching.* **2** *v.* To
be or become almost; resemble: His ability
approached genius. **3** *n.* A coming near or close.
4 *n.* A way or means of reaching a person or
thing: the *approach* to a bridge. **5** *n.* A method
of beginning or doing something: a new *approach*
to purifying salt water. **6** *v.* To come to with a
request or proposal: to *approach* someone about
a job.

ap·pro·ba·tion [ap′rə·bā′shən] *n.* **1** Approval.
2 Support and approval.

ap·pro·pri·ate [*adj.* ə·prō′prē·it, *v.* ə·prō′prē·
āt] *adj., v.* **ap·pro·pri·at·ed, ap·pro·pri·
at·ing 1** *adj.* Suitable; fitting. **2** *v.* To set
apart for a particular purpose: to *appropriate*
money for defense. **3** *v.* To take for one's own
use: The thief *appropriated* the necklace.
— ap·pro′pri·ate·ly *adv.*

ap·pro·pri·a·tion   [ə·prō′prē·ā′shən]   *n.*
1 Money set aside and made available for a
particular use. **2** The act of appropriating.

ap·prov·al [ə·prōō′vəl] *n.* **1** A favorable feeling
or opinion. **2** Consent as a result of such opinion:
He played without the doctor's *approval.* **— on
approval** For a customer to try or examine,
then decide about buying.

ap·prove [ə·prōōv′] *v.* **ap·proved, ap·prov·
ing 1** To have a good opinion: I *approve* of your
idea. **2** To accept as good; think well of: The
inspector *approved* the work. **3** To consent to;
authorize: The mayor *approved* the plan.

ap·prox·i·mate [*adj.* ə·prok′sə·mit, *v.* ə·prok′·
sə·māt] *adj., v.* **ap·prox·i·mat·ed, ap·prox·
i·mat·ing 1** *adj.* Almost exact, correct, or like:
an *approximate* 29,000 feet; the *approximate*
wording of the law. **2** *v.* To come close to:
Speed will *approximate* 650 mph.

ap·prox·i·mate·ly   [ə·prok′sə·mit·lē]   *adv.*
About; around: *approximately* an inch of rain.

ap·prox·i·ma·tion   [ə·prok′sə·mā′shən]   *n.*
1 The act of approximating. **2** An amount or
estimate nearly exact or correct.

ap·pur·te·nance [ə·pûr′tə·nəns] *n.* Something
that goes with a more important or main thing:
the farm, its barn, and other *appurtenances.*

Apr. Abbreviation of APRIL.

a·pri·cot [ā′pri·kot *or* ap′ri·kot] **1** *n.* A juicy,
orange-colored fruit similar to a small peach.
2 *n.* The tree bearing this small fruit. **3** *n.,
adj.* Yellowish orange.

A·pril [ā′prəl] *n.* The fourth month of the year,
having 30 days.

April Fools' Day April 1, a day when it is
customary to play practical jokes. The victim of
such a joke is called an **April fool.**

a·pron [ā′prən] *n.* **1** A garment worn to protect
the skirt or trousers in front, often with a bib
above. **2** An area in front of a garage, hangar,
etc. **3** The part of a theater stage in front of the
curtain. ◆ *Apron* was at one time spelled *napron,*

but when you say *a napron,* it sounds the same as
an apron [ənā′prən] and in the course of time
the word became *apron.*

ap·ro·pos [ap′rə·pō′] **1** *adj.* Timely; fitting;
appropriate: an   *apropos*   re-
mark. **2** *adv.* Fittingly; at
the right time. **— apropos
of** In connection with or
regard to.

apse [aps] *n.* A semicircular
recess with an arched or
domed ceiling, at the east end
of a church.

apt [apt] *adj.* **1** Having a
natural   tendency;   likely:
Fish are *apt* to be biting then.
2 Quick to learn: an *apt*
pupil. **3** To the point; fitting:
an *apt* suggestion. **— apt′ly**
adv. **— apt′ness** *n.*

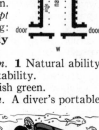

ap·ti·tude [ap′tə·t(y)ōōd] *n.* **1** Natural ability
or capacity. **2** Fitness; suitability.

aq·ua [ak′wə] *n., adj.* Bluish green.

aq·ua·lung [ak′wə·lung′] *n.* A diver's portable
breathing apparatus.
Tanks of compressed
air on the back supply
air through a mask.

aq·ua·ma·rine [ak′·
wə·mə·rēn′] **1** *n.* A
bluish green variety
of beryl. It is a pre-
cious stone. **2** *n., adj.* Bluish green.

Diver wearing an aqualung

aq·ua·plane [ak′wə·plān′] *n., v.* **aq·ua·
planed, aq·ua·plan·ing 1** *n.* A board on
which a person rides for sport while being towed
by a motorboat. **2** *v.* To ride an aquaplane.

a·quar·i·um [ə·kwâr′ē·əm] *n., pl.* **a·quar·i·
ums** or **a·quar·i·a** [ə·kwâr′ē·ə] **1** A tank, pond,
etc., for fish, water animals, or water plants, or all
three. **2** A building where such a collection is
displayed.

a·quat·ic [ə·kwat′ik] *adj.* **1** Living or growing
in or near water. **2** Performed on or in water:
aquatic sports.

aq·ue·duct [ak′wə·dukt] *n.* **1** A pipeline or
artificial channel for carrying water from a
distance. **2** A bridgelike structure used, where
needed, to bear such a channel.

a·que·ous [ā′kwē·əs *or* ak′wē·əs] *adj.* **1** Of, like,
or containing water; watery. **2** Composed of
matter deposited by water: *aqueous* rocks.

aqueous humor A clear fluid filling the space
in the eye between the cornea and the lens.

aq·ui·line [ak′wə·līn *or* ak′wə·lin] *adj.* **1** Of or
like an eagle. **2** Curving or hooked, like an eagle's
beak: an *aquiline* nose.

A·qui·nas [ə·kwī′nəs], **Thomas,** 1225?–1274,
Italian monk, famous philosopher and Christian
theologian, made a saint.

Ar The symbol for the element ARGON.

Ar·ab [ar′əb] **1** *n.* A person born or living in
Arabia. **2** *n.* A member of a people spread from
Arabia through sw Asia and parts of Africa.

A

3 *n.* A swift, graceful horse of a breed first developed in Arabia. **4** *adj.* Arabian.

ar·a·besque [ar′ə·besk′] **1** *n.* A fanciful design using geometric figures, leaves, flowers, etc., intertwined. **2** *adj.* Of or done in arabesque. **3** *adj.* Elaborate. **4** *n.* A position in ballet.

A·ra·bi·a [ə·rā′bē·ə] *n.* A large peninsula of sw Asia, between the Red Sea and the Persian Gulf.

A·ra·bi·an [ə·rā′bē·ən] **1** *adj.* Of or having to do with Arabia or its people. **2** *n.* An Arab.

Arabian Nights A collection of stories from Arabia, India, Persia, etc., dating from the tenth century.

Arabian Sea The part of the Indian Ocean between Arabia and India.

Ar·a·bic [ar′ə·bik] **1** *n.* The language of the Arabs. **2** *adj.* Of the Arabs or their language.

Arabic numerals The symbols 1, 2, 3, 4, 5, 6, 7, 8, 9, and 0.

ar·a·ble [ar′ə·bəl] *adj.* Fit for cultivating.

a·rach·nid [ə·rak′nid] *n.* Any of a class of animals including spiders, mites, and scorpions, with four pairs of legs but no antennae.

ar·bi·ter [är′bə·tər] *n.* **1** A person chosen to settle a dispute; arbitrator; umpire. **2** A person with full power to decide or judge.

ar·bi·trar·y [är′bə·trer′ē] *adj.* **1** Based only on one's own will, feelings, or notions: an *arbitrary* decision. **2** Not guided by rules or law: an *arbitrary* ruler. — **ar′bi·trar′i·ly** *adv.*

ar·bi·trate [är′bə·trāt] *v.* **ar·bi·trat·ed, ar·bi·trat·ing 1** To act as an arbitrator: to *arbitrate* between two nations. **2** To submit (a dispute) to arbitration: They agreed to *arbitrate* their differences. **3** To settle by arbitration.

ar·bi·tra·tion [är′bə·trā′shən] *n.* The settling of a dispute by the decision of someone accepted by both sides as umpire or arbiter.

ar·bi·tra·tor [är′bə·trā′tər] *n.* **1** A person chosen to settle a dispute. **2** A person with full power to decide or judge; arbiter.

ar·bor [är′bər] *n.* A place shaded by trees or by latticework covered with vines; bower.

ar·bo·re·al [är·bôr′ē·əl *or* är·bō′rē·əl] *adj.* **1** Of or like a tree. **2** Living in trees.

ar·bor·vi·tae [är′bər·vī′tē] *n.* or **arbor vitae** A small evergreen tree, often used for hedges.

ar·bu·tus [är·byōō′təs] *n.* A trailing evergreen plant that bears clusters of fragrant pink or white flowers in very early spring.

arc [ärk] *n., v.* **arced** [ärkt], **arc·ing** [är′·king] **1** *n.* A part of a curve, especially of a circle. **2** *v.* To make an arc: The rocket *arced* across the sky. **3** *n.* The bright glow made by an electric current as it passes through a gas, across the gap between two electrodes.

ar·cade [är·kād′] *n.* **1** A

covered passageway or street, often with an arched roof, especially one with small stores on both sides. **2** A row of arches held up by columns.

Ar·ca·di·a [är·kā′dē·ə] *n.* **1** A mountain region in ancient Greece remembered for the simple, pastoral life led by its inhabitants. **2** Any region of ideal rustic simplicity and complete contentment.

arch[1] [ärch] **1** *n.* A curved structure over an opening, capable of holding up material above it. Arches are used in windows, gateways, and bridges. **2** *n.* Anything shaped like an arch: the *arch* of a rainbow. **3** *v.* To bend or curve into an arch: to *arch* an eyebrow. **4** *v.* To make an arch: The bridge *arched* over the river.

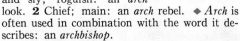

Arch

arch[2] [ärch] *adj.* **1** Playful and sly; roguish: an *arch* look. **2** Chief; main: an *arch* rebel. ◆ *Arch* is often used in combination with the word it describes: an *archbishop*.

ar·chae·o·log·i·cal [är′kē·ə·loj′i·kəl] *adj.* Of or having to do with archaeology.

ar·chae·ol·o·gist [är′kē·ol′ə·jist] *n.* An expert in archaeology.

ar·chae·ol·o·gy [är′kē·ol′ə·jē] *n.* The study of past times and cultures, mainly carried on by digging up and examining remains, as of the cities or tombs of ancient cultures.

ar·chae·op·ter·yx [är′kē·op′tər·iks] *n.* One of the first primitive birds, found as a fossil. It had some reptile features.

ar·cha·ic [är·kā′ik] *adj.* **1** No longer in ordinary use: Words or phrases such as "methinks," "soothly," and "I ween" are *archaic*. **2** Belonging to an earlier time; ancient: *archaic* armor.

arch·an·gel [ärk′ān′jəl] *n.* A chief angel; angel of a high rank.

arch·bish·op [ärch′bish′əp] *n.* A bishop of the highest station.

arch·dea·con [ärch′dē′kən] *n.* **1** Chief deacon. **2** A priest in the Episcopalian church who assists a bishop in supervising the clergy.

arched [ärcht] *adj.* Having an arch or arches.

arch·en·e·my [ärch′en′ə·mē] *n., pl.* **arch·en·e·mies** A chief or major enemy.

ar·che·o·log·i·cal [är′kē·ə·loj′i·kəl] *adj.* Another spelling of ARCHAEOLOGICAL.

ar·che·ol·o·gist [är′kē·ol′ə·jist] *n.* Another spelling of ARCHAEOLOGIST.

ar·che·ol·o·gy [är′kē·ol′ə·jē] *n.* Another spelling of ARCHAEOLOGY.

Ar·che·o·zo·ic [är′kē·ə·zō′ik] *adj.* Of or having to do with the oldest time in geological history, in which the first living things are supposed to have appeared.

---

add, āce, câre, pälm;   end, ēqual;   it, īce;   odd, ōpen, ôrder;   tŏŏk, pōōl;   up, bûrn;

ə = a in *above*, e in *sicken*, i in *possible*, o in *melon*, u in *circus*;   yōō = u in *fuse*;   oil;   pout;

check; ring; thin; this; zh in *vision*.   For ¶ reference, see page 64 · HOW TO

arch·er [är′chər] *n.* A person who shoots with a bow and arrow.

arch·er·y [är′chər·ē] *n.* The art or sport of shooting with a bow and arrow.

Archery

ar·che·type [är′kə·tīp] *n.* A first model from which others are derived or copied: The *Iliad* was regarded as the *archetype* of epic poetry.

Ar·chi·me·des [är′kə·mē′dēz] *n.*, 287?–212 B.C., Greek mathematician and inventor.

ar·chi·pel·a·go [är′kə·pel′ə·gō] *n.*, *pl.* **ar·chi·pel·a·goes** or **ar·chi·pel·a·gos** 1 A group of many islands. 2 A sea with many islands in it.

An archipelago

ar·chi·tect [är′kə·tekt] *n.* A person who designs and draws up plans for buildings or other structures, and sees that the plans are carried through by the builders.

ar·chi·tec·tur·al [är′kə·tek′chər·əl] *adj.* Of or having to do with architecture: *architectural* designs. **— ar′chi·tec′tur·al·ly** *adv.*

ar·chi·tec·ture [är′kə·tek′chər] *n.* 1 The science or profession of designing and putting up buildings or other structures. 2 Style or special method of building.

ar·chi·trave [är′kə·trāv] *n.* The beam or stone that rests directly on top of a column.

ar·chives [är′kīvz] *n.pl.* 1 A place for keeping public records and historical papers. 2 Such public records or papers.

arch·ly [ärch′lē] *adv.* In a playful manner.

arch·way [ärch′wā′] *n.* An entrance or passage under an arch.

arc light An electric lamp that produces a very strong light by means of an electric arc.

arc·tic [är(k)′tik] 1 *n.* (*usually written* **Arctic**) The region about the North Pole. 2 *adj.* (*usually written* **Arctic**) Of or living in this region: an *Arctic* plant. 3 *adj.* Extremely cold; freezing.

Arctic Circle A circle at about 66°33′ north latitude, beyond which the sun cannot be seen in the depth of winter, taken as the boundary of the north frigid zone.

Arctic Ocean The ocean surrounding the North Pole.

Arc·tu·rus [ärk·t(y)oor′əs] *n.* A very bright, orange-red star in the northern sky.

ar·dent [är′dənt] *adj.* Very enthusiastic and eager; fervent: an *ardent* supporter. **— ar′·dent·ly** *adv.*

ar·dor [är′dər] *n.* Great enthusiasm; strong feeling of warmth or passion: He loved his country with *ardor.* ¶1

ar·du·ous [är′joo·əs] *adj.* 1 Difficult to do; hard: an *arduous* task. 2 Taking much energy; strenuous: *arduous* efforts to climb the fence. **— ar′du·ous·ly** *adv.*

are [är] *v.* A form of the verb BE, in the present tense, used with *we, you, they,* and plural nouns: You *are* right; Eleven men *are* on a football team; *Are* we going?

ar·e·a [âr′ē·ə] *n.* 1 The amount or size of a surface: The *area* of a floor 10 feet by 10 feet is 100 square feet. 2 Region; section: the Chicago *area;* a tropical *area.* 3 An open space devoted to a special purpose: a parking *area;* a camping *area.*

a·re·na [ə·rē′nə] *n.* 1 The open space in a Roman stadium where combats were held, as between gladiators. 2 Any area of conflict or action: the political *arena.*

aren't [ärnt] A contraction of: Are not: *Aren't* you glad to see me? ◆ *Aren't I* is used to avoid both *ain't I* and *am I not.* It is ungrammatical, but sounds more correct than *ain't I* and less stuffy than *am I not.* It is even better to put the idea so none of the three is needed.

Ar·es [âr′ēz] *n.* The Greek god of war. He was called Mars by the Romans.

Ar·gen·ti·na [är′jən·tē′nə] *n.* A country in southern South America.

Ar·gen·tine [är′jən·tēn] 1 *adj.* Of or from Argentina. 2 *n.* A person born in or a citizen of Argentina.

ar·gon [är′gon] *n.* A colorless, gaseous chemical element. Small amounts are found in air. It is used in electric signs, light bulbs, etc.

Ar·go·naut [är′gə·nôt] *n.* In Greek legend, any of the men who sailed with Jason to find the Golden Fleece.

ar·go·sy [är′gə·sē] *n.*, *pl.* **ar·go·sies** 1 A large ship with a rich cargo. 2 A fleet of such ships.

ar·gue [är′gyoo] *v.* **ar·gued, ar·gu·ing** 1 To give reasons for or against something: He *argued* against going to the beach. 2 To dispute; disagree: They always *argue* about baseball. 3 To show; suggest: The big car *argued* a wealthy family. 4 To convince by giving reasons: He *argued* her into buying a new house.

ar·gu·ment [är′gyə·mənt] *n.* 1 The act of arguing; an angry discussion; dispute. 2 A reason or reasons offered for or against something. 3 A short statement telling what a story or poem is about.

ar·gu·men·ta·tive [är′gyə·men′tə·tiv] *adj.* 1 Liking argument; ready to argue. 2 Full of arguments: an *argumentative* essay. **— ar′gu·men′ta·tive·ly** *adv.*

Ar·gus [är′gəs] *n.* 1 In Greek myths, a giant with a hundred eyes. 2 A very watchful person.

a·ri·a [ä′rē·ə *or* är′ē·ə] *n.* A song, usually in an opera or oratorio, sung by a single person to musical accompaniment.

ar·id [ar′id] *adj.* **1** Without enough rainfall to grow things; dry; parched. **2** Dull; dry: an *arid* speech. **— a·rid·i·ty** [ə·rid′ə·tē] *n.*

a·right [ə·rīt′] *adv.* Correctly; rightly: I don't remember *aright.*

a·rise [ə·rīz′] *v.* **a·rose, a·ris·en** [ə·riz′(ə)n], **a·ris·ing 1** To get up: He *arose* and began his speech. **2** To rise up; ascend: Wild duck *arose* from the lake. **3** To start; come into being: New problems always *arise.* **4** To result: The argument *arose* from her stubbornness.

ar·is·toc·ra·cy [ar′is·tok′rə·sē] *n., pl.* **ar·is·toc·ra·cies 1** A class of society inheriting by birth a high position or rank, certain powers and privileges, and usually wealth. **2** Government by this upper class. **3** Any group of those thought to be the best: an *aristocracy* of rich men.

a·ris·to·crat [ə·ris′tə·krat] *n.* **1** A member of an aristocracy; nobleman. **2** A person with the opinions, manners, or appearance of the upper class. **3** A person who prefers an aristocratic form of government.

a·ris·to·crat·ic [ə·ris′tə·krat′ik] *adj.* **1** Fit for an aristocrat; superior; exclusive; snobbish. **2** Belonging to, having the characteristics of, or favoring an aristocracy: *aristocratic* government. **— a·ris′to·crat′i·cal·ly** *adv.*

Ar·is·tot·le [ar′is·tot′(ə)l] *n.,* 384–322 B.C., famous Greek philosopher, a pupil of Plato.

a·rith·me·tic [ə·rith′mə·tik] *n.* The study of working with numbers, mainly in addition, subtraction, multiplication, and division.

ar·ith·met·i·cal [ar′ith·met′i·kəl] *adj.* Of or having to do with arithmetic.

ar·ith·met·ic progression [ar′ith·met′ik] A sequence of numbers such that the difference between any two successive numbers is the same, as 3, 7, 11, 15.

Ariz. Abbreviation of ARIZONA.

Ar·i·zo·na [ar′ə·zō′nə] *n.* A state in the sw U.S.

ark [ärk] *n.* **1** In the Bible, the ship Noah built to save himself, his family, and two of every kind of animal from the Flood. **2** A chest in the ancient Jewish Temple that held the stone tablets on which the Ten Commandments were inscribed: also called **ark of the covenant.**

Ark. Abbreviation of ARKANSAS.

Ar·kan·sas [är′kən·sô] *n.* A state in the south central region of the U.S.

arm¹ [ärm] *n.* **1** The part of the body from the shoulder to the hand, or the forelimb of an animal. **2** Something for or like an arm: the *arm* of a coat; the *arm* of a crane.

arm² [ärm] **1** *n.* A weapon of any sort. **2** *v.* To supply with a weapon or weapons. **3** *v.* To supply with anything that strengthens or protects: to be *armed* with the facts.

ar·ma·da [är·mä′də] *n.* (*sometimes written* **Armada**) A fleet of warships: The Spanish *Armada* was defeated by the English in 1588. ◆ This word comes directly from a Spanish word, which in turn came from a Latin word meaning *armed.* It is closely related to the word *army.*

ar·ma·dil·lo [är′mə·dil′ō] *n., pl.* **ar·ma·dil·los** A small burrowing mammal found from South America north to Texas, having an armorlike shell of jointed plates. Some kinds can roll up, shell and all, into a ball when attacked.

Armadillo, about 28 in. long

ar·ma·ment [är′mə·mənt] *n.* **1** (*often pl.*) The military equipment, as guns, ships, bombs, used in war. **2** The armed forces of a nation, equipped for war.

ar·ma·ture [är′mə·chŏŏr] *n.* **1** The rotating part of an electric motor or generator, having a soft-iron core surrounded by coils of insulated wire. **2** The part of an electric relay, buzzer, or bell, that is moved by the electromagnet.

arm·chair [ärm′châr′] *n.* A chair with supports on both sides for the arms or elbows.

armed forces [ärmd] All the military, naval, and air forces of a nation.

arm·ful [ärm′fŏŏl′] *n., pl.* **arm·fuls** As much as can be held by one or both arms.

arm·hole [ärm′hōl′] *n.* An opening for the arm in clothes.

ar·mi·stice [är′mə·stis] *n.* An agreement to stop fighting for a short time; truce.

Armistice Day The former name for VETERANS DAY.

ar·mor [är′mər] *n.* **1** A covering worn when fighting, to protect the body. **2** Any protective covering, as the shell of a turtle, or plates of a tank. ¶1

ar·mored [är′mərd] *adj.* **1** Protected by armor. **2** Equipped with tanks and other armored vehicles: an *armored* division. ¶1

ar·mor·er [är′mər·ər] *n.* A maker or repairer of arms, especially a soldier or sailor who takes care of the small arms of his company or ship.

Armor of a mounted knight

ar·mo·ri·al [är·môr′ē·əl] *adj.* Of or having to do with coats of arms or heraldry.

ar·mor·y [är′mər·ē] *n., pl.* **ar·mor·ies 1** A

add, āce, câre, pälm; end, ēqual; it, īce; odd, ōpen, ôrder; tŏŏk, pŏŏl; up, bûrn;
ə = a in *above,* e in *sicken,* i in *possible,* o in *melon,* u in *circus;* yŏŏ = u in *fuse;* oil; pout;
check; ring; thin; this; zh in *vision.* For ¶ reference, see page 64 · HOW TO

place where arms are kept; arsenal. **2** A building where military units, as the National Guard, drill. **3** A factory for making weapons. ¶1

arm·pit [ärm′pit′] *n.* The hollow place under the arm at the shoulder.

arms [ärmz] *n.pl.* **1** Weapons. **2** Warfare; fighting. **3** The designs or emblems used in a coat of arms. **— up in arms** Excited and ready to fight.

ar·my [är′mē] *n.*, *pl.* **ar·mies 1** A large group of soldiers, organized, trained, and armed to fight. **2** All the soldiers in the land forces of a country. **3** Any group of people organized to advance a cause: The Salvation *Army*. **4** A great number of persons or things: an *army* of insects.

ar·ni·ca [är′ni·kə] *n.* **1** A perennial plant having large, yellow, daisylike flowers on tall stalks. **2** A medicine prepared from the flower heads of this plant, used for sprains and bruises.

Ar·nold [är′nəld], **Benedict,** 1741–1801, American general in the Revolutionary War, who became a traitor.

a·ro·ma [ə·rō′mə] *n.* A pleasant fragrance or smell, as of food or a plant.

ar·o·mat·ic [ar′ə·mat′ik] *adj.* Having a pleasant smell; fragrant; spicy: *aromatic* tobacco.

a·rose [ə·rōz′] Past tense of ARISE.

a·round [ə·round′] **1** *adv.* In a circle: The top spun *around*. **2** *prep.* About the circumference of: *around* the world. **3** *adv.* On all sides: The people crowded *around* to look. **4** *prep.* On all sides of; surrounding: The flowers grew *around* the pond. **5** *adv.* In the opposite direction; about: to turn *around*. **6** *adv.* Here and there; from place to place: to walk *around*. **7** *prep.* Here and there in: to wander *around* the house. **8** *adv.* Nearby; in the neighborhood: Stay *around* until he calls. **9** *prep.* Somewhere near or within: I'll be *around* the house. About; near: *around* midnight. **10** *prep.*

a·rouse [ə·rouz′] *v.* **a·roused, a·rous·ing 1** To stir up; awaken. **2** To excite or provoke: The cruel deed *aroused* our anger.

ar·que·bus [är′kwə·bəs] *n.* Another name for HARQUEBUS.

ar·raign [ə·rān′] *v.* **1** To call into court to answer "guilty" or "not guilty" to a charge. **2** To accuse; call in question. **— ar·raign′· ment** *n.*

ar·range [ə·rānj′] *v.* **ar·ranged, ar·rang· ing 1** To put into a certain order: to *arrange* the books on the shelf. **2** To make plans; prepare: Did he *arrange* to meet you here? **3** To come or bring to an agreement about: We can easily *arrange* terms. **4** To adapt (music) to a style or for performers not originally intended.

ar·range·ment [ə·rānj′mənt] *n.* **1** An arranging or placing in order. **2** The way in which something is arranged: the *arrangement* of pictures in an art gallery. **3** (*usually pl.*) A plan or preparation: the *arrangements* for the wedding. **4** Music changed to fit certain performers or a style of performance.

ar·rant [ar′ənt] *adj.* Out-and-out; thorough: an *arrant* coward.

ar·ray [ə·rā′] **1** *n.* Regular or proper order; arrangement. **2** *v.* To set in proper order: The soldiers were *arrayed* for an attack. **3** *n.* A large or impressive display: an *array* of gems. **4** *n.* Clothing; fine dress. **5** *v.* To dress; adorn: to be *arrayed* in silks.

ar·rears [ə·rirz′] *n.pl.* **1** A debt overdue and still unpaid. **2** Work already late but not finished: *arrears* of unanswered mail. **— in arrears** Behind in payment of a debt, or in one's work.

ar·rest [ə·rest′] **1** *v.* To stop suddenly; check: The medicine *arrested* his cold. **2** *v.* To attract and hold: The bright signs *arrested* our attention. **3** *v.* To capture by legal authority; take to jail or court. **4** *n.* The act of arresting. **—under arrest** Arrested; in custody.

ar·ri·val [ə·rī′vəl] *n.* **1** The act of arriving: the *arrival* of a train. **2** A person or thing that arrives: new *arrivals* to the country.

ar·rive [ə·rīv′] *v.* **ar·rived, ar·riv·ing 1** To reach a place after a journey: The boat *arrives* in London tomorrow. **2** To come: The hour has finally *arrived*. **3** To achieve success or fame: In this play she has *arrived*.

ar·ro·gance [ar′ə·gəns] *n.* Too much pride and too little regard for others.

ar·ro·gant [ar′ə·gənt] *adj.* Too proud and disdainful of others: an *arrogant* manner. **— ar′ro·gant·ly** *adv.*

ar·row [ar′ō] *n.* **1** A thin, straight rod, usually with a point at one end and feathers at the other. Arrows are used in shooting with a bow. **2** Anything shaped like an arrow. **3** A sign (→) used to indicate a direction, as in maps or road signs.

ar·row·head [ar′ō·hed′] *n.* The pointed tip or head of an arrow.

ar·row·root [ar′ō·rōōt′] *n.* **1** A nutritious starch from the roots of a tropical American plant. **2** This plant.

Indian arrowhead

target arrowhead

ar·roy·o [ə·roi′ō] *n.*, *pl.* **ar·roy·os** A small gulch cut out by a creek, usually dry.

hunting arrowhead

ar·se·nal [är′sə·nəl] *n.* A public building for making or keeping guns, ammunition, etc.

ar·se·nic [är′sə·nik] *n.* A grayish white metallic element. Compounds of arsenic, some very poisonous, are used in industry and medicine.

ar·son [är′sən] *n.* The crime of setting a building or other property afire on purpose.

art[1] [ärt] *n.* **1** Painting, drawing, or sculpture. **2** The making of arrangements of colors, lines, shapes, sounds, words, etc., that appeal to the taste and give pleasure through beauty or form. **3** Such an arrangement itself, as a piece of music or literature, a painting, etc. **4** (*usually pl.*) Fields of study including literature, philosophy, languages, etc., but not the sciences. **5** Rules or methods needed to make or do something; skill: the *art* of cooking. **6** Occupation; craft: the mariner's *art*. **7** (*usually pl.*) A sly trick; cunning or wile: She used her *arts* to entice him.

art² [ärt] *v*. The old form of ARE used with "thou": Thou *art* right.

Ar·te·mis [är′tə·mis] *n*. In Greek myths, the goddess of hunting and of the moon. Her Roman name is Diana.

ar·te·ri·al [är·tir′ē·əl] *adj*. **1** Of, having to do with, or carried in arteries or an artery. **2** Like an artery: an *arterial* highway.

ar·te·ri·o·scle·ro·sis [är·tir′ē·ō·sklə·rō′sis] *n*. A hardening of the walls of the arteries, making it hard for the blood to pass through.

ar·ter·y [är′tər·ē] *n*., *pl*. **ar·ter·ies** Any of the blood vessels that carry blood away from the heart to every part of the body.

ar·te·sian well [är·tē′zhən] A deep well so placed that under-ground pressure forces water to gush out of it.

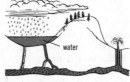

water

Artesian well

art·ful [ärt′fəl] *adj*. **1** Cunning; crafty: the *artful* dodges of the fox. **2** Skillful: an *artful* writer. — **art′·ful·ly** *adv*. — **art′ful·ness** *n*.

ar·thrit·ic [är·thrit′ik] *adj*. Of or brought about by arthritis: *arthritic* pains.

ar·thri·tis [är·thrī′tis] *n*. An inflammation of one or more joints.

ar·thro·pod [är′thrə·pod] *n*. Any of a large group of animals without backbones, having jointed legs and bodies, as insects, spiders, and crabs.

Ar·thur [är′thər] *n*. In many legends, a king of ancient Britain who gathered famous knights at his court in Camelot.

Ar·thur [är′thər], **Chester A.,** 1830–1886, 21st president of the United States, 1881–1885.

ar·ti·choke [är′tə·chōk] *n*. **1** A garden plant that looks like a large thistle. **2** Its flowering head, that is eaten as a vegetable.

Artichoke

ar·ti·cle [är′ti·kəl] *n*. **1** A particular thing; an individual item: an *article* of food. **2** A separate, often numbered section or clause in a law, constitution, contract, etc. **3** A complete piece of writing on a single topic, forming part of a magazine, newspaper, or book: an *article* on folk songs. **4** In English, any of the words *the, a,* or *an. The* is often used to make a noun definite and particular, as in *the* boy; *a* or *an* to make a noun indefinite and general, as in *a* boy.

ar·tic·u·late [*adj*. är·tik′yə·lit, *v*. är·tik′yə·lāt] *adj*., *v*. **ar·tic·u·lat·ed, ar·tic·u·lat·ing 1** *adj*. Using clear and distinct syllables or words: *articulate* speech. **2** *v*. To speak clearly and distinctly; enunciate. **3** *adj*. Having the power of speech; able to speak one's thoughts clearly: an *articulate* speaker. **4** *v*. To say or tell in words: He tried to *articulate* his gratitude. **5** *adj*. Having joints or segments: The arm is an *articulate* limb. **6** *v*. To connect by a joint: The leg is *articulated* to the body at the hip. — **ar·tic′u·late·ly** *adv*.

ar·tic·u·la·tion [är·tik′yə·lā′shən] *n*. **1** Manner of speaking or pronouncing. **2** The manner in which parts are joined together. **3** A joint.

ar·ti·fact [är′tə·fakt] *n*. Anything made by human work or art.

ar·ti·fice [är′tə·fis] *n*. A sly or clever trick; dodge: He used every *artifice* to get his way.

ar·ti·fi·cial [är′tə·fish′əl] *adj*. **1** Made by man rather than by nature: *artificial* flowers. **2** Not genuine; false: an *artificial* manner. — **ar′ti·fi′cial·ly** *adv*. — **ar·ti·fi·ci·al·i·ty** [är′tə·fish·ē·al′ə·tē] *n*.

artificial respiration The act or method of making a person breathe by forcing air in and out of his lungs, as after suffocation or shock.

ar·til·ler·y [är·til′ə·rē] *n*. **1** Large mounted guns; cannon. **2** A part of an army that makes use of such guns.

ar·ti·san [är′tə·zən] *n*. A workman, such as a plumber or carpenter, trained or skilled in some trade; craftsman.

ar·tist [är′tist] *n*. **1** A person who is skilled in any of the fine arts, as painting or sculpture. **2** A person who works with skill and originality: She is an *artist* at baking pies.

ar·tis·tic [är·tis′tik] *adj*. **1** Of art or artists. **2** Showing skill and good design, color, or form: an *artistic* job of decorating. **3** Showing or having a sense for the beautiful. — **ar·tis′ti·cal·ly** *adv*.

art·is·try [är′tis·trē] *n*. Artistic work or ability.

art·less [ärt′lis] *adj*. **1** Without cunning; simple; natural: the *artless* questions of children. **2** Not having skill or ability; clumsy. — **art′·less·ly** *adv*. — **art′less·ness** *n*.

-ary A suffix meaning: **1** Having to do with, as in *parliamentary*, having to do with parliament. **2** A person or thing connected with or engaged in, as in *revolutionary*, a person engaged in or connected with a revolution.

as [az] **1** *adv*. To the same degree; equally: Can you swim *as* well as your friend? **2** *conj*. To the same degree that: as fair *as* the sun. **3** *conj*. In the way that: Sing *as* I am singing. **4** *conj*. To the degree in which: He became gentler *as* he grew older. **5** *conj*. At the same time that; while: They waved *as* we sailed away. **6** *conj*. Because; since: *As* it rained, we stayed at home. **7** *conj*. That the result is, or was: Speak louder, so *as* to be heard. **8** *conj*. Though: Hungry *as* he was, he couldn't eat. **9** *conj*. For instance: We enjoy many sports, *as* tennis and swimming. **10** *pron.* That; who; which: such birds *as* swim; He has the same room *as* I had. **11** *pron.* A fact that: He is ill, *as* everyone knows. **12** *prep.* In the role or character of: to act *as* umpire. **— as for** or **as to** Concerning. **— as if** or **as though** The way it would be if: He looked *as though* he had cried. ◆ *As* used in place of "since" or "because" can cause confusion. The sentence *As it was raining, we covered our heads* can mean either that we covered our heads *because* it was raining or that we simply happened to cover our heads *while* it was raining. ◆ See LIKE.

As The symbol for ARSENIC.

as·bes·tos [as·bes′təs] *n.* A grayish white mineral that will not burn nor let much heat through. Mats of asbestos insulate furnace pipes, protect tables against hot dishes, etc.

as·cend [ə·send′] *v.* **1** To go upward; rise. **2** To climb: The climbers *ascended* the mountain.

as·cen·dan·cy [ə·sen′dən·sē] *n.* A position of power or control; domination: The tyrant lost his *ascendancy* over the people.

as·cen·dant [ə·sen′dənt] *adj.* **1** Rising; moving upward. **2** Dominant; in power. **— in the ascendant** Gaining in power or influence; on the rise.

as·cen·sion [ə·sen′shən] *n.* **1** An ascending; rise. **2** (*written* **Ascension**) In the Bible, the ascent of Jesus into heaven after the Resurrection.

as·cent [ə·sent′] *n.* **1** The act of rising or climbing: the *ascent* of a balloon. **2** Advancement; rise: *ascent* to the presidency. **3** A way going up; upward slope. ◆ *Ascent* and *assent* sound and look alike but are unrelated. *Ascent* comes from a Latin verb meaning *to climb to* and still means an upward climb: The *ascent* of the space rocket was shown on TV. *Assent* comes from Latin roots meaning *to feel* to and now means agreement or consent: Congress gave its *assent* to the policy outlined. You will come on both words in rather formal articles but you probably won't hear them often in conversation.

as·cer·tain [as′ər·tān′] *v.* To find out for certain; make sure of: He examined the book to *ascertain* its contents.

as·cet·ic [ə·set′ik] **1** *n.* A person who chooses not to have pleasures or comforts, as wealth or fine clothes, but prefers living plainly, usually for religious reasons. **2** *adj.* Holding back from pleasures or comforts; austere: *ascetic* life. — **as·cet·i·cism** [ə·set′ə·siz′əm] *n.*

a·scor·bic acid [ə·skôr′bik] Vitamin C. It is found in oranges, lemons, tomatoes, etc.

as·cribe [ə·skrīb′] *v.* **as·cribed, as·crib·ing** **1** To think of as coming from a cause or source: He *ascribes* his headache to too much television. **2** To think of as belonging; attribute: The work is *ascribed* to Shakespeare.

as·crip·tion [ə·skrip′shən] *n.* **1** The act of ascribing. **2** A sentence or statement that ascribes.

a·sex·u·al [ā·sek′shoo·əl] *adj.* **1** Lacking sex. **2** Without union of male and female reproductive cells: *asexual* reproduction. **— a·sex′u·al·ly** *adv.*

ash[1] [ash] *n.* The fine, grayish white powder left after a substance has been burned. See also ASHES.

ash[2] [ash] *n.* A shade tree related to the olive, having tough, springy wood, used for timber.

a·shamed [ə·shāmd′] *adj.* **1** Feeling shame; upset because something bad, silly, or improper was done: She was *ashamed* of her bad manners. **2** Not willing because of a fear of shame: She was *ashamed* to show her dirty notebook.

ash·en [ash′ən] *adj.* Of, like, or pale as ashes; gray: an *ashen* appearance.

ash·es [ash′iz] *n.pl.* **1** The grayish white particles and powder that remain after a substance has been burned. **2** A dead body, especially the remains of a body after cremation.

a·shore [ə·shôr′] *adj., adv.* **1** To or on the shore: A sailor *ashore* is homesick; He came *ashore*. **2** On land; aground.

Ash Wednesday The first day of Lent; the seventh Wednesday before Easter.

ash·y [ash′ē] *adj.* **ash·i·er, ash·i·est** **1** Of or covered with ashes. **2** Like ashes; pale: an *ashy* complexion.

A·sia [ā′zhə] *n.* The largest continent of the world, in the Eastern Hemisphere north of the equator.

Asia Minor A peninsula in western Asia, bounded by the Black Sea, the Aegean Sea, and the Mediterranean Sea.

A·sian [ā′zhən] **1** *adj.* Of or from Asia. **2** *n.* A person born or living in Asia.

A·si·at·ic [ā′zhē·at′ik] **1** *adj.* Of or from Asia. **2** *n.* An Asian.

a·side [ə·sīd′] **1** *adv.* To or on one side; away: Stand *aside!* **2** *adv.* Apart; away: Put some fruit *aside* for him. **3** *adv.* Out of thought: Put your worries *aside*. **4** *n.* Remarks spoken aside, as those of an actor not supposed to be heard by the other actors. **5** *adv.* Away from the general company; in seclusion. **— aside from** Apart from; excepting: *Aside from* one uncle, he had no relatives.

as·i·nine [as′ə·nīn] *adj.* Stupid; foolish.

ask [ask] *v.* **1** To put a question to: Don't *ask* me about her. **2** To use words to try to find out: to *ask* what time it is; to *ask* the price; I'll *ask* about it. **3** To say aloud: to *ask* questions. **4** To request or make a request: to *ask* permission. **5** To demand as a price; require: They are *asking* five dollars for the sweater. **6** To invite: Her aunt was *asked* to tea.

a·skance [ə·skans′] *adv.* **1** With distrust or doubt: They looked *askance* at the new plan. **2** With a look to the side; sidewise.

a·skew [ə·skyōō′] *adj.*, *adv.* On or to one side; out of line: The gate hung *askew*.

a·slant [ə·slant′] **1** *adj.* Slanting. **2** *adv.* At a slant. **3** *prep.* Across or over on a slant.

a·sleep [ə·slēp′] **1** *adj.* Sleeping. **2** *adj.* Numb: My foot is *asleep*. **3** *adv.* Into a sleep: to fall *asleep*.

Picture set askew

asp [asp] *n.* A small venomous snake of Africa and Europe; a viper.

as·par·a·gus [ə·spar′ə·gəs] *n.* **1** A perennial plant related to the lily. **2** Its young shoots, eaten as a vegetable.

as·pect [as′pekt] *n.* **1** Appearance; look: The dark street had a frightening *aspect*. **2** One way of looking at or approaching a subject, problem, etc.: There are many *aspects* to the problem. **3** The side or surface facing in a certain direction: The southern *aspect* of a house.

asp·en [as′pən] *n.* A poplar tree with leaves that tremble in the slightest breeze.

as·per·i·ty [as·per′ə·tē] *n.*, *pl.* **as·per·i·ties** **1** Roughness or harshness, as of weather or a surface. **2** Bitterness or sharpness of temper: The *asperity* in her voice surprised me.

as·per·sion [ə·spûr′zhən] *n.* A false or damaging remark or report; slander: to cast *aspersions* on his honesty.

as·phalt [as′fôlt] *n.* **1** A substance like tar, brown to black, found in natural beds or left over when petroleum is refined. **2** A mixture of this with crushed rock or sand used for pavement or roofing.

as·phyx·i·ate [as·fik′sē·āt] *v.* **as·phyx·i·at·ed, as·phyx·i·at·ing** To make unconscious or kill by keeping enough oxygen from reaching the blood; suffocate: Leaking gas may *asphyxiate* a person. **— as·phyx′i·a′tion** *n.*

as·pic [as′pik] *n.* A jelly of meat or vegetable juices, used in molded salads, as of meat or fish.

as·pir·ant [ə·spīr′ənt *or* as′pər·ənt] *n.* A person who aspires, or tries to achieve honors or high position: an *aspirant* to the governorship.

as·pi·rate [*v.* as′pə·rāt, *n.*, *adj.* as′pər·it] *v.* **as·pi·rat·ed, as·pi·rat·ing**, *n.*, *adj.* **1** *v.* To start a word or a vowel sound with the sound of *h*: You *aspirate* "hot" but not "honest." **2** *n.* This sound of *h*. **3** *adj.* Pronounced with this sound of *h*.

as·pi·ra·tion [as′pə·rā′shən] *n.* **1** A great hope or desire; ambition: to have *aspirations* to become a lawyer. **2** The act of breathing; breath. **3** An aspirating of a sound.

as·pire [ə·spīr′] *v.* **as·pired, as·pir·ing 1** To have great hope or ambition for something; seek: to *aspire* to be king. **2** *adj. use:* an *aspiring* author.

as·pi·rin [as′pər·in] *n.* A drug used to relieve headaches, pain, colds, or fever. ◆ The word *aspirin* was formed from an old chemical name and was at one time a trademark.

ass [as] *n.* **1** A donkey. **2** A stupid person; fool.

as·sail [ə·sāl′] *v.* **1** To attack violently, as with blows, weapons, or soldiers; assault. **2** To attack with words, arguments, or questions: to be *assailed* by doubts.

as·sail·ant [ə·sā′lənt] *n.* A person who assails; an attacker.

as·sas·sin [ə·sas′in] *n.* A murderer, especially a fanatic or a person hired to kill someone.

as·sas·si·nate [ə·sas′ə·nāt] *v.* **as·sas·si·nat·ed, as·sas·si·nat·ing** To murder by a secret or surprise attack. **— as·sas′si·na′tion** *n.*

as·sault [ə·sôlt′] **1** *n.* Any sudden, violent attack. **2** *n.* An illegal physical attack on another person, or a clear threat of one. **3** *v.* To attack with violence.

as·say [ə·sā′] **1** *v.* To analyze (an alloy or ore) to find out how much of a certain metal is in it. **2** *n.* A test such as this. **— as·say′er** *n.*

as·sem·blage [ə·sem′blij] *n.* **1** Any gathering of persons or things; collection; assembly: an *assemblage* of junk in the garage. **2** A fitting together, as of the parts of a machine.

as·sem·ble [ə·sem′bəl] *v.* **as·sem·bled, as·sem·bling 1** To come or bring together; collect: The team *assembled* for practice. **2** To fit together the parts of: He cleaned the rifle and *assembled* it.

as·sem·bly [ə·sem′blē] *n.*, *pl.* **as·sem·blies 1** A gathering or meeting together of persons: right of peaceful *assembly*. **2** A group of persons gathered together for a common purpose; meeting. **3** (*written* **Assembly**) The lower house of the legislature in some states. **4** A putting together of parts, as of a machine. **5** These parts put together. **6** The signal on a bugle or drum calling soldiers to fall into rank.

as·sent [ə·sent′] **1** *v.* To agree or consent: He *assented* to our scheme. **2** *n.* Consent or agreement. ◆ See ASCENT.

as·sert [ə·sûrt′] *v.* **1** To say in a clear, firm way; declare: The guide *asserted* that this was the spot. **2** To claim; insist on: He *asserted* his right to speak. **— assert oneself 1** To insist on one's rights. **2** To put oneself forward; demand attention.

as·ser·tion [ə·sûr′shən] *n.* **1** The asserting of something. **2** A firm, positive statement; claim.

as·ser·tive [ə·sûr′tiv] *adj.* Very bold and self-confident; aggressive. **— as·ser′tive·ly** *adv.* **— as·ser′tive·ness** *n.*

as·sess [ə·ses′] *v.* **1** To set a value on property as a basis for taxes. **2** To place a tax, fine, or other payment on: Each member was *assessed* five dollars. **3** To fix the amount of (a tax, fine, etc.).

---

add, āce, câre, pälm; end, ēqual; it, īce; odd, ōpen, ôrder; tŏŏk, pŏŏl; up, bûrn;
ə = a in *above*, e in *sicken*, i in *possible*, o in *melon*, u in *circus*; yōō = u in *fuse*; oil; pout;
check; ring; thin; this; zh in *vision*. For ¶ reference, see page 64 · HOW TO

as·sess·ment [ə·ses′mənt] *n*. **1** The act of assessing. **2** The amount that is assessed.

as·set [as′et] *n*. **1** (*often pl.*) Any item of property having value, as land or money: The business has *assets* of buildings, stocks, and machinery. **2** A valuable thing or quality: Beauty is her chief *asset*.

as·sev·er·ate [ə·sev′ə·rāt] *v*. **as·sev·er·at·ed, as·sev·er·at·ing** To declare or say in a firm, positive manner. — **as·sev·er·a′tion** *n*.

as·si·du·i·ty [as′ə·d(y)ōō′ə·tē] *n*., *pl*. **as·si·du·i·ties** Hard and constant effort; diligence: to study with *assiduity*.

as·sid·u·ous [ə·sij′ōō·əs] *adj*. Showing constant, steady attention and effort: *assiduous* work. — **as·sid′u·ous·ly** *adv*. — **as·sid′u·ous·ness** *n*.

as·sign [ə·sīn′] *v*. **1** To give as a task or share: to *assign* homework. **2** To put at some task or job: She was *assigned* to selling books. **3** To fix, name, or specify: Limits were *assigned* to the debate. **4** To transfer to another; hand over: He *assigned* his option rights to his son.

as·sign·ment [ə·sīn′mənt] *n*. **1** The act of assigning. **2** Something assigned, as a lesson: I spent two hours on the French *assignment*.

as·sim·i·late [ə·sim′ə·lāt] *v*. **as·sim·i·lat·ed, as·sim·i·lat·ing 1** To take in and make part of itself; absorb: His body cannot *assimilate* sugar. **2** To take in and understand: Have you *assimilated* all that information? **3** To make or become alike or similar: The new arrivals *assimilated* their customs to those of their new land. — **as·sim′i·la′tion** *n*.

as·sist [ə·sist′] **1** *v*. To give help or aid to: He *assisted* me in carrying the table. **2** *n*. Help given, as in scoring a goal in hockey.

as·sis·tance [ə·sis′təns] *n*. Help; aid; support.

as·sis·tant [ə·sis′tənt] **1** *n*. A person who assists; a helper. **2** *adj*. Aiding or assisting the person under whom one is employed: an *assistant* editor.

as·siz·es [ə·sīz′əz] *n.pl*. Court sessions held regularly in each county of England.

as·so·ci·ate [*v*. ə·sō′shē·āt, *n*., *adj*. ə·sō′shē·it] *v*. **as·so·ci·at·ed, as·so·ci·at·ing**, *n*., *adj*. **1** *v*. To make or see a connection between; connect in one's mind: to *associate* the color yellow with cowardice. **2** *n*. A person connected with another, as a fellow worker, companion, or partner. **3** *adj*. Joined with another or others in some common way: *associate* justices. **4** *v*. To combine with others for a common purpose. **5** *v*. To have dealings; keep company: Don't *associate* with such a rough crowd. **6** *adj*. Having a lower position; with less than full status: an *associate* professor.

as·so·ci·a·tion [ə·sō′s(h)ē·ā′shən] *n*. **1** The act of associating. **2** The state of being associated; fellowship; partnership. **3** An organization of persons with a common purpose; society. **4** The connection in the mind between two ideas or feelings: the *association* of tears with sadness.

as·so·ci·a·tive [ə·sō′shē·ā′tiv] *adj*. **1** Of or having to do with association. **2** Caused by association: an *associative* response. **3** Indicating an operation that can be performed on a set of three numbers by beginning with either of two pairs, as addition or multiplication: $2 + (3 + 4) = (2 + 3) + 4$, or $2 \times (3 \times 4) = (2 \times 3) \times 4$.

as·sort·ed [ə·sôr′tid] *adj*. **1** Of various sorts; of different kinds or varieties: a box of *assorted* chocolates. **2** Sorted into groups by size, type, color, etc.: a row of dresses *assorted* by size.

as·sort·ment [ə·sôrt′mənt] *n*. **1** A collection or group of various things; variety: an *assortment* of dresses. **2** A sorting into groups; classification.

as·suage [ə·swāj′] *v*. **as·suaged, as·suag·ing 1** To make less; make calmer or lighter: Her tears *assuaged* his anger. **2** To satisfy, as thirst: The sandwich *assuaged* his hunger.

as·sume [ə·sōōm′] *v*. **as·sumed, as·sum·ing 1** To take as or as if true; suppose: *Assume* that tides will be normal. **2** To take on (a shape, role, look, etc.): The cloud *assumed* a mushroom shape. **3** To take on or over: He *assumed* all responsibility. **4** To pretend; simulate; put on: He *assumed* an air of not caring.

as·sump·tion [ə·sump′shən] *n*. **1** The act of assuming. **2** Something supposed or taken for granted: a false *assumption*. **3** (*written* **Assumption**) The taking up of the Virgin Mary bodily into heaven, or the church festival on August 15 in honor of it.

as·sur·ance [ə·shŏŏr′əns] *n*. **1** A positive statement intended to give confidence: We had his *assurance* it was safe to go. **2** Certainty; guarantee: There is no *assurance* of his winning. **3** Self-confidence: She recited the poem with *assurance*. **4** Too much boldness; impudence. **5** The British word for insurance.

as·sure [ə·shŏŏr′] *v*. **as·sured, as·sur·ing 1** To make (a person) feel sure; convince: He *assured* me of his honesty. **2** To tell or declare to; promise: He *assured* us he would return. **3** To make certain; guarantee: This invention *assures* his fame.

as·sured [ə·shŏŏrd′] *adj*. **1** Guaranteed; sure: an *assured* salary. **2** Confident.

as·sur·ed·ly [ə·shŏŏr′id·lē] *adv*. **1** Surely; unquestionably. **2** With assurance; confidently.

As·syr·i·a [ə·sir′ē·ə] *n*. An ancient empire in sw Asia. — **As·syr′i·an** *adj*., *n*.

as·ter [as′tər] *n*. A plant with flowers like daisies, having white, pink, or purple petals and yellow centers.

Map caption: Black Sea · Caspian Sea · ASSYRIAN EMPIRE 7th CENTURY B.C. · Red Sea · Persian Gulf

as·ter·isk [as′tər·isk] *n*. A mark shaped like a star (*), used in printing and writing to indicate a note or show that something has been left out.

a·stern [ə·stûrn′] *adv*. **1** Behind a ship. **2** In or toward its rear end. **3** Backward.

as·ter·oid [as′tə·roid] *n.* Any of several hundred small planets between Mars and Jupiter.

asth·ma [az′mə] *n.* A chronic illness that makes breathing difficult and causes wheezing and sometimes coughing.

asth·mat·ic [az·mat′ik] **1** *adj.* Of asthma: an *asthmatic* attack. **2** *adj.* Having asthma. **3** *n.* A person having asthma.

a·stig·ma·tism [ə·stig′mə·tiz′əm] *n.* A defect of an eye or a lens which makes objects look out of shape or blurred. It prevents light rays from coming to a sharp focus.

a·stir [ə·stür′] *adj., adv.* Stirring; in motion: The forest was *astir* with life.

as·ton·ish [ə·ston′·ish] *v.* To surprise very much; amaze. **— as·ton′ish·ment** *n.*

If any of these lines look thin or blurred, you may have astigmatism.

as·ton·ish·ing [ə·ston′ish·ing] *adj.* Amazing. **— as·ton′ish·ing·ly** *adv.*

as·tound [ə·stound′] *v.* **1** To stun with amazement: The news *astounded* me. **2** *adj. use:* an *astounding* upset.

as·tra·khan [as′trə·kan] *n.* **1** Curly, furlike, black or gray wool, got from young lambs raised in SE Europe. **2** A fabric looking like this.

a·stray [ə·strā′] *adj., adv.* Away from the right path: The guide led the group *astray*.

a·stride [ə·strīd′] **1** *adj., adv.* With one leg on each side: Men usually ride *astride*. **2** *prep.* With one leg on each side of: He rode *astride* the horse.

as·trin·gent [ə·strin′jənt] **1** *n.* A substance that shrinks body tissues. It tightens skin, checks bleeding, etc. **2** *adj.* Able to shrink body tissue.

as·trol·o·ger [ə·strol′ə·jər] *n.* A person who studies or practices astrology.

Boy astride a fence

as·trol·o·gy [ə·strol′ə·jē] *n.* The study of the supposed influence of stars and planets on human lives.

as·tro·naut [as′trə·nôt] *n.* A person who travels in space. ◆ *Astronaut* is parallel to *aeronaut*, a balloon pilot, and is formed from the Greek roots *nautes*, meaning *sailor*, and *astro-*, meaning (*between or among*) *stars*.

as·tro·nau·tics [as′trə·nô′tiks] *n.* The science and art of flight in space. ◆ See -ICS.

as·tron·o·mer [ə·stron′ə·mər] *n.* A person who is an expert in astronomy.

as·tro·nom·i·cal [as′trə·nom′i·kəl] *adj.* **1** Of or having to do with astronomy. **2** Almost too large to imagine, like the numbers in astronomy; enormous: *astronomical* expenses. **— as′tro·nom′i·cal·ly** *adv.*

as·tron·o·my [ə·stron′ə·mē] *n.* The study of the stars, planets, and other heavenly bodies, their make-up, positions, motions, etc. ◆ *Astronomy* comes from two Greek words meaning *arrangement* or *distribution of the stars*, the early study having been mainly the mapping of stars.

as·tute [ə·st(y)ōot′] *adj.* Having a keen mind; shrewd. **— as·tute′ly** *adv.* **— as·tute′ness** *n.*

a·sun·der [ə·sun′dər] **1** *adv.* Apart; into pieces. **2** *adj.* Separated; apart.

a·sy·lum [ə·sī′ləm] *n.* **1** An institution for sheltering and taking care of orphans, the mentally ill, or other groups of unfortunate people. **2** A place of refuge or safety; shelter.

at [at] *prep.* **1** On; in; by: *at* sea; *at* home; *at* the door. **2** To or toward: Look *at* that sunset. **3** Engaged or occupied in: women *at* work. **4** In the condition or position of: countries *at* war; *at* an angle. **5** In the manner of: He rode *at* a trot. **6** Because of: He cried *at* the thought of leaving. **7** Amounting to; for: *at* two percent; *at* a dime apiece. **8** On the time or age of: *at* noon; He died *at* 60. **9** According to: proceed *at* your own pace.

ate [āt] Past tense of EAT.

a·the·ism [ā′thē·iz′əm] *n.* The belief that there is no God. **— a′the·ist** *n.* **— a′the·is′tic** *adj.*

A·the·ni·an [ə·thē′nē·ən] **1** *adj.* Of or from Athens. **2** *n.* A person born or living in Athens, or a citizen of Athens.

Ath·ens [ath′ənz] *n.* The capital of Greece, in the SE part. Ancient Athens was the center of Greek culture and art.

a·thirst [ə·thûrst′] *adj.* **1** Eager: *athirst* for power. **2** Thirsty: seldom used today.

ath·lete [ath′lēt] *n.* A person with skill in sports or games that take strength, speed, or dexterity, as football, tennis, or running.

athlete's foot A contagious disease caused by a fungus attacking the skin of the feet.

ath·let·ic [ath·let′ik] *adj.* **1** Of, for, or having to do with athletics or an athlete. **2** Strong and vigorous; active. **— ath·let′i·cal·ly** *adv.*

ath·let·ics [ath·let′iks] *n.pl.* Sports and games that take strength, speed, or dexterity, as football or wrestling. ◆ See -ICS.

a·thwart [ə·thwôrt′] **1** *adv.* From side to side; across. **2** *prep.* From side to side of; across: A ferry passed *athwart* our course. **3** *prep.* Contrary to; against: music *athwart* popular taste.

-ation A suffix meaning: **1** The act or process of, as in *creation*, the act of creating. **2** The condition or quality of, as in *affectation*, the quality of being affected. **3** The result of, as in *reformation*, the result of reforming.

add, āce, câre, pälm; end, ēqual; it, ice; odd, ōpen, ôrder; tŏŏk, pōōl; up, bûrn;
ə = a in *above*, e in *sicken*, i in *possible*, o in *melon*, u in *circus*; yōō = u in *fuse*; oil; pout;
check; ring; thin; this; zh in *vision*. For ¶ reference, see page 64 · HOW TO

-ative A suffix meaning: **1** Having to do with, as in *quantitative*, having to do with quantity. **2** Tending to, as in *talkative*, tending to talk.

At·lan·ta [at·lan′tə] *n.* The capital of Georgia.

At·lan·tic [at·lan′tik] **1** *n.* The ocean extending from the Arctic to the Antarctic between the Americas and Europe and Africa. **2** *adj.* Of, near, in, or having to do with the Atlantic.

Atlantic Charter A statement issued by Winston Churchill and Franklin D. Roosevelt in August, 1941, setting forth the basic aims for peace of the Allies after World War II.

At·lan·tis [at·lan′tis] *n.* In Greek myths, an island that was engulfed by the sea.

at·las [at′ləs] *n.* A book of maps.

At·las [at′ləs] *n.* In Greek myths, a giant who supported the heavens on his shoulders.

Atlas Mountains A mountain range in NW Africa.

at·mos·phere [at′məs·fir] *n.* **1** The air surrounding the earth. **2** The gases surrounding a heavenly body. **3** The air or climate in a place. **4** Surrounding influence; background: an *atmosphere* of gloom. ◆ This word comes from Greek words meaning *vapor sphere.*

at·mos·pher·ic [at′məs·fir′ik] *adj.* Occurring in, caused by, or having to do with the atmosphere.

atmospheric pressure The pressure exerted by the weight of the atmosphere, about 15 pounds per square inch at sea level, decreasing as one goes higher.

lagoon

An atoll

at·oll [at′ôl] *n.* An island of coral shaped something like a doughnut and enclosing a lagoon.

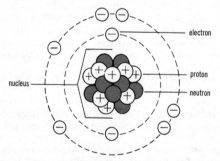
electron
proton
neutron
nucleus

Diagram of one atom of oxygen. The nucleus contains 8 protons, shown as white circles with plus signs, and 8 neutrons, shown as red circles. The 8 electrons are shown as white circles with minus signs.

at·om [at′əm] *n.* **1** The smallest unit of an element that is able to take part in chemical reactions. It is made up of smaller particles whose number and arrangement are different for each element. **2** A very small amount; the least bit. ◆ *Atom* comes from a Greek word meaning *indivisible.*

atom bomb An atomic bomb.

a·tom·ic [ə·tom′ik] *adj.* **1** Of or having to do with an atom or atoms. **2** Very small; minute; tiny.

atomic bomb A powerful bomb using the energy suddenly released when the nuclei of atoms of uranium or plutonium are split.

atomic energy The energy released by the splitting of heavy atoms or the fusion of light atoms.

atomic number The number of protons in the nucleus of an atom of each element.

atomic power Atomic energy used as a source of power.

atomic weight The weight of an atom of any element in relation to that of some standard element. Formerly, the standard was oxygen, taken as 16; now it is carbon, taken as 12.

at·om·ize [at′əm·īz] *v.* **at·om·ized, at·om·iz·ing** To reduce tiny bits or into a spray. ¶3

at·om·iz·er [at′əm·ī′zər] *n.* A device that reduces liquid, as perfume, to a fine spray. ¶3

a·tone [ə·tōn′] *v.* **a·toned, a·ton·ing** To make amends or make up: to *atone* for one's sins with prayer and good works; In art, sincerity cannot *atone* for lack of skill.

Atomizer

a·tone·ment [ə·tōn′mənt] *n.* **1** The act of atoning, as for a sin or crime; amends made. **2** (*written* **Atonement**) The reconciliation between God and man through Christ's suffering and death.

a·ton·ic [ə·ton′ik *or* ā·ton′ik] *adj.* Not accented, as a word or syllable.

a·top [ə·top′] **1** *adj., adv.* On or at the top. **2** *prep.* On the top of: snow *atop* a mountain.

a·tri·um [ā′trē·əm] *n., pl.* **a·tri·a** [ā′trē·ə] **1** One of the upper chambers of the heart, through which blood from the veins passes to the lower chambers. See picture at HEART. **2** The entrance hall or central court of an ancient Roman house.

a·tro·cious [ə·trō′shəs] *adj.* **1** Terribly wicked, criminal, vile, or cruel. **2** *informal* Very bad: an *atrocious* book. — **a·tro′cious·ly** *adv.*

a·troc·i·ty [ə·tros′ə·tē] *n., pl.* **a·troc·i·ties** **1** An extremely cruel or vicious act. **2** Terrible wickedness or cruelty.

at·ro·phy [at′rə·fē] *v.* **at·ro·phied, at·ro·phy·ing,** *n.* **1** *v.* To waste away or wither: Lack of exercise can cause muscles to *atrophy.* **2** *n.* A wasting away of a part of the body.

at·tach [ə·tach′] *v.* **1** To make fast; fasten; connect: to *attach* a button to a coat. **2** To add on, as a signature. **3** To connect in one's mind; ascribe: to *attach* importance to an event. **4** To seize by legal means: to *attach* a man's pay in collecting a debt. **5** To bind by feelings of love: She is *attached* to her sister. **6** To assign: He was *attached* to the general's staff.

at·ta·ché [at′ə·shā′] *n.* A person who is officially attached to the staff of a diplomatic mission.

attaché case A briefcase that resembles a box.

at·tach·ment [ə·tach′mənt] *n.* **1** The act of attaching. **2** An attached condition. **3** Something that attaches or joins; connection. **4** A part that fastens to or on something else, as on a machine. **5** Affection; fondness. **6** The legal seizure of a person or property.

at·tack [ə·tak′] **1** *v.* To set upon with violence; begin battle with: The cavalry *attacked* the fort. **2** *v.* To criticize harshly; condemn: to *attack* a policy. **3** *n.* The act of attacking; assault: an air *attack*. **4** *v.* To affect destructively: Acid *attacks* metal. **5** *v.* To begin work on; set about: to *attack* a problem. **6** *n.* A sudden onset of illness: an *attack* of fever.

at·tain [ə·tān′] *v.* **1** To gain or arrive at by hard work; achieve, as a desired end: to *attain* wealth. **2** To come to: to *attain* an old age.

at·tain·a·ble [ə·tā′nə·bəl] *adj.* Capable of being attained: Peace is an *attainable* goal.

at·tain·der [ə·tān′dər] *n.* The removal of all civil rights from a person who has been sentenced to death or declared an outlaw.

at·tain·ment [ə·tān′mənt] *n.* **1** The act of attaining. **2** Something attained, as a goal or a skill; achievement.

at·tar [at′ər] *n.* A fragrant oil from the petals of flowers, especially roses, used in perfume.

at·tempt [ə·tempt′] **1** *v.* To make an effort; try: He *attempted* to lift the trunk. **2** *n.* A putting forth of effort; a try. **3** *n.* An attack; assault: an *attempt* on the king's life. **4** *v.* To attack.

at·tend [ə·tend′] *v.* **1** To be present at; go to: I *attended* her party. **2** To go with or be useful to as a servant or helper: He *attends* the king. **3** To take care of: The nurse *attends* the sick man. **4** To follow or result from: Danger *attends* careless driving. **— attend to 1** To give careful attention to. **2** To do or carry out: to *attend to* the sweeping. **3** To dispose of, as a problem.

at·ten·dance [ə·ten′dəns] *n.* **1** The act of attending. **2** The number of people attending: The *attendance* was over 500.

at·ten·dant [ə·ten′dənt] **1** *n.* A person who attends, especially a servant or caretaker. **2** *adj.* Serving or attending: an *attendant* nursemaid. **3** *adj.* Following or accompanying: the *attendant* risks of having so many cars on our highways.

at·ten·tion [ə·ten′shən] *n.* **1** The act or power of directing the mind, as in noticing or concentrating on something: After listening for four hours, our *attention* began to falter. **2** Thought or care: to give *attention* to one's manners. **3** An act of courtesy or regard: the *attentions* of a gentleman. **4** The military position of readiness: to stand at *attention*.

at·ten·tive [ə·ten′tiv] *adj.* **1** Giving or showing attention: an *attentive* listener. **2** Courteous; thoughtful. **— at·ten′tive·ly** *adv.*

at·ten·u·ate [ə·ten′yoō·āt] *v.* **at·ten·u·at·ed, at·ten·u·at·ing 1** To make or become thin, small, or fine; draw out, as a wire. **2** To reduce in size or strength; weaken: to *attenuate* sound; His power was *attenuated* by the new court ruling. **— at·ten′u·a′tion** *n.*

at·test [ə·test′] *v.* **1** To state that something is true or genuine; vouch for: to *attest* to the quality of a new product. **2** To be proof of; confirm: Her shining hair *attests* the care it is given. **3** To bear witness; testify.

at·tic [at′ik] *n.* The uppermost story of a house, just under the roof; garret.

At·ti·ca [at′i·kə] *n.* In ancient and modern Greece, the region surrounding Athens.

At·ti·la [at′ə·lə *or* ə·til′ə] *n.*, 406?–453, the barbaric king of the Huns.

at·tire [ə·tīr′] *v.* **at·tired, at·tir·ing,** *n.* **1** *v.* To dress; clothe: *attired* in princely garments. **2** *n.* Dress; apparel: rich *attire*.

at·ti·tude [at′ə·t(y)oōd] *n.* **1** A position of the body, often suggesting some action: an *attitude* of thought. **2** A way of feeling or regarding; a mental view: a stubborn *attitude*; a humble *attitude*.

at·tor·ney [ə·tûr′nē] *n., pl.* **at·tor·neys 1** A person who has power to act in behalf of another person. **2** A lawyer.

attorney at law A lawyer.

attorney general *pl.* **attorneys general** or **attorney generals** The chief law officer of a government.

at·tract [ə·trakt′] *v.* **1** To cause to come near without visible connection: Magnets *attract* iron. **2** To draw or invite: Parades *attract* crowds.

at·trac·tion [ə·trak′shən] *n.* **1** The act or power of attracting. **2** Something that attracts: The main *attraction* was a juggler's act.

at·trac·tive [ə·trak′tiv] *adj.* **1** Attracting interest; tempting; pleasing: an *attractive* offer; an *attractive* girl. **2** Able to attract. **— at·trac′tive·ly** *adv.* **— at·trac′tive·ness** *n.*

at·trib·ut·a·ble [ə·trib′yoōt·ə·bəl] *adj.* Capable of being attributed: His death was *attributable* to natural causes.

at·trib·ute [*v.* ə·trib′yoōt, *n.* at′rə·byoōt] *v.* **at·trib·ut·ed, at·trib·ut·ing,** *n.* **1** *v.* To consider as belonging to or caused by: Many stories *attribute* slyness to foxes and wisdom to owls. **2** *n.* A quality or characteristic of a person or thing: Daring is an *attribute* of youth. **3** *n.* In art and mythology, a mark or symbol belonging to one character: The trident is an *attribute* of Neptune. **— at′tri·bu′tion** *n.*

at·tri·tion [ə·trish′ən] *n.* A gradual wearing down or wearing away; weakening: a disease of *attrition*; a war of *attrition*.

at·tune [ə·t(y)oōn′] *v.* **at·tuned, at·tun·ing 1** To bring into accord or harmony: They soon became *attuned* to city life. **2** To tune.

---

add, āce, câre, pälm; end, ēqual; it, īce; odd, ōpen, ôrder; toŏk, poōl; up, bûrn;
ə = a in *above*, e in *sicken*, i in *possible*, o in *melon*, u in *circus*; yoō = u in *fuse*; oil; pout;
check; ring; thin; this; zh in *vision*. For ¶ reference, see page 64 · HOW TO

a·typ·i·cal [ā·tip′i·kəl] *adj.* Not typical; without typical character; irregular.

Au The symbol for the element GOLD. ◆ The Latin word for gold is *aurum*.

au·burn [ô′bûrn] *n., adj.* Reddish brown.

auc·tion [ôk′shən] **1** *n.* A public sale at which each item is sold to the person offering the highest price for it. **2** *v.* To sell by or at an auction: to *auction* off used cars.

auc·tion·eer [ôk′shən·ir′] *n.* A person who conducts auctions as a business.

au·da·cious [ô·dā′shəs] *adj.* **1** Showing no fear; daring; bold. **2** Too daring or bold; impudent: an *audacious* child. **— au·da′cious·ly** *adv.*

au·dac·i·ty [ô·das′ə·tē] *n.* **1** Boldness; daring. **2** Impudence; indecency: He had the *audacity* to criticize his guests for being late.

au·di·ble [ô′də·bəl] *adj.* Capable of being heard. **— au′di·bil′i·ty** *n.* **— au′di·bly** *adv.*

au·di·ence [ô′dē·əns] *n.* **1** A group of listeners or watchers, as at a concert, play, etc. **2** The people who are reached by a book, television program, etc. **3** A formal hearing; interview: The queen granted him an *audience.* **4** An opportunity to be heard.

au·di·o [ô′dē·ō] *adj.* **1** Of or having to do with sound. **2** Used for producing or reproducing sound: Phonographs are *audio* equipment.

au·di·om·e·ter [ô′dē·om′ə·tər] *n.* An instrument to gauge and record the acuteness of hearing.

au·dit [ô′dit] **1** *v.* To examine for correctness, as the accounts of a business. **2** *n.* An examination of accounts, as of a business.

au·di·tion [ô·dish′ən] **1** *n.* A trial hearing to test the skill or suitability of an actor, singer, etc., for a job or role. **2** *v.* To give an audition to.

au·di·tor [ô′də·tər] *n.* **1** A person who examines accounts, as of a business. **2** A listener.

au·di·to·ri·um [ô′də·tôr′ē·əm] *n.* A building or a large room in a school, church, etc., in which an audience can assemble.

au·di·to·ry [ô′də·tôr′ē] *adj.* Of or having to do with hearing.

Au·du·bon [ô′də·bon], **John James,** 1785–1851, U.S. naturalist and artist, famous for his study and paintings of birds.

Aug. Abbreviation of AUGUST.

au·ger [ô′gər] *n.* A tool for boring holes in the earth or in wood.

aught[1] [ôt] **1** *n.* Anything at all: Have you *aught* to say? **2** *adv.* By any chance at all.

aught[2] [ôt] *n.* The figure zero; naught.

aug·ment [ôg·ment′] *v.* To make or become greater as in size, amount, etc.: increase: The army was *augmented* by calling up the reserves.

Auger

aug·men·ta·tion [ôg′men·tā′shən] *n.* **1** The act of augmenting. **2** A being augmented. **3** The amount by which something is increased.

au gra·tin [ô grä′tən] Sprinkled with bread crumbs or grated cheese and baked until brown.

au·gur [ô′gər] **1** *n.* In ancient Rome, an official who foretold the future by means of omens. **2** *n.* Anyone who foretells the future. **3** *v.* To foretell (the future). **4** *v.* To be a sign of; foreshadow: His earlier record *augurs* success for the future. **— augur ill** To be a bad omen. **— augur well** To be a good omen.

au·gu·ry [ô′gyə·rē] *n., pl.* **au·gu·ries 1** The art or practice of predicting the future by omens. **2** An omen or a prediction made from an omen.

au·gust [ô·gust′] *adj.* **1** Inspiring awe, admiration, etc.; majestic; imposing: an *august* dignitary. **2** Of high birth or rank; eminent.

Au·gust [ô′gəst] *n.* The eighth month of the year, having 31 days.

Au·gus·ta [ô·gus′tə] *n.* The capital of Maine.

Au·gus·tine [ô′gəs·tēn], **Saint,** died 604, Roman missionary to pagan England, the first archbishop of Canterbury.

Au·gus·tus Cae·sar [ô·gus′təs sē′zər], 63 B.C.–A.D. 14, the first Roman emperor.

auk [ôk] *n.* A diving bird having short wings and webbed feet, found in the northern seas.

aunt [ant] *n.* The sister or sister-in-law of one's father or mother.

au·ra [ôr′ə] *n.* A special air or quality that seems to surround or come from a particular source: There is an *aura* of kindness and humor about Robert Frost's poetry. ◆ *Aura* comes from the Greek word for *breath.*

Auk,
about 16 in. high

au·re·ole [ôr′ē·ōl] *n.* In art, a light shining around the head of a holy figure; halo.

Au·re·o·my·cin [ôr′ē·ō·mī′sin] *n.* The trade name of a strong antibiotic obtained from a soil bacillus, used against bacteria and viruses.

au re·voir [ō′rə·vwär′] A French expression for "good-by" or "until we meet again."

au·ri·cle [ôr′i·kəl] *n.* **1** An atrium of the heart. **2** The outside part of the ear.

au·ro·ra [ô·rôr′ə] *n.* **1** A richly colored display of lights seen in the skies close to the North and South Poles, caused by electrical disturbances in the air. **2** The dawn.

Au·ro·ra [ô·rôr′ə] *n.* In Roman myths, the goddess of the dawn.

aurora aus·tra·lis [ôs·trā′lis] The aurora seen near the South Pole.

aurora bo·re·al·is [bôr′ē·al′is] The aurora seen near the North Pole; northern lights.

aus·pi·ces [ôs′pə·siz] *n.pl.* **1** Helpful or guiding influence; sponsorship: under the *auspices* of a church. **2** Omens; signs.

aus·pi·cious [ôs·pish′əs] *adj.* Showing the likelihood of success in the future; favorable: an *auspicious* beginning. **— aus·pi′cious·ly** *adv.* **— aus·pi′cious·ness** *n.*

Aus·ten [ôs′tən], **Jane,** 1775–1817, English novelist.

aus·tere [ô·stir′] *adj.* **1** Stern, as in appearance or conduct; severe; strict: the *austere* habits of the Puritans. **2** Very plain and simple; without luxury or ornament: *austere* dress. **— aus·tere′ly** *adv.* **— aus·tere′ness** *n.*

aus·ter·i·ty [ôs·ter′ə·tē] *n.*, *pl.* **aus·ter·i·ties 1** The quality of being austere. **2** (*usually pl.*) Severe acts or practices of self-denial, as doing without food, water, sleep, comfort, etc.

Aus·tin [ôs′tən] *n.* The capital of Texas.

Aus·tral·a·sia [ôs′trəl·ā′zhə] *n.* The islands of the South Pacific, including Australia, New Zealand, New Guinea, and other nearby islands.

Aus·tral·ia [ô·strāl′yə] *n.* An island continent SE of Asia. It is a member of the British Commonwealth. **— Aus·tral′ian** *adj.*, *n.*

Australian ballot A ballot listing all candidates of all parties, voted on in secret.

Aus·tri·a [ôs′trē·ə] *n.* A country in central Europe. **— Aus′tri·an** *adj.*, *n.*

Aus·tri·a-Hun·ga·ry [ôs′trē·ə·hung′gə·rē] *n.* A former monarchy in central Europe, broken up at the end of World War I.

au·then·tic [ô·then′tik] *adj.* **1** Worthy of belief; trustworthy; reliable: an *authentic* record of events. **2** Genuine: an *authentic* painting by Van Gogh.

au·then·ti·cate [ô·then′ti·kāt] *v.* **au·then·ti·cat·ed, au·then·ti·cat·ing** To prove to be true or show to be genuine. **— au·then′ti·ca′·tion** *n.*

au·then·tic·i·ty [ô′thən·tis′ə·tē] *n.* The condition of being genuine or true; authentic nature.

au·thor [ô′thər] *n.* **1** A person who has written a book, story, article, etc. **2** A person who creates or originates: the *author* of an invention.

au·thor·i·tar·i·an [ə·thôr′ə·târ′ē·ən] *adj.* Favoring rule by authority rather than individual freedom: an *authoritarian* society.

au·thor·i·ta·tive [ə·thôr′ə·tā′tiv] *adj.* **1** Having or coming from proper authority. **2** Showing authority; commanding: an *authoritative* way of speaking. **3** Reliable, as if from an authority; trustworthy: an *authoritative* book. **— au·thor′i·ta′tive·ly** *adv.*

au·thor·i·ty [ə·thôr′ə·tē] *n.*, *pl.* **au·thor·i·ties 1** The right to command, act, make decisions, etc.: the *authority* to make arrests. **2** (*usually pl.*) A person who governs and enforces laws: He was brought before the *authorities*. **3** Personal influence that creates respect or confidence: to speak with *authority*. **4** A person who has special knowledge; expert: an *authority* on old coins.

au·thor·i·za·tion [ô′thər·ə·zā′shən] *n.* **1** The act of authorizing. **2** Legal right granted by someone who has authority. ¶3

au·thor·ize [ô′thə·rīz] *v.* **au·thor·ized, au·thor·iz·ing 1** To give authority or power to: The broker was *authorized* to sell the house. **2** To give permission for; approve: to *authorize* a loan. ¶3

au·thor·ship [ô′thər·ship] *n.* Origin or source, as of a book, idea, etc.

au·to [ô′tō] *n.*, *pl.* **au·tos** *informal* An automobile.

au·to·bi·o·graph·i·cal [ô′tə·bī′ə·graf′i·kəl] *adj.* Based on or having to do with one's own life: an *autobiographical* story.

au·to·bi·og·ra·phy [ô′tə·bī·og′rə·fē] *n.*, *pl.* **au·to·bi·og·ra·phies** The story of a person's life written by that person.

au·toc·ra·cy [ô·tok′rə·sē] *n.*, *pl.* **au·toc·ra·cies** A government or country ruled by one person with absolute authority.

au·to·crat [ô′tə·krat] *n.* **1** A ruler with absolute power. **2** A person who dictates to others in an arrogant manner.

au·to·crat·ic [ô′tə·krat′ik] *adj.* **1** Of or like an autocrat: His *autocratic* manner made him difficult to work with. **2** Having absolute power: an *autocratic* government.

au·to·graph [ô′tə·graf] **1** *n.* A person's name written in his own handwriting. **2** *v.* To write one's name on. **3** *n.* Something written in a person's own handwriting. ◆ *Autograph* comes from a Greek word meaning *self-written*.

au·to·harp [ô′tō·härp] *n.* A musical instrument resembling a zither, but having an arrangement of mutes enabling the player to produce the correct chords easily.

au·to·mate [ô′tə·māt] *v.* **au·to·mat·ed, au·to·mat·ing** To convert or adapt to automatic operation, as a factory, process, etc.: Computers have fully *automated* the processing of checks. ◆ See AUTOMATION.

au·to·mat·ic [ô′tə·mat′ik] **1** *adj.* Acting and regulated by itself, as machinery. **2** *adj.* Done without conscious thought or attention: Most of the movements in driving a car are *automatic*. **3** *n.* A pistol that fires, throws out the used cartridge, and puts in a new one when the trigger is pulled. **— au′to·mat′i·cal·ly** *adv.*

au·to·ma·tion [ô′tə·mā′shən] *n.* The automatic operation of a process, machine, etc., under the control of electronic or mechanical devices instead of human beings. ◆ This word comes from *autom(atic oper)ation*. The verb *automate* was formed from *automation*.

au·tom·a·ton [ô·tom′ə·ton] *n.* **1** A machine that operates by itself. **2** A person or animal whose actions seem too mechanical to be lifelike.

au·to·mo·bile [ô′tə·mə·bēl′] *n.* A four-wheeled vehicle propelled by its own engine, commonly designed to carry up to about six people. ◆ This word was formed in French from a Greek word meaning *self* and a Latin word meaning *moving*.

---

add, āce, câre, pälm;   end, ēqual;   it, īce;   odd, ōpen, ôrder;   tŏŏk, pŏŏl;   up, bûrn;
ə = a in *above*, e in *sicken*, i in *possible*, o in *melon*, u in *circus*;   yŏŏ = u in *fuse*;   oil;   pout;
check; ring; thin; this; zh in *vision*.   For ¶ reference, see page 64 · HOW TO

au·to·mo·tive [ô′tə·mō′tiv] *adj.* **1** Of or for automobiles, trucks, etc. **2** Moving under its own power.

au·to·nom·ic nervous system [ô′tə·nom′ik] The part of the nervous system that regulates the involuntary action of the heart, the digestive system, etc.

au·ton·o·mous [ô·ton′ə·məs] *adj.* Independent; self-governing: The Confederate States wanted to become an *autonomous* nation. **— au·ton′o·mous·ly** *adv.*

au·ton·o·my [ô·ton′ə·mē] *n.* An autonomous condition; self-government: to seek *autonomy.*

au·top·sy [ô′top·sē] *n., pl.* **au·top·sies** The examination of a human body after death, especially to find the cause of death.

au·tumn [ô′təm] *n.* **1** The season of the year between summer and winter. **2** *adj. use:* autumn leaves.

au·tum·nal [ô·tum′nəl] *adj.* Of or like autumn: The *autumnal* equinox is the time near September 21 when days and nights are of equal length.

aux·il·ia·ry [ôg·zil′yər·ē] *adj., n., pl.* **aux·il·ia·ries 1** *adj.* Giving help. **2** *adj.* Available if needed; extra: An *auxiliary* engine may be used if the power fails. **3** *adj.* Less important; not major. **4** *n.* Something auxiliary, as a woman's group attached to a men's organization.

auxiliary verb A verb that helps to form the meaning of other verbs in a sentence. In "I have seen," *have* is an auxiliary verb.

a·vail [ə·vāl′] **1** *v.* To be of use to; help or profit: All his cunning *availed* him nothing. **2** *n.* Usefulness; help; benefit: His efforts were of no *avail.* **— avail oneself of** To take advantage of; use: to *avail oneself of* an opportunity.

a·vail·a·ble [ə·vā′lə·bəl] *adj.* That can be used or had: *available* theater seats. **— a·vail′a·bil′i·ty** *n.*

av·a·lanche [av′ə·lanch] *n.* **1** The falling of a large mass of snow, ice, or rock down a slope. **2** The mass of snow, ice, or rock that so falls. **3** Something that suggests an avalanche: an *avalanche* of work.

An avalanche

av·a·rice [av′ə·ris] *n.* Too much eagerness for riches; greed. ◆ This word comes from the French.

av·a·ri·cious [av′ə·rish′əs] *adj.* Desiring wealth too much; greedy; grasping; miserly.

a·vast [ə·vast′] *interj.* Stop!; hold!: used by sailors.

a·vaunt [ə·vônt′] *interj.* Go away!: seldom used today.

Ave. Abbreviation of AVENUE.

A·ve Ma·ri·a [ä′vä mə·rē′ə] A Roman Catholic prayer to the Virgin Mary. ◆ The first words of this Latin prayer are *Ave Maria*, which mean *Hail, Mary.*

a·venge [ə·venj′] *v.* **a·venged, a·veng·ing** To get revenge for: They *avenged* his murder.

av·e·nue [av′ə·n(y)ōō] *n.* **1** A street, especially a broad one. **2** A road or path with trees along its borders. **3** A way of reaching or achieving something: an *avenue* of escape.

a·ver [ə·vûr′] *v.* **a·verred, a·ver·ring** To declare to be true; state positively.

av·er·age [av′rij] *adj., n., v.* **av·er·aged, av·er·ag·ing 1** *adj.* Of or like the ordinary or usual type; medium: an *average* housewife; an *average* football team. **2** *n.* Someone or something that is average. **3** *n.* The sum of the elements in a set of numbers divided by the number of elements in the set: The *average* of 4, 6, and 5 is 5. **4** *n.* A point between two extremes that shows a standing or accomplishment: a B *average.* **5** *v.* To calculate an average. **6** *v.* To amount to or get an average of: He *averages* three dollars an hour. **— on the average** As an average: He plays twice a week, *on the average.*

a·verse [ə·vûrs′] *adj.* Opposed by nature; not disposed: He was *averse* to staying up late.

a·ver·sion [ə·vûr′zhən] *n.* **1** Extreme dislike: an *aversion* to homework. **2** Something disliked.

a·vert [ə·vûrt′] *v.* **1** To turn or direct away: to *avert* the eyes. **2** To prevent or ward off, as a danger: A fight was narrowly *averted.*

a·vi·ar·y [ā′vē·er′ē] *n., pl.* **a·vi·ar·ies** A large cage or other enclosure for birds.

a·vi·a·tion [ā′vē·ā′shən] *n.* The science or techniques of building and flying aircraft.

a·vi·a·tor [ā′vē·ā′tər] *n.* A person who flies airplanes or other aircraft; pilot.

a·vi·a·trix [ā′vē·ā′triks] *n.* A female aviator.

av·id [av′id] *adj.* **1** Enthusiastic; eager: an *avid* stamp collector. **2** Greedy: *avid* for food. **— av′id·ly** *adv.*

a·vid·i·ty [ə·vid′ə·tē] *n.* Extreme eagerness; greediness.

av·o·ca·do [av′ə·kä′dō] *n., pl.* **av·o·ca·dos** The pear-shaped fruit of a West Indian tree, having a green skin and fleshy, edible pulp enclosing a single, large seed.

av·o·ca·tion [av′ə·kā′shən] *n.* An occupation that is not one's regular work; hobby: My teacher's *avocation* is sewing.

a·void [ə·void′] *v.* To keep away from; stay at a distance from; shun: Ever since the argument we have *avoided* each other. **— a·void′ance** *n.*

av·oir·du·pois [av′ər·də·poiz′] *n.* The ordinary system of weights in the U.S. and Great Britain in which 16 ounces make a pound.

a·vow [ə·vou′] *v.* To say openly as a fact; own up to; acknowledge: to *avow* one's guilt.

a·vow·al [ə·vou′əl] *n.* An open declaration; frank admission or acknowledgment.

a·vowed [ə·voud′] *adj.* Openly acknowledged or admitted; plainly declared: an *avowed* Communist. **— a·vow·ed·ly** [ə·vou′id·lē] *adv.*

a·wait [ə·wāt′] *v.* **1** To wait for; expect: She *awaited* the mail eagerly. **2** To be waiting or in store for: Final exams *await* you in June.

a·wake [ə·wāk′] *adj., v.* **a·woke** or **a·waked,**

a·wak·ing 1 *adj*. Not asleep; alert. **2** *v*. To stop sleeping; wake up. **3** *v*. To stir up; excite: to *awake* an interest in history. ◆ See WAKE.

a·wak·en [ə·wā′kən] *v*. To awake.

a·wak·en·ing [ə·wā′kən·ing] *n*. **1** The act of waking. **2** A stirring up of interest or attention.

a·ward [ə·wôrd′] **1** *n*. Something given for merit; prize. **2** *v*. To give after judging, as in a contest: She was *awarded* first prize for her tap dancing. **3** *v*. To judge to be due, as by legal decision: The judge *awarded* the plaintiff $5,000. **4** *n*. A legal decision that something is owed.

a·ware [ə·wâr′] *adj*. Realizing or knowing fully; conscious: I am *aware* of the difficulty. **— a·ware′ness** *n*.

a·way [ə·wā′] **1** *adv*. To a different place; off; forth: to drive *away*. **2** *adj*. In a different place; absent: to be *away*. **3** *adv*. To one side; aside: Put your books *away*. **4** *adv*. At or to a distance; far: The road stretches *away*. **5** *adj*. At a distance: Many miles *away*. **6** *adv*. Out of existence; at or to an end: to waste *away*. **7** *adv*. On and on; continuously: to work *away* at a task. **8** *adv*. Without hesitating or holding back: to swing *away*. **9** *adv*. Out of one's keeping: They took his hat *away*. **10** *adv*. Off from the whole: to cut rot *away*. **— do away with 1** To kill. **2** To put an end to: The store will *do away with* its delivery service.

awe [ô] *n*., *v*. **awed, aw·ing 1** *n*. A feeling of fear and wonder at the size, power, majesty, etc., of something. **2** *v*. To make feel awe: We were *awed* by the violence of the tropical thunderstorm.

awe·some [ô′səm] *adj*. **1** Causing awe: an *awesome* sight. **2** Full of awe: an *awesome* look.

awe-struck [ô′struk′] *adj*. Filled with awe.

aw·ful [ô′fəl] *adj*. **1** *informal* Very bad or unpleasant. **2** Causing awe; very striking: the *awful* destruction of a tornado. **3** *informal* Very great: an *awful* liar.

aw·ful·ly *adv*. **1** [ô′fəl·ē] In an awful way. **2** [ô′flē] *informal* Very: *awfully* rich.

a·while [ə·(h)wīl′] *adv*. For a short time.

awk·ward [ôk′wərd] *adj*. **1** Not graceful; clumsy; ungainly: an *awkward* movement. **2** Embarrassing: an *awkward* question. **3** Inconvenient or hard to use: an *awkward* place to reach. **4** Uncomfortable: an *awkward* position. **—awk′·ward·ly** *adv*. **— awk′ward·ness** *n*.

awl [ôl] *n*. A pointed tool for making small holes, as in wood or leather.

awn·ing [ô′ning] *n*. A cover often made of canvas on a frame used for protection from sun or rain over a window or door.

Awning

a·woke [ə·wōk′] Past tense of AWAKE.

AWOL or **A.W.O.L.** [ā′wôl] Absent without leave, chiefly from military service.

a·wry [ə·rī′] *adj*., *adv*. **1** Leaning or turned to one side; askew: Your cap is *awry*. **2** Not right; amiss: plans gone *awry*.

ax or **axe** [aks] *n*., *pl*. **ax·es** A tool with a heavy blade mounted on a handle, used for chopping wood, etc.

ax·i·al [ak′sē·əl] *adj*. Of, indicating, or forming an axis.

ax·i·om [ak′sē·əm] *n*. A self-evident statement whose truth is assumed without proof: "Things equal to the same thing are equal to each other" is an *axiom*.

ax·i·o·mat·ic [ak′sē·ə·mat′ik] *adj*. **1** Like an axiom; self-evident. **2** Full of or using axioms.

ax·is [ak′sis] *n*., *pl*. **ax·es** [ak′sēz] **1** The line around which a body turns or is imagined to turn. The earth's axis is a line connecting the North and South Poles. **2** A line around which an object is balanced or evenly divided. **3** A line on a graph along which distances are measured and in terms of which points are located. **4** (*written* **Axis**) The alliance of Germany, Italy, and Japan in World War II.

ax·le [ak′səl] *n*. A bar or spindle on or with which a wheel or wheels turn.

ax·le·tree [ak′səl·trē′] *n*. A fixed bar on which the opposite wheels of a car or wagon are mounted.

ax·on [ak′son] *n*. The long, slender part of a nerve cell that carries impulses away from the central body of the cell.

Axle

ay¹ [ā] *adv*. Ever; always: used mostly in poems.

ay² [ī] *n*., *adv*. Another spelling of AYE¹.

aye¹ [ī] **1** *n*. A vote of yes or a person who votes yes: The *ayes* win. **2** *adv*. Yes.

aye² [ā] *adv*. Another spelling of AY¹.

Ayr·shire [âr′shir *or* âr′shər] **1** *n*. One of a hardy breed of dairy cattle, brown and white or red and white in color. **2** *adj*. Of or having to do with this breed.

a·zal·ea [ə·zāl′yə] *n*. A shrub having pointed leaves and showy scarlet or orange flowers.

A·zores [ə·zôrz′ *or* ā′zôrz] *n.pl*. Three island groups west of and belonging to Portugal.

Az·tec [az′tek] **1** *n*. One of a nation of highly civilized Mexican Indians conquered by the Spanish under Cortés in 1519. **2** *n*. The language of the Aztecs. **3** *adj*. Of or having to do with the Aztecs, their language, culture, or empire.

az·ure [azh′ər] *n*., *adj*. Sky blue.

---

add, āce, câre, pälm;   end, ēqual;   it, īce;   odd, ōpen, ôrder;   tŏŏk, pōōl;   **u**p, bûrn;
ə = a in *above*, e in *sicken*, i in *possible*, o in *melon*, u in *circus*;   **y**ōō = u in *fuse*;   **oi**l;   **pou**t;
     check;   ri**ng**;   **th**in;   **th**is;   **zh** in *vision*.   For ¶ reference, see page 64 · HOW TO

B

b or **B** [bē] *n.*, *pl.* **b's** or **B's** The second letter of the English alphabet.

B The symbol for the element BORON.

Ba The symbol for the element BARIUM.

B.A. Abbreviation of BACHELOR OF ARTS.

baa [bä] *n.*, *v.* **baaed, baa·ing 1** *n.* The natural cry of a sheep or goat. **2** *v.* To make this cry; bleat.

Ba·al [bā′(ə)l] *n.*, *pl.* **Ba·al·im** [bā′(ə)l·im] **1** The sun god of the Phoenicians. **2** A false idol or god.

bab·ble [bab′əl] *v.* **bab·bled, bab·bling,** *n.* **1** *v.* To make meaningless speech sounds: The baby *babbled* happily. **2** *n.* Meaningless speech sounds. **3** *v.* To talk or say very fast or without thinking: to *babble* to a friend; to *babble* a secret. **4** *n.* Foolish or fast talk. **5** *v.* To make a murmuring or rippling sound, as a brook. **6** *n.* A rippling or bubbling sound; murmur. — **bab′bler** *n.*

babe [bāb] *n.* An infant; baby.

Ba·bel [bā′bəl *or* bab′əl] *n.* **1** In the Bible, a city where men tried to reach heaven by building the **Tower of Babel.** God stopped their work by suddenly causing them to speak different languages so they could not understand one another. **2** (*often written* **babel**) Noise and confusion, as when many people talk at once.

ba·boon [ba·bōōn′] *n.* A large, fierce monkey of Africa and Asia, with a dog-like head and a short tail.

ba·bush·ka [bə·bŏŏsh′kə] *n.* A woman's scarf, usually folded into a triangle, worn on the head and tied under the chin. ◆ *Babushka* comes from the Russian word for *grandmother.*

ba·by [bā′bē] *n.*, *pl.* **ba·bies,** *v.* **ba·bied, ba·by·ing 1** *n.* A very young child; infant. **2** *adj. use: baby* shoes;

Baboon, about 32 in. long

baby talk. **3** *v.* To treat like a baby; be gentle with; pamper. **4** *n.* A person who acts like a baby. **5** *adj.* Very small or young: a *baby* monkey. **6** *n.* The youngest or smallest member, as of a family.

ba·by·hood [bā′bē·hŏŏd] *n.* **1** The condition of being a baby. **2** The time when one is a baby.

ba·by·ish [bā′bē·ish] *adj.* Like a baby; childish.

Bab·y·lon [bab′ə·lən] *n.* The capital of ancient Babylonia, known as a city of wealth and of evil.

Bab·y·lo·ni·a [bab′ə·lō′nē·ə] *n.* An ancient empire of sw Asia. — **Bab′y·lo′ni·an** *adj.*, *n.*

ba·by-sit [bā′bē·sit′] *v.* **ba·by-sat, ba·by-sit·ting** To take care of a child while its parents are away for a short time.

baby sit·ter [sit′ər] *n.* A person who baby-sits.

Bac·chus [bak′əs] *n.* In Greek and Roman myths, the god of wine. His early Greek name was Dionysus.

Bach [bäk], **Johann Sebastian,** 1685–1750, German composer.

bach·e·lor [bach′(ə·)lər] *n.* **1** A man who has not married. **2** A person who has received his first college or university degree, such as a **Bachelor of Arts** or a **Bachelor of Science.**

bach·e·lor's-but·ton [bach′(ə·)lərz·but′(ə)n] *n.* Any of several plants having flowers shaped somewhat like buttons, as the cornflower.

ba·cil·lus [bə·sil′əs] *n.*, *pl.* **ba·cil·li** [bə·sil′ī] Any of a class of bacteria shaped like rods. Some cause serious diseases, such as tetanus and tuberculosis. ◆ *Bacillus* comes from a Latin word meaning *a little rod* or *staff,* the shape of the organism.

back [bak] **1** *n.* The section of the body that extends from the neck to the end of the spine and is opposite to the chest and abdomen. **2** *n.* The spine; backbone: His *back* is broken. **3** *n.* The section of a seat or chair that supports a person's back. **4** *v.* To support; aid: to *back* a plan. **5** *v.* To provide with a back, as a mirror. **6** *n.* The rear part: the *back* of the car. **7** *adj.* In the rear: a *back* room. **8** *adv.* At, to, or toward the rear: Slide *back* in your seat. **9** *v.* To move or cause to move backward: He *backed* away from the fire; *Back* the car into the garage. **10** *n.* The reverse side; other side: the *back* of the door. **11** *adj.* In a backward direction: a *back* stroke. **12** *n.* In football, a player whose position is behind the line. **13** *adv.* In, to, or toward a former place, time, or condition: Put it *back* on the shelf; to look *back* in history. **14** *adj.* Of or for a time earlier than the present: a *back* issue of a magazine. **15** *adv.* In return: Give him *back* his pencil. **16** *adv.* In reserve or concealment: to keep something *back.* — **back and forth** First in one direction and then in the opposite direction. — **back down** To abandon or retreat, as from an opinion. — **back out** To withdraw from: to *back out* of a contract.

back·bite [bak′bīt′] *v.* **back·bit** [bak′bit′], **back·bit·ten** [bak′bit·(ə)n], **back·bit·ing** To tell lies or say mean things about (a person who is not present).

back·bone [bak′bōn′] *n.* **1** The column of interlocking bones running down the middle of the back in man and many other animals; spine. **2** The main or strongest part: He was the *backbone* of the team. **3** Strength of character; courage.

back·drop [bak′drop′] *n.* A curtain, usually having a scene painted on it, that is hung at the back of a stage.

back·er [bak′ər] *n.* A person who supports another person's plan or idea, usually by giving or investing money.

back·field [bak′fēld′] *n.* In football, the players whose position is behind the line.

back·fire [bak′fīr′] *n., v.* **back·fired, back·fir·ing 1** *n.* An explosion of fuel that occurs too early or in the wrong place in an engine, making a loud bang. **2** *v.* To have such an explosion: The engine *backfired.* **3** *v.* To have an effect opposite to the expected or desired effect: The plot *backfired.* **4** *n.* A fire set to halt an advancing fire by clearing the area in front of it.

back·gam·mon [bak′gam′ən] *n.* A game played by two persons on a special board. Each player has 15 disks or counters, and a throw of the dice determines how they may be moved.

back·ground [bak′ground′] *n.* **1** An area or surface against which something is seen or represented: red polka dots on a dull, gray *background.* **2** The part of a picture or landscape that appears distant. **3** A position that does not attract notice: Carol's parents stayed in the *background* at her birthday party. **4** A person's education and experience: His *background* is well suited for newspaper work. **5** The events leading up to or causing a situation: the *background* of the Revolutionary War.

back·hand [bak′hand′] **1** *n.* A stroke, as in tennis, made with the back of the hand turned forward. **2** *adj. use:* a *backhand* stroke. **3** *adv.* With a backhand stroke. **4** *n.* Handwriting that slopes to the left.

A backhand stroke

back·hand·ed [bak′han′did] *adj.* **1** Done or made with the back of the hand moving forward, as a tennis stroke or a slap. **2** Roundabout, halfhearted, or insincere: "You're pretty good for a girl" is a *backhanded* way of saying that girls aren't as good as boys.

back·ing [bak′ing] *n.* **1** Help or support: His plan has the *backing* of the government. **2** Anything added at the back for strength or support: The rug has a *backing* of rubber.

back·log [bak′lôg′] *n.* **1** An accumulation, as of business orders, unfinished work, etc. **2** A large log at the back of a fireplace.

back·slide [bak′slīd′] *v.* **back·slid** [bak′slid′], **back·slid** or **back·slid·den** [bak′slid′(ə)n], **back·slid·ing** To slip back from good behavior to bad, or into indifference to religion. — **back′·slid′er** *n.*

back·stage [bak′stāj′] **1** *adv.* In or toward the part of a theater behind and to the sides of the stage. **2** *adj.* Situated or happening backstage.

back·stop [bak′stop′] *n.* In baseball and softball, a fence or net behind home plate that stops the ball from going too far.

back·stroke [bak′strōk′] *n.* **1** In swimming, a stroke made while on one's back. **2** A backhanded stroke.

Backstroke

back talk *informal* Rude or disrespectful answers.

back·ward [bak′wərd] **1** *adv.* Toward the back; to the rear: Go *backward.* **2** *adv.* With the back facing forward: The old clock hung *backward*, its face toward the wall. **3** *adv.* In a reverse order or direction: Movies run *backward* are funny. **4** *adv.* From better to worse: His health is going *backward* lately. **5** *adv.* To time past: to look *backward* into history. **6** *adj.* Turned or directed toward the rear: a *backward* look; a *backward* step. **7** *adj.* Slow in development; retarded. **8** *adj.* Hesitant; shy. — **back′ward·ness** *n.*

back·wards [bak′wərdz] *adv.* Backward.

back·wash [bak′wôsh′] *n.* **1** A backward movement of air or water caused by propellers, oars, etc. **2** An aftereffect or result.

back·wa·ter [bak′wô′tər] *n.* **1** Water turned or held back, as by a dam or an opposing current. **2** An isolated, backward place.

back·woods [bak′woodz′] *U.S.* **1** *n.pl.* Forest or country untouched by city customs, comforts, or ideas. **2** *adj. use:* a *backwoods* town.

back·woods·man [bak′woodz′mən] *n., pl.* **back·woods·men** [bak′woodz′mən] A person who lives in the backwoods.

ba·con [bā′kən] *n.* The salted and smoked back and sides of a hog.

bac·te·ri·a [bak·tir′ē·ə] *n.pl.* Organisms having only one cell each and visible only through a microscope. Some bacteria do such helpful things as enriching the soil and ripening cheese; others cause serious diseases. — **bac·te′ri·al** *adj.*

Bacteria, three main shapes

bac·te·ri·ol·o·gy [bak·tir′ē·ol′ə·jē] *n.* The branch of science that deals with bacteria.

---

add, āce, câre, pälm; end, ēqual; it, íce; odd, ōpen, ôrder; tŏŏk, pōōl; up, bûrn;
ə = a in *above*, e in *sicken*, i in *possible*, o in *melon*, u in *circus*; yōō = u in *fuse*; oil; pout;
check; ring; thin; this; zh in *vision*. For ¶ reference, see page 64 · HOW TO

Bac·tri·an camel [bak′trē·ən] A camel of sw Asia, having two humps. See picture at CAMEL.

bad [bad] *adj.* **worse, worst,** *n.* **1** *adj.* Not good; below standard: a *bad* road; *bad* marks. **2** *adj.* Evil; wicked: *bad* men. **3** *adj.* Faulty or incorrect: *bad* grammar. **4** *adj.* Unwelcome; unpleasant: a *bad* odor; *bad* news. **5** *adj.* Harmful: Candy is *bad* for your teeth. **6** *adj.* Spoiled; decayed: *bad* meat. **7** *adj.* Severe: a *bad* cold. **8** *adj.* Sorry; regretful: I felt *bad* about hurting her feelings. **9** *adj.* Sick; in ill health: I feel *bad* today. **10** *n.* People, things, or conditions that are bad: Separate the good from the *bad*. — **bad′ness** *n.*

bad blood A feeling of hatred or bitterness.

bade [bad] A past tense of BID.

badge [baj] *n.* **1** An emblem, pin, etc., worn to show that a person belongs to a certain group, has received an award, etc. **2** Any symbol: A doctor's bag is a *badge* of his profession.

badg·er [baj′ər] **1** *n.* A small animal with a broad back, short legs, and thick fur. Badgers live in burrows that they dig with the long claws on their forefeet. **2** *n.* The fur of the badger. **3** *v.* To nag at; pester; tease: They *badgered* him for autographs.

bad·ly [bad′lē] *adv.* **1** In a bad way: She dances *badly;* He behaves *badly*. **2** *informal* Very much: I need it *badly*.

bad·min·ton [bad′min·tən] *n.* A game in which a shuttlecock is hit back and forth over a high net with light rackets.

bad-tem·pered [bad′tem′pərd] *adj.* Easily angered; irritable; cross.

baf·fle [baf′əl] *v.* **baf·fled, baf·fling,** *n.* **1** *v.* To confuse; bewilder; perplex: The question *baffled* me. **2** *n.* A screen or partition used to control a flow, as of gases, liquids, or sound waves. **3** *v.* To control or slow the flow of, as with a baffle; hinder.

bag [bag] *n., v.* **bagged, bag·ging 1** *n.* A soft container, usually made of paper, cloth, or plastic, used to carry or hold something. **2** *v.* To put into a bag. **3** *n.* A suitcase, lady's handbag, etc. **4** *n.* A sag or bulge in the shape of a bag: trousers with *bags* in the knees. **5** *v.* To sag or bulge like a bag. **6** *n.* The amount of game caught or killed in hunting. **7** *v.* To catch or kill, as game. **8** *n.* In baseball, a base.

Bag·dad [bag′dad] *n.* Another spelling of BAGHDAD.

ba·gel [bā′gəl] *n.* A doughnut-shaped roll with a tough, glazed crust. ◆ *Bagel* comes directly from a Yiddish word, which in turn came from a word in an older German language meaning *ring*.

bag·gage [bag′ij] *n.* **1** The trunks, suitcases, packages, etc., of a person traveling; luggage. **2** An army's movable equipment.

bag·gy [bag′ē] *adj.* **bag·gi·er, bag·gi·est** Sagging or bulging like a bag; loose: *baggy* pants. — **bag′gi·ness** *n.*

Bagh·dad [bag′dad] *n.* The capital of Iraq, on the Tigris River.

bag·pipe [bag′pīp′] *n.* A shrill-toned musical instrument consisting of a leather bag and several pipes with reeds in them, played by blowing air into the bag and squeezing it.

Bagpipe

bah [bä *or* ba] *interj.* An exclamation of contempt or disgust.

Ba·ha·mas [bə·hä′məz *or* bə·hā′məz] *n.pl.* A group of islands in the West Indies. The Bahamas are a British colony. Also **Bahama Islands.**

bail[1] [bāl] **1** *n.* Money put up as a guarantee that an accused person will appear for trial, securing his release from jail pending the trial. **2** *v.* To provide bail for (an arrested person). — **jump bail** *informal* To run away and fail to appear for trial after being released on bail.

bail[2] [bāl] *v.* **1** To scoop (water) out of a boat, as with a bucket, pail, etc. **2** To scoop the water out of. — **bail out** To parachute from an aircraft that is in danger of crashing.

bail[3] [bāl] *n.* The curved handle of a bucket, kettle, etc.

bai·liff [bā′lif] *n.* **1** A court officer who is in charge of prisoners while they are in a courtroom. **2** A sheriff's deputy. **3** A person who manages an estate; steward.

bairn [bârn] *n.* A young child: a Scottish word.

bait [bāt] **1** *n.* Something, usually food, placed on a hook or in a trap to lure fish or animals. **2** *v.* To put food or some other lure in or on: to *bait* a trap. **3** *n.* Anything used as a lure or temptation. **4** *v.* To set dogs to attack: *Baiting* bulls was a cruel sport. **5** *v.* To torment or annoy; tease: They *baited* him by calling him names.

baize [bāz] *n.* A thick, fuzzy wool or cotton cloth.

bake [bāk] *v.* **baked, bak·ing 1** To cook in an oven: to *bake* a cake; The bread is *baking*. **2** To harden by heating: Bricks are *baked* in kilns.

bak·er [bā′kər] *n.* A person whose work is baking bread, cake, cookies, etc.

baker's dozen Thirteen. ◆ Bakers used to add an extra roll to every dozen they sold.

bak·er·y [bāk′(ə·)rē] *n., pl.* **bak·er·ies** A place where bread and cake are baked or sold.

bak·ing [bāk′ing] *n.* **1** Cooking or hardening by dry heat, as in an oven. **2** The amount baked at one time.

baking powder A powdered mixture of baking soda and acid salt used to make bread or cake rise.

baking soda Another name for SODIUM BICARBONATE.

Ba·laam [bā′ləm] *n.* In the Bible, a prophet who was reprimanded by the ass that he rode.

bal·ance [bal′əns] *n.*, *v.* **bal·anced, bal·anc·ing** **1** *n.* An instrument for weighing, especially a bar with two matched pans suspended from its ends, that pivots on a central point. **2** *n.* A condition of equality between opposing forces, amounts, values, etc.: the *balance* of power between two countries. **3** *v.* To bring into or keep in balance: He *balanced* the board by holding it up at its center. **4** *v.* To weigh or compare in a balance or as if in a balance: to *balance* two suggested ways of doing something. **5** *v.* To offset or counteract: The trip's inconvenience was *balanced* by the pleasure of seeing my old friends. **6** *n.* The ability to keep one's body in a desired position without falling: It takes *balance* to walk a tightrope. **7** *n.* A person's normal mental or emotional condition. **8** *n.* An arrangement in harmony and proportion. **9** *v.* To arrange in harmony and proportion: to *balance* colors in a room. **10** *n.* The amount of money in a bank account. **11** *n.* The amount a person still owes after a bill has been partly paid. **12** *n.* An amount left over; remainder: He ate four of the cookies and gave the *balance* to his sister. **13** *n.* The difference in an account between the amount a person owes and the amount owing to him. **14** *v.* To compute such a difference. **15** *v.* To adjust such a difference, as by paying a bill. **16** *n.* A wheel that regulates motion, as in a watch. — **in the balance** Undecided; not settled.

Balance

balance of power A distribution of power among nations such that no one nation is strong enough to overpower other nations.

balance of trade The difference in value between the exports and imports of a country.

bal·anc·er [bal′ən·sər] *n.* **1** A person or thing that balances. **2** An acrobat.

Bal·bo·a [bal·bō′ə], **Vasco de,** 1475–1517, Spanish explorer. He discovered the Pacific Ocean in 1513.

bal·co·ny [bal′kə·nē] *n.*, *pl.* **bal·co·nies 1** A platform that projects from the side of a building and has a low wall or railing around it. **2** An upper floor with seats, as in a theater.

bald [bôld] *adj.* **1** Without hair on all or part of the head. **2** Lacking a natural covering: a *bald* mountain. **3** Simple; plain: the *bald* facts. — **bald′ness** *n.*

bald eagle A large, dark brown North American eagle that has white feathers on its head, neck, and tail.

bal·der·dash [bôl′dər·dash] *n.* Nonsense.

bal·dric [bôl′drik] *n.* A belt used to hold a sword, bugle, etc. It is worn over one shoulder and across the chest.

bale [bāl] *n.*, *v.* **baled, bal·ing 1** *n.* A large, tightly packed bundle of hay, cotton, or other bulky material. **2** *v.* To gather together and tie into bales: to *bale* cotton.

bale·ful [bāl′fəl] *adj.* Evil or threatening; malicious: a *baleful* stare. — **bale′ful·ly** *adv.*

Bales

balk [bôk] **1** *v.* To stop and refuse to move or act. **2** *v.* To cause to stop; thwart; hinder: The crime was *balked* by the police. **3** *n.* Something that checks or hinders. **4** *n.* In baseball, an illegal breaking off of a pitching motion when there are runners on base.

Bal·kan [bôl′kən] *adj.* Of or from the Balkans.

Balkan States The countries of the **Balkan Peninsula** in SE Europe: Albania, Bulgaria, Greece, Rumania, Yugoslavia, and part of Turkey. Also **the Balkans.**

balk·y [bô′kē] *adj.* **balk·i·er, balk·i·est** Given to balking: a *balky* engine.

Balkan States

ball¹ [bôl] **1** *n.* Any round body; sphere: a *ball* of twine; a snow*ball*. **2** *n.* A round or oval object, often hollow, used in a number of games: a tennis *ball;* a foot*ball*. **3** *n.* A game played with a ball, as baseball. **4** *n.* A ball that has been thrown or hit so that it moves in a special way: a curve *ball;* a bouncing *ball*. **5** *n.* In baseball, a pitch that is not struck at by the batter and is not a strike. **6** *n.* A round bullet or a cannon ball. **7** *v.* To make into a ball.

ball² [bôl] *n.* A large, formal dance.

bal·lad [bal′əd] *n.* **1** A poem or song that tells a story in a series of short stanzas. **2** A sentimental song of two or more stanzas.

ball-and-sock·et joint [bôl′ən·sok′it] A joint made of a ball in a socket, as the hip.

bal·last [bal′əst] **1** *n.* Anything heavy, as sand, stone, or water carried in a ship, balloon, etc., to steady it. **2** *n.* Gravel or broken stone used as a bed for railroad tracks. **3** *n.* Something that gives steadiness to character, conduct, etc. **4** *v.* To steady or supply with ballast.

ball bearing 1 A bearing in which a shaft or revolving part is borne by hard metal balls that roll easily in a groove. **2** One of these balls.

bal·le·ri·na [bal′ə·rē′nə] *n.* A female ballet dancer.

bal·let [bal′ā *or* ba·lā′] *n.* **1** A dance in which formal steps and movements are performed by costumed dancers. A ballet often tells a story. **2** A group that performs ballets.

---

add, āce, câre, pälm;   end, ēqual;   it, īce;   odd, ōpen, ôrder;   tŏŏk, pool;   up, bûrn;
ə = a in *above*, e in *sicken*, i in *possible*, o in *melon*, u in *circus*;   yoo = u in *fuse*;   oil;   pout;
   check; ring; thin; this; zh in *vision*.   For ¶ reference, see page 64 · HOW TO

bal·lis·tic [bə·lis′tik] *adj.* Of or having to do with projectiles or ballistics.

ballistic missile A rocket guided while its fuel lasts but descending as any freely falling body.

bal·lis·tics [bə·lis′tiks] *n.* The science that deals with the motion of projectiles, missiles, and other objects thrown by force. ✦ See -ICS.

bal·loon [bə·loon′] **1** *n.* A large bag that rises and floats high in the air when filled with a gas lighter than air, often with a car or basket attached, for carrying people. **2** *n.* A small rubber bag that can be inflated and used as a toy. **3** *v.* To swell up like a balloon being filled.

bal·loon·ist [bə·loon′ist] *n.* A person who rides in or operates a balloon.

bal·lot [bal′ət] **1** *n.* A piece of paper used to cast a secret vote. **2** *n.* The total number of votes cast in an election. **3** *n.* The action or method of voting secretly. **4** *v.* To vote or decide by ballot.

ball-point pen [bôl′point′] A pen having as its point a tiny ball that transfers ink from a cartridge to the paper against which it is pressed.

ball·room [bôl′room′ *or* bôl′room′] *n.* A large room for dancing.

bal·ly·hoo [bal′ē·hoo′] *n., v.* **bal·ly·hooed, bal·ly·hoo·ing** *U.S. informal* **1** *n.* Sensational, noisy advertising or propaganda. **2** *v.* To advocate or promote by ballyhoo.

balm [bäm] *n.* **1** An oily substance taken from certain trees and used as a salve or ointment. **2** Anything that soothes or heals: *Darkness was balm to his tired eyes.*

balm·y [bä′mē] *adj.* **balm·i·er, balm·i·est** **1** Mild and soothing; pleasant: *balmy weather.* **2** Fragrant; aromatic. **— balm′i·ness** *n.*

bal·sa [bôl′sə] *n.* **1** A tree of tropical America and the West Indies that has a soft, lightweight wood. **2** The wood, used in rafts, model airplanes, etc.

bal·sam [bôl′səm] *n.* **1** A fragrant, oily substance obtained from certain trees and used in making varnishes, perfumes, and ointments. **2** Any tree from which balsam is obtained.

Bal·tic [bôl′tik] **1** *n.* A sea in northern Europe between Sweden and the Soviet Union. Also **Baltic Sea.** **2** *adj.* Of or having to do with the Baltic Sea or the Baltic States.

Baltic States Latvia, Lithuania, and Estonia, now included in the Soviet Union.

Bal·ti·more [bôl′tə·môr] *n.* A port city in northern Maryland.

bal·us·ter [bal′əs·tər] *n.* One of the small posts that supports the handrail of a staircase, etc.

bal·us·trade [bal′ə·strād′] *n.* A handrail supported by small posts, as on a staircase or balcony.

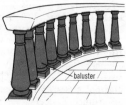

Balustrade

bam·boo [bam·boo′] *n.* A tall, treelike, tropical grass with hollow, jointed stems that are used in building and in making furniture, utensils, etc. ✦ *Bamboo* comes from a Malay word.

bam·boo·zle [bam·boo′zəl] *v.* **bam·boo·zled, bam·boo·zling** *informal* **1** To trick; hoodwink; cheat. **2** To puzzle or confuse: *Card tricks bamboozle me.*

ban [ban] *v.* **banned, ban·ning**, *n.* **1** *v.* To forbid, especially by law; prohibit: *to ban the sale of a book.* **2** *n.* A law or order forbidding something. **3** *n.* A curse: seldom used today.

ba·nal [bā′nəl *or* bə·nal′] *adj.* Boring or meaningless because it has been used too much; trite.

ba·nan·a [bə·nan′ə] *n.* **1** The fruit of a large, tropical plant. It has a red or yellow skin, sweet, creamy flesh, and grows in clusters on a stalk. **2** The plant. ✦ *Banana* comes from a Spanish or Portuguese word taken from an African language.

band [band] **1** *n.* A flat, flexible strip of any material, often used to bind or secure something: *A barrel has iron bands around it.* **2** *n.* A stripe: *The flag was white with a blue band.* **3** *v.* To put a band on or identify with a band, as a bird. **4** *n.* A specific range of radio frequencies: *the short-wave band.* **5** *n.* A group of persons united for a purpose: *a band of thieves.* **6** *v.* To unite in a band. **7** *n.* A group of musicians organized to play together.

band·age [ban′dij] *n., v.* **band·aged, band·ag·ing** **1** *n.* A strip of soft cloth or other material used to cover or bind up a wound or injury. **2** *v.* To cover or support with a bandage.

ban·dan·na *or* **ban·dan·a** [ban·dan′ə] *n.* A large, brightly colored, patterned handkerchief.

band·box [band′boks′] *n.* A round or oval box used to hold collars, hats, etc.

ban·deau [ban·dō′] *n., pl.* **ban·deaux** [ban·dōz′] A narrow band worn by women to hold their hair in place.

ban·dit [ban′dit] *n., pl.* **ban·dits** *or* **ban·dit·ti** [ban·dit′ē] A robber or outlaw; highwayman.

band·mas·ter [band′mas′tər] *n.* The leader of a musical band; conductor.

band·stand [band′stand′] *n.* A platform for a musical band, often roofed when out of doors.

band·wag·on [band′wag′ən] *n.* A decorated wagon used to carry a band in a parade. **— on the bandwagon** *informal* On the side that is popular or winning, as in an election: *Get on the bandwagon.*

ban·dy [ban′dē] *v.* **ban·died, ban·dy·ing**, *adj.* **1** *v.* To give and take; exchange: *to bandy stories.* **2** *adj.* Bent outward; bowed, as legs.

ban·dy-legged [ban′dē·legd′] *adj.* Bowlegged.

bane [bān] *n.* A cause of worry, ruin, or death.

bane·ful [bān′fəl] *adj.* Destructive; harmful: *a baneful climate.*

bang[1] [bang] **1** *n.* A hard, noisy blow or thump. **2** *v.* To beat or hit hard and noisily: *Who's banging on the door?* **3** *n.* A sudden, loud sound: *the bang of a gun.* **4** *v.* To make a loud sound: *I wish that drum would stop banging.*

5 *v.* To knock or thrust forcefully so as to make a sharp noise: to *bang* a door shut. **6** *adv.* Suddenly and loudly: He ran *bang* into the door. ◆ *Bang* comes from an old Scandinavian word meaning *to hammer.*

bang² [bang] *n.* (*often pl.*) A fringe of hair cut so that it hangs squarely across the forehead.

Bang·kok [bang'kok] *n.* The capital of Thailand.

ban·gle [bang'gəl] *n.* A hoop, chain, etc., worn around the wrist or ankle as jewelry.

Woman wearing bangs

ban·ish [ban'ish] *v.* **1** To compel to leave a country, as by political decree. **2** To drive away; get rid of; dismiss: He tried to *banish* the guilty feelings from his mind. — **ban'ish·ment** *n.*

ban·is·ter [ban'is·tər] *n.* **1** A post that supports a railing, as along a staircase. **2** A balustrade.

ban·jo [ban'jō] *n., pl.* **ban·jos** or **ban·joes** A stringed musical instrument that has a long neck attached to a shallow drum with a skin stretched over the top. It has four or five strings and is played by strumming or plucking.

Banjo

bank¹ [bangk] **1** *n.* A pile, mass, or mound: a cloud *bank.* **2** *v.* To heap up into a bank: The plow *banked* the snow at the side of the road. **3** *n.* The land along the edge of a river or stream. **4** *n.* A shallow place in a body of water: a sand *bank.* **5** *v.* To slant (a road or track on a curve) so the outer edge is higher. **6** *v.* To tilt an airplane so that one wing is higher than the other, as when turning. **7** *v.* To cover (a fire) with ashes, etc., so that it will burn more slowly.

bank² [bangk] **1** *n.* A place whose business is the lending, exchanging, and safeguarding of money. **2** *v.* To put or keep money in a bank. **3** *n.* A place where a supply of something is kept for future use: Many hospitals have blood *banks.* — **bank on** *informal* To rely on; be sure about.

bank³ [bangk] *n.* **1** A set of like objects in a row: a *bank* of organ keys. **2** A tier of oars in a galley.

bank·er [bangk'ər] *n.* A person who owns or runs a bank.

bank·ing [bangk'ing] *n.* The business of a bank or banker.

bank·rupt [bangk'rupt] **1** *n.* A person who has been declared unable to pay his debts by a court, his property being taken from him and distributed among his creditors. **2** *adj.* Declared a bankrupt by a court. **3** *v.* To make bankrupt.

bank·rupt·cy [bangk'rupt·sē] *n., pl.* **bank·rupt·cies** The condition of being bankrupt.

ban·ner [ban'ər] **1** *n.* A flag. **2** *n.* A piece of cloth with a motto or emblem on it. **3** *n.* A headline extending across a newspaper page. **4** *adj.* Leading; outstanding: a *banner* year.

ban·nock [ban'ək] *n.* A thin cake of meal baked on a griddle.

banns [banz] *n.pl.* An announcement in church that a man and woman are to be married.

ban·quet [bang'kwit] **1** *n.* A lavish feast. **2** *v.* To eat well; feast. **3** *n.* A formal dinner, often followed by speeches. **4** *v.* To give a banquet for.

ban·shee [ban'shē] *n.* In Gaelic myths, a female spirit whose wailing was supposed to warn that someone was going to die.

ban·tam [ban'təm] *n.* **1** (*often written* **Bantam**) A breed of small chickens, known for their fighting ability. **2** A small, aggressive person.

ban·tam·weight [ban'təm·wāt'] *n.* A boxer who weighs 118 pounds or less.

ban·ter [ban'tər] **1** *n.* Playful teasing; good-natured joking. **2** *v.* To tease or joke playfully.

Ban·ting [ban'ting], **Sir Frederick Grant,** 1891–1941, Canadian physician. He discovered the insulin treatment for diabetes.

Ban·tu [ban'tōō] *n., pl.* **Ban·tu** or **Ban·tus** [ban'tōōz], *adj.* **1** *n.* A member of any of a group of Negro tribes of central and southern Africa. **2** *n.* Any of the languages spoken by these tribes. **3** *adj.* Of or having to do with the Bantu or their languages.

ban·yan [ban'yən] *n.* A fig tree of the East Indies whose branches send down roots that develop into new trunks, producing a thick, shady grove.

Banyan

bap·tism [bap'tiz·əm] *n.* **1** A sacrament or rite in which a person is sprinkled with or dipped in water, used by most Christian churches when taking in a new member. **2** A first and often difficult experience: John received his *baptism* as an actor last night.

bap·tis·mal [bap·tiz'məl] *adj.* Of or having to do with baptism: a *baptismal* ceremony.

Bap·tist [bap'tist] **1** *n.* A member of a Christian church that baptizes only professed believers and only by immersing them in water. **2** *adj.* Of or having to do with Baptists or their church. **3** *n.* A person who baptizes: John the *Baptist.*

---

add, āce, câre, pälm; end, ēqual; it, īce; odd, ōpen, ôrder; tŏŏk, pōōl; up, bûrn;
ə = a in *above*, e in *sicken*, i in *possible*, o in *melon*, u in *circus*; yōō = u in *fuse*; oil; pout;
check; ring; thin; this; zh in *vision*. For ¶ reference, see page 64 · HOW TO

bap·tis·ter·y or **bap·tis·try** [bap′tis·trē] *n.*, *pl.* **bap·tis·ter·ies** or **bap·tis·tries** A place where baptisms are performed.

bap·tize [bap′tīz] *v.* **1** To admit someone into a Christian church by baptism. **2** To give a name to at baptism: He was *baptized* Thomas. ¶3

bar [bär] *n.*, *v.* **barred, bar·ring,** *prep.* **1** *n.* A straight, evenly shaped piece of wood, metal, etc., that is longer than it is wide or thick. Bars are used as levers, barriers, etc. **2** *v.* To fasten or shut off with a bar: to *bar* a door. **3** *n.* A solid, bar-shaped block: a *bar* of butter. **4** *n.* Something that blocks the way; obstacle: His lack of training was a *bar* to success. **5** *v.* To block the way; obstruct: The stalled car *barred* the road. **6** *v.* To exclude; prevent; forbid: Girls are *barred* from our club. **7** *n.* A band or stripe, as of color. **8** *v.* To mark with a band or stripe. **9** *n.* A court of law. **10** *n.* Something that acts like a court of law; an authority that passes judgment: the *bar* of conscience. **11** *n.* The railing around the place where a prisoner stands in court. **12** *n.* The legal profession: John was admitted to the *bar*. **13** *n.* Lawyers as a group. **14** *n.* Any of the vertical lines that divide a musical staff into measures. **15** *n.* The unit of music between two bars; measure. **16** *n.* A counter or room where drinks are served. **17** *prep.* Excepting, especially in the expression **bar none,** with no exceptions.

barb [bärb] **1** *n.* A point on an arrow, fishhook, etc., that sticks out and back from the main point. **2** *v.* To provide with a barb or barbs.

Bar·ba·dos [bär·bā′dōz] *n.* An island of the West Indies. It is a British Colony.

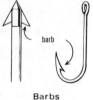

barb

Barbs

bar·bar·i·an [bär·bâr′ē·ən] **1** *n.* A member of a nation, group, or tribe whose way of life is considered primitive or backward. **2** *adj.* Of or like barbarians: *barbarian* manners. **3** *n.* A crude or brutal person. **4** *adj.* Brutal; crude. ◆ *Barbarian* and *barbarous* come from a Latin word taken from a Greek word meaning *foreign*. The ancient Greeks thought all foreigners uncivilized.

bar·bar·ic [bär·bar′ik] *adj.* **1** Of or like barbarians; uncivilized. **2** Wild; cruel.

bar·ba·rism [bär′bə·riz′əm] *n.* **1** An uncivilized condition. **2** Uncivilized action; brutality. **3** A word or phrase considered incorrect: "They is" is a *barbarism* for "they are."

bar·bar·i·ty [bär·bar′ə·tē] *n.*, *pl.* **bar·bar·i·ties** **1** Barbaric conduct. **2** A barbaric act. **3** Crudity or coarseness in style or taste.

bar·ba·rous [bär′bər·əs] *adj.* **1** Uncivilized. **2** Crude or coarse. **3** Cruel; brutal. **4** Using incorrect words or phrases. **— bar′ba·rous·ly** *adv.* ◆ See BARBARIAN.

Bar·ba·ry [bär′bər·ē] *n.* The largely Moslem region of North Africa west of Egypt.

bar·be·cue [bär′bə·kyōō] *n.*, *v.* **bar·be·cued, bar·be·cu·ing 1** *n.* *U.S.* A picnic or party at which meat is roasted over an open fire. **2** *n.* Meat roasted over an open fire, especially a whole animal carcass. **3** *n.* A grill, stove, or pit for outdoor cooking. **4** *v.* To roast over an open fire. **5** *v.* To cook (meat) with a highly seasoned sauce.

barbed [bärbd] *adj.* **1** Having a barb or barbs. **2** Pointed; wounding; painful: a *barbed* reply.

barbed wire Wire that has barbs on it, used for fences.

bar·ber [bär′bər] **1** *n.* A person whose work is giving haircuts, shaves, etc. **2** *v.* To cut the hair of, shave, or trim the beard of.

Barbed wire

bar·ber·ry [bär′ber′ē] *n.*, *pl.* **bar·ber·ries 1** A shrub that has yellow flowers and red berries. **2** Its berry.

bar·bit·u·rate [bär·bich′ər·it] *n.* Any of several drugs used to relieve pain and insomnia and to treat certain nervous conditions.

bar·ca·role or **bar·ca·rolle** [bär′kə·rōl] *n.* A Venetian gondolier's song or a melody imitating such a song.

Bar·ce·lo·na [bär′sə·lō′nə] *n.* A port city of Spain, on the Mediterranean Sea.

bard [bärd] *n.* **1** A writer or singer of narrative poems in ancient times. **2** A poet.

bare [bâr] *adj.* **bar·er, bar·est,** *v.* **bared, bar·ing 1** *adj.* Without clothing or covering; naked. **2** *adj.* Lacking the usual furnishings or supplies; empty: The cupboard is *bare*. **3** *adj.* Plain; unadorned: the *bare* truth. **4** *adj.* Nothing more than; mere: the *bare* necessities of life. **5** *v.* To make bare; uncover: He *bared* his chest. **— lay bare** To expose; reveal. **— bare′ness** *n.*

bare·back [bâr′bak′] **1** *adj.* Riding a horse without a saddle. **2** *adv.* Without a saddle.

bare·faced [bâr′fāst′] *adj.* Shameless; bold.

bare·foot [bâr′fŏŏt′] *adj.*, *adv.* With bare feet.

bare·foot·ed [bâr′fŏŏt′id] *adj.* Barefoot.

bare·head·ed [bâr′hed′id] *adj.*, *adv.* With the head uncovered or bare; without a hat.

bare·ly [bâr′lē] *adv.* **1** Only just; scarcely: We have *barely* enough food to last a week. **2** Plainly; openly. ◆ See HARDLY.

bar·gain [bär′gən] **1** *n.* An agreement between people about something to be done, traded, etc.: I made a *bargain* with Tom to trade him my skates for his baseball glove. **2** *n.* Something bought or offered for sale at less than its usual price. **3** *v.* To discuss a trade, sale, etc., in order to get a better price or better terms. **— bargain for** To expect; be prepared for: The work was harder than he had *bargained for*. **— into the bargain** In addition; besides: He's lazy, and stupid *into the bargain*.

barge [bärj] *n.*, *v.* **barged, barg·ing 1** *n.* A

large, flat-bottomed boat used to carry freight in harbors, rivers, and other inland waters. **2** *n.* Any large boat like this. **3** *v.* *informal* To enter or intrude quickly and rudely.

bar graph A graph using rectangles with lengths proportional to the numbers they represent.

bar·i·tone [bar′ə·tōn] **1** *n.* A male voice of a register higher than bass and lower than tenor. **2** *n.* A person having such a voice. **3** *adj.* *use:* *baritone* saxophone.

bar·i·um [bâr′ē·əm] *n.* A soft, silver-white metallic element. Many of its compounds are used in chemistry, industry, and medicine.

Bar graph showing population growth of the United States

bark[1] [bärk] **1** *n.* The short, abrupt, explosive cry of a dog. **2** *n.* Any sound like this: the *bark* of a rifle. **3** *v.* To utter a bark or a sound like a bark. **4** *v.* To say roughly and curtly: to *bark* a command. **5** *v.* *informal* To try to get people to go to a show, carnival attraction, etc., by talking about its attractions.

bark[2] [bärk] **1** *n.* The rind or covering of a tree or other plant. **2** *v.* To remove the bark from. **3** *v.* To rub off the skin of: to *bark* one's shins.

bark[3] [bärk] *n.* **1** A sailing vessel with three masts, all square-rigged except the mast farthest aft, which is fore-and-aft rigged. **2** In poetry, any sailing vessel.

Bark

bar·ken·tine [bär′kən·tēn] *n.* A sailing vessel having three masts, square-rigged on the foremast and fore-and-aft rigged on the other masts.

bark·er [bär′kər] *n.* *U.S. informal* A person who stands outside a show, carnival, etc., and gives a talk urging people to go in.

bar·ley [bär′lē] *n.* **1** A cereal grass whose grain is used in malt beverages, breakfast foods, food for stock, etc. **2** This grain.

bar mitz·vah [bär mits′və] In the Jewish religion, a ceremony in which a boy who is thirteen is publicly recognized as having reached the age of religious duty and responsibility.

barn [bärn] *n.* A farm building for storing hay, stabling livestock, etc.

bar·na·cle [bär′nə·kəl] *n.* A sea shellfish that attaches itself to rocks, ship bottoms, etc.

barn·storm [bärn′stôrm′] *v.* *U.S. informal* To tour rural districts giving shows, making speeches, or giving exhibitions of stunt flying.

barn·yard [bärn′yärd′] *n.* A yard around a barn.

ba·rom·e·ter [bə·rom′ə·tər] *n.* **1** An instrument for measuring air pressure, used in forecasting weather, determining height above sea level, etc. **2** Something that indicates changes, as of public opinion, business conditions, etc.

bar·o·met·ric [bar′ə·met′rik] *adj.* Of, having to do with, or measured by a barometer.

bar·on [bar′ən] *n.* The lowest ranking member of the nobility in many European countries.

bar·on·ess [bar′ən·is] *n.* **1** The wife or widow of a baron. **2** A woman who holds the rank of baron in her own right.

bar·on·et [bar′ən·it] *n.* **1** An English title, below that of baron and above that of knight. **2** A person who holds such a title.

ba·ro·ni·al [bə·rō′nē·əl] *adj.* Having to do with or suitable for a baron or his estate.

ba·roque [bə·rōk′] *adj.* **1** Much ornamented, massive, and sometimes grotesque: *baroque* architecture. **2** Irregular in shape: said of pearls. ◆ This word comes from a Portuguese word meaning *rough or imperfect pearl.*

ba·rouche [bə·rōōsh′] *n.* A four-wheeled carriage with a folding top, two seats facing each other, and an outside seat for the driver.

barque [bärk] Another spelling of BARK[3].

bar·racks [bar′əks] *n.pl.* (*sometimes used with singular verb*) A building or group of buildings where soldiers are housed.

bar·ra·cu·da [bar′ə·kōō′də] *n.*, *pl.* **bar·ra·cu·da** or **bar·ra·cu·das** A fierce, powerful fish of warm seas.

bar·rage [bə·räzh′] *n.* **1** A heavy curtain of gunfire to keep enemy troops from moving or to protect one's own. **2** Any overwhelming attack, as of words or blows.

bar·rel [bar′əl] *n.*, *v.* **bar·reled** or **bar·relled, bar·rel·ing** or **bar·rel·ling 1** *n.* A round container, flat at the top and base and bulging slightly in the middle, usually made of wood. **2** *n.* As much as a barrel will hold. The standard U.S. barrel contains 3.28 bushels dry measure or 31.5 gallons liquid measure.

Man hammering bung into the bunghole of a barrel

3 *v.* To put or pack in barrels. **4** *n.* In a gun, the tube through which the bullet or shell is shot.

barrel organ Another name for HAND ORGAN.

bar·ren [bar′ən] **1** *adj.* Unable to produce offspring; sterile. **2** *adj.* Not yielding fruit or

---

add, āce, câre, pälm;   end, ēqual;   it, īce;   odd, ōpen, ôrder;   tŏŏk, pōōl;   up, bûrn;

ə = a in *above*, e in *sicken*, i in *possible*, o in *melon*, u in *circus*;   yōō = u in *fuse*;   oil;   pout;

ch in **ch**eck;   ring;   thin;   this;   zh in *vision*.   For ¶ reference, see page 64 · HOW TO

crops: *barren* soil. **3** *adj.* Not producing results, profit, etc.: a *barren* plan. **4** *adj.* Empty; lacking: *barren* of ideas. **5** *n.* (*usually pl.*) A tract of barren land. — **bar'ren·ness** *n.*

bar·rette [bə·ret'] *n.* A small bar with a clasp used for holding hair in place.

bar·ri·cade [bar'ə·kād' *or* bar'ə·kād] *n.*, *v.* **bar·ri·cad·ed, bar·ri·cad·ing 1** *n.* An obstruction hastily built to bar passage or for defense. **2** *n.* Something that blocks passage; barrier. **3** *v.* To enclose, obstruct, or defend with a barricade.

bar·ri·er [bar'ē·ər] *n.* **1** Something that blocks the way or stops movement, as a wall, fence, dam, etc. **2** Something that acts as a barrier: Bad education is a *barrier* to success.

bar·ring [bär'ing] *prep.* Excepting; apart from: *Barring* snow, we will arrive at noon.

bar·ris·ter [bar'is·tər] *n. British* A lawyer who argues cases in court.

bar·row[1] [bar'ō] *n.* **1** A wheelbarrow. **2** A frame or tray with handles at each end by which it is carried, used for transporting loads.

bar·row[2] [bar'ō] *n.* A mound of earth and stones erected in early times to mark a grave.

Bart. Abbreviation of BARONET.

bar·tend·er [bär'ten·dər] *n.* A man who mixes and serves alcoholic drinks over a bar.

bar·ter [bär'tər] **1** *v.* To trade by exchanging goods or services without using money. **2** *v.* To trade or exchange: The trapper *bartered* his furs for a new rifle. **3** *n.* The act of bartering.

Bar·tók [bär'tôk], **Béla**, 1881–1945, Hungarian composer.

Bar·ton [bär'tən], **Clara,** 1821–1912, U.S. founder of the American Red Cross.

ba·sal [bā'səl] *adj.* **1** Of, at, or forming the base. **2** Basic; fundamental.

basal metabolism The smallest amount of energy required by a plant or animal at rest to maintain essential life activities.

bas·alt [bas'ôlt *or* bə·sôlt'] *n.* A dark, hard, fine-grained rock of volcanic origin.

base[1] [bās] *n.*, *v.* **based, bas·ing 1** *n.* The lowest supporting part of anything; bottom: the *base* of a monument. **2** *v.* To place on a foundation or on something serving as a support: They *based* their hopes on their only son. **3** *n.* A headquarters, especially one from which the men of an armed force, planes, ships, etc., are sent forth and in which supplies are stored. **4** *n.* The chief or fundamental part of something: Meat is the *base* of a stew. **5** *n.* A goal or stopping place in certain sports. **6** *n.* In chemistry, a substance that can combine with an acid to form a salt.

base[2] [bās] *adj.* **bas·er, bas·est 1** Dishonorable or cowardly; mean; low: a *base* fellow; *base* betrayal. **2** Suiting or typical of an inferior or unworthy person: *base* flattery. **3** Low in value: Lead is a *base* metal, not a precious one. — **base'ly** *adv.* — **base'ness** *n.*

base·ball [bās'bôl'] *n.* **1** A game played with a wooden bat and a hard ball by two teams of nine players each. To score, a player must run a diamond-shaped course, touching four bases. **2** The ball used in this game.

base·board [bās'bôrd'] *n.* A board running along the wall of a room, next to the floor.

base hit In baseball, a batted ball that enables the batter to reach a base safely, not helped by an error or the putout of another runner.

base·less [bās'lis] *adj.* Without reason; groundless; unfounded: *baseless* fears.

base·ment [bās'mənt] *n.* The lowest floor of a building, usually completely or partly underground.

bash [bash] *v. informal* To strike heavily.

bash·ful [bash'fəl] *adj.* Timid or uncomfortable with strangers; shy. — **bash'ful·ly** *adv.* — **bash'ful·ness** *n.*

ba·sic [bā'sik] *adj.* **1** Of, at, or forming a base or basis; fundamental: *basic* ingredients. **2** In chemistry, of, like, or producing a base. — **ba·si·cal·ly** [bā'sik·lē] *adv.*

bas·il [baz'(ə)l *or* bās'(ə)l] *n.* A plant with a sweet smell. Its leaves are used in cooking.

ba·sil·i·ca [bə·sil'i·kə] *n.* **1** A rectangular hall with a row of columns along each side and a semicircular section at one end. **2** An early Christian church in this style.

bas·i·lisk [bas'ə·lisk] *n.* **1** In myths, a lizard-like monster whose breath and look were said to kill. **2** A crested tropical American lizard with a pouch on its head that it can inflate.

ba·sin [bā'sən] *n.* **1** A wide, shallow bowl used for holding liquids. **2** The amount a basin will hold. **3** A sink or a bowl for washing. **4** A hollow containing water, as a bay. **5** The region drained by a river and its branches.

Basilisk, about 30 in. long

ba·sis [bā'sis] *n.*, *pl.* **ba·ses** [bā'sēz] The part supporting or essential to the whole; foundation: What is the *basis* for your belief?

bask [bask] *v.* **1** To enjoy a pleasant warmth: to *bask* in the sun. **2** To enjoy a warm feeling.

bas·ket [bas'kit] *n.* **1** A container made of interwoven rushes, cane, strips of wood, etc. **2** Something like a basket in shape or use. **3** The amount a basket will hold. **4** In basketball, the circular net through which the ball is thrown. **5** A goal scored in basketball.

bas·ket·ball [bas'kit·bôl'] *n.* **1** A game played with a large, inflated round ball by two teams of five players each. The object of the game is to toss the ball through the open net, or basket, at the opposing team's end of the court. **2** The round ball used in this game.

bas-re·lief [bä'ri·lēf'] *n.* A type of sculpture in which the figures stand out only slightly from the background.

bass[1] [bās] *n.* **1** The lowest pitched male singing voice. **2** A man with such a voice. **3** The lowest part in vocal or instrumental music. **4** *adj. use:* a *bass* viol.

bass[2] [bas] *n., pl.* **bass** or **bass·es** Any of various food fishes found in salt and fresh water.

bass clef [bās] The clef used in writing the notes for low-pitched instruments and voices.

bass drum [bās] A large drum having two surfaces for beating. It makes a deep sound.

bas·set [bas′it] *n.* A hound with a long body, long head and ears, and short, heavy legs.

bas·si·net [bas′ə·net′] *n.* A basket, often with a hood at one end, used as a baby's bed.

bas·soon [ba·sōōn′ *or* bə·sōōn′] *n.* A large, low-pitched woodwind instrument with a double reed.

bass viol [bās] Another name for DOUBLE BASS.

bass·wood [bas′-wŏŏd′] *n.* **1** The American linden tree. **2** The wood of this tree.

bas·tard [bas′tərd] *n.* A person born of parents not married

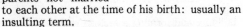
Bassoon

to each other at the time of his birth: usually an insulting term.

baste[1] [bāst] *v.* **bast·ed, bast·ing** To sew temporarily with long, loose stitches.

baste[2] [bāst] *v.* **bast·ed, bast·ing** To moisten (meat, etc.) while roasting, as by pouring drippings or melted butter over it.

Bas·tille [bas·tēl′] *n.* A fortress in Paris once used as a prison. It was attacked and destroyed during the French Revolution on July 14, 1789.

bas·tion [bas′chən] *n.* **1** In fortifications, a part of the rampart that juts out so that the main rampart can be protected. **2** A stronghold.

bat[1] [bat] *n., v.* **bat·ted, bat·ting** **1** *n.* A sturdy stick or a club, especially one used for hitting a ball. **2** *v.* To hit with or as if with a bat. **3** *n. informal* A sharp blow. **4** *v.* To use a bat. **5** *n.* In baseball, a turn at batting. **6** *v.* To take a turn at batting. **— at bat** In the act or position of batting: Each player sat on the bench until it was his turn *at bat.*

bat[2] [bat] *n.* A small, mouselike animal with wings of thin skin supported by bones of the forelimbs. Bats fly at night.

bat[3] [bat] *v.* **bat·ted, bat·ting** *informal* To wink, as in surprise.

batch [bach] *n.* **1** A quantity or number taken together: a *batch* of newspapers. **2** An amount of something produced at one time: a *batch* of bread.

Big brown bat, 4 in. long

bat·ed [bāt′id] *adj.* Held in; restrained, especially in the phrase **with bated breath,** barely breathing because of excitement or fear.

bath [bath] *n., pl.* **baths** [bathz] **1** A washing of the body with water. **2** The water used for this: Run my *bath.* **3** A bathtub or bathroom. **4** A public building for bathing. **5** A liquid in which something is treated by dipping or soaking, as metals, camera film, etc.

bathe [bāth] *v.* **bathed, bath·ing** **1** To give a bath to. **2** To take a bath. **3** To go into a pool, the sea, etc., to swim or cool off. **4** To apply a liquid to for healing or soothing: to *bathe* the forehead. **5** To cover as with a liquid: a hill *bathed* in light. **— bath′er** *n.*

bath·house [bath′hous′] *n.* **1** A building at a bathing resort used as a dressing room. **2** A building where people may take baths.

bath·robe [bath′rōb′] *n.* A long, loose garment worn before and after bathing and for lounging.

bath·room [bath′rōōm′] *n.* **1** A room in which to bathe. **2** A toilet.

bath·tub [bath′tub′] *n.* A tub to take baths in, usually a permanent fixture in a bathroom.

bath·y·scaph [bath′ə·skaf] *n.* A kind of submarine capable of propelling itself and designed for scientific explorations at great depths in the sea. It has a spherical cabin underneath.

bath·y·sphere [bath′ə·sfir] *n.* A hollow spherical steel structure with windows, used in underwater diving for deep-sea observations.

ba·tiste [bə·tēst′] *n.* A very fine linen or cotton fabric.

ba·ton [bə·ton′] *n.* **1** A slender stick or rod used by a conductor in leading an orchestra. **2** A short staff or rod carried as a symbol of authority. **3** A hollow, metal staff twirled rapidly for display, as by a drum majorette.

Bat·on Rouge [bat′(ə)n rōōzh′] The capital of Louisiana.

bats·man [bats′mən] *n., pl.* **bats·men** [bats′mən] A batter, especially in cricket.

bat·tal·ion [bə·tal′yən] *n.* **1** Two or more companies of soldiers led by a lieutenant colonel or major. **2** A large group of persons doing the same thing: a *battalion* of photographers.

bat·ten [bat′(ə)n] **1** *n.* A narrow strip of wood, as one used to fasten canvas over a ship's hatch in rough weather. **2** *v.* To fasten with such strips: *Batten* down the hatches!

bat·ter[1] [bat′ər] *n.* In baseball or cricket, a player who bats or whose turn it is to bat.

bat·ter[2] [bat′ər] *n.* A thick liquid mixture, as of milk, eggs, and flour, beaten up for making biscuits, cakes, etc.

bat·ter[3] [bat′ər] *v.* **1** To strike repeatedly; beat. **2** To break by striking hard again and again: Detectives *battered* down the door. **3** To damage with hard blows or by rough use.

add, āce, câre, pälm;   end, ēqual;   it, īce;   odd, ōpen, ôrder;   tŏŏk, pōōl;   up, bûrn;
ə = a in *above*, e in *sicken*, i in *possible*, o in *melon*, u in *circus*;   yōō = u in *fuse*;   oil;   pout;
check;   ring;   thin;   this;   zh in *vision*.   For ¶ reference, see page 64 · HOW TO

bat·ter·ing-ram [bat'ər·ing·ram'] *n.* A long, thick wooden beam, used in olden times in war for breaking down walls, gates, or doors. It sometimes had a ram's head of iron at the end.

Battering-ram

bat·ter·y [bat'ər·ē] *n., pl.* **bat·ter·ies** **1** Several electric cells operating together to give a required current or voltage. **2** An electric cell, as used in a flashlight. **3** A group of big guns used together in battle. **4** Any group of things or people connected or working together: a *battery* of photographers. **5** In baseball, the pitcher and catcher together. **6** The illegal beating or touching of another person: assault and *battery*.

battery jar A squarish glass container open at the top, used in science laboratories.

bat·ting [bat'ing] *n.* **1** Sheets or rolls of wadded cotton or wool used in quilts, as bandages, etc. **2** The act of a person who bats.

bat·tle [bat'(ə)l] *n., v.* **bat·tled, bat·tling** **1** *n.* A combat between enemy armies or fleets. **2** *n.* Any fight, conflict, or struggle. **3** *v.* To fight: He *battled* his way through the crowd.

bat·tle-ax or **bat·tle-axe** [bat'(ə)l·aks'] *n.* A large ax used long ago in battle.

bat·tle·dore [bat'(ə)l·dôr] *n.* A paddle or racket used to hit a shuttlecock over a net.

bat·tle·field [bat'(ə)l·fēld'] *n.* The land on which a battle is fought or has been fought.

bat·tle·ground [bat'(ə)l·ground'] *n.* A battlefield.

bat·tle·ment [bat'(ə)l·mənt] *n.* **1** A wall built at the top of a fort or tower providing openings through which men could shoot. **2** A low wall like this used to decorate a building.

bat·tle·ship [bat'·(ə)l·ship'] *n.* A large, armored warship equipped with heavy guns.

bau·ble [bô'bəl] *n.* A worthless, showy trinket.

Soldiers shooting from a battlement

baux·ite [bôk'sīt] *n.* A white to red claylike substance that is the main source of aluminum.

Ba·var·i·a [bə·vâr'ē·ə] *n.* A state in southern West Germany. **—Ba·var'i·an** *adj., n.*

bawd·y [bô'dē] *adj.* **bawd·i·er, bawd·i·est** Indecent; immoral; improper: a *bawdy* song.

bawl [bôl] *v.* **1** To cry or sob noisily. **2** To call out loudly and harshly; shout; bellow. **—bawl out** *U.S. slang* To scold severely.

bay[1] [bā] *n.* A body of water partly enclosed by land; an inlet of the sea or of a lake.

bay[2] [bā] *n.* **1** A recess, nook, or alcove of a room. **2** A bay window. **3** A main part or division of a structure, set off by screens, columns, pillars, etc.

bay[3] [bā] **1** *n.* A deep, prolonged bark or cry, as of dogs in hunting. **2** *v.* To utter such a bark or cry. **3** *n.* The position of a hunted animal forced to turn and fight its attackers: to stand at *bay*. **4** *n.* The condition of being kept off by or as if by an animal one has cornered: The bear held the attacking dogs at *bay*.

bay[4] [bā] *n.* **1** An evergreen tree with shiny, sweet-smelling leaves; laurel. **2** (*often pl.*) A laurel wreath with which poets and victors were once crowned as a sign of honor or fame.

bay[5] [bā] **1** *n., adj.* Reddish brown. **2** *n.* A reddish brown horse.

bay·ber·ry [bā'ber'ē] *n., pl.* **bay·ber·ries** **1** A shrub with sweet-smelling, waxy berries used in making a type of candle. **2** The berry itself.

bay·o·net [bā'ə·nit or bā'ə·net'] *n., v.* **bay·o·net·ed, bay·o·net·ing** **1** *n.* A daggerlike weapon that may be attached to the muzzle of a rifle. **2** *v.* To stab with this weapon.

bay·ou [bī'oo] *n.* In the southern U.S., a marshy inlet or outlet of a lake, river, etc.

bay window A window or set of windows jutting out from the wall of a building and forming a recess or alcove in the room within.

ba·zaar or **ba·zar** [bə·zär'] *n.* **1** An Oriental marketplace or street of shops. **2** A store for the sale of many kinds of goods. **3** A fair to raise money for some purpose: a church *bazaar*.

Bay window

ba·zoo·ka [bə·zoo'kə] *n.* A long, tube-shaped portable weapon that fires an explosive rocket.

BB [bē'bē] *n., pl.* **BB's** A lead ball that is shot from a **BB gun,** a type of air gun.

bbl. Abbreviation of: **1** BARREL. **2** (*usually written* **bbls.**) Barrels.

B.C. Abbreviation of *Before Christ*. It indicates dates before the birth of Christ: 23 B.C.

be [bē] *v.* **was** or **were, been, be·ing** **1** To have existence: Can such things *be*?; There *are* bears in the zoo. **2** To take place; happen: The parade *was* yesterday; Her birthday will *be* next month. **3** To stay or continue: I *was* in school all day. ◆ In addition to its use as a main verb, *be* is also a helping verb to show continuous action: I *am* working; She has *been* sleeping. It is also used with the past participle of transitive verbs to form the passive voice, and with the past participle of intransitive verbs to form the perfect tense: He *was* injured; I *am* finished. *Be* also may join a subject with an adjective, noun, or pronoun: You *were* late; We *are* friends; What *is* it? To show that something is expected to happen in the future, *be* is used with an infinitive or a present participle: He *is* to leave soon; They *are* returning Monday.

be- A prefix meaning: **1** Around; all over, as in *bestrew*, to strew all over. **2** Completely; thoroughly, as in *bedrench*, to drench completely.

3 Off; away from, as in *behead*, to cut off the head of. **4** To provide or cover with, as in *bejewel*, to cover with jewels. **5** To make; cause to be, as in *befoul*, to make foul. **6** About; because of, as in *bemoan*, to moan about.
Be The symbol for the element BERYLLIUM.
beach [bēch] **1** *n.* The sloping shore of a body of water, especially a sandy or pebbly shore. **2** *v.* To drive or haul up (a boat) on a beach.
beach·head [bēch′hed′] *n.* An area on a shore seized and held by an invading force.
bea·con [bē′kən] *n.* **1** A signal meant to warn or guide, as a light or fire. **2** A lighthouse. **3** Any place or height from which signals may be given. **4** A radio transmitter that sends out signals to guide ships and aircraft.
bead [bēd] **1** *n.* A small, usually round, piece of glass, wood, etc., with a hole in it to draw a thread through. **2** *v.* To decorate with beads. **3** *n.* (*pl.*) A string of beads. **4** *n.* (*pl.*) A rosary. **5** *n.* A bubble or a drop of moisture, as sweat. **6** *n.* A small knob on a gun used in aiming. **— draw a bead on** To aim at.
bead·ing [bē′ding] *n.* **1** A trimming made of beads. **2** Material of or covered with beads.
bea·dle [bēd′(ə)l] *n.* A church officer who kept order during the services in olden times.
bead·y [bē′dē] *adj.* **bead·i·er, bead·i·est** Small and glittering: *beady* eyes.
bea·gle [bē′gəl] *n.* A small hound with short legs and drooping ears, used in hunting.
beak [bēk] *n.* **1** The hooked bill of a bird of prey. **2** Any bird's bill. **3** Anything that looks like a bird's beak.
beak·er [bē′kər] *n.* **1** A large, wide-mouthed cup or goblet. **2** A glass or metal container with a lip for pouring, used by chemists.
beam [bēm] **1** *n.* A long, horizontal piece of wood or metal shaped for use, as in the frame of a building or ship. **2** *n.* The part where a ship is the widest. **3** *n.* The crossbar of a balance. **4** *n.* A ray of light. **5** *v.* To send out rays of light; shine. **6** *n.* A radiant, happy look; smile. **7** *v.* To smile very warmly: Her mother *beamed* when she heard the good news. **8** *n.* A continuous radio signal along a course to guide pilots. **9** *v.* To aim or transmit (a signal or broadcast) in a specific direction.

Beakers

bean [bēn] *n.* **1** The oval seed of certain plants, used as food: lima *beans.* **2** The pod containing such seeds. Both the beans and pod of the string bean are used as a vegetable. **3** A plant bearing beans. **4** A seed or plant resembling a bean or bean plant: a vanilla *bean.*
bean·ie [bē′nē] *n.* A small, brimless cap worn on the back of the head.

bear¹ [bâr] *v.* **bore, borne** (or **born** for def. 5), **bear·ing** **1** To hold up; support: The swing couldn't *bear* his weight. **2** To focus or exert force: to bring one's influence to *bear* on a case. **3** To show; display: to *bear* a scar. **4** To endure: to *bear* pain. **5** To give birth to: She has *borne* a son; He was *born* today. **6** To produce: The farm *bore* good crops. **7** To carry or convey: The horse *bore* two riders. **8** To take on: to *bear* all the costs. **9** To conduct or behave (oneself): He *bore* himself with confidence. **10** To go in a certain direction: *Bear* to the right. **11** To keep in the mind: to *bear* a grudge. **12** To require: His behavior *bears* watching. **13** To have: What relation does he *bear* to you? **14** To relate or apply to: This does not *bear* on the matter at hand. **— bear down 1** To apply pressure. **2** To try very hard. **— bear out** To confirm as true; prove. **— bear up** To keep up strength or spirits when under a strain. **— bear with** To endure patiently.
bear² [bâr] *n.* **1** A large, very strong mammal with a heavy, thickly furred body and a very short tail, as the grizzly bear, brown bear, or polar bear. **2** A gruff, clumsy person.
bear·a·ble [bâr′ə·bəl] *adj.* Endurable.
beard [bird] **1** *n.* The hair that grows on a man's face. **2** *n.* Any similar growth, as the tuft of hairs on a goat's chin or the slender, stiff bristles on some spikes of wheat. **3** *v.* To defy courageously. **— beard′ed** *adj.*
bear·er [bâr′ər] *n.* **1** A person or thing that bears, carries, or upholds. **2** A person who presents a check, money order, etc., for payment.
bear·ing [bâr′ing] *n.* **1** The way a person holds himself or behaves; posture, carriage, or manner: a manly *bearing.* **2** (*often pl.*) Position in relation to other, known points; direction: to lose one's *bearings.* **3** Relation; application: His remarks had no *bearing* on the subject. **4** A part of a machine on or in which another part slides or turns.
beast [bēst] *n.* **1** Any animal except man, especially a large, four-footed animal. **2** A cruel, rude, or filthy person.
beast of burden An animal used to carry loads.
beast·ly [bēst′lē] *adj.* **beast·li·er, beast·li·est** **1** Like a savage beast; cruel. **2** *informal* Disagreeable: *beastly* weather.
beat [bēt] *v.* **beat, beat·en** or **beat, beat·ing,** *n., adj.* **1** *v.* To strike over and over; pound. **2** *n.* A stroke or blow. **3** *v.* To punish by hitting again and again; thrash. **4** *v.* To defeat, as in a fight or contest. **5** *v.* To stir or mix rapidly: to *beat* eggs. **6** *v.* To flap or flutter, as wings. **7** *v.* To make, as one's way, by hitting or shoving. **8** *v.* To make flat by tramping or treading: to *beat* a path through the woods.

add, āce, câre, pälm; end, ēqual; it, īce; odd, ōpen, ôrder; tŏŏk, pōōl; up, bûrn; ə = a in *above*, e in *sicken*, i in *possible*, o in *melon*, u in *circus*; yōō = u in *fuse*; oil; pout; check; ring; thin; this; zh in *vision*. For ¶ reference, see page 64 · HOW TO

9 *n.* A route regularly walked or covered, as by a policeman or reporter. **10** *v.* To hunt through underbrush, etc., as for game. **11** *n.* A regular stroke, or its sound. **12** *n.* The basic unit of musical time. **13** *n.* Rhythm. **14** *v.* To give forth sound, as drums do when struck. **15** *n.* A throbbing, as of the heart. **16** *v.* To throb. **17** *adj. U.S. informal* Extremely tired. **18** *v. informal* To baffle; puzzle: It *beats* me. **— beat a retreat** To turn back; flee. **— beat time** To measure time in music, as by tapping the foot.

beat·en [bēt'(ə)n] **1** Past participle of BEAT. **2** *adj.* Shaped or made thin by beating: *beaten* gold. **3** *adj.* Mixed by beating: *beaten* eggs. **4** *adj.* Worn by use; customary: off the *beaten* track. **5** *adj.* Whipped or defeated.

beat·er [bē'tər] *n.* A person or thing that beats, as a utensil for stirring foods rapidly or a man who drives hunted game from hiding.

be·a·tif·ic [bē'ə·tif'ik] *adj.* Giving or expressing bliss or blessedness: a *beatific* smile.

be·at·i·fy [bē·at'ə·fī] *v.* **be·at·i·fied, be·at·i·fy·ing 1** To make supremely happy or blessed. **2** In the Roman Catholic Church, to declare publicly that (a certain dead person) is among the blessed in heaven. **— be·at·i·fi·ca·tion** [bē·at'ə·fi·kā'shən] *n.*

beat·ing [bē'ting] *n.* A whipping or defeat.

be·at·i·tude [bē·at'ə·t(y)ōōd] *n.* **1** Supreme blessedness; bliss. **2** (*written* **the Beatitudes**) In the Bible, the verses naming the kinds of people who are blessed.

beau [bō] *n., pl.* **beaus** or **beaux** [bōz] **1** A man courting a woman; lover. **2** A dandy.

Beau·fort scale [bō'fərt] An internationally accepted scale of wind speeds, ranging from 0 (calm) to 12 (hurricane).

beau·te·ous [byōō'tē·əs] *adj.* Beautiful.

beau·ti·ful [byōō'tə·fəl] *adj.* Giving pleasure or delight to the senses or the mind; very lovely: a *beautiful* day. **— beau'ti·ful·ly** *adv.*

beau·ti·fy [byōō'tə·fī] *v.* **beau·ti·fied, beau·ti·fy·ing** To make beautiful or lovelier. **— beau·ti·fi·ca·tion** [byōō'tə·fə·kā'shən] *n.*

beau·ty [byōō'tē] *n., pl.* **beau·ties 1** The quality in a person or thing that delights the eye, the ear, or the mind. **2** A person or thing that is beautiful, especially a woman.

beauty parlor or **beauty shop** A place of business where women have their hair dressed, nails manicured, and complexion cared for.

bea·ver [bē'vər] *n.* **1** A large rodent that can live on land or in water and has soft, brown fur and a broad, flat tail. It builds dams across streams from trees which it cuts down with its teeth. **2** The valuable fur of the beaver.

Beaver, about 3 ft. long, including tail

be·calmed [bi·kämd'] *adj.* Unable to move because of a lack of wind.

be·came [bi·kām'] Past tense of BECOME.

be·cause [bi·kôz'] *conj.* For the reason that; since. **— because of** On account of: The game was canceled *because of* rain. ◆ *Because* and *since* are often given identical meanings, but there is a distinction. *Because* introduces a direct cause: *Because* the day was cold, the snow did not melt. *Since* usually introduces only one step toward a reason, not the whole reason: *Since* it was raining hard, I did my homework.

beck [bek] *n.* A motion of the hand or head used to call someone closer. **— at one's beck and call** Subject to one's every order or wish.

beck·on [bek'ən] *v.* **1** To summon or signal by a movement of the hand or head. **2** To entice.

be·cloud [bi·kloud'] *v.* **1** To cover with clouds; darken. **2** To confuse, as an issue.

be·come [bi·kum'] *v.* **be·came, be·come, be·com·ing 1** To come to be or grow to be: The caterpillar *became* a butterfly. **2** To be suitable to or look nice on: Blue *becomes* you. **— become of** To happen to.

be·com·ing [bi·kum'ing] *adj.* Appropriate or suitable and attractive: a *becoming* hairdo.

bed [bed] *n., v.* **bed·ded, bed·ding 1** *n.* An article of furniture to rest or sleep on. **2** *n.* Any place or thing used for resting or sleeping. **3** *v.* To go to bed, put to bed, or prepare a place to sleep or lie: *Bed* down by the trail. **4** *n.* Sleep or sleeping: time for *bed*. **5** *n.* A place to stay: *bed* and board. **6** *n.* A layer in the earth, as of rock. **7** *n.* The ground beneath a body of water: a river *bed*. **8** *n.* A plot of ground for growing plants or flowers. **9** *n.* A level foundation: a driveway built on a *bed* of gravel. **— get up on the wrong side of the bed** To be grouchy.

be·daub [bi·dôb'] *v.* **1** To smear or daub; besmirch; soil. **2** To ornament vulgarly or excessively.

be·daz·zle [bi·daz'əl] *v.* **be·daz·zled, be·daz·zling 1** To confuse or blind by dazzling, as with a strong light. **2** To impress greatly; overwhelm: He was *bedazzled* by the wealthy people he met.

bed·bug [bed'bug'] *n.* A small, flat insect that bites. They sometimes get into beds.

bed·cham·ber [bed'chām'bər] *n.* A bedroom.

bed·clothes [bed'klō(th)z'] *n.pl.* Bed coverings, as blankets, sheets, spreads, etc.

bed·ding [bed'ing] *n.* **1** Bedclothes, including mattresses. **2** Straw as a bed for animals.

be·deck [bi·dek'] *v.* To ornament; adorn.

be·dew [bi·d(y)ōō'] *v.* To wet, as with dew.

bed·fel·low [bed'fel'ō] *n.* **1** A person who shares a bed with another. **2** An associate.

be·diz·en [bi·dī'zən] *v.* To dress or adorn with cheap, flashy splendor.

bed·lam [bed'ləm] *n.* **1** A place or scene of noisy confusion. **2** A lunatic asylum; madhouse. ◆ This word comes from *Bedlam*, a popular name for *St. Mary of Bethlehem*, an old hospital in London for the insane.

Bed·ou·in [bed'ōō·in] *n.* **1** One of the wandering Arabs living in the desert areas of Syria,

Arabia, and northern Africa. **2** Any nomad or vagabond.

be·drag·gled [bi·drag'əld] *adj.* Wet, dirty, and messy, as though dragged through mud.

bed·rid·den [bed'rid'(ə)n] *adj.* Confined to bed for a long time by sickness or injury.

bed·rock [bed'rok'] *n.* The solid rock under the looser materials of the earth's surface.

bed·roll [bed'rōl'] *n.* Bedding or a sleeping bag rolled up for carrying, as by a camper.

bed·room [bed'rōōm'] *n.* A room for sleeping.

bed·side [bed'sīd'] *n.* **1** The space beside a bed, especially a sick person's bed: His family remained at his *bedside* all day. **2** *adj. use:* a doctor with a cheerful *bedside* manner.

bed·spread [bed'spred'] *n.* A cover spread over a bed to hide the sheets or blankets.

bed·stead [bed'sted'] *n.* A framework for supporting the springs and mattress of a bed.

bed·time [bed'tīm'] *n.* Time to go to bed.

bee [bē] *n.* **1** An insect with four wings, a hairy body, and usually a sting. Some bees live and work together in large groups, and honeybees are raised in hives by man because they make honey from the nectar of flowers. **2** *U.S.* A social gathering of people for work, a contest, etc.: a spelling *bee.*

Bee gathering pollen

bee·bread [bē'bred'] *n.* A mixture of pollen and certain proteins stored by bees for food.

beech [bēch] *n.* **1** A tree with smooth, gray bark, dark green leaves, and small, sweet nuts that are good to eat. **2** The wood of this tree.

beech·nut [bēch'nut'] *n.* The edible, triangular nut of the beech tree.

beef [bēf] **1** *n.* The flesh of a cow, steer, or bull. **2** *n., pl.* **beeves** [bēvz] or **beefs** A full-grown cow, steer, or bull fattened for food. **3** *n., pl.* **beefs** *U.S. slang* A complaint. **4** *v. U.S. slang* To complain. — **beef up** *informal* To strengthen or reinforce: to *beef up* a team with new players. ◆ *Beef* comes from the French word *boeuf. Beef up* comes from the idea of supplying with more beef or muscle, as by giving a thin steer more to eat.

beef·steak [bēf'stāk'] *n.* A slice of beef suitable for broiling or frying.

beef·y [bē'fē] *adj.* **beef·i·er, beef·i·est** Muscular and heavy: a *beefy* arm.

bee·hive [bē'hīv'] *n.* **1** A shelter or container for a colony of honeybees, in which they live and store honey. **2** A place full of activity.

bee·line [bē'līn'] *n.* The shortest course from one place to another, as of a bee to its hive.

Be·el·ze·bub [bē·el'zə·bub] *n.* The Devil.

been [bin] Past participle of BE.

beep [bēp] **1** *n.* A short sound made by the horn of a car, etc. **2** *v.* To sound a horn. **3** *n.* A short, high-pitched sound coming at intervals, as in radio devices to help boats keep on course.

beer [bir] *n.* **1** An alcoholic drink made from malt and hops. **2** A soft drink made from roots or leaves of various plants, as ginger.

bees·wax [bēz'waks'] *n.* The yellow, fatty substance of which honeybees make their honeycombs. It is used in polishes, cosmetics, etc.

beet [bēt] *n.* The fleshy, edible root of a leafy plant. Red beets are used as vegetables and white beets are used to make sugar.

Bee·tho·ven [bā'tō·vən], **Ludwig van,** 1770–1827, German composer of music.

bee·tle¹ [bēt'(ə)l] *n.* Any of a large group of insects having biting mouth parts and two pairs of wings, of which the outside pair is hard and horny.

bee·tle² [bēt'(ə)l] *v.* **bee·tled, bee·tling 1** To jut out; overhang. **2** *adj. use:* beetling brows.

be·fall [bi·fôl'] *v.* **be·fell, be·fall·en, be·fall·ing 1**

Japanese beetle

To happen, as though by destiny. **2** To happen to: Some trouble had *befallen* them.

be·fit [bi·fit'] *v.* **be·fit·ted, be·fit·ting** To be suited to; be appropriate for.

be·fog [bi·fog'] *v.* **be·fogged, be·fog·ging 1** To wrap or envelop in fog. **2** To confuse; bewilder: His mind was *befogged* from fatigue.

be·fore [bi·fôr'] **1** *prep.* In front of; ahead of: He was *before* me in line. **2** *adv.* In front; ahead: His men followed while he rode *before.* **3** *prep.* Earlier or sooner than: *before* daybreak. **4** *adv.* Earlier; sooner: Go at noon, not *before.* **5** *adv.* In the past; previously: *Before,* things were different. **6** *conj.* Previous to the time when: They got here *before* we did. **7** *prep.* In preference to: They will die *before* surrendering. **8** *conj.* Rather than; sooner than: I will starve *before* I steal.

be·fore·hand [bi·fôr'hand'] *adv., adj.* In advance; ahead of time.

be·friend [bi·frend'] *v.* To act as a friend to; help: You should *befriend* the new girl.

be·fud·dle [bi·fud'(ə)l] *v.* **be·fud·dled, be·fud·dling** To confuse or cloud the mind of: The rapid questions *befuddled* him. — **be·fud'dle·ment** *n.*

beg [beg] *v.* **begged, beg·ging 1** To ask for (money, food, etc.) as a charity, especially to live as a beggar. **2** To ask for or of earnestly; beseech: We *begged* him to keep his promise. **3** To ask for politely: He *begged* my pardon. — **beg off** To ask to be excused from. — **beg**

add, āce, câre, pälm; end, ēqual; it, īce; odd, ōpen, ôrder; tŏŏk, pŏŏl; up, bûrn;
ə = a in *above,* e in *sicken,* i in *possible,* o in *melon,* u in *circus;* yōō = u in *fuse;* oil; pout;
check; ring; thin; this; zh in *vision.* For ¶ reference, see page 64 · HOW TO

the question To take for granted the very matter in dispute. **— go begging** To be unnoticed or unwanted.

be·gan [bi·gan′] Past tense of BEGIN.

be·get [bi·get′] *v.* **be·got** (or **be·gat**: seldom used today), **be·got·ten** or **be·got, be·get·ting** **1** To be the father of; produce. **2** To result in: Extravagance often *begets* misery. **— be·get′ter** *n.*

beg·gar [beg′ər] **1** *n.* A person who asks for charity or lives by begging. **2** *n.* A poor person; pauper. **3** *v.* To make poor; impoverish. **4** *v.* To make seem inadequate or useless: The scene that met our eyes *beggars* description.

beg·gar·ly [beg′ər·lē] *adj.* Appropriate for a beggar; extremely poor; miserable.

be·gin [bi·gin′] *v.* **be·gan, be·gun, be·gin·ning** **1** To take the first step in; start: to *begin* reading a new book. **2** To come or bring into being; originate: The river *begins* in the mountains; Two chemists *began* the company.

be·gin·ner [bi·gin′ər] *n.* **1** A person who has little experience or is doing something for the first time. **2** A person who begins something.

be·gin·ning [bi·gin′ing] *n.* **1** The first or earliest part: the *beginning* of a chapter; toward the *beginning* of his career. **2** The act of starting: *Beginning* is the hardest part. **3** Source; origin.

be·gone [bi·gôn′] *interj.* Go away! Leave!: seldom used today.

be·gon·ia [bi·gōn′yə] *n.* A plant with large, brightly colored leaves and small waxy flowers.

be·got [bi·got′] Past tense and alternative past participle of BEGET.

be·got·ten [bi·got′(ə)n] Alternative past participle of BEGET. Jacob was *begotten* by Isaac.

be·grime [bi·grīm′] *v.* **be·grimed, be·grim·ing** To make dirty with grime; soil.

be·grudge [bi·gruj′] *v.* **be·grudged, be·grudg·ing** **1** To envy another's enjoyment or possession of: to *begrudge* a neighbor his good luck. **2** To give or grant unwillingly: He *begrudged* every second away from his work.

be·guile [bi·gīl′] *v.* **be·guiled, be·guil·ing** **1** To mislead or trick; deceive: The king was *beguiled* into trusting the traitor. **2** To pass pleasantly; while away: to *beguile* the lonely hours with good books. **3** To charm; please: The puppy's tricks *beguiled* the children.

be·gun [bi·gun′] Past participle of BEGIN.

be·half [bi·haf′] *n.* Interest, part, or defense: My lawyer will act in my *behalf.* **— in behalf of** or **on behalf of 1** In the place of; for: The agent collects rent *in behalf of* the landlord. **2** In the defense of.

be·have [bi·hāv′] *v.* **be·haved, be·hav·ing** **1** To act; conduct oneself: The children *behaved* like angels. **2** To conduct oneself properly: He was told to *behave* and he did.

be·hav·ior [bi·hāv′yər] *n.* **1** Manner of conducting oneself; deportment. **2** The way a person or thing acts under certain conditions: to test the *behavior* of the new drug. ¶1

be·head [bi·hed′] *v.* To cut off the head of.

be·held [bi·held′] Past tense and past participle of BEHOLD.

be·he·moth [bi·hē′məth] *n.* **1** In the Bible, a huge animal. **2** Any huge thing.

be·hest [bi·hest′] *n.* A formal command: We are here at the *behest* of the government.

be·hind [bi·hīnd′] **1** *adv.* In, at, or toward the rear: to *lag* behind. **2** *prep.* At the back of; to the rear of: He sits *behind* me; Look *behind* you. **3** *adv.* To a position that is too slow or lagging: to fall *behind* in paying the rent. **4** *prep.* Later than or not up to the normal or expected time or position: The mail arrived *behind* schedule; She was *behind* other students of her own age. **5** *adv.* In a former place or time: He left his keys *behind.* **6** *prep.* Backing; supporting: We're *behind* the team 100 percent. **7** *n. informal* The part of the body one sits on; rump.

be·hind·hand [bi·hīnd′hand′] *adv., adj.* **1** Behind time; late. **2** Behind in development.

be·hold [bi·hōld′] *v.* **be·held, be·hold·ing** To look at or upon; view; see: to *behold* the Promised Land. **— be·hold′er** *n.*

be·hold·en [bi·hōl′dən] *adj.* Under obligation; indebted: We are *beholden* to you for your kindness.

be·hoove [bi·hōōv′] *v.* **be·hooved, be·hoov·ing** To be right or proper for; be expected of: It *behooves* all good citizens to accept their responsibilities.

beige [bāzh] *n., adj.* Grayish tan.

be·ing [bē′ing] **1** Present participle of BE. **2** *n.* Existence: The company came into *being* during the war. **3** *n.* A living thing, especially a person: a human *being.*

be·la·bor [bi·lā′bər] *v.* **1** To hit hard again and again. **2** To criticize severely; scold. ¶1

be·lat·ed [bi·lā′tid] *adj.* Late, or too late: a *belated* apology. **— be·lat′ed·ly** *adv.*

be·lay [bi·lā′] *v.* **be·layed, be·lay·ing**, *interj.* **1** *v.* To secure (a rope) by winding around a pin. **2** *interj.* Stop!: used mostly by sailors.

belaying pin A metal or wooden pin fitting in a hole, used on ships for making ropes secure.

Sailor belaying a rope around a belaying pin

belch [belch] **1** *v.* To let out wind from the stomach through the mouth. **2** *n.* The act of belching. **3** *v.* To throw out violently: The furnace *belched* smoke. **4** *v.* To gush; spurt.

bel·dam or **bel·dame** [bel′dəm] *n.* An old woman, especially one who is ugly or mean.

be·lea·guer [bi·lē′gər] *v.* **1** To surround or shut in with an armed force; besiege. **2** To beset; surround: *beleaguered* with problems.

Bel·fast [bel′fast] *n.* The capital of Northern Ireland, a seaport.

bel·fry [bel′frē] *n., pl.* **bel·fries** **1** A tower in which a bell is hung. **2** The part of a tower or steeple containing a bell. ◆ *Belfry* comes from the old French word *berfrei*, meaning *tower.* Because bells were associated with towers, and *belfrei* was easier for English-speaking people to pronounce, the word came to have its present sound and spelling.

Bel·gian [bel′jən] **1** *adj.* Of or from Belgium. **2** *n.* A person born in or a citizen of Belgium.

Bel·gium [bel′jəm] *n.* A country of NW Europe.

Belfry

Bel·grade [bel′grād] *n.* The capital of Yugoslavia.

be·lie [bi·lī′] *v.* **be·lied, be·ly·ing** **1** To give a false impression of: His shabby clothes *belied* his wealth. **2** To prove false; contradict: His good manners seemed to *belie* his bad reputation.

be·lief [bi·lēf′] *n.* **1** Acceptance of the truth or reality of something without certain proof. **2** Something believed: the *belief* that advances in medicine will continue to prolong lives; a *belief* in God. **3** Trust or faith; confidence.

be·liev·a·ble [bi·lēv′ə·bəl] *adj.* Capable of being believed: a *believable* story.

be·lieve [bi·lēv′] *v.* **be·lieved, be·liev·ing** **1** To accept as true or real: I *believe* your story. **2** To trust as having told the truth: I *believe* you. **3** To have faith or confidence; trust: I *believe* in my doctor's ability. **4** To have religious faith. **5** To think; suppose: I *believe* he's away on vacation. **— be·liev′er** *n.*

be·like [bi·līk′] *adv.* Perhaps; probably: seldom used today.

be·lit·tle [bi·lit′(ə)l] *v.* **be·lit·tled, be·lit·tling** To make seem small or less important: Jealous people *belittle* the success of others.

bell [bel] **1** *n.* A hollow, cup-shaped metal instrument that makes a ringing sound when its side is struck by a clapper or hammer. **2** *n.* The sound of a bell. **3** *v.* To put a bell on: to *bell* a cow. **4** *n.* Anything shaped like a bell, as the flaring end of a wind instrument. **5** *v.* To take the shape of a bell. **6** *n.* The time told by the striking of a ship's bell.

Bell [bel], **Alexander Graham,** 1847–1922, U.S. scientist born in Scotland, inventor of the telephone.

bel·la·don·na [bel′ə·don′ə] *n.* **1** A poisonous plant having black berries and purple-red flowers. **2** A drug made from this plant.

bell·boy [bel′boi′] *n.* U.S. A boy or man employed to serve hotel guests, as by carrying luggage, etc.

belle [bel] *n.* An attractive woman or girl, especially one most admired in a social group.

Bel·ler·o·phon [bə·ler′ə·fon] *n.* In Greek myths, the rider of the winged horse, Pegasus.

bel·li·cose [bel′ə·kōs] *adj.* Inclined to fight; warlike; belligerent.

bel·lig·er·ent [bə·lij′ər·ənt] **1** *adj.* Inclined to fight; warlike: a *belligerent* attitude. **2** *adj.* Engaged in war. **3** *n.* A person or nation engaged in warfare or fighting. **— bel·lig′er·ence** *n.* **— bel·lig′er·ent·ly** *adv.*

bell jar A bell-shaped glass container used as a cover for fragile articles, or in scientific experiments with gases and vacuums.

bel·low [bel′ō] **1** *v.* To utter a loud, hollow cry like that of a bull. **2** *n.* A loud cry or roar. **3** *v.* To cry out loudly; roar: to *bellow* orders.

bel·lows [bel′ōz] *n.pl.* (*used with singular or plural verb*) **1** An instrument that sucks in air when its sides are spread and blows it out, as to fan fires, when its sides are brought together. **2** The folding part of some cameras.

Bellows blowing into a fire

bel·ly [bel′ē] *n., pl.* **bel·lies,** *v.* **bel·lied, bel·ly·ing** **1** *n.* The part of the human body just below the ribs, containing the stomach and bowels; abdomen. **2** *n.* The under part of an animal. **3** *n.* The stomach. **4** *n.* Something that bulges out. **5** *v.* To swell out or fill, as a sail. **6** *n.* A deep, interior part: the *belly* of a ship.

be·long [bi·lông′] *v.* To have a proper place: The clean laundry *belongs* on this shelf. **— belong to** **1** To be the property of: This book *belongs to* me. **2** To be a part of: The orange blouse *belongs to* her new suit. **3** To be a member of: to *belong to* a club.

be·long·ings [bi·lông′ingz] *n.pl.* The things a person owns; possessions.

be·lov·ed [bi·luv′id *or* bi·luvd′] **1** *adj.* Greatly loved. **2** *n.* A person who is greatly loved.

be·low [bi·lō′] **1** *adv.* In or to a lower place: During the storm at sea, the sailors went *below*. **2** *prep.* Lower than in place, amount, or degree; under: The subway runs *below* the streets; a body temperature *below* normal.

belt [belt] **1** *n.* A strap or band worn around the waist to support clothing, weapons, etc., or as an ornament. **2** *v.* To put a belt on, or fasten with a belt. **3** *v. informal* To strike or hit, as with a belt. **4** *n.* An endless band for turning two or more wheels, as in a machine. **5** *n.* A broad area or region: the wheat *belt*.

be·moan [bi·mōn′] *v.* To moan about; lament.

bench [bench] **1** *n.* A long seat of wood, stone, or metal, with or without a back. **2** *n.* A sturdy

add, āce, câre, pälm;   end, ēqual;   it, īce;   odd, ōpen, ôrder;   toŏk, poōl;   up, bûrn;
ə = a in *above*, e in *sicken*, i in *possible*, o in *melon*, u in *circus*;   yoō = u in *fuse*;   oil;   pout;
check;   ring;   thin;   this;   zh in *vision*.   For ¶ reference, see page 64 · HOW TO

table for doing carpentry or other work with tools. **3** *n.* The seat for a judge in a courtroom. **4** *n.* The judge or judges in a courtroom. **5** *n.* The profession of a judge. **6** *n.* The substitute players on an athletic team. **7** *v.* To remove (a player) from a game, as for poor play.

bend [bend] *v.* **bent** (or **bend·ed:** seldom used today), **bend·ing,** *n.* **1** *v.* To cause to take the form of a curve: to *bend* a wire. **2** *v.* To become curved. **3** *n.* A curve or crook: a *bend* in the road. **4** *v.* To stoop or bow: He *bent* over to tie his shoelaces. **5** *v.* To yield or make yield: I *bent* him to my will. **6** *v.* To move or turn in a certain direction: to *bend* one's steps toward home. **7** *n.pl.* **(the bends)** Another name for CAISSON DISEASE.

be·neath [bi·nēth'] **1** *prep.* Under; below or directly below: *beneath* the stars; Put the coaster *beneath* the glass. **2** *adv.* In a lower place: Look *beneath.* **3** *prep.* Lower than in place, rank, etc.: Nobody ranks *beneath* a private. **4** *prep.* Unworthy of: That rude remark was *beneath* you.

Ben·e·dic·tine [ben'ə·dik'tin] **1** *n.* A member of a religious order founded by St. Benedict, an Italian monk. **2** *adj.* Of or having to do with St. Benedict or his order.

ben·e·dic·tion [ben'ə·dik'shən] *n.* **1** An asking of God's blessing at the end of a religious service. **2** A blessing.

ben·e·fac·tion [ben'ə·fak'shən] *n.* A kindly or generous act, especially a gift or endowment.

ben·e·fac·tor [ben'ə·fak'tər] *n.* A person who has given help or money.

ben·e·fice [ben'ə·fis] *n.* *British* A position in the church, and the income attached to it.

be·nef·i·cence [bə·nef'ə·səns] *n.* **1** The doing of good; kindness. **2** A charitable act; gift.

be·nef·i·cent [bə·nef'ə·sənt] *adj.* Bringing about or doing good; charitable.

ben·e·fi·cial [ben'ə·fish'əl] *adj.* Tending to help or benefit; useful or helpful: The treaty was *beneficial* to us because it increased our security.

ben·e·fi·ci·ar·y [ben'ə·fish'ē·er'ē or ben'ə·fish'· ər·ē] *n., pl.* **ben·e·fi·ci·ar·ies 1** A person who receives benefits or advantages. **2** A person entitled to receive an inheritance by a will or money from an insurance policy.

ben·e·fit [ben'ə·fit] *n., v.* **ben·e·fit·ed, ben· e·fit·ing 1** *n.* Something that is helpful; help; advantage: Give me the *benefit* of your advice. **2** *v.* To be helpful or useful to: Schools *benefit* the entire community. **3** *v.* To receive help or benefit; profit: to *benefit* from experience. **4** *n.* A public entertainment to raise money, especially for a charitable cause: The concert was a *benefit* for the flood victims. **5** *n.* (*usually pl.*) Money paid by insurance companies, welfare agencies, etc.: old-age *benefits.*

Ben·e·lux [ben'ə·luks] *n.* The economic union of Belgium, the Netherlands, and Luxembourg.

be·nev·o·lence [bə·nev'ə·ləns] *n.* **1** The desire to do good; kindliness. **2** An act of kindness; a charitable gift.

be·nev·o·lent [bə·nev'ə·lənt] *adj.* Desiring or showing the desire to do good; kindly: a *benevolent* look. — **be·nev'o·lent·ly** *adv.*

Ben·gal [ben·gôl' or ben'gəl] *n.* A former province of NE British India, divided into **East Bengal,** a Province of Pakistan, and **West Bengal,** a State of India.

Bengal, Bay of The part of the Indian Ocean between the east coast of India and the west coast of Burma.

be·night·ed [bi·nī'tid] *adj.* Mentally or morally ignorant; not enlightened.

be·nign [bi·nīn'] *adj.* **1** Pleasant and friendly; kind: a *benign* smile. **2** Not seriously harmful: a *benign* tumor. **3** Favorable to health; mild: a *benign* climate. — **be·nign'ly** *adv.*

be·nig·nant [bi·nig'nənt] *adj.* **1** Kind; gracious. **2** Favorable; mild.

be·nig·ni·ty [bi·nig'nə·tē] *n., pl.* **be·nig·ni· ties 1** Kindliness. **2** A kind action; favor.

ben·i·son [ben'ə·zən] *n.* A blessing.

Ben·ja·min [ben'jə·mən] *n.* **1** In the Bible, the youngest son of Jacob and Rachel. **2** The tribe of Israel descended from him.

bent [bent] **1** Past tense and past participle of BEND. **2** *adj.* Made crooked by bending: a *bent* nail. **3** *adj.* Set in purpose; determined: a man *bent* on success. **4** *n.* A liking or talent: She has a decided *bent* for music.

be·numb [bi·num'] *v.* To make numb; deaden.

ben·zene [ben'zēn or ben·zēn'] *n.* A colorless liquid compound of carbon and hydrogen, got from coal tar and used in making other chemicals or as a solvent.

ben·zine [ben'zēn or ben·zēn'] *n.* A clear, flammable liquid obtained from petroleum, used in dry cleaning and sometimes as a motor fuel.

be·queath [bi·kwēth' or bi·kwēth'] *v.* **1** To leave (property) to another when one dies, by means of a will. **2** To pass on; hand down: to *bequeath* a love for music to one's children.

be·quest [bi·kwest'] *n.* **1** Something bequeathed; legacy. **2** The act of bequeathing.

be·rate [bi·rāt'] *v.* **be·rat·ed, be·rat·ing** To scold sharply and severely.

be·reave [bi·rēv'] *v.* **be·reaved** or **be·reft, be·reav·ing** To deprive, especially by death: War *bereaved* the boy of his parents.

be·reave·ment [bi·rēv'· mənt] *n.* **1** A bereaved condition: lonely in her *bereavement.* **2** Loss by death, as of a relative.

be·reft [bi·reft'] **1** A past tense and past participle of BEREAVE. **2** *adj.* Deprived: refugees *bereft* of homes and property.

be·ret [bə·rā' or ber'ā] *n.* A soft, flat cap without a visor, usually made of wool.

Beret

berg [bûrg] *n.* Another name for ICEBERG.

ber·i·ber·i [ber'ē·ber'ē] *n.* A disabling disease caused by lack of vitamin B in the diet.

Ber·ing Sea [bâr'ing *or* bir'ing] A part of the northern Pacific Ocean between Alaska and Siberia.

Bering Strait The narrow waterway which connects the Bering Sea to the Arctic Ocean.

berke·li·um [bûrk'lē·əm] *n.* An unstable radioactive element.

Ber·lin [bər·lin'] *n.* A city in east central Germany, the former capital of Germany. It is now divided into **East Berlin,** the capital of East Germany, and **West Berlin,** associated with West Germany.

Ber·mu·da [bər·myoo'də] *n.* A group of British islands in the western Atlantic Ocean.

Bermuda shorts Shorts that reach down to just above the knees, worn by men and women.

Bern or **Berne** [bûrn *or* bern] *n.* The capital of Switzerland, in the west central part.

ber·ry [ber'ē] *n., pl.* **ber·ries,** *v.* **ber·ried, ber·ry·ing 1** *n.* A small, pulpy fruit containing many seeds, as the raspberry. **2** *v.* To gather berries. **3** *n.* Any fleshy fruit enclosed in a soft skin, as the banana.

ber·serk [bûr'sûrk *or* bər·sûrk'] *adj.* In a frenzy of wild rage: The wounded elephant was *berserk.*

berth [bûrth] **1** *n.* A space for sleeping on a ship, train, or airplane. **2** *n.* A place in which a ship may anchor or dock. **3** *v.* To put into or provide with a berth. **4** *n.* A job or position: He found a *berth* as a TV announcer. — **give a wide berth to** To keep safely out of the way of: to *give a wide berth to* a passing truck.

ber·yl [ber'əl] *n.* A mineral of great hardness. Some varieties, as the aquamarine and emerald, are used as gems.

be·ryl·li·um [bə·ril'ē·əm] *n.* A lightweight, very hard, gray metallic element. It is used chiefly in making alloys.

be·seech [bi·sēch'] *v.* **be·sought** or **be· seeched, be·seeching** To ask in a very serious way; beg: I *beseech* mercy of the court.

be·seem [bi·sēm'] *v.* To be suitable; be fitting: It ill *beseems* you to act like that.

be·set [bi·set'] *v.* **be·set, be·set·ting 1** To attack on all sides: *beset* by dozens of angry wasps. **2** *adj. use:* *besetting* sin. **3** To hem in; surround: The ship was *beset* by fields of ice.

be·side [bi·sīd'] *prep.* **1** At the side of; near: a chair *beside* the desk. **2** In comparison with: Our roses look poor *beside* yours. **3** Away or apart from: This discussion is *beside* the point. **4** Other than; over and above: I have no money with me *beside* this. — **beside oneself** Out of one's senses, as from anger or fear.

be·sides [bi·sīdz'] **1** *adv.* In addition; as well: He has a scooter and a bicycle *besides.* **2** *prep.* In addition to: He has a bicycle *besides* a scooter. **3** *adv.* Moreover; furthermore: Fresh fruit is good to eat, and *besides* it's good for you.

4 *prep.* Other than; apart from: I care for nothing *besides* this.

be·siege [bi·sēj'] *v.* **be·sieged, be·sieg·ing 1** To seek to capture by surrounding and wearing down resistance: to *besiege* the castle. **2** To crowd around: to *besiege* a movie star. **3** To bother; harass: to *besiege* a teacher with questions. — **be·sieg'er** *n.*

be·smear [bi·smir'] *v.* To smear over; sully.

be·smirch [bi·smûrch'] *v.* To soil; stain.

be·som [bē'zəm] *n.* A bundle of twigs used as a broom.

be·sot·ted [bi·sot'id] *adj.* Dull or stupefied, as from being foolishly in love or drunk.

be·sought [bi·sôt'] Alternative past tense and past participle of BESEECH.

be·spat·ter [bi·spat'ər] *v.* To cover or soil by spattering, as with mud or paint.

be·speak [bi·spēk'] *v.* **be·spoke** [bi·spōk'] or **be·spo·ken** [bi·spō'kən], **be·speak·ing 1** To ask for or order in advance: He had *bespoken* two seats for the play. **2** To show or indicate; signify: Your manners *bespeak* a good upbringing.

Bes·se·mer process [bes'ə·mər] A process of making steel, in which a blast of air is forced through molten iron to burn out carbon and impurities.

best [best] **1** Superlative of GOOD, WELL. **2** *adj.* Superior to all others; most excellent: I want to buy the *best* wrist watch in the store. **3** *adv.* In the most excellent way: Which watch keeps time *best?* **4** *n.* The best person, thing, part, etc.: If this watch is the *best,* I'll buy it. **5** *adj.* Most favorable; advantageous: Noon will be the *best* time to start our trip. **6** *adj.* Most; largest: He spent the *best* part of his lunch hour reading. **7** *adv.* To the greatest degree; most completely: Who is *best* able to finish this math problem? **8** *n.* Finest condition or quality: Be at your *best.* **9** *n.* Utmost: Do your *best.* **10** *v.* To do better than; defeat. — **at best** Under the most favorable circumstances: *At best* we can't get there before two o'clock. — **get the best of** To defeat or outwit. — **make the best of** To do as well as one can in spite of: He *made the best of* his handicap.

bes·tial [bes'chəl *or* best'yəl] *adj.* Having low, animal qualities; brutal; cruel. — **bes·ti·al· i·ty** [bes'chē·al'ə·tē *or* bes'tē·al'ə·tē] *n.*

be·stir [bi·stûr'] *v.* **be·stirred, be·stir·ring** To make (oneself) active: She *bestirred* herself and cleaned the house.

best man A friend chosen by the bridegroom to be his chief attendant at a wedding.

be·stow [bi·stō'] *v.* To present as a gift: to *bestow* money on a charity.

be·strew [bi·stroo'] *v.* **be·strewed, be· strewed** or **be·strewn, be·strew·ing** To spread at random; scatter: a sidewalk *bestrewed* with litter.

---

add, āce, câre, pälm; end, ēqual; it, īce; odd, ōpen, ôrder; took, pool; up, bûrn; ə = a in *above*, e in *sicken*, i in *possible*, o in *melon*, u in *circus*; yōō = u in *fuse*; oil; pout; check; ring; thin; this; zh in *vision*. For ¶ reference, see page 64 · HOW TO

be·stride [bi·strīd′] *v.* **be·strode** [bi·strōd′], **be·strid·den** [bi·strid′(ə)n], **be·strid·ing** To sit or stand with one leg on each side of; straddle: He *bestrode* his horse.

bet [bet] *v.* **bet** (or **bet·ted:** seldom used today), **bet·ting,** *n.* **1** *v.* To offer or agree to give (something specified) to another if one's guess is proved wrong and the other's right: I *bet* him a candy bar my grade would be higher than his. **2** *n.* The mutual agreement made. **3** *n.* Something risked in a bet, as money: My *bet* was a nickel against a dime. **4** *n.* The person, thing, or event on which a bet is made: Which runner is the best *bet* in the 100-yard dash? **5** *v.* To say positively as in a bet: I *bet* he doesn't come.

be·ta [bā′tə *or* bē′tə] *n.* The second letter of the Greek alphabet.

be·take [bi·tāk′] *v.* **be·took, be·tak·en, be·tak·ing** To take (oneself); go: He *betook* himself to bed.

beta particle An electrically charged particle having a mass equal to that of an electron. It is emitted from an atomic nucleus during radioactive decay.

be·ta·tron [bā′tə·tron] *n.* A device that uses a changing magnetic field to accelerate electrons.

Be·tel·geuse [bēt′(ə)l·jōōz] *n.* A very bright, reddish, giant star in the constellation Orion.

Beth·a·ny [beth′ə·nē] *n.* In the New Testament, a village near Jerusalem. It was the home of Lazarus, Martha, and Mary.

be·think [bi·thingk′] *v.* **be·thought** [bi·thôt′], **be·think·ing** To cause (oneself) to think or remember.

Beth·le·hem [beth′lē·əm *or* beth′lə·hem] *n.* The birthplace of Jesus, an ancient town now in Jordan, southwest of Jerusalem.

be·tide [be·tīd′] *v.* **be·tid·ed, be·tid·ing** To happen to or befall: Woe *betide* a lawbreaker.

be·times [bi·tīmz′] *adv.* Early: We'll rise *betimes* and start out.

be·to·ken [bi·tō′kən] *v.* To be a sign of; indicate: Her pale color *betokened* her troubled state.

be·took [bi·tŏŏk′] Past tense of BETAKE.

be·tray [bi·trā′] *v.* **1** To aid an enemy of; be a traitor to: Benedict Arnold *betrayed* his country. **2** To fail, desert, or be unfaithful to: Never *betray* a friend. **3** To give away; disclose: to *betray* secrets to spies. **4** To reveal without meaning to: She *betrayed* nervousness by stammering. **5** To indicate; show: Smoke *betrayed* the presence of another party. — **be·tray′er** *n.*

be·tray·al [bi·trā′əl] *n.* **1** The act of betraying. **2** A being betrayed.

be·troth [bi·trōth′ *or* bi·trôth′] *v.* To promise in marriage: Mary's father *betrothed* her to Jack.

be·troth·al [bi·trō′thəl *or* bi·trôth′əl] *n.* An engagement or mutual promise to marry.

be·trothed [bi·trōthd′ *or* bi·trôtht′] **1** *adj.* Engaged to be married. **2** *n.* A person engaged to be married.

bet·ter[1] [bet′ər] **1** Comparative of GOOD, WELL. **2** *adj.* Superior in quality, excellence, usefulness, operation, etc.: This coat is *better* than that one. **3** *adv.* In a more excellent manner: Which coat will wear *better*? **4** *n.* The better person or thing: John is the *better* of the two runners. **5** *v.* To make better; improve: Clean clothes *bettered* his appearance. **6** *v.* To improve on; surpass: He *bettered* the old record by two seconds. **7** *adj.* Larger; greater: I ate the *better* part of the cake. **8** *adj.* Improved in health: Ted feels *better* today. **9** *adv.* To a larger degree; more thoroughly: Pat is *better* informed than Henry. **10** *adv.* More: We spent *better* than a week traveling. **11** *n.* (*usually pl.*) One's superiors, as in ability or position: Always respect your *betters*. — **better off** In an improved condition. — **get the better of** To defeat. — **had better** Ought to; should: We *had better* leave.

bet·ter[2] [bet′ər] *n.* Another spelling of BETTOR.

bet·ter·ment [bet′ər·mənt] *n.* Improvement.

bet·tor [bet′ər] *n.* A person who bets.

be·tween [bi·twēn′] **1** *prep.* Within the time, space, range, or amount separating two things: *between* New York and Chicago; *between* the chair and the table; *between* noon and one o'clock; *between* sweet and sour. **2** *adv.* In a position or relation between two things: two classes with a study period *between*. **3** *prep.* Connecting: the plane *between* London and Paris. **4** *prep.* Involving: an agreement *between* nations. **5** *prep.* By the joint action of: *Between* them they finished the job. **6** *prep.* In the joint possession of: two dollars *between* them. **7** *prep.* After comparing: We must judge *between* right and wrong. — **between you and me** Confidentially. — **in between** In an intermediate position or condition. ◆ Although *between* is usually limited to two people or things (*between* you and me) and *among* is used for more than two, *between* is often used for more than two objects or persons, especially when they are considered as separate and individual: a choice *between* three candidates. *Among* suggests a group whose members are not necessarily considered individually: He lived *among* the Indians.

be·twixt [bi·twikst′] *prep.* Between: seldom used today. — **betwixt and between** Neither one thing nor the other.

bev·el [bev′əl] *n., v.* **bev·eled** or **bev·elled, bev·el·ing** or **bev·el·ling 1** *n.* A slanted or sloping edge, as on a mirror, chisel, ruler, etc. **2** *v.* To cut on a slant or angle other than a right angle: to *bevel* a printing plate.

beveled edges

bev·er·age [bev′rij *or* bev′·ər·ij] *n.* Any drink: Milk, coffee, and water are *beverages*.

bev·y [bev′ē] *n., pl.* **bev·ies** A group or flock, as of girls or quail.

be·wail [bi·wāl′] *v.* To express sorrow for; mourn; weep over: to *bewail* one's bad luck.

be·ware [bi·wâr′] *v.* **be·wared, be·war·ing**

1 To be careful: to *beware* of the dog. **2** To be on guard against: *Beware* the ides of March.

be·wil·der [bi·wil′dər] *v.* To puzzle and confuse; baffle. **— be·wil′der·ment** *n.*

be·witch [bi·wich′] *v.* **1** To gain power over by the use of magic or a spell. **2** To attract; charm; fascinate. **3** *adj. use: bewitching* ways.

be·yond [bi·yond′] **1** *prep.* On or to the far side of; farther on than: the hill *beyond* the forest. **2** *adv.* Farther on or away; at a distance: the hill lies *beyond.* **3** *prep.* Later than; past: to stay *beyond* noon. **4** *prep.* Outside the reach or scope of: *beyond* help. **5** *prep.* In an amount that surpasses: *beyond* belief. **6** *prep.* More than: *Beyond* that, we know nothing.

bi- A prefix meaning: **1** Twice; doubly; two; having two, as in *bilingual,* having two languages. **2** Once every two, as in *biennial,* once every two years. **3** Twice a, as in *biannual,* twice a year. ◆ *Bi-* in words like *bimonthly* may mean twice a (month, etc.) but more often means once every two (months, etc.). *Semi-* in words like *semimonthly* always means twice a (month, etc.). Use *semi-* for twice a ___, and use *bi-* for once every two ___.

Bi The symbol for the element BISMUTH.

bi·an·nu·al [bī·an′yoo·əl] *adj.* Occurring twice a year; semiannual. **— bi·an′nu·al·ly** *adv.* ◆ Notice that *biannual* means twice a year, four times as often as *biennial,* once every two years.

bi·as [bī′əs] *n., pl.* **bi·as·es,** *v.* **bi·ased** or **bi·assed, bi·as·ing** or **bi·as·sing 1** *n.* A line slanting across the weave of a fabric. **2** *n.* A leaning of the mind for or against a person or thing; prejudice. **3** *v.* To prejudice: A series of lies *biased* the jury. **4** *adj. use:* a *biased* judge. **— on the bias** On a slanting line across a fabric: The material must be cut *on the bias.* ◆ See PREJUDICE.

Cutting on the bias

bib [bib] *n.* **1** A cloth tied under a child's chin at meals to protect the clothing. **2** The upper front part of an apron or of overalls.

Bi·ble [bī′bəl] *n.* **1** The collection of writings which make up the Old Testament and the New Testament, held sacred in Christianity. **2** The Old Testament, held sacred in Judaism. **3** The sacred book or writings of any religion. ◆ *Bible* comes originally from the Greek word for *book* which

Bib

came from a word for *papyrus.* The ancient Greeks wrote on a kind of paper made from papyrus. *Bibliography* comes from the same root as *Bible* plus a Greek word meaning *a writing about.*

Bib·li·cal [bib′li·kəl] *adj.* (*sometimes written* **biblical**) Of or having to do with the Bible.

bib·li·o·graph·i·cal [bib′lē·ə·graf′ə·kəl] *adj.* Of or having to do with bibliography.

bib·li·og·ra·phy [bib′lē·og′rə·fē] *n., pl.* **bib·li·og·ra·phies 1** A list of the writings of an author, or of the writings about a certain subject. **2** The description and history of writings or books, including details, as of editions, dates, and typography. ◆ See BIBLE.

bi·cam·er·al [bī·kam′ər·əl] *adj.* Consisting of two chambers, houses, or branches: The U.S. Congress is a *bicameral* legislative body made up of the Senate and the House of Representatives.

bi·car·bo·nate of soda [bī·kär′bə·nit] Another name for SODIUM BICARBONATE. It is used in cooking and as a medicine.

bi·ceps [bī′seps] *n., pl.* **bi·ceps** A large muscle in the front part of the arm above the elbow.

bick·er [bik′ər] *v.* To argue in a mean way over a matter of little importance.

bi·cus·pid [bī·kus′pid] *n.* A tooth with two points on its biting surface. Adults have eight, two on each side of the upper and lower jaws.

bi·cy·cle [bī′sik·əl] *n., v.* **bi·cy·cled, bi·cy·cling 1** *n.* A vehicle with two large wheels, one behind the other. A rider moves it by foot pedals and steers with handlebars. **2** *v.* To ride a bicycle. **— bi′cy·clist** *n.*

bid [bid] *n., v.* **bade** or **bid, bid·den** or **bid, bid·ding 1** *n.* An offer to pay or accept a price: He made a number of *bids* at the auction. **2** *v.* To make an offer of (a price): He *bid* $20 for an antique sofa. **3** *n.* The amount offered: a $20 *bid.* **4** *v.* In some card games, to declare (the amount one proposes to win or make under specified conditions). **5** *n.* In some card games, the amount proposed. **6** *n.* An effort to obtain: He made a *bid* for the governorship. **7** *v.* To command; order: Do as I *bid* you. **8** *v.* To invite: Her mother *bade* her come to dinner. **9** *v.* To tell, as a greeting or farewell: I *bid* you good night. **— bid fair** To seem likely.

bid·der [bid′ər] *n.* A person who makes a bid, as at an auction or in a card game.

bid·ding [bid′ing] *n.* **1** Command; order: At the dentist's *bidding,* he opened his mouth. **2** Invitation: At her *bidding* I accepted a cooky. **3** The making of a bid or bids, as at an auction or in a card game.

bide [bīd] *v.* **bid·ed** or **bode, bid·ed, bid·ing** To wait; stay: seldom used today except in the phrase **bide one's time,** to wait for the best opportunity.

bi·en·ni·al [bī·en′ē·əl] **1** *adj.* Occurring every

add, āce, câre, pälm; end, ēqual; it, īce; odd, ōpen, ôrder; took, pool; up, bûrn;
ə = a in *above,* e in *sicken,* i in *possible,* o in *melon,* u in *circus;* yoo = u in *fuse;* oil; pout;
check; ring; thin; this; zh in *vision.* For ¶ reference, see page 64 · HOW TO

second year. **2** *n.* An event occurring every second year. **3** *adj.* Lasting or living for two years. **4** *n.* A plant that produces flowers and fruit in its second year, and then dies. **— bi·en'·ni·al·ly** *adv.* ◆ See BIANNUAL.

bier [bir] *n.* A framework on which a corpse or coffin is placed or carried to the grave.

bi·fo·cal [bī·fō'kəl] **1** *adj.* Having one part for seeing objects close up, and one for distant objects: said of eyeglass lenses. **2** *n.* (*pl.*) A pair of eyeglasses with bifocal lenses.

Bifocals

big [big] **big·ger, big·gest 1** *adj.* Of great size, amount, etc.; large: a *big* car. **2** *adj.* Full of self-importance; pompous: a *big* talker. **3** *adv. informal* Self-importantly; pompously: He talked *big.* **4** *adj.* Important; prominent: a *big* event. **5** *adj.* Loud: a *big* voice. **— big'ness** *n.*

big·a·my [big'ə·mē] *n.* The criminal act of marrying someone while legally married to another person. **— big'a·mist** *n.*

big·horn [big'hôrn] *n., pl.* **big·horns** or **big·horn** A large wild sheep of the Rocky Mountains, remarkable for its big, downward-curving horns.

bight [bīt] *n.* **1** A loop in a rope or cable. **2** A bend or curve, as in a shoreline. **3** A bay.

big·ot [big'ət] *n.* A person who is narrow-minded and intolerant in his attitudes, especially toward religion, politics, or race.

big·ot·ed [big'ət·id] *adj.* Having the characteristics of a bigot; narrow-minded; intolerant.

big·ot·ry [big'ə·trē] *n., pl.* **big·ot·ries** An attitude, belief, or action characteristic of a bigot.

big·wig [big'wig'] *n. informal* A person of importance.

bike [bīk] *n., v.* **biked, bik·ing** *informal* **1** *n.* A bicycle. **2** *v.* To ride a bicycle.

bi·ki·ni [bi·kē'nē] *n., pl.* **bi·ki·nis** A very brief bathing suit.

bi·lat·er·al [bī·lat'ər·əl] *adj.* **1** Of or having two sides. **2** Arranged on opposite sides of an axis, often symmetrically. **3** Affecting two sides: a *bilateral* treaty. **— bi·lat'er·al·ly** *adv.* **— bi·lat'er·al·ness** *n.*

bile [bīl] *n.* A bitter yellow or greenish liquid secreted by the liver. It aids digestion.

bilge [bilj] *n.* **1** A ship's bottom, inside or out. **2** The bulge of a barrel. **3** Bilge water. **4** *slang* Nonsense.

bilge water Foul, dirty water that collects in the bilge of a ship.

bi·lin·gual [bī·ling'gwəl] *adj.* **1** Written or expressed in two languages. **2** Able to speak two languages: a *bilingual* person. **— bi·lin'gual·ism** *n.* **— bi·lin'gual·ly** *adv.*

bil·ious [bil'yəs] *adj.* **1** Having or caused by trouble with the bile or liver: a *bilious* headache. **2** Ill-tempered; peevish.

bilk [bilk] *v.* To cheat, especially by evading payment of money owed.

bill¹ [bil] **1** *n.* A statement of money owed for work done or things supplied. **2** *v.* To send such a statement to: The store *billed* me for my purchases. **3** *n.* A list of items. **4** *n.* A piece of paper money: a dollar *bill.* **5** *n.* A proposed law offered to a legislative body. **6** *n.* A printed advertisement or notice. **7** *v.* To advertise by such bills. **8** *n.* The program of a theatrical performance, or the performance itself. **— fill the bill** To do or be what is wanted.

Bill

bill² [bil] **1** *n.* The horny mouth parts of a bird; beak. **2** *v.* To join beaks, as doves. **— bill and coo** To caress and speak in a loving way.

bill·board [bil'bôrd'] *n.* A large outdoor panel for notices or advertisements.

bil·let¹ [bil'it] *n.* **1** A short, thick stick, as of firewood. **2** A bar of iron or steel.

bil·let² [bil'it] **1** *n.* An order to lodge troops, as in private homes. **2** *n.* A lodging assigned to a person. **3** *v.* To order lodging for.

bil·let-doux [bil'ē·dōō'] *n., pl.* **bil·lets-doux** [bil'ē·dōōz'] A love letter.

bill·fold [bil'fōld'] *n.* A wallet or pocketbook for holding paper money, papers, etc.

bil·liards [bil'yərdz] *n.pl.* A game in which hard balls are hit by long, tapering rods called cues. Billiards is played on an oblong, cloth-covered table with cushioned edges.

Billiards

bil·lion [bil'yən] *n., adj.* **1** In the U.S., a thousand million, written as 1,000,000,000. **2** In Great Britain, a million million, written as 1,000,000,000,000.

bill of fare A list of the dishes provided at a meal; menu.

Bill of Rights The first ten amendments to the U.S. Constitution, guaranteeing certain rights to the people.

bill of sale A paper transferring ownership of something from seller to buyer.

bil·low [bil'ō] **1** *n.* A great wave or swell of the sea. **2** *n.* Anything that swells or surges like a wave: Great *billows* of sound came from the radio. **3** *v.* To rise or roll in waves; surge; swell. **— bil'low·y** *adj.*

bil·ly [bil'ē] *n., pl.* **bil·lies** A short club, such as those carried by some policemen.

billy goat *informal* A male goat.

bi·month·ly [bī·munth'lē] *adj., adv., n., pl.* **bi·month·lies 1** *adj.* Occurring every second month. **2** *adv.* Every second month. **3** *adj.* Occurring twice a month. **4** *adv.* Twice a month. **5** *n.* A bimonthly publication. ◆ See BI-.

bin [bin] *n.* An enclosed storage space for such things as grain or coal.

bi·na·ry [bī′nər·ē] *adj.* Made up of or having to do with two parts or elements: A *binary* number system uses two as a base and therefore has two numerals, 0 and 1.

bind [bīnd] *v.* **bound, bind·ing** **1** To tie or fasten, as with a band or cord. **2** To bandage. **3** To make stick together: gravel *bound* by tar. **4** To unite or hold together, as by love, duty, etc. **5** To force, as by legal or moral authority: He is *bound* by law to testify. **6** To fasten in a cover, as a book. **7** To cover the edge of, as with tape, for strength or decoration. **8** To constipate.

bind·er [bīn′dər] *n.* **1** A person who binds books. **2** Anything used to bind or tie, as a cord, or to hold together, as cement. **3** A cover in which sheets of paper may be fastened. **4** A machine that cuts and ties grain.

bind·er·y [bīn′dər·ē] *n.,* *pl.* **bind·er·ies** A place where books are bound.

bind·ing [bīn′ding] **1** *n.* The act of tying or joining. **2** *n.* Anything that binds; binder. **3** *adj.* Having the force to bind or oblige: a *binding* agreement. **4** *n.* The cover holding together and enclosing the pages of a book. **5** *n.* A strip sewed over an edge for protection.

bind·weed [bīnd′wēd′] *n.* A twining plant with trumpet-shaped flowers.

Binding of a book

bin·na·cle [bin′ə·kəl] *n.* A stand or case for a ship's compass, near the steering wheel.

bin·oc·u·lar [bə·nok′yə·lər] **1** *adj.* Having to do with, using, or used by both eyes at once. **2** *n.(pl.)* Two short telescopes fastened together, for seeing distant objects with both eyes. Field glasses are binoculars.

Binoculars

bi·no·mi·al [bī·nō′mē·əl] *n.* **1** In algebra, an expression made up of two terms joined by a plus or minus sign, as $a + b$ or $x - y$. **2** In biology, a name made up of two terms, one indicating the genus, the other indicating the species of some plant or animal, as *Homo sapiens*, modern man.

bi·o·chem·is·try [bī′ō·kem′is·trē] *n.* The science that studies the chemical processes that take place in living things, plant and animal.

bi·og·ra·pher [bī·og′rə·fər] *n.* A writer of biography.

bi·o·graph·i·cal [bī′ə·graf′i·kəl] *adj.* **1** Of or having to do with a person's life. **2** Of or having to do with biography.

bi·og·ra·phy [bī·og′rə·fē] *n.,* *pl.* **bi·og·ra·phies** An account of a person's life.

bi·o·log·i·cal [bī′ə·loj′i·kəl] *adj.* Of or having to do with biology. **— bi′o·log′i·cal·ly** *adv.*

biological magnification The gathering of huge amounts of a harmful substance such as DDT in a large animal. All of it in the plants and animals eaten in a food chain finally funnels into the top animal.

bi·ol·o·gy [bī·ol′ə·jē] *n.* The science of life and of the ways in which living things grow, develop, and reproduce. Its two chief divisions are zoology and botany. **— bi·ol′o·gist** *n.* ◆ This word comes from two Greek words meaning *study of life.*

bi·par·ti·san [bī·pär′tə·zən] *adj.* Of or supported by two parties: a *bipartisan* committee.

bi·ped [bī′ped] *n.* An animal having two feet.

bi·plane [bī′plān′] *n.* A type of airplane having two wings, one above the other.

Biplane

birch [bûrch] **1** *n.* A tree with thin bark that may be peeled off easily. Its wood is hard and is used in making furniture and other articles. **2** *n.* A rod from this tree, used as a whip. **3** *v.* To whip with a birch rod.

bird [bûrd] *n.* **1** A warm-blooded, feathered animal with two feet and wings. **2** A rounded piece of cork with a crown of feathers, used in badminton. **3** *slang* A person, especially one who is peculiar or remarkable. ◆ In Old English, this word was pronounced [brid] and spelled *bridd*; later on people began to pronounce it [bird] and the word came to be spelled *bird.*

bird·bath [bûrd′bath′] *n.* A shallow basin of water on a stand for birds to bathe in.

bird of paradise A bird of New Guinea noted for the brilliant colors of its feathers.

bird of prey Any of various birds, as the eagle or vulture, that eat the flesh of other animals.

bird's-eye [bûrdz′ī′] *adj.* **1** Marked with spots like birds' eyes. **2** Seen from above or afar.

bird watcher A person who observes or identifies wild birds in their natural surroundings as a hobby. **— bird watching**

bi·ret·ta [bi·ret′ə] *n.* A stiff, square cap worn by Roman Catholic clergymen.

Bir·ming·ham *n.* **1** [bûr′ming·əm] A city of central England. **2** [bûr′ming·ham] A manufacturing city in north central Alabama.

birth [bûrth] *n.* **1** The coming out from its mother's body of a new person or animal. **2** Beginning; origin: the *birth* of an idea. **3** Ancestry or descent: a man of humble *birth.* **— give birth to** **1** To bear: She *gave birth to* twins. **2** To create or originate, as an idea.

birth·day [bûrth′dā′] *n.* The day of one's birth or its anniversary.

birth·mark [bûrth′märk′] *n.* A mark or spot existing on the body from birth.

birth·place [bûrth′plās′] *n.* **1** Place of a

B

person's birth. **2** Place where something originates: New Orleans is the *birthplace* of jazz.

birth rate The number of births in proportion to a given number of persons in a certain area or group during a given time, commonly the number of births per thousand persons per year.

birth·right [bûrth′rīt′] *n.* A privilege or right a person has because of his birth.

birth·stone [bûrth′stōn′] *n.* A jewel identified with a particular month of the year and thought to bring good luck when worn by a person whose birthday falls in that month.

Bis·cay [bis′kā], **Bay of** A large, open bay of the Atlantic west of France and north of Spain.

bis·cuit [bis′kit] *n., pl.* **bis·cuits** or **bis·cuit** **1** A kind of bread baked in small cakes, raised with baking powder or soda. **2** The British word for a cracker.

bi·sect [bī·sekt′] *v.* To cut into two parts, especially of equal size.

bi·sec·tor [bī·sek′tər] *n.* **1** Something that bisects. **2** A line that divides an angle or a line segment into two equal parts.

bish·op [bish′əp] *n.* **1** A priest or minister of high position, usually in charge of a diocese or church district. **2** A piece that moves diagonally in the game of chess.

The red line bisects the angle.

bish·op·ric [bish′əp·rik] *n.* **1** The diocese of a bishop. **2** The position or rank of bishop.

Bis·marck [biz′märk] *n.* The capital of North Dakota, in the south central part.

bis·muth [biz′məth] *n.* A shiny, brittle, reddish white metallic element. It is used in making alloys and in medicine.

bi·son [bī′sən *or* bī′zən] *n., pl.* **bi·son** A large wild animal related to the ox, having a big, shaggy head, short horns, and a humped back. The North American bison is called a buffalo.

Bison, about 9 ft. long

bit[1] [bit] *n.* **1** A metal part of a bridle that fits in a horse's mouth, used to control its movements. **2** A tool for boring or drilling, used with a brace or drill. **3** The cutting part of a tool, as the blade of an ax. **4** That part of a key that enters a lock and moves the bolt.

bit[2] [bit] **1** *n.* A small quantity; a little: a *bit* of cake. **2** *n.* A short time: Wait a *bit.* **3** *n.* A small part, as in a play or movie. **4** *adj.* Small, unimportant: a *bit* part in a movie. **5** *n.* Twelve and one-half cents, used only in expressions like **two bits,** twenty-five cents. **— a bit** To a certain extent; somewhat: a *bit* tired.

bit[3] [bit] The past tense and a past participle of BITE.

bitch [bich] *n.* A female dog, fox, coyote, etc.

bite [bīt] *v.* **bit** [bit], **bit·ten** or **bit, bit·ing,** *n.* **1** *v.* To seize, cut, or wound with the teeth: *Bite* the orange; The dog *bites.* **2** *n.* The act of biting. **3** *n.* A wound inflicted by biting. **4** *v.* To sting, or have the effect of stinging: Mustard *bites* the tongue. **5** *n.* A painful sensation; sting: mosquito *bites.* **6** *v.* To take firm hold of; grip: The anchor *bit* the ground. **7** *v.* To take a bait, as fish. **8** *n.* A small bit of food; mouthful. **9** *n.* A light meal; snack.

bit·ing [bī′ting] *adj.* **1** Sharp; stinging: *biting* weather. **2** Sarcastic. **— bit′ing·ly** *adv.*

bit·ten [bit′(ə)n] Past participle of BITE.

bit·ter [bit′ər] *adj.* **1** Having a sharp, disagreeable taste. **2** Unpleasant to the mind: the *bitter* truth. **3** Painful to body or mind: a *bitter* wind. **4** Feeling or showing intense dislike: a *bitter* enemy. **5** Stinging; sharp: *bitter* criticism. **— bit′ter·ly** *adv.* **— bit′ter·ness** *n.*

bit·tern [bit′ərn] *n.* A long-legged bird related to the heron. It lives in marshy places and has a harsh, deep cry.

bit·ter·sweet [bit′ər·swēt′] **1** *n.* A poisonous plant with purple flowers and red berries whose taste is first bitter, then sweet. **2** *n.* A vine with green flowers and orange seedcases that open to show red seeds. **3** *adj.* Bitter and sweet. **4** *adj.* Pleasant and unpleasant.

bi·tu·men [bi·t(y)ōō′mən] *n.* Any of various mixtures of hydrocarbons, as naphtha, tar, or asphalt.

bi·tu·mi·nous coal [bi·t(y)ōō′mə·nəs] A soft coal containing bitumen but low in carbon. It burns with a yellow flame and much smoke.

bi·valve [bī′valv′] *n.* A mollusk having a soft body enclosed in two half shells hinged to open and close like doors. Clams are bivalves.

biv·ou·ac [biv′ōō·ak *or* biv′wak] *n., v.* **biv·ou·acked, biv·ou·ack·ing 1** *n.* A temporary camp, usually without shelter, especially for soldiers. **2** *v.* To camp out in a bivouac.

bi·week·ly [bī·wēk′lē] *adj., adv., n., pl.* **bi·week·lies 1** *adj.* Occurring once every two weeks. **2** *adv.* Once in two weeks. **3** *adj., adv.* Semiweekly. **4** *n.* A biweekly publication. ◆ See BI-.

bi·zarre [bi·zär′] *adj.* Very different from the usual style or manner; odd; fantastic.

blab [blab] *v.* **blabbed, blab·bing 1** To give away by talking too freely: to *blab* secrets. **2** To go on and on talking foolishly.

black [blak] **1** *n.* The opposite of white; the darkest of all colors. Black is the color of the printing on this page. **2** *adj.* Having the color black. **3** *adj.* Without light; in total darkness. **4** *v.* To make black; blacken. **5** *adj.* Gloomy; dismal: a *black* future. **6** *adj.* Angry; threatening: *black* looks. **7** *adj.* Evil; wicked: a *black* heart. **8** *v.* To put on blacking. **— black out 1** To lose vision or consciousness temporarily. **2** To put out or cover all lights, as during an air raid. **— black′ish** *adj.* **— black′ness** *n.*

Black [blak] **1** *n.* (also written **black**) A member of an ethnic division of man indigenous to Africa and now widespread; Negro. **2** *n.* Those desirable traits or qualities thought of as characteristic of Blacks or of their culture: *Black* is beautiful. **3** *adj.* (*usually written* **black**) Of, being, or having to do with a Black or Blacks: *black* history: Newark's *black* Mayor; Liberia is a *black* republic.

black-and-blue [blak′ən·blōō′] *adj.* Discolored by a bruise.

black·ball [blak′bôl′] **1** *v.* To vote against, especially to vote to keep out, as from a club. **2** *n.* A vote against; formerly, a small black ball placed in a ballot box to indicate such a vote.

black·ber·ry [blak′ber′ē] *n.*, *pl.* **black·ber·ries 1** The small, edible, black or dark purple fruit of certain prickly shrubs. **2** Any of the shrubs producing it.

black·bird [blak′bûrd′] *n.* **1** A common European thrush, the male of which is black with a yellow bill. **2** Any of several North American birds that have black or dark feathers.

black·board [blak′bôrd′] *n.* A dark surface for drawing and writing on with chalk.

Black Death A very destructive plague that was widespread in Europe and Asia during the 14th century.

black·en [blak′ən] *v.* **1** To make or become black or dark. **2** To hurt by evil talk or gossip.

black eye The flesh around an eye discolored by a bruise.

black-eyed Su·san [blak′īd′ sōō′z(ə)n] A North American plant that has yellow flowers with dark centers. It resembles the daisy.

black·guard [blag′ərd *or* blag′ärd] *n.* A person who has no principles; scoundrel; villain.

black·head [blak′hed′] *n.* A small piece of dried, fatty matter clogging a pore of the skin.

black·ing [blak′ing] *n.* A polish used to blacken or shine shoes, stoves, etc.

black·jack [blak′jak′] **1** *n.* A very short club with a flexible handle, used as a weapon. **2** *v.* To strike with a blackjack. **3** *n.* A large drinking cup. **4** *n.* A card game in which players try to get cards with a value under 22 and closer to 21 than the dealer's.

black·list [blak′list′] **1** *n.* A list of persons or organizations regarded as bad or dangerous. **2** *v.* To place on a blacklist.

black·mail [blak′māl′] **1** *v.* To get money or a service from, by threatening to tell something damaging. **2** *n.* The act of threatening for this purpose. **3** *n.* The money or service demanded. **— black′mail′er** *n.*

black market Illegal trade that violates regulations such as rationing or price controls.

black·out [blak′out′] *n.* **1** The putting out or covering of all lights, especially during an air raid. **2** Temporary unconsciousness or blindness due to lack of oxygen in the brain. It

may be caused by too much exertion or by sudden changes of speed or direction in an aircraft. **3** A loss of memory. **4** A ban, as on news.

Black Sea A large inland sea north of Turkey and south of the Soviet Union.

black sheep A person regarded as a disgrace by his family or group: He was the *black sheep* of an illustrious family.

black·smith [blak′smith′] *n.* **1** A person who works with iron by heating it in a forge and then hammering it into shape. **2** A person who makes, fits, and puts on horseshoes.

black·snake [blak′snāk′] *n.* **1** A harmless, dark-colored snake of the eastern U.S. **2** A heavy whip of braided leather or rawhide.

Blacksmith

black·thorn [blak′thôrn′] *n.* **1** A thorny European shrub having white flowers and a small fruit that looks like a plum and is called a sloe. **2** A cane made from its wood.

black widow A poisonous female spider, black with red markings on her belly, so named because she has the habit of eating her mate.

blad·der [blad′ər] *n.* **1** A baglike organ in the body that collects urine from the kidneys. **2** A bag, usually of rubber, that fits inside a football, basketball, etc., and holds the air.

blade [blād] *n.* **1** The flat, sharp-edged part of a knife, hoe, saw, saber, etc. **2** The thin, flat part of something: the *blade* of an oar. **3** The leaf of grasses or grains. **4** A sword. **5** A dashing young man. **6** The broad, flat part of a leaf or petal.

Blake [blāk], **William,** 1757–1827, English poet, artist, and mystic.

blam·a·ble [blā′mə·bəl] *adj.* Deserving blame.

blame [blām] *v.* **blamed, blam·ing,** *n.* **1** *v.* To hold responsible; accuse: I *blame* you for this mistake. **2** *n.* Responsibility: You deserve the *blame* for this mistake. **3** *v.* To find fault with: Don't *blame* me if your plan fails. **4** *n.* The act of finding fault. **— be to blame** To deserve to be criticized.

blame·less [blām′lis] *adj.* Not deserving blame; innocent. **— blame′less·ly** *adv.*

blanch [blanch] *v.* **1** To remove the color from; bleach: to *blanch* linen. **2** To turn pale. **3** To remove the skin of by scalding.

bland [bland] *adj.* **1** Gentle and pleasant: a *bland* smile. **2** Not irritating; mild: a *bland* diet. **— bland′ly** *adv.* **— bland′ness** *n.*

add, āce, câre, pälm; end, ēqual; it, īce; odd, ōpen, ôrder; tŏŏk, pōōl; up, bûrn;
ə = a in *above*, e in *sicken*, i in *possible*, o in *melon*, u in *circus*; yōō = u in *fuse*; oil; pout;
check; ring; thin; this; zh in *vision*. For ¶ reference, see page 64 · HOW TO

blan·dish·ment [blan′dish·mənt] *n.* Flattering speech or action; coaxing.

blank [blangk] **1** *adj.* Free from writing or printing: a *blank* page. **2** *adj.* Not completed or filled out: a *blank* check. **3** *n.* A space left empty in a printed form, to be filled in. **4** *n.* A paper or form with such spaces. **5** *adj.* Without expression; vacant: a *blank* stare. **6** *adj.* Without variety or interest: a *blank* prospect. **7** *adj.* Empty or void: a *blank* mind. **8** *n.* An empty space; void. **9** *n.* A cartridge loaded with powder but without a bullet. — **blank′ly** *adv.* — **blank′ness** *n.*

An application blank

blan·ket [blang′kit] **1** *n.* A large piece of soft, warm cloth, mainly used as a covering in bed. **2** *n.* Anything that covers, conceals, or protects: a *blanket* of fog. **3** *v.* To cover with or as if with a blanket: Snow *blanketed* the city. **4** *adj.* Covering many things: He issued a *blanket* order.

blank verse Poetry that is not rhymed, each line having five iambic feet.

blare [blâr] *v.* **blared, blar·ing,** *n.* **1** *v.* To sound loudly, as a trumpet. **2** *n.* A loud, brassy sound: the *blare* of a trumpet. **3** *v.* To speak loudly.

blar·ney [blär′nē] *n., v.* **blar·neyed, blar·ney·ing 1** *n.* Flattery. **2** *v.* To coax or wheedle. ◆ This word comes from *Blarney Stone*, a stone in a castle in Blarney, Ireland, that people kiss to get skill in flattery.

bla·sé [blä·zā′ *or* blä′zā] *adj.* Wearied or bored, as from too much pleasure.

blas·pheme [blas·fēm′] *v.* **blas·phemed, blas·phem·ing** To speak with a lack of respect for (God or sacred things). — **blas·phem′er** *n.*

blas·phe·mous [blas′fə·məs] *adj.* Showing lack of respect for God or sacred things.

blas·phe·my [blas′fə·mē] *n., pl.* **blas·phe·mies** Words or actions showing a lack of respect for God or sacred things.

blast [blast] **1** *n.* A strong wind or sudden rush of air. **2** *n.* A strong current of air, steam, etc., as in a furnace or from a tool for grinding, cleaning, etc. **3** *n.* A loud, sudden sound, as of a trumpet. **4** *n.* An explosion, as of dynamite. **5** *n.* The charge of dynamite or other explosive used. **6** *v.* To blow up or blow apart with an explosive. **7** *v.* To cause to wither or shrivel; blight; ruin: Age *blasted* her hopes. — **at full blast** In full operation or at top speed. — **blast off** To take off by means of a rocket.

blast furnace A furnace for separating iron from its ores, in which blasts of air blown through the fuel from the bottom make a very high heat.

bla·tant [blā′tənt] *adj.* **1** Loud or noisy in an offensive way. **2** Impossible to overlook: *blatant* stupidity. — **bla′tant·ly** *adv.*

blaze[1] [blāz] *n., v.* **blazed, blaz·ing 1** *n.* A bright, glowing flame; fire. **2** *v.* To burn with a bright, glowing flame. **3** *n.* A sudden outburst: a *blaze* of anger. **4** *v.* To burn, as with feeling: His eyes *blazed*. **5** *n.* Brightness; glow: the *blaze* of many lights. **6** *v.* To shine; glow: The painting *blazed* with color.

blaze[2] [blāz] *n., v.* **blazed, blaz·ing 1** *n.* A white spot on the face of a horse or other animal. **2** *n.* A mark chipped on a tree to indicate a trail. **3** *v.* To make such a mark. **4** *v.* To indicate, as a trail, by such marks.

blaze[3] [blāz] *v.* **blazed, blaz·ing** To make known: It was *blazed* on billboards everywhere.

blaz·er [blā′zər] *n.* A light sport jacket in solid colors or bright stripes.

bla·zon [blā′zən] **1** *v.* To display publicly; proclaim: A sign *blazoned* the names of the actors. **2** *v.* To describe or picture (a coat of arms) in its proper form. **3** *n.* A coat of arms.

bldg. Abbreviation of BUILDING.

bleach [blēch] **1** *v.* To make or become colorless or white by the use of chemicals or by the sun's action. **2** *n.* A fluid or powder used for bleaching.

bleach·ers [blē′chərz] *n.pl.* A section of seats, usually without a roof, for spectators at outdoor sports events.

Bleachers

bleak [blēk] *adj.* **1** Exposed to wind and weather; bare: *bleak* hills. **2** Cold and cutting: *bleak* winds. **3** Gloomy; dismal. — **bleak′ly** *adv.* — **bleak′ness** *n.*

blear·y [blir′ē] *adj.* **blear·i·er, blear·i·est 1** Made dim by or as if by tears: *bleary* eyes. **2** Blurred; dimmed; indistinct: *bleary* images.

bleat [blēt] **1** *v.* To utter the cry of a sheep, goat, or calf. **2** *v.* To speak in a voice like this. **3** *n.* Such a cry or sound.

bleed [blēd] *v.* **bled** [bled], **bleed·ing 1** To lose or shed blood. **2** To draw blood from: Doctors used to *bleed* their patients. **3** To exude sap or other fluid. **4** To feel great grief for: My heart *bleeds* for those poor children.

blem·ish [blem′ish] **1** *n.* A mark or defect, especially of the skin. **2** *n.* A moral fault or defect. **3** *v.* To spoil or mar the perfection of.

blench [blench] *v.* To shrink back; flinch.

blend [blend] *v.* **blend·ed** (or **blent:** seldom used today), **blend·ing,** *n.* **1** *v.* To combine or mix so that the separate parts cannot be distinguished: to *blend* two colors: These six kinds of tea *blend* well. **2** *v.* To pass or shade into each other, as the sky and sea at the horizon. **3** *n.* The result of blending; mixture. **4** *v.* To harmonize: Your tie *blends* well with your suit.

bless [bles] *v.* **blessed** or **blest, bless·ing 1** To bring happiness or prosperity to: The Lord *bless* thee. **2** To ask God's favor for: The priest *blessed* the congregation. **3** To make holy;

B

consecrate: This food has been *blessed*. **4** To endow: *blessed* with a great talent. **5** To glorify: *Bless* the Lord. **6** To guard; protect: used as an exclamation: *Bless* me!

bless·ed [bles′id *or* blest] *adj.* **1** Holy; sacred. **2** Blissful; happy. **— bless′ed·ness** *n.*

bless·ing [bles′ing] *n.* **1** A prayer or request for God's favor on someone or something. **2** Approval or favor: Give me your *blessing*. **3** Something that gives happiness or satisfaction: Her great talent was a *blessing* for us all.

blest [blest] An alternative past tense and past participle of BLESS.

blew [blōō] Past tense of BLOW¹ and BLOW³.

blight [blīt] **1** *n.* Any disease that harms or destroys plants. **2** *n.* Anything that harms or destroys: Crime is a *blight* on our nation. **3** *v.* To ruin, harm, or destroy: to *blight* one's prospects of success.

blimp [blimp] *n. informal* A small dirigible whose shape is not formed by a rigid framework.

blind [blīnd] **1** *adj.* Unable to see. **2** *v.* To make blind. **3** *n.* A thing to shut out light or hinder seeing, as a shutter or window shade. **4** *adj.* Done with instruments alone: *blind* flying. **5** *adj.* Hidden: a *blind* driveway. **6** *adj.* Lacking the ability to see or know the truth: to be *blind* to a person's faults. **7** *v.* To make unable to see or know the truth about someone or something: Her beauty *blinded* him to her selfishness. **8** *n.* A thing or person intended to deceive or mislead. **9** *adj.* Closed at one end: a *blind* alley. **10** *adj.* Having no opening or outlet: a *blind* wall. **— blind′ly** *adv.* **— blind′ness** *n.*

blind·er [blīn′dər] *n.* A flap, one of a pair, on the side of a horse's bridle, used to prevent the horse from looking sideways.

blind·fold [blīnd′fōld′] **1** *v.* To cover the eyes of with a cloth. **2** *adj.* Having the eyes so covered. **3** *n.* A cloth that is used to cover the eyes.

blind spot A small spot at the back of the eyeball where the optic nerve enters. It is insensitive to light.

blink [blingk] **1** *v.* To wink rapidly. **2** *n.* A blinking; wink. **3** *v.* To flash on and off. **4** *n.* A brief flash of light. **5** *v.* To ignore: You can't *blink* at that evidence! **— on the blink** *informal* Not working or not working right: The radio's *on the blink*.

blink·er [blingk′ər] *n.* A light that blinks, as in warning or for sending messages.

blip [blip] *n.* One of the luminous signals recorded on a radar screen.

bliss [blis] *n.* Great happiness or joy.

bliss·ful [blis′fəl] *adj.* Full of bliss. **— bliss′·ful·ly** *adv.*

blis·ter [blis′tər] **1** *n.* A small swelling on the skin full of watery matter. Blisters often result from burning or from rubbing. **2** *n.* A similar swelling on a plant, on steel, or on a painted surface. **3** *v.* To raise a blister or blisters on: The tight shoe *blistered* my heel. **4** *v.* To develop a blister or blisters.

blithe [blīth] *adj.* Joyous; gay; cheerful. **— blithe′ly** *adv.*

blitz [blits] *informal* **1** *n.* A sudden, violent attack. **2** *v.* To attack suddenly and overwhelmingly. ◆ This word comes from a German word, *Blitzkrieg*, meaning *lightning war*.

bliz·zard [bliz′ərd] *n.* A heavy snowstorm accompanied by strong, freezing wind.

bloat [blōt] *v.* **1** To puff up; swell. **2** *adj. use:* a *bloated* belly.

blob [blob] *n.* A lump or drop of soft or sticky matter: a *blob* of paint.

bloc [blok] *n.* A group, as of nations, united in promoting certain interests.

block [blok] **1** *n.* A solid piece of wood, metal, etc., usually with one or more flat surfaces. **2** *n.* A stand from which articles are sold at auction. **3** *n.* A support or form on which something is shaped or displayed: a hat *block*. **4** *v.* To shape with a block: to *block* a hat. **5** *n.* A set or section, as of tickets, seats, etc., considered as a unit. **6** *n. U.S.* The square or rectangular area enclosed by four streets, or the buildings in this area. **7** *n. U.S.* One side of such an area. **8** *n.* An obstacle or hindrance: a road *block*. **9** *v.* To hinder or obstruct: to *block* progress. **10** *n.* A pulley or set of pulleys in a frame with a hook or the like at one end. **— block out** To plan or sketch quickly and without great detail.

block·ade [blo·kād′] *n., v.* **block·ad·ed, block·ad·ing** **1** *n.* The shutting off of a coast city, etc., by enemy ships or troops. **2** *v.* To subject to a blockade. **3** *n.* Anything that hinders or obstructs. **4** *v.* To obstruct or hinder. **— run the blockade** To get through a blockade.

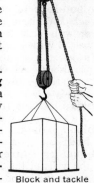

Block and tackle

block and tackle A set of pulley blocks and ropes for pulling or hoisting something.

block·house [blok′hous′] *n.* A small fortification with loopholes to shoot from.

bloke [blōk] *n. British slang* A fellow; guy.

blond or **blonde** [blond] **1** *adj.* Having light-colored hair, especially golden yellow hair, and a light skin. **2** *n.* A blond person. **3** *adj.* Light-colored: a chair of *blond* wood. **— blond′·**

Blockhouse

ness *n*. ◆ The spelling *blond* is always used for the adjective, and the noun *blond* can mean a blond person of either sex. *Blonde*, however, can only refer to a blond woman or girl.

blood [blud] *n*. **1** The dark red liquid that is pumped by the heart to every part of the body, bringing oxygen and digested food and carrying away waste materials. **2** *adj. use:* blood transfusions; a *blood* clot. **3** Descent from a common ancestor; kinship. **4** *adj. use:* a *blood* relative. **5** Temper; disposition: hot *blood*. **6** A dashing man: a young *blood*. **—in cold blood** Deliberately and without emotion: to kill *in cold blood*.

blood bank A place where human blood is stored for use in transfusions.

blood·cur·dling [blud′kûrd′ling] *adj*. Terrifying; horrifying.

blood·ed [blud′id] *adj*. **1** Having a certain blood, disposition, or character: often used in combination, as in *hot-blooded*. **2** Thoroughbred: *blooded* horses.

blood group One of several classes into which individuals are placed on the basis of chemical differences in the make-up of their blood.

blood·hound [blud′hound′] *n*. A large, smooth-coated hound with a keen sense of smell, often used to track escaped prisoners.

Bloodhound, 30 in. high

blood·less [blud′lis] *adj*. **1** Without blood or with little blood; pale. **2** Without vigor; listless. **3** Without bloodshed: a *bloodless* revolution. **—blood′·less·ly** *adv*.

blood·let·ting [blud′let′ing] *n*. **1** The opening of a vein to let out blood. **2** Bloodshed.

blood poisoning A diseased condition of the blood caused by toxins or bacteria.

blood pressure The pressure of the blood on the walls of the arteries. It varies in different people and in the same person at different times.

blood·shed [blud′shed′] *n*. The shedding of blood; killing; slaughter: the *bloodshed* of war.

blood·shot [blud′shot′] *adj*. Red, inflamed, and irritated: *bloodshot* eyes.

blood·suck·er [blud′suk′ər] *n*. **1** A small animal, as the leech, that sucks blood. **2** *informal* A person who sponges on others.

blood·thirst·y [blud′thûrs′tē] *adj*. Eager to kill or shed blood; murderous; cruel.

blood type Another name for BLOOD GROUP.

blood vessel An artery, vein, or capillary through which the blood circulates.

blood·y [blud′ē] *adj*. **blood·i·er, blood·i·est**, *v*. **blood·ied, blood·y·ing 1** *adj*. Full of, containing, or stained with blood: a *bloody* shirt. **2** *v*. To make bloody. **3** *adj*. Involving much bloodshed: a *bloody* fight. **4** *adj*. Bloodthirsty.

bloom [bloom] **1** *n*. A flower; blossom. **2** *n*. The condition or time of being in flower: lilacs in *bloom*. **3** *v*. To bear flowers; blossom. **4** *adj. use:* a *blooming* plant. **5** *n*. A condition or time of freshness and vigor: the *bloom* of youth. **6** *v*. To glow with freshness or health. **7** *n*. A healthy, youthful glow, as of the cheeks. **8** *n*. A powdery coating covering some fruits and leaves.

bloom·ers [bloo′mərz] *n.pl*. **1** Loose, wide trousers gathered at the knee, formerly worn by women for sports. **2** A woman's undergarment like these.

blos·som [blos′əm] **1** *n*. A flower, especially one of a plant or tree that bears edible fruit. **2** *n*. The condition or time of being in flower: cherry trees in *blossom*. **3** *v*. To bear blossoms; bloom. **4** *v*. To develop or grow.

blot [blot] *n., v*. **blot·ted, blot·ting 1** *n*. A spot or stain, as of ink. **2** *v*. To spot or stain. **3** *v*. To dry by absorbing: to *blot* ink with a blotter. **4** *v*. To erase or do away with: to *blot* out a memory. **5** *n*. A blemish or disgrace: These slums are a *blot* on our city.

blotch [bloch] **1** *n*. A spot or mark, especially on the skin. **2** *v*. To mark or cover with blotches. **3** *v*. To become blotched. **—blotch′y** *adj*.

blot·ter [blot′ər] *n*. **1** A sheet or pad of soft thick paper used to absorb wet ink. **2** A book for keeping temporary records, especially records of arrests in a police station.

blouse [blous *or* blouz] *n*. **1** A loose outer garment for women, extending from the neck to the waist. **2** A U.S. Army jacket.

blow¹ [blō] *v*. **blew, blown, blow·ing**, *n*. **1** *v*. To move rather strongly or forcefully, as wind or air. **2** *v*. To send out or emit (air, smoke, etc.), as through the mouth: *Blow* your breath on the hot coals. **3** *v*. To drive or move by blowing: The wind *blew* down the telephone lines. **4** *v*. To be carried or swept by the wind: Her hat *blew* off. **5** *v*. To produce or cause to produce sound by blowing or being blown: to *blow* a horn; The whistle *blew*. **6** *v*. To clear by forcing air into or through: to *blow* the nose. **7** *v*. To form by filling with air: to *blow* bubbles. **8** *n*. The act of blowing. **9** *n*. A windstorm or gale. **10** *v*. To pant or breathe hard. **—blow hot and cold** *informal* To be uncertain; vacillate. **—blow out 1** To extinguish or become extinguished by blowing. **2** To burst, as a tire. **3** To melt, as a fuse, from too much current. **—blow over** To pass by or away. **—blow up 1** To inflate. **2** To explode. **3** *informal* To lose one's temper. **4** To arise; become intense, as a storm.

blow² [blō] *n*. **1** A hard hit with the fist, a weapon, or the like. **2** A sudden and shocking event. **3** A sudden attack: a *blow* at the enemy. **—come to blows** To start fighting.

blow³ [blō] *v*. **blew, blown, blow·ing** To bloom: seldom used today except in *full-blown*.

blow·er [blō′ər] *n*. **1** A person or thing that blows. **2** A fan or other device for creating a current of air.

blow·gun [blō′gun′] *n*. A long tube through which darts or other missiles can be blown.

blown [blōn] Past participle of BLOW¹ and BLOW³.

blow·out [blō′out′] *n.* A blowing out, as of a tire.

blow·pipe [blō′pīp′] *n.* A tube used to blow a jet of air or gas into a flame to increase its heat and direct it to a point.

blow·torch [blō′tôrch′] *n.* An apparatus that burns a liquid fuel and shoots out a jet of very hot flame, used in soldering, removing paint, etc.

Blowtorch

blow·y [blō′ē] *adj.* **blow·i·er, blow·i·est** Windy.

blub·ber [blub′ər] **1** *n.* The layer of fat beneath the skin of a whale or other sea mammal, used as a source of oil. **2** *v.* To weep noisily.

bludg·eon [bluj′ən] **1** *n.* A short club, usually heavy at one end, used as a weapon. **2** *v.* To strike with or as if with a bludgeon. **3** *v.* To use force on; bully.

blue [bloo] *n., adj.* **blu·er, blu·est 1** *n.* The color of the clear sky in the daytime. **2** *adj.* Having this color. **3** *n.* Any blue dye, paint, etc. **4** *n.* Something having a blue color, as the sea or sky. **5** *adj.* Sad and melancholy. **— out of the blue** Very suddenly and unexpectedly. **— the blues** (*used with a singular or plural verb*) **1** Low spirits; melancholy. **2** A song, or songs, of a type originated by the American Negro, having a mournful melody and sad words.

blue·ber·ry [bloo′ber′ē] *n., pl.* **blue·ber·ries 1** A blue or black berry that is good to eat. **2** The shrub it grows on.

blue·bird [bloo′bûrd′] *n.* A small songbird with a blue back and wings, found in North America.

blue·bot·tle [bloo′bot′(ə)l] *n.* Any of various flies having large, hairy bodies of a metallic blue or greenish color.

blue·fish [bloo′fish′] *n., pl.* **blue·fish** or **blue·fish·es** A blue and silver food fish common along the Atlantic coast of the U.S.

blue·grass [bloo′gras′] *n.* A grass with bluish green stems, such as is found in Kentucky.

blue jay or **blue·jay** [bloo′jā′] *n.* A North American bird with a blue back, a crest on its head, and a noisy call.

blue law A law that forbids or strictly limits sports, motion pictures, etc., on Sunday.

blue·print [bloo′print′] *n.* A photographic print, as of an architectural plan, that shows white lines on a blue background.

blue ribbon The first prize in a contest.

bluff¹ [bluf] **1** *v.* To fool or frighten, usually by acting in a bold or confident manner. **2** *n.* The act or an instance of bluffing. **3** *n.* A person who bluffs. **— bluff′er** *n.*

bluff² [bluf] **1** *n.* A broad, steep bank or cliff.

2 *adj.* Having a broad, steep appearance: a *bluff* seacoast. **3** *adj.* Gruff but kindly.

blu·ing [bloo′ing] *n.* A blue liquid or powder added to water when rinsing clothes to keep white fabrics from turning yellow.

blu·ish [bloo′ish] *adj.* Somewhat blue.

blun·der [blun′dər] **1** *n.* A stupid mistake. **2** *v.* To make a blunder. **3** *v.* To act or move blindly, awkwardly, or stupidly; stumble.

blun·der·buss [blun′dər·bus] *n.* A short gun with a wide muzzle for scattering shot at close range, now no longer used.

blunt [blunt] **1** *adj.* Having a dull edge or end; not sharp: a *blunt* knife. **2** *v.* To make or become blunt or dull. **3** *adj.* Extremely frank and outspoken. **— blunt′·ly** *adv.* **— blunt′·ness** *n.*

Blunderbuss

blur [blûr] *v.* **blurred, blur·ring,** *n.* **1** *v.* To make less clear or distinct in form or outline: to *blur* a drawing. **2** *n.* A blurred condition or appearance. **3** *v.* To smudge; smear: The manuscript was *blurred* with ink. **4** *n.* A smudge; smear. **— blur′ry** *adv.*

blurt [blûrt] *v.* To say abruptly or without thinking: to *blurt* out a reply.

blush [blush] **1** *v.* To become red in the face, as from embarrassment or confusion. **2** *n.* Such a reddening of the face. **3** *n.* A red or rosy tint: the first *blush* of a rose. **— at first blush** At first sight; without thinking.

blus·ter [blus′tər] **1** *v.* To blow with a lot of force and noise, as the wind. **2** *n.* A noisy, blustering wind. **3** *v.* To speak in a noisy, boastful, or threatening manner. **4** *n.* Noisy bragging or talk. **— blus′ter·y** *adj.*

blvd. Abbreviation of BOULEVARD.

bo·a [bō′ə] *n.* **1** Any of several very large, nonpoisonous, tropical snakes that kill their prey by crushing it in their coils. **2** A long scarf of feathers or fur, worn by women.

boa constrictor A kind of boa found in South and Central America.

boar [bôr] *n., pl.* **boars** or **boar 1** A male swine. **2** A wild hog.

board [bôrd] **1** *n.* A flat, thin slab of sawed wood much longer than it is wide. **2** *v.* To cover or enclose with boards: to *board* up windows. **3** *n.* A thin slab of wood or other material having a specific purpose: an ironing *board*. **4** *n.* A table set for serving food. **5** *n.* Food or meals, especially meals furnished for pay: room and *board*. **6** *v.* To give or get meals, especially for pay. **7** *v.* To enter (a ship, train, bus, etc.). **8** *n.*

---

add, āce, câre, pälm; end, ēqual; it, īce; odd, ōpen, ôrder; took, pool; up, bûrn;
ə = a in *above*, e in *sicken*, i in *possible*, o in *melon*, u in *circus*; yoo = u in *fuse*; oil; pout;
check; ring; thin; this; zh in *vision*. For ¶ reference, see page 64 · HOW TO

A group of people who control or direct something: a school *board*. **9** *n.* The side of a ship. **— on board** On or in a ship, bus, etc.

board·er [bôr′dər] *n.* A person who pays for meals, lodging, or both at another's house.

boarding house or **board·ing·house** [bôr′-ding·hous′] *n.* A house where board, and usually lodging, is provided for pay.

boarding school A school which furnishes board and lodging to its students for pay.

board·walk [bôrd′wôk′] *n.* A walk made of boards or planks, especially along a beach.

boast [bōst] **1** *v.* To talk in a vain or bragging manner; brag. **2** *n.* Boastful talk; bragging. **3** *v.* To take pride in having. **4** *n.* Something that a person boasts about. **— boast′er** *n.*

boast·ful [bōst′fəl] *adj.* Given to boasting or bragging. **— boast′ful·ly** *adv.*

boat [bōt] **1** *n.* A small vessel for traveling on water by oars, sails, or an engine. **2** *n. informal* A ship of any size. **3** *v.* To travel by boat. **4** *v.* To transport in a boat. **5** *n.* Something, such as a dish, resembling a small boat in shape.

boat·man [bōt′mən] *n., pl.* **boat·men** [bōt′-mən] A man who rents boats, or is paid to operate or take care of a boat or boats.

boat·swain [bō′sən *or* bōt′swān′] *n.* The officer of a ship who supervises the crew in the care and maintenance of the hull, rigging, etc.

bob [bob] *v.* **bobbed, bob·bing,** *n.* **1** *v.* To move up and down or to and fro with short, jerky motions: to *bob* the head; The bottle *bobbed* on the waves. **2** *n.* A short, jerky motion up and down or to and fro. **3** *v.* To try to snatch with the teeth: to *bob* for apples. **4** *v.* To cut short, as hair. **5** *n.* A short haircut for a woman or child. **6** *n.* A small weight at the end of a line, as on a plumb line. **7** *n.* A cork or float on a fishing line.

bob·bin [bob′in] *n.* A reel or spool around which thread, yarn, or the like is wound for use in spinning, weaving, sewing with a machine, etc.

bob·by [bob′ē] *n., pl.* **bob·bies** *British informal* A policeman.

bobby pin A metal hairpin shaped so as to clasp and hold the hair tightly.

bob·cat [bob′kat′] *n.* A wildcat of North America. It is also called a lynx.

bob·o·link [bob′ə·lingk] *n.* A North American songbird, named from the sound of its call.

bob·sled [bob′sled′] *n., v.* **bob·sled·ded, bob·sled·ding 1** *n.* A long sled having two sets of runners, the front set pivoted so that the sled can be steered. **2** *v.* To ride on a bobsled.

bob·tail [bob′tāl′] *n.* **1** A short tail, or a tail cut short. **2** An animal, as a dog or cat, having such a tail. **3** *adj. use:* a *bobtail* cat.

Two-man bobsled

bob·white [bob′(h)wīt′] *n.* A North American quail that is gray with brown and white markings, named from the sound of its call.

bode[1] [bōd] *v.* **bod·ed, bod·ing** To be an omen or sign of: Thunder *bodes* a storm. **— bode ill** To be a bad sign. **— bode well** To be a good sign.

bode[2] [bōd] An alternative past tense and past participle of BIDE: seldom used today.

bod·ice [bod′is] *n.* **1** The upper portion of a woman's dress. **2** An ornamental vest for women and girls, held together by laces in front.

bod·i·less [bod′i·lis] *adj.* Having no body.

bod·i·ly [bod′ə·lē] **1** *adj.* Of or having to do with the body: *bodily* needs. **2** *adv.* In the flesh; in person: to appear *bodily*. **3** *adv.* All together; as a whole: The house was moved *bodily* to another town. ◆ See PHYSICAL.

Bodice

bod·kin [bod′kin] *n.* **1** A blunt needle for drawing tape through a hem or loop. **2** A stiletto: seldom used today.

bod·y [bod′ē] *n., pl.* **bod·ies 1** The entire physical part of a person, animal, or plant. **2** The main portion of a person or animal, not including the head and limbs; the trunk. **3** The principal part of anything: the *body* of a letter. **4** A distinct mass or portion of matter: a *body* of water; a heavenly *body*. **5** Density or substance: a soup with real *body*. **6** A group or collection of people or things taken as a whole: a student *body*. **7** *informal* A person.

bod·y·guard [bod′ē·gärd′] *n.* A guard whose job is to protect a particular person from harm.

Boer [bôr] *n.* **1** A South African of Dutch descent. **2** *adj. use:* the *Boer* War, a war between the Boers and Great Britain, 1899–1902.

bog [bog] *n., v.* **bogged, bog·ging 1** *n.* Wet and spongy ground, such as a marsh or swamp. **2** *v.* To sink or cause to sink in or as if in a bog: to *bog* down in difficulties. **— bog′gy** *adv.*

bo·gey [bō′gē] *n., pl.* **bo·geys** A bogy.

bo·gie [bō′gē] *n.* **1** A bogy. **2** One of the small rollers or wheels that support the weight of a tractor or tank, located inside the treads.

bo·gus [bō′gəs] *adj.* Counterfeit; fake; sham: a *bogus* ten-dollar bill.

bo·gy [bō′gē] *n., pl.* **bo·gies** Someone or something that startles or frightens, especially something imaginary, as a goblin.

Bo·he·mi·a [bō·hē′mē·ə] *n.* A region of western Czechoslovakia.

Bo·he·mi·an [bō·hē′mē·ən] **1** *adj.* Of or from Bohemia. **2** *n.* A person born or living in Bohemia. **3** *n.* The Czech language of Bohemia. **4** *n.* A person, usually an artist, musician, or writer, who lives in a very free, unconventional way. **5** *adj.* Of, having to do with, or leading the life of a Bohemian. **6** *n.* A gypsy.

B

boil[1] [boil] **1** *v.* To heat (a liquid) until bubbles are formed within it and rise to the surface as steam or vapor. **2** *v.* To become heated so as to form bubbles in this way: At sea level water *boils* at 212° F. **3** *n.* The condition of boiling. **4** *v.* To cook or cleanse by boiling: to *boil* rice; to *boil* shirts. **5** *v.* To be stirred up; be agitated: to *boil* with anger. — **boil away** To evaporate in boiling. — **boil down 1** To reduce the bulk of by boiling. **2** To shorten; summarize.

boil[2] [boil] *n.* A red, painful swelling on the skin enclosing a hard core surrounded by pus.

boil·er [boi′lər] *n.* **1** A container in which something is boiled. **2** A tank for hot water. **3** A large tank in which hot water is converted into steam for heating or power.

boiling point The temperature at which a liquid begins to boil.

Boi·se [boi′zē *or* boi′sē] *n.* The capital of Idaho.

bois·ter·ous [bois′tər·əs] *adj.* **1** Noisy and wild: a *boisterous* party. **2** Stormy: *boisterous* weather. — **bois′ter·ous·ly** *adv.*

bold [bōld] *adj.* **1** Having or requiring courage; daring: a *bold* warrior; a *bold* plan. **2** Very free or impudent in manner or character: a *bold* reply. **3** Distinct or striking, as in outline, color, etc. **4** Steep: a *bold* cliff. — **bold′ly** *adv.* — **bold′ness** *n.*

bold·face [bōld′fās′] *n.* A printing type in which the lines have been thickened to give a very black impression, like **this**.

bole [bōl] *n.* The trunk of a tree.

bo·le·ro [bō·lâr′ō] *n.*, *pl.* **bo·le·ros 1** A Spanish dance usually accompanied by castanets. **2** The music for this dance. **3** A kind of short, vestlike jacket, open at the front.

Bol·í·var [bō·lē′vär *or* bol′ə·vər], **Simón,** 1783–1830, Venezuelan general who helped free South America from Spanish rule.

Bo·liv·i·a [be·liv′ē·ə] *n.* A country in west central South America. — **Bo·liv′i·an** *adj.*, *n.*

boll [bōl] *n.* The seed pod of cotton, flax, and certain other plants.

boll weevil A small grayish beetle that lays its eggs in cotton bolls, thereby causing great damage to the cotton.

bo·lo·gna [bə·lō′nē *or* bə·lō′nə] *n.* A big sausage made of pork, beef, and veal.

Bol·she·vik [bōl′shə·vik] *n.* (*often written* **bolshevik**) **1** A member of the radical wing of the socialist party in Russia that seized power late in 1917, becoming the Communist Party in 1918. **2** A member of any Communist party. **3** Loosely, any radical.

Bol·she·vism [bōl′shə·viz′(ə)m] *n.* (*often written* **bolshevism**) The doctrine and policies of the Bolsheviks. — **Bol′she·vist** *adj.*, *n.*

bol·ster [bōl′stər] **1** *n.* A long, narrow pillow. **2** *v.* To support, prop, or make stronger: to *bolster* up someone's courage.

bolt [bōlt] **1** *n.* A pin or rod for holding something in place. It has a head at one end and a screw thread at the other for a nut. **2** *n.* A sliding bar or rod for fastening a door. **3** *n.* The part of a lock that shoots out or withdraws when the key is turned. **4** *v.* To fasten with a bolt. **5** *n.* A short arrow which was shot from a crossbow. **6** *n.* A stroke of lightning. **7** *n.* A sudden start or spring: He made a *bolt* for the door. **8** *v.* To move, go, or spring suddenly: The horse *bolted*. **9** *v.* To break away from (a political party or its candidates). **10** *v.* To gulp down (food or a meal). **11** *n.* A roll of cloth, wallpaper, or other material. — **bolt upright** Stiff and erect: to stand *bolt upright*.

Boards joined using a bolt and nut

bomb [bom] **1** *n.* A container filled with a material that explodes or burns violently when set off, as by a time fuse. **2** *v.* To attack with a bomb or bombs. **3** *n.* A receptacle containing a liquid under pressure: an insecticide *bomb*.

bom·bard [bom·bärd′] *v.* **1** To shell or bomb: to *bombard* a fort. **2** To attack with questions, requests, etc. **3** To subject (substances) to high-energy radiation or atomic particles. — **bom·bard′ment** *n.*

bom·bar·dier [bom′bər·dir′] *n.* The member of a bomber's crew who releases the bombs.

bom·bast [bom′bast] *n.* Talk or writing that sounds impressive but means little. — **bom·bas′tic** *adj.* — **bom·bas′ti·cal·ly** *adv.*

Bom·bay [bom·bā′] *n.* A large city in western India, on the Arabian Sea.

bomb·er [bom′ər] *n.* **1** A person who bombs. **2** An airplane designed to carry and drop bombs.

bomb·shell [bom′shel′] *n.* **1** A bomb (def. 1). **2** A complete surprise.

bo·na fide [bō′nə·fid′ *or* bō′nə·fi′dē] Made, being, or acting in good faith; genuine; sincere. ◆ This expression comes directly from the Latin.

bo·nan·za [bə·nan′zə] *n.* **1** A rich deposit of ore. **2** Something that provides great wealth.

Bo·na·parte [bō′nə·pärt], **Napoleon,** 1769–1821, French military leader and conqueror, emperor of France, 1804–1815.

bon·bon [bon′bon′] *n.* A small sugared candy.

bond [bond] **1** *n.* Something that binds or holds together. **2** *n.* A uniting force or influence: the *bonds* of friendship. **3** *n.* A written agreement to pay a sum of money at a specified time, subject to certain conditions. **4** *n.* A certificate, issued by a government or company, the purchase of which will pay for some project, job, cause, etc. The buyer is later paid back with interest. **5** *v.* To issue bonds on. **6** *n.* Bail. **7** *v.* To furnish bond for. **8** *n.* The way in which bricks or stones are overlapped in a building. **9** *v.* To lay (brick, stones, etc.) in interlocking patterns for strength.

bond·age [bon′dij] *n.* Slavery; serfdom.

bond·man [bond′mən] *n., pl.* **bond·men** [bond′mən] A male slave or serf.

bonds·man [bondz′mən] *n., pl.* **bonds·men** [bondz′mən] **1** A person who provides bail or bond for someone. **2** A bondman.

bone [bōn] *n., v.* **boned, bon·ing 1** *n.* One of the hard pieces that form the skeleton of a person or any vertebrate animal. **2** *n.* The hard, porous material of which a bone is made. **3** *v.* To remove the bones from: to *bone* fish. **4** *n.* A substance like bone, as whalebone.

bon·er [bō′nər] *n. slang* An error; blunder.

bon·fire [bon′fīr′] *n.* A fire built outdoors.

bon·go drums [bong′gō] A pair of joined drums held between the knees and played with the hands.

bo·ni·to [bə·nē′tō] *n., pl.* **bo·ni·to** or **bo·ni·toes** A salt-water fish related to the mackerel and tuna. Its flesh is canned for eating.

Bonn [bon] *n.* The capital of West Germany.

Bongo drums

bon·net [bon′it] *n.* **1** A hat for women and children covering most of the hair and held in place by ribbons tied under the chin. **2** A cap worn in Scotland by men and boys.

bon·ny or **bon·nie** [bon′ē] *adj.* **bon·ni·er, bon·ni·est 1** Good-looking, healthy, and cheerful: a *bonny* lad. **2** Fine; good. ◆ This word is used in Scotland and parts of England.

bo·nus [bō′nəs] *n.* Something extra given in addition to what is due or usual, as money given in addition to regular wages.

Bonnet

bon vo·yage [bôn vwä·yäzh′] Pleasant journey: a French expression often used as a farewell to someone going on a trip.

bon·y [bō′nē] *adj.* **bon·i·er, bon·i·est 1** Of or like bone: a *bony* material. **2** Full of bones. **3** Having prominent bones; thin: *bony* arms.

boo [bōō] *interj., n., v.* **booed, boo·ing 1** *interj., n.* A vocal sound made to show dislike or disapproval. **2** *v.* To shout this sound at (someone or something): to *boo* a play. **3** *interj., n.* A short sound made to frighten someone.

boo·by [bōō′bē] *n., pl.* **boo·bies 1** A stupid person; dunce. **2** A large sea bird; gannet.

booby prize An award for the worst score or performance in a game, contest, etc.

booby trap 1 A concealed bomb, mine, etc., set to explode when some harmless looking object to which it is attached is moved or touched. **2** Any trap for an unsuspecting person.

book [bōōk] *n.* **1** A bound set of printed sheets of paper, usually between covers. **2** *n.* A written work of some length, such as a novel, biography, etc., that has been or will be published as a book. **3** *n.* (*written* **Book**) The Bible. **4** *n.* A main division of a long literary work: a *book* of the Bible. **5** *n.* A volume of blank pages for entering things in writing, such as a notebook, ledger, etc. **6** *v.* To list charges against in a police register: to *book* a suspect for robbery. **7** *v.* To arrange for beforehand, as seats, reservations, etc. **8** *n.* Something like a book in shape, as a packet of matches or stamps. **— by the book** Strictly according to the rules. **— keep books** To keep business records or accounts. ◆ This word comes from an Old English word meaning *beech*, probably because letters and words were at one time carved on its wood.

book·case [bōōk′kās′] *n.* A cabinet containing shelves for books.

book end A support to hold books upright.

book·ish [bōōk′ish] *adj.* **1** Fond of reading and studying. **2** Knowing only what can be read in books. **3** Formal or literary.

book·keep·ing [bōōk′kē′ping] *n.* The work of recording business accounts and transactions. **— book′keep′er** *n.*

book·let [bōōk′lit] *n.* A small book or pamphlet.

book·mark [bōōk′märk′] *n.* An object, as a ribbon, inserted in a book to mark a place.

book·store [bōōk′stôr′] *n.* A store that sells books.

book·worm [bōōk′wûrm′] *n.* **1** A small worm that gnaws through books. **2** A person who is very fond of reading or studying.

boom¹ [bōōm] *n.* **1** A deep, reverberating sound, as of a supersonic airplane, a cannon, etc. **2** *v.* To make this sound. **3** *n. U.S.* A sudden increase, as in growth or prosperity. **4** *v. U.S.* To grow rapidly; flourish: The western towns *boomed*. **5** *v. U.S.* To praise or advertise vigorously.

boom² [bōōm] *n.* **1** The long pole or beam of a crane or derrick from which the objects to be lifted are suspended. **2** A long pole used to hold or extend the bottom of certain sails. **3** A chain, string of logs, etc., stretched across a body of water to keep things in or out. ◆ This word comes from the Dutch word *boom*, meaning *tree* or *beam*.

boom

boom·e·rang [bōō′mə·rang] **1** *n.* A curved wooden weapon used by the natives of Australia. Some forms of it, when thrown, will return to the thrower. **2** *n.* Something said or done against someone else which turns out to hurt the originator. **3** *v.* To return in this way: His plot *boomeranged*. ◆ This word comes from an Australian aborigine name for the weapon.

boon¹ [bōōn] *n.* **1** A blessing: Rain is a *boon* to farmers. **2** A request: seldom used today.

boon² [bōōn] *adj.* Jolly; merry: now used only in the expression **boon companion.**

Boone [bōōn], **Daniel,** 1735?–1820, American frontiersman in Kentucky and Missouri.

boor [bōōr] *n.* A crude, ill-mannered person. **— boor′ish** *adj.* **— boor′ish·ness** *n.*

boost [bŏost] **1** *v.* To raise by pushing from beneath or behind. **2** *n.* A lift; help: to give someone a *boost*. **3** *v.* To give support to: to *boost* a candidate or a team. **4** *v.* To increase: to *boost* prices. **5** *n.* An increase.

boost·er [bŏos'tər] *n.* **1** Anything used to increase or extend the force or operation of something, as an additional dose of a vaccine or serum or the first stage of a rocket which lifts and propels it in its early flight. **2** *informal* A person who gives enthusiastic support to a cause, organization, etc.

boot[1] [bŏot] **1** *n.* A covering, usually of leather, for the foot and part of the leg. **2** *v.* To put boots on. **3** *v.* To kick. **4** *n.* A kick. **5** *n.* A thick patch on the inside of an automobile tire.

boot[2] [bŏot] *n.* To benefit or avail: seldom used today. **— to boot** In addition: a turkey dinner and apple pie *to boot*.

boot·black [bŏot'blak'] *n.* A person whose business is shining boots and shoes.

Bo·ö·tes [bō-ō'tēz] *n.* A northern constellation near the Big Dipper.

booth [bŏoth] *n.* **1** A small compartment or space for privacy or keeping out sound: a voting *booth*; a telephone *booth*. **2** A place where goods are displayed or sold at an exhibition or fair.

boot·leg [bŏot'leg'] *v.* **boot·legged, boot·leg·ging** To make, sell, or transport illegally: to *bootleg* liquor. **— boot'leg'ger** *n.*

boot·less [bŏot'lis] *adj.* Useless; futile.

boo·ty [bŏo'tē] *n., pl.* **boo·ties 1** Goods taken from an enemy in war. **2** Goods taken by violence or robbery. **3** Any prize or gain.

booze [bŏoz] *n. informal* Alcoholic drink. ◆ This word was probably taken from an old Dutch word meaning *to drink*.

bo·rax [bôr'aks] *n.* A white crystalline mineral, used in cleaning, making glass, etc.

Bor·deaux [bôr-dō'] *n.* A white or red wine produced near Bordeaux, a city in France.

bor·der [bôr'dər] **1** *n.* A margin or edge. **2** *v.* To put a border on: to *border* a handkerchief. **3** *n.* The boundary line dividing one country or state from another. **4** *v.* To lie along the border of; bound: The park *borders* the lake. **— border on** or **border upon 1** To be next to. **2** To come close to being.

bor·der·land [bôr'dər·land'] *n.* **1** Land on or near the border of two adjoining countries. **2** A vague or uncertain area or condition.

bor·der·line [bôr'dər·līn'] **1** *n.* The boundary line between two countries or states; border. **2** *adj.* On a border: a *borderline* village. **3** *adj.* Hard to classify or rank; uncertain; doubtful: a *borderline* case.

bore[1] [bôr] *v.* **bored, bor·ing,** *n.* **1** *v.* To make a hole in or through, as with a drill. **2** *v.* To make (a hole, tunnel, etc.) by or as if by drilling. **3** *n.* A hole made by boring. **4** *n.* The hollow space

inside a tube or pipe, such as a gun barrel. **5** *n.* The inside diameter of a tube.

bore[2] [bôr] *v.* **bored, bor·ing,** *n.* **1** *v.* To make weary by being dull, tedious, etc.: This book *bores* me. **2** *n.* A boring person or thing.

bore[3] [bôr] The past tense of BEAR[1].

bore[4] [bôr] *n.* A very high wave caused by the rush of an incoming tide.

Bo·re·as [bôr'ē·əs] *n.* In Greek myths, the north wind.

bore·dom [bôr'dəm] *n.* The condition of being bored by something dull or tiresome.

bor·er [bôr'ər] *n.* **1** A tool used for boring, such as an auger or bit. **2** A beetle, moth, or worm that burrows in plants, wood, etc.

bo·ric acid [bôr'ik] A white powdery substance obtained from borax. Dissolved in water it is used as a mild antiseptic.

born [bôrn] **1** An alternative past participle of BEAR[1] meaning *given birth to*: a man *born* in May. **2** *adj.* Brought forth or into being: A nation was *born*. **3** *adj.* Natural; by birth: a *born* painter.

borne [bôrn] Past participle of BEAR[1]: The large crate was *borne* by two men.

Bor·ne·o [bôr'nē·ō] *n.* The third largest island in the world, in the East Indies.

bo·ron [bôr'on] *n.* A nonmetallic element obtained from borax and used in alloys, glass, reactors, rocket fuels, etc.

bor·ough [bûr'ō] *n.* **1** A village or town with a charter granting it the right of self-government. **2** One of the five administrative divisions of New York City.

bor·row [bôr'ō *or* bor'ō] *v.* **1** To take (something) from somebody else with the promise or understanding of returning it. **2** To adopt for one's own use, as words or ideas: We have *borrowed* many phrases from the French. **— borrow trouble** To worry before there is any need to. **— bor'row·er** *n.*

borsch [bôrsh] *n.* Borscht.

borscht [bôrsht] *n.* A Russian beet soup, eaten hot or cold. ◆ This word comes from the Russian word *borshch*.

bosh [bosh] *n. informal* Nonsense; rubbish.

bosk·y [bos'kē] *adj.* **1** Wooded; shady. **2** Shaded by or as by trees.

bo's'n [bō'sən] *n.* Another word for BOATSWAIN.

bos·om [bŏoz'əm *or* bŏo'zəm] **1** *n.* The breast of a human being, especially of a woman. **2** *n.* The portion of a dress or other garment covering the breast. **3** *n.* The breast as the seat of thought and emotion: Within his *bosom* Philip felt he was right. **4** *n.* Inner circle; midst: in the *bosom* of her family. **5** *adj.* Close; intimate: a *bosom* friend.

Bos·po·rus [bos′pə·rəs] *n.* A strait near Istanbul that divides the European part of Turkey from the Asian part.

boss[1] [bôs] *informal* **1** *n.* A person who employs or is in charge of workmen. **2** *n.* A person who controls a political organization. **3** *v.* To supervise; direct: to *boss* a project. ◆ This word comes from the Dutch word *baas*, meaning *master*.

boss[2] [bôs] *n.* An ornamental knob or stud.

boss·y [bôs′ē] *adj.* **boss·i·er, boss·i·est** *informal* Tending to boss or be domineering.

Bos·ton [bôs′tən] *n.* The capital of Massachusetts, an important seaport.

bo·sun [bō′sən] *n.* Another word for BOATSWAIN.

bo·tan·i·cal [bə·tan′i·kəl] *adj.* Having to do with plants or with botany.

botanical garden A place where many different plants and trees are grown and exhibited.

bot·a·ny [bot′ə·nē] *n.* The science that studies the growth, structure, and classification of plants. — **bot′an·ist** *n.*

botch [boch] **1** *v.* To spoil by carelessness or clumsiness; bungle: to *botch* a job. **2** *n.* A bungled piece of work; a bad job.

both [bōth] **1** *adj., pron.* The two together; one and the other: *Both* girls laughed; *Both* were there. **2** *adv., conj.* Equally; alike; as well: He is *both* kind and intelligent; The bill passed *both* the House and the Senate.

both·er [both′ər] **1** *v.* To annoy or trouble. **2** *n.* A person or thing that bothers. **3** *v.* To trouble or concern oneself.

both·er·some [both′ər·səm] *adj.* Annoying or troublesome: a very *bothersome* problem.

Bot·ti·cel·li [bot′ə·chel′ē], **Sandro**, 1447?–1515, Italian painter.

bot·tle [bot′(ə)l] *n., v.* **bot·tled, bot·tling 1** *n.* A vessel, usually of glass, for holding liquids, having a neck and a narrow mouth that can be stopped. **2** *n.* As much as a bottle will hold: a *bottle* of milk. **3** *v.* To put into a bottle or bottles. — **bottle up** To hold in check or under control: to *bottle up* one's temper.

bot·tle·neck [bot′(ə)l·nek′] *n.* **1** A narrow or congested passageway, road, etc. **2** A hindrance.

bot·tom [bot′əm] **1** *n.* The lowest part: the *bottom* of the page. **2** *adj.* Lowest: the *bottom* rung of the ladder. **3** *n.* The underside or under surface: the *bottom* of a box. **4** *n.* The ground beneath a body of water: The box fell into the lake and sank to the *bottom*. **5** *n.* (*often pl.*) Lowland along

Traffic bottleneck

a river. **6** *n.* The seat of a chair. **7** *n.* The basic facts, source, or cause: to get to the *bottom* of a matter.

bot·tom·less [bot′əm·lis] *adj.* **1** Having no bottom. **2** Infinitely deep, or so deep the distance can't be measured: a *bottomless* pit.

bot·u·lism [boch′ōō·liz′əm] *n.* Poisoning caused by bacteria sometimes found in spoiled food.

bou·doir [bōō′dwär *or* bōō·dwär′] *n.* A lady's private dressing room or bedroom.

bouf·fant [bōō·fänt′] *adj.* Puffed out, as a skirt or hairdo. ◆ This word comes directly from the French.

bough [bou] *n.* A large branch of a tree.

bought [bôt] Past tense and past participle of BUY: She *bought* a dress.

bouil·lon [bōol′yon] *n.* A clear soup made from beef, chicken, or other meat.

boul·der [bōl′dər] *n.* A large, detached rock or stone, worn or rounded as by water.

boul·e·vard [bōōl′ə·värd] *n.* A broad city avenue or main road, often lined with trees.

bounce [bouns] *v.* **bounced, bounc·ing,** *n.* **1** *v.* To strike or hit and spring back from a surface; rebound: to *bounce* on a sofa. **2** *v.* To cause to bounce: to *bounce* a ball. **3** *n.* A bound or rebound. **4** *n.* Ability or capacity to bounce or spring: a ball with *bounce*. **5** *v.* To jump or leap suddenly: to *bounce* out of bed. **6** *n.* A sudden jump or leap. **7** *n.* *informal* Pep and vitality.

bound[1] [bound] **1** *v.* To strike and spring back from a surface; bounce. **2** *v.* To move by a series of leaps. **3** *n.* A bounce, leap, or spring.

bound[2] [bound] **1** Past tense and past participle of BIND. **2** *adj.* Having a cover or binding: a *bound* book. **3** *adj.* Certain; sure: It's *bound* to rain. **4** *adj. informal* Resolved; determined: I'm *bound* on finishing this.

bound[3] [bound] *adj.* On the way; headed; going: *bound* for home.

bound[4] [bound] **1** *n.* (*usually pl.*) A boundary, edge, or limit: the *bounds* of space; Keep within the *bounds* of reason. **2** *v.* To form the boundary of; enclose: The jungle *bounds* the village. **3** *v.* To name the boundaries of (a state, country, etc.). — **out of bounds 1** Beyond the boundary or limits of a playing area, as in basketball. **2** Not to be entered, done, etc.

bound·a·ry [boun′də·rē *or* boun′drē] *n., pl.* **bound·a·ries** Something, as a line, mark, etc., that forms an outer limit, edge, or extent.

bound·en [boun′d(ə)n] *adj.* Required: seldom used today: our *bounden* duty.

bound·less [bound′lis] *adj.* Having no bounds or limits: *boundless* space; *boundless* sympathy.

boun·te·ous [boun′tē·əs] *adj.* Bountiful.

boun·ti·ful [boun′tə·fəl] *adj.* **1** Generous and free in giving; liberal: a *bountiful* ruler. **2** Abundant; plentiful: a *bountiful* harvest. — **boun′ti·ful·ly** *adv.*

boun·ty [boun′tē] *n., pl.* **boun·ties 1** Generosity in giving. **2** Something given freely and generously. **3** A reward from a government, as for killing a dangerous animal.

bou·quet *n.* **1** [bō·kā′ *or* boo·kā′] A bunch of flowers; nosegay. **2** [boo·kā′] A delicate odor, especially the odor of a good wine.

Bour·bon *n.* **1** [boor′bən] A family that formerly ruled France and Spain. **2** [bûr′bən] (*written* **bourbon**) A kind of whisky made chiefly of corn.

bour·geois [boor′zhwä *or* boor·zhwä′] *n., pl.* **bour·geois**, *adj.* **1** *n.* A member of the middle class. **2** *n.* The middle class. **3** *adj.* Of or like the ways or habits of the middle class.

bour·geoi·sie [boor′zhwä·zē′] *n.* The middle class, falling between the laboring class and the wealthy or noble class.

bourn[1] or **bourne**[1] [bôrn] *n.* **1** A goal or destination. **2** A boundary or limit. **3** A place.

bourn[2] or **bourne**[2] [bôrn] *n.* A brook.

bout [bout] *n.* **1** A contest or trial: a boxing *bout.* **2** A fit or spell, as of illness.

bo·vine [bō′vīn] **1** *adj.* Of or like a cow or ox. **2** *n.* A cow or ox. **3** *adj.* Dull, slow, or stupid.

bow[1] [bou] *v.* **bowed, bow·ing,** *n.* **1** *v.* To bend the head or body, as in greeting, worship, or saying yes. **2** *n.* A bending of the head or body, as in greeting, worship, etc. **3** *v.* To give up; yield: They *bowed* to the dictator's wishes. **4** *v.* To bend or curve: He was *bowed* by arthritis. — **bow out** To withdraw; resign. — **take a bow** To acknowledge the applause of an audience by returning to a stage after a performance.

bow[2] [bō] **1** *n.* A strip of springy wood bent by a string, used for shooting arrows. **2** *n.* A knot with loops in it. **3** *n.* Anything bent or curved, as a rainbow. **4** *n.* A rod holding tightly stretched horsehair, used to play a violin or related instrument. **5** *v.* To play with a bow.

bow[3] [bou] *n.* The forward part of a ship, boat, etc.

A violin bow

bow·el [bou′əl] *n.* **1** (*often pl.*) The part of the alimentary canal below the stomach; intestines. **2** (*pl.*) The inner part of anything: *bowels* of the earth.

bow·er [bou′ər] *n.* **1** A shady spot, as in a garden. **2** A bedroom or other private room.

bow·ie knife [bō′ē] A long, single-edged hunting knife.

bowl[1] [bōl] *n.* **1** A rounded, rather deep dish. **2** The amount a bowl will hold: a *bowl* of water. **3** Anything shaped like a bowl: the *bowl* of a pipe. — **bowl′ful′** *n.*

bowl[2] [bōl] **1** *v.* To play at bowling or bowls. **2** *n.* The ball used in bowls. **3** *v.* To move swiftly: to *bowl* along. — **bowl′er** *n.*

bowl·der [bōl′dər] *n.* Another spelling of BOULDER.

bow·leg·ged [bō′leg·id] *adj.* Having legs that are bowed out at the knee or just below.

bow·line [bō′lin *or* bō′līn] *n.* A knot tied so as to make a loop. One type will slip; another won't.

bowl·ing [bō′ling] *n.* A game in which each player rolls a heavy ball down a wooden path to try to knock down ten wooden pins at the other end.

Bowlegged man

bowling alley A long narrow wooden lane for bowling, or a building containing such lanes.

bowls [bōlz] *n.pl.* **1** A game played on a smooth lawn with slightly flattened balls. **2** A game of tenpins, ninepins, or skittles.

bow·man [bō′mən] *n., pl.* **bow·men** [bō′mən] An archer.

bow·sprit [bou′sprit′] *n.* A spar reaching forward from the bow of a sailing vessel. Wires from it brace the mast and hold jibs.

bow·string [bō′string′] *n.* **1** A strong cord used to string a bow. **2** Such a cord once used for strangling criminals.

bow tie A necktie worn tied in a bow.

box[1] [boks] **1** *n.* A container made of wood, leather, plastic, etc., often with a lid, to hold something. **2** *n.* The amount a box will hold: I ate half a *box* of candy. **3** *v.* To put into a box. **4** *n.* Anything like a box, as a railed space for a jury, a marked space for a batter in baseball, etc.

Bow tie

box[2] [boks] **1** *v.* To fight with one's fists. **2** *v.* To strike or slap with the hand; cuff: John *boxed* Tom's ear. **3** *n.* A blow given with the hand, especially on the ear.

box[3] [boks] *n.* Any of a family of evergreen shrubs or small trees, used for hedges, etc.

box·car [boks′kär′] *n.* A freight car with a roof and its sides closed in.

box·er[1] [bok′sər] *n.* A person who fights with his fists.

box·er[2] [bok′sər] *n.* A sturdy dog related to the bulldog, usually fawn or brindled in color.

box·ing [bok′sing] *n.* The sport or skill of fighting according to certain rules with the fists, using padded gloves.

boxing glove One of a pair of padded leather mitts used for fighting.

box office The place in a theater, stadium, etc., where tickets are sold.

box·wood [boks′wood′] *n.* **1** The hard, tough wood of the box. **2** The shrub.

boy [boi] *n.* **1** A male child; lad; youth. **2** *informal* Any man: The *boys* at the office have quit smoking. **3** A male servant.

boy·cott [boi'kot] **1** *v.* To unite in refusing to buy from, sell to, use, deal or associate with, etc.: The nationalist party *boycotting* all imported goods. **2** *n.* The act of boycotting.

boy·hood [boi'hŏŏd] *n.* The condition or time of being a boy.

boy·ish [boi'ish] *adj.* Of, like, or fitting for a boy. — **boy'ish·ly** *adv.* — **boy'ish·ness** *n.*

boy scout A member of the Boy Scouts.

Boy Scouts An organization for boys that trains them in self-reliance, camping skills, and good citizenship.

Br The symbol for the element BROMINE.

bra [brä] *n. informal* A brassiere.

brace [brās] *v.* **braced, brac·ing,** *n.* **1** *v.* To strengthen, support, or make firm: to *brace* a shelf with a bracket. **2** *n.* Something used to support, strengthen, or hold in place. **3** *v.* To prepare for a jerk, bump, or pressure: *Brace* yourself for a sharp turn. **4** *v.* To stimulate or refresh: A cold shower *braced* him. **5** *n.* A pair; couple: a *brace* of deer. **6** *n.* A tool like a handle, used to hold and turn a bit or drill. **7** *n.* Either of two marks { }, used to show that the words, numbers, etc., enclosed between them should be taken together. **8** *n.* (*pl.*) *British* Suspenders. — **brace up** *informal* To become again strong and resolute.

brace·let [brās'lit] *n.* A band or chain worn as an ornament around the wrist or arm.

brac·ing [brā'sing] *adj.* Giving energy; invigorating: a *bracing* wind.

brack·en [brak'ən] *n.* **1** A large hardy fern. **2** A clump of such ferns.

brack·et [brak'it] **1** *n.* A support, often a wooden triangle or a metal right angle, for a shelf or other weight sticking out from a wall. **2** *n.* A shelf supported by brackets. **3** *v.* To support with a bracket or brackets. **4** *n.* Either of two marks, [ ], used to enclose and separate inserted words or figures, or in mathematics, to enclose numbers or symbols that are to be treated as a single element. **5** *v.* To put between brackets. **6** *n.* A section of a numbered or graded series: the 18–25 age *bracket.* **7** *v.* To group together; associate: Radar and sonar are often *bracketed.*

Brackets

brack·ish [brak'ish] *adj.* **1** Somewhat salty. **2** Tasting unpleasant.

bract [brakt] *n.* A specialized leaf growing at the base of a flower or on the stem.

brad [brad] *n.* A thin nail with a small head.

brae [brā] *n.* The Scottish word for a hillside.

brag [brag] *v.* **bragged, brag·ging,** *n.* **1** *v.* To boast too much about what one has, has done, or can do: He *brags* constantly. **2** *n.* A boasting.

brag·gart [brag'ərt] *n.* A person who brags.

Brah·ma [brä'mə] *n.* In the Hindu religion, the creator of the universe.

Brah·man or **Brah·min** [brä'mən] *n.* **1** A member of the highest caste or social level in India. **2** A breed of humped cattle.

Brahms [brämz], **Johannes,** 1833–1897, German composer of music.

braid [brād] **1** *v.* To weave together three or more strands of; plait: to *braid* the hair. **2** *n.* Anything braided. **3** *v.* To ornament with braided cloth, ribbon, etc. **4** *n.* A strip of something braided, used for trimming.

Braille [brāl] *n.* (*sometimes written* **braille**) A system of printing and writing for blind people in which the letters are indicated by raised dots read by touch with the fingers.

brain [brān] **1** *n.* The complex mass of nerve tissue in the skull of man and vertebrate animals. It is the chief nerve center, controls voluntary movements, thinks, and remembers. **2** *n.* (*pl.*) Intelligence; intellect: He has *brains.* **3** *v. slang* To hit hard on the head.

cerebrum

brain·less [brān'lis] *adj.* Lacking intelligence; stupid; foolish.

medulla

brain·storm [brān'stôrm'] *n. informal* A sudden inspiration; brilliant idea.

cerebellum   spinal cord

Brain

brain·y [brā'nē] *adj.* **brain·i·er, brain·i·est** *informal* Having great intelligence; clever.

braise [brāz] *v.* To cook by first browning in fat and then simmering in a covered pan with a little liquid.

brake[1] [brāk] *n., v.* **braked, brak·ing 1** *n.* A device for slowing or stopping a turning wheel or a moving car, truck, etc., usually by friction. **2** *v.* To slow or stop by applying a brake.

brake[2] [brāk] *n.* Bracken.

brake[3] [brāk] *n.* An area covered with bushes, tall grass, briers, etc.; thicket.

brake·man [brāk'mən] *n., pl.* **brake·men** [brāk'mən] A man who helps the conductor manage a train. He used to put on the brakes.

bram·ble [bram'bəl] *n.* A prickly shrub, especially the blackberry.

bran [bran] *n.* The husks left when grains like wheat or rye are ground and the flour sifted out.

branch [branch] **1** *n.* A woody part of a tree growing out from the trunk or from a limb. **2** *n.* A part coming out like a branch of a tree from a main part: a *branch* of a railroad. **3** *n.* Any part or division of a system, subject, etc.: Geometry is a *branch* of mathematics; the Ohio *branch* of our family. **4** *n.* A store, office, etc., away from the main unit: Our bank has 18 *branches.* **5** *adj. use:* a *branch* office. **6** *v.* To separate or divide into branches: The highway *branches* here. — **branch out** To widen or add to one's activities, interests, etc.: The agency has *branched out* with a line of foreign cars. ◆ This word comes from a Latin word meaning *paw.*

brand [brand] **1** *n.* A trademark. **2** *n.* A kind, quality, or make: a good *brand* of tires. **3** *n.* A mark burned on with a hot iron, as on cattle to

B

show ownership or, long ago, on criminals as a sign of disgrace. **4** *v.* To put a mark on with a hot iron. **5** *n.* The iron used to make the mark. **6** *n.* A mark of disgrace or shame. **7** *v.* To mark or set apart as shameful or disgraced: He was *branded* a thief. **8** *n.* A burning stick of wood.

bran·dish [bran′dish] *v.* To wave triumphantly or threateningly: to *brandish* a knife.

brand-new [bran(d)′n(y)o͞o′] *adj.* Very new; not used.

bran·dy [bran′dē] *n.,* *pl.* **bran·dies,** *v.* **bran·died, bran·dy·ing 1** *n.* An alcoholic drink distilled from wine or other fermented fruit juice. **2** *v.* To mix or flavor with brandy.

brant [brant] *n.* A small wild goose.

brash [brash] *adj.* **1** Acting too hastily; rash. **2** Impudent and pert.

Bra·sí·lia [brə-zē′lyə] *n.* The capital of Brazil.

brass [bras] *n.* **1** An alloy of copper and zinc. **2** Ornaments, dishes, etc., made of this yellow metal. **3** (*sometimes pl.*) The brass instruments of an orchestra, taken together. **4** *informal* Barefaced boldness or impudence. **5** *informal* High-ranking officers in the armed forces.

bras·siere or **bras·sière** [brə-zir′] *n.* A woman's undergarment to support the breasts.

brass instrument A musical instrument consisting of a long, bent tube with a flare at one end, as a trumpet or tuba.

brass·y [bras′ē] *adj.* **brass·i·er, brass·i·est 1** Made of or decorated with brass. **2** Looking or sounding like brass. **3** *informal* Too bold.

brat [brat] *n.* An annoying or unpleasant child.

bra·va·do [brə-vä′dō] *n.* A show of bravery without much courage or confidence underneath.

brave [brāv] *adj.* **brav·er, brav·est,** *v.,* **braved, brav·ing,** *n.* **1** *adj.* Having or showing courage; not afraid. **2** *v.* To meet or face with courage; defy: to *brave* danger. **3** *adj.* Making a fine show; splendid: girls in *brave* new dresses. **4** *n.* A North American Indian warrior. **— brave′ly** *adv.*

brav·er·y [brā′vər·ē] *n.,* *pl.* **brav·er·ies 1** Valor; courage; fearlessness. **2** Fine appearance or showy display: to parade with a *bravery* of banners.

bra·vo [brä′vō] *interj.,* *n.,* *pl.* **bra·vos 1** *interj.* Well done. **2** *n.* A shout of bravo.

brawl [brôl] **1** *n.* A noisy argument or fight. **2** *v.* To fight roughly and noisily. **— brawl′er** *n.*

brawn [brôn] *n.* **1** Strong, well-developed muscles. **2** Power of muscles; strength.

brawn·y [brô′nē] *adj.* **brawn·i·er, brawn·i·est** Muscular; strong.

bray [brā] **1** *n.* The loud, harsh call of a donkey or a sound like it. **2** *v.* To make such a sound.

bra·zen [brā′z(ə)n] *adj.* **1** Made of or like brass. **2** Too bold; shameless; saucy: a *brazen* manner. **— brazen it out** To face something boldly as if not ashamed or afraid. **— bra′zen·ly** *adv.*

bra·zier [brā′zhər] *n.* An open pan for holding hot coals or burning charcoal.

Bra·zil [brə-zil′] *n.* A large country in South America. **— Bra·zil′ian** *adj., n.*

Brazil nut An edible South American nut with a white kernel and dark shell.

breach [brēch] **1** *n.* A hole; gap. **2** *v.* To make a hole in; break through: The flood *breached* the dam. **3** *n.* A breaking of a law, obligation, promise, etc.: a *breach* of contract. **4** *n.* A breaking up of friendship; quarrel.

bread [bred] **1** *n.* A baked food made of flour or meal, a liquid, and usually yeast. **2** *v.* To coat with bread crumbs before cooking: to *bread* veal cutlets. **3** *n.* Food or the needs of life. **— know which side one's bread is buttered on** To know where one's best interests lie.

bread·fruit [bred′fro͞ot′] *n.* A round, starchy fruit grown in the South Sea Islands. It tastes like bread when roasted.

breadth [bredth] *n.* **1** Distance from side to side; width. **2** Freedom from narrowness; broadness: *breadth* of vision.

bread·win·ner [bred′win′ər] *n.* A person who supports himself and others by his earnings.

break [brāk] *v.* **broke, brok·en, break·ing,** *n.* **1** *v.* To separate or crack into pieces, as by a blow or pull: Don't *break* the cup; The rope *broke.* **2** *n.* The act of breaking. **3** *n.* A gap, crack, or broken place. **4** *v.* To open the surface of, as with a plow; pierce: to *break* ground. **5** *v.* To put or get out of order; make or become useless: The clock *broke.* **6** *v.* To lessen the force or effect of: The snow *broke* his fall. **7** *v.* To overcome or defeat: to *break* a strike. **8** *n.* A stopping; interruption: to take a *break* from work. **9** *v.* To end or stop: to *break* a silence. **10** *v.* To fail to keep or obey; violate: to *break* a promise; to *break* the law. **11** *v.* To teach to obey; tame: to *break* a horse. **12** *v.* To lower in rank; demote: He was *broken* from corporal to private. **13** *v.* To give or get smaller units of money: to *break* a dollar. **14** *v.* To make or become poor; put or go into debt: Taxes will *break* me. **15** *v.* To make or become known: There may be trouble when the story *breaks.* **16** *v.* To do better than; exceed: The snowfall *broke* all records. **17** *v.* To change suddenly in tone or quality, as a singer's voice. **18** *v.* To dissolve and go away: The clouds *broke.* **19** *v.* To come into being; appear suddenly: The storm *broke;* Dawn is *breaking.* **20** *v.* To force one's way out of; escape from: He *broke* jail. **21** *n.* An escape, as from prison. **22** *n.* *informal* A chance or opportunity: a lucky *break.* **23** *v.* To change or fall off suddenly: The fever *broke.* **24** *n.* A sudden change: a *break* in a fever. **25** *v.* In baseball, to curve sharply near the plate: said of a pitch. **— break away** To leave or go away. **— break down 1** To stop

---

add, āce, câre, pälm; end, ēqual; it, īce; odd, ōpen, ôrder; to͝ok, po͞ol; up, bûrn;
ə = a in *above,* e in *sicken,* i in *possible,* o in *melon,* u in *circus;* y o͞o = u in *fuse;* oil; pout;
ch in *check;* ring; thin; this; zh in *vision.* For ¶ reference, see page 64 · HOW TO

working; undergo mechanical failure. **2** To have a physical or nervous collapse. **3** To lose one's self-control; begin to cry, etc.: The prisoners *broke down* under questioning. **4** To divide into smaller parts for study: Let us *break down* the problem. **— break in 1** To make ready for use; train. **2** To interrupt, as a conversation. **3** To enter by force. **— break into 1** To enter by force. **2** To interrupt. **— break off 1** To stop friendly relations. **2** To end suddenly: The diary *breaks off* here. **— break out 1** To have a rash, as on the skin. **2** To begin or appear suddenly, as a fire, riot, or epidemic. **3** To make an escape. **— break up 1** To spread out; scatter: to *break up* a crowd. **2** To take or fall to pieces. **3** To put an end to; stop. **— break with** To end relations with.

break·a·ble [brā′kə·bəl] *adj.* That can be or is easily broken: a *breakable* dish.

break·age [brā′kij] *n.* **1** A breaking or being broken; break. **2** Damage due to breaking. **3** The cost of or payment for such damage: The restaurant expected to have a certain amount of *breakage*.

break·down [brāk′doun′] *n.* **1** A collapse or failure, as of a machine, one's health, etc. **2** A separation into parts, as of facts, statistics, etc.; analysis. **3** The separation of a chemical compound into simpler compounds or elements.

break·er [brā′kər] *n.* **1** A person or thing that breaks. **2** A wave that breaks into foam on a shore, reef, etc.

break·fast [brek′fəst] **1** *n.* The first meal of the day. **2** *v.* To eat breakfast. ♦ This word was formed by combining *break* and *fast*, because the first meal of the day breaks the fast which has lasted all night.

break·neck [brāk′nek′] *adj.* Likely to break the neck; dangerous: He drove the car at *breakneck* speed.

break·wa·ter [brāk′wô′tər] *n.* A barrier or wall for protecting a harbor or beach from the force of waves.

bream [brēm] *n., pl.* **bream** or **breams 1** Any of several fresh-water fish commonly found in Europe. **2** Any of several fresh-water sunfishes.

Breakwater

breast [brest] **1** *n.* The front of the chest, from the neck to the belly. **2** *n.* One of the glands from which mothers give milk to babies. **3** *n.* The breast as the seat of emotions; heart: Joy filled his *breast*. **4** *v.* To face boldly; oppose: to *breast* the waves. **— make a clean breast of** To make a full confession of.

breast·bone [brest′bōn′] *n.* The long narrow bone in front of the chest, to which most of the ribs are attached.

breast·plate [brest′plāt′] *n.* A piece of armor to protect the breast.

breast stroke A swimming stroke made while lying face down by moving the hands forward together, then sweeping them outward and backward.

breast·work [brest′wûrk′] *n.* A low, temporary wall put up as a defense.

Breast stroke

breath [breth] *n.* **1** Air drawn into and sent out from the lungs. **2** Ability to breathe freely: I lost my *breath*. **3** Life; existence: We hope while *breath* remains. **4** A slight movement of air. **5** Air carrying a fragrance; hint: a *breath* of spring. **— in the same breath** At the same moment. **— under one's breath** In a whisper or mutter.

breathe [brēth] *v.* **breathed, breath·ing 1** To draw air into and let it out from the lungs; respire. **2** To be alive; live. **3** To stop for breath; rest. **4** To whisper: He *breathed* a secret in her ear. **5** To move gently, as a breeze. **6** To put into: to *breathe* life into a statue.

breath·er [brē′thər] *n.* **1** A person who breathes, especially in a certain manner: a heavy *breather*. **2** *informal* A short rest; rest period.

breath·less [breth′lis] *adj.* **1** Out of breath; panting. **2** Holding the breath from fear, excitement, etc. **3** Taking the breath away: *breathless* speed. **— breath′less·ly** *adv.*

breath·tak·ing [breth′tā′king] *adj.* Thrilling; exciting: a *breathtaking* trapeze act.

bred [bred] Past tense and past participle of BREED.

breech [brēch] *n.* **1** The part of a gun, cannon, etc., that is behind the barrel. **2** The lower, rear part of the body.

breech·cloth [brēch′klôth′] *n.* A loincloth.

breech·es [brich′iz] *n.pl.* **1** Short trousers that fasten below the knees. **2** Any trousers.

breed [brēd] *v.* **bred, breed·ing,** *n.* **1** *v.* To produce young; propagate. **2** *v.* To raise (plants or animals) to sell or to develop a new variety or strain: to *breed* roses. **3** *v.* To give rise to; produce: Speeding *breeds* accidents. **4** *v.* To bring up; train: He was *bred* to be a lawyer. **5** *n.* A particular kind, variety, or race of animals or plants. **— breed′er** *n.*

breeder reactor A nuclear reactor that produces more fissionable material than it uses.

breed·ing [brē′ding] *n.* **1** The producing of young. **2** Training or upbringing as displayed in one's manners and behavior. **3** The raising of plants or animals, especially to get new or better kinds.

breeze [brēz] *n., v.* **breezed, breez·ing 1** A light, gentle wind. **2** *v. informal* To move quickly and easily: She *breezed* through the door.

breeze·way [brēz′wā′] *n.* A passageway between two buildings, as a house and a garage, having a roof but no walls.

breez·y [brē′zē] *adj.* **breez·i·er, breez·i·est 1** Having breezes blowing. **2** Gay; lively: a *breezy* attitude. **— breez′i·ly** *adv.* **— breez′i·ness** *n.*

breth·ren [breth′rən] *n.pl.* **1** Brothers. **2** Members of the same church or society.

Bret·on [bret′(ə)n] **1** *adj.* Of or from Brittany. **2** *n.* A person from Brittany. **3** *n.* The language of Brittany.

breve [brev *or* brēv] *n.* A mark (˘) sometimes put over a vowel to indicate that it has a short sound or put over an unstressed syllable in verse.

bre·vi·ar·y [brē′vē·er′ē] *n., pl.* **bre·vi·ar·ies** In the Roman Catholic and Eastern Orthodox churches, a book containing the prayers that are to be said every day by priests.

brev·i·ty [brev′ə·tē] *n.* Briefness; shortness.

brew [brōō] **1** *v.* To make, as beer or ale, by soaking, boiling, and fermenting malt, hops, etc. **2** *n.* Something brewed, as beer or ale. **3** *v.* To prepare, as by boiling or soaking: to *brew* tea. **4** *n.* The amount brewed at one time. **5** *v.* To make up; devise: to *brew* mischief. **6** *v.* To be coming up; gather, as a storm, trouble, etc. **— brew′er** *n.*

brew·er·y [brōō′ər·ē] *n., pl.* **brew·er·ies** A place for brewing beer and ale.

Brezh·nev [brezh·nyev′], **Leonid,** born 1906, head of the Soviet Russian Communist Party.

bri·ar [brī′ər] *n.* **1** A tobacco pipe made from the root of a European shrub. **2** Another spelling of BRIER[1] and BRIER[2].

bribe [brīb] *n., v.* **bribed, brib·ing 1** *n.* A gift offered or given to persuade someone to do something wrong. **2** *v.* To give or offer a bribe.

brib·er·y [brī′bər·ē] *n.* The giving, offering, or taking of a bribe.

bric-a-brac [brik′ə·brak] *n.* Small objects, rare or beautiful, used to decorate a room.

brick [brik] **1** *n.* A block of clay that has been baked by the sun or in a kiln, used for building, paving, etc. **2** *n.* Bricks thought of together: a wall made of *brick.* **3** *adj. use:* a *brick* house. **4** *v.* To build with bricks. **5** *v.* To cover or wall up with bricks: We *bricked* up the fireplace. **6** *n.* Any object shaped like a brick.

brick·bat [brik′bat′] *n.* **1** A piece of brick used for throwing at someone or something. **2** *informal* An insulting remark.

brick·lay·er [brik′lā′ər] *n.* A man skilled in building with brick. **— brick′lay′ing** *n.*

brick·work [brik′wûrk′] *n.* Something that is made of or with bricks.

bri·dal [brīd′(ə)l] *adj.* Of or having to do with a bride or wedding: *bridal* flowers.

bride [brīd] *n.* A woman who is being married or who has been recently married.

bride·groom [brīd′grōōm′] *n.* A man who is being married or who has been recently married. ◆ This word was formed by combining two Old English words meaning *bride* and *man.* Thus the word meant *the bride's man.*

brides·maid [brīdz′mād′] *n.* A young woman who attends a bride at her wedding.

bridge[1] [brij] *n., v.* **bridged, bridg·ing 1** *n.* A structure built across water, a ravine, road, etc., on which people, cars, etc., cross over. **2** *v.* To build a bridge across: Engineers *bridged* the strait. **3** *v.* To extend across; span: A plank *bridged* the creek. **4** *n.* A platform raised above the deck of a ship for the officer in command, pilot, etc. **5** *n.* The upper, bony ridge of the nose. **6** *n.* The part of a pair of eyeglasses that rests on the nose. **7** *n.* A thin piece of wood that supports the strings of a violin, cello, etc. **8** *n.* A mounting for false teeth attached to real teeth.

bridge[2] [brij] *n.* A card game played by two pairs of partners.

bridge·head [brij′hed′] *n.* A position on the enemy's side of a river made or taken by advance troops of an attacking force.

bridge·work [brij′wûrk′] *n.* False teeth mounted and attached on each side to real teeth.

bri·dle [brīd′(ə)l] *n., v.* **bri·dled, bri·dling 1** *n.* The part of a harness for the head of a horse, including the bit and reins. **2** *v.* To put a bridle on. **3** *v.* To check or control: She *bridled* her anger. **4** *v.* To raise the head and draw in the chin as a way of showing anger, pride, etc.

Bridle

brief [brēf] **1** *adj.* Not long; short: a *brief* holiday. **2** *adj.* Of few words; concise: a *brief* talk. **3** *n.* In law, a summary of the facts, points of law, etc., of a case, for the use of lawyers in court. **4** *v.* To prepare in advance by instructing or advising: to *brief* salesmen. **— hold a brief for** To be on the side of; argue for. **— in brief** In short; briefly. **— brief′ly** *adv.*

brief·case [brēf′kās′] *n.* A flexible case or bag, usually of leather, for carrying books, papers, etc.

bri·er[1] [brī′ər] *n.* A prickly bush or shrub, as the sweetbrier.

bri·er[2] [brī′ər] *n.* A European shrub from whose roots briar pipes for tobacco are made.

brig [brig] *n.* **1** A square-rigged sailing vessel having two masts. **2** A prison on a ship.

bri·gade [bri·gād′] *n.* **1** A unit of troops smaller than a division but rather large. **2** A group of people organized for a purpose: a fire *brigade.*

brig·a·dier [brig′ə·dir′] *n.* A brigadier general.

brigadier general A military officer ranking next above a colonel and next below a major general.

Brig

---

add, āce, câre, pälm;   end, ēqual;   it, íce;   odd, ōpen, ôrder;   tŏŏk, pŏŏl;   up, bûrn;
ə = a in *above,* e in *sicken,* i in *possible,* o in *melon,* u in *circus;*   yōō = u in *fuse;*   oil;   pout;
check; ring; thin; this; zh in *vision.*   For ¶ reference, see page 64 · HOW TO

brig·and [brig′ənd] *n.* A robber or bandit, especially one of a band of outlaws.

brig·an·tine [brig′ən·tēn] *n.* A sailing vessel with the foremast square-rigged and the mainmast fore-and-aft-rigged.

bright [brīt] **1** *adj.* Giving off or reflecting much light; shining: a *bright* lamp. **2** *adj.* Vivid in color or sound; glowing: *bright* green. **3** *adj.* Having a quick, clever mind. **4** *adj.* Full of gladness or hope: a *bright* future. **5** *adj.* Splendid; glorious: *bright* fame. **6** *adv.* In a bright way; brightly: The sun shone *bright* all day. **— bright′ly** *adv.* **— bright′ness** *n.*

bright·en [brīt′(ə)n] *v.* To make or become bright or brighter.

bril·liance [bril′yəns] *n.* **1** Intense brightness or sparkle. **2** Very great intelligence. **3** Magnificence; excellence.

bril·lian·cy [bril′yən·sē] *n.* Brilliance.

bril·liant [bril′yənt] **1** *adj.* Sparkling or glowing with light; very bright. **2** *adj.* Very intelligent or able: a *brilliant* scientist. **3** *adj.* Splendid; illustrious: a *brilliant* performance. **4** *n.* A diamond or other gem cut so as to sparkle. **— bril′liant·ly** *adv.* **— bril′liant·ness** *n.*

brim [brim] *n., v.* **brimmed, brim·ming** **1** *n.* The upper edge of a cup, bowl, etc.; rim. **2** *n.* A rim that sticks out, as on a hat. **3** *n.* An edge or margin. **4** *v.* To fill or be filled to the brim.

brim·ful [brim′fool′] *adj.* Full to the brim.

brim·stone [brim′stōn′] *n.* Sulfur.

brin·dle [brin′dəl] **1** *n.* A brindled color. **2** *adj.* Brindled.

brin·dled [brin′dəld] *adj.* Tawny or grayish with darker streaks or spots: a *brindled* horse.

brine [brīn] *n.* **1** Water that has a great deal of salt in it, often used for pickling. **2** The ocean.

bring [bring] *v.* **brought, bring·ing** **1** To carry or cause to come with oneself or to or toward a place: *Bring* some milk home; *Bring* the dog. **2** To cause to happen or come about: War *brings* destruction. **3** To attract or draw; fetch: The knocking *brought* John to the door. **4** To sell for: The house *brought* a good price. **5** To influence or persuade: We *brought* him to our point of view. **6** To put before a court; start: to *bring* suit for damages. **— bring about** To make happen; cause; accomplish. **— bring around** or **bring round** **1** To win over gradually; persuade. **2** To bring back to consciousness; revive. **— bring forth** **1** To give birth to. **2** To produce: to *bring forth* an opinion. **— bring off** To do successfully. **— bring on** To cause; lead to. **— bring out** **1** To make known, as the truth. **2** To bring before the public; introduce, as a person, play, or book. **— bring to** To bring back to consciousness; revive. **— bring up** **1** To take care of through childhood; rear. **2** To call attention to: *Bring up* the subject at the next meeting. **3** To cough or vomit up. **4** To stop or make stop suddenly.

brink [bringk] *n.* The edge of a steep place, as a cliff. **— on the brink of** Very close to: *on the brink of* war.

brin·y [brī′nē] *adj.* **brin·i·er, brin·i·est** Of or like brine; salty.

brisk [brisk] *adj.* **1** Acting or moving quickly; lively: a *brisk* walk; Business is *brisk*. **2** Cool and stimulating: a *brisk* morning. **— brisk′ly** *adv.* **— brisk′ness** *n.*

bris·ket [bris′kit] *n.* Meat on or cut from the breast of an animal.

bris·tle [bris′(ə)l] *n., v.* **bris·tled, bris·tling** **1** *n.* A coarse, stiff hair on the back of a hog. **2** *n.* Any similar real or artificial hair, often used for brushes. **3** *v.* To stand on end, like bristles. **4** *v.* To make the bristles stand up, as in anger. **5** *v.* To show anger or annoyance. **6** *v.* To be thickly set or covered: The fort *bristled* with cannon. **— bris′tly** *adj.*

Brit·ain [brit′(ə)n] *n.* A shorter form for GREAT BRITAIN.

Bri·tan·ni·a [bri·tan′ē·ə] *n.* **1** The ancient Roman name for Great Britain. **2** In poetry, Great Britain.

A cat bristling

Brit·ish [brit′ish] **1** *adj.* Of, from, or having to do with Great Britain or its people. **2** *n.* **(the British)** The people of Great Britain.

British Columbia A province of Canada on the sw coast.

British Commonwealth of Nations An association formed of Great Britain, her colonies, and nations that were formerly her colonies, as Canada, Australia, India, etc.

British Empire Great Britain with its territories, colonies, and other possessions.

Brit·ish·er [brit′ish·ər] *n.* A person born in or a subject of Great Britain.

British Isles Great Britain, Ireland, and the small islands surrounding them.

British thermal unit The long form of BTU.

Brit·on [brit′(ə)n] *n.* **1** A member of a Celtic people who used to live in England before the Anglo-Saxon invasions. **2** A Britisher.

Brit·ta·ny [brit′ə·nē] *n.* A region of western France.

brit·tle [brit′(ə)l] **1** *adj.* Likely to break or snap; fragile: *brittle* bones. **2** *n.* A hard, crunchy kind of candy made with nuts.

British Isles

broach [brōch] *v.* **1** To mention for the first time; introduce: to *broach* a subject in a conversation. **2** To make a hole in so as to withdraw liquid: to *broach* a cask of wine.

broad [brôd] *adj.* **1** Large in width; wide. **2** Of considerable size; large and spacious: a *broad* plain. **3** Open and clear: *broad* daylight. **4** Wide in scope; not narrow or limited: a *broad* rule. **5** Liberal; tolerant. **6** General; main: a *broad* outline. **7** Easy to understand; obvious: a *broad* hint. **8** Vulgar: a *broad* joke. — **broad′ly** *adv.*

broad·cast [brôd′kast′] *v.* **broad·cast** or **broad·cast·ed, broad·cast·ing,** *n., adj., adv.* **1** *v.* To send by radio or television; transmit. **2** *n.* A sending by radio or television; transmission. **3** *n.* Music, words, etc., sent out by radio or television; program: Did you see last night's *broadcast?* **4** *adj.* Sent by radio or television. **5** *v.* To scatter, as seed, over a wide area. **6** *n.* A scattering or sowing over a wide area. **7** *adj.* Scattered, as seed. **8** *adv.* So as to scatter over a wide area: to sow wheat *broadcast.*

broad·cloth [brôd′klôth′] *n.* **1** A fine woolen cloth. **2** A closely woven, fine cloth of cotton, silk, etc., used for shirts, dresses, etc.

broad·en [brôd′(ə)n] *v.* To make or become broad or broader; widen.

broad jump In athletics, a contest to see who can jump the farthest, rather than the highest.

broad-mind·ed [brôd′mīn′did] *adj.* Without prejudice; tolerant: a *broadminded* attitude. — **broad′-mind′ed·ness** *n.*

broad·side [brôd′sīd′] **1** *n.* The side of a ship above the water line. **2** *n.* The firing of all the guns on one side of a ship at once, or the guns themselves. **3** *adv.* With the side turned or exposed: The car was hit *broadside.* **4** *n.* A sheet of paper printed on one side: a *broadside* advertising a sale.

broad·sword [brôd′sôrd′] *n.* A sword with a broad blade for cutting and slashing.

Broad·way [brôd′wā] *n.* A street in New York City noted for its theaters.

bro·cade [brō·kād′] *n.* A fabric woven with a raised design, often in gold or silver threads.

broc·co·li [brok′ə·lē] *n.* A variety of cauliflower. Its green stalks and tiny green flowers are eaten as a vegetable.

bro·chure [brō·shoor′] *n.* A pamphlet or booklet.

bro·gan [brō′gən] *n.* A heavy shoe.

brogue[1] [brōg] *n.* Speech characteristic of a certain region, especially an Irish accent in the pronunciation of English.

brogue[2] [brōg] *n.* A heavy oxford shoe, decorated with stitches and rows of holes.

broil [broil] *v.* **1** To cook, as meat, close to a flame or other source of heat. **2** To make or become very hot.

broil·er [broi′lər] *n.* **1** A pan, rack, or grill for broiling. **2** A tender young chicken for broiling.

broke [brōk] **1** Past tense of BREAK. **2** *adj. informal* Without money.

bro·ken [brō′kən] **1** Past participle of BREAK. **2** *adj.* Cracked or shattered into pieces; fractured. **3** *adj.* Out of order; damaged: a *broken* radio. **4** *adj.* Not kept or followed; violated: a *broken* law. **5** *adj.* Interrupted: *broken* sleep. **6** *adj.* Rough; uneven, as ground. **7** *adj.* Humbled; beaten: a *broken* man. **8** *adj.* Not properly spoken: *broken* English.

bro·ken-down [brō′kən·doun′] *adj.* **1** Out of order; not working: a *broken-down* machine. **2** Sick or disabled: a *broken-down* horse.

bro·ken·heart·ed [brō′kən·här′tid] *adj.* Full of grief or sorrow.

bro·ker [brō′kər] *n.* A person who buys and sells for others, as stocks, real estate, etc.

bro·ker·age [brō′kər·ij] *n.* The business of a broker, or the fee paid to him.

bro·mide [brō′mīd] *n.* **1** A compound of bromine with another element or group of elements. Some bromides are used as drugs to calm the nerves. **2** A dull, often heard remark, as "Keep smiling."

bro·mine [brō′mēn] *n.* A dark reddish brown liquid element that gives off suffocating fumes. Its chemical properties resemble those of chlorine and iodine.

bron·chi [brong′kī] *n., pl.* of **bron·chus** [brong′kəs] The two hollow tubes by which air passes from the windpipe to each of the lungs.

bron·chi·al [brong′·kē·əl] *adj.* Of or having to do with the bronchi or any of their smaller tubes or branches within the lungs.

windpipe (trachea)
bronchi
lungs

bron·chi·tis [brong·kī′tis] *n.* Acute inflammation of the bronchial tubes, marked by coughing.

bron·co or **bron·cho** [brong′kō] *n., pl.* **bron·cos** or **bron·chos** A small, wild or partly broken horse of the western U.S.

bron·to·sau·rus [bron′tə·sôr′əs] *n.* An extinct, very large dinosaur of North America.

bronze [bronz] *n., v.* **bronzed, bronz·ing, adj.** **1** *n.* A hard, reddish brown alloy of copper and tin. **2** *adj. use:* a *bronze* vase. **3** *v.* To coat with bronze. **4** *n., adj.* Reddish brown. **5** *v.* To make or become such a color. **6** *n.* A statue of bronze.

Bronze Age A time before history was written, after the Stone Age and before the Iron Age, when weapons and tools were made of bronze.

brooch [brōch] *n.* An ornamental pin secured by a catch, worn near the neck of a dress.

add, āce, câre, pälm; end, ēqual; it, īce; odd, ōpen, ôrder; toŏk, pool; up, bûrn;
ə = a in *above*, e in *sicken*, i in *possible*, o in *melon*, u in *circus*; yoō = u in *fuse*; oil; pout;
check; ring; thin; this; zh in *vision*. For ¶ reference, see page 64 · HOW TO

brood [brood] **1** *n.* All of the young produced at one time by a bird. **2** *v.* To hatch by sitting on, as eggs. **3** *n.* All of the young of the same mother. **4** *v.* To think deeply in a worried manner: He *brooded* over his low marks.

brood·er [brood′dər] *n.* **1** A heated shelter for raising young fowl, as chickens, ducks, etc. **2** A person or animal that broods.

brook[1] [brook] *n.* A natural stream smaller than a river.

brook[2] [brook] *v.* To put up with; stand for: He would *brook* no interference with his plan.

broom [broom] *n.* **1** A brush for sweeping, with a long handle. **2** A shrub with yellow flowers, small leaves, and stiff green branches.

broom·stick [broom′stik′] *n.* The handle of a broom.

broth [brôth] *n.* A soup made by boiling meat, vegetables, etc., in water and then straining.

broth·er [bruth′ər] *n., pl.* **broth·ers** or, *less frequently,* **breth·ren** **1** A boy or man having the same parents as another person of either sex. **2** A fellow member of the same organization, profession, etc. **3** A member of a religious order who is not a priest.

broth·er·hood [bruth′ər·hood] *n.* **1** The condition of being brothers. **2** A group of men organized for some purpose, as fellowship.

broth·er·in·law [bruth′ər·in·lô′] *n., pl.* **broth·ers·in·law** **1** A brother of one's husband or wife. **2** The husband of one's sister.

broth·er·ly [bruth′ər·lē] *adj.* **1** Of or like a brother. **2** Affectionate; kindly.

brougham [broom *or* broo′əm] *n.* A closed carriage or automobile with the driver's seat outside.

brought [brôt] Past tense and past participle of BRING.

brow [brou] *n.* **1** The front, upper part of the head; forehead. **2** The eyebrow. **3** The upper edge of a steep place: the *brow* of a hill.

Brougham

brow·beat [brou′bēt′] *v.* **brow·beat, brow·beat·en, brow·beat·ing** To bully or frighten by a stern or rough manner.

brown [broun] **1** *n.* The color of coffee, toast, or milk chocolate; a mixture of red, yellow, and black. **2** *adj.* Of this color. **3** *v.* To make or become brown. — **brown′ish** *adj.*

Brown [broun], **John,** 1800–1859, U.S. fighter against slavery.

brown·ie [brou′nē] *n.* **1** In folk tales, an elf or sprite who does good, useful deeds at night. **2** (*written* **Brownie**) A junior girl scout. **3** A small, flat chocolate cake with nuts.

Brown·ing [brou′ning], **Robert,** 1812–1889, English poet.

brown rice Unpolished rice.

brown·stone [broun′stōn′] *n.* A reddish brown sandstone used for buildings.

brown sugar Unrefined sugar, brown in color.

browse [brouz] *v.* **browsed, brows·ing 1** To feed on or nibble at leaves, shoots, etc.: Giraffes *browse* on trees. **2** To glance at a book or books, reading a little at one place or another.

bru·in [broo′in] *n.* A bear, especially a brown bear.

bruise [brooz] *v.* **bruised, bruis·ing,** *n.* **1** *v.* To injure a part of the body without breaking the skin, as by a blow. **2** *n.* An injury caused by bruising, as a black-and-blue mark. **3** *v.* To dent or hurt the outside of: Don't *bruise* these pears. **4** *v.* To hurt or offend, as feelings.

bruit [broot] *v.* To make known by talking, especially in the phrase **bruit about**: The rumor of their marriage was *bruited about.*

brunch [brunch] *n.* A meal, usually in the late morning, combining breakfast and lunch. ◆ This word is a blend of *br(eakfast)* and *(l)unch.*

bru·nette or **bru·net** [broo·net′] **1** *adj.* Having more or less dark skin, hair, and eyes. **2** *n.* A brunette person. ◆ *Brunette* usually refers to a girl or woman, whereas *brunet* is used only of a boy or man.

brunt [brunt] *n.* The main shock or force of a blow, attack, etc.; heaviest part: He bore the *brunt* of their accusations.

brush[1] [brush] **1** *n.* A tool having bristles, hairs, wires, etc., fastened to a back or handle, used for sweeping, scrubbing, painting, or grooming. **2** *v.* To use a brush on; paint, sweep, polish, etc., with a brush. **3** *n.* The act of brushing. **4** *n.* A light, grazing touch: a *brush* of the lips. **5** *v.* To touch lightly in passing. **6** *v.* To remove with or as if with a brush: He *brushed* the papers from the desk. **7** *n.* A brief encounter, especially a fight or skirmish: a *brush* with the law. **8** *n.* A conductor making contact between moving and stationary parts of an electric motor or generator. — **brush off** *informal* To dismiss or refuse abruptly. — **brush up** To refresh one's memory of; review: *Brush up* your Latin.

brush[2] [brush] *n.* **1** A growth of small trees and shrubs. **2** Wooded country where few people live. **3** Branches that have been cut off; brushwood.

brush·wood [brush′wood′] *n.* **1** Branches chopped or broken off. **2** A growth of small trees or shrubs.

brusque [brusk] *adj.* Blunt and abrupt in manner; curt: a *brusque* refusal. — **brusque′ly** *adv.*

Brus·sels [brus′əlz] *n.* The capital of Belgium, in the central part.

Brussels sprouts 1 A plant with heads like little cabbages along the stalk. **2** The small, edible heads on this plant.

bru·tal [broot′(ə)l] *adj.* **1** Of or like a brute; cruel; savage. **2** Unfeeling; rude; coarse. — **bru′tal·ly** *adv.*

bru·tal·i·ty [broo·tal′ə·tē] *n., pl.* **bru·tal·i·ties 1** A being brutal. **2** A brutal act.

brute [broot] **1** *n.* An animal. **2** *n.* A person who is stupid and cruel or coarse. **3** *adj.* Without mind or feeling: the *brute* force of the gale. — **brut′ish** *adj.*

Bry·ant [brī′ənt], **William Cullen,** 1794–1878, U.S. poet.

B.S. Abbreviation of BACHELOR OF SCIENCE.

BTU or **B.T.U.** Abbreviation of BRITISH THERMAL UNIT, the quantity of heat needed to raise the temperature of one pound of water one degree Fahrenheit.

bu. Abbreviation of: **1** BUSHEL. **2** Bushels.

bub·ble [bub′əl] *n., v.* **bub·bled, bub·bling** **1** *n.* A film of liquid in the form of a ball, filled with air or other gas. **2** *n.* A round space filled with air or other gas, as in a liquid or solid such as ice. **3** *v.* To form or give off bubbles; rise in bubbles, as boiling water. **4** *v.* To flow with a gurgling sound, as a brook. **5** *n.* An idea or plan that seems fine but turns out worthless and unsubstantial. **6** *v.* To express joy, delight, etc., in a happy way: He *bubbled* with glee. **— bubble over** To be unable to keep in one's excitement, joy, etc.

bubble chamber An apparatus in which movement of atomic particles leaves trails of bubbles.

bubble gum A kind of chewing gum that can be blown into large bubbles.

bu·bon·ic plague [byoo·bon′ik] A deadly contagious disease with fever, chills, and swollen lymph glands, spread by fleas mainly from rats.

buc·ca·neer [buk′ə·nir′] *n.* A pirate.

Bu·chan·an [byoo·kan′ən], **James,** 1791–1868, 15th president of the U.S., 1857–1861.

Bu·cha·rest [b(y)oo′kə·rest] *n.* The capital of Rumania, in the southern part.

buck[1] [buk] **1** *n.* The male of certain animals, as of antelope, deer, rabbits, goats, etc. **2** *v.* To jump suddenly with back arched up, as a horse trying to throw off its rider. **3** *n.* Such a jump by a horse. **4** *v.* To throw off (a rider) by bucking. **5** *v.* To charge or butt with the head lowered, as a football player, or an animal such as a goat. **— buck up** To take courage or cheer up.

A bucking horse

buck[2] [buk] *n. slang* A dollar.

buck·board [buk′bôrd′] *n.* A light, open carriage having, instead of springs, a flexible frame of long, springy boards.

buck·et [buk′it] *n.* **1** A deep, round container with a flat bottom and curved handle, used for carrying water, coal, etc.; pail. **2** As much as a bucket will hold: Add two *buckets* of water. **3** Something like a bucket, as the scoop on a dredge or steam shovel. **— buck′et·ful′** *n.*

bucket seat A single seat with a rounded back, used in racing and sports cars and some aircraft.

buck·eye [buk′ī′] *n.* **1** The horse chestnut tree. **2** Its glossy, brown seed or nut.

buck·le [buk′əl] *n., v.* **buck·led, buck·ling** **1** *n.* A clasp for fastening together two loose ends, as of a strap or belt. **2** *n.* Anything that looks like a buckle, used to decorate shoes, etc. **3** *v.* To fasten with or as if with a buckle. **4** *v.* To bend under pressure; crumple; warp: The dam *buckled,* then collapsed. **5** *n.* A bend, kink, or twist. **— buckle down** To work hard; apply oneself vigorously.

buck·ler [buk′lər] *n.* A small, round shield for defense.

buck·ram [buk′rəm] *n.* A coarse, stiffened fabric used in binding books, lining garments, etc.

buck·saw [buk′sô′] *n.* A saw set in an adjustable frame, used for cutting wood.

buck·shot [buk′shot′] *n.* A large size of lead shot, used in a shotgun for big game.

buck·skin [buk′skin′] *n.* **1** A soft, strong, grayish yellow leather made from skins of deer or sheep. **2** (*pl.*) Clothing made of such leather.

buck·wheat [buk′(h)wēt′] *n.* **1** A plant with three-sided brown seeds, ground into flour or fed to animals. **2** The flour, used to make pancakes.

bu·col·ic [byoo·kol′ik] *adj.* **1** Of or about shepherds; pastoral. **2** Of the country; rural; rustic: a *bucolic* scene.

bud [bud] *n., v.* **bud·ded, bud·ding** **1** *n.* A small swelling on a plant, that will grow into a flower, branch, or leaf. **2** *n.* A half-opened blossom. **3** *v.* To put forth buds. **4** *v.* To begin to grow or develop: His talents *budded* during early youth. **— nip in the bud** To stop in the early stages: to *nip* a rebellion *in the bud*.

Bu·da·pest [boo′də·pest] *n.* The capital of Hungary.

Bud·dha [boo′də *or* bood′ə] *n.,* 563?–483 B.C., a religious leader of India, the founder of Buddhism. ◆ The name *Buddha* in Sanskrit means *The Enlightened.*

Bud·dhism [bood′iz·əm *or* boo′diz·əm] *n.* An Asian religion, founded by Buddha, that holds that freedom from pain, suffering, and desire can be reached by right living, meditation, and self-control. **— Bud′dhist** *adj., n.*

bud·dy [bud′ē] *n., pl.* **bud·dies** *informal* Chum; pal; partner.

budge [buj] *v.* **budged, budg·ing** To move even slightly: The mule refused to *budge.*

budg·et [buj′it] **1** *n.* A plan for spending the money received for a given period: a household *budget.* **2** *v.* To draw up a budget. **3** *v.* To plan carefully for the use of: to *budget* time.

Bue·nos Ai·res [bwā′nəs ī′riz] A port city, the capital of Argentina.

buff [buf] **1** *n.* A thick, soft, brownish yellow leather, made from the skin of a buffalo or ox. **2** *n., adj.* Brownish yellow. **3** *n.* A stick or

add, āce, câre, pälm; end, ēqual; it, īce; odd, ōpen, ôrder; took, pool; up, bûrn;
ə = a in *above,* e in *sicken,* i in *possible,* o in *melon,* u in *circus;* yoo = u in *fuse;* oil; pout;
check; ring; thin; this; zh in *vision.* For ¶ reference, see page 64 · HOW TO

wheel covered with leather, used for polishing. **4** *v.* To clean or polish, as with a buff.

buf·fa·lo [buf′ə·lō] *n., pl.* **buf·fa·loes** or **buf·fa·los 1** A wild ox of Europe, Africa, and Asia, having a thick body and curved horns. Some are tamed to serve as work animals. **2** The bison of North America.

Cape buffalo, 54 in. high at shoulder

Buf·fa·lo [buf′ə·lō] *n.* A city in western New York, along Lake Erie.

Buffalo Bill, 1846–1917, U.S. army scout and showman. His real name was William F. Cody.

buff·er[1] [buf′ər] *n.* A person or thing that polishes or buffs, as a leather-covered stick.

buff·er[2] [buf′ər] *n.* Anything that lessens or cushions the shock of a blow.

buffer state A small country between two larger enemy countries, that serves as a barrier between them.

buf·fet[1] [boo·fā′] *n.* **1** A piece of dining-room furniture for holding silver, glassware, or table linen. **2** A meal at which guests serve themselves from platters of food.

buf·fet[2] [buf′it] **1** *n.* A blow or slap with the hand. **2** *n.* Any blow or upset: the *buffets* of fortune. **3** *v.* To strike over and over: The shore was *buffeted* by the waves.

buf·foon [bu·foon′] *n.* **1** A clown. **2** A person who tries to be funny and plays practical jokes. **— buf·foon′er·y** *n.*

bug [bug] *n.* **1** Any of a group of insects with biting and sucking mouth parts, usually wingless, but some having two pairs of wings. **2** *informal* Any insect. **3** *informal* A germ that causes disease.

bug·a·boo [bug′ə·boo] *n., pl.* **bug·a·boos** A bugbear.

bug·bear [bug′bâr′] *n.* **1** A make-believe person or thing, used in stories to frighten children. **2** Anything used to cause fear without good reason.

bug·gy [bug′ē] *n., pl.* **bug·gies 1** A light carriage with one large seat, drawn by one horse. **2** A baby's carriage.

bu·gle [byoo′gəl] *n., v.* **bu·gled, bu·gling 1** *n.* A kind of small trumpet, usually not having keys or valves. It is used to sound out orders and signals, as to soldiers. **2** *v.* To sound or call on a bugle. **— bu′gler** *n.*

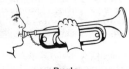
Bugle

◆ *Bugles* were originally made from the horns of oxen, and the word *bugle* comes from a Latin word for *ox.*

build [bild] *v.* **built** (or **build·ed**: seldom used today), **build·ing,** *n.* **1** *v.* To make by putting parts or materials together; construct; erect: to *build* a house. **2** *v.* To make; create:

to *build* a business. **3** *n.* The way a person or thing is constructed; form; figure: He has the *build* of an athlete.

build·er [bil′dər] *n.* A person who builds, especially one in charge of putting up houses or other buildings.

build·ing [bil′ding] *n.* **1** Something that is built; a structure, as a house, barn, or factory. **2** The act or business of someone who builds.

building block 1 One of a set of children's blocks used for building. **2** A basic or supporting unit: Atoms are the *building blocks* of matter.

built [bilt] Past tense of BUILD.

built-in [bilt′in′] *adj.* That cannot be taken out or removed: a *built-in* bookcase.

bulb [bulb] *n.* **1** The enlarged spherical underground bud of certain plants, as the lily and onion, from which the roots and upper parts grow. **2** Anything in the form of a bulb: an electric light *bulb.*

bul·bous [bul′bəs] *adj.* **1** Of or growing from bulbs. **2** Shaped like a bulb: a *bulbous* nose.

Bul·gar·i·a [bul·gâr′ē·ə] *n.* A country in SE Europe, along the Black Sea. **— Bul·gar′i·an** *adj., n.*

Onion bulb

bulge [bulj] *n., v.* **bulged, bulg·ing 1** *n.* A part that swells out: The candy made a *bulge* in his cheek. **2** *v.* To swell out.

bulk [bulk] **1** *n.* Great size or mass: The package's *bulk* made it hard to carry. **2** *n.* A greater or main part: The *bulk* of the work is finished. **3** *v.* To appear large or important; loom. **— in bulk 1** Not packaged; loose. **2** In large amounts.

bulk·head [bulk′hed′] *n.* Any of several upright partitions dividing a ship into watertight sections or compartments.

bulk·y [bul′kē] *adj.* **bulk·i·er, bulk·i·est** Having great size, especially so big and clumsy as to be hard to handle.

bull[1] [bool] *n.* **1** A male of the family that includes the ox. **2** The male of certain other animals, as the elephant or whale. **3** *adj. use:* *bull* moose.

bull[2] [bool] *n.* An official pronouncement or order from the Pope: a papal *bull.*

bull[3] [bool] *n.* A funny mistake in language, as in "The kitchen and dining room are the same size, especially the kitchen."

bull·dog [bool′dôg′] *n., v.* **bull·dogged, bull·dog·ging 1** *n.* A stocky dog with a large head and jaws that grip and hold. **2** *v. informal* To throw (a steer) down by gripping its horns and twisting its head.

bull·doze [bool′dōz′] *v.* **bull·dozed, bull·doz·ing 1** *slang* To frighten by using force or threats; bully. **2** To dig, level, scrape, etc., with a bulldozer.

Bulldog

bull·doz·er [bŏŏl′dō′zər] *n.* **1** A tractor with a broad, heavy steel blade in front, used for moving earth and rubble. **2** *informal* A person who bulldozes.

bul·let [bŏŏl′it] *n.* A metal ball or shaped cone, for shooting from a firearm.

bul·le·tin [bŏŏl′ə·tən] *n.* **1** A short account of the latest news.

Bulldozer

2 A magazine or paper put out at regular times, especially by a group for its members.

bulletin board A board, hung on a wall, on which announcements or notices are posted.

bull·fight [bŏŏl′fīt′] *n.* A contest in which a matador, using a cape and sword, shows his skill at handling and killing a bull. **— bull′fight′er** *n.* **— bull′fight′ing** *n.*

bull·finch [bŏŏl′finch′] *n.* A songbird of Europe with a short beak and red breast.

bull·frog [bŏŏl′frog′] *n.* A large frog with a deep, low croak.

bull·head [bŏŏl′hed′] *n.* Any of various American fishes with a broad head, as the catfish.

bull·head·ed [bŏŏl′hed′id] *adj.* Stubborn.

bul·lion [bŏŏl′yən] *n.* Bars of gold or silver, often later made into coins.

bul·lock [bŏŏl′ək] *n.* A steer or ox.

bull's-eye [bŏŏlz′ī] *n.* **1** The round, usually colored center of a target. **2** A shot that hits this center. **3** A small lantern with a lens formed like a half-sphere for making a stronger light.

bul·ly [bŏŏl′ē] *n., pl.* **bul·lies,** *v.* **bul·lied, bul·ly·ing,** *adj., interj.* **1** *n.* A person who likes frightening or hurting weaker people. **2** *v.* To act like a bully. **3** *adj. informal* Excellent; very good: a *bully* dinner. **4** *interj.* Excellent!

bul·rush [bŏŏl′rush′] *n.* A tall plant growing in shallow water or damp ground.

bul·wark [bŏŏl′wərk] *n.* **1** A sturdy wall of stone or earth, raised for defense against an enemy. **2** Any strong defense or safeguard: Democracy is a *bulwark* of liberty. **3** (*pl.*) The side of a ship above the deck.

bum [bum] *n., v.* **bummed, bum·ming,** *adj. informal* **1** *n.* A person who lives as a loafer and does no work; a worthless person; tramp. **2** *v.* To pass time idly; loaf. **3** *v.* To get by begging: to *bum* a cigarette. **4** *adj.* Bad: a *bum* knee; a *bum* check.

bum·ble·bee [bum′bəl·bē′] *n.* A large, hairy type of bee, with a loud buzz.

bump [bump] **1** *v.* To strike or knock, often heavily or with force: The ball *bumped* John on the head. **2** *n.* A sudden blow or jolt; knock. **3** *v.* To move with jerks or jolts: The car *bumped* down the road. **4** *n.* A part that sticks out, making an uneven surface; bulge: a road full of *bumps*. **5** *n.* A swelling caused by a blow or knock. **— bump into** *informal* To meet by chance: to *bump into* a friend.

bump·er[1] [bum′pər] *n.* Something that protects against bumps, as the metal bar across the front or back of a car.

bump·er[2] [bum′pər] **1** *n.* A cup or glass filled to the brim. **2** *adj.* Unusually large or full: a *bumper* crop of tomatoes.

bump·kin [bump′kin] *n.* An awkward or unsophisticated person from the country.

bump·y [bum′pē] *adj.* **bump·i·er, bump·i·est** Having or causing bumps; rough: a *bumpy* ride. **— bump′i·ly** *adv.*

bun [bun] *n.* **1** A small bread roll, sometimes sweetened. **2** Hair twisted into a coil on the back of a woman's head.

bunch [bunch] **1** *n.* A number of things of the same kind, growing or placed together: a *bunch* of bananas; a *bunch* of letters. **2** *n. informal* A group: a *bunch* of boys. **3** *v.* To gather in or form into a bunch: The flowers were *bunched* to make a bouquet.

bun·dle [bun′dəl] *n., v.* **bun·dled, bun·dling 1** *n.* A number of things bound or wrapped up together. **2** *n.* A package or parcel. **3** *v.* To make into a bundle: *Bundle* my old clothes together. **4** *v.* To send or put quickly: The children were *bundled* into bed. **— bundle up** To dress in lots of warm clothing.

bung [bung] **1** *n.* A stopper for the hole in a cask or barrel. **2** *n.* The hole in a cask or barrel; bunghole. **3** *v.* To close or stop with a bung.

bun·ga·low [bung′gə·lō] *n.* A small house or cottage, usually with one, or one and a half stories.

♦ *Bungalow* comes from a word in Hindustani meaning *of Bengal*, because it described a type of house found in Bengal.

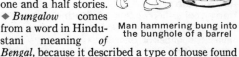
Man hammering bung into the bunghole of a barrel

bung·hole [bung′hōl′] *n.* A hole in a cask or barrel, through which liquid is drawn out.

bun·gle [bung′gəl] *v.* **bun·gled, bun·gling,** *n.* **1** *v.* To make or do clumsily or badly; botch: The nervous singer *bungled* her song in the opera. **2** *n.* The act of bungling. **3** *n.* A clumsy or bad piece of work. **— bun′gler** *n.*

bun·ion [bun′yən] *n.* A painful, inflamed swelling at the base of the big toe.

bunk[1] [bungk] **1** *n.* A narrow bed, built-in or set against a wall like a shelf. **2** *n. informal* Any narrow bed. **3** *v. informal* To sleep in a bunk. **4** *v. informal* To go to bed; sleep.

---

add, āce, câre, pälm; end, ēqual; it, īce; odd, ōpen, ôrder; tŏŏk, pōōl; up, bûrn;

ə = a in *above*, e in *sicken*, i in *possible*, o in *melon*, u in *circus*; yōō = u in *fuse*; oil; pout;

check; ring; thin; this; zh in *vision*. For ¶ reference, see page 64 · HOW TO

bunk[2] [bungk] *n. slang* Silly talk; nonsense.
◆ *Bunk* is short for *buncombe*, meaning *empty talk*, from the habit of a 19th-century congressman from North Carolina, of making windy, pointless speeches "for Buncombe," the name of the county he represented.

bun·ker [bung′kər] *n.* **1** A large bin, as for storing coal on a ship. **2** A hollow or a mound of earth serving as an obstacle on a golf course.

Bun·ker Hill [bung′kər] A hill in Charlestown, Massachusetts. A battle of the American Revolution took place near it in 1775.

bunk·house [bungk′hous′] *n.* A building having bunks, used as sleeping quarters by miners, ranch hands, etc.

bun·ny [bun′ē] *n., pl.* **bun·nies** A child's word for a rabbit.

Bun·sen burner [bun′sən] A type of burner in which a mixture of gas and air is burned at the top of a short metal tube. It produces a very hot flame.

bunt [bunt] **1** *v.* To strike or push as with horns; butt. **2** *n.* A push or shove; a butt. **3** *v.* To bat (a baseball) very lightly and low, so that it only reaches the infield. **4** *n.* A ball that has been bunted.

bunt·ing[1] [bun′ting] *n.* **1** Light, thin material, used for making flags. **2** Strips of material in the colors or designs of the flag, used as holiday decorations. **3** A blanket for a baby made like a sleeping bag with a hood.

Bunting

bunt·ing[2] [bun′ting] *n.* A type of bird related to finches and sparrows.

Bun·yan [bun′yən], **Paul** In American folklore, a huge lumberjack, famous for his amazing deeds of strength.

buoy [boi *or* bōō′ē] **1** *n.* A floating object, held in place by an anchor, used to mark a channel or dangerous spot in the water. It sometimes carries a bell or light. **2** *n.* A life preserver; life buoy. **3** *v.* To keep afloat. **4** *v.* To hold up or raise the spirits of: His new clothes *buoyed* him up.

buoy·an·cy [boi′ən·sē *or* bōō′yən·sē] *n.* **1** The ability to keep afloat: Plump people have more *buoyancy* in the water than thin ones. **2** The power to keep an object afloat. **3** Lightness of spirits; cheerfulness.

A bell buoy and a light buoy

buoy·ant [boi′ənt *or* bōō′yənt] *adj.* **1** Able to keep afloat or rise in liquid or air. **2** Able to keep an object afloat. **3** Cheerful and lighthearted: a *buoyant* wave of the hand. **— buoy′ant·ly** *adv.*

bur [bûr] *n.* **1** A rough or prickly flower head or seedcase, as of the chestnut. **2** A plant that bears burs. **3** A person or thing that clings like a bur.

Bur·bank [bûr′bangk], **Luther,** 1849–1926, U.S. grower of many new types of flowers, fruits, and vegetables.

bur·ble [bûr′bəl] *v.* **bur·bled, bur·bling** **1** To bubble; gurgle: The brooks *burbled.* **2** To talk with excitement and confusion.

bur·den[1] [bûr′dən] **1** *n.* Something carried; a load. **2** *n.* Something difficult to carry or bear: the *burden* of debts. **3** *v.* To load or overload; trouble: I won't *burden* you with my difficulties.

bur·den[2] [bûr′dən] *n.* **1** The chorus or refrain of a song. **2** The main idea or topic.

bur·den·some [bûr′dən·səm] *adj.* Hard to bear; heavy: a *burdensome* task.

bur·dock [bûr′dok] *n.* A plant with large, roundish leaves and round burs.

bu·reau [byoŏr′ō] *n., pl.* **bu·reaus** or **bu·reaux** [byoŏr′ōz] **1** A chest of drawers, usually with a mirror. **2** A government department: the Federal *Bureau* of Investigation. **3** An office or division of a business: a travel *bureau.*

bu·reauc·ra·cy [byoŏ·rok′rə·sē] *n., pl.* **bu·reauc·ra·cies** **1** Government with many departments made up of appointed officials, who follow set rules and regulations. **2** These departments and officials as a group. **3** Any system in which there are mix-ups and delays because of a too strict following of rules.

bu·reau·crat [byoŏr′ə·krat] *n.* **1** A member of a bureaucracy. **2** An official who follows the rules strictly and rigidly.

bu·reau·crat·ic [byoŏr′ə·krat′ik] *adj.* Of or like a bureaucrat or bureaucracy.

bur·geon [bûr′jən] *v.* To grow or flourish; blossom: a *burgeoning* community.

bur·gess [bûr′jis] *n.* **1** A citizen or officer of a borough. **2** During colonial times, a member of the lower house of the legislature of Virginia or Maryland.

burgh [bûrg] *n.* In Scotland, a town or borough.

burgh·er [bûr′gər] *n.* A citizen of a burgh or town.

bur·glar [bûr′glər] *n.* A person who breaks into a building or house to commit a theft or other crime.

bur·gla·ry [bûr′glər·ē] *n., pl.* **bur·gla·ries** The breaking into a building or house, especially in order to steal.

bur·go·mas·ter [bûr′gə·mas′tər] *n.* A mayor of a town in some European countries, as Austria or Germany.

Bur·gun·dy [bûr′gən·dē] *n.* **1** A region in eastern France, that at one time was a kingdom. **2** A red or white wine, first made in Burgundy.

bur·i·al [ber′ē·əl] *n.* The burying of a dead body.

bur·lap [bûr′lap] *n.* A coarse material, usually made of jute or hemp, used for making bags, wrappings, etc.

bur·lesque [bər·lesk′] *n., v.* **bur·lesqued, bur·les·quing** **1** *n.* A comic or sarcastic imitation of something serious, usually in the form of a play or book. **2** *v.* To imitate in a comic or sarcastic way. **3** *n.* A stage show with singing, dancing, and vulgar comedy.

bur·ly [bûr′lē] *adj.* **bur·li·er, bur·li·est** Big and sturdy; husky: a *burly* football player.

Bur·ma [bûr′mə] *n.* A country in SE Asia, between East Pakistan and Thailand.

Bur·mese [bər·mēz′] **1** *adj.* Of, having to do with, or from Burma. **2** *n., pl.* **Bur·mese** A person born in or a citizen of Burma. **3** *n.* The people of Burma. **4** *n.* The language of Burma.

burn[1] [bûrn] *v.* **burned** or **burnt, burn·ing,** *n.* **1** *v.* To be on fire; blaze: The forest *burned* for a week. **2** *v.* To set on fire so as to produce heat or light: to *burn* oil in a furnace. **3** *v.* To give off light or heat: The lamp *burns* in the window. **4** *v.* To destroy or be destroyed by fire. **5** *v.* To hurt or damage by fire, steam, acid, wind, etc. **6** *n.* An injury or damage from burning. **7** *v.* To produce by fire: The cigarette *burned* a hole in his jacket. **8** *v.* To cause to feel hot: Pepper *burns* his tongue. **9** *v.* To appear or feel hot. **10** *v.* To excite or be excited.

burn[2] [bûrn] *n.* A Scottish word for a brook.

burn·er [bûr′nər] *n.* **1** A person whose job is to burn something. **2** A device for burning something; incinerator. **3** The part of a stove, lamp, or furnace from which the flame comes.

bur·nish [bûr′nish] **1** *v.* To polish by rubbing: to *burnish* metal. **2** *n.* Polish; luster.

bur·noose or **bur·nous** [bər·nōōs′ or bûr′nōōs] *n.* A long, hooded cloak worn by Arabs.

Burns [bûrnz], **Robert,** 1759–1796, Scottish poet.

burnt [bûrnt] **1** An alternative past tense and past participle of BURN. **2** *adj.* Injured or charred by fire: *burnt* fingers; *burnt* toast.

burp [bûrp] *informal* **1** *v.* To belch. **2** *v.* To cause to belch: to *burp* a baby. **3** *n.* A belch.

burr[1] [bûr] *n.* Another spelling of BUR.

burr[2] [bûr] *n.* **1** A rough edge left on metal in drilling or cutting. **2** A cutting or drilling tool, as a dental drill. **3** The rough, trilled sound of "r," used by some Scotsmen. **4** A whirring sound; a buzz.

bur·ro [bûr′ō] *n., pl.* **bur·ros** A small donkey, used for riding or for carrying packs in the sw U.S.

bur·row [bûr′ō] **1** *n.* A hole made in the ground by certain animals: Rabbits live in *burrows.* **2** *v.* To dig a burrow. **3** *v.* To live or hide in a burrow. **4** *v.* To search deeply: He *burrowed* into his pile of reports.

Burro

bur·sa [bûr′sə] *n., pl.* **bur·sae** [bûr′sē] or **bur·sas** A pouch or saclike cavity in the body, especially one between the parts of a joint. It is filled with lubricating fluid to lessen friction.

bur·sar [bûr′sər] *n.* A treasurer, as of a college.

bur·si·tis [bər·sī′tis] *n.* Inflammation of a bursa.

burst [bûrst] *v.* **burst, burst·ing,** *n.* **1** *v.* To break open or apart suddenly; explode from a force inside: The balloon *burst* with a bang. **2** *v.* To give way to a sudden, strong feeling: to *burst* into tears. **3** *n.* A sudden explosion or outbreak: a *burst* of gunfire; a *burst* of laughter. **4** *v.* To be filled to overflowing: Our house is *bursting* with children. **5** *v.* To appear or enter suddenly: He *burst* into the hall. **6** *n.* A sudden rush or spurt: a *burst* of speed. ◆ Careful writers and speakers should avoid using *bust* when they mean *burst.*

bur·then [bûr′thən] *v., n.* An old-fashioned spelling of BURDEN.

bur·y [ber′ē] *v.* **bur·ied, bur·y·ing 1** To put (a dead body) in a grave, tomb, or the sea. **2** To hide or cover from view: He *buried* his face in his hands. **3** To put out of mind and forget: to *bury* a disagreement. **4** To absorb (oneself) deeply; engross: He *buried* himself in his studies.

bus [bus] *n., pl.* **bus·es** or **bus·ses,** *v.* **bused** or **bussed, bus·ing** or **bus·sing 1** *n.* A large, long motor vehicle with seats for carrying many passengers. **2** *v.* To bring or transport by bus. ◆ Originally *buses* were called *omnibuses,* because *omnibus* in Latin means "for all," and buses hold large numbers of passengers and are for the use of all. Later *omnibus* was shortened to *bus* and recently has come to be used as a verb as well: They *bussed* the children to school.

bush [bŏosh] **1** *n.* A low, treelike shrub with many branches or stems. **2** *v.* To grow or branch out like a bush. **3** *n.* Wild, uncleared land, with few settlers on it. **— beat about the bush** or **beat around the bush** To talk around a subject to avoid getting to the point.

bush·el [bŏosh′əl] *n.* **1** A unit of volume used to measure fruits, vegetables, or other dry things. It is equal to 4 pecks or 32 quarts. **2** A container, as a basket, holding this amount.

bush·ing [bŏosh′ing] *n.* A detachable metal lining used in a machine to prevent wearing down of parts.

Bush·man [bŏosh′mən] *n., pl.* **Bush·men** [bŏosh′mən] A member of a people of South Africa, who move from place to place and are related to the Pygmies.

bush·mas·ter [bŏosh′mas′tər] *n.* A large, very poisonous snake of tropical America.

bush·y [bŏosh′ē] *adj.* **bush·i·er, bush·i·est 1** Covered with or full of bushes. **2** Thick like a bush; shaggy: *bushy* hair and eyebrows.

bus·i·ly [biz′ə·lē] *adv.* In a busy manner.

---

add, āce, câre, pälm;   end, ēqual;   it, īce;   odd, ōpen, ôrder;   tŏŏk, pŏŏl;   up, bûrn;

ə = a in *above,* e in *sicken,* i in *possible,* o in *melon,* u in *circus;*   yŏŏ = u in *fuse;*   oil;   pout;

ch in *check;* ring; thin; this; zh in *vision.*   For ¶ reference, see page 64 · HOW TO

busi·ness [biz′nis] *n.* **1** A trade or occupation: My father's *business* is selling cars. **2** The buying, selling, and other details of trade or industry. **3** A place where the producing or selling of things is carried out: a shoe *business*. **4** *adj. use:* a *business* suit; a *business* card. **5** Matter or affair: Climbing mountains is a risky *business*. **6** Right; concern: It's not his *business* to tell me what to do. — **mean business** To be serious or determined. ◆ See OCCUPATION.

busi·ness·like [biz′nis·līk′] *adj.* Systematic and methodical; practical.

busi·ness·man [biz′nis·man′] *n., pl.* **busi·ness·men** [biz′nis·men′] A man who owns or manages a business.

busi·ness·wom·an [biz′nis·wŏŏm′ən] *n., pl.* **busi·ness·wom·en** [biz′nis·wim′in] A woman who owns or manages a business.

bus·kin [bus′kin] *n.* A type of boot worn long ago by Greek and Roman actors as a symbol of tragedy.

buss [bus] *n., v.* An old-fashioned word for KISS.

bust¹ [bust] *n.* **1** A piece of sculpture of the head, shoulders, and upper chest of a person. **2** The chest of a person, especially the bosom of a woman.

bust² [bust] *v. slang* To burst or break. ◆ See BURST.

bus·tle¹ [bus′(ə)l] *v.* **bus·tled, bus·tling,** *n.* **1** *v.* To move or hurry with much fuss and excitement. **2** *n.* Noisy activity and motion: the *bustle* of a crowded store.

Bust of Lincoln

bus·tle² [bus′(ə)l] *n.* A pad worn at the back of a woman's skirt to puff it out.

bus·y [biz′ē] *adj.* **bus·i·er, bus·i·est,** *v.* **bus·ied, bus·y·ing** **1** *adj.* Occupied; working: Mother is *busy* in the kitchen. **2** *adj.* Filled with activity: a *busy* morning. **3** *adj.* In use: The phone line is *busy*. **4** *v.* To keep or make busy: She *busied* herself cleaning the room.

bus·y·bod·y [biz′ē·bod′ē] *n., pl.* **bus·y·bod·ies** A person who pries into other people's affairs.

but [but] **1** *conj.* On the other hand: She is fat, *but* you are thin. **2** *conj.* Other than; except: I have no choice *but* to listen. **3** *prep.* With the exception of: owning nothing *but* his clothes. **4** *conj.* Yet; nevertheless: He was poor *but* honest. **5** *conj.* Without the result that: It never rains *but* it pours. **6** *conj.* That: We don't doubt *but* he'll be there. **7** *adv.* Only; just: She is *but* a child. — **all but** Almost.

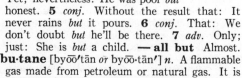
Bustle

bu·tane [byŏŏ′tān *or* byŏŏ·tān′] *n.* A flammable gas made from petroleum or natural gas. It is sometimes used as a fuel.

butch·er [bŏŏch′ər] **1** *n.* A person who kills

animals for market. **2** *n.* A person who cuts up and sells meat. **3** *v.* To kill or prepare for market. **4** *n.* A person who kills in a brutal way. **5** *v.* To kill in a brutal, bloody way; slaughter. **6** *v.* To ruin; botch.

butch·er·y [bŏŏch′ər·ē] *n., pl.* **butch·er·ies** Senseless and cruel killing; slaughter.

but·ler [but′lər] *n.* A manservant who directs other servants and is in charge of the dining room.

butt¹ [but] *n.* **1** The thicker or larger end of a weapon, tool, etc.: a rifle *butt*. **2** An unused end, as of a cigarette. **3** Someone who is ridiculed: The fat boy was the *butt* of all their jokes.

butt² [but] *n.* A large cask, especially for wine, beer, or water.

butt³ [but] **1** *v.* To strike, push, or bump with the head or horns; ram: The goat *butted* the man. **2** *n.* A blow or push with the head. — **butt in** or **butt into** To interrupt, or meddle in someone else's affairs.

butte [byŏŏt] *n.* A hill, standing alone, that has steep sides and sometimes a flat top.

but·ter [but′ər] **1** *n.* The yellowish fat that becomes separated from milk during churning. It is used as a spread and in cooking. **2** *v.* To spread butter on. **3** *n.* Something with the same use as butter: peanut *butter*. **4** *v. informal* To flatter: They *buttered* up the teacher. — **but′·ter·y** *adj.*

but·ter·cup [but′ər·kup′] *n.* A plant with small, yellow, cup-shaped flowers.

but·ter·fat [but′ər·fat′] *n.* The fatty substance in milk, from which butter is made.

but·ter·fly [but′ər·flī′] *n., pl.* **but·ter·flies** **1** A four-winged insect related to the moth, but having clubbed antennae and usually a more slender body and more brightly colored wings. **2** A type of swimming stroke.

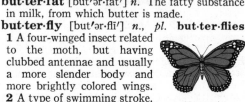
Monarch butterfly

but·ter·milk [but′ər·milk′] *n.* The sour liquid left after the butterfat is removed from milk.

but·ter·nut [but′ər·nut′] *n.* **1** The oily nut of a certain walnut tree. **2** This tree.

but·ter·scotch [but′ər·skoch′] **1** *n.* A hard, sticky candy, made with brown sugar and butter. **2** *adj.* Made of or flavored with butterscotch: *butterscotch* syrup.

but·tock [but′ək] *n.* Either of the two fleshy parts at the back of the hip, upon which human beings sit; rump.

but·ton [but′(ə)n] **1** *n.* A disk or knob sewn to a garment, serving as a fastening when passed through a narrow opening or buttonhole, or simply for decoration. **2** *v.* To fasten or enclose with buttons. **3** *n.* Anything like a button, as a small knob operating an electric bell.

but·ton·hole [but′(ə)n·hōl′] *n., v.* **but·ton·hol·ed, but·ton·hol·ing** **1** *n.* A slit to receive and hold a button. **2** *v.* To hold (a person) by the button of his coat so that he is forced to listen to what one says.

but·ton·wood [but′(ə)n·wŏŏd′] *n.* **1** The sycamore tree of North America. **2** Its wood.

but·tress [but′tris] **1** *n.* A structure built against a wall to strengthen it. **2** *v.* To prop up or sustain; support: to *buttress* a wall; to *buttress* one's hopes.

bux·om [buk′səm] *adj.* Plump and pleasant to look at. ◆ *Buxom* is used only of women.

buy [bī] *v.* **bought, buy·ing,** *n.* **1** *v.* To obtain in exchange for money or some other thing; purchase: He *bought* a balloon for a dime.

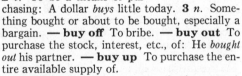

Flying buttresses

2 *v.* To be a means of purchasing: A dollar *buys* little today. **3** *n.* Something bought or about to be bought, especially a bargain. **— buy off** To bribe. **— buy out** To purchase the stock, interest, etc., of: He *bought out* his partner. **— buy up** To purchase the entire available supply of.

buy·er [bī′ər] *n.* **1** A person who buys. **2** A person whose work is buying merchandise for a department store.

buzz [buz] **1** *v.* To make the steady, humming sound of a bee. **2** *n.* The steady, humming sound made by a bee. **3** *v.* To talk with quiet excitement: The town *buzzed* with gossip. **4** *n.* A low, confused murmur, as of many voices. **5** *v.* To signal with a buzzer: He *buzzed* for his secretary. **6** *v.* To fly an airplane low over: to *buzz* a ship.

buz·zard [buz′ərd] *n.* **1** A kind of large, slow-flying hawk. **2** A sooty black vulture with a naked red head and neck; a turkey buzzard.

buzz·er [buz′ər] *n.* An electrical device that makes a buzzing sound.

Turkey buzzard, 30 in. long

by [bī] **1** *prep.* Next to; near: the tree *by* the river. **2** *adv.* At hand; near: Stay close *by*! **3** *prep.* Past and beyond: The train roared *by* us. **4** *adv.* Past: The years go *by*. **5** *prep.* By way of; through: Come *by* the nearest road. **6** *prep.* In the course of; during: to travel *by* night. **7** *prep.* According to a standard or fixed rate: to work *by* the day. **8** *prep.* Not later than: Be here *by* noon. **9** *prep.* After: day *by* day. **10** *prep.* Through the work of; by means of: to travel *by* plane. **11** *prep.* Regarding; for: to do well *by* one's friends. **12** *prep.* According to: *by* law. **13** *prep.* In accordance with: *by* your leave.

14 *prep.* In multiplication with: Multiply 6 *by* 8. **15** *prep.* In or to the amount of: insects *by* the hundreds. **16** *adv.* Aside, apart: to lay money *by*. **— by and by** After a time. **— by and large** On the whole; generally. **— by the by** or **by the bye** By the way; incidentally.

by-and-by [bī′ən·bī′] *n.* A future time: We shall meet in the *by-and-by*.

Bye·lo·rus·sia [bye′lə·rush′ə] *n.* A part of the Soviet Union in western Europe.

by·gone [bī′gôn′] **1** *adj.* Gone by; past: *bygone* days. **2** *n.* Something that is past or gone by. **— let bygones be bygones** To let past disagreements be forgotten.

by·law [bī′lô′] *n.* **1** A rule passed by a club or corporation for governing its own meetings and affairs. **2** A law that is secondary to the main set of laws.

by-line [bī′līn′] *n.* The line at the head of a newspaper article giving the writer's name.

by·pass [bī′pas′] **1** *n.* A road, route, or pipe that goes off the main course, so as to pass around an obstacle: We took a *by-pass* to avoid the traffic jam. **2** *v.* To go around or avoid: We *by-passed* the towns to save time.

by-path [bī′path′] *n.* A side or indirect path.

by-play [bī′plā′] *n.* Action or talking apart from the main action, as in a stage scene.

by-prod·uct [bī′prod′əkt] *n.* Anything else resulting from making a main product.

Byrd [bûrd], **Richard E.,** 1888–1957, U.S. admiral, explorer of the North and South poles.

byre [bīr] *n. British* A cow stable.

by·road [bī′rōd′] *n.* A back or side road.

By·ron [bī′rən], **George Gordon,** 6th Baron, 1788–1824, English poet, also called Lord Byron.

by·stand·er [bī′stan′dər] *n.* A person who is present but not taking part; onlooker: Many *bystanders* saw the fight.

by·way [bī′wā′] *n.* A side path; a path not often used.

by·word [bī′wûrd′] *n.* **1** A common saying or proverb. **2** An object of scorn: His dishonesty made him the *byword* of the whole school.

Byz·an·tine [biz′ən·tēn *or* biz′ən·tīn] *adj.* **1** Of or having to do with the eastern part of the later Roman Empire, from 395 to 1453. **2** Having to do with its style of architecture, which used round arches, rich mosaic art work, and many domes.

Byzantine architecture

Byz·an·ti·um [bi·zan′shē·əm *or* bi·zan′tē·əm] *n.* An ancient city which became the capital, Constantinople, of the Byzantine Empire. Constantinople is now called Istanbul.

C

c or **C** [sē] *n., pl.* **c's** or **C's 1** The third letter of the English alphabet. **2** (*written* **C**) The Roman numeral for 100.

C The symbol for the element CARBON.

c. or **C.** Abbreviation of: **1** CENT or CENTS. **2** CENTIGRADE. **3** CENTURY. **4** COPYRIGHT.

Ca The symbol for the element CALCIUM.

cab [kab] *n.* **1** A taxicab. **2** A one-horse carriage for public hire. **3** An enclosed compartment, as in a locomotive for the engineer, or in a truck or crane for the operator.

ca·bal [kə·bal′] *n.* **1** A group of persons who are secretly engaged in some scheme or plot. **2** The scheme or plot of such a group.

cab·al·le·ro [kab′əl·yâr′ō] *n., pl.* **cab·al·le·ros** A Spanish gentleman; cavalier.

ca·ban·a [kə·ban′ə] *n.* **1** A small cabin. **2** A small bathhouse for changing clothes at the beach.

cab·a·ret [kab′ə·rā′] *n.* A restaurant that provides entertainment for its customers.

cab·bage [kab′ij] *n.* A vegetable with closely folded leaves forming a hard, round head.

cab·in [kab′in] *n.* **1** A small, roughly built wooden house or hut. **2** A room equipped for sleeping on a ship. **3** The passengers' section in an aircraft.

cabin boy A boy who serves the officers and passengers on a ship.

cab·i·net [kab′ə·nit] *n.* **1** A piece of furniture fitted with shelves and drawers. **2** (*often written* **Cabinet**) A group of official advisers and assistants of a head of state.

cab·i·net·mak·er [kab′ə·nit·mā′kər] *n.* A person who makes fine wooden furniture and woodwork.

ca·ble [kā·bəl] *n., v.* **ca·bled, ca·bling 1** *n.* A heavy rope, now usually made of steel wire. **2** *n.* An insulated electric wire or group of wires, especially used to carry telephone and telegraph messages. **3** *n.* A cablegram. **4** *v.* To send a cablegram.

cable car A car moving along an overhead cable or pulled along tracks by an underground cable.

ca·ble·gram [kā′bəl·gram] *n.* A message sent across an ocean by a cable laid under the water.

ca·boose [kə·boos′] *n. U.S.* A car, usually the rear car, of a freight train, used by the crew.

ca·ca·o [kə·kā′ō] *n., pl.* **ca·ca·os 1** A tropical tree having large seeds from which cocoa and chocolate are made. **2** The seeds of this tree.

cach·a·lot [kash′ə·lot] *n.* Another name for SPERM WHALE.

cache [kash] *n., v.* **cached, cach·ing 1** *n.* A place for concealing or storing something. **2** *n.* The goods concealed or stored. **3** *v.* To hide or store away, as in a cache.

cack·le [kak′əl] *n., v.* **cack·led, cack·ling 1** *n.* A shrill, broken cry, as of a hen laying eggs. **2** *v.* To make such a cry. **3** *n.* A short, shrill laugh. **4** *v.* To utter such a laugh. **5** *n.* Idle, loud chatter: the *cackle* of old women.

cac·tus [kak′təs] *n., pl.* **cac·tus·es** or **cac·ti** [kak′tī] A plant of hot desert regions having a green pulpy trunk covered with spines or prickles instead of leaves and often bearing showy flowers.

cad [kad] *n.* An ill-bred, dishonorable man.

ca·dav·er [kə·dav′ər] *n.* A dead body, especially one awaiting dissection.

ca·dav·er·ous [kə·dav′ər·əs] *adj.* Resembling a dead person; pale, thin, and gloomy looking.

cad·die [kad′ē] *n., v.* **cad·died, cad·dy·ing 1** *n.* A person who carries clubs for golf players, usually for money. **2** *v.* To act as a caddie.

Saguaro cactus

cad·dy[1] [kad′ē] *n., pl.* **cad·dies** A small box or case, especially one in which to keep tea.

cad·dy[2] [kad′ē] *n., pl.* **cad·dies,** *v.* **cad·died, cad·dy·ing** Another spelling of CADDIE.

ca·dence [kād′əns] *n.* **1** A rhythmic flow or movement: the *cadence* of words in poetry. **2** The rise or fall in a speaker's voice. **3** A succession of harmonies ending a piece of music.

ca·den·za [kə·den′zə] *n.* A solo musical passage, usually near the end of a composition, intended to allow a performer to display his skill.

ca·det [kə·det′] *n.* **1** A young man in training to become an officer in any of the armed forces. **2** A student attending a military school.

cad·mi·um [kad′mē·əm] *n.* A soft, bluish white metallic element, used in making pigments, alloys, and for electroplating.

Cae·sar [sē′zər] *n.* **1** The title of any of the Roman emperors succeeding Augustus. **2** Any dictator or tyrant.

Cae·sar [sē′zər], **Julius,** 100–44 B.C., a Roman general, statesman, and historian.

cae·su·ra [si·zhoor′ə] *n., pl.* **cae·su·ras** or **cae·su·rae** [si·zhoor′ē] A pause or break in a line of poetry, usually near the middle.

ca·fé [ka·fā′] *n.* **1** A restaurant or barroom. **2** Coffee.

caf·e·te·ri·a [kaf′ə·tir′ē·ə] *n.* A restaurant where customers wait upon themselves.

caf·feine [kaf′ēn] *n.* A substance with a slightly bitter taste found in tea and coffee. It is used in medicine as a heart and nerve stimulant.

cage [kāj] *n., v.* **caged, cag·ing 1** *n.* A boxlike structure closed in with wire or bars for confining animals or birds. **2** *n.* Any cagelike structure, as an elevator car. **3** *v.* To shut up in or as if in a cage; imprison.

cage·y [kā′jē] *adj.* **cag·i·er, cag·i·est** *informal* Shrewd, sly, and careful. **— cag′i·ly** *adv.*

Cain [kān] *n.* In the Bible, the eldest son of Adam. He killed his brother Abel. **— raise Cain** *slang* To cause trouble, make noise, etc.

cairn [kârn] *n.* A mound or heap of stones set up as a memorial or a marker.

Cai·ro [kī′rō] *n.* The capital of Egypt.

cais·son [kā′sən] *n.* **1** A two-wheeled cart used to carry ammunition for a gun. **2** A large, watertight chamber in which men can work under water.

caisson disease A disease caused by too rapid a change from a high to a normal air pressure, often affecting divers; the bends.

cai·tiff [kā′tif] **1** *n.* A low scoundrel. **2** *adj.* Base. ◆ This word is seldom used today.

ca·jole [kə·jōl′] *v.* **ca·joled, ca·jol·ing** To coax or persuade by flattery or deceit; wheedle.

ca·jol·er·y [kə·jō′lər·ē] *n., pl.* **ca·jol·er·ies** The act of cajoling; coaxing.

cake [kāk] *n., v.* **caked, cak·ing 1** *n.* A baked mixture of flour, eggs, butter, etc., usually sweeter than bread. **2** *n.* A small, usually thin mass of dough or other food, baked or fried: a fish *cake*. **3** *n.* A mass of material compressed or hardened into a compact form: a *cake* of soap. **4** *v.* To form or harden into a cake.

Cal. An unofficial abbreviation of CALIFORNIA.

cal·a·bash [kal′ə·bash] *n.* **1** Either of two tropical American trees bearing a hard-shelled, gourdlike fruit. **2** This fruit. **3** A utensil made from this fruit, as a bowl, tobacco pipe, etc.

cal·a·mine [kal′ə·mīn] *n.* A pink powder prepared from a zinc compound, used in ointments or lotions for skin treatment.

ca·lam·i·tous [kə·lam′ə·təs] *adj.* Causing or resulting in a calamity; disastrous.

ca·lam·i·ty [kə·lam′ə·tē] *n., pl.* **ca·lam·i·ties 1** Any happening that causes great distress; a disaster: A flood is a *calamity.* **2** A condition or time of suffering or disaster.

cal·ci·fy [kal′sə·fī] *v.* **cal·ci·fied, cal·ci·fy·ing** To make or become hard or bony by the deposit of lime salts.

cal·ci·mine [kal′sə·mīn] *n., v.* **cal·ci·mined, cal·ci·min·ing 1** *n.* A watery mixture of chalk and glue, white or tinted, used to paint plastered walls, etc. **2** *v.* To apply calcimine to.

cal·cine [kal′sīn] *v.* **cal·cined, cal·cin·ing 1** To change into lime by prolonged heating. **2** To burn to ashes.

cal·ci·um [kal′sē·əm] *n.* A soft, silver-white, metallic element. It is an essential part of bones and is found in marble, chalk, etc.

calcium carbonate A compound forming the principle part of certain rocks and minerals, as marble. It is used in making lime.

cal·cu·late [kal′kyə·lāt] *v.* **cal·cu·lat·ed, cal·cu·lat·ing 1** To figure by using mathematics: to *calculate* expenses. **2** To think out; form an estimate of: to *calculate* the chance of success. **3** To plan or design: a move *calculated* to confuse the opposition.

cal·cu·lat·ing [kal′kyə·lā′ting] *adj.* Very sly and cautious; shrewd; scheming.

cal·cu·la·tion [kal′kyə·lā′shən] *n.* **1** The act of calculating. **2** The answer arrived at by calculating. **3** A forecast. **4** Careful planning.

cal·cu·la·tor [kal′kyə·lā′tər] *n.* **1** A person who calculates. **2** A machine that does mathematical problems, as an adding machine or computer.

cal·cu·lus [kal′kyə·ləs] *n.* An advanced form of algebra used to solve problems involving things that are changing at varying rates.

Cal·cut·ta [kal·kut′ə] *n.* A seaport in NE India, and the capital of West Bengal.

cal·dron [kôl′drən] *n.* A large kettle or pot.

cal·en·dar [kal′ən·dər] *n.* **1** An arrangement of time into years, months, weeks, and days. **2** A table showing the days, weeks, and months of a year. **3** A schedule or list of events or appointments: a social *calendar.*

cal·en·der [kal′ən·dər] **1** *n.* A machine for giving a gloss to cloth, paper, etc., by pressing between rollers. **2** *v.* To press in a calender.

calf[1] [kaf] *n., pl.* **calves** [kavz] **1** The young of the cow or other bovine animals. **2** The young of some other mammals, as the seal or whale. **3** Calfskin.

calf[2] [kaf] *n., pl.* **calves** [kavz] The muscular back part of the human leg below the knee.

calf·skin [kaf′skin′] *n.* **1** The skin or hide of young cattle. **2** Leather made from this.

Cal·i·ban [kal′ə·ban] *n.* A deformed, savage slave in Shakespeare's play *The Tempest.*

cal·i·ber [kal′ə·bər] *n.* **1** The diameter of the inside of a tube, especially of the barrel of a revolver, rifle, etc.: a .38 *caliber* pistol. **2** The diameter of a cartridge, shell, or other projectile fired from a gun. **3** Excellence, ability, etc. ¶2

cal·i·brate [kal′ə·brāt] *v.* **cal·i·brat·ed, cal·i·brat·ing 1** To mark, check, or adjust the scale of (a measuring instrument). **2** To determine the caliber of. **— cal·i·bra′tion** *n.*

cal·i·co [kal′i·kō] *n., pl.* **cal·i·coes** or **cal·i·cos 1** *n.* Cotton cloth printed with a figured design. **2** *adj. use:* a *calico* dress. **3** *adj.* Like calico; spotted or streaked: a *calico* cat.

---

ca·lif [kā′lif] *n.* Another spelling of CALIPH.

Calif. Abbreviation of CALIFORNIA.

Cal·i·for·nia [kal′ə·fôr′yə] *n.* A state in the western U.S. —**Cal′i·for′nian** *adj.*, *n.*

California, Gulf of An inlet of the Pacific Ocean between the main part of Mexico and Lower California.

cal·i·for·ni·um [kal′ə·fôr′nē·əm] *n.* An artificially produced radioactive chemical element.

cal·i·pers [kal′ə·pərz] *n.pl.* An instrument with two movable, hinged legs, used for measuring the diameter or thickness of an object.

ca·liph [kā′lif] *n.* Successor of Mohammed, a title of a Moslem ruler.

cal·is·then·ics [kal′is·then′iks] *n.pl.* Exercises done to promote grace and health.

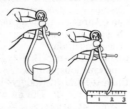
Measuring with calipers

calk¹ [kôk] Another spelling of CAULK.

calk² [kôk] *n.* **1** A pointed piece of metal on a horse's shoe to prevent slipping. **2** A device like this worn on the sole of a shoe or boot.

call [kôl] **1** *v.* To speak in a loud voice; shout: to *call* the roll. **2** *n.* A shout or cry: a *call* for help. **3** *v.* To summon: The principal *called* me to his office. **4** *n.* A summons or invitation. **5** *v.* To make a brief visit. **6** *n.* A brief visit. **7** *v.* To arouse, as from sleep: *Call* me early. **8** *v.* To make a telephone call to (someone). **9** *n.* A telephone message. **10** *v.* To name: They *called* him Shorty. **11** *v.* To consider or regard: I *call* such behavior disgraceful. **12** *v.* To insist upon payment of: to *call* a loan. **13** *v.* To stop or suspend: to *call* a baseball game. **14** *n.* A demand; claim: the *call* of duty. **15** *n.* An inward urge or attraction: a *call* to the ministry. **16** *n.* A need, occasion: You've no *call* to do that. **17** *n.* The special cry of an animal or bird. —**call for 1** To require; need. **2** To order. —**call off 1** To summon away. **2** To say or read aloud. **3** To cancel. —**call on 1** To visit. **2** To invite; request; ask. —**call up 1** To telephone. **2** To remember; recall. **3** To summon, especially for service in the armed forces. —**on call** Available when called for.
◆ *Call* comes from a Scandinavian word, *kalla*.

cal·la [kal′ə] *n.* A plant having a large milk-white leaf that resembles a flower. It is often called a **calla lily.**

call·er [kôl′ər] *n.* **1** A person making a brief visit. **2** A person who calls out the steps in a square dance.

call·ing [kôl′ing] *n.* **1** The act of speaking or crying aloud. **2** A profession; occupation. **3** A summons.

cal·li·o·pe [kə·lī′ə·pē *or* kal′ē·ōp] *n.* A musical instrument consisting of a series of steam whistles played by means of a keyboard.

cal·lis·then·ics [kal′is·then′iks] *n.pl.* Another spelling of CALISTHENICS.

call number A number given to a library book to indicate its general subject matter and its place on a shelf.

Call numbers

cal·lous [kal′əs] *adj.* **1** Thickened and hardened, as a callus. **2** Unfeeling; hard-hearted: a *callous* remark. —**cal′lous·ly** *adv.* —**cal′lous·ness** *n.*

cal·low [kal′ō] *adj.* Without experience; immature: a *callow* youth. —**cal′low·ness** *n.*

cal·lus [kal′əs] *n.*, *pl.* **cal·lus·es** A thickened and hardened part of the skin, as on the foot.

calm [käm] **1** *adj.* Quiet; peaceful; still: a *calm* sea; a *calm* manner. **2** *n.* Lack of wind or motion: the *calm* before a storm. **3** *v.* To make or become calm. —**calm′ly** *adv.* —**calm′ness** *n.*

cal·o·mel [kal′ə·mel] *n.* A heavy, white, tasteless compound of mercury and chlorine, formerly used as an antiseptic and laxative.

ca·lor·ic [kə·lôr′ik] *adj.* Of or having to do with heat or calories.

cal·o·rie [kal′ə·rē] *n.* **1** A unit of heat equal to the amount of heat needed to raise one gram of water one degree centigrade, used in the physical sciences. **2** (*often written* **Calorie**) A unit 1000 times larger, also used to measure the energy, or heat, food supplies to the body.

cal·u·met [kal′yə·met] *n.* A pipe smoked by American Indians when talking peace.

ca·lum·ni·ate [kə·lum′nē·āt] *v.* **ca·lum·ni·at·ed, ca·lum·ni·at·ing** To accuse falsely.

cal·um·ny [kal′əm·nē] *n.*, *pl.* **cal·um·nies** A false and spiteful accusation or report intended to harm another; slander.

Cal·va·ry [kal′vər·ē] *n.* The place near Jerusalem where Jesus was crucified.

calve [kav] *v.* **calved, calv·ing** To give birth to (a calf): Our cow *calved* this morning.

Cal·vin [kal′vin], **John,** 1509–1564, a French Protestant reformer.

Cal·vin·ism [kal′vin·iz′əm] *n.* The teachings of John Calvin, especially that salvation comes only by God's grace, and only those He has chosen will receive it. —**Cal′vin·ist** *adj.*, *n.*

ca·lyp·so [kə·lip′sō] *n.*, *pl.* **ca·lyp·sos** A type of West Indian song in which the singer gives the latest news or tells a story, making up the words as he sings.

ca·lyx [kā′liks *or* kal′iks] *n.*, *pl.* **ca·lyx·es** *or* **cal·y·ces** [kal′ə·sēz *or* kā′lə·sēz] The outer ring of leaves or sepals, usually green in color, which hold the petals of a flower.

cam [kam] *n.* A revolving part in a machine so shaped that its motion gives a to-and-fro or irregular motion to the part or parts it touches.

As the shaft turns, the cams move the valves up and down.

ca·ma·ra·de·rie [kä′mə·rä′dər·ē] *n.* The spirit of loyalty and friendship among comrades.

cam·bi·um [kam′bē·əm] *n.* A layer of tissue between the bark and wood of trees and woody plants, from which new bark and wood grow.

Cam·bo·di·a [kam·bō′dē·ə] *n.* A country in SE Asia, between Vietnam and Thailand.

Cam·bri·an [kam′brē·ən] *adj.* Having to do with a very early period in the earth's history. Rocks of this period yield fossils of the most primitive forms of life discovered so far.

cam·bric [kām′brik] *n.* **1** A fine white linen. **2** A cotton cloth made to look like linen.

cambric tea A drink made of sweetened hot water and milk and sometimes a little tea.

Cam·bridge [kām′brij] *n.* **1** A city in England, home of Cambridge University. **2** A city in Massachusetts, home of Harvard University.

came [kām] The past tense of COME.

cam·el [kam′əl] *n.* A large beast of burden of Asia and Africa that chews its cud and has one or two humps on its back. The **Arabian camel,** or dromedary, has one hump; the **Bactrian camel** has two humps. The camel has great powers of endurance in desert regions.

Bactrian camel, about 6ft. high at shoulder

ca·mel·lia [kə·mēl′yə] *n.* A tropical plant with green leaves and white, pink, or red flowers.

Cam·e·lot [kam′ə·lot] *n.* In English legend, the place where King Arthur had his court.

cam·e·o [kam′ē·ō] *n., pl.* **cam·e·os** A gem of sometimes differently colored layers, having a design carved in relief on the top layer with a lower layer serving as a background.

cam·er·a [kam′(ə·)rə] *n.* **1** A device for taking pictures in which light passes through a lens to form an image which is recorded on a film or plate. **2** An electronic device that forms an image and converts it into electrical impulses for television. ◆ Modern *camera* and *chamber* both came from Latin *camera*, which meant a room, as *chamber* still does.

cam·er·a·man [kam′(ə·)rə·man′] *n., pl.* **cam·er·a·men** [kam′(ə·)rə·men′] A person whose job is operating a camera, as for motion pictures or television.

cam·i·sole [kam′ə·sōl] *n.* A type of woman's undergarment with a fancy top, often worn under a sheer blouse.

cam·o·mile [kam′ə·mīl] *n.* A strongly scented plant from whose leaves and daisylike flowers a medicinal tea is brewed.

cam·ou·flage [kam′ə·fläzh] *n., v.* **cam·ou·** flaged, **cam·ou·flag·ing** **1** *n.* The act or technique of using paint, leaves, etc., to change the appearance of guns, troops, etc., so as to conceal them from the enemy. **2** *n.* The material used to do this. **3** *n.* Any disguise that hides or protects: Chameleons change color as a *camouflage*. **4** *v.* To change the appearance of, so as to hide.

camp [kamp] **1** *n.* A group of tents, cabins, or other structures, usually in the country, used for vacations or outings: a summer *camp*. **2** *n.* A similar place where soldiers and sailors live, usually used for training purposes. **3** *v.* To set up or live in a tent or camp: We'll *camp* by the river. — **break camp** To take down tents, etc., and move on. — **camp′er** *n.*

cam·paign [kam·pān′] **1** *n.* A series of connected military operations made to gain some special objective. **2** *n.* An organized series of activities designed to obtain a definite result: a *campaign* for funds; a *campaign* for the presidency. **3** *v.* To take part in, or go on, a campaign. — **cam·paign′er** *n.*

cam·pa·ni·le [kam′pə·nē′lē] *n.* A tower with bells in it, especially one that is not part of another building.

camp·fire [kamp′fīr′] *n.* A fire in an outdoor camp, used for cooking, warmth, etc.

Camp Fire Girls An organization for girls the purpose of which is to improve their health and welfare by encouraging outdoor life, etc.

cam·phor [kam′fər] *n.* A white, crystalline substance with a strong odor, obtained from an Asian tree or made synthetically. It is used in medicine, plastics, lacquers, and mothballs.

Campanile

cam·pus [kam′pəs] *n.* The grounds of a school, college, or university.

can¹ [kan] *v.* Present tense for all subjects **can,** past tense **could.** *Can* is a helping verb having the following senses: **1** To be able to: He *can* win the race. **2** To know how to: I *can* find my way. **3** To have the right to: You *can* drive in this state at eighteen. **4** *informal* To be permitted to: You *can* leave the room. ◆ In traditional usage *can* refers to ability and *may* to permission: He *can* climb very high walls; You *may* climb that wall if you're careful. In informal speech and writing, however, *can* is now often used to express permission: You *can* go now.

can² [kan] *n., v.* **canned, can·ning** **1** *n.* A metal container for holding, carrying, or preserving liquids or solids. **2** *n.* The contents of such a container: Add one *can* of corn. **3** *v.* To put in sealed cans or jars; preserve, as fruit. **4** *adj. use:* canned pears. — **can′ner** *n.*

Can. Abbreviation of: **1** CANADA. **2** CANADIAN.

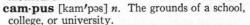

add, āce, câre, pälm; end, ēqual; it, īce; odd, ōpen, ôrder; tŏŏk, pōōl; up, bûrn; ə = a in *above*, e in *sicken*, i in *possible*, o in *melon*, u in *circus*; yŏŏ = u in *fuse*; oil; pout; check; ring; thin; this; zh in *vision*. For ¶ reference, see page 64 · HOW TO

Ca·naan [kā′nən] *n.* In the Bible, the name given by the Israelites to that part of Palestine between the Jordan River and the Mediterranean Sea; the Promised Land.

Ca·naan·ite [kā′nən·īt] *n.* A person who lived in Canaan before its conquest by the Israelites.

Can·a·da [kan′ə·də] *n.* A large country in northern North America, a member of the British Commonwealth of Nations.

Canada goose The common wild goose of North America, brownish gray with black head and neck.

Ca·na·di·an [kə·nā′dē·ən] **1** *adj.* Of or having to do with Canada or its people. **2** *n.* A person born in or a citizen of Canada.

ca·nal [kə·nal′] *n.* **1** A man-made waterway across land, used by ships or boats or for supplying water to dry areas. **2** A passage, duct, or tube in the body: the alimentary *canal.* **3** A long, narrow arm of the sea.

Canal Zone A strip of land extending five miles on each side of the Panama Canal. It is governed by the U.S. by treaty with Panama.

can·a·pé [kan′ə·pē *or* kan′ə·pā] *n.* A cracker or thin piece of toasted bread spread with cheese, fish, etc., and served as an appetizer.

ca·nard [kə·närd′] *n.* A false story; rumor.

ca·nar·y [kə·nâr′ē] *n., pl.* **ca·nar·ies,** *adj.* **1** *n.* A small, yellow songbird, popular as a pet. **2** *n., adj.* Light yellow. ◆ This word comes from the Canary Islands, from which canaries originally came.

Canary Islands A group of islands near the NW coast of Africa.

ca·nas·ta [kə·nas′tə] *n.* A card game based on rummy and using a double deck of cards.

Can·ber·ra [kan′bər·ə] *n.* The capital of Australia.

can·cel [kan′səl] *v.* **can·celed** or **can·celled, can·cel·ing** or **can·cel·ling 1** To cross out or mark (a postage stamp, check, etc.) to show it has been used or noted. **2** To call off, make impossible, or do away with: to *cancel* a trip; to *cancel* an order. **3** To have the same force, value, importance, etc., as; make up for: A good deed can often *cancel* a bad one.

can·cel·la·tion [kan′sə·lā′shən] *n.* **1** The act or process of canceling. **2** The marks used in canceling. **3** The thing that is canceled: Are there any *cancellations* for that flight?

can·cer [kan′sər] *n.* A serious, often fatal growth of abnormal cells in the body. It can destroy normal tissue and often spreads from its original location to other parts of the body. — **can′cer·ous** *adj.*

Can·cer [kan′sər] *n.* A constellation north of the equator.

can·de·la·brum [kan′də·lä′brəm] *n., pl.* **can·de·la·bra** [kan′də·lä′brə] or **can·de·la·brums** A candlestick branched to hold more than one candle.

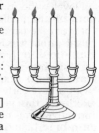

Candelabrum

can·did [kan′did] *adj.* Honest and direct; frank: a *candid* statement. — **can′did·ly** *adv.*

can·di·da·cy [kan′də·də·sē] *n., pl.* **can·di·da·cies** The fact or condition of being a candidate.

can·di·date [kan′də·dāt] *n.* A person who seeks, or is proposed for, an office or honor. ◆ This word comes from a Latin word meaning *wearing white* because candidates for office in ancient Rome wore white togas.

can·died [kan′dēd] *adj.* **1** Cooked in or coated with sugar: *candied* yams. **2** That has turned into sugar; crystallized: *candied* maple syrup.

can·dle [kan′dəl] *n., v.* **can·dled, can·dling 1** *n.* A stick of wax, tallow, or other solid fat, containing a wick that gives light when burning. **2** *v.* To examine, as eggs, by holding between the eye and a light. ◆ This word comes originally from the Latin verb *to gleam.*

can·dle·light [kan′dəl·līt′] *n.* **1** The light given by a candle. **2** The time for lighting candles; twilight.

can·dle·pow·er [kan′dəl·pou′ər] *n.* or **candle power** A standard measure of the strength of a light, based on a comparison with a standard light.

can·dle·stick [kan′dəl·stik′] *n.* A utensil with a socket on top for holding a candle.

can·dor [kan′dər] *n.* **1** Honesty; openness; frankness. **2** Fairness; impartiality. ¶1

can·dy [kan′dē] *n., pl.* **can·dies,** *v.* **can·died, can·dy·ing 1** *n.* A sweet food made of sugar or syrup, usually with flavorings, nuts, fruits, etc., added. **2** *v.* To form or cause to form into sugar. **3** *v.* To preserve by cooking in sugar. ◆ This word comes from an Arabic word meaning *made of sugar.*

cane [kān] *n., v.* **caned, can·ing 1** *n.* A walking stick. **2** *n.* Any rod, especially one used for flogging. **3** *v.* To strike or beat with a cane. **4** *n.* The slender, woody stem of certain plants, as bamboo and rattan, that is easily bent and is used as a weaving material in making baskets, furniture, etc. **5** *n.* A plant having such a stem. **6** *adj. use: cane* furniture. **7** *v.* To make or repair with cane, as furniture. **8** *n.* Sugar cane.

cane·brake [kān′brāk′] *n.* A thick growth of cane.

ca·nine [kā′nīn] **1** *adj.* Of, like, or having to do with the family of animals that includes dogs, wolves, foxes, etc. **2** *n.* A dog or other canine animal. **3** *n.* In humans, any of the four pointed teeth situated on either side of the upper and lower incisors.

can·is·ter [kan′is·tər] *n.* A container, usually metal, for coffee, tea, spices, etc.

can·ker [kang′kər] *n.* **1** An open sore, especially of the mouth and lips. **2** Anything that gradually decays and destroys: the *canker* of corrupt politics. — **can′ker·ous** *adj.*

can·ker·worm [kang′kər·wûrm′] *n.* Any of several caterpillars that destroy fruit trees and other plants.

can·na [kan′ə] *n.* A tropical plant with large leaves and red or yellow flowers.

canned [kand] *adj.* **1** Preserved in a sealed can or jar: *canned* tomatoes. **2** *informal* Recorded: *canned* music.

can·ner·y [kan′ər·ē] *n., pl.* **can·ner·ies** A factory where foods are canned.

can·ni·bal [kan′ə·bəl] *n.* **1** A human being who eats human flesh. **2** An animal that eats its own kind. ◆ This word comes through Spanish from a South American Indian word for *strong men.*

can·ni·bal·ism [kan′ə·bəl·iz′əm] *n.* The act or practice of eating the flesh of one's own kind. — **can′ni·bal·is′tic** *adj.*

can·non [kan′ən] *n., pl.* **can·nons** or **can·non** A large gun mounted on a fixed or movable base.

can·non·ade [kan′ən·ād′] *n., v.* **can·non·ad·ed, can·non·ad·ing** **1** *n.* A steady firing of cannons **2** *v.* To fire cannons repeatedly, as in an attack.

cannon ball A solid metal ball that formerly was used as ammunition for a cannon.

can·not [kan′ot *or* ka·not′] Can not. ◆ *Cannot* is usually preferred to *can not,* unless the writer wants to put a strong emphasis on the *not.*

can·ny [kan′ē] *adj.* **can·ni·er, can·ni·est** Careful; cautious; shrewd. — **can′ni·ly** *adv.*

ca·noe [kə·nōō′] *n., v.* **ca·noed, ca·noe·ing** **1** *n.* A small, light-weight boat, pointed at both ends and moved by paddles. **2** *v.* To paddle, sail, or travel in a canoe.

Canoe

can·on¹ [kan′ən] *n.* **1** A rule or law, especially a rule of faith and practice enacted by a church. **2** An established rule; an accepted principle. **3** A standard for judgment; criterion. **4** The sacred books of any sect or religion. **5** A list of such books. **6** The list of canonized saints.

can·on² [kan′ən] *n.* A clergyman who is on the staff of a cathedral or collegiate church.

ca·ñon [kan′yən] *n.* Another spelling of CANYON.

ca·non·i·cal [kə·non′i·kəl] *adj.* According to, or accepted by, church rule or law: *canonical* books of the Bible.

can·on·ize [kan′ən·īz] *v.* **can·on·ized, can·on·iz·ing** To declare (a dead person) to be a saint. — **can′on·i·za′tion** *n.* ¶3

can·o·py [kan′ə·pē] *n., pl.* **can·o·pies,** *v.* **can·o·pied, can·o·py·ing** **1** *n.* A covering hung over a throne, bed, entrance, etc., or carried on poles over high officials or sacred objects. **2** *n.* Any covering overhead, as the sky or a tree. **3** *v.* To cover with or as with a canopy.

Canopy

canst [kanst] A form of the verb CAN, used with *thou:* seldom used today.

cant¹ [kant] **1** *n.* A slope or tilt; incline. **2** *v.* To slant or tilt; tip.

cant² [kant] *n.* **1** Talk or statements that are insincere or stale; trite words or phrases. **2** Insincere religious talk. **3** Special words or phrases used by a particular group or profession; jargon: legal *cant;* political *cant.*

can't [kant] Cannot.

can·ta·loupe or **can·ta·loup** [kan′tə·lōp] *n.* A variety of muskmelon having a sweet, juicy, orange-colored pulp.

can·tank·er·ous [kan·tang′kər·əs] *adj.* Stubborn and contrary; troublesome: a *cantankerous* animal. — **can·tank′er·ous·ly** *adv.*

can·ta·ta [kən·tä′tə] *n.* A large musical composition to be sung. It often tells a story.

can·teen [kan·tēn′] *n.* **1** A small, usually metal container for carrying water or other liquids. **2** A store at a military post where servicemen can buy personal supplies, food, drink, etc.

can·ter [kan′tər] **1** *n.* A slow, gentle gallop. **2** *v.* To ride or go at a canter.

Can·ter·bur·y [kan′tər·ber′ē] *n.* A city in SE England with a famous cathedral.

can·ti·cle [kan′ti·kəl] *n.* A short hymn with words taken directly from the Bible.

can·ti·lev·er [kan′tə·lev′ər *or* kan′tə·lē′vər] *n.* A beam, slab, or similar structure firmly anchored at one end to a pier or wall, the other end extending free in space. A **cantilever bridge** is constructed of two cantilever arms, each supported on piers at one end and meeting at the center to complete the span.

can·tle [kan′təl] *n.* The hind part of a saddle that sticks up.

can·to [kan′tō] *n., pl.* **can·tos** A division of a long poem, similar to a chapter of a novel.

can·ton [kan′tən] *n.* A small division or district of a country, as of Switzerland.

can·ton·ment [kan·ton′mənt] *n.* A place for the temporary housing of troops.

can·tor [kan′tər] *n.* The chief singer in a synagogue.

can·vas [kan′vəs] **1** *n.* A heavy, strong cloth made of cotton, hemp, or flax, used for sails, tents, etc. **2** *adj.* use: *canvas* shoes. **3** *n.* A piece of canvas on which to paint, especially in oils. **4** *n.* A painting on canvas. — **under**

can·vas 1 With sails set, as a ship. **2** In tents.

can·vas·back [kan′vəs·bak′] *n.* A wild duck having a grayish white back.

can·vass [kan′vəs] **1** *v.* To go about (a district) or among (persons) seeking votes, orders, opinions, etc. **2** *v.* To examine, discuss, or debate (questions, plans, etc.). **3** *n.* The act of canvassing. **— can′vass·er** *n.*

can·yon [kan′yən] *n.* A deep, narrow valley or gorge with very steep sides.

caout·chouc [kōō′chŏŏk *or* kou·chōōk′] *n.* Raw, natural rubber as it comes from the tree.

cap [kap] *n., v.* **capped, cap·ping 1** *n.* A close-fitting covering for the head, made of a soft material without a brim but sometimes with a visor. **2** *n.* Any headgear designed to show one's rank or profession: a nurse's *cap.* **3** *n.* Something like a cap in appearance, position, or use: a *radiator* cap. **4** *v.* To put a cap on; cover. **5** *v.* To serve as a cap or cover to; lie on top of: Snow *capped* the trees. **6** *v.* To match or do better than: to *cap* a teammate's record. **7** *n.* A small amount of explosive material in a piece of paper, used in toy pistols.

cap. Abbreviation of CAPITAL.

ca·pa·bil·i·ty [kā′pə·bil′ə·tē] *n., pl.* **ca·pa·bil·i·ties** The quality of being capable; ability.

ca·pa·ble [kā′pə·bəl] *adj.* Having ability or skill; efficient; competent. **— capable of** In possession of the capacity, qualities, or nature needed for. **— ca′pa·bly** *adv.*

ca·pa·cious [kə·pā′shəs] *adj.* Able to contain much; roomy; large: a *capacious* closet.

ca·pac·i·tance [kə·pas′ə·təns] *n.* The ability of an electric circuit to store energy in the form of a charge built up across two points that are at different voltages.

ca·pac·i·tor [kə·pas′ə·tər] *n.* A device made of two electrical conductors with an insulator between them across which a charge builds up when they are at different voltages.

ca·pac·i·ty [kə·pas′ə·tē] *n., pl.* **ca·pac·i·ties 1** The ability, room, or space to contain, hold, etc.: a jar with a *capacity* of two pints. **2** The most something can contain, hold, or do: to operate below *capacity*; to be filled to *capacity*. **3** Ability, talent, or skill: a *capacity* for invention. **4** Specific position or function.

ca·par·i·son [kə·par′ə·sən] **1** *n.* A richly ornamented covering for a horse. **2** *n.* Showy or expensive clothing or ornaments. **3** *v.* To adorn with rich or showy clothing.

cape¹ [kāp] *n.* A sleeveless outer garment fastened at the neck and hanging loosely from the shoulders.

cape² [kāp] *n.* A point of land extending into the sea or a lake.

ca·per¹ [kā′pər] **1** *n.* A playful leap, skip, or jump. **2** *v.* To leap or skip playfully; frolic. **3** *n.* A wild, silly prank or trick. **— cut a caper** To caper, frolic, or play tricks.

ca·per² [kā′pər] *n. (usually pl.)* The green flower bud of a Mediterranean shrub, pickled and used as a relish or seasoning.

Cape Town *or* **Cape·town** [kāp′toun′] *n.* The legislative capital of the Republic of South Africa, a seaport.

cap·il·lar·y [kap′ə·ler′ē] *adj., n., pl.* **cap·il·lar·ies 1** *adj.* Like a hair; extremely fine. **2** *n.* Any very narrow tube, as the inside of a thermometer. **3** *n.* One of the very narrow, thread-like blood vessels that connect the arteries with the veins.

capillary attraction A force that causes a liquid to rise against gravity when enclosed in a very narrow tube or in contact with an absorbent material, as a blotter.

cap·i·tal¹ [kap′ə·təl] **1** *n.* The city or town in a country or state which is the seat of government. **2** *adj. use:* a *capital* city. **3** *n.* A capital letter. **4** *n.* The total amount of wealth, as money, property, stock, etc., owned or used by an individual or corporation. **5** *n.* Wealth, as money, property, etc., used or available for the production of more wealth. **6** *n.* People who have wealth, as a group: *capital* and labor. **7** *adj.* Of the first quality; chief; most important. **8** *adj.* Excellent: a *capital* idea. **9** *adj.* Punishable by or involving the penalty of death: a *capital* crime. **— make capital of** To turn to advantage. **— cap′i·tal·ly** *adv.* ◆ (def. 1) *Capital* and *capitol* both mean a seat of government, but a *capital* is a city, and a *capitol* is a building in which a legislature meets.

cap·i·tal² [kap′ə·təl] *n.* The top of a column.

cap·i·tal·ism [kap′ə·təl·iz′əm] *n.* A system in which the factories, materials, etc., for making and distributing goods are privately owned and operated for private profit rather than being owned or controlled by a state or government.

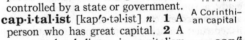

A Corinthian capital

cap·i·tal·ist [kap′ə·təl·ist] *n.* **1** A person who has great capital. **2** A person who believes in capitalism. **— cap′i·tal·is′tic** *adj.*

cap·i·tal·i·za·tion [kap′ə·təl·ə·zā′shən] *n.* **1** The act or process of capitalizing. **2** The total capital employed in a business. ¶3

cap·i·tal·ize [kap′ə·təl·īz′] *v.* **cap·i·tal·ized, cap·i·tal·iz·ing 1** To begin with or write in capital letters. **2** To provide capital for, as for a business. **3** To change into capital. **4** To profit or gain by turning something to one's own advantage: He *capitalized* on his father's fame. ¶3

capital letter The form of a letter used to begin a sentence, a proper name, etc.

capital punishment A penalty of death for a crime.

capital ship A warship of large size, as a battleship or aircraft carrier.

Cap·i·tol [kap'ə·təl] *n.* **1** The official building of the U.S. Congress in Washington, D.C. **2** (*written* **capitol**) The building in which a state legislature meets. ◆ See CAPITAL[1].

ca·pit·u·late [kə·pich'ŏŏ·lāt] *v.* **ca·pit·u·lat·ed, ca·pit·u·lat·ing** To surrender, especially on certain terms. — **ca·pit'u·la'tion** *n.*

ca·pon [kā'pon] *n.* A rooster from which the sex glands have been removed to improve its flesh for eating.

U.S. Capitol

ca·price [kə·prēs'] *n.* A sudden, unreasonable change of mind, mood, or opinion; whim.

ca·pri·cious [kə·prish'əs] *adj.* Likely to change without warning; fickle. — **ca·pri'cious·ly** *adv.*

Cap·ri·corn [kap'rə·kôrn] *n.* A constellation south of the equator.

cap·size [kap·sīz' *or* kap'sīz] *v.* **cap·sized, cap·siz·ing** To upset; tip over; overturn.

cap·stan [kap'stən] *n.* An upright cylinder resembling a large spool, turned by hand or motor-driven, and around which cables or ropes are wound to lift a weight, as an anchor.

Capstan

cap·sule [kap'səl *or* kap's(y)ŏŏl] *n.* **1** A small container made of gelatine, which is easily dissolved, used to hold one dose of medicine. **2** A covering or case for the seeds of some plants.

Capt. Abbreviation of CAPTAIN.

cap·tain [kap'tən] **1** *n.* A military rank. In the U.S. Army, Air Force, and Marine Corps, a captain is an officer ranking above a first lieutenant and below a major. In the U.S. Navy and Coast Guard, a captain is an officer ranking above a commander and below a rear admiral. **2** *n.* A person at the head or in command; leader. **3** *n.* The master or commander of a vessel. **4** *n.* A member of a team acting as leader. **5** *v.* To act as captain to; command; lead: Jim *captained* his team to victory.

cap·tain·cy [kap'tən·sē] *n.*, *pl.* **cap·tain·cies** The position, rank, or term of office of a captain.

cap·tion [kap'shən] **1** *n.* A heading, as of a chapter of a book or an article in a newspaper. **2** *n.* The title and written matter describing a picture. **3** *v.* To furnish with a caption.

cap·tious [kap'shəs] *adj.* **1** Apt or eager to find fault; critical: a *captious* teacher. **2** Intended only to stir up arguments: *captious* remarks.

cap·ti·vate [kap'tə·vāt] *v.* **cap·ti·vat·ed, cap·ti·vat·ing** To fascinate or charm, as by beauty or excellence: She *captivated* the audience.

cap·tive [kap'tiv] **1** *n.* A person or thing captured and held in confinement; prisoner. **2** *adj.* Held prisoner; not allowed to escape.

cap·tiv·i·ty [kap·tiv'ə·tē] *n.*, *pl.* **cap·tiv·i·ties** The condition of being held captive; confinement; imprisonment.

cap·tor [kap'tər] *n.* A person who takes or holds another captive.

cap·ture [kap'chər] *v.* **cap·tured, cap·tur·ing**, *n.* **1** *v.* To take captive by force, cleverness, etc.: to *capture* a lion; to *capture* a ship. **2** *n.* The act of capturing. **3** *n.* A being captured. **4** *n.* A person or thing captured.

cap·y·ba·ra [kap'i·bä'rə] *n.* A rodent of South America, about four feet long and having a stubby tail, often found near lakes and rivers.

car [kär] *n.* **1** Any vehicle used to carry people or goods, especially an automobile. **2** A vehicle for use on rails, as a railroad car or streetcar. **3** The enclosed platform on which people or things are carried in an elevator.

Ca·ra·cas [kə·rä'kəs] *n.* The capital of Venezuela, located in the northern part.

car·a·cul [kar'ə·kəl] *n.* **1** The black or gray, loosely curled fur made from the skin of an Asian lamb. **2** The animal producing this fur.

ca·rafe [kə·raf'] *n.* A bottle, usually of glass, used to hold water, hot coffee, or other drinks.

car·a·mel [kar'ə·mel] *n.* **1** A candy, usually cut in small cubes. **2** Burnt sugar, used to color and flavor foods.

car·a·pace [kar'ə·pās] *n.* The hard, bony covering of certain animals, as the turtle or lobster.

car·at [kar'ət] *n.* **1** A unit of weight for gems, equal to one fifth of a gram. **2** Karat.

car·a·van [kar'ə·van] *n.* **1** A group of traders, pilgrims, or nomads traveling together, especially through a desert. **2** A covered wagon or truck, especially one used as a house on wheels.

car·a·vel [kar'ə·vel] *n.* A small, fast sailing ship of the 15th and 16th centuries.

car·a·way [kar'ə·wā] *n.* A plant related to parsley, having small, spicy seeds.

car·bide [kär'bīd] *n.* A compound of carbon with another element.

car·bine [kär'bīn *or* kär'bēn] *n.* A light rifle with a short barrel.

Caravel

car·bo·hy·drate [kär'bō·hī'drāt] *n.* Any of a large group of compounds of carbon, hydrogen, and oxygen. Green plants make them out of carbon dioxide and water. Sugars and starches are carbohydrates.

car·bol·ic acid [kär·bol′ik] A poisonous compound obtained from coal tar.

car·bon [kär′bən] *n.* **1** A nonmetallic element found in all living things, and also in coal, charcoal, and petroleum. It occurs in pure form as diamond and graphite. **2** A piece of carbon paper, or a copy made with it.

carbon 14 A radioactive isotope of carbon whose presence in very old bones, fossils, etc., helps to determine their age.

car·bon·ate [kär′bə·nāt] *v.* **car·bon·at·ed, car·bon·at·ing,** *n.* **1** *v.* To charge with carbon dioxide: Ginger ale is *carbonated* so that it fizzes. **2** *n.* A salt of carbonic acid. **— car′· bon·a′tion** *n.*

carbon dioxide An odorless, colorless, gaseous compound of carbon and oxygen. It is breathed out by animals and taken up as food by plants.

car·bon·ic acid [kär·bon′ik] A compound formed from carbon dioxide and water. It produces a sharp taste in carbonated water.

car·bon·if·er·ous [kär′bə·nif′ər·əs] *adj.* **1** Containing or yielding carbon, especially in the form of coal. **2** (*written* **Carboniferous**) Of or having to do with the geological period in which large coal beds were formed.

car·bon·ize [kär′bən·īz] *v.* **car·bon·ized, car·bon·iz·ing 1** To reduce to carbon, as by burning or charring. **2** To overlay or coat with carbon. ¶3

carbon monoxide A colorless, odorless, very poisonous gas given off in the exhaust fumes of automobile engines.

carbon paper Thin paper coated with a waxy carbon substance. It is placed between sheets of paper so as to reproduce on the bottom sheets what has been typed or written on the top sheet.

car·bun·cle [kär′bung·kəl] *n.* **1** A painful, inflamed sore beneath the skin, larger than a boil. **2** A deep red precious stone, especially a garnet cut with a smooth surface.

car·bu·re·tor [kär′bə·rā′tər] *n.* A device for mixing air with the fuel of an internal combustion engine, as in an automobile.

car·cass or **car·case** [kär′kəs] *n.* **1** The dead body of an animal. **2** The human body: used in a joking way.

card¹ [kärd] *n.* **1** A small, usually rectangular piece of thin cardboard or stiff paper with something written or printed on it: A business *card* gives one's name, trade or profession, and business address; People often send good wishes in a birthday *card*. **2** A playing card. **3** A postal card. **4** *informal* A witty or funny person.

card² [kärd] **1** *n.* A tool with bent wire points used for combing and cleansing wool and other fibers. **2** *v.* To comb or cleanse with a card.

card·board [kärd′bôrd′] *n.* Thick, stiff paper used for making boxes, cards, etc.

car·di·ac [kär′dē·ak] *adj.* Of, having to do with, or near the heart: a *cardiac* patient.

car·di·gan [kär′də·gən] *n.* A jacket or sweater without a collar, and with long sleeves, that opens down the front. ◆ The garment was named after the Earl of *Cardigan*.

Cardigan

car·di·nal [kär′də·nəl] **1** *adj.* Of first importance; chief: the four *cardinal* virtues. **2** *adj., n.* Deep, rich red. **3** *n.* One of the high officials in the Roman Catholic Church who are appointed by the Pope. Cardinals wear scarlet robes and hats. **4** *n.* A red songbird.

cardinal number A number that tells how many elements there are in a set, as 6, 15, and 240.

cardinal point Any of the four principal points of the compass, north, south, east, and west.

card·ing [kär′ding] *n.* The cleaning and combing of wool, flax, or cotton fibers.

cards [kärdz] *n.pl.* (*often used with singular verb*) **1** Any game played with playing cards. **2** The act of playing games with cards.

Cardinal, 8–9 in. long

care [kâr] *n., v.* **cared, car·ing 1** *n.* A feeling of concern; worry: His face was full of *care* when his brother was ill. **2** *v.* To have or show interest and concern: John doesn't *care* if he fails history. **3** *n.* A cause of worry: He doesn't seem to have a *care* in the world. **4** *n.* Watchful attention; heed: Always handle matches with *care*. **5** *n.* A looking after; a tending: The farmer has the *care* of forty cows. **6** *v.* To feel inclined; like: Would you *care* to go to the movies? **— care for 1** To look after; provide for: Children should learn to *care for* their own pets. **2** To have a fondness for; like: Some people don't *care for* oysters. **— take care of 1** To look after; protect. **2** To attend to; do: to *take care of* the shopping.

ca·reen [kə·rēn′] *v.* **1** To lurch from side to side while moving, as if out of control: The truck *careened* around the curve. **2** To lean or cause to lean to one side, as a sailboat in the wind.

ca·reer [kə·rir′] **1** *n.* The course of a person's life, especially the part having to do with important activities: Ben Franklin had an interesting *career*. **2** *n.* A person's lifework; profession: Engineering is a good *career*. **3** *adj. U.S.* Planning to spend one's life in a certain kind of work: a *career* diplomat. **4** *n.* Great speed: The motorcycle passed in full *career*. **5** *v.* To move along at great speed: The bus *careered* down the highway, out of control.

care·free [kâr′frē′] *adj.* Free of troubles or worry; happy; lighthearted.

care·ful [kâr′fəl] *adj.* **1** Giving close attention to one's work or to what one is doing; painstaking: a *careful* typist. **2** Cautious: Be *careful* not to slip on the ice. **3** Done with care: a *careful* piece of work. — **care′ful·ly** *adv.* — **care′ful·ness** *n.*

care·less [kâr′lis] *adj.* **1** Not giving close attention to what one is doing or saying: a *careless* worker. **2** Due to or done with lack of care; thoughtless: a *careless* mistake; a *careless* remark. **3** Carefree; happy: a *careless* life. — **care′less·ly** *adv.* — **care′less·ness** *n.*

ca·ress [kə·res′] **1** *n.* A gentle, loving touch, as a kiss, embrace, or pat. **2** *v.* To touch or embrace gently and lovingly: to *caress* a kitten.

car·et [kar′ət] *n.* A sign (∧) placed below a line of writing or printing to show where something is to be inserted.

care·tak·er [kâr′tā′kər] *n.* A person employed to take care of and watch over a place or building, as an unoccupied house or a church.

care·worn [kâr′wôrn′] *adj.* Showing the effects of much care or worry: *careworn* eyes.

car·fare [kär′fâr′] *n.* The money a person pays to ride on a bus, subway, etc.

car·go [kär′gō] *n., pl.* **car·goes** or **car·gos** Freight carried by a ship, aircraft, etc.

Car·ib·be·an [kar′ə·bē′ən *or* kə·rib′ē·ən] **1** *n.*

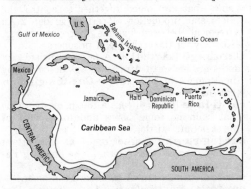

A sea that is part of the Atlantic Ocean between the West Indies and Central and South America. Also **Caribbean Sea. 2** *adj.* Of or having to do with the Caribbean Sea.

car·i·bou [kar′ə·bōō] *n., pl.* **car·i·bou** or **car·i·bous** Any of several kinds of reindeer found in North America. ◆ *Caribou* comes directly from Canadian French and goes back to an Algonquian Indian word meaning *a creature that paws or scratches.*

car·i·ca·ture [kar′i·kə·chŏŏr] *n., v.* **car·i·ca·tured, car·i·ca·tur·ing 1** *n.* A picture or description in which certain features or qualities are exaggerated or distorted so as to produce an absurd effect. **2** *n.* The art of caricaturing. **3** *v.* To make a caricature of.

car·ies [kâr′ēz] *n.* Decay of a bone or of a tooth.

car·il·lon [kar′ə·lon] *n.* A set of bells on which a melody can be played, often by hammers operated from a keyboard.

car·load [kär′lōd′] *n.* The amount that will fill a car, especially a railroad freight car.

car·mine [kär′min *or* kär′mīn] *n., adj.* Deep red or purplish red.

car·nage [kär′nij] *n.* A bloody killing of great numbers of people, as in war.

car·nal [kär′nəl] *adj.* **1** Of the body and bodily appetites. **2** Worldly; not spiritual.

car·na·tion [kär·nā′shən] *n.* **1** A white, yellow, or pink garden flower with a strong, spicy smell. **2** Its plant. **3** A pink or red color.

car·nel·ian [kär·nēl′yən] *n.* A clear, red stone.

car·ni·val [kär′nə·vəl] *n.* **1** An amusement show, typically having a merry-go-round, Ferris wheel, side shows, etc. **2** Any gay festival or celebration, including parades, dancing, and masquerades. **3** In some countries, the week of festivity just before Lent.

car·ni·vore [kär′nə·vôr] *n.* A carnivorous animal.

car·niv·o·rous [kär·niv′ə·rəs] *adj.* Eating or living on meat: Cats and dogs are *carnivorous.*

car·ol [kar′əl] *n., v.* **car·oled** or **car·olled, car·ol·ing** or **car·ol·ling 1** *n.* A song of joy or praise, especially a Christmas song. **2** *v.* To sing or praise in a joyous way with carols. — **car′ol·er** or **car′ol·ler** *n.*

Car·o·li·na [kar′ə·lī′nə] *n.* Either North Carolina or South Carolina.

car·om [kar′əm] **1** *n.* In billiards, a shot in which the cue ball strikes against two balls, one after the other. **2** *n.* A similar shot in other games. **3** *v.* To make a carom. **4** *v.* To strike and bounce off: The car *caromed* off the wall.

ca·rou·sal [kə·rou′zəl] *n.* A noisy, merry drinking party or banquet.

ca·rouse [kə·rouz′] *n., v.* **ca·roused, ca·rous·ing 1** *n.* A noisy, jolly party with much drinking and eating; carousal. **2** *v.* To join in such a party.

car·ou·sel [kar′ə·səl′] *n.* A merry-go-round.

carp[1] [kärp] *v.* To find fault in an unpleasant or nagging way; keep grumbling or whining.

carp[2] [kärp] *n., pl.* **carp** or **carps** An edible fresh-water fish, found in lakes and slow streams.

Car·pa·thi·ans [kär·pā′thē·ənz] *n.pl.* A range of mountains in central and eastern Europe.

car·pel [kär′pəl] *n.* A simple pistil, or seed-bearing organ of a flower.

car·pen·ter [kär′pən·tər] *n.* A workman whose trade is to cut and put in place the wood used in constructing buildings, ships, etc.

car·pen·try [kär′pən·trē] *n.* The work of a carpenter.

---

add, āce, câre, pälm; end, ēqual; it, īce; odd, ōpen, ôrder; tŏŏk, pōōl; up, bûrn;
ə = a in *above,* e in *sicken,* i in *possible,* o in *melon,* u in *circus;* yŏŏ = u in *fuse;* oil; pout;
check; ring; thin; this; zh in *vision.*

For ¶ reference, see page 64 · HOW TO

car·pet [kär′pit] **1** *n.* A covering for floors, usually made of a heavy, woven fabric. **2** *n.* Anything that covers like a carpet: a *carpet* of pine needles. **3** *v.* To cover with a carpet: to *carpet* a flight of stairs. **— on the carpet** Being scolded or criticized by someone in authority.

car·pet·bag [kär′pit·bag′] *n.* An old-fashioned suitcase or bag made of carpeting.

car·pet·bag·ger [kär′pit·bag′ər] *n.* One of the Northerners who went South right after the Civil War in order to profit financially from the confused, unsettled conditions there.

car·pet·ing [kär′pit·ing] *n.* **1** The act of covering with a carpet. **2** Material used for carpets. **3** Carpets: new *carpeting* for the halls.

car·port [kär′pôrt′] *n.* A shelter for a car, built against a building. It has a roof but is open at the sides.

car·riage [kar′ij; *for def. 7 also* kar′ē·ij] *n.* **1** A wheeled vehicle for carrying people. It is usually drawn by horses. **2** A perambulator; baby carriage. **3** A moving part of a

Carport

machine for carrying along another part or an object: a typewriter *carriage*. **4** A wheeled frame for carrying something heavy: a gun *carriage*. **5** The manner of carrying one's head and limbs; posture: a graceful *carriage*. **6** The act of carrying or transporting persons or goods. **7** The cost of transporting something.

car·ri·er [kar′ē·ər] *n.* **1** A person or thing that carries. **2** A person or company that carries persons or goods for a fee. **3** An aircraft carrier. **4** A person who is immune to a disease but carries the germs and may infect others.

carrier wave The radio wave produced by a broadcasting station or other radio transmitter. When modulated it carries the program or message.

car·ri·on [kar′ē·ən] **1** *n.* Dead and decaying flesh; meat not fit to be eaten by people: Buzzards live on *carrion*. **2** *adj.* Feeding on carrion: a *carrion* crow. **3** *adj.* Like carrion; dead and decaying.

Car·roll [kar′əl], **Lewis,** 1832–1898, English mathematician and author of *Alice in Wonderland*. His real name was Charles Dodgson.

car·rot [kar′ət] *n.* **1** The long, reddish yellow root of a plant related to parsley. It is eaten as a vegetable. **2** The plant itself.

car·rou·sel [kar′ə·sel′] *n.* Another word for MERRY-GO-ROUND.

car·ry [kar′ē] *v.* **car·ried, car·ry·ing 1** To bear from one place to another; transport: *Carry* the dishes to the sink; This pipe *carries* gas. **2** To hold up; support: The columns in this room *carry* the weight of the ceiling. **3** To wear on or about one's person: Policemen *carry* guns. **4** To bear (the body or part of it) in a certain way: *Carry* your shoulders straight. **5** To cause to go

or come: A love of animals *carries* him to the zoo every Sunday. **6** To reach to a distance: The sound *carried* for ten miles. **7** To win: Jonathan *carried* the election. **8** To have or keep for sale: A hardware store *carries* tools. **9** To bear in mind: to *carry* the memory of something. **10** To sing or play (a part or melody). **11** In adding up a row of figures, to transfer (a figure) from one column to the next. **12** To contain; include: His voice *carried* a note of warning. **— carry away** To move the feelings greatly: We were *carried away* by the music. **— carry out** To accomplish.

car·ry·all [kar′ē·ôl] *n.* A light, one-horse carriage with a top, holding several people. ◆ *Carryall* comes from the French word *cariole*. Apparently the sound and spelling of *cariole* were too un-English, because *carryall*, with its familiar English elements, *carry* and *all*, replaced it.

car·sick [kär′sik] *adj.* Dizzy or sick at one's stomach from riding in a car.

Car·son City [kär′sən] The capital of Nevada.

cart [kärt] **1** *n.* A heavy, two-wheeled vehicle for carrying heavy loads, usually pulled by a horse. **2** *n.* A light, usually two-wheeled vehicle for small loads or for riding: a pony *cart*; a grocery *cart*. **3** *v.* To carry in a cart.

carte blanche [kärt′blänsh′] Freedom to act as one thinks best; full authority.

car·tel [kär·tel′] *n.* **1** A large group of companies that are joined together to control the prices and production of certain goods. **2** An agreement between nations that are at war, especially for the exchange of prisoners.

Car·thage [kär′thij] *n.* A famous ancient city and state in North Africa. It was destroyed by the Romans in 146 B.C. **— Car·tha·gin·i·an** [kär′thə·jin′ē·ən] *adj., n.*

car·ti·lage [kär′tə·lij] *n.* A tough, elastic tissue that connects some bones and forms part of the skeleton; gristle.

car·tog·ra·phy [kär·tog′rə·fē] *n.* The art of making maps and charts. **— car·tog′ra·pher** *n.*

car·ton [kär′tən] *n.* A cardboard container.

car·toon [kär·tōōn′] *n.* **1** A drawing that influences or amuses by showing a person, political event, etc., in an exaggerated way. **2** Any humorous drawing. **3** A comic strip. **4** A motion picture film made by photographing a series of slightly different drawings so that the figures seem to move.

car·toon·ist [kär·tōōn′ist] *n.* A person who draws cartoons.

car·tridge [kär′trij] *n.* **1** A casing of metal or cardboard containing a charge of powder for a gun and usually the bullet or shot. **2** Any similar container, as that holding a phonograph needle and pickup or a cylinder for camera film.

cart·wheel [kärt′(h)wēl′] *n.* A sideways handspring, in which the body is supported first on one hand and then the other.

Ca·ru·so [kə·rōō′sō], **Enrico,** 1873–1921, Italian operatic tenor.

carve [kärv] *v.* **carved, carv·ing 1** To make by cutting or as if by cutting: to *carve* a statue; to *carve* one's name in history. **2** To cut figures or designs upon: to *carve* a table. **3** To cut up, as a piece of roasted meat. — **carv′er** *n.*

Car·ver [kär′vər], **George Washington,** 1864?–1943, U.S. botanist and chemist, known for the many products he developed from peanuts.

carv·ing [kär′ving] *n.* **1** The act of a person who carves. **2** A carved figure or design.

car·y·at·id [kar′ē·at′id] *n.,* *pl.* **car·y·at·ids** or **car·y·at·i·des** [kar′ē·at′ə·dēz] A supporting column made in the form of a sculptured woman.

cas·cade [kas·kād′] *n., v.* **cas·cad·ed, cas·cad·ing 1** *n.* A small waterfall over steep rocks. **2** *n.* Something that looks like a waterfall. **3** *v.* To fall in or as if in a cascade.

Cas·cade Mountains [kas·kād′] A range of mountains in Oregon, Washington, and British Columbia.

case[1] [kās] *n.* **1** A particular instance or example: a clear *case* of robbery. **2** The actual facts or state of affairs: Louise now loves to read, which was not the *case* last year. **3** An action or lawsuit in a court of law. **4** Someone being cared for, as by a doctor; patient. **5** In grammar, the form of a noun, pronoun, or adjective that expresses its relationship to the other words in the sentence. In "The cat scratched me with his sharp claws," *cat* is in the nominative *case*, *me* is in the objective *case*, and *his* is in the possessive *case*. **—in any case** No matter what; in spite of everything. **—in case** In the event that; if.

case[2] [kās] *n., v.* **cased, cas·ing 1** *n.* A box, bag, or other container for carrying or keeping things in: a jewel *case*; a pillow*case*. **2** *n.* A box and the containers or bottles it holds: a *case* of pop. **3** *v.* To put into or cover with a case. **4** *n.* A frame for a window or door.

ca·se·in [kā′sē·in *or* kā′sēn] *n.* A protein found in milk, used in making cheese, plastics, etc.

case·ment [kās′mənt] *n.* A window hung on side hinges and opening as a door does.

cash [kash] **1** *n.* Money in the form of bills and coins which a person has on hand. **2** *v.* To give or receive coins and bills for: to *cash* a check. **3** *n.* Money paid promptly when one makes a purchase: to buy a car for *cash*.

Casement

cash·ew [kash′ōō] *n.* **1** A soft, kidney-shaped nut that is very good to eat. It is grown on a tropical tree. **2** The tree itself.

cash·ier[1] [ka·shir′] *n.* A person who is employed to handle the money, as in a restaurant, store, or bank.

cash·ier[2] [ka·shir′] *v.* To dismiss from service in disgrace, especially a military officer.

cash·mere [kash′mir *or* kazh′mir] **1** *n.* A fine, soft wool obtained from a goat originally native in Kashmir. **2** *n.* A soft fabric woven from this wool. **3** *adj. use:* a *cashmere* sweater.

cas·ing [kā′sing] *n.* **1** A protective case or covering, as the outer part of an automobile tire. **2** The intestines of hogs and other animals that are cleaned and used as sausage skins. **3** A framework, as around a door or window.

ca·si·no [kə·sē′nō] *n., pl.* **ca·si·nos 1** A room or building for public amusement, especially for dancing or gambling. **2** A card game.

cask [kask] *n.* **1** A barrel-shaped wooden container for liquids. **2** The amount a cask will hold.

cas·ket [kas′kit] *n.* **1** A small box or chest, as for jewelry. **2** A coffin.

Cas·pi·an Sea [kas′pē·ən] The largest inland salt-water sea in the world. It lies between SE Europe and Asia.

casque [kask] *n.* A large helmet worn with armor.

Cas·san·dra [kə·san′drə] *n.* In Greek myths, a daughter of the king of Troy whose prophecies, although true, were never believed by anyone.

cas·sa·va [kə·sä′və] *n.* **1** A tropical American plant with starchy roots. **2** The starch made from this plant, used to make tapioca.

cas·se·role [kas′ə·rōl] *n.* **1** A dish, often with a cover, in which food may be baked and served. **2** Any food so prepared and served.

cas·si·no [kə·sē′nō] *n.* A card game.

Cas·si·o·pe·ia [kas′ē·ə·pē′ə] *n.* A northern constellation.

cas·sock [kas′ək] *n.* A close-fitting, usually black robe reaching to the feet. It is worn by the clergymen of some churches.

cast [kast] *v.* **cast, cast·ing,** *n.* **1** *v.* To throw or hurl with force; fling: to *cast* a spear; to *cast* a fishing line. **2** *n.* The act of casting or throwing: a *cast* of the dice. **3** *n.* The distance to which a thing may be thrown: a stone's *cast*. **4** *v.* To throw off; shed: Grasshoppers *cast* their hard shells as they grow. **5** *v.* To cause to fall upon or over something: to *cast* a shadow. **6** *v.* To let down; drop: to *cast* anchor. **7** *v.* To select actors for a play, motion picture, etc.: In the school play, Harold was *cast* as a fisherman. **8** *n.* All of the actors appearing in a play or motion picture. **9** *v.* To pour into a mold and let

add, āce, câre, pälm; end, ēqual; it, īce; odd, ōpen, ôrder; took, pool; up, bûrn;
ə = a in *above*, e in *sicken*, i in *possible*, o in *melon*, u in *circus*; yoo = u in *fuse*; oil; pout;
check; ring; thin; this; zh in *vision.* For ¶ reference, see page 64 · HOW TO

harden: to *cast* molten iron. **10** *v.* To shape in a mold: to *cast* a statue in bronze. **11** *n.* Something shaped or formed in a mold, as of metal, plaster, etc.; casting. **12** *n.* The appearance or form of something: a face with an Oriental *cast*. **13** *n.* A heavy bandage stiffened with plaster. It is wrapped around a broken bone to keep it from moving until it has healed. **14** *v.* To direct; cause to turn: to *cast* a glance up the street. **15** *v.* To deposit; give: to *cast* a vote. **16** *n.* A twist or turn of an eye to one side; squint. **17** *n.* A tinge or shade: a bluish *cast*. **— cast down 1** To overthrow; defeat. **2** To make discouraged; depress: to be *cast down* over a failure. **3** To throw or turn downward: *Cast down* your weapons.

cas·ta·nets [kas′tə·netz′] *n.pl.* A pair of small, shell-shaped disks of wood or ivory, clapped together with the fingers to beat time to music, especially to Spanish music or dances.

cast·a·way [kast′ə·wā′] **1** *adj.* Shipwrecked. **2** *adj.* Thrown away; discarded. **3** *n.* A person who has been shipwrecked.

caste [kast] *n.* **1** In India, one of the social classes into which Hindus are born. Formerly, Hindus of higher castes were forbidden to mix with or touch those of a lower caste. **2** Any social class to which a person belongs because of his money, occupation, rank, etc. **—lose caste** To lose one's social position.

cast·er [kas′tər] *n.* **1** A person or thing that casts. **2** One of a set of small, swiveling wheels fastened under each leg or corner of a piece of furniture to make it easier to move about. **3** A small container for vinegar, mustard, or other seasoning that is used at the table.

cas·ti·gate [kas′tə·gāt] *v.* **cas·ti·gat·ed, cas·ti·gat·ing** To scold or criticize harshly or severely. **— cas′·ti·ga′tion** *n.*

Casters

Cas·tile [kas·tēl′] *n.* A region and former kingdom in central and northern Spain.

Castile soap A pure soap made from olive oil.

Cas·til·ian [kas·til′yən] **1** *n.* A person born or living in Castile. **2** *n.* The standard and literary language of Spain. **3** *adj.* Of or from Castile.

cast·ing [kas′ting] *n.* **1** The act of a person or thing that casts. **2** Something that is cast, as a statue or other article formed in a mold.

cast-i·ron [kast′ī′ərn] *adj.* **1** Made of cast iron. **2** Like cast iron; strong and unyielding: The old man has a *cast-iron* will.

cast iron A hard, brittle kind of iron cast in molds. It contains a large amount of carbon.

cas·tle [kas′əl] *n.* **1** A large, fortified building or set of buildings, usually having a moat around it for defense. During the Middle Ages, kings and noblemen lived in castles. **2** Any large,

elegant house. **3** In chess, a rook. **— castle in the air** or **castle in Spain** A pleasing thought or daydream.

cast·off [kast′ôf′] **1** *adj.* Thrown away or laid aside because no longer wanted: a *castoff* coat. **2** *n.* A person or thing no longer wanted.

cas·tor [kas′tər] *n.* Another spelling for CASTER (*defs. 2* and *3*).

castor oil A thick, pale yellow oil extracted from the bean of a shrubby tropical tree. It is taken as a laxative and used to oil machinery.

cas·trate [kas′trāt] *v.* **cas·trat·ed, cas·trat·ing** To remove the male sex glands of. **— cas·tra′tion** *n.*

cas·u·al [kazh′oō·əl] **1** *adj.* Happening by chance; unexpected: a *casual* meeting. **2** *adj.* Done without thinking; not planned: a *casual* comment. **3** *adj.* Happening once in a while; not regular: a *casual* visit. **4** *n.* A person who works only occasionally. **5** *adj.* Not dressy; informal: *casual* clothes. **— cas′u·al·ly** *adv.*

cas·u·al·ty [kazh′oō·əl·tē] *n., pl.* **cas·u·al·ties** **1** A serious accident, especially one in which someone is killed. **2** Anyone who is injured or killed in an accident. **3** A soldier who is killed, wounded, or missing during a battle.

cat [kat] *n.* **1** A small domestic animal of various colors. ◆Adj., *feline*. **2** Any larger animal related to the cat, as the tiger, lion, leopard, bobcat, etc. **3** A woman who makes spiteful, mean remarks. **4** A cat-o′-nine-tails.

cat·a·clysm [kat′ə·kliz′əm] *n.* Any violent change or disturbance, as a war, flood, etc.

cat·a·comb [kat′ə·kōm] *n.* (*usually pl.*) An underground place of burial made up of passages and small rooms for tombs.

cat·a·log [kat′ə·lôg] *n., v.* **cat·a·loged, cat·a·log·ing** Another spelling of CATALOGUE.

cat·a·logue [kat′ə·lôg] *n., v.* **cat·a·logued, cat·a·logu·ing** **1** *n.* A list of names, objects, etc., usually in alphabetical order and often including descriptions. **2** *n.* A book or pamphlet including such a list: a sales *catalogue*; A college *catalogue* lists and describes the courses offered. **3** *n.* A card file showing the books, etc., in a library. **4** *v.* To place or describe in a catalogue. **— cat′a·logu′er** *n.*

ca·tal·pa [kə·tal′pə] *n.* A tree of North America having large, heart-shaped leaves and long pods that look like string beans.

cat·a·lyst [kat′ə·list] *n.* A substance that speeds up a chemical reaction without itself appearing to undergo permanent change.

cat·a·ma·ran [kat′ə·mə·ran′] *n.* **1** A long, narrow raft of logs. **2** A boat having twin hulls, side by side.

Catamaran

cat·a·mount [kat′ə·mount] *n.* Any of several wild cats, especially the puma and lynx.

cat·a·pult [kat′ə·pult] **1** *n*. An ancient military machine for throwing arrows, spears, or rocks with great force. **2** *n*. A device for helping an airplane to take off quickly into the air, as from the deck of a ship. **3** *v*. To hurl or be hurled from or as if from a catapult.

cat·a·ract [kat′ə·rakt] *n*. **1** A very large waterfall. **2** A heavy downpour or flood of water. **3** A disease in which the lens of the eye clouds over, causing partial or total blindness.

ca·tarrh [kə·tär′] *n*. An old-fashioned name for an inflammation of the nose and throat.

ca·tas·tro·phe [kə·tas′trə·fē] *n*. A sudden and widespread misfortune, calamity, or disaster.

Catapult

cat·a·stroph·ic [kat′ə·strof′ik] *adj*. Caused by, resulting in, or like a catastrophe.

cat·bird [kat′bûrd′] *n*. A small North American songbird whose cry is like the meow of a cat.

cat·boat [kat′bōt′] *n*. A sailboat that has a single mast set forward in the bow and only a single sail, with no jib.

cat·call [kat′kôl′] **1** *n*. A shrill call or whistle made in public to show dislike or impatience. **2** *v*. To make catcalls.

catch [kach] *v*. **caught, catch·ing,** *n*. **1** *v*. To seize or capture after pursuing: to *catch* a runaway dog. **2** *v*. To take in a trap or by means of a hook; ensnare: to *catch* rats; to *catch* fish. **3** *n*. Something that is caught: a fine *catch* of trout. **4** *v*. To entangle or become entangled: The thorns *caught* my sleeve. **5** *n*. Something that fastens or holds closed: a window *catch*. **6** *v*. To stop the motion of, as by grasping with the hands or arms: to *catch* a ball. **7** *n*. The act of catching, especially in baseball: a difficult *catch*. **8** *v*. In baseball, to act as a catcher. **9** *v*. To overtake: I *caught* him before he had gone very far. **10** *v*. To reach in time to board: to *catch* a bus at the corner. **11** *v*. To strike suddenly: The cat *caught* her kitten a blow on the ear. **12** *v*. To get (an infectious disease): to *catch* cold. **13** *v*. To become aware of through hearing, seeing, or understanding: I *caught* what my two friends were whispering. **14** *v*. To please or captivate: The puppy *caught* her fancy. **15** *v*. To start to burn: The house *caught* fire. **16** *v*. To surprise in the act; detect: The storekeeper *caught* the boys stealing. **17** *v*. To check suddenly: He *caught* himself just before blurting out the secret. **18** *n*. A break, as in the voice or breath from fear or strong feeling. **19** *n*. In music, a round. **20** *n*. *informal* A hidden trick or difficulty: There is a *catch* in this arithmetic problem. — **catch on** *informal* **1** To become popular or fashionable: Folk music has *caught on*.

2 To understand: to *catch on* to a new idea. — **catch up 1** To overtake: I *caught up* with him in the hall. **2** To pick up suddenly: He *caught up* his hat and left. ◆ See CHASE.

catch·er [kach′ər] *n*. **1** A person or thing that catches. **2** In baseball, the player behind home plate who catches balls that pass the batter.

catch·ing [kach′ing] *adj*. **1** Passing from person to person; contagious, as measles. **2** Attractive; charming: a *catching* dress.

catch·up [kach′əp *or* kech′əp] *n*. Another spelling of KETCHUP.

catch·y [kach′ē] *adj*. **catch·i·er, catch·i·est** **1** Easily remembered because pleasing: a *catchy* song. **2** Catching the fancy; attractive. **3** Likely to confuse; tricky: *catchy* questions. **4** Fitful; gusty: *catchy* winds.

cat·e·chism [kat′ə·kiz′əm] *n*. **1** A short book in the form of questions and answers for teaching the principles of a religion. **2** Any list of questions like this used for teaching.

cat·e·chize [kat′ə·kīz] *v*. **cat·e·chized, cat·e·chiz·ing** **1** To teach, as by questions and answers. **2** To question at length. ¶3

cat·e·gor·i·cal [kat′ə·gôr′i·kəl] *adj*. Positive and definite; without any question or condition: a *categorical* refusal — **cat′e·gor′i·cal·ly** *adv*.

cat·e·go·ry [kat′ə·gôr′ē] *n., pl.* **cat·e·go·ries** A division, class, or group in any system of classification: Drama is a *category* of literature.

ca·ter [kā′tər] *v*. **1** To furnish prepared food, drink, and services: to *cater* for a wedding. **2** To please by furnishing what is needed or wanted: That restaurant *caters* to families.

cat·er-cor·nered [kat′ər·kôr′nərd] **1** *adj*. Diagonal: a *cater-cornered* line. **2** *adv*. Diagonally: to walk *cater-cornered* across a street.

ca·ter·er [kā′tər·ər] *n*. A person who caters, especially one whose business is providing food and services for parties, banquets, etc.

cat·er·pil·lar [kat′ər·pil′ər] *n*. The wormlike form of certain insects, such as the butterfly or moth, after they hatch from the egg; larva.

Cat·er·pil·lar Tractor [kat′ər·pil′ər] *n*. A tractor that moves by means of two endless metal tracks running along each side, enabling it to be used on soft or rough ground: a trademark.

cat·er·waul [kat′ər·wôl] **1** *v*. To make a shrill yowl or shriek like that of a cat when fighting. **2** *n*. A sound like that of cats fighting.

Caterpillar

cat·fish [kat′fish′] *n., pl.* **cat·fish** *or* **cat·fish·es** Any of several fish having feelers about the mouth that look like a cat's whiskers.

cat·gut [kat′gut′] *n*. A tough cord made from

add, āce, câre, pälm;   end, ēqual;   it, īce;   odd, ōpen, ôrder;   tŏŏk, pōōl;   up, bûrn;
ə = a in *above*, e in *sicken*, i in *possible*, o in *melon*, u in *circus*;   yōō = u in *fuse*;   oil;   pout;
     check; **ri**ng; **th**in; **th**is; **zh** in *vision*.   For ¶ reference, see page 64 · HOW TO

the intestines of certain animals, as sheep, and used as strings for musical instruments, thread for sewing up surgical wounds, etc.

ca·thar·tic [kə·thär′tik] **1** *n.* A strong medicine, such as castor oil, used to empty the bowels. **2** *adj.* Cleansing; purifying.

ca·the·dral [kə·thē′drəl] *n.* **1** The main church of a diocese of some Christian churches, containing the bishop's throne. **2** Any large church.

cath·ode [kath′ōd] *n.* **1** The negative pole of a battery. **2** The electrode of an electron tube that gives off electrons.

cath·ode-ray tube [kath′- ōd·rā′] A special vacuum tube in which a beam of electrons strikes a fluorescent screen and makes it glow, as the picture tube of a television set.

Cath·o·lic [kath′ə·lik] **1** *adj.* Of or indicating the ancient Christian church or a church directly descended from it, especially the Roman Catholic Church. **2** *n.* A member of such a church, especially a Roman Catholic. **3** *adj.* (*written* **catholic**) Broad; extensive: a *catholic* taste in books.

A Gothic cathedral

Ca·thol·i·cism [kə·thol′ə·siz′əm] *n.* The beliefs and practices of the Roman Catholic Church.

cath·o·lic·i·ty [kath′ə·lis′ə·tē] *n.* The quality or condition of including many things; breadth.

cat·kin [kat′kin] *n.* A cluster of small flowers arranged like scales along a drooping spike, as in the willow.

cat·nip [kat′nip] *n.* A fragrant herb of the mint family. Cats love to sniff and nibble at it.

cat-o′-nine-tails [kat′ə·nīn′tālz′] *n.*, *pl.* **cat-o′-nine-tails** A whip with nine knotted lines and a handle, once used as a punishment.

cat's cradle A game played with a loop of string stretched in various arrangements over the fingers of both hands.

Cats·kill Mountains [kats′kil] A range of low mountains in SE New York. Also **the Cats·kills.**

cat's-paw or **cats·paw** [kats′pô′] *n.* A person tricked by another into doing something dangerous or wrong.

cat·sup [kat′səp *or* kech′əp] *n.* Another spelling of KETCHUP.

cat·tail [kat′tāl′] *n.* A marsh plant with long leaves and long, round, velvety spikes.

cat·tle [kat′(ə)l] *n. pl.* Domesticated cows, bulls, and steers; oxen.

cat·tle·man [kat′(ə)l·mən] *n.*, *pl.* **cat·tle·men** [kat′(ə)l·mən] A man who raises cattle.

cat·ty [kat′ē] *adj.* **cat·ti·er, cat·ti·est** **1** Having to do with or like a cat. **2** Spiteful.

cat·ty-cor·ner [kat′ē·kôr′nər] *adj.*, *adv.* Cater-cornered.

cat·walk [kat′wôk′] *n.* Any narrow walk, as along the side of a bridge.

Cau·ca·sian [kô·kā′zhən] **1** *n.* A member of the division of mankind that is the so-called white race. **2** *adj.* Of or having to do with this group. **3** *adj.* Of the Caucasus region.

Cau·ca·sus [kô′kə·səs] *n.* A mountain range between the Black Sea and the Caspian Sea, in the southernmost part of the Soviet Union.

cau·cus [kô′kəs] **1** *n.* A meeting of the leading members of a political party to choose candidates or to make plans, as for a campaign. **2** *v.* To meet in or hold a caucus.

cau·dal [kôd′(ə)l] *adj.* **1** Of or near the tail or hind part of the body. **2** Like a tail.

caught [kôt] Past tense of CATCH.

caul·dron [kôl′drən] *n.* Another spelling of CALDRON.

cau·li·flow·er [kô′lə·flou′ər] *n.* A variety of cabbage with a solid white head made up of clusters of flowers pressed tightly together.

caulk [kôk] *v.* To make tight, as the seams of a boat, by plugging with tar, putty, etc.

cause [kôz] *n.*, *v.* **caused, caus·ing 1** *n.* A person or thing that makes something happen: The driver was the *cause* of the accident. **2** *v.* To make happen; bring about: Fear *caused* his voice to tremble. **3** *n.* A reason for feeling or acting in a certain way: a *cause* for celebrating. **4** *n.* A movement or idea supported by an individual or group: the *cause* of freedom.

cause·way [kôz′wā′] *n.* **1** A raised road across marshy ground or shallow water. **2** A highway.

caus·tic [kôs′tik] **1** *adj.* Capable of eating or burning away living tissue, as lye or certain acids. **2** *n.* A caustic substance. **3** *adj.* Sarcastic; biting: *caustic* remarks.

cau·ter·ize [kô′tə·rīz] *v.* **cau·ter·ized, cau·ter·iz·ing** To burn (living tissue) with a hot iron or a caustic substance. ¶3

cau·tion [kô′shən] **1** *n.* Care to avoid injury or other mishaps; watchfulness: to use *caution* when walking on icy pavements. **2** *n.* A warning. **3** *v.* To advise to be careful; warn.

cau·tious [kô′shəs] *adj.* Using care; careful not to take chances or make mistakes; watchful: a *cautious* businessman. **— cau′tious·ly** *adv.*

cav·al·cade [kav′əl·kād′] *n.* **1** A procession of people on horseback or in carriages. **2** Any procession or series, as of shows.

cav·a·lier [kav′ə·lir′] **1** *n.* A horseman or knight. **2** *n.* A courtly or dashing gentleman. **3** *n.* A lady's escort. **4** *adj.* Free and easy; offhand: a *cavalier* attitude towards work. **5** *adj.* Haughty; scornful. **— cav′a·lier′ly** *adv.*

cav·al·ry [kav′əl·rē] *n.*, *pl.* **cav·al·ries 1** In the past, soldiers who were trained to fight on horseback. **2** In recent times, soldiers who fight and maneuver in armored motor vehicles.

cav·al·ry·man [kav′əl·rē·mən] *n.*, *pl.* **cav·al·ry·men** [kav′əl·rē·mən] A soldier who fought on horseback.

cave [kāv] *n.*, *v.* **caved, cav·ing 1** *n.* A natural hollow beneath the surface of the earth, having an opening to the outside. **2** *v.* To hollow out. **— cave in** To fall in or collapse, as when undermined: *The mine caved in on the men.*

cave-in [kāv′in′] *n.* A collapse or falling in, as of a tunnel or mine.

cave man 1 A human being who made his home in a cave in prehistoric times. 2 A man who is rough and brutal.

cav·ern [kav′ərn] *n.* A large cave.

cav·ern·ous [kav′ər·nəs] *adj.* 1 Like a cavern; deeply hollowed out: *a cavernous cellar.* 2 Full of caverns or caves.

cav·i·ar or **cav·i·are** [kav′ē·är] *n.* A salty appetizer made of the eggs, or roe, of the sturgeon or certain other fishes.

cav·il [ka′vəl] *v.* **cav·iled** or **cav·illed, cav·il·ing** or **cav·il·ling,** *n.* 1 *v.* To find fault unnecessarily; pick flaws: *to cavil at school rules instead of obeying them.* 2 *n.* A strong objection about something unimportant.

cav·i·ty [kav′ə·tē] *n., pl.* **cav·i·ties** 1 A hollow or sunken place; hole. 2 A natural hollow in the body: *the abdominal cavity.* 3 A hollow place in a tooth caused by decay.

ca·vort [kə·vôrt′] *v.* To prance about; caper.

caw [kô] 1 *v.* To make the high, harsh cry of a crow or raven. 2 *n.* This cry.

cay·enne [kī·en′] *n.* A hot, biting red pepper made by grinding up certain pepper plants.

cay·use [kī·yōōs′] *n.* An Indian pony.

cc Abbreviation of CUBIC CENTIMETER(S).

cease [sēs] *v.* **ceased, ceas·ing** To bring or come to an end: *Cease that noise.*

cease-fire [sēs′fīr′] *n.* 1 A military order to stop shooting at the enemy. 2 An armistice.

cease·less [sēs′lis] *adj.* Going on without pause; continual. — **cease′less·ly** *adv.*

ce·dar [sē′dər] *n.* 1 A large, broad evergreen tree of the pine family, with a fragrant, reddish wood. 2 This wood. 3 *adj. use: a cedar chest.*

cede [sēd] *v.* **ced·ed, ced·ing** To yield or give up; transfer the ownership of, as territory.

ce·dil·la [si·dil′ə] *n.* A hooklike mark placed under the letter *c* (ç) in some French words to show that the *c* is to be pronounced as an *s.*

ceil·ing [sē′ling] *n.* 1 The lining of the top side of a room. 2 The upper limit set, as on wages or prices. 3 The height of the lowest layers of clouds. 4 The greatest height at which a given type of airplane can fly.

cel·e·brant [sel′ə·brənt] *n.* 1 A person who celebrates something. 2 The priest who performs the main part of the Mass.

cel·e·brate [sel′ə·brāt] *v.* **cel·e·brat·ed, cel·e·brat·ing** 1 To observe or honor in a special manner: *to celebrate a holiday.* 2 To make known or famous; praise: *to celebrate a hero.* 3 To perform the ceremony of in a solemn manner: *A priest celebrates Mass.* — **cel′e·bra′tion** *n.*

cel·e·brat·ed [sel′ə·brā′tid] *adj.* Well-known; spoken of by many people: *a celebrated artist.*

ce·leb·ri·ty [sə·leb′rə·tē] *n., pl.* **ce·leb·ri·ties** 1 A famous or celebrated person. 2 The condition of being celebrated; fame.

ce·ler·i·ty [sə·ler′ə·tē] *n.* Quickness of motion or action; speed: *to work with celerity.*

cel·er·y [sel′ər·ē] *n.* A plant whose long, crisp stalks are eaten as a vegetable or in salads.

ce·les·ta [sə·les′tə] *n.* A small keyboard instrument with hammers that strike steel plates.

ce·les·tial [sə·les′chəl] *adj.* 1 Of or having to do with the sky or heavens. 2 Very beautiful; exquisite: *celestial music.*

cel·i·ba·cy [sel′ə·bə·sē] *n.* The state of being and remaining unmarried, especially by a religious vow: *the celibacy of monks.*

cel·i·bate [sel′ə·bit] 1 *n.* A person who remains unmarried, especially by a religious vow. 2 *adj.* Unmarried.

cell [sel] *n.* 1 The tiny basic structural unit of all living matter. Cells are usually enclosed by a membrane or wall and consist mostly of protoplasm with a nucleus in the middle. 2 A device that changes chemical energy into electricity. Several cells connected together make up a battery. 3 A small room, as for a prisoner or monk. 4 Any small space or cavity.

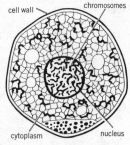

cell wall   chromosomes

cytoplasm   nucleus

Cell

cel·lar [sel′ər] *n.* A room or several rooms completely or partly underground, usually beneath a building.

cel·list or **'cel·list** [chel′ist] *n.* A person who plays the cello.

cel·lo or **'cel·lo** [chel′ō] *n., pl.* **cel·los** or **'cel·los** A large instrument like a violin but bigger, with a deep tone. It is held between the performer's knees when played.

cel·lo·phane [sel′ə·fān] *n.* A thin, transparent, waterproof substance made from cellulose, used as a wrapping, covering, etc.

cel·lu·lar [sel′yə·lər] *adj.* Of, having to do with, or made up of cells: *cellular tissue.*

Cel·lu·loid [sel′yə·loid] *n.* 1 A hard, very flammable plastic material made from cellulose combined with nitrogen and camphor: a trademark. Also written **celluloid.** 2 *adj. use: celluloid dolls.*

Cello

cel·lu·lose [sel′yə·lōs] *n.* A carbohydrate

C

forming the main part of cell walls of plants, widely used in making explosives, paper, etc.

Cel·si·us scale [sel′sē·əs] The centigrade temperature scale.

Celt [selt *or* kelt] *n.* A person belonging to a people who speak a Celtic language.

Celt·ic [sel′tik *or* kel′tik] **1** *n.* A family of European languages that include those now spoken by the Irish, the Welsh, the Scottish Highlanders, and the Bretons. **2** *adj.* Of or having to do with the Celts or their languages.

Celtic cross An upright cross having a circle behind the crossbeam.

ce·ment [si·ment′] **1** *n.* A substance made from limestone and clay burned together. **2** *n.* This substance mixed with water and sometimes sand, used in making mortar or concrete. **3** *n.* Any gluelike substance that will bind objects together. **4** *v.* To join or bind with or as if with cement. **5** *v.* To cover or coat with cement.

cem·e·ter·y [sem′ə·ter′ē] *n., pl.* **cem·e·ter·ies** A place for burying the dead; graveyard.

Ce·no·zo·ic [sē′nə·zō′ik *or* sen′ə·zō′ik] **1** *adj.* Of or having to do with the latest of the geological eras, beginning about 60 million years ago and including the present. **2** *n.* The Cenozoic era.

cen·ser [sen′sər] *n.* A container for burning incense, especially in religious ceremonies.

cen·sor [sen′sər] **1** *n.* A person who has the right to examine books, letters, news, plays, etc., and to cut out what he feels ought not to be read, heard, or seen. **2** *v.* To examine so as to cut out parts; act as a censor. **3** *n.* Any person who is very critical of what others do or say. **4** *n.* In ancient Rome, an official who took the census and supervised the manners and morals of the people. ◆ Both *censor* [sen′sər] and *censure* [sen′shər] come from the same Latin word, *censere*, meaning *to judge*, and both words as used today involve acts of judgment. To *censor* is to prevent something from being seen or heard. To *censure* is to blame someone formally for wrongdoing: Congress *censured* the senator for his improper conduct.

cen·so·ri·al [sen·sôr′ē·əl] *adj.* Of or having to do with censors.

cen·so·ri·ous [sen·sôr′ē·əs] *adj.* **1** Very critical: a *censorious* person. **2** Full of criticism: a *censorious* article. — **cen·so′ri·ous·ly** *adv.* — **cen·so′ri·ous·ness** *n.*

cen·sor·ship [sen′sər·ship] *n.* **1** The act, method, or system of censoring: There is a lot of strict *censorship* during a war. **2** The position or occupation of a censor.

cen·sure [sen′shər] *n., v.* **cen·sured, cen·sur·ing 1** *n.* Blame or criticism; a reprimand. **2** *v.* To blame or criticize. ◆ See CENSOR.

cen·sus [sen′səs] *n.* An official count of all the people in a city, district, or in the entire country, with additional information taken as to their age, sex, occupation, etc.

cent [sent] *n.* The hundredth part of a dollar; also, a coin of this value. Symbol: ¢.

cen·taur [sen′tôr] *n.* In Greek myths, one of a race of monsters having the head, arms, and upper body of a man united to the body and legs of a horse.

cen·ta·vo [sen·tä′vō] *n., pl.* **cen·ta·vos** A small coin of the Philippines and various Spanish-American countries.

cen·te·nar·y [sen′tə·ner′ē *or* sen·ten′ə·rē] *n., pl.* **cen·te·nar·ies 1** A period of 100 years. **2** A centennial.

Centaur

cen·ten·ni·al [sen·ten′ē·əl] **1** *adj.* Lasting or having an age of 100 years. **2** *adj.* Happening every 100 years. **3** *adj.* Having to do with a 100th anniversary. **4** *n.* A 100th anniversary or its celebration.

cen·ter [sen′tər] **1** *n.* In geometry, the point of a circle or sphere that is equally distant from every point on the circumference or surface. **2** *n.* The middle part or point of something: the *center* of a lake. **3** *v.* To place in or at the center. **4** *n.* A place or point where there is something special to see or do: a tourist *center*. **5** *v.* To direct toward one place; concentrate: *Center* your energy on your schoolbooks. **6** *n.* In some sports, a player stationed in the middle. ¶2

cen·ter·board [sen′tər·bôrd′] *n.* In certain sailboats, a keel that can be lowered through a watertight slot to prevent drifting to leeward.

center of gravity The point in an object around which its weight is equally distributed.

cen·ti·grade [sen′tə·grād] *adj.* Divided into 100 degrees, as the scale of a thermometer that shows the freezing point of water as 0 degrees and the boiling point as 100 degrees.

cen·ti·me·ter [sen′tə·mē′tər] *n.* A measure of length, equal to 1/100 of a meter. One inch is about 2.54 centimeters.

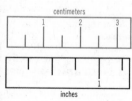

cen·ti·pede [sen′tə·pēd] *n.* Any of various wormlike animals having many pairs of legs and two poison fangs on the head.

cen·tral [sen′trəl] *adj.* **1** At, in, or near the center: the *central* part of the city. **2** Most important; principal; chief: the *central* character in a play. **3** Of or being the center. **4** Having but one unit or source located centrally: a *central* heating system. — **cen′tral·ly** *adv.*

Central African Republic A country in central Africa.

Central America The southernmost part of North America, including Guatemala on the north, Panama on the south, and the countries between.

cen·tral·ize [sen′trəl·īz] *v.* **cen·tral·ized,
cen·tral·iz·ing** **1** To bring or come to a center;
make central. **2** To bring under one central
authority: to *centralize* a government. — **cen′·
tral·i·za′tion** *n.* ¶3

central nervous system That part of the
nervous system consisting of the brain and
spinal cord.

cen·trif·u·gal [sen·trif′(y)ə·gəl] *adj.* **1** Moving
away from a center. **2** Using centrifugal force.

centrifugal force The force tending to pull
an object outward from a center about which it
is rotating.

cen·tri·fuge [sen′trə·fyo̅o̅j] *n.* A machine that
spins its contents, using centrifugal force to
remove moisture, separate liquids of different
densities, or for other purposes.

cen·trip·e·tal [sen·trip′ə·təl] *adj.* **1** Going
toward a center. **2** Using centripetal force.

centripetal force The force that tends to pull
an object inward toward the center about which
it is rotating.

cen·tu·ri·on [sen·t(y)o̅o̅r′ē·ən] *n.* In ancient
Rome, a captain of about 100 foot soldiers.

cen·tu·ry [sen′chə·rē] *n., pl.* **cen·tu·ries** **1** A
period of 100 years, counting from some particular time, such as the birth of Christ. From A.D. 1
to 100 was the first century; from 1901 to 2000 is
the twentieth. **2** Any period of 100 years. **3** In
ancient Rome, a group of 100 foot soldiers.

century plant A desert plant that is wrongly
believed to bloom once every 100 years.

ce·ram·ic [sə·ram′ik] *adj.* Made of baked clay.

ce·ram·ics [sə·ram′iks] *n.* The art or process of
making pottery, porcelain, etc., of baked clay.
◆ See -ICS.

Cer·ber·us [sûr′bər·əs] *n.* In Greek and
Roman myths, the three-headed dog that
guarded the door to Hades.

ce·re·al [sir′ē·əl] **1** *n.* Any edible grain that
comes from certain grasses, as rice, wheat, rye,
oats, etc. **2** *n.* The plants from which these
grains come. **3** *adj.* Of or having to do with such
edible grains or the plants that produce them.
4 *n.* A breakfast food made from grain.

cer·e·bel·lum [ser′ə·bel′əm] *n., pl.* **cer·e·
bel·lums** or **cer·e·bel·la**
[ser′ə·bel′ə] The part of the
brain that is at the back of
the head and that controls
coordination of the muscles.

cer·e·bral [ser′ə·brəl *or* sə·
rē′brəl] *adj.* **1** Of or having
to do with the brain or the
cerebrum. **2** Having or requiring great intelligence.

cerebral palsy An in-
ability to control one's movement and speech, caused by
damage to the brain before or during birth.

cerebrum

medulla

cerebellum   spinal cord

cer·e·brum [ser′ə·brəm *or* sə·rē′brəm] *n., pl.*
cer·e·brums or **cer·e·bra** [ser′ə·brə *or* sə·
rē′brə] The largest and most highly developed
part of the brain. It controls voluntary movement and all conscious mental activities.

cer·e·mo·ni·al [ser′ə·mō′nē·əl] **1** *adj.* Of, like,
or used in a ceremony: a *ceremonial* robe. **2** *adj.*
Very elaborate or formal: a *ceremonial* dinner.
3 *n.* A set of rules or actions for performing a
particular ceremony.

cer·e·mo·ni·ous [ser′ə·mō′nē·əs] *adj.* **1** Full of
or done with ceremony. **2** Extremely polite or
formal. — **cer′e·mo′ni·ous·ly** *adv.*

cer·e·mo·ny [ser′ə·mō′nē] *n., pl.* **cer·e·mo·
nies** **1** Any formal act or series of actions
performed in a definite, set manner: a graduation *ceremony*. **2** A formal or extremely polite
manner of acting: to serve tea with *ceremony*.
— **stand on ceremony** To act or insist that
others act in a very polite, formal manner.

Ce·res [sir′ēz] *n.* In Roman myths, the goddess
of grain and harvests. Her Greek name was
Demeter.

ce·rise [sə·rēs′] *n., adj.* Very bright red.

cer·tain [sûr′tən] *adj.* **1** Completely sure,
confident, or convinced: He is *certain* of success.
2 Sure as to results: To drive that way means
certain disaster. **3** Not named or stated, but
known: I saw a *certain* person buying you a gift.
4 Some: There is a *certain* improvement in his
work. — **for certain** Without doubt; surely.

cer·tain·ly [sûr′tən·lē] *adv.* Without doubt;
surely.

cer·tain·ty [sûr′tən·tē] *n., pl.* **cer·tain·ties**
1 The condition or fact of being certain: There
is no *certainty* of our winning the game. **2** Something that is positively true; a known fact.

cer·tif·i·cate [sər·tif′ə·kit] *n.* A printed or
written document stating officially that something is a fact: a marriage *certificate*.

cer·ti·fy [sûr′tə·fī] *v.* **cer·ti·fied, cer·ti·fy·
ing** **1** To testify, usually in writing, as to the
truth or correctness of; vouch for; verify: Your
statement will *certify* his correct age. **2** To
guarantee the quality or worth of: to *certify* a
check. **3** To furnish with a certificate: She is
certified to teach. — **cer′ti·fi·ca′tion** *n.*

cer·ti·tude [sûr′tə·t(y)o̅o̅d] *n.* Freedom from
any doubt; complete confidence and certainty.

ce·ru·le·an [sə·ro̅o̅′lē·ən] *n., adj.* Sky blue.

Cer·van·tes [sər·van′tēz], **Miguel de,** 1547–
1616, Spanish writer, author of *Don Quixote*.

ce·si·um [sē′zē·əm] *n.* A soft, grayish metallic
element. Because it is very sensitive to light,
it is used in photoelectric cells.

ces·sa·tion [se·sā′shən] *n.* A ceasing; stopping;
pause: a *cessation* of noise.

cess·pool [ses′po̅o̅l′] *n.* A deep, covered pit for
the drainage from sinks, toilets, etc.

ce·ta·cean [si·tā′shən] **1** *n.* Any of a group of

---

add, āce, câre, pälm;   end, ēqual;   it, īce;   odd, ōpen, ôrder;   to̅o̅k, po̅o̅l;   up, bûrn;
ə = a in *above*, e in *sicken*, i in *possible*, o in *melon*, u in *circus*;   yo̅o̅ = u in *fuse*;   oil;   pout;
check;   ring;   thin;   this;   zh in *vision*.   For ¶ reference, see page 64 · HOW TO

fish-shaped, aquatic mammals, as whales, dolphins, etc. **2** *adj.* Of or having to do with such mammals.

Cey·lon [si·lon'] *n.* An island south of India, an independent member of the British Commonwealth of Nations.

Cé·zanne [sā·zan'], **Paul,** 1839–1906, French painter.

ch. Abbreviation of CHAPTER.

cha-cha [chä'chä'] *n.* A rhythmic dance that originated in Latin America.

Chad [chad] *n.* A country in central Africa.

chafe [chāf] *v.* **chafed, chaf·ing 1** To make or become rough or sore by rubbing. **2** To make warm by rubbing: to *chafe* one's hands. **3** To make or become irritated or annoyed.

chaff[1] [chaf] **1** *v.* To tease good-naturedly. **2** *n.* Good-natured teasing or banter.

chaff[2] [chaf] *n.* **1** The outside husks or coverings of grain that are removed by threshing. **2** Any worthless or unimportant thing.

chaf·finch [chaf'inch] *n.* A songbird of Europe, popular as a pet and kept in a cage.

chafing dish A pan with a heating unit under it, to cook food or keep it warm at the table.

cha·grin [shə·grin'] *n., v.* **cha·grined** [shə·grind'], **cha·grin·ing** [shə·grin'ing] **1** *n.* A feeling of embarrassment or distress caused by a disappointment, failure, etc. **2** *v.* To annoy, embarrass, or distress.

Chafing dish

chain [chān] **1** *n.* A series of connected rings or links, usually of metal, used to bind, drag, or hold something, or often as an ornament. **2** *v.* To fasten or connect with a chain. **3** *n.* (*pl.*) Anything that binds or restrains. **4** *v.* To bind or restrain: His work *chains* him to his desk. **5** *n.* A series of things that are connected: a *chain* of lakes; a *chain* of events. **6** *n.* A measuring line like a chain: An engineer's *chain* is 100 feet long.

chain mail Very flexible armor that is made of small metal rings linked together.

chain reaction Any series of reactions or events, each of which develops from a preceding one. Atomic energy is produced by a chain reaction in which particles from the nuclei of certain atoms are set free, some of them striking the nuclei of other atoms, until the whole mass is used up.

chain store One of a number of retail stores all owned and run by the same company.

chair [châr] *n.* **1** A seat for one person, usually having four legs and a back. **2** A position of importance or authority, as the position of a bishop or professor. **3** A chairman.

chair·man [châr'mən] *n., pl.* **chair·men** [châr'mən] **1** A person who has charge of a meeting. **2** A person who is the head of a committee or other organization. **— chair'·man·ship** *n.*

chaise [shāz] *n.* A two-wheeled carriage, having a folding top and seating two persons.

chaise longue [shāz' lông'] A chair that has a long, couchlike seat on which one can sit and stretch out one's legs.

Chaise longue

Chal·de·a [kal·dē'ə] *n.* In Biblical times, a region in the Tigris and Euphrates valley in SW Asia. **— Chal·de'an** *adj., n.*

cha·let [sha·lā' *or* shal'ā] *n.* **1** A Swiss cottage with very wide eaves. **2** Any house built like this.

chal·ice [chal'is] *n.* **1** A goblet. **2** The cup used in the Communion service.

chalk [chôk] **1** *n.* A soft, grayish or yellowish limestone, largely made up of very small sea shells. **2** *n.* A stick of this or a similar material used for marking or drawing, as on a blackboard. **3** *v.* To write, draw, or mark with chalk. **— chalk up 1** To give as a score: *Chalk up* four points. **2** To give as a reason; credit: I *chalk up* the student's failure to laziness.

chalk·y [chôk'ē] *adj.* **chalk·i·er, chalk·i·est 1** Like chalk in color or texture: a *chalky* powder. **2** Made or full of chalk: *chalky* soil.

chal·lenge [chal'ənj] *v.* **chal·lenged, chal·leng·ing,** *n.* **1** *v.* To ask for a contest, duel, or fight with: They *challenged* us to a game. **2** *n.* An invitation or dare to do something, usually difficult or dangerous. **3** *v.* To question or dispute the truth or correctness of: I *challenge* your answer. **4** *n.* A questioning of the truth or correctness of something. **5** *v.* To dare or defy: I *challenge* you to try to find the treasure. **6** *v.* To stop and ask for identification, etc., before allowing to go ahead: The guards *challenged* us at every border. **7** *n.* A stopping in order to question, examine, etc. **— chal'leng·er** *n.*

chal·lis or **chal·lie** [shal'ē] *n.* A lightweight fabric, usually of printed wool, rayon, etc.

cham·ber [chām'bər] *n.* **1** A room in a house, especially a bedroom. **2** (*pl.*) The office of a judge or of a lawyer: a judge's *chambers.* **3** A hall where a group of lawmakers meet. **4** One house of a legislature or congress. **5** A group of men who meet together for some common purpose: a *chamber* of commerce. **6** A hollow or enclosed space, as in the body of an animal or plant. **7** An enclosed space in a gun or revolver for the shell or the cartridge. ◆ See CAMERA.

cham·ber·lain [chām'bər·lin] *n.* **1** A man who has charge of the household of a ruler or lord. **2** A very high officer in a royal court.

cham·ber·maid [chām'bər·mād'] *n.* A maid who makes beds and takes care of bedrooms.

chamber music Music composed for a small group of instruments, as for a string quartet.

chamber of commerce A group of merchants and businessmen who meet together regularly to try to promote business in their city or locality.

cham·bray [sham′brā] *n.* A lightweight fabric having a glistening surface created by the interweaving of white and colored threads.

cha·me·le·on [kə·mē′lē·ən] *n.* **1** A lizard having the ability to change color. **2** A person who often changes his mind or his habits.

cham·ois [sham′ē] *n., pl.* **cham·ois 1** An antelope found in the mountains of Europe and sw Asia. **2** A very soft leather originally made from the skin of the chamois but now from sheep, goats, deer, etc.

champ [champ] *v.* **1** To chew noisily; munch. **2** To make restless biting motions: to *champ* at the bit.

cham·pagne [sham·pān′] *n.* A fine white wine that sparkles and bubbles.

Chamois, about 30 in. high

cham·pi·on [cham′pē·ən] **1** *n.* A person who comes out ahead of all rivals, as in a sport. **2** *n.* Anything awarded first place. **3** *adj.* Having won first place; better than all others: a *champion* dog. **4** *n.* A person who fights for another person or for a cause. **5** *v.* To fight for; defend: to *champion* the cause of peace.

cham·pi·on·ship [cham′pē·ən·ship′] *n.* **1** The condition or honor of being champion: The *championship* meant much to him. **2** The act of defending or supporting.

Cham·plain [sham·plān′], **Lake** A lake between New York and Vermont, extending into Canada.

chance [chans] *n., v.* **chanced, chanc·ing, adj.** **1** *n.* The unknown cause of the way things often turn out; fate; luck. **2** *v.* To happen accidentally or by chance: I *chanced* to look down and there was my ring. **3** *adj.* Not planned or expected: a *chance* trip. **4** *n.* A possibility: There is a *chance* they won't come. **5** *n.* An opportunity: Now is your *chance* to study. **6** *n.* A risk or gamble: He'll take a *chance* on anything. **7** *v.* To take the chance of; risk: Let's *chance* it. — **chance on** or **chance upon** To find or meet unexpectedly or by chance: We *chanced* on a quiet, deserted park.

chan·cel [chan′səl] *n.* The area around the altar of a church, used by the clergy and choir.

chan·cel·lor [chan′s(ə)lər] *n.* **1** In some European countries, a chief minister of state. **2** The head of certain universities. **3** A judge of certain courts in the U.S.

chan·de·lier [shan′də·lir′] *n.* A lighting fixture that hangs from the ceiling and has supports or branches for a number of lights: a crystal *chandelier*.

Chandelier

chan·dler [chan′dlər] *n.* A dealer in groceries or supplies, especially for ships.

change [chānj] *v.* **changed, chang·ing, n.** **1** *v.* To make or become different; alter; vary: His facial expression *changed* when he saw us. **2** *n.* The act or result of changing: a *change* in the temperature. **3** *n.* Something new or different: Everyone likes a *change* now and then. **4** *v.* To exchange or substitute one thing for another: to *change* places. **5** *v.* To put other coverings, etc., on: to *change* a bed. **6** *v.* To put on other clothes: It will take me only a minute to *change*. **7** *n.* A clean or different set of clothes, coverings, etc. **8** *v.* To transfer from one train, bus, etc., to another. **9** *v.* To give or receive the equivalent of, usually in a different form: Can you *change* a dollar for me? **10** *n.* Money of smaller denominations given in exchange for the same amount of money in a higher denomination. **11** *n.* The amount returned when a person pays more than he owes. **12** *n.* Small coins. — **chang′er** *n.*

change·a·ble [chān′jə·bəl] *adj.* **1** Likely to change or vary: a *changeable* person. **2** Having different colors in different lights; iridescent: the *changeable* feathers of certain birds. — **change′a·ble·ness** *n.* — **change′a·bly** *adv.*

change·less [chānj′lis] *adj.* Free from change; constant; enduring.

change·ling [chānj′ling] *n.* A child secretly left in place of another who has been carried off.

chan·nel [chan′əl] *n., v.* **chan·neled** or **chan·nelled, chan·nel·ing** or **chan·nel·ling 1** *n.* The bed of a river or stream. **2** *n.* A body of water connecting two larger bodies of water: the English *Channel*. **3** *n.* The deep part of a river, harbor, etc. **4** *n.* A tubelike passage through which liquids can flow. **5** *v.* To cut or wear a channel in. **6** *n.* The way or route through which anything moves or passes: *channels* of information. **7** *n.* A path for communicating something by electronic means, as a band of frequencies assigned to a radio or television station by the government. **8** *v.* To send through or as if through a channel.

Channel Islands A group of British islands in the English Channel off the coast of Normandy.

chant [chant] **1** *n.* A very simple melody in which many words or syllables are sung on each note. Chants are used in the services of some churches. **2** *v.* To sing to a chant: to *chant* a psalm. **3** *v.* To recite or say in the manner of a chant: to *chant* a poem. **4** *n.* Any monotonous singing or shouting of words, as from spectators at a sports event. — **chant′er** *n.*

chant·ey or **chant·y** [shan′tē *or* chan′tē] *n., pl.* **chant·eys** or **chant·ies** A rhythmical song for sailors working together.

Cha·nu·kah [hä′nŏŏ·kə] *n.* Another spelling of HANUKKAH.

---

add, āce, câre, pälm;   end, ēqual;   it, īce;   odd, ōpen, ôrder;   took, pool;   up, bûrn;

ə = a in *above*, e in *sicken*, i in *possible*, o in *melon*, u in *circus*;   y**oo** = u in *fuse*;   oil;   pout;

ch in *check*; ring; thin; this; zh in *vision*.   For ¶ reference, see page 64 · HOW TO

cha·os [kā′os] *n.* Complete disorder and confusion.

cha·ot·ic [kā·ot′ik] *adj.* Completely disordered and confused. **— cha·ot′i·cal·ly** *adv.*

chap[1] [chap] *v.* **chapped, chap·ping** To make or become rough, reddened, or cracked: The cold has *chapped* my hands.

chap[2] [chap] *n. informal* A man or boy.

chap. Abbreviation of CHAPTER.

chap·el [chap′əl] *n.* **1** A building or place of Christian worship, usually smaller than a church. **2** A separate room or enclosed area in a larger building, used for religious services.

chap·er·on or **chap·er·one** [shap′ə·rōn] *n., v.* **chap·er·oned, chap·er·on·ing 1** *n.* An older person who goes with a group of young people, as to a party, to see that they behave. **2** *v.* To act as a chaperon for.

chap·lain [chap′lin] *n.* A priest, minister, or rabbi who conducts religious services for the army, Congress, a hospital, royal court, etc.

chap·let [chap′lit] *n.* **1** A wreath for the head. **2** A short rosary. **3** A string of beads.

chaps [chaps] *n.pl.* Leather trousers without any backs or seat, worn over regular trousers by cowboys to protect the legs.

chap·ter [chap′tər] *n.* **1** Any of the main divisions of a book, usually numbered. **2** Any period of time or experience: School began a happy *chapter* in her life. **3** A branch of a society or fraternity.

char [chär] *v.* **charred, char·ring 1** To burn or scorch slightly. **2** To change into charcoal by incomplete burning.

Chaps

char·ac·ter [kar′ik·tər] *n.* **1** All of the good as well as the bad qualities, habits, traits, etc., that go to make up the nature or worth of a particular person. **2** Good and noble qualities, habits, traits, etc.: He is a man of *character.* **3** Any special quality, look, or thing that makes one person, group, or thing different from all others: The jungle has a sinister *character.* **4** A person in a play, novel, poem, etc. **5** *informal* An odd, humorous, or unusual person: He's a *character.* **6** Any letter, figure, or mark used in writing or printing.

char·ac·ter·is·tic [kar′ik·tə·ris′tik] **1** *adj.* Indicating a special quality or character of a person or thing; typical: Sadness is the *characteristic* expression of a basset hound. **2** *n.* A very special feature, quality, or trait: A great curiosity was one of his *characteristics.* **— char′ac·ter·is′ti·cal·ly** *adv.*

char·ac·ter·ize [kar′ik·tə·rīz′] *v.* **char·ac·ter·ized, char·ac·ter·iz·ing 1** To describe the character or qualities of: to *characterize* someone as a hard worker. **2** To be a quality or characteristic of: Courage *characterizes* most dachshunds. **— char′ac·ter·i·za′tion** *n.* ¶3

cha·rades [shə·rādz′] *n.pl.* (*often used with singular verb*) A game in which the players try to guess what words or phrases are being acted out in pantomime, often syllable by syllable.

char·coal [chär′kōl′] *n.* A black substance made by heating wood in a container from which most of the air has been removed. Charcoal is used as a filter, drawing crayon, fuel, etc.

charge [chärj] *v.* **charged, charg·ing,** *n.* **1** *v.* To ask for as a price: to *charge* two dollars for tickets; Do you *charge* for checking the tires? **2** *n.* Cost; price: a *charge* for repairs. **3** *v.* To set down and record as a debt to be paid: to *charge* groceries. **4** *n.* A purchase that will be paid for later. **5** *v.* To attack or rush upon violently: to *charge* a fort. **6** *n.* An attack. **7** *v.* To load (a weapon). **8** *n.* Something used to load or fill: The gun's *charge* went off. **9** *v.* To fill with electricity, as a battery. **10** *n.* An amount of stored electricity, as in a battery or capacitor. **11** *v.* To accuse: He was *charged* with murder. **12** *n.* Something of which one is accused: a burglary *charge.* **13** *v.* To command or instruct: I *charge* you to tell the truth; The judge *charged* the jury. **14** *n.* An order, command, or instruction. **15** *v.* To entrust with a duty, task, etc.: He *charged* us to take care of the new student. **16** *n.* A person or thing under one's care: His mother is his *charge.* **17** *n.* Care and custody: to have *charge* of supplies. **— charge off 1** To look upon as a loss. **2** To think of as belonging: We *charged off* his behavior to his youthfulness. **— in charge** Having the care or control of: Who is *in charge* of this classroom?

charge·a·ble [chär′jə·bəl] *adj.* **1** That may be charged: This lunch is *chargeable* to my account. **2** Liable to be charged, as with a crime.

charge account A plan by which a store or business allows a customer to purchase and receive goods, but pay for them later.

charg·er[1] [chär′jər] *n.* **1** An apparatus for charging batteries. **2** A horse trained for battle.

charg·er[2] [chär′jər] *n.* A large, shallow dish or platter: seldom used today.

char·i·ly [châr′ə·lē] *adv.* **1** In a cautious or careful manner. **2** Sparingly; stingily.

char·i·ot [char′ē·ət] *n.* A two-wheeled vehicle pulled by horses, used in ancient times for racing, in war, processions, etc.

char·i·o·teer [char′ē·ə·tir′] *n.* A person who drives a chariot.

char·i·ta·ble [char′ə·tə·bəl] *adj.* **1** Generous in giving help of any kind to the poor and unfortunate. **2** Kind and understanding in judging others; lenient. **3** Of or concerned with charity: a *charitable* institution. **— char′i·ta·bly** *adv.*

Egyptian chariot

char·i·ty [char′ə·tē] *n., pl.* **char·i·ties 1** A

feeling of love or good will towards others. **2** Kindness and tolerance in judging others; forgiveness. **3** The giving of help, usually money, to the poor and unfortunate. **4** An organization, institution, or fund for helping those in need: They give to many *charities*.

char·la·tan [shär′lə·tən] *n.* A person who claims he has knowledge and skill which he does not possess; a fake; quack.

Char·le·magne [shär′lə·mān] *n.* 742?–814, king of the Franks, and from 800 until his death, emperor of the Holy Roman Empire. ◆ *Charlemagne* is old French for *Charles the Great.*

Charles·ton [chärl′stən] *n.* **1** The capital of West Virginia. **2** A port city in SE South Carolina. **3** A fast dance, very popular in the 1920's.

char·ley horse [chär′lē] *informal* A severe cramp or pain in the muscles of the arm or leg.

charm [chärm] **1** *n.* A pleasing or fascinating quality or feature: Her conversation has such *charm.* **2** *v.* To delight or fascinate. **3** *n.* Any word, phrase, action, or object supposed to bring good luck or keep away evil. **4** *v.* To protect, as if by magic. **5** *n.* A small ornament worn on a bracelet, necklace, etc. — **charmed life** A life that seems protected as if by a charm. — **charm′er** *n.*

charm·ing [chär′ming] *adj.* Very attractive, pleasing, or delightful: a *charming* person. — **charm′ing·ly** *adv.*

Char·on [kâr′ən] *n.* In Greek myths, the man who ferried the dead across the river Styx to Hades.

chart [chärt] **1** *n.* A map, especially one used by sailors, showing coastlines, lighthouses, currents, depth of water, etc. **2** *n.* A sheet or graph that shows facts such as the changes in temperature, population, prices, wages, etc. **3** *v.* To show, record, or map out on a chart: We *charted* the progress of the class in spelling.

char·ter [chär′tər] **1** *n.* An official document or paper given by a government and granting special rights or privileges to a person or company. **2** *n.* A document that states the laws and the purposes of an organization or government; a constitution. **3** *n.* A document giving the right to form a branch or chapter of a larger organization. **4** *v.* To give a charter to. **5** *v.* To hire (a bus, airplane, etc.) for some special purpose.

char·treuse [shär·trōōz′] *n., adj.* Pale, yellowish green.

char·wom·an [chär′wŏŏm′ən] *n., pl.* **char·wom·en** [chär′wim′ən] *British* A woman who is hired to clean a house, office building, etc.

char·y [châr′ē] *adj.* **char·i·er, char·i·est** **1** Cautious; careful; wary: *chary* of strangers. **2** Not generous; stingy: *chary* of praise.

Cha·ryb·dis [kə·rib′dis] *n.* In Greek myths, a whirlpool opposite the rock of Scylla. Ships

going between Italy and Sicily had to avoid both.

chase [chās] *v.* **chased, chas·ing,** *n.* **1** *v.* To go after or follow in order to catch, overtake, harm, etc. **2** *n.* The act of chasing or running after. **3** *n.* The sport of hunting, usually with dogs and horses. **4** *n.* That which is hunted; prey. **5** *v.* To put to flight; drive away: to *chase* mosquitoes. — **give chase** To go after; pursue. — **chas′er** *n.* ◆ Both *chase* and *catch* go back to the Latin word *captiare,* meaning *to strive after* or *seize.*

chasm [kaz′əm] *n.* **1** A deep crack or gorge in the surface of the earth. **2** A great difference of opinion, feeling, etc.

chas·sis [shas′ē *or* chas′ē] *n., pl.* **chas·sis** [shas′ēz *or* chas′ēz] **1** The frame that supports the body of an automobile and includes the wheels, springs, motor, etc. **2** The metal framework of a radio or

Chassis of an automobile

television set to which the tubes and other working parts are attached. **3** The frame that supports the main body of an airplane.

chaste [chāst] *adj.* **1** Pure or virtuous; moral. **2** Very simple or pure in style: the *chaste* lines of a building. — **chaste′ly** *adv.*

chas·ten [chā′sən] *v.* **1** To discipline or correct by some form of punishment: Those parents never *chastened* their unruly daughter. **2** To make more simple; purify; refine.

chas·tise [chas·tīz′] *v.* **chas·tised, chas·tis·ing** To punish, especially by beating. — **chas·tise·ment** [chas′tīz·mənt *or* chas·tīz′mənt] *n.*

chas·ti·ty [chas′tə·tē] *n.* The condition of being chaste or pure.

chat [chat] *v.* **chat·ted, chat·ting,** *n.* **1** *v.* To talk in a relaxed, informal manner. **2** *n.* A relaxed, informal conversation. **3** *n.* Any of several singing birds.

châ·teau *or* **cha·teau** [sha·tō′] *n., pl.* **châ·teaux** *or* **cha·teaux** [sha·tōz′] **1** A French castle. **2** A large country house resembling a French castle.

chat·e·laine [shat′ə·lān] *n.* **1** A woman who is the owner or wife of the owner of a castle or large estate. **2** A clasp or chain worn at the waist by women to hold keys, a purse, watch, etc.

chat·tel [chat′(ə)l] *n.* In law, any personal possession that can be moved. Furniture, clothing, automobiles, etc., are chattels.

chat·ter [chat′ər] **1** *v.* To click together rapidly, as the teeth when one is cold. **2** *n.* A rattling of the teeth. **3** *v.* To talk about nothing of any importance. **4** *n.* Foolish, unimportant talk. **5** *v.* To make many quick, sharp sounds, as a squirrel or monkey. **6** *n.* The sounds made by a squirrel or monkey. — **chat′ter·er** *n.*

---

add, āce, câre, pälm; end, ēqual; it, īce; odd, ōpen, ôrder; tŏŏk, pōōl; up, bûrn; ə = a in *above,* e in *sicken,* i in *possible,* o in *melon,* u in *circus;* yōō = u in *fuse;* oil; pout; check; ring; thin; this; zh in *vision.* For ¶ reference, see page 64 · HOW TO

chat·ty [chat′ē] *adj.* **chat·ti·er, chat·ti·est**
1 Fond of talking and chatting: *a chatty person.*
2 Relaxed and informal: *a chatty style of writing.*
— **chat′ti·ly** *adv.* — **chat′ti·ness** *n.*

Chau·cer [chô′sər] **Geoffrey,** 1340?–1400,
English poet. He wrote *The Canterbury Tales.*

chauf·feur [shō′fər *or* shō·fûr′] **1** *n.* A man
who is employed as the driver of an automobile.
2 *v.* To serve as a chauffeur for: *He chauffeured*
us all over the city.

cheap [chēp] **1** *adj.* Not costing much money;
inexpensive: *a cheap car.* **2** *adj.* Charging low
prices: *a cheap store.* **3** *adj.* Lower in price than
it is worth: *During the sale, this ring is cheap.*
4 *adv.* At a low price: *to sell cheap.* **5** *adj.*
Easily obtained: *He had a cheap success.*
6 *adj.* Of little value; poor; inferior: *a toy*
made of *cheap metal.* **7** *adj.* Vulgar; common:
She makes herself cheap by talking too loud.
— **cheap′ly** *adv.* — **cheap′ness** *n.* ◆ *Cheap*
was once used in the expression *good cheap,*
meaning a *bargain,* and comes originally from
the Old English word *cēap,* meaning *business* or
trade.

cheap·en [chē′pən] *v.* To make or become cheap
or cheaper.

cheap·skate [chēp′skāt′] *n. slang* A person
who is stingy or miserly.

cheat [chēt] **1** *v.* To trick or defraud; act in a
dishonest manner. **2** *v.* To get away from;
escape: *He cheated his captors.* **3** *n.* A person
who cheats. **4** *n.* The act of cheating; swindle.
— **cheat′er** *n.*

check [chek] **1** *v.* To bring to a stop; halt: *to*
check careless spending. **2** *n.* A sudden stop.
3 *v.* To hold back; curb: *to check angry words.*
4 *n.* A person, thing, or event that holds back.
5 *v.* To test or examine for accuracy, completeness, etc.: *to check a column of addition.* **6** *n.* A
comparison or examination to prove right, true,
etc. **7** *v.* To agree or correspond: *Does your*
list *check with mine?* **8** *n.* A mark (√) to show
that something is accurate or needs attention.
9 *v.* To mark with a check. **10** *adj.* Used to
verify or check: *a check list.* **11** *n.* An order in
writing to a bank asking that a certain sum of
money be paid out of
one's account. **12** *v.*
To deposit or put in
temporary safekeep-
ing: *to check one's*
luggage. **13** *n.* A
ticket given to a per-
son who has checked something for safekeeping.
14 *n.* A slip of paper listing the items one has
bought and the amount one owes: *a check for a*
meal. **15** *n.* A single, small square in a pattern
or design made up of many small squares. **16** *n.*
A fabric having a pattern or design of small
squares. **17** *adj. use: a check suit.* **18** *n.* In
chess, the position of a king that makes it possible
for him to be captured on the next opposing
move. **19** *v.* In chess, to put (an opponent's
king) in danger. **20** *interj.* In chess, a call warn-

Check

ing an opponent that his king is in check. —
check in To register and become a guest at a
hotel, motel, etc. — **check out 1** To pay one's
bill and leave, as from a hotel. **2** *informal* To
investigate: *to check out a rumor.* — **in check**
Under control: *Keep your temper in check.*

check·book [chek′book′] *n.* A book of forms
furnished by a bank for writing checks.

check·er [chek′ər] **1** *n.* One of the pieces used
in the game of checkers. **2** *n.* One of the squares
in a pattern or design made up of many squares.
3 *n.* A pattern or design of squares. **4** *v.* To
mark with squares or patches.

check·er·board [chek′ər·bôrd′] *n.* A board
divided into 64 squares in alternating colors,
used in playing checkers or chess.

check·ered [chek′ərd] *adj.* **1** Divided into
squares. **2** Marked by light and dark patches:
the *checkered* shade of the trees. **3** Full of ups
and downs; often changing: *a checkered career.*

check·ers [chek′ərz] *n.pl.* (*used with singular*
verb) A game played by two persons on a
checkerboard, each player starting with 12
pieces.

check·mate [chek′māt′] *v.* **check·mat·ed,**
check·mat·ing, *n.* **1** *v.* In chess, to put (an
opponent's king) in a position from which no
escape is possible, thus winning the game. **2** *n.*
In chess, the move that ends the game. **3** *v.* To
defeat by some skillful action. **4** *n.* Total defeat.

check·room [chek′room′] *n.* A room in which
packages, coats, etc., may be temporarily left
for safekeeping.

check·up [chek′up′] *n.* A thorough examination
or test, especially a medical examination.

cheek [chēk] *n.* **1** Either side of one's face
below the eyes and above the mouth. **2** *informal*
Impudent boldness or self-confidence.

cheek·y [chē′kē] *adj.* **cheek·i·er, cheek·i·est**
informal Impudent; saucy: *a cheeky reply.*

cheep [chēp] **1** *n.* A faint, shrill sound, as that
made by a young bird. **2** *v.* To make this sound.

cheer [chir] **1** *n.* A shout of encouragement, approval, etc. **2** *n.* A set form of words or phrases
shouted in a rhythmical manner as encouragement to the players in a sports contest. **3** *v.*
To urge, encourage, or greet
with cheers: *We cheered them*
on. **4** *n.* Gladness and joy;
happiness. **5** *v.* To make or
become happy and cheerful.
— **be of good cheer** To be
happy, hopeful, courageous,
etc.

cheer·ful [chir′fəl] *adj.*
1 Happy; joyous: *a cheerful*
mood. **2** Bright and pleasant:
a cheerful color. **3** Willing: *a*
cheerful helper. — **cheer′·**
ful·ly *adv.* — **cheer′ful·**
ness *n.*

cheer·lead·er [chir′lē′dər]
n. A person who directs the shouting of cheers at
a sports contest.

Cheerleader

cheer·less [chir'lis] *adj.* Sad and gloomy. — **cheer'less·ly** *adv.* — **cheer'less·ness** *n.*

cheer·y [chir'ē] *adj.* **cheer·i·er, cheer·i·est** Bright, gay, and cheerful: a *cheery* laugh. — **cheer'i·ly** *adv.* — **cheer'i·ness** *n.*

cheese [chēz] *n.* A food made of the curds of sour milk or cream that have been pressed into a more or less solid form.

cheese·cloth [chēz'klôth'] *n.* A very thin, loosely woven cotton cloth.

chee·tah [chē'tə] *n.* An animal like the leopard but smaller, often trained to hunt.

chef [shef] *n.* **1** A male cook in charge of a kitchen or of other cooks. **2** Any cook.

chem·i·cal [kem'i·kəl] **1** *adj.* Of, used in, or having to do with chemistry. **2** *n.* A substance made by or used in a chemical process.

che·mise [shə·mēz'] *n.* **1** A woman's loose undergarment resembling a short slip. **2** A woman's dress that hangs straight from the shoulder. ◆ *Chemise* comes directly from French.

chem·ist [kem'ist] *n.* **1** A person who is trained in chemistry. **2** The British word for a druggist.

chem·is·try [kem'is·trē] *n.* The science that deals with the structure, composition, and properties of substances and with the ways in which they react or interact under various conditions.

Che·ops [kē'ops] *n.* An Egyptian king of the fourth dynasty (about 2900 B.C.), builder of the largest of the pyramids.

cher·ish [cher'ish] *v.* **1** To hold dear; treat tenderly: to *cherish* a dear friend. **2** To think about with fondness and hope: a *cherished* hope.

Cher·o·kee [cher'ə·kē] *n., pl.* **Cher·o·kee** or **Cher·o·kees 1** A member of a great tribe of Indians who once lived in northern Georgia and North Carolina, but now mainly live in Oklahoma. **2** The language of these Indians.

cher·ry [cher'ē] *n., pl.* **cher·ries 1** A small, round, edible fruit, red, yellow, or nearly black in color, and having a single pit. **2** The tree bearing this fruit. **3** The wood of this tree. **4** *adj. use:* a *cherry* table. **5** A bright red color.

cher·ub [cher'əb] *n.* **1** *pl.* **cher·ubs** or **cher·u·bim** [cher'(y)ə·bim] An angel usually pictured as a beautiful child with wings. **2** *pl.* **cher·ubs** Any beautiful child.

che·ru·bic [chə·rōō'bik] *adj.* Beautiful, sweet, or plump, like a cherub: a *cherubic* face.

chess [ches] *n.* A game of skill played on a checkerboard by two players. Each player has 16 pieces and the winner of the game is the one who first checkmates his opponent's king.

Chess

chest [chest] *n.* **1** The part of the body that is enclosed by the ribs; thorax. **2** The front of this part of the body: to be tattooed on the *chest*. **3** A box with a lid, in which to keep or store things. **4** A chest of drawers.

chest·nut [ches'nut] **1** *n.* An edible nut that is enclosed by a prickly bur or husk. **2** *n.* The tree that bears this nut. **3** *n., adj.* Reddish brown. **4** *n.* A horse of this color. **5** *n. informal* A stale joke.

chest of drawers A piece of furniture having several drawers and used for storing clothing, linens, etc.; bureau.

chev·a·lier [shev'ə·lir'] *n.* **1** A member of an honorary society, especially in France. **2** A knight or cavalier: seldom used today.

chev·i·ot [shev'ē·ət] *n.* A rough cloth, usually having raised diagonal ribs or lines on its surface, used for suits, overcoats, etc.

chev·ron [shev'rən] *n.* An emblem made up of stripes meeting at a point and worn on the sleeve of a military, naval, or police uniform.

chew [chōō] **1** *v.* To crush or grind with the teeth: He *chewed* his food noisily. **2** *n.* Something that is chewed: a *chew* of tobacco.

chew·ing gum [chōō'ing] A gum, usually chicle, that is flavored and sweetened for chewing.

Chevrons

Chey·enne *n.* **1** [shī·en'] A member of a tribe of Indians living now in Montana and Oklahoma. **2** [shī·en' *or* shī·an'] The capital of Wyoming.

chic [shēk] **1** *adj.* Stylish; elegant: a *chic* dress. **2** *n.* Style, elegance, and taste, especially in dress: She has great *chic*.

Chi·ca·go [shə·kä'gō] *n.* A city in NE Illinois, on Lake Michigan.

chi·can·er·y [shi·kā'nər·ē] *n., pl.* **chi·can·er·ies** The use of tricky actions or clever arguing and quibbling, in order to deceive or outwit.

chick [chik] *n.* **1** A young chicken. **2** Any young bird. **3** *slang* A young woman; girl.

chick·a·dee [chik'ə·dē] *n.* A small bird having the top of its head and its throat of a darker color than the body.

chick·en [chik'ən] **1** *n.* The common domestic fowl. **2** *n.* The flesh of this fowl used as food. **3** *n.* Any young bird. **4** *adj. slang* Cowardly.

chick·en-heart·ed [chik'ən·här'tid] *adj.* Timid or cowardly.

chicken pox A contagious disease, especially of children, in which there is a slight fever and small blisters on the skin.

chick·weed [chik'wēd'] *n.* A plant whose seeds are used for feeding caged birds.

chic·le [chik'əl] *n.* The milky, gummy juice of a large, tropical evergreen tree. It is used as the main ingredient of chewing gum.

---

add, āce, câre, pälm; end, ēqual; it, īce; odd, ōpen, ôrder; tŏŏk, pōōl; up, bûrn; ə = a in *above*, e in *sicken*, i in *possible*, o in *melon*, u in *circus*; yōō = u in *fuse*; oil; pout; check; ring; thin; this; zh in *vision*. For ¶ reference, see page 64 · HOW TO

chic·o·ry [chik′ər·ē] *n.*, *pl.* **chic·o·ries 1** A plant whose leaves are often used in salads. **2** The roasted root of this plant which is often mixed with coffee or used in place of coffee.

chide [chīd] *v.* **chid·ed** or **chid** [chid], **chid·ed** or **chid** or **chid·den** [chid′ən], **chid·ing** To scold: He *chided* me for laughing.

chief [chēf] **1** *n.* The person who is highest in rank or authority, as the leader of a tribe, police force, etc. **2** *adj.* Having the highest authority or rank: the *chief* officer. **3** *adj.* Most important; principal. **— in chief** Having the highest rank or authority: commander *in chief*.

chief justice The judge who presides over a court composed of several judges.

chief·ly [chēf′lē] *adv.* **1** Most of all; above all: *Chiefly* he told us of the town. **2** Principally; mostly; mainly: a club *chiefly* of young people.

chief·tain [chēf′tən] *n.* **1** The head of a clan or tribe: an Aztec *chieftain*. **2** Any chief or leader.

chif·fon [shi·fon′ *or* shif′on] **1** *n.* A very thin silk or rayon cloth, used in dresses, scarves, etc. **2** *adj.* In cooking, light and fluffy: a *chiffon* custard. ◆ *Chiffon* comes directly from French and was formed from *chiffe*, meaning a *rag*.

chig·ger [chig′ər] *n.* The larva of certain mites. It attaches itself to the skin and causes great itching.

chi·gnon [shēn′yon] *n.* A tight ball or roll of hair worn at the back of the head by women.

Chi·hua·hua [chi·wä′wä] *n.* A small Mexican dog having a smooth coat and large ears.

chil·blain [chil′blān] *n.* A painful itching, swelling, and redness of the hands or feet, caused by exposure to extreme cold.

child [chīld] *n.*, *pl.* **chil·dren 1** A baby. **2** A young boy or girl. **3** A son or daughter. **4** A person from a certain family or country: the *children* of Israel. **— with child** Pregnant.

child·birth [chīld′bûrth′] *n.* The act of giving birth to a child.

child·hood [chīld′hŏŏd′] *n.* **1** The time during which one is a child. **2** The condition of being a child.

child·ish [chīl′dish] *adj.* **1** Of, like, or proper for a child. **2** Not proper to an adult; foolish, thoughtless, etc.: a *childish* temper tantrum. **— child′ish·ly** *adv.* **— child′ish·ness** *n.*

child·less [chīld′lis] *adj.* Having no children.

child·like [chīld′līk′] *adj.* Having certain of the best qualities of a child; trusting, lovable, refreshing, etc.: a *childlike* simplicity.

chil·dren [chil′drən] *n.* Plural of CHILD.

child's play [chīldz] Something that is very easy to do.

Chil·e [chil′ē] *n.* A country on the SW coast of South America. **— Chil′e·an** *adj.*, *n.*

chil·i [chil′ē] *n.*, *pl.* **chil·ies 1** A very hot and spicy red pepper, used as a seasoning. **2** A dish made with meat, chili, beans, spices, etc.

chill [chil] **1** *n.* A feeling of being cold, often with shivering. **2** *v.* To have a chill. **3** *n.* A moderate but uncomfortable coldness: There is a *chill* in this room. **4** *adj.* Moderately or unpleasantly cold: a *chill* wind. **5** *v.* To make or become cold: to *chill* food. **6** *v.* To harden (metal) by sudden cooling. **7** *adj.* Not friendly.

chill·y [chil′ē] *adj.* **chill·i·er, chill·i·est 1** Causing coldness or chill: a *chilly* rain. **2** Feeling cold: I am *chilly*. **3** Not friendly or warm: a *chilly* greeting. **— chill′i·ness** *n.*

chi·mae·ra [kə·mir′ə *or* kī·mir′ə] *n.* Another spelling of CHIMERA.

chime [chīm] *n.*, *v.* **chimed, chim·ing 1** *n.* (*often pl.*) A set of bells each of which has a different pitch. **2** *n.* The sounds or music produced by chimes. **3** *v.* To sound or ring: The bells *chimed* all over town. **4** *v.* To produce or indicate by chiming: The clock *chimed* three. **5** *n.* A metal tube or set of tubes making bell-like sounds when struck. **— chime in 1** To interrupt: He always *chimed in* on our conversations. **2** To agree or be in harmony.

chi·me·ra [kə·mir′ə *or* kī·mir′ə] *n.* **1** (*written* **Chimera**) In Greek myths, a fire-breathing monster, part lion, part goat, and part serpent. **2** Any horrible idea or fancy. **3** An absurd, impractical, or impossible idea.

chi·mer·i·cal [kə·mer′i·kəl *or* kī·mer′i·kəl] *adj.* **1** Fantastic; imaginary. **2** Wildly impossible.

chim·ney [chim′nē] *n.*, *pl.* **chim·neys 1** A tall, hollow structure that carries away smoke or fumes from fireplaces, stoves, furnaces, etc. **2** A glass tube for enclosing the flame of a lamp.

chimney sweep A person who makes his living by cleaning away the soot from inside chimneys.

chimney swift A bird that looks like a swallow and often builds its nest in an unused chimney.

chim·pan·zee [chim·pan·zē′ *or* chim·pan′zē] *n.* An ape of Africa that lives in trees, has large ears and dark brown hair, and is smaller and more intelligent than the gorilla. ◆ *Chimpanzee* comes from a native African name.

Chimpanzee, about 54 in. tall

chin [chin] *n.*, *v.* **chinned, chin·ning 1** *n.* The part of the face just below the mouth. **2** *v.* To hang by the hands and lift (oneself) until the chin is level with or above the hands.

chi·na [chī′nə] *n.* **1** A fine kind of glasslike porcelain, baked twice. **2** Dishes, vases, figurines, etc., made of china or porcelain. **3** Any earthenware dishes.

Chi·na [chī′nə] *n.* A country of eastern Asia, the most populous and second largest in the world. It is divided into **the People's Republic of China,** on the mainland, and **the Republic of China,** on Taiwan.

chinch [chinch] *n.* **1** A chinch bug. **2** A bedbug.

chinch bug A small black and white bug that is very destructive to grain.

chin·chil·la [chin·chil′ə] *n.* **1** A small rodent of the Andes, about the size of a squirrel. **2** Its

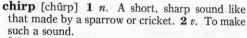

soft, valuable fur. **3** A heavy woolen cloth with a tufted surface.

chine [chīn] *n.* **1** The backbone or back. **2** A piece of meat including all or part of the backbone.

Chi·nese [chī·nēz'] *adj., n., pl.* **Chi·nese 1** *adj.* Of or from China. **2** *n.* A person born in or a citizen of China. **3** *n.* A person of Chinese ancestry. **4** *n.* **(the Chinese)** The people of China. **5** *n.* The language of China.

Chinese lantern A lantern made of thin paper, that can be folded flat.

chink[1] [chingk] **1** *n.* A crack: a *chink* in armor. **2** *v.* To fill the cracks of: to *chink* the walls with sticks and mud.

chink[2] [chingk] **1** *n.* A short, sharp metallic sound, as of coins hitting each other. **2** *v.* To make or cause to make this sound.

Chinese lantern

chi·nook [chi·nook'] *n.* **1** A warm, moist southwest wind that blows in from the sea along the coast of Oregon, Washington, and British Columbia. **2** A warm, dry wind blowing down the eastern slopes of the Rocky Mountains.

chintz [chints] *n.* A cotton fabric usually glazed and printed in bright colors: The slipcovers were made of flowered *chintz.*

chip [chip] *n., v.* **chipped, chip·ping 1** *n.* A small piece cut or broken off. **2** *v.* To break off a small piece or pieces of: to *chip* china. **3** *v.* To become chipped: This china *chips* easily. **4** *n.* A place where something has been chipped off: a *chip* on a glass. **5** *n.* A thinly sliced piece or morsel: a potato *chip.* **6** *n.* A small disk or counter used in certain games, as poker. **7** *v.* To chop or cut as with an ax. **8** *v.* To shape by cutting off pieces. — **chip in** To go along with others in giving money or help: We all *chipped in* to buy a new basketball. — **chip off the old block** A person who closely resembles either of his parents in behavior, looks, etc.

chip·munk [chip'mungk] *n.* A small North American ground squirrel with stripes down its back. ◆ *Chipmunk* comes from an Algonquian Indian word *chitmunk.* Perhaps it was changed because the animal's sharp, scolding call sounds like *chip, chip, chip,* or perhaps only because *chip* is easier for us to say before the sound of *m.*

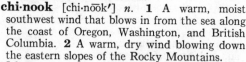
Chipmunk, 8–10 in. long

chip·per [chip'ər] *adj. U.S. informal* Feeling fine and spry or cheerful.

chi·rop·o·dist [kə·rop'ə·dist] *n.* A person who treats corns and other ailments of the feet.

chi·ro·prac·tor [kī'rə·prak'tər] *n.* A person who treats disease by pressing and manipulating the spine, the joints, etc.

chirp [chûrp] **1** *n.* A short, sharp sound like that made by a sparrow or cricket. **2** *v.* To make such a sound.

chir·rup [chir'əp] *v.* **1** To chirp continuously, as a bird. **2** To make a chirping sound with the lips, as in urging a horse.

chis·el [chiz'(ə)l] *n., v.* **chis·eled** or **chis·elled, chis·el·ing** or **chis·el·ling 1** *n.* A cutting tool with a sharp, beveled edge, used to cut or shape wood, metal, or stone. **2** *v.* To cut or shape with or as if with a chisel. **3** *v. slang* To cheat; swindle. — **chis'el·er** or **chis'el·ler** *n.*

chit·chat [chit'chat'] *n.* **1** Light conversation. **2** Gossip. ◆ *Chitchat* was formed when another syllable sounding like *chat* was put in front of it.

Chisel

chi·tin [kī'tin] *n.* A tough, colorless, horny substance forming the main part of the hard covering of insects and crustaceans. — **chi'·tin·ous** *adj.*

chiv·al·rous [shiv'əl·rəs] *adj.* **1** Gallant and brave, as an ideal knight; kind, courteous, generous, etc. **2** Of or having to do with chivalry. — **chiv'al·rous·ly** *adv.* — **chiv'al·rous·ness** *n.*

chiv·al·ry [shiv'əl·rē] *n.* **1** The beliefs and code of life of knights in the Middle Ages. **2** The ideal qualities of knighthood, as gallantry, courtesy, bravery, kindness, etc.

chive [chīv] *n.* A plant of the onion family whose long, slender leaves are chopped up and used for seasoning.

chlo·ride [klôr'īd] *n.* A compound of chlorine with another element or group of elements. Common salt is sodium chloride.

chlo·rin·ate [klôr'ə·nāt] *v.* **chlo·rin·at·ed, chlo·rin·at·ing** To add chlorine to, as in purifying water. — **chlo'rin·a'tion** *n.*

chlo·rine [klôr'ēn] *n.* A greenish yellow, poisonous gaseous element obtained chiefly from common salt, and widely used in medicine, industry, etc.

chlo·ro·form [klôr'ə·fôrm] **1** *n.* A colorless, volatile liquid used as an anesthetic and solvent. **2** *v.* To make unconscious or kill with an overdose of chloroform.

chlo·ro·phyll or **chlo·ro·phyl** [klôr'ə·fil] *n.* The green substance found in most plants. In the presence of sunlight it converts water and carbon dioxide from the air into sugars and starches.

chlo·ro·plast [klôr'ə·plast] *n.* A part of a plant cell where chlorophyll is found.

---

add, āce, câre, pälm; end, ēqual; it, īce; odd, ōpen, ôrder; took, pool; up, bûrn;
ə = a in *above,* e in *sicken,* i in *possible,* o in *melon,* u in *circus;* yoo = u in *fuse;* oil; pout;
check; ring; thin; this; zh in *vision.* For ¶ reference see page 64 · HOW TO

chock [chok] **1** *n.* A block or wedge placed to prevent something from moving or rolling. **2** *v.* To hold in position with a chock or chocks.

chock-full [chok′fōōl′] *adj.* Completely full.

choc·o·late [chôk′(ə·)lit *or* chok′(ə·)lit] **1** *n.* Cacao nuts that have been roasted and ground. **2** *n.* A drink or candy made from this. **3** *adj.* Made or flavored with chocolate: a *chocolate* cake. **4** *n., adj.* Dark, reddish brown. ◆ This word comes from a Mexican Indian word. Indians gave chocolate to Spanish explorers in South America and Mexico.

Chocks holding an airplane wheel

choice [chois] *n., adj.* **choic·er, choic·est** **1** *n.* The act of choosing; selection. **2** *n.* The right or privilege of choosing; option. **3** *n.* The person or thing chosen: the people's *choice*. **4** *n.* A number or variety from which to choose: a large *choice* of articles. **5** *n.* An alternative: He had no *choice*. **6** *adj.* Of very good quality; excellent: *choice* food.

choir [kwīr] *n.* **1** A trained group of singers, especially in a religious service. **2** The part of a church occupied by the choir.

choke [chōk] *v.* **choked, chok·ing,** *n.* **1** *v.* To stop the breathing of by squeezing or blocking the windpipe. **2** *v.* To become suffocated or stifled: to *choke* from smoke. **3** *n.* The act or sound of choking. **4** *v.* To keep back; suppress: to *choke* down anger. **5** *v.* To clog or become clogged: Filth *choked* the pipes. **6** *v.* To stop or hold back the progress, growth, or action of: to *choke* a fire. **7** *v.* To lessen the intake of air of (a gasoline engine). **8** *n.* A device that does this. **— choke up** To be overcome by emotion, nervousness, etc.

choke·cher·ry [chōk′cher′ē] *n., pl.* **choke·cher·ries** **1** A wild North American cherry with a bitter taste. **2** The tree it grows on.

chok·er [chō′kər] *n.* **1** A necklace worn high on the neck. **2** A person or thing that chokes.

chol·er [kol′ər] *n.* An excitable temper; anger.

chol·er·a [kol′ər·ə] *n.* An infectious bacterial disease that attacks the intestines, often causing death.

chol·er·ic [kol′ər·ik] *adj.* Easily made angry.

cho·les·ter·ol [kə·les′tə·rōl] *n.* A fatty crystalline substance present in animal fats, gallstones, bile, etc. It plays a part in metabolism.

choose [chōōz] *v.* **chose, cho·sen, choos·ing** **1** To select from a group: to *choose* a weapon; I *chose* in haste. **2** To decide or prefer (to do something): He *chose* to remain. **— choos′er** *n.*

choos·y [chōō′zē] *adj.* **choos·i·er, choos·i·est** *informal* Very fussy in choosing.

chop[1] [chop] *v.* **chopped, chop·ping,** *n.* **1** *v.* To cut by hitting with a sharp tool: to *chop* a tree down. **2** *n.* A cutting blow. **3** *v.* To cut into small pieces: to *chop* onions. **4** *n.* A slice of lamb, pork, etc., with part of its bone. **5** *v.* To make by

cutting: to *chop* a hole in ice. **6** *v.* To hit a ball with a downward slice, as in tennis. **— chop′·per** *n.*

chop[2] [chop] *v.* **chopped, chop·ping** To shift suddenly; veer, as the wind.

chop[3] [chop] *n.* (*usually pl.*) The jaw, or the part of the face that includes it.

Cho·pin [shō′pan], **Frédéric,** 1810–1849, Polish composer and pianist who lived in France.

chop·py[1] [chop′ē] *adj.* **chop·pi·er, chop·pi·est** Full of short, rough waves: a *choppy* sea.

chop·py[2] [chop′ē] *adj.* **chop·pi·er, chop·pi·est** Variable; changing, as the wind.

chop·sticks [chop′stiks′] *n.pl.* Slender rods of ivory or wood used in pairs by the Chinese, Japanese, etc., to lift food to the mouth.

chop su·ey [sōō′ē] A Chinese-American dish made of bits of meat, bean sprouts, onions, celery, mushrooms, etc., cooked in a sauce and served with rice. ◆ *Chop suey* is an American pronunciation and spelling of a Chinese term meaning *odds and ends*.

Chopsticks

cho·ral [*adj.* kôr′əl, *n.* kə·ral′ *or* kô·ral′] **1** *adj.* Of, for, by, or in the manner of a chorus. **2** *n.* Another spelling of CHORALE.

cho·rale [kə·ral′ *or* kô·ral′] *n.* A hymn having a simple melody and firm rhythm.

chord[1] [kôrd] *n.* A combination of three or more musical tones sounded together.

chord[2] [kôrd] *n.* **1** A straight line joining any two points of an arc. **2** A string of a musical instrument. **3** An emotional response or reaction: to touch a sympathetic *chord*.

chor·date [kôr′dāt] *n.* Any of the animals having backbones or having breathing organs and nervous systems placed as in vertebrates.

Chords

chore [chôr] *n.* *U.S.* **1** A routine task, as in housework. **2** An unpleasant or hard task.

cho·re·og·ra·phy [kôr′ē·og′rə·fē] *n.* The planning of movements for dance performances. **— cho′re·og′ra·pher** *n.*

chor·is·ter [kôr′is·tər] *n.* A member of a choir, especially a boy singer.

cho·roid [kôr′oid] **1** *n.* A membrane full of blood vessels between the retina and outer cover of the eye. **2** *adj.* Of or like this membrane.

chor·tle [chôr′təl] *v.* **chor·tled, chor·tling** To chuckle loudly or gleefully.

cho·rus [kôr′əs] **1** *n.* A group of singers, speakers, or dancers that perform together. **2** *n.* A musical or dramatic composition to be sung or spoken by a chorus. **3** *n.* A part of a song sung after each stanza; refrain. **4** *n.* Any group singing, speaking, etc., all at once. **5** *n.* A saying or shouting of something by many at once: a *chorus* of groans. **6** *v.* To sing, speak, etc., all at once. **— in chorus** All together; at one time.

chose [chōz] Past tense of CHOOSE.

cho·sen [chō′zən] Past participle of CHOOSE.

chow [chou] *n.* **1** A medium-sized dog native to China, having a thick brown or black coat and a blue-black tongue. **2** *slang* Food.

chow·der [chou′dər] *n.* A dish made of clams or fish stewed with vegetables, often in milk. ◆ *Chowder* comes from the French word *chaudière* [shō·dyâr′] meaning a *kettle or its contents*. People in New England changed it into *chowder.*

chow mein [chou′ mān′] A Chinese-American dish made of meat, onions, bean sprouts, etc., stewed and served with fried noodles.

Christ [krīst] *n.* **1** The promised savior of Israel, foretold by the prophets. **2** Jesus, regarded as fulfilling this prophecy. ◆ The name *Christ* comes from a Greek word meaning the *Anointed.* It is a translation of a Hebrew word.

chris·ten [kris′(ə)n] *v.* **1** To baptize or name in baptism. **2** To give a name to: to *christen* a boat.

Chris·ten·dom [kris′(ə)n·dəm] *n.* **1** Christian lands. **2** All Christians, as a group.

chris·ten·ing [kris′(ə)n·ing] *n.* A Christian baptism, especially of a baby.

Chris·tian [kris′chən] **1** *n.* A person who believes in Jesus, his teachings, or example. **2** *adj.* Of, having to do with, or believing in Jesus or his teachings. **3** *adj.* In keeping with the teachings of Jesus: *Christian* behavior.

Chris·ti·an·i·ty [kris′chē·an′ə·tē] *n.* **1** The religion taught by Jesus and his followers. **2** All Christians, as a group.

Chris·tian·ize [kris′chən·īz] *v.* **Chris·tian·ized, Chris·tian·iz·ing** To make Christian. ¶3

Christian name A given name, or first name.

Christian Science A religion and system of healing founded in 1866 by Mary Baker Eddy and based on her interpretation of the Bible. **— Christian Scientist**

Christ·like [krīst′līk′] *adj.* Like Christ; having the spirit of Christ.

Christ·mas [kris′məs] *n.* The celebration on December 25 of the birth of Jesus.

Christmas tree An evergreen tree decorated with ornaments and lights at Christmas.

chro·mat·ic [krō·mat′ik] *adj.* **1** Of, having, or having to do with color. **2** Of, using, or built on semitones: a *chromatic* scale.

chro·ma·tin [krō′mə·tin] *n.* The easily stained material of a cell nucleus in which the genes are located.

chro·ma·tog·ra·phy [krō′· mə·tog′rə·fē] *n.* A method for separating and analyzing the parts of a fluid mixture by adsorption.

Christmas tree

chrome [krōm] *n.* Chromium, especially when used to plate another metal.

chro·mi·um [krō′mē·əm] *n.* A grayish white, very hard metallic element that does not tarnish easily, much used in making alloys and pigments.

chro·mo·some [krō′mə·sōm] *n.* One of the rod-shaped or loop-shaped bodies that carry the genes in the cells of plants and animals.

chro·mo·sphere [krō′mə·sfir′] *n.* A flaming red gaseous envelope that surrounds the sun, visible during a total eclipse.

chron·ic [kron′ik] *adj.* **1** Continuing for a long time: *chronic* discontent. **2** Lasting or coming back again and again: *chronic* illness. **3** Long affected; habitual: a *chronic* alcoholic.

chron·i·cle [kron′i·kəl] *n., v.* **chron·i·cled, chron·i·cling** **1** *n.* A record of events as they happened in time. **2** *v.* To make a chronicle of.

Chron·i·cles [kron′i·kəlz] *n.pl. (used with singular verb)* Either of two historical books of the Old Testament.

chron·o·log·i·cal [kron′ə·loj′i·kəl] *adj.* **1** Arranged according to the order in which things happened. **2** Of or having to do with chronology. **— chron′o·log′i·cal·ly** *adv.*

chro·nol·o·gy [krə·nol′ə·jē] *n., pl.* **chro·nol·o·gies** **1** The science of determining the proper sequence and dating of historical events. **2** A chronological list, arrangement, etc.

chro·nom·e·ter [krə·nom′ə·tər] *n.* A very precise clock, used in science, navigation, etc.

chrys·a·lis [kris′ə·lis] *n., pl.* **chrys·a·lis·es** or **chry·sal·i·des** [kri·sal′ə·dēz] The form of an insect such as a butterfly when it is enclosed in a cocoon and before it becomes an adult.

chrys·an·the·mum [kri·san′thə·məm] *n.* Any of a group of plants cultivated in many varieties for their large, round, showy flowers.

chub·by [chub′ē] *adj.* **chub·bi·er, chub·bi·est** Plump; rounded. **— chub′bi·ness** *n.*

Chrysalis

chuck¹ [chuk] **1** *v.* To pat or tap playfully, as under the chin. **2** *n.* Such a pat or tap. **3** *v.* To throw or pitch: to *chuck* a baseball. **4** *n.* A throw; toss.

chuck² [chuk] *n.* **1** The cut of beef extending from the neck to the shoulder blade. **2** A clamp to hold a tool, drill, etc., in a machine.

chuck·le [chuk′əl] *v.* **chuck·led, chuck·ling,** *n.* **1** *v.* To laugh softly. **2** *n.* A soft laugh.

chuck wagon A wagon equipped to cook food for cowboys or other outdoor workers.

chug [chug] *n., v.* **chugged, chug·ging** **1** *n.* A dull explosive sound, as of the exhaust of an engine. **2** *v.* To move while making a series of such sounds: The old car *chugged* by.

chum [chum] *n., v.* **chummed, chum·ming**

add, āce, câre, pälm; end, ēqual; it, īce; odd, ōpen, ôrder; tŏŏk, pŏŏl; up, bûrn; ə = a in *above*, e in *sicken*, i in *possible*, o in *melon*, u in *circus*; yŏŏ = u in *fuse*; oil; pout; check; ring; thin; this; zh in *vision*. For ¶ reference, see page 64 · HOW TO

1 *n.* A close friend; buddy. **2** *v.* To have a close friendship with someone. **3** *n.* A roommate.

chum·my [chum′ē] *adj.* **chum·mi·er, chum·mi·est** *informal* Very friendly; intimate.

chump [chump] *n. informal* A foolish person.

Chung·king [chŏŏng′king′] *n.* A city on the Yangtze River, a former capital of China.

chunk [chungk] *n.* A short thick piece or lump.

chunk·y [chung′kē] *adj.* **chunk·i·er, chunk·i·est** Short and thickset; stocky.

church [chûrch] *n.* **1** A building for Christian worship. **2** Christian religious services. **3** (*usually written* **Church**) A distinct body of Christians having the same faith and discipline: the Lutheran *Church.* **4** (*usually written* **Church**) Christians, as a group. ◆ *Church* comes originally from a Greek word meaning *of the Lord.*

Church·ill [chûrch′il], **Sir Winston,** 1874–1965, British statesman and author, prime minister of Great Britain, 1940–1945, 1951–1955.

church·man [chûrch′mən] *n.,* *pl.* **church·men** [chûrch′mən] **1** A supporter or member of a church. **2** A clergyman.

Church of England The national church of England, established in the 16th century.

Church of Jesus Christ of Latter-day Saints The official name of the Mormon Church.

church·war·den [chûrch′wôr′dən] *n.* In the Episcopal Church, or the Church of England, a layman who helps to manage church property.

church·yard [chûrch′yärd′] *n.* The ground around a church, often used as a cemetery.

churl [chûrl] *n.* **1** In early England, a freeman of low birth. **2** A rude or surly person; boor. ◆ *Churl* comes from an Old English word meaning *man.* At first a *churl* was a free man, but after the Norman Conquest most of the common people were made serfs and *churl* began to mean *peasant of a low class.*

churl·ish [chûr′lish] *adj.* Rude; boorish. **—churl′ish·ly** *adv.* **—churl′ish·ness** *n.*

churn [chûrn] **1** *n.* A container or machine in which milk or cream is beaten to make butter. **2** *v.* To beat (milk or cream) in or as if in a churn. **3** *v.* To move or stir about violently.

chute [shŏŏt] *n.* **1** An inclined trough or vertical passage down which water, coal, laundry, etc., may pass. **2** A slide, as for toboggans. **3** A waterfall or rapid. **4** *informal* A parachute.

chut·ney [chut′nē] *n.,* *pl.* **chut·neys** A spicy relish of fruit, spices, etc.

ci·ca·da [si·kā′də] *n.* A large insect with four transparent wings. The male makes a shrill sound by rubbing its legs against a vibrating membrane on its abdomen.

Cic·e·ro [sis′ə·rō], **Marcus Tullius,** 106–43 B.C., Roman statesman, orator, and author.

ci·der [sī′dər] *n.* The juice of apples, used for drinking and for making vinegar.

ci·gar [si·gär′] *n.* A roll of tobacco leaves prepared and shaped for smoking.

cig·a·rette [sig′ə·ret′ *or* sig′ə·ret] *n.* A paper tube filled with shredded tobacco for smoking.

cil·i·a [sil′ē·ə] *n.pl., sing.* **cil·i·um** [sil′ē·əm] **1** Tiny hairlike outgrowths on some plant and animal cells. Some small water animals use them to move about or to set up currents. **2** The eyebrows.

cinch [sinch] *U.S.* **1** *n.* A strap that holds a pack or saddle on an animal. **2** *v.* To put a cinch on. **3** *v.* To tighten a cinch. **4** *n. informal* A strong grip. **5** *n. slang* Something easy or certain. **6** *v. slang* To make certain of.

cin·cho·na [sin·kō′nə] *n.* **1** A tree, originally of Peru, now cultivated in India and Java. **2** The bitter-tasting bark of this tree, from which quinine and related substances are obtained.

Cin·cin·nat·i [sin′sə·nat′ē] *n.* A city in sw Ohio, on the Ohio River.

cin·der [sin′dər] *n.* **1** A piece of partly burned wood, coal, etc., that is not flaming. **2** (*pl.*) Charred bits and ashes from a fire.

cinder block A block, usually hollow, of cement and pressed cinders, used in building.

Cin·der·el·la [sin′də·rel′ə] *n.* A girl in a fairy tale, treated cruelly by her stepmother and stepsisters, but finally married to a prince.

cin·e·ma [sin′ə·mə] *n.* **1** A motion picture. **2** A motion picture theater. **3** Motion pictures in general. ◆ *Cinema* comes from a Greek word meaning *movement.*

cin·na·bar [sin′ə·bär] *n.* A heavy red mineral, the principal ore of mercury.

cin·na·mon [sin′ə·mən] **1** *n.* The inner bark of various tropical trees, used as a spice. **2** *n.* Any of these trees. **3** *adj., n.* Reddish brown.

ci·on [sī′ən] *n.* A twig or shoot cut from a plant or tree, especially for grafting.

ci·pher [sī′fər] **1** *n.* Zero; naught. Symbol: 0. **2** *n.* An unimportant person or thing. **3** *v.* To work out (a problem), using arithmetic. **4** *n.* A system for writing secret messages; code. **5** *n.* A message in cipher. ◆ See ZERO.

cir·ca [sûr′kə] *prep.* About; around: a Latin word used before an approximate date or figure.

Cir·ce [sûr′sē] *n.* In Homer's *Odyssey,* an enchantress who changed Odysseus's companions into pigs by a magic drink.

cir·cle [sûr′kəl] *n., v.* **cir·cled, cir·cling** **1** *n.* A plane curve all of whose points are equally distant from a point in the plane, called the center. **2** *n.* The area enclosed by this curve. **3** *n.* Something resembling a circle, as a ring, etc. **4** *v.* To make or put a closed curve around: The fence *circled* the field. **5** *v.* To move about in or nearly in a circle: The lion *circled* its prey. **6** *n.* A complete series that repeats over and over: the *circle* of seasons. **7** *n.* A group of

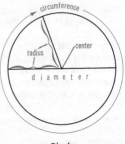

Circle

people with a common interest or purpose: a sewing *circle*.

cir·clet [sûr′klit] *n.* **1** A small circle. **2** A small circular object, as a ring.

cir·cuit [sûr′kit] *n.* **1** A route or path that turns back to where it began. **2** The line or distance around an area. **3** A periodic trip through a set of places, usually in a fixed order and in connection with one's work. **4** The route traveled in such a trip. **5** The path taken by an electric current. **6** The arrangement of parts in an electrical or electronic device or system. **7** A group of theaters presenting films, plays, etc., in turn.

cir·cu·i·tous [sər·kyoo′ə·təs] *adj.* Roundabout; indirect. **— cir·cu′i·tous·ly** *adv.*

circuit rider A minister who preaches at places on a circuit.

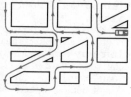
A circuitous route

cir·cu·lar [sûr′kyə·lər] **1** *adj.* Shaped like, moving in, or forming a circle. **2** *adj.* Of or having to do with circles. **3** *n.* A notice or advertisement sent to many people.

cir·cu·lar·ize [sûr′kyə·lə·rīz] *v.* **cir·cu·lar·ized, cir·cu·lar·iz·ing** To send circulars to.

cir·cu·late [sûr′kyə·lāt] *v.* **cir·cu·lat·ed, cir·cu·lat·ing 1** To move in a course that returns to its starting point, as the blood. **2** To spread or move about: Rumors *circulate*.

circulating library A library from which books can be borrowed or rented.

cir·cu·la·tion [sûr′kyə·lā′shən] *n.* **1** A moving around or through something back to the starting point. **2** The movement of the blood through the body. **3** A passing or spreading from one person or place to another. **4** The average number of copies of a magazine, newspaper, etc., distributed within a certain period of time.

cir·cu·la·to·ry [sûr′kyə·lə·tôr′ē] *adj.* Of or having to do with circulation, as of the blood.

cir·cum·cise [sûr′kəm·sīz] *v.* **cir·cum·cised, cir·cum·cis·ing** To cut off the foreskin of. **— cir·cum·ci·sion** [sûr′kəm·sizh′ən] *n.*

cir·cum·fer·ence [sər·kum′fər·əns] *n.* **1** The boundary of any closed curve, especially a circle. **2** The length of such a boundary.

cir·cum·flex [sûr′kəm·fleks] *n.* A mark (^) used over a vowel to show how to pronounce it.

cir·cum·lo·cu·tion [sûr′kəm·lō·kyoo′shən] *n.* A roundabout use of words: "to move from this place" is a *circumlocution* for "to go."

cir·cum·nav·i·gate [sûr′kəm·nav′ə·gāt] *v.* **cir·cum·nav·i·gat·ed, cir·cum·nav·i·gat·ing** To sail around. **— cir′cum·nav′i·ga′·tion** *n.*

cir·cum·po·lar [sûr′kəm·pō′lər] *adj.* **1** Near or around one of the earth's poles. **2** Seeming to circle one of the earth's poles, as a star.

cir·cum·scribe [sûr′kəm·skrīb′] *v.* **cir·cum·scribed, cir·cum·scrib·ing 1** To limit; confine: His powers were *circumscribed*. **2** To draw a line around; encircle. **3** To draw a circle so that it passes through each vertex of (a polygon). **4** To draw a polygon so that all its sides are tangent to (a circle).

cir·cum·spect [sûr′kəm·spekt] *adj.* Watchful and cautious; prudent.

cir·cum·spec·tion [sûr′kəm·spek′shən] *n.* Watchful caution; prudence.

cir·cum·stance [sûr′kəm·stans] *n.* **1** Something connected with an act, event, etc.: the *circumstances* of a crime. **2** An event, fact, or detail. **3** (*pl.*) Condition in life: a man in poor financial *circumstances*. **4** Formal display: pomp and *circumstance*. **— under the circumstances** Since such is the case.

cir·cum·stan·tial [sûr′kəm·stan′shəl] *adj.* **1** Having to do with or dependent on circumstances: *circumstantial* evidence. **2** Full of detail. **3** Not essential; incidental.

cir·cum·vent [sûr′kəm·vent′] *v.* **1** To trap or get the better of by cleverness or slyness. **2** To avoid or go around. **— cir′cum·ven′tion** *n.*

cir·cus [sûr′kəs] *n.* **1** A traveling show of acrobats, clowns, trained animals, etc. **2** *informal* A funny, entertaining person or thing. **3** In ancient Rome, a stadium for sports, etc.

cirque [sûrk] *n.* A half basin with steep walls, cut by a glacier at the head of a valley.

cir·rus [sir′əs] *n.,* *pl.* **cir·ri** [sir′ī] A kind of cloud seen as feathery bands in the sky.

cis·tern [sis′tərn] *n.* A tank for storing water or other liquids.

cit·a·del [sit′ə·dəl] *n.* A fortress overlooking a town or city.

ci·ta·tion [sī·tā′shən] *n.* **1** The act of quoting or mentioning someone or something. **2** A person or thing quoted or mentioned. **3** A public commendation or award. **4** A summons.

Cirrus clouds

cite [sīt] *v.* **cit·ed, cit·ing 1** To quote or mention as an example or authority. **2** To mention in a report, as for bravery. **3** To summon to a court of law. ◆ See SITE.

cit·i·zen [sit′ə·zən] *n.* **1** A person who is born in or made a member of a country or nation. He has certain rights and owes certain duties. **2** A resident of a city or town.

cit·i·zen·ry [sit′ə·zən·rē] *n.* Citizens as a group: an aroused local *citizenry*.

cit·i·zen·ship [sit′ə·zən·ship′] *n.* The condition of being a citizen, with its rights and duties.

cit·rate [sit′rāt] *n.* A salt of citric acid.

---

cit·ric acid [sit′rik] A weak acid found in citrus fruit.

cit·ron [sit′rən] *n.* **1** A fruit like a lemon, but larger and less acid. **2** The tree it grows on. **3** The rind of this fruit, candied and used in cakes, puddings, etc.

cit·ron·el·la [sit′rə·nel′ə] *n.* **1** An oil used in making perfumes, in cooking, and to keep mosquitoes away. **2** The grass it comes from.

cit·rus [sit′rəs] *n.* **1** Any tree that bears oranges, lemons, grapefruit, limes, or related fruit. **2** The fruit of any such tree. **3** *adj. use: citrus* trees.

cit·y [sit′ē] *n., pl.* **cit·ies** **1** A large town that takes care of its own affairs. **2** In the U.S., a local government organized and operated on the basis of a charter from its state. **3** The people of a city, as a group. **4** *adj. use: city* politics.

city hall The building where the government of a city is located.

city manager A person appointed by a city government to take charge of managing the city.

civ·et [siv′it] *n.* **1** A small, spotted animal of Africa and Asia, often called **civet cat. 2** A musky substance secreted by the civet, used in making perfume.

civ·ic [siv′ik] *adj.* Of or having to do with a city, a citizen, or citizenship.

civ·ics [siv′iks] *n.pl.* The study of citizenship and government. ◆ See -ICS.

civ·il [siv′əl] *adj.* **1** Of or having to do with citizens or citizenship. **2** Not connected with the armed forces or the church. **3** Within a state or nation: a *civil* war. **4** Civilized; polite: a *civil* answer. — **civ′il·ly** *adv.*

civil engineer An engineer trained to plan and build roads, harbors, bridges, tunnels, dams, etc. — **civil engineering**

ci·vil·ian [sə·vil′yən] *n.* **1** A person who is not in active military service. **2** *adj. use: civilian* life; *civilian* clothes.

ci·vil·i·ty [sə·vil′ə·tē] *n., pl.* **ci·vil·i·ties** **1** Courtesy; politeness. **2** A polite action.

civ·i·li·za·tion [siv′ə·lə·zā′shən] *n.* **1** A stage of human society in which there is a high level of culture and well-developed industry and science. **2** Civilized countries or peoples. **3** The society and culture of a particular people, place, or period.

civ·i·lize [siv′ə·līz] *v.* **civ·i·lized, civ·i·liz·ing** **1** To bring into a state of civilization. **2** *adj. use:* a *civilized* nation. ¶3

civil liberties Freedom within the law to think, speak, and act as one likes.

civil rights The rights and privileges of a citizen, especially, in the U.S., the rights guaranteed by the 13th, 14th, 15th, and 19th amendments to the Constitution.

civil service The administrative services of a government, excluding the armed forces, the courts, and the legislature.

Civil War 1 The war between the Union and the Confederacy from 1861 to 1865. **2** (*written* **civil war**) A war between groups of citizens of the same country.

Cl The symbol for the element CHLORINE.

clack [klak] **1** *v.* To make or cause to make a sharp, dry sound: to *clack* sticks together. **2** *n.* Such a sound.

clad [klad] An alternative past tense and past participle of CLOTHE: He was *clad* in white.

claim [klām] **1** *v.* To demand what is one's own or one's right: to *claim* one's wages. **2** *n.* A demand for what is rightfully due to one. **3** *n.* A basis for claiming something: a *claim* to greatness. **4** *n.* Something that is claimed, as a piece of land. **5** *v.* To declare or maintain: to *claim* the truth of a report. **6** *n.* A declaration or statement: a *claim* of innocence. **7** *v.* To require or deserve: The problem *claims* our careful attention.

claim·ant [klā′mənt] *n.* A person who makes a claim.

clair·voy·ance [klâr·voi′əns] *n.* The supposed ability to see things that are out of sight.

clair·voy·ant [klâr·voi′ənt] **1** *adj.* Having clairvoyance. **2** *n.* A clairvoyant person.

clam [klam] *n., v.* **clammed, clam·ming 1** *n.* A soft-bodied animal something like an oyster, having a shell in two hinged halves. Clams live in sand along the shore of the ocean or rivers and lakes. Some are good to eat. **2** *v.* To hunt or dig for clams.

clam·bake [klam′bāk′] *n. U.S.* A picnic where clams and other foods are baked.

clam·ber [klam′bər] *v.* To climb up or down with effort, using both hands and feet.

clam·my [klam′ē] *adj.* **clam·mi·er, clam·mi·est** Stickily soft and damp, and usually cold.

clam·or [klam′ər] **1** *n.* A loud and continuous noise, especially a loud protest or outcry. **2** *v.* To make a clamor. — **clam′or·ous** *adj.* ¶1

clamp [klamp] **1** *n.* A device having parts that can be brought together by a screw or spring to hold something. **2** *v.* To hold or bind with or as if with a clamp. — **clamp down** *U.S. informal* To become more strict.

clan [klan] *n.* **1** A group of families claiming descent from a common ancestor. **2** A group of people bound by a common interest.

Clamp

clan·des·tine [klan·des′tin] *adj.* Kept secret, often for an evil reason: a *clandestine* plot.

clang [klang] **1** *v.* To make or cause to make a loud, ringing, metallic sound. **2** *n.* This sound.

clan·gor [klang′(g)ər] *n.* **1** A clang. **2** Repeated clanging. — **clan′gor·ous** *adj.* ¶1

clank [klangk] **1** *v.* To make or cause to make a short, harsh, metallic sound. **2** *n.* This sound.

clan·nish [klan′ish] *adj.* **1** Of or having to do with a clan. **2** Closely united, like a family; bound by family traditions, prejudices, etc.

clans·man [klanz′mən] *n., pl.* **clans·men** [klanz′mən] A member of a clan.

clap [klap] *v.* **clapped, clap·ping,** *n.* **1** *v.* To strike (the hands) together with a sharp sound.

2 *n.* A loud, sharp sound: a *clap* of thunder. **3** *v.* To make or cause to make a clap by striking: to *clap* books together. **4** *v.* To slap with the palm of the hand: to *clap* someone on the back. **5** *n.* A slap. **6** *v.* To put or place quickly: They *clapped* him into jail.

clap·board [klab'ərd *or* klap'bôrd'] *n.* A thin board having one edge thinner than the other, used as siding on wooden buildings.

clap·per [klap'ər] *n.* **1** The tongue of a bell. **2** A person or thing that claps.

clap·trap [klap'trap] *n.* Nonsense.

clar·et [klar'ət] *n.* **1** A dry, red wine. **2** *adj.*, *n.* Deep purplish red.

clar·i·fy [klar'ə·fī] *v.* **clar·i·fied, clar·i·fy·ing** **1** To make or become clear or pure, as a liquid. **2** To make or become understandable. — **clar'·i·fi·ca'tion** *n.*

clar·i·net [klar'ə·net'] *n.* A high-pitched wood-wind musical instrument having a cylindrical body and a single-reed mouthpiece.

clar·i·on [klar'ē·ən] **1** *n.* An old-fashioned kind of trumpet. **2** *n.* The sound of a clarion. **3** *adj.* Clear and piercing, as a trumpet's sound.

clar·i·ty [klar'ə·tē] *n.* Clearness.

Clark [klärk], **William,** 1770–1838, U.S. explorer who worked with Meriwether Lewis.

clash [klash] **1** *v.* To hit or cause to hit with a harsh, metallic sound: The cymbals *clashed.* **2** *n.* A harsh, metallic sound. **3** *v.* To be in opposition; conflict. **4** *n.* A conflict.

Clarinet

clasp [klasp] **1** *n.* A fastening, as a hook, by which things or parts are held together. **2** *v.* To fasten with or as if with a clasp. **3** *n.* A firm grasp or embrace. **4** *v.* To grasp or embrace.

class [klas] **1** *n.* A group of persons or things that have something in common: the working *class*; the *class* of odd numbers. **2** *v.* To put in a class; classify. **3** *n.* A division of people, objects, etc., according to quality or rank: to travel in first *class.* **4** *n.* A group of students who are taught or who graduate together. **5** *n.* A meeting at which a group of students is taught. **6** *n. slang* High quality or elegance; excellence: a dress with *class.*

clas·sic [klas'ik] **1** *adj.* Being in the first class or highest rank, as in literature or art. **2** *n.* A novel, symphony, etc., of such quality. **3** *n.* A person who creates works of such quality. **4** *adj.* Following strict or formal rules, principles, etc. **5** *adj.* Of or characteristic of the art, literature, or culture of ancient Greece and Rome. **6** *adj.* Customary; traditional: a *classic* holiday meal.

7 *n.* A well-known or traditional event: a football *classic.* — **the classics** Ancient Greek and Roman literature.

clas·si·cal [klas'i·kəl] *adj.* **1** Of or characteristic of the arts or culture of ancient Greece and Rome. **2** Following a strict, established form, as a fugue. **3** Formal or serious in nature, form, etc. **4** High in quality; first-rate. — **clas'si·cal·ly** *adv.*

clas·si·cism [klas'ə·siz'əm] *n.* **1** The principles of simplicity, balance, etc., found in classical art. **2** Observance of these principles. — **clas'si·cist** *n.*

clas·si·fi·ca·tion [klas'ə·fə·kā'shən] *n.* The act, process, or result of classifying.

clas·si·fy [klas'ə·fī] *v.* **clas·si·fied, clas·si·fy·ing** To put or divide into classes or groups: to *classify* books. — **clas'si·fi'er** *n.*

class·mate [klas'māt] *n.* A member of the same class in school or college.

class·room [klas'rōōm'] *n.* A room in a school or college where classes are held.

clat·ter [klat'ər] **1** *v.* To move with or make a clashing noise. **2** *n.* A clashing noise, as of horses' hoofs on pavement. **3** *v.* To talk or chatter noisily. **4** *n.* Noisy chatter.

clause [klôz] *n.* **1** A group of words having a subject and predicate and forming part of a sentence. Some clauses can stand alone; others cannot. **2** A single point or article of a law, will, treaty, contract, etc.

claus·tro·pho·bi·a [klôs'trə·fō'bē·ə] *n.* A fear of being in a small, closed space.

clav·i·cle [klav'ə·kəl] *n.* The bone connecting the shoulder blade and breast-bone; collarbone.

clav·ier [klə·vir'] *n.* **1** A musical keyboard. **2** An early type of keyboard instrument.

claw [klô] **1** *n.* A sharp, hooked nail on the toe of an animal or bird. **2** *n.* A foot with claws. **3** *v.* To tear, scratch, dig, pull, etc., with or as if with claws. **4** *n.* A pincer of a lobster, crab, scorpion, etc. **5** *n.* Something shaped like a claw, as the forked end of a hammer.

Clavicles

clay [klā] *n.* **1** A fine-grained earth that can be molded when wet, used in making bricks, tiles, pottery, etc. **2** The human body: used in this sense in the Bible.

clay·ey [klā'ē] *adj.* **clay·i·er, clay·i·est** Of, like, full of, or covered with clay.

clean [klēn] **1** *adj.* Free from dirt or stain. **2** *v.* To make clean. **3** *v.* To do cleaning: We *clean* on Saturdays. **4** *adv.* To a condition of cleanness: to wash a cup *clean.* **5** *adj.* Complete: a *clean* miss. **6** *adv.* Wholly; completely: You're *clean* wrong. **7** *adj.* Wholesome; virtuous: a *clean* life. **8** *adj.* Free of faults or flaws: a *clean*

---

add, āce, câre, pälm;   end, ēqual;   it, īce;   odd, ōpen, ôrder;   tŏŏk, pōōl;   up, bûrn;
ə = a in *above*, e in *sicken*, i in *possible*, o in *melon*, u in *circus*;   yōō = u in *fuse*;   oil;   pout;
    check; ring; thin; this; zh in *vision*.   For ¶ reference, see page 64 · HOW TO

record. **9** *adj.* Neat in habits or work. **10** *adj.* Skillfully or properly made or done: a *clean* hit. **11** *adj.* Of pleasing proportions: *clean* features. **—clean out 1** To empty of contents, occupants, etc. **2** *informal* To use up all the money of. **—clean up 1** To clean completely. **2** *informal* To finish. **3** *slang* To make a large profit. **—clean′ness** *n.*

clean-cut [klēn′kut′] *adj.* **1** Sharply outlined; distinct. **2** Pleasing in appearance.

clean·er [klē′nər] *n.* **1** A person whose work is cleaning. **2** A substance or machine used for cleaning.

clean·ly [*adv.* klēn′lē, *adj.* klen′lē] *adv.*, *adj.* **clean·li·er, clean·li·est 1** *adv.* In a clean way. **2** *adj.* Clean and neat by habit: a *cleanly* person. **—clean·li·ness** [klen′lē·nis] *n.*

cleanse [klenz] *v.* **cleansed, cleans·ing** To make clean or pure.

cleans·er [klen′zər] *n.* A cleaning substance, as a detergent.

clear [klir] **1** *adj.* Easily seen through; transparent: a *clear* glass. **2** *adj.* Not blocked: a *clear* road. **3** *adj.* Free of clouds, fog, etc.: a *clear* day. **4** *adj.* With no blemish, scar, etc.: a *clear* skin. **5** *adj.* Distinct and without blurs: a *clear* picture. **6** *v.* To make clear. **7** *v.* To become clear. **8** *adj.* Plain and understandable: *clear* instructions. **9** *adv.* In a clear way: Shout loud and *clear*. **10** *adj.* Obvious; plain: a *clear* case of fraud. **11** *adj.* Keen and alert: a *clear* head. **12** *v.* To remove; get rid of: to *clear* away junk. **13** *v.* To get by, under, or over without touching: The ball *cleared* the fence. **14** *adv. informal* Completely: to go *clear* over a fence. **15** *adj.* Free from guilt or shame: a *clear* conscience. **16** *v.* To free of blame or suspicion: to *clear* a defendant. **17** *adj.* Net: a *clear* profit of $500. **18** *v.* To receive after all expenses, taxes, etc., have been deducted: to *clear* $50. **—clear up 1** To make clear. **2** To become clear, as weather. **3** To free from confusion or mystery. **—in the clear 1** In the open; not blocked or confined. **2** Free from guilt or suspicion. **3** Not in code. **—clear′ly** *adv.* **clear′ness** *n.*

clear·ance [klir′əns] *n.* **1** The act of clearing. **2** A clear space, especially between a moving thing and a stationary thing. **3** Disposal of goods, as in a sale. **4** Permission or approval.

clear-cut [klir′kut′] *adj.* **1** Sharply outlined. **2** Plain; obvious.

clear·ing [klir′ing] *n.* An area that is free of trees but surrounded by them.

Clearance

cleat [klēt] *n.* **1** A piece of wood, metal, etc., fastened to a surface to provide strength or secure footing. **2** A wood or metal fixture with arms to which a rope may be fastened.

cleav·age [klē′vij] *n.* **1** A cleaving. **2** A split.

3 A tendency in some rocks or crystals to split in certain planes.

cleave[1] [klēv] *v.* **cleft** or **cleaved** or **clove, cleft** or **cleaved** or **clo·ven, cleav·ing 1** To split, as with an ax or wedge. **2** To cut through; penetrate: The destroyer *cleaved* the waves.

cleave[2] [klēv] *v.* **cleaved, cleav·ing** To stick fast; cling: to *cleave* to a principle.

cleav·er [klē′vər] *n.* A butcher's chopper, with a broad, heavy blade and short handle.

clef [klef] *n.* In music, a sign that indicates the pitch of the notes written on each of the lines and spaces of a staff.

cleft [kleft] **1** Past tense and past participle of CLEAVE[1]. **2** *adj.* Divided or split, wholly or partly. **3** *n.* A division between two parts; crack or dent, as in the chin.

clem·a·tis [klem′ə·tis] *n.* A climbing vine usually having purple or white flowers.

treble clef

bass clef

clem·en·cy [klem′ən·sē] *n.* **1** Mildness in judging; mercy. **2** Mildness of weather, etc.

Clem·ens [klem′ənz], **Samuel Langhorne** The real name of Mark Twain. ◆ See TWAIN.

clem·ent [klem′ənt] *adj.* **1** Merciful or lenient; not harsh. **2** Mild: said about weather.

clench [klench] **1** *v.* To grasp or grip firmly. **2** *n.* A tight grip. **3** *v.* To close tightly or lock, as the fist or teeth.

Cle·o·pat·ra [klē′ə·pat′rə *or* klē′ə·pät′rə] *n.*, 69–30 B.C., last queen of ancient Egypt.

cler·gy [klûr′jē] *n.*, *pl.* **cler·gies** All the people ordained for the service of God, as ministers, priests, and rabbis.

cler·gy·man [klûr′jē·mən] *n.*, *pl.* **cler·gy·men** [klûr′jē·mən] A member of the clergy.

cler·ic [kler′ik] *n.* A member of the clergy.

cler·i·cal [kler′i·kəl] *adj.* **1** Of or related to clerks in offices or their work: a *clerical* error. **2** Having to do with the clergy.

clerk [klûrk] **1** *n.* An office worker who keeps records or accounts, attends to letters, etc. **2** *n.* An official or employee of a court, government, etc., who keeps records and performs other duties. **3** *n. U.S.* A person who sells goods in a store. **4** *v.* To work as a clerk.

Cleve·land [klēv′lənd] *n.* A city in NE Ohio.

Cleve·land [klēv′lənd], **(Stephen) Grover,** 1837–1908, 22nd and 24th president of the U.S., 1885–1889 and 1893–1897.

clev·er [klev′ər] *adj.* **1** Good at learning, solving problems, etc.; bright; ingenious. **2** Skillful, as in work with the hands. **3** Exhibiting skill, wit, or sharp thinking: a *clever* remark. **—clev′er·ly** *adv.* **—clev′er·ness** *n.*

clew [kloo] *n.* **1** A ball of yarn, thread, or cord. **2** Another spelling of CLUE. **3** A lower corner of a sail or a loop at the corner.

cli·ché [klē·shā′] *n.* An expression that has lost its original point and freshness from too much use. *As busy as a bee* is a cliché.

click [klik] **1** *n.* A short, sharp sound: the *click*

C

of knitting needles. **2** *v.* To make or cause to make a click or clicks: heels *clicking* across the floor. **3** *v. slang* To succeed.

cli·ent [klī′ənt] *n.* **1** A person consulting a professional man, as a lawyer. **2** A customer.

cli·en·tele [klī′ən·tel′] *n.* One's group of clients or customers: an exclusive *clientele*.

cliff [klif] *n.* A high, steep face of rock rising sharply above the ground or water below.

cli·mate [klī′mit] *n.* **1** The kind of weather a place usually has over a long period. **2** A region having given weather conditions: to go to a cool, dry *climate*. **3** An atmosphere or trend among people: the *climate* of opinion.

cli·mat·ic [klī·mat′ik] *adj.* Of or having to do with climate.

cli·max [klī′maks] *n.* The point of highest interest or greatest effect, coming at or near the end of an action, a series of events, etc.

climb [klīm] **1** *v.* To go up or down by means of the feet and sometimes the hands: to *climb* a mountain; to *climb* down from a ledge. **2** *n.* The action of climbing. **3** *n.* A place to be climbed: a steep *climb*. **4** *v.* To rise in position: The kite *climbed* higher. **5** *v.* To grow up, as certain vines, by twining around or clinging to a support.

climb·er [klī′mər] *n.* **1** A person or thing that climbs. **2** A plant that climbs, as a vine.

clime [klīm] *n.* A country, region, or climate: used mostly in poems.

clinch [klinch] **1** *v.* To fix firmly in place, as a driven nail or staple, by bending over the part that sticks out. **2** *v.* To make sure; settle: His offer to reduce the price *clinched* the sale. **3** *v.* To grip an opponent closely, as in boxing. **4** *n.* The act of clinching.

cling [kling] *v.* **clung, cling·ing** To hold tight; stick: His wet coat *clung* to his back.

clin·ic [klin′ik] *n.* **1** A special department of a hospital or medical school where people can come in for medical treatment, often at little or no cost. **2** A place where patients are studied and treated by specialists. **3** The teaching of medicine by treating patients in front of a class. **4** A place where advice on specific problems is given: a sales *clinic*.

clin·i·cal [klin′i·kəl] *adj.* **1** Of, like, or having to do with a clinic. **2** Used for sick people. **3** Coldly objective. — **clin′i·cal·ly** *adv.*

clink [klingk] **1** *v.* To make or cause to make a short, ringing sound, as of glasses struck together lightly. **2** *n.* A clinking sound.

clink·er [kling′kər] *n.* A stony mass of rough cinder sometimes left after coal burns.

clip¹ [klip] *v.* **clipped, clip·ping,** *n.* **1** *v.* To cut, cut short, or cut out, as with scissors or shears: to *clip* hair; to *clip* a coupon. **2** *v.* To trim the wool, hair, or excess growth of: to *clip* a sheep; to *clip* a hedge. **3** *n.* The act of clipping.

4 *v. informal* To strike with a quick, sharp blow: He was *clipped* on the chin. **5** *n. informal* A quick, sharp blow. **6** *v. informal* To move swiftly. **7** *n. informal* A quick pace: to go at a good *clip*.

clip² [klip] *n., v.* **clipped, clip·ping 1** *n.* A device that clasps or holds things together, especially papers. **2** *v.* To fasten with a clip: *Clip* the check to the letter.

clip·board [klip′bôrd′] *n.* A board with a clip at the top, used to hold papers for writing.

clip·per [klip′ər] *n.* **1** (*usually pl.*) A tool for clipping. **2** A person who clips. **3** A sailing ship of the 19th century, built for speed, having slender lines and an overhanging bow.

Clipboard

clip·ping [klip′ing] *n.* A part clipped off or out, as an article cut from a newspaper or a branch of a plant to form a new plant.

clique [klēk *or* klik] *n.* A small group whose members stick together and shut out outsiders.

cloak [klōk] **1** *n.* A loose outer garment, usually without sleeves. **2** *v.* To cover with a cloak. **3** *n.* Something that covers or hides: Darkness is a *cloak* for thieves. **4** *v.* To conceal: She *cloaked* her heartbreak under a smile.

cloak·room [klōk′rōōm′] *n.* A room where coats, hats, luggage, etc., are left for a short time.

clock¹ [klok] **1** *n.* An instrument for measuring and telling the time, usually by pointers, or hands, moving around a dial. A clock is not made to be worn or carried on the person as a watch is. **2** *v.* To measure the speed or time of: to *clock* a race.

clock² [klok] *n.* An ornamental design on the side of a sock or stocking at the ankle.

clock·wise [klok′wīz′] *adv., adj.* In the direction traveled by the hands of a clock: We skated around the pond *clockwise*.

clock·work [klok′wûrk′] *n.* A machine driven by a spring, used to run a clock, mechanical toy, etc. — **like clockwork** In a regular, precise, orderly way: The convention was well planned and everything went off *like clockwork*.

clod [klod] *n.* **1** A lump of earth, clay, etc. **2** A dull, stupid person; dolt.

clod·hop·per [klod′hop′ər] *n.* **1** *informal* A rustic person; hick. **2** (*pl.*) Big, heavy shoes.

clog [klog] *v.* **clogged, clog·ging,** *n.* **1** *v.* To make or become stopped up or blocked up: Hair had *clogged* the drain. **2** *v.* To slow down or hold back; hinder. **3** *n.* Anything interfering with movement. **4** *n.* A shoe with a wooden sole.

---

add, āce, câre, pälm; end, ēqual; it, īce; odd, ōpen, ôrder; tŏŏk, pōōl; up, bûrn; ə = a in *above*, e in *sicken*, i in *possible*, o in *melon*, u in *circus*; yōō = u in *fuse*; oil; pout; check; ring; thin; this; zh in *vision*. For ¶ reference, see page 64 · HOW TO

clois·ter [klois′tər] **1** *n.* A covered walk, often around a courtyard, as of a monastery or college. **2** *n.* A place of religious retirement; monastery or convent. **3** *v.* To put away from the world, as in a convent or monastery. **4** *n.* Any quiet, solitary place.

Cloister

close [*adj., adv.* klōs, *v., n.* klōz] *adj.* **clos·er, clos·est,** *adv., v.* **closed, clos·ing,** *n.* **1** *adj.* Near or near together in space, time, or relationship: *close* associates. **2** *adv.* Near: Stay *close* to home. **3** *adv.* In a close way; closely: following too *close.* **4** *v.* To bring together; join, as parts of an electric circuit. **5** *adj.* Having the parts near to each other; compact: a *close* weave. **6** *adj.* Lacking extra space; cramped: *close* quarters. **7** *adj.* Stuffy, stifling, or muggy, as a room or the weather. **8** *n.* [klōs] An enclosed place. **9** *v.* To shut, as a door. **10** *v.* To fill or block up: to *close* a gap. **11** *v.* To bring or come to an end: to *close* a prayer. **12** *n.* The end: the *close* of day. **13** *adj.* Near to the surface, as a shave or haircut. **14** *adj.* Very near to an original: a *close* resemblance. **15** *adj.* Near and dear: a *close* friend. **16** *adj.* Almost even: said about contests. **17** *adj.* Strict or careful: *close* attention. **18** *adj.* Stingy, as with money. **19** *adj.* Strictly guarded or hidden: *close* secrecy. **20** *adj.* Secretive: to be *close* about one's plans. **— close down** To stop operating; shut down. **— close in** To advance from all sides so as to prevent escape. **— close out** *U.S.* To sell all of, as merchandise, usually at reduced prices. **— close·ly** [klōs′lē] *adv.* **— close·ness** [klōs′·nis] *n.*

close call [klōs] *informal* A narrow escape.

clos·et [kloz′it] **1** *n.* *U.S.* A small room or alcove for storing clothes, linens, etc. **2** *n.* A small, private room. **3** *v.* To shut up in a room for a talk in private: The candidate was *closeted* with his campaign manager.

close-up [klōs′up′] *n.* **1** A picture or movie shot taken with the camera close to the subject. **2** A close look or view.

clo·sure [klō′zhər] *n.* **1** A closing or shutting up. **2** A way of putting an end to debate in a legislature in order to get a vote on an issue.

clot [klot] *n., v.* **clot·ted, clot·ting** **1** *n.* A mass resulting from a thickening of a liquid, as blood. **2** *v.* To form into clots or a clot.

cloth [klôth] *n., pl.* **cloths** [klôthz *or* klôths] **1** A fabric made of fibers, as wool, cotton, rayon, etc. **2** A piece of such material for a special use, as a tablecloth. **3** *adj.* use: a *cloth* coat. **— the cloth** The clergy.

clothe [klōth] *v.* **clothed** *or* **clad, cloth·ing** **1** To cover or provide with clothes; dress. **2** To cover: Spring *clothed* the trees in blossoms.

clothes [klō(th)z] *n.pl.* **1** The articles of dress worn by people, as dresses, suits, shirts, etc.; garments. **2** Bedclothes.

clothes·line [klō(th)z′līn′] *n.* A cord, rope, or wire on which to hang clothes to dry.

clothes·pin [klō(th)z′pin′] *n.* A forked peg or clamp used to fasten clothes on a line.

cloth·ier [klōth′yər] *n.* A person who makes or sells clothes or cloths.

cloth·ing [klō′thing] *n.* Clothes in general.

cloud [kloud] **1** *n.* A white or dark mass floating up in the air, made up of tiny particles of water or ice. **2** *n.* A visible mass of dust, smoke, or steam. **3** *n.* A cloudlike mass of things in motion: a *cloud* of gnats. **4** *n.* Something that darkens or threatens: a *cloud* of gloom. **5** *v.* To cover or become covered with or as if with clouds; dim or darken. **6** *n.* A dark vein, as in marble. **7** *n.* A milkiness, as in liquids.

cloud·burst [kloud′bûrst′] *n.* A sudden, heavy downpour of rain.

cloud chamber A closed vessel containing air or gas overloaded with water vapor that forms dense fog along the paths taken by charged particles. Cloud chambers are used for observing the behavior of atomic radiation.

cloud·less [kloud′lis] *adj.* Free of clouds.

cloud·y [klou′dē] *adj.* **cloud·i·er, cloud·i·est** **1** Overcast with clouds. **2** Of or like clouds. **3** Not clear; misty, murky, etc. **4** Streaked, as marble. **5** Gloomy. **— cloud′i·ness** *n.*

clout [klout] *informal* **1** *n.* A heavy blow. **2** *n.* In baseball, a long hit. **3** *v.* To hit hard.

clove[1] [klōv] *n.* A dried flower bud of a tropical evergreen tree used as a spice in cookery.

clove[2] [klōv] *n.* One of the small inner sections of a large plant bulb, as of garlic.

clove[3] [klōv] An alternative past tense of CLEAVE[1].

clo·ven [klō′vən] **1** An alternative past participle of CLEAVE[1]. **2** *adj.* Split, as a hoof.

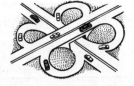

Cloven hoof

clo·ver [klō′vər] *n.* A low-growing plant with leaves normally having three leaflets but on rare occasions, four. It has fragrant white, red, yellow, or purple blossoms. It is grown as rich food for horses and cattle. **— in clover** Enjoying prosperity or luxuries without working.

clo·ver·leaf [klō′vər·lēf′] *n., pl.* **clo·ver·leafs** An intersection in which two highways crossing at different levels are connected by a system of curving ramps that allow a vehicle to change roads without interference.

Cloverleaf

clown [kloun] **1** *n.* A man in a circus or pantomime who entertains by jokes, tricks, etc.; jester; buffoon. **2** *v.* To behave like a clown, as by acting silly or playing tricks. **3** *n.* A coarse or rude person; boor. — **clown'ish** *adj.*

cloy [kloi] *v.* To displease with too much of a good thing: appetites *cloyed* with sweets.

club [klub] *n.*, *v.* **clubbed, club·bing 1** *n.* A heavy wooden stick for use as a weapon, generally thicker at one end. **2** *v.* To beat, as with a club. **3** *n.* A stick or bat used to hit a ball: a golf *club*. **4** *n.* A figure like this: ♣. **5** *n.* A playing card of the suit marked with black club figures. **6** *n.* (*pl.*) The suit so marked. **7** *n.* A group of people organized for enjoyment or for some purpose: a social *club*. **8** *n.* The building or room where such a group meets. **9** *v.* To unite for some purpose.

club·foot [klub'foot'] *n.*, *pl.* **club·feet** [klub'·fēt'] A deformity, usually present from birth, in which the foot is twisted out of shape.

club sandwich A sandwich with many layers.

cluck [kluk] **1** *v.* To make a low, throaty, clicking sound such as a hen makes when calling her chicks. **2** *n.* Such a sound.

clue [kloo] *n.* A hint, piece of evidence, etc., helpful in solving a problem or mystery.

clump [klump] **1** *n.* A group of similar things very close together; tight cluster: a *clump* of bushes. **2** *n.* An irregular mass; lump: a *clump* of earth. **3** *n.* A heavy, dull sound, as of tramping. **4** *v.* To walk heavily and noisily.

clum·sy [klum'zē] *adj.* **clum·si·er, clum·si·est 1** Lacking control; not graceful; awkward: a *clumsy* child. **2** Not well made, said, or done: a *clumsy* raft; *clumsy* excuses. — **clum'si·ly** *adv.* — **clum'si·ness** *n.*

clung [klung] Past tense and past participle of CLING: The monkey *clung* to the cage.

clus·ter [klus'tər] **1** *n.* A group of things of the same kind growing or found together: a flower *cluster*. **2** *v.* To form into a cluster or clusters: The campers *clustered* around the fire.

clutch [kluch] **1** *v.* To grasp and hold firmly. **2** *n.* A tight grip or grasp. **3** *n.* (*pl.*) Power or control: in the *clutches* of the police. **4** *v.* To seize or reach for eagerly or desperately; snatch: **5** *n.* A device in a machine for connecting or disconnecting driving and driven parts. Many cars have clutches to permit the shifting of gears or stopping.

clut·ter [klut'ər] **1** *n.* A collection of things scattered without order; litter. **2** *v.* To fill or cover with disordered or worthless things: to *clutter* up a closet or a shelf.

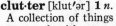

A cluttered desk

cm. Abbreviation of: **1** CENTIMETER. **2** Centimeters.

co- A prefix meaning: **1** Together, as in *coexist*, to exist together. **2** With another; joint, as in *copartner*, a joint partner. **3** Equally, as in *coextensive*, equally extensive.

c/o or **c.o.** Abbreviation of *in care of:* I wrote him a letter *c/o* the Jones family.

Co The symbol for the element COBALT.

Co. Abbreviation of COMPANY.

coach [kōch] **1** *n.* An old-fashioned, closed carriage pulled by horses. **2** *n.* A bus or railroad car in which passengers sit. **3** *n.* A teacher or trainer for pupils, athletes, actors, etc. **4** *v.* To instruct, train, or direct. **5** *v.* To tutor, as for a test.

coach·man [kōch'mən] *n.*, *pl.* **coach·men** [kōch'mən] A man who drives a coach.

co·ag·u·late [kō·ag'yə·lāt] *v.* **co·ag·u·lat·ed, co·ag·u·lat·ing** To change from a liquid to a thick mass; clot. — **co·ag'u·la'tion** *n.*

coal [kōl] **1** *n.* A black or dark brown mineral, mostly carbon, which gives off heat when burned. Coal was formed by decaying plants covered by land or water and under great pressure. **2** *n.* A glowing piece of coal, wood, etc.; ember. **3** *v.* To supply with or take on coal.

co·a·lesce [kō'ə·les'] *v.* **co·a·lesced, co·a·lesc·ing** To grow or come together into one; fuse, blend, or unite: Five groups of wagons *coalesced* to make a big train.

co·a·li·tion [kō'ə·lish'ən] *n.* A temporary alliance of leaders, parties, or nations.

coal·scut·tle [kōl'skut'(ə)l] A pail for carrying coal.

coal tar A black, gummy substance produced by the distillation of soft coal. It is the raw material for dyes, explosives, drugs, etc.

coarse [kôrs] *adj.* **coars·er, coars·est 1** Composed of large particles; not fine: *coarse* salt. **2** Rough: *coarse* skin. **3** Not refined; vulgar: *coarse* talk. **4** Inferior in quality: *coarse* food. — **coarse'ly** *adv.* — **coarse'ness** *n.*

coars·en [kôr'sən] *v.* To make or become coarse.

coast [kōst] **1** *n.* The land next to the sea; seashore. **2** *v.* To sail along a coast or the coast of. **3** *n.* A region near the sea. **4** *v.* To slide or ride down a slope, as on a sled or bicycle, with no force applied.

coast·al [kōs'təl] *adj.* Of, on, or near a coast: *coastal* waters.

coast·er [kōs'tər] *n.* **1** A person or ship that trades along a coast. **2** A sled, toboggan, etc., for coasting. **3** A small tray set under a glass to protect the surface of a table, etc.

coast guard 1 A naval or military group that patrols coasts, saves lives, prevents smuggling, etc. **2** (*written* **Coast Guard**) In the U.S., such a group that operates in peacetime under

add, āce, câre, pälm; end, ēqual; it, īce; odd, ōpen, ôrder; took, pool; up, bûrn;
ə = a in *above*, e in *sicken*, i in *possible*, o in *melon*, u in *circus*; yoo = u in *fuse*; oil; pout.
check; ring; thin; this; zh in *vision*. For ¶ reference, see page 64 · HOW TO

the Treasury Department and in wartime under the U.S. Navy.

coast·line [kōst′līn′] *n.* The outline or boundary of a coast.

coast·wise [kōst′wīz′] *adj.*, *adv.* Along the coast: a *coastwise* trade.

coat [kōt] **1** *n.* An outer garment with sleeves, as the jacket of a suit, an overcoat, etc. **2** *n.* A natural covering or skin, as the fur of an animal. **3** *n.* Any layer covering a surface, as paint, ice, etc. **4** *v.* To cover with a layer: *Coat* the walls with paint.

coat·ing [kō′ting] *n.* **1** A covering; layer; coat. **2** Cloth for coats.

coat of arms A design, as on a shield, used as the symbol of a family, nation, etc.

coat of mail *pl.* **coats of mail** A suit of armor made of metal chain or plates.

coax [kōks] *v.* **1** To ask or persuade in a gentle, flattering manner; wheedle: She *coaxed* her mother to bake a cake. **2** To obtain by coaxing: to *coax* a promise from someone.

co·ax·i·al cable [kō·ak′sē·əl] An electrical cable made up of pairs of conductors arranged so that one of each pair surrounds the other and is separated from it by an insulator, used to carry radio and television signals.

Coat of arms

cob [kob] *n.* **1** The center of an ear of corn, on which the kernels grow. **2** A male swan. **3** A heavy horse with short legs.

co·balt [kō′bôlt] *n.* A hard, glossy, pinkish gray metallic element, used in making alloys and a brilliant blue pigment.

cob·ble¹ [kob′əl] *n.* A cobblestone.

cob·ble² [kob′əl] *v.* **cob·bled, cob·bling** To make or repair, as boots or shoes.

cob·bler¹ [kob′lər] *n.* A shoemaker.

cob·bler² [kob′lər] *n.* A fruit pie baked in a deep dish, with no bottom crust.

cob·ble·stone [kob′əl·stōn′] *n.* A rounded stone formerly used for paving streets.

co·bra [kō′brə] *n.* A very poisonous snake of Asia and Africa that can swell its neck into a hood when excited.

cob·web [kob′web′] *n.* **1** The delicate web spun by a spider. **2** Anything delicate like a cobweb.

co·caine [kō·kān′ *or* kō′kān] *n.* A white, bitter substance, used as a drug to deaden pain.

coc·cus [kok′əs] *n.*, *pl.* **coc·ci** [kok′sī] Any of a large group of bacteria having an oval shape.

coch·le·a [kok′lē·ə] *n.*, *pl.* **coch·le·ae** [kok′·li·ē] A small, hollow organ in the inner ear shaped like a snail shell, containing the sensory ends of the auditory nerve.

cock¹ [kok] **1** *n.* A male bird, especially a rooster. **2** *n.* A faucet or tap. **3** *n.* The hammer of a gun or its position when set for firing. **4** *v.*

To put the cock of (a gun) into firing position. **5** *v.* To put into a ready position: He *cocked* his fists. **6** *v.* To turn up or to one side alertly or inquisitively: to *cock* the head. **7** *n.* A tipping or turning up, as of a hat brim: a jaunty *cock.*

cock² [kok] *n.* A cone-shaped pile of hay or straw.

cock·ade [kok·ād′] *n.* A rosette or decoration worn on the hat, lapel, etc.

cock·a·too [kok′ə·tōō′ *or* kok′ə·tōō] *n.*, *pl.* **cock·a·toos** Any of several brightly colored parrots with crests, found in Australasia.

cock·a·trice [kok′ə·tris] *n.* In folk tales, a serpent hatched from a bird's egg, whose look was said to be deadly.

cock·er·el [kok′ər·əl] *n.* A young rooster.

cock·er spaniel [kok′ər] A small dog with long ears and silky hair, used as a house pet and for hunting. It is also called a **cocker.**

cock·eyed [kok′īd′] *adj.* **1** Cross-eyed. **2** *slang* Off center; crooked. **3** *slang* Ridiculous.

cock·le¹ [kok′əl] *n.* **1** An edible shellfish with ridged shells. **2** A cockleshell. **3** A wrinkle; pucker. — **warm the cockles of one's heart** To give heartfelt joy or pleasure.

Cocker spaniel, 15 in. high at shoulder

cock·le² [kok′əl] *n.* A weed that grows among grain.

cock·le·bur [kok′əl·bûr′] *n.* A coarse weed having prickly burs.

cock·le·shell [kok′əl·shel′] *n.* **1** The shell of a cockle. **2** A frail, light boat.

cock·ney [kok′nē] *n.*, *pl.* **cock·neys 1** (*often written* **Cockney**) A person born or living in the East End of London, England. **2** The dialect of this section of London. **3** *adj. use:* cockney speech.

cock·pit [kok′pit′] *n.* **1** A compartment in some airplanes where the pilot and others sit. **2** A low part aft of the decked area of a sailboat or motorboat.

cock·roach [kok′rōch′] *n.* An insect with a flat, oval, dark brown body that is a household pest.

cocks·comb [koks′kōm′] *n.* **1** The fleshy, red growth on a rooster's head. **2** A plant with showy red or yellowish flowers. **3** A jester's cap.

cock·sure [kok′shŏŏr′] *adj.* **1** Absolutely sure. **2** Too sure of oneself; too self-confident.

cock·tail [kok′tāl′] *n.* **1** Any of various mixed alcoholic drinks. **2** An appetizer served at the start of a meal, as seafood in a sauce.

cock·y [kok′ē] *adj.* **cock·i·er, cock·i·est** *informal* Too sure of oneself; boldly conceited. — **cock′i·ly** *adv.*

co·co [kō′kō] *n.*, *pl.* **co·cos 1** The coconut palm. **2** Its fruit, the coconut.

co·coa [kō′kō] *n.* **1** A powder made from the seeds of the cacao; chocolate. **2** A beverage made from cocoa. **3** *adj.*, *n.* Light, reddish brown.

co·co·nut [kō′kə·nut′] *n.* The large fruit of the

coconut palm with a hard shell, white meat, and a center filled with a sweet liquid.

coconut palm A tropical palm bearing coconuts.

co·coon [kə·kōōn′] *n.* The envelope spun by the larvae of certain insects for protection while they are undergoing changes, as from a caterpillar to a moth.

coco palm Another name for the COCONUT PALM.

cod [kod] *n., pl.* **cod** or **cods** An important food fish of the northern Atlantic.

Cod [kod], **Cape** A peninsula projecting into the Atlantic Ocean from SE Massachusetts.

Cape Cod Bay
CAPE COD
Atlantic Ocean

C.O.D. or **c.o.d.** Abbreviation of: **1** Cash on delivery. **2** Collect on delivery.

cod·dle [kod′(ə)l] *v.* **cod·dled, cod·dling 1** To treat gently, as a baby or sick person; pamper. **2** To cook in hot water, as eggs.

code [kōd] *n., v.* **cod·ed, cod·ing 1** *n.* A body of laws, arranged in a systematic way. **2** *n.* Any set of rules or principles: the *code* of honor. **3** *v.* To arrange, as laws, in an orderly way. **4** *n.* A set of signals used in communication: the Morse *code.* **5** *n.* A set of letters, words, or symbols that has a secret meaning, used in transmitting messages. **6** *v.* To put (a message, etc.) into code.

co·deine [kō′dēn] *n.* A drug obtained from opium and used as a mild narcotic to deaden pain.

cod·fish [kod′fish] *n., pl.* **cod·fish** or **cod·fish·es** Another word for COD.

codg·er [koj′ər] *n. informal* An odd or grouchy man, especially if he is old.

cod·i·fy [kod′ə·fī or kō′də·fī] *v.* **cod·i·fied, cod·i·fy·ing** To put into a code, as laws. **— cod′i·fi·ca′tion** *n.*

cod·ling moth [kod′ling] A moth whose larvae feed on the insides of apples, pears, etc.

cod-liv·er oil [kod′liv′ər] Oil from the livers of cod, used as a source of vitamins A and D.

Co·dy [kō′dē], **William F.** See BUFFALO BILL.

co·ed or **co-ed** [kō′ed′] *n. informal* A girl or woman student at a coeducational college.

co·ed·u·ca·tion·al [kō′ej·ōō·kā′shən·əl] *adj.* Indicating a school or college to which both boys and girls are admitted and allowed to attend classes together.

co·ef·fi·cient [kō′ə·fish′ənt] *n.* A number placed in front of an algebraic expression and multiplying it: In the expression $3y = 9$, 3 is the *coefficient* of *y.*

co·erce [kō·ûrs′] *v.* **co·erced, co·erc·ing** To

force or compel into doing something, as by threats or violence: They *coerced* him into paying. **— co·er·cion** [kō·ûr′shən] *n.*

co·er·cive [kō·ûr′siv] *adj.* Tending to coerce.

co·ex·ist [kō′ig·zist′] *v.* To live or exist together in the same place or at the same time.

co·ex·ist·ence [kō′ig·zis′təns] *n.* **1** The state of coexisting. **2** The living together in peace of nations with different political systems or ways of thinking.

cof·fee [kôf′ē] **1** *n.* A beverage made from the roasted and ground seeds or beans of a tropical shrub. **2** *n.* These seeds or beans. **3** *n.* The shrub on which they grow. **4** *n., adj.* Brown, as the color of coffee with cream. ♦ *Coffee* comes from an Arabic word.

coffee bean The berry or seed of a tropical shrub from which coffee is made.

cof·fer [kôf′ər] *n.* **1** A chest or box, especially one for keeping money or valuables. **2** *(pl.)* Financial resources; a treasury.

cof·fin [kôf′in] *n.* The box or case in which a dead body is buried.

cog [kog] *n.* **1** A tooth or one of a series of teeth on the edge of a wheel, used to transmit or receive motion or power. **2** A cogwheel. **3** A person who plays a small but necessary part in a large process or business.

co·gent [kō′jənt] *adj.* Causing belief, agreement, or action; forceful; convincing: a *cogent* speech. **— co′gen·cy** *n.* **— co′gent·ly** *adv.*

cog·i·tate [koj′ə·tāt] *v.* **cog·i·tat·ed, cog·i·tat·ing** To think with care; ponder; meditate. **— cog′i·ta′tion** *n.*

co·gnac [kōn′yak or kon′yak] *n.* **1** A kind of brandy from western France. **2** Any brandy.

cog·nate [kog′nāt] *adj.* Related, as by blood or by common source: French and Spanish are *cognate* languages since both come from Latin.

cog·ni·zance [kog′nə·zəns] *n.* The knowing or understanding of something; attention; notice. **— take cognizance of** To notice; perceive.

cog·ni·zant [kog′nə·zənt] *adj.* Having knowledge; aware: Are you *cognizant* of the situation?

cog·wheel [kog′(h)wēl′] *n.* A wheel with cogs or teeth, used to transmit or receive motion.

co·here [kō·hir′] *v.* **co·hered, co·her·ing 1** To stick or hold together: Grains of salt often *cohere* into a lump. **2** To show a logical connection, as among the parts: The story *coheres.*

Cogwheels

co·her·ent [kō·hir′ənt] *adj.* **1** Having logical order or connection; consistent: a *coherent* essay. **2** Sticking or holding together, as particles of the same substance. **— co·her′·ence** *n.* **— co·her′ent·ly** *adv.*

co·he·sion [kō·hē′zhən] *n.* **1** The act or

add, āce, câre, pälm; end, ēqual; it, īce; odd, ōpen, ôrder; tŏŏk, pōōl; up, bûrn;
ə = a in *above,* e in *sicken,* i in *possible,* o in *melon,* u in *circus;* yōō = u in *fuse;* oil; pout;
check; ring; thin; this; zh in *vision.* For ¶ reference, see page 64 · HOW TO

condition of cohering. **2** In physics, the force by which similar molecules are held together.

co·he·sive [kō·hē′siv] *adj.* Having or showing cohesion. **— co·he′sive·ness** *n.*

co·hort [kō′hôrt] *n.* **1** The tenth part of an ancient Roman legion of soldiers, from 300 to 600 men. **2** A band or group, especially of warriors. **3** A companion or follower: He was led in by his *cohorts.*

coif [koif] *n.* A close-fitting cap or hood, as worn by certain nuns under the veil.

coif·fure [kwä·fyŏor′] *n.* A lady's hairdo.

coil [koil] **1** *n.* A ring or spiral formed by twisting or winding: He caught his leg in a *coil* of the rope. **2** *n.* A series of coils: He wound the rope into a *coil.* **3** *v.* To wind into a coil. **4** *n.* A wire wound in a spiral, usually used for an electromagnetic effect.

coin [koin] **1** *n.* A piece of metal stamped by a government for use as money. **2** *v.* To make (coins) of metal. **3** *n.* Metal money as a whole: the *coin* of the realm. **4** *v.* To make up or invent, as a word or phrase.

coin·age [koi′nij] *n.* **1** The act or right of making coins. **2** The coins made. **3** Something newly invented or created, as a word or phrase.

co·in·cide [kō′in·sīd′] *v.* **co·in·cid·ed, co·in·cid·ing** **1** To be the same size and take up the same space: If one of these two circles OO were placed on the other, the two would coincide. **2** To occur at the same time: The holiday *coincides* with my vacation. **3** To agree exactly: His idea *coincided* with mine.

co·in·ci·dence [kō·in′sə·dəns] *n.* **1** A seemingly remarkable chance occurrence or appearance of two things at the same place or time: It was a *coincidence* that our coats were exactly alike. **2** The act or condition of coinciding.

co·in·ci·den·tal [kō·in′sə·den′təl] *adj.* Involving coincidence; happening at the same time purely by chance. **— co·in′ci·den′tal·ly** *adv.*

coke [kōk] *n.* A solid fuel made from coal that has been heated to remove gases.

Col. Abbreviation of COLONEL.

col·an·der [kul′ən·dər *or* kol′ən·dər] *n.* A kitchen utensil with holes, for draining off liquids from foods.

cold [kōld] **1** *adj.* Having little heat or a low temperature: a *cold* night; a *cold* iron; *cold* hands. **2** *n.* The lack of heat: The *cold* invigorates me. **3** *adj.* Feeling cold or chilled: I'm *cold.* **4** *adj.*

Colander

Lacking the usual heat: Eat your soup before it gets *cold.* **5** *adj.* Lacking affection or sympathy: She's a *cold* person. **6** *adj.* Not new or fresh; stale: a *cold* trail. **7** *n.* A mild illness with symptoms of sneezing, running nose, coughing, and sometimes fever. **— catch cold** To become ill with a cold. **— cold′ly** *adv.* **— cold′·ness** *n.*

cold-blood·ed [kōld′blud′id] *adj.* **1** Heartless

and cruel: a *cold-blooded* crime. **2** Having blood whose temperature changes with that of the surrounding air or water: Snakes and fish are *cold-blooded* creatures.

cold cream A cleansing salve for the skin.

cold front The forward edge of a cold mass of air coming forward against a warm air mass.

cold shoulder *informal* A snub or show of indifference.

cold sore A blister or sore on the mouth that often comes with a cold or fever.

cold war An international conflict expressed in diplomatic and economic rivalry rather than war.

Cole·ridge [kōl′rij], **Samuel Taylor,** 1772–1834, English poet.

cole·slaw [kōl′slô′] or **cole slaw** *n.* A salad made of finely shredded raw cabbage.

col·ic [kol′ik] *n.* A pain in the abdomen that comes from muscular spasms. **— col′ick·y** *adj.*

col·i·se·um [kol′ə·sē′əm] *n.* **1** A building or stadium for exhibitions, sports events, etc. **2** (*written* **Coliseum**) A spelling of COLOSSEUM.

col·lab·o·rate [kə·lab′ə·rāt] *v.* **col·lab·o·rat·ed, col·lab·o·rat·ing** **1** To work together, as on literary or scientific efforts: They *collaborated* on the play. **2** To work against one's country by helping the enemy. **— col·lab′o·ra′tion** *n.* **— col·lab′o·ra′tor** *n.*

col·lage [kə·läzh′] *n.* A decorative composition of bits of paper, cloth, or other materials attached to a surface.

A collage

col·lapse [kə·laps′] *v.* **col·lapsed, col·laps·ing,** *n.* **1** *v.* To give way; cave in: The old barn *collapsed.* **2** *v.* To fail completely: Our plans *collapsed.* **3** *v.* To lose health or strength: to *collapse* from overwork. **4** *n.* The act of collapsing. **5** *n.* A collapsed condition: a mental *collapse.* **6** *v.* To fold together compactly: He *collapsed* the table.

col·laps·i·ble [kə·laps′ə·bəl] *adj.* Capable of being folded: a *collapsible* chair.

col·lar [kol′ər] **1** *n.* A part of a garment or a separate piece of fabric worn at the neck. **2** *v.* To put a collar on. **3** *v.* To grab by the collar. **4** *n.* A metal or leather piece placed around an animal's neck: a dog *collar.* **5** *n.* The part of a harness that fits over a horse's neck. **6** *n.* A ring-shaped part in a machine encircling a rod or a shaft and used to limit motion.

col·lar·bone [kol′ər·bōn′] *n.* The clavicle.

col·lat·er·al [kə·lat′ər·əl] **1** *adj.* Aside from the main subject; secondary: a *collateral* argument. **2** *adj.* Going with the main part; parallel. **3** *adj.* Additional; supporting: *collateral* evidence. **4** *n.* Money or property used as security for a loan. **5** *adj.* Descended from the same ancestors but in a different line or branch: A cousin is a *collateral* relative.

col·la·tion [kə·lā′shən] *n.* A light meal.

col·league [kol'ēg] *n.* A fellow worker in a profession or organization; associate.

col·lect [kə·lekt'] **1** *v.* To gather together; assemble: *Collect* all the papers; A crowd *collected*. **2** *v.* To accumulate, as sand or dust. **3** *v.* To bring together, as for study or as a hobby: He *collects* stamps. **4** *v.* To seek and receive as payments: to *collect* taxes. **5** *adv., adj.* To be paid for by the receiver: a *collect* call. **6** *v.* To regain control of: to *collect* one's wits.

col·lect·ed [kə·lek'tid] *adj.* Calm and composed.

col·lec·tion [kə·lek'shən] *n.* **1** The act of collecting. **2** The things collected: a *collection* of stamps. **3** A pile that has gathered: a *collection* of dirt. **4** An asking for and gathering of money, as for a church or charity.

col·lec·tive [kə·lek'tiv] **1** *adj.* Formed or gathered together by collecting: the *collective* result of wear. **2** *adj.* Of, having to do with, run by, or coming from a group: a *collective* effort; a *collective* farm. **3** *n.* An enterprise in which a group works together, especially a farm. **4** *adj.* Indicating a group of individuals, but in the singular form: "Audience" is a *collective* noun. **— col·lec'tive·ly** *adv.*

collective bargaining Negotiation between an employer and workers organized as a group, as to wages, hours, etc.

col·lec·tor [kə·lek'tər] *n.* A person or thing that collects: The government is the *collector* of taxes; a *collector* of paintings.

col·leen [kol'ēn *or* kə·lēn'] *n.* An Irish girl.

col·lege [kol'ij] *n.* **1** A school of higher learning that gives a bachelor's degree to students who have completed a course of study. **2** A school for instruction in a special field or profession, often attached to a university: a *college* of medicine. **3** A group of people who have certain duties and rights: the electoral *college.*

col·le·giate [kə·lē'jit] *adj.* **1** Of, like, or having to do with a college. **2** Of or for college students.

col·lide [kə·līd'] *v.* **col·lid·ed, col·lid·ing** **1** To come together with a strong or violent impact; crash: The two cars *collided*. **2** To come into conflict; disagree; clash.

col·lie [kol'ē] *n.* A breed of large dog, sometimes used to herd sheep. It has a long head and a heavy coat.

col·lier [kol'yər] *n.* *British* **1** A coal miner. **2** A ship used to carry coal.

col·lier·y [kol'yər·ē] *n., pl.* **col·lier·ies** A coal mine.

col·li·sion [kə·lizh'ən] *n.* **1** A violent colliding: The *collision*

Collie, about 25 in. high at shoulder

involved four cars. **2** A clash of views; conflict: a *collision* of ideas.

col·loid [kol'oid] *n.* A substance formed when small particles are suspended in a liquid or gas, neither dissolved nor sinking, as blood, gelatin, etc. **— col·loi·dal** [kə·loid'(ə)l] *n.*

col·lo·qui·al [kə·lō'kwē·əl] *adj.* Used in or appropriate to ordinary, informal talk; not formal. **— col·lo'qui·al·ly** *adv.*

col·lo·qui·al·ism [kə·lō'kwē·əl·iz'əm] *n.* A word or phrase used in conversation but not in formal speech or writing.

col·lo·quy [kol'ə·kwē] *n., pl.* **col·lo·quies** A talk or conference, especially a formal one.

col·lu·sion [kə·lōō'zhən] *n.* A secret agreement for a wrongful purpose, as to cheat or deceive.

Colo. Abbreviation of COLORADO.

co·logne [kə·lōn'] *n.* A scented toilet water.

Co·lom·bi·a [kə·lum'bē·ə] *n.* A country in NW South America. **— Co·lom'bi·an** *adj., n.*

co·lon[1] [kō'lən] *n.* The largest part of the large intestine, above the rectum.

co·lon[2] [kō'lən] *n.* A punctuation mark (:) used to introduce a long quotation, a series, an example, etc.

colo·nel [kûr'nəl] *n.* A military rank. In the U.S. Army, a colonel is a commissioned officer ranking below a brigadier general.

co·lo·ni·al [kə·lō'nē·əl] **1** *adj.* Of, having to do with, or living in a colony or colonies, especially the 13 British colonies that became the U.S. **2** *n.* A person who lives in a colony. **3** *adj.* Of a style of architecture or furniture used originally in the American colonies.

col·o·nist [kol'ə·nist] *n.* **1** A person who lives in a colony. **2** A settler or founder of a colony.

col·o·nize [kol'ə·nīz] *v.* **col·o·nized, col·o·niz·ing** **1** To set up a colony in; settle: The British *colonized* New England. **2** To settle in colonies. **— col'o·ni·za'tion** *n.* **— col'o·niz'er** *n.* ¶3

col·on·nade [kol'ə·nād'] *n.* A row of regularly spaced columns.

col·o·ny [kol'ə·nē] *n., pl.* **col·o·nies** **1** A group of people who live in a land separate from, but under the control of, the country from which they came. **2** The region where they settle. **3** Any territory governed by a distant state. **4** A group of people from the same country or who have the same occupation, living together in one area: a writers' *colony*. **5** A group of organisms of the same kind that live or grow together: Sponges grow in *colonies*.

Colonnade

col·or [kul'ər] **1** *n.* The visual sensation produced when light of particular wavelengths strikes the retina of the eye. It ranges from bright red for the longest to deep violet for the shortest wavelength, and includes all tones from

add, āce, câre, pälm; end, ēqual; it, īce; odd, ōpen, ôrder; tŏŏk, pōōl; up, bûrn; ə = a in *above*, e in *sicken*, i in *possible*, o in *melon*, u in *circus*; yōō = u in *fuse*; oil; pout; **ch**eck; **r**ing; **th**in; **th**is; **zh** in *vision*. For ¶ reference, see page 64 · HOW TO

white to black. **2** *n.* Any paint, dye, etc., capable of giving color. **3** *v.* To apply or give color to. **4** *v.* To take on or change color, as fruit. **5** *n.* The hue of the skin; complexion. **6** *v.* To blush. **7** *n.* Appearance; aspect: His argument had the *color* of reason. **8** *v.* To change or distort: Envy *colored* his statement. **9** *n.* (*pl.*) Nature; beliefs, especially in the expression **show one's true colors,** to show one's real nature. **10** *n.* Liveliness: to speak with *color.* **11** *n.* (*pl.*) The flag or banner of a country, military unit, etc. **— change color 1** To turn pale. **2** To blush. **— with flying colors** Very successfully. ¶1

Col·o·ra·do [kol′ə·rä′dō *or* kol′ə·rad′ō] *n.* **1** A state in the western U.S. **2** A river flowing from Colorado through Utah and Arizona.

col·or·a·tion [kul′ə·rā′shən] *n.* The arrangement of colors, as of an animal or plant; coloring.

col·or·blind [kul′ər·blīnd′] *adj.* Incapable of telling the difference between two or more colors because of some defect in the eyes. ¶1

col·ored [kul′ərd] *adj.* **1** Having color. **2** Of a race not white: often used to mean BLACK: *colored* people. **3** Influenced; biased. ¶1

col·or·ful [kul′ər·fəl] *adj.* **1** Full of colors. **2** Vivid; interesting: a *colorful* story. **— col′·or·ful·ly** *adv.* **— col′or·ful·ness** *n.* ¶1

col·or·ing [kul′ər·ing] *n.* **1** The act or style of applying colors. **2** Something that gives color, as a dye or paint: food *coloring.* **3** The appearance of something in respect to its color. ¶1

col·or·less [kul′ər·lis] *adj.* **1** Without color. **2** Lacking brightness or variety; dull: a *colorless* existence; a *colorless* speech. ¶1

co·los·sal [kə·los′əl] *adj.* **1** Of enormous size; huge. **2** *informal* Beyond belief: *colossal* nerve. **— co·los′sal·ly** *adv.*

Col·os·se·um [kol′ə·sē′əm] *n.* A stadium built in Rome A.D. 75–80 and still partly standing.

co·los·sus [kə·los′əs] *n., pl.* **co·los·si** [kə·los′ī] *or* **co·los·sus·es 1** A gigantic statue. **2** Anything large or great.

Colossus of Rhodes A gigantic statue of Apollo that was set at the entrance to the harbor of Rhodes about 285 B.C.

colt [kōlt] *n.* A young horse or donkey, especially a male.

Co·lum·bi·a [kə·lum′bē·ə] *n.* **1** The capital of South Carolina. **2** A river in sw Canada and the NW U.S. **3** The U.S.: used only in poems.

col·um·bine [kol′əm·bīn] *n.* **1** A plant with variously colored flowers of five petals. **2** (*written* **Columbine**) A stock character in pantomimes, the sweetheart of Harlequin.

Co·lum·bus [kə·lum′bəs], **Christopher,** 1446?–1506, Italian explorer who discovered America for Spain in 1492.

col·umn [kol′əm] *n.* **1** A tall post or pillar shaped like a cylinder, used as a support in or around a building or for decoration. **2** Something shaped like a column: the spinal *column.* **3** A tall, narrow section of a page, set off by a line or space at the side: This page has two *columns.* **4** A feature article, usually by one person, that appears regularly in a newspaper or magazine: a society *column;* a bridge *column.* **5** A military or naval formation of men, rows of men, ships, etc., one behind another.

Columns

col·um·nist [kol′əm·nist] *n.* A person who writes a column in a newspaper or magazine.

com- A prefix meaning: **1** With, as in *combat,* to fight with. **2** Together, as in *compare,* to bring together.

co·ma [kō′mə] *n.* A state of deep and lasting unconsciousness, caused by injury, disease, or poison.

comb [kōm] **1** *n.* A strip of hard material with teeth, used to arrange or clean hair, or to keep it neat. **2** *n.* A thing like this used to clean and straighten wool or other fibers. **3** *v.* To arrange or clean, as hair or wool, with a comb. **4** *v.* To search carefully: He *combed* the old town for the house where he was born. **5** *n.* The fleshy, red outgrowth on the head of a fowl. **6** *n.* Something like a fowl's comb in shape or position, as the top of a breaking wave. **7** *n.* A honeycomb.

com·bat [*n.* kom′bat, *v.* kəm·bat′] *n., v.* **com·bat·ed** *or* **com·bat·ted, com·bat·ing** *or* **com·bat·ting 1** *n.* A battle or fight: *combat* between soldiers. **2** *v.* To battle or fight with: Doctors are *combating* cancer. **3** *v.* To fight or struggle: The candidates *combated* fiercely for the election.

com·bat·ant [kəm·bat′ənt *or* kom′bə·tənt] **1** *n.* A person fighting or prepared to fight: The *combatants* entered the ring. **2** *adj.* Fighting: *combatant* troops. **3** *adj.* Combative.

com·bat·ive [kəm·bat′iv *or* kom′bə·tiv] *adj.* Eager or ready to fight: His *combative* disposition often gets him into trouble.

comb·er [kō′mər] *n.* **1** A person or thing that combs wool or other fibers. **2** A wave that breaks or is topped with foam.

com·bi·na·tion [kom′bə·nā′shən] *n.* **1** The act of joining: *Combination* of oil with water is impossible. **2** A combined condition: Working in *combination,* the two men finished the job easily. **3** The thing that is formed by combining: A *combination* of bright colors can be very unpleasant. **4** A group, as of people, joined for a special purpose: Six colleges formed a *combination* to do the research. **5** A series of numbers or letters used in opening certain locks.

com·bine [*v.* kəm·bīn′, *n.* kom′bīn] *v.* **com·bined, com·bin·ing,** *n.* **1** *v.* To bring together;

unite; join. **2** *v*. To come together: Oxygen and carbon *combine* readily. **3** *n*. A combination.

combining form The stem of a word, or an entire word, that is combined with other forms to create compound words. *Tele-* and *-phone* are combining forms.

com·bus·ti·ble [kəm·bus′tə·bəl] **1** *adj*. Capable of catching fire; easily burned: Magnesium is highly *combustible*. **2** *n*. Any substance that will burn easily. **3** *adj*. Excitable; fiery.

com·bus·tion [kəm·bus′chən] *n*. The action or process of burning: Quick *combustion* produces heat and often light; Slow *combustion* of food gives the body energy.

come [kum] *v*. **came, come, com·ing 1** To approach the speaker; move toward where he is or is going: *Come* here. **2** To arrive: We *came* yesterday. **3** To happen; occur: Labor Day *came* late last year. **4** To originate; be born: to *come* from a good background. **5** To result: Nothing *comes* of wasting time. **6** To become: The wheel *came* loose. **7** To be obtainable: The car *comes* in four colors. **8** To turn out to be: His prediction *came* true. **9** To reach or extend: Her skirt *came* to her knees. **10** To amount; add up: The bill *comes* to a dollar. **11** To arrive at some state or condition: to *come* to one's senses. **— come about** To take place; happen: How did this *come about?* **— come around** To recover; revive: She fainted but soon *came around.* **— come back 1** To return: *Come back* soon. **2** To return to a former state or position: After a bad season, he *came back.* **— come by** To get: How did you *come by* that beautiful sweater? **— come into** To inherit: I *came into* some money from my grandfather. **— come off 1** To happen; occur: What time does the race *come off?* **2** To act so as to be judged: In the contest I *came off* as a second-rate speller. **— come out 1** To be made known: Wait till the inside story *comes out.* **2** To be published: My book *came out* last week. **3** To make one's debut. **4** To speak out in support: Whom did you *come out* for in the school election? **5** To try out: Did you *come out* for the debating team? **6** To end: How did the movie *come out?* **— come to** To recover; revive: How soon did he *come to* after the accident? **— come up** To come into discussion.

co·me·di·an [kə·mē′dē·ən] *n*. **1** An actor or entertainer who tries by his performance to make people laugh. **2** A person who writes comedy.

com·e·dy [kom′ə·dē] *n*., *pl*. **com·e·dies 1** An entertainment, as a play or movie, that tells a story in a light and humorous way, and has a happy ending. **2** The branch of drama that tells such stories. **3** Any writing that tells such stories. **4** Any happening in real life that is like the happenings in such stories.

come·ly [kum′lē] *adj*. **come·li·er, come·li·est**

1 Pleasant looking; handsome: *comely* men and women. **2** Suitable; proper. **— come′li·ness** *n*.

com·er [kum′ər] *n*. **1** A person who comes or arrives. **2** *informal* A person who gives signs of future success.

com·et [kom′it] *n*. A bright celestial body moving in elliptical orbit around the sun, usually having a tail of luminous gaseous matter pointing away from the sun.

com·fit [kum′fit] *n*. A piece of candy.

com·fort [kum′fərt] **1** *v*. To make feel better in time of grief or trouble: John's sister *comforted* him when his dog died. **2** *n*. Anything that eases grief or trouble: My mother gave me *comfort* when I was sad. **3** *n*. A pleasant condition, free from pain, want, or worry: Everyone likes to live in *comfort*. **4** *n*. A person or thing that gives ease, freedom from pain or worry, etc.

com·fort·a·ble [kum′fər·tə·bəl *or* kumf′tə·bəl] *adj*. **1** Giving comfort and satisfaction: Is that hat *comfortable*, or is it too small? **2** Free from physical or mental trouble; at ease: Are you *comfortable?* **— com′fort·a·bly** *adv*.

com·fort·er [kum′fər·tər] *n*. **1** A person who comforts. **2** A thick, quilted cover for a bed.

com·fort·less [kum′-fərt·lis] *adj*. **1** Giving no comfort: His advice was *comfortless*. **2** Having no comfort: His life was hard and *comfortless*.

com·ic [kom′ik] **1** *adj*. Of or having to do with comedy. **2** *adj*. Funny; entertaining: I just heard a *comic* story. **3** *n*. A funny person, especially an actor. **4** *n*. (*pl*.) Comic strips.

Comforter

com·i·cal [kom′i·kəl] *adj*. Causing laughter; funny: Punch and Judy's quarrel was *comical*.

comic book A booklet of comic strips.

comic strip A group of drawings that tell a story which is comical or adventurous.

com·ing [kum′ing] **1** *adj*. Approaching, especially in time: the *coming* year. **2** *adj*. On the way to success: a *coming* writer. **3** *n*. Approach; arrival.

com·ma [kom′ə] *n*. A punctuation mark (,) that indicates a short pause between words, phrases, or clauses in a sentence.

com·mand [kə·mand′] **1** *v*. To order; direct: to *command* planes to search the area. **2** *n*. An order: a *command* to march. **3** *v*. To be in control of or authority over: to *command* a ship. **4** *n*. The power or authority to give orders. **5** *n*. The men or area under a commander. **6** *v*. To overlook and dominate: These hills *command* the town. **7** *v*. To deserve and call for: His knowl-

---

add, āce, câre, pälm;　end, ēqual;　it, īce;　odd, ōpen, ôrder;　tŏŏk, pool;　up, bûrn;
ə = a in *above*, e in *sicken*, i in *possible*, o in *melon*, u in *circus*;　yōō = u in *fuse*;　oil;　pout;
check; ring; thin; this; zh in *vision*.　For ¶ reference, see page 64 · HOW TO

edge *commands* our respect. **8** *v.* To have or surely get for use: He can't *command* the support of city voters. **9** *n.* The ability to make use: a good *command* of English.

com·man·dant [kom′ən·dant′] *n.* The officer in charge of a navy yard, military school, etc.

com·man·deer [kom′ən·dir′] *v.* **1** To take control of for public use, especially because of military necessity: The army *commandeered* all trucks in the city. **2** To force into military service.

com·man·der [kə·man′dər] *n.* **1** A person who is in command, as of a ship or military force. **2** A naval rank. In the U.S. Navy, a commander is a commissioned officer ranking next above a lieutenant commander and next below a captain.

commander in chief *pl.* **commanders in chief** **1** (*often written* **Commander in Chief**) The person who is in command of all the armed forces of a nation. In the U.S., the President is the Commander in Chief. **2** The officer who is in command of a major military force, as an army or a fleet.

com·mand·ing [kə·man′ding] *adj.* **1** In charge or control: the *commanding* general. **2** That must be obeyed; powerful: *Commanding* necessity forces this step. **3** Authoritative: a *commanding* manner. **4** Dominating, as from a height: a *commanding* view.

com·mand·ment [kə·mand′mənt] *n.* **1** A command or law. **2** (*sometimes written* **Commandment**) One of the Ten Commandments.

com·man·do [kə·man′dō] *n., pl.* **com·man·dos** or **com·man·does** **1** A soldier trained for quick raids and hand-to-hand fighting. **2** A group of such soldiers.

com·mem·o·rate [kə·mem′ə·rāt] *v.* **com·mem·o·rat·ed, com·mem·o·rat·ing** To honor or keep fresh the memory of: The monument *commemorates* the landing of the Pilgrims.

com·mem·o·ra·tion [kə·mem′ə·rā′shən] *n.* **1** The act of commemorating. **2** Something that commemorates, as a ceremony or service in honor of someone or something. **—in commemoration of** As a reminder of; in honor of.

com·mem·o·ra·tive [kə·mem′ə·rā′tiv *or* kə·mem′ə·rə·tiv] *adj.* Serving to commemorate.

com·mence [kə·mens′] *v.* **com·menced, com·menc·ing** To start; initiate; begin.

com·mence·ment [kə·mens′mənt] *n.* **1** A commencing; beginning. **2** The ceremony at a school or college of giving out diplomas or degrees to graduating students. **3** The day on which such a ceremony takes place.

com·mend [kə·mend′] *v.* **1** To speak highly of; praise: The teacher *commended* her pupils on their homework. **2** To mention with approval; recommend. **3** To give over with confidence: The mother *commended* her boy to the nurse.

com·mend·a·ble [kə·men′də·bəl] *adj.* Deserving credit or approval: a *commendable* job.

com·men·da·tion [kom′ən·dā′shən] *n.* **1** Praise or recommendation. **2** The entrusting of something to another.

com·men·su·rate [kə·men′shə·rit *or* kə·men′· sə·rit] **1** Having the same measure or size. **2** In proper proportion: The result is not *commensurate* with the effort.

com·ment [kom′ent] **1** *n.* A note or remark explaining or giving an opinion of a person or thing, as a play, book, etc. **2** *v.* To give an opinion or explanation. **3** *n.* Talk; conversation; gossip: The speaker's unusual clothes caused much *comment.*

com·men·tar·y [kom′ən·ter′ē] *n., pl.* **com·men·tar·ies** **1** A series of notes that explain a book or other writing. **2** A description, with comment and explanation, of some event while it is going on, as a political convention. **3** A comment.

com·men·ta·tor [kom′ən·tā′tər] *n.* **1** A person who writes or reads commentaries. **2** A person who reports, analyzes, and explains the news on radio or television.

com·merce [kom′ərs] *n.* The buying and selling of goods, especially on a large scale between different places or nations; trade.

com·mer·cial [kə·mûr′shəl] **1** *adj.* Of or having to do with commerce. **2** *adj.* Created or made to be sold, with profit as the object: He wrote a *commercial* novel. **3** *n.* An advertisement on radio or television.

com·mer·cial·ize [kə·mûr′shəl·īz] *v.* **com·mer·cial·ized, com·mer·cial·iz·ing** To put on a commercial basis for profit; treat as a business: Some art galleries are *commercialized.* ¶3

com·min·gle [kə·ming′gəl] *v.* **com·min·gled, com·min·gling** To mix or blend together: Nine scents are *commingled* in this perfume.

com·mis·er·ate [kə·miz′ə·rāt] *v.* **com·mis·er·at·ed, com·mis·er·at·ing** **1** To feel or express sympathy for; pity: to *commiserate* the condition of the poor and needy. **2** To sympathize: to *commiserate* with a worried mother.

com·mis·er·a·tion [kə·miz′ə·rā′shən] *n.* A feeling or expression of sympathy; pity.

com·mis·sar [kom′ə·sär] *n.* A Communist official assigned to a Soviet military unit to teach Communist principles and check on loyalty.

com·mis·sar·i·at [kom′ə·sâr′ē·ət] *n.* The department of an army that is responsible for providing food and daily supplies.

com·mis·sar·y [kom′ə·ser′ē] *n., pl.* **com·mis·sar·ies** A store that sells food and daily supplies, as at a camp or military post.

com·mis·sion [kə·mish′ən] **1** *n.* A written paper giving certain powers, rights, and duties. **2** *n.* A written order giving a certain rank to an officer in any of the armed services. **3** *n.* The rank and powers given by such an order. **4** *v.* To give a specified rank and powers to by such an order. **5** *v.* To give authority to act as an agent: He *commissioned* a dealer in London to buy a painting for him. **6** *n.* The authority given, limited or complete. **7** *n.* The thing which a person is authorized and trusted to do. **8** *n.* A group of people chosen to do certain things: a *commission* to study air pollution. **9** *n.* Pay consisting of a percentage of the business done or arranged by an agent or salesman. **10** *n.* A performance or doing: the *commission* of a crime. **11** *v.* To have composed, written, or created: The concerto was *commissioned* by a famous violinist. **12** *v.* To put into active service, as a ship. **—in commission** In active use, or ready for use, as a ship or an aircraft; usable. **—out of commission** Not in active use; not usable.

com·mis·sion·er [kə·mish′ən·ər] *n.* **1** A member of a commission. **2** A public official in charge of a department: a fire *commissioner.* **3** One of a group chosen to govern in some cities or counties.

com·mit [kə·mit′] *v.* **com·mit·ted, com·mit·ting 1** To do; perform: to *commit* a crime. **2** To give over for safekeeping; entrust: He *committed* his papers to the university. **3** To hand over for custody, as to a prison or mental institution. **4** To pledge (oneself); make known one's view: He has *committed* himself in favor of the bill. **5** To refer, as to a committee, for consideration. **—commit to memory** To learn by heart; memorize. **—commit to writing** To write down.

com·mit·ment [kə·mit′mənt] *n.* **1** A committing or being committed. **2** An order sending someone to prison or a mental hospital. **3** A sending to or placement in a prison or mental hospital. **4** A pledge; promise.

com·mit·tee [kə·mit′ē] *n.* A group of people chosen to do certain specified things: a *committee* to study housing problems.

com·mode [kə·mōd′] *n.* **1** A low chest of drawers. **2** A movable washstand with a bowl and pitcher.

com·mo·di·ous [kə·mō′dē·əs] *adj.* Having plenty of room; spacious: a *commodious* house.

com·mod·i·ty [kə·mod′ə·tē] *n., pl.* **com·mod·i·ties 1** Something that is bought and sold: Corn, steel, and lumber are *commodities.* **2** Anything useful.

com·mo·dore [kom′ə·dôr] *n.* **1** A naval rank. In the U.S. Navy, an officer next above a captain and next below a rear admiral: no longer used. **2** A title given to the chief officer of a yacht club.

com·mon [kom′ən] **1** *adj.* Frequent or usual: a *common* happening. **2** *adj.* Widespread; general: *common* knowledge. **3** *adj.* Shared equally by each or by all: Cousins have a *common* ancestor. **4** *adj.* Of, for, from, by, or to all; general: the *common* welfare. **5** *n.* Land owned or used by all the people of a community. **6** *adj.* Of low rank: a *common* soldier. **7** *adj.* Vulgar; low; coarse. **—in common** Equally with another or others: We have tastes *in common.* **—com′mon·ness** *n.*

common denominator A number that may be evenly divided by each of the denominators of a given group of fractions: 6, 12, and 18 are all *common denominators* of $\frac{1}{3}$ and $\frac{1}{2}$.

com·mon·er [kom′ən·ər] *n.* One of the common people; a person who is not a noble.

com·mon·ly [kom′ən·lē] *adv.* Ordinarily; usually: Philip is *commonly* known as Red.

Common Market A group of European nations that is working toward freer trade among its members.

common noun A noun that names a class of persons or things rather than a particular person or thing: Not *George,* but *boy* is a *common noun.*

com·mon·place [kom′ən·plās′] **1** *adj.* Not remarkable or interesting; ordinary. **2** *n.* Something ordinary and familiar: Traffic jams are a *commonplace* on city streets. **3** *n.* A flat or ordinary remark.

com·mons [kom′ənz] *n.pl.* **1** The common people; those not of a noble class. **2** (*written* **The Commons**) The House of Commons. **3** (*often used with singular verb*) A dining hall where food is provided at a common table, as in a college. **4** Food; rations.

common sense Ordinary intelligence; the understanding a person gets from practical experience.

com·mon·weal [kom′ən·wēl′] *n.* The general welfare.

com·mon·wealth [kom′ən·welth′] *n.* **1** The whole people of a state or nation. **2** A democratic state or nation; republic. **3** A group of states or nations linked by common ties and interests.

com·mo·tion [kə·mō′shən] *n.* Great confusion; excitement; disturbance: Boos and *commotion* interrupted the speech.

com·mu·nal [kom′yə·nəl *or* kə·myōō′nəl] *adj.* Of, having to do with, or belonging to a community; public: a *communal* playground.

com·mune[1] [kə·myōōn′] *v.* **com·muned, com·mun·ing 1** To talk privately. **2** To receive Holy Communion.

com·mune[2] [kom′yōōn] *n.* The smallest political division that is locally governed in several European countries.

com·mu·ni·ca·ble [kə·myōō′ni·kə·bəl] *adj.* That can be passed on or communicated from person to person, as a contagious disease.

com·mu·ni·cant [kə·myōō′nə·kənt] *n.* **1** A person who receives or has a right to receive Holy Communion. **2** A person who communicates.

com·mu·ni·cate [kə·myōō′nə·kāt] *v.* **com·mu·ni·cat·ed, com·mu·ni·cat·ing 1** To give or exchange thoughts, information, or messages. **2** To express or exchange (ideas, information, etc.). **3** To pass on; transmit: to *communicate* a disease. **4** To be joined; connect: The den *communicates* with the living room. **5** To receive Holy Communion.

---

a**dd**, **ā**ce, c**â**re, p**ä**lm;   **e**nd, **ē**qual;   **i**t, **ī**ce;   **o**dd, **ō**pen, **ô**rder;   t**oo**k, p**ool**;   **u**p, b**û**rn; ə = a in *above*, e in *sicken*, i in *possible*, o in *melon*, u in *circus*;   y**oo** = u in *fuse*;   **oil**;   p**ou**t; **ch**eck; **ri**n**g**; **th**in; **th**is; **zh** in *vision*.   For ¶ reference, see page 64 · HOW TO

com·mu·ni·ca·tion [kə·myōō′nə·kā′shən] *n.*
1 The act of passing on; transmitting. **2** The giving or exchange of ideas or information, as by speech or writing: All our *communication* was by mail. **3** The ideas or information given. **4** A message or letter carrying information. **5** A connection or means of passage from one place to another.

com·mu·ni·ca·tive [kə·myōō′nə·kā′tiv *or* kə·myōō′nə·kə·tiv] Tending to talk freely.

com·mun·ion [kə·myōon′yən] *n.* **1** A having or sharing in common: a *communion* of ideas. **2** A fellowship or intimate association: In the mountains he felt a *communion* with nature. **3** A body of people having common religious beliefs. **4** (*written* **Communion**) A Christian ceremony in which bread and wine are blessed and consumed in memory of the death of Christ. **5** (*written* **Communion**) The consecrated bread and wine used in the ceremony. **6** (*written* **Communion**) *adj. use:* a *Communion* service.

com·mu·nism [kom′yə·niz′əm] *n.* **1** A social system in which the means for producing economic goods belong to the entire community or the state, not to individuals. **2** (*written* **Communism**) A political organization in which a single political party controls the state and manages the production and distribution of goods, as in the Soviet Union.

com·mu·nist [kom′yə·nist] **1** *n.* A person who supports or is in favor of communism. **2** *n.* (*written* **Communist**) A member of a political party that advocates Communism. **3** *adj.* Communistic.

com·mu·nis·tic [kom′yə·nis′tik] *adj.* Having to do with or favoring communism.

com·mu·ni·ty [kə·myōō′nə·tē] *n., pl.* **com·mu·ni·ties** **1** A group of people living together in one locality: a rural *community*. **2** A group of people living together who share common interests: a religious *community*. **3** The public; society in general: What the *community* wants it usually gets. **4** Sameness or likeness: a *community* of interests.

community chest A fund made up of individual contributions to help local welfare organizations.

com·mu·ta·tion [kom′yə·tā′shən] *n.* **1** A substitution, as of one kind of payment for another. **2** A reduction or lightening of punishment: a *commutation* of life imprisonment to twelve years in jail. **3** Regular travel to and from work, usually of some distance.

com·mu·ta·tive [kə·myōō′tə·tiv] *adj.* Indicating a mathematical operation in which the order of the numbers or quantities does not affect the result, as addition, $a + b = b + a$, or multiplication, $a \times b = b \times a$.

com·mu·ta·tor [kom′yə·tā′tər] *n.* A device, as in an electric motor or generator, that makes the current flow in the right direction at the right time.

com·mute [kə·myōot′] *v.* **com·mut·ed, com·mut·ing** **1** To change for something less severe: to *commute* a prison term. **2** To make regular, rather long trips to and from work.

com·mut·er [kə·myōō′tər] *n.* A person who makes regular trips of some distance to and from work.

com·pact[1] [*adj.* kəm·pakt′ *or* kom′pakt, *v.* kəm·pakt′, *n.* kom′pakt]
1 *adj.* Closely and firmly put together: The magazines were stacked in a *compact* pile. **2** *v.* To pack or press closely and firmly. **3** *adj.* Brief and to the point: a *compact* speech. **4** *n.* A small box for carrying face powder. **5** *n.* A small automobile. **— com·pact′ly** *adv.* **— com·pact′ness** *n.*

A compact car

com·pact[2] [kom′pakt] *n.* An agreement or contract: a *compact* between two nations to promote trade.

com·pan·ion [kəm·pan′yən] *n.* **1** A person who goes with another person; comrade; associate: Mary and Louise were constant *companions*. **2** A person employed to live or travel with and help another. **3** One of a pair of things that match: These two chairs are *companions*. ◆ *Companion* comes from the Latin *com-*, meaning *together*, and *panis*, meaning *bread*, because *companions* "break bread"—that is, share meals—together.

com·pan·ion·a·ble [kəm·pan′yən·ə·bəl] *adj.* Fitted to be a companion; friendly. **— com·pan′ion·a·bly** *adv.*

com·pan·ion·ship [kəm·pan′yən·ship] *n.* A being companions; fellowship: Jim liked the *companionship* of his fraternity brothers.

com·pan·ion·way [kəm·pan′yən·wā′] *n.* A staircase leading from the deck of a ship to the area below.

com·pa·ny [kum′pə·nē] *n., pl.* **com·pa·nies** **1** A group of people. **2** A group of people who have come together because of some common purpose or interest: an insurance *company*. **3** Companionship: Julie enjoyed her mother's *company*. **4** Companions: Don't associate with bad *company*. **5** A guest or guests: We're having *company* tonight. **6** A body of soldiers commanded by a captain. **7** The officers and sailors of a ship. **— keep company 1** To be with or go with: *Keep* me *company* tonight. **2** To go together, as an engaged couple; court. **— part company** To end friendship or association: After vacation, Joe and Ted *parted company*.

com·pa·ra·ble [kom′pər·ə·bəl] *adj.* **1** Similar enough to be compared: Are the men *comparable* in size? **2** Fit to be compared: A bow is not *comparable* to a rifle. **— com′pa·ra·bly** *adv.*

com·par·a·tive [kəm·par′ə·tiv] **1** *adj.* Having to do with or using comparison: *comparative* studies. **2** *adj.* Estimated by comparison; relative: His work is of *comparative* importance.

3 *adj.* In the higher but not highest degree of comparison of an adjective or adverb. **4** *n.* A form or phrase showing this degree: *Greener* and *more clearly* are comparatives of *green* and *clearly*. — **com·par′a·tive·ly** *adv.*

com·pare [kəm·pâr′] *v.* **com·pared, com·par·ing,** *n.* **1** *v.* To describe as similar; liken: to *compare* a laugh to music. **2** *v.* To examine so as to find similarities or differences: to *compare* one student's work with another's. **3** *n.* Comparison. **4** *v.* To be suitable for comparison: Few composers can be *compared* with Beethoven. **5** *v.* To form or state the degrees of comparison of (an adjective or adverb). — **beyond compare** Above comparison; without equal.

com·par·i·son [kəm·par′ə·sən] *n.* **1** A comparing or being compared: Would you make a *comparison* between the two books? **2** Enough likeness to make things worth comparing: There's no *comparison* between the two books. **3** In grammar, the change in form of an adjective or adverb that indicates differences of degree. There are three degrees of comparison, the positive, the comparative, and the superlative: The *comparison* of *new* is *new, newer, newest.* — **in comparison with** Compared with.

com·part·ment [kəm·pärt′mənt] *n.* Any one of the separate sections into which an enclosed area is divided: a *compartment* in a desk drawer.

com·pass [kum′pəs *or* kom′pəs] **1** *n.* An instrument that shows direction, usually by a magnetic needle that always points to magnetic north. **2** *n.* The reach or extent; scope: the *compass* of a lifetime. **3** *n.* The limits: Stay within the *compass* of the school playground. **4** *n.* The range of tones of a voice or instrument. **5** *n.* (*sometimes pl.*) An

Compasses

instrument with two legs that are hinged at one end, used for taking measurements and drawing circles. **6** *v.* To go round; circle: to *compass* the schoolyard. **7** *v.* To surround; encircle; encompass. **8** *v.* To grasp mentally; understand: to *compass* a problem. **9** *v.* To attain or accomplish: to *compass* one's wishes.

com·pas·sion [kəm·pash′ən] *n.* Pity for the suffering or distress of another and the desire to help.

com·pas·sion·ate [kəm·pash′ən·it] *adj.* Feeling compassion or pity; sympathetic; merciful. — **com·pas′sion·ate·ly** *adv.*

com·pat·i·ble [kəm·pat′ə·bəl] *adj.* Able to get along together; agreeable. — **com·pat′i·bil′·i·ty** *n.* — **com·pat′i·bly** *adv.*

com·pa·tri·ot [kəm·pā′trē·ət] *n.* A fellow countryman.

com·peer [kəm·pir′] *n.* An equal, peer, or companion.

com·pel [kəm·pel′] *v.* **com·pelled, com·pel·ling 1** To force; drive: The flood *compelled* us to seek high ground. **2** To obtain by force; demand: The law *compels* obedience.

com·pen·sate [kom′pən·sāt] *v.* **com·pen·sat·ed, com·pen·sat·ing 1** To make suitable payment or reward to or for: to *compensate* a man for work. **2** To be a balance; make up: The girl's hard work *compensated* for her lack of intelligence.

com·pen·sa·tion [kom′pən·sā′shən] *n.* **1** The act of compensating. **2** Something paid, given, or done to balance something else.

com·pete [kəm·pēt′] *v.* **com·pet·ed, com·pet·ing 1** To take part in a contest. **2** To be a rival or contender: Six teams *competed* in all.

com·pe·tence [kom′pə·təns] *n.* **1** Ability; capability: He has the *competence* to do the work. **2** Enough money to live comfortably.

com·pe·ten·cy [kom′pə·tən·sē] *n.* Competence.

com·pe·tent [kom′pə·tənt] *adj.* Having enough ability; capable: a *competent* teacher. — **com′·pe·tent·ly** *adv.*

com·pe·ti·tion [kom′pə·tish′ən] *n.* **1** Effort to get something wanted by others or to excel others: *Competition* in the classroom is good for most students. **2** A contest: a swimming *competition.*

com·pet·i·tive [kəm·pet′ə·tiv] *adj.* Having to do with or decided by competition. — **com·pet′·i·tive·ly** *adv.*

com·pet·i·tor [kəm·pet′ə·tər] *n.* A person who competes, as in games or in business.

com·pi·la·tion [kom′pə·lā′shən] *n.* **1** The act of compiling. **2** Something that is compiled, as an encyclopedia.

com·pile [kəm·pīl′] *v.* **com·piled, com·pil·ing 1** To put together in a list, book, or account: to *compile* statistics of population. **2** To make or compose (a book) from various materials: to *compile* a recipe book. — **com·pil′er** *n.*

com·pla·cence [kəm·plā′səns] *n.* Complacency.

com·pla·cen·cy [kəm·plā′sən·sē] *n.* A being pleased or satisfied with oneself; smugness.

com·pla·cent [kəm·plā′sənt] *adj.* Satisfied with oneself, one's possessions, or one's accomplishments.

com·plain [kəm·plān′] *v.* **1** To find fault or say that something is bad, wrong, or uncomfortable: to *complain* about bad weather. **2** To make a charge or report of something bad: to *complain* to the police about a noisy party next door.

com·plain·ant [kəm·plā′nənt] *n.* A person who starts a lawsuit against another.

com·plaint [kəm·plānt′] *n.* **1** An expression of dissatisfaction or discomfort; a finding fault.

2 The thing complained about: "No hot water" is a common *complaint*. **3** A sickness or physical disorder. **4** A charge or accusation.

com·plai·sant [kəm·plā′zənt] *adj.* Showing a desire to please; agreeable. **— com·plai′· sance** *n.*

com·ple·ment [*n.* kom′plə·mənt, *v.* kom′plə· ment] **1** *n.* Something that completes or perfects. **2** *n.* Full or complete number, allowance, or amount: The ship has her *complement* of men. **3** *v.* To make complete; supply a lack in: His drawings *complement* her funny verses. **4** *n.* In grammar, a word or phrase used to complete a predicate. *Gray* in "The sky was gray" is a complement. ◆ See COMPLIMENT.

com·ple·men·ta·ry [kom′plə·men′tər·ē] *adj.* Serving to fill up or complete.

complementary angle Either one of two angles whose sum is a right angle.

com·plete [kəm·plēt′] *adj.*, *v.* **com·plet·ed, com·plet· ing 1** *adj.* Having all needed or normal parts; entire; whole: a *complete* set of dishes. **2** *v.* To make whole, with no part missing: A viola *completed* the quartet. **3** *adj.* Wholly finished; ended: My review for the test is *complete*. **4** *v.* To finish; end: I'll *complete* the housework at noon. **5** *adj.* Full; thorough: She has a *complete* command of French.

a + b = 90°
a and b are complementary angles

com·plete·ly [kəm·plēt′lē] *adv.* In a complete manner or degree; entirely; wholly.

com·ple·tion [kəm·plē′shən] *n.* **1** The act of completing. **2** A completed condition; finish: At the *completion* of the school year we go on vacation.

com·plex [*adj.* kəm·pleks′ or kom′pleks, *n.* kom′pleks] **1** *adj.* Complicated; intricate; not simple: a *complex* mathematical problem. **2** *adj.* Made up of a number of parts. **3** *n.* A complicated or intricate whole: The railroad yard is a *complex* of tracks. **4** *n.* An unreasonable dislike or fear caused by memories and emotions which a person may not be aware are in his mind. **— com·plex′ly** *adv.*

com·plex·ion [kəm·plek′shən] *n.* **1** The color and appearance of the skin, especially of the face. **2** Character; quality: The *complexion* of my friendship with Paul was changed by an argument.

com·plex·i·ty [kəm·plek′sə·tē] *n., pl.* **com· plex·i·ties 1** The state of being complex. **2** A complex thing.

complex sentence A sentence that is made up of a main clause and one or more subordinate clauses. "Recess ends when the bell rings" is a complex sentence.

com·pli·ance [kəm·plī′əns] *n.* **1** The act of yielding or giving in: The law demands *compliance*. **2** A tendency to yield or give in. **— in compliance with** In agreement with.

com·pli·ant [kəm·plī′ənt] *adj.* Complying; yielding.

com·pli·cate [kom′plə·kāt] *v.* **com·pli·cat· ed, com·pli·cat·ing** To make or become hard to understand, use, solve, cure, etc.: Problems *complicate* a person's life.

com·pli·cat·ed [kom′plə·kā′tid] *adj.* Involved; complex; not simple: a *complicated* engine.

com·pli·ca·tion [kom′plə·kā′shən] *n.* **1** An involved, difficult, or confusing state. **2** Anything that complicates: Our trip turned out to be full of annoying *complications*. **3** The act of complicating.

com·plic·i·ty [kəm·plis′ə·tē] *n., pl.* **com·plic· i·ties** Connection with a wrong act as a partner or accomplice.

com·pli·ment [*n.* kom′plə·mənt, *v.* kom′plə· ment] **1** *n.* An expression of admiration, praise, or congratulation: John paid Madge a *compliment* on her new dress. **2** *n.* An expression of courtesy: The students paid the teacher the *compliment* of complete silence during her lecture. **3** *n.* (*usually pl.*) A formal greeting. **4** *v.* To pay a compliment. ◆ Originally a *compliment* was thought of as completing or fulfilling an act of courtesy. Now it refers to any expression of praise or admiration. *Complement* is a part added to something else to make it complete: Long white gloves are the perfect *complement* to an evening dress.

com·pli·men·ta·ry [kom′plə·men′tər·ē] *adj.* **1** Paying or like a compliment. **2** Given free: a *complimentary* copy of a book.

com·ply [kəm·plī′] *v.* **com·plied, com·ply·ing** To act in agreement: *Comply* with my request.

com·po·nent [kəm·pō′nənt] **1** *n.* One main part, ingredient, or constituent of a whole: Tuner, amplifier, and speaker are major *components* of a radio. **2** *adj.* Helping to form: *component* parts.

com·port [kəm·pôrt′] *v.* **1** To conduct or behave: He *comported* himself with great dignity. **2** To agree; suit: Her solemn look did not *comport* with the gaiety of the occasion.

com·pose [kəm·pōz′] *v.* **com·posed, com· pos·ing 1** To make up; form: Water is *composed* of hydrogen and oxygen. **2** To create: to *compose* music. **3** To make calm: *Compose* yourself before you speak. **4** *adj. use:* a *composed* manner. **5** To settle, as differences. **6** To arrange, as elements in a painting. **7** To arrange; set: to *compose* type.

com·pos·er [kəm·pō′zər] *n.* A person who composes, especially one who composes music.

com·pos·ite [kəm·poz′it] **1** *adj.* Made up of separate parts; compound. **2** *adj.* Belonging to a group of plants that have heads made up of many tiny flowers, as asters and dandelions. **3** *n.* Something that is made up of parts.

com·po·si·tion [kom′pə·zish′ən] *n.* **1** The make-up of something. **2** The act of putting together: The *composition* of the symphony took two years. **3** The thing that is put together, as a piece of music. **4** A short essay, especially one written as an exercise for school. **5** A mixture, as of metals.

com·post [kom'pōst] *n.* **1** A mixture of rotted leaves, grass, manure, etc., used for fertilizing. **2** A mixture; compound.

com·po·sure [kəm·pō'zhər] *n.* Calmness; self-control.

com·pound[1] [*n., adj.* kom'pound, *v.* kəm·pound' *or* kəm·pound'] **1** *n.* A combination or mixture of two or more ingredients or parts. **2** *adj.* Having or made up of more than one part: a *compound* leaf. **3** *v.* To mix; put together: to *compound* a medicine. **4** *n.* A word composed of two or more words joined with a hyphen or written in solid form, as *forget-me-not* and *shoestring.* **5** *n.* A substance formed by chemical combination of two or more elements: Salt is a *compound* of sodium and chlorine. **6** *v.* To settle by compromise, as a debt.

com·pound[2] [kom'pound] *n.* A fenced or walled yard with buildings in it.

compound interest Interest on both the original sum of money and the accumulated interest.

compound sentence A sentence consisting of two or more main clauses.

com·pre·hend [kom'pri·hend'] *v.* **1** To understand; grasp: I don't *comprehend* spoken German. **2** To take in; include: The list *comprehends* all the dealers in the city.

com·pre·hen·si·ble [kom'pri·hen'sə·bəl] *adj.* Understandable: a *comprehensible* problem.

com·pre·hen·sion [kom'pri·hen'shən] *n.* **1** The act of understanding. **2** The power to understand: His *comprehension* of foreign languages was poor.

com·pre·hen·sive [kom'pri·hen'siv] *adj.* **1** Of wide scope; including much: a *comprehensive* study of literature. **2** Having a broad understanding: His mind is *comprehensive.* **— com'·pre·hen'sive·ly** *adv.*

com·press [*v.* kəm·pres', *n.* kom'pres] **1** *v.* To press together; condense; squeeze: to *compress* gas. **2** *n.* A folded cloth or pad, used to stop bleeding, to apply moisture, heat, or cold, etc.

com·press·i·ble [kəm·pres'ə·bəl] *adj.* Capable of being compressed. **— com·press'i·bil'·i·ty** *n.*

com·pres·sion [kəm·presh'ən] *n.* **1** The act of compressing. **2** The state of being compressed.

com·pres·sor [kəm·pres'ər] *n.* **1** A person or thing that compresses. **2** A machine for compressing a gas or air.

com·prise [kəm·prīz'] *v.* **com·prised, com·pris·ing** To consist of; contain; include: The state *comprises* 29 counties.

com·pro·mise [kom'prə·mīz] *n., v.* **com·pro·mised, com·pro·mis·ing 1** *n.* An adjustment or settlement in which each side gives up part of its demands: He was offered $2.00 an hour,

asked for $3.00, but accepted $2.50 as a *compromise.* **2** *v.* To settle a dispute by such an adjustment. **3** *v.* To expose to risk, suspicion, or disgrace: to *compromise* one's reputation.

comp·trol·ler [kən·trō'lər] *n.* Another spelling of CONTROLLER. ◆ *Comptroller* is a word based on the French word *compte,* meaning *an account,* because a *controller* managed the accounts and expenditures of a large household.

com·pul·sion [kəm·pul'shən] *n.* **1** The act of forcing or compelling: The *compulsion* of hunger drove them on. **2** A being forced: Under *compulsion* they went into exile.

com·pul·so·ry [kəm·pul'sər·ē] *adj.* **1** Required; enforced: *compulsory* education. **2** Using force.

com·punc·tion [kəm·pungk'shən] *n.* A feeling of guilt or regret: John had a slight *compunction* about missing a class.

com·pu·ta·tion [kom'pyə·tā'shən] *n.* **1** The act or method of computing; calculation; reckoning: By my *computation* we are nine miles offshore. **2** The amount or number arrived at by computing.

com·pute [kəm·pyoot'] *v.* **com·put·ed, com·put·ing** To figure by using mathematics; calculate; reckon: *Compute* the cost of a new roof. ◆ See COUNT.

com·put·er [kəm·pyoo'tər] *n.* An electronic device capable of doing arithmetic with great speed and accuracy, widely used in industry and business for handling masses of information automatically and for timing and controlling other devices.

com·rade [kom'rad *or* kom'rid] *n.* **1** A close companion or friend. **2** A person who shares one's occupation or interests. **— com'rade·ship** *n.*

con[1] [kon] *v.* **conned, con·ning** To study with care; learn: to *con* a book.

con[2] [kon] **1** *n.* A vote, argument, or person against something. **2** *adv.* Against: to discuss a matter pro and *con.*

con- A prefix meaning: with; together, as in *connect,* to join with.

con·cave [kon·kāv' *or* kon'kāv] *adj.* Hollow and curved like the inner curve of a crescent or bowl. **— con·cav·i·ty** [kon·kav'ə·tē] *n.*

concave lens   convex lens

con·ceal [kən·sēl'] *v.* To keep secret or out of sight; hide.

con·ceal·ment [kən·sēl'mənt] *n.* **1** The act of concealing. **2** A place or means of hiding.

con·cede [kən·sēd'] *v.* **con·ced·ed, con·ced·ing 1** To admit as true; acknowledge: to *concede* a point in an argument. **2** To grant; yield: I'll *concede* you your short putt.

con·ceit [kən·sēt'] *n.* **1** Too high an opinion of oneself or one's accomplishments: John's *conceit* about his intelligence is unpleasant.

add, āce, câre, pälm;   end, ēqual;   it, īce;   odd, ōpen, ôrder;   took, pool;   up, bûrn;
ə = a in *above,* e in *sicken,* i in *possible,* o in *melon,* u in *circus;*   yoo = u in *fuse;*   oil;   pout;
check;   ring;   thin;   this;   zh in *vision.*   For ¶ reference, see page 64 · HOW TO

2 A fanciful idea; a clever thought or expression. ◆ *Conceit* was formed from *conceive* in imitation of *deceit* and *deceive*.

con·ceit·ed [kən·sē′tid] *adj.* Having too high an opinion of oneself or one's accomplishments; vain. **— con·ceit′ed·ly** *adv.* **— con·ceit′ed·ness** *n.*

con·ceiv·a·ble [kən·sē′və·bəl] *adj.* Capable of being thought of; imaginable: the best plan *conceivable*. **— con·ceiv′a·bly** *adv.*

con·ceive [kən·sēv′] *v.* **con·ceived, con·ceiv·ing 1** To form or develop as an idea; imagine: a new nation, *conceived* in liberty; He *conceived* an ideal solution to the problem. **2** To understand; grasp: I can't fully *conceive* a million years. **3** To become pregnant with.

con·cen·trate [kon′sən·trāt] *v.* **con·cen·trat·ed, con·cen·trat·ing,** *n.* **1** *v.* To gather or focus one's entire attention: to *concentrate* on a book. **2** *v.* To gather or collect closely together: to *concentrate* our troops. **3** *v.* To make less diluted or mixed: to *concentrate* a solution of sugar by boiling off water. **4** *n.* A concentrated substance, as frozen juice.

con·cen·tra·tion [kon′sən·trā′shən] *n.* **1** The act of concentrating. **2** A concentrated condition. **3** Complete attention: Odd noises broke his *concentration*. **4** Strength, as of a solution.

concentration camp A fenced and guarded camp for confining political enemies, aliens, or prisoners of war.

con·cen·tric [kən·sen′trik] *adj.* Having a common center, as circles.

concentric circles   concentric triangles

con·cept [kon′sept] *n.* A general idea or notion: the *concept* of natural rights.

con·cep·tion [kən·sep′shən] *n.* **1** The act of forming an idea. **2** An idea, notion, or concept: He has no *conception* of punctuality. **3** The beginning of pregnancy.

con·cern [kən·sûrn′] **1** *v.* To relate to; be the business of: Your affairs don't *concern* me. **2** *n.* Anything that relates to one; affair; business. **3** *v.* To enage, involve or interest (oneself): He *concerns* himself with minor matters. **4** *v.* To worry; trouble: Her poor health *concerns* me. **5** *n.* Interest; worry: Your *concern* over my health is touching. **6** *n.* A business firm: Her father is with a manufacturing *concern*.

con·cerned [kən·sûrnd′] *adj.* **1** Interested or involved: Mary is more *concerned* with music than with painting. **2** Uneasy; worried: I'm *concerned* about my brother's health.

con·cern·ing [kən·sûr′ning] *prep.* Relating to; about; regarding: a book *concerning* dinosaurs.

con·cert [*n.* kon′sûrt, *v.* kən·sûrt′] **1** *n.* A musical program or performance. **2** *n.* Agreement; harmony; unity; accord: to work in *concert*. **3** *adj. use: concerted* effort. **4** *v.* To arrange or work out by agreement: Plans were *concerted* for the next season. **— in concert** In unison; all together.

con·cer·ti·na [kon′sər·tē′nə] *n.* A small musical instrument like an accordion.

con·cer·to [kən·cher′tō] *n.,* *pl.* **con·cer·tos** or **con·cer·ti** [kən·cher′tē] A musical composition, usually of three movements, for a solo instrument or instruments accompanied by an orchestra.

Concertina

con·ces·sion [kən·sesh′ən] *n.* **1** The act of granting or yielding: *Concession* by both sides led to agreement. **2** The thing that is granted or yielded. **3** A right, privilege, or property granted by a government or other authority: a *concession* to sell coffee at the stadium.

conch [kongk *or* konch] *n., pl.* **conchs** [kongks] or **conch·es** [kon′chiz] **1** A marine animal that lives in a large, spiral shell. **2** The shell itself.

con·cil·i·ate [kən·sil′ē·āt] *v.* **con·cil·i·at·ed, con·cil·i·at·ing 1** To overcome the unfriendliness of; win over; soothe: to *conciliate* an enemy. **2** To reconcile; make compatible: to *conciliate* conflicting stories. **— con·cil′i·a′tion** *n.*

Conch

con·cil·i·a·to·ry [kən·sil′ē·ə·tôr′ē] *adj.* Tending to soothe or win over.

con·cise [kən·sīs′] *adj.* Expressing much in brief form; short: a *concise* summary. **— con·cise′ly** *adv.* **— con·cise′ness** *n.*

con·clude [kən·klōōd′] *v.* **con·clud·ed, con·clud·ing 1** To end; finish: How did he *conclude* his speech? **2** To arrange or settle finally: to *conclude* a treaty. **3** To form an opinion; infer.

con·clu·sion [kən·klōō′zhən] *n.* **1** The end of something; finish; close: the *conclusion* of a play. **2** A closing part, as the summing up of a speech. **3** The result of an act or process; outcome. **4** A judgment or opinion reached by reasoning: My *conclusion* is that a tube is weak. **5** A final arrangement; settlement. **— in conclusion** In closing; finally.

con·clu·sive [kən·klōō′siv] *adj.* Putting an end to doubt; decisive: His reasons were *conclusive* and sound.

con·coct [kon·kokt′ *or* kən·kokt′] *v.* **1** To make by mixing ingredients, as food. **2** To make up; devise: to *concoct* a plan.

con·coc·tion [kon·kok′shən *or* kən·kok′shən] *n.* **1** The act of concocting. **2** Something concocted: a *concoction* of ice cream and fruit juice.

con·com·i·tant [kon·kom′ə·tənt *or* kən·kom′ə·tənt] **1** *adj.* Going along with; accompanying: hotel service and *concomitant* comforts. **2** *n.* Something that goes along with something else.

con·cord [kon′kôrd *or* kong′kôrd] *n.* **1** Peace; harmonious agreement. **2** A treaty establishing this: a *concord* between nations.

Con·cord [kong′kərd] *n.* **1** The capital of New Hampshire, in the south central part. **2** A town in NE Massachusetts, scene of a Revolutionary War battle, April 19, 1775.

con·cor·dance [kon·kôr′dəns *or* kən·kôr′dəns] *n.* **1** Agreement; concord. **2** An alphabetical index of the important words in a book with references to the places where they occur: a *concordance* to the Bible.

con·course [kon′kôrs *or* kong′kôrs] *n.* **1** A coming or moving together; confluence: a *concourse* of waterways. **2** A crowd; assembly. **3** An open place where crowds gather or through which they pass, as in a railroad station.

con·crete [kon′krēt *or* kon·krēt′] **1** *n.* A hard substance formed of cement, sand, gravel, and water, used as a building and paving material. **2** *adj. use:* a *concrete* floor. **3** *adj.* Actually existing; real: A chair is *concrete*, but a dream is not. **4** *adj.* Specific; particular: Give me a *concrete* example. **— con·crete′ness** *n.*

con·cu·bine [kong′kyə·bīn *or* kon′kyə·bīn] *n.* **1** A woman who lives with a man without being married to him. **2** A secondary wife, in certain countries where a man is allowed to have more than one wife.

con·cur [kən·kûr′] *v.* **con·curred, con·cur·ring** **1** To agree or approve: I *concur* with you in your decision. **2** To cooperate; work together: Reading, study, and reflection had *concurred* to make him wise. **3** To happen at the same time.

con·cur·rence [kən·kûr′əns] *n.* **1** Agreement: He and I are in *concurrence* on this matter. **2** A working or happening together.

con·cur·rent [kən·kûr′ənt] *adj.* **1** Happening at the same time; existing in close association: The earliest birds and mammals had *concurrent* developments. **2** In agreement; consistent: The views brought out were not identical but *concurrent*. **— con·cur′rent·ly** *adv.*

con·cus·sion [kən·kush′ən] *n.* **1** A violent shaking; a shock, as an earthquake. **2** A violent shock to some organ, especially to the brain, by a fall, blow, or blast.

con·demn [kən·dem′] *v.* **1** To speak against as being wrong: to *condemn* dishonesty. **2** To declare the guilt of; convict: to *condemn* a prisoner. **3** To pass sentence on: to *condemn* someone to prison. **4** To declare unfit or unsafe for use: to *condemn* a hospital. **5** To take over for public use: to *condemn* land for a highway. **— con′dem·na′tion** *n.*

con·den·sa·tion [kon′den·sā′shən] *n.* **1** The act of condensing. **2** A being condensed. **3** Any product of condensing: Dew is a *condensation* of water vapor from the air. **4** The changing of a vapor or gas to a liquid, or of a liquid to a solid.

Condensation on a glass

con·dense [kən·dəns′] *v.* **con·densed, con·dens·ing** **1** To make or become denser, thicker, or more compressed, as by removing water: to *condense* orange juice before freezing it. **2** To shorten; make concise, as a speech or essay. **3** To change (a gas or vapor) into a liquid, or (a liquid) into a solid.

con·dens·er [kən·den′sər] *n.* **1** A person or thing that condenses. **2** Any device for reducing a vapor to liquid or solid form. **3** A capacitor.

con·de·scend [kon′di·send′] *v.* **1** To come down willingly to one's inferiors or show kindness to them: The star pitcher *condescended* to talk to the boys' club. **2** To behave as if superior; patronize. **3** *adj. use:* a *condescending* snob.

con·de·scen·sion [kon′di·sen′shən] *n.* **1** Pleasant or gracious treatment of an inferior. **2** Proud, patronizing behavior.

con·di·ment [kon′də·mənt] *n.* Something used to season food, as a sauce, pepper, or spice.

con·di·tion [kən·dish′ən] **1** *n.* The state of being of a person or thing: This book is in good *condition*. **2** *n.* Physical fitness; healthy state: The team is in *condition* for a hard game. **3** *v.* To put into a good state; make fit: Running two miles a day *conditioned* his legs. **4** *n.* Rank in life; social status: He rose above his family's *condition*. **5** *n.* Something on which another thing depends: A dry track is a *condition* of a fast race. **6** *v.* To be a necessary factor of: A fast or slow track *conditions* the speed of a race. **7** *n.* A requirement or stipulation: He set up *conditions* before he would accept. **8** *v.* To make conditional or dependent. **9** *v.* To accustom or train: Poverty *conditioned* him to hunger. **— on condition that** Provided that; if.

con·di·tion·al [kən·dish′ən·əl] *adj.* **1** Dependent on or subject to a condition. **2** Expressing or implying a condition: If I can come in "If I can come, I will" is a *conditional* clause.

con·dole [kən·dōl′] *v.* **con·doled, con·dol·ing** To grieve or express sympathy.

con·do·lence [kən·dō′ləns] *n.* An expression of sympathy.

con·done [kən·dōn′] *v.* **con·doned, con·don·ing** To forgive or pass over: Many mothers *condone* the mistakes of their children.

con·dor [kon′dôr *or* kon′dər] *n.* A large vulture having no feathers on its head and neck. Condors are found in the mountains of South America and California. ◆ *Condor* comes from a South American Indian name.

Condor, wingspread 9 ft.

add, āce, câre, pälm; **end, ēqual;** **it, ice;** **odd, ōpen, ôrder;** **tŏŏk, pōōl;** **up, bûrn;**
ə = a in *above*, e in *sicken*, i in *possible*, o in *melon*, u in *circus*; **yōō** = u in *fuse*; **oil;** **pout;**
check; ring; thin; this; zh in *vision.* For ¶ reference, see page 64 · HOW TO

con·duce [kən·d(y)o͞os′] *v.* **con·duced, con·duc·ing** To help or tend toward a result; contribute: Fresh air *conduces* to good health.

con·du·cive [kən·d(y)o͞o′siv] *adj.* Helpful: Good lighting is *conducive* to good vision.

con·duct [*n.* kon′dukt, *v.* kən·dukt′] **1** *n.* The way a person acts or lives; behavior. **2** *v.* To act or behave: He *conducts* himself well. **3** *n.* Management, as of a business; direction; control. **4** *v.* To manage; direct; control: How does she *conduct* her class? **5** *v.* To guide or lead: He *conducted* the orchestra brilliantly. **6** *v.* To pass on; carry (heat, electricity, etc.): Wood *conducts* heat badly.

con·duc·tion [kən·duk′shən] *n.* **1** A carrying: the *conduction* of water through a pipe. **2** The passage of heat, light, sound, or electricity through a material that does not appear to move.

con·duc·tiv·i·ty [kon′duk·tiv′ə·tē] *n.* The ability of a substance to act as a conductor.

con·duc·tor [kən·duk′tər] *n.* **1** A person who leads or guides. **2** A person in charge of a railroad train, streetcar, or bus. **3** The director of an orchestra or chorus. **4** A material that allows light, heat, sound, or electricity to pass through.

con·duit [kon′do͞o·it *or* kon′dit] *n.* **1** A channel or pipe for carrying water or other liquid. **2** A covered passage or tube for electric wires.

cone [kōn] *n.* **1** A surface formed by the set of points on all the lines joining the points of a given curve to a fixed point. **2** A figure consisting of such a surface bounded by two planes that intersect all its lines and form closed curves. **3** Any object having such a shape. **4** A dry, scaly fruit, as of the pine tree.

cone   pine cone   ice cream cone

con·fec·tion [kən·fek′shən] *n.* Any of various sweet preparations, as candy or preserves.

con·fec·tion·er [kən·fek′shən·ər] *n.* A person who makes or has to do with confectionery.

con·fec·tion·er·y [kən·fek′shən·er′ē] *n., pl.* **con·fec·tion·er·ies 1** All kinds of sweets, as ice cream, candies, and cakes. **2** The shop or business of a confectioner.

con·fed·er·a·cy [kən·fed′ər·ə·sē] *n., pl.* **con·fed·er·a·cies 1** A union or league of persons or states who have joined together for mutual support or action. **2** An unlawful combination; conspiracy. **3** (*written* **the Confederacy**) The Confederate States of America.

con·fed·er·ate [*n., adj.* kən·fed′ər·it, *v.* kən·fed′ə·rāt] *n., adj., v.* **con·fed·er·at·ed, con·fed·er·at·ing 1** *n.* A partner or accomplice, as in a crime. **2** *adj.* Joined or allied for some purpose. **3** *v.* To bring together or join in a league or alliance. **4** *n.* (*written* **Confederate**) A supporter of the Confederate States of America. **5** *adj.* (*written* **Confederate**) Having to do with the Confederate States of America.

Confederate States of America A league of eleven southern states that seceded from the United States in 1860 and 1861.

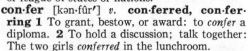

con·fed·er·a·tion [kən·fed′ə·rā′shən] *n.* **1** The act of confederating. **2** A being confederated. **3** A union or league of states or nations.

con·fer [kən·fûr′] *v.* **con·ferred, con·fer·ring 1** To grant, bestow, or award: to *confer* a diploma. **2** To hold a discussion; talk together: The two girls *conferred* in the lunchroom.

con·fer·ence [kon′fər·əns *or* kon′frəns] *n.* **1** A discussion or consultation on a particular subject. **2** A meeting at which such a discussion is held: The teachers are in an important *conference* in the principal's office. **3** A league or association, as of athletic teams.

con·fess [kən·fes′] *v.* **1** To admit, concede, or acknowledge: I *confess* I wasn't listening. **2** To admit guilt or error: Will you *confess*? **3** To declare; profess: I *confess* my belief in God. **4** To admit or make known (one's sins) to a priest. **5** To hear the confession of: The priest *confessed* the old lady.

con·fes·sion [kən·fesh′ən] *n.* **1** The act of confessing; acknowledgment; admission, especially of faults or guilt. **2** The thing that is admitted.

con·fes·sion·al [kən·fesh′ən·əl] *n.* A booth or stall where a priest hears confessions.

con·fes·sor [kən·fes′ər] *n.* **1** A priest who hears confessions. **2** A person who confesses.

con·fet·ti [kən·fet′ē] *n.pl.* (*used with singular verb*) Small pieces of colored paper thrown at weddings, carnivals, etc.: *Confetti* is colorful.

con·fi·dant [kon′fə·dant′ *or* kon′fə·dant] *n.* A friend whom one trusts with one's secrets.

con·fide [kən·fīd′] *v.* **con·fid·ed, con·fid·ing 1** To tell in trust or confidence: I *confided* my secret to my mother. **2** To have trust; place confidence: I *confided* in her. **3** To hand over for safekeeping; entrust: The will had been *confided* to a lawyer.

con·fi·dence [kon′fə·dəns] *n.* **1** A feeling of trust; reliance; faith: I have *confidence* in my parents. **2** A relationship of trust and intimacy: We spoke in *confidence*. **3** Faith in oneself; self-reliance: He has *confidence* in his own ability. **4** Something told in trust; a secret: The two girls exchanged *confidences*. ◆ See TRUST.

con·fi·dent [kon′fə·dənt] *adj.* Having confidence; assured: *confident* of success. — **con′·fi·dent·ly** *adv.*

con·fi·den·tial [kon′fə·den′shəl] *adj.* **1** Given in confidence; secret: *confidential* information. **2** Having another's confidence; trusted. **3** Showing readiness to confide: a *confidential* tone. — **con′·fi·den′·tial·ly** *adv.*

con·fig·u·ra·tion [kən·fig′yə·rā′shən] *n.* The form, shape, and arrangement of parts of a thing: the *configuration* of a leaf.

con·fine [*v.* kən·fīn′, *n.* kon′fīn] *v.* **con·fined, con·fin·ing,** *n.* **1** *v.* To shut in or keep shut in: He was *confined* in a prison camp; to be *confined* to his room by flu. **2** *v.* To limit: to *confine* a telephone call to five minutes. **3** *n.* (*usually pl.*) A boundary or border; limit: Keep within the *confines* of your subject.

con·fine·ment [kən·fīn′mənt] *n.* **1** The act of confining. **2** A being confined.

con·firm [kən·fûrm′] *v.* **1** To make certain of; verify: to *confirm* a report. **2** To approve; ratify: to *confirm* a treaty. **3** To receive into the church by confirmation.

con·fir·ma·tion [kon′fər·mā′shən] *n.* **1** The act of confirming. **2** Something that proves or makes certain. **3** A ceremony in which a person is admitted to full membership in a church.

con·firmed [kən·fûrmd′] *adj.* **1** Fixed; firmly established. **2** Habitual: a *confirmed* liar.

con·fis·cate [kon′fis·kāt] *v.* **con·fis·cat·ed, con·fis·cat·ing 1** To take or seize for the public treasury: The new government *confiscated* properties owned abroad. **2** To take by authority: The smuggled watches were *confiscated*. — **con′fis·ca′tion** *n.*

con·fla·gra·tion [kon′flə·grā′shən] *n.* A great fire.

con·flict [*n.* kon′flikt, *v.* kən·flikt′] **1** *n.* A struggle, fight, or battle. **2** *v.* To be opposed; clash; disagree: The views of Jefferson and Hamilton often *conflicted*. **3** *n.* An opposition or disagreement, as of ideas or interests.

con·flu·ence [kon′flōō·əns] *n.* **1** A flowing together: a *confluence* of streams. **2** A flocking together; crowd: a *confluence* of people.

con·flu·ent [kon′flōō·ənt] *adj.* Running together.

con·form [kən·fôrm′] *v.* **1** To make similar; adapt: *Conform* your behavior to that of the other students. **2** To be or act in accord with customs, rules, or accepted ideas: *Conform* to the rules. — **con·form′ist** *n.*

con·form·a·ble [kən·fôr′mə·bəl] *adj.* **1** Similar; corresponding; adapted: a schedule *conformable* to your wishes. **2** Obedient; submissive.

con·for·ma·tion [kon′fôr·mā′shən] *n.* The structure, shape, or way in which a thing is formed: the *conformation* of a glacier.

con·form·i·ty [kən·fôr′mə·tē] *n., pl.* **con·form·i·ties 1** Similarity or correspondence: the *conformity* of the dress to the pattern. **2** The following of the customs, fashions, tastes, and accepted ideas of others.

con·found [kon·found′] *v.* **1** To confuse, amaze, or bewilder: The puzzle *confounded* him. **2** To mix up; not to know apart: to *confound* rights and privileges.

con·front [kən·frunt′] *v.* **1** To stand face to face with; face boldly: to *confront* a storm at sea. **2** To put face to face: to *confront* a liar with the truth. — **con′fron·ta′tion** *n.*

Con·fu·cius [kən·fyōō′shəs] *n.,* 551?–478? B.C., Chinese philosopher and teacher.

con·fuse [kən·fyōōz′] *v.* **con·fused, con·fus·ing 1** To perplex; mix up: The traffic *confused* me. **2** To mix up; jumble: Don't *confuse* the papers on my desk. **3** To fail to distinguish; mistake: You are *confusing* me with my brother.

con·fu·sion [kən·fyōō′zhən] *n.* **1** A mixed-up or disordered state of mind or of things: thoughts in *confusion*. **2** The taking of one thing for another by mistake; failure to distinguish: His *confusion* of the chemicals caused an explosion. **3** Commotion; turmoil.

con·fute [kən·fyōōt′] *v.* **con·fut·ed, con·fut·ing 1** To prove (an argument, statement, etc.) wrong or false. **2** To prove (a person) wrong: to *confute* one's critics. — **con′fu·ta′tion** *n.*

con·geal [kən·jēl′] *v.* To thicken or change to a solid condition, as by growing cooler: The melted candle wax *congealed*.

con·gen·ial [kən·jēn′yəl] *adj.* **1** Getting along well with one another: *congenial* associates. **2** Suited to one's nature; agreeable: a *congenial* job. — **con·gen′ial·ly** *adv.*

con·gen·i·tal [kən·jen′ə·təl] *adj.* Existing at or before the time of birth: a *congenital* deformity. — **con·gen′i·tal·ly** *adv.*

con·gest [kən·jest′] *v.* **1** To make too full or very crowded: The sidewalks were *congested* with people watching the parade. **2** To fill too full of blood: said about a part of the body. — **con·ges′tion** *n.*

con·glom·er·ate [*v.* kən·glom′ə·rāt, *adj., n.* kən·glom′ər·it] *v.* **con·glom·er·at·ed, con·glom·er·at·ing,** *adj., n.* **1** *v.* To gather into a mass that holds together; cluster. **2** *adj.* Made up of various materials or parts gathered into a whole: a *conglomerate* mass. **3** *n.* A collection of things that are not alike. **4** *n.* A rock made up of pebbles and other rounded stones stuck together, as by hardened clay. — **con·glom′er·a′tion** *n.*

Con·go [kong′gō] *n.* **1** A very long river in central Africa, flowing into the Atlantic Ocean. **2** A country in central Africa east of the Congo River, formerly a colony of Belgium. **3** A country in central Africa west of the Congo River, formerly a colony of France.

con·grat·u·late [kən·grach′ōō·lāt] *v.* **con·grat·u·lat·ed, con·grat·u·lat·ing** To express pleasure to (someone) on his good fortune or success: I *congratulate* you on your victory.

con·grat·u·la·tion [kən·grach′ōō·lā′shən] *n.* **1** The act of congratulating. **2** (*pl.*) Good wishes

Mississippi River

Missouri River

Confluence of the Mississippi and Missouri rivers

add, āce, câre, pälm;   end, ēqual;   it, īce;   odd, ōpen, ôrder;   tŏŏk, pōōl;   up, bûrn;
ə = a in *above,* e in *sicken,* i in *possible,* o in *melon,* u in *circus;   yōō = u in *fuse*;   oil;   pout;*
check;   ring;   thin;   this;   zh in *vision.*   For ¶ reference, see page 64 · HOW TO

expressing pleasure at another's good fortune or success: to offer *congratulations*.

con·gre·gate [kong′grə·gāt] *v.* **con·gre·gat·ed, con·gre·gat·ing** To bring or come together into a crowd; assemble: A group of tourists *congregated* around the statue.

con·gre·ga·tion [kong′grə·gā′shən] *n.* **1** A group of people, especially those who meet together for worship. **2** A collection of things. **3** A collecting together into one group or mass.

con·gre·ga·tion·al [kong′grə·gā′shən·əl] *adj.* **1** Of or done by a congregation. **2** (*written* **Congregational**) Of a Protestant denomination in which each local congregation governs itself.

con·gress [kong′gris] *n.* **1** An assembly or conference, especially a formal meeting of representatives. **2** (*written* **Congress**) In the U.S., the assembly of elected representatives that meets to make the laws for the nation. It is divided into the Senate and the House of Representatives. **3** A coming together; meeting.

con·gres·sion·al [kən·gresh′ən·əl] *adj.* Having to do with Congress or with a congress.

con·gress·man [kong′gris·mən] *n.,* *pl.* **con·gress·men** [kong′gris·mən] A member of the U.S. Congress, especially of the House of Representatives.

con·gru·ent [kong′grōō·ənt] *adj.* Coinciding exactly when one is placed on another, as two triangles. —**con′·gru·ence** *n.*

con·i·cal [kon′i·kəl] *adj.* Of or like a cone, as in shape. — **con′·i·cal·ly** *adv.*

Congruent triangles

con·i·fer [kon′ə·fər *or* kō′nə·fər] *n.* Any tree or shrub that bears cones, as the pine, fir, and spruce. — **co·nif·er·ous** [kō·nif′ər·əs] *adj.*

conj. Abbreviation of CONJUNCTION.

con·jec·ture [kən·jek′chər] *n., v.* **con·jec·tured, con·jec·tur·ing** **1** *n.* A guess made when there is not enough evidence to be sure. **2** *v.* To guess: The major *conjectured* that the missing men were alive. **3** *n.* The making of conjectures. — **con·jec′tur·al** *adj.*

con·join [kən·join′] *v.* To join together; associate: Wit and memory are often *conjoined*.

con·joint·ly [kən·joint′lē] *adv.* In association; together: They acted *conjointly*.

con·ju·gal [kon′jōō·gəl] *adj.* Having to do with marriage: *conjugal* bliss.

con·ju·gate [kon′jōō·gāt] *v.* **con·ju·gat·ed, con·ju·gat·ing** To list in regular order the various forms of (a verb): To conjugate *to have,* begin with "I have, you have, he has."

con·ju·ga·tion [kon′jōō·gā′shən] *n.* **1** A listing or arrangement in regular order of the various forms of a verb. **2** A joining together; union.

con·junc·tion [kən·jungk′shən] *n.* **1** Combination; association: The FBI worked in *conjunction* with local police. **2** A word that is used to connect other words, phrases, clauses, or sen-

tences, as *or* in "day or night," *and* in "over the hill and across the bridge," and *when* in "He waved when he saw me."

con·jure [kon′jər *or* kun′jər] *v.* **con·jured, con·jur·ing** **1** To summon (a spirit) by magic words or a magic spell: to *conjure* up a devil. **2** To perform a magician's puzzling tricks. **3** To cause to come to mind as if by magic: He *conjured* up the scene in the story. **4** [kən·jŏŏr′] To appeal to seriously: I *conjure* you to heed my advice.

con·jur·er *or* **con·jur·or** [kon′jər·ər *or* kun′·jər·ər] *n.* A magician.

Conn. Abbreviation of CONNECTICUT.

con·nect [kə·nekt′] *v.* **1** To join together; link: A canal *connects* the lake with Puget Sound. **2** To join by association or relationship: to *connect* two thoughts; He is *connected* with the government. **3** To place in an electric circuit: to *connect* a telephone.

Con·nect·i·cut [kə·net′ə·kət] *n.* A state in the NE U.S.

con·nec·tion [kə·nek′shən] *n.* **1** The act of connecting. **2** The condition of being connected; union. **3** A thing or part that connects, or a means for connecting; link; bond: The hose *connection* was bent. **4** An association or relationship: There is no *connection* between the two events. **5** (*usually pl.*) A group of persons with whom one is associated: to have good *connections*. **6** A relative, especially by marriage. **7** A transfer from one train, bus, etc., to another: We missed our *connection* at Richmond.

con·nec·tive [kə·nek′tiv] **1** *adj.* Serving to connect: *Connective* tissue unites and supports the various parts of the body. **2** *n.* A thing or word that connects, as a conjunction.

con·niv·ance [kə·nī′vəns] *n.* The act of conniving, as silent consent to wrongdoing.

con·nive [kə·nīv′] *v.* **con·nived, con·niv·ing** **1** To allow something wrong to go on by pretending not to see it or by not telling about it. **2** To join secretly in wrongdoing. — **con·niv′er** *n.* ◆ *Connive* comes from a Latin word meaning *to wink* or *shut the eyes.*

con·nois·seur [kon′ə·sûr′] *n.* An expert qualified to judge in some field of art or taste: a *connoisseur* of old china. ◆ See AMATEUR.

con·no·ta·tion [kon′ə·tā′shən] *n.* What a word or expression suggests or may be associated with, not what it actually means. ◆ See DENOTATION.

con·note [kə·nōt′] *v.* **con·not·ed, con·not·ing** To suggest or imply along with the actual meaning: The word "summer" may *connote* swimming.

con·nu·bi·al [kə·n(y)ōō′bē·əl] *adj.* Having to do with marriage; matrimonial.

con·quer [kong′kər] *v.* **1** To defeat or win control of by use of force, as in war: to *conquer* an enemy nation. **2** To be victorious. **3** To overcome by effort: to *conquer* a bad habit. — **con′·quer·or** *n.*

con·quest [kon(g)′kwest] *n.* **1** The act of winning over or defeating by force. **2** Something conquered, as territory.

con·quis·ta·dor [kon·k(w)is′tə·dôr] *n.*, *pl.* **con·quis·ta·dors** or **con·quis·ta·do·res** [kon·k(w)is′tə·dôr′ās] Any of the Spanish conquerors of Mexico and Peru in the 16th century.

Con·rad [kon′rad], **Joseph**, 1857–1924, English author born in Poland.

con·science [kon′shəns] *n.* The inner understanding that lets a person know when he is doing right and when he is doing wrong: Her guilty *conscience* led her to confess.

con·sci·en·tious [kon′shē·en′shəs] *adj.* **1** Trying to do right; guided by conscience: a *conscientious* student. **2** Done carefully and thoroughly: *conscientious* work. — **con′sci·en′tious·ly** *adv.* — **con′sci·en′tious·ness** *n.*

conscientious objector A person who refuses to serve in the armed forces because of religious or moral beliefs that war is wrong.

con·scious [kon′shəs] *adj.* **1** Able to hear, see, feel, etc.; awake: Is the patient *conscious*? **2** Aware of some object, fact, or feeling: *conscious* of a low hum. **3** Felt or known by oneself: *conscious* superiority. **4** Deliberate; intended: a *conscious* rebuke. — **con′scious·ly** *adv.*

con·scious·ness [kon′shəs·nis] *n.* **1** A conscious condition; awareness: to regain *consciousness*; *consciousness* of danger. **2** One's conscious thoughts, feelings, etc.

con·script [*v.* kən·skript′, *adj.*, *n.* kon′skript] **1** *v.* To force into military, naval, or other service; draft. **2** *adj.* Forced into service. **3** *n.* A person drafted into the armed forces or forced to do some job. — **con·scrip′tion** *n.*

con·se·crate [kon′sə·krāt] *v.* **con·se·crat·ed, con·se·crat·ing** **1** To dedicate to sacred uses: to *consecrate* a church. **2** To devote to a special purpose: She *consecrated* her life to caring for the sick. — **con′se·cra′tion** *n.*

con·sec·u·tive [kən·sek′yə·tiv] *adj.* Following each other without a break: five *consecutive* months. — **con·sec′u·tive·ly** *adv.*

con·sen·sus [kən·sen′səs] *n.* Agreement of a majority or of everyone; general opinion. ◆ The phrase *consensus of opinion* is widely used, although it is actually repetitious, since *consensus* by itself means *general opinion*.

con·sent [kən·sent′] **1** *v.* To give approval; agree: She *consented* to marry him. **2** *n.* Permission or approval; agreement: You may not go without your parents' *consent*.

con·se·quence [kon′sə·kwens] *n.* **1** A result or effect: He did not consider the *consequences* of his acts. **2** Importance: an event of no *consequence*.

con·se·quent [kon′sə·kwent] *adj.* Following as a result: excitement and *consequent* confusion.

con·se·quen·tial [kon′sə·kwen′shəl] *adj.* **1** Important. **2** Self-important. **3** Consequent.

con·se·quent·ly [kon′sə·kwent′lē] *adv.* As a result; therefore.

con·ser·va·tion [kon′sər·vā′shən] *n.* The protecting or preserving from waste, injury, or loss: the *conservation* of natural resources such as forests. — **con′ser·va′tion·ist** *n.*

con·ser·va·tism [kən·sûr′və·tiz′əm] *n.* Opposition to change; the desire to keep things as they have been: political *conservatism*.

con·ser·va·tive [kən·sûr′və·tiv] **1** *adj.* Wishing to keep things as they have been; opposed to change: a *conservative* politician. **2** *adj.* Moderate; cautious: a *conservative* estimate. **3** *n.* A conservative person. **4** *adj.* Conserving.

con·ser·va·to·ry [kən·sûr′və·tôr′ē] *n.*, *pl.* **con·ser·va·to·ries** **1** A small greenhouse for growing plants. **2** A school of music.

con·serve [*v.* kən·sûrv′, *n.* kən·sûrv′ or kon′·sûrv] *v.* **con·served, con·serv·ing**, *n.* **1** *v.* To keep from becoming lost, spoiled, or used up: to *conserve* water. **2** *n.* (*often pl.*) A jam made of fruits stewed with sugar.

con·sid·er [kən·sid′ər] *v.* **1** To think about carefully: I will *consider* your request. **2** To believe to be: They *consider* her a genius. **3** To take into account; make allowance for: He does well, if you *consider* his lack of training. **4** To be thoughtful of; respect: to *consider* other people's feelings.

con·sid·er·a·ble [kən·sid′ər·ə·bəl] *adj.* Rather large; worth noticing: *considerable* talent.

con·sid·er·a·bly [kən·sid′ər·ə·blē] *adv.* Much.

con·sid·er·ate [kən·sid′ər·it] *adj.* Thoughtful of others; kind. — **con·sid′er·ate·ly** *adv.*

con·sid·er·a·tion [kən·sid′ə·rā′shən] *n.* **1** The act of thinking carefully: After long *consideration*, he refused the job offer. **2** Thoughtful concern, as for the feelings or interests of others. **3** A reason, as for an action: Your safety was my major *consideration* in refusing to let you go. **4** A payment given for a service; fee. — **in consideration of 1** Because of. **2** In return for. — **take into consideration** To take into account; allow for. — **under consideration** Being thought about or discussed.

con·sid·ered [kən·sid′ərd] *adj.* Carefully thought about: a *considered* opinion.

con·sid·er·ing [kən·sid′ər·ing] *prep.* In view of; taking into account: *Considering* his illness, he has achieved a great deal.

con·sign [kən·sīn′] *v.* **1** To give or hand over: He *consigned* his pictures to a museum. **2** To send: to *consign* goods to an agent.

con·sign·ment [kən·sīn′mənt] *n.* **1** The act of consigning. **2** Something consigned, as goods.

con·sist [kən·sist′] *v.* **1** To be made up or composed: The program *consisted* of folk songs. **2** To be found or contained; lie: For him, happiness *consisted* in helping others.

con·sis·ten·cy [kən·sis′tən·sē] *n.*, *pl.* **con·sis·ten·cies** **1** The degree of firmness or stiffness: egg whites beaten to the *consistency* of

---

add, āce, câre, pälm; end, ēqual; it, īce; odd, ōpen, ôrder; took, pool; up, bûrn; ə = a in *above*, e in *sicken*, i in *possible*, o in *melon*, u in *circus*; yoo = u in *fuse*; oil; pout; check; ring; thin; this; zh in *vision*. For ¶ reference, see page 64 · HOW TO

whipped cream. **2** A sticking to the same principles, ways of acting, etc.: He voted with *consistency* against all taxes. **3** Agreement or accord.

con·sis·tent [kən·sis′tənt] *adj.* **1** Sticking to the same principles, ways of acting, etc.: a *consistent* supporter of higher pay for teachers. **2** In agreement or accord: actions *consistent* with promises. — **con·sis′tent·ly** *adv.*

con·sis·to·ry [kən·sis′tər·ē] *n., pl.* **con·sis·to·ries** A court or council of a church.

con·so·la·tion [kon′sə·lā′shən] *n.* **1** The act of consoling. **2** A person or thing that consoles. **3** The condition of being consoled.

con·sole[1] [kən·sōl′] *v.* **con·soled, con·sol·ing** To comfort in sorrow or disappointment; cheer.

con·sole[2] [kon′sōl] *n.* **1** The part of an organ containing the keyboards, pedals, and stops. **2** A radio, phonograph, or television cabinet made to stand on the floor.

con·sol·i·date [kən·sol′ə·dāt] *v.* **con·sol·i·dat·ed, con·sol·i·dat·ing** **1** To combine or unite: to *consolidate* three school districts to form one big school. **2** To make or become firm; strengthen: The prize *consolidated* his rating as a star. — **con·sol′i·da′tion** *n.*

con·som·mé [kon′sə·mā′] *n.* A clear soup made of meat boiled in water.

con·so·nance [kon′sə·nəns] *n.* **1** Agreement. **2** Harmony of sounds, especially of consonants.

con·so·nant [kon′sə·nənt] **1** *n.* A speech sound made when the breath is partly or completely blocked by the teeth, tongue, or lips. **2** *n.* A letter representing such a sound, as *b, f, k, s;* any letter that is not a vowel. **3** *adj.* In agreement or accord: His acts are *consonant* with his character.

con·sort [*n.* kon′sôrt, *v.* kən·sôrt′] **1** *n.* A husband or wife, especially of a ruler. **2** *v.* To associate: Don't *consort* with strangers. **3** *n.* A ship sailing with another.

con·spic·u·ous [kən·spik′yo͞o·əs] *adj.* **1** Easily or clearly seen: a *conspicuous* poster. **2** Attracting attention because remarkable: *conspicuous* courage. — **con·spic′u·ous·ly** *adv.* — **con·spic′u·ous·ness** *n.*

con·spir·a·cy [kən·spir′ə·sē] *n., pl.* **con·spir·a·cies** A secret plan of two or more

This is a conspicuous error.

persons to do an evil or unlawful act; plot.

con·spir·a·tor [kən·spir′ə·tər] *n.* A person involved in a conspiracy; plotter.

con·spire [kən·spīr′] *v.* **con·spired, con·spir·ing** **1** To plan with one another secretly to commit an evil or unlawful act; plot. **2** To act together: Winds and currents *conspired* to speed the voyage.

con·sta·ble [kon′stə·bəl] *n.* A policeman.

con·stan·cy [kon′stən·sē] *n.* Faithfulness or firmness in purpose, action, affections, etc.

con·stant [kon′stənt] **1** *adj.* Remaining the same; not changing: a *constant* factor. **2** *n.* A number or other thing that never changes: The speed of light is a *constant.* **3** *adj.* Faithful;

true: a *constant* friend. **4** *adj.* Happening over and over; endless; continual: *constant* interruptions. — **con′stant·ly** *adv.*

Con·stan·ti·no·ple [kon′stan·tə·nō′pəl] *n.* An old name for Istanbul, a city in Turkey.

con·stel·la·tion [kon′stə·lā′shən] *n.* A group of stars to which a definite name has been assigned, as Orion or the Big Dipper.

con·ster·na·tion [kon′stər·nā′shən] *n.* Great fear or dismay that makes one feel helpless.

The Big Dipper

con·sti·pate [kon′stə·pāt] *v.* **con·sti·pat·ed, con·sti·pat·ing** To cause constipation in.

con·sti·pa·tion [kon′stə·pā′shən] *n.* A condition in which bowel movements are difficult or do not occur often enough.

con·stit·u·en·cy [kən·stich′o͞o·ən·sē] *n., pl.* **con·stit·u·en·cies** **1** All of the voters in an election district. **2** The district itself.

con·stit·u·ent [kən·stich′o͞o·ənt] **1** *adj.* Necessary in making up a whole: a *constituent* part or element. **2** *n.* A necessary part or element: Hydrogen is a *constituent* of water. **3** *n.* A voter represented by an elected representative. **4** *adj.* Entitled to vote for a representative or to make or change a constitution: a *constituent* assembly.

con·sti·tute [kon′stə·t(y)o͞ot] *v.* **con·sti·tut·ed, con·sti·tut·ing** **1** To make up; compose: Two pints *constitute* a quart. **2** To set up; establish: a government *constituted* by the people. **3** To select or appoint.

con·sti·tu·tion [kon′stə·t(y)o͞o′shən] *n.* **1** The fundamental laws and principles set up to govern a nation, state, or association. **2** (*written* **the Constitution**) The fundamental law of the U.S. **3** The way in which a person or thing is put together; make-up: The sickly girl had a weak *constitution.* **4** The act of constituting.

con·sti·tu·tion·al [kon′stə·t(y)o͞o′shən·əl] **1** *adj.* Of, in agreement with, or subject to the constitution of a nation or state: a *constitutional* right; a *constitutional* monarchy. **2** *adj.* Of or found in the make-up of a person or thing: a *constitutional* weakness. **3** *n.* A walk taken for the health. — **con′sti·tu′tion·al·ly** *adv.*

con·sti·tu·tion·al·i·ty [kon′stə·t(y)o͞o′shən·al′ə·tē] *n.* Agreement with a constitution: to question a law's *constitutionality.*

con·strain [kən·strān′] *v.* **1** To force; compel: Honesty *constrained* him to agree. **2** *adj. use:* a *constrained* smile. **3** To hold back; restrain.

con·straint [kən·strānt′] *n.* **1** Force, either to compel or to hold back and restrain. **2** The holding back of feelings.

con·strict [kən·strikt′] *v.* To draw together; make narrower; squeeze: A corset *constricted* her waist. — **con·stric′tion** *n.*

con·stric·tor [kən·strik′tər] *n.* A snake that coils about and crushes its prey.

con·struct [kən·strukt′] *v.* To make by putting parts together; build: to *construct* a garage.

con·struc·tion [kən·struk′shən] *n.* **1** The act of constructing: The *construction* of a house takes time. **2** The business of building. **3** Something built or put together; structure. **4** The way in which a thing is formed or built: a table of sturdy *construction*. **5** Explanation; interpretation: What *construction* do you put on his behavior? **6** The arrangement of words in a sentence.

con·struc·tive [kən·struk′tiv] *adj.* **1** Helping to build up or improve: *constructive* criticism. **2** Having to do with construction. —**con·struc′tive·ly** *adv.*

con·strue [kən·strōō′] *v.* **con·strued, con·stru·ing** **1** To interpret; explain: We *construed* his gesture as a signal. **2** To show how the parts of (a clause or sentence) are arranged.

con·sul [kon′səl] *n.* **1** An official living in a foreign city to protect the people and business interests of the country he represents: the American *consul* in Venice. **2** Either of the two chief magistrates ruling the ancient Roman republic. —**con·su·lar** [kon′sə·lər] *adj.* —**con′sul·ship** *n.* ◆ See COUNCIL.

con·su·late [kon′sə·lit] *n.* **1** The official place of business of a consul. **2** The position or term of office of a consul.

con·sult [kən·sult′] *v.* **1** To turn to for advice, aid, or information: to *consult* a doctor or a dictionary. **2** To compare views: to *consult* with others. **3** To take into account; consider: to *consult* one's best interests.

con·sult·ant [kən·sul′tənt] *n.* A person who provides expert or professional advice.

con·sul·ta·tion [kon′səl·tā′shən] *n.* **1** A meeting to discuss something or to share opinions; conference. **2** The act of consulting.

con·sume [kən·sōōm′] *v.* **con·sumed, con·sum·ing** **1** To destroy, as by burning. **2** To use up or waste, as money or time. **3** To eat or drink. **4** To take up all the attention or interest of: Curiosity *consumed* her.

con·sum·er [kən·sōō′mər] *n.* A person who uses goods or services for his own needs.

con·sum·mate [*adj.* kən·sum′it, *v.* kon′sə·māt] *adj., v.* **con·sum·mat·ed, con·sum·mat·ing** **1** *adj.* Of the highest degree; perfect; complete: *consummate* wisdom. **2** *v.* To make complete or perfect; fulfill: The award *consummated* his career. —**con′sum·ma′tion** *n.*

con·sump·tion [kən·sump′shən] *n.* **1** The act of using up or destroying. **2** The amount used up: a rise in the *consumption* of fuel. **3** An old-fashioned word for tuberculosis of the lungs.

con·sump·tive [kən·sump′tiv] **1** *adj.* Suffering from tuberculosis of the lungs. **2** *n.* A person suffering from this disease. **3** *adj.* Of or like consumption. **4** *adj.* Wasteful; destructive.

con·tact [kon′takt] **1** *n.* A coming together, touching, or meeting: The bomb exploded on *contact.* **2** *n.* The relation of touching or being in touch: They kept in *contact* by writing. **3** *v. informal* To get in touch with: Try to *contact* him at his office. **4** *n.* Connection: to maintain radio *contact* with an astronaut. **5** *n.* The connection of two electric conductors, as in a switch or relay.

contact lens A thin lens worn directly on the eyeball to aid vision.

con·ta·gion [kən·tā′jən] *n.* **1** The passing on of disease from person to person by contact. **2** A disease spread in this manner. **3** The passing on of an influence: the *contagion* of laughter.

con·ta·gious [kən·tā′jəs] *adj.* Easily spread from person to person, as by contact; catching: a *contagious* disease; Laughter is *contagious.*

con·tain [kən·tān′] *v.* **1** To have inside; hold or include: Each carton *contains* 12 cans. **2** To be able to hold: This basket *contains* a bushel. **3** To be equal to: A pound *contains* 16 ounces. **4** To hold back; restrain: He could not *contain* his laughter.

con·tain·er [kən·tā′nər] *n.* A box, jar, cup, can, etc., used to hold something.

con·tam·i·nate [kən·tam′ə·nāt] *v.* **con·tam·i·nat·ed, con·tam·i·nat·ing** To make impure or spoil by mixing with or getting into: Smoke *contaminates* city air. —**con·tam′i·na′tion** *n.*

con·tem·plate [kon′təm·plāt] *v.* **con·tem·plat·ed, con·tem·plat·ing** **1** To look at or consider thoughtfully for a long time: to *contemplate* a painting. **2** To intend or plan; expect: We don't *contemplate* moving before next fall. **3** To meditate. —**con′tem·pla′tion** *n.*

con·tem·pla·tive [kən·tem′plə·tiv *or* kon′təm·plā′tiv] *adj.* Given to meditation, especially religious; thoughtful: a *contemplative* mind.

con·tem·po·ra·ne·ous [kən·tem′pə·rā′nē·əs] *adj.* Living or happening at the same time: *contemporaneous* discoveries.

con·tem·po·rar·y [kən·tem′pə·rer′ē] *adj., n., pl.* **con·tem·po·rar·ies** **1** *adj.* Living or happening during the same period of time. **2** *n.* A person living at the same time as another: Byron and Keats were *contemporaries.* **3** *adj.* Modern; current.

con·tempt [kən·tempt′] *n.* **1** The feeling that a person, act, or thing is low, dishonorable, or disgusting: to have *contempt* for a traitor. **2** The condition of being despised; disgrace: to hold a liar in *contempt.* **3** Disrespect for or disregard of the rules or orders of a court or legislature: jailed for *contempt* of Congress. ◆ *Contempt, disdain,* and *scorn* all suggest a looking down on others. *Contempt* is the strongest term, and is reserved for those whom, if we regarded them as equals, we would loathe or hate. *Disdain* suggests more an unwillingness to touch or get involved with than a feeling as intense as hate. A wealthy aristocrat may feel *disdain* for a beggar, but he reserves his *contempt* for swindlers and thieves. A person who feels *disdain* must have a high opinion of himself, but one who feels *scorn* need only have a low opinion of others. *Scorn* is closer to ridicule: The *scorn* with which he greeted my request made me ashamed.

con·tempt·i·ble [kən·temp′tə·bəl] *adj.* Deserving contempt or scorn: a *contemptible* bully.

con·temp·tu·ous [kən·temp′chōō·əs] *adj.* Full of contempt or scorn; disdainful: a *contemptuous* attitude. **— con·temp′tu·ous·ly** *adv.*

con·tend [kən·tend′] *v.* **1** To struggle; fight: to *contend* with prejudice. **2** To engage in a contest or competition; compete: to *contend* for a trophy. **3** To argue; maintain: I *contend* that you are wrong. **— con·tend′er** *n.*

con·tent[1] [kon′tent] *n.* **1** (*usually pl.*) All that a thing contains: the *contents* of a box; a book's table of *contents*. **2** The amount of a particular substance contained: the silver *content* of ore. **3** Facts, ideas, or meaning expressed in speaking or writing: the style and *content* of a novel.

con·tent[2] [kən·tent′] **1** *adj.* Happy enough not to complain or to want something else; satisfied: She was *content* to stay at home. **2** *v.* To satisfy: *Content* yourself with what you have. **3** *n.* Ease of mind; satisfaction.

con·tent·ed [kən·ten′tid] *adj.* Satisfied with things as they are. **— con·tent′ed·ly** *adv.*

con·ten·tion [kən·ten′shən] *n.* **1** Argument, strife, or dispute. **2** A point or belief for which someone argues: It was his *contention* that I was at fault.

con·ten·tious [kən·ten′shəs] *adj.* Liking to argue; quarrelsome. **— con·ten′tious·ly** *adv.*

con·tent·ment [kən·tent′mənt] *n.* Calm satisfaction; peaceful happiness.

con·test [*n.* kon′test, *v.* kən·test′] **1** *n.* A game, race, or competition that is to be won or lost. **2** *v.* To fight for: The two teams *contested* every yard. **3** *n.* A struggle, fight, or quarrel. **4** *v.* To question or challenge: to *contest* a decision.

con·test·ant [kən·tes′tənt] *n.* A person who enters a contest or who contests something.

con·text [kon′tekst] *n.* The phrase or passage in which a word or group of words is found and which affects or suggests its meaning: "Affects" means "influences" in this *context*.

con·tig·u·ous [kən·tig′yōō·əs] *adj.* **1** Touching at the edge: *contiguous* back yards. **2** Close, but not touching: *contiguous* buildings.

con·ti·nence [kon′tə·nəns] *n.* Self-restraint.

con·ti·nent [kon′tə·nənt] **1** *n.* One of the major land areas of the earth. Europe, Asia, Africa, Australia, North America, South America, and Antarctica are the continents. **2** *n.* (*written* **the Continent**) Europe, apart from the British Isles. **3** *adj.* Able to control one's desires; showing self-restraint.

con·ti·nen·tal [kon′tə·nen′təl] **1** *adj.* Of or resembling a continent. **2** *adj.* (*often written* **Continental**) Of, on, or having to do with the European continent. **3** *n.* (*usually written* **Continental**) A European. **4** *adj.* (*written* **Con-**

tinental) Having to do with the 13 American colonies during and just after the Revolutionary War. **5** *n.* (*written* **Continental**) An American soldier in the Revolutionary War.

Continental Divide The high ridge of the Rocky Mountains which separates streams flowing into the Atlantic or the Arctic from those flowing into the Pacific.

con·tin·gen·cy [kən·tin′jən·sē] *n., pl.* **con·tin·gen·cies 1** A possible happening or chance event: equipped for every *contingency*. **2** The condition of being subject to chance or accident.

con·tin·gent [kən·tin′jənt] **1** *adj.* Likely, but not sure, to happen; possible: a *contingent* result. **2** *adj.* Occurring by chance; accidental. **3** *adj.* Dependent upon an uncertain event or condition: A good crop is *contingent* on summer rains. **4** *n.* A possible happening or accident; contingency. **5** *n.* A group making up part of a larger group. **6** *n.* A share or quota of troops, workers, etc.: a *contingent* of Irish troops.

con·tin·u·al [kən·tin′yōō·əl] *adj.* **1** Repeated very often; frequent: *continual* complaints. **2** Going on without a pause; continuous. **— con·tin′u·al·ly** *adv.* ◆ Something *continual* starts and stops, as the dripping of a faucet. Something *continuous*, however, continues without any interruptions: a *continuous* flow of water.

con·tin·u·ance [kən·tin′yōō·əns] *n.* **1** A continuing, lasting, or remaining: The *continuance* of this privilege depends on how you behave. **2** A putting off of a legal action to a future time.

con·tin·u·a·tion [kən·tin′yōō·ā′shən] *n.* **1** The act of going on, keeping up, or carrying further, as after a break: the *continuation* of our studies after lunch. **2** An added part: Look for a *continuation* of this story next month.

con·tin·ue [kən·tin′yōō] *v.* **con·tin·ued, con·tin·u·ing 1** To go on or persist in an action or condition: They *continued* to try. **2** To go on or begin again after a break; resume: The story *continues* on the next page. **3** To go or carry further; extend: to *continue* a history. **4** To remain in the same place or condition: He will *continue* in this present job. **5** To keep on; retain: The mayor was *continued* in office. **6** To postpone, as a case for trial.

con·ti·nu·i·ty [kon′tə·nōō′ə·tē *or* kon′tə·nyōō′ə·tē] *n., pl.* **con·ti·nu·i·ties 1** The condition or quality of being continuous. **2** An unbroken sequence of thoughts, actions, etc.

con·tin·u·ous [kən·tin′yōō·əs] *adj.* Going on without pause or interruption: a *continuous* flow. **— con·tin′u·ous·ly** *adv.* ◆ See CON-TINUAL.

con·tort [kən·tôrt′] *v.* To twist or wrench out of the normal shape: Rage *contorted* his face.

con·tor·tion [kən·tôr′shən] *n.* **1** The act of twisting. **2** A twisted condition. **3** A twisted shape or position, as one taken by an acrobat.

con·tour [kon′tŏŏr] **1** *n.* The outline of a figure or body, or a line representing it. **2** *adj.* Following a line crosswise to any slope, as in plowing, to prevent erosion: *contour* farming.

contour map A map showing altitudes in a region by use of **contour lines** which connect points of equal altitude.

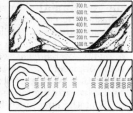

Contour map

con·tra·band [kon′trə·band] **1** *n.* Goods that cannot legally be imported or exported; smuggled goods. **2** *adj. use:* contraband goods. **3** *n.* Illegal trade; smuggling. **4** *n.* Goods such as arms, called **contraband of war,** that can be legally seized by either party in a war if they are shipped to the other.

con·tract [*n.* kon′trakt, *v.* kən·trakt′ *or in def.* 2 kon′trakt] **1** *n.* A binding agreement between two or more parties, especially a written one. **2** *v.* To enter into or arrange by such an agreement: He *contracted* to do the work; to *contract* marriage. **3** *v.* To acquire or catch: to *contract* debts; to *contract* a disease. **4** *v.* To draw together into a smaller space: to *contract* a muscle; When cooled, metals *contract.* **5** *n.* The now usual form of the game of bridge.

con·trac·tion [kən·trak′shən] *n.* **1** The action of drawing together or contracting: *Contraction* of the heart drives blood to the arteries. **2** A contracted condition. **3** A shortened form of a word or phrase made by leaving out letters or sounds: "Isn't" is a *contraction* of "is not."
◆ See ABBREVIATION.

con·trac·tor [kon′trak·tər] *n.* A person or firm that agrees to supply materials or perform services for a stated price.

con·tra·dict [kon′trə·dikt′] *v.* **1** To deny (a statement); state the opposite of. **2** To deny what is stated by: Don't *contradict* me. **3** To be opposite or contrary to: Her testimony *contradicted* his.

con·tra·dic·tion [kon′trə·dik′shən] *n.* **1** Denial of a statement. **2** A statement or action contradicting another. **3** Lack of agreement.

con·tra·dic·to·ry [kon′trə·dik′tər·ē] *adj.* Expressing the opposite; contradicting. ◆ Two statements are *contradictory* if one must be true and the other false. *I am an American* and *I am not an American* are *contradictory* statements. *Contrary* statements cannot both be true, but they can both be false. *I am an American* and *I am a Frenchman* are *contrary* statements.

con·tral·to [kən·tral′tō] *n., pl.* **con·tral·tos** **1** The lowest female singing voice. **2** *adj. use:* a *contralto* voice; the *contralto* part. **3** A singer having a contralto voice.

con·trap·tion [kən·trap′shən] *n. informal* An odd or puzzling device or gadget.

con·trar·y [kon′trer·ē *or for def.* 4 kən·trâr′ē] *adj., n., pl.* **con·trar·ies** **1** *adj.* Entirely different; opposite: *contrary* beliefs. **2** *n.* The opposite: The *contrary* is true. **3** *adj.* Opposed: a claim *contrary* to the facts. **4** *adj.* Stubbornly determined to oppose or contradict: a *contrary* girl. **— on the contrary** The reverse is true.
◆ See CONTRADICTORY.

con·trast [*v.* kən·trast′, *n.* kon′trast] **1** *v.* To compare in order to show differences: *Contrast* city life with country life. **2** *n.* A difference revealed when things are compared: the sharp *contrast* between light and shadow. **3** *v.*

slight contrast   strong contrast

To show differences when compared: Blue and white *contrast* attractively. **4** *n.* A person or thing showing such differences: His antique car is quite a *contrast* to a new one.

con·trib·ute [kən·trib′yo͞ot] *v.* **con·trib·ut·ed, con·trib·ut·ing** **1** To join others in giving to some cause: to *contribute* to a charity. **2** To furnish (an article, story, etc.) to a newspaper or magazine. **— contribute to** To share in bringing about: Many causes *contribute to* the growth of suburbs. **— con·trib′u·tor** *n.*

con·tri·bu·tion [kon′trə·byo͞o′shən] *n.* **1** The act of contributing. **2** Anything contributed, as money to a fund or a story to a magazine.

con·trib·u·to·ry [kən·trib′yə·tôr′ē] *adj.* Helping toward a result; contributing: Poor diet was a *contributory* cause of his illness.

con·trite [kən·trīt′ *or* kon′trīt] *adj.* **1** Deeply and humbly sorry for having done wrong. **2** Resulting from such a feeling: *contrite* tears.

con·tri·tion [kən·trish′ən] *n.* Sincere sorrow for sin or wrongdoing; repentance; penitence.

con·triv·ance [kən·trī′vəns] *n.* **1** A mechanical device, clever plan, or other invention: That new can opener is an odd looking *contrivance.* **2** The act, power, or manner of contriving.

con·trive [kən·trīv′] *v.* **con·trived, con·triv·ing** **1** To figure out; plan or plot: He *contrived* a way to trick them. **2** To manage, as by a plan: We *contrived* to leave early. **3** To design; invent: They *contrived* a boat of hides.

con·trol [kən·trōl′] *v.* **con·trolled, con·trol·ling,** *n.* **1** *v.* To have power or authority to direct or manage: Each principal *controls* his own school. **2** *n.* Power or authority to direct or manage: to win *control* of a company. **3** *v.* To hold back; restrain; check: He tried to *control* his temper. **4** *n.* A controlled or guided condition; restraint: Everything is under *control*; a car out of *control.* **5** *n.* (*often pl.*) A device used to operate a machine: The copilot took the *controls.* **6** *n.* A standard of comparison used in checking the results of a scientific experiment.

con·trol·ler [kən·trō′lər] *n.* **1** An official who decides about making proposed expenditures. **2** A person or thing that controls or regulates.

---

add, āce, câre, pälm;   end, ēqual;   it, īce;   odd, ōpen, ôrder;   to͝ok, po͞ol;   up, bûrn;
ə = a in *above*, e in *sicken*, i in *possible*, o in *melon*, u in *circus*;   yo͞o = u in *fuse*;   oil;   pout;
    check;   ring;   thin;   this;   zh in *vision*.   For ¶ reference, see page 64 · HOW TO

control tower A building at an airport where take-offs and landings are directed.

con·tro·ver·sial [kon'trə·vûr'shəl] *adj.* **1** Tending to stir up argument: a *controversial* issue. **2** Fond of arguing.

con·tro·ver·sy [kon'trə·vûr'sē] *n., pl.* **con·tro·ver·sies 1** Argument or debate on a matter about which opinions differ. **2** A dispute.

Inside an airport control tower

con·tro·vert [kon'trə·vûrt] *v.* **1** To argue against; contradict; deny: The facts *controvert* your testimony. **2** To argue about.

con·tu·me·ly [kon't(y)oo·mə·lē] *n.* **1** Insulting rudeness; scorn. **2** An insult.

con·tu·sion [kən·too'zhən] *n.* A bruise.

co·nun·drum [kə·nun'drəm] *n.* A riddle whose answer depends on a pun. Example: "When is a horse not a horse?" "When he's turned into a pasture."

con·va·lesce [kon'və·les'] *v.* **con·va·lesced, con·va·lesc·ing** To get well gradually: He *convalesced* at the seashore after his illness.

con·va·les·cence [kon'və·les'əns] *n.* Gradual recovery from illness, or the recovery period.

A black eye is a contusion.

con·va·les·cent [kon'və·les'ənt] **1** *adj.* Recovering from illness. **2** *n.* A person recovering from illness. **3** *adj.* Of convalescence.

con·vec·tion [kən·vek'shən] *n.* **1** The transfer of heat within a gas or liquid by means of movement of warmer parts. **2** The act of conveying.

con·vene [kən·vēn'] *v.* **con·vened, con·ven·ing 1** To come together; assemble: Congress *convenes* every year. **2** To summon to meet: The governor *convened* the legislature.

con·ven·ience [kən·vēn'yəns] *n.* **1** Personal comfort; benefit: The motel has a restaurant for the *convenience* of guests. **2** Anything that increases comfort or saves work: Television sets and freezers are modern *conveniences*. **3** The condition of being convenient: the *convenience* of the arrangement. **— at one's convenience** At a time that suits one's plans or preference.

con·ven·ient [kən·vēn'yənt] *adj.* **1** Suited to one's purpose, plans, or comfort: We went at a *convenient* hour. **2** Within easy reach; handy: a *convenient* store. **— con·ven'ient·ly** *adv.*

con·vent [kon'vent] *n.* **1** A group of nuns who live together, following set religious rules. **2** The house or buildings which they occupy.

con·ven·tion [kən·ven'shən] *n.* **1** A meeting or assembly for some purpose: a *convention* of the Democratic Party. **2** The established way of doing things; accepted custom: The artist defied *convention* and lived as he pleased. **3** An established practice, rule, or form; a custom: Placing the fork to the left of the plate is a con-

vention. **4** An agreement on minor matters, as between nations.

con·ven·tion·al [kən·ven'shən·əl] *adj.* **1** Established by custom; customary; usual: It is *conventional* to say "Hello" when answering the telephone. **2** Behaving in an expected way: a highly *conventional* woman. **3** Not original; commonplace: a *conventional* painting. **4** In accordance with set rules rather than with nature: In early Egyptian art, it was *conventional* to paint the king much larger than his subjects. **— con·ven'tion·al·ly** *adv.*

con·ven·tion·al·i·ty [kən·ven'shən·al'ə·tē] *n., pl.* **con·ven·tion·al·i·ties 1** The condition of being conventional; allegiance to custom. **2** A rule, custom, or conventional practice.

con·verge [kən·vûrj'] *v.* **con·verged, con·verg·ing** To move toward one point or place; come or draw together: The rails seemed to *converge* in the distance; A crowd *converged*.

con·ver·gence [kən·vûr'jəns] *n.* **1** The act or fact of converging. **2** The point at which things come together. **— con·ver'gent** *adj.*

con·ver·sant [kən·vûr'sənt *or* kon'vər·sənt] *adj.* Well acquainted or familiar, as by study: He is *conversant* with American history.

con·ver·sa·tion [kon'vər·sā'shən] *n.* An exchange of ideas by informal talk; a talk. **— con'ver·sa'tion·al** *adj.*

con·verse[1] [*v.* kən·vûrs', *n.* kon'vûrs] *v.* **con·versed, con·vers·ing,** *n.* **1** *v.* To take part in conversation; talk. **2** *n.* A conversation.

con·verse[2] [kon'vûrs] **1** *adj.* Turned about or reversed; opposite; contrary. **2** *n.* The opposite or contrary: "Happy" is the *converse* of "sad." **— con·verse'ly** *adv.*

con·ver·sion [kən·vûr'zhən] *n.* **1** A changing into another form or substance: the *conversion* of ice into water. **2** A winning over or changing to a new religion or belief.

con·vert [*v.* kən·vûrt', *n.* kon'vûrt] **1** *v.* To change, turn, or transform: to *convert* wool into yarn; to *convert* a garage into an apartment. **2** *v.* To exchange for equal value: to *convert* merchandise into cash. **3** *v.* To win over or change to a new religion or belief: to *convert* the heathen. **4** *n.* A person who has been won over to a new religion or belief. **5** *v.* In football, to score one or two extra points after a touchdown.

con·vert·i·ble [kən·vûr'tə·bəl] **1** *adj.* Capable of being changed into something else: Fuel is *convertible* into heat. **2** *n.* Something convertible, as a car with a folding top.

con·vex [kon·veks' *or* kon'veks] *adj.* Curving outward, as the outside of a globe: a *convex* surface. **— con·vex'i·ty** *n.*

con·vey [kən·vā'] *v.* **1** To carry from one place to another; transport: Trucks *convey* supplies to a city. **2** To serve as a medium or path for; transmit: Pipes *convey* water and gas. **3** To make known; communicate: to *convey* ideas. **4** To transfer ownership of, as land.

concave lens

convex lens

con·vey·ance [kən·vā′əns] *n.* **1** The act of conveying. **2** Something used for conveying, as a truck or bus.

con·vey·er or **con·vey·or** [kən·vā′ər] *n.* A person or thing that conveys, as an endless belt that moves things about in a factory.

con·vict [*v.* kən·vikt′, *n.* kon′vikt] **1** *v.* To prove or find guilty, as in a trial: He was *convicted* of the crime. **2** *n.* A person found guilty of a crime and serving a prison sentence.

Conveyor

con·vic·tion [kən·vik′shən] *n.* **1** A strong, firm belief: a *conviction* that her missing son was safe. **2** The condition of being judged guilty. **3** The act of proving or declaring guilt.

con·vince [kən·vins′] *v.* **con·vinced, con·vinc·ing** **1** To make feel certain; cause to believe; persuade: Her smile *convinced* me that all was well. **2** *adj. use:* a *convincing* argument.

con·viv·i·al [kən·viv′ē·əl] *adj.* **1** Fond of feasting and good company; sociable. **2** Festive; merry. — **con·viv′i·al·ly** *adv.*

con·vo·ca·tion [kon′vō·kā′shən] *n.* **1** An assembly; meeting: a religious *convocation.* **2** The act of calling together for a meeting.

con·voke [kən·vōk′] *v.* **con·voked, con·vok·ing** To summon to meet: to *convoke* a church council.

con·vo·lu·tion [kon′və·loo′shən] *n.* **1** A winding or coiling together. **2** A fold or twist, as one of the folds or ridges of the surface of the brain.

con·voy [*v.* kon′voi *or* kən·voi′, *n.* kon′voi] **1** *v.* To go with to protect; escort: Destroyers were *convoying* the freighters. **2** *n.* A protecting escort. **3** *n.* A group of ships, trucks, etc., traveling with an escort. **4** *n.* The act of convoying. **5** *n.* The condition of being convoyed.

A naval convoy

con·vulse [kən·vuls′] *v.* **con·vulsed, con·vuls·ing** **1** To disturb with violent movements; shake: a world *convulsed* by war. **2** To cause to jerk or shake, as in a fit: A spasm of coughing *convulsed* him. **3** To cause to shake with laughter.

con·vul·sion [kən·vul′shən] *n.* **1** (*often pl.*) A sudden, violent drawing up or jerking of the muscles that a person cannot stop: epileptic *convulsions.* **2** A violent disturbance, as an earthquake. **3** A violent fit of laughter.

con·vul·sive [kən·vul′siv] *adj.* **1** Like a convulsion: *convulsive* rage. **2** Causing or marked by convulsions. — **con·vul′sive·ly** *adv.*

co·ny [kō′nē] *n., pl.* **co·nies** **1** A rabbit. **2** Rabbit fur.

coo [koo] *v.* **cooed, coo·ing,** *n., pl.* **coos** **1** *v.* To make the soft, murmuring sound of a dove: The baby *cooed.* **2** *n.* The sound itself. **3** *v.* To talk or say in low, loving murmurs.

cook [kook] **1** *v.* To use heat to prepare (food) to be eaten. Boiling, frying, and baking are ways of cooking. **2** *n.* A person who cooks or otherwise prepares food for eating. **3** *v.* To undergo cooking: The turkey *cooked* all morning. — **cook up** *informal* To make up; invent.

cook·book [kook′book′] *n.* A book containing recipes, instructions for cooking, etc.

cook·er·y [kook′ər·ē] *n.* The art of cooking.

cook·ie [kook′ē] *n.* Another spelling of COOKY.

cook·y [kook′ē] *n., pl.* **cook·ies** *U.S.* A small, thin, dry, sweet cake. ◆ *Cooky* comes from a Dutch word meaning *little cake.*

cool [kool] **1** *adj.* Slightly cold; lacking warmth: a *cool* breeze. **2** *v.* To make or become less warm: to *cool* drinks with ice; The hot chocolate *cooled.* **3** *n.* A cool time, thing, place, etc.: the *cool* of dawn. **4** *adj.* Comfortable and not heating in hot weather: a *cool* suit. **5** *adj.* Suggesting coolness: Blue, green, and violet are *cool* colors. **6** *adj.* Not excited; calm: He remained *cool* and collected. **7** *adj.* Calmly bold or daring. **8** *adj.* Not enthusiastic; unfriendly: a *cool* answer. **9** *adj. informal* Actual: a *cool* million. — **cool′ly** *adv.* — **cool′ness** *n.*

cool·er [koo′lər] *n.* A container, device, or room used for cooling something: a water *cooler.*

Coo·lidge [koo′lij], **Calvin,** 1872–1933, 30th president of the U.S., 1923–1929.

coo·lie or **coo·ly** [koo′lē] *n., pl.* **coo·lies** A poorly paid, unskilled Oriental laborer.

coon [koon] *n.* A raccoon.

coop [koop] **1** *n.* A cage or enclosed house for keeping fowl or small animals: a chicken *coop.* **2** *v.* To shut up in or as if in a coop: The sick boy was *cooped* up in his room.

co-op [kō′op] *n. informal* A cooperative.

coop·er [koo′pər *or* koop′ər] *n.* A person who makes or mends barrels, casks, etc.

A chicken coop

Coop·er [koo′pər *or* koop′ər], **James Fenimore,** 1789–1851, U.S. novelist.

co·op·er·ate [kō·op′ə·rāt] *v.* **co·op·er·at·ed, co·op·er·at·ing** To work together or with others for a common purpose: The fifth and sixth grades *cooperated* in giving the play.

co·op·er·a·tion [kō·op′ə·rā′shən] *n.*   **1** A working together for a common purpose; joint action. **2** Assistance: I need your *cooperation*.

co·op·er·a·tive [kō·op′rə·tiv *or* kō·op′ə·rā′tiv] **1** *adj.* Acting or willing to act with others; giving assistance. **2** *n.* A store, apartment house, etc., owned and managed by an association of people. **3** *adj.* Owned and operated in this way: a *cooperative* store.

co·or·di·nate [*v.* kō·ôr′də·nāt, *adj., n.* kō·ôr′də·nit] *v.*   **co·or·di·nat·ed, co·or·di·nat·ing,** *adj., n.*   **1** *v.* To bring or come into the right relation for working together: to *coordinate* the plans of four groups. **2** *adj.* Of equal importance or rank: *coordinate* branches of the armed forces. **3** *v.* To put or be in the same rank or order. **4** *n.* A person or thing of the same rank; an equal. **5** *n.* One of a set of numbers used to locate a point, line, etc., in space, as on a graph.

coordinating conjunction A word such as *and, but,* or *or,* used to join words or groups of words of equal rank.

co·or·di·na·tion [kō·ôr′də·nā′shən] *n.*   **1** The act of coordinating. **2** A being coordinated. **3** A smooth working together, as of parts of the body: The athlete has good *coordination*.

coot [kōot] *n.*   A web-footed water bird having short wings.

cop [kop] *n. informal* A policeman.

cope[1] [kōp] *v.*   **coped, cop·ing** To deal successfully; handle: to *cope* with a problem.

cope[2] [kōp] *n.*   **1** A cape worn by bishops or priests on ceremonial occasions. **2** Something that arches overhead; canopy: the *cope* of heaven.

Co·pen·ha·gen [kō′pən·hā′gən] *n.*   The capital and largest city of Denmark.

Co·per·ni·cus [kō·pûr′nə·kəs], **Nicholas,** 1473–1543, Polish astronomer.

cop·ied [kop′ēd] Past tense and past participle of COPY.

co·pi·lot [kō′pī′lət] *n.*   The assistant pilot of an aircraft.

cop·ing [kō′ping] *n.*   The top layer of a brick or stone wall, usually sloping so as to shed water.

coping saw A narrow blade in a U-shaped frame, used to saw curves.

co·pi·ous [kō′pē·əs] *adj.*   **1** Abundant; plentiful: a *copious* harvest. **2** Wordy; not brief: a *copious* apology. **— co′pi·ous·ly** *adv.*

Coping saw

Cop·land [kōp′lənd], **Aaron,** born 1900, U.S. composer.

cop·per [kop′ər] **1** *n.* A reddish brown metal, one of the chemical elements. It is easy to work and is a good conductor of electricity. **2** *adj. use: copper* wire. **3** *v.* To cover or coat with copper. **4** *n.* A coin of copper or bronze. **5** *n., adj.* Reddish brown.

cop·per·head [kop′ər·hed′] *n.*   A poisonous snake of North America, with copper-colored markings on its head and body.

cop·per·smith [kop′ər·smith′] *n.* A person who makes things of copper.

cop·pice [kop′is] *n.*   A copse.

cop·ra [kop′rə *or* kō′prə] *n.* Dried coconut meat. It yields coconut oil.

copse [kops] *n.*   A thicket of bushes and small trees.

cop·ter [kop′tər] *n. informal* A helicopter.

cop·y [kop′ē] *n., pl.* **cop·ies,** *v.* **cop·ied, cop·y·ing** **1** *n.* A likeness or reproduction of something: a *copy* of a drawing; Make two *copies* of this letter. **2** *v.* To make a copy or copies of. **3** *v.* To follow as a model. **4** *n.* A model or pattern to be imitated, especially a sample of penmanship. **5** *n.* A single specimen of an issue of a newspaper, magazine, book, etc. **6** *n.* Written material to be set in type and printed.

cop·y·right [kop′ē·rīt] **1** *n.* The exclusive right to publish or sell any part or all of a literary, musical, or art work. In the U.S., copyright lasts for 28 years with the right of renewal for another 28 years. **2** *v.* To protect by copyright.

co·quet·ry [kō′kə·trē *or* kō·ket′rē] *n., pl.* **co·quet·ries** **1** Flirtation. **2** A flirtatious act.

co·quette [kō·ket′] *n.*   A woman or girl who flirts with men. **— co·quet′tish** *adj.*

co·qui·na [kō·kē′nə] *n.*   A soft limestone formed from sea shells, used as a building material.

cor·a·cle [kôr′ə·kəl] *n.*   A small, rounded boat made of wickerwork covered with a waterproof material, used in some parts of the British Isles.

cor·al [kor′əl *or* kôr′əl] **1** *n.* A stony substance formed by great numbers of the skeletons of tiny sea animals. **2** *adj. use:* a *coral* reef. **3** *n.* Coral, especially red coral, made into jewelry. **4** *adj. use:* a *coral* necklace. **5** *n.* The animal whose skeleton forms coral. **6** *n., adj.* Pinkish or yellowish red.

Coral

coral snake A poisonous snake with brilliant red, black, and yellow rings, found in Mexico and the SW and southern U.S.

cord [kôrd] **1** *n.* A thick string or very thin rope made of several strands twisted together. **2** *v.* To bind with a cord or cords: to *cord* a box for shipping. **3** *n.* A part of the body that is like a cord: the spinal *cord.* **4** *n.* A pair of insulated wires used to connect a lamp, appliance, etc., to an electric outlet. **5** *n.* A ridge or rib in a cloth such as corduroy. **6** *n.* A cloth having ridges or ribs. **7** *n.* A measure for a pile of cut firewood. A cord is 8 feet long, 4 feet wide, and 4 feet high. **8** *v.* To pile wood into cords.

cord·age [kôr′dij] *n.*   **1** The ropes and cords of a ship's rigging. **2** An amount of wood, in cords.

cor·dial [kôr′jəl] **1** *adj.* Warm and hearty; sincere. **2** *n.* A liqueur. **— cor′dial·ly** *adv.*

cor·dial·i·ty [kôr·jal′ə·tē] *n.*, *pl.* **cor·dial·i·ties** Cordial quality; warm, friendly feeling.

cor·dil·le·ra [kôr′dil·yâr′ə] *n.* A very long mountain chain, such as the one that includes the Rocky Mountains and the Andes.

cor·don [kôr′dən] *n.* **1** A line of men, ships, fortresses, etc., enclosing an area to guard it. **2** A cord or ribbon worn as an emblem of honor or rank.

cor·do·van [kôr′də·vən] **1** *n.* A fine, soft leather, now usually made of split horsehide. **2** *adj. use: cordovan* shoes.

cor·du·roy [kôr′də·roi] *n.*, *pl.* **cor·du·roys** **1** *n.* A strong cloth, usually made of cotton, having raised, velvety ridges or ribs. **2** *adj. use:* a *corduroy* suit. **3** *n.* (*pl.*) Trousers made of corduroy. ◆ *Corduroy* may come from the French *corde du roi* meaning *king's cord*, "cord" being a ribbed fabric.

corduroy road A road made from logs laid crosswise over wet or muddy ground.

cord·wood [kôrd′wŏŏd′] *n.* Wood cut in 4-foot lengths, to be sold by the cord.

core [kôr] *n.*, *v.* **cored, cor·ing 1** *n.* The hard central part of certain fruits, such as apples or pears. The core contains the seeds. **2** *v.* To remove the core from: to *core* a pear. **3** *n.* The central or innermost part of anything. **4** *n.* The most important part of anything.

Cor·inth [kôr′inth] *n.* An ancient city in Greece, noted for its art and luxurious living.

Co·rin·thi·an [kə·rin′thē·ən] **1** *adj.* Of or from ancient Corinth. **2** *n.* A person born or living in Corinth. **3** *adj.* Of or having to do with a highly ornamented style of Greek architecture.

Co·rin·thi·ans [kə·rin′thē·ənz] *n.* In the New Testament, either of two letters of Paul to the Christians at Corinth.

cork [kôrk] **1** *n.* The thick but light outer bark of a type of oak tree that grows in the Mediterranean region. Cork has many uses. **2** *n.* A stopper made of cork for a bottle, barrel, etc. **3** *n.* A stopper made of other material, as glass, rubber, etc. **4** *v.* To stop with a cork, as a bottle. **5** *n.* A small float used on a fishing net or line.

cork·screw [kôrk′skrŏŏ′] **1** *n.* A tool, basically a pointed metal spiral attached to a handle, for drawing corks from bottles. **2** *adj.* Spiral; twisted: *corkscrew* curls. **3** *v.* To move

Corkscrew

or cause to move in a winding or spiral course.

corm [kôrm] *n.* A bulblike swelling of the underground stem of certain plants, as the crocus.

cor·mo·rant [kôr′mər·ənt] *n.* A large web-footed sea bird having a hooked beak with a pouch under it for holding fish.

corn[1] [kôrn] **1** *n.* A tall, cultivated plant bearing kernels on a large ear. It is also called maize or Indian corn. **2** *n.* The kernels, an important food for people and domestic animals. **3** *n.* In Great Britain, any grain or grain plant, especially wheat or oats. **4** *v.* To preserve (beef, tongue, etc.) in dry salt or brine.

corn[2] [kôrn] *n.* A painful growth of hard, thick skin, as on a toe, usually caused by a shoe that rubs or binds.

corn bread Bread made from cornmeal.

corn·cob [kôrn′kob′] *n.* The woody part of an ear of corn, on which the kernels grow.

corn·crib [kôrn′krib′] *n.* A bin or small building for storing ears of corn.

cor·ne·a [kôr′nē·ə] *n.* The transparent outer layer of the eyeball covering the iris and pupil.

corned [kôrnd] *adj.* Preserved and kept from spoiling in salt or salt water: *corned* beef.

cor·ner [kôr′nər] **1** *n.* The place where two lines or surfaces meet and form an angle. **2** *n.* The area around such a place: Put your name in the upper right-hand *corner* of the page. **3** *n.* The place where two or more streets meet. **4** *adj.* Located in or on a corner: the *corner* grocery store. **5** *n.* A difficult or embarrassing position. **6** *v.* To drive into a corner or into a position hard to get out of: They *cornered* the escaped lion in an alley. **7** *n.* A place that is far from the center of things: the far *corners* of the earth. **8** *n.* The buying of all or most of a certain stock or product in order to control its price: a *corner* in cotton. **9** *v.* To buy such control: to *corner* rye. — **cut corners 1** To take a short cut by going across corners instead of around them. **2** To economize; reduce expenses. — **turn a corner** To pass a critical point and begin to get better.

cor·ner·stone [kôr′nər·stōn′] *n.* **1** A stone at the corner of a building, especially one laid during a ceremony to mark the start of construction. **2** The main support; foundation: Free speech is the *cornerstone* of liberty.

cor·net [kôr·net′] *n.* A brass musical instrument like a trumpet. — **cor·net′ist** or **cor·net′·tist** *n.*

corn·field [kôrn′fēld′] *n.* A field used for growing corn.

corn·flow·er [kôrn′flou′ər] *n.* Any of several plants with blue, purple, pink, or white flowers, especially the bachelor's-button.

corn·husk [kôrn′husk′] *n.* The tough leaves or husk enclosing an ear of corn.

cor·nice [kôr′nis] *n.* **1** The molding that juts out from the top of a building or pillar. **2** A molding high on the walls of a room.

Cor·nish [kôr′nish] **1** *adj.* Of or from Cornwall. **2** *n.* The old Celtic language of Cornwall, now no longer spoken.

corn·meal [kôrn′mēl′] *n.* Meal ground from corn.

---

add, āce, câre, pälm; end, ēqual; it, īce; odd, ōpen, ôrder; tŏŏk, pŏŏl; up, bûrn; ə = a in *above*, e in *sicken*, i in *possible*, o in *melon*, u in *circus*; yŏŏ = u in *fuse*; oil; pout; check; ring; thin; this; zh in *vision*. For ¶ reference, see page 64 · HOW TO

corn·starch [kôrn'stärch'] *n.* A floury starch made from corn, used in cooking.

cor·nu·co·pi·a [kôr'nə·kō'pē·ə] *n.* **1** A curved goat's horn overflowing with fruits and flowers, symbolizing abundance. It is also called horn of plenty. **2** Any horn-shaped container.

Corn·wall [kôrn'wôl] *n.* A county in sw England.

Corn·wal·lis [kôrn·wôl'is], **Charles,** 1738–1805, British general.

corn·y [kôr'nē] *adj.* **corn·i·er, corn·i·est** *slang* Trite, silly, or sentimental.

Cornucopia

co·rol·la [kə·rol'ə] *n.* The petals of a flower.

cor·ol·lar·y [kôr'ə·ler'ē] *n., pl.* **cor·ol·lar·ies** **1** Something that clearly follows once something else is shown to be true. **2** Something that is a natural consequence or result.

co·ro·na [kə·rō'nə] *n., pl.* **co·ro·nas** or **co·ro·nae** [kə·rō'nē] A luminous ring surrounding the sun, seen during a total eclipse of the sun.

Co·ro·na·do [kôr'ə·nä'dō], **Francisco,** 1510–1544, Spanish explorer.

cor·o·nar·y [kôr'ə·ner'ē] *adj., n., pl.* **cor·o·nar·ies** **1** *adj.* Having to do with either of the two main arteries (**coronary arteries**) that supply blood to the heart muscle. **2** *n.* Coronary thrombosis.

coronary thrombosis A blocking of the flow of blood to the heart muscle. It is caused by a clot in a coronary artery.

cor·o·na·tion [kôr'ə·nā'shən] *n.* The crowning of a king or queen.

cor·o·ner [kôr'ə·nər] *n.* An official in charge of investigating the cause of any death not clearly due to natural causes.

cor·o·net [kôr'ə·net] *n.* **1** A small crown worn by princes, princesses, and nobles. **2** A circlet of jewels, flowers, or the like, worn on the head.

Corp. Abbreviation of CORPORATION.

cor·po·ral[1] [kôr'pə·rəl] *n.* A military rank. In the U.S. Army, a corporal is the lowest ranking noncommissioned officer, below a sergeant.

cor·po·ral[2] [kôr'pə·rəl] *adj.* Of the body; bodily: Spanking is *corporal* punishment.

cor·po·rate [kôr'pə·rit] *adj.* **1** Formed by law into one body, as a business; incorporated. **2** Of or related to a corporation. **3** United; collective: *corporate* efforts.

cor·po·ra·tion [kôr'pə·rā'shən] *n.* A group of people who have been given the legal power to act as one person. Businesses, universities, towns, etc., may all be organized as corporations.

cor·po·re·al [kôr·pôr'ē·əl] *adj.* **1** Of, for, or related to the body; bodily. **2** Tangible; real: Land is *corporeal* property.

corps [kôr] *n., pl.* **corps** [kôrz] **1** A large section or special branch of the armed forces: the Marine *Corps;* a medical *corps.* **2** A group of people united in some special work: a *corps* of accountants.

corpse [kôrps] *n.* The dead body of a human being.

cor·pu·lent [kôr'pyə·lənt] *adj.* Having a fleshy body; fat. **— cor'pu·lence** *n.*

cor·pus·cle [kôr'pəs·əl] *n.* One of the red or white cells forming part of the blood.

cor·ral [kə·ral'] *n.,v.* **cor·ralled, cor·ral·ling** **1** *n.* An enclosed space or pen for livestock. **2** *v.* To drive into a corral: to *corral* horses. **3** *v. U.S. informal* To seize or capture. **4** *n.* A circle of covered wagons surrounding a camp to protect it from attack. **5** *v.* To arrange (wagons) in the form of a corral.

cor·rect [kə·rekt'] **1** *adj.* Exact; right: the *correct* amount of change. **2** *adj.* Proper: *correct* behavior. **3** *v.* To change so as to make right; eliminate faults or errors from: *Correct* your spelling. **4** *v.* To mark for errors: to *correct* tests. **5** *v.* To punish or rebuke so as to improve. **— cor·rect'ly** *adv.* **— cor·rect'ness** *n.*

cor·rec·tion [kə·rek'shən] *n.* **1** The act of correcting. **2** A change, made or suggested, that removes an error or makes an improvement. **3** Punishment or rebuke.

cor·rec·tive [kə·rek'tiv] **1** *adj.* That corrects or tends to correct: *corrective* measures. **2** *n.* Something that corrects: Exercise can be a *corrective* for poor posture.

cor·re·late [kôr'ə·lāt] *v.* **cor·re·lat·ed, cor·re·lat·ing** **1** To place or put in relation one to the other: to *correlate* art with history. **2** To be mutually related: Crime and poverty often *correlate.* **— cor're·la'tion** *n.*

cor·rel·a·tive [kə·rel'ə·tiv] **1** *adj.* Mutually related, as a pair of words: *Either* and *or* are *correlative* conjunctions. **2** *n.* Either of two mutually related things.

cor·re·spond [kôr'ə·spond'] *v.* **1** To be in agreement with each other: Their answers *correspond.* **2** To be similar in function or character: A bird's beak *corresponds* to a man's mouth. **3** To write or exchange letters.

cor·re·spon·dence [kôr'ə·spon'dəns] *n.* **1** A being alike or in agreement. **2** Letter writing, or letters written.

cor·re·spon·dent [kôr'ə·spon'dənt] **1** *n.* A person who writes letters to someone else and receives letters in return. **2** *n.* A reporter who regularly sends news to his newspaper or magazine from a distant place. **3** *n.* A person or company that carries on business with another at a distance. **4** *adj.* Corresponding; agreeing.

cor·re·spond·ing [kôr'ə·spon'ding] *adj.* Similar or equivalent. **— cor're·spond'ing·ly** *adv.*

cor·ri·dor [kôr'ə·dər] *n.* A long hallway or passageway with rooms opening onto it.

cor·rob·o·rate [kə·rob'ə·rāt] *v.* **cor·rob·o·rat·ed, cor·rob·o·rat·ing** To bear out; confirm: His friends *corroborated* his story. **— cor·rob'o·ra'tion** *n.*

cor·rode [kə·rōd'] *v.* **cor·rod·ed, cor·rod·ing** **1** To eat away or destroy gradually: Rust and acid *corrode* metal. **2** To become eaten away; rust: Iron *corrodes* in damp air.

C

cor·ro·sion [kə·rō′zhən] *n.* A corroding; an eating or wearing away.

cor·ro·sive [kə·rō′siv] **1** *adj.* That corrodes; corroding. **2** *n.* A corrosive substance.

cor·ru·gate [kôr′ə·gāt] *v.* **cor·ru·gat·ed, cor·ru·gat·ing** To shape or bend into ridges and hollows like waves. — **cor′ru·ga′tion** *n.*

cor·ru·gat·ed [kôr′ə·gā′tid] *adj.* Having a ridged or wrinkled surface: *Corrugated* cardboard is used in making cartons; *Corrugated* iron is used for roofs.

A corrugated roof

cor·rupt [kə·rupt′] **1** *adj.* Depraved, wicked, or dishonest: the *corrupt* government of a city. **2** *v.* To make wicked or dishonest, as by bribery. **3** *adj.* Rotten; decayed. **4** *v.* To make or become rotten or decayed. **5** *v.* To change from the original; debase: to *corrupt* a language by adding words from other languages. **6** *adj.* Made worse by changes or errors: a *corrupt* translation of Homer's *Odyssey*. — **cor·rupt′ly** *adv.*

cor·rupt·i·ble [kə·rup′tə·bəl] *adj.* Capable of being corrupted.

cor·rup·tion [kə·rup′shən] *n.* **1** Evil or dishonest behavior. **2** Bribery. **3** Decay; rottenness. **4** The changing of a text or language.

cor·sage [kôr·säzh′] *n.* A small bouquet of flowers for a woman to wear, especially at the shoulder or waist.

cor·sair [kôr′sâr] *n.* **1** A privateer. **2** A pirate. **3** A pirate ship.

corse·let *n.* **1** [kôrs′lit] A type of armor worn on the upper part of the body. **2** [kôr′sə·let′] A light corset.

cor·set [kôr′sit] *n.* A close-fitting undergarment worn, usually by women, to give support and shape to the hips and waist.

Corsage

Cor·si·ca [kôr′si·kə] *n.* A French island in the Mediterranean, off the NW coast of Italy. — **Cor′si·can** *adj., n.*

cor·tege or **cor·tège** [kôr·tezh′ or kôr·tāzh′] *n.* **1** A ceremonial procession: a funeral *cortege.* **2** A train of attendants; retinue.

Cor·tés [kôr·tez′], **Hernando,** 1485–1547, Spanish conqueror of Mexico.

cor·tex [kôr′teks] *n., pl.* **cor·ti·ces** [kôr′tə·sēz] **1** The bark of a tree. **2** The outer layers of an organ or gland. **3** The layer of gray matter covering most of the surface of the brain.

Cor·tez [kôr·tez′] Another spelling of CORTÉS.

cor·ti·cal [kôr′tə·kəl] *adj.* Of or having to do with a cortex, especially of the brain.

cor·ti·sone [kôr′tə·sōn] *n.* A powerful hormone from the adrenal glands, sometimes used in treating arthritis, rheumatic fever, etc.

co·run·dum [kə·run′dəm] *n.* A very hard mineral used for grinding. Transparent varieties include the ruby and the sapphire.

cor·vette [kôr·vet′] *n.* A small warship used against submarines and to escort other ships.

co·sine [kō′sīn] *n.* In a right triangle, the length of the shorter side next to an acute angle divided by the length of the hypotenuse. This quotient changes with the size of the angle and is a function of the angle.

Cosine x = $\frac{a}{c}$

cos·met·ic [koz·met′ik] **1** *n.* A preparation for beautifying the complexion, hair, eyes, or nails. Lipstick, powder, and nail polish are cosmetics. **2** *adj.* Used to beautify.

cos·mic [koz′mik] *adj.* **1** Of or having to do with the universe or cosmos. **2** Vast; tremendous.

cosmic rays Very powerful rays that hit the earth from outer space.

cos·mo·naut [koz′mə·nôt] *n.* An astronaut.

cos·mo·pol·i·tan [koz′mə·pol′ə·tən] **1** *adj.* Common to all the world; not local or limited. **2** *adj.* At home in all parts of the world. **3** *n.* A person who feels at home anywhere.

cos·mos [koz′məs *or* koz′mōs′] *n.* **1** The universe thought of as a complete and harmonious system. **2** Any complete and ordered system. **3** A tall, flowering garden plant, related to the dahlia.

Cos·sack [kos′ak] *n.* One of a people of southern Russia noted as horsemen and soldiers.

cost [kôst] *n., v.* **cost, cost·ing 1** *n.* Price: The *cost* of this coat is $35. **2** *v.* To have as its price; be sold for: Popcorn *costs* twenty cents a bag. **3** *n.* Loss; sacrifice: We won the war at the *cost* of many lives. **4** *v.* To cause to lose: The boy's lateness *cost* him his job. **5** *n.* (*pl.*) The expenses of conducting a lawsuit, usually paid by the loser. — **at all costs** or **at any cost** Regardless of cost or trouble.

Cos·ta Ri·ca [kos′tə rē′kə] A country in Central America. — **Cos′ta Ri′can** *adj., n.*

cos·ter·mon·ger [kos′tər·mung′gər] *n. British* A street vendor of vegetables, fruits, etc.

cost·ly [kôst′lē] *adj.* **cost·li·er, cost·li·est** Costing very much; expensive.

cos·tume [kos′t(y)ōōm] *n., v.* **cos·tumed, cos·tum·ing 1** *n.* The clothing, ornaments, and arrangement of hair worn in a particular time or place or by a certain group of people: an Arab *costume.* **2** *n.* Clothing worn by an actor or a masquerader. **3** *n.* A special set of clothes for a certain time or activity: a summer *costume;* a riding *costume.* **4** *v.* To furnish with costumes.

cos·tum·er [kos·t(y)ōō′mər] *n.* A person who makes, sells, or rents costumes.

co·sy [kō′zē] Another spelling of COZY.

---

add, āce, câre, pälm; end, ēqual; it, īce; odd, ōpen, ôrder; tŏŏk, pōōl; up, bûrn;
ə = a in *above*, e in *sicken*, i in *possible*, o in *melon*, u in *circus*; yōō = u in *fuse*; oil; pout;
check; ring; thin; this; zh in *vision*. For ¶ reference, see page 64 · HOW TO

cot[1] [kot] *n.* A light, narrow bed usually made of a piece of canvas stretched on a folding frame.

cot[2] [kot] *n.* **1** A cottage: used mostly in poems. **2** A cote. **3** A covering for an injured finger.

cote [kōt] *n.* A shelter for birds or other small animals.

co·te·rie [kō′tə·rē] *n.* A small circle of people who share the same interests or activities.

co·til·lion [kə·til′yən] *n.* **1** An elaborate dance in which the dancers change partners often. **2** *U.S.* A formal ball.

cot·tage [kot′ij] *n.* **1** A small house. **2** A house, as at a beach, for use on a vacation.

cottage cheese A soft white cheese made of strained milk curds.

cot·ter or **cot·tar** [kot′ər] *n.* A Scottish worker on a farm, allowed the use of a cottage and plot of land there.

cot·ter pin [kot′ər] A metal pin inserted to hold machinery parts together. It is split lengthwise so that the ends may be spread apart to keep it in its hole.

cot·ton [kot′(ə)n] *n.* **1** The soft white fibers that surround the seeds of the cotton plant. **2** The plant itself. It is a low shrub. **3** Cloth or thread made from cotton fibers. **4** *adj. use: cotton* socks. **5** A crop of cotton plants. — **cot·ton·y** *adj.*

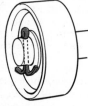

Cotter pin

cotton gin A machine that separates the seeds from the fibers of cotton.

cot·ton·mouth [kot′(ə)n·mouth′] *n., pl.* **cot·ton·mouths** [kot′(ə)n·mouthz′] Another name for the WATER MOCCASIN, a snake.

cot·ton·seed [kot′(ə)n·sēd′] *n.* The seed of the cotton plant. It yields an oil and is used as fodder or fertilizer.

cottonseed oil A yellow oil pressed from cottonseed, used for cooking, in soaps, etc.

cot·ton·tail [kot′(ə)n·tāl′] *n.* The common rabbit of America, having a little white tail.

cot·ton·wood [kot′(ə)n·wŏŏd′] *n.* **1** An American poplar tree having seeds covered with cottony tufts of hair. **2** The wood of this tree.

cot·y·le·don [kot′ə·lēd′(ə)n] *n.* The first leaf, or either one of the first pair of leaves, sprouting from a seed.

couch [kouch] **1** *n.* A sofa or upholstered bed. **2** *n.* Any place for resting or sleeping, as the burrow of an animal. **3** *v.* To lie down or cause to lie down, as on a bed. **4** *v.* To put into words: Keats *couched* his thoughts in poetry. **5** *v.* To lower (a weapon) for attack: to *couch* a lance.

cou·gar [kōō′gər] *n.* A large wildcat of North and South America. It is also called a mountain lion or puma.

cough [kôf] **1** *v.* To force air from the lungs with a sudden harsh noise. **2** *n.* The act of coughing. **3** *n.* Frequent coughing as an ailment: a bad *cough.* **4** *v.* To expel by coughing: to *cough* up phlegm.

could [kŏŏd] Past tense of CAN.

could·n't [kŏŏd′(ə)nt] Could not.

couldst [kŏŏdst] *v.* A form of the verb CAN, used with *thou*: seldom used today.

cou·lee [kōō′lē] *n.* **1** A ravine or gulch, often dry in summer. **2** A sheet of solidified lava.

coun·cil [koun′səl] *n.* **1** A group of people called together for discussion. A council makes plans or decisions or gives advice. **2** A group of people elected to make laws for a city or town. ◆ *Council, counsel,* and *consul* are pronounced similarly, but their meanings are different. A *council* is a group of people meeting to discuss something or make decisions: a city *council. Counsel* may mean either *advice* or *a lawyer* (because you hire a lawyer to give you advice): In the U.S. every person accused of a crime has the right to *counsel.* A *consul* [kon′səl] is a person who lives in a foreign city to protect the people and business interests of the country he represents: the American *consul* in Venice.

coun·cil·man [koun′səl·mən] *n., pl.* **coun·cil·men** [koun′səl·mən] A member of a council, especially of a city or town council.

coun·cil·or or **coun·cil·lor** [koun′səl·ər *or* koun′slər] *n.* A member of a council.

coun·sel [koun′səl] *n., v.* **coun·seled** or **coun·selled, coun·sel·ing** or **coun·sel·ling** **1** *n.* Talk and exchange of ideas between or among people. **2** *n.* Advice: wise *counsel.* **3** *n.* A lawyer or group of lawyers handling one side of a case. **4** *v.* To give advice to: to *counsel* a child. **5** *v.* To recommend; advise in favor of. ◆ See COUNCIL.

coun·sel·or or **coun·sel·lor** [koun′səl·ər *or* koun′slər] *n.* **1** An adviser. **2** A lawyer. **3** A children's supervisor in a camp.

count[1] [kount] **1** *v.* To list or call off numbers in a regular order: to *count* to 100. **2** *v.* To add up; find the total of: Tony *counted* 20 pencils in the box. **3** *n.* The act of counting or reckoning. **4** *n.* The amount found by counting; total: a *count* of 50. **5** *v.* To include: *Counting* Mrs. Smith, there were nine people. **6** *v.* To be taken into account: The mark in this test will *count* toward your final grade. **7** *v.* To be important: Every vote *counts.* **8** *v.* To consider to be; judge: I *count* myself fortunate. **9** *n.* A separate charge against an accused person: guilty on two *counts* of fraud. — **count off** To divide into equal groups by counting: to *count off* in groups of three. — **count on** To rely on. ◆ *Count* and *compute* come from French words, both of which go back to the same Latin word, *computare. Count* comes through the Old French word *conter.*

count[2] [kount] *n.* In some European countries, a nobleman having a rank equal to that of an earl in England.

count·down [kount′doun′] *n.* A downward counting of the time left before a scheduled act, as the firing of a rocket. Zero marks the doing of the act.

coun·te·nance [koun′tə·nəns] *n., v.* **coun·te·nanced, coun·te·nanc·ing** **1** *n.* The expression of the face: a sad *countenance*. **2** *n*. A face. **3** *n*. Approval; encouragement: John's parents gave *countenance* to his playing football. **4** *v*. To approve; encourage: I will not *countenance* bad manners. **5** *n*. Self-control; calmness. **— out of countenance** Embarrassed; abashed: The laughter put her *out of countenance*.

coun·ter¹ [koun′tər] **1** *adv*. In an opposite manner or direction; contrary: to act *counter* to orders. **2** *adj*. Opposing; contrary: a *counter* proposal. **3** *v*. To oppose: He *countered* my suggestions with some of his own. **4** *n*. In boxing, a blow given while receiving or blocking another. **5** *v*. To give such a blow.

coun·ter² [koun′tər] *n*. **1** A long board or table in a restaurant, store, etc., on which meals are served or goods sold: a lunch *counter*. **2** Something used for counting or keeping score in games, as a disk or chip.

count·er³ [koun′tər] *n*. A person or thing that counts.

counter- A prefix meaning: **1** Opposite; contrary, as in *counterbalance*. **2** In return, as in *counterattack*. **3** Corresponding; being duplicate or parallel, as in *counterpart*.

coun·ter·act [koun′tər·akt′] *v*. To act against; check: Penicillin *counteracts* infection.

coun·ter·at·tack [koun′tər·ə·tak′] **1** *n*. An attack made in return for or to stop an enemy's attack. **2** *v*. To make a counterattack.

coun·ter·bal·ance [*n*. koun′tər·bal′əns, *v*. koun′tər·bal′əns] *n*., *v*. **coun·ter·bal·anced, coun·ter·bal·anc·ing** **1** *n*. A power or force that balances and offsets another. **2** *n*. A weight that balances another. **3** *v*. To act as a counterbalance to; offset.

coun·ter·claim [koun′tər·klām′] *n*. A claim that opposes another claim, as in a lawsuit.

coun·ter·clock·wise [koun′tər·klok′wīz′] *adj*., *adv*. In the opposite direction from that in which the hands of a clock turn.

coun·ter·feit [koun′tər·fit] **1** *adj*. Copied to look like and pass as something genuine; false: a *counterfeit* ten-dollar bill. **2** *n*. A counterfeit thing; forgery. **3** *v*. To make a counterfeit of: to *counterfeit* money, stamps, etc. **4** *v*. To sham: to *counterfeit* sympathy. **— coun′ter·feit′er** *n*. ◆ *Counterfeit* once meant simply an *imitation*: She is the *counterfeit* of my sister. Now, however, it almost always implies an evil motive.

coun·ter·mand [koun′tər·mand′] *v*. To cancel (an order), often by giving a contrary one.

coun·ter·pane [koun′tər·pān′] *n*. A bedspread or quilt.

coun·ter·part [koun′tər·pärt′] *n*. **1** A person or thing that closely resembles another: Tokyo is a *counterpart* of New York. **2** Something that

goes with or completes another, as one of a pair of gloves. **3** A copy or duplicate.

coun·ter·point [koun′tər·point′] *n*. **1** Music in which two or more parts or voices contribute melodic material at the same time. **2** Any of these parts. **3** The art of writing counterpoint.

coun·ter·poise [koun′tər·poiz′] *n*., *v*. **coun·ter·poised, coun·ter·pois·ing** **1** *n*. A weight that balances another weight. **2** *n*. A counterbalancing force or power. **3** *n*. A being in balance. **4** *v*. To offset.

coun·ter·rev·o·lu·tion [koun′tər·rev′ə·lōō′·shən] *n*. A revolution to overthrow the government set up by a previous revolution.

coun·ter·sign [koun′tər·sīn′] **1** *n*. A password or signal that must be given to a sentry in order to pass. **2** *n*. A person's signature showing that he confirms someone else's signature. **3** *v*. To put a countersign on: to *countersign* a check.

coun·ter·sink [koun′tər·singk′] *v*. **coun·ter·sunk, coun·ter·sink·ing** **1** To widen the top of a hole so the head of a screw or bolt will lie flush with or below the surface. **2** To sink (a screw or bolt) into such a hole.

A countersunk screw

coun·ter·weight [koun′tər·wāt′] *n*. A weight that offsets another; counterpoise.

count·ess [koun′tis] *n*. **1** The wife or widow of a count or earl. **2** A woman equal in rank to a count or an earl.

counting house or **count·ing·house** [koun′ting·hous′] An office or building in which a firm keeps its accounts and transacts business.

counting number Any whole number but 0. 24 and 231 are counting numbers but $\frac{1}{2}$ is not.

count·less [kount′lis] *adj*. Too numerous to be counted: *countless* centuries.

coun·tri·fied [kun′tri·fīd] *adj*. Looking or behaving like simple country people.

coun·try [kun′trē] *n*., *pl*. **coun·tries**, *adj*. **1** *n*. An area, district, or region: mountain *country*; farm *country*. **2** *n*. The land of a nation: France is a beautiful *country*. **3** *n*. A nation: the prosperous *countries* of Europe. **4** *n*. The people of a nation. **5** *n*. The land of one's birth or allegiance. **6** *n*. The land outside cities and towns. **7** *adj*. Of or having to do with the country; rural: *country* dances.

coun·try·man [kun′trē·mən] *n*., *pl*. **coun·try·men** [kun′trē·mən] **1** A man of one's own country. **2** A man who lives in the country.

coun·try·side [kun′trē·sīd′] *n*. **1** A rural area. **2** The people living in it.

coun·try·wom·an [kun′trē·wŏŏm′ən] *n*., *pl*. **coun·try·wom·en** [kun′trē·wim′in] **1** A woman of one's own country. **2** A woman living in the country.

coun·ty [koun′tē] *n.*, *pl.* **coun·ties** **1** One of the sections into which a country or, in the U.S., a state is divided. A county has its own local government, courts, roads, etc. **2** The people living in it.

coup [kōō] *n.*, *pl.* **coups** [kōōz] A sudden and brilliant maneuver; a clever or lucky move.

coup d'état [kōō′dā·tä′] A sudden change in the political affairs of a country, often involving the seizing of the government by force.

coupe [kōōp] *n.* A closed automobile with two doors, seating up to six people.

cou·pé [kōō·pā′] *n.* **1** A coupe. **2** A low, closed carriage having a seat for two persons and a seat outside for the driver.

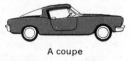

A coupe

cou·ple [kup′əl] *n.*, *v.* **cou·pled, cou·pling** **1** *n.* Two things of the same kind; a pair. **2** *n.* A man and woman who are married, engaged, partners in a dance, etc. **3** *v.* To join two things together: to *couple* two railroad cars; talent *coupled* with hard work.

cou·plet [kup′lit] *n.* Two lines of verse that go together, usually rhymed and having the same meter. Example:
"Know then thyself, presume not God to scan; The proper study of mankind is man."

coup·ling [kup′ling] *n.* **1** A joining together of two things. **2** A device that connects parts together, especially one that links one railroad car to another.

cou·pon [k(y)ōō′pon] *n.* **1** A ticket, certificate, advertisement, etc., that entitles the holder to something; They are saving soap *coupons* for a set of dishes. **2** One of the parts of a bond that are clipped off at regular times and turned in for interest payments.

cour·age [kûr′ij] *n.* The ability to meet danger or pain without giving in to fear; bravery.

cou·ra·geous [kə·rā′jəs] *adj.* Having or showing courage. — **cou·ra′geous·ly** *adv.*

cou·ri·er [kōōr′ē·ər *or* kûr′ē·ər] *n.* **1** A messenger required to deliver a message quickly. **2** A person who accompanies travelers to take care of tickets, baggage, reservations, etc.

course [kôrs] *n.*, *v.* **coursed, cours·ing** **1** *n.* A moving onward in space or time: the *course* of a journey; the *course* of time. **2** *v.* To move swiftly: The blood *coursed* through his veins. **3** *n.* The path, ground, etc., passed over: the *course* of a river; a golf *course*. **4** *n.* Line of motion; direction: The ship's *course* was due west. **5** *n.* A way of proceeding: What *course* should we take? **6** *n.* A series of like things having a certain order: a *course* of exercises. **7** *n.* A program of study leading to a degree or diploma: a high school *course*. **8** *n.* A particular subject or study: a history *course*. **9** *n.* A part of a meal served by itself: the dessert *course*. **10** *n.* A horizontal row, as of brick or stones in a wall. **11** *v.* To hunt with hounds: to *course* rabbits. **— of course** Naturally; certainly.

cours·er [kôr′sər] *n.* A swift, spirited horse: used mostly in poems.

court [kôrt] **1** *n.* An open space surrounded by buildings or walls; courtyard. **2** *n.* A short street open at only one end. **3** *n.* A space laid out for a game: a tennis *court*. **4** *n.* A palace. **5** *n.* Those who serve or attend a ruler. **6** *n.* A group of persons made up of a ruler and his council. **7** *n.* A formal meeting held by a ruler. **8** *n.* A place where law cases are tried. **9** *n.* A person or group of persons who lawfully decide cases; a judge or judges. **10** *n.* A meeting in which a law case is conducted: *Court* is adjourned until two o'clock. **11** *adj. use*: *court* sessions; *court* fees. **12** *n.* An attempt to win a woman or to gain someone's favor; courtship. **13** *v.* To seek the love of; woo. **14** *v.* To try to gain the favor of: to *court* voters in an election. **15** *v.* To act in such a way that one will probably get: to *court* disaster.

cour·te·ous [kûr′tē·əs] *adj.* Polite and considerate. — **cour′te·ous·ly** *adv.*

cour·te·sy [kûr′tə·sē] *n.*, *pl.* **cour·te·sies** **1** Politeness and consideration for others; good manners. **2** A courteous act. **3** A curtsy.

court·house [kôrt′hous′] *n.*, *pl.* **court·hous·es** [kôrt′hou′zəz] **1** A building occupied by courts of law. **2** The main building used for the offices of a county government.

cour·ti·er [kôr′tē·ər] *n.* **1** A member of a ruler's court. **2** A person who seeks favor by flattering or trying to please.

court·ly [kôrt′lē] *adj.* **court·li·er, court·li·est** Having elegant, polished manners: a *courtly* gentleman. — **court′li·ness** *n.*

court-mar·tial [kôrt′mär′shəl] *n.*, *pl.* **courts-mar·tial**, *v.* **court-mar·tialed** or **court-mar·tialled, court-mar·tial·ing** or **court-mar·tial·ling** **1** *n.* A military court that tries soldiers, sailors, or others coming under military law. **2** *n.* A trial by such a court. **3** *v.* To try by court-martial.

court·room [kôrt′rōōm′] *n.* A room in which the sessions of a law court are held.

court·ship [kôrt′ship′] *n.* A man's courting of a woman in order to marry her; wooing.

court·yard [kôrt′yärd′] *n.* An open space surrounded by buildings or walls; a court.

cous·in [kuz′(ə)n] *n.* **1** A son or daughter of one's uncle or aunt. **2** A less close relative.

cove [kōv] *n.* A small, sheltered bay or inlet in a shoreline.

cov·e·nant [kuv′ə·nənt] **1** *n.* An agreement entered into by two or more persons; pact. **2** *v.* To promise by or in such an agreement.

Cov·en·try [kuv′ən·trē] *n.* A city in central England. — **send to Coventry** To refuse to talk to or associate with.

cov·er [kuv′ər] **1** *v.* To place over or upon something else so as to protect or hide: to *cover* a person with a blanket. **2** *v.* To lie over or upon: Snow *covered* the ground. **3** *v.* To hide: to *cover* an error. **4** *v.* To protect, as against loss: His family is *covered* by insurance. **5** *n.* Anything that covers, conceals, or protects: a *cover* of topsoil. **6** *n.* The binding of a book or magazine. **7** *v.* To travel or pass over: to *cover* 300 miles a day. **8** *v.* To include or deal with: This book *covers* the Civil War. **9** *v.* To get news of or photograph, as for a newspaper: to *cover* a trial. **10** *v.* To provide for: Is this *covered* by the rules? **11** *v.* To keep a gun pointed at: to *cover* a prisoner. **12** *v.* In sports, to guard (an opponent). **13** *v.* In sports, to defend (a position, base, etc.).

cov·er·age [kuv′ər·ij] *n.* The extent or amount to which anything is covered: the *coverage* of an insurance policy.

cov·er·all [kuv′ər·ôl] *n.* (*usually pl.*) A one-piece work garment combining pants and a shirt with long sleeves.

cover crop A crop planted to protect the soil during the winter and to enrich it.

covered wagon A large wagon covered with canvas stretched over hoops, used especially by American pioneers; prairie schooner.

cover glass A thin piece of glass put over a specimen on a slide for examination under a microscope.

cov·er·ing [kuv′ər·ing] *n.* Anything that covers or protects.

Coveralls

cov·er·let [kuv′ər·lit] *n.* A bedspread.

cov·ert [kuv′ərt *or* kō′vərt] **1** *adj.* Secret; concealed: a *covert* smile. **2** *n.* A shelter or hiding place, especially underbrush where wild animals are likely to hide. **— cov′ert·ly** *adv.*

cov·et [kuv′it] *v.* To desire strongly (something belonging to someone else).

cov·et·ous [kuv′ə·təs] *adj.* Strongly desiring what belongs to someone else. **— cov′et·ous·ly** *adv.* **— cov′et·ous·ness** *n.*

cov·ey [kuv′ē] *n., pl.* **cov·eys** **1** A flock of quail or partridge. **2** A small group of people.

cow[1] [kou] *n.* **1** A full-grown female of domestic cattle. Cows are kept for their milk, have cloven hoofs, and chew their cud. **2** A full-grown female of certain other animals, as the elephant, moose, seal, and whale.

cow[2] [kou] *v.* To make afraid or timid.

cow·ard [kou′ərd] *n.* A person who lacks the courage to meet pain, danger, or difficulty.

cow·ard·ice [kou′ər·dis] *n.* Lack of courage when facing pain, danger, or difficulty.

cow·ard·ly [kou′ərd·lē] **1** *adj.* Of or like a coward. **2** *adv.* In a cowardly way.

cow·bell [kou′bel′] *n.* A bell hung around a cow's neck to make her easy to find.

cow·bird [kou′bûrd′] *n.* A small American blackbird often found with cattle. It lays its eggs in smaller birds' nests.

cow·boy [kou′boi′] *n. U.S.* A man, usually working on horseback, who handles cattle on a ranch.

cow·catch·er [kou′kach′ər] *n.* An iron frame on the front of a locomotive or streetcar to clear off anything on the track.

cow·er [kou′ər] *v.* To crouch, as in fear or shame; tremble.

cow·hand [kou′hand′] *n.* A cowboy.

cow·herd [kou′hûrd′] *n.* A person who tends cattle.

cow·hide [kou′hīd′] *n.* **1** The skin of a cow. **2** Leather made from it. **3** A heavy, flexible whip, usually of braided leather.

Cowcatcher

cowl [koul] *n.* **1** A monk's robe having a hood. **2** The hood itself. **3** The part of an automobile that holds the windshield and dashboard. **4** A cowling.

cow·lick [kou′lik′] *n.* A tuft of hair that sticks up and will not easily lie flat.

cowl·ing [kou′ling] *n.* A metal covering for an engine of an aircraft.

cow·pox [kou′poks′] *n.* A mild contagious disease of cattle. The virus of cowpox is used to make smallpox vaccine.

Cowlick

cow·punch·er [kou′pun′chər] *n. informal* A cowboy.

cow·slip [kou′slip′] *n.* A wild marigold with yellow flowers, found in swampy places.

cox·comb [koks′kōm′] *n.* A conceited, foolish man, often vain about his appearance.

cox·swain [kok′sən *or* kok′swān′] *n.* A person who steers a racing shell or other boat.

coy [koi] *adj.* **1** Shy; bashful. **2** Pretending to be shy in order to be flirtatious. **— coy′ly** *adv.* **— coy′ness** *n.*

coy·o·te [kī·ō′tē] *n., pl.* **coy·o·tes** *or* **coy·o·te** A small wolf of the western prairies of North America. ◆ *Coyote* comes directly from a Mexican Spanish word, which in turn came from a Mexican Indian word for the animal, *coyotl.*

Coyote, about 4 ft. long

coz·en [kuz′ən] *v.* To cheat or deceive, especially in small ways.

add, āce, câre, pälm; end, ēqual; it, īce; odd, ōpen, ôrder; took, pool; up, bûrn;
ə = a in *above*, e in *sicken*, i in *possible*, o in *melon*, u in *circus*; yōō = u in *fuse*; oil; pout;
check; ring; thin; this; zh in *vision*. For ¶ reference, see page 64 · HOW TO

co·zy [kō′zē] *adj.* **co·zi·er, co·zi·est,** *n.,* *pl.* **co·zies 1** *adj.* Warm and comfortable; snug: to be *cozy* in bed on a cold night. **2** *n.* A padded cover for a teapot to keep the tea warm. — **co′·zi·ly** *adv.* — **co′zi·ness** *n.*

Cpl. Abbreviation of CORPORAL.

Cr The symbol for the element CHROMIUM.

crab¹ [krab] *n., v.* **crabbed, crab·bing 1** *n.* A sea animal related to the lobster, having a flat shell, eight legs, and two pincerlike front claws. Crabs usually move sideways. **2** *v.* To catch or try to catch crabs.

Blue crab, about 6 in. wide

crab² [krab] *n., v.* **crabbed, crab·bing 1** *n.* *informal* A cross, disagreeable person. **2** *v.* *informal* To complain ill-naturedly. **3** *n.* A crab apple.

crab apple 1 A small, sour apple usually used for making jelly or preserves. **2** The small tree on which these apples grow.

crab·bed [krab′id] *adj.* **1** Complaining; surly; disagreeable. **2** Crowded, uneven, and difficult to figure out, as handwriting.

crab·by [krab′ē] *adj.* **crab·bi·er, crab·bi·est** Ill-tempered; peevish; cross.

crab grass A rapidly spreading grass with broad leaves, considered a pest in lawns.

crack [krak] **1** *n.* A break that shows as a fine line or narrow opening in a surface. **2** *v.* To break so as to form such lines or split apart: to *crack* an egg; The dish *cracked* when it fell. **3** *n.* A narrow space: Open the door a *crack*. **4** *n.* A sharp, snapping sound: the *crack* of a rifle. **5** *v.* To make or cause to make such a sound: to *crack* one's knuckles. **6** *v.* To change abruptly in tone: Her voice *cracked* on a high note. **7** *v.* *informal* To strike sharply or with a sharp sound: She *cracked* her elbow against the wall. **8** *n.* *informal* A sudden, sharp blow: a *crack* on the nose. **9** *v.* *informal* To tell or say humorously: to *crack* jokes. **10** *n.* *informal* A funny or sarcastic remark. **11** *v.* *informal* To find the solution of: to *crack* a code. **12** *n.* *informal* A try; chance: Let him have a *crack* at pitching. **13** *adj.* *informal* Very good; first-class: a *crack* regiment. **14** *v.* To break down mentally or physically: to *crack* under pressure. **15** *v.* To break up (petroleum) into simpler compounds. — **crack down** *informal* To become harsh or strict, especially to enforce discipline. — **crack up** *informal* **1** To be in a crash or collision, as of an airplane. **2** To have a nervous breakdown. **3** To praise.

cracked [krakt] *adj.* **1** Having a crack or cracks. **2** Broken apart or into pieces: *cracked* ice. **3** Harsh and uneven in tone: a high, *cracked* voice. **4** *informal* Crazy.

crack·er [krak′ər] *n.* **1** A thin, brittle biscuit, usually unsweetened. **2** A firecracker.

crack·er·jack [krak′ər·jak′] *informal* **1** *adj.* Of exceptional quality; excellent. **2** *n.* A person or thing of exceptional merit or skill.

crack·ing [krak′ing] *n.* A process in which the molecules of petroleum are changed by heat and pressure into smaller ones. It is used in making gasoline.

crack·le [krak′əl] *v.* **crack·led, crack·ling,** *n.* **1** *v.* To make sudden, snapping sounds: The twigs *crackled* as they burned. **2** *n.* A snapping or rustling sound: the *crackle* of dry leaves under our feet. **3** *n.* A network of fine cracks in the surface of china, porcelain, etc.

crack·ling [krak′ling] *n.* **1** The crisp, browned skin of roasted pork. **2** The sound of something that crackles.

crack-up [krak′up′] *n.* **1** A crash, as of an automobile or an airplane. **2** *informal* A breakdown of the mind or body.

cra·dle [krād′(ə)l] *n., v.* **cra·dled, cra·dling 1** *n.* A small bed for a baby, that can be rocked from side to side. **2** *v.* To hold or rock as if in a cradle: She *cradled* her doll in her lap. **3** *n.* A place where something originated: the *cradle* of freedom. **4** *n.* A rack or framework, as a support for a ship being built or repaired, or a frame attached to a scythe to catch cut grain.

Cradle

craft [kraft] *n.* **1** Skill, especially in work done with the hands. **2** An occupation or trade requiring skillful or artistic work: Making pottery is a *craft*. **3** Cleverness in deceiving others; cunning. **4** *pl.* **craft** A boat, ship, airplane, etc.

crafts·man [krafts′mən] *n.,* *pl.* **crafts·men** [krafts′mən] **1** A person skilled in a craft. **2** Anyone skilled in his work: This author is a fine *craftsman*. — **crafts′man·ship** *n.*

craft·y [kraf′tē] *adj.* **craft·i·er, craft·i·est** Clever at deceiving others; sly; wily. — **craft′·i·ly** *adv.* — **craft′i·ness** *n.* ◆ *Crafty* originally meant *able* or *skillful*. A *crafty* workman was a good workman, not a sly one. Only in more recent times has *crafty* come to mean *skillful in deceiving*.

crag [krag] *n.* A rough mass of rock jutting out from a cliff.

crag·gy [krag′ē] *adj.* **crag·gi·er, crag·gi·est 1** Full of crags. **2** Like a crag; jutting: *craggy* eyebrows. — **crag′gi·ness** *n.*

cram [kram] *v.* **crammed, cram·ming 1** To push or stuff into a tight or crowded space: to *cram* papers into a drawer. **2** To fill completely; pack: a closet *crammed* with clothes. **3** To eat fast and greedily. **4** To study hard for a short time: to *cram* before a history test.

cramp [kramp] **1** *n.* A sudden, painful tightening of a muscle, often in the leg or foot. **2** *v.* To hold or confine so as to prevent free action; hamper: Tight shoes *cramp* the toes. **3** *n.* (*pl.*) Twinges of pain in the abdomen.

cran·ber·ry [kran′ber′·ē] *n.,* *pl.* **cran·ber·ries 1** A glossy, sour, red berry used to make sauce and jelly. **2** The shrub it grows on.

C

crane [krān] *n., v.* **craned, cran·ing 1** *n.* A wading bird with long legs, a long neck, and a long, pointed bill. **2** *v.* To stretch out (one's neck), especially to try to see something. **3** *n.* A machine with a long, movable arm, used to lift and move heavy objects. **4** *n.* A swinging metal rod, as one used to hold a pot over a fire.

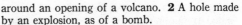

Crane

cra·ni·al [krā′nē·əl] *adj.* Of or having to do with the skull or cranium.

cra·ni·um [krā′nē·əm] *n., pl.* **cra·ni·ums** or **cra·ni·a** [krā′nē·ə] The skull, especially the upper part, in which the brain is enclosed.

crank [krangk] **1** *n.* A part or handle that sticks out at a right angle from another part and transmits motion by turning. **2** *v.* To start, move, or turn by means of a crank. **3** *n. informal* A grouchy, ill-tempered person. **4** *n. informal* A person with strong and unreasonable feelings about a particular subject.

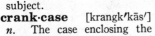

Crank

crank·case [krangk′kās′] *n.* The case enclosing the crankshaft of an engine, as of an automobile.

crank·shaft [krangk′shaft′] *n.* A shaft turned by or turning one or more cranks.

crank·y [krangk′ē] *adj.* **crank·i·er, crank·i·est** Peevish; irritable. — **crank′i·ness** *n.*

cran·ny [kran′ē] *n., pl.* **cran·nies** A narrow opening, crack, or chink, as in a wall.

crape [krāp] *n.* Another spelling of CREPE, used chiefly to mean black crepe worn as a sign of mourning.

crash[1] [krash] **1** *n.* A loud noise, as of something being violently broken or struck. **2** *v.* To fall, strike, or break with a loud noise. **3** *v.* To be damaged or destroyed by falling or colliding. **4** *n.* A destructive fall or collision. **5** *v.* To move noisily and violently: Elephants *crashed* through the jungle. **6** *n.* Failure or collapse, as of a business. **7** *v. informal* To come to (a party, meeting, etc.) without being invited.

crash[2] [krash] *n.* Cloth woven from thick, uneven threads, used for towels, curtains, etc.

crass [kras] *adj.* Vulgar and ignorant; crude: *crass* stupidity. — **crass′ly** *adv.* — **crass′ness** *n.*

crate [krāt] *n., v.* **crat·ed, crat·ing 1** *n.* A wooden box or frame for packing goods to be shipped. **2** *v.* To pack in a crate.

cra·ter [krā′tər] *n.* **1** A bowl-shaped hollow around an opening of a volcano. **2** A hole made by an explosion, as of a bomb.

cra·vat [krə·vat′] *n.* An old-fashioned word for a necktie.

crave [krāv] *v.* **craved, crav·ing 1** To need or want very much; long for: The starving man *craved* food. **2** To ask for earnestly; beg: to *crave* forgiveness.

cra·ven [krā′vən] **1** *adj.* Cowardly. **2** *n.* A coward. — **cra′ven·ly** *adv.*

crav·ing [krā′ving] *n.* A very strong desire; a hankering: a *craving* for candy.

craw [krô] *n.* **1** The enlarged part of a bird's gullet; crop. **2** The stomach of any animal.

craw·fish [krô′fish′] *n., pl.* **craw·fish** or **craw·fish·es 1** A fresh-water animal that looks like a small lobster. **2** Any of several similar salt-water animals. ◆ *Crevice*, from the French, was the earlier English name for *crawfish*. Because the animal lived in the water, people began substituting *fish* for *-vice* [pronounced vēs], and the main stress shifted to the first syllable, changing *cre-* [krə] to *craw-* [krô] or *cray-* [krā].

crawl [krôl] **1** *v.* To move along slowly with the body on or close to the ground; creep. **2** *v.* To move very slowly: Traffic *crawled* on the crowded road. **3** *n.* The action of crawling; a slow or creeping motion. **4** *v.* To be covered with things that crawl. **5** *v.* To feel as if covered with crawling things. **6** *n.* A speedy overhand swimming stroke in which the legs are kicked rapidly.

cray·fish [krā′fish′] *n., pl.* **cray·fish** or **cray·fish·es** Another word for CRAWFISH, used by biologists. ◆ See CRAWFISH.

cray·on [krā′on *or* krā′ən] **1** *n.* A stick of colored wax, chalk, etc., used for drawing or writing. **2** *v.* To draw, color, or write with crayons. **3** *n.* A drawing made with crayons.

craze [krāz] *v.* **crazed, craz·ing,** *n.* **1** *v.* To make insane; cause to go mad: *crazed* by fear. **2** *n.* A short-lived fashion or enthusiasm; fad. **3** *v.* To become or cause to become covered with fine, crisscrossing cracks, as in the glaze of pottery.

cra·zy [krā′zē] *adj.* **cra·zi·er, cra·zi·est 1** Out of one's mind; insane. **2** Foolish; senseless; absurd: *crazy* plans. **3** *informal* Very enthusiastic; extremely fond: He's *crazy* about her. **4** Shaky; rickety. — **cra′zi·ly** *adv.* — **cra′zi·ness** *n.*

crazy quilt A patchwork quilt made of pieces of various sizes, colors, and shapes.

creak [krēk] **1** *v.* To make a sharp, squeaking sound: The gate *creaked* in the wind. **2** *n.* A sharp, squeaking sound.

creak·y [krē′kē] *adj.* **creak·i·er, creak·i·est 1** Likely to creak: a *creaky* door. **2** Creaking.

Crazed vase

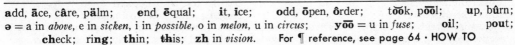

cream [krēm] **1** *n.* The yellowish, oily part of milk. It can be removed and used separately or churned into butter. **2** *n.* A yellowish white color. **3** *n.* A food that is made from cream or is soft and creamy. **4** *v.* To stir together, as butter and sugar, so as to make soft and creamy. **5** *n.* A soft, oily substance used to clean or protect the skin. **6** *n.* The best part: the *cream* of the senior class. **7** *v.* To remove the cream from. **8** *v.* To add cream to (coffee, tea, etc.).

cream cheese Soft, white cheese made from cream or a mixture of cream and milk.

cream·er [krē′mər] *n.* A small pitcher used for serving cream.

cream·er·y [krē′mər·ē] *n., pl.* **cream·er·ies** A place where butter and cheese are made, sold, or stored.

cream of tartar A white powder with an acid taste, used as an ingredient of baking powder.

cream·y [krē′mē] *adj.* **cream·i·er, cream·i·est 1** Full of cream; rich and moist as cream. **2** Having the color or appearance of cream: a *creamy* complexion. — **cream′i·ness** *n.*

crease [krēs] *n., v.* **creased, creas·ing 1** *n.* A mark or line made by folding, pressing, or wrinkling. **2** *v.* To form or become marked with a crease or creases.

cre·ate [krē·āt′] *v.* **cre·at·ed, cre·at·ing 1** To cause to come into existence; originate; make. **2** To be the cause of: His speech *created* much interest.

cre·a·tion [krē·ā′shən] *n.* **1** The act of creating or forming. **2** Anything that is created, especially something that shows great originality. **3** (*written* **Creation**) The act of God in creating the universe. **4** The world or the universe, including all living things.

cre·a·tive [krē·ā′tiv] *adj.* **1** Having the power or ability to create. **2** Having or showing originality and imagination: *creative* writing. — **cre·a′tive·ly** *adv.*

cre·a·tor [krē·ā′tər] *n.* **1** A person or thing that creates. **2** (*written* **Creator**) God.

crea·ture [krē′chər] *n.* **1** A living being, animal or human. **2** A person who is dominated by and carries out the wishes of another.

crèche [kresh *or* krāsh] *n.* A group of figures representing the scene in the stable when Jesus was born.

cre·dence [krēd′-(ə)ns] *n.* Belief in the truth of; trust: to give *credence* to an unlikely story.

cre·den·tials [kri·den′shəlz] *n.pl.* A letter, certificate, etc., that identifies the bearer and shows his position, authority, or right to be trusted.

Crèche

cred·i·ble [kred′ə·bəl] *adj.* **1** Believable: a *credible* excuse. **2** Deserving belief or confidence; reliable: a *credible* witness. — **cred·i·bil·i·ty** [kred′ə·bil′ə·tē] *n.* — **cred′i·bly** *adv.* ◆ A *credible* explanation is one that can be believed. It may or may not be true, but there are good grounds for believing it. A *credulous* person is someone who is ready to believe almost anything, no matter how unlikely. Only people can be *credulous*, but both people and statements can be *credible*.

cred·it [kred′it] **1** *n.* Belief in the truth or reliability of; faith; trust: to place *credit* in his story. **2** *v.* To believe to be true or reliable: to *credit* a story. **3** *n.* Admiration and approval; honor: He deserves *credit* for his bravery. **4** *n.* A source of honor or praise: to be a *credit* to one's family. **5** *n.* Reputation for paying bills or meeting obligations: His *credit* is good. **6** *n.* Confidence in a person's ability to pay for something: to extend *credit* for a week's supply of groceries. **7** *n.* Time allowed for payment: a month's *credit.* **8** *n.* A balance in one's favor, as in an account: She has a *credit* of ten dollars. **9** *v.* To make a record of money due to: *Credit* me with this amount. **10** *n.* Recognition or certification, as in some official record: to get *credit* for an art course. — **credit with** To believe or declare that (someone) has: *Credit* him *with* good intentions. — **on credit** With the agreement to pay later.

cred·it·a·ble [kred′it·ə·bəl] *adj.* Deserving credit or respect: a *creditable* effort.

cred·i·tor [kred′i·tər] *n.* A person to whom money is owed.

cre·do [krē′dō *or* krā′dō] *n., pl.* **cre·dos** A set of beliefs; creed.

cre·du·li·ty [krə·d(y)oo′lə·tē] *n.* Thoughtless or foolish readiness to believe anything.

cred·u·lous [krej′oo·ləs] *adj.* Believing without question; easily misled. — **cred′u·lous·ly** *adv.* ◆ See CREDIBLE.

creed [krēd] *n.* **1** A summary or formal statement of religious beliefs. **2** A set of personal beliefs or principles.

creek [krēk *or* krik] *n.* **1** *U.S.* A stream, especially one smaller than a river and larger than a brook. **2** *British* [krēk] A narrow inlet.

creel [krēl] *n.* A wicker basket used by fishermen to hold fish.

creep [krēp] *v.* **crept, creep·ing,** *n.* **1** *v.* To move on hands and knees, or with the body close to or on the ground; crawl. **2** *v.* To move cautiously and slyly; sneak. **3** *v.* To move very slowly: The glacier *crept* down the mountainside. **4** *n.* The action of creeping. **5** *v.* To trail along the ground or cling to something for support, as a vine. **6** *v.* To feel as if covered by creeping things: to make one's flesh *creep.* **7** *n.* (*pl.*) *informal* A feeling of horror and disgust: Snakes give me the *creeps.*

Creel

creep·er [krē′pər] *n.* **1** A person or thing that creeps. **2** A trailing or clinging plant, as ivy.

creep·y [krē′pē] *adj.* **creep·i·er, creep·i·est** Having or producing a feeling of horror or disgust. — **creep′i·ly** *adv.* — **creep′i·ness** *n.*

cre·mate [krē′māt *or* kri·māt′] *v.* **cre·mat·ed, cre·mat·ing** To cause (a dead body) to be burned to ashes. — **cre·ma′tion** *n.*

cre·ma·to·ry [krē′mə·tôr′ē *or* krem′ə·tôr′ē] *n., pl.* **cre·ma·to·ries** A place where dead bodies are cremated.

Cre·ole [krē′ōl] **1** *n.* A descendant of the original French settlers of Louisiana. **2** *n.* A person of European descent born in the West Indies or Latin America. **3** *n.* The French dialect spoken in Louisiana. **4** *adj.* Having to do with or typical of Creoles: *Creole* manners. **5** *adj.* (*written* **creole**) Cooked with tomatoes, peppers, spices, etc.: shrimp *creole.* ◆ *Creole* comes through the French from the Spanish word *criollo,* meaning a *native.*

cre·o·sote [krē′ə·sōt] *n.* An oily liquid with a strong odor, used to preserve wood from rot.

crepe or **crêpe** [krāp] *n.* A thin fabric, of silk, rayon, or other fiber, with a crinkled surface.

crepe paper Thin paper with a crinkled texture, used for decorations.

crept [krept] Past tense of CREEP.

cre·scen·do [krə·shen′dō] *n., pl.* **cre·scen·dos** A gradual increase in loudness or strength: The symphony ended with a *crescendo.*

cres·cent [kres′ənt] *n.* **1** The curved shape of the moon seen in its first or last quarter. **2** *adj. use:* the *crescent* moon. **3** Anything having the curved shape of the crescent moon. ◆ *Crescent* comes from a Latin word meaning *increasing.*

cress [kres] *n.* One of several related plants, many of whose leaves have a peppery taste and are used in salads.

cres·set [kres′it] *n.* A metal holder for burning oil, wood, etc., for illumination.

Crescent

crest [krest] *n.* **1** A tuft or projection on the head, especially one of feathers on a bird's head. **2** Something resembling this in shape or position: waves with foamy *crests.* **3** A plume or similar decoration on the top of a helmet. **4** The top or highest point of something: the *crest* of the flood. **5** A design or symbol at the top of a coat of arms, often used on stationery, silver, etc.

crest·ed [kres′tid] *adj.* Having a crest.

crest·fall·en [krest′fô′lən] *adj.* Low in spirits; downcast; dejected.

Cre·ta·ceous [kri·tā′shəs] **1** *adj.* Of or having to do with a geological period in which the dinosaurs became extinct. **2** *n.* The Cretaceous period or time.

Crete [krēt] *n.* A Greek island in the eastern part of the Mediterranean Sea. — **Cre′·tan** *adj., n.*

cre·tonne [kri·ton′ *or* krē′ton] *n.* A strong cotton or linen fabric printed in colored patterns, used for curtains, covering furniture, etc.

cre·vasse [krə·vas′] *n.* **1** A deep crack or gap, as in a glacier. **2** A break in a levee or dam.

crev·ice [krev′is] *n.* A narrow opening due to a crack or split, as in a rock, wall, etc.

crew[1] [krōo] *n.* **1** The company of men who work together on a ship. **2** A group of people working together to do a particular job: a repair *crew.* **3** The oarsmen and coxswain of a racing boat. **4** Any gang, band, or set: a *crew* of tramps.

crew[2] [krōo] A past tense of CROW (def. 1).

crew cut A man's very short, bristly haircut.

crib [krib] *n., v.* **cribbed, crib·bing 1** *n.* A small bed enclosed by railings for a baby. **2** *n.* A bin or building for storing grain, corn, etc. **3** *n.* A rack or box from which cattle or horses eat. **4** *n.* A supporting wooden or metal framework, as in a mine. **5** *v. informal* To copy someone else's words or ideas and use them as one's own. **6** *n. informal* A copy, translation, etc., used to cheat in doing school work.

crib·bage [krib′ij] *n.* A card game in which the score is kept by moving pegs in holes on a board.

crick [krik] *n.* A pain or cramp: a *crick* in the neck.

crick·et[1] [krik′it] *n.* An insect related to the grasshopper. The male makes a chirping sound by rubbing its front wings together.

crick·et[2] [krik′it] *n.* **1** An outdoor game popular in the British Commonwealth, played with bats, a ball, and wickets, by two teams of eleven players. **2** *informal* Fair, gentlemanly behavior; sportsmanship.

cried [krīd] Past tense and past participle of CRY: I *cried* when I stubbed my toe.

cri·er [krī′ər] *n.* In former times, an official who called out news and information.

crime [krīm] *n.* **1** An action that is against the law, especially a serious wrongdoing for which one can be severely punished. Murder and robbery are crimes. **2** Any very wrong or improper act.

Cri·me·a [krī·mē′ə *or* kri·mē′ə] *n.* A peninsula in the Soviet Union, on the north coast of the Black Sea. — **Cri·me′an** *adj., n.*

crim·i·nal [krim′ə·nəl] **1** *n.* A person who has committed a crime. **2** *adj.* Consisting of or guilty

add, āce, câre, pälm;   end, ēqual;   it, īce;   odd, ōpen, ôrder;   tŏŏk, pōōl;   up, bûrn;
ə = a in *above,* e in *sicken,* i in *possible,* o in *melon,* u in *circus;*   yōō = u in *fuse;*   oil;   pout;
check;   ring;   thin;   this;   zh in *vision.*   For ¶ reference, see page 64 · HOW TO

of crime; wicked and unlawful. **3** *adj.* Having to do with crime or enforcement of laws against crime: a *criminal* court. **— crim′i·nal·ly** *adv.*

crimp [krimp] **1** *v.* To press or bend into small, regular ridges or folds. **2** *n.* A fold or wavy surface produced by crimping.

crim·son [krim′zən] **1** *n., adj.* Deep red. **2** *v.* To make or become crimson.

cringe [krinj] *v.* **cringed, cring·ing 1** To shrink, cower, or crouch in fear or submission. **2** To behave too humbly; fawn.

crin·kle [kring′kəl] *v.* **crin·kled, crin·kling,** *n.* **1** *v.* To form a ridged, wrinkled, or roughened surface: The corners of his eyes *crinkle* when he smiles. **2** *adj.* *use:* a *crinkled* fabric. **3** *v.* To rustle or crackle. **4** *n.* A wrinkling or crumpling. **— crin′kly** *adj.*

crin·o·line [krin′ə·lin] *n.* **1** A stiff material used to line or spread out part of a garment. **2** A petticoat of this material, worn under a full skirt to make it flare. **3** A hoop skirt.

crip·ple [krip′əl] *n., v.* **crip·pled, crip·pling 1** *n.* Someone unable to move normally because part of the body is lost, damaged, or deformed; a lame person. **2** *v.* To make a cripple of. **3** *v.* To make unable to function well; disable: Ignorance *cripples* the mind.

cri·sis [krī′sis] *n., pl.* **cri·ses** [krī′sēz] **1** A very important or decisive moment in the course of any series of events: The battle at Gettysburg was a *crisis* in the Civil War. **2** The climax of an illness, when a change for better or worse occurs. **3** A time of worry or danger.

crisp [krisp] **1** *adj.* Dry, brittle, and easily broken: *crisp* bacon. **2** *adj.* Fresh and firm: *crisp* vegetables. **3** *adj.* Brisk; fresh: a *crisp* breeze. **4** *adj.* Short and forceful: a *crisp* answer. **5** *adj.* Wiry and waved or curled tightly: *crisp* curls. **6** *v.* To make or become crisp. **— crisp′· ly** *adv.* **— crisp′ness** *n.*

criss·cross [kris′krôs′] **1** *n.* A network or pattern of crossing lines. **2** *adj.* Forming such a pattern: *crisscross* lines. **3** *adv.* In different crossing directions. **4** *v.* To move in or form a pattern of crossing lines.

cri·te·ri·on [krī·tir′ē·ən] *n., pl.* **cri·te·ri·a** [krī·tir′ē·ə] or **cri·te·ri·ons** A standard or rule by which a judgment can be made: Make good taste your *criterion* in choosing clothes.

crit·ic [krit′ik] *n.* **1** A person who judges the quality or value of books, art, plays, opera, music, or the like. **2** A person whose occupation is to form or write such judgments: a music *critic*. **3** A person who shows disapproval and finds fault: a *critic* of the mayor.

crit·i·cal [krit′i·kəl] *adj.* **1** Apt to find fault; disapproving. **2** Typical of or suitable for a critic; expressing thoughtful judgment: a *critical* discussion of a new book. **3** Of, related to, or causing a crisis; crucial: a *critical* period in history. **4** Likely to cause trouble or danger; risky: a *critical* water shortage. **— crit′i·cal·ly** *adv.*

crit·i·cism [krit′ə·siz′əm] *n.* **1** The opinions or judgment of a critic: favorable *criticism*. **2** Un-

favorable comment; severe judgment of faults. **3** A book, article, etc., expressing critical opinion.

crit·i·cize [krit′ə·sīz] *v.* **crit·i·cized, crit·i· ciz·ing 1** To find fault with; judge severely. **2** To pass judgment on the qualities of. ¶3

cri·tique [kri·tēk′] *n.* A review, as of a work of art or literature, expressing critical judgment.

croak [krōk] **1** *v.* To make a hoarse, throaty sound, as a frog or crow does. **2** *v.* To speak in a low, hoarse voice. **3** *n.* The sound made by croaking. **4** *v.* To talk gloomily and predict misfortune.

cro·chet [krō·shā′] *v.* **cro·cheted** [krō·shād′], **cro·chet·ing** [krō·shā′ing], *n.* **1** *v.* To make or trim (sweaters, afghans, etc.) by forming connected loops of thread or yarn with a hooked needle. **2** *n.* Something crocheted.

crock [krok] *n.* A pot or jar made of baked clay.

crock·er·y [krok′ər·ē] *n.* Dishes or similar articles made of baked clay; earthenware.

croc·o·dile [krok′ə·dīl] *n.* A large reptile resembling the alligator, with thick, armorlike skin, and a long head. Crocodiles live in and near rivers in warm parts of Africa, the Americas, Asia, and Australia.

Crocodile, about 8 ft. long

crocodile tears Pretended tears; insincere grief. ◆ This expression comes from an old belief that crocodiles pity their prey and cry as they eat it.

cro·cus [krō′kəs] *n.* A small plant having cup-shaped yellow, purple, or white flowers. Crocuses bloom very early in the spring.

Croe·sus [krē′səs] *n.* **1** A very wealthy king who lived in Asia Minor in the sixth century B.C. **2** Any very wealthy man.

Cro-Mag·non [krō·mag′non] *adj.* Of or belonging to a race of men who lived in Europe in prehistoric times and were very similar to modern man.

Crom·well [krom′wel], **Oliver,** 1599–1658, English general, statesman, and ruler of England from 1653 to 1658.

crone [krōn] *n.* A withered old woman.

cro·ny [krō′nē] *n., pl.* **cro·nies** A close friend or constant companion.

crook [krook] **1** *n.* A bend or curve; bent or curved part: The old man leaned on the *crook* of his cane. **2** *n.* A long staff with a crook at the top, as one carried by shepherds. **3** *v.* To bend into a curve or hook: to beckon by *crooking* one's finger. **4** *n. informal* A thief or cheat.

crook·ed [krook′id] *adj.* **1** Bent, twisted, or uneven; not straight. **2** Dishonest; deceitful. **— crook′ed·ly** *adv.* **— crook′ed·ness** *n.*

croon [kroon] *v.* **1** To sing or hum in a low, murmuring tone: to *croon* a baby to sleep. **2** To sing (popular songs) in a soft, sentimental manner. **— croon′er** *n.*

crop [krop] *n., v.* **cropped, crop·ping 1** *n.*

Any farm product, growing or harvested, as cotton, corn, hay, or apples. **2** *n.* The amount of one product grown in one season: the Minnesota wheat *crop.* **3** *n.* A collection or quantity of anything produced: a new *crop* of school graduates. **4** *v.* To cut off very closely, as hair. **5** *n.* A cropped condition; short haircut. **6** *n.* To bite off or nibble, as grass. **7** *n.* An enlarged part of a bird's digestive tract, where food is partly digested before reaching the stomach. **8** *n.* A short whip with a loop at one end. **— crop out** To appear above the surface. **— crop up** To appear or come up unexpectedly: That old rumor *cropped up* again.

crop·per [krop′ər] *n.* A bad fall, as from a horse, especially in the expression **come a cropper,** to fail badly or meet with misfortune.

cro·quet [krō·kā′] *n.* An outdoor game in which the players use mallets with long handles to drive wooden balls through a series of wickets.

Croquet

cro·quette [krō·ket′] *n.* A ball or patty consisting chiefly of finely chopped cooked meat, fish, etc., fried in deep fat.

cro·sier [krō′zhər] *n.* A bishop's staff resembling a shepherd's crook, carried in religious ceremonies.

cross [krôs] **1** *n.* Any mark or object formed by two straight lines or parts across one another. **2** *v.* To place or put crosswise: to *cross* one's legs. **3** *v.* To go or pass across or over: *Cross* the street carefully. **4** *v.* To pass going in different directions: Their planes *crossed* in flight; Our paths *crossed* while we were hiking. **5** *adj.* Going across; crosswise: *cross* currents. **6** *n.* A tall upright post with a shorter horizontal piece near the top. In ancient times a cross was used to crucify those convicted of crime. **7** *n.* (*often written* **Cross**) The symbol of the Christian religion, representing the cross on which Jesus was crucified. **8** *v.* To make motions of forming a cross over, especially as a sign of religious faith: to *cross* oneself; to *cross* one's heart. **9** *n.* Any burdensome trouble or suffering. **10** *v.* To draw a line or lines through or across: *Cross* my name off the list; *Cross* your t's carefully. **11** *adj.* Bad-tempered; irritable. **12** *v.* To interfere with; oppose: She hates to be *crossed.* **13** *n.* A breeding together of related kinds of animals or plants, or the result of such breeding: A mule is a *cross* between a donkey and a horse. **14** *v.* To breed to produce such a plant or animal.

— cross one's mind To enter one's thoughts.
— cross′ly *adv.*

cross·bar [krôs′bär′] *n.* A crosswise bar, strip, or line.

cross·bones [krôs′bōnz′] *n.pl.* A picture of two bones crossed to form an X. ◆ See SKULL AND CROSSBONES.

cross·bow [krôs′bō′] *n.* A weapon consisting of a bow fastened crosswise at the front of a grooved stock, used in the Middle Ages.

Crossbow

cross·breed [krôs′brēd′] *v.* **cross·bred** [krôs′bred′], **cross·breed·ing,** *n.* **1** *v.* To produce (a cross) by breeding related kinds of plants or animals. **2** *n.* The product of such breeding.

cross·coun·try [krôs′kun′trē] *adj.* Across fields or open countryside rather than by roads or paths: a *cross-country* hike.

cross·cut [krôs′kut′] *v.* **cross·cut, cross·cut·ting,** *adj., n.* **1** *v.* To cut crosswise, as through the grain of wood. **2** *adj.* Used or made for cutting across something: a *crosscut* saw. **3** *n.* A direct way across; short cut.

cross·ex·am·ine [krôs′ig·zam′in] *v.* **cross·ex·am·ined, cross·ex·am·in·ing** To question (a witness called and questioned by the other side) usually to test or discredit answers already given by him. **— cross′-ex·am′i·na′tion** *n.*

cross·eyed [krôs′īd′] *adj.* Having one or both eyes turned toward the bridge of the nose.

cross·grained [krôs′grānd′] *adj.* **1** Having the grain twisted or crosswise: *cross-grained* lumber. **2** Stubborn and contrary: a *cross-grained* fellow.

cross·ing [krôs′ing] *n.* **1** A place where a road, stream, etc., may be crossed. **2** A place where roads, railroad tracks, etc., cross one another. **3** A going across.

cross·piece [krôs′pēs′] *n.* Any piece, as of wood, metal, etc., placed across another.

cross·pur·pose [krôs′pûr′pəs] *n.* A purpose or aim in conflict with another, especially in the expression **at cross-purposes,** opposing or blocking each other's aims without meaning to.

cross·ques·tion [krôs′kwes′chən] *v.* To cross-examine.

cross·ref·er·ence [krôs′ref′ər·əns *or* krôs′ref′-rəns] *n.* A note or statement directing a reader from one part of a book, index, etc., to another part for additional information.

cross·road [krôs′rōd′] *n.* **1** A road that connects two main roads or crosses one. **2** *pl.* (*used with singular verb*) A place where roads meet.

---

add, āce, câre, pälm;   end, ēqual;   it, īce;   odd, ōpen, ôrder;   took, pool;   up, bûrn;

ə = a in *above*, e in *sicken*, i in *possible*, o in *melon*, u in *circus*;   yōo = u in *fuse*;   oil;   pout;

check;   ring;   thin;   this;   zh in *vision*.   For ¶ reference, see page 64 · HOW TO

cross section   **1** A slice or piece cut straight across something: a *cross section* of an airplane wing. **2** A cut made in this way. **3** A sample or selection considered typical of a whole: a *cross section* of public opinion.

cross·tie [krôs′tī′] *n.* One of the beams laid crosswise under railroad tracks to support them.

Cross section of a watermelon

cross·trees [krôs′trēz′] *n.pl.* Two crosswise pieces at the top of a ship's lower mast, for spreading the shrouds of the mast above.

cross·walk [krôs′wôk′] *n.* A lane marked off for people to use when crossing a street on foot.

cross·wise [krôs′wīz′] *adv.* **1** Across; athwart. **2** So as to form a cross.

cross·word puzzle [krôs′wûrd′] A puzzle calling for words to be guessed and spelled out on a pattern of numbered squares, crosswise and downward as specified. For each direction a list of clues suggests the words.

crotch [kroch] *n.* **1** The fork where a trunk, limb, etc., divides into two limbs or branches. **2** The place where the body divides into legs.

crotch·et [kroch′it] *n.* An odd notion or whim.

crotch·et·y [kroch′ə·tē] *adj.* **1** Full of odd notions; queer. **2** Cranky; peevish.

crouch [krouch] **1** *v.* To stoop down with the knees bent, as an animal about to spring. **2** *v.* To bend in a shrinking or cowering position. **3** *n.* The action or position of crouching.

croup[1] [kroop] *n.* A children's throat disease accompanied by a hoarse cough and difficulty in breathing. **— croup′y** *adj.*

croup[2] [kroop] *n.* The part of a horse's back above the hind legs.

crow[1] [krō] *v.* **crowed** or sometimes for def. 1 **crew, crow·ing,** *n.* **1** *v.* To make the high, shrill cry of a rooster. **2** *n.* The cry itself. **3** *v.* To make cries or squeals of delight, as a baby. **4** *n.* Such a cry of pleasure. **5** *v.* To rejoice loudly and triumphantly; boast.

crow[2] [krō] *n.* A large black bird with a harsh, cawing voice. **— eat crow** *informal* To humble oneself, as by publicly admitting a mistake.

crow·bar [krō′bär′] *n.* A straight metal bar used as a lever for lifting or prying.

crowd [kroud] **1** *n.* A large number of people gathered closely together. **2** *v.* To gather in large numbers. **3** *n.* People in general, considered as acting or thinking alike. **4** *v.* To fill too full; cram; pack. **5** *v.* To press or force forward. **6** *v.* To shove or push: They *crowded* us to the wall. **7** *n.* *informal* A group of people who do things together; set: He belongs to our *crowd*.

crown [kroun] **1** *n.* An ornament, often of precious metal set with jewels, worn encircling the head as a sign of royal power. **2** *n.* (*often written* **Crown**) The ruling sovereign, or the power of the sovereign. **3** *adj. use:* *crown* jewels; *crown* land. **4** *n.* A wreath or similar object worn on the head, especially as a sign of victory or honor. **5** *v.* To honor or install as a ruler by placing a crown on the head of. **6** *n.* The top part of the head. **7** *n.* The part or place at the top of something: the *crown* of a hat; the *crown* of the hill. **8** *v.* To be at or cover the top of; cap: peaks *crowned* with snow. **9** *v.* To make complete or perfect; climax: a career *crowned* with honors. **10** *n.* A British coin worth five shillings. **11** *v.* In checkers, to make (a piece) a king by placing another piece upon it. **12** *n.* The part of a tooth covered with enamel, outside the gum, or an artificial substitute for it. **13** *v.* To place an artificial crown on (a tooth).

crown prince A man or boy next in line to inherit the title and rank of king.

crow's-feet [krōz′fēt′] *n.pl.* The wrinkles spreading from the outer corner of the eye.

crow's-nest [krōz′nest′] *n.* A high, partly sheltered platform on a ship's mast for a lookout.

cru·cial [krōō′shəl] *adj.* Likely to have a very important or decisive result or effect; critical: a *crucial* decision. **— cru′cial·ly** *adv.*

Crow's-nest

cru·ci·ble [krōō′sə·bəl] *n.* **1** A container that can withstand great heat, used for melting metals, ore, etc. **2** A severely trying test.

cru·ci·fix [krōō′sə·fiks] *n.* A cross with an image of Christ crucified on it, used as a Christian symbol.

cru·ci·fix·ion [krōō′sə·fik′shən] *n.* **1** The act of crucifying. **2** A being crucified. **3** (*written* **Crucifixion**) The execution of Jesus on the cross. **4** A painting or sculpture of this.

cru·ci·fy [krōō′sə·fī] *v.* **cru·ci·fied, cru·ci·fy·ing 1** To put to death by nailing the hands and feet to a cross. **2** To cause to suffer greatly.

crude [krōōd] *adj.* **crud·er, crud·est 1** In an unrefined state; not processed: *crude* oil. **2** Roughly made; not well finished: a *crude* shack. **3** Lacking refinement or good taste; uncouth. **— crude′ly** *adv.* **— crude′ness** *n.*

cru·di·ty [krōō′də·tē] *n., pl.* **cru·di·ties 1** A crude condition. **2** A crude act or remark.

cru·el [krōō′əl] *adj.* **1** Eager or willing to give pain to others; brutal. **2** Not caring whether others suffer; pitiless. **3** Resulting in great pain or suffering; harsh: *cruel* neglect; *cruel* treatment. **— cru′el·ly** *adv.*

cru·el·ty [krōō′əl·tē] *n., pl.* **cru·el·ties 1** Cruel behavior, feelings, treatment, etc. **2** Harshness; severity: the *cruelty* of the wind.

cru·et [krōō′it] *n.* A small glass bottle with a stopper, for holding oil, vinegar, etc.

cruise [krōōz] *n., v.* **cruised, cruis·ing 1** *n.* A sea voyage stopping at several ports, often taken for pleasure. **2** *v.* To sail or ride about, as for pleasure or business. **3** *v.* To go at the speed found most efficient, as for the use of fuel.

cruis·er [krōō′zər] *n.* **1** A power boat with a cabin equipped for living aboard. **2** A fast, rather large warship. **3** A person or thing that cruises.

crul·ler [krul′ər] *n.* A cake made from a strip or twist of sweetened dough fried in deep fat.

crumb [krum] **1** *n.* A tiny broken piece of bread, cake, etc. **2** *n.* A bit or scrap: *crumbs* of learning. **3** *v.* To break into crumbs; crumble. **4** *v.* To coat with crumbs, as for frying. **5** *n.* The soft part of bread, enclosed by the crust.

crum·ble [krum′bəl] *v.* **crum·bled, crum·bling** **1** To break into crumbs or tiny pieces. **2** To fall apart or into pieces: a *crumbling* wall.

A crumbling wall

crum·bly [krum′blē] *adj.* **crum·bli·er, crum·bli·est** Crumbling easily; likely to crumble.

crum·pet [krum′pit] *n.* A flat, unsweetened cake baked on a griddle, and usually split and toasted.

crum·ple [krum′pəl] *v.* **crum·pled, crum·pling** **1** To crush so as to form wrinkles: *crumpled* paper; a dress that won't *crumple*. **2** *informal* To collapse: to *crumple* with weariness.

crunch [krunch] **1** *v.* To chew with a crushing or crackling sound. **2** *v.* To grind or crush noisily. **3** *v.* To move with or make a crushing or crackling sound: We *crunched* over the gravel; Gravel *crunched* under us. **4** *n.* The sound or act of crunching.

crunch·y [krun′chē] *adj.* **crunch·i·er, crunch·i·est** Crisp and easily crunched, as cookies.

crup·per [krup′ər] *n.* One of the straps of a horse's harness, forming a loop under the tail.

cru·sade [krōō·sād′] *n., v.* **cru·sad·ed, cru·sad·ing** **1** *n.* (*often written* **Crusade**) One of a series of wars fought by European Christians during the Middle Ages in an attempt to capture the Holy Land from the Moslems. **2** *n.* A vigorous struggle against an evil or in favor of a cause. **3** *v.* To take part in a crusade. **— cru·sad′er** *n.*

cruse [krōōz *or* krōōs] *n.* A small pottery jar or jug: seldom used today.

crush [krush] **1** *v.* To press or squeeze so as to break, injure, or force out of shape. **2** *v.* To grind or smash into small pieces: to *crush* ore. **3** *v.* To rumple or wrinkle: Linen *crushes* easily. **4** *v.* To put down; subdue; quell: to *crush* a rebellion. **5** *v.* To press together; cram. **6** *n.* A closely pressed crowd; jam. **7** *n.* The act of crushing; very strong pressure. **8** *n. informal* A strong, often silly liking for another person.

Cru·soe [krōō′sō], **Robinson** In Daniel Defoe's novel *Robinson Crusoe*, the hero, a sailor shipwrecked on a desert island.

crust [krust] **1** *n.* The hard outer part of bread. **2** *n.* Any dry, hard piece of bread: He had only a few *crusts* to eat. **3** *n.* A shell or cover of pastry, as for a pie. **4** *n.* Any hard, crisp surface, as of snow. **5** *n.* The solid outer part of the earth. **6** *v.* To have, cover with, or form into a crust: rocks *crusted* with lichens.

crus·ta·cean [krus·tā′shən] **1** *n.* One of a large class of animals having a tough outer shell and generally living in water. Lobsters, crabs, and crawfish are crustaceans. **2** *adj.* Belonging to this class of animals.

crust·y [krus′tē] *adj.* **crust·i·er, crust·i·est** **1** Having a crust: *crusty* rolls. **2** Gruff and irritable in manner: a *crusty* old fellow.

crutch [kruch] *n.* **1** A support, usually one of a pair, to help the lame walk. It usually has a grip for the hand and a crosspiece at the top under the armpit. **2** Something used to give support or a feeling of security.

Crutches

crux [kruks] *n.* The most important or significant point: the *crux* of the argument.

cry [krī] *v.* **cried, cry·ing,** *n., pl.* **cries** **1** *v.* To weep or sob, especially with sounds of unhappiness, pain, or fear. **2** *n.* A spell of weeping: to have a good *cry*. **3** *v.* To call out loudly; shout. **4** *v.* To say loudly; exclaim: "How lovely!" she *cried*. **5** *n.* A shout, call, or exclamation: a *cry* for help. **6** *n.* The characteristic sound made by some animal or bird: the *cry* of the owl. **7** *v.* To make such a sound. **8** *v.* To beg with emotion; plead: to *cry* for mercy. **9** *v.* To need very much; demand: a situation that *cries* for attention. **10** *n.* A strong appeal or demand: a *cry* for justice. **11** *n.* A slogan or rallying call. **12** *v.* To advertise by calling or shouting: to *cry* one's wares. **— a far cry** A long way: It's *a far cry* from poverty to riches. **— in full cry** In noisy pursuit, as a pack of hounds.

cry·ing [krī′ing] *adj.* Calling for immediate action or remedy: a *crying* need.

crypt [kript] *n.* An underground vault or chamber, especially one beneath a church used as a burial place. ◆ *Crypt* and *grotto* both come from Latin *crypta* which comes from a Greek word meaning *hidden*. *Crypt* came directly from *crypta*, but *grotto* was changed by coming through Italian.

cryp·tic [krip′tik] *adj.* Having a secret or hidden meaning; mysterious: *cryptic* remarks; a *cryptic* message. — **cryp′ti·cal·ly** *adv.*

cryp·to·gram [krip′tə·gram] *n.* A message or puzzle written in a secret code.

crys·tal [kris′təl] **1** *n.* A body formed when a substance solidifies, having flat surfaces and angles in a regular, characteristic pattern: salt *crystals*; ice *crystals*. **2** *n.* Colorless, transparent quartz. **3** *n.* A type of fine, clear glass. **4** *adj. use:* a *crystal* goblet. **5** *adj.* Resembling crystal; very clear: a *crystal* stream. **6** *n.* A transparent covering for the dial of a watch: The jeweler had to replace the *crystal*.

crys·tal·line [kris′tə·lin] *adj.* **1** Made of crystal. **2** Resembling crystal; transparent; clear. **3** Composed of or typical of crystals.

crys·tal·lize [kris′tə·liz] *v.* **crys·tal·lized, crys·tal·liz·ing** **1** To form or cause to form into crystals: Diamonds are *crystallized* carbon. **2** To become or cause to become clear and definite: to allow one's plans to *crystallize*. — **crys′·tal·li·za′tion** *n.* ¶3

Cs The symbol for the element CESIUM.

cu. Abbreviation of CUBIC.

Cu The symbol for the element COPPER. ◆ The Latin word for COPPER is *cuprum*.

cub [kub] *n.* **1** The young of certain animals, such as the bear, fox, wolf, or lion. **2** A clumsy or ill-mannered boy.

Cu·ba [kyōō′bə] *n.* A country, the largest of the islands in the Caribbean Sea. — **Cu′ban** *adj., n.*

cub·by·hole [kub′ē·hōl′] *n.* A snug, enclosed space, such as a closet or storage compartment.

cube [kyōōb] *n., v.* **cubed, cub·ing** **1** *n.* A solid object with six equal square sides. **2** *v.* To multiply a number by itself and multiply the result by the original number: Two *cubed* equals eight, or $2 \times 2 \times 2 = 8$. **3** *n.* A number obtained in this way: The *cube* of 4 is 64. **4** *v.* To cut or form into cubes; dice: to *cube* potatoes.

Cube

cube root A number which, cubed, equals the number given: The *cube root* of 125 is 5.

cu·bic [kyōō′bik] *adj.* **1** Shaped like a cube. **2** Having or measured in the three dimensions length, breadth, and thickness: A *cubic* foot is the amount of space in a cube one foot long, one foot broad, and one foot high.

cu·bi·cle [kyōō′bi·kəl] *n.* Any small room or partly enclosed section of a room. ◆ This word comes from the Latin word *cubare*, meaning *to lie down*, and originally meant a bedroom.

cu·bit [kyōō′bit] *n.* An old measure of length, originally the length of the forearm, but usually 18 to 20 inches. ◆ *Cubit* comes from the Latin word *cubitum*, meaning *elbow*.

cub scout A member of a junior division of Boy Scouts for boys eight to ten years of age.

cuck·oo [kŏok′ōō *or* kōo′kōo] *n., pl.* **cuck·oos,** *adj.* **1** Any of several birds with a whistle or call that sounds like the word "cuckoo." Some

European cuckoos lay their eggs in the nests of other birds. **2** *adj. slang* Crazy; silly.

cu·cum·ber [kyōō′kum·bər] *n.* **1** A long vegetable with tough, green skin and crisp, moist, whitish flesh, used in salads and for making pickles. **2** The creeping plant it grows on.

cud [kud] *n.* Food forced back up into the mouth from the first stomach of certain animals, as the cow, and chewed over again.

cud·dle [kud′(ə)l] *v.* **cud·dled, cud·dling** **1** To hold and caress gently in one's arms: to *cuddle* a furry rabbit. **2** To lie or nestle snugly: *Cuddle* up under the covers.

cudg·el [kuj′əl] *n., v.* **cudg·eled** or **cudg·elled, cudg·el·ing** or **cudg·el·ling** **1** *n.* A short, thick club. **2** *v.* To beat with a cudgel. — **cudgel one's brains** To think hard, as if trying to remember something.

cue[1] [kyōō] *n., v.* **cued, cu·ing** **1** *n.* In theatrical performances, an action, word, etc., that serves as a signal or reminder to another actor: Wait for your *cue* before you start your speech. **2** *v.* To give a cue to (a performer). **3** *n.* Any signal to begin: The conductor gave his *cue* to the orchestra. **4** *n.* A helpful hint or indication, as when one is uncertain what to do.

cue[2] [kyōō] *n., v.* **cued, cu·ing** **1** *n.* A long, tapering stick used in billiards to strike the ball. **2** *n., v.* Another spelling of QUEUE.

cuff[1] [kuf] *n.* **1** A band or fold at the wrist of a sleeve. **2** A folded piece at the bottom of a trouser leg. **3** A handcuff.

cuff[2] [kuf] **1** *v.* To strike with the open hand; box. **2** *n.* A blow, especially with the open hand.

cui·rass [kwi·ras′] *n.* A piece of armor, especially a breastplate, protecting the upper part of the body.

cui·sine [kwi·zēn′] *n.* **1** A style or type of cooking: French *cuisine*. **2** The food prepared: The *cuisine* is excellent. ◆ This word comes from the French word meaning *kitchen*.

cu·li·nar·y [kyōō′lə·ner′ē *or* kul′ə·ner′ē] *adj.* Of or having to do with cooking or the kitchen: *culinary* art.

cull [kul] **1** *v.* To pick out; select: to *cull* the best specimens. **2** *v.* To sort out and take the poor or worthless ones from. **3** *n.* Something of poor quality picked out to be discarded, as damaged fruit or spoiled vegetables.

cul·mi·nate [kul′min·āt] *v.* **cul·mi·nat·ed, cul·mi·nat·ing** To reach the highest point or climax: The ceremonies *culminated* in the presentation of awards. — **cul′mi·na′tion** *n.*

cul·pa·ble [kul′pə·bəl] *adj.* Deserving blame; at fault: *culpable* negligence. — **cul·pa·bil·i·ty** [kul′pə·bil′ə·tē] *n.* — **cul′pa·bly** *adv.*

cul·prit [kul′prit] *n.* **1** A person guilty of a crime or misdeed; offender. **2** A person accused of a crime, as in court.

cult [kult] *n.* **1** Religious worship of someone or something: a *cult* of the sun. **2** A great liking or enthusiasm for an activity, idea, person, etc.: the *cult* of folk singing. **3** The people who share such a liking or enthusiasm.

cul·ti·vate [kul′tə·vāt] *v.* **cul·ti·vat·ed, cul·ti·vat·ing** **1** To prepare (land) for the growing of plants by loosening the soil, putting on fertilizer, etc.: to *cultivate* the fields. **2** To plant and care for: to *cultivate* roses. **3** To loosen the soil around (plants) so as to help them grow, kill weeds, etc. **4** To improve and develop by study, exercise, or training: to *cultivate* one's mind. **5** *adj. use:* a *cultivated* mind. **6** To make an effort to get to know or be friendly with.

cul·ti·va·tion [kul′tə·vā′shən] *n.* **1** The work of cultivating plants or the ground around them. **2** The development of something by study or effort. **3** Culture and refinement.

cul·ti·va·tor [kul′tə·vā′tər] *n.* **1** A person who cultivates. **2** A tool or machine used to loosen the soil around plants.

cul·tur·al [kul′chər·əl] *adj.* Having to do with or resulting in culture: *cultural* traditions. — **cul′tur·al·ly** *adv.*

cul·ture [kul′chər] *n., v.* **cul·tured, cul·tur·ing** **1** *n.* The entire way of life of a particular people, including its customs, religions, ideas, inventions, tools, etc.: ancient Egyptian *culture*. **2** *n.* The training or care of the mind or body: physical *culture*. **3** *n.* The knowledge, refinement, and good taste acquired through training the mind and faculties: a woman of *culture*. **4** *n.* The growing or improvement of animals, plants, etc.: the *culture* of bees. **5** *n.* A colony or growth of bacteria, viruses, etc., in a prepared medium, as for study. **6** *v.* To grow and improve; cultivate: to *culture* roses. **7** *n.* The cultivation of the soil.

cul·tured [kul′chərd] *adj.* **1** Having or showing culture or refinement: a *cultured* person. **2** Produced by special methods: *cultured* bacteria.

cul·vert [kul′vərt] *n.* A covered channel for water crossing under a road, railroad, etc.

cum·ber [kum′bər] *v.* **1** To obstruct; clutter. **2** To burden or weigh down. **3** *adj. use:* an old man *cumbered* with cares.

cum·ber·some [kum′bər·səm] *adj.* Hard to move or manage; unwieldy: a *cumbersome* package.

cum·brous [kum′brəs] *adj.* Cumbersome.

Culvert

cu·mu·la·tive [kyōōm′yə·lā′tiv *or* kyōōm′yə·lə·tiv] *adj.* Increasing by being added to: *cumulative* knowledge. — **cu′mu·la′tive·ly** *adv.*

cu·mu·lus [kyōōm′yə·ləs] *n., pl.* **cu·mu·li** [kyōōm′yə·lī] **1** A large cloud having a flat base and rounded masses piled up on top. **2** A mass; pile.

cu·ne·i·form [kyōō·nē′ə·fôrm] **1** *adj.* Shaped like a wedge, as the characters used in the writings of ancient Assyria, Babylonia, and Persia. **2** *n.* Ancient writing in cuneiform characters.

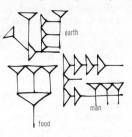

earth

man

food

Cuneiform characters

cun·ning [kun′ing] **1** *adj.* Clever or tricky. **2** *n.* Slyness or cleverness in getting something wanted: Cats use great *cunning* to catch their prey. **3** *adj. U.S.* Cute and appealing: a *cunning* toy. — **cun′ning·ly** *adv.* ◆ If you called someone *cunning* today, he probably wouldn't like it, but in former times he would have taken it as a compliment. A *cunning* craftsman was very skillful with his hands.

cup [kup] *n., v.* **cupped, cup·ping** **1** *n.* A small, open bowl, usually with a handle, used mainly for drinking. **2** *n.* The amount a cup will hold; cupful; in measuring, half a pint. **3** *n.* A cuplike bowl or vessel awarded as a prize. **4** *n.* Something shaped like a cup, as certain parts of a flower. **5** *n.* One of the holes, or its metal lining, on a golf course. **6** *v.* To shape like a cup: to *cup* one's hands. **7** *v.* To place in or as if in a cup: He *cupped* his ear with his hand. **8** *n.* One's lot or fate in life: The exile's *cup* is bitter.

cup·bear·er [kup′bâr′ər] *n.* In former times, a person who served cups of wine at banquets.

cup·board [kub′ərd] *n.* A closet or cabinet, usually with shelves for dishes, food, etc.

cup·cake [kup′kāk′] *n.* A small cake baked in a cup-shaped container.

cup·ful [kup′fŏŏl′] *n., pl.* **cup·fuls** As much as a cup will hold.

Cu·pid [kyōō′pid] *n.* **1** The Roman god of love, usually shown as a winged boy with a bow and arrow. **2** (*usually written* **cupid**) The picture of a winged baby carrying a bow and arrow, often seen on valentines.

cu·pid·i·ty [kyōō·pid′ə·tē] *n.* Greedy desire to possess something.

cu·po·la [kyōō′pə·lə] *n.* **1** A circular, dome-shaped roof. **2** A small tower built on a roof and having a dome-shaped top.

cur [kûr] *n.* **1** A scrubby mongrel dog. **2** A nasty, ill-tempered, or cowardly person.

cur·a·ble [kyŏŏr′ə·bəl] *adj.* Capable of being cured: a *curable* disease.

cu·rate [kyŏŏr′it] *n.* A clergyman who acts as assistant to a parish priest, rector, or vicar.

cur·a·tive [kyŏŏr′ə·tiv] **1** *adj.* Having the power or tendency to cure. **2** *n.* A remedy: She tried all the known *curatives* for migraine.

cu·ra·tor [kyŏŏ·rā′tər] *n.* A person in charge of

add, āce, câre, pälm;   end, ēqual;   it, īce;   odd, ōpen, ôrder;   tŏŏk, pōōl;   up, bûrn;
ə = a in *above,* e in *sicken,* i in *possible,* o in *melon,* u in *circus;*   yōō = u in *fuse;*   oil;   pout;
check; ring; thin; this; zh in *vision.*   For ¶ reference, see page 64 · HOW TO

a museum, zoo, or other place where things are collected or exhibited.

curb [kûrb] **1** *v.* To control or restrain: to *curb* one's excitement. **2** *n.* Anything that controls or restrains; a check. **3** *n.* A raised border of concrete or stone along the edge of a street or pavement. **4** *n.* A chain or strap connected to the bit of a horse and used to control the horse when the reins are pulled.

curd [kûrd] *n.* (*often pl.*) The thick clots that separate from the watery part when milk sours. Many cheeses are made from curd.

cur·dle [kûr′dəl] *v.* **cur·dled, cur·dling 1** To turn into or form curds. **2** To thicken; clot: The sauce *curdled.* — **curdle one's blood** To fill with terror; frighten badly.

cure [kyŏŏr] *v.* **cured, cur·ing,** *n.* **1** *v.* To restore to good health; make well: to *cure* a sick person. **2** *v.* To get rid of or correct: to *cure* a sore throat. **3** *n.* A medicine, diet, treatment, or other means of curing; remedy. **4** *n.* A recovery from an illness or harmful condition. **5** *v.* To preserve (meat) by salting, smoking, drying, etc.

cu·ré [kyŏŏ-rā′] *n.* The French word for a parish priest.

cure-all [kyŏŏr′ôl′] *n.* A remedy supposed to cure everything.

cur·few [kûr′fyŏŏ] *n.* **1** A rule or law requiring certain persons, especially children, to keep off the streets after a certain hour in the evening. **2** The sounding of a bell or other signal to announce that the curfew is in effect. ◆ This word comes from two French words meaning *to cover the fire.* In a medieval town people had to put out or cover all fires when a bell rang in the evening. Gradually *curfew* came to mean the bell or the hour at which it rang.

Cu·rie [kyŏŏr′ē], **Marie,** 1867–1934, French scientist born in Poland. She and her husband Pierre discovered radium.

cu·ri·o [kyŏŏr′ē-ō] *n., pl.* **cu·ri·os** Any object that is thought to be rare or unusual.

cu·ri·os·i·ty [kyŏŏr′ē-os′ə-tē] *n., pl.* **cu·ri·os·i·ties 1** Eager desire to know or find out. **2** Too much interest in other people's affairs. **3** Something strange, rare, or unusual.

cu·ri·ous [kyŏŏr′ē-əs] *adj.* **1** Eager to know or learn more. **2** Odd or unusual; strange: a *curious* old Chinese coin. — **cu′ri·ous·ly** *adv.*

cu·ri·um [kyŏŏr′ē-əm] *n.* A radioactive chemical element artificially produced from uranium and plutonium.

curl [kûrl] **1** *v.* To twist into or form curves or ringlets. **2** *n.* A coiled or rounded lock of hair; ringlet. **3** *v.* To become or cause to become curved or twisted: He *curled* his lips in scorn. **4** *v.* To move in rings or spirals: The fog *curled* over the town. **5** *n.* Anything having a curled, rounded, or spiral shape.

curl·er [kûr′lər] *n.* A device on which a lock of hair is rolled and fastened for curling.

cur·lew [kûr′lŏō] *n., pl.* **cur·lews** or **cur·lew** A bird that lives along the shore and has long legs and a very long bill curving downward.

curl·i·cue [kûr′li·kyŏō] *n.* Any fancy curl or twist: handwriting with many *curlicues.*

curl·y [kûr′lē] *adj.* **curl·i·er, curl·i·est 1** Curling or tending to curl: *curly* hair. **2** Having curls. — **curl′i·ness** *n.*

Curlicues in a signature

cur·rant [kûr′ənt] *n.* **1** A small, sour, red, white, or black berry, used for jelly. **2** The bush on which this berry grows. **3** A small seedless raisin used in cooking.

cur·ren·cy [kûr′ən·sē] *n., pl.* **cur·ren·cies 1** Money in general use. **2** General acceptance or use; popularity: Many new fads lose *currency* quickly. **3** A circulating or spreading from one person to another: That story enjoyed wide *currency.* ◆ *Money* and *currency* have almost the same meaning. *Money* is the common word. *Currency* is likely to mean many people's money, as the money used in another country is foreign *currency.*

cur·rent [kûr′ənt] **1** *n.* That part of any body of water or air that flows more or less in a definite direction: an ocean *current.* **2** *n.* A flow of electricity through a wire or other conductor. **3** *adj.* Belonging to the present time; now in effect: *current* fashions; the *current* year. **4** *adj.* Generally accepted or practiced; common. **5** *n.* Any noticeable course, trend, or tendency: a *current* of revolt. — **cur′rent·ly** *adv.*

cur·ric·u·lum [kə·rik′yə·ləm] *n., pl.* **cur·ric·u·lums** or **cur·ric·u·la** [kə·rik′yə·lə] All of the subjects or courses taught in a school or in any particular grade.

cur·ry[1] [kûr′ē] *v.* **cur·ried, cur·ry·ing** To rub down and clean (a horse or other animal) with a currycomb. — **curry favor** To try to get favors from someone by flattering him in an insincere way.

cur·ry[2] [kûr′ē] *n., pl.* **cur·ries,** *v.* **cur·ried, cur·ry·ing 1** *n.* A sauce or powder made of finely ground spices and used to season food. **2** *n.* A dish of meat, fish, etc., seasoned with this sauce or powder. **3** *v.* To season food with curry: to *curry* rice and shrimp. ◆ *Curry* comes from a word meaning *sauce* in a language of southern India and Ceylon.

cur·ry·comb [kûr′ē·kōm′] **1** *n.* A comb having rows of metal teeth or ridges used to groom horses. **2** *v.* To groom with a currycomb.

curse [kûrs] *n., v.* **cursed** [kûrst] or **curst, cur·sing 1** *n.* A wish for evil or harm to befall someone or something, often made by calling on God or gods. **2** *v.* To wish harm or punishment on: The prophet *cursed* the wicked people. **3** *n.* The harm or evil asked for. **4** *v.* To use profane language; swear or swear at. **5** *n.* A word used in cursing or swearing. **6** *n.* A source of harm, evil, or trouble: That ring was always a *curse.* **7** *v.* To cause to suffer; afflict: He was *cursed* with ill health.

curs·ed [kûr′sid *or* kûrst] *adj.* **1** Deserving a curse; wicked; hateful. **2** Under a curse.

cur·sive [kûr′siv] *adj.* Written or printed so that the letters are joined together, as in *This is cursive writing* handwriting.

cur·so·ry [kûr′sər·ē] *adj.* Not thorough; hasty: *a cursory reading.* **— cur′so·ri·ly** *adv.*

curt [kûrt] *adj.* Short and somewhat rude in tone or manner: *a curt nod; a curt answer.* **— curt′ly** *adv.* **— curt′ness** *n.*

cur·tail [kər·tāl′] *v.* To cut short or cut back; reduce: *to curtail a meeting.* **— cur·tail′· ment** *n.*

cur·tain [kûr′tən] **1** *n.* A piece of cloth hung in or over a window, door, or other opening, as a decoration or screen, usually capable of being drawn to the sides or raised. **2** *n.* Such a screen used to hide the stage of a theater from the audience. **3** *n.* Something like a curtain that covers, hides, or screens: *a curtain of mist.* **4** *v.* To cover, hide, or screen with or as if with a curtain: *to curtain a window.*

cur·sey [kûrt′sē] *n., pl.* **curt·seys,** *v.* **curt· seyed, curt·sey·ing** Curtsy.

curt·sy [kûrt′sē] *n., pl.* **curt·sies,** *v.* **curt· sied, curt·sy·ing 1** *n.* A bow made by bending the knees and inclining the upper part of the body forward, used by women and girls as a sign of respect. **2** *v.* To make such a bow.

A girl curtsying

cur·va·ture [kûr′və·chər] *n.* A curve or a curved condition: *curvature of the earth.*

curve [kûrv] *n., v.* **curved, curv·ing 1** *n.* In mathematics, a connected set of points such that a part of it would be separated by the omission of a single point. Popularly, it is a continuous set of points with no straight line segment. **2** *n.* Something shaped like a curve: *a curve in the road.* **3** *v.* To bend into or take the form of a curve: *One track curved off to the west.* **4** *n.* In baseball, a ball pitched with a spin that causes it to swerve. **5** *v.* To throw or move in a curve: *Smoke curved from the chimney.*

cur·vet [*n.* kûr′vit, *v.* kər·vet′ or kûr′vit] *n., v.* **cur·vet·ted** or **cur·vet·ed, cur·vet·ting** or **cur·vet·ing 1** *n.* A light, low leap of a horse, made so that all four legs are off the ground at one time. **2** *v.* To make a curvet.

cush·ion [kŏosh′ən] **1** *n.* A case or bag filled with a soft, springy material and used to sit, kneel, or lie on; pillow. **2** *n.* Anything like a cushion in appearance or use. **3** *v.* To provide or support with or as if with a cushion: *She cushioned the child's head in her lap.* **4** *v.* To absorb the shock or effect of: *to cushion a blow.*

cusp [kusp] *n.* **1** A pointed end formed by the meeting of two curves. Either end of a crescent moon is a cusp. **2** A point on the crown of a tooth.

cus·pid [kus′pid] *n.* A tooth having one cusp; canine tooth.

cus·pi·dor [kus′pə·dôr] *n. U.S.* A container for spitting into; spittoon. ◆ *Cuspidor* comes directly from Portuguese.

cuss [kus] *U.S. informal* **1** *v.* To swear or curse. **2** *n.* A person; fellow.

cus·tard [kus′tərd] *n.* A dessert made of sweetened milk and eggs, baked or boiled.

cus·to·di·an [kus·tō′dē·ən] *n.* A guardian or keeper: *He was custodian of a building.*

cus·to·dy [kus′tə·dē] *n., pl.* **cus·to·dies** Care and control; guardianship: *The foster parents were given custody of the child.* **— in custody** Under arrest; in prison or jail. **— take into custody** To arrest.

cus·tom [kus′təm] **1** *n.* A usual way of acting or doing something; habit: *It was his custom to walk to work.* **2** *n.* Something that has become an accepted practice by many people: *the custom of decorating Christmas trees.* **3** *n.* Business given by a steady customer: *We gave our custom to the neighborhood grocery.* **4** *n.* (*pl.*) The tax which a government collects on goods brought into a country from abroad; also, the agency of the government that collects such taxes. **5** *adj.* Made specially for an individual customer; made-to-order: *custom shoes.* **6** *adj.* Dealing or specializing in made-to-order goods: *a custom tailor.* ◆ *Custom, habit,* and *fashion* refer to a way of doing or behaving that has become usual. *Custom* is used especially for rules of conduct followed by a group: *the Mexican custom of taking a midday siesta. Habit* usually refers to one person's behavior: *Mary has the bad habit of biting her fingernails. Fashions* are styles, as of dress, taken up by many but often not for long: *Tall silk hats were then the fashion.*

cus·tom·ar·y [kus′tə·mer′ē] *adj.* Based on custom; usual: *at the customary time.* **— cus′· tom·ar′i·ly** *adv.*

cus·tom·er [kus′təm·ər] *n.* **1** A person who buys something, as from a store. **2** *informal* A person unusual in some way: *a tough customer.*

cus·tom·house [kus′təm·hous′] *n.* The government office where customs are collected on goods brought into a country from abroad.

cus·tom-made [kus′təm·mād′] *adj.* Made for an individual customer; made-to-order.

cut [kut] *v.* **cut, cut·ting,** *n.* **1** *v.* To make an opening in (something) with a sharp edge or instrument: *to cut one's foot.* **2** *n.* An opening made with something having a sharp edge: *to bandage a cut.* **3** *n.* A stroke, slice, or blow with something having a sharp edge. **4** *v.* To divide, separate, or break up into parts: *to cut paper;*

---

add, āce, câre, pälm; end, ēqual; it, īce; odd, ōpen, ôrder; tŏŏk, pōōl; up, bûrn; ə = a in *above,* e in *sicken,* i in *possible,* o in *melon,* u in *circus;* yōō = u in *fuse;* oil; pout; check; ring; thin; this; zh in *vision.* For ¶ reference, see page 64 · HOW TO

Tender meat *cuts* easily. **5** *v.* To remove a part or parts by cutting: to *cut* hair. **6** *n.* A part removed by cutting: a *cut* of meat. **7** *v.* To make, shape, or ornament by or as if by cutting: to *cut* a diamond. **8** *adj. use:* finely *cut* features. **9** *v.* To make less; reduce: to *cut* prices. **10** *n.* A reduction: a *cut* in salary. **11** *v.* To take a direct route; go straight: to *cut* through the woods. **12** *n.* A passage or channel made by cutting: The road goes through a *cut* there. **13** *n.* A route or way that is straight and direct: a short *cut.* **14** *v.* To pierce like a knife: Her words *cut* me to the heart. **15** *n.* Something that hurts one's feelings. **16** *v.* To pretend not to see or recognize (someone); snub: I nodded to her, but she *cut* me. **17** *v.* To have (a new tooth) grow through the gum. **18** *n.* The fashion or style of anything: the *cut* of a suit. **19** *n.* An engraved block or plate used in printing; also, a picture, etc., made from this. **20** *v.* To hit a ball so that it will spin or swerve to one side. **21** *n. slang* A part; portion; share: a *cut* of the loot. **— cut in 1** To move or swerve into a line suddenly: to *cut in* ahead of someone. **2** To break in, as on a conversation; interrupt. **— cut off 1** To remove a part or parts by cutting. **2** To shut off; stop: to *cut off* the water supply. **3** To disinherit: She *cut* her grandchild *off* without a cent. **— cut out 1** To remove or shape by cutting: to *cut out* pictures. **2** Suited: He's not *cut out* to be a soldier. **3** *slang* To stop doing; cease: *Cut out* that nonsense. **— cut up 1** To divide or separate into pieces. **2** *informal* To show off; act silly. **3** To upset or distress.

cut·a·way [kut′ə·wā′] *n.* A man's formal coat for daytime wear, cut slopingly away from the waist in front down to the tails at the back.

cut·back [kut′bak′] *n.* A sharp reduction: a *cutback* in prices.

cute [kyoot] *adj.* **cut·er, cut·est** *informal* **1** Charming and appealing: a *cute* puppy. **2** Clever or shrewd. ◆ *Cute* was first used, mostly in the U.S., only with the second meaning, a sense now not common. It is a shortened form of *acute.*

cu·ti·cle [kyoo′ti·kəl] *n.* **1** The hardened skin around the base of a fingernail or toenail. **2** The outer layer of skin.

cut·lass or **cut·las** [kut′ləs] *n.* A short, curved sword, used in former days chiefly by sailors.

cut·ler·y [kut′lər·ē] *n.* **1** Tools or utensils used for cutting: Knives and scissors are *cutlery.* **2** Knives, forks, and spoons used in eating and serving food.

Cuticle

cut·let [kut′lit] *n.* **1** A thin piece of meat, such as veal, for frying or broiling. **2** A flat cake of chopped meat or fish, usually fried.

cut·off [kut′ôf′] **1** *n.* A stopping or shutting off of something: The water *cutoff* will last two hours. **2** *adj. use:* The *cutoff* hour is two o'clock. **3** *n. U.S.* A shorter, more direct way; short cut.

cut·purse [kut′pûrs′] *n.* A pickpocket.

cut·ter [kut′ər] *n.* **1** A person or instrument that cuts: a paper *cutter.* **2** A small, armed ship, especially one used by the Coast Guard. **3** A boat carried by a ship to go to and from the ship. **4** A small sleigh. **5** A sailboat having a single mast.

cut·throat [kut′thrōt′] **1** *n.* A murderer. **2** *adj.* Merciless; ruthless: The *cutthroat* competition forced him out of business.

cut·ting [kut′ing] **1** *adj.* Able to cut; sharp: a *cutting* blade. **2** *adj.* Cold and piercing: a *cutting* wind. **3** *adj.* Able to wound the feelings; sarcastic: a *cutting* reply. **4** *n.* The action of a person or thing that cuts. **5** *n.* An excavation made through a hill or high piece of ground for the construction of a railroad, canal, etc. **6** *n.* A shoot cut from a plant to form a new plant.

cut·tle·fish [kut′(ə)l·fish′] *n., pl.* **cut·tle·fish** or **cut·tle·fish·es** A sea animal having ten arms with suckers on them and a hard inner shell. Some kinds squirt an inky fluid to hide in when attacked.

cut·worm [kut′wûrm′] *n.* A caterpillar that cuts off plants near the surface of the ground.

cwt. Abbreviation of HUNDREDWEIGHT. ◆ This abbreviation comes from the Latin word *centum,* meaning *hundred,* and the English word *weight.*

-cy A suffix meaning: **1** Quality, state, or condition of being, as in *secrecy,* the state of being secret. **2** Rank, grade, or position of, as in *presidency,* the position of being president.

cy·a·nide [sī′ə·nīd] *n.* Any of various very poisonous chemical compounds.

cy·ber·net·ics [sī′bər·net′iks] *n.* The comparative study of machines such as computers and the nervous system of man or animals, to gain better understanding of the functioning of the brain. ◆ See -ICS.

cyc·la·men [sik′lə·mən] *n.* A plant having large pink, red, or white flowers.

cy·cle [sī′kəl] *n., v.* **cy·cled, cy·cling 1** *n.* A series of events that always happen in the same order and return to the original position, as the waxing and waning of the moon. **2** *n.* A series of predictable stages in the growth of a plant or animal or the completion of a process, as the erosion of a river valley. **3** *n.* The time needed for such series. **4** *n.* A long period of time; an eon. **5** *n.* A collection of poems, songs, or stories handed down about a certain hero, period, or event. **6** *n.* A bicycle, motorcycle, etc. **7** *v.* To ride a bicycle, motorcycle, etc.

cy·clic [sī′klik *or* sik′lik] *adj.* **1** Of a cycle. **2** Returning or occurring in cycles.

cy·clist [sī′klist] *n.* A person who rides a bicycle, motorcycle, etc.

cy·clone [sī′klōn] *n.* **1** A storm in which winds whirl spirally in toward a center of low pressure, which also moves. **2** Any violent windstorm; a tornado: used chiefly in the Middle West.

cy·clon·ic [sī·klon′ik] *adj.* **1** Of a cyclone. **2** Like a cyclone; violent; destructive.

cy·clo·pe·di·a [sī′klə·pē′dē·ə] *n.* Another word for ENCYCLOPEDIA.

D

Cy·clops [sī′klops] *n.*, *pl.* **Cy·clo·pes** [sī·klō′pēz] or **Cy·clops** In Greek legend, any of a race of giants having one eye in the middle of the forehead.

Cyclops

cy·clo·tron [sī′klə·tron] *n.* An apparatus that whirls charged particles through a strong magnetic field to such high speeds that they can enter and change the nuclei of certain atoms.

cyg·net [sig′nit] *n.* A young swan. ◆ *Cygnet* comes from the French word *cygne*, meaning *swan*, and *-et*, meaning *small*.

cyl·in·der [sil′in·dər] *n.* **1** A geometric figure bounded by two circles in parallel planes and the parallel lines joining them. The lines may or may not be perpendicular to the planes. **2** Any object or container having this shape.

Cylinder

cy·lin·dri·cal [si·lin′dri·kəl] *adj.* Shaped like a cylinder.

cym·bal [sim′bəl] *n.* A round metal plate that makes a ringing sound when struck, often used in pairs in a band or orchestra.

cyn·ic [sin′ik] **1** *n.* A sneering, faultfinding person who distrusts the goodness and sincerity of others. **2** *adj.* Cynical.

cyn·i·cal [sin′i·kəl] *adj.* **1** Having no belief in the goodness and sincerity of others. **2** Sneering; sarcastic. — **cyn′i·cal·ly** *adv.*

cyn·i·cism [sin′ə·siz′əm] *n.* **1** The thoughts and feelings of a cynic. **2** A cynical remark, act, etc.

cy·no·sure [sī′nə·shoor *or* sin′ə·shoor] *n.* A person or object that is the center of attention, attraction, or admiration: The bride was the *cynosure* of all eyes.

cy·press [sī′prəs] *n.* **1** An evergreen tree with hard wood and dark, scalelike leaves. **2** The wood of this tree.

Cyp·ri·ot [sip′rē·ət] *n.*, *adj.* Cypriote.

Cyp·ri·ote [sip′rē·ōt] **1** *n.* A person born in or a citizen of Cyprus. **2** *adj.* Of or from Cyprus.

Cy·prus [sī′prəs] *n.* A country, an island in the Mediterranean Sea, south of Turkey.

Cy·rus [sī′rəs] *n.*, died 529 B.C., king of Persia who made it an empire. He was called Cyrus the Great.

cyst [sist] *n.* An abnormal baglike growth in some part of the body, in which liquid or solid material may collect and remain.

cy·tol·o·gy [sī·tol′ə·jē] *n.* The scientific study of the structure and workings of living cells. — **cy·tol′o·gist** *n.*

cy·to·plasm [sī′tə·plaz′əm] *n.* All of the protoplasm of a cell, except for that in the nucleus.

czar [zär] *n.* **1** One of the former emperors of Russia. **2** Someone having great power or authority in a certain activity: a baseball *czar*.

cza·ri·na [zä·rē′nə] *n.* A former empress of Russia.

Czech [chek] **1** *n.* A person born in or a citizen of Czechoslovakia, especially one from the western part of the country. **2** *n.* A language of Czechoslovakia. **3** *adj.* Having to do with Czechoslovakia, the Czechs, or their language.

Czech·o·slo·vak [chek′ə·slō′vak *or* chek′ə·slō′väk] **1** *n.* A person born in or a citizen of Czechoslovakia. **2** *adj.* Of or from Czechoslovakia.

Czech·o·slo·va·ki·a [chek′ə·slō·vä′kē·ə] *n.* A country in east central Europe. — **Czech′o·slo·va′ki·an** *adj.*, *n.*

D

d or **D** [dē] *n.*, *pl*, **d's** or **D's** **1** The fourth letter of the English alphabet. **2** (*written* **D**) The Roman numeral for 500. **3** *U.S.* A school grade indicating the student's work is poor.

d. Abbreviation of PENCE. ◆ *d.* comes from the Latin word *denarius*, an ancient Roman coin.

D.A. Abbreviation of DISTRICT ATTORNEY.

dab [dab] *n.*, *v.* **dabbed, dab·bing** **1** *n.* A quick, gentle stroke; pat. **2** *v.* To stroke quickly and gently: to *dab* one's eyes. **3** *n.* A small lump of something soft and moist.

dab·ble [dab′əl] *v.* **dab·bled, dab·bling** **1** To splash gently, as with the hands: to *dabble* in a brook. **2** To spatter lightly: a dress *dabbled* with mud. **3** To do something but not seriously: to *dabble* at chess. — **dab′bler** *n.*

---

add, āce, câre, pälm; end, ēqual; it, īce; odd, ōpen, ôrder; took, pool; up, bûrn;

ə = a in *above*, e in *sicken*, i in *possible*, o in *melon*, u in *circus*; yoo = u in *fuse*; oil; pout;

check; **r**ing; **th**in; **th**is; **zh** in *vision*. For ¶ reference, see page 64 · HOW TO

dace [dās] *n., pl.* **dac·es** or **dace** A small freshwater fish related to carp and goldfish.

dachs·hund [däks′hoont′ or daks′hoond′] *n.* A breed of small hound dog native to Germany, having a long, compact body, very short legs, and short hair, usually red, tan, or black and tan in color.

Dachshund, 8 in. high at shoulder

Da·cron [dā′kron or dak′ron] *n.* A synthetic fiber or cloth that does not wrinkle or stretch easily: a trademark. Also written **dacron.**

dad [dad] *n. informal* Father.

dad·dy [dad′ē] *n., pl.* **dad·dies** *informal* Father: used mostly by children: My *daddy* is away on a trip.

dad·dy-long·legs [dad′ē·lông′legz′] *n., pl.* **dad·dy-long·legs** An animal that looks like a spider with long thin legs and a small body.

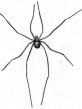

Daddy-longlegs

Daed·a·lus [ded′ə·ləs] *n.* In Greek myths, the architect of the labyrinth at Crete. He and his son Icarus were imprisoned there and escaped by using artificial wings.

daf·fo·dil [daf′ə·dil] *n.* A plant with yellow flowers and long, bladelike leaves. It grows from a bulb.

daf·fy [daf′ē] *adj.* **daf·fi·er, daf·fi·est** *informal* Crazy or silly.

daft [daft] *adj. British* Crazy or foolish.

dag·ger [dag′ər] *n.* A short, pointed weapon used for stabbing.

da·guerre·o·type [də·ger′ə·tīp′] *n.* An old-fashioned kind of photograph made on a silver-coated metal plate sensitive to light.

dahl·ia [dal′yə] *n.* A plant that has bright, showy flowers in red, purple, yellow, or white.

Da·ho·mey [də·hō′mē] *n.* A country in western Africa.

dai·ly [dā′lē] *adj., adv., n., pl.* **dai·lies 1** *adj.* Done, occurring, or appearing every day: *daily* exercise; a *daily* newspaper. **2** *adv.* Every day; day after day: to walk *daily* in the park. **3** *n.* A newspaper published every day.

dain·ty [dān′tē] *adj.* **dain·ti·er, dain·ti·est,** *n., pl.* **dain·ties 1** *adj.* Delicately pretty or graceful: a *dainty* little girl. **2** *adj.* Very particular or fussy: a *dainty* eater. **3** *n.* A delicious food; delicacy. **4** *adj.* Delicious; tasty. **— dain′ti·ly** *adv.* **— dain′ti·ness** *n.*

dair·y [dâr′ē] *n., pl.* **dair·ies 1** A place where milk and cream are stored or made into butter, cheese, etc. **2** A farm or store that specializes in milk products.

dair·y·maid [dâr′ē·mād′] *n.* A girl or woman who works on a dairy farm.

da·is [dā′is] *n.* A platform in a room or hall for a speaker, a throne, or seats of honor.

dai·sy [dā′zē] *n., pl.* **dai·sies 1** A flower with a central yellow disk surrounded by white or pink rays. **2** The plant.

dale [dāl] *n.* A small valley.

Dal·las [dal′əs] *n.* A city in NE Texas.

dal·li·ance [dal′ē·əns] *n.* **1** Trifling or wasting of time. **2** Flirting or playing.

dal·ly [dal′ē] *v.* **dal·lied, dal·ly·ing 1** To treat lightly or playfully; trifle: to *dally* with danger. **2** To waste time; dawdle; linger: He *dallied* on the way to school. ◆ *Dally* comes from an old French word meaning *to chat.*

Dal·ma·tian [dal·mā′shən] *n.* A large, short-haired dog, white with black spots.

dam¹ [dam] *n., v.* **dammed, dam·ming 1** *n.* A wall or other barrier to hold back or control flowing water. **2** *v.* To hold back by or as if by a dam: to *dam* a river.

Dam

dam² [dam] *n.* The female parent of a horse, sheep, or cow, and of some other animals.

dam·age [dam′ij] *n., v.* **dam·aged, dam·ag·ing 1** *n.* Injury or harm that reduces value or usefulness: The drought did much *damage* to the crops; *damage* to one's reputation. **2** *n.* The resulting loss: The *damage* was estimated at $750. **3** *v.* To cause injury to: to *damage* a library book. **4** *n.* (*pl.*) Money asked for or paid under law to make up for an injury or wrong.

Da·mas·cus [də·mas′kəs] *n.* The capital of Syria, one of the most ancient cities in the world.

dam·ask [dam′əsk] **1** *n.* A fine table linen with a pattern woven into it. **2** *adj. use:* a *damask* tablecloth. **3** *n.* A rich, reversible silk fabric with an elaborate woven design. **4** *n.* A steel with wavy markings. **5** *n., adj.* Deep pink or rose.

dame [dām] *n.* **1** A lady: seldom used today except as a British title of honor. **2** An old woman. **3** *slang* A woman or girl.

damn [dam] **1** *v.* In some religions, to condemn to eternal punishment. **2** *v.* To pronounce as bad or worthless: to *damn* a book or a movie. **3** *interj.* An exclamation or curse expressing annoyance, disappointment, etc. **4** *v.* To curse by saying "damn."

dam·na·ble [dam′nə·bəl] *adj.* That ought to be damned; hateful; detestable.

dam·na·tion [dam·nā′shən] *n.* **1** The act of damning. **2** The condition of being damned.

Dam·o·cles [dam′ə·klēz] *n.* In Greek myths, a man who flattered his king and was forced to sit at a banquet table under a sword hung by a single hair to teach him how insecure rulers are.

Da·mon and Pyth·i·as [dā′mən; pith′ē·əs] In Roman myths, two devoted friends. Damon served as a hostage so that Pythias, condemned to die, could visit his home one last time.

damp [damp] **1** *adj.* Slightly wet; moist: a *damp* day; *damp* shoes. **2** *n.* Moisture; vapor: The cellar is full of *damp.* **3** *v.* To dampen; moisten: to *damp* clothes. **4** *v.* To discourage or dull: to *damp* enthusiasm. **5** *n.* A discouragement; chill. **6** *n.* Foul air or poisonous gas, especially in a mine. **— damp′ness** *n.*

damp·en [dam′pən] *v.* **1** To make or become damp; moisten: Dew *dampened* the grass. **2** To check or dull: Nothing could *dampen* our spirits.

damp·er [dam′pər] *n.* **1** A flat plate in the flue of a stove, furnace, etc., that can be tilted to control the draft. **2** A person or thing that dulls, depresses, or checks.

dam·sel [dam′zəl] *n.* A young girl: seldom used today.

dam·son [dam′zən] *n.* **1** A small, oval purple plum. **2** The tree it grows on.

dance [dans] *v.* **danced, danc·ing,** *n.* **1** *v.* To move the body and feet rhythmically, usually to music. **2** *n.* The act of dancing. **3** *n.* A round of dancing: the next *dance.* **4** *n.* A particular form of dance, as the waltz, polka, etc. **5** *v.* To perform (a dance): to *dance* the polka. **6** *n.* A piece of music for dancing. **7** *n.* A gathering of people for dancing; a ball. **8** *v.* To move up and down; leap about: *dancing* waves; to *dance* for joy. **— dance attendance on** To wait upon (another) constantly and eagerly.

danc·er [dan′sər] *n.* A person who dances, especially a paid performer.

dan·de·li·on [dan′də·lī′ən] *n.* A common weed with a yellow flower and toothed leaves.

dan·dle [dan′dəl] *v.* **dan·dled, dan·dling 1** To move up and down lightly on the knee or in the arms: to *dandle* a baby. **2** To pamper; coddle.

dan·druff [dan′drəf] *n.* Small scales of dead skin formed on the scalp.

dan·dy [dan′dē] *n., pl.* **dan·dies,** *adj.* **dan· di·er, dan·di·est 1** *n.* A man who is greatly interested in fine clothes and an elegant appearance. **2** *n. slang* Something very good. **3** *adj. slang* Very good; excellent.

Dane [dān] *n.* A person born in or a citizen of Denmark.

dan·ger [dān′jər] *n.* **1** A being exposed to harm, trouble, etc.: A fireman's life is full of *danger.* **2** Something that may cause harm: Smoking is a *danger* to health.

dan·ger·ous [dān′jər·əs] *adj.* Likely to cause harm; unsafe. **— dan′ger·ous·ly** *adv.*

dan·gle [dang′gəl] *v.* **dan·gled, dan·gling 1** To hang loosely and swing to and fro: The light cord *dangled* from the ceiling. **2** To hold or carry so as to swing loosely: to *dangle* a piece of string in front of a kitten. **3** To follow or hover about: My sister kept her boy friend *dangling* for a year before she agreed to marry him.

dan·gling [dang′gling] *adj.* **1** That dangles. **2** In grammar, without or not near a logical word to modify. In "After driving all day, the mountains rose up before us," *driving* is a dangling participle.

Dan·iel [dan′yəl] *n.* **1** In the Bible, a Hebrew prophet whose faith was so great that he stood in a den of lions and was not harmed. **2** A book of the Old Testament named after him.

Dan·ish [dā′nish] **1** *adj.* Of or from Denmark. **2** *n.* **(the Danish)** The people of Denmark. **3** *n.* The language of the Danes.

dank [dangk] *adj.* Unpleasantly cold and wet.

Dan·te [dän′tä *or* dan′tē] *n.*, 1265–1321, Italian poet, author of the *Divine Comedy.*

Dan·ube [dan′yōōb] *n.* A long river flowing from Germany eastward into the Black Sea.

dap·per [dap′ər] *adj.* **1** Smartly dressed; trim. **2** Small and lively: a *dapper* elf.

dap·ple [dap′əl] *adj., v.* **dap·pled, dap·pling 1** *adj.* Spotted; mottled. **2** *v.* To make spotted or mottled: Clouds *dappled* the sky. **3** *adj. use:* a *dappled* horse.

Dar·da·nelles [där′də·nelz′] *n.* A narrow strait connecting the Sea of Marmara with the Aegean Sea. It was once called the Hellespont.

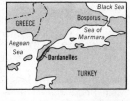

dare [dâr] *v.* **dared** (or **durst**: seldom used today), **dar· ing,** *n.* **1** *v.* To have the courage or boldness to do something: I wouldn't *dare* fight him. **2** *v.* To have the courage to face: He *dared* the dangers of the deep. **3** *v.* To challenge to do something: He *dared* me to climb the tree. **4** *n.* A challenge: I took his *dare* and climbed the tree. **— I dare say** Very likely; probably. ◆ *Dare,* when used with *he, she,* or *it* in the present tense, sometimes takes the form *dare* rather then *dares*: He *dare* not go; *Dare* he do it?

dare·dev·il [dâr′dev′əl] **1** *n.* A recklessly bold person. **2** *adj.* Reckless; rash.

dar·ing [dâr′ing] **1** *n.* Adventurous courage; bravery. **2** *adj.* Brave and adventurous; fearless.

Da·ri·us I [də·rī′əs] *n.*, 558?–486? B.C., king of Persia.

dark [därk] **1** *adj.* Without light, or having little light: a *dark* night; a *dark* cave. **2** *n.* Darkness: He is afraid of the *dark.* **3** *adj.* Having a deep shade; nearly black: *dark* blue. **4** *adj.* Gloomy: to look on the *dark* side of things. **5** *adj.* Evil: *dark* deeds. **6** *adj.* Having little knowledge or understanding; ignorant. **— in the dark** In ignorance. **— dark′ness** *n.*

Dark Ages A name given to the early Middle Ages because the period was thought to be one of little knowledge or progress.

---

add, āce, câre, pälm;   end, ēqual;   it, īce;   odd, ōpen, ôrder;   took, pool;   up, bûrn;

ə = a in *above,* e in *sicken,* i in *possible,* o in *melon,* u in *circus;*   yōō = u in *fuse;*   oil;   pout;

check; ring; thin; this; zh in *vision.*   For ¶ reference, see page 64 · HOW TO

dark·en [där′kən] *v.* To make or become dark.

dark horse A contestant who wins unexpectedly, especially in a political campaign.

dark·ling [därk′ling] **1** *adj.* Dark, or occurring in the dark. **2** *adv.* In the dark. ◆ This word is used mostly in poems.

dark·ly [därk′lē] *adv.* **1** Gloomily: He looked *darkly* at me. **2** Mysteriously: to hint *darkly*.

dark·room [därk′rōōm′] *n.* A dark room where film may be processed.

dar·ling [där′ling] **1** *n.* A person very dearly loved: often used as a form of address. **2** *adj.* Dearly loved: my *darling* child.

darn [därn] **1** *v.* To mend (cloth) by filling the hole or tear with crossing stitches. **2** *n.* A place mended by darning.

dart [därt] **1** *n.* A small arrow that can be thrown by hand, shot from a blowgun, etc. It is used in a game, **darts,** or as a weapon. **2** *n.* A sudden, quick movement: The deer made a *dart* across the road. **3** *v.* To move suddenly and swiftly: Fish *dart* through the water. **4** *v.* To throw or send out suddenly or swiftly: She *darted* an angry look at him.

Dar·win [där′win], **Charles Robert,** 1809–1882, English naturalist.

dash [dash] **1** *v.* To throw violently so as to break or shatter: Angrily he *dashed* the vase to pieces. **2** *v.* To strike; hit: Waves *dashed* against the rocks. **3** *n.* A striking against; blow: the *dash* of rain on a windowpane. **4** *v.* To splash or sprinkle: After she fainted, we *dashed* water on her face. **5** *v.* To destroy; ruin: to *dash* hopes. **6** *v.* To rush: The children *dashed* out onto the playground. **7** *n.* A short race; sprint: a 50-yard *dash*. **8** *n.* A small bit: a *dash* of salt. **9** *n.* Spirit; zest: The Johnsons always add *dash* to a party. **10** *n.* A horizontal line (—) used as a punctuation mark, usually to show a pause or break in a sentence.

dash·board [dash′bôrd′] *n.* The panel below the windshield of an automobile or other vehicle that holds the dials and controls.

Dashboard of an automobile

dash·er [dash′ər] *n.* The plunger of a churn.

dash·ing [dash′ing] *adj.* **1** Full of spirit; energetic: a *dashing* horseman. **2** Colorful; gay: a *dashing* outfit.

das·tard [das′tərd] **1** *n.* A mean, sneaky coward. **2** *adj.* Dastardly.

das·tard·ly [das′tərd·lē] *adj.* Cowardly and mean: a *dastardly* act.

da·ta [dā′tə] *n.pl.* Facts or figures; information. ◆ *Data* comes from a plural Latin word meaning *things given*. Its singular form, *datum*, is rarely used today, and *data* is now commonly used with either a plural or a singular verb.

date¹ [dāt] *n., v.* **dat·ed, dat·ing 1** *n.* The time of some event: The *date* of the landing of the Mayflower was 1620. **2** *n.* The day of the month: What's today's *date*? **3** *n.* A date written or inscribed on something: The *date* is part of the heading of a letter. **4** *v.* To mark with a date: to *date* a painting. **5** *v.* To find out the age of; give a date to: to *date* a fossil. **6** *n.* A certain period of time: At that *date* women wore bustles. **7** *v.* To belong to a certain period: This picture *dates* from the 14th century. **8** *n. informal* A social appointment for a certain time. **9** *n. informal* A person of the opposite sex with whom such an appointment is made. **10** *v. informal* To have a date or dates with: Joe *dates* my sister. **— out of date** Old-fashioned. **— up to date 1** In fashion; modern. **2** Up to the present time; till now.

date² [dāt] *n.* **1** The sweet fruit of a type of palm tree. **2** The tree bearing this fruit, often called **date palm.**

date·less [dāt′lis] *adj.* **1** Bearing no date. **2** Ageless; enduring: a jewel's *dateless* beauty.

date line Another name for INTERNATIONAL DATE LINE.

da·tive [dā′tiv] **1** *adj.* Showing the case of or indicating the indirect object of a verb. In "I gave Jerry the book," *Jerry* is in the dative case. **2** *n.* A word in the dative case. **3** *n.* The dative case. ◆ In Latin, Greek, etc., datives have special endings.

daub [dôb] **1** *v.* To smear or coat with a sticky or greasy substance: to *daub* plaster on a wall. **2** *n.* Something daubed on. **3** *v.* To smear on or paint without skill: to *daub* colors on a canvas. **4** *n.* A poor painting. **— daub′er** *n.*

daugh·ter [dô′tər] *n.* **1** A girl or woman, considered in relation to either or both of her parents. **2** A girl or woman regarded as an offspring or descendant: a *daughter* of Spain.

daugh·ter-in-law [dô′tər·in·lô′] *n., pl.* **daugh·ters-in-law** The wife of one's son.

daunt [dônt] *v.* To frighten or discourage.

daunt·less [dônt′lis] *adj.* Fearless; brave.

dau·phin [dô′fin] *n.* The eldest son of the king of France, a title no longer used.

dav·en·port [dav′ən·pôrt] *n. U.S.* A large upholstered sofa. Some open out to form beds.

Da·vid [dā′vid] *n.* In the Bible, the second king of Israel, father of Solomon.

da Vin·ci [də vin′chē], **Leoardo,** 1452–1519 Italian painter, sculptor, and architect. He was also a pioneer in biology, geology, engineering, and military science.

Da·vis [dā′vis], **Jefferson,** 1808–1889, U.S. statesman and president of the Confederacy.

Davits

dav·it [dav′it] *n.* One of a pair of small cranes on a ship's side for raising and lowering small boats.

Da·vy Jones [dā′vē jōnz′] The spirit of the sea: a humorous name used by sailors. **— Davy Jones's locker** The bottom of the sea, especially as the graveyard of those drowned or buried at sea.

daw [dô] *n.* Another name for JACKDAW.

daw·dle [dôd′(ə)l] *v.* **daw·dled, daw·dling** To waste time; idle: to *dawdle* away the hours. **— daw′dler** *n.*

dawn [dôn] **1** *n.* The first appearance of light in the morning. **2** *v.* To begin to grow light in the morning. **3** *n.* An awakening; beginning: the *dawn* of a new period in history. **4** *v.* To begin to appear or develop: New hope *dawned* on his face. **5** *v.* To begin to be clear to the mind: The truth just *dawned* on me.

day [dā] *n.* **1** The time between sunrise and sunset. **2** The period of 24 hours from one midnight to the next. **3** The time of the day a person spends on his job: an eight-hour *day.* **4** A time or period; age: the present *day;* in Caesar's *day.* **5** (*pl.*) A lifetime, or part of one: A doctor spends his *days* treating the sick.

day·break [dā′brāk′] *n.* Dawn: The farmer was up at *daybreak* to milk the cows.

day·dream [dā′drēm′] **1** *n.* A pleasant, dreamlike thought, as of something one wishes would happen. **2** *v.* To have daydreams. **— day′· dream′er** *n.*

day·light [dā′līt′] *n.* **1** Light from the sun; light of day. **2** Dawn; daybreak.

day·light-sav·ing time [dā′līt′sā′ving] Time which is an hour ahead of standard time, usually used in the summer. Nine o'clock standard time is 10 o'clock daylight-saving time.

Day of Atonement Another name for YOM KIPPUR.

day school A school that has classes only during the day and does not board its pupils.

day·time [dā′tīm′] *n.* The time of the day between sunrise and sunset.

daze [dāz] *v.* **dazed, daz·ing,** *n.* **1** *v.* To confuse or bewilder; stun: to be *dazed* by a blow on the head. **2** *n.* A dazed condition.

daz·zle [daz′(ə)l] *v.* **daz·zled, daz·zling,** *n.* **1** *v.* To blind or dim the vision of by too much light. **2** *v.* To charm or bewilder, as with a brilliant display: The violinist *dazzled* the audience with his skill. **3** *adj. use:* a *dazzling* performance. **4** *n.* A dazzling brightness or thing.

D.C. Abbreviation of: **1** DISTRICT OF COLUMBIA. **2** (*often written* **d.c.**) DIRECT CURRENT.

DDT A powerful chemical used to kill insects.

de- A prefix meaning: **1** Away; off, as in *decapitate,* to cut off the head of. **2** To remove or reverse (a condition, action, etc.), as in *deodorize,* to take the bad smell from. **3** Down, as in *descend,* to go down. **4** Completely, as in *denude,* to strip the covering from.

dea·con [dē′kən] *n.* **1** A clergyman who is next below a priest in rank. **2** A church official who helps a clergyman in things not connected with actual worship.

dead [ded] **1** *adj.* Without life: *dead* leaves. **2** *n. use:* Dead people: *The dead* are remembered on Memorial Day. **3** *adj.* Not having interest or excitement; dull: a *dead* town. **4** *adj.* Not working or operating: a *dead* battery. **5** *adj.* No longer used: a *dead* language. **6** *n.* The coldest or darkest part: the *dead* of night. **7** *adj.* Sure; accurate: a *dead* shot. **8** *adj.* Absolute; complete: a *dead* certainty. **9** *adv.* Absolutely: You are *dead* right. **10** *adv.* Directly: *dead* ahead.

dead·en [ded′(ə)n] *v.* **1** To take away the sensation of; make numb: to *deaden* a nerve with anesthetic. **2** To lessen the force of; weaken: Thick carpets *deaden* noise.

dead end A passage, street, etc., having no outlet at one end.

dead heat A race in which two or more finish together; a tie.

dead letter **1** A letter that is not claimed or cannot be delivered because of an incorrect address. **2** A law that is not enforced.

dead·line [ded′līn′] *n.* A date or time by which something must be done or finished.

dead·lock [ded′lok′] **1** *n.* A stopping of activity because opposing sides are equally strong and neither one will give in. **2** *v.* To cause or reach a deadlock.

dead·ly [ded′lē] *adj.* **dead·li·er, dead·li·est,** *adv.* **1** *adj.* Likely or certain to cause death: a *deadly* poison. **2** *adj.* Filled with enough hatred and violence to kill: a *deadly* fight; a *deadly* enemy. **3** *adj.* Deathlike: When she fainted, she had a *deadly* pallor. **4** *adj. informal* Very boring or lifeless. **5** *adv. informal* Very: *deadly* dull. **— dead′li·ness** *n.*

dead reckoning The locating of a ship's position without observing the sun or stars, by charting the direction and distance traveled.

Dead Sea A salt lake on the boundary between Israel and Jordan.

deaf [def] *adj.* **1** Completely or partially unable to hear. **2** Unwilling to listen: Some people are *deaf* to good advice. **— deaf′ness** *n.*

deaf·en [def′ən] *v.* **1** To make deaf. **2** To confuse or overwhelm with noise: The noise of the truck *deafened* him.

deaf-mute [def′myōōt′] *n.* A deaf person unable to speak. Early deafness may have kept him from learning to talk.

deal [dēl] *v.* **dealt, deal·ing,** *n.* **1** *v.* To be concerned with; have to do with: Biology *deals* with plants and animals. **2** *v.* To consider, discuss, or take action: to *deal* with a problem; to *deal* justly with a criminal. **3** *v.* To do business; trade: This store *deals* in furniture. **4** *n.*

informal A bargain or transaction: a business *deal*. **5** *v*. To give: The cat *dealt* the dog a sharp blow on the nose. **6** *v*. To distribute among a number of persons: to *deal* playing cards. **7** *n*. A distributing of cards, or the cards dealt. **— a good deal** or **a great deal 1** A large amount; a lot. **2** Much; a lot: Go *a good deal* faster.

deal·er [dē′lər] *n*. **1** A person whose business it is to buy and sell; a trader. **2** In card games, the player who deals the cards.

deal·ing [dē′ling] *n*. **1** (*usually pl*.) Relations with others: business *dealings*. **2** A way of acting: honest *dealing*.

dealt [delt] Past tense and past participle of DEAL: He *dealt* in TV sets; They *dealt* the cards.

dean [dēn] *n*. **1** A person in a college or university who is in charge of students, teachers, or a division of study: *dean* of men; *dean* of the law school. **2** A clergyman who has charge of a cathedral. **3** The person who has been a member of a class or group the longest.

dear [dir] **1** *adj*. Beloved; precious: my *dear* child. **2** *n*. A loved person: *Dear*, will you help me make a cake? **3** *adj*. Highly regarded: used at the opening of letters: *Dear* Sir. **4** *adj*. Expensive: Food was *dear* during the war. **5** *adv*. At great cost; dearly. **6** *interj*. An exclamation of surprise, regret, etc.: Oh, *dear*! **— dear′ness** *n*.

dear·ly [dir′lē] *adv*. **1** With much affection. **2** At great cost: He paid *dearly* for his crime.

dearth [dûrth] *n*. A great scarcity; lack.

death [deth] *n*. **1** The ending of life. **2** The condition of being dead. **3** A cause of death: This blizzard will be the *death* of us. **4** A wiping out; destruction: the *death* of a city. **— put to death** To kill; execute.

death·bed [deth′bed′] **1** *n*. The bed on which a person dies or has died. **2** *adj*. Made or done while dying: a *deathbed* confession.

death·less [deth′lis] *adj*. That will live forever; immortal: *deathless* poetry.

death·ly [deth′lē] **1** *adj*. Like death: a *deathly* silence. **2** *adv*. As in death: *deathly* pale. **3** *adj*. Deadly; fatal. **4** *adv*. Very: *deathly* ill.

death rate The number of persons per thousand of population who die within a given time.

death's-head [deths′hed′] *n*. A human skull, thought of as a symbol of death.

Death Valley A desert valley in SE California. It contains the lowest point in the Western Hemisphere.

de·ba·cle [dā·bäk′əl *or* di·bak′əl] *n*. A sudden, complete disaster or collapse; downfall: the *debacle* of the stock market in 1929.

de·bar [di·bär′] *v*. **de·barred, de·bar·ring** To bar; exclude: A man under 35 is *debarred* from being president.

Death's-head

de·bark [di·bärk′] *v*. To disembark.

de·base [di·bās′] *v*. **de·based, de·bas·ing** To lower in character or worth: Cheating *debases* a person; High prices cut down what a dollar will buy, and thus they *debase* it. **— de·base′·ment** *n*.

de·bat·a·ble [di·bā′tə·bəl] *adj*. Open to doubt or disagreement: The wisdom of your plan to raise funds is *debatable*.

de·bate [di·bāt′] *v*. **de·bat·ed, de·bat·ing,** *n*. **1** *v*. To discuss or argue for or against, especially in a formal way between persons taking opposite sides of a question. **2** *v*. To try to decide; consider: to *debate* whether to go home. **3** *n*. The act of debating. **— de·bat′er** *n*.

de·bauch [di·bôch′] **1** *v*. To lead away from right and good conduct; corrupt. **2** *n*. An act or period of giving in too much to one's appetites or desires.

de·bauch·er·y [di·bô′chər·ē] *n*., *pl*. **de·bauch·er·ies** Too much giving in to physical desires and appetites; dissipation.

de·bil·i·tate [di·bil′ə·tāt] *v*. **de·bil·i·tat·ed, de·bil·i·tat·ing** To weaken; make feeble: A long illness *debilitated* the boy.

de·bil·i·ty [di·bil′ə·tē] *n*. Great weakness; feebleness or languor.

deb·it [deb′it] **1** *n*. An entry in an account of an amount owed. **2** *v*. To enter (a debt) in an account. **3** *v*. To charge with a debt. ◆ See DEBT.

deb·o·nair or **deb·o·naire** [deb′ə·nâr′] *adj*. Lively and pleasant; gracious; airy: a *debonair* young fellow in a top hat.

de·bris or **dé·bris** [də·brē′ *or* dā′brē] *n*. Scattered fragments or remains; rubble: The explosion left much *debris*.

debt [det] *n*. **1** That which a person owes to another: a *debt* of ten dollars; a *debt* of gratitude. **2** The condition of owing; indebtedness: Mr. Larkin is in *debt* to the bank. ◆ *Debt* comes

Debris

from an old French word *dette*. The "b" was added later because the Latin word for "something owed" was *debitum*, from which the English word *debit* is also derived.

debt·or [det′ər] *n*. A person who owes something to another, as money, services, etc.

de·bunk [di·bungk′] *v*. To expose the nonsense or false sentiment in: to *debunk* witchcraft.

De·bus·sy [də·byoo′sē], **Claude,** 1862–1918, French composer.

de·but or **dé·but** [di·byoo′ *or* dā′byoo] *n*. **1** A first public appearance: an actor's *debut*. **2** The formal entrance of a young woman into society, made at a party.

deb·u·tante or **dé·bu·tante** [deb′yoo·tänt′ *or* deb′yə·tänt] *n*. A young woman making a debut into society.

Dec. Abbreviation of DECEMBER.

deca- A prefix meaning: Ten, as in *decagon*, a plane figure having ten sides.

dec·ade [dek′ād] *n.* A period of ten years.

dec·a·dence [di·kād′(ə)ns *or* dek′ə·dəns] *n.* A process or period of decay or decline, especially in morals or art: The bribery trials reveal shocking moral *decadence*.

dec·a·dent [di·kād′(ə)nt *or* dek′ə·dənt] **1** *adj.* Falling into or indicating decay or decline. **2** *n.* A decadent person.

dec·a·gon [dek′ə·gon] *n.* A closed plane figure bounded by ten line segments.

de·cal [dē′kal *or* di·kal′] *n.* A shortened form of DECALCOMANIA.

de·cal·co·ma·ni·a [di·kal′kə·mā′nē·ə] *n.* A design or picture transferred from specially prepared paper to glass, porcelain, etc.

Decalcomania

Dec·a·logue [dek′ə·lôg] *n.* (*sometimes written* **deca-logue**) Another name for the TEN COMMANDMENTS.

de·camp [di·kamp′] *v.* **1** To leave suddenly or secretly. **2** To leave a camping ground.

de·cant [di·kant′] *v.* **1** To pour off (a liquid) without disturbing its sediment: to *decant* vinegar. **2** To pour into another container.

de·cant·er [di·kan′tər] *n.* A decorative, stoppered glass bottle for serving wine or liquor.

de·cap·i·tate [di·kap′ə·tāt] *v.* **de·cap·i·tat·ed, de·cap·i·tat·ing** To cut off the head of; behead. **— de·cap′i·ta′tion** *n.*

de·cath·lon [di·kath′lon] *n.* An athletic contest like a track meet in which each contestant must take part in all ten events.

de·cay [di·kā′] **1** *v.* To rot or cause to rot: Fruit *decays* in a hot room; Too much candy can *decay* teeth. **2** *n.* A rotting. **3** *v.* To decline in health, power, beauty, etc. **4** *n.* A falling into ruin.

de·cease [di·sēs′] *n., v.* **de·ceased, de·ceas·ing** **1** *n.* Death. **2** *v.* To die. ◆ See DECEASED.

Decanter

de·ceased [di·sēst′] **1** *adj.* Dead. **2** *n. use* The dead person or persons: *The deceased* left his money to charity. ◆ *Deceased* and *decease* are formal words which are used mainly in legal documents.

de·ceit [di·sēt′] *n.* **1** The act of deceiving; lying or cheating. **2** A lie or a dishonest trick. **3** A tendency or readiness to deceive.

de·ceit·ful [di·sēt′fəl] *adj.* Tending to deceive; lying or treacherous: a *deceitful* person. **— de·ceit′ful·ly** *adv.* **— de·ceit′ful·ness** *n.*

de·ceive [di·sēv′] *v.* **de·ceived, de·ceiv·ing** To cause to take as true something that is not true; fool or mislead, as by lying: She *deceived* us about her age. **— de·ceiv′er** *n.* ◆ *Deceive, lie,* and *mislead* all mean to cause someone to believe something that is not true. *Lie* usually refers to statements that are the direct opposite of truth: "I haven't taken a cooky," Tom *lied.* *Deceive* refers to the giving of a false impression: Her pretended illness *deceived* everybody. When you *deceive* someone you intend to fool him, but you may *mislead* quite unintentionally, as by giving someone the wrong directions. Situations can *mislead* too: The clues at the scene of the crime *misled* him into thinking that the butler was the chief suspect.

De·cem·ber [di·sem′bər] *n.* The 12th month of the year, having 31 days.

de·cen·cy [dē′sən·sē] *n., pl.* **de·cen·cies 1** The quality of being decent; proper character or behavior: He didn't even have the *decency* to thank us. **2** (*usually pl.*) Things needed for a pleasant, proper life.

de·cent [dē′sənt] *adj.* **1** Proper; respectable: *decent* clothes. **2** Reasonably good; fair; adequate: He makes a *decent* living, but he'll never be rich. **3** Kind or kindhearted; generous: a *decent* fellow. **— de′cent·ly** *adv.* ◆ *Decent, descent,* and *dissent* look and sound rather alike but are not related. *Decent* [dē′sənt] is from a Latin word meaning *fitting* and still means *fitting* or *proper. Descent* [di·sent′] comes from a Latin verb meaning *to climb down,* and it still means *a coming down. Dissent* [di·sent′] is from a Latin verb meaning *to feel opposed* or *apart.* It is now either a noun meaning *disagreement* or a verb meaning *to disagree.*

de·cen·tral·ize [dē·sen′trəl·īz] *v.* **de·cen·tral·ized, de·cen·tral·iz·ing** To lessen the central authority, as of a government, by giving local groups more power. **— de·cen′tral·i·za′tion** *n.* ¶3

de·cep·tion [di·sep′shən] *n.* **1** The act of deceiving or tricking: a magician's *deception* of an audience. **2** A being deceived. **3** Something that deceives; an illusion; fraud.

de·cep·tive [di·sep′tiv] *adj.* That deceives or is meant to deceive; misleading: Statistics can be *deceptive.* **— de·cep′tive·ly** *adv.* **— de·cep′tive·ness** *n.*

de·cide [di·sīd′] *v.* **de·cid·ed, de·cid·ing 1** To make up one's mind; come to a decision: She *decided* to become a teacher. **2** To determine or settle: The jury will *decide* whether he is guilty.

de·cid·ed [di·sī′did] *adj.* **1** Definite: There is a *decided* improvement in John's reading. **2** Showing that one's mind is made up; determined: a *decided* manner. **— de·cid′ed·ly** *adv.*

de·cid·u·ous [di·sij′ōō·əs] *adj.* **1** Falling off at a certain time of year or when fully developed:

deciduous leaves; *deciduous* antlers. **2** Shedding leaves every year: *deciduous* trees. ◆ See EVERGREEN.

dec·i·mal [des′ə·məl] **1** *n.* A fraction written using base ten and place values to show 10 or 10 multiplied by itself some number of times as its denominator, as 0.3 ($\frac{3}{10}$), 0.27 ($\frac{27}{100}$), 0.034 ($\frac{34}{1000}$), etc. **2** *adj.* Of or based on the number 10: a *decimal* system; a *decimal* fraction. ◆ *Decimal* comes from a Latin word meaning *tenth.*

decimal point A dot used before a decimal fraction, as in 0.3 ($\frac{3}{10}$) or 3.27 ($3 + \frac{27}{100}$).

dec·i·mate [des′ə·māt] *v.* **dec·i·mat·ed, dec·i·mat·ing** To destroy or kill a large part of: The invaders *decimated* the town. — **dec′i·ma′tion** *n.*

de·ci·pher [di·sī′fər] *v.* **1** To translate from cipher or code into plain language; decode. **2** To determine the meaning of: to *decipher* a garbled telegram; to *decipher* hieroglyphics.

de·ci·sion [di·sizh′ən] *n.* **1** A making up of one's mind. **2** A conclusion or judgment. **3** Firmness; determination: to act with *decision.*

de·ci·sive [di·sī′siv] *adj.* **1** Putting an end to doubt: a *decisive* victory. **2** Showing decision; firm: a *decisive* statement. — **de·ci′sive·ly** *adv.* — **de·ci′sive·ness** *n.*

deck [dek] **1** *n.* Any floor or platform extending from side to side of a ship. It may be open or roofed over by another deck. **2** *n.* A pack of playing cards. **3** *v.* To dress or adorn: She *decked* her poodle with a rhinestone collar.

de·claim [di·klām′] *v.* To speak loudly and forcefully in the manner of an orator.

dec·la·ma·tion [dek′lə·mā′shən] *n.* **1** The act or art of declaiming. **2** Something that is or may be declaimed, as a formal speech.

A room decked out for a party

de·clam·a·to·ry [di·klam′ə·tôr′ē] *adj.* **1** Having to do with or used for declamation. **2** Loud and forceful: *declamatory* speech.

dec·la·ra·tion [dek′lə·rā′shən] *n.* A formal statement or announcement: a *declaration* of war.

Declaration of Independence The formal proclamation that the thirteen American colonies were free and independent of Great Britain. It was adopted on July 4, 1776.

de·clar·a·tive [di·klar′ə·tiv] *adj.* Making a statement: "I'll be home at five o'clock" is a *declarative* sentence.

de·clare [di·klâr′] *v.* **de·clared, de·clar·ing** **1** To make known to be; announce formally; proclaim: to *declare* war; The company was *declared* bankrupt. **2** To say forcefully; assert: The thief *declared* he would never steal again. **3** To describe or make a list of (taxable things): We *declared* everything we bought overseas.

de·clen·sion [di·klen′shən] *n.* **1** The changing of the forms or endings of nouns, pronouns, or adjectives according to case. The declension of *they* consists of *they, their* or *theirs, them.* **2** A class of words having similar endings or forms in each case.

dec·li·na·tion [dek′lə·nā′shən] *n.* **1** An inclining or bending downward. **2** The deviation of a compass needle from true north or true south. **3** A polite or formal refusal.

de·cline [di·klīn′] *v.* **de·clined, de·clin·ing,** *n.* **1** *v.* To refuse in a polite way: to *decline* an invitation. **2** *v.* To lessen or fail gradually: His health *declined* over the years. **3** *n.* A gradual lessening or failing: the *decline* of a nation's power. **4** *v.* To slope or bend downward: The land gently *declines* to the sea. **5** *n.* A downward slope. **6** *v.* To give the declension of (a noun, pronoun, or adjective).

de·cliv·i·ty [di·kliv′ə·tē] *n., pl.* **de·cliv·i·ties** **1** A surface, as of a hill, that slopes downward. **2** A sloping downward.

de·code [dē·kōd′] *v.* **de·cod·ed, de·cod·ing** To translate from code into plain language.

de·com·pose [dē′kəm·pōz′] *v.* **de·com·posed, de·com·pos·ing** **1** To decay; rot. **2** To separate into its basic parts or elements: to *decompose* water into hydrogen and oxygen.

de·com·po·si·tion [dē′kom·pə·zish′ən] *n.* **1** The process or result of decay. **2** A separating into basic parts or elements.

de·com·pres·sion [dē′kəm·presh′ən] *n.* The lowering or removing of pressure, especially of air.

dec·o·rate [dek′ə·rāt] *v.* **dec·o·rat·ed, dec·o·rat·ing** **1** To make more fancy, pretty, or attractive by adding ornaments or frills: to *decorate* a street with colored lights. **2** To paint, paper, or add new furnishings to (a room, house, etc.). **3** To honor with a medal or ribbon.

dec·o·ra·tion [dek′ə·rā′shən] *n.* **1** The act of decorating. **2** Something used for decorating; ornament. **3** A medal or other sign given as a mark of honor.

Decoration Day Another name for MEMORIAL DAY.

dec·o·ra·tive [dek′(ə)rə·tiv *or* dek′ə·rā′tiv] *adj.* Serving to decorate; ornamental.

dec·o·ra·tor [dek′ə·rā′tər] *n.* A person who decorates, especially an interior decorator.

dec·o·rous [dek′ə·rəs *or* di·kôr′əs] *adj.* Proper or dignified; decent. — **dec′o·rous·ly** *adv.*

de·co·rum [di·kôr′əm] *n.* Proper behavior, speech, dress, etc.; seemliness.

de·coy [*n.* di·koi′ *or* dē′koi. *v.* di·koi′] **1** *n.* A bird or animal trained to lure game into a trap or into shooting range. **2** *n.* An imitation duck used to lure real ducks. **3** *n.* A person or thing used as a lure. **4** *v.* To lure or entice into danger or a trap.

A decoy duck

de·crease [*v.* di·krēs′, *n.* dē′krēs *or* di·krēs′] *v.* **de·creased, de·creas·ing,** *n.* **1** *v.* To make or become less: to *decrease* the amount of sugar in a recipe for cookies; His influence *decreased.* **2** *n.* A lessening; reduction: a *decrease* in population.

de·cree [di·krē′] *n., v.* **de·creed, de·cree·ing 1** *n.* A formal order or decision, as by a government or court. **2** *v.* To proclaim by a decree: The governor *decreed* a state holiday.

de·crep·it [di·krep′it] *adj.* Worn out or feeble from old age or much use: a *decrepit* old man.

de·cry [di·krī′] *v.* **de·cried, de·cry·ing** To speak critically of; condemn: to *decry* bribery in government.

ded·i·cate [ded′ə·kāt] *v.* **ded·i·cat·ed, ded·i·cat·ing 1** To set apart for or devote to a special purpose: to *dedicate* one's life to science. **2** To write or say publicly that one has written (a book, symphony, etc.) as a sign of affection or respect for a person named.

ded·i·ca·tion [ded′ə·kā′shən] *n.* **1** The act of dedicating. **2** A being dedicated. **3** The words dedicating a book or other work to someone.

ded·i·ca·to·ry [ded′ə·kə·tôr′ē] *adj.* That is or serves as a dedication: a *dedicatory* inscription.

de·duce [di·d(y)o͞os′] *v.* **de·duced, de·duc·ing** To arrive at by reasoning; infer: Sherlock Holmes *deduced* the thief's identity.

de·duct [di·dukt′] *v.* To take away; subtract: If you *deduct* 7 from 10, you get 3.

de·duct·i·ble [di·duk′tə·bəl] *adj.* That can be deducted, especially from taxable income.

de·duc·tion [di·duk′shən] *n.* **1** A conclusion based on reasoning; inference: If everyone who took the test passed, and I took the test, then it is a simple *deduction* that I passed. **2** This form of reasoning. **3** An amount deducted: a $30 *deduction.* **4** A taking away; subtraction.

de·duc·tive [di·duk′tiv] *adj.* Of, based on, or reached by deduction.

deed [dēd] **1** *n.* Anything done; an act: a heroic *deed.* **2** *n.* A legal document showing ownership of property. **3** *v.* To give over ownership of by a deed: to *deed* a house to one's nephew.

deem [dēm] *v.* To judge; consider: It was *deemed* advisable to accept his offer at once.

deep [dēp] **1** *adj.* Extending far below a surface: *deep* water; a *deep* cut. **2** *adj.* Extending far in or back: a *deep* dresser drawer. **3** *adj.* Being or reaching a certain distance down, in, or back: The hole is four feet *deep.* **4** *adv.* Far down, in, or back: to dig *deep.* **5** *n.* A very deep place, especially the ocean: used mostly in poems. **6** *adj.* Having a low pitch: a *deep* voice. **7** *adj.* Difficult to understand; complicated: a *deep* person. **8** *adj.* Having the mind occupied; absorbed: He was *deep* in thought. **9** *adj.* Intense; great; profound: *deep* feelings; a *deep* sleep.

10 *adj.* Vivid and dark: *deep* red. **11** *n.* The darkest or most intense part: the *deep* of night. — **deep′ly** *adv.* — **deep′ness** *n.*

deep·en [dē′pən] *v.* To make or become deep or deeper: to *deepen* a well; The darkness *deepens.*

deep-root·ed [dēp′ro͞o′tid] *adj.* **1** Rooted deep in the ground. **2** Firmly held: a *deep-rooted* loyalty.

deep-sea [dēp′sē′] *adj.* In or having to do with the deeper parts of the sea: *deep-sea* fish.

deep-seat·ed [dēp′sē′tid] *adj.* Firmly established; hard to root out or change: *deep-seated* prejudice.

deer [dir] *n., pl.* **deer** A swift, graceful wild animal that chews its cud. The male usually has antlers which are shed yearly. ♦ *Deer* comes from an Old English word meaning *beast.* Gradually, over the years, *deer* came to be the name of one special kind of beast.

deer·skin [dir′skin′] *n.* **1** A deer's hide. **2** Leather made from it.

def. Abbreviation of DEFINITION.

de·face [di·fās′] *v.* **de·faced, de·fac·ing** To spoil the looks of; mar: to *deface* a statue. — **de·face′ment** *n.*

de fac·to [dē fak′tō] Actual or functioning, whether legal or not: a *de facto* government.

def·a·ma·tion [def′ə·mā′shən] *n.* The act of defaming; slander or libel.

de·fam·a·to·ry [di·fam′ə·tôr′ē] *adj.* That defames: a *defamatory* newspaper article.

de·fame [di·fām′] *v.* **de·famed, de·fam·ing** To say untrue or harmful things about the character or reputation of; slander or libel.

A defaced poster

de·fault [di·fôlt′] **1** *n.* A failure to do something required or expected, as to appear in court or take part in or finish a game or contest: to lose by *default.* **2** *v.* To fail to pay (money) or fail to do (something expected or required): to *default* a loan.

de·feat [di·fēt′] **1** *v.* To gain a victory over; conquer; beat: to *defeat* a nation in war. **2** *n.* A defeating: Rutgers' *defeat* of Columbia. **3** *n.* A being defeated: Columbia's *defeat* by Rutgers. **4** *v.* To keep from succeeding; thwart; frustrate.

de·feat·ist [di·fē′tist] **1** *n.* A person who gives up too easily because he expects defeat or failure. **2** *adj.* Of, like, or held by a defeatist. — **de·feat′ism** *n.*

de·fect [*n.* di·fekt′ *or* dē′fekt, *v.* di·fekt′] **1** *n.* A fault, flaw, or lack of something necessary: a speech *defect.* **2** *v.* To desert one's country, side, etc., especially in order to go over to an opposing group.

de·fec·tion [di·fek′shən] *n.* A deserting of one's country, side, etc., especially to go over to an opposing group.

de·fec·tive [di·fek′tiv] *adj.* Having a fault, flaw, or lack; not perfect.

de·fend [di·fend′] *v.* **1** To guard against harm or attack; protect: Learn how to *defend* yourself. **2** To justify: He *defended* the new rule as fair to all. **3** To act as a lawyer for (a person prosecuted in court). **4** To fight (a legal charge, suit, or claim). — **de·fend′er** *n.*

de·fen·dant [di·fen′dənt] *n.* A person who is accused or sued in a court of law.

de·fense [di·fens′] *n.* **1** A defending against danger or attack: the *defense* of one's country. **2** Something that guards, protects, or defends: A levee is a *defense* against floods. **3** An argument that justifies or supports: He gave a *defense* of his actions. **4** The answer to charges or claims brought against a defendant. **5** A defendant and his lawyers, as a group.

de·fense·less [di·fens′lis] *adj.* Without any defense or means of protection; helpless.

de·fen·sive [di·fen′siv] **1** *adj.* Defending or suitable for defense. **2** *n.* A defensive attitude or position. — **de·fen′sive·ly** *adv.*

de·fer[1] [di·fûr′] *v.* **de·ferred, de·fer·ring** To put off until later; delay: to *defer* payment of money owed.

de·fer[2] [di·fûr′] *v.* **de·ferred, de·fer·ring** To yield to the opinions, wishes, or decisions of another out of respect.

def·er·ence [def′ər·əns] *n.* Respect and consideration for the wishes and opinions of another. — **in deference to** Out of consideration or respect for.

def·er·en·tial [def′ə·ren′shəl] *adj.* Full of deference; respectful. — **def′er·en′tial·ly** *adv.*

de·fer·ment [di·fûr′mənt] *n.* A putting off, especially of induction into military service.

de·fi·ance [di·fī′əns] *n.* Bold opposition to power or authority; refusal to submit or obey.

de·fi·ant [di·fī′ənt] *adj.* Full of defiance; resisting. — **de·fi′ant·ly** *adv.*

de·fi·cien·cy [di·fish′ən·sē] *n., pl.* **de·fi·cien·cies** **1** A deficient condition. **2** An amount that is lacking and needed.

deficiency disease A disease, as rickets or scurvy, caused by a lack or shortage in the diet of some substance needed by the body.

de·fi·cient [di·fish′ənt] *adj.* Not sufficient or complete; lacking: mentally *deficient*.

def·i·cit [def′ə·sit] *n.* The amount by which money available falls short of money needed: With $100 on hand and bills for $300, the *deficit* is $200.

de·file[1] [di·fīl′] *v.* **de·filed, de·fil·ing** **1** To make dirty or disgusting: to *defile* a clear pond. **2** To spoil the purity or sacredness of: to *defile* a temple. — **de·file′ment** *n.*

de·file[2] [di·fīl′] *v.* **de·filed, de·fil·ing**, *n.* **1** *v.* To march one behind the other in a line. **2** *n.* A long, narrow pass, as between mountains.

de·fine [di·fīn′] *v.* **de·fined, de·fin·ing** **1** To give the exact meaning of (a word or term). **2** To describe; explain: to *define* the duties of a job. **3** To set or mark the limits of: to *define* the area of a farm.

def·i·nite [def′ə·nit] *adj.* **1** Having fixed limits. **2** Known for certain: It is *definite* that he won. **3** Plain and clear in meaning: *definite* rules.

definite article The word *the*, put before a noun to show that the noun refers to one or more particular persons or things.

def·i·nite·ly [def′ə·nit·lē] *adv.* **1** Without question; positively. **2** In a definite way.

def·i·ni·tion [def′ə·nish′ən] *n.* **1** The act of defining. **2** A being defined. **3** A statement giving the meaning of a word or term. **4** A being clearly or sharply outlined.

de·fin·i·tive [di·fin′ə·tiv] *adj.* Ending uncertainty; conclusive; final: a *definitive* statement.

de·flate [di·flāt′] *v.* **de·flat·ed, de·flat·ing** **1** To let the air or gas out of; collapse: to *deflate* a balloon. **2** To take the conceit or confidence out of: to *deflate* a pompous person. **3** To reduce (the supply of money or amount of spending) so that prices go down.

A deflated tire

de·fla·tion [di·flā′shən] *n.* **1** The act of deflating. **2** A deflated condition. **3** A reduction in the amount of available money or of spending, resulting in lower prices.

de·flect [di·flekt′] *v.* To turn aside from its regular course: Wind *deflected* the bullet. — **de·flec′tion** *n.*

De·foe [di·fō′], **Daniel,** 1660?–1731, English writer, the author of *Robinson Crusoe*.

de·for·est [dē·fôr′ist] *v.* To clear (land) of trees or forests. — **de·for′es·ta′tion** *n.*

de·form [di·fôrm′] **1** *v.* To mar the shape or appearance of; disfigure: Arthritis had *deformed* her hands. **2** *adj. use:* a *deformed* toe. — **de·for·ma·tion** [dē′·fôr·mā′shən] *n.*

de·form·i·ty [di·fôr′mə·tē] *n., pl.* **de·form·i·ties** **1** A deformed condition. **2** A part that is not normal in shape, as a clubfoot.

de·fraud [di·frôd′] *v.* To take money, rights, etc., away from by tricking or deceiving.

de·fray [di·frā′] *v.* To pay or furnish the money for (costs or expenses).

A deformed tree

de·frost [dē·frôst′] *v.* To remove ice or frost from, as a refrigerator.

de·frost·er [dē·frôs′tər] *n.* A device for melting or removing ice, as from a windshield.

deft [deft] *adj.* Quick and skillful: a *deft* tennis stroke. — **deft′ly** *adv.* — **deft′ness** *n.*

de·funct [di·fungkt′] *adj.* No longer in existence; dead or extinct: a *defunct* magazine.

de·fy [di·fī′] *v.* **de·fied, de·fy·ing** **1** To resist openly and boldly; refuse to submit to: He *defied* the doctor's orders. **2** To resist successfully; withstand: a situation so complicated that it *defies* explanation. **3** To challenge (someone) to do something; dare.

De·gas [də·gä′], **Edgar,** 1834–1917, French artist.

de Gaulle [də·gōl′ or də·gôl′], **Charles,** 1890–1970, French general and president of France.

de·gen·er·a·cy [di·jen′ər·ə·sē] *n.* **1** The process of degenerating. **2** A being degenerate.

de·gen·er·ate [*v.* di·jen′ə·rāt, *n., adj.* di·jen′ər·it] *v.* **de·gen·er·at·ed, de·gen·er·at·ing,** *n., adj.* **1** *v.* To become worse, inferior, or lower in quality, condition, character, etc. **2** *n.* A person who has low moral standards and does evil things. **3** *adj.* Having grown worse, inferior, or lower in quality, condition, character, etc. **4** *v.* To go back to a simpler type or earlier stage of development, as some animals, plants, or organs of the body. **— de·gen′er·a′tion** *n.*

deg·ra·da·tion [deg′rə·dā′shən] *n.* **1** The act of degrading. **2** A degraded condition.

de·grade [di·grād′] *v.* **de·grad·ed, de·grad·ing** **1** To bring down from a higher to a lower condition; corrupt; debase: Telling lies *degrades* a person. **2** To reduce in rank; demote.

de·gree [di·grē′] *n.* **1** A step in a series or stage in a process. **2** A unit for measuring temperature: The normal temperature of the body is 98.6 *degrees* Fahrenheit (98.6° F). Symbol: ° **3** A unit used for measuring arcs and angles: There are 360 *degrees* (360°) in a circle. **4** The number of times variables, as *x* and *y*, are used as factors in a term, or the largest such number in an equation: x^2, xy, and y^2 are of the second *degree*. **5** A measure of damage done to bodily tissue: a burn of the second *degree*. **6** A measure of guilt as fixed by law: murder in the first *degree*. **7** Amount, extent, or measure: There is only a small *degree* of difference between the twins. **8** Station; rank: a lady of high *degree*. **9** A title awarded to a student who has completed a course of study or to a person as an honor: a B.S. *degree*. **10** Any of the three forms that an adjective or adverb takes in comparison. The adjective *bright* is in the positive degree, *brighter* is in the comparative degree, and *brightest* is in the superlative degree.

de·hy·drate [dē·hī′drāt] *v.* **de·hy·drat·ed, de·hy·drat·ing** **1** To take water out of: to *dehydrate* vegetables to preserve them. **2** To lose water; dry up. **— de′hy·dra′tion** *n.*

de·ic·er [dē·ī′sər] *n.* A device for removing ice, as from an airplane wing.

de·i·fy [dē′ə·fī] *v.* **de·i·fied, de·i·fy·ing** To make a god of; treat as sacred: to *deify* a ruler. **— de·i·fi·ca·tion** [dē′ə·fə·kā′shən] *n.*

deign [dān] *v.* To lower oneself; think fit: The king did not *deign* to answer.

de·ist [dē′ist] *n.* A person who believes that the orderly workings of nature prove the existence of God, but who does not follow a formal religion. **— de′ism** *n.*

de·i·ty [dē′ə·tē] *n., pl.* **de·i·ties** **1** (*written* the **Deity**) God. **2** A god or goddess: Mars was a Roman *deity*. **3** Divine nature: They believed in the *deity* of their emperor.

de·jec·ted [di·jek′tid] *adj.* Low in spirits; unhappy; downcast. **— de·ject′ed·ly** *adv.*

de·jec·tion [di·jek′shən] *n.* Lowness of spirits; depression; sadness.

de Koo·ning [də kōō′ning], **Willem,** born 1904, U.S. painter, born in the Netherlands.

Del. Abbreviation of DELAWARE.

De·la·croix [də·lä·krwä′], **Eugène,** 1799–1863, French painter.

Del·a·ware [del′ə·wâr] *n.* **1** A state in the eastern U.S. **2** A river separating Pennsylvania and Delaware from New York and New Jersey.

de·lay [di·lā′] **1** *v.* To make late by stopping or slowing up: The traffic jam *delayed* me. **2** *v.* To put off until later: They *delayed* the game because of rain. **3** *v.* To go slow; linger: Don't *delay* along the way. **4** *n.* The act of delaying. **5** *n.* A putting off, waiting, or going slow.

de·lec·ta·ble [di·lek′tə·bəl] *adj.* Giving pleasure; delightful: a *delectable* dish.

de·lec·ta·tion [dē′lek·tā′shən] *n.* Delight; enjoyment; amusement: They had a concert for the *delectation* of their guests.

del·e·gate [*n.* del′ə·gāt *or* del′ə·git, *v.* del′ə·gāt] *n., v.* **del·e·gat·ed, del·e·gat·ing** **1** *n.* A person sent with authority to act for a group to which he belongs; representative. **2** *v.* To choose or send as a representative. **3** *v.* To give or entrust (duties, authority, rights, etc.) to another.

del·e·ga·tion [del′ə·gā′shən] *n.* **1** The act of delegating. **2** A being delegated. **3** A group of delegates.

de·lete [di·lēt′] *v.* **de·let·ed, de·let·ing** To remove or mark out (something written or printed). **— de·le′tion** *n.*

He wore a blue ~~cloth~~ shirt

The word "cloth" is deleted.

del·e·te·ri·ous [del′ə·tir′ē·əs] *adj.* Causing injury; physically or morally harmful.

Del·hi [del′ē] *n.* A large city in northern India. It used to be the capital.

de·lib·er·ate [*adj.* di·lib′ər·it, *v.* di·lib′ə·rāt] *adj., v.* **de·lib·er·at·ed, de·lib·er·at·ing** **1** *adj.* Thought about and intended: a *deliberate* insult. **2** *adj.* Slow and careful about deciding: He is *deliberate*, not reckless. **3** *v.* To consider carefully; ponder: He always *deliberates* before taking action. **4** *v.* To talk things over in order to reach a decision: They have been *deliberating* for hours. **5** *adj.* Not hurried; slow and steady: a *deliberate* trot. **— de·lib′er·ate·ly** *adv.*

---

add, āce, câre, pälm;   end, ēqual;   it, īce;   odd, ōpen, ôrder;   tŏŏk, pōōl;   up, bûrn;

ə = a in *above*, e in *sicken*, i in *possible*, o in *melon*, u in *circus*;   yōō = u in *fuse;*   oil;   pout;

check; ring; thin; this; zh in *vision*.   For ¶ reference, see page 64 · HOW TO

de·lib·er·a·tion [di·lib′ə·rā′shən] *n.* **1** Long and careful thought: She decided at once, without *deliberation*. **2** (*often pl.*) Discussion of the arguments for and against an action: The jury interrupted its *deliberations* to have lunch. **3** Slowness and care: He climbed the stairs with *deliberation*.

de·lib·er·a·tive [di·lib′ə·rā′tiv *or* di·lib′ə·rə·tiv] *adj.* Involved in or concerned with the careful consideration of issues.

del·i·ca·cy [del′ə·kə·sē] *n.*, *pl.* **del·i·ca·cies** **1** Fineness of structure, design, or make: the *delicacy* of a butterfly's wing. **2** Refinement of feeling, manner, etc.; sensitivity. **3** Weakness of body or health. **4** Need of careful, tactful treatment: a situation of great *delicacy*. **5** Ability to appreciate fine differences: a *delicacy* of taste. **6** A choice food: Frogs' legs are a *delicacy*. **7** Consideration for other people's feelings.

del·i·cate [del′ə·kit] *adj.* **1** Fine in structure, design, shape, etc.: a *delicate* snowflake. **2** Pleasing, as in taste, aroma, or color: a *delicate* shade of blue. **3** Weak or easily injured: a *delicate* child; a *delicate* vase. **4** Requiring cautious, tactful treatment: *delicate* diplomatic relations. **5** Barely felt or seen; subtle; slight: a *delicate* distinction. **6** Reacting quickly to slight differences or changes: a *delicate* thermometer. **— del′i·cate·ly** *adv.*

del·i·ca·tes·sen [del′ə·kə·tes′(ə)n] *n.* **1** A store selling prepared foods, such as cooked meats, salads, cheese, etc. **2** The foods which such a store sells. ◆ *Delicatessen* comes from a German word meaning *delicacies*.

de·li·cious [di·lish′əs] *adj.* Highly pleasing, especially to the taste; extremely good.

de·light [di·līt′] **1** *n.* Great pleasure or joy: full of *delight* at hearing the good news. **2** *v.* To please extremely: The praise *delighted* her. **3** *adj. use:* a *delighted* smile. **4** *v.* To take great pleasure: They *delighted* in their victory. **5** *n.* Something that gives great joy or pleasure.

de·light·ful [di·līt′fəl] *adj.* Giving joy or pleasure. **— de·light′ful·ly** *adv.*

de·lin·e·ate [di·lin′ē·āt] *v.* **de·lin·e·at·ed, de·lin·e·at·ing** **1** To outline, sketch, or draw; portray: The artist faithfully *delineated* the scene. **2** To describe or show in words: to *delineate* character. **— de·lin′e·a′tion** *n.*

de·lin·quen·cy [di·ling′kwən·sē] *n.*, *pl.* **de·lin·quen·cies** **1** The doing of things that are wrong or that break the law: juvenile *delinquency*. **2** Failure to do what is required; neglect of duty. **3** A fault; offense.

de·lin·quent [di·ling′kwənt] **1** *n.* A person who neglects his duty, does wrong things, or breaks the law: a juvenile *delinquent*. **2** *adj.* Guilty of doing wrong or of breaking the law: a *delinquent* boy. **3** *adj.* Guilty of neglect or lateness: *delinquent* in payment of a debt. **4** *adj.* Due but not paid: *delinquent* taxes.

de·lir·i·ous [di·lir′ē·əs] *adj.* **1** Temporarily out of one's mind; wild and raving. **2** Wildly excited. **— de·lir′i·ous·ly** *adv.*

de·lir·i·um [di·lir′ē·əm] *n.* **1** A disturbance of the mind marked by restlessness, excitement, and wild, confused thoughts and speech. It occurs only at times, as during fever or drunkenness. **2** Extreme excitement.

de·liv·er [di·liv′ər] *v.* **1** To hand over; give up; transfer: to *deliver* a message. **2** To carry and distribute: to *deliver* groceries. **3** To speak or utter: to *deliver* a speech. **4** To give forth; strike: He *delivered* a blow. **5** To throw. **6** To set free; rescue, as from danger. **7** To aid in the birth of, or in childbirth. **— de·liv′er·er** *n.*

de·liv·er·ance [di·liv′ər·əns] *n.* Freedom; rescue: thankful for their *deliverance*.

de·liv·er·y [di·liv′ər·ē] *n.*, *pl.* **de·liv·er·ies** **1** The action of handing over or distributing: the *delivery* of mail. **2** Way of speaking: His *delivery* made his jokes funny. **3** The action or manner of throwing, striking, etc.: a fast *delivery*. **4** Rescue or release: The captives still hoped for *delivery*. **5** The act of giving birth.

dell [del] *n.* A small, protected valley, usually full of trees; dale; glen.

Del·phi [del′fī] *n.* An ancient city of Greece where people went to consult the famous oracle of Apollo.

Del·phic [del′fik] *adj.* **1** Having to do with Delphi or the oracle there. **2** Having more than one possible meaning; puzzling.

del·ta [del′tə] *n.* **1** The fourth letter of the Greek alphabet (Δ or δ). **2** A piece of low land shaped like a Greek delta or like a fan, formed at the mouths of some rivers by deposits of soil or sand.

A river delta

de·lude [di·lood′] *v.* **de·lud·ed, de·lud·ing** To mislead the mind or judgment of; deceive; fool.

del·uge [del′yooj] *v.* **del·uged, del·ug·ing,** *n.* **1** *v.* To flood with water: Rain *deluged* the area. **2** *n.* A great flood or fall of rain. **3** *v.* To swamp or overwhelm: He was *deluged* with mail. **4** *n.* A great flow or stream of anything. **— the Deluge** The great flood in the time of Noah.

de·lu·sion [di·loo′zhən] *n.* **1** A false, fixed belief, especially one held by a person who is mentally ill. **2** The act of deluding or deceiving.

de·lu·sive [di·loo′siv] *adj.* Apt to delude; misleading: a *delusive* promise of help. **— de·lu′sive·ly** *adv.*

de luxe (di looks′ *or* di luks′) Of the very highest quality; elegant and expensive.

delve [delv] *v.* **delved, delv·ing** **1** To make a careful search for information: to *delve* into a crime. **2** To dig: seldom used today.

Dem. Abbreviation of: **1** DEMOCRAT. **2** DEMOCRATIC.

de·mag·net·ize [dē·mag′nə·tīz] *v.* **de·mag·net·ized, de·mag·net·iz·ing** To treat (a magnetized object) so that it is no longer a magnet. ¶3

dem·a·gogue [dem′ə·gôg] *n.* A leader or

politician who stirs up the feelings and fears of people in order to gain power for himself.

de·mand [di·mand′] **1** *v.* To ask for boldly; claim as a right: The man *demanded* a lawyer. **2** *v.* To ask for forcefully: The teacher *demanded* an answer. **3** *n.* The act of demanding: a *demand* for silence. **4** *v.* To need; require: This job *demands* skill. **5** *n.* A claim or requirement: The work made great *demands* on his health. **—in demand** Sought after; wanted.

de·mar·ca·tion [dē′mär·kā′shən] *n.* **1** The fixing or marking of boundaries or limits. **2** A setting apart; separation.

de·mean[1] [di·mēn′] *v.* To lower in dignity or worth; degrade: to *demean* oneself by lying.

de·mean[2] [di·mēn′] *v.* To behave or conduct (oneself): She *demeans* herself like a lady.

de·mean·or [di·mē′nər] *n.* Behavior or bearing; manner: a meek *demeanor*. ¶1

de·ment·ed [di·men′tid] *adj.* Out of one's mind; crazy; insane.

de·mer·it [di·mer′it] *n.* **1** A fault or weakness. **2** A mark set down against someone for poor work or bad conduct.

de·mesne [di·mān′ *or* di·mēn′] *n.* **1** A house and land on an estate kept for the owner's use. **2** A region or district; domain.

De·me·ter [di·mē′tər] *n.* In Greek myths, the goddess of agriculture and marriage. Her Roman name was Ceres.

dem·i·god [dem′ē·god′] *n.* In myths, a lesser god or a hero who is half god and half human.

dem·i·john [dem′ē·jon′] *n.* A large jug with a narrow neck. It is often enclosed in wicker.

de·mil·i·ta·rize [dē·mil′ə·tə·rīz′] *v.* **de·mil·i·ta·rized, de·mil·i·ta·riz·ing** To remove or do away with the army and the military power of: to *demilitarize* a zone. **—de·mil·i·ta·ri·za·tion** [dē·mil′ə·tə·rə·zā′shən] *n.* ¶3

de·mise [di·mīz′] *n.* Death.

dem·i·tasse [dem′ē·tas′ *or* dem′ē·täs′] *n.* **1** A small cup in which coffee is served after dinner. **2** Such a cup of coffee.

de·mo·bi·lize [dē·mō′bə·līz] *v.* **de·mo·bi·lized, de·mo·bi·liz·ing 1** To break up or disband (an army or troops), as after a war. **2** To free from military duty. **—de·mo·bi·li·za·tion** [dē·mō′bə·lə·zā′shən] *n.* ¶3

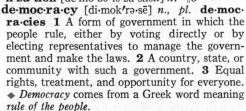

A demitasse

de·moc·ra·cy [di·mok′rə·sē] *n., pl.* **de·moc·ra·cies 1** A form of government in which the people rule, either by voting directly or by electing representatives to manage the government and make the laws. **2** A country, state, or community with such a government. **3** Equal rights, treatment, and opportunity for everyone.
◆ *Democracy* comes from a Greek word meaning *rule of the people.*

dem·o·crat [dem′ə·krat] *n.* **1** A person who believes in government by the people. **2** A person who holds that all people should have equal rights and social treatment. **3** (*written* **Democrat**) A member of the Democratic Party.

dem·o·crat·ic [dem′ə·krat′ik] *adj.* **1** Of, favoring, or like a democracy. **2** Treating all people the same way, regardless of their social class: a *democratic* school system. **3** (*written* **Democratic**) Of or belonging to the Democratic Party. **—dem′o·crat′i·cal·ly** *adv.*

Democratic Party One of the two major political parties in the U.S., dating from 1828.

de·moc·ra·tize [di·mok′rə·tīz] *v.* **de·moc·ra·tized, de·moc·ra·tiz·ing** To make or become democratic. ¶3

de·mol·ish [di·mol′ish] *v.* To tear down completely; wreck; ruin.

dem·o·li·tion [dem′ə·lish′ən] *n.* The act or result of demolishing; destruction.

de·mon [dē′mən] *n.* **1** An evil spirit; devil. **2** A person or thing that is very cruel or evil. **3** A person having great energy or skill. **4** A lesser Greek god or guardian spirit.

de·mo·ni·ac [di·mō′nē·ak] **1** *adj.* Of or like a demon or evil spirit. **2** *n.* A person thought to be possessed by an evil spirit. **3** *adj.* Violent, furious, or frantic.

de·mo·ni·a·cal [dē′mə·nī′ə·kəl] *adj.* Demoniac.

de·mon·stra·ble [di·mon′strə·bəl] *adj.* That can be demonstrated, shown, or proved: a *demonstrable* error. **—de·mon′stra·bly** *adv.*

dem·on·strate [dem′ən·strāt] *v.* **dem·on·strat·ed, dem·on·strat·ing 1** To show clearly; exhibit. **2** To explain or prove by reasoning or by the use of examples or experiments: Our teacher *demonstrated* that helium does not burn. **3** To show how a product works: to *demonstrate* a new car. **4** To make a public show of feeling, as by meeting, marching, or picketing.

dem·on·stra·tion [dem′ən·strā′shən] *n.* **1** A showing or expressing outwardly: a *demonstration* of anger. **2** An explanation or proof, as by the use of reasoning, examples, or experiments: a *demonstration* of the weight of air. **3** A public showing of how a product works: a *demonstration* of a sewing machine. **4** Expression of public feeling by a meeting, march, or other gathering.

Demonstration for a lower voting age

de·mon·stra·tive [di·mon′strə·tiv] *adj.* **1** Serving to point out or show. *This* and *those* are demonstrative pronouns. **2** Freely and openly showing one's feelings, especially love: a *demonstrative* parent.

dem·on·stra·tor [dem′ən·strā′tər] *n.* A person or thing that demonstrates.

de·mor·al·ize [di·môr′əl·īz] *v.* **de·mor·al·ized, de·mor·al·iz·ing 1** To destroy the morals of; corrupt. **2** To weaken or destroy the spirit or discipline of: Hunger *demoralized* the explorers. — **de·mor·al·i·za′tion** *n.* ¶3

de·mote [di·mōt′] *v.* **de·mot·ed, de·mot·ing** To reduce to a lower grade, rank, or position. — **de·mo′tion** *n.*

de·mur [di·mûr′] *v.* **de·murred, de·mur·ring,** *n.* **1** *v.* To raise an objection: to *demur* at being sent to bed. **2** *n.* An objection or protest.

de·mure [di·myŏŏr′] *adj.* **de·mur·er, de·mur·est** Quiet, modest, and shy, or seeming so.

den [den] *n.* **1** The cave or resting place of a wild animal; lair. **2** A place where criminals gather secretly. **3** A private room to relax or study in. **4** A patrol of cub scouts.

de·na·tured [dē·nā′chərd] *adj.* **1** Changed in nature. **2** Made unfit for drinking or eating, although not spoiled for other purposes.

den·drite [den′drīt] *n.* One of the long, branching filaments that conduct impulses to the body of a nerve cell.

de·ni·al [di·nī′əl] *n.* **1** A saying that something is false: He issued a *denial* of the charges against him. **2** A refusal to grant or allow: *denial* of a permit. **3** A refusal to recognize or claim a connection with: the man's *denial* of his father.

den·im [den′əm] *n.* **1** A strong twilled cotton cloth used for overalls, play clothes, etc. **2** (*pl.*) Clothes made of this material.

den·i·zen [den′ə·zən] *n.* **1** A person, plant, or animal that lives or is found in a particular place: A bird is a *denizen* of the air. **2** A person, animal, or thing at home in a place not native to it.

Den·mark [den′märk] *n.* A small country in northern Europe, between the North Sea and the Baltic Sea.

de·nom·i·nate [*v.* di·nom′ə·nāt, *adj.* di·nom′ə·nit] *v.* **de·nom·i·nat·ed, de·nom·i·nat·ing,** *adj.* **1** *v.* To give a name to; call. **2** *adj.* Made up of units of a specified kind: *3 pounds* and *5 feet* are *denominate* numbers.

de·nom·i·na·tion [di·nom′ə·nā′shən] *n.* **1** The name by which a thing or class of things is known. **2** A particular religious group; sect. **3** A specific class of units, as in a system of measures, weights, or money.

de·nom·i·na·tor [di·nom′ə·nā′tər] *n.* The lower or second number in a fraction, as 5 in $\frac{3}{5}$ or 3/5. It is the number by which the numerator is divided.

de·no·ta·tion [dē′nō·tā′shən] *n.* **1** What a word or statement actually means or says, not what it suggests or may be associated with. **2** The act of denoting; indi-

The denominator is in red.

cation. ◆ *Denotation* and *connotation* both have to do with meaning. The *denotation* of a word is its exact, literal meaning. The *connotation* is what it suggests in one's mind. The *denotation* of *book* is a bound set of pages, whereas its *connotations* may include a whole world of romance and adventure.

de·note [di·nōt′] *v.* **de·not·ed, de·not·ing 1** To be a sign or symbol of; show; indicate: Red spots on the face may *denote* measles. **2** To be the name for; mean: The word "dell" *denotes* a small, sheltered valley.

de·nounce [di·nouns′] *v.* **de·nounced, de·nounc·ing 1** To speak against openly and strongly; call bad; condemn. **2** To inform against; tell on: The arrested robber *denounced* his partners. **3** To give formal notice of the ending of (a treaty or pact).

dense [dens] *adj.* **dens·er, dens·est 1** Having its parts crowded together; thick: a *dense* jungle. **2** Stupid; dull. **3** In mathematics, indicating a set that always has a member between any two other members. — **dense′ly** *adv.*

den·si·ty [den′sə·tē] *n., pl.* **den·si·ties 1** A dense condition; closeness; compactness: the *density* of the fog. **2** The amount of something per unit of volume or area: the *density* of population. **3** The mass of a substance per unit of its volume: the *density* of a gas. **4** Stupidity.

dent [dent] **1** *n.* A small hollow made in a hard surface by a blow or by pressure. **2** *v.* To make or become dented: Tin *dents* easily.

den·tal [den′təl] *adj.* **1** Of, for, or having to do with the teeth or with a dentist's work: *dental* hygiene. **2** Pronounced with the tip of the tongue against or near the upper front teeth.

den·ti·frice [den′tə·fris] *n.* A substance, such as toothpaste, used to clean the teeth.

den·tin [den′tin] *n.* Dentine.

den·tine [den′tēn] *n.* The hard, bony substance that makes up the main part of a tooth. It is under the enamel.

den·tist [den′tist] *n.* A doctor whose job is caring for and treating the teeth. He cleans teeth, fills cavities, fits braces, pulls diseased teeth, and fits false teeth.

den·tist·ry [den′tis·trē] *n.* The profession or work of a dentist.

den·ture [den′chər] *n.* A full or partial set of false teeth; plate.

de·nude [di·n(y)ōōd′] *v.* **de·nud·ed, de·nud·ing** To strip the covering from; make bare: The garden is *denuded* of flowers.

Denture

de·nun·ci·a·tion [di·nun′sē·ā′shən] *n.* An act or instance of denouncing.

Den·ver [den′vər] *n.* The capital of Colorado.

de·ny [di·nī′] *v.* **de·nied, de·ny·ing 1** To declare to be untrue or not right: Columbus *denied* that the world was flat. **2** To refuse to give, grant, or allow: They *denied* us our rights. **3** To refuse (someone) a request: It is hard to *deny* a sick friend. **4** To refuse to recognize or claim a connection with: to *deny* one's church.

— deny oneself To make oneself do without things one wants.

de·o·dor·ant [dē·ō′dər·ənt] *n.* Any substance used to prevent or cover up bad odors.

de·o·dor·ize [dē·ō′dər·īz] *v.* **de·o·dor·ized, de·o·dor·iz·ing** To take away or prevent the smell of. ¶3

de·ox·y·ri·bo·nu·cle·ic acid [dē·ok′sē·rī′bō·nōō·klē′ik] A complex substance found in the genes of plants and animals and having much to do with the passing on of inherited characteristics. It is also called DNA.

de·part [di·pärt′] *v.* **1** To go away; leave: The expedition *departed* in early May. **2** To turn away or aside; change: to *depart* from the usual custom. **3** To die.

de·part·ed [di·pär′tid] **1** *adj.* Gone; past: *departed* time. **2** *n. use* A dead person or persons: to pray for *the departed.*

de·part·ment [di·pärt′mənt] *n.* A separate part or division, as of a business, government, school, etc. **— de′part·men′tal** *adj.*

department store A large store having separate sections for selling different kinds of goods.

de·par·ture [di·pär′chər] *n.* **1** A going away; leaving: a *departure* for unknown regions. **2** A change or turning away, as from an accepted thought, practice, or pattern, to a new one: Taking care of a new baby will be a *departure* for her. **3** Death: seldom used today.

de·pend [di·pend′] *v.* **1** To trust; rely: You can *depend* on me to do it. **2** To rely for support or aid: The old lady *depends* on her son. **3** To be controlled or determined by: Crops here *depend* on the amount of rain. **4** To hang down: Lanterns *depended* from the ceiling.

de·pend·a·bil·i·ty [di·pen′də·bil′ə·tē] *n.* The quality of being dependable; reliability.

de·pend·a·ble [di·pen′də·bəl] *adj.* Worthy of trust; reliable. **— de·pend′a·bly** *adv.*

de·pen·dant [di·pen′dənt] *adj., n.* Dependent.

de·pen·dence [di·pen′dəns] *n.* **1** A depending on someone or something, as for support, help, or direction. **2** Trust or reliance: He put his *dependence* in his teacher. **3** A being determined by something else: Safe speed varies because of its *dependence* on traffic conditions.

de·pen·den·cy [di·pen′dən·sē] *n., pl.* **de·pen·den·cies 1** A dependent condition; dependence. **2** A territory or state governed by another country geographically separated from it.

de·pen·dent [di·pen′dənt] **1** *adj.* Depending on someone or something for support or aid: *dependent* children. **2** *n.* A person who depends on another for support. **3** *adj.* That cannot stand alone as a sentence; subordinate: said about a clause. In "This is the house that Jack built," *that Jack built* is a dependent clause. **4** *adj.* Determined or controlled by something

else: How soon you finish is *dependent* upon how fast you go. **5** *adj.* Subject to outside control: *dependent* territories.

de·pict [di·pikt′] *v.* **1** To show by a picture; portray. **2** To describe in words: The poet *depicted* a sunset. **— de·pic′tion** *n.*

de·plete [di·plēt′] *v.* **de·plet·ed, de·plet·ing 1** To make less; reduce: The fever *depleted* his strength. **2** To empty: to *deplete* a club's treasury. **— de·ple′tion** *n.*

de·plor·a·ble [di·plôr′ə·bəl] *adj.* **1** That causes or should cause regret: a *deplorable* temper. **2** Wretched. **— de·plor′a·bly** *adv.*

de·plore [di·plôr′] *v.* **de·plored, de·plor·ing** To feel or express strong regret over; be extremely sorry about: The mayor *deplored* the shortage of water.

de·ploy [di·ploi′] *v.* To spread out in or as if in battle formation.

de·pop·u·late [dē·pop′yə·lāt] *v.* **de·pop·u·lat·ed, de·pop·u·lat·ing** To remove many or all of the people from. **— de·pop′u·la′tion** *n.*

de·port [di·pôrt′] *v.* **1** To expel (a person, usually an alien) from a country by legal order; banish. **2** To behave (oneself) in a particular way: to *deport* oneself like a soldier.

de·por·ta·tion [dē′pôr·tā′shən] *n.* The expulsion of a person from a country.

de·port·ment [di·pôrt′mənt] *n.* The way a person acts or behaves; conduct.

de·pose [di·pōz′] *v.* **de·posed, de·pos·ing 1** To remove or oust from high office. **2** To give testimony under oath, especially in writing.

de·pos·it [di·poz′it] **1** *v.* To set down; place; put: She *deposited* the silverware on the table. **2** *v.* To put down in the form of a layer: The river had *deposited* soil and sand to form a delta. **3** *n.* Material laid down by natural forces: a *deposit* of silt; a mineral *deposit.* **4** *v.* To give over or entrust for safekeeping: to *deposit* money in a savings account.

5 *n.* Something given over or entrusted for safekeeping, especially money in a bank. **6** *v.* To put down money as partial payment or as a pledge: She *deposited* $10 on a new radio. **7** *n.* The

Name**	Julie Newman	
deposits	withdrawals	balance
6/1/65 $35.00		$35.00
7/3/65	$12.00	$23.00
7/9/65 $10.00		$33.00
`		

A record of bank deposits

money put down as a partial payment for something, or as a pledge.

dep·o·si·tion [dep′ə·zish′ən] *n.* **1** The action of removing from high office or rank. **2** The giving of testimony before a court. **3** The testimony given by a witness under oath, especially written testimony. **4** The action of depositing, or the material deposited.

de·pos·i·tor [di·poz′ə·tər] *n.* A person who makes a deposit, especially in a bank.

---

add, āce, câre, pälm; end, ēqual; it, īce; odd, ōpen, ôrder; tŏŏk, pōōl; up, bûrn;

ə = a in *above*, e in *sicken*, i in *possible*, o in *melon*, u in *circus*; yōō = u in *fuse*; oil; pout;

check; ring; thin; this; zh in *vision*. For ¶ reference, see page 64 · HOW TO

de·pos·i·to·ry [di·poz'ə·tôr'ē] *n.*, *pl.* **de·pos·i·to·ries** A place where something is put for safekeeping or storage.

de·pot [dē'pō *for defs. 1, 2,* dep'ō *for def. 3*] *n.* **1** *U.S.* A railroad station. **2** A place for storing things; warehouse. **3** A place for storing military equipment and supplies, or for receiving and training troops.

de·praved [di·prāvd'] *adj.* Completely wicked.

de·prav·i·ty [di·prav'ə·tē] *n.*, *pl.* **de·prav·i·ties** A wicked and corrupt condition, action, or habit; sin or vice.

dep·re·cate [dep'rə·kāt] *v.* **dep·re·cat·ed, dep·re·cat·ing** To express disapproval of or regret for. — **dep're·ca'tion** *n.*

de·pre·ci·ate [di·prē'shē·āt] *v.* **de·pre·ci·at·ed, de·pre·ci·at·ing 1** To lessen the value of: to *depreciate* currency. **2** To become less valuable: Fruit *depreciates* quickly. **3** To make seem small; belittle: My brother *depreciated* the prize I won. — **de·pre'ci·a'tion** *n.*

dep·re·da·tion [dep'rə·dā'shən] *n.* An act of robbing or plundering, as in war.

de·press [di·pres'] *v.* **1** To lower the spirits of; make gloomy or sad: Loneliness *depresses* many people. **2** To make less active or strong: The highway has *depressed* travel on the railroad. **3** To press or push down; lower.

de·pres·sant [di·pres'ənt] *n.* A drug or other substance which calms or soothes; a sedative.

de·pressed [di·prest'] *adj.* **1** Gloomy or sad: a *depressed* person. **2** Suffering from unemployment and a low standard of living: a *depressed* area. **3** Reduced in activity, energy, power, amount, or value. **4** Pressed down; lowered or flattened, especially below the general surface.

de·pres·sion [di·presh'ən] *n.* **1** Low spirits; gloom or sadness. **2** A pressing down: the *depression* of a piano key. **3** A low or sunken place in a surface; hollow. **4** A time when business is sharply cut down and many people are out of work.

dep·ri·va·tion [dep'rə·vā'shən] *n.* **1** The action of depriving or taking away. **2** The condition of being deprived, as of something needed or wanted: the *deprivation* of civil rights.

de·prive [di·prīv'] *v.* **de·prived, de·priv·ing 1** To take away from: to *deprive* a child of his favorite toy. **2** To keep from getting, having, or enjoying: to *deprive* them of rest.

dept. Abbreviation of DEPARTMENT.

depth [depth] *n.* **1** Distance to the bottom or to the back; deepness: the *depth* of a pool; the *depth* of a cave. **2** (*usually pl.*) The part deepest down or farthest in: the *depths* of the sea. **3** (*sometimes pl.*) The part of anything that is most intense: the *depth* of night. **4** Deepness of thought: This book has great *depth*. **5** Lowness

of pitch. **6** Understanding or ability: Higher mathematics is beyond my *depth*.

dep·u·ta·tion [dep'yə·tā'shən] *n.* **1** The act of deputing. **2** A group of persons sent to act for a larger group; delegation: A *deputation* of tenants demanded lower rents.

de·pute [di·pyoōt'] *v.* **de·put·ed, de·put·ing 1** To appoint to act for one or to do one's work: The leader *deputed* an assistant to serve in his absence. **2** To transfer (duties, powers, or authority) to another.

dep·u·tize [dep'yə·tīz] *v.* **dep·u·tized, dep·u·tiz·ing 1** To appoint as a deputy: to *deputize* a man. **2** To act as a deputy. ¶3

dep·u·ty [dep'yə·tē] *n.*, *pl.* **dep·u·ties** A person given the power to do another's job or to act in his place: a sheriff's *deputy*.

de·rail [dē·rāl'] *v.* To run or cause to run off a track: to *derail* a train. — **de·rail'ment** *n.*

de·range [di·rānj'] *v.* **de·ranged, de·rang·ing 1** To upset, confuse, or disturb the arrangement of: The delay *deranged* his schedule. **2** To cause to go crazy; make insane. — **de·range'·ment** *n.*

der·by [dûr'bē] *n.*, *pl.* **der·bies** A man's stiff felt hat having a curved, narrow brim and a round crown.

Der·by *n.* **1** [där'bē] A famous horse race run each year in England, founded in 1780 by the Earl of Derby. **2** [dûr'bē] Any similar horse race, as the Kentucky Derby.

der·e·lict [der'ə·likt] **1** *n.* A ship left abandoned at sea. **2** *adj.* Abandoned; deserted. **3** *n.* A poor, homeless person;

Derby

bum. **4** *adj.* Guilty of neglect or carelessness.

der·e·lic·tion [der'ə·lik'shən] *n.* **1** Failure to do what is required; neglect of duty: The guard's *dereliction* allowed the prisoner to escape. **2** A deliberate abandonment; desertion.

de·ride [di·rīd'] *v.* **de·rid·ed, de·rid·ing** To laugh at with contempt; make fun of.

de·ri·sion [di·rizh'ən] *n.* Mocking laughter; ridicule: to greet someone with *derision*.

de·ri·sive [di·rī'siv] *adj.* Full of contempt; mocking: a *derisive* smile. — **de·ri'sive·ly** *adv.*

der·i·va·tion [der'ə·vā'shən] *n.* **1** A getting from a source. **2** Descent or origin: to be of Spanish *derivation*. **3** The history of a word, showing how it was formed and how it developed.

de·riv·a·tive [di·riv'ə·tiv] **1** *adj.* That is derived from something else. **2** *n.* Something that is derived: The word "functional" is a *derivative* of "function." **3** *n.* A chemical compound formed from another compound by certain chemical processes: a benzine *derivative*.

de·rive [di·rīv'] *v.* **de·rived, de·riv·ing 1** To get or receive: to *derive* satisfaction from one's work. **2** To trace or come from a particular source: The word "zoo" *derives* from the Greek.

der·ma [dûr'mə] *n.* Another word for DERMIS.

der·ma·tol·o·gist [dûr′mə·tol′ə·jist] *n.* A doctor who specializes in the skin and its diseases. ◆ See EPIDERMIS.

der·mis [dûr′mis] *n.* The sensitive layer of skin lying under the outer skin.

de·rog·a·to·ry [di·rog′ə·tôr′ē] *adj.* Meant to lessen the value or merit of someone or something; belittling: a *derogatory* remark.

der·rick [der′ik] *n.* **1** A machine for lifting heavy weights and swinging them into place. It has a long arm hinged at an angle from the foot of an upright pole and is raised or lowered by ropes or cables. **2** The framework over the mouth of an oil well or similar deep hole made by drilling. It holds machinery for drilling, hoisting, and pumping. ◆ *Derrick* comes from the name of *Derrick*, a London hangman in the 1600's.

Derrick

der·ring-do [der′ing·dōō′] *n.* Brave or daring action: a deed of *derring-do*.

der·vish [dûr′vish] *n.* A member of any of various Moslem religious orders. Some dervishes worship by whirling or howling.

des·cant [des·kant′] *v.* To talk at length; hold forth: to *descant* upon baseball.

Des·cartes [dā·kärt′], **René,** 1596–1650, French philosopher and mathematician.

de·scend [di·send′] *v.* **1** To go or move from a higher to a lower point; go down: to *descend* a stairway; to *descend* to the town. **2** To lower oneself; stoop: to *descend* to lying. **3** To come or derive by birth from a certain source: He is *descended* from a duke. **4** To be passed down by inheritance: His property will *descend* to his children. **5** To make a sudden attack; swoop.

de·scen·dant [di·sen′dənt] *n.* The child, grandchild, etc., of an ancestor; offspring.

de·scent [di·sent′] *n.* **1** The action of going or coming down to a lower point: the *descent* of an airplane. **2** A slope or way going down: a steep *descent*. **3** Family origin; ancestry: She is of Italian *descent*. **4** A sudden attack; assault. ◆ See DECENT.

de·scribe [di·skrīb′] *v.* **de·scribed, de·scrib·ing** **1** To tell about in words, either in speaking or writing: to *describe* a house; to *describe* one's emotions. **2** To draw or form the outline of: His arm *described* an arc.

de·scrip·tion [di·skrip′shən] *n.* **1** The act of describing. **2** An account given in words: the *description* of the accident. **3** Sort, kind, or variety: birds of every *description*.

de·scrip·tive [di·skrip′tiv] *adj.* Telling what a person or thing is like; describing: a *descriptive* passage. **— de·scrip′tive·ly** *adv.*

de·scry [di·skrī′] *v.* **de·scried, de·scry·ing** To catch sight of, as something far off or hard to make out: to *descry* a boat.

des·e·crate [des′ə·krāt] *v.* **des·e·crat·ing** To treat something sacred without reverence, or use it in an unworthy way: to *desecrate* an altar. **— des′e·cra′tion** *n.*

de·seg·re·gate [dē·seg′rə·gāt] *v.* **de·seg·re·gat·ed, de·seg·re·gat·ing** To abolish the separation of races in: to *desegregate* a school. **— de′seg·re·ga′tion** *n.* ◆ *Desegregate* was formed from the word *segregate* and the prefix *de-*, which means *do the opposite of*.

des·ert¹ [dez′ərt] **1** *n.* An extremely dry region, often covered with sand, where few or no plants will grow: the Gobi *Desert*. **2** *adj.* Of or like a desert; barren or remote.

de·sert² [di·zûrt′] *v.* **1** To leave a person, place, or thing, especially if one has a duty to stay; abandon: to *desert* one's family. **2** To leave one's military duty or post without leave and without intending to return. **— de·sert′er** *n.*

de·sert³ [di·zûrt′] *n.* (*often pl.*) Reward or punishment that is deserved, especially in the phrase **just deserts**: They got their *just deserts*.

de·ser·tion [di·zûr′shən] *n.* **1** The action of deserting. **2** A deliberate abandoning of a person or persons toward whom one has a duty, as one's family. **3** The leaving of one's military duty without permission and without intending to return. **4** A being deserted.

de·serve [di·zûrv′] *v.* **de·served, de·serv·ing** To be worthy of or entitled to; merit: She *deserves* a second chance.

de·serv·ed·ly [di·zûr′vid·lē] *adv.* According to what is fair and right; justly: That scientist is *deservedly* famous.

de·serv·ing [di·zûr′ving] *adj.* Worthy of help, praise, or reward: a *deserving* composer.

des·ic·cate [des′ə·kāt] *v.* **des·ic·cat·ed, des·ic·cat·ing** **1** To dry completely; dry up. **2** To dry (a food) in order to preserve.

de·sign [di·zīn′] **1** *n.* A plan or sketch to be used as a pattern for making something: a *design* for a theater. **2** *v.* To work out and draw plans or sketches for: to *design* an evening dress. **3** *n.* The arrangement of parts, features, shape, etc., of something: The new *design* has two carburetors. **4** *n.* A visible pattern or arrangement: cloth having a floral *design*. **5** *n.* The art of making designs. **6** *v.* To plan or

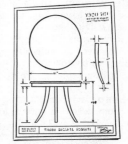
Design for a table

---

add, āce, câre, pälm;   end, ēqual;   it, īce;   odd, ōpen, ôrder;   tŏŏk, pōōl;   up, bûrn;

ə = a in *above*, e in *sicken*, i in *possible*, o in *melon*, u in *circus*;   **yōō** = u in *fuse*;   **oil;**   pout;

check; **r**ing; **th**in; **th**is; **zh** in *vision*.   For ¶ reference, see page 64 · HOW TO

set aside, as for a certain purpose: clothes *designed* for skiing. **7** *n.* (*often pl.*) A sly and wicked plot or scheme to get or take something: He has *designs* on my job. **8** *v.* To form (plans or schemes) in the mind.

des·ig·nate [dez′ig·nāt] *v.* **des·ig·nat·ed, des·ig·nat·ing 1** To point out; indicate: Signs *designate* the places where you may park. **2** To stand for; represent: Names *designate* persons, places, or things. **3** To choose or appoint for a definite duty or purpose: Jones was *designated* to pitch. **— des′ig·na′tion** *n.*

de·sign·er [di·zī′nər] *n.* A person who creates designs, as for dresses or machinery.

de·sign·ing [di·zī′ning] **1** *n.* The act or art of making designs. **2** *adj.* Scheming; crafty: a *designing* woman.

de·sir·a·ble [di·zīr′ə·bəl] *adj.* Worth wanting because good, helpful, or very pleasing: a *desirable* job. **— de·sir′a·bil′i·ty** *n.*

de·sire [di·zīr′] *v.* **de·sired, de·sir·ing,** *n.* **1** *v.* To long for; want very badly: to *desire* freedom. **2** *n.* A longing or craving: a *desire* for gold. **3** *v.* To express a wish for; request: You may have milk if you *desire* it. **4** *n.* A request or wish. **5** *n.* The thing one wishes.

de·sir·ous [di·zīr′əs] *adj.* Having a desire; wanting; eager: to be *desirous* of sleep.

de·sist [di·zist′] *v.* To stop what one is doing; cease: He *desisted* from teasing the cat.

desk [desk] *n.* **1** A piece of furniture at which a person sits to study, read, or write. Many desks have drawers or a compartment for storage. **2** A division or department in an organization: the copy *desk* of a newspaper.

Des Moines [də moin′] The capital of Iowa.

des·o·late [*adj.* des′ə·lit, *v.* des′ə·lāt] *adj.*, *v.* **des·o·lat·ed, des·o·lat·ing 1** *adj.* Dreary; barren: a *desolate* prairie. **2** *v.* To ruin or destroy: The flood *desolated* the valley. **3** *adj.* Laid waste; ruined: a *desolate* tangle of fallen trees. **4** *adj.* Lacking people; deserted. **5** *v.* To empty of inhabitants. **6** *adj.* Lonely; miserable: The lost dog looked hungry and *desolate*. **7** *v.* To make sorrowful or miserable.

des·o·la·tion [des′ə·lā′shən] *n.* **1** A lonely or deserted condition: the *desolation* of the moors. **2** Destruction; ruin: The army left *desolation* in its wake. **3** Sorrow that comes from loss or loneliness. **4** A desolate region.

De So·to [də sō′tō], **Hernando,** 1500?–1542, Spanish explorer. He discovered the Mississippi River.

de·spair [di·spâr′] **1** *n.* The heavy feeling that comes when all hope is lost or given up: to feel *despair*. **2** *v.* To lose or give up all one's hopes: She *despaired* of being rescued. **3** *n.* A person or thing that causes a feeling of hopelessness: He is the *despair* of his family.

des·patch [di·spach′] *v., n.* Another spelling of DISPATCH.

des·per·a·do [des′pə·rä′dō *or* des′pə·rā′dō] *n., pl.* **des·per·a·does** or **des·per·a·dos** A reckless or violent criminal; outlaw.

des·per·ate [des′pər·it] *adj.* **1** Reckless because all hope or choice seems gone: a *desperate* effort to escape. **2** Considered almost hopeless; dangerous; critical: a *desperate* illness. **3** Very great; extreme: in *desperate* need of money. **— des′per·ate·ly** *adv.*

des·per·a·tion [des′pə·rā′shən] *n.* Reckless willingness to dare anything because no hope seems left: He swung his ax in *desperation*.

des·pi·ca·ble [des′pi·kə·bəl *or* di·spik′ə·bəl] *adj.* Deserving to be despised; mean; contemptible: a *despicable* liar. **— des′pi·ca·bly** *adv.*

de·spise [di·spīz′] *v.* **de·spised, de·spis·ing** To look on with contempt; to dislike and scorn: Brave men *despise* cowards.

de·spite [di·spīt′] **1** *prep.* In spite of; notwithstanding: They kept cheerful *despite* hardships. **2** *n.* A harmful or defiant act.

de·spoil [di·spoil′] *v.* To rob of possessions or of value; plunder or spoil: to *despoil* a landscape by cutting down trees.

de·spon·den·cy [di·spon′dən·sē] *n.* Lowness of spirits caused by loss of hope or courage.

de·spon·dent [di·spon′dənt] *adj.* In low spirits; discouraged or depressed: *despondent* over his bad health. **— de·spon′dent·ly** *adv.*

des·pot [des′pət] *n.* A person with absolute power over the people under him, especially a ruler; tyrant.

des·pot·ic [di·spot′ik] *adj.* Exercising power in a harsh or bullying way; tyrannical: a *despotic* ruler. **— des·pot′i·cal·ly** *adv.*

des·pot·ism [des′pə·tiz′əm] *n.* **1** Absolute authority; unlimited power; tyranny. **2** A state ruled by a despot.

des·sert [di·zûrt′] *n.* A sweet food, such as pie, cake, pudding, or fruit, served at the end of a meal.

des·ti·na·tion [des′tə·nā′shən] *n.* The place towards which someone or something is traveling; goal: Their *destination* is Chicago.

des·tine [des′tin] *v.* **des·tined, des·tin·ing 1** To intend, as if by fate, for some special purpose: to be *destined* to become a hero. **2** To cause by fate. **— destined for** Bound or intended for: The plane was *destined for* France.

des·ti·ny [des′tə·nē] *n., pl.* **des·ti·nies 1** The outcome or fate that is bound to come; one's lot: It was his *destiny* to be a poet. **2** The power which is believed to decide the course of events in advance; fate.

des·ti·tute [des′tə·t(y)ōōt] *adj.* **1** Without the necessities of life; in great need; extremely poor. **2** Not having; lacking: a pond *destitute* of fish.

des·ti·tu·tion [des′tə·t(y)ōō′shən] *n.* **1** The condition of being without the necessities of life; extreme poverty. **2** Lack; deficiency.

de·stroy [di·stroi′] *v.* **1** To ruin completely; wreck; smash: A tornado *destroyed* five houses. **2** To put an end to; kill: Frost *destroyed* the plants.

de·stroy·er [di·stroi′ər] *n.* **1** A person or thing that destroys. **2** A small warship equipped with guns, depth charges, and other weapons.

de·struc·tion [di·struk′shən] *n.* **1** The action of destroying. **2** Ruin or great damage: *destruction* caused by a hurricane.

de·struc·tive [di·struk′tiv] *adj.* **1** Causing destruction or apt to destroy: *destructive* floods. **2** Intended to tear down or discredit: *destructive* criticism. — **de·struc′tive·ly** *adv.*

des·ul·to·ry [des′əl·tôr′ē] *adj.* Passing abruptly from one thing to another; lacking order or purpose: *desultory* conversation.

de·tach [di·tach′] *v.* **1** To unfasten and remove; disconnect: *Detach* and mail the coupon. **2** To send off for special duty: A squad of soldiers was *detached* to blow up the bridge.

de·tach·a·ble [di·tach′ə·bəl] *adj.* That can be unfastened and taken off or out: a *detachable* hood on a coat.

de·tached [di·tacht′] *adj.* **1** Not connected to something else; standing alone; separate: a *detached* house. **2** Not favoring a certain side; impartial: a *detached* attitude.

de·tach·ment [di·tach′mənt] *n.* **1** The act of detaching or separating. **2** Troops or ships sent off for special duty. **3** A permanent military unit that serves a specific purpose: a medical *detachment*. **4** A feeling of not being personally involved; freedom from prejudice: *Detachment* is necessary for a judge. **5** Aloofness.

de·tail [di·tāl′ *or* dē′tāl *for defs. 1, 2, 4,* di·tāl′ *for def. 3,* dē′tāl *for defs. 5, 6*] **1** *n.* A small, secondary part of something: The artist paid attention to *details*. **2** *n.* A minor piece of information; particular: Please write and give further *details*. **3** *v.* To tell item by item; give particulars about: The union *detailed* its demands. **4** *n.* A dealing with small items one by one: Avoid going into *detail*. **5** *n.* A small group of soldiers, policemen, etc., selected for a special duty. **6** *v.* To select for special duty: to *detail* soldiers to guard the prisoners. — **in detail** Item by item.

de·tain [di·tān′] *v.* **1** To keep from going ahead or leaving; hold back; delay: A phone call *detained* her. **2** To hold in custody; confine.

de·tect [di·tekt′] *v.* To discover, as something hidden or hard to perceive: to *detect* a slight movement in the bushes. — **de·tec′tion** *n.*

de·tec·tive [di·tek′tiv] **1** *n.* A person, often a policeman, whose work is to investigate crimes, find out hidden information, and watch suspected persons. **2** *adj.* Of, for, or about detectives and their work: a *detective* story.

de·tec·tor [di·tek′tər] *n.* **1** A person or device that detects or discovers something: a lie *detector*. **2** In a radio or television receiver, a device that separates the sound or other signal from the carrier wave.

de·ten·tion [di·ten′shən] *n.* **1** The act of detaining or confining: the police's *detention* of the suspect. **2** A being detained, delayed, or held: a suspected spy's *detention* for questioning.

3 Forced legal confinement, as in a jail: a house of *detention*.

de·ter [di·tûr′] *v.* **de·terred, de·ter·ring** To prevent from doing something through fear or doubt; discourage.

de·ter·gent [di·tûr′jənt] **1** *n.* A synthetic cleansing substance, like soap, used for washing and cleaning. **2** *adj.* Having cleansing qualities.

de·te·ri·o·rate [di·tir′ē·ə·rāt′] *v.* **de·te·ri·o·rat·ed, de·te·ri·o·rat·ing** To make or become worse or less valuable: the building *deteriorated*. — **de·te′ri·o·ra′tion** *n.*

de·ter·mi·na·tion [di·tûr′mə·nā′shən] *n.* **1** The act of deciding or settling finally: the *determination* of a new government policy. **2** Firmness of purpose; courage: His *determination* never wavered. **3** A decision reached on the basis of judgment or analysis. **4** The act or result of finding out exactly, as by measuring or calculating: a *determination* of the position of an aircraft.

de·ter·mine [di·tûr′min] *v.* **de·ter·mined, de·ter·min·ing** **1** To decide firmly; resolve: He *determined* to do far better in school. **2** To settle or decide: The court *determined* the case in his favor. **3** To find out by investigation; discover: to *determine* the salt content of sea water. **4** To have a direct effect on; define the limits of: Hereditary factors *determine* the color of one's eyes. **5** To fix in advance: to *determine* the date for a parade.

de·ter·mined [di·tûr′mind] *adj.* Firmly decided; resolute: a *determined* effort to win.

de·ter·min·er [di·tûr′min·ər] *n.* A word such as *a*, *his*, *six*, or *that*, used before a noun and descriptive adjectives modifying it.

de·ter·rent [di·tûr′ənt] **1** *n.* Something that deters. **2** *adj.* Serving to deter.

de·test [di·test′] *v.* To dislike strongly; hate. — **de·tes·ta·tion** [dē′tes·tā′shən] *n.* ◆ See HATE.

de·test·a·ble [di·tes′tə·bəl] *adj.* Deserving to be strongly disliked or disapproved; abominable.

de·throne [dē·thrōn′] *v.* **de·throned, de·thron·ing** To remove from the throne or from any high position. — **de·throne′ment** *n.*

det·o·nate [det′ə·nāt] *v.* **det·o·nat·ed, det·o·nat·ing** To explode suddenly and violently: A clockwork *detonated* the bomb. — **det′o·na′tion** *n.* — **det′o·na′tor** *n.*

de·tour [dē′tŏŏr *or* di·tŏŏr′] **1** *n.* A roundabout way, as a road used temporarily when a more direct route is closed off. **2** *v.* To follow or direct to follow a detour: to *detour* incoming traffic.

de·tract [di·trakt′] v. To take away a part; withdraw something: Losing a game does not *detract* from the fun of playing. — **de·trac′tion** n.

de·trac·tor [di·trak′tər] n. A person who speaks ill of or belittles someone.

det·ri·ment [det′rə·mənt] n. 1 Damage; loss; impairment: To the *detriment* of his health, he worked seven days a week. 2 Something that injures or damages. — **det′ri·men′tal** adj.

de·tri·tus [di·trī′təs] n. 1 Loose particles of rock separated by erosion, etc., from masses of rock. 2 Any mass of crumbly material; debris.

De·troit [di·troit′] n. A large city in SE Michigan.

deuce¹ [d(y)ōōs] n. 1 Something standing for the number two, as a playing card having two spots. 2 In tennis, the score when both sides are tied after having won three or more points each in a game, or five or more games each in a set.

deuce² [d(y)ōōs] n. informal The devil or bad luck: used as a mild oath: What the *deuce* is that?

deu·te·ri·um [d(y)ōō·tir′ē·əm] n. An isotope of hydrogen in which each atom contains a neutron. Deuterium is about twice as heavy as ordinary hydrogen.

Deu·ter·on·o·my [d(y)ōō′tə·ron′ə·mē] n. The fifth book of the Old Testament.

dev·as·tate [dev′ə·stāt] v. **dev·as·tat·ed, dev·as·tat·ing** To leave in ruins; destroy: An earthquake *devastated* Tokyo. — **dev′as·ta′tion** n.

de·vel·op [di·vel′əp] v. 1 To expand or increase gradually, as if by natural growth: to *develop* one's talent; The cold *developed* into pneumonia. 2 To start having: to *develop* good manners. 3 To work out in detail; unfold: to *develop* a topic sentence into a paragraph. 4 To bring or come into existence: to *develop* a new TV program; Some tastes *develop* slowly. 5 In photography, to treat (a film, plate, etc.) with chemicals to bring out a picture.

de·vel·op·er [di·vel′əp·ər] n. 1 A person or thing that develops. 2 A chemical solution used to develop photographs.

de·vel·op·ment [di·vel′əp·mənt] n. 1 A growing or causing to grow larger or better: the *development* of one's mind. 2 The result of such growth: a fine muscular *development*. 3 A stage in the developing of something; event: a political *development*.

de·vi·ate [dē′vē·āt] v. **de·vi·at·ed, de·vi·at·ing** To turn aside or away from a course, rule, etc.: His research *deviated* from all earlier studies. — **de′vi·a′tion** n.

de·vice [di·vīs′] n. 1 Something built for a specific purpose; an instrument or tool: A thermometer is a *device* for measuring temperature. 2 A scheme or plan: a *device* to bring in customers. — **leave someone to his own devices** To let someone do as he pleases.

dev·il [dev′əl] n., v. **dev·iled** or **dev·illed, dev·il·ing** or **dev·il·ling** 1 n. An evil spirit; demon. 2 n. A mean or wicked person. 3 n. An unfortunate person: poor *devil*. 4 n. A person

who is bold, lively, and carefree. 5 v. To bother or annoy. — **the Devil** or **the devil** In the Jewish and Christian religions, the prince and ruler of the kingdom of evil; Satan.

dev·iled [dev′əld] adj. Highly seasoned and usually chopped fine: *deviled* eggs.

dev·il·fish [dev′əl·fish′] n., pl. **dev·il·fish** or **dev·il·fish·es** 1 A large ray having a flat body and wide pectoral fins. 2 An octopus.

dev·il·ish [dev′əl·ish] adj. Of or like a devil; evil: a *devilish* plot. — **dev′il·ish·ly** adv.

dev·il·try [dev′əl·trē] n., pl. **dev·il·tries** 1 Reckless and spiteful mischief: to be up to some *deviltry*. 2 Wickedness or cruelty.

de·vi·ous [dē′vē·əs] adj. 1 Not direct, straight, or simple; roundabout: a *devious* route. 2 Untrustworthy; dishonest: *devious* conduct. — **de′vi·ous·ly** adv. — **de′vi·ous·ness** n.

de·vise [di·vīz′] v. **de·vised, de·vis·ing** 1 To figure out; invent; plan: to *devise* a means of escape. 2 To pass on (real estate) by will.

de·void [di·void′] adj. Entirely without; empty: a situation *devoid* of hope; a sea *devoid* of fish.

de·volve [di·volv′] v. **de·volved, de·volv·ing** 1 To pass over; be transferred: Direction of meetings *devolves* on a student committee. 2 To hand over, as to a successor; transfer.

Dev·on [dev′ən] n. A county in SW England.

de·vote [di·vōt′] v. **de·vot·ed, de·vot·ing** To give over (oneself, one's time, etc.) to a person or activity: to *devote* hours to music.

de·vot·ed [di·vō′tid] adj. Feeling or showing love or devotion; true: a *devoted* wife. — **de·vot′ed·ly** adv.

dev·o·tee [dev′ə·tē′] n. A person who is deeply interested in or devoted to something: a *devotee* of folk music.

de·vo·tion [di·vō′shən] n. 1 A strong, loyal affection. 2 Dedication: a lifelong *devotion* to the arts. 3 (pl.) Prayers; worship.

de·vo·tion·al [di·vō′shən·əl] adj. Of or having to do with devotion; used in worship: *devotional* music.

de·vour [di·vour′] v. 1 To eat up greedily. 2 To eat away, consume, or destroy: Fever *devoured* him. 3 To take in eagerly, as by reading: My father *devours* the paper each day.

de·vout [di·vout′] adj. 1 Religious; reverent; pious: a *devout* Catholic. 2 Heartfelt; sincere: a *devout* hope. — **de·vout′ly** adv.

dew [d(y)ōō] 1 n. Moisture condensed from the air in small drops upon cool surfaces. Dew forms overnight on grass, trees, etc. 2 v. To wet with or as if with dew. 3 n. Anything fresh, pure, or young.

dew·drop [d(y)ōō′drop′] n. A drop of dew.

Dew·ey Decimal System [d(y)ōō′ē] A code of numbers used to classify books by subject.

dew·lap [d(y)ōō′lap′] n. The loose skin hanging under the throat of some animals, as cattle.

dew point The temperature at which dew forms or vapor condenses to drops of liquid.

dew·y [d(y)oo′ē] *adj.* **dew·i·er, dew·i·est**
1 Moist with or as if with dew: *dewy* eyes.
2 Fresh; clear: a *dewy* complexion.

dex·ter·i·ty [dek·ster′ə·tē] *n.* **1** Skill in using
the hands or body; agility. **2** Mental quickness.

dex·ter·ous [dek′strəs *or* dek′stər·əs] *adj.* **1**
Skillful in using the hands or body; adroit: a
dexterous billiard player. **2** Mentally quick; keen.
— **dex′ter·ous·ly** *adv.* ◆ *Dexterous* comes from
a Latin word meaning *skillful*, which in turn
comes from a Latin root meaning *on the right* or
right-handed.

dex·trose [dek′strōs] *n.* A natural sugar found
in plants and animals; glucose.

dex·trous [dek′strəs] *adj.* Another spelling of
DEXTEROUS.

di·a·be·tes [dī′ə·bē′tis *or* dī′ə·bē′tēz] *n.* A
disease in which sugar that has been eaten
cannot be absorbed into the system because of
too little natural insulin.

di·a·bet·ic [dī′ə·bet′ik *or* dī′ə·bē′tik] **1** *adj.* Of
or having to do with diabetes. **2** *adj.* Having
diabetes. **3** *n.* A person who has diabetes.

di·a·bol·ic [dī′ə·bol′ik] *adj.* Diabolical.

di·a·bol·i·cal [dī′ə·bol′ə·kəl] *adj.* Of or like the
devil; fiendish; wicked: a *diabolical* plot.
— **di′a·bol′i·cal·ly** *adv.*

di·a·crit·ic [dī′ə·krit′ik] **1** *n.* A diacritical
mark. **2** *adj.* Diacritical.

di·a·crit·i·cal [dī′ə·krit′i·kəl] *adj.* Used to
indicate a difference: *diacritical* marks.

diacritical mark A mark, point, or sign
placed near or attached to a letter or letters to
indicate special pronunciation, as ē, oo, ô, ä.

di·a·dem [dī′ə·dem] *n.* A crown or band worn
on the head as a sign of royalty or honor.

di·ag·nose [dī′əg·nōs′ *or* dī′əg·nōs′] *v.* **di·ag·**
nosed, di·ag·nos·ing To determine by
diagnosis.

di·ag·no·sis [dī′əg·nō′sis] *n., pl.* **di·ag·no·ses**
[dī′əg·nō′sēz] **1** The act or process of recognizing
a disease by its symptoms. Diagnosis begins
with examination of the patient, and often
includes tests of his blood and urine, X-rays, etc.
2 A conclusion reached as to the nature of a
disease: The tests confirmed the doctor's *diag-*
nosis. **3** A critical study of any condition or
situation; conclusion based on analysis: a
diagnosis of the country's economic troubles.

di·ag·o·nal [dī·ag′ə·nəl] **1** *adj.* Crossing in a
slanting direction from corner
to corner or from side to side.
2 *adj.* In geometry, connecting any two vertices of a
closed plane figure that do not
have a common side. **3** *n.* A
diagonal line. — **di·ag′o·**
nal·ly *adv.*

horizontal
diagonal
vertical

diagonal cloth A fabric with diagonal ridges
or lines.

di·a·gram [dī′ə·gram] *n., v.* **di·a·gramed** or
di·a·grammed, di·a·gram·
ing or **di·a·gram·ming 1** *n.*
An outline or drawing of
something, not intended to
look like it but to explain how
its parts are arranged, how it
works, etc.: a *diagram* of an
internal-combustion engine.
2 *n.* A graph or chart: a
diagram showing population
growth. **3** *v.* To show by
diagram; make a diagram of.

START
Diagram
of a dance

di·a·gram·mat·ic [dī′ə·grə·
mat′ik] *adj.* **1** Having the
form of a diagram. **2** Lacking detail; sketchy.

di·al [dī′(ə)l] *n., v.* **di·aled** or **di·alled,**
di·al·ing or **di·al·ling 1** *n.* A flat surface
marked with numbers or other signs so that a
movable pointer can indicate time, pressure,
temperature, etc. The face of a watch or clock
is a dial. **2** *n.* A knob, disk, etc., on a radio or
television set for turning it on and off or regulating its operation. **3** *v.* To turn to or indicate
by means of a dial: *Dial* the station you like
best. **4** *n.* A disk on some telephones that can
be rotated over a numbered or lettered guide in
making a call. **5** *v.* To call by means of the dial
on a telephone: I *dialed* 611-7248. **6** *v.* To use
a dial, as in telephoning. **7** *n.* A sundial.

di·a·lect [dī′ə·lekt] *n.* A form of speech characteristic of a particular region or class, different
in some of its words, idioms, and pronunciations
from the standard language: "Auld lang syne"
is Scottish *dialect* for "long ago."

di·a·logue [dī′ə·lôg *or* dī′ə·log] *n.* **1** A conversation in which two or more speakers take part.
2 The conversation in a play, novel, etc.: The
dialogue didn't sound natural to me. ◆ *Dialogue*
comes originally from two Greek roots that mean
across or *between* and *word* or *speech.*

dial tone A low, steady, humming sound
indicating to the user of a telephone that a call
may be made.

di·am·e·ter [dī·am′ə·tər] *n.* **1** A line segment
joining two points on a circle
or sphere and passing through
its center. **2** The length of
such a segment, especially
when used to measure something: The *diameter* of the
tube was 16 inches.

Diameters

di·a·met·ric [dī′ə·met′rik]
adj. Diametrical.

di·a·met·ri·cal [dī′ə·met′ri·
kəl] *adj.* **1** Of a diameter: *diametrical* distance.
2 Directly opposite: *diametrical* opinions.

di·a·met·ri·cal·ly [dī′ə·met′rik·lē] *adv.* **1**
Completely; exactly: *diametrically* opposed
points of view. **2** Along a diameter.

add, āce, câre, pälm; end, ēqual; it, īce; odd, ōpen, ôrder; took, pool; up, bûrn;
ə = a in *above,* e in *sicken,* i in *possible,* o in *melon,* u in *circus;* yoo = u in *fuse;* oil; pout;
check; ring; thin; this; zh in *vision.* For ¶ reference, see page 64 · HOW TO

dia·mond [dī′(ə·)mənd] *n.* **1** A mineral consisting of carbon in crystal form, which when cut and polished is highly valued as a gem. Because of their great hardness, diamonds are used in industry in cutting tools and for grinding. **2** A figure like this ♦. **3** A playing card of the suit marked with red diamond figures. **4** (*pl.*) The suit so marked. **5** The infield of a baseball field. **6** The entire field.

dia·mond·back [dī′(ə·)mənd·bak′] *n.* A large rattlesnake of the SE U.S. having diamond-shaped marks on its back.

Di·an·a [dī·an′ə] *n.* In Roman myths, the goddess of hunting and of the moon. Her Greek name was Artemis.

di·a·pa·son [dī′ə·pā′sən *or* dī′ə·pā′zən] *n.* **1** Either of two principal stops in an organ. **2** A fixed standard of musical pitch. **3** The entire range of a voice or instrument. **4** A great rush of sound or harmony.

di·a·per [dī′(ə·)pər] **1** *n.* A piece of cloth or other absorbent material pinned around the loins of a baby, worn as an undergarment. **2** *v.* To put a diaper on. **3** *n.* A decorative pattern of repeated designs. **4** *n.* A silk or linen cloth having such a pattern.

di·aph·a·nous [dī·af′ə·nəs] *adj.* Thin enough to be seen through; transparent: a *diaphanous* veil.

di·a·phragm [dī′ə·fram] *n.* **1** A muscular wall separating the chest and abdominal cavities in mammals. **2** Any partition or membrane that divides. **3** A disk with an adjustable opening that can control the amount of light passing through the lens of a camera. **4** A disk that responds to sound by vibrating, used in telephones, etc.

A diaphanous scarf

di·ar·rhe·a [dī′ə·rē′ə] *n.* A condition in which the bowels move too often and too loosely.

di·a·ry [dī′(ə·)rē] *n., pl.* **di·a·ries 1** A personal record kept day by day of what happens or what one thinks about each day. **2** A book with space for writing down each day's record: June and her friend received *diaries* for Christmas. ♦ *Diary* comes from a Latin word meaning *day.*

di·as·to·le [dī·as′tə·lē] *n.* The rhythmic expansion of the heart that draws the blood into its chambers. ♦ See SYSTOLE.

di·a·tom [dī′ə·tom *or* dī′ə·təm] *n.* Any of various tiny, single-celled plants with hard cell walls, largely of silica, found in fresh or salt water.

di·a·ton·ic [dī′ə·ton′ik] *adj.* Using or having to do with the tones of an ordinary major or minor scale without alteration or added tones.

di·a·tribe [dī′ə·trīb] *n.* A very strong spoken or written criticism, often bitter or malicious: The speech turned out to be a *diatribe* against the tax bill.

dib·ble [dib′əl] *n.* A pointed tool that makes holes in soil for seeding and planting.

dice [dīs] *n.pl. of* **die,** *v.* **diced, dic·ing 1** *n.* Small cubes marked on each side with from one to six spots, used in games of chance. **2** *n.* A game played with dice. **3** *v.* To cut into cubes: to *dice* potatoes.

Dibble

Dick·ens [dik′ənz], **Charles,** 1812–1870, English novelist.

dick·er [dik′ər] **1** *v.* To bargain, especially over a petty trade: to *dicker* over the price of a dozen eggs. **2** *n.* A petty agreement or deal. ♦ This word is used mostly in the U.S.

dick·ey [dik′ē] *n., pl.* **dick·eys** An article of clothing that circles the neck and sometimes covers part of the chest, worn under a shirt, blouse, jacket, etc.

Dick·in·son [dik′ən·sən], **Emily,** 1830–1886, U.S. poet.

di·cot·y·le·don [dī′kot·ə·lēd′(ə)n] *n.* A plant having two cotyledons, or first leaves sprouting from a seed. — **di′·cot·y·le′do·nous** *adj.*

dic·tate [dik′tāt] *v.* **dic·tat·ed, dic·tat·ing,** *n.* **1** *v.* To say or read aloud (something to be written down or recorded): to *dictate* a long letter. **2** *v.* To order or require with authority: Fog *dictated* postponement of the flight. **3** *v.* To give orders. **4** *n.* (*often pl.*) Something established with authority; a rule or order: the *dictates* of the heart.

Dickey

dic·ta·tion [dik·tā′shən] *n.* **1** The act of speaking or reading something aloud to be written down or recorded. **2** Whatever is so spoken or read; dictated material: Do you take *dictation*? **3** The giving of orders that must be obeyed.

dic·ta·tor [dik′tā·tər *or* dik·tā′tər] *n.* **1** A person who rules a country with absolute power. **2** Any person who rules with authority: a *dictator* of fashion. **3** A person who dictates words to be written down or recorded. — **dic·ta′tor·ship′** *n.*

dic·ta·to·ri·al [dik′tə·tôr′ē·əl] *adj.* **1** Of or suited to a dictator: a *dictatorial* policy. **2** Overbearing; bossy. — **dic′ta·to′ri·al·ly** *adv.*

dic·tion [dik′shən] *n.* **1** The way in which one expresses oneself in words; the use, choice, and arrangement of words in talking and writing. "I ain't got none" is an example of poor diction. **2** A manner of saying or pronouncing words; enunciation: clear *diction*.

dic·tion·ar·y [dik′shən·er′ē] *n., pl.* **dic·tion·ar·ies** A reference book that lists words in a language or languages in alphabetical order and tells what they mean, how they are pronounced, etc. This dictionary, a general English-language dictionary, explains its words with other words in the same language. Bilingual dictionaries translate words of one language into those of another. Specialized dictionaries include only words that are related to a particular subject, like sports, cooking, or chemistry.

dic·tum [dik′təm] *n., pl.* **dic·tums** or **dic·ta** [dik′tə] Something said with authority; formal pronouncement: the *dicta* of the Church.

did [did] Past tense of DO[1].

di·dac·tic [dī·dak′tik *or* di·dak′tik] *adj.* **1** Suitable or intended for teaching or for guiding moral conduct: a *didactic* story. **2** Inclined to teach or lecture: His was a *didactic* nature.

did·n't [did′(ə)nt] Did not.

die[1] [dī] *v.* **died, dy·ing 1** To stop living; suffer death. **2** To lose force or power; fade away: The fire *died* out; The noise *died* down. **3** To stop working: The engine *died*.

die[2] [dī] *n.* **1** *pl.* **dies** A hard metal block or plate for stamping, shaping, or cutting out some object. Dies cut the threads on nuts and bolts, stamp designs on coins, and shape wire. **2** *pl.* **dice** A small marked cube. ◆ See DICE. **—the die is cast** The choice has been made and cannot be undone.

Die for stamping nickels

die-hard [dī′härd′] **1** *adj.* Refusing to give up or change one's views: a *die-hard* segregationist. **2** *n.* A person who resists to the end.

di·er·e·sis [dī·er′ə·sis] *n., pl.* **di·er·e·ses** [dī·er′ə·sēz] Two dots (¨) placed over the second of two vowels that are next to one another to indicate that two separate vowel sounds are to be pronounced, as in *naïve.*

die·sel [dē′zəl] *n.* (*sometimes written* **Diesel**) **1** An internal-combustion engine used in ships, locomotives, trucks, etc., burning oil injected into hot compressed air. **2** *adj. use:* a *diesel* engine. **3** A vehicle powered by a diesel, as a locomotive. **4** *adj. use:* a *diesel* locomotive. ◆ *Diesel* comes from the name of *Rudolf Diesel,* the inventor of the *diesel* engine.

di·et[1] [dī′ət] **1** *n.* The food and drink that a person or animal is used to; daily fare: The *diet* of most Americans includes meat at least once a day. **2** *n.* Food and drink specially selected for someone's health, appearance, etc.: a salt-free *diet;* a *diet* of liquids. **3** *v.* To eat and drink according to a special diet: She *dieted* to lose weight.

di·et[2] [dī′ət] *n.* **1** In some countries, the national legislature: the Japanese *Diet.* **2** An official meeting or assembly.

di·e·tar·y [dī′ə·ter′ē] *adj.* Having to do with diet: *dietary* rules; *dietary* habits.

di·e·tet·ic [dī′ə·tet′ik] *adj.* **1** Suitable for use in special diets: *dietetic* cookies. **2** Having to do with diet.

di·e·tet·ics [dī′ə·tet′iks] *n.* The science that deals with how much and what kinds of food a person or group needs to maintain health. ◆ See -ICS.

di·e·ti·tian or **di·e·ti·cian** [dī′ə·tish′ən] *n.* A person who is trained in the planning of meals or diets necessary for good health.

dif·fer [dif′ər] *v.* **1** To be unlike; have different content, form, etc.: His version of the story *differed* from ours. **2** To have a difference of opinion; disagree: They *differed* over who was the best teacher.

dif·fer·ence [dif′rəns] *n.* **1** A being unlike or different: the *difference* between right and wrong; a *difference* in price. **2** A particular way in which things are different: The only *difference* between our cars is color. **3** The amount by which things are different, as the amount remaining after subtracting one number from another: The *difference* between 22 and 8 is 14. **4** A disagreement; quarrel. **—make a difference** To be important; matter: Having a seat in the front row *made a* big *difference.*

dif·fer·ent [dif′rənt] *adj.* **1** Not the same; separate; distinct: He went to two *different* parties on the same day. **2** Not similar; not alike: The U.S. has citizens of many *different* backgrounds. **3** Out of the ordinary; unusual: You may not like her hat but you must admit it's *different.* **—dif′fer·ent·ly** *adv.* ◆ *Different* is usually followed by *from* in American speech and writing: John's book is *different from* Tom's. *Different than,* when a clause follows, is also widely used, but is best avoided in formal writing: The weather was *different than* what we had expected. In Great Britain, *different to* is sometimes used as a substitute for *different from:* She is *different to* her sister.

dif·fer·en·tial [dif′ə·ren′shəl] **1** *adj.* Indicating, showing, or based on a difference: *differential* tax rates. **2** *n.* An arrangement of gears in an automobile, bus, etc., that lets one wheel powered by the engine turn faster than its opposite, as on curves.

dif·fer·en·ti·ate [dif′ə·ren′shē·āt] *v.* **dif·fer·en·ti·at·ed, dif·fer·en·ti·at·ing 1** To recognize a difference: to *differentiate* between common sense and intelligence. **2** To distinguish from something similar: color of skin, eyes, and hair *differentiates* albinos from other people. **3** To become different or specialized, as cells developing into organs. **—dif′fer·en′ti·a′tion** *n.*

dif·fi·cult [dif′ə·kult *or* dif′ə·kəlt] *adj.* **1** Hard to do: a *difficult* job. **2** Not easy to understand: a *difficult* chapter. **3** Hard to please, handle, or get along with: a *difficult* person. ◆ *Difficult* was formed from the noun *difficulty*, which comes from a Latin word meaning *not easy to do*.

dif·fi·cul·ty [dif′ə·kul′tē *or* dif′ə·kəl·tē] *n.*, *pl.* **dif·fi·cul·ties** **1** A being difficult; difficult nature: the *difficulty* of a problem. **2** Something that is not easy to do, understand, or overcome; obstacle: to face many *difficulties*. **3** A good deal of effort: to walk with *difficulty*. **4** Trouble or worry, especially involving money.

dif·fi·dent [dif′ə·dənt] *adj.* Lacking confidence in oneself; timid; shy. **— dif′fi·dence** *n.* **— dif′fi·dent·ly** *adv.*

dif·frac·tion [di·frak′shən] *n.* **1** A breaking up of light rays into light and dark or colored bands, caused by interference. **2** A similar breaking up of sound waves, X-rays, etc.

dif·fuse [*v.* di·fyōoz′, *adj.* di·fyōos′] *v.* **dif·fused, dif·fus·ing,** *adj.* **1** *v.* To spread out in all directions; circulate in a wider area: The heat *diffused* throughout the house. **2** *adj.* Spread out; dispersed: a *diffuse* light. **3** *v.* To mix together or spread by mixing: said about gases and liquids. **4** *adj.* Using more words than necessary; wordy. **— dif·fu′sion** *n.*

dig [dig] *v.* **dug** (or **digged**: seldom used today), **dig·ging,** *n.* **1** *v.* To break up, turn over, or remove (earth, etc.), as with a spade, claws, or the hands: They *dug* for gold; to *dig* the ground. **2** *v.* To make or form by digging: to *dig* a trench. **3** *v.* To make a way by digging: to *dig* through a mountain. **4** *v.* To find and remove by digging: to *dig* clams. **5** *v.* To discover by painstaking effort or study: to *dig* up the facts. **6** *v.* To stick or thrust; jab: He *dug* his finger into my chest. **7** *n.* A thrust; poke. **8** *n. informal* A sarcastic remark; gibe. **9** *v. U.S. informal* To study hard.

di·gest [*v.* di·jest′ *or* dī·jest′, *n.* dī′jest] **1** *v.* To change (food) chemically in the stomach and intestines into a form that can be absorbed by the body. **2** *v.* To change into form usable by the body. **3** *v.* To take in by the mind; let sink in. **4** *n.* A summary or condensed account of what is in one or more books, articles, etc.: a *digest* of recent discoveries in medicine.

di·gest·i·ble [di·jes′tə·bəl *or* dī·jes′tə·bəl] *adj.* Capable of being digested; easy to digest.

di·ges·tion [di·jes′chən *or* dī·jes′chən] *n.* **1** The act or process of digesting, as food. **2** The ability or power to digest: a good *digestion*.

di·ges·tive [di·jes′tiv *or* dī·jes′tiv] *adj.* Having to do with digestion: the *digestive* system.

dig·ger [dig′ər] *n.* A person or thing that digs.

dig·gings [dig′ingz] *n.pl.* **1** Materials dug out, as from a mine. **2** A mining region.

dig·it [dij′it] *n.* **1** A finger or toe. **2** Any of the numerals from 0 through 9, so named from counting on the fingers.

dig·ni·fied [dig′nə·fīd] *adj.* Having dignity; proud; calm and stately: a *dignified* manner.

dig·ni·fy [dig′nə·fī] *v.* **dig·ni·fied, dig·ni·fy·ing** To give dignity to: make or make seem more honorable or worthy.

ies A person having a high position, as in a government, church, or university.

dig·ni·ty [dig′nə·tē] *n.*, *pl.* **dig·ni·ties** **1** The quality of character, worth, or nobility that commands respect: Washington had great *dignity*. **2** Proper pride in one's worth or position: beneath his *dignity* to complain. **3** A grave, stately manner: His *dignity* was unruffled. **4** High position, rank, or office.

di·graph [dī′graf] *n.* A combination of two letters having one sound, as *oa* in *boat*.

di·gress [di·gres′ *or* dī·gres′] *v.* To turn aside from the main subject. **— di·gres′sion** *n.*

dike [dīk] *n.*, *v.* **diked, dik·ing** **1** *n.* A dam or wall to keep back a river or sea from low land. **2** *v.* To provide with a dike.

di·lap·i·dat·ed [di·lap′ə·dā·tid] *adj.* Half ruined by neglect; falling to pieces: a *dilapidated* old farmhouse.

A dilapidated house

di·lap·i·da·tion [di·lap′ə·dā′shən] *n.* A rundown or ruined condition.

di·late [dī·lāt′ *or* di·lāt′] *v.* **di·lat·ed, di·lat·ing** **1** To make or become wider or larger: Fear caused her eyes to *dilate*. **2** To enlarge in all directions; swell: to *dilate* the heart muscle. **— di·la′tion** *n.*

The pupil dilates in the dark.

dil·a·to·ry [dil′ə·tôr′ē] *adj.* **1** Inclined to delay or put off; not prompt: *dilatory* in making payments. **2** Intended to cause delay: a *dilatory* legal measure.

di·lem·ma [di·lem′ə] *n.* A position where either of two choices is as bad and unpleasant as the other.

dil·et·tante [dil′ə·tänt′ *or* dil′ə·tan′tē] *n.*, *pl.* **dil·et·tantes** or **dil·et·tan·ti** [dil′ə·tan′tē] A person whose interest in an art or science is not serious; dabbler.

dil·i·gence[1] [dil′ə·jəns] *n.* **1** Hard, careful work. **2** Willingness or ability to work steadily and carefully.

dil·i·gence[2] [dil′ə·jəns] *n.* A public stagecoach used in France in the 18th century.

dil·i·gent [dil′ə·jənt] *adj.* Hard-working: a *diligent* worker. **— dil′i·gent·ly** *adv.*

dill [dil] *n.* An herb whose spicy seeds are used as a seasoning.

dill pickle A cucumber pickled in vinegar and seasoned with dill.

dil·ly-dal·ly [dil′ē-dal′ē] *v.* **dil·ly-dal·lied, dil·ly-dal·ly·ing** To take one's time; dawdle; loiter: Don't *dilly-dally* over your lunch.

di·lute [di·lōot′ *or* dī·lōot′, *adj. also* dī′lōot′] *v.* **di·lut·ed, di·lut·ing,** *adj.* **1** *v.* To make weaker or thinner by adding a liquid, as water.

2 *v.* To weaken by adding something else: He *diluted* a strong speech with too many jokes. **3** *adj.* Weak; diluted: a *dilute* solution. — **di·lu′tion** *n.*

dim [dim] *adj.* **dim·mer, dim·mest,** *v.* **dimmed, dim·ming 1** *adj.* Lacking enough light; not bright: a *dim* lamp. **2** *adj.* Not clearly seen; shadowy: a *dim* figure in the distance. **3** *adj.* Not clearly understood or remembered; vague: a *dim* recollection. **4** *adj.* Lacking brilliance; faint: a *dim* sound; a *dim* yellow. **5** *v.* To make or grow dim. — **dim′ly** *adv.* — **dim′ness** *n.*

dime [dīm] *n.* A coin of the United States and Canada worth ten cents.

di·men·sion [di·men′shən] *n.* **1** A measurement along a straight line of the length, width, or thickness of a thing. **2** (*usually pl.*) Size, bulk, or importance: a project of large *dimensions.*

di·men·sion·al [di·men′shən·əl] *adj.* Having dimensions: a three-*dimensional* figure.

di·min·ish [di·min′ish] *v.* **1** To make smaller or less; decrease: A sandwich *diminished* his hunger. **2** To grow smaller or weaker; lessen; dwindle: The winds *diminished.*

di·min·u·en·do [di·min′yōō·en′dō] *n., pl.* **di·min·u·en·dos** A gradual decrease in loudness or strength.

dim·i·nu·tion [dim′ə·n(y)ōō′shən] *n.* A lessening or reduction in size, amount, or degree: a *diminution* of polio cases.

di·min·u·tive [di·min′yə·tiv] *adj.* **1** Of very small size; tiny. **2** Expressing diminished size: said of certain suffixes as -*ette* or -*let.*

dim·i·ty [dim′ə·tē] *n., pl.* **dim·i·ties** A sheer cotton cloth with raised stripes or patterns, used to make curtains and dresses.

dim·ple [dim′pəl] *n., v.* **dim·pled, dim·pling 1** *n.* A slight hollow on the cheek or chin or on any smooth surface. **2** *v.* To mark with or form dimples: A smile *dimpled* her face.

din [din] *n., v.* **dinned, din·ning 1** *n.* A loud, harsh, confused noise or clamor; uproar: the *din* of the machine shop. **2** *v.* To make a din. **3** *v.* To keep saying over and over: The rules were *dinned* into our ears.

Dimple

dine [dīn] *v.* **dined, din·ing** To eat the principal meal of the day: to *dine* out.

din·er [dī′nər] *n.* **1** A person who dines. **2** A railroad dining car. **3** Any restaurant resembling a dining car.

din·ette [dī·net′] *n.* An alcove or a small room used as a dining room.

ding [ding] *v.* **1** To sound, as a bell; ring. **2** To keep saying over and over.

ding-dong [ding′dông′ *or* ding′dong′] *n.* The sound of a bell when it is struck repeatedly.

din·ghy [ding′gē *or* ding′ē] *n., pl.* **din·ghies** A small boat used with oars as a tender for a larger craft or with jib and mainsail for sailing.

din·gle [ding′gəl] *n.* A narrow, wooded valley; dell.

din·go [ding′gō] *n., pl.* **din·goes** A wild dog native to Australia.

din·gy [din′jē] *adj.* **din·gi·er, din·gi·est** Looking dirty; dull; shabby: *dingy* wallpaper. — **din′gi·ness** *n.*

dining car A railway car in which meals are served while the train is moving.

dining room A room designed and furnished for serving and eating meals.

dink·y [ding′kē] *adj.* **dink·i·er, dink·i·est** *informal* Small and unimportant.

din·ner [din′ər] *n.* **1** The principal meal of the day. **2** A banquet given in honor of a person or event: a *dinner* for the astronauts.

di·no·saur [dī′nə·sôr] *n.* Any of a large group of reptiles that died off millions of years ago. They had four limbs. They were of all sizes, some being the largest land animals ever known.

dint [dint] **1** *n.* Means; force: The spy escaped by *dint* of trickery. **2** *n.* A dent. **3** *v.* To make a dent in.

di·o·cese [dī′ə·sēs *or* dī′ə·sis] *n.* The district under a bishop's authority.

Di·og·e·nes [dī·oj′ə·nēz] *n.,* 412–323 B.C., Greek philosopher.

Dinosaur, about 45 ft. long

Di·o·ny·sus [dī′ə·nī′səs] *n.* In Greek myths, the god of wine. He was later called Bacchus.

di·o·ra·ma [dī′ə·rä′mə *or* dī′ə·ram′ə] *n.* An exhibit made up of lifelike figures in natural surroundings in the foreground with a painting for the background.

di·ox·ide [dī·ok′sīd *or* dī·ok′sid] *n.* An oxide containing two atoms of oxygen to the molecule.

dip [dip] *v.* **dipped, dip·ping,** *n.* **1** *v.* To put into a liquid and take out again at once: to *dip* a foot in hot water. **2** *v.* To lower and then raise: to *dip* a flag. **3** *v.* To dye by immersion. **4** *n.* A brief plunge into water: a *dip* in the pool. **5** *n.* A liquid or sauce into which something is dipped: a cream cheese *dip.* **6** *n.* A hollow or depression: a *dip* in the road. **7** *v.* To make by dipping into tallow or wax: to *dip* candles.

diph·the·ri·a [dif·thir′ē·ə *or* dip·thir′ē·ə] *n.* A serious contagious disease of the throat, usually with high fever, caused by a bacillus. It blocks air passages and makes breathing difficult.

---

add, āce, câre, pälm; end, ēqual; it, īce; odd, ōpen, ôrder; tōok, pōol; up, bûrn;
ə = a in *above,* e in *sicken,* i in *possible,* o in *melon,* u in *circus;* yōo = u in *fuse;* oil; pout;
check; ring; thin; this; zh in *vision.* For ¶ reference, see page 64 · HOW TO

diph·thong [dif′thông *or* dip′thông] *n.* A blend of two vowel sounds in one syllable, as *oi* in *coil*.

di·plo·ma [di·plō′mə] *n.* A certificate given by a school or college to a student who has successfully completed a course of study.

di·plo·ma·cy [di·plō′mə·sē] *n.*, *pl.* **di·plo·ma·cies** 1 The handling of relations, friendly or unfriendly, short of war, between nations. 2 Skill or tact in dealing with others.

dip·lo·mat [dip′lə·mat] *n.* 1 A person engaged in diplomacy. 2 A person having skill and tact in dealing with others.

dip·lo·mat·ic [dip′lə·mat′ik] *adj.* 1 Of or having to do with diplomacy: a *diplomatic* mission. 2 Tactful: to be *diplomatic* and efficient. — **dip′lo·mat′i·cal·ly** *adv.*

dip·per [dip′ər] *n.* 1 A long-handled cup used to dip liquids. 2 Either of two northern groups of stars (the **Big Dipper** and the **Little Dipper**) so arranged as to resemble dippers.

A dipper and the Big Dipper

dire [dīr] *adj.* **dir·er, dir·est** Dreadful; terrible: *dire* distress; *dire* poverty.

di·rect [di·rekt′ *or* dī·rekt′] 1 *v.* To control; manage: to *direct* a company's affairs. 2 *v.* To instruct; order; command: to *direct* soldiers to attack. 3 *v.* To tell or show the way: *Direct* me to the office. 4 *adj.* Straight; shortest: a *direct* road. 5 *adj.* Straightforward; clear: a speech that was *direct* and to the point. 6 *adj.* Having nothing between; immediate: a *direct* plea to the president. 7 *adj.* From parent to child to grandchild, etc., in unbroken line: a *direct* descendant. 8 *adv.* In a direct line or manner; directly. — **di·rect′ness** *n.*

direct current An electrical current flowing in one direction at all times.

di·rec·tion [di·rek′shən *or* dī·rek′shən] *n.* 1 Control or management: research under the *direction* of Dr. Black. 2 A command or order. 3 (*usually pl.*) Instructions on how to do something, operate something, or reach a place: *directions* for knitting a sock. 4 The line along which something moves or the point toward which it faces. South, east, and down are directions. 5 A tendency or line of development: to change the *direction* of a discussion.

di·rec·tion·al [di·rek′shən·əl] *adj.* 1 Of or having to do with a direction. 2 Sending or receiving radio waves mainly in or from one direction, as an antenna.

di·rec·tive [di·rek′tiv *or* dī·rek′tiv] *n.* An order or regulation.

di·rect·ly [di·rekt′lē *or* dī·rekt′lē] *adv.* 1 In a direct line or manner; straight: *directly* west; Go *directly* to the shelter. 2 Without anything or anyone between: taken *directly* from nature; I am *directly* responsible to the captain. 3 Exactly: *directly* opposite.

direct object The person or thing that receives the direct action of a verb. In "Mary boiled an egg," *egg* is the direct object.

di·rec·tor [di·rek′tər *or* dī·rek′tər] *n.* 1 A person who directs, as one in charge of the production of a play or movie. 2 One of a group chosen to direct the affairs of a corporation, society, etc. — **di·rec′tor·ship** *n.*

di·rec·to·ry [di·rek′tər·ē *or* dī·rek′tər·ē] *n.*, *pl.* **di·rec·to·ries** An alphabetical list of names and addresses: a telephone *directory*.

dirge [dûrj] *n.* A slow, sad song or piece of music, as for a funeral.

dir·i·gi·ble [dir′ə·jə·bəl] *n.* A type of balloon driven by motors and steered by rudders. It is shaped like a cigar.

Dirigible

dirk [dûrk] *n.* A dagger.

dirt [dûrt] *n.* 1 Loose earth. 2 Anything filthy or unclean; anything that soils. 3 Something despised or of little value.

dirt·y [dûr′tē] *adj.* **dirt·i·er, dirt·i·est,** *v.* **dirt·ied, dirt·y·ing** 1 *adj.* Unclean; soiled: *dirty* hands. 2 *adj.* Unpleasant; stormy: a *dirty* job; *dirty* weather. 3 *adj.* Despicable; mean: a *dirty* trick. 4 *adj.* Lacking brightness; muddy: a *dirty* yellow. 5 *v.* To make or become dirty. — **dirt′i·ness** *n.*

dis- A prefix used with verbs, adjectives, and nouns to give the opposite sense to or to reverse the action or effect expressed in the rest of the word, as *disorder*, lack of order; *dishonest*, not honest; *disability*, lack of ability; *disallow*, refuse to allow; *disloyal*, not loyal.

dis·a·bil·i·ty [dis′ə·bil′ə·tē] *n.*, *pl.* **dis·a·bil·i·ties** 1 Something that disables. 2 Lack of ability to function normally.

dis·a·ble [dis·ā′bəl] *v.* **dis·a·bled, dis·a·bling** To make unfit or unable; incapacitate; cripple.

dis·a·buse [dis′ə·byooz′] *v.* **dis·a·bused, dis·a·bus·ing** To free from false or mistaken ideas.

dis·ad·van·tage [dis′ad·van′tij] *n.* 1 Something that hinders success; handicap: A poor education is a *disadvantage*. 2 An unfavorable condition or situation: His weak ankle put him at a *disadvantage* in the race.

dis·ad·van·taged [dis′ad·van′tijd] *adj.* Lacking advantages; underprivileged.

dis·ad·van·ta·geous [dis′ad·vən·tā′jəs] *adj.* Hindering success; unfavorable: in a *disadvantageous* position.

dis·af·fect·ed [dis′ə·fek′tid] *adj.* No longer contented or friendly; disloyal: spies hidden by *disaffected* farmers. — **dis′af·fec′tion** *n.*

dis·a·gree [dis′ə·grē′] *v.* **dis·a·greed, dis·a·gree·ing** 1 To have a different opinion; differ: I *disagree* with the speaker. 2 To quarrel; argue. 3 To be unsuitable or upsetting: The medicine *disagreed* with him.

dis·a·gree·a·ble [dis′ə·grē′ə·bəl] *adj.* 1 Not agreeable; unpleasant. 2 Having a bad temper; irritable. — **dis′a·gree′a·bly** *adv.*

dis·a·gree·ment [dis/ə·grē/mənt] *n.* **1** A difference in views; failure to agree. **2** An angry dispute; quarrel. **3** A difference; discrepancy: a *disagreement* between your answer and mine.

dis·al·low [dis/ə·lou/] *v.* **1** To refuse to allow or permit. **2** To reject or deny, as a petition.

dis·ap·pear [dis/ə·pir/] *v.* **1** To pass from sight; fade away; vanish. **2** To pass out of existence: The snow *disappeared.* — **dis/ap·pear/ance** *n.*

dis·ap·point [dis/ə·point/] *v.* **1** To fail to meet the hope, expectation, or wishes of: The dress *disappointed* me. **2** To fail to do something promised to: You promised to sing; don't *disappoint* us.

dis·ap·point·ment [dis/ə·point/mənt] *n.* **1** The state or feeling of being disappointed: His *disappointment* was hard to forget. **2** Something that disappoints: The new house was a *disappointment.*

dis·ap·pro·ba·tion [dis/ap·rə·bā/shən] *n.* Disapproval.

dis·ap·prov·al [dis/ə·proo/vəl] *n.* A feeling, judgment, or opinion against something; refusal to approve: a look of *disapproval.*

dis·ap·prove [dis/ə·proov/] *v.* **dis·ap·proved, dis·ap·prov·ing** To have a feeling, judgment, or opinion against; think of as bad or wrong: to *disapprove* of a child's behavior.

dis·arm [dis·ärm/] *v.* **1** To take away the weapons of: to *disarm* a soldier. **2** To lay aside weapons: We agreed to *disarm.* **3** To reduce fighting forces and equipment: said about nations. **4** To take away unfriendliness or suspicion from: His charming manner *disarmed* us.

dis·arm·a·ment [dis·är/mə·mənt] *n.* The cutting down, limiting, or getting rid of a nation's fighting forces and equipment.

dis·ar·range [dis/ə·rānj/] *v.* **dis·ar·ranged, dis·ar·rang·ing** To disturb the order or arrangement of; disorder: to *disarrange* hair.

dis·ar·ray [dis/ə·rā/] **1** *n.* A very untidy state; confusion; disorder. **2** *v.* To put out of orderly arrangement; throw into confusion. **3** *n.* Disordered or incomplete clothing: to escape from a fire in *disarray.*

dis·as·ter [di·zas/tər] *n.* An event causing great distress or ruin, as fires, floods, etc.

dis·as·trous [di·zas/trəs] *adj.* Causing great distress or damage: a *disastrous* fire. — **dis·as/trous·ly** *adv.*

dis·a·vow [dis/ə·vou/] *v.* To say that one does not know about, approve of, or have any responsibility for: He *disavowed* the statement quoted as his.

dis·a·vow·al [dis/ə·vou/əl] *n.* The act of disavowing; denial of responsibility or knowledge.

dis·band [dis·band/] *v.* To break up as an organization; scatter or become scattered: The club *disbanded;* The army was *disbanded.*

dis·bar [dis·bär/] *v.* **dis·barred, dis·bar·ring** To take away the right to practice law from: to *disbar* a dishonest lawyer. — **dis·bar/ment** *n.*

dis·be·lief [dis/bi·lēf/] *n.* A conviction that something is untrue.

dis·be·lieve [dis/bi·lēv/] *v.* **dis·be·lieved, dis·be·liev·ing** To refuse to believe; consider untrue.

dis·bur·den [dis·bûr/dən] *v.* To relieve of a burden; unburden.

dis·burse [dis·bûrs/] *v.* **dis·bursed, dis·burs·ing** To pay out or spend.

dis·burse·ment [dis·bûrs/mənt] *n.* **1** The act of disbursing. **2** Money paid out.

disc [disk] *n.* Another spelling of DISK.

dis·card [*v.* dis·kärd/, *n.* dis/kärd] **1** *v.* To throw away or get rid of as useless or not wanted. **2** *n.* A person or thing that is discarded. **3** *v.* To play (a card not a trump and not of the suit led). **4** *v.* To lay aside from one's hand (one or more unwanted cards).

dis·cern [di·sûrn/ *or* di·zûrn/] *v.* To pick out or recognize with the eye or the mind: to *discern* a deer on the hilltop; to *discern* the truth. — **dis·cern/i·ble** *adj.*

dis·cern·ing [di·sûr/ning *or* di·zûr/ning] *adj.* Quick to discern; discriminating.

dis·cern·ment [di·sûrn/mənt] *n.* **1** Keenness of judgment; insight. **2** The act of discerning.

dis·charge [dis·chärj/, *n. also* dis/chärj] *v.* **dis·charged, dis·charg·ing,** *n.* **1** *v.* To shoot or fire, as a weapon. **2** *v.* To remove; unload: to *discharge* a cargo. **3** *v.* To dismiss: to *discharge* an employee. **4** *v.* To release or set free: to *discharge* a soldier or a patient. **5** *n.* A certificate of release: a military *discharge.* **6** *v.* To fulfill the requirements of: to *discharge* a duty. **7** *v.* To give or send forth contents: The wound *discharges* constantly. **8** *n.* Something that is discharged, as pus. **9** *v.* To pay (a debt). **10** *n.* Payment.

dis·ci·ple [di·sī/pəl] *n.* **1** A person who accepts and follows a teacher. **2** A follower of Jesus.

dis·ci·pli·nar·i·an [dis/ə·plə·nâr/ē·ən] *n.* A person who disciplines or believes in the use of dicipline.

dis·ci·pli·nar·y [dis/ə·plə·ner/ē] *adj.* Of or for discipline: *disciplinary* training.

dis·ci·pline [dis/ə·plin] *n., v.* **dis·ci·plined, dis·ci·plin·ing 1** *n.* Strict, systematic training that teaches obedience and orderly conduct. **2** *n.* The obedience, self-control, and orderly conduct that result from such training: The *discipline* of the children prevented panic when the school burned. **3** *v.* To train to obedience, self-control, and order: to *discipline* a squad of recruits. **4** *n.* Punishment for the sake of training or correcting. **5** *v.* To punish: to *discipline* anyone who lies.

---

add, āce, câre, pälm;   end, ēqual;   it, īce;   odd, ōpen, ôrder;   tŏŏk, pōŏl;   up, bûrn;
ə = a in *above*, e in *sicken*, i in *possible*, o in *melon*, u in *circus*;   yōō = u in *fuse*;   oil;   pout;
check; ring; thin; this; zh in *vision.*   For ¶ reference, see page 64 · HOW TO

dis·claim [dis·klām′] v. **1** To deny any knowledge of or connection with; disavow. **2** To give up any right or claim to: He *disclaimed* a share in his father's estate.

dis·close [dis·klōz′] v. **dis·closed, dis·closing 1** To expose to sight; uncover. **2** To make known: to *disclose* a secret.

dis·clo·sure [dis·klō′zhər] n. **1** The act of disclosing. **2** The thing that is disclosed.

dis·col·or [dis·kul′ər] v. **1** To change or harm the color of: Dampness *discolored* the walls. **2** To become changed, spoiled, faded, etc., in color: The fabric *discolored* with age. ¶1

dis·col·or·a·tion [dis·kul′ə·rā′shən] n. **1** The act of discoloring. **2** A stain or discolored spot. ¶1

dis·com·fit [dis·kum′fit] v. To frustrate, confuse, or embarrass, as by thwarting plans. — **dis·com·fi·ture** [dis·kum′fi·chər] n.

dis·com·fort [dis·kum′fərt] n. **1** An uncomfortable condition; distress. **2** Something that causes discomfort.

dis·com·pose [dis′kəm·pōz′] v. **dis·composed, dis·com·pos·ing** To make uneasy and nervous; upset the calmness of: The pianist was *discomposed* by the loud whispers of the audience. — **dis·com·po·sure** [dis′·kəm·pō′zhər] n.

dis·con·cert [dis′kən·sûrt′] v. To upset or embarrass, as by unexpected difficulty or unfriendliness: His rude stare *disconcerted* me.

dis·con·nect [dis′kə·nekt′] v. To break or undo the connection of or between: *Disconnect* the hose from the faucet.

dis·con·nect·ed [dis′kə·nek′tid] adj. **1** Not connected. **2** Not in logical order; wandering: *disconnected* ideas. — **dis′con·nect′ed·ly** adv.

dis·con·so·late [dis·kon′sə·lit] adj. Full of sadness or despair; unhappy; forlorn.

dis·con·tent [dis′kən·tent′] **1** n. An unhappy, dissatisfied feeling: *discontent* over the new rules. **2** v. To cause to become discontented.

dis·con·tent·ed [dis′kən·ten′tid] adj. Unhappy and dissatisfied. — **dis′con·tent′ed·ly** adv.

dis·con·tin·ue [dis′kən·tin′yōō] v. **dis·con·tin·ued, dis·con·tin·u·ing** To stop having, using, making, etc.; break off or end: to *discontinue* weekly meetings.

dis·con·tin·u·ous [dis′kən·tin′yōō·əs] adj. Not continuous; having breaks or interruptions.

dis·cord [dis′kôrd] n. **1** Angry or quarrelsome disagreement; lack of harmony: *discord* between North and South. **2** A combination of clashing or disagreeable sounds. **3** In music, a sounding together of notes that do not seem to harmonize. ◆ *Discord* comes from a Latin word whose elements mean literally *apart from the heart.*

dis·cor·dant [dis·kôr′dənt] adj. **1** Not agreeing or fitting together; clashing: *discordant* opinions. **2** Not in harmony; disagreeable; jarring: *discordant* tones. — **dis·cor′dant·ly** adv.

dis·count [n. dis′kount, v. dis·kount′ or dis′·kount] **1** n. A reduction in an amount charged:

Students get a *discount* on tickets. **2** v. To deduct (a part) of a bill, price, etc. **3** v. To disregard, doubt, or consider exaggerated: *Discount* the stories of his heroism.

dis·coun·te·nance [dis·koun′tə·nəns] v. **dis·coun·te·nanced, dis·coun·te·nanc·ing 1** To disapprove of; frown on: to *discountenance* lateness. **2** To make uneasy; embarrass.

dis·cour·age [dis·kûr′ij] v. **dis·cour·aged, dis·cour·ag·ing 1** To cause to lose courage or confidence: Harsh criticism can be *discouraging*. **2** To try to prevent, as by expressing disapproval: Her parents *discourage* late hours. **3** To interfere with; hinder: Poor eating habits *discourage* growth. — **dis·cour′age·ment** n.

dis·course [n. dis′kôrs, v. dis·kôrs′] n., v. **dis·coursed, dis·cours·ing 1** n. A formal speech or written treatment of a subject. **2** v. To speak at length; make a long, formal speech. **3** n. Conversation or talk. **4** v. To talk.

dis·cour·te·ous [dis·kûr′tē·əs] adj. Impolite; rude. — **dis·cour′te·ous·ly** adv.

dis·cour·te·sy [dis·kûr′tə·sē] n., pl. **dis·cour·te·sies 1** Lack of courtesy; rudeness. **2** A discourteous act, remark, etc.

dis·cov·er [dis·kuv′ər] v. **1** To find out, get knowledge of, or come upon before anyone else: Balboa *discovered* the Pacific; Roentgen *discovered* X-rays. **2** To learn or find out, especially for the first time: We *discovered* that reading is fun. — **dis·cov′er·er** n.

dis·cov·er·y [dis·kuv′ər·ē] n., pl. **dis·cov·er·ies 1** The act of discovering: the *discovery* of an ancient city. **2** Something discovered.

dis·cred·it [dis·kred′it] **1** v. To cause to be doubted; consider unacceptable or untrustworthy: to *discredit* a rumor; He was *discredited* as a reliable witness. **2** n. Doubt; disbelief: a theory fallen into *discredit*. **3** n. Loss of reputation or honor; disgrace. **4** n. A cause of disgrace or loss of honor: A traitor is a *discredit* to his country. **5** v. To harm the reputation of; bring dishonor to.

dis·cred·it·a·ble [dis·kred′it·ə·bəl] adj. Resulting in or causing discredit.

dis·creet [dis·krēt′] adj. Tactful, cautious, and wise: *discreet* inquiries. — **dis·creet′ly** adv.

dis·crep·an·cy [dis·krep′ən·sē] n., pl. **dis·crep·an·cies** A difference or inconsistency; contradiction: a *discrepancy* between two answers to the same problem.

dis·cre·tion [dis·kresh′ən] n. **1** Good judgment; prudence: Use *discretion* in confiding secrets. **2** Individual judgment, or freedom to use it: Use your own *discretion* in choosing.

dis·cre·tion·ar·y [dis·kresh′ən·er′ē] adj. Left to one's own judgment or discretion: the *discretionary* powers of the President.

dis·crim·i·nate [dis·krim′ə·nāt] v. **dis·crim·i·nat·ed, dis·crim·i·nat·ing 1** To recognize a difference between; distinguish: to *discriminate* between right and wrong. **2** To show prejudice or partiality: In 1917 we *discriminated* against anything German, even old operas.

dis·crim·i·na·tion [dis·krim′ə·nā′shən] *n.* **1** Prejudice in one's attitude or actions: to show *discrimination* against foreigners. **2** The noticing of differences or the making of distinctions. **3** The ability to note small differences.

dis·crim·i·na·to·ry [dis·krim′ə·nə·tôr′ē] *adj.* Showing prejudice or partiality.

dis·cur·sive [dis·kûr′siv] *adj.* Going from subject to subject and often wandering from the main point: a *discursive* lecture.

dis·cus [dis′kəs] *n.* A heavy disk, now usually of metal and wood, used in athletic contests to see who can throw it the greatest distance.

dis·cuss [dis·kus′] *v.* **1** To talk over or consider; exchange ideas or opinions about: to *discuss* a proposed law. **2** To have or treat as a subject: This chapter *discusses* the American Revolution.

dis·cus·sion [dis·kush′ən] *n.* Argument on or consideration of a subject.

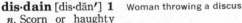

Woman throwing a discus

dis·dain [dis·dān′] **1** *n.* Scorn or haughty contempt, especially toward someone or something considered inferior. **2** *v.* To regard as beneath one; scorn; spurn: a rich man who *disdains* his poor relatives; a poor man who *disdains* gifts of charity. ◆ See CONTEMPT.

dis·dain·ful [dis·dān′fəl] *adj.* Filled with or expressing disdain; scornful. — **dis·dain′ful·ly** *adv.*

dis·ease [di·zēz′] *n.* A sickness or illness, usually of a particular kind. People, animals, and plants may have diseases: Chicken pox is a contagious *disease;* elm trees dying of *disease.*

dis·eased [di·zēzd′] *adj.* **1** Having or affected by a disease. **2** Seriously disordered: a *diseased* mind.

dis·em·bark [dis′em·bärk′] *v.* To go or put ashore from a ship; land: The Pilgrims *disembarked* at Plymouth Rock; to *disembark* troops.

dis·em·bod·ied [dis′em·bod′ēd] *adj.* Existing apart from a body: a *disembodied* spirit.

dis·en·chant [dis′en·chant′] *v.* To free from a pleasant but false belief; disillusion: He was expecting luxury, but his first meal *disenchanted* him. — **dis′en·chant′ment** *n.*

dis·en·gage [dis′en·gāj′] *v.* **dis·en·gaged, dis·en·gag·ing 1** To loosen, detach, or free from something that holds: to *disengage* the clutch of a car; She *disengaged* her scarf from a thorn. **2** To free, as from an obligation.

dis·en·tan·gle [dis′en·tang′gəl] *v.* **dis·en·tan·gled, dis·en·tan·gling** To free from a tangled or confused condition; untangle.

dis·fa·vor [dis·fā′vər] **1** *n.* Disapproval; dislike: to regard someone with *disfavor.* **2** *n.* A being disapproved of or opposed: a theory now in *disfavor.* **3** *v.* To disapprove of; oppose. ¶1

dis·fig·ure [dis·fig′yər] *v.* **dis·fig·ured, dis·fig·ur·ing** To mar or destroy the appearance of; make unattractive: A broken nose *disfigured* the statue. — **dis·fig′ure·ment** *n.*

dis·fran·chise [dis·fran′chīz] *v.* **dis·fran·chised, dis·fran·chis·ing** To take a right or privilege away from, especially the right to vote. — **dis·fran′chise·ment** *n.*

dis·gorge [dis·gôrj′] *v.* **dis·gorged, dis·gorg·ing** To throw out; vomit forth: a volcano *disgorging* streams of lava.

dis·grace [dis·grās′] *n.*, *v.* **dis·graced, dis·grac·ing 1** *n.* A condition of shame or dishonor: Our boy is in *disgrace* for a school prank. **2** *n.* A person or thing that causes shame or dishonor: That untidy room is a *disgrace*! **3** *v.* To bring shame or dishonor to: to *disgrace* one's family by cheating. — **dis·grace′ful** *adj.*

dis·grun·tled [dis·grun′təld] *adj.* Resentful and dissatisfied; discontented.

dis·guise [dis·gīz′] *v.* **dis·guised, dis·guis·ing,** *n.* **1** *v.* To change in appearance or manner so as not to be known or to appear as someone else: a king *disguised* as a shepherd. **2** *n.* Something that disguises, as a costume. **3** *v.* To conceal or give a false idea of: to *disguise* one's voice. **4** *n.* The condition of being disguised: Great clowns are masters of *disguise.*

dis·gust [dis·gust′] **1** *v.* To fill with a sickening feeling of intense distaste or dislike: The sight of blood *disgusts* her. **2** *n.* Strong dislike caused by something offensive.

dis·gust·ing [dis·gus′ting] *adj.* Arousing disgust; offensive. — **dis·gust′ing·ly** *adv.*

dish [dish] **1** *n.* A container for serving or holding food, as a plate, a bowl, etc. **2** *n.* The amount held or served in a dish: He ate four *dishes* of pudding. **3** *n.* A food prepared for eating: Peach pie is a delicious *dish.* **4** *v.* To put (food to be served) in a dish or dishes: to *dish* out scrambled eggs.

A disheveled boy

dis·heart·en [dis·här′tən] *v.* To cause to lose one's hope or confidence; discourage.

di·shev·eled or **di·shev·elled** [di·shev′əld] *adj.* Rumpled and untidy, as hair or clothing.

dis·hon·est [dis-on′ist] *adj.* **1** Not honest, as a person who lies, steals, or cheats. **2** Showing a lack of honesty: a *dishonest* act. **— dis·hon′est·ly** *adv.* **— dis·hon′es·ty** *n.*

dis·hon·or [dis-on′ər] **1** *n.* Loss of honor, respect, or good reputation; disgrace or humiliation. **2** *n.* Something that causes loss of honor or respect. **3** *v.* To bring shame to; disgrace. **4** *v.* To treat shamefully; insult. ¶1

dis·hon·or·a·ble [dis-on′ər-ə-bəl] *adj.* Not honorable; dishonest or deceitful. **— dis·hon′or·a·bly** *adv.* ¶1

dish·wash·er [dish′wosh′ər *or* dish′wôsh′ər] *n.* **1** A machine for washing dishes. **2** A person hired to wash dishes.

dis·il·lu·sion [dis′i·lōō′zhən] **1** *v.* To take a false idea, hope, etc., away from; disenchant: We were *disillusioned* to discover that the cake didn't taste as good as it looked. **2** *n.* A freeing or release from illusion. **— dis·il·lu′sion·ment** *n.*

dis·in·clined [dis′in·klīnd′] *adj.* Not inclined; not wi'ling: *disinclined* to talk. **— dis·in·cli·na·tion** [dis·in′klə·nā′shən] *n.*

dis·in·fect [dis′in·fekt′] *v.* To destroy or prevent the growth of disease germs in or on: to *disinfect* a cut with an antiseptic.

dis·in·fec·tant [dis′in·fek′tənt] *n.* A substance used to destroy disease germs.

dis·in·her·it [dis′in·her′it] *v.* To keep from inheriting; deprive of an inheritance: He *disinherited* his son, leaving his money to charity.

dis·in·te·grate [dis·in′tə·grāt] *v.* **dis·in·te·grat·ed, dis·in·te·grat·ing** To break apart into small pieces or fragments; crumble: Rain *disintegrated* the children's mud pies; His alibi began to *disintegrate* after hours of questioning. **— dis·in′te·gra′tion** *n.*

dis·in·ter [dis′in·tûr′] *v.* **dis·in·terred, dis·in·ter·ring** To dig up or remove from or as if from a grave. **— dis′in·ter′ment** *n.*

dis·in·ter·est·ed [dis·in′tər·is·tid *or* dis·in′tris·tid] *adj.* Free from prejudice or a desire for personal advantage; impartial: *disinterested* advice. ◆ *Disinterested* is sometimes inaccurately used to mean not interested or indifferent.

dis·joint [dis·joint′] **1** *v.* To take apart or separate at the joints: to *disjoint* a roasted turkey. **2** *adj.* In mathematics, indicating or describing sets in which none of the members of one set appear in any other: 1, 3, 5, 7 and 2, 4, 6, 8 and $\frac{1}{10}$, $\frac{1}{11}$, $\frac{1}{12}$ are *disjoint* sets.

dis·joint·ed [dis·join′tid] *adj.* Rambling and disorganized: a composition full of *disjointed* ideas. **— dis·joint′ed·ly** *adv.*

disk [disk] *n.* **1** Any flat, circular object, such as a plate, coin, phonograph record, etc. **2** Something appearing to have this form: The *disk* of the moon darkens the sun in an eclipse.

dis·like [dis·līk′] *v.* **dis·liked, dis·lik·ing,** *n.* **1** *v.* To have no liking for; consider disagreeable: She is fond of cats, but *dislikes* dogs. **2** *n.* A feeling of not liking; distaste.

dis·lo·cate [dis′lō·kāt] *v.* **dis·lo·cat·ed, dis·lo·cat·ing 1** To put or force out of joint, as a

bone: The fall *dislocated* his shoulder. **2** To throw into disorder: to *dislocate* the nation's economy. **— dis′lo·ca′tion** *n.*

dis·lodge [dis·loj′] *v.* **dis·lodged, dis·lodg·ing** To move or force out from a firm or settled position: The plow *dislodged* buried rocks.

dis·loy·al [dis·loi′əl] *adj.* Not loyal; betraying one's allegiance. **— dis·loy′al·ty** *n.*

dis·mal [diz′məl] *adj.* **1** Dark, gloomy, and depressing: a *dismal* day. **2** Sad and miserable. **3** Very bad: a *dismal* failure. **— dis′mal·ly** *adv.* ◆ *Dismal* comes from the Latin words *dies mali*, meaning *evil days*, from the days that were marked as unlucky on medieval calendars.

dis·man·tle [dis·man′təl] *v.* **dis·man·tled, dis·man·tling 1** To remove all equipment or furnishings from; strip bare: to *dismantle* a battleship. **2** To take apart: to *dismantle* a stove in order to clean it.

dis·may [dis·mā′] **1** *n.* A feeling of alarm, uneasiness, and confusion: The girls squealed in *dismay* when the lights went out. **2** *v.* To fill with uneasiness and alarm: a teacher *dismayed* by his students' lack of discipline.

dis·mem·ber [dis-mem′bər] *v.* **1** To cut into pieces or separate limb from limb: to *dismember* a chicken. **2** To divide into separate parts, as a conquered nation. **— dis·mem′ber·ment** *n.*

dis·miss [dis·mis′] *v.* **1** To tell or permit to leave: to *dismiss* a class. **2** To discharge from a job; fire. **3** To put aside or refuse to consider: to *dismiss* a suggestion. **4** To get rid of; forget: *Dismiss* your fears. **5** To put out of a law court without further hearing: The judge *dismissed* the case. **— dis·miss′al** *n.*

dis·mount [dis·mount′] *v.* **1** To get off or get down, as from a horse. **2** To knock off or throw down; unseat: to *dismount* an enemy horseman. **3** To take apart or remove from a support: to *dismount* a gun.

dis·o·be·di·ent [dis′ə·bē′dē·ənt] *adj.* Not obedient; refusing or failing to obey. **— dis′o·be′di·ence** *n.* **— dis′o·be′di·ent·ly** *adv.*

dis·o·bey [dis′ə·bā′] *v.* To refuse or fail to obey.

dis·or·der [dis·ôr′dər] **1** *n.* A condition of untidiness or confusion: a room left in *disorder*. **2** *n.* Unhealthy or unsound condition; illness: a digestive *disorder*. **3** *n.* Disturbance of the peace; riot; uproar. **4** *v.* To cause disorder in; upset or disarrange.

dis·or·der·ly [dis·ôr′dər·lē] *adj.* **1** Lacking neatness or order: a *disorderly* bed. **2** Undisciplined, unruly, and likely to cause trouble: *disorderly* conduct. **— dis·or′der·li·ness** *n.*

dis·or·gan·ize [dis·ôr′gən·īz] *v.* **dis·or·gan·ized, dis·or·gan·iz·ing** To throw into disorder; upset the arrangement or working of: Fog *disorganized* plane schedules. **— dis·or·gan·i·za·tion** [dis·ôr′gən·ə·zā′shən] *n.* ¶3

dis·own [dis·ōn′] *v.* To refuse to regard as one's own; deny responsibility for: The man *disowned* his only son; to *disown* one's former beliefs.

dis·par·age [dis·par′ij] *v.* **dis·par·aged, dis·par·ag·ing** To speak of as having little value or importance; belittle: to *disparage* a rival's success. — **dis·par'age·ment** *n.*

dis·par·i·ty [dis·par'ə·tē] *n., pl.* **dis·par·i·ties** A noticeable difference; inequality: a *disparity* between the wrestlers' weights.

dis·pas·sion·ate [dis·pash'ən·it] *adj.* Not affected by strong feelings or prejudices; calm and impartial. — **dis·pas'sion·ate·ly** *adv.*

dis·patch [dis·pach'] **1** *v.* To send off, as on a route or errand, to a destination: to *dispatch* a messenger; to *dispatch* buses; to *dispatch* mail. **2** *n.* A message or report, especially from an official source: a news *dispatch*. **3** *v.* To finish or get rid of quickly: to *dispatch* one's business for the day. **4** *n.* Speed and efficiency: to finish a job with *dispatch*. **5** *n.* The act or process of dispatching. **6** *v.* To kill quickly.

dis·patch·er [dis·pach'ər] *n.* A person who sends out scheduled trains, buses, etc.

dis·pel [dis·pel'] *v.* **dis·pelled, dis·pel·ling** To drive away by or as if by scattering: A breeze *dispelled* the smoke; to *dispel* fears.

dis·pen·sa·ry [dis·pen'sər·ē] *n., pl.* **dis·pen·sa·ries** A place where medicine or first-aid treatment is given free or at a low cost.

dis·pen·sa·tion [dis'pən·sā'shən] *n.* **1** The act of dispensing or dealing out; distribution: the *dispensation* of funds. **2** What is given out or distributed. **3** An official permission to disregard a rule in a particular case. **4** Management or rule, especially the ordering of earthly affairs by nature or God. **5** A system of religious laws: the Christian *dispensation*.

dis·pense [dis·pens'] *v.* **dis·pensed, dis·pens·ing 1** To give out, especially in separate portions; distribute: a machine that *dispenses* candy bars. **2** To carry out; administer: to *dispense* justice. **3** To prepare and distribute or sell (medicines). — **dispense with** To do without. — **dis·pen'ser** *n.*

dis·perse [dis·pûrs'] *v.* **dis·persed, dis·pers·ing 1** To scatter or spread in many directions: The guests *dispersed* after the party. **2** To drive away: The sun *dispersed* the mist. — **dis·per'·sal** *n.* — **dis·per·sion** [dis·pûr'zhən] *n.*

dis·pir·it [dis·pir'it] *v.* To make discouraged or depressed: *dispirited* by bad news.

dis·place [dis·plās'] *v.* **dis·placed, dis·plac·ing 1** To remove or shift from the usual or proper place: to *displace* a lock of hair. **2** To take the place of; supplant: Electric lights have *displaced* candles and oil lamps.

displaced person A person forced to

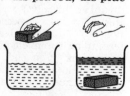

The brick has displaced the water colored red.

leave his home and country by war, famine, persecution, etc.

dis·place·ment [dis·plās'mənt] *n.* **1** The act of displacing. **2** A being displaced. **3** The amount of fluid displaced by a floating object, as by a ship in water, equal to the weight of the object itself.

dis·play [dis·plā'] **1** *v.* To show in a way that attracts notice; exhibit: to *display* goods. **2** *n.* An arrangement for public viewing: an attractive *display* of women's hats. **3** *n.* A show of something simply to attract notice: an elaborate *display* of courtesy. **4** *v.* To show openly; reveal: to *display* skill. **5** *n.* A show or exhibition: a *display* of anger. — **on display** Out for people to see; on view.

dis·please [dis·plēz'] *v.* **dis·pleased, dis·pleas·ing** To annoy, vex, or offend.

dis·pleas·ure [dis·plezh'ər] *n.* Disapproval, dislike, or an annoyed or angry feeling.

dis·port [dis·pôrt'] *v.* To amuse (oneself) or play: a kitten *disporting* itself on the rug.

dis·pos·a·ble [dis·pō'zə·bəl] *adj.* Made to be thrown away after use: *disposable* napkins.

dis·po·sal [dis·pō'zəl] *n.* **1** A getting rid of something, as by throwing away, selling, etc.: the *disposal* of garbage. **2** A settling of something: the *disposal* of a case by a judge. **3** A particular arrangement: the *disposal* of the pictures on the wall. — **at one's disposal** Freely available for one's use or service: He had time *at his disposal*.

dis·pose [dis·pōz'] *v.* **dis·posed, dis·pos·ing 1** To put in the mood or condition for; make inclined: His apology *disposes* me to forgive him. **2** To set in a certain order; arrange: to *dispose* books about the room. — **dispose of 1** To get rid of, as by throwing away, selling, etc.: to *dispose of* property. **2** To attend to or settle: Let's *dispose of* this matter first.

dis·po·si·tion [dis'pə·zish'ən] *n.* **1** A person's usual mood or spirit; nature; temperament: a sweet *disposition*. **2** A tendency or inclination: a *disposition* to loaf. **3** A particular arrangement: the *disposition* of troops in the field. **4** Settlement: *disposition* of a case in court. **5** Transfer of something to another, as by gift or sale.

dis·pos·sess [dis'pə·zes'] *v.* To deprive of possession: The debtors were *dispossessed* of their house and land. — **dis'pos·ses'sion** *n.*

dis·proof [dis·prōōf'] *n.* **1** The act of disproving. **2** Evidence that disproves something.

dis·pro·por·tion [dis'prə·pôr'shən] *n.* Lack of proportion or balance.

dis·pro·por·tion·ate [dis'prə·pôr'shən·it] *adj.* Out of proportion to something else, as in size. — **dis'pro·por'tion·ate·ly** *adv.*

dis·prove [dis·prōōv'] *v.* **dis·proved, dis·prov·ing** To prove to be false or wrong: His theory was *disproved* by the evidence.

dis·pu·tant [dis'pyōō·tənt *or* dis·pyōō'tənt] *n.* A person engaged in a dispute or argument.

add, āce, câre, pälm; end, ēqual; it, īce; odd, ōpen, ôrder; tŏŏk, pōōl; up, bûrn; ə = a in *above*, e in *sicken*, i in *possible*, o in *melon*, u in *circus*; yōō = u in *fuse*; oil; pout; check; ring; thin; this; zh in *vision*. For ¶ reference, see page 64 · HOW TO

dis·pu·ta·tion [dis′pyoo·tā′shən] *n.* **1** The act of disputing. **2** A formal debate.

dis·pute [dis·pyoot′] *v.* **dis·put·ed, dis·put·ing,** *n.* **1** *v.* To argue or challenge in debate: to *dispute* a point; to *dispute* over one's legal rights. **2** *v.* To quarrel: to *dispute* over a boundary. **3** *n.* An argument, debate, or quarrel. **4** *v.* To question the truth or justice of, as a claim. **5** *v.* To fight over or for; contest.

dis·qual·i·fy [dis·kwol′ə·fī] *v.* **dis·qual·i·fied, dis·qual·i·fy·ing 1** To make unqualified or unfit: Lack of education *disqualified* him for the job. **2** To declare not qualified, as to exercise a right or to receive a prize: to *disqualify* a winner for breaking rules.

dis·qui·et [dis·kwī′ət] **1** *v.* To make uneasy; disturb; worry. **2** *adj. use:* a *disquieting* suspicion. **3** *n.* An anxious or uneasy feeling.

dis·qui·e·tude [dis·kwī′ə·t(y)ood] *n.* Disquiet.

dis·qui·si·tion [dis′kwi·zish′ən] *n.* A long, formal writing or speech about some subject.

dis·re·gard [dis′ri·gärd′] **1** *v.* To pay no attention to; ignore: People who *disregard* traffic regulations endanger the lives of others. **2** *n.* Lack of attention or regard, especially when deliberate; neglect.

dis·re·pair [dis′ri·pâr′] *n.* A run-down condition due to neglect: The deserted house fell into *disrepair.*

dis·rep·u·ta·ble [dis·rep′yə·tə·bəl] *adj.* Having or giving a bad reputation; not respectable or decent: a *disreputable* tavern.

dis·re·pute [dis′ri·pyoot′] *n.* Low regard; disfavor: That idea is now in *disrepute.*

dis·re·spect [dis′ri·spekt′] *n.* A lack of proper respect or courtesy: to show *disrespect* for your elders.

dis·re·spect·ful [dis′ri·spekt′fəl] *adj.* Lacking in proper respect or politeness; rude. **— dis′re·spect′ful·ly** *adv.*

dis·robe [dis·rōb′] *v.* **dis·robed, dis·rob·ing** To undress.

dis·rupt [dis·rupt′] *v.* To break up or interfere with: The accident *disrupted* railway service. **— dis·rup′tion** *n.* **— dis·rup′tive** *adj.*

dis·sat·is·fac·tion [dis′sat·is·fak′shən] *n.* A displeased feeling; discontent.

dis·sat·is·fy [dis·sat′is·fī] *v.* **dis·sat·is·fied, dis·sat·is·fy·ing** To fail to satisfy or suit; leave discontented.

dis·sect [di·sekt′ *or* dī·sekt′] *v.* **1** To cut apart so as to study the structure: to *dissect* an earthworm. **2** To examine or analyze part by part: to *dissect* a problem. **— dis·sec′tion** *n.*

dis·sem·ble [di·sem′bəl] *v.* **dis·sem·bled, dis·sem·bling 1** To cover or disguise (true thoughts, feelings, or intentions): He *dissembled* his rage with an easy laugh. **2** To be a hypocrite. **3** To pretend in order to deceive; feign. **— dis·sem′bler** *n.*

dis·sem·i·nate [di·sem′ə·nāt] *v.* **dis·sem·i·nat·ed, dis·sem·i·nat·ing 1** To scatter, as seeds. **2** To spread widely, as ideas, news, or knowledge. **— dis·sem′i·na′tion** *n.*

dis·sen·sion [di·sen′shən] *n.* Quarrelsome disagreement, often within a group; conflict.

dis·sent [di·sent′] **1** *v.* To hold or express a different opinion or belief; disagree: One justice *dissented* from the Supreme Court decision. **2** *n.* Difference of opinion; disagreement: religious *dissent.* **— dis·sent′er** *n.* ◆ See DECENT.

dis·sent·ing [di·sen′ting] *adj.* Expressing disagreement: a *dissenting* opinion.

dis·ser·ta·tion [dis′ər·tā′shən] *n.* **1** A long, formal treatment of some subject. **2** A thesis written for the university degree of doctor.

dis·ser·vice [dis·sûr′vis] *n.* A bad turn, especially where a service was intended; harm: You did the team a *disservice* by playing with an injury.

dis·sev·er [di·sev′ər] *v.* To separate into parts; divide; sever.

dis·sim·i·lar [di·sim′ə·lər] *adj.* Not similar or alike; different: *dissimilar* styles. **— dis·sim·i·lar·i·ty** [di·sim′ə·lar′ə·tē] *n.*

dis·sim·u·la·tion [di·sim′yə·lā′shən] *n.* False pretense; hypocrisy.

dis·si·pate [dis′ə·pāt] *v.* **dis·si·pat·ed, dis·si·pat·ing 1** To break up and scatter or dissolve: The sun *dissipated* the mist; Her grief gradually *dissipated.* **2** To use up or spend foolishly; waste, as one's energies or money. **3** To indulge in harmful pleasures.

dis·si·pat·ed [dis′ə·pā′tid] *adj.* Weakened in character and health from indulging in harmful pleasures: a *dissipated* young man.

dis·si·pa·tion [dis′ə·pā′shən] *n.* **1** Too much indulgence in harmful pleasures. **2** Useless or foolish waste. **3** A scattering or dissolving.

dis·so·ci·ate [di·sō′sē·āt *or* di·sō′shē·āt] *v.* **dis·so·ci·at·ed, dis·so·ci·at·ing** To break the connection with; separate: to *dissociate* oneself from a club. **— dis·so′ci·a′tion** *n.*

dis·sol·u·ble [di·sol′yə·bəl] *adj.* Capable of being dissolved or decomposed.

dis·so·lute [dis′ə·loot] *adj.* Lacking moral principles or restraint: a *dissolute* life.

dis·so·lu·tion [dis′ə·loo′shən] *n.* **1** A breaking up, ending, or dissolving: the *dissolution* of a marriage. **2** Separation into parts; disintegration. **3** Decay or death.

dis·solve [di·zolv′] *v.* **dis·solved, dis·solv·ing 1** To make or become liquid; form a solution with a liquid: Salt *dissolves* in water. **2** To seem to melt from emotion: to *dissolve* in tears. **3** To break up or end: to *dissolve* parliament. **4** To fade away or vanish.

dis·so·nance [dis′ə·nəns] *n.* **1** A mingling together or combination of sounds that are not in harmony; discord. **2** Any lack of agreement.

dis·so·nant [dis′ə·nənt] *adj.* **1** Not in harmony; clashing: *dissonant* sounds. **2** Not in agreement; conflicting.

dis·suade [di·swād′] *v.* **dis·suad·ed, dis·suad·ing** To persuade not to take some step or do something: He was *dissuaded* from quitting his job by the promise of a raise.

dis·taff [dis′taf] *n.* A stick from which flax or wool was drawn off in spinning by hand or using an old-fashioned spinning wheel.

distaff side The maternal or female side of a family.

dis·tance [dis′təns] *n., v.* **dis·tanced, dis·tanc·ing 1** *n.* The extent of space between two points: to walk a *distance* of three miles. **2** *n.* A point or place far away: We could barely make out a steeple in the *distance.* **3** *n.* The condition of being far off. **4** *n.* The interval between points of time. **5** *v.* To leave behind, as in a race; excel. **— keep one's distance** To be unfriendly; hold aloof.

Twisting fibers from a distaff onto a spindle

dis·tant [dis′tənt] *adj.* **1** Far off or remote in space or time: a *distant* star; a *distant* era. **2** Away: She lives 15 miles *distant.* **3** Not closely related: *distant* kin. **4** Unfriendly or reserved; aloof. **— dis′tant·ly** *adv.*

dis·taste [dis·tāst′] *n.* Dislike.

dis·taste·ful [dis·tāst′fəl] *adj.* Unpleasant, disagreeable, or offensive: a *distasteful* duty.

dis·tem·per [dis·tem′pər] *n.* A contagious disease of dogs and other animals.

dis·tend [dis·tend′] *v.* To stretch out; expand.

dis·till or **dis·til** [dis·til′] *v.* **dis·tilled, dis·till·ing 1** To heat (a liquid or solid) until it gives off a vapor that is then condensed by cooling into a purer liquid form. Distilled water is produced in this way. **2** To obtain by distilling: to *distill* whisky from fermented rye. **3** To find and draw out, as if by distilling: to *distill* the moral from a fable.

dis·til·la·tion [dis′tə·lā′shən] *n.* **1** The act or process of distilling. **2** Anything obtained by distilling.

dis·til·ler [dis·til′ər] *n.* A person or firm that makes alcoholic liquors by distilling.

dis·til·ler·y [dis·til′ər·ē] *n., pl.* **dis·til·ler·ies** A place where alcoholic liquors are made by distilling.

dis·tinct [dis·tingkt′] *adj.* **1** Not alike or not the same; clearly different; separate: The chapter dealt with four *distinct* topics. **2** Easy to perceive or understand; sharp and clear: a *distinct* outline or scent; a *distinct* difference. **3** Definite: a *distinct* possibility. **— dis·tinct′ly** *adv.* **— dis·tinct′ness** *n.*

dis·tinc·tion [dis·tingk′shən] *n.* **1** A difference that may be distinguished: a *distinction* between two brands of soap. **2** Attention to differences: All are invited without *distinction.* **3** The act of distinguishing. **4** Exceptional merit; honor: to serve one's country with *distinction.* **5** A mark of honor, as a medal.

dis·tinc·tive [dis·tingk′tiv] *adj.* Serving to mark out as different or special; characteristic: a *distinctive* style of writing. **— dis·tinc′tive·ly** *adv.*

dis·tin·guish [dis·ting′gwish] *v.* **1** To mark as different, or characterize: A very long neck *distinguishes* the giraffe. **2** To recognize as different: to *distinguish* one twin from the other. **3** To recognize or point out a difference: to *distinguish* between truth and falsehood. **4** To perceive clearly or make out: He could not *distinguish* the shape in the fog. **5** To bring fame or honor upon: He *distinguished* himself in battle. **— dis·tin′guish·a·ble** *adj.*

dis·tin·guished [dis·ting′gwisht] *adj.* **1** Famous; prominent: a *distinguished* author. **2** Having the look of a notable person; dignified.

dis·tort [dis·tôrt′] *v.* **1** To twist or bend out of the normal shape: Rage *distorted* his features. **2** To alter in a way that creates a false impression: to *distort* the facts.

dis·tor·tion [dis·tôr′shən] *n.* **1** The act of distorting: a *distortion* of the facts. **2** A distorted condition. **3** Something distorted.

dis·tract [dis·trakt′] *v.* **1** To draw (the mind, etc.) from something claiming attention: The radio *distracts* her from her homework. **2** To confuse or bother, as by dividing the attention. **3** To amuse; entertain; divert.

dis·trac·tion [dis·trak′shən] *n.* **1** The act of distracting. **2** A being distracted. **3** Something that draws the attention away, as an amusement: The movie was a pleasant *distraction* after the test. **4** A condition of being extremely upset; mental distress: Pain was driving him to *distraction.*

dis·traught [dis·trôt′] *adj.* Extremely upset; crazed: *distraught* with fear and worry.

dis·tress [dis·tres′] **1** *n.* Extreme suffering or its cause; pain; trouble. **2** *v.* To cause to suffer, worry, or be sorry: Her child's illness *distressed* her. **3** *n.* A condition of needing help badly: a ship in *distress.*

dis·trib·ute [dis·trib′yo͞ot] *v.* **dis·trib·ut·ed, dis·trib·ut·ing 1** To divide and deal out in shares; hand out: *Distribute* the drawing materials to the class. **2** To scatter or spread out: Animals are *distributed* over the earth. **3** To divide and classify or arrange: to *distribute* letters throughout a file.

A distraught woman

dis·tri·bu·tion [dis′trə·byo͞o′shən] *n.* **1** The act of distributing: the *distribution* of gifts. **2** The way in which something is distributed: an even *distribution.* **3** Something distributed.

dis·trib·u·tive [dis·trib′yə·tiv] *adj.* **1** Having

add, **ā**ce, c**â**re, p**ä**lm;   **e**nd, **ē**qual;   **i**t, **ī**ce;   **o**dd, **ō**pen, **ô**rder;   t**o͞o**k, p**o͞o**l;   **u**p, b**û**rn;
ə = a in *above*, e in *sicken*, i in *possible*, o in *melon*, u in *circus*;   **y**o͞o = u in *fuse*;   **oi**l;   p**ou**t;
check;   **r**ing;   **th**in;   **th**is;   **zh** in *vision.*   For ¶ reference, see page 64 · HOW TO

to do with distribution. **2** Singling out separate individuals. *Each* in "Each boy gets a gift" is a distributive adjective. **3** Indicating an operation that when performed on the sum of a set of numbers gives a result equal to the sum of the results of performing the operation on each member of the set. Multiplication is distributive in respect to addition, since $2 \times (3 + 4) = (2 \times 3) + (2 \times 4)$.

dis·trib·u·tor [dis·trib′yə·tər] *n.* **1** A person, thing, or group that distributes something or sells merchandise. **2** In a gasoline engine, a device that connects each of the spark plugs into an electric circuit in turn.

dis·trict [dis′trikt] *n.* **1** A particular region or locality. **2** An area, as within a city or state, marked out for a particular purpose: a school *district;* an election *district.*

district attorney A lawyer who acts for the government in a district. He prosecutes persons accused of crime.

District of Columbia A Federal district in the eastern part of the U.S. that is wholly occupied by the capital city of Washington.

dis·trust [dis·trust′] **1** *n.* Lack of trust or confidence; suspicion; doubt. **2** *v.* To feel no trust for; suspect. **— dis·trust′ful** *adj.*

dis·turb [dis·tûrb′] *v.* **1** To break in on or interrupt, especially with noise or disorder: to *disturb* someone's rest. **2** To bother or annoy. **3** To worry, trouble, or upset: The bad news *disturbed* her. **4** To upset the order of: A leaping trout *disturbed* the calm pool.

dis·tur·bance [dis·tûr′bəns] *n.* **1** The act of disturbing. **2** A being disturbed. **3** Something that disturbs. **4** Confusion; tumult; commotion.

dis·un·ion [dis·yōōn′yən] *n.* **1** Division or separation. **2** Disagreement or conflict.

dis·u·nite [dis′yōō·nīt′] *v.* **dis·u·nit·ed, dis·u·nit·ing** To break the union or harmony of; divide; separate.

dis·use [dis·yōōs′] *n.* A condition of not being used; lack of use: Some words fall into *disuse.*

ditch [dich] **1** *n.* A long, narrow hole dug in the ground, often used as a channel for water; trench. **2** *v.* To dig a ditch around or in. **3** *v.* To run, send, or drive into a ditch. **4** *v. slang* To get rid of.

dith·er [dith′ər] *n.* A condition of nervous excitement or agitation: to be in a *dither.*

dit·to [dit′ō] *n., pl.* **dit·tos,** *adv.* **1** *n.* The same thing (as something just mentioned). **2** *n.* A ꞏark (") placed beneath something written to show that it is to be repeated. Example:

     2 dozen cookies at $.60 a dozen
     1   "   eggs   " .73 "

3 *adv.* As written above or as mentioned before. ◆ *Ditto* comes directly from an Italian word meaning *said.*

dit·ty [dit′ē] *n., pl.* **dit·ties** A short, simple song or poem meant for singing.

di·van [di·van′ *or* dī′van] *n.* A long, low sofa or couch, often without arm rests or back.

dive [dīv] *v.* **dived** or **dove, dived, div·ing,** *n.* **1** *v.* To plunge into water, especially head-first. **2** *n.* A plunge, as into water. **3** *v.* To plunge into something suddenly or deeply, as with the body or mind: to *dive* into bed. **4** *v.* To plunge sharply downward, as an airplane. **5** *n.* A sudden, steep descent. **6** *n. informal* A tavern, nightclub, etc., considered cheap and vulgar.

div·er [dī′vər] *n.* **1** A person who dives into water. **2** Someone who works under water, often wearing a waterproof suit and a helmet supplied with air. **3** A bird that dives, as a loon.

di·verge [di·vûrj′] *v.* **di·verged, di·verg·ing** **1** To branch off, lie, or move in different directions from a common point: Two paths *diverged* in a forest. **2** To depart from a given or normal course. **3** To differ, as in opinion.

di·ver·gence [di·vûr′jəns] *n.* **1** A moving apart; difference: a serious *divergence* of opinion. **2** Departure from a set course or standard. **— di·ver′gent** *adj.*

Diverging roads

di·vers [dī′vərz] *adj.* Several or various.

di·verse [di·vûrs′ *or* dī′vûrs] *adj.* Distinctly different; not alike. **— di·verse′ly** *adv.*

di·ver·si·fy [di·vûr′sə·fī] *v.* **di·ver·si·fied, di·ver·si·fy·ing** To give variety to, as by adding different things or changing; vary: to *diversify* one's meals with new foods.

di·ver·sion [di·vûr′zhən] *n.* **1** The act of diverting or turning aside: the *diversion* of a stream into a new channel. **2** An amusement, game, or pastime as a change or relaxation.

di·ver·si·ty [di·vûr′sə·tē] *n., pl.* **di·ver·si·ties** **1** A being unlike; difference: The two talked despite *diversity* of language. **2** Variety: He has a *diversity* of interests.

di·vert [di·vûrt′] *v.* **1** To turn aside: to *divert* someone from a purpose or goal. **2** To amuse or entertain: The game *diverted* us. **3** *adj. use:* a *diverting* comedy.

di·vest [di·vest′] *v.* **1** To strip, as of clothing: He *divested* himself of his raincoat and boots. **2** To deprive, as of rights or possessions: The king was *divested* of his power.

di·vide [di·vīd′] *v.* **di·vid·ed, di·vid·ing,** *n.* **1** *v.* To split or separate into parts: to *divide* a room with a partition. **2** *v.* To find a number by which one given number must be multiplied to get (a second given number). Thus, 6 divided by 2 equals 3 because $3 \times 2 = 6$. **3** *v.* To cause to be or keep apart: A hedge *divides* the two yards. **4** *n.* A ridge or area of high land between two regions drained by separate river systems. **5** *v.* To split up into opposed sides: The jury *divided* on the question of his guilt. **6** *v.* To separate into groups; classify: These jewels are *divided* into two kinds, the real ones and the false ones. **7** *v.* To give out portions of; distribute: to *divide* candy among children.

div·i·dend [div′ə·dend] *n.* **1** In mathematics,

a number that is to be divided by another number. In 9 ÷ 3, 9 is the dividend. **2** A sum of money to be distributed, as profits to be divided among the owners of a company. **3** One share of such a sum.

di·vid·er [di·vī′dər] *n.* **1** A person or thing that divides. **2** (*pl.*) A pair of compasses used for measuring or marking off short intervals.

A room divider

div·i·na·tion [div′ə·nā′shən] *n.* **1** The act of foretelling the future or finding out secret knowledge, as by interpreting omens or using magic. **2** A prophecy. **3** A clever guess.

di·vine [di·vīn′] *adj., n., v.* **di·vined, di·vin·ing 1** *adj.* Of, coming from, or having to do with God or a god: *divine* might; *divine* inspiration. **2** *adj.* Devoted to God or a god; religious: *divine* worship. **3** *n.* A clergyman or theologian. **4** *adj.* Almost godlike in excellence or perfection: *divine* singing. **5** *v.* To foretell or discover through magic, the interpretation of omens, etc. **6** *v.* To know instinctively; guess: From her guilty blush her mother *divined* the truth. **— di·vine′ly** *adv.* **— di·vin′er** *n.*

diving bell A container open at the bottom and supplied with air. Men work in it under water.

divining rod A forked twig believed to bend down when carried over water, oil, or ore.

Divining rod

di·vin·i·ty [di·vin′ə·tē] *n., pl.* **di·vin·i·ties 1** The quality of being divine; divine nature. **2** (*written* **the Divinity**) God. **3** A god or goddess; deity. **4** The study of religion; theology.

di·vis·i·ble [di·viz′ə·bəl] *adj.* **1** Capable of being divided. **2** That can be divided by a certain number and leave no remainder: 9 is *divisible* by 3. **— di·vis·i·bil·i·ty** [di·viz′ə·bil′ə·tē] *n.*

di·vi·sion [di·vizh′ən] *n.* **1** The act of dividing; separation. **2** A divided condition. **3** In mathematics, the process of determining the number which, used as a multiplier of a given number, will lead to another given number. When 15 is divided by 3, division determines the number 5, for 5 × 3 = 15. **4** Something that divides, as a boundary line. **5** A separate part, section, or unit: the research *division* of a company. **6** A major unit of an army, larger than a regiment.

7 A difference in opinion or interest; disagreement. **— di·vi′sion·al** *adj.*

division sign The sign (÷) placed between two numbers or quantities to show that the first is to be divided by the second, as 8 ÷ 2 = 4.

di·vi·sor [di·vī′zər] *n.* A number by which another number is divided. In 8 ÷ 2, 2 is the divisor.

di·vorce [di·vôrs′] *n., v.* **di·vorced, di·vorc·ing 1** *n.* The ending of a marriage by process of law. **2** *v.* To free legally from the marriage relationship: They were *divorced*. **3** *v.* To free oneself from (one's husband or wife) by divorce. **4** *v.* To separate: He could not *divorce* his mind from his emotions. **5** *n.* Total separation: the *divorce* of body and soul at death.

di·vor·cee [di·vôr′sē′] *n.* A divorced person, especially a woman.

di·vot [div′ət] *n.* A piece of turf torn from the sod by the stroke of a golf club.

di·vulge [di·vulj′] *v.* **di·vulged, di·vulg·ing** To tell; reveal; disclose: to *divulge* military secrets to the enemy.

Dix·ie [dik′sē] *n.* The southern states of the U.S., especially the Confederacy.

diz·zy [diz′ē] *adj.* **diz·zi·er, diz·zi·est,** *v.* **diz·zied, diz·zy·ing 1** *adj.* Affected by a whirling sensation in the head and apt to weave about or fall; giddy: Swinging makes her *dizzy*. **2** *adj.* Causing a dizzy feeling: a *dizzy* height. **3** *v.* To make dizzy: Dancing around *dizzied* her. **— diz′zi·ly** *adv.* **— diz′zi·ness** *n.*

DNA Abbreviation of DEOXYRIBONUCLEIC ACID.

Dnie·per [nē′pər] *n.* A river in the sw Soviet Union, flowing into the Black Sea.

do[1] [do͞o] *v.* **did, done, do·ing 1** To carry out in action; perform: He *did* his duty. **2** To work at: What does she *do* for a living? **3** To deal with or take care of: Who's going to *do* the dishes? **4** To finish or complete: He has *done* the exercises. **5** To cause or produce; bring about: He went about *doing* good. **6** To put forth: She *did* her best. **7** To get along or behave oneself: How did Tom *do* at school? **8** To give; render: You aren't *doing* him justice. **9** To be enough or be right; serve: Two pounds of apples will *do*. **— do away with 1** To get rid of; throw away. **2** To kill. **— do up 1** To wrap up, as a package. **2** To roll up or arrange, as the hair. **— have to do with** To deal with or concern. **— make do** To get along with whatever is available. ◆ Apart from its use as a main verb, *do* is often used as a helping verb in questions and negative statements: *Do* you *want* it? I *did*n't *want* it. It is also sometimes used in affirmative statements, where it is usually spoken with extra heavy stress: I *did want* it! *Do* may also substitute for another verb: He will go home when I *do*.

do[2] [dō] *n.* In music, a syllable used to represent

the first tone of a major scale or the third tone of a minor scale, or in a fixed system the tone C.

dob·bin [dob′in] *n.* A slow, good-natured horse.

doc·ile [dos′(ə)l] *adj.* Easy to teach, manage, or handle; obedient: a *docile* pupil. — **doc′ile·ly** *adj.* — **do·cil·i·ty** [do·sil′ə·tē] *n.*

dock[1] [dok] **1** *n.* A platform built beside or out from a shore where ships or boats tie up; wharf; pier. **2** *n.* The water between two wharves. **3** *v.* To bring or come into a dock: to *dock* a ship; The ship *docked* at the pier. **4** *n.* Short for DRY DOCK. **5** *n.* A raised platform for loading trucks, freight cars, etc.

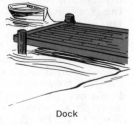
Dock

dock[2] [dok] *v.* **1** To cut off the end of (a tail). **2** To take away from: to *dock* one's wages.

dock[3] [dok] *n.* A weed with bitter or sour leaves, sometimes used as a food or seasoning.

dock[4] [dok] *n.* An enclosed space in a law court where an accused person stands or sits.

dock·age [dok′ij] *n.* **1** A charge for docking a ship. **2** Facilities for docking a ship.

dock·et [dok′it] **1** *n.* A schedule listing cases to be tried in court. **2** *n.* Any schedule of things to be done or dealt with; agenda. **3** *v.* To enter in a docket. **4** *n.* A tag or label put on a package, listing contents, directions, etc. **5** *v.* To put such a tag or label on.

dock·yard [dok′yärd′] *n.* A waterfront area where ships are built, repaired, or fitted out.

doc·tor [dok′tər] **1** *n.* A person trained and licensed to treat disease, illness, or injury, and to preserve health. **2** *v. informal* To try to cure or heal by treatment: to *doctor* a cut. **3** *n.* A person who holds one of the highest degrees awarded by a university. **Doctor of Philosophy** is such a degree. **4** *v. informal* To tamper with or alter: to *doctor* evidence.

doc·trine [dok′trin] *n.* Something taught, as a principle or belief of a religious or political group. — **doc′tri·nal** [dok′trə·nəl] *adj.*

doc·u·ment [*n.* dok′yə·mənt, *v.* dok′yə·ment′] **1** *n.* A written or printed paper that gives information or serves as evidence of something. Licenses and maps are documents. **2** *v.* To prove by documents. — **doc′u·men·ta′tion** *n.*

doc·u·men·ta·ry [dok′yə·men′tər·ē] *adj., n., pl.* **doc·u·men·ta·ries 1** *adj.* Consisting of or based on documents: *documentary* proof. **2** *adj.* Dealing with facts rather than telling an invented story. **3** *n.* A movie, novel, etc., that deals with factual rather than invented material.

dod·der [dod′ər] *v.* To tremble or walk in a feeble, unsteady way, as from old age.

dodge [doj] *v.* **dodged, dodg·ing,** *n.* **1** *v.* To move aside suddenly. **2** *v.* To get out of the path of: Jaywalkers *dodged* the cars. **3** *n.* An act of dodging. **4** *v.* To avoid by tricks or cunning: to *dodge* a duty. **5** *n.* A trick used to avoid or deceive. — **dodg′er** *n.*

do·do [dō′dō] *n., pl.* **do·does** or **do·dos 1** A large, heavy, pigeonlike bird that could not fly and no longer exists. **2** *informal* A silly, stupid, or senile person. ◆ *Dodo* comes from a Portuguese word meaning *silly* or *stupid.*

doe [dō] *n.* The female of the deer, antelope, rabbit, kangaroo, and certain other animals.

do·er [dōō′ər] *n.* A person who does or acts: a *doer* of deeds; He is a *doer,* not a thinker.

does [duz] *v.* The third person form of DO, in the present tense, used with *he, she, it,* and singular nouns: *Does* your dog bite?

doe·skin [dō′skin′] *n.* **1** The skin of the female deer. **2** Soft leather made from this. **3** A heavy, smooth, woolen cloth.

does·n't [duz′ənt] Does not.

doff [dof] *v.* **1** To take off (the hat) as a greeting. **2** To take off, as clothing.

dog [dôg] *n., v.* **dogged, dog·ging 1** *n.* A tame, flesh-eating animal kept as a pet or used to guard, guide, hunt, herd, etc. ◆ Adj., *canine.* **2** *v.* To follow like a hunting dog; hound: Misfortune *dogged* his steps. **3** *n.* A device for gripping or holding logs, etc.

Man doffing his hat

dog days The hot, sultry days of July and early August when the heat causes discomfort.

doge [dōj] *n.* The elected chief magistrate in the former republics of Venice and Genoa.

dog-eared [dôg′ird′] *adj.* Having the corners of the pages turned down: said about a book.

dog·fish [dôg′fish′] *n., pl.* **dog·fish** or **dog·fish·es** A type of small shark.

dog·ged [dôg′id] *adj.* Continuing stubbornly despite difficulties; persistent: *dogged* determination. — **dog′ged·ly** *adv.* — **dog′ged·ness** *n.*

A dog-eared book

dog·ger·el [dôg′ər·əl] *n.* Badly-written verse, often having singsong rhythm.

do·gie [dō′gē] *n.* A motherless or stray calf: used chiefly in the western U.S.

dog·ma [dôg′mə] *n., pl.* **dog·mas 1** Teaching to be taken as true on the word of one's church or other authority. **2** Any unquestioned belief.

dog·mat·ic [dôg·mat′ik] *adj.* **1** Holding or asserting opinions as if one were the final authority. **2** Stated without proof or evidence. **3** Having to do with dogma. — **dog·mat′i·cal·ly** *adv.*

Dog Star Another name for the star SIRIUS.

dog·trot [dôg′trot′] *n.* A regular, easy trot.

dog·wood [dôg′wŏŏd′] *n.* A tree whose small flower is enclosed by four white or pink petallike leaves, notched at the tips.

doi·ly [doi′lē] *n., pl.* **doi·lies** A thin, ornamental mat, often lace, used under a dish or vase.

do·ings [doō′ingz] *n.pl.* Activities; events.

Doily

dol·drums [dol′drəmz *or* dōl′drəmz] *n.pl.* **1** The parts of the ocean near the equator where there is often little or no wind. **2** A dull, sad, or bored condition of mind: in the *doldrums*.

dole [dōl] *n., v.* **doled, dol·ing 1** *n.* The giving or distributing of money, food, or clothing to the poor. **2** *n.* Anything given out or distributed, as money or food for the poor. In Great Britain, government relief for the poor and unemployed is called *dole*. **3** *v.* To distribute in small quantities: to *dole* out cookies.

dole·ful [dōl′fəl] *adj.* Sorrowful; mournful. **— dole′ful·ly** *adv.*

doll [dol] *n.* **1** A toy made to look like a baby or a grown-up person. **2** A pretty or adorable child, especially a little girl. **— doll up** *informal* To dress stylishly or formally: We all *dolled up* for the wedding. ◆ *Doll* comes from a nickname for Dorothy.

dol·lar [dol′ər] *n.* **1** 100 cents, the basic unit of money in the United States. Symbol: $. **2** A silver coin or a piece of paper currency equal to 100 cents. **3** A similar unit of money in certain other countries: the Canadian or Mexican *dollar*.

dol·ly [dol′ē] *n.* **1** A doll: a child's term. **2** A low, flat frame set on small wheels or rollers, used for moving heavy loads.

do·lor·ous [dō′lər·əs *or* dol′ər·əs] *adj.* **1** Very sad or mournful: *dolorous* moaning. **2** Wretched and painful: a *dolorous* condition. **— do′lor·ous·ly** *adv.*

dol·phin [dol′fin] *n.* **1** A salt-water mammal, related to the whale but smaller, having a snout like a bird's beak. **2** A large, edible, oceanic fish which changes colors when taken from the water.

Dolphin, 6–12 ft. long

dolt [dōlt] *n.* A stupid person; blockhead; dunce. **— dolt′ish** *adj.*

-dom A suffix meaning: **1** The realm of, as in *kingdom*, the realm of a king. **2** The position or rank of, as in *earldom*, the position or rank of an earl. **3** The state or condition of being, as in *freedom*, the state or condition of being free. **4** The whole group or class of, as in *officialdom*, the whole group or class of officials.

do·main [dō·mān′] *n.* **1** A land or territory owned or controlled by a government or ruler: the king's *domain*. **2** Any field of action, interest, or knowledge: the *domain* of chemistry.

dome [dōm] *n.* **1** A round roof shaped somewhat like an upside-down cup or hemisphere. **2** Something like a dome in shape: the *dome* of a hill.

Dome

do·mes·tic [də·mes′tik] **1** *adj.* Of or having to do with the home or family: *domestic* affairs. **2** *adj.* Fond of home and family affairs: a *domestic* person. **3** *n.* A household servant. **4** *adj.* Tame: *domestic* animals. **5** *adj.* Produced in or having to do with one's own country: *domestic* goods; *domestic* laws.

do·mes·ti·cate [də·mes′tə·kāt] *v.* **do·mes·ti·cat·ed, do·mes·ti·cat·ing 1** To tame or cultivate for domestic use: to *domesticate* a wild animal or plant. **2** To make happy with domestic life: to *domesticate* a husband. **3** To make feel at ease or at home: to *domesticate* a foreigner.

do·mes·tic·i·ty [dō′mes·tis′ə·tē] *n., pl.* **do·mes·tic·i·ties 1** Life at home or with one's family. **2** Devotion to home and family. **3** (*pl.*) Domestic matters: She found the *domesticities* of her new life very tiring.

dom·i·cile [dom′ə·sīl *or* dom′ə·səl] *n., v.* **dom·i·ciled, dom·i·cil·ing 1** *n.* A person's home or residence. **2** *n.* A person's legal residence. **3** *v.* To provide with a home or residence: The soldiers were *domiciled* in that old castle.

dom·i·nance [dom′ə·nəns] *n.* The state or condition of being dominant; authority; control.

dom·i·nant [dom′ə·nənt] **1** *adj.* Most powerful, influential, or important: a *dominant* nation; a *dominant* place in history. **2** *adj.* Higher than or rising above its surroundings: a *dominant* cliff. **3** *n.* The fifth note of a musical scale: D is the *dominant* in the key of G.

dom·i·nate [dom′ə·nāt] *v.* **dom·i·nat·ed, dom·i·nat·ing 1** To control or rule over: to *dominate* one's students. **2** To tower over; loom above. **— dom′i·na′tion** *n.*

dom·i·neer [dom′ə·nir′] *v.* To rule in an arrogant or insolent manner; bully.

dom·i·neer·ing [dom′ə·nir′ing] *adj.* Overbearing; tyrannical; bullying.

Do·min·i·can [də·min′ə·kən] **1** *adj.* Of or having to do with Saint Dominic or the religious order founded by him. **2** *n.* A Dominican friar or nun. **3** *adj.* Of or from the Dominican Republic. **4** *n.* A person born in or a citizen of the Dominican Republic.

Dominican Republic A country in the eastern part of Hispaniola, an island of the West Indies.

dom·i·nie [dom′ə·nē] *n.* **1** *U.S. informal* A clergyman. **2** A Scottish word for a schoolmaster.

do·min·ion [də·min'yən] *n.* **1** Supreme power or authority; rule. **2** A country under a particular government. **3** (*often written* **Dominion**) A self-governing member of the British Commonwealth of Nations. **— the Dominion** Canada.

dom·i·no [dom'ə·nō] *n., pl.* **dom·i·noes** or **dom·i·nos** **1** A small, rectangular piece of wood, plastic, etc., one side of which is either blank or marked with dots. **2** (*pl., used with a singular verb*) A game played with a set of these pieces. **3** A small, half mask worn over the eyes.

don[1] [don] *v.* **donned, don·ning** To put on (a piece or pieces of clothing).

don[2] [don] *n.* **1** (*written* **Don**) A Spanish title of respect used before a man's first name; Sir; Mr.: *Don Diego.* **2** *informal* In Great Britain, the head of a college or a tutor in one.

Don [don] *n.* A river in the sw Soviet Union.

do·nate [dō'nāt *or* dō·nāt'] *v.* **do·nat·ed, do·nat·ing** To give, as to a charity. ◆ *Donate* comes from the noun *donation.*

Don·a·tel·lo [don'ə·tel'ō] *n.*, 1386–1466, Italian sculptor.

do·na·tion [dō·nā'shən] *n.* **1** The act of giving, as to a charity. **2** A gift or contribution.

done [dun] **1** Past participle of DO: We have *done* the job. **2** *adj.* Completed; finished. **3** *adj.* Cooked enough. **4** *adj. informal* Tired out; exhausted.

Don Juan [don hwän'] In Spanish legend, a nobleman famous for his many love affairs.

don·key [dong'kē *or* dung'kē] *n., pl.* **don·keys** **1** A long-eared animal related to the horse but smaller and used throughout the world as a beast of burden. It is also called an ass. **2** A stupid or stubborn person.

do·nor [dō'nər] *n.* A person who gives or donates something.

Don Quix·ote [don kē·hō'tē *or* don kwik'sət] The hero of a Spanish novel by Cervantes. He is an idealistic but often foolish knight.

don't [dōnt] Do not.

doo·dle [dōōd'(ə)l] *v.* **doo·dled, doo·dling,** *n.* **1** *v.* To draw or scribble aimlessly, without thinking of what one is doing. **2** *n.* Something drawn or scribbled in this manner. **— doo'dler** *n.*

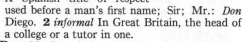

Doodles on a letter

doom [dōōm] **1** *n.* A terrible or tragic fate or destiny: It was his *doom* to die young. **2** *n.* Death or ruin: A sense of *doom* came over us. **3** *n.* A severe judgment or punishment:

The judge pronounced the prisoner's *doom.* **4** *v.* To condemn to a terrible fate: He was *doomed* from birth. **5** *adj. use:* a *doomed* man. ◆ *Doom* comes from an Old English word meaning *judgment.*

dooms·day [dōōmz'dā'] *n.* **1** Another name for JUDGMENT DAY. **2** Any day of final judgment.

door [dôr] *n.* **1** A hinged, sliding, folding, or rotating structure, as of wood, used for closing or opening an entrance to a house, room, car, etc. **2** A doorway. **3** A house or building: three *doors* down the street. **4** A way or means of achieving something: the *door* to success.

door·knob [dôr'nob'] *n.* A handle for opening a door.

door·man [dôr'man'] *n., pl.* **door·men** [dôr'men'] A man at the entrance of a hotel, apartment house, etc., to guard it or to help people coming in or going out.

door mat A mat at an entrance for wiping the shoes.

door·step [dôr'step'] *n.* A step up to an outside door.

door·way [dôr'wā'] *n.* **1** An opening, as into a room or building, that a door closes. **2** Any means of getting into or to: the *doorway* to fame.

door·yard [dôr'yärd'] *n.* A yard in front of or about the door of a house.

Doorman

dope [dōp] *n., v.* **doped, dop·ing 1** *n. slang* A stupid person. **2** *n. slang* A drug or narcotic. **3** *v. slang* To give a drug or narcotic to. **4** *n.* A thick lubricant, varnish, etc. **5** *n. slang* Information; news. **— dope out** *slang* To plan or figure out: to *dope out* a new idea for the party.

Dop·pler effect [dop'lər] The change in the frequency of a sound wave or light wave as the distance between the source of the waves and the observer increases or decreases.

Dor·ic [dôr'ik] *adj.* Of or having to do with the oldest and simplest of the three types of ancient Greek architecture.

dor·mant [dôr'mənt] *adj.* **1** Asleep or as if asleep. **2** Inactive: a *dormant* volcano.

dor·mer [dôr'mər] *n.* **1** A small, roofed structure extending out from a sloping roof and containing an upright window. **2** The window. It is often called a dormer window.

dor·mi·to·ry [dôr'mə·tôr'ē] *n., pl.* **dor·mi·to·ries 1** A building, as at a school or college, that has many rooms for sleeping. **2** A large room with many beds for sleeping.

Dormer window

dor·mouse [dôr'mous'] *n., pl.* **dor·mice** [dôr'mīs'] A small European animal that is related to the mouse but lives in trees like a squirrel.

dor·sal [dôr′səl] *adj.* Having to do with, on, or near the back.

do·ry [dôr′ē] *n., pl.* **do·ries** A flat-bottomed rowboat having high sides and well adapted to rough weather, used by fishermen.

dos·age [dō′sij] *n.* **1** A specified amount of medicine to be given or taken: *a dosage of one tablespoon every hour.* **2** The giving of medicine in certain quantities or doses.

dose [dōs] *n., v.* **dosed, dos·ing 1** *n.* A specified amount of medicine or other treatment to be given at one time. **2** *v.* To give a dose or doses to. **3** *n.* A particular amount of anything, especially something unpleasant: *a large dose of studying.*

dost [dust] A form of DO used with *thou*: seldom used today.

Dos·to·ev·ski [dôs′tô·yef′skē], **Feodor,** 1821–1881, Russian novelist.

dot [dot] *n., v.* **dot·ted, dot·ting 1** *n.* A round, usually very small mark or spot. **2** *v.* To mark with or as with a dot or dots: *Dot your i's; Trees dotted the countryside.* **3** *n.* A very short, clicklike sound used in Morse code to form letters. — **on the dot** *informal* At exactly the specified time: *to arrive on the dot.*

do·tage [dō′tij] *n.* The condition of being feeble-minded or childish as the result of old age.

do·tard [dō′tərd] *n.* A very old person who is feeble-minded and childish.

dote [dōt] *v.* **dot·ed, dot·ing 1** To lavish or show too much love or affection: *They doted on their pets.* **2** To be feeble-minded as a result of old age.

doth [duth] A form of DOES: seldom used today.

dot·ted swiss [dot′id] A thin, crisp cotton fabric, having a pattern of dots.

doub·le [dub′əl] *adj., v.* **doub·led, doub·ling, n., adv. 1** *adj.* Twice as large, as many, as much, etc.: *a double portion; double fare.* **2** *v.* To make or become twice as much or as great: *to double an amount; The membership doubled.* **3** *n.* Something that is twice as much: *18 is the double of 9.* **4** *adv.* Twice as much, as in amount or size: *We paid double what we did before.* **5** *adj.* Having or made of two parts, like or unlike: *a double yolk in an egg; a double meaning.* **6** *n.* A person or thing that closely resembles another: *She is my double.* **7** *v.* To have or serve two purposes: *This sofa doubles as a bed.* **8** *adv.* Two at a time; in pairs: *to march double.* **9** *adj.* Made for two: *a double bed.* **10** *v.* To bend or fold: *to double the blanket back over the bed.* **11** *v.* To clench (the fist). **12** *v.* To turn and go back on one's course or trail: *He doubled back on his tracks.* **13** *v.* To sail around: *to double a cape.* **14** *n.* In baseball, a hit that enables a batter to get to second base. **15** *v.* In baseball, to hit a double. **16** *n.* (*pl.*) A game of tennis, etc., in which each side has two players.

— **double up 1** To bend over or cause to bend over, as from pain or laughter. **2** *U.S. informal* To share a room, bed, etc., with someone else. — **on the double** *informal* Quickly.

double bass [bās] The largest stringed instrument, having a deep bass tone. It is also called a bass viol.

double boiler Two pots, one fitting into the other. Food in the upper pot is cooked by the heat from water boiling in the lower pot.

Double bass

doub·le-breast·ed [dub′əl·bres′tid] *adj.* Of a coat or vest, with sides overlapping clear across the breast, usually with two rows of buttons.

doub·le-cross [*v.* dub′əl·krôs′, *n.* dub′əl·krôs′] *slang* **1** *v.* To betray by failing to act as promised. **2** *n.* An act that betrays or cheats someone. — **doub′le-cross′er** *n.*

double date A social engagement in which two couples go out together.

doub·le-deal·ing [dub′əl·dē′ling] **1** *n.* A dishonest or treacherous way of dealing with others. **2** *adj.* Dishonest; deceitful. — **doub′·le-deal′er** *n.*

doub·le-head·er [dub′əl·hed′ər] *n.* In sports, two games played one after the other on the same day, usually by the same two teams.

doub·le-joint·ed [dub′əl·join′tid] *adj.* Having joints so flexible that the arms, legs, fingers, etc., can be bent in unusual ways.

double play In baseball, a play in which two base runners are put out.

doub·le-quick [dub′əl·kwik′] **1** *adj.* Very quick. **2** *adv.* Very quickly: *to run double-quick.* **3** *n.* A very fast marching step. **4** *v.* To march or run or cause to march or run very quickly.

doub·let [dub′lit] *n.* A short, tight-fitting jacket, with or without long sleeves, worn by men from about 1400 to 1660.

doub·loon [du·blōōn′] *n.* A former Spanish gold coin, originally worth about 16 dollars.

doub·ly [dub′lē] *adv.* In twice the quantity or degree: *doubly successful.*

doubt [dout] **1** *v.* To feel uncertain about the truthfulness or rightness of (someone or something): *We doubted her; I doubt that it will fit.* **2** *n.* A lack of trust, confidence, or certainty: *to have many doubts.* **3** *n.* The state or condition of being uncertain

Doublet

add, āce, câre, pälm; end, ēqual; it, īce; odd, ōpen, ôrder; tŏŏk, pōōl; up, bûrn;
ə = a in *above*, e in *sicken*, i in *possible*, o in *melon*, u in *circus*; yōō = u in *fuse*; oil; pout;
ch in *check*; ring; thin; this; zh in *vision*.   For ¶ reference, see page 64 · HOW TO

or undecided: The exact date is in *doubt*. **— no doubt 1** Most likely; probably: *No doubt* she went home. **2** Certainly. **— without doubt** or **beyond doubt** Surely; certainly: It is *without doubt* the worst play I've seen. **— doubt′er** *n.* ◆ *Doubt* comes from a French word, *douter*, meaning *to doubt*. The "b" was added later because the Latin word for *doubt* has a "b" in it.

doubt·ful [dout′fəl] *adj.* **1** Uncertain or undecided: It is *doubtful* whether or not we'll go. **2** Open to doubt: a *doubtful* reputation. **— doubt′ful·ly** *adv.*

doubt·less [dout′lis] **1** *adv.* Probably: She will *doubtless* arrive late. **2** *adv.* Without doubt; certainly: *Doubtless* she was pretty then. **3** *adj.* Free from uncertainty; sure.

dough [dō] *n.* **1** A soft, thick mass of flour and a liquid mixed together with other ingredients, used for making bread, biscuits, pastry, etc. **2** *slang* Money.

dough·nut [dō′nut′] *n.* A small cake, usually shaped like a ring, of sweetened dough fried in deep fat.

dough·ty [dou′tē] *adj.* **dough·ti·er, dough·ti·est** Strong and brave: now rarely used except humorously. **— dough′ti·ly** *adv.*

dough·y [dō′ē] *adj.* **dough·i·er, dough·i·est 1** Like dough. **2** Not fully baked: *doughy* bread.

dour [dŏŏr *or* dour] *adj.* **1** Gloomy and sullen: a *dour* nature. **2** Severe; stern: a *dour* look.

douse [dous] *v.* **doused, dous·ing 1** To thrust into water or other liquid. **2** To throw water or other liquid on: We *doused* him with the hose. **3** *informal* To put out: *Douse* the light.

dove[1] [duv] *n.* A pigeon, especially any of a number of small, usually wild pigeons.

dove[2] [dōv] A past tense of DIVE.

dove·cote [duv′kōt′ *or* duv′kot′] *n.* A house or box for pigeons or doves.

Do·ver [dō′vər] *n.* **1** The capital of Delaware. **2** A strait between England and France, the narrowest part of the English Channel. **3** An English city and port on this strait.

dove·tail [duv′tāl′] **1** *v.* To join (two boards, etc.) by fitting wedge-shaped projections on one into corresponding openings in the other. **2** *n.* One of these projections. **3** *n.* A joint formed by this method. **4** *v.* To fit together perfectly: Our schedules *dovetailed*.

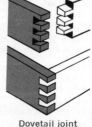
Dovetail joint

dow·a·ger [dou′ə·jər] *n.* **1** A widow who holds a title or property from her dead husband. **2** *informal* Any dignified old lady.

dow·dy [dou′dē] *adj.* **dow·di·er, dow·di·est,** *n.*, *pl.* **dow·dies 1** *adj.* Lacking style; unfashionable. **2** *adj.* Sloppy; untidy. **3** *n.* A dowdy woman. **— dow′di·ly** *adv.*

dow·el [dou′əl] *n.* A peg that fits tightly into corresponding holes in two pieces of wood or metal to hold them together.

Dowels

dow·er [dou′ər] **1** *n.* The part of a dead man's estate given by law to his widow for life. **2** *n.* A dowry. **3** *n.* A natural or inborn talent or gift. **4** *v.* To give a dower to.

down[1] [doun] **1** *adv.* In, on, or to a lower place, level, position, etc.: Come *down*; Sit *down*. **2** *adv.* To or in a place, position, etc., regarded as lower or more distant: The sun went *down*. **3** *adj.* Directed, going, or brought downward: a *down* curve; The champion is *down*! **4** *prep.* In a descending direction along, upon, through, or in: The store is *down* the street. **5** *v.* To knock, throw, shoot, or put down: to *down* a plane. **6** *v. informal* To swallow: *Down* your milk. **7** *adv.* To a smaller or lower amount, size, rate, etc.: The swelling went *down*; to boil *down* syrup; Prices have gone *down*. **8** *adv.* Actually; seriously: Let's get *down* to work. **9** *n.* (*usually pl.*) Bad luck, used chiefly in the phrase **have ups and downs,** to have both good and bad luck. **10** *adj.* Ill: She is *down* with a cold. **11** *adj. informal* Downcast; depressed: to be *down*. **12** *adv.* From an earlier time or individual: This sword came *down* from my grandfather. **13** *adv.* Completely; fully: loaded *down* with work. **14** *adv.* When something is bought: to pay five dollars *down*. **15** *adj.* Made when something is bought: a *down* payment. **16** *adv.* In writing: Take *down* his name. **17** *adj.* In football, not in play. **18** *n.* In football, an opportunity to move the ball forward, one of a series of four in which a team must advance the ball at least ten yards or give it to the other team. **— down and out** In a miserable state of poverty, ill health, etc. **— down on** *informal* Angry with: to be *down on* someone. **— down with** (Let's) do away with; overthrow: *Down with* the king!

down[2] [doun] *n.* **1** The fine, soft feathers of birds, especially of young birds. **2** Fine, soft hair, as on a baby's head.

down·cast [doun′kast′] *adj.* **1** Directed downward: *downcast* eyes. **2** Low in spirits; sad.

down·fall [doun′fôl′] *n.* **1** Ruin; collapse: the *downfall* of a government. **2** A heavy, usually sudden fall of rain or snow.

down·grade [doun′grād′] *n.*, *v.* **down·grad·ed, down·grad·ing 1** *n.* A descending slope, as of a hill or road. **2** *v.* To make less in amount or importance: to *downgrade* wages; to *downgrade* a person's work. **— on the downgrade** Becoming less or worse: His health is *on the downgrade*.

down·heart·ed [doun′här′tid] *adj.* Sad; dejected; discouraged.

down·hill [*adv.* doun′hil′, *adj.* doun′hil′] **1** *adv.* Down a hill: to run *downhill*. **2** *adj.* Downward: a *downhill* path. **— go downhill** To become worse: The town has *gone downhill*.

down·pour [doun′pôr′] *n.* A heavy fall of rain.
down·right [doun′rīt′] **1** *adj.* Absolute; complete; utter: *downright* nonsense. **2** *adv.* Thoroughly; extremely: *downright* scared. **3** *adj.* Straightforward; frank: a *downright* answer.
downs [dounz] *n.pl.* Small, rolling hills usually covered with grass.
down·stairs [*adv.* doun′stârz′, *adj., n.* doun′stârz′] **1** *adv.* On or to a lower floor: to go *downstairs.* **2** *adj.* Situated on a lower or main floor: a *downstairs* room. **3** *n.* The ground or main floor of a house or building,
down·stream [*adv.* doun′strēm′, *adj.* doun′strēm′] *adv., adj.* In the direction of the current of a stream: to row *downstream.*
down·town [*adv.* doun′toun′, *adj.* doun′toun′] *adv., adj.* To, toward, or in the lower or the chief business section of a town or city: to move *downtown;* a *downtown* store.
down·trod·den [doun′trod′(ə)n] *adj.* Abused or oppressed by those in power.
down·ward [doun′wərd] **1** *adv., adj.* From a higher to a lower place or position: to fly *downward;* a *downward* movement. **2** *adv.* From an earlier to a more recent time: to go *downward* in history.
down·wards [doun′wərdz] *adv.* Downward.
down·y [dou′nē] *adj.* **down·i·er, down·i·est** **1** Of or covered with down. **2** Soft like down.
dow·ry [dou′rē] *n., pl.* **dow·ries** The money or property a bride brings to her husband when they marry.
dox·ol·o·gy [dok·sol′ə·jē] *n., pl.* **dox·ol·o·gies** A hymn or verse praising God.
doz. Abbreviation of: **1** DOZEN. **2** Dozens.
doze [dōz] *v.* **dozed, doz·ing,** *n.* **1** *v.* To sleep lightly; nap. **2** *n.* A brief, light sleep; nap.
doz·en [duz′ən] *n., pl.* **doz·ens** or, after a number, **doz·en** **1** A group or set of twelve: two *dozen* eggs. **2** (*pl.*) A fairly large number: *Dozens* of people attended the show.
DP or **D.P.** Abbreviation of DISPLACED PERSON.
Dr. Abbreviation of DOCTOR.
drab [drab] *adj.* **drab·ber, drab·best,** *n.* **1** *adj.* Dull and monotonous in appearance or quality: a *drab* painting; a *drab* city. **2** *adj., n.* Dull, yellowish or grayish brown.
draft [draft] **1** *v.* To select for service in the armed forces or for some other purpose or job: to *draft* young men into the Army; to *draft* baseball players. **2** *n.* The act of selecting an individual for service in the armed forces or for some other purpose or job. **3** *n.* The persons so selected. **4** *n.* A current of air: There is a *draft* coming in the window. **5** *n.* A device for controlling the flow of air, as in a furnace. **6** *n.* A sketch, plan, or design of something that is to be made or written: a *draft* of a speech. **7** *v.* To make a plan, outline, or rough copy of: to *draft* a sermon. **8** *n.* A written order, as made

by an individual or bank, directing the payment of money to a person, bank, or business: a *draft* for $100.00. **9** *n.* The pulling or drawing of a load. **10** *adj.* Used for pulling heavy loads: a *draft* animal. **11** *n.* The drawing in of a fishing net, or the amount of fish drawn in. **12** *n.* The depth of water needed for a ship to float, or the depth reached by the lowest part of a fully loaded ship. **13** *n.* The act of drinking or inhaling something. **14** *n.* The amount drunk or inhaled. **15** *n.* A drink: a *draft* of ale.
draft·ee [draf·tē′] *n.* A person who is drafted for military service.
drafts·man [drafts′mən] *n., pl.* **drafts·men** [drafts′mən] **1** A person who draws designs or sketches of buildings, machinery, etc. **2** A person who writes out documents, speeches, etc.
draft·y [draf′tē] *adj.* **draft·i·er, draft·i·est** Having or being exposed to drafts of air: a *drafty* room. **— draft′i·ness** *n.*
drag [drag] *v.* **dragged, drag·ging,** *n.* **1** *v.* To haul or pull along: to *drag* a log through the water. **2** *v.* To be pulled or hauled along: His coat *dragged* behind him. **3** *n.* Some device or tool that works by being dragged or pulled along, as a harrow. **4** *v.* To search the bottom of with a net or hooklike device: We *dragged* the lake for old tires. **5** *v.* To go or continue too slowly: Time *drags* at a dull party. **6** *n.* Any person or thing that hinders or slows down something: War is a *drag* on man's progress.
drag·gle [drag′əl] *v.* **drag·gled, drag·gling** **1** To make or become soiled or wet by dragging. **2** To follow slowly; lag.
drag·net [drag′net′] *n.* **1** A net for dragging along the bottom of the water or along the ground in order to find or capture something. **2** Any device or plan for catching or gathering: The *dragnet* caught a gang of thieves.
drag·on [drag′ən] *n.* In old legends, a huge monster, shaped like a serpent with claws and wings, often said to breathe out fire.
drag·on·fly [drag′ən·flī′] *n., pl.* **drag·on·flies** An insect having a long, slender body and four long, very thin wings. It eats flies and mosquitoes.
dra·goon [drə·gōōn′] **1** *n.* In former times, a soldier who served on horseback. **2** *v.* To force or browbeat: We *dragooned* the farmers into helping us.

Dragonfly, 2–3 in. long

drain [drān] **1** *v.* To draw off (a liquid) gradually: to *drain* water from a pool. **2** *v.* To draw water or other liquid from: to *drain* a pool. **3** *v.* To flow off: The water in our new sink *drains* very quickly. **4** *v.* To let liquid flow off;

add, āce, câre, pälm; end, ēqual; it, īce; odd, ōpen, ôrder; tŏŏk, pŏŏl; up, bûrn;
ə = a in *above*, e in *sicken*, i in *possible*, o in *melon*, u in *circus*; yŏŏ = u in *fuse*; oil; pout;
check; ring; thin; this; zh in *vision*. For ¶ reference, see page 64 · HOW TO

become empty or dry: Many rivers *drain* into
the sea. **5** *n.* A pipe, ditch, or other device for
draining: The basement *drain* is clogged up.
6 *v.* To use up gradually; exhaust: Hunger
drained his strength. **7** *n.* Something that
gradually uses up or exhausts another thing.

drain·age [drā′nij] *n.* **1** The act or method of
draining. **2** A system of drains: The town's
drainage is bad. **3** Something drained off.

drain·pipe [drān′pīp′] *n.* A pipe used for
draining.

drake [drāk] *n.* A male duck.

dram [dram] *n.* **1** A small weight equaling $\frac{1}{8}$ of
an ounce in apothecaries' weight or $\frac{1}{16}$ of an
ounce in avoirdupois weight. **2** A small drink.

dra·ma [drä′mə *or* dram′ə] *n.* **1** A play written
to be performed by actors. **2** The art or profession of writing or putting on plays. **3** A series of
exciting actions or events: the *drama* of exploring
outer space.

dra·mat·ic [drə·mat′ik] *adj.* **1** Of or having to
do with plays or with the theater: a *dramatic*
critic. **2** Exciting; thrilling: a *dramatic* race.
— **dra·mat′i·cal·ly** *adv.*

dra·mat·ics [drə·mat′iks] *n.* **1** The art or
study of acting or of putting on plays. **2** An
exaggerated or dramatic manner of behaving or
of expressing oneself: I get tired of her *dramatics*.
◆ See -ICS.

dram·a·tist [dram′ə·tist] *n.* A person who
writes plays.

dram·a·tize [dram′ə·tīz] *v.* **dram·a·tized,
dram·a·tiz·ing 1** To make a play or movie out
of: to *dramatize* the life of Lincoln. **2** To make
seem exciting or unusual: to *dramatize* one's
troubles. — **dram′a·ti·za′tion** *n.* ¶3

drank [drangk] Past tense of DRINK.

drape [drāp] *v.* **draped, drap·ing,** *n.* **1** *v.* To
cover or decorate with cloth or clothing: to
drape a window or statue. **2** *v.* To arrange in
graceful folds: to *drape* a cloth. **3** *n.* (*usually pl.*)
Cloth arranged in long, loose folds, especially
when used as a curtain; drapery.

dra·per·y [drā′pər·ē] *n., pl.* **dra·per·ies
1** (*usually pl.*) Curtains or other hangings
arranged in loose folds. **2** Clothing that hangs
in loose folds, especially as seen in painting or
sculpture.

dras·tic [dras′tik] *adj.* Very forceful or severe;
extreme: Teachers must sometimes use *drastic*
methods. — **dras′ti·cal·ly** *adv.*

draught [draft] *n., v., adj.* Another spelling of
DRAFT.

draughts [drafts] *n.pl.* (*used with a singular
verb*) *British* The game of checkers.

draught·y [draf′tē] *adj.* **draught·i·er,
draught·i·est** Another spelling of DRAFTY.

draw [drô] *v.* **drew, drawn, draw·ing,** *n.*
1 *v.* To pull; drag: to *draw* a cart. **2** *v.* To pull
off, on, down, out, together, or back: to *draw* a
gun; to *draw* the curtains; to *draw* gloves on.
3 *v.* To pull tight; stretch: to *draw* a bowstring
taut. **4** *v.* To inhale: to *draw* a breath. **5** *v.* To
obtain or get: to *draw* money from the bank;

to *draw* water from a well; to *draw* an audience.
6 *v.* To result in: Their exciting acts *drew* praise
from the audience. **7** *v.* To move: to *draw* near.
8 *v.* To make (a picture, design, cartoon, etc.)
with lines and sometimes shading. **9** *v.* To make
a picture, sketch, or likeness of with lines and
sometimes shading. **10** *v.* To describe: A novelist must *draw* his characters well. **11** *v.* To
write (a check). **12** *v.* To produce a current of
air: The chimney *draws* well. **13** *v.* To sink to
when floating: This ship *draws* 25 feet. **14** *n.*
The act or action of drawing, especially the act
of pulling out a weapon: to be quick on the *draw*.
15 *n.* The part of a drawbridge that is moved
out of the way. **16** *n.* Something pulled or
drawn, as a ticket in a lottery. **17** *n.* A tie in a
game or contest: to end in a *draw*. **18** *n. U.S.*
A gully or ravine. — **draw out 1** To make
longer; prolong: You must *draw out* the ending
of your story. **2** To cause to talk freely: A
newspaper reporter must be able to *draw* people
out. — **draw up 1** To write out in a correct
or legal form: to *draw up* a deed. **2** To stop:
The car *drew up* near us.

draw·back [drô′bak′] *n.* Any unpleasant or
objectionable feature or characteristic: Heat is
one *drawback* to living in the tropics.

draw·bridge [drô′brij′] *n.* A bridge so built
that all or part of it
can be raised, lowered,
or drawn aside. Now,
opened, it lets ships
pass; formerly, it
kept enemies from
crossing over it.

Drawbridge

draw·er [drô′ər *for
def. 1*, drôr *for def. 2*]
n. **1** A person who draws. **2** A sliding, boxlike
container, as in a bureau or desk, that can be
drawn out and pushed back.

draw·ers [drôrz] *n.pl.* An undergarment
covering the lower part of the body and having
either long or short legs.

draw·ing [drô′ing] *n.* **1** The act or art of
making a picture, sketch, design, etc., by means
of lines and sometimes shading. **2** The picture,
design, or sketch made by this method. **3** A
lottery.

drawing room A room in which visitors are
received and entertained; parlor. ◆ *Drawing
room* is short for *withdrawing room*, which was so
called because people withdrew to it from another room, as from a dining room after dinner.

drawl [drôl] **1** *v.* To speak or pronounce
slowly, especially by making the vowel sounds
long. **2** *n.* A drawling manner of speaking.

drawn [drôn] Past participle of DRAW.

dray [drā] *n.* A low, strong cart with removable
sides, used for carrying heavy loads.

dread [dred] **1** *v.* To look forward to with fear
or uneasiness. **2** *n.* Great fear or uneasiness,
especially over something in the future: She
has a *dread* of the dentist. **3** *adj.* Dreadful.

dread·ful [dred′fəl] *adj.* **1** Causing dread or

awe; terrible: a *dreadful* threat. **2** *informal*
Very bad; shocking; awful: a *dreadful* book.
— **dread′ful·ly** *adv.*

dread·nought or **dread·naught** [dred′·
nôt′] *n.* A type of large battleship having many
big guns and much used in World War I.

dream [drēm] *n., v.* **dreamed** or **dreamt,**
dream·ing **1** *n.* A series of thoughts or
pictures passing through the mind during sleep.
2 *v.* To see or imagine in a dream. **3** *v.* To have a
dream. **4** *n.* An imaginary and usually pleasant
thought or reverie one has while awake; daydream. **5** *v.* To have daydreams or imaginary
reveries: She *dreams* too much during class.
— **dream of** To think or consider possible;
imagine: Our grandfathers never *dreamed of* such
things. — **dream′er** *n.*

dream·land [drēm′land′] *n.* An imaginary
land that exists in dreams.

dreamt [drem(p)t] Alternative past tense and
past participle of DREAM: I *dreamt* I was flying.

dream·y [drē′mē] *adj.* **dream·i·er, dream·**
i·est **1** Like a dream; vague; dim. **2** Given to
daydreaming: a *dreamy* girl. **3** Soothing; soft:
dreamy music. — **dream′i·ly** *adv.* — **dream′·**
i·ness *n.*

drear [drir] *adj.* Dreary: used mostly in poems.

drear·y [drir′ē] *adj.* **drear·i·er, drear·i·est**
Full of or causing sadness or gloom: a *dreary*
day. — **drear′i·ly** *adv.* — **drear′i·ness** *n.*

dredge[1] [drej] *n., v.* **dredged, dredg·ing**
1 *n.* A large machine
used to scoop out or
suck up mud, sand,
etc., from the bottom
of a body of water.
2 *n.* Something like a
net that is used to
gather shellfish, etc.,
from under the water.
3 *v.* To clear, widen,
or remove with a
dredge: to *dredge* a harbor; to *dredge* oysters.
— **dredg′er** *n.*

Dredge

dredge[2] [drej] *v.* **dredged, dredg·ing** To
sprinkle or dust (food), as with flour or sugar.

dregs [dregz] *n.pl.* **1** Bits of solid matter that
settle to the bottom of a liquid, as coffee grounds.
2 The most undesirable part of anything: the
dregs of society.

drench [drench] *v.* To wet completely; soak.

Dres·den [drez′dən] *n.* A city in southern
East Germany.

dress [dres] **1** *n.* The outer garment worn by a
woman or girl, usually in one piece; frock. **2** *n.*
Clothes; apparel. **3** *v.* To put clothes on: to
dress a doll; We must *dress* quickly. **4** *v.* To
trim or decorate: to *dress* a store window. **5** *v.*
To comb and arrange (hair). **6** *v.* To clean or
prepare for use or sale: to *dress* a chicken; to

dress leather. **7** *v.* To treat with medicine and
bandages: to *dress* a wound. **8** *v.* To line up in a
straight line, as soldiers.

dress·er[1] [dres′ər] *n.* **1** A person who dresses
something or someone. **2** A tool for dressing
leather, stone, etc.

dress·er[2] [dres′ər] *n.* A chest of drawers for
clothing, usually with a mirror above it.

dress·ing [dres′ing] *n.* **1** Bandages and medicine put on a wound or sore. **2** A sauce, as for
salads or vegetables. **3** A mixture of bread
crumbs and seasonings, used for stuffing chickens,
turkeys, etc., before roasting.

dressing gown A loose gown or robe worn
while resting at home or before dressing.

dressing room A room for dressing, as
backstage in a theater.

dressing table A small table with a mirror,
used while putting on makeup, arranging the
hair, etc.

dress·mak·er [dres′mā′kər] *n.* A person who
makes dresses or other articles of clothing for
women — **dress′mak′ing** *n.*

dress rehearsal A final rehearsal of a play,
opera, etc., done with all the costumes, properties, and the lighting to be used in the actual
performance.

dress·y [dres′ē] *adj.* **dress·i·er, dress·i·est**
informal **1** Very stylish or fancy: a *dressy*
blouse. **2** Fond of dressing up: a *dressy* crowd.

drew [drōō] Past tense of DRAW: He *drew* a map.

drib·ble [drib′əl] *v.* **drib·bled, drib·bling,**
n. **1** *v.* To fall or let fall in drops; drip: The
faucets *dribbled* water. **2** *v.* To come in small
amounts: Contributions *dribbled* in slowly.
3 *n.* A small quantity of water, usually falling in
drops. **4** *v.* To drool: The baby *dribbled* saliva.
5 *v.* To move (a ball) either by bouncing or by
short kicks: In both basketball and soccer the
ball is *dribbled*. **6** *n.* The act of dribbling a ball.
— **drib′bler** *n.*

drib·let [drib′lit] *n.* A small amount or bit.

dried [drīd] Past tense and past participle of
DRY: The clothes were *dried* by the wind.

dri·er [drī′ər] **1** Comparative of DRY: This
sheet is *drier* than that one. **2** *n.* A person or
thing that dries. **3** *n.* Another spelling of
DRYER.

dri·est [drī′ist] Superlative of DRY.

drift [drift] **1** *v.* To move or float along in a
current of water or air: We let the boat *drift*;
Leaves *drifted* down. **2** *v.* To become piled up
by water or wind: The snow *drifted* as high as
the door. **3** *n.* Something piled or heaped up by
the wind or water: a *drift* of snow. **4** *v.* To move
or live without any particular goal or purpose:
He *drifted* from city to city. **5** *n.* The act of
drifting, or the direction or speed of drifting:
a westward *drift*. **6** *n.* The meaning of something: the *drift* of a speech. — **drift′er** *n.*

add, āce, câre, pälm;   end, ēqual;   it, īce;   odd, ōpen, ôrder;   took, pool;   up, bûrn;

ə = a in *above*, e in *sicken*, i in *possible*, o in *melon*, u in *circus*;   **yōō** = u in *fuse*;   **oil**;   **pout**;

check;   **ring**;   **thin**;   **th**is;   **zh** in *vision*.   For ¶ reference, see page 64 · HOW TO

drift·wood [drift′wŏŏd′] *n.* Wood drifting in water or washed up on the shore.

drill¹ [dril] **1** *n.* A tool or machine used for boring holes. **2** *v.* To make (a hole) with or as with a drill: We *drilled* holes for rivets. **3** *v.* To make a hole in with a drill: The dentist *drilled* my tooth. **4** *n.* A kind of instruction based on the repetition of physical or mental exercises. **5** *n.* Such an exercise, aimed at perfecting a skill or kind of knowledge: a piano *drill.* **6** *v.* To teach or learn by this method: to *drill* recruits. **drill′er** *n.* ◆ See PRACTICE.

Electric drill

drill² [dril] *n.* A machine that plants seeds in rows by digging holes, dropping the seed, and then covering the seeds with soil.

dri·ly [drī′lē] *adv.* Another spelling of DRYLY.

drink [dringk] *v.* **drank, drunk, drink·ing,** *n.* **1** *v.* To swallow (a liquid): We have *drunk* too much pop. **2** *n.* Any liquid that one can drink. **3** *n.* A portion of liquid for drinking, as a glassful. **4** *n.* Alcoholic liquor. **5** *v.* To drink alcoholic liquor. **6** *v.* To drink alcoholic liquor too much or too often. **— drink in** To take in eagerly with the senses or the mind. **— drink to** To drink a toast to. **— drink′er** *n.*

drip [drip] *v.* **dripped, drip·ping,** *n.* **1** *v.* To fall or cause to fall in drops: Rain *dripped* from the trees; The faucet *drips* water. **2** *n.* The forming and falling of drops of liquid, or the sound made by this. **3** *n.* Liquid that falls in drops. **4** *n. slang* A stupid and irritating person.

drip·pings [drip′ingz] *n.pl.* The fat and juices that drip from meat when it is roasted or broiled.

drive [drīv] *v.* **drove, driv·en, driv·ing,** *n.* **1** *v.* To direct and control the movement of (a car or other vehicle). **2** *v.* To go or carry in a car or other vehicle: to *drive* to town; to *drive* someone home. **3** *n.* A trip in a car or other vehicle. **4** *n.* A road, street, or driveway. **5** *v.* To move or cause to move: The car *drove* slowly; We *drove* cattle all day. **6** *n.* Something that is being driven along, as a herd of cattle. **7** *n.* The means by which the power of a machine is passed on to where it takes effect, as in an automobile. **8** *v.* To move by striking: to *drive* a nail or a ball. **9** *n.* In certain games, the act of hitting a ball or the flight of a ball when hit: a hard *drive;* a *drive* to center field. **10** *v.* To produce or form by drilling: to *drive* a well. **11** *v.* To force into some act or condition: to *drive* someone mad. **12** *v.* To force to work hard: The boss *drove* them all day. **13** *v.* To bring about with force and energy: He *drives* a hard bargain. **14** *n. informal* Energy: He has a lot of *drive.* **15** *n.* A planned effort of a group for getting something done: a *drive* for charity. **16** *n.* A strong force or need. **— drive at** To try to say; mean: What are you *driving at?* —

let drive To aim or hit: to *let drive* with both fists.

drive-in [drīv′in′] *n.* **1** Any establishment serving or entertaining people seated in their cars, as a bank, restaurant, or motion-picture theater. **2** *adj. use:* a *drive-in* movie.

driv·el [driv′əl] *v.* **driv·eled** or **driv·elled, driv·el·ing** or **driv·el·ling,** *n.* **1** *v.* To drool; slobber. **2** *n.* A flow of saliva from the mouth. **3** *v.* To talk or write foolishly. **4** *n.* Foolish talk or writing. **— driv′el·er** or **driv′el·ler** *n.*

driv·en [driv′ən] Past participle of DRIVE.

driv·er [drī′vər] *n.* **1** A person or thing that drives. **2** A golf club having a wooden head, used to drive the ball from the tee.

drive·way [drīv′wā′] *n.* A private road leading from a street or highway to a house, garage, or other building.

driz·zle [driz′əl] *v.* **driz·zled, driz·zling,** **1** *v.* To rain steadily in tiny drops like mist. **2** *n.* A mistlike rain: It's only a light *drizzle.* **— driz′zly** *adj.*

droll [drōl] *adj.* Comically strange, odd, or quaint: a *droll* little man.

droll·er·y [drō′lər·ē] *n., pl.* **droll·er·ies 1** An amusing way of acting or talking. **2** Something droll, as a story.

drom·e·dar·y [drom′ə·der′ē] *n., pl.* **drom·e·dar·ies** A swift camel of Arabia, having only one hump, used for riding.

drone¹ [drōn] *v.* **droned, dron·ing,** *n.* **1** *v.* To make a deep humming or buzzing sound. **2** *n.* Such a sound: the *drone* of bees. **3** *v.* To speak in a dull, monotonous manner: Our teacher *droned* on.

Dromedary, 6–7 ft. high at shoulder

drone² [drōn] *n.* **1** A male bee. Drones have no sting and do no work. **2** A person who won't work but lives by the work of others.

drool [drŏŏl] **1** *v.* To let saliva flow from the mouth. **2** *n. informal* Foolish talk; drivel.

droop [drŏŏp] **1** *v.* To sink or hang down: The flowers *drooped* in the sun. **2** *n.* A drooping condition or position. **3** *v.* To become tired, sad, or discouraged.

droop·y [drŏŏ′pē] *adj.* **droop·i·er, droop·i·est 1** Drooping or tending to droop. **2** Sad; gloomy.

drop [drop] *n., v.* **dropped** or **dropt, drop·ping 1** *n.* A small amount of liquid shaped like a tiny ball or pear. **2** *n.* Something like this in size or shape: a chocolate *drop.* **3** *v.* To fall in drops, as a liquid. **4** *n.* A very small amount of anything, especially of a liquid: a *drop* of coffee. **5** *n.* A sudden or quick fall or downward movement. **6** *n.* The distance straight down from a higher place to a lower place: a 50-foot *drop.* **7** *v.* To fall or let fall: We *dropped* to the ground; Don't *drop* your books. **8** *n.* A sudden decrease or decline: a *drop* in prices. **9** *v.* To decline or decrease in amount, volume, etc.: His voice *dropped* to a whisper. **10** *v.* To fall down dead, injured, or exhausted: After the race, he *dropped* to the ground. **11** *v.* To cause to fall: to *drop* a deer. **12** *v.* To fall into some state or condition: to *drop* into a sound sleep. **13** *v.* To have no more to do with: to *drop* a friend or an argument. **14** *v.* To fire (a worker): used chiefly in the U.S. and Canada. **15** *v.* To send, give, or say casually: to *drop* a hint; to *drop* a letter to a friend. **16** *v.* To leave out or omit. **17** *v.* To let out or leave: *Drop* your friend off at my house. **— drop back** or **drop behind** To fall or lag behind. **— drop in** or **drop over** To make an informal or surprise visit. **— drop out** To leave or quit some activity: to *drop out* of a game.

drop·let [drop′lit] *n.* A tiny drop.

drop·out [drop′out′] *n.* A person who drops out, especially a student who leaves school before he graduates or who leaves a course of study before he finishes it.

drop·per [drop′ər] *n.* A glass tube with one narrowed end from which a rubber bulb at the other end, when squeezed, releases a liquid drop by drop.

drop·sy [drop′sē] *n.* A diseased condition in which too much liquid collects in certain parts of the body.

dropt [dropt] A past tense and past participle of DROP.

drosh·ky [drosh′kē] *n., pl.* **drosh·kies** An open, four-wheeled Russian carriage.

dross [drôs] *n.* **1** Scum that rises to the surface of melted metal. **2** Any worthless matter; rubbish.

Dropper

drought [drout] *n.* A lack of rain for a long period; severe dry spell.

drouth [drouth] *n.* Another word for DROUGHT.

drove[1] [drōv] Past tense of DRIVE.

drove[2] [drōv] *n.* **1** A herd or flock of animals driven or moving along together. **2** A crowd of people moving along together.

drov·er [drō′vər] *n.* **1** A person who drives cattle, sheep, or other animals to market in droves. **2** A cattle or sheep dealer.

drown [droun] *v.* **1** To die or kill by suffocation in water or other liquid. **2** To cover with or as if with a liquid: He *drowned* his potatoes in butter. **3** To overwhelm the sound of by a louder sound; keep from being heard.

drowse [drouz] *v.* **drowsed, drows·ing,** *n.* **1** *v.* To be only half asleep; doze. **2** *n.* A nap or doze.

drow·sy [drou′zē] *adj.* **drow·si·er, drow·si·est 1** Sleepy. **2** Causing sleepiness: a *drowsy* day. **— drow′si·ly** *adv.* **— drow′si·ness** *n.*

drub [drub] *v.* **drubbed, drub·bing** To beat or thrash, as with a stick.

drudge [druj] *n., v.* **drudged, drudg·ing 1** *n.* A person whose work is hard and boring. **2** *v.* To do hard, tiresome work.

drudg·er·y [druj′ər·ē] *n., pl.* **drudg·er·ies** Dull, hard, unpleasant work.

drug [drug] *n., v.* **drugged, drug·ging 1** *n.* Any substance, other than food, used as a medicine or in the preparation of medicines. **2** *n.* A substance that relieves pain or makes one sleep; narcotic. **3** *v.* To give a drug to. **4** *v.* To add drugs to: They *drugged* our food. **5** *v.* To make sleepy or unconscious: The wine seemed to *drug* the wedding guests. **— drug on the market** A product that nobody wants to buy.

drug·gist [drug′ist] *n.* **1** A person who sells drugs, medicines, toilet articles, etc. **2** A pharmacist.

drug·store [drug′stôr′] *n.* Formerly, a place where drugs and medicines were sold. In modern drugstores, however, a person can buy many other things.

dru·id [drōō′id] *n.* (*often written* **Druid**) A priest of a Celtic religion that was formerly practiced in ancient Britain, Ireland, and Gaul.

drum [drum] *n., v.* **drummed, drum·ming 1** *n.* A hollow musical instrument, usually shaped like a cylinder or hemisphere with skin or other material stretched tightly over one or both ends. It is played by striking with sticks or with the hands. **2** *n.* A thumping or tapping sound made by or as if by a drum. **3** *v.* To beat a drum. **4** *v.* To tap or thump over and over again: to *drum* on the table with one's fingers. **5** *v.* To force a person to learn or remember by constant repetition: to *drum* rules into a person's head. **6** *n.* Something shaped like a drum, as a large metal container for oil. **— drum up 1** To try to get: to *drum up* business. **2** To bring together: We couldn't *drum up* enough people for cards.

drum·head [drum′hed′] *n.* The skin or other material stretched over the end or ends of a drum.

drum·lin [drum′lin] *n.* A long or oval hill made up of dirt and stones left behind by glaciers.

drum major The person who leads a marching band, usually twirling a baton.

drum ma·jor·ette [mā′jə·ret′] A girl or woman who marches with a band, twirls a baton, does acrobatics, etc.

drum·mer [drum′ər] *n.* **1** A person who plays a drum. **2** *U.S. informal* A traveling salesman.

drum·stick [drum′stik′] *n.* **1** A stick used for beating a drum. **2** The lower half of the leg of a cooked chicken, turkey, or other fowl.

---

add, āce, câre, pälm; end, ēqual; it, īce; odd, ōpen, ôrder; tŏŏk, pōōl; up, bûrn; ə = a in *above*, e in *sicken*, i in *possible*, o in *melon*, u in *circus*; yōō = u in *fuse*; oil; pout; check; ring; thin; this; zh in *vision*. For ¶ reference, see page 64 · HOW TO

drunk [drungk] **1** Past participle of DRINK: We have *drunk* our last toast. **2** *adj.* Having alcohol enough in the body to make mental and physical reactions less accurate than normal; intoxicated. **3** *n. informal* A drunkard.

drunk·ard [drungk′ərd] *n.* A person who is drunk a great part of the time.

drunk·en [drungk′ən] *adj.* **1** Drunk; intoxicated. **2** Resulting from or showing the effects of being drunk: a *drunken* act; a *drunken* look. — **drunk′en·ly** *adv.* — **drunk′en·ness** *n.*

dry [drī] *adj.* **dri·er, dri·est,** *v.* **dried, dry·ing 1** *adj.* Not wet or damp. **2** *v.* To make or become dry: *Dry* your hands; The clothes will *dry* quickly today. **3** *adj.* Not lying under water: *dry* land. **4** *adj.* Having little or no water or moisture: a *dry* stream; a *dry* well. **5** *adj.* Having little or no rain: a *dry* season. **6** *adj.* Shriveled or withered from lack of water: The plants are *dry*. **7** *adj.* No longer giving milk: a *dry* cow. **8** *adj.* Thirsty: to feel *dry*. **9** *adj.* Having no tears: *dry* eyes. **10** *adj.* Eaten or served without butter, jam, etc.: *dry* toast. **11** *adj.* Dull and boring: a *dry* lecture. **12** *adj.* Having no warmth, excitement, or feeling: a *dry* welcome. **13** *adj.* Plain and bare: the *dry* facts. **14** *adj.* Not sweet: said about wine. **15** *adj. informal* Not allowing the sale of alcoholic liquor: a *dry* county. — **dry′ness** *n.*

dry·ad [drī′əd] *n.* (*often written* **Dryad**) In mythology, a nymph that lives in the woods or in trees.

dry cell A battery cell that produces an electric current, as for a flashlight. Its electrolyte is a paste rather than a liquid.

dry-clean [drī′klēn′] *v.* To clean (clothing, etc.) with a liquid other than water.

dry cleaner 1 A person who dry-cleans. **2** An establishment whose business is dry cleaning. — **dry cleaning**

dry dock A floating or stationary dock from which the water can be emptied, used for building, repairing, or cleaning ships.

Dry dock

dry·er [drī′ər] *n.* **1** A mechanical device used for drying, as by heat, whirling, etc.: a clothes *dryer*. **2** Another spelling of DRIER.

dry goods Clothing, cloth, ribbon, needles, thread, etc.

Dry Ice Solidified carbon dioxide at −78.5 degrees centigrade or less: a trademark. It is used to keep things cold, especially because, on warming, it changes directly to gas. Also written **dry ice.**

dry·ly [drī′lē] *adv.* In a dry manner.

dry measure A system for measuring the volume of dry commodities, such as fruits or grains.

DST or **D.S.T.** Abbreviation of DAYLIGHT-SAVING TIME.

du·al [d(y)ōō′əl] *adj.* Of, having, or consisting of two parts, sets, etc.; double: a car with *dual* controls.

dub[1] [dub] *v.* **dubbed, dub·bing 1** To make (someone) a knight by tapping his shoulder with a sword. **2** To give a name or nickname to: They *dubbed* him "Tiny." **3** To make smooth, usually by rubbing: to *dub* wood.

dub[2] [dub] *v.* **dubbed, dub·bing** To substitute or add sound or language to a motion picture, phonograph record, etc.

du·bi·ous [d(y)ōō′bē·əs] *adj.* **1** Not sure or certain; doubtful: She was *dubious* about going out without permission. **2** Causing doubt, question, or suspicion: a *dubious* reputation. — **du′bi·ous·ly** *adv.* — **du′bi·ous·ness** *n.*

Dub·lin [dub′lin] *n.* The capital of Ireland, in the eastern part.

du·cal [d(y)ōō′kəl] *adj.* Of or having to do with a duke or a duchy.

duc·at [duk′ət] *n.* Any of several gold or silver coins formerly used in Europe.

duch·ess [duch′is] *n.* **1** The wife or widow of a duke. **2** A woman holding a rank equal to that of a duke; female ruler of a duchy.

duch·y [duch′ē] *n.,* *pl.* **duch·ies** The territory that a duke or duchess rules; dukedom.

duck[1] [duk] *n.* **1** A swimming bird, either wild or tame, having short legs, webbed feet, and a broad bill. **2** The female of this bird. The male is called a drake. **3** The flesh of the duck used as food.

duck[2] [duk] **1** *v.* To thrust or plunge under water suddenly and briefly: to *duck* someone in a swimming pool. **2** *v.* To lower the head or stoop down quickly. **3** *n.* The act of ducking. **4** *v.* To dodge, as by lowering the head or bending the body: to *duck* a punch.

Mallard, 20–28 in. long

duck[3] [duk] *n.* A strong, tightly woven linen or cotton cloth similar to canvas but of a lighter weight: slacks made of *duck*.

duck[4] [duk] *n.* A military truck which can travel on land and on water.

duck·bill [duk′bil′] *n.* Another name for the PLATYPUS.

duck hawk A swift falcon of North and South America.

duck·ling [duk′ling] *n.* A young duck.

duck·weed [duk′wēd′] *n.* A small, stemless water plant that floats on the surface of ponds and streams.

duct [dukt] *n.* **1** A tube, channel, or other passage through which fluid, gas, electric cables, etc., can pass. **2** A tube in the body that carries fluid: tear *ducts.*

duc·tile [duk′təl] *adj.* **1** Capable of being hammered into thin layers or drawn out into wire, as certain metals. **2** Easily molded or shaped, as plastic. **3** Easily led or managed.

duct·less gland [dukt′lis] A gland that has no duct but releases its fluids directly into the blood or lymph, as the thyroid gland.

dud [dud] *n.* **1** A bomb or shell that fails to explode. **2** *informal* A person, thing, or event that proves a failure.

dude [d(y)ōōd] *n.* **1** A man whose clothes are always too dressy or showy. **2** *informal* A city man in the country, especially in the West.

dude ranch A vacation resort that entertains guests with horseback riding and the activities of a cattle ranch.

dudg·eon [duj′ən] *n.* Anger or resentment, now used mainly in the phrase **in high dudgeon**, in a very angry or resentful mood.

due [d(y)ōō] **1** *adj.* Owed and expected to be paid: The rent is *due* May 1st. **2** *n.* Something that is owed or should be given; a right: Respect is a teacher's *due*. **3** *adj.* Proper or sufficient: *due* caution; in *due* time. **4** *n.* (*pl.*) Money charged or paid for belonging to a union, club, etc.: We pay *dues* twice a year. **5** *adj.* Expected to arrive or be ready: When is the bus *due*? **6** *adv.* Directly; exactly: *due* east. **— due to** Caused by: His success was *due to* hard work. ◆ Careful writers will avoid *due to* as a substitute for *because of* or *on account of:* We were delayed *because of* (or *on account of*) rain, NOT *due to* rain. It is, however, correct to use *due* as an adjective: The delay was *due to* rain.

du·el [d(y)ōō·əl] *n., v.* **du·eled** or **du·elled, du·el·ing** or **du·el·ling** **1** *n.* A combat between two persons, fought with deadly weapons according to set rules and before witnesses. **2** *n.* Any conflict or contest: a *duel* of words. **3** *v.* To fight in a duel. **— du′el·ist** or **du′el·list** *n.*

du·en·na [d(y)ōō·ən′ə] *n.* **1** An elderly woman who is governess and companion of the girls in a Spanish family. **2** A chaperon.

du·et [d(y)ōō·et′] *n.* A piece of music to be played or sung by two performers.

duf·fel [duf′əl] *n.* **1** A coarse woolen fabric napped on both sides. **2** Equipment or supplies, especially for camping.

duffel bag A sack, usually made of canvas or duck, used to carry clothing and personal possessions.

duffel coat A heavy, outer coat, usually knee-length and having a hood.

dug [dug] Past tense and past participle of DIG.

dug·out [dug′out′] *n.* **1** A boat made by hollowing out a log. **2** A shelter hollowed out in the earth. **3** A low, covered shelter at a baseball diamond, in which players sit when not on the field.

duke [d(y)ōōk] *n.* **1** A nobleman having the highest rank below that of a royal prince. **2** A prince who rules over a duchy.

duke·dom [d(y)ōōk′dəm] *n.* **1** A duchy. **2** The rank or title of a duke.

dul·cet [dul′sit] *adj.* Pleasing to the ear; sweet, melodious, or soothing: *dulcet* tones.

dul·ci·mer [dul′sə·mər] *n.* A musical instrument having wire strings that are struck with two padded hammers held in the hands.

Dulcimer

dull [dul] **1** *adj.* Not sharp or piercing: a *dull* blade; a *dull* pain. **2** *adj.* Not bright or clear: *dull* colors; a *dull* sound. **3** *adj.* Slow to learn; stupid: a *dull* student. **4** *adj.* Not interesting; tedious; boring: a *dull* book. **5** *adj.* Not active; listless or slow: Trade is dull. **6** *v.* To make or become dull: to *dull* the appetite; The old man's eyesight *dulled*. **— dull′ness** *n.* **— dul′ly** *adv.*

dull·ard [dul′ərd] *n.* A stupid person.

Du·luth [də·lōōth′] *n.* A city in Minnesota, on Lake Superior.

du·ly [d(y)ōō′lē] *adv.* **1** In the proper manner or degree: *duly* respectful. **2** At the proper time: bills *duly* paid.

Du·mas [dōō·mä′ or dōō′mä], **Alexandre,** 1802–1870, and his son **Alexandre,** 1824–1895 French writers of novels and plays.

dumb [dum] *adj.* **1** Lacking the power of speech; mute: a deaf and *dumb* child. **2** Speechless for a time; silent: to be *dumb* with horror. **3** *U.S. informal* Stupid. **— dumb′ly** *adv.* **— dumb′ness** *n.*

dumb·bell [dum′bel′] *n.* **1** A wood or metal bar with a heavy knob at each end, used in pairs to exercise the muscles. **2** *U.S. slang* A stupid person.

dumb·found [dum′found′] *v.* Another spelling of DUMFOUND.

dumb show Gestures without words; pantomime: He acted it out in *dumb show.*

dumb·wait·er [dum′wā′tər] *n.* **1** A small elevator used to hoist food, dishes, etc., from one floor to another. **2** A movable stand for serving food.

Dumbbells

dum·found [dum′found′] *v.* To strike speechless with surprise; astonish; amaze: I was *dumfounded* when I heard of it. ◆ *Dumfound* comes from the blending of parts of the two words *dum(b)* and *(con)found.*

dum·my [dum′ē] *n., pl.* **dum·mies,** *adj.* **1** *n.* A figure made to look like a real person, used for displaying clothing, for tackling in football practice, etc. **2** *n.* Any imitation object made to look like the real thing, as a false drawer or a model of a book. **3** *adj.* Imitation; artificial: a *dummy* door. **4** *n. slang* A stupid person. **5** *n.* In bridge, the inactive player who lays his cards face up for his partner to play; also, his hand of cards. **6** *adj.* Acting for another while seeming to act for oneself: a *dummy* stockholder.

dump [dump] **1** *v.* To throw down or away: to *dump* packages on the bed; to *dump* trash. **2** *v.* To empty out; unload: to *dump* gravel on the road. **3** *n.* A place used for dumping: a garbage *dump.* **4** *n.* A temporary storage place for military supples: a munitions *dump.* **5** *n. U.S. slang* A shabby, poorly kept place.

dump·ling [dump′ling] *n.* **1** A ball of dough filled with fruit and baked. **2** A small mass of dough cooked in soup or stew.

dumps [dumps] *n.pl.* A gloomy state of mind, especially in the phrase **in the dumps,** sad and gloomy.

dump truck A truck with a back part that tilts to slide out the load at the rear.

dump·y [dump′ē] *adj.* **dump·i·er, dump·i·est** Short and plump: a *dumpy* little woman.

dun[1] [dun] *v.* **dunned, dun·ning,** *n.* **1** *v.* To ask over and over for payment of a debt: He *dunned* me for the money I owed him. **2** *n.* A repeated demand for payment of a debt.

dun[2] [dun] *n., adj.* Grayish or reddish brown.

dunce [duns] *n.* A dull, slow student; stupid person.

dune [d(y)ōōn] *n.* A hill or bank of loose sand heaped up by the wind.

dung [dung] *n.* The solid waste matter eliminated from the body by animals; manure.

dun·ga·ree [dung′gə·rē′] *n.* **1** (*pl.*) Trousers or overalls made from a coarse, heavy, usually blue, cotton cloth. **2** This kind of cloth.

dun·geon [dun′jən] *n.* A dark underground prison or cell: the *dungeon* of a castle.

dung·hill [dung′hil′] *n.* A heap of manure.

dunk [dungk] *v.* To dip or soak (doughnuts, bread, etc.) in a liquid, as coffee or soup.

du·o [d(y)ōō′ō] *n., pl.* **du·os 1** A duet, especially instrumental. **2** A pair.

du·o·dec·i·mal system [dōō′ō·des′ə·məl] A system of counting and of arithmetic based on 12. Each successive digit tells the number of ones, twelves, 144's, etc., instead of ones, tens, hundreds, etc.

Dunking a doughnut

du·o·de·nal [dōō′ə·dē′nəl *or* dōō·od′ə·nəl] *adj.* Of, having to do with, or located in the duodenum.

du·o·de·num [dōō′ə·dē′nəm *or* dōō·od′ə·nəm] *n., pl.* **du·o·de·na** [dōō′ə·dē′nə *or* dōō·od′ə·nə] The part of the small intestine that connects with the stomach.

dupe [d(y)ōōp] *n., v.* **duped, dup·ing 1** *n.* A

person who is easily deceived or made a fool of. **2** *v.* To make a fool of; deceive, trick, or cheat: He is easily *duped.*

du·ple [d(y)ōō′pəl] *adj.* **1** Double. **2** Having two beats to the measure, as music: *duple* time.

du·plex [d(y)ōō′pleks] **1** *adj.* Double; twofold. **2** *n.* A house for two families. **3** *n.* An apartment having rooms on two floors.

du·pli·cate [*v.* d(y)ōō′plə·kāt, *n., adj.* d(y)ōō′plə·kit] *v.* **du·pli·cat·ed, du·pli·cat·ing,** *n., adj.* **1** *v.* To copy exactly or do again: That work of art could not be *duplicated.* **2** *n.* An exact copy: a *duplicate* of a letter. **3** *adj.* Made like or exactly corresponding to something else: a *duplicate* key. **4** *adj.* In pairs; double. **—in duplicate** In two identical copies: Submit your application *in duplicate.* **—du′·pli·ca′tion** *n.*

du·pli·ca·tor [d(y)ōō′plə·kā′tər] *n.* A machine that makes copies of printed or written matter.

du·plic·i·ty [d(y)ōō·plis′ə·tē] *n., pl.* **du·plic·i·ties** An acting contrary to one's real feelings and beliefs in order to deceive; deceitfulness.

du·ra·ble [d(y)ōōr′ə·bəl] *adj.* Lasting a long time without wearing out: a *durable* material. **—du′·ra·bil′i·ty** *n.*

dur·ance [d(y)ōōr′əns] *n.* Imprisonment, especially in the phrase **in durance vile,** in confinement.

du·ra·tion [d(y)ōō·rā′shən] *n.* The time during which anything goes on or lasts: the *duration* of the winter.

Dü·rer [door′ər], **Albrecht,** 1471–1528, German painter and engraver.

du·ress [d(y)ōō·res′] *n.* The use of threats or force to compel a person to do something: to confess under *duress.*

dur·ing [d(y)ōōr′ing] *prep.* **1** Throughout the time of: That school is closed *during* the summer. **2** In the course of: *During* today's game he hit a home run. ◆ *During* comes from the present participle of the verb *dure,* seldom used today, meaning *to last. During* thus meant *lasting.*

durst [dûrst] Past tense of DARE: seldom used today: *Durst* he do so dastardly a thing?

dusk [dusk] *n.* The darkest part of twilight, just before night falls.

dusk·y [dus′kē] *adj.* **dusk·i·er, dusk·i·est 1** Dim or gloomy: The room grew *dusky.* **2** Somewhat dark in color or complexion.

dust [dust] **1** *n.* Any substance, as earth, that is in the form of very fine, light, dry particles: *dust* in the air; gold *dust.* **2** *v.* To wipe dust from (furniture, etc.): to *dust* a table; *Dust* well today. **3** *v.* To sprinkle with powder, insecticide, etc.: to *dust* crops. **4** *n.* A dead human body or the earth in which it is buried: used in the Bible and in literary works. **— bite the dust** To fall down dead or injured. **— throw dust in someone's eyes** To deceive or mislead on purpose.

dust bowl A very dry region where the topsoil is blown away in clouds of dust.

dust·er [dus′tər] *n.* **1** A cloth or brush for

removing dust. **2** A woman's dress-length house-coat. **3** A woman's lightweight, loose-fitting coat. **4** A lightweight jacket or coat to protect one's clothes from dust. **5** A device for sprinkling powder or insecticide.

dust jacket The removable paper cover that comes on new books.

dust storm A windstorm of dry regions that carries clouds of dust with it.

dust·y [dus'tē] *adj.* **dust·i·er, dust·i·est** **1** Full of or covered with dust: a *dusty* room. **2** Like dust; powdery: a light, *dusty* snow. **3** Grayish or dull, as a color. — **dust'i·ness** *n.*

Dutch [duch] **1** *adj.* Of or from the Netherlands. **2** *n.* **(the Dutch)** The people of the Netherlands. **3** *n.* The language of the Netherlands. — **go Dutch** *U.S. informal* To have each person pay his own expenses, as on a date. — **in Dutch** *U.S. informal* In trouble, disfavor, or disgrace.

Dutch·man [duch'mən] *n., pl.* **Dutch·men** [duch'mən] **1** A person who was born in or is a citizen of the Netherlands. **2** A German. ◆ The German word for *German* is *Deutsch.* Perhaps this is why Germans are sometimes called "Dutchmen."

Dutch treat *U.S. informal* A meal or entertainment at which each person pays his own bill.

du·ti·ful [d(y)o͞o'ti·fəl] *adj.* Having or showing a sense of duty; obedient or respectful: a *dutiful* child. — **du'ti·ful·ly** *adv.*

du·ty [d(y)o͞o'tē] *n., pl.* **du·ties** **1** That which a person ought to do because it is right or required: It is a soldier's *duty* to obey. **2** Any work or task that is part of a particular job or occupation: the *duty* of a doctor. **3** A tax on goods brought into a country and sometimes on goods sent out.

dwarf [dwôrf] **1** *n.* A person, animal, or plant that is much less than normal size. **2** *n.* In fairy tales, a tiny man having some special skill or magical power. **3** *v.* To keep from growing to normal size; stunt the growth of: to *dwarf* trees. **4** *v.* To cause to appear small or less by comparison: That great hill *dwarfs* all the others around it. **5** *adj.* Small; stunted: a *dwarf* tree. **6** *n.* A star of medium or less than medium brightness and mass. Astronomers class the sun as a dwarf.

dwarf·ish [dwôr'fish] *adj.* Like a dwarf; small; stunted. — **dwarf'ish·ly** *adv.* — **dwarf'ish·ness** *n.*

dwell [dwel] *v.* **dwelt** or **dwelled, dwell·ing** **1** To live; reside: to *dwell* by the sea. **2** To talk, write, or think about something for a long time: Don't *dwell* too much on your mistakes. — **dwell'er** *n.*

dwell·ing [dwel'ing] *n.* A place where someone lives; a house or other home: Some American Indians live in adobe *dwellings.*

dwelt [dwelt] A past tense and past participle of DWELL.

dwin·dle [dwin'dəl] *v.* **dwin·dled, dwin·dling** To grow steadily smaller or less; shrink; diminish: Hope of rescue *dwindled.*

dye [dī] *v.* **dyed, dye·ing,** *n.* **1** *v.* To give lasting color to by soaking in liquid coloring matter: to *dye* a dress. **2** *n.* A colored preparation, often dissolved in a liquid, used for dyeing. **3** *n.* The color produced by dyeing. **4** *v.* To take color: Wool *dyes* well. **5** *v.* To color or stain. — **dy'er** *n.*

dyed-in-the-wool [dīd'in·thə·wo͞ol'] *adj.* Complete; thoroughgoing: a *dyed-in-the-wool* scoundrel.

dye·stuff [dī'stuf'] *n.* A natural or artificial substance used for dyeing or making dye.

dy·ing [dī'ing] Present participle of DIE¹.

dyke [dīk] *n., v.* **dyked, dyk·ing** Another spelling of DIKE.

dy·nam·ic [dī·nam'ik] *adj.* **1** Having to do with physical force or energy. **2** Causing or marked by change or action: a *dynamic* period in history. **3** Full of energy and forcefulness: a *dynamic* man.

dy·nam·ics [dī·nam'iks] *n.* **1** The science concerned with things in motion and how forces act to cause or change this motion. **2** The forces causing or controlling activity of any kind: the *dynamics* of progress. ◆ See -ICS.

dy·na·mite [dī'nə·mīt] *n., v.* **dy·na·mit·ed, dy·na·mit·ing** **1** *n.* A powerful explosive made from nitroglycerin, used for blasting. **2** *v.* To blow up with dynamite; blast. **3** *n.* Anything having an explosive effect.

dy·na·mo [dī'nə·mō] *n., pl.* **dy·na·mos** A machine used to change mechanical energy into electricity; generator.

dy·nas·tic [dī·nas'tik] *adj.* Of or having to do with a dynasty: *dynastic* power.

dy·nas·ty [dī'nəs·tē] *n., pl.* **dy·nas·ties** **1** A ruling family whose members reign one after another over a long period of time. **2** The period during which one ruling family is in power: the Ming *dynasty* of China.

dyne [dīn] *n.* In physics, a unit of force equal to the force needed to accelerate a mass of one gram at the rate of one centimeter per second per second.

dys·en·ter·y [dis'ən·ter·ē] *n.* A disease of the intestines, marked by the passing of blood and mucus in loose bowel movements.

dys·pep·sia [dis·pep'shə *or* dis·pep'sē·ə] *n.* Difficulty in digesting food; indigestion. ◆ *Dyspepsia* comes from a Greek word meaning *bad* or *hard to digest.*

dys·pep·tic [dis·pep'tik] **1** *adj.* Suffering from indigestion. **2** *n.* A person suffering from indigestion. **3** *adj.* Cross; irritable.

dz. Abbreviation of DOZEN.

---

add, **ā**ce, **câ**re, **pä**lm;   **e**nd, **ē**qual;   **i**t, **ī**ce;   **o**dd, **ō**pen, **ô**rder;   t**oo**k, p**o͞o**l;   **u**p, b**û**rn;
ə = a in *above*, e in *sicken*, i in *possible*, o in *melon*, u in *circus*;   **yo͞o** = u in *fuse*;   **oi**l;   p**ou**t;
check;   **r**i**ng**;   **th**in;   **th**is;   **zh** in *vision*.   For ¶ reference, see page 64 · HOW TO

E

e or **E** [ē] *n.*, *pl.* **e's** or **E's** The fifth letter of the English alphabet.

E. Abbreviation of EAST or EASTERN.

each [ēch] **1** *adj.* Being one of two or more persons or things, considered as separate from the others; every: *Each* child had a pencil. **2** *pron.* Every one of any group or number taken singly: *Each* of them had his own pencil. **3** *adv.* For or to each person or thing; apiece: The toys cost a dollar *each.* **— each other** One another: They saw *each other* at the same time. ◆ The pronoun *each* is usually treated as a singular: *Each* does *his* own work. For a discussion of *each other, one another* see ONE.

ea·ger [ē′gər] *adj.* **1** Impatiently anxious: *eager* for a chance; He was *eager* to go. **2** Extremely interested: an *eager* collector of stamps. **— ea′ger·ly** *adv.* **— ea′ger·ness** *n.*

ea·gle [ē′gəl] **1** *n.* A very large bird of prey with powerful wings and sharp eyesight. **2** *n.* A design or picture of an eagle used as an emblem, etc. **3** *n.* A former gold coin of the U.S. **4** *adj.* Like an eagle, especially in keenness of sight: an *eagle* eye.

ea·glet [ē′glit] *n.* A young eagle.

ear¹ [ir] *n.* **1** The organ of hearing in man and in animals, especially the outer part of the ear on either side of the head. **2** The ability to hear: to have a good *ear.* **3** An ability to appreciate or understand something that is heard: an *ear* for music. **4** Careful attention. **5** Something like an ear in shape. **— be all ears** To be eagerly attentive.

Bald eagle, wingspread about 6 ft.

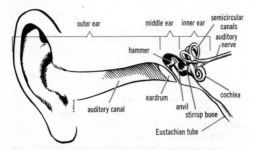

outer ear   middle ear inner ear   semicircular canals
                                     auditory nerve
hammer
eardrum   cochlea
auditory canal   anvil
                      stirrup bone
            Eustachian tube

ear² [ir] **1** *n.* The part of a cereal plant, as corn, rice, wheat, etc., on which the edible grains grow. **2** *v.* To form ears: This corn will *ear* late.

ear·ache [ir′ak′] *n.* Pain in the inner part of the ear.

ear·drum [ir′drum′] *n.* A thin membrane stretched tight inside the ear, which transmits sound waves to the inner part of the ear.

earl [ûrl] *n.* A member of the British nobility next above a viscount, and below a marquis.

earl·dom [ûrl′dəm] *n.* **1** The lands of an earl or countess. **2** The rank or title of an earl.

ear·ly [ûr′lē] *adj.* **ear·li·er, ear·li·est,** *adv.* **1** *adj.* Coming or happening near the beginning: The *early* reports were better than the later ones; *early* evening. **2** *adv.* At or near the beginning: It happened *early* in this century. **3** *adv., adj.* Before the usual or arranged time: The guests came *early; an early* dinner. **4** *adj.* About to be; soon to occur: An *early* truce is expected.

ear·mark [ir′märk′] **1** *n.* A mark on the ear of an animal that tells who the owner is. **2** *v.* To put an earmark on: to *earmark* cattle. **3** *n.* Any quality, sign, or feature that tells something about a person or thing: It has all the *earmarks* of a good car. **4** *v.* To set aside: to *earmark* money for a college education.

earn [ûrn] *v.* **1** To receive in payment of work or service done: to *earn* a good salary. **2** To gain through effort; win or deserve: He *earned* a promotion because of his outstanding record.

ear·nest¹ [ûr′nist] *adj.* Very serious, determined, or sincere: an *earnest* apology; an *earnest* student. **— in earnest 1** With great determination. **2** Serious; sincere: You can't be *in earnest* when you say that. **— ear′nest·ly** *adv.* **— ear′nest·ness** *n.* ◆ See SERIOUS.

ear·nest² [ûr′nist] *n.* Anything given as a pledge or token of something more to come later: Money is a good *earnest* to bind a bargain.

earn·ings [ûr′ningz] *n.pl.* Money earned, as wages or profits.

ear·phone [ir′fōn′] *n.* A listening device, as a telephone receiver, held against the ear.

ear·ring [ir′ring′] *n.* An ornament worn at the lobe of the ear.

ear·shot [ir′shot′] *n.* The distance at which sounds may be heard: Stay within *earshot* of the camp.

ear·split·ting [ir′split′ing] *adj.* Painfully loud; deafening: an *earsplitting* shriek.

earth [ûrth] *n.* **1** (*often written* **Earth**) The planet of the solar system on which man lives, the fifth in size and third in distance from the sun. **2** The dry land of the earth, considered as separate from the oceans, lakes, and rivers. **3** The softer, loose part of land; soil; dirt:

Plant the trees in rich *earth.* **— down to earth** Simple and natural in behavior.

earth·en [ûr′thən] *adj.* Made of earth or baked clay: an *earthen* jug.

earth·en·ware [ûrth′ən·wâr′] *n.* Dishes, pots, pans, and the like, made of baked clay.

earth·ly [ûrth′lē] *adj.* **1** Of or having to do with the earth and this present life rather than with heaven or some imaginary world. **2** Possible: of no *earthly* use.

earth·quake [ûrth′kwāk′] *n.* A shaking or vibration of a part of the earth's surface, caused by an underground shift, volcanic action, etc.

earth·work [ûrth′wûrk′] *n.* A wall or high earthen bank, used for protection or defense.

earth·worm [ûrth′wûrm′] *n.* A very common worm that lives and burrows in the earth, loosening up the soil; angleworm.

earth·y [ûr′thē] *adj.* **earth·i·er, earth·i·est 1** Of or like earth or soil: an *earthy* color. **2** Natural and simple; not refined: an *earthy* dance.

ease [ēz] *n., v.* **eased, eas·ing 1** *n.* Freedom from discomfort or worry: a life of *ease.* **2** *v.* To relieve of mental or physical pain: to *ease* a person of his suffering. **3** *v.* To make less painful: to *ease* a toothache. **4** *n.* Freedom from effort or difficulty: to jump with *ease.* **5** *n.* Freedom from embarrassment or nervousness. **6** *v.* To lessen the pressure or strain on: We must *ease* the chain before it breaks. **7** *v.* To move or put in place slowly and carefully: to *ease* a car into a parking space. **— at ease 1** In a relaxed position: Stand *at ease.* **2** Free from nervousness; relaxed: *at ease* before an audience.

ea·sel [ē′zəl] *n.* A folding frame resting on three legs, used for holding an artist's canvas, chart, etc.

eas·i·ly [ē′zə·lē] *adv.* **1** Without effort, difficulty, or discomfort: to do something *easily.* **2** Without a doubt; certainly: This is *easily* his best work. **3** Very possibly: He may *easily* be correct.

east [ēst] **1** *n.* The direction opposite west; one of the four main points of the compass. If you face the sun at sunrise, you are facing east. **2** *adj.* To, toward, or in the east; eastern. **3** *adj.* Coming from the east: the *east* wind. **4** *adv.* In or toward the east; eastward. **— east of** Farther east than: Illinois is *east of* Iowa. **— the East 1** Asia and its neighboring lands; the Orient. **2** The eastern part of the U.S., especially the part east of the Allegheny Mountains and north of Maryland.

Easel

north

west ←——→ east

south

East·er [ēs′tər] *n.* A Christian festival commemorating the resurrection of Christ. It is celebrated on the first Sunday **(Easter Sunday)** after the first full moon that occurs on or after March 21st.

east·er·ly [ēs′tər·lē] **1** *adj.* In or of the east. **2** *adj., adv.* Toward or from the east.

east·ern [ēs′tərn] *adj.* **1** Of, to, or in the east: an *eastern* bird. **2** From the east: an *eastern* wind. **3** *(often written* **Eastern***)* Of or in the Orient or the eastern part of the U.S.

Eastern Church 1 The official Christian church of the Byzantine Empire. **2** Another name for the EASTERN ORTHODOX CHURCH.

east·ern·er [ēs′tərn·ər] *n.* **1** A person born or living in the east. **2** *(usually written* **Easterner***)* A person born or living in the East, especially in the eastern U.S.

Eastern Hemisphere The half of the earth that lies east of the Atlantic Ocean, including Europe, Africa, Asia, and Australia.

east·ern·most [ēs′tərn·mōst′] *adj.* Farthest east.

Eastern Orthodox Church A group of modern Christian churches, including the Greek Orthodox, that are derived from the Eastern Church of the Byzantine Empire.

East Germany The eastern part of Germany, now a separate state called the **German Democratic Republic,** whose capital is **East Berlin.**

East Indies 1 An island group in the Indian and Pacific Oceans, southeast of Asia. The Philippines, Java, Borneo, and Sumatra are part of this group. **2** The islands of Indonesia.

east·ward [ēst′wərd] **1** *adj., adv.* To or toward the east. **2** *n.* An eastward direction or point.

east·wards [ēst′wərdz] *adv.* Another word for EASTWARD.

eas·y [ē′zē] *adj.* **eas·i·er, eas·i·est,** *adv.* **1** *adj.* Requiring little work or effort; not difficult: an *easy* task. **2** *adj.* Free from worry or trouble: an *easy* mind. **3** *adj.* Comfortable: an *easy* chair. **4** *adj.* Not strict; lenient: an *easy* teacher. **5** *adj.* Not stiff or formal; relaxed: an *easy* manner. **6** *adj.* Not strained or rushed; unhurried: an *easy* pace. **7** *adv. informal* Easily or slowly: Go *easy.* **— take it easy** *informal* To avoid hurry, anger, strain, etc.

eas·y·go·ing [ē′zē·gō′ing] *adj.* Not hurried, strained, or upset about things; relaxed.

eat [ēt] *v.* **ate, eat·en, eat·ing 1** To take in as nourishment; chew and swallow: to *eat* fruit. **2** To have a meal: to *eat* three times a day. **3** To destroy or wear away: His body was *eaten* by disease. **4** To use up: Sodas *ate* up his allowance. **— eat′er** *n.*

eat·a·ble [ēt′ə·bəl] **1** *n. (often pl.)* Food: to have good *eatables.* **2** *adj.* Fit to be eaten.

---

add, āce, câre, pälm;   end, ēqual;   it, īce;   odd, ōpen, ôrder;   tŏŏk, pōōl;   up, bûrn;

ə = a in *above,* e in *sicken,* i in *possible,* o in *melon,* u in *circus;*   yōō = u in *fuse;*   oil;   pout;

check;   ring;   thin;   this;   zh in *vision.*   For ¶ reference, see page 64 · HOW TO

eaves [ēvz] *n.pl.* The lower border or edge of a roof that hangs over the side of the building.

Eaves

eaves·drop [ēvz′drop′] *v.* **eaves·dropped, eaves·drop·ping** To listen secretly to things being said in private. — **eaves′drop′per** *n.*

ebb [eb] **1** *v.* To flow out or recede, as the tide. **2** *n.* The flowing back of the tide to the ocean. **3** *v.* To decline or weaken: His courage *ebbed.* **4** *n.* A condition or period of decline or decay: to reach a low *ebb.*

ebb tide The tide that flows back to the sea.

eb·on [eb′ən] *n., adj.* Ebony: used mostly in poems.

eb·on·y [eb′ə·nē] *n., pl.* **eb·on·ies,** *adj.* **1** *n.* A hard, heavy wood, usually black. **2** *adj. use:* an *ebony* cabinet. **3** *adj.* Black, like ebony.

ec·cen·tric [ek·sen′trik] **1** *adj.* Very different in behavior, appearance, or opinions; odd; peculiar: The *eccentric* old woman carried an open umbrella regardless of the weather. **2** *n.* An eccentric person. **3** *adj.* Not having the same center, as two circles, one within the other. **4** *n.* A wheel set off center turning within a ring or collar to change circular motion into motion up and down.

ec·cen·tric·i·ty [ek′sen·tris′ə·tē] *n., pl.* **ec·cen·tric·i·ties** **1** Something that is odd, peculiar, or eccentric, as a manner of speaking or dressing. **2** The condition of being eccentric: The old man's *eccentricity* caused comment.

Ec·cle·si·as·tes [i·klē′zē·as′tēz] *n.* A book of the Old Testament.

ec·cle·si·as·tic [i·klē′zē·as′tik] **1** *adj.* Ecclesiastical. **2** *n.* A clergyman.

ec·cle·si·as·ti·cal [i·klē′zē·as′ti·kəl] *adj.* Of, having to do with, or suitable for a church.

ech·e·lon [esh′ə·lon] *n.* **1** A steplike formation of troops, ships, or airplanes in which each unit is behind and slightly to one side of the one in front. **2** A level or grade of command: the top *echelon.* **3** A section of a military unit: the rear *echelon.* ◆ *Echelon* comes from a French word meaning *ladder.*

e·chi·no·derm [i·kī′nə·dûrm] *n.* Any of a class of sea animals having a radial arrangement of its parts and often a spiny shell.

ech·o [ek′ō] *n., pl.* **echoes,** *v.* **ech·oed, ech·o·ing** **1** *n.* The repetition of a sound caused by sound waves striking an obstacle and being thrown back toward their starting point. **2** *v.* To repeat or send back the sound of: The walls *echoed* the shot. **3** *v.* To be sounded again as an echo: His shouts *echoed* throughout the house. **4** *v.* To repeat the words, opinions, or actions of: to *echo* great men.

é·clair [ā·klâr′ *or* i·klâr′] *n.* A small, oblong shell of pastry filled with custard or whipped cream and usually topped with chocolate icing.

é·clat [ā·klä′ *or* i·klä′] *n.* **1** Brilliance of action or effect: The musicians performed with *éclat.* **2** Fame; renown; glory.

e·clipse [i·klips′] *n., v.* **e·clipsed, e·clips·ing** **1** *n.* A complete or partial hiding of the sun **(solar eclipse)** as the moon passes between the sun and an observer on the earth. **2** *n.* A complete or partial hiding of the moon **(lunar eclipse)** as the moon passes through the earth's shadow. **3** *v.* To cause an eclipse of; darken. **4** *v.* To surpass; outshine: She *eclipses* her mother in beauty.

Progress of a solar eclipse

e·clip·tic [i·klip′tik] *n.* The great circular path the sun seems to travel among the stars during one revolution of the earth around it.

e·col·o·gy [i·kol′ə·jē *or* ē·kol′ə·jē] *n.* The study of the relationships between living things and their surroundings. — **e·col′o·gist** *n.*

ec·o·nom·ic [ek′ə·nom′ik *or* ē′kə·nom′ik] *adj.* **1** Of or having to do with the science of economics. **2** Of or having to do with money or with the managing of money: They have many *economic* problems.

ec·o·nom·i·cal [ek′ə·nom′i·kəl *or* ē′kə·nom′i·kəl] *adj.* Not wasteful; thrifty: an *economical* little car to operate. — **ec′o·nom′i·cal·ly** *adv.*

ec·o·nom·ics [ek′ə·nom′iks *or* ē′kə·nom′iks] *n.* The science that deals with the production, distribution, and use of goods and services. It includes the study of money, wages, taxes, etc. — **e·con·o·mist** [i·kon′ə·mist] *n.* ◆ See -ICS.

e·con·o·mize [i·kon′ə·mīz] *v.* **e·con·o·mized, e·con·o·miz·ing** **1** To be thrifty and sparing: In the desert, one must *economize* on water. **2** To spend or use with care and thrift. ¶3

e·con·o·my [i·kon′ə·mē] *n., pl.* **e·con·o·mies** **1** Careful and thrifty use of money, food, resources, etc., to avoid waste. **2** The management of the resources or finances of a country, business, home, or other organization.

e·co·sys·tem [ē′kō·sis′təm] *n.* An ecological community along with its nonliving environment thought of as a functioning unit.

ec·ru [ek′rōō] *n., adj.* Light, yellowish brown.

ec·sta·sy [ek′stə·sē] *n., pl.* **ec·sta·sies** A feeling of great happiness or delight; rapture.

ec·stat·ic [ek·stat′ik] *adj.* Full of or marked by ecstasy. — **ec·stat′i·cal·ly** *adv.*

Ec·ua·dor [ek′wə·dôr′] *n.* A country in NW South America. — **Ec′ua·do′ri·an** *adj., n.*

ec·ze·ma [ek′sə·mə *or* eg·zē′mə] *n.* A skin condition marked by red, scaly pimples and severe itching.

-ed A suffix meaning: **1** Taking place in the past, and used to form the past tense and past participle of regular verbs, as in *walked, washed, mended, clothed.* **2** Having, as in *bearded,* having a beard. **3** Like, as in *bigoted,* like a bigot.

ed·dy [ed′ē] *n., pl.* **ed·dies,** *v.* **ed·died,**

ed·dy·ing 1 *n.* A current of water or air moving against a main current, often in circles; a whirlpool or whirlwind. **2** *v.* To move or cause to move in an eddy.

Ed·dy [ed′ē], **Mary Baker,** 1821–1910, U.S. religious leader and founder of Christian Science.

E·den [ēd′(ə)n] *n.* **1** In the Bible, the garden that was the first home of Adam and Eve. **2** Any place of joy and happiness; paradise.

edge [ej] *n., v.* **edged, edg·ing 1** *n.* The line or place where an object or area ends; margin: the *edge* of a table. **2** *v.* To put an edge or border on: to *edge* a collar with lace. **3** *n.* A brink or rim: the *edge* of a cup; the *edge* of a cliff. **4** *n.* The thin, sharp, cutting side of a blade. **5** *v.* To sharpen: to *edge* an ax. **6** *v.* To move sideways or little by little: to *edge* into a crowded room. **— on edge** Too nervous or impatient to sit still; jumpy.

edge·ways [ej′wāz′] Another spelling of EDGEWISE.

edge·wise [ej′wīz′] *adv.* **1** With the edge forward. **2** On or in the direction of the edge.

edg·ing [ej′ing] *n.* Something that forms an edge or is attached to an edge: an *edging* of lace.

edg·y [ej′ē] *adj.* **edg·i·er, edg·i·est** Tense, nervous, or irritable; on edge.

ed·i·ble [ed′ə·bəl] **1** *adj.* Suitable for food; fit to eat. **2** *n.* (*usually pl.*) Something fit to eat.

Edging on a shelf

e·dict [ē′dikt] *n.* An official order, rule, or law that is made known to the public by a formal announcement; decree.

ed·i·fice [ed′ə·fis] *n.* A building, especially a large and impressive structure.

ed·i·fy [ed′ə·fī] *v.* **ed·i·fied, ed·i·fy·ing** To instruct or improve, especially morally or spiritually: A good book *edifies* the mind. **— ed·i·fi·ca·tion** [ed′ə·fə·kā′shən] *n.*

Ed·in·burgh [ed′(ə)n·bûr′ə] *n.* The capital of Scotland, in the eastern part.

Ed·i·son [ed′ə·sən], **Thomas Alva,** 1847–1931, U.S. inventor.

ed·it [ed′it] *v.* **1** To arrange, correct, or in any way prepare for publication: to *edit* a new novel. **2** To direct the publication of: to *edit* a paper.

e·di·tion [i·dish′ən] *n.* **1** The particular form in which a literary work is published: a three-volume *edition*. **2** The total number of copies of a publication issued at any one time and printed from the same plates. **3** A copy belonging to this printing: a first *edition*. ◆ See ADDITION.

ed·i·tor [ed′i·tər] *n.* **1** A person who edits. **2** A person in charge of a newspaper or magazine or of one of its departments: a sports *editor*. **3** A writer of editorials. **— ed′i·tor·ship′** *n.*

ed·i·to·ri·al [ed′i·tôr′ē·əl] **1** *n.* An article in a newspaper or magazine expressing an opinion held by the editor or publisher. **2** *adj.* Of or having to do with an editor or editing: *editorial* policy.

ed·u·cate [ej′ōō·kāt] *v.* **ed·u·cat·ed, ed·u·cat·ing 1** To teach, develop, or train: to *educate* one's ear to appreciate good music. **2** To provide schooling for: to *educate* one's children.

ed·u·ca·tion [ej′ōō·kā′shən] *n.* **1** The development of a person's mind, body, or natural talents through study and training: *Education* ought not to end with school. **2** Instruction or training: a college *education*. **3** All of the things a person learns by study or training.

ed·u·ca·tion·al [ej′ōō·kā′shən·əl] *adj.* **1** Of or having to do with education: an *educational* meeting. **2** That instructs or gives information: an *educational* trip. **— ed′u·ca′tion·al·ly** *adv.*

ed·u·ca·tor [ej′ōō·kā′tər] *n.* **1** A teacher. **2** A person skilled in the field of education.

-ee A suffix meaning: **1** A person who undergoes or benefits from an action, as in *payee*, a person who receives payment. **2** A person who is or does something, as in *absentee*, a person who is absent, or in *employee*, a person who is employed.

eel [ēl] *n., pl.* **eels** or **eel** A fish having a long, snakelike body and a smooth skin.

e'en [ēn] *adv.* Even: used mostly in poems.

e'er [âr] *adv.* Ever: used mostly in poems.

ee·rie or **ee·ry** [ir′ē or ē′rē] *adj.* **ee·ri·er, ee·ri·est** Causing or arousing fear; weird; strange: an *eerie* feeling; an *eerie* sound.

Eel, 30 in. long

ef·face [i·fās′] *v.* **ef·faced, ef·fac·ing 1** To rub or blot out; get rid of; destroy: Time had *effaced* the words carved on the ancient pillar; to *efface* old memories. **2** To hide or keep (oneself) from the notice or attention of others.

ef·fect [i·fekt′] **1** *n.* Something brought about by some action or cause; result: the *effect* of an explosion. **2** *n.* The ability or power to produce some result: Punishment had little *effect* on her. **3** *v.* To bring about or cause; accomplish: The prisoners *effected* an escape. **4** *n.* An impression or reaction made on the mind or body: the *effect* of music; the *effect* of drugs. **5** *n.* (*pl.*) Personal goods or belongings. **— for effect** In order to be noticed or make an impression. **— in effect 1** In actual fact; really: *In effect* she refused the offer. **2** In active force or operation: The law is now *in effect*. **— take effect** To begin to act upon something or bring about a result. ◆ *Effect* and *affect* are often confused because they sound alike, but their meanings are different. *To effect* means *to bring about* or *cause to happen*: Good treatment should *effect* a cure. *To affect* means *to influence* or *have an effect upon*:

The accident *affected* his outlook on life. Both words are based on the Latin word for *to do*, but *effect* comes from elements meaning *to do out*, and *affect* from elements meaning *to do to*.

ef·fec·tive [i·fek′tiv] *adj.* **1** Producing or able to produce the proper result; efficient: an *effective* weapon. **2** Producing a great impression; impressive: an *effective* speaker. **3** In effect or in force: This law is only *effective* in July. — **ef·fec′tive·ly** *adv.* — **ef·fec′tive·ness** *n.* ◆ *Effective* and *effectual* both refer to the ability to achieve a desired result. *Effective* is the more general term, and may apply to both persons and things: an *effective* leader; an *effective* strategy. *Effectual* is usually limited to things: an *effectual* remedy; an *effectual* plan.

ef·fec·tu·al [i·fek′cho̅o̅·əl] *adj.* Producing or able to produce a desired result or effect. — **ef·fec′tu·al·ly** *adv.* ◆ See EFFECTIVE.

ef·fec·tu·ate [i·fek′cho̅o̅·āt] *v.* **ef·fec·tu·at·ed, ef·fec·tu·at·ing** To bring about, accomplish; effect.

ef·fem·i·nate [i·fem′ə·nit] *adj.* Having qualities, traits, or ways usually found in a woman; unmanly. — **ef·fem·i·na·cy** [i·fem′ə·nə·sē] *n.*

ef·fer·ent [ef′ər·ənt] *adj.* Carrying or carried outward. Efferent nerves carry impulses from the brain or spinal cord to the muscles.

ef·fer·vesce [ef′ər·ves′] *v.* **ef·fer·vesced, ef·fer·vesc·ing** **1** To give off bubbles, as soda water. **2** To be lively and enthusiastic. — **ef′·fer·ves′cence** *n.*

ef·fer·ves·cent [ef′ər·ves′ənt] *adj.* **1** Bubbling up. **2** Full of life and high spirits; lively: an *effervescent* personality.

ef·fete [i·fēt′] *adj.* **1** Having lost strength and vigor; worn-out. **2** Unable to produce anything new or original; decadent: an *effete* society.

ef·fi·ca·cious [ef′ə·kā′shəs] *adj.* Producing the desired effect or result; effective: an *efficacious* medicine. — **ef′fi·ca′cious·ly** *adv.* — **ef′fi·ca′cious·ness** *n.*

ef·fi·ca·cy [ef′ə·kə·sē] *n.* Power to produce an effect wanted; effectiveness: I doubted the *efficacy* of the new medicine.

ef·fi·cien·cy [i·fish′ən·sē] *n.* The ability to produce results without any waste of time, effort, money, etc.

ef·fi·cient [i·fish′ənt] *adj.* Producing results with the least effort or waste; capable: an *efficient* motor. — **ef·fi′cient·ly** *adv.*

ef·fi·gy [ef′ə·jē] *n., pl.* **ef·fi·gies** **1** A painting or statue of a person. **2** A crude, often stuffed figure of a person who is disliked: The dictator was burnt in *effigy*.

ef·fort [ef′ərt] *n.* **1** The use of physical or mental energy or power to get something done: Playing tennis requires *effort*. **2** Something produced by work and effort: A new play is a theatrical *effort*. **3** An attempt: He made no *effort* to see us.

ef·fort·less [ef′ərt·lis] *adj.* Requiring or showing little or no effort: His *effortless* playing of the violin is amazing. — **ef′fort·less·ly** *adv.*

ef·front·er·y [i·frun′tər·ē] *n.* Shameless or insolent boldness; audacity; impudence: While a guest at my house, he had the *effrontery* to criticize the food.

ef·ful·gence [i·ful′jəns] *n.* Great brightness or radiance of light.

ef·ful·gent [i·ful′jənt] *adj.* Shining brilliantly; radiant; splendid.

ef·fu·sion [i·fyo̅o̅′zhən] *n.* **1** The action of pouring forth or out: The *effusion* of blood was finally checked. **2** A very free, unrestrained outpouring of emotion or words.

ef·fu·sive [i·fyo̅o̅′siv] *adj.* Overly emotional and enthusiastic; gushing: an *effusive* greeting. — **ef·fu′sive·ly** *adv.*

eft [eft] *n.* A newt or small lizard.

e.g. For example: birds, *e.g.* starlings, robins, sparrows, etc. ◆ *e.g.* is an abbreviation of a Latin phrase.

egg¹ [eg] *n.* **1** The round or oval body produced by female birds, insects, and most reptiles and fishes, and containing the material from which the young bird, fish, etc., develops. An egg is covered by a thin shell or skin. **2** The egg of the domestic hen, raw or cooked.

egg² [eg] *v.* To urge or coax into doing something: We *egged* him on to jump.

egg·beat·er [eg′bē′tər] *n.* A cooking utensil having blades that whirl, used to beat eggs, whip cream, etc.

egg·head [eg′hed′] *n. informal* A person mostly interested in intellectual things; a highbrow.

egg·nog [eg′nog′] *n.* A drink made of beaten eggs, milk, sugar, and sometimes whisky, brandy, or wine.

egg·plant [eg′plant′] *n.* A plant bearing a large egg-shaped, usually purple-skinned fruit that is cooked and eaten as a vegetable.

egg·shell [eg′shel′] **1** *n.* The hard, brittle covering of the egg of a bird. **2** *adj.* Thin and easily broken. **3** *adj.* Pale yellow or ivory: *eggshell* satin.

eg·lan·tine [eg′lən·tīn *or* eg′lən·tēn] *n.* Another name for SWEETBRIER, a wild rose.

e·go [ē′gō] *n., pl.* **e·gos** **1** The part of a person's mind or self by which he is aware that he is different from all other people in his thoughts, feelings, and actions. **2** *informal* Egotism. ◆ *Ego* comes from the Latin word for *I*.

e·go·ism [ē′gō·iz′əm] *n.* **1** The tendency to think mainly of one's own welfare; selfishness. **2** Egotism. — **e′go·ist** *n.*

e·go·tism [ē′gə·tiz′əm] *n.* **1** The habit of talking or writing about oneself, often boastfully; conceit. **2** Egoism. — **e′go·tist** *n.*

e·go·tis·ti·cal [ē′gə·tis′ti·kəl] *adj.* Inclined to think too highly of oneself; conceited. — **e′go·tis′ti·cal·ly** *adv.*

e·gre·gious [i·grē′jəs *or* i·grē′jē·əs] *adj.* Extremely bad; glaring: an *egregious* mistake.

e·gress [ē′gres] *n.* **1** A way of getting out; exit. **2** A going out: The fire department requires all buildings to have a ready means of *egress*.

e·gret [ē′grit] *n.* **1** A white heron, valued for its long, beautiful white plumes. **2** One of its plumes; aigrette.

E·gypt [ē′jipt] *n.* A country of NE Africa, officially called the United Arab Republic.

E·gyp·tian [ē·jip′shən] **1** *adj.* Of or from Egypt. **2** *n.* A person born in or a citizen of Egypt. **3** *n.* The language of ancient Egypt.

Egret, about 2 ft. high

eh [ā *or* e] *interj.* What; isn't that so: usually spoken with the voice rising: He had a bad fall, *eh*?

ei·der [ī′dər] *n.* A large sea duck found in northern waters.

ei·der·down [ī′dər·doun′] *n.* **1** The soft feathers of the eider duck, used for stuffing pillows and quilts. **2** A quilt stuffed with eiderdown.

eight or **8** [āt] *n.*, *adj.* One more than seven.

eight·een or **18** [ā′tēn′] *n., adj.* One more than seventeen.

eight·eenth or **18th** [ā′tēnth′] **1** *adj.* Next after the seventeenth. **2** *n.* The eighteenth one. **3** *adj.* Being one of eighteen equal parts. **4** *n.* An eighteenth part.

eighth or **8th** [ātth *or* āth] **1** *adj.* Next after the seventh. **2** *n.* The eighth one. **3** *adj.* Being one of eight equal parts. **4** *n.* An eighth part.

eighth note In music, a note having one eighth the time value of a whole note.

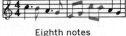

Eighth notes

eight·i·eth or **80th** [ā′tē·ith] **1** *adj.* Tenth in order after the seventieth. **2** *n.* The eightieth one. **3** *adj.* Being one of eighty equal parts. **4** *n.* An eightieth part.

eight·y or **80** [ā′tē] *n., pl.* **eight·ies 1** *n., adj.* Ten more than seventy. **2** *n.* (*pl.*) The years between the age of 80 and the age of 90.

Ein·stein [īn′stīn], **Albert,** 1879–1955, U.S. physicist born in Germany.

Eir·e [âr′ə] *n.* The Irish Gaelic name for the Republic of Ireland.

Ei·sen·how·er [ī′zən·hou′ər], **Dwight David,** 1890–1969, U.S. general and 34th president of the U.S., 1953–1961.

ei·ther [ē′thər *or* ī′thər] **1** *adj.* One or the other of two: Use *either* hand. **2** *pron.* One or the other; one of two: *Either* will do. **3** *adj.* Each of two; one and the other: They sat on *either* side of him. **4** *conj.* In one of two or more

cases: used before two or more choices joined by *or: Either* you will buy it *or* you won't. **5** *adv.* Any more so; in addition; besides: If he can't speak, I won't *either*. ◆ *Either* and *neither* in formal writing both take a singular verb: *Either* of the boys *has* a chance to win. In informal speech and writing, a plural verb is often used: *Are either* of them going to the party? When there are two subjects, one singular and one plural, the verb agrees with the subject closest to it: *Neither* he nor *they are* going.

e·jac·u·late [i·jak′yə·lāt] *v.* **e·jac·u·lat·ed, e·jac·u·lat·ing** To say or utter suddenly: "No!" he *ejaculated*.

e·jac·u·la·tion [i·jak′yə·lā′shən] *n.* A brief utterance or exclamation.

e·ject [i·jekt′] *v.* To throw or put out; expel: to *eject* steam; The police *ejected* the unruly people at the fair. **— e·jec′tion** *n.*

e·jec·tor [i·jek′tər] *n.* **1** A person or thing that ejects. **2** A device that ejects used material, as shells or cartridges from a gun.

eke [ēk] *v.* **eked, ek·ing 1** To make with difficulty and effort: to *eke* out a living. **2** To add to little by little: to *eke* out one's income.

e·lab·o·rate [*v.* i·lab′ə·rāt, *adj.* i·lab′ər·it] *v.* **e·lab·o·rat·ed, e·lab·o·rat·ing,** *adj.* **1** *v.* To work out or develop very carefully: to *elaborate* an idea. **2** *adj.* Worked out or developed carefully and thoroughly: an *elaborate* plan. **3** *adj.* Fancy and usually costly or luxurious in its details or parts: an *elaborate* dress; an *elaborate* dinner. **4** *v.* To add more details: He always *elaborates* on his stories. **— e·lab′o·rate·ly** *adv.* **— e·lab′o·ra′tion** *n.*

e·land [ē′lənd] *n.* A large, oxlike antelope of Africa, having twisted horns.

e·lapse [i·laps′] *v.* **e·lapsed, e·laps·ing** To slip by; pass away: said about time: Six months *elapsed* before we met again.

e·las·tic [i·las′tik] **1** *adj.* Able to return to a former size or shape after being pulled or pressed: an *elastic* rubber ball. **2** *n.* Any elastic material or fabric. **3** *adj.* Springy; lively: an *elastic* stride. **4** *adj.* Easily adaptable or adjustable, so as to fit changes, new circumstances, etc.: an *elastic* schedule.

e·las·tic·i·ty [i·las′tis′ə·tē] *n.* The quality of being elastic.

e·late [i·lāt′] *v.* **e·lat·ed, e·lat·ing** To cause to feel full of joy or pride.

e·lat·ed [i·lā′tid] *adj.* Filled with joy or pride, as over success or good fortune.

e·la·tion [i·lā′shən] *n.* A feeling of joy or triumph.

El·ba [el′bə] *n.* An island off the west coast of Italy, where Napoleon was held in exile in 1814 and 1815.

El·be [el′bə] *n.* A river in central Europe, flowing into the North Sea.

---

add, āce, câre, pälm;   end, ēqual;   it, īce;   odd, ōpen, ôrder;   tŏŏk, pool;   up, bûrn;

ə = a in *above*, e in *sicken*, i in *possible*, o in *melon*, u in *circus*;   yōō = u in *fuse*;   oil;   pout;

check; ring; thin; this; zh in *vision*.   For ¶ reference, see page 64 · HOW TO

el·bow [el′bō] **1** *n.* The joint at the bend of the arm between the forearm and the upper arm. **2** *n.* Something having an angle or bend like an elbow, as a curved length of pipe. **3** *v.* To push or jostle, as if with the elbows: to *elbow* one's way through a crowd.

Elbow joint

elbow grease *informal* Physical effort; hard work: Use some *elbow grease* on that dirty pan.

el·bow·room [el′bō-rōōm′] *n.* Enough room to work or move about in.

eld·er[1] [el′dər] **1** *adj.* Older: an *elder* sister. **2** *n.* An older person. **3** *n.* A church official.

el·der[2] [el′dər] *n.* A shrub with white flowers and dark purple or red berries.

el·der·ber·ry [el′dər·ber′ē] *n., pl.* **el·der·ber·ries 1** The berry of the elder, used to make wine. **2** Another name for ELDER[2].

eld·er·ly [el′dər·lē] *adj.* Approaching old age; rather old. ◆ See OLD.

eld·est [el′dist] *adj., n.* Oldest.

El Do·ra·do or **El·do·ra·do** [el′də·rä′dō] *n.* **1** An imaginary South American city long sought by early Spanish explorers because it was believed to be rich in gold and jewels. **2** Any region that is rich in gold or in opportunities.

e·lect [i·lekt′] **1** *v.* To choose for an office by vote; select: to *elect* a mayor. **2** *adj.* Elected to office but not yet sworn in: a president *elect*. **3** *v.* To choose; decide: to *elect* to remain behind. **— the elect** A specially favored group: She thinks she is one of *the elect*.

e·lec·tion [i·lek′shən] *n.* **1** The selecting of a person or persons for any position or honor, especially by voting. **2** A choice.

e·lec·tion·eer [i·lek′shən·ir′] *v.* To work to get votes for a candidate or political party.

e·lec·tive [i·lek′tiv] **1** *adj.* Settled by an election: an *elective* position. **2** *adj.* Selected by vote: an *elective* official. **3** *n.* A school subject that may be chosen or not as the student prefers. **4** *adj.* Left to choice; optional: an *elective* course.

e·lec·tor [i·lek′tər] *n.* **1** A person who is qualified to vote in an election. **2** *U.S.* A member of the electoral college. **— e·lec′tor·al** *adj.*

electoral college In the U.S., a group of persons chosen by the voters of each State to elect formally the President and Vice-President.

e·lec·tor·ate [i·lek′tər·it] *n.* Those persons who are eligible to vote in an election.

e·lec·tric [i·lek′trik] *adj.* **1** Consisting of or having to do with electricity. **2** Producing or carrying electricity: an *electric* generator; *electric* cable. **3** Operated by electricity: an *electric* train. **4** Thrilling or sparkling: an *electric* personality. **— e·lec′tri·cal·ly** *adv.*

e·lec·tri·cal [i·lek′tri·kəl] *adj.* Electric: *electrical* engineering; an *electrical* connection.

electric current A flow of electrons through a conductor, as through a wire.

electric eel An eellike, fresh-water fish found in South America, capable of delivering powerful electric shocks.

electric eye Another name for PHOTOELECTRIC CELL.

e·lec·tri·cian [i·lek·trish′ən] *n.* A person who designs, installs, operates, or repairs electrical equipment or machinery.

e·lec·tric·i·ty [i·lek·tris′ə·tē] *n.* **1** A property of matter by which some atomic particles (electrons and protons) attract and repel each other and by their movements create magnetic fields. **2** Energy in the form of an excess or shortage of electrons, as caused by rubbing glass with silk. **3** Energy in the form of electrons flowing through a conductor; an electric current. Electricity provides power for lighting, heating, and operating machines and devices.

e·lec·tri·fy [i·lek′trə·fī] *v.* **e·lec·tri·fied, e·lec·tri·fy·ing 1** To charge with or expose to electricity: to *electrify* steel. **2** To equip for using electricity: to *electrify* a barn. **3** To arouse; startle; thrill: to *electrify* a crowd. **— e·lec′tri·fi·ca′tion**, *n.*

electro- A combining form meaning: Electric; by, with, or of electricity, as in *electroplate*, to plate by means of electricity. ◆ See ELECTRO-MAGNET.

e·lec·tro·cute [i·lek′trə·kyōōt] *v.* **e·lec·tro·cut·ed, e·lec·tro·cut·ing** To execute or kill by electricity. **— e·lec′tro·cu′tion** *n.*

e·lec·trode [i·lek′trōd] *n.* Any of the points at which current enters or leaves an electrical device; terminal.

e·lec·trol·y·sis [i·lek·trol′ə·sis] *n.* The process of separating an electrolyte into its elements by passing an electric current through it. Electrolysis deposits a metal in electroplating.

e·lec·tro·lyte [i·lek′trə·līt] *n.* A liquid that can conduct electricity and which will be decomposed by the electric current. **— e·lec·tro·lyt·ic** [i·lek′trə·lit′ik] *adj.*

e·lec·tro·mag·net [i·lek′trō·mag′nit] *n.* A device made of a soft iron core surrounded by a coil of insulated wire. The core becomes a magnet while an electric current is passing through the wire. **— e·lec·tro·mag·net·ic** [i·lek′trō·mag·net′ik] *adj.* ◆ *Electromagnet* is formed by combining *electro-*, meaning *electric*, with *magnet*. *Electro-* comes from a Greek word meaning *amber*.

An electromagnet made from a nail and a coil of wire.

electromagnetic wave Any wave made up of electrical and magnetic pulsations moving through space at about 186,000 miles per second. Light, radio waves, X-rays, and cosmic rays are electromagnetic waves.

e·lec·tro·mag·net·ism [i·lek′trō·mag′nə·tiz′·

əm] *n.* **1** Magnetism that is developed by a current of electricity. **2** A branch of science that deals with the relationship between electricity and magnetism.

e·lec·tro·mo·tive [i·lek′trə·mō′tiv] *adj.* Producing or tending to produce an electric current.

e·lec·tron [i·lek′tron] *n.* One of the negatively charged particles that surround the central core (nucleus) of an atom.

e·lec·tron·ic [i·lek′tron′ik] *adj.* Of or having to do with electrons or electronics. — **e·lec′tron′·i·cal·ly** *adv.*

e·lec·tron·ics [i·lek′tron′iks] *n.* The branch of engineering that deals with the design and manufacture of radios, television sets, and other devices that use electron tubes, transistors, and similar parts. ◆ See -ICS.

electron microscope An instrument that uses a beam of electrons instead of light rays to magnify very tiny objects.

electron tube A glass or metal tube containing a vacuum or a small amount of gas, in which electrons are emitted by a heated cathode and their flow to the anode is controlled.

e·lec·tro·plate [i·lek′trə·plāt′] *v.* **e·lec·tro·plat·ed, e·lec·tro·plat·ing** To deposit a metal film or coating upon by means of an electric current: to *electroplate* a ring.

e·lec·tro·type [i·lek′trə·tīp] *n.* A metallic copy of something to be printed, made by electroplating a wax or plastic mold of the original page of type.

el·e·gance [el′ə·gəns] *n.* Good taste and luxuriousness in clothes, household furnishings or decorations, etc.

el·e·gant [el′ə·gənt] *adj.* **1** Tasteful, luxurious, and beautiful: an *elegant* evening gown. **2** Graceful and refined in style, manners, or taste: an *elegant* old gentleman. — **el′e·gant·ly** *adv.*

el·e·gy [el′ə·jē] *n., pl.* **el·e·gies** A melancholy or sad poem, often expressing sorrow for a dead person.

el·e·ment [el′ə·mənt] *n.* **1** Any of a limited number of substances of which all matter is made. An element is made up of atoms that are all alike and that cannot be changed by chemical means. Some elements are gold, silver, carbon, oxygen, and iron. **2** A necessary or basic part of anything: Hard work is an *element* of success; the *elements* of French. **3** A quality or trait: an *element* of mischief. **4** A condition or environment that is natural or pleasing to a person or thing: to be out of one's *element*. **5** (*pl.*) Weather conditions, especially if violent or severe: the fury of the *elements*. **6** One of the four substances (earth, air, fire, water) which the ancients believed made up the universe.

el·e·men·tal [el′ə·men′təl] *adj.* **1** Of or having to do with an element. **2** Simple; basic; fundamental: an *elemental* principle. **3** Of or having

to do with the powerful forces at work in nature: The storm broke with *elemental* fury.

el·e·men·ta·ry [el′ə·men′tər·ē] *adj.* **1** Of or dealing with simple, beginning rules or principles: an *elementary* course in arithmetic. **2** Simple and undeveloped: an *elementary* knowledge of chemistry.

elementary school A school having six or eight grades, where elementary subjects such as reading, writing, spelling, and arithmetic are taught.

el·e·phant [el′ə·fənt] *n.* The largest of all animals that live on land, having a long, tubelike snout or trunk and two ivory tusks. It is found in both Africa and Asia.

el·e·phan·tine [el′ə·fan′tēn *or* el′ə·fən·tēn *or* el′ə·fan′tīn *or* el′ə·fən·tīn] *adj.* **1** Of an elephant or elephants. **2** Huge, clumsy, and heavy, like an elephant.

el·e·vate [el′ə·vāt] *v.* **el·e·vat·ed, el·e·vat·ing** **1** To raise;

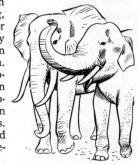

An African elephant and an Indian elephant

lift up: a building *elevated* on stilts. **2** To raise to a higher position: He was *elevated* to the presidency. **3** To raise the spirits or improve the quality of: to *elevate* the mind.

el·e·va·tion [el′ə·vā′shən] *n.* **1** The act of elevating. **2** An elevated place, as a hill. **3** Height above the ground or above sea level.

el·e·va·tor [el′ə·vā′tər] *n.* **1** A movable, usually enclosed platform or cage for carrying passengers or freight up and down, as inside a building. **2** A large warehouse for storing grain. **3** A movable flat piece attached to the tail of an airplane, used to make the airplane go up or down.

e·lev·en or **11** [i·lev′ən] *n., adj.* One more than ten: *Eleven* will attend; *eleven* trees.

e·lev·enth or **11th** [i·lev′ənth] **1** *adj.* Next after the tenth. **2** *n.* The eleventh one. **3** *adj.* Being one of eleven equal parts. **4** *n.* An eleventh part. — **eleventh hour** The latest possible time: saved at the *eleventh hour*.

elf [elf] *n., pl.* **elves** A small, usually mischievous fairy. — **elf′ish** *adj.*

elf·in [el′fin] *adj.* Of or like an elf; mischievous; impish: an *elfin* smile.

El Grec·o [el grek′ō], 1548?–1614, Spanish painter born in Crete. ◆ *El Greco* is the Spanish term for *The Greek*.

e·lic·it [i·lis′it] *v.* To draw out or call forth: to *elicit* a reply; to *elicit* the truth. ◆ *Elicit* and *illicit*, although pronounced alike, have different

---

add, āce, câre, pälm; end, ēqual; it, īce; odd, ōpen, ôrder; took, pool; up, bûrn;
ə = a in *above*, e in *sicken*, i in *possible*, o in *melon*, u in *circus*; yōō = u in *fuse*; oil; pout;
check; ring; thin; this; zh in *vision*. For ¶ reference, see page 64 · HOW TO

meanings. *Elicit* is a verb meaning *to draw out:* The sharp cross-examination of the district attorney *elicited* a confession. *Illicit* is an adjective meaning *not legal* or *not allowed*: an *illicit* trade in smuggled goods.

el·i·gi·ble [el′ə·jə·bəl] *adj.* **1** Capable of or legally qualified for something: Minors are not *eligible* to vote. **2** Fit; suitable; desirable, as for marriage. — **el′i·gi·bil′i·ty** *n.*

E·li·jah [i·lī′jə] *n.* A Hebrew prophet who lived during the ninth century B.C.

e·lim·i·nate [i·lim′ə·nāt] *v.* **e·lim·i·nat·ed, e·lim·i·nat·ing 1** To get rid of: Sunglasses *eliminate* glare. **2** To take out or omit: to *eliminate* a sentence. **3** To remove from competition, as by defeating: to be *eliminated* from a tennis tournament. — **e·lim′i·na′tion** *n.* — **e·lim′i·na′tor** *n.*

El·i·ot [el′ē·ət], **George,** 1819–1880, English woman novelist whose real name was Mary Ann Evans.

El·i·ot [el′ē·ət], **Thomas Stearns,** 1888–1965, British poet and critic who was born in the U.S., usually called T. S. Eliot.

E·li·sha [i·lī′shə] *n.* A Hebrew prophet of the ninth century B.C., successor of Elijah.

e·lite or **é·lite** [i·lēt′ *or* ā·lēt′] *n.* The social or professional group considered to be the best: Only the *elite* were invited.

e·lix·ir [i·lik′sər] *n.* **1** An imaginary substance sought by medieval alchemists, who believed it could change ordinary metals to gold, restore youth, and prolong life indefinitely. **2** A sweetened liquid containing alcohol and drugs or herbs, used as a medicine and as a flavoring.

E·liz·a·beth I [i·liz′ə·bəth], 1533–1603, Queen of England, 1558–1603.

E·liz·a·beth II [i·liz′ə·bəth], born 1926, Queen of England, 1952– .

E·liz·a·be·than [i·liz′ə·bē′thən *or* i·liz′ə·beth′·ən] **1** *adj.* Of or having to do with Queen Elizabeth I or the time during which she reigned. **2** *n.* An Englishman, especially a writer or statesman, who lived during the reign of Elizabeth I.

elk [elk] *n., pl.* **elks** or **elk 1** A large deer of North America. It is also called a wapiti. **2** A large deer of Europe and Asia, similar to the moose of North America.

ell [el] *n.* An old measure of length, in England equal to 45 inches.

el·lipse [i·lips′] *n.* A closed curve which is a set of points so located that the sum of the distances from any point to two interior points, called the foci, is constant. See diagram in next column.

Elk, 5 ft. high at shoulder

el·lip·tic [i·lip′tik] *adj.* Elliptical.

el·lip·ti·cal [i·lip′tə·kəl] *adj.* Shaped like an ellipse. — **el·lip′ti·cal·ly** *adv.*

F, F′ are the foci
FA + F′A = FB + F′B
Ellipse

elm [elm] *n.* **1** A large shade tree having arching branches. **2** The wood of this tree.

el·o·cu·tion [el′ə·kyōo′shən] *n.* A way or style of making speeches or reciting, especially an old-fashioned style.

e·lon·gate [i·lông′gāt] *v.* **e·lon·gat·ed, e·lon·gat·ing** To increase in length; lengthen; stretch out: He lost so much weight that he seemed *elongated*. — **e′lon·ga′tion** *n.*

e·lope [i·lōp′] *v.* **e·loped, e·lop·ing** To run away in secret, especially to get married. — **e·lope′ment** *n.*

el·o·quence [el′ə·kwəns] *n.* **1** A moving and skillful use of language, especially in speaking: The orator's *eloquence* stirred us all. **2** Expressiveness: the *eloquence* of her glance.

el·o·quent [el′ə·kwənt] *adj.* **1** Effective or skillful in expressing feelings, ideas, etc.; moving: an *eloquent* speaker. **2** Showing much feeling; expressive. — **el′o·quent·ly** *adv.*

El Sal·va·dor [el sal′və·dôr] A small country in western Central America.

else [els] **1** *adj.* Other; different or more: I want something *else;* What *else* could I do? **2** *adv.* In a different place, time, or manner: How *else* can I do it? **3** *adv.* If not; otherwise: Run fast or *else* he will catch you! ◆ Today, the expressions *someone else, anyone else,* etc., are usually treated as compound pronouns. This means that the possessive, instead of being *anyone's else,* is *anyone else's:* Let's go to *someone else's* house.

else·where [els′(h)wâr′] *adv.* In or to another place or places.

e·lu·ci·date [i·lōō′sə·dāt] *v.* **e·lu·ci·dat·ed, e·lu·ci·dat·ing** To explain; clarify: The ambassador was asked to *elucidate* his proposal. — **e·lu′ci·da′tion** *n.*

e·lude [i·lōōd′] *v.* **e·lud·ed, e·lud·ing 1** To escape from or avoid by quickness or cleverness: The fugitive *eluded* the police. **2** To escape the understanding of: The meaning *eludes* me.

e·lu·sive [i·lōō′siv] *adj.* **1** Escaping or avoiding capture. **2** Hard to understand, remember, or recognize: *elusive* ideas; an *elusive* melody.

E·ly·sian [i·lizh′ən] *adj.* **1** Of or like Elysium. **2** Heavenly; delightful.

E·ly·si·um [i·lizh′ē·əm *or* i·liz′ē·əm] *n.* **1** In Greek myths, a pleasant region of the underworld where the souls of good people went after death. It is often called the **Elysian Fields. 2** Any heavenly or delightful place or condition.

'em [əm] *pron. informal* Them.

e·ma·ci·ate [i·mā′shē·āt] *v.* **e·ma·ci·at·ed, e·ma·ci·at·ing 1** To make abnormally thin: *emaciated* by hunger or disease. **2** *adj. use:* an *emaciated* old woman. — **e·ma′ci·a′tion** *n.*

em·a·nate [em′ə·nāt] *v.* **em·a·nat·ed, em·a·nat·ing** To come or flow forth from a source;

issue: Heat *emanated* from the lighted stove; News *emanates* from Washington.

em·a·na·tion [em′ə·nā′shən] *n.* **1** The action of emanating. **2** Something that emanates.

e·man·ci·pate [i·man′sə·pāt] *v.* **e·man·ci·pat·ed, e·man·ci·pat·ing** To set free, as from slavery or oppression. **— e·man′ci·pa′tion** *n.* **— e·man′ci·pa′tor** *n.*

e·mas·cu·late [i·mas′kyə·lāt] *v.* **e·mas·cu·lat·ed, e·mas·cu·lat·ing** **1** To castrate. **2** To deprive of strength or force; make weak: The amendments to the bill *emasculated* it.

em·balm [im·bäm′] *v.* To preserve (a dead body) from decay by treatment with chemicals and other steps. **— em·balm′er** *n.*

em·bank·ment [im·bangk′mənt] *n.* A mound or bank of stone, cement, earth, etc., built usually to hold back water or support a roadway.

em·bar·go [im·bär′gō] *n., pl.* **em·bar·goes,** *v.* **em·bar·goed, em·bar·go·ing** **1** *n.* An order by a government that prohibits certain ships from entering or leaving its ports. **2** *n.* Any official restriction, rule, etc., that prevents or interferes with trade. **3** *v.* To place an embargo on.

em·bark [im·bärk′] *v.* **1** To go or put on board a ship for a voyage. **2** To begin, as an adventure, project, etc.; set forth: to *embark* on a new career. **— em′bar·ka′tion** *n.*

em·bar·rass [im·bar′əs] *v.* **1** To make self-conscious and uneasy or confused. **2** To hinder; hamper: *embarrassed* by lack of funds.

em·bar·rass·ment [im·bar′əs·mənt] *n.* **1** An embarrassed condition or feeling. **2** Something that embarrasses.

em·bas·sy [em′bə·sē] *n., pl.* **em·bas·sies** **1** The official home or headquarters of an ambassador in a foreign country. **2** An ambassador and the people working with him. **3** The assignment or duties entrusted to an ambassador.

em·bat·tled [im·bat′(ə)ld] *adj.* **1** Prepared for and awaiting battle. **2** Fortified against attack.

em·bed [im·bed′] *v.* **em·bed·ded, em·bed·ding** To set firmly in a surrounding substance.

em·bel·lish [im·bel′ish] *v.* To make more attractive by adding something; decorate: to *embellish* a cake with icing; to *embellish* a story with vivid details. **— em·bel′lish·ment** *n.*

em·ber [em′bər] *n.* **1** A coal, piece of wood, etc., no longer in flames but still glowing. **2** (*pl.*) A fire that has died down but is still glowing.

em·bez·zle [im·bez′əl] *v.* **em·bez·zled, em·bez·zling** To take (someone else's money, etc.) that has been entrusted to one's care: The treasurer *embezzled* large sums from his company. **— em·bez′zle·ment** *n.* **— em·bez′zler** *n.*

Glowing embers

em·bit·ter [im·bit′ər] *v.* To make bitter or resentful: a woman *embittered* by hardships.

em·bla·zon [em·blā′zən] *v.* **1** To mark or decorate with brilliant colors or designs: The title was *emblazoned* in gold on the cover; a banner *emblazoned* with the royal arms. **2** To honor with praise; celebrate: events *emblazoned* in history.

em·blem [em′bləm] *n.* **1** Something that stands for an idea, belief, nation, etc.; symbol: The lily is the *emblem* of purity. **2** A seal, badge, etc.: He wore his club's *emblem*.

em·blem·at·ic [em′blə·mat′ik] *adj.* Used or considered as an emblem; symbolic. **— em′·blem·at′i·cal·ly** *adv.*

em·bod·i·ment [im·bod′i·mənt] *n.* **1** A person or thing thought of as representing an idea or quality: She is the *embodiment* of kindness. **2** The act of embodying. **3** A being embodied.

em·bod·y [im·bod′ē] *v.* **em·bod·ied, em·bod·y·ing** **1** To put or represent (an idea, belief, quality, etc.) in real or definite form: The Bill of Rights *embodies* our individual freedoms. **2** To bring together in a single form or system; incorporate: The information you need is *embodied* in this leaflet.

em·bold·en [im·bōl′dən] *v.* To make bold or bolder; encourage: His early successes *emboldened* the young salesman.

em·bo·lism [em′bə·liz′əm] *n.* The blocking of the flow of blood in a vein or artery, as by a clot.

em·boss [im·bôs′] *v.* To form or decorate with raised designs: a gold bracelet *embossed* with birds and butterflies.

em·bow [em·bō′] *v.* To bend or curve like a bow; arch. **— em·bow′ment** *n.*

em·brace [im·brās′] *v.* **em·braced, em·brac·ing,** *n.* **1** *v.* To clasp or enfold in the arms; hug. **2** *n.* The act of embracing. **3** *v.* To hug each other. **4** *v.* To surround or encircle: Dense woods *embraced* the village. **5** *v.* To include; contain: Astronomy *embraces* the study of all the heavenly bodies. **6** *v.* To accept or take up willingly: He discarded the old theory and *embraced* the new one.

em·bra·sure [em·brā′zhər] *n.* **1** An opening with slanted sides, in a thick wall, widening from outside to inside, for a door or window. **2** An opening, as in the wall of a fort, through which a gun may be fired.

em·broi·der [im·broi′dər] *v.* **1** To decorate with or make designs in needlework: to *embroider* flowers on a blouse. **2** To add fanciful details to (a description, story, etc.).

em·broi·der·y [im·broi′dər·ē] *n., pl.* **em·broi·der·ies** **1** Stitches or decoration made by embroidering. **2** The art of embroidering.

em·broil [em·broil′] *v.* To involve in disagreement or conflict: *embroiled* in a war, *embroiled* in a struggle for political power.

---

add, āce, câre, pälm; end, ēqual; it, īce; odd, ōpen, ôrder; took, pool; up, bûrn; ə = a in *above*, e in *sicken*, i in *possible*, o in *melon*, u in *circus*; yoo = u in *fuse*; oil; pout; check; ring; thin; this; zh in *vision*. For ¶ reference, see page 64 · HOW TO

em·bry·o [em′brē·ō] *n., pl.* **em·bry·os** **1** A plant or animal in its earliest stages, as a plant within its seed, a mammal not yet born, or a bird within an egg. **2** An early, undeveloped stage of anything: The committee's report is still in *embryo.*

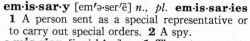

embryo

endosperm

A plant embryo

em·bry·on·ic [em′brē·on′ik] *adj.* **1** Just beginning to develop. **2** Of an embryo.

em·er·ald [əm′ər·əld] **1** *n.* A bright green precious stone. **2** *n., adj.* Bright green.

e·merge [i·mûrj′] *v.* **e·merged, e·merg·ing** **1** To come forth or come out, especially so as to be visible: The woodchuck *emerged* from its burrow. **2** To become known; come to light: New facts *emerged* during the trial.

e·mer·gence [i·mûr′jəns] *n.* A coming out or becoming known; appearance.

e·mer·gen·cy [i·mûr′jən·sē] *n., pl.* **e·mer·gen·cies** A sudden and unexpected turn of events calling for immediate action.

e·mer·i·tus [i·mer′ə·təs] *adj.* Retired from active work but still retaining one's rank or title as an honor: a professor *emeritus.*

Em·er·son [em′ər·sən], **Ralph Waldo,** 1803–1882, U.S. philosopher and writer.

em·er·y [em′ər·ē] *n.* A very hard mineral used, usually in powdered form, for polishing, smoothing, or sharpening metal, stone, etc.

e·met·ic [i·met′ik] **1** *n.* Something that causes vomiting, as a medicine given to someone who has swallowed poison. **2** *adj.* Causing vomiting.

em·i·grant [em′ə·grənt] *n.* A person who leaves a place or country to settle in another.

em·i·grate [em′ə·grāt] *v* **em·i·grat·ed, em·i·grat·ing** To move from one country or section of a country to settle in another: to *emigrate* from Italy to the U.S. **— em′i·gra′·tion** *n.*

em·i·nence [em′ə·nəns] *n.* **1** Superiority or importance because of high rank, great achievement, etc. **2** A high place, as a hill. **3** (*written* **Eminence**) A title of honor used when formally addressing or speaking of a cardinal of the Roman Catholic Church: His *Eminence.*

em·i·nent [em′ə·nənt] *adj.* Important or respected because of high rank or quality; outstanding: an *eminent* musician; *eminent* achievements. ◆ *Eminent* and *imminent* have completely different meanings, although they come from similar Latin roots. An *eminent* person is one who stands out above others, and the Latin roots of *eminent* literally mean *to stand out. Imminent* was formed from elements that mean *to lean over,* and *imminent* means *hanging over* or *threatening to happen at any moment:* The river rose, and a flood was *imminent.*

em·i·nent·ly [em′ə·nənt·lē] *adv.* Notably; outstandingly: She is *eminently* suited to the job.

e·mir [ə·mir′] *n.* **1** A Moslem prince or chief, especially in Arabia. **2** A high Turkish official.

em·is·sar·y [em′ə·ser′ē] *n., pl.* **em·is·sar·ies** **1** A person sent as a special representative or to carry out special orders. **2** A spy.

e·mis·sion [i·mish′ən] *n.* **1** The act or process of emitting. **2** Something emitted.

e·mit [i·mit′] *v.* **e·mit·ted, e·mit·ting** To send forth or give off: Fireflies *emit* light; The child *emitted* a loud squeal. ◆ See TRANSMIT.

e·mol·u·ment [i·mol′yə·mənt] *n.* The salary or fees connected with one's occupation or position.

e·mo·tion [i·mō′shən] *n.* A strong feeling, such as love, anger, fear, sorrow, or joy.

e·mo·tion·al [i·mō′shən·əl] *adj.* **1** Of or related to the emotions: an *emotional* problem. **2** Having one's emotions easily aroused: an *emotional* child. **3** Expressing or arousing emotion: an *emotional* appeal. **— e·mo′tion·al·ly** *adv.*

em·per·or [em′pər·ər] *n.* A man who reigns over an empire or has the title of ruler of an empire.

em·pha·sis [em′fə·sis] *n., pl.* **em·pha·ses** [em′fə·sēz] **1** A stressing by the voice of a particular syllable, word, or phrase. **2** Special significance or importance given to something; stress: The *emphasis* here is on achievement.

em·pha·size [em′fə·sīz] *v.* **em·pha·sized, em·pha·siz·ing** To point out for special notice; stress: to *emphasize* the value of education. ¶3

em·phat·ic [em·fat′ik] *adj.* **1** Spoken or done with emphasis. **2** Striking; decisive: an *emphatic* success. **— em·phat′i·cal·ly** *adv.*

em·pire [em′pīr] *n.* **1** A group of different, often widespread states, nations, or territories under a single ruler or government: the Roman *Empire.* **2** A country reigned over by an emperor or empress. **3** Wide power or range of influence, as of a person, industry, etc.

em·pir·i·cal [em·pir′i·kəl] *adj.* **1** Based entirely on direct experience or observation: *empirical* knowledge. **2** Relying on practical experience rather than on science or theory: *empirical* medicine. **— em·pir′i·cal·ly** *adv.*

em·ploy [im·ploi′] **1** *v.* To give work and payment to; hire: This store *employs* six salesmen. **2** *n.* Paid service; employment: in the *employ* of the government. **3** *v.* To make use of: to *employ* force. **4** *v.* To keep occupied: to *employ* oneself in a hobby. ◆ See IMPLY.

em·ploy·ee or **em·ploy·e** [im·ploi′ē or em′·ploi·ē′] *n.* A person who is employed for pay.

em·ploy·er [im·ploi′ər] *n.* A person, business firm, etc., that employs a person or people.

em·ploy·ment [im·ploi′mənt] *n.* **1** A person's job or occupation. **2** The condition of being employed. **3** The act of employing; use.

em·po·ri·um [em·pôr′ē·əm] *n., pl.* **em·po·ri·ums** or **em·po·ri·a** [em·pôr′ē·ə] A large store selling many different kinds of merchandise.

em·pow·er [im·pou′ər] *v.* To give the power or right to do something; authorize: The President is *empowered* to appoint judges.

em·press [em′pris] *n.* **1** A woman who reigns over an empire. **2** The wife of an emperor.

emp·ty [emp′tē] *adj.* **emp·ti·er, emp·ti·est,** *n.,* *pl.* **emp·ties,** *v.* **emp·tied, emp·ty·ing** **1** *adj.* Containing or holding nothing: an *empty* jar; *empty* hands. **2** *n.* An empty bottle, freight car, etc. **3** *adj.* Not filled; vacant: an *empty* seat. **4** *v.* To make or become empty. **5** *v.* To pour out; drain: *Empty* the milk from the pitcher; The river *empties* into the bay. **6** *adj.* Having no real value or significance; idle: *empty* boasts or promises. **— emp′ti·ness** *n.*

emp·ty-hand·ed [emp′tē-han′did] *adj.* Without something sought or needed: to go fishing and come home *empty-handed.*

em·pyr·e·al [em·pir′ē·əl *or* em′pə·rē′əl] *adj.* Of or from the heavens; celestial.

em·py·re·an [em′pə·rē′ən] **1** *n.* The highest heaven. **2** *adj.* Empyreal; heavenly.

e·mu [ē′myōō] *n.* An Australian bird similar to the ostrich, but somewhat smaller.

em·u·late [em′yə·lāt] *v.* **em·u·lat·ed, em·u·lat·ing** To try to equal or surpass; imitate so as to excel: to *emulate* the success of great men. **— em′u·la′tion** *n.*

Emu, about 5 ft. high

e·mul·si·fy [i·mul′sə·fī] *v.* **e·mul·si·fied, e·mul·si·fy·ing** To make into an emulsion.

e·mul·sion [i·mul′shən] *n.* A mixture in which many small droplets or globules of one liquid remain evenly distributed throughout another.

en- A prefix meaning: **1** In, into, or within, as in *entrap,* to catch in or within a trap. **2** To make, as in *enrich,* to make rich. **3** Very much or completely, as in *entangle,* to tangle completely in something. ◆ Many words beginning with *en-* can also be written with the prefix *in-*[1], as *incase,* another word for *encase.*

en·a·ble [in·ā′bəl] *v.* **en·a·bled, en·a·bling** To give the means, ability, or opportunity to; make able: Telescopes *enable* us to see far into space.

en·act [in·akt′] *v.* **1** To make into or approve officially, as a statute, edict, etc.: Congress *enacts* laws. **2** To act or perform, as a part in a play.

en·act·ment [in·akt′mənt] *n.* **1** The act or process of enacting into law. **2** A law.

en·am·el [in·am′əl] *n., v.* **en·am·eled** or **en·am·elled, en·am·el·ing** or **en·am·el·ling** **1** *n.* A glassy, often colorful substance that is fused by heat to a surface of metal, porcelain, etc., for protection or decoration. **2** *n.* A paint or varnish that dries to form a hard, glossy surface. **3** *v.* To cover or inlay with enamel. **4** *n.* The hard, outer layer of the teeth.

en·am·ored [in·am′ərd] *adj.* In love, especially in the phrase **enamored of,** in love with: The prince was *enamored of* Cinderella.

en·camp [in·kamp′] *v.* To set up and move into a camp: The scouts *encamped* near the river.

en·camp·ment [in·kamp′mənt] *n.* **1** The act of encamping. **2** A camp or the people in it.

en·case [in·kās′] *v.* **en·cased, en·cas·ing** To enclose in or as if in a case: a caterpillar *encased* in a cocoon.

-ence A suffix meaning: **1** The condition or quality of being, as in *independence,* the condition of being independent. **2** The act of, as in *emergence,* the act of emerging.

en·chant [in·chant′] *v.* **1** To put under a magic spell; bewitch: A wave of her wand *enchanted* the princess. **2** To charm; delight. **3** *adj. use:* an *enchanting* smile. **— en·chant′er** *n.*

en·chant·ment [in·chant′mənt] *n.* **1** The use or effect of charms or spells; magic. **2** Something enchanting. **3** Great charm or fascination.

en·chant·ress [in·chant′ris] *n.* **1** A witch or sorceress. **2** A charming, fascinating woman.

en·cir·cle [en·sûr′kəl] *v.* **en·cir·cled, en·cir·cling** **1** To form a circle around; surround: A ribbon *encircled* her waist. **2** To move in a circle around; go around: We *encircled* the lake on our hike. **— en·cir′cle·ment** *n.*

en·close [in·klōz′] *v.* **en·closed, en·clos·ing** **1** To close in on all sides; surround: A fence *enclosed* the yard. **2** To put in an envelope or container along with whatever is being sent.

en·clo·sure [in·klō′zhər] *n.* **1** An enclosed area, as a yard or pen. **2** Something that encloses, as a fence. **3** Something enclosed in an envelope or container. **4** The act or process of enclosing. **5** A being enclosed.

en·co·mi·um [en·kō′mē·əm] *n.* High praise, especially when expressed formally; tribute.

en·com·pass [in·kum′pəs] *v.* **1** To encircle; surround. **2** To include; contain: The social sciences *encompass* psychology and sociology.

en·core [än(g)′kôr] **1** *interj.* Once more! Again! **2** *n.* A call by an audience to perform again, as by shouting "Encore!" or applauding steadily. **3** *n.* A performance in response to such a call.

en·coun·ter [in·koun′tər] **1** *v.* To meet unexpectedly; come upon: to *encounter* an old friend at a party. **2** *n.* A meeting, especially when unexpected. **3** *v.* To be faced with; have to contend with: to *encounter* difficulties. **4** *v.* To face in battle. **5** *n.* A battle; contest.

en·cour·age [in·kûr′ij] *v.* **en·cour·aged, en·cour·ag·ing** **1** To give courage or hope to; inspire with confidence or the wish to do well. **2** To be favorable for; help or foster: Watering *encourages* plant growth.

en·cour·age·ment [in·kûr′ij·mənt] *n.* **1** Something that encourages: His father's praise served as *encouragement.* **2** The act of encouraging. **3** An encouraged condition.

en·croach [in·krōch′] *v.* **1** To advance beyond the usual or proper limits; overrun: weeds *encroached* upon the garden. **2** To intrude upon the rights or property of another; trespass: troops *encroaching* upon the territory of a neighboring country. **— en·croach′ment** *n.*

en·crust [in·krust′] *v.* **1** To cover with a crust or hard coating: dirty dishes *encrusted* with food. **2** To decorate or cover with jewels or other ornamentation: a scepter *encrusted* with rubies.

en·cum·ber [in·kum′bər] *v.* **1** To weigh down with or as if with a burden: a horse *encumbered* with a heavy load; a man *encumbered* with troubles. **2** To interfere with; hinder: *encumbered* with galoshes and an umbrella. **3** To crowd or fill with obstacles: a staircase *encumbered* with scattered toys.

en·cum·brance [in·kum′brəns] *n.* Something that encumbers, as a burden or added difficulty.

-ency A suffix meaning: The condition or quality of being, as in *decency*, the condition of being decent.

en·cyc·li·cal [en·sik′li·kəl] *n.* A letter about important religious matters, sent by the Pope to bishops of the Roman Catholic Church.

en·cy·clo·pe·di·a or **en·cy·clo·pae·di·a** [en·sī′klə·pē′dē·ə] *n.* A book or set of books containing information arranged in alphabetical order according to subjects, and covering a wide range of knowledge. Some encyclopedias are limited to one field, as science or art.

en·cy·clo·pe·dic [en·sī′klə·pē′dik] *adj.* **1** Having or covering information on a wide range of subjects: an *encyclopedic* mind. **2** Of, like, or suitable for an encyclopedia.

end [end] **1** *n.* The last or outermost part of something long: the *end* of the road; the *end* of a log. **2** *n.* The last or final part: the *end* of a story; the *end* of October. **3** *v.* To come or bring to an end; terminate: *End* a sentence with a period. **4** *n.* Final state or condition. **5** *adj. use:* the *end* result; an *end* product. **6** *n.* Aim; purpose: to work toward good *ends*. **7** *n.* Death: He met a hero's *end*. **8** *n.* A leftover part; remnant: odds and *ends*. **9** *n.* In football, either of the two outermost players in the line. **— make ends meet** To manage to get along on the money one has or earns. **— on end** In an upright position.

en·dan·ger [in·dān′jər] *v.* To expose to danger: Faulty brakes *endanger* people's lives.

en·dear [in·dir′] *v.* To make dear; cause to be well liked: He has *endeared* himself to us all.

en·dear·ment [in·dir′mənt] *n.* An expressing of love or affection, as by a word or action: "Darling" is a term of *endearment*.

en·deav·or [in·dev′ər] **1** *v.* To try hard; make an earnest effort; attempt: to *endeavor* to succeed. **2** *n.* An earnest effort. ¶1

en·dem·ic [en·dem′ik] *adj.* Usually found in a certain region or among certain people: an *endemic* disease.

end·ing [end′ing] *n.* The last part; conclusion: a play with a sad *ending*.

en·dive [en′dīv *or* än′dēv] *n.* A plant with crisp white or green leaves used in salads.

end·less [end′lis] *adj.* **1** Having no end; lasting or going on forever. **2** Seeming to have no end; going on too long: *endless* complaints. **3** Forming a closed loop or circle: the *endless* chain on a bicycle. **— end′less·ly** *adv.*

en·do·crine gland [en′dō·krin *or* en′dō·krēn] *n.* Any of several glands, as the pituitary or thyroid, whose secretions enter the blood or lymph directly instead of through a duct.

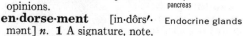
Endocrine glands

en·dorse [in·dôrs′] *v.* **en·dorsed, en·dors·ing 1** To sign the back of (a check or similar paper), especially so that it may be cashed. **2** To give support or approval to: to *endorse* a man's political opinions.

en·dorse·ment [in·dôrs′mənt] *n.* **1** A signature, note, etc., written on the back of a check or similar paper. **2** Approval, especially formal approval. **3** The act or process of endorsing.

en·do·sperm [en′dō·spûrm] *n.* The substance within a seed that nourishes a plant embryo.

en·dow [in·dou′] *v.* **1** To equip or supply, as with talents or natural gifts: Nature *endowed* her with genius. **2** To provide money or property to earn income for (a college, hospital, etc.).

en·dow·ment [in·dou′mənt] *n.* **1** Something with which a person is endowed, such as beauty or talent. **2** A fund to earn income for a college, museum, etc. **3** The act of endowing.

en·due [in·d(y)oo′] *v.* **en·dued, en·du·ing 1** To provide or endow with some power or quality: His faith *endued* him with strength and wisdom. **2** To clothe; garb.

en·dur·a·ble [in·d(y)oor′ə·bəl] *adj.* Capable of being endured; bearable.

en·dur·ance [in·d(y)oor′əns] *n.* The ability or power to bear up or last under continued effort, hardship, or strain.

en·dure [in·d(y)oor′] *v.* **en·dured, en·dur·ing 1** To bear up under; stand firm against: to *endure* pain or suffering. **2** To put up with; bear; tolerate. **3** To last for a long time; continue to exist. **4** *adj. use: enduring* art.

end·ways [end′wāz′] *adv.* Endwise.

end·wise [end′wīz′] *adv.* **1** On end: logs stacked *endwise*. **2** With the end forward or toward something else: a table placed *endwise* against a wall. **3** End to end; lengthwise.

en·e·ma [en′ə·mə] *n.* The injection of a liquid by means of a tube or nozzle into the rectum, especially to empty the bowels.

en·e·my [en′ə·mē] *n., pl.* **en·e·mies 1** A person, nation, etc., who hates and tries to harm, destroy, or triumph over another. **2** Anyone strongly opposed to or trying to combat something: The policeman is an *enemy* of crime. **3** Anything harmful or destructive.

en·er·get·ic [en/ər·jet/ik] *adj.* Full of energy; forceful; vigorous.

en·er·get·i·cal·ly [en/ər·jet/ik·lē] *adv.* In an energetic manner; vigorously.

en·er·gize [en/ər·jīz] *v.* **en·er·gized, en·er·giz·ing** To give energy, force, or strength to; make active or effective. ¶3

en·er·gy [en/ər·jē] *n., pl.* **en·er·gies** **1** Lively force or activity; vigor; vitality. **2** (*often pl.*) Power forcefully and effectively used: All their *energies* were thrown into the campaign. **3** The capacity for doing work or supplying power: the *energy* of steam or electricity.

en·er·vate [en/ər·vāt] *v.* **en·er·vat·ed, en·er·vat·ing** To drain the strength or vigor of; weaken: The heat *enervated* the players.

en·fee·ble [en·fē/bəl] *v.* **en·fee·bled, en·fee·bling** To make feeble.

en·fold [in·fōld/] *v.* **1** To wrap in or as if in folds; envelop. **2** To hug; embrace.

en·force [in·fôrs/] *v.* **en·forced, en·forc·ing** **1** To require to be obeyed: to *enforce* rules. **2** To impose by the use of force or severity: to *enforce* discipline.

en·force·a·ble [in·fôr/sə·bəl] *adj.* Capable of being enforced: Some rules are not *enforceable*.

en·force·ment [in·fôrs/mənt] *n.* A putting into force: *Enforcement* of the new tax law starts next year.

en·fran·chise [in·fran/chīz] *v.* **en·fran·chised, en·fran·chis·ing** **1** To allow to vote. **2** To set free, as from slavery. **— en·fran·chise·ment** [in·fran/chiz·mənt] *n.*

Eng. Abbreviation of **1** ENGLISH. **2** ENGLAND.

en·gage [in·gāj/] *v.* **en·gaged, en·gag·ing** **1** To hire; employ: to *engage* a piano teacher. **2** To occupy; keep busy: to be *engaged* in doing one's homework. **3** To take part; enter into: to *engage* in conversation or battle. **4** To attract; gain: to *engage* someone's attention. **5** To reserve the use of: to *engage* a room at a hotel. **6** To pledge, promise, or agree to do something: to *engage* to do certain chores; to be *engaged* to marry someone. **7** To meet in battle; attack: to *engage* the enemy. **8** To fit together or interlock, as gear wheels.

en·gaged [in·gājd/] *adj.* **1** Pledged to marry; betrothed: Joe and Winnie are *engaged.* **2** Busy; occupied: The doctor is *engaged.*

en·gage·ment [in·gāj/mənt] *n.* **1** A promise to marry; betrothal. **2** The period of being engaged to be married: a long *engagement.* **3** An arrangement to meet someone; appointment. **4** A pledge or obligation. **5** A job or employment, as an appearance in a theater. **6** A battle. **7** The act of engaging. **8** A being engaged.

en·gag·ing [in·gā/jing] *adj.* Pleasing; charming: *engaging* manners. **— en·gag·ing·ly** *adv.*

en·gen·der [in·jen/dər] *v.* To be the cause or source of; produce: Poverty can *engender* crime.

en·gine [en/jin] *n.* **1** A machine that uses energy, such as that produced by burning fuel, to do work, as by causing wheels or other mechanical parts to move. **2** A locomotive. **3** Any device or apparatus used for a special purpose: an *engine* of war.

en·gi·neer [en/jə·nir/] **1** *n.* A person who works or is trained in any branch of engineering. **2** *n.* A person who operates an engine, such as the driver of a locomotive. **3** *n.* A soldier who builds or repairs bridges, roads, etc. **4** *v.* To manage or accomplish cleverly or skillfully: to *engineer* a scheme. **5** *v.* To plan, build, or supervise as an engineer.

en·gi·neer·ing [en/jə·nir/ing] *n.* The work, skill, or profession in which scientific knowledge is put to practical use, as in the planning, designing, and building of roads, bridges, machinery, etc.

Eng·land [ing/glənd] *n.* The largest and southernmost division of the island of Great Britain.

Atlantic Ocean — SCOTLAND — *North Sea* — NORTHERN IRELAND — IRELAND — *Irish Sea* — WALES — ENGLAND — *English Channel*

Eng·lish [ing/glish] **1** *adj.* Of or having to do with England, its people, or its language, customs, etc. **2** *n.* **(the English)** The people of England. **3** *n.* The language of England and also of the United States and most parts of the British Commonwealth of Nations. **4** *n.* A course of study dealing with the English language or English literature. **5** *n.* (*sometimes written* **english**) A spinning motion given to a ball, as in billiards.

English Channel A strait between England and France, connecting the North Sea with the Atlantic Ocean.

English horn A musical instrument resembling the oboe, but larger and lower in pitch.

Eng·lish·man [ing/glish·mən] *n., pl.* **Eng·lish·men** [ing/glish·mən] A man born in or a citizen of England.

Eng·lish·wom·an [ing/glish·wŏŏm/ən] *n., pl.* **Eng·lish·wom·en** [ing/glish·wim/in] A woman born in or a citizen of England.

en·graft [en·graft/] *v.* **1** To graft (a shoot or branch) onto a tree or plant. **2** To add as if by grafting; implant.

en·grave [in·grāv/] *v.* **en·graved, en·grav·ing** **1** To carve or cut letters, designs, etc., into: to *engrave* a ring. **2** To print with a block or plate of metal, stone, wood, etc., into which pictures, letters, or marks have been cut: to *engrave* wedding invitations. **3** To fix or impress deeply, as in the memory. **— en·grav/er** *n.*

en·grav·ing [in·grā′ving] *n.* **1** A picture or print made from an engraved plate or surface. **2** The art or process of making engraved designs, printing plates, etc. **3** An engraved design.

Printing from an engraving

en·gross [in·grōs′] *v.* To occupy completely; take up the attention of: to be *engrossed* in a new hobby. **2** *adj. use:* an *engrossing* story.

en·gulf [in·gulf′] *v* To swallow up; overwhelm completely: Night *engulfed* the city.

en·hance [in·hans′] *v.* **en·hanced, en·hanc·ing** To add to; increase: Good grooming *enhances* good looks. **— en·hance′ment** *n.*

e·nig·ma [i·nig′mə] *n.* Something or someone that is baffling, mysterious, or hard to understand.

en·ig·mat·ic [en′ig·mat′ik] *adj.* Puzzling; baffling: *enigmatic* answers. **— en′ig·mat′i·cal·ly** *adv.*

en·join [in·join′] *v.* **1** To order or direct, especially officially: The policeman *enjoined* the crowd to leave. **2** To forbid or prohibit: They were *enjoined* from trespassing.

en·joy [in·joi′] *v.* **1** To receive pleasure or delight from: I *enjoy* a good book. **2** To have the benefit or satisfaction of: to *enjoy* continued prosperity. **— enjoy oneself** To have a pleasant time.

en·joy·a·ble [in·joi′ə·bəl] *adj.* Giving pleasure; pleasant; satisfying: an *enjoyable* dinner.

en·joy·ment [in·joi′mənt] *n.* **1** Pleasure or great satisfaction. **2** Satisfying possession; benefit: the *enjoyment* of good health.

en·large [in·lärj′] *v.* **en·larged, en·larg·ing** To make or become larger; expand. **— enlarge on** or **enlarge upon** To tell about in great detail: to *enlarge upon* one's adventures.

en·large·ment [in·lärj′mənt] *n.* **1** A making or becoming larger. **2** Something enlarged, especially a photograph made larger than its negative.

en·light·en [in·līt′(ə)n] *v.* To give knowledge and understanding to; inform.

en·light·en·ment [in·līt′(ə)n·mənt] *n.* **1** The condition of being enlightened; knowledge. **2** The act of enlightening; instruction.

en·list [in·list′] *v.* **1** To join or cause to join a branch of the armed forces without being drafted. **2** To join any activity or cause: to *enlist* in the fight against poverty. **3** To obtain (help, support, aid, etc.). **— en·list′ment** *n.*

enlisted man A man in the armed forces who is not a commissioned officer, warrant officer, or in training to become a commissioned officer.

en·li·ven [in·lī′vən] *v.* To make lively, cheerful, or more spirited: to *enliven* a speech.

en masse [en mas′ *or* än mas′] In a group or mass; all together: They marched *en masse* to the auditorium.

en·mesh [en·mesh′] *v.* To entangle in or as if in a net: to be *enmeshed* in difficulties.

en·mi·ty [en′mə·tē] *n., pl.* **en·mi·ties** Deep hatred, mistrust, or dislike.

en·no·ble [i·nō′bəl *or* en·nō′bəl] *v.* **en·no·bled, en·no·bling** To make noble; give greatness, honor, or dignity to.

en·nui [än′wē] *n.* A feeling of discontented weariness or boredom.

e·nor·mi·ty [i·nôr′mə·tē] *n., pl.* **e·nor·mi·ties** **1** Tremendous wickedness: the *enormity* of his crime. **2** An exceedingly wicked act or crime.

e·nor·mous [i·nôr′məs] *adj.* Unusually large or great; immense. **— e·nor′mous·ly** *adv.*

e·nough [i·nuf′] **1** *adj.* Sufficient for what is needed or wanted: There is *enough* cake for everyone. **2** *n.* As much as is required: You've had *enough.* **3** *adv.* Sufficiently: Are you well *enough* to go? **4** *adv.* Fairly; quite; somewhat: Strangely *enough,* we had no rain last month.

en·quire [in·kwīr′] *v.* **en·quired, en·quir·ing** Another spelling of INQUIRE.

en·quir·y [in·kwīr′ē *or* in′kwər·ē] *n., pl.* **en·quir·ies** Another spelling of INQUIRY.

en·rage [in·rāj′] *v.* **en·raged, en·rag·ing** To fill with rage; make angry or furious.

en·rap·ture [in·rap′chər] *v.* **en·rap·tured, en·rap·tur·ing** To fill with rapture; delight greatly: *enraptured* by the sound of her voice.

en·rich [in·rich′] *v.* **1** To make wealthy. **2** To improve by adding something: to *enrich* flour with extra vitamins. **— en·rich′ment** *n.*

en·roll or **en·rol** [in·rōl′] *v.* **en·rolled, en·roll·ing** **1** To put one's name on a list, as for membership; register. **2** To join as a member; enlist: to *enroll* in an art class.

en·roll·ment or **en·rol·ment** [in·rōl′mənt] *n.* **1** The act or process of enrolling. **2** A being enrolled. **3** The number of people enrolled.

en route [än rŏŏt′] On the way: I pass the police station *en route* to school.

en·sconce [en·skons′] *v.* **en·sconced, en·sconc·ing** To settle or place firmly or snugly: She *ensconced* herself among the cushions.

en·sem·ble [än·säm′bəl] *n.* **1** All the parts of a thing considered as a whole. **2** A costume made up of parts that match or harmonize. **3** A group of players, singers, etc., performing together.

en·shrine [in·shrīn′] *v.* **en·shrined, en·shrin·ing** **1** To place in or as if in a shrine. **2** To cherish as precious or sacred: His words are *enshrined* in our hearts.

en·sign [en′sīn *or* en′sən] *n.* **1** A flag or banner, especially a national banner or naval flag. **2** [en′sən] In the U.S. Navy, a commissioned officer of the lowest rank. **3** Any badge, symbol, etc.

en·si·lage [en′sə·lij] *n.* Fodder made from green plants stored in a silo.

en·slave [in·slāv′] *v.* **en·slaved, en·slav·ing** **1** To force into slavery. **2** To dominate or control completely. **— en·slave′ment** *n.*

en·snare [en·snâr′] *v.* **en·snared, en·snar·ing** To catch in or as if in a snare; trap.

en·sue [en·sōō′] *v.* **en·sued, en·su·ing** **1** To follow in time; come next: A long correspondence *ensued* after their trip. **2** To follow as a consequence: We disagreed, and an argument *ensued.*

en·sure [in·shŏŏr′] *v.* **en·sured, en·sur·ing** **1** To make sure or certain; guarantee: Winning this game will *ensure* our final victory. **2** To make safe or secure: to *ensure* liberty.

-ent A suffix meaning: **1** Showing, having, or doing something, as in *independent,* showing or having independence. **2** A person or thing that does something, as in *superintendent,* a person who superintends.

en·tail [in·tāl′] **1** *v.* To require or necessitate: This project will *entail* much research. **2** *v.* To restrict the inheritance of (property) to a certain succession of heirs, thus preventing its being willed or disposed of in any other way. **3** *n.* A legal restriction by which property is entailed. **4** *n.* Something entailed, as property.

en·tan·gle [in·tang′gəl] *v.* **en·tan·gled, en·tan·gling** **1** To catch in or as if in something tangled; snarl: The kitten became *entangled* in the yarn. **2** To trap or involve, as in difficulties. **— en·tan′gle·ment** *n.*

en·tente [än·tänt′] *n.* **1** An agreement or understanding, as between nations. **2** The alliance formed by such an agreement.

en·ter [en′tər] *v.* **1** To come or go in or into: to *enter* a building. **2** To pierce; penetrate: The nail *entered* his shoe. **3** To join; take part in: to *enter* a discussion. **4** To cause to join or be admitted: to *enter* a child in school. **5** To write down; record: to *enter* one's name on a list. **6** To list or offer for competition in a contest. **7** To cause to be recorded, as evidence in a law court. **— enter on** or **enter upon** To start out on; begin: to *enter on* a new career.

en·ter·prise [en′tər·prīz] *n.* **1** A project, undertaking, or venture requiring effort, ability, or daring. **2** Energy and spirit for starting new or difficult undertakings.

en·ter·pris·ing [en′tər·prīz′ing] *adj.* Full of energy, daring, and willingness to embark on new undertakings.

en·ter·tain [en′tər·tān′] *v.* **1** To hold the attention of and give enjoyment to: to *entertain* an audience. **2** To have as a guest or guests: to *entertain* friends. **3** To have guests: They rarely *entertain.* **4** To take into or have in one's mind: to *entertain* doubts. ◆ *Entertain* and *amuse* both mean to hold the attention of others in an enjoyable way, but *amuse* often adds the idea of being funny. A musician and a comedian would both like to *entertain* an audience, but the musician might be displeased if his listeners were *amused.*

en·ter·tain·er [en′tər·tān′ər] *n.* A person who entertains, especially one who earns money by entertaining audiences.

en·ter·tain·ment [en′tər·tān′mənt] *n.* **1** Something that entertains, as a performance for an audience. **2** The act of entertaining. **3** A being entertained; amusement.

en·thrall or **en·thral** [in·thrôl′] *v.* **en·thralled, en·thrall·ing** **1** To keep spellbound; fascinate: The play *enthralled* us. **2** To enslave.

en·throne [in·thrōn′] *v.* **en·throned, en·thron·ing** **1** To place on a throne. **2** To place in a position of very high rank or esteem.

en·thuse [in·thōōz′] *v.* **en·thused, en·thus·ing** *informal* **1** To make or become very enthusiastic. **2** To say with enthusiasm; gush.

en·thu·si·asm [in·thōō′zē·az′əm] *n.* Keen interest or liking: *enthusiasm* for a hobby.

en·thu·si·ast [in·thōō′zē·ast] *n.* A person filled with enthusiasm.

en·thu·si·as·tic [in·thōō′zē·as′tik] *adj.* Full of enthusiasm; expressing eager interest or approval. **— en·thu′si·as′ti·cal·ly** *adv.*

en·tice [in·tīs′] *v.* **en·ticed, en·tic·ing** To attract or lure by offering or tempting with something attractive, desirable, etc. **— en·tice′ment** *n.*

en·tire [in·tīr′] *adj.* **1** All the members or parts of; whole: The *entire* family was there. **2** Complete; full; total: He has *entire* control of the business. **3** Not divided, broken, or in parts: Put the *entire* mass of dough in one pan. **— en·tire′ly** *adv.*

en·tire·ty [in·tīr′tē] *n., pl.* **en·tire·ties** **1** Complete state, with nothing missing or omitted. **2** Something entire; a whole.

en·ti·tle [in·tīt′(ə)l] *v.* **en·ti·tled, en·ti·tling** **1** To give the right to receive, demand, or do something: Your ticket *entitles* you to a seat. **2** To give a title to: The novel was *entitled* "Treasure Island."

en·ti·ty [en′tə·tē] *n., pl.* **en·ti·ties** Something that exists or can be thought of as a real and recognizable thing, individual, or whole, such as a person, a building, or an orchestra.

en·tomb [in·tōōm′] *v.* To place or confine in or as if in a tomb; bury. **— en·tomb′ment** *n.*

en·to·mol·o·gy [en′tə·mol′ə·jē] *n.* The scientific study of insects. **— en′to·mol′o·gist** *n.*

en·trails [en′trālz] *n.pl.* The inner parts of the body, especially the intestines.

en·train [en·trān′] *v.* To board or put on board a train.

en·trance[1] [en′trəns] *n.* **1** A passage, doorway, etc., used for entering something. **2** The act of entering: No one noticed his late *entrance.* **3** The right, privilege, or ability to enter.

en·trance[2] [in·trans′] *v.* **en·tranced, en·tranc·ing** **1** To fill with wonder or delight; charm; fascinate. **2** To put in a trance.

---

add, āce, câre, pälm; end, ēqual; it, īce; odd, ōpen, ôrder; tŏŏk, pōōl; up, bûrn; ə = a in *above,* e in *sicken,* i in *possible,* o in *melon,* u in *circus;* yōō = u in *fuse;* oil; pout; check; ring; thin; this; zh in *vision.* For ¶ reference, see page 64 · HOW TO

en·trant [en′trənt] *n.* A person who enters or is entered, especially in a race, contest, etc.

en·trap [in·trap′] *v.* **en·trapped, en·trap·ping 1** To catch in or as if in a trap. **2** To lure or trick into a troublesome situation.

en·treat [in·trēt′] *v.* To ask earnestly; implore; beg: I *entreat* you to forgive me.

en·treat·y [in·trē′tē] *n., pl.* **en·treat·ies** An earnest request or plea.

en·trée or **en·tree** [än′trā] *n.* **1** A dish served as the main course of a meal. **2** The means or privilege of entering or visiting: to have *entrée* to a private club.

en·trench [in·trench′] *v.* **1** To protect in a trench, or surround with trenches for defense: The soldiers were *entrenched* on the battlefield. **2** To establish firmly: The idea was *entrenched* in his mind. **— en·trench′ment** *n.*

en·trust [in·trust′] *v.* **1** To give or turn over for care, safekeeping, etc.: to *entrust* money to someone. **2** To make responsible for something: to *entrust* a pilot with one's safety.

en·try [en′trē] *n., pl.* **en·tries 1** The act of entering. **2** A place for entering, as a hallway. **3** A word, phrase, number, etc., entered in a list or series, as in a dictionary or ledger. **4** A person or thing entered in a contest, race, etc.

en·twine [in·twīn′] *v.* **en·twined, en·twin·ing** To twine around; twist or twine together.

en·u·mer·ate [i·n(y)ōō′mər·āt] *v.* **e·nu·mer·at·ed, e·nu·mer·at·ing 1** To name one by one: to *enumerate* the presidents of the United States. **2** To count. **— e·nu′·mer·a′tion** *n.*

e·nun·ci·ate [i·nun′sē·āt] *v.* **e·nun·ci·at·ed, e·nun·ci·at·ing 1** To pronounce words; speak: *Enunciate* clearly. **2** To state in precise language: to *enunciate* a theory. **— e·nun′ci·a′tion** *n.*

Vines entwined around a column

en·vel·op [in·vel′əp] *v.* To wrap, cover, or surround: Clouds *enveloped* the mountain peak. **— en·vel′op·ment** *n.*

en·ve·lope [en′və·lōp *or* än′və·lōp] *n.* **1** A flat paper case or wrapper, usually with a flap that folds over and is sealed at the back, used chiefly to mail letters. **2** Any surrounding outer covering or wrapping.

en·ven·om [en·ven′əm] *v.* **1** To put poison in or on: to *envenom* arrows. **2** To fill with hatred or resentment: a mind *envenomed* by misfortune.

en·vi·a·ble [en′vē·ə·bəl] *adj.* So excellent as to be envied or much desired: *enviable* talent.

en·vi·ous [en′vē·əs] *adj.* Full of envy: an *envious* rival. **— en′vi·ous·ly** *adv.*

en·vi·ron·ment [in·vī′rən·mənt] *n.* The conditions and surroundings that have an effect on the development of a person, animal, or plant. **— en·vi·ron·men·tal** [in·vī′rən·men′təl] *adj.*

en·vi·rons [in·vī′rənz] *n.pl.* Surrounding area or neighborhoods: Chicago and its *environs*.

en·vis·age [en·viz′ij] *v.* **en·vis·aged, en·vis·ag·ing** To form a mental image of; visualize: He *envisaged* himself as a pilot.

en·vi·sion [en·vizh′ən] *v.* To see or predict in the imagination: to *envision* the future.

en·voy [en′voi] *n.* **1** A government representative sent to a foreign country, ranking just below an ambassador. **2** A messenger on a special mission.

en·vy [en′vē] *n., pl.* **en·vies,** *v.* **en·vied, en·vy·ing 1** *n.* A feeling of discontent or jealousy aroused by the good fortune or superior abilities of another. **2** *n.* A desire to have in equal amount or degree the possessions, good qualities, etc., of another. **3** *v.* To have a feeling of envy toward or because of: She *envied* him because of his high marks; He *envied* her popularity. **4** *n.* A person or thing that is envied: He is the *envy* of the team. ◆ *Envy* comes from a Latin word meaning *to look at in a bad way*.

en·wrap [en·rap′] *v.* **en·wrapped, en·wrap·ping** To wrap up; envelop.

en·zyme [en′zīm] *n.* A protein substance produced by living cells, and capable of causing a specific chemical reaction in the body without being changed itself. Some enzymes play an important part in the digestion of food.

e·on [ē′on *or* ē′ən] *n.* An extremely long time; hundreds of thousands of years: Dinosaurs lived *eons* ago.

ep·au·let or **ep·au·lette** [ep′ə·let] *n.* An ornament worn on each shoulder of a naval or military officer's uniform.

e·phem·er·al [i·fem′ər·əl] *adj.* Living or lasting for a brief time only: *ephemeral* flowers that bloom but for a day; *ephemeral* sorrows.

Epaulets

E·phe·sians [i·fē′zhənz] *n.* A book of the New Testament, a letter written in the name of St. Paul to Christians in Asia Minor.

ep·ic [ep′ik] **1** *n.* A long poem that tells of the wanderings and adventures of a great hero or heroes: The *Iliad* by Homer is an ancient Greek *epic*. **2** *n.* A novel, play, etc., that resembles an epic. **3** *adj.* Heroic; impressive: *epic* courage.

ep·i·cure [ep′ə·kyŏor] *n.* A person who is very interested in good and often unusual food and drink; a gourmet. ◆ *Epicure* comes from the name of *Epicurus*, an ancient Greek philosopher.

ep·i·cu·re·an [ep′ə·kyŏo·rē′ən] **1** *adj.* Of or suitable for an epicure: Some people consider snails an *epicurean* delight. **2** *n.* An epicure.

ep·i·dem·ic [ep′ə·dem′ik] **1** *n.* The sudden spread of a disease among many people: a measles *epidemic*. **2** *adj.* Occurring in many places at once.

ep·i·der·mis [ep′ə·dûr′mis] *n.* The outer, protective layer of the skin. ◆ The Greek word for *skin* is *derma*, and many English words, such as *epidermis, pachyderm,* and *dermatology,* are derived partly from it. *Epidermis* literally means *upon the skin, pachyderm* means *thick skin,* and *dermatology* means *the science or study of the skin.*

ep·i·glot·tis [ep′ə·glot′is] *n.* A lidlike piece of cartilage that keeps food from entering the windpipe during swallowing.

ep·i·gram [ep′ə·gram] *n.* A brief, witty verse or statement that makes a clever point: "I can resist everything except temptation" is an *epigram.*

ep·i·gram·mat·ic [ep′i·grə·mat′ik] *adj.* 1 Brief and witty, like an epigram. 2 Full of or using epigrams: an *epigrammatic* speaker.

ep·i·lep·sy [ep′ə·lep′sē] *n.* A disorder of the nervous system, attacks of which sometimes cause loss of consciousness and convulsions.

ep·i·lep·tic [ep′ə·lep′tik] 1 *n.* A person who suffers from epilepsy. 2 *adj.* Of, like, or having epilepsy.

ep·i·logue [ep′ə·lôg] *n.* 1 A short section at the end of a book, poem, etc. 2 A speech to the audience by an actor at the end of a play.

ep·i·neph·rine [ep′ə·nef′rin *or* ep′ə·nef′rēn] *n.* Another name for ADRENALINE.

E·piph·a·ny [i·pif′ə·nē] *n.* January 6th, the day Christians celebrate the visit of the Wise Men to adore the baby Jesus.

e·pis·co·pal [i·pis′kə·pəl] *adj.* 1 (*written* **Episcopal**) Of or having to do with the Protestant Episcopal Church. 2 Having to do with or ruled by bishops.

E·pis·co·pa·li·an [i·pis′kə·pā′lē·ən *or* i·pis′kə·pāl′yən] 1 *n.* A member of the Protestant Episcopal Church. 2 *adj.* Of or having to do with Episcopalians or their church.

ep·i·sode [ep′ə·sōd] *n.* Any incident or event that is part of a story, a person's life, etc.

e·pis·tle [i·pis′əl] *n.* 1 A long, formal letter. 2 (*written* **Epistle**) Any of the books of the New Testament that are written in the form of a letter by the Apostles.

ep·i·taph [ep′ə·taf *or* ep′ə·täf] *n.* The writing on a monument or gravestone in remembrance of the person who has died.

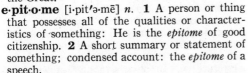
John Hale
1879–1939
May he rest
in peace

Epitaph

ep·i·thet [ep′ə·thet] *n.* A descriptive word or phrase used to indicate some outstanding characteristic or feature of a person or thing, as "the Great" in Alexander the Great.

e·pit·o·me [i·pit′ə·mē] *n.* 1 A person or thing that possesses all of the qualities or characteristics of something: He is the *epitome* of good citizenship. 2 A short summary or statement of something; condensed account: the *epitome* of a speech.

e·pit·o·mize [i·pit′ə·mīz] *v.* **e·pit·o·mized,**

e·pit·o·miz·ing 1 To have or represent the chief qualities of. 2 To summarize briefly. ¶3

e plu·ri·bus u·num [ē′ plŏŏr′ə·bəs yōō′nəm] One out of many: a Latin expression used as a motto of the United States.

ep·och [ep′ək] *n.* 1 A period of time remembered for great events, new discoveries, etc.: Recent years may be remembered as the atomic *epoch.* 2 A period that is part of a longer period of the earth's history: a geological *epoch.*

ep·och-mak·ing [ep′ək·mā′king] *adj.* 1 Bringing in a new period of knowledge or discovery: The airplane was an *epoch-making* invention. 2 Having important results: an *epoch-making* decision to go to war.

Ep·som salts [ep′səm] A compound found in certain mineral springs, used as a laxative or to reduce swelling.

eq·ua·ble [ek′wə·bəl *or* ē′kwə·bəl] *adj.* 1 Not changing or varying greatly: *equable* temperature. 2 Not easily upset; peaceful; calm: an *equable* nature. **— eq′ua·bly** *adv.*

e·qual [ē′kwəl] *adj., v.* **e·qualed** *or* **e·qualled, e·qual·ing** *or* **e·qual·ling** *n.* 1 *adj.* Of or having the same elements, size, amount, etc. 2 *adj.* Having the same rights, privileges, rank, etc. 3 *v.* To be equal to: 10×2 equals 20; His swimming speed *equaled* mine. 4 *n.* A person or thing equal to another: She is his *equal* in ability. 5 *v.* To do or produce something equal to. **— be equal to** To have the necessary ability, power, etc., for: He is *equal to* the race.

e·qual·i·ty [i·kwol′ə·tē] *n., pl.* **e·qual·i·ties** The condition or quality of being equal: an *equality* of size or amount.

e·qual·ize [ē′kwəl·īz] *v.* **e·qual·ized, e·qual·iz·ing** To make equal, uniform, or even. ¶3

e·qual·iz·er [ē′kwəl·ī′zər] *n.* 1 A person or thing that equalizes. 2 A device for equalizing pressure or strain between parts of a structure. ¶3

e·qual·ly [ē′kwəl·ē] *adv.* 1 In equal amounts or parts: Divide the gold *equally.* 2 To the same extent: You and I are *equally* wrong.

equal sign In mathematics, a sign ($=$) that means "is equal to," as in $4 + 3 = 7$.

e·qua·nim·i·ty [ē′kwə·nim′ə·tē *or* ek′wə·nim′·ə·tē] *n.* Evenness of mind and disposition.

e·quate [i·kwāt′] *v.* **e·quat·ed, e·quat·ing** 1 To consider or treat as equal: Some people *equate* old age with wisdom. 2 To make or set equal.

e·qua·tion [i·kwā′zhən] *n.* 1 In mathematics, a statement that two or more quantities or groups of quantities are equal, usually made with an equal sign: "$9 \times 3 - 1 = 26$" and "$a + b = c$" are *equations.* 2 In chemistry, a way of showing results of chemical reaction, as $CO_2 + H_2O \rightarrow H_2CO_3$. 3 The act of making things equal.

---

add, āce, câre, pälm; end, ēqual; it, īce; odd, ōpen, ôrder; tŏŏk, pōōl; up, bûrn; ə = a in *above,* e in *sicken,* i in *possible,* o in *melon,* u in *circus;* yōō = u in *fuse;* oil; pout; check; ring; thin; this; zh in *vision.* For ¶ reference, see page 64 · HOW TO

e·qua·tor [i·kwā′tər] *n.* An imaginary line that encircles the earth exactly halfway between the North Pole and the South Pole.

The equator

e·qua·to·ri·al [ē′·kwə·tôr′e·əl] *adj.* **1** Of or close to the equator. **2** Like or related to conditions at the equator: *equatorial* heat.

eq·uer·ry [ek′wər·ē] *n., pl.* **eq·uer·ries** **1** An officer who works for any member of the royal family of England. **2** In former times, an officer in charge of the horses of a prince or nobleman.

e·ques·tri·an [i·kwes′trē·ən] **1** *n.* A skilled rider of horses. **2** *adj.* Having to do with horses or with the riding of horses. **3** *adj.* Showing a person mounted on horseback: an *equestrian* portrait.

equi- A prefix meaning: Equal or equally, as in *equidistant*, equally distant.

e·qui·dis·tant [ē′kwə·dis′tənt] *adj.* Equally distant: The midpoint of a line is *equidistant* from either end.

e·qui·lat·er·al [ē′kwə·lat′ər·əl] *adj.* Having all the sides of the same length: an *equilateral* triangle.

e·qui·lib·ri·um [ē′kwə·lib′rē·əm] *n.* A state of balance: A beginning skater finds it hard to keep his *equilibrium*; Identical weights on each side of a scale will be in *equilibrium*.

Equilateral triangle

e·quine [ē′kwīn] *adj.* Of, related to, or like a horse: The zebra is an *equine* animal.

e·qui·nox [ē′kwə·noks] *n.* Either of two times of the year when the sun crosses the equator, so that the days and the nights are of equal length. The **vernal equinox** takes place about March 21, the **autumnal equinox** about September 21. ◆ *Equinox* comes from a Latin word meaning *equal night*.

Weights in equilibrium

e·quip [i·kwip′] *v.* **e·quipped, e·quip·ping** To supply or fit out with something needed: to *equip* an automobile with seat belts.

eq·ui·page [ek′wə·pij] *n.* **1** A carriage, especially a showy one with horses, footmen, etc. **2** The equipment for a camp, army, etc.

e·quip·ment [i·kwip′mənt] *n.* **1** A thing or things needed for some special use or purpose: football *equipment*. **2** The act of equipping.

e·qui·poise [ē′kwə·poiz *or* ek′wə·poiz] *n.* **1** Equal weight or balance; equilibrium. **2** A thing that balances another in weight or force.

eq·ui·ta·ble [ek′wə·tə·bəl] *adj.* Just, fair, and reasonable: *equitable* laws. — **eq′ui·ta·bly** *adv.*

eq·ui·ty [ek′wə·tē] *n., pl.* **eq·ui·ties** **1** Fairness; justice. **2** Something that is fair or just.

e·quiv·a·lent [i·kwiv′ə·lənt] **1** *adj.* Equal in worth, force, amount, etc.: One dollar is *equivalent* to four quarters. **2** *n.* Something that is equivalent. — **e·quiv′a·lence** *n.*

e·quiv·o·cal [i·kwiv′ə·kəl] *adj.* **1** Having a double meaning; puzzling: Her *equivocal* reply left me confused. **2** Uncertain or unreliable in value, results, etc.: Our *equivocal* findings did not solve the mystery at all. **3** Causing suspicion; not to be trusted: *equivocal* politeness.

e·quiv·o·cate [i·kwiv′ə·kāt] *v.* **e·quiv·o·cat·ed, e·quiv·o·cat·ing** To use language that can have two or more meanings, so as to mislead, confuse, or deceive. — **e·quiv′o·ca′tion** *n.*

-er[1] A suffix meaning: **1** A person or thing that does something, as in *runner*, a person who runs, or in *grater*, a thing that grates. **2** A person who lives in or comes from, as in *Northerner*, a person who lives in or comes from the North. **3** A person practicing a trade or profession, as in *geographer*, a person who specializes in geography.

-er[2] A suffix meaning: more, as in *larger*, more large, or in *faster*, more fast. It is added to adjectives and adverbs to form the comparative.

e·ra [ir′ə *or* ē′rə] *n.* **1** A period of time that dates from some important event, discovery, etc.: the atomic *era*. **2** A period of time noted for certain characteristics or accomplishments: the Elizabethan *era*. **3** One of the major divisions of geological time.

e·rad·i·cate [i·rad′ə·kāt] *v.* **e·rad·i·cat·ed, e·rad·i·cat·ing** To remove or get rid of completely: to *eradicate* a disease; to *eradicate* ink stains. — **e·rad′i·ca′tion** *n.*

e·rase [i·rās′] *v.* **e·rased, e·ras·ing** **1** To remove (writing, drawing, etc.), especially by rubbing or scraping: *Erase* the second line. **2** To remove written or recorded matter from: *Erase* the tape and we will record it again.

e·ras·er [i·rā′sər] *n.* Something used for erasing, as a small piece of rubber for removing pencil or ink marks.

e·ra·sure [i·rā′shər] *n.* **1** The act of erasing. **2** Something erased, as a word or letter. **3** The place where something has been erased.

ere [âr] *prep., conj.* Before: seldom used today.

e·rect [i·rekt′] **1** *adj.* Upright; not stooping or leaning: an *erect* posture; The tree remained *erect* in the wind. **2** *v.* To put or raise into an upright position: to *erect* a flagpole. **3** *v.* To build or construct: to *erect* a hospital.

e·rec·tion [i·rek′shən] *n.* **1** The act or process of erecting something. **2** Something erected, as a building.

erg [ûrg] *n.* In physics, a unit of work and energy equal to the work done by one dyne acting through a distance of one centimeter. ◆ *Erg* comes from a Greek word meaning *work*.

er·go [ûr′gō] *conj., adv.* Hence; therefore: a Latin word.

Er·ic·son [er′ik·sən], **Leif,** Norwegian sailor who lived in the eleventh century and probably discovered North America about the year 1000.

E·rie [ir′ē], **Lake** The fourth largest of the five Great Lakes.

Erie Canal A historic waterway in New York State, connecting Albany and Buffalo.

Er·in [âr′in] *n.* Ireland: used mostly in poems.

er·mine [ûr′min] *n.* **1** A weasel having brown fur that in winter turns white with a black tip on the tail. **2** The white fur of the ermine, used for garments and, in Europe, for trimming on certain royal and judicial ceremonial robes.

e·rode [i·rōd′] *v.* **e·rod·ed, e·rod·ing** To wear away or gradually destroy by the constant action of water, wind, friction, acid, etc

Er·os [ir′os *or* er′os] *n.* In Greek myths, the god of love. His Roman name was Cupid.

e·ro·sion [i·rō′zhən] *n.* The wearing away or gradual destruction of something by the action of wind, water, acid, etc.: the *erosion* of land.

err [ûr *or* er] *v.* **erred, err·ing** **1** To make an error; be wrong. **2** To do what is not right; sin.

er·rand [er′ənd] *n.* **1** A short trip made to carry out some task, usually for someone else. **2** The purpose of such a trip.

er·rant [er′ənt] *adj.* **1** Roving or wandering in search of adventure: an *errant* knight. **2** Straying from what is right or correct: *errant* behavior.

er·rat·ic [i·rat′ik] *adj.* **1** Uneven or irregular in action, progress, etc.: *erratic* growth. **2** Unusual; odd: *erratic* behavior. **— er·rat′i·cal·ly** *adv.*

er·ro·ne·ous [ə·rō′nē·əs] *adj.* Not correct or true; mistaken; false: *erroneous* opinions.

er·ror [er′ər] *n.* **1** Something done, said, or believed incorrectly; a mistake: an *error* in addition. **2** The condition of being incorrect or mistaken: He is in *error* about the dates of the Civil War. **3** In baseball, a misplay, such as a fumble or wild throw, that allows a runner to reach base or to advance safely.

erst·while [ûrst′(h)wīl′] *adj.* Previous; former: an *erstwhile* companion.

er·u·dite [er′yoo·dīt] *adj.* Having or displaying much knowledge; scholarly: an *erudite* teacher.

er·u·di·tion [er′yoo·dish′ən] *n.* Great knowledge or learning: His *erudition* impressed us.

e·rupt [i·rupt′] *v.* **1** To cast forth lava, steam, etc.: Mount Etna *erupts* frequently. **2** To cast forth (lava, steam, etc.). **3** To become covered with pimples or a rash. **4** Of new teeth, to break through the gums.

e·rup·tion [i·rup′shən] *n.* **1** The act or process of erupting. **2** A breaking out in a rash.

Volcano erupting

-ery A suffix meaning: **1** A business or place where something is done, as in *bakery*, a place where baked goods are made or sold. **2** A place or residence for, as in *nunnery*, a residence for nuns. **3** A collection of things, as in *finery*, a collection of fine clothes, decorations, etc. **4** The actions or attitudes of, as in *snobbery*, the actions or attitudes of snobs. **5** An act, art, trade, or profession, as in *cookery*, the act or art of cooking. **6** A state of being, as in *bravery*, the state of being brave.

E·sau [ē′sô] *n.* In the Bible, the oldest son of Isaac. He sold his birthright to his brother Jacob in exchange for a dish of food.

es·ca·late [es′kə·lāt] *v.* **es·ca·la·ted, es·ca·lat·ing** To develop, increase, or expand, especially by stages: These small skirmishes could *escalate* into a war.

es·ca·la·tor [es′kə·lā′tər] *n.* A moving stairway for carrying people from one floor to another.

Escalator

es·cal·lop [e·skol′əp *or* e·skal′əp] *v.* To bake in a sauce, usually of milk, flour, butter, etc.

es·ca·pade [es′kə·pād] *n.* A reckless or mischievous act or prank; fling; spree.

es·cape [ə·skāp′] *v.* **es·caped, es·cap·ing,** *n.* **1** *v.* To break out or get free. **2** *v.* To get or keep free from: to *escape* notice. **3** *v.* To avoid or remain untouched by: to *escape* chicken pox. **4** *n.* The act of escaping. **5** *n.* A way of escaping. **6** *v.* To leak out little by little: Fumes *escaped* from the pipe. **7** *v.* To slip by the notice, memory, or understanding of: Your meaning *escapes* me. **8** *v.* To slip out from unintentionally: A groan *escaped* his lips. **9** *n.* A means of forgetting troubles, boredom, etc.

es·cape·ment [ə·skāp′mənt] *n.* **1** A device in clocks and watches that keeps the movement regular. It consists of a wheel having notches around its rim, each notch of which is held back briefly by a catch and then allowed to escape at regular intervals. **2** A device in a typewriter that controls the sideways movement of the carriage.

escape velocity The velocity that an object, as a rocket, must reach in order to escape the pull of gravity of the earth or other body.

es·cap·ism [ə·skā′piz·əm] *n.* A desire or tendency to escape something unpleasant by daydreaming or by some form of entertainment.

es·carp·ment [es·kärp′mənt] *n.* **1** A steep, man-made slope that surrounds a fortification. **2** Any steep slope or cliff.

es·cort [*n.* es′kôrt, *v.* es·kôrt′] **1** *n.* A person or

---

add, āce, câre, pälm; end, ēqual; it, īce; odd, ōpen, ôrder; tŏŏk, pōōl; up, bûrn;
ə = a in *above*, e in *sicken*, i in *possible*, o in *melon*, u in *circus*; yōō = u in *fuse*; oil; pout;
check; ring; thin; this; zh in *vision*. For ¶ reference, see page 64 · HOW TO

group of persons attending someone so as to protect, guide, or honor: The Queen was given a military *escort.* **2** *n.* A man who takes a young girl or woman to a party, dance, etc. **3** *n.* One or more planes, ships, cars, etc., moving along with another so as to protect, guide, or honor. **4** *v.* To accompany as an escort.

es·cutch·eon [i·skuch′ən] *n.* A shield on whose surface there is a coat of arms.

-ese A suffix meaning: **1** A native or inhabitant of, as in *Japanese,* a native or inhabitant of Japan. **2** The language of, as in *Portuguese,* the language of Portugal. **3** The manner or style of, as in *journalese,* the manner or style of writing in newspapers, etc.

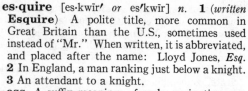

Escutcheon

Es·ki·mo [es′kə·mō] *n.,* *pl.* **Es·ki·mos** or **Es·ki·mo 1** Any of a stocky, flat-faced race of people living along the Arctic coasts of North America, Greenland, and NE Siberia. **2** The language of these people. **3** *adj. use:* an *Eskimo* village. ◆ *Eskimo* comes from a North American Indian word meaning *eaters of raw flesh.*

Eskimo dog Another name for HUSKY.

e·soph·a·gus [i·sof′ə·gəs] *n.* The tube through which food passes from the throat to the stomach.

es·o·ter·ic [es′ə·ter′ik] *adj.* **1** Known or understood by only a few special people: the *esoteric* initiation rites of a secret society. **2** Private; confidential.

esp. or **espec.** Abbreviation of ESPECIALLY.

es·pe·cial [es·pesh′əl] *adj.* Very special or particular: It is of *especial* importance. — **in especial** In particular; especially.

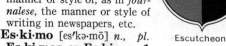

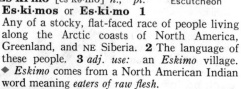

esophagus

stomach

large intestine small intestine

es·pe·cial·ly [es·pesh′əl·ē] *adv.* To a very special degree; particularly: I like all pies, but *especially* apple; an *especially* good pie.

es·pi·o·nage [es′pē·ə·nij′ *or* es′pē·ə·näzh′] *n.* **1** The act of spying. **2** The work of a spy, especially the attempt to learn the military or political secrets of other nations.

es·pou·sal [es·pou′zəl] *n.* **1** The taking up or support of a cause, idea, etc. **2** An engagement to marry. **3** *(usually pl.)* A marriage ceremony.

es·pouse [es·pouz′] *v.* **es·poused, es·pous·ing 1** To take up or back a cause or idea; support: to *espouse* civil rights. **2** To marry.

es·prit [es·prē′] *n.* Spirit; wit: a French word.

esprit de corps [es·prē′ də kôr′] A sense of pride in and devotion to a group to which one belongs: a French phrase.

es·py [es·pī′] *v.* **es·pied, es·py·ing** To catch sight of (something hidden or distant); see.

Esq. Abbreviation of ESQUIRE.

es·quire [es·kwīr′ *or* es′kwīr] *n.* **1** *(written* **Esquire***)* A polite title, more common in Great Britain than the U.S., sometimes used instead of "Mr." When written, it is abbreviated, and placed after the name: Lloyd Jones, *Esq.* **2** In England, a man ranking just below a knight. **3** An attendant to a knight.

-ess A suffix meaning: female, as in *tigress,* a female tiger.

es·say 1 *n.* [es′ā] A short composition, in which the writer gives his own ideas on a single subject. **2** *n.* [es′ā *or* e·sā′] An attempt; endeavor. **3** *v.* [e·sā′] To attempt; try.

es·say·ist [es′ā·ist] *n.* A writer of essays.

es·sence [es′əns] *n.* **1** That which makes something what it is; basic quality: The *essence* of mercy is love. **2** A substance that has in concentrated form the special qualities, as of smell and taste, of the plant or drug from which it was taken: *essence* of peppermint. **3** A perfume.

es·sen·tial [ə·sen′shəl] **1** *adj.* Of, having to do with, or forming a basis or foundation; basic: Learning to read is an *essential* part of education. **2** *adj.* Extremely important or necessary; vital: It is *essential* to keep alert while driving. **3** *n.* Something extremely important or basic: Good balance is an *essential* in bicycling. — **es·sen′·tial·ly** *adv.*

-est[1] A suffix meaning: most, as in *softest,* the most soft. *-est* is used with many adjectives and adverbs for the superlative form.

-est[2] An ending once used for the present tense of verbs with "thou": "Thou *singest*" is the old form of "you sing."

es·tab·lish [ə·stab′lish] *v.* **1** To set up, found, or institute on a firm or lasting basis: to *establish* a government, colony, or business. **2** To put or settle permanently or securely in a particular place, business, etc.: to *establish* oneself as a lawyer. **3** To introduce and cause to last (a law, custom, habit, etc.). **4** To clear from doubt; show to be true; prove: The lawyer sought to *establish* his client's innocence.

established church A church set up as the official church of a nation, and supported by the government.

es·tab·lish·ment [ə·stab′lish·mənt] *n.* **1** The act of establishing. **2** A being established. **3** Something established, as a company, store, household, church, etc.

es·tate [ə·stāt′] *n.* **1** A large piece of land, usually with a home on it. **2** Everything a person possesses, as money, land, or property: He willed his *estate* to his son. **3** A stage in life: to reach a man's *estate* at 21 years.

es·teem [ə·stēm′] **1** *v.* To have a high opinion of; value: We *esteem* bravery. **2** *n.* Respect or regard; appreciation: to hold bravery in high *esteem.* **3** *v.* To think; consider; deem: We *esteem* it an honor to know you.

Es·ther [es′tər] *n.* **1** In the Bible, the Jewish wife of a Persian king. She saved her people from being slaughtered. **2** A book of the Old Testament containing her story.

es·thet·ic [es·thet′ik] *adj.* Another spelling of AESTHETIC. — **es·thet′i·cal·ly** *adv.*

es·thet·ics [es·thet′iks] *n.* Another spelling of AESTHETICS.

es·ti·ma·ble [es′tə·mə·bəl] *adj.* Worthy of respect and esteem: an *estimable* deed.

es·ti·mate [*v.* es′tə·māt, *n.* es′tə·mit] *v.* **es·ti·mat·ed, es·ti·mat·ing,** *n.* **1** *v.* To make a close guess about (size, number, cost, etc.): He *estimates* the cost to be 20 dollars. **2** *n.* A general but careful guess about size, value, cost, etc. **3** A judgment or opinion: In your *estimate*, is this book worth reading?

es·ti·ma·tion [es′tə·mā′shən] *n.* **1** The act of estimating. **2** Opinion; judgment. **3** Esteem; regard: I hold him in high *estimation*.

Es·to·ni·a [es·tō′nē·ə] *n.* A country in NE Europe, part of the Soviet Union. — **Es·to′· ni·an** *adj., n.*

es·trange [es·trānj′] *v.* **es·tranged, es· trang·ing** To make (someone once friendly) unfriendly or hostile. — **es·trange′ment** *n.*

es·tu·ar·y [es′choo·er′ē] *n., pl.* **es·tu·ar·ies 1** The broad meeting place of a river and sea, where the tide flows in. **2** An arm of a sea.

etc. Abbreviation of ET CETERA.

et cet·er·a [et set′ər·ə] And other things; and so on: a Latin phrase.

etch [ech] *v.* To engrave (a design) on a metal plate. The surface of the plate is coated with a substance, as wax, and the desired design is drawn on the wax with a sharp instrument. Acid is then used to eat into the parts of the metal not protected by the wax.

etch·ing [ech′ing] *n.* **1** A process of engraving a design, as on metal or glass. **2** A plate that is etched. **3** An etched design. **4** A print that is made from an etched plate.

e·ter·nal [i·tûr′nəl] *adj.* **1** Having no beginning or end; lasting forever. **2** Unchanging; always the same: *eternal* truths. **3** Seeming to last forever; continual: *eternal* bickering. — **e·ter′· nal·ly** *adv.*

e·ter·ni·ty [i·tûr′nə·tē] *n., pl.* **e·ter·ni·ties 1** All time, with no beginning or ending. **2** A seemingly endless period of time: It was an *eternity* before she answered my letter. **3** The unending time that follows death.

-eth¹ An ending used after a vowel to form an ordinal number, as in *twentieth.*

-eth² An ending once used in the third person singular for the present tense of some verbs. "He *goeth*" is an old-fashioned way of saying "He goes."

e·ther [ē′thər] *n.* **1** A colorless liquid whose fumes, when inhaled, can make a person unconscious, as before an operation. **2** An elastic substance once believed to fill all space. **3** The upper, clear regions of the sky.

e·the·re·al [i·thir′ē·əl] *adj.* **1** Like air or ether; light; delicate: *ethereal* beauty. **2** Not belonging to earth; heavenly: *ethereal* spirits.

eth·i·cal [eth′i·kəl] *adj.* **1** Of or having to do with ethics and morality. **2** Conforming to certain rules of behavior. — **eth′i·cal·ly** *adv.*

eth·ics [eth′iks] *n.* **1** The study of right and wrong in human behavior. **2** Rules of right behavior, especially with reference to a particular profession, way of life, etc. ◆ See -ICS.

E·thi·o·pi·a [ē′thē·ō′pē·ə] **1** A country, once also called Abyssinia, in eastern Africa, south of Egypt. **2** An ancient country south of Egypt. — **E′thi·o′pi·an** *adj., n.*

eth·nic [eth′nik] *adj.* Of, having to do with, or belonging to a specific group of mankind, whose members share the same culture, language, or customs.

eth·nol·o·gy [eth·nol′ə·jē] *n.* The science that deals with the racial and ethnic groups of mankind, their origins, characteristics, distribution, and cultures.

eth·yl [eth′əl] *adj.* In chemistry, indicating the radical C_2H_5, found only as a part of some chemical compounds: *ethyl* ether.

et·i·quette [et′ə·ket] *n.* The rules established for behavior in polite society or in official or professional life.

Et·na [et′nə] *n.* A volcano in eastern Sicily.

E·ton [ē′t(ə)n] *n.* A boy's school in England.

E·tru·ri·a [i·troor′ē·ə] *n.* An ancient country in what is now west central Italy.

E·trus·can [i·trus′kən] **1** *adj.* Of or from Etruria. **2** *n.* A person who was born or lived in Etruria. **3** *n.* The extinct language of Etruria.

-ette A suffix meaning: **1** Little; small, as in *kitchenette*, a small kitchen. **2** Female, as in *farmerette*, a female farmer. **3** Imitation, as in *leatherette*, imitation leather.

é·tude [ā′t(y)ood] *n.* A piece of music, used for developing or showing off certain skills on an instrument.

et·y·mol·o·gy [et′ə·mol′ə·jē] *n., pl.* **et·y·mol· o·gies 1** The history of a word, showing how the word developed into its present form and meaning. **2** The science that deals with the history of words.

eu·ca·lyp·tus [yoo′kə·lip′təs] *n., pl.* **eu·ca· lyp·tus·es** or **eu·ca·lyp·ti** [yoo′kə·lip′tī] An evergreen tree, common in Australia, that is valuable for its oil and wood.

Eu·char·ist [yoo′kə·rist] *n.* **1** Another name for HOLY COMMUNION. **2** The consecrated bread and wine used in this. — **Eu′cha·ris′tic** *adj.*

Eu·clid [yoo′klid] *n.* A Greek mathematician who lived about the third century B.C. He wrote a famous book on geometry.

eu·gen·ics [yoo·jen′iks] *n.* The science that deals with improving the human race through control of the factors influencing heredity, as by careful selection of parents. ◆ See -ICS.

---

add, āce, câre, pälm; end, ēqual; it, īce; odd, ōpen, ôrder; tŏŏk, pool; up, bûrn;
ə = a in *above*, e in *sicken*, i in *possible*, o in *melon*, u in *circus*; yoo = u in *fuse*; oil; pout;
check; ring; thin; this; zh in *vision.* For ¶ reference, see page 64 · HOW TO

eu·lo·gize [yōō′lə·jīz] *v.* **eu·lo·gized, eu·lo·giz·ing** To praise highly; extol. ¶3

eu·lo·gy [yōō′lə·jē] *n., pl.* **eu·lo·gies** A speech or writing in praise of a person or thing, especially when presented formally and in public. — **eu′lo·gis′tic** *adj.*

eu·nuch [yōō′nək] *n.* **1** A castrated man employed as an attendant in an Oriental harem. **2** Any castrated man or boy.

eu·phe·mism [yōō′fə·miz′əm] *n.* **1** A mild or agreeable expression used in place of another felt to be harsh or crude: "The departed" is a *euphemism* for "the dead." **2** The use of such words or expressions. — **eu′phe·mis′tic** *adj.*

eu·pho·ni·ous [yōō·fō′nē·əs] *adj.* Having an agreeable and pleasant sound.

eu·pho·ny [yōō′fə·nē] *n., pl.* **eu·pho·nies** Pleasant sound or combination of sounds.

Eu·phra·tes [yōō·frā′tēz] *n.* A river in sw Asia that flows from eastern Turkey through Syria and Iraq into the Persian Gulf.

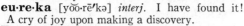

Eur·a·sia [yōō·rā′zhə] *n.* The body of land making up Europe and Asia.

Eur·a·sian [yōō·rā′zhən] *n.* A person of mixed European and Asian ancestry.

eu·re·ka [yōō·rē′kə] *interj.* I have found it! A cry of joy upon making a discovery.

Eu·rip·i·des [yōō·rip′ə·dēz] *n.*, 480?–406? B.C., Greek writer of tragic plays.

Eu·rope [yōŏr′əp] *n.* The continent that is east of the Atlantic Ocean and west of Asia.

Eu·ro·pe·an [yōŏr′ə·pē′ən] **1** *adj.* Of or from Europe. **2** *n.* A person born or living in Europe.

Eu·sta·chi·an tube [yōō·stā′kē·ən *or* yōō·stā′shən] A narrow canal between the pharynx and middle ear, that helps make the air pressure equal on both sides of the eardrum.

eu·tro·phi·ca·tion [yōō′trə·fə·kā′shən] *n.* A natural or pollution-caused increase of dissolved nutrients in a lake, causing excessive plant growth and often also shortages of the free oxygen needed for animal life.

e·vac·u·ate [i·vak′yōō·āt] *v.* **e·vac·u·at·ed, e·vac·u·at·ing** **1** To remove; withdraw: to *evacuate* troops from the besieged town. **2** To move out of; vacate: to *evacuate* a firetrap. **3** To remove the contents of; empty: to *evacuate* the stomach. — **e·vac′u·a′tion** *n.*

e·vade [i·vād′] *v.* **e·vad·ed, e·vad·ing** To get or keep away from by tricks or cleverness; avoid; elude: to *evade* a bill collector.

e·val·u·ate [i·val′yōō·āt] *v.* **e·val·u·at·ed, e·val·u·at·ing** To judge or find the amount, worth, etc., of: to *evaluate* a student's compositions. — **e·val′u·a′tion** *n.*

ev·a·nes·cent [ev′ə·nes′ənt] *adj.* Soon passing away; not lasting; fleeting: Their anger was *evanescent.* — **ev′a·nes′cence** *n.*

e·van·gel·i·cal [ē′van·jel′i·kəl] *adj.* **1** Of, having to do with, or according to the New Testament, especially the four Gospels. **2** Of, related to, or holding the belief that the Bible is the most important rule of faith and that the soul is saved only through faith in Jesus.

e·van·gel·ism [i·van′jə·liz′əm] *n.* Enthusiastic preaching or spreading of the gospel.

e·van·gel·ist [i·van′jə·list] *n.* **1** (*usually written* **Evangelist**) One of the four writers of the Gospels: Matthew, Mark, Luke, or John. **2** A person who preaches the gospel, especially a traveling preacher or minister.

e·vap·o·rate [i·vap′ə·rāt] *v.* **e·vap·o·rat·ed, e·vap·o·rat·ing** **1** To turn into vapor: Boiling *evaporates* water. **2** To remove moisture from: to *evaporate* fruit. **3** To give off vapor. **4** To vanish; disappear: His courage *evaporated* in battle. — **e·vap′o·ra′tion** *n.*

evaporated milk Milk, in cans, that has been made thick by removal of some of its water.

e·va·sion [i·vā′zhən] *n.* The act of evading, especially the avoiding of something unpleasant or difficult by cleverness or tricks: Income tax *evasion* is a serious offense.

e·va·sive [i·vā′siv] *adj.* Tending to evade; not direct or frank: an *evasive* reply. — **e·va′sive·ly** *adv.*

eve [ēv] *n.* **1** The evening or day before a holiday or festival: Christmas *Eve.* **2** The time just before some event: on the *eve* of the election. **3** Evening: used mostly in poems.

Eve [ēv] *n.* In the Bible, the first woman, Adam's wife. ◆ The name *Eve* comes from a Hebrew word meaning *life.*

e·ven¹ [ē′vən] **1** *adj.* Flat and smooth: an *even* sheet of ice. **2** *adj.* Steady; not changing: to hold an *even* speed. **3** *v.* To make or become even: to *even* up accounts; The road *evens* off here. **4** *adj.* The same in quantity, number, measure, etc.; equal: *even* portions. **5** *adj.* On the same line or level: The speeding cars were *even.* **6** *adj.* Not easily excited; calm: an *even* disposition. **7** *adj.* Not owing or being owed anything: You owe me a dime and I owe you a dime, so we're *even.* **8** *adj.* Precise; exact: to walk an *even* mile. **9** *adv.* Precisely; exactly; just: Do *even* as I say. **10** *adj.* Exactly divisible by 2: 6, 8, and 10 are *even* numbers. **11** *adv.* Still: an *even* better plan. **12** *adv.* At the very same time; while: *Even* as they watched, the ship sank. **13** *adv.* Indeed; in fact: to feel glad, *even* delighted. **14** *adv.* Unlikely as it may seem: He was kind *even* to his enemies. **15** *adv.* All the same; notwithstanding: *Even* with a broken toe, he won. — **even if** Although; notwithstanding. — **even with** To get revenge upon. — **e′ven·ly** *adv.* — **e′ven·ness** *n.*

e·ven² [ē′vən] *n.* Evening: seldom used today.

eve·ning [ēv′ning] *n.* The end of the day and the first part of night, or the time from sunset until bedtime.

evening star A bright planet, as Venus, visible in the western sky just after sunset.

e·ven·song [ē′vən·sông′] *n.* A service in some churches, said or sung in the evening.

e·vent [i·vent′] *n.* **1** A happening; occurrence, especially an important one: historical *events.* **2** One of the items that make up a sports program. **3** Final outcome; result. **— in any event** In any case; anyhow. **— in the event of** If there should be; in case of.

e·vent·ful [i·vent′fəl] *adj.* **1** Full of events, usually important ones: an *eventful* day. **2** Having significant results; important: an *eventful* decision.

e·ven·tide [ē′vən·tīd′] *n.* Evening: used mostly in poems.

e·ven·tu·al [i·ven′chōo·əl] *adj.* Happening or resulting in the future: *eventual* victory.

e·ven·tu·al·i·ty [i·ven′chōo·al′ə·tē] *n.,* *pl.* **e·ven·tu·al·i·ties** Something that may or may not take place; a possible occurrence.

e·ven·tu·al·ly [i·ven′chōo·əl·ē] *adv.* In the course of time; in the end; ultimately.

ev·er [ev′ər] *adv.* **1** At any time: Did you *ever* see it? **2** At all times; always: They remained *ever* on guard. ◆ *Ever* is often used in informal talk to make what is being said more forceful: How did you *ever* manage it? **— ever so** *informal* So very; extremely.

Ev·er·est [ev′ər·ist], **Mount** A mountain on the border between Tibet and Nepal in Asia. It is the highest mountain in the world.

ev·er·glade [ev′ər·glād′] *n.* A swamp covered with tall grass. **— The Everglades** A large, swampy region in southern Florida.

ev·er·green [ev′ər·grēn′] **1** *adj.* Having leaves that stay green all through the year. **2** *n.* An evergreen tree or plant, as ivy.

ev·er·last·ing [ev′ər·las′ting] **1** *adj.* Lasting forever; eternal. **2** *adj.* Seeming to last forever; constant: *everlasting* chatter. **3** *n.* Eternity. **— the Everlasting** God.

ev·er·more [ev′ər·môr′] *adv.* Always: used mostly in poems. **— for evermore** Forever.

eve·ry [ev′rē or ev′ər·ē] *adj.* **1** Each of all that form a group: *Every* guest is here now. **2** All that is possible; each possible: He had *every* chance to escape. **3** Each: *every* tenth man; *every* four hours. **— every now and then** or **every so often** From time to time; occasionally. **— every other** Skipping one each time, as first, third, fifth, etc., in a series: They won *every other* game. **— every which way** In all directions and ways; without order.

ev·er·y·bod·y [ev′rē·bod′ē] *pron.* Every person: *Everybody* saw her. ◆See EVERYONE.

ev·er·y·day [ev′rē·dā′] *adj.* **1** Happening each day; daily. **2** Suitable for ordinary or common use: *everyday* clothes.

ev·er·y·one [ev′rē·wun′] *pron.* Every person; everybody. ◆ Although *everyone* and *everybody* are followed by a singular verb, the pronouns

they, them, and *their* are often used informally as substitutes for these two words, but not in formal writing. *Everyone* was there; Call *everybody* and tell them to come tonight.

eve·ry·thing [ev′rē·thing′] *n.* **1** All things: to have *everything* one needs. **2** The only thing that matters: Tennis was *everything* to him.

eve·ry·where [ev′rē·(h)wâr′] *adv.* In or at all places; all about: The grass grew *everywhere.*

e·vict [i·vikt′] *v.* To make (a person) by law move out from a building or house: They were *evicted* for not having paid the rent. **— e·vic′· tion** *n.*

ev·i·dence [ev′ə·dəns] *n., v.* **ev·i·denced, ev·i·denc·ing** **1** *n.* Something that proves what is true or not true or that provides reason or support for believing the truth or falsity of something: Good grades are usually *evidence* that one has studied. **2** *v.* To show clearly or unmistakably: Her laughter *evidenced* her joy. **— in evidence** Readily seen; in plain view.

ev·i·dent [ev′ə·dənt] *adj.* Easily seen or understood; apparent: It is *evident* that she is ill.

ev·i·dent·ly [ev′ə·dənt·lē or ev′ə·dent′lē] *adv.* So far as can be seen; apparently: *Evidently* he is her son.

e·vil [ē′vəl] **1** *adj.* Bad; depraved; wicked: to say *evil* things. **2** *n.* Something that is wicked or bad. **3** *adj.* Causing pain or misfortune: *evil* times. **4** *n.* Anything that causes harm or suffering: Poverty is an *evil.* **— e′vil·ly** *adv.*

e·vil·do·er [ē′vəl·dōo′ər] *n.* A person who does evil.

e·vil-mind·ed [ē′vəl·mīn′did] *adj.* Having evil thoughts or ideas.

e·vince [i·vins′] *v.* **e·vinced, e·vinc·ing** To show clearly; make plain: Her tears *evinced* her unhappiness.

e·voke [i·vōk′] *v.* **e·voked, e·vok·ing** To bring forth; call up: This photograph *evokes* pleasant memories.

ev·o·lu·tion [ev′ə·lōo′shən] *n.* **1** The changes that take place in the gradual development of something: the *evolution* of the seed into a plant. **2** The theory that all living things developed from earlier, simpler forms, through changes that were passed through generations over long periods of time. **3** One of a series of movements, as in dancing. **— ev′o·lu′tion·ar′y** *adj.*

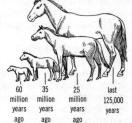

60 million years ago   35 million years ago   25 million years ago   last 125,000 years

Evolution of the horse

e·volve [i·volv′] *v.* **e·volved, e·volv·ing** To work out; develop gradually: to *evolve* a new theory in psychology.

---

add, **ā**ce, **c**â**re, **p**ä**lm;   end, **ē**qual;   it, **ī**ce;   **o**dd, **ō**pen, **ô**rder;   t**ŏŏ**k, p**ōō**l;   **u**p, **b**û**rn;**
ə = a in *above,* e in *sicken,* i in *possible,* o in *melon,* u in *circus;*   **y**ōō = u in *fuse;*   **oi**l;   **pout;**
check;   **r**i**ng;   **th**in;   **th**is;   zh in *vision.*   For ¶ reference, see page 64 · HOW TO

ewe [yōō] *n*. A female sheep.

ew·er [yōō′ər] *n*. A large water pitcher with a wide mouth.

ex- A prefix meaning: **1** Out, as in *exit*, to go out. **2** Former, written with a hyphen, as in *ex-president*, a former president.

Ewer

ex·act [ig·zakt′] **1** *adj*. Completely accurate; precise: the *exact* amount necessary. **2** *v*. To insist upon and get: to *exact* obedience. **3** *adj*. Very strict and correct: *exact* in his behavior toward ladies. **— ex·act′ness** *n*.

ex·act·ing [ig·zak′ting] *adj*. **1** Strict; demanding a lot: an *exacting* teacher. **2** Requiring hard work and attention: an *exacting* profession.

ex·ac·tion [ig·zak′shən] *n*. **1** The exacting or requiring of something, especially by wrongful means. **2** Something required or exacted.

ex·act·i·tude [ig·zak′tə·t(y)ōōd] *n*. Exactness.

ex·act·ly [ig·zakt′lē] *adv*. **1** In an exact manner; precisely: to cut a cake *exactly* in half. **2** Precisely right; just so.

ex·ag·ger·ate [ig·zaj′ə·rāt] *v*. **ex·ag·ger·at·ed, ex·ag·ger·at·ing 1** To make appear greater than is really true; overstate: to *exaggerate* one's own importance. **2** To make greater in size than is normal or expected: She *exaggerates* her eyebrows by blackening them heavily.

ex·ag·ger·a·tion [ig·zaj′ə·rā′shən] *n*. **1** The act of exaggerating. **2** The condition of being exaggerated. **3** A statement, story, etc., that is exaggerated.

ex·alt [ig·zôlt′] *v*. **1** To praise or honor: to *exalt* the glory of God. **2** To raise up in position, power, or honor. **3** To fill with delight, pride, etc.; elate: He was *exalted* by the singing. **— ex·al·ta·tion** [eg′zôl·tā′shən] *n*.

ex·alt·ed [ig·zôl′tid] *adj*. **1** High in position or rank. **2** Lofty or noble: an *exalted* ideal.

ex·am [ig·zam′] *n. informal* An examination.

ex·am·i·na·tion [ig·zam′ə·nā′shən] *n*. **1** The act of examining; careful inspection. **2** A formal test of what a person has learned or has the skill to do.

ex·am·ine [ig·zam′in] *v*. **ex·am·ined, ex·am·in·ing 1** To look at with care and attention: to *examine* an injured leg; to *examine* fruit for spots. **2** To ask questions of in order to get information or to test a person's knowledge or skill. **— ex·am′in·er** *n*.

ex·am·ple [ig·zam′pəl] *n*. **1** Something used to show what others of the same kind or group are like; sample: an *example* of modern art. **2** A model or pattern deserving to be imitated: A father should set a good *example* for his children. **3** A warning: Let this be an *example* to you. **4** A problem, as in arithmetic, that is to be worked out. **— for example** For instance.

ex·as·per·ate [ig·zas′pə·rāt] *v*. **ex·as·per·at·ed, ex·as·per·at·ing** To annoy or irritate almost to the point of anger: Her constant

lateness *exasperated* him. **— ex·as′per·a′·tion** *n*.

Ex·cal·i·bur [eks·kal′ə·bər] *n*. In legend, the name of King Arthur's sword.

ex·ca·vate [eks′kə·vāt] *v*. **ex·ca·vat·ed, ex·ca·vat·ing 1** To make a hole or cavity in by digging: to *excavate* the side of a mountain. **2** To make by digging out: to *excavate* a tunnel. **3** To remove by digging or scooping out. **4** To uncover by digging: Archaeologists *excavate* ancient ruins. **— ex′ca·va′tor** *n*.

ex·ca·va·tion [eks′kə·vā′shən] *n*. **1** The act or process of excavating. **2** A hole or hollow made by digging.

An excavation

ex·ceed [ik·sēd′] *v*. **1** To be greater or better than: Crops *exceeded* estimates. **2** To go beyond the limits of: The task *exceeds* his abilities.

ex·ceed·ing [ik·sē′·ding] **1** *adj*. Unusual; very great; extreme. **2** *adv*. Exceedingly: seldom used today.

ex·ceed·ing·ly [ik·sē′ding·lē] *adv*. Extremely; very: He is *exceedingly* busy.

ex·cel [ik·sel′] *v*. **ex·celled, ex·cel·ling** To be better than; surpass: He *excels* them in sports.

ex·cel·lence [ek′sə·ləns] *n*. Very high quality; great goodness or superiority: They praised the *excellence* of his performance.

ex·cel·len·cy [ek′sə·lən·sē] *n*., *pl*. **ex·cel·len·cies 1** (*usually written* **Excellency**) A title of honor used when formally addressing or speaking of certain high officials, as governors, ambassadors, or bishops: Your *Excellency*. **2** Excellence.

ex·cel·lent [ek′sə·lənt] *adj*. Extremely good; superior: He is an *excellent* skater and won a prize. **— ex′cel·lent·ly** *adv*.

ex·cel·si·or [*n*. ik·sel′sē·ər, *interj*. ek·sel′sē·ôr] **1** *n*. Fine shavings of wood used for packing breakable goods, as dishes or glassware. **2** *interj*. (*usually written* **Excelsior**) A Latin word meaning: Ever higher; upward: used as a motto.

ex·cept [ik·sept′] **1** *prep*. With the exception of; leaving out; but: any color *except* blue. **2** *v*. To leave out; exclude: Medicines are *excepted* from the tax. **3** *conj*. Only; but: I would write *except* I have no paper. ◆ *Except* and *accept* are often confused. Though they have the same root, from a Latin verb meaning *to take*, the prefixes are different. Latin *ex-* means *out*, and Latin *ac-* (or *ad-*) means *to*. *Except* is often a preposition meaning *taking out* or *leaving out*, less often a verb meaning *to take out*. *Accept* is a verb meaning *to take to* oneself, or *receive*.

ex·cept·ing [ik·sep′ting] *prep*. Except.

ex·cep·tion [ik·sep′shən] *n*. **1** A leaving out; exclusion: With the *exception* of Tom, everyone was there. **2** A person or thing that is different in some way from others of its class; an instance that does not fit the general rule: *Auks*, not able to fly, are *exceptions* among sea birds. **3** An objection or complaint: a statement open to *exception.* **— take exception** To feel angry or resentful; object.

ex·cep·tion·al [ik·sep′shən·əl] *adj.* Not ordinary; unusual. **— ex·cep′tion·al·ly** *adv.*

ex·cerpt [*n.* ek′sûrpt, *v.* ik·sûrpt′] **1** *n.* A passage or section taken from a piece of writing: They acted out *excerpts* from several plays. **2** *v.* To pick out and quote (a passage from a book, etc.).

ex·cess [*n.* ik·ses′ *or* ek′ses, *adj.* ek′ses] **1** *n.* An amount or degree of something over what is needed, wanted, used, or proper: *an excess of rain; an excess of emotion.* **2** *adj.* Over the usual, allowed, or necessary amount; extra: *excess baggage.* **3** *n.* The amount by which one thing is more than another: *The excess of 25 over 13 is 12.* **— in excess of** Over; above: *weight in excess of five pounds.* **— to excess** More than is proper: *Don't eat to excess.*

ex·ces·sive [ik·ses′iv] *adj.* Too great or too much: *It took an excessive amount of time.* **— ex·ces′sive·ly** *adv.*

ex·change [iks·chānj′] *v.* **ex·changed, ex·chang·ing,** *n.* **1** *v.* To give and receive in return; interchange: *to exchange gifts.* **2** *n.* The act of giving and receiving in return: *an exchange of compliments.* **3** *v.* To give one thing for something else; trade; swap: *to exchange a red shirt for a blue one.* **4** *n.* A trade or substitution: *What will you give me in exchange for this marble?* **5** *n.* A place where brokers, merchants, etc., buy, sell, or trade: *a stock exchange.* **6** *n.* A central office in a telephone system.

ex·cheq·uer [eks′chek·ər *or* iks·chek′ər] *n.* **1** The treasury of a state, nation, etc. **2** (*written* **Exchequer**) The department of the British government that has charge of all public revenue and finance. **3** *informal* The amount of money a person has for everyday use.

ex·cise[1] [ek′sīz *or* ik·sīz′] *n.* A tax within a country on the production, sale, or use of certain goods, such as tobacco.

ex·cise[2] [ik·sīz′] *v.* **ex·cised, ex·cis·ing** To remove by cutting out: *to excise a growth from the body.* **— ex·ci·sion** [ik·sizh′ən] *n.*

ex·cit·a·ble [ik·sī′tə·bəl] *adj.* Easily excited: *An excitable horse may be dangerous.* **— ex·cit′a·bil′i·ty** *n.*

ex·cite [ik·sīt′] *v.* **ex·cit·ed, ex·cit·ing 1** To stir up strong or lively feelings in: *The fireworks excited them.* **2** To stir up (a feeling, reaction, etc.); arouse: *That story excited our interest.* **3** To arouse to activity or motion: *The loud noise excited the horse.*

ex·cit·ed [ik·sī′tid] *adj.* Full of strong or lively feelings; stirred up; aroused: *I'm so excited about the trip!* **— ex·cit′ed·ly** *adv.*

ex·cite·ment [ik·sīt′mənt] *n.* **1** The condition of being excited: *to be full of excitement.* **2** The act of exciting. **3** Something that excites.

ex·cit·ing [ik·sī′ting] *adj.* Causing excitement; thrilling: *an exciting movie.*

ex·claim [iks·klām′] *v.* To cry out suddenly or speak with force, as in surprise or anger: "The supper's burning!" she *exclaimed.*

ex·cla·ma·tion [eks′klə·mā′shən] *n.* A word or words cried out suddenly or said with force. "Oh!" and "Stop it!" are exclamations.

exclamation point or **exclamation mark** A punctuation mark (!) used to show that the word, phrase, or sentence which it follows is an exclamation.

ex·clam·a·to·ry [iks·klam′ə·tôr′ē] *adj.* Expressing, using, or having to do with exclamation: *an exclamatory phrase.*

ex·clude [iks·klōōd′] *v.* **ex·clud·ed, ex·clud·ing 1** To shut out or bar, as from a group or place: *Don't exclude the new girl from your club.* **2** To refuse to notice, think about, or allow: *Don't exclude the possibility of his coming back.*

ex·clu·sion [iks·klōō′zhən] *n.* **1** An act or instance of excluding. **2** The condition of being excluded: *Exclusion from our group hurt him.*

ex·clu·sive [iks·klōō′siv] *adj.* **1** Very particular about admitting or including friends, members, etc.: *an exclusive club.* **2** Not shared with any other; belonging to only one: *That magazine has exclusive rights to the story.* **3** Complete and undivided: *my exclusive attention.* **4** Excluding all others: *His family is his exclusive concern.* **— exclusive of** Not including: *The price exclusive of tax is $2.00.* **— ex·clu′sive·ly** *adv.*

ex·com·mu·ni·cate [eks′kə·myōō′nə·kāt] *v.* **ex·com·mu·ni·cat·ed, ex·com·mu·ni·cat·ing** To expel officially from membership in a church; cut off from the sacraments of a church. **— ex′com·mu′ni·ca′tion** *n.*

ex·cre·ment [eks′krə·mənt] *n.* Waste matter eliminated from the body, especially solid waste matter.

ex·cres·cence [iks·kres′əns] *n.* An unnatural growth, as a wart or corn.

ex·crete [iks·krēt′] *v.* **ex·cret·ed, ex·cret·ing** To throw off or eliminate (waste matter) from the body: *to excrete sweat.*

ex·cre·tion [iks·krē′shən] *n.* **1** Elimination of waste matter, as from the body. **2** Waste matter eliminated, as sweat and urine.

ex·cre·to·ry [eks′krə·tôr′ē] *adj.* Of, having to do with, or adapted for excreting: *an excretory organ.*

ex·cru·ci·at·ing [iks·krōō′shē·ā′ting] *adj.* Causing great pain or anguish.

ex·cur·sion [ik·skûr′zhən] *n.* **1** A short pleasure trip or outing. **2** A short trip on a boat, train, etc., at reduced prices. **3** *adj. use:* an *excursion* boat.

---

add, āce, câre, pälm; end, ēqual; it, īce; odd, ōpen, ôrder; tŏŏk, pōōl; up, bûrn; ə = a in *above*, e in *sicken*, i in *possible*, o in *melon*, u in *circus*; yōō = u in *fuse*; oil; pout; check; ring; thin; this; zh in *vision*. For ¶ reference, see page 64 · HOW TO

ex·cus·a·ble [ik·skyōō′zə·bəl] *adj.* That can be excused; pardonable: an *excusable* error.

ex·cuse [*v.* ik·skyōōz′, *n.* ik·skyōōs′] *v.* **ex·cused, ex·cus·ing,** *n.* **1** *v.* To pardon or forgive: *Excuse* me, would you let me by? **2** *v.* To offer an apology for (oneself): She *excused* herself for being late. **3** *v.* To understand and overlook: to *excuse* a mistake. **4** *v.* To serve as a reason for; explain: Nothing can *excuse* such rude behavior. **5** *n.* A reason given to explain or justify: What is your *excuse* for this mistake? **6** *v.* To free from some duty or obligation: to *excuse* a sick pupil from homework. **7** *n.* A note or statement explaining an absence, freeing someone from a duty, etc.: He brought an *excuse* from home. **8** *v.* To allow to leave: She asked to be *excused* from the room.

ex·e·cra·ble [ek′sə·krə·bəl] *adj.* **1** Extremely wicked; hateful: an *execrable* crime. **2** Extremely bad or poor: an *execrable* speller.

ex·e·crate [ek′sə·krāt] *v.* **ex·e·crat·ed, ex·e·crat·ing** **1** To hate; detest; abominate. **2** To curse; denounce.

ex·e·cra·tion [ek′sə·krā′shən] *n.* **1** The act of cursing or denouncing. **2** A curse. **3** A person or thing that is cursed or hated.

ex·e·cute [ek′sə·kyōōt] *v.* **ex·e·cut·ed, ex·e·cut·ing** **1** To follow or carry out; do: to *execute* an order. **2** To put into force or effect; administer: to *execute* a law. **3** To put to death by legal order: to *execute* a condemned man. **4** To produce, following a plan or design: to *execute* a portrait. **5** To make (a will, deed, etc.) legal by signing and meeting other requirements.

ex·e·cu·tion [ek′sə·kyōō′shən] *n.* **1** The act of doing or carrying out something: the *execution* of plans. **2** The act of putting to death as legally ordered. **3** The manner in which something is done or performed: Their *execution* of the dance was wonderful. **4** The act of making something legal: the *execution* of a will.

ex·e·cu·tion·er [ek′sə·kyōō′shən·ər] *n.* A person who puts to death those sentenced to die.

ex·ec·u·tive [ig·zek′yə·tiv] **1** *n.* One of the persons responsible for directing and managing a business, institution, etc. **2** *adj.* Of, for, or having to do with an executive: an *executive* decision. **3** *n.* A person or group responsible for directing a government and putting its laws into effect: The President is the chief *executive* of the U.S. **4** *adj.* Having the authority and the duty of managing the affairs of a nation and of putting its laws into effect.

ex·ec·u·tor [ig·zek′yə·tər] *n.* A person appointed to carry out the directions of another person's will after he has died.

ex·em·pla·ry [ig·zem′plər·ē] *adj.* **1** Deserving to be imitated; model: an *exemplary* career. **2** Serving as a warning: *exemplary* discipline. **3** Serving as a typical example.

ex·em·pli·fy [ig·zem′plə·fī] *v.* **ex·em·pli·fied, ex·em·pli·fy·ing** To show by example; illustrate: Benedict Arnold *exemplifies* the traitor. **— ex·em′pli·fi·ca′tion** *n.*

ex·empt [ig·zempt′] **1** *v.* To free or excuse, as from a duty or obligation: He was *exempted* from jury duty. **2** *adj.* Freed or excused, as from a duty or obligation: bonds *exempt* from taxes.

ex·emp·tion [ig·zemp′shən] *n.* **1** The act of exempting. **2** The condition of being exempted. **3** A portion of a person's income that is not taxed. **4** Someone claimed as a dependent.

ex·er·cise [ek′sər·sīz] *v.* **ex·er·cised, ex·er·cis·ing,** *n.* **1** *v.* To develop or train by active use or repeated movement: Running *exercises* the legs. **2** *n.* Active movement of the body to improve health or strength.

Man exercising

3 *n.* (*usually pl.*) A series of movements, problems, etc., that give training, skill, or strength: to play *exercises* on the piano; arithmetic *exercises*. **4** *v.* To use; employ: to *exercise* a right; to *exercise* patience. **5** *n.* The act of using: the *exercise* of authority. **6** *n.* (*usually pl.*) A ceremony or program: A song opened the *exercises*. ◆ See PRACTICE.

ex·ert [ig·zûrt′] *v.* To put forth or use: to *exert* one's influence. **— exert oneself** To put forth effort; try hard.

ex·er·tion [ig·zûr′shən] *n.* **1** Active use or employment: the *exertion* of will power. **2** Great effort: The *exertions* of the UN stopped the war.

ex·hale [eks·hāl′] *v.* **ex·haled, ex·hal·ing** **1** To breathe out. **2** To give off, as air, vapor, or an odor: The woods *exhaled* a musty odor. **— ex·ha·la·tion** [eks′hə·lā′shən] *n.*

ex·haust [ig·zôst′] **1** *v.* To make extremely tired: to *exhaust* oneself. **2** *v.* To use up entirely: We *exhausted* our supply of wood. **3** *v.* To draw off; empty: to *exhaust* the air from a jar. **4** *n.* The escape of waste gases or fumes from an engine, or the waste gases or fumes that escape. **5** *n.* In an engine,

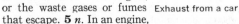

Exhaust from a car

a pipe or opening through which waste gases or fumes escape. **6** *v.* To study or discuss thoroughly and completely.

ex·haus·tion [ig·zôs′chən] *n.* **1** Extreme weariness or fatigue. **2** The act of exhausting. **3** The condition of being exhausted.

ex·haus·tive [ig·zôs′tiv] *adj.* Thoroughly covering all details or possibilities; complete: an *exhaustive* study. **— ex·haus′tive·ly** *adv.*

Outdoor art exhibit

ex·hib·it [ig·zib′it] **1** *v.* To display or show publicly; put on view: to *exhibit* art. **2** *n.*

A public showing; display. **3** *n.* A thing or things put on display: Their *exhibit* was a 1908 car. **4** *v.* To show signs of; reveal: to *exhibit* patience. **5** *n.* Something submitted as evidence in a court of law.

ex·hib·it·er [ig·zib′ə·tər] *n.* Another spelling of EXHIBITOR.

ex·hi·bi·tion [ek′sə·bish′ən] *n.* **1** An open showing; display: an *exhibition* of bad temper. **2** A public display, as of art. **3** Something displayed; exhibit.

ex·hib·i·tor [ig·zib′ə·tər] *n.* A person or group that exhibits: an *exhibitor* of motion pictures.

ex·hil·a·rate [ig·zil′ə·rāt] *v.* **ex·hil·a·rat·ed, ex·hil·a·rat·ing** To fill with happiness or high spirits; stimulate. **— ex·hil′a·ra′tion** *n.*

ex·hort [ig·zôrt′] *v.* To advise or urge earnestly: to *exhort* a team to play better.

ex·hor·ta·tion [eg′zôr·tā′shən *or* ek′sôr·tā′·shən] *n.* A very earnest plea or request: His talk in chapel was an *exhortation* to do better.

ex·hume [ig·zyo͞om′ *or* iks·hyo͞om′] *v.* **ex·humed, ex·hum·ing** To dig up from a grave.

ex·i·gen·cy [ek′sə·jən·sē] *n., pl.* **ex·i·gen·cies** **1** A situation requiring immediate action; emergency. **2** (*usually pl.*) An urgent need or demand: The *exigencies* of staying alive took all his attention.

ex·i·gent [ek′sə·jənt] *adj.* **1** Demanding immediate aid or action; urgent: an *exigent* situation. **2** Hard to satisfy or meet: *exigent* demands.

ex·ile [eg′zīl *or* ek′sīl] *v.* **ex·iled, ex·il·ing,** *n.* **1** *v.* To send (someone) away from his native land and forbid him to return; banish. **2** *n.* A person who is exiled. **3** *n.* The condition of an exile: to be driven into *exile.*

ex·ist [ig·zist′] *v.* **1** To have actual being or reality; be: Dinosaurs once *existed.* **2** To continue to live: People can't *exist* without oxygen. **3** To be present; be found: Does life *exist* on Mars?

ex·is·tence [ig·zis′təns] *n.* **1** The fact or condition of being. **2** Life: a fight for *existence.* **3** Manner of living: a lonely *existence.* **4** Presence; occurrence: the *existence* of life on Mars.

ex·is·tent [ig·zis′tənt] *adj.* **1** Having existence. **2** Now existing; present.

ex·it [eg′zit *or* ek′sit] *n.* **1** A way out, as a door or passage: Leave by the nearest *exit.* **2** A departure, especially the departure of an actor from the stage.

ex·o·dus [ek′sə·dəs] *n.* **1** A departure or going away: a mass *exodus* from the flooded city. **2** (*written* **Exodus**) The second book of the Old Testament, describing the departure of Moses and the Israelites from Egypt. **— the Exodus** This departure.

ex of·fi·ci·o [eks ə·fish′ē·ō] Because of one's office or position: a Latin term: The mayor is, *ex officio*, on the committee.

ex·on·er·ate [ig·zon′ə·rāt] *v.* **ex·on·er·at·ed, ex·on·er·at·ing** To free from blame; find innocent: Witnesses *exonerated* the driver. **— ex·on′er·a′tion** *n.*

ex·or·bi·tant [ig·zôr′bə·tənt] *adj.* Much greater than is usual or proper; unreasonably excessive: *exorbitant* prices; *exorbitant* demands.

ex·or·cise [ek′sôr·sīz] *v.* **ex·or·cised, ex·or·cis·ing** **1** To get rid of (an evil spirit) by religious or magical rites. **2** To rid (a person, place, etc.) of an evil spirit.

ex·ot·ic [ig·zot′ik] **1** *adj.* Belonging to or growing in another part of the world; foreign: an *exotic* fruit. **2** *adj.* Strangely different and fascinating: an *exotic* custom. **3** *n.* Anything exotic. **— ex·ot′i·cal·ly** *adv.*

ex·pand [ik·spand′] *v.* **1** To make or become larger: Heat makes air *expand.* **2** To spread out by unfolding: The eagle *expanded* its wings. **3** To make longer or more complete: to *expand* a speech.

ex·panse [ik·spans′] *n.* A wide and open area or space: a blue *expanse* of sky.

ex·pan·sion [ik·span′shən] *n.* **1** The act of expanding: *expansion* due to heat. **2** An expanded condition. **3** The part, surface, etc., that results from expanding: an *expansion* of a short article.

ex·pan·sive [ik·span′siv] *adj.* **1** Able or tending to expand: Air is *expansive.* **2** Wide; broad; extensive: an *expansive* view. **3** Very friendly and outgoing: an *expansive* personality.

ex·pa·ti·ate [ik·spā′shē·āt] *v.* **ex·pa·ti·at·ed, ex·pa·ti·at·ing** To speak or write at length; hold forth: to *expatiate* upon a topic.

ex·pa·tri·ate [*v.* eks·pā′trē·āt, *n.* eks·pā′trē·it] *v.* **ex·pa·tri·at·ed, ex·pa·tri·at·ing,** *n.* **1** *v.* To drive (a person) from his native land; exile. **2** *v.* To withdraw (oneself) from one's native land to live in another country. **3** *n.* An expatriated person. **— ex·pa′tri·a′tion** *n.*

ex·pect [ik·spekt′] *v.* **1** To be sure or almost sure of the coming or happening of: We *expect* them tonight. **2** To look for as right, proper, or necessary; require: Our teacher *expects* the best from us. **3** *informal* To suppose; imagine: I *expect* so.

ex·pec·tan·cy [ik·spek′tən·sē] *n., pl.* **ex·pec·tan·cies** Expectation.

ex·pec·tant [ik·spek′tənt] *adj.* Feeling or showing expectation; looking forward to something: an *expectant* look. **— ex·pec′tant·ly** *adv.*

ex·pec·ta·tion [ek′spek·tā′shən] *n.* **1** A looking forward to something; anticipation: to wait in *expectation.* **2** Something expected. **3** (*often pl.*) A reason or ground for expecting something.

ex·pec·to·rate [ik·spek′tə·rāt] *v.* **ex·pec·to·rat·ed, ex·pec·to·rat·ing** To spit. **— ex·pec′to·ra′tion** *n.*

ex·pe·di·ence [ik·spē′dē·əns] *n.* Expediency.

ex·pe·di·en·cy [ik·spē′dē·ən·sē] *n., pl.* **ex·pe·**

di·en·cies **1** The usefulness or suitability of an action or plan: the *expediency* of returning to port before a storm. **2** Selfishness or self-interest in one's thoughts, actions, plans, etc.: The politician was guided only by *expediency*.

ex·pe·di·ent [ik·spē′dē·ənt] **1** *adj.* Helpful; useful; suitable: It is *expedient* to be early. **2** *n.* A way of doing or achieving something: He tried various *expedients* before one worked. **3** *adj.* Selfish or easy rather than right or proper: purely *expedient* plans. **— ex·pe′di·ent·ly** *adv.*

ex·pe·dite [ek′spə·dīt] *v.* **ex·pe·dit·ed, ex·pe·dit·ing** To make go faster or more easily; speed up: Please *expedite* this order.

ex·pe·di·tion [ek′spə·dish′ən] *n.* **1** A journey, march, or voyage made for a definite purpose: a scientific *expedition.* **2** The group of people making such a journey, or their ships, planes, etc. **3** Speed: with great *expedition.*

ex·pe·di·tion·ar·y [ek′spə·dish′ən·er′ē] *adj.* Of, for, or going on an expedition: *expeditionary* forces sent abroad to fight.

ex·pe·di·tious [ek′spə·dish′əs] *adj.* Quick and efficient; prompt: *expeditious* handling of a complaint. **— ex′pe·di′tious·ly** *adv.*

ex·pel [ik·spel′] *v.* **ex·pelled, ex·pel·ling** **1** To drive out or force out: to *expel* air from the lungs. **2** To put out permanently; dismiss: For some prank he was *expelled* from school.

ex·pend [ik·spend′] *v.* To use up; spend.

ex·pend·a·ble [ik·spen′də·bəl] *adj.* **1** Available for spending: *expendable* funds. **2** Worth giving up or losing to gain some end or military objective: *expendable* equipment.

ex·pen·di·ture [ik·spen′də·chər] *n.* **1** The act of spending or using up: *expenditure* of energy. **2** The amount spent or used.

ex·pense [ik·spens′] *n.* **1** Cost; price: at the *expense* of a phone call. **2** (*pl.*) Money needed or spent to cover costs or charges: traveling *expenses.* **3** A cause or reason for spending: A car is an *expense.* **4** Loss, cost, or sacrifice: at the *expense* of one's health.

ex·pen·sive [ik·spen′siv] *adj.* Costing a great deal; costly: an *expensive* purchase; an *expensive* mistake. **— ex·pen′sive·ly** *adv.*

ex·pe·ri·ence [ik·spir′ē·əns] *n., v.* **ex·pe·ri·enced, ex·pe·ri·enc·ing** **1** *n.* The actual doing or undergoing of something: to learn from *experience.* **2** *n.* Something one has actually done or gone through: Our trip was a most unusual *experience.* **3** *n.* Knowledge or skill gained by doing or undergoing something: This job requires no previous *experience.* **4** *v.* To feel or undergo: to *experience* fear.

ex·pe·ri·enced [ik·spir′ē·ənst] *adj.* **1** Having had experience: an *experienced* worker. **2** Skilled or able through experience: an *experienced* guide.

ex·per·i·ment [*n.* ik·sper′ə·mənt, *v.* ik·sper′ə·ment] **1** *n.* Any test or trial that one makes in order to gain knowledge, try out a theory, etc.: a chemical *experiment.* **2** *v.* To make experiments: to *experiment* with mice. **— ex·per′i·ment′er** *n.*

ex·per·i·men·tal [ik·sper′ə·men′təl] *adj.* **1** Having to do with, based on, or using experiment: an *experimental* vaccine. **2** Like an experiment; early; tentative: His first swim was *experimental.* **— ex·per′i·men′tal·ly** *adv.*

ex·per·i·men·ta·tion [ik·sper′ə·men·tā′shən] *n.* The act or practice of experimenting: to learn through *experimentation.*

ex·pert [*n.* ek′spûrt, *adj.* ek′spûrt *or* ik·spûrt′] **1** *n.* A person who has special skill or knowledge in a certain field: an *expert* in chemistry. **2** *adj.* Highly skillful: an *expert* skater. **3** *adj.* Of or done by an expert: *expert* cooking. **— ex·pert′·ly** *adv.*

ex·pi·ate [ek′spē·āt] *v.* **ex·pi·at·ed, ex·pi·at·ing** To make up for (a sin, offense, failure, etc.); atone for. **— ex′pi·a′tion** *n.*

ex·pi·ra·tion [ek′spə·rā′shən] *n.* **1** The running out of something; ending: the *expiration* of a license. **2** The breathing out of air from the lungs.

ex·pire [ik·spīr′] *v.* **ex·pired, ex·pir·ing** **1** To end its term; run out: When does his driver's license *expire*? **2** To die. **3** To breathe out; exhale.

ex·plain [ik·splān′] *v.* **1** To make plain or understandable: He *explained* the problem to us. **2** To give the meaning of; interpret: to *explain* a poem. **3** To give reasons for: *Explain* your conduct.

ex·pla·na·tion [ek′splə·nā′shən] *n.* **1** The act or process of explaining something: Is an *explanation* needed? **2** A reason that explains: Slow reading is the *explanation* of his trouble.

ex·plan·a·to·ry [ek·splan′ə·tôr′ē] *adj.* That explains: a brief, *explanatory* statement.

ex·ple·tive [eks′plə·tiv] **1** *n.* An exclamation or an oath. *Gee!* and *Darn!* are expletives. **2** *n.* A word having no particular meaning of its own used to fill out the pattern of a clause. *It* in "It is cold today," and *there* in "Upstairs there are five rooms" are expletives.

ex·plic·it [ik·splis′it] *adj.* Clearly and plainly expressed; definite: He gave *explicit* orders not to go out. **— ex·plic′it·ly** *adv.*

ex·plode [ik·splōd′] *v.* **ex·plod·ed, ex·plod·ing** **1** To burst or cause to burst violently and with noise: to watch fireworks *explode;* to *explode* a bomb. **2** To prove completely wrong: The experiment *exploded* his theory. **3** To burst out suddenly: to *explode* with laughter.

ex·ploit [*n.* eks′ploit, *v.* ik·sploit′] **1** *n.* A brave or daring act: the *exploits* of Robin Hood. **2** *v.* To make good use of: to *exploit* a coal mine. **3** *v.* To use selfishly or unfairly: He became wealthy by *exploiting* poor, immigrant workers.

ex·ploi·ta·tion [eks′ploi·tā′shən] *n.* **1** A using or utilizing. **2** Improper or selfish use: a ruthless *exploitation* of natural resources.

ex·plo·ra·tion [eks′plə·rā′shən] *n.* **1** The exploring of a new or strange region in order to learn about it: *exploration* of outer space. **2** A careful examination or study: *exploration* of various solutions to a problem.

ex·plor·a·to·ry [ik·splôr′ə·tôr′ē] *adj.* Of, for, or having to do with exploration: an *exploratory* voyage.

ex·plore [ik·splôr′] *v.* **ex·plored, ex·plor·ing** **1** To travel in or through in order to learn or discover something: to *explore* an island. **2** To look through or examine closely: to *explore* the contents of a drawer. — **ex·plor′er** *n.*

ex·plo·sion [ik·splō′zhən] *n.* **1** A sudden blowing up or bursting: the *explosion* of dynamite. **2** The loud noise caused by exploding: a deafening *explosion.* **3** A sudden noisy outburst: an *explosion* of laughter. **4** A sudden expansion or increase: the population *explosion.*

An explosion

ex·plo·sive [ik·splō′·siv] **1** *adj.* Able to explode or to cause an explosion: an *explosive* charge. **2** *n.* A substance that explodes: TNT is an *explosive.* **3** *adj.* Apt to burst out suddenly in noise or violence: The quarrel created an *explosive* atmosphere.

ex·po·nent [ik·spō′nənt] *n.* **1** A person who explains or interprets something: an *exponent* of modern art. **2** A person or thing that represents or is an example of something: an *exponent* of fair play. **3** A number placed as a superscript to show how many times another number is to be used as a factor. In $a^2 = a \times a$ and $4^3 = 4 \times 4 \times 4 = 64$, 2 and 3 are exponents.

ex·port [*v.* ik·spôrt′ *or* eks′pôrt, *n. and adj. use* eks′pôrt] **1** *v.* To send to other countries for sale or trade: Germany *exports* many cars. **2** *n.* Something that is exported: Brazil's chief *export* is coffee. **3** *adj. use:* the *export* trade. **4** *n.* The act of exporting: These goods are for *export.* — **ex·port′er** *n.*

ex·por·ta·tion [ek′spôr·tā′shən] *n.* **1** The act of exporting. **2** Something that is exported.

ex·pose [ik·spōz′] *v.* **ex·posed, ex·pos·ing** **1** To put in an open or unprotected position: to *expose* oneself to danger, laughter, etc. **2** To display or uncover: He opened his coat and *exposed* the gun. **3** To make known or reveal: to *expose* a crime. **4** To bring into contact with something; subject: to *expose* a child to good music. **5** To let light come into contact with (a sensitive photographic film).

ex·po·sé [ek′spō·zā′] *n.* The making known to the public of a crime, fraud, or scandal.

ex·po·si·tion [eks′pə·zish′ən] *n.* **1** A large public display or exhibition: an *exposition* of farm products. **2** A written or spoken explanation of an idea or process.

ex·pos·i·to·ry [ik·spoz′ə·tôr′ē] *adj.* That explains; explanatory: *expository* writing.

ex·pos·tu·late [ik·spos′chŏŏ·lāt] *v.* **ex·pos·tu·lat·ed, ex·pos·tu·lat·ing** To argue earnestly with a person in objection to his plans, opinions, or actions: We *expostulated* with him on his behavior. — **ex·pos′tu·la′tion** *n.*

ex·po·sure [ik·spō′zhər] *n.* **1** The act of exposing. **2** The condition of being exposed: to suffer from *exposure* to the cold. **3** The position of something with regard to the sun, weather, or points of a compass: a room with a northern *exposure.* **4** The time required for light to produce the desired effect on a photographic film: Astronomers often use long *exposures.* **5** A section of film that makes a single picture: There are 12 *exposures* on this roll.

exposure meter Another name for a LIGHT METER.

ex·pound [ik·spound′] *v.* To explain or interpret; set forth in detail: to *expound* a theory.

ex·press [ik·spres′] **1** *v.* To tell in words; state: He *expressed* his opinion. **2** *v.* To show without words, as by a look or sign: His frown *expressed* his disapproval. **3** *adj.* Clearly stated or expressed; explicit: Her *express* request was to wake her at seven. **4** *n.* A fast train, bus, etc., that takes a direct route and makes few stops. **5** *adj.* Designed for fast travel: an *express* highway. **6** *adj.* Operating at a fast speed: an *express* train. **7** *n.* A system for moving goods, parcels, money, etc., very rapidly from one point to another. **8** *n.* Something sent by this system. **9** *adj.* Rapid; quick: to send goods by *express* delivery. **10** *v.* To send by rapid delivery: to *express* a parcel. **11** *adv.* By express: The package went *express.* — **express oneself** To say or communicate what one thinks or feels: The ability to *express oneself* is an asset.

ex·pres·sion [ik·spresh′ən] *n.* **1** The saying or putting into words of something: the *expression* of an opinion. **2** A word or group of words used together: "Ahoy" is a sailors' *expression.* **3** Something that indicates what one is thinking or feeling: We sent flowers as an *expression* of sympathy. **4** A look on the face that shows a feeling or mood: a gay *expression.*

Helpless expression

5 Emotional warmth and feeling: She sings with great *expression.*

ex·pres·sive [ik·spres′iv] *adj.* **1** Serving to express or indicate: a frown *expressive* of anger. **2** Full of feeling or special meaning; significant: an *expressive* sigh. — **ex·pres′sive·ly** *adv.* — **ex·pres′sive·ness** *n.*

ex·press·ly [ik·spres′lē] *adv.* **1** With the definite purpose; particularly: I came here *expressly* to see her. **2** Clearly and plainly: We were *expressly* warned against going.

---

add, āce, câre, pälm; end, ēqual; it, īce; odd, ōpen, ôrder; tŏŏk, pōōl; up, bûrn;
ə = a in *above*, e in *sicken*, i in *possible*, o in *melon*, u in *circus*; yōō = u in *fuse*; oil; pout;
check; ring; thin; this; zh in *vision.* For ¶ reference, see page 64 · HOW TO

ex·press·way [ik·spres′wā′] *n.* A highway designed for rapid travel.

ex·pro·pri·ate [eks·prō′prē·āt] *v.* **ex·pro·pri·at·ed, ex·pro·pri·at·ing** To take (private property) away from the owner, by or as if by government authority: to *expropriate* factories owned abroad. — **ex·pro′pri·a′tion** *n.*

ex·pul·sion [ik·spul′shən] *n.* **1** The act of expelling: the *expulsion* of a student. **2** A being forced or driven out: Gases on *expulsion* from a jet engine are very hot.

ex·punge [ik·spunj′] *v.* **ex·punged, ex·pung·ing** To remove (something written); delete: to *expunge* a paragraph from a speech.

ex·pur·gate [eks′pər·gāt] *v.* **ex·pur·gat·ed, ex·pur·gat·ing** To remove from (a book, etc.) words or passages thought to be improper.

ex·qui·site [eks′kwi·zit *or* ik·skwiz′it] *adj.* **1** Finely and delicately made: an *exquisite* bracelet. **2** Extremely beautiful: an *exquisite* gown. **3** Of great excellence; admirable: *exquisite* skill; *exquisite* taste. **4** Very sharp; keen: *exquisite* pain. — **ex′qui·site·ly** *adv.*

ex·tant [ek′stənt *or* ik·stant′] *adj.* Still in existence: All of his works are *extant*.

ex·tem·po·ra·ne·ous [ik·stem′pə·rā′nē·əs] *adj.* Done, made, or given with little or no advance preparation: *extemporaneous* verses. — **ex·tem′po·ra′ne·ous·ly** *adv.*

ex·tem·po·re [ik·stem′pə·rē] *adv.* With little or no advance preparation; offhand: to speak *extempore*.

ex·tend [ik·stend′] *v.* **1** To stretch out: *Extend* your arm. **2** To lengthen or prolong in time or space: to *extend* a lease; to *extend* a pier. **3** *adj. use:* an *extended* journey; an *extended* inquiry. **4** To stretch, reach, or last: The desert *extends* for miles; The trial *extended* over five weeks. **5** To make greater or broader; increase: to *extend* one's knowledge. **6** *adj. use:* *extended* knowledge. **7** To give or offer: to *extend* hospitality.

ex·ten·sion [ik·sten′shən] *n.* **1** The act of extending. **2** The condition of being extended. **3** That which extends something: an *extension* to a house; a telephone *extension*. **4** *adj. use:* an *extension* cord. **5** Additional time allowed in which to do something: We got an *extension* on the payment of our loan.

ex·ten·sive [ik·sten′siv] *adj.* **1** Spreading over a wide area: *extensive* damage. **2** Large in amount: *extensive* funds. **3** Wide or far-reaching: *extensive* reading. — **ex·ten′sive·ly** *adv.*

ex·ten·sor [ik·sten′sər *or* ik·sten′sôr] *n.* A muscle that straightens out a limb, as an arm, leg, or wing.

ex·tent [ik·stent′] *n.* **1** The size, amount, or degree to which something extends: the *extent* of the damage; To what *extent* can he be trusted? **2** An extended space; expanse.

ex·ten·u·ate [ik·sten′yōō·āt] *v.* **ex·ten·u·at·ed, ex·ten·u·at·ing** **1** To make (a fault or bad action) seem less serious; partially excuse: Poor eyesight *extenuated* his bad spelling. **2** *adj.*

use: *extenuating* circumstances. — **ex·ten′u·a′tion** *n.*

ex·te·ri·or [ik·stir′ē·ər] **1** *n.* The outside: the *exterior* of the building. **2** *adj.* Of, situated on, or for the outside: *exterior* damage to a house. **3** *n.* Outward appearance: a meek *exterior*. **4** *adj.* Coming from or happening outside: *exterior* events.

ex·ter·mi·nate [ik·stûr′mə·nāt] *v.* **ex·ter·mi·nat·ed, ex·ter·mi·nat·ing** To destroy (living things) entirely; kill: to *exterminate* harmful insects. — **ex·ter′mi·na′tion** *n.* — **ex·ter′mi·na′tor** *n.*

ex·ter·nal [ik·stûr′nəl] **1** *adj.* Of, on, or for the outside: Weeping is an *external* sign of grief; an *external* covering of paint. **2** *adj.* Of or for the outside part of the body: for *external* use only. **3** *adj.* Coming from the outside: *external* causes. **4** *adj.* Not real or genuine; on the surface only: an *external* appearance of amusement. **5** *n.* (*usually pl.*) An outer appearance, act, etc.: Don't judge a person by *externals*. — **ex·ter′nal·ly** *adv.*

ex·tinct [ik·stingkt′] *adj.* **1** No longer in existence: an *extinct* animal. **2** No longer active; extinguished: an *extinct* volcano.

ex·tinc·tion [ik·stingk′shən] *n.* **1** The condition of no longer existing: The bald eagle is in danger of *extinction*. **2** The destruction or wiping out of something: the *extinction* of all one's hopes. **3** The act of extinguishing something: the *extinction* of a flame.

ex·tin·guish [ik·sting′gwish] *v.* **1** To put out: *Extinguish* the lights. **2** To wipe out; destroy: to *extinguish* life. ◆ *Extinguish* comes from a Latin word meaning *to quench completely.*

ex·tin·guish·er [ik·sting′gwish·ər] *n.* A fire extinguisher.

ex·tol *or* **ex·toll** [ik·stōl′] *v.* **ex·tolled, ex·tol·ling** To praise highly: to *extol* a new play.

ex·tort [ik·stôrt′] *v.* To get (money, a confession, etc.) from a person by force or threats.

Fire extinguisher

ex·tor·tion [ik·stôr′shən] *n.* **1** The getting of money, a confession, etc., by force or threats. **2** Something extorted. — **ex·tor′tion·ist** *n.*

ex·tra [eks′trə] **1** *adj.* In addition to what is usual, required, or expected; additional: an *extra* phone. **2** *n.* A person, thing, or charge in addition to what is needed or expected: We need six, but get an *extra*. **3** *adv.* Extremely; unusually: *extra* good. **4** *n.* A special edition of a newspaper telling of some important event. **5** *n.* An actor hired by the day to play in a motion picture, as part of a crowd, army, etc.

ex·tract [*v.* ik·strakt′, *n.* eks′trakt] **1** *v.* To take out, as by pulling, squeezing, etc.: to ex-

tract a tooth; to *extract* juice. **2** *n.* A concentrated preparation taken from a plant, drug, etc.: Vanilla *extract* is used as flavoring. **3** *v.* To get by using force or effort: to *extract* the truth from a prisoner. **4** *v.* To draw or derive; get: to *extract* satisfaction from one's work. **5** *v.* To figure out; deduce: to *extract* a principle. **6** *v.* To calculate (a root of a number). **7** *v.* To choose or copy for quoting, etc.: to *extract* a passage from a poem. **8** *n.* A passage taken from a piece of writing.

ex·trac·tion [ik·strak′shən] *n.* **1** The act of extracting: the *extraction* of a tooth. **2** Origin or descent; ancestry: a person of German *extraction.*

ex·tra·cur·ric·u·lar [eks′trə·kə·rik′yə·lər] *adj.* Connected with a school but not part of its regular course of study.

ex·tra·dite [eks′trə·dīt] *v.* **ex·tra·dit·ed, ex·tra·dit·ing** **1** To hand over (a prisoner or fugitive) to the authorities of another state or country. **2** To obtain the transfer of (a prisoner). — **ex·tra·di·tion** [eks′trə·dish′ən] *n.*

ex·tra·ne·ous [ik·strā′nē·əs] *adj.* Coming from without; foreign: Static and *extraneous* noises spoiled the broadcast.

ex·traor·di·nar·y [ik·strôr′də·ner′ē *or* eks′·trə·ôr′də·ner′ē] *adj.* **1** Remarkable; unusual; surprising: *extraordinary* strength. **2** Employed for a special purpose or mission: an envoy *extraordinary.* — **ex·traor′di·nar′i·ly** *adv.*

ex·trav·a·gance [ik·strav′ə·gəns] *n.* **1** Wasteful spending of money. **2** A great lack of reason or moderation in one's behavior, speech, dress, etc. **3** Any extravagant action, purchase, etc.

ex·trav·a·gant [ik·strav′ə·gənt] *adj.* **1** Spending too much; wasteful: an *extravagant* person. **2** Going beyond reason or proper limits: *extravagant* praise. — **ex·trav′a·gant·ly** *adv.*

ex·treme [ik·strēm′] **1** *adj.* Very great or severe: *extreme* weakness; *extreme* danger. **2** *n.* The greatest or highest degree: He was angry in the *extreme.* **3** *adj.* Far beyond the usual or average; exaggerated: to take *extreme* measures; *extreme* opinions. **4** *n.* One of two things that are completely different from each other: the *extremes* of joy and sorrow. **5** *adj.* Most distant; farthest out: the *extreme* frontier outposts. — **go to extremes** To do or say more than is usual or expected: He *goes to extremes* to prove he is right.

ex·treme·ly [ik·strēm′lē] *adv.* Much more than usual or common; very: Be *extremely* careful.

ex·trem·ist [ik·strē′mist] *n.* A person who holds extreme opinions, favors extreme measures, or who goes to extremes in his actions.

ex·trem·i·ty [ik·strem′ə·tē] *n., pl.* **ex·trem·i·ties** **1** The most distant point or part; end or edge: the western *extremity* of the state. **2** The utmost degree: the *extremity* of despair. **3** An extreme distress, need, danger, etc.: to be in *extremity.* **4** An extreme action or measure:

Extremities such as blowing up buildings failed to halt the fire. **5** (*pl.*) The hands or feet.

ex·tri·cate [eks′trə·kāt] *v.* **ex·tri·cat·ed, ex·tri·cat·ing** To free from something that tangles, holds back, endangers, or embarrasses: to *extricate* a car stuck in sand.

ex·tro·vert [eks′trə·vûrt] *n.* A person chiefly interested in things outside himself rather than in his own thoughts and feelings.

ex·trude [ik·strood′] *v.* **ex·trud·ed, ex·trud·ing** **1** To push or thrust out. **2** To shape (plastic, metal, etc.) by forcing through special openings. **3** To stick out.

ex·tru·sion [ik·stroo′zhən] *n.* The act or process of extruding, especially the shaping of plastic, metal, etc., by forcing it through special openings.

ex·u·ber·ance [ig·zoo′bər·əns] *n.* Joy and energy; high spirits: He greeted us with great *exuberance.*

ex·u·ber·ant [ig·zoo′bər·ənt] *adj.* **1** Full of high spirits, joy, and energy. **2** Growing in great abundance: *exuberant* foliage. — **ex·u′ber·ant·ly** *adv.*

ex·ude [ig·zood′ *or* ik·syood′] *v.* **ex·ud·ed, ex·ud·ing** **1** To give off in small amounts or in drops, as through pores: The skin *exudes* sweat; The ground *exuded* oil. **2** To give forth or show; radiate: to *exude* confidence.

ex·ult [ig·zult′] *v.* To be extremely joyful; rejoice greatly: to *exult* in victory.

ex·ul·tant [ig·zul′tənt] *adj.* Full of great joy, as in triumph: The team gave an *exultant* cheer. — **ex·ul′tant·ly** *adv.*

ex·ul·ta·tion [eg′zul·tā′shən] *n.* Great joy and jubilation: The crowd yelled in *exultation.*

eye [ī] *n., v.* **eyed, ey·ing** *or* **eye·ing** **1** *n.* The organ of the body with which men and other animals see. In man it includes the cornea, iris, pupil, lens, and retina. **2** *n.* The area around the eye: a black *eye.* **3** *n.* The colored part of the eye; iris: brown *eyes.* **4** *n.* The power of sight; eyesight; vision: He has good *eyes.* **5** *v.* To look at or watch carefully: They *eyed* each other with distrust. **6** *n.* A gaze or glance; look: Cast an *eye* in this direction. **7** *n.* Sight; view: in the public *eye.* **8** *n.* Attention; notice: to try to catch a waiter's *eye.* **9** *n.* The ability to recognize, judge, or appreciate: to have an *eye* for beauty. **10** *n.* (*often pl.*) A way of regarding something; judgment; opinion: That is a sin in the *eyes* of the church. **11** *n.* Anything resembling the human eye in some way, as the hole in a needle or the

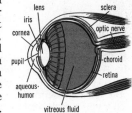

Diagram of a human eye

---

add, āce, câre, pälm; end, ēqual; it, īce; odd, ōpen, ôrder; took, pool; up, bûrn; ə = a in *above*, e in *sicken*, i in *possible*, o in *melon*, u in *circus*; yoo = u in *fuse*; oil; pout; check; ring; thin; this; zh in *vision*. For ¶ reference, see page 64 · HOW TO

loop through which a hook fastens. — **keep an
eye on** To watch closely or tend carefully:
Keep an eye on your little sister. — **lay eyes on**
or **set eyes on** To see: I've never *laid eyes on*
her. — **make eyes at** To look at in an ad-
miring or flirting way. — **see eye to eye** To
agree in all respects: He and I don't *see eye to eye*
on that issue.

eye·ball [ī′bôl′] *n.* The entire globe or ball of
the eye.

eye·brow [ī′brou′] *n.* The bony ridge above
each eye or the arch of small hairs growing on it.

eye·glass [ī′glas′] *n., pl.* **eye·glass·es 1**
(*pl.*) A pair of glass lenses fitted into a frame and
worn over the eyes to help a person see more
clearly. **2** Any lens used to aid the vision, as a
monocle.

eye·lash [ī′lash′] *n.* One of the stiff, curved
hairs growing from the edge of the eyelids.
◆ *Eyelash* was formed by
combining the words *eye*
and *lash.*

eye·let [ī′lit] *n.* **1** A small
hole to hold a cord, lace,
or other fastening: Shoe-
laces are put through the
eyelets of a shoe. **2** A metal
ring that lines and strengthens such a hole. **3** A small
opening in embroidery edged with fancy stitches.

Eyelets

eye·lid [ī′lid′] *n.* Either of the folds of skin that
move to cover or uncover the eyes.

eye·piece [ī′pēs′] *n.* The lens or lenses nearest
the eye of someone looking through a telescope,
microscope, etc.

eye·sight [ī′sīt′] *n.* **1** The power of seeing;
vision: weak *eyesight.* **2** The distance that the
eye can see: to be within *eyesight.*

eye·sore [ī′sôr′] *n.* A disagreeable or ugly thing
to see: That billboard is an *eyesore.*

eye·spot [ī′spot′] *n.* One of the small, often
colored spots by which many invertebrate
animals see.

eye·strain [ī′strān′] *n.* A tired or uncomfortable condition of the eyes caused by using them
too much or in the wrong way.

eye·tooth [ī′tooth′] *n., pl.* **eye·teeth** [ī′tēth′]
One of the two canine teeth of the upper jaw.
It is the third tooth from the middle on either
side.

eye·wit·ness [ī′wit′nis] *n.* **1** A person who saw
something happen, as a crime or accident. **2** *adj.
use:* an *eyewitness* account.

ey·rie [âr′ē *or* ir′ē] *n.* Another spelling of AERIE.

E·ze·ki·el [i·zē′kē·əl] *n.* **1** In the Bible, a Hebrew prophet who lived during the sixth century
B.C. **2** A book of the Old Testament.

Ez·ra [ez′rə] *n.* **1** In the Bible, a Hebrew priest
who lived during the fifth century B.C. **2** A book
of the Old Testament.

F

f or **F** [ef] *n., pl.* **f's** or **F's** The sixth letter of
the English alphabet.

F The symbol for the element FLUORINE.

F. Abbreviation of FAHRENHEIT.

fa [fä] *n.* In music, a syllable used to represent
the fourth tone in a major scale, the sixth tone
in a minor scale, or in a fixed system the tone F.

fa·ble [fā′bəl] *n.* **1** A short story teaching a
lesson. It is often about animals who behave like
people. **2** A story that is not true, as a lie or
falsehood.

fa·bled [fā′bəld] *adj.* **1** Told of in legends or
stories: *fabled* sea monsters. **2** Not real.

fab·ric [fab′rik] *n.* **1** A material, as cloth, lace,
or felt, made of woven, knitted, or matted
fibers. **2** A thing formed of different parts, or its
structure: the social *fabric.*

fab·ri·cate [fab′rə·kāt] *v.* **fab·ri·cat·ed,
fab·ri·cat·ing 1** To make or build by joining
parts; construct; manufacture. **2** To make up;
invent: to try to *fabricate* a clever excuse.
◆ *Fabricate* comes from a Latin word meaning
to construct or *build,* and this was once its only
meaning in English. Nowadays, however, it

usually refers to making up or "constructing" a
story or a lie. — **fab′ri·ca′tion** *n.*

fab·u·lous [fab′yə·ləs] *adj.* **1** Unbelievable;
astonishing: a *fabulous* fortune. **2** Of, like, or
found in fables; imaginary: The unicorn is a
fabulous animal. — **fab′u·lous·ly** *adv.*

fa·çade [fə·säd′] *n.* The front of a building,
especially if more impressive than the rest.

face [fās] *n., v.* **faced, fac·ing 1** *n.* The front
of the head, extending from the forehead to the
chin and from ear to ear. **2** *n.* A look or expression: happy *faces.* **3** *n.* An exaggerated expression made by twisting or pulling at the features:
He made a *face.* **4** *n.* Outward appearance; look:
Her claim seems false on the *face* of it. **5** *n.* The
front, top, outer, or most important side or
surface: to turn a card *face* up; the *face* of a
clock or watch. **6** *v.* To cover with another
material: to *face* a lapel with velvet. **7** *v.* To
turn or be turned with the front side toward:
Face the flag. **8** *v.* To confront: to be *faced* with
a problem. **9** *v.* To meet with courage: to *face*
the fact of defeat. **10** *n.* Respect, dignity, or
reputation: to lose *face.* **11** *n. informal* Shame-

less or disrespectful boldness. **— face to face
1** Turned toward each other at close range: We stood *face to face*. **2** In the presence of: *face to face* with danger. **— in the face of 1** In the presence of. **2** In spite of.

fac·et [fas′it] *n.* **1** One of the small, smooth surfaces cut upon a gem. **2** A side or aspect: the many *facets* of his talent.

fa·ce·tious [fə·sē′shəs] *adj.* Meant or trying to be funny or flippant. **— fa·ce′tious·ly** *adv.* **— fa·ce′-tious·ness** *n.*

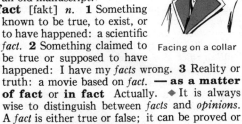

Facets of a jewel

fa·cial [fā′shəl] **1** *adj.* Of, near, or for the face: a *facial* expression. **2** *n. informal* A massage or other treatment for the face.

fac·ile [fas′(ə)l] *adj.* **1** Requiring little effort; easy: *facile* work. **2** Too easy; superficial: a *facile* solution. **3** Quick and skillful in performance: a *facile* tongue.

fa·cil·i·tate [fə·sil′ə·tāt] *v.* **fa·cil·i·tat·ed, fa·cil·i·tat·ing** To make easier or more convenient: Good roads *facilitate* travel.

fa·cil·i·ty [fə·sil′ə·tē] *n., pl.* **fa·cil·i·ties 1** Ease or skill in performance: to write with *facility*. **2** (*usually pl.*) A thing that makes some action or work easier: good library *facilities*. **3** (*often pl.*) A place used by or serving people, as a school, restaurant, etc.

fac·ing [fā′sing] *n.* **1** A covering in front for decoration, protection, etc.: a brick house with a stucco *facing*. **2** (*sometimes pl.*) The lining of a garment on parts exposed by being turned back, as the collar and cuffs.

fac·sim·i·le [fak·sim′ə·lē] *n.* An exact copy: a *facsimile* of an old manuscript.

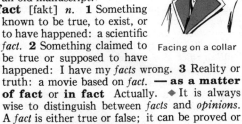

Facing on a collar

fact [fakt] *n.* **1** Something known to be true, to exist, or to have happened: a scientific *fact*. **2** Something claimed to be true or supposed to have happened: I have my *facts* wrong. **3** Reality or truth: a movie based on *fact*. **— as a matter of fact** or **in fact** Actually. ◆ It is always wise to distinguish between *facts* and *opinions*. A *fact* is either true or false; it can be proved or disproved. An *opinion*, though it may be based upon *facts*, is a judgment or conclusion. The statement "Tom is six feet tall" is a *fact*, but the conclusion that Tom is a tall person is an *opinion*.

fac·tion [fak′shən] *n.* **1** A distinct group of people within a larger group, working against other parts of the main group to gain its own ends. **2** Angry disagreement or strife among group or party members. **— fac′tion·al** *adj.*

fac·tor [fak′tər] **1** *n.* One of the elements or causes that help to produce a result: Luck was a *factor* in our victory. **2** *n.* A number that when multiplied by one or more other numbers gives a certain result. 3 is a *factor* of 18. a is a *factor* of ab + ac. **3** *v.* To find the factors of. **4** *n.* A business agent.

fac·to·ri·al [fak·tôr′ē·əl] *n.* The product of all the positive whole numbers from 1 to a given number. The factorial of 4 (written 4!) equals $1 \times 2 \times 3 \times 4 = 24$.

fac·to·ry [fak′tər·ē] *n., pl.* **fac·to·ries** A building or group of buildings where goods are manufactured or assembled: a shoe *factory*.

fac·to·tum [fak·tō′təm] *n.* A person employed to take care of extra work, do odd jobs, etc.

fac·tu·al [fak′chōō·əl] *adj.* Based on or made up of facts; literal. **— fac′tu·al·ly** *adv.*

fac·ul·ty [fak′əl·tē] *n., pl.* **fac·ul·ties 1** *U.S.* The entire teaching staff at a college or school. **2** A department of learning at a university: the English *faculty*. **3** A natural or acquired ability or talent: a *faculty* for writing. **4** An ability or power of the body or mind: the *faculties* of seeing and reasoning.

fad [fad] *n.* A style, amusement, or fashion that is very popular for a short time; craze.

fade [fād] *v.* **fad·ed, fad·ing 1** To lose or cause to lose brightness or color: The yellow rug *faded*; Washing *faded* the blouse. **2** To lose freshness; wither. **3** To grow dimmer and slowly disappear: His smile *faded*.

fade-out [fād′out′] *n.* The gradual disappearance or fading away of a motion-picture, television, or radio scene.

fag [fag] *v.* **fagged, fag·ging** To tire out by hard work: By evening he was *fagged* out.

fag end 1 The frayed or untwisted end of a piece of cloth or rope. **2** A last part or remnant of anything, almost worthless in itself.

fag·ot or **fag·got** [fag′ət] *n.* A bound bundle of sticks or twigs used for fuel, etc.

Fahr·en·heit [far′ən·hīt] *adj.* Of or indicating the temperature scale used for ordinary purposes in the U.S. and Great Britain. In this system water freezes at 32 degrees and boils at 212 degrees.

Woman holding fagot

fail [fāl] **1** *v.* To turn out to be unsuccessful or not good enough: to *fail* in an effort. **2** *v.* To be lacking, missing, or too little: The electricity *failed*. **3** *v.* To neglect or omit: Don't *fail* to return my book. **4** *n.* Failure, especially in the phrase **without fail**: Be here *without fail*. **5** *v.* To prove of no help to when needed: His friends *failed* him. **6** *v.* To receive a grade too low to pass (a test, course, etc.). **7** *v.* To give (a student) such a grade.

8 *v.* To weaken or decline: Her health was *failing*. **9** *v.* To become bankrupt, as a business.

fail·ing [fā′ling] **1** *n.* A minor fault; weakness. **2** *n.* Failure. **3** *prep.* In the absence of; lacking: *Failing* your reply, we left.

faille [fīl] *n.* A very finely ribbed silk or rayon fabric used mainly to make dresses.

fail·ure [fāl′yər] *n.* **1** A turning out to be unsuccessful. **2** A person or thing that has failed. **3** A failing to pass in school work. **4** Neglect, as of something expected: *failure* to obey the law. **5** A falling short or giving out: *failure* of the food supply. **6** A breaking down or weakening: the *failure* of his hearing. **7** A becoming bankrupt, as a business or bank.

fain [fān] **1** *adv.* Gladly: *Fain* would he depart. **2** *adj.* Willing, glad, or eager: *fain* to go. ◆ This word is used mostly in poems.

faint [fānt] **1** *n.* A condition in which one suddenly loses consciousness and is unaware of things for a time. **2** *v.* To fall into such a condition; swoon. **3** *adj.* Weak enough to faint: She felt *faint*. **4** *adj.* Weak, slight, or dim: a *faint* glow; a *faint* noise. **5** *adj.* Timid: a *faint* heart. **—faint′ly** *adv.*

faint·heart·ed [fānt′här′tid] *adj.* Cowardly or undecided; timid: a *fainthearted* effort.

fair¹ [fâr] **1** *adj.* Not favoring one above another; just. **2** *adj.* Following the right rules; honest: *fair* play. **3** *adv.* In a fair manner: Play *fair* with me. **4** *adj.* Less than good but better than poor; average: a *fair* student. **5** *adj.* Clear and bright; sunny: a *fair* day. **6** *adj.* Light in coloring: *fair* hair. **7** *adj.* Beautiful: a *fair* lady. **8** *adj.* Gracious and pleasant: *fair* words. **9** *adj.* Not soiled or spoiled; clean: Write a *fair* copy. **10** *adj.* Not foul: a *fair* ball. **11** *adj.* Properly open to attack: He is *fair* game. **— bid fair** To appear likely. **—fair′. ness** *n.*

fair² [fâr] *n.* **1** An exhibition of goods, products, machinery, etc. **2** A regularly held gathering of buyers and sellers. **3** A sale of articles, often with entertainment, as to benefit a charity.

fair·ly [fâr′lē] *adv.* **1** In a fair, just way: He dealt *fairly* with me. **2** Not extremely; somewhat: a *fairly* fast trip. **3** Positively; really: They *fairly* raced for the door.

fair·way [fâr′wā′] *n.* In golf, a strip from tee to green where the grass is kept short.

fair·y [fâr′ē] *n., pl.* **fair·ies,** *adj.* **1** *n.* An imaginary being able to work magic, often tiny with a graceful human form. **2** *adj.* Of fairies. **3** *adj.* Like a fairy, as in delicacy.

fair·y·land [fâr′ē·land′] *n.* **1** The place where the fairies are supposed to live. **2** Any delightful and enchanting place.

fairy tale 1 A story involving fairies. **2** A story that is or sounds made up; lie or fib.

faith [fāth] **1** *n.* Confidence, trust, or belief: I have *faith* in you. **2** *n.* Belief in God or in religious teachings. **3** *n.* A system of religious belief: the Christian *faith*. **4** *n.* A promise, as of loyalty: He broke *faith* with us. **5** *n.* Allegiance:

a pledge of *faith*. **6** *interj.* In truth; indeed. **— bad faith** Dishonesty or falseness. **— good faith** Honesty, sincerity, or loyalty. ◆ See TRUST.

faith·ful [fāth′fəl] *adj.* **1** Loyal, true, and constant: a *faithful* friend. **2** *n. use* The followers of a religion or loyal members of any group: She is one of *the faithful*. **3** True in detail; accurate: Give a *faithful* account. **—faith′. ful·ly** *adv.* **—faith′ful·ness** *n.*

faith·less [fāth′lis] *adj.* **1** Not true to one's word or duty. **2** Lacking religious faith.

fake [fāk] *n., adj., v.* **faked, fak·ing** *informal* **1** *n.* A person or thing passed off as something it is not; fraud. **2** *adj.* Not genuine; false: *fake* jewels. **3** *v.* To try to pass off as genuine: to *fake* a painting; to *fake* gratitude. **— fak′er** *n.*

fa·kir [fə·kir′ *or* fā′kər] *n.* A Moslem or Hindu holy man who is a beggar.

fal·con [fal′kən *or* fô(l)′kən] *n.* **1** A swift hawk trained to hunt and kill other birds and small animals. **2** Any of various related hawks with long, pointed wings and a notched bill.

fal·con·er [fal′kən·ər *or* fô(l)′kən·ər] *n.* **1** A person who breeds falcons or trains them to hunt. **2** A person who hunts with falcons.

fal·con·ry [fal′kən·rē *or* fô(l)′kən·rē] *n.* **1** The art of training falcons to hunt small game. **2** The sport of hunting with falcons.

Falcon

fall [fôl] *v.* **fell, fall·en, fall·ing,** *n.* **1** *v.* To drop to a lower place, position, or level: A tear *fell* from her eye; to *fall* off a horse. **2** *v.* To drop suddenly from an erect position: to slip and *fall*. **3** *n.* The act of falling or dropping down: the silent *fall* of snow; injured in a *fall*. **4** *n.* Something that falls, or the amount that falls: a light *fall* of rain. **5** *n.* The distance anything falls: a long *fall*. **6** *n.* *U.S.* The season when leaves fall; autumn. **7** *adj. use: fall* weather. **8** *n.* (*usually pl.*) A waterfall. **9** *v.* To slope downward: The land *falls* away gradually eastward. **10** *n.* A downward slope. **11** *v.* To hang down: Her veil *fell* about her shoulders. **12** *v.* To become lower or less: Prices *fell*; The wind has *fallen*. **13** *n.* A lowering or lessening; decrease: a sudden *fall* in temperature. **14** *v.* To hit; land: Bombs *fell* on the city. **15** *v.* To be wounded or killed, as in combat. **16** *v.* To be taken, captured, or overthrown: The fort *fell*. **17** *n.* Overthrow or collapse: the *fall* of the Roman Empire. **18** *v.* To collapse: The bridge *fell*. **19** *n.* Loss of innocence through wrongdoing: the *fall* of man. **20** *v.* To pass into a given condition: to *fall* asleep. **21** *v.* To show or experience sadness: His face *fell*. **22** *v.* To happen or come: The holiday *falls* on a Monday. **23** *v.* To come as though descending: Night *fell*. **24** *v.* To come by chance, right, etc.: Suspicion *fell* on him; The estate *fell* to the oldest son. **25** *v.* To be divided: His speech *fell* into three parts. **—fall back** To move back; retreat. **—fall back on** To turn to for help or security. **—fall behind** To fail to keep up, as in work, meeting payments, etc. **—fall in 1** To get into a military line. **2** To meet or go along, as with others. **—fall off** To become less, as attendance. **—fall on** or **fall upon** To attack. **—fall out 1** To quarrel. **2** To drop out of a military line. **—fall short** To fail, as in reaching a goal. **—fall through** To come to nothing; fail. **—fall to 1** To begin. **2** To begin eating or fighting. **—fall under** To come under.

fal·la·cious [fə·lā′shəs] *adj.* **1** Not logical or correct: a *fallacious* conclusion. **2** Deceptive or misleading: *fallacious* evidence.

fal·la·cy [fal′ə·sē] *n.*, *pl.* **fal·la·cies 1** A false or misleading notion: the *fallacy* that age always brings wisdom. **2** Faulty reasoning.

fall·en [fô′lən] **1** Past participle of FALL. **2** *adj.* Having dropped down: *fallen* leaves. **3** *adj.* Overthrown, captured, or ruined: a *fallen* empire. **4** *adj.* Killed: a *fallen* soldier.

fal·li·ble [fal′ə·bəl] *adj.* Liable to make errors, to be deceived, or to be wrong. **—fal·li·bil·i·ty** [fal′ə·bil′ə·tē] *n.*

fall·out [fôl′out′] *n.* Radioactive dust that falls from the atmosphere as a result of a nuclear explosion.

fal·low [fal′ō] **1** *adj.* Plowed but not planted for a season: *fallow* land. **2** *n.* Land allowed to lie unplanted so as to make it more fertile.

fallow deer A small European deer whose yellowish coat has white spots on it in summer.

false [fôls] **1** *adj.* Not true, right, or correct; wrong. **2** *adj.* Based on mistaken ideas: *false* economy. **3** *adj.* Not real or genuine; artificial: *false* teeth. **4** *adj.* Meant to deceive or trick: *false* pretenses. **5** *adj.* Not truthful; lying: a *false* witness. **6** *adj.* Not faithful; disloyal: *false* friends. **7** *adv.* In a false manner. **8** *adj.* Not properly so called: used in names of plants, etc. **—play (someone) false** To mislead, cheat, or betray (someone). **—false′ly** *adv.* **—false′ness** *n.*

Fallow deer, about 3 ft. high at shoulder

false colors 1 The flag of another country flown as though one's own: The ship was sailing under *false colors.* **2** False pretenses.

false·hood [fôls′hŏŏd] *n.* **1** A lie or act of lying. **2** Untruthfulness. **3** An untrue belief.

false teeth 1 Artificial teeth made to replace real ones. **2** A set of artificial teeth.

fal·set·to [fôl·set′ō] *n.*, *pl.* **fal·set·tos,** *adv.*, *adj.* **1** *n.* A way of singing that makes the voice high but thin: The high notes in a yodel are in *falsetto.* **2** *adv.* In falsetto. **3** *adj.* Sung or to be sung in falsetto.

fal·si·fy [fôl′sə·fī] *v.* **fal·si·fied, fal·si·fy·ing 1** To change or give a wrong idea of so as to deceive: to *falsify* results. **2** To tell lies. **3** To prove to be false; disprove. **—fal·si·fi·ca·tion** [fôl′sə·fə·kā′shən] *n.*

fal·si·ty [fôl′sə·tē] *n.*, *pl.* **fal·si·ties 1** The quality of being false. **2** A lie.

fal·ter [fôl′tər] **1** *v.* To hesitate, be uncertain, or give way: His determination never *faltered.* **2** *v.* To move or speak in an unsteady or stumbling way. **3** *n.* An uncertainty or hesitation in voice or action.

fame [fām] *n.* **1** The fact or condition of being well known and highly regarded; renown. **2** Reputation: of ill *fame.*

famed [fāmd] *adj.* Widely known; famous.

fa·mil·iar [fə·mil′yər] **1** *adj.* Well acquainted, as through experience or study: *familiar* with modern art. **2** *adj.* Well-known because often encountered: a *familiar* voice. **3** *adj.* Intimate or friendly: We are on *familiar* terms. **4** *n.* A good friend. **5** *adj.* Improperly friendly; forward: Don't be *familiar* with strangers. **6** *n.* A spirit said to take animal form to serve a witch. **—fa·mil′iar·ly** *adv.*

fa·mil·i·ar·i·ty [fə·mil′ē·ar′ə·tē *or* fə·mil′yar′·ə·tē] *n.*, *pl.* **fa·mil·i·ar·i·ties 1** Thorough acquaintance, as with a subject. **2** Absence of formality. **3** Friendly closeness. **4** (*often pl.*) Impertinent speech or manner.

fa·mil·i·ar·ize [fə·mil′yə·rīz] *v.* **fa·mil·i·ar·ized, fa·mil·i·ar·iz·ing 1** To make well acquainted: *Familiarize* yourself with the traffic laws. **2** To make (something) well known. ¶3

fam·i·ly [fam′ə·lē *or* fam′lē] *n.*, *pl.* **fam·i·lies 1** A unit consisting of parents and their children. **2** One's group of children: They reared a large *family.* **3** A group of persons forming a household. **4** One's entire group of relatives. **5** A group of people descended from the same ancestor. **6** In biology, a group of related animals or plants: The wolf belongs to the dog *family.* **7** Any class or group of related things: a *family* of languages.

family tree A diagram giving the ancestors of a family and showing all their descendants.

fam·ine [fam′in] *n.* **1** A widespread lack of food which causes many to starve. **2** Starvation. **3** Any serious scarcity: a water *famine.*

fam·ished [fam′isht] *adj.* Extremely hungry.

fa·mous [fā′məs] *adj.* **1** Very well known and

add, āce, câre, pälm; end, ēqual; it, īce; odd, ōpen, ôrder; tŏŏk, pōōl; up, bûrn; ə = a in *above,* e in *sicken,* i in *possible,* o in *melon,* u in *circus;* yōō = u in *fuse;* oil; pout; **ch**eck; **r**ing; **th**in; **th**is; **zh** in *vision.* For ¶ reference, see page 64 · HOW TO

often mentioned or praised; celebrated; renowned. **2** *informal* Excellent; splendid. —**fa′·mous·ly** *adv.*

fan¹ [fan] *n., v.* **fanned, fan·ning 1** *n.* A device for stirring the air, so as to create a cool breeze. A hand fan folds up and opens out into a wedgelike shape, while an electric fan has revolving blades. **2** *v.* To stir (the air) with or as if with a fan. **3** *v.* To direct air upon, as by using a fan: to *fan* the face. **4** *v.* To stir to action: to *fan* the flames of hatred. **5** *n.* Anything like an open fan, as a peacock's tail. **6** *v.* To spread like a fan.

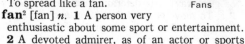

Fans

fan² [fan] *n.* **1** A person very enthusiastic about some sport or entertainment. **2** A devoted admirer, as of an actor or sports star.

fa·nat·ic [fə·nat′ik] *n.* A person whose exaggerated enthusiasm or zeal makes his beliefs unreasonable: a religious *fanatic*.

fa·nat·i·cal [fə·nat′i·kəl] *adj.* Unreasonably enthusiastic. —**fa·nat′i·cal·ly** *adv.*

fa·nat·i·cism [fə·nat′ə·siz′əm] *n.* Devotion, zeal, or enthusiasm that goes beyond the bounds of reason.

fan·cied [fan′sēd] *adj.* Imagined; unreal: *fancied* insults.

fan·ci·er [fan′sē·ər] *n.* A person with a special interest in something, as in breeding a certain kind of animal: a poodle *fancier*.

fan·ci·ful [fan′si·fəl] *adj.* **1** Full of pleasantly odd, imaginative ideas: a *fanciful* mind. **2** Created by the fancy; not real: *fanciful* notions. **3** Pleasantly odd in appearance; quaint: a *fanciful* costume. —**fan′ci·ful·ly** *adv.*

fan·cy [fan′sē] *n., pl.* **fan·cies,** *v.* **fan·cied, fan·cy·ing,** *adj.* **fan·ci·er, fan·ci·est 1** *n.* The ability to picture odd, whimsical, or unreal things in the mind; imagination. **2** *v.* To imagine or picture: *Fancy* that! **3** *n.* An imagined idea, notion, etc.: Was it a fact or a *fancy*? **4** *v.* To believe without being positive; suppose: I *fancy* she is tired. **5** *n.* A liking: He took a *fancy* to the child. **6** *v.* To like; enjoy: to *fancy* special foods. **7** *adj.* Decorated or elegant: a *fancy* shirt. **8** *adj.* Of unusually high quality; choice: *fancy* peaches. **9** *adj.* Extremely high: *fancy* prices. **10** *adj.* Showy and elaborate: a dancer's *fancy* footwork.

fan·cy·work [fan′sē·wûrk′] *n.* Ornamental needlework, as embroidery.

fan·fare [fan′fâr′] *n.* **1** A lively phrase of music played on trumpets or bugles to attract attention. **2** Any noisy or showy display: The candidate slipped into town without *fanfare*.

fang [fang] *n.* **1** A long, pointed tooth by which an animal seizes and tears its prey. **2** One of the long, hollow or grooved teeth with which a poisonous snake injects its poison.

fan·light [fan′līt′] *n.* A semicircular window resembling an open fan, as over a door.

fan·tail [fan′tāl′] *n.* **1** Any end, tail, or part shaped like an open fan. **2** A domestic pigeon or fancy goldfish with a fanlike tail.

fan·tas·tic [fan·tas′tik] *adj.* **1** Odd, original, weird, or unreal, like a creation of the fancy: *fantastic* shapes and forms. **2** Amazing; unbelievable: His progress has been *fantastic*.

Fanlight

fan·tas·ti·cal [fan·tas′ti·kəl] *adj.* Fantastic or eccentric. —**fan·tas′ti·cal·ly** *adv.*

fan·ta·sy [fan′tə·sē] *n., pl.* **fan·ta·sies 1** Imagination or wild fancy. **2** A creation of the imagination, as a story or daydream very different from reality.

far [fär] *adv., adj.* **far·ther** or **fur·ther, far·thest** or **fur·thest 1** *adv.* At, to, or from a great distance: *far* from town; to come *far*. **2** *adj.* Very distant in space or time: a *far* country. **3** *adj.* More distant: the *far* side of the moon. **4** *adv.* To or at a particular distance, point, or degree: How *far* will he go to help us? **5** *adv.* Very much: *far* wiser. — **as far as** To the extent, distance, or degree that. — **by far** or **far and away** Very much; decidedly. — **far and wide** Over a considerable area; everywhere. — **so far 1** To that extent; up to that point. **2** Up to now.

far·a·way [fär′ə·wā′] *adj.* **1** Distant: *faraway* islands. **2** Absent-minded: a *faraway* look.

farce [färs] *n.* **1** A comedy using exaggeration and ridiculous situations to be funny. **2** A ridiculous action or empty pretense that deceives no one: The investigation was a *farce*.

far·ci·cal [fär′si·kəl] *adj.* **1** Like a farce; laughable; absurd; ridiculous. **2** Of farce.

far cry A long way.

fare [fâr] *n., v.* **fared, far·ing 1** *n.* The money charged or paid to ride in a bus, train, etc. **2** *n.* A passenger who pays a fare. **3** *v.* To get along; manage; do: He *fared* poorly in the race. **4** *v.* To turn out; happen or go: Things *fared* well with us. **5** *n.* Food and drink.

Far East The countries of eastern Asia, including China, Japan, Korea, etc.

fare·well [fâr′wel′] **1** *interj.* Good-by and may you get on well. **2** *n.* A saying good-by. **3** *adj.* Parting: a *farewell* speech.

far-fetched [fär′fecht′] *adj.* Not natural or probable: a *far-fetched* excuse.

far-flung [fär′flung′] *adj.* Extending over great distances: *far-flung* business interests.

farm [färm] **1** *n.* An area of land used for growing crops or raising cattle, sheep, pigs, chickens, etc. **2** *v.* To grow crops or raise livestock. **3** *v.* To prepare or use (land) for crops: to *farm* 80 acres. **4** *n.* Land or water used to grow other products: an oyster *farm*. — **farm**

out **1** To send (an athlete) to a minor league for experience. **2** To send out (work) from an office or shop to be done by others.

farm·er [fär′mər] *n.* A person who works on, manages, or owns a farm.

farm·house [färm′hous′] *n.* A home on a farm.

farm·ing [fär′ming] *n.* The business of running a farm and raising crops or livestock.

farm·stead [färm′sted] *n.* A farm and the buildings on it.

farm·yard [färm′yärd′] *n.* The yard around farm buildings; barnyard.

far-off [fär′ôf′] *adj.* Distant; remote.

far-reach·ing [fär′rē′ching] *adj.* Having a wide influence or range: *far-reaching* changes.

far·ri·er [far′ē·ər] *n.* **1** A man who shoes horses; blacksmith. **2** A doctor for animals.

far·row [far′ō] **1** *n.* A litter of pigs. **2** *v.* To give birth to (young): said about pigs.

far·see·ing [fär′sē′ing] *adj.* **1** Able to see far. **2** Good at planning ahead for the future.

far·sight·ed [fär′sī′tid] *adj.* **1** Able to see distant things more clearly than things near at hand. **2** Showing good judgment in looking and planning ahead. **— far′sight′·ed·ness** *n.*

The focus of light rays entering a farsighted eye is behind the retina. A convex lens corrects this.

far·ther [fär′thər] **1** Comparative of FAR. **2** *adv.* At or to a more distant point: *farther* down the road; I can go no *farther*. **3** *adj.* More distant or remote: the *farther* shore. **4** *adj.* Additional; more. ◆ *Farther* is preferred for distance in space: ten miles *farther*; Don't go any *farther* away. *Further* is preferred in relation to time, degree, or quantity: *further* information; My memory goes back no *further*. In conversation, however, *further* is often used for distance in space as well.

far·ther·most [fär′thər·mōst′] *adj.* Most distant; farthest: the *farthermost* point.

far·thest [fär′thist] **1** Superlative of FAR. **2** *adv.* To or at the greatest distance: Who jumped *farthest*? **3** *adj.* Most distant: the *farthest* island in the chain. **4** *adj.* Longest or most extended: the *farthest* way home.

far·thing [fär′thing] *n.* A small coin once used in England, worth about half a cent.

fas·ci·nate [fas′ə·nāt] *v.* **fas·ci·nat·ed, fas·ci·nat·ing** **1** To attract and interest extremely, as by novelty, mystery, or charm: The magician's tricks *fascinated* us. **2** To hold paralyzed and helpless, as by a strange influence: a bird *fascinated* by a snake.

fas·ci·na·tion [fas′ə·nā′shən] *n.* **1** The act of fascinating. **2** Great interest or charm.

fas·cism [fash′iz·əm] *n.* A form of government in which a dictator and his party support private property but strictly control industry and labor,

and ruthlessly suppress criticism or opposition. **— fas′cist** *adj., n.*

fash·ion [fash′ən] **1** *n.* The style, as of dress or behavior, popular at any given time: new spring *fashions*. **2** *n.* A current practice. **3** *n.* Manner; way: He spoke in a forceful *fashion*. **4** *v.* To make, shape, or form: to *fashion* a snowman. **5** *n.* Outward appearance. **— after a fashion** In a way; not well. ◆ See CUSTOM.

fash·ion·a·ble [fash′ən·ə·bəl] *adj.* **1** In style; stylish: a *fashionable* coat. **2** Of or attracting socially prominent people: a *fashionable* neighborhood. **— fash′ion·a·bly** *adv.*

fast¹ [fast] **1** *adj.* Moving or acting with speed; quick; swift; rapid: a *fast* worker. **2** *adv.* Quickly; swiftly; rapidly: to walk *fast*. **3** *adj.* Ahead of the correct time: The clock is *fast*. **4** *adj.* Devoted to harmful pleasures; wild: a *fast* life. **5** *adv.* In a firm manner; firmly: Stand *fast* and don't yield. **6** *adj.* Firmly fastened, attached, or fixed: a boat made *fast* to the dock. **7** *adj.* Faithful; loyal: *fast* friends. **8** *adj.* Not apt to fade: *fast* colors. **9** *adv.* Soundly: *fast* asleep.

fast² [fast] **1** *v.* To go without food or avoid certain foods, as for religious reasons. **2** *n.* The act of fasting. **3** *n.* A period of fasting.

fas·ten [fas′(ə)n] *v.* **1** To close up or make secure: *Fasten* my dress; *Fasten* the door. **2** To attach, as by tying, pinning, etc.: *Fasten* the boat to the dock. **3** To direct steadily: He *fastened* his gaze on me. **— fas′ten·er** *n.*

fas·ten·ing [fas′(ə)n·ing] *n.* Something used to fasten, as a bolt, zipper, or clasp.

fas·tid·i·ous [fas·tid′ē·əs] *adj.* Extremely particular; hard to suit or please: He is a *fastidious* dresser. **— fas·tid′i·ous·ly** *adv.*

fast·ness [fast′nis] *n.* **1** A fortress; stronghold. **2** A firm or fixed condition. **3** Swiftness.

fat [fat] *n., adj.* **fat·ter, fat·test** **1** *n.* Any of a large class of yellowish to white, greasy substances found in plant and animal tissues. **2** *n.* Any such substance used in cooking, as butter, oil, or lard. **3** *adj.* Containing much oil, grease, etc.: *fat* meat. **4** *adj.* Rounded in body from having more flesh than is needed. **5** *adj.* Profitable: a *fat* job. **6** *n.* The richest or most desirable part: the *fat* of the land. **— fat′ness** *n.*

fa·tal [fāt′(ə)l] *adj.* **1** Causing death: a *fatal* illness. **2** Causing ruin or disaster: a *fatal* mistake. **3** Having important consequences: the *fatal* hour. **— fa′tal·ly** *adv.*

fa·tal·ism [fāt′(ə)l·iz′əm] *n.* **1** The belief that all events are determined by fate, not by men's efforts. **2** Resigned acceptance of fate. **— fa′tal·ist** *n.* **— fa′tal·is′tic** *adj.*

fa·tal·i·ty [fā·tal′ə·tē] *n., pl.* **fa·tal·i·ties** **1** A death brought about through some disaster or accident: Reduce traffic *fatalities*. **2** The

---

add, āce, câre, pälm;   end, ēqual;   it, īce;   odd, ōpen, ôrder;   tŏŏk, pōōl;   up, bûrn;
ə = a in *above*, e in *sicken*, i in *possible*, o in *melon*, u in *circus*;   yōō = u in *fuse*;   oil;   pout;
check; **r**ing; **th**in; **th**is; **zh** in *vision*.   For ¶ reference, see page 64 · HOW TO

capability of causing death or disaster; deadliness: the *fatality* of cancer.

fate [fāt] *n.* **1** A power supposed to determine in advance the way things happen; destiny: to defy *fate*. **2** What happens to a person; fortune; lot: It was her *fate* to die young. **3** Final outcome; end: The jury will decide his *fate*. **— the Fates** In Greek myths, the three goddesses who controlled human destiny.

fat·ed [fā'tid] *adj.* Destined, doomed, or marked by fate: They were *fated* never to meet.

fate·ful [fāt'fəl] *adj.* **1** Having a serious effect on the future: a *fateful* choice. **2** Warning about the future; ominous: a prophet's *fateful* words. **3** Bringing death or disaster: the *fateful* shot. **4** Brought about by fate.

fa·ther [fä'thər] **1** *n.* The male parent of a child. **2** *v.* To become the father of: He *fathered* twin sons. **3** *n.* Any male ancestor. **4** *n.* A man or a thing to which something else owes its existence; creator or source: the founding *fathers* of our nation. **5** *v.* To originate, create, or claim as one's own: to *father* new legislation. **6** *n.* (written **Father**) God. **7** *n.* (usually written **Father**) A priest. **8** *n.* (usually *pl.*) A leader: the city *fathers*.

fa·ther·hood [fä'thər·hŏŏd] *n.* The condition of being a father.

fa·ther-in-law [fä'thər·in·lô'] *n., pl.* **fa·thers-in-law** The father of one's husband or wife.

fa·ther·land [fä'thər·land'] *n.* The land of one's birth; one's native country.

fa·ther·less [fä'thər·lis] *adj.* **1** Having no father living. **2** Not having a known father.

fa·ther·ly [fä'thər·lē] *adj.* Of or like a father: *fatherly* pride. **— fa'ther·li·ness** *n.*

fath·om [fath'əm] **1** *n.* A measure of length equal to six feet, used mainly in measuring the depth of water. **2** *v.* To find the depth of. **3** *v.* To understand; puzzle out.

fath·om·less [fath'əm·lis] *adj.* Too deep to measure or to understand; unfathomable.

fa·tigue [fə·tēg'] *n., v.* **fa·tigued, fa·ti·guing** **1** *n.* A tired condition resulting from hard work, effort, or strain; weariness. **2** *v.* To tire out; weary.

fat·ten [fat'(ə)n] *v.* To make or become fat.

fat·ty [fat'ē] *adj.* **fat·ti·er, fat·ti·est** **1** Made of fat. **2** Containing fat or too much fat, as bodily tissues. **3** Like fat; greasy.

fat·u·ous [fach'ŏŏ·əs] *adj.* Foolish or stupid in a self-satisfied way. **— fat'u·ous·ly** *adv.*

fau·cet [fô'sit] *n.* A device with an adjustable valve used to start, stop, or regulate the flow of a liquid, as from a pipe; spigot.

Faulk·ner [fôk'nər], **William,** 1897–1962, U.S. novelist.

Fault

fault [fôlt] *n.* **1** Something that makes a person or thing less than perfect; defect, weakness, or flaw. **2** A mistake or blunder.

3 Responsibility for wrongdoing or neglect; blame: It wasn't our *fault* that we lost. **4** A break in the earth's crust causing rock layers to shift. **— at fault** In the wrong. **— find fault** To look for and complain about mistakes. **— find fault with** To criticize.

fault·less [fôlt'lis] *adj.* Free from any fault or flaw; perfect. **— fault'less·ly** *adv.*

fault·y [fôl'tē] *adj.* **fault·i·er, fault·i·est** Having faults; imperfect. **— fault'i·ly** *adv.*

faun [fôn] *n.* In Roman myths, a woodland god represented as a man having the ears, horns, tail, and hind legs of a goat.

fau·na [fô'nə] *n.* The animals living within a certain area or during a certain period.

fa·vor [fā'vər] **1** *n.* A kind act or service: He did me a *favor*. **2** *v.* To oblige. **3** *v.* To help along; aid: The thick fog *favored* their escape. **4** *v.* To approve of or support: I *favor* his suggestion. **5** *n.* Good will, liking, or approval. **6** *v.* To prefer in a prejudiced way: Grandmother *favors* my sister. **7** *n.* A little gift; keepsake: party *favors*. **8** *v.* To look like: The boy *favors* his father. **9** *v.* To treat gently; spare: to *favor* a hurt foot. **— in favor of 1** On the side of; for. **2** To the advantage of. **— in one's favor** To one's advantage or profit. ¶1

A faun

fa·vor·a·ble [fā'vər·ə·bəl] *adj.* **1** Helping: a *favorable* wind. **2** Encouraging or supporting: a *favorable* reply. **— fa'vor·a·bly** *adv.* ¶1

fa·vor·ite [fā'vər·it] **1** *n.* A person or thing preferred over others. **2** *adj.* Best loved: my *favorite* song. ¶1

fa·vor·it·ism [fā'vər·ə·tiz'əm] *n.* An unfair favoring of one or a few out of a group. ¶1

fawn¹ [fôn] *v.* **1** To show affection as a dog does by crouching, licking the hands, etc. **2** To seek favor or advantage by humbling oneself and flattering: to *fawn* over a celebrity.

fawn² [fôn] *n.* **1** A young deer not yet a year old. **2** Its color, a light yellowish brown.

fay [fā] *n.* A fairy.

faze [fāz] *v.* **fazed, faz·ing** U.S. *informal* To disturb or upset: Nothing *fazes* him.

FBI or **F.B.I.** The Federal Bureau of Investigation, an agency of the U.S. government that investigates violations of Federal law.

Fe The symbol for the element IRON. ◆ The Latin word for iron is *ferrum*.

Fawn

fe·al·ty [fē'əl·tē] *n.* **1** The loyalty owed to a feudal lord by his vassal. **2** Faithfulness; allegiance; loyalty.

fear [fir] **1** *n.* A frightening feeling that danger

or trouble is close; dread; terror. **2** *v*. To feel dread or terror. **3** *v*. To be frightened of: to *fear* the dark. **4** *n*. A cause of dread: His worst *fear* is failure. **5** *v*. To be uneasy or worried: I *fear* that he won't come. **6** *n*. An uneasy feeling.

fear·ful [fir′fəl] *adj*. **1** Full of fear; frightened: *fearful* of strangers; a *fearful* look. **2** Causing fear; frightening: a *fearful* storm. **3** *informal* Extremely bad; dreadful. **—fear′ful·ly** *adv*.

fear·less [fir′lis] *adj*. Without fear; not at all afraid; brave. **—fear′less·ly** *adv*.

fear·some [fir′səm] *adj*. Causing fear; alarming: a *fearsome* monster.

fea·si·ble [fē′zə·bəl] *adj*. **1** Capable of being done or put into effect: a *feasible* plan. **2** Fairly probable; likely: a *feasible* explanation. **—fea·si·bil·i·ty** [fē′zə·bil′ə·tē] *n*.

feast [fēst] **1** *n*. A great meal at which there is an abundance of food; banquet. **2** *v*. To entertain with such a meal: The rich man *feasted* his friends. **3** *v*. To eat heartily. **4** *v*. To delight; gratify: to *feast* the eyes on a loved one. **5** *n*. A joyous religious celebration.

feat [fēt] *n*. A remarkable act or deed, as one showing great skill, endurance, or daring.

feath·er [feth′ər] **1** *n*. One of the growths that cover a bird's skin, made up of a hollow quill with fanlike webs of light, soft filaments growing out on each side of it. **2** *n*. A thing like a feather. **3** *v*. To furnish or cover with feathers. **4** *v*. To grow feathers. **5** *n*. The same class or sort; kind: birds of a *feather*. **6** *v*. To turn edgewise, or flat: to *feather* an oar; to *feather* propeller blades. **— a feather in one's cap** An achievement to be proud of.

feather bed A soft mattress stuffed with feathers and used on a bed or as a bed.

feath·er·bed·ding [feth′ər·bed′ing] *n*. The practice, used by some labor unions, of requiring employers to hire more workers than are actually needed. ◆ *Featherbedding* was made up, or "coined," from a bed of feathers to describe the soft life of the workers involved.

feath·er·y [feth′ər·ē] *adj*. **1** Provided with or suggesting feathers. **2** Light as a feather.

fea·ture [fē′chər] *n*., *v*. **fea·tured, fea·tur·ing 1** *n*. A part of the face, as the eyes, nose, or mouth. **2** *n*. A prominent characteristic or quality: The snow was the worst *feature* of our trip. **3** *n*. A special attraction, as at a sale, exhibit, etc. **4** *n*. A full-length motion picture. **5** *n*. A special article, story, or column, as in a newspaper. **6** *v*. To present as worthy of special attention: to *feature* a story on page one.

Feb. Abbreviation of FEBRUARY.

Feb·ru·ar·y [feb′rōō·er′ē *or* feb′yōō·er′ē] *n*. The second month of the year, having 28, or, in leap years, 29 days.

fe·ces [fē′sēz] *n.pl*. Solid waste matter discharged from the intestines.

fe·cund [fē′kənd *or* fek′ənd] *adj*. Fruitful; fertile. **—fe·cun·di·ty** [fi·kun′də·tē] *n*.

fed [fed] Past tense and past participle of FEED. **—fed up** *slang* Bored or weary.

fed·er·al [fed′ər·əl] **1** *adj*. Of, having to do with, or based on an agreement between two or more states to unite under one central government: a *federal* union. **2** *adj*. (*often written* **Federal**) Of, having, or belonging to such a union of states: *federal* troops; the *Federal* government. **3** *adj*. (*written* **Federal**) Of, having to do with, or loyal to the Union cause in the Civil War. **4** *n*. (*written* **Federal**) A supporter of the Union during the Civil War. **5** *adj*. (*written* **Federal**) Of or supporting the Federalist Party.

fed·er·al·ist [fed′ər·əl·ist] **1** *n*. A person who favors a federal government. **2** *n*. (*written* **Federalist**) A member of the Federalist Party. **3** *adj*. (*often written* **Federalist**) Of or having to do with a federal government or the Federalist Party. **—fed′er·al·ism** *n*.

Federalist Party A political party (1787–1830) that favored the adoption of the U.S. Constitution and a strong central government.

fed·er·ate [fed′ə·rāt] *v*. **fed·er·at·ed, fed·er·at·ing** To unite in a federation.

fed·er·a·tion [fed′ə·rā′shən] *n*. The union of two or more states or groups under one governing body: a *federation* of churches.

fe·do·ra [fə·dôr′ə] *n*. A soft hat, usually of felt, with a curved brim and a crown creased lengthwise.

fee [fē] *n*. **1** A charge, as for services, rights, etc.: a membership *fee;* a doctor's *fee*. **2** A piece of land or an estate that has been or can be inherited. **A fee simple** is land that can be sold to or inherited by anyone.

Fedora

fee·ble [fē′bəl] *adj*. **fee·bler, fee·blest 1** Lacking strength; weak. **2** Not adequate or effective: *feeble* efforts. **—fee′ble·ness** *n*. **—fee′bly** *adv*.

fee·ble-mind·ed [fē′bəl·mīn′did] *adj*. Lacking normal mental ability; mentally deficient.

feed [fēd] *v*. **fed, feed·ing,** *n*. **1** *v*. To give food to: to *feed* the family. **2** *v*. To give as food: to *feed* carrots to rabbits. **3** *v*. To eat: Goats *feed* on grass. **4** *n*. Food, especially for animals: chicken *feed*. **5** *n*. *informal* A meal. **6** *v*. To supply or furnish with something: to *feed* a fire with fuel; to *feed* suspicions. **—feed′er** *n*.

feed·back [fēd′bak′] *n*. A sample of or information about what a machine or system is producing, returned to it in a way that modifies operation: A thermostat provides *feedback* for a heater.

feel [fēl] *v*. **felt, feel·ing,** *n*. **1** *v*. To get an impression of by touching: *Feel* the material. **2** *n.* Quality as perceived by touch: a soft *feel.* **3** *v.* To be aware of: to *feel* sweat on one's forehead. **4** *n.* A sense or impression. **5** *v.* To be or seem to be to the body, touch, or mind: The room *feels* cold. **6** *v.* To move along or explore by touching: to *feel* one's way in the dark. **7** *v.* To have the sensation of being: He *feels* cold. **8** *v.* To experience: to *feel* joy. **9** *v.* To experience sympathy: I *feel* for you. **10** *v.* To believe or be convinced: I *feel* that I should go. — **feel like** *informal* To have an inclination for: I *feel like* swimming. — **feel (like) oneself** To seem to oneself to be in one's usual or normal state of health, spirits, etc. — **feel out 1** To try to learn indirectly and cautiously the viewpoint, opinions, etc. of (a person). **2** To try to find out about (a situation) in a cautious way. — **feel up to** *informal* To think one is capable of.

feel·er [fē′lər] *n.* **1** A special part of an animal for touching, as a tentacle or an insect's antenna. **2** A question or remark made in order to find out the opinions, attitudes, or plans of others.

feel·ing [fē′ling] **1** *n.* The sense of touch, through which one experiences heat, cold, contact, etc. **2** *n.* A sensation or awareness of something: a *feeling* of dizziness. **3** *n.* An emotion: the *feeling* of joy or sadness. **4** *n.* Sympathy or compassion. **5** *n.* (*pl.*) The sensitive or emotional side of

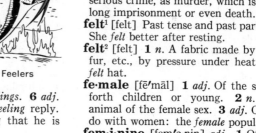

Feelers

a person's nature: He hurt my *feelings.* **6** *adj.* Full of emotion or sympathy: a *feeling* reply. **7** *n.* An opinion: I have a *feeling* that he is wrong. — **feel′ing·ly** *adv.*

feet [fēt] Plural of FOOT.

feign [fān] *v.* To pretend: to *feign* interest.

feigned [fānd] *adj.* **1** Purely imaginary; made up: *feigned* illness. **2** Meant to deceive; false: *feigned* sympathy.

feint [fānt] **1** *n.* A pretended blow or attack made in order to distract an opponent from the real blow or attack. **2** *n.* An appearance or action meant to deceive or mislead: to make a *feint* of studying. **3** *v.* To make a feint.

feld·spar [feld′spär] *n.* A hard, crystalline mineral containing silicon and aluminum.

fe·lic·i·tate [fə·lis′ə·tāt] *v.* **fe·lic·i·tat·ed, fe·lic·i·tat·ing** To congratulate.

fe·lic·i·tous [fə·lis′ə·təs] *adj.* Particularly well chosen; apt: a *felicitous* phrase.

fe·lic·i·ty [fə·lis′ə·tē] *n., pl.* **fe·lic·i·ties 1** Very great happiness; bliss. **2** A pleasant or effective manner or style: a *felicity* of phrasing. **3** A pleasant and appropriate remark.

fe·line [fē′līn] **1** *n.* An animal of the cat family, which also includes lions, tigers, and leopards. **2** *adj.* Of the cat family. **3** *adj.* Like a cat: *feline* grace.

fell¹ [fel] Past tense of FALL.

fell² [fel] *v.* **1** To knock down: to *fell* an opponent. **2** To cut down (timber). **3** To hem one edge of (a seam) down flat over another.

fell³ [fel] *adj.* Cruel; vicious; fierce: to kill with one *fell* blow.

fell⁴ [fel] *n.* The skin of an animal; hide.

fel·low [fel′ō] **1** *n.* A man or boy. **2** *n.* A companion, associate, or equal: *fellows* in crime. **3** *adj.* Joined through some common condition: one's *fellow* man. **4** *n.* A member of certain scholarly societies. **5** *n.* A graduate student awarded a fellowship. **6** *n.* Either one of a pair; mate: the *fellow* to a boot. ◆ *Fellow* goes back to a Scandinavian word meaning *a business partner.*

fel·low·ship [fel′ō·ship] *n.* **1** Warm companionship; friendship. **2** Association, as with others. **3** A group sharing the same interests. **4** A position or sum of money given to a student to finance his graduate study.

fel·on¹ [fel′ən] *n.* A person guilty of a serious crime, such as murder or burglary.

fel·on² [fel′ən] *n.* A painful inflammation of a finger or toe, generally near the nail.

fe·lo·ni·ous [fə·lō′nē·əs] *adj.* Having to do with a felony; criminal: *felonious* assault.

fel·o·ny [fel′ə·nē] *n., pl.* **fel·o·nies** A very serious crime, as murder, which is punishable by long imprisonment or even death.

felt¹ [felt] Past tense and past participle of FEEL: She *felt* better after resting.

felt² [felt] **1** *n.* A fabric made by matting wool, fur, etc., by pressure under heat. **2** *adj. use:* a *felt* hat.

fe·male [fē′māl] **1** *adj.* Of the sex that brings forth children or young. **2** *n.* A person or animal of the female sex. **3** *adj.* Of or having to do with women: the *female* population.

fem·i·nine [fem′ə·nin] *adj.* **1** Of or having to do with the female sex. **2** Like, typical of, or appropriate to women. **3** In grammar, of the gender that includes words for females: *She, duchess,* and *mare* are in the *feminine* gender.

fe·mur [fē′mər] *n.* The long bone of the thigh, extending from the pelvis to the knee.

fen [fen] *n.* A swamp; marsh; bog.

fence [fens] *n., v.* **fenced, fenc·ing 1** *n.* A structure, as of wooden rails, steel mesh, or wire, built as an enclosure, barrier, or boundary. **2** *v.* To enclose with a fence: to *fence* in cattle; to *fence* off a garden. **3** *v.* To practice the art of fencing with foils or swords. **4** *n.* A dealer who buys and sells stolen goods. — **on the fence** Undecided on some issue; not committed to one side or the other.

femur
patella
fibula
tibia

fenc·er [fen′sər] *n.* A person who fences with a foil or sword.

fenc·ing [fen′sing] *n.* **1** The art or sport of using a foil or sword in attack and defense. **2** Material used in making or repairing fences. **3** Fences.

fend [fend] *v.* To ward off: to *fend* off a blow or an attack. **—fend for one-self** To get along on one's own: An alley cat *fends for itself.*

fend·er [fen′dər] *n.* **1** A metal part projecting over each wheel of a car, etc., to keep mud from being thrown upwards. **2** A part on the front of a locomotive to push away objects blocking the tracks. **3** A metal frame or screen set in front of a fireplace to keep in sparks or hot coals.

Men fencing

fen·nel [fen′əl] *n.* A tall herb with bright yellow flowers. Its seeds are used in medicines and as a flavoring in cooking.

fer·ment [*v.* fər·ment′, *n.* fûr′mənt] **1** *v.* To undergo or bring about the slow decomposition of organic substances by the action of yeast, bacteria, or enzymes: Wine is formed when grape juice *ferments.* **2** *n.* Any substance that is used to bring about fermenting. **3** *n.* Fermentation. **4** *v.* To excite or be excited with emotion. **5** *n.* Agitation; excitement: the *ferment* of a battle.

fer·men·ta·tion [fûr′mən·tā′shən] *n.* The chemical change brought about in a substance by the action of a ferment, such as yeast, bacteria, or enzymes.

Fer·mi [fer′mē], **Enrico,** 1901–1954, U.S. nuclear physicist, born in Italy.

fern [fûrn] *n.* Any of a large class of plants that have no flowers or seeds. They reproduce by means of spores growing on the undersides of their featherlike leaves, or fronds.

fe·ro·cious [fə·rō′shəs] *adj.* **1** Extremely fierce or savage. **2** *informal* Very intense or great: *ferocious* heat. **—fe·ro′cious·ly** *adv.*

Fern

fe·roc·i·ty [fə·ros′ə·tē] *n.* Extreme fierceness; savagery; cruelty.

fer·ret [fer′it] **1** *n.* A small animal related to the weasel that is sometimes tamed and used in hunting rabbits, rats, etc. **2** *v.* To drive out of hiding or to hunt with a ferret. **3** *v.* To uncover with difficulty by determined investigation: to *ferret* out a secret.

fer·ric [fer′ik] *adj.* Containing or having to do with iron in its higher valence.

Fer·ris wheel [fer′is] A giant wheel that revolves around a fixed axle and has seats in which passengers ride for amusement.

fer·rous [fer′əs] *adj.* Containing or having to do with iron in its lower valence.

fer·rule [fer′əl *or* fer′ool] *n.* A metal ring or cap put around the end of a cane, handle, etc., to strengthen it or to prevent splitting.

fer·ry [fer′ē] *v.* **fer·ried, fer·ry·ing,** *n., pl.* **fer·ries** **1** *v.* To transport (people, cars, or goods) across a river or other narrow body of water by boat or other craft. **2** *n.* A boat or other craft used for ferrying. **3** *n.* A place where a ferry docks or crosses a body of water. **4** *v.* To deliver (an airplane, boat, etc.) under its own power to the place where it is needed or wanted.

Ferris wheel

fer·ry·boat [fer′ē·bōt′] *n.* A boat used as a ferry.

fer·tile [fûr′təl] *adj.* **1** Producing or able to produce abundant crops or vegetation: *fertile* soil. **2** Capable of producing seeds, fruit, young, etc.; not sterile. **3** Able to grow into a new animal or plant: *fertile* eggs; *fertile* seeds. **4** Able to produce many ideas or thoughts: a *fertile* mind. **—fer·til·i·ty** [fər·til′ə·tē] *n.*

fer·til·ize [fûr′təl·īz] *v.* **fer·til·ized, fer·til·iz·ing** **1** To make (soil) more fertile by applying fertilizer. **2** To cause (a female cell) to start growing into a new animal or plant by union with a male cell: to *fertilize* an egg; Bumblebees *fertilize* clover by carrying pollen from one blossom to another. **—fer·til·i·za·tion** [fûr′təl·ə·zā′shən] *n.* ¶3

fer·til·iz·er [fûr′təl·ī′zər] *n.* A substance, such as manure or certain chemicals, applied to soil to furnish food for plants. ¶3

fer·ule[1] [fer′əl *or* fer′ool] *n., v.* **fer·uled, fer·ul·ing** **1** *n.* A flat stick or ruler sometimes used for punishing children, usually by hitting them on the hand. **2** *v.* To punish with a ferule.

fer·ule[2] [fer′əl *or* fer′ool] *n.* Another spelling of FERRULE.

fer·vent [fûr′vənt] *adj.* **1** Very eager and earnest; ardent: a *fervent* hope of winning. **2** Very hot; burning or glowing: *fervent* heat: used mostly in poems. **—fer′vent·ly** *adv.*

fer·vid [fûr′vid] *adj.* Afire with feeling; fiery: a *fervid* speech. **—fer′vid·ly** *adv.*

fer·vor [fûr′vər] *n* Very strong emotion or enthusiasm; zeal. ¶1

fes·tal [fes′təl] *adj.* Of or having to do with a feast or a festival: *festal* songs.

fes·ter [fes′tər] **1** *v.* To become full of pus: A

neglected wound or cut may *fester*. **2** *n*. A festering sore or wound. **3** *v*. To remain or grow in the mind as a constant source of bad feeling: Jealousy *festered* within her.

fes·ti·val [fes′tə·vəl] *n*. **1** A time or occasion for rejoicing or feasting. **2** A particular feast, holiday, or celebration, especially an annual one: a spring *festival*. **3** A special series of performances: a drama *festival*.

fes·tive [fes′tiv] *adj*. Of, having to do with, or suitable for a joyous celebration; gay.

fes·tiv·i·ty [fes·tiv′ə·tē] *n*., *pl*. **fes·tiv·i·ties** **1** Gladness and rejoicing typical of a joyous occasion. **2** (*pl*.) The activities accompanying such an occasion: birthday *festivities*.

fes·toon [fes·tōōn′] **1** *n*. A length of flowers, leaves, colored paper, or other material hung in a curve as a decoration. **2** *v*. To decorate with festoons. **3** *v*. To fashion into festoons.

A festoon

fetch [fech] *v*. **1** To go for, get, and bring back: to *fetch* a package for one's mother. **2** To draw forth: The announcement of the test *fetched* a groan from the class. **3** To give forth (a sigh, groan, etc.). **4** To cost or sell for: The material will *fetch* a good price.

fetch·ing [fech′ing] *adj*. *informal* Very attractive or pleasing: a *fetching* dress.

fete or **fête** [fāt *or* fet] *n*., *v*. **fet·ed** or **fêt·ed**, **fet·ing** or **fêt·ing** **1** *n*. A festival, party, or entertainment, often held outdoors. **2** *v*. To honor, as with a party or dinner; entertain: to *fete* a visiting celebrity.

fet·id [fet′id] *adj*. Having a bad odor, as of rot or decay; stinking: *fetid* garbage.

fet·ish [fet′ish *or* fē′tish] *n*. **1** An object worshipped by primitive peoples as being the dwelling place of a spirit or having magical powers to protect its owner. **2** Anything to which a person is excessively and unreasonably devoted: He makes a *fetish* of being on time.

fet·lock [fet′lok′] *n*. **1** A tuft of hair growing at the back of the leg of a horse or similar animal just above the hoof. **2** The part or joint of the leg where this tuft grows.

Fetlock

fet·ter [fet′ər] **1** *n*. A chain or other bond put about the ankles to restrain movement. **2** *n*. (*usually pl*.) Anything that checks freedom of movement or expression. **3** *v*. To bind with fetters or as if with fetters; shackle; hamper.

fet·tle [fet′(ə)l] *n*. Condition of health and spirits: to be in fine *fettle*.

fe·tus [fē′təs] *n*., *pl*. **fe·tus·es** An unborn baby or animal in the later stages of its development in the womb.

feud [fyōōd] **1** *n*. A long, bitter quarrel between families, sometimes leading to bloodshed. **2** *n*. A lasting quarrel between two or more people or groups. **3** *v*. To take part in a feud.

feu·dal [fyōōd′(ə)l] *adj*. Of or having to do with feudalism.

feu·dal·ism [fyōōd′(ə)l·iz′əm] *n*. An economic and political system of medieval Europe in which vassals were given land and protection by their lords in return for military service or the performance of other duties.

feudal system Feudalism.

fe·ver [fē′vər] *n*. **1** A body temperature higher than normal, usually indicating illness. **2** A sickness characterized by high fever: scarlet *fever*. **3** A highly restless, eager, or excited condition: in a *fever* of anticipation.

fe·ver·ish [fē′vər·ish] *adj*. **1** Having a fever, especially a low fever. **2** Showing signs of fever: *feverish* eyes. **3** Tending to cause fever: a *feverish* swamp. **4** Excited; restless: a *feverish* desire for speed. —**fe′ver·ish·ly** *adv*. —**fe′ver·ish·ness** *n*.

few [fyōō] *adj*. **few·er, few·est,** *n*., *pron*. **1** *adj*. Small in number; not many: a *few* books. **2** *n*., *pron*. A small number; not very many: Many applied for jobs, but only a *few* were chosen. —**quite a few** A fairly large number. ◆ *Few, several,* and *various* all indicate a quantity that is not large. *Few* stresses *not many*, whereas *several* stresses *more than two*: Note the difference in emphasis between "Only a *few* good apples were left out of the entire bushel" and "*Several* good apples were left." *Various* refers mainly to things that are not alike: *various* duties. ◆ See LESS.

fez [fez] *n*., *pl*. **fez·zes** A felt cap worn by Egyptian men and formerly by Turkish men, usually red and having a black tassel.

ff. Abbreviation of *and those that follow*. Pages 56 *ff*. means page 56 and following pages.

fi·an·cé [fē′än·sā′] *n*. A man to whom a woman is engaged to be married.

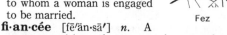

Fez

fi·an·cée [fē′än·sā′] *n*. A woman or girl to whom a man is engaged to be married.

fi·as·co [fē·as′kō] *n*., *pl*. **fi·as·coes** or **fi·as·cos** A complete or humiliating failure: The hoarse singer's recital was a *fiasco*.

fi·at [fī′at] *n*. An official order; decree.

fib [fib] *n*., *v*. **fibbed, fib·bing** **1** *n*. A lie about something of little importance told without any bad intention. **2** *v*. To tell a fib. —**fib′ber** *n*.

fi·ber [fī′bər] *n*. **1** A thread or threadlike part, as of a fabric or of animal or plant tissue: silk *fibers*; muscle *fibers*. **2** A material made up of fibers, or the fibers themselves as a group: hemp *fiber*. **3** Character; nature: Cowards are people of weak moral *fiber*. ¶2

fi·ber·board [fī′bər·bôrd′] *n*. A tough, flexible building material made of wood or plant fiber pressed into sheets. ¶2

Fi·ber·glas [fī′bər·glas′] *n.* A trademark for a flexible, fireproof material made of glass spun into filaments. Also written **fiberglass.**

fi·brin [fī′brin] *n.* A strong, elastic substance in the blood. It promotes clotting by becoming a network of fibers.

fi·brous [fī′brəs] *adj.* Made up of, having, or resembling fiber: *fibrous* tissue.

fib·u·la [fib′yoo·lə] *n., pl.* **fib·u·lae** [fib′yoo·lē] or **fib·u·las** The outer and smaller of the two bones forming the lower part of the human leg between the knee and the ankle.

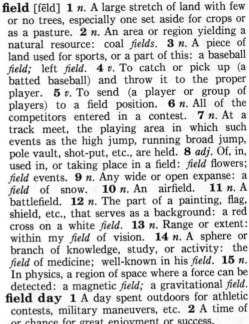
femur
patella
fibula
tibia

-fication A suffix meaning: The act of or the condition of being. It is added to some verbs ending in *-fy* to form nouns, as in *glorification,* the act of glorifying or the condition of being glorified.

fick·le [fik′əl] *adj.* Not constant in feeling, purpose, or nature; apt to change without warning: a *fickle* woman. — **fick′le·ness** *n.*

fic·tion [fik′shən] *n.* **1** Stories whose characters and incidents are entirely or partly imaginary; a form of prose literature. **2** An example of such literature, as a novel or short story. **3** Something made up; an invention or lie: His excuse is a *fiction.* — **fic′tion·al** *adj.*

fic·ti·tious [fik·tish′əs] *adj.* Not real; made-up: a *fictitious* name. — **fic·ti′tious·ly** *adv.*

fid·dle [fid′(ə)l] *n., v.* **fid·dled, fid·dling** **1** *n. informal* A violin. **2** *v. informal* To play a violin. **3** *v.* To make restless movements with the fingers; fidget or play: to *fiddle* with a rubber band. — **fid·dler** [fid′lər] *n.*

fiddler crab A small crab found mostly off the Atlantic coast of the U.S. One of the claws in the male is much larger than the other.

fid·dle·sticks [fid′(ə)l·stiks′] *interj.* Nonsense!

fi·del·i·ty [fī·del′ə·tē *or* fə·del′ə·tē] *n.* **1** Faithfulness in carrying out one's duties, responsibilities, etc.; loyalty. **2** Accuracy; correctness: a translation done with *fidelity.*

Fiddler crab, body up to 1 in. wide

fidg·et [fij′it] **1** *v.* To stir about in an impatient, nervous, or restless way: Children often *fidget* on rainy days. **2** *n.* (*usually pl.*) A restless condition causing constant impatient or nervous movements: He had the *fidgets* and couldn't sit still. — **fidg′et·y** *adj.*

fie [fī] *interj.* Shame! For shame!: rarely used today except humorously.

fief [fēf] *n.* In the feudal system, land held by a vassal from a lord.

field [fēld] **1** *n.* A large stretch of land with few or no trees, especially one set aside for crops or as a pasture. **2** *n.* An area or region yielding a natural resource: coal *fields.* **3** *n.* A piece of land used for sports, or a part of this: a baseball *field;* left *field.* **4** *v.* To catch or pick up (a batted baseball) and throw it to the proper player. **5** *v.* To send (a player or group of players) to a field position. **6** *n.* All of the competitors entered in a contest. **7** *n.* At a track meet, the playing area in which such events as the high jump, running broad jump, pole vault, shot-put, etc., are held. **8** *adj.* Of, in, used in, or taking place in a field: *field* flowers; *field* events. **9** *n.* Any wide or open expanse: a *field* of snow. **10** *n.* An airfield. **11** *n.* A battlefield. **12** *n.* The part of a painting, flag, shield, etc., that serves as a background: a red cross on a white *field.* **13** *n.* Range or extent: within my *field* of vision. **14** *n.* A sphere or branch of knowledge, study, or activity: the *field* of medicine; well-known in his *field.* **15** *n.* In physics, a region of space where a force can be detected: a magnetic *field;* a gravitational *field.*

field day **1** A day spent outdoors for athletic contests, military maneuvers, etc. **2** A time of or chance for great enjoyment or success.

field·er [fēl′dər] *n.* In baseball or cricket, a player in the field.

field glasses Two small, portable telescopes fastened together for use outdoors; binoculars.

field goal In football, a goal worth three points, scored by kicking the ball over the crossbar of the goal post during regular play.

field magnet The magnet used to create a magnetic field in a generator or electric motor.

field marshal In some European armies, an officer ranking just below the commander in chief.

field trip An educational trip by a class to a place away from school.

fiend [fēnd] *n.* **1** An evil spirit; demon; devil. **2** A terribly wicked or cruel person. **3** *informal* A person very much devoted or addicted to a thing: a tennis *fiend.* — **fiend′ish** *adj.*

fierce [firs] *adj.* **fierc·er, fierc·est** Frighteningly savage, cruel, violent, or intense: a *fierce* tiger; *fierce* anger. — **fierce′ly** *adv.*

fier·y [fir′ē *or* fī′ər·ē] *adj.* **fier·i·er, fier·i·est** **1** Containing or composed of fire: a *fiery* furnace. **2** Hot as fire; burning: the *fiery* sun. **3** Very passionate; intense: a *fiery* speech; a *fiery* temper.

fi·es·ta [fē·es′tə] *n.* A festival, especially a religious one in Spain and Latin America.

fife [fīf] *n., v.* **fifed, fif·ing** **1** *n.* A small flute having a shrill tone, used with drums in military music. **2** *v.* To play on a fife.

fif·teen or **15** [fif′tēn′] *n., adj.* One more than fourteen.

fif·teenth or **15th** [fif′tēnth′] **1** adj. Next after the fourteenth. **2** n. The fifteenth one. **3** adj. Being one of fifteen equal parts. **4** n. A fifteenth part.

fifth or **5th** [fifth] **1** adj. Next after the fourth. **2** n. The fifth one. **3** adj. Being one of five equal parts. **4** n. A fifth part.

fifth column In war, a civilian group working secretly within their country for the enemy.

fif·ti·eth or **50th** [fif′tē·ith] **1** adj. Tenth in order after the fortieth. **2** n. The fiftieth one. **3** adj. Being one of fifty equal parts. **4** n. A fiftieth part.

fif·ty or **50** [fif′tē] n., pl. **fif·ties** or **50's**, adj. **1** n., adj. Ten more than forty. **2** n. (pl.) The years between the age of 50 and the age of 60: He's in his *fifties*.

fif·ty-fif·ty [fif′tē·fif′tē] informal **1** adj. Equal. **2** adv. Equally. **3** adj. Half favorable and half not favorable.

fig [fig] n. **1** A small, sweet, pear-shaped fruit, often dried or canned but also eaten fresh. **2** The tree that bears this fruit. **3** The least bit; trifle: I don't care a *fig*.

fig. Abbreviation of FIGURE (def. 15).

Figs

fight [fīt] v. **fought, fight·ing,** n. **1** v. To try to beat or conquer by struggling with, hitting, etc. **2** v. To take part in angry, violent, or determined struggle. **3** n. A struggle or battle involving physical combat or weapons. **4** v. To carry on or engage in (a war, duel, etc.). **5** v. To make (one's way) by struggling. **6** v. To put forth efforts in order to overcome: to *fight* crime. **7** n. Any struggle or contest. **8** n. Power or willingness to fight: The old man still has *fight* in him. **— fight′er** n.

fig·ment [fig′mənt] n. An unreal creation of the mind: only a *figment* of your imagination.

fig·ur·a·tive [fig′yər·ə·tiv] adj. Departing from the actual, or literal, meaning of a word to create a vivid effect. *Blazing* in "The tiger had blazing eyes" is a word used in a figurative way. **— fig′ur·a·tive·ly** adv.

fig·ure [fig′yər] n., v. **fig·ured, fig·ur·ing** **1** n. A character or symbol representing a number: the *figure* 4. **2** n. (pl.) The use of numbers in arithmetic: a good head for *figures*. **3** n. An amount expressed in numbers, as a price: The paintings sold at a high *figure*. **4** v. To use arithmetic to find; calculate: Given the distance and the rate of speed, *figure* the time. **5** v. informal To think or predict: I *figure* that conditions will improve. **6** n. A visible outline or form; shape: A rectangle is a four-sided *figure*; She has a good *figure*. **7** n. A human form: to glimpse a ghostly *figure*. **8** n. A person in terms of his appearance, conduct, or the impression he makes: a fine *figure* of a man. **9** n. A personage or character: a well-known *figure* in the theater. **10** v. To have a part: Determination as well as

talent *figured* in his success. **11** n. A pattern or design, as on a fabric. **12** v. To decorate or mark with a design. **13** adj. use: a *figured* fabric. **14** n. A movement or series of movements in dancing or skating, or a pattern traced by such movements: a *figure* 8. **15** n. A picture, drawing, or diagram, as in a textbook; illustration. **16** n. A figure of speech. **— figure on** U.S. informal To rely on or plan on. **— figure out** To solve or understand: I can't *figure* it *out*.

fig·ure·head [fig′yər·hed′] n. **1** A carved figure decorating the prow of a sailing ship. **2** A leader in name only, with no real power.

figure of speech An expression, as a metaphor, which cannot be taken literally but is used to create a vivid picture or striking effect, as in "The fog crept in" or "Lightning streaked the sky."

fig·u·rine [fig′yə·rēn′] n. A small molded or carved statue; statuette.

Figurehead

Fi·ji Islands [fē′jē] A group of islands about 1500 miles north of New Zealand.

fil·a·gree [fil′ə·grē] n. Another spelling of FILIGREE.

fil·a·ment [fil′ə·mənt] n. A very thin thread or a threadlike structure, as the fine wire that produces light in an electric bulb.

fil·bert [fil′bərt] n. Another name for HAZELNUT.

filch [filch] v. To steal slyly and in small amounts; pilfer: to *filch* cookies from a jar.

file¹ [fīl] n., v. **filed, fil·ing** **1** n. A cabinet, drawer, box, or folder in which papers are systematically arranged. **2** n. The papers, cards, or other documents so arranged. **3** v. To arrange and put in a file: to *file* school records. **4** v. To enter or have entered in an official record: to *file* a complaint. **5** n. A line of persons, animals, or things, one behind the other. **6** v. To move in a file: The players *filed* onto the field. **— on file** Stored in a file for quick reference.

file² [fīl] n., v. **filed, fil·ing** **1** n. A tool of hard steel with rough teeth or ridges, used to grind, smooth, or polish. **2** v. To cut, smooth, sharpen, or remove with a file.

fi·let [fi·lā′ or fil′ā] n. **1** Net lace having a square mesh. **2** A fish or meat fillet.

fil·i·al [fil′ē·əl] adj. Suitable to or expected of a son or daughter: *filial* respect; *filial* devotion.

Files

fil·i·bus·ter [fil′ə·bus′tər] U.S. **1** n. In a legislative body, the making of long, often pointless speeches or the use of other delaying tactics in order to prevent a bill from being passed. **2** *v.* To block passage of (legislation) by means of long speeches and delay. ◆ *Filibuster* comes from a Spanish word, which in turn came from the Dutch word for *freebooter.* Originally a *filibuster* was a person who organized an attack in a foreign country. Later the word came to mean a person in a legislature who tried to obstruct the will of the majority, and finally switched from the man to his actions or methods.

fil·i·gree [fil′ə·grē] *n.* Delicate ornamental work, as of intertwined gold or silver wire.

fil·ings [fī′lingz] *n.pl.* Bits or particles rubbed off with a file: brass *filings.*

Fil·i·pi·no [fil′ə·pē′nō] *adj., n., pl.* **Fil·i·pi·nos 1** *adj.* Philippine. **2** *n.* A person born in or a citizen of the Philippines.

Filigree

fill [fil] **1** *v.* To put as much into (a space, container, etc.) as it can hold; make full: to *fill* a pitcher with lemonade. **2** *v.* To become full: Soon the dry ravine will *fill* with water. **3** *v.* To occupy the whole of: Guests *filled* the ballroom. **4** *v.* To stop up; plug: to *fill* a cavity in a tooth. **5** *v.* To satisfy or meet, as a need or requirement. **6** *n.* An amount sufficient to fill or satisfy: to eat one's *fill.* **7** *n.* Material used to fill, as gravel or dirt used to build up low ground. **8** *v.* To supply what is called for in: to *fill* a prescription. **9** *v.* To occupy or put someone into (an office or position): to *fill* the governorship. **10** *v.* To cause (a sail) to swell out: said about wind. **— fill in 1** To insert: *Fill in* the answer. **2** To complete or fill by putting in something: *Fill in* the blanks. **3** To be a substitute. **— fill out 1** To make or become fuller or more rounded. **2** To complete by adding the requested information: to *fill out* a form. **— fill up** To make or become full.

fill·er [fil′ər] *n.* **1** A person who fills. **2** A thing that fills, as a brief piece of writing used to fill space in a newspaper, or paper packaged for use in loose-leaf notebooks.

fil·let [fil′it *for defs.* 1, 2, fil′ā *or* fi·lā′ *for defs.* 3, 4] **1** *n.* A narrow band or ribbon for binding the hair. **2** *v.* To bind or adorn with a fillet. **3** *n.* A slice of boneless meat or fish. **4** *v.* To cut into fillets.

fill·ing [fil′ing] *n.* A substance used to fill something: a custard *filling* for a pie; a silver *filling* for a cavity in a tooth.

filling station A gas station.

fil·lip [fil′ip] **1** *n.* An outward snap of a finger that has been pressed against the thumb and suddenly released. **2** *v.* To strike or toss with a fillip. **3** *n.* Something that arouses or stirs up: The sight of a deer gave a *fillip* to our hike.

Fill·more [fil′môr], **Millard,** 1800–1874, 13th president of the U.S., 1850–1853.

fil·ly [fil′ē] *n., pl.* **fil·lies** A young mare.

film [film] **1** *n.* A thin coating or layer: a *film* of dust on the table. **2** *v.* To cover or become covered with a film. **3** *n.* A sheet, roll, or strip of material having a thin coating of a chemical substance that is sensitive to light, used for making photographs. **4** *n.* A motion picture. **5** *v.* To make or take motion pictures of: to *film* a novel. **6** *n.* A thin haze or blur: a *film* of mist.

film·strip [film′strip′] *n.* A series of still pictures on film that are projected on a screen, often used as an aid in teaching.

film·y [fil′mē] *adj.* **film·i·er, film·i·est 1** Made up of or like a film; gauzy: a *filmy* scarf. **2** Covered with a film; clouded; dim.

fil·ter [fil′tər] **1** *n.* Any device containing a porous substance, as paper, charcoal, or sand, used to strain out impurities from a liquid or gas. **2** *n.* The porous substances used in such a device. **3** *v.* To pass or cause to pass through a filter. **4** *v.* To act as a filter for: Charcoal *filters* air. **5** *n.* In physics, any of various devices that allow waves or electric currents of certain frequencies to pass through while stopping all others. **6** *v.* To leak out slowly.

fil·ter·a·ble [fil′tər·ə·bəl] *adj.* **1** Capable of being filtered. **2** Small enough to pass through a filter: A *filterable* virus passes through a filter that stops bacteria.

filth [filth] *n.* **1** Anything that soils or makes foul; disgusting dirt. **2** Something indecent, as dirty words, pictures, or books.

filth·y [fil′thē] *adj.* **filth·i·er, filth·i·est 1** Covered with filth; foul; dirty. **2** Indecent or obscene. **— filth′i·ness** *n.*

fil·trate [fil′trāt] *v.* **fil·trat·ed, fil·trat·ing,** *n.* **1** *v.* To filter. **2** *n.* Liquid that has been passed through a filter. **— fil·tra′tion** *n.*

fin [fin] *n.* **1** A fanlike or winglike part sticking out on a fish's body, used as a balance or to propel the fish. **2** Any finlike part, as on an aircraft or missile, used for steadiness in flight.

fi·nal [fī′nəl] **1** *adj.* Coming at the end; last: the *final* page of a newspaper. **2** *adj.* That cannot be changed; definite: a *final* decision. **3** *n.* (*pl.*) The last examinations in a school term. **4** *n.* (*pl.*) The last games in a tournament. **— fi′nal·ly** *adv.*

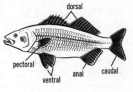

Fins

fi·na·le [fə·nä′lē] *n.* The last part of something, as the final scene of a play or the concluding section of a musical composition.

fi·nal·ist [fī′nəl·ist] *n.* A contestant who has reached the finals of a contest.

add, āce, câre, pälm;   end, ēqual;   it, īce;   odd, ōpen, ôrder;   tŏŏk, pool;   up, bûrn;
ə = a in *above,* e in *sicken,* i in *possible,* o in *melon,* u in *circus;*   yoo = u in *fuse;*   oil;   pout;
check; ring; thin; this; zh in *vision.*   For ¶ reference, see page 64 · HOW TO

fi·nal·i·ty [fi·nal′ə·tē] *n.*, *pl.* **fi·nal·i·ties**
1 A final or definite condition or quality: to speak with *finality*. **2** Something final or definite, as an act, remark, or decision.

fi·nance [fi·nans′ *or* fi′nans] *n.*, *v.* **fi·nanced, fi·nanc·ing 1** *n.* (*pl.*) Available money; funds: family *finances;* government *finances.* **2** *n.* The use or management of money, especially in large amounts. **3** *v.* To provide or get the necessary money for: to *finance* a new car.

fi·nan·cial [fi·nan′shəl *or* fi·nan′shəl] *adj.* Of or having to do with money or the use or management of money. — **fi·nan′cial·ly** *adv.*

fin·an·cier [fin′ən·sir′] *n.* A person who is an expert in financial affairs, as a banker.

finch [finch] *n.* Any of a large group of small songbirds, having a short bill adapted for eating seeds. Sparrows and canaries are finches.

find [fīnd] *v.* **found, find·ing,** *n.* **1** *v.* To come upon unexpectedly: to *find* a ring. **2** *v.* To search for and discover: Please *find* my glasses. **3** *v.* To recover or get back (something lost): Harry *found* his wallet. **4** *n.* Something found, especially something valuable. **5** *v.* To learn; discover: We *found* that Dan was a good jumper. **6** *v.* To reach a decision and declare: The jury *found* for the defendant. **7** *v.* To arrive at; reach: The bullet *found* its mark. — **find oneself 1** To discover one's special abilities. **2** To discover that one is in a certain place or condition: He *found himself* alone. — **find out** To learn with certainty: to *find out* the truth.

find·er [fīn′dər] *n.* **1** A person or thing that finds. **2** An attachment on a camera that shows the user what will appear in the picture.

find·ing [fīn′ding] *n.* **1** The action of finding; discovery. **2** Something found. **3** (*usually pl.*) A conclusion arrived at, as by a law court, after careful investigation of the facts.

fine¹ [fīn] *adj.* **fin·er, fin·est,** *adv.* **1** *adj.* Very good; excellent: a *fine* dinner. **2** *adv.* *informal* Very well: Cold weather suits me *fine.* **3** *adj.* Free from impurities; pure: *fine* gold. **4** *adj.* Not cloudy; clear: *fine* weather. **5** *adj.* Made up of very small particles: *fine* powder. **6** *adj.* Very thin; slender: a *fine* thread. **7** *adj.* Keen; sharp: a sword with a *fine* edge. **8** *adj.* Delicate: *fine* lace. **9** *adj.* Very refined; elegant: *fine* manners. **10** *adj.* Not obvious; subtle; clever: a *fine* point in an argument. — **fine′ness** *n.*

fine² [fīn] *n.*, *v.* **fined, fin·ing 1** *n.* A sum of money that has to be paid as a penalty for breaking a law or rule. **2** *v.* To punish by a fine.

fine arts The arts having to do with the creation of beautiful things, as painting, drawing, sculpture, and architecture. Fine arts may include music, literature, drama, and dancing.

fin·er·y [fī′nər·ē] *n.*, *pl.* **fin·er·ies** Fine or showy clothes or decorations.

fi·nesse [fi·nes′] *n.* **1** Delicate skill: The pianist plays with *finesse.* **2** Skill in handling a difficult situation without offending anyone.

fin·ger [fing′gər] **1** *n.* Any of the five separate parts forming the end of the hand, especially the four besides the thumb. **2** *n.* The part of a glove that covers a finger. **3** *v.* To touch or handle with the fingers: to *finger* a bracelet. **4** *v.* To play (music) by using the fingers on a musical instrument in a certain way: to *finger* a scale. **5** *n.* Anything that looks like or serves as a finger. **6** *n.* The width of a finger, about ¾ of an inch.

finger bowl A small bowl holding water to be used to rinse the fingers at a formal meal.

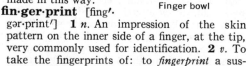

fin·ger·nail [fing′gər·nāl′] *n.* The horny plate growing at the end of each finger.

finger painting 1 The act of painting pictures on wet paper using the fingers and palms rather than a brush. **2** A picture made in this way.

Finger bowl

fin·ger·print [fing′gər·print′] **1** *n.* An impression of the skin pattern on the inner side of a finger, at the tip, very commonly used for identification. **2** *v.* To take the fingerprints of: to *fingerprint* a suspected robber.

fin·ick·y [fin′i·kē] *adj.* Too particular or fussy.

fin·ish [fin′ish] **1** *v.* To bring to or reach an end: The poet finally *finished* his poem; The movie *finished* at midnight. **2** *v.* *informal* To kill, destroy, or defeat. **3** *v.* To use or consume completely: to *finish* the cake. **4** *n.* The last stage of anything; end: the *finish* of a race. **5** *v.* To give a particular kind of surface to: to *finish* a table with shellac. **6** *n.* The type of surface something has: a bright *finish.* **7** *n.* A material or substance used in finishing: an oil *finish* on a painting. **8** *n.* Perfection or polish in speech, manners, or education.

fin·ished [fin′isht] *adj.* **1** Ended; completed. **2** Perfected; polished: a *finished* work of art. **3** Highly skilled: a *finished* musician.

fi·nite [fī′nīt] *adj.* Having a limit or boundary; not infinite: a *finite* quantity.

Fin·land [fin′lənd] *n.* A country in northern Europe.

Finn [fin] *n.* A person born in or a citizen of Finland.

fin·nan had·die [fin′ən had′ē] Smoked haddock.

Finn·ish [fin′ish] **1** *adj.* Of or from Finland. **2** *n.* (**the Finnish**) The people of Finland. **3** *n.* The language of Finland.

Fiord

fiord [fyôrd] *n.* In Norway, a long, narrow inlet of the sea between high cliffs or banks.

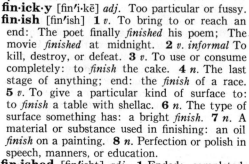

fir [fûr] *n.* **1** Any of several kinds of evergreen trees related to the pine, often used as Christmas trees. **2** The wood of a fir tree.

fire [fīr] *n., v.* **fired, fir·ing 1** *n.* The flame and heat caused by something burning. **2** *n.* A burning mass of fuel, as in a fireplace. **3** *n.* A destructive burning, as of a building. **4** *v.* To feed or tend the fire of. **5** *v.* To bake in a kiln: to *fire* a piece of pottery. **6** *n.* Strong feeling; excitement; ardor: Her eyes were full of *fire.* **7** *v.* To inspire or excite: to *fire* a boy's imagination with adventure stories. **8** *v.* To shoot, as a gun. **9** *n.* Shooting: enemy *fire;* Cease *fire!* **10** *v. informal* To hurl: to *fire* stones; to *fire* questions. **11** *n.* A rapid series or an outburst of something: a *fire* of questions. **12** *v. informal* To discharge from a job; dismiss. **— between two fires** Under attack or criticism from both sides. **— catch fire** To start to burn. **— hang fire** To be delayed or undecided, as an event or decision. **— on fire** **1** Burning. **2** Full of fervor or excitement. **— under fire 1** Exposed to gunfire. **2** Being severely criticized.

fire·arm [fīr′ärm′] *n.* A weapon, especially one small enough to be carried, that shoots a bullet or other missile.

fire·brand [fīr′brand′] *n.* **1** A piece of burning wood. **2** A person who stirs up trouble or strife.

fire·break [fīr′brāk′] *n.* A strip of land that has been plowed or cleared to stop the spread of a forest or brush fire.

fire·brick [fīr′brik′] *n.* A type of brick able to withstand great heat, used for lining fireplaces and some types of furnaces.

fire·crack·er [fīr′krak′ər] *n.* A paper cylinder containing an explosive and used as a noise-maker, as on the Fourth of July.

fire·damp [fīr′damp′] *n.* A dangerous gas that collects in coal mines and is explosive when mixed with certain proportions of air.

fire engine A truck with special equipment for putting out fires, especially one having powerful pumps for throwing water or chemicals.

fire escape A metal stairway, ladder, or chute along the outside of a building to be used as a means of escape in case of fire.

fire extinguisher A portable metal container from which a chemical may be sprayed to put out a fire.

fire·fly [fīr′flī′] *n., pl.* **fire·flies** An insect having, in the lower part of its body, a phosphorescent substance that glows on and off as it flies at night.

fire·house [fīr′hous′] *n.* A building where firemen are stationed and fire engines are kept.

fire·light [fīr′līt′] *n.* The light cast from a fire, as from a campfire or a fireplace.

fire·man [fīr′mən] *n., pl.* **fire·men** [fīr′mən]
1 A man who is trained and employed to put out fires. **2** A man who feeds fuel to a furnace, as for a steam engine or power plant.

fire·place [fīr′plās′] *n.* A structure or opening in which a fire is built, especially one connected with a chimney and opening into a room.

fire·plug [fīr′plug′] *n.* A hydrant.

fire·proof [fīr′proof′] **1** *adj.* Resisting fire; not likely to catch fire. **2** *v.* To make fireproof, as with chemicals, etc.

fire·side [fīr′sīd′] *n.* **1** The hearth or space about a fireplace. **2** Home or home life.

fire station A firehouse.

Fireplace

fire tower A watchtower in which a lookout is stationed to watch for forest fires.

fire·trap [fīr′trap′] *n.* A building which can easily burn down or which does not have adequate means of escape or protection from fire.

fire·wa·ter [fīr′wô′tər] *n.* Whisky or other strong alcoholic drink: a term first used by the North American Indian.

fire·wood [fīr′wood′] *n.* Wood suitable for making a fire, as in a fireplace.

fire·works [fīr′wûrks′] *n.pl.* Things that burn brightly or explode with a loud noise, as firecrackers, rockets, or sparklers. They are used during celebrations, often to create spectacular displays at night.

firm[1] [fûrm] *adj.* **1** That does not readily give in to touch or pressure; solid or unyielding: *firm* snow; *firm* muscle. **2** Difficult to move or loosen: a *firm* structure; a *firm* fastening. **3** Constant; steadfast: a *firm* friend. **4** Strong; vigorous; steady: a *firm* friendship. **— firm′ly** *adv.* **— firm′ness** *n.*

firm[2] [fûrm] *n.* A partnership of two or more persons for conducting business.

fir·ma·ment [fûr′mə·mənt] *n.* The expanse of the heavens; sky: used mostly in poems.

first [fûrst] **1** *adj.* (*sometimes written* **1st**) Coming before another or all others in time, position, or quality: a *first* child; to be *first* in one's class. **2** *adv.* Before all others or anything else: to go *first; First* put your books away. **3** *n.* A person or thing that is first. **4** *n.* The beginning: from the *first.* **5** *n.* (*sometimes written* **1st**) The first day of the month. **6** *adv.* For the first time: I met him *first* ten years ago. **7** *adv.* In preference to anything else; sooner: rather: He would die *first.* **8** *adj.* In music,

---

add, āce, câre, pälm; end, ēqual; it, īce; odd, ōpen, ôrder; took, pool; up, bûrn; ə = a in *above,* e in *sicken,* i in *possible,* o in *melon,* u in *circus;* y**oo** = u in *fuse;* oil; pout; check; ring; thin; **th**is; zh in *vision.* For ¶ reference, see page 64 · HOW TO

playing or singing the higher or principal part: *first* violin.

first aid Treatment given in an emergency to an injured person before full medical attention can be had.

first-born [fûrst′bôrn′] **1** *adj.* Born before any other children in the family; oldest. **2** *n.* A first-born child.

first-class [fûrst′klas′] **1** *adj.* Of the highest type or best quality: a *first-class* store; *first-class* accommodations on a ship. **2** *adj.* Of or having to do with a class of sealed mail, especially letters, made up mostly of written matter. **3** *adv.* By first-class means: to travel *first-class*.

first-hand [fûrst′hand′] *adj., adv.* Directly from the person involved: a *first-hand* report.

first lady (*often written* **First Lady**) The wife of the chief executive of a nation, state, etc.

first lieutenant A military rank. In the U.S. Army, a first lieutenant is a commissioned officer ranking next above a second lieutenant and next below a captain.

first person The form of a pronoun or verb which refers to the speaker. *I, me, we, us, am,* etc., are words in the first person.

first-rate [fûrst′rāt′] **1** *adj.* Of the finest class, quality, or character; excellent. **2** *adv. informal* Excellently; very well: He sings *first-rate*.

firth [fûrth] *n.* An inlet of the sea.

fis·cal [fis′kəl] *adj.* Of or having to do with money matters; financial. A **fiscal year** is any twelve-month period at the end of which business accounts are balanced.

fish [fish] *n., pl.* **fish** or **fish·es,** *v.* **1** *n.* Any of a group of animals that have backbones, live in water, and have gills to breathe with. Fish are usually covered with scales and have fins for moving themselves. **2** *n.* The flesh of a fish used as food. **3** *v.* To catch or try to catch fish. **4** *v.* To grope for and bring out: to *fish* money out of one's pockets. **5** *v.* To try to get or uncover in an indirect manner: to *fish* for information. ◆ *Fish* is the usual plural: There are many *fish* in the stream. However, when different kinds are meant, *fishes* is often used: We saw many fresh-water *fishes* in the market.

fish·er [fish′ər] *n.* **1** A person or animal that fishes. **2** A kind of marten found in North America. **3** The dark brown fur of this animal.

fish·er·man [fish′ər·mən] *n., pl.* **fish·er·men** [fish′ər·mən] A man who fishes for sport or as work.

fish·er·y [fish′ə·rē] *n., pl.* **fish·er·ies 1** The business of catching fish. **2** A place where this is done. **3** A place where fish are bred.

Fisher, about 3 ft. long

fish hawk Another name for OSPREY.

fish·hook [fish′hook′] *n.* A hook, usually barbed, for catching fish.

fish·ing [fish′ing] *n.* The catching of fish, either for a living or for pleasure.

fishing rod A slender pole with a hook, a line, and often a reel, used to catch fish.

fish·mon·ger [fish′mung′gər] *n. British* A person who deals in fish.

fish·wife [fish′wīf′] *n., pl.* **fish·wives** [fish′wīvz′] **1** A woman who sells fish. **2** A woman who uses loud, abusive language.

fish·y [fish′ē] *adj.* **fish·i·er, fish·i·est 1** Having to do with or like fish: a *fishy* smell. **2** Abounding in fish. **3** *informal* Unlikely; improbable; doubtful: a *fishy* story. **4** Without expression; vacant: *fishy* eyes.

fis·sion [fish′ən] *n.* **1** A splitting or breaking apart. **2** The division of a cell or small organism into new cells or organisms, especially as a means of reproduction. **3** In physics, nuclear fission.

fis·sion·a·ble [fish′ən·ə·bəl] *adj.* Capable of undergoing nuclear fission.

fis·sure [fish′ər] *n.* A narrow split or crack, as in a rock.

fist [fist] *n.* A hand that is tightly closed: He punched the bag with his *fist*.

fist·i·cuffs [fis′ti·kufs′] *n.pl.* **1** A fight with the fists. **2** The art of boxing.

fit[1] [fit] *adj.* **fit·ter, fit·test,** *v.* **fit·ted** or **fit, fit·ting,** *n.* **1** *adj.* Right or satisfactory; suitable: This house isn't *fit* to live in. **2** *adj.* Proper or appropriate: It is not *fit* for people to laugh in church. **3** *v.* To be proper or suitable for: The tune of this song *fits* the words. **4** *v.* To provide with what is suitable or necessary: to *fit* a library with book shelves. **5** *v.* To be the right size and shape for: Does Laura's dress *fit* well? Yes, it *fits* her perfectly. **6** *v.* To cause to fit by altering or adjusting: to *fit* a wedding dress. **7** *n.* The way something fits: a loose *fit*. **8** *v.* To put in place carefully or exactly: to *fit* an arrow to a bow. **9** *adj.* In good physical condition; healthy: Andy will soon be *fit* enough to play ball. — **fit′ly** *adv.* — **fit′ness** *n.*

fit[2] [fit] *n.* **1** A sudden attack marked by convulsion or unconsciousness. **2** A sudden attack of something such as coughing or sneezing. **3** A sudden show of feeling that is too strong to be held back: a *fit* of rage.

fit·ful [fit′fəl] *adj.* Ceasing from time to time; not steady; irregular: a *fitful* breeze. — **fit′ful·ly** *adv.*

fit·ter [fit′ər] *n.* **1** A person who checks and adjusts the fit of a garment. **2** A person who puts together pipe or parts of a machine.

fit·ting [fit′ing] **1** *adj.* Suitable; proper: a *fitting* answer. **2** *n.* A trying on of clothes to find out how much altering has to be done to make them fit. — **fit′ting·ly** *adv.*

fit·tings [fit′ingz] *n.pl.* Furnishings, fixtures, or decorations, as for a house.

Fitz·ger·ald [fits′jer′əld], **F. Scott,** 1896–1940, U.S. novelist and short-story writer.

five or **5** [fiv] *n., adj.* One more than four.

Five Nations A confederacy of five Iroquois Indian tribes in New York State.

fix [fiks] **1** *v.* To make or become firm or secure: to *fix* a picture to the wall. **2** *v.* To hold or direct steadily: to *fix* one's eyes on someone. **3** *v.* To settle or decide definitely: to *fix* a date for a party. **4** *v.* To arrange properly; put in order: to *fix* one's hair. **5** *v.* To restore to good condition; repair: to *fix* a rickety table. **6** *v.* To prepare: to *fix* breakfast. **7** *v. informal* To use bribery or other dishonest methods to get a certain result: to *fix* a basketball game. **8** *v. informal* To punish or get even with: I'll *fix* him if he bothers me again. **9** *v.* To place (blame, responsibility, etc.) on a person. **10** *v.* In photography, to bathe (a film) in chemicals so as to prevent fading. **11** *n. informal* An embarrassing or difficult situation: When Jim lost his money he was in a *fix*. — **fix on** To decide upon: We *fixed on* twenty dollars as a reasonable price. — **fix up** *informal* **1** To repair. **2** To arrange or put in order: We *fixed up* the room for the party. **3** To supply the needs of: The manager will *fix* you *up* with a uniform.

fix·a·tion [fik·sā′shən] *n.* **1** The act of fixing. **2** The condition of being fixed or unchanging.

fix·a·tive [fik′sə·tiv] **1** *n.* A substance that fixes or makes permanent. Varnish sprayed on a pastel or crayon drawing to prevent smudging is called a fixative. **2** *adj.* Making permanent.

fixed [fikst] *adj.* **1** Firm; steady: a *fixed* gaze. **2** Agreed upon; set: a *fixed* price. — **fix·ed·ly** [fik′sid·lē] *adv.*

fixed star Any star so far away that it seems to keep the same position in relation to the stars around it.

fix·ings [fik′singz] *n.pl. informal* The things that usually go with a more important thing; trimmings: broiled steak and all the *fixings*.

fix·ture [fiks′chər] *n.* **1** Anything securely fixed or fastened into a permanent position, especially in a building: light *fixtures*. **2** A person or thing thought of as being fixed in a particular place because of having been there so long: Mr. Ogden has become a *fixture* at the club.

Light fixtures

fizz [fiz] **1** *n.* A hissing or bubbling sound. **2** *v.* To bubble and hiss like soda water. — **fizz′y** *adj.*

fiz·zle [fiz′əl] *v.* **fiz·zled, fiz·zling,** *n.* **1** *v.* To make a hissing or sputtering sound. **2** *n.* Such a sound. **3** *v. informal* To fail, especially after a good start: His attempt to paint pictures *fizzled* out. **4** *n. informal* A failure.

fjord [fyôrd] *n.* Another spelling of FIORD.

fl. Abbreviation of FLUID.

Fl A symbol for the element FLUORINE.

Fla. Abbreviation of FLORIDA.

flab·ber·gast [flab′ər·gast] *v. informal* To amaze greatly; astound.

flab·by [flab′ē] *adj.* **flab·bi·er, flab·bi·est** Lacking strength or firmness; soft: Exercise will tone up *flabby* muscles. — **flab′bi·ly** *adv.* — **flab′bi·ness** *n.*

flac·cid [flak′sid] *adj.* Lacking firmness or elasticity; flabby.

flag[1] [flag] *n., v.* **flagged, flag·ging 1** *n.* A piece of cloth, usually rectangular, having certain colors and designs on it. A flag is used as a symbol of a country, state, etc., or as a signal. **2** *v.* To cause to stop by signaling with or as if with a flag: to *flag* a taxi. **3** *v.* To send (information) by signals.

flag[2] [flag] *v.* **flagged, flag·ging** To grow tired or weak; lose vigor; droop: Their spirits *flagged* when no one came to rescue them.

flag[3] [flag] *n.* Either of two plants with sword-shaped leaves, an iris or a marsh plant.

Flag Day June 14th, the anniversary of the day in 1777 when Congress made the Stars and Stripes the flag of the United States.

flag·el·late [flaj′ə·lāt] *v.* **flag·el·lat·ed, flag·el·lat·ing,** *adj.* **1** *v.* To whip; flog; scourge. **2** *adj.* Shaped like a flagellum or whip. — **flag′·el·la′tion** *n.*

fla·gel·lum [flə·jel′əm] *n., pl.* **fla·gel·la** [flə·jel′ə] or **fla·gel·lums 1** A whiplike part, such as one on a one-celled animal, bacterium, etc., which it uses for moving about. **2** A whip.

flag·eo·let [flaj′ə·let′] *n.* A small musical instrument resembling a flute or recorder.

flag·on [flag′ən] *n.* **1** A container with a handle and spout and often a lid on hinges, used for serving liquids. **2** A large wine bottle.

flag·pole [flag′pōl′] *n.* A pole on which a flag is displayed and flown. ◆ *Flagpole* was created by putting together as one word what had been written as two: *flag + pole*.

fla·grant [flā′grənt] *adj.* Openly disgraceful; shockingly bad: a *flagrant* contempt for the law. — **fla′grant·ly** *adv.*

flag·ship [flag′ship′] *n.* The ship carrying the commander of a fleet and displaying his flag.

A flagrant violation

flag·staff [flag′staf′] *n., pl.* **flag·staffs** or **flag·staves** [flag′stāvz′] A flagpole.

flag·stone [flag′stōn′] *n.* A broad, flat stone used in paving footpaths, terraces, etc.

---

add, āce, câre, pälm; end, ēqual; it, īce;   odd, ōpen, ôrder;   tŏŏk, pōol; up, bûrn;

ə = a in *above*, e in *sicken*, i in *possible*, o in *melon*, u in *circus*;   yŏŏ = u in *fuse*; oil; pout;

check; ring; thin; this; zh in *vision*.   For ¶ reference, see page 64 · HOW TO

flail [flāl] **1** *n.* A tool for beating off, or threshing, the heads of ripened grain. It has a long handle to which a shorter, freely swinging bar is attached. **2** *v.* To beat with or as if with a flail.

flair [flâr] *n.* **1** A natural ability or talent; knack: a *flair* for drawing. **2** Sharp perception.

flake [flāk] *n.*, *v.* **flaked, flak·ing 1** *n.* A small, thin chip or fluffy bit of a substance: a *flake* of paint; snow *flakes*. **2** *v.* To form or peel off in flakes: Paint *flaked* from the ceiling.

Flail

flak·y [flā'kē] *adj.* **flak·i·er, flak·i·est 1** Consisting of or like flakes. **2** Easily separated into flakes. **— flak'i·ness** *n.*

flam·boy·ant [flam·boi'ənt] *adj.* **1** Brilliant in color, glowing: a *flamboyant* sunrise. **2** Too gaudy or showy: a *flamboyant* hat. **— flam·boy'ance** *n.* ◆ *Flamboyant* comes from a French word that means *flaming* or *blazing*.

flame [flām] *n.*, *v.* **flamed, flam·ing 1** *n.* The burning gas rising from a fire, usually in glowing orange or yellow tongues. **2** *n.* A single tongue of flame. **3** *v.* To give out flame; blaze. **4** *n.* (*often pl.*) A burning condition: in *flames*. **5** *n.* Something bright, hot, etc., like a flame. **6** *v.* To light up or burn as if on fire: to *flame* with rage. **7** *adj. use* Fervent; passionate: *flaming* courage.

fla·min·go [flə·ming'gō] *n.*, *pl.* **fla·min·gos** or **fla·min·goes** A pink or red wading bird that lives in tropical areas and has a long neck and long legs.

Flamingo, 4 ft. bill to tail

flam·ma·ble [flam'ə·bəl] *adj.* Likely to catch fire easily and burn quickly.

Flan·ders [flan'dərz] *n.* A region in western Europe that includes western Belgium and northern France. It was once a separate country.

flange [flanj] *n.* An edge or ridge on a wheel, pipe, girder, etc., used to attach it to something else or to keep it in place.

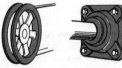

Flanges

flank [flangk] **1** *n.* The side of an animal or person between the ribs and the hip. **2** *n.* The right or left part, as of an army, fleet, football team, etc. **3** *v.* To be located at the

side or sides of: Trees *flanked* the driveway. **4** *v.* To move around the flank of.

flan·nel [flan'əl] **1** *n.* A very soft cotton or wool fabric with a nap. **2** *adj. use: flannel* pajamas. **3** *n.* (*pl.*) Clothing made of flannel, especially trousers.

flap [flap] *v.* **flapped, flap·ping,** *n.* **1** *v.* To cause to move rapidly up and down: The eagle *flapped* its wings. **2** *v.* To have a waving or fluttering motion, as a flag in the wind. **3** *n.* The action or sound of flapping. **4** *n.* A loosely hanging part, often used to cover an opening: Tuck the *flap* inside the envelope; the *flap* of a pocket.

flap·jack [flap'jak'] *n.* A pancake.

flare [flâr] *v.* **flared, flar·ing,** *n.* **1** *v.* To blaze up suddenly with a glaring, unsteady light: If you fan glowing embers, they will *flare* up. **2** *n.* A bright, flickering light lasting for a short time: the *flare* of a match. **3** *n.* A brilliant light used for signaling, lighting up an airfield, etc. **4** *v.* To burst out in sudden anger: to *flare* up at someone. **5** *v.* To widen out in the shape of a bell. **6** *n.* A widening or spreading outward.

flash [flash] **1** *n.* A sudden blaze of brilliant light or fire: a *flash* of lightning. **2** *v.* To give out a sudden blaze; gleam brightly: The searchlight *flashed* across the sky. **3** *v.* To cause to shine brightly: to *flash* a lantern. **4** *n.* A sudden feeling or thought: a *flash* of hope. **5** *v.* To move or appear suddenly or quickly: The train *flashed* by; An idea *flashed* into his mind. **6** *n.* A very short time; instant: He had the answer in a *flash*. **7** *n.* A short news report sent by radio or telegraph. **8** *v.* To send at great speed: to *flash* a message by telegraph. **9** *v. informal* To show suddenly or abruptly: The policeman *flashed* his badge.

flash bulb A light bulb on a camera that flashes a brilliant light as a picture is being taken.

flash card A card bearing a word, letters, numbers, pictures, etc., shown briefly to a class during learning drills.

flash flood A sudden, rushing flood of a river, lake, etc., usually caused by heavy rains.

flash·light [flash'līt'] *n.* **1** A small portable electric light that uses batteries. **2** The burst of bright light from a flash bulb. **3** A bright, flashing light, as in a lighthouse.

flash·y [flash'ē] *adj.* **flash·i·er, flash·i·est 1** Dazzling for a short time. **2** Too showy or gaudy: a *flashy* car. **— flash'i·ly** *adv.*

flask [flask] *n.* A small container with a narrow neck, usually made of glass or metal.

flat¹ [flat] *adj.* **flat·ter, flat·test,** *n.*, *v.* **flat·ted, flat·ting,** *adv.* **1** *adj.* Having a level surface; smooth: The top of a table is *flat*. **2** *n.* The flat part: the *flat* of a sword. **3** *n.* (*pl.*) A level piece of land, as a marsh. **4** *adj.* Stretched or spread out horizontally: *flat* on one's back. **5** *adj.* Not very deep; shallow: a *flat* dish. **6** *n.* A shallow box of earth

Flask

for holding young plants. **7** *adj.* Having lost all or most of its air: a *flat* tire. **8** *n* A flat tire. **9** *adj.* Without much flavor or liveliness: *flat* soda. **10** *adj.* Having little or no gloss: said about paint. **11** *adj.* Not changing; fixed: to charge a *flat* rate **12** *n.* A musical tone half a step below a natural tone of the same name. **13** *n.* The sign (♭) indicating that the note following is a flat. **14** *adv.* Below the proper pitch: to sing *flat*. **15** *v.* To make or become flat. **16** *adv.* In a flat position or way: to fall *flat*. **17** *adv.* Exactly: ten pounds *flat*. **— flat′ly** *adv.* **— flat′ness** *n.*

flat² [flat] *n.* A set of rooms on one floor used as a dwelling; apartment.

flat·boat [flat′bōt′] *n.* A large boat with a flat bottom, used on rivers.

flat·car [flat′kär′] *n.* A railroad car with no sides or roof, used for large pieces of freight.

flat·fish [flat′fish′] *n.*, *pl.* **flat·fish** or **flat·fish·es** A fish having a flattened body and both eyes on the upper side, as a flounder.

flat·foot·ed [flat′fŏŏt′id] *adj.* Having feet with the arches flattened.

flat·i·ron [flat′ī′ərn] *n.* Another name for IRON, a device for pressing clothes, etc.

flat·ten [flat′(ə)n] *v.* To make or become flat.

flat·ter [flat′ər] *v.* **1** To praise insincerely or too much, usually to gain favor. **2** To make appear more attractive than is actually so: That hat *flatters* her. **3** To please: I'm *flattered* that you think so. **— flat′ter·er** *n.*

flat·ter·y [flat′ər·ē] *n.*, *pl.* **flat·ter·ies** **1** The act of flattering. **2** Too much or insincere praise: He used *flattery* to get ahead.

flat·worm [flat′wûrm′] *n.* Any of several kinds of thin, flat worms. Many live in water, and some, as the tapeworm, live in other animals as parasites.

flaunt [flônt] *v.* **1** To wave or flutter freely, as flags. **2** To call too much attention to; show off: to *flaunt* one's knowledge.

fla·vor [flā′vər] **1** *n.* The special taste and smell of something: the *flavor* of cinnamon. **2** *v.* To give flavor to, as by adding spices. **3** *n.* A distinctive quality; aura: the *flavor* of spring. ¶1

fla·vor·ing [flā′vər·ing] *n.* Something added, as to food or drink, to give a certain taste. ¶1

flaw [flô] **1** *n.* A crack, blemish, or other defect: a *flaw* in a gem; Your plan has one *flaw*. **2** *v.* To make a flaw in: His argument was *flawed* by poor reasoning. **3** *v.* To become marred, cracked, etc.

flaw·less [flô′lis] *adj.* Having no defects or blemishes; perfect. **— flaw′less·ly** *adv.*

flax [flaks] *n.* **1** A plant with blue flowers and a slender stem that yields the fiber used in making linen. Linseed oil is produced from its seeds. **2** The fibers of this plant when ready to be spun into thread.

flax·en [flak′sən] *adj.* **1** Having the pale yellow color of flax: *flaxen* hair. **2** Of flax.

flax·seed [flaks′sēd′ *or* flak′sēd′] *n.* The seeds of flax, used to make linseed oil and in medicines.

flay [flā] *v.* **1** To strip off the skin or hide from. **2** To scold or criticize very harshly.

flea [flē] *n.* A tiny, leaping insect without wings. Fleas suck the blood of animals and live on their bodies as parasites.

fleck [flek] **1** *n.* A spot or speck, as of color, dust, etc. **2** *v.* To mark or sprinkle with flecks: Stars *flecked* the evening sky.

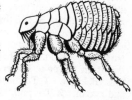

Dog flea, one tenth in. long

fled [fled] Past tense and past participle of FLEE: They *fled* the approaching storm.

fledge [flej] *v.* **fledged, fledg·ing** **1** To grow enough feathers for flying: said about a young bird. **2** To furnish with feathers.

fledg·ling or **fledge·ling** [flej′ling] *n.* **1** A young bird just learning to fly. **2** A young, inexperienced person; beginner.

flee [flē] *v.* **fled, flee·ing** **1** To run away, as from danger or enemies: People *fled* to shelters during the air raid. **2** To run away from: When the fire started, they *fled* the house. **3** To move swiftly: cars *fleeing* by.

fleece [flēs] *n.*, *v.* **fleeced, fleec·ing** **1** *n.* The coat of wool covering a sheep or similar animal. **2** *v.* To shear or clip the fleece from. **3** *v. slang* To rob or cheat: to *fleece* a person of his money.

fleec·y [flē′sē] *adj.* **fleec·i·er, fleec·i·est** Made of or like fleece; downy and soft.

fleet¹ [flēt] *n.* **1** All of the ships belonging to one country, or sailing under one command: the U.S. *fleet*. **2** A group of ships, aircraft, motor vehicles, etc., used together or belonging to one company: a *fleet* of taxicabs.

fleet² [flēt] *adj.* Rapid in movement; swift: to be *fleet* of foot. **— fleet′ness** *n.*

fleet·ing [flē′ting] *adj.* Passing quickly: a *fleeting* moment. **— fleet′ing·ly** *adv.*

Flem·ing [flem′ing] *n.* **1** A person born in Flanders. **2** A Belgian who speaks Flemish.

Flem·ing [flem′ing], **Alexander,** 1881–1955, British scientist. He discovered penicillin.

Flem·ish [flem′ish] **1** *adj.* Of or from Flanders. **2** *n.* **(the Flemish)** The people of Flanders. **3** *n.* The language of Flanders.

flesh [flesh] *n.* **1** The soft parts that cover the bones in a human or animal body. **2** The parts of an animal used for food; meat. **3** The human body, as distinguished from the mind or spirit. **4** Mankind; humanity: the way of all *flesh*. **5** The pulpy, solid part of fruits or vegetables. **— in the flesh 1** Actually present;

in person. **2** Alive. **— one's own flesh and blood** One's blood relatives.

flesh·ly [flesh′lē] *adj.* **flesh·li·er, flesh·li·est** **1** Of the body; bodily. **2** Sensual.

flesh·y [flesh′ē] *adj.* **flesh·i·er, flesh·i·est** Having much flesh; plump or fat.

fleur-de-lis [floŏr′də·lē′] *n., pl.* **fleurs-de-lis** [floŏr′də·lēz′] A design that looks like the iris flower. The fleur-de-lis was the emblem of the former kings of France.

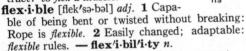

Fleur-de-lis

flew [floŏ] Past tense and past participle of FLY: The butterfly *flew* from flower to flower.

flex [fleks] *v.* **1** To bend: to *flex* one's arm. **2** To pull tight; contract: to *flex* a muscle.

flex·i·ble [flek′sə·bəl] *adj.* **1** Capable of being bent or twisted without breaking: Rope is *flexible*. **2** Easily changed; adaptable: *flexible* rules. **— flex′i·bil′i·ty** *n.*

flick [flik] **1** *n.* A light, snapping movement or blow, as of a whip. **2** *n.* A slight, cracking sound. **3** *v.* To strike at or remove with a quick, light snap: to *flick* crumbs from one's lap. **4** *v.* To cause to move with a snap: to *flick* a dust cloth over furniture.

flick·er¹ [flik′ər] **1** *v.* To gleam or burn with an unsteady, wavering light: The moon's reflection *flickered* among the waves. **2** *n.* A fluttering, unsteady light. **3** *v.* To flutter or quiver; wave to and fro: The leaves are *flickering* in the wind. **4** *n.* A quivering motion or feeling: the *flicker* of a cat's ear; a *flicker* of fear.

flick·er² [flik′ər] *n.* A large woodpecker of North America with a brown back. The undersides of its wings are brightly colored.

flied [flīd] Alternative past tense and past participle of FLY¹ (def. 7): I *flied* out to left field.

fli·er [flī′ər] *n.* **1** Something that can fly, as a bird or insect. **2** A pilot of an airplane. **3** *U.S.* A leaflet or handbill.

flight¹ [flīt] *n.* **1** The act or manner of flying: the *flight* of a bee; a bird of swift *flight*. **2** The distance traveled by an airplane, bird, bullet, etc. **3** A trip in an airplane. **4** A group flying together: a *flight* of swallows; a *flight* of arrows. **5** A soaring above or beyond usual bounds: a *flight* of imagination. **6** A set of stairs, as between floors of a building.

flight² [flīt] *n.* The act of running away; escape. **— put to flight** To cause to run away: Our shouts *put* the dogs *to flight*.

flight·less [flīt′lis] *adj.* Unable to fly: The ostrich is a *flightless* bird.

flight·y [flī′tē] *adj.* **flight·i·er, flight·i·est** Unable to keep one's mind or attention fixed on any one thing; whimsical; frivolous.

flim·sy [flim′zē] *adj.* **flim·si·er, flim·si·est** **1** Ready to fall apart or tear; easily damaged or broken: a *flimsy* old chair; *flimsy* cloth. **2** Not very convincing; weak: She gave a *flimsy* excuse for being late. **— flim′si·ly** *adv.*

◆ *Flimsy* probably comes from the word *film*

plus *-sy* as in *clumsy*. The *i* and the *l* may have been reversed because *flimsy* was somehow easier to pronounce than *filmsy*.

flinch [flinch] **1** *v.* To shrink back, as from anything unpleasant or dangerous; wince: She *flinched* at the sight of the dentist's drill. **2** *n.* The act of drawing back or wincing.

Boy flinching

fling [fling] *v.* **flung, fling·ing,** *n.* **1** *v.* To throw, especially with force; hurl: He *flung* his coat on the floor. **2** *n.* The act of flinging; a throw. **3** *v.* To rush headlong: to *fling* out the door in a rage. **4** *n.* A brief time of freedom and fun: George had a last *fling* before school opened. **5** *n.* A Scottish dance with rapid steps and flinging arm movements. **6** *n. informal* An attempt; try: to have a *fling* at painting.

flint [flint] *n.* A hard, dark stone which produces sparks when struck against steel.

flint·lock [flint′lok′] *n.* **1** A gunlock in which a piece of flint is struck against steel in order to light the gunpowder. **2** An old-fashioned type of gun having such a lock.

flint·y [flin′tē] *adj.* **flint·i·er, flint·i·est** **1** Made of or containing flint: *flinty* soil. **2** Like flint; very hard or cruel: a *flinty* heart.

flip [flip] *v.* **flipped, flip·ping,** *n., adj.* **1** *v.* To move suddenly or jerkily: He *flipped* over in a somersault. **2** *n.* A quick snap or jerk. **3** *v.* To toss up and over, often with a snapping movement of the thumb: to *flip* a coin. **4** *adj. informal* Impertinent; flippant.

flip·pant [flip′ənt] *adj.* Not respectful or serious; too smart or pert: a *flippant* remark. **— flip′pan·cy** *n.* **— flip′pant·ly** *adv.*

flip·per [flip′ər] *n.* **1** A broad, flat limb, as of a seal, adapted for swimming. **2** A broad, flat shoe like a fin, worn by skin divers.

flirt [flûrt] **1** *v.* To act in an affectionate or loving way without being serious; play at love. **2** *n.* A person who flirts. **3** *v.* To expose oneself to something, often carelessly or not seriously: to *flirt* with danger. **4** *v.* To snap or move quickly; flick: Mockingbirds *flirt* their tails. **5** *n.* A sudden, jerky movement.

flir·ta·tion [flûr·tā′shən] *n.* **1** The act of flirting. **2** A brief and casual love affair.

flir·ta·tious [flûr·tā′shəs] *adj.* **1** Having to do with flirtation: a *flirtatious* look. **2** Having the habit of flirting: Sheila is a very *flirtatious* girl. **— flir·ta′tious·ly** *adv.*

flit [flit] *v.* **flit·ted, flit·ting** **1** To move or fly rapidly and lightly; dart: Birds *flitted* among the trees. **2** To pass rapidly: Vacation days seem to *flit* by.

flitch [flich] *n.* A salted and smoked cut of meat from the side of a pig: a *flitch* of bacon.

float [flōt] **1** *v.* To rest or cause to rest on the surface of a liquid, such as water, without sinking: A life preserver *floats*. **2** *n.* An object that floats or holds up something else in a liquid, as an anchored raft at a beach, a piece of cork attached to a fishing line, etc. **3** *v.* To be carried along gently on the surface of a liquid or through the air; drift: Fog *floated* over the city. **4** *v.* To move lightly and without effort: The dancer *floated* across the stage. **5** *n.* A wheeled platform or truck on which an exhibit is carried in a parade.

flock [flok] **1** *n.* A group of animals of the same kind herded, feeding, or moving together: a *flock* of sheep; a *flock* of pigeons. **2** *n.* A large number or group: a *flock* of people. **3** *v.* To come or move together in a flock or crowd: to *flock* together; People *flock* to the beaches in hot weather. **4** *n.* The people belonging to the congregation of a church.

floe [flō] *n.* A large, almost flat field of floating ice.

flog [flog] *v.* **flogged, flog·ging** To beat hard with a whip, stick, etc.

flood [flud] **1** *n.* A great flow of water, especially over land not usually covered with water. **2** *v.* To cover, fill, or pour into, as with a flood: The water from the broken dam *flooded* the town; Sunshine *flooded* the porch. **3** *v.* To overflow: After the storm, the lake *flooded*. **4** *n.* The coming in of the tide; high tide. **5** *n.* Any great flow or stream: a *flood* of words. **— the Flood** The deluge in the time of Noah, as told in the Old Testament.

flood·gate [flud′gāt′] *n.* **1** A gate or valve that controls the flow of water in a canal, stream, etc. **2** Anything that restrains or holds back: to open the *floodgates* of anger.

flood·light [flud′līt′] *n.* **1** A lamp that gives a very bright, wide beam of light. **2** The light from such a lamp.

floor [flôr] **1** *n.* The surface in a room or building upon which one walks. **2** *v.* To cover or provide with a floor: The kitchen was *floored* with tiles. **3** *n.* A story of a building: We live on the third *floor*. **4** *n.* The lowest surface; bottom: the *floor* of the sea. **5** *n.* The right to speak at a meeting: John has the *floor* now. **6** *v.* To knock down, as to the floor. **7** *v. informal* To bewilder or surprise; flabbergast.

Floodlights

floor·ing [flôr′ing] *n.* **1** Material for the making of a floor. **2** A floor or floors.

floor·walk·er [flôr′wôk′ər] *n.* A person who supervises sales people and assists customers in a department of a large store.

flop [flop] *v.* **flopped, flop·ping,** *n.* **1** *v.* To move about heavily and clumsily: The seal *flopped* across the stage. **2** *v.* To fall or cause to drop heavily: He *flopped* into bed. **3** *v.* To flap loosely, as in a wind. **4** *n.* The act or sound of flopping. **5** *n. informal* A total failure.

flop·py [flop′ē] *adj.* **flop·pi·er, flop·pi·est** *informal* Flapping loosely; likely to bounce around: Dachshunds have *floppy* ears.

flo·ra [flôr′ə] *n.* All the plants of a particular place or period of time.

flo·ral [flô′rəl] *adj.* Of, like, or having to do with flowers: a *floral* wreath.

Flor·ence [flôr′əns] *n.* A city in central Italy.

Flor·en·tine [flôr′ən·tēn] **1** *adj.* Of or coming from Florence. **2** *n.* A person born or living in Florence.

flor·id [flôr′id] *adj.* **1** Having a ruddy, flushed color: a *florid* complexion. **2** Decorated very much; flowery: *florid* architecture.

Flor·i·da [flôr′ə·də] *n.* A state in the SE U.S.

flor·in [flôr′in] *n.* Any of several gold or silver coins used at different times in various countries of Europe.

flo·rist [flôr′ist] *n.* A person who sells flowers or raises them to sell.

floss [flôs] *n.* **1** Soft, silky fibers, as those produced by the milkweed. **2** Glossy, untwisted silk thread used in embroidery. **3** A similar, waxed thread used to clean between teeth.

flo·til·la [flō·til′ə] *n.* **1** A fleet of boats or small ships. **2** A small fleet of ships.

flot·sam [flot′səm] *n.* Parts of a wrecked ship or its cargo drifting on the water.

flounce[1] [flouns] *v.* **flounced, flounc·ing,** *n.* **1** *v.* To move or go with exaggerated tosses of the body. **2** *n.* The act of flouncing.

flounce[2] [flouns] *n., v.* **flounced, flounc·ing** **1** *n.* A gathered or pleated ruffle used for trimming skirts, etc., sewn on by one edge. **2** *v.* To decorate with a flounce or flounces.

floun·der[1] [floun′dər] *v.* **1** To struggle clumsily; move awkwardly, as through mud or snow. **2** To struggle in speech or action as if confused: He forgot his lines but *floundered* along.

floun·der[2] [floun′dər] *n., pl.* **floun·der** or **floun·ders** A flatfish valued as food.

Dress with flounces

flour [flour] **1** *n.* A fine, soft powder made by grinding wheat or other grain, and used in making bread, cake, etc. **2** *v.* To cover or sprinkle with flour. **— flour′y** *adj.*

flour·ish [flûr′ish] **1** *v.* To grow or fare well or prosperously; thrive: Chrysanthemums *flourish* in cool weather. **2** *v.* To wave about or brandish: The lawyer *flourished* the photograph before the jury. **3** *n.* The act of waving about or shaking. **4** *n.* Showy display in doing anything: She sang the song with a *flourish.* **5** *n.* A curve or decorative stroke in handwriting. **6** *n.* A showy, lively passage of music; fanfare.

flout [flout] *v.* To treat with open contempt; scoff at; defy: to *flout* tradition.

flow [flō] **1** *v.* To move along or pour steadily and smoothly: said about water or other fluids. **2** *n.* Something that flows: a *flow* of blood. **3** *v.* To move steadily and freely: The children *flowed* through the gates. **4** *v.* To hang or ripple down loosely: Hair *flowed* over her shoulders. **5** *n.* The way something flows: the elegant *flow* of a long dress. **6** *n.* The amount of something that flows: a daily *flow* of 500 barrels of oil. **7** *n.* The coming in of the tide.

flow·er [flou′ər *or* flour] **1** *n.* The part of a plant or tree that encloses the seeds; blossom. A flower usually has brightly colored petals. **2** *n.* Any plant that produces such blossoms. **3** *v.* To produce flowers; bloom: to *flower* in the spring. **4** *n.* The finest part or result of anything: the *flower* of our youth. **5** *n.* The time when something is at its finest: when knighthood was in *flower.* **6** *v.* To reach fullest growth or development: His musical talent *flowered* early.

flow·ered [flou′ərd] *adj.* Covered or decorated with flowers or a floral pattern: a *flowered* fabric.

flow·er·pot [flou′ər·pot′] *n.* A pot to be filled with earth and used for growing plants.

flow·er·y [flou′ər·ē *or* flour′ē] *adj.* **flow·er·i·er, flow·er·i·est 1** Covered or decorated with flowers. **2** Full of fancy words and showy language: a *flowery* poem.

flown [flōn] Past participle of FLY[1].

flu [flōo] *n. informal* Influenza.

fluc·tu·ate [fluk′chŏo·āt] *v.* **fluc·tu·at·ed, fluc·tu·at·ing** To change or move in an irregular manner or up and down: His temperature *fluctuated* often. **— fluc′tu·a′tion** *n.*

flue [flōo] *n.* A tube, as in a chimney, through which smoke or hot air is drawn off.

flu·en·cy [flōo′ən·sē] *n.* Smoothness and ease in speech or writing.

flu·ent [flōo′ənt] *adj.* **1** Able to speak or write with smoothness or ease. **2** Spoken or written with smoothness or ease: She speaks *fluent* German. **— flu′ent·ly** *adv.*

fluff [fluf] **1** *n.* A very soft, light mass of wool, fur, feathers, or other downy substance. **2** *v.* To make (pillows, hair, feathers, etc.) soft and light by shaking or patting.

fluff·y [fluf′ē] *adj.* **fluff·i·er, fluff·i·est 1** Like fluff; light and frothy: Beaten egg whites are *fluffy.* **2** Covered or filled with fluff: *fluffy* kittens; *fluffy* blankets. **— fluff′i·ly** *adv.* **— fluff′i·ness** *n.*

flu·id [flōo′id] **1** *n.* Any substance able to flow easily; a liquid or gas. Water, air, and steam are fluids. **2** *adj.* Able to flow or pour easily; not solid. **3** *adj.* Changing or flowing, as a fluid: *fluid* opinions. **— flu·id·i·ty** [flōo·id′ə·tē] *n.*

fluke[1] [flōok] *n.* **1** Any of several kinds of flat, parasitic worms living in the livers of some animals. **2** Another name for a FLATFISH or FLOUNDER.

fluke[2] [flōok] *n.* **1** The triangular head at the end of either arm of an anchor. A fluke sticks into the ground to hold the anchor fast. **2** A barb on an arrow head or harpoon. **3** Either of the two parts of a whale's tail.

fluke[3] [flōok] *n. informal* Any piece of good luck, especially a lucky stroke in a game.

flume [flōom] *n.* **1** A narrow gap in a mountain through which a torrent passes. **2** A long, sloping trough filled with running water. It is used to carry logs or supply water.

flung [flung] Past tense and past participle of FLING: Jack *flung* his coat on a chair.

flunk [flungk] *informal* **1** *v.* To fail, as a school subject or examination. **2** *v.* To give a failing grade to: The teacher *flunked* him. **3** *n.* A failure in school work. **— flunk out** To leave or cause to leave a class, school, or college because of failure.

flunk·y [flung′kē] *n., pl.* **flunk·ies 1** A manservant or footman: no longer used. **2** A person who fawns upon or flatters others, especially those in authority.

flu·o·res·cent [flōo′ə·res′ənt] *adj.* Giving off light when acted upon by certain forms of energy, as by ultraviolet rays. A **fluorescent lamp** has a **fluorescent tube** filled with mercury vapor and coated with fluorescent material on the inside. When an electric current passes through the mercury vapor, ultraviolet rays strike the coating and cause it to give off light. **— flu′o·res′cence** *n.*

fluor·i·date [flŏor′ə·dāt] *v.* **fluor·i·dat·ed, fluor·i·dat·ing** To add a fluoride to (drinking water), especially to prevent tooth decay. **— fluor′i·da′tion** *n.*

flu·o·ride [flōo′(ə·)rīd] *n.* In chemistry, a compound of fluorine and another element.

flu·o·rine [flōo′(ə·)rēn] *n.* In chemistry, a greenish, poisonous, extremely active gaseous element that forms many compounds.

fluor·o·scope [flŏor′ə·skōp] *n.* A device for looking at the shadows on a fluorescent screen made by objects put between the screen and a direct beam of X-rays. A fluoroscope is often used to examine the bones and inner organs of the body.

flur·ry [flûr′ē] *n., pl.* **flur·ries,** *v.* **flur·ried, flur·ry·ing 1** *n.* A sudden, brief gust of wind. **2** *n.* A light, brief rain or snowfall, often with wind. **3** *n.* A sudden commotion; stir. **4** *v.* To confuse or excite; fluster: The crowd's noise *flurried* the players.

flush[1] [flush] **1** *v.* To become or cause to become red in the face; redden: He *flushed* with embarrassment. **2** *n.* A warm, rosy glow; blush. **3** *v.* To wash out or purify, as a sewer, with a gush of water or other liquid. **4** *v.* To flow or rush suddenly; flood. **5** *n.* A sudden gush, as of water. **6** *v.* To stir with a sudden, strong feeling: The winning team was *flushed* with pride. **7** *n.* A warm feeling of excitement or pleasure.

flush[2] [flush] **1** *adj.* Even or level with another surface: The tiles are all *flush.* **2** *adv.* In a flush manner; on an even level: The door should fit *flush* with the frame. **3** *adj.* Having plenty of money on hand.

flush[3] [flush] *v.* To drive or rush from a cover or hiding place: to *flush* rabbits from their burrows.

flus·ter [flus′tər] **1** *v.* To make confused or upset: Big crowds *fluster* some people. **2** *n.* A confused or excited condition.

flute [floot] *n., v.* **flut·ed, flut·ing 1** *n.* A musical wind instrument having a high, clear pitch and made in the shape of a narrow tube. A flute is played by blowing across a mouthpiece at one end and by opening and closing holes along its length with the fingers or with keys. **2** *v.* To play on the flute. **3** *v.* To make flutelike sounds by whistling or singing. **4** *n.* In architecture, one of the rounded grooves cut from the top to the bottom of a column. **5** *n.* A small ruffle or pleat in cloth. **6** *v.* To make flutes in (columns or cloth).

Flute

flut·ing [floo′ting] *n.* **1** Rounded grooves in a column. **2** Small ruffles or pleats made in cloth.

flut·ist [floo′tist] *n.* A person who plays the flute.

flut·ter [flut′ər] **1** *v.* To wave back and forth irregularly: The line of clothes *fluttered* in the wind. **2** *v.* To flap the wings without really flying, or fly clumsily. **3** *v.* To move or cause to move rapidly or unevenly; quiver: Her heart *fluttered* as she walked out on the stage. **4** *n.* A waving or quivering motion; fluttering. **5** *v.* To excite or fluster. **6** *n.* Excitement; stir: The new boy caused a *flutter* among the girls.

flux [fluks] *n.* **1** A flowing or pouring out. **2** Constant change or movement: in a state of *flux.* **3** An abnormal flow of fluid from the body during an illness. **4** A substance used to help melt or solder metals together.

fly[1] [flī] *v.* **flew,** *for def. 7* **flied, flown,** *for def. 7* **flied, fly·ing,** *n., pl.* **flies 1** *v.* To move through the air on wings, as birds or insects. **2** *v.* To move or travel through the air in an aircraft. **3** *v.* To cause to fly in the air: to *fly* a kite. **4** *v.* To move very fast: Summer *flies* by. **5** *v.* To wave or flutter in the air, as a flag. **6** *v.* To run away; flee: to *fly* for one's life. **7** *v.* In baseball, to bat the ball high over the field. **8** *n.* A baseball batted high over the field. **9** *n.* A flap covering a zipper or buttons on the opening of a garment, especially on a pair of pants. **— on the fly 1** While still in the air: to catch a ball *on the fly.* **2** *informal* In motion; very busy.

fly[2] [flī] *n., pl.* **flies 1** One of a large group of small, two-winged insects, especially the housefly. **2** Any of several other flying insects, as the dragonfly, May fly, etc. **3** A fishhook to which bits of colored cloth or feathers are tied so that it looks like an insect. **— fly in the ointment** Any small, annoying thing that spoils one's enjoyment.

fly·catch·er [flī′kach′ər] *n.* A bird that catches and eats insects as it flies.

fly·er [flī′ər] *n.* Another spelling of FLIER.

flying buttress A support built out from a wall, connecting with it by an arch to brace it against outward pressure.

flying fish A fish with large, flat, winglike fins that enable it to jump out of the water and glide through the air for short distances.

flying saucer Any of various strange, moving objects shaped like a disk which some people have reported seeing in the sky.

Flying buttresses

flying squirrel A squirrel having a wide fold of skin connecting its front and back legs on both sides, enabling it to make gliding leaps.

fly·leaf [flī′lēf′] *n., pl.* **fly·leaves** [flī′lēvz′] An extra blank page at the beginning or end of a book.

fly·pa·per [flī′pā′pər] *n.* A strip of paper coated with a sticky, often poisonous substance. It is placed so as to catch and kill flies.

fly·speck [flī′spek′] **1** *n.* A small speck of dirt left by a fly. **2** *n.* Any small speck. **3** *v.* To mark with flyspecks.

fly·wheel [flī′(h)wēl] *n.* A heavy wheel attached to a revolving shaft to keep the speed of the shaft from changing suddenly.

FM or **F.M.** Abbreviation for FREQUENCY MODULATION, a form of radio transmission.

f number In photography, a number that shows the effectiveness of a lens in admitting light to a camera. The lower the f number, the more light the lens admits.

foal [fōl] **1** *n.* A young horse, donkey, zebra, etc. **2** *v.* To give birth to (a foal).

foam [fōm] **1** *n.* A white, frothy mass of small bubbles. Foam forms on a liquid when it is shaken or on the crest of a wave. **2** *v.* To form or give off foam; froth.

foam rubber A firm, spongy rubber, used especially in mattresses, pillows, and cushions.

foam·y [fō'mē] *adj.* **foam·i·er, foam·i·est 1** Full of or consisting of foam: *foamy* milk. **2** Like foam. — **foam'i·ness** *n.*

fob [fob] *n.* **1** A small pocket for a watch. **2** A short chain or ribbon attached to a watch and dangling from such a pocket. **3** An ornament worn on the dangling end of such a chain.

F.O.B. or **f.o.b.** Abbreviation of *free on board,* put after a price to show that an article will be delivered without charge onto the train, ship, etc., which is to transport it. The buyer must pay all other shipping costs.

fo·cal [fō'kəl] *adj.* Of or having to do with a focus. **Focal distance** (or **focal length**) is the distance from the center of a lens or curved mirror to its focus.

fo·ci [fō'sī] Plural of FOCUS.

fo'c's'le [fōk'səl] *n.* A contraction of FORE-CASTLE.

fo·cus [fō'kəs] *n., pl.* **fo·cus·es** or **fo·ci** [fō'sī], *v.* **fo·cused** or **fo·cussed, fo·cus·ing** or **fo·cus·sing 1** *n.* In physics, a point at which light rays, sound waves, radio waves, etc., come together after passing through something that bends them,

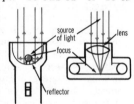

Foci in flashlight and camera

as a lens, or after bouncing off a curved reflector. **2** *v.* To bring (light rays, sound waves, etc.) to a focus. **3** *n.* Focal distance. **4** *n.* An adjustment, as of the eye, a lens, etc., that produces a clear image: to bring binoculars into *focus.* **5** *v.* To adjust the focus of (the eye, a lens, etc.) to receive a clear image. **6** *n.* The place where a visual image is clearly formed, as in a camera. **7** *v.* To become focused: Our eyes *focused* on the door. **8** *n.* Any central point, as of interest or importance: The new girl was the *focus* of attention. **9** *v.* To fix; concentrate: to *focus* one's mind on a problem. **10** *n., pl.* **fo·ci** Either of two points inside an ellipse, the sum of whose distances to any point on the curve is always the same.

fod·der [fod'ər] *n.* Coarse feed for horses, cattle, etc., as hay or stalks of corn.

foe [fō] *n.* An enemy: friend or *foe?*

foe·tus [fē'təs] *n.* Another spelling of FETUS.

fog [fog] *n., v.* **fogged, fog·ging 1** *n.* Condensed, watery vapor suspended in the air; dense mist through which it is hard to see. **2** *v.* To cover or become covered with or as if with fog; cloud or blur: The photograph was *fogged* during development; His glasses *fogged* up. **3** *n.* A bewildered, confused condition: to be in a *fog.* **4** *v.* To make or become confused.

fog·gy [fog'ē] *adj.* **fog·gi·er, fog·gi·est 1** Full of fog. **2** Dim, cloudy, or confused: not even a *foggy* notion. — **fog'gi·ness** *n.*

fog·horn [fog'hôrn'] *n.* A horn or loud whistle to warn ships during a fog.

fo·gy [fō'gē] *n., pl.* **fo·gies** A person who is fussy and old-fashioned in his ideas or ways.

foi·ble [foi'bəl] *n.* A slight, easily excusable fault or weak point in a person's nature.

foil[1] [foil] *v.* To keep from succeeding in some purpose; outwit and thwart.

foil[2] [foil] *n.* A light, narrow sword used in fencing. It has a button at its tip to prevent injury.

foil[3] [foil] *n.* **1** Metal that has been hammered or rolled into thin, flexible sheets: aluminum *foil.* **2** Something that by contrast shows up the qualities of something else: The clumsy puppy was a *foil* for the graceful kitten.

foist [foist] *v.* To pass off or present wrongfully as being good or genuine: to *foist* a bad check on someone.

fold[1] [fōld] **1** *v.* To turn, bend, or crease so that one part covers another: to *fold* a blanket. **2** *n.* A part of a thing folded over another part: the *folds* of a curtain. **3** *n.* The crease made by folding. **4** *v.* To place or twine together, especially against the body: to *fold* one's arms. **5** *v.* To embrace or hug gently: She *folded* the puppy in her arms. **6** *v.* To wrap up: *Fold* the picture in paper.

fold[2] [fōld] *n.* **1** A pen for sheep. **2** The congregation of a church.

-fold A suffix meaning: **1** Having a certain number of parts: a *threefold* piece of luck. **2** An amount multiplied by a certain number: increased a *hundredfold.*

fold·er [fōl'dər] *n.* **1** A sheet of heavy paper folded double or an envelope for holding loose papers. **2** A booklet made of folded sheets. **3** A person or machine that folds something.

fo·li·age [fō'lē·ij *or* fō'lij] *n.* The leaves on a tree or other plant.

fo·li·a·tion [fō'lē·ā'shən] *n.* The process of sprouting leaves.

fo·lic acid [fō'lik] One of the vitamins of the B complex group, found in green leaves, mushrooms, etc., and used in treating anemia.

fo·li·o [fō'lē·ō] *n., pl.* **fo·li·os,** *adj.* **1** *n.* A sheet of paper folded once to form four pages of a book. **2** *n.* A book of the largest size, with pages made by folding large sheets once. **3** *n.* Any page number of a book. **4** *adj.* Having to do with or being the size of a folio.

folk [fōk] *n., pl.* **folk** or **folks,** *adj.* **1** *n.* A people, nation, or race. **2** *adj.* Having to do with or coming from the common people: *folk* songs. **3** *n.* People in general or as a group: old *folk*; young *folk.* **4** *n.* (*pl.*) *informal* One's family or relatives: his wife's *folks.*

folk dance A dance that was started among the common people of a region or country.

folk·lore [fōk'lôr'] *n.* The beliefs, stories, and customs preserved among a people or tribe.

F

folk singer A person or entertainer who sings folk songs. **— folk singing**

folk song A song originating and passed down among the common people of a region or country.

folk·sy [fōk'sē] *adj.* **folk·si·er, folk·si·est** *U.S. informal* Friendly, neighborly, or casual.

fol·li·cle [fol'i·kəl] *n.* A small cavity or sac in the body. Hair grows from follicles.

fol·low [fol'ō] *v.* **1** To go or come after: The dog *followed* me home; Summer *follows* spring. **2** To keep to the course of: to *follow* a path. **3** To come after as a result: Fresh, cool air *follows* a thunderstorm. **4** To act in accordance with; obey: to *follow* orders. **5** To watch or observe closely: to *follow* a tennis match. **6** To understand clearly: I don't *follow* your line of thought. **7** To engage in as one's work: to *follow* a trade. **— follow through** In games, to continue a stroke after having struck the ball. **— follow up 1** To pursue closely. **2** To add to the effect of by further action.

fol·low·er [fol'ō·ər] *n.* **1** A person or thing that follows, as a person who follows the beliefs of another. **2** A servant or attendant.

fol·low·ing [fol'ō·ing] **1** *adj.* Coming next in order: the *following* week. **2** *n.* A group of disciples or followers. **— the following** The persons or things about to be mentioned.

fol·ly [fol'ē] *n., pl.* **fol·lies 1** Lack of sense; foolishness. **2** A foolish idea or act.

fo·ment [fō·ment'] *v.* To stir up or promote (trouble): to *foment* rebellion.

fond [fond] *adj.* **1** Loving or affectionate: a *fond* father; a *fond* farewell. **2** Foolishly loving and indulgent. **3** Cherished: *fond* hopes. **— fond of** Having a liking for or love of: *fond of* animals. **— fond'ly** *adv.* **— fond'·ness** *n.*

fon·dle [fon'dəl] *v.* **fon·dled, fon·dling** To handle lovingly; caress: to *fondle* a baby.

font¹ [font] *n.* **1** A basin for holy water or for water used in baptism. **2** A source, as a spring or fountain: a *font* of knowledge.

font² [font] *n.* A complete assortment of printing type of a particular size and style.

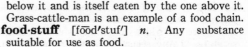

Girl fondling a kitten

food [fōōd] *n.* **1** Anything that is eaten, drunk, or absorbed by plants, animals, or people to make them grow and go on living. **2** Nourishment taken in solid form, as distinguished from drink. **3** Anything that feeds or nourishes: His speech gave us *food* for thought.

food chain A group of plants and animals connected with each other in such a way that each member of the group feeds upon the one below it and is itself eaten by the one above it. Grass-cattle-man is an example of a food chain.

food·stuff [fōōd'stuf'] *n.* Any substance suitable for use as food.

fool [fōōl] **1** *n.* A silly, stupid person who can be easily tricked. **2** *n.* A clown formerly kept by noblemen or princes to entertain the household; jester. **3** *v.* To behave as a fool; tease or joke. **4** *v.* To make a fool of; deceive.

fool·har·dy [fōōl'här'dē] *adj.* **fool·har·di·er, fool·har·di·est** Daring in a foolish, reckless way. **— fool'har'di·ness** *n.*

fool·ish [fōō'lish] *adj.* Showing lack of good sense; unwise; silly. **— fool'ish·ly** *adv.* **— fool'ish·ness** *n.*

fool·proof [fōōl'prōōf'] *adj.* So simple, strong, or trustworthy that even a fool could not cause it to fail: a *foolproof* plan.

fools·cap [fōōlz'kap'] *n.* A size of writing paper about 13 inches wide and 16 inches long.

fool's gold Iron pyrites, a mineral sometimes mistaken for gold.

foot [fōōt] *n., pl.* **feet,** *v.* **1** *n.* The end part of the leg of a person or animal, upon which it stands or moves. **2** *v. informal* To walk: They had to *foot* it home. **3** *n.* Infantry. **4** *n.* The part farthest from the top or head; base, bottom, or end: the *foot* of a ladder; the *foot* of a list. **5** *n.* The end of a bed where one's feet go. **6** *n.* The part of a stocking or boot that covers the foot. **7** *n.* A measure of length equal to 12 inches. **8** *n.* In poetry, one of the rhythmic parts into which a line is divided. "Upŏn/thŏse boughs/thăt shāke/ăgāinst/thĕ cōld"/ is a line having five feet. **9** *v. informal* To pay: to *foot* a bill. **10** *v.* To add: *Foot* up the bill. **— on foot 1** Walking or standing. **2** In progress. **— put one's foot down** *informal* To act firmly.

foot·ball [fōōt'bôl'] *n.* **1** An inflated, leather-covered ball used in various games. The U.S. football is oval. **2** A game played in the U.S. by two teams on a field, the object being to carry the ball over the opponent's goal line or kick it over the goal.

foot·bridge [fōōt'brij'] *n.* A bridge for persons on foot.

foot·can·dle [fōōt'kan'dəl] *n.* A unit used in measuring how well a surface is lighted.

foot·ed [fōōt'id] *adj.* **1** Having a foot or feet. **2** Having a certain kind or number of feet: often used in combination: a *flatfooted* man; a *four-footed* animal.

foot·fall [fōōt'fôl'] *n.* The sound of a footstep.

foot·hill [fōōt'hil'] *n.* A low hill at the base of a mountain or a range of mountains.

foot·hold [fōōt'hōld'] *n.* **1** A place on which the foot can rest securely, as in climbing. **2** A firm position from which one can carry forward some action: to get a *foothold* in politics.

---

add, āce, câre, pälm; end, ēqual; it, īce; odd, ōpen, ôrder; tŏŏk, pōōl; up, bûrn;
ə = a in *above*, e in *sicken*, i in *possible*, o in *melon*, u in *circus*; yōō = u in *fuse*; oil; pout;
check; ring; thin; this; zh in *vision*. For ¶ reference, see page 64 · HOW TO

foot·ing [foot′ing] *n.* **1** A secure position or placing of the feet: to lose one's *footing* and slip. **2** A place on which to stand, walk, or climb securely. **3** Any secure position or foundation. **4** Relationship; standing: to be on a friendly *footing* with one's classmates.

foot·lights [foot′līts′] *n.pl.* Lights in a row along the very front of a stage floor.

foot·man [foot′mən] *n.*, *pl.* **foot·men** [foot′· mən] A male servant who answers the door, waits on table, or attends a rider in a carriage,

foot·note [foot′nōt′] *n.* A note at the bottom of a page explaining something on the page or telling where the information came from.

foot·pad [foot′pad′] *n.* A highwayman who goes on foot: seldom used today.

foot·path [foot′path′] *n.* A path to be used only by persons on foot.

foot-pound [foot′pound′] *n.* The amount of energy needed to raise a mass of one pound a distance of one foot. This is used as a unit of energy.

foot·print [foot′print′] *n.* The mark left by a foot or shoe in sand, mud, snow, etc.

foot·rest [foot′rest′] *n.* A small stool or other support on which the feet may be placed.

foot soldier An infantryman.

foot·sore [foot′sôr′] *adj.* Having sore or tired feet, as from walking.

foot·step [foot′step′] *n.* **1** A step made by a foot in walking, or its sound. **2** The distance covered in a single step. **3** A footprint.

foot·stool [foot′stool′] *n.* A low stool on which to rest the feet when sitting down.

foot·work [foot′wûrk′] *n.* Use or control of the feet, as in boxing, tennis, or dancing.

fop [fop] *n.* A man very vain about his clothes and looks; a dandy. **—fop′pish** *adj.*

for [fôr] **1** *prep.* To the distance of: The land is flat *for* many miles. **2** *prep.* For the period of time of: We waited *for* an hour. **3** *prep.* To the amount of: a check *for* six dollars. **4** *prep.* At the cost of: to buy a ticket *for* fifty cents. **5** *prep.* As the equivalent of in exchange: You will get ten points *for* each correct answer. **6** *prep.* On account of; because of: He is liked *for* his pleasant smile. **7** *conj.* Because; as: I am thirsty, *for* the sun is very hot. **8** *prep.* In spite of: I believe in it *for* all your arguments. **9** *prep.* To be used at, in, on, or by: tickets *for* a play; a time *for* work; a collar *for* a dog. **10** *prep.* Appropriate to: It's time *for* a change. **11** *prep.* In favor, support, or approval of: We voted *for* the proposal. **12** *prep.* Directed toward; with regard to: love *for* one's country; an eye *for* bargains. **13** *prep.* As affecting: good *for* your health. **14** *prep.* Sent or given to: a package *for* you. **15** *prep.* In honor of: He was named *for* his grandfather. **16** *prep.* In proportion to: big *for* his age. **17** *prep.* Considering the usual qualities of: She is strong *for* a girl. **18** *prep.* As being: I took him *for* his twin brother. **19** *prep.* In place of: to use a mat on the floor *for* a bed. **20** *prep.* With the purpose of: She reads *for* pleasure. **21** *prep.* In order to go to: to leave *for* school. **22** *prep.* In order to find, get, keep, etc.: He was looking *for* his coat. **— O for** I wish I had: *O for* a place to sit down!

for·age [fôr′ij] *n.*, *v.* **for·aged, for·ag·ing 1** *n.* Food suitable for horses, cattle, etc. **2** *v.* To search about for something, as for food or supplies: Pigs like to *forage* in the farmyard; He was *foraging* in the closet for his shoe. **3** *v.* To plunder in order to get supplies, as soldiers do during war. **—for′ag·er** *n.*

for·ay [fôr′ā] **1** *n.* A raid or expedition, as for plunder or in a war: a brief *foray* behind enemy lines. **2** *v.* To raid.

for·bade or **for·bad** [fər·bad′] Past tense of FORBID.

for·bear[1] [fôr·bâr′] *v.* **for·bore, for·borne, for·bear·ing 1** To refrain or hold back from (doing something): to *forbear* answering a silly question. **2** To show patience or self-control.

for·bear[2] [fôr′bâr′] *n.* Another spelling of FOREBEAR.

for·bear·ance [fôr·bâr′əns] *n.* **1** The act of forbearing or holding back. **2** Patience; self-control.

for·bid [fər·bid′] *v.* **for·bade** or **for·bad, for·bid·den, for·bid·ding** To refuse to allow; keep from doing or being done: Eating is *forbidden* during class; Joey's mother *forbade* him to cross the street alone.

for·bid·ding [fər·bid′ing] *adj.* Grim and unfriendly; frightening: a *forbidding* swamp.

for·bore [fôr·bôr′] Past tense of FORBEAR[1].

for·borne [fôr·bôrn′] Past participle of FOR-BEAR[1].

force [fôrs] *n.*, *v.* **forced, forc·ing 1** *n.* Power or energy; strength: the *force* of the waves. **2** *n.* Power used to overcome the resistance of a person or thing: They dragged him in by *force*. **3** *v.* To drive or move in spite of resistance: to *force* the enemy back into the hills. **4** *v.* To bring forth with an effort: He *forced* a smile to his lips. **5** *v.* To compel to do something by using power or persuasion: He *forced* me to tell the truth. **6** *n.* The quality that affects the thinking or feelings of people: the *force* of one's argument. **7** *v.* To break open, as a door or lock. **8** *n.* A group of people organized to do certain work: a police *force*; the armed *forces*. **9** *n.* Anything that changes or tends to change the state of rest or motion in a body: the *force* of gravitation. **10** *v.* To make grow faster by artificial means, as the plants in a hothouse. **11** *v.* In baseball, to put out (a base runner who must move up to the next base). **—in force 1** In effect or being applied, as a law. **2** In full strength.

forced [fôrst] *adj.* **1** Compelled or required by force: *forced* labor. **2** Strained; affected: a *forced* smile. **3** Done in an emergency: the *forced* landing of an airplane.

force·ful [fôrs′fəl] *adj.* Full of or done with force; vigorous; strong: a *forceful* blow; a *forceful* speech. **—force′ful·ly** *adv.*

for·ceps [fôr′səps] *n.*, *pl.* **for·ceps** Pincers for grasping or handling small or delicate objects. Forceps are used by doctors, dentists, jewelers, etc.

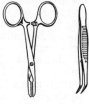
Surgical forceps

for·ci·ble [fôr′sə·bəl] *adj.* **1** Brought about or done by force: the *forcible* removal of demonstrators. **2** Having or displaying force; vigorous; effective: a *forcible* speech. **—for′ci·bly** *adv.*

ford [fôrd] **1** *n.* A shallow place in a stream, river, etc., that can be crossed by wading. **2** *v.* To cross (a river, stream, etc.) at a shallow place.

fore [fôr] **1** *adv.* In or toward the front part or bow of a boat; forward. **2** *adj.* At or toward the front or beginning. **3** *n.* The front part, foremost position, or forefront. **4** *interj.* A cry which a golfer shouts before hitting the ball, to warn anyone in the way.

fore- A prefix meaning: **1** Before, earlier, or in advance, as in *forewarn*, to warn in advance. **2** At the front, as in *forepaw*, a front paw.

fore-and-aft [fôr′ən·aft′] *adj.* Lying or going from bow to stern on a ship; lengthwise.

fore and aft **1** In a line extending from the bow to the stern of a boat. **2** In, at, or toward both the front and the back of a boat.

fore·arm¹ [fôr′ärm′] *n.* The part of the arm between the elbow and the wrist.

fore·arm² [fôr·ärm′] *v.* To prepare in advance, as for coming trouble; arm beforehand.

fore·bear [fôr′bâr] *n.* An ancestor.

fore·bode [fôr·bōd′] *v.* **fore·bod·ed, fore·bod·ing** **1** To be a warning sign of. **2** To sense beforehand, as some coming evil.

fore·bod·ing [fôr·bō′ding] *n.* A feeling that something bad is going to happen; premonition.

fore·cast [fôr′kast′] *v.* **fore·cast** or **fore·cast·ed, fore·cast·ing,** *n.* **1** *v.* To predict after studying available facts: to *forecast* election results. **2** *n.* A prediction, as of coming weather conditions. **—fore′cast′er** *n.*

fore·cas·tle [fōk′səl] *n.* **1** That part of the upper deck of a ship in front of the foremast. **2** Sailors' quarters in a merchant ship, usually in the forward section.

fore·close [fôr·klōz′] *v.* **fore·closed, fore·clos·ing** To end a mortgage agreement and claim the mortgaged property, as when payments on the original loan are not met. **—fore·clo·sure** [fôr·klō′zhər] *n.*

fore·fa·ther [fôr′fä·thər] *n.* An ancestor.

fore·fin·ger [fôr′fing′gər] *n.* The finger next to the thumb; index finger.

Forefinger

fore·foot [fôr′foot′] *n.*, *pl.* **fore·feet** [fôr′fēt′] A front foot of an animal or insect.

fore·front [fôr′frunt′] *n.* **1** The very front. **2** The position of most activity, importance, etc.: He was in the *forefront* of the battle.

fore·gath·er [fôr·gath′ər] *v.* Another spelling of FORGATHER.

fore·go [fôr·gō′] *v.* **fore·went, fore·gone, fore·go·ing** Another spelling of FORGO.

fore·go·ing [fôr·gō′ing] *adj.* Going before; previous: The *foregoing* statement is correct.

fore·gone [fôr·gôn′] *adj.* **1** Certain enough to be known in advance: a *foregone* conclusion. **2** Previous or past: *foregone* eras.

fore·ground [fôr′ground′] *n.* The part of a landscape or picture that is nearest or seems nearest to the person looking at it.

fore·hand [fôr′hand′] **1** *n.* A stroke, as in tennis, in which the player holds the racket with his palm turned forward. **2** *adj.* Done with the palm turned forward: a powerful *forehand* stroke.

A forehand stroke

fore·head [fôr′id *or* fôr′hed′] *n.* The part of the face between the eyebrows and the natural hairline.

for·eign [fôr′in] *adj.* **1** Located or coming from outside one's own country; not native: a *foreign* city; a *foreign* language. **2** Carried on or concerned with other countries: *foreign* trade; *foreign* affairs. **3** Not belonging naturally or normally: a *foreign* substance in the body; behavior *foreign* to his character.

for·eign·er [fôr′in·ər] *n.* **1** A native or citizen of a foreign country. **2** An outsider.

fore·knowl·edge [fôr′nol′ij] *n.* Knowledge of something before it exists or takes place.

fore·leg [fôr′leg′] *n.* One of the front legs of an animal or insect.

fore·lock [fôr′lok′] *n.* A lock of hair growing over the forehead.

fore·man [fôr′mən] *n.*, *pl.* **fore·men** [fôr′mən] **1** A worker in charge of a group of workmen. **2** A jury chairman, who announces the verdict.

fore·mast [fôr′mast′] *n.* The mast that is closest to the bow of a ship.

fore·most [fôr′mōst′] **1** *adj.* First in place, time, rank, or order; chief: the *foremost* artist of his day. **2** *adv.* Before everything else; first: He put his duty *foremost*.

fore·noon [fôr′noon′] *n.* The period of daylight before noon; morning.

fore·or·dain [fôr′ôr·dān′] *v.* To order or decide in advance; determine beforehand.

fore·paw [fôr′pô′] *n.* A front paw.

fore·run·ner [fôr′run′ər] *n.* **1** A person who goes ahead to tell that another is coming. **2** A

add, āce, câre, pälm;   end, ēqual;   it, íce;   odd, ōpen, ôrder;   took, pool;   up, bûrn;
ə = a in *above*, e in *sicken*, i in *possible*, o in *melon*, u in *circus*;   yoo = u in *fuse*;   oil;   pout;
check;   ring;   thin;   this;   zh in *vision*.   For ¶ reference, see page 64 · HOW TO

sign of some coming thing: The first robin is a *forerunner* of spring. **3** A predecessor.

fore·sail [fôr′sāl′] *n.* **1** The lowest sail on the foremast of a square-rigged vessel. **2** The main fore-and-aft sail on a schooner's foremast.

fore·see [fôr·sē′] *v.* **fore·saw, fore·seen, fore·see·ing** To see or know in advance.

fore·shad·ow [fôr·shad′ō] *v.* To give an advance indication or warning of: Her bad grades *foreshadowed* her failure.

fore·short·en [fôr·shôr′tən] *v.* To draw (a line, surface, etc.) less than true length to create a sense of distance or depth.

fore·sight [fôr′sīt′] *n.* **1** The act or power of foreseeing or looking ahead. **2** Preparation or concern for the future. **— fore′sight′ed** *adj.*

Foreshortened legs

fore·skin [fôr′skin′] *n.* A fold of skin that covers the end of the male sex organ.

for·est [fôr′ist] **1** *n.* A thick growth of trees spreading over a large tract of land. **2** *adj.* Of, in, or having to do with a forest. **3** *v.* To plant with many trees: to *forest* ground.

fore·stall [fôr·stôl′] *v.* To prevent, keep out, or get ahead of by taking action first: to *forestall* criticism by doing a good job.

for·est·a·tion [fôr′is·tā′shən] *n.* The planting or care of forests.

for·est·er [fôr′is·tər] *n.* A person who is trained and skilled in forestry.

for·est·ry [fôr′is·trē] *n.* The science of planting, developing, and managing forests.

fore·taste [fôr′tāst′] *n.* A taste or brief experience of something to come later.

fore·tell [fôr·tel′] *v.* **fore·told, fore·tell·ing** To tell about in advance; predict: A computer *foretold* these figures a year ago.

fore·thought [fôr′thôt′] *n.* Careful planning or attention ahead of time; thought in advance.

fore·told [fôr·tōld′] Past tense and past participle of FORETELL.

for·ev·er [fôr·ev′ər] *adv.* **1** To the end of time; throughout eternity. **2** Again and again; always: He is *forever* telling me what to do.

fore·warn [fôr·wôrn′] *v.* To warn in advance.

fore·went [fôr·went′] Past tense of FOREGO.

fore·word [fôr′wûrd′] *n.* An introduction to a book; preface.

for·feit [fôr′fit] **1** *v.* To lose or give up as a penalty for an offense, mistake, etc.: By failing to register, he *forfeited* his right to vote. **2** *n.* The giving up or loss of something as a penalty: the *forfeit* of a privilege. **3** *n.* Something that is forfeited; penalty.

for·fei·ture [fôr′fi·chər] *n.* **1** The act of forfeiting. **2** Something given up as a penalty.

for·gath·er [fôr·gath′ər] *v.* **1** To meet; assemble. **2** To meet by chance. **3** To meet socially.

for·gave [fər·gāv′] Past tense of FORGIVE.

forge[1] [fôrj] *n., v.* **forged, forg·ing 1** *n.* A fireplace or furnace for heating metal so it can be hammered into shape. **2** *n.* A blacksmith's shop; smithy. **3** *v.* To work (metal) into shape by heating and hammering. **4** *v.* To produce or form; shape: to *forge* armor. **5** *n.* A furnace or factory for melting or refining metals. **6** *v.* To make an imitation of to be passed off as genuine: to *forge* a signature. **7** *v.* To be guilty of forgery.

Colonial forge

forge[2] [fôrj] *v.* **forged, forg·ing** To move slowly but steadily forward, as by effort: to *forge* through the mud.

forg·er [fôr′jər] *n.* **1** A person who commits forgery. **2** A man who forges metal; smith.

forg·er·y [fôr′jər·ē] *n., pl.* **forg·er·ies 1** The act of making an imitation, as of a signature or document, to be passed off as genuine. **2** An imitation meant to deceive.

for·get [fər·get′] *v.* **for·got, for·got·ten** or **for·got, for·get·ting 1** To cease or fail to remember; lose from memory: I *forgot* the answer. **2** To neglect (to do something), fail to think of, or leave behind accidentally: You *forgot* to feed the cat; to *forget* your lunch.

for·get·ful [fər·get′fəl] *adj.* **1** Inclined to forget easily. **2** Neglectful; careless: *forgetful* of one's duty. **— for·get′ful·ness** *n.*

for·get-me-not [fər·get′mē·not′] *n.* A small herb bearing clusters of blue or white flowers.

for·giv·a·ble [fər·giv′ə·bəl] *adj.* Capable of being forgiven: a *forgivable* error.

for·give [fər·giv′] *v.* **for·gave, for·giv·en, for·giv·ing 1** To stop blaming or being angry with: I have *forgiven* you. **2** To excuse; pardon: to *forgive* a mistake.

for·give·ness [fər·giv′nis] *n.* **1** Pardon, as for an offense. **2** A willingness to forgive.

for·giv·ing [fər·giv′ing] *adj.* **1** Willing or ready to forgive. **2** Showing pardon; pardoning.

for·go [fôr·gō′] *v.* **for·went, for·gone, for·go·ing** To give up; go without: to *forgo* cake when one is dieting.

for·got [fər·got′] Past tense and past participle of FORGET: We *forgot* to ask him.

for·got·ten [fər·got′(ə)n] Past participle of FORGET: She has *forgotten* her lines.

fork [fôrk] **1** *n.* A small eating utensil, large farm tool, or other instrument with a handle at one end and two or more prongs at the other. **2** *v.* To lift or toss with a fork: to *fork* hay into a wagon. **3** *n.* A dividing of something, as a road, into branches. **4** *n.* One such branch: Follow the right *fork* at the crossroads. **5** *v.* To divide into branches: The river *forks* upstream.

forked [fôrkt] *adj.* Having a fork or a part that branches: a *forked* road; *forked* lightning.

fork lift A hoisting machine with fingerlike prongs that slide under heavy objects to lift, move, or stack them.

Fork lift

for·lorn [fôr·lôrn′] *adj.* Sad or pitiful because alone or neglected. **—for·lorn′ly** *adv.*

form [fôrm] **1** *n.* An outline or outward shape: the shifting *forms* of clouds. **2** *n.* A mold, frame, or model that gives shape to something, as wet cement. **3** *v.* To make, shape, or fashion: to *form* clay into a ball; to *form* a plan. **4** *v.* To shape by training: Education *forms* the mind. **5** *v.* To develop or acquire, as a habit. **6** *v.* To take shape or form; come to be: A scab *formed* over the sore. **7** *n.* Any of the shapes given to a word to show special meaning: "Men" is the plural *form* of "man." **8** *n.* A specific type; kind: Democracy is a *form* of government. **9** *n.* Condition of body or mind for performance: an athlete in top *form*. **10** *n.* Arrangement or organization: the sonata *form* in music. **11** *n.* A manner of proceeding or behaving: to show good *form* in diving; Showing anger in public is bad *form*. **12** *n.* Outward ceremony or formality: He nodded as a matter of *form*. **13** *n.* A formula, or draft, as of a letter, used as a model. **14** *adj. use:* a *form* letter. **15** *n.* A document with blanks to be filled in. **16** *v.* To make up: Guesswork *forms* a part of his theory. **17** *v.* To combine or organize into: to *form* a club. **18** *n. British* A grade in school. **19** *n. British* A long bench without a back.

for·mal [fôr′məl] **1** *adj.* Strictly or stiffly following set rules or patterns: a *formal* greeting; a *formal* garden; a *formal* agreement. **2** *adj.* Requiring elaborate dress and manners. **3** *n. informal* A formal dance. **4** *adj.* Suiting elaborate occasions. **5** *n. informal* An evening dress. **6** *adj.* Concerning outward form. **—for′mal·ly** *adv.* ◆ See FORMERLY.

for·mal·de·hyde [fôr·mal′də·hīd] *n.* A colorless gas used in a liquid solution to kill germs and to preserve dead animals for study.

for·mal·i·ty [fôr·mal′ə·tē] *n., pl.* **for·mal·i·ties 1** Formal character or quality. **2** Strict politeness; ceremony. **3** A proper or customary act or ceremony: the *formalities* of a christening. **4** A required outward gesture.

for·mat [fôr′mat] *n.* The form, size, arrangement, and style of a printed publication.

for·ma·tion [fôr·mā′shən] *n.* **1** The act of forming: the *formation* of rust on iron. **2** Something formed, as a mass of rock. **3** An arrangement, as of troops.

form·a·tive [fôr′mə·tiv] *adj.* Of or related to formation or development: *formative* stages.

for·mer [fôr′mər] *adj.* **1** Belonging to the past; previous; earlier: a *former* mayor; *former* ages. **2** Being the first of two persons or things referred to. **3** *n. use* The first one referred to: I prefer *the former* to the latter.

for·mer·ly [fôr′mər·lē] *adv.* In the past; once. ◆ *Formerly* and *formally*, though pronounced similarly, have entirely different meanings. *Formerly* means *once* or *in the past*: Our ambassador to Mexico was *formerly* a teacher. *Formally* means *in a formal way*: She was dressed *formally* for the royal ball.

for·mi·da·ble [fôr′mi·də·bəl] *adj.* **1** Causing fear or dread, as because of strength or size: a *formidable* opponent. **2** Extremely difficult: a *formidable* assignment. **—for′mi·da·bly** *adv.*

form·less [fôrm′lis] *adj.* Lacking form or structure; shapeless. **—form′less·ly** *adv.*

For·mo·sa [fôr·mō′sə] *n.* An island off the SE coast of China, now called Taiwan.

for·mu·la [fôr′myə·lə] *n., pl.* **for·mu·las** or **for·mu·lae** [fôr′myə·lē] **1** A set of words used by custom. "Dear Sir" is a formula for beginning a letter. **2** A statement expressing some belief or principle. **3** An established method or rule. **4** A statement of some fact or relationship in mathematical terms. The formula $s = 16t^2$ gives the distance in feet, s, that an object falls in the time t seconds. **5** A prescription or recipe. **6** A mixture prepared by prescription or recipe. **7** A set of symbols showing the elements making up a chemical compound. The formula for carbon dioxide is CO_2.

for·mu·late [fôr′myə·lāt] *v.* **for·mu·lat·ed, for·mu·lat·ing 1** To express in or as a formula. **2** To work out and state in an exact, orderly way.

for·sake [fôr·sāk′] *v.* **for·sook** [fôr·sŏŏk′], **for·sak·en, for·sak·ing** To leave completely; desert; give up: He has *forsaken* his family.

for·sooth [fôr·sŏŏth′] *adv.* In truth; in fact: seldom used today.

for·swear [fôr·swâr′] *v.* **for·swore, for·sworn, for·swear·ing 1** To swear to give up completely. **2** To swear falsely; commit perjury.

for·syth·i·a [fôr·sith′ē·ə] *n.* A shrub bearing bell-shaped yellow flowers early in spring.

fort [fôrt] *n.* A structure or enclosed area strong enough to be defended against attack.

forte[1] [fôrt] *n.* Something one does with excellence; strong point: Singing is her *forte*.

for·te[2] [fôr′tā] *adj., adv.* In music, loud.

forth [fôrth] *adv.* **1** Forward; on: from this day *forth*. **2** Out, as from hiding or a place of origin: Come *forth!*; to put *forth* effort.

forth·com·ing [fôrth′kum′ing] *adj.* **1** About to appear, arrive, or happen; approaching: our *forthcoming* vacation. **2** Available when expected or needed: Money will be *forthcoming*.

forth·right [fôrth′rīt′] *adj.* Coming straight to the point; frank; direct: *forthright* advice.

---

a**dd**, **ā**ce, c**â**re, p**ä**lm;   **e**nd, **ē**qual;   **i**t, **ī**ce;   **o**dd, **ō**pen, **ô**rder;   t**ŏŏ**k, p**ōō**l;   **u**p, b**û**rn;

ə = a in *above*, e in *sicken*, i in *possible*, o in *melon*, u in *circus*;   **y**ōō = u in *fuse*;   **oi**l;   p**ou**t;

check;   **r**i**ng**;   **th**in;   **th**is;   **zh** in *vision*.   For ¶ reference, see page 64 · HOW TO

forth·with [fôrth′with′] *adv.* Immediately.

for·ti·eth or **40th** [fôr′tē·ith] **1** *adj.* Tenth in order after the thirtieth. **2** *n.* The fortieth one. **3** *adj.* Being one of forty equal parts. **4** *n.* A fortieth part.

for·ti·fi·ca·tion [fôr′tə·fə·kā′shən] *n.* **1** The act of fortifying. **2** A wall, ditch, etc., for defense. **3** A military place of defense.

for·ti·fy [fôr′tə·fī] *v.* **for·ti·fied, for·ti·fy·ing** **1** To make strong enough to resist attack, as by building walls and forts. **2** To give added strength to; strengthen: Our support *fortified* his will. **3** To add minerals or vitamins to (a food, as milk).

for·tis·si·mo [fôr·tis′ə·mō] *adj., adv.* In music, very loud.

for·ti·tude [fôr′tə·t(y)ood] *n.* Courage to meet and endure pain, hardship, or danger: the amazing *fortitude* of the pioneer women.

fort·night [fôrt′nīt′] *n.* A period of two weeks.

for·tress [fôr′tris] *n.* A fort, a series of forts, or a fortified town; stronghold.

for·tu·i·tous [fôr·t(y)oo′ə·təs] *adj.* Coming about by chance; accidental, and often lucky. **— for·tu′i·tous·ly** *adv.*

for·tu·nate [fôr′chə·nit] *adj.* Having, happening by, or bringing good luck; lucky: a *fortunate* person or event. **— for′tu·nate·ly** *adv.*

for·tune [fôr′chən] *n.* **1** A power supposed to determine the course of men's lives; destiny; fate. **2** A person's future fate: to claim to tell *fortunes.* **3** Luck or chance, whether good or bad: *Fortune* favored him. **4** Favorable luck; success. **5** A great sum of money; wealth.

for·tune·tell·er [fôr′chən·tel′ər] *n.* A person claiming to foretell the future.

for·ty or **40** [fôr′tē] *n., pl.* **for·ties** or **40's,** *adj.* **1** *n., adj.* Ten more than thirty. **2** *n.* (*pl.*) The years between the age of 40 and the age of 50: She is in her *forties.*

for·ty-nin·er [fôr′tē·nī′nər] *n.* A pioneer who went to California in the 1849 gold rush.

fo·rum [fôr′əm] *n.* **1** The public market place of an ancient Roman city, where assemblies met and most legal and political business was carried on. **2** A court of law. **3** An assembly for the discussion of public affairs.

for·ward [fôr′wərd] **1** *adj.* At, near, or toward the front. **2** *adv.* To or toward the front or forefront: to move *forward;* to bring *forward* an idea. **3** *n.* A player in the front line or one who leads the offensive play, as in basketball. **4** *v.* To send onward, as to another address: *Forward* my mail. **5** *v.* To help to advance: to *forward* someone's hopes. **6** *adj.* Ahead of the usual; advanced: a boy *forward* for his age. **7** *adv.* To the future: to look *forward* to retirement. **8** *adj.* Ready or prompt: He is *forward* in speaking out. **9** *adj.* Too bold; rude.

for·ward·ness [fôr′wərd·nis] *n.* **1** Improper boldness in behavior: It was difficult to forgive such *forwardness.* **2** Willing readiness.

for·wards [fôr′wərdz] *adv.* Forward; ahead.

for·went [fôr·went′] Past tense of FORGO.

fos·sil [fos′əl] **1** *n.* The remains of a plant or animal of an earlier age, hardened and preserved in earth or rock. **2** *adj. use* Like or being a fossil: a *fossil* fern. **3** *n. informal* A person with old-fashioned notions or ways.

A fossil fern

fos·ter [fôs′tər] **1** *v.* To bring up (a child); rear. **2** *adj.* Having a given relationship as the result of rearing only, not by birth or adoption. Foster parents rear a foster child, one entrusted to their care but not legally their own. **3** *v.* To promote the growth or development of: to *foster* talent.

Fos·ter [fôs′tər], **Stephen Collins,** 1826–1864, U.S. song writer.

fought [fôt] Past tense and past participle of FIGHT: The team *fought* hard to win.

foul [foul] **1** *adj.* Very dirty, disgusting, stinking, or rotten: *foul* water; *foul* smells. **2** *v.* To make or become foul or dirty: Gasoline fumes *fouled* the air. **3** *v.* To stop up; clog: Dirt *fouled* the gun barrel. **4** *adj.* Clogged or packed with dirt, etc.: a *foul* chimney. **5** *adj.* Not decent; profane or abusive: *foul* language. **6** *adj.* Evil; wicked: *foul* deeds. **7** *adj.* Not fair; rainy or stormy: *foul* weather. **8** *v.* To tangle or become tangled up: The fishing lines *fouled.* **9** *adj.* Caught or entangled: a *foul* anchor. **10** *v.* To hit against or hit together, as two boats. **11** *adj.* Against the rules; unfair: a *foul* blow. **12** *n.* An action that breaks the rules of a game. **13** *v.* To commit a foul, as against an opponent. **14** *adj.* In baseball, landing first outside the foul lines or passing outside these lines before reaching first or third base: a *foul* ball. **15** *n.* A foul ball. **16** *v.* To bat (a baseball) outside the foul lines. **— foul′ly** *adv.*

fou·lard [foo·lärd′] *n.* A lightweight fabric, as of silk, usually with a printed design.

foul line In baseball, either of the two lines extending from home plate past first and third bases to the limits of the playing field.

foul play **1** Unfair or dishonest action, as in sports. **2** A violent, evil action, as murder.

found[1] [found] *v.* **1** To set up; establish; start: to *found* a school. **2** To base, as for support: suspicions *founded* on rumors. **— found′er** *n.*

found[2] [found] Past tense and past participle of FIND: The boys have *found* the lost dog.

foun·da·tion [foun·dā′shən] *n.* **1** A base, as of a building, which supports everything above it. **2** An underlying basis, as for a belief. **3** The act of founding. **4** The condition of being founded. **5** An organization set up and endowed to carry on or pay for some worthy purpose, as charity or research.

foun·der [foun′dər] *v.* **1** To fill with water and sink, as a ship. **2** To fall or cave in. **3** To fail completely. **4** To stumble or go lame.

found·ling [found′ling] *n.* A baby found after having been deserted by its unknown parents.

foun·dry [foun′drē] *n., pl.* **foun·dries** **1** A

place where molten metal is shaped in molds. **2** The act of casting metal to make things.

fount [fount] *n.* **1** A fountain. **2** Any source.

foun·tain [foun′tən] *n.* **1** A natural spring of water. **2** A jet of water thrown into the air from a pipe and caught in a basin, for ornament or drinking. **3** The basinlike structure in which this water rises and falls. **4** A soda fountain. **5** A source, as of wisdom.

foun·tain·head [foun′tən·hed′] *n.* A source, as a spring from which a stream originates.

fountain pen A pen holding a supply of ink which automatically flows to the writing end.

four or **4** [fôr] *n., adj.* One more than three. **—on all fours 1** On hands and knees. **2** On all four feet.

four-foot·ed [fôr′foot′id] *adj.* Having four feet; quadruped: *four-footed* animals.

Four-H Club [fôr′āch′] A club training boys and girls in farming and home management.

four-post·er [fôr′pōs′tər] *n.* A bed with four tall posts at the corners which may be used to support a canopy or curtains.

four·score [fôr′skôr′] *adj.* Four times twenty; eighty.

four·some [fôr′səm] *n.* A group of four, as four persons joining together to play golf.

four·square [fôr′skwâr′] **1** *adj.* Square in shape. **2** *adj.* Frank; direct. **3** *adj.* Not giving way; firm. **4** *adv.* Firmly.

four·teen or **14** [fôr′tēn′] *n., adj.* One more than thirteen.

four·teenth or **14th** [fôr′tēnth′] **1** *adj.* Next after the thirteenth. **2** *n.* The fourteenth one. **3** *adj.* Being one of fourteen equal parts. **4** *n.* A fourteenth part.

fourth or **4th** [fôrth] **1** *adj.* Next after the third. **2** *n.* The fourth one. **3** *adj.* Being one of four equal parts. **4** *n.* A fourth part.

Fourth of July Independence Day.

fowl [foul] *n., pl.* **fowl** or **fowls 1** A hen or rooster. **2** Any similar large bird, as the duck or turkey. **3** The flesh of such birds used as food. **4** Birds as a group: wild *fowl*.

fowl·ing piece [fou′ling] A light gun for shooting birds.

fox [foks] *n.* **1** A small wild animal kin to the dog and wolf and noted for its cunning. It has a long, pointed muzzle and bushy tail. **2** The fur of the fox. **3** A sly, crafty person.

Gray fox, about 3 ft. long

fox·glove [foks′gluv′] *n.* A tall plant bearing flowers shaped something like a bell.

fox·hole [foks′hōl′] *n.* A shallow pit dug by a soldier for shelter against enemy gun-fire.

Soldier in a foxhole

fox·hound [foks′hound′] *n.* A large, swift breed of dog with a keen sense of smell, trained to hunt foxes.

fox terrier A small, lively white dog with dark markings, once used to hunt foxes.

fox trot 1 A ballroom dance combining fast steps and slow steps. **2** A piece of music used for this dance.

fox·y [fok′sē] *adj.* **fox·i·er, fox·i·est** Having the cunning of a fox; sly; shrewd.

foy·er [foi′ər] *n.* **1** A public lobby, as in a hotel or theater. **2** An entrance room or hall.

fra·cas [frā′kəs] *n.* A noisy fight or quarrel.

frac·tion [frak′shən] *n.* **1** A part taken from a whole. **2** A little bit. **3** A rational number that is more than zero and less than 1, or the sum of a whole number and such a quantity. In the fraction ⅔, the 3 tells into how many equal parts a whole is divided, and the 2 tells how many of those parts the fraction contains.

frac·tion·al [frak′shən·əl] *adj.* **1** Having to do with or making up a fraction. **2** Small in size or importance. **— frac′tion·al·ly** *adv.*

fractional distillation The separating of a substance, as petroleum, by boiling off one component of it at a time.

frac·tious [frak′shəs] *adj.* **1** Hard to control; unruly. **2** Easily annoyed; irritable.

frac·ture [frak′chər] *n., v.* **frac·tured, frac·tur·ing 1** *n.* The act of breaking, as the breaking or cracking of a bone. **2** *n.* A break, crack, or rupture. **3** *v.* To break or crack: to *fracture* a rib. **4** *n.* A broken condition.

frag·ile [fraj′əl] *adj.* Easily shattered or broken; delicate: *fragile* dishes. **— fra·gil·i·ty** [frə·jil′ə·tē] *n.* ◆ Both *fragile* and *frail* come from a Latin word meaning *to break.*

frag·ment [frag′mənt] *n.* A part broken off or incomplete: *fragments* of a broken mirror.

frag·men·tar·y [frag′mən·ter′ē] *adj.* Made up of fragments; not complete: *fragmentary* pieces of a broken vase; *fragmentary* evidence.

fra·grance [frā′grəns] *n.* **1** Sweetness of scent or smell. **2** A sweet or delicate smell.

fra·grant [frā′grənt] *adj.* Sweet in smell.

frail [frā(ə)l] *adj.* **1** Easily damaged in body or structure; weak: a *frail* old lady; a *frail* scaffold. **2** Weak in character. ◆ See FRAGILE.

frail·ty [frāl′tē] *n., pl.* **frail·ties 1** Weakness. **2** A fault or moral weakness.

frame [frām] *n., v.* **framed, fram·ing 1** *n.* A basic inner structure which gives support and shape to the thing built around it; framework:

the *frame* of a building. **2** *n.* The bone structure or build of the body. **3** *v.* To plan and put together; make or construct: to *frame* a question; to *frame* a law. **4** *n.* The arrangement or structure of a thing. **5** *n.* A case or border made to hold or surround something, as a window. **6** *v.* To put within such a case or border: to *frame* a picture. **7** *v. slang* To cause (an innocent person) to look guilty by furnishing false evidence. **8** *n.* One of the divisions of a game of bowling. — **frame of mind** Condition of mind or feeling; mood.

frame-up [frām'up'] *n. slang* **1** A plot to make a person look guilty of a thing he did not do. **2** A scheme to bring about a dishonest result.

frame·work [frām'wûrk'] *n.* The basic structure around which a thing is built: the *framework* of a ship; the *framework* of society.

Framework of a barn

franc [frangk] *n.* The basic unit of money in France, Belgium, Switzerland, Luxembourg, etc.

France [frans] *n.* A country in western Europe.

fran·chise [fran'chīz] *n.* **1** The right to vote. **2** A right or special privilege granted by a government: a *franchise* to operate a bus line. **3** Permission given to a dealer to market a certain company's products or services.

Fran·cis·can [fran·sis'kən] **1** *adj.* Of Saint Francis of Assisi or the religious order which he founded. **2** *n.* A Franciscan friar or nun.

Fran·cis of As·si·si [fran'sis əv ə·sē'zē], 1182?–1226, Italian friar and saint. He founded the Franciscan order in 1209.

frank¹ [frangk] *adj.* Completely honest in saying or showing what one really thinks or feels. — **frank'ly** *adv.* — **frank'ness** *n.*

frank² [frangk] **1** *n.* The right to send mail free of charge. **2** *n.* The mark used to indicate this right. **3** *v.* To send (mail) without postage by marking it with an official sign.

Frank [frangk] *n.* A member of the Germanic tribes that conquered Gaul in the fifth century A.D. and gave their name to France. — **Frank'ish** *adj., n.*

Frank·fort [frangk'fərt] *n.* The capital of Kentucky.

frank·furt·er [frangk'fər·tər] *n.* A smoked, reddish sausage of beef or of beef and pork.

frank·in·cense [frangk'in·sens] *n.* A gum or resin from various trees of East Africa, burned as incense for its sweet, spicy smell.

Frank·lin [frangk'lin], **Benjamin,** 1706–1790, American patriot, writer, and scientist.

fran·tic [fran'tik] *adj.* Wild with fear, worry, pain, rage, etc.: Her family was *frantic* until they heard from her. — **fran'ti·cal·ly** *adv.*

fra·ter·nal [frə·tûr'nəl] *adj.* **1** Of or characteristic of brothers; brotherly. **2** Made up of men with mutual interests: *fraternal* organizations. **3** Describing twins of the same or the opposite sex that develop from two separately fertilized egg cells and so are not identical.

fra·ter·ni·ty [frə·tûr'nə·tē] *n., pl.* **fra·ter·ni·ties** **1** Brotherly unity or affection; brotherhood. **2** A club of men or boys, especially one made up of college students. **3** A group of people sharing the same interests, profession, etc.: the legal *fraternity.*

frat·er·nize [frat'ər·nīz] *v.* **frat·er·nized, frat·er·niz·ing** To associate in a friendly way: Don't *fraternize* with the enemy. ¶3

Frau [frou] *n.* The German title of courtesy for a married woman, equivalent to *Mrs.*

fraud [frôd] *n.* **1** The deceiving of another for one's own gain; dishonest deception. **2** A thing that deceives or is not genuine; trick or deception. **3** *U.S. informal* A person who is not what he represents himself as being.

fraud·u·lent [frô'jə·lənt] *adj.* **1** Employing fraud; dishonest. **2** Acquired or done by fraud. **3** Based on fraud; false: *fraudulent* claims.

fraught [frôt] *adj.* Filled; loaded: Man's exploration of space is *fraught* with danger.

Fräu·lein or **Frau·lein** [froi'līn] *n.* The German title of courtesy for an unmarried woman or girl, equivalent to *Miss.*

fray¹ [frā] *n.* A noisy quarrel; fight; brawl.

fray² [frā] *v.* To wear down so that loose threads or fibers show; make or become ragged: His shirt cuffs were *frayed.*

fraz·zle [fraz'(ə)l] *v.* **fraz·zled, fraz·zling,** *n. informal* **1** *v.* To make or become ragged; fray. **2** *v.* To tire out; exhaust. **3** *n.* A ragged, worn-out, or exhausted condition.

A frayed collar

freak [frēk] **1** *n.* A person, animal, or plant that is not normal, as a dog with five legs. **2** *adj.* Not normal; highly unusual: a *freak* flood. **3** *n.* A sudden strange notion or action or an odd change of mind. — **freak'ish** *adj.*

freck·le [frek'əl] *n., v.* **freck·led, freck·ling** **1** *n.* A small brownish spot on the skin. **2** *v.* To mark or become marked with such spots.

free [frē] *adj.* **fre·er, fre·est,** *v.* **freed, free·ing,** *adv.* **1** *adj* Not under any other's control; enjoying liberty. **2** *adj.* Not tied, held, or shut up; loose: the *free* end of a rope. **3** *v.* To set at liberty; release: to *free* a prisoner. **4** *adv.* In a free manner; without restraint: Let him go *free.* **5** *adj.* Allowed; permitted: *free* to go. **6** *adj.* Having the right to think, act, vote, express oneself, and worship as one wishes. **7** *adj.* Not influenced by any outside power: to have *free* choice. **8** *adj.* Not held back or slowed down: a *free* fall. **9** *adj.* Not blocked; clear; open: a *free* drain. **10** *v.* To clear or rid: to *free* a drain of grease. **11** *adj.* Having or containing no: used in combination, as in *salt-free,* containing no salt. **12** *adj.* Not restricted, as by taxes or limitations: *free* trade; *free* debate. **13** *adj.* Not following set rules of form: *free* verse. **14** *adj.*

Not chemically combined: *free* hydrogen. **15** *adj.* Not occupied or busy: *free* time. **16** *adj.* Costing no money: a *free* sample. **17** *adv.* Without cost or charge: to get tickets *free*. **18** *adj.* Generous in giving; liberal: to be *free* with advice. **19** *adj.* Honest and frank. **20** *adj.* Bold and not polite or proper. — **free from** or **free of** Without any: *free from* care; *free of* infection. — **set free** To release. — **free·ly** *adv.*

free-and-easy [frē′ən(d)·ē′zē] *adj.* Not bound by convention; casual; informal.

free·boot·er [frē′boō′tər] *n.* A person who plunders, as a pirate or buccaneer.

free·born [frē′bôrn′] *adj.* **1** Born free, not in slavery. **2** Of or suiting those born free.

freed·man [frēd′mən] *n.*, *pl.* **freed·men** [frēd′mən] A former slave who has been freed.

free·dom [frē′dəm] *n.* **1** The condition of being free. **2** Frankness or familiarity, often improper: The *freedom* of the waiter's manner offended them. **3** Ease, as in acting: The leash hampered the dog's *freedom* of movement. **4** The right to enter or use all parts: to give a cat the *freedom* of one's apartment.

free enterprise An economic system based upon private ownership and operation of business with little or no governmental control.

free-for-all [frē′fər·ôl′] *n.* **1** A noisy or disorderly fight in which anyone can become involved. **2** A contest, game, etc., open to anyone who wishes to take part.

free·hand [frē′hand′] *adj.* Drawn by hand without the help of instruments, as rulers.

free·hand·ed [frē′han′did] *adj.* Generous.

free-lance [frē′lans′] *v.* **free-lanced, free-lanc·ing,** *adj.* **1** *v.* To work independently, as some artists or writers do, often for different employers. **2** *adj.* Working in this way: a *free-lance* illustrator.

free·man [frē′mən] *n.*, *pl.* **free·men** [frē′mən] A person who is free, not a slave, and who has the rights of a free man or a citizen.

Free·ma·son [frē′mā′sən] *n.* A member of a widespread secret order or fraternity; Mason.

free·stone [frē′stōn′] **1** *n.* A stone that can be cut in any direction without breaking, as sandstone. **2** *adj.* Having a pit from which the fruit pulp easily separates: a *freestone* peach. **3** *n.* A fruit having a pit or stone like this.

free·style [frē′stīl′] **1** *n.* An event in which a contestant, as a swimmer or skater, may use any style he chooses. **2** *adj.* Having no restrictions as to the style used.

free·think·er [frē′thing′kər] *n.* A person who forms his own opinions, as about religion, not accepting anything solely on authority.

free verse Verse without regular meter or rhyme, having its own special form and rhythm.

free·way [frē′wā′] *n.* A highway for fast travel with no toll charges.

free·will [frē′wil′] *adj.* Made, done, or given of one's own free choice; voluntary.

free will The power to choose on one's own, free of outside influence or interference: He confessed of his own *free will*.

freeze [frēz] *v.* **froze, fro·zen, freez·ing,** *n.* **1** *v.* To change into ice by the action of cold: to *freeze* water; The milk *froze*. **2** *v.* To become or cause to be covered or filled with ice: The pond *froze* over; Cold *froze* the water pipes. **3** *n.* A period of weather marked by freezing temperatures. **4** *v.* To damage, kill, or be damaged or killed by great cold: The crops *froze* during the night. **5** *v.* To make or be extremely cold. **6** *v.* To stick because of cold or ice: The paper cover *froze* to the ice cream. **7** *v.* To stick or tighten, as by the heat of friction. **8** *v.* To make or become motionless, as with fear, or unfriendly, as with dislike. **9** *v.* To hold (prices, wages, etc.) at a fixed level. **10** *n.* The act of freezing. **11** *n.* A frozen condition.

freez·er [frē′zər] *n.* **1** A refrigerator made to freeze food quickly and preserve frozen food. **2** A device for freezing ice cream.

freezing point The temperature at which a liquid freezes. The freezing point for fresh water at sea level is 32° F. or 0° C.

freight [frāt] **1** *n.* The service of shipping goods by train, truck, ship, or plane at regular rates: Ship it by *freight*. **2** *n.* Goods shipped in this way, or the charge for shipping them: The customer refused to pay the *freight*. **3** *v.* To send or carry as or by freight. **4** *v.* To load, as with goods to be transported. ◆ *Freight* comes from an old Dutch word.

freight·er [frā′tər] *n.* A ship used chiefly for carrying loads of goods, or cargo.

French [french] **1** *adj.* Of or from France. **2** *n.* **(the French)** The people of France. **3** *n.* The language of France.

French-Ca·na·di·an [french′kə·nā′dē·ən] **1** *n.* A French settler or a descendant of French settlers in Canada. **2** *adj.* Of, concerning, or occupied mainly by Canadians who speak French.

French fried Cooked by frying crisp in deep fat: *French fried* potatoes.

French Gui·a·na [gē·an′ə] A region on the NE coast of South America, administered as an overseas part of France.

French horn

French horn A brass musical instrument with a long, coiled tube, flaring widely at the end and producing a mellow tone.

---

add, āce, câre, pälm; end, ēqual; it, īce; odd, ōpen, ôrder; toŏk, poōl; up, bûrn; ə = a in *above*, e in *sicken*, i in *possible*, o in *melon*, u in *circus*; yoō = u in *fuse*; oil; pout; check; ring; thin; this; zh in *vision*. For ¶ reference, see page 64 · HOW TO

French leave A stealthy or hurried departure.

Frenchman [french′mən] *n., pl.* **French·men** [french′mən] A person born in or a citizen of France.

French Revolution The revolution in France from 1789 to 1799, during which the monarchy was overthrown and replaced with a republic.

fren·zied [fren′zēd] *adj.* **1** Madly excited; wild: A *frenzied* mob attacked the factory. **2** Very enthusiastic: *frenzied* applause.

fren·zy [fren′zē] *n., pl.* **fren·zies 1** A wild, excited fit or condition suggesting madness: He was angry to the point of *frenzy*. **2** Very great or intense work or effort: He attacked the weeds with *frenzy*.

fre·quen·cy [frē′kwən·sē] *n., pl.* **fre·quen·cies 1** The fact of being frequent; a repeated occurrence. **2** Rate of occurrence, as within a given time or group. **3** The number of times a recurring event happens in a given time, often expressed in cycles per second.

frequency modulation The changing of the frequency of a radio wave in a way that corresponds with the sound or other signal to be broadcasted.

fre·quent [*adj.* frē′kwənt, *v.* fri·kwent′] **1** *adj.* Happening again and again; often occurring: *frequent* interruptions. **2** *v.* To go to regularly; be often at or in: a man who *frequents* his club. **— fre′quent·ly** *adv.*

fres·co [fres′kō] *n., pl.* **fres·coes** or **fres·cos**, *v.* **fres·coed, fres·co·ing 1** *n.* The art of painting on a surface of moist plaster. **2** *v.* To paint in fresco, as a ceiling. **3** *n.* A picture so painted. ◆ *Fresco* comes directly from an Italian word meaning *fresh*, because a *fresco* is made while the plaster is fresh.

fresh¹ [fresh] *adj.* **1** Newly made, gotten, or gathered: *fresh* orange juice; *fresh* fruit. **2** Having just come: vegetables *fresh* from the garden. **3** Not stale or spoiled: *fresh* rolls; *fresh* cream. **4** Not dirty; clean: *fresh* sheets. **5** Pure and clear: *fresh* air. **6** Free of salt: *fresh* water. **7** New or original: *fresh* ideas. **8** Recent: *fresh* news. **9** Appearing young or healthy. **10** Rested and lively: a *fresh* horse. **— fresh′ly** *adv.* **— fresh′ness** *n.*

fresh² [fresh] *adj. U.S. informal* So bold as to offend; rude or disrespectful.

fresh·en [fresh′ən] *v.* To make or become fresh, as by washing oneself: to *freshen* up.

fresh·et [fresh′it] *n.* **1** A sudden overflow of a stream when snow melts or it rains a lot. **2** A fresh-water stream emptying into the sea.

fresh·man [fresh′mən] *n., pl.* **fresh·men** [fresh′mən] A student during the first year of studies in a high school or college.

fresh·wa·ter [fresh′wô′tər] *adj.* Of or living in water free of salt: *fresh-water* fish.

fret¹ [fret] *v.* **fret·ted, fret·ting,** *n.* **1** *v.* To make or be cross, irritated, or worried: Small cares *fret* us; Don't *fret*. **2** *n.* A cross or worried condition: He is in a *fret* over the delay. **3** *v.* To wear away, as by much rubbing.

fret² [fret] *n.* Any of the ridges across the top of the neck of a guitar, ukulele, etc.

fret·ful [fret′fəl] *adj.* Cross, restless, or peevish: a *fretful* baby. **— fret′ful·ly** *adv.*

fret·work [fret′wûrk′] *n.* Ornamental openwork, as in wood, usually composed of bands of lines or bars arranged in balanced patterns.

Frets on a guitar

Freud [froid], **Sigmund,** 1856–1939, Austrian doctor. He developed a theory of psychoanalysis.

Freu·di·an [froi′dē·ən] *adj.* Of, having to do with, or following the teachings of Freud.

Fri. Abbreviation of FRIDAY.

fri·a·ble [frī′ə·bəl] *adj.* Easily crumbled or reduced to powder or dust: Pumice is *friable*.

fri·ar [frī′ər] *n.* A man who belongs to any of certain Roman Catholic religious orders.

fric·as·see [frik′ə·sē′] *v.* **fric·as·seed, fric·as·see·ing 1** *n.* A dish of meat, especially chicken, cut up into small pieces, stewed, and served with gravy. **2** *v.* To make (meat) into a fricassee.

fric·tion [frik′shən] *n.* **1** The rubbing of one object against another. **2** The resistance to movement of a body that is in contact with another body. **3** A conflict or disagreement.

Fri·day [frī′dē] *n.* The sixth day of the week.

fried [frīd] **1** *adj.* Cooked by frying in hot fat. **2** Past tense and past participle of FRY².

friend [frend] *n.* **1** A person who knows another well, likes him, and is willing to help him. **2** A person who helps; supporter: *friends* of the college. **3** Someone on the same side, as contrasted with a foe. **4** (*written* **Friend**) A member of the Society of Friends; a Quaker.

friend·less [frend′lis] *adj.* Without friends.

friend·ly [frend′lē] *adj.* **friend·li·er, friend·li·est 1** Of or typical of a friend: a *friendly* suggestion. **2** Showing friendship or kindness: a *friendly* town. **3** Showing no ill will: a *friendly* rival. **— friend′li·ness** *n.*

friend·ship [frend′ship] *n.* **1** The condition or fact of being friends. **2** Mutual liking or friendly relationship. **3** Friendly feelings.

frieze [frēz] *n.* A decorated or sculptured horizontal band, as along the top of a wall.

frig·ate [frig′it] *n.* **1** A fast, square-rigged sailing warship of medium size, in use in the 18th and early 19th centuries. **2** A modern ship used on escort and patrol missions.

Frigate

frigate bird Either of two types of large sea birds noted for great powers of flight.

fright [frīt] *n.* **1** Sudden, violent alarm or fear. **2** *informal* Any-

F

thing ugly, ridiculous, or shocking: Her matted wig was a *fright!*

fright·en [frīt′(ə)n] *v.* **1** To fill with sudden fear; make or become afraid; scare. **2** To force or drive by scaring: He *frightened* us into agreeing; to *frighten* a thief away.

fright·ful [frīt′fəl] *adj.* **1** Alarming or terrifying: a *frightful* experience. **2** Shocking or horrible: a *frightful* sight. **3** *informal* Very bad or very great: a *frightful* headache; a *frightful* bore. **— fright′ful·ly** *adv.*

frig·id [frij′id] *adj.* **1** Bitterly cold: a *frigid* region. **2** Lacking warmth of feeling; formal and unfriendly: a *frigid* greeting.

frill [fril] **1** *n.* A pleated or gathered strip, as of lace, used as a fancy trimming or edging; ruffle. **2** *v.* To put frills on: to *frill* a dress. **3** *n. U.S. informal* An unnecessary thing added because it is fancy: to live simply, without *frills.* **— frill′y** *adj.*

fringe [frinj] *n., v.* **fringed, fring·ing 1** *n.* An ornamental border or trimming of hanging cords, threads, etc. **2** *n.* Any border, outer edge, or edging: He lives on the *fringe* of town. **3** *v.* To border with or as if with a fringe: Flowers *fringed* the path.

Fringe

frip·per·y [frip′ər·ē] *n., pl.* **frip·per·ies 1** Cheap, flashy dress or decoration. **2** A showing off or putting on airs, as in speech.

frisk [frisk] *v.* **1** To move or leap about playfully: Lambs *frisk* in the field. **2** *U.S. slang* To search (someone), as for weapons.

frisk·y [fris′kē] *adj.* **frisk·i·er, frisk·i·est** Lively or playful. **— frisk′i·ness** *n.*

frit·ter[1] [frit′ər] *v.* To waste or squander little by little: He *fritters* away his time.

frit·ter[2] [frit′ər] *n.* A small, fried cake of batter, often having corn, fruit, etc., in it.

fri·vol·i·ty [fri·vol′ə·tē] *n., pl.* **fri·vol·i·ties 1** The quality or condition of being frivolous. **2** A frivolous action or thing.

friv·o·lous [friv′ə·ləs] *adj.* **1** Not important or worthwhile; trivial: *frivolous* comment. **2** Not serious or responsible; silly or giddy: *frivolous* girls. **— friv′o·lous·ly** *adv.*

friz·zle[1] [friz′(ə)l] *v.* **friz·zled, friz·zling** To fry or cook with a sizzling noise.

friz·zle[2] [friz′(ə)l] *v.* **friz·zled, friz·zling,** *n.* **1** *v.* To curl tightly; kink, as the hair. **2** *n.* A crisp curl. **— friz′zly** *adj.*

frizz·y [friz′ē] *adj.* **frizz·i·er, frizz·i·est** Having tight curls; kinky: *frizzy* hair.

fro [frō] *adv.* Back again, especially in the phrase **to and fro,** back and forth.

frock [frok] *n.* **1** A woman's or girl's dress. **2** A long, loose robe worn by monks.

frog [frog] *n.* **1** A small, tailless, web-footed animal that lives in water or on land. It has large, strong hind legs for leaping. **2** An ornamental piece of braid or cord, as on a jacket, looped so as to fasten over a button.

frog·man [frog′man′] *n., pl.* **frog·men** [frog′men′] A skin diver, often in the armed forces, equipped with an independent supply of air so that he can swim and work under water.

frol·ic [frol′ik] *n., v.* **frol·icked, frol·ick·ing 1** *n.* An occasion full of playful fun. **2** *n.* Merriment. **3** *v.* To play about in a frisky way: The dog *frolicked* in the yard.

frol·ic·some [frol′ik·səm] *adj.* Playful.

from [frum, from, *or* frəm] *prep.* **1** Beginning at: the plane *from* New York; *from* May to June. **2** Sent, made, or given by: a letter *from* mother. **3** Because of: to faint *from* weakness. **4** Out of: She took a coin *from* her purse; Subtract 3 *from* 8. **5** Out of the control or reach of: He escaped *from* his enemies. **6** At a distance in relation to: far *from* home. **7** Protected against: He kept her *from* falling. **8** In respect to: His injured ankle prevented him *from* running. **9** As being other than: to know right *from* wrong.

frond [frond] *n.* A large leaf or leaflike part, as of a palm tree or fern.

front [frunt] **1** *n.* The part or side that faces forward. **2** *v.* To face in the direction of: This room *fronts* the ocean. **3** *n.* A position directly ahead: He sits in *front* of me. **4** *n.* The part coming before the rest: I was at the *front* of the line. **5** *adj.* In, at, on, of, or toward the front: a *front* seat. **6** *n.* The forward edge of a moving mass of warm or cold air. **7** *n.* In war, one of the areas where armies are fighting. **8** *n.* Land bordering a lake, road, etc.: a hotel on the ocean *front.* **9** *n.* Look, manner, or attitude: The frightened boy put on a bold *front.* **10** *v.* To meet boldly face to face; confront. **11** *n. informal* An outward pretense, as of wealth or success: to keep up a *front.* **12** *n.* A person, business, etc., used as a cloak for hidden actions.

front·age [frun′tij] *n.* **1** The front part of a lot or building. **2** The length of this part. **3** Land next to a road, body of water, etc. **4** The land lying between the front of a building and a road, river, etc.

fron·tal [frun′təl] *adj.* **1** Of, in, or on the front: a *frontal* assault. **2** Of or for the forehead: the *frontal* bone.

fron·tier [frun·tir′] *n.* **1** The part of a country lying along another country's border. **2** The edge of a settled region that borders on unsettled territory. **3** A new or unexplored area, as of knowledge: the *frontiers* of biology.

---

add, **ā**ce, **câ**re, **pä**lm; **e**nd, **ē**qual; **i**t, **ī**ce; **o**dd, **ō**pen, **ô**rder; t**oŏ**k, p**oōl**; **u**p, **bû**rn; ə = a in *above*, e in *sicken*, i in *possible*, o in *melon*, u in *circus*; **y**oō = u in *fuse*; **oi**l; p**ou**t; **ch**eck; **r**ing; **th**in; **th**is; **zh** in *vision*. For ¶ reference, see page 64 · HOW TO

fron·tiers·man [frun·tirz′mən] *n.,* *pl.* **fron·tiers·men** [frun·tirz′mən] A person who lives on the frontier, next to the wilderness.

fron·tis·piece [frun′tis·pēs′] *n.* A picture or drawing facing the title page of a book.

front·let [frunt′lit] *n.* **1** Something worn on or across the forehead. **2** An animal's forehead.

frost [frôst] **1** *n.* Dew or water vapor that has frozen into many fine, white ice crystals: *frost* on a window. **2** *n.* Weather cold enough to freeze things: A *frost* in summer ruins fruit trees. **3** *v.* To cover with frost. **4** *v.* To cover with frosting: to *frost* a cake.

Frost [frôst], **Robert Lee,** 1875–1963, U.S. poet.

frost·bite [frôst′bīt′] *n., v.* **frost·bit, frost·bit·ten, frost·bit·ing** **1** *n.* An injury to some part of the body caused by freezing. **2** *v.* To injure (some part of the body) by freezing: The cold wind *frostbit* his ears. **3** *adj. use: frostbitten* noses.

frost·ed [frôs′tid] *adj.* **1** Covered with frost. **2** Covered with frosting. **3** Having a roughened, frostlike surface, as some glass.

frost·ing [frôs′ting] *n.* A sweet, smooth mixture of eggs, sugar, etc., used to decorate cakes; icing.

frost·y [frôs′tē] *adj.* **frost·i·er, frost·i·est** **1** Cold enough to produce frost: *frosty* weather. **2** Covered with frost: *frosty* ground. **3** Cool and unfriendly: a *frosty* look.

froth [frôth] **1** *n.* A mass of very small bubbles; foam. **2** *n.* Something light and rather empty: Most of the music was *froth.* **3** *v.* To foam or cause to foam: The wind *frothed* the sea.

froth·y [frô′thē] *adj.* **froth·i·er, froth·i·est** **1** Covered with or full of froth. **2** Light or unimportant, as chatter. **— froth′i·ness** *n.*

frown [froun] **1** *v.* To wrinkle the forehead as in thinking, disapproval, or anger; scowl: The unhappy boy *frowns* often. **2** *n.* A sign of anger or worry made by frowning. **3** *v.* To be displeased; express disapproval: Mother *frowns* upon eating between meals.

frow·zy [frou′zē] *adj.* **frow·zi·er, frow·zi·est** **1** Dirty and messy; slovenly. **2** Having a bad smell; musty. **— frow′zi·ness** *n.*

froze [frōz] Past tense of FREEZE.

fro·zen [frō′zən] **1** Past participle of FREEZE. **2** *adj.* Changed into or covered with ice: a *frozen* lake. **3** *adj.* Killed or damaged by great cold: a *frozen* sparrow. **4** *adj.* Describing a place with very cold weather: the *frozen* North Pole. **5** *adj.* Preserved by freezing: *frozen* vegetables. **6** *adj.* Cold and cruel: a *frozen* look. **7** *adj.* Unable to move from fright, astonishment, etc.: *frozen* with fear.

fruc·tose [fruk′tōs *or* frŏŏk′tōs] *n.* A very sweet sugar found mainly in fruits and honey.

fru·gal [frŏŏ′gəl] *adj.* **1** Avoiding waste; using thrift: a *frugal* housekeeper. **2** Costing little

money; meager: a *frugal* meal. **— fru·gal·i·ty** [frŏŏ·gal′ə·tē] *n.* **— fru′gal·ly** *adv.*

fruit [frŏŏt] **1** *n.* An eatable part of a plant that develops from a flower, as a peach, apple, or grape. **2** *n.* The part of a plant that encloses the seeds, as a peach or nut. **3** *v.* To produce fruit. **4** *n.* Any useful plant product. **5** *n.* An outcome or result of some effort: the *fruit* of one's labor.

fruit·age [frŏŏ′tij] *n.* **1** The state or process of fruiting: the time of *fruitage.* **2** A harvest of fruit; fruits: a season's *fruitage.* **3** An outcome or successful result.

fruit·cake [frŏŏt′kāk′] *n.* A rich, spicy cake filled with nuts, raisins, and candied fruits.

fruit·er·er [frŏŏ′tər·ər] *n.* A fruit dealer.

fruit fly A type of fly that in its larval stage of development feeds on fruit.

fruit·ful [frŏŏt′fəl] *adj.* **1** Bearing much fruit. **2** Producing a great deal; abundant. **3** Having useful results; productive: a *fruitful* discussion. **— fruit′ful·ness** *n.*

fru·i·tion [frŏŏ·ish′ən] *n.* **1** The bearing of fruit. **2** An achievement worked or hoped for: The design was the *fruition* of hard work. **3** Enjoyment found in having or using something.

fruit·less [frŏŏt′lis] *adj.* **1** Yielding no fruit; barren. **2** Useless or unsuccessful.

fruit sugar Another name for FRUCTOSE.

fruit·y [frŏŏ′tē] *adj.* **fruit·i·er, fruit·i·est** Tasting or smelling like fruit.

frus·trate [frus′trāt] *v.* **frus·trat·ed, frus·trat·ing** To baffle the efforts of or bring to nothing; foil: The low grade *frustrated* his goal of being first in his class; The long delay *frustrated* him. **— frus·tra′tion** *n.*

fry¹ [frī] *n., pl.* **fry** A very young fish.

fry² [frī] *v.* **fried, fry·ing,** *n., pl.* **fries** **1** *v.* To cook in hot fat, usually over direct heat. **2** *n.* An outing at which foods are fried and eaten. **3** *n.* A dish of anything fried.

ft. Abbreviation of: **1** FOOT (12 inches). **2** Feet.

fuch·sia [fyŏŏ′shə] **1** *n., adj.* Bluish red. **2** *n.* A plant with handsome drooping flowers.

fud·dle [fud′(ə)l] *v.* **fud·dled, fud·dling** To make stupid with or as if with liquor; confuse: Too much champagne *fuddled* him.

fudge [fuj] *n.* A rich, soft candy made from butter, chocolate, sugar, and sometimes nuts.

Fueh·rer [fyŏŏr′ər] *n.* Another spelling of FÜHRER.

fu·el [fyŏŏ′əl] *n., v.* **fu·eled** or **fu·elled, fu·el·ing** or **fu·el·ling** **1** *n.* Something that readily produces energy in the form of heat when burnt, as wood, coal, oil, etc. **2** *n.* Anything that feeds a desire or emotion: The insult was *fuel* to her anger. **3** *v.* To supply or be supplied with fuel: to *fuel* an engine.

fuel cell A device that makes electricity directly from the reaction of two chemicals.

fu·gi·tive [fyŏŏ′jə·tiv] **1** *adj.* Fleeing, as from danger or arrest. **2** *n.* A fugitive person: a *fugitive* from justice. **3** *adj.* Quickly passing; not lasting: a *fugitive* hope.

fugue [fyŏŏg] *n.* A musical piece in which

Froth

elaborate counterpoint is developed from one or sometimes more themes.

Füh·rer [fyo͞or′ər] *n.* Leader: a German word.

Fu·ji [fo͞o′jē] *n.* The highest mountain of Japan.

Fu·ji·ya·ma [fo͞o′jē·yä′mä] *n.* Another name for FUJI.

-ful A suffix meaning: **1** Full of, as in *hopeful,* full of hope. **2** Tending to; able to, as in *helpful,* tending to help. **3** Having the character of, as in *manful,* being manly. **4** The amount or number that will fill, as in *cupful,* the amount that will fill a cup.

ful·crum [fo͞ol′krəm] *n.* A support on which a lever rests or turns when raising or moving a weight. ◆ *Fulcrum* comes from the Latin word for *bedpost,* which in turn comes from a word meaning *to prop up.*

Fulcrum

ful·fill or **ful·fil** [fo͞ol′fil′] *v.* **ful·filled, ful·fill·ing** **1** To carry out, as a promise, prediction, etc. **2** To do or perform (a duty) or obey (a law, request, etc.): to *fulfill* an obligation. **3** To meet or satisfy (a requirement, quota, etc.). **4** To finish up: to *fulfill* a task. **—ful·fill′·ment** or **ful·fil′ment** *n.*

full [fo͞ol] **1** *adj.* Filled with as much as is possible: a *full* barrel. **2** *adj.* Containing much or many: a book *full* of pictures. **3** *adj.* Whole or complete: a *full* day's work. **4** *adv.* To a complete degree: to know *full* well; a *full*-grown lion. **5** *adv.* Directly; straight: I looked him *full* in the eye. **6** *adj.* At the greatest point in size, degree, etc.: a *full* moon. **7** *n.* The greatest size or degree: the *full* of the moon. **8** *adj.* Having had much food and drink. **9** *adj.* Well-rounded; plump: a *full* figure. **10** *adj.* Clear and rich: the *full* tones of a cello. **11** *adj.* Having many wide folds: a *full* cape. **—in full 1** To the entire amount: a bill paid *in full.* **2** Not shortened or cut down: a speech printed *in full.* **—full′ness** *n.*

full·back [fo͞ol′bak′] *n.* A football player who stands farthest behind the front line.

full-blown [fo͞ol′blōn′] *adj.* At the peak of bloom or development: a *full-blown* rose.

full-fledged [fo͞ol′flejd′] *adj.* **1** Completely developed or mature: a *full-fledged* bird. **2** Having full standing: a *full-fledged* doctor.

full-grown [fo͞ol′grōn′] *adj.* Having reached full growth: a *full-grown* lion.

full moon The phase of the moon when its face appears as a full circle.

ful·ly [fo͞ol′ē] *adv.* **1** Totally and entirely: *fully* proved. **2** Sufficiently; adequately: *fully* fed. **3** At least: *fully* 50 miles away.

ful·mi·nate [ful′mə·nāt] *v.* **ful·mi·nat·ed, ful·mi·nat·ing** **1** To talk, argue, or utter violently and loudly: to *fulminate* against taxes. **2** To explode noisily. **—ful′mi·na′tion** *n.* ◆ *Fulminate* comes from the Latin word meaning *lightning.*

ful·some [fo͞ol′səm] *adj.* So much or so false as to be disgusting. ◆ *Fulsome* once meant *full* or *abundant,* but in time began to mean *too full* or *full in a false or insincere way,* and this is its meaning today. *Fulsome* flattery is so exaggerated that it is disgusting.

Ful·ton [fo͞ol′tən], **Robert,** 1765–1815, U.S. inventor, developed the first profitable steamboat.

fum·ble [fum′bəl] *v.* **fum·bled, fum·bling,** *n.* **1** *v.* To search about blindly or clumsily: to *fumble* for a key. **2** *v.* To handle or let drop clumsily, as a ball. **3** *n.* The act of fumbling.

fume [fyo͞om] *n., v.* **fumed, fum·ing 1** *n.* (*usually pl.*) Unpleasant smoke, gas, or vapor. **2** *v.* To give off fumes. **3** *v.* To darken with fumes: *fumed* oak. **4** *n.* A state of rage. **5** *v.* To complain angrily.

fu·mi·gate [fyo͞o′mə·gāt] *v.* **fu·mi·gat·ed, fu·mi·gat·ing** To subject to or disinfect with fumes or smoke. **—fu′mi·ga′tion** *n.*

fun [fun] *n.* **1** Pleasant amusement: The dance was *fun.* **2** Playfulness: full of *fun.* **3** Joking or jest: They fought only in *fun.* **— make fun of** To ridicule: They *made fun of* his strange ways.

func·tion [fungk′shən] **1** *n.* The proper action, use, or purpose: The *function* of a clock is to keep time. **2** *v.* To operate or work properly: Oiled machines *function* best. **3** *n.* A social affair. **4** *n.* A mathematical quantity whose value depends on the value of another quantity.

func·tion·al [fungk′shən·əl] *adj.* **1** Of or having to do with a function. **2** Affecting the proper function of an organ or part: a *functional* illness. **—func′tion·al·ly** *adv.*

func·tion·ar·y [fungk′shən·er′ē] *n., pl.* **func·tion·ar·ies** A public official.

fund [fund] **1** *n.* A sum of money set aside for a purpose: a building *fund.* **2** *v.* To set up a fund. **3** *v.* To pay off (a debt). **4** *n.* (*pl.*) Money available for use: insufficient *funds.* **5** *n.* A ready supply or stock: a *fund* of jokes.

fun·da·men·tal [fun′də·men′təl] **1** *adj.* Having to do with or serving as a foundation; essential; basic. **2** *n.* Anything basic to a system; an essential part. **—fun′da·men′tal·ly** *adv.*

Fun·dy [fun′dē], **Bay of** An inlet of the Atlantic Ocean between NW Nova Scotia and New Brunswick, famous for its high tides.

fu·ner·al [fyo͞o′nər·əl] **1** *n.* The ceremony at a burial or cremation, usually including a religious service and a procession to the cemetery. **2** *adj.* Of or suitable for a funeral.

---

add, āce, câre, pälm;   end, ēqual;   it, īce;   odd, ōpen, ôrder;   toͦok, poͦol;   up, bûrn;
ə = a in *above,* e in *sicken,* i in *possible,* o in *melon,* u in *circus;*   yoͦo = u in *fuse;*   oil;   pout;
check;   ring;   thin;   this;   zh in *vision.*   For ¶ reference, see page 64 · HOW TO

fu·ne·re·al [fyo͞o·nir′ē·əl] *adj.* Depressing and sad; gloomy: a *funereal* expression.

fun·gous [fung′gəs] *adj.* **1** Of or like a fungus. **2** Caused by a fungus: a *fungous* disease.

fun·gus [fung′gəs] *n., pl.* **fun·gi** [fun′jī] or **fun·gus·es** A plant with no chlorophyll, flowers, or leaves, as a mold, mushroom, etc. ◆ *Fungus* comes from the Latin word for *mushroom*.

Fungi

funk [fungk] *informal* **1** *n.* A panic; fear. **2** *v.* To shrink from or avoid. **3** *v.* To terrify.

fun·nel [fun′əl] *n., v.* **fun·neled** or **fun·nelled, fun·nel·ing** or **fun·nel·ling** **1** *n.* A cone-shaped utensil for pouring liquids, powders, etc., through a small opening. **2** *v.* To pour through or as if through a funnel. **3** *n.* A smokestack or chimney on a ship or steam locomotive.

fun·nies [fun′ēz] *n.pl. informal* The comic strips in a newspaper.

fun·ny [fun′ē] *adj.* **fun·ni·er, fun·ni·est** **1** Amusing or comical: a *funny* story. **2** *informal* Strange; peculiar: a *funny* look.

funny bone The place at the back of the elbow where a nerve is located close to the surface of the skin. When struck, the nerve causes an unpleasant tingling.

Funnel

fur [fûr] *n., v.* **furred, fur·ring** **1** *n.* The soft, hairy coat of many animals, as foxes, seals, squirrels, etc. **2** *n.* A cleaned animal skin covered with such a coat. **3** *adj. use:* a *fur* hat. **4** *n.* A coat, cape, etc., made of fur. **5** *v.* To trim, cover, or line with fur. **6** *n.* A fuzzy layer on the tongue, often accompanying illness. **7** *v.* To coat, as the tongue, with a layer of foul matter.

fur·be·low [fûr′bə·lō] **1** *n.* A fancy trimming: a hat with frills and *furbelows*. **2** *v.* To trim with ruffles and frills. ◆ Originally the English word for *furbelow* was *falbala*, which comes from the French. Apparently the grouping of sounds seemed too foreign to American ears, because the word gradually came to be pronounced and written as if it were composed of the familiar words *fur* and *below*.

fur·bish [fûr′bish] *v.* **1** To make bright by rubbing. **2** To renovate: to *furbish* up antiques.

Fu·ries [fyo͝or′ēz] *n.pl.* In Greek and Roman myths, three goddesses who avenged crimes that had gone unpunished.

fu·ri·ous [fyo͝or′ē·əs] *adj.* **1** Very angry. **2** Very strong or fierce: a *furious* wind. **3** Very great: a *furious* speed. **—fu′ri·ous·ly** *adv.* **—fu′ri·ous·ness** *n.*

furl [fûrl] **1** *v.* To roll up and fasten: to *furl* a sail to the yard. **2** *n.* Something furled.

fur·long [fûr′lông] *n.* A measure of length, equal to ⅛ of a mile, or 220 yards.

fur·lough [fûr′lō] **1** *n.* An official leave of absence, especially one granted to a sailor, soldier, etc. **2** *v.* To give a furlough to.

fur·nace [fûr′nis] *n.* A large structure with a chamber in which a fire of such intense heat may be made as to heat a building or melt metals.

fur·nish [fûr′nish] *v.* **1** To provide with furniture, as a room. **2** To provide or supply: to *furnish* each child with a ruler.

fur·nish·ings [fûr′nish·ingz] *n.pl.* **1** Clothing and accessories: men's *furnishings*. **2** Furniture or appliances, as for a room, office, etc.

fur·ni·ture [fûr′nə·chər] *n.* The movable articles in a house or office, as chairs, beds, etc.

fu·ror [fyo͝or′ôr] *n.* **1** Great rage or fury: the mob's *furor*. **2** Intense enthusiasm or excitement: The movie caused a *furor*. **3** Craze or mania.

fur·ri·er [fûr′ē·ər] *n.* **1** A dealer in furs. **2** A person who makes or restores fur garments.

fur·row [fûr′ō] **1** *n.* A long, deep groove made in land by a plow. **2** *n.* A wrinkle on the face or forehead. **3** *v.* To make furrows in.

fur·ry [fûr′ē] *adj.* **fur·ri·er, fur·ri·est** **1** Covered with fur. **2** Of or like fur.

Furrows

fur·ther [fûr′thər] **1** Comparative of FAR. **2** *adv.* At or to a more distant point. **3** *adj.* More distant or advanced. **4** *adv.* To a greater degree: We must question her *further*. **5** *adj.* Additional: *further* news. **6** *adv.* In addition; besides. **7** *v.* To promote or help forward: to *further* one's aims. ◆ See FARTHER.

fur·ther·ance [fûr′thər·əns] *n.* **1** Advancement or promotion. **2** Something that helps advancement.

fur·ther·more [fûr′thər·môr′] *adv.* Moreover.

fur·ther·most [fûr′thər·mōst′] *adj.* Furthest and most distant: the *furthermost* point on a map.

fur·thest [fûr′thist] **1** Superlative of FAR. **2** *adv.* At or to the most distant or advanced point; farthest: He fell *furthest* behind in spelling. **3** *adj.* Most distant or advanced.

fur·tive [fûr′tiv] *adj.* **1** Done in secret; stealthy: a *furtive* glance. **2** Sly: a *furtive* manner. **—fur′tive·ly** *adv.* ◆ See STEALTHY.

fu·ry [fyo͝or′ē] *n., pl.* **fu·ries** **1** Wild or extreme anger; rage. **2** A fit of such anger. **3** Great force or violence. **4** A person with a violent or raging temper.

furze [fûrz] *n.* Another name for GORSE.

fuse¹ [fyo͞oz] *n.* **1** The wick on a firecracker, or a mechanical or electric device that will set off a bomb, missile, etc. **2** A small, enclosed strip of metal that completes an electrical circuit. If the current gets too strong the fuse melts and breaks the connection.

fuse² [fyo͞oz] *v.* **fused, fus·ing** **1** To melt or join by melting together. **2** To unite.

fu·se·lage [fyōō′sə·lij *or* fyōō′sə·läzh] *n.* The body of an airplane, excluding the wings and tail.

Fuselage

fu·si·ble [fyōō′zə·bəl] *adj.* Capable of being fused or melted by heat: a *fusible* metal.

fu·sil·lade [fyōō′sə·läd′] *n.* **1** A burst of fire from guns, cannons, etc. **2** Anything like a fusillade: a *fusillade* of complaints.

fu·sion [fyōō′zhən] *n.* **1** A blending or melting together. **2** The condition of being blended or melted together. **3** Something formed by a joining or coming together, especially a joining together or union of political parties or factions. **4** Nuclear fusion.

fusion bomb Another name for HYDROGEN BOMB.

fuss [fus] **1** *n.* Bother over small details; needless nervous activity. **2** *v.* To bother with tiny details: He kept *fussing* with his tie. **3** *n.* A protest or complaint: Why does she always make a *fuss* about the heating? **4** *v.* To complain, scold, or grumble: He was constantly *fussing* about the way the students behaved. **5** *n.* A quarrel or dispute: a loud *fuss* in the hall.

fuss·y [fus′ē] *adj.* **fuss·i·er, fuss·i·est 1** Hard to please; particular; finicky: a *fussy* eater. **2** Elaborately trimmed: a *fussy* hat. **— fuss′i· ly** *adv.* **— fuss′i·ness** *n.*

fus·tian [fus′chən] *n.* **1** A coarse, twilled, cotton fabric, as corduroy. **2** High-flown speech or writing; bombast.

fust·y [fus′tē] *adj.* **fust·i·er, fust·i·est 1** Moldy; musty: *fusty* old books. **2** Old-fashioned: a *fusty* old man. **— fust′i·ly** *adv.* **— fust′i·ness** *n.*

fu·tile [fyōō′təl] *adj.* **1** Done in vain; useless: *futile* efforts. **2** Having no importance; trivial: *futile* chatter. **— fu′tile·ly** *adv.*

fu·til·i·ty [fyōō·til′ə·tē] *n., pl.* **fu·til·i·ties 1** Complete lack of effectiveness; uselessness: the *futility* of our efforts to stop the flood. **2** Unimportance, insignificance, or triviality: the *futility* of arguing over such silly matters. **3** A futile act, event, thing, etc.

fu·ture [fyōō′chər] **1** *n.* The time yet to come; time that is to be. **2** *adj.* Occurring in the future: a *future* date. **3** *adj.* Having to do with or expressing time to come. **4** *n.* The future tense of a language. **5** *n.* Chance for success; prospect: a job with a *future*.

future tense In some languages, a form of a verb used to express meanings of future time. In English, such meanings are expressed by verb phrases that include *shall* or *will*.

fu·tu·ri·ty [fyōō·t(y)ŏŏr′ə·tē] *n., pl.* **fu·tu·ri·ties 1** The future. **2** The state or quality of being future. **3** A future act, thing, etc.

fuze [fyōōz] *n.* Another spelling of FUSE[1].

fuzz [fuz] *n.* Short light hairs or fibers; fine down: Peaches have *fuzz.*

fuzz·y [fuz′ē] *adj.* **fuzz·i·er, fuzz·i·est 1** Of, like, or having fuzz. **2** Blurry; not clear: *fuzzy* images. **— fuzz′i·ness** *n.*

-fy A suffix meaning: **1** To make or cause to be, as in *simplify*, to make simple or simpler. **2** To become, as in *liquefy*, to become liquid.

G

g or **G** [jē] *n., pl.* **g's** or **G's** The seventh letter of the English alphabet.

g. Abbreviation of: **1** GRAM. **2** Grams.

G The symbol for gravity.

Ga. Abbreviation of GEORGIA.

gab [gab] *v.* **gabbed, gab·bing,** *n. informal* **1** *v.* To chatter; talk a great deal. **2** *n.* Idle talk.

gab·ar·dine or **gab·er·dine** [gab′ər·dēn] *n.* **1** A firm, twilled fabric used for coats, suits, etc. **2** A long, loose, coarse cloak worn in medieval times.

gab·ble [gab′əl] *v.* **gab·bled, gab·bling,** *n.* **1** *v.* To talk or utter quickly, making little or no sense; jabber: They *gabbled* away, like so many geese. **2** *n.* Rapid, senseless talk.

ga·ble [gā′bəl] *n.* The triangular top part of an outer wall, under a ridged roof and above its eaves.

ga·bled [gā′bəld] *adj.* Built with or forming a gable or gables: a *gabled* house.

Ga·bon [ga·bon′] *n.* A country in western Africa.

Ga·bri·el [gā′brē·əl] *n.* In the Bible, one of the archangels, chosen as the special messenger of God.

Gables

add, āce, câre, pälm;   end, ēqual;   it, īce;   odd, ōpen, ôrder;   tŏŏk, pōōl;   up, bûrn;
ə = a in *above*, e in *sicken*, i in *possible*, o in *melon*, u in *circus*;   yōō = u in *fuse*;   oil;   pout;
check; ring; thin; this; zh in *vision*.   For ¶ reference, see page 64 · HOW TO

gad [gad] *v.* **gad·ded, gad·ding** To roam about idly or looking for fun and excitement.

gad·a·bout [gad′ə·bout′] *n.* A person who gads about aimlessly or restlessly.

gad·fly [gad′flī′] *n., pl.* **gad·flies 1** A large fly that bites cattle, horses, etc. **2** An irritating, bothersome person.

gadg·et [gaj′it] *n. informal* A small device or contrivance, especially a mechanical one.

Gael·ic [gā′lik] **1** *n.* The Celtic language of the Irish or Scottish Highlanders. **2** *adj.* Of or having to do with these Celts or their language.

gaff [gaf] **1** *n.* A spear or iron hook used to land large fish. **2** *v.* To hook or land with a gaff. **3** *n.* A spar to hold the upper edge of a fore-and-aft sail.

gaf·fer [gaf′ər] *n.* An old man: used in humor.

gag [gag] *n., v.* **gagged, gag·ging 1** *n.* Something, as a cloth, put in or across the mouth to muffle the voice. **2** *v.* To prevent speaking by applying a gag to. **3** *v.* To retch or cause to retch. **4** *n. slang* A joke or playful hoax.

gage[1] [gāj] *n.* **1** Something given as security; a pledge. **2** Anything offered in challenge, as a glove for a duel, etc. **3** Any challenge.

gage[2] [gāj] *n., v.* Another spelling of GAUGE.

gai·e·ty [gā′ə·tē] *n., pl.* **gai·e·ties 1** Gay liveliness. **2** Gay activity. **3** Colorful brightness.

gai·ly [gā′lē] *adv.* In a gay manner.

gain [gān] **1** *v.* To obtain, earn, or win: to *gain* the advantage. **2** *v.* To increase in: to *gain* momentum. **3** *n.* An increase in size, amount, etc. **4** *n.* (*often pl.*) Profit, winnings, etc.: small *gains*. **5** *v.* To profit or advance: to *gain* by an action. **6** *n.* An advantage or lead: a *gain* of one mile. **7** *v.* To reach or draw nearer: to *gain* port; to *gain* on an opponent. **8** *v.* To put on, as weight. **9** *v.* To grow better or stronger: The invalid was *gaining*. **10** *n.* The act of gaining.

gain·ful [gān′fəl] *adj.* Yielding or bringing gain; profitable. — **gain′ful·ly** *adv.*

gain·say [gān′sā′] *v.* **gain·said, gain·say·ing 1** To deny. **2** To contradict. **3** To oppose.

Gains·bor·ough [gānz′bûr·ō] **Thomas,** 1727–1788, English painter.

'gainst or **gainst** [genst] *prep.* Against: used mostly in poems.

gait [gāt] *n.* A way of walking, stepping, or running.

gai·ter [gā′tər] *n.* **1** A covering as of cloth or leather, for the lower leg or ankle. **2** A high shoe with an elastic strip in each side.

gal. Abbreviation of: **1** GALLON. **2** Gallons.

ga·la [gā′lə *or* gal′ə] **1** *adj.* Festive and gay. **2** *n.* A lively celebration; festival.

Gal·a·had [gal′ə·had] *n.* The noblest knight of the Round Table, who found the Grail.

Ga·la·tians [gə·lā′shənz] *n.* A book of the New Testament written by Saint Paul.

gal·ax·y [gal′ək·sē] *n., pl.* **gal·ax·ies 1** (*written* **Galaxy**) The Milky Way. **2** A large system of celestial bodies. **3** Any brilliant group.

gale [gāl] *n.* **1** A strong wind. **2** An outburst, as of laughter.

ga·le·na [gə·lē′nə] *n.* A metallic, dull gray mineral from which lead is extracted.

Gal·i·le·an [gal′ə·lē′ən] **1** *adj.* Of or from Galilee. **2** *n.* A person born or living in Galilee. — **the Galilean** Jesus Christ.

Gal·i·lee [gal′ə·lē] *n.* A region in northern Palestine. — **Sea of Galilee** A fresh-water lake in northern Palestine.

Gal·i·le·o [gal·ə·lē′ō] *n.*, 1564–1642, Italian astronomer and physicist who developed the first practical telescope and showed that the earth goes around the sun.

gall[1] [gôl] *n.* **1** The bitter fluid produced by the liver; bile. **2** Bitter feeling; malice. **3** Anything bitter. **4** *U.S. slang* Impudence.

gall[2] [gôl] **1** *n.* A sore made by rubbing. **2** *v.* To make sore by rubbing; chafe. **3** *v.* To annoy; irritate; vex.

gall[3] [gôl] *n.* A lump or growth on a part of a plant that has been injured by insects, fungi, or bacteria.

gal·lant [gal′ənt *or* gə·lant′] **1** *adj.* [gal′ənt] Bold and courageous; brave. **2** *adj.* [gə·lant′] Courteous and respectful to women; chivalrous. **3** *n.* A brave or chivalrous man. **4** *n.* A fashionable young man. **5** *adj.* Showy or imposing: *gallant* attire. — **gal′lant·ly** *adv.*

gal·lant·ry [gal′ən·trē] *n., pl.* **gal·lant·ries 1** Bravery and nobility. **2** Chivalrous behavior. **3** A courteous act or speech.

gall bladder A small, pear-shaped sac beneath the liver, in which excess bile is stored.

gal·le·on [gal′ē·ən] *n.* A large sailing ship of former times, having many decks.

gal·ler·y [gal′ər·ē] *n., pl.* **gal·ler·ies 1** A long corridor or passageway, sometimes with one open side. **2** An indoor balcony, especially the highest one in a theater. **3** The people who sit in this balcony. **4** A place where works of art are displayed. **5** A long room used for a special purpose: a shooting *gallery*.

Galleon

gal·ley [gal′ē] *n., pl.* **gal·leys 1** In ancient and medieval times, a long, narrow ship with sails and oars, usually rowed by prisoners or slaves. **2** The kitchen of a ship.

Gal·lic [gal′ik] *adj.* **1** Of or having to do with Gaul or the Gauls. **2** French.

Galley

gall·ing [gôl′ing] *adj.* Very irritating: It was a *galling* experience to have to ask for help.

gal·li·vant [gal′ə·vant] *v.* To roam about in search of fun and excitement.

gal·lon [gal′ən] *n.* A liquid measure equal to 4 quarts or 8 pints.

gal·lop [gal′əp] **1** *n.* The fastest gait of a four-footed animal. Once in each stride all four feet are off the ground at the same time. **2** *v.* To ride or go at this gait. **3** *n.* Such a ride. **4** *v.* To go at a fast pace.

Horse galloping

gal·lows [gal′ōz] *n.*, *pl.* **gal·lows·es** or **gal·lows** **1** A wooden framework used for hanging criminals. **2** The punishment of executing criminals by hanging.

gall·stone [gôl′stōn′] *n.* A hard, stonelike substance sometimes formed in the gall bladder.

ga·lore [gə·lôr′] *adv.* In great abundance.

ga·losh [gə·losh′] *n.* (*usually pl.*) A high, rubber overshoe worn in wet or snowy weather.

ga·lumph [gə·lumf′] *v.* To walk or bound clumsily and noisily.

gal·van·ic [gal·van′ik] *adj.* **1** Of or having to do with electricity produced by chemical action. **2** Sudden or startling: *galvanic* news.

gal·va·nize [gal′və·nīz] *v.* **gal·va·nized, gal·va·niz·ing 1** To shock or stimulate with electricity. **2** To rouse; startle. **3** To coat (iron, etc.) with a protective layer of zinc. ¶3

gal·va·nom·e·ter [gal′və·nom′ə·tər] *n.* A device that measures the strength and direction of an electric current.

gam·bit [gam′bit] *n.* In chess, an opening in which a piece is risked to gain an advantage.

gam·ble [gam′bəl] *v.* **gam·bled, gam·bling,** *n.* **1** *v.* To risk (something, as money) by betting on the outcome of an event, game, etc. **2** *v.* To take a risk, as on a chance for gain. **3** *n.* An act of gambling; wager; bet. **4** *n.* A risky or uncertain act or venture. **5** *v.* To lose by gambling. **— gam·bler** [gam′blər] *n.*

gam·bol [gam′bəl] *v.* **gam·boled** or **gam·bolled, gam·bol·ing** or **gam·bol·ling,** *n.* **1** *v.* To skip or run about in play: lambs *gamboling* about the field. **2** *n.* A frolic; play.

gam·brel roof [gam′brəl] A ridged roof with its slope broken on each side so that the lower section is steeper than the upper.

game [gām] *n.*, *adj.*, *v.* **gamed, gam·ing 1** *n.* A contest or sport involving chance, skill, endurance, etc., governed by set rules. **2** *n.* A set used in playing a game. **3** *n.* A form of play. **4** *n.* A plan; scheme. **5** *n.* Animals or birds hunted for food or sport. **6** *n.* The flesh of such game used as food. **7** *adj.* Of or having to do with such game. **8** *adj.* Spirited;

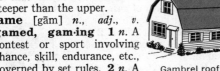

Gambrel roof

plucky. **9** *adj. informal* Ready; willing. **10** *v.* To gamble. **11** *n.* A score needed to win, as in tennis. **— make game of** To ridicule.

game·cock [gām′kok′] *n.* A rooster bred and trained to fight other roosters.

game·keep·er [gām′kē′pər] *n.* A person who tends and protects wild game, as on an estate.

game·some [gām′səm] *adj.* Playful; sportive.

game·ster [gām′stər] *n.* A gambler.

gam·ete [gam′ēt] *n.* Either of the two reproductive cells, a sperm or ovum, that unite to form a new plant or animal.

gam·in [gam′in] *n.* A homeless, neglected child who wanders about the streets.

gam·ing [gām′ing] *n.* Gambling.

gam·ma [gam′ə] *n.* The third letter of the Greek alphabet.

gamma glob·u·lin [glob′yə·lin] The part of blood plasma that has most of the antibodies.

gamma ray A type of electromagnetic radiation of short wavelength and great penetrating power.

gam·ut [gam′ət] *n.* **1** The whole range of anything. **2** The entire range of musical tones.

gam·y [gā′mē] *adj.* **gam·i·er, gam·i·est 1** Having the odor or flavor of game that has been aged before cooking. **2** Plucky.

gan·der [gan′dər] *n.* A male goose.

Gan·dhi [gän′dē *or* gan′dē], **Mohandas K.,** 1869–1948, Hindu political and spiritual leader, widely known as Mahatma Gandhi.

gang [gang] *n.* **1** A group of people, as friends, laborers, criminals, etc., who work or pass the time together. **2** A set of similar tools or machines that work together: a *gang* of saws. **— gang up** or **gang up on** To attack or act against as a group.

Gan·ges [gan′jēz] *n.* A river in northern India flowing 1,500 miles SE to the Bay of Bengal.

gan·gling [gang′gling] *adj.* Awkward, tall, and lanky: a *gangling* youth.

gan·gli·on [gang′glē·ən] *n.*, *pl.* **gan·gli·ons** or **gan·gli·a** [gang′glē·ə] **1** A collection of nerve cells, located elsewhere than in the brain or spinal cord. **2** Any center of activity or strength.

gang·plank [gang′plangk′] *n.* A movable bridge which persons cross to get on or off a ship.

gan·grene [gang′grēn] *n.*, *v.* **gan·grened, gan·gren·ing 1** *n.* The decay of tissue in part of the body, caused by a failure in circulation of the blood, as from injury or disease. **2** *v.* To cause or be affected by gangrene. **— gan′·gre·nous** [gang′grə·nəs] *adj.*

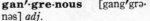

Gangplank

gang·ster [gang′stər] *n.* A member of a gang of criminals or racketeers.

---

add, āce, câre, pälm; end, ēqual; it, īce; odd, ōpen, ôrder; took, pool; up, bûrn; ə = a in *above*, e in *sicken*, i in *possible*, o in *melon*, u in *circus*; yoo = u in *fuse*; oil; pout; check; ring; thin; this; zh in *vision*. For ¶ reference, see page 64 · HOW TO

gang·way [gang′wā] **1** *n.* A passageway or gangplank. **2** *interj.* Move aside!

gan·net [gan′it] *n.* Any of several large sea birds related to the pelican.

gant·let[1] [gônt′lit] *n.* A punishment in which the victim runs between and is hit by two lines of people with clubs. **— run the gantlet 1** To run between and be hit by two lines of people with clubs. **2** To undergo an ordeal of any kind.

gant·let[2] [gônt′lit] *n.* Another spelling of GAUNTLET[1].

gaol [jāl] *n. British* A jail. **— gaol′er** *n.*

gap [gap] *n.* **1** A crack or opening, as in a wall. **2** A mountain pass. **3** An empty space. **4** A difference: a wide *gap* in their ages.

gape [gāp] *v.* **gaped, gap·ing,** *n.* **1** *v.* To stare with the mouth open, as in surprise. **2** *v.* To open the mouth wide, as in yawning. **3** *n.* The act of gaping. **4** *v.* To be or become wide open. **5** *n.* A wide opening; gap.

ga·rage [gə·räzh′] *n.* A place where automobiles are housed or repaired. ◆ When the French word *garage,* meaning *a storing away,* came into use in English, its meaning became narrower, referring only to a place where automobiles, trucks, etc., were stored.

garb [gärb] **1** *n.* Clothing; manner of dress: the *garb* of a sailor. **2** *v.* To clothe; dress.

gar·bage [gär′bij] *n.* Worthless or offensive material, especially waste from a kitchen.

gar·ble [gär′bəl] *v.* **gar·bled, gar·bling 1** To mix up or confuse (a story, facts, etc.) by mistake. **2** To deliberately change or leave out, as parts of a story, so that a false or unclear presentation is given.

gar·den [gär′dən] **1** *n.* A plot of land where flowers, vegetables, etc., are grown. **2** *v.* To work in a garden. **— gar′den·er** *n.*

gar·de·nia [gär·dēn′yə] *n.* A large, white flower with a very sweet scent.

Gar·field [gär′fēld], **James A.,** 1831–1881, 20th president of the U.S., 1881. He was assassinated.

gar·gle [gär′gəl] *v.* **gar·gled, gar·gling,** *n.* **1** *v.* To rinse (the throat and mouth) with a liquid kept in motion by expelling air. **2** *n.* A liquid used for gargling.

gar·goyle [gär′goil] *n.* A carved figure of a grotesque animal or human being that juts out from a building and usually contains a channel for draining off rain water.

gar·ish [gâr′ish] *adj.* Too showy or bright; gaudy. **— gar′ish·ly** *adv.*

gar·land [gär′lənd] **1** *n.* A wreath or rope of flowers or leaves. **2** *v.* To decorate with, or make into a garland.

Gargoyle

gar·lic [gär′lik] *n.* **1** A plant of the onion family.

2 The bulb of this plant, used as a seasoning. It has a strong, penetrating smell.

gar·ment [gär′mənt] *n.* An article of clothing.

gar·ner [gär′nər] **1** *v.* To gather and store (grain, etc.). **2** *n.* A storage place, especially for grain.

gar·net [gär′nit] **1** *n.* A hard, deep red mineral, often used as a gem. **2** *adj., n.* Deep red.

gar·nish [gär′nish] **1** *n.* A small piece of fruit, a bit of spice, etc., added to a main dish to improve its taste or appearance. **2** *n.* A decoration; ornament. **3** *v.* To add garnishes to.

gar·nish·ee [gär′nish·ē′] *v.* **gar·nish·eed, gar·nish·ee·ing** To seize (a part of a person's wages) by legal means, in payment of a debt.

gar·ret [gar′it] *n.* A small room or set of rooms in an attic, under a sloping roof.

gar·ri·son [gar′ə·sən] **1** *n.* The troops stationed in a fort or town. **2** *v.* To station (troops) in a fort or town. **3** *n.* The place where the troops are stationed. **4** *v.* To station troops in (a town, fort, etc.).

gar·ru·lous [gar′ə·ləs] *adj.* Talking a lot, especially about trifles. **— gar′ru·lous·ly** *adv.* **— gar′ru·lous·ness** *n.*

gar·ter [gär′tər] **1** *n.* An elastic band or strap, used to hold up a stocking or sock. **2** *v.* To support or fasten with a garter.

Gar·ter [gär′tər], **Order of the** The most honored badge and award of knighthood given in Great Britain.

garter snake A small, harmless American snake with long yellow lines on the back.

gas [gas] *n., pl.* **gas·es,** *v.* **gassed, gas·sing 1** *n.* A substance that is not solid or liquid but is fluid and able to expand indefinitely: Oxygen and hydrogen are *gases* at normal temperatures. **2** *n.* Any gas, considered with respect to its use, effect, origin, etc.: cooking *gas;* poison *gas;* swamp *gas.* **3** *v.* To kill or injure with poison gas: to *gas* a hamster. **4** *n. informal* Gasoline. **5** *v. informal* To fill with gasoline. **6** *v. slang* To talk idly and boastfully. ◆ *Gas* was coined about 350 years ago by a Belgian chemist, either from the Dutch word *geest,* meaning *a spirit,* or the Greek word *chaos,* meaning *a formless mass.* Later the suffix *-eous,* a form of *-ous,* was added to *gas* to make *gaseous.*

gas·e·ous [gas′ē·əs *or* gash′əs] *adj.* Of or like gas; in the form of gas. ◆ See GAS.

gash [gash] **1** *v.* To make a long, deep cut in. **2** *n.* A long, deep cut or flesh wound.

gas·ket [gas′kit] *n.* A ring or packing, as of rubber or metal, tightly fitted around the edges of two joined parts to prevent leaking.

gas mask A protective mask with an air filter worn to prevent poisoning or irritation by harmful gases, radioactive dust, etc.

Gas mask

gas·o·line or **gas·o·lene** [gas′ə·lēn] *n.* An almost colorless liquid made from petroleum, used mainly as a motor fuel.

gasp [gasp] **1** *n.* A sudden catching of the breath; a pant. **2** *v.* To breathe in gasps. **3** *v.* To utter (sounds or words) between gasps.

gas station A place where gasoline and other supplies for motor vehicles are sold.

gas·tric [gas′trik] *adj.* Of or having to do with the stomach.

gas·tru·la [gas′troo·lə] *n.,* *pl.* **gas·tru·las** or **gas·tru·lae** [gas′troo·lē] A stage in the development of an animal when the embryo is a hollow sac formed by two layers of cells.

gate [gāt] *n.* **1** A part of a fence or wall, that opens and shuts like a door. **2** An opening in a fence or wall with a gate in it. **3** Something that controls a flow, as a valve or sluice. **4** The number of people who pay to attend a play, sporting event, etc. **5** The total amount of money collected from these people.

gate·way [gāt′wā′] *n.* **1** An entrance or archway, often fitted with a gate. **2** A way of entering, exiting, or getting at: the *gateway* to wisdom.

gath·er [gath′ər] **1** *v.* To bring together or come together; collect; assemble: *Gather* your books; They *gathered* to celebrate. **2** *v.* To pick or harvest: to *gather* flowers. **3** *v.* To collect over a period of time; accumulate: The storm *gathered* force. **4** *v.* To draw (cloth) into folds. **5** *n.* A pleat or fold in cloth. **6** *v.* To draw as a conclusion: I *gather* that you're unhappy. **7** *v.* To swell and fill with pus: The boil *gathered*.

gath·er·ing [gath′ər·ing] *n.* **1** A meeting or assembly. **2** A boil or abscess.

gauche [gōsh] *adj.* Awkward or crude.

Gau·cho [gou′chō] *n.,* *pl.* **Gau·chos** A cowboy of the South American pampas or plains.

gaud·y [gô′dē] *adj.* **gaud·i·er, gaud·i·est** Showy or bright in a way that lacks taste.

gauge [gāj] *v.* **gauged, gaug·ing,** *n.* **1** *v.* To make an accurate measurement. **2** *n.* Any of various systems or standards for measuring. **3** *n.* A measurement made according to such a system or standard: the *gauge* of a wire. **4** *n.* Any of various instruments for measuring: a pressure *gauge*. **5** *n.* The distance between rails of a railway. **6** *v.* To estimate or judge: to *gauge* a person's character.

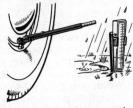

The tire gauge measures air pressure in the tire. The rain gauge measures rainfall.

Gaul [gôl] *n.* **1** The ancient name for France and some regions around it. **2** A person who lived in or was born in Gaul. **3** A Frenchman.

gaunt [gônt] *adj.* **1** Very thin and bony, as from illness or hunger; worn. **2** Gloomy and barren; desolate: a *gaunt,* deserted region.

gaunt·let[1] [gônt′lit] *n.* **1** A glove covered with metal plates, worn by knights as part of their armor. **2** A heavy glove with a long, wide cuff, flaring past the wrist. — **throw down the gauntlet** To challenge to fight.

gaunt·let[2] [gônt′lit] *n.* Another spelling of GANTLET[1].

gauze [gôz] *n.* A thin, loosely-woven fabric.

gauz·y [gô′zē] *adj.* **gauz·i·er, gauz·i·est** **1** Of or like gauze. **2** Thin enough to be seen through.

gave [gāv] Past tense of GIVE.

gav·el [gav′əl] *n.* A small, wooden mallet used by the person in charge of a meeting to call for attention or order.

ga·votte [gə·vot′] *n.* A 17th-century French dance, like the minuet, but somewhat quicker.

Gavel

Ga·wain [gä′win] *n.* One of the knights of the Round Table, nephew of King Arthur.

gawk [gôk] *informal* **1** *v.* To stare stupidly; gape. **2** *n.* An awkward, stupid person.

gawk·y [gô′kē] *adj.* **gawk·i·er, gawk·i·est** Awkward or clumsy. — **gawk′i·ness** *n.*

gay [gā] *adj.* **1** Joyful; full of fun. **2** Colorful and bright: *gay* decorations.

gay·e·ty [gā′ə·tē] *n.* Another spelling of GAIETY.

gay·ly [gā′lē] *adv.* Another spelling of GAILY.

gaze [gāz] *v.* **gazed, gaz·ing,** *n.* **1** *v.* To look steadily; stare, as in wonder or awe. **2** *n.* A steady or fixed look. — **gaz′er** *n.*

ga·zelle [gə·zel′] *n.* A small, graceful antelope of Africa and Arabia with curved horns and large eyes.

ga·zette [gə·zet′] *n.,* *v.* **ga·zet·ted, ga·zet·ting** **1** *n.* A newspaper: used mainly in the names of newspapers. **2** *n.* An official journal. **3** *v.* To publish or announce in a gazette.

Gazelle, about 4 ft. long

gaz·et·teer [gaz′ə·tir′] *n.* A book or part of a dictionary giving names and descriptions of countries, cities, mountains, rivers, etc.

gear [gir] **1** *n.* A toothed wheel that meshes with another such wheel. A smaller wheel turns faster than a larger one meshed with it. **2** *n.* One of several alternative systems of such wheels in an automobile, each delivering a range of speed and power: low *gear*. **3** *n.* A mechanism to do

---

add, āce, câre, pälm; end, ēqual; it, īce; odd, ōpen, ôrder; took, pool; up, bûrn; ə = a in *above,* e in *sicken,* i in *possible,* o in *melon,* u in *circus;* yoo = u in *fuse;* oil; pout; check; ring; thin; this; zh in *vision.* For ¶ reference, see page 64 · HOW TO

something: a steering *gear*. **4** *v*. To connect (machine parts) by gears. **5** *v*. To adjust or regulate: to *gear* a plan to necessity. **6** *n*. Equipment for a special purpose: camping *gear*. **7** *v*. To provide with gear; equip.
— in gear Connected, as to a motor. **— out of gear 1** Disconnected, as from a motor. **2** Unable to operate corectly; fouled.

Gears

gear·ing [gir'ing] *n*. Any system of gears or parts that transmits power or motion.

gear·shift [gir'shift'] *n*. A device that allows speed to be varied by the connection of different sets of gears.

gear·wheel [gir'(h)wēl'] *n*. A toothed wheel in a gear.

geck·o [gek'ō] *n.*, *pl*. **geck·os** or **geck·oes** A small lizard having suction pads on its toes that enable it to walk on walls, ceilings, etc.

gee[1] [jē] *interj*. A command meaning "turn to the right," given to an ox or horse.

gee[2] [jē] *interj*. An exclamation of surprise, sympathy, wonder, etc.

geese [gēs] Plural of GOOSE.

Gei·ger counter [gi'gər] An instrument for detecting and measuring radioactivity.

gei·sha [gā'sha] *n.*, *pl*. **gei·sha** or **gei·shas** A Japanese girl trained to entertain by singing and dancing.

gel·a·tin or **gel·a·tine** [jel'ə·tin] *n*. A protein obtained by boiling the bones, skins, hooves, etc., of animals. It forms a jelly when mixed with hot water and cooled, and is used in foods, photographic films, etc.

ge·lat·i·nous [ji·lat'ə·nəs] *adj* Of or resembling gelatin or jelly.

geld·ing [gel'ding] *n*. A castrated horse.

gem [jem] *n.*, *v*. **gemmed, gem·ming 1** *n*. A cut and polished precious or semiprecious stone; jewel. **2** *v*. To decorate or set with or as with gems. **3** *n*. A person or thing that is greatly admired or prized. **4** *n*. A kind of muffin.

Gen. Abbreviation of: **1** GENERAL. **2** GENESIS.

gen·darme [zhän'därm] *n.*, *pl*. **gen·darmes** [zhän'därmz] An armed policeman, especially in France.

gen·der [jen'dər] *n*. Any of the classes into which nouns, pronouns, and sometimes adjectives are divided. In English, *boy* and *he* are of the masculine gender, *girl* and *she* are of the feminine gender, *stone* and *it* are of the neuter gender, and *child* and *they* are of the common gender.

gene [jēn] *n*. One of the protein molecules in the chromosomes of all plants and animals that govern the passing on of hereditary traits.

ge·ne·al·o·gy [jē'nē·al'ə·jē *or* jē'nē·ol'ə·jē] *n.*, *pl*. **ge·ne·al·o·gies 1** A record of the ancestors and descent of a person or family. **2** Direct descent from an ancestor or ancestors. **3** The study of family descent.

gen·er·a [jen'ər·ə] Plural of GENUS.

gen·er·al [jen'ər·əl] **1** *adj*. Of, for, from, or having to do with everyone or with the whole: the *general* welfare; a *general* election. **2** *adj*. Common among the majority; prevalent: a *general* opinion. **3** *adj*. Not limited or specialized: a *general* principle. **4** *adj*. Not precise or detailed: a *general* idea. **5** *n*. Any of several military ranks higher than colonel. **— in general** On the whole; usually; commonly.

General Assembly 1 The main body of the United Nations, in which every member nation is represented. **2** The legislature in some states.

gen·er·al·i·ty [jen'ə·ral'ə·tē] *n.*, *pl*. **gen·er·al·i·ties 1** The condition or quality of being general. **2** A general statement or idea. **3** The greater number; majority.

gen·er·al·i·za·tion [jen'ər·əl·ə·zā'shən] *n*. **1** The act of generalizing. **2** A general statement, rule, or principle. ¶3

gen·er·al·ize [jen'ər·əl·īz'] *v*. **gen·er·al·ized, gen·er·al·iz·ing 1** To make (a statement, conclusion, rule, etc.) general or more general. **2** To form a general conclusion from particular facts or data. **3** To make general statements in speaking or writing. **4** To make widespread. ¶3

gen·er·al·ly [jen'ər·əl·ē *or* jen'rəl·ē] *adv*. **1** Usually; ordinarily: We *generally* close at six. **2** Widely; commonly: The song became *generally* popular. **3** In a general way.

General of the Air Force An officer of the highest rank in the U.S. Air Force.

General of the Army An officer of the highest rank in the U.S. Army.

gen·er·al·ship [jen'ər·əl·ship] *n*. **1** The rank, authority, or term of office of a general. **2** The military skill of a general. **3** Leadership; skill in management.

gen·er·ate [jen'ə·rāt] *v*. **gen·er·at·ed, gen·er·at·ing** To produce or cause to be: A flame *generates* heat; Insults *generate* anger.

gen·er·a·tion [jen'ə·rā'shən] *n*. **1** The act or process of generating. **2** One step or stage in the history of a family: My father and I are of two *generations*. **3** The average time between any two such successive steps, about 30 years. **4** The people born around a certain time.

gen·er·a·tive [jen'ə·rā'tiv] *adj*. **1** Of or having to do with generation. **2** Able to generate.

gen·er·a·tor [jen'ə·rā'tər] *n*. **1** A person or thing that generates. **2** A machine that changes mechanical energy to electricity.

ge·ner·ic [ji·ner'ik] *adj*. **1** Characteristic of or indicating a whole group, genus, or class: a *generic* trait. **2** General; not specific. **— ge·ner'i·cal·ly** *adv*.

gen·er·os·i·ty [jen'ə·ros'ə·tē] *n.*, *pl*. **gen·er·os·i·ties 1** The quality of being generous. **2** A generous act.

gen·er·ous [jen'ər·əs] *adj*. **1** Quick to give or share; unselfish. **2** Large or abundant: a *generous* portion of meat. **3** Not mean or narrow-minded; forgiving. **— gen'er·ous·ly** *adv*.

gen·e·sis [jen'ə·sis] *n*. Origin; beginning.

Gen·e·sis [jen′ə·sis] *n.* The first book of the Old Testament, describing the creation of the world.

ge·net·ic [jə·net′ik] *adj.* **1** Of or having to do with genetics. **2** Having to do with origin or development. — **ge·net′i·cal·ly** *adv.*

ge·net·ics [jə·net′iks] *n.pl.* The science that studies heredity and variation, and their causes, in organisms of the same or related kinds. ◆ See -ICS.

Ge·ne·va [jə·nē′və] *n.* A city in sw Switzerland on a large lake.

gen·ial [jēn′yəl] *adj.* **1** Friendly and kind; cheerful: a *genial* smile. **2** Giving warmth and comfort; helping life or growth: the *genial* rays of the sun. — **ge·ni·al·i·ty** [jē′nē·al′ə·tē] *n.* — **gen′ial·ly** *adv.*

ge·nie [jē′nē] *n.*, *pl.* **ge·ni·i** [jē′nē·ī] In Arabian stories, a supernatural being having great magical powers.

gen·i·tal [jen′ə·təl] *adj.* **1** Of or related to the sex organs. **2** Related to sexual reproduction.

gen·i·tals [jen′ə·təlz] *n.pl.* The external sex organs.

gen·i·tive [jen′ə·tiv] **1** *adj.* In grammar, showing possession or origin; possessive. **2** *n.* The genitive case, or a word in the genitive case. ◆ In English grammar, the term *possessive* is used more often than *genitive*.

gen·ius [jēn′yəs] *n.* **1** *pl.* **gen·ius·es** An extremely high degree of mental power or talent. **2** *pl.* **gen·ius·es** A person who possesses such talent or mental power. **3** *pl.* **gen·ius·es** A special talent or knack: He has a *genius* for persuasion. **4** *pl.* **ge·ni·i** [jē′nē·ī] In Roman myths, a spirit that watched over a person or place. **5** *pl.* **gen·ius·es** The spirit, thought, or character of a people, place, time, etc. **6** *pl.* **ge·ni·i** A person who has great influence over another for good or evil.

Gen·o·a [jen′ō·ə] *n.* A seaport in NW Italy.

gen·o·cide [jen′ə·sīd] *n.* The extermination of an entire people or cultural or political group.

Gen·o·ese [jen′ō·ēz′] **1** *adj.* Of or from Genoa. **2** *n.*, *pl.* **Gen·o·ese** A person born or living in Genoa.

gen·teel [jen·tēl′] *adj.* **1** Polite or well-bred; refined. **2** Making a pretence of elegance.

gen·tian [jen′shən] *n.* A plant with showy, usually blue flowers.

Gen·tile [jen′tīl] **1** *n.* (*often written* **gentile**) A heathen; pagan. **2** *n.* A person who is not Jewish. **3** *adj.* Of, having to do with, or being a Gentile.

gen·til·i·ty [jen·til′ə·tē] *n.* **1** The condition of being well-born. **2** Well-born people as a group. **3** Refinement and good manners.

gen·tle [jen′tl] *adj.* **gen·tler, gen·tlest** **1** Quiet or kindly; mild: a *gentle* manner; a *gentle* nature. **2** Soft or mild: a *gentle* touch; a *gentle* voice. **3** Of or fit for a person of wealth and breeding. **4** Easily managed; tame: a *gentle* animal. **5** Not steep; gradual: a *gentle* slope. — **gen′tle·ness** *n.*

gen·tle·folk [jen′təl·fōk′] *n.pl.* People of good family and good breeding.

gen·tle·man [jen′təl·mən] *n.*, *pl.* **gen·tle·men** [jen′təl·mən] **1** A man of high social standing. **2** A courteous, refined, and honorable man. **3** Any man: a polite term.

gen·tle·man·ly [jen′təl·mən·lē] *adj.* Of, like, or fit for a gentleman.

gen·tle·wom·an [jen′təl·wŏŏm′ən] *n.*, *pl.* **gen·tle·wom·en** [jen′təl·wim′in] **1** A woman of high social standing. **2** A polite, refined woman; lady.

gen·tly [jen′tlē] *adv.* **1** In a gentle or mild way. **2** Gradually: a *gently* sloping hillside.

gen·try [jen′trē] *n.* **1** People who are well-born, but not of the nobility. **2** Persons of a particular area, profession, etc.

gen·u·flect [jen′yə·flekt] *v.* To bend one knee, as in worship.

gen·u·ine [jen′yŏŏ·in] *adj.* **1** Being as it appears; not false: a *genuine* pearl. **2** Sincere; frank: *genuine* pity. — **gen′u·ine·ly** *adv.*

ge·nus [jē′nəs] *n.*, *pl.* **gen·e·ra** or **ge·nus·es** A group of closely related animals or plants, composed of one or more species.

ge·o·cen·tric [jē′ō·sen′trik] *adj.* **1** As seen or measured from the earth's center: *geocentric* distance. **2** Considering the earth the center of the universe: a *geocentric* theory.

ge·og·ra·pher [jē·og′rə·fər] *n.* A person who specializes in geography.

ge·o·graph·ic [jē′ə·graf′ik] *adj.* Geographical.

ge·o·graph·i·cal [jē′ə·graf′i·kəl] *adj.* Of or having to do with geography. — **ge′o·graph′i·cal·ly** *adv.*

ge·og·ra·phy [jē·og′rə·fē] *n.* **1** The study of the features of the earth's surface, sometimes also including its peoples, natural resources, climates, etc. **2** The natural features of a place.

ge·o·log·ic [jē′ə·loj′ik] *adj.* Geological.

ge·o·log·i·cal [jē′ə·loj′ə·kəl] *adj.* Of or having to do with geology. — **ge′o·log′i·cal·ly** *adv.*

ge·ol·o·gist [jē·ol′ə·jist] *n.* A person who specializes in geology.

ge·ol·o·gy [jē·ol′ə·jē] *n.* The study of the history and structure of the earth's crust, especially as recorded in rocks. ◆ *Geology* comes from Greek words meaning *study of the earth.*

ge·o·met·ric [jē′ə·met′rik] *adj.* **1** Of or according to the principles of geometry. **2** Consisting of straight lines and simple curves: a *geometric* shape. — **ge′o·met′ri·cal·ly** *adv.*

ge·o·met·ri·cal [jē′ə·met′rə·kəl] *adj.* Geometric.

geometric progression A sequence of terms in which every pair of consecutive terms is in the same ratio, as 2, 4, 8, 16, etc.

---

add, āce, câre, pälm;   end, ēqual;   it, īce;   odd, ōpen, ôrder;   tŏŏk, pŏŏl;   up, bûrn;

ə = a in *above*, e in *sicken*, i in *possible*, o in *melon*, u in *circus*;   yŏŏ = u in *fuse*;   oil;   pout;

check; ring; thin; this; zh in *vision.*   For ¶ reference, see page 64 · HOW TO

ge·om·e·try [jē·om′ə·trē] *n.* The branch of mathematics that studies the relations among points, lines, angles, surfaces, and solids.

ge·o·phys·i·cal [jē′ō·fiz′i·kəl] *adj.* Of or having to do with geophysics.

ge·o·phys·ics [jē′ō·fiz′iks] *n.* The study of the physics of the earth, including its magnetism, volcanoes, movements of air and water, etc. ◆ See -ICS.

George [jôrj], **Saint,** died about 303, patron saint of England.

George III [jôrj], 1738–1820, King of England 1760–1820. He ruled at the time of the American Revolution.

George V [jôrj], 1865–1936, King of England 1910–1936.

George VI [jôrj], 1895–1952, King of England 1936–1952.

Geor·gia [jôr′jə] *n.* **1** A state in the SE U.S. **2** A republic in the SW Soviet Union.

Geor·gian [jôr′jən] **1** *adj.* Of or from Georgia. **2** *n.* A person born in or living in Georgia. **3** *n.* The language of the Soviet republic of Georgia. **4** *adj.* Of or having to do with the reigns of the first four King Georges of England, 1714–1830, or with that of George V, 1910–1936.

ge·ot·ro·pism [jē·ot′rə·piz′əm] *n.* A reaction in response to gravity, especially by a plant.

ge·ra·ni·um [ji·rā′nē·əm] *n.* **1** A plant with showy pink, scarlet, or white flowers. **2** A plant related to it, having pink or purple flowers.

ger·bil [jûr′bil] *n.* A small, furry rodent having long hind legs and short forelegs, popular as a pet.

ger·fal·con [jûr′fal′kən *or* jûr′fôl′kən] *n.* Another spelling of GYRFALCON.

ger·i·at·rics [jer′ē·at′riks] *n.* The branch of medicine dealing with old people and their diseases. ◆ See -ICS.

germ [jûrm] *n.* **1** A microscopic animal or plant that can cause disease; a microbe, especially one of the bacteria that cause disease. **2** A seed, bud, etc., that will develop into a plant or animal. **3** Something in its beginning form: the *germ* of an idea.

Ger·man [jûr′mən] **1** *adj.* Of or from Germany. **2** *n.* A person born in or a citizen of Germany. **3** *n.* The language of Germany and Austria.

ger·mane [jər·mān′] *adj.* Having to do with what is being discussed or considered; pertinent.

Ger·man·ic [jər·man′ik] *adj.* **1** Of or having to do with a large group of people of northern and central Europe, as the Germans, Dutch, Flemings, Scandinavians, Swiss of German descent, and the English. **2** Of or having to do with the languages these people speak. **3** Of Germany or the people of Germany.

ger·ma·ni·um [jər·mā′nē·əm] *n.* A grayish white metallic element which is used in electronics, metallurgy, and optics.

German measles A contagious disease marked by fever, sore throat, and a skin rash.

German shepherd A breed of dog with a large, strong body, thick, smooth coat, and high intelligence, often used as a guide for the blind.

Ger·ma·ny [jûr′mə·nē] *n.* A former country of central Europe. See EAST GERMANY and WEST GERMANY.

germ cell A cell from which a new individual can develop.

ger·mi·cide [jûr′mə·sīd] *n.* Something used to kill germs. — **ger·mi·ci·dal** [jûr′mə·sī′dəl] *adj.*

ger·mi·nate [jûr′mə·nāt] *v.* **ger·mi·nat·ed, ger·mi·nat·ing** **1** To sprout or cause to sprout: Seeds *germinate* in warm weather. **2** To develop or evolve, as an idea. — **ger′mi·na′tion** *n.*

ger·ry·man·der [jer′i·man′dər] **1** *v.* To alter (a voting area) so as to give an unfair advantage to one political party. **2** *n.* The act or result of gerrymandering.

ger·und [jer′ənd] *n.* A form of a verb, ending in *-ing*, which is used as a noun. In "Playing baseball is fun" *playing* is a gerund.

ges·ta·tion [jes·tā′shən] *n.* **1** A carrying of the unborn young in the womb; pregnancy: The period of *gestation* for elephants is about 20 months. **2** The development of an idea, etc., in the mind.

ges·tic·u·late [jes·tik′yə·lāt] *v.* **ges·tic·u·lat·ed, ges·tic·u·lat·ing** To make emphatic or expressive gestures. — **ges·tic′u·la′tion** *n.*

ges·ture [jes′chər] *n., v.* **ges·tured, ges·tur·ing** **1** *n.* A motion of the hands, head, or other part of the body expressing or emphasizing some feeling or idea. **2** *v.* To make gestures. **3** *n.* Something done, offered, or said as a formality, courtesy, or for effect: a polite *gesture.*

get [get] *v.* **got, got** *or U.S.* **got·ten, get·ting** **1** To obtain: to *get* money. **2** To go for and bring back: Please *get* my hat. **3** To arrive: When does the train *get* here? **4** To carry away; take: *Get* this out of the house! **5** To make ready; prepare: to *get* lunch. **6** To cause to be: to *get* the work done. **7** To prevail on; persuade: *Get* him to play for us. **8** To receive (reward or punishment): to *get* a whipping. **9** To learn, master, or understand: to *get* a lesson. **10** To be or become: to *get* rich. **11** To become sick with: to *get* a cold. **12** To communicate with: I'll *get* him on the phone. **13** *informal* To possess: He has *got* quite a temper. **14** *informal* To be obliged or forced: I have *got* to go home. **15** *informal* To strike, hit, or kill: That shot *got* him. **16** *slang* To puzzle; baffle: The remark *got* me. **17** *slang* To notice; observe: *Get* the blush on her face! — **get along** **1** To leave; go. **2** To manage or be successful, as in business. **3** To be friendly or compatible. — **get away with** *slang* To do (something) without being caught, criticized, or punished. — **get behind** To support (a person or cause). — **get by** **1** To pass. **2** *informal* To manage to survive or succeed. **— get off 1** To descend from; come off. **2** To depart. **3** To be relieved or freed, as of a duty. **4** To escape or help to escape from consequences at small cost, or none at all. **5** To take off; remove. **— get on 1** To go onto or into. **2** To get along. **3** To put on. **4** To grow older. **5** To upset. **6** To proceed. **— get out 1** To depart or leave. **2** To escape. **3** To become known, as a secret. **4** To publish. **5** To express or utter with difficulty. **6** To take out. **— get over 1** To recover from. **2** To get across. **— get up 1** To rise, as from sleep. **2** To mount; climb. **3** To devise. **4** To acquire, develop, or work up.

get·a·way [get′ə·wā′] *n.* **1** An escape, as by a criminal. **2** A start, as in a race.

Geth·sem·a·ne [geth·sem′ə·nē] *n.* A garden near Jerusalem where Jesus began his sufferings and was betrayed and arrested.

Get·tys·burg [get′iz·bûrg] *n.* A town in southern Pennsylvania, scene of a great Civil War battle, July 1–3, 1863.

get-up [get′up′] *n. informal* **1** Dress; costume: an actor's *get-up.* **2** Appearance or style.

gew·gaw [gyōō′gô] *n.* A showy, usually worthless trinket or bauble.

gey·ser [gī′zər] *n.* A natural spring which at intervals sends up a fountain of hot water, steam, or mud.

Gha·na [gä′nə] *n.* A country in western Africa, a member of the British Commonwealth.

ghast·ly [gast′lē] *adj.* **ghast·li·er, ghast·li·est 1** Horrible; terrifying. **2** Deathlike in appearance; pale; wan. **3** *informal* Very bad or unpleasant: a truly *ghastly* book. **— ghast′li·ness** *n.*

A geyser

gher·kin [gûr′kin] *n.* A very small cucumber used for pickling.

ghet·to [get′ō] *n., pl.* **ghet·tos 1** The section of some cities or towns where, in former times, Jews were forced to live. **2** Any section of a city or town crowded with a minority group or the very poor.

ghost [gōst] *n.* **1** The spirit of a dead person that supposedly appears to the living. **2** A mere trace or suggestion: the *ghost* of a smile.

ghost·ly [gōst′lē] *adj.* **ghost·li·er, ghost·li·est** Of, having to do with, or like a ghost.

ghost town A deserted town, especially an abandoned mining town in the West.

ghost·writ·er [gōst′rī′tər] *n.* A person who writes articles, speeches, etc., for other people who take credit for the writing.

ghoul [gōōl] *n.* **1** In Moslem legend, an evil spirit who robs graves and eats corpses. **2** A person who robs graves. **3** A person who enjoys disgusting things. **— ghoul′ish** *adj.*

GI or **G.I.** [jē′ī′] *n., pl.* **GIs** or **GI's, G.I.s** or **G.I.'s,** *adj. U.S. informal* **1** *n.* An enlisted man in the U.S. Army. **2** *adj.* Of or having to do with GIs. **3** *adj.* Issued by the U.S. government for the armed forces. ◆ This term is the abbreviation of *government issue,* supplies or clothing issued by the government to soldiers.

gi·ant [jī′ənt] **1** *n.* An imaginary being in human form but a great deal larger and more powerful than a real man. **2** *n.* Any person, animal, or thing of great size, strength, intelligence, ability, etc. **3** *adj.* Huge or great.

gib·ber [jib′ər] **1** *v.* To jabber rapidly and apparently without meaning, as monkeys do. **2** *n.* Gibberish.

gib·ber·ish [jib′ər·ish] *n.* Rapid and senseless talk or chatter.

gib·bet [jib′it] *n., v.* **gib·bet·ed** or **gib·bet·ted, gib·bet·ing** or **gib·bet·ting 1** *n.* An upright post with a projecting arm at the top, formerly used to hang criminals or to display them after being executed, as a warning to others. **2** *v.* To hang or execute on a gibbet.

gib·bon [gib′ən] *n.* A slender, long-armed ape of SE Asia and the East Indies, that lives in trees.

gib·bous [gib′əs *or* jib′əs] *adj.* Having a nearly circular form, as the moon when it is more than half full but less than full.

gibe [jīb] *v.* **gibed, gib·ing,** *n.* **1** *v.* To make jeering remarks; scoff. **2** *n.* A sneering remark; jeer.

gib·let [jib′lit] *n. (usually pl.)* Any of the parts of a fowl that are usually cooked separately, as the heart, liver, or gizzard.

Gibbon, about 30 in. long

Gi·bral·tar [ji·brôl′tər] *n.* A British colony, fortress, and naval base located on a huge rock at the southern tip of Spain.

gid·dy [gid′ē] *adj.* **gid·di·er, gid·di·est 1** Dizzy. **2** Causing or tending to cause dizziness: a *giddy* height. **3** Frivolous; flighty: a *giddy* girl. **— gid′di·ly** *adv.* **— gid′di·ness** *n.*

gift [gift] *n.* **1** Something that is given; a present. **2** A natural ability; talent: a *gift* for music.

gift·ed [gif′tid] *adj.* Very talented: a *gifted* young painter.

gig [gig] *n.* **1** A light, open, two-wheeled carriage drawn by a single horse. **2** A small boat used by a captain to get to and from his ship.

gi·gan·tic [jī·gan′tik] *adj.* Like a giant; huge; mighty.

gig·gle [gig′əl] *v.* **gig·gled, gig·gling,** *n.* **1** *v.* To laugh in a silly or nervous manner with high fluttering sounds. **2** *n.* Such a laugh.

---

add, āce, câre, pälm;   end, ēqual;   it, īce;   odd, ōpen, ôrder;   tŏŏk, pōōl;   up, bûrn;
ə = a in *above,* e in *sicken,* i in *possible,* o in *melon,* u in *circus;*   yōō = u in *fuse;*   oil;   pout;
check; ring; thin; this; zh in *vision.*   For ¶ reference, see page 64 · HOW TO

Gi·la monster [hē′lə] A large, poisonous lizard of the sw U.S. and northern Mexico. It is covered with black and orange scales.

Gila monster, 20 in. long

Gil·bert [gil′bərt], **Sir William S.,** 1836–1911, English poet and collaborator with Sir Arthur Sullivan on comic operas.

gild [gild] v. **gild·ed** or **gilt, gild·ing 1** To cover or coat with a thin layer of gold. **2** To brighten or adorn. **3** To make (something) seem better or more pleasing than it is.

Gil·e·ad [gil′ē·əd] n. A mountainous region of ancient Palestine.

gill¹ [gil] n. The organ for breathing of fishes and other animals that live under water. Oxygen is removed from water as it passes through the gills, and carbon dioxide is discharged.

gill² [jil] n. A liquid measure equal to ¼ pint, or half a cup.

gilt [gilt] **1** Alternative past tense and past participle of GILD. **2** n. Gold or a gold-colored material used in gilding. **3** adj. Covered with gilt; gilded.

gim·crack [jim′krak] **1** n. A useless, gaudy object; knickknack. **2** adj. Cheap and gaudy.

gim·let [gim′lit] n. A small, sharp tool with a handle at one end and a pointed spiral tip at the other for boring holes.

gin¹ [jin] n. A strong alcoholic drink, flavored usually with juniper berries.

gin² [jin] n., v. **ginned, gin·ning 1** n. Another name for COTTON GIN. **2** v. To remove the seeds from (cotton) in a gin.

gin·ger [jin′jər] n. **1** A spice made from the root of a tropical plant. Ginger is used in cooking and in medicine. **2** This root. **3** This plant. **4** informal Liveliness; pep.

ginger ale A bubbly soft drink flavored with ginger.

gin·ger·bread [jin′jər·bred′] n. **1** A dark ginger-flavored cake sweetened with molasses, often cut into fancy shapes. **2** Gaudy decoration, as showy carving on furniture.

gin·ger·ly [jin′jər·lē] **1** adv. In a cautious, careful, or reluctant manner: to step gingerly around the broken pavement. **2** adj. Cautious; careful: gingerly movements.

gin·ger·snap [jin′jər·snap′] n. A small, flat, brittle cooky flavored with ginger and molasses.

ging·ham [ging′əm] n. A cotton fabric woven in solid colors, stripes, checks, or plaids. ◆ Gingham goes back to a Malay word meaning striped.

gink·go [ging′kō or jing′kō] n., pl. **gink·goes** A large tree with fan-shaped leaves native to China and grown in the U.S.

gin rummy A card game for two players, a variety of rummy.

gin·seng [jin′seng] n. **1** A plant native to China and North America, from whose root a bitter medicine is made by the Chinese. **2** This root. **3** The medicine made from it.

Giot·to [jôt′tō] n., 1266?–1337, Italian painter, architect, and sculptor.

gip·sy [jip′sē] n., pl. **gip·sies** Another spelling of GYPSY.

gi·raffe [jə·raf′] n. An African animal that chews its cud. The tallest of all animals living today, it has a very long neck, long slender legs, and a spotted skin.

Giraffe, about 18 ft. tall

gird [gûrd] v. **gird·ed** or **girt, gird·ing 1** To surround or fasten, as with a belt or girdle. **2** To encircle; surround: Trees girded the fields. **3** To get ready for action: He girded himself for battle.

gird·er [gûr′dər] n. A long heavy beam, as of steel or wood, that acts as a horizontal support for the framework of a bridge, building, etc.

gir·dle [gûr′dəl] n., v. **gir·dled, gir·dling 1** n. A belt or cord worn around the waist; sash. **2** n. An elastic corset worn to support and shape the waist and hips. **3** v. To fasten a girdle or belt around: to girdle the waist. **4** n. Something that encircles like a belt: the girdle of the sea. **5** v. To encircle; surround.

girl [gûrl] n. **1** A female baby or child. **2** A young unmarried woman. **3** informal A sweetheart. **4** informal Any woman. **5** A female servant.

girl·hood [gûrl′hŏŏd] n. **1** The condition or time of being a girl. **2** Girls as a group.

girl·ish [gûr′lish] adj. Of, like, or proper for a girl. **— girl·ish·ly** adv.

girl scout A member of the Girl Scouts.

Girl Scouts An organization founded in the U.S. in 1912 for girls between 7 and 17. Its purpose is to develop character, health, and domestic skills.

girt [gûrt] An alternative past tense and past participle of GIRD.

girth [gûrth] **1** n. The circumference of anything: the girth of a tree. **2** v. To measure in girth. **3** n. A band or strap around a horse or other animal to hold a saddle, pack, etc., in place. **4** v. To bind with a girth. **5** n. A girdle or band. **6** v. To encircle; girdle.

gist [jist] n. The main idea or substance of an argument, question, or the like.

give [giv] v. **gave, giv·en, giv·ing,** n. **1** v. To hand over freely as a gift or present: I gave my old skates to my brother. **2** v. To make donations; make free gifts: to give to a charity. **3** v. To hand over in exchange for something: I gave him a quarter for this pen. **4** v. To hand over freely for a time: Give me your newspaper to read. **5** v. To put into the grasp of another: Give me your hand. **6** v. To make available; offer: to give help and advice. **7** v. To be a source of; yield: Fire gives warmth. **8** v. To grant: to give permission. **9** v. To administer: to *give* medicine. **10** *v.* To deal or deliver: to *give* someone a beating. **11** *v.* To perform or do: to *give* a nod of the head. **12** *v.* To utter or speak: to *give* a cry. **13** *v.* To put on or present: to *give* a play. **14** *v.* To part with; yield: He *gave* his life for his country. **15** *v.* To move down, back, etc., as under pressure: The door *gave* when they pushed it. **16** *v.* To be springy, flexible, etc.: This mattress *gives*. **17** *n.* The quality of yielding under pressure: Rubber has more *give* than metal. **— give a good account of** To conduct (oneself) well in a difficult situation: The battle was lost but the men *gave a good account of* themselves. **— give and take** To exchange on equal terms. **— give away 1** To hand over as a gift. **2** To hand over (the bride) to the bridegroom at a wedding. **3** *informal* To make known; reveal: to *give away* a secret. **— give in** To yield; surrender. **— give off** To send out or emit, as an odor. **— give out 1** To send forth; emit. **2** To hand out or distribute. **3** To make known; publish or announce. **4** To become used up or exhausted. **— give over 1** To hand over, as into someone else's care. **2** To cease; stop. **— give rise to** To cause or produce; result in. **— give to understand** To cause to understand or know. **— give up 1** To yield; surrender. **2** To stop; cease. **3** To stop trying. **4** To lose all hope for. **5** To devote completely: He *gave* himself *up* to art. **— give way 1** To yield or collapse under pressure. **2** To draw back. **— giv′er** *n.*

give-and-take [giv′ən·tāk′] *n.* A smooth, good-natured exchange of ideas, talk, etc.

give·a·way [giv′ə·wā′] *n.* *informal* **1** Something that one tells, as a secret or clue, usually without meaning to. **2** Something given for nothing or for a very low price.

giv·en [giv′ən] **1** The past participle of GIVE. **2** *adj.* Inclined; disposed: He is *given* to eating between meals. **3** *adj.* Stated; specified: a *given* date or address.

given name A name given to a child in addition to his family name; the first name, as *Ralph* in *Ralph Johnson.*

giz·zard [giz′ərd] *n.* A second stomach in birds, where the food is ground to bits.

gla·cial [glā′shəl] *adj.* Of, having to do with, or marked by the presence of ice or glaciers.

gla·cier [glā′shər] *n.* A large mass or field of ice that moves very slowly down a mountain valley or across land until it either melts or breaks off in the sea to form icebergs.

glad [glad] *adj.* **glad·der, glad·dest 1** Having a feeling of joy or pleasure. **2** Giving joy or happiness: *glad* tidings. **3** Bright and cheerful: a *glad* face. **4** More than willing: I'm *glad* to do it. **— glad′ly** *adv.* **— glad′ness** *n.*

glad·den [glad′(ə)n] *v.* To make glad.

glade [glād] *n.* An open place in a forest.

glad·i·a·tor [glad′ē·ā′tər] *n.* **1** In ancient Rome, a slave, captive, or paid freeman who fought other men or wild animals with weapons as public entertainment. **2** A person who takes part in any kind of struggle.

Gladiators

glad·i·o·lus [glad′ē·ō′ləs] *n., pl.* **glad·i·o·lus·es** or **glad·i·o·li** [glad′ē·ō′lī] A plant related to the iris, having sword-shaped leaves and spikes of colored flowers.

glam·or [glam′ər] *n.* *U.S.* Another spelling of GLAMOUR.

glam·or·ize [glam′ər·īz] *v.* **glam·or·ized, glam·or·iz·ing** To make glamorous.

glam·or·ous [glam′ər·əs] *adj.* Full of glamour: a *glamorous* woman. **— glam′or·ous·ly** *adv.*

glam·our [glam′ər] *n.* A charm, beauty, or fascination: the *glamour* of Paris; the *glamour* of a movie star.

glance [glans] *v.* **glanced, glanc·ing,** *n.* **1** *v.* To take a quick look: to *glance* around; to *glance* at a building. **2** *n.* A quick look. **3** *v.* To strike slantwise and go off at an angle: Bullets *glanced* off the wall. **4** *n.* A grazing hit and slanting off. **5** *v.* To flash; glint: The water *glanced* in the sun. **6** *n.* A flash or glint.

gland [gland] *n.* Any of several organs of the body that have to do with the production, storage, or secretion of certain substances, either for elimination as waste or for use elsewhere in the body. The liver, pancreas, thyroid, and adrenals are glands.

glan·du·lar [glan′jə·lər] *adj.* Of, like, or affecting a gland or glands.

glare [glâr] *n., v.* **glared, glar·ing 1** *n.* A bright, blinding light. **2** *v.* To give off such a light. **3** *n.* An angry, hostile stare. **4** *v.* To stare in anger or hostility.

glar·ing [glâr′ing] *adj.* **1** Shining with a glare. **2** Staring with anger or hostility. **3** Showy; gaudy: a *glaring* array of colors. **4** Plainly or unpleasantly conspicuous: a *glaring* mistake.

Glas·gow [glas′gō] *n.* A large seaport in sw Scotland.

glass [glas] **1** *n.* A hard substance that breaks easily and is usually transparent. Glass is made by melting together sand and other materials, as soda, lime, etc., and then rapidly cooling them. **2** *adj.* *use:* a *glass* door; a *glass* jar. **3** *n.* Something made of glass, such as a container for drinking, a mirror, or a lens. **4** *n.* (*pl.*) A pair of eyeglasses; spectacles. **5** *n.* The amount a drinking glass holds: a *glass* of water. **6** *v.* To cover or enclose with glass: Last summer we *glassed* in our porch.

glass·ful [glas′fŏŏl] *n.*, *pl.* **glass·fuls** The amount a drinking glass holds.

glass·ware [glas′wâr′] *n.* Articles made of glass.

glass·y [glas′ē] *adj.* **glass·i·er, glass·i·est** **1** Like glass; clear, shiny, brittle, etc. **2** Fixed, blank, and lifeless: a *glassy* stare.

glaze [glāz] *v.* **glazed, glaz·ing,** *n.* **1** *v.* To fit or cover with glass: to *glaze* a window. **2** *v.* To coat with a glassy surface: to *glaze* pottery. **3** *n.* A glassy surface or coating, or a substance used to produce such a surface or coating. **4** *v.* To make or become covered with or as if with a thin coating of film: His eyes *glazed* with pain. **5** *v.* To cover (food) with a thin coating, as of syrup. **6** *n.* A substance used to coat foods, as syrup or egg white.

gla·zier [glā′zhər] *n.* A person whose job is to put glass in windows, doors, etc.

gleam [glēm] **1** *n.* A ray or beam of light that is faint or that shines for only a short time. **2** *n.* The shine of reflected light upon a surface. **3** *v.* To shine with a gleam. **4** *n.* A faint trace: a *gleam* of hope.

glean [glēn] *v.* **1** To gather (grain) left in a field after it has been reaped: to *glean* corn. **2** To collect (facts, etc.) by patient effort. **— glean′·er** *n.*

glee [glē] *n.* **1** Joy or merriment. **2** A song for three or more voices, usually unaccompanied.

glee club A group organized to sing songs.

glee·ful [glē′fəl] *adj.* Full of glee; mirthful; joyous; merry. **— glee′ful·ly** *adv.*

glen [glen] *n.* A small secluded valley.

glib [glib] *adj.* **glib·ber, glib·best** Speaking or spoken easily but without much thought or sincerity: a *glib* person; a *glib* answer. **— glib′·ly** *adv.* **— glib′ness** *n.*

glide [glīd] *v.* **glid·ed, glid·ing,** *n.* **1** *v.* To move smoothly and without effort. **2** *v.* To pass quietly and unnoticed, as time. **3** *v.* To move in a downward slant without using power, as an airplane. **4** *n.* A gliding movement. ◆ *Glide* comes from the Old English word *glīdan*.

glid·er [glī′dər] *n.* **1** A person or thing that glides. **2** A light air-craft like an airplane but without an engine. It is kept aloft by air currents. **3** A swing made of a seat hung in a metal frame so it can glide back and forth.

Glider

glim·mer [glim′ər] **1** *v.* To shine with a faint, unsteady light. **2** *n.* A faint, unsteady light. **3** *n.* A faint hint or trace: a *glimmer* of hope; a *glimmer* of the truth.

glimpse [glimps] *n.*, *v.* **glimpsed, glimps·ing** **1** *n.* A momentary view or look. **2** *v.* To see for a moment: to *glimpse* someone in a passing car. **3** *v.* To look for an instant: to *glimpse* at a picture. **4** *n.* A faint hint; inkling.

glint [glint] **1** *n.* A gleam; flash. **2** *v.* To gleam or flash; glitter.

glis·san·do [gli·sän′dō] *n.*, *pl.* **glis·san·di** [gli·sän′dē] or **glis·san·dos** A sliding effect, as that made by running a finger across a group of piano keys.

glis·ten [glis′(ə)n] **1** *v.* To shine or sparkle, as with reflected light. **2** *n.* A shine; sparkle.

glit·ter [glit′ər] **1** *v.* To sparkle brightly, as a diamond. **2** *n.* A bright or brilliant sparkle. **3** *v.* To be showy, attractive, or outstanding. **4** *n.* Showiness; brilliance.

gloam·ing [glō′ming] *n.* Twilight; dusk.

gloat [glōt] *v.* To experience an intense, often malicious or evil delight: to *gloat* over someone else's misfortune.

glob·al [glō′bəl] *adj.* **1** Of or having to do with the whole world or a large part of it: a *global* war. **2** Shaped like a globe; spherical.

globe [glōb] *n.* **1** A sphere; ball. **2** Something having a shape like this. **3** The earth. **4** A sphere on which is drawn a map of the earth or the heavens.

glob·u·lar [glob′yə·lər] *adj.* **1** Shaped like a globe; round; spherical. **2** Made up of globules.

glob·ule [glob′yōōl] *n.* A tiny sphere of matter or drop of liquid.

glock·en·spiel [glok′ən·spēl] *n.* A musical instrument made up of a series of metal bars in a frame, each sounding a different note when struck with a small, light hammer.

gloom [glōōm] **1** *n.* Partial or total darkness; heavy shadow. **2** *n.* Low spirits; dejection; sadness. **3** *v.* To make or become gloomy.

gloom·y [glōō′mē] *adj.* **gloom·i·er, gloom·i·est** **1** Dark; dismal. **2** Sad; dejected. **3** Causing gloom. **— gloom′i·ly** *adv.* **— gloom′i·ness** *n.*

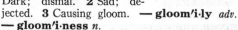
Glockenspiel

glo·ri·fy [glôr′ə·fī] *v.* **glo·ri·fied, glo·ri·fy·ing** **1** To make glorious. **2** To honor or exalt; worship. **3** To make seem more splendid or glorious than is actually so: Movies sometimes *glorify* crime. **— glo′ri·fi·ca′tion** *n.*

glo·ri·ous [glôr′ē·əs] *adj.* **1** Full of or deserving glory: a *glorious* work. **2** Bringing glory: a *glorious* victory. **3** Magnificently beautiful: a *glorious* sunset. **4** *informal* Very pleasant; delightful. **— glo′ri·ous·ly** *adv.*

glo·ry [glôr′ē] *n.*, *pl.* **glo·ries,** *v.* **glo·ried, glo·ry·ing** **1** *n.* Great honor and praise; very high renown. **2** *n.* A person or thing bringing praise or honor: Shakespeare's plays are his *glory*. **3** *n.* Splendor; magnificence: the *glory* of Rome. **4** *n.* A condition of happiness, prosperity, pride, etc.: to be in one's *glory*. **5** *v.* To rejoice proudly; take pride: to *glory* in one's accomplishments. **6** *n.* Worship; adoration: to give *glory* to God. **7** *n.* The bliss of heaven: to dwell in *glory* with the saints.

gloss [glôs] **1** *n.* The luster or shine of a polished surface. **2** *v.* To make shiny or lustrous. **3** *n.* A nice surface appearance that hides something wrong. **4** *v.* To conceal or make little of: He tried to *gloss* over his error.

glos·sa·ry [glos′ə·rē] *n., pl.* **glos·sa·ries** A list of difficult or special words of a book or subject, together with their meanings.

gloss·y [glôs′ē] *adj.* **gloss·i·er, gloss·i·est** Smooth and shiny; lustrous. — **gloss′i·ness** *n.*

glot·tis [glot′is] *n.* The cleft or opening between the vocal cords in the larynx.

Glouces·ter [glos′tər] *n.* **1** A city in SW England. **2** A fishing port in NE Massachusetts.

glove [gluv] *n., v.* **gloved, glov·ing 1** *n.* A covering for the hand, having a separate part for each finger and thumb. **2** *n.* Such an article specially padded for protection of the hand: a baseball *glove*. **3** *n.* A boxing glove. **4** *v.* To cover or furnish with gloves.

glow [glō] **1** *v.* To shine because of great heat, especially without a flame: An ember *glows*. **2** *v.* To shine without a flame or heat: A glowworm *glows*. **3** *n.* The light from something that glows. **4** *n.* Brightness or warmth of color. **5** *v.* To show a bright, warm color: Her cheeks *glowed*. **6** *v.* To be eager, excited, ardent, etc.: to *glow* with love. **7** *n.* Warm emotion.

glow·er [glou′ər] **1** *v.* To stare angrily: to *glower* at someone. **2** *n.* An angry stare.

glow·worm [glō′wûrm′] *n.* The larva of a firefly, or a firefly, that glows in the dark.

glu·cose [glōō′kōs] *n.* **1** A kind of sugar found in fruits, not as sweet as cane sugar. **2** A thick, yellowish syrup made from starch.

glue [glōō] *n., v.* **glued, glu·ing 1** *n.* A substance made from the hoofs, bones, and other parts of animals and used to stick things together. **2** *n.* Any substance like this. **3** *v.* To stick together or attach with glue: to *glue* a notice to a wall. **4** *v.* To fasten or hold as if with glue: We were *glued* to our seats with suspense.

glue·y [glōō′ē] *adj.* **glu·i·er, glu·i·est 1** Like glue; sticky. **2** Covered with glue.

glum [glum] *adj.* **glum·mer, glum·mest** Gloomy and silent. — **glum′ly** *adv.* — **glum′·ness** *n.*

glut [glut] *v.* **glut·ted, glut·ting,** *n.* **1** *v.* To stuff, as with food; gorge: to *glut* oneself with pastry. **2** *v.* To supply with too much: The market was *glutted* with cotton dresses. **3** *n.* A supply that is too great.

glu·ten [glōōt′(ə)n] *n.* A sticky substance left in flour after the starch has been removed.

glu·ti·nous [glōōt′(ə)n·əs] *adj.* Sticky.

glut·ton [glut′(ə)n] *n.* **1** A person who eats greedily. **2** A person with a great liking or capacity for something: a *glutton* for work. — **glut′ton·ous** *adj.*

glut·ton·y [glut′(ə)n·ē] *n., pl.* **glut·ton·ies** The habit of eating too much; greediness.

glyc·er·in or **glyc·er·ine** [glis′ər·in] *n.* A clear, sweet, oily liquid obtained from natural fats and used in ointments, explosives, etc.

gly·co·gen [glī′kə·jən] *n.* A white, starchlike substance found in the liver and muscles of animals. Glucose is stored in the form of glycogen.

G-man [jē′man′] *n., pl.* **G-men** [jē′men′] An agent of the FBI.

gnarled [närld] *adj.* Knotty or twisted: His hands were *gnarled* from hard work.

gnash [nash] *v.* To grind or strike (the teeth) together, as in rage.

gnat [nat] *n.* A small biting or stinging fly.

gnaw [nô] *v.* **gnawed, gnawed** or **gnawn** [nôn], **gnaw·ing 1** To bite or eat away little by little with or as if with teeth: to *gnaw* at a bone. **2** To make by gnawing: to *gnaw* a hole. **3** To trouble persistently: Poverty *gnawed* at the family's happiness.

gneiss [nīs] *n.* A rock similar to granite, having a coarse grain.

gnome [nōm] *n.* In folklore, a dwarf who lives in a cave and guards a treasure.

gnu [n(y)ōō] *n., pl.* **gnus** or **gnu 1** A large antelope of South Africa with a head like an ox's, curved horns, a mane, and a long tail.

go [gō] *v.* **went, gone, go·ing,** *third person singular present* **goes,** *n.* **1** *v.* To proceed or pass along; move: We *went* on the highway. **2** *v.* To move from a place; pass away; leave; depart: *Go* home!; I wish my toothache would *go*. **3** *v.* To have a regularly scheduled route or specific destination: This train *goes* to Chicago daily. **4** *v.* To move for some specific purpose: She *went* to dress for dinner. **5** *v.* To be in motion or operation; work; function: The motor is *going*. **6** *v.* To extend or reach: This pipe *goes* to the cellar. **7** *v.* To produce a certain sound, movement, etc.: The chain *goes* "clank." **8** *v.* To fail, give way, or collapse: His hearing *went*. **9** *v.* To have a specific place or position; belong: The plates *go* on that shelf. **10** *v.* To pass into someone's possession; be given, sold, etc.: The cake *goes* to John. **11** *v.* To be, continue, or become: to *go* unpunished; to *go* insane. **12** *v.* To proceed, happen, or end in a specific way: The election *went* badly for him. **13** *v.* To be about or intending: I am *going* to ask her tonight. **14** *v.* To be suitable; fit: These colors *go* well together. **15** *v.* To be phrased, expressed, sung, etc.: How does that tune *go*? **16** *v.* To pass: A weekend *goes* fast. **17** *v.* To put or subject oneself: He *went* to great pains to do it. **18** *n. informal* A try; attempt: to have a *go* at something. **19** *n. informal* A success: He made a *go* of it. — **go around 1** To enclose; encircle. **2** To satisfy

---

add, āce, câre, pälm;   end, ēqual;   it, īce;   odd, ōpen, ôrder;   tŏŏk, pōōl;   up, bûrn;

ə = a in *above*, e in *sicken*, i in *possible*, o in *melon*, u in *circus*;   yōō = u in *fuse*;   oil;   pout;

check; ring; thin; this; zh in *vision*.   For ¶ reference, see page 64 · HOW TO

the demand or need. **— go at** 1 To attack. 2 To work at. **— go back on** 1 To break (a promise or the like). 2 To betray or forsake. **— go for** 1 To try to get. 2 *informal* To attack. 3 To favor or support. 4 *informal* To be strongly attracted by. **— go in for** *informal* To take part in or be interested in. **— go into** 1 To investigate. 2 To be contained in: *4 goes into 12 three times.* **— go off** 1 To leave. 2 To explode. 3 *informal* To happen in a certain way. **— go out** 1 To go to a party, to the theater, etc. 2 To be extinguished. **— go over** 1 To examine. 2 To review or rehearse. 3 To treat or cover again. 4 *informal* To succeed. **— go through** 1 To be accepted or approved. 2 To experience; undergo. 3 To search. **— go together** 1 To suit each other; harmonize. 2 To keep steady company as sweethearts. **— let go** 1 To set free or let escape. 2 To give up a hold. **— let oneself go** To give in to one's feelings or desires; throw off restraint. **— no go** *informal* Hopeless; useless. **— on the go** *informal* Very busy: *The tourists were on the go every minute.*

goad [gōd] 1 *n.* A pointed stick for driving oxen or other animals by pricking them. 2 *n.* Something that drives or spurs; incentive: *a goad to study.* 3 *v.* To drive with or as if with a goad.

goal [gōl] *n.* 1 The end of a race or journey. 2 An end; aim; objective: *What is your goal in life?* 3 In hockey, soccer, and certain other games, a place or structure where a score can be made. 4 A score made in these games.

goal·ie [gō′lē] *n. informal* Another word for GOALKEEPER.

goal·keep·er [gōl′kē′pər] *n.* In hockey, soccer, etc., a player who guards his team's goal.

goal post One of two posts joined by a crosspiece to form a goal, as in football.

goat [gōt] *n.* 1 An animal, related to the sheep, that chews its cud. It has hollow horns that curve backward, usually straight hair, a lean body, and a short tail. 2 *informal* A person who is the butt of a joke or on whom blame is placed; scapegoat.

goat·ee [gō·tē′] *n.* A man's beard trimmed short to a pointed end below the chin.

goat·herd [gōt′hûrd′] *n.* A person who tends goats.

goat·skin [gōt′skin′] *n.* 1 The skin of a goat. 2 Leather made from this. 3 Something made from this leather, as a container for liquid.

gob¹ [gob] *n. informal* A sailor in the U.S. Navy.

gob² [gob] *n. informal* A lump or mass, as of something soft or sticky: *a gob of mud.*

gob·ble¹ [gob′əl] *v.* **gob·bled, gob·bling** To eat greedily and in gulps: *The boys had so little time they gobbled their sandwiches and ran.*

Goatee

gob·ble² [gob′əl] *n., v.* **gob·bled, gob·bling** 1 *n.* The throaty sound made by a male turkey. 2 *v.* To make this sound.

gob·bler [gob′lər] *n.* A male turkey.

go-be·tween [gō′bə·twēn′] *n.* A person who goes back and forth between two people or sides, making arrangements, proposals, etc.

Go·bi [gō′bē] *n.* A large desert in central Asia.

gob·let [gob′lit] *n.* A drinking glass with a base and stem and no handles.

gob·lin [gob′lin] *n.* In folklore, an ugly, mischievous, elflike creature.

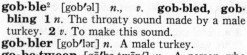
Goblets

go-cart [gō′kärt′] *n.* A small carriage or wagon for little children to ride in or pull.

god [god] *n.* 1 (*written* **God**) In certain religions, as Judaism, Christianity, and Islam, the one supreme being, creator, protector, and ruler of the world. 2 In myths, primitive religions, etc., any of various beings whose supposed immortality and supreme powers are or were considered worthy of man's worship. 3 A statue, image, or symbol of such beings. 4 Any person or thing greatly loved or considered most important: *Money is his god.*

god·child [god′chīld′] *n., pl.* **god·chil·dren** A baby or child for whom, at baptism, an older person promises a religious education.

god·daugh·ter [god′dô′tər] *n.* A female godchild.

god·dess [god′is] *n.* 1 A female god. 2 A woman or girl of great beauty or charm.

god·fa·ther [god′fä′thər] *n.* A male godparent.

god·fear·ing [god′fir′ing] *adj.* (*often written* **God-fearing**) 1 Having reverence for God. 2 Pious; devout.

god·head [god′hed′] *n.* 1 Divine nature; divinity. 2 (*written* **Godhead**) God (def. 1).

god·less [god′lis] *adj.* 1 Having or believing in no god. 2 Wicked.

god·like [god′līk′] *adj.* Like or proper for a god or God; very great, holy, or beautiful.

god·ly [god′lē] *adj.* **god·li·er, god·li·est** Filled with reverence and love for God; devout. **— god′li·ness** *n.*

god·moth·er [god′muth′ər] *n.* A female godparent.

god·par·ent [god′pâr′ənt] *n.* A person who, at the baptism of a baby or child, promises to be responsible, if necessary, for the child's religious training.

god·send [god′send′] *n.* Something unexpected that comes or happens when it is badly needed: *The inheritance was a godsend to the family.*

god·son [god′sun′] *n.* A male godchild.

God·speed [god′spēd′] *n.* An expression used to wish a person a successful journey or undertaking. It is short for *God speed you.*

Goe·the [gû′tə], **Johann Wolfgang von,** 1749–1832, German writer.

go-get·ter [gō′get′ər] *n. U.S. informal* A very bold, ambitious, energetic person.

gog·gle [gog′əl] *n.*, *v.* **gog·gled, gog·gling,**
adj. **1** *n.* (*pl.*) Large glasses
that protect the eyes from
dust, wind, sparks, etc. **2** *v.*
To stare with the eyes wide
open and bulging: We all
goggled as the jet plane took
off. **3** *adj.* Staring or bulging:
goggle eyes.

Goggles

go·ing [gō′ing] **1** Present
participle of GO. **2** *adj.* Mov-
ing ahead successfully: a *going* business. **3** *n.* A
departing; leaving: his coming and *going*. **4** *n.*
A condition of something as it affects moving or
getting along: The *going* was bad on these rutted
roads; Old age is often rough *going*.

goi·ter [goi′tər] *n.* An abnormal enlargement of
the thyroid gland. It is visible as a swelling in
the front of the neck. ¶2

gold [gōld] **1** *n.* A heavy, yellow, metallic
element, used in making coins, jewelry, etc.
2 *adj. use:* a *gold* cup. **3** *adj.* Producing gold:
a *gold* mine. **4** *n.* Gold coins. **5** *n.* Wealth;
riches. **6** *n.*, *adj.* Bright yellow.

gold·en [gōl′dən] *adj.* **1** Made of or containing
gold: a *golden* statue. **2** Having the color of gold.
3 Very good, happy, prosperous, or valuable: a
golden opportunity.

Golden Fleece In Greek myth, a fleece of gold
guarded by a dragon. It was taken away by Jason
and the Argonauts with Medea's help.

Golden Gate A strait connecting the Pacific
Ocean and San Francisco Bay.

gold·en·rod [gōl′dən·rod′] *n.* A North American plant with small, usually yellow, flowers that
bloom in the late summer or early fall.

golden rule A rule stating that a person should
treat other people in the way that he himself
would like to be treated.

gold-filled [gōld′fild′] *adj.* Covered over with
a layer of gold: *gold-filled* jewelry.

gold·finch [gōld′finch] *n.* A small American
songbird. In the summer the male goldfinch has
a yellow body and a black tail.

gold·fish [gōld′fish′] *n.*, *pl.* **gold·fish** or
gold·fish·es A small fish, usually gold or
orange, often kept in ponds or small aquariums.

gold leaf Sheets of gold hammered until they
are extremely thin, used in gilding.

gold rush A large migration of people to an
area where gold has been discovered.

gold·smith [gōld′smith′] *n.* A person who
makes or deals in articles of gold.

golf [golf] **1** *n.* An outdoor game played on a
large course with a small hard ball and a set of
clubs. The object of the game is to hit the ball
into a series of holes, 9 or 18, in as few strokes
as possible. **2** *v.* To play golf. **— golf′·er** *n.*

Gol·go·tha [gol′gə·thə] *n.* Another name for
CALVARY.

Go·li·ath [gə·li′əth] *n.* In the Bible, a giant
killed by David with a stone from a sling.

Go·mor·rah or **Go·mor·rha** [gə·môr′ə] *n.* In
the Bible, a city destroyed by God because of the
wickedness of its people.

go·nad [gō′nad] *n.* A male or female sex gland in
which germ cells develop.

gon·do·la [gon′də·lə] *n.* **1** A long, narrow boat
with a high point at
each end, used on the
canals of Venice. **2** A
railroad freight car
that has low sides and
no top. **3** A car
attached to the bot-
tom of a dirigible.

Gondola

gon·do·lier [gon′də·
lir′] *n.* A man who
moves a gondola by rowing or poling.

gone [gôn] **1** The past participle of GO. **2** *adj.*
Moved away; left. **3** *adj.* Ruined; lost. **4** *adj.*
Dead. **5** *adj.* Used up. **6** *adj.* Weak; failing.

gon·er [gôn′ər] *n. informal* A person or thing
that is dying, ruined, or beyond help.

gong [gông] *n.* A heavy metal disk giving a deep,
resonant tone when struck.

goo [gōō] *n. U.S. slang* Any sticky substance.

goo·ber [gōō′bər] *n. U.S.* A peanut. ◆ *Goober*
may come from *nguba*, an African Bantu word
for *peanut*.

good [gŏŏd] *adj.* **bet·ter, best,** *n.* **1** *adj.*
Having the proper qualities; admirable. **2** *adj.*
Skillful: a *good* pianist. **3** *adj.* Kind: a *good*
turn. **4** *adj.* Well-behaved; polite: a *good*
child. **5** *adj.* Proper; desirable: *good* manners.
6 *adj.* Favorable: a *good* opinion. **7** *adj.* Pleasant; agreeable: *good* company. **8** *adj.* Beneficial; helpful: *good* advice. **9** *n.* Benefit;
advantage: for the *good* of mankind. **10** *adj.*
Genuine; valid: a *good* excuse. **11** *adj.* Above
the average in quality, degree, or kind: *good*
food; a really *good* fur coat. **12** *adj.* Unspoiled;
fresh: *good* meat. **13** *adj.* In a sound or satisfactory condition: *good* eyesight; a *good* chair.
14 *adj.* Satisfactory or appropriate, as for a
particular purpose: *good* weather for flying.
15 *adj.* Great or fairly great in amount, extent,
etc.: a *good* share. **16** *adj.* Thorough; sufficient:
a *good* spanking. **17** *adj.* Full: a *good* mile away.
18 *n.* A thing that is good. **— as good as**
Almost; nearly; practically. **— for good** For
the last time; permanently. **— good and**
informal Very; extremely: This chili is *good and*
hot. **— good for 1** Capable of lasting or remaining valid or in operation (for a certain period
of time). **2** *informal* Able or willing to pay, give,
or produce (something). **— make good 1** To
be successful. **2** To replace; repay. **3** To fulfill
(a promise, threat, etc.). **4** To prove. **— to the
good** To the credit, profit, or advantage of

---

add, **ā**ce, c**â**re, p**ä**lm;   **e**nd, **ē**qual;   **i**t, **ī**ce;   **o**dd, **ō**pen, **ô**rder;   t**ŏŏ**k, p**ōō**l;   **u**p, b**û**rn;
ə = a in *above*, e in *sicken*, i in *possible*, o in *melon*, u in *circus*;   **y**oo = u in *fuse*;   **oi**l;   p**ou**t;
check; ri**ng**; **th**in; **th**is; **zh** in *vision*.   For ¶ reference, see page 64 · HOW TO

someone or something. ◆ The word *good* is primarily an adjective describing a person or thing, and as such it often follows a verb telling how a person or thing is or appears, as in "This pie tastes *good*," or "I feel *good* today," or "Your singing sounded *good* to me." However, *good* should not be used adverbially to modify a verb, as in "He doesn't play *good*," or "This watch doesn't run *good* any more." In these last two examples, *well* is the proper word to use.

good-by or **good-bye** [good′bī′] *interj., n., pl.* **good-bys** or **good-byes** [good′bīz′] What a person says at parting; farewell. ◆ *Good-by* is a contraction of *God be with you.*

good-for-noth·ing [good′fər·nuth′ing] **1** *n.* A worthless person. **2** *adj.* Worthless.

Good Friday The Friday before Easter, commemorating the crucifixion of Jesus.

good-heart·ed [good′här′tid] *adj.* Kind; generous.

Good Hope, Cape of A cape at the southern tip of Africa.

good-hu·mored [good′(h)yoo′mərd] *adj.* Cheerful; amiable; pleasant. — **good′-hu′·mored·ly** *adv.*

good-look·ing [good′look′ing] *adj.* Handsome or pretty; attractive.

good·ly [good′lē] *adj.* **good·li·er, good·li·est 1** Handsome or pleasing. **2** Excellent. **3** Large; considerable. — **good′li·ness** *n.*

good·man [good′mən] *n., pl.* **good·men** [good′mən] **1** A man who is the head of a household. **2** A title, similar to *Mr.* ◆ This word is seldom used today.

good morning A greeting made in the morning.

good-na·tured [good′nā′chərd] *adj.* Friendly, pleasant, and kindly: a *good-natured* reply; *good-natured* joking. — **good′-na′tured·ly** *adv.* — **good′-na′tured·ness** *n.*

good·ness [good′nis] **1** *n.* The condition of being good, especially of being virtuous or generous. **2** *n.* The best or most nourishing part of anything. **3** *interj.* A word used to express surprise or emphasis: *Goodness*, but you're late!

goods [goodz] *n.pl.* **1** Anything made to be sold; merchandise. **2** Cloth; material: dress *goods.* **3** Personal property capable of being moved.

Good Samaritan 1 In a parable of Jesus, a man who helps another man who has been robbed and beaten. **2** Any person who voluntarily helps someone else in trouble.

good-sized [good′sīzd′] *adj.* Quite large.

good-tem·pered [good′tem′pərd] *adj.* Having a good disposition; not easily angered: a *good-tempered*, pleasant person.

good·wife [good′wīf′] *n.* **1** The female head of a household. **2** A title, similar to *Mrs.* ◆ This word is seldom used today.

good will 1 Good feeling toward others. **2** The advantage a business develops over the years because of its good reputation and its friendly relationship with its customers.

good·y [good′ē] *n., pl.* **good·ies,** *interj.*

informal **1** *n.* Something tasty, as a piece of candy or a cooky. **2** *interj.* A word showing delight, which is used mostly by children.

goo·ey [goo′ē] *adj.* **goo·i·er, goo·i·est** *U.S. slang* Sticky and messy.

goo·gol [goo′gol] *n.* An enormous number, 1 followed by a hundred zeros.

goose [goos] *n., pl.* **geese** [gēs] **1** A swimming bird, tame or wild, that is like a duck but is larger and has a longer neck. **2** The female of this bird. The male is called a gander. **3** A silly person. **—cook one's goose** *informal* To ruin one's chances, plans, etc.

Canada goose, about 40 in. long

goose·ber·ry [goos′ber′ē] *n., pl.* **goose·ber·ries 1** A sour berry that grows on a prickly shrub, used in making pies, tarts, jams, etc. **2** The shrub itself.

goose flesh A condition of the skin in which many tiny bumps appear. It is caused usually by fear or cold.

goose·neck [goos′nek′] *n.* Any of various mechanical devices curved like a goose's neck, as a flexible shaft between the base and the bulb of a desk lamp.

goose pimples Goose flesh.

goose step A marching step in which the leg is swung forward high with the knee stiff.

G.O.P. or **GOP** Abbreviation of Grand Old Party, a name for the Republican Party.

go·pher [gō′fər] *n.* **1** A rodent of North America that burrows into the ground and has large cheek pouches for storing food. **2** Any of various ground squirrels of western North America.

gore[1] [gôr] *n.* Blood that has come from wounds, especially when thick or partly clotted.

gore[2] [gôr] *n., v.* **gored, gor·ing 1** *n.* A triangular piece of cloth sewn into a garment or a sail to provide a fuller shape. **2** *v.* To put gores into: She *gored* her skirt.

gore[3] [gôr] *v.* **gored, gor·ing** To wound or pierce with a horn or tusk: The horse was *gored* by the enraged bull.

gorge [gôrj] *n., v.* **gorged, gorg·ing 1** *n.* A narrow, very deep ravine; canyon. **2** *v.* To stuff (oneself) with food: A hungry dog will *gorge* himself. **3** *n.* The throat; gullet: seldom used today.

gor·geous [gôr′jəs] *adj.* Brilliantly colorful; dazzling; very beautiful: a *gorgeous* sunset. — **gor′geous·ly** *adv.*

Gorge

Gor·gon [gôr′gən] *n.* In Greek myths, any of the three sisters, with snakes for hair, who were so frightening that the sight of them turned the viewer to stone.

go·ril·la [gə·ril′ə] *n.* The largest and most powerful of the apes, living in the African jungles.

gorse [gôrs] *n.* A spiny shrub having many branches and yellow flowers, common in Europe.

go·ry [gôr′ē] *adj.* **gor·i·er, gor·i·est** **1** Covered or marked with gore; bloody. **2** Like gore.

gos·hawk [gos′hôk′ or gôs′hôk′] *n.* A large, short-winged hawk.

Gorilla, 5–6 ft. tall

Go·shen [gō′shən] *n.* **1** In the Bible, the part of Egypt where the Israelites lived. **2** Any place of peace or plenty.

gos·ling [goz′ling] *n.* A young goose.

gos·pel [gos′pəl] *n.* **1** The teaching of Christ and his apostles. **2** Something thought to be true. **3** (*written* **Gospel**) Any of the first four books of the New Testament. Matthew, Mark, Luke, and John wrote the Gospels. **4** (*written* **Gospel**) A lesson taken from the Gospel, read as part of a church service.

gos·sa·mer [gos′ə·mər] **1** *n.* The fine strands of a spider's web. **2** *n.* A flimsy, delicate material or fabric. **3** *adj.* Like gossamer; filmy.

gos·sip [gos′əp] *n., v.* **gos·siped, gos·sip·ing** **1** *n.* Idle, often malicious talk about others; chatter or tales. **2** *v.* To spread gossip. **3** *n.* A person who spreads gossip; a busybody.

got [got] Past tense and past participle of GET. ◆ See GOTTEN.

Goth [goth] *n.* A member of a Germanic tribe that invaded the Roman Empire in the third, fourth, and fifth centuries.

Goth·ic [goth′ik] **1** *adj.* Having to do with the Goths or their language. **2** *n.* The language of the Goths. **3** *adj.* Belonging to a style of architecture marked by pointed arches and flying buttresses, used in Europe from about 1200 to 1500. **4** *n.* Gothic architecture.

got·ten [got′(ə)n] Past participle of GET. ◆ *Gotten* is no longer used in Great Britain, but it is still widely used in the U.S.: It has *gotten* cold since last night. With the meaning of "must" or "possess," however, only the past participle *got* is used: I've *got* to go; He's *got* a fine library.

Gothic architecture

gouge [gouj] *n., v.* **gouged, goug·ing** **1** *n.* A chisel with a scoop-shaped blade, used to carve wood. **2** *n.* A groove made by or as if by a gouge. **3** *v.* To make a gouge in or scoop out: to *gouge* the eyes. **4** *v. informal* To cheat.

gou·lash [gōō′läsh] *n.* A stew of beef or veal with vegetables and paprika and other spices. ◆ *Goulash* comes from two Hungarian words meaning *shepherd's meat.*

gourd [gôrd *or* gōōrd] *n.* **1** A fruit related to the pumpkin, with a hard outer shell. **2** A ladle, drinking cup, etc., made from a dried gourd. **3** The plant bearing this fruit.

gour·mand [gōōr′mənd *or* gōōr·mān′] *n.* A person who takes great joy in eating. ◆ *Gourmand* comes from a French word meaning *glutton.*

gour·met [gōōr·mā′] *n.* A person who appreciates the finest food and drink. ◆ *Gourmet* comes from an old French word meaning *wine taster.*

gout [gout] *n.* A painful inflammation of the joints, especially of the big toe.

Gov. Abbreviation of GOVERNOR.

gov·ern [guv′ərn] *v.* To rule or guide; manage.

gov·ern·ess [guv′ər·nis] *n.* A woman who cares for and teaches children in a private home.

gov·ern·ment [guv′ər(n)·mənt] *n.* **1** Control or administration of the affairs of a nation, state, city, etc. **2** The system of such administration. **3** The officials in a government. — **gov·ern·men·tal** [guv′ər(n)·men′təl] *adj.*

gov·er·nor [guv′ər·nər] *n.* **1** The elected chief executive of any state of the U.S. **2** A person who governs, especially an official appointed to govern a colony, territory, etc. **3** A device that regulates the speed of a motor.

gov·er·nor·ship [guv′ər·nər·ship] *n.* The position, powers, or time of service of a governor.

govt. Abbreviation of GOVERNMENT.

gown [goun] **1** *n.* A woman's dress worn mainly on formal occasions. **2** *n.* Any long, flowing garment, as a nightgown. **3** *n.* A flowing outer robe, as worn by a judge. **4** *v.* To dress in a gown.

Go·ya [gô′yə], **Francisco de,** 1746–1828, Spanish painter.

grab [grab] *v.* **grabbed, grab·bing,** *n.* **1** *v.* To grasp suddenly and forcefully; snatch: He *grabbed* up a basket. **2** *n.* The act of grabbing.

grab bag A bag filled with various objects, as toys, from which one draws without looking.

grace [grās] *n., v.* **graced, grac·ing** **1** *n.* Beauty or delicacy of movement or form. **2** *n.* Pleasing manners and behavior: social *graces.* **3** *n.* Extra time allowed in which to do something, as pay a debt: ten days of *grace.* **4** *n.* A short prayer

Man wearing cap and gown

add, āce, câre, pälm;   end, ēqual;   it, īce;   odd, ōpen, ôrder;   tŏŏk, pōōl;   up, bûrn;
ə = a in *above*, e in *sicken*, i in *possible*, o in *melon*, u in *circus*;   **yōō** = u in *fuse*;   **oil**;   **pout**;
check; ring; thin; this; zh in *vision*.   For ¶ reference, see page 64 · HOW TO

of thanks said at a meal. **5** *n.* The love and favor of God for man: to fall from *grace.* **6** *n.* (*often pl.*) Esteem; regard: She stayed in his good *graces.* **7** *v.* To dignify; honor: He *graced* us with a visit. **8** *v.* To beautify: Flowers *grace* a room. **— Your Grace** A title of honor used in speaking to an archbishop, duke, or duchess. In speaking about the person **His Grace** or **Her Grace** is used. **— the Graces** In Greek myths, three sister goddesses who gave joy, beauty, charm, and grace to people and nature.

grace·ful [grās′fəl] *adj.* Having or showing grace, especially of form, movement, or manner: a *graceful* dancer. **— grace′ful·ly** *adv.*

grace·less [grās′lis] *adj.* **1** Without grace; clumsy; awkward. **2** Having no sense of good manners or decency: a *graceless* boor.

grace note In music, a note written smaller than the other notes and played in a very short period of time taken from the note that follows it.

gra·cious [grā′shəs] **1** *adj.* Kind and polite. **2** *adj.* Elegant; refined: *gracious* living. **3** *interj.* A cry of surprise. **— gra′cious·ly** *adv.*

grack·le [grak′əl] *n.* A variety of blackbird.

gra·da·tion [grā-dā′shən] *n.* **1** A gradual change by steps: a *gradation* from loud to soft. **2** Any of the steps or degrees in a series: *gradations* between light and dark.

grade [grād] *n., v.* **grad·ed, grad·ing 1** *n.* A degree or step in a scale, as of quality, rank, or worth: This meat is of a low *grade.* **2** *v.* To divide into groups by quality or size: to *grade* lumber. **3** *n. U.S.* Any regular stage of study in a school: the third *grade.* **4** *n.* A group of people or things that are alike in some way. **5** *n. U.S.* A mark showing the merit of someone's work, as at school: Poor *grades* mean failure. **6** *v.* To assign a grade or mark to: The teacher *graded* the test. **7** *n.* A slope, as of a road or track. **8** *v.* To adjust or improve the slope of, as a road or track. **9** *v.* To change gradually: Day *grades* into dusk. **— make the grade** *informal* To be successful.

grade crossing A crossing of railroad tracks or of a road and a railroad at the same level.

grade school Another name for ELEMENTARY SCHOOL.

gra·di·ent [grā′dē·ənt] *n.* **1** Degree of slope: a steep *gradient.* **2** A ramp or incline. **3** In physics, the rate at which something changes: a temperature *gradient.*

grad·u·al [graj′ōō·əl] *adj.* Happening slowly and in small steps; bit by bit: *gradual* changes. **— grad′u·al·ly** *adv.*

grad·u·ate [*v.* graj′ōō·āt, *n., adj.* graj′ōō·it] *v.* **grad·u·at·ed, grad·u·at·ing,** *n., adj.* **1** *v.* To complete a course of study, as at a school or college; earn a diploma. **2** *n.* A person who has graduated. **3** *adj. use: graduate* students; *graduate* studies. **4** *v.* To mark off for use in measuring: Rulers are *graduated.* ◆ *He graduated from college* is now more widely used than the older form, *He was graduated from college. He graduated college* is not considered good usage.

grad·u·a·tion [graj′ōō·ā′shən] *n.* **1** The act of graduating. **2** The ceremonies performed when students graduate. **3** Any of the marks on a measuring instrument: *graduations* on a ruler.

graft[1] [graft] **1** *n.* A shoot from a plant joined to the stem and roots of another plant. **2** *n.* A piece of skin or bone transferred from one part of the body to another, or from one person to another. **3** *n.* The joining of a graft to a plant or body. **4** *v.* To transfer as a graft: Some plants *graft* well; to *graft* skin.

graft[2] [graft] *U.S.* **1** *n.* The getting of money or unfair advantage by dishonest use of a position, especially in a government. **2** *n.* Money obtained in this way. **3** *v.* To obtain by graft.

gra·ham [grā′əm] *adj.* Made of unsifted whole-wheat flour: *graham* crackers.

Grail [grāl] *n.* (*sometimes written* **grail**) In medieval legends, the cup or dish used by Christ at the Last Supper, and in which some of the blood shed at the Crucifixion was caught. It is sometimes called the Holy Grail.

grain [grān] *n.* **1** A small, hard seed, especially from a cereal plant, as wheat or rye. **2** Any cereal plant. **3** A small bit of something: a *grain* of sand; a *grain* of truth. **4** A small unit of weight. There are 7,000 grains in one pound. **5** The arrangement of the fibers or particles in wood, stone, etc.: Oak has a fine *grain.* **6** Basic nature; temperament: His attitude goes against my *grain.*

Grain

grain alcohol Ethyl alcohol, often made from grain.

grain elevator A building for storing grain.

grain·y [grā′nē] *adj.* **grain·i·er, grain·i·est 1** Full of or made up of grains. **2** Having many small bumps; rough: a *grainy* surface. **3** Rough in tone and showing details poorly, as a photograph. **4** Like the grain of wood.

gram [gram] *n.* The unit of weight or mass in the metric system. There are about 28⅓ grams in an ounce.

gram·mar [gram′ər] *n.* **1** The study of the forms, structure, and arrangement of words as used in a language. **2** A set of rules telling how to use words and how to form sentences in a particular language. **3** A way of speaking or writing as judged by how closely it follows these rules: poor *grammar.* **4** A book about grammar.

gram·mar·i·an [grə·mâr′ē·ən] *n.* A person who specializes in grammar.

grammar school 1 Another name for an ELEMENTARY SCHOOL. **2** *British* A school similar to a high school, especially one in which Latin and Greek are taught.

gram·mat·i·cal [grə·mat′i·kəl] *adj.* **1** Having to do with grammar: a *grammatical* mistake. **2** Following the rules of grammar; correct: a *grammatical* sentence; *grammatical* speech. **— gram·mat′i·cal·ly** *adv.*

gramme [gram] *n.* Another spelling of GRAM.

gram·pus [gram′pəs] *n.* **1** A large, dolphinlike creature. **2** A relatively small but ferocious whale, sometimes called the killer whale.

Gra·na·da [grə·nä′də] *n.* A city in southern Spain that was once capital of a Moorish kingdom.

gran·a·ry [gran′ə·rē *or* grā′nə·rē] *n., pl.* **gran·a·ries** A storehouse for grain.

grand [grand] **1** *adj.* Remarkable because of great size or splendor; magnificent; impressive. **2** *adj.* Of high rank or position: a *grand* duke; a *grand* jury. **3** *adj.* First in size or importance: a *grand* ballroom. **4** *adj.* Respected; honored: a *grand* old man. **5** *adj.* Too conscious of being important; haughty. **6** *adj.* Including everything; complete: the *grand* total. **7** *adj. informal* Very pleasing; excellent. **8** *n. U.S. slang* A thousand dollars. **— grand′ly** *adv.*

gran·dam [gran′dam] *n.* **1** A grandmother. **2** An old woman. ◆ This word is seldom used today.

Grand Canyon A large gorge formed by the Colorado River in NW Arizona.

grand·child [gran(d)′chīld′] *n., pl.* **grand·chil·dren** [gran(d)′chil′drən] A child, considered in relation to any of his grandparents.

grand·daugh·ter [gran(d)′dô′tər] *n.* A girl or woman, considered in relation to any of her grandparents.

gran·dee [gran·dē′] *n.* **1** A Spanish or Portuguese nobleman of the highest rank. **2** A person of high rank or status.

gran·deur [gran′jər] *n.* **1** Largeness and splendor; magnificence. **2** Nobility of character.

grand·fa·ther [gran(d)′fä′thər] *n.* A man, considered in relation to a child of his son or daughter.

grandfather clock A clock having a pendulum and enclosed in a tall cabinet.

gran·dil·o·quent [gran·dil′ə·kwənt] *adj.* Speaking in a very fancy and pretentious way; pompous.

gran·di·ose [gran′dē·ōs *or* gran′dē·ōs′] *adj.* **1** Very grand and magnificent; imposing. **2** Making a show of being grand; pompous.

grand jury A group of from 12 to 23 persons that hears the evidence of suspected crime and decides if the accused person should be tried.

grand·ma [gran(d)′mä′] *n. informal* Grandmother.

grand·moth·er [gran(d)′muth′·ər] *n.* A woman, considered in relation to a child of her son or daughter.

grand·neph·ew [gran(d)′nef′·yōo] *n.* A boy or man, considered in relation to his great aunt or great uncle.

grand·niece [gran(d)′nēs′] *n.* A girl or woman,

Grandfather clock

considered in relation to her great aunt or great uncle.

grand·pa [gran(d)′pä′ *or* gram′pä′] *n. informal* Grandfather.

grand·par·ent [gran(d)′pâr′ənt] *n.* A grandmother or a grandfather.

grand piano A large piano whose strings extend from the front to the back of its case.

grand·sire [grand′·sīr′] *n.* **1** A grandfather. **2** An ancestor. **3** A respected old man. ◆ This word is seldom used today.

Grand piano

grand·son [gran(d)′·sun′] *n.* A boy or man, considered in relation to any of his grandparents.

grand·stand [gran(d)′stand′] *n.* The main seating place for spectators at sports events.

grange [grānj] *n.* **1** (*often written* **Grange**) An association of U.S. farmers. **2** *British* A farm and its buildings.

gran·ite [gran′it] *n.* A hard, igneous rock that will take a high polish and is often used as a building material.

gran·ny [gran′ē] *n., pl.* **gran·nies** *informal* **1** Grandmother. **2** An old woman.

granny knot A square knot with the second part crossed the wrong way, so that it often slips and is hard to untie.

grant [grant] **1** *v.* To give; bestow: We *grant* him pardon; The king *granted* permission. **2** *v.* To accept as true; concede: I *grant* it will be hard. **3** *n.* Something that is granted, as a sum of money, a piece of land, etc. **4** *n.* The act of granting. **— take for granted** To accept or assume without question, as an idea.

Grant [grant], **Ulysses Simpson**, 1822–1885, U.S. general in the Civil War and 18th president of the U.S., 1869–1877.

gran·u·lar [gran′yə·lər] *adj.* **1** Made up of, like, or containing grains or granules. **2** Having a granulated surface.

gran·u·late [gran′yə·lāt] *v.* **gran·u·lat·ed, gran·u·lat·ing** **1** To reduce or form into grains or granules. **2** *adj. use: granulated* sugar.

gran·u·la·tion [gran′yə·lā′shən] *n.* The act or process of granulating.

gran·ule [gran′yōol] *n.* A small grain; particle.

grape [grāp] *n.* **1** A smooth-skinned, juicy berry that grows in bunches on some vines. Grapes are edible, and their juice is used to make wine. **2** A vine that bears grapes. **3** Grapeshot.

grape·fruit [grāp′frōot′] *n.* **1** A large, round citrus fruit having a yellow rind and sour, juicy pulp. **2** The tree that bears this fruit.

---

add, āce, câre, pälm;   end, ēqual;   it, īce;   odd, ōpen, ôrder;   tŏŏk, pōol;   up, bûrn;

ə = a in *above*, e in *sicken*, i in *possible*, o in *melon*, u in *circus*;   yōo = u in *fuse*;   oil;   pout;

check;   ring;   thin;   this;   zh in *vision*.   For ¶ reference, see page 64 · HOW TO

grape·shot [grāp′shot′] *n.* A cluster of small iron balls, formerly fired from cannons.

grape·vine [grāp′vīn′] *n.* **1** A vine on which grapes grow. **2** *U.S.* A secret or informal way of passing news from person to person: He heard by the *grapevine* that he had won the prize.

graph [graf] **1** *n.* A diagram that shows the relation between the elements of two sets, by a series of points, or by a curve, or by lines or bars of different lengths. **2** *v.* To express or present in the form of a graph.

Graph of average temperature in Washington, D.C.

graph·ic [graf′ik] *adj.* **1** Giving an exact picture or report; vivid; detailed: a *graphic* news story. **2** Having to do with graphs. **3** Having to do with painting, drawing, engraving, etc.: *graphic* arts. **4** Having to do with or expressed in writing: *graphic* symbols. — **graph′i·cal·ly** *adv.*

graph·ite [graf′īt] *n.* A soft, black, slippery form of carbon, used as lead for pencils and to make moving parts of machines slide against each other more easily.

graph paper Paper marked with many intersecting lines, usually into small, equal squares, and used for drawing graphs, curves, etc.

grap·nel [grap′nəl] *n.* **1** A shaft with several hooks at one end, often attached to a rope and thrown so as to hook something and pull it closer. **2** A similar object used as an anchor.

grap·ple [grap′əl] *v.* **grap·pled, grap·pling,** *n.* **1** *v.* To take hold of; grab firmly. **2** *n.* A hold or grip, as in wrestling. **3** *v.* To struggle closely; contend: The wrestlers *grappled*; She *grappled* with the problem. **4** *n.* A grapnel.

Grapnel

grappling iron A type of grapnel used to find sunken objects and pull them from the water.

grasp [grasp] **1** *v.* To take hold of firmly, as with the hand. **2** *n.* A hold, or the ability to hold; grip: Get a good *grasp*. **3** *v.* To understand; comprehend: He can *grasp* French. **4** *n.* Understanding; comprehension: a poor *grasp* of English. **5** *n.* Complete control; domination: the *grasp* of a tyrant. — **grasp at 1** To try to grab. **2** To accept eagerly: He *grasped at* the chance to escape.

grasp·ing [gras′ping] *adj.* Greedy; acquisitive.

grass [gras] *n.* **1** A green plant with narrow leaves that covers fields and lawns. Cows, sheep, and other grazing animals eat grass. **2** Ground on which grass grows, as a lawn or pasture. **3** Any of various other plants with jointed stems, as grains, bamboo, and sugar cane.

grass·hop·per [gras′hop′ər] *n.* Any of a large group of insects having strong hind legs for leaping and two pairs of wings. They often destroy plants and crops.

grass·land [gras′land′] *n.* Land with grass growing on it; a pasture or prairie.

grass·y [gras′ē] *adj.* **grass·i·er, grass·i·est** **1** Covered with or full of grass. **2** Like or having to do with grass.

grate¹ [grāt] *v.* **grat·ed, grat·ing** **1** To reduce to small pieces by rubbing against a rough surface: to *grate* onions; Cheese *grates* easily. **2** To rub together so as to make a scraping sound: The bent fender *grated* on the wheel. **3** To cause irritation: His conceit *grates* on us.

grate² [grāt] *n., v.* **grat·ed, grat·ing** **1** *n.* A framework of crossed or parallel bars placed over a window, door, drain, etc. **2** *n.* A metal framework used to hold burning fuel, in a furnace or fireplace. **3** *n.* A fireplace. **4** *v.* To fit with a grate: to *grate* a window.

grate·ful [grāt′fəl] *adj.* **1** Thankful or expressing thanks: a *grateful* man; a *grateful* nod. **2** Giving pleasure; welcome; agreeable: a *grateful* warmth. — **grate′ful·ly** *adv.*

grat·er [grā′tər] *n.* **1** A person or thing that grates. **2** A kitchen utensil with sharp teeth, holes, etc., used to grate food: a cheese *grater*.

grat·i·fy [grat′ə·fī] *v.* **grat·i·fied, grat·i·fy·ing** **1** To give pleasure or satisfaction to: The boy's eagerness to learn *gratified* his teachers. **2** To satisfy, as a want or need; indulge: to *gratify* a wish. **3** *adj. use:* a *gratifying* meal. — **grat·i·fi·ca·tion** [grat′ə·fə·kā′shən] *n.*

grat·ing¹ [grā′ting] *n.* An arrangement of bars or slats, as over a window or opening; grate.

grat·ing² [grā′ting] *adj.* **1** Harsh or unpleasant in sound; rasping. **2** Irritating; annoying.

gra·tis [grā′tis *or* gra′tis] *adj., adv.* Free of charge: a dinner *gratis*; Admit them *gratis*.

grat·i·tude [grat′ə·t(y)ood] *n.* Thankfulness for a gift or favor; appreciation.

gra·tu·i·tous [grə·t(y)oo′ə·təs] *adj.* **1** Given or accepted without payment; free: a *gratuitous* ticket. **2** Lacking cause; needless; uncalled-for: *gratuitous* advice. — **gra·tu′i·tous·ly** *adv.*

gra·tu·i·ty [grə·t(y)oo′ə·tē] *n., pl.* **gra·tu·i·ties** A gift, usually money, given in return for some service; tip: a generous *gratuity*.

grave¹ [grāv] *adj.* **grav·er, grav·est** **1** Of great importance; weighty: a *grave* responsibility. **2** Filled with or showing danger: a *grave* problem. **3** Solemn and dignified; sober; heavy: a *grave* mood. — **grave′ly** *adv.*

grave² [grāv] *n.* **1** A burial place for a dead body, usually a hole in the ground. **2** Any final resting place: The ship went down to a watery *grave*. **3** Death.

grave³ [grāv] *v.* **graved, grav·en** *or* **graved, grav·ing** **1** To make by carving; sculpture: to *grave* a statue. **2** To engrave or inscribe: to *grave* words in stone.

grav·el [grav′əl] *n., v.* **grav·eled** *or* **grav·elled, grav·el·ing** *or* **grav·el·ling** **1** *n.* A mixture of small, rounded pebbles and pieces of stone. **2** *v.* To put gravel on, as a road.

grav·el·ly [grav′əl·ē] *adj.* **1** Made of or containing gravel. **2** Like gravel. **3** Harsh, as a voice.

grav·en [grāv′ən] **1** An alternative past participle of GRAVE³. **2** *adj. use:* A sculptured idol is sometimes called a *graven* image.

grave·stone [grāv′stōn′] *n.* A stone used to mark a grave and tell who the dead person was.

grave·yard [grāv′yärd′] *n.* A burial place; cemetery.

grav·i·tate [grav′ə·tāt] *v.* **grav·i·tat·ed, grav·i·tat·ing 1** To move or tend to move as a result of the force of gravity. **2** To move as though pulled by a powerful force; be attracted: Crowds *gravitate* to the exhibit. **3** To sink or settle: Mud *gravitates* to the bottom of a jar of water.

grav·i·ta·tion [grav′ə·tā′shən] *n.* **1** In physics, the force by which any two bodies attract each other. **2** The act or process of gravitating. **3** A movement, as to a source of attraction.

grav·i·ty [grav′ə·tē] *n., pl.* **grav·i·ties 1** In physics, gravitation, especially as shown by the tendency of objects to fall toward the center of the earth. **2** Weight; heaviness: the center of *gravity*. **3** Seriousness: the *gravity* of the situation; the *gravity* of her manner.

gra·vy [grā′vē] *n., pl.* **gra·vies 1** The juice and melted fat given off by meat while it is cooking. **2** A sauce made from this liquid, often thickened with flour.

gray [grā] **1** *n.* A shade or color made up of a mixture of white and black. **2** *adj.* Of or having this color or shade. **3** *adj.* Dark or dull; dismal; gloomy: a *gray* day. **4** *adj.* Having gray hair. **5** *v.* To make or become gray. — **gray′ness** *n.*

gray·beard [grā′bird′] *n.* An old man.

gray·ling [grā′ling] *n., pl.,* **gray·ling** or **gray·lings** A troutlike fish having a large, colorful dorsal fin.

gray matter 1 The reddish gray nerve tissue of the brain and spinal cord. **2** *informal* Brains; intelligence.

graze¹ [grāz] *v.* **grazed, graz·ing 1** To feed on growing grass: Cattle *graze* when hungry. **2** To let or put to graze: The farmer *grazed* sheep in the field.

graze² [grāz] *v.* **grazed, graz·ing,** *n.* **1** *v.* To brush against or scrape lightly in passing: A truck *grazed* his car. **2** *n.* A light contact. **3** *n.* A mark or scrape made by grazing.

grease [*n.* grēs, *v.* grēs *or* grēz] *n., v.* **greased, greas·ing 1** *n.* Animal fat in a soft state. **2** *n.* Any thick, fatty, or oily substance; lubricant. **3** *v.* To apply grease to: to *grease* a car.

grease paint A waxy substance used for theatrical make-up.

greas·y [grē′sē *or* grē′zē] *adj.* **greas·i·er,**

greas·i·est 1 Smeared or spotted with grease. **2** Containing much grease or fat; oily. **3** Like grease; slick; *greasy* mud. — **greas′i·ly** *adv.* — **greas′i·ness** *n.*

great [grāt] *adj.* **1** Very large in size, quantity, amount, extent, expanse, etc.; immense; big. **2** More than ordinary; remarkable: *great* pain. **3** Of unusual importance: a *great* writer; a *great* victory. **4** Enthusiastic: a *great* hiker. **5** One generation further away in relationship: used in combination: *great-aunt; great-uncle.* **6** *informal* Excellent; first-rate; fine: He's a *great* fellow. — **great′ness** *n.*

great-aunt [grāt′ant′] *n.* An aunt of either of one's parents.

Great Barrier Reef A chain of coral reefs 1,260 miles long, off the NE coast of Australia.

Great Bear A constellation of the northern sky, containing seven bright stars.

Great Britain The main island of the United Kingdom, containing England, Scotland, and Wales.

great circle 1 In geometry, a circle formed on the surface of a sphere by a plane that passes through the center of the sphere. It is the largest circle that can be drawn on a sphere. **2** In geography, a similar circle on the surface of the earth. The shortest distance between any two places is on a great circle.

great·coat [grāt′kōt′] *n.* A heavy overcoat.

Great Dane One of a breed of large, strong, smooth-haired dogs.

Great Divide Another name for the CONTINENTAL DIVIDE.

great·er [grāt′ər] **1** Comparative of GREAT. **2** *adj.* (*usually written* **Greater**) Indicating a city and its suburbs: *Greater* London.

Great Dane, about 32 in. high at shoulder

great-grand·child [grāt′gran(d)′child] *n., pl.* **great-grand·chil·dren** [grāt′gran(d)′chil′drən] A great-grandson or great-granddaughter.

great-grand·daugh·ter [grāt′gran(d)′dô′tər] *n.* A woman or girl, considered in relation to any of her great-grandparents.

great-grand·fa·ther [grāt′gran(d)′fä′thər] *n.* A man, considered in relation to any of the grandchildren of his children.

great-grand·moth·er [grāt′gran(d)′muth′ər] *n.* A woman, considered in relation to any of the grandchildren of her children.

great-grand·par·ent [grāt′gran(d)′pâr′ənt] *n.* A person, considered in relation to any of the grandchildren of his or her children.

great-grand·son [grāt′gran(d)′sun′] *n.* A

add, āce, câre, pälm;   end, ēqual;   it, īce;   odd, ōpen, ôrder;   tŏŏk, pōōl;   up, bûrn;
ə = a in *above*, e in *sicken*, i in *possible*, o in *melon*, u in *circus*;   yōō = u in *fuse*;   oil;   pout;
check;   ri**ng**;   **th**in;   **th**is;   zh in *vision*.   For ¶ reference, see page 64 · HOW TO

man or boy, considered in relation to any of his great-grandparents.

great·heart·ed [grāt′här′tid] *adj.* **1** Noble or generous in spirit. **2** Brave; courageous.

Great Lakes A chain of five large lakes in central North America, on the border between the U.S. and Canada. They are Lakes Superior, Michigan, Huron, Erie, and Ontario.

great·ly [grāt′lē] *adv.* **1** In or to a great degree; very much. **2** In a great manner.

Great Plains A sloping plateau in western North America just east of the Rocky Mountains.

Great Salt Lake A salt lake in NW Utah, having no outlet.

great-un·cle [grāt′ung′kəl] *n.* An uncle of either of one's parents.

greave [grēv] *n.* (*usually pl.*) Armor that protects the leg from knee to ankle.

grebe [grēb] *n.* A swimming and diving bird, having flaps on its toes but not webbed feet.

Gre·cian [grē′shən] *n., adj.* Greek.

Greece [grēs] *n.* A country in SE Europe.

greed [grēd] *n.* A selfish and grasping desire for possessions, especially for money: His *greed* for more money ruined his life.

greed·y [grē′dē] *adj.* **greed·i·er, greed·i·est** **1** Wanting selfishly to get more, especially more money: a *greedy* landlord. **2** Wanting to eat and drink a lot; gluttonous. **— greed′i·ly** *adv.* **— greed′i·ness** *n.*

Greek [grēk] **1** *adj.* Of or from Greece. **2** *n.* A person born in or a citizen of Greece. **3** *n.* The language of Greece.

Greek Orthodox Church A branch of the Eastern Orthodox Church.

green [grēn] **1** *n.* The color of growing grass and foliage. **2** *adj.* Of or having this color. **3** *adj.* Not cured or ready for use: *green* lumber. **4** *adj.* Not fully developed; immature; unripe: *green* fruit. **5** *adj.* Not fully trained; inexperienced: *green* troops. **6** *adj.* Thriving; flourishing: a *green* garden. **7** *n.* A plot of land covered with turf: a large putting *green*; the village *green*. **8** *n.* (*pl.*) The leaves and stems of certain plants used as food, such as spinach, beets, etc. **— green′ness** *n.*

green·back [grēn′bak′] *n.* Any U.S. paper money that is printed in green ink on the back.

green·er·y [grēn′ər·ē] *n.* Green plants; foliage.

green·gage [grēn′gāj′] *n.* A type of sweet plum having green skin and flesh.

green·gro·cer [grēn′grō′sər] *n.* *British* A dealer in fresh fruits and vegetables.

green·horn [grēn′hôrn′] *n.* An inexperienced person; beginner. ◆*Greenhorn* comes from *green*, meaning *immature*, plus *horn*. The word originally referred to a young animal whose horns were not yet fully grown.

green·house [grēn′hous′] *n.* A heated building used for growing delicate plants, having its roof and sides made partly of glass; hothouse.

Greenhouse

Green·land [grēn′·lənd] *n.* An island belonging to Denmark. It is the largest island in the world and is off the coast of NE North America.

green·sward [grēn′swôrd′] *n.* Ground covered with green grass; turf.

green thumb A special knack for making plants grow very well.

Green·wich [gren′ich] *n.* A borough of SE London, England. The meridian at 0° longitude (prime meridian) passes through Greenwich.

green·wood [grēn′wŏŏd′] *n.* A forest when the trees have leaves.

greet [grēt] *v.* **1** To show friendly recognition to, as when meeting; welcome: He *greeted* us warmly. **2** To meet or receive in a certain way: She *greeted* us with flowers. **3** To present itself to: The glow of the fire *greeted* us.

greet·ing [grē′ting] *n.* **1** The act of a person who greets; welcome. **2** (*sometimes pl.*) A message showing friendship or regard.

gre·gar·i·ous [gri·gâr′ē·əs] *adj.* **1** Living together in flocks, herds, or groups: Cattle are *gregarious*. **2** Enjoying the company of others; sociable: Our friends are very *gregarious*.

Gre·go·ri·an calendar [gri·gôr′ē·ən] The calendar now used in most parts of the world, prescribed by Pope Gregory XIII in 1582.

Gregorian chant A type of music sung in the services of the Roman Catholic and some other churches. It was started by Pope Gregory I.

Greg·o·ry I [greg′ər·ē], 540?–604, pope 590–604, later made a saint. He reformed the church service and was called Gregory the Great.

grem·lin [grem′lin] *n.* An imaginary, elflike creature jokingly said to cause mechanical troubles in airplanes and other devices.

gre·nade [gri·nād′] *n.* **1** A small bomb thrown by hand or fired from a rifle. **2** A glass container that breaks and releases chemicals when thrown, as to put out a fire.

gren·a·dier [gren′ə·dir′] *n.* **1** In earlier times, a soldier assigned to throw grenades. **2** A member of a special regiment in the British army.

grew [grōō] Past tense of GROW.

grey [grā] *n., adj.* Another spelling of GRAY.

grey·hound [grā′hound′] *n.* One of a breed of tall, slender dogs, used in dog races.

grid [grid] *n.* **1** An arrangement of evenly spaced parallel or intersecting bars, wires, etc.; grate. **2** An arrangement of lines that divides a map into small squares. **3** The metal framework that supports the active material in a storage battery. **4** An electrode of a vacuum tube, made of closely spaced wires and located between the cathode and anode.

grid·dle [grid′(ə)l] *n.* A flat pan, often with no raised rim, used for cooking pancakes, etc.

grid·dle·cake [grid′(ə)l·kāk′] *n.* A pancake.

grid·i·ron [grid′ī′ərn] *n.* **1** A metal grating in a frame, used to hold meat or other food during broiling. **2** Something that looks like a cooking gridiron, as a structure of beams or pipes. **3** A football field.

grief [grēf] *n.* **1** Deep sorrow or mental distress. **2** A cause of deep sorrow. **— come to grief** To end badly; meet with disaster; fail.

Grieg [grēg], **Edvard,** 1843–1907, Norwegian composer.

griev·ance [grē′vəns] *n.* A real or imagined wrong thought of as a cause for anger or complaint: Tell your *grievance* to the judge.

grieve [grēv] *v.* **grieved, griev·ing** To feel or cause to feel grief: They *grieved* over the dog's death; His absence *grieves* us.

griev·ous [grē′vəs] *adj.* **1** Causing grief or sorrow; distressing: a *grievous* occasion. **2** Deserving severe punishment; very bad; grave: a *grievous* sin. **3** Showing grief; mournful: a *grievous* wail. **4** Extremely painful; severe: a *grievous* wound.

grif·fin [grif′ən] *n.* In Greek myths, a beast with the head and wings of an eagle and the body of a lion.

grill [gril] **1** *n.* A gridiron or similar cooking utensil. **2** *v.* To cook, as on a grill. **3** *n.* A meal or serving of grilled food. **4** *n.* A restaurant where grilled food is served. **5** *v.* To torment with great heat. **6** *v. U.S. informal* To question hard and thoroughly: The police *grilled* him.

Griffin

grille [gril] *n.* A grating, often decorative, used as a covering or screen in a door, window, etc.

grim [grim] *adj.* **grim·mer, grim·mest 1** Stern or forbidding: a *grim* expression. **2** Unyielding; fixed: *grim* determination. **3** Cruel; fierce: a *grim* war. **4** Repulsive or ghastly: *grim* tales of murder. **— grim′ly** *adv.* **— grim′ness** *n.*

gri·mace [gri·mās′ *or* grim′əs] *n., v.* **gri·maced, gri·mac·ing 1** A twisting of the face expressing pain, annoyance, disgust, etc. **2** *v.* To make a grimace; make faces.

grime [grīm] *n., v.* **grimed, grim·ing 1** *n.* Dirt, especially soot, rubbed into or coating a surface. **2** *v.* To make dirty: to *grime* a floor.

Grimm [grim], **Jakob,** 1785–1863, and his brother **Wilhelm,** 1786–1859, German philologists, noted for their collection of fairy tales.

grim·y [grī′mē] *adj.* **grim·i·er, grim·i·est** Full of or covered with grime; dirty.

grin [grin] *v.* **grinned, grin·ning,** *n.* **1** *v.* To smile broadly and sometimes foolishly, showing the teeth. **2** *v.* To pull back the lips and show the teeth, as in a snarl or grimace. **3** *n.* An expression made by grinning, especially a broad smile.

grind [grīnd] *v.* **ground, grind·ing,** *n.* **1** *v.* To crush or undergo crushing into small pieces or fine powder: to *grind* coffee; Meat *grinds* easily. **2** *n.* The degree of fineness to which something is ground: a coarse *grind* of hominy. **3** *v.* To sharpen, shape, or polish by rubbing with something rough: to *grind* a chisel. **4** *v.* To press together with a scraping motion; grate: to *grind* the teeth. **5** *v.* To operate by turning a crank. **6** *n.* The act of grinding. **7** *v.* To produce mechanically, or with effort: He *grinds* out bad stories. **8** *v.* To reduce to misery, as by harsh treatment: Injustice *grinds* people down. **9** *v. U.S. informal* To work or study hard or long. **10** *n. U.S. informal* Long and hard work or study. **11** *n. U.S. informal* A student who studies constantly.

grind·er [grīn′dər] *n.* **1** A person who grinds, especially one who sharpens tools. **2** A device that grinds, as a mill for coffee. **3** A tooth that grinds food; a molar.

grind·stone [grīnd′stōn′] *n.* A flat, circular stone that is rotated and is used for grinding tools. **— keep one's nose to the grindstone** To work hard and steadily.

grip [grip] *v.* **gripped** or **gript, grip·ping,** *n.* **1** *v.* To grasp or hold on firmly. **2** *n.* The act of gripping. **3** *n.* The ability to grip: a good *grip*. **4** *n.* Control: in the *grip* of fear. **5** *v.* To capture the imagination of: The story *gripped* us. **6** *n.* Understanding; mastery: a good *grip* of

Grindstone

history. **7** *n.* The part of an object to be held in the hand; handle. **8** *n.* The way in which a tool, bat, etc., is held. **9** *n.* The strength of a handshake: a strong *grip*. **10** *n.* A secret handshake, as one used by members of a fraternity or society. **11** *n. U.S.* A small suitcase. **— come to grips 1** To struggle in combat. **2** To face bravely, as a difficulty or problem.

gripe [grīp] *v.* **griped, grip·ing,** *n.* **1** *v.* To cause cramps or sharp pains in the bowels. **2** *n. (usually pl.)* Cramps in the bowels. **3** *v. U.S. informal* To anger or annoy: His lies *gripe* me. **4** *v. U.S. informal* To complain or grumble: to *gripe* about the weather. **5** *n. U.S. informal* A complaint; grievance.

grippe [grip] *n.* Influenza, or a bad cold.

gris·ly [griz′lē] *adj.* **gris·li·er, gris·li·est** Causing fear or horror; gruesome: I shivered when I heard his *grisly* story.

---

add, āce, câre, pälm;   end, ēqual;   it, īce;   odd, ōpen, ôrder;   took, pool;   up, bûrn;

ə = a in *above,* e in *sicken,* i in *possible,* o in *melon,* u in *circus;*   yoo = u in *fuse;*   oil;   pout;

check;   ring;   thin;   this;   zh in *vision.*   For ¶ reference, see page 64 · HOW TO

grist [grist] *n.* **1** Grain that is to be ground. **2** Ground grain; meal.

gris·tle [gris'(ə)l] *n.* A tough, stringy substance found in meat; cartilage.

gris·tly [gris'lē] *adj.* **gris·tli·er, gris·tli·est 1** Like gristle. **2** Containing gristle.

grist·mill [grist'mil'] *n.* A mill for grinding grain.

grit [grit] *n., v.* **grit·ted, grit·ting 1** *n.* Small hard particles of sand, stone, etc. **2** *n.* A hard, coarse sandstone, used for making grindstones. **3** *n.* Determined courage; pluck. **4** *v.* To grind or press together: He *gritted* his teeth.

grits [grits] *n.pl.* Coarse meal made from grain, especially corn, with the husks removed.

grit·ty [grit'ē] *adj.* **grit·ti·er, grit·ti·est 1** Like, containing, or made of grit. **2** Bravely determined; plucky: *a gritty* soldier.

griz·zled [griz'əld] *adj.* **1** Streaked or mixed with gray. **2** Having gray hair.

griz·zly [griz'lē] *adj.* **griz·zli·er, griz·zli·est,** *n., pl.* **griz·zlies 1** *adj.* Grayish; grizzled. **2** *n.* A grizzly bear.

grizzly bear A large, brownish or grayish bear of western North America.

groan [grōn] **1** *v.* To make a long, low sound that shows pain, anguish, displeasure, boredom, etc.: We *groaned* at the extra homework. **2** *v.* To make a rough, creaking sound, especially from being overloaded: The chair *groaned* under his weight. **3** *n.* Any groaning sound.

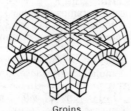
Grizzly bear

groat [grōt] *n.* **1** An old English silver coin worth four pennies. **2** Any very small, trivial sum.

gro·cer [grō'sər] *n* A person who deals in foods and other household goods.

gro·cer·y [grō'sər·ē *or* grōs'rē] *n., pl.* **gro·cer·ies 1** *U.S.* A store selling foods and other household goods. **2** (*pl.*) The food, etc., sold by a grocer.

grog [grog] *n.* **1** Alcoholic liquor, especially rum, mixed with water. **2** Any alcoholic drink.

grog·gy [grog'ē] *adj.* **grog·gi·er, grog·gi·est 1** Dazed or not fully conscious, as from a blow or exhaustion. **2** Drunk. — **grog'gi·ly** *adv.* — **grog'gi·ness** *n.*

groin [groin] **1** *n.* The fold or crease formed where either of the thighs joins the abdomen. **2** *n.* A curved line formed on a ceiling where two vaults meet. **3** *v.* To build with or form into groins.

Groins

groom [grōōm] **1** *v.* To attend to the feeding, cleaning, and brushing of (a horse). **2** *n.* A man or boy who tends horses. **3** *v.* To make neat, tidy, etc.: Cats *groom* themselves daily. **4** *v.* To prepare by giving special training to. **5** *n.* A bridegroom.

groove [grōōv] *n., v.* **grooved, groov·ing 1** *n.* A long, narrow cut or furrow made in a surface, especially by a tool. **2** *n.* Any long, narrow depression, channel, or rut. **3** *n.* A thin spiral track cut into the surface of a phonograph record. **4** *v.* To make a groove or grooves in: to *groove* wood. **5** *n.* A fixed or habitual routine: He is in the same old *groove.*

grope [grōp] *v.* **groped, grop·ing 1** To feel or reach around blindly and clumsily: to *grope* for a light. **2** To search in a confused, uncertain way: to *grope* for truth. **3** To find by groping: He *groped* his way in the dark.

gros·beak [grōs'bēk'] *n.* Any of various finch-like birds with a short, stout beak.

gros·grain [grō'grān] *n.* A strong silk or rayon fabric with horizontal ribs, usually woven as ribbon.

gross [grōs] **1** *adj.* Having nothing subtracted; total: *gross* income. **2** *adj.* Clearly bad or wrong; flagrant: *gross* errors. **3** *adj.* Too large or fat; hulking. **4** *adj.* Coarse or improper; vulgar; obscene: *gross* conduct. **5** *n., pl.* **gross·es** The entire amount; total: ten percent of the *gross.* **6** *n., pl.* **gross** Twelve dozen; 144. — **gross'ly** *adv.* — **gross'ness** *n.*

gro·tesque [grō·tesk'] *adj.* Distorted or very strange or ugly in appearance or style: The hyena is a *grotesque* animal. — **gro·tesque'ness** *n.*

grot·to [grot'ō] *n., pl.* **grot·toes** *or* **grot·tos 1** A cave. **2** An artificial cavelike structure, as a shrine. ◆ See CRYPT.

grouch [grouch] *U.S. informal* **1** *v.* To complain and find fault. **2** *n.* A discontented, grumbling person. **3** *n.* A sulky, grouchy mood.

grouch·y [grouch'ē] *adj.* **grouch·i·er, grouch·i·est** *U.S. informal* Cross or ill-humored. — **grouch'i·ly** *adv.* — **grouch'i·ness** *n.*

ground[1] [ground] **1** *n.* The part of the earth's surface that is solid; land. **2** *n.* A tract of land used for a particular purpose: a burial *ground.* **3** *n.* (*pl.*) Land surrounding and belonging to a building: a house and *grounds.* **4** *v.* To put or place on the ground. **5** *n.* A connection of an electric circuit with the earth. **6** *v.* To connect with the ground, as an electric circuit. **7** *adj.* On, near, or level with the ground. **8** *v.* To run aground, as a ship. **9** *n.* (*often pl.*) A basic cause, reason, or justification: What were the *grounds* for that accusation? **10** *v.* To base, as on a foundation or idea; establish: to *ground* a theory on facts. **11** *v.* To teach basic principles to: to *ground* students in grammar. **12** *n.* (*pl.*) Sediment, especially if remaining after a beverage has been brewed: coffee *grounds.* **13** *n.* Background, as in various arts and crafts. **14** *v.* To confine to the ground, as an airplane: The airline *grounded* the plane. **15** *v.* In baseball, to hit a ball so that it bounces or rolls on the ground: He *grounded* to first base. — **break ground 1** To dig into the earth, as in plowing or building. **2** To make a start in doing something. — **cover**

ground 1 To travel, especially over a long distance. **2** To make progress. **— gain ground** To advance; make headway. **— give ground** To give up a position or advantage; retreat. **— lose ground** To fall behind or weaken.

ground² [ground] **1** Past tense and past participle of GRIND. **2** *adj. use*: *ground* meat.

ground cover Plants that form a dense and extensive growth close to the ground.

ground·er [groun′dər] *n.* In baseball, a ball hit so that it bounces or rolls on the ground.

ground hog The woodchuck. In popular tradition the animal comes out of hibernation on February 2, or **ground-hog day.** If he sees his shadow, winter remains for another six weeks; and if he does not see it, spring comes early.

ground·less [ground′lis] *adj.* Having no reason or cause; baseless.

ground·nut [ground′nut′] *n.* Any of various plants having edible underground parts, as the peanut.

ground pine Any of various creeping evergreens.

ground squirrel A chipmunk or similar small rodent that lives on or in the ground.

ground swell Broad, deep ocean waves caused by an often distant storm or earthquake.

ground water Water that seeps into the earth and collects, serving to supply wells and springs.

ground·work [ground′wûrk′] *n.* A foundation; basis.

group [groop] **1** *n.* A number of persons or things. **2** *n.* A number of people or things that have one or more things in common; class. **3** *v.* To gather or arrange in a group or groups: *Group* yourselves around me.

grouse [grous] *n., pl.* **grouse** A plump bird, often hunted for sport.

grove [grōv] *n.* **1** A small group of trees. **2** An orchard: an orange *grove.*

grov·el [gruv′əl *or* grov′əl] *v.* **grov·eled** or **grov·elled, grov·el·ing** or **grov·el·ling 1** To kneel, crawl, or lie face downward in fear or humility. **2** To act in a very humble and fearful way; cringe. **— grov′el·er** or **grov′el·ler** *n.*

Ruffed grouse, about 17 in. long

grow [grō] *v.* **grew, grown, grow·ing 1** To increase in size, age, or maturity: Our kitten *grew.* **2** To increase in size or amount: The debt *grew* rapidly. **3** To exist in a live or flourishing condition: Bananas *grow* in the tropics. **4** To make grow; cultivate: to *grow* roses. **5** To develop naturally: His interest in science *grew.* **6** To become: to *grow* angry; to *grow* older. **— grow on** To become increasingly pleasing or necessary to. **— grow out of 1** To become too big or mature for; outgrow. **2** To result

from. **— grow up** To reach full growth; become adult. **— grow′er** *n.*

growl [groul] **1** *n.* A deep, rumbling, threatening sound, as that of an angry dog. **2** *v.* To make a growl. **3** *v.* To speak gruffly and angrily.

grown [grōn] **1** Past participle of GROW. **2** *adj.* Fully developed; mature; adult: a *grown* man.

grown-up [*n.* grōn′up′, *adj.* grōn′up′] **1** *n.* An adult. **2** *adj.* Fully grown; adult. **3** *adj.* Of or suited for adults.

growth [grōth] *n.* **1** The action of growing. **2** The amount grown: a season's *growth.* **3** Something grown or growing: a *growth* of weeds.

grub [grub] *v.* **grubbed, grub·bing,** *n.* **1** *v.* To dig or dig up: to *grub* for food; to *grub* potatoes. **2** *v.* To work hard and live miserably: The poor *grub* along from day to day. **3** *n.* A fat, wormlike larva of an insect. **4** *n. slang* Food.

grub·by [grub′ē] *adj.* **grub·bi·er, grub·bi·est** Dirty or sloppy: a *grubby* little boy.

grudge [gruj] *n., v.* **grudged, grudg·ing 1** *n.* A feeling of hatred or resentment: He had a *grudge* against the man who sued him. **2** *v.* To be envious of or angry at (someone) because of what he has: They *grudge* him his wealth. **3** *v.* To give or allow unwillingly: He *grudged* what his wife spent. **4** *adj. use*: *grudging* admiration; a *grudging* contribution.

gru·el [groo′əl] *n.* A thin, liquid food made by boiling cereal in water or milk.

gru·el·ing or **gru·el·ling** [groo′əl·ing] *adj.* Very tiring or exhausting: a *grueling* trip.

grue·some [groo′səm] *adj.* Causing disgust or horror; repulsive; frightful.

gruff [gruf] *adj.* **1** Harsh or hoarse: a *gruff* voice. **2** Rude or surly; unfriendly: a *gruff* fellow. **— gruff′ly** *adv.* **— gruff′ness** *n.*

grum·ble [grum′bəl] *v.* **grum·bled, grum·bling,** *n.* **1** *v.* To complain in a grumpy way; mutter unhappily. **2** *n.* A low, muttered complaint. **3** *v.* To make a low, rumbling sound. **4** *n.* A low, rumbling sound: the *grumble* of thunder. **— grum′bler** *n.*

grump·y [grum′pē] *adj.* **grump·i·er, grump·i·est** Cranky or grouchy: a *grumpy* old man.

grunt [grunt] **1** *n.* A short, deep, hoarse sound made in the throat. **2** *v.* To make such a sound: He *grunted* as he lifted the heavy stone. **3** *v.* To say or express by grunting: He *grunted* his approval.

gry·phon [grif′ən] *n.* Another spelling of GRIFFIN.

Guam [gwäm] *n* A U.S. territory consisting of an island in the western Pacific.

gua·no [gwä′nō] *n.* The manure, or dung, of sea birds, bats, etc., used as fertilizer.

guar·an·tee [gar′ən·tē′] *n., v.* **guar·an·teed, guar·an·tee·ing 1** *n.* A pledge to repair, replace, or refund payment for an article sold if anything goes wrong with it before a certain

add, āce, câre, pälm; end, ēqual; it, īce; odd, ōpen, ôrder; tŏŏk, pōōl; up, bûrn; ə = a in *above*, e in *sicken*, i in *possible*, o in *melon*, u in *circus*; yōō = u in *fuse*; oil; pout; check; ring; thin; this; zh in *vision*. For ¶ reference, see page 64 · HOW TO

time has passed. **2** *n.* A promise that something will be done or happen. **3** *v.* To give a guarantee for or of: to *guarantee* a product. **4** *n.* A guaranty (defs. 1, 2). **5** *n.* Someone who gives a guarantee.

guar·an·tor [gar′ən·tər *or* gar′ən·tôr] *n.* Someone who gives or makes a guarantee or guaranty.

guar·an·ty [gar′ən·tē] *n., pl.* **guar·an·ties** **1** A promise to make good someone's debt or obligation if he should fail to do so himself. **2** Something given or taken as security for a debt or obligation. **3** A guarantee (defs. 1, 2).

guard [gärd] **1** *v.* To watch over and keep from harm; protect; defend: to *guard* a herd. **2** *v.* To keep under control or from escaping: to *guard* prisoners. **3** *n.* A person or group that guards. **4** *v.* To be alert; watch out: to *guard* against errors. **5** *n.* The act of guarding; watchful care: Keep a *guard* against prowlers. **6** *n.* Something that protects against injury or damage: the *guard* on the handle of a sword. **7** *n.* In football, either of the linemen that play next to the center. **8** *n.* In basketball, either of two players whose main duty is to defend the basket. **9** *n.* A position for defense, as in boxing or fencing. **— on guard** Watchful and ready to protect or defend; cautious.

guard cell Either of the two cells that control the opening and closing of a pore in plants.

guard·ed [gär′did] *adj.* **1** Carefully protected or defended; closely watched. **2** Prudent; cautious: a *guarded* answer. **— guard′·ed·ly** *adv.*

guard·house [gärd′hous′] *n.* **1** A headquarters for military guards. **2** An army jail.

guard·i·an [gär′dē·ən] *n.* **1** A person who guards or watches over; protector: the *guardians* of justice. **2** A person chosen by a court to care for someone who is young or unable to care for himself. **3** *adj. use: guardian* angel. **— guard′·i·an·ship** *n.* ◆ See WARDEN.

guards·man [gärdz′mən] *n., pl.* **guards·men** [gärdz′mən] **1** A guard. **2** A member of a national guard or any military body called a guard.

Gua·te·ma·la [gwä′tə·mä′lä] *n.* A country in northern Central America. **— Gua′te·ma′·lan** *adj., n.*

gua·va [gwä′və] *n.* The sweet, yellow fruit of a tropical American tree, used to make jelly.

gu·ber·na·to·ri·al [gōō′bər·nə·tôr′ē·əl] *adj.* Of or having to do with a governor.

gudg·eon [guj′ən] *n.* A small, European, freshwater fish that is very easy to catch.

gue·ril·la [gə·ril′ə] *n.* Another spelling of GUERRILLA.

Guern·sey [gûrn′zē] *n.* **1** *pl.* **Guern·seys** One of a breed of white and tan dairy cattle first bred on the island of Guernsey. **2** An island of Great Britain in the English Channel.

guer·ril·la [gə·ril′ə] *n.* **1** One of a group of fighters, usually not part of a regular army, that harasses the enemy with surprise raids and sabotage. **2** *adj. use: guerrilla* warfare.

guess [ges] **1** *v.* To judge or decide without

knowing enough to be sure: *Guess* how much I weigh. **2** *v.* To decide correctly in this way: to *guess* an answer. **3** *n.* A judgment made in this way. **4** *v.* To believe; think; suppose: I *guess* it will rain later. ◆ *Guess* comes from an older English word *gessen*, which probably came from a Scandinavian language.

guess·work [ges′wûrk′] *n.* **1** The action of guessing. **2** A judgment made by guessing.

guest [gest] *n.* **1** A person received or entertained by another or others, especially at a meal or party, or for a visit. **2** *adj. use:* a *guest* room; a *guest* speaker. **3** Someone who pays for lodging, food, or both in a hotel, etc.

guf·faw [gə·fô′] **1** *n.* A loud burst of laughter. **2** *v.* To utter such a laugh.

Gui·an·a [gē·an′ə] *n.* A coastal region of NE South America, including British, French, and Dutch territories.

gui·dance [gīd′(ə)ns] *n.* **1** The act of guiding. **2** Something that guides, as the automatic control system of a missile. **3** Advice or supervision.

guide [gīd] *v.* **guid·ed, guid·ing**, *n.* **1** *v.* To show the way to; lead; conduct. **2** *n.* A person who conducts or leads others, as on a trip or tour. **3** *v.* To lead or direct the affairs, standards, opinions, etc., of. **4** *n.* Something that shows the way, controls, or gives an example: to use a star as a *guide*. **5** *n.* A guidebook.

guide·book [gīd′bŏŏk′] *n.* A book of useful information for travelers or tourists.

guided missile A missile propelled toward its target by a rocket and kept on the correct course by an automatic system.

guide·post [gīd′pōst′] *n.* A post, usually at an intersection, with a sign giving the places, and often the distances to them, on each road.

guide word One of the two words or phrases at the upper right and left of a dictionary page, indicating the first and last main entries on the page.

guild [gild] *n.* **1** A group of people who meet regularly for some purpose. **2** In the Middle Ages, an organization formed to protect the interest of workers in one craft or trade.

guil·der [gil′dər] *n.* **1** The basic unit of money in the Netherlands. **2** Any of several gold or silver coins formerly used in Europe.

guild·hall [gild′hôl′] *n.* **1** The hall where a guild meets. **2** *British* A town hall.

guile [gīl] *n.* The use of cunning; craft; slyness.

guile·ful [gīl′fəl] *adj.* Full of guile; crafty.

guile·less [gīl′lis] *adj.* Free from guile; innocent; sincere. **— guile′less·ly** *adv.*

guil·lo·tine [*n.* gil′ə·tēn, *v.* gil′ə·tēn′] *n., v.* **guil·lo·tined, guil·lo·tin·ing 1** *n.* A device for beheading condemned persons by means of a heavy blade that falls between vertical guides. **2** *v.* To behead with a guillotine.

guilt [gilt] *n.* **1** The condition or fact of having committed a crime or sin.

2 An act of wrongdoing; crime; sin. **3** A feeling of remorse or regret for wrongdoing.

guilt·less [gilt′lis] *adj.* Without guilt; free from sin or crime; innocent.

guilt·y [gil′tē] *adj.* **guilt·i·er, guilt·i·est** **1** Having done wrong; deserving blame or punishment: The court found him *guilty*. **2** Having to do with guilt: a *guilty* act. **3** Showing guilt: a *guilty* expression. **4** Feeling guilt: a *guilty* conscience. **— guilt′i·ly** *adv.*

guimpe [gamp] *n.* A woman's or girl's short-sleeved blouse worn under a jumper.

guin·ea [gin′ē] *n.* **1** A former gold coin of Great Britain, worth 21 shillings. **2** The sum of 21 shillings, or 105 new pence.

Guin·ea [gin′ē] *n.* A country in western Africa.

guinea hen A chickenlike fowl raised for food, having gray feathers with white specks.

guinea pig **1** A small, ratlike animal with a short tail, used in laboratory experiments. **2** A person used in an experiment.

Guin·e·vere [gwin′ə·vir] *n.* In legends about King Arthur, his wife and queen.

Guinea pig,
9–14 in. long

guise [gīz] *n.* **1** Outward appearance, especially if false: The *guise* of boldness often hides fear. **2** A type or manner of dress; costume.

gui·tar [gi·tär′] *n.* A stringed musical instrument played by plucking the strings with the fingers or a pick.

gulch [gulch] *n.* A deep, narrow valley or ravine formed by a rushing stream.

gul·den [gōōl′dən] *n.*, *pl.*, **gul·den** or **gul·dens** Another word for GUILDER.

gulf [gulf] *n.* **1** A large bay or arm of the sea partially enclosed by land. **2** A deep hole; chasm. **3** A great separation, as between people or ideas: a *gulf* of misunderstanding.

Gulf States Florida, Alabama, Mississippi, Louisiana, and Texas, the states bordering on the Gulf of Mexico.

Gulf Stream The warm ocean current that flows out of the Gulf of Mexico and northward along the east coast of the U.S., then in a northeasterly direction toward Europe.

gull[1] [gul] *n.* A gray and white bird with webbed feet and long wings living on or near a large body of water.

gull[2] [gul] **1** *v.* To trick or cheat. **2** *n.* A person who is easily cheated or fooled.

gul·let [gul′it] *n.* **1** The tube for the passage of food from the mouth to the stomach; esophagus. **2** The throat or something resembling it.

gul·li·ble [gul′ə·bəl] *adj.* Easily fooled or cheated; ready to believe almost anything.

Gul·li·ver [gul′ə·vər], **Lemuel** The hero of *Gulliver's Travels*, a book written by Jonathan Swift.

gul·ly [gul′ē] *n.*, *pl.* **gul·lies** A channel, ravine, or ditch, especially one cut in the earth by running water.

gulp [gulp] **1** *n.* A large, often noisy swallow. **2** *v.* To drink in large swallows: to *gulp* down a glass of milk. **3** *n.* The quantity swallowed at one time; mouthful. **4** *v.* To choke back or stifle by, or as if by, swallowing: to *gulp* down a cry. **5** *v.* To swallow hard, as if surprised or out of breath.

gum[1] [gum] *n.*, *v.* **gummed, gum·ming** **1** *n.* A sticky or rubbery substance, obtained from plants, that hardens when exposed to the air. **2** *n.* A substance used to make paper stick to something else; mucilage. **3** *n.* A gum tree. **4** *v.* To stick together or clog with or as if with gum: The valve *gummed* up. **5** *n.* Chewing gum.

gum[2] [gum] *n.* (*often pl.*) The firm, fleshy tissue around the teeth.

gum·bo [gum′bō] *n.*, *pl.* **gum·bos** **1** A thick soup or stew containing okra. **2** The okra. **3** A soil that gets very sticky when wet. ♦ *Gumbo* comes from an African Bantu word.

gum·drop [gum′drop′] *n.* A small, round piece of jellylike candy, usually colored and dipped in sugar.

gum·my [gum′ē] *adj.* **gum·mi·er, gum·mi·est** **1** Of or like gum; sticky. **2** Clogged or covered with gum or something like gum.

gump·tion [gump′shən] *n. informal* **1** Aggressive energy; initiative: He lacked the *gumption* to be a success. **2** Common sense.

gum tree Any tree that produces gum.

gun [gun] *n.*, *v.* **gunned, gun·ning** **1** *n.* A weapon that shoots bullets, shot, or shells from a metal tube at high speed, usually by an explosion. In military language only heavy mounted weapons, not rifles or pistols, are called guns. **2** *n.* The firing of a gun as a salute or signal. **3** *v.* To shoot or hunt with a gun: to *gun* ducks. **4** *n.* A device that is like a gun in shape or use: a grease *gun.* **— stick to one's guns** To be steadfast despite opposition or pressure.

gun·boat [gun′bōt′] *n.* A small naval ship armed with one or more guns, used for patrolling rivers and coastal waters.

gun·cot·ton [gun′kot′(ə)n] *n.* An explosive made of cotton or wood shavings soaked in nitric and sulfuric acids.

gun·fire [gun′fīr′] *n.* The firing of a gun or guns.

gun·lock [gun′lok′] *n.* The parts in some guns that control the hammer and make the charge explode.

gun·man [gun′mən] *n.*, *pl.* **gun·men** [gun′-mən] A man who carries a gun, especially a criminal.

gun·met·al [gun′met′(ə)l] *adj.*, *n.* Dark, bluish gray.

gun·ner [gun′ər] *n.* **1** A person who aims, operates, or fires a gun, especially a member of

add, āce, câre, pälm; end, ēqual; it, īce; odd, ōpen, ôrder; took, pool; up, bûrn;
ə = a in *above*, e in *sicken*, i in *possible*, o in *melon*, u in *circus*; yoō = u in *fuse*; oil; pout;
check; ring; thin; this; zh in *vision*. For ¶ reference, see page 64 · HOW TO

the armed forces. **2** In the U.S. Navy, an officer in charge of guns.

gun·ner·y [gun′ər-ē] *n.* **1** The techniques of making and firing guns. **2** The firing of guns.

gun·ny·sack [gun′ē-sak′] *n.* A sack made from a coarse, heavy material such as burlap.

gun·pow·der [gun′pou′dər] *n.* **1** An early explosive powder used in guns, fireworks, etc. **2** Any powder used to fire guns.

gun·run·ning [gun′run′ing] *n.* The smuggling of guns and ammunition into a country. — **gun′run′ner** *n.*

gun·shot [gun′shot′] *n.* **1** The shooting of a gun, or the noise made by this. **2** A shot fired from a gun. **3** The range or reach of a gun.

gun·smith [gun′smith′] *n.* A person who makes or repairs rifles, shotguns, etc.

gun·wale [gun′əl] *n.* The upper edge of the side of a ship or boat.

gup·py [gup′ē] *n.,* *pl.* **gup·pies** A small, colorful, tropical fresh-water fish, born alive, not hatched.

Gunwales

gur·gle [gûr′gəl] *v.* **gur·gled, gur·gling,** *n.* **1** *v.* To flow irregularly and with a bubbling sound: Water *gurgled* from the jug. **2** *v.* To make a bubbling sound: The infant *gurgled* happily in his crib. **3** *n.* The sound of gurgling.

gush [gush] **1** *v.* To pour forth with sudden force: Blood *gushed* from the cut. **2** *n.* A sudden flow or rush, as of a liquid or of sound. **3** *v.* *informal* To talk with silly or insincere feeling and enthusiasm. **4** *n.* *informal* Gushing talk.

gush·er [gush′ər] *n.* An oil well that spurts oil without the need of pumps.

gush·y [gush′ē] *adj.* **gush·i·er, gush·i·est** *informal* Full of silly feeling or enthusiasm.

gus·set [gus′it] *n.* A piece of material, usually shaped like a triangle, put into a garment, glove, shoe, etc., for roomier fit or for more strength.

gust [gust] *n.* **1** A sudden, violent rush of wind, or something driven by the wind. **2** A short outburst, as of laughter.

gus·to [gus′tō] *n.* Great relish; keen enjoyment: He ate with *gusto.*

gust·y [gus′tē] *adj.* **gust·i·er, gust·i·est** Full of gusts, as of wind or rain.

gut [gut] *n.,* *v.* **gut·ted, gut·ting** **1** *n.* The alimentary canal or a part of it; intestine. **2** *n.* (*pl.*) The intestines; entrails. **3** *n.* (*pl.*) *slang* Raw courage; grit. **4** *n.* The dried intestines of certain animals made into strings for musical instruments, tennis rackets, etc.; catgut. **5** *v.* To take out the intestines or inner organs of: to *gut* a chicken. **6** *v.* To destroy the inside of: The bomb *gutted* the building.

Gu·ten·berg [gōot′ən·bûrg], **Johann,** 1400?–1468?, German printer, supposedly the first European to print with movable type.

gut·ta-per·cha [gut′ə·pûr′chə] *n.* A rubber-like material from the sap of certain tropical trees, used in insulation, dentistry, etc.

gut·ter [gut′ər] **1** *n.* A channel or ditch at the side of a street or road into which water drains and runs off. **2** *n.* A channel along the lower edge of a roof to drain off water. **3** *n.* Any narrow channel or groove, as at either side of a bowling alley. **4** *v.* To burn rapidly and drip wax in narrow channels, as a candle.

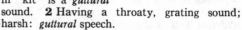

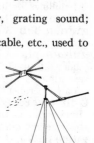

Gutter

gut·tur·al [gut′ər·əl] *adj.* **1** Of or produced in the throat: The *k* in "kit" is a *guttural* sound. **2** Having a throaty, grating sound; harsh: *guttural* speech.

guy[1] [gī] **1** *n.* A rope, wire, cable, etc., used to steady or support something. **2** *v.* To support with or as if with a guy.

guy[2] [gī] *n.,* *v.* **guyed, guy·ing** **1** *n.* *informal* A man or boy; fellow. **2** *n.* *British* A person who appears strange in dress or manner. **3** *v.* *informal* To ridicule or tease.

guz·zle [guz′(ə)l] *v.* **guz·zled, guz·zling** To drink greedily or in too large amounts.

gym [jim] *n.* *informal* **1** A gymnasium. **2** A class in physical training in a school.

Guys

♦ *Gym* is a shortened form of *gymnasium.*

gym·na·si·um [jim·nā′zē·əm] *n.,* *pl.* **gym·na·si·ums** or **gym·na·si·a** [jim·nā′zē·ə] A building or large room equipped for athletic training and certain indoor sports. ♦ *Gymnasium* comes from a Greek word meaning *to exercise,* which goes back to a word meaning *naked,* because Greek athletes stripped for sports or exercise.

gym·nast [jim′nast] *n.* A person who is skilled in gymnastics.

gym·nas·tic [jim·nas′tik] *adj.* Having to do with physical exercises: My brother worked hard to perfect his *gymnastic* skills.

gym·nas·tics [jim·nas′tiks] *n.* **1** (*pl.*) Exercises that develop, and stunts that use, muscular strength and control. **2** The practice of such exercises and stunts. ♦ See -ICS.

gym·no·sperm [jim′nə·spûrm′] *n.* A plant whose seeds are not covered by a seedcase, as the ginkgo.

gy·ne·col·o·gy [gī′nə·kol′ə·jē *or* jī′nə·kol′ə·jē] *n.* The branch of medicine dealing with the treatment of women's diseases. — **gy′ne·col′o·gist** *n.*

gyp [jip] *v.* **gypped, gyp·ping,** *n.* *informal* **1** *v.* To cheat or swindle. **2** *n.* A use of trickery; swindle. **3** *n.* Someone who cheats; swindler.

gyp·sum [jip′səm] *n.* A common mineral used chiefly in the form of a white powder in making plaster of Paris, and as fertilizer.

Gyp·sy [jip′sē] *n.,* *pl.* **Gyp·sies** **1** *n.* A member of a wandering tribe of people with swarthy skin and dark hair, believed to have come from India long ago. **2** *n.* (*usually written* **gypsy**) A person who looks like or leads the life of a Gypsy. **3** *adj. use: gypsy* ways; *Gypsy* music.

gypsy moth A brown or white moth whose larvae eat leaves, doing much damage to plants.

gy·rate [ji′rāt] *v.* **gy·rat·ed, gy·rat·ing** To move with a circular or spiral motion; spin around; rotate; whirl. **— gy·ra′tion** *n.*

gyr·fal·con [jûr′fal′kən *or* jûr′fôl′kən] *n.* A large falcon found mainly in the Arctic regions.

gy·ro·com·pass [ji′rō·kum′pəs] *n.* A compass that uses a gyroscope to keep its indicator pointing north.

gy·ro·scope [ji′rə·skōp] *n.* A heavy wheel that is made to rotate at high speed. While rotating it resists forces that tend to move its axis of rotation, and is used to steady ships and aircraft, indicate direction, etc.

gyve [jīv] *n., v.* **gyved, gyv·ing** **1** *n.* (*usually pl.*) A shackle or fetter, as for the legs. **2** *v.* To shackle. ◆ This word is seldom used today.

H

h or **H** [āch] *n., pl.* **h's** or **H's** The eighth letter of the English alphabet.

H The symbol for the element HYDROGEN.

ha [hä] *interj.* An exclamation expressing surprise, discovery, triumph, or joy.

ha·be·as cor·pus [hā′bē·əs kôr′pəs] A legal order demanding that a prisoner be produced in court to determine if his being held is lawful. ◆ *Habeas corpus* comes directly from Latin, where it literally means *you shall have the body.*

hab·er·dash·er [hab′ər·dash′ər] *n.* A dealer in men's shirts, ties, hats, etc.

hab·er·dash·er·y [hab′ər·dash′ər·ē] *n., pl.* **hab·er·dash·er·ies** **1** The goods sold by a haberdasher. **2** A haberdasher's shop.

ha·bil·i·ment [hə·bil′ə·mənt] *n.* (*usually pl.*) Clothing; attire; garb.

hab·it [hab′it] *n.* **1** An act or practice done so often that it becomes almost automatic and is difficult to stop. **2** A usual form, way of developing, etc., of a plant or animal: *Ivy is of a creeping habit.* **3** The clothing worn by people in certain activities or religious orders: *a nun's habit; a riding habit.* ◆ See CUSTOM.

hab·it·a·ble [hab′it·ə·bəl] *adj.* Fit to be lived in: *The cabins were soon made habitable.*

hab·i·tat [hab′ə·tat] *n.* **1** The place where a plant, animal, etc., normally grows or lives. **2** A place where something lives; dwelling.

hab·i·ta·tion [hab′ə·tā′shən] *n.* **1** A dwelling place. **2** The act or state of inhabiting or living in: *unfit for human habitation.*

ha·bit·u·al [hə·bich′ōō·əl] *adj.* **1** Done or happening by habit; customary: *habitual* politeness. **2** Expected from habit; usual: her *habitual* way home. **— ha·bit′u·al·ly** *adv.* **— ha·bit′u·al·ness** *n.*

ha·bit·u·ate [hə·bich′ōō·āt] *v.* **ha·bit·u·at·ed, ha·bit·u·at·ing** To accustom; make used: to *habituate* oneself to high altitudes.

ha·ci·en·da [hä′sē·en′də] *n.* In Spanish America, a large estate or plantation, or the main house on such an estate.

hack[1] [hak] **1** *v.* To cut or chop crudely or irregularly, as with an ax. **2** *n.* A crude gash or notch. **3** *n.* A short, dry cough. **4** *v.* To give forth such a cough.

hack[2] [hak] **1** *n.* A carriage for hire. **2** *n.* A worn-out horse. **3** *n.* A taxicab. **4** *n.* A person who does dull, tedious work, especially a writer. **5** *adj.* Done only for money: *hack* writing.

hack·le [hak′əl] *n.* **1** One of the long, narrow feathers on the neck of a rooster, pigeon, etc. **2** (*pl.*) The hairs on the neck and back of a dog that stand up when he is angry or attacked.

hack·ney [hak′nē] *n., pl.* **hack·neys** **1** A horse used to ride or drive. **2** A carriage for hire.

hack·neyed [hak′nēd] *adj.* Made ordinary or dull by too much use; trite: *a hackneyed* plot.

hack·saw [hak′sô] *n.* A saw with a fine-toothed, narrow blade set in a frame, used to cut metal.

had [had] The past tense and past participle of HAVE. ◆ *Had* is used in certain phrases showing obligation or preference. "You *had* better hurry" means "You ought to hurry." "I *had* rather stay home" means "I prefer to stay home."

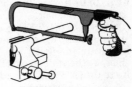

Hacksaw

had·dock [had′ək] *n., pl.* **had·dock** or

had·docks A food fish of the northern Atlantic, related to but not so big as the cod.

Ha·des [hā′dēz] *n.* **1** In Greek myths, the underground kingdom of the dead. **2** *informal* Hell.

had·n't [had′(ə)nt] Had not.

hadst [hadst] *v.* A form of HAD, used with *thou*: seldom used today.

haft [haft] *n.* A handle, especially of a knife, sword, or ax; hilt.

hag [hag] *n.* An ugly and usually spiteful old woman; crone.

Hag·ga·dah [hə·gä′də] *n.* In Judaism, the story of the Exodus from Egypt, read at Passover services.

Hag·ga·i [hag′ē·ī′] *n.* In the Bible, a Hebrew prophet who lived during the sixth century B.C.

hag·gard [hag′ərd] *adj.* Looking as if ill, starved, exhausted, or in pain.

hag·gle [hag′əl] *v.* **hag·gled, hag·gling,** *n.* **1** *v.* To bargain in a petty way: to *haggle* over a dime. **2** *n.* The act of haggling. **— hag′gler** *n.*

Hague [hāg], **The** The political capital of the Netherlands, in the western part.

hah [hä] *interj.* Another spelling of HA.

hail[1] [hāl] **1** *n.* Drops of ice that fall during a storm; hailstones. **2** *n.* A rapid or heavy showering: a *hail* of bullets. **3** *v.* To fall or shower like hail. **4** *v.* To pour down hail.

hail[2] [hāl] **1** *n.* A shout to attract attention; greeting. **2** *v.* To call loudly to in greeting; salute. **3** *v.* To call to so as to attract attention: to *hail* a cab. **4** *interj.* An exclamation of greeting or tribute: *Hail* to Caesar! **— hail from** To come from as a birthplace or point of origin: He *hails from* Arkansas.

hail·stone [hāl′stōn′] *n.* A pellet of frozen rain.

hair [hâr] *n.* **1** A fine, threadlike structure growing from the skin of most mammals. **2** The thick growth of hairs, as on the human head. **3** A small measure, as of space, degree, etc.: to miss by a *hair*. **— split hairs** To search for small differences; raise petty objections.

hair·breadth [hâr′bredth′] **1** *n.* An extremely small space or margin. **2** *adj.* Very narrow or close: a *hairbreadth* escape.

hair·brush [hâr′brush′] *n.* A brush for grooming the hair.

hair·cloth [hâr′klôth′] *n.* A wiry fabric used for stiffening, upholstering, etc.

hair·cut [hâr′kut′] *n.* The act of cutting the hair, or the style in which it is cut.

hair·do [hâr′dōō′] *n.*, *pl.* **hair·dos** **1** A style of fixing a woman's hair. **2** The hair thus styled. ◆ The word *hairdo* was made up or "coined" in the 1930's. The two words *hair* and *do* (meaning *to arrange* or *set*, as in "to do one's hair") were simply stuck together to form one word.

19th-century hairdo

hair·dress·er [hâr′dres′ər] *n.* A person who cuts or arranges women's hair.

hair·less [hâr′lis] *adj.* Without hair.

hair·line [hâr′līn′] *n.* **1** The edge of the growth of hair on the head, as at the forehead. **2** A very thin line.

hair·pin [hâr′pin′] **1** *n.* A thin, U-shaped piece of wire, bone, etc., for holding a hairdo. **2** *adj.* Shaped like a hairpin: a *hairpin* turn.

hair-rais·ing [hâr′rā′zing] *adj.* Causing fright or terror: The leader of the expedition gave a *hair-raising* account of the avalanche.

hairs·breadth [hârz′bredth′] *n.*, *adj.* Another spelling of HAIRBREADTH.

hair·split·ting [hâr′split′ing] **1** *n.* The making of distinctions too fine to matter. **2** *adj.* Inclined to quibble about details.

hair·spring [hâr′spring′] *n.* The very fine spring that regulates the balance wheel in a watch or clock.

hair·y [hâr′ē] *adj.* **hair·i·er, hair·i·est** **1** Covered with hair; having much hair. **2** Made of or resembling hair. **— hair′i·ness** *n.*

Hai·ti [hā′tē] *n.* **1** A country in the western part of the West Indian island of Hispaniola. **2** A former name of Hispaniola. **— Hai·ti·an** [hā′-tē·ən *or* hā′shən] *adj., n.*

hake [hāk] *n., pl.* **hake** or **hakes** A food fish related to the cod.

hal·berd [hal′bərd] *n.* A weapon used about 400 years ago, with a spear point and an ax blade on a long shaft.

hal·cy·on [hal′sē·ən] *adj.* Calm; peaceful. ◆ In myths, the *halcyon* was a bird supposed to build its nest in the water and make the winds become calm while it was nesting.

hale[1] [hāl] *v.* **haled, hal·ing** To compel to go: to *hale* into court.

hale[2] [hāl] *adj.* **hal·er, hal·est** Vigorous and healthy; robust: He felt *hale* and hearty.

Hale [hāl], **Nathan,** 1755–1776, American patriot, hanged as a spy by the British.

half [haf] *n., pl.* **halves** [havz] **1** *n.* Either of two equal or almost equal parts into which a thing may be divided, or a quantity equal to such a part: Give me *half.* **2** *adj.* Having half of a standard value: a *half* teaspoon. **3** *adj.* Not complete; partial. **4** *adv.* To the extent of a half; partially. **5** *adv.* Nearly: I was *half* inclined to refuse. **6** *adv. informal* To any extent at all: not *half* good enough.

Halberd

half·back [haf′bak] *n.* In football, either of two players who play behind the line of scrimmage.

half-baked [haf′bākt′] *adj.* **1** Not completely baked. **2** *informal* Badly or insufficiently thought out; poorly planned: a *half-baked* idea.

half-breed [haf′brēd′] *n.* A person having parents of different races.

half brother A brother related through only one parent.

half-caste [haf′kast′] *n.* **1** A person having one Asian and one European parent; Eurasian. **2** A half-breed.

half crown A British silver coin worth $2\frac{1}{2}$ shillings, being withdrawn from use.

half dollar A U.S. or Canadian coin worth 50 cents.

half gainer A dive in which the diver, facing forward, does half of a back somersault and hits the water head first and facing back.

half-heart·ed [haf′här′tid] *adj.* Having or showing little interest or enthusiasm.

half life The period of time it takes for half the atoms of a radioactive substance to disintegrate.

half-mast [haf′mast′] *n.* The position of a flag about halfway up a mast, used to show respect to the dead or to signal distress.

half nelson A wrestling hold in which an arm is placed under an opponent's armpit from the back and the hand is pressed against the back of his neck.

half note A note in music having half the time value of a whole note.

half·pen·ny [hā′- pən·ē] *n., pl.* **half- pence** [hā′pəns] or **half·pen·nies,** *adj.*

Half notes

1 *n.* A British bronze coin worth half of a penny. **2** *adj.* Almost worthless.

half sister A sister related through only one parent.

half step or **half tone** A semitone.

half-track [haf′trak′] *n.* A military vehicle with wheels in front and short endless tracks in the rear.

half·way [haf′wā′] **1** *adj.* Midway between two points: a *halfway* house. **2** *adj.* Partial; incomplete: *halfway* measures. **3** *adv.* At or to half the distance: to go *halfway* home. **— meet halfway** To be willing to give in to on some points so as to reach an agreement.

half-wit [haf′wit′] *n.* **1** A feeble-minded person. **2** A foolish or silly person.

half-wit·ted [haf′wit′id] *adj.* **1** Feeble-minded. **2** Foolish; silly.

hal·i·but [hal′ə·bət] *n., pl.* **hal·i·but** or **hal· i·buts** A large flatfish of northern seas, used widely as a food.

Hal·i·fax [hal′ə·faks] *n.* A seaport in SE Canada, capital of Nova Scotia.

hall [hôl] *n.* **1** A passage or corridor in a building. **2** A room at the entry of a house or building; lobby. **3** A large building or room used for public business or entertainment: a concert *hall.* **4** In England, the main house on the estate of a landowner. **5** A building or dormitory on a college campus.

hal·lah [hä′lə] *n.* A loaf of bread shaped in the form of a braid, traditionally eaten by Jews on the Sabbath.

hal·le·lu·jah or **hal·le·lu·iah** [hal′ə·lōō′yə] **1** *interj.* Praise ye the Lord. **2** *n.* A song of praise or thanksgiving. ◆ *Hallelujah* comes from two Hebrew words meaning *Praise Jehovah!*

Hal·ley's Comet [hal′ēz] A comet that reappears every 75 or 76 years.

hall·mark [hôl′märk′] **1** *n.* In England, an official mark placed upon articles of gold or silver to indicate purity. **2** *v.* To stamp with a hallmark. **3** *n.* Any mark or proof that something is genuine or of high quality.

hal·loo [hə·lōō′] *n., pl.* **hal·loos,** *v.* **hal·looed, hal·loo·ing,** *interj.* **1** *n.* A loud call or shout. **2** *v.* To shout or call. **3** *interj.* An exclamation to attract attention.

hal·low [hal′ō] *v.* **1** To make holy; consecrate. **2** *adj. use:* hallowed ground.

Hal·low·een or **Hal·low·e'en** [hal′ō·ēn′ *or* hôl′ō·ēn′] *n.* The evening of October 31, celebrated by masquerading.

hal·lu·ci·na·tion [hə·lōō′sə·nā′shən] *n.* **1** The impression of seeing or hearing something that is not really present. **2** The thing supposedly seen or heard.

hall·way [hôl′wā′] *n.* A passageway between rooms; hall or corridor.

ha·lo [hā′lō] *n., pl.* **ha·los** or **ha·loes** **1** A shining circle, as around the moon. **2** In art, a shining circle around the head of a holy person. **3** An aura of glory or splendor.

Halo

hal·o·gen [hal′ə·jən] *n.* Any of the group of nonmetallic chemical elements that includes chlorine, bromine, fluorine, and iodine.

halt[1] [hôlt] **1** *n.* A complete but temporary stop in an activity. **2** *v.* To stop. **— call a halt** To demand that something be stopped.

halt[2] [hôlt] **1** *v.* To be in doubt; hesitate. **2** *adj. use:* slow and *halting* speech. **3** *v.* To walk with a limp. **4** *adj.* Lame: seldom used today.

hal·ter [hôl′tər] *n.* **1** A strap or rope used to lead or hold a horse or other animal. **2** A hangman's rope. **3** A woman's blouse held up by a band around the neck, leaving the arms and most of the back bare.

halve [hav] *v.* **halved, halv·ing** **1** To divide into halves. **2** To lessen by half: to *halve* one's expenses.

Halter

halves [havz] Plural of HALF. **— go halves** To share equally: to go *halves* on expenses.

hal·yard [hal′yərd] *n.* A rope used on ships to raise or lower a sail, yard, or flag.

ham [ham] *n.* **1** The upper part of a hog's hind leg, salted and smoked. **2** The back of the thigh and the buttock. **3** *informal* An amateur radio operator. **4** *slang* An actor who overdoes his part and exaggerates feelings.

Ha·man [hā′mən] *n.* In the Bible, a Persian official who persecuted the Jews and was hanged.

Ham·burg [ham′bûrg] *n.* A large seaport in northern West Germany.

ham·burg·er [ham′bûr′gər] *n.* **1** Ground or chopped beef. **2** A sandwich made with a broiled or fried patty of this meat.

Ham·il·ton [ham′əl·tən], **Alexander,** 1757–1804, American statesman, first secretary of the treasury.

ham·let [ham′lit] *n.* A small village.

Ham·let [ham′lit] *n.* **1** A play by William Shakespeare. **2** The hero of this play.

ham·mer [ham′ər] **1** *n.* A hand tool with a solid metal head and a handle, used for driving nails, pounding, or flattening. **2** *n.* A mechanical part that strikes or beats: the *hammer* of a gun. **3** *v.* To strike, beat, or drive with or as if with a hammer. **4** *v.* To form or shape with a hammer; forge. **5** *v.* To form by steady mental labor: to *hammer* out a solution. **6** *v.* To work hard or steadily: to *hammer* away at a job. **7** *v.* To have the sound or feeling of pounding: My heart *hammered* with excitement. **8** *v.* To force or impress by repeated efforts: to *hammer* a lesson into a boy's head.

ham·mer·head [ham′ər·hed′] *n.* A shark with a head resembling a hammer.

ham·mock [ham′ək] *n.* A bed or couch formed by hanging a strong fabric between two supports.

Ham·mu·ra·bi [hä′·moo·rä′bē] *n.* King of Babylonia about 2000 B.C., who issued a code of law.

ham·per[1] [ham′pər] *v.* To interfere with the movements of; hinder; obstruct.

ham·per[2] [ham′pər] *n.* A large covered basket, as for storing laundry or carrying food.

Hammock

ham·ster [ham′stər] *n.* A small rodent with a short, hairy tail and large cheek pouches, often used in laboratory experiments.

ham·string [ham′string′] *n., v.* **ham·strung, ham·string·ing 1** *n.* A tendon at the back of the human knee. **2** *n.* In animals with four legs, the large sinew at the back of the hock. **3** *v.* To cut the hamstring of; cripple. **4** *v.* To frustrate: The project was *hamstrung* by a lack of funds.

Han·cock [han′kok], **John,** 1737–1793, American patriot. He was the first to sign the Declaration of Independence.

hand [hand] **1** *n.* The end part of the arm from the wrist down, including the palm, fingers, and thumb. ◆ *adj., manual.* **2** *adj.* Of or suited for the hand. **3** *n.* The use of the hand: He did it by *hand.* **4** *adj.* Worked or done by hand: a *hand* loom; *hand* sewing. **5** *n.* A group or bunch of something: a *hand* of bananas. **6** *n.* One of the pointers on a clock. **7** *v.* To give, pass, or transmit by hand. **8** *v.* To assist or lead with the hand. **9** *n.* Help: to lend a *hand.* **10** *n.* A part or role in doing something: to have a *hand* in the victory. **11** *n.* A laborer: a farm *hand.* **12** *n.* A characteristic mark: The painting showed the *hand* of a true artist. **13** *n.* A round of applause. **14** *n.* A style of handwriting: a broad *hand.* **15** *n.* A measure for the height of a horse, equal to four inches: a horse 15 *hands* high. **16** *n.* (*pl.*) Possession; control: a fort in enemy *hands.* **17** *n.* A side: the house on the left *hand.* **18** *n.* A source: to get a story at second *hand.* **19** *n.* A pledge or promise of marriage: to ask for one's *hand.* **20** *n.* The cards held by a player at one deal, or the player. **21** *n.* One deal in a card game. **— at hand 1** Close by. **2** About to happen. **— change hands** To pass from one person to another: The store *changed hands.* **— hand down** To pass along; bequeath. **— hand in glove** In close contact; intimately: to work *hand in glove* with a partner. **— in hand 1** Under control. **2** In one's possession: to have money *in hand.* **— keep one's hand in** To continue an activity; keep in practice. **— lay hands on** To get hold of; seize. **— on hand 1** Available for use: enough food *on hand* for a week. **2** Present: Be *on hand* for the speech. **— out of hand 1** Not under control: The children were cross and *out of hand.* **2** At once; immediately. **— upper hand** The controlling advantage.

hand·bag [hand′bag′] *n.* **1** A woman's purse for holding money and small articles. **2** A small suitcase.

hand·ball [hand′bôl′] *n.* **1** A game in which a ball is hit by hand so as to strike a wall on the fly. **2** The small ball used in this game.

hand·bill [hand′bil′] *n.* A small printed notice distributed by hand.

hand·book [hand′book′] *n.* A small guidebook, reference book, or book of instructions.

hand·craft·ed [hand′kraf′tid] *adj.* Made by hand.

hand·cuff [hand′kuf′] **1** *n.* (*often pl.*) One of a pair of metal rings joined by a chain, designed to lock around the wrist; manacle. **2** *v.* To put handcuffs on.

Han·del [han′dəl], **George Frederick,** 1685–1759, British composer born in Germany.

hand·ful [han(d)′fool] *n., pl.* **hand·fuls 1** As much or as many as a hand can hold at once. **2** A small number. **3** *informal* A thing or person hard to control: The cat was a *handful.*

Handcuffs

hand·i·cap [han'dē·kap] *n.*, *v.* **hand·i·capped, hand·i·cap·ping** **1** *n.* A race or contest in which some competitors are given advantages or disadvantages so that all have an equal chance of winning. **2** *n.* Such an advantage or disadvantage: a twenty-pin *handicap* in a bowling tournament. **3** *v.* To assign handicaps for a race or contest. **4** *n.* Any disadvantage. **5** *v.* To put at a disadvantage: We were *handicapped* by poor equipment.

hand·i·craft [han'dē·kraft'] *n.* **1** Skill in working with the hands. **2** A trade, occupation, or art requiring such skill.

hand·i·work [han'dē·wûrk'] *n.* **1** Work done by the hands. **2** Work done personally.

hand·ker·chief [hang'kər·chif] *n.* A square piece of cloth used for wiping the face or nose, or as an ornament.

han·dle [han'dəl] *v.* **han·dled, han·dling,** *n.* **1** *v.* To touch, feel, or hold with the hand. **2** *n.* A part of a tool, cup, pail, etc. made to be grasped by the hand. **3** *v.* To manage, control, or operate: to *handle* a tractor. **4** *v.* To deal with or treat: to *handle* customers. **5** *v.* To buy and sell; deal in: to *handle* used cars. **6** *v.* To respond to control: This car *handles* well. — **han·dler** [hand'lər] *n.*

han·dle·bar [han'dəl·bär'] *n.* (*often pl.*) The curved steering bar on a bicycle, etc.

hand·made [hand'mād'] *adj.* Made by hand or by hand tools.

hand·maid [hand'mād'] *n.* Another word for HANDMAIDEN: seldom used today.

hand·maid·en [hand'mād'(ə)n] *n.* A female servant or attendant: seldom used today.

hand organ A large music box with a hand crank, once used by street musicians.

hand·out [hand'out'] *n.* *slang* **1** Money or food given to a tramp or beggar. **2** A prepared statement distributed as publicity or information.

hand·rail [hand'rāl'] *n.* A railing used to support or protect, as on a balcony or staircase.

hand·shake [han(d)'shāk'] *n.* The act of clasping and shaking a person's hand, as in greeting.

hand·some [han'səm] *adj.* **hand·som·er, hand·som·est** **1** Pleasing in appearance, especially in a stately or manly way. **2** Of generous size; ample: a *handsome* gift. — **hand'some·ly** *adv.*

hand·spike [han(d)'spīk'] *n.* A bar used as a lever, as on a ship.

hand·spring [han(d)'spring'] *n.* An acrobatic turn like a somersault, but with only one or both hands touching the ground.

Handspring

hand-to-hand [han(d)'tə·hand'] *adj.* In close contact: *hand-to-hand* combat.

hand-to-mouth [han(d)'tə·mouth'] *adj.* Having nothing in reserve; using at once whatever is obtained: a *hand-to-mouth* existence.

hand·writ·ing [hand'rī'ting] *n.* **1** Writing done by hand, not printed or typewritten. **2** The form of writing peculiar to a certain person: I recognized my friend's *handwriting*.

hand·y [han'dē] *adj.* **hand·i·er, hand·i·est** **1** Within easy reach; nearby. **2** Skillful with the hands. **3** Easy to use; useful: a *handy* tool. — **hand'i·ly** *adv.* — **hand'i·ness** *n.*

hang [hang] *v.* **hung** or **hanged, hang·ing,** *n.* **1** *v.* To fasten or be attached to something above: to *hang* pictures; A lamp *hangs* in the hall. **2** *v.* To attach or be attached, as to hinges, so as to swing freely: to *hang* a door. **3** *v.* To decorate with hangings: a wall *hung* with tapestries. **4** *n.* The manner in which something hangs: the *hang* of a dress. **5** *v.* To die or put to death by hanging with a rope around the neck. **6** *v.* To cause to droop: The boy *hung* his head. **7** *v.* To fasten (wallpaper, etc.) to walls with paste. **8** *v.* To deadlock: The jury was *hung*. **9** *v.* To depend: The decision *hangs* on your vote. **10** *n.* *informal* The manner in which something is done or controlled: He soon got the *hang* of sailing. — **hang back** To be unwilling. — **hang on** **1** To keep a hold. **2** To pay close attention to. **3** To linger: Her cold *hangs* on. — **hang together** **1** To stay united. **2** To remain intact, coherent, or unchanged. — **hang up** **1** To finish using a telephone. **2** To place on a hanger or hook: *Hang up* your clothes. **3** To delay; hold back. ◆ *Hanged* is used when referring to putting to death by hanging: The traitor will be *hanged* at dawn. In the other meanings, *hung* is the more common form: They *hung* the picture from the molding.

han·gar [hang'ər] *n.* A shelter or shed for storing aircraft.

hang·dog [hang'dôg'] *adj.* Guilty, ashamed, or sneaky: a *hangdog* expression.

hang·er [hang'ər] *n.* **1** A device on which or from which something may be hung, as a light frame for hanging garments. **2** A person who hangs something.

hang·er-on [hang'ər·on'] *n.*, *pl.* **hang·ers-on** [hang'ərz·on'] A person who attaches himself to others in the hope of receiving favors.

hang·ing [hang'ing] **1** *n.* Death by hanging with a rope tight around the neck. **2** *n.* (*often pl.*) Curtains, drapes, etc. **3** *adj.* Suspended or dangling. **4** *n.* The act of suspending.

hang·man [hang'mən] *n.*, *pl.* **hang·men** [hang'mən] An official who hangs condemned people.

hang·nail [hang'nāl'] *n.* Skin partially torn loose at the side or root of a fingernail.

add, āce, câre, pälm; end, ēqual; it, īce; odd, ōpen, ôrder; took, pool; up, bûrn;
ə = a in *above*, e in *sicken*, i in *possible*, o in *melon*, u in *circus*; yoo = u in *fuse*; oil; pout;
check; ring; thin; this; zh in *vision*. For ¶ reference, see page 64 · HOW TO

hang·out [hang′out′] *n. slang* A place where a person or group spends much time.

hank [hangk] *n.* **1** A skein of yarn or thread. **2** A loop or curl: a *hank* of hair.

han·ker [hang′kər] *v.* To have a strong desire; wish: to *hanker* for roast turkey.

Han·ni·bal [han′ə·bəl] *n.*, 247?–183? B.C., Carthaginian general who invaded Italy by crossing the Alps.

han·som [han′səm] *n.* A low, two-wheeled, one-horse carriage with the driver's seat perched at the rear.

Hansom

Ha·nuk·kah [hä′·nōō·kə] *n.* A Jewish festival lasting eight days, commemorating the dedication of the Temple in Jerusalem in 165 B.C.

hap·haz·ard [hap′·haz′ərd] **1** *adj.* Happening by chance; accidental. **2** *n.* Mere chance. **3** *adv.* By chance; at random: to choose *haphazard*. **— hap′haz′ard·ly** *adv.*

hap·less [hap′lis] *adj.* Having no luck; unfortunate.

hap·pen [hap′ən] *v.* **1** To come about; occur: What *happened* while I was gone? **2** To occur by chance: Anything can *happen*. **3** To have the fortune: We *happened* to be home. **4** To come or go by chance: He *happened* along. **— happen on** To meet or find by chance.

hap·pen·ing [hap′ən·ing] *n.* Something that happens; an event.

hap·pi·ness [hap′ē·nis] *n.* **1** A being pleased and contented. **2** Good fortune; good luck.

hap·py [hap′ē] *adj.* **hap·pi·er, hap·pi·est** **1** Enjoying or showing pleasure; joyous; contented. **2** Timely; lucky: By some *happy* chance we found her. **— hap′pi·ly** *adv.*

hap·py-go-luck·y [hap′ē·gō·luk′ē] *adj.* Trusting to luck; without a care.

Haps·burg [haps′bûrg] *n.* A German family which once ruled many European countries.

ha·rangue [hə·rang′] *n., v.* **ha·rangued, ha·rangu·ing** **1** *n.* A long, loud, emotional speech. **2** *v.* To address in or deliver a harangue.

har·ass [har′əs *or* hə·ras′] *v.* **1** To trouble with cares, worries, etc.: Mothers are sometimes *harassed* by their children. **2** To annoy with small, repeated attacks: to *harass* an enemy. **— har·ass·ment** [har′əs·mənt *or* hə·ras′·mənt] *n.*

har·bin·ger [här′bin·jər] **1** *n.* A person or thing that goes ahead and announces the coming of something. **2** *v.* To announce; herald.

har·bor [här′bər] **1** *n.* A place or port where ships can anchor or be protected in a storm. **2** *n.* Any place of refuge. **3** *v.* To take shelter in or as if in a harbor. **4** *v.* To give refuge or shelter to: to *harbor* an escaped convict. **5** *v.* To keep in the mind: to *harbor* a grudge. ¶1

har·bor·age [här′bər·ij] *n.* **1** A shelter or refuge for ships. **2** Any shelter. ¶1

hard [härd] **1** *adj.* Solid and firm; not easily dented or broken; not soft. **2** *adj.* Difficult to solve, do, or understand: a *hard* problem. **3** *adj.* Difficult to manage or deal with: a *hard* man in business. **4** *adj.* Strict; harsh: a *hard* taskmaster. **5** *adj.* Energetic: a *hard* worker. **6** *adv.* With much continued effort: to study *hard*. **7** *adv.* With great vigor: to fight *hard*. **8** *adv.* With difficulty: to breathe *hard*. **9** *adv.* Close; near. **10** *adj.* Describing the sound of *c* and *g* in *car* and *good*, as opposed to soft *c* and *g* in *cent* and *age*. **11** *adj.* Involving suffering; severe: *hard* times. **12** *adj.* Containing much alcohol: *hard* cider. **13** *adj.* Containing minerals that keep soap from working: *hard* water. **14** *adv.* Securely; tightly: to hold on *hard*. **— hard of hearing** Deaf or partially deaf. **— hard up** *informal* **1** Poor; broke. **2** In need of something. **— hard′ness** *n.*

hard-and-fast [härd′(ə)n(d)·fast′] *adj.* Fixed and unchangeable: a *hard-and-fast* rule.

hard-bit·ten [härd′bit′(ə)n] *adj.* Tough; unyielding: a *hard-bitten* group of defenders.

hard-boiled [härd′boild′] *adj.* **1** Boiled until cooked through: a *hard-boiled* egg. **2** *informal* Tough; unfeeling: a *hard-boiled* politician.

hard coal Coal that burns slowly and with little flame; anthracite.

hard·en [här′dən] *v.* To make or become hard or harder.

hard·head·ed [härd′hed′id] *adj.* **1** Possessing common sense; shrewd. **2** Willful; stubborn.

hard·heart·ed [härd′här′tid] *adj.* Lacking pity or sympathy; unfeeling.

har·di·hood [här′dē·hood] *n.* Unflinching courage; boldness; daring.

Har·ding [här′ding], **Warren Gamaliel,** 1865–1923, 29th president of the U.S., 1921–1923.

hard·ly [härd′lē] *adv.* **1** Only just; scarcely; barely: She could *hardly* speak. **2** Not quite; probably not: That is *hardly* the true story. **3** In a harsh, cruel, or severe way. ◆*Hardly, barely,* and *scarcely* all have negative force. "I hardly saw him" means "I almost did *not* see him." Therefore, it is not necessary or correct to use another negative with any of the three, as in "I didn't hardly see him."

hard·ship [härd′ship] *n.* Something that is hard to endure.

hard·tack [härd′tak′] *n.* A hard, unsalted, crackerlike biscuit.

hard·top [härd′top′] *n.* A car with the body design of a convertible, but with a rigid top.

hard·ware [härd′wâr′] *n.* Manufactured articles of metal, as utensils or tools.

hard·wood [härd′wood′] *n.* **1** Any hard, heavy wood, as oak. **2** *adj. use:* *hardwood* floors.

har·dy [här′dē] *adj.* **har·di·er, har·di·est** **1** Able to endure hardship; robust; tough. **2** Able to endure a winter outdoors, as some plants. **3** Having courage; bold; daring. **— har′di·ly** *adv.* **— har′di·ness** *n.*

hare [hâr] *n.*, *pl.* **hare** or **hares** A timid, rabbitlike animal having a split upper lip, and noted for its great speed.

hare·bell [hâr′bel′] *n.* A slender herb with blue, bell-shaped flowers.

hare·brained [hâr′brānd′] *adj.* Foolish; flighty; giddy.

hare·lip [hâr′lip′] *n.* A split upper lip, a deformity some people are born with.

har·em [hâr′əm] *n.* **1** The part of a Moslem household reserved for women. **2** The women living there.

hark [härk] *v.* To listen. **— hark back** To go back, as in one's memory, to a previous time.

hark·en [här′kən] *v.* Another spelling of HEARKEN.

har·le·quin [här′lə·kwin] **1** *n.* (*written* **Harlequin**) A pantomime character who wears a mask and a costume of contrasting colors. **2** *adj.* Checkered in many colors. **3** *adj.* Shaped like Harlequin's mask: *harlequin* eyeglasses. **4** *n.* A clown.

har·lot [här′lət] *n.* A prostitute.

harm [härm] **1** *n.* Injury; damage: The storm did great *harm.* **2** *v.* To do harm to.

harm·ful [härm′fəl] *adj.* Able to harm; doing harm.

harm·less [härm′lis] *adj.* Not harmful; meaning no harm. **— harm′less·ly** *adv.*

har·mon·ic [här·mon′ik] **1** *adj.* Related to or marked by harmony. **2** *n.* An overtone closely related to its primary or fundamental tone.

Harlequin

har·mon·i·ca [här·mon′i·kə] *n.* A small wind instrument played by blowing in and out on metal reeds fixed within a frame; mouth organ.

har·mo·ni·ous [här·mō′nē·əs] *adj.* **1** Made up of things that harmonize. **2** Free from disagreement; in accord. **3** Pleasing to the senses. **— har·mo′ni·ous·ly** *adv.*

har·mo·nize [här′mə·nīz] *v.* **har·mo·nized, har·mo·niz·ing 1** To arrange or be in musical harmony. **2** To bring into or be in agreement or harmony. ¶3

har·mo·ny [här′mə·nē] *n.*, *pl.* **har·mo·nies 1** An orderly and pleasing arrangement of simultaneous musical sounds. **2** The method of arranging music into harmony. **3** Any orderly and pleasing arrangement, as of colors, parts, etc. **4** An orderly, peaceful condition; agreement in feeling, ways of acting, etc.: different peoples living in *harmony.*

har·ness [här′nis] **1** *n.* Leather straps, bands, etc., used to hitch a horse or mule to a cart, plow, etc. **2** *v.* To put a harness on. **3** *n.* Any similar arrangement of straps, cords, etc., as one used to attach a parachute to the body. **4** *v.* To make use of the power of: to *harness* a waterfall.

harp [härp] **1** *n.* A stringed musical instrument played by plucking with the fingers. **2** *v.* To play on a harp. **— harp on** To keep on endlessly talking or writing about. **— harp′er** *n.*

Harp

harp·ist [här′pist] *n.* A person who plays the harp.

har·poon [här·pōōn′] **1** *n.* A pointed and barbed weapon with a rope attached, used to spear whales or large fish. **2** *v.* To strike with a harpoon. **— har·poon′er** *n.*

harp·si·chord [härp′sə·kôrd] *n.* A keyboard instrument resembling a piano but having its strings mechanically plucked instead of struck.

Har·py [här′pē] *n.*, *pl.* **Har·pies 1** In Greek myths, a greedy, nasty creature, in part a woman, in part a bird. **2** (*written* **harpy**) Any greedy, mean person, especially a woman.

har·que·bus [här′kwə·bəs] *n.* An early portable gun, fired resting on a hooked stick.

har·ri·er [har′ē·ər] *n.* **1** A small hound used for hunting hares. **2** A cross-country runner.

Har·ris·burg [har′is·bûrg] *n.* The capital of Pennsylvania.

Har·ri·son [har′ə·sən], **Benjamin**, 1833–1901, 23rd president of the U.S., 1889–1893.

Har·ri·son [har′ə·sən], **William Henry**, 1773–1841, ninth president of the U.S., for one month in 1841.

har·row [har′ō] **1** *n.* A frame with spikes or upright disks used to level or break up soil. **2** *v.* To work (land) with a harrow. **3** *v.* To agitate or distress; torment. **4** *adj. use:* a *harrowing* experience.

har·ry [har′ē] *v.* **har·ried, har·ry·ing 1** To make raids upon. **2** To disturb or agitate.

Disk harrow

harsh [härsh] *adj.* **1** Grating, rough, or unpleasant to the senses. **2** Severe; cruel; unfeeling: a *harsh* judgment. **— harsh′ly** *adv.* **— harsh′ness** *n.*

hart [härt] *n.*, *pl.* **hart** or **harts** The male of the red deer, especially after its fifth year.

Hart·ford [härt′fərd] *n.* The capital of Connecticut.

harts·horn [härts′hôrn′] *n.* A preparation of ammonia used as smelling salts.

har·um-scar·um [hâr′əm·skâr′əm] **1** *adj.* Reckless; wild. **2** *adv.* Wildly. **3** *n.* A reckless, careless person.

har·vest [här′vist] **1** *n.* The gathering and bringing in of a crop. **2** *v.* To gather and bring in a crop of: to *harvest* apples. **3** *n.* The time of year for harvesting. **4** *n.* One season's yield of any product grown. **5** *n.* The consequences or natural outcome: He is enjoying the *harvest* of the good will he created.

har·vest·er [här′vis·tər] *n.* **1** A person who harvests. **2** A machine used in harvesting.

Har·vey [här′vē], **William,** 1578–1657, English physician. He discovered circulation of the blood.

has [haz] The third person form of HAVE, in the present tense, used with *he, she, it,* and singular nouns: He *has* luck; The girl *has* more work than she can finish.

hash [hash] **1** *n.* A dish of cooked meat, potatoes, etc., chopped fine and fried or baked. **2** *v.* To cut or chop into small pieces. **3** *n.* A jumble; mess: to make a *hash* of a project. **4** *v. informal* To discuss at length and in detail: We'll *hash* the plan over later.

hash·ish or **hash·eesh** [hash′ēsh or hash′ish] *n.* A drug made from Indian hemp.

has·n't [haz′ənt] Has not.

hasp [hasp] *n.* A hinged fastening or flap that fits over a staple and is fastened by a padlock or peg.

has·sle [has′(ə)l] *n. slang* An argument; fight.

has·sock [has′ək] *n.* **1** An upholstered stool or cushion used to sit or kneel on or as a foot rest. **2** A tuft of coarse grass.

hast [hast] A form of HAVE, used with *thou:* seldom used today.

Hasp

haste [hāst] *n.* **1** Swiftness of movement or action. **2** Reckless hurry: *Haste* makes waste. — **make haste** To hurry.

has·ten [hā′sən] *v.* **1** To move or act with speed; hurry. **2** To cause to hasten: The rain *hastened* our departure.

hast·y [hās′tē] *adj.* **hast·i·er, hast·i·est 1** Quick: a *hasty* retreat. **2** Acting or done on impulse; rash: a *hasty* decision. **3** Showing impatience: *hasty* words. — **hast′i·ly** *adv.* — **hast′i·ness** *n.*

hasty pudding Porridge made of cornmeal.

hat [hat] *n., v.* **hat·ted, hat·ting 1** *n.* A covering for the head, usually with a brim. **2** *v.* To supply or cover with a hat. — **pass the hat** To ask for donations. — **under one's hat** *informal* Secret: You must promise to keep what I tell you *under your hat.*

hat·band [hat′band′] *n.* A ribbon or band of cloth around a hat just above the brim.

hat·box [hat′boks′] *n.* A box or piece of luggage for holding a hat or hats.

hatch¹ [hach] *n.* **1** A hatchway. **2** The cover on a hatchway.

hatch² [hach] *v.* **1** To produce young from (an egg), or (young) from an egg: Hens *hatch* eggs; She *hatched* 11 chicks. **2** To come out of an egg. **3** To think out or invent, as a plot or plan.

hatch·er·y [hach′ər·ē] *n., pl.* **hatch·er·ies** A place for hatching eggs of fish or poultry.

hatch·et [hach′it] *n.* **1** A small ax with a short handle, held in one hand. **2** A tomahawk. — **bury the hatchet** To make peace.

hatch·way [hach′wā′] *n.* An opening in a deck, floor, or roof, leading to spaces beneath.

hate [hāt] *n., v.* **hat·ed, hat·ing 1** *n.* A deep, strong dislike; hostility. **2** *v.* To dislike intensely; detest. **3** *v.* To dislike; want to avoid: I *hate* to bother you. — **hat′er** *n.* ◆ *Hate, detest,* and *abhor* all mean to dislike greatly. *Hate* often refers to a deep, personal feeling that may make someone try to hurt another or be happy at another's misfortune: Cain *hated* Abel. *Detest* is not so strong. It is intense, but often leads to avoiding rather than damaging the person or thing detested: I *detest* people who gossip. *Abhor* suggests a disgust that makes one shrink away from something: Many people who like realistic painting *abhor* abstract art.

hate·ful [hāt′fəl] *adj.* **1** Arousing or worthy of hatred. **2** Feeling or showing hate. — **hate′·ful·ly** *adv.* — **hate′ful·ness** *n.*

hath [hath] A form of HAS, used with *he, she,* or *it:* seldom used today.

hat·pin [hat′pin′] *n.* A long pin used to attach a woman's hat to her hair.

ha·tred [hā′trid] *n.* Bitter dislike; hate.

hat·ter [hat′ər] *n.* A person who makes or deals in hats.

Hat·ter·as [hat′ər·əs], **Cape** A cape on an island off the eastern coast of North Carolina.

hau·berk [hô′bûrk] *n.* A long coat of chain mail.

haugh·ty [hô′tē] *adj.* **haugh·ti·er, haugh·ti·est** Satisfied with oneself and scornful of others; arrogant: a *haughty* manner. — **haugh′ti·ly** *adv.* — **haugh′ti·ness** *n.*

haul [hôl] **1** *v.* To pull with force; drag. **2** *n.* A strong pull; tug. **3** *v.* To move or carry, as in a truck. **4** *n.* The load hauled. **5** *n.* The distance over which something is hauled: a short *haul.* **6** *n.* The amount of something caught or taken at one time: a *haul* of fish. **7** *v.* To change the course of (a ship). — **haul off** To draw back the arm to punch.)

Hauberk

haunch [hônch] *n.* **1** The fleshy part of the hip and buttock. **2** The leg and loin of an animal, considered as meat: a *haunch* of beef.

haunt [hônt] **1** *v.* To visit often: He *haunted* the library for the whole summer. **2** *n.* A place often visited: a favorite *haunt* of students. **3** *v.* To stay in or appear to, as a ghost: Ghosts and demons *haunted* his dreams. **4** *v.* To trouble or molest. **5** *v.* To disturb by returning to the mind or memory: The song *haunts* me.

Man on his haunches

haunt·ed [hôn′tid] *adj.* Often visited by ghosts or spirits: The story took place in a *haunted* castle.

haunt·ing [hôn′ting] *adj.* Difficult to forget: a *haunting* tune. — **haunt′ing·ly** *adv.*

haut·boy [hō′boi] *n.* An oboe.

hau·teur [hō·tûr′] *n.* A haughty manner or spirit; arrogance.

Ha·van·a [hə·van′ə] *n.* The capital of Cuba.

have [hav] *v.* **had, hav·ing,** *n.* **1** *v.* To be in possession of; own: to *have* a new car; to *have* blue eyes. **2** *v.* To hold; contain: The well *has* little water; The hotel *has* 200 rooms. **3** *v.* To hold in the mind: to *have* an opinion. **4** *v.* To be obliged or compelled: People *have* to eat. **5** *v.* To get; take: to *have* a nap. **6** *v.* To experience; suffer or enjoy: to *have* a headache. **7** *v.* To allow: I'll *have* no interruptions. **8** *v.* To cause to do or be done: Please *have* my order delivered; *Have* the bellboy bring up the bags. **9** *v.* To carry on; accomplish: to *have* a talk. **10** *v.* To possess in some relationship, as in a family: I *have* two brothers. **11** *n. informal* A comparatively rich person or country: the *haves* and the have-nots. — **have at** To attack. — **have done** To stop; desist. — **have it out** To continue a fight or discussion to a final settlement. — **have to do with** To be concerned with; be related to. ◆ *Have* is used as a helping verb with the past participles of other verbs to show that an action is completed: We *have* worked all day; Charles *had* gone before they arrived; We will *have* lived here three years next month.

ha·ven [hā′vən] *n.* **1** A harbor; port. **2** A safe place; refuge; shelter.

have-not [hav′not′] *n. informal* A person or country lacking in wealth.

have·n't [hav′ənt] Have not.

hav·er·sack [hav′ər·sak] *n.* A bag for carrying provisions on a march or hike.

hav·oc [hav′ək] *n.* Widespread destruction of life and property; ruin; devastation. — **play havoc with** To ruin; destroy; devastate: The war *played havoc with* his quiet life.

Haversack

haw[1] [hô] *n.* **1** The hawthorn. **2** The hawthorn's red berry.

haw[2] [hô] **1** *n., interj.* A word used by a driver to make a horse or ox turn left. **2** *v.* To turn to the left.

haw[3] [hô] **1** *v.* To make short, grunting sounds while fumbling for words: to hem and *haw.* **2** *interj.* A word that represents such sounds.

Ha·wai·i [hə·wī′ē] *n.* **1** The fiftieth State of the U.S., composed of the Hawaiian Islands. **2** The largest of the Hawaiian Islands. — **Ha·wai·ian** [hə·wī′yən] *n., adj.*

Hawaiian Islands A group of islands in the central Pacific Ocean.

hawk[1] [hôk] **1** *n.* A large bird with a strong, hooked beak, very powerful talons, short, rounded wings, and a long tail, that captures and eats smaller birds and animals. **2** *v.* To use trained hawks in hunting birds. — **hawk′er** *n.*

Hawaiian Islands

hawk[2] [hôk] *v.* To announce (goods) for sale in the streets by shouting; peddle. — **hawk′er** *n.*

hawk[3] [hôk] **1** *v.* To cough or cough up, as in clearing the throat. **2** *n.* A loud cough.

haw·ser [hô′zər] *n.* A rope or cable used for mooring or towing ships.

haw·thorn [hô′thôrn] *n.* A small, thorny tree of the rose family having white or pink flowers and red berries.

Haw·thorne [hô′thôrn], **Nathaniel,** 1804–1864, U.S. novelist and short-story writer.

hay [hā] **1** *n.* Grass, clover, etc., that is cut, dried, and used for animal feed. **2** *v.* To make (grass, etc.) into hay: to *hay* for a week; to *hay* clover. **3** *v.* To feed with hay: to *hay* cows.

hay·cock [hā′kok′] *n.* A pile of hay in a field.

Hay·dn [hīd′(ə)n], **Franz Joseph,** 1732–1809, Austrian composer.

Hayes [hāz], **Rutherford Birchard,** 1822–1893, 19th president of the U.S., 1877–1881.

hay fever A disease caused by an allergy to certain pollens. Sneezing, a running nose, itching eyes, etc., are common symptoms.

---

add, āce, câre, pälm;   end, ēqual;   it, īce;   odd, ōpen, ôrder;   tŏŏk, pōōl;   up, bûrn;
ə = a in *above*, e in *sicken*, i in *possible*, o in *melon*, u in *circus*;   yōō = u in *fuse*;   oil;   pout;
check; ring; thin; this; zh in *vision*.   For ¶ reference, see page 64 · HOW TO

hay·loft [hā′lôft′] *n.* An upper section of a barn or stable, used for storing hay.

hay·mow [hā′mou′] *n.* **1** A mass of stored hay. **2** A place in a barn or stable for storing hay.

hay·stack [hā′stak′] *n.* A large pile of hay stacked outdoors, sometimes covered.

Haystack

hay·wire [hā′wīr′] **1** *n.* Wire for binding hay into bales. **2** *adj. slang* Broken down or messed up. **3** *adj. slang* Confused or crazy.

haz·ard [haz′ərd] **1** *n.* A chance of injury or loss; danger; peril: the *hazards* of war. **2** *v.* To put in danger; risk: to *hazard* one's life. **3** *v.* To take a chance on; venture: to *hazard* an opinion. **4** *n.* Chance; accident. **5** *n.* In golf, an obstacle, as a sand trap.

haz·ard·ous [haz′ər·dəs] *adj.* Full of danger or risk. — **haz′ard·ous·ly** *adv.*

haze¹ [hāz] *n.* **1** Fine droplets of water, dust particles, etc., suspended in the air, making seeing difficult. **2** Mental confusion or fogginess; a muddle.

haze² [hāz] *v.* **hazed, haz·ing** *U.S.* To force (newcomers) to do silly or humiliating things; bully: to *haze* freshmen.

ha·zel [hā′zəl] **1** *n.* A small tree or bushy shrub related to the birch. **2** *n., adj.* Light, yellowish brown

ha·zel·nut [hā′zəl·nut′] *n.* The small, edible nut of the hazel.

haz·y [hā′zē] *adj.* **haz·i·er, haz·i·est** **1** Full of or blurred by haze; misty: a *hazy* sky; a *hazy* view. **2** Unclear; confused: *hazy* thoughts. — **haz′i·ly** *adv.* — **haz′i·ness** *n.*

H-bomb [āch′bom′] *n.* A hydrogen bomb.

he [hē] *pron., n., pl.* **hes** **1** *pron.* The man, boy, or male animal that has been mentioned: The prisoner knew *he* was doomed. **2** *pron.* That person; one: *He* who reads learns. **3** *n.* A male person or animal: Is it a *he* or a she?

He The symbol for the element HELIUM.

head [hed] **1** *n.* In animals having a backbone, the part of the body at the top or front of the spinal column, containing the brain, eyes, mouth, etc. **2** *n.* A similar part of other animals and organisms. **3** *n.* A sculpture of a head. **4** *n.* The top or front part: the *head* of a nail; Go to the *head* of the line. **5** *adj.* Located at the top or front: the *head* seat. **6** *adj.* Hitting or striking against the front: *head* winds. **7** *n.* The part of a tool or weapon that strikes: the *head* of a hammer. **8** *n.* The skin stretched across a drum, tambourine, etc. **9** *n.* A leader or boss; chief: the *head* of a firm. **10** *adj.* Principal; chief: a *head* waiter. **11** *n.* The most outstanding position: to be at the *head* of the class. **12** *v.* To lead or command: to *head* an army. **13** *v.* To be the first or the most prominent or outstanding on or in: to *head* the class. **14** *n., pl.* **head** A single person or individual: Admission is a dime a *head*; ten *head* of cattle. **15** *n.* Something shaped like a head: a *head* of lettuce. **16** *n.* Mind or intelligence: Use your *head!*; a good *head* for figures. **17** *n.* A source, as of a river. **18** *n. (pl.)* The top side of a coin, often bearing a likeness of a person's head. **19** *v.* To move or turn in a specified direction: to *head* toward shore. **20** *n.* Progress against something that opposes: to make *head* against the wind. **21** *n.* The tip of a boil, abscess, etc., where pus may break through. **22** *n.* A climax or crisis: Things came to a *head*. — **head off** To get in front of and block the way; intercept. — **keep one's head** To remain calm and under self-control in a distressing situation. — **lose one's head** To lose self-control; become excited. — **out of one's head** or **off one's head** Not reasonable; crazy; insane. — **over one's head** **1** Too difficult to understand. **2** Beyond one's ability to control or cope with. — **turn someone's head** To spoil or make vain with praise.

head·ache [hed′āk′] *n.* **1** Discomfort or pain in the head. **2** *U.S. informal* A difficulty or trouble.

head·band [hed′band′] *n.* A band worn around the head.

head·dress [hed′dres′] *n.* A covering or ornament for the head.

head·er [hed′ər] *n. informal* A fall or plunge with the head leading, especially in the expression **take a header,** to fall headfirst.

head·first [hed′fûrst′] *adv.* **1** With the head first. **2** Without caution; recklessly.

head·gear [hed′gir′] *n.* A covering for the head, as a hat, helmet, etc.

head·ing [hed′ing] *n.* **1** Something written or printed at the top of a page, as a name, address, etc. **2** Something serving as the top or front part of anything. **3** A title, as of a chapter, new topic, etc. **4** A direction of travel: Take a *heading* due north.

Indian headdress

head·land [hed′lənd] *n.* A point of high land extending out into water.

head·less [hed′lis] *adj.* **1** Without a head. **2** Without a leader. **3** Stupid; brainless.

head·light [hed′līt′] *n.* A powerful lamp placed at the front of a motor vehicle, train, etc., to allow the operator to see ahead at night.

head·line [hed′līn′] *n., v.* **head·lined, head·lin·ing** **1** *n.* Several words set in bold type at the top of a newspaper article, serving to introduce it and tell what it is about. **2** *v.* To give a headline to, as a news article. **3** *v.* To be or be listed as the main attraction of a show.

head·long [hed′lông′] *adv., adj.* **1** With the head leading: He fell *headlong* from the tree; a *headlong* plunge. **2** With reckless speed or energy: to burst *headlong* into a meeting.

head·mas·ter [hed′mas′tər] *n.* The principal of a school, especially a private school.

head-on [hed′on′] *adj., adv.* With the front ends striking: a *head-on* crash; to collide *head-on.*

head·phone [hed′fōn′] *n.* An earphone held to the ear by a band that fits over the head.

head·piece [hed′pēs′] *n.* A hat, helmet, or other covering for the head.

head·quar·ters [hed′kwôr′tərz] *n.pl. (usually used with singular verb)* **1** The place from which the operations of an organization, military unit, police force, etc., are directed. **2** The person or persons who direct the operations: *Headquarters* says to attack at dawn.

head·stone [hed′stōn′] *n.* **1** The stone placed at the head of a grave. **2** A cornerstone.

head·strong [hed′strông′] *adj.* Stubbornly set upon having one's own way; obstinate: The *headstrong* boy insisted on quitting school.

John Hale
1879-1939
May he rest
in peace

Headstone

head·wa·ters [hed′wô′tərz] *n.pl.* The streams or other waters that form the source of a river.

head·way [hed′wā′] *n.* **1** Forward motion or progress: They could make little *headway* in the dark without a lantern; to make *headway* against ignorance. **2** The height clear under a bridge, arch, etc.; clearance.

head wind A wind in a direction opposite to the course of a ship, airplane, etc.

head·y [hed′ē] *adj.* **head·i·er, head·i·est** **1** Apt to make one lightheaded or dizzy; intoxicating: a *heady* perfume. **2** Headstrong; rash.

heal [hēl] *v.* **1** To return to soundness or health: His cuts have all *healed*; The ointment *healed* the burn. **2** To remedy, repair, or mend: Time *healed* their quarrel. **— heal′er** *n.*

health [helth] *n.* **1** Freedom in body and mind from any disease, defect, or disorder. **2** General condition of the body and mind: good *health*; poor *health.*

health·ful [helth′fəl] *adj.* **1** Promoting health or well-being: a *healthful* sport. **2** Healthy.

health·y [hel′thē] *adj.* **health·i·er, health·i·est** **1** Having or showing good health: a *healthy* woman. **2** Promoting good health. **— health′i·ly** *adv.* **— health′i·ness** *n.*

heap [hēp] **1** *n.* A collection of things piled up; a pile or mound. **2** *v.* To pile or collect into a heap: *Heap* the wood here. **3** *v.* To fill full or more than full: to *heap* a plate with food. **4** *v.* To give or give something to in large amounts: to *heap* abuse on a dog; to *heap* someone with praise. **5** *n. informal* A large amount: He has a *heap* of money.

hear [hir] *v.* **heard** [hûrd], **hear·ing** **1** To experience (sounds) in the ears: The deaf cannot *hear*; I *hear* thunder. **2** To listen to: *Hear* what I say! **3** To learn or come to know: Did you *hear* about the fire? **4** To receive a message: Have you *heard* from him? **5** To listen to officially or legally: to *hear* a case in court. **6** To answer, as a prayer. **— hear′er** *n.*

hear·ing [hir′ing] *n.* **1** The sense by which sounds are experienced; the ability to hear. **2** The act or process of experiencing sound. **3** A chance to be heard: New ideas deserve a *hearing*. **4** An official examination, as by a court. **5** The range or distance within which a sound may be heard; earshot.

hearing aid A small electronic device that makes sounds strong enough for partially deaf people to hear them.

heark·en [här′kən] *v.* To listen or pay attention: seldom used today: *Hearken* to my words.

hear·say [hir′sā′] *n.* Something heard from others; rumor.

hearse [hûrs] *n.* A vehicle for carrying a dead person to the place of burial.

heart [härt] *n.* **1** The hollow muscular organ that by rhythmically contracting and expanding acts as a pump to keep blood flowing through the body. **2** The heart regarded as the source of feelings and emotions, especially of love, affection, sorrow, etc.: to pour out one's *heart*; a heavy *heart*. **3** The ability to be kind and gentle: a good *heart*. **4** Courage or strength: to gain *heart*. **5** Energy or enthusiasm: His *heart* was not in it. **6** Someone loved or respected: a brave *heart*. **7** The central or inner part: the *heart* of the city. **8** The main or essential part: the *heart* of the problem. **9** A figure like this ♥. It is often used as a symbol of love. **10** A playing card of the suit marked with red heart figures. **11** (*pl.*) The suit so marked. **— after one's heart** or **after one's own heart** Exactly to one's liking. **— at heart** By nature; basically. **— by heart** By memory. **— take to heart** To be seriously concerned with. **— with all one's heart** With full sincerity or enthusiasm.

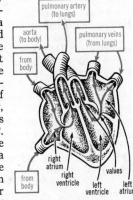

pulmonary artery (to lungs)

aorta (to body)

pulmonary veins (from lungs)

from body

right atrium

right ventricle

left ventricle

left atrium

valves

from body

Blood flow in a human heart

heart·ache [härt′āk′] *n.* Grief or great sorrow.

heart·beat [härt′bēt′] *n.* **1** A single contraction and relaxation of the heart. **2** The rhythmic sound that the heart makes.

heart·break [härt′brāk′] *n.* Great disappointment or sorrow. **— heart′break′ing** *adj., n.*

heart·bro·ken [härt′brō′kən] *adj.* Overcome by grief or sorrow.

add, āce, câre, pälm;   end, ēqual;   it, īce;   odd, ōpen, ôrder;   tŏŏk, pōol;   up, bûrn;
ə = a in *above*, e in *sicken*, i in *possible*, o in *melon*, u in *circus*;   yŏŏ = u in *fuse*;   oil;   pout;
check;   ring;   thin;   this;   zh in *vision*.   For ¶ reference, see page 64 · HOW TO

heart·burn [härt′bûrn′] *n.* Discomfort caused by too much acid in the stomach.

heart·ed [här′tid] *adj.* Having a particular kind of heart: used in combination, as in *heavy-hearted*, having a heart heavy with sadness or grief.

heart·en [här′tən] *v.* To give courage or cheer to: The news *heartened* her.

heart·felt [härt′felt′] *adj.* Deeply felt; sincere: Please accept my *heartfelt* thanks.

hearth [härth] *n.* **1** The floor of a fireplace, furnace, etc. **2** The fireside; home. **3** The bottom of a blast furnace, where molten metal collects.

hearth·stone [härth′stōn′] *n.* **1** The stone that forms a hearth. **2** The fireside; home.

heart·i·ly [här′tə·lē] *adv.* **1** Sincerely and enthusiastically: to greet friends *heartily*. **2** Eagerly and abundantly: to eat *heartily*. **3** Completely; thoroughly: *heartily* disgusted.

heart·less [härt′lis] *adj.* Without sympathy or kindness; cruel; pitiless: a *heartless* jibe. **— heart′less·ly** *adv.* **— heart′less·ness** *n.*

heart-rend·ing [härt′ren′ding] *adj.* Causing much grief and sorrow: a *heart-rending* tale.

heart·sick [härt′sik′] *adj.* Very disappointed or depressed: He's *heartsick* over losing his job.

heart·strings [härt′stringz′] *n.pl.* Deep or strong feelings, as of sympathy or pity: His gloom touched my *heartstrings*.

heart·y [här′tē] *adj.* **heart·i·er, heart·i·est,** *n., pl.* **heart·ies 1** *adj.* Full of warmth; friendly: a *hearty* welcome. **2** *adj.* Strongly felt; intense: *hearty* disgust. **3** *adj.* Healthy and strong: a *hearty* old man; a *hearty* appetite. **4** *adj.* Abundant and satisfying: a *hearty* meal. **5** *n.* A hearty fellow or sailor. **— heart′i·ness** *n.*

heat [hēt] **1** *n.* The condition of being hot or the degree to which something is hot. Scientifically, heat is the energy possessed by an object or substance due to the vibration of its molecules. **2** *n.* Warmth supplied to the air in a building, as from a furnace, etc. **3** *v.* To make or become hot or less cold. **4** *n.* Hot weather. **5** *n.* Excitement or intensity of feeling: in the *heat* of debate. **6** *v.* To make or become excited or intense. **7** *adj. use:* a *heated* argument; a *heated* contest. **8** *n.* A single trial or effort, as in a race.

heat·er [hē′tər] *n.* A device that produces heat.

heath [hēth] *n.* **1** A low, hardy evergreen shrub with narrow leaves and small red, white, or yellow flowers. **2** *British* An open area overgrown with heath or coarse plants.

hea·then [hē′thən] *n., pl.* **hea·thens** or **hea·then 1** A member of a tribe of people that is neither Christian, Jewish, nor Islamic, especially a worshiper of idols or spirits. **2** *adj. use:* *heathen* worship; *heathen* lands; *heathen* tribes. **3** A person whose religion is thought to be false.

heath·er [heth′ər] *n.* A low evergreen shrub related to the heath, having small pinkish flowers.

heat shield A barrier of heat-resistant material used to protect a space vehicle as it reenters the atmosphere.

heat wave A period of very hot weather.

heave [hēv] *v.* **heaved** or **hove, heav·ing,** *n.* **1** *v.* To lift or throw with great effort: to *heave* a sack onto a platform. **2** *v.* To pull or haul up or on: *Heave* in the net; to *heave* a rope. **3** *v.* To pitch and toss about: The boat *heaved* in the waves. **4** *v.* To move or proceed, as a ship. **5** *v.* To utter painfully: to *heave* a sigh. **6** *v.* To vomit; retch. **7** *v.* To breathe hard; pant. **8** *v.* To expand and contract rhythmically: His chest *heaved*. **9** *n.* The act of heaving. **— heave to 1** To bring (a ship) to a halt. **2** To stop.

Men heaving a log

heav·en [hev′ən] *n.* **1** In various religions, the place where God, the angels, the blessed souls, etc., are located. **2** (*written* **Heaven**) God: *Heaven* protect you. **3** (*pl.*) The stars, planets, etc., and the apparent background in which they are located. **4** Something very pleasant: Listening to good music is *heaven*.

heav·en·ly [hev′ən·lē] *adj.* **1** Of or belonging to heaven: *heavenly* choirs of angels. **2** Located in the heavens: *heavenly* bodies. **3** Delightful: *heavenly* weather.

heav·en·ward [hev′ən·wərd] *adj., adv.* Towards heaven: The angel flew *heavenward*.

Heav·i·side layer [hev′i·sīd] A region of the atmosphere about 60 miles above the earth that reflects radio waves of certain frequencies.

heav·y [hev′ē] *adj.* **heav·i·er, heav·i·est,** *adv.* **1** *adj.* Having great weight or mass; hard to move or hold up. **2** *adj.* Having relatively great weight compared to size or volume: a *heavy* oil. **3** *adj.* Greater in amount, size, number, etc., than what is usual: a *heavy* snow; a *heavy* vote. **4** *adj.* Giving an impression of thickness; coarse; broad: *heavy* features. **5** *adj.* Weighted down; burdened: a tree *heavy* with fruit. **6** *adj.* Lacking grace; clumsy: a *heavy* style. **7** *adj.* Forceful and severe: a *heavy* blow. **8** *adj.* Of great importance; serious: a *heavy* responsibility. **9** *adj.* Affected by grief or misery: a *heavy* heart. **10** *adj.* Hard to do or bear; oppressive: *heavy* labor; *heavy* taxes. **11** *adj.* Overcast; gloomy: The sky was *heavy*. **12** *adj.* Hard to digest; rich: a *heavy* meal. **13** *adv.* In a heavy or thick manner: The snow lay *heavy* on the ground. **— heav′i·ly** *adv.* **— heav′i·ness** *n.*

heavy hydrogen Another name for DEUTERIUM.

heavy water Water made from deuterium and oxygen.

heav·y·weight [hev′ē·wāt′] *n.* **1** An unusually

heavy person or thing. **2** A boxer or wrestler who weighs more than 175 pounds.

He·bra·ic [hi·brā′ik] *adj.* Of, having to do with, or characteristic of the Hebrews, their language, or their culture.

He·brew [hē′brōō] **1** *n.* One of the Semitic people that claim descent from Abraham; Jew. **2** *n.* An ancient Semitic language in which most of the Old Testament was first written. **3** *n.* The modern form of this language, used officially in Israel. **4** *adj.* Of or having to do with the Hebrews, their language, or their culture.

Heb·ri·des [heb′rə·dēz] *n.pl.* The islands off the west coast of Scotland.

Hec·a·te [hek′ə·tē] *n.* In Greek myths, a goddess of the earth, moon, and underworld, associated with witchcraft and magic.

heck·le [hek′əl] *v.* **heck·led, heck·ling** To try to confuse or annoy with insults, mocking questions, etc.: to *heckle* a speaker. — **heck·ler** [hek′lər] *n.*

hec·tic [hek′tik] *adj.* **1** Marked by or full of excitement, confusion, haste, etc.: a *hectic* trip. **2** Flushed and feverish, as if from illness.

hec·tor [hek′tər] **1** *v.* To bully, as by ranting or blustering. **2** *n.* A bully or boor.

Hec·tor [hek′tər] *n.* In the *Iliad*, the leading Trojan warrior, killed by Achilles.

he'd [hēd] **1** He had. **2** He would.

hedge [hej] *n., v.* **hedged, hedg·ing 1** *n.* A fence formed by bushes planted close together. **2** *n.* Any boundary or barrier. **3** *v.* To surround with a hedge: to *hedge* a patio. **4** *v.* To restrict the movement or action of: to *hedge* someone in. **5** *v.* To avoid frank or direct answers: The mayor *hedged* when asked if taxes would be raised. **6** *n.* The act of hedging.

hedge·hog [hej′hog′] *n.* **1** A small European animal with spines on its back. **2** *U.S.* A porcupine.

hedge·row [hej′rō′] *n.* A dense row of trees or bushes planted as a hedge.

heed [hēd] **1** *v.* To pay close attention to: *Heed* my advice. **2** *n.* Careful attention: Give *heed* to what she says. — **heed′ful** *adj.*

Hedgehog, about 10 in. long

heed·less [hēd′lis] *adj.* Not caring or paying attention; reckless: *heedless* of the consequences. — **heed′less·ly** *adv.* — **heed′less·ness** *n.*

heel[1] [hēl] **1** *n.* The rounded back part of the human foot, below the ankle. **2** *n.* The part of a shoe, sock, or stocking that covers the heel. **3** *n.* The built-up part of a shoe or boot on which the heel rests. **4** *v.* To supply (a shoe) with a heel. **5** *n.* Something that suggests a heel, as by shape or position: the *heel* of a golf club. **6** *v.* To follow closely. **7** *n.* *slang* A low or dishonorable person. — **down at the heel 1** Having the heels of one's shoes worn down. **2** Shabby;

rundown. — **take to one's heels** To run away; flee.

heel[2] [hēl] **1** *v.* To lean or cause to lean: The boat *heeled*. **2** *n.* The act or extent of heeling.

heft [heft] *informal* **1** *v.* To lift up; heave. **2** *n.* Heaviness. **3** *v.* To test the weight of by lifting.

heft·y [hef′tē] *adj.* **heft·i·er, heft·i·est** *informal* **1** Heavy or weighty. **2** Large and powerful: a *hefty* man.

heif·er [hef′ər] *n.* A young cow that has not produced a calf.

heigh-ho [hī′hō′ *or* hā′hō′] *interj.* An expression of weariness, disappointment, surprise, etc.

height [hīt] *n.* **1** The condition of being high. **2** The distance upward from the bottom to the top: the *height* of a tree. **3** (*often pl.*) A high place: to ascend to the *heights*. **4** Distance from the ground or sea level: clouds at a *height* of 20,000 feet. **5** The highest part; summit; peak. **6** The greatest degree: the *height* of stupidity.

height·en [hīt′(ə)n] *v.* **1** To make or become high or higher. **2** To increase or intensify: Seasoning *heightens* the taste of food.

hei·nous [hā′nəs] *adj.* Extremely wicked; terrible: a *heinous* crime.

heir [âr] *n.* A person who inherits or is likely to inherit rank or property upon the death of the person who possesses it: *heir* to the throne.

heir apparent *pl.* **heirs apparent** A person who must by law become the heir to rank or property if the person possessing it dies before he does.

heir·ess [âr′is] *n.* A female heir, especially one who has or will come into great wealth.

heir·loom [âr′lōōm] *n.* An object that has been passed through several generations of a family.

held [held] Past tense and past participle of HOLD: She *held* the doll upside down.

Hel·e·na [hel′ə·nə] *n.* The capital of Montana.

Hel·en of Troy [hel′ən] In the *Iliad*, the beautiful wife of the king of Sparta. Her elopement with Paris caused the Trojan War.

hel·i·cop·ter [hel′ə·kop′tər] *n.* An aircraft that is lifted and propelled by big, motor-driven, horizontal rotors and is able to hover and to fly in any direction. ◆ *Helicopter* comes from two Greek words meaning *spiral wing*.

Helicopter

he·li·o·cen·tric [hē′lē·ō·sen′trik] *adj.* Having or regarding the sun as the center: a *heliocentric* universe; a *heliocentric* theory.

he·li·o·graph [hē′lē·ə·graf′] **1** *n.* A device used in photographing the sun. **2** *n.* A device with a movable mirror, used to signal by reflecting flashes of sunlight. **3** *v.* To signal by heliograph.

He·li·os [hē′lē·ōs] *n.* In Greek myths, the sun god.

he·li·o·trope [hē′lē·ə·trōp′] **1** *n.* A plant with fragrant white or purplish flowers. **2** *adj.*, *n.* Soft, rosy purple.

he·li·ot·ro·pism [hē′lē·ot′rə·piz′əm] *n.* A response to sunlight, especially the tendency of some plants to turn toward it.

hel·i·port [hel′ə·pôrt′] *n.* An airport for helicopters. ◆ *Heliport* is a combination of *heli-* (*copter*) and (*air*)*port*.

he·li·um [hē′lē·əm] *n.* A gaseous element, light, odorless, and inert. Because it will not burn, it is used to fill balloons, dirigibles, etc.

he·lix [hē′liks] *n.*, *pl.* **he·lix·es** or **hel·i·ces** [hel′ə·sēz] A spiral coil like the thread of a screw.

hell [hel] *n.* **1** (*often written* **Hell**) In various religions, the realm of devils and the place where wicked souls are punished after death. **2** Any evil place. **3** A condition of suffering: He went through *hell* with an inflamed foot.

he′ll [hēl] **1** He will. **2** He shall.

Hel·las [hel′əs] *n.* Ancient or modern Greece.

Helix

hel·le·bore [hel′ə·bôr] *n.* A flowering plant whose roots are used in medicines and in insecticides.

Hel·lene [hel′ēn] *n.* A Greek.

Hel·len·ic [he·len′ik *or* he·lē′nik] **1** *adj.* Greek; Grecian. **2** *n.* The family of languages that includes ancient and modern Greek.

Hel·les·pont [hel′əs·pont] *n.* The ancient name for the DARDANELLES.

hell·ish [hel′ish] *adj.* **1** Of or like hell. **2** Horrible; fiendish: a *hellish* plan.

hel·lo [hə·lō′] *interj.*, *n.*, *pl.* **hel·los**, *v.* **hel·loed, hel·lo·ing 1** *interj.* An exclamation of greeting. **2** *interj.* An exclamation of surprise, interest, etc.: "*Hello!* What's happened here?" **3** *n.* A saying or shouting of "hello." **4** *v.* To say or greet with "hello."

helm¹ [helm] *n.* **1** A wheel or lever for steering a vessel. **2** A position of control: He took over the *helm* of his father's business.

helm² [helm] *n.* A helmet: seldom used today.

hel·met [hel′mit] *n.* A protective covering for the head: a football *helmet*.

helms·man [helmz′-mən] *n.*, *pl.* **helms·men** [helmz′mən] The person who steers a ship.

hel·ot [hel′ət *or* hē′lət] *n.* **1** A slave or serf; bondman. **2** (*usually written* **Helot**) A member of a class of serfs in ancient Sparta.

A knight's helmet and a construction worker's helmet

help [help] **1** *v.* To be of use or service to; assist or support: to *help* an old woman across a street; to *help* our country. **2** *v.* To be of use or service; lend a hand: Will you come and *help*?; to *help* with the dishes. **3** *interj.* A cry of fear, terror, etc., calling for assistance. **4** *v.* To improve or cure: Rest *helps* a cold. **5** *n.* The act of helping; assistance: Thanks for the *help*. **6** *n.* A person or thing that helps: You were a great *help*. **7** *n.* The condition of being helped. **8** *n.* A hired worker or workers. — **help oneself to 1** To serve oneself, as with food. **2** To take without requesting or being offered: He *helped himself to* my typewriter while I was away. — **help′er** *n.*

help·ful [help′fəl] *adj.* Useful or beneficial. — **help′ful·ly** *adv.* — **help′ful·ness** *n.*

help·ing [help′ing] *n.* A single portion of food.

helping verb See at VERB.

help·less [help′lis] *adj.* **1** Unable to help oneself; defenseless: When a knight was unseated from his horse, the weight of his armor made him *helpless*. **2** Having no help available. — **help′less·ly** *adv.* — **help′less·ness** *n.*

help·mate [help′māt′] *n.* A partner or helper, especially a wife or husband.

Hel·sin·ki [hel′sing·kē] *n.* The capital of Finland, in the southern part of the country.

hel·ter-skel·ter [hel′tər·skel′tər] **1** *adj.* Hurried and confused. **2** *adv.* In a hurried or confused manner: to run *helter-skelter*.

helve [helv] *n.* The handle of a tool, as of an ax, hatchet, etc.

hem¹ [hem] *n.*, *v.* **hemmed, hem·ming 1** *n.* A smooth edge on cloth or a garment, made by turning the rough edge under and sewing it down. **2** *v.* To provide with a hem: to *hem* a coat. **3** *v.* To shut in; surround: to *hem* in an enemy.

hem² [hem] *interj.*, *n.*, *v.* **hemmed, hem·ming 1** *interj.*, *n.* A coughlike sound made in clearing the throat. **2** *v.* To make this sound, as in clearing the throat, attracting attention, etc. — **hem and haw** To hesitate in speaking, so as to avoid making a clear statement.

Hem

hem·a·tite [hem′ə·tīt] *n.* A common mineral that is an important ore of iron.

Hem·ing·way [hem′ing·wā], **Ernest,** 1899–1961, U.S. novelist and short-story writer.

hem·i·sphere [hem′ə·sfir] *n.* **1** A half of a sphere. **2** (*often written* **Hemisphere**) One half of the earth's surface. See EASTERN HEMISPHERE, WESTERN HEMISPHERE, NORTHERN HEMISPHERE, and SOUTHERN HEMISPHERE.

hem·lock [hem′lok] *n.* **1** An evergreen tree with drooping branches, related to the pine. **2** A large plant that yields a poison.

he·mo·glo·bin [hē′mə·glō′bin] *n.* A red pigment that contains iron, found in red blood corpuscles, where it serves to carry oxygen.

he·mo·phil·i·a [hē′mə·fil′ē·ə] *n.* An inherited

tendency to bleed without stopping, because the blood does not clot properly.

hem·or·rhage [hem′ər·ij] **1** *n.* A flow of blood, usually a heavy flow from a broken blood vessel. **2** *v.* To lose blood; bleed.

hemp [hemp] *n.* **1** A tall plant with small green flowers. **2** The tough, strong fibers of this plant, used to make rope and cloth. **3** A drug from the flowers and leaves of this plant.

hemp·en [hem′pən] *adj.* Like or made of hemp.

hem·stitch [hem′stich′] **1** *n.* A decorative stitch made by pulling out many threads of a fabric and then stitching together in groups the remaining cross threads so as to form a design. **2** *v.* To decorate with a hemstitch.

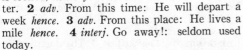

Hemstitching

hen [hen] *n.* The female of various birds, especially of the chicken and related birds.

hence [hens] **1** *adv.* Consequently; therefore: The door is locked, *hence* you can't enter. **2** *adv.* From this time: He will depart a week *hence*. **3** *adv.* From this place: He lives a mile *hence*. **4** *interj.* Go away!: seldom used today.

hence·forth [hens′fôrth′] *adv.* From this time on: *Henceforth* you will be more careful!

hence·for·ward [hens′fôr′wərd] *adv.* Henceforth.

hench·man [hench′mən] *n., pl.* **hench·men** [hench′mən] A faithful and devoted helper or follower, especially of a wicked person or cause.

hen·na [hen′ə] *n., v.* **hen·naed, hen·na·ing,** *adj.* **1** *n.* An Oriental shrub with slender leaves and white flowers. **2** *n.* A reddish brown dye made from this plant. **3** *v.* To dye with henna. **4** *adj., n.* Reddish brown.

hen·peck [hen′pek′] *v.* **1** To dominate (one's husband) by nagging, abuse, etc. **2** *adj. use:* a *henpecked* husband.

Hen·ry [hen′rē], **O.** See O. HENRY.

Hen·ry [hen′rē], **Patrick,** 1736–1799, American Revolutionary statesman and public speaker.

Henry IV, 1553–1610, King of France, 1589–1610.

Henry VIII, 1491–1547, King of England, 1509–1547.

he·pat·i·ca [hi·pat′ə·kə] *n.* A small plant having pink, white, or purple flowers and blooming early in the spring.

hep·a·ti·tis [hep′ə·tī′tis] *n.* Inflammation of the liver.

her [hûr] *pron.* **1** The pronoun *she* when used as an object of a verb or preposition: Please tell *her* now; I gave the book to *her*. **2** Of or belonging to her: the possessive form of *she*: *her* dress; *her* rescue.

He·ra [hir′ə] *n.* In Greek myths, the wife of Zeus and queen of the gods. Her Roman name was Juno.

Her·a·cles or **Her·a·kles** [her′ə·klēz] *n.* Hercules.

her·ald [her′əld] **1** *n.* A bearer of important news; messenger. **2** *n.* A person or thing that announces something to come. **3** *v.* To announce or foretell: Autumn frosts *herald* winter.

he·ral·dic [hi·ral′dik] *adj.* Of or having to do with heralds or heraldry.

her·ald·ry [her′əl·drē] *n., pl.* **her·ald·ries 1** The study of coats of arms and family descent. **2** A coat of arms. **3** Formal pageantry and pomp.

herb [(h)ûrb] *n.* A plant that withers and dies away after its yearly flowering, especially such a plant used as a seasoning, medicine, etc.

Heraldic emblem

her·ba·ceous [(h)ûr·bā′shəs] *adj.* Of, like, or having to do with an herb or herbs.

herb·age [(h)ûr′bij] *n.* Grass and green plants for grazing animals.

her·biv·o·rous [(h)ûr·biv′ə·rəs] *adj.* Feeding entirely on plants: Cows are *herbivorous* animals.

Her·cu·le·an [hûr·kyōō′lē·ən *or* hûr′kyə·lē′ən] *adj.* **1** Of or having to do with Hercules. **2** (*often written* **herculean**) Having or requiring great strength, courage, endurance, etc.: a *herculean* task.

Her·cu·les [hûr′kyə·lēz] *n.* In Greek and Roman myths, a hero of great strength who successfully performed twelve gigantic tasks.

herd [hûrd] **1** *n.* A large group of animals of one kind, moving about or kept together in a group: a *herd* of cattle. **2** *v.* To take care of in a herd: to *herd* goats. **3** *n.* A person who herds a specified kind of animal: used in combination, as in *swineherd*. **4** *v.* To gather or form into a herd. **5** *n.* The common people; the masses.

herds·man [hûrdz′mən] *n., pl.* **herds·men** [hûrdz′mən] Someone who tends a herd.

here [hir] **1** *adv.* In, at, or about this place or time: We'll start *here*; We'll camp *here*; *Here* you start to sing. **2** *adv.* To or into this place: They ran *here*; *Here* comes the train. **3** *adv.* From this place: He left *here* earlier. **4** *adv.* Now or about to be seen, indicated, etc.: *Here* are my reasons. **5** *adv.* In the present life. **6** *n.* This place: the *here* and now. **7** *interj.* An exclamation used to answer a roll call, attract attention, call an animal, etc. **— here and there 1** In or to one place or another; scattered or all about. **2** Now and then. **— neither here nor there** Having nothing to do with what is being considered; beside the point.

here·a·bout [hir′ə·bout′] *adv.* Hereabouts.

---

add, āce, câre, pälm;   end, ēqual;   it, īce;   odd, ōpen, ôrder;   tŏŏk, pōōl;   up, bûrn;
ə = a in *above*, e in *sicken*, i in *possible*, o in *melon*, u in *circus*;   yōō = u in *fuse*;   oil;   pout;
check;   ring;   thin;   this;   zh in *vision*.   For ¶ reference, see page 64 · HOW TO

here·a·bouts [hir′ə·bouts′] *adv.* In or about this place; in this vicinity.

here·af·ter [hir·af′tər] **1** *adv.* After this time; from now on: *Hereafter* keep silent! **2** *adv.* In the future. **3** *n.* A life after death.

here·by [hir·bī′ *or* hir′bī] *adv.* With or by means of this: You are *hereby* permitted to go.

he·red·i·tar·y [hə·red′ə·ter′ē] *adj.* **1** Left to one by an ancestor; inherited: a *hereditary* title. **2** Holding office by inheritance: a *hereditary* monarch. **3** Transmitted from parents to their offspring: a *hereditary* disease. **4** Of or having to do with heredity or inheritance.

he·red·i·ty [hə·red′ə·tē] *n.* **1** The passing on of characteristics from parents to offspring by means of genes. **2** The total of the qualities passed on in this way.

Here·ford [hûr′fərd *or* her′ə·fərd] *n.* One of a breed of beef cattle having a white face and a red coat with white markings.

here·in [hir·in′ *or* hir′in] *adv.* In or into this place, thing, matter, case, etc.: Payment is included *herein; Herein* is your mistake.

here·of [hir·uv′] *adv.* Of or concerning this.

here·on [hir·on′] *adv.* On this.

her·e·sy [her′ə·sē] *n., pl.* **her·e·sies 1** A belief different from or contrary to an accepted belief of a church, profession, science, etc. **2** The holding of such a belief.

her·e·tic [her′ə·tik] *n.* A person who believes or teaches heresy.

he·ret·i·cal [hə·ret′i·kəl] *adj.* Made up of, having in it, or having to do with heresy.

here·to·fore [hir′tə·fôr′] *adv.* Before this; up to now.

here·up·on [hir′ə·pon′] *adv.* At this; immediately after this.

here·with [hir·with′] *adv.* **1** Along with this: I am enclosing *herewith* my passport. **2** By means of this.

her·i·ta·ble [her′ə·tə·bəl] *adj.* That can be inherited: a *heritable* trait.

her·i·tage [her′ə·tij] *n.* **1** Inherited things, as property, characteristics, etc. **2** A tradition, belief, attitude, etc., handed down from the past.

her·maph·ro·dite [hûr·maf′rə·dīt] *n.* An animal or plant that shows both male and female physical characteristics.

Her·mes [hûr′mēz] *n.* In Greek myths, the messenger of the gods, and the god of science, commerce, travel, eloquence, and cunning. His Roman name was Mercury.

her·met·ic [hûr·met′ik] *adj.* Preventing gases or liquids from getting in or out; airtight: a *hermetic* seal. **— her·met′i·cal·ly** *adv.*

her·mit [hûr′mit] *n.* A person who lives alone and apart from others, as for religious reasons.

her·mit·age [hûr′mə·tij] *n.* The place where a hermit lives.

Hermes

hermit crab A crab that has a soft abdomen and lives in abandoned shells of other creatures.

hermit thrush A North American thrush having a spotted breast, red tail, and a lovely song.

her·ni·a [hûr′nē·ə] *n.* A bulging out of an organ or tissue through a break in its surrounding walls; rupture.

he·ro [hir′ō *or* hē′rō] *n., pl.* **he·roes 1** A man or boy who is known for his courage, nobility, great deeds, etc. **2** The principal male character in a story, play, etc.

Her·od [her′əd] *n.* In the Bible, the king of Judea at the time of Christ's birth.

He·rod·o·tus [hi·rod′ə·təs] *n.* A Greek historian of the fifth century B.C.

he·ro·ic [hi·rō′ik] *adj.* **1** Of, like, or proper for a hero: a *heroic* person; a *heroic* deed. **2** Telling or describing the deeds or lives of heroes: a *heroic* play. **— he·ro′i·cal·ly** *adv.*

he·ro·i·cal [hi·rō′i·kəl] *adj.* Heroic.

he·ro·ics [hi·rō′iks] *n.pl.* Words or deeds not truly grand or noble but meant to seem so.

her·o·in [her′ō·in] *n.* A habit-forming drug, made from morphine, now illegal in the U.S.

her·o·ine [her′ō·in] *n.* **1** A heroic woman or girl. **2** The principal female character of a story, play, etc.

her·o·ism [her′ō·iz′əm] *n.* **1** The qualities of a hero or heroine. **2** Heroic behavior or deeds.

her·on [her′ən] *n.* Any of several wading birds having a long bill, a long neck, and long legs.

her·pe·tol·o·gy [hûr′pə·tol′ə·jē] *n.* The science that studies reptiles.

Herr [her] *n., pl.* **Her·ren** [her′ən] **1** A gentleman: a German word. **2** The German title of courtesy for a man, equivalent to the English *Mr.*: *Herr* Kraus.

her·ring [her′ing] *n., pl.* **her·rings** or **her·ring** A food fish common in the North Atlantic Ocean, the

Great blue heron, about 4 ft. high

young of which are canned as sardines, and the adults eaten cooked, smoked, salted, etc.

her·ring·bone [her′ing·bōn′] *n.* **1** A design something like the bones of a herring, or like rows of closely spaced v's one above another. This design is often used in fabrics, embroidery, etc. **2** *adj. use: herringbone* tweed.

hers [hûrz] *pron.* **1** The one or ones belonging to her. **2** Of or belonging to her: That book is *hers*.

her·self [hər·self′] *pron.* **1** A form of *her* that refers back to the subject: She dressed *herself.* **2** A form of *her* that makes the word it goes with stronger or more intense: She *herself* told me. **3** Her normal, healthy, usual, or proper condition: She's *herself* again.

Hertz·i·an wave [hûr′tsē·ən] An artificially produced radio wave.

he's [hēz] **1** He is. **2** He has.

hes·i·tan·cy [hez′ə·tən·sē] *n.* The act or condition of hesitating; hesitation.

hes·i·tant [hez′ə·tənt] *adj.* Lacking certainty; hesitating; doubtful: He appeared *hesitant* in asking for the raise. **— hes′i·tant·ly** *adv.*

hes·i·tate [hez′ə·tāt] *v.* **hes·i·tat·ed, hes·i·tat·ing 1** To be slow or doubtful in acting, making a decision, etc.; pause or falter: He *hesitated* before giving the order; Don't *hesitate* to call me. **2** To be unwilling or reluctant: I *hesitate* to say what's really on my mind. **3** To stammer in speech.

hes·i·ta·tion [hez′ə·tā′shən] *n.* **1** The act of hesitating; wavering or doubt: She said "I do" without the slightest *hesitation.* **2** A pause or faltering in speech.

Hes·per·i·des [hes·per′ə·dēz] *n.pl.* In Greek myths, the nymphs who together with a dragon guarded the golden apples of Hera.

Hes·per·us [hes′pər·əs] *n.* The evening star.

Hes·sian [hesh′ən] *n.* One of the German soldiers hired to fight for the British in the American Revolution.

het·er·o·dox [het′ə·rə·doks′] *adj.* **1** Different from an accepted view or standard. **2** Rejecting accepted views or standards.

het·er·o·ge·ne·ous [het′ər·ə·jē′nē·əs] *adj.* Consisting of parts or units that are not alike: a *heterogeneous* collection of rubbish; Ours is a *heterogeneous* society.

hew [hyoō] *v.* **hewed, hewed** or **hewn** [hyoōn], **hew·ing 1** To cut or strike with an ax, sword, etc.: to *hew* branches. **2** To make or shape with blows of a knife, ax, etc.: to *hew* railings. **— hew′er** *n.*

hex [heks] *U.S. informal* **1** *n.* An evil spell. **2** *v.* To bewitch. ◆ *Hex* comes from the German word for *witch.*

hex·a·gon [hek′sə·gon] *n.* A closed plane figure having six sides and six angles.

hex·ag·o·nal [hek·sag′ə·nəl] *adj.* Having the form of a hexagon: a *hexagonal* building.

hex·a·he·dron [hek′sə·hē′drən] *n., pl.* **hex·a·he·dra** [hek′sə·hē′drə] or **hex·a·he·drons** A solid figure bounded by six plane faces.

Hexagons (the red one is regular)

hex·am·e·ter [hek·sam′ə·tər] *n.* A line of verse having six rhythmic feet, as "Thĕn mūl | tĭ tūdes | pässed bȳ | thĕir vōi | cĕs rāised | ĭn sŏng."

hey [hā] *interj.* A cry used to attract attention or express interest, surprise, pleasure, etc.

hey·day [hā′dā] *n.* The time of greatest vigor, power, etc.: In his *heyday* he was a champion.

Hg The symbol for the element MERCURY. ◆ The Latin word for mercury is *hydrargyrum.*

hi [hī] *interj. U.S. informal* Hello.

hi·a·tus [hī·ā′təs] *n., pl.* **hi·a·tus·es** or **hi·a·tus** A space where something is missing, as in a manuscript; gap.

Hi·a·wath·a [hī′ə·woth′ə or hī′ə·wô′thə] *n.* In Longfellow's poem *The Song of Hiawatha,* the hero, a young Indian brave.

hi·ber·nate [hī′bər·nāt] *v.* **hi·ber·nat·ed, hi·ber·nat·ing** To spend the winter sleeping or dormant, as bears and certain other animals do. **— hi·ber·na′tion** *n.*

hi·bis·cus [hī·bis′kəs] *n.* A plant having large showy flowers of various colors.

hic·cough [hik′əp] *n., v.* Another spelling of HICCUP.

hic·cup [hik′əp] *n., v.* **hic·cuped** or **hic·cupped, hic·cup·ing** or **hic·cup·ping 1** *n.* A sudden, involuntary gasp of breath which is immediately cut off by a spasm in the throat. **2** *v.* To undergo these spasms; have the hiccups.

hick·o·ry [hik′ə·rē] *n., pl.* **hick·o·ries 1** Any of several North American trees related to the walnut and having a hard wood and edible nuts. **2** The wood of this tree. ◆ *Hickory* comes from an Algonquian Indian word.

hide[1] [hīd] *v.* **hid** [hid], **hid·den** [hid′(ə)n] or **hid, hid·ing 1** To put or keep out of sight; conceal: to *hide* a key; Smoke *hid* the building. **2** To go or remain out of sight. **3** To keep secret: to *hide* one's fears. **4** *adj. use: hidden* treasure.

hide[2] [hīd] *n.* **1** The skin of an animal, especially when stripped from its carcass. **2** *informal* The human skin: I'll tan your *hide!*

hide-and-seek [hīd′(ə)n·sēk′] *n.* A game in which a person who is "it" has to find others who have hid and touch home base before they do.

hide·bound [hīd′bound′] *adj.* Narrow-minded, obstinate, and with little imagination.

hid·e·ous [hid′ē·əs] *adj.* Very ugly; horrible. **— hid′e·ous·ly** *adv.* **— hid′e·ous·ness** *n.*

hide-out [hīd′out′] *n. informal* A hiding place, especially for criminals.

hid·ing[1] [hī′ding] *n.* **1** The act of a person or thing that hides. **2** A place out of sight.

hid·ing[2] [hī′ding] *n. informal* A whipping or flogging.

hie [hī] *v.* **hied, hy·ing** or **hie·ing** To hasten; hurry: I *hied* myself home.

hi·er·ar·chy [hī′ə·rär′kē] *n., pl.* **hi·er·ar·chies 1** A group of persons or things arranged in successive classes, each class subject to or dependent on the ones above it. **2** A group of clergymen organized in this way.

hi·er·o·glyph·ic [hī′ər·ə·glif′ik or hī′rə·glif′ik] *n.* **1** A picture or symbol representing an object, idea, or sound. **2** (*pl.*) A system of writing using such pictures or symbols: ancient Egyptian *hieroglyphics.* **3** (*pl.*) Any writing that is hard to read or make out. **4** *adj. use: hieroglyphic* writ-

Hiero-
glyphics

add, **ā**ce, **c**âre, **p**älm;   **e**nd, **ē**qual;   **i**t, **ī**ce;   **o**dd, **ō**pen, **ô**rder;   t**oŏ**k, p**oō**l;   **u**p, b**û**rn;

ə = a in *above,* e in *sicken,* i in *possible,* o in *melon,* u in *circus;*   **y**o**ō** = u in *fuse;*   **oi**l;   **p**out;

check;   **r**i**ng**;   **th**in;   **th**is;   **zh** in *vision.*   For ¶ reference, see page 64 · HOW TO

ing. ◆ *Hieroglyphic* comes from Greek words meaning *sacred, carved* (writing), because the symbols were originally found on temple walls and in tombs.

hi-fi [hī′fī′] *n., pl.* **hi-fis,** *adj.* **1** *n.* High fidelity. **2** *n.* Equipment for reproducing sound with high fidelity. **3** *adj.* Of or having to do with high fidelity. ◆ *Hi-fi* is a shortened or "clipped" form of *hi(gh) fi(delity).*

hig·gle·dy-pig·gle·dy [hig′əl·dē·pig′əl·dē] **1** *adv.* In great confusion or disorder: His things were tossed about *higgledy-piggledy.* **2** *adj.* Jumbled.

high [hī] **1** *adj.* Reaching upward a great distance: a *high* mountain. **2** *adj.* At a good distance from the floor or ground: The kite was *high.* **3** *adj.* Having a certain height: ten feet *high.* **4** *adj.* To or from a great height: a *high* jump; a *high* dive. **5** *adj.* Great or large, as in amount or degree: *high* speeds; *high* voltage. **6** *adj.* Raised in pitch; shrill: a *high* sound. **7** *adj.* Superior in rank, quality, etc.: a *high* office. **8** *adj.* Very favorable: a *high* opinion of someone. **9** *adj.* Gay and joyful: *high* spirits. **10** *n.* A high level, position, degree, etc.: a *high* in prices. **11** *adv.* In or to a high level, position, degree, etc.: He jumps *high.* **12** *adj.* Most important; chief: a *high* court. **13** *adj.* Serious or grave: *high* treason. **14** *adj.* Having a bad odor, as spoiled meat, etc. **15** *adj.* Giving the greatest speed, as an arrangement of gears. **16** *n.* Such an arrangement of gears. **— high and dry 1** Completely out of water, as a stranded ship. **2** Helpless and alone; stranded. **— high and low** All around: to look *high and low.* **— high and mighty** Too proud or arrogant; haughty. **— on high 1** In or at a high place. **2** In heaven.

high·born [hī′bôrn′] *adj.* Of noble ancestry.

high·boy [hī′boi′] *n.* A tall chest of drawers, usually in two sections, the lower one on legs.

high·brow [hī′brou′] *informal* **1** *n.* A person claiming to be mainly interested in knowledge, serious ideas, and culture. **2** *adj.* Of or suitable for a highbrow: *highbrow* music.

high chair A baby's chair standing on tall legs and having a tray.

high·fa·lu·tin [hī′fə·lōōt′(ə)n] *adj.* *informal* Too grand or pompous.

high fidelity The reproduction of sound with no noticeable change or distortion from the original, as on a phonograph.

high-flown [hī′flōn′] *adj.* Too grand or pretentious; not simple: *high-flown* talk.

high frequency A radio wave frequency between 3 and 30 megacycles.

high-grade [hī′grād′] *adj.* Of superior quality.

high·hand·ed [hī′han′did] *adj.* Acting or done in an arrogant manner without any thought for the wishes or desires of other people. **— high′hand′ed·ly** *adv.* **— high′·hand′ed·ness** *n.*

high jump 1 A contest to see who can jump highest. **2** A jump in such a contest.

high·land [hī′lənd] *n.* **1** Land that is high above sea level. **2** (*pl., written* **Highlands**) A mountainous region of northern and western Scotland.

High·land·er [hī′lən·dər] *n.* A person born or living in the Highlands.

Highland fling A lively Scottish dance.

high·light [hī′līt′] **1** *n.* A bright area in a painting, photograph, etc. **2** *n.* An especially important or excellent part of something. **3** *v.* To have as or make into a highlight.

highlights

high·ly [hī′lē] *adv.* **1** Very much; extremely: *highly* agreeable. **2** Very favorably: to think *highly* of someone. **3** In a high position or rank: a *highly* placed diplomat. **4** At a high price or rate: *highly* paid.

High Mass A Mass celebrated with full ceremony.

high-mind·ed [hī′mīn′did] *adj.* Having noble thoughts or ideals.

High·ness [hī′nis] *n.* A title used in formally addressing or speaking of a person of royal rank: Your *Highness;* Her *Highness.*

high-pres·sure [hī′presh′ər] *adj., v.* **high-pres·sured, high-pres·sur·ing 1** *adj.* Having, using, or able to withstand high pressure: a *high-pressure* boiler; a *high-pressure* area. **2** *adj. informal* Forceful in trying to persuade: *high-pressure* sales tactics. **3** *v. informal* To try to persuade in a forceful way.

high·road [hī′rōd′] *n.* A main road.

high school A school which in the U.S. covers grades 9 or 10 through 12.

high seas The open waters of an ocean or sea that do not belong to any nation.

high-spir·it·ed [hī′spir′it·id] *adj.* Having a courageous, vigorous, or fiery spirit.

high-strung [hī′strung′] *adj.* Very nervous.

high tide 1 The highest level that the tide reaches. **2** The time when this occurs.

high time So late as to be nearly too late: It's *high time* he did some work.

high·way [hī′wā′] *n.* A main road; thoroughfare.

high·way·man [hī′wā′mən] *n.* A man who holds up and robs travelers on a road.

hike [hīk] *n., v.* **hiked, hik·ing 1** *n.* A long walk or march. **2** *v.* To take a hike: We *hiked* through the woods. **3** *v. informal* To raise or rise: to *hike* up prices; His jacket *hiked* up in back. **— hik′er** *n.*

hi·lar·i·ous [hi·lâr′ē·əs] *adj.* **1** Noisily cheerful and gay; merry: a *hilarious* party. **2** Very humorous: a *hilarious* story. **— hi·lar′i·ous·ly** *adv.* **— hi·lar′i·ous·ness** *n.*

hi·lar·i·ty [hi·lar′ə·tē] *n.* Boisterous gaiety or laughter.

hill [hil] *n.* **1** A piece of ground higher than the surrounding land, but not as high as a mountain.

2 Any heap or pile. **3** A small mound of earth placed over or around certain plants: a *hill* of corn.

hill·bil·ly [hil′bil′ē] *n.*, *pl.* **hill·bil·lies** *U.S. informal* A person coming from or living in the mountains or backwoods.

hill·ock [hil′ək] *n.* A small hill or mound.

hill·side [hil′sīd′] *n.* The slope of a hill.

hill·top [hil′top′] *n.* The top of a hill.

hill·y [hil′ē] *adj.* **hill·i·er, hill·i·est 1** Having many hills: *hilly* country. **2** Steep: a *hilly* slope. **— hill′i·ness** *n.*

hilt [hilt] *n.* The handle of a sword or dagger. **— to the hilt** To tne full extent; thoroughly; fully.

hi·lum [hī′ləm] *n.*, *pl.* **hi·la** [hī′lə] or **hi·lums** The scar on a seed at the point where it was attached to the seed vessel.

him [him] *pron.* The form of *he* used as the object of a verb or preposition: Help *him;* Give it to *him.*

Hi·ma·la·yan [him′ə·lā′ən *or* hi·mäl′yən] *adj.* Of or having to do with the Himalayas.

Hilt

Hi·ma·la·yas [him′ə·lā′əz *or* hi·mäl′yəz] *n.pl.* A chain of mountains between Tibet and India containing the highest mountains in the world.

him·self [him·self′] *pron.* **1** A form of *him* that refers back to the subject: He cut *himself;* He talked to *himself.* **2** A form of *him* that makes the word it goes with stronger or more intense: He *himself* will come. **3** His usual or proper self: He wasn't *himself.*

hind[1] [hīnd] *n.*, *pl.* **hinds** or **hind** A female red deer, especially one fully grown.

hind[2] [hīnd] *adj.* **hind·er, hind·most** or **hind·er·most** Back; rear: a *hind* leg.

hin·der[1] [hin′dər] *v.* To interfere with; retard, obstruct, or thwart: to *hinder* a person.

hind·er[2] [hin′dər] Comparative of HIND[2].

hind·er·most [hīn′dər·mōst′] *adj.* Hindmost.

Hin·di [hin′dē] *n.* The main language of northern India.

hind·most [hīnd′mōst′] Superlative of HIND[2].

Hin·doo [hin′dōō] *n.*, *pl.* **Hin·doos**, *adj.* Another spelling of HINDU.

hind·quar·ter [hīnd′kwôr′tər] *n.* A large cut of meat including a hind leg and loin.

hin·drance [hin′drəns] *n.* **1** A person or thing that hinders; obstacle or impediment: Lack of confidence is a *hindrance* to getting ahead. **2** A hindering or being hindered.

hind·sight [hīn(d)′sīt′] *n.* Realization of what should have been done when it is too late.

Hin·du [hin′dōō] *n.*, *pl.* **Hin·dus**, *adj.* **1** *n.* A native of India descended from an ancient race that conquered it. **2** *n.* A person whose religion is Hinduism. **3** *adj.* Of, having to do with, or characteristic of Hindus or Hinduism.

Hin·du·Ar·a·bic numerals [hin′dōō·ar′ə·bik] Arabic numerals.

Hin·du·ism [hin′dōō·iz′əm] *n.* A religion, chiefly of India, in which Brahma is the main god.

Hin·du·sta·ni [hin′dōō·stä′nē] **1** *n.* An important and probably the commonest language of India, based on Hindi. **2** *adj.* Of or having to do with India, its people, or Hindustani.

hinge [hinj] *n.*, *v.* **hinged, hing·ing 1** *n.* A joint on which a door, lid, etc., pivots or turns. **2** *v.* To equip with a hinge or hinges. **3** *v.* To hang or swing on a hinge. **4** *v.* To depend: Success *hinges* on his actions.

hint [hint] **1** *n.* A slight suggestion that is made with delicacy or tact. **2** *v.* To make a hint or hints. **3** *n.* A small piece of advice: household *hints.* **4** *n.* A slight bit or trace: Put a *hint* of garlic in the sauce.

Hinge

hin·ter·land [hin′tər·land′] *n.* **1** A region behind a coast; inland region. **2** A region far from cities and towns.

hip[1] [hip] *n.* **1** The projecting part on either side of the human body where the thigh is jointed to the body. **2** A similar part of an animal where the hind leg is attached.

hip[2] [hip] *n.* The ripened fruit of a rose.

hip·bone [hip′bōn] *n.* Either of two bones that form the sides of the pelvis.

hip·po·drome [hip′ə·drōm] *n.* **1** In ancient Greece and Rome, an oval track for horse and chariot racing surrounded by seats for spectators. **2** An arena for horse shows, circuses, etc.

hip·po·pot·a·mus [hip′ə·pot′ə·məs] *n.*, *pl.* **hip·po·pot·a·mus·es** or **hip·po·pot·a·mi** [hip′ə·pot′ə·mī] A large four-footed mammal with thick skin that lives in and around African rivers. Its diet consists of plants. ◆ *Hippopotamus* comes from two Greek words meaning *river horse.*

Hippopotamus, 13 ft. long

hire [hīr] *v.* **hired, hir·ing,** *n.* **1** *v.* To agree to pay for the work or use of; employ or rent: to *hire* a helper; to *hire* a car. **2** *v.* To allow the use of in return for payment: to *hire* out boats. **3** *v.* To accept employment: to *hire* on as a guide. **4** *n.* Payment received for work or services; wages or fee. **— for hire** Available to be hired: The livery stable had some spirited horses *for hire* last year.

hire·ling [hīr′ling] *n.* A person who works for hire and cares for little besides his pay.

Hi·ro·shi·ma [hir′ə·shē′mə] *n.* A city in sw

---

add, **ā**ce, **câ**re, **pä**lm; **e**nd, **ē**qual; **i**t, **ī**ce; **o**dd, **ō**pen, **ô**rder; t**oo**k, p**oo**l; **u**p, b**û**rn; ə = a in *above*, e in *sicken*, i in *possible*, o in *melon*, u in *circus*; y**oo** = u in *fuse*; **oi**l; p**ou**t; **ch**eck; **r**ing; **th**in; **th**is; **zh** in *vision*. For ¶ reference, see page 64 · HOW TO

Japan where the first atomic bomb used in war was dropped on August 6, 1945.

his [hiz] *pron.* **1** Of or belonging to him: the possessive form of *he*: *his* book; *his* work; *his* sister. **2** The one or ones belonging to or having to do with him: The book is *his*.

His·pa·ni·o·la [his'pə·nyō'lə] *n.* A large island in the West Indies divided into Haiti and the Dominican Republic.

hiss [his] **1** *n.* A prolonged sound like *ss*, or like a gas passing through a small opening. **2** *v.* To make such a sound, often as a sign of anger or dislike: The snake *hissed;* The crowd *hissed* at the umpire.

hist [hist] *interj.* An exclamation meaning "Be quiet! Listen!"

his·to·ri·an [his·tôr'ē·ən] *n.* A writer of or authority on history.

his·tor·ic [his·tôr'ik] *adj.* Important or famous in history: a *historic* place or event.

his·tor·i·cal [his·tôr'ə·kəl] *adj.* **1** Of, having to do with, or belonging to history: *historical* documents. **2** Historic. **3** That really happened or existed: *historical* evidence. **4** Based on people and events in history: a *historical* novel. **— his·tor'i·cal·ly** *adv.*

his·to·ry [his'tə·rē] *n., pl.* **his·to·ries 1** Past events, or a record of them, often concerning a particular nation, people, activity, etc.: European *history;* the *history* of art; the *history* of his life. **2** The branch of knowledge that deals with past events. **3** An interesting past: That house has quite a *history.*

his·tri·on·ic [his'trē·on'ik] *adj.* **1** Having to do with actors or acting. **2** Affected; insincere.

hit [hit] *v.* **hit, hit·ting,** *n.* **1** *v.* To give a blow to or make forceful contact with; strike: to *hit* a snake; The car *hit* the tree. **2** *v.* To reach or strike, as with a shot from a gun, an arrow, etc.: He *hit* the target. **3** *n.* A blow, shot, etc., that reaches its target. **4** *v.* To have a bad effect on; cause to suffer: Misfortune *hit* him hard. **5** *v.* To come upon or discover: to *hit* the main road; to *hit* upon an idea. **6** *n.* A great success: The song was a *hit.* **7** *n.* In baseball, a base hit. **8** *v.* To bat. **— hit it off** To get on well together. **— hit'ter** *n.*

hit-and-run [hit'(ə)n·run'] *adj.* Having to do with or involved in an accident in which the driver of the motor vehicle that caused the accident simply drives away: a *hit-and-run* victim.

hitch [hich] **1** *v.* To fasten or tie: to *hitch* a rope to a post; to *hitch* up a horse. **2** *n.* A thing used to hitch, as one of various knots. **3** *n.* A coupling; fastening. **4** *v.* To become fastened or snarled: Moorings fouled and *hitched.* **5** *n.* An obstacle or delay: a *hitch* in a plan. **6** *v.* To move, pull, raise, etc., with a jerk: He *hitched* up his pants. **7** *n.* A quick jerking movement. **8** *v.* *U.S. slang* To seek or get (a ride or rides) in hitchhiking.

hitch·hike [hich'hīk'] *v.* **hitch·hiked, hitch·hik·ing** To travel by asking for and receiving rides in passing cars. **— hitch'hik'er** *n.*

hith·er [hith'ər] **1** *adv.* To or toward this place. **2** *adj.* Situated toward this side; nearer.

hith·er·to [hith'ər·tōō' *or* hith'ər·tōō'] *adv.* Up to now: A *hitherto* unknown man was chosen to develop recreation areas for the city.

Hit·ler [hit'lər], **Adolf,** 1889–1945, leader of Nazi Germany, 1933–1945.

hit-or-miss [hit'ər·mis'] *adj.* Haphazard; random; careless.

Hit·tite [hit'īt] *n.* A member of a people that established a powerful empire in Asia Minor and northern Syria from about 2000 to 1200 B.C.

hive [hīv] *n., v.* **hived, hiv·ing 1** *n.* A shelter or container for a colony of honeybees. **2** *n.* A colony of bees living in a hive. **3** *v.* To put or gather into a hive. **4** *v.* To live close together in or as if in a hive. **5** *n.* A place full of people or animals busily working or moving about.

hives [hīvz] *n.* A skin disease caused by an allergy, in which the skin itches and breaks out in swollen patches.

ho [hō] *interj.* An exclamation to get attention, show surprise, joy, etc.

hoar [hôr] *adj.* Hoary.

hoard [hôrd] **1** *v.* To save and store away, often greedily: to *hoard* food. **2** *n.* Something hoarded: a *hoard* of gold. **— hoard'er** *n.*

hoar·frost [hôr'frôst'] *n.* White frost.

hoarse [hôrs] *adj.* **hoars·er, hoars·est** Rough, deep, and husky in sound: a *hoarse* voice; to become *hoarse* from cheering. **— hoarse'ly** *adv.* **— hoarse'ness** *n.*

hoar·y [hôr'ē] *adj.* **hoar·i·er, hoar·i·est 1** White or whitish. **2** Gray or white with age. **3** Very old; ancient. **— hoar'i·ness** *n.*

hoax [hōks] **1** *n.* A trick or deception, often intended to fool the public: The news of war was a *hoax.* **2** *v.* To fool by a hoax.

hob¹ [hob] *n.* A hobgoblin or elf. **— play hob** To cause mischief or confusion.

hob² [hob] *n.* A shelf in the interior of a fireplace for keeping things warm.

hob·ble [hob'əl] *v.* **hob·bled, hob·bling,** *n.* **1** *v.* To walk lamely. **2** *n.* A limping walk. **3** *v.* To tie the legs of (an animal) together to limit movement. **4** *n.* Something used to hobble an animal. **5** *v.* To hinder or hamper.

hob·by [hob'ē] *n., pl.* **hob·bies** Something a person works at for pleasure in his spare time: His *hobby* is building model airplanes.

hob·by·horse [hob'ē·hôrs'] *n.* **1** A stick with the figure of a horse's head at one end, used as a toy. **2** A rocking horse.

hob·gob·lin [hob'gob'lin] *n.* **1** A goblin or imp. **2** An imaginary cause of fear or dread.

hob·nail [hob'nāl'] *n.* A short nail with a large head. Hobnails are put into the soles of heavy shoes so that they won't slip or wear out.

hob·nob [hob'nob'] *v.* **hob·nobbed, hob·nob·bing** To be on friendly terms: to *hobnob* with the neighbors.

ho·bo [hō'bō] *n., pl.* **ho·boes** or **ho·bos** A tramp who lives by odd jobs and begging.

hock¹ [hok] *n.* A joint on the hind leg of a horse, ox, sheep, etc., corresponding to the ankle in man.

hock² [hok] *U.S. informal* **1** *v.* To pawn. **2** *n.* The condition of being pawned: My guitar is in *hock*.

hock·ey [hok′ē] *n.* **1** A game played on ice in which the players wear skates and use large sticks curved at one end to try to drive a small disk or puck into the goal of the opponent. **2** A similar game played on a field with a ball.

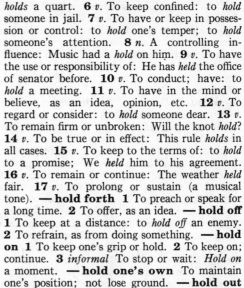

Horse's hock

ho·cus-po·cus [hō′kəs-pō′kəs] *n.* **1** An expression used in conjuring and performing magic tricks. **2** Trickery or deception.

hod [hod] *n.* **1** A trough set on a long handle, used to carry bricks, cement, etc. **2** A pail or scuttle for carrying coal.

hodge·podge [hoj′poj′] *n.* A confused mixture.

hoe [hō] *n., v.* **hoed, hoe·ing** **1** *n.* A tool having a flat blade set across the end of a long handle, used to clear weeds, loosen soil, etc. **2** *v.* To use a hoe on (weeds, soil, etc.).

Hod

hog [hog *or* hôg] *n., v.* **hogged, hog·ging** **1** *n.* A pig, especially a large one raised for meat. **2** *n.* *informal* A gluttonous, selfish, or filthy person. **3** *v.* *slang* To take more than one's proper share of: He *hogs* everything in sight.

ho·gan [hō′gən] *n.* A Navaho Indian hut made of sticks and branches covered with earth.

Ho·garth [hō′gärth], **William,** 1697–1764, English painter and engraver.

hog·gish [hog′ish] *adj.* **1** Very greedy. **2** Filthy.

Hogan

hogs·head [hogz′hed′ *or* hôgz′hed′] *n.* **1** A cask that holds from 63 to 140 gallons. **2** A measure of volume for liquids equal to 63 gallons.

hoist [hoist] **1** *v.* To raise or lift, especially by mechanical means. **2** *n.* A machine that hoists. **3** *n.* A lift or boost.

Hol·bein [hōl′bīn *or* hôl′bīn], **Hans,** 1465?–1524, and his son **Hans,** 1497?–1543, German painters.

hold¹ [hōld] *v.* **held, hold·ing,** *n.* **1** *v.* To take and keep in the hands, arms, etc.; grip or clasp. **2** *n.* An act or method of holding: a firm *hold.* **3** *v.* To support or keep fixed: The beams hold the roof up. **4** *n.* Something grasped for support. **5** *v.* To contain or have room for: The bottle *holds* a quart. **6** *v.* To keep confined: to *hold* someone in jail. **7** *v.* To have or keep in possession or control: to *hold* one's temper; to *hold* someone's attention. **8** *n.* A controlling influence: Music had a *hold* on him. **9** *v.* To have the use or responsibility of: He has *held* the office of senator before. **10** *v.* To conduct; have: to *hold* a meeting. **11** *v.* To have in the mind or believe, as an idea, opinion, etc. **12** *v.* To regard or consider: to *hold* someone dear. **13** *v.* To remain firm or unbroken: Will the knot *hold?* **14** *v.* To be true or in effect: This rule *holds* in all cases. **15** *v.* To keep to the terms of: to *hold* to a promise; We *held* him to his agreement. **16** *v.* To remain or continue: The weather *held* fair. **17** *v.* To prolong or sustain (a musical tone). — **hold forth 1** To preach or speak for a long time. **2** To offer, as an idea. — **hold off 1** To keep at a distance: to *hold* off an enemy. **2** To refrain, as from doing something. — **hold on 1** To keep one's grip or hold. **2** To keep on; continue. **3** *informal* To stop or wait: *Hold on* a moment. — **hold one's own** To maintain one's position; not lose ground. — **hold out 1** To continue resisting. **2** To last: Our supplies *held out.* — **hold over 1** To put off until later; postpone. **2** To remain or keep beyond the expected time. — **hold up 1** To prevent from falling. **2** To show; display. **3** *informal* To last or endure: to *hold up* under wear. **4** To delay or stop: The storm *held* us *up.* **5** To rob by using force or threats. — **hold with** To approve of or support.

hold² [hōld] *n.* The compartment where cargo is carried in a ship or airplane.

hold·er [hōl′dər] *n.* **1** A person or thing that holds. **2** A device used in holding something.

hold·ing [hōl′ding] *n.* **1** The act of a person or thing that holds. **2** (*often pl.*) Property that is owned, as stocks, bonds, etc.

hold·up [hōld′up′] *n.* **1** A stopping or delay. **2** *informal* A robbing by force or threats.

hole [hōl] *n., v.* **holed, hol·ing** **1** *n.* An opening in or through anything: a *hole* in a shoe, fence, etc. **2** *n.* A pit, hollow, or cavity: a *hole* in the sand. **3** *v.* To make a hole or holes in. **4** *n.* An animal's burrow: a rat's *hole.* **5** *n.* A dark, miserable place, as a dungeon. **6** *n.* In golf, a small opening into which the ball is to be hit. **7** *n.* One of the divisions of a golf course, each one having a hole. **8** *v.* To putt or hit (a ball) into a hole. **9** *n.* A defect or fault: a *hole* in an argument. — **hole up 1** To hibernate in a cave. **2** To hide or seclude oneself.

hol·i·day [hol′ə-dā] *n.* **1** A day on which most business is stopped in remembrance of an important event. **2** A holyday. **3** *adj. use:* holiday clothes; *holiday* joy. ◆ *Holiday* once referred

add, **ā**ce, **cā**re, **pä**lm;   **e**nd, **ē**qual;   **i**t, **ī**ce;   **o**dd, **ō**pen, **ô**rder;   **t**o͡ok, **p**o�<u>o</u>l;   **u**p, **b**ûrn;

ə = a in *above*, e in *sicken*, i in *possible*, o in *melon*, u in *circus*;   y**oo** = u in *fuse*;   **oi**l;   **p**ou**t**;

check;   **r**i**ng**;   **th**in;   **th**is;   **zh** in *vision*.   For ¶ reference, see page 64 · HOW TO

only to days set aside to celebrate religious events. They were thus literally *holy days*, as the term is still sometimes spelled. Now, however, *holiday* is more often used for any day, religious or not, on which business or school is suspended.

ho·li·ness [hō′lē·nis] *n.* **1** The condition of being holy. **2** (*written* **Holiness**) A title used when addressing or speaking of the Pope: Your *Holiness*; His *Holiness*.

Hol·land [hol′ənd] *n.* Another name for the NETHERLANDS. **— Hol′land·er** *n.*

hol·ler [hol′ər] *U.S. informal* **1** *v.* To shout: He *hollered* for help. **2** *n.* A shout.

hol·low [hol′ō] **1** *adj.* Empty on the inside; not solid: a *hollow* log. **2** *n.* An empty space in something; hole. **3** *adj.* Having the shape of a dish or bowl; concave. **4** *adj.* Sunken or fallen in: *hollow* cheeks. **5** *v.* To make or become hollow: to *hollow* out a log. **6** *n.* A valley. **7** *adj.* Deep and muffled as though echoing in a cave: a *hollow* voice. **8** *adj.* Meaningless and empty: *hollow* praise. **— hol′low·ness** *n.*

hol·ly [hol′ē] *n., pl.* **hol·lies** An evergreen tree or shrub with shining, dark green, pointed leaves and scarlet berries, often used as a Christmas decoration.

hol·ly·hock [hol′ē·hok] *n.* A tall plant with large rounded leaves and showy flowers.

Hol·ly·wood [hol′ē·wŏŏd] *n.* **1** An area in Los Angeles regarded as the center of the U.S. movie industry. **2** The U.S. movie industry.

Holmes [hōlmz *or* hōmz], **Oliver Wendell,** 1809–1894, U.S. writer and doctor; and his son **Oliver Wendell,** 1841–1935, a justice of the U.S. Supreme Court, 1902–1932.

Holmes [hōlmz *or* hōmz], **Sherlock** A fictional detective created by the English author Sir Arthur Conan Doyle.

hol·o·caust [hol′ə·kôst] *n.* Great destruction and loss of life, especially by fire.

Hol·stein [hōl′stīn *or* hōl′stēn] *n.* One of a breed of large black and white dairy cattle.

hol·ster [hōl′stər] *n.* A leather case for a pistol, often worn on a belt.

ho·ly [hō′lē] *adj.* **ho·li·er, ho·li·est** **1** Regarded with reverence because it comes from or has to do with God; sacred: *holy* Scripture. **2** Saintly: a *holy* man; *holy* love. **3** Thought of with devotion and respect: a *holy* cause.

Holster

Holy Communion The sacrament in which consecrated bread and wine are eaten and sipped in memory of the death of Christ; the Eucharist.

ho·ly·day [hō′lē·dā′] *n.* or **holy day** A day set aside for a special religious reason. ◆ See HOLIDAY.

Holy Ghost In Christianity, the third person of the Trinity; the spirit of God.

Holy Grail The Grail.

Holy Land Palestine.

holy of holies **1** The most sacred part of the Jewish temple at Jerusalem, where the Ark of the Covenant was kept. **2** Any very holy place.

Holy Roman Empire The empire in central and western Europe from 962 to 1806, whose spiritual head was the Pope.

Holy See The Pope's office or authority.

Holy Spirit Another name for HOLY GHOST.

ho·ly·stone [hō′lē·stōn′] *n., v.* **ho·ly·stoned, ho·ly·ston·ing** **1** *n.* A flat piece of soft sandstone used to scrub the wooden decks of a ship. **2** *v.* To scrub with a holystone.

Holy Week The week before Easter.

Holy Writ The Bible.

hom·age [(h)om′ij] *n.* **1** Respect or honor given or shown: to pay *homage* to a queen. **2** In the Middle Ages, the allegiance sworn by a vassal to his lord.

hom·bre [om′brā *or* om′brē] *n. slang* Man; guy.

home [hōm] *n., v.* **homed, hom·ing,** *adv.* **1** *n.* The place where a person or animal lives. **2** *adj. use: home* furnishings. **3** *n.* The place or region where a person was born or raised. **4** *adv.* To, in, or at one's home: to fly *home*; to stay *home*. **5** *v.* To have a home: Deer *home* in the woods. **6** *v.* To return home, as a pigeon. **7** *n.* A family or household. **8** *n.* A shelter for the care of the poor, sick, aged, etc. **9** *n.* A place of comfort, security, etc. **10** *n.* The place where something originates, develops, or is mainly located. **11** *adj. use:* the *home* office. **12** *adv.* In or at the place intended: to strike *home*. **13** *n.* The goal or base that one must reach in order to score, as in baseball. **14** *v.* To go or be guided toward a destination: The missile *homed* in on its target. **— at home 1** At or in one's home. **2** At one's ease; in a familiar or comfortable place. **3** Prepared to receive visitors.

home economics The study of how to manage a home, including cooking, budgets, etc.

home·land [hōm′land′] *n.* The country in which a person has his home or was born.

home·less [hōm′lis] *adj.* Having no home.

home·like [hōm′līk′] *adj.* Like or typical of home; comfortable or familiar.

home·ly [hōm′lē] *adj.* **home·li·er, home·li·est** **1** Not good-looking; plain or ugly. **2** Plain and familiar: *homely* truths. **3** Simple; plain; ordinary: *homely* meals. **— home′li·ness** *n.*

home·made [hōm′mād′] *adj.* Made at home or in a nonprofessional way.

home·mak·er [hōm′mā′kər] *n.* A housewife.

home plate In baseball, the rubber slab beside which a player stands in batting and to which he must return in order to score.

hom·er [hō′mər] *n. U.S. informal* A home run.

Ho·mer [hō′mər] *n.* A Greek epic poet who lived in about the ninth century B.C. He is regarded as the author of the *Iliad* and the *Odyssey*.

home room The school room in which a class meets for a check of attendance, dismissal, etc.

H

home run In baseball, a hit by which a batter circles the bases and scores a run.

home·sick [hōm′sik′] *adj.* Unhappy or ill because of longing for home. **—home′sick′· ness** *n.*

home·spun [hōm′spun′] **1** *adj.* Spun at home. **2** *n.* Cloth made of homespun yarn or a strong, loose fabric like it. **3** *adj. use;* a *homespun* gown. **4** *adj.* Plain; simple: *homespun* humor.

home·stead [hōm′sted] *n.* **1** A house and its land, etc., used as a home. **2** A piece of land given to a settler by the U.S. government to farm, improve, and eventually own.

home·stretch [hōm′strech′] *n.* **1** The straight section of a racetrack between the final turn and the finish line. **2** The last stage of any journey or effort.

home·ward [hōm′wərd] *adv., adj.* Toward home: to go *homeward*; a *homeward* journey.

home·wards [hōm′wərdz] *adv.* Homeward.

home·work [hōm′wûrk′] *n.* Work done at home, especially school work.

home·y [hō′mē] *adj.* **hom·i·er, hom·i·est 1** Homelike. **2** Plain and simple.

hom·i·ci·dal [hom′ə·sīd′(ə)l] *adj.* **1** Of or having to do with homicide. **2** Murderous: a *homicidal* maniac.

hom·i·cide [hom′ə·sīd] *n.* **1** The killing of a person by another, on purpose or accidentally. **2** A person who kills someone.

hom·i·ly [hom′ə·lē] *n., pl.* **hom·i·lies 1** A sermon, especially about something in the Bible. **2** A long lecture on morals and conduct.

homing pigeon A pigeon that can make its way home from great distances, often used for carrying messages.

hom·i·ny [hom′ə·nē] *n.* Kernels of dried corn with the hulls removed, usually crushed, and boiled in milk or water. ◆ *Hominy* comes from an Algonquian Indian word meaning *parched corn.*

ho·mo·ge·ne·ous [hō′mə·jē′nē·əs] *adj.* Alike or made of like parts: a *homogeneous* fishing village. **—ho′mo·ge′ne·ous·ly** *adv.*

ho·mog·en·ize [hə·moj′ə·nīz] *v.* **ho·mog·en· ized, ho·mog·en·iz·ing 1** To mix the cream throughout (milk) so that it cannot separate. **2** To make homogeneous. ¶3

hom·o·graph [hom′ə·graf] *n.* Any of two or more words that are spelled alike but have different meanings and origins, as *wind* (moving air) and *wind* (coil around).

hom·o·nym [hom′ə·nim] *n.* Any of two or more words that sound and may be spelled alike but have different meanings and origins, as *cleave* (split) and *cleave* (stick to).

hom·o·phone [hom′ə·fōn] *n.* Any of two or more words that are pronounced alike but have different meanings, origins, and usually spellings, as *sun* and *son.*

Ho·mo sa·pi·ens [hō′mō sā′pē·enz] The scientific name for modern man.

Hon. Abbreviation of HONORABLE.

Hon·du·ras [hon·d(y)ŏŏr′əs] *n.* A country in Central America.

hone [hōn] *n., v.* **honed, hon·ing 1** *n.* A stone used for sharpening tools, razors, etc. **2** *v.* To sharpen with a hone: to *hone* an ax.

hon·est [on′ist] *adj.* **1** Acting honorably and justly; not lying, stealing, or cheating: *honest* men. **2** Truthful, genuine, or fair: an *honest* answer. **3** Fairly done or earned: *honest* wages. **4** Belonging to or indicating an honest person: an *honest* face; an *honest* manner.

hon·est·ly [on′ist·lē] *adv.* **1** In an honest manner. **2** Really; indeed: *Honestly,* that's right.

hon·es·ty [on′is·tē] *n.* The condition or quality of being honest.

hon·ey [hun′ē] *n., pl.* **hon·eys, v. hon·eyed** or **hon·ied, hon·ey·ing 1** *n.* A sweet, syrup-like substance made by bees from nectar gathered from flowers. **2** *v.* To sweeten with or as if with honey. **3** *n.* Anything like honey. **4** *n.* Sweetness. **5** *n.* Darling; dear. **6** *v.* To speak or speak to in a loving or flattering way. **7** *adj. use: honeyed* words.

hon·ey·bee [hun′ē·bē′] *n.* A bee that makes honey.

hon·ey·comb [hun′ē·kōm′] **1** *n.* A wax structure of many six-sided cells made by bees for storing honey, their eggs, etc. **2** *n.* Anything like a honeycomb. **3** *adj. use:* a *honeycomb* pattern. **4** *v.* To fill with many small holes: Termites *honey-combed* the woodwork.

Honeycomb

hon·ey·dew [hun′ē·d(y)ŏŏ′] *n.* **1** A sweet liquid given off by the leaves of certain plants in warm weather. **2** A sweet substance secreted on leaves and stems by aphids.

honeydew melon A kind of melon having a smooth white skin and a sweet greenish pulp.

hon·ey·moon [hun′ē·mŏŏn′] **1** *n.* A vacation spent by a couple who have just been married. **2** *v.* To have or spend a honeymoon.

hon·ey·suck·le [hun′ē·suk′əl] *n.* A climbing shrub with white, buff, or crimson flowers that give off a fragrant smell.

Hong Kong [hong kong *or* hông kông] *n.* A British colony in SE China.

honk [hôngk *or* hongk] **1** *n.* The sound made by a goose or a sound like it, as that of an automobile horn. **2** *v.* To make such a sound.

Ho·no·lu·lu [hon′ə·lŏŏ′lŏŏ] *n.* The capital of Hawaii, on the island of Oahu.

hon·or [on′ər] **1** *n.* Respect and admiration: to give *honor* to our heroes. **2** *v.* To give or show

add, āce, câre, pälm;　end, ēqual;　it, īce;　odd, ōpen, ôrder;　tŏŏk, pŏŏl;　up, bûrn;
ə = a in *above*, e in *sicken*, i in *possible*, o in *melon*, u in *circus*;　yŏŏ = u in *fuse*;　oil;　pout;
ch in *check*; ring; thin; this; zh in *vision*.　For ¶ reference, see page 64 · HOW TO

respect and admiration for: to *honor* a great man.
3 *n.* An act or sign of respect. **4** *n.* Glory, reputation, or credit for fine or heroic acts: The *honor* must go to him. **5** *n.* A person or thing that brings honor: This promotion is a great *honor.* **6** *v.* To bring honor to: His works *honor* his name. **7** *n.* Fairness, rightness, and honesty: to act with *honor.* **8** *n.* Reputation; standing: His *honor* is at stake. **9** *n.* (*pl.*) Special mention or credit given to a student for excellent work: to graduate with *honors.* **10** *n.* (*written* **Honor**) A title of respect used in formally addressing or speaking of a judge, mayor, etc.: Your *Honor*; His *Honor.* **11** *v.* To accept as good for payment or credit: to *honor* a check. **— do the honors 1** To act as a host or hostess. **2** To perform a social courtesy, as offering a toast, etc. ¶1

hon·or·a·ble [on′ər·ə·bəl] *adj.* **1** Worthy of honor or respect. **2** Fair; honest; upright: an *honorable* man. **3** Bringing honor or credit: *honorable* work. **4** (*written* **Honorable**) A title of respect used in speaking of important officials: the *Honorable* Robert Hickok. **— hon′or·a·bly** *adv.* ¶1

hon·or·ar·y [on′ə·rer′ē] *adj.* **1** Given as an honor: an *honorary* degree. **2** As an honor, without duties, powers, or pay: an *honorary* chairman.

Hon·shu [hon′shoo] *n.* The largest island of Japan.

hood[1] [hŏŏd] **1** *n.* A covering for the head and back of the neck, often part of a coat, robe, etc. **2** *n.* Something that looks like or is used like a hood, as the cover of an automobile engine. **3** *v.* To cover or furnish with a hood.

hood[2] [hŏŏd] *n. U.S. slang* A hoodlum.

-hood A suffix meaning: **1** The condition, time, or quality of being, as in *babyhood*, the condition, time, or quality of being a baby. **2** The whole group or class of, as in *priesthood*, the whole group or class of priests.

hood·ed [hŏŏd′id] *adj.* **1** Having or covered with a hood. **2** Shaped like a hood.

hood·lum [hŏŏd′ləm] *n. U.S.* A gangster or thug.

hoo·doo [hoo′doo] *n., pl.* **hoo·doos**, *v.* **hoo·dooed, hoo·doo·ing 1** *n.* Voodoo. **2** *n. informal* Bad luck. **3** *n. informal* A bringer of bad luck. **4** *v. informal* To bring bad luck to.

hood·wink [hŏŏd′wingk′] *v.* **1** To trick; mislead; deceive. **2** To blindfold.

hoof [hŏŏf *or* hŏŏf] *n., pl.* **hoofs** or **hooves** [hŏŏvz *or* hŏŏvz], *v.* **1** *n.* The horny covering of the foot of certain animals, as horses, cattle, and pigs. **2** *n.* A foot of such an animal. **3** *v. informal* To walk or dance. **— on the hoof** Not butchered; alive, as cattle.

hoofed [hŏŏft *or* hŏŏft] *adj.* Having hoofs.

hook [hŏŏk] **1** *n.* A curved piece of metal, wood, etc., used to hold up, fasten, catch, or drag things. **2** *v.* To catch, fasten, etc., with a hook or hooks: to *hook* a fish. **3** *n.* Something shaped like or suggesting a hook, as a punch thrown with a bent elbow. **4** *v.* To curve or bend

like a hook. **5** *v. informal* To swindle; hoodwink: He was *hooked* into a bad deal. **6** *v. slang* To steal. **— by hook or by crook** By any means available. **— hook up 1** To put together or connect the parts of: to *hook up* a dress. **2** To connect (a device) to a source, as of power, water, etc. **— on one's own hook** *informal* By or for oneself; independently.

hook·ah [hŏŏk′ə] *n.* An Oriental smoking pipe that passes the smoke through water.

hook and ladder A fire engine carrying long ladders, axes, hooked poles, etc.

hooked [hŏŏkt] *adj.* **1** Curved like a hook. **2** Having a hook or hooks. **3** Made by looping yarn through canvas or burlap with a hook: a *hooked* rug.

hook·up [hŏŏk′up′] *n.* The arrangement of parts used in a radio, phonograph, etc.

Hookah

hook·worm [hŏŏk′wûrm′] *n.* A small worm with hooked mouth parts that invades the intestines of man and some animals and sucks blood.

hook·y [hŏŏk′ē] *n. U.S. informal* Absence without permission, especially in the phrase **play hooky,** to be absent from school without permission.

hoop [hoop *or* hŏŏp] **1** *n.* A circular band of metal, wood, etc., used to bind barrels, to extend a skirt, or as a toy. **2** *v.* To surround or fasten with a hoop or hoops.

hoop skirt A skirt puffed out with hoops.

hoo·ray [hŏŏ·rā′] *interj., n., v.* Another word for HURRAH.

hoot [hŏŏt] **1** *n.* The cry of an owl. **2** *n.* A sound like it. **3** *n.* A loud outcry, especially one showing contempt. **4** *v.* To make a hoot or hoots. **5** *v.* To drive off with hoots: The audience *hooted* him from the stage.

Hoo·ver [hŏŏ′vər], **Herbert,** 1874–1964, 31st president of the U.S., 1929–1933.

Hoover Dam A dam on the Colorado River between Arizona and Nevada.

Hoop skirt

hooves [hŏŏvz *or* hŏŏvz] A plural of HOOF.

hop[1] [hop] *v.* **hopped, hop·ping,** *n.* **1** *v.* To move with short leaps on both, or all four, feet, as a bird or rabbit. **2** *v.* To make short leaps on one foot. **3** *n.* A short leap. **4** *v. informal* To jump over or on: to *hop* a hedge; to *hop* a bus.

hop[2] [hop] *n.* **1** A climbing vine with clusters of small yellow flowers. **2** (*pl.*) These clusters when ripe and dried, used to flavor beer, ale, etc.

hope [hōp] *n., v.* **hoped, hop·ing 1** *n.* A feeling that what one wishes for may happen. **2** *v.* To want and expect: We *hope* to be back soon. **3** *n.* Something that is hoped for: His *hope* is to succeed. **4** *n.* A person or thing that is a cause for hope: He is the *hope* of our team.

hope·ful [hōp′fəl] *adj.* **1** Having or showing hope: a *hopeful* attitude. **2** Giving or allowing hope: a *hopeful* situation. **— hope′ful·ly** *adv.* **— hope′ful·ness** *n.*

hope·less [hōp′lis] *adj.* **1** Without hope: a *hopeless* feeling. **2** Giving or allowing no hope: a *hopeless* situation. **— hope′less·ly** *adv.* **— hope′less·ness** *n.*

Ho·pi [hō′pē] *n.*, *pl.* **Ho·pi** or **Ho·pis** A member of a tribe of Indians now living in towns built of stone in NE Arizona.

hop·per [hop′ər] *n.* **1** A person or thing that hops. **2** A container for coal, grain, etc., that narrows toward the bottom, through which the contents can be dropped or fed slowly.

hop·scotch [hop′-skoch′] *n.* A children's game in which a player hops on one foot over the lines of a diagram marked on the ground to pick up something thrown into an area of the diagram.

Hopper

horde [hôrd] *n.* **1** A great crowd; swarm: a *horde* of people. **2** A wandering tribe or clan: *Hordes* from the east swept into Spain.

hore·hound [hôr′hound′] *n.* **1** A plant related to the mint. **2** A substance extracted from it, used to make a candy that helps stop coughing.

ho·ri·zon [hə·rī′zən] *n.* **1** The line where the earth and sky seem to meet. **2** The limits of one's observation, knowledge, or experience.

hor·i·zon·tal [hôr′ə·zon′təl] **1** *adj.* Parallel to the horizon; level. **2** *n.* A horizontal line, plane, bar, etc. **3** *adj.* Measured parallel to the horizon: *horizontal* distance. **— hor′i·zon′tal·ly** *adv.*

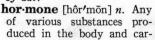

hor·mone [hôr′mōn] *n.* Any of various substances produced in the body and carried by its fluids, each controlling the activity of a specific organ or of a related group.

horn [hôrn] *n.* **1** One of a pair of hard, hollow, permanent growths, usually curved and pointed, on the heads of cattle, sheep, goats, etc. **2** One of a pair of branched, solid growths on the heads of deer, shed each year; antler. **3** The material of a horn. **4** Something made from a horn: a powder *horn*. **5** A musical wind instrument, originally made from a horn, now usually of brass.

6 A device for sounding a warning: an automobile *horn*. **— horn in** *slang* To meddle or intrude.

Horn, Cape A cape on an island at the southern tip of South America.

horn·blende [hôrn′blend′] *n.* A common mineral found in granite and other rocks.

horn·book [hôrn′bŏŏk′] *n.* A leaf or page on which was printed the alphabet, etc., covered with transparent horn and framed, formerly used in teaching reading to children.

horned [hôrnd] *adj.* Having a horn or horns.

horned toad A small harmless lizard with a flat body and hornlike spines.

hor·net [hôr′nit] *n.* A large wasp with a very severe and painful sting.

horn of plenty Another name for CORNUCOPIA.

Hornet

horn·pipe [hôrn′pīp′] *n.* **1** A lively English dance for one or more people, originally danced by sailors. **2** Music for it.

horn·y [hôr′nē] *adj.* **horn·i·er, horn·i·est** **1** Made of horn or a similar substance. **2** Having horns or hornlike projections. **3** Calloused; rough: *horny* hands.

hor·o·scope [hôr′ə·skōp] *n.* **1** The position of the sun, moon, and planets in the zodiac at a certain time, especially the time of a person's birth. **2** A chart showing this, used in predicting a person's future by astrology.

hor·ren·dous [hô·ren′dəs] *adj.* Horrible; frightful: It was a truly *horrendous* crime.

hor·ri·ble [hôr′ə·bəl] *adj.* **1** Causing horror; frightful. **2** *informal* Very unpleasant or very bad: a *horrible* day. **— hor′ri·bly** *adv.*

hor·rid [hôr′id] *adj.* **1** Frightful; horrible. **2** *informal* Very unpleasant or offensive: a *horrid* odor. **— hor′rid·ly** *adv.*

hor·ri·fy [hôr′ə·fī] *v.* **hor·ri·fied, hor·ri·fy·ing** **1** To fill with horror. **2** *informal* To shock or surprise in an annoying way: His manners *horrified* everyone.

hor·ror [hôr′ər] *n.* **1** A feeling of extreme fear, dread, loathing, etc. **2** Something that causes this feeling. **3** The quality of being horrible: the *horror* of war. **4** A strong dislike or hatred: a *horror* of cats.

hors d'oeuvre [ôr dûrv′] *n.*, *pl.* **hors d'oeuvres** An appetizer, as celery, olives, radishes, etc., generally served before a meal.

horse [hôrs] *n.*, *v.* **horsed, hors·ing** **1** *n.* A large, four-legged animal with hoofs and a long tail and mane, used for riding or to pull loads. ◆ *Adj.*, *equine.* **2** *v.* To mount a horse. **3** *n.* Mounted soldiers: a unit of *horse*. **4** *v.* To supply with a horse or horses. **5** *n.* A frame with four legs, used as a support. **6** *n.* A padded block on legs, used in gymnastics. **— horse**

around *slang* To play in a boisterous or rough way; fool.

horse·back [hôrs′bak′] **1** *n.* A horse's back. **2** *adv.* On a horse's back: to ride *horseback*.

horse chestnut 1 A shade tree having large leaves, clusters of white flowers, and large, glossy brown nuts. **2** The nut of this tree.

horse·fly [hôrs′flī′] *n.*, *pl.* **horse·flies** A large fly that bites horses and cattle.

horse·hair [hôrs′hâr′] *n.* **1** The hair from the mane or tail of horses. **2** A cloth made from this. **3** *adj. use:* a *horsehair* mattress.

horse·hide [hôrs′hīd′] *n.* **1** The hide of a horse. **2** Leather made from horsehide.

horse·laugh [hôrs′laf′] *n.* A loud, scornful laugh; guffaw.

horse·man [hôrs′mən] *n.*, *pl.* **horse·men** [hôrs′mən] **1** A man skilled in riding or handling horses. **2** A man riding a horse.

horse·man·ship [hôrs′mən·ship] *n.* The skill of riding and managing horses.

horse·play [hôrs′plā′] *n.* Rough, boisterous play or fun.

horse·pow·er [hôrs′pou′ər] *n.* A unit of power equal to that needed to lift 550 pounds one foot in one second.

horse·rad·ish [hôrs′rad′ish] *n.* **1** A plant related to mustard. **2** A sharp-tasting relish made from the white, grated root of this plant.

horse sense *informal* Ordinary common sense.

horse·shoe [hôr(s)′shoo′] *n.*, *v.* **horse·shoed, horse·shoe·ing 1** *n.* A U-shaped piece of metal nailed to the bottom of a horse's hoof for protection. **2** *v.* To furnish with horseshoes. **3** *n.* Something shaped like a horseshoe. **4** *n.* (*pl.*) A game in which the object is to toss horseshoes onto or near a stake. **— horse′sho′er** *n.*

horseshoe crab A crablike sea animal with a spiny tail and a shell shaped like a horseshoe.

horse·tail [hôrs′tāl′] *n.* **1** The tail of a horse. **2** A flowerless plant with hollow, jointed stems.

horse·whip [hôrs′(h)wip′] *n.*, *v.* **horse·whipped, horse·whip·ping 1** *n.* A whip for managing horses. **2** *v.* To flog with a horsewhip.

horse·wom·an [hôrs′woom′ən] *n.*, *pl.* **horse·wom·en** [hôrs′wim′in] **1** A woman skilled in riding or handling horses. **2** A woman riding a horse.

Horseshoe crab, about 20 in. long

hors·y [hôr′sē] *adj.* **hors·i·er, hors·i·est 1** Of or having to do with a horse or horses: a *horsy* odor. **2** Fond of horses, horse racing, fox hunting, etc. **3** Like a horse: *horsy* features.

hor·ti·cul·ture [hôr′tə·kul′chər] *n.* **1** The cultivation of a garden. **2** The science of growing garden vegetables, flowers, etc. **— hor′ti·cul′tur·al** *adj.* **— hor′ti·cul′tur·ist** *n.*

ho·san·na [hō·zan′ə] *interj.* A cry of praise and adoration to God.

hose [hōz] *n.*, *v.* **hosed, hos·ing 1** *n.*, *pl.* **hose** Stockings or socks; hosiery. **2** *n.*, *pl.* **hose** An outer garment once worn by men, fitting like tight trousers. **3** *n.*, *pl.* **hos·es** An easily bending tube, often of rubber, through which water, etc., may be forced. **4** *v.* To water with a hose.

Ho·se·a [hō·zē′ə] *n.* **1** A Hebrew prophet who lived during the 8th century B.C. **2** A book of the Old Testament which he wrote.

ho·sier·y [hō′zhər·ē] *n.* Stockings or socks.

hos·pice [hos′pis] *n.* A place of rest or shelter for travelers, especially one maintained by a religious group or order.

hos·pi·ta·ble [hos′pi·tə·bəl *or* hos·pit′ə·bəl] *adj.* **1** Fond of having guests, or showing welcome and generosity toward guests. **2** Showing an open mind: *hospitable* to new ideas. **— hos′pi·ta·bly** *adv.*

hos·pi·tal [hos′pi·təl] *n.* A place where injured or sick people are taken care of. ◆ See HOTEL.

hos·pi·tal·i·ty [hos′pə·tal′ə·tē] *n.*, *pl.* **hos·pi·tal·i·ties** Friendly, welcoming treatment of guests or strangers.

hos·pi·tal·ize [hos′pi·təl·īz′] *v.* **hos·pi·tal·ized, hos·pi·tal·iz·ing** To put into a hospital for treatment and care. **— hos·pi·tal·i·za·tion** [hos′pi·təl·ə·zā′shən] *n.* ¶3

host[1] [hōst] *n.* **1** A man who entertains guests. **2** A person in charge of a hotel or inn. **3** A living plant or animal on or in which a parasite lives.

host[2] [hōst] *n.* **1** A large number of men or things: a *host* of children. **2** An army.

Host [hōst] *n.* (*sometimes written* **host**) The bread or wafer used in the Mass of the Roman Catholic Church and in some other churches.

hos·tage [hos′tij] *n.* **1** A person given up to or held by an enemy until certain promises or conditions are fulfilled. **2** A pledge; security.

hos·tel [hos′təl] *n.* A supervised shelter, as for youths on hikes, tours, etc. ◆ See HOTEL.

hos·tel·ry [hos′təl·rē] *n.*, *pl.* **hos·tel·ries** An inn; lodging place: seldom used today.

host·ess [hōs′tis] *n.* **1** A woman who entertains guests. **2** A woman hired to seat people at tables in a restaurant. **3** A woman who runs an inn or hotel.

hos·tile [hos′təl] *adj.* **1** Of, having to do with, or belonging to an enemy: *hostile* acts; *hostile* forces. **2** Showing dislike; unfriendly: a *hostile* glance. **— hos′tile·ly** *adv.*

hos·til·i·ty [hos·til′ə·tē] *n.*, *pl.* **hos·til·i·ties 1** An unfriendly feeling; dislike or hate. **2** (*pl.*) Warfare, or acts of war. **3** Opposition: *hostility* to Darwin's theory of evolution.

hos·tler [(h)os′lər] *n.* A man who cares for horses in a stable or at an inn.

hot [hot] *adj.* **hot·ter, hot·test,** *adv.* **1** *adj.* Having a high temperature or great heat; very warm: a *hot* day; a *hot* oven. **2** *adv.* With heat: Desert winds blow *hot*. **3** *adj.* Causing a burning sensation in the mouth: *hot* pepper. **4** *adj.* Showing great activity or feeling: a *hot* battle; *hot* words. **5** *adj.* Not far behind; close: in *hot*

pursuit. **6** *adj.* Fresh or strong: a *hot* scent.
7 *adj.* Dangerously radioactive. — **hot′ly** *adv.*

hot·bed [hot′bed′] *n.* **1** A bed of rich earth,
warmed by manure and protected by glass, for
growing plants. **2** A place or condition favoring
growth, as of something bad: a *hotbed* of disease.

hot·blood·ed [hot′blud′id] *adj.* Easily excited;
passionate.

hot cake A pancake or griddlecake.

hot dog *informal* A cooked frankfurter, usually
served in a long roll.

ho·tel [hō·tel′] *n.* A place where travelers and
others go for food and lodging; inn. ◆ *Hotel*,
hostel, and *hospital* all refer to places that give
lodging to strangers, and all three words come
originally from the same Latin word, *hospes*,
meaning *guest* or *stranger*. *Hotels* are usually in
cities, and are often large and luxurious, whereas
hostels, which are designed for students and
others traveling on low budgets, may be found
everywhere in Europe, are often small and
humble, and are always inexpensive. *Hospitals*,
of course, are specially designed for the ill.

hot·head·ed [hot′hed′id] *adj.* **1** Quick-tempered; easily angered. **2** Impetuous; rash.

hot·house [hot′hous′] *n.*, *pl.* **hot·hous·es** A
heated building with glass roof and sides, in
which delicate plants are grown.

hot plate A small, portable gas or electric
cooking stove.

hot rod *slang* An automobile, usually old, with
an engine rebuilt for
greater speeds.

Hot·ten·tot [hot′(ə)n-
tot] *n.* **1** A member
of a South African
people. **2** Their lan-
guage.

hound [hound] **1** *n.*
A dog with droopy
ears and short hair,
used in hunting be-
cause of its keen sense
of smell. **2** *v. informal*

A hot rod

To follow or pester: The actress was *hounded* by
newsmen.

hour [our] *n.* **1** Any of the 24 equal periods
making up a day; 60 minutes. **2** A definite or
particular time of day: The *hour* is
6:15. **3** (*pl.*) A regularly fixed time,
as for school, work, etc.: office
hours. **4** The present time: the topic of the *hour.* **5** The distance measured by the time it takes to cover
it: to live two *hours* away.

hour·glass [our′glas′] *n.* An old-
fashioned device for measuring time.
It is made up of two glass bulbs   Hourglass
connected by a narrow neck through
which a quantity of sand runs from the upper

bulb to the lower during a certain time, usually
an hour.

hou·ri [hoo′rē *or* hour′ē] *n.*, *pl.* **hou·ris** One
of the maidens of the Moslem paradise, remaining forever young and beautiful.

hour·ly [our′lē] **1** *adj.* Done, taken, or hap-
pening every hour: an *hourly* news report. **2** *adj.*
Of or for an hour: an *hourly* wage rate. **3** *adj.*
Continual; frequent: *hourly* rumors. **4** *adv.* Fre-
quently: Telephone calls came *hourly.* **5** *adv.*
Almost at once: We expect him *hourly.*

house [*n.* hous, *v.* houz] *n.*, *pl.* **hous·es**
[hou′zəz], *v.* **housed, hous·ing** **1** *n.* A
building for one or a few persons or families to
live in. **2** *v.* To give shelter to; lodge: The building *houses* 50 families. **3** *n.* A building for holding
anything: a carriage *house.* **4** *v.* To put away;
store. **5** *n.* A family, especially of the nobility: a
house of royal blood. **6** *n.* A building in which
people meet for a special purpose: a *house* of worship. **7** *n.* A business firm: a publishing *house.*
8 *n.* An audience, as in a theater. **9** *n.* An assembly of people who make the laws for a country, or
the place where they meet. — **keep house** To
do housework; manage a home.

house·boat [hous′bōt′] *n.* A boat or barge
used as a home.

house·break [hous′-
brāk′] *v.* **house·**
broke, house·bro·
ken, house·break·
ing **1** To train (a pet
animal) in habits of
excretion for indoor
living. **2** *adj. use:*
a *housebroken* dog.

Houseboat

house·break·ing
[hous′brā′king] *n.* The act of breaking into
another's home so as to steal or commit some
other crime. — **house′break′er** *n.*

house·coat [hous′kōt′] *n.* A woman's lightweight, loose-fitting garment for informal wear
about the house.

house·fly [hous′flī′] *n.*, *pl.* **house·flies** A
small, two-winged insect that lives about houses
and feeds on garbage.

house·hold [hous′hōld′] *n.* **1** All the persons
who live in one house, especially a family. **2** The
home and its domestic affairs. **3** *adj. use:* house-
hold tasks.

house·hold·er [hous′hōl′dər] *n.* **1** A person
dwelling in a house. **2** The head of a family.

house·keep·er [hous′kē′pər] *n.* A woman hired
to manage and take care of a home.

house·keep·ing [hous′kē′ping] *n.* The doing
or managing of household tasks; housework.

house·maid [hous′mād′] *n.* A woman or girl
servant, hired to do housework.

House of Commons The lower house of the
British Parliament. Its members are elected.

---

add, **ā**ce, c**â**re, p**ä**lm;   end, **ē**qual;   it, **ī**ce;   odd, **ō**pen, **ô**rder;   t**oo**k, p**ōō**l;   up, b**û**rn;

ə = a in *above,* e in *sicken,* i in *possible,* o in *melon,* u in *circus;*   y**oo** = u in *fuse;*   oil;   pout;

check; **ri**ng; **th**in; **th**is; **zh** in *vision.*   For ¶ reference, see page 64 · HOW TO

House of Lords The upper house of the British Parliament, made up of members of the nobility and clergymen of high rank.

House of Representatives The lower house of the U.S. Congress and of many state legislatures.

house·top [hous′top′] *n.* The roof or top of a house.

house·wares [hous′wârz′] *n.pl.* Household or kitchen appliances or utensils.

house·warm·ing [hous′wôr′ming] *n.* A party given when a family first moves into a home.

house·wife [hous′wīf′] *n.*, *pl.* **house·wives** [hous′wīvz′] A woman who manages a household for her family; homemaker.

house·work [hous′wûrk′] *n.* The work done in a home, as cleaning, cooking, etc.

hous·ing[1] [hou′zing] *n.* **1** The providing of shelter or lodgings. **2** Houses or dwellings: low-cost *housing.* **3** Something that protects or shelters, as a cover, casing, etc.

hous·ing[2] [hou′zing] *n.* An ornamental covering or blanket worn by a horse.

Hous·ton [hyōōs′tən] *n.* A city in SE Texas.

Hous·ton [hyōōs′tən], **Samuel,** 1793–1863, U.S. general and Texas statesman.

hove [hōv] A past tense and past participle of HEAVE.

hov·el [huv′əl *or* hov′əl] *n.* **1** An old, dirty hut or small house. **2** A low, open shed for sheltering cattle, tools, etc.

hov·er [huv′ər *or* hov′ər] *v.* **1** To remain in or near one place in the air, as birds, etc. **2** To linger or remain nearby: to *hover* over a sick child. **3** To remain in an uncertain condition; waver: to *hover* between laughter and tears.

Hov·er·craft [huv′ər·kraft′ *or* hov′ər·kraft′] *n.* A vehicle that travels over land or water a little above the surface, supported on a cushion of air produced by powerful fans: a trademark.

how [hou] *adv.* **1** In what way: *How* does the tune go? **2** To what degree, amount, or extent: *How* far is it? **3** In what state or condition: *How* are you? **4** For what reason; why: *How* could he have done it? **5** *informal* What: *How* about coming? **— how come** *informal* Why?

how·be·it [hou·bē′it] *adv.* Nevertheless: seldom used today.

how·dah [hou′də] *n.* A seat for people riding on an elephant's back, often with a canopy.

how·ev·er [hou·ev′ər] **1** *adv.* In whatever way; by whatever means: *However* did you fix that car? **2** *adv.* To whatever degree, amount, or extent: Spend *however* much it costs. **3** *conj.* Nevertheless; yet; but: He smiled; *however,* he was unhappy.

Howdah

how·it·zer [hou′it·sər] *n.* A short cannon that fires off shells at a high angle.

howl [houl] **1** *v.* To make one or more loud, drawn-out cries: Dogs and wolves often *howl* at night. **2** *v.* To make sounds like this: The wind *howls.* **3** *n.* A loud, drawn-out cry. **4** *v.* To cry out or shout loudly: to *howl* with laughter. **5** *v.* To force or drive away by howling: They *howled* the singer off the platform.

Howitzer

how·so·ev·er [hou′sō·ev′ər] *adv.* No matter how; in whatever manner.

hoy·den [hoid′(ə)n] *n.* A bold, boisterous girl; tomboy.

h.p. or **hp** Abbreviation of HORSEPOWER.

H.Q. or **hq** Abbreviation of HEADQUARTERS.

hr. Abbreviation of: **1** HOUR. **2** (*usually written* **hrs.**) Hours.

hub [hub] *n.* **1** The center part of a wheel, that turns on or with an axle. **2** A center of great activity or interest: Washington, D.C., is the *hub* of U.S. politics.

hub·bub [hub′ub] *n.* A loud, confused noise; uproar.

huck·le·ber·ry [huk′əl·ber′ē] *n.*, *pl.* **huck·le·ber·ries** **1** A dark blue or black berry like a blueberry. **2** The bush it grows on.

Hub of a wheel

huck·ster [huk′stər] *n.* **1** A peddler of small articles or of provisions, such as fruits and vegetables. **2** *U.S. slang* A person who works in the advertising business.

hud·dle [hud′(ə)l] *v.* **hud·dled, hud·dling,** *n.* **1** *v.* To crowd or nestle together closely: The girls *huddled* together in fear. **2** *v.* To bring, push, or crowd together: The hen *huddled* her chicks under her wings. **3** *n.* A number of persons or things crowded or jumbled together. **4** *n.* A small, private conference, especially the gathering together of a football team to receive instructions for the next play.

Hud·son [hud′sən] *n.* A river in eastern New York, flowing south to a bay in New York City.

Hudson Bay A large inland sea in NE Canada.

Hud·son [hud′sən], **Henry,** died 1611?, English explorer, discovered the Hudson for the Dutch, 1609, and Hudson Bay for the English, 1610.

hue [hyōō] *n.* A color, or a shade of a color: the red and yellow *hues* of autumn.

hue and cry A loud protest or outcry: The mayor joined in the *hue and cry* against crime.

huff [huf] *n.* A fit of anger: He left in a *huff.*

huff·y [huf'ē] *adj.* **huff·i·er, huff·i·est**
1 Touchy; quickly offended. **2** Sulky; peevish.
— **huff'i·ly** *adv.*

hug [hug] *v.* **hugged, hug·ging,** *n.* **1** *v.* To
clasp in the arms; embrace: The girl kissed and
hugged her mother. **2** *n.* A close embrace or tight
clasping with the arms. **3** *v.* To keep close to:
The ship *hugged* the shore. **4** *v.* To cling to, as a
belief or principle.

huge [(h)yōōj] *adj.* Extremely large; vast: a
huge mountain. — **huge'ly** *adv.*

Hu·go [hyōō'gō], **Victor,** 1802–1885, French
poet, novelist, and dramatist.

Hu·gue·not [hyōō'gə·not] *n.* Any French
Protestant of the 16th or 17th century.

hu·la [hōō'lə] *n.* A Hawaiian dance characterized by sinuous motions of the arms, hands, and
hips, which often pantomime a story.

hulk [hulk] *n.* **1** The hull of an old, broken-down
ship. **2** A large, clumsy person or thing.

hulk·ing [hul'king] *adj.* Large and clumsy: a
hulking young fellow.

hull [hul] **1** *n.* The outer covering of certain
fruits or seeds, as a husk or pod. **2** *n.* The green,
leaflike parts around the base of some fruits, as
the strawberry; calyx. **3** *v.* To remove the hull
of. **4** *n.* The body or frame of a ship, seaplane,
dirigible, etc. **5** *n.* Any outer covering.

hul·la·ba·loo [hul'ə·bə·lōō'] *n.,* *pl.* **hul·la·ba·**
loos An uproar; tumult.

hum [hum] *v.* **hummed, hum·ming,** *n.* **1** *v.*
To make a low, steady droning or buzzing sound,
as a bee or mosquito. **2** *n.* Such a sound. **3** *v.* To
sing with closed lips, using no words. **4** *n.* The
act of humming. **5** *n.* The sound made by
humming. **6** *v.* To put into a certain condition
by humming: to *hum* a child to sleep. **7** *v.*
informal To be very busy or active: The office
hummed.

hu·man [(h)yōō'mən] **1** *n.* A man, woman, or
child; person. The more formal term is **human**
being. 2 *adj.* Of or having to do with people:
human events. **3** *adj.* Having or showing traits
that are natural to people: It is *human* to make
mistakes.

hu·mane [(h)yōō·mān'] *adj.* Kind; compassionate: a *humane* interest in the care of animals.

hu·man·ist [(h)yōō'mən·ist] *n.* **1** A scholar of
classical humanities. **2** A person concerned with
human problems who believes in man's ability to
improve himself by using reason.

hu·man·i·tar·i·an [(h)yōō·man'ə·târ'ē·ən] **1** *n.*
A person concerned with or working for the
welfare of mankind. **2** *adj.* Helpful to people.

hu·man·i·ty [(h)yōō·man'ə·tē] *n.,* *pl.* **hu·man·**
i·ties 1 The human race; mankind. **2** The
state or quality of being human; human nature.
3 Kindness: *humanity* to animals. **4** (*pl.*) The
study of classical Greek and Roman literature.

5 (*pl.*) The area of learning that includes literature, history, the arts, etc., as distinguished from
the sciences.

hu·man·ize [(h)yōō'mə·nīz] *v.* **hu·man·ized,**
hu·man·iz·ing To make or become humane,
gentle, kindly, etc. ¶3

hu·man·ly [(h)yōō'mən·lē] *adv.* **1** In a human
manner. **2** Within human knowledge or power:
That's not *humanly* possible.

hum·ble [hum'bəl] *adj.* **hum·bler, hum·**
blest, *v.* **hum·bled, hum·bling 1** *adj.* Not
proud or vain; modest; meek. **2** *adj.* Low in
station, rank, etc. **3** *v.* To lower in power, pride,
etc.; humiliate. — **hum'ble·ness** *n.* — **hum'·**
bly *adv.*

humble pie In former times, a pie containing
the less choice parts of a deer, made for servants
after a hunt. It is now used mainly in the phrase
eat humble pie, to be forced to make apologies
or admit that one is wrong.

hum·bug [hum'bug] *n.,* *v.* **hum·bugged,**
hum·bug·ging 1 *n.* A person who seeks to
deceive others; fake. **2** *n.* Something used to
trick or deceive others; fraud; sham. **3** *v.* To
trick or cheat.

hum·drum [hum'drum'] *adj.* Dull; monotonous.

hu·mer·us [hyōō'mər·əs] *n.,* *pl.* **hu·mer·i**
[hyōō'mər·ī] or **hu·mer·us·es 1** The long
bone in the upper part of the arm, extending
from the shoulder to the elbow. **2** The part of
the arm containing this bone.

hu·mid [(h)yōō'mid] *adj.* Containing water
vapor; damp; moist: *humid* air.

hu·mid·i·fy [(h)yōō·mid'ə·fī] *v.* **hu·mid·i·fied,**
hu·mid·i·fy·ing To make (the air) moist or
humid. — **hu·mid'i·fi·er** *n.*

hu·mid·i·ty [(h)yōō·mid'ə·tē] *n.* Moisture;
dampness, especially of the air.

hu·mil·i·ate [(h)yōō·mil'ē·āt] *v.* **hu·mil·i·at·ed,**
hu·mil·i·at·ing To strip of pride or self-respect;
humble; embarrass: Winning no votes at all
humiliated him. — **hu·mil'i·a'tion** *n.*

hu·mil·i·ty [(h)yōō·mil'ə·tē] *n.* The condition
or quality of being humble.

hum·ming·bird [hum'ing·bûrd'] *n.* A tiny,
brightly colored bird
with a long bill. It
moves its wings so
rapidly that they
hum.

hum·mock [hum'ək]
1 A low mound. **2** A
ridge or mound in an
ice field.

Hummingbird,
about 4 in. long

hu·mor [(h)yōō'mər]
1 *n.* The quality of
being funny or amusing: His conversation is
full of *humor.* **2** *n.* Speech, writing, or actions
that are amusing. **3** *n.* The ability to see or bring

add, āce, câre, pälm;   end, ēqual;   it, īce;   odd, ōpen, ôrder;   tŏŏk, pōŏl;   up, bûrn;
ə = a in *above,* e in *sicken,* i in *possible,* o in *melon,* u in *circus;*   **yōō** = u in *fuse;*   oil;   pout;
check; ring; thin; this; zh in *vision.*   For ¶ reference, see page 64 · HOW TO

out the funny side of things: a sense of *humor*.
4 *n.* A state of mind; mood: to be in a good *humor*. **5** *n.* A whim; caprice. **6** *v.* To give in to the whims or caprices of; indulge: A nurse often *humors* her patients. **— out of humor** Temporarily cross or ill-tempered. ¶1

hu·mor·ist [(h)yoo'mər·ist] *n.* A person who tells or writes funny stories, anecdotes, etc.

hu·mor·ous [(h)yoo'mər·əs] *adj.* Full of or using humor; funny; amusing: a *humorous* situation. **— hu'mor·ous·ly** *adv.*

hump [hump] **1** *n.* A rounded lump, especially on the back, as of a buffalo or camel. **2** *n.* A low mound of earth; hummock. **3** *v.* To raise or rise into a hump: Cats *hump* their backs when frightened.

hump·backed [hump'bakt'] *adj.* Hunchbacked.

humph [humf] *interj.* An exclamation of doubt, annoyance, contempt, etc.

Hum·phrey [hum'frē], **Hubert H.,** born 1911, vice-president of the U.S., 1965–1969.

hu·mus [(h)yoo'məs] *n.* Rich, dark soil containing decayed plant and animal matter.

Hun [hun] *n.* A member of a warlike Asian tribe that invaded Europe in the fourth and fifth centuries.

hunch [hunch] **1** *n.* A hump. **2** *v.* To bend or draw, as into a hump: to *hunch* one's shoulders. **3** *v.* To move or thrust oneself forward jerkily. **4** *n. informal* A vague feeling or notion: He had a *hunch* that he had not done well in his test.

hunch·back [hunch'bak'] *n.* **1** A deformed back with a hump at or just below the shoulders. **2** A person with such a back.

hunch·backed [hunch'bakt'] *adj.* Having a hunchback.

hun·dred or **100** [hun'drid] *n., adj.* Ten more than ninety.

hun·dred·fold [hun'drid·fōld'] **1** *adj.* Being a hundred times as much or as many. **2** *n.* A hundred times as much or as many. **3** *adv.* By a hundred times.

hun·dredth [hun'dridth] **1** *n.* One of a hundred equal parts. **2** *adj.* Being one of a hundred equal parts. **3** *adj.* Next after 99 others; coming after the 99th. **4** *n.* The hundredth person or thing.

hun·dred·weight [hun'drid·wāt'] *n., pl.* **hun·dred·weight** or **hun·dred·weights** A weight of 100 pounds in the U.S., or 112 pound in England.

hung [hung] A past tense and past participle of HANG: We *hung* the painting on the wall.

Hun·gar·i·an [hung·gâr'ē·ən] **1** *adj.* Of or from Hungary. **2** *n.* A person born in or a citizen of Hungary. **3** *n.* The language of Hungary.

Hun·ga·ry [hung'gə·rē] *n.* A country in central Europe.

hun·ger [hung'gər] **1** *n.* The discomfort or weakness caused by eating too little or nothing. **2** *n.* A desire or need for food. **3** *n.* Any strong desire or craving: a *hunger* for wealth. **4** *v.* To have or experience a hunger.

hun·gry [hung'grē] *adj.* **hun·gri·er, hun·gri·est 1** Wanting or needing food. **2** Having or showing a desire or need: He has always been *hungry* for fame. **— hun'gri·ly** *adv.* **— hun'gri·ness** *n.*

hunk [hungk] *n. informal* A large piece or lump; chunk: a *hunk* of meat.

hunt [hunt] **1** *v.* To try to find and kill (deer, wild duck, etc.). **2** *v.* To chase and try to catch (a fox, coon, etc.) with dogs and often horses. **3** *n.* A group of huntsmen. **4** *v.* To try to track and catch (a criminal, spy, etc.). **5** *v.* To look carefully; make a search: to *hunt* for one's glasses. **6** *n.* The act of hunting.

hunt·er [hun'tər] *n.* A person or animal that hunts or takes part in a hunt.

hunt·ress [hun'tris] *n.* A female hunter.

hunts·man [hunts'mən] *n., pl.* **hunts·men** [hunts'mən] A man who hunts or directs a hunt.

hur·dle [hûr'dəl] *n., v.* **hur·dled, hur·dling 1** *n.* A small frame or fence to be jumped over in a race. **2** *n.* (*pl.*) A race in which hurdles are used. **3** *v.* To leap over: to *hurdle* a gate. **4** *n.* A movable fence woven from branches. **5** *v.* To fence in with hurdles. **6** *n.* A difficulty or obstacle to be overcome. **7** *v.* To overcome (a difficulty or obstacle). **— hur'dler** *n.*

Runner going over a hurdle

hur·dy-gur·dy [hûr'dē·gûr'dē] *n., pl.* **hur·dy-gur·dies** Another name for a HAND ORGAN.

hurl [hûrl] *v.* **1** To throw (an object) with force. **2** To say with force: to *hurl* abuse. **— hurl'er** *n.*

hur·ly-bur·ly [hûr'lē·bûr'lē] *n.* Uproar; commotion.

Hu·ron [hyoor'ən], **Lake** The second largest of the Great Lakes, between Michigan and Canada.

hur·rah [hə·rä'] **1** *n., interj.* A cry of joy or applause. **2** *v.* To applaud by shouts; cheer.

hur·ray [hoo·rā'] *n., interj., v.* Hurrah.

hur·ri·cane [hûr'ə·kān] *n.* A storm with heavy rains and whirling winds of 75 miles per hour or more, usually beginning in the tropics, often the West Indies. ◆ *Hurricane* comes from a Spanish word taken from an Indian language in the West Indies.

hur·ried [hûr'ēd] *adj.* Made, done, or acting in haste: a *hurried* departure. **— hur'ried·ly** *adv.*

hur·ry [hûr'ē] *v.* **hur·ried, hur·ry·ing,** *n.* **1** *v.* To act or move unusually quickly in order to save time. **2** *n.* The act of hurrying; haste. **3** *v.* To cause to act or move too hastily: If you *hurry* me, I'll make mistakes. **4** *v.* To cause to move or act quickly or more quickly: *Hurry* him to a doctor. **5** *v.* To cause to occur or be done sooner: Please *hurry* lunch. **6** *n.* Need or desire for haste: He's in a *hurry* to get home.

hurt [hûrt] *v.* **hurt, hurt·ing,** *n.* **1** *v.* To cause pain, injury, or damage to: The fall *hurt* his back. **2** *v.* To be painful or uncomfortable: My neck *hurts*. **3** *n.* Pain, injury, or damage. **4** *v.* To cause grief or mental suffering to: Being called bad names *hurt* her.

hurt·ful [hûrt′fəl] *adj.* Causing or tending to cause hurt; harmful; injurious.

hur·tle [hûr′təl] *v.* **hur·tled, hur·tling** To move or cause to move with great speed or force.

hus·band [huz′bənd] **1** *n.* The man in a married couple; married man. **2** *v.* To manage wisely; save part of: to *husband* one's energies.

hus·band·man [huz′bənd·mən] *n.,* *pl.* **hus·band·men** [huz′bənd·mən] A farmer: seldom used today.

hus·band·ry [huz′bən·drē] *n.* **1** The business of farming. **2** Careful, efficient management.

hush [hush] **1** *v.* To make or become quiet or silent: to *hush* a noisy dog; At dusk the birds *hushed*. **2** *n.* Stillness; quiet: in the *hush* of the night. **3** *v.* To keep hidden: to *hush* up a scandal.

husk [husk] **1** *n.* The dry outer covering of various seeds or fruits. **2** *v.* To strip the husk from: to *husk* corn. **3** *n.* Any outer covering, especially when worthless.

husk·y [hus′kē] *adj.* **husk·i·er, husk·i·est,** *n.,* *pl.* **husk·ies 1** *adj.* Full of, like, or made of husks. **2** *adj.* Rough and somewhat hoarse in sound, as a voice. **3** *adj. informal* Large and strong. **4** *n. informal* A strong or powerfully built person. — **husk′i·ly** *adv.* — **husk′i·ness** *n.*

Husk·y [hus′kē] *n.,* *pl.* **Huskies** (*often written* **husky**) A large, strong dog with thick fur, used by the Eskimos and others to pull sleds.

hus·sar [hoo·sär′] *n.* In some European armies, a cavalryman, often wearing a showy uniform.

hus·sy [huz′ē *or* hus′ē] *n.,* *pl.* **hus·sies 1** An immoral woman. **2** A girl who is too bold or saucy. ◆ *Hussy* is a native English word formed from *housewife*. Only later on did it come to mean a bold or evil woman.

hus·tle [hus′(ə)l] *v.* **hus·tled, hus·tling,** *n.* **1** *v.* To force one's way: to *hustle* through a mob. **2** *v.* To push or carry with force: to *hustle* an intruder out. **3** *v. U.S. informal* To work with drive and energy. **4** *n.* Energy and drive. **5** *n.* Great activity: the *hustle* of a bus station.

hut [hut] *n.* A small, crude house or cabin.

hutch [huch] *n.* **1** A pen or coop for keeping small animals: a rabbit *hutch*. **2** A chest, box, or cupboard used for storage.

Hwang Ho [hwäng′hō′] A river that flows across northern China into the Yellow Sea.

hy·a·cinth [hī′ə·sinth] *n.* A plant related to the lily, having a spikelike cluster of fragrant, bell-shaped flowers.

hy·brid [hī′brid] **1** *n.* The offspring of parents that are of different species or strains. **2** *adj. use:*

hybrid corn. **3** *n.* Something that combines elements from different sources. **4** *adj. use:* a *hybrid* word.

hy·brid·ize [hī′brid·īz] *v.* **hy·brid·ized, hy·brid·iz·ing** To produce or cause to produce hybrids; crossbreed. — **hy′brid·i·za′tion** *n.* ¶3

hy·dra [hī′drə] *n.,* *pl.* **hy·dras** or **hy·drae** [hī′drē] **1** (*usually written* **Hydra**) In Greek myths, a serpent with nine heads. It grew two new heads for each one that was cut off. **2** A tiny, tubelike, fresh-water animal having a ring of tentacles surrounding its mouth.

hy·dran·gea [hī·drān′jə] *n.* A shrub with large clusters of white, blue, or pink flowers.

hy·drant [hī′drənt] *n.* A large upright pipe coming from a water main, from which water may be drawn for fighting fires or washing streets.

Hydra

hy·drate [hī′drāt] *n.,* *v.* **hy·drat·ed, hy·drat·ing 1** *n.* A chemical compound that contains water. **2** *v.* To cause (a chemical compound) to combine with water. — **hy·dra′tion** *n.*

hy·drau·lic [hī·drô′lik] *adj.* **1** Of or having to do with a liquid in motion. **2** Operated by the force of a moving liquid: a *hydraulic* jack. **3** Hardening under water, as a cement.

hydro- A prefix meaning: **1** Of or having to do with water, as in *hydrosphere*, all the water covering or near the earth's surface. **2** Containing hydrogen, as in *hydrocarbon*, a compound containing only hydrogen and carbon.

hy·dro·car·bon [hī′drə·kär′bən] *n.* A chemical compound containing only hydrogen and carbon.

hy·dro·chlo·ric acid [hī′drə·klôr′ik] A strong acid composed of hydrogen and chlorine.

hy·dro·e·lec·tric [hī′drō·i·lek′trik] *adj.* Of or having to do with electricity produced by water power: a *hydroelectric* power plant.

hy·dro·foil [hī′drə·foil] *n.* **1** A device similar to a short airplane wing, attached to a boat below the water line in order to lift the hull out of the water to allow for greater speeds. **2** A boat equipped with hydrofoils.

Hydrofoils

hy·dro·gen [hī′drə·jən] *n.* The lightest of the elements, a colorless, odorless, highly flammable gas, found mainly in combination with oxygen as water.

hy·dro·gen·ate [hī′drə·jə·nāt′ *or* hī·droj′ə·nāt] *v.* **hy·dro·gen·at·ed, hy·dro·gen·at·ing** To combine or treat with hydrogen.

---

add, āce, câre, pälm; end, ēqual; it, īce; odd, ōpen, ôrder; tŏŏk, pŏŏl; up, bûrn; ə = a in *above*, e in *sicken*, i in *possible*, o in *melon*, u in *circus*; yŏŏ = u in *fuse*; oil; pout; check; ring; thin; this; zh in *vision*. For ¶ reference, see page 64 · HOW TO

hydrogen bomb A very powerful bomb that gets its energy from the fusion of atomic nuclei of light weight, often those of lithium, and an isotope of hydrogen.

hy·drol·y·sis [hī·drol′ə·sis] *n.*, *pl.* **hy·drol·y·ses** [hī·drol′ə·sēz] A chemical reaction in which a molecule of water and another molecule break apart and exchange components to form two new molecules.

hy·drom·e·ter [hī·drom′ə·tər] *n.* An instrument for measuring the density of liquids.

hy·dro·pho·bi·a [hī′drə·fō′bē·ə] *n.* Another name for RABIES.

hy·dro·plane [hī′drə·plān′] *n.* **1** A small motorboat whose hull skims over the water when driven at high speeds. **2** A seaplane.

hy·dro·pon·ics [hī′drə·pon′iks] *n.* The growing of plants in solutions of special salts and water rather than in soil. ◆ See -ICS.

hy·dro·sphere [hī′drə·sfir′] *n.* **1** All of the water, both salt and fresh, on the earth. **2** The moisture in the earth's atmosphere.

hy·drox·ide [hī·drok′sīd] *n.* A chemical compound that contains the radical made up of one hydrogen atom and one oxygen atom.

hy·e·na [hī·ē′nə] *n.* A wolflike animal of Africa and Asia that feeds on decaying carcasses.

hy·giene [hī′jēn] *n.* **1** The science of health. **2** Healthful rules or practices.

hy·gi·en·ic [hī′j(ē)en′ik] *adj.* **1** Of or having to do with hygiene. **2** Very clean; sanitary.

Hyena, about 5 ft. long

hy·grom·e·ter [hī·grom′ə·tər] *n.* An instrument for measuring the humidity in the air.

hy·ing [hī′ing] Present participle of HIE.

Hy·men [hī′mən] *n.* In Greek myths, the god of marriage.

hymn [him] *n.* A song of praise, especially to God.

hym·nal [him′nəl] *n.* A book of church hymns.

hyper- A prefix meaning: **1** Overly; too, as in *hypersensitive*, too sensitive. **2** More than normal, as in *hypertension*, blood pressure that is much higher than normal.

hy·per·bo·le [hī·pûr′bə·lē] *n.* An obviously exaggerated statement made for dramatic effect, as in "He's as tough as nails."

hy·per·crit·i·cal [hī′pər·krit′i·kəl] *adj.* Too critical; very difficult to please.

hy·per·ten·sion [hī′pər·ten′shən] *n.* Blood pressure that is much higher than normal.

hy·phen [hī′fən] *n.* A mark (-) used between parts of a compound word, as in "full-blown," or to show that a word has been divided at the end of a line.

hy·phen·ate [hī′fən·āt] *v.* **hy·phen·at·ed hy·phen·at·ing** To write with or connect by a hyphen. — **hy′phen·a′tion** *n.*

hyp·no·sis [hip·nō′sis] *n.* An artificially induced condition like sleep in which a person responds to suggestions or instructions made by the person who has induced the condition.

hyp·not·ic [hip·not′ik] **1** *adj.* Of, causing, or having to do with hypnosis. **2** *n.* A hypnotized or easily hypnotized person. **3** *adj.* Tending to cause sleep. **4** *n.* A drug that puts one to sleep. — **hyp·not′ic·al·ly** *adv.*

hyp·no·tism [hip′nə·tiz′əm] *n.* The act or practice of producing hypnosis. — **hyp′no·tist** *n.*

hyp·no·tize [hip′nə·tīz] *v.* **hyp·no·tized, hyp·no·tiz·ing 1** To produce hypnosis in. **2** To control the feelings and will of; fascinate or charm: His words *hypnotized* me. ¶3

hy·po[1] [hī′pō] *n.* A chemical used as a fixing agent in developing or printing photographs.

hy·po[2] [hī′pō] *n.*, *pl.* **hy·pos** *informal* A hypodermic injection or syringe.

hy·po·chon·dri·ac [hī′pə·kon′drē·ak] *n.* A person who is too concerned with his health and imagines that he has symptoms of various diseases.

hy·poc·ri·sy [hi·pok′rə·sē] *n.*, *pl.* **hy·poc·ri·sies 1** A pretending to have attitudes, good qualities, etc., that one really does not have; insincerity. **2** A hypocritical act.

hyp·o·crite [hip′ə·krit] *n.* A person who pretends to have attitudes, good qualities, etc., that he really does not have; an insincere person.

hyp·o·crit·i·cal [hip′ə·krit′ə·kəl] *adj.* **1** Being a hypocrite. **2** Characteristic of a hypocrite: insincere; deceitful: a *hypocritical* remark.

hy·po·der·mic [hī′pə·dûr′mik] **1** *adj.* Beneath the skin. **2** *n.* An injection of a substance beneath the skin. **3** *n.* A syringe (**hypodermic syringe**) having a sharp, hollow needle for injecting substances beneath the skin.

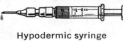
Hypodermic syringe

hy·pot·e·nuse [hī·pot′ə·n(y)ōōs] *n.* In a right triangle, the side opposite the right angle.

hy·poth·e·sis [hī·poth′ə·sis] *n.*, *pl.* **hy·poth·e·ses** [hī·poth′ə·sēz] An idea assumed to be true for the sake of argument or further study.

Hypotenuse

hy·po·thet·i·cal [hī′pə·thet′i·kəl] *adj.* **1** Based on a hypothesis; theoretical: a *hypothetical* question. **2** Based on supposition; imaginary: a *hypothetical* situation. — **hy′po·thet′i·cal·ly** *adv.*

hys·te·ri·a [his·tir′ē·ə *or* his·ter′ē·ə] *n.* **1** Uncontrolled excitement or emotion; frenzy. **2** A mental disease marked by disorders of the body for which no physical causes exist.

hys·ter·i·cal [his·ter′ə·kəl] *adj.* **1** Showing or caused by hysteria: a *hysterical* symptom. **2** Affected with hysteria. — **hys·ter′i·cal·ly** *adv.*

hys·ter·ics [his·ter′iks] *n.pl.* A fit of uncontrolled, wild laughing and crying. ◆ See -ICS.

i or **I** [ī] *n., pl.* **i's** or **I's** [īz] **1** The ninth letter of the English alphabet. **2** The Roman numeral for 1.

I The symbol for the element IODINE.

I [ī] *pron., pl.* **we** A speaker or writer when referring to himself: *I* asked him to help me.

Ia. An unofficial abbreviation of IOWA.

i·am·bic [ī·am′bik] *adj.* Marked by rhythm in which an unaccented syllable is followed by an accented one. The line "Hĭs flēēce / wăs whīte / ăs snōw" has three iambic feet.

-ian Another form of the suffix -AN, as in *amphibian* and *Grecian.*

I·be·ri·a [ī·bir′ē·ə] *n.* The peninsula in sw Europe, occupied by Spain and Portugal. **—I·be′ri·an** *adj., n.*

i·bex [ī′beks] *n., pl.* **i·bex** or **i·bex·es** A wild goat of Europe, Asia, and Africa, with long horns that curve backwards.

i·bis [ī′bis] *n., pl.* **i·bis** or **i·bis·es** A wading bird related to the heron, having a long bill that curves downward. The ancient Egyptians looked on it as sacred.

Ibis, 22 in. long

-ible A suffix meaning: **1** Capable of being or tending to, as in *flexible*, capable of being bent or tending to bend. **2** Worthy of, as in *contempt-ible*, worthy of contempt. **3** Full of, as in *forcible*, full of force. **4** Causing, as in *horrible*, causing horror.

-ic A suffix meaning: **1** Of, like, or having to do with, as in *metallic*, of or like metal. **2** Caused or produced by, as in *allergic*, caused or produced by an allergy. **3** Consisting of or containing, as in *alcoholic*, containing alcohol.

-ical Another form of the suffix -IC. ◆ Some twin adjectives ending in *-ic* and *-ical* differ in meaning, as *economic* and *economical.*

ice [īs] *n., v.* **iced, ic·ing 1** *n.* Frozen water; water in solid form. **2** *v.* To chill by adding ice: to *ice* juice. **3** *v.* To cover or become covered with ice: The windshield *iced* up. **4** *v.* To turn to ice; freeze: The pond *iced* over. **5** *n.* The

Iceberg

frozen surface of a body of water. **6** *n.* A substance resembling ice in form. **7** *n.* A frozen dessert made of fruit juice, sugar, and water. **8** *n.* Frosting. **9** *v.* To spread icing over (a cake, etc.).

Ice Age or **ice age** A period in the earth's development when icecaps and glaciers covered large parts of the surface of the earth.

ice·berg [īs′bûrg′] *n.* A thick mass of ice separated from a glacier and floating in the ocean.

ice·boat [īs′bōt′] *n.* **1** A light framework with skatelike runners and sails for sailing over ice. **2** An icebreaker.

ice·box [īs′boks′] *n.* A cabinet kept cool by putting ice in it, and used for storing food.

ice·break·er [īs′brā′kər] *n.* A boat with a very strong prow and powerful engines, used to open channels through ice for ships.

Icebreaker

ice·cap [īs′kap′] *n.* A field of ice and snow permanently covering an area of land and moving in all directions from the center.

ice cream A frozen mixture of sweetened and flavored cream, milk, or custard.

Ice·land [īs′lənd] *n.* A country, a large island in the North Atlantic. **—Ice′land′er** *n.*

Ice·land·ic [īs·lan′dik] **1** *adj.* Of or from Iceland. **2** *n.* The language of Iceland.

ich·neu·mon [ik·n(y)ōō′mən] *n.* **1** A fly whose larvae feed on other insects' larvae. It is often called an ichneumon fly. **2** A type of mongoose.

i·ci·cle [ī′si·kəl] *n.* A hanging rod of ice formed by the freezing of dripping water.

ic·ing [ī′sing] *n.* A smooth mixture of sugar, egg whites, etc., spread over cakes; frosting.

i·con [ī′kon] *n.* **1** An image; picture. **2** In some churches, a picture treated as sacred, as one of Christ, the Virgin Mary, or a saint.

i·con·o·clast [ī·kon′ə·klast] *n.* **1** A person who opposes the worship of images. **2** A person who attacks popular beliefs or established customs, calling them wrong. **—i·con′o·clas′tic** *adj.*

add, **ā**ce, c**â**re, p**ä**lm;   **e**nd, **ē**qual;   **i**t, **ī**ce;   **o**dd, **ō**pen, **ô**rder;   t**ŏŏ**k, p**ōō**l;   **u**p, b**û**rn;

ə = a in *above,* e in *sicken,* i in *possible,* o in *melon,* u in *circus;*   y**ōō** = u in *fuse;*   **oi**l;   p**ou**t;

check; **r**i**ng**; **th**in; **th**is; **zh** in *vision.*   For ¶ reference, see page 64 · HOW TO

◆ **Iconoclast** comes from two Greek words meaning *breaker of images*.

-ics A suffix meaning: **1** An art, science, or field of study, as in *mathematics*. **2** Methods, systems, or activities, as in *acrobatics, athletics*. ◆ Nouns ending in *-ics* that refer to arts, sciences, or fields of activity were originally plural, meaning things relating to a field. Later they came to mean all such things relating to a field, taken as a single collection, and they became singular: *Politics* is exciting; *Physics* is his favorite subject. Such words seldom take *a, an,* or *the*. Nouns in *-ics* that refer to specific details, qualities, or methods within a field are plural and often take articles: The *acoustics* in this hall are bad; These *statistics* are from the last census.

i·cy [ī′sē] *adj.* **i·ci·er, i·ci·est 1** Covered with or having a lot of ice: *icy* steps. **2** Like ice; cold as ice: *icy* hands; an *icy* greeting. —**i·ci·ly** [ī′sə·lē] *adv.* —**i′ci·ness** *n.*

I'd [īd] **1** I would. **2** I should. **3** I had.

Ida. An unofficial abbreviation of IDAHO.

I·da·ho [ī′də·hō] *n.* A state in the NW U.S.

i·de·a [ī·dē′ə] *n.* **1** A way of seeing, understanding, or solving things that is formed in or grasped by the mind; a thought. **2** An impression or notion: I have no *idea* where he is. **3** An opinion or belief: What are your *ideas* on the subject? **4** An intention, plan, or purpose: He has the *idea* of becoming a writer. ◆ *Idea* comes from a Greek word meaning *to see*.

i·de·al [ī·dē′əl *or* ī·dēl′] **1** *n.* A standard, principle, or goal of perfection: to live up to high *ideals*. **2** *n.* A perfect model or example. **3** *adj.* Perfect or excellent: an *ideal* pupil; an *ideal* location. **4** *adj.* Existing only in the mind as a concept: an *ideal* government.

i·de·al·ism [ī·dē′əl·iz′əm] *n.* **1** The tendency to see things as one would like to have them rather than as they are. **2** The following of ideals of conduct which one has set up. **3** Any system of philosophy which teaches that things do not exist except as ideas in the mind.

i·de·al·ist [ī·dē′əl·ist] *n.* **1** A person who has high ideals of conduct and tries to live according to them. **2** An impractical dreamer. **3** In philosophy, a believer in idealism. —**i′de·al·is′tic** *adj.*

i·de·al·ize [ī·dē′əl·īz] *v.* **i·de·al·ized, i·de·al·iz·ing** To regard or represent as perfect: She tends to *idealize* the past. ¶3

i·den·ti·cal [ī·den′ti·kəl] *adj.* **1** The very same: the *identical* spot where it happened. **2** Exactly alike: *identical* dresses. **3** Describing twins of the same sex that develop from a single fertilized egg cell. —**i·den′ti·cal·ly** *adv.*

i·den·ti·fi·ca·tion [ī·den′tə·fə·kā′shən] *n.* **1** The action of identifying. **2** A being identified. **3** A means of proving identity, as an official card or document telling who one is.

i·den·ti·fy [ī·den′tə·fī] *v.* **i·den·ti·fied, i·den·ti·fy·ing 1** To recognize, claim, or prove to be a certain person or thing: to *identify* a lost dog. **2** To regard as the same: to *identify* change with

progress. **3** To associate closely: People *identify* Edison with the electric light.

i·den·ti·ty [ī·den′tə·tē] *n., pl.* **i·den·ti·ties 1** The fact of being a specific person or thing and no other: His passport established his *identity*. **2** Individuality: to lose one's *identity*. **3** Sameness or oneness: the *identity* of the handwriting in two letters. **4** A mathematical statement of equality that is true for all values of the variables involved, shown by the sign $\equiv$, as, $(a + b)^2 \equiv a^2 + 2ab + b^2$.

i·de·ol·o·gy [ī′dē·ol′ə·jē] *n., pl.* **i·de·ol·o·gies** The ideas or beliefs held by a class or group.

ides [īdz] *n.pl.* In the ancient Roman calendar, the 15th of March, May, July, and October, and the 13th of the other months.

id·i·o·cy [id′ē·ə·sē] *n., pl.* **id·i·o·cies 1** The condition of being or acting like an idiot. **2** Extreme stupidity or foolishness.

id·i·om [id′ē·əm] *n.* **1** An expression having a special meaning different from the usual meanings of the words. "To put up with" is an idiom meaning "to tolerate or endure." **2** The language or dialect of a region, profession, or social class: Scottish *idiom*; legal *idiom*.

id·i·o·mat·ic [id′ē·ə·mat′ik] *adj.* **1** Using or containing an idiom or idioms. **2** Showing a language's characteristic way of putting things: *idiomatic* French. —**id′i·o·mat′i·cal·ly** *adv.*

id·i·o·syn·cra·sy [id′ē·ō·sing′krə·sē] *n., pl.* **id·i·o·syn·cra·sies** A way of thinking, behaving, etc., peculiar to an individual; quirk: Refusing to wait in lines was one of his *idiosyncrasies*.

id·i·ot [id′ē·ət] *n.* **1** A person so feeble-minded that he cannot learn or understand and needs constant care. **2** A very foolish person.

id·i·ot·ic [id′ē·ot′ik] *adj.* Very foolish.

i·dle [īd′(ə)l] *adj.* **i·dler** [īd′lər], **i·dlest** [īd′list], *v.* **i·dled, i·dling 1** *adj.* Not busy: *idle* hands; *idle* moments. **2** *adj.* Unwilling to work; lazy. **3** *adj.* Not operating: *idle* machines. **4** *v.* To waste (time) doing nothing: to *idle* away a morning. **5** *v.* To operate without transmitting power: to let the motor *idle* in a car. **6** *adj.* Of no worth or importance; useless; meaningless: *idle* chatter; *idle* threats. —**i′dle·ness** *n.* —**i·dly** [īd′lē] *adv.*

i·dler [īd′lər] *n.* A lazy person; loafer.

i·dol [ī′d(ə)l] *n.* **1** An image of a god which is worshiped as sacred. **2** A person or thing greatly loved or admired: a sports *idol*.

i·dol·a·trous [ī·dol′ə·trəs] *adj.* **1** Having to do with or practicing idolatry. **2** Blindly devoted.

i·dol·a·try [ī·dol′ə·trē] *n., pl.* **i·dol·a·tries 1** The worship of idols. **2** Extreme admiration or love for a person or thing. —**i·dol′a·ter** *n.*

i·dol·ize [īd′(ə)l·īz] *v.* **i·dol·ized, i·dol·iz·ing 1** To love or admire blindly or too much. **2** To worship as an idol. ¶3

Idol

i·dyl or **i·dyll** [īd′(ə)l] *n.* **1** A short work in poetry or prose describing simple, peaceful scenes of country life. **2** Any scene or event whose simple charm might inspire an idyl.

i·dyl·lic [ī·dil′ik] *adj.* Full of simple charm and contentment: an *idyllic* cruise to Brazil.

i.e. An abbreviation of *id est*, a Latin phrase meaning *that is*: He is the Queen's consort, *i.e.*, her husband.

if [if] *conj.* **1** In the event that; in case that: *If you come home early, call me.* **2** Even though; although: an enjoyable *if* rather tiring day. **3** Whether: See *if* I have any mail. **—if only** I wish that: *If only* I were rich!

ig·loo [ig′lōō] *n., pl.* **ig·loos** A dome-shaped hut built by Eskimos, usually of blocks of hard snow. ◆ *Igloo* comes from an Eskimo word meaning a *house.*

Igloo

ig·ne·ous [ig′nē·əs] *adj.* Formed, as rocks, by great heat within the earth: Granite is an *igneous* rock.

ig·nite [ig·nīt′] *v.* **ig·nit·ed, ig·nit·ing 1** To set on fire; make burn. **2** To catch fire.

ig·ni·tion [ig·nish′ən] *n.* **1** The act of igniting or of being ignited. **2** The electrical system that sets fire to the fuel in a gasoline engine.

ig·no·ble [ig·nō′bəl] *adj.* Dishonorable; shameful: an *ignoble* betrayal. **—ig·no′bly** *adv.*

ig·no·min·i·ous [ig′nə·min′ē·əs] *adj.* Deserving or bringing disgrace; shameful: an *ignominious* defeat. **—ig′no·min′i·ous·ly** *adv.*

ig·no·min·y [ig′nə·min′ē] *n., pl.* **ig·no·min·ies** Public disgrace or dishonor.

ig·no·ra·mus [ig′nə·rā′məs] *n.* An ignorant person.

ig·no·rance [ig′nər·əns] *n.* The condition of being ignorant; lack of knowledge.

ig·no·rant [ig′nər·ənt] *adj.* **1** Having little or no learning or knowledge: an *ignorant* man. **2** Indicating a lack of knowledge: *ignorant* remarks. **3** Not informed; unaware: *ignorant* of what has happened. **—ig′no·rant·ly** *adv.*

ig·nore [ig·nôr′] *v.* **ig·nored, ig·nor·ing** To refuse to notice; pay no attention to: She *ignored* the witch's warning and entered the palace.

Iguana, about 5 ft. long

i·gua·na [i·gwä′nə] *n.* A large, climbing lizard of tropical America, fringed along its spine.

il- Another form of the prefix IN-², meaning *not*, used before words beginning with *l*, as in *illiterate*, not literate.

Il·i·ad [il′ē·əd] *n.* An ancient Greek epic poem written by Homer, describing the siege of Troy by the Greeks.

Il·i·um [il′ē·əm] *n.* Ancient Troy.

ilk [ilk] *n.* Family; kind; sort; class. **—of that ilk** *informal* **1** Of the same name, place, or estate. **2** Of the same kind or sort.

ill [il] *adj.* **worse, worst,** *n.*, *adv.* **1** *adj.* Not in good health; sick. **2** *n.* A sickness: childhood *ills.* **3** *adj.* Bad or harmful: an *ill* omen; an *ill* wind. **4** *n.* Evil, wrong, injury, or harm: Do good in return for *ill.* **5** *adv.* Badly or wrongly: a job *ill* done. **6** *adv.* Unkindly: Don't speak *ill* of the dead. **7** *adj.* Unfriendly; bitter: *ill* feeling. **8** *adv.* With difficulty; hardly: I can *ill* afford the expense. **—ill at ease** Uncomfortable; nervous.

Ill. Abbreviation of ILLINOIS.

I'll [īl] **1** I will. **2** I shall.

ill-ad·vised [il′əd·vīzd′] *adj.* Unwise; rash: His hasty reply was *ill-advised.*

ill-bred [il′bred′] *adj.* Showing a lack of good training in the home; impolite; rude.

il·le·gal [i·lē′gəl] *adj.* Not legal; forbidden by law. **—il·le′gal·ly** *adv.*

il·leg·i·ble [i·lej′ə·bəl] *adj.* Not printed or written clearly enough to be read; hard or impossible to read. **—il·leg′i·bly** *adv.*

il·le·git·i·mate [il′i·jit′ə·mit] *adj.* **1** Born of parents who were not married to each other. **2** Contrary to the law or rules. **—il′le·git′i·mate·ly** *adv.*

ill-fat·ed [il′fā′tid] *adj.* Doomed to end in or to bring disaster or woe: an *ill-fated* voyage.

ill-fa·vored [il′fā′vərd] *adj.* Ugly.

ill-got·ten [il′got′(ə)n] *adj.* Obtained by dishonest or evil means: *ill-gotten* gains.

ill-hu·mored [il′(h)yōō′mərd] *adj.* Irritable.

il·lib·er·al [i·lib′ər·əl] *adj.* **1** Not generous; stingy. **2** Narrow-minded; intolerant.

il·lic·it [i·lis′it] *adj.* Not permitted; unlawful: *illicit* trading. ◆ See ELICIT.

il·lim·it·a·ble [i·lim′it·ə·bəl] *adj.* Having no limits; limitless: an *illimitable* capacity.

Il·li·nois [il′ə·noi′] *n.* A state in the north central U.S.

il·lit·er·a·cy [i·lit′ər·ə·sē] *n.* **1** Inability to read and write. **2** Lack of education.

il·lit·er·ate [i·lit′ər·it] **1** *adj.* Lacking the ability to read and write. **2** *n.* A person who cannot read and write. **3** *adj.* Showing lack of education; ignorant: an *illiterate* writer.

ill-man·nered [il′man′ərd] *adj.* Impolite; rude.

ill-na·tured [il′nā′chərd] *adj.* Cross; grumpy.

ill·ness [il′nis] *n.* **1** Poor health; sickness. **2** An ailment; disease.

---

add, āce, câre, pälm;   end, ēqual;   it, īce;   odd, ōpen, ôrder;   tŏŏk, pōōl;   up, bûrn;
ə = a in *above*, e in *sicken*, i in *possible*, o in *melon*, u in *circus*;   yōō = u in *fuse*;   oil;   pout;
    check; ri**ng**; **th**in; **th**is; zh in *vision*.   For ¶ reference, see page 64 · HOW TO

il·log·i·cal [i·loj′i·kəl] *adj.* Showing a lack of sound reasoning. **—il·log′i·cal·ly** *adv.*

ill-starred [il′stärd′] *adj.* Unlucky.

ill-tem·pered [il′tem′pərd] *adj.* Having a bad temper; ill-natured.

ill-treat [il′trēt′] *v.* To treat cruelly or roughly; abuse. **—ill′-treat′ment** *n.*

il·lu·mi·nate [i·lōō′mə·nāt] *v.* **il·lu·mi·nat·ed, il·lu·mi·nat·ing** **1** To light up: to *illuminate* a room. **2** To make clear; clarify: Her explanation *illuminated* the lesson for us. **3** To decorate, as the first letter or the margin of a page, with designs in gold and colors. **4** *adj. use:* an *illuminated* manuscript.

il·lu·mi·na·tion [i·lōō′mə·nā′shən] *n.* **1** The act of illuminating. **2** An illuminated condition. **3** An amount of light: adequate *illumination* for reading. **4** A public display of lights. **5** Enlightenment. **6** Decoration, as of a manuscript, with designs in gold and colors.

il·lu·mine [i·lōō′min] *v.* **il·lu·mined, il·lu·min·ing** To light up.

ill-us·age [il′yōō′sij] *n.* Bad treatment.

ill-use [il′yōōz′] *v.* **ill-used, ill-us·ing** To treat badly or cruelly; abuse.

il·lu·sion [i·lōō′zhən] *n.* **1** A false, mistaken idea or belief: to lose childish *illusions*. **2** A deceiving appearance or the false impression it gives: an optical *illusion*.

The flickering gray spots at the intersections of the white lines are an illusion.

il·lu·sive [i·lōō′siv] *adj.* Illusory.

il·lu·so·ry [i·lōō′sər·ē] *adj.* Coming from or causing an illusion; not real; deceptive.

il·lus·trate [il′ə·strāt or i·lus′trāt] *v.* **il·lus·trat·ed, il·lus·trat·ing** **1** To explain or make clear by examples, comparisons, etc.: He told a story to *illustrate* his point. **2** To furnish with pictures or drawings that explain or decorate. **3** *adj. use:* an *illustrated* book.

il·lus·tra·tion [il′ə·strā′shən] *n.* **1** A picture used in a book, etc., to explain or decorate. **2** An example or comparison used to explain: He gave the ant as an *illustration* of a social insect. **3** The process of illustrating.

il·lus·tra·tive [i·lus′trə·tiv or il′ə·strā′tiv] *adj.* Serving to illustrate or explain: An *illustrative* phrase shows how a word is used.

il·lus·tra·tor [il′ə·strā′tər] *n.* An artist who makes illustrations, as for books.

il·lus·tri·ous [i·lus′trē·əs] *adj.* Very famous; distinguished: an *illustrious* statesman.

ill will Unfriendly feeling; hostility.

im-¹ A prefix meaning: In, into, or on, as in *import*, to bring into, or *imprint*, to print on.

im-² A form of the prefix IN-², meaning *not*, used before words beginning with *b*, *m*, and *p*, as in *imbalance*, *immoderate*, and *impossible*.

I'm [īm] I am.

im·age [im′ij] *n.* **1** A statue or other likeness of some person or thing: a graven *image*. **2** A picture such as is formed in a mirror or by a lens. **3** A person or thing very much like another: He is the *image* of his father. **4** A mental picture: *images* in daydreams. **5** An expression, as a metaphor or simile, that calls up a picture or other sense impression to the mind. "The curtain of night" is an image.

im·age·ry [im′ij·rē] *n.* Images, especially word pictures or figures of speech in poetry.

im·ag·i·na·ble [i·maj′ə·nə·bəl] *adj.* Capable of being imagined; conceivable.

im·ag·i·nar·y [i·maj′ə·ner′ē] *adj.* Existing only in the imagination; unreal.

im·ag·i·na·tion [i·maj′ə·nā′shən] *n.* **1** The power to picture absent, unknown, or unreal things in the mind: In his *imagination* his hobbyhorse was a great white steed prancing at the head of a parade. **2** The power to see things in new ways, form new ideas, or create new things from thought: the *imagination* of an artist.

im·ag·i·na·tive [i·maj′ə·nə·tiv or i·maj′ə·nā′tiv] *adj.* Full of or showing imagination.

im·ag·ine [i·maj′in] *v.* **im·ag·ined, im·ag·in·ing** **1** To form a mental picture or idea of: Try to *imagine* how the cave men must have lived; *Imagine* the earth revolving around the sun. **2** To suppose; guess: I *imagine* I'll be able to go.

i·ma·go [i·mā′gō] *n., pl.* **i·ma·goes** or **i·mag·i·nes** [i·maj′ə·nēz] An insect in its adult stage.

im·bal·ance [im·bal′əns] *n.* The condition of lacking balance or being out of balance.

im·be·cile [im′bə·səl] *n.* **1** A feeble-minded person not quite so helpless as an idiot. **2** A very foolish or stupid person.

im·be·cil·i·ty [im′bə·sil′ə·tē] *n., pl.* **im·be·cil·i·ties** **1** The condition of being or acting like an imbecile. **2** Utter stupidity or foolishness. **3** A stupid or foolish action.

im·bed [im·bed′] *v.* **im·bed·ded, im·bed·ding** Another spelling of EMBED.

im·bibe [im·bīb′] *v.* **im·bibed, im·bib·ing** **1** To drink, especially liquor. **2** To take in as if drinking; absorb: soil *imbibing* water. **3** To absorb in the mind: to *imbibe* learning.

im·bro·glio [im·brōl′yō] *n., pl.* **im·bro·glios** A confused state of affairs, complicated misunderstanding, or other difficult situation.

im·bue [im·byōō′] *v.* **im·bued, im·bu·ing** **1** To fill, as with emotions or ideals: He was *imbued* with the ideals of democracy. **2** To fill or saturate, as with color or moisture.

im·i·tate [im′ə·tāt] *v.* **im·i·tat·ed, im·i·tat·ing** **1** To try to act or look the same way as: Boys often *imitate* their fathers. **2** To copy or mimic: to *imitate* the call of a bird. **3** To have or take on the appearance of: a plastic material made to *imitate* leather. **—im′i·ta·tor** *n.*

im·i·ta·tion [im′ə·tā′shən] *n.* **1** The act of imitating: *Imitation* is a form of flattery. **2** Something made or done by imitating an original; copy: *The drawing was an* imitation *of a famous painting.* **3** *adj. use:* imitation *gems.*

im·i·ta·tive [im′ə·tā′tiv] *adj.* Copying or imitating. *Buzz and swish are imitative words.*

im·mac·u·late [i·mak′yə·lit] *adj.* **1** Completely clean; spotless: *Her clothes were always immaculate.* **2** Without sin or blemish.

im·ma·te·ri·al [im′ə·tir′ē·əl] *adj.* **1** Of no importance. **2** Not made of material substance.

im·ma·ture [im′ə·chŏŏr′ *or* im′ə·t(y)ŏŏr′] *adj.* Not fully grown, ripened, or developed. **—im′·ma·ture′ly** *adv.* **—im′ma·tur′i·ty** *n.*

im·meas·ur·a·ble [i·mezh′ər·ə·bəl] *adj.* Not capable of being measured; very great. **—im·meas′ur·a·bly** *adv.*

im·me·di·ate [i·mē′dē·it] *adj.* **1** Done or happening without delay; at once. **2** Near, in time or space: *the* immediate *future; my* immediate *neighborhood.* **3** Closest: *your* immediate *family.* **4** Direct: in immediate *contact.*

im·me·di·ate·ly [i·mē′dē·it·lē] *adv.* **1** Without delay; instantly: *Come home* immediately. **2** In close relation; with nothing between: *Immediately beyond our yard is a parking lot.*

im·me·mo·ri·al [im′ə·môr′ē·əl] *adj.* Reaching back beyond everybody's memory; very old. **—im′me·mo′ri·al·ly** *adv.*

im·mense [i·mens′] *adj.* Very large; huge: an immense *ship.* **—im·mense′ly** *adv.*

im·men·si·ty [i·men′sə·tē] *n.* **1** The condition of being immense; hugeness; vastness. **2** Boundless space; infinity.

im·merse [i·mûrs′] *v.* **im·mersed, im·mers·ing** **1** To dip into liquid so as to cover completely. **2** To involve deeply: *to be* immersed *in a book.* **3** To baptize by dipping the entire body under water. **—im·mer·sion** [i·mûr′shən *or* i·mûr′zhən] *n.*

im·mi·grant [im′ə·grənt] *n.* A person who comes into a country or region where he was not born, in order to live there.

im·mi·grate [im′ə·grāt] *v.* **im·mi·grat·ed, im·mi·grat·ing** To come into a country or region where one was not born, in order to live there. **—im′mi·gra′tion** *n.*

im·mi·nent [im′ə·nənt] *adj.* Likely to happen soon; probable: in imminent *danger.* **—im′mi·nence** *n.* **—im′mi·nent·ly** *adv.* ◆ See EMINENT.

im·mo·bile [i·mō′bəl] *adj.* **1** Not movable; fixed tightly. **2** Not moving; motionless.

im·mo·bi·lize [i·mō′bə·līz] *v.* **im·mo·bi·lized, im·mo·bi·liz·ing** To make immobile. ¶3

im·mod·er·ate [i·mod′ər·it] *adj.* More than is reasonable or proper; too much.

im·mod·est [i·mod′ist] *adj.* **1** Not modest; indecent. **2** Not humble; bold. **—im·mod′·est·ly** *adv.*

im·mod·est·y [i·mod′is·tē] *n.* **1** A lack of modesty or decency. **2** A lack of humility.

im·mor·al [i·môr′əl] *adj.* **1** Morally bad; wicked. **2** Indecent; lewd. **—im·mor·al·i·ty** [im′·ə·ral′ə·tē] *n.* **—im·mor′al·ly** *adv.*

im·mor·tal [i·môr′təl] **1** *adj.* Living, lasting, or remembered forever: *Patrick Henry's immortal words;* immortal *gods.* **2** *n.* A person who lives forever. **3** *n.* A person worthy of being remembered forever. **—im·mor′tal·ly** *adv.*

im·mor·tal·i·ty [im′ôr·tal′ə·tē] *n.* Life or fame lasting forever.

im·mor·tal·ize [i·môr′təl·īz] *v.* **im·mor·tal·ized, im·mor·tal·iz·ing** To give eternal life or fame to; make immortal. ¶3

im·mov·a·ble [i·mŏŏ′və·bəl] *adj.* **1** Not movable; fixed tightly. **2** Unchangeable; steadfast. **—im·mov′a·bly** *adv.*

im·mune [i·myōon′] *adj.* **1** Protected against a disease, as by inoculation: immune *to measles.* **2** Not to be affected by; protected from: *immune from doubt;* immune *to corruption.* **—im·mun′i·ty** *n.*

im·mu·nize [im′yə·nīz] *v.* **im·mu·nized, im·mu·niz·ing** To make immune, especially against a disease. **—im′mu·ni·za′tion** *n.* ¶3

im·mure [i·myōor′] *v.* **im·mured, im·mur·ing** To enclose within walls; imprison; confine.

im·mu·ta·ble [i·myōō′tə·bəl] *adj.* That cannot change or be changed: *the* immutable *laws of nature.* **—im·mu′ta·bly** *adv.*

imp [imp] *n.* **1** A young or minor demon; evil spirit. **2** A mischievous child.

im·pact [im′pakt] *n.* A striking together; collision: *Some bombs explode at the moment of* impact.

im·pair [im·pâr′] *v.* To make worse; damage; injure: *Overwork can* impair *the health.* **—im·pair′ment** *n.*

im·pale [im·pāl′] *v.* **im·paled, im·pal·ing** **1** To pierce with or as if with something sharp and pointed. **2** To torture or put to death by thrusting a sharp stake through the body.

im·pal·pa·ble [im·pal′pə·bəl] *adj.* **1** Not capable of being felt by the sense of touch, as a shadow. **2** Not marked enough to be grasped: impalpable *differences.* **—im·pal′pa·bly** *adv.*

im·pan·el [im·pan′əl] *v.* **im·pan·eled** *or* **im·pan·elled, im·pan·el·ing** *or* **im·pan·el·ling** **1** To add to a list, as for jury duty. **2** To select (a jury) from such a list.

im·part [im·pärt′] *v.* **1** To make known; disclose: *to* impart *a secret.* **2** To give a degree or measure of; give: *Flowers* impart *freshness to a room.*

im·par·tial [im·pär′shəl] *adj.* Not favoring one person, side, etc.; unbiased: *a jury's* impartial *verdict.* **—im·par·ti·al·i·ty** [im′pär·shē·al′ə·tē] *n.* **—im·par′tial·ly** *adv.*

im·pass·a·ble [im·pas′ə·bəl] *adj.* That cannot be passed over or traveled through: impassable *jungle.* **—im·pass′a·bly** *adv.*

---

add, āce, câre, pälm; end, ēqual; it, īce; odd, ōpen, ôrder; tŏŏk, pōōl; up, bûrn;
ə = a in *above*, e in *sicken*, i in *possible*, o in *melon*, u in *circus*; yōō = u in *fuse*; oil; pout;
check; ring; thin; this; zh in *vision.* For ¶ reference, see page 64 · HOW TO

im·passe [im′pas *or* im·pas′] *n.* A position or situation from which there is no way out; deadlock.

im·pas·sioned [im·pash′ənd] *adj.* Filled with strong feeling; fervent: an *impassioned* plea.

im·pas·sive [im·pas′iv] *adj.* Not affected by emotion; showing no feeling: He remained *impassive*, but I was sympathetic. **—im·pas′·sive·ly** *adv.*

im·pa·tience [im·pā′shəns] *n.* The quality or condition of being impatient.

im·pa·tient [im·pā′shənt] *adj.* **1** Lacking patience; easily annoyed at delay, discomfort, etc. **2** Caused by or showing a lack of patience: an *impatient* sigh. **3** Very eager: *impatient* for success. **—im·pa′tient·ly** *adv.*

im·peach [im·pēch′] *v.* **1** To challenge or bring discredit upon: to *impeach* a man's honor. **2** To accuse of doing wrong. **3** To formally charge (a public official) with wrongdoing in office: to *impeach* a governor for bribery. **—im·peach′ment** *n.*

im·pec·ca·ble [im·pek′ə·bəl] *adj.* Free from fault or flaw. **—im·pec′ca·bly** *adv.*

im·pe·cu·ni·ous [im′pə·kyōō′nē·əs] *adj.* Having no money; poor; penniless.

im·pede [im·pēd′] *v.* **im·ped·ed, im·ped·ing** To put obstacles in the way of; obstruct: Snowstorms *impeded* the explorers' march.

im·ped·i·ment [im·ped′ə·mənt] *n.* **1** A hindrance; obstacle. **2** A physical defect, especially one that makes normal speech difficult.

im·pel [im·pel′] *v.* **im·pelled, im·pel·ling** **1** To force or drive to an action; urge on: Pride *impelled* him to refuse the gift. **2** To push or drive forward; propel.

im·pend [im·pend′] *v.* **1** To be about to occur: Disaster *impended*, but she did not know it. **2** To be suspended; hang; overhang. **3** *adj. use: impending* cliffs.

im·pen·e·tra·ble [im·pen′ə·trə·bəl] *adj.* **1** Not capable of being pierced, seen through, entered, etc.: an *impenetrable* jungle. **2** Not capable of being understood: an *impenetrable* mystery.

im·pen·i·tent [im·pen′ə·tənt] *adj.* Not sorry, as for doing wrong; not penitent. **—im·pen′i·tence** *n.* **—im·pen′i·tent·ly** *adv.*

im·per·a·tive [im·per′ə·tiv] **1** *adj.* Urgently necessary; unavoidable: Speed is *imperative*. **2** *n.* Something that is imperative, as a command. **3** *adj.* In grammar, expressing a command. In "Go at once!" *go* is in the imperative mood. **4** *n.* In grammar, the form of a verb which expresses command.

im·per·cep·ti·ble [im·pər·sep′tə·bəl] *adj.* Too small or slight to be noticed: an *imperceptible* movement. **—im′per·cep′ti·bly** *adv.*

im·per·fect [im·pûr′fikt] *adj.* **1** Having a fault or faults; not perfect. **2** Incomplete or inadequate: an *imperfect* grasp of a situation. **3** In grammar, designating a tense that indicates a state or action, usually past, as continuing or uncompleted, as *was speaking* in "He was speaking when I came in." **—im·per′fect·ly** *adv.*

im·per·fec·tion [im′pər·fek′shən] *n.* **1** An imperfect condition. **2** A defect; flaw.

im·pe·ri·al [im·pir′ē·əl] **1** *adj.* Of or having to do with an empire, an emperor, or an empress. **2** *adj.* Superior, as in size or quality; magnificent. **3** *n.* A small pointed beard just under the lower lip. **—im·pe′ri·al·ly** *adv.*

im·pe·ri·al·ism [im·pir′ē·əl·iz′əm] *n.* **1** The policy of increasing the power or dominion of a nation by conquering other nations, exerting influence in political and economic areas, etc. **2** An imperial form of government. **—im·pe′·ri·al·ist** *n., adj.* **—im·pe′ri·al·is′tic** *adj.*

im·per·il [im·per′il] *v.* **im·per·iled** or **im·per·illed, im·per·il·ing** or **im·per·il·ling** To place in peril; put in danger.

im·pe·ri·ous [im·pir′ē·əs] *adj.* **1** Proud and haughty; domineering; arrogant. **2** Urgent; imperative. **—im·pe′ri·ous·ly** *adv.*

im·per·ish·a·ble [im·per′ish·ə·bəl] *adj.* Not liable to decay, perish, or pass away.

im·per·me·a·ble [im·pûr′mē·ə·bəl] *adj.* **1** Not allowing anything to pass through or into. **2** Impervious to liquids or moisture.

im·per·son·al [im·pûr′sən·əl] *adj.* **1** Not being a person: the *impersonal* forces of nature. **2** Without reference to a particular person or persons: an *impersonal* observation. **3** In grammar, designating a verb having no specific subject. In "It will rain," the verb *rain* is an impersonal verb. **—im·per′son·al·ly** *adv.*

im·per·son·ate [im·pûr′sən·āt] *v.* **im·per·son·at·ed, im·per·son·at·ing** **1** To play the part of: She *impersonates* Cleopatra. **2** To adopt or mimic the appearance or mannerisms of: He wore a uniform and badge to *impersonate* a policeman. **—im·per′son·a′tion** *n.*

im·per·son·a·tor [im·pûr′sən·ā′tər] *n.* **1** A person who pretends to be someone else. **2** An entertainer who imitates famous people.

im·per·ti·nence [im·pûr′tə·nəns] *n.* Deliberate disrespect; insolence; impudence.

im·per·ti·nent [im·pûr′tə·nənt] *adj.* Deliberately disrespectful; insolent; impudent: The *impertinent* fellow held out his hand for a tip.

im·per·turb·a·ble [im′pər·tûr′bə·bəl] *adj.* Almost never upset or excited; calm.

im·per·vi·ous [im·pûr′vē·əs] *adj.* **1** Permitting no passage through or into: a hat *impervious* to rain. **2** Unreceptive or indifferent: to be *impervious* to reason. **—im·per′vi·ous·ness** *n.*

im·pe·ti·go [im′pə·tī′gō] *n.* A contagious skin disease marked by pimples filled with pus.

im·pet·u·os·i·ty [im·pech′ōō·os′ə·tē] *n., pl.* **im·pet·u·os·i·ties** **1** The quality of being impetuous. **2** An impetuous act.

im·pet·u·ous [im·pech′ōō·əs] *adj.* **1** Acting on impulse and without thought; hasty; rash. **2** Moving with violent force: an *impetuous* storm. **—im·pet′u·ous·ly** *adv.*

im·pe·tus [im′pə·təs] *n.* **1** The force with which an object moves; momentum. **2** Any force that leads to action: Good grades can serve as an *impetus* to learning.

im·pi·e·ty [im·pī′ə·tē] *n.*, *pl.* **im·pi·e·ties** 1 Lack of respect, especially for God or sacred things. 2 An impious act.

im·pinge [im·pinj′] *v.* **im·pinged, im·ping·ing** 1 To strike or collide: a beam of light *impinging* on the retina of the eye. 2 To intrude upon; encroach; infringe: to *impinge* on a teacher's authority.

im·pi·ous [im′pē·əs] *adj.* Lacking respect or reverence, as for God. —**im′pi·ous·ly** *adv.*

imp·ish [imp′ish] *adj.* Like an imp; full of mischief: an *impish* grin. —**imp′ish·ly** *adv.* —**imp′ish·ness** *n.*

im·pla·ca·ble [im·plā′kə·bəl *or* im·plak′ə·bəl] *adj.* Not capable of being pacified or soothed: *implacable* foes. —**im·pla′ca·bly** *adv.*

im·plant [im·plant′] *v.* 1 To plant firmly, as seeds in the ground; embed. 2 To fix in the mind: to *implant* new ideas. 3 To insert (living tissue), as in skin grafting.

im·plau·si·ble [im·plô′zə·bəl] *adj.* Not plausible; hard to believe: an *implausible* excuse.

im·ple·ment [*n.* im′plə·mənt, *v.* im′plə·ment] 1 *n.* A thing used in work; utensil; tool. 2 *v.* To furnish with implements. 3 *v.* To put into effect; carry out; fulfill: to *implement* a tax reform law.

im·pli·cate [im′plə·kāt] *v.* **im·pli·cat·ed, im·pli·cat·ing** To show to be involved or connected, as in a plot or a crime: He was *implicated* in the robbery by two eyewitnesses.

im·pli·ca·tion [im′plə·kā′shən] *n.* 1 The act of implicating. 2 The condition of being implicated. 3 The act of implying or suggesting. 4 Something that is implied: The *implication* was that she was late on purpose.

im·plic·it [im·plis′it] *adj.* 1 Absolute; complete: *implicit* confidence. 2 Implied, although not expressed: an *implicit* agreement. —**im·plic′it·ly** *adv.*

im·plore [im·plôr′] *v.* **im·plored, im·plor·ing** 1 To beg; entreat; beseech: He *implored* his captors to free him. 2 To beg for urgently: I *implore* your mercy.

im·ply [im·plī′] *v.* **im·plied, im·ply·ing** To hint at or suggest without actually stating: His silence *implied* approval. ◆ See INFER.

im·po·lite [im′pə·līt′] *adj.* Not polite; discourteous; rude. —**im′po·lite′ly** *adv.* —**im′·po·lite′ness** *n.*

im·pol·i·tic [im·pol′ə·tik] *adj.* Not wise, prudent, or expedient: It is *impolitic* to offend one's employer.

im·port [*v.* im·pôrt′, *n.* im′pôrt] 1 *v.* To bring into a country from abroad: The U.S. *imports* silk from Japan. 2 *n.* Something brought in from another country. 3 *n.* A bringing in from abroad; importation. 4 *v.* To have as its meaning: What did his remark *import*? 5 *n.* Meaning; significance. 6 *n.* Importance: a matter of no *import*.

im·por·tance [im·pôr′təns] *n.* A being important; significance; consequence.

im·por·tant [im·pôr′tənt] *adj.* 1 Having much significance, value, or influence: an *important* occasion. 2 Deserving special attention or notice: an *important* project. 3 Having power, authority, prestige, high social rank, etc.: an *important* executive. 4 Giving the impression of importance; pretentious; pompous.

im·por·ta·tion [im′pôr·tā′shən] *n.* 1 The act of importing goods. 2 The goods imported.

im·port·er [im·pôr′tər] *n.* A person or company in the business of importing merchandise.

im·por·tu·nate [im·pôr′chə·nit] *adj.* 1 Asking or demanding again and again: an *importunate* beggar. 2 Made again and again, as a request.

im·por·tune [im′pôr·t(y)ōōn′ *or* im·pôr′chən] *v.* **im·por·tuned, im·por·tun·ing** To request or urge again and again.

im·por·tu·ni·ty [im′pôr·t(y)ōō′nə·tē] *n.*, *pl.* **im·por·tu·ni·ties** An urging or requesting over and over again.

im·pose [im·pōz′] *v.* **im·posed, im·pos·ing** 1 To levy or exact: to *impose* taxes. 2 To inflict or enforce by influence or force: to *impose* one's wishes on others. 3 To take advantage; make unfair use: to *impose* on a friend by asking for too big a loan. 4 To palm off as genuine.

im·pos·ing [im·pō′zing] *adj.* Impressive in appearance, manner, size, etc.

im·po·si·tion [im′pə·zish′ən] *n.* 1 A taking advantage of someone, as by asking for too great a favor. 2 The act of imposing or imposing on. 3 Something imposed, as a tax, punishment, etc.

im·pos·si·bil·i·ty [im·pos′ə·bil′ə·tē] *n.*, *pl.* **im·pos·si·bil·i·ties** 1 The condition of being impossible. 2 Something impossible.

im·pos·si·ble [im·pos′ə·bəl] *adj.* 1 Not capable of being, being done, or taking place; not possible: It is *impossible* to be in two places at the same time. 2 Not to be endured; intolerable: an *impossible* situation. —**im·pos′si·bly** *adv.*

im·post [im′pōst] *n.* A tax, especially a tax on things imported into a country.

im·pos·tor [im·pos′tər] *n.* A person who deceives, especially one who pretends to be someone else.

im·pos·ture [im·pos′chər] *n.* Deception, especially the act of pretending to be someone else.

im·po·tent [im′pə·tənt] *adj.* Lacking power or strength; helpless; weak. —**im′po·tence** *n.*

im·pound [im·pound′] *v.* 1 To shut up in a pound, as a stray dog. 2 To seize and place in the custody of a court: to *impound* a company's files pending an investigation.

im·pov·er·ish [im·pov′ər·ish] *v.* 1 To make poor: Business losses *impoverished* me. 2 To take away the richness or strength of; make infertile, as the soil. —**im·pov′er·ish·ment** *n.*

---

add, āce, câre, pälm; end, ēqual; it, īce; odd, ōpen, ôrder; tŏŏk, pōōl; up, bûrn; ə = a in *above*, e in *sicken*, i in *possible*, o in *melon*, u in *circus*; yōō = u in *fuse*; oil; pout; check; ring; thin; this; zh in *vision*. For ¶ reference, see page 64 · HOW TO

im·prac·ti·ca·ble [im·prak′ti·kə·bəl] *adj.* **1** Not capable of being carried out: *impracticable* schemes. **2** Not suitable for use. **—im·prac′·ti·ca·bil′i·ty** *n.*

im·prac·ti·cal [im·prak′ti·kəl] *adj.* Not practical; not useful or sensible.

im·pre·ca·tion [im′prə·kā′shən] *n.* **1** The act of cursing. **2** A curse.

im·preg·na·ble [im·preg′nə·bəl] *adj.* Not capable of being conquered or overcome; unassailable: an *impregnable* defense.

im·preg·nate [im·preg′nāt] *v.* **im·preg·nat·ed, im·preg·nat·ing 1** To make pregnant or fertile. **2** To saturate or fill: Pickles are *impregnated* with brine. **—im′preg·na′tion** *n.*

im·pre·sa·ri·o [im′prə·sä′rē·ō] *n., pl.* **im·pre·sa·ri·os** A person who manages a performer or performance, especially one who directs an opera or ballet company.

im·press¹ [*v.* im·pres′, *n.* im′pres] **1** *v.* To affect the mind or feelings of: His sincerity *impressed* me. **2** *n.* An effect on the mind or feelings; impression. **3** *v.* To fix firmly in the mind, as ideas, beliefs, etc.: to *impress* a fact on one's memory. **4** *v.* To make (a mark) by pressure; stamp: to *impress* the title in gold on the spine of a book. **5** *n.* A mark made by pressing or stamping. **6** *n.* Distinctive character or mark: Frost's *impress* shows in every line of his poetry.

im·press² [im·pres′] *v.* **1** To compel to enter public service: to *impress* men into the navy. **2** To seize (property) for public use.

im·pres·sion [im·presh′ən] *n.* **1** An effect on the mind, senses, or feelings. **2** A feeling, notion, or idea: I got the *impression* that he is very shy. **3** Any mark made by pressing: the *impression* of a hand. **4** The act of impressing.

im·pres·sion·a·ble [im·presh′ən·ə·bəl] *adj.* Quickly and easily influenced; sensitive: an *impressionable* young girl.

im·pres·sion·ism [im·presh′ən·iz′əm] *n.* **1** A style of painting popular in the late 19th century. A visual impression of the subject was represented instead of photographic details. **2** A musical style of the same period in which the effect of the music on the senses was considered more important than formal structure. **—im·pres′sion·ist** *n.* **—im·pres′sion·is′tic** *adj.*

im·pres·sive [im·pres′iv] *adj.* Producing a strong impression of admiration or awe: an *impressive* man; an *impressive* accomplishment. **—im·pres′sive·ly** *adv.*

im·print [*v.* im·print′, *n.* im′print] **1** *v.* To make (a mark, figure, etc.) by pressure. **2** *n.* A mark made by printing, stamping, or pressing: the *imprint* of a boot in the snow. **3** *v.* To fix firmly or impress, as in the mind: The final scene in the play is *imprinted* in my memory. **4** *n.* An effect or influence: the *imprint* of suffering. **5** *n.* A publisher's or printer's name, place of business, etc., on the title leaf of a book.

im·pris·on [im·priz′(ə)n] *v.* **1** To put into prison. **2** To shut in closely; confine. **—im·pris′on·ment** *n.*

im·prob·a·ble [im·prob′ə·bəl] *adj.* Not probable; not likely to be true or to happen. **—im′·prob·a·bil′i·ty** *n.* **—im·prob′a·bly** *adv.*

im·promp·tu [im·promp′t(y)ōō] **1** *adj.* Not prepared in advance; offhand: *impromptu* remarks. **2** *adv.* Without preparation: to speak *impromptu.* **3** *n.* Anything produced on the impulse of the moment.

im·prop·er [im·prop′ər] *adj.* **1** Not proper; unsuitable: It is *improper* to shout on a bus. **2** Indecent; unseemly. **3** Incorrect: an *improper* address. **—im·prop′er·ly** *adv.*

improper fraction A fraction in which the numerator is larger than or equal to the denominator, as $\frac{4}{3}$ or $\frac{5}{5}$.

im·pro·pri·e·ty [im′prə·prī′ə·tē] *n., pl.* **im·pro·pri·e·ties 1** The quality of being improper. **2** Something improper, as an exhibition of bad taste. **3** An error in speech or writing.

im·prove [im·prōōv′] *v.* **im·proved, im·prov·ing 1** To make or become better, as in condition, quality, value, etc. **2** To use to good purpose: to *improve* one's leisure time.

im·prove·ment [im·prōōv′mənt] *n.* **1** The act of making better. **2** A becoming better. **3** Something that increases value or efficiency. **4** A person or thing superior to another: His new hat is an *improvement* over the old one.

im·prov·i·dent [im·prov′ə·dənt] *adj.* Not planning for the future; lacking foresight or thrift. **—im·prov′i·dence** *n.*

im·pro·vi·sa·tion [im′prə·vi·zā′shən] *n.* **1** The act of improvising. **2** Something improvised.

im·pro·vise [im′prə·vīz] *v.* **im·pro·vised, im·pro·vis·ing 1** To make up (music, verse, etc.) at the time of performance and without preparation. **2** To make offhand from whatever material is available: to *improvise* a shelter from old boards.

An improvised bench

im·pru·dent [im·prōōd′(ə)nt] *adj.* Not prudent; lacking foresight; unwise. **—im·pru′dence** *n.* **—im·pru′dent·ly** *adv.*

im·pu·dence [im′pyə·dəns] *n.* Offensive boldness; lack of shame; rudeness.

im·pu·dent [im′pyə·dənt] *adj.* Offensively bold; rude; insolent. **—im′pu·dent·ly** *adv.*

im·pugn [im·pyōōn′] *v.* To attack with criticism; call into question: Do you *impugn* his honesty?

im·pulse [im′puls] *n.* **1** A sudden desire or feeling which makes one want to act: an *impulse* of pity. **2** A driving force; push; thrust: the *impulse* of a strong wind. **3** The transference of a stimulus through a nerve fiber. **4** In radio and electricity, a pulse.

im·pul·sive [im·pul′siv] *adj.* **1** Acting suddenly and without careful thought: The *impulsive* girl bought six new hats. **2** Prompted by impulse: an *impulsive* act. **3** Driving; pushing. —**im·pul′sive·ly** *adv.* —**im·pul′sive·ness** *n.*

im·pu·ni·ty [im·pyoo′nə·tē] *n.* Freedom from punishment or harmful result: You cannot neglect school work with *impunity*.

im·pure [im·pyoor′] *adj.* **1** Not pure or clean. **2** Containing some foreign or less valuable substance; adulterated: *impure* copper. **3** Immoral; immodest; sinful.

im·pu·ri·ty [im·pyoor′ə·tē] *n., pl.* **im·pu·ri·ties 1** The condition of being impure. **2** Something that is impure or makes impure: *impurities* in the air.

im·pu·ta·tion [im′pyoo·tā′shən] *n.* **1** The charging of a wrongdoing or fault to someone; accusation. **2** Something imputed; a slur.

im·pute [im·pyoot′] *v.* **im·put·ed, im·put·ing** To lay the blame or responsibility for; blame: to *impute* the theft to someone.

in [in] **1** *adv.* From the outside to the inside: Come *in*. **2** *prep.* Into: Get *in* the car. **3** *adv.* At home, indoors, or inside a place: On rainy weekends we stay *in*. **4** *adj.* Being within or leading toward the inside: the *in* door. **5** *prep.* Held by or found within: a child *in* her arms. **6** *prep.* Surrounded by: buried *in* the mud. **7** *prep.* Within the range or limits of: *in* my hearing; *in* the city. **8** *prep.* Belonging to: *in* the navy. **9** *adv.* In or into some activity, place, etc.: to join *in*; to move *in*. **10** *n.* (*pl.*) The group in public office or in power. **11** *adj.* Having power or status: the *in* group. **12** *n. informal* A position of favor or influence: to have an *in* with the boss. **13** *prep. U.S.* At or before the end of: I'll come *in* a minute. **14** *prep.* During: *in* the evening. **15** *prep.* Wearing: a man *in* a hat. **16** *prep.* Experiencing or showing the effects of: *in* doubt; *in* tears. **17** *prep.* Arranged or proceeding so as to form: *in* a row; to go *in* circles. **18** *prep.* Engaged at: *in* business. **19** *prep.* For the purpose of: to run *in* pursuit. **20** *prep.* By means of: to draw *in* crayon. **21** *prep.* According to: *in* my opinion. **22** *prep.* Regarding: I have faith *in* his ability. —**in for** *informal* Certain to experience: He's *in for* trouble. —**ins and outs** All the details and particulars. —**in that** Because; since.

in-¹ A prefix meaning: **1** In, as in *inhabit*, to live in. **2** Into, as in *inflammable*, capable of bursting into flame. **3** Within, as in *indoors*, within a building. **4** Toward, as in *inshore*, toward shore. **5** On, as in *inscribe*, to write on. ◆ See EN-.

in-² A prefix meaning: Not, as in *insane*, not sane. ◆ See UN-.

in. Abbreviation of: **1** INCH. **2** Inches.

in·a·bil·i·ty [in′ə·bil′ə·tē] *n.* The condition of being unable; lack of means or power.

in·ac·ces·si·ble [in′ak·ses′ə·bəl] *adj.* Not possible or not easy to reach or approach.

in·ac·cu·ra·cy [in·ak′yər·ə·sē] *n., pl.* **in·ac·cu·ra·cies 1** The condition of being inaccurate. **2** An error.

in·ac·cu·rate [in·ak′yər·it] *adj.* Not accurate; incorrect. —**in·ac′cu·rate·ly** *adv.*

in·ac·tion [in·ak′shən] *n.* Lack of action.

in·ac·tive [in·ak′tiv] *adj.* Not active; idle; inert. —**in′ac·tiv′i·ty** *n.*

in·ad·e·qua·cy [in·ad′ə·kwə·sē] *n., pl.* **in·ad·e·qua·cies 1** A being inadequate; insufficiency. **2** A defect.

in·ad·e·quate [in·ad′ə·kwit] *adj.* Less than is needed or required; not adequate. —**in·ad′e·quate·ly** *adv.*

in·ad·mis·si·ble [in′əd·mis′ə·bəl] *adj.* Not to be considered, approved, or allowed; not admissible: Such evidence is *inadmissible* in a court of law.

in·ad·ver·tent [in′əd·vûr′tənt] *adj.* **1** Not using good judgment; negligent; careless. **2** Unintentional: an *inadvertent* snub. —**in·ad·ver′tence** *n.* —**in′ad·ver·tent·ly** *adv.*

in·ad·vis·a·ble [in′əd·vī′zə·bəl] *adj* Not advisable; unwise.

in·al·ien·a·ble [in·āl′yən·ə·bəl] *adj.* That cannot be taken away or transferred: the *inalienable* rights of a citizen. —**in·al′ien·a·bly** *adv.*

in·ane [in·ān′] *adj.* Senseless; silly: an *inane* remark. —**in·ane′ly** *adv.*

in·an·i·mate [in·an′ə·mit] *adj.* **1** Lacking life; lifeless: A chair is an *inanimate* object. **2** Without spirit; dull: *inanimate* talk.

in·an·i·ty [in·an′ə·tē] *n., pl.* **in·an·i·ties 1** Foolishness; silliness. **2** A foolish remark, action, etc. **3** Emptiness.

in·ap·pli·ca·ble [in·ap′li·kə·bəl] *adj.* Not suitable or applicable; irrelevant.

in·ap·pro·pri·ate [in′ə·prō′prē·it] *adj.* Not right, proper, or suitable.

in·ap·ti·tude [in·ap′tə·t(y)ood] *n.* **1** Lack of skill. **2** Lack of fitness or suitability.

in·ar·tic·u·late [in′är·tik′yə·lit] *adj.* **1** Uttered but not in distinct sounds of spoken language: an *inarticulate* moan. **2** Not able to speak; mute. **3** Not able to express oneself fully or clearly. **4** Not segmented or jointed, as certain worms. —**in′ar·tic′u·late·ly** *adv.*

in·ar·tis·tic [in′är·tis′tik] *adj.* Not artistic in skill, taste, execution, etc.: an *inartistic* picture. —**in′ar·tis′ti·cal·ly** *adv.*

in·as·much as [in′əz·much′] **1** Seeing that; since; because: We left early *inasmuch as* we had to be home for dinner. **2** In so far as; as much as: *Inasmuch* as he is able, let him help.

in·at·ten·tion [in′ə·ten′shən] *n.* Lack of attention; carelessness.

in·at·ten·tive [in′ə·ten′tiv] *adj.* Not paying attention. —**in′at·ten′tive·ly** *adv.*

in·au·di·ble [in·ô′də·bəl] *adj.* Incapable of being heard. —**in·au′di·bly** *adv.*

add, āce, câre, pälm; end, ēqual; it, īce; odd, ōpen, ôrder; tŏŏk, pool; up, bûrn; ə = a in *above*, e in *sicken*, i in *possible*, o in *melon*, u in *circus*; yoo = u in *fuse*; oil; pout; check; ring; thin; this; zh in *vision*. For ¶ reference, see page 64 · HOW TO

in·au·gu·ral [in·ô′gyər·əl] **1** *adj.* Of or having to do with an inauguration. **2** *n.* An inaugural address, especially by a president.

in·au·gu·rate [in·ô′gyə·rāt] *v.* **in·au·gu·rat·ed, in·au·gu·rat·ing** **1** To install in an office with a formal ceremony: to *inaugurate* a president. **2** To commence or begin: to *inaugurate* important changes. **3** To celebrate the public opening or first use of: to *inaugurate* a bridge.

in·au·gu·ra·tion [in·ô′gyə·rā′shən] *n.* **1** A ceremony installing a person in an office: a president's *inauguration*. **2** The act of inaugurating.

in·aus·pi·cious [in′ô·spish′əs] *adj.* Not favorable or lucky. **—in′aus·pi′cious·ly** *adv.*

in·born [in′bôrn′] *adj.* That seems to have existed from birth; natural: an *inborn* trait.

in·bred [in′bred′] **1** Past tense and past participle of INBREED. **2** *adj.* Inborn. **3** *adj.* Produced by inbreeding.

in·breed [in′brēd′] *v.* **in·bred, in·breed·ing** To breed (new animals) by mating animals that are closely related.

inc. Abbreviation of INCORPORATED.

In·ca [ing′kə] *n.* A member of a very advanced group of Indian tribes which ruled Peru at the time of the Spanish conquest.

in·cal·cu·la·ble [in·kal′kyə·lə·bəl] *adj.* **1** Too numerous or great to be calculated: *incalculable* stars. **2** That cannot be predicted; uncertain. **—in·cal′cu·la·bly** *adv.*

in·can·des·cent [in′kən·des′ənt] *adj.* **1** Hot enough to give off light. **2** Very bright; brilliant. **—in′can·des′cence** *n.*

incandescent lamp A type of lamp in which an electric current heats a small wire or filament until it gives off light.

in·can·ta·tion [in′kan·tā′shən] *n.* **1** The uttering of words or syllables supposed to produce magical results. **2** Such words or syllables.

in·ca·ble [in·kā′pə·bəl] *adj.* Lacking the necessary ability, skill, capacity, etc.: an *incapable* driver. **—incapable of** Not open or susceptible to: a problem *incapable of* solution.

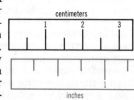

Incandescent lamp

in·ca·pac·i·tate [in′kə·pas′ə·tāt] *v.* **in·ca·pac·i·tat·ed, in·ca·pac·i·tat·ing** To make unfit, especially for normal physical activity; disable: *incapacitated* with a broken back.

in·ca·pac·i·ty [in′kə·pas′ə·tē] *n., pl.* **in·ca·pac·i·ties** A lack of ability, power, or fitness.

in·car·cer·ate [in·kär′sə·rāt] *v.* **in·car·cer·at·ed, in·car·cer·at·ing** To put in prison; imprison. **—in·car′cer·a′tion** *n.*

in·car·nate [*adj.* in·kär′nit *or* in·kär′nāt, *v.* in·kär′nāt] *adj., v.* **in·car·nat·ed, in·car·nat·ing** **1** *adj.* Having a body, especially a human body: a god *incarnate*. **2** *adj.* Appearing or being represented in some recognizable form or shape: He is cruelty *incarnate*. **3** *v.* To represent in some concrete form or shape: to

incarnate one's hopes in a picture. **4** *v.* To be a type or example of; typify: Joan of Arc *incarnated* saintly courage.

in·car·na·tion [in′kär·nā′shən] *n.* **1** A taking on of human form. **2** (*written* **Incarnation**) The taking on of a human form by Jesus. **3** A person or thing that is an example or symbol of some quality, idea, etc.: Hitler was an *incarnation* of evil tyranny.

in·case [in·kās′] *v.* **in·cased, in·cas·ing** Another spelling of ENCASE.

in·cau·tious [in·kô′shəs] *adj.* Not cautious; reckless; heedless.

in·cen·di·ar·y [in·sen′dē·er′ē] *adj., n., pl.* **in·cen·di·ar·ies** **1** *adj.* Of or having to do with the malicious burning of property. **2** *n.* A person who maliciously sets fire to property. **3** *adj.* Causing or producing fire: an *incendiary* bomb. **4** *adj.* Stirring up trouble, rebellion, or the like: an *incendiary* speech.

in·cense[1] [in′sens] *n.* **1** A substance that gives off a fragrant odor when burned. **2** The odor or smoke produced in burning it. **3** Any pleasing odor: the *incense* of lilacs.

in·cense[2] [in·sens′] *v.* **in·censed, in·cens·ing** To make angry; enrage: He was *incensed* at having to wait in line for two hours.

in·cen·tive [in·sen′tiv] *n.* Something that makes a person want to work, put forth effort, etc.: an *incentive* to study.

in·cep·tion [in·sep′shən] *n.* A beginning; start; origin: the *inception* of a new business.

in·ces·sant [in·ses′ənt] *adj.* Not ceasing; continuing without letup: *incessant* noise. **—in·ces′sant·ly** *adv.*

in·cest [in′sest] *n.* Sexual intercourse between persons so closely related that marriage between them is forbidden by law.

inch [inch] **1** *n.* A measure of length equal to $\frac{1}{12}$ of a foot. **2** *n.* A very small bit or amount: Neither runner could gain an *inch* on the other. **3** *v.* To move a very short distance at a time: The prisoner *inched* along the tunnel. **—every inch** In every way; completely: *every inch* a lady. **—within an inch of** Exceedingly close to: *within an inch of* death. ◆*Inch* comes from a Latin word meaning *inch, ounce,* or *the twelfth part* — in other words, a basic unit of measurement. It goes back to the Latin *unus,* which means *one.*

inch·worm [inch′wûrm′] *n.* A worm, the larva of a moth, that moves by bringing its rear end forward and arching its back up in the middle, then moving its front end forward.

in·ci·dence [in′sə·dəns] *n.* **1** The rate or degree of occurrence or effect: a high *incidence* of crime. **2** The striking of a surface by a body, by radiation, etc.

in·ci·dent [in′sə·dənt] **1** *n*. An event, often one of little importance. **2** *adj*. Naturally or usually belonging or having to do with: the dangers *incident* to flying.

in·ci·den·tal [in′sə·den′təl] **1** *adj*. Happening by chance or in the course of something else: an *incidental* remark. **2** *adj*. Naturally or usually belonging or having to do with: problems *incidental* to adolescence. **3** *n.pl*. Minor items or expenses.

in·ci·den·tal·ly [in′sə·den′təl·ē] *adv*. **1** As a secondary, casual, or chance occurrence along with something else: The book *incidentally* contains some historical data. **2** By the way: *Incidentally*, where were you last night?

in·cin·er·ate [in·sin′ə·rāt] *v*. **in·cin·er·at·ed, in·cin·er·at·ing** To burn to ashes. —**in·cin′- er·a′tion** *n*.

in·cin·er·a·tor [in·sin′ə·rā′tər] *n*. A furnace for burning rubbish or waste.

in·cip·i·ent [in·sip′ē·ənt] *adj*. Just beginning; not fully developed: an *incipient* revolt; an *incipient* sore throat.

in·cise [in·sīz′] *v*. **in·cised, in·cis·ing** **1** To cut into with a sharp instrument. **2** To make by cutting; engrave: to *incise* a design.

in·ci·sion [in·sizh′ən] *n*. **1** A cut or gash, especially one made in surgery. **2** The act of incising.

in·ci·sive [in·sī′siv] *adj*. Sharp; keen; penetrating: an *incisive* mind; *incisive* wit. —**in· ci′sive·ly** *adv*. —**in·ci′sive·ness** *n*.

in·ci·sor [in·sī′zər] *n*. A front tooth with a sharp edge for cutting. Man has eight incisors, the front four upper and lower teeth.

Incisors

in·cite [in·sīt′] *v*. **in·cit·ed, in·cit·ing** To stir up; rouse to action. —**in·cite′ment** *n*.

in·ci·vil·i·ty [in′sə·vil′ə·tē] *n., pl*. **in·ci·vil·i·ties** **1** Rudeness. **2** A rude act or remark.

in·clem·en·cy [in·klem′ən·sē] *n., pl*. **in·clem· en·cies** Severity; cruelty; harshness.

in·clem·ent [in·klem′ənt] *adj*. **1** Stormy; bad: said about the weather. **2** Without mercy; harsh.

in·cli·na·tion [in′klə·nā′shən] *n*. **1** A personal liking or preference: an *inclination* for study. **2** A tendency: the *inclination* of prices to rise. **3** A slant or slope: the *inclination* of a roof. **4** A bending or bowing: a slight *inclination* of the head.

in·cline [*v*. in·klīn′, *n*. in′klīn or in·klīn′] *v*. **in· clined, in·clin·ing**, *n*. **1** *v*. To lean; slant; slope: The land *inclined* gently to the sea. **2** *adj. use*: an *inclined* surface. **3** *n*. A sloping surface; slope: a steep *incline*. **4** *v*. To bend or bow: to *incline* the head. **5** *v*. To have a preference or tendency: Ruth *inclines* to talk a great deal. **6** *adj. use*: a person *inclined* to loaf.

inclined plane A plane surface, as a plank, track, etc., set at an oblique angle with the horizontal plane. It is used for raising heavy objects.

in·close [in·klōz′] *v*. Another spelling of ENCLOSE.

in·clo·sure [in·klō′zhər] *n*. Another spelling of ENCLOSURE.

It is much harder to lift the barrel than to roll it up an inclined plane.

in·clude [in·klōōd′] *v*. **in·clud·ed, in·clud·ing** **1** To put, shut up, or enclose: *Include* your address. **2** To hold or contain as a part or parts: The area *includes* many lakes. **3** To put into a group, total, or reckoning.

in·clu·sion [in·klōō′zhən] *n*. **1** The act of including. **2** The condition of being included. **3** Something included.

in·clu·sive [in·klōō′siv] *adj*. Including, especially including the limits specified or mentioned: Lincoln was president from 1861 to 1865 *inclusive*, a period of five years. —**in·clu′sive·ly** *adv*.

in·cog·ni·to [in·kog′nə·tō or in′kog·nē′tō] *adv., adj., n., pl*. **in·cog·ni·tos** **1** *adv., adj*. Under an assumed name or identity; in disguise: to travel *incognito*; to be *incognito*. **2** *n*. The condition of being incognito. **3** *n*. A person who is incognito. **4** *n*. An assumed name.

in·co·her·ent [in′kō·hir′ənt] *adj*. **1** Not clear; confused; disjointed: *incoherent* talk; an *incoherent* account. **2** Not sticking together; loose: an *incoherent* mass. —**in′co·her′ence** *n*. —**in′co·her′ent·ly** *adv*.

in·com·bus·ti·ble [in′kəm·bus′tə·bəl] *adj*. Not capable of being burned; fireproof.

in·come [in′kum] *n*. Money received by a person in return for labor, services, investment, rental of property, etc.

income tax A yearly tax on a person's income.

in·com·ing [in′kum′ing] **1** *adj*. Coming in or about to come in: *incoming* ships. **2** *n*. Entrance or arrival: the *incoming* of the tide.

in·com·men·su·rate [in′kə·men′shər·it] *adj*. **1** Not matched or on a par: a salary *incommensurate* with the job. **2** Not having a common measure or standard of comparison: Inches and ounces are *incommensurate*.

in·com·mode [in′kə·mōd′] *v*. **in·com·mod·ed, in·com·mod·ing** To bother or disturb.

in·com·mu·ni·ca·ble [in′kə·myōō′ni·kə·bəl] *adj*. That can't be communicated or passed on: an *incommunicable* disease; *incommunicable* secrets.

in·com·mu·ni·ca·do [in′kə·myōō′nə·kä′dō] *adv., adj*. Shut off from communication with anyone: The tourist was arrested and held *incommunicado*.

in·com·pa·ra·ble [in·kom′pər·ə·bəl] *adj.* **1** That can't be equaled or surpassed; matchless: Homer was an *incomparable* poet. **2** That can't be compared. **—in·com′pa·ra·bly** *adv.*

in·com·pat·i·ble [in′kəm·pat′ə·bəl] *adj.* **1** Not able to agree or get along well together: an *incompatible* couple. **2** Not able to exist together or be combined logically or harmoniously: *incompatible* colors. **—in·com·pat·i·bil·i·ty** [in′kəm·pat′ə·bil′ə·tē] *n.*

in·com·pe·tent [in·kom′pə·tənt] **1** *adj.* Lacking ability or skill; not competent. **2** *adj.* Not legally qualified: an *incompetent* witness. **3** *n.* A person who is incompetent. **—in·com′pe·tence** *n.* **—in·com′pe·tent·ly** *adv.*

in·com·plete [in′kəm·plēt′] *adj.* Not complete; unfinished or imperfect: an *incomplete* song; *incomplete* growth. **—in′com·plete′ly** *adv.*

in·com·pre·hen·si·ble [in′kom·pri·hen′sə·bəl] *adj.* Incapable of being understood.

in·com·press·i·ble [in′kəm·pres′ə·bəl] *adj.* That cannot be compressed.

in·con·ceiv·a·ble [in′kən·sē′və·bəl] *adj.* Impossible to imagine or believe; unthinkable. **—in′con·ceiv′a·bly** *adv.*

in·con·clu·sive [in′kən·kloo′siv] *adj.* Not leading to a conclusion or result: *inconclusive* evidence. **—in′con·clu′sive·ly** *adv.*

in·con·gru·i·ty [in′kən·groo′ə·tē] *n., pl.* **in·con·gru·i·ties 1** The condition of being incongruous. **2** Something incongruous.

in·con·gru·ous [in·kong′groo·əs] *adj.* **1** Not suitable or appropriate: a tugboat is *incongruous* among sleek yachts. **2** Not consistent or harmonious. **—in·con′gru·ous·ly** *adv.*

in·con·se·quen·tial [in′kon·sə·kwen′shəl] *adj.* Unimportant. **—in′con·se·quen′tial·ly** *adv.*

in·con·sid·er·a·ble [in′kən·sid′ər·ə·bəl] *adj.* Not worth considering; insignificant.

in·con·sid·er·ate [in′kən·sid′ər·it] *adj.* Lacking concern for the rights and feelings of others.

in·con·sis·ten·cy [in′kən·sis′tən·sē] *n., pl.* **in·con·sis·ten·cies 1** The condition of being inconsistent. **2** Something that is inconsistent.

in·con·sis·tent [in′kən·sis′tənt] *adj.* **1** Not in agreement or harmony; contrary: His words are *inconsistent* with his actions. **2** Not always the same in behavior or thought; changeable: an *inconsistent* person. **—in′con·sis′tent·ly** *adv.*

in·con·sol·a·ble [in′kən·sō′lə·bəl] *adj.* Not to be comforted or cheered; broken-hearted. **—in′con·sol′a·bly** *adv.*

in·con·spic·u·ous [in′kən·spik′yoo·əs] *adj.* Not very noticeable; not attracting attention. **—in′con·spic′u·ous·ly** *adv.*

in·con·stan·cy [in·kon′stən·sē] *n.* Fickleness.

in·con·stant [in·kon′stənt] *adj.* Changeable; fickle: an *inconstant* girl friend.

in·con·test·a·ble [in′kən·tes′tə·bəl] *adj.* That cannot be disputed or questioned. **—in′con·test′a·bly** *adv.*

in·con·ti·nent [in·kon′tə·nənt] *adj.* Having no self-control or restraint: an *incontinent* eater. **—in·con′ti·nence** *n.*

in·con·tro·vert·i·ble [in′kon·trə·vûr′tə·bəl] *adj.* Undeniable. **—in′con·tro·vert′i·bly** *adv.*

in·con·ven·ience [in′kən·vēn′yəns] *n., v.* **in·con·ven·ienced, in·con·ven·ienc·ing 1** *n.* Trouble or bother: the *inconvenience* of a traffic jam. **2** *n.* Something that is inconvenient; a trouble or bother. **3** *v.* To trouble or bother.

in·con·ven·ient [in′kən·vēn′yənt] *adj.* Troublesome or bothersome: He called at an *inconvenient* time. **—in′con·ven′ient·ly** *adv.*

in·cor·po·rate [in·kôr′pə·rāt] *v.* **in·cor·po·rat·ed, in·cor·po·rat·ing 1** To take in or include as a part of something else: He *incorporated* his latest findings in a report. **2** To form into or become a corporation. **3** To combine or merge into a larger organization, plan, etc.: All the small groups were *incorporated* into one large fellowship. **—in·cor′po·ra′tion** *n.*

in·cor·po·re·al [in′kôr·pôr′ē·əl] *adj.* Not consisting of or made of matter; spiritual.

in·cor·rect [in′kə·rekt′] *adj.* Not correct, proper, true, suitable, etc.: an *incorrect* answer; *incorrect* behavior. **—in′cor·rect′ly** *adv.*

in·cor·ri·gi·ble [in·kôr′ə·jə·bəl] **1** *adj.* That cannot be corrected, improved, or reformed: an *incorrigible* thief. **2** *n.* An incorrigible person.

in·cor·rupt·i·ble [in′kə·rup′tə·bəl] *adj.* **1** That cannot be bribed; steadfastly honest: an *incorruptible* judge. **2** That cannot decay: It is built of hard, *incorruptible* stone.

in·crease [*v.* in·krēs′, *n.* in′krēs] *v.* **in·creased, in·creas·ing,** *n.* **1** *v.* To make or become greater or larger: *Increase* the number of exercises you do; The population *increases* daily. **2** *n.* A growing or becoming greater in size, amount, etc. **3** *n.* The amount added by an increase. **—on the increase** Increasing; growing.

in·creas·ing·ly [in·krēs′ing·lē] *adv.* To an increasing degree; more and more.

in·cred·i·ble [in·kred′ə·bəl] *adj.* So strange, unusual, or extraordinary as to be unbelievable: an *incredible* tale. **—in·cred′i·bly** *adv.*

in·cre·du·li·ty [in′krə·d(y)oo′lə·tē] *n.* Doubt; disbelief.

in·cred·u·lous [in·krej′ə·ləs] *adj.* Feeling, having, or showing doubt or disbelief: an *incredulous* person; an *incredulous* look. **—in·cred′u·lous·ly** *adv.*

in·cre·ment [in′krə·mənt] *n.* **1** An increase or addition: an *increment* in one's salary. **2** The amount by which a quantity increases: an *increment* of $40.

in·crim·i·nate [in·krim′ə·nāt] *v.* **in·crim·i·nat·ed, in·crim·i·nat·ing** To declare or show to be guilty: The killer's fingerprints *incriminated* him. **—in·crim′i·na′tion** *n.*

in·crust [in·krust′] *v.* Another spelling of ENCRUST.

in·cu·bate [in(g)′kyə·bāt] *v.* **in·cu·bat·ed, in·cu·bat·ing 1** To hatch (eggs) by sitting on them. **2** To hatch (eggs) in an incubator. **3** To grow or develop gradually, as a plan or idea in the mind. **—in′cu·ba′tion** *n.*

in·cu·ba·tor [in(g)′kyə·bā′tər] *n.* **1** A container in which eggs are hatched artificially. It is kept at a warm temperature. **2** A container for keeping warm a prematurely born baby.

Incubator

in·cu·bus [in(g)′kyə·bəs] *n., pl.* **in·cu·bus·es** or **in·cu·bi** [in(g)′·kyə·bī] **1** A nightmare. **2** Anything that tends to oppress or discourage.

in·cul·cate [in·kul′kāt *or* in′kul·kāt] *v.* **in·cul·cat·ed, in·cul·cat·ing** To teach or impress upon the mind by frequent and forceful repetition: The army *inculcates* obedience in new soldiers. — **in′cul·ca′tion** *n.*

in·cum·bent [in·kum′bənt] **1** *n.* A person who holds an office or performs official duties. **2** *adj.* That is an incumbent: A candidate running for reelection is an *incumbent* candidate. **3** *adj.* Resting as a duty or moral obligation: It is *incumbent* on all to vote.

in·cum·brance [in·kum′brəns] *n.* Another spelling of ENCUMBRANCE.

in·cur [in·kûr′] *v.* **in·curred, in·cur·ring** To bring (something unpleasant) on oneself: to *incur* debts; to *incur* a penalty.

in·cur·a·ble [in·kyŏŏr′ə·bəl] **1** *adj.* Not curable. **2** *n.* A person who has an incurable disease. — **in·cur′a·bly** *adv.*

in·cur·sion [in·kûr′zhən] *n.* An invasion or raid, especially a sudden and brief one: an *incursion* into enemy territory.

Ind. Abbreviation of INDIANA.

in·debt·ed [in·det′id] *adj.* **1** Owing money. **2** Owing gratitude or thanks, as for a benefit or favor: We are *indebted* for your hospitality.

in·debt·ed·ness [in·det′id·nis] *n.* **1** The condition of being indebted. **2** That which is owed: His family can take care of his *indebtedness*.

in·de·cen·cy [in·dē′sən·sē] *n., pl.* **in·de·cen·cies** **1** The condition of being indecent. **2** Something indecent, as an action or remark.

in·de·cent [in·dē′sənt] *adj.* **1** Not decent or proper: *indecent* pride. **2** Not moral or modest; obscene: *indecent* behavior. — **in·de′cent·ly** *adv.*

in·de·ci·sion [in′di·sizh′ən] *n.* Inability to make a decision; vacillation.

in·de·ci·sive [in′di·sī′siv] *adj.* **1** Not able to decide; hesitant or wavering. **2** Not bringing about a definite conclusion or solution: an *indecisive* fight. — **in′de·ci′sive·ly** *adv.*

in·dec·o·rous [in·dek′ər·əs] *adj.* Not fitting, proper, or in good taste.

in·deed [in·dēd′] **1** *adv.* In fact; truly: I am *indeed* sorry. **2** *interj.* Is that true?

in·de·fat·i·ga·ble [in′də·fat′ə·gə·bəl] *adj.* Never tired or lacking energy.

in·de·fen·si·ble [in′di·fen′sə·bəl] *adj.* **1** That cannot be defended from attack: an *indefensible* outpost. **2** That cannot be justified or excused: an *indefensible* mistake. **3** That cannot be proved or supported: an *indefensible* theory.

in·de·fin·a·ble [in′di·fī′nə·bəl] *adj.* That cannot be defined or described: an *indefinable* feeling of joy. — **in′de·fin′a·bly** *adv.*

in·def·i·nite [in·def′ə·nit] *adj.* **1** Not definite or precise; vague: an *indefinite* answer. **2** Not precisely known, determined, or limited: an *indefinite* amount of money. **3** Not precise about the number, quantity, etc., of the person or thing referred to, as *some, few,* or *any.* — **in·def′i·nite·ly** *adv.*

indefinite article The word *a* or the word *an.*

in·del·i·ble [in·del′ə·bəl] *adj.* **1** That cannot be erased or blotted out: *indelible* memories. **2** Capable of making marks that are hard to get out: *indelible* pencils. — **in·del′i·bly** *adv.*

in·del·i·ca·cy [in·del′ə·kə·sē] *n., pl.* **in·del·i·ca·cies** **1** The quality of being indelicate. **2** Something that is indelicate.

in·del·i·cate [in·del′ə·kit] *adj.* **1** Not proper or decent: an *indelicate* remark. **2** Crude; coarse.

in·dem·ni·fy [in·dem′nə·fī] *v.* **in·dem·ni·fied, in·dem·ni·fy·ing** **1** To repay or compensate for loss, injury, or damage: The company *indemnified* him for the loss of his house. **2** To protect against future loss, injury, or damage; insure.

in·dem·ni·ty [in·dem′nə·tē] *n., pl.* **in·dem·ni·ties** **1** Payment to cover loss, injury, or damage. **2** Insurance against loss or damage.

in·dent¹ [in·dent′] *v.* **1** To set in from the margin, as the first line of a paragraph. **2** To cut notches like teeth into the edge of: a shore *indented* with inlets. **3** To form a notch or bay.

in·dent² [in·dent′] *v.* To press or push in so as to make a dent; dent.

in·den·ta·tion [in′den·tā′shən] *n.* **1** A notch or recess. **2** The act of indenting. **3** A dent.

in·den·ture [in·den′chər] *n., v.* **in·den·tured, in·den·tur·ing** **1** *n.* A written contract or agreement, especially a contract in which a person agrees to work for another for a certain period of time. **2** *v.* To bind by an indenture.

in·de·pen·dence [in′di·pen′dəns] *n.* The condition of being independent; freedom.

Independence Day In the U.S., July 4, a holiday commemorating the adoption of the Declaration of Independence on July 4, 1776.

in·de·pen·dent [in′di·pen′dənt] **1** *adj.* Not subject to the authority of another; free: an *independent* country. **2** *adj.* Not affected, influenced, or guided by others: an *independent* voter. **3** *n.* A person who is independent, especially an independent voter. **4** *adj.* Not dependent on

add, āce, câre, pälm; end, ēqual; it, īce; odd, ōpen, ôrder; tŏŏk, pŏŏl; up, bûrn;
ə = a in *above,* e in *sicken,* i in *possible,* o in *melon,* u in *circus;* yŏŏ = u in *fuse;* oil; pout;
check; ring; thin; this; zh in *vision.* For ¶ reference, see page 64 · HOW TO

someone else for financial help; self-supporting. **5** *adj.* Big enough to live on without other support: an *independent* income. **6** *adj.* Not part of some larger group, system, etc.: an *independent* company. **7** *adj.* In grammar, capable of being a complete sentence: an *independent* clause. **—in′de·pen′dent·ly** *adv.*

in·de·scrib·a·ble [in′di·skrī′bə·bəl] *adj.* Not capable of being described: the *indescribable* horror of war. **—in′de·scrib′a·bly** *adv.*

in·de·struc·ti·ble [in′di·struk′tə·bəl] *adj.* Not capable of being destroyed. **—in·de·struc′ti·bly** *adv.*

in·de·ter·mi·nate [in′di·tûr′mə·nit] *adj.* **1** Not definite. **2** Not clear; vague. **3** Not settled.

in·dex [in′deks] *n.*, *pl.* **in·dex·es** or **in·di·ces**, *v.* **1** *n.* A list in alphabetical order of topics, names, etc., at the end of a book, showing on which page or pages each appears. **2** *v.* To put (a topic, name, etc.) in an index. **3** *v.* To supply (a book) with an index. **4** *n.* Anything that serves to indicate or show something: One *index* of skill is speed. **5** *n.* An index finger. **6** *n.* Something that points, as the needle on a dial.

index finger The finger next to the thumb; forefinger.

In·di·a [in′dē·ə] *n.* **1** A large country in southern Asia. It is a member of the British Commonwealth of Nations. **2** A large peninsula which includes India, Pakistan, and several smaller states.

India ink A thick, black ink used in printing signs, drawing, etc.

In·di·an [in′dē·ən] **1** *n.* A member of any of the races of people inhabiting North and South America when European explorers came to the New World. **2** *adj.* Of or having to do with these people or any of their languages. **3** *n.* A person born in or a citizen of India. **4** *adj.* Of or having to do with India.

In·di·an·a [in′dē·an′ə] *n.* A north central state of the U.S., east of Illinois and west of Ohio.

In·di·an·ap·o·lis [in′dē·ə·nap′ə·lis] *n.* The capital of Indiana.

Indian club A bottle-shaped wooden club used in gymnastic exercises, usually in pairs.

Indian corn Another name for CORN (def. 1).

Indian file Single file.

Indian Ocean An ocean west of Australia, east of Africa, and south of Asia.

Indian summer A period of mild warm weather in the fall, usually after the first frost.

India paper A thin but opaque paper used for Bibles or other long books.

India rubber Rubber (def. 1).

in·di·cate [in′də·kāt] *v.* **in·di·cat·ed, in·di·cat·ing** **1** To point out; show: to *indicate* the right page or road. **2** To be or give a sign of; signify: The red spots *indicate* measles.

in·di·ca·tion [in′də·kā′shən] *n.* **1** The act of indicating. **2** Something that indicates; sign.

in·dic·a·tive [in·dik′ə·tiv] **1** *adj.* Suggestive of or pointing out: His playing is *indicative* of a great musical talent. **2** *adj.* In grammar, des-

ignating the mood of a verb in which an act or condition is stated or questioned as an actual fact. In "They went to the beach" and "Did he throw the stone?" the verbs *went* and *throw* are in the indicative mood. **3** *n.* The indicative mood or a verb in this mood.

in·di·ca·tor [in′də·kā′tər] *n.* A person or thing that indicates or points out.

in·di·ces [in′də·sēz] A plural of INDEX.

in·dict [in·dīt′] *v.* **1** To charge with a crime or offense; accuse. **2** To bring an indictment against: The grand jury *indicted* him for fraud. ◆ *Indict* comes from an old French word, *enditer*, meaning *to make known*. The English spelling was influenced by the Latin form, *indictare*.

in·dict·ment [in·dīt′mənt] *n.* **1** The act of indicting. **2** The condition of being indicted. **3** A formal, written charge delivered by a grand jury, accusing someone of a crime for which he should be tried in court.

In·dies [in′dēz] *n.pl.* **1** The East Indies. **2** The West Indies.

in·dif·fer·ence [in·dif′rəns *or* in·dif′ər·əns] *n.* **1** Lack of interest; unconcern. **2** Unimportance: This is a matter of *indifference* to me.

in·dif·fer·ent [in·dif′rənt *or* in·dif′ər·ənt] *adj.* **1** Not caring; unconcerned: *indifferent* to danger. **2** Not good nor bad; so-so: an *indifferent* singer. **3** Not important or vital: an *indifferent* matter. **4** Having no preference; unbiased. **—in·dif′fer·ent·ly** *adv.*

in·dig·e·nous [in·dij′ə·nəs] *adj.* Native to the place where found; not brought in or exotic: The eucalyptus is *indigenous* to Australia.

in·di·gent [in′də·jənt] *adj.* Needy; poor. **—in′di·gence** *n.*

in·di·gest·i·ble [in′də·jes′tə·bəl] *adj.* Hard or impossible to digest.

in·di·ges·tion [in′də·jes′chən] *n.* Difficulty in digesting food.

in·dig·nant [in·dig′nənt] *adj.* Angry because of something that is not right, just, fair, etc. **—in·dig′nant·ly** *adv.*

in·dig·na·tion [in′dig·nā′shən] *n.* Anger aroused by something that is not right, just, fair, etc.: to feel *indignation* at cruelty.

in·dig·ni·ty [in·dig′nə·tē] *n.*, *pl.* **in·dig·ni·ties** Something that humiliates one or injures one's self-respect.

in·di·go [in′də·gō] *n.*, *pl.* **in·di·gos** or **in·di·goes**, *adj.* **1** *n.* A blue dye obtained from certain plants related to the pea, or made artificially. **2** *n.*, *adj.* Deep violet blue.

in·di·rect [in′də·rekt′] *adj.* **1** Not following a direct path or line; roundabout: an *indirect* route. **2** Not directly connected with or resulting from something else: *indirect* benefits. **3** Not frank or straightforward: an *indirect* answer. **—in′di·rect′ly** *adv.*

indirect object The person or thing indirectly affected by the action expressed by the verb. Something is usually done for or given to the indirect object, as *him* in "Give him the book" or *idea* in "Give the idea some thought."

in·dis·creet [in′dis·krēt′] *adj*. Not careful, wise, prudent, etc. — **in′dis·creet′ly** *adv*.

in·dis·cre·tion [in′dis·kresh′ən] *n*. **1** The condition of being indiscreet. **2** An indiscreet act, remark, etc.

in·dis·crim·i·nate [in′dis·krim′ə·nit] *adj*. **1** Not seeing differences; showing no discrimination: He has an *indiscriminate* love of art, praising both the good and bad alike. **2** Confused; jumbled: an *indiscriminate* collection of things. — **in′dis·crim′i·nate·ly** *adv*.

in·dis·pen·sa·ble [in′dis·pen′sə·bəl] *adj*. Absolutely necessary; essential.

in·dis·posed [in′dis·pōzd′] *adj*. **1** Mildly ill; unwell. **2** Not willing: *indisposed* to act.

in·dis·po·si·tion [in′dis·pə·zish′ən] *n*. **1** A slight illness. **2** Unwillingness.

in·dis·put·a·ble [in′dis·pyoo′tə·bəl] *adj*. Incapable of being disputed; unquestionable.

in·dis·sol·u·ble [in′di·sol′yə·bəl] *adj*. Incapable of being dissolved, separated into its parts, or destroyed: an *indissoluble* vow; a large, *indissoluble* mass.

in·dis·tinct [in′dis·tingkt′] *adj*. Not clear or distinct; vague, dim, faint, etc.: an *indistinct* picture. — **in′dis·tinct′ly** *adv*.

in·dis·tin·guish·a·ble [in′dis·sting′gwish·ə·bəl] *adj*. Incapable of being clearly seen, perceived, or known as separate or different: Colors are *indistinguishable* in a very dim light.

in·dite [in·dīt′] *v*. **in·dit·ed, in·dit·ing** To write; compose: seldom used today.

in·di·vid·u·al [in′də·vij′oo·əl] **1** *adj*. Single: each *individual* person or thing. **2** *n*. A single human being, animal, or thing. **3** *n*. A person: She's a funny *individual*! **4** *adj*. Of or meant for a single person, animal, or thing: *individual* rooms. **5** *adj*. Characteristic of a certain person, animal, or thing; unique; special: Mark Twain's *individual* sense of humor.

in·di·vid·u·al·ism [in′də·vij′oo·əl·iz′əm] *n*. **1** A theory that lays stress on individual rights and independence of action, declaring these things to be as important as the community or nation. **2** Complete interest in oneself, without regard for others. — **in′di·vid′u·al·ist** *n*. — **in′di·vid′u·al·is′tic** *adj*.

in·di·vid·u·al·i·ty [in′də·vij′oo·al′ə·tē] *n*. **1** A quality or trait that makes a person or thing different from all others. **2** The condition of being special or different.

in·di·vid·u·al·ly [in′də·vij′oo·əl·ē] *adv*. **1** One at a time; as individuals: Mr. Mitchell spoke to each member of the club *individually*. **2** One from another: to differ *individually*.

in·di·vis·i·ble [in′də·viz′ə·bəl] *adj*. Not divisible. — **in′di·vis′i·bly** *adv*.

In·do·chi·na [in′dō·chī′nə] *n*. **1** The area of Asia east of India and south of China and including the Malay Peninsula. **2** The states of Cambodia, Laos, North Vietnam, and South Vietnam, formerly called French Indochina.

in·doc·tri·nate [in·dok′trə·nāt] *v*. **in·doc·tri·nat·ed, in·doc·tri·nat·ing** To teach (a person or persons) certain doctrines, principles, or beliefs. — **in·doc′tri·na′tion** *n*.

in·do·lent [in′də·lənt] *adj*. Lazy. — **in′do·lence** *n*. — **in′do·lent·ly** *adv*.

in·dom·i·ta·ble [in·dom′i·tə·bəl] *adj*. Not easily defeated or overcome; persevering: an *indomitable* leader. — **in·dom′i·ta·bly** *adv*.

In·do·ne·sia [in′də·nē′zhə] *n*. A country of SE Asia which includes over 100 large and small islands of the Malay Archipelago and part of New Guinea. — **In′do·ne′sian** *adj*., *n*.

in·door [in′dôr′] *adj*. That is, belongs, or takes place indoors: *indoor* equipment; *indoor* work.

in·doors [in′dôrz′] *adv*. Into or inside a house or other building: to play or go *indoors*.

in·dorse [in·dôrs′] *v*. **in·dorsed, in·dors·ing** Another spelling of ENDORSE. — **in·dorse′ment** *n*. — **in·dors′er** *n*.

in·du·bi·ta·ble [in·d(y)oo′bə·tə·bəl] *adj*. Not to be doubted; unquestionable: an *indubitable* fact. — **in·du′bi·ta·bly** *adv*.

in·duce [in·d(y)oos′] *v*. **in·duced, in·duc·ing** **1** To influence (someone) to do something; persuade: They *induced* him to accept. **2** To cause; produce: Her illness was *induced* by damp weather. **3** To reach (a conclusion, principle, etc.) by observing particular facts or examples. **4** To produce by electric or magnetic induction: to *induce* an electric current.

in·duce·ment [in·d(y)oos′mənt] *n*. **1** The act of inducing. **2** Something that induces or persuades; an incentive: The reward was an *inducement* to return the lost diamond ring.

in·duct [in·dukt′] *v*. **1** To bring into military service: to *induct* a draftee. **2** To install formally in an office, society, etc.: to *induct* a new governor.

in·duc·tance [in·duk′təns] *n*. The ability of an electric circuit to produce induction.

in·duc·tion [in·duk′shən] *n*. **1** The act of inducting. **2** The condition of being inducted. **3** The process of arriving at a general principle or conclusion by observing a number of particular facts or examples. **4** The creation of a magnetic or electric field by the nearness of another magnetic or electric field. **5** The creation of an electric field by a moving magnetic field, or of a magnetic field by a moving electric field.

in·duc·tive [in·duk′tiv] *adj*. **1** Of, having to do with, or resulting from induction: *inductive* reasoning. **2** Produced by or causing electrical or magnetic induction. — **in·duc′tive·ly** *adv*.

in·due [in·doo′] *v*. Another spelling of ENDUE.

in·dulge [in·dulj′] *v*. **in·dulged, in·dulg·ing** **1** To yield to or give free rein to (a pleasure,

add, āce, câre, pälm; end, ēqual; it, īce; odd, ōpen, ôrder; took, pool; up, bûrn;
ə = a in *above*, e in *sicken*, i in *possible*, o in *melon*, u in *circus*; yoo = u in *fuse*; oil; pout;
check; ring; thin; this; zh in *vision*. For ¶ reference, see page 64 · HOW TO

desire, etc.): to *indulge* a love of ice cream. **2** To permit oneself to take pleasure in something: to *indulge* in daydreaming. **3** To give in to the desires, whims, etc., of: to *indulge* a sick child.

in·dul·gence [in·dul′jəns] *n.* **1** The act of indulging in something. **2** That which is indulged in: Expensive hats were her great *indulgence*. **3** The condition of being indulgent. **4** Something granted as a favor, such as extra time allowed for payment of a debt. **5** In the Roman Catholic Church, a freeing from the punishment still due in purgatory for a sin after it has been forgiven through the sacrament of penance.

in·dul·gent [in·dul′jənt] *adj.* Very kind and lenient; not strict or critical: an *indulgent* mother. **—in·dul′gent·ly** *adv.*

In·dus [in′dəs] *n.* A river flowing through Tibet, Kashmir, and Pakistan.

in·dus·tri·al [in·dus′trē·əl] *adj.* **1** Of, engaged in, or having to do with industry: an *industrial* product; *industrial* workers. **2** Of or having to do with the people working in industries. **3** Having many industries: an *industrial* area. **—in·dus′tri·al·ly** *adv.*

in·dus·tri·al·ist [in·dus′trē·əl·ist] *n.* A person who owns or manages an industry.

in·dus·tri·al·ize [in·dus′trē·əl·īz] *v.* **in·dus·tri·al·ized, in·dus·tri·al·iz·ing** To make or become industrial: to *industrialize* a town. **—in·dus·tri·al·i·za·tion** [in·dus′trē·əl·i·zā′shən] *n.* ¶3

in·dus·tri·ous [in·dus′trē·əs] *adj.* Working hard and diligently. **—in·dus′tri·ous·ly** *n.*

in·dus·try [in′dəs·trē] *n., pl.* **in·dus·tries** **1** Any branch of manufacturing or business. **2** Manufacturing and business activity as a whole. **3** Hard, diligent work or effort: to live by one's own *industry*.

in·e·bri·ate [*v.* in·ē′brē·āt, *n.* in·ē′brē·it] *v.* **in·e·bri·at·ed, in·e·bri·at·ing,** *n.* **1** *v.* To make drunk; intoxicate. **2** *adj. use: inebriated* guests. **3** *n.* A drunkard.

in·ed·i·ble [in·ed′ə·bəl] *adj.* Unfit to eat.

in·ef·fa·ble [in·ef′ə·bəl] *adj.* Too great to be described or expressed: *ineffable* joy.

in·ef·fec·tive [in′i·fek′tiv] *adj.* **1** Not producing the effect expected or wanted; not effective. **2** Not competent; incapable: an *ineffective* teacher. **—in′ef·fec′tive·ly** *adv.*

in·ef·fec·tu·al [in′i·fek′chŏo·əl] *adj.* Not effective; useless. **—in′ef·fec′tu·al·ly** *adv.*

in·ef·fi·cien·cy [in′i·fish′ən·sē] *n.* The condition or quality of being inefficient.

in·ef·fi·cient [in′i·fish′ənt] *adj.* **1** Lacking ability or skill; incompetent: an *inefficient* secretary. **2** Not able to do something without waste of energy, time, etc.: an *inefficient* engine. **—in′ef·fi′cient·ly** *adv.*

in·e·las·tic [in′i·las′tik] *adj.* Not elastic or adaptable; inflexible.

in·el·e·gant [in·el′ə·gənt] *adj.* **1** Not having elegance; plain: an *inelegant* meal. **2** Coarse; crude: *inelegant* manners or speech.

in·el·i·gi·ble [in·el′ə·jə·bəl] *adj.* Not eligible, suitable, or qualified: to be *ineligible* to vote. **—in·el·i·gi·bil·i·ty** [in·el′ə·jə·bil′ə·tē] *n.*

in·ept [in·ept′] *adj.* **1** Not suitable or appropriate: an *inept* compliment. **2** Clumsy; awkward: an *inept* worker. **—in·ept′ly** *adv.*

in·e·qual·i·ty [in′i·kwol′ə·tē] *n., pl.* **in·e·qual·i·ties** **1** The condition of being unequal in size, position, quantity, etc. **2** The condition of being unequal in social position, opportunity, justice, etc.: the *inequalities* that exist between the rich and the poor.

inequality sign Any of various mathematical signs that indicate that numbers or quantities are not equal. $\neq$ means "is not equal to," (a $\neq$ b), $>$ means "is greater than," (a $>$ b), $<$ means "is smaller than," (a $<$ b), $\geqq$ means "is greater than or equal to," (a $\geqq$ b), $\leqq$ means "is smaller than or equal to," (a $\leqq$ b).

in·eq·ui·ta·ble [in·ek′wə·tə·bəl] *adj.* Unfair.

in·e·rad·i·ca·ble [in′i·rad′ə·kə·bəl] *adj.* Impossible to remove or root out.

in·ert [in·ûrt′] *adj.* **1** Lacking the power to move or act: *inert* material. **2** Slow to move or act; sluggish. **3** Unable or unlikely to unite with another chemical element or substance: Helium and neon are *inert* gases. **—in·ert′ly** *adv.*

in·er·tia [in·ûr′shə] *n.* **1** The continuance of a body or mass in its particular state of rest or motion unless acted upon by some force. **2** A not wanting to act, move, or change.

in·es·cap·a·ble [in′ə·skā′pə·bəl] *adj.* Impossible to escape or avoid: an *inescapable* fate. **—in′es·cap′a·bly** *adv.*

in·es·ti·ma·ble [in·es′tə·mə·bəl] *adj.* Too great or valuable to be counted or measured.

in·ev·i·ta·ble [in·ev′ə·tə·bəl] *adj.* Unavoidable; certain. **—in·ev′i·ta·bly** *adv.*

in·ex·act [in′ig·zakt′] *adj.* Not exact; not completely accurate or true.

in·ex·cus·a·ble [in′ik·skyŏo′zə·bəl] *adj.* Impossible to excuse or justify: *inexcusable* behavior. **—in′ex·cus′a·bly** *adv.*

in·ex·haust·i·ble [in′ig·zôs′tə·bəl] *adj.* **1** Incapable of being used up; unending: an almost *inexhaustible* supply of food. **2** Never getting tired; tireless: an *inexhaustible* speaker.

in·ex·o·ra·ble [in·ek′sər·ə·bəl] *adj.* Inflexible; relentless: the *inexorable* coming of winter.

in·ex·pe·di·ent [in′ik·spē′dē·ənt] *adj.* Not wise, suitable, or advisable.

in·ex·pen·sive [in′ik·spen′siv] *adj.* Not expensive; costing little. **—in′ex·pen′sive·ly** *adv.*

in·ex·pe·ri·ence [in′ik·spir′ē·əns] *n.* Lack of experience or of the skill and knowledge gained from experience.

in·ex·pe·ri·enced [in′ik·spir′ē·ənst] *adj.* Lacking experience or the skill and knowledge gained from experience.

in·ex·pert [in·ek′spûrt] *adj.* Not expert.

in·ex·pli·ca·ble [in·eks′pli·kə·bəl *or* in′iks·plik′ə·bəl] *adj.* Impossible to explain.

in·ex·press·i·ble [in′ik·spres′ə·bəl] *adj.* Impossible to express or put into words.

in·ex·tin·guish·a·ble [in′ik·sting′gwish·ə·bəl] *adj.* Incapable of being put out or extinguished.

in·ex·tri·ca·ble [in·eks′tri·kə·bəl] *adj.* **1** Impossible to get out of: an *inextricable* situation. **2** Impossible to solve or make clear: an *inextricable* problem. **3** Impossible to undo or disentangle, as a knot.

in·fal·li·ble [in·fal′ə·bəl] *adj.* **1** Free from error: an *infallible* judgment. **2** Not liable to fail; sure. **—in·fal·li·bil·i·ty** [in·fal′ə·bil′ə·tē] *n.* **—in·fal′li·bly** *adv.*

in·fa·mous [in′fə·məs] *adj.* **1** Having a notoriously bad reputation: an *infamous* liar. **2** Shamefully wicked or evil: an *infamous* act.

in·fa·my [in′fə·mē] *n., pl.* **in·fa·mies** **1** A notoriously bad reputation; public disgrace: His name will live in *infamy*. **2** Extreme wickedness. **3** A shamefully wicked act.

in·fan·cy [in′fən·sē] *n., pl.* **in·fan·cies** **1** The condition or time of being an infant; babyhood. **2** The earliest stage of anything.

in·fant [in′fənt] **1** *n.* A child in the earliest stages of life; baby. **2** *adj.* Of, like, or for an infant or infancy. **3** *adj.* Just beginning to exist or develop: an *infant* country.

in·fan·tile [in′fən·tīl] *adj.* **1** Of or having to do with infants or infancy. **2** Babyish; childish: an *infantile* remark. **3** Being at the earliest stage of its development: an *infantile* river.

Infant

infantile paralysis Another name for POLIOMYELITIS.

in·fan·try [in′fən·trē] *n., pl.* **in·fan·tries** Soldiers, or a branch of the army, trained and equipped to fight on foot. ◆*Infantry* comes from a Latin word meaning *boy, page,* or *foot soldier,* and goes back to the Latin *infans, infantis,* meaning *child.*

in·fan·try·man [in′-fən·trē·mən] *n., pl.* **in·fan·try·men** [in′-fən·trē·mən] An infantry soldier.

in·fat·u·ate [in-fach′oo·āt] *v.* **in·fat·u·at·ed, in·fat·u·at·ing** **1** To inspire with a foolish or exaggerated love or passion. **2** *adj. use:* an *infatuated* youth. **—in·fat′u·a′tion** *n.*

Infantry

in·fect [in·fekt′] *v.* **1** To make ill or diseased by the introduction of a germ or virus: Dirt *infected* the cut on his knee; She *infected* us all with her cold. **2** To have an influence on: His courage *infected* us.

in·fec·tion [in·fek′shən] *n.* **1** The act of infecting. **2** The condition of being infected. **3** Something that infects. **4** A disease or other harmful condition caused by an invasion of germs.

in·fec·tious [in·fek′shəs] *adj.* **1** Spread by infection: an *infectious* disease. **2** Producing infection: an *infectious* germ. **3** Likely to spread to other people: *infectious* laughter. **—in·fec′tious·ly** *adv.*

in·fer [in·fûr′] *v.* **in·ferred, in·fer·ring** **1** To come to by reasoning: From your smile I *infer* that you are amused. **2** To lead to as a conclusion; imply: Smoke *infers* something burning. **3** To indicate without saying outright; imply. ◆Both *infer* and *imply* are common in this sense, but *imply* has far better standing.

in·fer·ence [in′fər·əns] *n.* **1** The act of inferring. **2** Something inferred; conclusion.

in·fe·ri·or [in·fir′ē·ər] **1** *adj.* Not so good in quality, worth, usefulness, etc.: an *inferior* car. **2** *adj.* Lower in rank, position, or importance: In diplomacy, a minister is *inferior* to an ambassador. **3** *n.* A person or thing that is inferior in some way.

in·fe·ri·or·i·ty [in·fir′ē·ôr′ə·tē] *n.* The quality or condition of being inferior.

inferiority complex A strong feeling of being inferior to other people.

in·fer·nal [in·fûr′nəl] *adj.* **1** Of or having to do with Hell: the *infernal* regions. **2** Horrible; terrible: *infernal* cruelty.

in·fer·no [in·fûr′nō] *n., pl.* **in·fer·nos** **1** Hell. **2** A place like hell, full of fire or great heat: The furnace was a roaring *inferno.*

in·fer·tile [in·fûr′til] *adj.* Not fertile or productive: *infertile* fields.

in·fest [in·fest′] *v.* To overrun or occupy in large numbers so as to be annoying or dangerous: The swamp was *infested* with mosquitoes.

in·fi·del [in′fə·dəl] **1** *n.* A person who has no religious beliefs. **2** *n.* Among Christians, a person who is not a Christian. **3** *n.* Among Moslems, a person who is not a Moslem. **4** *adj.* Rejecting all religions, especially rejecting Christianity or Islam: an *infidel* writer.

in·fi·del·i·ty [in′fə·del′ə·tē] *n., pl.* **in·fi·del·i·ties** **1** Unfaithfulness to a person, promise, obligation, etc.; especially, unfaithfulness to one's husband or wife. **2** A disloyal act. **3** Lack of belief in religion or in a particular religion.

in·field [in′fēld′] *n.* **1** The part of a baseball field defended by the infielders. **2** The infielders as a group.

in·field·er [in′fēld′ər] *n.* In baseball, the first

baseman, second baseman, shortstop, or third baseman.

in·fil·trate [in-fil′trāt *or* in′fil·trāt] *v.* **in·fil·trat·ed, in·fil·trat·ing** To pass through or enter into (a substance, an organization, an area, etc.) by or as if by filtering: Enemy spies *infiltrated* our troops. **—in′fil·tra′tion** *n.*

in·fi·nite [in′fə·nit] **1** *adj.* Having no limits; endless or boundless. **2** *adj.* Very great: *infinite* patience. **3** *n.* Something infinite. **—in′fi·nite·ly** *adv.*

in·fin·i·tes·i·mal [in′fin·ə·tes′ə·məl] *adj.* So small or insignificant as to be close to nothing. **—in′fin·i·tes′i·mal·ly** *adv.*

in·fin·i·tive [in·fin′ə·tiv] *n.* A verb form which has no person or number and is often preceded by *to.* It is used in verb phrases (He will *go.*), as a noun (*To go* to Europe was his great desire.), and in other uses.

in·fin·i·tude [in·fin′ə·t(y)ōōd] *n.* **1** The quality of being infinite. **2** An unlimited quantity.

in·fin·i·ty [in·fin′ə·tē] *n., pl.* **in·fin·i·ties 1** The condition or quality of being infinite. **2** Something considered infinite, as space or time. **3** A distance, extent, or number greater than any definite equivalent.

in·firm [in·fûrm′] *adj.* **1** Feeble or weak, as from old age or illness. **2** Not resolute.

in·fir·ma·ry [in·fûr′mə·rē] *n., pl.* **in·fir·ma·ries** A place for treating the sick, as in a school, factory, etc.

in·fir·mi·ty [in·fûr′mə·tē] *n., pl.* **in·fir·mi·ties** Any weakness or illness: The old man tried to work despite his *infirmity.*

in·flame [in·flām′] *v.* **in·flamed, in·flam·ing 1** To make or become excited, angry, etc.: to *inflame* a crowd. **2** To increase (anger, hatred, etc.). **3** To make or become hot, swollen, or sore: Tight shoes can *inflame* toes.

in·flam·ma·ble [in·flam′ə·bəl] *adj.* **1** Capable of easily catching fire; flammable. **2** Easily excited or aroused.

in·flam·ma·tion [in′flə·mā′shən] *n.* **1** The act of inflaming. **2** An inflamed condition. **3** A red and painful swelling caused by infection or irritation.

in·flam·ma·to·ry [in·flam′ə·tôr′ē] *adj.* **1** Tending or meant to arouse anger, violence, etc.: an *inflammatory* speech. **2** Of, having to do with, or causing an inflammation.

in·flate [in·flāt′] *v.* **in·flat·ed, in·flat·ing 1** To swell or puff out by filling with air or gas: to *inflate* a tire. **2** To puff up, as with pride or importance. **3** To increase (prices or the like) a great deal.

in·fla·tion [in·flā′shən] *n.* **1** The act of inflating. **2** An inflated condition. **3** A rise in price levels resulting from an increase in the amount of money or credit relative to available goods.

Inflating a balloon

in·fla·tion·ar·y [in·flā′shə·ner′ē] *adj.* Of, related to, causing, or caused by inflation.

in·flect [in·flekt′] *v.* **1** To vary the tone or pitch of (the voice). **2** To change the form of (a word) by inflection. **3** To bend or curve.

in·flec·tion [in·flek′shən] *n.* **1** A change in the tone, pitch, or loudness of the voice. **2** The changes made in a word in order to show case, number, gender, tense, comparison, etc. The adjective *cold* is changed by inflection to *colder* or *coldest,* depending on the degree of comparison required. **3** An angle, bend, or curve. **—in·flec′tion·al** *adj.*

in·flex·i·ble [in·flek′sə·bəl] *adj.* That cannot be bent, altered, or changed; rigid; unyielding: *inflexible* metal; an *inflexible* mind. **—in·flex·i·bil·i·ty** [in·flek′sə·bil′ə·tē] *n.* **—in·flex′i·bly** *adv.*

in·flict [in·flikt′] *v.* **1** To strike; give; deal: to *inflict* a blow. **2** To impose: to *inflict* a heavy tax. **—in·flic′tion** *n.*

in·flow [in′flō′] *n.* **1** The act of flowing in or into. **2** Something that flows in.

in·flu·ence [in′flōō·əns] *n., v.* **in·flu·enced, in·flu·enc·ing 1** *n.* The power of a person or thing to have an effect on others: The moon has a strong *influence* on the tides. **2** *n.* Such a power working without any direct force: Use your *influence* to get them to help. **3** *n.* A person or thing having this power. **4** *v.* To alter the nature, thoughts, or behavior of: He *influenced* his students to read some good novels.

in·flu·en·tial [in′flōō·en′shəl] *adj.* Having or using influence.

in·flu·en·za [in′flōō·en′zə] *n.* A contagious virus disease causing inflammation of the nose, throat, and bronchial tubes, or of the intestines, and accompanied by fever, weakness, and discomfort.

in·flux [in′fluks] *n.* A continuous flowing or coming in, as of people or things: an *influx* of gas; an *influx* of new students.

in·fold [in·fōld′] *v.* Another spelling of ENFOLD.

in·form [in·fôrm′] *v.* **1** To let know; tell; notify: *Inform* him that we are here. **2** To furnish with facts or knowledge: to *inform* oneself about a subject. **3** To tell on; tattle: The criminal *informed* on his gang. **4** To animate; fill: His speech was *informed* with sincerity.

in·for·mal [in·fôr′məl] *adj.* **1** Not bound by a set form or rule; relaxed, casual, or friendly: *informal* manners; an *informal* agreement. **2** Not requiring formal dress: an *informal* dance. **3** Proper for daily conversation or familiar writing but not for formal speaking or writing. **—in·for′mal·ly** *adv.*

in·for·mal·i·ty [in′fôr·mal′ə·tē] *n., pl.* **in·for·mal·i·ties 1** Informal nature or quality: the *informality* of the gathering. **2** An informal act or proceeding.

in·form·ant [in·fôr′mənt] *n.* A person who gives information about something to another.

in·for·ma·tion [in′fər·mā′shən] *n.* **1** The act of informing or an informed condition: a handbook for the *information* of students. **2** Facts about a subject or subjects; knowledge or news: Textbooks and newspapers are sources of *information*.

in·form·a·tive [in·fôr′mə·tiv] *adj.* Giving information or knowledge: an *informative* book.

in·form·er [in·fôr′mər] *n.* A person who gives information against someone who has broken a rule or law; tattletale.

in·frac·tion [in·frak′shən] *n.* An act or instance of breaking a rule or law; violation: He was found guilty of a minor *infraction* of the town's building code.

in·fra·red [in′frə·red′] *adj.* Describing invisible electromagnetic waves that are longer than those of red light and shorter than radio waves.

in·fre·quen·cy [in·frē′kwən·sē] *n.* A being infrequent; rarity: The *infrequency* of his visits upset his family.

in·fre·quent [in·frē′kwənt] *adj.* Not coming or happening often; not common; rare: an *infrequent* visitor. —**in·fre′quent·ly** *adv.*

in·fringe [in·frinj′] *v.* **in·fringed, in·fring·ing** **1** To break; violate: to *infringe* a law. **2** To trespass; encroach: to *infringe* on someone's rights. —**in·fringe′ment** *n.*

in·fu·ri·ate [in·fyŏŏr′ē·āt] *v.* **in·fu·ri·at·ed, in·fu·ri·at·ing** To make furious or extremely angry; enrage.

in·fuse [in·fyōōz′] *v.* **in·fused, in·fus·ing** **1** To pour in; instill: The coach *infused* the will to win into his team. **2** To inspire: He *infused* them with determination. **3** To soak; steep, as tea leaves. —**in·fu·sion** [in·fyōō′zhən] *n.*

-ing¹ A suffix meaning: **1** The act or practice of, as in *hunting*, the act of someone who hunts. **2** Something made or created by, as a *painting*, something made by a person who paints. **3** Something used to make or do, as *flooring*, something used to make a floor, or a *lining*, something used to line.

-ing² A suffix used to form the present participle of verbs: *talking; eating.*

in·gen·ious [in·jēn′yəs] *adj.* **1** Skillful or clever: an *ingenious* architect. **2** Worked out, made, or done in a clever way: an *ingenious* solution. —**in·gen′ious·ly** *adv.*

in·gé·nue or **in·ge·nue** [an′zhə·nōō′] *n.* **1** The role of a young woman or girl in a play, film, etc. **2** An actress who plays such a part. **3** Any ingenuous young woman or girl.

in·ge·nu·i·ty [in′jə·n(y)ōō′ə·tē] *n.* Skill or cleverness, as shown in inventing or solving things: a detective's *ingenuity*.

in·gen·u·ous [in·jen′yōō·əs] *adj.* Showing artless innocence, trust, or sincerity; simple or frank: an *ingenuous* person. —**in·gen′u·ous·ly** *adv.* —**in·gen′u·ous·ness** *n.*

in·gest [in·jest′] *v.* To take or put (food, etc.) into the body. —**in·ges′tion** *n.*

in·gle·nook [ing′gəl·nŏŏk′] *n. British* A corner by the fire.

in·glo·ri·ous [in·glôr′ē·əs] *adj.* **1** Not bringing glory or honor; shameful; disgraceful: an *inglorious* war. **2** Not famous; unknown; humble: rarely used today.

in·got [ing′gət] *n.* A mass of metal cast into the shape of a bar or block.

Inglenook

in·graft [in·graft′] *v.* Another spelling of ENGRAFT.

in·grain [in·grān′] *v.* **1** To fix firmly and deeply on the mind or character. **2** *adj. use:* an *ingrained* trait.

in·grate [in′grāt] *n.* An ungrateful person.

in·gra·ti·ate [in·grā′shē·āt] *v.* **in·gra·ti·at·ed, in·gra·ti·at·ing** **1** To bring (oneself) into someone's favor by trying to please: He tried to *ingratiate* himself with his boss. **2** *adj. use:* an *ingratiating* manner.

in·grat·i·tude [in·grat′ə·t(y)ōōd] *n.* Lack of gratitude or appreciation.

in·gre·di·ent [in·grē′dē·ənt] *n.* **1** Something put into a mixture as a part of it: the *ingredients* of a cake. **2** A part in the make-up of anything: the *ingredients* of success.

in·gress [in′gres] *n.* **1** The act of going in or the right to go in: Reporters demanded *ingress*. **2** A place for going in; an entrance.

in·grown [in′grōn′] *adj.* Grown into the flesh: an *ingrown* toenail.

in·hab·it [in·hab′it] *v.* **1** To live in as a home; occupy: Deer *inhabit* the forest. **2** *adj. use* Occupied by someone: an *inhabited* area.

in·hab·it·a·ble [in·hab′it·ə·bəl] *adj.* Suitable for being lived in.

in·hab·i·tant [in·hab′ə·tənt] *n.* A person or animal that lives in a particular place; resident: He is an *inhabitant* of the city.

in·hale [in·hāl′] *v.* **in·haled, in·hal·ing** To draw (air, smoke, a scent, or vapor) into the lungs; breathe in: to *inhale* fumes.

in·har·mo·ni·ous [in′här·mō′nē·əs] *adj.* Lacking harmony; conflicting or clashing: *inharmonious* opinions; *inharmonious* sounds.

in·her·ent [in·hir′ənt *or* in·her′ənt] *adj.* Being in something as a built-in quality or element: the *inherent* strength of steel. —**in·her′ent·ly** *adv.*

in·her·it [in·her′it] *v.* **1** To get from someone after he dies, by will or law: to *inherit* an estate. **2** To get from a parent or ancestor as a characteristic: to *inherit* red hair. **3** To get from someone who has gone before: to *inherit* a problem.

---

add, āce, câre, pälm; end, ēqual; it, īce; odd, ōpen, ôrder; tŏŏk, pōōl; up, bûrn;
ə = a in *above*, e in *sicken*, i in *possible*, o in *melon*, u in *circus*; yōō = u in *fuse*; oil; pout;
check; ring; thin; this; zh in *vision*. For ¶ reference, see page 64 · HOW TO

in·her·i·tance [in·her′ə·təns] *n.* **1** The act, fact, or right of inheriting: He is wealthy by *inheritance.* **2** Something inherited, as money.

in·her·i·tor [in·her′ə·tər] *n.* Someone who inherits something; heir.

in·hib·it [in·hib′it] *v.* To hold back, check, or restrain (an act, impulse, etc.): Her words were *inhibited* by shyness.

in·hi·bi·tion [in′(h)i·bish′ən] *n.* **1** The act of inhibiting. **2** An inhibited condition. **3** A belief, feeling, fear, or other force within that keeps a person from acting or thinking freely: to overcome one's *inhibitions.*

in·hos·pi·ta·ble [in·hos′pi·tə·bəl *or* in′hos·pit′·ə·bəl] *adj.* **1** Not kind and generous towards guests; not hospitable. **2** Providing no shelter or comfort: an *inhospitable* climate.

in·hu·man [in·(h)yōō′mən] *adj.* **1** Cruel, brutal, or monstrous: *inhuman* treatment. **2** Not human in nature or form. — **in·hu′man·ly** *adv.*

in·hu·man·i·ty [in′(h)yōō·man′ə·tē] *n., pl.* **in·hu·man·i·ties** **1** Extreme cruelty. **2** A cruel action or word.

in·im·i·cal [in·im′i·kəl] *adj.* **1** Unfavorable; opposed: Rust is *inimical* to machines. **2** Not friendly: an *inimical* nation.

in·im·i·ta·ble [in·im′ə·tə·bəl] *adj.* That cannot be copied or imitated; matchless: her *inimitable* grace. — **in·im′i·ta·bly** *adv.*

in·iq·ui·tous [in·ik′wə·təs] *adj.* Extremely wicked or unjust; sinful: an *iniquitous* act.

in·iq·ui·ty [in·ik′wə·tē] *n., pl.* **in·iq·ui·ties** **1** Great evil or injustice; wickedness. **2** An evil or unjust action; sin.

in·i·tial [in·ish′əl] *adj., n., v.* **in·i·tialed** or **in·i·tialled, in·i·tial·ing** or **in·i·tial·ling** **1** *adj.* Of or coming at the beginning; earliest; first: his *initial* attempt. **2** *n.* (often *pl.*) The first letter of a name or word. **3** *v.* To mark or sign with one's initials: The teacher *initialed* the note.

in·i·tial·ly [in·ish′əl·lē] *adv.* At the beginning; at first.

Initial Teaching Alphabet An alphabet of 43 characters representing the sounds of English, for use in teaching beginners to read.

in·i·ti·ate [*v.* in·ish′ē·āt, *n.* in·ish′ē·it] *v.* **in·i·ti·at·ed, in·i·ti·at·ing,** *n.* **1** *v.* To set up or set going; start; begin: to *initiate* changes. **2** *v.* To make (someone) a member of a club or society, usually by putting him through special ceremonies or tests. **3** *n.* A person who has recently been admitted to a club or society. **4** *v.* To instruct or introduce: We *initiated* her into the art of cooking. — **in·i′ti·a′tion** *n.* — **in·i′ti·a·tor** *n.*

in·i·ti·a·tive [in·ish′(ē·)ə·tiv] *n.* **1** The first step in starting or doing something: to take the *initiative.* **2** The power, ability, or right to take the first step: to have the *initiative.* **3** The right or procedure by which citizens may introduce bills in a legislature by petition.

in·ject [in·jekt′] *v.* **1** To drive or shoot in, especially to force (a fluid) into the body with a

hypodermic needle or syringe: to *inject* an antitoxin. **2** To treat with injections: to *inject* a dog with serum. **3** To put or throw in (a comment, suggestion, quality, etc.): to *inject* humor into a play. — **in·jec′tion** *n.*

in·ju·di·cious [in′jōō·dish′əs] *adj.* Not showing good judgment; thoughtless; unwise: an *injudicious* remark. — **in′ju·di′cious·ly** *adv.*

in·junc·tion [in·jungk′shən] *n.* **1** An order, direction, or command. **2** An order issued by a court of law forbidding or requiring someone to do something.

in·jure [in′jər] *v.* **in·jured, in·jur·ing** To hurt, harm, or damage: She *injured* her arm; The gossip *injured* his reputation.

in·ju·ri·ous [in·jōōr′ē·əs] *adj.* Causing hurt or damage; harmful: *injurious* insects.

in·ju·ry [in′jər·ē] *n., pl.* **in·ju·ries** Hurt, harm, or damage done to someone or something: a head *injury;* an *injury* to one's pride.

in·jus·tice [in·jus′tis] *n.* **1** Lack of justice, fairness, or equal treatment: the *injustice* of an innocent man's being punished. **2** An unjust action; a wrong: to do an *injustice.*

ink [ingk] **1** *n.* A black or colored liquid substance, used for writing, drawing, and printing. **2** *v.* To put ink on or over: to *ink* out a word. **3** *n.* The dark liquid that octopuses, squids, and cuttlefish shoot out into the water to hide themselves.

ink·ling [ingk′ling] *n.* A slight suggestion or hint: to give an *inkling* of one's plans.

ink·stand [ingk′stand′] *n.* **1** A rack for holding pens and ink. **2** A container for ink.

ink·well [ingk′wel′] *n.* A container for ink, sometimes set into the surface of a desk.

ink·y [ing′kē] *adj.* **ink·i·er, ink·i·est** **1** Dark as black ink: the *inky* night. **2** Covered or stained with ink: *inky* fingers.

Inkwells

in·laid [in′lād *or* in·lād′] **1** Past tense and past participle of INLAY. **2** *adj.* Set into and even with the surface of something to form a design: a box with *inlaid* ivory. **3** *adj.* Decorated with pieces of contrasting material set evenly into the surface of something: an *inlaid* wall panel.

in·land [*adj.* in′lənd, *n., adv.* in′lənd *or* in′·land′] **1** *adj.* Not near the coast or the borders of a country; of or in the interior: *inland* population; an *inland* state. **2** *n.* The inner part of a country; the interior. **3** *adv.* In or towards an interior region: We live *inland;* They traveled *inland.*

in-law [in′lô′] *n. informal* A relative by marriage instead of by blood.

in·lay [*v.* in·lā′ *or* in′lā′, *n.* in′lā′] *v.* **in·laid, in·lay·ing,** *n.* **1** *v.* To set into a surface so as to form a decoration or design: to *inlay* dark wood in light wood. **2** *v.* To decorate by inserting such designs: to *inlay* a wooden cabinet with tortoise shell. **3** *n*. Material or a design that has been inlaid. **4** *n*. A filling, as of gold, made to fit a cavity in a tooth and cemented into it.

in·let [in′let′ *or* in′lət] *n*. **1** A narrow strip of water leading into the land from a larger body of water. **2** An entrance or opening.

Inlets

in·mate [in′māt′] *n*. **1** A person confined in a prison, asylum, or other such institution. **2** An inhabitant or resident.

in·most [in′mōst′] *adj*. Farthest in, deepest, or most secret: the *inmost* layer.

inn [in] *n*. A restaurant or hotel, usually located by a road and serving travelers.

in·nate [i·nāt′ *or* in′āt] *adj*. Natural; inborn; inherent: *innate* ability. **—in·nate′ly** *adv*.

in·ner [in′ər] *adj*. **1** Farther inside; interior: the *inner* halls. **2** Of the mind or spirit: his *inner* life. **3** Private; intimate; secret: her *inner* feelings.

inner ear In human beings, a place in the bone of the ear that contains organs that function in hearing and balance. See picture at EAR.

in·ner·most [in′ər·mōst′] *adj*. Farthest within; inmost.

in·ning [in′ing] *n*. **1** A division of a baseball game during which each team has a turn at bat until it makes three outs. A regular baseball game has nine innings. **2** (*often pl.*) A chance for action, as by a person or party: Now the Democrats have their *innings*.

inn·keep·er [in′kē′pər] *n*. A person who owns or operates an inn.

in·no·cence [in′ə·səns] *n*. **1** Freedom from sin, guilt, or blame. **2** Natural simplicity; purity: a baby's *innocence*.

in·no·cent [in′ə·sənt] **1** *adj*. Free from sin, blame, or evil; guiltless: He was *innocent* of the crime. **2** *adj*. Showing a lack of worldly wisdom; simple; naive: an *innocent* girl. **3** *n*. An innocent person. **4** *adj*. Having no bad or evil effect or intention; harmless: an *innocent* pastime. **—in′no·cent·ly** *adv*.

in·noc·u·ous [i·nok′yōō·əs] *adj*. Not causing injury or harm; harmless: an *innocuous* snake; an *innocuous* remark. **—in·noc′u·ous·ly** *adv*.

in·no·va·tion [in′ə·vā′shən] *n*. **1** A change in the usual way of doing things: to make *innovations*. **2** Something newly introduced: Television was an *innovation* in 1945.

in·no·va·tor [in′ə·vā′tər] *n*. A person who introduces new ideas, methods, or devices.

in·nu·en·do [in′yōō·en′dō] *n., pl.* **in·nu·en·does** A sly hint, usually one that hurts somebody's reputation: to accuse by *innuendoes*.

in·nu·mer·a·ble [i·n(y)ōō′mər·ə·bəl] *adj*. Too many to be counted; countless.

in·oc·u·late [in·ok′yə·lāt] *v*. **in·oc·u·lat·ed, in·oc·u·lat·ing** **1** To give a mild and harmless form of a disease to (a person or animal) by injecting vaccines, serums, or other prepared substances into the body. This builds up immunity that prevents a serious attack of the disease later. **2** To put ideas or opinions into the mind of. **—in·oc′u·la′tion** *n*.

in·of·fen·sive [in′ə·fen′siv] *adj*. Giving no offense; not annoying; harmless: an *inoffensive* little man. **—in′of·fen′sive·ly** *adv*.

in·op·er·a·tive [in·op′ər·ə·tiv] *adj*. Not in force, effect, or operation: an *inoperative* regulation: an *inoperative* mine.

in·op·por·tune [in·op′ər·t(y)ōōn′] *adj*. Not coming at a good or a convenient time: an *inopportune* request.

in·or·di·nate [in·ôr′də·nit] *adj*. Too great; excessive: an *inordinate* fondness for sweets. **—in·or′di·nate·ly** *adv*.

in·or·gan·ic [in′ôr·gan′ik] *adj*. **1** Lacking the organized physical structure of animal or vegetable life; not alive. Minerals are inorganic. **2** Not made by or derived from the activities of plants or animals: *inorganic* fertilizers.

in·put [in′pōot′] *n*. **1** Something that is put in, as electric current or other power put into a machine, or food taken into the body. **2** A point where something is put into a system.

in·quest [in′kwest] *n*. A legal investigation, especially one held before a jury, as that conducted by a coroner to determine the cause of a death.

in·quire [in·kwīr′] *v*. **in·quired, in·quir·ing** **1** To ask in order to find out: He *inquired* the way. **2** To make an investigation or search: to *inquire* into the causes of heart disease. **—in·quir′er** *n*.

in·quir·y [in·kwīr′ē *or* in′kwər·ē] *n., pl.* **in·quir·ies** **1** An investigation, especially of some public matter. **2** A question: to reply to *inquiries*.

in·qui·si·tion [in′kwə·zish′ən] *n*. **1** (*written* **Inquisition**) A court set up by the Roman Catholic Church during the 13th century for the discovery and punishment of heretics. **2** An official investigation or inquiry, often judicial; inquest. **3** A thorough, searching investigation.

in·quis·i·tive [in·kwiz′ə·tiv] *adj*. **1** Full of questions; eager for knowledge; curious. **2** Too curious; prying. **—in·quis′i·tive·ly** *adv*. **—in·quis′i·tive·ness** *n*.

in·quis·i·tor [in·kwiz′ə·tər] *n*. A person who makes an official investigation.

in·road [in′rōd′] *n*. **1** (*usually pl.*) A destructive invasion or encroachment: Overwork and strain made *inroads* on his health. **2** A raid.

in·rush [in′rush′] *n*. A sudden rushing in.

in·sane [in·sān′] *adj*. **1** Suffering from mental illness; not sane; crazy: an *insane* person.

---

add, **ā**ce, **c**â**re, **p**ä**lm;   **e**nd, **ē**qual;   **i**t, **ī**ce;   **o**dd, **ō**pen, **ô**rder;   t**ŏŏ**k, p**ōō**l;   **u**p, b**û**rn;

ə = a in *above*, e in *sicken*, i in *possible*, o in *melon*, u in *circus*;   **yōō** = u in *fuse*;   **oi**l;   p**ou**t;

check;   **r**i**ng**;   **th**in;   **th**is;   **zh** in *vision*.   For ¶ reference, see page 64 · HOW TO

2 For insane people: an *insane* asylum. **3** Mad; wild: *insane* schemes. —**in·sane′ly** *adv.*

in·san·i·ty [in·san′ə·tē] *n., pl.* **in·san·i·ties** **1** The condition of being insane: now mainly a legal term meaning unable to distinguish right from wrong, as because of mental illness. **2** Extreme foolishness: That plan is sheer *insanity.*

in·sa·tia·ble [in·sā′shə·bəl] *adj.* Not able to be satisfied; never getting enough; greedy: an *insatiable* appetite. —**in·sa′tia·bly** *adv.*

in·scribe [in·skrīb′] *v.* **in·scribed, in·scrib·ing** **1** To write, mark, or engrave: to *inscribe* a monument with the names of heroes. **2** To put (a name) on an official list or roll. **3** To establish firmly, as in the mind or memory.

in·scrip·tion [in·skrip′shən] *n.* **1** Words, letters, etc., that are inscribed: an *inscription* on an ancient vase. **2** The act of inscribing. **3** A written dedication, as of a book.

in·scru·ta·ble [in·skrōō′tə·bəl] *adj.* Incapable of being understood; mysterious; puzzling: an *inscrutable* smile. —**in·scru′ta·bly** *adv.*

in·sect [in′sekt] *n.* Any of a large class of small animals with a head, thorax, and abdomen, six legs, and usually two pairs of wings. Bees, beetles, flies, and mosquitoes are true insects. Small animals such as spiders are often loosely called insects. ◆ *Insect* goes back to a Latin word meaning *to notch* or *cut into*, because the bodies of insects are divided or "cut" into three segments.

in·sec·ti·cide [in·sek′tə·sīd] *n.* A poisonous substance for killing insects.

in·sec·tiv·o·rous [in′sek·tiv′ər·əs] *adj.* Feeding on insects: *insectivorous* plants.

in·se·cure [in′sə·kyŏŏr′] *adj.* **1** Apt to break, fall, or fail; not safe: an *insecure* bolt. **2** Not confident; anxious; uncertain: to feel *insecure.* —**in′se·cure′ly** *adv.*

in·se·cu·ri·ty [in′sə·kyŏŏr′ə·tē] *n., pl.* **in·se·cu·ri·ties** **1** Lack of safety; dangerous condition. **2** A condition of worry, anxiety, and uncertainty. **3** Something that is insecure.

in·sen·sate [in·sen′sāt] *adj.* **1** Not able to feel; not alive: *insensate* stone. **2** Showing no mercy, pity, or sympathy; hard. **3** Without reason; senseless; stupid: *insensate* rage.

in·sen·si·ble [in·sen′sə·bəl] *adj.* **1** Unconscious: He lay *insensible* on the floor. **2** Unable to feel, perceive, or notice: *insensible* to pain; *insensible* to the troubles of others. **3** Not aware; not realizing: *insensible* of the risk. **4** So slight or gradual as to be hardly noticed: Daylight diminished by *insensible* stages. —**in·sen′si·bil′i·ty** *n.* —**in·sen′si·bly** *adv.*

in·sen·si·tive [in·sen′sə·tiv] *adj.* Not feeling, noticing, or responding; not sensitive: an *insensitive* person.

in·sep·a·ra·ble [in·sep′ər·ə·bəl] *adj.* Incapable of being separated: *inseparable* companions. —**in·sep′a·ra·bly** *adv.*

in·sert [*v.* in·sûrt′, *n.* in′sûrt] **1** *v.* To put or place in something: to *insert* a key in a lock. **2** *n.* Something inserted, as pages of illustrations in a book.

in·ser·tion [in·sûr′shən] *n.* **1** The action of inserting. **2** Something inserted, as lace or embroidery sewn into cloth.

in·set [*v.* in·set′, *n.* in′set] *v.* **in·set, in·set·ting,** *n.* **1** *v.* To set in; insert. **2** *n.* Something inserted, as material in a garment.

in·shore [in′shôr′] *adj., adv.* Near or toward the shore: *inshore* fishing; to drift *inshore.*

in·side [*n., adj.* in′sīd′ *or* in·sīd′, *adv., prep.* in·sīd′] **1** *n.* The part, space, or surface that lies within; interior: the *inside* of a house. **2** *adv.* In or into the interior; within: Come *inside.* **3** *prep.* In or within: Put it *inside* the drawer. **4** *adj.* Found within; inner; internal: an *inside* part. **5** *n. (pl.) informal* The inner parts or organs of the body. **6** *adj.* Known only by a few; private; secret: *inside* information. **7** *adj.* Used or working indoors: *inside* clothing. —**inside out** So that the inside part is on the outside: He turned his pockets *inside out.*

in·sid·er [in′sī′dər] *n.* Someone who has special information or influence.

in·sid·i·ous [in·sid′ē·əs] *adj.* **1** Slyly treacherous, evil, or deceitful: an *insidious* plan to win. **2** Working in a hidden but dangerous way: an *insidious* disease. —**in·sid′i·ous·ly** *adv.*

in·sight [in′sīt′] *n.* The ability to see into the heart or inner nature of something or someone: to have *insight* into a problem.

in·sig·ni·a [in·sig′nē·ə] *n.pl.* Badges or emblems used as special marks of membership, office, or honor: the various royal *insignia.* ◆ *Insignia* was originally the plural of *insigne* in English as it had been in Latin. Now it is often used in the singular, with *insignias* as its accepted plural form: a display of *insignias.*

Insignia

in·sig·nif·i·cance [in′sig·nif′ə·kəns] *n.* Lack of importance, meaning, size, or worth.

in·sig·nif·i·cant [in′sig·nif′ə·kənt] *adj.* Lacking importance, meaning, size, or worth; trifling; trivial: an *insignificant* difference. —**in′sig·nif′i·cant·ly** *adv.*

in·sin·cere [in′sin·sir′] *adj.* Not expressing true feelings; not sincere or genuine. —**in′sin·cere′ly** *adv.*

in·sin·cer·i·ty [in′sin·ser′ə·tē] *n., pl.* **in·sin·cer·i·ties** **1** Lack of sincerity or honesty. **2** Something insincere.

in·sin·u·ate [in·sin′yŏŏ·āt] *v.* **in·sin·u·at·ed, in·sin·u·at·ing** **1** To suggest slyly without saying; hint: They *insinuated* that he was a fool. **2** To get or bring in gradually by indirect and subtle means: to *insinuate* oneself into someone's favor.

in·sin·u·a·tion [in·sin′yŏŏ·ā′shən] *n.* **1** A sly hint; innuendo. **2** The act of insinuating.

in·sip·id [in·sip′id] *adj.* **1** Lacking flavor or taste; flat: *insipid* food. **2** Not lively or interesting; dull: an *insipid* speech.

in·sist [in·sist′] *v.* **1** To demand with determination: I *insist* that you do it. **2** To stand up strongly for a belief or opinion: He *insisted* that he was right.

in·sis·tent [in·sis′tənt] *adj.* **1** Insisting or persistent: *insistent* demands. **2** Demanding or holding the attention: *insistent* colors. **—in·sis′tence** *n.* **—in·sis′tent·ly** *adv.*

in·sole [in′sōl′] *n.* **1** The fixed inner sole of a shoe. **2** An extra inside sole, as one put in to make a shoe fit better.

in·so·lent [in′sə·lənt] *adj.* Deliberately rude; insulting; sneering: an *insolent* manner. **—in′so·lence** *n.* **—in′so·lent·ly** *adv.*

in·sol·u·ble [in·sol′yə·bəl] *adj.* **1** Incapable of being dissolved: an *insoluble* salt. **2** Incapable of being solved: an *insoluble* problem.

in·sol·vent [in·sol′vənt] *adj.* Unable to pay one's debts; bankrupt. **—in·sol′ven·cy** *n.*

in·som·ni·a [in·som′nē·ə] *n.* Difficulty in sleeping; sleeplessness.

in·so·much [in′sō·much′] *adv.* **1** To such a degree; so much: The brake is worn *insomuch* that it is unsafe. **2** Because; seeing that: *Insomuch* as he was busy, we decided to postpone the meeting.

in·spect [in·spekt′] *v.* **1** To look at or examine carefully: to *inspect* a car for defects. **2** To review officially: to *inspect* troops.

in·spec·tion [in·spek′shən] *n.* **1** Careful or critical examination of something. **2** An official examination or review, as of troops.

in·spec·tor [in·spek′tər] *n.* **1** A person who inspects, especially in an official capacity: a meat *inspector*. **2** A police officer usually ranking next below the superintendent.

in·spi·ra·tion [in′spə·rā′shən] *n.* **1** A good idea or impulse that comes to someone, usually suddenly: I had an *inspiration*. **2** The power to inspire: the *inspiration* of his words. **3** An inspired condition: to lose one's *inspiration*. **4** A person or thing that inspires: His life is an *inspiration*. **5** The action of drawing in the breath. **—in′spi·ra′tion·al** *adj.*

in·spire [in·spīr′] *v.* **in·spired, in·spir·ing** **1** To fill with a certain thought, feeling, or desire to do something: He *inspired* us to work harder. **2** To arouse (a feeling, idea, etc.) in someone: He inspired *fear* in them. **3** To direct or guide, as if by some divine influence: The writers of the Bible were *inspired*. **4** *adj. use:* an *inspired* effort. **5** To inhale.

in·spir·it [in·spir′it] *v.* To fill with new spirit, life, or courage; cheer.

in·sta·bil·i·ty [in′stə·bil′ə·tē] *n.* Lack of stability, firmness, or steadiness.

in·stall [in·stôl′] *v.* **1** To fix in position and adjust for service or use: to *install* an air conditioner. **2** To establish in a place; settle: She *installed* herself in the new chair. **3** To place officially in office with a ceremony: to *install* a new mayor.

in·stal·la·tion [in′stə·lā′shən] *n.* **1** The act of installing. **2** A mechanical device or system fixed in place for use. **3** A large, fixed military base, fort, or the like.

in·stall·ment[1] or **in·stal·ment**[1] [in·stôl′mənt] *n.* **1** One of several payments made on a debt at definite times until the whole debt is paid. **2** *adj. use:* *installment* buying. **3** One of several parts presented at different times, as one chapter of a serial in a newspaper.

in·stall·ment[2] or **in·stal·ment**[2] [in·stôl′mənt] *n.* The act of installing, or an installed condition.

in·stance [in′stəns] *n., v.* **in·stanced, in·stanc·ing** **1** *n.* An example or illustration: for *instance*. **2** *v.* To give as an example: He *instanced* thrift as a good habit. **3** *n.* A particular case or occasion: In that *instance*, I was wrong. **4** *n.* Request or urging: Mary did the task at the *instance* of her teacher.

in·stant [in′stənt] **1** *n.* A very short time; moment. **2** *adj.* Without delay; immediate: *instant* recognition. **3** *adj.* Demanding quick attention; urgent: an *instant* need. **4** *adj.* Prepared quickly, as by adding water or milk: *instant* coffee. **5** *n.* A specific point in time: at the same *instant*. **6** *adj.* Of the present month: the 13th *instant*: seldom used today.

in·stan·ta·ne·ous [in′stən·tā′nē·əs] *adj.* Happening, done, or over in an instant: an *instantaneous* reaction; Death was *instantaneous*. **—in′stan·ta·ne·ous·ly** *adv.*

in·stant·ly [in′stənt·lē] *adv.* Immediately.

in·stead [in·sted′] *adv.* **1** Rather than; in place: a friend *instead* of an enemy. **2** In the place of someone or something else: to look for silver and find gold *instead*.

in·step [in′step′] *n.* **1** The arched upper part of the human foot, extending from the toes to the ankle. **2** The part of a shoe or stocking covering this.

in·sti·gate [in′stə·gāt] *v.* **in·sti·gat·ed, in·sti·gat·ing** **1** To spur or urge on to some action: She *instigated* him to murder. **2** To bring about by stirring up: to *instigate* treason. **—in′sti·ga′tion** *n.* **—in′sti·ga′tor** *n.*

in·still or **in·stil** [in·stil′] *v.* **in·stilled, in·still·ing** **1** To introduce gradually, as by teaching: to *instill* courage in one's son. **2** To pour in drop by drop: to *instill* a few drops of oil into a sauce.

in·stinct [*n.* in′stingkt, *adj.* in·stingkt′] **1** *n.* A natural tendency or impulse that causes animals to act in characteristic ways: Bees make honey by *instinct*. **2** *n.* A natural talent, skill, or ability; knack: She has an *instinct* for knowing what to do. **3** *adj.* Filled; abounding: a heart *instinct* with good will.

in·stinc·tive [in·stingk′tiv] *adj.* Of, having to do with, or coming from instinct: *instinctive* fear. **—in·stinc′tive·ly** *adv.*

---

add, āce, câre, pälm; end, ēqual; it, īce; odd, ōpen, ôrder; tŏŏk, pōōl; up, bûrn;
ə = a in *above*, e in *sicken*, i in *possible*, o in *melon*, u in *circus*; yōō = u in *fuse*; oil; pout;
check; ring; thin; **th**is; zh in *vision*. For ¶ reference, see page 64 · HOW TO

in·sti·tute [in′stə·t(y)ōōt] *v.* **in·sti·tut·ed,
in·sti·tut·ing,** *n.* **1** *v.* To set up or establish;
found: The county *instituted* an annual fair.
2 *v.* To set going; start: to *institute* an investigation. **3** *n.* An organization, school, or society
devoted to a special study or cause: an art
institute.

in·sti·tu·tion [in′stə·t(y)ōō′shən] *n.* **1** An
established organization with a special purpose.
Schools, banks, hospitals, and prisons are
institutions. **2** An established principle, practice,
law, or custom: Freedom of the press is a
democratic *institution.* **3** An establishing or
starting. **—in′sti·tu′tion·al** *adj.*

in·struct [in·strukt′] *v.* **1** To teach or train.
2 To order, direct, or command: He *instructed*
us to wait. **3** To give information to; inform:
They *instructed* the prisoner of his legal rights.

in·struc·tion [in·struk′shən] *n.* **1** The act of
instructing or teaching. **2** Something that trains
or gives knowledge, as a lesson. **3** (*pl.*) Directions or orders: to follow *instructions.*

in·struc·tive [in·struk′tiv] *adj.* Giving knowledge or information: an *instructive* speech.

in·struc·tor [in·struk′tər] *n.* **1** A teacher. **2** A
teacher in an American college who ranks below
all of the professors.

in·stru·ment [in′strə·mənt] *n.* **1** A tool or
implement, especially one used for work requiring great accuracy: a surgical *instrument.*
2 A person or thing used to accomplish a
purpose; means: He used his friends as *instruments* in gaining power. **3** A device or system
for measuring, recording, or controlling, as one
found in a car or airplane. **4** *adj.* *use:* an
instrument panel. **5** A device for producing
musical sounds, as a piano or trumpet. **6** A legal
document, as a will.

in·stru·men·tal [in′strə·men′təl] *adj.* **1** Serving as a means; helpful; useful: He was
instrumental in getting the law passed. **2** Of,
composed for, or performed on musical instruments: an *instrumental* concert.

in·stru·men·tal·i·ty [in′strə·men·tal′ə·tē] *n.,*
pl. **in·stru·men·tal·i·ties** Means, agency, or
assistance: He got the job through the *instru-
mentality* of his father.

in·sub·or·di·nate [in′sə·bôr′də·nit] *adj.* Refusing to submit to authority; disobedient.

in·sub·or·di·na·tion [in′sə·bôr′də·nā′shən] *n.*
Refusal to obey or submit; disobedience.

in·sub·stan·tial [in′səb·stan′shəl] *adj.* **1** Not
real; imaginary: A daydream is *insubstantial.*
2 Not firm or solid; flimsy or fragile.

in·suf·fer·a·ble [in·suf′ər·ə·bəl] *adj.* That
cannot be put up with; unbearable: *insufferable*
rudeness. **—in·suf′fer·a·bly** *adv.*

in·suf·fi·cien·cy [in′sə·fish′ən·sē] *n., pl.* **in-
suf·fi·cien·cies** A lack of enough of something;
deficiency: an *insufficiency* of air.

in·suf·fi·cient [in′sə·fish′ənt] *adj.* Not enough;
not adequate. **—in′suf·fi′cient·ly** *adv.*

in·su·lar [in′s(y)ə·lər] *adj.* **1** Of, located on, or
forming an island. **2** Of or like people living on

an island; isolated. **3** Not broad-minded or
liberal; narrow: *insular* attitudes. **—in·su·
lar·i·ty** [in′s(y)ə·lar′ə·tē] *n.*

in·su·late [in′sə·lāt] *v.* **in·su·lat·ed, in·su·
lat·ing** **1** To surround with material that
keeps electricity, heat, sound, etc., from leaking
out or in: to *insulate* a wire with plastic. **2** To
set apart from someone or something: They
insulated him from society.

in·su·la·tion [in′sə·lā′shən] *n.* **1** Material used
for insulating. **2** The act of insulating. **3** An
insulated condition.

in·su·la·tor [in′sə·lā′tər] *n.* Something that
insulates, especially a material, as glass, that
does not conduct electricity.

in·su·lin [in′sə·lin] *n.* **1** A hormone produced in
the pancreas which enables the body to break
down sugar and use it. **2** A preparation of this
hormone obtained from animals and taken by
people suffering from diabetes.

in·sult [*v.* in·sult′, *n.* in′sult] **1** *v.* To treat
with scorn and contempt, as by saying or doing
something rude: She *insulted* us by making fun
of our gift. **2** *n.* A rude action or remark: a
deliberate *insult.*

in·su·per·a·ble [in·s(y)ōō′pər·ə·bəl] *adj.* Not
capable of being overcome: *insuperable* obstacles.
—in·su′per·a·bly *adv.*

in·sup·port·a·ble [in′sə·pôr′tə·bəl] *adj.* Not
bearable or to be put up with; intolerable:
insupportable insolence.

in·sur·ance [in·shoor′əns] *n.* **1** Protection
against damage, injury, or loss. This protection
is provided by a contract, or **insurance policy,**
which guarantees that if regular payments are
made, money up to a specific amount will be
paid in the event of death, accident, fire, or
some other special cause of loss. **2** The business
of providing such protection. **3** The amount
regularly paid for insurance; premium: His
automobile *insurance* is $200 a year. **4** The
amount for which anything is insured: She
has $5000 *insurance* on her life.

in·sure [in·shoor′] *v.* **in·sured, in·sur·ing** **1**
To buy, give, or get insurance on: The insurance
company won't *insure* our house against hurricanes; The pianist *insured* his hands. **2** To make
certain; guarantee: To *insure* good results,
follow directions. **3** To make safe; guard or
protect: This checking *insures* us against error.

in·sur·gent [in·sûr′jənt] **1** *adj.* Rising in revolt
against authority. **2** *n.* A rebel.

in·sur·mount·a·ble [in′sər·moun′tə·bəl] *adj.*
Incapable of being overcome: an *insurmountable*
difficulty.

in·sur·rec·tion [in′sə·rek′shən] *n.* A rebellion
or uprising: to put down an *insurrection.*
—in′sur·rec′tion·ist *n.*

in·tact [in·takt′] *adj.* Whole or entire, with no
part taken away or damaged: He kept the
family fortune *intact.*

in·take [in′tāk′] *n.* **1** The act of taking in: a
sudden *intake* of breath. **2** A thing or amount
taken in: our *intake* of liquids. **3** The place

where water, air, or gas goes into a pipe, channel, etc. **4** The amount of energy or power taken into a machine.

in·tan·gi·ble [in·tan′jə·bəl] **1** *adj.* Not capable of being touched; not material: Darkness is *intangible.* **2** *adj.* Not definite; vague: an *intangible* fear. **3** *n.* (*usually pl.*) Something intangible: the *intangibles* of success.

in·te·ger [in′tə·jər] *n.* A positive or negative whole number or zero. 3, 130, and −18 are integers; ½ and 4¼ are not integers.

in·te·gral [in′tə·grəl] *adj.* **1** Necessary if a whole thing is to be complete; essential: Legs are *integral* parts of a table. **2** Whole or entire; complete. **3** Having to do with a whole number, or integer.

in·te·grate [in′tə·grāt] *v.* **in·te·grat·ed, in·te·grat·ing** **1** To fit or bring together into a whole: He *integrated* the various episodes into a narrative. **2** *U.S.* To make the use or occupancy of (a school, park, neighborhood, etc.) available to persons of all races. **3** To make complete. —**in′te·gra′tion** *n.* —**in′te·gra′tion·ist** *n.*

in·teg·ri·ty [in·teg′rə·tē] *n.* **1** Great sincerity, honesty, and virtue; strength of character. **2** The condition of being whole and entire; completeness: the lost *integrity* of Germany.

in·teg·u·ment [in·teg′yə·mənt] *n.* An outer covering, as a skin, shell, husk, or rind.

in·tel·lect [in′tə·lekt] *n.* **1** The power of the mind to understand, think, and know; reason: the human *intellect.* **2** Mental power; great intelligence: to show signs of *intellect.* **3** A highly intelligent person.

in·tel·lec·tu·al [in′tə·lek′chōō·əl] **1** *adj.* Of or having to do with the intellect; mental: *intellectual* ability. **2** *adj.* Requiring intelligence: *intellectual* work. **3** *adj.* Having or showing great intelligence: an *intellectual* author. **4** *n.* An intelligent or learned person. —**in′tel·lec′tu·al·ly** *adv.*

in·tel·li·gence [in·tel′ə·jəns] *n.* **1** The ability to understand and learn or to work out problems requiring thought. **2** *adj. use:* an *intelligence* test. **3** News or secret information: *intelligence* obtained by a spy. **4** The collecting of secret information or the agency that collects it: He works for enemy *intelligence.* ◆ *Intelligence* comes from Latin roots meaning *to choose between.*

intelligence quotient A number meant to show the level of a person's mental development; the IQ. To obtain this number, the mental age, as determined by standard tests, is multiplied by 100 and then divided by the real age.

in·tel·li·gent [in·tel′ə·jənt] *adj.* Having or showing intelligence; smart; bright. —**in·tel′li·gent·ly** *adv.*

in·tel·li·gent·si·a [in·tel′ə·jent′sē·ə] *n.pl.* Intellectual or educated people considered as a group.

in·tel·li·gi·ble [in·tel′ə·jə·bəl] *adj.* Capable of being understood; clear: an *intelligible* reply. —**in·tel′li·gi·bly** *adv.*

in·tem·per·ance [in·tem′pər·əns] *n.* A failure to use self-control or restraint, especially in drinking alcoholic liquor.

in·tem·per·ate [in·tem′pər·it] *adj.* **1** Lacking restraint; too strong: *intemperate* words. **2** Using too much alcoholic liquor. **3** Not mild; severe, as a climate or the weather. —**in·tem′per·ate·ly** *adv.*

in·tend [in·tend′] *v.* **1** To have as a purpose; plan: What do you *intend* to do? **2** To make or set aside for a purpose; mean; design: That remark was *intended* for George.

in·tend·ed [in·ten′did] *n. informal* The person someone plans to marry.

in·tense [in·tens′] *adj.* **1** Very strong, great, or deep: *intense* cold. **2** Full of strong emotion or deep feelings: an *intense* look. **3** Done with effort and concentration; hard: *intense* study. —**in·tense′ly** *adv.*

in·ten·si·fy [in·ten′sə·fī] *v.* **in·ten·si·fied, in·ten·si·fy·ing** To make or become intense or more intense: Moving *intensified* the pain. —**in·ten′si·fi·ca′tion** *n.*

in·ten·si·ty [in·ten′sə·tē] *n., pl.* **in·ten·si·ties** **1** The quality of being intense; extreme force or strength: the *intensity* of the sunlight. **2** Degree of strength: a pain of low *intensity.* **3** The amount of force or energy, as of light, sound, heat, or radiation, for each unit of volume, area, mass, etc.

in·ten·sive [in·ten′siv] **1** *adj.* Done with energy and concentration; thorough and complete: an *intensive* effort. **2** *adj.* Adding emphasis or force: said about a word: an *intensive* pronoun. **3** *n.* A word, phrase, particle, or prefix that adds emphasis or force. *Herself* in "She herself did it" is an intensive. —**in·ten′sive·ly** *adv.*

in·tent [in·tent′] **1** *n.* Purpose, aim, or intention: with *intent* to steal. **2** *adj.* Directing all one's efforts or attention: *intent* upon a problem. **3** *adj.* Firmly directed or fixed; earnest: an *intent* gaze. **4** *n.* Meaning: the *intent* of a remark. —**in·tent′ly** *adv.*

in·ten·tion [in·ten′shən] *n.* Plan, purpose, or intent: I have no *intention* of waiting.

in·ten·tion·al [in·ten′shən·əl] *adj.* Done on purpose; deliberate; intended: an *intentional* snub. —**in·ten′tion·al·ly** *adv.*

in·ter [in·tûr′] *v.* **in·terred, in·ter·ring** To place in a grave or tomb; bury.

inter- A prefix meaning: **1** With or on one another, as in *intermingle*, to mingle with one another, or *interdependent*, dependent on one another. **2** Between or among, as in *intercollegiate*, between or among colleges.

in·ter·act [in′tər·akt′] *v.* To act on each other. —**in′ter·ac′tion** *n.*

---

add, āce, câre, pälm; **end, ēqual;** **it, īce;** **odd, ōpen, ôrder;** **tŏŏk, pōōl;** **up, bûrn;**
ə = a in *above*, e in *sicken*, i in *possible*, o in *melon*, u in *circus*; **yōō** = u in *fuse*; **oil;** **pout;**
check; **ring**; **th**in; **th**is; **zh** in *vision*. For ¶ reference, see page 64 · HOW TO

in·ter·breed [in′tər·brēd′] *v.* **in·ter·bred, in·ter·breed·ing** To breed together (different species or varieties of animals or plants).

in·ter·cede [in′tər·sēd′] *v.* **in·ter·ced·ed, in·ter·ced·ing** 1 To speak or plead on behalf of another: They *interceded* for him with the police. 2 To come between persons or sides that disagree, in an effort to reconcile them.

in·ter·cept [in′tər·sept′] *v.* 1 To seize or stop on the way to a destination: to *intercept* a message. 2 To meet and block the passage of: to *intercept* enemy aircraft. 3 In mathematics, to mark off or bound, as by two points, lines, etc. **—in·ter·cep′tion** *n.*

in·ter·cep·tor [in′tər·sep′tər] *n.* A person or thing that intercepts, especially a fighter plane.

in·ter·ces·sion [in′tər·sesh′ən] *n.* 1 The act of interceding: Through his *intercession* we were saved. 2 Prayer on behalf of others.

in·ter·ces·sor [in′tər·ses′ər] *n.* Someone who intercedes.

in·ter·change [*v.* in′tər·chānj′, *n.* in′tər·chānj′] *v.* **in·ter·changed, in·ter·chang·ing,** *n.* 1 *v.* To change or substitute one for another: You can *interchange* the first and last letters of "are" and get "era." 2 *v.* To give and receive in return; exchange: to *interchange* gifts. 3 *n.* The act of interchanging; an exchange: an *interchange* of ideas. 4 *n.* An intersection of two highways designed so that cars can change roads without crossing other traffic.

in·ter·change·a·ble [in′tər·chān′jə·bəl] *adj.* Capable of being put in place of one another: *interchangeable* parts. **— in′ter·change′a·bly** *adv.*

Interchange

in·ter·col·le·giate [in′tər·kə·lē′jit] *adj.* Between colleges: *intercollegiate* sports.

in·ter·com [in′tər·kom′] *n. informal* A telephone or radio system for communicating within a limited space, as between offices or in a plane.

in·ter·com·mu·ni·ca·tion [in′tər·kə·myoo′nə·kā′shən] *n.* Communication with one another, as by means of a telephone or radio system.

in·ter·con·ti·nen·tal [in′tər·kon′tə·nen′təl] *adj.* Between or able to travel between continents: an *intercontinental* missile.

in·ter·course [in′tər·kôrs] *n.* 1 Dealings or relations between individuals or nations. 2 Mating, as of animals.

in·ter·de·pen·dent [in′tər·di·pen′dənt] *adj.* Dependent on one another. **—in′ter·de·pend′ence** *n.*

in·ter·dict [*v.* in′tər·dikt′, *n.* in′tər·dikt′] 1 *v.* To prohibit or forbid by authority. 2 *v.* In the Roman Catholic Church, to forbid (a person or group) to take part in certain sacraments and services. 3 *n.* A ban, especially one forbidding holy sacraments and services. **—in′ter·dic′tion** *n.*

in·ter·est [in′tər·ist *or* in′trist] 1 *n.* A desire to learn, know, have, do, see, or join in something: to have an *interest* in music. 2 *v.* To stir up or hold the curiosity, attention, or concern of: The play *interested* us. 3 *n.* The power to stir up attention: That subject has *interest* for me. 4 *n.* Something that stirs up attention: Baseball is his chief *interest*. 5 *n.* Attention: Does the story hold your *interest*? 6 *n.* What helps or profits someone; advantage; benefit: to consider one's own *interest*. 7 *v.* To cause to care about or join in; involve or concern: He tried to *interest* them in the club project. 8 *adj. use:* an *interested* party in a dispute. 9 *n.* A share or part, as in a business or estate: He owns an *interest* in that company. 10 *n.* Something in which someone has a share, as a business. 11 *n.* (*usually pl.*) A group of persons involved in a certain business or cause: the dairy *interests*. 12 *n.* The money paid, as by a bank or borrower, for the use of money: He gets 4% *interest* on his savings account. **—in the interest of** For the sake or purpose of: *In the interest of* safety, cross only at the corners.

in·ter·est·ing [in′tər·is·ting *or* in′tris·ting] *adj.* Stirring up or holding the interest or attention. **—in′ter·est·ing·ly** *adv.*

in·ter·fere [in′tər·fir′] *v.* **in·ter·fered, in·ter·fer·ing** 1 To meddle or intervene in other people's business: Don't *interfere* in their quarrel. 2 To get in the way; be an obstacle: The radio *interferes* with my studying.

in·ter·fer·ence [in′tər·fir′əns] *n.* 1 The act of interfering. 2 Something that interferes. 3 In sports, the act of hindering an opponent's play. Some ways are against the rules; others are allowable. 4 A disturbance in the reception of radio or television signals.

in·ter·fold [in′tər·fold′] *v.* To fold together or one within another.

in·ter·fuse [in′tər·fyooz′] *v.* **in·ter·fused, in·ter·fus·ing** To mix; combine; blend.

in·ter·im [in′tər·im] 1 *n.* A temporary period between times or events: in the *interim*. 2 *adj.* Temporary: an *interim* appointment.

in·te·ri·or [in·tir′ē·ər] 1 *n.* Inside part: the *interior* of a house. 2 *adj.* Of, situated on, or done on the inside; internal; inner: *interior* decorating. 3 *n.* The part of a country back from a border or coastline. 4 *adj.* Inland: an *interior* region. 5 *n.* The internal or domestic affairs of a country. The U.S. Department of the Interior has charge of mining, forestry, national parks, public lands, etc.

interior decorator A person whose job is decorating and furnishing rooms, homes, etc.

interj. Abbreviation of INTERJECTION.

in·ter·ject [in′tər·jekt′] *v.* To throw in abruptly; insert: to *interject* a comment.

in·ter·jec·tion [in′tər·jek′shən] *n.* 1 A word that is used as an exclamation, often expressing surprise, shock, etc., as *Oh!* in "Oh! You stepped on my foot." 2 The act of interjecting. 3 Something interjected.

in·ter·lace [in′tər·lās′] v. **in·ter·laced, in·ter·lac·ing** 1 To join (threads, strips, or other parts) by passing them over and under one another: to *interlace* rushes to make a mat. 2 To cross one another as if woven together: The vines *interlaced*.

Interlaced fingers

in·ter·lard [in′tər·lard′] v. To give variety to by adding something different here and there: to *interlard* a lecture with jokes.

in·ter·line¹ [in′tər·līn′] v. **in·ter·lined, in·ter·lin·ing** To write between the lines of (a book, manuscript, etc.).

in·ter·line² [in′tər·līn′] v. **in·ter·lined, in·ter·lin·ing** To put in an extra lining under the regular lining of (a garment).

in·ter·lin·ing [in′tər·lī′ning] n. An extra lining beneath the usual lining of a garment.

in·ter·lock [in′tər·lok′] v. To join or lock together firmly: Our hands *interlocked*.

in·ter·lo·per [in′tər·lō′pər] n. Someone who meddles in other people's business; intruder.

in·ter·lude [in′tər·lōōd] n. 1 A short interval of time that interrupts something: an *interlude* of calm in the storm. 2 A short, often funny, performance presented between the acts of a play. 3 A brief piece of music such as is played between stanzas of a song or acts of a play.

in·ter·mar·riage [in′tər·mar′ij] n. Marriage between members of different families, religions, races, etc.

in·ter·mar·ry [in′tər·mar′ē] v. **in·ter·mar·ried, in·ter·mar·ry·ing** 1 To marry someone of a different religion, race, class, etc. 2 To become connected through marriage: The two royal families *intermarried*.

in·ter·me·di·ar·y [in′tər·mē′dē·er′ē] n., pl. **in·ter·me·di·ar·ies,** adj. 1 n. Someone who goes between persons or sides in trying to settle something; go-between: an *intermediary* in a dispute. 2 adj. Acting as a go-between: an *intermediary* agent. 3 adj. Intermediate.

in·ter·me·di·ate [in′tər·mē′dē·it] 1 adj. Being or coming between two things, levels, stages, or events; in the middle: an *intermediate* course of study. 2 n. Something intermediate.

in·ter·ment [in·tûr′mənt] n. A burial.

in·ter·mez·zo [in′tər·met′sō] n., pl. **in·ter·mez·zos** or **in·ter·mez·zi** [in′tər·met′sē] A short musical composition performed between the main parts of a long work.

in·ter·mi·na·ble [in·tûr′mə·nə·bəl] adj. Never ending or seeming never to end: an *interminable* wait. **—in·ter′mi·na·bly** adv.

in·ter·min·gle [in′tər·ming′gəl] v. **in·ter·min·gled, in·ter·min·gling** To mix or mingle together; mingle with one another.

in·ter·mis·sion [in′tər·mish′ən] n. A pause for a time between periods of activity; recess: an *intermission* between acts of a play.

in·ter·mit·tent [in′tər·mit′ənt] adj. Stopping and starting or coming and going from time to time: *intermittent* activity; an *intermittent* fever. **—in·ter·mit′tent·ly** adv.

in·ter·mix [in′tər·miks′] v. To mix together.

in·ter·mix·ture [in′tər·miks′chər] n. 1 The act of intermixing. 2 A mixture.

in·tern [n. in′tûrn, v. in·tûrn′] 1 n. A graduate of medical school who lives in a hospital and assists in treating patients, to get practical experience under supervision. 2 v. To serve as an intern. 3 v. To confine in or keep from leaving a country or place during a war: to *intern* a warship or an enemy alien.

in·ter·nal [in·tûr′nəl] adj. 1 Of, on, or having to do with the inside; inner: *internal* medicine. 2 Having to do with the domestic affairs of a country: *internal* revenue. **—in·ter′nal·ly** adv.

in·ter·nal-com·bus·tion engine [in·tûr′nəl·kəm·bus′chən] An engine in which a mixture of fuel and air is exploded inside the cylinders to drive the pistons. It is the engine used in automobiles.

in·ter·na·tion·al [in′tər·nash′ən·əl] adj. 1 For or existing between or among nations: *international* trade agreements. 2 Having to do with the relations between nations: an *international* peace plan. **—in·ter·na′tion·al·ly** adv.

International Date Line An imaginary line approximately along the 180th meridian where, by international agreement, each calendar day begins. When it is Monday just east of the line, it is Tuesday just west of it.

in·ter·na·tion·al·ize [in′tər·nash′ən·əl·īz′] v. **in·ter·na·tion·al·ized, in·ter·na·tion·al·iz·ing** To place under the control of several different nations: The Suez Canal was *internationalized* by an agreement in 1888. ¶3

in·terne [in′tûrn] n. Another spelling of INTERN.

in·ter·ne·cine [in′tər·nē′sin or in′tər·nē′sīn] adj. Very destructive, especially to both sides in a conflict; bloody: *internecine* warfare.

in·tern·ment [in·tûrn′mənt] n. 1 The act of confining or holding: the *internment* of warships by a neutral country. 2 A being interned.

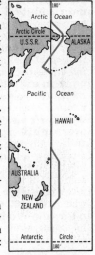
International Date Line

in·ter·plan·e·tar·y [in′tər·plan′ə·ter′ē] adj. Between or among planets: *interplanetary* space.

---

add, āce, câre, pälm;   end, ēqual;   it, īce;   odd, ōpen, ôrder;   tŏŏk, pōōl;   up, bûrn;
ə = a in *above*, e in *sicken*, i in *possible*, o in *melon*, u in *circus*;   yŏŏ = u in *fuse*;   oil;   pout;
check; ring; thin; this; zh in *vision*.   For ¶ reference, see page 64 · HOW TO

in·ter·play [in′tər·plā′] *n.* Action or influence of persons or things on each other.

in·ter·po·late [in·tûr′pə·lāt] *v.* **in·ter·po·la·ted, in·ter·po·lat·ing** To add to a text or discourse, often with the aim of distorting its meaning: to *interpolate* incorrect statistics in a report. **—in·ter′po·la′tion** *n.*

in·ter·pose [in′tər·pōz′] *v.* **in·ter·posed, in·ter·pos·ing** **1** To put between: to *interpose* a line of police. **2** To come between, as if to settle an argument; intervene. **3** To put in or introduce (a question, comment, etc.) in a conversation or speech. **—in′ter·po·si′tion** *n.*

in·ter·pret [in·tûr′prit] *v.* **1** To explain or make clear: to *interpret* a story. **2** To judge in a personal way: I *interpret* your inquiry as a sign of interest. **3** To give or put forth one's own impression or understanding of: to *interpret* a piece of music. **4** To translate aloud: to *interpret* for the U.N.

in·ter·pre·ta·tion [in·tûr′prə·tā′shən] *n.* The act, process, or result of interpreting: He gave a fine *interpretation* of the role.

in·ter·pret·er [in·tûr′prit·ər] *n.* A person who interprets or translates.

in·ter·pre·tive [in·tûr′prə·tiv] *adj.* Of or having to do with an interpretation.

in·ter·ra·cial [in′tər·rā′shəl] *adj.* Of, for, or among people of different races: an *interracial* gathering; *interracial* misunderstanding.

in·ter·reg·num [in′tər·reg′nəm] *n.* **1** The time between the end of a monarch's rule and the beginning of the next monarch's. **2** A pause.

in·ter·re·lat·ed [in′tər·ri·lā′tid] *adj.* Having a connection or relation to each other: *interrelated* problems.

in·ter·re·la·tion [in′tər·ri·lā′shən] *n.* The relation of one person or thing to another: the *interrelation* of family and friends.

in·ter·ro·gate [in·ter′ə·gāt] *v.* **in·ter·ro·gat·ed, in·ter·ro·gat·ing** To question, usually in a formal examination: to *interrogate* a prisoner. **—in·ter′ro·ga′tion** *n.*

interrogation mark or **interrogation point** Alternative names of QUESTION MARK.

in·ter·rog·a·tive [in′tə·rog′ə·tiv] **1** *adj.* Asking or expressing a question: an *interrogative* sentence. **2** *n.* A word used to ask a question.

in·ter·ro·ga·tor [in·ter′ə·gā′tər] *n.* A person who asks questions; examiner.

in·ter·rog·a·to·ry [in′tə·rog′ə·tôr′ē] *adj.* Asking or suggesting a question.

in·ter·rupt [in′tə·rupt′] *v.* **1** To cause (a speech, person working or talking, etc.) to stop by breaking in: to *interrupt* a broadcast; Don't *interrupt* me. **2** To interfere or get in the way of: The wall *interrupts* the view. **3** To break the course or continuity of.

in·ter·rup·tion [in′tə·rup′shən] *n.* **1** The act of interrupting. **2** A being interrupted: He spoke without any *interruption.* **3** Something that interrupts.

in·ter·scho·las·tic [in′tər·skə·las′tik] *adj.* Between or among schools: an *interscholastic* game.

in·ter·sect [in′tər·sekt′] *v.* **1** To divide by cutting across or passing through: No streets *intersect* the elevated highway. **2** To cross each other: Lines on graph paper *intersect.*

in·ter·sec·tion [in′tər·sek′shən] *n.* **1** A crossing, especially a place where streets cross. **2** An intersecting.

in·ter·sperse [in′tər·spûrs′] *v.* **in·ter·spersed, in·ter·spers·ing** **1** To put here and there among other things: to *intersperse* FBI men in the crowd. **2** To change or vary by putting in things here and there: red *interspersed* with gray.

in·ter·state [in′tər·stāt′] *adj.* Between, among, or having to do with different states of the U.S.

in·ter·stel·lar [in′tər·stel′ər] *adj.* Between or among the stars.

in·ter·stice [in·tûr′stis] *n., pl.* **in·ter·sti·ces** [in·tûr′stə·sēz] A small opening; narrow space; chink: Moss filled *interstices* between logs.

in·ter·twine [in′tər·twīn′] *v.* **in·ter·twined, in·ter·twin·ing** To unite by twining or twisting together: to *intertwine* strands of hair.

in·ter·ur·ban [in′tər·ûr′bən] *adj.* Between or among cities: an *interurban* railroad.

in·ter·val [in′tər·vəl] *n.* **1** The time between two events: the *interval* between school terms. **2** The distance or space between two objects or points: an *interval* of 20 feet. **3** In music, the difference in pitch between two tones. **—at intervals** **1** From time to time. **2** With spaces between.

in·ter·vene [in′tər·vēn′] *v.* **in·ter·vened, in·ter·ven·ing** **1** To come in to change a situation: to *intervene* to prevent a fight. **2** To come or be between two places or times.

in·ter·ven·tion [in′tər·ven′shən] *n.* **1** The act of intervening. **2** Interference in the affairs of one country by another: armed *intervention.*

in·ter·view [in′tər·vyōō′] **1** *n.* A meeting of two or more people arranged for a special purpose: an *interview* with a new student. **2** *n.* A meeting in which one or more reporters seek information for publication from another person. **3** *v.* To have an interview with: to *interview* a job applicant. **—in′ter·view′er** *n.*

in·ter·weave [in′tər·wēv′] *v.* **in·ter·wove** or **in·ter·weaved, in·ter·wo·ven, in·ter·weav·ing** **1** To weave together: to *interweave* fibers. **2** To connect closely; blend. **3** *adj. use: interwoven* fibers.

in·tes·tate [in·tes′tāt *or* in·tes′tit] *adj.* Not having made a will before death.

in·tes·ti·nal [in·tes′tə·nəl] *adj.* Of, in, or affecting the intestine: *intestinal* pain.

in·tes·tine [in·tes′tin] *n.* (*often pl.*) A long, coiled tube extending from the stomach to the anus and helping to digest food and eliminate waste matter from the body.

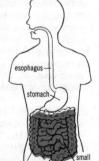

esophagus

stomach

large intestine

small intestine

Intestines

It has two parts, the **small intestine** and the **large intestine.**

in·ti·ma·cy [in'tə·mə·sē] *n., pl.* **in·ti·ma·cies** An intimate condition or close relationship.

in·ti·mate[1] [in'tə·mit] **1** *adj.* Very close or friendly; familiar: an *intimate* companion. **2** *n.* A close friend. **3** *adj.* Deeply personal; private: *intimate* thoughts. **4** *adj.* Resulting from first-hand knowledge or familiarity: *intimate* knowledge of the crime. **—in'ti·mate·ly** *adv.*

in·ti·mate[2] [in'tə·māt] *v.* **in·ti·mat·ed, in·ti·mat·ing** To hint; suggest; imply: He *intimated* that there might be trouble. **—in'ti·ma'tion** *n.*

in·tim·i·date [in·tim'ə·dāt] *v.* **in·tim·i·dat·ed, in·tim·i·dat·ing 1** To make timid; frighten: The bully *intimidated* us. **2** To frighten into doing or not doing something: to *intimidate* a witness. **—in·tim'i·da'tion** *n.*

in·to [in'tōō] *prep.* **1** To or toward the inside of: to go *into* the forest; Cut *into* the melon. **2** To the form or state of: to change water *into* steam. **3** Dividing: Two *into* six is three.

in·tol·er·a·ble [in·tol'ər·ə·bəl] *adj.* **1** Too hard or painful to be endured. **2** More than one can be expected to put up with: *intolerable* noise.

in·tol·er·ance [in·tol'ər·əns] *n.* **1** Unwillingness to let others live, think, believe, or worship as they choose. **2** An inability to bear or stand; excessive sensitivity: an *intolerance* to penicillin.

in·tol·er·ant [in·tol'ər·ənt] *adj.* Unwilling to accept the right of others to live or worship as they choose. **—intolerant of** Not able or willing to endure. **—in·tol'er·ant·ly** *adv.*

in·to·na·tion [in'tō·nā'shən] *n.* **1** A reciting or chanting, as of a prayer. **2** The pattern the voice follows in rising and falling in pitch during speech: an American *intonation.*

in·tone [in·tōn'] *v.* **in·toned, in·ton·ing** To say or recite in a singing tone; chant: to *intone* the Lord's Prayer.

in·tox·i·cant [in·tok'sə·kənt] *n.* Something that intoxicates, as an alcoholic drink.

in·tox·i·cate [in·tok'sə·kāt] *v.* **in·tox·i·cat·ed, in·tox·i·cat·ing 1** To make drunk. **2** *adj. use:* An *intoxicated* person staggered by. **3** To make very excited or elated; overjoy: He was *intoxicated* by his success in business.

in·tox·i·ca·tion [in·tok'sə·kā'shən] *n.* **1** Drunkenness. **2** Wild excitement or joy. **3** In medicine, a poisoned condition.

in·trac·ta·ble [in·trak'tə·bəl] *adj.* Not easily controlled; stubborn: an *intractable* horse.

in·tra·mu·ral [in'trə myōō'rəl] *adj.* Happening between or among members of the same school or organization: *intramural* football.

in·tran·si·tive [in·tran'sə·tiv] *adj.* Referring to a verb that is not used with a direct object, as *lives* in "She lives in Wyoming" or *ran* in "He ran fast." **—in·tran'si·tive·ly** *adv.*

in·tra·ve·nous [in'trə·vē'nəs] *adj.* Into or within a vein: *intravenous* injections.

in·treat [in·trēt'] *v.* Another spelling of ENTREAT.

in·trench [in·trench'] *v.* Another spelling of ENTRENCH.

in·trep·id [in·trep'id] *adj.* Very brave; fearless. **—in·tre·pid·i·ty** [in'trə·pid'ə·tē] *n.*

in·tri·ca·cy [in'tri·kə·sē] *n., pl.* **in·tri·ca·cies 1** The condition of being intricate. **2** Something intricate: the *intricacies* of the law.

in·tri·cate [in'tri·kit] *adj.* **1** Complicated or involved: *intricate* machinery. **2** Requiring close attention to follow or understand: an *intricate* problem. **—in'tri·cate·ly** *adv.*

in·trigue [*n.* in·trēg' or in'trēg, *v.* in·trēg'] *n., v.* **in·trigued, in·tri·guing 1** *n.* Sly, secret scheming or plotting. **2** *n.* A secret, crafty plot or scheme. **3** *v.* To plot

An intricate maze

or carry out an intrigue: to *intrigue* against the emperor. **4** *n.* A secret love affair. **5** *v.* To arouse the interest or curiosity of; fascinate. **6** *adj. use:* an *intriguing* opportunity.

in·trin·sic [in·trin'sik] *adj.* Belonging to the inner or real nature of a thing; essential: Collectors prize stamps for rarity, not for *intrinsic* value. **—in·trin'si·cal·ly** *adv.*

in·tro·duce [in'trə·d(y)ōōs'] *v.* **in·tro·duced, in·tro·duc·ing 1** To make acquainted face to face; present: Let me *introduce* you to my sister. **2** To turn the attention of (someone) to a thing for the first time: He *introduced* us to the world of science. **3** To bring into use or notice first: to *introduce* a new patent medicine. **4** To begin: to *introduce* a noun clause with the conjunction *that.* **5** To bring in as something added: The rabbit was *introduced* into Australia. **6** To put forward; propose: to *introduce* a resolution. **7** To put in; insert: to *introduce* a feeding tube into a patient's nostril.

in·tro·duc·tion [in'trə·duk'shən] *n.* **1** The act of introducing: Ladies used to curtsy at formal *introductions*; the *introduction* of a new drug. **2** A being introduced: Her *introduction* to the wonders of nature was a turning point in her life. **3** Something introduced. **4** The opening part, as of a book or speech, which serves to lead up to what follows.

in·tro·duc·to·ry [in'trə·duk'tər·ē] *adj.* Serving as an introduction: *introductory* remarks.

in·tro·spec·tion [in'trə·spek'shən] *n.* The examining of one's own thoughts and emotions.

in·tro·spec·tive [in'trə·spek'tiv] *adj.* Having to do with or tending toward introspection.

---

add, āce, câre, pälm;   end, ēqual;   it, īce;   odd, ōpen, ôrder;   tŏŏk, pōōl;   up, bûrn;

ə = a in *above*, e in *sicken*, i in *possible*, o in *melon*, u in *circus*;   **yōō** = u in *fuse*;   **oil**;   p**ou**t;

check;   **r**i**ng**;   **th**in;   **th**is;   **zh** in *vision.*   For ¶ reference, see page 64 · HOW TO

in·tro·vert [in'trə·vûrt] *n.* A person whose main interest is directed toward himself and his own thoughts and feelings rather than toward the world about him. —**in'tro·vert·ed** *adj.*

in·trude [in·trōōd'] *v.* **in·trud·ed, in·trud· ing** **1** To come in without being invited or wanted: I hope I am not *intruding.* **2** To thrust or force in. —**in·trud'er** *n.*

in·tru·sion [in·trōō'zhən] *n.* The act of intruding: an unwelcome *intrusion.*

in·tru·sive [in·trōō'siv] *adj.* Coming or thrusting in without being wanted; intruding.

in·trust [in·trust'] *v.* Another spelling of ENTRUST.

in·tu·i·tion [in't(y)ōō·ish'ən] *n.* **1** Direct knowledge or awareness that is based not on conscious reasoning but on an inner feeling: Her *intuition* told her he would come back. **2** Something known in this way.

in·tu·i·tive [in·t(y)ōō'ə·tiv] *adj.* **1** Knowing or working by intuition. **2** Known by intuition: *intuitive* knowledge. —**in·tu'i·tive·ly** *adv.*

in·un·date [in'un·dāt] *v.* **in·un·dat·ed, in· un·dat·ing** To cover by overflowing; flood.

in·un·da·tion [in'un·dā'shən] *n.* A flooding.

in·ure [in·yŏŏr'] *v.* **in·ured, in·ur·ing** To make accustomed; harden: Living in a city *inures* one to street noises.

in·vade [in·vād'] *v.* **in·vad·ed, in·vad·ing** **1** To enter by force with the purpose of conquering: Hitler's armies *invaded* Poland. **2** To get inside and spread throughout: Germs *invaded* his blood stream. **3** To rush or swarm into; overrun. **4** To intrude or trespass upon: to *invade* someone's privacy. —**in·vad'er** *n.*

in·va·lid[1] [in'və·lid] **1** *n.* A sickly person who cannot live an active life the way a healthy person can: The disease confined him to a wheel chair as an *invalid.* **2** *adj.* Of or for an invalid. **3** *v.* To make an invalid. **4** *adj.* Weak and sickly: an *invalid* neighbor. **5** *v.* To release from active military duty because of ill health.

in·val·id[2] [in·val'id] *adj.* Not valid; not true or sound; worthless: an *invalid* conclusion.

in·val·i·date [in·val'ə·dāt] *v.* **in·val·i·dat·ed, in·val·i·dat·ing** To make worthless or invalid: The erasure *invalidated* the check.

in·val·u·a·ble [in·val'y(ōō)ə·bəl] *adj.* Worth more than can be estimated; priceless.

in·var·i·a·ble [in·vâr'ē·ə·bəl] *adj.* Not changing or liable to change; constant: an *invariable* truth. —**in·var'i·a·bly** *adv.*

in·va·sion [in·vā'zhən] *n.* **1** The act of invading: The armed *invasion* started a war. **2** An attack or spreading out of something harmful: an *invasion* of Japanese beetles. **3** An intruding.

in·vec·tive [in·vek'tiv] *n.* A harsh and ruthless attack in words; violent denunciation.

in·veigh [in·vā'] *v.* To make a harsh or bitter attack in words: to *inveigh* against high taxes.

in·vei·gle [in·vē'gəl *or* in·vā'gəl] *v.* **in·vei· gled, in·vei·gling** To coax or entice by flattery or trickery: He *inveigled* me into lending him ten dollars.

in·vent [in·vent'] *v.* **1** To think out or bring into being for the first time: The Wright brothers *invented* the airplane. **2** To think up as a matter of convenience: to *invent* a reason.

in·ven·tion [in·ven'shən] *n.* **1** Something invented: to patent an *invention.* **2** The act of inventing: the *invention* of a new synthetic fiber. **3** The power of inventing: The poet's *invention* was faulty. **4** A false, made-up story: His alibi was a mere *invention.*

in·ven·tive [in·ven'tiv] *adj.* **1** Skillful at inventing; original: an *inventive* mind. **2** Showing invention: an *inventive* novel.

in·ven·tor [in·ven'tər] *n.* A person who invents.

in·ven·to·ry [in'vən·tôr'ē] *n., pl.* **in·ven·to· ries,** *v.* **in·ven·to·ried, in·ven·to·ry·ing** **1** *n.* A complete list and valuation of goods: Some stores take *inventory* every summer. **2** *n.* The making of such a list: closed for *inventory.* **3** *n.* The available stock of goods: The sale reduced the store's *inventory.* **4** *v.* To make a detailed list or inventory of: The clerks stayed late to *inventory* the stock.

in·verse [in·vûrs' *or* in'vûrs] **1** *adj.* Opposite or reversed in order, direction, or effect. **2** *n.* The direct opposite; reverse: Addition is the *inverse* of subtraction. —**in·verse'ly** *adv.*

in·ver·sion [in·vûr'zhən] *n.* **1** Something inverted. **2** The act of inverting: the *inversion* of subject and verb, as "Am I" for "I am." **3** A being inverted.

in·vert [in·vûrt'] *v.* **1** To turn upside down. **2** *adj.* use: The British call quotation marks *inverted* commas. **3** To reverse the order of.

in·ver·te·brate [in·vûr'tə·brit *or* in·vûr'tə· brāt] **1** *adj.* Without a backbone. **2** *n.* An animal without a backbone. Worms and insects are invertebrates.

in·vest [in·vest'] *v.* **1** To put (money) to use in order to make a profit. Buying a business, a property, or stocks are ways of investing. **2** To use or spend with the hope of getting some later advantage or profit: to *invest* time and effort on one's education. **3** To give power, authority, or rank to: Policemen are *invested* with the authority to make arrests. **4** To give a particular quality to; endow: The cobwebs *invested* the room with a gloomy air. **5** To clothe or cover. —**in·vest'or** *n.*

in·ves·ti·gate [in·ves'tə·gāt] *v.* **in·ves·ti·gat· ed, in·ves·ti·gat·ing** To look into thoroughly in order to find out the facts or details: to *investigate* an alleged robbery; to *investigate* the effects of a drug. —**in·ves'ti·ga·tor** *n.*

in·ves·ti·ga·tion [in·ves'tə·gā'shən] *n.* A thorough search or inquiry; examination to find out facts or details.

in·vest·ment [in·vest'mənt] *n.* **1** The investing of something, as money or time, in order to get a profit or advantage. **2** Invested money. **3** Something in which money is invested: a good *investment.*

in·vet·er·ate [in·vet'ər·it] *adj.* **1** Firmly established by long use; deep-rooted: an *inveterate* custom. **2** Fixed in a particular habit or opinion; confirmed: an *inveterate* gambler.

in·vid·i·ous [in·vid′ē·əs] *adj.* Likely to create ill will or resentment by unfairness: an *invidious* comparison of religious groups.

in·vig·or·ate [in·vig′ər·āt] *v.* **in·vig·or·at·ed, in·vig·or·at·ing** To give vigor and energy to: Walking in the fresh air *invigorates* him. **—in·vig′or·a′tion** *n.*

in·vin·ci·ble [in·vin′sə·bəl] *adj.* Not to be overcome or conquered: an *invincible* warrior. **—in·vin′ci·bil′i·ty** *n.* **—in·vin′ci·bly** *adv.*

in·vi·o·la·ble [in·vī′ə·lə·bəl] *adj.* Not to be violated or profaned: an *inviolable* pledge; an *inviolable* shrine. **—in·vi′o·la·bil′i·ty** *n.*

in·vi·o·late [in·vī′ə·lit] *adj.* Not violated; not profaned or broken; intact.

in·vis·i·ble [in·viz′ə·bəl] *adj.* Not visible; not capable of being seen: Air is *invisible*; The image on film is *invisible* until developed. **—in·vis′i·bil′i·ty** *n.* **—in·vis′i·bly** *adv.*

in·vi·ta·tion [in′və·tā′shən] *n.* **1** An asking of someone to come to a place or do something: a formal *invitation*. **2** The act of inviting.

in·vite [in·vīt′] *v.* **in·vit·ed, in·vit·ing 1** To ask (someone) courteously to come to a place or perform some action: She *invited* twenty friends to her party. **2** To make a polite request for: to *invite* suggestions. **3** To make more likely; tend to bring forth: Speeding *invites* accidents. **4** To tempt; entice.

in·vo·ca·tion [in′və·kā′shən] *n.* **1** An appeal or prayer for help, inspiration, etc., to God or gods. **2** The words used to call up evil spirits.

in·voice [in′vois] *n., v.* **in·voiced, in·voic·ing 1** *n.* A list sent to a customer describing the items shipped and including prices and delivery charges. **2** *v.* To list on an invoice.

in·voke [in·vōk′] *v.* **in·voked, in·vok·ing 1** To call upon for help or protection, as in a prayer: to *invoke* the gods. **2** To ask or appeal for: to *invoke* revenge. **3** To call into operation; apply: to *invoke* the power of the court. **4** To call up by magic: to *invoke* spirits.

in·vol·un·tar·y [in·vol′ən·ter′ē] *adj.* **1** Done without conscious control: an *involuntary* stammer. **2** Not done by one's own will or wish; unwilling. **—in·vol′un·tar′i·ly** *adv.*

in·volve [in·volv′] *v.* **in·volved, in·volv·ing 1** To include as a necessary part; have to do with: The job *involves* hard work; Biology *involves* all living things. **2** To associate; implicate: His abrupt departure *involved* him in the scandal. **3** To absorb; engross: *involved* in making a dress. **—in·volve′ment** *n.*

in·volved [in·volvd′] *adj.* Complicated; intricate: directions too *involved* to follow.

in·vul·ner·a·ble [in·vul′nər·ə·bəl] *adj.* Not capable of being wounded or overcome by attack; impregnable: an *invulnerable* fortress.

in·ward [in′wərd] **1** *adv., adj.* Toward the inside: He pushed the door *inward*; an *inward* thrust. **2** *adj.* Inner; interior: an *inward* part of an animal. **3** *adj., adv.* Of or toward one's inner self: *inward* thoughts. **—in′ward·ly** *adv.*

i·o·dine [ī′ə·dīn *or* ī′ə·din] *n.* **1** An element related to chlorine and occurring as crystals. It is used in medicine and in photography. **2** Iodine in alcohol, used to kill germs.

i·on [ī′ən] *n.* An atom or group of atoms having a positive or negative electric charge due to a gain or loss of electrons.

-ion A suffix meaning: **1** The act or process of, as in *union*, the act or process of uniting. **2** The result of, as in *invention*, the result of inventing. **3** The condition of being, as in *relation*, the condition of being related.

I·on·ic [ī·on′ik] *adj.* Of or indicating a style of Greek architecture marked by columns having scroll-like decorations carved at the top.

i·on·ize [ī′ən·īz] *v.* **i·on·ized, i·on·iz·ing** To make or be made, fully or in part, into ions. **—i′on·i·za′tion** *n.* ¶3

i·on·o·sphere [ī·on′ə·sfir] *n.* Several layers of the earth's atmosphere where radiation from the sun and outer space has ionized the air.

i·o·ta [ī·ō′tə] *n.* **1** The ninth letter of the Greek alphabet. **2** A very small amount.

IOU or **I.O.U.** A note having on it these letters (meaning *I owe you*), to acknowledge a debt.

I·o·wa [ī′ə·wə] *n.* A state in the north central U.S.

IQ or **I.Q.** Abbreviation of INTELLIGENCE QUOTIENT.

ir- A form of the prefix IN- meaning *not*, used before words beginning with *r*, as in *irresponsible*.

I·ran [i·ran′ *or* ē·rän′] *n.* A country, once called Persia, in sw Asia. **— I·ra′ni·an** *adj., n.*

I·raq [i·rak′ *or* ē·räk′] *n.* A country in sw Asia between Iran and Saudi Arabia.

i·ras·ci·ble [i·ras′ə·bəl] *adj.* Quickly angered; irritable.

i·rate [ī′rāt *or* ī·rāt′] *adj.* Angry.

ire [īr] *n.* Wrath; anger.

Ire·land [īr′lənd] *n.* **1** A large island, the westernmost of the British Isles, containing the country of Ireland in the south and the smaller **Northern Ireland** in the north. **2** A country in the southern part of this island.

ir·i·des·cent [ir′ə·des′ənt] *adj.* Showing the colors of the rainbow in changing patterns, as mother-of-pearl and some gems. **—ir′i·des′·cence** *n.*

i·ris [ī′ris] *n.* **1** The colored part of the eye that encircles the pupil. **2** A plant with long, sword-shaped leaves and colorful flowers. **3** The flower. **4** The rainbow.

I·rish [ī′rish] **1** *adj.* Of or from Ireland. **2** *n.* **(the Irish)** The people of Ireland. **3** *n.* The

---

add, āce, câre, pälm; end, ēqual; it, īce; odd, ōpen, ôrder; tŏŏk, pōōl; up, bûrn; ə = a in *above*, e in *sicken*, i in *possible*, o in *melon*, u in *circus*; yōō = u in *fuse*; oil; pout; check; ring; thin; this; zh in *vision*. For ¶ reference, see page 64 · HOW TO

dialect of English spoken in Ireland. **4** *n.* Irish Gaelic. ◆ Historically the Irish spoke a Celtic language called *Gaelic,* related to the old language of Scotland. A modern version of Gaelic is still spoken, but English is now more widespread.

I·rish·man [ī′rish·mən] *n., pl.* **I·rish·men** [ī′rish·mən] A man born in or a citizen of Ireland or Northern Ireland.

Irish potato The common white potato.

Irish Sea The part of the Atlantic Ocean separating Ireland from Great Britain.

irk [ûrk] *v.* To annoy or irritate; vex.

irk·some [ûrk′səm] *adj.* Tiresome; tedious: Waxing a car can be an *irksome* job.

i·ron [ī′ərn] **1** *n.* A tough, abundant, metallic element that is easily worked, highly magnetic, and widely used to make steel. **2** *n.* Something made of iron. **3** *adj. use:*

iron doors. **4** *adj.* Like iron; firm; strong: an *iron* constitution. **5** *n.* Something firm or unyielding, like iron: a will of *iron.* **6** *n.* (*pl.*) Iron chains or shackles. **7** *n.* A device, usually of iron, with a handle and smooth bottom that is heated and used to press clothes, etc. **8** *v.* To press with an iron, as clothing. **— iron out** To clear up or smooth over: to *iron out* differences.

Iron Age A period in man's early history, after the Stone Age and the Bronze Age, when man's weapons and tools were made of iron.

i·ron·clad [ī′ərn·klad′] **1** *adj.* Covered with iron or armor. **2** *n.* An armored warship. **3** *adj.* Very firm; strict: an *ironclad* rule.

iron curtain A barrier of censorship, secrecy, etc., that isolates a country from others.

i·ron·ic [ī·ron′ik] *adj.* **1** Of, related to, expressing, or full of irony: an *ironic* comment. **2** Odd because so unexpected: It was *ironic* that the minute he gave up the search, he found the missing clue. **— i·ron′i·cal·ly** *adv.*

i·ron·i·cal [ī·ron′i·kəl] *adj.* Ironic.

ironing board A padded board, often with folding legs, on which to iron clothing, etc.

iron lung A large machine for giving artificial respiration over long periods, as to a polio patient with lungs affected.

i·ron·wood [ī′ərn·wŏŏd′] *n.* **1** Any of various trees having very hard wood. **2** This wood.

i·ro·ny [ī′rə·nē] *n., pl.* **i·ro·nies** **1** A way of implying the opposite of what the words expressed literally mean, often in an effort to be humorous or sarcastic, as when one says "Thanks" after being insulted. **2** A fact, result, or happening that

Iron lung

seems the opposite of what one would naturally expect: the *irony* of being at sea with "Water, water everywhere | Nor any drop to drink."

Ir·o·quois [ir′ə·kwoi(z)] *n., pl.* **Ir·o·quois** A member of a group of Indian tribes that lived in the NE U.S.

ir·ra·di·ate [i·rā′dē·āt] *v.* **ir·ra·di·at·ed, ir·ra·di·at·ing** **1** To light up; illuminate: The moon *irradiated* the sky. **2** To make or be radiant. **3** To send forth like rays of light: to *irradiate* happiness. **4** To treat with or subject to radiation, especially X-rays, ultraviolet light, etc. **— ir·ra′di·a′tion** *n.*

ir·ra·tion·al [i·rash′ən·əl] *adj.* Not rational; not reasonable; senseless: an *irrational* fear of water. **— ir·ra′tion·al·ly** *adv.*

irrational number A number which cannot be exactly expressed as a whole number or as the quotient of two whole numbers. $\sqrt{3}$ and π are irrational numbers.

ir·rec·on·cil·a·ble [i·rek′ən·sī′lə·bəl] *adj.* Not able or willing to be reconciled: *irreconcilable* rivals.

ir·re·cov·er·a·ble [ir′i·kuv′ər·ə·bəl] *adj.* Not capable of being recovered or regained: the *irrecoverable* past.

ir·re·deem·a·ble [ir′i·dē′mə·bəl] *adj.* **1** Not capable of being recovered or exchanged: Postmarked stamps are *irredeemable.* **2** Beyond redeeming; past help: an *irredeemable* criminal.

ir·re·duc·i·ble [ir′i·d(y)ŏŏ′sə·bəl] *adj.* Not capable of being reduced or made simpler.

ir·ref·u·ta·ble [i·ref′yə·tə·bəl *or* ir′i·fyŏŏ′tə·bəl] *adj.* Not capable of being disproved: *irrefutable* evidence.

ir·reg·u·lar [i·reg′yə·lər] *adj.* **1** Not evenly shaped or arranged; following no pattern: an *irregular* outline. **2** Not conforming to established rules; improper or unusual: a highly *irregular* motion. **3** Having forms that do not fit the usual pattern: "Be" is an *irregular* verb. **— ir·reg′u·lar·ly** *adv.*

ir·reg·u·lar·i·ty [i·reg′yə·lar′ə·tē] *n., pl.* **ir·reg·u·lar·i·ties** **1** The condition of being irregular. **2** Something irregular or improper.

ir·rel·e·vant [i·rel′ə·vənt] *adj.* Not related to the subject or topic; not applicable or pertinent: an *irrelevant* objection. **— ir·rel′e·vance** *n.* **— ir·rel′e·vant·ly** *adv.*

ir·re·li·gious [ir′i·lij′əs] *adj.* Not religious.

ir·re·me·di·a·ble [ir′i·mē′dē·ə·bəl] *adj.* Not capable of being remedied or corrected.

ir·rep·a·ra·ble [i·rep′ər·ə·bəl] *adj.* Not capable of being repaired, fixed, or set right: *irreparable* harm. **— ir·rep′a·ra·bly** *adv.*

ir·re·place·a·ble [ir′i·plā′sə·bəl] *adj.* Not capable of being replaced; having no substitute: an *irreplaceable* antique chair.

ir·re·pres·si·ble [ir′i·pres′ə·bəl] *adj.* Not capable of being controlled or held back: *irrepressible* humor. **— ir′re·pres′si·bly** *adv.*

ir·re·proach·a·ble [ir′i·prō′chə·bəl] *adj.* Not capable of being blamed or found fault with; blameless: *irreproachable* behavior.

ir·re·sis·ti·ble [ir′i·zis′tə·bəl] *adj*. Incapable of being resisted or opposed: an *irresistible* smile. **—ir′re·sis′ti·bly** *adv*.

ir·res·o·lute [i·rez′ə·lōot] *adj*. Not firm or resolute in acting or in making up one's mind.

ir·res·o·lu·tion [i·rez′ə·lōo′shən] *n*. A lack of firmness or resolution in acting or in making up one's mind; hesitation.

ir·re·spec·tive [ir′i·spek′tiv] *adj*. Regardless: Anyone can join, *irrespective* of age.

ir·re·spon·si·ble [ir′i·spon′sə·bəl] *adj*. Not responsible or reliable; having no sense of duty. **—ir′re·spon′si·bil′i·ty** *n*. **—ir′re·spon′si·bly** *adv*.

ir·re·triev·a·ble [ir′i·trē′və·bəl] *adj*. That cannot be recovered or repaired: an *irretrievable* loss. **—ir′re·triev′a·bly** *adv*.

ir·rev·er·ent [i·rev′ər·ənt] *adj*. Having or showing a lack of awe, reverence, or respect: an *irreverent* attitude toward the flag. **—ir·rev′·er·ence** *n*. **—ir·rev′er·ent·ly** *adv*.

ir·re·vers·i·ble [ir′i·vûr′sə·bəl] *adj*. Incapable of being reversed, changed, or undone: an *irreversible* decision.

ir·rev·o·ca·ble [i·rev′ə·kə·bəl] *adj*. Incapable of being brought back, undone, or altered: an *irrevocable* decision; the *irrevocable* past. **—ir·rev′o·ca·bly** *adv*.

ir·ri·gate [ir′ə·gāt] *v*. **ir·ri·gat·ed, ir·ri·gat·ing** **1** To furnish (land) with water, by using pipes, ditches, or canals: The fruit growers of the west *irrigate* their crops. **2** To wash out, by applying a stream of water or other liquid: to *irrigate* a wound; to *irrigate* the nasal passages. **—ir′ri·ga′tion** *n*.

Irrigation system

ir·ri·ta·bil·i·ty [ir′ə·tə·bil′ə·tē] *n*. **1** The condition of being irritable. **2** The capacity of a plant or animal to respond to an external or internal stimulus.

ir·ri·ta·ble [ir′ə·tə·bəl] *adj*. **1** Easily annoyed or angered; snappish. **2** Very sensitive or sore. **—ir′ri·ta·bly** *adv*.

ir·ri·tant [ir′ə·tənt] **1** *adj*. Causing irritation: an *irritant* gas. **2** *n*. Something that irritates.

ir·ri·tate [ir′ə·tāt] *v*. **ir·ri·tat·ed, ir·ri·tat·ing** **1** To annoy; bother: Her constant laughter *irritated* him. **2** To make sore or inflamed: The rough wool *irritates* her skin. **—ir′ri·ta′tion** *n*.

ir·rup·tion [i·rup′shən] *n*. A breaking or rushing in with great force: an *irruption* of water through the broken dike.

Ir·ving [ûr′ving], **Washington**, 1783–1859, U.S. writer and humorist.

is [iz] A form of the verb BE. It indicates the present time and is used with "he," "she," or "it," or with singular nouns: He *is* a lawyer.

One man *is* arriving now. **— as is** Just as it is; with no change: Keep everything *as is*.

I·saac [ī′zək] *n*. In the Bible, the father of Jacob and Esau, and the son of Abraham and Sarah.

I·sa·iah [ī·zā′ə] *n*. **1** A Hebrew prophet who lived during the eighth century B.C. **2** A book of the Old Testament, containing his teachings.

Is·car·i·ot [is·kar′ē·ət] *n*. See JUDAS ISCARIOT.

-ise *suffix* Alternate spelling of -IZE, used chiefly in Great Britain. ¶ 3

-ish A suffix meaning: **1** Of or belonging to, as in a *Polish* church, a church of Poland. **2** Like, as in *childish*, like a child. **3** Somewhat; rather, as in *bluish*, somewhat blue. **4** Fond of or inclined to, as in *bookish*, fond of books.

i·sin·glass [ī′zing·glass′] *n*. **1** A type of gelatin made from fish bladders, used in jelly or glue. **2** Another name for MICA.

I·sis [ī′sis] *n*. In Egyptian myths, the goddess of fertility.

Is·lam [is·läm′ *or* is′ləm] *n*. **1** The religion of the Moslems, founded by Mohammed and in which there is only one God, called Allah. **2** All Moslems as a group. **3** The countries of the world where Islam is the chief religion. ◆ *Islam* comes from the Arabic word meaning *submission* (to the will of Allah).

Is·lam·ic [is·lam′ik *or* is·läm′ik] *adj*. Moslem.

is·land [ī′lənd] *n*. **1** A body of land entirely surrounded by water. The major continents of the world, however, are not usually considered islands. **2** Any place set apart from its surroundings: The park was an *island* of quiet in the city. ◆ *Island* comes from the Old English word *igland*. The *s* was added in the 15th century because of a mistaken association with *isle*. *Isle* actually has nothing to do with the Old English word; it came into English from the old French and goes back to the Latin *insula*.

is·land·er [ī′lən·dər] *n*. A person who comes from or lives on an island.

isle [īl] *n*. An island, especially a small one. ◆ See ISLAND.

is·let [ī′lit] *n*. A very small island.

-ism A suffix meaning: **1** A system, practice, or belief, as in *socialism*, a system of or a belief in socialist ideas. **2** The act or result of, as in *baptism*, the act or result of baptizing. **3** The quality or behavior of, as in *heroism*, the quality or behavior of a hero. **4** The condition of being, as in *skepticism*, the condition of being skeptical. **5** An example of, as in *colloquialism*, an example of a colloquial saying.

is·n't [iz′ənt] Is not.

i·so·bar [ī′sə·bär] *n*. A line on a weather map or chart drawn so that all points on the line have equal barometric pressures.

i·so·late [ī′sə·lāt] *v*. **i·so·lat·ed, i·so·lat·ing** **1** To place apart or alone; separate from others:

---

add, āce, câre, pälm;   end, ēqual;   it, īce;   odd, ōpen, ôrder;   tŏŏk, pōōl;   up, bûrn; ə = a in *above*, e in *sicken*, i in *possible*, o in *melon*, u in *circus*;   yōō = u in *fuse*;   oil;   pout; check;   ring;   thin;   this;   zh in *vision*.   For ¶ reference, see page 64 · HOW TO

His unfriendliness *isolated* him from the team. **2** *adj. use*: an *isolated* village. —**i'so·la'tion** *n.*
◆ The verb *isolate* was formed from the adjective *isolated*, which goes back to the Latin word *insula*, meaning *island.*

i·so·la·tion·ism [ī'sə·lā'shən·iz'əm] *n.* A belief that a country should keep apart from other nations and not take part in international alliances or affairs. —**i'so·la'tion·ist** *n.*

i·so·mer [ī'sə·mər] *n.* Any of a group of chemical compounds that are made up of the same elements in the same proportions but with different arrangements of their atoms.

i·sos·ce·les [ī·sos'ə·lēz] *adj.* Indicating a triangle having two of its sides equal.

i·so·therm [ī'sə·thûrm] *n.* A line on a weather map drawn so that all points on the line have the same average temperature.

i·so·tope [ī'sə·tōp] *n.* Any of two or more forms of an element that have the same atomic number and chemical properties but which have different atomic weights.

Isosceles triangles

Is·ra·el [iz'rē·əl] *n.* **1** A small country in western Asia, on the Mediterranean Sea. **2** An ancient Jewish kingdom in Palestine. **3** The Jewish people, as descended from Jacob.

Is·rae·li [iz·rā'lē] *adj., n., pl.* **Is·rae·lis 1** *adj.* Of or from modern Israel. **2** *n.* A person born in or a citizen of modern Israel.

Is·ra·el·ite [iz'rē·əl·īt] *n.* Any of the people of ancient Israel or their descendants; a Hebrew or Jew.

is·su·ance [ish'ōō·əns] *n.* The act of issuing.

is·sue [ish'ōō] *n., v.* **is·sued, is·su·ing 1** *n.* A sending out or supplying: an emergency *issue* of food. **2** *n.* Something supplied, distributed, or sent out, as a magazine, stamps, etc. **3** *v.* To give out; distribute: the army *issued* new rifles. **4** *v.* To send forth or out; publish: The book was first *issued* in England. **5** *n.* A going out; outflow: an *issue* of hot water from the faucet. **6** *v.* To come forth; flow out: Blood *issued* from the cut. **7** *n.* The outcome; result: The *issue* of the game was in doubt. **8** *v.* To come as a result or consequence: What *issued* from your efforts? **9** *n.* A topic or problem under discussion: the *issues* of the meeting. **10** *n.* Offspring; a child or children: The woman died without *issue.* — **at issue** To be resolved; under discussion. — **take issue** To disagree.

-ist A suffix meaning: **1** A person who makes or does, as in *tourist*, a person who tours. **2** A person whose work or job is, as in *pharmacist*, a person whose work is pharmacy. **3** A person who knows about, performs on, or is skilled in, as in *pianist*, a person who performs on a piano. **4** A person who believes in or advocates, as in *communist*, a person who believes in or advocates communism.

Is·tan·bul [is'tän·bool'] *n.* A city in the NW part of Turkey.

isth·mus [is'məs] *n.* A narrow strip of land, with water on each side, that connects two larger masses of land.

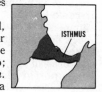

ISTHMUS

it [it] **1** *pron.* The animal, thing, happening, place, or idea being talked about: He took a cooky and bit *it* in two; I don't believe *it.* **2** *pron.* The apparent subject of a verb when the real subject follows: *It* was decided that we should go. **3** *pron.* The subject of an impersonal verb: *It* rained last night. **4** *pron.* An object having no definite meaning, used with certain verbs: He brazened *it* out. **5** *n.* The person in certain children's games who must catch or find another.

I·tal·ian [i·tal'yən] **1** *adj.* Of or from Italy. **2** *n.* A person born in or a citizen of Italy. **3** *n.* The language of Italy.

i·tal·ic [i·tal'ik] **1** *n.* (*usually pl.*) A kind of printing type in which the letters slant to the right. It is used to stress or call attention to words. *These words are printed in italics.* **2** *adj.* Describing or printed in this type.

i·tal·i·cize [i·tal'ə·sīz] *v.* **i·tal·i·cized, i·tal·i·ciz·ing 1** To print in italics. **2** To underline (something written) to show that it should be printed in italics. ¶3

It·a·ly [it'ə·lē] *n.* A country in southern Europe, also including the islands of Sardinia and Sicily.

itch [ich] **1** *v.* To have a tickling feeling on the skin that makes one want to scratch. **2** *n.* Such a tickling feeling. **3** *n.* A skin disease that causes this feeling. **4** *v.* To have a restless desire: He's *itching* to get moving again. **5** *n.* A restless desire: an *itch* to travel. —**itch'i·ness** *n.* —**itch'y** *adj.*

-ite A suffix meaning: **1** A person of or from, as in *Israelite*, a person from Israel. **2** A believer in or follower of, as in *Darwinite*, a believer in Darwin's theories.

i·tem [ī'təm] *n.* **1** Any one thing in a group of things: many *items* on a list. **2** A single piece of news or information.

i·tem·ize [ī'təm·īz] *v.* **i·tem·ized, i·tem·iz·ing** To list each item of: Please *itemize* the bill. ¶3

it·er·ate [it'ə·rāt] *v.* **it·er·at·ed, it·er·at·ing** To state or utter again; repeat.

Ith·a·ca [ith'ə·kə] *n.* A small island near the west coast of Greece, said to have been the home of Ulysses.

i·tin·er·ant [ī·tin'ər·ənt] **1** *adj.* Going from place to place; traveling: an *itinerant* farm worker. **2** *n.* A person who travels from place to place, especially one who moves from job to job.

i·tin·er·ar·y [ī·tin'ə·rer'ē] *n., pl.* **i·tin·er·ar·ies 1** The plan or route of a journey. **2** A detailed record of a journey.

it'll [it'(ə)l] **1** It will. **2** It shall.

its [its] *pron.* The possessive form of *it*: The dog had *its* dinner; This is *its* bed; *its* tricks.

it's [its] **1** It is. **2** It has.

it·self [it·self′] *pron.* Its own self. *Itself* is used: **1** As the object of a verb or preposition, referring, in both cases, back to the subject: The baby hurt *itself*; The motor started by *itself*. **2** To give emphasis to a noun: This drawing is simplicity *itself*. **3** To describe a normal or usual condition: The house isn't *itself* with the children gone.

-ity A suffix meaning: The condition or quality of being, as in *brutality*, the condition or quality of being brutal.

I've [īv] I have.

-ive A suffix meaning: **1** Likely to; tending to, as in *descriptive*, tending to describe. **2** Having the nature, character, or quality of, as in *instinctive*, having the character of instinct.

i·vied [ī′vēd] *adj.* Covered or overgrown with ivy: an *ivied* cottage.

i·vo·ry [ī′vər·ē] *n., pl.* **i·vo·ries**, *adj.* **1** *n.* The hard, smooth, white substance of which the tusks of elephants and walruses are composed. **2** *adj. use:* an *ivory* box. **3** *n.* Any hard, white substance like ivory. **4** *n.* (*pl.*) *slang* The keys of a piano. **5** *adj., n.* Creamy white.

Ivory Coast **1** A part of the coast of western Africa. **2** A country in West Africa. Its full name is **Republic of the Ivory Coast.**

i·vy [ī′vē] *n., pl.* **i·vies** **1** A climbing vine with shiny, evergreen leaves. **2** Any of the various other plants like this.

-ize A suffix meaning: **1** To cause to be, as in *legalize*, to cause to be legal. **2** To make or become, as in *brutalize*, to make or become brutal. **3** To make or change into, as in *crystallize*, to change into crystals. **4** To subject to the action of; affect with, as in *oxidize*, to subject to the action of oxygen. ¶3

Ivy

J

j or **J** [jā] *n., pl.* **j's** or **J's** The tenth letter of the English alphabet.

jab [jab] *n., v.* **jabbed, jab·bing** **1** *n.* A sharp poke or nudge. **2** *v.* To poke or nudge sharply. **3** *n.* A rapid punch. **4** *v.* To punch or strike with short, quick blows.

jab·ber [jab′ər] **1** *v.* To speak rapidly without making sense; chatter. **2** *n.* Rapid, senseless talk; chatter. **—jab′ber·er** *n.*

ja·bot [zha·bō′] *n., pl.* **ja·bots** [zha·bōz′] A ruffle or frill falling from the neckline of a blouse, dress, or, formerly, a man's shirt.

jack [jak] **1** *n.* A device or tool using a screw, lever, etc., to raise a heavy weight a short distance, as part of a car when a tire must be changed. **2** *v.* To lift with a jack. **3** *n.* A boy or man; fellow: seldom used today. **4** *n.* The male of certain animals. **5** *n.* A jackass. **6** *n.* A playing card bearing the face of a young man. It usually ranks just below the queen. **7** *n.* One of a set of stones or small metal pieces used in a children's game. **8** *n.* (*pl., used with a singular verb*) The game played with these pieces. **9** *n.* A small flag flown from a ship as a signal or an indication of nationality. **—jack up** **1** To raise with or as if with a jack: to *jack up* a car. **2** To raise (prices, fees, etc.).

Jack

jack·al [jak′əl] *n.* A doglike mammal of Asia and Africa which feeds on small animals and decaying carcasses.

jack·a·napes [jak′ə·nāps] *n.* An impudent or mischievous fellow; rascal.

jack·ass [jak′as′] *n.* **1** A male ass; donkey. **2** A stupid person; fool.

jack·boot [jak′bo͞ot′] *n.* A strong, heavy boot reaching above the knee.

jack·daw [jak′dô′] *n.* A glossy, black, crowlike bird of Europe, sometimes tamed as a pet.

jack·et [jak′it] *n.* **1** A short coat. **2** A wrapper or outer covering, as a removable paper covering for a book, the skin of a cooked potato, etc.

jack-in-the-box [jak′in·thə·boks′] *n.* A child's toy consisting of a box with a figure that springs up when the lid is unfastened.

jack-in-the-pul·pit [jak′in·thə·po͞ol′pit] *n.* A woodland plant having a flower stalk partly covered by a green or purplish hood.

add, āce, câre, pälm;   end, ēqual;   it, īce;   odd, ōpen, ôrder;   to͝ok, po͞ol;   up, bûrn;
ə = a in *above*, e in *sicken*, i in *possible*, o in *melon*, u in *circus*;   y o͞o = u in *fuse*;   oil;   pout;
check; ring; thin; this; zh in *vision*.   For ¶ reference, see page 64 · HOW TO

jack·knife [jak′nīf′] *n.*, *pl.* **jack·knives** [jak′· nīvz′], *v.* **jack·knifed, jack·knif·ing** **1** *n.* A large knife with folding blades, carried in the pocket. **2** *n.* A dive in which the diver bends over and touches his ankles with his hands while in the air and then straightens out and enters the water head first. **3** *v.* To double up like a jackknife.

jack-of-all-trades [jak′əv-ôl′trādz′] *n.* A person who is able to do many kinds of work.

jack-o'-lan·tern [jak′ə-lan′tərn] *n.* A lantern made of a hollowed pumpkin carved into a grotesque face.

jack·pot [jak′pot′] *n.* The big prize in a contest or game of chance.

jack rabbit A large American hare with very long ears and long hind legs.

Jack·son [jak′sən] *n.* The capital of Mississippi.

Jack·son [jak′sən], **Andrew,** 1767–1845, seventh president of the U.S., 1829–1837.

Jack·son [jak′sən], **Thomas Jona·than,** 1824–1863, Confederate general in the Civil War. He was called Stonewall Jackson.

Jack rabbit, 20 in. long

Jack·son·ville [jak′sən-vil] *n.* A city in NE Florida.

jack·stone [jak′stōn′] *n.* **1** A jack (*def. 7*). **2** (*pl.*, *used with a singular verb*) The game of jacks.

jack·straw [jak′strô′] *n.* **1** One of a set of thin rods used in a game. They must be picked out of a heap one at a time without moving any of the others. **2** (*pl.*, *used with a singular verb*) The game itself.

Ja·cob [jā′kəb] *n.* In the Bible, a son of Isaac and father of the founders of the twelve Hebrew tribes.

jade¹ [jād] **1** *n.* A hard, usually green mineral used as a gem. **2** *adj.*, *n.* Pale to dark green.

jade² [jād] *v.* **jad·ed, jad·ing,** *n.* **1** *v.* To tire through hard work or overuse; weary. **2** *adj. use:* a *jaded* appetite. **3** *n.* An old or useless horse. **4** *n.* A coarse or bad-tempered woman; hussy.

jag [jag] *n.* **1** A sharp, projecting point; notch. **2** A rough, pointed tear, as in cloth.

jagged [jag′id] *adj.* Having sharp points or notches.

Jaguar, 5–6 ft. long

jag·uar [jag′war] *n.* A large, spotted cat resembling a leopard, found in Central and South America. ◆ *Jaguar* comes from a Portuguese word derived from a South American Indian word.

jail [jāl] **1** *n.* A place for confining persons guilty of minor offenses or those awaiting trial. **2** *v.* To put or hold in jail.

jail·er or **jail·or** [jā′lər] *n.* The officer in charge of a jail or of the prisoners in it.

Ja·kar·ta [jä-kär′tä] *n.* The capital of Indonesia.

ja·lop·y [jə-lop′ē] *n.*, *pl.* **ja·lop·ies** *U.S. informal* An old automobile in bad shape.

jal·ou·sie [jal′ŏŏ-sē] *n.* A screen or shutter consisting of overlapping horizontal slats that can be tilted to keep out sun and rain while admitting light and air.

jam¹ [jam] *v.* **jammed, jam·ming,** *n.* **1** *v.* To press or squeeze into a tight space: to *jam* things into a box. **2** *v.* To block up, as by crowding: People *jammed* the halls. **3** *n.* A number of people or things crowded together: a traffic *jam.* **4** *v.* To make or become wedged or stuck, as a machine, door, part, etc. **5** *v.* To interfere with (radio signals) by broadcasting on the same frequency. **6** *v.* To injure by force or pressure: His foot was *jammed* in the door. **7** *v.* To push with force: to *jam* on the brakes. **8** *n. informal* An embarrassing or dangerous situation.

jam² [jam] *n.* A preserve of fruit boiled with sugar until the mixture is thick.

Ja·mai·ca [jə-mā′kə] *n.* An island in the West Indies, a member of the British Commonwealth. **— Ja·mai′can** *adj.*, *n.*

jamb [jam] *n.* A side post or side of a doorway or window.

jam·bo·ree [jam′bə-rē′] *n.* **1** *informal* A loud, lively party. **2** A large assembly of Boy Scouts, often from many countries.

James [jāmz] *n.* **1** Either of two disciples of Jesus. **2** A book of the New Testament.

James [jāmz], **Henry,** 1843–1916, U.S. writer and critic, active in England, and his brother **William,** 1842–1910, U.S. philosopher and psychologist.

James I, 1566–1625, King of England, 1603–1625.

James·town [jāmz′toun] *n.* A restored village in eastern Virginia. It was the first permanent English settlement in the U.S.

Jan. Abbreviation of JANUARY.

jan·gle [jang′gəl] *n.*, *v.* **jan·gled, jan·gling** **1** *n.* A harsh, unmusical sound. **2** *v.* To make or cause to make harsh, unmusical sounds. **3** *n.* A quarrel; wrangling. **4** *v.* To quarrel.

jan·i·tor [jan′i-tər] *n.* A person hired to clean and take care of a building.

Jan·u·ar·y [jan′yŏŏ-er′ē] *n.*, *pl.* **Jan·u·ar·ies** The first month of the year, having 31 days.

Ja·nus [jā′nəs] *n.* In Roman myths, the god of gates and doors, who watched over beginnings and endings. He is pictured as having two faces looking in opposite directions.

ja·pan [jə-pan′] *n.*, *v.* **ja·panned, ja·pan·ning** **1** *n.* A hard black varnish originally made in Japan. **2** *v.* To cover or lacquer with japan. **3** *adj. use:* a *japan* vase. **4** *n.* Objects lacquered or decorated in the Japanese manner.

Ja·pan [jə·pan′] *n.* A country made up of several islands east of the Asian mainland.

Jap·a·nese [jap′ə·nēz′] **1** *adj.* Of or from Japan. **2** *n.* A person born in or a citizen of Japan. **3** *n.* The language of Japan.

Japanese beetle A beetle that destroys crops, introduced into the U.S. from Japan.

jar¹ [jär] *n., v.* **jarred, jar·ring 1** *n.* A shaking, as from a sudden shock. **2** *v.* To cause to tremble or shake; jolt. **3** *v.* To strike with unpleasant or painful effect: Her voice *jars* on my nerves. **4** *n.* A harsh, grating sound. **5** *v.* To clash; conflict: The rumors *jarred* with the facts.

Japanese beetle

jar² [jär] *n.* **1** A deep earthenware or glass container with a wide opening at the top. **2** The quantity a jar contains.

jar·gon [jär′gən] *n.* **1** Confused speech which cannot be understood; gibberish. **2** A mixture of two or more languages. **3** The special words or terms used by the members of a particular profession or class: legal *jargon.*

jas·mine [jas′min *or* jaz′min] *n.* A shrub with fragrant white, yellow, or red flowers.

Ja·son [jā′sən] *n.* In Greek myths, the leader of the Argonauts in their search for the Golden Fleece.

jas·per [jas′pər] *n.* A variety of quartz, usually red, brown, or yellow in color.

jaun·dice [jôn′dis] *n., v.* **jaun·diced, jaun·dic·ing 1** *n.* A diseased condition of the liver in which there is a yellowness of the skin and the whites of the eyes caused by bile in the blood stream. **2** *v.* To affect with jaundice. **3** *n.* A state of mind caused by prejudice, envy, gloom, etc. **4** *v.* To affect the judgment of by prejudice or envy. **5** *adj. use:* a *jaundiced* view of the world.

jaunt [jônt] **1** *n.* A short journey for pleasure. **2** *v.* To make such a journey.

jaunt·y [jôn′tē] *adj.* **jaunt·i·er, jaunt·i·est 1** Having a lively or self-confident air or manner. **2** Dashing; perky: a *jaunty* little hat. —**jaunt′i·ly** *adv.* —**jaunt′i·ness** *n.*

Ja·va [jä′və *or* jav′ə] *n.* **1** An island of Indonesia. **2** A type of coffee grown there.

Java man A forerunner of modern man. His fossil bones were found in central Java.

Throwing a javelin

jave·lin [jav′(ə)lin] *n.* A light spear once used as a weapon, but now thrown for distance in athletic contests.

jaw [jô] **1** *n.* Either of the two bony parts of the skull in which the teeth grow; the framework of the mouth. **2** *n.* A jawbone. **3** *n.* The mouth, including the jaws and teeth. **4** *n.* (*often plural*) Anything resembling the mouth and its actions, as the gripping parts of a vise or the narrow opening of a canyon. **5** *v. Slang* To talk or gossip, especially in a dull, long-winded way.

jaw·bone [jô′bōn′] *n.* One of the bones forming the framework of the mouth, especially the lower jaw.

jay [jā] *n.* A noisy bird related to the crow but highly colored, as the blue jay.

jay·walk [jā′wôk′] *v. informal* To walk across a street carelessly and in violation of traffic rules or signals. —**jay′walk′er** *n.*

jazz [jaz] **1** *n.* A kind of popular music that originated with Negroes in the southern U.S. It uses strongly syncopated rhythms and has a characteristic style of melody and harmony. **2** *adj. use:* a *jazz* band; *jazz* musicians.

jeal·ous [jel′əs] *adj.* **1** Fearful of losing someone's love to a rival. **2** Caused by this fear: *jealous* actions. **3** Begrudging someone what he has; envious. **4** Careful in protecting; watchful: He was *jealous* of his reputation. **5** Demanding absolute loyalty, faithfulness, or worship: a *jealous* God. —**jeal′ous·ly** *adv.*

jeal·ous·y [jel′ə·sē] *n., pl.* **jeal·ous·ies** The condition or quality of being jealous.

jean [jēn] *n.* **1** A strong cotton cloth used in making workclothes. **2** (*pl.*) Trousers or overalls made of this material.

Jeanne d'Arc [zhän därk] The French spelling of JOAN OF ARC.

jeep [jēp] *n.* A small, sturdy automobile first used by the U.S. Army.

jeer [jir] **1** *v.* To make fun of with insulting words; ridicule; mock. **2** *n.* A bitter and sarcastic remark.

Jef·fer·son [jef′ər·sən], **Thomas,** 1743–1826, American states-

Jeep

man, writer, and philosopher; third president of the U.S., 1801–1809.

Jefferson City The capital of Missouri.

Je·ho·vah [ji·hō′və] *n.* In the Old Testament, one of the names for God.

jell [jel] *v.* **1** To thicken and turn to jelly. **2** *informal* To assume or cause to assume definite form: He can't leave until his plans *jell.*

jel·lied [jel′ēd] *adj.* **1** Made into a jelly or jellylike substance, as by chilling: a *jellied* consommé. **2** Covered with a jellylike substance.

jel·ly [jel′ē] *n., pl.* **jel·lies,** *v.* **jel·lied, jel·ly·ing 1** *n.* A thick, sticky substance that quivers when shaken but will not flow, as a spread made from fruit juice boiled with sugar. **2** *v.* To make into or become jelly. **3** *n.* Any substance like jelly.

jel·ly·bean [jel'ē·bēn'] *n.* A bean-shaped candy with a hard covering and a gummy center.

jel·ly·fish [jel'ē·fish'] *n.,* *pl.* **jel·ly·fish** *or* **jel·ly·fish·es** A sea animal with a jellylike, umbrella-shaped body and long trailing tentacles that capture and poison its prey.

Jen·ner [jen'ər], **Edward,** 1749–1823, English doctor. He discovered vaccination.

jen·net [jen'it] *n.* A small Spanish horse.

jen·ny [jen'ē] *n.,* *pl.* **jen·nies** **1** A machine for spinning yarn. **2** The female of some birds and animals: a *jenny* wren.

Jellyfish

jeop·ard·ize [jep'ər·dīz] *v.* **jeop·ard·ized, jeop·ard·iz·ing** To put in danger; place in jeopardy. ¶3

jeop·ard·y [jep'ər·dē] *n.* Danger of death, loss, or injury; peril.

jer·bo·a [jər·bō'ə] *n.* A small rodent of Asia and North Africa, having very long hind legs that enable it to move by great leaps.

Jer·e·mi·ah [jer'ə·mī'ə] *n.* **1** A Hebrew prophet who lived during the seventh century B.C. **2** A book of the Old Testament containing his prophecies.

Jer·i·cho [jer'ə·kō] *n.* In the Bible, a fortified city in ancient Palestine whose walls fell down miraculously when trumpets were blown.

jerk¹ [jûrk] **1** *n.* A sudden, sharp pull or twist: a *jerk* of the wrist. **2** *v.* To give a sharp, sudden pull or twist to; pull or tug at: to *jerk* a rope. **3** *n.* An involuntary tightening of a muscle; twitch. **4** *n.* A sudden, sharp movement: She turned with a *jerk*. **5** *v.* To move in a sudden or uneven way: to *jerk* one's head.

jerk² [jûrk] *v.* **1** To cure (meat, especially beef) by cutting into strips and drying. **2** *adj. use:* *jerked* beef.

jer·kin [jûr'kin] *n.* A man's tight jacket or vest, usually sleeveless, popular in the 16th and 17th centuries.

jerk·y [jûr'kē] *adj.* **jerk·i·er, jerk·i·est** Moving with sudden starts and stops: a *jerky* train. —**jerk'i·ly** *adv.* —**jerk'i·ness** *n.*

Je·rome [jə·rōm'] *n.,* 340?–420, Christian saint who prepared the Vulgate or Latin Bible.

jer·sey [jûr'zē] *n.,* *pl.* **jer·seys** **1** A cloth knitted by machine. **2** A knitted shirt or sweater pulled on over the head. **3** (*written* **Jersey**) One of a breed of small cattle giving rich milk.

Jerkin

Jersey City A city in NE New Jersey.

Je·ru·sa·lem [ji·roo'sə·ləm] *n.* A city in central Palestine, the capital of the ancient Jewish nation and present capital of Israel. Part of the city is in Jordan.

jes·sa·mine [jes'ə·min] *n.* Another name for JASMINE.

jest [jest] **1** *n.* Something said or done to provoke laughter; joke. **2** *n.* An object of laughter; laughingstock. **3** *v.* To tell jokes. **4** *v.* To speak or act in a playful way.

jest·er [jes'tər] *n.* A person who jests, especially, in former times, a clown whose job was to amuse a king.

Jes·u·it [jezh'oo·it *or* jez'yoo·it] *n.* A member of the Society of Jesus, a Roman Catholic religious order founded in 1534.

Je·sus [jē'zəs] *n.* The person whose life, teachings, and death are the basis of the Christian religion. He is also called **Jesus Christ.**

jet¹ [jet] **1** *n.* A hard, black mineral used for jewelry, buttons, etc. **2** *adj. use:* *jet* buttons. **3** *adj., n.* Deep, glossy black.

jet² [jet] *n., v.* **jet·ted, jet·ting 1** *n.* A gush or spurt of gas or liquid from a small opening. **2** *v.* To shoot out in a jet or jets. **3** *n.* A nozzle or spout. **4** *n.* A jet-propelled aircraft.

jet engine An engine that draws in air, mixes it with fuel, and ignites the mixture, producing a blast of hot gases to the rear and creating a strong forward thrust by reaction.

jet propulsion Propulsion, as of an airplane, by means of jets or jet engines.

jet·sam [jet'səm] *n.* **1** Goods thrown into the sea to lighten a ship in danger of sinking. **2** Such goods washed ashore.

jet stream 1 A current of winds blowing from the west at speeds often above 250 miles an hour, usually 30,000 to 45,000 feet up. **2** The blast of gases from a jet engine.

jet·ti·son [jet'ə·sən] *v.* **1** To throw (cargo or goods) overboard. **2** To throw away; discard.

jet·ty [jet'ē] *n., pl.* **jet·ties 1** A structure of stone or piles extending into a body of water to divert a current or protect a harbor. **2** A wharf or pier.

Jew [joo] *n.* **1** A member of the Hebrew people; Israelite. **2** A person who believes in and practices Judaism.

Jetty

jew·el [joo'əl] *n., v.* **jew·eled** *or* **jew·elled, jew·el·ing** *or* **jew·el·ling 1** *n.* A precious stone; gem. **2** *n.* Anything of rare excellence or value. **3** *v.* To set or adorn with jewels or something like a jewel: The grass was *jeweled* with dew. **4** *n.* A bit of ruby or other hard mineral used as a bearing, as in a watch.

jew·el·er [jōō′əl·ər] *n.* A person who sells or makes jewelry.

jew·el·ry [jōō′əl·rē] *n.* Personal ornaments, as rings, bracelets, etc., often made from precious metals and with precious stones.

Jew·ish [jōō′ish] *adj.* Of or having to do with the Jews, their religion, or their customs.

jew's-harp or **jews'-harp** [jōōz′harp′] *n.* A small metal musical instrument that is held between the teeth and played by striking a bent piece of metal with the finger.

Jez·e·bel [jez′ə·bəl] *n.* **1** In the Bible, a very wicked woman, the wife of King Ahab. **2** Any bold or wicked woman.

jib [jib] *n.* A triangular sail set forward of the foremast.

jibe¹ [jīb] *v.* **jibed, jib·ing** **1** To swing to the other side of a boat sailing before the wind: said about a sail. **2** To cause (a sail) to shift in this way, on purpose.

jibe² [jīb] *v.* **jibed, jib·ing** Another spelling of GIBE.

jibe³ [jīb] *v.* **jibed, jib·ing** *informal* To agree: Their stories appeared to *jibe*.

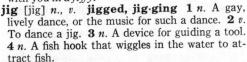
Jib

jif·fy [jif′ē] *n., pl.* **jif·fies** *informal* An instant: I'll be with you in a *jiffy*.

jig [jig] *n., v.* **jigged, jig·ging** **1** *n.* A gay, lively dance, or the music for such a dance. **2** *v.* To dance a jig. **3** *n.* A device for guiding a tool. **4** *n.* A fish hook that wiggles in the water to attract fish.

jig·gle [jig′əl] *v.* **jig·gled, jig·gling,** *n.* **1** *v.* To vibrate with short, quick jerks. **2** *n.* A jerky, unsteady movement.

jig·saw [jig′sô′] *n.* A saw with a slim blade set vertically in a frame and moved up and down, used for cutting curved or irregular lines.

jigsaw puzzle A puzzle consisting of a picture mounted on cardboard or wood and then cut into irregularly shaped pieces to be fitted together again.

jilt [jilt] **1** *v.* To cast off or discard, as a lover or sweetheart. **2** *n.* A woman who jilts.

jim·my [jim′ē] *n., pl.* **jim·mies,** *v.* **jim·mied, jim·my·ing** **1** *n.* A burglar's crowbar. **2** *v.* To break or pry open, as with a jimmy.

jim·son·weed [jim′sən·wēd′] *n.* A tall, very poisonous weed having a rank odor and large, funnel-shaped flowers.

jin·gle [jing′gəl] *n., v.* **jin·gled, jin·gling** **1** *n.* A tinkling, clinking, or rapid ringing. **2** *v.* To make or cause to make light, ringing or tinkling sounds: to *jingle* coins. **3** *n.* A catchy song or poem, especially for advertising purposes.

jin·ni [jin′ē *or* ji·nē′] *n., pl.* **jinn** [jin] Another spelling of GENIE.

jin·rik·sha or **jin·rik·i·sha** [jin·rik′shə *or* jin·rik′shô] *n.* A small two-wheeled carriage pulled by one or two men, used in some parts of the Orient.

jinx [jingks] *informal* **1** *n.* A person or thing supposed to bring bad luck. **2** *v.* To bring bad luck to.

jit·ney [jit′nē] *n., pl.* **jit·neys** *informal* A small bus or car that follows a regular route and carries passengers for a small fare.

Jinriksha

jit·ters [jit′ərz] *n.pl. U.S. slang* Nervousness, or nervous fear: a case of the *jitters*.

jit·ter·y [jit′ər·ē] *adj.* Nervous; fearful.

jiu·jit·su [jōō·jit′sōō] *n.* Another spelling of JUJITSU.

Joan of Arc [jōn], 1412?–1431, French heroine martyr, and saint who led the French army against the English in 1429.

job [job] **1** *n.* Anything that is to be done; a task or piece of work. **2** *adj.* Done by, or working by, the single job: a *job* printer. **3** *n.* A position or situation of employment.

Job [jōb] *n.* **1** In the Bible, a patient man who despite much suffering kept his faith in God. **2** A book of the Old Testament concerning him.

job·ber [job′ər] *n.* A person who buys in quantity from a manufacturer and sells to retail dealers.

jock·ey [jok′ē] *n., pl.* **jock·eys,** *v.* **1** *n.* A person employed to ride horses in races. **2** *v.* To ride as a jockey. **3** *v.* To manipulate or trick: to *jockey* someone into a bad position. **4** *v.* To maneuver in a tricky or skillful way.

jo·cose [jō·kōs′] *adj.* Merry; humorous; joking: a *jocose* manner. **—jo·cose′ly** *adv.*

joc·u·lar [jok′yə·lər] *adj.* **1** Making jokes; given to joking. **2** Intended as a joke. **—joc·u·lar·i·ty** [jok′yə·lâr′ə·tē] *n.* **—joc′u·lar·ly** *adv.*

jo·cund [jok′ənd *or* jō′kənd] *adj.* Cheerful; gay; jovial: seldom used today.

jodh·purs [jod′pərz] *n.pl.* Riding breeches that fit tightly from ankle to knee and loosely from the knee upward.

jog [jog] *v.* **jogged, jog·ging,** *n.* **1** *v.* To push or shake lightly, as though to get the attention of; nudge. **2** *n.* A nudge. **3** *v.* To urge on; stimulate: to *jog* one's memory. **4** *n.* An urging or stimulation. **5** *v.* To move slowly or monotonously: to *jog* along. **6** *v.* To move with a slow, jolting pace or trot. **7** *n.* A slow,

Jodhpurs

add, āce, câre, pälm;   end, ēqual;   it, īce;   odd, ōpen, ôrder;   tŏŏk, pŏŏl;   up, bûrn;
ə = a in *above*, e in *sicken*, i in *possible*, o in *melon*, u in *circus*;   yŏŏ = u in *fuse*;   oil;   pout;
check;   ring;   thin;   this;   zh in *vision*.   For ¶ reference, see page 64 · HOW TO

jolting pace; a jogging. **8** *n.* An angle or projection in a surface, as a wall.

jog·gle [jog′əl] *v.* **jog·gled, jog·gling,** *n.* **1** *v.* To shake slightly; jog. **2** *n.* A mild jolt.

John [jon] *n.* **1** In the Bible, one of the twelve Apostles of Jesus. **2** The Fourth Gospel or any of three other books of the New Testament ascribed to him.

John [jon] *n.* 1167–1216, King of England, 1199–1216. He signed the Magna Carta in 1215.

John Bull 1 The English people. **2** A typical Englishman.

John Hancock *U.S. informal* A signature: Put your *John Hancock* on the deed.

john·ny·cake [jon′ē·kāk′] *n.* A flat cornmeal cake baked on a griddle.

John·son [jon′sən], **Andrew,** 1808–1875, 17th president of the U.S., 1865–1869.

John·son [jon′sən], **Lyndon Baines,** born 1908, 36th president of the U.S., 1963–1969.

John·son [jon′sən], **Samuel,** 1709–1784, English lexicographer, poet, and writer.

John the Baptist In the Bible, the prophet who baptized Jesus, his cousin.

join [join] **1** *v.* To connect or combine; make or become one or as one; unite: to *join* two wires. **2** *n.* A point where things connect; joint. **3** *v.* To become a member of (a group, club, etc.): to *join* the navy. **4** *v.* To keep company with: *Join* us for supper. **5** *v.* To take part: Come *join* in the fun. **6** *v.* To return to or meet: *Join* us here later. **—join battle** To start to fight.

join·er [joi′nər] *n.* **1** A person or thing that joins. **2** A carpenter who finishes woodwork.

joint [joint] **1** *n.* The place, point, line, or surface where two things are joined. **2** *v.* To fasten by means of a joint. **3** *n.* A point in an animal's body where two or more parts or bones are joined, usually in a way that allows them to move. **4** *n.* A large cut of meat that contains a bone. **5** *v.* To divide into joints or cut apart at the joints. **6** *adj.* Done, owned, or shared by two or more persons: a *joint* effort. **7** *adj.* Sharing with another or others: *joint* owners. **8** *n. informal* A dingy or disreputable place, often a cheap bar. **— out of joint** Out of position at a joint, as a bone; dislocated. **—joint′ly** *adv.*

joist [joist] *n.* A horizontal beam of a floor.

joke [jōk] *n., v.* **joked, jok·ing 1** *n.* Something said or done for the purpose of creating laughter or amusement; jest. **2** *v.* To make jokes; jest. **3** *n.* Something humorous.

jok·er [jō′kər] *n.* **1** A person who jokes. **2** An extra playing card, used in some games. **3** A hidden difficulty, as a clause of a legislative bill that weakens its effectiveness.

Joists

Jo·li·et [jō′lē·et], **Louis,** 1645–1700, French-Canadian explorer in America.

jol·ly [jol′ē] *adj.* **jol·li·er, jol·li·est 1** Full of life and merriment; jovial. **2** Arousing gaiety; festive; merry. **—jol′li·ty** (jol′ə·tē) *n.*

Jolly Roger [roj′ər] The pirate flag bearing a skull and crossbones.

jolt [jōlt] **1** *n.* A sudden shock. **2** *v.* To shake roughly: The bump *jolted* us. **3** *v.* To move with jerks: The bus *jolted* along.

Jolly Roger

Jo·nah [jō′nə] *n.* **1** In the Bible, a Hebrew prophet who was thrown overboard, swallowed by a great fish, and cast up on shore alive three days later. **2** A book of the Old Testament concerning him. **3** (*written* **jonah**) A person whose presence is thought to bring ill fortune.

Jon·a·than [jon′ə·thən] *n.* In the Bible, the son of Saul and close friend of David.

Jones [jōnz], **John Paul,** 1747–1792, American naval commander in the Revolutionary War.

jon·quil [jon′kwil *or* jong′kwil] *n.* A type of narcissus related to the daffodil, having fragrant white or yellow flowers.

Jor·dan [jôr′dən] *n.* **1** A country in western Asia. **2** A river in Palestine flowing to the Dead Sea.

Jo·seph [jō′zəf] *n.* **1** In the New Testament, husband of Mary the mother of Jesus. **2** In the Old Testament, the favorite son of Jacob, sold into slavery in Egypt by his brothers.

josh [josh] *v. slang* To make good-humored fun of (someone).

Josh·u·a [josh′ōō·ə] *n.* **1** In the Bible, an Israelite leader and successor to Moses. **2** A book of the Old Testament relating his story.

jos·tle [jos′(ə)l] *v.* **jos·tled, jos·tling,** *n.* **1** *v.* To push or crowd against; elbow; shove; bump. **2** *n.* A hard shove or bump.

jot [jot] *v.* **jot·ted, jot·ting,** *n.* **1** *v.* To make a hasty and brief note of: to *jot* down a phone number. **2** *n.* The least bit; iota.

jounce [jouns] *n., v.* **jounced, jounc·ing 1** *n.* A shake; bump. **2** *v.* To shake or move roughly up and down; bounce; jolt: The wagon *jounced* along the old dirt road.

jour·nal [jûr′nəl] *n.* **1** A daily record or account, as of events, business transactions, thoughts, etc. **2** A newspaper, magazine, or other periodical. **3** The part of a shaft or axle that turns in or against a bearing.

jour·nal·ism [jûr′nəl·iz′əm] *n.* The occupation of writing, editing, or managing a newspaper or other periodical.

jour·nal·ist [jûr′nəl·ist] *n.* A person whose occupation is journalism.

jour·nal·is·tic [jûr′nəl·is′tik] *adj.* Of or having to do with journalism or journalists.

jour·ney [jur′nē] **1** *n.* Travel from one place to another; trip. **2** *n.* The distance traveled. **3** *v.* To make a trip; travel.

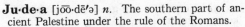

jour·ney·man [jûr′nē·mən] *n., pl.* **jour·ney·men** [jûr′nē·mən] A worker who has completed his apprenticeship in a skilled trade or craft.

joust [joust *or* just] **1** *n.* A formal combat between two mounted knights armed with lances; tilt. **2** *v.* To take part in a joust.

Jove [jōv] *n.* In Roman myths, the god Jupiter.

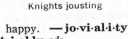

Knights jousting

jo·vi·al [jō′vē·əl] *adj.* Possessing or showing good nature; jolly; happy. —**jo·vi·al·i·ty** [jō′vē·al′ə·tē] *n.* —**jo′vi·al·ly** *adv.*

jowl [joul] *n.* The fleshy part under the lower jaw, especially when fat.

joy [joi] *n.* **1** A strong feeling of happiness, contentment, or satisfaction. **2** Something that causes this feeling.

Joyce [jois], **James,** 1882–1941, Irish poet and writer of novels and short stories.

joy·ful [joi′fəl] *adj.* **1** Full of joy. **2** Showing or causing joy. —**joy′ful·ly** *adv.*

joy·less [joi′lis] *adj.* Lacking in joy; dreary; sad.

joy·ous [joi′əs] *adj.* Joyful. —**joy′ous·ly** *adv.*

Jr. or **jr.** Abbreviation of JUNIOR.

ju·bi·lant [jōō′bə·lənt] *adj.* Expressing great joy; joyful; exultant. —**ju′bi·lant·ly** *adv.*

ju·bi·la·tion [jōō′bə·lā′shən] *n.* Rejoicing; gladness.

ju·bi·lee [jōō′bə·lē] *n.* **1** An anniversary celebration, especially for a twenty-fifth, fiftieth, or seventy-fifth anniversary. **2** A time of festivity or rejoicing. ◆ In Jewish history a *jubilee* year was a year during which Hebrew slaves were to be freed and the land left uncultivated. The word *jubilee* comes from a Hebrew word for a *ram's horn* or *trumpet* with which the beginning of a jubilee year was announced.

Ju·dae·a [jōō·dē′ə] *n.* Another spelling of JUDEA.

Ju·dah [jōō′də] *n.* **1** In the Bible, the fourth son of Jacob and Leah. **2** The tribe of Israel descended from him. **3** The kingdom made up of the tribes of Judah and Benjamin.

Ju·da·ic [jōō·dā′ik] *adj.* Of or having to do with the Jews.

Ju·da·ism [jōō′dē·iz′əm] *n.* The religion of the Jews, taught by Moses and the Hebrew prophets.

Ju·das Is·car·i·ot [jōō′dəs is·car′ē·ət] In the Bible, the disciple who betrayed Jesus.

Ju·de·a [jōō·dē′ə] *n.* The southern part of ancient Palestine under the rule of the Romans.

judge [juj] *n., v.* **judged, judg·ing 1** *n.* An official who administers justice by hearing and deciding cases in a court of law. **2** *v.* To hear and decide the merits of (a case) or the guilt of (a person); try. **3** *n.* A person appointed to make decisions, as in a contest. **4** *v.* To decide officially, as a contest. **5** *v.* To form a judgment or opinion about (something): Don't *judge* people without sympathy; to *judge* wisely. **6** *n.* A person having expert knowledge: a good *judge* of art. **7** *v.* To act as a judge. **8** *v.* To consider; suppose: How old do you *judge* that man to be?

Judg·es [juj′iz] *n.pl.* A book in the Old Testament containing a history of the Jews from the death of Joshua to the beginning of the monarchy.

judge·ship [juj′ship] *n.* The office, functions, or period in office of a judge.

judg·ment [juj′mənt] *n.* **1** The act of judging. **2** The ability to decide wisely. **3** The result of judging, especially the decision or sentence of a court. **4** Blame or condemnation: to pass *judgment.* **5** A disaster or misfortune thought to come as punishment from God.

Judgment Day In some religions, the day on which God makes final judgment of mankind.

ju·di·cial [jōō·dish′əl] *adj.* **1** Of or having to do with the administration of justice: *judicial* procedure. **2** Of or having to do with judges or courts of law: *judicial* duties. **3** Capable of forming fair and impartial judgments: a *judicial* mind. —**ju·di′cial·ly** *adv.*

ju·di·ci·ar·y [jōō·dish′ē·er′ē *or* jōō·dish′ə·rē] *n., pl.* **ju·di·ci·ar·ies,** *adj.* **1** *n.* The branch of government that interprets and applies the law. **2** *n.* The system of courts of law. **3** *n.* Judges collectively. **4** *adj.* Of or having to do with courts, judges, and their judgments: He was appointed to a *judiciary* committee.

ju·di·cious [jōō·dish′əs] *adj.* Having, showing, or using good judgment; prudent; wise. —**ju·di′cious·ly** *adv.*

Ju·dith [jōō′dith] *n.* In the Bible, a Jewish widow who saved her countrymen by charming, tricking, and killing an Assyrian general.

ju·do [jōō′dō] *n.* A method of defending oneself against physical attack, developed from jujitsu. ◆ *Judo* comes from two Japanese words meaning *gentle art* or *soft way.*

jug [jug] *n., v.* **jugged, jug·ging 1** *n.* A glass or earthenware container for liquids, having a narrow neck and a handle. **2** *n.* A pitcher or similar container. **3** *v.* To put into a jug. **4** *v.* To cook in a jug: to *jug* a hare.

jug·ger·naut [jug′ər·nôt] *n.* A slow and irresistible force or object that destroys everything in its path.

jug·gle [jug′əl] v. **jug·gled, jug·gling 1** To keep a number of objects continuously moving in the air by skillful tossing and catching. **2** To perform as a juggler. **3** To manipulate in a dishonest way: to *juggle* financial accounts. — **jug′gler** n.

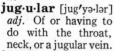
Man juggling

jug·u·lar [jug′yə·lər] adj. Of or having to do with the throat, neck, or a jugular vein.

jugular vein One of the two large veins in the neck that return blood from the brain and head to the heart.

juice [jōōs] n. **1** The liquid part of vegetable or animal matter: grapefruit *juice*; meat *juice*. **2** (*often pl.*) Body fluids: digestive *juices*. **3** *U.S. slang* Electricity.

juic·y [jōō′sē] adj. **juic·i·er, juic·i·est 1** Full of juice; moist. **2** Interesting; colorful; spicy: a *juicy* tale. — **juic′i·ness** n.

ju·jit·su [jōō·jit′sōō] n. A Japanese system of hand-to-hand fighting or wrestling in which one's opponent is made to use his strength to his own disadvantage.

juke box [jōōk] An automatic phonograph that allows records to be selected for playing after one or more coins are deposited.

Ju·li·et [jōō′lē·et *or* jōōl′yit] n. In Shakespeare's *Romeo and Juliet*, the heroine.

Ju·ly [jōō·lī′ *or* jōō·lī′] n. The seventh month of the year, having 31 days.

jum·ble [jum′bəl] n., v. **jum·bled, jum·bling 1** n. A confused mixture or collection. **2** v. To throw together in a confused mass; mix up. **3** v. To mix up in the mind; muddle.

jum·bo [jum′bō] n., pl. **jum·bos 1** n. A very large person, animal, or thing. **2** adj. Very large; extra large: a *jumbo* ice cream cone.

jump [jump] **1** v. To spring from the ground, floor, or other surface by bending and quickly straightening the legs: to *jump* up and touch the ceiling; The dog *jumped* off the chair. **2** v. To move in this way; bounce: to *jump* into bed. **3** v. To pass over or across (an object or obstacle) in this way: to *jump* a fence. **4** n. Something that is jumped over, as a fence or hurdle. **5** v. To cause to leap over an obstacle: to *jump* a horse. **6** n. The action of jumping; leap. **7** n. The height or distance covered by jumping: a six-foot *jump*. **8** n. A sporting contest in jumping: the high *jump*. **9** v. To move suddenly or jerkily, as though startled or surprised: When the floor creaked, she *jumped*. **10** n. A startled movement. **11** v. To increase or cause to increase suddenly: The temperature *jumped* sharply. **12** n. A sudden increase: a *jump* in prices. **13** v. To make a sudden shift, as in thought or conversation: to *jump* from one topic to another.

14 v. *informal* To attack (a person or group) by surprise; ambush. — **jump at** To accept with haste: to *jump at* a chance. — **jump the gun** *slang* To begin before the correct time.

jump·er¹ [jum′pər] n. A person, animal, or thing that jumps.

jum·per² [jum′pər] n. **1** A sleeveless dress, usually worn over a blouse or sweater. **2** A loose jacket or smock worn over other clothes.

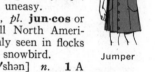
Jumper

jump·ing jack [jump′ing] A toy figure of a man, whose jointed limbs are moved by strings.

jump·y [jum′pē] adj. **jump·i·er, jump·i·est 1** Moving with jumps; jerky. **2** Nervous; uneasy.

jun·co [jung′kō] n., pl. **jun·cos** or **jun·coes** A small North American finch, commonly seen in flocks during the winter; snowbird.

junc·tion [jungk′shən] n. **1** A point where things meet or join. **2** The act of joining. **3** The condition of being joined.

junc·ture [jungk′chər] n. **1** A joint or union. **2** A particular, often critical, point in time or circumstances, especially in the phrase **at this juncture,** at this moment, or at this particular turn of events.

June [jōōn] n. The sixth month of the year, having 30 days.

Ju·neau [jōō′nō] n. The capital of Alaska.

June bug A large brown or greenish beetle that begins to fly early in June.

jun·gle [jung′gəl] n. **1** A dense, tropical forest, usually filled with wild animals. **2** Anything that seems like such a forest: the *jungle* of a city slum.

jun·ior [jōōn′yər] **1** adj. Younger, lower in rank, or having served for a shorter time: a *junior* member of a law firm. **2** n. The one who is younger or lower in rank. **3** n. The younger: written after the name of a son whose father has the same name, and usually abbreviated: John Snead, *Jr.* **4** adj. Indicating the next to last year of high school or college. **5** n. A student in his next to last year of high school or college.

junior high school In the U.S., a school coming between elementary and high school, and usually covering grades 7, 8, and 9.

ju·ni·per [jōō′nə·pər] n. An evergreen shrub or tree with dark blue berries.

junk¹ [jungk] **1** n. Worthless or worn-out things; trash; rubbish. **2** v. *informal* To discard as worthless: Let's *junk* this old sofa.

Junk

junk² [jungk] n. A large Chinese ship with lugsails, a high stern, and a flat bottom.

jun·ket [jung′kit] **1** *n.* Curdled, sweetened, and flavored milk, sometimes served as a dessert. **2** *n.* A feast, picnic, or banquet. **3** *n.* A pleasure trip, often at public expense. **4** *v.* To go on a pleasure trip.

Ju·no [jōō′nō] *n.* In Roman myths, the wife of Jupiter and the goddess of marriage. She was called Hera by the Greeks.

jun·ta [jun′tə *or* hŏōn′tə] *n.* **1** A group or council that runs a government, especially a small group that has seized power by force. **2** A group involved in political plotting.

Ju·pi·ter [jōō′pə·tər] *n.* **1** In Roman myths, the god ruling over all other gods and all men. He was called Zeus by the Greeks. **2** The largest planet in the solar system, the fifth in distance from the sun.

ju·ris·dic·tion [jōōr′is·dik′shən] *n.* **1** The legal right to exercise official authority. **2** The area or the affairs over which such authority may be exercised. **3** The power of those in authority.

ju·ris·pru·dence [jōōr′is·prōōd′əns] *n.* **1** The science of law. **2** A system of laws.

ju·rist [jōōr′ist] *n.* A person trained and skilled in the science of law.

ju·ror [jōōr′ər] *n.* A member of a jury.

ju·ry [jōōr′ē] *n.,* *pl.* **ju·ries 1** A qualified group of people sworn to give a true verdict after hearing the evidence in a trial in a court of law. It is sometimes called a *trial jury* to distinguish it from a *grand jury*, which decides whether or not a person should be brought to trial. **2** A group chosen to select a winner in a competition.

ju·ry·man [jōōr′ē·mən] *n.,* *pl.* **ju·ry·men** [jōōr′ē·mən] A juror.

just¹ [just] **1** *adj.* Fair and impartial in dealing with people, making decisions, etc.: a *just* teacher. **2** *adj.* True; accurate: a *just* picture of world events. **3** *adj.* Well deserved; fairly earned: a *just* reward. **4** *adj.* Felt with good reason: *just* indignation. **5** *adv.* Not long ago; very recently: He *just* left; You *just* missed the train. **6** *adv.* Only; merely: He's *just* sleepy. **7** *adv.* *informal* Really; very: Your party was *just* great. **— just′ly** *adv.*

just² [just] *n.,* *v.* Another spelling of JOUST.

jus·tice [jus′tis] *n.* **1** The condition or quality of being just; a being fair and impartial according to the principles of right and wrong: *Justice* demands that the guilty be punished; There is *justice* in his plea for equal treatment. **2** What is due or deserved: to receive *justice* in court. **3** The administration of law. **4** A judge, especially one of high rank. **— do justice 1** To act or treat fairly. **2** To show appreciation for.

justice of the peace A local judge able to try minor offenses, send cases to higher courts, perform marriages, etc.

jus·ti·fi·a·ble [jus′tə·fī′ə·bəl] *adj.* Capable of being shown to be just or proper: *justifiable* pride in one's work. **— jus′ti·fi′a·bly** *adv.*

jus·ti·fi·ca·tion [jus′tə·fə·kā′shən] *n.* **1** The act of justifying. **2** The fact of being justified. **3** An acceptable excuse or defense: Ignorance of the law is not a *justification* for breaking it.

jus·ti·fy [jus′tə·fī] *v.* **jus·ti·fied, jus·ti·fy·ing 1** To show to be just, right, or reasonable: The boy's achievements *justified* his teachers' confidence in him. **2** To provide good reason for: His bad conduct *justified* his being dismissed.

jut [jut] *v.* **jut·ted, jut·ting** To extend outward; project: The shelf *juts* out too far.

jute [jōōt] *n.* **1** A tall plant that grows in Asia. **2** The tough fiber from the bark of this plant, used for making burlap, cord, etc.

Jute [jōōt] *n.* A member of a Germanic tribe that invaded Britain in the fifth century.

ju·ve·nile [jōō′və·nəl *or* jōō′və·nīl] **1** *adj.* Young, youthful, or immature. **2** *adj.* Of, like, or for young persons. **3** *n.* A young person; youth. **4** *n.* A book for children. **5** *n.* An actor who plays youthful roles.

juvenile delinquency The illegal or destructive behavior of juvenile delinquents.

juvenile delinquent A person who has broken the law or behaved destructively, but is too young to be punished as an adult criminal.

jux·ta·po·si·tion [juks′tə·pə·zish′ən] *n.* **1** The act of placing close together or side by side. **2** A being close together or side by side.

K

k or **K** [kā] *n.,* *pl.* **k's** or **K's** The 11th letter of the English alphabet.

K The symbol for the element POTASSIUM. ◆ The Latin word for potassium is *kalium*.

kai·ak [kī′ak] *n.* Another spelling of KAYAK.

Kai·ser [kī′zər] *n.* An emperor, especially an emperor of Austria or Germany before 1918.

kale [kāl] *n.* A cabbage with loose, curled leaves that do not form a head.

ka·lei·do·scope [kə·lī′də·skōp] *n.* **1** A tubelike device containing loose bits of colored glass and a set of mirrors. When it is held to the eye and turned, the bits of glass move and are reflected in constantly changing patterns. **2** Any changing pattern, view, scene, etc.

ka·lei·do·scop·ic [kə·lī'/də·skop'ik] *adj*. Of or like a kaleidoscope; always changing.

kan·ga·roo [kang'/gə·rōō'] *n.*, *pl.* **kan·ga·roos** An Australian animal that has short, weak forelegs, strong hind legs used for leaping, and a long, thick tail. The female has a pouch in which it carries its young.

Kangaroo, 6–7 ft. high

◆ *Kangaroo* comes from a native Australian language.

Kans. Abbreviation of KANSAS.

Kan·sas [kan'zəs] *n.* A state in the central U.S.

Kansas City 1 A city in western Missouri. **2** A city in NE Kansas.

ka·o·lin [kā'ə·lin] *n.* A fine, white clay, widely used to make porcelain.

Ka·ra·chi [kə·rä'chē] *n.* A seaport in Pakistan on the Arabian Sea, the former capital.

kar·a·kul [kar'ə·kəl] *n.* Another spelling of CARACUL.

kar·at [kar'ət] *n.* The 24th part by weight of pure gold in an alloy. Pure gold has 24 karats.

Kash·mir [kash·mir' *or* kash'mir] *n.* A region adjoining India and Pakistan and claimed by both.

ka·ty·did [kā'tē·did] *n.* A green insect that looks like a grasshopper. The male makes a shrill sound by rubbing its wings together.

kay·ak [kī'ak] *n.* An Eskimo canoe made of a light frame fully enclosed by skins, with an opening for the user.

Keats [kēts], **John,** 1795–1821, English poet.

keel [kēl] *n.* **1** The main structural timber or steel bar running along the center of a ship's bottom. **2** Any part or object

Kayak

that resembles or functions like a keel. **— keel over 1** To turn upside down. **2** To fall, as in a swoon. **— on an even keel** In equilibrium; steady.

keel·boat [kēl'bōt'] *n.* A shallow freight boat with no sails, propelled by poles or oars.

keel·son [kēl'sən] *n.* A beam fastened along the top of the keel of a ship to stiffen it.

keen [kēn] *adj*. **1** Able to cut easily; very sharp: a *keen* knife. **2** Acute or sensitive, as in vision, mental perception, etc.: a *keen* mind; *keen* hearing. **3** Eager; enthusiastic; intense: a *keen* interest; He's *keen* about meeting you. **4** Pierc-

ing or cutting in force; sharp: a *keen* wind. **5** *slang* Fine; excellent: We had a *keen* time. **— keen'ly** *adv*. **— keen'ness** *n.*

keep [kēp] *v.* **kept, keep·ing,** *n.* **1** *v.* To retain possession or control of; hold, hold back, or hold on to: to *keep* a secret; to *keep* one's earnings. **2** *v.* To prevent or restrain: The rope *kept* him from falling down the mountain. **3** *v.* To save; reserve: to *keep* a piece of cake for later. **4** *v.* To take care of; tend: to *keep* the flock. **5** *v.* To stay or cause to stay in good condition, as food. **6** *v.* To remain; stay: *Keep* away. **7** *v.* To continue or maintain: *Keep* the game going; *Keep* dancing. **8** *v.* To be faithful to, observe, or fulfill: to *keep* a promise; to *keep* holydays. **9** *v.* To write down or maintain a regular record in: to *keep* a journal. **10** *v.* To have a supply of for use or sale: The baker *keeps* rolls. **11** *n.* The food and shelter one needs to live: He earns his *keep* by chopping wood. **12** *v.* To employ for service: to *keep* a servant. **13** *n.* A castle or fortress, or the stronghold of a castle. **— for keeps** *informal* **1** With all winnings kept: to play *for keeps*. **2** Forever: It's yours *for keeps*. **— keep to oneself 1** To stay away from others. **2** To avoid revealing (a secret, etc.). **— keep up 1** To maintain in good condition. **2** To continue: *Keep up* the good work. **3** To make stay awake. **— keep up with 1** To stay informed about: to *keep up with* the news. **2** To stay even with, as in speed.

keep·er [kē'pər] *n.* A person who guards or takes care of people, animals, or things; attendant, guardian, overseer, warden, etc.

keep·ing [kē'ping] *n.* **1** Charge; custody: He's in a doctor's *keeping*. **2** Observing or maintaining: the *keeping* of a holiday. **3** Agreement; conformity: conduct in *keeping* with the rules.

keep·sake [kēp'sāk'] *n.* Something kept as a remembrance of the person who gave it.

keg [keg] *n.* A small barrel, usually one that holds up to ten gallons.

kelp [kelp] *n.* **1** A coarse, brown seaweed. **2** Its ash, a source of iodine.

Kel·vin scale [kel'vin] A temperature scale that places zero at absolute zero and uses degrees of the same size as the centigrade scale.

ken [ken] *v.* **kenned, ken·ning,** *n.* **1** *v.* To know: used chiefly in Scotland. **2** *n.* Range of sight or knowledge: It's beyond my *ken.*

Ken·ne·dy [ken'ə·dē], **Cape** A cape of eastern Florida, site of a U.S. rocket-launching base.

Ken·ne·dy [ken'ə·dē], **John Fitzgerald,** 1917–1963, 35th president of the U.S., 1961–1963, assassinated while in office.

ken·nel [ken'əl] *n.*, *v.* **ken·neled** *or* **kennelled, ken·nel·ing** *or* **ken·nel·ling 1** *n.* A house for a dog or a pack of dogs. **2** *n.* (*often pl.*) A place where dogs are bred, housed, etc.: Our dog will stay at a *kennel* while we are away. **3** *v.* To place or keep in a kennel.

Kent [kent] *n.* A county in SE England.

Ken·tuck·y [kən·tuk'ē] *n.* A state in the east central U.S.

Ken·ya [kĕn′yə *or* ken′yə] *n.* A country in eastern Africa, a member of the British Commonwealth of Nations.

Kep·ler [kep′lər], **Johann,** 1571–1630, German astronomer.

kept [kept] Past tense and past participle of KEEP: He *kept* his cash in a wallet.

ker·chief [kûr′chif] *n.* **1** A piece of fabric, usually square, worn over the head or around the neck. **2** A handkerchief.

ker·nel [kûr′nəl] *n.* **1** A seed or grain, as of wheat or corn. **2** The soft, often edible part inside a nut or fruit pit. **3** The central part, as of a plan or theory; nucleus; gist.

ker·o·sene [ker′ə·sēn] *n.* A thin oil made from petroleum, used as fuel in lamps, stoves, etc.

Kerchief

ketch [kech] *n.* A vessel with a tall mast forward and a shorter one aft.

ketch·up [kech′əp] *n.* A thick red sauce made with tomatoes and spices.

ket·tle [ket′(ə)l] *n.* **1** A metal vessel for boiling or stewing. **2** A teakettle. **— kettle of fish** A difficult or awkward situation.

ket·tle·drum [ket′(ə)l·drum′] *n.* A large drum, a metal hemisphere with a head that adjusts to pitch.

key¹ [kē] *n., pl.* **keys**, *v* **keyed, key·ing**, *adj.* **1** *n.* A small metal instrument for moving the bolt or tumblers of a lock, as in locking, or unlocking a door, drawer, padlock, etc. **2** *n.* A wedge or pin to lock parts together. **3** *n.* An instrument like a key in form or function, as the winding mechanism on a clock.

Kettledrums

4 *n.* Anything that opens, explains, identifies, or solves something, as a set of answers to problems, a translation of a book in a foreign language, etc. **5** *v.* To prepare or provide with such a key. **6** *n.* A person, place, or thing that controls or is important to something else: Hard work is one of the *keys* to success. **7** *adj.* Controlling or important: a *key* man in the steel industry. **8** *n.* One of the parts pressed down with the fingers in playing a piano, using a typewriter, etc. **9** *n.* In music, a system of tones, chiefly of a major or minor scale, in which a particular tone predominates and after which the system is named. **10** *v.* To regulate the pitch or tone of. **11** *v.* To harmonize or fit: decor *keyed* to the room. **12** *n.* A style, tone, or manner: a play written in a somber *key*. **— key up** To cause excitement, nervousness, expectancy, etc., in.

key² [kē] *n., pl.* **keys** A low island, especially one of coral, along a coast: the Florida *Keys*.

key·board [kē′bôrd′] *n.* The row or rows of keys, as in a piano or typewriter.

key·hole [kē′hōl′] *n.* A hole for a key, as in a lock or door.

key·note [kē′nōt′] *n.* **1** The note that a musical key is named after and based upon. **2** The basic idea or principle of a speech, philosophy, policy, etc.: Brotherhood was the *keynote*.

key·stone [kē′stōn′] *n.* **1** The middle stone at the top of an arch, serving to lock the other stones in place. **2** A basic or fundamental part, as of a science.

keystone

khak·i [kak′ē] *n., pl.* **khak·is,** *adj.* **1** *n., adj.* Yellowish brown. **2** *n.* A strong cotton cloth of this color. **3** *n.* (*pl.*) A uniform made of khaki.

◆ *Khaki,* which describes an earthy color, comes from a Persian word meaning *dust.*

khan [kän] *n.* **1** A title once used by Mongol rulers. **2** A title for a ruler or high ranking official in central Asia, Afghanistan, and Iran.

Khrush·chev [krōōsh·chôf′], **Nikita,** born 1894, Soviet statesman and premier, 1958–1964.

kib·itz·er [kib′it·sər] *n. informal* A person who looks on and offers advice, as at a card game.

kick [kik] **1** *v.* To strike forcefully with the foot: She *kicked* her sister. **2** *v.* To strike out with the foot or feet: This horse *kicks.* **3** *n.* A blow with the foot. **4** *v.* To cause to move by striking with the foot: to *kick* a ball. **5** *v.* To snap back suddenly, as a gun does when fired. **6** *n.* A sudden recoil, as of a gun when fired. **7** *v. informal* To complain or object. **8** *n. informal* A complaint or objection. **9** *n.* The act of kicking. **10** *n. slang* An excited sensation; thrill: They went to the carnival for *kicks.* **— kick′er** *n.*

kick·off [kik′ôf′] *n.* In football and soccer, the kick that puts the ball into play.

kid [kid] *n., v.* **kid·ded, kid·ding 1** *n.* A young goat. **2** *n.* The leather made from its skin. **3** *adj. use:* **kid** gloves. **4** *n. informal* A child. **5** *v. slang* To make fun of; tease.

kid·nap [kid′nap] *v.* **kid·naped** or **kid·napped, kid·nap·ing** or **kid·nap·ping** To carry off, as by force or fraud, usually so as to demand a ransom. **— kid′nap·er** or **kid′·nap·per** *n.*

kid·ney [kid′nē] *n., pl.* **kid·neys 1** Either of a pair of organs close to the spinal cord, that separate excess water and waste products from the blood, and pass them out as urine. **2** The kidneys of certain animals, used as food. **3** Temperament, nature, or kind: a man of my own *kidney.*

Kidneys

add, **ā**ce, **câ**re, **pä**lm;   **e**nd, **ē**qual;   **i**t, **ī**ce;   **o**dd, **ō**pen, **ô**rder;   t**ŏŏ**k, p**ōō**l;   **u**p, b**û**rn;
ə = a in *above*, e in *sicken*, i in *possible*, o in *melon*, u in *circus*;   **y ōō** = u in *fuse*;   **oi**l;   p**ou**t;
check;   **r**i**ng**;   **th**in;   **th**is;   **zh** in *vision*.   For ¶ reference, see page 64 · HOW TO

Ki·ev [kē′ev *or* kē·ev′] *n*. The capital of the Ukraine, in the sw Soviet Union.

kill [kil] **1** *v*. To cause the death of or put an end to life. **2** *v*. To slaughter for food. **3** *n*. The act of killing. **4** *n*. The animal or animals killed as prey or in a hunt. **5** *v*. To bring to an end; destroy; ruin. **6** *v*. To spoil the effect of. **7** *v*. To veto or defeat (legislation). **8** *v*. To pass (time) aimlessly. **9** *v*. *slang* To overwhelm, as with laughter or pain. **— kill′er** *n*.

kill·deer [kil′dir] *n.*, *pl.* **kill·deers** or **kill·deer** A North American wading bird related to the plover, having a loud cry.

kill-joy [kil′joi′] *n*. A person who spoils other people's fun or pleasure.

kiln [kil(n)] *n*. An oven or furnace for baking, burning, or drying bricks, pottery, lime, etc.

kil·o [kil′ō *or* kē′lō] *n.*, *pl.* **kil·os 1** A kilogram. **2** A kilometer.

kilo- A prefix meaning: One thousand, as in *kilometer*, one thousand meters.

kil·o·cy·cle [kil′ə·sī′kəl] *n*. In physics, 1,000 cycles, especially 1,000 cycles per second.

kil·o·gram [kil′ə·gram′] *n*. In the metric system, a unit of weight equal to 1,000 grams, and equivalent to about 2.2 pounds.

kil·o·me·ter [kil′ə·mē′tər *or* ki·lom′ə·tər] *n*. In the metric system, 1,000 meters, a unit of length equal to about ⅝ of a mile.

kil·o·watt [kil′ə·wat′] *n*. A unit of power equal to 1,000 watts.

kil·o·watt-hour [kil′ə·wat·our′] *n*. The work done or the energy delivered by one kilowatt acting for one hour. Electric power is usually sold by the kilowatt-hour.

Kilt

kilt [kilt] *n*. A short pleated skirt, often plaid, worn by men in the Scottish highlands.

kil·ter [kil′tər] *n*. *informal* Proper working order, especially in the phrase **out of kilter:** My old car is *out of kilter.*

ki·mo·no [kə·mō′nə] *n.*, *pl.* **ki·mo·nos 1** A loose robe worn as an outer garment in Japan. **2** A woman's dressing gown resembling this.

kin [kin] **1** *n*. Relatives; family. **2** *adj.* Related by blood: I am *kin* to him. — **next of kin** The nearest relative or relatives.

kind[1] [kīnd] *n*. **1** Sort; type; variety: He buys all *kinds* of clothes. **2** A natural grouping or class; species. **— in kind 1** With goods rather than money: to pay taxes *in kind.* **2** With the same sort of thing: to return an insult *in kind.* **— kind of** *informal* Somewhat. **— of**

Kimono

a kind Of the same sort or kind. ◆ *Kind of* (or *sort of*), when used before a singular noun, as in *this kind of book*, is generally accepted in formal speaking and writing. *Kind of*, when used after *these* and before a plural noun, as in *these kind of books*, is not accepted in formal English, the correct form being *these kinds of books* followed by a plural verb.

kind[2] [kīnd] *adj.* **1** Always ready to do good; helpful; gentle; friendly; sympathetic: a *kind* old man. **2** Coming from or showing goodness, sympathy, friendliness, etc.: It was *kind* of her to give the hungry kitten some milk.

kin·der·gar·ten [kin′dər·gär′tən] *n*. A school or class for young children, usually from the ages of four to six, which develops basic skills and serves as a preparation for regular school work. ◆ *Kindergarten* comes directly from German, where it means *children's garden.*

kind·heart·ed [kīnd′här′tid] *adj.* Kind and sympathetic.

kin·dle [kin′dəl] *v*. **kin·dled, kin·dling 1** To set fire to; light: They *kindled* the paper with a match. **2** To catch fire; start to burn: The wet paper did not *kindle.* **3** To excite or arouse: The brutal deed *kindled* our rage. **4** To brighten or glow: His eyes *kindled* with excitement.

kin·dling [kind′ling] *n*. Small pieces of dry wood, twigs, etc., for starting a fire.

kind·ly [kīnd′lē] *adj.* **kind·li·er, kind·li·est,** *adv.* **1** *adj.* Kind; sympathetic. **2** *adv.* In a kind or sympathetic way. **3** *adj.* Pleasant or favorable: a *kindly* wind. **4** *adv.* So as to please or oblige: *Kindly* leave. **— kind′li·ness** *n*.

kind·ness [kīnd′nis] *n*. **1** The condition of being kind. **2** A kind act or service.

kin·dred [kin′drid] **1** *n*. A person's relatives by blood. **2** *adj.* Belonging to the same family. **3** *n*. A family, clan, or other group related by blood. **4** *adj.* Having a similar nature: *kindred* souls. **5** *n*. Kinship.

kine [kīn] *n.pl.* Cattle: seldom used today.

ki·net·ic [ki·net′ik] *adj.* Of or having to do with motion: *kinetic* energy.

king [king] *n*. **1** A male ruler of a country, especially one whose position is inherited. **2** A person, animal, or thing that holds a chief position, as in some field or class. **3** A playing card marked with a picture of a king. **4** In chess, the principal piece. When a king is in danger of being captured and cannot move out of danger, the game is ended. **5** A piece in checkers that has reached the opponent's end of the board.

King [king], **Martin Luther, Jr.,** 1929–1968, U.S. civil rights leader; assassinated.

king·bird [king′bûrd′] *n*. A flycatcher of North America that eats insects and attacks larger birds, as crows and hawks.

king·dom [king′dəm] *n*. **1** A country ruled by a king or queen. **2** An area or sphere where someone or something is dominant: the *kingdom* of the sea. **3** A primary division in the natural world: the animal, vegetable, and mineral *kingdoms.*

king·fish·er [king′fish′ər] *n*. A brightly-colored bird with a short tail and strong bill, that usually feeds on fish.

king·ly [king′lē] *adj*. **king·li·er, king·li·est** Of, having to do with, or fit for a king; regal; royal.

Kings [kingz] *n*. **1** Either of two books of the Old Testament that give the history of the Hebrew kings after David. **2** Any of four books in the Roman Catholic Bible corresponding to I and II Samuel and the two above.

Kingfisher, about 1 ft. long

king·ship [king′ship] *n*. **1** The office or power of a king. **2** Government by a king; monarchy.

king-size [king′sīz′] *adj*. *informal* Extra large or long: a *king-size* package.

kink [kingk] **1** *n*. A sharp bend, twist, or curl, as in a hair or wire. **2** *v*. To form a kink or kinks. **3** *n*. A painful muscular cramp; crick. **4** *n*. A queer idea; odd notion.

kink·y [kingk′ē] *adj*. **kink·i·er, kink·i·est** Full of kinks. — **kink′i·ness** *n*.

kins·folk [kinz′fōk′] *n*. Family; kin.

kin·ship [kin′ship] *n*. Relationship, especially by blood.

kins·man [kinz′mən] *n*., *pl*. **kins·men** [kinz′-mən] A relative, especially a male relative.

kins·wom·an [kinz′woŏm′ən] *n*., *pl*. **kins·wom·en** [kinz′wim′ən] A female relative, as an aunt.

ki·osk [kē·osk′] *n*. **1** A small structure, with one or more open sides, used especially as a newsstand, booth, bandstand, etc. **2** In Turkey, an open pavilion used as a shady resting place.

Kiosk

Kip·ling [kip′ling], **Rud·yard,** 1865–1936, English writer and poet.

kip·per [kip′ər] **1** *v*. To split and salt (a fish), and then dry or smoke it. **2** *n*. A fish that is kippered, especially a herring.

kirk [kûrk] *n*. A church: a Scottish word.

kir·tle [kûr′t(ə)l] *n*. **1** A skirt or petticoat. **2** A man's tunic. ◆ This word is seldom used today.

kiss [kis] **1** *v*. To touch with the lips as a token of love, respect, greeting, etc. **2** *n*. The act of kissing. **3** *v*. To meet or touch lightly: The marbles just *kissed*. **4** *n*. A light or gentle touch. **5** *n*. A small candy.

kit [kit] *n*. **1** A collection of tools or equipment for some special purpose: a repair *kit*. **2** A box or bag for equipment or gear. **3** A packaged set of parts from which an article may be assembled:

a furniture *kit*. **4** A collection of articles carried for a person's own use: a soldier's *kit*.

kitch·en [kich′ən] *n*. A room where food is prepared and cooked.

kitch·en·ette [kich′ən·et′] *n*. A small kitchen or area used as a kitchen.

kitch·en·ware [kich′ən·wâr′] *n*. Kitchen utensils, as pots or pans.

kite [kīt] *n*. **1** A light frame, as of wood, covered with paper or cloth, designed to be flown in the wind on a long string. **2** A hawk with long, pointed wings and a forked tail.

kith [kith] *n*. Friends, now used only in the phrase **kith and kin,** friends and relatives.

kit·ten [kit′(ə)n] *n*. A young cat.

kit·ty [kit′ē] *n*., *pl*. **kit·ties** A cat or kitten: often used as a pet name for a cat.

Klon·dike [klon′dīk] *n*. A region of NW Canada where gold was discovered in 1896.

km. Abbreviation of: **1** KILOMETER. **2** Kilometers.

knack [nak] *n*. Ability or skill; talent: He has the *knack* of saying the right thing at the right time.

knap·sack [nap′sak′] *n*. A large bag for supplies, etc., worn strapped to the back.

knave [nāv] *n*. **1** A sly, dishonest person; rogue. **2** The jack, a playing card. — **knav′ish** *adj*.

knav·er·y [nā′vər·ē] *n*., *pl*. **knav·er·ies 1** The behavior of a knave. **2** An act of trickery.

knead [nēd] *v*. **1** To mix and work (dough, clay, etc.) into a mass by pressing, squeezing, etc. **2** To work upon by pressing or squeezing with the hands; massage: to *knead* a sprained muscle. **3** To make by or as if by kneading.

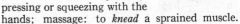

Knapsack

knee [nē] *n*. **1** The joint between the upper and lower bones of the leg. **2** The area around this joint. **3** Anything shaped like a bent knee. **4** The part of a garment that covers the knee.

knee·cap [nē′kap′] *n*. The flat, movable bone in the front of the knee.

kneel [nēl] *v*. **knelt** or **kneeled, kneel·ing** To sink down or rest on one or both knees: They *knelt* to pray.

knell [nel] **1** *n*. The sound of a bell slowly ringing, as at a funeral. **2** *v*. To ring a bell slowly and solemnly. **3** *v*. To announce, summon, or warn by or as if by a bell. **4** *n*. A warning of the passing or end of something: Electric lights sounded the *knell* of gas lamps.

knelt [nelt] A past tense and past participle of KNEEL.

knew [n(y)ōō] Past tense of KNOW.

K

knick·er·bock·ers [nik′ər·bok′erz] *n.pl.* Loose-fitting, short trousers, gathered in below the knee.

knick·ers [nik′ərz] *n.pl.* Knicker-bockers.

knick·knack [nik′nak′] *n.* A small ornament or article of trifling value.

knife [nīf] *n., pl.* **knives** [nīvz], *v.* **knifed, knif·ing 1** *n.* A cutting tool having a sharp, often pointed blade set in a handle. **2** *v.* To stab or cut with a knife. **3** *n.* A cutting blade in a machine.

Knicker-bockers

knight [nīt] **1** *n.* In the Middle Ages, a man having the rank and duties of a mounted officer, usually after service as a page and squire. **2** *n.* In the British Commonwealth, a man given an honorary rank and the title "Sir" before his name in recognition of his merits or service. **3** *v.* To make into a knight. **4** *n.* A chess piece having a horse's head.

knight-er·rant [nīt′er′ənt] *n., pl.* **knights-er·rant** In the Middle Ages, a knight who traveled in search of adventure.

knight-er·rant·ry [nīt′er′ən·trē] *n., pl.* **knight-er·rant·ries 1** The conduct and customs of the knights-errant. **2** Action that is brave and romantic but impractical.

knight·hood [nīt′hŏŏd] *n.* **1** The character, rank, or profession of a knight. **2** Knights as a group. **3** The customs and conduct of knights.

knight·ly [nīt′lē] **1** *adj.* Of, having to do with, or befitting a knight. **2** *adv.* In a manner befitting a knight. — **knight′li·ness** *n.*

knit [nit] *v.* **knit·ted** or **knit, knit·ting 1** To make (cloth or clothing) by interlocking loops of yarn or thread with special needles. **2** To fasten or unite closely and firmly: The broken bone *knit* well. **3** To draw (the brows) together, as in a frown. — **knit′ter** *n.*

knob [nob] *n.* **1** A rounded handle, as on a door, radio, etc. **2** A rounded, projecting part: the *knobs* on a tree trunk. **3** A rounded hill.

knob·by [nob′ē] *adj.* **knob·bi·er, knob·bi·est 1** Full of knobs: a *knobby* tree trunk. **2** Shaped like a knob: *knobby* knees.

knock [nok] **1** *v.* To strike with a sharp blow; hit: John *knocked* the bully on the back of his head. **2** *v.* To strike so as to make fall: The blow *knocked* him down. **3** *v.* To strike together: They *knocked* heads. **4** *v.* To make by striking: to *knock* a hole in a wall. **5** *v.* To make a sharp pounding or rapping noise, especially by striking with the knuckles: to *knock* on a door. **6** *n.* A sharp blow or rap, or the sound accompanying it. **7** *v. informal* To find fault with; be critical of. — **knock about** *informal* To wander around. — **knock down 1** To take apart for shipping or storage. **2** At auctions, to sell to the highest bidder. — **knock off** *informal* **1** To stop (work, talking, etc.). **2** To deduct. — **knock out 1** To defeat by a knockout in boxing. **2** To make unconscious. **3** *informal* To make very tired; exhaust.

knock·er [nok′ər] *n.* **1** A person or thing that knocks. **2** A ring, knob, etc., hinged to a door and used in knocking.

knock-kneed [nok′nēd′] *adj.* Having legs that curve inward at the knees.

knock·out [nok′out′] **1** *n.* In boxing, the knocking of a fighter to the floor with a blow that makes him unconscious or so hurt that he cannot stand up before the referee counts to ten. **2** *n.* The blow that knocks out a fighter. **3** *adj.* Forcible enough to cause a knockout; overpowering; stunning.

knoll [nōl] *n.* A small round hill; mound.

Knock-kneed

knot [not] *n., v.* **knot·ted, knot·ting 1** *n.* A fastening made by the tying or looping together of one or more ropes, cords, etc. There are many types of knots. **2** *n.* A lump or tangle like a knot. **3** *n.* An ornamental bow of silk, lace, braid, etc. **4** *v.* To tie in or form a knot. **5** *v.* To fasten with a knot. **6** *v.* To become knotted or tangled. **7** *n.* A group or cluster, as of people or things. **8** *n.* A bond or union: the marriage *knot.* **9** *n.* A difficulty; problem. **10** *n.* A hard, gnarled lump on the trunk of a tree where a branch grows out. **11** *n.* A cross section of such a lump in a piece of sawed lumber. **12** *n.* A speed equal to one nautical mile (6,076.1 feet) per hour.

knot·hole [not′hōl′] *n.* A hole in a board where a knot has fallen out.

knot·ty [not′ē] *adj.* **knot·ti·er, knot·ti·est 1** Full of knots: a *knotty* board; *knotty* rope. **2** Difficult or complex: a *knotty* puzzle.

know [nō] *v.* **knew, known, know·ing 1** To be certain of or have the facts about: I *know* that the sun will rise tomorrow; Do you *know* his problem? **2** To have knowledge, understanding, or command of: to *know* the facts. **3** To be acquainted or familiar with: Do you *know* her?; to *know* a song. **4** To be able to identify; recognize: I'll *know* it if I see it. **5** To be aware of; understand or realize: Do you *know* what you're saying? **6** To distinguish between: Do you *know* him from his brother?

know-how [nō′hou′] *n. informal* Knowledge or skill: engineering *know-how*; American *know-how*.

know·ing [nō′ing] *adj.* **1** Having knowledge or information; informed. **2** Showing secret or sly knowledge: a *knowing* smile. **3** Shrewd or alert. — **know′ing·ly** *adv.*

knowl·edge [nol′ij] *n.* **1** The fact or condition of knowing or being aware: *Knowledge* of the tragedy stunned her. **2** What a person knows: He has a good *knowledge* of physics. **3** All that is or may be known by man. — **to one's knowledge** As far as a person knows.

known [nōn] Past participle of KNOW.

knuck·le [nuk′əl] *n., v.* **knuck·led, knuck·ling 1** *n.* One of the joints of the fingers, especially one connecting a finger to the hand. **2** *n.* The knee or hock joint of a pig, calf, etc., the flesh of which is used as food. **3** *v.* To rub, press, or hit with the knuckles. **— knuckle down** To apply oneself seriously. **— knuckle under** To give in; submit.

ko·a·la [kō·ä′lə] *n.* A small, bearlike animal of Australia that lives in trees.

kohl·ra·bi [kōl·rä′bē *or* kōl′·rä·bē] *n., pl.* **kohl·ra·bies** A kind of cabbage with an edible, turnip-shaped stem.

koo·doo [kōō′dōō] *n., pl.* **koo·doos** A large, striped antelope of Africa.

ko·peck or **ko·pek** [kō′pek] *n.* A Russian coin equal to one hundredth of a ruble.

Ko·ran [kō·rän′] *n.* The sacred book of Islam.

Ko·re·a [kō·rē′ə *or* kō·rē′ə] *n.* A peninsula in eastern Asia, divided into two countries, **North Korea** and **South Korea. — Ko·re′an** *adj., n.*

ko·sher [kō′shər] *adj.* Clean or proper, according to Jewish religious laws: *kosher* food.

Koala, 30 in. long

kow·tow [kou′tou] *v.* **1** To kneel and touch the ground with the forehead as a sign of respect or obedience. **2** To be slavish or submissive, as in seeking favor.

Krem·lin [krem′lin] *n.* A large fortress in the central part of Moscow, that houses the government offices of the Soviet Union.

Men kowtowing

Kriss Krin·gle [kris kring′gəl] Santa Claus.

kryp·ton [krip′ton] *n.* A colorless, inert, gaseous element found in small amounts in the air. It is used in certain light bulbs.

ku·du [kōō′dōō] Another spelling of KOODOO.

kum·quat [kum′kwot] *n.* A sour, tangy citrus fruit resembling a small orange, used mainly for preserves.

kwh or **K.W.H.** Abbreviation of: **1** KILOWATT-HOUR. **2** Kilowatt-hours.

Ky. Abbreviation of KENTUCKY.

Kyo·to [kē·ō′tō] *n.* A city in central Japan.

L

l or **L** [el] *n., pl.* **l's** or **L's** **1** The 12th letter of the English alphabet. **2** (*written* **L**) The Roman numeral for 50.

L (*often written* £) An abbreviation of the English POUND, roughly equivalent to $2.80.

la [lä] *n.* In music, a syllable used to represent the sixth tone of a major scale or the first tone of a minor scale, or in a fixed system the tone A.

La. Abbreviation of LOUISIANA.

lab [lab] *n. U.S. informal* Laboratory.

la·bel [lā′bəl] *n., v.* **la·beled** or **la·belled, la·bel·ing** or **la·bel·ling** **1** *n.* A slip of paper, strip of cloth, etc., fastened to a thing to tell what it is, who made it, whom it belongs to, or where it is going, etc. **2** *v.* To fasten a label to: to *label* a jar or box. **3** *v.* To classify; call: to be *labeled* a poor sport.

Labels

la·bi·al [lā′bē·əl] **1** *adj.* Of or having to do with the lips. **2** *adj.* Formed by the lips, as the sounds for the letters *p*, *b*, and *m*. **3** *n.* A sound formed by the lips.

la·bor [lā′bər] **1** *n.* Work, especially hard work: manual *labor*. **2** *v.* To work hard: to *labor* in the fields. **3** *n.* A piece of work; task. **4** *n.* Working people as a group: Unions represent *labor*. **5** *v.* To move slowly and with difficulty. **6** *n.* The process of giving birth to a child. ¶1

lab·o·ra·to·ry [lab′rə·tôr′ē] *n., pl.* **lab·o·ra·to·ries** A building or room equipped for doing scientific work or experiments.

Labor Day The first Monday in September, in the U.S. and Canada a legal holiday in honor of working people. ¶1

la·bored [lā′bərd] *adj.* Done with effort, not with ease; forced: *labored* breathing. ¶1

la·bor·er [lā′bər·ər] *n.* A person who does physical or manual work, especially work that calls for strength rather than skill. ¶1

la·bo·ri·ous [lə·bôr′ē·əs] *adj.* **1** Requiring great effort; hard: a *laborious* task. **2** Hard-working; diligent. **—la·bo′ri·ous·ly** *adv.*

labor union An association of workers organized to improve working conditions and to protect the interests of members. ¶1

Lab·ra·dor [lab′rə·dôr] *n.* **1** The northernmost district of Newfoundland. **2** A peninsula of NE North America between the St. Lawrence River and Hudson Bay.

add, āce, câre, pälm;   end, ēqual;   it, īce;   odd, ōpen, ôrder;   tŏŏk, pōōl;   up, bûrn;
ə = a in *above*, e in *sicken*, i in *possible*, o in *melon*, u in *circus*;   yōō = u in *fuse*;   oil;   pout;
check;   ri**ng**;   **th**in;   **th**is;   **zh** in *vision*.   For ¶ reference, see page 64 · HOW TO

la·bur·num [lə·bûr′nəm] *n.* A small tree with yellow flowers that hang in clusters.

lab·y·rinth [lab′ə·rinth] *n.* An arrangement of winding passages or paths designed to confuse anyone trying to find his way through; maze. ◆ This word comes from the name of the maze in Greek myths which Daedalus made to confine the Minotaur.

lab·y·rin·thine [lab′ə·rin′thin] *adj.* Like a labyrinth; highly complicated; intricate.

lace [lās] *n., v.* **laced, lac·ing 1** *n.* A delicate network of threads of linen, silk, etc., worked into a pattern. **2** *adj. use:* a *lace* dress. **3** *v.* To trim with lace. **4** *n.* A cord or string passed through holes or over hooks to pull and hold together the edges of a shoe, garment, etc. **5** *v.* To fasten with a lace or laces: to *lace* up ice skates. **6** *v.* To twist together; intertwine: They *laced* arms.

lac·er·ate [las′ər·āt] *v.* **lac·er·at·ed, lac·er·at·ing 1** To tear in a ragged way so as to wound: His legs had been *lacerated* by briars. **2** To hurt painfully: to *lacerate* the feelings.

lac·er·a·tion [las′ər·ā′shən] *n.* **1** The act of lacerating. **2** A ragged wound made by tearing.

lach·ry·mal [lak′rə·məl] *adj.* Of, having to do with, or producing tears: *lachrymal* glands.

lack [lak] **1** *n.* A deficiency or complete absence of something needed or desired. **2** *v.* To be without or have too little: to *lack* talent. **3** *v.* To be short by: He *lacks* three inches of the required height. **4** *v.* To be absent or insufficient: Vitamins were *lacking* in her diet. **5** *n.* A thing needed; a need.

lack·a·dai·si·cal [lak′ə·dā′zi·kəl] *adj.* Without interest, energy, or concern; listless.

lack·ey [lak′ē] *n., pl.* **lack·eys 1** A male servant in a uniform; footman. **2** Anyone who takes orders from another as a servant does.

lack·lus·ter [lak′lus′tər] *adj.* Lacking brightness; dim; dull.

la·con·ic [lə·kon′ik] *adj.* Using no unnecessary words; brief and concise: a *laconic* answer.

lac·quer [lak′ər] **1** *n.* A varnish made by dissolving shellac or various resins in alcohol. **2** *n.* A natural varnish obtained from an oriental tree. **3** *v.* To coat with lacquer. **4** *n.* Wooden articles coated with lacquer.

la·crosse [lə·krôs′] *n.* A ball game played with long, racketlike implements by two teams of ten men each. The object is to advance the ball down the field, into the opponents' goal.

lac·ta·tion [lak·tā′shən] *n.* **1** The forming and secreting of milk by mammals. **2** The period during which milk is produced.

lac·te·al [lak′tē·əl] *adj.* Of or like milk.

lac·tic [lak′tik] *adj.* Of, having to do with, or derived from milk.

lactic acid An acid present in sour milk.

lac·tose [lak′tōs] *n.* A white, odorless sugar present in milk.

lac·y [lā′sē] *adj.* **lac·i·er, lac·i·est** Made of or resembling lace: a *lacy* collar.

lad [lad] *n.* A boy or youth.

lad·der [lad′ər] *n.* **1** A device for climbing up or down, usually consisting of two side pieces connected by crosspieces placed at regular intervals to serve as steps. **2** A means by which one can move upward: at the bottom of the social *ladder.*

lade [lād] *v.* **lad·ed, lad·ed** or **lad·en, lad·ing 1** To load. **2** To dip or ladle (a liquid).

lad·en [lād′(ə)n] **1** Alternative past participle of LADE. **2** *adj.* Weighed down; loaded; burdened: *laden* with gifts; *laden* with cares.

lad·ing [lā′ding] *n.* A load or cargo, often used in the term **bill of lading,** a receipt listing goods received for transportation.

la·dle [lād′(ə)l] *n., v.* **la·dled, la·dling 1** *n.* A cup-shaped spoon with a long handle for dipping out or serving liquids. **2** *v.* To dip out and pour with a ladle: *Ladle* out the soup.

Ladle

la·dy [lā′dē] *n., pl.* **la·dies 1** A woman who has good manners, good character, and refinement. **2** A woman having the rights and powers of a lord; mistress. **3** (*written* **Lady**) In Great Britain, a title used with the last or first name of certain women of high rank, as countesses, the wives of knights, or the daughters of dukes. **4** A man's wife or sweetheart. **5** A term of reference or address for any woman. **— Our Lady** The Virgin Mary. ◆ When you want simply to indicate a person's sex, *woman* is better than *lady. Lady* doctor should not be used for *woman* doctor, because all you mean to say is that the doctor is of the female sex.

la·dy·bird [lā′dē·bûrd′] *n.* Another name for LADYBUG.

la·dy·bug [lā′dē·bug′] *n.* A small, brightly colored beetle, usually red spotted with black.

lady in waiting A lady appointed to serve or wait upon a queen or princess.

la·dy·like [lā′dē·līk′] *adj.* Like or suitable to a lady; gentle, polite, or refined.

la·dy·slip·per [lā′dē·slip′ər] *n.* A kind of wild orchid, having a flower that resembles a slipper.

Ladybug

La·fay·ette [lä′fē·et′ *or* laf′ē·et′], **Marquis de,** 1757–1834, French general. He fought for the Americans in the American Revolution.

lag [lag] *v.* **lagged, lag·ging,** *n.* **1** *v.* To move slowly; stay or fall behind: to *lag* behind. **2** *n.* The condition or act of falling behind. **3** *n.* The amount by which or time during which there is a falling behind or delay: a *lag* between the idea and the accomplishment.

lag·gard [lag′ərd] **1** *n.* A person who lags; loiterer. **2** *adj.* Falling behind; slow.

la·goon [lə·gōōn′] *n.* **1** A body of shallow water, as a pond or inlet, usually connecting with a river, a larger lake, or the sea. **2** The water enclosed by a ring-shaped coral island.

laid [lād] Past tense and past participle of LAY[1]: I *laid* the board down on the ground; She had *laid* the book on the table.

lain [lān] Past participle of LIE[1]: He had just *lain* on the bed when the phone rang.

lair [lâr] *n.* The den of a wild animal.

laird [lârd] *n.* The Scottish word for the owner of a landed estate.

lais·sez faire [les′ā·fâr′] The doctrine that government should exercise as little control as possible in economic affairs.

la·i·ty [lā′ə·tē] *n.* **1** The people who are not members of the clergy; laymen. **2** All of those outside a specific profession or occupation.

lake [lāk] *n.* **1** A body of fresh or salt water enclosed by land. **2** A large pool of any liquid.

Lake, Lake of, etc. See the specific name.

la·ma [lä′mə] *n.* A Buddhist priest or monk in Tibet or Mongolia.

la·ma·ser·y [lä′mə·ser′ē] *n., pl.* **la·ma·ser·ies** A Buddhist monastery in Tibet or Mongolia.

lamb [lam] **1** *n.* A young sheep. **2** *v.* To give birth to a lamb. **3** *n.* The meat of a lamb used as food. **4** *n.* Any gentle or innocent person.

Lamb [lăm], **Charles,** 1775–1834, English critic and writer of essays.

lam·baste [lam·bāst′] *v.* **lam·bast·ed, lam·bast·ing** *slang* **1** To beat or thrash. **2** To lash with harsh words; scold severely.

lam·bent [lam′bənt] *adj.* **1** Playing over a surface with a flickering movement, as a flame. **2** Softly radiant. **3** Playfully brilliant, as wit.

lamb·kin [lam′kin] *n.* A little lamb.

lame [lām] *adj.* **lam·er, lam·est,** *v.* **lamed, lam·ing 1** *adj.* Crippled or disabled, especially in a leg or foot. **2** *v.* To make lame; cripple. **3** *adj.* Sore; stiff; painful: a *lame* back. **4** *adj.* Weak and not effective: a *lame* attempt at humor. **—lame′ly** *adv.* **—lame′ness** *n.*

la·mé [la·mā′] *n.* A cloth woven of flat gold or silver thread mixed with silk or other fiber.

la·ment [lə·ment′] **1** *v.* To feel or express great sorrow over: to *lament* a death. **2** *v.* To mourn. **3** *n.* An expression of grief or remorse, as wailing, words, or a song expressing sorrow.

lam·en·ta·ble [lam′ən·tə·bəl *or* lə·ment′ə·bəl] *adj.* Bad or unfortunate enough to inspire regret or pity: a *lamentable* failure. **—lam′en·ta·bly** *adv.*

lam·en·ta·tion [lam′ən·tā′shən] *n.* **1** The act of lamenting. **2** A lament; wail; moan.

lam·i·nate [lam′ə·nāt] *v.* **lam·i·nat·ed, lam·i·nat·ing 1** To beat, roll, or press into thin layers. **2** To form by uniting separate layers. **3** *adj. use: laminated* glass; *laminated* wood. **4** To cover with thin layers. **—lam′i·na′tion** *n.*

lamp [lamp] *n.* A device for producing light, as a holder or stand with a socket for an electric light bulb, or a vessel in which oil is burned through a wick.

lamp·black [lamp′blak′] *n.* A fine black soot of almost pure carbon, obtained by burning oil, tar, or gas, used in ink, paints, etc.

lam·poon [lam·pōōn′] **1** *n.* A written attack on an individual, using humor to make fun of him. **2** *v.* To attack or ridicule in a lampoon.

lam·prey [lam′prē] *n., pl.* **lam·preys** A water animal resembling an eel and having a round, sucking mouth lined with sharp teeth.

lance [lans] *n., v.* **lanced, lanc·ing 1** *n.* A weapon with a long shaft and a sharp metal head. **2** *v.* To pierce with a lance. **3** *n.* A soldier armed with a lance. **4** *n.* A slender, sharp instrument resembling a lance, as a whaler's spear or a surgeon's lancet. **5** *v.* To cut open with a lancet: to *lance* an abscess.

Lance

Lan·ce·lot [lan′sə·lot] *n.* In English legend, the bravest knight at King Arthur's court.

lanc·er [lan′sər] *n.* A soldier on horseback armed with a lance.

lan·cet [lan′sit] *n.* A small knife with two sharp edges, used by doctors, as to open boils.

land [land] **1** *n.* The solid, exposed surface of the earth. **2** *n.* A country or region. **3** *n.* Ground considered with reference to its uses, location, value, etc.: pasture *land*; His wealth is in *land*. **4** *v.* To move from a ship to the shore: to *land* cargo; The passengers *landed*. **5** *v.* To touch at a port; come to shore, as a ship. **6** *v.* To bring or come to rest on the surface below after a flight, jump, or fall: to *land* a plane; The acrobat *landed* on his feet. **7** *v.* To arrive or cause to arrive: to *land* in jail; My friend's car *landed* me at my home. **8** *v.* To pull (a fish) out of the water; catch: It took me three hours to *land* that trout. **9** *v. informal* To obtain; win: to *land* a good job.

land·ed [lan′did] *adj.* **1** Owning land: *landed* gentry. **2** Consisting of land: *landed* property.

land·hold·er [land′hōl′dər] *n.* An owner or occupant of land.

---

add, āce, câre, pälm;   end, ēqual;   it, īce;   odd, ōpen, ôrder;   tŏŏk, pōōl;   up, bûrn;

ə = a in *above*, e in *sicken*, i in *possible*, o in *melon*, u in *circus*;   yōō = u in *fuse*;   oil;   pout;

check; ring; thin; this; zh in *vision*.   For ¶ reference, see page 64 · HOW TO

land·ing [lan′ding] *n.* **1** The act of going or putting on shore from a ship. **2** The place where a ship lands; wharf; pier. **3** The act of bringing or coming down after a flight, jump, or fall. **4** A platform at the head of a staircase or between flights of stairs.

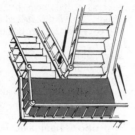

Landing

landing field A level strip of land prepared so that planes may land on it and take off from it.

land·la·dy [land′lā′dē] *n.*, *pl.* **land·la·dies 1** A woman who owns and rents out buildings, apartments, or land. **2** A woman who keeps an inn, boarding house, or rooming house.

land·locked [land′lokt′] *adj.* **1** Entirely or nearly shut in by land. **2** Confined to fresh water shut off from the sea: *landlocked* salmon.

land·lord [land′lôrd′] *n.* **1** A man who owns and rents out buildings, apartments, or land. **2** A man who keeps an inn, rooming house, etc.

land·lub·ber [land′lub′ər] *n.* A sailor's term for someone new to sailing and clumsy on ships.

land·mark [land′märk′] *n.* **1** A fixed object marking the boundary of a piece of land. **2** A familiar or outstanding object in a landscape which may serve as a guide to aircraft, ships, or travelers. **3** A fact or event marking an important change or a new advance: The discovery of penicillin was a medical *landmark*.

land·own·er [land′ō′nər] *n.* A person who owns land.

land·scape [land′skāp] *n.*, *v.* **land·scaped, land·scap·ing 1** *n.* A stretch of natural scenery on land as seen from a single point. **2** *n.* A picture representing such scenery. **3** *v.* To change or improve the appearance of (a piece of land) by adding or arranging trees, flowers, etc. ◆ The word *landscape* comes from Dutch.

land·slide [land′slīd′] *n.* **1** The slipping down of a mass of loose soil or rock on a mountain side or other steep slope. **2** The mass that slips down. **3** A great majority of votes for one party or candidate in an election.

land·ward [land′wərd] **1** *adv.* Toward the land. **2** *adj.* Being, facing, or moving toward land.

land·wards [land′wərdz] *adv.* Toward the land.

lane [lān] *n.* **1** A narrow path or road, as one between fences, walls, hedges, etc.: a country *lane*. **2** A wooden pathway down which bowling balls are rolled. **3** Any narrow way or passage: a *lane* through a crowd of people. **4** A marked division of a road, to be used by vehicles going in the same direction. **5** A set route followed by ships at sea or airplanes in the sky. **6** On a racetrack, any of several parallel courses in which the contestants must stay while racing.

lan·guage [lang′gwij] *n.* **1** The sounds spoken and heard or the symbols written and read by human beings to express emotions and ideas or to record facts. **2** The words which a certain nation or group uses in speaking and writing: the French *language*. **3** The study of a language or of languages. **4** Any means of expressing ideas or emotions: sign *language*. **5** The special words used in a certain field: scientific *language*. **6** A particular style or manner of expression: Milton's *language*; strong *language*.

lan·guid [lang′gwid] *adj.* Lacking energy or spirit; listless; weak. **—lan′guid·ly** *adv.*

lan·guish [lang′gwish] *v.* **1** To become weak or feeble. **2** To droop from restless longing; pine or suffer: to *languish* in prison. **3** To put on a sad, tender, or weary look in order to gain sympathy. **4** *adj. use:* a *languishing* look.

lan·guor [lang′gər] *n.* **1** A weak, tired, or listless condition. **2** A tender or dreamy mood. **3** Inactivity or stillness. **—lan′guor·ous** *adj.*

lank [langk] *adj.* **1** Very lean: a *lank* lad. **2** Long and straight; not curly: *lank* hair.

lank·y [lang′kē] *adj.* **lank·i·er, lank·i·est** Ungracefully tall and thin. **—lank′i·ness** *n.*

Lan·sing [lan′sing] *n.* The capital of Michigan.

lan·tern [lan′tərn] *n.* A case to hold and protect a light, having sides of glass, paper, etc., through which the light can be seen.

lan·yard [lan′yərd] *n.* **1** A short rope used on a ship to fasten things. **2** A cord worn around the neck. A sailor may attach a knife to it. **3** A cord used in firing certain cannons.

La·os [lous, lā′os, *or* lä′ōs] *n.* A country in SE Asia, in the NW part of Indochina.

lap¹ [lap] *n.* **1** The front part from waist to knees of a person sitting down. **2** The part of the clothing covering the lap, as the front of a skirt. **3** An environment that holds or protects: in the *lap* of luxury.

Lantern

lap² [lap] *v.* **lapped, lap·ping,** *n.* **1** *v.* To wrap, fold. or wind: to *lap* a bandage around the leg. **2** *v.* To lay (one thing) so that it partly covers something else: to *lap* each shingle over another in repairing a roof. **3** *v.* To lie partly over (another or each other); overlap. **4** *v.* To extend over, into, or beyond something else. **5** *n.* The amount by which one thing overlaps another, or the overlapping part. **6** *n.* One of several trips made around a race track.

lap³ [lap] *v.* **lapped, lap·ping,** *n.* **1** *v.* To drink as an animal does by licking up with the tongue. **2** *v.* To wash with a licking sound, as waves. **3** *n.* The act or sound of lapping.

lap dog A dog small enough to hold on the lap.

la·pel [lə·pel′] *n.* Either part of the front of a coat that is folded back below the collar.

lap·i·dar·y [lap′ə·der′ē] *n.*, *pl.* **lap·i·dar·ies** A person whose work or hobby is to cut, engrave, or polish precious stones.

L

lap·is laz·u·li [lap′is laz′yo͞o·lī] **1** A deep blue mineral sometimes used as a semiprecious stone. **2** Deep blue; sky blue.

Lap·land [lap′land] *n.* A region of northern Norway, Sweden, and Finland, and the NW Soviet Union, that is inhabited by Lapps.

Lapp [lap] *n.* **1** A member of a wandering people living in Lapland. **2** Their language.

lapse [laps] *n., v.* **lapsed, laps·ing 1** *n.* A minor, momentary slip or mistake: a *lapse* of judgment. **2** *n.* A slip or fall, as from a better to a worse condition: a *lapse* into despair. **3** *v.* To fall away from good behavior: to *lapse* into bad habits. **4** *v.* To pass gradually; slip: to *lapse* into a coma. **5** *n.* A gradual passing away: a *lapse* of time. **6** *n.* The ending of a right, benefit, etc., through failure to fill certain conditions: the *lapse* of an insurance policy. **7** *v.* To become void; end: He had let his membership *lapse.*

lap·wing [lap′wing′] *n.* A bird of Europe and Asia noted for its awkward way of flying and its shrill cry.

lar·board [lär′bərd] **1** *adj.* Being on or toward the left side of a ship as one faces forward. **2** *n.* The left side of a ship; port.

lar·ce·ny [lär′sə·nē] *n., pl.* **lar·ce·nies** The unlawful taking of another's goods; theft.

larch [lärch] *n.* **1** A tree bearing cones and having needlelike leaves that drop off in the autumn. **2** The strong wood of this tree.

lard [lärd] **1** *n.* The fat of a hog after being melted and made clear. **2** *v.* To cover or smear with lard. **3** *v.* To insert strips of bacon or fat in (meat) before cooking. **4** *v.* To fill or enrich with: to *lard* a speech with quotations.

lar·der [lär′dər] *n.* **1** A place where food is stored; pantry. **2** A stock or supply of food.

large [lärj] *adj.* **larg·er, larg·est 1** Big in size, amount, extent, etc.: a *large* refrigerator. **2** Bigger than usual or than the average: Give me the *large* size. **— at large 1** Free; loose: A killer is *at large.* **2** Elected from the whole state, not from a particular district: a congressman *at large.* **3** In general: the people *at large.*

large intestine The short, thick, lower part of the intestine, leading from the small intestine to the anus.

large·ly [lärj′lē] *adv.* To a great extent; chiefly: Her success was *largely* due to luck.

lar·gess or **lar·gesse** [lär·jes′ *or* lär′jis] *n.* **1** Generous giving. **2** A generous gift.

lar·go [lär′gō] *n., pl.* **lar·gos,** *adv., adj.* **1** *n.* A slow movement or passage in music. **2** *adj.* Slow. **3** *adv.* In a slow tempo.

lar·i·at [lar′ē·ət] *n.* **1** A lasso. **2** A rope used to tie grazing animals to a stake.

lark¹ [lärk] *n.* **1** Any of various small European songbirds, especially the skylark. **2** A similar bird, as the meadowlark of America.

lark² [lärk] **1** *n.* A carefree adventure; good time. **2** *v.* To have fun or play pranks; frolic.

lark·spur [lärk′spûr] *n.* A tall plant with loose clusters of flowers that resemble a bird's foot in shape.

lar·va [lär′və] *n., pl.* **lar·vae** [lär′vē] or **lar·vas** An insect in its early stage as a caterpillar, grub, or maggot, between hatching from an egg and becoming a pupa: *Larvae* of moths are caterpillars.

moth

lar·val [lär′vəl] *adj.* **1** Of or having to do with larvae. **2** In the stage of a larva.

lar·yn·gi·tis [lar′ən·jī′tis] *n.* Inflammation of the larynx, as during a cold, when the voice becomes faint or hoarse.

larva

lar·ynx [lar′ingks] *n., pl.* **la·ryn·ges** [lə·rin′jēz] or **lar·ynx·es** The upper part of the windpipe, containing the vocal cords.

La Salle [lə sal′], **Robert,** 1643–1687, French explorer of America.

las·civ·i·ous [lə·siv′ē·əs] *adj.* Having or causing lust; lewd. **—las·civ′i·ous·ly** *adv.*

la·ser [lā′zər] *n.* A device that produces an intense beam of light whose waves are parallel, of the same wavelength, and exactly in step.

lash¹ [lash] **1** *n.* A whip, especially the flexible cord or its tip. **2** *v.* To strike, punish, or command with or as if with a lash; whip; flog. **3** *n.* A single stroke with a whip: to receive twenty *lashes.* **4** *v.* To move back and forth in a whiplike manner: The dog *lashed* his tail in excitement. **5** *v.* To beat or dash against violently: The waves *lashed* the rocks. **6** *v.* To scold in speech or writing: A newspaper editorial *lashed* the governor. **7** *v.* To stir or arouse. **8** *n.* An eyelash.

lash² [lash] *v.* To bind or tie, especially with rope or cord: to *lash* a bicycle to the top of a car.

lass [las] *n.* A young woman; girl.

las·sie [las′ē] *n.* A young or small girl.

las·si·tude [las′ə·t(y)o͞od] *n.* A feeling of weariness; lack of energy; languor.

las·so [las′ō] *n., pl.* **las·sos** or **las·soes 1** *n.* A long rope having a loop with a slipknot at one end, used for catching horses and cattle. **2** *v.* To catch with or as if with a lasso.

last¹ [last] **1** *adj.* Coming after all others; being at the end; final: the *last* page of a book. **2** *adv.* After all others in time or order: to be served *last.* **3** *n.* A person or thing that is last: He was the *last* to arrive. **4** *adj.* Nearest before the present time: *last* month. **5** *adv.* At the time nearest to the present: He was *last* seen boarding a bus. **6** *adj.* Being the only one remaining: his *last* dollar. **7** *adj.* Least suitable or likely. **8** *adv.* In conclusion; finally. **9** *n.* The final part or portion; the end. **— at last** Finally.

last² [last] *v.* **1** To continue; go on: How long does the movie *last*? **2** To remain in good condition. **3** To hold out: Our food *lasted* a week.

last³ [last] **1** *n.* A wood or metal model of a human foot on which to make or repair a shoe or boot. **2** *v.* To fit to or form on a last.

last·ing [las′ting] *adj.* Continuing for a long time; durable: a *lasting* friendship.

last·ly [last′lē] *adv.* In the last place; in conclusion; finally.

Last Supper The last meal Jesus had with his disciples, on the night before his Crucifixion.

latch [lach] **1** *n.* A movable bar of metal or wood that slides or drops into a notch to fasten a window, door, or gate. **2** *v.* To fasten by means of a latch; close.

latch·key [lach′kē′] *n.* A key for unfastening a latch, especially on an outside or front door.

latch·string [lach′string′] *n.* A string on a latch that is passed through a hole in a door so that the latch can be unfastened from the outside.

Latch

late [lāt] *adj.* **lat·er** or **lat·ter, lat·est** or **last,** *adv.* **1** *adj.* Appearing or coming after the expected time; tardy. **2** *adv.* After the expected time; tardily. **3** *adj.* Occurring at an unusually advanced time: a *late* marriage. **4** *adv.* At or until an advanced time of the day, year, etc.: to sleep *late*. **5** *adj.* Toward the end or close, as of a period, season, etc.: in *late* spring. **6** *adj.* Recent or fairly recent: the *late* elections. **7** *adj.* Having died recently: my *late* uncle. **8** *adj.* Having left office a short time ago: our *late* mayor. **— of late** Recently. **— late′ness** *n.*

late·com·er [lāt′kum·ər] *n.* A person who arrives later than he is expected to.

la·teen sail [lə·tēn′] A triangular sail held by a slanting yard and usually a boom.

late·ly [lāt′lē] *adv.* Not long ago; recently.

la·tent [lā′tənt] *adj.* Hidden or not active, but present: *latent* musical ability.

lat·er·al [lat′ər·əl] *adj.* Of, situated at, coming from, or directed toward the side. **— lat′er·al·ly** *adv.*

la·tex [lā′teks] *n.* The sticky, milky juice secreted by various plants, especially the rubber tree, used to make rubber, gutta-percha, chicle, etc.

Lateen sails

lath [lath] **1** *n.* One of the thin strips of wood used as a base for plaster, tile, etc. **2** *n.* Sheet metal with holes in it, used in place of wooden laths. **3** *v.* To cover or line with laths.

lathe [lāth] *n.* A machine that holds and turns an article against the edge of a cutting tool so as to shape it.

lath·er [lath′ər] **1** *n.* The suds or foam formed by soap or detergents moistened with water. **2** *v.* To spread over with lather. **3** *n.* The froth formed in sweating, as on a racehorse. **4** *v.* To become covered with or form lather. **— in a lather** *U.S. slang* Very excited or upset.

Lat·in [lat′(ə)n] **1** *n.* The language of ancient Rome. **2** *adj.* Having to do with ancient Rome, its language, or its people. **3** *adj.* Of or having to do with the people or countries, such as France, Italy, and Spain, whose language and culture are derived from ancient Rome. **4** *n.* A person whose language is derived from Latin, as a Spaniard or an Italian.

Latin America The countries in the Western Hemisphere south of the Rio Grande River, in which the official languages developed from Latin.

lat·i·tude [lat′ə·t(y)ōōd] *n.* **1** Distance north or south of the equator, measured as an angle at the earth's center and expressed in degrees. **2** A particular region north or south of the equator. **3** Freedom from narrow restrictions or limitations: He wants *latitude* to choose for himself.

lat·ter [lat′ər] **1** *adj.* Later or nearer to the end: the *latter* part of his life. **2** *adj.* Being the second of two things referred to. **3** *n. use* The second of two things referred to: I prefer the *latter* to the former.

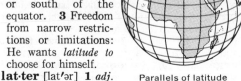
Parallels of latitude

Lat·ter-day Saint [lat′ər·dā′] Another name for MORMON.

lat·ter·ly [lat′ər·lē] *adv.* Recently; lately.

lat·tice [lat′is] *n., v.* **lat·ticed, lat·tic·ing** **1** *n.* A structure made of strips of metal, wood, etc., crossed or interlaced to form regularly spaced openings. **2** *v.* To form into or cover with a lattice.

lat·tice·work [lat′is·wûrk′] *n.* Openwork made of or like a lattice.

Lat·vi·a [lat′vē·ə] *n.* A country on the Baltic Sea, part of the Soviet Union.

laud [lôd] **1** *v.* To praise highly; extol. **2** *n.* A hymn of praise or honor.

laud·a·ble [lô′də·bəl] *adj.* Deserving praise or

Lattice fence

approval; praiseworthy. **—laud′a·bly** *adv.*

lau·da·num [lô′də·nəm] *n.* A solution of opium in alcohol, used in former times as a medicine.

laud·a·to·ry [lô′də·tôr′ē] *adj.* Expressing praise and approval: a *laudatory* review of a play.

laugh [laf] **1** *v.* To make the sounds and those movements of the mouth, eyes, etc., that show joy, amusement, happiness, or, sometimes, scorn. **2** *n.* An act or sound of laughing. **3** *v.* To bring to a certain condition, drive away, etc., by laughing: I *laughed* myself sick. **4** *v.* To be bright and sparkling. **— have the last laugh** To succeed or win after seeming to fail or lose. **—laugh at 1** To express amusement. **2** To ridicule; mock.

laugh·a·ble [laf′ə·bəl] *adj.* Causing or likely to cause laughter; ridiculous; funny.

laugh·ing·stock [laf′ing·stok′] *n.* A person or thing that is the object of ridicule.

laugh·ter [laf′tər] *n.* The characteristic sound, facial expression, or action of laughing.

launch[1] [lônch] *v.* **1** To move or push (a boat, etc.) into the water, especially for the first time. **2** To start; open: to *launch* a campaign. **3** To hurl; fling: to *launch* a rocket.

launch[2] [lônch] *n.* **1** A large, open motorboat used for pleasure, as a patrol boat, etc. **2** In former times, the largest boat carried by a ship.

laun·der [lôn′dər] *v.* To wash, or wash and iron (clothing, linens, etc.).

laun·dress [lôn′dris] *n.* A woman paid to launder clothing, linens, etc.

laun·dro·mat [lôn′drə·mat] *n. U.S.* A place where customers bring laundry to be washed and dried in automatic machines operated by coins. ◆ The word *laundromat* was taken from a trademark, *Laundromat.*

laun·dry [lôn′drē] *n.,* *pl.* **laun·dries 1** A room in a home, or a place of business, where clothes are washed and ironed. **2** Articles to be laundered or that have just been laundered.

laun·dry·man [lôn′drē·mən] *n.,* *pl.* **laun·dry·men** [lôn′drē·mən] **1** A man who works in or manages a commercial laundry. **2** A man who calls for and delivers laundry.

lau·re·ate [lô′rē·it] **1** *adj.* Singled out for special honor. **2** *adj.* Crowned or decked with laurel as a mark of honor. **3** *n.* A poet laureate.

lau·rel [lôr′əl] *n.* **1** An evergreen shrub of southern Europe with fragrant lance-shaped leaves, used by the ancients to make wreaths for heroes. **2** Any of various trees or shrubs resembling the laurel. **3** (*pl.*) Honor; fame. **— rest on one's laurels** To be content with what one has already achieved or accomplished.

la·va [lä′və *or* lav′ə] *n.* **1** Molten rock that flows from an active volcano. **2** Solid rock formed when this substance cools.

lav·a·to·ry [lav′ə·tôr′ē] *n.,* *pl.* **lav·a·to·ries 1** A room with a basin, sink, etc., for washing, and usually with a toilet. **2** A basin, small sink, etc., used for washing the hands and face.

lave [lāv] *v.* **laved, lav·ing** To wash or bathe: used mostly in poems.

lav·en·der [lav′ən·dər] **1** *n.* A plant related to mint, cultivated for its flowers and aromatic oils. **2** *n.* The dried flowers and leaves of this plant, used to scent linen, clothing, etc. **3** *n., adj.* Pale, reddish violet.

lav·ish [lav′ish] **1** *adj.* Generous or too generous: a man *lavish* with his gifts to others. **2** *adj.* Provided or used up in great abundance: He gave me a *lavish* helping of turkey. **3** *v.* To give freely; squander. **—lav′ish·ly** *adv.*

law [lô] *n.* **1** A rule of action or conduct set down by custom or authority and followed by a nation or group of people. **2** A system or body of such rules: civil *law.* **3** The condition of society when such rules are observed: *law* and order. **4** All such rules relating to a specified subject, area, etc.: criminal *law.* **5** The system, as a court or its magistrates, which enforces such rules. **6** The profession of a lawyer, judge, etc. **7** A scientific statement of what always happens in the natural world under certain conditions. **8** Any generally accepted rule: the *laws* of golf.

law-a·bid·ing [lô′ə·bī′ding] *adj.* Obedient to the law: a *law-abiding* citizen.

law·break·er [lô′brā′kər] *n.* A person who violates the law. **—law′break′ing** *n., adj.*

law·ful [lô′fəl] *adj.* **1** Permitted or not forbidden by law. **2** Recognized by the law: a *lawful* debt. **—law′ful·ly** *adv.*

law·giv·er [lô′giv′ər] *n.* A person who makes or sets up a law or system of laws.

law·less [lô′lis] *adj.* **1** Refusing to obey or pay attention to the law: a *lawless* gang of thieves. **2** Difficult to keep orderly; unruly. **3** Having no laws: a *lawless* town of the old West. **—law′less·ly** *adv.* **—law′less·ness** *n.*

law·mak·er [lô′mā′kər] *n.* A person who makes or helps to make laws, especially a legislator. **—law′mak′ing** *adj.*

lawn[1] [lôn] *n.* A piece of ground covered with grass that is kept short by mowing.

lawn[2] [lôn] *n.* A fine, thin linen or cotton fabric, used for handkerchiefs, etc.

Lawn mower

lawn mower A machine operated by a motor or pushed with the hands, used to cut grass.

lawn tennis Another name for TENNIS.

law·suit [lô′sōōt′] *n.* A case brought to a court of law to settle a claim.

law·yer [lô′yər] *n.* A member of the legal profession, especially one qualified to advise clients about laws and act for them in court.

lax [laks] *adj.* **1** Not strict or forceful; weak: a *lax* teacher; *lax* conduct. **2** Not precise or exact; vague: a *lax* interpretation of the law. **3** Not taut or firm; slack. **—lax′ness** *n.*

lax·a·tive [lak′sə·tiv] **1** *n.* A medicine taken to empty the bowels. **2** *adj.* Causing the bowels to move.

lax·i·ty [lak′sə·tē] *n., pl.* **lax·i·ties** The condition or quality of being lax.

lay[1] [lā] *v.* **laid, lay·ing,** *n.* **1** *v.* To place in a horizontal or reclining position: to *lay* a sleeping child down. **2** *v.* To put or place, especially in a specified position, order, etc.: to *lay* a rug on the floor; to *lay* bricks. **3** *v.* To produce (an egg or eggs) as a hen or fish does. **4** *v.* To think out; devise: to *lay* plans. **5** *v.* To place: to *lay* great importance on good manners. **6** *v.* To set forth; present: to *lay* a claim before a court. **7** *v.* To knock down; level: to *lay* someone low in a fight. **8** *v.* To cause to settle: to *lay* the dust. **9** *v.* To make ineffective; quiet down: to *lay* a ghost. **10** *v.* To set, place, or locate: to *lay* the scene of a play in Italy. **11** *v.* To offer as a wager; bet. **12** *n.* The manner in which something lies or is placed: the *lay* of the land. **—lay aside** To save for future use. **—lay away** To store up; save. **—lay by** To save or reserve, as money. **—lay down 1** To give up; sacrifice: to *lay down* one's life. **2** To state firmly: to *lay down* the rules. **—lay in** To get and store: to *lay in* a supply of food. **—lay off 1** *U.S.* To dismiss from a job. **2** To mark out; plan. **—lay open 1** To cut deeply; gash: The blow *laid open* his cheek. **2** To leave exposed, as to attack or blame. **—lay out 1** To set out or arrange for use, inspection, etc. **2** To arrange according to a plan. **3** To spend or supply: to *lay out* the room rent. **4** To prepare (a corpse) for burial. **—lay up 1** To save or store away. **2** To confine, as by illness or injury: Pneumonia *laid* him *up* for six weeks. ◆ The verbs *lay* and *lie* should always be distinguished in formal writing. *Lay* takes an object: She *is laying the book* on the table. *Lie,* meaning *to recline* or *be located,* does not take an object: The book *will lie* there until someone picks it up. The past tense of *to lie* is *lay:* He *lay* there all last night. The past tense of *to lay* is *laid:* She *laid* it on the table.

lay[2] [lā] *adj.* **1** Of or having to do with people other than the clergy. **2** Not belonging to or coming from a particular profession: We have a *lay* opinion on the case as well as one from a lawyer.

A piece of three-layer cake

lay[3] [lā] Past tense of LIE[1].

lay[4] [lā] *n.* **1** A song, ballad, or poem that tells a story. **2** A melody or song.

lay·er [lā′ər] **1** *n.* A single thickness, coating, covering, etc.: a *layer* of cloth. **2** *v.* To form a layer or layers. **3** *n.* A person or thing that lays: These hens are good *layers.*

lay·ette [lā·et′] *n.* The supply of clothing, bedding, etc., provided for a newborn infant.

lay·man [lā′mən] *n., pl.* **lay·men** [lā′mən] **1** A person who does not belong to a particular profession. **2** A person who is not a clergyman.

lay·out [lā′out′] *n.* **1** The act of laying out or planning. **2** A planned arrangement; design: a *layout* of the new playground. **3** The thing that is arranged or designed.

lay·o·ver [lā′ō′vər] *n.* A short stop or interruption in a journey; a stopover.

Laz·a·rus [laz′ə·rəs] *n.* In the Bible: **1** The brother of Martha and Mary, raised from the dead by Jesus. **2** A sick beggar in the parable of the rich man and the poor man.

la·zy [lā′zē] *adj.* **laz·i·er, laz·i·est 1** Unwilling to work or to keep busy; indolent. **2** Moving or acting slowly; sluggish. **—la′zi·ly** *adv.* **—la′zi·ness** *n.*

lb. Abbreviation of: **1** POUND. **2** (*often written* **lbs.**) Pounds.

lea [lē] *n.* A meadow: used mostly in poems.

leach [lēch] *v.* **1** To make water or other liquid run or filter through (something) in order to remove certain materials: to *leach* ore. **2** To remove or be removed by such a filtering action: to *leach* alkali out of ashes.

lead[1] [lēd] *v.* **led, lead·ing,** *n.* **1** *v.* To guide or conduct: We *led* her by the hand; This path *led* him to the hut. **2** *v.* To be in command or control of; direct: to *lead* a discussion. **3** *n.* Guidance; example: Follow his *lead.* **4** *v.* To be first among; be at the head of: She *led* the class with a 98% average. **5** *v.* To be first or in advance: Our runners *led* all the way. **6** *n.* Position in advance or at the head. **7** *n.* The amount or distance by which one is ahead: a *lead* of three runs. **8** *n.* The opening part of a news story or magazine article, as the first paragraph. **9** *adj. use:* a *lead* article. **10** *n.* The principal role in a play, motion picture, etc. **11** *v.* To begin or start: He *led* with a wild swing. **12** *n.* In games, sports, etc., the first play or the right to play first. **13** *v.* To influence the ideas or actions of: Her encouragement *led* me to work harder. **14** *v.* To result in: Such actions can *lead* to crime. **15** *v.* To go or extend: These wires *lead* to the barn. **16** *v.* To experience or cause to experience: to *lead* a merry life. **17** *n.* A clue: Give me a *lead.*

lead[2] [led] **1** *n.* A soft, heavy, dull gray, metallic element, used to make pipes, printing type, etc. **2** *adj. use:* a *lead* pipe. **3** *n.* Any object made of lead, especially a weight at the end of a line used to measure the depth of water. **4** *v.* To cover, join, fasten, or make heavier with lead: to *lead* stained glass windows. **5** *n.* Thin rods or sticks of graphite, used in pencils. **6** *n.* Bullets or shot.

lead·en [led′(ə)n] *adj.* **1** Dull gray. **2** Made of lead. **3** Heavy or feeling heavy: *leaden* legs. **4** Dark and gloomy: a *leaden* spirit.

lead·er [lē′dər] *n.* A person or thing that leads, as by going ahead or guiding.

lead·er·ship [lē′dər·ship] *n.* **1** The condition of being a leader. **2** The ability to lead. **3** Control or guidance: They lack *leadership*.

lead·ing [lē′ding] *adj.* **1** Located or going at the front; first: the *leading* car in the parade. **2** Most important; chief; principal: the town's *leading* citizen. **3** Guiding; controlling.

leaf [lēf] *n., pl.* **leaves** [lēvz], *v.* **1** *n.* One of the flat, thin, usually green parts of a plant or tree that grow from a stem or root. **2** *n.* A petal: the pressed *leaves* of a rose. **3** *v.* To grow or produce leaves. **4** *n.* One of the sheets of paper in a book, magazine, etc., each side being a single page. **5** *v.* To turn over or glance at the pages of a book, etc.: to *leaf* through a magazine. **6** *n.* Metal in a very thin sheet: gold *leaf*. **7** *n.* A flat, movable piece attached or fitted to a table to make it larger.

leaf·hop·per [lēf′hop′ər] *n.* A leaping insect that sucks the juices of plants.

leaf·less [lēf′lis] *adj.* Having no leaves.

leaf·let [lēf′lit] *n.* **1** A small leaf or leaflike part. **2** A small, printed sheet of paper, usually folded: to slip a *leaflet* under a door.

leaf·y [lē′fē] *adj.* **leaf·i·er, leaf·i·est 1** Bearing or covered with many leaves: Lettuce is a *leafy* vegetable. **2** Like a leaf.

league¹ [lēg] *n., v.* **leagued, lea·guing 1** *n.* A number of persons, groups, countries, etc., united for some common purpose. **2** *n.* A group of athletic teams that compete mostly among themselves. **3** *v.* To form or unite in a league. **—in league** Working or acting closely together.

league² [lēg] *n.* An old measure of length, usually equal to about three miles.

League of Nations A group of nations established in 1920 to preserve world peace. In 1946 it was replaced by the United Nations.

Le·ah [lē′ə] *n.* In the Bible, the first wife of Jacob and the older sister of Rachel.

leak [lēk] **1** *n.* An opening, as a crack or hole, that accidentally lets something in or out: a *leak* in a gas tank. **2** *v.* To let a liquid, gas, etc., accidentally get in or out through a hole or crack: The rowboat *leaked* badly. **3** *v.* To pass or let pass through a hole or crack: Air *leaked* out of the balloon; Your car is *leaking* oil. **4** *n.* Any way by which something is accidentally allowed to escape or become known: a *leak* in our secret files. **5** *v.* To become known despite efforts at secrecy: The plans *leaked* out. **6** *n.* The act of leaking; leakage: a slow *leak*.

leak·age [lē′kij] *n.* **1** The act of leaking. **2** That which leaks. **3** The amount leaked.

leak·y [lē′kē] *adj.* **leak·i·er, leak·i·est** Having a leak: a *leaky* roof. **—leak′i·ness** *n.*

lean¹ [lēn] *v.* **leaned** or **leant, lean·ing 1** To rest or incline for support: He *leaned* against the tree; I *leaned* the hoe on the wall. **2** To bend or slant from an upright position: The trees *leaned* in the wind. **3** To rely or depend for help, comfort, advice, etc.: She *leaned* too much on her mother for help. **4** To favor or prefer: She *leans* toward strictness in the classroom.

lean² [lēn] **1** *adj.* Having little fat or none: *lean* meat; a *lean* person. **2** *n.* Meat or flesh having little or no fat. **3** *adj.* Not plentiful; meager: a *lean* crop of corn. **—lean′ness** *n.*

lean·ing [lē′ning] *n.* An inclination or tendency.

leant [lent] Alternative past tense and past participle of LEAN¹.

lean-to [lēn′tōō′] *n., pl.* **lean-tos 1** A rough shelter, sloping to the ground at one end. **2** A low building built against one wall of a taller one, from which its roof slopes out and down.

Lean-to

leap [lēp] *v.* **leaped** or **leapt, leap·ing,** *n.* **1** *v.* To rise by a sudden thrust of the legs; jump or spring: He *leaped* up from the ground. **2** *v.* To jump over: to *leap* a fence. **3** *v.* To cause to jump: to *leap* a horse. **4** *n.* The act of leaping; a jump. **5** *n.* The space covered by leaping: a long *leap*.

leap·frog [lēp′frog′] *n.* A game in which each player puts his hands on the back of another player, who is bending over, and leaps over him in a straddling position.

leapt [lept *or* lēpt] Alternative past tense and past participle of LEAP.

leap year A year of 366 days, the extra day being the 29th of February. If a year can be divided by 4 and have no remainder (as 1972 ÷ 4 = *exactly* 493), it is a leap year. But if it completes a century it must be exactly divisible by 400 (as the years 1600 and 2000).

learn [lûrn] *v.* **learned** or **learnt, learn·ing 1** To get knowledge of or skill in: He *learned* reading at an early age; to *learn* to swim. **2** To gain knowledge or skill: He *learns* easily. **3** To find out; come to know or realize: We *learned* that the train was late. **4** To memorize: to *learn* poems. **5** To get by example or experience: to *learn* good habits. **—learn′er** *n.* ◆ See TEACH.

learn·ed [lûr′nid] *adj.* Full of or characterized by much learning or knowledge; erudite: a *learned* man; a *learned* profession.

learn·ing [lûr′ning] *n.* **1** The process of getting knowledge or skill. **2** Knowledge gotten by study or instruction.

learnt [lûrnt] Alternative past tense and past participle of LEARN: I *learnt* how to spell.

lease [lēs] *n., v.* **leased, leas·ing 1** *n.* A contract in which an owner agrees to let someone else live in or use his property for a certain time in return for money paid as rent. **2** *v.* To rent or use by means of a lease: We *leased* the garage for a year.

leash [lēsh] **1** *n.* A cord, rope, chain, etc., by which a dog or other animal is led or held. **2** *v.* To hold or control with a leash: to *leash* a dog. **3** *v.* To control or hold back: She learned to *leash* her emotions in public.

Leash

least [lēst] **1** A superlative of LITTLE. **2** *adj.* Smallest in size, amount, value, importance, etc.: The *least* piece of pie is better than none. **3** *n.* Some person or thing that is the smallest, slightest, or most unimportant. **4** *adv.* In the smallest degree or amount: He was *least* tired of them all. **— at least 1** At the lowest possible estimate. **2** At any rate: *At least* we now know the truth.

least common denominator The least common multiple of the denominators of a set of fractions. 24 is the least common denominator of $\frac{3}{4}$, $\frac{1}{8}$, and $\frac{1}{12}$.

least common multiple The smallest counting number that is evenly divisible by each member of a set of counting numbers. The least common multiple of 2, 3, 4, and 6 is 12.

least·wise [lēst′wīz′] *adv. informal* At least; at any rate: *Leastwise* we'll know next time.

leath·er [leth′ər] **1** *n.* Animal skin or hide, usually with the hair or fur removed, and made ready for many uses by cleaning and tanning. **2** *adj. use: leather* gloves; a *leather* strap.

leath·ern [leth′ərn] *adj.* Made of leather.

leath·er·y [leth′ər·ē] *adj.* Like leather in appearance or toughness: *leathery* hands.

leave[1] [lēv] *v.* **left, leav·ing 1** To go or depart from: We *left* him on the corner. **2** To go away: We *left* late. **3** To end one's connection with: He *left* his brother's firm. **4** To abandon; desert: He *left* his family. **5** To allow to be or remain: He *left* his bicycle on the porch. **6** To have or cause as a result: Oil *leaves* stains. **7** To give to another to do, decide, solve, etc.: *Leave* your problem to me. **8** To have remaining after one's death: He *left* a wife and child. **9** To give in a will at one's death: She *left* a large fortune. **10** In arithmetic, to have as a difference: 12 minus 8 *leaves* 4. **— leave alone** To refrain from annoying, interfering with, etc. **— leave off 1** To stop; cease. **2** To stop using. **— leave out 1** To take out or omit. **2** To decide not to include. ◆ *Leave* (def. **5**) means *to permit to remain*: He *left* his hat in the closet. *Let* means simply *to permit*: *Let* him speak (Permit him to speak).

leave[2] [lēv] *n.* **1** Permission: Give him *leave* to buy what he needs. **2** Permission to be absent, as from one's job, the armed forces, etc., often called **leave of absence. 3** The length of time for which such permission is given: a three-month *leave.* **4** Departure, especially in the expression **take one's leave,** to say good-by and depart.

leave[3] [lēv] *v.* **leaved, leav·ing** To put forth leaves; leaf.

leav·en [lev′ən] **1** *n.* A substance, as yeast, that when added to dough or batter helps it to rise and become light and fluffy. **2** *v.* To make rise by using leaven. **3** *n.* Anything that lightens, improves, or otherwise changes the character of something else: Wit is a *leaven* to good talk. **4** *v.* To change the character of.

leave-tak·ing [lēv′tā′king] *n.* The act of saying good-by; a farewell.

leav·ings [lē′vingz] *n.pl.* The leftover parts of anything that have not been used, eaten, etc.

Leb·a·non [leb′ə·nən] *n.* A country of sw Asia, at the eastern end of the Mediterranean Sea.

lec·tern [lek′tərn] *n.* A stand having an inclined top on which a speaker, teacher, etc., may put the books or papers he wants to read from.

lec·ture [lek′chər] *n., v.* **lec·tured, lec·tur·ing 1** *n.* A speech on a particular subject, usually given to instruct or inform. **2** *v.* To give a lecture or teach by lectures. **3** *n.* A long or severe scolding. **4** *v.* To scold. **— lec′tur·er** *n.*

Lectern

led [led] Past tense and past participle of LEAD[1]: I *led* my baby sister home.

ledge [lej] *n.* **1** A narrow, shelflike piece of land or rock jutting out from the side of a mountain, cliff, etc. **2** A shelf, sill, or other surface jutting out from a wall, window, etc.

led·ger [lej′ər] *n.* A book in which a business keeps a record of money spent and received.

ledger line A short line used to locate notes above or below a musical staff.

lee [lē] **1** *n.* Shelter or protection, especially from the wind. **2** *n.* A place or side, usually of a ship, that is sheltered from the wind: the *lee* of the rock. **3** *adj. use:* the *lee* side of the ship.

Lee [lē], **Robert E.,** 1807–1870, the commander in chief of the Confederate army in the Civil War.

leech [lēch] *n.* **1** A worm that lives in the water and sucks the blood of animals and humans. **2** A person who sticks close to another person in order to gain something. ◆ *Leeches* were formerly used by physicians to draw the blood of patients in the treatment of certain diseases. In fact the Old English word for this worm originally meant *physician.*

leek [lēk] *n.* A vegetable similar to an onion but having a smaller bulb and milder taste.

leer [lir] **1** *n.* A sly, knowing look or glance, usually made out of the corner of the eye. **2** *v.* To look with a leer: He *leered* at us.

leer·y [lir′ē] *adj.* **leer·i·er, leer·i·est** *informal* Suspicious; doubtful; wary: We were *leery* of his strange voice and actions.

lees [lēz] *n.pl.* Sediment, as of wine; dregs.

Man leering

Leeu·wen·hoek [lā′vən·hook], **Anton van,** 1632–1723, Dutch naturalist and one of the first men to use a microscope in his work.

lee·ward [lē′wərd *or* loo′ərd] **1** *adj.* In the direction toward which the wind is blowing. **2** *n.* The leeward side or direction. **3** *adj., adv.* On or toward the side sheltered from the wind.

lee·way [lē′wā′] *n.* **1** Extra space, time, money, etc., to be used if needed: The high ceilings gave us *leeway* to move the ladders. **2** The drifting of a ship or plane to the side.

left[1] [left] **1** *adj.* On, to, or indicating the side of the body that is toward the north when one faces east: a *left* arm; a *left* shoe. **2** *adv.* To or toward the left hand or side: Turn *left.* **3** *n.* The left side, direction, or hand. **4** *adj.* Nearer to the left side: Go through the *left* door. **5** *adj.* Liberal or radical in political views. **6** *n.* A group or party having liberal or radical political views.

left[2] [left] Past tense and past participle of LEAVE[1]: I *left* three hours ago.

left-hand [left′hand′] *adj.* **1** Of, for, or on the left side or the left hand: a *left-hand* glove. **2** Left-handed: a *left-hand* pitcher.

left-hand·ed [left′han′did] **1** *adj.* Using the left hand more easily and more often than the right. **2** *adj.* Done with or meant to be used by the left hand: a *left-handed* pitch; a *left-handed* golf club. **3** *adj.* Turning from right to left. **4** *adv.* With the left hand. **5** *adj.* Insincere or doubtful: a *left-handed* compliment.

left·o·ver [left′ō′vər] *n.* **1** (*usually pl.*) An unused part, especially food that has not been eaten. **2** *adj. use: leftover* potatoes.

leg [leg] *n., v.* **legged, leg·ging 1** *n.* One of the limbs of animals and man that serve as supports in standing and walking. **2** *n.* The part of an article of clothing meant to cover a leg. **3** *n.* Anything like a leg in shape or use: a table *leg.* **4** *n.* A section or part, as of a journey. **5** *v. informal* To walk or run: Let's *leg* it from here. **— on one's last legs** Nearly worn out or dead. **— pull one's leg** *informal* To fool or tease a person.

leg·a·cy [leg′ə·sē] *n., pl.* **leg·a·cies 1** Money, property, etc., that has been left to one by a will; bequest. **2** Something inherited.

le·gal [lē′gəl] *adj.* **1** Of or having to do with law: *legal* papers. **2** Permitted by or based on law. **3** Of, for, or characteristic of lawyers: a *legal* mind. **— le′gal·ly** *adv.*

le·gal·i·ty [li·gal′ə·tē] *n.* The condition of being lawful.

le·gal·ize [lē′gəl·īz] *v.* **le·gal·ized, le·gal·iz·ing** To make legal. ¶ 3

legal tender Money that may be legally offered to pay a debt and which a creditor must accept.

leg·ate [leg′it] *n.* A person who officially represents a government or ruler, especially a person who represents the Pope.

leg·a·tee [leg′ə·tē′] *n.* A person who inherits money or property in a will.

le·ga·tion [li·gā′shən] *n.* **1** The residence or offices of an official who represents his government in a foreign country and has a lower rank than an ambassador. **2** The official and his staff.

le·ga·to [li·gä′tō] **1** *adj.* In music, smooth and flowing: a *legato* passage. **2** *adv.* In a legato style or manner: Play *legato.*

leg·end [lej′ənd] *n.* **1** A story that has come down from earlier times and is often thought by many people to be partly true: The tales about Robin Hood are *legends.* **2** A group of such stories. **3** The writing on a coin, monument, banner, etc. **4** A short explanation or title accompanying a picture, map, chart, etc.

leg·en·dar·y [lej′ən·der′ē] *adj.* **1** Of, having to do with, or like a legend. **2** Famous in or as in a legend: a *legendary* hero.

leg·er·de·main [lej′ər·də·mān′] *n.* **1** Tricks of magic or sleight of hand. **2** Trickery; deception. ◆ *Legerdemain* comes from the French words *leger de main*, meaning *light of hand*.

leg·ged [leg′id *or* legd] *adj.* Having a certain number or kind of legs: often used in combination, as in *four-legged*, having four legs.

leg·ging [leg′ing] *n.* (*usually pl.*) A covering for the leg, usually reaching from the ankle to the knee.

Leg·horn [leg′hôrn] *n.* (*sometimes written* **leghorn**) A breed of small domestic chicken.

leg·i·ble [lej′ə·bəl] *adj.* Easy to read: *legible* handwriting. **— leg′i·bil′i·ty** *n.* **— leg′i·bly** *adv.*

le·gion [lē′jən] *n.* **1** In ancient Rome, a large military unit of foot soldiers and cavalry, numbering up to 6,000 men. **2** Any large military force; army. **3** A great number; multitude.

le·gion·ar·y [lē′jən·er′ē] *adj., n., pl.* **le·gion·ar·ies 1** *adj.* Of or making up a legion. **2** *n.* A member of a legion.

leg·is·late [lej′is·lāt] *v.* **leg·is·lat·ed, leg·is·lat·ing 1** To make laws. **2** To create or change by passing laws: to *legislate* new taxes.

leg·is·la·tion [lej′is·lā′shən] *n.* **1** The act of making laws. **2** The laws made.

add, āce, câre, pälm; end, ēqual; it, īce; odd, ōpen, ôrder; took, pool; up, bûrn;
ə = a in *above*, e in *sicken*, i in *possible*, o in *melon*, u in *circus*; yoo = u in *fuse*; oil; pout;
check; ring; thin; this; zh in *vision.* For ¶ reference, see page 64 · HOW TO

leg·is·la·tive [lej′is·lā′tiv] *adj.* **1** Of or having to do with laws or with making laws: *legislative* duties. **2** Having the power to make laws: the *legislative* branch of government.

leg·is·la·tor [lej′is·lā′tər] *n.* A member of a law-making body, as a member of Congress.

leg·is·la·ture [lej′is·lā′chər] *n.* A group of persons who make the laws of a nation or state.

le·git·i·ma·cy [lə·jit′ə·mə·sē] *n.* The condition of being legitimate.

le·git·i·mate [lə·jit′ə·mit] *adj.* **1** Permitted or approved by law; lawful: He has a *legitimate* right to sue. **2** Logical; reasonable; justified: a *legitimate* fear. **3** Born of parents who are married to each other.

leg·ume [leg′yo͞om *or* lə·gyo͞om′] *n.* **1** The edible fruit or seed of various plants that bear pods, as the bean, pea, or lentil. **2** A pod containing such seeds, or the plant itself.

le·gu·mi·nous [lə·gyo͞o′mə·nəs] *adj.* **1** Of or belonging to various plants having legumes, as the bean or pea. **2** Of or bearing legumes.

lei [lā *or* lā′ē] *n., pl.* **leis** In Hawaii, a garland of flowers, leaves, etc., often worn around the neck.

lei·sure [lē′zhər *or* lezh′ər] **1** *n.* Time free from work, study, or any duties: a day of *leisure.* **2** *adj.* Free from work or duties: *leisure* hours. — **at one's leisure** Whenever one has the time or the chance: Call me *at your leisure.*

Lei

lei·sure·ly [lē′zhər·lē *or* lezh′ər·lē] **1** *adj.* Relaxed and unhurried: a *leisurely* stroll. **2** *adv.* In a slow, relaxed manner.

lem·ming [lem′ing] *n.* Any of several small ratlike animals living in arctic regions and having a short tail and furry feet. Lemmings are noted for migrating in vast numbers and often throwing themselves into the sea to drown.

lem·on [lem′ən] **1** *n.* An oval-shaped citrus fruit, having a juicy, sour pulp and a yellow skin, used to flavor foods and in perfumes. **2** *n.* The tree bearing this fruit. **3** *n., adj.* Pale or bright yellow. **4** *n. slang* A failure; disappointment.

lem·on·ade [lem′ən·ād′] *n.* A drink made of lemon juice, sugar, and water.

le·mur [lē′mər] *n.* A small animal that lives in trees and is related to the monkey. It is found chiefly in Madagascar.

Ring-tailed lemur, about 33 in. long, including tail

lend [lend] *v.* **lent, lend·ing 1** To permit the use of with the understanding that the thing, or its equivalent, will be returned: to *lend* a book; to *lend* a cup of flour. **2** To permit the use of (money) to be returned later, sometimes with interest. **3** To give; add; contribute: Fog *lent* an air of mystery to the scene. — **lend′er** *n.*

length [leng(k)th] *n.* **1** The longest part or side of something rather than its width or thickness: the *length* of a car. **2** The measure of something from end to end: The *length* is just 25 feet. **3** The condition of being long. **4** The size, extent, or period covered from beginning to end: the *length* of a book; a short *length* of time. **5** A piece of something, usually of a standard size: a *length* of pipe. — **at length 1** After a while; finally. **2** Without leaving anything out; fully. — **go to great lengths** or **go to any length** To do all that is possible: He *went to great lengths* to impress his friends.

length

length·en [leng(k)′thən] *v.* To make or grow longer: She *lengthened* her dress.

length·ways [leng(k)th′wāz′] *adv.* Lengthwise.

length·wise [leng(k)th′wīz′] *adj., adv* In the direction of the length: a *lengthwise* path across the field; to swim the pool *lengthwise.*

length·y [leng(k)′thē] *adj.* **length·i·er, length·i·est** Unusually long; too long: a *lengthy* voyage. — **length′i·ly** *adv.*

le·ni·ence [lē′nē·əns *or* lēn′yəns] *n.* Leniency.

le·ni·en·cy [lē′nē·ən·sē *or* lēn′yən·sē] *n.* Gentleness; mildness.

le·ni·ent [lē′nē·ənt *or* lēn′yənt] *adj.* Gentle or merciful; not stern or severe; mild: a *lenient* punishment. — **le′ni·ent·ly** *adv.*

Le·nin [len′in], **V. I. (Nikolai),** 1870–1924, chief leader of the Russian Revolution of 1917 and head of the Soviet Union from 1917 to 1924.

Le·nin·grad [len′in·grad] *n.* A city in the NW Soviet Union.

len·i·ty [len′ə·tē] *n.* Leniency; mercifulness.

lens [lenz] *n.* **1** A piece of glass or other transparent material having one surface or two opposite surfaces curved in such a way that light rays passing through it are bent apart or together. Lenses are used to magnify things, bring images into focus, etc. **2** A transparent part of the eye located behind the iris and serving to focus an image on the retina.

lent [lent] Past tense and past participle of LEND: I *lent* him a dime three weeks ago.

Lent [lent] *n.* The forty days (not including Sundays), from Ash Wednesday to Easter. Lent is a Christian season of fasting and self-denial.

Lent·en [len′tən] *adj.* (*sometimes written* **lenten**) Of, occurring in, or suitable for Lent.

len·til [len′təl] *n.* **1** A plant having large pods that contain flat, edible, pealike seeds. **2** The seed of this plant.

Le·o·nar·do [lē′ə·när′dō] *n.* See DA VINCI.

le·o·nine [lē′ə·nīn] *adj.* Of or like a lion.

leop·ard [lep′ərd] *n.* A ferocious animal of the cat family, found in Asia and Africa and having a brownish yellow coat with black spots.

lep·er [lep′ər] *n.* A person who has leprosy.

lep·re·chaun [lep′rə·kôn] *n.* In Irish folk stories, a tiny elf, often a cobbler, supposed to tell where treasure is, if caught.

lep·ro·sy [lep′rə·sē] *n.* A mildly contagious disease marked by sores and scales on the skin and a gradual rotting away of parts of the body.

lep·rous [lep′rəs] *adj.* 1 Having leprosy. 2 Of, caused by, or like leprosy: a *leprous* sore.

lese ma·jes·ty [lēz′ maj′is·tē] A crime against a king or ruler or against his authority.

le·sion [lē′zhən] *n.* A harmful change to an organ or tissue of the body, as an injury.

less [les] 1 A comparative of LITTLE. 2 *adj.* Not as much or as great in size, amount, value, importance, etc.: *less* candy; *less* speed. 3 *n.* Something smaller or less important or valuable: You gave us *less* than you gave her. 4 *adv.* To a smaller or not so great degree, amount, extent, etc.: *less* loudly. 5 *prep.* Minus: 8 *less* 5 is 3. ◆ *Less* and *fewer* are both used to compare unequal things. *Less* is usually used for things that cannot be counted or measured separately: There was less rain this year than last year. *Fewer* is used for things that can be counted or measured in separate units: *fewer* people. Thus we speak of *less* time but *fewer* hours.

-less A suffix meaning: 1 Not having; without, as in *motherless*, not having a mother, or *harmless*, without harm. 2 Not able to do or not capable of being, as in *restless*, not able to rest, or *countless*, not capable of being counted.

les·see [les·ē′] *n.* A person who has a lease to rent or use property; a tenant.

less·en [les′(ə)n] *v.* To make or become less: His anger *lessened* as we talked. ◆ See LESSON.

less·er [les′ər] *adj.* Not as large, great, or important, etc.: the *lesser* crime of the two.

les·son [les′(ə)n] *n.* 1 A regular part of a course of study; period of instruction: a history *lesson*; a driving *lesson*. 2 Something to be studied or learned, as by a student; assignment. 3 An action or experience from which something can be learned: Let that be a *lesson* to you! 4 A portion of the Bible meant to be read at a religious service. ◆ *Lesson* and *lessen*, although pronounced alike, are not related in meaning. *Lessen* is a verb meaning *to make less*: Stiff competition *lessened* his chances of winning. *Lesson* is a noun meaning *something to be learned*: a *lesson* in manners.

less·or [les′ôr] *n.* A person who gives another person a lease to rent property; landlord.

lest [lest] *conj.* 1 For fear that: We hid *lest* he should see us. 2 That: used after expressions of fear or anxiety: We worried *lest* it should rain.

let¹ [let] *v.* **let, let·ting** 1 To allow or permit: We *let* her do it. 2 To permit to pass, come, go, etc.: *Let* him by. 3 To cause; make: *Let* me know when you arrive. 4 To cause to flow: to *let* blood. 5 To rent or be rented: We *let* our cottage for the summer; rooms to *let*. ◆ *Let* may also be used with other verbs in order to give a command, as in *Let us go*, to express willingness or assent, as in *Let it rain*, or to assume or suppose, as in *Let X equal the sum of two numbers*. **—let alone** 1 To leave undisturbed. 2 *informal* Not to mention; and surely not: He can't even float, *let alone* swim. **—let be** To refrain from disturbing or tampering with: *Let* the camera *be*. **—let down** 1 To lower. 2 To disappoint: You *let* me *down*. **—let loose** To set free; release. **—let off** 1 To let go; release. 2 To dismiss or excuse, as from a punishment or from work. **—let on** *informal* 1 To pretend: *Let on* you don't know. 2 To make known; reveal: Don't *let on* that I told you. **—let out** 1 To give forth: to *let out* a yell. 2 To set free; release. 3 To unfasten so as to make wider or longer: to *let out* a hem. **—let up** To grow or cause to grow less: The noise *let up* a bit. ◆ See LEAVE.

let² [let] *n.* 1 An obstacle, often used in the phrase **without let or hindrance,** without anything to hinder, prevent, or stand in the way. 2 In tennis, interference with the ball's flight that requires playing the point again.

-let A suffix meaning: 1 Small; little, as in *booklet*, a small book. 2 A band or ornament for, as in *anklet*, a band for the ankle.

let·down [let′doun′] *n.* 1 A decrease or slackening, as of energy, speed, etc. 2 *informal* Disappointment: The story's end was a *letdown*.

le·thal [lē′thəl] *adj.* Causing death; deadly: a *lethal* gas.

le·thar·gic [li·thär′jik] *adj.* 1 Drowsy, listless, and dull: Fever made him *lethargic*. 2 Causing lethargy: a *lethargic* climate.

leth·ar·gy [leth′ər·jē] *n.* The condition of feeling tired, dull, and listless.

Le·the [lē′thē] *n.* In Greek myths, a river in Hades whose waters, when drunk, made a person forget the past.

let's [lets] Let us.

let·ter [let′ər] 1 *n.* A sign or mark used in writing or printing to represent a speech sound; a character in an alphabet. 2 *v.* To form letters, as by hand: He *letters* very well. 3 *v.* To make or mark with letters: to *letter* a name. 4 *n.* A written or printed message, usually sent by mail. 5 *n.* (*pl.*) Literature in general: a man of *letters*. 6 *n.* An emblem in the form of the first letter of the name of a school or college, given as an award for achievement in athletics or other activities. 7 *n.* The absolute and exact meaning of something as opposed to the general inter-

add, āce, câre, pälm;   end, ēqual;   it, īce;   odd, ōpen, ôrder;   tŏŏk, pōōl;   up, bûrn;
ə = a in *above*, e in *sicken*, i in *possible*, o in *melon*, u in *circus*;   yōō = u in *fuse*;   oil;   pout;
check;   ring;   thin;   this;   zh in *vision*.   For ¶ reference, see page 64 · HOW TO

pretation: the *letter* of the law. **— to the letter** Precisely as written or directed: Follow my instructions *to the letter*.

let·ter·head [let′ər·hed′] *n.* **1** The name and usually the address of a person or business printed at the top of a sheet of stationery. **2** A sheet of paper with such a heading.

RODGERS ELECTRONICS INC. 23 State Street Troy, New York

Letterhead

let·ter·ing [let′ər·ing] *n.* **1** The act or art of forming letters. **2** Letters formed in this way.

let·ter-per·fect [let′ər·pûr′fikt] *adj.* Correct in every detail: a *letter-perfect* recitation.

let·tuce [let′is] *n.* A plant having crisp, green, edible leaves, used in salads.

let·up [let′up′] *n. informal* A pausing, relaxing, or brief stopping of some activity, effort, etc.

leu·co·cyte [loo′kə·sīt] *n.* A white or colorless corpuscle of the blood, which helps to destroy harmful bacteria, etc.

leu·ke·mi·a [loo·kē′mē·ə] *n.* A disease of the blood in which there is a very great increase in the number of leucocytes formed.

Le·vant [lə·vant′] *n.* The countries that border on the eastern Mediterranean Sea, between western Greece and western Egypt.

lev·ee[1] [lev′ē] *n.* **1** A bank built along the shore of a river to keep it from flooding. **2** A landing place for boats on a river.

lev·ee[2] [lev′ē *or* lə·vē′] *n.* An official morning reception held in former times by a king or other person of high rank.

lev·el [lev′əl] *adj., n., v.* **lev·eled** or **lev·elled, lev·el·ing** or **lev·el·ling 1** *adj.* Having a flat surface, with each part at the same height: a *level* board. **2** *adj.* Equal in height; even: Make this pile of bricks *level* with that one. **3** *n.* Height; depth: The snowfall reached a *level* of 10 feet. **4** *n.* A position that is at the same height: The bookcase is on a *level* with the desk. **5** *v.* To give an even, horizontal, or level surface to: *Level* the board. **6** *adj.* Being parallel to the horizon; horizontal: *level* flight. **7** *n.* An instrument, as a glass tube of liquid containing an air bubble, used to see if a surface is level. **8** *n.* A flat expanse, as of land. **9** *n.* A degree or stage: a high reading *level*. **10** *v.* To bring to a common state or condition: The war *leveled* all social classes. **11** *adj.* Not excited; calm; sensible: a *level* head. **12** *v.* To destroy or knock down: The bomb *leveled* the entire block; The boxer *leveled* his opponent.

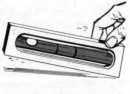

Level

13 *v.* To aim or direct: He *leveled* the gun at me. **— level off 1** To move or fly horizontally after gaining or losing altitude: The plane *leveled off* at 15,000 feet. **2** To give a level, even surface to. **— on the level** *informal* Fair and honest: Be *on the level* with us. **— lev′el·er** *n.* **— lev′el·ness** *n.*

lev·el·head·ed [lev′əl·hed′id] *adj.* **1** Not easily excited; calm. **2** Sensible; reasonable.

lev·er [lev′ər *or* lē′vər] **1** *n.* A mechanical device for lifting or prying up heavy objects. It consists of a straight bar that rests on a fixed support called a fulcrum. When force is applied at one end of the bar, the weight at the other end is moved or lifted. **2** *n.* Any bar used to turn, move, or control something: Pull that *lever* and the machinery will stop. **3** *v.* To move or pry with or as if with a lever.

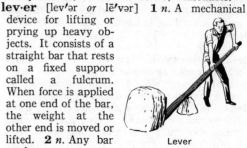

Lever

lev·er·age [lev′ər·ij *or* lē′vər·ij] *n.* **1** The use of a lever. **2** The advantage or extra force gained by using a lever.

Le·vi [lē′vī] *n.* In the Bible, a son of Jacob. The Levites were descended from him.

le·vi·a·than [lə·vī′ə·thən] *n.* **1** A gigantic water beast mentioned in the Bible. **2** Any enormous creature or thing, as a whale or large ship.

Le·vite [lē′vīt] *n.* In the Bible, one of the tribe of Levi. The Levites were chosen to assist the priests in the Jewish temple.

lev·i·ty [lev′ə·tē] *n., pl.* **lev·i·ties** Joking and gaiety, especially at the wrong time or in the wrong place.

lev·y [lev′ē] *v.* **lev·ied, lev·y·ing,** *n., pl.* **lev·ies 1** *v.* To demand and collect by law: to *levy* a tax or a fine. **2** *v.* To draft for military service: to *levy* troops. **3** *v.* To prepare for or wage (war). **4** *n.* The act of levying. **5** *n.* Something that is levied, as money or troops.

lewd [lood] *adj.* Vulgar and obscene; indecent. **— lewd′ly** *adv.* **— lewd′ness** *n.*

Lew·is [loo′is], **Meriwether,** 1774–1809, U.S. explorer who with William Clark led the first U.S. expedition overland to the Pacific Ocean.

Lew·is [loo′is], **Sinclair,** 1885–1951, U.S. novelist.

lex·i·cog·ra·phy [lek′sə·kog′rə·fē] *n.* The act or profession of writing dictionaries. **— lex′i·cog′ra·pher** *n.*

lex·i·con [lek′sə·kon] *n.* **1** A dictionary, especially of Latin, Greek, or Hebrew. **2** A list of words used in or having to do with a particular subject or occupation.

Lex·ing·ton [lek′sing·tən] *n.* **1** A town in NE Massachusetts where the first battle of the American Revolution was fought, April 19, 1775. **2** A city in north central Kentucky.

Li The symbol for the element LITHIUM.

li·a·bil·i·ty [lī′ə·bil′ə·tē] *n., pl.* **li·a·bil·i·ties**
1 The condition of being liable. **2** (*pl.*) The
money a person or business owes; debts. **3** A
hindrance or drawback; disadvantage.

li·a·ble [lī′ə·bəl] *adj.* **1** Subject or susceptible,
as to illness, injury, etc.: He is *liable* to colds.
2 Likely; apt: It is *liable* to rain; He is *liable* to
fall. **3** Legally responsible; answerable: They
are *liable* for the damage done.

li·ai·son [lē′ā·zon′ *or* lē·ā′zon *or* lē′ə·zon] *n.*
Contacts and communication between units or
groups of an army, government, etc., to secure
better cooperation.

li·ar [lī′ər] *n.* A person who lies.

li·ba·tion [lī·bā′shən] *n.* **1** The act of pouring
out a liquid, as wine, in honor of a god. **2** The
liquid poured out.

li·bel [lī′bəl] *n., v.* **li·beled** *or* **li·belled, li·**
bel·ing *or* **li·bel·ling 1** *n.* A written statement
or a picture, especially if published, that damages
a person's reputation or dignity. **2** *n.* The act or
crime of making or publishing such a statement
or picture. **3** *v.* To make or publish a libel
against. **— li′bel·er** *n.* **— li′bel·ous** *adj.*

lib·er·al [lib′ər·əl *or* lib′rəl] **1** *adj.* Very generous: a *liberal* gift to the museum. **2** *adj.* Abundant; ample: Put in a *liberal* amount of detergent. **3** *adj.* Not narrow-minded or prejudiced;
tolerant; broad. **4** *adj.* Based on the liberal arts:
a *liberal* education. **5** *adj.* Favoring progress or
reform, as in politics. **6** *n.* A person who favors
progress or reform. **— lib′er·al·ly** *adv.*

liberal arts A group of college courses, as
literature, philosophy, history, and languages,
giving a broad, general education rather than a
scientific or technical one.

lib·er·al·ism [lib′ər·əl·iz′əm] *n.* **1** The condition of being liberal. **2** Liberal beliefs or actions,
especially in politics and religion.

lib·er·al·i·ty [lib′ə·ral′ə·tē] *n., pl.* **lib·er·al·**
i·ties 1 Generosity in giving. **2** Tolerance and
understanding; broad-mindedness.

lib·er·al·ize [lib′ər·əl·īz′] *v.* **lib·er·al·ized,**
lib·er·al·iz·ing To make or become liberal.
— lib′er·al·i·za′tion *n.* ¶ 3

lib·er·ate [lib′ə·rāt] *v.* **lib·er·at·ed, lib·er·**
at·ing To set free; release: to *liberate* a conquered country; to *liberate* hydrogen. **— lib′·**
er·a′tion *n.* **— lib′er·a′tor** *n.*

Li·be·ri·a [lī·bir′ē·ə] *n.* A country on the west
coast of Africa, founded in 1847 by freed slaves
from the U.S. **— Li·be′ri·an** *adj., n.*

lib·er·tine [lib′ər·tēn] *n.* A man who lives an
immoral life without restraining himself.

lib·er·ty [lib′ər·tē] *n., pl.* **lib·er·ties 1** Freedom from any arbitrary control by others.
2 Freedom to think or act as one wishes, regarded
as a very important human right. **3** Permission
to be in and make use of a particular place: Our

class was given *liberty* of the entire beach. **4** In
the Navy, permission to be absent from one's
ship or one's place of duty. **— at liberty 1**
Permitted or free to do something. **2** Not busy:
The doctor will see you when he's *at liberty*.
— take liberties To behave with too much
boldness, friendliness, or familiarity.

li·brar·i·an [lī·brâr′ē·ən] *n.* A person in charge
of a library or trained in library work.

li·brar·y [lī′brer′ē *or* lī′brə·rē] *n., pl.* **li·brar·**
ies 1 A collection of books, magazines, newspapers, etc., especially when arranged and
catalogued for public use. **2** A building, room,
etc., in which such a collection is kept.

li·bret·to [li·bret′ō] *n., pl.* **li·bret·tos** *or* **li·**
bret·ti [li·bret′ē] **1** The words of an opera or
other big vocal work. **2** A book or pamphlet
containing these words.

Lib·y·a [lib′ē·ə] *n.* A country in northern Africa.
— Lib′y·an *adj., n.*

lice [līs] Plural of LOUSE.

li·cense [lī′səns] *n., v.* **li·censed, li·cens·ing**
1 *n.* An official card or paper giving permission
to do something: a driver's *license*. **2** *v.* To give
a license to or for: They *licensed* him to fish.
3 *n.* Too much freedom or laxity in one's
conduct. **4** *n.* The breaking or ignoring of usual
or established rules, especially for artistic effect:
to use poetic *license*.

li·cen·tious [lī·sen′shəs] *adj.* Not held back
by rules or decency; immoral; lewd. **— li·**
cen′tious·ly *adv.* **— li·cen′tious·ness** *n.*

li·chen [lī′kən] *n.* A mosslike plant, made up
of a fungus and an alga, which grows in patches
on rocks, trees, etc.

lick [lik] **1** *v.* To pass the tongue over the
surface of: The dog *licked* his sore paw. **2** *v.* To
move or pass over or about: The flames *licked*
the coals. **3** *n.* The act of licking: My dog gave
me a *lick* on my face. **4** *n. informal* A quick or
careless action or effort. **5** *n. informal* A bit or
small amount: He hasn't done a *lick* of work all
day. **6** *v. informal* To defeat or thrash: We
licked them easily. **7** *n. informal* A sharp blow
or hit. **8** *n.* A salt lick.

lic·o·rice [lik′ə·ris *or* lik′rish] *n.* **1** A plant that
grows in central or southern Europe. **2** Its root,
used in medicine or to flavor things. **3** A candy
flavored with licorice. ◆ *Licorice* comes from
two Greek words meaning *sweet root*.

lid [lid] *n.* **1** A hinged or removable cover for a
box, pot, etc. **2** An eyelid. **3** *slang* A hat.

lie[1] [lī] *v.* **lay, lain, ly·ing 1** To be in a flat,
horizontal position: The tree *lay* on the ground.
2 To put oneself in a horizontal position: She
lay down on the bed. **3** To be buried: Juliet *lay*
in her tomb. **4** To be or remain in some particular condition: The seeds *lay* dormant all
winter. **5** To exist: Our strength *lies* in our
numbers. **6** To be in a certain location; be

situated: New York *lies* northeast of Philadelphia. **7** To continue or extend: The future *lies* before us. ◆ See LAY.

lie² [lī] *n.*, *v.* **lied, ly·ing** **1** *n.* Something said or written that is not true and is meant to deceive; falsehood. **2** *v.* To tell or write a lie; deceive on purpose. **3** *v.* To give a wrong impression; be inaccurate: Figures don't *lie*. **— give the lie to 1** To show or prove the falseness of: His public speech *gave the lie to* rumors that he was dead. **2** To accuse (someone) of lying. ◆ See DECEIVE.

Liech·ten·stein [lik′tən·stīn] *n.* A small country between Switzerland and Austria.

lief [lēf] *adv.* Willingly; gladly, now used only in the phrase **would as lief:** He *would as lief* knock you down as look at you.

liege [lēj] **1** *n.* In the Middle Ages, a lord or ruler to whom feudal service or allegiance was due. **2** *n.* A vassal or subject who owed such services. **3** *adj.* Entitled to receive feudal allegiance: a *liege* lord. **4** *adj.* Owing feudal allegiance: a *liege* vassal.

liege·man [lēj′mən] *n.*, *pl.* **liege·men** [lēj′·mən] **1** A feudal vassal. **2** A loyal follower or subject.

lien [lēn] *n.* A legal right to claim or hold the property of a person who owes one money.

lieu [lōō] *n.* Place; stead, now used only in the phrase **in lieu of:** I will send her *in lieu of* you.

Lieut. Abbreviation of LIEUTENANT.

lieu·ten·ant [lōō·ten′ənt] *n.* **1** A military rank. In the U.S. Army, either of two commissioned officers, a **first lieutenant** ranking next below a captain, or a **second lieutenant** ranking next below a first lieutenant. **2** A naval rank. In the U.S. Navy, either of two commissioned officers, a **lieutenant** ranking next below a lieutenant commander, or a **lieutenant (junior grade)** ranking next above an ensign. **3** A person able to perform the duties of his superior, either in the latter's absence or under his direction. ◆ *Lieutenant* comes from the French words *lieu* and *tenant* that mean *holding the place* (of a superior).

lieutenant colonel A military rank. In the U.S. Army, Air Force, and Marine Corps, an officer ranking next above a major and next below a colonel.

lieutenant commander A naval rank. In the U.S. Navy and Coast Guard, an officer ranking next above a lieutenant and next below a commander.

lieutenant general A military rank. In the U.S. Army, Air Force, and Marine Corps, an officer ranking next above a major general and next below a general.

lieutenant governor An elected official who performs the duties of a governor of a state during his absence or who replaces the governor in case he dies or resigns.

life [līf] *n.*, *pl.* **lives** [līvz] **1** The form of existence marked by growth, metabolism, reproduction, and adaptation to the environment. Life is what makes people, plants, and ani-

mals different from rocks, the earth, water, etc. **2** A living being; person: to save a *life*. **3** Living organisms as a group: *life* on Mars. **4** The period of a person's existence: a long, happy *life*. **5** The period of time during which something continues to work, be useful, etc.: the *life* of an engine. **6** The way or manner in which a person, group, etc., lives: city *life*. **7** Energy; vitality; spirit: He is certainly full of *life*. **8** An account of the events of a person's lifetime; a biography.

life belt A life preserver in the form of a belt.

life·blood [līf′blud′] *n.* **1** The blood necessary to life. **2** Any source of strength, vigor, or power.

life·boat [līf′bōt′] *n.* A boat equipped for saving lives at sea or along a shore, especially such a boat carried aboard a ship.

life buoy A life preserver, often in the form of a ring.

life cycle The entire series of biological processes and stages through which an organism passes from birth to death: the *life cycle* of a butterfly.

Lifeboat

life·guard [līf′gärd′] *n.* An expert swimmer employed at a beach, etc., to protect the safety of bathers.

life insurance Insurance on the life of an individual who pays regular payments or premiums during his lifetime. At his death a sum of money is given to his family or to whomever he names.

life·less [līf′lis′] *adj.* **1** Having lost life; dead. **2** Not ever having had life: A toy bear is *lifeless*. **3** Lacking vitality; dull: a *lifeless* book. **— life′less·ly** *adv.* **— life′less·ness** *n.*

life·like [līf′līk′] *adj.* **1** Looking like a person or thing that is or was alive: a *lifelike* picture. **2** Accurately representing actual events or circumstances: a *lifelike* movie.

life·line [līf′līn′] *n.* **1** A rope used to lower or raise an underwater diver. **2** Any rope giving support or aid, as to bathers in surf. **3** Any land, air, or sea route used for transporting supplies necessary for life.

life·long [līf′lông′] *adj.* Lasting or continuing throughout one's life: a *lifelong* friendship.

life preserver Any of various devices, often in the form of a belt, jacket, or ring, used to keep afloat a person who is in danger of drowning.

life·sav·ing [līf′sāv′ing] *n.* **1** The act of saving a life. **2** Any of various methods used to save the lives of those who are drowning or have been injured in some way. **3** *adj. use: lifesaving* equipment. **— life′sav′er** *n.*

Life preserver

life-size [līf′sīz′] *adj.* Having the same size as

the thing or person represented or portrayed: a *life-size* replica of a dinosaur.

life-sized [līf′sīzd′] *adj.* Life-size.

life·time [līf′tīm′] *n.* **1** The period of time during which a person, animal, or plant has life. **2** The period of time during which something lasts.

life·work [līf′wûrk′] *n.* **1** The chief things produced by a person during his lifetime: These few paintings are his entire *lifework*. **2** The work that a person does during his life.

lift [lift] **1** *v.* To take hold of and raise to a higher position: *Lift* the table. **2** *v.* To bring to a higher or better condition: His talk *lifted* the team's spirits. **3** *v.* To rise or ascend: His brows *lifted* in surprise. **4** *v.* To go or move away: The fog *lifted*. **5** *v.* To cancel, end, or revoke: He *lifted* the ban on Sunday games. **6** *n.* The act of lifting or raising. **7** *n.* An amount lifted; load. **8** *n.* The height or distance to which something is lifted. **9** *n.* Assistance; aid: Please give me a *lift* with this trunk. **10** *n.* A feeling of happiness or well-being: The good news gave us a *lift*. **11** *n.* A ride given a traveler to help him along the way. **12** *v. informal* To steal. **13** *n.* The British word for an elevator. **—lift′er** *n.*

lig·a·ment [lig′ə·mənt] *n.* A band of firm, strong tissue that connects bones or helps to support an organ of the body.

li·gate [lī′gāt] *v.* **li·gat·ed, li·gat·ing** To tie up or bind with a ligature.

lig·a·ture [lig′ə·chŏŏr *or* lig′ə·chər] *n.* **1** A band, strip, etc., used to tie or bind something. **2** In surgery, a thread or wire tied around a blood vessel to prevent bleeding. **3** In printing and writing, a character made up of two or more connected letters, as æ, fi, ffi.

light¹ [līt] *n., v.* **light·ed** or **lit, light·ing,** *adj.* **1** *n.* A form of energy that stimulates the eyes and makes it possible to see things. **2** *n.* Brightness: A lot of *light* comes in this window. **3** *v.* To make or become light or bright. **4** *v.* To cause to give off light: *Light* the bulb on the cellar stairs. **5** *n.* A source of light or brightness, as an electric light bulb, a candle, etc. **6** *adj.* Full of light; not dark; bright: a *light* room. **7** *n.* Daylight or dawn. **8** *n.* Something that admits light, as a window or skylight. **9** *v.* To guide or conduct with light: The fires *lit* him home. **10** *adj.* Pale: a *light* blue scarf. **11** *v.* To cause or start to burn: *Light* the kindling in the fireplace; It *lights* quickly. **12** *n.* Something that ignites or sets fire to something else: a *light* for a cigarette. **13** *n.* A lively or intense expression on the face or in the eyes. **14** *v.* To make or become radiant or cheerful: A smile *lit* her face; Their eyes *lit* up with joy. **15** *n.* Knowledge or understanding: Get all the *light* you can on this subject. **16** *n.* Public attention or knowledge:

to bring new facts to *light*. **17** *n.* The way in which something impresses or appears to one: to see things in a new *light*. **18** *n.* An outstanding or famous person: a lesser *light*. **— bring to light** To expose or reveal: The trial *brought to light* enough evidence to clear the defendant of the charge of libel. **— in the light of** In view of; considering: *In the light of* what we heard about his past job performance, we decided not to hire the young man. **— see the light 1** To come into being; be born. **2** To be brought to the attention of the public. **3** To get knowledge or understanding. **— shed light on** or **throw light on** To explain or make clear.

light² [līt] *adj., v.* **light·ed** or **lit, light·ing 1** *adj.* Having little weight, especially in relation to size or bulk: a *light* cotton cloth; a *light* plane. **2** *adj.* Not heavy; easily carried or done: a *light* package; *light* work. **3** *adj.* Intended as entertainment: *light* reading. **4** *adj.* Not great in amount, force, etc.: a *light* rain. **5** *adj.* Cheerful; gay: a *light* laugh. **6** *adj.* Not clumsy; graceful: to be *light* on one's feet. **7** *adj.* Dizzy; giddy: a *light* head. **8** *adj.* Gentle: a *light* tap on the door. **9** *adj.* Not coarse or heavy in texture, feel, etc.: *light* biscuits. **10** *adj.* Not rich or heavy: a *light* meal; a *light* wine. **11** *adj.* Not carrying huge or heavy weapons, armor, etc.: a *light* tank. **12** *v.* To come down and settle, as after flight. **13** *v.* To happen or come, as by chance: We *lighted* upon the best bargains in town. **14** *v.* To fall; strike: The heavy branch *lighted* on his head. **15** *v.* To get down, as from a horse; dismount. **— light into** *informal* To attack: We *lit into* him with our arguments. **— light out** *informal* To leave or go in haste. **— make light of** To consider or treat as unimportant, silly, or trivial: He *made light* of our troubles.

light·en¹ [līt′(ə)n] *v.* **1** To make or become light or bright. **2** To give off or display lightning flashes: The sky *lightened* in the west.

light·en² [līt′(ə)n] *v.* **1** To make or become less heavy: *Lighten* your luggage. **2** To make or become less troublesome, severe, etc.: The judge *lightened* the sentence. **3** To make or become more cheerful; gladden: to *lighten* one's spirits.

light·er¹ [līt′ər] *n.* A person or thing that lights, especially a device to light cigarettes, etc.

light·er² [līt′ər] *n.* A bargelike vessel used in loading or unloading ships.

light-foot·ed [līt′fŏŏt′id] *adj.* Stepping or running lightly and gracefully. **— light′-foot′·ed·ly** *adv.*

light·head·ed [līt′hed′id] *adj.* **1** Silly and giddy in manner or behavior. **2** Slightly faint or dizzy.

light·heart·ed [līt′här′tid] *adj.* Free from care or trouble; happy. **— light′heart′ed·ly** *adv.*

---

add, āce, câre, pälm;   end, ēqual;   it, īce;   odd, ōpen, ôrder;   tŏŏk, pōōl;   up, bûrn;

ə = a in *above*, e in *sicken*, i in *possible*, o in *melon*, u in *circus*;   yōō = u in *fuse*;   oil;   pout;

check; ring; thin; this; zh in *vision*.   For ¶ reference, see page 64 · HOW TO

light·house [līt′hous′] *n.* A tower equipped
with a powerful light and used
to guide ships or warn them
of rocks or similar dangers.

light·ly [līt′lē] *adv.* **1** With
little weight or pressure;
softly; gently: I pushed him
lightly. **2** In a small amount
or degree; moderately: He
was *lightly* armed. **3** With a
swift, light step or motion: to
skim *lightly* over the water.
4 In a carefree manner: to
laugh *lightly.* **5** Without seriousness; frivolously. **6** In a
slighting or almost insulting
manner: to speak *lightly* of
someone.

Lighthouse

light meter An instrument that indicates how
much light is entering it, used by photographers
to determine correct exposure for films.

light·ness[1] [līt′nis] *n.* **1** The condition of being
bright or illuminated: the *lightness* of a room.
2 Paleness of color: the *lightness* of the sky.

light·ness[2] [līt′nis] *n.* **1** The condition of
having little weight, especially in relation to size,
bulk, etc.: The *lightness* of this car is a drawback.
2 Ease of motion; agility; grace: the *lightness*
of her dancing. **3** Freedom from sorrow or care.
4 Lack of seriousness; levity.

light·ning [līt′ning] *n.* A sudden flash of light
caused by a discharge of electricity between two
clouds or between a cloud and the earth.

lightning bug Another word for FIREFLY.

lightning rod A pointed metal rod that
protects a building by conducting lightning
from above it into the ground.

light·ship [līt′ship′] *n.* A vessel equipped with
a bright light, signals, etc., and moored in
dangerous waters as a guide to ships.

light·some [līt′səm] *adj.* **1** Cheerful and gay;
carefree. **2** Easy and graceful in movement.
3 Not serious; frivolous; flighty.

light·weight [līt′wāt′] **1** *n.* A person or animal
of much less than average weight. **2** *adj.* Of
less than average or required weight. **3** *n.* A
boxer weighing between 127 and 135 pounds.

light-year [līt′yir′] *n.* The distance traveled
by light in one year, about six trillion miles.

lig·nite [lig′nīt] *n.* A soft, brownish coal, still
showing the structure of wood.

lik·a·ble [lī′kə·bəl] *adj.* Easy to like; pleasant,
cheerful, etc. **—lik′a·ble·ness** *n.*

like[1] [līk] **1** *prep.* Having a close resemblance to;
similar to: She is *like* her mother. **2** *prep.* In the
same way or manner of: to swim *like* a fish.
3 *prep.* Typical or characteristic of: How *like*
him to say that. **4** *adj.* Similar: He had a *like*
answer to mine. **5** *adj.* Equal or nearly equal:
He gave a *like* quantity of blood. **6** *n.* A person
or thing of equal value, importance, size, etc.:
We shall not see his *like* again. **7** *prep.* Likely to
result in: It looks *like* rain. **8** *prep.* In need of;
desirous of: I feel *like* resting. **9** *conj. informal*

The same as; as: It turned out *like* you said.
10 *conj. informal* As if: It looks *like* it's going
to rain. **11** *adv. informal* Probably: *Like* enough
he'll go. **— and the like** And other similar
things, qualities, etc.: He talked of good
manners, sportsmanship, *and the like.* **— like
anything, like mad, like crazy,** etc. *slang*
With great force, speed, energy, etc. ◆ *Like*
is not used as a conjunction in place of *as* or *as if*
in formal speech: *not* The machine works *like* it
should *but* The machine works *as* it should; *not*
He bats *like* he was (*or* were) Babe Ruth *but* He
bats *as if* he were Babe Ruth. *Like* is used as a
preposition when no verb is expressed: He looks
like his father; He bats *like* Babe Ruth. *Like* is
also acceptable in place of *as if* when followed by
a short expression containing no verb: It looks
like new.

like[2] [līk] *v.* **liked, lik·ing,** *n.* **1** *v.* To take
pleasure in; enjoy: I *like* swimming. **2** *v.* To
feel affection for: She *likes* him. **3** *v.* To wish or
desire; prefer: Do as you *like.* **4** *n.* (*usually pl.*)
Those things one enjoys or prefers, especially in
the phrase **likes and dislikes.**

-like A suffix meaning: **1** Resembling or
similar to, as in *ironlike,* resembling or similar to
iron. **2** Characteristic of; proper to or for, as in
childlike, characteristic of or proper for a child.
◆ Compound words formed with *-like* are usually
written as one word, except those that would
bring three *l*'s together, which are hyphenated,
as in *shell-like.*

like·a·ble [lī′kə·bəl] *adj.* Likable.

like·li·hood [līk′lē·hŏŏd] *n.* The possibility or
probability that something will happen: Is there
any *likelihood* that they will arrive early?

like·ly [līk′lē] *adj.* **like·li·er, like·li·est,** *adv.*
1 *adj.* Having or showing a tendency or possibility to do, be, etc.; apt: He is *likely* to go.
2 *adv.* Probably: She will *likely* go shopping.
3 *adj.* Probably about to happen: His promotion seems *likely.* **4** *adj.* Probably true; believable: a *likely* story. **5** *adj.* Suitable; appropriate: a *likely* spot for a picnic. **6** *adj.* Able to
please, be successful, etc.; promising: a *likely*
lad.

lik·en [lī′kən] *v.* To represent as alike or similar;
compare.

like·ness [līk′nis] *n.* **1** The condition or fact of
being alike or similar: There is a real *likeness*
between the two dogs. **2** A painting, photograph, etc., of a person or thing. **3** Form; guise:
She appeared in the *likeness* of a witch.

like·wise [līk′wīz′] *adv.* **1** In like manner; the
same: She recited so well; now you do *likewise.*
2 In addition; besides: He coaches football and
likewise track. ◆ *Likewise* was formed by
combining *like* with *wise,* an old word meaning
manner or *way of doing.*

lik·ing [lī′king] *n.* **1** A feeling of affection;
fondness: to have a *liking* for someone. **2** Preference: to have a *liking* for classical music.

li·lac [lī′lak *or* lī′lək] **1** *n.* A large shrub having
clusters of numerous tiny, fragrant flowers,

usually purple or white in color. **2** *n.*, *adj.* Light purple. ◆ *Lilac* comes from an Arabic word derived from a Persian word meaning *bluish*.

lilt [lilt] **1** *n.* A lively or rhythmical way of speaking or singing: She has a *lilt* in her voice. **2** *n.* A cheerful tune. **3** *v.* To speak, sing, move, etc., in a cheerful, rhythmic way.

lil·y [lil′ē] *n.*, *pl.* **lil·ies**, *adj.* **1** *n.* A wild or cultivated plant growing from a bulb and having white or colored flowers shaped like a funnel. **2** *n.* Any flower like the lily, as the water lily. **3** *adj.* Like a lily in beauty, whiteness, etc.

lily of the valley *pl.* **lilies of the valley** A plant having two large green leaves and small, fragrant white flowers arranged along a stem.

Li·ma [lē′mə] *n.* The capital of Peru, in the western part.

li·ma bean [lī′mə] (*often written* **Lima bean**) A large, flat, edible bean.

limb [lim] *n.* **1** An arm, leg, or wing. **2** A large branch, as of a tree.

lim·ber [lim′bər] **1** *adj.* Flexible; pliant: a *limber* twig. **2** *adj.* Agile or supple: a *limber* body. **3** *v.* To make or become limber: Exercise *limbers* up the body. **— lim′ber·ness** *n.*

lim·bo [lim′bō] *n.*, *pl.* **lim·bos 1** (*often written* **Limbo**) In some Christian belief, a region on the edge of hell for the souls of unbaptized infants and those of the righteous who died before the coming of Christ. **2** A place or condition for unwanted or forgotten people or things.

Lim·burg·er [lim′bûr·gər] *n.* A soft, white cheese with a strong odor.

lime¹ [līm] *n.*, *v.* **limed, lim·ing 1** *n.* A white material made by heating limestone, chalk, shells, etc., to a high temperature. It is used in making mortar, cement, and fertilizer. **2** *v.* To treat, mix, or spread with lime.

lime² [līm] *n.* **1** A small, green, citrus fruit whose sour juice is used for flavoring, in drinks, etc. **2** The tree on which it grows.

lime³ [līm] *n.* A type of linden tree.

lime·light [līm′līt′] *n.* **1** A bright light used on the stage as a spotlight. **2** Public attention or notice: Her book was in the *limelight*.

lim·er·ick [lim′rik *or* lim′ər·ik] *n.* A humorous, five-line poem. Example:

> For beauty I'm surely no star;
> There are others more handsome by far.
> But my face I don't mind it
> Because I'm behind it
> It's those out in front that I jar.

lime·stone [līm′stōn′] *n.* A type of rock, as marble, that contains mainly calcium carbonate.

lime·wa·ter [līm′wô′tər] *n.* A solution of lime and water, used in medicine.

lim·it [lim′it] **1** *n.* The furthest or utmost point, line, etc., beyond which something does not or cannot go. **2** *n.* (*usually pl.*) The bounds

of a certain area: the city *limits*. **3** *n.* The largest permissible quantity or amount. **4** *v.* To set a limit to; restrict.

lim·i·ta·tion [lim′ə·tā′shən] *n.* **1** A limiting or being limited. **2** Something that limits, especially a shortcoming.

lim·it·ed [lim′it·id] **1** *adj.* Confined within a limit or limits; restricted: *limited* space. **2** *adj.* Making few stops and carrying a limited number of people. **3** *n.* A limited train, bus, etc.

lim·it·less [lim′it·lis] *adj.* Boundless.

limn [lim] *v.* **1** To draw or paint. **2** To describe in words.

lim·ou·sine [lim′ə·zēn′] *n.* A large, closed automobile often having a glass partition between the driver in front and the passengers in back.

limp¹ [limp] **1** *v.* To walk with a halting or irregular step, as with an injured leg or foot. **2** *n.* Such a walk or step.

limp² [limp] *adj.* **1** Lacking stiffness; flabby. **2** Lacking strength; weak. **— limp′ly** *adv.*

lim·pet [lim′pit] *n.* A small shellfish that clings fast to rocks and timbers.

lim·pid [lim′pid] *adj.* Clear; transparent. **— lim·pid′i·ty** *n.* **— lim′pid·ly** *adv.*

Lin·coln [ling′kən] *n.* The capital of Nebraska.

Lin·coln [ling′kən], **Abraham,** 1809–1865, 16th president of the U.S., 1861–1865.

Lind·bergh [lind′bûrg], **Charles Augustus,** born 1902, U.S. aviator who in 1927 made the first solo flight across the Atlantic.

lin·den [lin′dən] *n.* Any of a number of trees having soft, white wood, heart-shaped leaves, and fragrant, cream-colored flowers.

line¹ [līn] *n.*, *v.* **lined, lin·ing 1** *n.* A slender, continuous mark, as that drawn by a pen. **2** *n.* A crease, as in the skin. **3** *v.* To mark or cover with lines: to *line* paper; Age *lined* her brow. **4** *n.* Something that is shaped like a line, as a rope, string, etc.: a fishing *line*. **5** *n.* A pipe or a system of pipes: a gas *line*. **6** *n.* A wire, or system of wires, used to carry electric power, telephone messages, etc. **7** *n.* A row: a *line* of people. **8** *v.* To form a row or line along: Statues *lined* the walk. **9** *n.* A succession of related people or things: a family *line*. **10** *n.* An arrangement of soldiers, troops, weapons, etc., aligned abreast, or nearly so: the front *line*. **11** *n.* In football, the linemen, collectively. **12** *n.* A boundary or border: the state *line*. **13** *n.* A transportation company having an established route or routes: a bus *line*. **14** *n.* One of these routes: the main *line*. **15** *n.* A path; course: the *line* of fire. **16** *n.* A course of action or thought: the Communist *line*. **17** *n.* (*often pl.*) A general plan or concept: a work on modern *lines*. **18** *n.* A short letter; note: Drop me a *line*. **19** *n.* (*pl.*) The words of an actor's or performer's part. **20** *n.* A verse in poetry. **21** *n.* All the words in one row in one column of

add, āce, câre, pälm;　　end, ēqual;　　it, īce;　　odd, ōpen, ôrder;　　tŏŏk, pŏŏl;　　up, bûrn;
ə = a in *above*, e in *sicken*, i in *possible*, o in *melon*, u in *circus*;　　yŏŏ = u in *fuse*;　　oil;　　pout;
check; ring; thin; this; zh in *vision.*　　For ¶ reference, see page 64 · HOW TO

printed material: Read the next *line*. **22** *n.* In mathematics, a set of points in a row, that could be represented by a straight pencil mark, but extending indefinitely in both directions, without width or thickness. **23** *n.* A straight line: to be in a *line* with each other. **24** *n.* The equator: The ship crossed the *line*. **25** *n.* A business; occupation: His *line* is insurance. **26** *n.* A make or brand of goods. **27** *v.* In baseball, to hit hard and on a more or less flat course, as a ball: to *line* a ball to center field. **— all along the line** At every point; everywhere. **— get a line on** *U.S. informal* To get information about. **— in line** **1** Forming a line or row. **2** In agreement; conforming. **— into line** **1** Into a line or row. **2** Into conformity with something. **— line up** To form or bring into a line or row. **— out of line** **1** Not in a line or row. **2** Not conforming. **— read between the lines** To find a hidden meaning.

line² [līn] *v.* **lined, lin·ing** **1** To put a covering or layer on the inner surface of: to *line* a jacket with wool. **2** To serve as a lining of.

lin·e·age [lin′ē·ij] *n.* **1** Line of descent; ancestry. **2** A family or stock.

lin·e·al [lin′ē·əl] *adj.* **1** In the direct line of descent. **2** Linear. **— lin′e·al·ly** *adv.*

lin·e·a·ment [lin′ē·ə·mənt] *n.* A feature or contour of the face.

lin·e·ar [lin′ē·ər] *adj.* **1** Of, having to do with, like, or in a line or lines. **2** Of length.

line·man [līn′mən] *n.,* *pl.* **line·men** [līn′mən] **1** A man who installs or repairs telephone or electric power lines. **2** In football, a player on the forward line; a center, guard, tackle, or end.

lin·en [lin′ən] **1** *n.* Thread or cloth made of flax fibers. **2** *adj.* Made of linen. **3** *n.* Articles made or formerly made of linen: table *linen*.

line of force A line that shows the direction of a force in a magnetic or other field.

lin·er [lī′nər] *n.* **1** A ship or airplane operated by a transportation line. **2** In baseball, a hard-hit ball that stays close to the ground.

line segment Two points on a line and all the points between them.

lines·man [līnz′mən] *n.,* *pl.* **lines·men** [līnz′·mən] **1** A lineman who works on power lines, etc. **2** In football, the official who marks the distance gained or lost on each play.

line·up or **line-up** [līn′up′] *n.* **1** A list of starting players on a team for a game. **2** These players. **3** A row of possible criminal suspects displayed for purposes of identification.

lin·ger [ling′gər] *v.* To stay on as if unwilling to go; loiter: The twilight *lingered*.

lin·ge·rie [län′zhə·rē *or* län′zhə·rā′] *n.* Women's underwear.

lin·go [ling′gō] *n.,* *pl.* **lin·goes** A language or talk that seems outlandish or is not understood: jazz *lingo*; a foreign *lingo*. ◆ This word is used in humor or contempt.

lin·guist [ling′gwist] *n.* **1** A person who speaks several languages. **2** An expert or student in linguistics.

lin·guis·tic [ling·gwis′tik] *adj.* Of or having to do with language or linguistics.

lin·guis·tics [ling·gwis′tiks] *n.* The scientific study of language. ◆ See -ICS.

lin·i·ment [lin′ə·mənt] *n.* A liquid rubbed on the skin to relieve sprains, stiffness, etc.

lin·ing [lī′ning] *n.* A covering of an inner surface: the *lining* of a jacket.

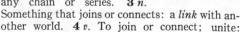

Lining

link [lingk] **1** *n.* One of the rings or loops of a chain. **2** *n.* A single part or element of any chain or series. **3** *n.* Something that joins or connects: a *link* with another world. **4** *v.* To join or connect; unite: to *link* arms. **5** *n.* A sausage in a string of sausages.

linking verb A verb that merely connects the subject and a noun or adjective that follows, as *be, become,* etc. *Am* and *feels* are linking verbs in "I am fine" and "He feels good."

Girls with arms linked

links [lingks] *n.pl.* A golf course.

lin·net [lin′it] *n.* A small finch of Europe, Asia, and Africa.

li·no·le·um [li·nō′lē·əm] *n.* A floor covering made by pressing a mixture of ground cork and linseed oil on canvas or burlap.

lin·seed [lin′sēd′] *n.* Flaxseed.

linseed oil A yellowish oil obtained from flax-seed, used in paints, printing inks, linoleum, etc.

lin·sey-wool·sey [lin′zē-wŏŏl′zē] *n.* A coarse cloth woven of linen and wool or cotton and wool.

lint [lint] *n.* **1** A soft material made by scraping linen, used to dress wounds. **2** Bits of thread, fluff, etc., from yarn or fabric.

lin·tel [lin′təl] *n.* The horizontal part above the opening of a door or window, supporting the wall above it.

Lintel

li·on [lī′ən] *n.* **1** A large, tawny, powerful animal related to the cat, found in Africa and sw Asia. The adult male lion has a shaggy mane. **2** A man of noble courage, great strength, etc. **3** A celebrity.

li·on·ess [lī′ən·is] *n.* A female lion.

lip [lip] **1** *n.* One of the two folds of flesh that border the mouth. **2** *n.* Any rim or edge, as of an opening, cavity, or container: the *lip* of a cup. **3** *adj.* Merely spoken; insincere, as in **lip service,** devotion or regard

Lion, about 6 ft. long

L

expressed in words but not really felt or acted upon.

lip·ase [lip′ās *or* lī′pās] *n.* A digestive enzyme that breaks down fats.

lip reading The act or skill of finding out what a person is saying by watching the movement of his lips, used especially by the deaf.

lip·stick [lip′stik′] *n.* A stick of waxy cosmetic, usually in a tube, used to color the lips.

liq·ue·fac·tion [lik′wə·fak′shən] *n.* **1** The process of becoming liquid, **2** The condition of being liquid.

liq·ue·fy [lik′wə·fī] *v.* **liq·ue·fied, liq·ue·fy·ing** To make or become liquid.

li·queur [li·kûr′] *n.* A strong, sweet, flavored alcoholic liquor: cherry *liqueur.*

liq·uid [lik′wid] **1** *n.* A substance that flows more or less freely and may be poured from its container, as water, oil, etc.; a fluid that is not a gas. **2** *adj.* Able to flow. **3** *adj.* Graceful and flowing. **4** *adj.* Sweet and clear. **5** *adj.* Readily converted into cash: *liquid* assets.

liquid air Air changed into a liquid by great compression and cooling.

liq·ui·date [lik′wə·dāt] *v.* **liq·ui·dat·ed, liq·ui·dat·ing** **1** To settle, as debts. **2** To settle accounts and finish up the operation of. **3** To wipe out. **— liq′ui·da′tion** *n.*

liquid measure A unit or system of units for measuring liquids.

liq·uor [lik′ər] *n.* **1** An alcoholic drink, especially a distilled spirit, as whisky, rum, etc. **2** Any liquid, as broth, juice, etc.

li·ra [lir′ə] *n., pl.* **li·re** [lir′ə] or **li·ras** The basic unit of money in Italy.

Lis·bon [liz′bən] *n.* The capital of Portugal.

lisle [lil] *n.* **1** A fine twisted cotton thread or a fabric made from it. **2** *adj. use: lisle* socks.

lisp [lisp] **1** *n.* A speech defect in which the sounds of *s* and *z* are pronounced like *th* and *th,* as "yeth" for "yes" and "eathy" for "easy." **2** *v.* To say or speak with a lisp.

lis·some or **lis·som** [lis′əm] *adj.* Lithe.

list[1] [list] **1** *n.* An itemized series of names, words, etc., usually set down in a certain order. **2** *v.* To make a list of or enter in a list.

list[2] [list] **1** *v.* To lean or tilt to one side: said about a ship. **2** *n.* Such a lean or tilt.

list[3] [list] *v.* To listen or listen to: used mostly in poems.

lis·ten [lis′(ə)n] *v.* To pay attention so as to hear or understand what is heard: to *listen* to a song. **— listen in 1** To listen to a radio program: There were millions of people *listening in* and the performers were extremely nervous. **2** To eavesdrop. **— lis′ten·er** *n.*

Listing ship

list·less [list′lis] *adj.* Lacking energy or interest in anything. **— list′less·ly** *adv.* **— list′less·ness** *n.*

lists [lists] *n.pl.* The field where knights fought in medieval tournaments. **— enter the lists** To engage in a contest or controversy.

Liszt [list], **Franz,** 1811–1886, Hungarian composer and pianist.

lit[1] [lit] An alternate past tense and past participle of LIGHT[1]: He *lit* the lamp.

lit[2] [lit] An alternate past tense and past participle of LIGHT[2]: The weary bird *lit* on a rock.

lit·a·ny [lit′ə·nē] *n., pl.* **lit·a·nies** A prayer consisting of a series of supplications by the minister with responses by the people.

li·ter [lē′tər] *n.* In the metric system, a measure of volume equal to that of one kilogram of water or of 1.0567 quarts liquid measure. ¶ 2

lit·er·a·cy [lit′ər·ə·sē] *n.* The ability to read and write.

lit·er·al [lit′ər·əl] *adj.* **1** Following the exact words and order of an original: a *literal* translation. **2** Based on or following exactly what is said: a *literal* meaning; a *literal* mind. **3** Straightforward; unembellished: the *literal* truth. **— lit′er·al·ly** *adv.*

lit·er·ar·y [lit′ə·rer′ē] *adj.* **1** Having to do with literature. **2** Knowing or devoted to literature. **3** Having literature as a profession.

lit·er·ate [lit′ə·rit] **1** *adj.* Able to read and write. **2** *n.* An educated person.

lit·er·a·ture [lit′ər·ə·chər] *n.* **1** Written works collectively, especially those showing imagination and artistic skill. **2** The writings on a particular subject: medical *literature.* **3** Writing as a profession. **4** *informal* Any printed matter for advertising, publicity, etc.: campaign *literature.*

lithe [līth] *adj.* Supple; limber: *lithe* as a cat.

lith·i·um [lith′ē·əm] *n.* A soft, silver-white metallic element, the lightest of the metals.

lith·o·graph [lith′ə·graf] **1** *n.* A print made by lithography. **2** *v.* To produce or reproduce by lithography.

li·thog·ra·phy [li·thog′rə·fē] *n.* The act or process of producing printed matter from a flat stone or a metal plate on which a drawing or design has been made. **— li·thog′ra·pher** *n.*

lith·o·sphere [lith′ə·sfir] *n.* The solid crust of the earth.

Lith·u·a·ni·a [lith′ōō·ā′nē·ə] *n.* A country on the Baltic Sea, part of the Soviet Union. **— Lith′u·a′ni·an** *adj., n.*

lit·i·gant [lit′ə·gənt] *n.* A person taking part in a lawsuit.

lit·i·ga·tion [lit′ə·gā′shən] *n.* **1** The bringing or carrying on of a lawsuit. **2** A lawsuit.

lit·mus [lit′məs] *n.* A dyestuff made from certain lichens. It is turned red by acids and blue by alkalis.

litmus paper Paper dyed with litmus, used to test solutions for acidity or alkalinity.

lit·ter [lit′ər] **1** *n.* Scraps or other things strewn about; clutter. **2** *v.* To make untidy or unsightly with litter: to *litter* the sidewalk with trash. **3** *n.* The young brought forth at one birth by a mammal normally having several offspring at a time. **4** *v.* To give birth to (young). **5** *v.* To have a litter. **6** *n.* Straw, hay, etc., spread as bedding for animals. **7** *n.* A stretcher for carrying sick or wounded persons. **8** *n.* A vehicle consisting of a couch on two poles carried by men or animals.

Litter

lit·tle [lit′(ə)l] *adj.* **lit·tler** or for defs. 3 and 6 **less** or **less·er, lit·tlest** or for defs. 3 and 6 **least,** *n., adv.* **less, least 1** *adj.* Not big; small: a *little* dog. **2** *n.* A small amount: Give me a *little.* **3** *adj., adv.* Not much: *little* power; He sleeps *little.* **4** *n.* A very small amount: *Little* can be done. **5** *adv.* Not at all: She *little* suspects what happened. **6** *adj.* Short or brief: in a *little* time. **7** *n.* A short time or distance: We walked a *little.* **8** *adj.* Trivial: *little* details. **8** *adj.* Petty or mean: a *little* mind. **— little by little** Gradually. **— make little of** To treat or regard as of no importance. **— not a little** Quite a bit; much: *not a little* influence. **— think little of** To regard as unimportant or almost worthless. **— lit′tle·ness** *n.*

Little America A U.S. base in Antarctica.

Little Rock The capital of Arkansas.

lit·ur·gy [lit′ər·jē] *n., pl.* **lit·ur·gies** In various religions, the form of public worship.

liv·a·ble [liv′ə·bəl] *adj.* **1** Fit or pleasing to live in. **2** Tolerable: *livable* conditions.

live¹ [liv] *v.* **lived, liv·ing 1** To be alive. **2** To remain alive: while I *live.* **3** To pass life in a certain way: to *live* in peace. **4** To enjoy a varied or satisfying life. **5** To reside: We *live* in Maine. **6** To maintain life; feed: to *live* on meat. **7** To maintain or support oneself: to *live* on one's income. **8** To continue: The custom *lives* on. **9** To put into practice in one's life: to *live* one's religion. **— live down** To behave so as to erase the memory of, as a crime, mistake, etc. **— live up to** To satisfy or fulfill.

live² [līv] *adj.* **1** Having life; alive. **2** Energetic; dynamic: a *live* personality. **3** Of present interest and importance: a *live* issue. **4** Burning or glowing: a *live* coal. **5** Charged with electricity: a *live* wire. **6** Capable of being exploded: a *live* firecracker. **7** Actually being performed as it is being broadcast: a *live* show.

live·li·hood [līv′lē·hŏod] *n.* Food, shelter, etc., needed to live: to earn one's *livelihood.*

live·long [liv′lông′] *adj.* Whole; entire: the *livelong* day.

live·ly [līv′lē] *adj.* **live·li·er, live·li·est,** *adv.* **1** *adj.* Full of life; spirited: a *lively* song; a

lively man. **2** *adj.* Full of activity or excitement: a *lively* season. **3** *adj.* Bright; cheerful: *lively* colors. **4** *adj.* Full of bounce: a *lively* ball. **5** *adv.* Briskly: Step *lively.* **— live′li·ness** *n.*

liv·en [lī′vən] *v.* To make or become lively.

liv·er¹ [liv′ər] *n.* **1** A large gland in man and other vertebrates that produces bile and regulates digestive processes. **2** Food prepared from or consisting of animal liver.

liv·er² [liv′ər] *n.* **1** A person who lives in a certain manner: a quiet *liver.* **2** A dweller.

liv·er·ied [liv′ər·ēd] *adj.* Dressed in livery.

Position of liver

Liv·er·pool [liv′ər·pōol] *n.* A seaport in NW England.

liv·er·wort [liv′ər·wûrt′] *n.* **1** A small, moss-like plant found in shady places. **2** A hepatica.

liv·er·y [liv′ər·ē] *n., pl.* **liv·er·ies 1** The uniform worn by servants. **2** The stabling and care of horses for pay.

livery stable A stable where horses and vehicles are cared for or kept for hire.

lives [līvz] Plural of LIFE.

live·stock [līv′stok′] *n.* Domestic farm animals, as horses, cattle, sheep, and pigs.

liv·id [liv′id] *adj.* **1** Purplish, bluish, or ashen from a bruise, anger, etc. **2** *informal* Extremely angry.

liv·ing [liv′ing] **1** *adj.* Not dead; alive. **2** *n.* A being alive. **3** *n. use* Those who are or were alive: *The living* rebuilt the town. **4** *adj.* Still existing or used: within *living* memory. **5** *n.* Manner or conduct of life: virtuous *living.* **6** *adj.* Of or having to do with everyday life: *living* conditions. **7** *n.* A livelihood. **8** *adj.* Used or intended for a livelihood: a *living* wage. **9** *adj.* Lifelike: the *living* image of his father.

living room A room in a house for talking, reading, entertainment, and general use.

liz·ard [liz′ərd] *n.* Any of certain reptiles, most of them small, with slender, scaly bodies, long tails, and four legs.

lla·ma [lä′mə] *n.* A South American beast of burden, like a small camel with no hump.

lla·no [lä′nō] *n., pl.* **lla·nos** A flat, tree-less plain of Spanish America.

lo [lō] *interj.* See! behold!: seldom used today.

load [lōd] **1** *n.* What a person or thing is carrying; burden. **2** *n.* The quantity usually carried at one time, taken as a unit: to deliver a *load* of gravel. **3** *v.* To put in or on something for carrying: to *load* furniture

Llama, about 4 ft. long

on a truck. **4** *v*. To put a load in or on: to *load* a ship, aircraft, etc. **5** *v*. To take on a load: The ship was *loading* at the pier. **6** *v*. To burden or overburden: He is *loaded* with too many responsibilities. **7** *v*. To supply abundantly or excessively: They *loaded* him with honors. **8** *n*. The charge or ammunition for a firearm, shell, etc. **9** *v*. To fill with something necessary for working: to *load* a pistol with cartridges, a camera with film, etc. **10** *n*. The electricity supplied by a generator. **11** *n*. (*pl.*) *informal* Lots: *loads* of fun. — **load'er** *n*.

load·star [lōd'stär'] *n*. Another spelling of LODESTAR.

load·stone [lōd'stōn'] *n*. Another spelling of LODESTONE.

loaf¹ [lōf] *n*., *pl*. **loaves** **1** A shaped portion of bread baked in a single piece. **2** Any shaped mass of food: a meat *loaf*; a sugar *loaf*.

loaf² [lōf] *v*. To do nothing; idle.

loaf·er [lōf'ər] *n*. **1** An idler. **2** An informal shoe like a moccasin but with a sole and heel.

loam [lōm] *n*. Rich soil made up of sand, clay, and much humus. — **loam'y** *adj*.

loan [lōn] **1** *n*. The act of lending: a *loan* of a book. **2** *n*. Something lent, especially a sum of money. **3** *v*. *U.S.* To lend. ◆ *Loan*, as a verb, is not accepted by the British but is standard in the U.S., especially in business English.

loath [lōth] *adj*. Unwilling: I'm *loath* to go.

loathe [lōth] *v*. **loathed, loath·ing** To detest; abhor: to *loathe* snakes.

loath·ing [lō'thing] *n*. Extreme dislike or disgust: a *loathing* for greasy food.

loath·some [lōth'səm] *adj*. Detestable; repulsive. — **loath'some·ness** *n*.

loaves [lōvz] Plural of LOAF¹.

lob [lob] *v*. **lobbed, lob·bing,** *n*. **1** *v*. To hit (a ball) in a high, arching curve, as in tennis. **2** *n*. A ball hit in a high, arching curve, as in tennis. **3** *v*. To throw or toss (a ball) slowly.

lo·bar [lō'bər *or* lō'bär] *adj*. **1** Of or having to do with a lobe. **2** Affecting one or more lobes of the lung: *lobar* pneumonia.

lob·by [lob'ē] *n*., *pl*. **lob·bies,** *v*. **lob·bied, lob·by·ing** **1** *n*. An entrance hall, vestibule, or public lounge. **2** *v*. *U.S.* To try to influence legislators in favor of some special interest. **3** *v*. *U.S.* To work for or against (a bill) by lobbying. **4** *n*. *U.S.* A group that lobbies: a farmers' *lobby*.

lob·by·ist [lob'ē·ist] *n*. A person who lobbies.

lobe [lōb] *n*. A curved or rounded projecting part, as of a leaf or an organ of the body: an ear *lobe*; a *lobe* of the lung.

lo·be·li·a [lō·bē'lē·ə *or* lō·bēl'yə] *n*. A plant with flower clusters in any of several colors.

lob·lol·ly [lob'lol·ē] *n*., *pl*. **lob·lol·lies** **1** A pine tree of the southern U.S. with long needles and heavy bark. **2** Its coarse wood.

lob·ster [lob'stər] *n*. **1** A large crustacean with a pair of pincers in front, and four pairs of legs behind them. **2** Its flesh eaten as food.

lobster pot A cagelike trap to catch lobsters.

lo·cal [lō'kəl] **1** *adj*. Of or having to do with a neighborhood, region, or relatively small area: the *local* people. **2** *adj*. Affecting only a certain part of the body. **3** *adj*. Stopping at all or almost all stations along its run. **4** *n*. A train, bus, etc., that does this. **5** *n*. A branch or chapter of an organization, as a trade union.

lo·cale [lō·kal'] *n*. The setting of an event, dramatic action, etc.; scene.

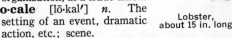

Lobster, about 15 in. long

lo·cal·ism [lō'kəl·iz'əm] *n*. A local custom, word, etc., not used elsewhere.

lo·cal·i·ty [lō·kal'ə·tē] *n*., *pl*. **lo·cal·i·ties** A certain place, area, region, or the like.

lo·cal·ize [lō'kəl·īz] *v*. **lo·cal·ized, lo·cal·iz·ing** To make or keep local; limit to a particular place: to keep a forest fire *localized*. ¶3

lo·cal·ly [lō'kə·lē] *adv*. **1** In a local area. **2** In only a few places; not everywhere.

lo·cate [lō'kāt] *v*. **lo·cat·ed, lo·cat·ing** **1** To place; situate: The phone is *located* here. **2** *U.S. informal* To settle: to *locate* in Boston. **3** To discover the position of; find: to *locate* a missing person. **4** To show or indicate the position of.

lo·ca·tion [lō·kā'shən] *n*. **1** A place or site: a good *location* for a camp. **2** The act of locating: The *location* of the stolen jewels took a month. **3** The state of being located.

loch [lok] *n*. A Scottish word for: **1** A lake. **2** A bay or arm of the sea.

lock¹ [lok] **1** *n*. A device for fastening a door, safe, etc. It is usually opened only by a key with a special shape. **2** *v*. To fasten with a lock. **3** *v*. To become locked. **4** *v*. To shut in or out; keep: to *lock* money in a safe; A barge was *locked* in the ice; He was *locked* out of the house. **5** *n*. Anything that fastens, secures, or holds something else in place. **6** *v*. To join, link, or jam: to *lock* bumpers. **7** *n*. An enclosed section of a canal in which ships can be raised or lowered by letting water in or out. **8** *n*. The mechanism that fires the charge of a gun.

lock² [lok] *n*. **1** A curl or strand of hair. **2** A small tuft of cotton, wool, etc.

lock·er [lok'ər] *n*. A closet, cabinet, etc., often metal, and fastened by a lock: a gym *locker*.

lock·et [lok'it] *n*. A small case for a picture or keepsake, worn on a chain around the neck.

lock·jaw [lok'jô'] *n*. A form of tetanus causing rigid locking of the jaws.

lock·out [lok′out′] *n.* The closing of a business by an employer in order to make employees agree to his terms.

lock·smith [lok′smith′] *n.* A person who makes and repairs locks and keys.

lock·up [lok′up′] *n.* A jail or prison cell.

lo·co·mo·tion [lō′kə·mō′shən] *n.* The act or power of moving from one place to another.

lo·co·mo·tive [lō′kə·mō′tiv] **1** *n.* An engine that moves by its own power, used to pull trains on a railroad. **2** *adj.* Of, capable of, or used in moving by its own power.

lo·cus [lō′kəs] *n., pl.* **lo·ci** [lō′sī] **1** A place; locality; area. **2** In mathematics, the set of all the points that satisfy a given set of conditions. A circle is the locus of all the points in a plane that are at a certain distance from a given point.

lo·cust [lō′kəst] *n.* **1** An insect like a grasshopper that often moves in swarms and destroys crops. **2** A cicada. **3** A tree having compound leaves made up of leaflets, and clusters of fragrant, white flowers.

lode [lōd] *n.* A vein of ore of a metal.

lode·star [lōd′stär′] *n.* A guiding star, especially the North Star.

lode·stone [lōd′stōn′] *n.* A naturally magnetized piece of magnetite, an iron ore.

lodge [loj] *n., v.* **lodged, lodg·ing 1** *n.* A small house, cabin, etc., where a person may stay, as for a vacation. **2** *n.* An inn or hotel. **3** *v.* To house for a time: to *lodge* a guest. **4** *v.* To live temporarily, especially as a paying guest. **5** *n.* The shelter or den of a beaver, otter, or certain other animals. **6** *n.* A local branch of any of certain societies: a Masonic *lodge.* **7** *n.* Its meeting place. **8** *v.* To place or implant firmly: to *lodge* a stake in the ground. **9** *v.* To become fixed or embedded: The bullet had *lodged* in his chest. **10** *v.* To submit or enter formally: to *lodge* a complaint with the police.

lodg·er [loj′ər] *n.* A person who lives in one or more rented rooms in someone else's house.

lodg·ing [loj′ing] *n.* **1** A temporary place to live. **2** (*pl.*) Living quarters consisting of a rented room or rooms in someone else's house.

lodg·ment [loj′mənt] *n.* **1** The act of lodging. **2** The condition of being lodged. **3** Something lodged or deposited: a *lodgment* of driftwood on a shoal.

lo·ess [lō′is] *n.* A yellowish loam deposited by wind in some places.

loft [lôft] **1** *n.* An attic or other space just under a roof. **2** *n.* An upper story of a warehouse, storehouse, or factory. **3** *n.* An upper section or gallery in a church, theater, etc. **4** *v.* To hit or send high up: to *loft* a ball over the trees.

loft·y [lôf′tē] *adj.* **loft·i·er, loft·i·est 1** Very high. **2** Exalted: *lofty* poetry. **3** Proud; arrogant. **—loft′i·ly** *adv.* **—loft′i·ness** *n.*

log¹ [lôg *or* log] *n., v.* **logged, log·ging 1** *n.* Part of the trunk or a limb of a felled tree, stripped of branches. **2** *adj. use:* a *log* cabin. **3** *v.* To cut the timber on (land). **4** *v.* To cut (trees) into logs. **5** *n.* A daily record of a ship's voyage. **6** *n.* Any record of operation or progress: the *log* of an airplane flight. **7** *n.* Any of various devices used to measure a ship's speed and the distance traveled. **—log′ger** *n.*

log² [lôg *or* log] *n.* A logarithm.

lo·gan·ber·ry [lō′gən·ber′ē] *n., pl.* **lo·gan·ber·ries 1** A plant obtained by crossing the red raspberry plant with a blackberry plant. **2** Its edible, purple berry.

log·a·rithm [lôg′ə·rith·əm *or* log′ə·rith·əm] *n.* The exponent that must be applied to a fixed number, usually 10, in order to make some other number. $100 = 10^2$, so log $100 = 2$. $125 = 10^{2.09691}$, so log $125 = 2.09691$. Using logarithms simplifies calculation since log a + log b = log ab, and log a − log b = log a/b. ◆ *Logarithm* comes from two Greek words, one meaning *word* or *ratio* and the other meaning *number.*

logarithm table A table that gives the fractional parts of the logarithms of numbers.

log·book [lôg′book′ *or* log′book′] *n.* The book in which a record, as of a voyage, is entered.

log·ger·head [lôg′ər·hed′ *or* log′ər·hed′] *n.* **1** A large sea turtle found in tropical Atlantic waters. **2** A stupid person; blockhead. **—at loggerheads** Quarreling.

log·gi·a [loj′(ē·)ə] *n.* A roofed gallery or arcade open to air on one or more sides.

log·ging [lôg′ing *or* log′ing] *n.* The business or job of felling timber and getting the logs out of the woods.

log·ic [loj′ik] *n.* **1** The science of reasoning and of proving. **2** The proper rules of reasoning. **3** Sound reasoning. **4** A way or method of reasoning: poor *logic.*

log·i·cal [loj′ə·kəl] *adj.* **1** Of or based on logic: a *logical* argument. **2** Using clear reasoning: a *logical* writer. **3** Reasonably to be expected: To such treatment the *logical* response is anger. **—log′i·cal·ly** *adv.*

lo·gi·cian [lō·jish′ən] *n.* A person skilled in logic.

log·roll·ing [lôg′rōl′ing *or* log′rōl′ing] *n. U.S.* **1** A contest in which two men balance on a floating log and roll it until one falls off. **2** The trading of votes and influence between politicians.

lo·gy [lō′gē] *adj.* **lo·gi·er, lo·gi·est** *U.S.* Dull; lethargic: Hot weather makes me *logy.*

loin [loin] *n.* **1** (*usually pl.*) The part of the back on each side of the backbone between the lower ribs and the hipbone. **2** Such a section of meat, with the flank removed: a *loin* of beef.

loin·cloth [loin′klôth′] *n.* A piece of cloth worn around the hips and between the legs.

loi·ter [loi′tər] *v.* **1** To linger or dawdle. **2** To pass idly: to *loiter* time away. **—loi′ter·er** *n.*

Lo·ki [lō′kē] *n.* In Norse myths, the god of mischief and destruction.

loll [lol] *v.* **1** To lounge: He *lolled* around the house. **2** To hang loosely; droop. **3** To allow to droop: Spot *lolled* out his tongue.

lol·li·pop or **lol·ly·pop** [lol′ē·pop′] *n.* A lump or piece of candy on the end of a stick.

Lon·don [lun′dən] *n.* The capital of the United Kingdom, in SE England.

Lon·don [lun′dən], **Jack,** 1876–1916, U.S. author.

lone [lōn] *adj.* Single; alone: a *lone* bird.

lone·ly [lōn′lē] *adj.* **lone·li·er, lone·li·est 1** Feeling alone and longing for the presence of friends. **2** Without others nearby; solitary. **3** Deserted; desolate. — **lone′li·ness** *n.*

lone·some [lōn′səm] *adj.* **1** Feeling lonely. **2** Causing or expressing loneliness.

long[1] [lông] **1** *adj.* Extending quite far between ends, in space or time: a *long* tunnel. **2** *adj.* Having a specified extent or duration: ten miles *long*; three days *long*. **3** *adv.* For a long time: an improvement *long* needed. **4** *adv.* At a time far from another time indicated: *long* ago; *long* since. **5** *n.* A long time: The danger will not last for *long*. **6** *adv.* Throughout the whole duration of: It rained all day *long*. **7** *adj.* Taking rather a long time to sound, as the vowel sounds in *ace* [ās], *ice* [īs], and *hope* [hōp]. — **as long as** or **so long as 1** For or during the time that. **2** Seeing that; since. **3** Provided; if: *As long as* he does it, I'll be happy. — **before long** Soon.

long[2] [lông] *v.* To want greatly; yearn.

long·boat [lông′bōt′] *n.* The longest boat carried by a sailing ship.

lon·gev·i·ty [lon·jev′ə·tē] *n.* Long life.

Long·fel·low [lông′fel·ō], **Henry Wadsworth,** 1807–1882, U.S. poet.

long·hand [lông′hand′] *n.* Ordinary handwriting with the words spelled out in full.

long·horn [lông′hôrn′] *n.* One of a former breed of beef cattle with long horns.

long·ing [lông′ing] *n.* Great desire; yearning: a *longing* for peace. — **long′ing·ly** *adv.*

Long Island A large island south of Connecticut, part of the state of New York.

lon·gi·tude [lon′jə·t(y)ood] *n.* Distance east or west of a given meridian, usually the one running through Greenwich, England, measured as an angle at the earth's center and expressed in degrees.

lon·gi·tu·di·nal [lon′·jə·t(y)oo′də·nəl] *adj.* **1** Of or having to do with longitude or length. **2** Running lengthwise: *longitudinal* bars. — **lon′gi·tu′di·nal·ly** *adv.*

Lines of longitude

long-play·ing [lông′plā′ing] *adj.* Having small grooves and played at a speed of 33⅓ revolutions per minute: said about a phonograph record.

long-range [lông′rānj′] *adj.* **1** Designed to shoot or travel over a long distance: a *long-range* missile. **2** Covering a long span of time, usually partly in the future: *long-range* plans.

long·shore·man [lông′shôr′mən] *n., pl.* **long·shore·men** [lông′shôr′mən] A man who loads and unloads ships; stevedore.

long-suf·fer·ing [lông′suf′ər·ing] *adj.* Quietly enduring pain or misfortune for a long time.

long-wind·ed [lông′win′did] *adj.* Long and tiresome in speech or writing.

look [look] **1** *v.* To turn or direct the eyes to see or try to see something. **2** *v.* To keep the eyes fixed on: to *look* someone in the face. **3** *n.* The act of looking: a *look* at a picture. **4** *v.* To face in a certain direction: The house *looks* on the park. **5** *v.* To turn one's attention; consider: *Look* at his record. **6** *v.* To search: *Look* for the ball. **7** *v.* To seem: It *looks* safe. **8** *n.* An aspect or expression: a saintly *look*. **9** *n.* (*often pl.*) *informal* General appearance: I like the *looks* of this place. **10** *n.* (*pl.*) *informal* Personal appearance: good *looks*. — **look after** To take care of. — **look back** To think about the past; recall. — **look down on** To despise. — **look for** To expect. — **look forward to** To anticipate with pleasure. — **look into** To examine or investigate. — **look on 1** To be a spectator. **2** To regard: I *look on* this as trash. — **look out** To be careful; watch out. — **look over** To inspect. — **look up 1** To search for and find, as in a dictionary or file. **2** *informal* To locate and pay a visit to: to *look up* an old friend. **3** *informal* To become better: Things are *looking up*. — **look up to** To have great respect for.

look·er-on [look′ər·on′] *n., pl.* **look·ers-on** [look′ərz·on′] A person watching but not taking part.

looking glass A glass mirror.

look·out [look′out′] *n.* **1** A close watch: Be on the *lookout* for the enemy. **2** The place where such a watch is kept. **3** A watchman; sentry.

loom[1] [loom] *n.* A machine on which thread or yarn is woven into cloth.

loom[2] [loom] *v.* To appear indistinctly but seeming large or ominous: The mountains *loomed* up in the distance; Trouble *looms* ahead.

An Indian hand loom

loon[1] [loon] *n.* A web-footed diving bird resembling a duck, but with a pointed bill and a weird, laughing cry.

loon[2] [loon] *n.* A stupid or crazy person.

add, āce, câre, pälm;   end, ēqual;   it, īce;   odd, ōpen, ôrder;   took, pool;   up, bûrn;
ə = a in *above*, e in *sicken*, i in *possible*, o in *melon*, u in *circus*;   yoo = u in *fuse*;   oil;   pout;
check; ring; thin; this; zh in *vision*.   For ¶ reference, see page 64 · HOW TO

loon·y [lōō′nē] *adj.* **loon·i·er, loon·i·est** *slang* Insane; crazy.

loop [lōōp] **1** *n.* The shape of a curved line that crosses back over itself, as in a written *h.* **2** *v.* To make a loop or loops: The gull *looped* through the sky. **3** *n.* Something having the shape of a loop: a *loop* of string. **4** *v.* To form a loop in or of: to *loop* a cord. **5** *n.* A round or oval opening: He caught his leg in a *loop* of the rope. **6** *v.* To fasten or encircle with a loop: to *loop* a halter around a post.

loop·hole [lōōp′hōl′] *n.* **1** A small hole or slit in a wall, to look or shoot through. **2** A means of getting out of the intended meaning of a law, agreement, etc.: His lawyer found a *loophole* and he avoided paying the tax.

loose [lōōs] *adj.* **loos·er, loos·est,** *v.* **loosed, loos·ing,** *adv.* **1** *adj.* Not fastened or confined: *loose* hair. **2** *v.* To release: to *loose* an arrow. **3** *adj.* Not drawn tight; slack: a *loose* knot. **4** *adj.* Not firmly fitted, embedded, or packed: a *loose* window; a *loose* tooth. **5** *v.* To make less tight; loosen: to *loose* a knot. **6** *adj.* Not bound or fastened together: *loose* sheets of paper. **7** *adj.* Not in a package or container: *loose* salt. **8** *adv.* In a loose manner: to hang *loose.* **9** *adj.* Immoral: *loose* living. **10** *adj.* Not precise: a *loose* translation. **— at loose ends** In a confused state. **— cast loose** To untie, as a boat from a dock. **— set loose** or **turn loose** To set free. **— loose′ly** *adv.* **— loose′· ness** *n.* ◆ The verbs *loose* [lōōs] and *lose* [lōōz] both mean to part with. To *loose* is to release intentionally: You can *loose* your dog for a run in the woods by taking off his leash. To *lose* is to mislay or be unable to find: If your dog runs too far away, you may *lose* him. *Loose,* of course, is more commonly used as an adjective: a *loose* hinge. *Lose* is always a verb.

loose-leaf [lōōs′lēf′] *adj.* Designed so that pages can be easily inserted or removed: a *loose-leaf* notebook.

loos·en [lōō′sən] *v.* To make or become loose or looser: to *loosen* a belt.

loot [lōōt] **1** *n.* Spoils; booty. **2** *v.* To plunder.

lop[1] [lop] *v.* **lopped, lop·ping 1** To cut off: to *lop* off the sleeves at the elbows. **2** To cut or trim the branches, etc., from: to *lop* a tree.

lop[2] [lop] *v.* **lopped, lop·ping,** *adj.* **1** *v.* To droop or flop. **2** *adj.* Drooping: *lop* ears.

lope [lōp] *v.* **loped, lop·ing,** *n.* **1** *v.* To run with a steady swinging stride or gallop. **2** *n.* Such a stride or gallop.

lop·sid·ed [lop′sī′did] *adj.* Heavier, larger, or sagging on one side. **— lop′sid′ed·ly** *adv.* **— lop′sid′ed·ness** *n.*

lo·qua·cious [lō·kwā′shəs] *adj.* Talkative.

lo·quac·i·ty [lō·kwas′ə·tē] *n.* A tendency to talk a great deal.

lo·ran [lôr′an] *n.* An electronic device that uses signals from two radio stations to give a navigator his exact location.

lord [lôrd] **1** *n.* A ruler or master. **2** *n.* A member of the House of Lords. **3** *n.* A feudal landlord. **4** *v.* To rule as or like a lord, especially in the expression **lord it over,** to treat in a domineering or arrogant way.

Lord [lôrd] *n.* **1** God. **2** Jesus. **3** A title used in Great Britain in speaking to or of a nobleman who is a baron or higher. **4** (*pl.*) The House of Lords.

lord·ly [lôrd′lē] *adj.* **lord·li·er, lord·li·est 1** Suitable for a lord; splendid. **2** Arrogant; haughty: *lordly* airs.

lord·ship [lôrd′ship] *n.* **1** The power or authority of a lord. **2** (*often written* **Lordship**) The title used in speaking of or addressing a lord when his name is not used: your *Lordship.*

Lord's Prayer The prayer beginning "Our Father," taught by Christ to his disciples.

Lord's Supper 1 The Last Supper. **2** Holy Communion.

lore [lôr] *n.* **1** Facts or stories about a subject: Scottish *lore;* bird *lore.* **2** Knowledge or learning.

lor·gnette [lôr·nyet′] *n.* A pair of eyeglasses or opera glasses with a handle.

lorn [lôrn] *adj.* Forlorn: seldom used today.

lor·ry [lôr′ē] *n., pl.* **lor·ries 1** A low wagon without sides. **2** *British* A truck.

Los An·ge·les [lôs an′jə·lēz *or* los ang′g(ə)ləs] A large city in sw California, on the Pacific.

Lorgnette

lose [lōōz] *v.* **lost, los·ing 1** To be unable to find or discover; mislay. **2** To fail to keep, control, or maintain: to *lose* one's balance. **3** To be deprived of by accident, death, change, etc.: to *lose* a leg. **4** To be defeated or fail to win: We *lost;* to *lose* a game. **5** To fail to use; waste: to *lose* a chance. **6** To fail to see or hear; miss: I *lost* what he was saying. **7** To bring to death or destruction: The ship was *lost.* **8** To cause to lose: One fumble *lost* the game. **9** To gain or win less than is risked, spent, or given up, as in business. **10** To wander from so as to be unable to find: He *lost* his way. **— lose oneself 1** To let oneself stray and not know where one is. **2** To become engrossed: to *lose oneself* in thought. **— los′er** *n.* ◆ See LOOSE.

los·ing [lōō′zing] *adj.* That cannot or does not win: a *losing* venture; a *losing* team.

loss [lôs] *n.* **1** The act of losing. **2** The state of being lost. **3** A person, thing, number, or amount that is lost. **4** The harm or cost caused by losing someone or something. **— at a loss** In a state of confusion.

lost [lôst] **1** The past tense and past participle of LOSE. **2** *adj.* Missing: a *lost* shoe. **3** *adj.* No longer held or possessed: *lost* good looks. **4** *adj.* Having gone astray: a *lost* child. **5** *adj.* Not won: a *lost* fight. **6** *adj.* Confused or helpless. **7** *adj.* Wasted: a *lost* chance. **8** *adj.* Ruined or destroyed. **9** *adj.* No longer known: *lost* arts. **— be lost in** To be engrossed in.

lot [lot] *n.* **1** A small object chosen at random from a group of similar objects to determine something by chance: to draw *lots*. **2** The fact or process of deciding something in this way: The winner was chosen by *lot*. **3** A choice or decision made in this way: The *lot* fell to our team to begin the game. **4** A share or portion received by lot. **5** A person's portion in life, ascribed to chance or fate: A soldier's *lot* is a hard one. **6** A number of things or persons considered as a single group or unit: the best of the *lot*. **7** A small plot of land: a vacant *lot*. **8** (*often pl.*) *informal* A great deal: *lots* of money; a *lot* of trouble. ◆ *A lot* and *lots* are acceptable in informal writing and in speech, but in formal writing they should be avoided, as by using *a great many* or *a great deal* instead.

Lot [lot] *n.* In the Bible, a nephew of Abraham. His wife, disobeying a warning, was turned into a pillar of salt when she looked back on burning Sodom from which they were fleeing.

loth [lōth] *adj.* Another spelling of LOATH.

lo·tion [lō′shən] *n.* A liquid containing medicine, for cleaning, soothing, or healing the skin or eyes.

lot·ter·y [lot′ər·ē] *n., pl.* **lot·ter·ies** A type of gambling in which numbered tickets are sold, numbers drawn by lot, and prizes awarded to the tickets so chosen.

lo·tus [lō′təs] *n.* **1** A water lily of Asia and Egypt. **2** A plant related to the pea, with red, pink, or white flowers. **3** A tree whose fruit was thought by the ancient Greeks to cause dreaminess.

loud [loud] **1** *adj.* Strong or intense in sound; not soft or quiet: *loud* thunder. **2** *adj.* Noisy: a *loud* party. **3** *adj.* Insistent and clamorous: *loud* demands. **4** *adv.* In a loud manner. **5** *adj. informal* Crude; vulgar: a *loud* person. **6** *adj. informal* Too showy; flashy: a *loud* tie. **— loud′ly** *adv.* **— loud′ness** *n.*

loud·speak·er [loud′spē′kər] *n.* A device that changes a varying electric current into sound loud enough to be heard throughout a room or area, as in a radio, phonograph, etc.

Lou·is XIV [lōō′ē *or* lōō′is], 1638–1715, king of France, 1643–1715.

Louis XVI, 1754–1793, king of France, 1774–1792. He was guillotined during the French Revolution.

lou·is d'or [lōō′ē dôr′] **1** An old French coin worth about four dollars. **2** A later French coin, no longer used, worth 20 francs.

Lou·i·si·an·a [lōō·ē′zē·an′ə] *n.* A state in the southern U.S., on the Gulf of Mexico.

lounge [lounj] *v.* **lounged, loung·ing,** *n.* **1** *v.* To recline or lean in a relaxed way. **2** *v.* To pass time in a lazy manner; loaf. **3** *n.* A room in a hotel, theater, etc., containing comfortable furniture where people can relax. **4** *n.* A sofa.

lour [lour] *v., n.* Another spelling of LOWER[1].

louse [lous] *n., pl.* **lice** [līs] **1** A small, wingless insect that infests the skin or hair of man and other animals. It lives by sucking their blood. **2** Any similar insect living on plants.

lous·y [lou′zē] *adj.* **lous·i·er, lous·i·est** **1** Infested or covered with lice. **2** *slang* Unpleasant or worthless: a *lousy* play. **3** *slang* Having plenty or too much: *lousy* with money.

lout [lout] *n.* An awkward, stupid person. **— lout′ish** *adj.*

lou·ver [lōō′vər] *n.* **1** One of a series of overlapping slats in a window or opening, sloped downward to shed rain while still admitting light and air. **2** A window provided with louvers.

Lou·vre [lōō′vr(ə)] *n.* A famous art museum in Paris, built as a palace for French kings.

lov·a·ble [luv′ə·bəl] *adj.* Worthy of affection or love; charming; dear. **— lov′a·bly** *adv.*

Louver

love [luv] *n., v.* **loved, lov·ing** **1** *n.* A deep, passionate affection, as for a sweetheart. **2** *v.* To be in love with. **3** *v.* To have a deep devotion for: to *love* one's mother. **4** *n.* A very great interest in or enjoyment of something: a *love* of the theater. **5** *v.* To enjoy very much: He *loves* the out-of-doors. **6** *n.* A person or thing that is loved: She was the only *love* of his life; John's *love* is science. **7** *n.* In tennis, a score of nothing. **— fall in love** To begin to feel love for someone or something. **— for the love of** For the sake of. **— in love** Experiencing love for someone or something. **— make love** To kiss and embrace, as lovers.

love·a·ble [luv′ə·bəl] *adj.* Another spelling o LOVABLE.

love·bird [luv′bûrd′] *n.* One of several kinds of small parrots kept in cages. They like to nestle up against their mates.

love·less [luv′lis] *adj.* Receiving no love; unloved.

love·lorn [luv′lôrn] *adj.* Longing hopelessly for love; abandoned by the person one loves.

love·ly [luv′lē] *adj.* **love·li·er, love·li·est** **1** Having qualities that make people love one: a *lovely* child. **2** Beautiful: a *lovely* rose. **3** *informal* Enjoyable; pleasant: to have a *lovely* time at a party. **— love′li·ness** *n.*

lov·er [luv′ər] *n.* **1** A person who is in love, especially a man in love with a woman. **2** A person who is very fond of something: a *lover* of animals.

love·sick [luv′sik′] *adj.* So strongly affected by love that one is not his usual self.

lov·ing [luv′ing] **1** Present participle of LOVE.

add, āce, câre, pälm;   end, ēqual;   it, īce;   odd, ōpen, ôrder;   took, pool;   up, bûrn;
ə = a in *above*, e in *sicken*, i in *possible*, o in *melon*, u in *circus*;   yōō = u in *fuse*;   oil;   pout;
check; ring; thin; this; zh in *vision*.   For ¶ reference, see page 64 · HOW TO

2 *adj.* Experiencing or showing love: a *loving* parent; *loving* words. **—lov′ing·ly** *adv.*

low¹ [lō] **1** *v.* To make the hollow, mournful sound of a cow; moo. **2** *n.* This sound.

low² [lō] **1** *adj.* Not high or tall: a *low* hill; a *low* tree. **2** *adj.* Lying or situated below the usual height: a *low* marsh; a *low* table. **3** *adj.* Close to the ground: *low* clouds. **4** *adj.* Fitted so as to show part of the wearer's chest and back: a *low* neckline. **5** *n.* A low position, level, degree, etc.: The stock market reached a new *low* this week. **6** *adv.* In or to a low level, position, or degree: to bow *low*. **7** *adj.* Not good in quality: a *low* grade of meat. **8** *adj.* Inexpensive; economical: a *low* price. **9** *adj.* Poor or humble in position, rank, etc.: of *low* birth. **10** *adj.* Unfavorable; poor: to have a *low* opinion of oneself. **11** *adj.* Not refined; vulgar: *low* companions. **12** *adj.* Not high or shrill in pitch: the *low* notes of a cello. **13** *adj.* Not loud; faint: a *low* moan. **14** *adv.* Softly: Please speak *low*. **15** *adj.* Depressed; sad: Ron is *low* because he lost his wallet. **16** *adj.* Without much strength; weak: The fire is *low*. **17** *adj.* Having a small supply of: to be *low* on groceries. **18** *n.* An arrangement of gears, as in an automobile, that gives the greatest power but the slowest speed. **—lay low** To strike down; defeat. **—lie low** *informal* To remain in hiding: Thieves *lie low* after they have committed a robbery. **—low′ness** *n.*

low·brow [lō′brou′] *informal* **1** *n.* A person who does not have refined or cultured tastes in art, music, literature, etc. **2** *adj.* Of or suited to such a person: *lowbrow* amusements.

Low Countries The region of NW Europe that includes the Netherlands, Belgium, and Luxembourg.

low-down [*adj.* lō′doun′, *n.* lō′doun′] *slang* **1** *adj.* Mean or contemptible: a *low-down* trick. **2** *n.* The truth, especially the secret facts: to get the *low-down* on a dishonest politician.

low·er¹ [lou′ər] **1** *v.* To look angry; scowl. **2** *n.* A frown or scowl. **3** *v.* To appear dark and threatening, as the sky before a storm.

low·er² [lō′ər] **1** Comparative of LOW: His grades are *lower* than mine. **2** *adj.* Situated below something else: the *lower* jaw. **3** *v.* To let down or pull down: to *lower* a lifeboat. **4** *adj.* Having less importance; inferior in rank: the *lower* house of a legislature. **5** *v.* To make or become less in amount, quality, pitch, etc.: He *lowered* the price; The volume *lowered*. **6** *v.* To weaken: Lack of sleep *lowers* the body's resistance.

Lower California A long peninsula of NW Mexico, situated just below California.

low·er·most [lō′ər·mōst′] *adj.* Lowest.

low·land [lō′lənd] *n.* **1** (*usually pl.*) Land lying lower than the country around it. **2** (*pl.*) (*written* **Lowlands**) The less mountainous regions of southern and eastern Scotland.

Low·land·er [lō′land/ər] *n.* A person born or living in the Scottish Lowlands.

low·ly [lō′lē] *adj.* **low·li·er, low·li·est 1** *adj.* Humble or low in rank, position, etc.: a *lowly* peasant. **2** *adj.* Humble; meek: a *lowly* penitent. **3** *adv.* Modestly; humbly. **—low′li·ness** *n.*

low-spir·it·ed [lō′spir′it·id] *adj.* Sad and unhappy; depressed: He felt *low-spirited*.

low tide 1 The outgoing tide at its lowest point. **2** The time when this happens.

lox¹ [loks] *n.* Liquid oxygen.

lox² [loks] *n.* Salty smoked salmon. ◆ *Lox* comes from a Yiddish word derived from a German word for *salmon*.

loy·al [loi′əl] *adj.* **1** Faithful to one's country: a *loyal* soldier. **2** Constant and faithful to one's family, friends, obligations, work, etc.: a *loyal* servant. **—loy′al·ly** *adv.*

loy·al·ist [loi′əl·ist] *n.* A person who remains loyal to a certain government or political party during a revolution or other uprising.

loy·al·ty [loi′əl·tē] *n.*, *pl.* **loy·al·ties** The condition or fact of being loyal.

loz·enge [loz′inj] *n.* **1** A small tablet of candy or a medicated cough drop, formerly made in the shape of a diamond. **2** A figure in the shape of a diamond.

Lt. Abbreviation of LIEUTENANT.

lub·ber [lub′ər] *n.* **1** An awkward, clumsy fellow. **2** A clumsy, inexperienced sailor on a ship.

lu·bri·cant [loo′brə·kənt] *n.* A substance, as oil or grease, used to coat moving parts of a machine so that they will slide smoothly against each other and not wear out so quickly.

lu·bri·cate [loo′brə·kāt] *v.* **lu·bri·cat·ed, lu·bri·cat·ing** To apply a lubricant to: to *lubricate* an engine. **—lu′bri·ca′tion** *n.*

lu·cent [loo′sənt] *adj.* **1** Giving off radiance; bright. **2** Clear; transparent.

lu·cid [loo′sid] *adj.* **1** Easily understood; clear; plain: a *lucid* explanation. **2** Thinking clearly; mentally sound: a *lucid* mind. **3** Clear; transparent, as water. **4** Shining; bright: used in poems. **—lu·cid′i·ty** *n.* **—lu′cid·ly** *adv.*

Lu·ci·fer [loo′sə·fər] *n.* The archangel who led the revolt of the angels and was thrown from Heaven; Satan; the Devil.

luck [luk] *n.* **1** Good fortune; success: He had *luck* in finding a good job. **2** Something that happens by chance; fortune: John always seems to have bad *luck* in sports. **—in luck** Successful; lucky. **—out of luck** Unlucky.

luck·i·ly [luk′ə·lē] *adv.* By good fortune; fortunately: *Luckily* he saw us.

luck·less [luk′lis] *adj.* Having bad luck.

luck·y [luk′ē] *adj.* **luck·i·er, luck·i·est 1** Having good fortune: to be *lucky* at cards. **2** Resulting in good fortune: to make a *lucky* move in checkers. **3** Believed to bring good fortune: a *lucky* penny. **—luck′i·ness** *n.*

lu·cra·tive [loo′krə·tiv] *adj.* Bringing in lots of money; profitable: a *lucrative* business.

lu·cre [loo′kər] *n.* Money or wealth, usually used in the phrase **filthy lucre**.

lu·di·crous [lōō′də·krəs] *adj.* Causing laughter, scorn, or ridicule; ridiculous; absurd: a *ludicrous* action. **—lud′i·crous·ly** *adv.*

luff [luf] **1** *n.* The turning of a ship closer to the wind. **2** *n.* The foremost edge of a fore-and-aft sail. **3** *v.* To bring the head of a sailing vessel toward or into the wind.

lug¹ [lug] *n.* An earlike part that sticks out, used for holding or supporting something.

lug² [lug] *v.* **lugged, lug·ging** To carry or pull with effort: to *lug* large rocks.

Ludicrous antics

lug·gage [lug′ij] *n.* Suitcases, bags, and trunks used in traveling; baggage.

lug·ger [lug′ər] *n.* A boat having lugsails. It may have one, two, or three masts.

lug·sail [lug′sāl′ *or* lug′səl] *n.* A four-cornered sail having no boom. It is hung from a yard that slants across the mast.

lu·gu·bri·ous [lōō·gōō′brē·əs] *adj.* Sad, mournful, or pretending sadness: Hounds often have *lugubrious* faces. **—lu·gu′bri·ous·ly** *adv.*

lugsails

Lugger

Luke [lōōk] *n.* **1** An early Christian and saint who was a physician and a companion of St. Paul. **2** The third book of the New Testament, which he is believed to have written.

luke·warm [lōōk′wôrm′] *adj.* **1** Barely warm; tepid: No one likes *lukewarm* soup. **2** Lacking in warmth or enthusiasm: a *lukewarm* greeting.

lull [lul] **1** *v.* To quiet or put to sleep by soothing sounds or motions. **2** *v.* To make or become quiet or calm: to *lull* someone's distrust; The wind *lulled.* **3** *n.* A time of calm or quiet during a period of noise or activity: a *lull* in business.

lull·a·by [lul′ə·bī] *n., pl.* **lull·a·bies 1** A song to soothe a baby to sleep. **2** A piece of instrumental music that sounds like a lullaby.

lum·ba·go [lum·bā′gō] *n.* A form of rheumatism that affects the lower part of the back.

lum·bar [lum′bər] *adj.* Of or near the lower part of the back: a *lumbar* nerve.

lum·ber¹ [lum′bər] **1** *n.* Timber that has been sawed into boards, planks, and beams. **2** *v.* To cut down and saw (timber) for marketing. **3** *n.* *British* Household articles and furniture no longer used and usually stored away.

lum·ber² [lum′bər] *v.* **1** To move along clumsily and heavily: The elephant *lumbered* through the jungle. **2** To move with a rumbling noise, as a heavy truck.

lum·ber·ing [lum′bər·ing] *n.* The business of cutting down timber and sawing it into lumber for the market.

lum·ber·jack [lum′bər·jak] *n.* A man whose work it is to saw down trees and transport them to the sawmill.

lum·ber·man [lum′bər·mən] *n., pl.* **lum·ber·men** [lum′bər·mən] **1** A lumberjack. **2** A person who is in the business of lumbering.

lu·mi·nar·y [lōō′mə·ner′ē] *n., pl.* **lu·mi·nar·ies 1** A body that gives out light, especially the sun or moon. **2** A person who has achieved great fame.

lu·mi·nes·cent [lōō′mə·nes′ənt] *adj.* Giving out light at a temperature below that of incandescence. Fluorescent lights and fireflies are luminescent because they give off light, though cool to the touch. **—lu′mi·nes′cence** *n.*

lu·mi·nos·i·ty [lōō′mə·nos′ə·tē] *n., pl.* **lu·mi·nos·i·ties 1** The quality of being luminous. **2** Something luminous.

lu·mi·nous [lōō′mə·nəs] *adj.* **1** Full of light; glowing: The room was *luminous* with moonlight. **2** Giving off light: *luminous* insects. **3** Easily understood: a *luminous* remark.

lump [lump] **1** *n.* A shapeless mass, especially a small one: a *lump* of dough. **2** *n.* A swelling on the body: His fall caused a *lump* on his head. **3** *v.* To form lumps in or on. **4** *v.* To put in one mass or group: to *lump* all the facts together. **5** *v. slang* To put up with; bear: You can like it or *lump* it. **—lump sum** A full or single amount of money paid at one time: to pay for something in one *lump sum.*

lump·ish [lump′ish] *adj.* **1** Like a lump; thick and shapeless. **2** Clumsy and stupid.

lump·y [lum′pē] *adj.* **lump·i·er, lump·i·est 1** Full of lumps. **2** Covered with or having lumps: a *lumpy* bed. **—lump′i·ness** *n.*

Lu·na [lōō′nə] *n.* In Roman myths, the goddess of the moon.

lu·na·cy [lōō′nə·sē] *n., pl.* **lu·na·cies 1** Unwise or reckless conduct: It is *lunacy* to drive so fast. **2** Mental illness; insanity.

lu·nar [lōō′nər] *adj.* **1** Of or having to do with the moon: A *lunar* eclipse is caused by the moon's passing through the earth's shadow. **2** Round or crescent-shaped like the moon.

lunar month The time it takes for the moon to go once around the earth, equal to 29.53 days.

lu·na·tic [lōō′nə·tik] **1** *adj.* Wildly foolish; senseless. **2** *adj.* Mentally ill; insane. **3** *adj.* For or having to do with mentally ill persons. **4** *n.* A mentally ill person. ◆ *Lunatic* comes from *luna,* the Latin word for *moon.* People used to believe that insanity increased and decreased with the phases of the moon.

lunch [lunch] **1** *n.* A light meal, especially the noonday meal. **2** *n.* The food provided for such a meal. **3** *v.* To eat lunch.

lunch·eon [lun′chən] *n.* A noonday meal, especially a formal one.

lung [lung] *n.* Either of the two saclike organs of breathing found in the chest of man and other vertebrate animals that breathe air. The lungs bring oxygen to and remove carbon dioxide from the blood.

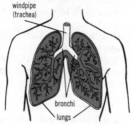

windpipe (trachea)

bronchi

lungs

lunge [lunj] *n., v.* **lunged, lung·ing 1** *n.* A quick movement or plunge forward, as a thrust with a sword. **2** *v.* To make a lunge.

lu·pine [loo′pin] *n.* A plant related to the pea, having long spikes of flowers and bean-shaped seeds in flat pods.

lurch¹ [lûrch] **1** *v.* To roll or pitch suddenly to one side, as from loss of balance: The sailor *lurched* across the tilting deck. **2** *n.* A rolling or pitching motion.

lurch² [lûrch] *n.* An embarrassing or difficult position or situation, now used only in the phrase **leave in the lurch,** to abandon (someone) having difficulties and needing help.

lure [loor] *n., v.* **lured, lur·ing 1** *n.* Anything that invites or attracts, as by offering pleasure or gain: the *lure* of a big city. **2** *v.* To attract or entice, especially into danger: to *lure* birds into traps. **3** *n.* Artificial bait made of feathers, wood, etc., used in catching fish.

lu·rid [loor′id] *adj.* **1** Causing horror or fear; shocking: a *lurid* crime. **2** Lighted up or glowing with a yellowish red glare, especially as seen through smoke or darkness.

lurk [lûrk] *v.* **1** To lie hidden; stay out of sight. **2** To creep along stealthily; slink: Snakes *lurk* in the long grass.

Fishing lure

lus·cious [lush′əs] *adj.* **1** Very good to taste and smell; delicious: a *luscious*, ripe pear. **2** Pleasing to any sense or to the mind: a *luscious* red rose. **—lus′cious·ly** *adv.*

lush [lush] *adj.* **1** Full of a healthy growth of trees, plants, etc.: *lush* jungles. **2** Growing with vigor: *lush* grass. **3** Elaborate or ornate: *lush* prose. **4** Delicious; savory: *lush* fruit. **5** Appealing to the eyes, ears, or other senses: a *lush* sound. **6** Prosperous: a *lush* business.

lust [lust] **1** *n.* A strong desire or craving: a *lust* for money. **2** *n.* A strong sexual appetite. **3** *v.* To have a strong desire or craving: to *lust* after power. **—lust′ful** *adj.*

lus·ter [lus′tər] *n.* **1** Soft, reflected light playing over a surface; sheen: the *luster* of polished wood. **2** Brightness; radiance: The lights had lost their *luster*. **3** Brilliance or glory, as of achievement, beauty, etc. **4** A glossy, often iridescent finish baked on the surface of certain kinds of pottery.

lus·trous [lus′trəs] *adj.* Having a luster or gleam; glossy; shiny: a cat's *lustrous* fur.

lust·y [lus′tē] *adj.* **lust·i·er, lust·i·est** Full of health and vigor; robust: a *lusty* infant. **—lust′i·ly** *adv.* **—lust′i·ness** *n.*

lute [loot] *n.* An old stringed instrument somewhat like a guitar. It is played by plucking with the fingers.

Lu·ther [loo′thər], **Martin,** 1483–1546, German monk and leader in the Reformation and formation of Protestant Churches.

Lute

Lu·ther·an [loo′thər·ən] **1** *n.* A member of the Protestant church founded by Martin Luther in Germany in the 16th century. **2** *adj.* Of or having to do with Martin Luther, Lutherans, or with their church or doctrines.

Lux·em·bourg or **Lux·em·burg** [luk′səm·bûrg] *n.* **1** A very small country in central Europe, between Belgium, France, and Germany. **2** Its capital.

lux·u·ri·ant [lug·zhoor′ē·ənt] *adj.* **1** Growing thickly and abundantly; lush: *luxuriant* plants. **2** Very rich, fancy, or elaborate, as in decorations, furnishings, ornaments, etc. **— lux·u′ri·ance** *n.* **—lux·u′ri·ant·ly** *adv.*

lux·u·ri·ate [lug·zhoor′ē·āt] *v.* **lux·u·ri·at·ed, lux·u·ri·at·ing 1** To take great pleasure; enjoy oneself fully: to *luxuriate* in a soft bed. **2** To live the way rich people do. **3** To grow thickly and abundantly, as plants.

lux·u·ri·ous [lug·zhoor′ē·əs] *adj.* **1** Characterized by luxury or great comfort; costly: a *luxurious* palace. **2** Loving luxury. **— lux·u′ri·ous·ly** *adv.* **—lux·u′ri·ous·ness** *n.*

lux·u·ry [luk′shər·ē] *n., pl.* **lux·u·ries 1** Anything costly that gives comfort or pleasure, but is not necessary to life or health: A diamond necklace is a *luxury*. **2** A way of life in which one has great ease and comfort: to live in *luxury*. **3** Any pleasure.

Lu·zon [loo·zon′] *n.* The largest island of the Philippine Islands.

-ly¹ A suffix meaning: **1** Like or suited to, as in *motherly*, like or suited to a mother. **2** Toward or from a certain direction, as in *northerly*, toward or from the north. **3** Happening at regular intervals of time, as in *daily*, happening or appearing every day. **4** Of or having to do with, as in *earthly*, of or having to do with the earth or the world. This suffix is used mainly to form adjectives.

-ly² A suffix meaning: **1** In a certain manner, as in *carefully*, in a careful manner. **2** To a certain degree or extent, as in *highly*, to a high degree. **3** In certain respects or ways, as in *mentally*, in mental ways. **4** At or in a certain order or time, as in *recently*, at a recent time, or in *fourthly*, in fourth place or position. This suffix is used to form adverbs.

ly·cée [lē·sā′] *n.* In France, a secondary school financed by the government, that prepares its students for a university.

ly·ce·um [lī·sē′əm] *n.* **1** An organization that gives lectures, concerts, etc., for the public. **2** A hall where such lectures and concerts are held.

lye [lī] *n.* A strong, alkaline solution, now usually sodium hydroxide, used in making soap, refining oil, etc.

ly·ing¹ [lī′ing] Present participle of LIE¹: The dog is *lying* in the shade.

ly·ing² [lī′ing] **1** Present participle of LIE²: The boy is *lying* about his absence from class. **2** *n.* The act of telling lies. **3** *adj.* Telling lies; untruthful: a *lying* witness.

lymph [limf] *n.* A watery, yellowish liquid containing lymphocytes and similar to blood plasma.

lym·phat·ic [lim·fat′ik] *adj.* **1** Containing or carrying lymph: the *lymphatic* vessels. **2** Lacking energy; listless: a *lymphatic* boy.

lymph gland or **lymph node** Any of numerous glandlike bodies through which lymph flows to be cleansed of waste matter and bacteria.

lym·pho·cyte [lim′fə·sīt] *n.* A type of white blood cell produced in the lymph nodes.

lym·phoid [lim′foid] *adj.* Of, having to do with, or like lymph or the tissues of a lymph gland.

lynch [linch] *v.* To kill (a person accused of a crime) by mob action, as by hanging, without a legal trial.

lynx [lingks] *n., pl.* **lynx** or **lynx·es** A wildcat of North America, having a short tail, tufted ears, and rather long legs.

Lynx, about 32 in. long

ly·on·naise [lī′ə·nāz′] *adj.* Cooked with finely chopped onions: *lyonnaise* potatoes.

Ly·ra [lī′rə] *n.* A constellation, the Lyre, containing the star Vega.

lyre [līr] *n.* An ancient stringed instrument like a harp. It was used by the ancient Greeks to accompany singing or poetry.

lyre·bird [līr′bûrd′] *n.* A large bird of Australia, the male of which spreads its long tail feathers into the shape of a lyre.

lyr·ic [lir′ik] **1** *n.* A poem expressing the writer's personal feelings or experiences, as a poem about love or grief. **2** *adj.* Of or having to do with such poems. **3** *adj.* Describing a singing voice that is light, graceful, and melodic: a *lyric* soprano. **4** *n.* (*pl.*) The words of a popular song. **5** *adj.* Meant to be sung; like a song.

Lyre

lyr·i·cal [lir′ə·kəl] *adj.* **1** Lyric. **2** Full of emotion, excitement, or enthusiasm: a *lyrical* account of a vacation. —**lyr′i·cal·ly** *adv.*

ly·sin [lī′sin] *n.* Any of a class of substances that are formed in the body and which have the power to destroy blood cells, bacteria, etc.

M

m or **M** [em] *n., pl.* **m's** or **M's 1** The 13th letter of the English alphabet. **2** (*written* **M**) The Roman numeral for 1,000.

ma [mä] *n. informal* Mama. ◆ See MAMA.

M.A. Abbreviation of MASTER OF ARTS.

ma'am [mam, mäm, *or* məm] *n.* Madam. ◆ See MADAM.

mac·ad·am [mə·kad′əm] *n.* **1** Small, broken stones used to cover a road. **2** A road made from such stones.

mac·ad·am·ize [mə·kad′ə·mīz] *v.* **mac·ad·am·ized, mac·ad·am·iz·ing** To surface or cover a road with macadam, and often tar. ¶3

ma·caque [mə·käk′] *n.* Any of several monkeys, found chiefly in Asia and North Africa.

mac·a·ro·ni [mak′ə·rō′nē] *n.* A dried flour paste in tubular shape that is boiled and eaten.

mac·a·roon [mak′ə·rōōn′] *n.* A small cooky made chiefly of egg whites, sugar, and almonds or coconut.

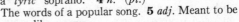

add, āce, câre, pälm; end, ēqual; it, īce; odd, ōpen, ôrder; tŏŏk, pōōl; up, bûrn; ə = a in *above*, e in *sicken*, i in *possible*, o in *melon*, u in *circus*; yōō = u in *fuse*; oil; pout; check; ring; thin; **t**his; zh in *vision*.   For ¶ reference, see page 64 · HOW TO

Mac·Ar·thur [mək·är′thər], **Douglas,** 1880–1964, U.S. general.

ma·caw [mə·kô′] *n.* Any of various large parrots of South and Central America, having a long tail, harsh voice, and brilliant plumage.

Mac·beth [mək·beth′] *n.* **1** A play by Shakespeare. **2** The Scottish general in it who murdered his king and took the throne.

mace[1] [mās] *n.* **1** A heavy, medieval, clublike weapon, usually with a spiked metal head. **2** An ornamental staff carried before or by an official to symbolize his power or authority.

mace[2] [mās] *n.* A fragrant spice made from the covering of the nutmeg seed.

Mac·e·don [mas′ə·don] *n.* An ancient country north of Greece which became a leading world power under Alexander the Great.

Mac·e·do·ni·a [mas′ə·dō′nē·ə] *n.* **1** A region of SE Europe, divided among Bulgaria, Greece, and Yugoslavia. **2** The ancient kingdom of Macedon. **— Mac′e·do′ni·an** *adj., n.*

ma·chet·e [mə·shet′ē *or* mə·shet′] *n.* A heavy knife used as a tool and as a weapon, especially in South America and the West Indies.

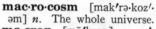
Mace

Mach·i·a·vel·li [mäk′ē·ə·vel′ē], **Niccolò,** 1469–1527, Italian statesman and writer on politics who believed that a ruler should use craft and deceit, if useful, to keep his power and carry out his aims.

Mach·i·a·vel·li·an [mak′ē·ə·vel′ē·ən] *adj.* Having to do with or resembling the theories of Niccolò Machiavelli.

mach·i·na·tion [mak′ə·nā′shən] *n.* (*usually pl.*) A secret scheming and working for a purpose, usually an evil or improper one.

ma·chine [mə·shēn′] *n., v.* **ma·chined, ma·chin·ing** **1** *n.* An arrangement of parts that transmits energy so as to produce a desired result. **2** *v.* To make, shape, mill, etc., by means of a machine. **3** *n.* An airplane, automobile, or other mechanical vehicle. **4** *n.* Any of various simple devices by which a small amount of energy can be made to exert a maximum force. **5** *n.* A person whose actions are machinelike, showing no evidence of thought or will. **6** *n.* The people who control a political party.

machine gun An automatic gun that fires many bullets rapidly and continuously.

ma·chin·er·y [mə·shēn′(ə·)rē] *n.* **1** A collection of machines: a shop filled with *machinery*. **2** The parts of a machine: the *machinery* of a watch. **3** The principles or processes by which something works: the *machinery* of the law.

Machine gun

machine shop A shop where metals or other materials are cut, shaped, or finished.

machine tool A power-driven tool, partly or fully automatic, for cutting or shaping.

ma·chin·ist [mə·shē′nist] *n.* **1** A person who is skilled in the operation of machine tools. **2** A person who is skilled in the construction, operation, or repair of machinery.

mach number [mäk] (*often written* **Mach number**) The ratio of the speed of an object traveling in a fluid, as air, to the speed of sound in that fluid.

mack·er·el [mak′ər·əl] *n., pl.* **mack·er·el** or **mack·er·els** A fish of the Atlantic Ocean, used for food.

mackerel sky Small, fleecy, white clouds in rows like the markings on a mackerel's back.

Mack·i·nac [mak′ə·nô], **Straits of** A strait between Lake Michigan and Lake Huron.

mack·i·naw [mak′ə·nô] *n.* A heavy, short, woolen coat, usually with a plaid pattern.

mack·in·tosh [mak′ən·tosh] *n.* A waterproof coat or cloak; a raincoat. ◆ The word *mackintosh* was named after Charles *Macintosh*, a Scottish chemist who invented the cloth.

Mackinaw

mac·ro·cosm [mak′rə·koz′əm] *n.* The whole universe.

ma·cron [mā′kron] *n.* A straight line (¯) placed over a vowel to show that it is pronounced in a certain way, as *ā* in *made*.

mad [mad] *adj.* **mad·der, mad·dest** **1** Suffering from or showing severe mental disorder; insane: When the woman went *mad*, she was committed to an asylum. **2** Uncontrollably excited by strong feeling; wildly emotional: He was *mad* with jealousy. **3** *informal* Angry: I was so *mad* at him that we fought. **4** Foolish; rash: It was a *mad* idea. **5** Confused; disorderly: We'd thrown everything into a *mad* jumble. **6** *informal* Very enthusiastic or fond: to be *mad* about singing folk songs. **7** *informal* Very gay or funny; hilarious: a *mad* time. **8** Having rabies: a *mad* dog.

Mad·a·gas·car [mad′ə·gas′kər] *n.* An island in the Indian Ocean off the SE coast of Africa, the main part of the Malagasy Republic.

mad·am [mad′əm] *n., pl.* **mes·dames** [mā·däm′] or **mad·ams** My lady: a title of courtesy originally addressed to a woman of rank or high position, but now addressed to any woman, as at the beginning of a letter, question, etc.: *Madam*, may I help you? ◆ *Madam* is the English spelling of the French *madame*, although the French spelling is itself often used in English. *Madam* is proper in the salutation of a letter to a woman, just as *sir* is when writing to a man, but in speaking, *madam* often sounds too proper and affected. *Ma'am* is less formal. *Madame* in French literally means *my lady*, going back to the

Latin words *mea*, meaning *my*, and *domina, a mistress of a household.*

mad·ame [mad'əm] *n.,* *pl.* **mes·dames** [mā·däm'] The French title of courtesy for a married woman, equivalent to the English *Mrs.*: often used in English, especially in the plural. ◆ See MADAM.

mad·cap [mad'kap'] **1** *adj.* Wild; rash: a *madcap* adventure. **2** *n.* A person who acts wildly or rashly.

mad·den [mad'(ə)n] *v.* To make or become mad; infuriate: John's actions *maddened* me.

made [mād] Past tense and past participle of MAKE.

Ma·dei·ra [mə·dir'ə] *n.* **1** A group of Portuguese islands in the Atlantic Ocean, west of Morocco. **2** The principal island in the group. **3** A strong white wine made in Madeira.

mad·e·moi·selle [mad'ə·mə·zel'] *n.,* *pl.* **mad·e·moi·selles** or **mes·de·moi·selles** [mād·mwä·zel'] The French title of courtesy for an unmarried woman or girl, equivalent to the English *Miss.*

made-up [mād'up'] *adj.* **1** Not real; invented; false: a *made-up* name. **2** Changed or made more attractive by cosmetics or make-up: her carefully *made-up* face.

mad·house [mad'hous'] *n.* **1** A hospital for the mentally ill; insane asylum. **2** A place of disorder and uproar: The gym was a *madhouse.*

Mad·i·son [mad'ə·sən] *n.* The capital of Wisconsin, in the south central part.

Mad·i·son [mad'ə·sən], **James,** 1751–1836, fourth president of the U.S., 1809–1817.

mad·ly [mad'lē] *adv.* In a mad manner; insanely; angrily; rashly.

mad·man [mad'man'] *n.,* *pl.* **mad·men** [mad'men'] A person who is mad; a maniac.

mad·ness [mad'nis] *n.* **1** Insanity. **2** Great anger or fury. **3** Extreme foolishness; folly.

Ma·don·na [mə·don'ə] *n.* **1** The Virgin Mary. **2** A painting or statue of the Virgin Mary.

ma·dras [mə·dras' *or* mad'rəs] *n.* A cotton cloth in woven checked, plaid, or striped patterns. ◆ *Madras* was named after *Madras,* a city and province of southern India, where it was originally made.

Ma·drid [mə·drid'] *n.* The capital of Spain, in the central part.

mad·ri·gal [mad'rə·gəl] *n.* **1** An unaccompanied song, with parts for several voices. **2** A short poem, usually about love or rural life, that is suitable for such a song.

mael·strom [māl'strəm] *n.* **1** (written **Maelstrom**) A violent and dangerous whirlpool off the NW coast of Norway. **2** Any whirlpool. **3** A dangerous and irresistible force that resembles a maelstrom in its action: the destructive *maelstrom* of hatred.

maes·tro [mīs'trō] *n.* A master in any art,

especially an important conductor, composer, or performer of music.

mag·a·zine [mag'ə·zēn' *or* mag'ə·zēn] *n.* **1** A publication that appears at regular intervals, containing articles, stories, and other features by various writers. **2** A storage place, especially for military supplies. **3** A building for storing explosives, or a room in a ship or a fort for such a purpose. **4** A container in a rifle, pistol, etc., that holds cartridges and feeds them into the chamber. **5** The enclosed space in a camera that holds the film.

Ma·gel·lan [mə·jel'ən], **Ferdinand,** 1480?–1521, Portuguese navigator in the service of Spain. He led the first expedition to sail around the world.

Magellan, Strait of The channel between the Atlantic and the Pacific Oceans, separating the South American mainland from Tierra del Fuego.

ma·gen·ta [mə·jen'tə] *n., adj.* Purplish rose or purplish red.

mag·got [mag'ət] *n.* The legless larva of an insect, as the housefly, usually found in decaying matter.

Ma·gi [mā'jī] *n.pl.* In the Bible, the three wise men who came with gifts for the baby Jesus.

mag·ic [maj'ik] *n.* **1** The use of formulas, charms, rites, etc., to gain supposed supernatural power. **2** *adj. use:* a *magic* charm. **3** Any unusual or powerful influence or effect: the *magic* of her smile. **4** Tricks performed by a magician; sleight of hand. ◆ *Magic, witchcraft,* and *voodoo* all have to do with man dealing in powers that are apparently supernatural. *Magic* is the common term and includes everything from pulling rabbits out of hats to black magic, used for evil purposes. *Witchcraft* is magic used for personal or evil motives (*black magic*), and is supposedly practiced by witches—women possessed by demons. *Voodoo* is a religion that originated in Africa and involves a belief in black magic and the use of charms, fetishes, etc.

mag·i·cal [maj'i·kəl] *adj.* Of, having to do with, or produced by magic. **— mag'i·cal·ly** *adv.*

ma·gi·cian [mə·jish'ən] *n.* A person who performs magic, especially an entertainer who performs magical tricks.

magic lantern An old-fashioned term for a slide projector.

mag·is·te·ri·al [maj'is·tir'ē·əl] *adj.* **1** Of or having to do with a magistrate: *magisterial* duties. **2** Dictatorial; pompous; authoritative: a *magisterial* manner of speaking.

mag·is·tra·cy [maj'is·trə·sē] *n.,* *pl.* **mag·is·tra·cies** **1** The office, duties, or term of a magistrate. **2** Magistrates as a group.

add, āce, câre, pälm; end, ēqual; it, īce; odd, ōpen, ôrder; took, pool; up, bûrn; ə = a in *above*, e in *sicken*, i in *possible*, o in *melon*, u in *circus*; yoo = u in *fuse*; oil; pout; check; ring; thin; this; zh in *vision*. For ¶ reference, see page 64 · HOW TO

mag·is·trate [maj′is·trāt *or* maj′is·trit] *n.*
1 A high public official having many executive or legal powers, as the president of a nation. **2** A minor judge, as a justice of the peace.

mag·ma [mag′mə] *n., pl.* **mag·ma·ta** [mag′-mə·tə] The hot, partly liquid mass of rock material within the earth from which igneous rocks are formed.

Mag·na Char·ta *or* **Mag·na Car·ta** [mag′-nə kär′tə] **1** The document that guaranteed certain liberties to the English people which the barons of England forced King John to sign in 1215. **2** Any document that secures liberty and rights.

mag·na·nim·i·ty [mag′nə·nim′ə·tē] *n., pl.* **mag·na·nim·i·ties** **1** The quality of being magnanimous. **2** A magnanimous act.

mag·nan·i·mous [mag·nan′ə·məs] *adj.* Showing generosity in forgiving insults or injuries; not given to resentment. — **mag·nan′i·mous·ly** *adv.*

mag·nate [mag′nāt] *n.* A person of rank or importance: an industrial *magnate*.

mag·ne·sia [mag·nē′zhə *or* mag·nē′shə] *n.* A white, powdery magnesium compound, used in making firebrick and as a laxative.

mag·ne·si·um [mag·nē′zē·əm *or* mag·nē′zhē·əm *or* mag·nē′shē·əm] *n.* A silvery white metallic element that burns with a brilliant white light.

mag·net [mag′nit] *n.* An object that creates a magnetic field around itself and so is able to attract iron or steel, especially an object that does this without using electric power.

mag·net·ic [mag·net′ik] *adj.* **1** Capable of being attracted by a magnet: a *magnetic* metal. **2** Acting as a magnet: *magnetic* scissors. **3** Capable of being magnetized, as iron. **4** Of, related to, or operating by magnetism. **5** Exercising a strong attraction or personal power: She has a *magnetic* personality.

magnetic field A region surrounding a magnet, an electromagnet, or a moving electric charge, in which magnetism may be detected.

magnetic needle A magnet in the form of a slender bar which, when able to move freely, points its poles toward the magnetic poles of the earth, roughly indicating north and south.

magnetic pole **1** One of the points of a magnet or electromagnet where the magnetic field is strongest. **2** One of the points where the earth's magnetic field is strongest, close to but not at the geographical North and South Poles.

mag·net·ism [mag′nə·tiz′əm] *n.* **1** An effect seen in the attraction of iron by a magnet and in the ability of magnetic poles to attract and repel each other. This effect occurs in connection with moving electricity. **2** The science that deals with such effects. **3** The personal quality that attracts or influences: My sister's *magnetism* won her many friends.

mag·net·ite [mag′nə·tīt] *n.* A heavy, strongly magnetic mineral, an important iron ore.

mag·net·ize [mag′nə·tīz] *v.* **mag·net·ized, mag·net·iz·ing** **1** To make into a magnet: to *magnetize* a steel bar. **2** To attract by strong, personal influence; captivate. ¶3

mag·ne·to [mag·nē′tō] *n., pl.* **mag·ne·tos** A type of electrical generator with permanent magnets, often used to produce the electrical spark in certain internal-combustion engines.

magni- A prefix meaning great or large, as in *magnify*, to make greater or larger.

mag·nif·i·cence [mag·nif′ə·səns] *n.* Impressive splendor, beauty, or grandeur.

mag·nif·i·cent [mag·nif′ə·sənt] *adj.* **1** Grand and stately; splendid: a *magnificent* palace. **2** Exalted; superb: a *magnificent* poem.

mag·ni·fy [mag′nə·fī] *v.* **mag·ni·fied, mag·ni·fy·ing** **1** To make (something) look larger than its actual or normal size: Telescopes *magnify* images of stars. **2** To cause to seem greater or more important; exaggerate: He *magnifies* his problems. — **mag′ni·fi·ca′tion** *n.* — **mag′ni·fi′er** *n.*

magnifying glass A lens or system of lenses that makes objects seen through it look larger.

mag·nil·o·quent [mag·nil′-ə·kwənt] *adj.* Speaking or spoken in a pompous, showy way: His speech was *magniloquent*. — **mag·nil′o·quence** *n.*

mag·ni·tude [mag′nə-t(y)ood] *n.* **1** Size or extent: an art collection of great *magnitude*.

Magnifying glass

2 Greatness or importance: a problem of no *magnitude*. **3** A number indicating the relative brightness of a star. A star with a magnitude of 6 can barely be seen; a star with a magnitude of 1 is a hundred times brighter.

mag·no·li·a [mag·nō′lē·ə *or* mag·nōl′yə] *n.* An ornamental flowering shrub or tree with large, fragrant, white, pink, purple, or yellow flowers.

mag·pie [mag′pī] *n.* **1** Any of various large, noisy birds, having a long tapering tail and black and white plumage. **2** A person who talks a lot.

Mag·yar [mag′yär] **1** *n.* A member of the main group of the population of Hungary. **2** *n.* The Hungarian language of these people. **3** *adj.* Of or having to do with the Magyars or their language.

ma·ha·ra·ja *or* **ma·ha·ra·jah** [mä′hə·rä′jə] *n.* A title of certain princes of India, particularly one ruling an Indian state.

ma·ha·ra·ni *or* **ma·ha·ra·nee** [mä′hə·rä′nē] *n.* **1** The wife of a maharaja. **2** An Indian princess.

ma·hat·ma [mə·hat′mə *or* mə·hät′mə] *n.* In some Asian religions, a holy man who has special knowledge and power.

mah·jong *or* **mah·jongg** [mä′zhong′] *n.* A game of Chinese origin, usually played by four persons with 144 tiles.

ma·hog·a·ny [mə·hog′ə·nē] *n., pl.* **ma·hog·a·nies** **1** Any of various tropical trees yielding reddish brown hardwood, used for furniture. **2** The wood itself. **3** *adj., n.* Reddish brown.

Ma·hom·et [mə·hom′it] *n.* Another spelling of MOHAMMED. — **Ma·hom′e·tan** *adj., n.*

maid [mād] *n.* **1** A young, unmarried woman or girl; maiden. **2** A female servant.

maid·en [mād′(ə)n] **1** *n.* An unmarried woman, especially if young. **2** *adj. use: maiden* charm. **3** *adj.* Unmarried: a *maiden* aunt. **4** *adj.* Of or having to do with the first use, trial, or experience: a ship's *maiden* voyage.

maid·en·hair [mād′(ə)n·hâr′] *n.* A very delicate and graceful fern with a thin black stem, common in damp, rocky woods.

maid·en·hood [mād′(ə)n·hŏŏd] *n.* The state or time of being a maiden.

maid·en·ly [mād′(ə)n·lē] *adj.* Of, having to do with, or suiting a maiden: *maidenly* grace.

maiden name A woman's last name before she is married.

maid of honor **1** The chief unmarried woman attendant of a bride at a wedding. **2** An unmarried woman, usually of noble birth, attendant upon an empress, queen, or princess.

maid·ser·vant [mād′sûr′vənt] *n.* A female servant.

mail[1] [māl] **1** *n.* Letters or parcels sent or received through a governmental postal system. **2** *n.* The postal system itself. **3** *n.* Postal matter collected or delivered at a certain time: the morning *mail*. **4** *adj. use:* a *mail* truck. **5** *v.* To send by mail; put into the mail.

mail[2] [māl] *n.* Flexible armor made of linking rings or overlapping scales.

mail·box [māl′boks′] *n.* **1** A box in which mail is deposited for collection. **2** A private box into which mail is delivered.

mail·man [māl′man′] *n., pl.* **mail·men** [māl′men′] A man who carries and delivers mail.

mail order An order sent by mail for goods to be shipped to the buyer.

maim [mām] *v.* To take away a part of the body or the use of it; cripple: The accident *maimed* him.

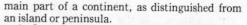

Mail armor

main [mān] **1** *adj.* First or chief, as in size, rank, importance, etc.; principal; leading: the *main* building; the *main* event. **2** *n.* A principal pipe in a system conveying gas, water, etc. **3** *n.* The open sea: used mostly in poems. — **by main force** or **by main strength** By full effort or exertion. — **in the main** For the most part; on the whole; chiefly; principally. — **with might and main** With utmost effort.

Maine [mān] *n.* A state in the NE U.S.

main·land [mān′land *or* mān′lənd] *n.* The main part of a continent, as distinguished from an island or peninsula.

main·ly [mān′lē] *adv.* Chiefly; principally.

main·mast [mān′məst *or* mān′mast′] *n.* The principal mast of a vessel, usually the second mast from the bow.

main·sail [mān′səl *or* mān′sāl′] *n.* The principal sail on a mainmast.

main·spring [mān′spring′] *n.* **1** The principal spring of a mechanism, as a watch. **2** The principal cause or motive: a *mainspring* of crime.

main·stay [mān′stā′] *n.* **1** The rope leading forward from the mainmast, used to steady the mast. **2** A chief support: the *mainstay* of a family.

main·tain [mān·tān′] *v.* **1** To carry on or continue: to *maintain* a constant speed. **2** To preserve or keep: to *maintain* an open mind. **3** To keep in proper condition: to *maintain* roads. **4** To supply with means of support; provide for: to *maintain* a family. **5** To claim to be true; insist or state: He *maintains* he saw a light. **6** To hold or defend, as a position or place: to *maintain* an outpost against attack.

main·te·nance [mān′tə·nəns] *n.* **1** The act of maintaining. **2** A being maintained; support: to provide for *maintenance*. **3** Means of support; livelihood.

maize [māz] *n.* Corn, the plant or its seeds; Indian corn.

Maj. Abbreviation of MAJOR.

ma·jes·tic [mə·jes′tik] *adj.* Having or showing majesty; stately; royal: a *majestic* manner. — **ma·jes′ti·cal·ly** *adv.*

maj·es·ty [maj′is·tē] *n., pl.* **maj·es·ties** **1** Great dignity, beauty, and grandeur: the *majesty* of the sea. **2** Supreme authority: the *majesty* of the law. **3** (*written* **Majesty**) A title or form of address for a king, queen, etc.

ma·jor [mā′jər] **1** *adj.* Greater in quantity, number, extent, etc.: The *major* part of my work is done. **2** *adj.* Having great importance, excellence, or rank: He's a *major* writer. **3** *adj.* Indicating or based on a musical scale that has semitones between the third and fourth and seventh and eighth tones and whole tones between all the others. **4** *adj.* Indicating a chord that could be formed from the first, third, and fifth or fifth, seventh, and second tones of a major scale. **5** *n.* A military rank. In the U.S. Army, a major is an officer ranking next above a captain and next below a lieutenant colonel. **6** *n.* The subject or field of study which a student chooses as his main one: John's *major* is chemistry. **7** *n.* The student himself: a chemistry *major*. **8** *v.* To study a subject as a major.

ma·jor-do·mo [mā′jər·dō′mō] *n., pl.* **ma·jor-do·mos** The chief steward or butler, especially of a royal or noble household.

add, āce, câre, pälm;   end, ēqual;   it, īce;   odd, ōpen, ôrder;   tŏŏk, pōōl;   up, bûrn;
ə = a in *above*, e in *sicken*, i in *possible*, o in *melon*, u in *circus*;   yōō = u in *fuse*;   oil;   pout;
check;   ring;   thin;   this;   zh in *vision*.   For ¶ reference, see page 64 · HOW TO

major general A military rank. In the U.S. Army, a major general is an officer ranking next above a brigadier general and next below a lieutenant general.

ma·jor·i·ty [mə·jôr′ə·tē] *n.*, *pl.* **ma·jor·i·ties** **1** More than half of a given number or group; the greater part: The *majority* of students voted for her. **2** The number of votes for a person or measure in excess of the sum of the votes for others: When a vote comes out 60, 40, and 10, the winner has a *majority* of 10 or a plurality of 20. **3** The legal age for assuming adult rights and responsibilities.

make [māk] *v.* **made, mak·ing,** *n.* **1** *v.* To form, produce, or bring into existence, as by putting parts together, shaping, etc.: to *make* a car; to *make* a new dress. **2** *n.* Type or brand: What *make* of car is that? **3** *n.* The manner or style in which something is made: Is the *make* becoming to me? **4** *v.* To bring about; cause: to *make* trouble; to *make* a sound. **5** *v.* To cause to be: The wind *makes* him cold. **6** *v.* To appoint: They *made* him president. **7** *v.* To form in the mind: Let's *make* plans. **8** *v.* To understand: What do you *make* of his story? **9** *v.* To utter: to *make* an announcement. **10** *v.* To engage in: to *make* war. **11** *v.* To get, earn, or acquire: to *make* a fortune. **12** *v.* To act so as to gain: to *make* new friends. **13** *v.* To add up or amount to: Four quarts *make* a gallon. **14** *v.* To bring the total to: That *makes* four times he's tried to do that. **15** *v.* To draw up, enact, or establish: to *make* a will; to *make* a treaty. **16** *v.* To prepare for use: to *make* a bed. **17** *v.* To force; compel: The teacher *made* him leave the room. **18** *v.* To be the essential part of: Fresh meat and vegetables *make* a nourishing diet. **19** *v.* To provide: *Make* a place in the line for John. **20** *v.* To become through development: He will *make* a good student. **21** *v.* To cause the success of: His last book *made* him. **22** *v.* To perform; do: to *make* a gesture. **23** *v.* To act or behave in a certain manner: to *make* merry. **24** *v.* To travel at the rate of: to *make* sixty miles an hour. **25** *v.* To arrive at; reach: We'll *make* Boston by noon. **26** *v.* To arrive in time for: He barely *made* his train. **27** *v. informal* To win a place on: to *make* the track team. **28** *v. informal* To attain the rank or position of: to *make* colonel in the army. — **make after** To pursue; follow. — **make away with 1** To carry off; steal. **2** To kill. **3** To get rid of. — **make believe** To pretend. — **make for 1** To go toward: Let's *make for* the city. **2** To bring about: Fighting doesn't *make for* happiness. — **make good 1** To succeed. **2** To carry out: to *make good* a threat. **3** To compensate for: Will your insurance company *make good* your losses in the robbery? — **make it** *informal* To succeed in doing something. — **make off with** To steal. — **make out 1** To see: I can't quite *make out* the road ahead. **2** To understand. **3** To succeed: How are you *making out* in school? **4** To fill out, as a paper with blanks. **5** To portray or represent as being: She *made* us *out* to be brave. — **make over 1** To put into a changed form: to *make over* a dress. **2** To transfer title or possession of: to *make over* an estate. — **make time** To travel with speed. — **make up 1** To compound, as a prescription. **2** To be the parts of: What *makes up* this prescription? **3** To settle differences and be friendly again. **4** To invent: to *make up* an answer. **5** To supply the lack in: Will you *make up* the money we need? **6** To compensate: How can you *make up* for all the wrong you did? **7** To settle; decide: to *make up* one's mind. **8** To arrange lines of type or illustrations, as for a book. **9** To put cosmetics on. — **make up to** *informal* To make a show of friendliness and affection toward; flatter. — **mak′er** *n.*

make-be·lieve [māk′bi·lēv′] **1** *n.* Something not true or real; sham; pretense. **2** *adj.* Pretended; unreal: a *make-believe* fight with toy soldiers.

make·shift [māk′shift′] *n.* **1** A temporary substitute. **2** *adj. use:* a *makeshift* table.

make-up [māk′up′] *n.* **1** The arrangement or combination of parts of anything: the *make-up* of a chemical compound. **2** The powder and paint, wigs, pads, etc., used by an actor in a specific role.

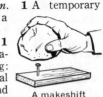
A makeshift hammer

3 Cosmetics used by a woman. **4** The physical or mental characteristics or qualities of a person: a slim *make-up*; a nasty streak in his *make-up*. **5** The arrangement of type, illustrations, etc., in a magazine, newspaper, etc.

mal·a·chite [mal′ə·kīt] *n.* A brittle, green mineral, often used to make ornamental articles.

mal·ad·just·ed [mal′ə·jus′tid] *adj.* Badly adjusted, especially badly suited to or in conflict with the persons, things, and conditions that surround one in life. — **mal′ad·just′ment** *n.*

mal·a·droit [mal′ə·droit′] *adj.* Lacking skill; clumsy; awkward. — **mal′a·droit′ly** *adv.* — **mal′a·droit′ness** *n.*

mal·a·dy [mal′ə·dē] *n.*, *pl.* **mal·a·dies** A disease, sickness, or illness.

Mal·a·gas·y Republic [mal′ə·gas′ē] A country mainly consisting of the island of Madagascar.

ma·lar·i·a [mə·lâr′ē·ə] *n.* A disease spread by the bite of an infected mosquito and marked by recurrent attacks of chills, fever, and sweating. — **ma·lar′i·al** *adj.* ♦ *Malaria* comes from the Italian *mala aria*, meaning *bad air*. Later it came to mean the disease which was supposed to be caused by foul air coming from swamps.

Ma·la·wi [mä′lä·wē] *n.* A country in SE Africa, a member of the British Commonwealth of Nations.

Ma·lay [mā′lā *or* mə·lā′] **1** *n.* One of a people living on the Malay Peninsula or in the East Indies. **2** *n.* Their language. **3** *adj.* Of or having to do with the Malays.

Ma·lay·a [mə·lā′ə], **Federation of** A part of Malaysia consisting of nine Malay states.

Malay Archipelago An island group in the Indian and Pacific Oceans southeast of Asia, including Java, Borneo, Sumatra, and the Philippines.

Malay Archipelago

Malay Peninsula A peninsula of SE Asia, including Malaya and part of Thailand.

Ma·lay·sia [mə·lā′·zhə] *n.* A federation consisting of Malaya and a large section of Borneo. **—Ma·lay′sian** *adj., n.*

mal·con·tent [mal′kən·tent] **1** *adj.* Discontented or dissatisfied; rebellious. **2** *n.* A person who is malcontent; a rebel.

male [māl] **1** *adj.* Of the sex that can fertilize eggs or, in plants, produce pollen. **2** *n.* An animal or plant of this sex. **3** *adj.* Of or suitable for this sex: *male* characteristics.

mal·e·dic·tion [mal′ə·dik′shən] *n.* A calling for evil or injury to happen to another person.

mal·e·fac·tor [mal′ə·fak′tər] *n.* **1** A person who commits a crime. **2** A person who does evil.

ma·lev·o·lent [mə·lev′ə·lənt] *adj.* Wishing evil to others; spiteful. **—ma·lev′o·lence** *n.* **—ma·lev′o·lent·ly** *adv.*

mal·fea·sance [mal·fē′zəns] *n.* A wrong or dishonest act, especially by a public official.

mal·for·ma·tion [mal′fôr·mā′shən] *n.* A wrong or defective formation, especially of some part of the body.

mal·formed [mal·fôrmd′] *adj.* Badly formed.

Ma·li [mä′lē], **Republic of** A country in western Africa.

mal·ice [mal′is] *n.* An intention or desire to hurt or injure someone; ill will; spite.

ma·li·cious [mə·lish′əs] *adj.* Showing or having malice; spiteful. **—ma·li′cious·ly** *adv.*

ma·lign [mə·līn′] **1** *v.* To speak evil of; slander. **2** *adj.* Evil; malicious. **3** *adj.* Harmful; injurious. **—ma·lign′er** *n.*

ma·lig·nan·cy [mə·lig′nən·sē] *n., pl.* **ma·lig·nan·cies 1** The condition of being malignant. **2** A very bad tumor, often fatal.

ma·lig·nant [mə·lig′nənt] *adj.* **1** Tending to do great harm; evil; injurious: *malignant* forces. **2** Very harmful physically, as a disease that grows progressively worse. **—ma·lig′·nant·ly** *adv.*

ma·lig·ni·ty [mə·lig′nə·tē] *n., pl.* **ma·lig·ni·ties 1** Intense ill will; malice. **2** Harmfulness; injuriousness.

ma·lin·ger [mə·ling′gər] *v.* To pretend sickness so as to avoid work or duty. **—ma·lin′ger·er** *n.*

mall [môl] *n.* A promenade or walk, usually public and often shaded.

mal·lard [mal′ərd] *n., pl.* **mal·lard** or **mal·lards** A common wild duck having brownish plumage and, in the male, a bright green head.

mal·le·a·ble [mal′ē·ə·bəl] *adj.* **1** Capable of being hammered or rolled out without breaking: Gold is *malleable.* **2** Easily adapted or influenced: a *malleable* personality. **—mal′le·a·bil′i·ty** *n.*

mal·let [mal′it] *n.* **1** A hammer, usually with a wooden head. **2** A long-handled wooden hammer, used in croquet and in polo.

mal·low [mal′ō] *n.* A type of herb having rounded leaves and pale pink, purplish, or white flowers.

Mallet

mal·nu·tri·tion [mal′n(y)oo·trish′ən] *n.* A harmful condition of the body caused by lack of enough or proper food or nourishment.

mal·prac·tice [mal·prak′tis] *n.* **1** In medicine, harmful treatment or neglect of a patient. **2** Improper conduct in any profession.

malt [môlt] **1** *n.* Grain, usually barley, that is soaked in water, allowed to sprout, and then dried in a kiln, used to make beer, ale, or whisky. **2** *v.* To cause (grain) to become malt. **3** *v.* To mix with malt: a *malted* milk.

Mal·ta [môl′tə] *n.* **1** An island in the Mediterranean Sea. **2** A country including this and nearby islands, a member of the British Commonwealth of Nations. **—Mal·tese** [môl·tēz′] *adj., n.*

Maltese cat A cat with long, silky, bluish gray fur.

Maltese cross An eight-pointed cross.

malt·ose [môl′tōs] *n.* A white crystalline sugar formed by the action of an enzyme on starch.

mal·treat [mal·trēt′] *v.* To treat badly, roughly, or unkindly; abuse. **—mal·treat′·ment** *n.*

Maltese cross

ma·ma or **mam·ma** [mä′mə or mə·mä′] *n.* Mother: used especially by or in talking to children. ◆ *Mama* is a baby's word for mother. It is just a repetition of the sound [mä].

mam·mal [mam′əl] *n.* Any of the vertebrate animals the females of which produce milk for their young. People, cows, cats, mice, and whales are mammals.

mam·ma·li·an [ma·mā′lē·ən *or* ma·māl′yən] *adj.* Of or having to do with mammals.

mam·ma·ry [mam′ər·ē] *adj.* Of or having to do with the breast.

add, āce, câre, pälm;   end, ēqual;   it, īce;   odd, ōpen, ôrder;   tŏŏk, pool;   up, bûrn;
ə = a in *above*, e in *sicken*, i in *possible*, o in *melon*, u in *circus*;   yoo = u in *fuse*;   oil;   pout;
check;   ring;   thin;   this;   zh in *vision*.   For ¶ reference, see page 64 · HOW TO

mam·mon [mam′ən] *n.* Wealth thought of as an evil influence and a bad thing to strive for.

mam·moth [mam′əth] **1** *n.* A large, now extinct animal related to the elephant. It had long tusks that curved upward and a hairy skin. **2** *adj.* Huge; colossal.

Mammoth, 9–12 ft. high at shoulder

man [man] *n., pl.* **men** [men], *v.* **manned, man·ning 1** *n.* An adult male human being. **2** *v.* To supply with men, as for work or defense: to *man* a fort. **3** *n.* Any person: All *men* should be free. **4** *n.* Human beings in general; the human race: *man's* efforts toward conquering disease. **5** *n.* A male employee, servant, or follower: the foreman and his *men.* **6** *n.* A husband: *man* and wife. **7** *n.* A piece used in certain games, as chess or checkers. **8** *v.* To take a place on, at, or in for work, defense, etc. **— as one man** Unanimously. **— to a man** Unanimously.

man·a·cle [man′ə·kəl] *n., v.* **man·a·cled, man·a·cling 1** *n.* A handcuff. **2** *v.* To put handcuffs on. **3** *v.* To restrain or hamper.

man·age [man′ij] *v.* **man·aged, man·ag·ing 1** To direct or control; have charge of: to *manage* a hotel. **2** To accomplish somehow; contrive. **3** To cause to do what one wants: to *manage* a crowd. **4** To use; handle: to *manage* a gun. **5** To make out; get by.

man·age·a·ble [man′ij·ə·bəl] *adj.* Capable of being managed, controlled, or directed.

man·age·ment [man′ij·mənt] *n.* **1** The act or practice of managing. **2** The person or persons who manage a business, institution, etc. **3** People who manage business, as a group.

man·ag·er [man′ij·ər] *n.* A person who manages a business, institution, or enterprise.

man·a·ge·ri·al [man′ə·jir′ē·əl] *adj.* Of or having to do with a manager or management.

man-at-arms [man′ət·ärmz′] *n., pl.* **men-at-arms** [men′ət·ärmz′] A soldier, especially a heavily armed soldier of medieval times who rode horseback.

man·a·tee [man′ə·tē′] *n.* A sluggish, clumsy mammal that lives off Florida and in the Gulf of Mexico. It has flippers, a broad flat tail, and eats only plants.

Man·ches·ter [man′ches·tər] *n.* **1** A city in NW England. **2** A city in southern New Hampshire.

Manatee, about 10 ft. long

Man·chu [man·choō′ or man′choō] *n.* **1** A member of a people from Manchuria that con-

quered China. They ruled it from 1644 to 1912. **2** The language of this people.

Man·chu·ri·a [man·choor′ē·ə] *n.* A region in NE China. — **Man·chu′ri·an** *adj., n.*

man·da·rin [man′də·rin] *n.* **1** A member of any of nine grades of public officials who served the emperors of China until 1912. **2** (*written* **Mandarin**) The most widespread dialect of the Chinese language. **3** A tangerine.

man·date [man′dāt *or* man′dit] *n.* **1** A formal, usually written command from someone in authority. **2** In politics, the will of the voters as expressed in an election.

man·da·to·ry [man′də·tôr′ē] *adj.* Demanded or required by custom, duty, someone in authority, etc.

man·di·ble [man′də·bəl] *n.* **1** The lower jawbone. **2** Either the upper or lower part of a bird's beak or an insect's jaws.

man·do·lin [man′də·lin *or* man′də·lin′] *n.* A musical instrument with a pear-shaped body and eight to twelve metal strings.

man·drake [man′·drāk] *n.* A plant related to belladonna, having roots sometimes resembling the human form.

man·drill [man′dril] *n.* A powerful baboon of West Africa, having strong teeth and bright scarlet and blue patches on the face and rump.

Mandolin

mane [mān] *n.* The long hair growing on and about the neck of some animals, as the horse and lion.

ma·neu·ver [mə·n(y)oō′vər] **1** *n.* A planned movement or action, as of troops or warships. **2** *v.* To put (troops, warships, etc.) through a maneuver or maneuvers. **3** *n.* Any skillful move or action. **4** *v.* To use planned moves skillfully. **5** *v.* To force or trick by skillful moves.

man·ful [man′fəl] *adj.* Brave and resolute; manly. — **man′ful·ly** *adv.*

man·ga·nese [mang′gə·nēs *or* mang′gə·nēz] *n.* A grayish white, hard, but very brittle metallic element, used in various alloys.

mange [mānj] *n.* A skin disease of animals marked by itching and loss of hair.

man·ger [mān′jər] *n.* A trough or box for feeding horses or cattle.

man·gle¹ [mang′gəl] *v.* **man·gled, man·gling 1** To tear or disfigure by cutting, bruising, crushing, etc.: Our dog *mangled* the neighbor's cat in a fight. **2** To mar or ruin; spoil; botch: to *mangle* one's part in a play.

man·gle² [mang′gəl] *n., v.* **man·gled, man·gling 1** *n.* A machine for smoothing and pressing fabrics by passing them between rollers. **2** *v.* To smooth with a mangle: to *mangle* sheets.

M

man·go [mang′gō] *n.*, *pl.* **man·goes** or **man·gos** 1 A juicy tropical fruit having a slightly acid taste. 2 The tree it grows on.

man·grove [mang′grōv] *n.* An evergreen tree or shrub of warm, marshy regions, having thick, leathery leaves and branches that take root and form a dense tangle of new growths.

man·gy [mān′jē] *adj.* **man·gi·er, man·gi·est** 1 Having mange: a *mangy* animal. 2 Dirty; shabby: a *mangy* tramp. — **man′gi·ness** *n.*

man·han·dle [man′han′dəl] *v.* **man·han·dled, man·han·dling** To handle with rough force.

Man·hat·tan [man·hat′ən] *n.* An island in the Hudson River. It is a borough of New York City.

man·hole [man′hōl] *n.* A usually circular and covered opening by which a man may enter a sewer, boiler, etc.

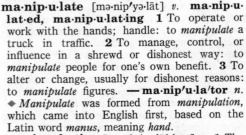
MEN AT WORK

Manhole

man·hood [man′hŏŏd] *n.* 1 The condition or the time of being a man. 2 Manly qualities, as physical strength or bravery. 3 Men as a group.

ma·ni·a [mā′nē·ə *or* mān′yə] *n.* 1 A mental disorder marked by excessive excitement, sometimes violence, and often swift changes of mood. 2 An exaggerated interest, desire, or enthusiasm: She has a *mania* for parties.

ma·ni·ac [mā′nē·ak] 1 *n.* A person who is violently insane; madman. 2 *adj.* Maniacal.

ma·ni·a·cal [mə·nī′ə·kəl] *adj.* 1 Violently insane; mad. 2 Suggesting madness or insanity: a *maniacal* laugh. — **ma·ni′a·cal·ly** *adv.*

man·ic-de·pres·sive [man′ik-di·pres′iv] 1 *adj.* Having to do with a mental illness in which periods of depression alternate with periods of excitement. 2 *n.* A person suffering from this illness.

man·i·cure [man′ə·kyŏŏr] *n.*, *v.* **man·i·cured, man·i·cur·ing** 1 *n.* The care of the hands and fingernails. 2 *v.* To take care of (the hands and fingernails). — **man′i·cur′ist** *n.*

man·i·fest [man′ə·fest] 1 *adj.* Easy to see or understand; evident: a *manifest* error. 2 *v.* To make apparent; reveal; show: to *manifest* a desire. 3 *n.* A list, as of cargo or passengers, for a ship or airplane.

man·i·fes·ta·tion [man′ə·fes·tā′shən] *n.* 1 A display, show, or demonstration: He gave no *manifestation* of his joy. 2 Something that manifests or shows: Tears are a *manifestation* of sorrow.

man·i·fes·to [man′ə·fes′tō] *n.*, *pl.* **man·i·fes·toes** or **man·i·fes·tos** An official statement or explanation of principles, plans, motives, etc., usually by a government or political group.

man·i·fold [man′ə·fōld] 1 *adj.* Having many forms, kinds, or types; varied: *manifold* tasks. 2 *adj.* Having many parts or features: the *manifold* themes in a novel. 3 *v.* To make more than one copy of, as with carbon paper. 4 *n.* A copy made in this way. 5 *n.* A pipe having several openings, so as to connect it with other pipes, etc.

man·i·kin [man′ə·kin] *n.* 1 A model of the human body used for demonstrating anatomy. 2 A little man; dwarf. 3 Another spelling of MANNEQUIN.

Manikin

Ma·nil·a [mə·nil′ə] *n.* A port city on sw Luzon; former capital of the Philippines.

Manila hemp The tough, inner fiber of a plant related to the banana, much used in making ropes, cords, etc.

Manila paper A heavy, brown paper made from Manila hemp and similar plant fibers. It is used for making wrapping paper, envelopes, etc.

man·i·oc [man′ē·ok] *n.* Another name for CASSAVA, a tropical plant.

ma·nip·u·late [mə·nip′yə·lāt] *v.* **ma·nip·u·lat·ed, ma·nip·u·lat·ing** 1 To operate or work with the hands; handle: to *manipulate* a truck in traffic. 2 To manage, control, or influence in a shrewd or dishonest way: to *manipulate* people for one's own benefit. 3 To alter or change, usually for dishonest reasons: to *manipulate* figures. — **ma·nip′u·la′tor** *n.*
◆ *Manipulate* was formed from *manipulation*, which came into English first, based on the Latin word *manus*, meaning *hand*.

ma·nip·u·la·tion [mə·nip′yə·lā′shən] *n.* 1 The act of manipulating. 2 The condition of being manipulated. 3 An instance or example of manipulating: a dishonest *manipulation* of the figures.

Man·i·to·ba [man′ə·tō′bə] *n.* A province in central Canada.

man·kind *n.* 1 [man′kīnd *or* man′kīnd′] The whole human race; every human being. 2 [man′kīnd] Men as a group, as distinguished from women.

man·ly [man′lē] *adj.* **man·li·er, man·li·est** 1 Having the qualities and virtues a man should have, as courage, determination, honesty, etc. 2 Having to do with or appropriate for a man: a *manly* voice. — **man′li·ness** *n.*

man-made [man′mād′] *adj.* Produced by man rather than by nature.

man·na [man′ə] *n.* 1 In the Bible, the food miraculously given to the Israelites in the wilderness as they fled from Egypt. **2** Any unexpected help or gift.

man·ne·quin [man'ə·kin] *n.* **1** A life-sized model of a complete or partial human figure used for cutting, fitting, or displaying garments. **2** A woman who models clothing; model.

man·ner [man'ər] *n.* **1** A way of doing, being done, or occurring: Fold it in this *manner*. **2** A way of behaving: a cheerful *manner*. **3** (*pl.*) Behavior judged by rules of politeness: good *manners*. **4** (*pl.*) Polite behavior: He has no *manners*. **5** (*pl.*) Social customs. **6** Kind; sort: What *manner* of creature is this?

man·nered [man'ərd] *adj.* **1** Having (a certain kind of) manner or manners: often used in combination, as in *mild-mannered*. **2** Having mannerisms in writing, speaking, etc.

man·ner·ism [man'ər·iz'əm] *n.* **1** An excessive or artificial use of a special manner or style: His writing has many *mannerisms*. **2** A personal habit, as of speech or behavior.

man·ner·ly [man'ər·lē] **1** *adj.* Having good manners; polite. **2** *adv.* With good manners; politely.

man·nish [man'ish] *adj.* Resembling, characteristic of, or suitable to a man; masculine: said about women: Susie had a *mannish* way of walking.

ma·noeu·ver [mə·n(y)ōō'vər] *n., v.* Another spelling of MANEUVER. ¶2

man-of-war [man'ə(v)·wôr'] *n., pl.* **men-of-war** [men'ə(v)·wôr'] An armed ship of any recognized navy; a warship.

ma·nom·e·ter [mə·nom'ə·tər] *n.* An instrument used to measure the pressure of a fluid.

man·or [man'ər] *n.* **1** In Europe of the Middle Ages, an estate which belonged to a lord and was partly divided among peasants who paid for the use of the land in money, goods, or labor. **2** The house found on a manor; a mansion.

ma·no·ri·al [mə·nôr'ē·əl] *adj.* Of, like, or having to do with a manor.

man·sard [man'särd] *n.* **1** A four-sided roof having two different slopes on each of the four sides. **2** *adj. use:* a *mansard* roof.

manse [mans] *n.* A clergyman's house; parsonage.

man·ser·vant [man'sûr'vənt] *n., pl.* **men·ser·vants** [men'sûr'vənts] An adult male servant.

Mansard roof

man·sion [man'shən] *n.* A large and impressive house, as of a wealthy person or family.

man·slaugh·ter [man'slô'tər] *n.* The killing of a human being unlawfully but without malice, as in an automobile accident.

man·tel [man'təl] *n.* **1** The shelf above a fireplace. **2** The wood, brick, stone, etc., that surrounds and decorates a fireplace.

man·tel·piece [man'təl·pēs'] *n.* Another name for MANTEL.

man·tis [man'tis] *n.* An insect with a long body and swiveling head, that folds its forelegs as if in prayer. It feeds on other insects.

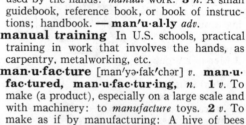
Praying mantis, 3–4 in. long

man·tle [man'təl] *n., v.* **man·tled, man·tling 1** *n.* A loose and usually sleeveless garment worn over other garments; a cloak. **2** *n.* Anything that clothes, covers, or conceals: a *mantle* of ice. **3** *v.* To cover with or as if with a mantle; conceal. **4** *n.* A cylindrical device made of a special, screen-like material that glows when a gas flame is lit inside of it. **5** *v.* To blush.

man·u·al [man'yōō·əl] **1** *adj.* Of or having to do with the hands. **2** *adj.* Done, operated, or used by the hands: *manual* work. **3** *n.* A small guidebook, reference book, or book of instructions; handbook. **— man'u·al·ly** *adv.*

manual training In U.S. schools, practical training in work that involves the hands, as carpentry, metalworking, etc.

man·u·fac·ture [man'yə·fak'chər] *v.* **man·u·fac·tured, man·u·fac·tur·ing,** *n.* **1** *v.* To make (a product), especially on a large scale and with machinery: to *manufacture* toys. **2** *v.* To make as if by manufacturing: A hive of bees *manufactures* honey. **3** *n.* The act of manufacturing. **4** *n.* Something that is manufactured. **5** *v.* To make up; invent: to *manufacture* a story. **— man'u·fac'tur·er** *n.*

ma·nure [mə·n(y)ōōr'] *n., v.* **ma·nured, ma·nur·ing 1** *n.* Any substance used to fertilize soils, as dung. **2** *v.* To apply manure to.

man·u·script [man'yə·skript] *n.* A book, article, document, etc., written by hand or with a typewriter: The writer sent his *manuscript* to a publisher.

man·y [men'ē] *adj.* **more, most,** *n., pron.* **1** *adj.* Adding up to a large number; numerous: There are *many* children in the school. **2** *n., pron.* A large number: *Many* applied for the job. **3** *n.* The majority of people; masses: He was a hero to the *many*. **— a good many** (*used with plural verb*) A rather large number: *A good many* of our high school students go on to college.

Ma·o·ri [mou'rē *or* mä'ō·rē] *n., pl.* **Ma·o·ris 1** One of an aboriginal light brown people of New Zealand. **2** The language of these people.

Mao Tse-tung [mou' dzu'dŏŏng], born 1893, Chinese Communist leader.

map [map] *n., v.* **mapped, map·ping 1** *n.* A drawing or representation, usually on a flat surface, of any region, as of a country, city, etc. **2** *n.* A representation of the sky, showing the location of the stars, planets, etc. **3** *v.* To make a map of. **4** *v.* To plan in detail: We *mapped* out our vacation.

ma·ple [mā′pəl] *n.* **1** Any of various trees of north temperate regions, having hard wood used for flooring and furniture. One variety yields sugar. **2** The light-colored wood of any of these trees. **3** The flavor of the sap of the maple that yields sugar.

maple sugar Sugar made from the sap of a variety of the maple.

maple syrup The syrup of the sugar maple after it has been boiled down and refined.

mar [mär] *v.* **marred, mar·ring** To do harm or injury to; to hurt the appearance of; damage: to *mar* furniture.

Mar. Abbreviation of MARCH.

ma·ra·ca [mə·rä′kə] *n.* A musical instrument made of a gourd or gourd-shaped rattle with pebbles in it.

mar·a·schi·no cherry [mar′ə·skē′·nō *or* mar′ə·shē′nō] A cherry preserved in a sweet syrup and used in drinks, salads, and desserts.

Maracas

Mar·a·thon [mar′ə·thon] *n.* **1** A plain near Athens, Greece; scene of battle in which the Athenians defeated the Persians in 490 B.C. **2** (*written* **marathon**) A foot race of 26 miles, 385 yards, a feature of the Olympic Games: so called from a messenger's run from Marathon to Athens to announce the victory over the Persians. **3** (*written* **marathon**) Any contest of endurance.

ma·raud [mə·rôd′] *v.* **1** To roam or raid in search of plunder: Danes *marauded* the English coast. **2** *adj. use:* a vicious, *marauding* tiger. **— ma·raud′er** *n.*

mar·ble [mär′bəl] *n., adj., v.* **mar·bled, mar·bling** **1** *n.* A hard, partly crystallized limestone occurring in many colors, used for building, sculpture, etc. **2** *adj. use:* a *marble* statue. **3** *adj.* Like marble as to coldness, hardness, lack of feeling, etc. **4** *n.* A small ball of glass, stone, etc. **5** *n.* (*pl.*) A boys' game played with small balls of glass, etc. **6** *v.* To color or streak in imitation of marble, as book edges.

mar·cel [mär·sel′] *v.* **mar·celled, mar·cel·ling**, *n.* **1** *v.* To arrange the hair in even, continuous waves with a special machine. **2** *n.* This hair style.

march[1] [märch] **1** *v.* To walk with even, rhythmic steps, as a soldier. **2** *n.* A marching, as of soldiers. **3** *n.* The distance passed over in marching. **4** *v.* To walk in a solemn or dignified way, as a bride. **5** *v.* To cause to march. **6** *n.* A musical composition with a strong, steady beat to march to. **7** *v.* To advance or progress steadily: Science *marches* on. **8** *n.* Onward

progress or advance. **— steal a march on** To win an advantage over, especially secretly or slyly. **— mar′cher** *n.*

march[2] [märch] *n.* A region lying along a boundary line; border; frontier.

March [märch] *n.* The third month of the year, having 31 days.

mar·chion·ess [mär′shən·is] *n. British* **1** The wife or widow of a marquis. **2** A woman with a rank equal to that of a marquis.

Mar·co·ni [mär·kō′nē], **Guglielmo,** 1874–1937, Italian inventor who developed the wireless telegraph.

Mar·co Po·lo [mär′kō pō′lō] See POLO, MARCO.

Mar·di gras [mär′dē grä′] The Tuesday before Ash Wednesday, the first day of Lent. It is celebrated as a carnival in some cities.

mare [mâr] *n.* The female of the horse and other animals like it, as the donkey.

mar·ga·rine [mär′jə·rin] *n.* A substitute for butter, made of vegetable oils and skim milk.

mar·gin [mär′jin] *n.* **1** The blank part of a page around the written or printed text. **2** An edge or border. **3** An extra amount or allowance of something, beyond what is needed: to win by a safe *margin*.

mar·gi·nal [mär′jə·nəl] *adj.* **1** Of, having to do with, or near a margin. **2** Written or printed on a margin. **3** At the point below which something stops being worth using or doing.

mar·gue·rite [mär′gə·rēt′] *n.* Any of several flowers, especially a kind of daisy.

Ma·rie An·toi·nette [mə·rē′ än·twä·net′], 1755–1793, queen of France, guillotined during the French Revolution.

mar·i·gold [mar′ə·gōld] *n.* A plant with golden yellow flowers that have a pungent smell.

mar·i·jua·na or **mar·i·hua·na** [mar′ə·wä′nə] *n.* The dried leaves and flower tops of the hemp plant, which contain a narcotic.

ma·rim·ba [mə·rim′bə] *n.* A kind of xylophone.

ma·ri·na [mə·rē′nə] *n.* A place where small boats and yachts can dock, get supplies, etc.

mar·i·nade [mar′ə·nād′] *n.* A brine or pickle sometimes flavored with wine, oil, spices, etc., in which meat and fish are soaked before cooking, to improve their flavor.

mar·i·nate [mar′ə·nāt] *v.* **mar·i·nat·ed, mar·i·nat·ing** To soak (meat, fish, etc.) in brine, spiced vinegar and oil, wine, or the like.

ma·rine [mə·rēn′] **1** *adj.* Of, having to do with, formed by, or found in the sea: *marine* fish; *marine* salt. **2** *adj.* Having to do with shipping or sailing; maritime: *marine* laws. **3** *adj.* Used at sea: a *marine* compass. **4** *n.* (*sometimes written* **Marine**) A member of the Marine Corps.

Marine Corps A service within the U.S. Navy department having combat troops, air forces, etc.

mar·i·ner [mar′ə·nər] *n.* A sailor; seaman.

---

add, āce, câre, pälm;   end, ēqual;   it, īce;   odd, ōpen, ôrder;   took, pool;   up, bûrn;

ə = a in *above*, e in *sicken*, i in *possible*, o in *melon*, u in *circus*;   yoo = u in *fuse*;   oil;   pout;

check; ring; thin; this; zh in *vision*.   For ¶ reference, see page 64 · HOW TO

mar·i·o·nette [mar′ē·ə·net′] *n.* A jointed figure or doll made to move by pulling strings, used in shows on small stages; puppet.

mar·i·tal [mar′ə·təl] *adj.* Of or having to do with marriage or the married state.

mar·i·time [mar′ə·tīm] *adj.* **1** Located on or near the sea. **2** Of or having to do with the sea, its shipping, trade, laws, etc.

Maritime Provinces New Brunswick, Nova Scotia, and Prince Edward Island, on the Atlantic coast of Canada.

mar·jo·ram [mär′jər·əm] *n.* An herb related to mint, used as a seasoning in cooking.

Marionette

mark¹ [märk] **1** *n.* A line, spot, stain, etc., visible on a surface. **2** *v.* To make a mark or marks on: to *mark* the walls with chalk. **3** *n.* A symbol, seal, or label; trademark. **4** *v.* To write or draw: He *marks* his initials on all his books. **5** *n.* A sign made by a person who cannot write his name. **6** *n.* A grade; rating: She got high *marks* in school. **7** *v.* To give a grade or rating to. **8** *n.* A written or printed symbol: a punctuation *mark.* **9** *n.* A sign that shows a quality or trait: Rosy cheeks are a *mark* of health. **10** *v.* To set apart; distinguish: a year *marked* by great events. **11** *n.* A target: His arrow split the thin sapling chosen as a *mark.* **12** *n.* A line, point, etc., that shows position: The flood reached this *mark.* **13** *v.* To show by making a mark or marks: *Mark* all the rivers in New York on this map. **14** *n.* An object, point, sign, etc., that serves to guide or indicate. **15** *v.* To make known or clear: His strong build *marks* him as an athlete. **16** *n.* Notice; attention: This play is worthy of *mark.* **17** *v.* To pay attention to: *Mark* his warning! **18** *n.* A standard of quality or performance: His behavior in school was below the *mark.* **19** *n.* Influence: Shakespeare left his *mark* on the English language. **20** *n.* Fame; distinction: an artist of *mark.* **21** *n.* The starting line of a race or contest. **— hit the mark 1** To be accurate. **2** To reach one's goal; be successful. **— make one's mark** To achieve fame and success. **— mark down 1** To note in writing. **2** To put a lower price on, as for a sale. **— mark off** or **mark out** To mark the boundaries of, as by drawing lines. **— mark time 1** To keep time by moving the feet as in marching, but without going forward. **2** To pass time without making any progress. **— mark up 1** To make marks on. **2** To raise the price of. **— miss the mark 1** To fail in something. **2** To be incorrect.

mark² [märk] *n.* The basic unit of money in Germany.

Mark [märk] *n.* **1** A Christian evangelist and saint who wrote the second Gospel of the New Testament. **2** The second Gospel of the New Testament.

marked [märkt] *adj.* **1** Very obvious; evident: with *marked* disgust. **2** Singled out as an object of suspicion, vengeance, etc.: a *marked* man. **3** Having a mark or marks. **— mark·ed·ly** [mär′ked·lē] *adv.*

mark·er [mär′kər] *n.* **1** Something that marks, as a bookmark, a milestone, or a gravestone. **2** A person who marks, as one who gives grades, a scorekeeper, etc.

mar·ket [mär′kit] **1** *n.* A coming together of people for buying and selling. **2** *n.* The people who come together in this way. **3** *n.* A place where many kinds of goods are sold, especially a space outdoors or a building with stalls. **4** *n.* A store where food is sold. **5** *v.* To buy groceries, meat, etc., in a market. **6** *n.* A country or region where one can buy or sell: the Canadian *market.* **7** *n.* A special group of people who are buyers: the college *market.* **8** *n.* A demand: There is no *market* for heavy woolens in the summer. **9** *v.* To sell: Farmers *market* their crops. **— be in the market for** To want or seek to buy. **— put on the market** To offer for sale.

mar·ket·a·ble [mär′kit·ə·bəl] *adj.* **1** Fit to be put on sale in a market. **2** In demand by buyers. **— mar·ket·a·bil·i·ty** [mär′kit·ə·bil′ə·tē] *n.*

market place A place where goods are bought and sold, especially an open space or a hall with stalls, counters, etc.

mark·ing [mär′king] *n.* **1** A mark. **2** (*often pl.*) The color pattern of a bird's feathers, an animal's fur, etc.

marks·man [märks′mən] *n., pl.* **marks·men** [märks′mən] A person who is good at hitting a target, as with a weapon. **— marks′man·ship** *n.*

Mark Twain [märk twān] See TWAIN, MARK.

marl [märl] *n.* Crumbly soil containing clay and calcium carbonate, used as fertilizer.

mar·lin [mär′lin] *n.* Any of several large game fishes of the Atlantic and Pacific Oceans, related to the sailfish.

mar·line·spike or **mar·lin·spike** [mär′lin·spīk′] *n.* A sharp-pointed iron tool used for separating strands of rope or wire, as in splicing.

mar·ma·lade [mär′mə·lād] *n.* A jam, usually of citrus fruits, with pieces of peel in it.

Mar·ma·ra [mär′mə·rə], **Sea of** A sea between Europe and Asia leading to the Aegean Sea and to the Black Sea.

mar·mo·set [mär′-mə·zet] *n.* A small monkey of South and Central America, with soft, woolly hair and a long tail.

mar·mot [mär′mət] *n.* Any of various rodents, as the woodchuck.

ma·roon¹ [mə·rōōn′] *v.* **1** To put ashore and leave on a barren island or coast. **2** To desert or leave helpless.

ma·roon² [mə·rōōn′] *n., adj.* Dull, dark red.

mar·quee [mär·kē′] *n.* A canopy, usually made of metal, projecting over the entrance of a theater, hotel, etc.

Marquee

mar·quess [mär′-kwis] *n. British* Another spelling of MAR-QUIS.

Mar·quette [mär·ket′], **Jacques,** 1637–1675, French Jesuit missionary who explored the Mississippi River. He was called Père (Father) Marquette.

mar·quis [mär′kwis *or* mär·kē′] *n.* The title of a nobleman next in rank below a duke.

mar·quise [mär·kēz′] *n.* **1** The wife or widow of a marquis. **2** A woman with the rank of a marquis.

mar·qui·sette [mär′ki·zet′ *or* mär′kwi·zet′] *n.* A loosely woven fabric of cotton, silk, nylon, etc., used especially for curtains.

mar·riage [mar′ij] *n.* **1** The act of marrying. **2** The ceremony of marrying; a wedding. **3** The condition of being married; wedlock.

mar·riage·a·ble [mar′ij·ə·bəl] *adj.* Fitted or suitable for marriage: a *marriageable* girl.

mar·ried [mar′ēd] *adj.* **1** Having a husband or wife. **2** United by marriage: a *married* couple. **3** Of or having to do with marriage or married persons.

mar·row [mar′ō] *n.* **1** A soft, spongy substance contained in the hollow interiors of many bones. **2** The main substance or essence; pith: the *marrow* of a story.

marrow

mar·ry [mar′ē] *v.* **mar·ried, mar·ry·ing 1** To accept as husband or wife; take in marriage: My sister *married* her childhood sweetheart. **2** To join as husband and wife in marriage: A clergyman *married* them. **3** To give in marriage: The Joneses were happy to *marry* off their eldest daughter. **4** To take a husband or wife: Mr. Thomas *married* late in life. **5** To join or unite closely: Fact and fiction have been *married* in this book.

Mars [märz] *n.* **1** In Roman myths, the god of war. His Greek name was Ares. **2** A planet of the solar system, the seventh in size and the fourth in distance from the sun.

Mar·seil·laise [mär′sə·lāz′ *or* mär·sā·yez′] *n.* The national anthem of France.

Mar·seille *or* **Mar·seilles** [mär·sā′] *n.* A seaport in SE France.

marsh [märsh] *n.* An area of low, wet land; swamp; bog. **— marsh′y** *adj.*

mar·shal [mär′shəl] *n., v.* **mar·shaled** or

mar·shalled, mar·shal·ing *or* **mar·shal·ling 1** *n.* In some foreign countries, a military officer of very high rank. **2** *n.* An officer of the Federal courts, having duties like those of a sheriff. **3** *n.* In some cities, the chief of the police or fire department. **4** *n.* An officer who organizes and is in charge of parades and other ceremonies. **5** *v.* To lead or usher. **6** *v.* To arrange or draw up, as troops for battle. **7** *v.* To arrange in order, as facts, thoughts, etc. ◆ A *marshal* did not always refer to someone so high up in the world. The word comes from two old German words meaning *horse servant*, and actually once meant a man in charge of stables.

Mar·shall [mär′shəl], **George Catlett,** 1880–1959, U.S. general and diplomat, secretary of state, 1947–1949.

Mar·shall [mär′shəl], **John,** 1755–1835, chief justice of the Supreme Court, 1801–1835.

marsh gas Methane, a gas found in marshes.

marsh·mal·low [märsh′mel′ō] *n.* A white, spongy candy made of starch, gelatin, sugar, etc., and coated with powdered sugar.

mar·su·pi·al [mär·soo′pē·əl] *n.* Any of various animals, the females of which carry their undeveloped young in a pouch. The opossum, the wombat, and the kangaroo are marsupials. **— mar·su′pi·an** *adj., n.*

mart [märt] *n.* A place where goods are bought and sold; market.

mar·ten [mär′tən] *n., pl.* **mar·ten** *or* **mar·tens 1** An animal like a weasel. **2** Its valuable, dark brown fur.

Mar·tha [mär′thə] *n.* In the Bible, the sister of Lazarus and Mary.

mar·tial [mär′shəl] *adj.* **1** Of or having to do with war or military life. **2** Liking or experienced in war; warlike. **— mar′tial·ly** *adv.* ◆ *Martial* comes from *Mars*, the god of war.

Marten, about 18 in. long

martial law Temporary rule by the military instead of by civilian authorities, as during a war or crisis.

Mar·tian [mär′shən] **1** *adj.* Of or having to do with the planet Mars. **2** *n.* One of the supposed inhabitants of Mars.

mar·tin [mär′tən] *n.* A bird related to the swallow, especially a North American species having a bluish black body and a square or forked tail.

mar·ti·net [mär′tə·net′] *n.* A person who always enforces rules strictly and exactly, as some army officers.

Mar·ti·nique [mär′ti·nēk′] *n.* A French island of the West Indies.

mar·tyr [mär′tər] **1** *n.* A person who accepts death or torture rather than give up his religion or beliefs. **2** *n.* A person who suffers a great deal. **3** *v.* To torture, persecute, or kill for not giving up one's beliefs, religion, etc.

mar·tyr·dom [mär′tər·dəm] *n.* **1** The sufferings of a martyr. **2** Long, terrible suffering.

mar·vel [mär′vəl] *v.* **mar·veled** or **mar·velled, mar·vel·ing** or **mar·vel·ling,** *n.* **1** *v.* To be astonished or awestruck; wonder. **2** *n.* Something that excites wonder.

mar·vel·ous or **mar·vel·lous** [mär′vəl·əs] *adj.* **1** Causing astonishment and wonder; amazing. **2** *informal* Very good; excellent. **—mar′·vel·ous·ly** or **mar′vel·lous·ly** *adv.*

Marx [märks], **Karl,** 1818–1883, German philosopher who wrote about socialism.

Mar·y [mâr′ē] *n.* **1** In the Bible, the mother of Jesus, often called the Virgin Mary. **2** In the Bible, the sister of Lazarus and Martha.

Mar·y·land [mâr′i·lənd *or* mer′i·lənd] *n.* A state in the eastern U.S.

Mary Mag·da·lene [mag′də·lin *or* mag′də·lēn] In the Bible, a repentant sinner whom Jesus forgave.

Mary, Queen of Scots, 1542–1587, queen of Scotland, 1542–1567, beheaded by the orders of Queen Elizabeth I.

Ma·sac·cio [mä·sät′chō], 1401–1429?, Italian painter.

mas·car·a [mas·kar′ə] *n.* A cosmetic used to color the eyelashes and eyebrows.

mas·cot [mas′kot] *n.* A person, animal, or thing thought to bring good luck by its presence.

mas·cu·line [mas′kyə·lin] *adj.* **1** Of or having to do with men; male. **2** Of, related to, like, or fit for men or boys. **3** In grammar, of the gender to which words denoting males belong. **—mas·cu·lin·i·ty** [mas′kyə·lin′ə·tē] *n.*

mash [mash] **1** *n.* A soft, pulpy mixture or mass. **2** *v.* To crush into a mash. **3** *n.* A mixture of meal or bran and water fed to horses and cattle. **4** *n.* Crushed grain or malt steeped in hot water and used in making beer.

mask [mask] **1** *n.* A covering used to hide or protect all or part of the face: a fencing *mask.* **2** *n.* A copy of a person's face, usually of plaster. **3** *v.* To put on a mask: We *mask* ourselves on Halloween. **4** *n.* Something that hides or conceals: a *mask* of kindness. **5** *v.* To hide or conceal; disguise: He *masked* his anger with a grin.

Mask

ma·son [mā′sən] *n.* A person who is skilled in building with stone, brick, concrete, etc.

Ma·son [mā′sən] *n.* A Freemason.

Ma·son-Dix·on line [mā′sən·dik′sən] The boundary between Pennsylvania and Maryland, thought of as dividing the North from the South.

ma·son·ic [mə·son′ik] *adj.* **1** Of or having to do with masons or masonry. **2** (*usually written* **Masonic**) Of or related to the Freemasons.

ma·son·ry [mā′sən·rē] *n., pl.* **ma·son·ries 1** The art or work of a mason. **2** A thing of stone, brick, etc., built by a mason.

masque [mask] *n.* **1** An entertainment with music, costumes, dancing, etc., popular in the 16th and 17th centuries. **2** A masquerade (def. 1).

mas·quer·ade [mas′kə·rād′] *n., v.* **mas·quer·ad·ed, mas·quer·ad·ing 1** *n.* A party at which the guests wear masks and fancy costumes. **2** *n.* A costume or disguise for such a party. **3** *v.* To take part in a masquerade. **4** *n.* A false show; pretense: a *masquerade* of wealth. **5** *v.* To disguise oneself; pose: The girl *masqueraded* as a boy. **—mas′quer·ad′er** *n.*

mass [mas] **1** *n.* A body of matter with no definite shape or size: a *mass* of clay. **2** *n.* A large number or amount; great quantity: a *mass* of evidence. **3** *v.* To form into a mass. **4** *n.* The main or greater part: the *mass* of voters. **5** *adj.* Of or having to do with a large number of persons or things: *mass* education; This news magazine has a *mass* circulation. **6** *adj.* On a large scale: *mass* production of cars. **7** *n.* Great size; volume; bulk: the *mass* of a huge mountain. **8** *n.* The amount of matter in a body as measured by its resistance to change of motion or by the gravitational force it exerts. Mass is independent of weight. **—in the mass** As a whole. **—the masses** Ordinary people as a group.

Mass [mas] *n.* (*sometimes written* **mass**) **1** In the Roman Catholic and some Anglican churches the service at which Holy Communion takes place. **2** Music written for some parts of this service.

Mass. Abbreviation of MASSACHUSETTS.

Mas·sa·chu·setts [mas′ə·chōō′sits] *n.* A state in the NE U.S.

mas·sa·cre [mas′ə·kər] *n., v.* **mas·sa·cred, mas·sa·cring 1** *n.* A brutal, pitiless killing of a large number of people or animals. **2** *v.* To kill or slaughter in large numbers.

mas·sage [mə·säzh′] *n., v.* **mas·saged, mas·sag·ing 1** *n.* A rubbing or kneading of parts of the body to stimulate circulation, relax muscles, etc. **2** *v.* To give a massage to.

mas·sive [mas′iv] *adj.* Large, heavy, or bulky: a *massive* wall. **—mas′sive·ness** *n.*

Mast

mast [mast] *n.* A long pole set upright in a sailing ship to hold up the sails, yards, etc. **—sail before the mast** To serve as a common sailor.

mas·ter [mas′tər] **1** *n.* A person who has control or authority, as over workers, a household, a ship, etc. **2** *v.* To bring under control; defeat: to *master* one's shyness. **3** *n.* A person who is especially gifted or skilled: a *master* of the violin. **4** *adj. use:* a *master* chef. **5** *v.* To become an expert in: to *master* Greek. **6** *n. British* A male teacher. **7** *adj.* Principal; main; controlling: a *master* switch; a *master* copy. **8** *n.* The title of respect given to a young boy: *Master* Edward Smith. **9** *n.* A person who has received an academic degree more advanced than a bachelor's, but less advanced than a doctor's, such as a **Master of Arts** or a **Master of Science.**

mas·ter·ful [mas′tər-fəl] *adj.* **1** Like a master; positive or domineering. **2** Having or showing great skill. **— mas′ter·ful·ly** *adv.*

mas·ter·ly [mas′tər-lē] *adj.* Characteristic of or from a master: a *masterly* performance.

master of ceremonies A person who presides over an entertainment or dinner and introduces the performers or speakers.

mas·ter·piece [mas′tər-pēs′] *n.* **1** Something of outstanding excellence; great achievement. **2** The greatest thing done by its creator: The painting was his *masterpiece.*

mas·ter·y [mas′tər-ē] *n.* **1** The state of being master; control: He tried to gain *mastery* over his shortcomings. **2** Great knowledge or skill: a *mastery* of languages. **3** Victory, as in a contest.

mast·head [mast′hed′] *n.* **1** The top of a mast. **2** The part of a newspaper or magazine that gives the names of the editors, staff, and owners, tells where it is published, etc.

mas·tic [mas′tik] *n.* A gummy resin obtained from certain evergreen trees of the Mediterranean that are related to the cashew. It is used in varnishes and chewing gum, and sometimes as a flavoring agent.

mas·ti·cate [mas′tə-kāt] *v.* **mas·ti·cat·ed, mas·ti·cat·ing** To chew. **— mas′ti·ca′·tion** *n.*

mas·tiff [mas′tif] *n.* A breed of large hunting dog with strong jaws and drooping ears.

mas·to·don [mas′tə-don] *n.* A large, extinct mammal much like the elephant but having differently shaped molar teeth.

mas·toid [mas′toid] *n.* A small, conelike projection of the bone just back of the human ear.

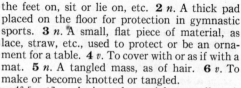
Mastiff, about 30 in. high at shoulder

mat¹ [mat] *n., v.* **mat·ted, mat·ting** **1** *n.* A rough, flat piece of material made of hemp, straw, rope, etc., and used to cover floors, to wipe the feet on, sit or lie on, etc. **2** *n.* A thick pad placed on the floor for protection in gymnastic sports. **3** *n.* A small, flat piece of material, as lace, straw, etc., used to protect or be an ornament for a table. **4** *v.* To cover with or as if with a mat. **5** *n.* A tangled mass, as of hair. **6** *v.* To make or become knotted or tangled.

mat² [mat] *n.* A piece of material, as cardboard, serving as the frame or border of a picture.

mat·a·dor [mat′ə-dôr] *n.* In bullfighting, the man who kills the bull with a sword.

match¹ [mach] *n.* **1** A small, thin piece of wood or cardboard tipped with a substance that catches fire quickly when rubbed against a chemically treated or rough surface. **2** A wick or cord formerly used for firing cannon.

match² [mach] **1** *n.* A person or thing that is like or equal to another: He met his *match* in tennis when he played Ted. **2** *v.* To be like or in agreement with: His looks *match* his mood. **3** *n.* Either of two persons or things that go with each other: Your hat is a good *match* for my coat. **4** *n.* A suitable or fit pair: The hat and coat are a good *match.* **5** *v.* To be alike or go with: The colors of the hat and coat *match.* **6** *v.* To make or select as equals or as fit to go together: to *match* a hat and coat. **7** *n.* A game or contest: a boxing *match.* **8** *v.* To set against one another in a game or contest: to *match* two boxers. **9** *v.* To equal, as in a contest. **10** *v.* To test or oppose: They *matched* wits in a guessing game. **11** *n.* A marriage or an agreement to marry: a *match* between a princess and a commoner. **12** *n.* A possible marriage partner: Sue is a good *match* for my brother. **13** *v.* To marry.

match·less [mach′lis] *adj.* Having no match or equal; peerless. **— match′less·ly** *adv.*

match·lock [mach′lok′] *n.* An old-fashioned type of musket, fired by igniting the powder with a slow-burning wick or match.

mate [māt] *n., v.* **mat·ed, mat·ing** **1** *n.* One of a pair: a robin and its *mate*; a shoe and its *mate.* **2** *v.* To join or match closely together; pair. **3** *n.* A husband or wife. **4** *v.* To marry. **5** *v.* To join or be joined for breeding, as animals. **6** *n.* A companion; comrade. **7** *n.* An officer of a merchant ship ranking next below the captain. **8** *n.* A petty officer in the navy.

ma·té [mä′tā *or* mat′ā] *n.* A plant related to the holly. It grows in South America and its leaves are used to make a beverage like tea.

ma·te·ri·al [mə-tir′ē-əl] **1** *n.* The stuff or substance of which a thing is made. **2** *adj.* Of or having to do with matter: the *material* universe. **3** *n.* Cloth or fabric. **4** *adj.* Of or having to do with the body or its needs: *material* well-being. **5** *adj.* Of or having to do with physical or worldly rather than spiritual things. **6** *adj.* Important or pertinent: There are *material* differences between cats and dogs.

add, āce, câre, pälm;   end, ēqual;   it, īce;   odd, ōpen, ôrder;   tŏŏk, pōōl;   up, bûrn;
ə = a in *above*, e in *sicken*, i in *possible*, o in *melon*, u in *circus*;   yōō = u in *fuse*;   oil;   pout;
check;   ring;   thin;   this;   zh in *vision*.   For ¶ reference, see page 64 · HOW TO

ma·te·ri·al·ism [mə·tir′ē·əl·iz′əm] *n.* **1** Too much regard for the material or physical side of life, rather than for the mind or the spirit. **2** The philosophical idea that nothing exists except matter and everything can be explained in terms of physical laws. **—ma·te′ri·al·ist** *n.* **—ma·te′ri·al·is′tic** *adj.*

ma·te·ri·al·ize [mə·tir′ē·əl·īz′] *v.* **ma·te·ri·al·ized, ma·te·ri·al·iz·ing** **1** To make or become material or actual; to be carried out: My plans for a vacation did not *materialize*. **2** To take on visible form; appear: The mountain top *materialized* from behind the clouds. **3** To appear or cause to appear, as a spirit. **—ma·te′ri·al·i·za′tion** *n.* ¶3

ma·te·ri·al·ly [mə·tir′ē·əl·ē] *adv.* **1** In an important way or to a large degree: It did not affect us *materially*. **2** With regard to what is physical or material.

ma·te·ri·el or **ma·té·ri·el** [mə·tir′ē·el′] *n.* The equipment and supplies of an army.

ma·ter·nal [mə·tûr′nəl] *adj.* **1** Of or having to do with a mother; motherly. **2** Related through or inherited from one's mother: *maternal* grandparents. **—ma·ter′nal·ly** *adv.* ◆ *Maternal* and *matrimony* both are based on the Latin word *mater*, meaning *a mother*.

ma·ter·ni·ty [mə·tûr′nə·tē] *n.* The state of being a mother; motherhood.

math [math] *n. informal* Mathematics. ◆ *Math* is a shortened or "clipped" form of *mathematics*.

math·e·mat·i·cal [math′ə·mat′i·kəl] *adj.* **1** Of, related to, or like mathematics. **2** Very exact or precise. **—math′e·mat′i·cal·ly** *adv.*

math·e·ma·ti·cian [math′ə·mə·tish′ən] *n.* A person who is an expert in mathematics.

math·e·mat·ics [math′ə·mat′iks] *n.* The science that deals with size, position, form, magnitude, etc., in terms of numbers and symbols that stand for numbers, using operations that are derived in a logical and consistent way. Arithmetic, algebra, geometry, and calculus are branches of mathematics. ◆ See -ICS.

mat·i·nee or **mat·i·née** [mat′ə·nā′] *n.* A performance, as of a play, movie, concert, etc., held in the daytime, usually in the afternoon.

mat·ins [mat′inz] *n.pl.* The prayers that are said in the Roman Catholic church at midnight or dawn and in the Church of England in the morning.

Ma·tisse [ma·tēs′], **Henri**, 1869–1954, French painter.

ma·tri·arch [mā′trē·ärk] *n.* A woman who is the ruler or head of her family, tribe, community, etc. **—ma′tri·ar′chal** *adj.*

ma·tric·u·late [mə·trik′yə·lāt] *v.* **ma·tric·u·lat·ed, ma·tric·u·lat·ing** To enroll as a student, especially in a college or university. **—ma·tric′u·la′tion** *n.*

mat·ri·mo·ni·al [mat′rə·mō′nē·əl] *adj.* Of or having to do with marriage.

mat·ri·mo·ny [mat′rə·mō′nē] *n., pl.* **mat·ri·mo·nies** **1** A being married; marriage. **2** The act or ceremony of marriage. ◆ See MATERNAL.

ma·trix [mā′triks] *n., pl.* **ma·trix·es** or **ma·tri·ces** [mā′trə·sēz] A place in which anything originates, develops, takes shape, or is contained. A mold for casting is a matrix.

ma·tron [mā′trən] *n.* **1** A married woman or widow, especially one no longer young. **2** A woman in charge of others, as at an institution.

ma·tron·ly [mā′trən·lē] *adj.* Of, like, or suitable for a matron.

mat·ted [mat′id] *adj.* **1** Covered with or made from a mat or matting. **2** Tangled or twisted.

mat·ter [mat′ər] **1** *n.* The substance of anything, especially of materially existing things. **2** *n.* Anything physically existing and occupying space, as solids, liquids, or gases. **3** *n.* A specific kind or form of material: organic *matter*. **4** *n.* A subject, event, or situation about which there is concern, feeling, talk, etc. **5** *n.* Importance: It's of no *matter*. **6** *v.* To be of concern or importance; signify: It *matters* little. **7** *n.* An unpleasant or unfortunate condition; trouble: What's the *matter* with you? **8** *n.* The ideas, facts, or meaning of a book, speech, etc., apart from the style. **9** *n.* Anything sent or to be sent by mail: third-class *matter*. **10** *n.* An amount, quantity, or extent: a *matter* of a few dollars. **11** *n.* Pus. **—as a matter of fact** In truth; really. **—for that matter** As far as that goes. **—no matter** **1** It isn't important; never mind. **2** In spite of.

Mat·ter·horn [mat′ər·hôrn] *n.* A mountain in the Alps on the Swiss-Italian border.

mat·ter-of-fact [mat′ər·əv·fakt′] *adj.* Closely sticking to facts; not emotional or imaginative.

Mat·thew [math′yōō] *n.* **1** In the Bible, one of the twelve apostles of Jesus, and a saint. **2** The first book of the New Testament, written by him.

mat·ting [mat′ing] *n.* A fabric of fiber, straw, or other material, used as a floor covering.

mat·tock [mat′ək] *n.* A garden tool, somewhat like a pickax, used for cutting roots, breaking up soil, etc.

mat·tress [mat′rəs] *n.* A large pad made of a strong fabric and filled with cotton, foam rubber, springs, etc., used on a bed.

ma·ture [mə·t(y)oor′ or mə·choor′] *adj., v.* **ma·tured, ma·tur·ing** **1** *adj.* Completely developed, grown, or ripened, as plants, fruit, animals, etc. **2** *v.* To make or

Mattock

become ripe or completely developed. **3** *adj.* Highly developed or advanced in intelligence: a *mature* thinker. **4** *adj.* Fully worked out or perfected: a *mature* scheme. **5** *v.* To perfect or complete. **6** *adj.* Having reached its time limit; due and payable: a *mature* bond. **7** *v.* To become due, as a note or a bond.

ma·tur·i·ty [mə·t(y)o͞or′ə·tē *or* mə·cho͞or′ə·tē] *n.* **1** The condition of being mature or fully developed. **2** The time at which a note, bill, etc., becomes due.

mat·zo [mät′sə] *n., pl.* **mat·zos** A flat piece of unleavened bread eaten during Passover.

maud·lin [môd′lin] *adj.* Tearfully emotional or too sentimental, as from too much liquor.

maul [môl] **1** *n.* A heavy mallet. **2** *v.* To beat and bruise. **3** *v.* To handle roughly.

maun·der [môn′dər] *v.* **1** To talk aimlessly; ramble. **2** To wander idly or in confusion.

Mau·pas·sant [mō·pa·sän′], **Guy de,** 1850–1893, French author.

Mau·ri·ta·ni·a [môr′ə·tā′nē·ə] *n.* A country in western Africa.

mau·so·le·um [mô′sə·lē′əm] *n.* A large tomb.

mauve [mōv] *n., adj.* Purplish rose.

mav·er·ick [mav′ər·ik] *n.* **1** An animal, especially a lost calf, that has not been branded by its owner. **2** *informal* A person who thinks and acts independently. ◆ *Maverick* comes from Samuel *Maverick,* a Texan of the 1800's who did not brand his cattle.

maw [mô] *n.* **1** The jaws, mouth, or gullet of some animals, as the lion. **2** The craw of a bird. **3** The stomach.

mawk·ish [mô′kish] *adj.* **1** Full of sickening sentimentality or false emotion. **2** Nauseating or insipid in taste. **— mawk′ish·ness** *n.*

max·im [mak′sim] *n.* A brief statement of a rule of conduct or a general principle.

max·i·mum [mak′sə·məm] *n., pl.* **max·i·mums** or **max·i·ma** [mak′sə·mə] **1** *n.* The greatest possible quantity, number, degree, etc.: *Two hundred pounds was the maximum the horse could carry.* **2** *n.* The greatest quantity, number, degree, etc., reached or recorded: *The month's maximum was 76°.* **3** *adj.* Greatest; highest possible: *The maximum grade is 100.*

may [mā] *v. Present tense for all subjects* **may,** *past tense* **might** *May* is a helping verb having the following senses: **1** To have permission or be allowed to: *May I go?* **2** To be able to as a consequence: *He died that we might live.* **3** To be possible: *It may snow. May* is also used to express: Desire, prayer, or wish, as in *"May you always be happy."* ◆ See CAN.

May [mā] *n.* The fifth month of the year, having 31 days.

Ma·ya [mä′yə] *n.* **1** A member of a tribe of Indians of southern Mexico and parts of Central America who had an advanced civilization before they were conquered by the Spanish in the 16th century. **2** Their language. **— Ma′yan** *n., adj.*

may·be [mā′bē] *adv.* Perhaps; possibly.

May Day The first day of May, celebrated by crowning a May queen, dancing around a Maypole, etc. In some countries it is a holiday in honor of laboring people.

may·flow·er [mā′flou′ər] *n.* Any of several plants that blossom in the spring, especially the arbutus.

May·flow·er [mā′flou′ər] *n.* The ship on which the Pilgrims came to America in 1620.

May fly An insect with large, transparent front wings.

may·hem [mā′hem] *n.* The crime of hurting someone very badly, so as to cripple or maim him.

may·on·naise [mā′ə·nāz′ *or* mī′ə·nāz′] *n.* A creamy dressing, as for salads, made with egg yolk, oil, lemon juice or vinegar, and seasonings.

may·or [mā′ər] *n.* The chief governing official of a city or town.

may·or·al·ty [mā′ər·əl·tē] *n., pl.* **may·or·al·ties** The position or term of office of a mayor.

May·pole [mā′pōl′] *n. (often written* **maypole***)* A pole decorated with flowers and streamers around which people dance on May Day.

mayst [māst] *v.* A form of the verb MAY, used with *thou*: seldom used today.

maze [māz] *n.* **1** A complicated network of paths or passages in which it is hard to find one's way. **2** A state of bewilderment or confusion.

ma·zur·ka or **ma·zour·ka** [mə·zûr′kə] *n.* **1** A lively Polish dance. **2** The music for this dance.

Maze

M.C. Abbreviation of MASTER OF CEREMONIES.

Mc·Kin·ley [mə·kin′lē], **Mount** The highest mountain in North America, located in Alaska.

Mc·Kin·ley [mə·kin′lē], **William,** 1843–1901, 25th president of the U.S., 1897–1901.

Md. Abbreviation of MARYLAND.

M.D. Abbreviation of DOCTOR OF MEDICINE, used after a doctor's name: *Harold Davies, M.D.*

me [mē] *pron.* The form of *I* that serves as the object of verbs and prepositions: *Talk to me; Take me with you.* ◆ Nowadays many people would regard "It is I," in answer to the question "Who's there?" as a little stuffy. Although in formal speech and writing *It is I* (or *It is we,* etc.) is the preferred form, *It's me* (or *It's us,* etc.) is now acceptable in informal conversation.

Me. Abbreviation of MAINE (not official).

mead¹ [mēd] *n.* An alcoholic drink made of fermented honey, water, and spices.

mead² [mēd] *n.* A meadow: used mostly in poems.

mead·ow [med′ō] *n.* A tract of land where grass is grown for hay or for grazing.

mead·ow·lark [med′ō·lärk′] *n.* Any of various

songbirds of North America, usually having black markings on a yellow breast.

mea·ger or **mea·gre** [mē′gər] *adj.* **1** Lacking in quality or quantity; not adequate; inferior. **2** Thin; lean: a *meager* frame.

meal[1] [mēl] *n.* **1** The edible seeds of any grain, coarsely ground: a sack of *meal*. **2** Any powdery material produced by grinding.

meal[2] [mēl] *n.* **1** The food served or eaten at certain times during the day. **2** The time or occasion of eating.

meal·y [mē′lē] *adj.* **meal·i·er, meal·i·est** **1** Like meal; dry; powdery. **2** Made of, containing, or covered with meal. **3** Pale or anemic.

mean[1] [mēn] *v.* **meant, mean·ing** **1** To have in mind as a purpose; intend: I *mean* to visit him. **2** To intend for some purpose, target, etc.: Was that remark *meant* for me? **3** To intend to express or convey: That's not what I *mean*. **4** To have as the sense; signify; denote: Dictionaries tell what words *mean*. **5** To be of a specified importance: Her work *means* everything to her. **— mean well** To intend to do good.

mean[2] [mēn] *adj.* **1** Poor or inferior in grade or quality: *mean* garments. **2** Humble in rank; lowly: a person of *mean* birth. **3** Poor in appearance; shabby: a *mean* house. **4** Not noble in mind or character; base: It's *mean* to lie. **5** Having the qualities of a miser; stingy: to be *mean* with money. **6** *informal* Selfish or nasty: a *mean* child. **7** *informal* Vicious or dangerous, as an animal. **— mean′ly** *adv.*

mean[3] [mēn] **1** *n.* The middle point or state between two extremes: The *mean* between stinginess and being a spendthrift is moderation. **2** *adj.* Coming halfway between two limits or extremes; average: The *mean* rainfall is the average rainfall over a certain period of time. **3** *n.* A number that is considered to be typical and representative of a whole set of numbers; an average. **4** *n.* (*pl.*) A way in which something is accomplished or brought about: Travel is a *means* of enjoyment. **5** *n.* (*pl.*) Money, property, or other wealth: a man of *means*. **— by all means** Of course; certainly. **— by any means** In any way possible; somehow. **— by means of** With the help of; by using. **— by no means** Most certainly not.

me·an·der [mē·an′dər] **1** *v.* To wind and turn in a course, as a river. **2** *n.* A winding or rambling course or movement. **3** *v.* To wander aimlessly, without purpose.

mean·ing [mē′ning] **1** *n.* Something meant or to be understood; significance: the *meaning* of a word. **2** *adj.* Showing or having meaning; expressive: a *meaning* glance.

mean·ing·ful [mē′ning·fəl] *adj.* Full of meaning. **— mean′ing·ful·ly** *adv.*

mean·ing·less [mē′ning·lis] *adj.* Having no meaning or importance; senseless. **— mean′ing·less·ly** *adv.*

mean·ness [mēn′nis] *n.* **1** The condition of being mean. **2** A mean act.

meant [ment] Past tense and past participle of MEAN[1].

mean·time [mēn′tīm′] **1** *n.* The time between. **2** *adv.* In or during the time between. **3** *adv.* At the same time.

mean·while [mēn′(h)wīl′] *n., adv.* Meantime.

mea·sles [mē′zəlz] *n.pl.* (*used with singular verb*) A contagious virus disease marked by fever and an outbreak of small red spots on the skin, particularly common among children.

meas·ur·a·ble [mezh′ər·ə·bəl] *adj.* Capable of being measured. **— meas′ur·a·bly** *adv.*

meas·ure [mezh′ər] *n., v.* **meas·ured, meas·ur·ing** **1** *n.* A unit or standard, as a foot, ounce, pint, minute, etc., used for comparison. **2** *n.* A ruler, scale, or other device for using standard units. **3** *v.* To find out, in standard units, the extent, contents, weight, time, or degree of: *Measure* the wire in yards. **4** *n.* The extent, weight, time, etc., found in this way. **5** *v.* To set apart, mark off, allot, etc., by or as if by measuring: *Measure* off two pints of milk. **6** *v.* To have a certain measurement: The table *measures* two feet by four feet. **7** *v.* To serve as an instrument for measuring: Thermometers *measure* temperature. **8** *n.* A system of measurement: liquid *measure*. **9** *v.* To make or take measurements. **10** *n.* A standard or criterion of comparison, judgment, etc.: Is strength a true *measure* of manliness? **11** *v.* To find out or estimate by a standard or criterion: Ted *measured* his running speed against his brother's. **12** *n.* A fixed limit or bound: talkative beyond all *measure*. **13** *n.* A certain amount or degree: The prisoners had a *measure* of freedom. **14** *n.* (*pl.*) Actions or steps: We have taken *measures* to make him behave. **15** *n.* A bill or law. **16** *n.* The portion of music between two bar lines; bar. **17** *n.* Rhythm or meter, as in poetry or music. **— beyond measure** More than can be measured. **—**

Four measures of music

for good measure As something added or extra. **— measure up to** To meet or satisfy, as expectations.

meas·ured [mezh′ərd] *adj.* **1** Set or determined by some standard: the *measured* form of classical architecture. **2** Slow and stately; rhythmical: a *measured* step. **3** Carefully thought out: *measured* speech.

meas·ure·less [mezh′ər·lis] *adj.* Too big to be measured; very great; immense.

meas·ure·ment [mezh′ər·mənt] *n.* **1** The act of measuring anything. **2** The size, quantity, amount, etc., found by measuring. **3** A system of measures: linear *measurement*.

measuring worm The larva of certain moths. It moves by advancing its rear end, humping up in the middle, then advancing its front end.

meat [mēt] *n.* **1** The flesh of animals used as food, especially the flesh of mammals, as the cow or pig, and not of fish or fowl. **2** The part of anything that can be eaten: the *meat* of a coconut. **3** Anything used as food, now used mainly in the phrase **meat and drink. 4** The main idea; gist: the *meat* of the story.

meat·y [mē′tē] *adj.* **meat·i·er, meat·i·est 1** Of, having to do with, or like meat. **2** Full of meat. **3** Full of meaning; significant.

Mec·ca [mek′ə] *n.* **1** A city in Saudi Arabia, the birthplace of Mohammed and a holy city of Islam. **2** (*written* **mecca**) A place or attraction visited by many people.

me·chan·ic [mə·kan′ik] *n.* A person who is skilled in the making, operating, or repairing of tools or machinery.

me·chan·i·cal [mə·kan′i·kəl] *adj.* **1** Of or having to do with a machine or machinery: *Mechanical* engineers created new tools. **2** Operated or produced by a machine. **3** Having to do with the science of mechanics. **4** Made or done as if by a machine; automatic: a *mechanical* speech. **— me·chan′i·cal·ly** *adv.*

mechanical advantage A number equal to the force a machine applies to its load divided by the force supplied to the machine.

mechanical drawing A drawing, usually of mechanical parts or objects, done with the aid of compasses, squares, and other instruments.

me·chan·ics [mə·kan′iks] *n.* The branch of physics that deals with motion and with the action of forces on bodies. ◆ See -ICS.

mech·a·nism [mek′ə·niz′əm] *n.* **1** The parts or the arrangement of parts of a machine. **2** Something like a machine in the working of its parts: the *mechanism* of the human body; the *mechanism* of government.

mech·a·nize [mek′ə·nīz] *v.* **mech·a·nized, mech·a·niz·ing 1** To make mechanical. **2** To convert, as an industry, to machine production. **3** To equip, as an army, with tanks, trucks, etc. ¶3

med·al [med′(ə)l] *n.* **1** A small piece of metal with an image, writing, etc., on it, given as an award for an outstanding act or service. **2** Such a piece of metal bearing a religious image or inscription.

me·dal·lion [mə·dal′yən] *n.* **1** A large medal. **2** A round or oval design or ornament that looks like a large medal.

med·dle [med′(ə)l] *v.* **med·dled, med·dling** To interfere or tamper without being asked or wanted. **— med′dler** *n.*

Medals

med·dle·some [med′(ə)l·səm] *adj.* Tending to meddle; interfering.

Mede [mēd] *n.* A person born in or a citizen of ancient Media.

Me·de·a [mə·dē′ə] *n.* In Greek myths, the woman who helped Jason obtain the Golden Fleece.

Me·di·a [mē′dē·ə] *n.* An ancient country of SW Asia.

me·di·ae·val [mē′dē·ē′vəl] *adj.* Another spelling of MEDIEVAL.

me·di·al [mē′dē·əl] *adj.* **1** Of, related to, or in the middle; median. **2** Average; mean.

me·di·an [mē′dē·ən] **1** *adj.* In the middle; medial. **2** *n.* The middle number in a series, as 5 in 1, 2, 5, 6, 9.

me·di·ate [*v.* mē′dē·āt, *adj.* mē′dē·it] *v.* **me·di·at·ed, me·di·at·ing,** *adj.* **1** *v.* To settle, as a quarrel, by acting as a peacemaker or a go-between. **2** *v.* To act between disputing parties as a peacemaker. **3** *v.* To bring about (a settlement, etc.) by acting as a go-between. **4** *adj.* Acting as a go-between; indirect. **— me′di·a′tion** *n.* **— me′di·a′tor** *n.*

med·ic [med′ik] *n. informal* **1** A medical doctor or intern. **2** A soldier or sailor trained in medical work.

med·i·cal [med′i·kəl] *adj.* Of or having to do with medicine. **— med′i·cal·ly** *adv.*

med·i·ca·ment [med′ə·kə·mənt *or* mə·dik′ə·mənt] *n.* A medicine.

med·i·care [med′i·kâr] *n. U.S.* A program of health insurance sponsored by the national government.

med·i·cate [med′ə·kāt] *v.* **med·i·cat·ed, med·i·cat·ing 1** To treat medically. **2** To put medicine on or in. **3** *adj. use:* a *medicated* bandage.

med·i·ca·tion [med′ə·kā′shən] *n.* **1** The act or process of medicating. **2** A medicine.

me·dic·i·nal [mə·dis′ə·nəl] *adj.* Being or acting as a medicine; healing; curative.

med·i·cine [med′ə·sən] *n.* **1** Any substance used in treating disease, in healing, or in relieving pain. **2** The science of restoring and preserving health and of preventing and treating disease. **3** The profession of medicine. **4** Among American Indians, any object or ceremony supposed to have magic power, curative effects, etc.

medicine man Among North American Indians, a man believed to have magic powers of healing, of keeping away evil spirits, etc.

me·di·e·val [mē′dē·ē′vəl *or* med′ē·ē′vəl] *adj.* Of, relating to, or belonging to the Middle Ages.

me·di·o·cre [mē′dē·ō′kər] *adj.* Of only average quality; neither good nor bad; ordinary.

me·di·oc·ri·ty [mē′dē·ok′rə·tē] *n., pl.* **me·di·oc·ri·ties 1** The condition of being mediocre or ordinary. **2** Mediocre ability or performance. **3** A mediocre person.

med·i·tate [med′ə·tāt] *v.* **med·i·tat·ed, med·i·tat·ing 1** To think quietly and deeply over a period of time; muse. **2** To think about doing; plan: to *meditate* mischief. **— med·i·ta′tion** *n.* **— med′i·ta′tive** *adj.*

Med·i·ter·ra·ne·an [med′ə·tə·rā′nē·ən] **1** *n.* A great inland sea between Europe, Asia, and Africa. **2** *adj.* Of or having to do with this sea or the lands around it.

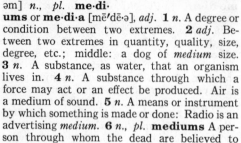

me·di·um [mē′dē·əm] *n., pl.* **me·di·ums** or **me·di·a** [mē′dē·ə], *adj.* **1** *n.* A degree or condition between two extremes. **2** *adj.* Between two extremes in quantity, quality, size, degree, etc.; middle: a dog of *medium* size. **3** *n.* A substance, as water, that an organism lives in. **4** *n.* A substance through which a force may act or an effect be produced. Air is a medium of sound. **5** *n.* A means or instrument by which something is made or done: Radio is an advertising *medium.* **6** *n., pl.* **mediums** A person through whom the dead are believed to speak, as at a seance.

med·ley [med′lē] *n., pl.* **med·leys** **1** A mixture of unlike or unrelated things; jumble. **2** A series of songs or tunes arranged to be played as a single piece.

me·dul·la [mə·dul′ə] *n.* **1** The soft, inner portion of an organ or part, as of the adrenal gland or spinal cord. **2** The pith of a plant.

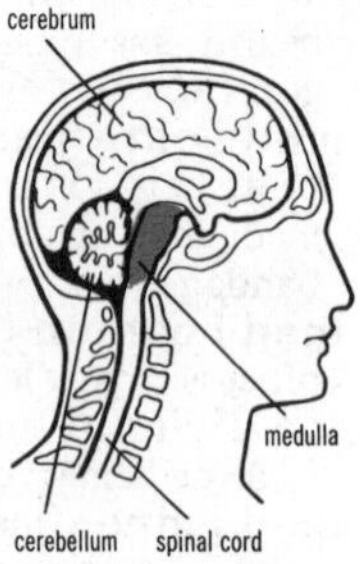

medulla ob·lon·ga·ta [ob′·lông·gā′tə] The lowest part of the brain, topping the spinal chord. It controls circulation, breathing, etc.

Me·du·sa [mə·d(y)ōō′sə] *n.* In Greek myths, one of the Gorgons, killed by Perseus.

meek [mēk] *adj.* **1** Having a patient, gentle disposition; mild. **2** Lacking spirit or courage; submissive. **— meek′ly** *adv.* **— meek′ness** *n.*

meer·schaum [mir′shəm] *n.* **1** A soft, lightweight, white, claylike mineral. **2** A pipe for smoking, made of this mineral. ◆ *Meerschaum,* which resembles froth or foam in color, comes from two German words meaning *sea foam.*

meet[1] [mēt] *v.* **met, meet·ing,** *n.* **1** *v.* To come upon; come face to face with: He happened to *meet* a friend. **2** *v.* To become acquainted with: Have you *met* Jane? **3** *v.* To be introduced or become acquainted: We've already *met.* **4** *v.* To keep an appointment with: I'll *meet* you there. **5** *v.* To be waiting for on arrival: She *met* my plane. **6** *v.* To come together and join or merge: where two streams *meet.* **7** *v.* To come into contact with: where the path *meets* the road. **8** *v.* To assemble: How often does the club *meet*? **9** *n.* A meeting, as for a sports event: a track *meet.* **10** *v.* To experience; undergo: to *meet* difficulties. **11** *v.* To deal or cope with: He *met* and overcame our objections. **12** *v.* To satisfy or fulfill, as requirements or a need. **13** *v.* To pay (a bill, debt, etc.). **— meet with** **1** To come upon; encounter. **2** To experience: to *meet with* hardships.

meet[2] [mēt] *adj.* Suitable; proper.

meet·ing [mē′ting] *n.* **1** A coming together. **2** A gathering of persons, as for religious worship or some other common purpose; assembly.

meeting house A building used for public worship, especially for Quaker meetings.

meg·a·cy·cle [meg′ə·sī′kəl] *n.* One million cycles, especially one million cycles per second.

meg·a·phone [meg′ə·fōn] *n.* A funnel-shaped tube which one talks or yells through to make the voice sound loud and go far. ◆ See OMEGA.

Megaphone

mel·an·chol·y [mel′ən·kol′ē] **1** *adj.* Very gloomy; sad; dejected. **2** *n.* Low spirits; depression; sadness. **3** *adj.* Causing or suggesting sadness: the *melancholy* sound of a cello.

Mel·a·ne·sia [mel′ə·nē′zhə] *n.* The islands of the western Pacific Ocean that lie south of the equator. **— Mel′a·ne′sian** *adj., n.*

Mel·bourne [mel′bərn] *n.* A large seaport in SE Australia.

me·lee [mā′lā *or* mā·lā′] *n.* A confused, hand-to-hand fight in which many people take part.

mel·lif·lu·ous [mə·lif′lōō·əs] *adj.* Flowing in a sweet, smooth way: *mellifluous* speech.

mel·low [mel′ō] **1** *adj.* Soft, sweet, and full of flavor; ripe, as fruit. **2** *adj.* Soft and pleasant to the taste; well aged: *mellow* wine. **3** *adj.* Rich and soft in quality, as colors or sounds. **4** *adj.* Made gentle and sympathetic by age or experience. **5** *v.* To make or become mellow: Age *mellowed* the rebel. **— mel′low·ness** *n.*

me·lod·ic [mə·lod′ik] *adj.* **1** Having to do with or containing melody. **2** Melodious.

me·lo·di·ous [mə·lō′dē·əs] *adj.* **1** Producing melody or full of melody; tuneful. **2** Pleasant to hear; musical. **— me·lo′di·ous·ly** *adv.*

mel·o·dra·ma [mel′ə·drä′mə] *n.* **1** A play using exaggeration or shocking events to stir up the feelings. It is often too full of violence, emotion, or sentimentality to be true to life. **2** Action, language, etc., suiting such a play.

mel·o·dra·mat·ic [mel′ə·drə·mat′ik] *adj.* Of, suitable to, or like melodrama, as in being too dramatic, too emotional, or violent. **— mel′o·dra·mat′i·cal·ly** *adv.*

mel·o·dy [mel′ə·dē] *n., pl.* **mel·o·dies** **1** A meaningful succession of musical tones in a single part or voice; tune. **2** The leading part or voice in a harmonic composition. **3** Any pleasant series or succession of sounds.

mel·on [mel′ən] *n.* A large, juicy fruit growing on vines, as the watermelon or cantaloupe.

melt [melt] *v.* **1** To change from a solid to a liquid condition by heat: The candle wax *melted*; to *melt* ice. **2** To fill with warm, tender feelings; soften: Sympathy *melted* his hard heart. **3** To dissolve, as in water: food so tender it seems to

melt in the mouth. **4** To fade away or disappear: Her shyness *melted* away. **5** To blend little by little; merge: red *melting* into gold in a sunset.

Mel·ville [mel′vil], **Herman,** 1819–1891, U.S. novelist.

mem·ber [mem′bər] *n.* **1** A person who belongs to a group, as a family, club, legislature, etc. **2** A part of the body, especially an arm or leg. **3** An element of a set or of any whole thing.

mem·ber·ship [mem′bər·ship] *n.* **1** The condition of being a member. **2** All of the members of some group. **3** The total number of members.

mem·brane [mem′brān] *n.* A thin, flexible layer of tissue that covers or lines certain organs or parts of plants and animals. **— mem·bra· nous** [mem′brə·nəs] *adj.*

me·men·to [mə·men′tō] *n., pl.* **me·men·tos** or **me·men·toes** Anything kept or given as a reminder of the past; souvenir.

mem·o [mem′ō] *n., pl.* **mem·os** *informal* A memorandum.

mem·oir [mem′wär] *n.* **1** (*usually pl.*) The story of a person's own life and experiences. **2** An account of a person written by someone else, usually someone who knew him. **3** (*often pl.*) A written account or report based on what the writer has experienced, observed, or learned.

mem·o·ra·ble [mem′ər·ə·bəl] *adj.* Worth remembering; hard to forget. **— mem′o·ra· bly** *adv.*

mem·o·ran·dum [mem′ə·ran′dəm] *n., pl.* **mem·o·ran·dums** or **mem·o·ran·da** [mem′· ə·ran′də] **1** A brief note of a thing or things to be remembered. **2** An informal letter, usually sent between departments in an office.

me·mo·ri·al [mə·môr′ē·əl] **1** *adj.* Devoted to the memory of a person or event: a *memorial* library. **2** *n.* Something designed to remind people of a person or event, as a monument.

Memorial Day *U.S.* A day for honoring the dead of American wars. It is May 30 in most states.

mem·o·rize [mem′ə·rīz] *v.* **mem·o·rized, mem·o·riz·ing** To commit to memory; learn by heart. **— mem·o·ri·za·tion** [mem′ə·rə· zā′shən] *n.* ¶3

mem·o·ry [mem′ər·ē] *n., pl.* **mem·o·ries 1** The mental act of or capacity for remembering: a good *memory* for names. **2** The total of what a person remembers: to commit a poem to *memory.* **3** Something remembered: *memories* of childhood. **4** The period of time covered by the ability to remember: beyond the *memory* of man. **— in memory of** As a reminder of or memorial to.

Mem·phis [mem′fis] *n.* **1** A city in sw Tennessee. **2** The capital of Egypt in ancient times.

men [men] Plural of MAN.

men·ace [men′is] *v.* **men·aced, men·ac·ing,** *n.* **1** *v.* To threaten with evil or harm: a beach

menaced by a hurricane. **2** *n.* A threat. **3** *n. informal* A troublesome person; pest.

me·nag·er·ie [mə·naj′ər·ē] *n.* **1** A collection of caged wild animals kept for exhibition. **2** The enclosure in which they are kept.

mend [mend] **1** *v.* To repair: to *mend* a broken toy. **2** *n.* A mended place, as in a garment. **3** *v.* To correct faults in; improve. **4** *v.* To get or make better, as in health. **— on the mend** Getting well. **— mend′er** *n.*

men·da·cious [men·dā′shəs] *adj.* **1** Lying or likely to tell lies. **2** Not true; false.

men·dac·i·ty [men·das′ə·tē] *n., pl.* **men· dac·i·ties 1** The tendency to tell lies. **2** A lie.

Men·del [men′dəl], **Gregor Johann,** 1822– 1884, Austrian botanist, formulated laws of genetics.

Men·dels·sohn [men′dəl·sən], **Felix,** 1809– 1847, German composer of music.

men·di·cant [men′də·kənt] **1** *adj.* Depending on charity for a living; begging: a *mendicant* friar. **2** *n.* A beggar. **3** *n.* A begging friar.

men·ha·den [men·hād′(ə)n] *n.* A fish related to the herring, common off the Atlantic coast. It is used as a source of oil and as fertilizer.

me·ni·al [mē′nē·əl *or* mēn′yəl] **1** *adj.* Having to do with or appropriate to servants: a *menial* job. **2** *n.* A servant. **— me′ni·al·ly** *adv.*

men·in·gi·tis [men′ən·jī′tis] *n.* A serious disease in which the membranes covering the brain or spinal cord become inflamed, usually by infection.

Men·non·ite [men′ən·īt] *n.* A member of a Christian sect that is opposed to taking oaths, holding public office, and military service.

Me·no·rah [mə·nôr′ə] *n.* In Judaism, a candelabrum used during religious ceremonies.

men·stru·ate [men′strōō·āt] *v.* **men·stru· at·ed, men·stru·at·ing** To have a discharge of blood from the uterus about every 28 days. This is a normal occurrence in women from puberty until some time in middle age. **— men· stru·a′tion** *n.*

men·su·ra·tion [men′shə·rā′shən] *n.* **1** The art, act, or process of measuring. **2** The branch of mathematics having to do with determining length, area, and volume.

-ment A suffix meaning: **1** The act of, as in *development,* the act of developing. **2** The result of, as in *achievement,* the result of achieving. **3** A means of or thing that, as in *punishment,* a means of punishing or being punished. **4** The condition of being, as in *astonishment,* the condition of being astonished.

men·tal [men′təl] *adj.* **1** Of or having to do with the mind: *mental* ability; *mental* illness. **2** Done by or in the mind: *mental* arithmetic. **3** Having a sick or disordered mind: a *mental* patient. **4** For the care of people with sick or disordered minds: a *mental* hospital.

add, āce, câre, pälm;   end, ēqual;   it, īce;   odd, ōpen, ôrder;   tŏŏk, pōōl;   up, bûrn;
ə = a in *above,* e in *sicken,* i in *possible,* o in *melon,* u in *circus;*   yōō = u in *fuse;*   oil;   pout;
check;   ring;   thin;   this;   zh in *vision.*   For ¶ reference, see page 64 · HOW TO

mental age A level of mental development equal to that of the average child of a given age: She is only nine but her *mental age* is twelve.

men·tal·i·ty [men·tal′ə·tē] *n.*, *pl.* **men·tal·i·ties** Mental capacity or power; intelligence.

men·tal·ly [men′tə·lē] *adv.* In or with the mind: *mentally* retarded; to add *mentally*.

men·thol [men′thôl] *n.* A white crystalline substance obtained from the oil of peppermint. It has a cooling taste and is used in medicine, perfumery, and cigarettes.

men·tion [men′shən] **1** *v.* To refer to briefly or name in passing. **2** *n.* A brief remark or statement about or a reference to something. — **make mention of** To refer to; mention.

men·tor [men′tər] *n.* A wise, devoted adviser.

men·u [men′yōō] *n.* **1** A list of the foods provided for a meal. **2** The foods provided.

me·ow [mē·ou′] **1** *n.* The crying sound made by a cat. **2** *v.* To make this sound.

mer·can·tile [mûr′kən·tēl′ *or* mûr′kən·tīl′] *adj.* Having to do with merchants or commerce.

mer·ce·nar·y [mûr′sə·ner′ē] *adj.*, *n.*, *pl.* **mer·ce·nar·ies 1** *adj.* Influenced only by the desire for money or reward; greedy: They showed a *mercenary* concern over the rich old lady's health. **2** *n.* A soldier who serves for pay in the army of a foreign government.

mer·cer·ize [mûr′sə·rīz] *v.* **mer·cer·ized, mer·cer·iz·ing** To treat (cotton fiber or fabrics) with a chemical that makes the fibers stronger, glossy, and better able to take dyes.

mer·chan·dise [*n.* mûr′chən·dīz *or* mûr′chən·dīs, *v.* mûr′chən·dīz] *n.*, *v.* **mer·chan·dised, mer·chan·dis·ing 1** *n.* Goods bought and sold for profit. **2** *v.* To buy and sell for profit. **3** *v.* To promote the sale of (goods).

mer·chant [mûr′chənt] **1** *n.* A person who buys and sells things for profit; trader. **2** *adj.* Of, having to do with, or used in trade; commercial: *merchant* ships. **3** *n.* A storekeeper.

mer·chant·man [mûr′chənt·mən] *n.*, *pl.* **mer·chant·men** [mûr′chənt·mən] A ship used in trade.

merchant marine Those ships and sailors of a nation that are engaged in trade, not defense.

mer·ci·ful [mûr′sə·fəl] *adj.* Full of or showing mercy; kind. — **mer′ci·ful·ly** *adv.*

mer·ci·less [mûr′sə·lis] *adj.* Having or showing no mercy. — **mer′ci·less·ly** *adv.*

mer·cu·ri·al [mər·kyŏŏr′ē·əl] *adj.* **1** Lively; clever; changeable. **2** Of, having to do with, containing, or caused by the element mercury.

mer·cu·ry [mûr′kyə·rē] *n.*, *pl.* **mer·cu·ries 1** A heavy, silver-white, metallic element that is liquid at ordinary temperatures; quicksilver. It is used in thermometers, and its compounds and amalgams have many uses in industry and medicine. **2** (*written* **Mercury**) In Roman myths, the messenger of the gods and the god of commerce, eloquence, and skill. ◆ See the picture at HERMES, his Greek name. **3** (*written* **Mercury**) A planet of the solar system, the smallest one and the one nearest to the sun.

mer·cy [mûr′sē] *n.*, *pl.* **mer·cies 1** Kind treatment or mildness where severity is expected or deserved. **2** The power to show kindness or pity: The prisoner threw himself on his captor's *mercy*. **3** A thing to be thankful for: It's a *mercy* I got here in time. — **at the mercy of** Completely in the power of.

mere[1] [mir] *adj.* **mer·est** Being nothing more or less than; being nothing but: a *mere* trifle.

mere[2] [mir] *n.* A lake, pond, or marsh: seldom used today.

mere·ly [mir′lē] *adv.* Nothing more than; only.

mer·e·tri·cious [mer′ə·trish′əs] *adj.* Showy and meant to attract but really false or cheap. — **mer′e·tri′cious·ly** *adv.* — **mer′e·tri′cious·ness** *n.*

mer·gan·ser [mər·gan′sər] *n.*, *pl.* **mer·gan·ser** *or* **mer·gan·sers** A diving duck with a long, slender bill and usually a crest.

merge [mûrj] *v.* **merged, merg·ing** To combine or be combined so as to lose separate identity: The two lanes of traffic *merged*, becoming one.

merg·er [mûr′jər] *n.* The act of merging, as the combining of separate companies into one.

me·rid·i·an [mə·rid′ē·ən] *n.* **1** Any imaginary semicircle drawn on the earth's surface from the North to the South Pole. Meridians are used in measuring longitude. **2** The highest point that the sun or a star seems to climb to. **3** The highest point of anything, as of a life.

Meridians

me·ringue [mə·rang′] *n.* The stiffly beaten whites of eggs, blended with sugar and usually baked on a pie or as a small cake or shell.

me·ri·no [mə·rē′nō] *n.*, *pl.* **me·ri·nos 1** A breed of sheep with fine, silky wool. The male has heavy, curled horns. **2** The wool of this sheep. **3** A fine, soft, woolen fabric originally made of this wool. **4** A fine yarn.

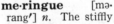
Merino, about 30 in. high at shoulder

mer·it [mer′it] **1** *n.* Worth or value; high quality; excellence: an idea with *merit*; That scheme has little *merit*. **2** *n.* (*pl.*) The actual rights or wrongs of a matter: Consider the case on its *merits*. **3** *v.* To be entitled to; deserve: Parents *merit* respect.

mer·i·to·ri·ous [mer′ə·tôr′ē·əs] *adj.* Having merit; worthy; commendable.

Mer·lin [mûr′lin] *n.* In English legend, a magician and prophet at King Arthur's court.

mer·maid [mûr′mād′] *n.* A legendary sea creature having the head and upper body of a woman and the tail of a fish.

mer·man [mûr′man′] *n., pl.* **mer·men** [mûr′men′] A legendary sea creature having the head and upper body of a man and the tail of a fish.

mer·ri·ment [mer′i·mənt] *n.* Laughter; fun.

mer·ry [mer′ē] *adj.* **mer·ri·er, mer·ri·est** Full of fun and laughter; joyous; gay; zestful: a *merry* dance. — **mer′ri·ly** *adv.*

Mermaid

mer·ry-an·drew [mer′ē·an′drōō] *n.* A clown.

mer·ry-go-round [mer′i·gō·round′] *n.* **1** A revolving platform fitted with wooden horses, seats, etc., on which children and sometimes grown-ups ride for amusement. **2** A rapid going around or whirl, as of social events.

mer·ry·mak·ing [mer′ē·mā′king] **1** *n.* Fun and gaiety; laughter, joking, etc. **2** *adj.* Festive and gay. **3** *n.* A merry time. — **mer′·ry·mak′er** *n.*

me·sa [mā′sə] *n.* A hill or small plateau with a flat top and steep sides, common in the sw U.S. ◆ *Mesa* comes directly from Spanish and goes back to the Latin word *mensa*, meaning *table*.

Mesa

mesh [mesh] **1** *n.* One of the open spaces between the cords of a net or the wires of a screen. **2** *n.* (*pl.*) The cords or wires that make up a network. **3** *v.* To trap or ensnare, as in a net. **4** *v.* To fit into place, as the teeth of interlocking gears. — **in mesh** In gear.

mes·mer·ism [mes′mə·riz′əm] *n.* Hypnotism.

mes·mer·ize [mes′mə·rīz] *v.* **mes·mer·ized, mes·mer·iz·ing** To hypnotize. ¶3

mes·on [mē′son *or* mes′on] *n.* Any of a class of short-lived atomic particles having a mass between those of the electron and the proton.

Mes·o·po·ta·mi·a [mes′ə·pə·tā′mē·ə] *n.* An ancient country in Asia between the Tigris and Euphrates rivers, part of modern Iraq.

Mes·o·zo·ic [mes′ə·zō′ik] **1** *adj.* Of or having to do with the geological era between the Paleozoic and the Cenozoic. In this era the reptiles were dominant and the first mammals appeared. **2** *n.* The Mesozoic era.

mes·quite [mes·kēt′] *n.* A spiny shrub or small tree found in the sw U.S., Mexico, and Central America. Its pods are fed to cattle.

mess [mes] **1** *n.* A state of disorder, especially a condition of dirty or untidy confusion: The place was in a *mess* after the party. **2** *n.* An unpleasant or confused mixture; jumble; muddle: a *mess* of clothes piled in the corner; He made a *mess* of his homework. **3** *v.* To make a mess of: Don't *mess* up my hair. **4** *v.* To busy oneself; putter: Stop *messing* with that ash tray. **5** *n.* A number of persons who regularly take their meals together, as in the army. **6** *n.* A meal taken by them, or the place where the meal is served. **7** *n.* A portion, as of food. **8** *n.* A serving of soft, partly liquid food.

mes·sage [mes′ij] *n.* **1** Advice, news, instructions, or other communication sent to another person. **2** A lesson or idea contained in a speech, story, etc.

mes·sen·ger [mes′ən·jər] *n.* A person sent with a message or on an errand.

Mes·si·ah [mə·sī′ə] *n.* **1** In the Jewish religion, the awaited deliverer of the Jewish people promised by God. **2** In the Christian religion, Jesus. **3** (*written* **messiah**) An expected liberator of a country or people.

Mes·si·an·ic [mes′ē·an′ik] *adj.* **1** Of or having to do with the Messiah. **2** (*written* **messianic**) Of or having to do with a messiah.

Messrs. [mes′ərz] An abbreviation used as the plural of MR. ◆ *Messrs.* is an abbreviation of the French word *messieurs*, plural of *monsieur*.

mess·y [mes′ē] *adj.* **mess·i·er, mess·i·est** Dirty, sloppy, or disorderly. — **mess′i·ly** *adv.* — **mess′i·ness** *n.*

met [met] Past tense and past participle of MEET[1].

me·tab·o·lism [mə·tab′ə·liz′əm] *n.* All of the processes by which a plant or animal converts materials taken from its environment into the energy required to maintain itself, grow, and carry on all vital activities. — **met·a·bol·ic** [met′ə·bol′ik] *adj.*

met·al [met′(ə)l] *n.* **1** Any of a class of chemical elements having a shiny appearance, as aluminum, copper, and iron. They can be hammered, stretched, or rolled, and are conductors of heat and electricity. Their atoms usually lose electrons in forming chemical compounds. **2** *adj. use*: *metal* shelves. **3** Inner quality; substance; mettle: A soldier's *metal* is tested in battle.

me·tal·lic [mə·tal′ik] *adj.* **1** Of or having to do with metal. **2** Like or suggesting metal: a sharp, *metallic* noise.

met·al·lur·gy [met′ə·lûr′jē] *n.* The science of removing metals from their ores, refining them, and using them, as in alloys. — **met′al·lur′·gist** *n.*

met·a·mor·phic [met′ə·môr′fik] *adj.* Of or resulting from a change in form or structure.

met·a·mor·phose [met′ə·môr′fōz] *v.* **met·a·mor·phosed, met·a·mor·phos·ing** To change or be changed from one form or structure into another: A silkworm *metamorphoses* into a moth.

met·a·mor·pho·sis [met′ə·môr′fə·sis] *n.*, *pl.* **met·a·mor·pho·ses** [met′ə·môr′fə·sēz] **1** A change from one form, shape, or substance into another, as the development of a tad-pole into a frog. **2** A complete change, as in someone's character: the *metamorphosis* of a shy girl into a popular belle.

Metamorphosis of a fly

eggs larva pupa adult

met·a·phor [met′ə·fôr] *n.* A figure of speech which suggests, without saying so, that one thing is like another. It applies a word or phrase to something to which it does not actually or ordinarily apply, as in *"silver* moonlight" or "He was a *lion* in battle."

met·a·phor·i·cal [met′ə·fôr′i·kəl] *adj.* Of or using a metaphor. **— met′a·phor′i·cal·ly** *adv.*

met·a·phys·i·cal [met′ə·fiz′i·kəl] *adj.* **1** Of or having to do with metaphysics. **2** Highly abstract and often difficult to understand.

met·a·phys·ics [met′ə·fiz′iks] *n.* The branch of philosophy that investigates reality, being, and knowledge. ◆ See -ICS.

mete [mēt] *v.* **met·ed, met·ing** To give according to measure or one's judgment: to *mete* out five dollars per person; to *mete* out justice.

me·te·or [mē′tē·ər] *n.* A small fragment of matter from outer space that is heated white-hot by friction with the earth's atmosphere and appears briefly as a streak of light; shooting star.

me·te·or·ic [mē·tē·ôr′ik] *adj.* **1** Of or made up of meteors. **2** Brilliant, rapid, and dazzling, like a meteor: a *meteoric* career.

me·te·or·ite [mē′tē·ə·rīt′] *n.* A part of a meteor that is not burned up and strikes the earth as a lump of stone or metal.

me·te·or·oid [mē′tē·ə·roid′] *n.* One of the pieces of matter in outer space that form meteors upon entering the earth's atmosphere.

me·te·or·o·log·i·cal [mē′tē·ôr′ə·loj′i·kəl] *adj.* Of or having to do with the atmosphere, winds, and weather, or with meteorology.

me·te·or·ol·o·gy [mē′tē·ə·rol′ə·jē] *n.* The science that studies the atmosphere, winds, and weather. **— me′te·or·ol′o·gist** *n.*

me·ter[1] [mē′tər] *n.* An instrument used to measure and often record a quantity or an amount used: a gas *meter*.

me·ter[2] [mē′tər] *n.* **1** The standard unit of length in the metric system, equal to 39.37 inches. **2** The measured rhythm used in poetry, a pattern of accented and unaccented syllables. **3** The pattern of beats and accents in a measure of music. ¶2

meth·ane [meth′ān] *n.* A colorless, odorless gas that burns easily and is a main part of the gas used for cooking. It is formed by decaying plants and found in coal mines, oil wells, etc.

me·thinks [mē·thingks′] *v.* **me·thought** It seems to me: seldom used today.

meth·od [meth′əd] *n.* **1** A way of doing or ac-complishing something: Flying by airplane is a *method* of traveling. **2** System, order, or regularity: To study without *method* is a waste of time.

me·thod·i·cal [mə·thod′i·kəl] *adj.* Using or showing the use of a strict, orderly system: a *methodical* search. **— me·thod′i·cal·ly** *adv.*

Meth·od·ism [meth′əd·iz′əm] *n.* The doctrines, practice, and way of worship of the Methodists.

Meth·od·ist [meth′əd·ist] **1** *n.* A member of a Christian church that grew out of the religious movement started by John Wesley. **2** *adj.* Of or having to do with Methodists or their church.

me·thought [mē·thôt′] Past tense of ME-THINKS.

Me·thu·se·lah [mə·th(y)ōō′zə·lə] *n.* **1** In the Bible, a man who was said to have lived for 969 years. **2** Any very old man.

meth·yl alcohol [meth′əl] A highly poisonous form of alcohol; wood alcohol.

me·tic·u·lous [mə·tik′yə·ləs] *adj.* Extremely careful or too careful about minor details.

met·ric [met′rik] *adj.* **1** Of, in, having to do with, or using the metric system. **2** Metrical. ◆ *Metric* comes from the French *métrique*, which was formed by combining *mètre*, meaning *meter*, with the suffix *-ique*.

met·ri·cal [met′ri·kəl] *adj.* **1** Of, arranged in, or using meter: Blank verse is written in *metrical* feet; *metrical* music. **2** Of, having to do with, or used in measurement.

metric system A system of weights and measures in which all units are formed by multiplying or dividing a standard unit by 10, 100, 1000, etc. The standard unit of length in the metric system is the meter, the unit of weight is the gram, and the unit of volume is the liter.

met·ro·nome [met′rə·nōm] *n.* An instrument that makes clicks at an even but adjustable rate, used to set a tempo in practicing music.

me·trop·o·lis [mə·trop′ə·lis] *n.* **1** The largest or most important city of a country, state, or area. **2** Any large city or center of activity.

met·ro·pol·i·tan [met′rə·pol′ə·tən] **1** *adj.* Of, having to do with, or making up a large city or metropolis: the *metropolitan* area. **2** *n.* A person who lives in a large city or who has characteristics associated with city people. **3** *n.* In various churches, an archbishop.

Metronome

met·tle [met′(ə)l] *n.* Spirit, courage, or resolu-tion: to test a man's *mettle*. **— on one's mettle** Ready to do the best one can.

mew[1] [myōō] *n.* A sea gull.

mew[2] [myōō] **1** *n.* A cage in which hawks are

kept when they are shedding their feathers.
2 *v.* To confine in or as if in a cage.

mew[3] [myo͞o] **1** *n.* The crying sound typical of a cat. **2** *v.* To make the crying sound of a cat.

mewl [myo͞ol] **1** *v.* To whimper or cry feebly, as a baby does. **2** *n.* A whimper or feeble cry.

Mex·i·can [mek′sə·kən] **1** *adj.* Of or from Mexico. **2** *n.* A person born in or a citizen of Mexico.

Mex·i·co [mek′sə·kō] *n.* A country in North America, south of the U.S.

Mexico City The capital of Mexico.

Mexico, Gulf of An inlet of the Atlantic Ocean nearly enclosed by the U.S., Mexico, and Cuba.

mez·za·nine [mez′ə·nēn] *n.* **1** A story in a building between two main floors, usually just above the ground floor and sometimes extending over it like a balcony. **2** In a theater, the first balcony or the front rows of the balcony.

mez·zo [met′sō] *adj.* Half; medium; moderate.

mez·zo-so·pran·o [met′sō·sə·pran′ō] *n., pl.* **mez·zo-so·pran·os 1** A female singing voice of a quality and range between soprano and contralto. **2** A singer having such a voice.

Mg The symbol for the element MAGNESIUM.

mi [mē] *n.* In music, a syllable used to represent the third tone of a major scale or the fifth tone of a minor scale, or in a fixed system the tone E.

mi. Abbreviation of: **1** MILE. **2** Miles.

Mi·am·i [mī·am′ē] *n.* A city in SE Florida.

mi·as·ma [mī·az′mə] *n.* A heavy vapor rising from the earth, especially from decaying matter in swamps, formerly thought to cause disease.

mi·ca [mī′kə] *n.* A shiny mineral that is easily split into thin, flexible, partly transparent layers. It is also called isinglass.

mice [mīs] Plural of MOUSE.

Mich. Abbreviation of MICHIGAN.

Mi·chael [mī′kəl] *n.* One of the archangels.

Mich·ael·mas [mik′əl·məs] *n.* September 29, a church feast honoring the archangel Michael.

Mi·chel·an·ge·lo [mī′kəl·an′jə·lō] *n.* 1475–1564, Italian sculptor, painter, architect, and poet.

Mich·i·gan [mish′ə·gən] *n.* A state in the north central U.S.

Michigan, Lake The third in size of the Great Lakes.

mi·crobe [mī′krōb] *n.* An organism too tiny to be seen except with a microscope, especially one of the bacteria that cause disease; a germ.

mi·cro·bi·ol·o·gy [mī′krō·bī·ol′ə·jē] *n.* The branch of biology concerned with the study of microorganisms. — **mi′cro·bi·ol′o·gist** *n.*

mi·cro·film [mī′krə·film] **1** *n.* Film used to take tiny photographs of papers, records, pages of books, etc., for storage in small space. **2** *v.* To photograph on microfilm: The company will *microfilm* all personnel records.

mi·crom·e·ter [mī·krom′ə·tər] *n.* **1** A caliper used to make very precise measurements. **2** An instrument used with a microscope or telescope to measure very small distances. ◆ See OMEGA.

Micrometer caliper

Mi·cro·ne·sia [mī′krə·nē′zhə] *n.* A group of islands in the western Pacific Ocean north of the equator.

mi·cro·or·gan·ism [mī′krō·ôr′gən·iz′əm] *n.* An organism so small that it can be seen only through a microscope, especially one of the bacteria, a protozoan, or a virus.

mi·cro·phone [mī′krə·fōn] *n.* A device that converts sound waves into alternating electric currents, used for broadcasting, amplifying, etc.

mi·cro·scope [mī′krə·skōp] *n.* An instrument, usually consisting of a combination of lenses, used to magnify objects too small to be seen or clearly observed by the naked eye.

mi·cro·scop·ic [mī′krə·skop′ik] *adj.* **1** So small as to be visible only under a microscope. **2** Very small; minute. **3** Of, like, having to do with, or performed with a microscope: a *microscopic* examination. **4** Showing very close observation or attention to details: a *microscopic* search. — **mi′cro·scop′i·cal·ly** *adv.*

Microscope

mi·cro·wave [mī′krə·wāv] *n.* An electromagnetic wave having a frequency between about 1,000 and 30,000 megacycles.

mid [mid] *adj.* Middle.

mid or **'mid** [mid] *prep.* Amid; among: used mostly in poems.

mid- A prefix meaning: **1** The middle or the middle part of, as in *midwinter*, the middle of winter. **2** Being in, at, or near the middle or center, as in *midpoint*, a point at the center.

Mi·das [mī′dəs] *n.* In Greek legend, a king whose magic touch would turn anything to gold.

mid·day [mid′dā′] *n.* **1** The middle of the day; noon. **2** *adj. use*: a *midday* snack.

mid·dle [mid′(ə)l] **1** *n.* The part, point, position, or area in the center, equally distant from the ends, sides, or edges: the *middle* of the night; in the *middle* of a group; I want to sit in the *middle*. **2** *adj.* Being in, at, or near the middle: a *middle* position. **3** *adj.* Coming halfway between others; in between: the *middle* child in a family. **4** *n.* The waist.

---

add, āce, câre, pälm;   end, ēqual;   it, īce;   odd, ōpen, ôrder;   to͝ok, po͞ol;   up, bûrn;
ə = a in *above*, e in *sicken*, i in *possible*, o in *melon*, u in *circus*;   yo͞o = u in *fuse*;   oil;   pout;
check; ring; thin; this; zh in *vision*.   For ¶ reference, see page 64 · HOW TO

mid·dle-aged [mid′(ə)l·ājd′] *adj.* Being no longer young but not yet old: said about people.

Middle Ages The period in European history between the downfall of Rome and the Renaissance, extending from 476 to about 1450.

middle class The part of a society in a social or economic position between the laboring class and the very wealthy or the nobility.

middle ear A small cavity between the eardrum and the inner ear where three small bones pass sound waves along to the inner ear; tympanum.

Middle East Egypt and the countries of sw Asia west of Pakistan and India.

mid·dle·man [mid′(ə)l·man′] *n., pl.* **mid·dle·men** [mid′(ə)l·men′] **1** A go-between or agent. **2** A person who buys in large quantities from producers and sells to retailers or consumers.

mid·dle·weight [mid′(ə)l·wāt′] *n.* **1** A person or animal of average weight. **2** A boxer weighing between 147 and 160 pounds.

Middle West The section of the U.S. between the Rocky Mountains and the Allegheny Mountains, and north of the Ohio River and the southern borders of Kansas and Missouri.

mid·dling [mid′ling] **1** *adj.* Of middle or average size, quality, or condition; ordinary. **2** *n.* (*pl.*) Various products of medium size, quality, etc. **3** *n.* (*pl.*) The coarser part of ground grain.

mid·dy [mid′ē] *n., pl.* **mid·dies 1** A loose blouse (also called a **middy blouse**) having a large collar that is square in back, worn by women and children. **2** *informal* A midshipman.

midge [mij] *n.* A gnat or small fly.

midg·et [mij′it] *n.* **1** A person of much less than normal size but with normal physical proportions. **2** Anything very small of its kind.

mid·land [mid′lənd] **1** *n.* The central or inland part of a country or region; the interior. **2** *adj.* Of or in an inland or interior region.

Middy blouse

mid·most [mid′mōst′] *adj.* Situated exactly or most nearly in the middle.

mid·night [mid′nīt′] **1** *n.* The middle of the night; twelve o'clock at night. **2** *adj. use:* a *midnight* snack. **3** *adj.* As dark as midnight.

midnight sun The sun when visible at midnight in summer in the arctic or antarctic.

mid·point [mid′point′] *n.* A point halfway between the ends, as of a line segment.

mid·rib [mid′rib′] *n.* The central vein of a leaf.

mid·riff [mid′rif] *n.* **1** The part of the body between the chest and the abdomen. **2** The diaphragm.

mid·ship·man [mid′ship′mən] *n., pl.* **mid·ship·men** [mid′ship′mən] **1** In the U.S. Navy, a student at the U.S. Naval Academy. **2** In the British Navy, an officer ranking between a naval cadet and the lowest commissioned officer.

midst [midst] **1** *n.* The central or inner part; middle. **2** *prep.* Amid. **—in the midst of 1** Surrounded by or occupied with. **2** During.

mid·sum·mer [mid′sum′ər] *n.* **1** The middle of summer. **2** The summer solstice, around June 21.

mid·way [mid′wā′] **1** *adj., adv.* In, to, or at the middle; halfway. **2** *n. U.S.* The amusement area at a fair or exposition.

Mid·west [mid′west′] *n.* The Middle West.

Mid·west·ern [mid′wes′tərn] *adj.* Of, having to do with, or located in the Middle West.

mid·wife [mid′wīf′] *n., pl.* **mid·wives** [mid′·wīvz′] A woman whose occupation is assisting women in childbirth.

mid·win·ter [mid′win′tər] *n.* **1** The middle of winter. **2** The winter solstice, around Dec. 22

mien [mēn] *n.* A person's air, manner, facial expression, or way of carrying himself.

might[1] [mīt] *n.* Great power; force; strength.

might[2] [mīt] Past tense of MAY.

might·i·ly [mī′tə·lē] *adv.* **1** With might, force, energy, or effort: to strive *mightily.* **2** Greatly; extremely: I was *mightily* relieved.

might·y [mī′tē] *adj.* **might·i·er, might·i·est,** *adv.* **1** *adj.* Extremely strong; powerful. **2** *adj.* Very great in size, influence, force, etc.: a *mighty* gale. **3** *adv. informal* Extremely; very: a *mighty* fine person. **— might′i·ness** *n.*

mi·gnon·ette [min′yən·et′] *n.* A plant having small, very fragrant, yellowish green flowers.

mi·graine [mī′grān] *n.* A very bad kind of headache, usually in one side of the head, and often accompanied by nausea.

mi·grant [mī′grənt] **1** *n.* A person, animal, bird, etc., that migrates. **2** *adj.* Moving regularly from place to place: *migrant* workers.

mi·grate [mī′grāt] *v.* **mi·grat·ed, mi·grat·ing 1** To move from one country or region to settle in another. **2** To move from one region or climate to another at the change of season: Birds *migrate* in autumn and spring. **— mi·gra′tion** *n.*

mi·gra·to·ry [mī′grə·tôr′ē] *adj.* Migrating or moving regularly from place to place.

mi·ka·do [mi·kä′dō] *n., pl.* **mi·ka·dos** The emperor of Japan.

Mi·lan [mi·lan′] *n.* A city in northern Italy.

milch [milch] *adj.* Giving milk, as a cow.

mild [mīld] *adj.* **1** Kind and gentle: She was meek and *mild.* **2** Gentle or moderate; not rough or severe: a *mild* rebuke; *mild* weather. **3** Not strong, sharp, or bitter, as in taste: *mild* cheese. **— mild′ly** *adv.* **— mild′ness** *n.*

mil·dew [mil′d(y)oo] **1** *n.* A whitish or discolored coating deposited by a fungus on plants, damp cloth or paper, etc. **2** *n.* The fungus itself. **3** *v.* To coat or become coated with mildew. ◆ Today *mildew* brings to mind an unpleasant, musty odor. But the Old English form of the word referred to the sweet-tasting *honeydew,* whose whitish color served to link it with the whitish coating now called *mildew.*

mile [mīl] *n*. A measure of distance equal to 5,280 feet. A nautical mile, air mile, or geographical mile is about 6076 feet. ◆ *Mile* goes back to the Latin word for *thousand*, as the mile in ancient Rome was a thousand paces.

mile·age [mī'lij] *n*. **1** The number of miles traveled or to be traveled: *Did you record the* mileage *from Philadelphia to New York?* **2** The approximate number of miles a vehicle can travel on a gallon of fuel. **3** *U.S.* An allowance of money given for traveling, usually figured at a fixed amount per mile.

mile·post [mīl'pōst'] *n*. A signpost giving the distance in miles to a stated point.

mile·stone [mīl'stōn'] *n*. **1** A stone, post, or pillar set up to indicate the distance in miles to a stated point. **2** An important event or a turning point in a lifetime, career, etc.

An old milestone

mil·i·tant [mil'ə·tənt] *adj*. Taking or ready to take aggressive action, as on behalf of beliefs or rights; fighting or ready to fight. **— mil'i·tan·cy** *n*. **— mil'i·tant·ly** *adv*.

mil·i·ta·rism [mil'ə·tə·riz'əm] *n*. **1** A national policy favoring the maintenance of a powerful military force and constant preparation for war. **2** Emphasis on military ideals. **— mil'i·ta·rist** *n*. **— mil'i·ta·ris'tic** *adj*.

mil·i·ta·rize [mil'ə·tə·rīz] *v*. **mil·i·ta·rized, mil·i·ta·riz·ing 1** To prepare or equip for war: to *militarize* a nation by strengthening the power of its armies. **2** To make military in nature. **3** To fill with warlike fervor. **— mil·i·ta·ri·za·tion** [mil'ə·tə·rə·zā'shən] *n*. ¶3

mil·i·tar·y [mil'ə·ter'ē] **1** *adj*. Of or having to do with the army, the armed forces, or warfare: *military* police; a *military* objective. **2** *adj*. Of, suitable to, or done by soldiers: a *military* bearing; *military* maneuvers. **3** *n*. The armed forces of a nation, or sometimes a group of officers who are leaders in the armed forces: *The* military *took over control of the government.*

mil·i·tate [mil'ə·tāt] *v*. **mil·i·tat·ed, mil·i·tat·ing** To have influence or effect; work: *The evidence* militated *against the defendant.*

mi·li·tia [mə·lish'ə] *n*. A body of citizens given military training outside the regular armed forces and called up only in emergencies.

milk [milk] **1** *n*. A white liquid secreted by female mammals for nourishing their young, especially cow's milk drunk or used by human beings. **2** *v*. To draw milk from: to *milk* a cow or goat. **3** *v*. To draw everything useful or valuable from, as if by milking: to *milk* someone of information. **4** *n*. Any milklike liquid or juice, as the liquid contained in a coconut.

milk·man [milk'man'] *n*., *pl*. **milk·men** [milk'men'] A man who sells or delivers milk.

milk of magnesia A white, powdery magnesium compound suspended in water, used as a laxative or to counteract stomach acidity.

milk shake A drink made of chilled, flavored milk, and often ice cream, mixed thoroughly.

milk·sop [milk'sop'] *n*. A weak, timid fellow.

milk·weed [milk'wēd'] *n*. Any of various plants having stems filled with a milky juice.

milk·y [mil'kē] *adj*. **milk·i·er, milk·i·est 1** Like milk, as in whiteness: *milky* glass. **2** Of or containing milk. **— milk'i·ness** *n*.

Milky Way A band of soft light seen across the sky at night, made up of stars and nebulae too far away for the eye to see them separately.

mill¹ [mil] **1** *n*. A machine or device for grinding or crushing corn, coffee, etc. **2** *n*. A building, establishment, etc., in which grain is ground into meal or flour. **3** *n*. Any of various machines that prepare materials, perform a continuous operation, etc.: often used in combination, as in saw*mill* or wind*mill*. **4** *n*. A factory equipped with machinery: a steel *mill*. **5** *v*. To grind, make, shape, prepare, etc., in or with a mill. **6** *v*. To raise, indent, or ridge the edge of (a coin, etc.). **7** *v*. To move or circle about without order or method: *The audience was* milling *about in the lobby.*

mill² [mil] *n*. In the U.S., one tenth of a cent, not a coin but a unit used in figuring.

Mil·lay [mi·lā'], **Edna St. Vincent,** 1892–1950, U.S. poet.

mil·len·ni·um [mi·len'ē·əm] *n*., *pl*. **mil·len·ni·a** [mi·len'ē·ə] or **mil·len·ni·ums 1** A period of a thousand years. **2** According to the New Testament, the thousand years during which Christ is to rule the world. **3** Any period in which life seems ideal. **— mil·len'ni·al** *adj*.

mill·er [mil'ər] *n*. **1** A person who operates or works in a flour mill. **2** A moth whose wings seem to have been dusted with flour.

mil·let [mil'it] *n*. **1** A grass grown in the U.S. for use as hay. **2** The seeds of this grass used as food in Asia and Europe.

mil·li·me·ter [mil'ə·mē'tər] *n*. A unit of length in the metric system equal to one thousandth of a meter or .03937 inch. ¶2

mil·li·ner [mil'ə·nər] *n*. A person who designs, makes, trims, or sells women's hats.

mil·li·ner·y [mil'ə·ner'ē] *n*. **1** Women's hats. **2** The business or occupation of a milliner.

mil·lion or **1,000,000** [mil'yən] *n*., *adj*. A thousand thousands.

mil·lion·aire [mil'yən·âr'] *n*. **1** A person whose wealth is valued at a million or more dollars, pounds, etc. **2** A very rich person.

mil·lionth [mil'yənth] **1** *adj*. Next after the 999,999th. **2** *n*. The millionth one. **3** *adj*. Being one of a million equal parts. **4** *n*. A millionth part.

mill·race [mil'rās'] *n*. **1** The current of water

that turns or drives a mill wheel. **2** The channel through which such a current runs.

mill·stone [mil′stōn′] *n.* **1** One of a pair of heavy, flat, round stones used for grinding grain. **2** A heavy burden, as one that weighs on a person.
◆ *Mill* and *stone* were combined to form the compound word *millstone*.

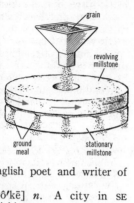
grain
revolving millstone
ground meal
stationary millstone

mill wheel A water wheel that furnishes the power to operate a mill.

Mil·ton [mil′tən], **John,** 1608–1674, English poet and writer of essays.

Mil·wau·kee [mil·wô′kē] *n.* A city in SE Wisconsin, on Lake Michigan.

mime [mīm] *n., v.* **mimed, mim·ing 1** *n.* An actor who does mimicry or pantomime. **2** *v.* To perform as a mime, usually without words.

mim·e·o·graph [mim′ē·ə·graf′] **1** *n.* A machine that prints copies from a usually typewritten stencil. **2** *v.* To print (copies) with this machine.

mim·ic [mim′ik] *v.* **mim·icked, mim·ick·ing,** *n., adj.* **1** *v.* To imitate the speech or actions of, usually in order to make fun of someone. **2** *n.* A person who mimics, especially one skillful at it. **3** *v.* To copy closely; ape. **4** *adj.* Of mimicry; imitative: *mimic* gestures. **5** *adj.* Simulated; mock: a *mimic* battle. **6** *v.* To have or assume the appearance of: Some insects *mimic* twigs.

mim·ic·ry [mim′ik·rē] *n., pl.* **mim·ic·ries 1** The act, practice, or art of mimicking. **2** The resemblance of a living thing to its surroundings or to another living thing for the purpose of concealment or protection.

mi·mo·sa [mi·mō′sə] *n.* A plant or tree of warm regions having feathery leaves and clusters of small yellow, pink, or white flowers.

min. Abbreviation of: **1** MINUTE. **2** Minutes.

min·a·ret [min′ə·ret′] *n.* A tower on a mosque from which a crier summons the people to prayer.

mince [mins] *v.* **minced, minc·ing 1** To cut or chop (food) into small bits. **2** To lessen the force or strength of (language, ideas, etc.): He didn't *mince* words. **3** To say or express with affected elegance or daintiness. **4** To walk with dainty steps.

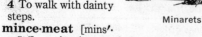
Minarets

mince·meat [mins′mēt′] *n.* A mixture of chopped apples, raisins, spices, etc., used as a pie filling.

minc·ing [min′sing] *adj.* Affectedly dainty or elegant: a *mincing* walk. **— minc′ing·ly** *adv.*

mind [mīnd] **1** *n.* All of the processes by which a person thinks, feels, remembers, imagines, etc., consciously or unconsciously. **2** *n.* Capability for thought or reasoning; intelligence: a good *mind.* **3** *n.* Way of thinking: a logical *mind.* **4** *n.* A person's opinions, ideas, plans, etc.: to change one's *mind.* **5** *n.* Memory; recall: Within the *mind* of man this has never happened. **6** *n.* Sanity; reason: to lose one's *mind.* **7** *n.* Attention: Put your *mind* on the test. **8** *v.* To pay attention to: *Mind* what he says. **9** *v.* To be careful about: *Mind* your appearance. **10** *v.* To obey: *Mind* the teacher. **11** *v.* To look after; tend: *Mind* the bonfire. **12** *v.* To object to: to *mind* the heat. **— a piece of one's mind** A severe scolding. **— bear in mind** or **keep in mind** To be sure to remember. **— be of one mind** To agree. **— have a mind to** To be tempted to: I *have a* good *mind to* punch him. **— have in mind** To be thinking about. **— make up one's mind** To decide. **— on one's mind** In one's thoughts or concern. **— out of one's mind 1** Insane; mad. **2** Frantic.

mind·ed [mīn′did] *adj.* **1** Having a specified kind of mind: used in combination: evil-*minded.* **2** Disposed: He was *minded* to argue.

mind·ful [mīnd′fəl] *adj.* Keeping in mind; aware: Be *mindful* of the needs of the poor.

mind·less [mīnd′lis] *adj.* **1** Having little or no intelligence. **2** Heedless; thoughtless.

mind's eye The imagination.

mine¹ [mīn] *pron.* **1** The one or ones that belong to or have to do with me: That ball is *mine*; Those are older than *mine*. **2** My: *mine* eyes: seldom used today.

mine² [mīn] *n., v.* **mined, min·ing 1** *n.* A large hole or deep tunnel made for removing minerals from the earth. **2** *v.* To dig from a mine: to *mine* coal. **3** *v.* To dig for minerals; work in a mine. **4** *v.* To dig a mine or mines in: to *mine* the earth. **5** *n.* An abundant source: a *mine* of ideas. **6** *n.* A hidden explosive set to go off when an enemy ship, tank, soldier, etc., comes near it. **7** *v.* To hide such explosives in or under: to *mine* a field.

min·er [mīn′ər] *n.* A person who works digging minerals from the earth.

min·er·al [min′ər·əl] **1** *n.* A natural substance that is not a plant or animal and has a fairly definite physical and chemical make-up, as quartz, coal, diamond, etc. **2** *adj.* Like, being, or containing a mineral or minerals.

min·er·al·o·gy [min′ə·ral′ə·jē *or* min′ə·rol′ə·jē] *n.* The scientific study of minerals. **— min′er·al′o·gist** *n.*

mineral water Any water that contains, either artificially or naturally, mineral salts or gases. It is thought to be healthful.

Mi·ner·va [mi·nûr′və] *n.* In Roman myths, the goddess of wisdom, invention, and handicraft. Her Greek name was Athena.

min·gle [ming'gəl] *v.* **min·gled, min·gling**
1 To bring or come together; mix or join: to
mingle different ingredients. **2** To associate or
mix: to *mingle* with a group or crowd.

min·i·a·ture [min'(ē·)ə·chər] **1** *n.* Something
made or represented on a small scale: a *miniature*
of a ship. **2** *n.* A tiny painting, most often a
portrait. **3** *adj.* Very small; tiny.

min·i·a·tur·ize [min'(ē·)ə·chər·iz'] *v.* **min·i·a·**
tur·ized, min·i·a·tur·iz·ing To make in an
unusually small size, as a radio, machine, etc.

min·i·mize [min'ə·miz] *v.* **min·i·mized, min·**
i·miz·ing 1 To reduce to the smallest possible
amount or degree: to *minimize* a danger. **2** To
make as little of as possible: to *minimize* the
importance of something. ¶3

min·i·mum [min'ə·məm] *n., pl.* **min·i·mums**
or **min·i·ma** [min'ə·mə] **1** The least amount
possible or allowed. **2** The lowest point or
smallest amount reached. **3** *adj. use:* a *mini-*
mum wage; a *minimum* temperature.

min·ing [mi'ning] *n.* **1** The extracting of coal,
ore, etc., from a mine or mines. **2** The laying of
an explosive mine or mines.

min·ion [min'yən] *n.* A servant or follower,
especially one who is slavish.

min·is·ter [min'is·tər] **1** *n.* A clergyman, especially a Protestant clergyman who is pastor
of a church. **2** *v.* To give help or attention: to
minister to a sick person. **3** *n.* The head of a
department of a government: the *Minister* of
Finance. **4** *n.* A diplomat who represents his
government in a foreign country. **— min·is·te·**
ri·al [min'is·tir'ē·əl] *adj.*

min·is·trant [min'is·trənt] **1** *adj.* Ministering.
2 *n.* A person who ministers.

min·is·tra·tion [min'is·trā'shən] *n. (usually pl.)*
Help or aid given to others.

min·is·try [min'is·trē] *n., pl.* **min·is·tries**
1 The profession, duties, or service of a clergyman. **2** The clergy. **3** A body of government
ministers. **4** A department of government headed
by a minister. **5** The act of ministering.

mink [mingk] *n.* **1** An animal like, but slightly
larger than, a weasel,
found in North
America. **2** The valu-
able brown fur of this
animal.

Minn. Abbreviation
of MINNESOTA.

Min·ne·ap·o·lis
[min'ē·ap'ə·lis] *n.* A
city in eastern Minne-
sota, on the Mississippi River.

Mink, about 17 in. long

Min·ne·so·ta [min'ə·sō'tə] *n.* A state in the
north central U.S.

min·now [min'ō] *n.* **1** A small, fresh-water fish
related to the carp, common in North America
and much used for bait. **2** Any small fish.

mi·nor [mi'nər] **1** *adj.* Smaller; lesser: Compared to Jupiter, Earth is a *minor* planet. **2** *adj.*
Not important: a *minor* problem. **3** *n.* A person
below the legal age for adult rights and responsibilities. **4** *n.* A subject or field of study second
in importance to a major. **5** *v.* To spend time
and study with a minor: to *minor* in physics.
6 *adj.* Indicating or based on a musical scale
that has a semitone between its second and third
tones and whole tones between the first and
second, third and fourth, and fourth and fifth,
the remaining tones varying with the direction
of the melody. **7** *adj.* Indicating a chord that
could be formed from the first, third, and fifth
tones of a minor scale.

mi·nor·i·ty [mə·nôr'ə·tē] *n., pl.* **mi·nor·i·ties**
1 The smaller in number of two parts or parties.
2 A group of people different in some way from
the larger group of which it is a part. **3** The
condition or time of being a minor.

Min·o·taur [min'ə·tôr] *n.* In Greek myths, a
monster with a man's body and a bull's head.
It was kept in a labyrinth at Crete where it ate
human captives until slain by Theseus.

min·strel [min'strəl] *n.* **1** In the Middle Ages,
a wandering musician, poet, and entertainer.
2 A performer in a minstrel show.

minstrel show A stage show of songs, jokes,
dances, etc., put on by actors disguised as
Negroes, popular in the 19th century.

min·strel·sy [min'strəl·sē] *n., pl.* **min·strel·**
sies 1 The art or occupation of a minstrel.
2 A collection of ballads or lyrics. **3** A troupe
of minstrels.

mint¹ [mint] *n.* **1** Any of several sweet-smelling
plants whose leaves are used for flavoring,
especially peppermint and spearmint. **2** A candy
flavored with mint.

mint² [mint] **1** *n.* A place where coins are lawfully made. **2** *v.* To make (coins). **3** *n.* A large
amount: a *mint* of money. **4** *adj.* In original
condition; brand-new; unused.

min·u·end [min'yoo·end] *n.* A number from
which another number is to be subtracted. In
$10 - 4 = 6$, 10 is the *minuend.*

min·u·et [min'yoo·et'] *n.* **1** A stately dance
popular in the 18th century. **2** Music for it, in
moderate $\frac{3}{4}$ time.

mi·nus [mi'nəs] **1** *prep.* Made less by; less:
ten *minus* five. **2** *n.* A minus sign. **3** *adj.* Less
than zero; negative: a *minus* score. **4** *prep.*
informal Lacking; without: *minus* two teeth.

minus sign A sign (−) indicating subtraction
or a negative quantity: $6 - 2 = 4$.

min·ute¹ [min'it] *n.* **1** The 60th part of an hour;
60 seconds. **2** A very brief time; moment. **3** A
specific instant of time: Do it this *minute!* **4** The
60th part of a degree of an arc or angle. **5** (*pl.*)
An official record of the events and discussions of
a particular meeting.

---

add, āce, câre, pälm;   end, ēqual;   it, īce;   odd, ōpen, ôrder;   took, pool;   up, bûrn;
ə = a in *above*, e in *sicken*, i in *possible*, o in *melon*, u in *circus*;   yoo = u in *fuse*;   oil;   pout;
check; ring; thin; this; zh in *vision*.   For ¶ reference, see page 64 · HOW TO

mi·nute[2] [mĭ·n(y)ōōt′] *adj.* **1** Tiny. **2** Very careful and precise in small details: a *minute* examination. — **mi·nute′ly** *adv.* — **mi·nute′·ness** *n.*

min·ute·man [mĭn′it·man′] *n.,* *pl.* **min·ute·men** [mĭn′it·men′] During the Revolutionary War, one of the armed citizens that pledged to be ready to fight the British at a minute's notice.

mi·nu·ti·ae [mĭ·n(y)ōō′shi·ē] *n.pl.* Small or unimportant details.

minx [mĭngks] *n.* A bold or flirtatious girl.
◆ *Minx,* which once meant simply a pet dog, later came to mean a playful or bold woman, and later still a bad or lewd woman. This last meaning is no longer used.

mir·a·cle [mĭr′ə·kəl] *n.* **1** A happy or wondrous event that cannot be explained by any known natural or scientific law. **2** Any wonderful thing or person: a *miracle* of foresight.

mi·rac·u·lous [mĭ·rak′yə·ləs] *adj.* **1** Seeming contrary to natural law. **2** Amazing or wondrous. — **mi·rac′u·lous·ly** *adv.*

mi·rage [mĭ·räzh′] *n.* An optical illusion, as of a lake and palm trees in a desert or an upside-down ship at sea, appearing quite close, but actually being images of distant objects reflected by the atmosphere.

mire [mīr] *n., v.* **mired, mir·ing** **1** *n.* Swampy ground or deep mud. **2** *v.* To sink or stick in mire. **3** *v.* To soil or smear with mud.

mir·ror [mĭr′ər] **1** *n.* A smooth surface that reflects light, especially a surface of glass backed with a coating of metal. **2** *v.* To reflect or show an image of: The pond *mirrored* her face. **3** *n.* Something that reflects or pictures truly: The book is a *mirror* of modern times.

mirth [mûrth] *n.* Spirited fun and gaiety.

mirth·ful [mûrth′fəl] *adj.* Full of mirth; merry. — **mirth′ful·ly** *adv.*

mirth·less [mûrth′lis] *adj.* Joyless; sad. — **mirth′less·ly** *adv.*

mis- A prefix meaning: **1** Bad or wrong, as in *misbehavior,* bad behavior. **2** Badly or wrongly, as in *misunderstand,* to understand wrongly.

mis·ad·ven·ture [mĭs′əd·ven′chər] *n.* An unlucky happening or accident; a bit of bad luck.

mis·an·thrope [mĭs′ən·thrōp] *n.* A person who hates or mistrusts his fellow men.

mis·ap·ply [mĭs′ə·plī′] *v.* **mis·ap·plied, mis·ap·ply·ing** To use or apply wrongly.

mis·ap·pre·hend [mĭs′ap·ri·hend′] *v.* To misunderstand. — **mis′ap·pre·hen′sion** *n.*

mis·ap·pro·pri·ate [mĭs′ə·prō′prē·āt] *v.* **mis·ap·pro·pri·at·ed, mis·ap·pro·pri·at·ing** To use or take improperly or dishonestly: The politician was accused of *misappropriating* public funds. — **mis′ap·pro′pri·a′tion** *n.*

mis·be·have [mĭs′bi·hāv′] *v.* **mis·be·haved, mis·be·hav·ing** To behave badly.

mis·be·hav·ior [mĭs′bi·hāv′yər] *n.* Bad or improper conduct.

misc. Abbreviation of MISCELLANEOUS.

mis·cal·cu·late [mĭs·kal′kyə·lāt] *v.* **mis·cal·cu·lat·ed, mis·cal·cu·lat·ing** To calculate or plan wrongly. — **mis′cal·cu·la′tion** *n.*

mis·call [mĭs·kôl′] *v.* To call by a wrong name.

mis·car·riage [mĭs·kar′ij] *n.* **1** The birth of a baby before it is well enough developed to live. **2** Failure to reach a proper conclusion or destination: a *miscarriage* of justice.

mis·car·ry [mĭs·kar′ē] *v.* **mis·car·ried, mis·car·ry·ing** **1** To reach a wrong conclusion or destination: The plan *miscarried*; The freight has *miscarried*. **2** To have a miscarriage.

mis·cel·la·ne·ous [mĭs′ə·lā′nē·əs] *adj.* **1** Composed of many different things or elements: a *miscellaneous* mixture. **2** Various: *miscellaneous* details. — **mis′cel·la′ne·ous·ly** *adv.*

mis·cel·la·ny [mĭs′ə·lā′nē] *n., pl.* **mis·cel·la·nies** A miscellaneous collection, especially of written things in a single book.

mis·chance [mĭs·chans′] *n.* Bad luck or a mishap.

mis·chief [mĭs′chif] *n.* **1** Thoughtless conduct that may cause harm: Don't get into *mischief* with matches. **2** Harm, trouble, or injury: High winds can cause great *mischief*. **3** Teasing or pranks. **4** A person or animal that teases or does harm in play.

mis·chie·vous [mĭs′chi·vəs] *adj.* **1** Inclined to or full of mischief: a *mischievous* child. **2** Slightly troubling or annoying: a *mischievous* act. **3** Causing or tending to cause harm or injury: a *mischievous* rumor. — **mis′chie·vous·ly** *adv.* — **mis′chie·vous·ness** *n.*

mis·con·ceive [mĭs′kən·sēv′] *v.* **mis·con·ceived, mis·con·ceiv·ing** To understand wrongly; misunderstand.

mis·con·cep·tion [mĭs′kən·sep′shən] *n.* A false or mistaken notion, idea, concept, etc.

mis·con·duct [*n.* mĭs·kon′dukt, *v.* mĭs′kən·dukt′] **1** *n.* Improper or immoral behavior. **2** *v.* To behave (oneself) improperly. **3** *n.* Mismanagement. **4** *v.* To manage badly or wrongly.

mis·con·struc·tion [mĭs′kən·struk′shən] *n.* **1** The act of misconstruing. **2** A wrong interpretation or understanding of something.

mis·con·strue [mĭs′kən·strōō′] *v.* **mis·con·strued, mis·con·stru·ing** To interpret wrongly; misunderstand: to *misconstrue* a signal.

mis·count [mĭs·kount′] **1** *v.* To count incorrectly. **2** *n.* An incorrect count.

mis·cre·ant [mĭs′krē·ənt] **1** *n.* An evildoer; villain. **2** *adj.* Doing evil; wicked.

mis·deal [mĭs·dēl′] *v.* **mis·dealt, mis·deal·ing,** *n.* **1** *v.* To deal (cards) incorrectly. **2** *n.* An incorrect deal of cards.

mis·deed [mĭs·dēd′] *n.* A wrong or evil act.

mis·de·mean·or [mĭs′di·mē′nər] *n.* Any legal offense less serious than a felony, as disorderly conduct or littering a public place. ¶1

mis·di·rect [mĭs′di·rekt′] *v.* To direct or guide wrongly: to *misdirect* a person.

mis·do·ing [mĭs·dōō′ing] *n.* A misdeed.

mi·ser [mī′zər] *n.* A greedy, stingy person who hoards money because he loves it.

mis·er·a·ble [miz′ər·ə·bəl] *adj.* **1** In misery; very unhappy or wretched. **2** Causing misery or great discomfort: a *miserable* toothache. **3** Very poor; awful: a *miserable* play. **— mis′· er·a·bly** *adv.*

mi·ser·ly [mī′zər·lē] *adj.* Like a miser; greedy and stingy. **— mi′ser·li·ness** *n.*

mis·er·y [miz′ər·ē] *n., pl.* **mis·er·ies 1** A condition of great wretchedness or suffering. **2** A cause or source of such suffering.

mis·fire [*v.* mis·fīr′, *n.* mis′fīr] *v.* **mis·fired, mis·fir·ing,** *n.* **1** *v.* To fail to fire, ignite, or explode at the right time, as a gun or an engine. **2** *n.* A misfiring. **3** *v.* To go wrong; fail: His plan *misfired.*

mis·fit [*v.* mis·fit′, *n.* mis′fit′] *v.* **mis·fit·ted, mis·fit·ting,** *n.* **1** *v.* To fail to fit or make fit. **2** *n.* Something that fits badly. **3** *n.* A person that gets on badly with those around him or in a given situation.

mis·for·tune [mis·fôr′chən] *n.* **1** Ill fortune; bad luck. **2** A mishap or calamity.

mis·giv·ing [mis·giv′ing] *n.* (*often pl.*) A feeling of doubt, distrust, or worry.

mis·gov·ern [mis·guv′ərn] *v.* To govern or administer badly. **— mis·gov′ern·ment** *n.*

mis·guid·ed [mis·gī′did] *adj.* Led by or resulting from bad advice or wrong ideas: a *misguided* person; a *misguided* effort.

mis·han·dle [mis·han′dəl] *v.* **mis·han·dled, mis·han·dling** To handle, treat, or manage badly.

mis·hap [mis′hap] *n.* An unfortunate accident.

mis·in·form [mis′in·fôrm′] *v.* To give wrong or false information to. **— mis′in·for·ma′tion** *n.*

mis·in·ter·pret [mis′in·tûr′prit] *v.* To interpret or understand incorrectly. **— mis′in·ter′pre·ta′tion** *n.*

mis·judge [mis·juj′] *v.* **mis·judged, mis·judg·ing** To judge wrongly or unfairly.

mis·lay [mis·lā′] *v.* **mis·laid, mis·lay·ing 1** To put in a place not remembered later: to *mislay* a book. **2** To place or put down incorrectly: to *mislay* tiles.

mis·lead [mis·lēd′] *v.* **mis·led, mis·lead·ing 1** To guide or lead in the wrong direction. **2** To lead into wrongdoing: The gang *misled* him into stealing. **3** To lead into an error or wrong judgment: He *misled* me as to the price. **4** *adj. use:* a *misleading* report. ◆ See DECEIVE.

mis·man·age [mis·man′ij] *v.* **mis·man·aged, mis·man·ag·ing** To manage badly or improperly. **— mis·man′age·ment** *n.*

mis·name [mis·nām′] *v.* **mis·named, mis·nam·ing** To give a wrong name to.

mis·no·mer [mis·nō′mər] *n.* **1** An incorrect name: "Insect" is a *misnomer* for a spider, which is really an arachnid. **2** The act of misnaming.

mis·place [mis·plās′] *v.* **mis·placed, mis·plac·ing 1** To put in a wrong place. **2** To put aside and forget where; mislay. **3** To give or place (love, faith, etc.) wrongly or unwisely.

mis·play [mis·plā′] **1** *v.* In games and sports, to play wrongly or badly. **2** *n.* A bad play or move.

mis·print [*n.* mis′print′, *v.* mis·print′] **1** *n.* An error in printing. **2** *v.* To print incorrectly.

mis·pro·nounce [mis′prə·nouns′] *v.* **mis·pro·nounced, mis·pro·nounc·ing** To pronounce incorrectly.

mis·pro·nun·ci·a·tion [mis′prə·nun′sē·ā′shən] *n.* An incorrect pronunciation.

mis·quote [mis·kwōt′] *v.* **mis·quot·ed, mis·quot·ing** To quote incorrectly. **— mis·quo·ta·tion** [mis′kwō·tā′shən] *n.*

mis·read [mis·rēd′] *v.* **mis·read, mis·read·ing** To read incorrectly or with a wrong meaning.

mis·rep·re·sent [mis′rep·ri·zent′] *v.* To give a false or misleading idea of: to *misrepresent* facts. **— mis′rep·re·sen·ta′tion** *n.*

mis·rule [mis·rool′] *v.* **mis·ruled, mis·rul·ing,** *n.* **1** *v.* To rule unwisely or unjustly. **2** *n.* Bad or unjust rule or government. **3** *n.* Disorder or confusion, as from lawlessness.

miss [mis] **1** *v.* To fail to hit, strike, reach, or land upon (an object): to *miss* a target; to swing and *miss.* **2** *n.* Such a failure. **3** *v.* To fail to meet or catch: to *miss* a train. **4** *v.* To fail to see, hear, notice, or understand: I *missed* that remark; You *missed* the point. **5** *v.* To fail to attend, keep, perform, etc.: to *miss* an appointment. **6** *v.* To overlook or not take advantage of: to *miss* a chance. **7** *v.* To discover the absence of: to *miss* one's watch. **8** *v.* To be sad about the absence of: to *miss* a pet. **9** *v.* To escape; avoid: He barely *missed* falling.

Miss [mis] *n.* **1** A title for an unmarried girl or woman. **2** (*written* **miss**) A young, unmarried girl. ◆ In speaking of two or more unmarried women of the same last name, either *the Misses Clark* or *the Miss Clarks* is acceptable, although the first is more formal.

Miss. Abbreviation of MISSISSIPPI.

mis·sal [mis′əl] *n.* A book containing all the prayers, responses, etc., for celebrating Mass.

mis·shap·en [mis·shā′pən] *adj.* Deformed.

mis·sile [mis′əl] *n.* An object, especially a weapon, intended to be thrown or shot, as a bullet, arrow, stone, or guided missile. ◆ *Missile* comes from the Latin word *missus,* meaning *sent.*

mis·sing [mis′ing] *adj.* **1** Absent or lost. **2** Lacking; minus: *missing* an arm.

mis·sion [mish′ən] *n.* **1** The task, business, or duty that a person or group is sent forth to do. **2** A group of people sent out to perform some task. **3** A group of persons sent to represent their government in a foreign country. **4** A group of missionaries, the work they do, or their living and working quarters. **5** One's chief purpose or task in life; calling.

---

add, āce, câre, pälm; end, ēqual; it, īce; odd, ōpen, ôrder; tŏŏk, pōōl; up, bûrn;
ə = a in *above,* e in *sicken,* i in *possible,* o in *melon,* u in *circus;* yōō = u in *fuse;* oil; pout;
check; ring; thin; this; zh in *vision.* For ¶ reference, see page 64 · HOW TO

mis·sion·ar·y [mish′ən·er′ē] **1** *n.* A person sent out to convert people to his religion. **2** *adj.* Of or having to do with religious missions or missionaries.

Mis·sis·sip·pi [mis′ə·sip′ē] *n.* **1** A state in the south central U.S. **2** A river in the central U.S. flowing about 2330 miles to the Gulf of Mexico.

Mis·sis·sip·pi·an [mis′ə·sip′ē·ən] **1** *adj.* Of or from Mississippi. **2** *n.* A person born or living in Mississippi. **3** *adj.* Of or having to do with the Mississippi River.

mis·sive [mis′iv] *n.* A written message.

Mis·sou·ri [mi·zŏŏr′ē] *n.* **1** A state in the central U.S. **2** A river in the west central U.S., flowing 2,714 miles from the Rocky Mountains to the Mississippi River. — **Mis·sou′ri·an** *adj., n.*

mis·spell [mis·spel′] *v.* **mis·spelled** or **mis·spelt, mis·spell·ing** To spell incorrectly.

mis·spell·ing [mis·spel′ing] *n.* An incorrect spelling.

mis·spent [mis·spent′] *adj.* Spent or used foolishly or wastefully, as time.

mis·state [mis·stāt′] *v.* **mis·stat·ed, mis·stat·ing** To state wrongly or falsely. — **mis·state′ment** *n.*

mis·step [mis′step′] *n.* **1** A false step; stumble. **2** An error or blunder, as in conduct.

mist [mist] **1** *n.* A cloud of fine droplets of water. **2** *v.* To rain in fine droplets: It's *misting* out. **3** *v.* To make or become misty. **4** *n.* A film or haze that blurs the vision: a *mist* of tears. **5** *n.* Something that clouds the mind, memory, thoughts, etc.: the *mists* of time.

mis·take [mis·tāk′] *n., v.* **mis·took, mis·tak·en, mis·tak·ing 1** *n.* An error or blunder. **2** *v.* To take to be another: to *mistake* a friend for an enemy. **3** *v.* To misunderstand; misinterpret: to *mistake* someone's purpose.

mis·tak·en [mis·tā′kən] **1** Past participle of MISTAKE. **2** *adj.* Wrong: a *mistaken* notion. — **mis·tak′en·ly** *adv.*

Mis·ter [mis′tər] *n.* **1** A title for a man: used before his name or position and abbreviated to **Mr.** in writing. **2** (*written* **mister**) *informal* Sir: used without the name.

mis·tle·toe [mis′əl·tō] *n.* A small evergreen plant that grows as a parasite on certain trees. It bears white, waxy berries and is often used as a Christmas decoration.

mis·took [mis·tŏŏk′] Past tense of MISTAKE.

mis·treat [mis·trēt′] *v.* To treat badly or improperly. — **mis·treat′ment** *n.*

mis·tress [mis′tris] *n.* **1** A woman in a position of authority or control: the *mistress* of a household. **2** (*sometimes written* **Mistress**) Anything considered feminine that has rule or power over something else: England was *mistress* of the seas. **3** A woman who lives intimately for a period of time with a man who is not her husband. **4** (*written* **Mistress**) A former title for any woman.

mis·tri·al [mis·trī′əl] *n.* **1** A trial that is set aside because of a legal defect or error. **2** A trial in which the jury cannot reach a verdict.

mis·trust [mis·trust′] **1** *v.* To regard with suspicion or doubt. **2** *n.* Lack of trust.

mis·trust·ful [mis·trust′fəl] *adj.* Having mistrust; suspicious. — **mis·trust′ful·ly** *adv.*

mist·y [mis′tē] *adj.* **mist·i·er, mist·i·est 1** Of or like mist: a *misty* haze. **2** Covered with or obscured by mist: a *misty* glass; a *misty* landscape. **3** Not clear; vague: *misty* ideas or concepts. — **mist′i·ness** *n.*

mis·un·der·stand [mis′un·dər·stand′] *v.* **mis·un·der·stood, mis·un·der·stand·ing** To understand wrongly.

mis·un·der·stand·ing [mis′un·dər·stan′ding] *n.* **1** A failure to understand someone or something correctly. **2** A disagreement or quarrel.

mis·use [*v.* mis·yōōz′, *n.* mis·yōōs′] *v.* **mis·used, mis·us·ing,** *n.* **1** *v.* To use or apply wrongly or improperly. **2** *n.* An incorrect use or usage: a *misuse* of a noun. **3** *v.* To mistreat.

mite¹ [mīt] *n.* **1** Something very small; tiny bit. **2** A very small coin or sum of money.

mite² [mīt] *n.* Any of a number of small, spiderlike animals, such as chiggers, mainly living on plants or other animals or in certain foods.

mi·ter [mī′tər] **1** *n.* A tall headdress worn by a pope, bishop, or abbot. **2** *n.* A joint made of two pieces of material whose ends have been beveled at equal angles, as at the corner of a picture frame. **3** *v.* To join with a miter.

Miter

mit·i·gate [mit′ə·gāt] *v.* **mit·i·gat·ed, mit·i·gat·ing** To make or become milder or less severe: to *mitigate* pain. — **mit′i·ga′tion** *n.*

mi·to·sis [mī·tō′sis] *n.* The series of changes by which the body cells of a plant or animal divide in two.

mi·tre [mī′tər] *n., v.* **mi·tred** [mī′tərd], **mi·tring** [mī′tər·ing] Another spelling of MITER.

mitt [mit] *n.* **1** In baseball, a covering something like a mitten to protect the hand in catching the ball: a catcher's *mitt*. **2** A woman's glove sometimes extending to or above the elbow but without fully covering the fingers. **3** A mitten. **4** *slang* (*usually pl.*) A hand. **5** *slang* A boxing glove.

mit·ten [mit′ən] *n.* A glove encasing four fingers together and the thumb separately.

Mitt

mix [miks] *v.* **mixed** or **mixt, mix·ing,** *n.* **1** *v.* To combine or add so as to blend: to *mix* fuel with air; Oil and water won't *mix*; *Mix* in two eggs. **2** *v.* To make by mixing: to *mix* a drink. **3** *n.* A mixture, especially one containing the ingredients for something except for certain liquids: a biscuit *mix*. **4** *v.* To combine or join: to *mix* age and wisdom. **5** *v.* To get along or

associate: to *mix* with strangers. **—mix up**
1 To confuse. **2** To involve or implicate.

mixed [mikst] *adj.* **1** Composed of different elements, qualities, types, etc.: a *mixed* basket of fruit. **2** Made up of or involving people of both sexes: a *mixed* chorus. **3** Confused. We got our signals *mixed*.

mixed number The sum of an integer and a fraction, as 6⅝ or 2¼.

mix·er [mik′sər] *n.* **1** A person or thing that mixes. **2** *informal* A person who gets along well socially with others.

mix·ture [miks′chər] *n.* **1** The act of mixing. **2** The result of mixing. **3** A combination of things mixed or blended together.

mix-up [miks′up′] *n.* **1** A muddle; confusion. **2** *informal* A fight or melee.

miz·zen [miz′(ə)n] *n.* **1** A principal sail set on the mizzenmast. **2** A mizzenmast.

A hand mixer

miz·zen·mast [miz′(ə)n·mast′ *or* miz′(ə)n·məst] *n.* In a ship with three or more masts, the third mast from the bow.

Mlle. Abbreviation of MADEMOISELLE.

mm. Abbreviation of: **1** MILLIMETER. **2** Millimeters.

Mme. Abbreviation of MADAME.

Mn The symbol for the element MANGANESE.

Mo The symbol for the element MOLYBDENUM.

mo. Abbreviation of: **1** MONTH. **2** Months.

Mo. Abbreviation of MISSOURI.

Mo·ab [mō′ab] *n.* An ancient country east of the Dead Sea.

moan [mōn] **1** *n.* A low, sustained, mournful sound, as from grief or pain. **2** *n.* Any similar sound: the *moan* of the wind. **3** *v.* To produce a moan or moans. **4** *v.* To lament; mourn: to *moan* for the dead. **5** *v.* To complain; whine. **6** *v.* To speak or say with moans.

moat [mōt] *n.* A ditch, usually full of water, around a castle, fortress, etc., used as a defense against attackers.

mob [mob] *n.,* *v.* **mobbed, mob·bing** **1** *n.* A large or disorderly crowd. **2** *v.* To crowd around or attack in or as if in a mob: to *mob* a jail; to *mob* a bargain counter. **3** *n.* The ordinary mass of people: used to show contempt. **4** *n. informal* A gang of criminals.

Moat

◆ *Mob* comes from the Latin *mob(ile vulgus)* meaning *a movable,* or *excitable, crowd.*

mo·bile [*adj.* mō′bəl *or* mō′bēl, *n.* mō′bēl] **1** *adj.* Easily transported or movable: a *mobile* hospital; *mobile* troops. **2** *adj.* Changing quickly in response to feelings, situations, etc.: a *mobile* face. **3** *n.* A sculpture made of movable parts hung from or balanced on rods, wires, etc., so as to move with slight air currents. **—mo·bil·i·ty** [mō·bil′ə·tē] *n.*

mo·bi·lize [mō′bə·līz] *v.* **mo·bi·lized, mo·bi·liz·ing** **1** To prepare for war: to *mobilize* troops; The nation *mobilized.* **2** To assemble and organize for use: to *mobilize* resources. **—mo′·bi·li·za′tion** *n.* ¶3

moc·ca·sin [mok′ə·sin] *n.* **1** A shoe or slipper with soft soles and no heels, formerly worn by North American Indians. **2** A shoe or slipper resembling it. **3** The water moccasin, a snake. ◆ *Moccasin* comes from an Algonquian Indian word.

Moccasin

mo·cha [mō′kə] *n.* A choice coffee originally from Arabia.

mock [mok] **1** *v.* To ridicule or make fun of, often by mimicking or imitating: to *mock* someone's stutter. **2** *n.* An act of mocking. **3** *n.* A person or thing that is mocked. **4** *adj.* Not real but made to look so: a *mock* wedding. **5** *v.* To disappoint or thwart; frustrate. **—mock′er** *n.*

mock·er·y [mok′ər·ē] *n., pl.* **mock·er·ies** **1** A mocking; ridicule. **2** A mocking speech or act. **3** A person or thing that is mocked or deserves to be mocked. **4** A ridiculously poor imitation: a *mockery* of a trial. **5** Something very poor and disappointing.

mock·ing·bird [mok′ing·bûrd′] *n.* A bird of the southern U.S. that mimics other bird calls.

mode [mōd] *n.* **1** A way; method: a *mode* of living. **2** Prevailing or current style or fashion, as in dress. **3** A mood, as of a verb.

mod·el [mod′əl] *n., v.* **mod·eled** *or* **mod·elled, mod·el·ing** *or* **mod·el·ling** **1** *n.* A miniature copy or replica of an object: a *model* of a building. **2** *adj. use:* a *model* automobile. **3** *n.* A representation of something that is to be copied later in a more lasting material: a wax *model* of a statue. **4** *v.* To make a model of (an object, figure, etc.): to *model* a head. **5** *v.* To make (a material) into a

A model ship

add, āce, câre, pälm;   end, ēqual;   it, īce;   odd, ōpen, ôrder;   took, pool;   up, bûrn;
ə = a in *above,* e in *sicken,* i in *possible,* o in *melon,* u in *circus;   yoo = u in *fuse;*   oil;   pout;
check; ring; thin; this; zh in *vision.*   For ¶ reference, see page 64 · HOW TO

model: He *modeled* the clay into a small statue.
6 *n.* A person or thing that is worth imitating:
a *model* of good taste. **7** *adj. use:* a *model*
student. **8** *v.* To plan or form after a model:
a table *modeled* on an antique. *Model* yourself
on him. **9** *n.* A particular style, plan, or design:
a new *model* of boat. **10** *n.* Someone who poses
for a painter, sculptor, or photographer. **11** *v.*
To pose for an artist or photographer. **12** *n.* A
person hired to wear and display clothing. **13** *v.*
To wear and display (clothing). **— mod′el·er**
or **mod′el·ler** *n.*

mod·er·ate [*adj., n.* mod′ər·it, *v.* mod′ə·rāt]
adj., n., v. **mod·er·at·ed, mod·er·at·ing**
1 *adj.* Not extreme or excessive: There will be a
moderate delay; These are *moderate* prices. **2** *adj.*
Not extreme or radical in beliefs, actions, etc.:
He is a *moderate* spender; They have *moderate*
political views. **3** *n.* A person who has moderate
ideas or opinions, especially in politics or
religion. **4** *adj.* Not exceptional; average: a
moderate intelligence. **5** *v.* To make or become
moderate or more moderate: You must *moderate*
some of your more extreme opinions. **6** *v.* To be a
moderator. **7** *v.* To preside over as a moderator:
to *moderate* a debate. **— mod′er·ate·ly** *adv.*

mod·er·a·tion [mod′ə·rā′shən] *n.* **1** The condition or quality of being moderate. **2** The act
of moderating.

mod·er·a·tor [mod′ə·rā′tər] *n.* The chairman
of a meeting, forum, or debate.

mod·ern [mod′ərn] **1** *adj.* Of or having to do
with present or recent time. **2** *adj.* Not old-
fashioned; up-to-date. **3** *n.* A modern person.

mod·ern·is·tic [mod′ər·nis′tik] *adj.* Modern in
looks, design, ideas, etc.

mod·ern·ize [mod′ərn·īz] *v.* **mod·ern·ized,
mod·ern·iz·ing** To make or become modern
or more modern. **— mod′ern·i·za′tion** *n.* ¶3

mod·est [mod′ist] *adj.* **1** Not boastful; humble:
a *modest* hero. **2** Quietly decent and proper in
behavior, manner, speech, etc.: a *modest* girl.
3 Not elaborate, showy, or gaudy: a *modest*
meal. **4** Not excessive or extreme; moderate: a
modest price. **5** Bashful; shy. **— mod′est·ly**
adv.

mod·es·ty [mod′is·tē] *n.* The condition or
quality of being modest.

mod·i·cum [mod′ə·kəm] *n.* A moderate or
small amount: a *modicum* of bother.

mod·i·fi·ca·tion [mod′ə·fə·kā′shən] *n.* **1** The
act of modifying. **2** The condition of being
modified. **3** A qualification or mild change:
The plan needs *modification.* **4** Something made
by modifying: a *modification* of an old model.

mod·i·fi·er [mod′ə·fī′ər] *n.* A person or thing
that modifies, especially a word or group of
words that limits the meaning of another word
or group of words, as an adjective or adverb.

mod·i·fy [mod′ə·fī] *v.* **mod·i·fied, mod·i·fy·
ing** **1** To change moderately. **2** To make less
extreme or severe; moderate: to *modify* one's
views. **3** To qualify or limit the meaning of:
Adjectives *modify* nouns.

mod·ish [mō′dish] *adj.* Fashionable; stylish.
— mod′ish·ly *adv.*

mod·u·late [moj′ŏŏ·lāt] *v.* **mod·u·lat·ed,
mod·u·lat·ing** **1** To vary the tone, inflection,
pitch, or volume of: to *modulate* one's voice.
2 To regulate or adjust; modify: to *modulate*
air pressure. **3** To change some characteristic
of (a radio wave) in a way that corresponds to
a sound or other signal transmitted. **4** In music,
to go from one key to another.

mod·u·la·tion [moj′ŏŏ·lā′shən] *n.* **1** The act of
modulating. **2** The condition of being modulated. **3** In music, a change from one key to
another.

Mo·gul [mō′gul] *n.* **1** A Mongol, especially one
of the Mongolian conquerors of India or a
descendant of one of them. **2** (*written* **mogul**)
A very important person.

mo·hair [mō′hâr] *n.* **1** The hair of the Angora
goat. **2** A cloth made of mohair, usually in
combination with other materials, as with
cotton or wool.

Mo·ham·med [mō·ham′id] *n.*, 570?–632, Arabian founder of Islam and its chief prophet.

Mo·ham·me·dan [mō·ham′ə·dən] **1** *adj.* Of or
having to do with Mohammed or Islam. **2** *n.* A
Moslem.

Mo·ham·me·dan·ism [mō·ham′ə·dən·iz′əm] *n.*
Islam.

Mo·hawk [mō′hôk] *n.* One of a tribe of Indians
that lived in central New York State.

Mo·hi·can [mō·hē′kən] *n.* One of a tribe of
Indians that lived in NE New York State.

Mohs scale [mōz] A scale of hardness for
minerals, based on their ability to scratch or be
scratched by any of a set of standard minerals.

moi·dore [moi′dôr] *n.* An old Portuguese coin.

moi·e·ty [moi′ə·tē] *n., pl.* **moi·e·ties 1** A
half. **2** Any portion, part, or share.

moist [moist] *adj.* Slightly wet or damp.
— moist′ness *n.*

mois·ten [mois′ən] *v.* To make or become moist.

mois·ture [mois′chər] *n.* Water or other liquid
in very small drops causing dampness in the air
or through or on the surface of something.

mo·lar [mō′lər] *n.* A tooth with a broad crown,
adapted for grinding. An adult person has
three on each side at the back of each jaw.

mo·las·ses [mə·las′iz] *n.* A sweet, dark-colored
syrup obtained in making sugar, especially from
sugar cane.

mold[1] [mōld] **1** *n.* A hollow form that gives a
particular shape to
something in a soft or
fluid condition. **2** *v.*
To shape or form in a
mold. **3** *n.* Some-
thing shaped or made
in a mold: a *mold* of
wax. **4** *n.* The shape
or pattern formed by
a mold. **5** *v.* To
shape, form, or direct:
Newspapers often *mold* public opinion. **6** *n.* A

mold

special or distinctive nature, character, or type: an aristocratic *mold*.

mold² [mōld] **1** *n.* A furry fungous growth found on a surface of decaying food or other decaying organic matter. **2** *v.* To become moldy.

mold³ [mōld] *n.* Soft, loose earth that is good for plants because it is rich in decaying organic matter.

mold·er [mōl′dər] *v.* To decay gradually and turn to dust; crumble.

mold·ing [mōl′ding] *n.* **1** The act of molding or shaping. **2** Something that is molded. **3** A decorative strip of wood or other material fastened around a wall, door frame, window, etc.

Baseboard molding

mold·y [mōl′dē] *adj.* **mold·i·er, mold·i·est** **1** Of, covered with, or containing mold: *moldy* cake. **2** Musty; stale: a *moldy* room. **— mold′i·ness** *n.*

mole¹ [mōl] *n.* A small, often dark and hairy spot on the skin.

mole² [mōl] *n.* A small mammal that lives in underground burrows. It has tiny, weak eyes, soft fur, and forefeet adapted for digging.

mole³ [mōl] *n.* A massive, usually stone barricade in the sea, serving as a breakwater or pier.

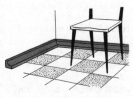

Mole, about 5 in. long

mo·lec·u·lar [mə·lek′yə·lər] *adj.* Of, produced by, or having to do with molecules.

mol·e·cule [mol′ə·kyōōl] *n.* **1** The smallest part of an element or compound that can exist separately without loss of its chemical properties: A *molecule* of water is made up of two atoms of hydrogen and one of oxygen. **2** A very small particle.

mole·hill [mōl′hil′] *n.* **1** A small mound of earth raised by a burrowing mole. **2** Something trivial, especially in the expression **make a mountain out of a molehill,** to make a fuss over nothing.

mo·lest [mə·lest′] *v.* To interfere with in a bad or wrong way; harm or bother. **— mo·les·ta·tion** [mō′les·tā′shən] *n.*

Mo·lière [mô·lyâr′] *n.,* 1622–1673, French comic dramatist and actor.

mol·li·fy [mol′ə·fī] *v.* **mol·li·fied, mol·li·fy·ing** To soothe or soften: to *mollify* someone's anger.

mol·lusk [mol′əsk] *n.* Any of a large group of animals having soft bodies that are not divided into segments, usually protected by a hard shell, as snails, oysters, squids, etc.

mol·ly·cod·dle [mol′ē·kod′(ə)l] *n., v.* **mol·ly·cod·dled, mol·ly·cod·dling** **1** *n.* A pampered boy or man; sissy. **2** *v.* To pamper; coddle. ◆ *Mollycoddle* comes from *Molly*, a girl's name, plus *coddle.*

molt [mōlt] *v.* To shed (feathers, horns, skin, etc.) in preparation for a new growth, as do certain animals such as snakes or birds.

mol·ten [mōl′tən] *adj.* **1** Made liquid, as by great heat: *molten* metal. **2** Made by melting and casting in a mold: a *molten* statue.

mo·lyb·de·num [mə·lib′də·nəm] *n.* A heavy, silver-white, metallic element, used in alloys to harden steel.

mom [mom] *n. informal* Mother.

mo·ment [mō′mənt] *n.* **1** A very short period of time; instant. **2** A particular point in time, often the present time: He is busy at the *moment.* **3** Importance: matters of great *moment.*

mo·men·tar·i·ly [mō′mən·ter′ə·lē *or* mō′mən·ter′ə·lē] *adv.* **1** For a moment: We saw the sun *momentarily.* **2** At any moment: The attack was expected *momentarily.* **3** Moment by moment: Our fear grew *momentarily.*

mo·men·tar·y [mō′mən·ter′ē] *adj.* Lasting for a moment.

mo·men·tous [mō·men′təs] *adj.* Very important: a *momentous* event.

mo·men·tum [mō·men′təm] *n.* **1** The amount of force that can be exerted by a moving body, equal to its mass multiplied by its speed. **2** Force, speed, or impetus, usually growing in strength or intensity: The uprising of the peasants gained *momentum* with the king's death.

Mon. Abbreviation of MONDAY.

Mon·a·co [mon′ə·kō *or* mə·nä′kō] *n.* A small independent country in SE France, ruled by a prince.

Mo·na Li·sa [mō′nə lē′zə] A portrait by Leonardo da Vinci of a Neapolitan woman. The painting is famous for the mysterious expression, often regarded as a smile, on the woman's face.

mon·arch [mon′ärk] *n.* **1** A ruler, as a king, queen, etc. **2** A large orange and brown North American butterfly.

mo·nar·chi·cal [mə·när′ki·kəl] *adj.* **1** Of, having to do with, or like a monarch or monarchy. **2** Governed by a monarch. **3** Favoring monarchy.

mon·arch·ist [mon′ər·kist] *n.* A person who believes in or supports a monarchy.

mon·ar·chy [mon′ər·kē] *n., pl.* **mon·ar·chies** **1** Government by a monarch. **2** A government or country ruled by a monarch.

mon·as·ter·y [mon′əs·ter′ē] *n., pl.* **mon·as·ter·ies** A place where monks live in seclusion.

mo·nas·tic [mə·nas′tik] *adj.* Of, having to do with, or like monasteries, monks, or the religious life as practiced in a monastery.

Mon·day [mun′dē *or* mun′dā] *n.* The second day of the week.

Mon·dri·an [môn′drē·än], **Piet,** 1872–1944, Dutch painter.

Mo·net [mō·nā′], **Claude,** 1840–1926, French painter.

mon·e·tar·y [mon′ə·ter′ē] *adj.* Of or in money: The dollar is the *monetary* unit of the U.S.; to receive a *monetary* reward.

mon·ey [mun′ē] *n., pl.* **mon·eys** or **mon·ies** 1 Coins and paper currency issued by a government to be used in paying debts and obligations. 2 Anything used in this way. 3 Wealth; riches: a person of *money*. ◆ See CURRENCY.

mon·eyed [mun′ēd] *adj.* 1 Having a lot of money; wealthy. 2 Made up of, coming from, or representing money or wealth: *moneyed* interests.

money order An order for the payment of a specified sum of money, issued at one bank, post office, etc., and payable at another. It is a safe way of sending money by mail.

Mon·gol [mong′gəl] 1 *n.* A native of Mongolia. 2 *n.* The language of Mongolia. 3 *n.* A Mongoloid person. 4 *adj.* Mongolian.

Mon·go·li·a [mong·gō′lē·ə] *n.* A region of east central Asia. It is divided into the **Mongolian People's Republic** and **Inner Mongolia,** a part of northern China.

Mon·go·li·an [mong·gō′lē·ən] 1 *n.* A person born in or a citizen of Mongolia. 2 *adj.* Of or having to do with Mongolia, its people, or its language. 3 *n.* Any person belonging to the Mongoloid division of mankind. 4 *adj.* Mongoloid. 5 *n.* The language of Mongolia.

Mon·go·loid [mong′gə·loid] *adj.* Of, having to do with, or belonging to a major ethnic division of mankind, characterized by a yellowish skin, slanting eyes, straight hair, high cheekbones, etc. Chinese, Japanese, Eskimos, etc., are Mongoloid people.

mon·goose [mong′gōos] *n., pl.* **mon·goos·es** A small animal of Asia and Africa. It resembles the ferret and preys on snakes and rats.

Mongoose, about 3 ft. long, including tail

mon·grel [mung′grəl *or* mong′grəl] *n.* A dog or any animal or plant of mixed breed.

mon·i·tor [mon′ə·tər] 1 *n.* A pupil chosen to assist a teacher in administrative tasks, maintaining order, etc. 2 *n.* A person or thing that warns or reminds. 3 *n.* A device that allows the operation or activity of a thing or person to be observed constantly. 4 *v.* To observe with or as if with a monitor: to *monitor* a broadcast.

mon·i·to·ry [mon′ə·tôr′ē] *adj.* Giving a warning; admonitory.

monk [mungk] *n.* A man who is a member of a religious order and lives usually in a monastery under a rule and is vowed to poverty, chastity, and obedience.

mon·key [mung′kē] *n., pl.* **mon·keys,** *v.* 1 *n.* Any of a large group of animals resembling the ape, but smaller and more agile and having long tails by which many of them can hang. 2 *n.* A mischievous child. 3 *v. informal* To play or trifle; meddle: Don't *monkey* with matches.

monkey wrench A wrench having an adjustable jaw for grasping nuts, bolts, etc., of various sizes.

Monkey wrench

monk·ish [mung′kish] *adj.* Of or like a monk or monks.

monks·hood [mungks′hŏŏd′] *n.* A poisonous plant having hood-shaped flowers; aconite.

mon·o·cle [mon′ə·kəl] *n.* An eyeglass for only one eye.

mon·o·cot·y·le·don [mon′-ə·kot′ə·lēd′(ə)n] *n.* A plant whose seeds contain but one cotyledon, as grasses, palms, etc.

Monocle

mo·nog·a·my [mə·nog′ə·mē] *n.* The condition or practice of having only one husband or wife at a time.

mon·o·gram [mon′ə·gram] *n.* A design made from the initials of a name.

mon·o·graph [mon′ə·graf] *n.* A book, pamphlet, or long article on a single subject.

A monogram

mon·o·lith [mon′ə·lith] *n.* A single block of stone, usually very large, or a statue, column, etc., made of such a block.

mon·o·lith·ic [mon′ə·lith′ik] *adj.* 1 Of, having to do with, or like a monolith. 2 Having a massive, uniform structure; unvarying.

mon·o·logue [mon′ə·lôg] *n.* 1 A long speech by one person, especially one that interrupts conversation. 2 A dramatic work for one actor. 3 A poem, part of a play, etc., performed by one actor.

mon·o·ma·ni·a [mon′ə·mā′nē·ə] *n.* 1 A mental disorder in which a person, otherwise rational, is obsessed with one idea or subject. 2 An extreme and irrational interest in one thing.

mo·no·mi·al [mō·nō′mē·əl] 1 *adj.* Being a single algebraic term. 2 *n.* A monomial expression.

mon·o·plane [mon′ə·plān] *n.* An airplane having a single pair of wings, one wing on each side of the airplane.

mo·nop·o·lize [mə·nop′ə·līz] *v.* **mo·nop·o·lized, mo·nop·o·liz·ing** 1 To get or have a monopoly of. 2 To possess, use, or control: She *monopolizes* all of his time. ¶3

mo·nop·o·ly [mə·nop′ə·lē] *n., pl.* **mo·nop·o·lies** 1 Exclusive control of a product or service in a certain area by a single person or group, with a resulting power over prices and competition. **2** Such control granted and supervised by a government. **3** A company, group, or person that holds a monopoly. **4** A product or service controlled by a monopoly. **5** Exclusive possession or control.

mon·o·rail [mon'ō·rāl'] *n.* **1** A railway whose cars run on or are suspended from a single track or rail. **2** This track or rail.

mon·o·syl·lab·ic [mon'ə·si·lab'ik] *adj.* **1** Having only one syllable. **2** Using or composed of monosyllables: a *monosyllabic* answer.

mon·o·syl·la·ble [mon'ə·sil'ə·bəl] *n.* A word of one syllable.

mon·o·the·ism [mon'ə·thē·iz'əm] *n.* The doctrine or belief that there is but one God.

A monorail train

mon·o·tone [mon'ə·tōn] *n.* **1** A succession of syllables, words, etc., uttered in a single tone. **2** Boring sameness, as of color.

mo·not·o·nous [mə·not'ə·nəs] *adj.* **1** Not changing in pitch, tone, etc.: *monotonous* talk. **2** Boring because of lack of variety or change: a *monotonous* task. — **mo·not'o·nous·ly** *adv.*

mo·not·o·ny [mə·not'ə·nē] *n.* The condition or quality of being monotonous; sameness.

mon·ox·ide [mon·ok'sīd] *n.* An oxide containing a single atom of oxygen in each molecule.

Mon·roe [mən·rō'], **James,** 1758–1831, fifth president of the U.S., 1817–1825.

Monroe Doctrine President Monroe's statement, in his message to Congress in 1823, that any attempt by a European nation to interfere or acquire territory in the Western Hemisphere would be regarded as an unfriendly act by the U.S.

mon·sieur [mə·syûr'] *n., pl.* **mes·sieurs** [mes'ərz] The French title of courtesy for a man, equivalent to the English *Mr.* and *sir.*

Mon·si·gnor [mon·sēn'yər] *n.* **1** In the Roman Catholic Church, a title of honor of certain priests. **2** A priest having this title.

mon·soon [mon·sōōn'] *n.* **1** A seasonal wind of southern Asia and the Indian Ocean, blowing from the northeast in winter and from the southwest in summer. **2** The rainy season in India and adjacent countries, extending from June to September.

mon·ster [mon'stər] *n.* **1** A plant or animal that is abnormal in form or structure, as a calf with two heads. **2** Any of various mythical, often terrifying beasts, as dragons, griffins, etc. **3** A

person who is very cruel, evil, or ugly. **4** An extremely large person, animal, or thing.

mon·stros·i·ty [mon·stros'ə·tē] *n., pl.* **mon·stros·i·ties** **1** The condition or quality of being monstrous. **2** A monster.

mon·strous [mon'strəs] *adj.* **1** Differing greatly from the natural or normal, as in form, looks, character, etc. **2** Horrible; atrocious: *monstrous* deeds. **3** Completely or strikingly wrong; absurd: a *monstrous* error. **4** Huge; enormous.

Mont. Abbreviation of MONTANA.

Mon·tan·a [mon·tan'ə] *n.* A state in the NW U.S.

Mont Blanc [mont blangk' *or* môn blän] *n.* The highest mountain in the Alps, on the border between France and Italy.

Mon·te·vi·de·o [mon'tə·vi·dā'ō] *n.* The capital of Uruguay.

Mont·gom·er·y [mont·gum'ər·ē *or* mən(t)·gum'ər·ē] *n.* The capital of Alabama.

month [munth] *n.* **1** Any of the parts, usually 12 in number, into which a year is divided. **2** A period of 30 days or of 4 weeks. **3** The time the moon takes to revolve completely around the earth, about 29½ days.

month·ly [munth'lē] *adv., adj., n., pl.* **month·lies** **1** *adv.* Once a month; every month. **2** *adj.* Of or having to do with a month. **3** *adj.* Happening, done, payable, etc., monthly. **4** *adj.* Lasting for a month. **5** *n.* A magazine that appears monthly.

Mont·pel·ier [mont·pēl'yər] *n.* The capital of Vermont.

Mon·tre·al [mon'trē·ôl'] *n.* The largest city in Canada, in the SE part.

mon·u·ment [mon'yə·ment] *n.* **1** A thing built in memory of a person or event. **2** A work of art, literature, scholarship, etc., thought to have lasting value: His work in chemistry is a *monument* of science.

mon·u·men·tal [mon'yə·men'təl] *adj.* **1** Of, like, or being a monument. **2** Impressive or important; great; grand: *monumental* art. **3** Huge; enormous: a *monumental* fraud. — **mon'u·men'tal·ly** *adv.*

moo [mōō] *n., pl.* **moos,** *v.* **mooed, moo·ing** **1** *n.* The sound made by a cow. **2** *v.* To make this sound.

mood[1] [mōōd] *n.* A state of mind or emotion.

mood[2] [mōōd] *n.* The form of a verb used to express a speaker's attitude toward what he says. In English there are three moods, the indicative, the subjunctive, and the imperative.

mood·y [mōō'dē] *adj.* **mood·i·er, mood·i·est** **1** Often falling into sad, gloomy moods. **2** Showing or expressing such moods: a *moody* reply. — **mood'i·ly** *adv.* — **mood'i·ness** *n.*

moon [mōōn] **1** *n.* A large natural satellite of the earth that often shines at night by reflecting sunlight. ◆ *Adj., lunar.* **2** *n.* Any satellite, especially a natural one. **3** *n.* Something suggesting the visible shape of the moon. **4** *n.* Moonlight. **5** *v.* To behave or move about as though dazed. **6** *n.* A month.

moon·beam [mōōn′bēm′] *n.* A ray of moonlight.

moon·light [mōōn′līt′] *n.* **1** Light from the moon. **2** *adj. use:* a *moonlight* excursion.

moon·lit [mōōn′lit′] *adj.* Lighted by the moon.

moon·shine [mōōn′shīn′] *n.* **1** *informal* Smuggled or illegally distilled liquor. **2** Moonlight. **3** Empty, foolish talk, ideas, etc.; nonsense.

moon·stone [mōōn′stōn′] *n.* A milky white, lustrous mineral, often used as a gemstone.

moon·struck [mōōn′struk′] *adj.* Crazed; dazed.

moor¹ [mōōr] *n. British* A stretch of wasteland, often marshy and covered with heather.

moor² [mōōr] *v.* To secure or fasten with cables, ropes, anchors, etc., as a ship.

Moor [mōōr] *n.* One of a Moslem people of NW Africa who conquered Spain in the 8th century and lived there until they were driven out in the late 15th century. **— Moor′ish** *adj.*

moor·ings [mōōr′ingz] *n.pl.* **1** A place where a thing is moored. **2** The line, cable, anchor, etc., that holds something in place: Our boat had slipped its *moorings* during the night.

moose [mōōs] *n., pl.* **moose** A large mammal related to the deer, found in North America. ◆ *Moose* comes from an Algonquian Indian word meaning *he strips off,* because the animal eats bark from trees.

Moose, about 5 ft. high at shoulder

moot [mōōt] **1** *adj.* Open to argument; debatable: a *moot* point. **2** *v.* To debate. **3** *v.* To bring up for discussion.

mop [mop] *n., v.* **mopped, mop·ping 1** *n.* A handle with rags, yarn, or a sponge attached to the end for cleaning floors, etc. **2** *v.* To clean with or as if with a mop. **3** *n.* Something that suggests a mop, as thick, matted hair.

mope [mōp] *n.* **moped, mop·ing** To be gloomy and depressed.

mo·raine [mə·rān′] *n.* A mass of rocks, gravel, etc., carried and deposited by a glacier.

mor·al [môr′əl] **1** *adj.* Good or virtuous in behavior or character: a thoughtful, *moral* man. **2** *adj.* Having to do with standards of right and wrong: a *moral* problem. **3** *adj.* Able to distinguish between right and wrong: A wolf is not a *moral* being. **4** *n.* (*pl.*) Behavior or habits in respect to right and wrong: His *morals* are poor. **5** *adj.* Teaching standards of right and wrong: a *moral* tale. **6** *n.* The lesson contained in a fable, story, etc. **7** *adj.* Mental or spiritual but not physical or concrete: *moral* support; a *moral*

victory. **8** *adj.* Being almost or practically: a *moral* certainty. **— mor′al·ly** *adv.*

mor·ale [mə·ral′] *n.* State of mind, especially in terms of confidence, courage, hope, etc.

mor·al·ist [môr′əl·ist] *n.* **1** A person who leads a moral life. **2** A person who moralizes.

mo·ral·i·ty [mə·ral′ə·tē] *n., pl.* **mo·ral·i·ties 1** The quality of an action, in terms of good and evil. **2** A system of standards or rules of conduct. **3** Virtuous conduct.

mor·al·ize [môr′əl·īz] *v.* **mor·al·ized, mor·al·iz·ing 1** To discuss morals. **2** To draw a moral from. **3** To improve the morals of. ¶3

mo·rass [mə·ras′] *n.* A stretch of soft, wet ground; marsh; bog.

mor·a·to·ri·um [môr′ə·tôr′ē·əm] *n.* **1** A legal authorization to delay payments on a debt. **2** The period for which the delay is granted.

mor·bid [môr′bid] *adj.* **1** Having or showing an abnormal interest in gruesome or unwholesome matters. **2** Grisly; gruesome: a *morbid* fantasy. **3** Caused by or affected with disease: a *morbid* growth. **— mor′bid·ly** *adv.*

mor·dant [môr′dənt] **1** *adj.* Biting; sarcastic: a *mordant* wit. **2** *n.* A substance that makes color fast in dyeing.

more [môr] **1** Comparative of MUCH, MANY. **2** *adj.* Greater in number, degree, or amount: I have *more* books than you. **3** *adj.* Additional; extra: We have to buy *more* books today. **4** *n.* A larger or additional portion, number, or amount: *More* of the books are now available. **5** *adv.* In or to a greater extent or degree: He reads *more* now. ◆ *More* may be used to form the comparative of some adjectives and adverbs: *more* sensible; *more* quickly. **6** *adv.* In addition; further; again: Read it once *more.* **7** *n.* Something that exceeds or excels something else: This is *more* than enough. **— more or less 1** Somewhat. **2** Approximately.

more·o·ver [môr·ō′vər] *adv.* Also; besides.

morgue [môrg] *n.* **1** A place where the bodies of unknown dead persons and of those dead of violence or unknown causes are kept to be examined, identified, etc. **2** In a newspaper, a reference library and its books, files, etc.

Mor·mon [môr′mən] *n.* A member of the Mormon Church, founded in the U.S. by Joseph Smith in 1830, and having its own book of prophecy.

morn [môrn] *n.* Morning: used mostly in poems.

morn·ing [môr′ning] *n.* **1** The early part of the day, from midnight to noon, or from sunrise to noon. **2** *adj. use: morning* exercises.

morn·ing-glo·ry [môr′ning·glôr′ē] *n., pl.* **morn·ing-glo·ries** A climbing plant with funnel-shaped flowers of various colors.

morning star A planet, usually Venus, that appears in the eastern sky before sunrise.

Mo·roc·co [mə·rok′ō] *n.* **1** A country in NW Africa. **2** (*written* **morocco**) A soft, fine leather made from goatskin, and first produced in Morocco.

mo·ron [môr′on] *n.* **1** An adult having a mental

ability equal to that of a normal 12-year-old child. **2** A stupid or very foolish person.

mo·rose [mə·rōs'] *adj.* Gloomy or sullen: a *morose* mood; a *morose* person. **— mo·rose·ly** *adv.* **— mo·rose·ness** *n.*

mor·pheme [môr'fēm] *n.* The smallest unit of meaning in speech. It may be a whole word, as *car*, or part of a word, as *car* and *s* in *cars.*

Mor·phe·us [môr'fē·əs *or* môr'fyōōs] *n.* In Greek myths, the god of dreams.

mor·phine [môr'fēn] *n.* A bitter, crystalline substance extracted from opium, used in medicine to cause sleep or lessen pain.

mor·ris dance [môr'is] An old English dance, usually performed on May Day, in which the performers wear costumes and bells.

mor·row [môr'ō] *n.* **1** The following day. **2** Morning. ◆ This word is seldom used today.

Morse [môrs], **Samuel F. B.,** 1791–1872, U.S. artist and inventor who made the first telegraph.

Morse code A system of dots and dashes or short and long sounds that represent letters and numerals, used in telegraphy.

mor·sel [môr'səl] *n.* **1** A small piece or bite of food. **2** A small piece or bit: a choice *morsel* of gossip.

mor·tal [môr'təl] **1** *adj.* Certain to die eventually. **2** *n.* A human being. **3** *adj.* Of or related to man as a being subject to death; human. **4** *adj.* Of or related to death. **5** *adj.* Causing physical or spiritual death: a *mortal* blow; *mortal* sin. **6** *adj.* Lasting or remaining until death: *mortal* combat; *mortal* enemies. **7** *adj. informal* Very great: *mortal* terror.

mor·tal·i·ty [môr·tal'ə·tē] *n., pl.* **mor·tal·i·ties** **1** The condition or quality of being mortal. **2** The death of many people: the *mortality* due to war. **3** The number of deaths in proportion to the population; death rate.

mor·tal·ly [môr'təl·lē] *adv.* **1** Fatally: *mortally* hurt. **2** Extremely: *mortally* offended.

mor·tar¹ [môr'tər] *n.* A bowl in which materials are crushed with a pestle.

mor·tar² [môr'tər] *n.* A mixture of lime, cement, etc., with sand and water, used to keep bricks together, to plaster walls, etc.

mor·tar³ [môr'tər] *n.* A short cannon, loaded through the muzzle and fired at a high angle.

Mortar and pestle

mor·tar·board [môr'tər·bôrd'] *n.* **1** A square board, often with a handle, for holding mortar. **2** A cap with a flat, stiff, square top, worn in some school or college ceremonies, as at graduation.

mort·gage [môr'gij] *n., v.* **mort·gaged, mort·gag·ing** **1** *n.* A claim on property, given as security for a loan. **2** *n.* The contract that establishes such a claim. **3** *v.* To give a claim on (property) as security for a loan. **4** *v.* To risk; hazard: to *mortgage* one's future.

mort·ga·gee [môr'gi·jē'] *n.* The lender to whom a mortgage is given.

mort·ga·gor [môr'gi·jər] *n.* A borrower who mortgages property as security for a loan.

mor·tice [môr'tis] *n., v.* **mor·ticed, mor·tic·ing** Another spelling of MORTISE.

mor·ti·cian [môr·tish'ən] *n. U.S.* A funeral director; undertaker.

mor·ti·fi·ca·tion [môr'tə·fə·kā'shən] *n.* **1** A feeling of loss of self-respect or pride; humiliation. **2** An act or situation that causes this. **3** The use of strict disciplines, as fasting, etc., to subdue one's appetites and strengthen one's will. **4** The death of one part of a living body, as by gangrene.

mor·ti·fy [môr'tə·fī] *v.* **mor·ti·fied, mor·ti·fy·ing** **1** To deprive of self-respect or pride; humiliate. **2** To subject (one's body, desires, etc.) to severe discipline. **3** To make or become dead or decayed, as with gangrene.

mor·tise [môr'tis] *n., v.* **mor·tised, mor·tis·ing** **1** *n.* A hole cut in a piece of wood, stone, etc., to fit a tenon of another piece and form a joint. **2** *v.* To join by a mortise.

tenon

mor·tu·ar·y [môr'chŏō·er'ē] *n., pl.* **mor·tu·ar·ies** A place for keeping corpses before burial.

mortise

mo·sa·ic [mō·zā'ik] *n.* **1** A picture or design made from bits of colored stone, glass, etc. **2** A picture or design that is like a mosaic. **3** *adj. use:* *mosaic* tiles; *mosaic* tables. **4** The art or craft of constructing or building mosaics.

Mo·sa·ic [mō·zā'ik] *adj.* Of or having to do with Moses or the laws and writings ascribed to him.

Mos·cow [mos'kou *or* mos'kō] *n.* The capital of the Soviet Union, in the western part.

Mo·ses [mō'zis] *n.* In the Old Testament, a man who led the Israelites from bondage in Egypt, received the Ten Commandments from God, and made laws for the people.

A mosaic

Mos·lem [moz'ləm] *n.* **1** A believer in Islam; Mohammedan. **2** *adj. use:* the *Moslem* faith.

mosque [mosk] *n.* A Moslem temple of worship.

add, āce, câre, pälm; end, ēqual; it, īce; odd, ōpen, ôrder; tŏŏk, pōōl; up, bûrn;
ə = a in *above*, e in *sicken*, i in *possible*, o in *melon*, u in *circus*; yōō = u in *fuse*; oil; pout;
check; ring; thin; this; zh in *vision*. For ¶ reference, see page 64 · HOW TO

mos·qui·to [məs·kē′tō] *n.*, *pl.* **mos·qui·toes**
or **mos·qui·tos** A small fly-
ing insect with two wings, the
female of which bites and
sucks blood from people or
animals. Some kinds spread
malaria, yellow fever, or
other diseases.

Mosquito

moss [môs] *n.* A tiny,
delicate, flowerless plant that grows in clumps
on trees, rocks, etc.

moss·y [môs′ē] *adj.* **moss·i·er, moss·i·est**
Like or covered with moss.

most [mōst] **1** Superlative of MANY, MUCH.
2 *adj.* Being the greatest in number: *Most* dogs
bark. **3** *n.* The greatest number: *Most* of the
children are here. **4** *adj.* Being the greatest in
amount or degree: to have the *most* power.
5 *n.* The greatest amount, quantity, or degree:
Most of the air is out. **6** *adv.* In or to the
greatest or highest degree, quantity, or extent:
But who suffered *most*? ◆ *Most* may be used to
form the superlative of some adjectives and
adverbs: *most* sensible; *most* quickly. **7** *adv.*
Very: a *most* pleasing gift. **8** *adv. informal*
Almost: It grows *most* anywhere. **— for the
most part** Generally or usually.

-most A suffix meaning: In or to the greatest
extent or degree, as in *outmost*, out to the
greatest degree.

most·ly [mōst′lē] *adv.* Principally; chiefly.

mote [mōt] *n.* A tiny particle, as of dust.

mo·tel [mō·tel′] *n. U.S.* A hotel designed to
accommodate motorists. ◆ *Motel* was formed by
combining *mo*(tor) and (*ho*)*tel*.

moth [môth] *n.*, *pl.* **moths** [môthz *or* môths]
An insect like a
butterfly, but with
smaller wings and
duller coloring, active
mainly at night. The
larvae of one variety
feed on wool, fur, etc.

moth·ball [môth′·
bôl′] *n.* A round
pellet whose odor
drives moths away
from stored clothing, blankets, etc.

Cecropia moth

moth-eat·en [môth′ēt′(ə)n] *adj.* **1** Damaged
by moth larvae, as clothing. **2** Worn out or
old-fashioned: a *moth-eaten* joke.

moth·er[1] [muth′ər] **1** *n.* A female parent,
especially a woman considered in relation to her
child or children. **2** *adj. use:* a *mother* cat. **3** *adj.*
Of, like, or from a mother: *mother* love. **4** *v.* To
take care of or protect as a mother does. **5** *adj.*
Native: one's *mother* tongue. **6** *adj.* Having a
relation like that of a mother: the *mother* church.
7 *n.* The source or cause of something: Repetition is the *mother* of memory. **8** *n.* (*written*
Mother) A mother superior.

moth·er[2] [muth′ər] *n.* A slimy film formed of
the bacteria that make vinegar.

moth·er·hood [muth′ər·hood] *n.* **1** The condi-

tion of being a mother. **2** The character or
qualities of a mother. **3** Mothers as a group.

moth·er-in-law [muth′ər·in·lô′] *n.*, *pl.*
moth·ers-in-law The mother of one's spouse.

moth·er·land [muth′ər·land′] *n.* One's own or
one's ancestors' native country.

moth·er·ly [muth′ər·lē] *adj.* Of or like a
mother; protective; warm: *motherly* care.

moth·er-of-pearl [muth′ər·əv·pûrl′] *n.* The
pearly, lustrous inside layer of certain sea-
shells, used to make buttons, ornaments, etc.

mother superior A nun who heads a religious
community of women, as a convent.

mo·tif [mō·tēf′] *n.* **1** A main idea or central
theme in a work of art or literature. **2** A distinct
design in a decoration.

mo·tion [mō′shən] **1** *n.* Any change in position
or location; movement. **2** *n.* An expressive
movement of some part of the body; gesture.
3 *v.* To signal by a gesture. **4** *n.* A proposal to be
discussed and voted on, as by an assembly.

mo·tion·less [mō′shən·lis] *adj.* Not moving.

motion picture **1** A series of pictures flashed
on a screen in rapid succession, creating the
illusion that things in them are moving. **2** A
story told by the use of such pictures; a film.

mo·ti·vate [mō′tə·vāt] *v.* **mo·ti·vat·ed, mo·
ti·vat·ing** To provide with a motive.

mo·ti·va·tion [mō′tə·vā′shən] *n.* **1** The act of
motivating. **2** A motive; incentive.

mo·tive [mō′tiv] **1** *n.* A reason or cause that
makes a person act. **2** *n.* A motif. **3** *adj.* Of or
having to do with motion. ◆ See REASON.

mot·ley [mot′lē] **1** *adj.* Having a mixture of
colors. **2** *n.* A motley fabric or garment, as that
of a jester. **3** *adj.* Containing very different and
often clashing elements: a *motley* gang of boys.

mo·tor [mō′tər] **1** *n.* A machine that transforms
electrical energy into mechanical energy, as in a
vacuum cleaner. **2** *n.* An internal-combustion
engine, as in a tractor. **3** *adj.* Having or driven
by a motor: a *motor* scooter. **4** *adj.* Of, for, or
having to do with a motor: *motor* power. **5** *v.* To
travel by automobile. **6** *adj.* Of, for, or by a
motor vehicle: a *motor* trip. **7** *adj.* Having to
do with movements of the muscles.

mo·tor·boat [mō′tər·bōt′] *n.* A boat powered
by a motor.

mo·tor·car [mō′tər·kär′] *n.* An automobile.

mo·tor·cy·cle [mō′tər·sī′kəl] *n.* A vehicle like
a large, heavy bicycle
powered by a gasoline
engine.

mo·tor·ist [mō′tər·
ist] *n.* A person who
drives or travels by
automobile.

mo·tor·man [mō′tər·
mən] *n.*, *pl.* **mo·tor·
men** [mō′tər·mən] A
man who operates an
electric streetcar or
subway train.

Motorcycle

mot·tle [mot′(ə)l] *v.* **mot·tled, mot·tling,** *n.*

1 *v.* To mark with spots of different colors; blotch. **2** *adj. use: mottled* skin. **3** *n.* A spotted or blotched appearance or design.

mot·to [mot′ō] *n., pl.* **mot·toes** or **mot·tos** **1** A word or short saying expressing a rule of conduct or action. **2** A word or phrase that expresses a principle or slogan, inscribed on a seal, coins, etc.

mould [mōld] *n., v.* Another spelling of MOLD.

mould·er [mōld′ər] *v.* Another spelling of MOLDER.

mould·ing [mōld′ing] *n.* Another spelling of MOLDING.

mould·y [mōld′ē] *adj.* **mould·i·er, mould·i· est** Another spelling of MOLDY.

moult [mōlt] *n., v.* Another spelling of MOLT.

mound [mound] **1** *n.* A small hill or pile of earth, debris, rocks, etc. **2** *v.* To heap up or enclose in a mound. **3** *n.* The slightly raised ground from which a baseball pitcher pitches.

mount¹ [mount] **1** *v.* To climb (a slope, stairs, etc.). **2** *v.* To get up on (a horse, camel, etc.). **3** *n.* A horse or other animal used for riding. **4** *v.* To furnish with such a mount. **5** *v.* To set or fix, as in a frame, support, or setting, as for display. **6** *n.* A support or setting for something. **7** *v.* To increase in amount, degree, etc. **8** *v.* To prepare and begin (an attack, etc.). **9** *v.* To be equipped with (weapons): a plane *mounting* eight rockets. **10** *v.* To furnish with costumes, scenery, etc.: to *mount* a play.

mount² [mount] *n.* A mountain or hill: used mostly in poems or as part of a name: *Mount Olympus.*

moun·tain [moun′tən] *n.* **1** A mass of land, higher than a hill, rising far above its surroundings. **2** *adj. use: mountain* greenery. **3** A pile; heap: a *mountain* of work.

moun·tain·eer [moun′tən·ir′] **1** *n.* A person who lives in a mountainous area. **2** *n.* A person who climbs mountains. **3** *v.* To climb mountains.

mountain goat A goatlike antelope of the Rocky Mountains, with white hair and black horns.

mountain laurel An evergreen shrub of the eastern U.S., with pink or white flowers.

mountain lion Another name for COU-GAR.

moun·tain·ous [moun′tən·əs] *adj.* **1** Full of mountains. **2** Huge; gigantic.

mountain range A group or row of mountains.

moun·te·bank [moun′tə·bangk] *n.* **1** A person

Mountain goat, about 4 ft. long

who draws a crowd by tricks and jokes and sells quack remedies. **2** Any cheap swindler.

mount·ing [moun′ting] *n.* A frame or support.

Mount Ver·non [vûr′nən] The home and burial place of George Washington, in Virginia, near Washington, D.C.

mourn [môrn] *v.* To be sad or show sorrow over (someone dead, a loss, etc.). — **mourn′er** *n.*

mourn·ful [môrn′fəl] *adj.* Showing or causing grief; sorrowful. — **mourn′ful·ly** *adv.*

mourn·ing [môr′ning] *n.* **1** A sorrowing; grieving. **2** An expression of sorrow for the dead, such as the wearing of black. **3** Black clothes or other symbols of sorrow.

mourning dove A dove of North America, that has a mournful cry.

mouse [*n.* mous, *v.* mouz] *n., pl.* **mice** [mīs], *v.* **moused, mous·ing** **1** *n.* A small rodent with a long tail, often found in fields and houses. **2** *v.* To hunt or catch mice. **3** *v.* To prowl, as a cat does. **4** *n. U.S. informal* A timid person.

mouse·trap [mous′trap′] *n.* A trap for mice.

mousse [moos] *n.* A frozen dessert made of whipped cream, gelatin, sugar, etc.

mous·tache [mus′tash *or* məs·tash′] *n.* Another spelling of MUSTACHE.

mous·y [mou′sē] *adj.* **mous·i·er, mous·i·est** Shy, timid, drab, etc.

mouth [*n.* mouth, *v.* mouᵺ] *n., pl.* **mouths** [mouᵺz], *v.* **1** *n.* The opening at which food is taken into the body and through which sounds are uttered. **2** *n.* The space between the lips and the throat, containing the tongue and teeth. **3** *v.* To take in, hold, or rub with the mouth. **4** *v.* To form with the mouth, as words or letters. **5** *v.* To speak in an insincere or affected way: to *mouth* a greeting. **6** *n.* Something like a mouth in shape or function, as the opening of a bottle or the part of a stream where its waters enter a larger body of water.

mouth·ful [mouth′fool′] *n., pl.* **mouth·fuls** **1** As much as can be held in the mouth. **2** As much as is usually taken or put in the mouth at one time. **3** A small quantity.

mouth organ Another name for HARMONICA.

mouth·piece [mouth′pēs′] *n.* **1** The part put in or near the mouth, as of a trumpet, a telephone, etc. **2** A person used by another or others to express views, beliefs, etc.; spokesman.

mov·a·ble [moo′və·bəl] *adj.* Capable of being moved; not fixed: *movable* furniture.

move [moov] *v.* **moved, mov·ing**, *n.* **1** *v.* To change position or place: Don't *move* yet. **2** *v.* To change the position or place of: *Move* the bed to the window. **3** *v.* To change one's residence. **4** *n.* An act of moving; a change in position, residence, etc.; movement. **5** *v.* To make act or operate: A breeze *moved* the branches. **6** *v.* To begin to take action; act: to *move* on the matter. **7** *n.* An act toward some purpose or goal; step: a clever *move*. **8** *v*. To progress; advance: The play *moves* quickly. **9** *v*. *informal* To depart; go: to *move* on. **10** *v*. To change (a chess piece, checker, etc.) from one position to another. **11** *n*. A turn to play in a game such as chess, or the play made. **12** *v*. To cause; influence: What *moved* him to change his mind? **13** *v*. To affect the emotions of; touch: The story *moved* us to tears. **14** *v*. To make a suggestion or proposal, as at a meeting: to *move* to adjourn. **— be on the move** *informal* To move about constantly.

move·a·ble [mōō′və·bəl] *adj*. Another spelling of MOVABLE.

move·ment [mōōv′mənt] *n*. **1** The act of moving; motion: the *movement* of the waves. **2** A particular manner of moving: a dance *movement*. **3** A series of actions, efforts, etc., directed toward some end: a peace *movement*. **4** An arrangement of moving parts, as of a clock. **5** A rhythm or tempo. **6** One of the sections of a sonata, symphony, or other long musical piece. **7** An emptying of the bowels.

mov·er [mōō′vər] *n*. A person or thing that moves, especially one whose job is moving household goods from one place to another.

mov·ie [mōō′vē] *n*. *informal* **1** A motion picture. **2** A motion picture theater.

mov·ing [mōōv′ing] *adj*. **1** In motion or capable of movement. **2** Causing movement or change. **3** Affecting the feelings; touching: a *moving* appeal for peace.

moving picture A motion picture.

mow[1] [mou] *n*. **1** Stored hay or grain. **2** The place where hay or grain is stored.

mow[2] [mō] *v*. **mowed, mowed** or **mown** [mōn], **mow·ing 1** To cut down (grass or grain), as with a scythe. **2** To cut the grass or grain of: to *mow* the lawn. **3** *informal* To knock down or kill: to *mow* the enemy down. **— mow′er** *n*.

Mo·zam·bique [mō′zam·bēk′] *n*. A Portuguese territory in SE Africa.

Mo·zart [mō′tsärt], **Wolfgang Amadeus,** 1756–1791, Austrian composer of music.

MP Abbreviation of Military Police.

M.P. Abbreviation of Member of Parliament.

mph or **m.p.h.** Abbreviation of miles per hour.

Mr. Abbreviation of MISTER.

Mrs. [mis′iz]. A title of a married woman: used before her name.

ms. or **MS.** Abbreviation of: **1** MANUSCRIPT. **2** (*written* **mss.** or **MSS.**) Manuscripts.

mt. Abbreviation of: **1** MOUNT. **2** MOUNTAIN. **3** (*written* **mts.**) Mounts. **4** (*written* **mts.**) Mountains.

much [much] *adj*. **more, most,** *n*., *adv*. **1** *adj*. Great in amount, extent, etc.: *much* noise. **2** *n*. A great amount, extent, etc.: *Much* of the story is badly written. **3** *adv*. To a great degree; greatly: *much* obliged. **4** *n*. A remarkable or important thing: It isn't *much*. **5** *adv*. Nearly or almost: I feel *much* the same as you.

mu·ci·lage [myōō′sə·lij] *n*. A sticky substance, used to glue things together.

muck [muk] *n*. **1** Moist animal manure. **2** Rich, dark brown soil with decaying vegetable matter, as leaves, in it. **3** Mud or filth.

muck·rake [muk′rāk′] *v*. **muck·raked, muck·rak·ing** To search out and make public graft or misconduct in politics or business. **— muck′rak′er** *n*.

mu·cous [myōō′kəs] *adj*. **1** Giving off mucus. **2** Of or like mucus; slimy.

mucous membrane The thin, moist lining of the nose, throat, and other cavities that open to the outside.

mu·cus [myōō′kəs] *n*. A thick, slimy liquid secreted by the mucous membranes to keep them moist.

mud [mud] *n*. Soft and sticky wet earth.

mud·dle [mud′(ə)l] *v*. **mud·dled, mud·dling,** *n*. **1** *v*. To confuse or mix up: to *muddle* the message. **2** *v*. To think or act in a confused manner. **3** *n*. A condition of confusion; mix-up.

mud·dy [mud′ē] *adj*. **mud·di·er, mud·di·est,** *v*. **mud·died, mud·dy·ing 1** *adj*. Spattered or filled with mud: a *muddy* path. **2** *adj*. Not clear or bright: a *muddy* stream. **3** *adj*. Confused or obscure: a *muddy* style of writing. **4** *v*. To make or become muddy.

muff [muf] **1** *n*. A tubelike covering, often of fur, open at both ends, for warming the hands. **2** *n*. A clumsy action, especially dropping a ball one should have caught. **3** *v*. To perform (some act) clumsily, especially to fail to catch (a ball).

Muff

muf·fin [muf′in] *n*. A bread that is shaped like a cupcake and is usually eaten hot.

muf·fle [muf′əl] *v*. **muf·fled, muf·fling,** *n*. **1** *v*. To wrap up in order to hide or keep warm: He *muffled* up in a scarf against the wind. **2** *v*. To deaden the sound of by, or as if by, wrapping: to *muffle* a cry. **3** *n*. Something used for muffling. **4** *v*. To deaden (a sound).

muf·fler [muf′lər] *n*. **1** A device used to reduce noise, as from the exhaust of an engine. **2** A heavy scarf worn around the neck.

muf·ti [muf′tē] *n*. Ordinary civilian clothes worn by someone who usually wears a uniform.

mug[1] [mug] *n*. **1** A large drinking cup usually with a handle. **2** As much as will fill a mug.

mug[2] [mug] *v*. **mugged, mug·ging,** *n*. *slang* **1** *v*. To assault and rob. **2** *n*. The face, especially the mouth.

mug·gy [mug′ē] *adj*. **mug·gi·er, mug·gi·est** Warm, humid, and close: *muggy* weather.

Mug

mug·wump [mug′wump′] *n*. A person who is independent, especially in politics.

mu·lat·to [mə·lat′ō *or* myŏŏ·lat′ō] *n.*, *pl.* **mu·lat·toes** A person with one white and one Negro parent.

mul·ber·ry [mul′ber′ē] *n.*, *pl.* **mul·ber·ries**, *adj.* **1** *n.* Any of various trees bearing a juicy, edible fruit resembling the blackberry. Silkworms feed on the leaves of some mulberries. **2** *n.* The purplish red, berrylike fruit of this tree. **3** *adj.*, *n.* Purplish red.

mulch [mulch] **1** *n.* Any loose material, as straw or leaves, spread on the ground around plants to protect their roots from drying out or freezing. **2** *v.* To cover with mulch.

mulct [mulkt] **1** *v.* To cheat or swindle: The rascal *mulcted* me of $30. **2** *v.* To punish with a fine. **3** *n.* A fine or penalty.

mule[1] [myōol] *n.* **1** The offspring of an ass and a horse. **2** *informal* A stubborn person. **3** A machine that spins fibers into yarn and winds it on spindles.

mule[2] [myōol] *n.* A lounging slipper with no back.

mu·le·teer [myōo′lə·tir′] *n.* A mule driver.

mul·ish [myōo′lish] *adj.* Like a mule; stubborn.

mull[1] [mul] *v.* To think at length; ponder: to *mull* over the problem.

mull[2] [mul] *v.* To heat and spice, as wine.

mul·lein or **mul·len** [mul′ən] *n.* A tall, weedy herb with coarse, woolly leaves and spikes of yellow, red, purple, or white flowers.

mul·let [mul′it] *n.*, *pl.* **mul·let** or **mul·lets** A fish with a reddish or silvery color, living in either fresh or salt water.

multi- A prefix meaning: **1** Having many or much, as in *multicolored*, having many colors. **2** Many times over, as in *multimillionaire*, a millionaire many times over.

mul·ti·far·i·ous [mul′tə·fâr′ē·əs] *adj.* Having many forms or much variety.

mul·ti·lat·er·al [mul′ti·lat′ər·əl] *adj.* **1** Having many sides. **2** Involving more than two nations: a *multilateral* agreement.

mul·ti·mil·lion·aire [mul′ti·mil′yən·âr′] *n.* A person who has a fortune of many millions.

mul·ti·ple [mul′tə·pəl] **1** *adj.* Of, like, or having more than one part, element, etc. **2** *n.* A number which has a given number as one of its factors: 64 is a *multiple* of 16.

mul·ti·pli·cand [mul′tə·plə·kand′] *n.* A number multiplied or to be multiplied by another.

mul·ti·pli·ca·tion [mul′tə·plə·kā′shən] *n.* **1** The act of increasing in number or degree. **2** The state of being increased in number or degree. **3** The process of adding one or more of the same number together, that is, finding the sum of $n_1 + n_2 + n_3 \ldots + n_x$, where n is any number and x tells how many n's there are. $5 \times 2 = 2 + 2 + 2 + 2 + 2 = 10$.

multiplication sign The symbol (×) placed between two numbers to show that the first number is to be multiplied by the second, as $4 \times 2 = 8$.

mul·ti·plic·i·ty [mul′tə·plis′ə·tē] *n.*, *pl.* **mul·ti·plic·i·ties** A large number or variety.

mul·ti·pli·er [mul′tə·plī′ər] *n.* **1** A person or thing that multiplies. **2** The number by which another number is multiplied.

mul·ti·ply [mul′tə·plī] *v.* **mul·ti·plied, mul·ti·ply·ing 1** To make or become more in number or degree; increase: His sorrows *multiplied*. **2** To add (a whole number) a specified number of times: 2 *multiplied* by 3 is 6 because $2 + 2 + 2 = 6$; To *multiply* numbers represented by fractions, *multiply* their numerators and *multiply* their denominators. **3** To apply multiplication to: to *multiply* 2 by 5.

mul·ti·tude [mul′tə·t(y)ōod] *n.* A great number of persons or things; crowd; throng.

mul·ti·tu·di·nous [mul′tə·t(y)ōo′də·nəs] *adj.* In great numbers; very many: *multitudinous* stars.

mum [mum] *adj.* Silent: He kept *mum* about the deed. **—mum's the word** Keep silent.

mum·ble [mum′bəl] *v.* **mum·bled, mum·bling** To speak in a low, unclear way, as with lips nearly closed: He *mumbled* his thanks. **—mum′bler** *n.*

mum·mer [mum′ər] *n.* **1** A person who acts or frolics in a mask or costume. **2** An actor.

mum·mer·y [mum′ər·ē] *n.*, *pl.* **mum·mer·ies 1** A performance by mummers. **2** A ridiculous, pretentious, or hypocritical ritual.

mum·mi·fy [mum′ə·fī] *v.* **mum·mi·fied, mum·mi·fy·ing 1** To make a mummy of. **2** To dry up or shrivel up. **—mum′mi·fi·ca′tion** *n.*

mum·my [mum′ē] *n.*, *pl.* **mum·mies** A dead body, wrapped in cloth and preserved from decay by certain chemical preparations, as was done by the ancient Egyptians. ◆ *Mummy* comes from an Arabic word derived from the Persian word for *wax*, which was used in embalming.

mumps [mumps] *n.pl.* (*used with a singular verb*) A contagious virus disease that causes inflammation and swelling of certain glands, particularly below the ear.

Mummy case and wrapped mummy

munch [munch] *v.* To chew with a crunching noise: to *munch* popcorn. **—munch′er** *n.*

mun·dane [mun·dān′ *or* mun′dān] *adj.* **1** Practical or ordinary: the *mundane* problems of cooking a meal. **2** Of the world; earthly.

Mu·nich [myoo′nik] *n.* A city in SE West Germany.

mu·nic·i·pal [myoo·nis′ə·pəl] *adj.* Of or having to do with a town or city or its local government: *municipal* parks. **— mu·nic′i·pal·ly** *adv.*

mu·nic·i·pal·i·ty [myoo·nis′ə·pal′ə·tē] *n., pl.* **mu·nic·i·pal·i·ties** A town or city with the power of self-government in local affairs.

mu·nif·i·cent [myoo·nif′ə·sənt] *adj.* Very generous; liberal: a *munificent* donation. **— mu·nif′i·cence** *n.* **— mu·nif′i·cent·ly** *adv.*

mu·ni·tion [myoo·nish′ən] **1** *n.* (*usually pl.*) Materials and supplies for war, as ammunition, guns, etc. **2** *v.* To supply with munitions.

mu·ral [myoor′əl] *n.* A painting done on a wall.

mur·der [mûr′dər] **1** *n.* The unlawful and intentional killing of one person by another. **2** *v.* To kill (someone) unlawfully and intentionally. **3** *v.* To spoil or ruin, as by a bad performance or improper pronunciation, etc.

mur·der·er [mûr′dər·ər] *n.* A person who is guilty of committing murder.

mur·der·ess [mûr′dər·is] *n.* A female murderer.

mur·der·ous [mûr′dər·əs] *adj.* **1** Of, like, or involving murder: a *murderous* plot. **2** Capable of murdering or likely to murder: a *murderous* fiend. **— mur′der·ous·ly** *adv.*

murk [mûrk] *n.* Darkness; gloom.

murk·y [mûr′kē] *adj.* **murk·i·er, murk·i·est** Dark, gloomy, or obscure: the *murky* depths.

mur·mur [mûr′mər] **1** *n.* A low, unclear, steady sound, as of many voices, a quiet brook, etc. **2** *v.* To make a low, unclear, steady sound. **3** *n.* A mumbled complaint. **4** *v.* To complain, utter, or speak in a murmur. ◆ The sound [mûr] suggests the low, muffled sound of an actual murmur. The sound was simply repeated to form the word.

mur·rain [mûr′in] *n.* Any of several contagious diseases that attack cattle.

mus·ca·tel [mus′kə·tel′] *n.* A sweet wine.

mus·cle [mus′əl] *n.* **1** One of the bundles of fibrous tissue in the body that, by contraction and stretching, produce the body's voluntary and involuntary movements. **2** An organ or structure made up of this tissue: leg *muscles*. **3** Muscular strength; brawn. ◆ *Muscle* comes from a Latin word that means *a little mouse*, because a bunched muscle can look like a little mouse.

mus·cu·lar [mus′kyə·lər] *adj.* **1** Of, using, or made of muscle: *muscular* tissue; *muscular* activity. **2** Having strong, well-developed muscles; powerful.

muse [myooz] *v.* **mused, mus·ing** To ponder or contemplate thoughtfully.

Muse [myooz] *n.* **1** In Greek myths, any of the nine goddesses of the arts and sciences. **2** (*often written* **muse**) A spirit or power thought to inspire poets, artists, etc.

mu·se·um [myoo·zē′əm] *n.* A place for keeping and exhibiting works of nature and art, scientific objects, curiosities, etc.

mush¹ [mush] *n.* **1** A porridge made with cornmeal. **2** Anything soft, thick, and pulpy.

mush² [mush] *v.* To travel, especially over snow with a dog team.

mush·room [mush′room] **1** *n.* A fungus, shaped like an umbrella or a cone, that grows very quickly. Some kinds, often called toadstools, are poisonous. **2** *adj.* Of, like, or shaped like a mushroom. **3** *v.* To grow or spread out quickly.

mush·y [mush′ē] *adj.* **mush·i·er, mush·i·est** **1** Soft; spongy: *mushy* ground. **2** *informal* Too sentimental or emotional.

mu·sic [myoo′zik] *n.* **1** The art of combining sounds, usually of voices or instruments, into patterns that are organized and expressive. **2** A composition consisting of such patterns. **3** The notation in which music is written: to read *music*. **4** Any pleasing series of sounds. **— face the music** To accept the consequences of one's actions.

mu·si·cal [myoo′zi·kəl] **1** *adj.* Of, related to, or used to make music. **2** *adj.* Fond of or skilled in music: a *musical* society. **3** *adj.* Like music; melodious; harmonious: a *musical* voice. **4** *adj.* Set to, accompanied by, or containing music. **5** *n.* A musical comedy. **— mu′si·cal·ly** *adv.*

musical comedy A show with music, songs, and dances, often based on a slight plot.

mu·si·cale [myoo′zə·kal′] *n.* A private concert or recital, as in a home.

music box A box fitted with a mechanism that plays a tune when activated, as by clockwork.

mu·si·cian [myoo·zish′ən] *n.* A person who is skilled in music, especially a professional composer or performer of music.

mu·si·col·o·gy [myoo′zə·kol′ə·jē] *n., pl.* **mu·si·col·o·gies** The science and historical study of the forms, theory, methods, etc., of music.

musk [musk] *n.* **1** A substance with a strong scent, used in perfumes, obtained from a male musk deer. **2** Any similar substance from some other animals, as the civet or the muskrat. **3** This scent. **— musk′y** *adj.*

musk deer A small deer without horns, of central Asia. The male secretes musk.

mus·kel·lunge [mus′kə·lunj] *n., pl.* **mus·kel·lunge** or **mus·kel·lunges** A large North American, fresh-water fish, a kind of pike.

mus·ket [mus′kit] *n.* An old type of firearm, now replaced by the rifle.

mus·ket·eer [mus′kə·tir′] *n.* In former times, a soldier armed with a musket.

mus·ket·ry [mus′kit·rē] *n.* **1** Muskets or musket fire. **2** The art of firing small arms.

musk·mel·on [musk′mel′ən] *n.* **1** Any of several varieties of melon with sweet, juicy meat and tough rind, as the cantaloupe. **2** The plant bearing this melon.

Musket

musk ox *pl.* **musk oxen** An arctic animal with a musky smell, shaggy hair, and curved horns, resembling both the sheep and the ox.

musk·rat [musk′rat] *n., pl.* **musk·rats** or **musk·rat** 1 A rodent with glossy, brown fur and a musky odor that lives in the marshes and ponds of North America. 2 Its fur.
◆ The word *muskrat* was formed because the original Algonquian Indian name

Musk ox, about 7 ft. long

for this animal, *musquash*, apparently sounded too un-English, and because the animal does have a musky odor and does resemble a rat.

Mus·lem or **Mus·lim** [muz′ləm] *n., adj.* Other spellings of MOSLEM.

mus·lin [muz′lin] *n.* A strong cotton cloth, often used for sheets or curtains.

muss [mus] *informal* 1 *n.* A state of disorder; mess. 2 *v.* To make messy; rumple.

mus·sel [mus′əl] *n.* A shellfish like a small clam with a shell of two hinged parts. Some saltwater mussels are eaten.

Mus·so·li·ni [mo̅o̅s′ə·lē′nē], **Benito**, 1883–1945, Fascist leader, premier of Italy, 1922–1943.

Mus·sul·man [mus′əl·mən] *n., pl.* **Mus·sul·mans** or **Mus·sul·men** [mus′əl·mən] A Moslem.

muss·y [mus′ē] *U.S. informal adj.* **muss·i·er, muss·i·est** Rumpled; messy.

must [must] *v.* A helping verb used to express: 1 Necessity or obligation: *Must* you go? I *must.* 2 Probability: He *must* have been tired. 3 Certainty or conviction: War *must* follow.
◆ *Must* has only this one form, used for all tenses and persons.

mus·tache [mus′tash *or* məs·tash′] *n.* 1 The hair on a man's upper lip, especially when cultivated or groomed. 2 The hair or bristles growing near an animal's mouth.

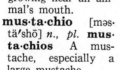

mus·ta·chio [məs·tä′shō] *n., pl.* **mus·ta·chios** A mustache, especially a large mustache.

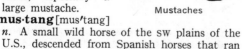
Mustaches

mus·tang [mus′tang] *n.* A small wild horse of the sw plains of the U.S., descended from Spanish horses that ran away.

mus·tard [mus′tərd] *n.* 1 A plant with yellow flowers and small seed pods. 2 A sharp, brownish yellow seasoning made by grinding the seeds of this plant into a powder or paste.

mus·ter [mus′tər] 1 *v.* To call or bring together; assemble. 2 *n.* A gathering or assembling, as of troops for inspection. 3 *n.* The persons or things assembled together. 4 *v.* To gather or collect: to *muster* up courage. 5 *n.* A list of officers and men in a military unit. — **muster out** To discharge from military service. — **pass muster** To pass an inspection.

must·n't [mus′ənt] Must not.

must·y [mus′tē] *adj.* **must·i·er, must·i·est** 1 Having a moldy odor or taste. 2 Stale or old: *musty* humor. — **must′i·ness** *n.*

mu·ta·ble [myo̅o̅′tə·bəl] *adj.* 1 Frequently changing; fickle. 2 Capable of or subject to change. — **mu·ta·bil·i·ty** [myo̅o̅′tə·bil′ə·tē] *n.*

mu·tant [myo̅o̅′tənt] *n.* 1 A new variety of plant or animal differing from its parents as a result of mutation. 2 A person or thing that changes or is capable of change.

mu·tate [myo̅o̅′tāt] *v.* **mu·tat·ed, mu·tat·ing** To undergo or cause to undergo mutation.

mu·ta·tion [myo̅o̅·tā′shən] *n.* 1 A change or variation. 2 A sudden variation by which an organism differs from its parents in one or more characteristics that can be inherited.

mute [myo̅o̅t] *adj., n., v.* **mut·ed, mut·ing** 1 *adj.* Lacking the power of speech; dumb. 2 *n.* A mute person, especially a deaf-mute. 3 *adj.* Not making noise or speaking; silent. 4 *adj.* Not pronounced; silent, as the *e* in *gone.* 5 *n.* A device used to muffle the tone of a musical instrument. 6 *v.* To make softer in sound. — **mute′ly** *adv.* — **mute′ness** *n.*

mu·ti·late [myo̅o̅′tə·lāt] *v.* **mu·ti·lat·ed, mu·ti·lat·ing** 1 To cut or tear off a leg, arm, or other part of (a person, animal, etc.). 2 To damage, disfigure, or spoil (a book, song, etc.) by cutting out parts. — **mu·ti·la′tion** *n.*

mu·ti·neer [myo̅o̅′tə·nir′] *n.* A person who takes part in a mutiny.

mu·ti·nous [myo̅o̅′tə·nəs] *adj.* Stirring up or involved in a mutiny; rebellious.

mu·ti·ny [myo̅o̅′tə·nē] *n., pl.* **mu·ti·nies, *v.*** **mu·ti·nied, mu·ti·ny·ing** 1 *n.* A rebellion against authority, as by a group of soldiers or sailors against their commanders. 2 *v.* To take part in a mutiny; rebel; revolt.

mut·ter [mut′ər] 1 *v.* To speak in a low tone with half-closed lips. 2 *n.* A low, unclear utterance or tone. 3 *v.* To complain; grumble.

mut·ton [mut′(ə)n] *n.* The flesh of sheep, especially an adult sheep, used as food.

mu·tu·al [myo̅o̅′cho̅o̅·əl] *adj.* 1 Felt, shown, or done by two or more persons, sides, etc., for or toward each other: *mutual* dislike. 2 Having the same attitude toward or relationship with each other or others: *mutual* friends. 3 Held in common: *mutual* interests. — **mu′tu·al·ly** *adv.*

add, āce, câre, pälm;   end, ēqual;   it, īce;   odd, ōpen, ôrder;   to̅o̅k, po̅o̅l;   up, bûrn;
ə = a in *above*, e in *sicken*, i in *possible*, o in *melon*, u in *circus*;   y o̅o̅ = u in *fuse*;   oil;   pout;
check;   ring;   thin;   this;   zh in *vision*.   For ¶ reference, see page 64 · HOW TO

muz·zle [muz′(ə)l] *n., v.* **muz·zled, muz·zling 1** *n.* The snout of an animal, as a dog or horse. **2** *n.* A guard for a snout that prevents an animal from biting. **3** *v.* To fasten a muzzle to the snout of. **4** *v.* To prevent from speaking or giving an opinion. **5** *n.* The front end of a firearm.

Muzzle

my [mī] **1** *pron.* Of, belonging to, done by, or having to do with me: the possessive form of *I*: *my* book; *my* work. **2** *interj.* A word used to show surprise or dismay: Oh *my*! What a shame!

my·ce·li·um [mī·sē′lē·əm] *n., pl.* **my·ce·li·a** [mī·sē′lē·ə] The mass of threadlike structures that form the main body of a fungus.

my·col·o·gy [mī·kol′ə·jē] *n.* The branch of botany that deals with fungi.

my·na or **my·nah** [mī′nə] *n.* An Asian bird related to the starling, often taught to speak.

my·o·pi·a [mī·ō′pē·ə] *n.* A visual defect in which distant objects are not seen clearly; nearsightedness.

myr·i·ad [mir′ē·əd] *n.* **1** Ten thousand. **2** A vast indefinite number.

myr·mi·don [mûr′mə·don] *n.* **1** A faithful follower, especially one who follows orders without question. **2** (*written* **Myrmidon**) In Greek myths, any of the warriors who fought under their king, Achilles, in the Trojan War.

myrrh [mûr] *n.* A fragrant gum resin obtained from certain small trees of Arabia and Africa, used in perfumes, incense, etc.

myr·tle [mûr′təl] *n.* **1** An evergreen shrub of southern Europe, with white or rose-colored flowers and black berries. **2** Any of several evergreen plants, as the periwinkle.

my·self [mī·self′] *pron.* **1** The one that I really am; my very own self. ◆ *Myself* in this sense is used to refer back to the subject *I* or to make the *I* more emphatic: I cut *myself*; I saw him *myself*. **2** My normal, healthy, usual, or proper condition: I was *myself* in no time at all.

mys·te·ri·ous [mis·tir′ē·əs] *adj.* Filled with or suggesting mystery; unexplained: *mysterious* events. **— mys·te′ri·ous·ly** *adv.*

mys·ter·y [mis′tər·ē] *n., pl.* **mys·ter·ies 1** Something that is not known, understood, or explained. **2** Any action, affair, etc., that arouses curiosity because it is not understood or explained. **3** A story, play, etc., about such an action, affair, etc. **4** A quality of secrecy or obscurity. **5** A play of a type popular in medieval times, based on a Biblical incident.

mys·tic [mis′tik] **1** *n.* A person who believes that knowledge of God and spiritual truth is best obtained through devotion and contemplation rather than by reason. **2** *adj.* Of or related to mystics or mysticism. **3** *adj.* Mysterious; uncanny: *mystic* abilities.

mys·ti·cal [mis′ti·kəl] *adj.* **1** Of or having a quality or meaning that is spiritual and beyond human reason. **2** Of or related to mystics or mysticism. **3** Mysterious or secret. **— mys′ti·cal·ly** *adv.*

mys·ti·cism [mis′tə·siz′əm] *n.* **1** The beliefs and practices of mystics; the search for God and truth through contemplation and love, with no use of reason. **2** Vague or confused thinking.

mys·ti·fi·ca·tion [mis′tə·fi·kā′shən] *n.* **1** The act of mystifying. **2** The condition of being mystified. **3** Something mystifying.

mys·ti·fy [mis′tə·fī] *v.* **mys·ti·fied, mys·ti·fy·ing 1** To puzzle or baffle; bewilder. **2** To make obscure or mysterious; complicate.

myth [mith] *n.* **1** A traditional story, usually about gods, heroes, etc., often offering an explanation of something in nature or of past events. **2** Any made-up story, person, event, etc.

myth·i·cal [mith′ə·kəl] *adj.* **1** Of, like, in, or having to do with a myth or myths. **2** Imaginary. **— myth′i·cal·ly** *adv.*

myth·o·log·i·cal [mith′ə·loj′i·kəl] *adj.* Of or having to do with mythology. **— myth′o·log′i·cal·ly** *adv.*

my·thol·o·gy [mi·thol′ə·jē] *n., pl.* **my·thol·o·gies 1** A group or collection of myths, especially of a particular people. **2** The study of myths.

N

n or **N** [en] *n., pl.* **n's** or **N's 1** The 14th letter of the English alphabet. **2** In mathematics, an indefinite number or quantity.

n. Abbreviation of NOUN.

N The symbol for the element NITROGEN.

N. Abbreviation of NORTH.

Na The symbol for the element SODIUM. ◆ The Latin word for sodium is *natrium*.

NAACP Abbreviation of NATIONAL ASSOCIA-

TION FOR THE ADVANCEMENT OF COLORED PEOPLE, a civil rights organization.

nab [nab] *v.* **nabbed, nab·bing** *informal* **1** To catch or arrest: They *nabbed* the thief at the airport. **2** To take or grab suddenly; snatch.

na·dir [nā′dər] *n.* **1** The point in the sky directly opposite the zenith. It is on the other side of the earth, straight below the observer. **2** The lowest possible point: the *nadir* of despair.

nag[1] [nag] *n.* Any horse, especially an old, broken-down, or worthless one.

nag[2] [nag] *v.* **nagged, nag·ging** To bother with urging, complaints, etc.; scold; pester: His sister often *nags* him. **— nag'ger** *n.*

Na·ga·sa·ki [nä'gə·sä'kē] *n.* A city in southern Japan. It was the second of the two cities struck by atomic bombs in 1945.

nai·ad [nā'ad *or* nī'ad] *n.*, *pl.* **nai·ads** or **nai·ad·es** [nā'ə·dēz *or* nī'ə·dēz] In Greek and Roman myths, one of the nymphs that lived in and guarded bodies of water, as fountains, rivers, etc.

nail [nāl] **1** *n.* A slender, pointed piece of metal, usually with a head at the top end, to be driven into or through pieces of wood, etc., to fasten them together. **2** *v.* To fasten in place by a nail or nails. **3** *n.* A thin, horny substance that grows at the ends of the fingers and toes. **4** *v. informal* To catch: to *nail* someone in a lie. **— hit the nail on the head** To be exactly right.

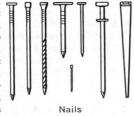

Nails

nain·sook [nān'sŏŏk] *n.* A soft, lightweight cotton cloth.

na·ive or **na·ïve** [nä·ēv'] *adj.* **1** Simple and unaffected; childlike. **2** Foolish or inexperienced. **3** Not carefully thought out: a *naive* idea. **— na·ive'ly** *adv.* ◆ See NATIVE.

na·ive·té or **na·ïve·té** [nä·ēv'tā'] *n.* **1** Childlike innocence or inexperience. **2** A naive remark or act.

na·ked [nā'kid] *adj.* **1** Not wearing any clothes; nude. **2** Not covered; stripped bare: a *naked* tree. **3** Not protected; exposed: the *naked* mountain top. **4** Having nothing added; stark; plain: *naked* truth. **— na'ked·ness** *n.*

naked eye The human eye, not helped by glasses, a microscope, telescope, or other instrument.

name [nām] *n.*, *v.* **named, nam·ing** **1** *n.* A word or group of words by which a person, animal, place, etc., is known or spoken of. **2** *v.* To give a name to: to *name* a cat. **3** *v.* To speak or write the name of; mention: *Name* five stars. **4** *n.* A reputation: to have a bad *name*. **5** *n.* An insulting word or phrase: They called him *names*. **6** *v.* To designate for a particular job or office; appoint: Mr. Smith was *named* coach. **— in the name of 1** For the sake of: *in the name of* peace. **2** By the authority of: *in the name of* Congress. **— make a name for oneself** To become famous. **— to one's name** In one's possession: I haven't a cent *to my name*.

name·less [nām'lis] *adj.* **1** Having no name. **2** Not known by name; anonymous: a *nameless* crowd. **3** Not fit or able to be spoken of; unmentionable: *nameless* terror; *nameless* crimes. **4** Not mentioned by name.

name·ly [nām'lē] *adv.* That is to say; to wit: Two metals, *namely* copper and gold, are used.

name·sake [nām'sāk'] *n.* A person given or having the same name as another person.

nan·keen or **nan·kin** [nan·kēn'] *n.* A buff-colored, Chinese cotton fabric.

Nan·king [nan·king'] *n.* A city in eastern China, on the Yangtze River, the capital from 1928–1937.

Na·o·mi [nā·ō'mē] *n.* In the Bible, the mother-in-law of Ruth.

nap[1] [nap] *n.*, *v.* **napped, nap·ping** **1** *n.* A short sleep. **2** *v.* To sleep for a short time; doze. **3** *v.* To be unprepared or off guard: to be caught *napping*.

nap[2] [nap] *n.* The short fibers forming a fuzzy surface, as on flannel or velvet.

nape [nāp] *n.* The back part of the neck.

naph·tha [naf'thə *or* nap'·thə] *n.* An oily substance distilled from petroleum, used as a fuel, a solvent, and a cleaning fluid.

nap·kin [nap'kin] *n.* **1** A small cloth or paper used at meals to protect clothing and to wipe the hands and mouth. **2** A small towel or piece of cloth.

nape

Na·ples [nāp'əlz] *n.* A port in sw Italy.

Na·po·le·on [nə·pō'lē·ən] See BONAPARTE.

Na·po·le·on·ic [nə·pō'lē·on'ik] *adj.* Of or having to do with Napoleon Bonaparte.

nar·cis·sus [när·sis'əs] *n.*, *pl.* **nar·cis·sus·es** or **nar·cis·si** [när·sis'ī] **1** A spring plant that grows from a bulb and bears white or yellow flowers. Daffodils and jonquils are species of narcissus. **2** (*written* **Narcissus**) In Greek myths, a youth who was made to fall in love with his own reflection in water and who pined for it until he died and was turned into a narcissus.

nar·cot·ic [när·kot'ik] **1** *n.* A drug, as morphine, that produces sleep and dulls pain when taken in small doses but may be poisonous in large doses. **2** *adj.* Of, like, or having the effects of a narcotic.

nar·rate [na·rāt' *or* nar'āt] *v.* **nar·rat·ed, nar·rat·ing** **1** To tell or relate, as a story. **2** To talk along with in order to explain: to *narrate* a film.

nar·ra·tion [na·rā'shən] *n.* **1** A telling, as of a story or event. **2** A talk given to explain a film, etc.

nar·ra·tive [nar'ə·tiv] **1** *n.* An account, story, or tale. **2** *n.* The act of narrating; narration. **3** *adj.* Telling a story: a *narrative* poem.

nar·rat·or [na·rāt′ər *or* nar′ā·tər] *n.* **1** A person who tells a story. **2** A person who talks along with a film, television program, etc., and explains it or comments on it.

nar·row [nar′ō] **1** *adj.* Having little width or less than a standard or expected width; not broad: a *narrow* bridge; *narrow* ribbon. **2** *v.* To make or become less wide: The brook *narrows* to a trickle. **3** *n.* (*usually pl.*) A narrow part, as of a strait. **4** *adj.* Limited in breadth of vision, tolerance, etc.: *narrow* views. **5** *adj.* Limited or small: a family of *narrow* means. **6** *adj.* Nearly unsuccessful or disastrous; close: a *narrow* escape. **— nar′row·ly** *adv.* **— nar′row·ness** *n.*

nar·row-mind·ed [nar′ō·mīn′did] *adj.* Having or showing narrow ideas; not liberal; bigoted.

nar·whal [när′(h)wəl] *n.* A small whale of arctic waters. The male has a long, spiral tusk.

na·sal [nā′zəl] **1** *adj.* Of or having to do with the nose: *nasal* congestion. **2** *adj.* Produced with the voice passing through the nose, as [m], [n], or [ng]. **3** *n.* A nasal sound.

Nash·ville [nash′vil] *n.* The capital of Tennessee.

Narwhal, 13 ft. long; tusk about 7 ft. long

na·stur·tium [nə·stûr′shəm] *n.* A garden plant with a strong odor and funnel-shaped flowers of red, orange, or yellow. ◆ *Nasturtium* comes from a Latin phrase *nasus tortus*, meaning *twisted nose*, describing how the flower's sharp odor makes a person draw up his nose.

nas·ty [nas′tē] *adj.* **nas·ti·er, nas·ti·est** **1** Disgusting to smell or taste. **2** Filthy. **3** Indecent; foul: *nasty* language. **4** Disagreeable, unpleasant, or painful: a *nasty* cut. **5** Mean or vicious: a *nasty* temper. **— nas′ti·ly** *adv.* **— nas′ti·ness** *n.*

na·tal [nā′təl] *adj.* Of or having to do with one's birth; dating from birth. ◆ See NATIVE.

Na·tal [nə·täl′ *or* nə·tal′] *n.* A province in the eastern part of the Republic of South Africa.

na·tion [nā′shən] *n.* **1** A group of people who live in a particular area, have a distinctive way of life, and are organized under a central government. They usually speak the same language. **2** A tribe or federation: the Iroquois *nation*. ◆ See NATIVE.

na·tion·al [nash′ən·əl] **1** *adj.* Of, belonging to, or having to do with a nation as a whole: a *national* law; a *national* crisis. **2** *n.* A citizen of a nation: a Danish *national.* **— na′tion·al·ly** *adv.*

National Guard A military force of a state, paid for in part by the U.S. government and subject to federal service in times of emergency.

na·tion·al·ism [nash′ən·əl·iz′əm] *n.* **1** Patriotic feelings for one's own nation. **2** A desire or movement for national independence. **— na′tion·al·ist** *n.* **— na′tion·al·is′tic** *adj.*

na·tion·al·i·ty [nash′ən·al′ə·tē] *n., pl.* **na·tion·al·i·ties** **1** A group of people who form a nation. **2** The condition of belonging to a particular nation, as by birth or naturalization. **3** The condition of existing as a nation.

na·tion·al·ize [nash′ən·əl·īz′] *v.* **na·tion·al·ized, na·tion·al·iz·ing** **1** To place (the industries, resources, etc., of a nation) under the control or ownership of the state. **2** To make national, as in character or scope. **3** To make into a nation. **— na′tion·al·i·za′tion** [nash′ən·əl·ə·zā′shən] *n.* ¶3

na·tion-wide [nā′shən·wīd′] *adj.* Extending throughout or across a nation.

na·tive [nā′tiv] **1** *adj.* Born, grown, or living naturally in a particular area. **2** *n.* A person, plant, animal, etc., native to an area. **3** *n.* One of the original inhabitants of a place; aborigine. **4** *adj.* Related or belonging to a person by birth or place of birth: one's *native* language. **5** *adj.* Not learned; inborn: *native* charm. **6** *adj.* Found in a pure state in nature: *native* gold. ◆ *Native* and *naive* come from two different French words that were both derived from one Latin word, *nativus*, meaning *natural* or *inborn*. *Nativus* is based on the Latin word *nasci*, meaning *to be born*, from which such words as *nation* and *natal* are also derived.

na·tive-born [nā′tiv·bôrn′] *adj.* Born in the area or country stated: a *native-born* Mexican.

na·tiv·i·ty [nə·tiv′ə·tē] *n., pl.* **na·tiv·i·ties** Birth. **— the Nativity 1** The birth of Jesus. **2** Christmas Day.

NATO [nā′tō] The North Atlantic Treaty Organization, a military alliance of Belgium, Canada, Denmark, France, Great Britain, Greece, Iceland, Italy, Luxemburg, the Netherlands, Norway, Portugal, Turkey, the U.S. and West Germany.

nat·ty [nat′ē] *adj.* **nat·ti·er, nat·ti·est** Smart in looks or dress; neat. **— nat′ti·ly** *adv.*

nat·u·ral [nach′ər·əl] **1** *adj.* Produced by or existing in nature; not artificial: a *natural* bridge. **2** *adj.* Having to do with the study of nature: *natural* sciences. **3** *adj.* Inborn; native: *natural* talent. **4** *adj.* Being so by nature: a *natural* athlete. **5** *adj.* Happening in a normal or expected way: a *natural* death. **6** *adj.* Resembling nature closely; lifelike: a *natural* pose. **7** *adj.* Not forced or affected: *natural* behavior. **8** *adj.* Felt by instinct to be just: *natural* rights. **9** *adj.* In music, not sharp or flat, as a note. **10** *n.* A natural note. **11** *n.* A sign (♮) used to cancel sharps and flats. **12** *n. U.S. informal* A person or thing that is well suited for some job or purpose. **— nat′u·ral·ness** *n.*

natural history The study of nature, especially as related to the earth and living things.

nat·u·ral·ist [nach′ər·əl·ist] *n.* A person who is trained in natural history.

nat·u·ral·ize [nach′ər·əl·īz′] *v.* **nat·u·ral·ized, nat·u·ral·iz·ing 1** To make into or accept as a citizen: to *naturalize* an immigrant. **2** To adopt into common use, as a foreign word or custom. **3** To adapt to a country or place, as a foreign plant or animal. — **nat′u·ral·i·za′·tion** [nach′ər·əl·ə·zā′shən] *n.* ¶3

nat·u·ral·ly [nach′ər·əl·ē] *adv.* **1** In a natural, normal, or usual manner. **2** By nature: He was *naturally* clever. **3** Of course; certainly.

natural number A positive integer, as 1, 2, etc.

natural resource (*often pl.*) A source of raw material, power, or wealth provided by nature, as forests, minerals, water supply, etc.

natural science 1 Any science that deals with the physical world, such as biology, chemistry, or physics. **2** All such sciences together.

na·ture [nā′chər] *n.* **1** The overall pattern or system of objects, forces, events, etc., in the universe: laws of *nature.* **2** The world, except for those things made by man: In the country people enjoy *nature.* **3** The basic qualities and character of a thing or person: the *nature* of war; his gentle *nature.* **4** The natural tendencies directing conduct: Suicide is against *nature.* **5** Sort; kind; variety: nothing of that *nature.*

naught [nôt] *n.* **1** Nothing. **2** The numeral 0; zero.

naugh·ty [nô′tē] *adj.* **naugh·ti·er, naugh·ti·est 1** Badly behaved; mischievous; disobedient: a *naughty* child. **2** A little improper: a *naughty* word. — **naugh′ti·ly** *adv.* — **naugh′ti·ness** *n.*

nau·se·a [nô′zē·ə *or* nô′zhə] *n.* **1** A sick feeling that comes along with an urge to vomit. **2** Disgust or loathing. ◆ *Nausea* comes originally from a Greek word meaning *seasickness.*

nau·se·ate [nô′zē·āt *or* nô′sē·āt] *v.* **nau·se·at·ed, nau·se·at·ing** To feel or cause to feel nausea or disgust: The filth *nauseated* her.

nau·seous [nô′shəs *or* nô′sē·əs] *adj.* Causing nausea; nasty to taste or smell: *nauseous* fumes.

nau·ti·cal [nô′ti·kəl] *adj.* Of or having to do with ships, sailors, or navigation. — **nau′ti·cal·ly** *adv.*

nautical mile A measure of distance equal to about 6,076 feet.

Chambered nautilus and cross section of its shell

nau·ti·lus [nô′tə·ləs] *n.* **1** A small sea animal that lives in the largest and outermost chamber of a spiral shell having many chambers. **2** An eight-armed sea creature related to the octopus, the female of which has a thin, delicate shell.

Nav·a·ho [nav′ə·hō] *n., pl.* **Nav·a·hos** or

Nav·a·hoes A member of a tribe of North American Indians, now living in Arizona, New Mexico, and Utah.

na·val [nā′vəl] *adj.* **1** Of, for, or performed by a navy: a *naval* hospital; a *naval* battle. **2** Having a navy; a *naval* power.

nave [nāv] The main part of a church, located between the side aisles.

na·vel [nā′vəl] *n.* **1** The scar at the center of the abdomen where the umbilical cord was attached. **2** A central part or point.

navel orange An orange without seeds that has a navel-like depression at one end.

nav·i·ga·ble [nav′ə·gə·bəl] *adj.* **1** Deep and wide enough for ships to sail on: a *navigable* river. **2** Capable of being steered, as a dirigible. — **nav·i·ga·bil·i·ty** [nav′ə·gə·bil′ə·tē] *n.*

nav·i·gate [nav′ə·gāt] *v.* **nav·i·gat·ed, nav·i·gat·ing 1** To travel or travel on, through, or over, as by boat. **2** To chart or control the course and position of, as a ship or aircraft.

nav·i·ga·tion [nav′ə·gā′shən] *n.* **1** The act or practice of navigating. **2** The art of charting the position or course of a ship or aircraft.

nav·i·ga·tor [nav′ə·gā′tər] *n.* **1** A person who navigates. **2** A person trained in charting the position and course of a ship, aircraft, etc.

na·vy [nā′vē] *n., pl.* **na·vies 1** (*often written* **Navy**) The entire military sea force of a country, including its ships, its officers and men, and the government department that supervises them. **2** Navy blue. **3** A fleet of ships: seldom used today.

navy blue A very dark blue.

nay [nā] **1** *adv.* No: seldom used today. **2** *adv.* No, rather; not only that, but also: He is somewhat odd, *nay,* insane. **3** *n.* A negative vote. **4** *n.* A denial or refusal.

Naz·a·rene [naz′ə·rēn] *n.* A person born or living in Nazareth. — **the Nazarene** Jesus.

Naz·a·reth [naz′ə·rəth] *n.* A town in northern Israel where Jesus spent his childhood.

Na·zi [nä′tsē] *n.* A member of the fascist political party that controlled Germany from 1933 to 1945 under Adolf Hitler. — **Naz′ism** or **Na′zi·ism** *n.*

N.B. Abbreviation of *nota bene,* a Latin phrase meaning "note well."

N.C. Abbreviation of NORTH CAROLINA.

N. Dak. Abbreviation of NORTH DAKOTA.

Ne The symbol for the element NEON.

NE or **N.E.** Abbreviation of: **1** NORTHEAST. **2** NORTHEASTERN.

---

add, āce, câre, pälm; end, ēqual; it, īce; odd, ōpen, ôrder; tŏŏk, pōōl; up, bûrn; ə = a in *above,* e in *sicken,* i in *possible,* o in *melon,* u in *circus;* yōō = u in *fuse;* oil; pout; check; ring; thin; this; zh in *vision.* For ¶ reference, see page 64 · HOW TO

Ne·an·der·thal man [nē·an'dər·täl *or* nē·an'·dər·thôl] An extinct species of man that lived in caves and used stone tools.

Ne·a·pol·i·tan [nē'ə·pol'ə·tən] **1** *adj.* Of or coming from Naples. **2** *n.* A person born or living in Naples.

neap tide [nēp] The tide soon after the first and third quarters of the moon, when the difference between high tide and low tide is very slight.

Neanderthal man

near [nir] **1** *adv., adj.* Not distant in place, time, or degree; close: He came *near*; The town is *near*. **2** *prep.* Close by or to. **3** *v.* To come near; approach: My arrow *neared* the target. **4** *adv. informal* Nearly; almost: *near* perfect weather. **5** *adj.* Barely escaped or avoided; close: a *near* tragedy. **6** *adj.* Close in relationship or affection: a *near* and dear person. **7** *adj.* Saving distance or time; short: 20 miles by the *nearest* route. **8** *adj.* Stingy; cheap. — **near'ness** *n.* ◆ In Old English *near* was the comparative of *nēah*, meaning *nigh* or *close*. Now, however, *near* has pretty much taken the place of *nigh*, and *nearer* has become the comparative form.

near·by [*adj.* nir'bī', *adv.* nir'bī'] *adj., adv.* Close by; near: a *nearby* hut; to fly *nearby*.

Near East 1 *U.S.* The region, mainly in sw Asia, surrounding the eastern Mediterranean Sea, from Egypt to the Balkans. **2** *British* The Balkans.

near·ly [nir'lē] *adv.* **1** Almost; practically; approximately: It is *nearly* bedtime. **2** Closely.

near·sight·ed [nir'sī'tid] *adj.* Able to see clearly at short distances only. — **near'·sight'ed·ness** *n.*

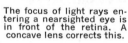

neat [nēt] *adj.* **1** Orderly, tidy, and clean: a *neat* house; Cats are *neat* animals.

The focus of light rays entering a nearsighted eye is in front of the retina. A concave lens corrects this.

2 Precise: *neat* work. **3** Not mixed or diluted, as liquor. **4** *slang* Cleverly done: a *neat* trick. — **neat'ly** *adv.* — **neat'ness** *n.*

'neath *or* **neath** [nēth] *prep.* Beneath; under: used mostly in poems.

Nebr. Abbreviation of NEBRASKA.

Ne·bras·ka [nə·bras'kə] *n.* A state in the central U.S.

Neb·u·chad·nez·zar [neb'yōō·kəd·nez'ər] *n.*, died 562 B.C., king of Babylonia, 605–562 B.C., conquered Judea and destroyed Jerusalem.

neb·u·la [neb'yōō·lə] *n., pl.* **neb·u·las** *or* **neb·u·lae** [neb'yōō·lē] **1** A shining or dark celestial mass consisting of a cloud of gases and cosmic dust, sometimes enveloping one or more stars. **2** A very distant system of stars; galaxy.

neb·u·lous [neb'yōō·ləs] *adj.* **1** Vague or unclear: a *nebulous* feeling. **2** Of, having to do with, or like a nebula. **3** Cloudlike; misty.

nec·es·sar·y [nes'ə·ser'ē] *adj., n., pl.* **nec·es·sar·ies 1** *adj.* Not to be done without; essential: Your help is *necessary*. **2** *n.* (*often pl.*) Something that cannot be done without, as food. **3** *adj.* Bound to happen; inevitable: Heat is a *necessary* result of friction. — **nec'es·sar'i·ly** *adv.*

ne·ces·si·tate [nə·ses'ə·tāt] *v.* **ne·ces·si·tat·ed, ne·ces·si·tat·ing** To make necessary; force: The rain *necessitated* a delay.

ne·ces·si·ty [nə·ses'ə·tē] *n., pl.* **ne·ces·si·ties 1** (*often pl.*) Something that cannot be done without, such as food: They could barely afford *necessities*. **2** Extreme need: Wake me in case of *necessity*. **3** A need or force that compels: *Necessity* made him learn to cook. **4** Great poverty: to live in *necessity*. — **of necessity** With no possibility of being otherwise.

neck [nek] *n.* **1** The part of an animal that connects the head with the trunk. **2** The part of a garment that comes nearest to or touches the neck. **3** Something thought to resemble a neck, as the narrow part of a violin or bottle, or a narrow piece of land between two bodies of water. — **neck and neck** Abreast or even, as in a race.

neck·er·chief [nek'ər·chif] *n.* A kerchief worn around the neck.

neck·lace [nek'lis] *n.* An ornament, as a string of beads, gems, etc., worn around the neck.

neck·line [nek'līn'] *n.* The line or shape formed by the neck of a garment.

neck·tie [nek'tī'] *n.* A narrow strip of cloth worn around the neck under a collar and tied in front.

Neckerchief

nec·ro·man·cy [nek'rə·man'sē] *n.* **1** The telling of the future by supposedly consulting the dead. **2** Magic; witchcraft. — **nec'ro·man'cer** *n.*

nec·tar [nek'tər] *n.* **1** In Greek myths, the drink of the gods. **2** A delicious or satisfying drink. **3** A sweet liquid found in flowers, collected by bees to make honey.

nec·tar·ine [nek'tə·rēn'] *n.* A type of peach having a smooth skin and a firm pulp.

née *or* **nee** [nā] *adj.* Born with the name of: used to indicate the maiden name of a married woman: Mrs. Mary Lincoln, *née* Todd. ◆ *Née* comes directly from the French, in which it is the feminine form of *né*, meaning *born*.

need [nēd] **1** *v.* To require; find necessary: Everyone *needs* food. **2** *n.* A lack of something required or wanted: a *need* for nurses. **3** *n.* The thing wanted or required but lacking: Our great *need* was money. **4** *n.* A condition of requiring help: a friend in *need*. **5** *n.* Poverty: My neighbor is in great *need*. **6** *v.* To have to; ought to: He *needs* to study more. **7** *n.* Obligation; necessity: Is there any *need* to hurry? ◆ *Need* is sometimes used in negative statements and in questions as an unchanging helping verb:

He *need* not go; *Need* he come? **— if need be** If necessary.

need·ful [nēd′fəl] *adj.* Needed; necessary.

nee·dle [nēd′(ə)l] *n., v.* **nee·dled, nee·dling** **1** *n.* A small, thin, steel rod with a hole in one end, used to carry thread through cloth in sewing. **2** *n.* The thin, hollow tube at the end of a hypodermic syringe. **3** *n.* A pointer, as in a gauge or compass. **4** *n.* A short rod, often tipped with a hard material, as diamond, used to pick up vibrations from a phonograph record. **5** *n.* A slender rod used in knitting. **6** *n.* Something that suggests the shape of a needle, as a leaf of a pine, an obelisk, etc. **7** *v. informal* To tease or heckle.

need·less [nēd′lis] *adj.* Not needed or necessary; useless. **— need′less·ly** *adv.*

nee·dle·work [nēd′(ə)l·wûrk′] *n.* Work done using a needle, as embroidery, sewing, etc.

need·n't [nēd′(ə)nt] Need not.

needs [nēdz] *adv.* Necessarily: seldom used to-day: A woman must *needs* be a good manager to run a household.

need·y [nē′dē] *adj.* **need·i·er, need·i·est** In need or want; very poor. **— need′i·ness** *n.*

ne'er [nâr] *adv.* Never: used mostly in poems.

ne'er-do-well [nâr′doo·wel′] *n.* A worthless, good-for-nothing person.

ne·far·i·ous [ni·fâr′ē·əs] *adj.* Extremely wicked.

ne·gate [ni·gāt′] *v.* **ne·gat·ed, ne·gat·ing 1** To cancel the effect of; abolish; nullify. **2** To deny or contradict.

ne·ga·tion [ni·gā′shən] *n.* **1** The act of denying. **2** The absence or reverse of something: Silence is the *negation* of sound.

neg·a·tive [neg′ə·tiv] *adj., n., v.* **neg·a·tived, neg·a·tiv·ing 1** *adj.* Expressing refusal, denial, or opposition: a *negative* answer. **2** *n.* A negative word or expression: *No* is a *negative.* **3** *adj.* Contrary or resisting; not helpful: a

negative

positive

negative attitude. **4** *v.* To negate or veto. **5** *n.* The group that argues against a point, as in a debate. **6** *adj.* Opposite from positive; minus: a *negative* number. **7** *adj.* Indicating or having the kind of electricity that repels electrons and attracts protons. **8** *adj.* Indicating that something looked for or tested for is not there or does not happen: *negative* results. **9** *adj.* In photography, having the light and dark areas reversed. **10** *n.* A negative picture or film. **— double negative** A sentence or phrase that uses two negatives, as "He hasn't got none." ◆ In Old English the double negative was standard English, but in modern English it is unacceptable and is usually taken to be a sign of ignorance.

Such statements as *I am not unhappy,* however are standard and have the effect of weak affirmatives. **— in the negative 1** In denial or refusal. **2** Opposed. **— neg′a·tive·ly** *adv.*

neg·lect [ni·glekt′] **1** *v.* To fail to care for or attend to: to *neglect* a child; to *neglect* one's homework. **2** *v.* To omit or fail to do: He *neglected* to wear his rubbers. **3** *v.* To pay no attention to; ignore: They *neglected* his advice. **4** *n.* The act of neglecting. **5** *n.* A neglected condition; want of attention or care.

neg·lect·ful [ni·glekt′fəl] *adj.* Heedless; careless: She was *neglectful* of her appearance.

neg·li·gee or **neg·li·gée** [neg′li·zhā′ or neg′li·zhā] *n.* A loose dressing gown worn by women.

neg·li·gent [neg′lə·jənt] *adj.* **1** Failing to do what one should; showing neglect. **2** Failing to use proper caution; reckless. **— neg′li·gence** *n.* **— neg′li·gent·ly** *adv.*

neg·li·gi·ble [neg′lə·jə·bəl] *adj.* Not worth considering; too small to bother with.

ne·go·ti·a·ble [ni·gō′shē·ə·bəl or ni·gō′shə·bəl] *adj.* Capable of being sold or transferred to another person: a *negotiable* check.

ne·go·ti·ate [ni·gō′shē·āt] *v.* **ne·go·ti·at·ed, ne·go·ti·at·ing 1** To bargain and talk with others in hope of reaching an agreement. **2** To arrange by negotiating: to *negotiate* a treaty. **3** To sell or transfer ownership of, as a bond. **4** *informal* To manage to climb, cross, etc.: to *negotiate* a steep hill. **— ne·go′ti·a′tion** *n.* **— ne·go′ti·a′tor** *n.*

Ne·gro [nē′grō] *adj., n., pl.* **Ne·groes 1** *n.* A member of a people of African origin; Black. **2** *n.* A person with any Negro ancestors. **3** *adj.* Of or having to do with Negroes.

Ne·groid [nē′groid] *adj.* Having to do with, like, or characteristic of Negroes.

Ne·he·mi·ah [nē′hə·mī′ə] *n.* **1** A fifth-century B.C. Hebrew statesman and historian. **2** A book of the Old Testament named after him.

Neh·ru [nā′roo], **Jawaharlal,** 1899–1964, Indian nationalist leader, first prime minister, 1947–1964.

neigh [nā] **1** *v.* To make the cry of a horse. **2** *n.* The cry made by a horse.

neigh·bor [nā′bər] **1** *n.* A person or thing that is near another. **2** *n.* A person living near another. **3** *v.* To be near to; border on: His land *neighbors* mine. **4** *n.* A fellow human being. ¶1

neigh·bor·hood [nā′bər·hŏŏd] *n.* **1** A small area or section of a city or town, often having a distinctive quality or character. **2** The people living in such a section. **— in the neighborhood of 1** Near; close to. **2** *informal* About; approximately: *in the neighborhood of* $10,000. ¶1

neigh·bor·ing [nā′bər·ing] *adj.* Located or living nearby; adjacent. ¶1

neigh·bor·ly [nā′bər·lē] *adj.* Being or like a

add, āce, câre, pälm; end, ēqual; it, īce; odd, ōpen, ôrder; tŏŏk, pōōl; up, bûrn;
ə = a in *above,* e in *sicken,* i in *possible,* o in *melon,* u in *circus;* yōō = u in *fuse;* oil; pout;
check; ring; thin; this; zh in *vision.* For ¶ reference, see page 64 · HOW TO

good or pleasant neighbor; friendly; considerate. **— neigh′bor·li·ness** *n.* ¶1

nei·ther [nē′thər *or* nī′thər] **1** *adj.*, *pron.* Not one nor the other; not either: *Neither* plan is any good; *Neither* will do. **2** *conj.* Not either; not: *neither* rain nor snow. **3** *conj.* Nor yet: He can't read; *neither* can he write. ◆ See EITHER.

nem·e·sis [nem′ə·sis] *n.*, *pl.* **nem·e·ses** [nem′·ə·sēz] **1** (*written* **Nemesis**) In Greek myths, the goddess of vengeance. **2** A problem or opponent that one cannot overcome or master: Arithmetic is her *nemesis.* **3** Just punishment or vengeance.

Ne·o·lith·ic [nē′ə·lith′ik] *adj.* Of or having to do with the late Stone Age, when men were making and using polished stone weapons and tools.

ne·on [nē′on] *n.* A colorless, odorless gaseous element that does not combine easily with other elements, and occurs in small amounts in air.

neon sign A sign or display in which glass tubes filled with neon or other gases are bent into the shapes of letters, etc., and made to glow in colors by passing electricity through them.

ne·o·phyte [nē′ə·fit] *n.* A beginner or novice, especially someone new to a religion or a religious order.

Ne·pal [nə·päl′] *n.* A small country between Tibet and India.

neph·ew [nef′yōō] *n.* A son of one's brother or sister, or of one's brother-in-law or sister-in-law.

nep·o·tism [nep′ə·tiz′əm] *n.* The practice of giving jobs or special favors to relatives, especially when done by government officials.

Nep·tune [nep′t(y)ōōn] *n.* **1** In Roman myths, the god of the sea. His Greek name was Poseidon. **2** A planet of the solar system, the fourth in size and eighth in distance from the sun.

nep·tu·ni·um [nep·t(y)ōō′nē·əm] *n.* A radioactive element made by bombarding uranium with neutrons. The neptunium nucleus emits a beta particle and becomes plutonium.

Ne·re·id [nir′ē·id] *n.*, *pl.* **Ne·re·i·des** [ni·rē′ə·dēz] *or* **Ne·re·ids** In Greek myths, one of the 50 sea nymphs who attended the god Poseidon.

Neptune

Ne·ro [nir′ō] *n.*, 37–68, emperor of Rome, 54–68. He was known for his cruelty and vices.

nerve [nûrv] *n.*, *v.* **nerved, nerv·ing 1** *n.* Any of the fibers or bundles of fibers that carry impulses between the brain or spinal cord and all parts of the body. **2** *n.* Courage: to lose one's *nerve.* **3** *n. informal* Offensive boldness;

impudence: He has some *nerve* to say that. **4** *v.* To make strong or courageous: He *nerved* himself to go to the dentist. **5** *n.* (*usually pl.*) Self-control: cool *nerves.* **6** *n.* (*usually pl.*) A feeling of being very upset: a bad case of *nerves.* **7** *n.* A vein in a leaf. **— get on one's nerves** *informal* To annoy or upset. **— strain every nerve** To try with all of one's strength.

nerve cell Another name for NEURON.

nerve fiber Any of the threadlike axons and dendrites that make up a nerve.

nerve·less [nûrv′lis] *adj.* **1** Lacking strength; feeble; slack: His *nerveless* arm fell to his side. **2** Having no nerves, as the hair or nails.

nerve-rack·ing *or* **nerve-wrack·ing** [nûrv′rak′ing] *adj.* Extremely irritating, annoying, or trying: a *nerve-racking* ordeal.

ner·vous [nûr′vəs] *adj.* **1** Showing unusual or abnormal restlessness, anxiety, tension, etc. **2** Fearful; timid. **3** Energetic or forceful: a *nervous* style of writing. **4** Of or having to do with nerves: a *nervous* disorder. **— ner′vous·ly** *adv.* **— ner′vous·ness** *n.*

nervous system In vertebrates, the network of neurons and nerve fibers, with the brain and spinal cord as centers, by which impulses are carried throughout the body.

-ness A suffix meaning: **1** The condition or quality of being, as in *darkness,* the quality or condition of being dark. **2** An instance of being, as in *kindness,* an instance of being kind. ◆ -NESS is a suffix that may be attached to many adjectives to form nouns.

nest [nest] **1** *n.* A structure built by a bird for laying its eggs and raising its young. **2** *n.* A place in which insects, mice, squirrels, etc., live and raise their young. **3** *v.* To build or occupy a nest: Rats *nested* in the cellar. **4** *n.* The group of birds, animals, insects, etc., that live in a nest. **5** *n.* A snug or cozy place. **6** *n.* A place full of something bad or dangerous: a *nest* of pirates. **7** *n.* A set of similar objects of different sizes, made to fit into one another: a *nest* of mixing bowls.

wasp's nest

blackbird's nest

nest egg A sum of money saved up for the future.

nes·tle [nes′əl] *v.* **nes·tled, nes·tling 1** To lie closely or snugly; cuddle: The kittens *nestled* together. **2** To place or press snugly or with affection: The little girl *nestled* her head on her mother's shoulder. **3** To settle down in comfort: to *nestle* among pillows. **4** To lie sheltered or partly hidden: The hut *nestled* in a shady valley.

nest·ling [nes(t)′ling] *n.* A bird too young to leave the nest.

net¹ [net] *n., v.* **net·ted, net·ting** **1** *n.* A fabric of thread, cord, rope, etc., knotted or woven together in an open pattern. **2** *v.* To make into a net. **3** *n.* An object made from fabric that is netted: a fish *net*; a tennis *net*. **4** *v.* To catch in or as in a net. **5** *n.* A delicate, meshed, lacelike fabric. **6** *v.* To cover or shelter with a net. **7** *n.* Anything that traps: a *net* of falsehoods.

Net

net² [net] *adj., n., v.* **net·ted, net·ting** **1** *adj.* Remaining after all necessary subtractions have been made, as of losses, taxes, expenses, weight of container, etc. **2** *n.* A net profit, weight, etc. **3** *v.* To earn or produce as a net amount.

neth·er [neth'ər] *adj.* Located beneath or below: seldom used today.

Neth·er·lands [neth'ər·ləndz] *n.* A country in NW Europe, on the North Sea; Holland.

neth·er·most [neth'ər·mōst'] *adj.* Lowest.

net·ting [net'ing] *n.* A fabric or material having large open spaces in it; net.

net·tle [net'(ə)l] *n., v.* **net·tled, net·tling** **1** *n.* A plant with hairlike needles that sting when touched. **2** *v.* To annoy or irritate: He was *nettled* by the delay.

net·work [net'wûrk'] *n.* **1** Netting. **2** Any system having parts that cross or are connected somewhat like the cords of a net. **3** A chain of radio or television broadcasting stations. ◆ *Network*, formed by combining *net* and *work*, originally referred only to actual netting, but now is more commonly used of things that crisscross and connect in many places like netting: a *network* of roads; a radio *network*.

neu·ral·gi·a [n(y)ŏŏ·ral'jə] *n.* A sharp pain along the course of a nerve.

neu·ri·tis [n(y)ŏŏ·rī'tis] *n.* Inflammation of a nerve.

neu·rol·o·gy [n(y)ŏŏ·rol'ə·jē] *n.* The branch of medicine that deals with the nervous system and its disorders. — **neu·rol'o·gist** *n.*

neu·ron [n(y)ŏŏr'on] *n.* The basic cell unit of nerves, having a nucleus and many nerve fibers.

neu·ro·sis [n(y)ŏŏ·rō'sis] *n., pl.* **neu·ro·ses** [n(y)ŏŏ·rō'sēz] A mental or emotional disturbance marked by unusual anxiety, depression, fear, etc., usually not very serious.

neu·rot·ic [n(y)ŏŏ·rot'ik] **1** *adj.* Of, resulting from, or suffering from a neurosis. **2** *n.* A neurotic person. — **neu·rot'ic·al·ly** *adv.*

neu·ter [n(y)ŏŏ'tər] **1** *adj.* Neither masculine nor feminine, as a noun or pronoun. **2** *n.* A neuter word. **3** *n.* The neuter gender: The pronoun *it* is in the *neuter*. **4** *adj.* Having no sex or having neither sex developed: Worker bees are *neuter*. **5** *n.* A neuter plant or animal.

neu·tral [n(y)ŏŏ'trəl] **1** *adj.* Not interfering or taking sides, as in a dispute, contest, war, etc. **2** *adj.* Belonging to none of the opposing sides: *neutral* territory. **3** *adj.* Belonging to neither one category nor the other; in the middle. **4** *adj.* Neither acid nor alkaline. **5** *adj.* Having neither a positive nor negative electric charge. **6** *adj.* Not strongly defined; middling: a *neutral* color. **7** *n.* A neutral person or thing. **8** *n.* The position of gearwheels in which the teeth are not meshed: Put the car in *neutral*.

neu·tral·i·ty [n(y)ŏŏ·tral'ə·tē] *n.* A neutral condition, attitude, policy, etc., especially of a nation in time of war.

neu·tral·ize [n(y)ŏŏ'trəl·īz] *v.* **neu·tral·ized, neu·tral·iz·ing** **1** To declare (a nation, area, etc.) neutral in time of war. **2** To offset or make ineffective by an opposite force: Vinegar *neutralizes* an alkali. — **neu'tral·i·za'tion** [n(y)ŏŏ'· trəl·ə·zā'shən] *n.* ¶3

neu·tron [n(y)ŏŏ'tron] *n.* A particle found in the nucleus of most atoms, having no electrical charge and a mass about equal to that of a proton.

Nev. Abbreviation of NEVADA.

Ne·vad·a [nə·vad'ə *or* nə·vä'də] *n.* A state in the western U.S.

nev·er [nev'ər] *adv.* **1** Not at any time; not ever. **2** Not at all; certainly not: *Never* fear.

nev·er·more [nev'ər·môr'] *adv.* Never again.

nev·er·the·less [nev'ər·thə·les'] **1** *adv.* In any case; anyhow: It rained, but we went *nevertheless*. **2** *conj.* But; however: It was cold; *nevertheless* the game was played.

new [n(y)ŏŏ] **1** *adj.* Recently made, grown, or constructed: *new* leaves. **2** *adj.* Found, invented, or arrived at for the first time: a *new* theory. **3** *adj.* Having been in a place, condition, or relationship for only a short time: a *new* partner. **4** *adj.* Not used or worn: a *new* piano. **5** *adj.* Changed for the better; renewed: *new* courage. **6** *adj.* Not trained or experienced: *new* at a job. **7** *adj.* Following an earlier one; beginning over: a *new* moon. **8** *adj.* Additional; further: a *new* supply. **9** *adv.* Newly; recently: used only in combination, as in *newborn* lamb. — **new'· ness** *n.*

New·ark [n(y)ŏŏ'ərk] *n.* A city in NE New Jersey.

new·born [n(y)ŏŏ 'bôrn'] *adj.* **1** Just lately born. **2** Born again; renewed: *newborn* hope.

New Bruns·wick [brunz'wik] A province of SE Canada.

new·com·er [n(y)ŏŏ'kum'ər] *n.* A person who has recently arrived.

New Deal The political, economic, and social policies and measures advocated by President Franklin D. Roosevelt.

New Del·hi [del'ē] The capital of India, in the northern part.

---

add, āce, câre, pälm; end, ēqual; it, īce; odd, ōpen, ôrder; tŏŏk, pōōl; up, bûrn; ə = a in *above*, e in *sicken*, i in *possible*, o in *melon*, u in *circus*; yŏŏ = u in *fuse*; oil; pout; check; ring; thin; this; zh in *vision*. For ¶ reference, see page 64 · HOW TO

new·el [n(y)ōō′əl] *n.* The post that supports an end of the handrail of a staircase.

New England The NE part of the U.S., including Maine, New Hampshire, Vermont, Massachusetts, Rhode Island, and Connecticut. **— New Eng′land·er** *n.*

new·fan·gled [n(y)ōō′fang′gəld] *adj.* New and modern; too modern to be of much worth.

New·found·land [n(y)ōō′fənd·lənd] *n.* **1** A large island off the eastern coast of Canada. **2** A province of eastern Canada that includes this island and Labrador. **3** A breed of large dog having a thick coat, usually black.

New Guin·ea [gin′ē] A large island just north of Australia.

New Hamp·shire [hamp′shər] A state in the NE U.S.

New Jer·sey [jûr′zē] A state in the eastern U.S.

new·ly [n(y)ōō′lē] *adv.* Very recently; lately: a *newly* bought radio.

New Mexico A state in the SW U.S.

new moon The phase of the moon when it is invisible or is seen as a small, thin crescent.

New Or·le·ans [ôr′lē·ənz *or* ôr′lənz] A city in SE Louisiana.

new penny *pl.* **new pence** A British unit of money equal to $\frac{1}{100}$ pound, the base of a new decimal coinage system, with six coins worth $\frac{1}{2}$, 1, 2, 5, 10, and 50 new pence.

news [n(y)ōōz] *n.pl.* (*used with singular verb*) **1** Information about events that have just taken place, as reported regularly in a newspaper, on the radio, etc. **2** Any new information: Today we heard the *news* of his illness.

news·cast [n(y)ōōz′kast′] *n.* A radio or television broadcast of news. ◆ *Newscast* comes from combining *news* (*broad*)*cast.*

news·man [n(y)ōōz′man′] *n., pl.* **news·men** [n(y)ōōz′men′] **1** A newspaperman. **2** A man who sells newspapers, magazines, etc.

New South Wales A state in SE Australia.

news·pa·per [n(y)ōōz′pā′pər] *n.* A publication, usually put out daily or weekly, containing news, editorials, advertisements, etc.

news·pa·per·man [n(y)ōōz′pā′pər·man] *n., pl.* **news·pa·per·men** [n(y)ōōz′pā′pər·men] **1** A writer for or an editor of a newspaper. **2** A person who owns or manages a newspaper.

news·reel [n(y)ōōz′rēl′] *n.* A news report in the form of a motion picture.

news·stand [n(y)ōōz′stand′] *n.* *U.S.* A stand at which newspapers and magazines are sold.

news·y [n(y)ōō′zē] *adj.* **news·i·er, news·i·est** *informal* Full of news.

newt [n(y)ōōt] *n.* A small salamander that lives both on land and in the water.

Newt, about 3 in. long

New Testament The part of the Bible containing the life and teaching of Jesus as told by his followers, and their acts and teachings.

New·ton [n(y)ōō′tən], **Sir Isaac,** 1642–1727, English philosopher and mathematician.

New World North America and South America.

New Year or **New Year's Day** January 1, the first day of the year.

New York [yôrk] **1** A state in the NE U.S. **2** A city in SE New York, the largest city in the U.S.

New Zea·land [zē′lənd] A country on two main islands in the South Pacific SE of Australia, a member of the British Commonwealth.

next [nekst] **1** *adj.* Following immediately in time, order, position, etc. **2** *adv.* In the nearest place or time: My brother sits *next* to me; the teacher called on me *next.* **3** *adj.* Adjoining or nearest in space: the *next* town. **4** *prep.* Nearest to: *next* his heart. **5** *adv.* On the nearest following occasion: when *next* we see them. **— next door 1** The next house, building, or apartment. **2** In, at, or to the next house, etc.

N.H. Abbreviation of NEW HAMPSHIRE.

Ni The symbol for the element NICKEL.

ni·a·cin [nī′ə·sin] *n.* A member of the vitamin B complex, found in meat, eggs, milk, wheat germ, etc. Lack of it causes pellagra.

Ni·ag·a·ra (nī·ag′(ə·)rə] *n.* A river that flows along the U.S.-Canadian border, from Lake Erie to Lake Ontario. In its course is **Niagara Falls,** a very large waterfall.

nib [nib] *n.* **1** The point of a pen. **2** The pointed part of anything; tip. **3** The beak of a bird.

nib·ble [nib′əl] *v.* **nib·bled, nib·bling,** *n.* **1** *v.* To eat or bite in a quick, gentle way: to *nibble* grass. **2** *n.* The act of nibbling. **3** *n.* A small bit of food; small bite.

Nic·a·ra·gua [nik′ə·rä′gwə] *n.* A small country in Central America. **— Nic′a·ra′guan** *adj., n.*

nice [nīs] *adj.* **nic·er, nic·est 1** Pleasing or suitable; agreeable: *nice* manners. **2** Friendly or kind: *nice* neighbors. **3** Precise or needing exactness; fine: a *nice* distinction; a *nice* fit. **— nice′ly** *adv.* ◆ *Nice*, which refers to something attractive or pleasant, originally meant *ignorant, foolish,* or *stupid.* Later, *nice* meant *precise* or *accurate,* and it still does, although it is now more often used loosely to indicate general approval: *nice* people; *nice* weather.

ni·ce·ty [nī′sə·tē] *n., pl.* **ni·ce·ties 1** (*usually pl.*) A fine or delicate point; detail: the *niceties* of grammar. **2** (*usually pl.*) A delicacy or refinement: *niceties* of living. **3** Great refinement or delicacy, as of taste; fussiness. **4** Exactness; precision or accuracy. **— to a nicety** Exactly right: cooked *to a nicety.*

niche [nich] *n.* **1** A recess or hollow in a wall, as for a statue. **2** A position or job that suits someone very well: to find one's *niche*.

Nich·o·las [nik′ə·ləs] *n.* **1** A fourth-century Christian bishop, patron saint of Russia, of seamen, and of children. **2** Santa Claus.

nick [nik] **1** *n.* A slight cut, notch, or dent in a surface or edge. **2** *v.* To make a nick on or in. **3** *v.* To barely make contact with, graze: The ball *nicked* his ear. **— in the nick of time** Barely soon enough; just in time.

Niche

nick·el [nik′əl] *n.* **1** A hard metallic element, having the color of silver and used in making alloys and in electroplating metals. **2** A five-cent coin of the U.S.

nick·name [nik′·nām′] *n., v.* **nick· named, nick·nam· ing 1** *n.* A familiar or shortened form of a proper name, as *Bill* for *William*. **2** *n.* A descriptive name, as *Honest Abe*. **3** *v.* To give a nic's name to.

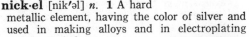

A badly nicked table

nic·o·tine [nik′ə·tēn] *n.* A bitter, oily, poisonous compound obtained from dried tobacco leaves.

niece [nēs] A daughter of one's brother or sister, or of one's brother-in-law, or sister-in-law.

Nie·tzsche [nē′chə], **Friedrich Wilhelm,** 1844–1900, German philosopher.

nif·ty [nif′tē] *adj.* **nif·ti·er, nif·ti·est** *slang* Stylish; pleasing; attractive.

Ni·ger [nī′jər *or* nī′gər] *n.* **1** A very long river of western Africa. **2** A country in west central Africa.

Ni·ge·ri·a [nī·jir′ē·ə] *n.* A country in west Africa, a member of the British Commonwealth.

nig·gard [nig′ərd] **1** *n.* A stingy person; miser. **2** *adj.* Stingy; miserly.

nig·gard·ly [nig′ərd·lē] **1** *adj.* Very stingy. **2** *adj.* Small or scanty: a *niggardly* piece of cake. **3** *adv.* In a stingy way. **— nig′gard·li·ness** *n.*

nigh [nī] *prep., adv., adj.* **nigh·er, nigh·est** *or* **next 1** *prep.* Near: *nigh* home. **2** *adv.* Near: as summer draws *nigh*. **3** *adv.* Nearly; almost: *nigh* a year. **4** *adj.* Close; near. ◆ *Nigh* is seldom used except in some dialects and poems.

night [nīt] *n.* **1** The period from sunset to sunrise, especially when it is dark. **2** *adj. use: night* clothes. **3** Darkness; the dark. **4** A condition of darkness, misery, or ignorance.

night·cap [nīt′kap′] *n.* **1** A cap worn in bed at night. **2** A relaxing drink taken at bedtime.

night club A restaurant open until late at night and providing music, dancing, and other entertainment.

night·fall [nīt′fôl′] *n.* The close of day.

night·gown [nīt′goun′] *n.* A loose garment worn by women and children in bed.

Nightcap

night·hawk [nīt′hôk′] *n.* **1** Any of several birds with long wings, related to the whippoorwill, that fly mostly at night. **2** A person who likes to stay up late at night.

night·in·gale [nīt′ən·gāl] *n.* A small, reddish brown, European bird. The male, who sings until late at night, is noted for its song.

Night·in·gale [nīt′ən·gāl], **Florence,** 1820–1910, English nurse born in Italy. She was a pioneer of modern nursing.

Nighthawk, about 9 in. long

night-light [nīt′līt′] *n.* A dim light kept burning all night, as at a bedside.

night·ly [nīt′lē] **1** *adj.* Done at or happening each night: a *nightly* task. **2** *adv.* Every night or at night: He flies *nightly*.

night·mare [nīt′mâr′] *n.* **1** A horrible and frightening dream. **2** Any horrible or frightening experience: the *nightmare* of war.

night·shade [nīt′shād′] *n.* Any of several plants related to the potato and tomato and bearing black or red berries. Some are poisonous, especially belladonna.

night·shirt [nīt′shûrt′] *n.* A long, loose garment worn in bed, usually by men and boys.

night·time [nīt′tīm′] *n.* The time from sunset to sunrise, or from dark to dawn.

nil [nil] *n.* Nothing: The profits are *nil*.

Nile [nīl] *n.* The longest river in Africa, rising in Lake Victoria and flowing north into the Mediterranean Sea in Egypt.

nim·ble [nim′bəl] *adj.* **nim·bler, nim·blest 1** Light and quick in movement; lively: a *nimble* dancer. **2** Quick to grasp or understand; keen: a *nimble* mind. **— nim′ble· ness** *n.* **— nim′bly** *adv.*

nim·bus [nim′bəs] *n., pl.* **nim· bus·es** *or* **nim·bi** [nim′bī] **1** A halo, as shown behind the head of a holy person in a painting. **2** Any atmosphere of glory or

Nightshirt

fame about a person or thing. **3** A rain or snow cloud.

Nim·rod [nim′rod] *n.* **1** In the Bible, a great hunter, the grandson of Noah. **2** Any hunter.

nin·com·poop [nin′kəm·pōōp] *n.* An idiot or fool; a stupid person.

nine or **9** [nīn] *n.*, *adj.* One more than eight.

nine·pins [nīn′pinz′] *n.pl.* (*often used with singular verb*) A bowling game somewhat like tenpins, using nine large wooden pins.

nine·teen or **19** [nīn′tēn′] *n.*, *adj.* One more than eighteen.

nine·teenth or **19th** [nīn′tēnth′] **1** *adj.* Next after the eighteenth. **2** *n.* The nineteenth one. **3** *adj.* Being one of nineteen equal parts. **4** *n.* A nineteenth part.

nine·ti·eth or **90th** [nīn′tē·ith] **1** *adj.* Tenth in order after the eightieth. **2** *n.* The ninetieth one. **3** *adj.* Being one of ninety equal parts. **4** *n.* A ninetieth part.

nine·ty or **90** [nīn′tē] *n.*, *pl.* **nine·ties** or **90's**, *adj.* **1** *n.*, *adj.* Ten more than eighty. **2** *n.* (*pl.*) The years between the age of 90 and 100.

Nin·e·veh [nin′ə·və] *n.* An ancient city on the Tigris River, capital of Assyria.

nin·ny [nin′ē] *n.*, *pl.* **nin·nies** A fool; dunce.

ninth or **9th** [nīnth] **1** *adj.* Next after the eighth. **2** *n.* The ninth one. **3** *adj.* Being one of nine equal parts. **4** *n.* A ninth part.

Ni·o·be [nī′ə·bē] *n.* In Greek myths, a weeping mother whose great pride in her children had led the gods to kill them. Zeus turned her to stone, from which her tears continued to flow.

nip¹ [nip] *v.* **nipped, nip·ping**, *n.* **1** *v.* To pinch or bite sharply with the fingers, the teeth, or with claws, as a crab. **2** *n.* A sudden, sharp pinch or bite. **3** *v.* To remove by pinching or clipping: to *nip* off dead blossoms from a plant. **4** *v.* To injure or pain as by cold: A sharp wind *nipped* his ears; The frost *nipped* our plants. **5** *n.* Severe cold or frost: the *nip* of winter.
— **nip and tuck** Very close, even, or uncertain: It was *nip and tuck* as to who would win.
— **nip in the bud** To stop at the very beginning or outset.

nip² [nip] *n.* A small drink or sip of liquor.

nip·per [nip′ər] *n.* **1** A person or thing that nips. **2** The claw of a crab or lobster. **3** (*pl.*) Any of various tools used for nipping or grasping, as pliers or pincers.

nip·ple [nip′əl] *n.* **1** The pointed projection on the breast or udder of a mammal through which the milk passes to the baby or young animal.

Nippers

2 The rubber mouthpiece through which a baby sucks milk from a bottle.

Nip·pon [nip′on or nip·on′] *n.* The Japanese name for Japan.

nip·py [nip′ē] *adj.* **nip·pi·er, nip·pi·est** Biting and sharp, as cold weather.

nir·va·na [nir·vä′nə] *n.* **1** In Buddhism, a state of complete bliss that is free from all passion, desire, suffering, etc. **2** Any completely happy condition.

Ni·sei [nē′sā] *n.* A native-born American whose parents were Japanese immigrants.

nit [nit] *n.* **1** The egg of a louse or other parasitic insect. **2** A young louse.

ni·ter [nī′tər] *n.* Either of two minerals containing nitrates, once much used in manufacturing fertilizer and explosives.

ni·trate [nī′trāt] *n.* Any of a large group of chemical compounds derived from nitric acid, especially its salts.

ni·tre [nī′tər] Another spelling of NITER.

ni·tric acid [nī′trik] A strong, colorless liquid containing nitrogen, that fumes in air and eats into cloth, flesh, and most metals.

ni·tro·gen [nī′trə·jən] *n.* An odorless, colorless, gaseous element that makes up nearly four-fifths of the earth's atmosphere. It forms many useful compounds and is a necessary element in all living things.

ni·tro·gen-fix·ing bacteria [nī′trə·jən·fik′-sing] Any of the bacteria in the soil that take nitrogen from the air and make it into compounds that can be used by living things.

ni·trog·e·nous [nī·troj′ə·nəs] *adj.* Having to do with or containing nitrogen.

ni·tro·glyc·er·in or **ni·tro·glyc·er·ine** [nī′-trō·glis′ər·in] *n.* A thick, oily, highly explosive liquid, used in medicine and in making dynamite.

ni·trous oxide [nī′trəs] A gas sometimes used as an anesthetic, especially by dentists.

nit·wit [nit′wit′] *n.* A silly or stupid person.

Nix·on [nik′sən], **Richard Milhous,** born 1913, 37th president of the U.S., 1969–

N.J. Abbreviation of NEW JERSEY.

N. Mex. Abbreviation of NEW MEXICO.

no [nō] *adv.*, *adj.*, *n.*, *pl.* **noes 1** *adv.* A word used to show that one disagrees, denies, or doesn't want something: Don't you like this hat? *No.* Are you feeling ill? *No.* **2** *n.* A negative reply: He simply won't take *no* for an answer. **3** *n.* A negative vote or voter: The *noes* have it. **4** *adj.* Not any: *No* seats are left. **5** *adv.* Not at all: He feels *no* better today.

No. or **no.** Abbreviation of NUMBER.

No·ah [nō′ə] *n.* In the Bible, a good man who, at God's command, built an ark that saved him, his family, and two of every kind of animal from the Flood.

No·bel prize [nō·bel′] One of the five prizes awarded each year for great work in physics, chemistry, literature, medicine, and the advancement of world peace.

no·bil·i·ty [nō·bil′ə·tē] *n.*, *pl.* **no·bil·i·ties 1** In certain countries, a group of people who have hereditary titles and rank, as kings, queens, princes, dukes, counts, etc. **2** The condition or quality of being noble.

no·ble [nō′bəl] *adj.* **nob·ler, nob·lest**, *n.* **1** *adj.* Having or showing outstandingly good or moral qualities: a *noble* soul; a *noble* ambition. **2** *adj.* Of or having a high rank or title; aristocratic. **3** *n.* A member of the nobility. **4** *adj.*

Impressive and handsome: a *noble* face; a *noble* tree. **— no′ble·ness** *n.* **— no′bly** *adv.*

no·ble·man [nō′bəl·mən] *n.,* *pl.* **no·ble·men** [nō′bəl·mən] A man of noble rank; peer.

no·bod·y [nō′bod′ē] *pron., n., pl.* **no·bod·ies** **1** *pron.* Not anybody; no one at all. **2** *n.* A person of no importance or influence.

noc·tur·nal [nok·tûr′nəl] *adj.* **1** Of or happening at night: *nocturnal* noises. **2** Active or blooming at night, as certain animals or plants. **— noc·tur′nal·ly** *adv.*

noc·turne [nok′tûrn] *n.* In music, a dreamy or melancholy composition, often for the piano.

nod [nod] *n., v.* **nod·ded, nod·ding** **1** *v.* To lower the head forward briefly, as in agreement or greeting. **2** *v.* To let the head fall forward, as when sleepy. **3** *n.* The act of nodding the head. **4** *v.* To sway or bend at the top or upper part.

node [nōd] *n.* **1** A swelling or knob of tissue: a lymph *node.* **2** A knot or joint on the stem of a plant from which leaves grow. **— no′dal** *adj.*

nod·ule [noj′ool *or* nod′yool] *n.* A little knob or node, especially on a plant stem.

No·ël or **No·el** [nō·əl′] *n.* **1** Christmas. **2** (*often written* **noël** or **noel**) A Christmas carol.

nog·gin [nog′in] *n.* **1** *informal* A person's head. **2** A small mug or cup. **3** A small drink equal to one fourth of a pint.

noise [noiz] *n., v.* **noised, nois·ing** **1** *n.* A loud, confused, disturbing sound. **2** *n.* A sound of any kind. **3** *n.* In electronics, anything that interferes with a signal in an unpredictable way; static. **4** *v.* To spread, report, or rumor: It was *noised* about that the mayor was dishonest.

noise·less [noiz′lis] *adj.* Causing or making little or no noise; quiet; silent: a *noiseless* motor. **— noise′less·ly** *adv.*

noise·mak·er [noiz′mā′kər] *n.* Something used to make noise at parties, etc., as a horn or rattle.

noi·some [noi′səm] *adj.* **1** Foul or disgusting, especially in smell; stinking: a *noisome* sewer. **2** Harmful; injurious.

nois·y [noi′zē] *adj.* **nois·i·er, nois·i·est** **1** Making a loud noise: a *noisy* dog; a *noisy* truck. **2** Full of noise: a *noisy* street. **3** Accompanied by noise: a *noisy* argument. **— nois′i·ly** *adv.* **— nois′i·ness** *n.*

no·mad [nō′mad] *n.* **1** A member of a people moving constantly from place to place to find food and

Noisemakers

pasture. **2** *adj. use: nomad* tribes. **3** A person who keeps wandering aimlessly from place to place. **— no·mad′ic** *adj.*

nom de plume [nom′ də ploom′] A name used by a writer in place of his real name.

no·men·cla·ture [nō′mən·klā′chər] *n.* The system of names used to describe the various elements in a particular science or art: the *nomenclature* of zoology.

nom·i·nal [nom′ə·nəl] *adj.* **1** Existing in name only; not actual or real: a *nominal* peace. **2** Small or trifling: a *nominal* sum. **— nom′i·nal·ly** *adv.*

nom·i·nate [nom′ə·nāt] *v.* **nom·i·nat·ed, nom·i·nat·ing** **1** To name as a candidate for an elective office: We *nominated* John for class president. **2** To appoint to some office, duty, honor, etc.: We *nominated* him to be chairman of the dance committee.

nom·i·na·tion [nom′ə·nā′shən] *n.* **1** The act of nominating. **2** A being nominated.

nom·i·na·tive [nom′ə·nə·tiv] **1** *adj.* Indicating the case of a noun or pronoun that is a subject or complement. In "My dog, whose name is Max, is a dachshund," *dog, name, Max,* and *dachshund* are all in the nominative case. **2** *n.* The nominative case, or a word in the nominative case.

nom·i·nee [nom′ə·nē] *n.* A person who is nominated for some elective office, duty, etc.

non- A prefix meaning: Not, as in *nonheroic,* not heroic. If *non-* is combined with a capitalized word, it is hyphenated, as in *non-American.* Otherwise, no hyphen is used.

non·ag·gres·sion [non′ə·gresh′ən] *n.* A holding back from aggression or attack.

non·al·co·hol·ic [non′al·kə·hôl′ik] *adj.* With no alcohol in it, as a drink.

nonce [nons] *n.* The present time or occasion: now mostly used in the phrase **for the nonce,** for the time being; for the present.

non·cha·lant [non′shə·länt′] *adj.* Showing a jaunty coolness; not excited or concerned: She accepted the prize with a *nonchalant* air. **— non′cha·lance′** *n.* **— non′cha·lant′ly** *adv.*

non·com·bat·ant [non′kom·bat′ənt *or* non′·kom′bə·tənt] *n.* **1** A member of the armed forces whose duties do not involve fighting, as a medical officer or chaplain. **2** A civilian in wartime.

non·com·mis·sioned officer [non′kə·mish′·ənd] In the U.S. armed services, an enlisted man who ranks above a private but has no commission. Corporals and sergeants are noncommissioned officers.

non·com·mit·tal [non′kə·mit′(ə)l] *adj.* Not binding one to an opinion, attitude, or plan of action: "Maybe" is a *noncommittal* answer.

non·con·duc·tor [non′kən·duk′tər] *n.* A substance that does not easily conduct certain forms

add, āce, câre, pälm;   end, ēqual;   it, īce;   odd, ōpen, ôrder;   took, pool;   up, bûrn; ə = a in *above,* e in *sicken,* i in *possible,* o in *melon,* u in *circus;*   yoo = u in *fuse;*   oil;   pout; check; ring; thin; this; zh in *vision.*   For ¶ reference, see page 64 · HOW TO

of energy, as heat, sound, and electricity. Glass and rubber are nonconductors of electricity.

non·con·form·ist [non'kən·fôr'mist] *n.* **1** A person who thinks and acts in a way unlike that of most people. **2** (*often written* **Non-conformist**) In England, a Protestant who does not belong to the Church of England.

non·de·script [non'də·skript] *adj.* Not easy to describe because of no distinctive kind or type: a *nondescript* little man.

none [nun] **1** *pron.* Not one; no one: *None* will arrive today. **2** *pron.* Not any: *None* of the cake is left. **3** *adv.* Not at all; by no means: He is *none* too bright.

non·en·ti·ty [non·en'tə·tē] *n., pl.* **non·en·ti·ties** A person or thing that is of little or no importance or interest; a nothing.

non·es·sen·tial [non'ə·sen'shəl] **1** *adj.* Not essential; not really needed. **2** *n.* A person or thing that is nonessential.

none·the·less [nun'thə·les'] or **none the less** *adv.* In spite of everything; nevertheless.

non·ex·is·tent [non'ig·zis'tənt] *adj.* Not existing; not real or actual: He boasts about his *nonexistent* wealth. **— non'ex·is'tence** *n.*

non·fic·tion [non·fik'shən] *n.* Writing that does not tell a story of made-up people or events. Books on science, history, etc., are nonfiction. **— non'fic'tion·al** *adj.*

non·me·tal·lic [non'mə·tal'ik] *adj.* Not metal; not having the properties of a metal. Carbon, oxygen, and nitrogen are nonmetallic elements.

non·pa·reil [non'pə·rel'] **1** *adj.* Having no equal; matchless. **2** *n.* A person or thing that has no equal; a model of excellence.

non·par·ti·san [non·pär'tə·zən] *adj.* Not strongly supporting a person, cause, or party, especially not one political party.

non·pay·ment [non·pā'mənt] *n.* A failure to pay money that is owed.

non·plus [non·plus' *or* non'plus] *v.* **non·plused** or **non·plussed, non·plus·ing** or **non·plus·sing** To place in a state of bewilderment or confusion: We were *nonplused* at the news.

non·poi·son·ous [non·poi'zən·əs] *adj.* Not poisonous; harmless: a *nonpoisonous* snake.

non·pro·duc·tive [non'prə·duk'tiv] *adj.* **1** Not producing that which is wanted or needed: a *nonproductive* farm. **2** Not directly producing goods: Office workers are *nonproductive* labor.

non·prof·it [non·prof'it] *adj.* Not organized or run to make money: a *nonprofit* organization.

non·res·i·dent [non·rez'ə·dənt] **1** *adj.* Not living in the place where one works, owns property, or goes to school. **2** *n.* A person who is nonresident.

non·re·stric·tive [non'ri·strik'tiv] *adj.* In grammar, describing a word or group of words, usually an adjective clause set off by commas, that can be omitted from a sentence without changing its essential meaning, as *which is for sale*, in *Our house, which is for sale, needs repairs.*

non·sec·tar·i·an [non'sek·târ'ē·ən] *adj.* Not connected with or run by a particular religious sect: a *nonsectarian* school.

non·sense [non'sens] *n.* Words or actions that are meaningless or silly; foolishness: Let's stop the *nonsense.*

non·stop [non'stop'] *adj., adv.* Without making a stop: a *nonstop* train; to fly *nonstop.*

non·un·ion [non·yōon'yən] *adj.* **1** Not belonging to a trade union: a *nonunion* plumber. **2** Not hiring union workers: a *nonunion* shop. **3** Not produced by union labor.

noo·dle [nōod'(ə)l] *n.* A thin strip of dried dough, usually made with eggs. ◆ *Noodle* comes from the German word *nudel.*

nook [nŏok] *n.* **1** A corner or alcove set off from the main part of a room: a chimney *nook.* **2** Any cozy, sheltered place: a shady *nook.*

noon [nōon] *n.* Twelve o'clock in the daytime, written 12 A.M. or 12 M.

noon·day [nōon'dā'] *adj.* Of or happening at noon: the *noonday* meal.

noon·tide [nōon'tīd'] *n.* Noon; midday.

noon·time [nōon'tīm'] *n.* Noon; midday.

noose [nōos] *n.* **1** A loop, as of rope, with a slipknot that binds more closely as it is pulled. **2** Anything that traps or binds.

nor [nôr] *conj.* And not; likewise not. ◆ *Nor* is usually paired with a negative word that precedes it, as *neither, not, no,* or *never*: He is neither fat *nor* thin; He has not offered us any of his candy, *nor* will he; I have never seen a dragon, *nor* do I expect to see one.

Nor·dic [nôr'dik] **1** *adj.* Describing or belonging to a type of tall, blond, usually blue-eyed people chiefly from northern Europe. Norwegians are Nordic people. **2** *n.* A Nordic person.

Noose

norm [nôrm] *n.* A pattern, standard, or model considered typical or average: He is above the *norm* in height for boys of his age.

nor·mal [nôr'məl] **1** *adj.* Agreeing with the usual standard; natural: *normal* tides; *normal* eyesight; a *normal* way of acting. **2** *adj.* Not ill or defective in body or mind: a *normal* baby. **3** *n.* A typical or average amount, condition, degree, etc.: a temperature above *normal.* **— nor·mal·i·ty** [nôr·mal'ə·tē] *n.*

nor·mal·ly [nôr'mə·lē] *adv.* **1** In a normal way. **2** As a rule; usually: *Normally* we eat early.

normal school A school that prepares high-school graduates to become teachers.

Nor·man [nôr'mən] **1** *n.* A person born or living in Normandy. **2** *n.* One of the people of mixed Scandinavian and French descent who conquered England in 1066. **3** *adj.* Of or having to do with Normandy or the Normans.

Norman Conquest The conquest of England in 1066 by the Normans under the leadership of William the Conqueror.

Nor·man·dy [nôr′mən·dē] *n.* A region and former province of NW France.

Norse [nôrs] **1** *adj.* Of or from Scandinavia. **2** *n.* (**the Norse**) The people of Scandinavia. **3** *n.* The language of Scandinavia, especially Norwegian. **4** *n.* The language of ancient Scandinavia.

Norse·man [nôrs′mən] *n.*, *pl.* **Norse·men** [nôrs′mən] A Scandinavian of ancient times.

north [nôrth] **1** *n.* The direction opposite south, one of the four main points of the compass. If you face the sun at sunrise, the north is to your left. **2** *adj.* To, toward, or in the north; northern. **3** *adj.* Coming from the north: the *north* wind. **4** *adv.* In or toward the north; northward. — **north of** Farther north than: Vermont is *north of* Connecticut. — **the North 1** In the U.S., the states north of Maryland, the Ohio River, and Missouri. **2** (*often written* **the north**) The parts of the world that are farthest north; the arctic regions.

North America The northern continent of the Western Hemisphere, including the U.S., Canada, Mexico, and Central America. — **North American** *adj.*, *n.*

north·bound [nôrth′bound′] *adj.* Going north.

North Carolina A state in the SE U.S.

North Da·ko·ta [də·kō′tə] A state in the north central U.S.

north·east [nôrth′ēst′] **1** *n.* The direction midway between north and east. **2** *n.* Any region lying in or toward this direction. **3** *adj.* To, toward, or in the northeast; northeastern. **4** *adj.* Coming from the northeast: a *northeast* breeze. **5** *adv.* In or toward the northeast. — **northeast of** Farther northeast than: Boston is *northeast* of New York.

north·east·er [nôrth′ēs′tər] *n.* A gale or storm from the northeast.

north·east·er·ly [nôrth′ēs′tər·lē] *adj.*, *adv.* **1** To, toward, or in the northeast. **2** From the northeast.

north·east·ern [nôrth′ēs′tərn] *adj.* **1** To, toward, or in the northeast: *northeastern* New Jersey. **2** Coming from the northeast: a *northeastern* wind.

north·er·ly [nôr′thər·lē] *adj.*, *adv.* **1** To, toward, or in the north. **2** From the north.

north·ern [nôr′thərn] *adj.* **1** To, toward, or in the north. **2** Coming from the north: a *northern* mass of cold, dry air.

north·ern·er [nôr′thər·nər] *n.* **1** A person born or living in the north. **2** (*sometimes written* **Northerner**) A person born or living in the North.

Northern Hemisphere The half of the earth situated north of the equator.

Northern Ireland A part of the United Kingdom, occupying the northeastern part of Ireland.

northern lights Another name for the AURORA BOREALIS.

north·ern·most [nôr′thərn·mōst′] *adj.* Farthest north: the *northernmost* point in Europe.

North Korea See KOREA.

North·man [nôrth′mən] *n.*, *pl.* **North·men** [nôrth′mən] One of a fair, tall people of ancient Scandinavia, especially a viking.

North Pole The northernmost point on the earth; the north end of the earth's axis.

North Sea The part of the Atlantic Ocean between Great Britain and northern Europe.

North Star A bright star that is almost directly above the North Pole; Polaris.

North·um·bri·a [nôr·thum′brē·ə] *n.* An ancient Anglo-Saxon kingdom in England.

North Vietnam See VIETNAM.

north·ward [nôrth′wərd] **1** *adj.*, *adv.* To, toward, or in the north. **2** *n.* A northward direction or location.

north·wards [nôrth′wərdz] *adv.* Northward.

north·west [nôrth′west′] **1** *n.* The direction midway between north and west. **2** *n.* Any region lying in or toward this direction. **3** *adj.* To, toward, or in the northwest; northwestern. **4** *adj.* Coming from the northwest. **5** *adv.* In or toward the northwest. — **northwest of** Farther northwest than: Detroit is *northwest of* Cleveland.

north·west·er [nôrth′wes′tər] *n.* A gale or storm from the northwest.

north·west·er·ly [nôrth′wes′tər·lē] *adj.*, *adv.* **1** To, toward, or in the northwest. **2** From the northwest.

north·west·ern [nôrth′wes′tərn] *adj.* **1** To, toward, or in the northwest. **2** Coming from the northwest.

Northwest Passage A water route from the Atlantic Ocean to the Pacific Ocean along the northern coast of North America.

Nor·way [nôr′wā] *n.* A Scandinavian country of northern Europe, west of Sweden.

Nor·we·gian [nôr·wē′jən] **1** *adj.* Of or from Norway. **2** *n.* A person born in or a citizen of Norway. **3** *n.* The language of Norway.

nose [nōz] *n.*, *v.* **nosed, nos·ing 1** *n.* The projecting part in the middle of the face that contains two air passages for breathing and the organ of smell. ◆ Adj., *nasal.* **2** *n.* The sense of smell; power of smelling: This hunting dog has a good *nose.* **3** *v.* To sniff or smell. **4** *v.* To

add, āce, câre, pälm;   end, ēqual;   it, īce;   odd, ōpen, ôrder;   tŏŏk, pōōl;   up, bûrn;
ə = a in *above*, e in *sicken*, i in *possible*, o in *melon*, u in *circus*;   yōō = u in *fuse*;   oil;   pout;
check;   ring;   thin;   this;   zh in *vision*.   For ¶ reference, see page 64 · HOW TO

touch or rub with the nose; nuzzle. **5** *n*. Something that looks like a nose because of its shape or position, as the forward part of an aircraft or a boat. **6** *v*. To move forward cautiously with the front end foremost: The bus *nosed* its way through traffic. **7** *n*. The ability to find or recognize: a *nose* for news. **8** *v*. To meddle; pry; snoop: He can *nose* out a scandal anywhere. **— pay through the nose** *slang* To pay much too high a price for something.

nose·bleed [nōz′blēd′] *n*. Bleeding from the nose.

nose cone The cone-shaped front section of a spacecraft, where cargo or people are carried.

nose-dive [nōz′dīv′] *v*. **nose-dived, nose-div·ing** To take a nose dive; plunge downward.

nose dive 1 A steep, downward plunge of an aircraft, nose end first. **2** Any steep fall.

nose·gay [nōz′gā′] *n*. A small bunch of flowers.

nos·ey [nō′zē] *adj*. **nos·i·er, nos·i·est** Another spelling of NOSY.

nos·tal·gi·a [nos-tal′jə] *n*. A longing for some pleasant place, happening, or condition that is past or far away: *nostalgia* for one's childhood.

nos·tal·gic [nos-tal′jik] *adj*. Having, showing, or coming from nostalgia: a *nostalgic* mood.

nos·tril [nos′tril] *n*. Either of the two openings in the nose for letting in air and smells. ◆ *Nostril* comes from two Old English words meaning *nose hole.*

nos·trum [nos′trəm] *n*. **1** A medicine invented and prepared by the person who is selling it; a quack medicine. **2** A favorite remedy or plan for solving some problem or correcting an evil.

nos·y [nō′zē] *adj*. **nos·i·er, nos·i·est** *informal* Prying and snooping into other people's affairs.

not [not] *adv*. In no way or to no extent or degree: I will *not* go; She is *not* a good student.

no·ta·ble [nō′tə·bəl] **1** *adj*. Worthy of note; remarkable; famous: a *notable* poet. **2** *n*. A person who is notable. **— no′ta·bly** *adv*.

no·ta·rize [nō′tə·rīz] *v*. **no·ta·rized, no·ta·riz·ing** To sign and put an official seal on (a legal document).

no·ta·ry [nō′tə·rē] *n*., *pl*. **no·ta·ries** A public official authorized to witness the signing of contracts or other documents, to certify that a certain person swears he is making true statements, etc. Also **notary public.**

no·ta·tion [nō·tā′shən] *n*. **1** A set of symbols or abbreviations used to represent numbers, quantities, words, notes, etc.: $K = \frac{1}{2} m(gt + v_0)^2$ is an example of algebraic *notation*. **2** A brief note made to help a person remember something. **3** The act of making a notation.

notch [noch] **1** *n*. A V-shaped cut made in an edge or curve. **2** *v*. To cut a notch or notches in. **3** *n*. A narrow pass between mountains. **4** *n*. *informal* A degree; level: As an athlete, he is a *notch* above his classmates.

Notches

note [nōt] *n*., *v*. **not·ed, not·ing 1** *n*. A brief record or jotting down of a word, sentence, fact, etc., that one wishes to remember: to make *notes* on a lecture. **2** *v*. To record or set down in writing: *Note* the date of his birthday. **3** *n*. Close attention; heed: What he said is worthy of *note*. **4** *v*. To pay careful attention to: *Note* how I do this. **5** *v*. To become aware of; observe: I *noted* her absence. **6** *v*. To mention. **7** *n*. A written comment, as at the bottom of a page or at the back of a book, explaining or adding more information to something: Shakespeare's plays have many *notes* to help the student. **8** *n*. A short letter. **9** *n*. A formal or official letter from one country or government to another. **10** *n*. In music, a symbol whose position on a staff indicates the pitch of the tone and whose form indicates its length. **11** *n*. Any more or less musical sound: the *notes* of a bird. **12** *n*. Any of the keys on a piano, etc. **13** *n*. A sign or quality: a *note* of winter in the air. **14** *n*. A piece of paper money issued by a government or a bank. **15** *n*. A written agreement to pay a sum of money at a certain time. **16** *n*. Importance; fame: He is a scientist of great *note*. **— compare notes** To exchange ideas about something.

note·book [nōt′book′] *n*. A book in which one may write notes on things one wants to remember.

not·ed [nō′tid] **1** Past participle of NOTE. **2** *adj*. Well-known; famous: a *noted* statesman.

note·wor·thy [nōt′wûr′thē] *adj*. Deserving of attention; remarkable; important.

noth·ing [nuth′ing] **1** *n*. Not anything; not something: *Nothing* interesting happened today. **2** *n*. A person or thing that is of little or no importance. **3** *adv*. Not at all; to no degree: *Nothing* daunted, he jumped on the horse and rode away. **— for nothing 1** Without charge; free. **2** To no avail; in vain: All our hard work was *for nothing*. **3** For no reason; without cause.

noth·ing·ness [nuth′ing·nis] *n*. **1** The condition of being nothing; nonexistence: At noon, the mist faded into *nothingness*. **2** Complete worthlessness or uselessness.

no·tice [nō′tis] *n*., *v*. **no·ticed, no·tic·ing 1** *n*. Observation; attention; heed: Bring this book to his *notice*. **2** *v*. To pay attention to; observe; see: Did you *notice* his leaving? **3** *n*. Announcement; warning; information: *notice* of an approaching storm. **4** *n*. A written or printed announcement: a wedding *notice* in the paper. **5** *n*. A formal announcement that one is leaving a job, a rented place, etc.: Landlords like 30 days' *notice*. **6** *n*. A short critical article or review: Did the book get good *notices*? **7** *v*. To refer to; mention, as in a speech or article. **8** *n*. Polite or respectful treatment.

no·tice·a·ble [nō′tis·ə·bəl] *adj*. **1** Attracting one's attention; easily seen: a *noticeable* difference. **2** Worthy of notice: The dancer was *noticeable* for her grace. **— no′tice·a·bly** *adv*.

no·ti·fi·ca·tion [nō′tə·fə·kā′shən] *n*. **1** The act of notifying or giving notice. **2** The notice given: We received *notification* of a sale.

no·ti·fy [nō′tə·fī] *v.* **no·ti·fied, no·ti·fy·ing**
To give notice to; inform: The teacher *notified*
Peter that he had passed the test.

no·tion [nō′shən] *n.* **1** A general idea or impression: I have a *notion* that he'll go. **2** An opinion or belief: to have the *notion* that cold baths are healthful. **3** A whim, inclination, or fancy: I took a *notion* to stand on my head. **4** (*pl.*) Small articles for sale, as ribbons, thread, pins, etc.

no·to·chord [nō′tə·kôrd] *n.* A tough, flexible rod of supporting tissue that runs along the back of certain primitive animals and of the embryos of higher vertebrate animals.

no·to·ri·e·ty [nō′tə·rī′ə·tē] *n., pl.* **no·to·ri·e·ties** The condition of being widely known or notorious, usually in an unfavorable sense.

no·to·ri·ous [nō·tôr′ē·əs] *adj.* Widely known, especially for bad reasons: a *notorious* thief. — **no·to′ri·ous·ly** *adv.*

not·with·stand·ing [not′with·stan′ding] **1** *adv.* All the same; nevertheless: Although closely guarded, he escaped *notwithstanding*. **2** *prep.* In spite of: *Notwithstanding* his tendency to catch cold, he won't wear a coat. **3** *conj.* Although: They had to push on, *notwithstanding* they were exhausted.

nou·gat [nōō′gət] *n.* A candy made of chopped nuts, fruits, etc., mixed with a sugar paste.

nought [nôt] *n.* **1** Nothing; naught: His efforts came to *nought*. **2** The character 0; zero.

noun [noun] *n.* **1** A word used as the name of a person, thing, place, action, quality, condition, class, etc., as *John, bat, Ohio, attack, kindness, illness,* and *plants.* Nouns commonly function as subjects of verbs, complements, and objects of verbs or prepositions. **2** *adj. use:* a *noun* clause.

nour·ish [nûr′ish] **1** *v.* To keep alive and healthy or help to grow with food: This diet will *nourish* a growing boy. **2** *adj. use: nourishing* food. **3** *v.* To keep up; maintain: to *nourish* feelings of anger.

nour·ish·ment [nûr′ish·mənt] *n.* **1** The act of nourishing. **2** Something that nourishes; food: Fish has a lot of *nourishment*. **3** The condition of being nourished.

Nov. Abbreviation of NOVEMBER.

no·va [nō′və] *n., pl.* **no·vas** or **no·vae** [nō′vē] A star that suddenly flares up, shines, and then fades away after a few weeks or months.

No·va Sco·tia [nō′və skō′shə] A province of SE Canada.

nov·el [nov′əl] **1** *n.* A long piece of fiction, usually of book length. Novels tell a story of imaginary people, their feelings, thoughts, and adventures. **2** *adj.* New, strange, or unusual: Using the elbows is a *novel* way to play the piano.

nov·el·ette [nov′əl·et′] *n.* A short novel.

nov·el·ist [nov′əl·ist] *n.* A person who writes novels.

nov·el·ty [nov′əl·tē] *n., pl.* **nov·el·ties 1** Something new or different: It was a *novelty* to sleep late. **2** The quality of being new and unusual; newness: the *novelty* of sending rockets into space. **3** (*usually pl.*) Any small, inexpensive article, as a toy, piece of jewelry, etc.

No·vem·ber [nō·vem′bər] *n.* The 11th month of the year, having 30 days.

nov·ice [nov′is] *n.* **1** A beginner or inexperienced person. **2** A person taken into a religious order on trial before being allowed to become a monk or nun.

no·vi·ti·ate or **no·vi·ci·ate** [nō·vish′ē·it] *n.* **1** The condition or period of being a novice, especially in a religious order. **2** The quarters occupied by novices, as in a monastery.

now [nou] **1** *adv.* At once; immediately: Please do it *now*. **2** *adv.* At or during the present time: *Now* he is coming up the walk. **3** *n.* The present time: Until *now*, he didn't study well. **4** *adv.* Under such circumstances; with things being what they are: *Now* we'll never get home. **5** *conj.* Seeing that; since: *Now* he has finished school, he wants to go to work. **6** *adv.* Sometimes: *now* this, *now* that. **7** *interj. Now* is often used to make a command or request stronger: Come, *now,* you'd better hurry; *Now, now,* don't think about it. —**just now 1** In the immediate past: He said so *just now.* **2** In the immediate future: He is going *just now.* — **now and again** or **now and then** From time to time; once in a while.

now·a·days [nou′ə·dāz′] *adv.* In the present time or age: *Nowadays* people live longer.

no·way [nō′wā′] *adv.* In no way, manner, or degree; not at all.

no·ways [nō′wāz′] *adv.* Noway.

no·where [nō′(h)wâr′] **1** *adv.* In or to no place; not anywhere: I can find my boots *nowhere*. **2** *n.* No place: We were miles from *nowhere*.

no·wise [nō′wīz′] *adv.* In no manner; not at all: He is *nowise* guilty of this crime.

nox·ious [nok′shəs] *adj.* Harmful to health or morals: *noxious* slums; *noxious* smells.

noz·zle [noz′əl] *n.* A spout or small opening, as at the end of a hose or pipe.

nth [enth] *adj.* Extremely or indefinitely large or small, especially in the phrase **to the nth degree** To the most extreme degree.

nu·ance [nōō·äns′] *n.* A very slight variation of color, tone, meaning, etc.: There are many *nuances* of meaning in his poems.

nub [nub] *n.* **1** A knob or swelling. **2** *informal* The point, core, or gist of anything: the *nub* of a joke.

Nozzle

add, āce, câre, pälm; end, ēqual; it, īce; odd, ōpen, ôrder; tŏŏk, pōōl; up, bûrn;
ə = a in *above*, e in *sicken*, i in *possible*, o in *melon*, u in *circus*; yōō = u in *fuse*; oil; pout;
check; ring; thin; this; zh in *vision*. For ¶ reference, see page 64 · HOW TO

Nu·bi·a [n(y)ōō'bē·ə] *n.* A region and ancient country in NE Africa. — **Nu'bi·an** *adj.*, *n.*

nu·cle·ar [n(y)ōō'klē·ər] *adj.* **1** Of, having to do with, or like a nucleus or nuclei. **2** Of, having to do with, or using atomic energy.

nuclear energy Another name for ATOMIC ENERGY.

nuclear fission The splitting that takes place when the nucleus of a heavy atom absorbs a neutron. The split forms nuclei of lighter atoms and releases great energy. The rate of fission may increase rapidly, as in a bomb, or be controlled to provide power for practical use.

nuclear fusion The union at very high temperatures of nuclei of light atoms, forming nuclei of heavier atoms and releasing enormous energy.

nu·cle·on [n(y)ōō'klē·on] *n.* Any particle found in the nucleus of an atom, as the proton, neutron, meson, etc.

nu·cle·us [n(y)ōō'klē·əs] *n.*, *pl.* **nu·cle·i** [n(y)ōō'klē·ī] *or* **nu·cle·us·es** **1** The small central mass embedded in the cytoplasm of most plant and animal cells. It is surrounded by a membrane and contains the chromatin, chromosomes, and other structures essential to the cell's growth, reproduction, etc. **2** The central core of an atom, carrying a positive electric charge and around which the negatively charged electrons revolve. **3** Any central point or part around which other things are gathered: Four novels form the *nucleus* of his work.

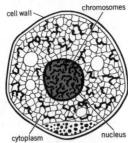

cell wall · chromosomes · cytoplasm · nucleus

nude [n(y)ōōd] **1** *adj.* Wearing no clothing or covering; naked; bare. **2** *n.* A nude figure of a person, especially as represented in painting, sculpture, etc. — **nu'di·ty** *n.*

nudge [nuj] *v.* **nudged, nudg·ing,** *n.* **1** *v.* To touch or push gently, as with the elbow so as to attract attention. **2** *n.* A gentle push, as with the elbow.

nug·get [nug'it] *n.* **1** A lump, especially of gold in its natural state. **2** Any valuable bit or piece: *nuggets* of information.

nui·sance [n(y)ōō'səns] *n.* Any person, thing, condition, etc., that annoys, bothers, or irritates.

null [nul] *adj.* **1** Having no legal force or effect. **2** Having no value; useless. — **null and void** Without legal force or effect: This contract is *null and void.*

nul·li·fy [nul'ə·fī] *v.* **nul·li·fied, nul·li·fy·ing** **1** To make useless; bring to nothing: During the day, the light of the sun *nullifies* that of the stars. **2** To take away the legal force or effect of; annul: to *nullify* a will. — **nul'li·fi·ca'tion** *n.*

numb [num] **1** *adj.* Having no sensation or feeling: fingers *numb* with cold; to be *numb* with fear. **2** *v.* To make numb: The dentist *numbed* my jaw. — **numb'ly** *adv.* — **numb'ness** *n.*

num·ber [num'bər] **1** *n.* An element of arithmetic on which operations such as addition and multiplication are performed and which tells how many elements there are in a set; cardinal number. **2** *v.* To count; make a total of: I *number* the stamps in my collection at 2,000. **3** *n.* A quantity or amount of things or persons; sum or total: The *number* of players on a baseball team is nine. **4** *v.* To amount to; total: Our club *numbers* twenty members. **5** *n.* (*usually pl.*) A rather large group of persons or things: *Numbers* of library books are lost each year. **6** *n.* A number given to a person or piece of merchandise for identification: All cars have serial *numbers.* **7** *v.* To give or assign a number to: to *number* the pages of a long letter. **8** *n.* One of a series of things: the July *number* of a magazine; Her last *number* on the program was very short. **9** *v.* To include as one of a collection or group: She *numbers* dancing among her talents. **10** *v.* To set or limit the number of: His days on this job are *numbered.* **11** *n.* In grammar, the form of a noun, pronoun, verb, and adjective that shows whether one thing or more is being spoken of. The word *has* shows a singular number, and the word *they* shows a plural number. — **any number of** A good many; quite a lot of. — **beyond number** or **without number** Too many to be counted. ◆ A *number* is the idea or concept; a *numeral* is a symbol used to express a *number.* Forty, 40, and XL are all *numerals* for the same *number.*

num·ber·less [num'bər·lis] *adj.* Very numerous; countless: *numberless* flakes of snow.

Num·bers [num'bərz] *n.pl.* (*used with singular verb*) The fourth book of the Old Testament.

nu·mer·al [n(y)ōō'mər·əl] *n.* **1** A symbol, letter, or word used alone or with others to express a number. Arabic numerals 24 and 190 show the same numbers as the Roman numerals XXIV and CXC. **2** (*pl.*) Figures of cloth showing the year a student will graduate, awarded for playing on a class team in a sport. ◆ See NUMBER.

nu·mer·a·tion [n(y)ōō'mə·rā'shən] *n.* The act, process, or system of reading or naming numbers.

nu·mer·a·tor [n(y)ōō'mə·rā'tər] *n.* In a fraction, the number above the line, which is divided by the denominator. In ⅔, 2 is the numerator.

The red numeral is the numerator.

nu·mer·i·cal [n(y)ōō·mer'i·kəl] *adj.* **1** Of or having to do with numbers. **2** By numbers: to put in *numerical* order. **3** Expressed in numerals. — **nu·mer'i·cal·ly** *adv.*

nu·mer·ous [n(y)ōō'mə·rəs] *adj.* **1** Very many: *numerous* mistakes. **2** Consisting of a great number: a *numerous* collection of books.

nu·mis·mat·ics [n(y)ōō'miz·mat'iks] *n.* The study or collecting of coins and medals. — **nu·mis·ma·tist** [n(y)ōō·miz'mə·tist] *n.* ◆ See -ICS.

num·skull [num′skul′] *n.* A very stupid person.

nun [nun] *n.* A woman who has taken religious vows, belongs to a religious order, and commonly lives in a convent. Many nuns serve as teachers or nurses, or do charitable work.

nun·ci·o [nun′shē·ō *or* nun′sē·ō] *n.*, *pl.* **nun·ci·os** An ambassador whom the Pope sends to represent him in other countries.

nun·ner·y [nun′ə·rē] *n.*, *pl.* **nun·ner·ies** A place where nuns live together; convent.

Nun's habit

nup·tial [nup′shəl] **1** *adj.* Of or having to do with marriage or a wedding. **2** *n.* (*pl.*) A wedding, or the wedding ceremonies.

nurse [nûrs] *n.*, *v.* **nursed, nurs·ing 1** *n.* A specially trained person who cares for the sick, injured, or aged, and assists doctors in hospitals. **2** *v.* To give skilled or special care to (a sick person, an illness, etc.) so as to cure: She *nursed* us carefully; He *nursed* his headache. **3** *n.* A nursemaid. **4** *v.* To feed (a baby or young animal) at the breast or udder: The dog *nursed* her puppies. **5** *v.* To take nourishment from the breast or udder: The kittens were *nursing*. **6** *n.* A person who feeds or protects. **7** *v.* To hold or embrace fondly. **8** *v.* To cause to grow in the mind; cherish: to *nurse* ambitions.

nurse·maid [nûrs′mād′] *n.* A girl or woman employed to care for children.

nurs·er·y [nûr′sər·ē] *n.*, *pl.* **nurs·er·ies 1** A baby's bedroom or a room for children's use. **2** A place where trees or other plants are raised for sale or transplanting. **3** A nursery school.

nurs·er·y·man [nûr′sər·ē·mən] *n.*, *pl.* **nurs·er·y·men** [nûr′sər·ē·mən] A man who raises or cultivates plants in a nursery.

nursery rhyme A simple, short poem or jingle for little children.

nursery school A place where children too young for kindergarten regularly meet for training and play.

nurs·ling [nûrs′ling] *n.* **1** A baby or young animal that is being nursed. **2** Any person or thing receiving watchful care.

nur·ture [nur′chər] *v.* **nur·tured, nur·tur·ing,** *n.* **1** *v.* To bring up; care for and educate, as a child. **2** *n.* A bringing up and educating, as of a child. **3** *v.* To provide with food; nourish. **4** *n.* Something that nourishes; food.

Nut

nut [nut] *n.* **1** A dry fruit consisting of a kernel or seed enclosed in a woody shell. Pecans and cashews are nuts. **2** The kernel of such a fruit, especially when edible. **3** A small block of metal with a hole in it, having a screw thread inside, used to hold a bolt in place. **4** *slang* A person who does silly or crazy things.

nut·crack·er [nut′krak′ər] *n.* **1** A tool used to crack the hard, outer shells of nuts. **2** Any of several birds related to the crow. They live on nuts.

nut·hatch [nut′hach′] *n.* A small, short-tailed bird that feeds on nuts and insects.

Nutcracker

nut·meg [nut′meg] *n.* A hard, sweet-smelling seed of a tropical evergreen tree. It is grated and used as a spice.

nu·tri·a [n(y)ōō′trē·ə] *n.* **1** A large, beaverlike animal of South America. **2** Its light-brown fur, like beaver, but not so thick.

nu·tri·ent [n(y)ōō′trē·ənt] **1** *adj.* Giving nourishment; nourishing. **2** *n.* Food.

nu·tri·ment [n(y)ōō′trə·mənt] *n.* Something that nourishes; food.

nu·tri·tion [n(y)ōō·trish′ən] *n.* **1** Food; nourishment. **2** The process by which a plant or animal takes in and uses food for its growth, maintenance, and repair. **— nu·tri′tion·al** *adj.*

nu·tri·tious [n(y)ōō·trish′əs] *adj.* Giving nourishment; nourishing. **— nu·tri′tious·ly** *adv.*

nu·tri·tive [n(y)ōō′trə·tiv] *adj.* **1** Nutritious; nourishing. **2** Having to do with nutrition.

nut·shell [nut′shel′] *n.* The shell of a nut. **— in a nutshell** In as few words as possible.

nut·ting [nut′ing] *n.* Searching for and gathering nuts.

nut·ty [nut′ē] *adj.* **nut·ti·er, nut·ti·est 1** Having the flavor of nuts. **2** Containing nuts: *nutty* candy. **3** *slang* Crazy or foolish.

nuz·zle [nuz′əl] *v.* **nuz·zled, nuz·zling 1** To push or rub with or as if with the nose: My dog *nuzzled* my hand. **2** To nestle or lie close.

NW or **N.W.** Abbreviation of: **1** NORTHWEST. **2** NORTHWESTERN.

N.Y. Abbreviation of NEW YORK.

ny·lon [nī′lon] *n.* **1** A strong, elastic, man-made material, used to make clothes, rope, brushes, plastics, etc. **2** (*pl.*) *informal* Stockings for women, made of nylon.

A horse nuzzling a girl

nymph [nimf] *n.* **1** In Greek and Roman myths, any of a group of lesser goddesses who lived in woods, fountains, trees, etc. **2** Any beautiful young woman or girl. **3** The young of certain insects just before they become adult.

O

o or **O** [ō] *n.*, *pl.* **o's** or **O's** The 15th letter of the English alphabet.

O [ō] *interj.* **1** A word used in direct address, as in prayer or earnest appeal: *O* Lord, help me. **2** A word expressing surprise, disappointment, fear, etc.; oh: *O* dear!; *O* to be twenty-one!

o' [ō *or* ə] *prep.* Of: one *o'*clock; jack-*o'*-lantern.

O The symbol for the element OXYGEN.

O. Abbreviation of OHIO.

oaf [ōf] *n.* A stupid, clumsy person; bungler. **— oaf'ish** *adj.*

O·a·hu [ō·ä′hōō] *n.* The third largest of the Hawaiian Islands. Honolulu, the capital of Hawaii, is on Oahu.

oak [ōk] *n.* **1** A tree bearing nuts called acorns. **2** The hard, durable wood of this tree.

oak·en [ō′kən] *adj.* Made or consisting of oak.

Oak Ridge A town in eastern Tennessee. It is the site of an atomic research center.

oak·um [ō′kəm] *n.* Hemp fiber obtained by untwisting and picking out the fibers of old rope. It is used for plugging up cracks and seams in wooden boats and ships.

oar [ôr] **1** *n.* A wooden pole with a blade at one end, used for rowing or steering a boat. **2** *v.* To propel with oars; row. **3** *n.* A person who rows with an oar; oarsman.

oar·lock [ôr′lok′] *n.* A U-shaped device attached to a boat for keeping an oar in place.

oars·man [ôrz′mən] *n.*, *pl.* **oars·men** [ôrz′·mən] A person who rows, especially in a racing boat.

o·a·sis [ō·ā′sis] *n.*, *pl.* **o·a·ses** [ō·ā′sēz] **1** An area in a desert made fertile by a water supply. **2** Any place of shelter or relief; refuge.

oat [ōt] *n.* (*usually pl.*) A tall cereal grass cultivated for its edible grain. **— feel one's oats** To act in a lively or high-spirited way.

oat·en [ōt′ən] *adj.* Of or made of oats or oatmeal.

oath [ōth] *n.*, *pl.* **oaths** [ōths *or* ōᵺz] **1** A formal appeal to God or other authority to witness to the truth of a promise or statement. **2** The use of the name of God or some sacred person or thing to show anger or to add emphasis. **3** A vulgar or disrespectful utterance; curse. **—**

take an oath To make a promise or statement with a solemn oath. **— under oath** Morally or legally bound by an oath.

oat·meal [ōt′mēl′] *n.* **1** Meal made by grinding or rolling oats. **2** A breakfast cereal made by boiling such meal.

ob·du·rate [ob′d(y)ə·rit] *adj.* **1** Unmoved by pity; hardhearted; unfeeling: an *obdurate* murderer. **2** Stubborn: an *obdurate* denial. **— ob′·du·rate·ly** *adv.*

o·be·di·ence [ō·bē′dē·əns] *n.* The act or habit of obeying; submission to commands, laws, etc.: The first thing a soldier learns is *obedience* to his officers.

o·be·di·ent [ō·bē′dē·ənt] *adj.* Obeying or submitting to commands, laws, etc.: an *obedient* soldier; an *obedient* pet. **— o·be′di·ent·ly** *adv.*

o·bei·sance [ō·bā′səns *or* ō·bē′səns] *n.* **1** An act of courtesy or reverence, as bowing or a bending of the knee. **2** Homage; respect: As king, he demanded *obeisance* from all.

ob·e·lisk [ob′ə·lisk] *n.* A square shaft of stone that tapers to a top shaped like a pyramid.

O·ber·on [ō′bə·ron] *n.* In medieval legends, the king of the fairies, husband of Titania.

o·bese [ō·bēs′] *adj.* Very fat; exceedingly stout. **— o·bes·i·ty** [ō·bē′sə·tē *or* ō·bes′ə·tē] *n.*

o·bey [ō·bā′] *v.* **1** To do the bidding of; submit to: to *obey* one's superiors. **2** To comply with or carry into effect: to *obey* the law. **3** To be guided or controlled by: to *obey* one's impulses. **4** To follow a command or request.

o·bit·u·ar·y [ō·bich′ōō·er′ē] *n.*, *pl.* **o·bit·u·ar·ies**, *adj.* **1** *n.* Published notice of a person's death, often including a brief biography. **2** *adj.* Of or recording a death: an *obituary* column in a newspaper.

ob·ject [*n.* ob′jikt *or* ob′jekt, *v.* əb·jekt′] **1** *n.* Anything that is or may be seen or touched. **2** *n.* The purpose of an action: What was your *object* in coming here? **3** *n.* A person or thing toward which some action, thought, or feeling is directed: Mary is the *object* of his love. **4** *n.* In grammar, a word or group of words which receives the action of a verb or follows a preposition which relates it to another word. In "Put some cream in your coffee," *cream* is the object of *put* and *coffee* the object of *in.* **5** *v.* To be opposed: Mother *objects* to our trip. **6** *v.* To offer as a

Obelisk

reason for opposition: We wanted to go to a movie, but Mother *objected* that it was too late to go. **— ob·jec′tor** *n.*

ob·jec·tion [əb·jek′shən] *n.* **1** A statement or feeling of disagreement, opposition, etc. **2** The cause or reason for disagreement, etc.: His *objections* to our plan were that it was too difficult.

ob·jec·tion·a·ble [əb·jek′shən·ə·bəl] *adj.* Deserving or causing disapproval; offensive.

ob·jec·tive [əb·jek′tiv] **1** *adj.* Free from personal feelings or opinions; detached: A jury must be *objective*. **2** *adj.* Having to do with what is external and real rather than what is in the mind. **3** *adj.* Indicating the case of the object of a verb or preposition. In "I want a book for my brother" both *book* and *brother* are in the objective case. **4** *n.* A goal or end: My *objective* is to attend college. **5** *n.* The objective case. **— ob·jec′tive·ly** *adv.*

ob·jec·tiv·i·ty [ob′jek·tiv′ə·tē] *n.* A being objective: *Objectivity* must be a jury's goal.

ob·la·tion [ob·lā′shən] *n.* **1** The act of offering worship or sacrifice to God or a god. **2** The thing that is offered, especially the bread and wine of Holy Communion.

ob·li·gate [ob′lə·gāt] *v.* **ob·li·gat·ed, ob·li·gat·ing** To bind or compel, as by contract, law, or conscience: We are *obligated* to pay taxes.

ob·li·ga·tion [ob′lə·gā′shən] *n.* **1** A duty required by law, a promise, or one's conscience: the *obligation* to pay taxes. **2** A debt of gratitude for a service or favor. **3** A debt: He is paying off his *obligations*.

ob·lig·a·to·ry [ə·blig′ə·tôr′ē *or* ob′lə·gə·tôr′ē] *adj.* Binding by law, conscience, etc.; required: Obedience in the army is *obligatory*.

o·blige [ə·blīj′] *v.* **o·bliged, o·blig·ing 1** To place under obligation, as for a service or a favor: I am *obliged* to you for the work you have done. **2** To compel; bind; force: The traffic laws *oblige* us to drive carefully. **3** To do a favor or service for: Will you *oblige* me by closing the window?

o·blig·ing [ə·blī′jing] *adj.* Inclined to do favors; good-natured; kind. **— o·blig′ing·ly** *adv.*

ob·lique [ə·blēk′] *adj.* **1** Neither level nor straight up and down; slanting. **2** Not direct or straightforward: an *oblique* answer. **— ob·lique′ly** *adv.*

oblique angle An angle that is not a right angle.

ob·lit·er·ate [ə·blit′ə·rāt] *v.* **ob·lit·er·at·ed, ob·lit·er·at·ing 1** To destroy completely; leave no trace of: A bomb had *obliterated* the chapel. **2** To blot or wipe out; erase, as writing. **— ob·lit′er·a′tion** *n.*

ob·liv·i·on [ə·bliv′ē·ən] *n.* **1** The state or fact of being completely forgotten: Even famous people sometimes fade into *oblivion*. **2** The fact of forgetting; forgetfulness.

ob·liv·i·ous [ə·bliv′ē·əs] *adj.* **1** Not conscious or aware: He was *oblivious* to his surroundings. **2** Causing forgetfulness: *oblivious* sleep.

ob·long [ob′lông] **1** *adj.* Longer in one dimension than in another: A football field is *oblong*. **2** *n.* An oblong figure, object, etc.

Oblongs

ob·lo·quy [ob′lə·kwē] *n., pl.* **ob·lo·quies 1** Abusive and critical language, especially when directed against a person by the public. **2** Disgrace; shame.

ob·nox·ious [əb·nok′shəs] *adj.* Highly disagreeable; hateful; offensive. **— ob·nox′ious·ly** *adv.*

o·boe [ō′bō] *n.* A high-pitched woodwind instrument that has a conical body and a double reed. ◆ *Oboe* comes from the French word *hautbois*, meaning *high wood*. It was originally written *hautbois* in English too, and was pronounced [hō′boi *or* ō′boi], but the spelling and pronunciation now used came through Italian.

ob·scene [əb·sēn′ *or* ob·sēn′] *adj.* Offensive to accepted standards of morality or decency; indecent; immodest; disgusting. **— ob·scene′ly** *adv.*

Oboe

ob·scen·i·ty [əb·sen′ə·tē *or* əb·sē′nə·tē] *n., pl.* **ob·scen·i·ties** An obscene act, word, etc.

ob·scure [əb·skyoor′] *adj.* **ob·scur·er, ob·scur·est,** *v.* **ob·scured, ob·scur·ing 1** *adj.* Not clear to the mind; hard to understand: an *obscure* statement. **2** *adj.* Not clear to the senses: *obscure* sounds; *obscure*, shadowy figures. **3** *v.* To make vague, hard to understand, etc.: Her elaborate way of speaking *obscured* the meaning of what she said. **4** *v.* To make dim or indistinct: Fog *obscured* the mountains. **5** *adj.* Not easily found; hidden: an *obscure* country path. **6** *adj.* Without fame: an *obscure* artist. **7** *adj.* Having little or no light; dark: *obscure* cellar stairs. **— ob·scure′ly** *adv.*

The veil obscures the woman's eyes.

ob·scu·ri·ty [əb·skyoor′ə·tē] *n., pl.* **ob·scu·ri·ties** The condition or quality of being obscure.

ob·se·quies [ob′sə·kwēz] *n.pl.* Funeral rites; burial services.

ob·se·qui·ous [əb·sē′kwē·əs] *adj.* Too ready to please, praise, or obey; fawning; flattering; servile. **— ob·se′qui·ous·ly** *adv.*

---

add, āce, câre, pälm; end, ēqual; it, īce; odd, ōpen, ôrder; took, pool; up, bûrn;
ə = a in *above*, e in *sicken*, i in *possible*, o in *melon*, u in *circus*; yoo = u in *fuse*; oil; pout;
check; ring; thin; this; zh in *vision*. For ¶ reference, see page 64 · HOW TO

ob·serv·a·ble [əb·zûr′və·bəl] *adj.* **1** Readily seen; noticeable: an *observable* change. **2** That may or must be observed or celebrated, as a holiday. — **ob·serv′a·bly** *adv.*

ob·ser·vance [əb·zûr′vəns] *n.* **1** The act of observing, as a command, law, holiday, etc. **2** A customary ceremony, act, or rite: the *observance* of a wedding anniversary.

ob·ser·vant [əb·zûr′vənt] *adj.* **1** Quick to observe or notice; alert. **2** Strict or careful in observing, as a custom, law, holiday, etc.

ob·ser·va·tion [ob′zər·vā′shən] *n.* **1** The act, ability, or habit of observing. **2** The fact of being observed: We wanted to avoid *observation*. **3** The act of observing scientifically and making notes on what is observed: He is famous for his astronomical *observations*. **4** A comment or incidental remark.

ob·ser·va·to·ry [əb·zûr′və·tôr′ē] *n., pl.* **ob·ser·va·to·ries** A building equipped with telescopes and other instruments for studying the stars, weather conditions, and other natural phenomena.

ob·serve [əb·zûrv′] *v.* **ob·served, ob·serv·ing** **1** To see or notice: I *observed* you when you came in. **2** To watch attentively: to *observe* the enemy. **3** To make careful examination of, especially for scientific purposes: to *observe* the cells of a plant under a microscope. **4** To comment or remark: I *observed* that it was a very warm day. **5** To follow or comply with: to *observe* the law. **6** To celebrate in the proper way, as a holiday. — **ob·serv′er** *n.*

ob·sess [əb·ses′] *v.* To fill or trouble the mind of excessively; haunt: Worries about his health have *obsessed* Jack lately.

ob·ses·sion [əb·sesh′ən] *n.* **1** A thought, feeling, or idea that fills the mind and cannot be driven out: It was an *obsession* with her that she would fail the course. **2** The condition of being obsessed by such a thought, feeling, etc.

ob·sid·i·an [əb·sid′ē·ən] *n.* A hard, glassy rock, usually black, formed by the cooling of hot lava.

ob·so·les·cent [ob′sə·les′ənt] *adj.* Passing out of use or fashion. — **ob′so·les′cence** *n.*

ob·so·lete [ob′sə·lēt *or* ob′sə·lēt′] *adj.* **1** Old; out-of-date: an *obsolete* automobile. **2** No longer used or practiced: an *obsolete* word.

ob·sta·cle [ob′stə·kəl] *n.* Something that stands in the way or interferes; hindrance; obstruction: Lack of education was an *obstacle* to his success.

ob·ste·tri·cian [ob′stə·trish′ən] *n.* A doctor who specializes in obstetrics.

ob·stet·rics [əb·stet′riks] *n.* The branch of medicine that deals with the care and treatment of women in the time leading up to, during, and just after the birth of a child. ◆ See -ICS.

ob·sti·na·cy [ob′stə·nə·sē] *n., pl.* **ob·sti·na·cies** **1** A being obstinate; stubbornness. **2** An obstinate act, feeling, etc.

ob·sti·nate [ob′stə·nit] *adj.* **1** Stubbornly holding to one's opinions or purposes; unyielding: He's so *obstinate* he will never change his mind. **2** Hard to overcome, control, or cure: an *obsti-*

nate habit. — **ob′sti·nate·ly** *adv.* ◆ *Obstinate* and *stubborn* both mean fixed and unchanging in opinion or action. A person who is *obstinate* seems unreasonably determined not to change his mind, whereas a *stubborn* person may stick to his course for good reasons: a *stubborn* refusal to give up; He *obstinately* defied the law.

ob·strep·er·ous [əb·strep′ər·əs] *adj.* Unruly or noisy: *Obstreperous* boys are hard to teach.

ob·struct [əb·strukt′] *v.* **1** To stop or retard movement through; block; clog: The water pipes are *obstructed* by rust. **2** To hinder: to *obstruct* the work on the new bridge. **3** To cut off or be in the way of: Tall buildings *obstruct* the view. — **ob·struc′tive** *adj.*

ob·struc·tion [əb·struk′shən] *n.* **1** Something that obstructs; obstacle; hindrance: Some *obstruction* was blocking the drain. **2** The act of obstructing. **3** The condition of being obstructed: the *obstruction* of a blood vessel.

ob·tain [əb·tān′] *v.* **1** To gain possession of, especially by effort; get; acquire: I *obtained* a good knowledge of French in Europe. **2** To be in effect: Old customs still *obtain* here.

ob·tain·a·ble [əb·tān′ə·bəl] *adj.* Capable of being obtained.

ob·trude [əb·trōōd′] *v.* **ob·trud·ed, ob·trud·ing** **1** To force upon another without request: to *obtrude* an unwanted opinion. **2** To intrude oneself: to *obtrude* upon another's happiness. **3** To push forward or out.

ob·tru·sive [əb·trōō′siv] *adj.* Having a tendency to obtrude or push oneself forward.

ob·tuse [əb·t(y)ōōs′] *adj.* **1** Slow to understand; dull; stupid: She was too *obtuse* to follow instructions. **2** Not having a sharp edge or point; blunt. — **ob·tuse′ness** *n.*

obtuse angle An angle greater than a right angle and less than 180°.

ob·verse [ob′vûrs] *n.* The front or principal side of anything, especially the side of a coin that has the main design on it.

obtuse angle   right angle

ob·vi·ate [ob′vē·āt] *v.* **ob·vi·at·ed, ob·vi·at·ing** To anticipate and prevent; provide for in advance: to *obviate* risks; to *obviate* difficulties.

ob·vi·ous [ob′vē·əs] *adj.* Easily perceived; clear; visible: an *obvious* error. — **ob′vi·ous·ly** *adv.* — **ob′vi·ous·ness** *n.*

oc·a·ri·na [ok′ə·rē′nə] *n.* A small musical instrument in the shape of a sweet potato, with a mouthpiece and finger holes. ◆ *Ocarina* comes from the Italian word for *little goose*, because its shape suggested a goose ready for cooking.

oc·ca·sion [ə·kā′zhən] **1** *n.* The particular time of a happening: I met her on one *occasion*. **2** *n.* The happening itself: The *occasion* of our meeting was not a happy one. **3** *n.* An impor-

Ocarina

tant event: *The party was quite an occasion.*
4 *n.* A favorable time; opportunity. **5** *n.* An
immediate cause; reason: *He gave me occasion
to complain.* **6** *v.* To cause or bring about: *His
accident occasioned us great worry.* **— on occa·
sion** Now and then.

oc·ca·sion·al [ə·kā′zhən·əl] *adj.* **1** Occurring
now and then: *an occasional visit.* **2** Made, intended, or suitable for a special occasion: *occasional verse.*

oc·ca·sion·al·ly [ə·kā′zhən·əl·ē] *adv.* Now and
then; sometimes: *We see them occasionally.*

Oc·ci·dent [ok′sə·dənt] *n.* (*sometimes written
occident*) The countries west of Asia, especially
those of Europe and the Americas; the West.

Oc·ci·den·tal [ok′sə·den′təl] **1** *n.* A member of
any of the peoples native to the Occident. **2** *adj.*
(*sometimes written* **occidental**) Of or from the
Occident.

oc·ci·put [ok′sə·put] *n., pl.* **oc·cip·i·ta** [ok·
sip′ə·tə] The lower back part of the skull.
— oc·cip·i·tal [ok·sip′ə·təl] *adj.*

oc·clude [ə·klōōd′] *v.* **oc·clud·ed, oc·clud·ing**
1 To shut up or close, as pores or openings. **2** To
shut in, out, or off. **3** To meet with the cusps
fitting closely: *His upper and lower teeth occlude
properly.* **4** To take up (gases or liquids); absorb
or adsorb. **— oc·clu·sion** [ə·klōō′zhən] *n.*

oc·cult [ə·kult′ *or* ok′ult] *adj.* **1** Of or having to
do with various magical or mysterious arts and
practices, as astrology and spiritualism. **2** Beyond human understanding; mysterious: *He
claims to have occult powers.*

oc·cu·pan·cy [ok′yə·pən·sē] *n.* The act of occupying or holding possession of land, buildings,
etc.

oc·cu·pant [ok′yə·pənt] *n.* A person who occupies a house, lands, a position, etc.: *the occupant
of the building next door.*

oc·cu·pa·tion [ok′yə·pā′shən] *n.* **1** Any activity
with which a person busies himself, especially
the regular work by which he earns a living.
2 The act of occupying. **3** The taking and holding of land by a military force. **— oc′cu·pa′·
tion·al** *adj.* ◆ *Occupation, vocation,* and *business*
all refer to one's work. An *occupation* is what one
does for a living or how one spends most of one's
time. A *vocation* has more to do with one's abilities and desires: *She is a librarian by occupation,
but her real vocation is teaching.* One's *business*
refers to the field in which one makes his living:
He is in the insurance business.

oc·cu·py [ok′yə·pī] *v.* **oc·cu·pied, oc·cu·py·
ing** **1** To take and hold possession of, as by
conquest. **2** To fill or take up: *The estate occupies ten acres.* **3** To live in; inhabit: *We
occupy this house.* **4** To hold; fill: *He occupies
a minor government position.* **5** To busy or engage; employ: *He occupies himself with unimportant matters.*

oc·cur [ə·kûr′] *v.* **oc·curred, oc·cur·ring** **1**
To happen or take place. **2** To be found; appear:
Meteors occur frequently in August. **3** To sug-
gest itself; come to mind.

oc·cur·rence [ə·kûr′əns] *n.* **1** The act or fact
of occurring: *In this weather, the occurrence of
a tornado is possible.* **2** Something that occurs;
an event; incident: *an unusual occurrence.*

o·cean [ō′shən] *n.* **1** The great body of salt
water that covers about 70 percent of the earth's
surface. **2** (*often written* **Ocean**) Any one of its
divisions having a distinct basin, as the Atlantic,
Pacific, Indian, and Arctic.

O·ce·an·i·a [ō′shē·an′ē·ə] *n.* The islands of the
central and southern Pacific Ocean, including
Melanesia, Micronesia, and Polynesia, and sometimes the Malay Archipelago and Australasia.

o·ce·an·ic [ō′shē·an′ik] *adj.* **1** Of or living in
the ocean. **2** Like an ocean; vast.

o·ce·an·og·ra·phy [ō′shē·ən·og′rə·fē *or* ō′shən-
og′rə·fē] *n.* The science that studies the oceans,
their physical features, their chemistry, the life
in them, etc. **— o′ce·an·og′ra·pher** *n.*

o·ce·lot [ō′sə·lət *or* os′ə·lot] *n.* A wildcat of Central and
South America, hav-
ing a spotted, yellow-
ish coat.

o·cher or **o·chre** [ō′-
kər] **1** *n.* An earthy
material containing
iron. It varies in color
from light yellow to
deep orange or red and
is used as a pigment.
2 *n., adj.* Dark yellow.

Ocelot, about 3 ft. long

o′clock [ə·klok′] Of or according to the clock:
six o'clock.

Oct. Abbreviation of OCTOBER.

oc·ta·gon [ok′tə·gon] *n.* A closed plane figure
bounded by eight straight lines
that form eight interior angles.

oc·tane [ok′tān] *n.* A liquid hydrocarbon found in petroleum and
chemically related to methane.

oc·tave [ok′tiv *or* ok′tāv] *n.* **1**
The shortest distance between two   Octagon
musical tones that have the same
name. The higher tone has twice the frequency
of vibration of the lower tone. **2** A tone at this
distance above or below any other, considered in
relation to that other. **3** Two tones at this distance, sounded together. **4** The series of tones
within this distance. **5** Any group or series of
eight.

oc·ta·vo [ok·tā′vō] *n., pl.* **oc·ta·vos** **1** The size
of a page, usually $6 \times 9\frac{1}{2}$ inches, made from
printer's sheets folded and cut into eight leaves.
2 A book made up of pages of this size. **3** *adj.*
use: octavo pages.

---

add, āce, câre, pälm;   end, ēqual;   it, īce;   odd, ōpen, ôrder;   tŏŏk, pōōl;   up, bûrn;
ə = a in *above*, e in *sicken*, i in *possible*, o in *melon*, u in *circus*;   yōō = u in *fuse*;   oil;   pout;
check;   ring;   thin;   this;   zh in *vision*.   For ¶ reference, see page 64 · HOW TO

Oc·to·ber [ok·tō′bər] *n.* The tenth month of the year, having 31 days. ◆ In the Roman calendar, *October* was the eighth month.

oc·to·ge·nar·i·an [ok′tə·jə·nâr′ē·ən] **1** *adj.* Between eighty and ninety years of age. **2** *n.* A person between eighty and ninety years of age.

oc·to·pus [ok′tə·pəs] *n., pl.* **oc·to·pus·es** or **oc·to·pi** [ok′tə·pī] **1** A soft-bodied sea animal related to the squid, having a large oval head, prominent eyes, and eight long arms each having two rows of suckers. **2** Anything like an octopus, as a powerful organization that is far-reaching and possibly dangerous.

Octopus, up to 3 ft. long

oc·u·lar [ok′yə·lər] *adj.* **1** Of or having to do with the eye: an *ocular* weakness. **2** Of or having to do with sight; visual: *ocular* proof.

oc·u·list [ok′yə·list] *n.* A physician skilled in treating faulty vision and diseases of the eye; ophthalmologist.

odd [od] *adj.* **1** Strange or unusual; peculiar; queer: The *odd* old lady wears men's shoes. **2** Not part of a routine; casual: *odd* jobs. **3** Being part of an incomplete pair, set, etc.: an *odd* sock. **4** Leaving a remainder when divided by two; not even: Five is an *odd* number. **5** Having an odd number: The *odd* addresses are on the north side of the street. **6** And a little extra; a few more: I have seventy-*odd* dollars in the bank. **— odd′ness** *n.*

odd·i·ty [od′ə·tē] *n., pl.* **odd·i·ties 1** A person or thing that is odd or peculiar. **2** The condition of being odd; strangeness; queerness.

odd·ly [od′lē] *adv.* Strangely; queerly.

odds [odz] *n.pl.* (*sometimes used with singular verb*) **1** An advantage given to a weaker opponent: Bill gave Fred *odds* in the golf tournament. **2** In betting, the ratio of the amount that can be won to the amount bet: The *odds* are three to one. **3** A chance or probability: *Odds* are that it won't rain. **4** Advantage; benefit, especially in a contest: The *odds* are in his favor. **— at odds** In disagreement. **— odds and ends** A number of different things left over: *odds and ends* from today's lunch.

ode [ōd] *n.* A poem that deals with a dignified theme in a lofty, exalted style.

O·des·sa [ō·des′ə] *n.* A seaport in the southern Soviet Union, on the Black Sea.

O·din [ō′din] *n.* In Norse myths, the supreme god. He was the god of war, art, and wisdom.

o·di·ous [ō′dē·əs] *adj.* Arousing hate or disgust; offensive; detestable: *odious* crimes.

o·di·um [ō′dē·əm] *n.* **1** Extreme dislike or hatred, especially widespread hatred. **2** Disgrace or shame: the *odium* of being a criminal.

o·dom·e·ter [ō·dom′ə·tər] *n.* A device for measuring the distance traveled by a vehicle.

o·dor [ō′dər] *n.* **1** A smell or scent, whether pleasing or not: the *odor* of flowers; the *odor* of sour milk. **2** Regard or reputation: The senator is in bad *odor* since the scandal. ¶1

o·dor·if·er·ous [ō′də·rif′ər·əs] *adj.* Having or giving off an odor, especially a pleasant odor.

o·dor·less [ō′dər·lis] *adj.* Having no odor.

o·dor·ous [ō′dər·əs] *adj.* Having or giving off an odor, especially a fragrant odor.

O·dys·seus [ō·dis′yoos *or* ō·dis′ē·əs] *n.* In Greek legends, one of the leaders in the Greek war against Troy and the hero of Homer's *Odyssey*. His Latin name is Ulysses.

Od·ys·sey [od′ə·sē] *n.* **1** An ancient Greek poem by Homer, describing the wanderings of Odysseus after the fall of Troy. **2** (*written* **odyssey**, *pl.* **od·ys·seys**) Any long, adventurous wandering or journey.

Oed·i·pus [ed′ə·pəs *or* ē′də·pəs] *n.* In Greek legend, a king who, without knowing who they were, killed his father and married his mother.

o′er [ôr] *prep., adv.* Over: used mostly in poems.

of [uv, ov, *or* əv] *prep.* **1** Coming from: Saint Francis *of* Assisi. **2** Connected with: Is he *of* your party? **3** Located at: the Colossus *of* Rhodes. **4** Away from: We're within six miles *of* home. **5** Specified as; named: the city *of* Newark. **6** Having as a quality: a man *of* strength. **7** In reference to: sharp *of* tongue. **8** About; concerning: Don't speak *of* it. **9** Owing to: I'm tired *of* your complaints. **10** Possessing: a lady *of* great wealth. **11** Belonging to: the lid *of* a box. **12** Made with or from: a ship *of* steel. **13** Containing: a glass *of* water. **14** Taken from: six *of* the seven students; most *of* my time. **15** So as to be without: relieved *of* trouble. **16** Created by: the plays *of* Shakespeare. **17** Directed toward: a love *of* music. **18** During: *of* recent years. **19** Devoted to: a program *of* folk music. **20** Before; until: used in telling time: It's ten minutes *of* ten.

off [ôf *or* of] **1** *prep.* Away from: The pencil rolled *off* the desk; The plane rose *off* the runway. **2** *adv.* Away, in space, time, etc.: The dog trotted *off*; The tower is a mile *off*; The holiday is a week *off*. **3** *prep.* Not on; not in: *off* the street; *off* duty; *off* balance; *off* key. **4** *adv.* So as to make or become smaller or fewer: to wear *off*; die *off*. **5** *adv.* Away from the usual position or contact: Peel *off* the rind; Take your coat *off*. **6** *adj.* Not in the usual position; not attached: My coat button is *off*. **7** *adv.* So as not to work or happen: Turn the radio *off*. **8** *adj.* Not working or happening: The gas is *off*. **9** *prep.* Less than; below: ten cents *off* the regular price. **10** *adj.* Not up to a standard; not busy: an *off* season for business. **11** *adv.* So as to be below standard: His business dropped *off*. **12** *prep.* Below standard in: to be *off* one's golf game. **13** *adj.* Free from work or duty: my day *off*. **14** *adj.* Not likely; remote: an *off* chance. **15** *adj.* Provided for; situated: to be well *off*. **16** *adj.* Not correct; wrong. **17** *adj.* On the right: said of one of a team of horses. **18** *prep.* On or from: living *off* nuts and berries. **19** *prep. informal* No longer using, doing, etc.: to be *off* smoking. **20** *interj.* Go away! — **be off** To leave; depart. — **off and on** Now and then; occasionally. — **off with** Take off; remove: *Off with* his head! ◆ The *of* in sentences like *He fell off of the horse* serves no purpose and should be left out.

of·fal [ô′fəl] *n.* **1** The waste parts of a butchered animal. **2** Rubbish or refuse of any kind.

of·fend [ə·fend′] *v.* **1** To give offense to; displease; anger: Your hasty refusal *offended* me. **2** To be disagreeable or unpleasant to: The bright colors in the room *offended* my eyes. **3** To commit an offense, crime, or sin. — **of·fend′· er** *n.*

of·fense [ə·fens′] *n.* **1** Any violation, as of a rule, duty, or law. **2** The act of offending: He meant no *offense*. **3** A being offended: I felt *offense* at his words. **4** Something that offends or causes displeasure: The noise was an *offense* to the ears. **5** [*also* ô′fens] The act of attacking: *offense* against the enemy. **6** [*also* ô′fens] In football, hockey, etc., the team possessing the ball, puck, etc. — **give offense** To offend or cause anger, resentment, etc. — **take offense** To be offended; feel angry, hurt, etc.

of·fen·sive [ə·fen′siv] **1** *adj.* Unpleasant or disagreeable: an *offensive* odor; an *offensive* remark. **2** *adj.* Of or having to do with attack: Today our troops began an *offensive* operation; A rifle is an *offensive* weapon. **3** *n.* An attack or an arrangement of forces for attacking. — **of·fen′sive·ly** *adv.* — **of·fen′sive·ness** *n.*

of·fer [ô′fər] **1** *v.* To present for taking if wanted; volunteer: to *offer* a loan. **2** *v.* To suggest or propose: to *offer* a plan of action. **3** *v.* To present solemnly, as in worship: to *offer* up a prayer. **4** *v.* To show readiness or willingness: I *offered* to go with him. **5** *v.* To attempt or try: The enemy *offered* only minor resistance. **6** *v.* To suggest as payment; bid: I *offered* three dollars for the vase. **7** *n.* The act of offering: an *offer* of money; an *offer* to help.

of·fer·ing [ô′fər·ing] *n.* **1** The act of making an offer. **2** The thing that is offered, as a contribution or a gift.

of·fer·to·ry [ô′fər·tôr′ē] *n., pl.* **of·fer·to·ries 1** A part of a church service during which money is collected from the congregation. **2** The prayers said or the music played or sung during this part of the church service.

off·hand [ôf′hand′] **1** *adv.* Without preparation or thought: He could not remember her name *offhand*. **2** *adj.* Done, said, or made casually; informal: He made some *offhand* remarks.

of·fice [ôf′is] *n.* **1** A place in which a business or profession is carried on: a doctor's *office*; an accounting *office*. **2** The people who work as a group in an office. **3** Any position, especially a public position of authority: the *office* of president. **4** The duties or responsibilities a person

has in his position. **5** (*usually pl.*) Any act or service done for another: The trip was arranged through John's kind *offices*. **6** A religious ceremony or service.

of·fice·hold·er [ôf′is·hōl′dər] *n.* A person who holds an office under a government.

of·fi·cer [ôf′ə·sər] *n.* **1** In the armed forces, a person who has the rank to command others. **2** A person who holds an office or post, as in a corporation, government, or club. **3** A policeman. **4** The captain of a merchant or passenger ship or any of his chief assistants.

of·fi·cial [ə·fish′əl] **1** *n.* A person who holds an office or position, as in the government or a business. **2** *adj.* Of or having to do with a position of authority: his last *official* act. **3** *adj.* Coming from or supported by authority; authorized: an *official* request. **4** *adj.* Authorized to carry out some special duty: the *official* timekeeper. **5** *adj.* Appropriate for a person or persons in office: *official* robes. — **of·fi′cial·ly** *adv.*

of·fi·ci·ate [ə·fish′ē·āt] *v.* **of·fi·ci·at·ed, of·fi·ci·at·ing 1** To conduct a service, as a priest or minister: to *officiate* at a wedding. **2** To perform the functions of any office or position: to *officiate* as referee at a boxing match.

of·fi·cious [ə·fish′əs] *adj.* Too forward in offering service or advice; meddlesome. — **of·fi′· cious·ly** *adv.*

off·ing [ôf′ing] *n.* **1** That part of the sea which is distant but visible from the shore. **2** A position some distance from the shore. — **in the offing 1** In sight and not very distant. **2** Ready or soon to happen, arrive, etc.: Big things are *in the offing*.

off·ish [ôf′ish] *adj.* Distant in manner; aloof.

off·set [*v.* ôf′set′, *n.* ôf′set′] *v.* **off·set, off·set· ting,** *n.* **1** *v.* To make up for; compensate for: to *offset* a defeat by a victory. **2** *n.* Something that compensates for or balances. **3** *n.* An offshoot. **4** *n.* A method of printing in which the inked impression is transferred to a rubber-covered cylinder and from that to the paper.

off·shoot [ôf′shoot′] *n.* **1** A shoot or branch from the main stem of a plant. **2** Anything that comes from or branches off from a principal source.

off·shore [ôf′shôr′] **1** *adj.* Moving or located away from the shore: an *offshore* breeze. **2** *adv.* At a distance from the shore: The boat is anchored *offshore*. **3** *adv.* From or away from the shore.

off·side [ôf′sīd′] *adj.* In football or ice hockey, crossing a line too soon.

off·spring [ôf′spring′] *n., pl.* **off·spring** or **off·springs** Something that is descended from a person, animal, or plant; progeny; young.

oft [ôft] *adv.* Often: used mostly in poems.

oft·en [ôf′ən] *adv.* Frequently or repeatedly; many times: We go there *often*.

---

oft·en·times [ôf′ən·tīmz′] *adv.* Often: seldom used today.

oft·times [ôf′tīmz′] *adv.* Often: seldom used today.

o·gle [ō′gəl *or* og′əl] *v.* **o·gled, o·gling,** *n.* **1** *v.* To look or stare at with admiration. **2** *n.* An ogling look or glance. **— o′gler** *n.*

o·gre [ō′gər] *n.* **1** In fairy tales, a man-eating giant or monster. **2** A brutal person.

oh [ō] *interj.* A word expressing surprise, sudden emotion, etc.: *Oh! How could you?*

O. Hen·ry [ō hen′rē] The pen name of William Sydney Porter, 1862–1910, U.S. short-story writer.

O·hi·o [ō·hī′ō] *n.* **1** A north central state of the U.S., on Lake Erie. **2** A river flowing from sw Pennsylvania southwest to the Mississippi.

ohm [ōm] *n.* A unit of electrical resistance, equal to the resistance of a conductor across which one volt is developed when a current of one ampere flows through it. ◆ *Ohm* comes from Georg Simon *Ohm*, a German physicist who studied electric current.

oil [oil] **1** *n.* Any of various fatty or greasy liquids that are obtained from plants, animals, or minerals. Oils will dissolve in alcohol but not in water, are sometimes volatile, and usually burn easily. Mineral oils are used mainly for fuel and to lubricate machinery. Vegetable and animal oils are used in cooking, soaps, perfumes, etc. **2** *adj. use:* an *oil* slick; an *oil* burner. **3** *n.* Petroleum. **4** *n.* An oil color. **5** *n.* An oil painting. **6** *v.* To smear, lubricate, or supply with oil: to *oil* the mainspring of a watch.

oil burner A furnace or heating unit that operates on oil fuel.

oil·can [oil′kan′] *n.* A can with a spout, used for applying oil to machinery.

oil·cloth [oil′klôth′] *n.* A cloth made waterproof by a coating of oil or paint, used as a covering for tables, shelves, etc.

oil color A paint made of pigment ground in linseed or other oil, used chiefly by artists.

oil·er [oi′lər] *n.* **1** A person or thing that oils, especially a person who oils engines or machinery. **2** A ship that carries oil as its cargo; tanker.

oil painting 1 A painting done in oil colors. **2** The art of painting in oil colors.

oil·skin [oil′skin′] *n.* **1** Cloth made waterproof with oil. **2** A garment of such cloth.

oil well A well that is dug or drilled to obtain petroleum.

oil·y [oi′lē] *adj.* **oil·i·er, oil·i·est 1** Of or like oil. **2** Full of, smeared with, or soaked with oil: *oily* rags; *oily* salad dressing. **3** Too smooth or unctuous, as in behavior or speech. **— oil′i·ness** *n.*

oint·ment [oint′mənt] *n.* A preparation, usually oily, used as a medicine for the skin.

OK or **O.K.** *adj., adv., interj., n., v.* **OK'd** or **O.K.'d, OK'ing** or **O.K.'ing 1** *adj., adv., interj.* [ō′kā′] All correct; all right. **2** *n.* [ō′kā′] Approval; agreement: Give me your *OK.* **3** *v.* [ō·kā′] To approve; agree.

o·ka·pi [ō·kä′pē] *n.* An African mammal related to the giraffe, but smaller and with a shorter neck.

o·kay [*adj., adv., interj., n.* ō′kā′; *v.* ō·kā′] *adj., adv., interj., n., v.* **o·kayed, o·kay·ing** Another spelling of OK.

Okla. Abbreviation of OKLAHOMA.

O·kla·ho·ma [ō′klə·hō′mə] *n.* A state in the south central U.S.

Oklahoma City The capital of Oklahoma.

Okapi, about 5 ft. high at shoulder

o·kra [ō′krə] *n.* The sticky green pods of an annual plant, used in soups and as a vegetable. ◆ *Okra* comes from a west African language.

old [ōld] *adj.* **old·er** or **eld·er, old·est** or **eld·est,** *n.* **1** *adj.* Living or existing for a long time: an *old* woman; *old* cities. **2** *n. use* Old people: *The old* are easily tired. **3** *adj.* Showing the characteristics of an aged person: When John is tired he looks *old.* **4** *adj.* Of age; in existence: He is two years *old.* **5** *n.* Past time: days of *old.* **6** *adj.* Belonging to the past: *old* superstitions. **7** *adj.* Worn with age or use: an *old* suit of clothes. **8** *adj.* Known or familiar for a long time: an *old* friend. **9** *adj.* Of former times: my father's *old* high school. **10** *adj.* Skilled through long experience: an *old* hand at politics. **11** *adj.* (*usually written* **Old**) Indicating the earlier or earliest of two or more things: the *Old* Testament. **12** *adj. informal* Good; dear: *old* buddy of mine. **— old′ness** *n.* ◆ *Old, aged* [ā′jid], and *elderly* all refer to persons who have lived a long time, but *old* may refer also to things not alive: an *old* house. An *aged* person is very *old,* and often feeble. *Elderly* suggests someone who is approaching *old* age but is still fairly vigorous. The word is sometimes used as a pleasant substitute (or *euphemism*) for *old.*

old country The native country of an immigrant, especially a European country.

old·en [ōl′dən] *adj.* Old; ancient: used mostly in poems: *olden* times.

Old English The language of England from about 450 to 1050; Anglo-Saxon.

old-fash·ioned [ōld′fash′ənd] *adj.* **1** Out of fashion; out-of-date; antiquated: *old-fashioned* furniture. **2** Of or having to do with former times: *old-fashioned* ideas. **3** Attached to or favoring old customs, ways, behavior, etc.: an *old-fashioned* mother.

Old Glory The flag of the U.S.

old·ish [ōl′dish] *adj.* Somewhat old.

old maid 1 An older woman who has never married. **2** A simple game involving the matching of pairs of cards.

Old Testament The first of the two main divisions of the Bible, dealing with the history of the

Hebrews, the laws of Moses, and the writings of the prophets.

old-time [ōld′tīm′] *adj.* Of, having to do with, or like a former time.

old-tim·er [ōld′tī′mər] *n. informal* A person who has been a member, resident, etc., for a long time.

old-world [ōld′wûrld′] *adj.* **1** (*often written* **Old-World**) Of or having to do with the Old World: *old-world* customs. **2** Ancient; antique.

Old World The Eastern Hemisphere, including Europe, Asia, and Africa, especially Europe.

o·le·an·der [ō′lē·an′dər] *n.* An evergreen shrub with poisonous leaves and clusters of white, pink, or red flowers.

o·le·o·mar·ga·rine [ō′lē·ō·mär′jə·rin] *n.* An early substitute for butter, similar to margarine but with more animal fat.

ol·fac·to·ry [ol·fak′tər·ē] *adj.* Of or having to do with the sense of smell: *olfactory* nerves.

ol·i·garch [ol′ə·gärk] *n.* A ruler in an oligarchy.

ol·i·gar·chy [ol′ə·gär′kē] *n., pl.* **ol·i·gar·chies** **1** A form of government in which the ruling power is held by a few persons. **2** A state or country governed in this way. **3** The few persons who rule.

ol·ive [ol′iv] **1** *n.* A small, oily fruit eaten green or ripe as a relish. Olives are grown in southern Europe and the Middle East. **2** *n.* The evergreen tree that produces this fruit. **3** *n., adj.* Dull yellowish green or brown. **4** *adj.* Tinged with this color: an *olive* complexion.

olive branch **1** A branch of the olive tree considered as a symbol of peace. **2** Anything offered as a symbol of peace.

olive oil A yellow oil pressed from olives. It is used in cooking, making soap, etc.

O·lym·pi·a [ō·lim′pē·ə] *n.* **1** In ancient Greece, a plain where the Olympic games were held. **2** The capital of Washington, at the south end of Puget Sound.

O·lym·pi·an [ō·lim′pē·ən] **1** *adj.* Of or having to do with Mount Olympus or with Olympia. **2** *n.* Any of the twelve chief gods who dwelt on Mount Olympus. **3** *adj.* Godlike in manner; majestic. **4** *n.* A contestant in the Olympic games.

O·lym·pic games [ō·lim′pik] **1** In ancient Greece, athletic games, races, and contests in poetry held every four years at the plain of Olympia as a festival in honor of Zeus. **2** A modern international athletic competition held every four years in a different country. Also **the Olympics.**

O·lym·pus [ō·lim′pəs], **Mount** The highest mountain in Greece, regarded in Greek myths as the home of the gods. Also **Olympus.**

O·ma·ha [ō′mə·hä] *n.* A city in eastern Nebraska.

o·me·ga [ō·mē′gə *or* ō·meg′ə] *n.* **1** The last letter in the Greek alphabet. **2** The end; the

last. ◆ The Greek word for *big* is *mega*. The Greek word for *little* or *small* is *micron*. Therefore *omega* and *omicron*, which are names of letters in the Greek alphabet, mean simply *big o* (o + mega) and *little o* (o + micron). You can find these Greek roots in many English words, such as *megaphone* (literally, *big sound*) and *micrometer* (literally, *small measure*).

om·e·let or **om·e·lette** [om′lit *or* om′ə·lit] *n.* Eggs beaten together with water or milk and cooked by frying or sometimes by baking.

o·men [ō′mən] *n.* Something that is looked on as a prophetic sign of what is going to happen: Breaking a mirror is regarded as a bad *omen*.

om·i·nous [om′ə·nəs] *adj.* Threatening or foreboding, like a bad omen: an *ominous* look. **— om′i·nous·ly** *adv.*

o·mis·sion [ō·mish′ən] *n.* **1** The act of leaving out or omitting: the *omission* of a name from a list. **2** A being omitted. **3** Anything omitted: a serious *omission*.

o·mit [ō·mit′] *v.* **o·mit·ted, o·mit·ting** **1** To leave out; fail to include: I *omitted* a section of my speech. **2** To fail to do, make, etc.; neglect: Never *omit* an opportunity to learn.

om·ni·bus [om′nə·bəs *or* om′nə·bus] **1** *n.* A bus. **2** *n.* A printed collection: an *omnibus* of short stories. **3** *adj.* Covering many things: Congress passed an *omnibus* tax bill.

om·nip·o·tent [om·nip′ə·tənt] *adj.* Not limited in power or authority; almighty. **— the Omnipotent** God. **— om·nip′o·tence** *n.*

om·ni·pres·ent [om′nə·prez′ənt] *adj.* Present everywhere at the same time. **— om′ni·pres′ence** *n.*

om·nis·cient [om·nish′ənt] *adj.* Knowing all things. **— om·nis′cience** *n.*

om·niv·o·rous [om·niv′ər·əs] *adj.* **1** Eating both animal and vegetable food. **2** Eating food of all kinds. **3** Eagerly taking in everything: an *omnivorous* reader. **— om·niv′o·rous·ly** *adv.*

on [on] **1** *prep.* Above and supported by: lying *on* the ground. **2** *prep.* In or to the surface of: a blow *on* the head. **3** *prep.* Attached to or suspended from: a marionette *on* a string. **4** *prep.* Along the course of: Be *on* your way. **5** *prep.* Near; next to: the town *on* the river. **6** *prep.* At the time of: He arrived *on* my birthday. **7** *prep.* In a condition of: The building is *on* fire. **8** *prep.* By means of; using: We came *on* foot; Lions live *on* meat. **9** *prep.* Confirmed by or based on: *on* my honor. **10** *prep.* With reference to: to bet *on* a race. **11** *prep.* Concerning; about: a book *on* physics. **12** *prep.* Occupied with: The nurse is *on* duty all night. **13** *prep.* As a result of: to make a profit *on* tips. **14** *prep.* Toward: We marched *on* the enemy's camp. **15** *prep.* Directed against: to make war *on* crime. **16** *prep.* In the number of; among: Are you *on* the team? **17** *adv.* In a position of contact, covering, etc: He has his new jacket *on*. **18** *adv*. In the direction of something: He looked *on* while they argued. **19** *adv*. Ahead in time or space: further *on*. **20** *adv*. Continuously: The music played *on*. **21** *adv*. In or into existence or operation: Turn the fan *on*. **22** *adj*. Being in operation, progress, etc.: The radio is *on*. **— and so on** And like what has gone before; et cetera. **— on and off** Now and then; occasionally. **— on and on** Without interruption; continuously. ◆ See notes under ONTO and UPON.

once [wuns] **1** *adv*. One time; without repetition: I saw her *once*. **2** *n*. One time: For *once* I'm right. **3** *adv*. At any time; ever: If *once* you visit New York, you will never forget it. **4** *conj*. As soon as; whenever: *Once* he gets here, we can start the meeting. **5** *adv*. Formerly: a *once* handsome man. **— all at once 1** All at the same time. **2** All of a sudden. **— at once 1** Immediately. **2** At the same time. **— once and for all** or **once for all** Finally. **— once in a while** Occasionally. **— once upon a time** At a time long past; long ago.

on·com·ing [on′kum′ing] **1** *adj*. Approaching: an *oncoming* storm. **2** *n*. An approach: the *oncoming* of spring.

one [wun] **1** *n*. (*sometimes written* **l, i,** *or* **1**) A single unit, the first and lowest whole number. **2** *adj*. Being a single person or thing: *one* child; *one* book. **3** *n*. A single person or thing: Choose either the red *one* or the black *one*. **4** *pron*. Someone or something; anyone or anything: *One* of us will go; *One* of the dresses will fit you. **5** *adj*. Indicating a single person or thing not specified: *one* day in June. **6** *adj*. Indicating a person or thing as contrasted with another: from *one* end of the street to the other. **7** *adj*. Closely united or alike: They were *one* in spirit. **8** *pron*. Anyone; any person, including the speaker: *One* hopes for a solution to the problem. **— all one 1** Of equal importance. **2** Of no importance. **— at one** In agreement or harmony. **— one and all** Everybody. **— one another** Each other. **— one by one** One following another. ◆ See note under ANY. ◆ Most people today use *one another* and *each other* interchangeably, but traditionally *each other* applies to only two people and *one another* to more than two.

one·ness [wun′nis] *n*. **1** The quality or condition of being one; unity; sameness. **2** Agreement: a *oneness* of purpose.

on·er·ous [on′ər·əs] *adj*. Hard to bear; burdensome; oppressive: *onerous* work; *onerous* duties.

one·self [wun′self′] *pron*. One's very own self: used as the object of a verb or preposition when *one* is the subject: One should apply *oneself* in school; to look out for *oneself*.

one-sid·ed [wun′sī′did] *adj*. **1** Having only one side. **2** Favoring one side; biased; unfair: a *one-sided* news report. **3** Having unequal or unbalanced sides.

one-way [wun′wā′] *adj*. Moving or permitting movement in one direction only: *one-way* traffic.

on·ion [un′yən] *n*. The juicy bulb of a plant of the lily family, having a strong odor and taste. Onions are eaten raw or used in cooking.

on·look·er [on′look′ər] *n*. A person who looks on but takes no part; spectator.

on·ly [ōn′lē] **1** *adv*. By oneself or itself alone: It is *only* by hard work that we'll succeed. **2** *adv*. Without others: He has *only* two helpers. **3** *adv*. Simply; just: I'd be *only* too happy to come. **4** *adv*. Exclusively; solely: The cake is meant *only* for you. **5** *adj*. Alone in its class; sole: an *only* child; her *only* doll. **6** *adj*. Standing alone because of excellence: This is the *only* ship to take to Europe. **7** *conj*. Except that; but: The weather is fine, *only* it is too cold.

on·rush [on′rush′] *n*. A forward rush or flow.

on·set [on′set′] *n*. **1** An attack: an enemy *onset*. **2** An initial stage: the *onset* of an illness.

on·shore [on′shôr′] *adv*., *adj*. To, toward, or on the shore.

on·slaught [on′slôt′] *n*. A very violent attack.

On·tar·i·o [on·târ′ē·ō] *n*. A province in SE Canada.

Ontario, Lake The smallest of the five Great Lakes.

on·to [on′tōō] *prep*. **1** Upon the top of: The cat jumped *onto* the table. **2** To and upon: The team came *onto* the field. **3** *informal* Aware of; informed about: I'm *onto* your tricks. ◆ In most cases either *onto* or *on* may be used when motion into position is indicated, but sometimes *onto* makes the meaning clearer. Compare *They moved onto the dance floor* with *They moved on the dance floor*.

on·ward [on′wərd] **1** *adv*. Forward in space or time; ahead: They moved *onward*. **2** *adj*. Moving or tending to be forward or ahead: an *onward* rush.

on·wards [on′wərdz] *adv*. Onward.

on·yx [on′iks] *n*. A variety of quartz having layers of different colors, used as a gem and for other ornaments.

Onyx

ooze [ōōz] *v*. **oozed, ooz·ing,** *n*. **1** *v*. To flow or leak out slowly or gradually: Water *oozed* through the crack in the dam. **2** *v*. To escape little by little: My courage *oozed* away. **3** *n*. A slow, gradual leak. **4** *n*. Something that oozes. **5** *n*. Slimy mud or moist, spongy soil, as that which is found on the bottom of a body of water.

Ketchup oozing from a hamburger

oo·zy [ōō′zē] *adj*. **oo·zi·er, oo·zi·est** Of or resembling ooze; slimy.

o·pal [ō′pəl] *n*. A mineral found in many varieties, some of which reflect light in an iridescent play of color and are used as gems. ◆ *Opal* comes from a Sanskrit word meaning *precious stone*.

o·pal·es·cent [ō′pəl·es′ənt] *adj*. Having an iridescent play of colors, as an opal. **— o′pal·es′·cence** *n*.

o·paque [ō·pāk′] *adj.* **1** Not allowing light to pass through; not transparent. **2** Having no shine or luster; dull. **3** Hard to understand; not simple. **4** Dull-witted; dense. **— o·paque′ly** *adv.* **— o·paque′ness** *n.*

ope [ōp] *v.* **oped, op·ing** To open: used mostly in poems.

o·pen [ō′pən] **1** *adj.* Not fastened, shut, covered, or closed: an *open* door; an *open* drawer; an *open* book. **2** *adj.* Allowing people or things to pass through, enter, or leave: an *open* street; an *open* drain pipe. **3** *adj.* Having no obstacles or barriers; not enclosed or hemmed in: an *open* field. **4** *n. use* A clear space, as the outdoors: to be in *the open.* **5** *adj.* Having no covering, top, roof, etc.: an *open* car. **6** *adj.* Available to all; public: an *open* golf tournament. **7** *adj.* Not filled; available: The job is *open.* **8** *v.* To make or become open: *Open* the book to page 70; The door *opened* quickly. **9** *v.* To spread out, expand, or unfold: The parachute *opened.* **10** *v.* To begin: He *opened* the meeting with a brief welcome. **11** *v.* To be an entrance; lead: The door *opened* onto a courtyard. **12** *adj.* Not settled or decided: an *open* question. **13** *v.* To make ready for business, use, etc.: to *open* a charge account. **14** *adj.* Having spaces, holes, or openings between parts: an *open* weave. **15** *adj.* Not secret or hidden: *open* hostility. **16** *n. use* A condition in which nothing is hidden or secret: Get the facts out into *the open.* **17** *adj.* Ready or willing to consider other views, opinions, etc.: an *open* mind. **18** *adj.* Generous: to give with an *open* hand. **19** *adj.* In hunting or fishing, having no limits or prohibitions: an *open* season on rabbits. **20** *adj.* Ending in a vowel or diphthong: said about a syllable, as the final syllable in *tomato.* **— open one's eyes** To make very clear to one the real meaning or significance of an action or situation. **— open to** To be willing to think about or consider opinions, etc.: He is not *open to* all your ideas. **— o′pen·er** *n.* **— o′pen·ly** *adv.* **— o′pen·ness** *n.*

open air The outdoors. **— o′pen-air** [ō′pən·âr′] *adj.*

o·pen-eyed [ō′pən·īd′] *adj.* **1** Having the eyes open; watchful. **2** Amazed: in *open-eyed* wonder.

o·pen-hand·ed [ō′pən·han′did] *adj.* Generous.

o·pen-heart·ed [ō′pən·här′tid] *adj.* Disclosing thoughts and feelings freely; frank.

o·pen-hearth [ō′pən·härth′] *adj.* **1** Having to do with a process of making steel in which the materials are melted in a shallow furnace open at each end to admit fuel and air. **2** Describing steel made by this process.

open house A social or somewhat festive occasion when a house, school, etc., is open to all who wish to visit it.

o·pen·ing [ō′pən·ing] *n.* **1** The act of becoming open or causing to be open. **2** A hole, passage, or vacant space. **3** The first part or beginning: The *opening* of the novel was dull. **4** An opportunity or chance: He waited for an *opening* to tell his story. **5** A job that is available: There are *openings* now.

o·pen-mind·ed [ō′pən·mīn′did] *adj.* Willing to consider new views, opinions, etc.

o·pen·work [ō′pən·wûrk′] *n.* Any product or ornamental work containing many holes or openings as part of its pattern or design.

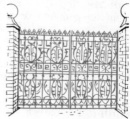
An openwork gate

op·er·a [op′ər·ə *or* op′rə] *n.* A kind of play set to music in which all or most of the lines are sung rather than spoken. The singers in an opera are usually accompanied by an orchestra ◆ *Opera* and *opus* come from the same Latin word, *opus*, meaning *work*, but whereas English *opus* comes directly from the Latin, *opera* comes through Italian, in which it developed a new meaning.

opera glasses Small binoculars for use in a theater.

op·er·ate [op′ə·rāt] *v.* **op·er·at·ed, op·er·at·ing 1** To work or run: Can you *operate* this machine?; The pump *operates* by hand. **2** To manage or be in charge of: to *operate* a business. **3** To produce a certain result: This cleaner *operates* mostly on grease spots. **4** To perform surgery: to *operate* on an animal.

Opera glasses

op·er·at·ic [op′ə·rat′ik] *adj.* Of, like, or suitable for opera: an *operatic* voice.

op·er·a·tion [op′ə·rā′shən] *n.* **1** The act, method, or process of operating: The engine's *operation* was complicated. **2** The condition of working or being in action: The train had been in *operation* for 20 years. **3** A series of actions that bring about a certain result: There are three *operations* in making this drawing. **4** An act performed on the body, usually with instruments, to cure or remedy a disease or injury. **5** A military or naval activity or campaign.

op·er·a·tive [op′ər·ə·tiv *or* op′ə·rā′tiv] **1** *adj.* In operation or in force: The law is not yet *operative.* **2** *adj.* Having to do with work or with mechanical operations: a new *operative* schedule. **3** *n.* A skilled worker or operator. **4** *n.* A detective or secret agent.

op·er·a·tor [op′ə·rā′tər] *n.* **1** A person who works or operates a machine or mechanism. **2** A person who owns or runs a business, factory, etc.

3 A symbol that indicates a mathematical process: +, −, and √ are *operators*.

op·e·ret·ta [op'ə·ret'ə] *n.* A form of light, often humorous opera with some spoken lines.

oph·thal·mol·o·gy [of'thal·mol'ə·jē] *n.* The medical science that deals with the structure, function, and diseases of the eye. **— oph'thal·mol'o·gist** *n.*

o·pi·ate [ō'pē·it *or* ō'pē·āt] **1** *n.* A medicine containing opium or a drug derived from it, used to make one sleepy or to lessen pain. **2** *adj.* Containing opium. **3** *n.* Anything that brings relaxation or sleepiness. **4** *adj.* Bringing about sleep or freedom from pain.

o·pine [ō·pīn'] *v.* **o·pined, o·pin·ing** To have or express as an opinion; think: now used only in humorous writing or talking.

o·pin·ion [ə·pin'yən *or* ō·pin'yən] *n.* **1** Something a person believes to be true but of which he is not absolutely certain: It is his *opinion* that we will win the game. **2** A judgment or estimate of the excellence or value of a person or thing: What is your *opinion* of him? **3** A more or less formal judgment made by an expert. ◆ See FACT.

o·pin·ion·at·ed [ə·pin'yən·ā'tid] *adj.* Holding very stubbornly to one's own opinions.

o·pi·um [ō'pē·əm] *n.* The thickened juice of a special kind of poppy, used as a drug to cause sleep and dull pain. Opium contains morphine.

o·pos·sum [ə·pos'əm *or* pos'əm] *n., pl.* **o·pos·sums** or **o·pos·sum** A small animal common in the southern U.S. that lives in trees, pretends to be dead when threatened, and carries its young in a pouch. ◆ *Opossum* comes from an American Indian word meaning *white animal*.

Opossum, about 17 in. long

op·po·nent [ə·pō'nənt] *n.* A person who opposes another, as in sports, war, debating, etc.

op·por·tune [op'ər·t(y)ōōn'] *adj.* **1** Fortunate; suitable: the *opportune* coming of darkness. **2** Timely: an *opportune* remark. ◆ *Opportune* comes from a Latin word meaning *toward port*, because in the age of sailboats, winds that blew toward port were considered a good omen.

op·por·tu·nist [op'ər·t(y)ōō'nist] *n.* A person who uses any means or opportunity to get what he wants done, not caring if what he does is right or wrong. **— op'por·tu'nism** *n.*

op·por·tu·ni·ty [op'ər·t(y)ōō'nə·tē] *n., pl.* **op·por·tu·ni·ties** A right or convenient time, occasion, or circumstance; good chance: an *opportunity* to appear on TV.

op·pose [ə·pōz'] *v.* **op·posed, op·pos·ing 1** To act or be in opposition to; resist; fight: to *oppose* a suggestion. **2** To set against or put in contrast: Strength is *opposed* to weakness.

op·po·site [op'ə·zit] **1** *adj.* Located or placed on the other side or on each side of a space or object: *opposite* ends of the room. **2** *adj.* Facing or moving the other way; contrary: *opposite*

directions. **3** *adj.* Completely different in all ways: *opposite* opinions. **4** *n.* Someone or something that is opposite: He is the *opposite* of his brother. **5** *prep.* Across from; facing: The store is *opposite* the school. **— op'po·site·ly** *adv.*

op·po·si·tion [op'ə·zish'ən] *n.* **1** The act of opposing or being against something; resistance. **2** The condition of being opposite or contrary: the *opposition* of left to right. **3** An obstacle or hindrance. **4** (*often written* **Opposition**) A political party opposed to the party in power.

op·press [ə·pres'] *v.* **1** To burden or keep down by unjust use of force or authority: Tyranny *oppressed* the country. **2** To make sad or uneasy; depress; worry: His gloomy predictions *oppressed* us all. **— op·pres'sor** *n.*

op·pres·sion [ə·presh'ən] *n.* **1** The act of oppressing: the bully's *oppression* of a small boy. **2** A hardship, privation, or cruelty. **3** The condition of being oppressed: the *oppression* of the slaves. **4** A feeling of being overloaded with burdens, problems, or worry.

op·pres·sive [ə·pres'iv] *adj.* **1** Burdensome; harsh; cruel: *oppressive* laws. **2** Producing a state of oppression: *oppressive* heat. **— op·pres'sive·ly** *adv.* **— op·pres'sive·ness** *n.*

op·pro·bri·ous [ə·prō'brē·əs] *adj.* **1** Expressing scorn, abuse, or hate: *opprobrious* language. **2** Deserving hate or contempt; shameful: *opprobrious* conduct. **— op·pro'bri·ous·ly** *adv.*

op·pro·bri·um [ə·prō'brē·əm] *n.* **1** Disgrace or scorn brought about by vicious, shameful conduct. **2** A cause of such disgrace or scorn.

op·tic [op'tik] *adj.* Of or having to do with the eye or vision: the *optic* nerve.

op·ti·cal [op'ti·kəl] *adj.* **1** Made to improve vision: an *optical* glass. **2** Having to do with the act of seeing. **3** Of or related to optics. **— op'ti·cal·ly** *adv.*

op·ti·cian [op·tish'ən] *n.* A person who makes or sells optical goods, as eyeglasses, etc.

optic nerve The nerve that carries the sensations of seeing from the eye to the brain.

op·tics [op'tiks] *n.* The science that deals with light, vision, and sight. ◆ See -ICS.

op·ti·mism [op'tə·miz'əm] *n.* **1** The tendency to see things on their bright side. **2** The belief that everything in life works out to a good end. **3** The doctrine that the world we live in is the best of all possible worlds.

op·ti·mist [op'tə·mist] *n.* A person who always looks on the bright side of things, believing that everything works out well in the end.

op·ti·mis·tic [op'tə·mis'tik] *adj.* **1** Full of hope and cheerfulness: an *optimistic* person. **2** Having to do with optimism: an *optimistic* theory. **— op'ti·mis'ti·cal·ly** *adv.*

op·ti·mum [op'tə·məm] *n., pl.* **op·ti·ma** [op'tə·mə] *or* **op·ti·mums,** *adj.* **1** *n.* The condition, amount, or degree producing the best result. **2** *adj.* Producing the best results: an *optimum* situation.

op·tion [op'shən] *n.* **1** The act of choosing. **2** The right or freedom to choose. **3** The privilege of buying or selling something at a certain price within a certain time.

op·tion·al [op′shən·əl] *adj.* Left to a person's own choice or preference; not required.

op·tom·e·trist [op·tom′ə·trist] *n.* A person whose work or profession is optometry.

op·tom·e·try [op·tom′ə·trē] *n.* Measurement of the range and power of sight and the prescription of glasses to correct eye defects.

op·u·lence [op′yə·ləns] *n.* **1** Great riches; wealth. **2** A great plenty or abundance.

op·u·lent [op′yə·lənt] *adj.* **1** Possessing great wealth; rich: an *opulent* businessman. **2** Showing great wealth; luxurious; costly; rich: He owns an *opulent* summer home. **3** Plentiful; abundant: an *opulent* supply of water.

o·pus [ō′pəs] *n., pl.* **op·er·a** [op′ər·ə] or **o·pus·es** Any work or composition, especially a musical work. ◆ See OPERA.

or [ôr] *conj.* A word that: **1** Introduces an alternative: stop *or* go; red *or* white. **2** Offers a choice of a series: Do you want milk *or* tea *or* chocolate? **3** Introduces a word or phrase that has the same meaning as the word or phrase immediately before it: a culinary school *or* a school of cooking. **4** Indicates uncertainty: He lives in Chicago *or* thereabouts. **5** Introduces an alternative when the first of two choices comes after *either* or *whether*: It must be either you *or* he.

-or A suffix meaning: The person or thing that, as in *competitor*, a person who competes.

or·a·cle [ôr′ə·kəl] *n.* **1** A priest through whom the gods were supposed to speak or prophesy to the ancient Greeks and Romans. **2** The place where this occurred. The oracle of Apollo was at Delphi. **3** The prophecy thus given. **4** Any person thought of as having great wisdom.

o·rac·u·lar [ô·rak′yə·lər] *adj.* **1** Of, having to do with, or like an oracle. **2** Difficult to understand. **3** Wise or prophetic.

o·ral [ôr′əl *or* ō′rəl] **1** *adj.* Uttered through the mouth; spoken. **2** *adj.* Of, given through, or situated near the mouth. **3** *n.* (*usually pl.*) An examination taken by a student working for an advanced degree, in which the student speaks his answers aloud. **— o′ral·ly** *adv.*

or·ange [ôr′inj *or* or′inj] **1** *n.* A round, reddish yellow, juicy fruit. **2** *n.* The tree it grows on, having shiny evergreen leaves and fragrant white flowers. **3** *n., adj.* Reddish yellow. ◆ *Orange* comes originally from a Persian word.

or·ange·ade [ôr′inj·ād′ *or* or′inj·ād′] *n.* A drink made of orange juice, sugar, and water.

orange blossom The white, fragrant blossom of the orange tree, often carried by brides.

orange pe·koe [pē′kō] A very fine black tea of India, Ceylon, and Java.

o·rang-ou·tang [ō·rang′ə·tang *or* ō·rang′ōō·tang] *n.* Another word for ORANG-UTAN.

o·rang-u·tan [ō·rang′ə·tan *or* ō·rang′ōō·tan] *n.* A large ape having brownish red hair and extremely long arms, found in Borneo and Sumatra. ◆ *Orang-utan* comes from two Malay words meaning *forest man.*

Orang-utan, about 54 in. high

o·rate [ôr′āt *or* ô·rāt′] *v.* **o·rat·ed, o·rat·ing** To speak in a pompous manner.

o·ra·tion [ô·rā′shən] *n.* A serious public speech, usually given at a formal occasion.

or·a·tor [ôr′ə·tər] *n.* **1** A person who delivers an oration. **2** Any good public speaker.

or·a·tor·i·cal [ôr′ə·tôr′i·kəl] *adj.* Of, like, or having to do with an orator or oratory.

or·a·to·ri·o [ôr′ə·tôr′ē·ō] *n., pl.* **or·a·to·ri·os** A large musical composition for solo voices, chorus, and orchestra, usually dramatizing a sacred story but without scenery or acting.

or·a·to·ry[1] [ôr′ə·tôr′ē] *n.* The art of speaking before an audience.

or·a·to·ry[2] [ôr′ə·tôr′ē] *n., pl.* **or·a·to·ries** A place for prayer, as a private chapel.

orb [ôrb] *n.* **1** A sphere or globe. **2** A heavenly body, as the sun or a planet. **3** The eye: used mostly in poems.

or·bit [ôr′bit] **1** *n.* The path taken by a planet, comet, satellite, space vehicle, etc., as it moves around its center of attraction. Orbits are usually in the form of ellipses. **2** *n.* The probable position of an electron in relation to its atomic nucleus. **3** *v.* To move or cause to move in or as if in an orbit.

satellite at apogee —

— earth

satellite at perigee

Orbit of a satellite

or·bi·tal [ôr′bit·əl] *adj.* Of, related to, or moving in an orbit: an *orbital* electron.

or·chard [ôr′chərd] *n.* **1** A large group of trees, planted and cultivated for their products. **2** The ground on which these trees grow.

or·ches·tra [ôr′kəs·trə] *n.* **1** A group of musicians playing together, especially a large group including violinists, cellists, etc. **2** The instruments such musicians play. **3** In a theater, the place just in front of the stage where the musicians sit. **4** The seats and seating area on the main floor of a theater. **— or·ches·tral** [ôr·kes′trəl] *adj.*

or·ches·trate [ôr′kəs·trāt] *v.* **or·ches·trat·ed, or·ches·trat·ing** To arrange (music) for an orchestra. **— or′ches·tra′tion** *n.*

or·chid [ôr′kid] **1** *n.* Any of a large number of plants bearing often beautiful and irregular flowers, usually having three petals of which one is large and shaped differently from the others. **2** *n.*, *adj.* Pale, rosy purple.

or·dain [ôr·dān'] *v.* **1** To order; decree: The king *ordained* a great council. **2** To arrange to happen; predestine: said of God, fate, etc.: Fate *ordained* that he should be famous. **3** To make (someone) a minister or priest.

or·deal [ôr·dēl' *or* ôr·dē'əl *or* ôr'dēl] *n.* **1** A very difficult or trying experience. **2** A former method of trying a person for a crime. The accused was put through some painful physical tests which were supposed to do him no harm if he were innocent.

or·der [ôr'dər] **1** *n.* A condition in which everything is in its proper or logical place: This messy room must be put in *order*. **2** *n.* A special or particular arrangement or placement of things one after the other: List the pupils in *order* of age. **3** *v.* To put in a proper or particular condition or arrangement: You must *order* your life. **4** *n.* The customary or set method, form, or procedure for doing something: the *order* of conducting a meeting. **5** *n.* An existing state; condition: This machine is not in working *order*. **6** *n.* A social condition of peace and harmony: to restore *order* after a riot. **7** *n.* A command or direction to do something: Here are your *orders*. **8** *v.* To give a command or direction to: I *order* you to stay. **9** *v.* To demand or ask for: She *ordered* more homework from us all. **10** *n.* A demand or request, usually written, to buy, sell, or supply something: an *order* for groceries. **11** *n.* That which is bought or received. **12** *v.* To give an order for: to *order* a new suit. **13** *n.* (*often written* **Order**) A body of persons united by some common bond or purpose: the Masonic *Order*. **14** *n.* A monastic or religious body: an *order* of monks. **15** *n.* (*often written* **Order**) A group of persons honored in some way, or the ribbon, medal, etc., they are entitled to wear: The *Order* of the Garter is the highest *order* of knighthood in Great Britain. **16** *n.* (*usually pl.*) Any of the various ranks or grades of the Christian ministry: Is he in *orders*? **17** *n.* In biology, a grouping of related animals or plants ranking below the class and above the family. **18** *n.* A kind or degree: She has talent of a high *order*. **19** *n.* A style of ancient architecture, usually known by the style or character of its columns: Doric, Ionic, and Corinthian are the main *orders* of ancient buildings. **— by order** In accordance with an order given by someone in authority. **— call to order** To ask for quiet, so as to begin work, start a meeting, etc. **— in order 1** In accordance with the rules. **2** In a proper or working condition. **3** Neat; tidy. **— in order that** So that; to the end that. **— in order to** For the purpose of. **— in short order** Quickly; without delay. **— on the order of** Similar to; like. **— order about** *or* **order around** To command to do this or that or go here or there. **— out of order 1** Not working; broken. **2** Not according to rules or proper procedure. **3** Not in its proper place, arrangement, or se-

quence. **4** Not suitable or proper. **— to order** According to the wishes or specifications of the buyer. **— take orders 1** To obey. **2** To become a minister or priest.

or·der·ly [ôr'dər·lē] *adj.*, *n.*, *pl.* **or·der·lies** **1** *adj.* Neat and tidy: an *orderly* kitchen. **2** *adj.* Peaceful and well-behaved: an *orderly* assembly. **3** *adj.* Characterized by or liking order or method: He has an *orderly* mind. **4** *n.* A soldier who performs various services for an officer. **5** *n.* A male worker in a hospital who helps the doctors and nurses. **— or'der·li·ness** *n.*

or·di·nal number [ôr'də·nəl] A number that shows place or order in a series: Second, third, and fifth are *ordinal numbers*, two, three, and five the corresponding cardinal numbers.

or·di·nance [ôr'də·nəns] *n.* An order, law, or decree, especially one made by a city government: Our town has an *ordinance* against Sunday movies.

or·di·nar·i·ly [ôr'də·ner'ə·lē *or* ôr'də·nâr'ə·lē] *adv.* Commonly; usually; normally.

or·di·nar·y [ôr'də·ner'ē] *adj.* **1** Of common or everyday occurrence; usual: an *ordinary* problem. **2** Average in quality or ability; not special: an *ordinary* play. **3** Normal; regular: The *ordinary* tuition is very high. **— out of the ordinary** Not common or usual; very special.

or·di·nate [ôr'də·nit] *n.* On a graph, the distance of a point from the horizontal axis.

or·di·na·tion [ôr'də·nā'shən] *n.* **1** The act or ceremony of ordaining a minister or priest. **2** The condition of being ordained.

ord·nance [ôrd'nəns] *n.* **1** Military equipment, as weapons, ammunition, etc. **2** Cannon or artillery.

The ordinate of *P* is 3. The ordinate of *Q* is −5.

ore [ôr *or* ōr] *n.* A natural substance, as a rock or mineral, that contains a valuable metal or other substance: gold *ore*; sulfur *ore*.

Ore. or **Oreg.** Abbreviations of OREGON.

Or·e·gon [ôr'ə·gən *or* ôr'ə·gon] *n.* A state in the NW U.S., on the Pacific Ocean.

or·gan [ôr'gən] *n.* **1** A musical instrument consisting of a collection of pipes that are made to sound when, by pressing down a key or pedal, compressed air is sent through them. **2** Any musical instrument similar to this in sound or in some aspect of its mechanism. **3** Any part of a plant or animal that performs some definite function: The heart is a body *organ*; The stamen is a plant *organ*. **4** A newspaper or magazine. **5** An agency for or a means of getting something done: Congress is an *organ* of government.

or·gan·dy *or* **or·gan·die** [ôr'gən·dē] *n.*, *pl.* **or·gan·dies** A thin, crisp, cotton cloth, used for dresses, collars, cuffs, etc.

organ grinder A street musician who plays a small, portable hand organ.

or·gan·ic [ôr·gan′ik] *adj.* **1** Of, having, or related to bodily organs. **2** Affecting or altering the shape of an organ or part: *organic* disease. **3** Of, like, or produced by animals or plants: an *organic* substance. **4** Of or related to compounds containing carbon. **5** Having parts that are arranged according to a system. **6** Basic or fundamental. **— or·gan′i·cal·ly** *adv.*

Organ grinder

organic chemistry The branch of chemistry that studies compounds of carbon.

or·gan·ism [ôr′gən·iz′əm] *n.* **1** An animal or plant considered as a structure of interdependent organs or parts. **2** Any structure or thing made up of many smaller, interdependent parts: A city is a social *organism*.

or·gan·ist [ôr′gən·ist] *n.* A person who plays an organ.

or·gan·i·za·tion [ôr′gən·ə·zā′shən] *n.* **1** The act of organizing. **2** The condition of being organized. **3** The manner in which something is organized: the complicated *organization* of an ant hill. **4** A number of people systematically united for some special work or purpose. ¶3

or·gan·ize [ôr′gən·īz] *v.* **or·gan·ized, or·gan·iz·ing 1** To form or be formed as a whole: to *organize* a club. **2** To come or bring together for some special work or purpose: to *organize* workers into a union. **3** To arrange or put in good order: He *organizes* his time well. **4** To cause to have an organic unity or structure. **— or′gan·iz′er** *n.* ¶3

or·gy [ôr′jē] *n., pl.* **or·gies** A wild, drunken party or festivity.

o·ri·el [ôr′ē·əl] *n.* A bay window, especially one built out from a wall and resting on a support.

o·ri·ent [*v.* ôr′ē·ent, *n. and adj.* ôr′ē·ənt] **1** *v.* To place, set, or adjust in some position, especially in relation to the points of the compass. **2** *v.* To adjust or set right according to the facts or a particular situation: He *oriented* himself quickly to college life. **3** *n.* The East: used mostly in poems. **4** *adj.* Resembling sunrise; bright: used mostly in poems. **— the Orient** The countries east of Europe; Asia, especially eastern Asia. ◆ *Orient* comes from a Latin word meaning *rising,* because the sun rises in the east.

O·ri·en·tal [ôr′ē·en·təl] **1** *adj.* (*sometimes written* oriental) Of or from the Orient. **2** *n.* A member of one of the peoples native to the Orient. **3** *n.* A person of Chinese or Japanese ancestry.

o·ri·en·tate [ôr′ē·en·tāt′] *v.* **o·ri·en·tat·ed, o·ri·en·tat·ing** To orient.

o·ri·en·ta·tion [ôr′ē·en·tā′shən] *n.* **1** The act of orienting: His *orientation* to army life was difficult. **2** An oriented condition.

or·i·fice [ôr′ə·fis] *n.* An opening or hole, as into a larger space: The tube has two *orifices*.

or·i·gin [ôr′ə·jin] *n.* **1** The beginning of the existence of anything: the *origin* of baseball. **2** The primary cause or source: the *origin* of a fire. **3** Parentage; ancestry.

o·rig·i·nal [ə·rij′ə·nəl] **1** *adj.* Of or belonging to the beginning of something; earliest; first: The *original* rules of the game were different. **2** *adj.* Produced by one's own mind and work; not copied: an *original* poem. **3** *n.* The original creation or model from which a copy, reproduction, or translation is made. **4** *n.* The first form of anything. **5** *adj.* Able to produce things without copying or imitating others; creative; fresh; inventive: an *original* student. **6** *n.* A person or thing represented in a painting, novel, etc. **7** *n.* An unusual or odd person.

o·rig·i·nal·i·ty [ə·rij′ə·nal′ə·tē] *n.* **1** The ability to be new and original in what one does or thinks: *Originality* is important in her job. **2** Newness or freshness of design, style, idea, etc.: The *originality* of the new cars is startling.

o·rig·i·nal·ly [ə·rij′ə·nəl·ē] *adv.* **1** At the beginning; at first: *Originally,* there were no flowers in our yard. **2** In a manner that is new, fresh, or unusual.

o·rig·i·nate [ə·rij′ə·nāt] *v.* **o·rig·i·nat·ed, o·rig·i·nat·ing** To bring or come into existence: to *originate* an idea; The rumor *originated* with me. **— o·rig′i·na′tion** *n.*

o·rig·i·na·tor [ə·rij′ə·nā′tər] *n.* A person who begins or creates something.

O·ri·no·co [ôr′ə·nō′kō] *n.* A river in Venezuela, flowing into the Atlantic Ocean.

o·ri·ole [ôr′ē·ōl] *n.* Any of various European and American songbirds having brilliant black and yellow or black and orange plumage.

O·ri·on [ō·rī′ən] *n.* **1** In Greek and Roman myths, a giant hunter who pursued the Pleiades and was killed by Diana. **2** A constellation near the equator, pictured by the ancients as a hunter with a belt and sword.

or·i·son [ôr′i·zən] *n.* (*usually pl.*) A prayer: used mostly in poems.

Ork·ney Islands [ôrk′nē] A group of islands north of Scotland.

Or·lon [ôr′lon] *n.* A synthetic fiber, not badly affected by heat, light, or common chemicals. It is widely used for clothing, sails, curtains, etc.: a trademark. Also written **orlon.**

or·na·ment [*n.* ôr′nə·mənt, *v.* ôr′nə·ment] **1** *n.* Something that makes another thing more beautiful; a decoration. **2** *v.* To furnish with ornaments; decorate. **3** *n.* A person thought of as bringing honor or credit to his school, town, country, etc.

---

add, āce, câre, pälm;   end, ēqual;   it, īce;   odd, ōpen, ôrder;   to͝ok, po͞ol;   up, bûrn;
ə = a in *above,* e in *sicken,* i in *possible,* o in *melon,* u in *circus;*   yo͞o = u in *fuse;*   oil;   pout;
check;   ring;   thin;   this;   zh in *vision.*   For ¶ reference, see page 64 · HOW TO

or·na·men·tal [ôr′nə·men′təl] *adj.* Like or serving as an ornament: *ornamental* lace.

or·na·men·ta·tion [ôr′nə·men·tā′shən] *n.* **1** The act of ornamenting. **2** The condition of being ornamented. **3** Something that ornaments.

or·nate [ôr·nāt′] *adj.* **1** Having much or too much decoration. **2** Fancy or showy: An *ornate* style of dress. **— or·nate′ly** *adv.*

or·ner·y [ôr′nər·ē *or* ôrn′rē] *adj.* *U.S. informal* **1** Hard to manage; stubborn: an *ornery* mule. **2** Mean; ugly; low: an *ornery* trick.

or·ni·thol·o·gy [ôr′nə·thol′· ə·jē] *n.* A branch of zoology dealing with birds. **— or′· ni·thol′o·gist** *n.*

An ornate bed

o·ro·tund [ôr′ə·tund] *adj.* **1** Full, clear, and resonant: an *orotund* voice. **2** Pompous and elaborate: an *orotund* speaking style.

or·phan [ôr′fən] **1** *n.* A child whose parents are dead. **2** *adj. use:* an *orphan* asylum. **3** *n.* A child who has only one parent living. **4** *v.* To make an orphan of: The plague *orphaned* all four children.

or·phan·age [ôr′fən·ij] *n.* An institution for the care of orphans or other abandoned children.

Or·phe·us [ôr′fē·əs] *n.* In Greek myths, a musician whose singing to the lyre could charm beasts and even rocks and trees.

or·tho·don·tics [ôr′thə·don′tiks] *n.* The branch of dentistry that deals with straightening or adjusting the teeth to improve occlusion. **— or′· tho·don′tist** *n.* ◆ See -ICS.

or·tho·dox [ôr′thə·doks] *adj.* **1** Believing in or adhering to long-established and commonly accepted doctrines or practices, especially of a religion: an *orthodox* person. **2** Proper, generally accepted, or traditional: an *orthodox* vacation at the beach. ◆ See ORTHOPEDICS.

Orthodox Church Another name for EAST-ERN ORTHODOX CHURCH.

or·tho·dox·y [ôr′thə·dok′sē] *n., pl.* **or·tho· dox·ies** **1** The quality or condition of being orthodox. **2** An orthodox belief or practice.

or·tho·graph·ic [ôr′thə·graf′ik] *adj.* **1** Of or having to do with orthography. **2** Correctly spelled.

or·thog·ra·phy [ôr·thog′rə·fē] *n., pl.* **or·thog· ra·phies** **1** The study of spelling. **2** Correct spelling or spelling according to common usage.

or·tho·pe·dics [ôr′thə·pē′diks] *n.pl.* The treatment, correction, or prevention of deformities of the bones or joints, especially of the spine. ◆ See -ICS. *Orthopedics* and *orthodox* depend on the Greek word *orthos*, meaning *right* or *correct*, and *orthopedics* and *pediatrics* on the Greek root *paid-*, meaning *child*. Thus *orthopedics* originally referred to the correction of deformities in children. *Orthodox* literally means *right opinion*, and *pediatrics* is the art of healing as it relates to children.

-ory A suffix meaning: **1** A place or thing for, as in *reformatory*, a place for reforming. **2** Of, re-

lated to, or like, as in *circulatory*, of, related to, or like circulation.

o·ryx [ôr′iks] *n., pl.* **o·ryx·es** *or* **o·ryx** An antelope of Africa, having long, slender horns pointing straight back from the head.

O·sa·ka [ō·sä′kä] *n.* A city and port in Japan.

os·cil·late [os′ə·lāt] *v.* **os·cil·lat·ed, os·cil· lat·ing** **1** To move back and forth in a regular way, as a pendulum. **2** To cause an electric current to move back and forth. **3** To be unable to make up one's mind about what to do or think. **— os′cil·la′tion** *n.*

os·cil·la·tor [os′ə·lā′tər] *n.* **1** A person who oscillates. **2** A device that oscillates or produces oscillation, especially one of various electronic devices.

os·cil·lo·scope [ə·sil′ə·skōp] *n.* An instrument having a viewing screen similar to that of a television receiver on which the oscillations of alternating currents and electromagnetic waves can be made visible.

os·cu·late [os′kyə·lāt] *v.* **os· cu·lat·ed, os·cu·lat·ing** To kiss. **— os′cu·la′tion** *n.*

o·sier [ō′zhər] *n.* A kind of willow tree whose long, flexible twigs are used in making wicker baskets and furniture.

Oscilloscope

O·si·ris [ō·sī′ris] *n.* In Egyptian myths, the god of the underworld and lord of the dead.

Os·lo [os′lō *or* oz′lō] *n.* The capital of Norway, in the SE part.

os·mo·sis [oz·mō′sis *or* os·mō′sis] *n.* **1** The tendency of fluids separated by a somewhat porous membrane to move through it and become mixed. **2** The intermingling of fluids in this manner until they are mixed. **3** The gradual process of a person's taking on certain habits, ideas, etc., without being conscious of it.

os·mot·ic [oz·mot′ik *or* os·mot′ik] *adj.* Of, related to, or resulting from osmosis.

os·prey [os′prē] *n., pl.* **os·preys** *or* **os·prey** An American hawk, brown above and white below, that preys on fish.

Os·sa [os′ə] *n.* A mountain in Greece. ◆ See PELION.

os·si·fy [os′ə·fī] *v.* **os·si·fied, os·si·fy· ing** **1** To change or be changed into bone: Age had *ossified* some of the cartilage of his body. **2** To make or become rigid or stubborn in habits, beliefs, etc. **— os′si·fi·ca′tion** *n.*

Osprey, about 23 in. long

os·ten·si·ble [os·ten′sə·bəl] *adj.* Apparently real but actually not. **— os·ten′si·bly** *adv.*

os·ten·ta·tion [os′tən·tā′shən] *n.* Too much or uncalled-for display of something in order to attract attention, admiration, etc.: She lives quietly, without *ostentation*.

os·ten·ta·tious [os′ten·tā′shəs] *adj.* Showing or tending toward ostentation: an *ostentatious* person or party. **— os′ten·ta′tious·ly** *adv.*

os·te·o·path [os′tē·ə·path] *n.* A person who practices osteopathy.

os·te·op·a·thy [os′tē·op′ə·thē] *n.* A system of treating disease by manipulating bones and muscles thought to be displaced. Medicines and surgery are also used as needed.

ost·ler [os′lər] *n.* Another word for HOSTLER.

os·tra·cism [os′trə·siz′əm] *n.* **1** The act of banishing or shutting out someone **2** The condition of being shut out or excluded. **3** In ancient Greece, the temporary banishment of someone by popular vote.

os·tra·cize [os′trə·sīz] *v.* **os·tra·cized, os·tra·ciz·ing** To shut out, banish, or exclude, as from a certain group: He was *ostracized* from the team because of his temper. ¶3

os·trich [ôs′trich] *n., pl.* **os·trich·es** or **os·trich** A tall, two-toed bird of Africa and Arabia with feathers valued as ornaments. The largest living bird, it cannot fly but runs very fast.

Ostrich, 6–8 ft. high

O·thel·lo [ō·thel′ō] *n.* The hero of Shakespeare's play of the same name, a Moor of Venice who kills his wife because of jealousy.

oth·er [uth′ər] **1** *adj.* Not the same as that which was just mentioned; different: not on Tuesday but some *other* time. **2** *adj.* Noting or being the remaining one of two persons or things: Close your *other* eye. **3** *pron.* Another or different person or thing: Besides this book, what *others* have you read? **4** *pron.* The other person or thing: Use this hand, not the *other*. **5** *adj.* Additional; more: Have you no *other* children? **6** *adj.* Different in quality, character, condition, etc.: The truth is *other* than what you think. **7** *adv.* In a different way or manner; otherwise: I cannot feel *other* than I do toward him. **— every other** Every alternate or second: We go *every other* day. **— the other day, night,** etc. A day, night, etc., not long ago; recently.

oth·er·wise [uth′ər·wīz′] **1** *adv.* In a different manner; by other means: I would do it *otherwise*. **2** *adv.* In other circumstances or conditions: I had to do it; we might have lost *otherwise*. **3** *adj.* Other than supposed; different: The facts are *otherwise*. **4** *adv.* In all other ways: He is a good person *otherwise*.

Ot·ta·wa [ot′ə·wə] *n.* The capital of Canada, in SE Ontario.

ot·ter [ot′ər] *n., pl.* **ot·ter** or **ot·ters 1** Any of several fish-eating, swimming animals, related to the weasel and mink. They have long, flattened tails. **2** Their valuable, dark brown fur.

ot·to·man [ot′ə·mən] *n., pl.* **ot·to·mans 1** An upholstered, armless seat or sofa, usually without a back. **2** A cushioned footrest.

Ot·to·man [ot′ə·mən] *n., pl.* **Ot·to·mans,** *adj.* **1** *n.* A Turk. **2** *adj.* Turkish.

Ottoman

ouch [ouch] *interj.* A cry or sound expressing sudden pain.

ought [ôt] A helping verb followed by an infinitive and meaning: **1** To have a duty or obligation: He *ought* to keep his promises. **2** To be advised or what is sensible: You *ought* to be more careful. **3** To be expected, likely, or logical: The engine *ought* to run. ◆ *Ought* was originally the past tense of an Old English verb meaning *to have*. It is never used as a main verb, and it has no infinitive, past, etc. It is used only as a helping or auxiliary verb before an infinitive.

ounce [ouns] *n.* **1** A unit of weight, equal to $\frac{1}{16}$ pound avoirdupois or to $\frac{1}{12}$ pound troy. **2** A unit of liquid measure, equal to $\frac{1}{16}$ pint. **3** Any small amount: an *ounce* of courage.

our [our] *pron.* Of or by us; belonging to us: the possessive form of *we*: *our* play; *our* house; *our* vacation.

ours [ourz] *pron.* The one or ones belonging to us or having to do with us: The victory was all *ours*; *Ours* is broken.

our·self [our·self′] *pron.* Myself or ourselves: used in formal or legal situations, as by a king, queen, judge, etc.: The king said, "We *ourself* shall see that he is punished."

our·selves [our·selvz′] *pron.* **1** The ones that we really are; our very own selves. *Ourselves* in this sense is used to refer back to the subject *we* or to make the subject *we* more emphatic: We helped *ourselves*; We *ourselves* want to know. **2** Our normal, healthy, proper, or usual condition: We weren't *ourselves*.

-ous A suffix meaning: Full of, having, given to, or like, as in *joyous*, full of joy.

ou·sel [ōō′zəl] *n.* Another spelling of OUZEL.

oust [oust] *v.* To force out or remove: We *ousted* them from the party.

oust·er [ous′tər] *n.* The act of forcing out or removing; ejection; expulsion.

out [out] **1** *adv., adj.* Away from the inside, center, etc.: Go *out* into the street; Paul isn't *out* because of the bad weather. **2** *adv., adj.* Away from a particular or usual place, as one's home, office, etc.: to go *out* to work; Fred is *out* to lunch. **3** *prep.* Forth from; through; out of: He jumped *out* the window. **4** *prep.* Along or on: Walk *out* the old dirt road. **5** *adv.* From a bottle or other container: Pour *out* the coffee. **6** *adv.* From among others: to pick *out* a shirt. **7** *adv.* So as to remove, use up, extinguish, or end: Sweep *out* the dust. **8** *adj.* Removed, used up, extinguished, or ended: The fire is *out*. **9** *adv.* Completely; thoroughly: I am tired *out*. **10** *adv.* To a result or end: They fought it *out*. **11** *adv.* So as to extend or project: to lean *out*. **12** *adv.* Into being or activity: The sun came *out*. **13** *adv.* So as to be known publicly: The secret leaked *out*. **14** *adj.* Known to the public: The news is *out*. **15** *v.* To become known publicly: Murder will *out*. **16** *adv.* In or into circulation: He brought *out* a new edition of the book. **17** *adv.* Loudly: Speak *out*. **18** *adv.* Boldly or frankly: Tell it *out*! **19** *adv.* Into the possession or care of others: Pass *out* the books. **20** *n.* In baseball, the failure of a player to get on base or to get to the next base safely. **21** *adv.* In baseball, so as to cause an out: to strike *out*. **22** *adj.* Having failed to get on base or to get to the next base safely. **23** *adv. informal* Into unconsciousness: to pass *out*. **24** *n. informal* A way or means of avoiding doing something: She is always looking for an *out* in gym class. **25** *adj.* Not in use or working order: The bridge is *out*. **26** *adj.* At a financial loss: We were *out* five dollars. **27** *adj.* In error; mistaken: I am *out* in my count. **28** *interj.* Get out! Away! **— go all out** To make every possible effort: Bud *went all out* to be elected president of his class. **— on the outs** or **at outs** Involved in a quarrel or disagreement: Fred and Susan are *on the outs* because she refused to go to the prom with him. **— out and away** By far: It is *out and away* his best film. **— out and out** Completely; thoroughly. **— out for** Looking for; trying to get: He is *out for* a high grade. **— out into the open** Known or admitted publicly. **— out of 1** From or beyond the inside of; from within: We ran *out of* the house; It fell *out of* the window. **2** Beyond the limits, range, or usual position of: They flew *out of* sight. **3** From among others of: Take a shirt *out of* that pile. **4** From (a material, etc.): It was made *out of* tin. **5** Caused or influenced by; because of: *out of* pity. **6** Without: *out of* breath. **7** So as not to have: We were cheated *out of* our money. **— out to** With the intention of: trying to: He is *out to* get a good job.

out- A prefix meaning: **1** Away from the center or inside; outside, as in *outlying*, lying away from the center or inside. **2** Going forth or out; outward, as in *outbound*, bound or going outward. **3** More or better than, as in *outplay*, to play more or better than.

out-and-out [out′(ə)n(d)·out′] *adj.* Complete; thoroughgoing: an *out-and-out* fool.

out·bid [out·bid′] *v.* **out·bid, out·bid·den** or **out·bid, out·bid·ding** To make a higher bid than: We *outbid* them yesterday.

out·board [out′bôrd′] *adj., adv.* In aircraft, boats, or ships, outside the hull or away from the center or fuselage: an *outboard* jet engine.

outboard motor A portable gasoline or electric motor equipped with a propeller and tiller and attached to the stern of a small boat.

out·bound [out′bound′] *adj.* Bound or going away from a a place: an *outbound* train.

Outboard motor

out·break [out′brāk′] *n.* A sudden bursting or breaking forth, as of an emotion, disease, rioting, etc.

out·build·ing [out′bil′ding] *n.* A building separate from a main building, as a woodshed or barn.

out·burst [out′bûrst′] *n.* A sudden and violent bursting out, as of anger, flame, or noise.

out·cast [out′kast′] **1** *adj.* Rejected or cast out by society, family, friends, etc. **2** *n.* An outcast person or thing.

out·class [out·klas′] *v.* To be better than in skill, quality, talent, etc.

out·come [out′kum′] *n.* A result or conclusion.

out·crop [*n.* out′krop′, *v.* out·krop′] *n., v.* **out·cropped, out·crop·ping 1** *n.* The coming out at or above the ground of a mineral. **2** *n.* The part so exposed. **3** *v.* To appear at the surface.

out·cry [out′krī′] *n., pl.* **out·cries 1** A loud cry or clamor. **2** A strong outburst of alarm, anger, protest, etc.

out·dat·ed [out·dā′tid] *adj.* Out-of-date; old-fashioned: Muskets are *outdated*.

out·dis·tance [out·dis′təns] *v.* **out·dis·tanced, out·dis·tanc·ing** To run or move far ahead of: We *outdistanced* them easily.

out·do [out·dōō′] *v.* **out·did, out·done, out·do·ing** To be better than; surpass.

out·door [out′dôr′] *adj.* **1** Being or done in the open air: an *outdoor* concert. **2** Open to the sky; without a roof: an *outdoor* theater.

out·doors [out·dôrz′] **1** *adv.* Outside of the house; in the open air: Go *outdoors*. **2** *n.pl.* (*used with singular verb*) The world that is outside the house or other buildings; the open air: The *outdoors* is a good place to paint.

out·er [ou′tər] *adj.* **1** Being on the exterior side; external: the *outer* door. **2** Farther from a center or from the inside: the *outer* part of the harbor.

out·er·most [ou′tər·mōst] *adj.* Farthest away or out from the inside or inner part.

outer space The space beyond the earth's atmosphere.

out·field [out′fēld′] *n.* **1** The part of a baseball field beyond the infield, defended by three players. **2** The three players who defend the outfield.

out·field·er [out′fēl′dər] *n.* In baseball, any of the three players assigned to defend the outfield.

out·fit [out′fit′] *n., v.* **out·fit·ted, out·fit·ting 1** *n.* The clothing, tools, or other equipment needed for some particular purpose, as traveling or sports. **2** *v.* To furnish or equip with an outfit. **3** *n.* Any organized group or team of persons who do some particular work: a construction *outfit.* **4** *n.* A military unit, as a regiment, division, etc. — **out′fit′ter** *n.*

out·flank [out·flangk′] *v.* To get around and in back of the flank or side of (an opposing force or army).

out·flow [out′flō′] *n.* **1** Something that flows out. **2** The act or process of flowing out.

out·gen·er·al [out·jen′ər·əl] *v.* **out·gen·er·aled** or **out·gen·er·alled, out·gen·er·al·ing** or **out·gen·er·al·ling** To outdo by better strategy and leadership.

out·go [out′gō′] *n., pl.* **out·goes** That which goes out, especially money that is paid out.

out·go·ing [out′gō′ing] *adj.* **1** Going out; leaving; departing: an *outgoing* bus. **2** Easy to meet and talk to; friendly: an *outgoing* person.

out·grow [out·grō′] *v.* **out·grew, out·grown, out·grow·ing** **1** To grow too large for: He *outgrew* his shirts. **2** To grow larger than: He has *outgrown* his sister. **3** To lose or get rid of as one grows older: to *outgrow* a habit.

out·growth [out′grōth′] *n.* **1** Something that grows out of something else. **2** A natural result or development: Revolutions are often an *outgrowth* of poverty and oppression. **3** The act or process of growing out.

out·guess [out·ges′] *v.* To be more clever than; outwit.

out·house [out′hous′] *n., pl.* **out·hous·es** [out′hou·zəz] **1** An outdoor toilet. **2** Any outbuilding.

out·ing [ou′ting] *n.* A short pleasure trip or excursion, often with a picnic.

out·land·ish [out·lan′dish] *adj.* **1** Strange or unfamiliar: *outlandish* customs. **2** *informal* Crazy; ridiculous: an *outlandish* notion. — **out·land′ish·ness** *n.*

out·last [out·last′] *v.* To last longer than.

out·law [out′lô′] **1** *n.* A person who constantly breaks or defies the law; a criminal. **2** *n.* A person denied the rights and protection of law: Robin Hood was an *outlaw.* **3** *v.* To declare to be an outlaw. **4** *v.* To make illegal; prohibit; ban: a treaty to *outlaw* war.

out·lay [out′lā′] *n., v.* **out·laid, out·lay·ing** **1** *n.* The act of spending money. **2** *n.* The amount of money spent: There was a large *outlay* involved in the deposit on my new piano. **3** *v.* To lay out or spend (money).

out·let [out′let] *n.* **1** A place or means of exit; passage; vent: The Niagara River is the *outlet* of Lake Erie. **2** The point in an electrical wiring system where electrical appliances are plugged in. **3** A means of release or expression: Painting was an *outlet* for his imagination. **4** A market for any commodity.

out·line [out′līn′] *n., v.* **out·lined, out·lin·ing** **1** *n.* The line formed by the real or apparent outer edges of an object and defining its shape. **2** *n.* A sketch or drawing made only of the outer lines of an object without any shading. **3** *n.* A written plan of the most important points of a speech, essay, story, etc. **4** *v.* To make, draw, or give an outline of.

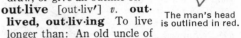

out·live [out·liv′] *v.* **out· lived, out·liv·ing** To live longer than: An old uncle of mine *outlived* several of his children.

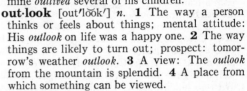

The man's head is outlined in red.

out·look [out′look′] *n.* **1** The way a person thinks or feels about things; mental attitude: His *outlook* on life was a happy one. **2** The way things are likely to turn out; prospect: tomorrow's weather *outlook.* **3** A view: The *outlook* from the mountain is splendid. **4** A place from which something can be viewed.

out·ly·ing [out′lī′ing] *adj.* Far or remote from the center or main part; remote: the *outlying* parts of town.

out·mod·ed [out·mōd′id] *adj.* Out-of-date; old-fashioned: an *outmoded* way to dance.

out·most [out′mōst′] *adj.* Farthest out.

out·num·ber [out′num′bər] *v.* To be greater in number than.

out-of-date [out′əv·dāt′] *adj.* No longer stylish or in use; old-fashioned.

out-of-door [out′əv·dôr′] *adj.* Outdoor.

out-of-doors [out′əv·dôrz′] **1** *adj.* Outdoor. **2** *n.pl.* (*used with singular verb*) Outdoors. **3** *adv.* Outdoors: Go play *out-of-doors.*

out-of-the-way [out′əv·thə·wā′] *adj.* **1** Remote; secluded: an *out-of-the-way* beach. **2** Unusual; odd: an *out-of-the-way* happening.

out·pa·tient [out′pā′shənt] *n.* A patient who is treated at a hospital but does not stay there as an inmate.

out·play [out·plā′] *v.* To play better than.

out·post [out′pōst′] *n.* **1** A group of soldiers stationed at a distance from the main body as a guard against surprise attack. **2** The place occupied by such troops. **3** An outlying village or settlement, as at a frontier.

out·put [out′poot′] *n.* **1** The amount of anything produced: the electrical *output* of a generator; a factory's *output*; a writer's *output.* **2** The act of putting forth: an *output* of energy.

out·rage [*n.* out′rāj′, *v.* out·rāj′] *n., v.* **out· raged, out·rag·ing** **1** *n.* An act of great violence or cruelty. **2** *n.* A very great insult or injury: Her words were an *outrage* to all present. **3** *v.* To commit an outrage upon. **4** *v.* To treat (rules, moral laws, principles, etc.) as of no value: He *outraged* all rules of decency by his

add, āce, câre, pälm; end, ēqual; it, īce; odd, ōpen, ôrder; tŏŏk, pōōl; up, bûrn;
ə = a in *above*, e in *sicken*, i in *possible*, o in *melon*, u in *circus*; yōō = u in *fuse*; oil; pout;
check; ring; thin; this; zh in *vision*. For ¶ reference, see page 64 · HOW TO

conduct. **5** *n.* Anger or resentment over unjust or insulting behavior. **6** *v.* To make angry.

out·ra·geous [out·rā′jəs] *adj.* **1** Violently cruel or wrong: an *outrageous* act. **2** Very rude or insulting: an *outrageous* thing to say. **3** Fantastic; unbelievable: an *outrageous* exaggeration. — **out·ra′geous·ly** *adv.*

out·rank [out·rangk′] *v.* To be higher in rank than: That general *outranks* all the others.

out·rig·ger [out′rig′ər] *n.* **1** A frame holding a float extended beyond the side of a canoe to prevent it from tipping over. **2** A canoe equipped with such a framework.

Outrigger

out·right [*adj.* out′·rīt′, *adv.* out′rīt′] **1** *adj.* Complete; entire; thoroughgoing: an *outright* lie. **2** *adv.* Completely; entirely; utterly: I gave him everything *outright*. **3** *adv.* With no holding back; openly: to cry *outright*. **4** *adv.* Without delay: It was accepted *outright*.

out·run [out·run′] *v.* **out·ran, out·run, out·run·ning** **1** To run faster or farther than. **2** To be greater than; exceed: His dreams *outran* his talent.

out·sell [out·sel′] *v.* **out·sold, out·sell·ing** **1** To sell more goods than: I *outsold* him quickly. **2** To sell more easily or for a higher price than: These shirts have always *outsold* those.

out·set [out′set′] *n.* The beginning, start, or opening of something.

out·shine [out·shīn′] *v.* **out·shone, out·shin·ing** **1** To shine brighter than. **2** To be better than; surpass: His playing *outshone* mine.

out·side [*n., adj., adv.* out′sīd′, *prep.* out′·sīd′] **1** *n.* The outer or exterior part of a thing: the *outside* of the house. **2** *adj.* Of, located on, or having to do with the outer or exterior part or surface: an *outside* pocket. **3** *adv.* On or to the outside; outdoors: Let's go *outside* now. **4** *n.* A place or part that is beyond a boundary line or enclosure; outer region. **5** *prep.* On or to the exterior or outside of: *outside* the park. **6** *adj.* Not belonging to or connected with a certain group, organization, person, etc.: *outside* influences. **7** *adj.* Slight; slim: an *outside* possibility of rain. **8** *adj.* Reaching the limit or maximum; extreme: an *outside* estimate. — **at the outside** At the farthest, longest, or most. — **outside of 1** *informal* Except; besides. **2** Outside: *outside of* the building.

out·sid·er [out′sī′dər] *n.* A person who does not come from a certain place or belong to a certain group, set, organization, etc.

out·skirts [out′skûrts′] *n.pl.* The outer edges or areas far from the center, as of a city.

out·smart [out·smärt′] *v. informal* To fool or trick; outwit.

out·spo·ken [out′spō′kən] *adj.* **1** Bold or frank in speech. **2** Spoken boldly or frankly: an *outspoken* statement. — **out′spo′ken·ly** *adv.*

out·spread [*v.* out·spred′, *adj.* out′spred′] *v.* **out·spread, out·spread·ing,** *adj.* **1** *v.* To spread out; extend. **2** *adj.* Spread out: *outspread* wings.

out·stand·ing [out·stan′ding] *adj.* **1** More excellent or important than others of its kind: an *outstanding* book. **2** Not paid or settled, as a debt or claim. — **out·stand′ing·ly** *adv.*

out·stretched [out′strecht′] *adj.* Stretched out; extended: *out-stretched* wings.

Outstretched arms

out·strip [out·strip′] *v.* **out·stripped, out·strip·ping** **1** To outrun or leave behind. **2** To be better than; surpass; excel.

out·ward [out′wərd] **1** *adj.* Of or having to do with the outside; outer; external. **2** *adj.* Toward or directed toward the outside or away from the center: an *outward* road. **3** *adv.* Toward the outside or away from the center: The cars moved *outward* from the city. **4** *adj.* Readily seen or apparent; clear: no *outward* sign of trouble. **5** *adj.* Of or having to do with the body rather than with the mind or inner self: his *outward* ease of manner. — **out′ward·ly** *adv.*

out·wards [out′wərdz] *adv.* Outward.

out·wear [out·wâr′] *v.* **out·wore, out·worn, out·wear·ing** **1** To wear or stand use longer than: This material *outwore* all the others. **2** To use up; exhaust: to *outwear* a welcome.

out·weigh [out·wā′] *v.* **1** To weigh more than. **2** To be more important, valuable, etc., than: His idea seems to *outweigh* the others.

out·wit [out·wit′] *v.* **out·wit·ted, out·wit·ting** To beat or get the better of by being smarter or more clever.

out·work [*v.* out·wûrk′, *n.* out′wûrk′] **1** *v.* To work more, faster, or better than: He *outworked* all of us. **2** *n.* A small defensive position built outside a fort, etc.

out·worn [out·wôrn′] *adj.* **1** Worn out: *outworn* machinery. **2** Old-fashioned; out-of-date: an *outworn* method of working.

ou·zel [ōō′zəl] *n.* The blackbird of Europe.

o·val [ō′vəl] **1** *adj.* Having the shape of an egg or an ellipse. **2** *n.* Something with this shape.

o·va·ry [ō′və·rē] *n., pl.* **o·va·ries** **1** The organ in females in which eggs are produced. **2** The part of a plant where seeds are formed.

Ovals

o·vate [ō′vāt] *adj.* Egg-shaped; oval: *ovate* leaves.

o·va·tion [ō·vā′shən] *n.* A burst of loud, enthusiastic, continuing applause, through which a crowd expresses great approval.

ov·en [uv′ən] *n.* An enclosed chamber in which

things are heated, cooked, or dried, as the part of a stove used for baking and roasting.

ov·en·bird [uv′ən·bûrd′] *n.* A bird that builds an ovenlike nest with a roof like a dome.

o·ver [ō′vər] **1** *prep.* In or to a place or position above; higher than: a light *over* the door. **2** *adv.* Above; overhead: A helicopter just went *over*. **3** *prep.* Above in power or authority: A captain is *over* a lieutenant. **4** *prep.* Upon: said about an effect: to have influence *over* someone. **5** *prep.* In preference to: chosen *over* all the others. **6** *prep.* So as to close or cover: Put the lid *over* the jar. **7** *adv.* So as to cover the surface: to board windows *over*. **8** *adv.* So as to be covered: The pond froze *over*. **9** *prep.* Upon the surface of: a layer of varnish *over* wood. **10** *adv.* Through from beginning to end: Think it *over*. **11** *prep.* During or throughout the time of: to visit *over* the holidays. **12** *prep.* Through all or many parts of: The guide took us *over* the building. **13** *prep.* From one side or end of to the other; across or along: to climb *over* a fence; to ride *over* a scenic stretch of road. **14** *adj.* On the other side: Is the swimmer *over* yet? **15** *prep.* On the other side of: *over* the ocean. **16** *adv.* At or on the other side: He is *over* in England. **17** *adv.* From one side, opinion, or attitude to another: Her charm won him *over*. **18** *adv.* Across some space or barrier: Let's go *over* to Mary's. **19** *adv.* To a specified place: Bring *over* a friend. **20** *prep.* More than: *over* a million. **21** *adv.* More: six years old or *over*. **22** *adv.* Beyond some amount or limit; as a surplus: food left *over*. **23** *adv.* Beyond and down from the edge or brim: The water in the tub is running *over*. **24** *prep.* Downward beyond: She fell *over* the side of the boat. **25** *adv.* From an upright position to a lower one: The statue toppled *over*. **26** *adv.* So as to bring the underside up: to turn a boat *over*. **27** *prep.* Concerning or because of; about: an argument *over* nothing. **28** *prep.* By means of: to talk *over* the telephone. **29** *adv.* Again: Do your homework *over*. **30** *adj.* Finished; done; past: The storm is *over*. **— all over 1** Past and gone; finished. **2** On or in all parts; everywhere. **— over again** Once more. **— over against 1** Opposite to. **2** As contrasted with: *Over against* the others, he stands out as a leader. **— over all** Including or considering everything: *Over all*, he's not a bad boy. **— over and above** In addition to; besides. **— over and over** Again and again.

over- A prefix meaning: **1** Above, as in *overhead*, above one's head. **2** On or across, as in *overspread*, to spread across. **3** Covering, as in *overshoe*, a covering shoe. **4** Past some limit, as in *overdue*, past due. **5** Too or too much, as in *overweight*, too much weight. **6** Over, as in *overturn*, to turn over.

o·ver·all [ō′vər·ôl′] *adj.* **1** From one end to the other: the *overall* span of a bridge. **2** Including everything: the *overall* charges.

o·ver·alls [ō′vər·ôlz′] *n.pl.* Loose, coarse trousers, often with suspenders and a piece extending over the chest, worn over other clothing to keep it from becoming soiled.

o·ver·awe [ō′vər·ô′] *v.* **o·ver·awed, o·ver·aw·ing** To subdue or restrain by filling with awe or fear: The stern schoolmaster *over-awed* Tom.

o·ver·bal·ance [ō′vər·bal′əns] *v.* **o·ver·bal·anced, o·ver·bal·anc·ing 1** To exceed in weight, importance, etc.: The good points *overbalance* the bad points. **2** To cause to lose balance.

o·ver·bear·ing [ō′vər·bâr′ing] *adj.* Imposing one's will on others in a very bossy, conceited way; domineering. **— o′ver·bear′ing·ly** *adv.*

Overalls

o·ver·board [ō′vər·bôrd′] *adv.* Over the side of a ship into the water: to fall *overboard*.

o·ver·bur·den [ō′vər·bûr′dən] *v.* To cause to carry too great a burden; weigh down.

o·ver·cast [ō′vər·kast′] *adj., v.* **o·ver·cast, o·ver·cast·ing 1** *adj.* Clouded over and dark, as the sky. **2** *v.* To cover or darken, as with clouds. **3** *adj.* Gloomy, as a face. **4** *v.* To sew (the edge of a fabric) with long, wrapping stitches to prevent raveling.

o·ver·charge [*v.* ō′vər·chärj′, *n.* ō′vər·chärj′] *v.* **o·ver·charged, o·ver·charg·ing,** *n.* **1** *v.* To charge too high a price: The butcher *overcharged* me for the chops. **2** *v.* To load or fill with too great a charge: to *overcharge* an old gun; to *overcharge* a battery. **3** *n.* Too high or too great a charge, as of money or electricity.

o·ver·coat [ō′vər·kōt′] *n.* A warm coat worn over one's regular clothing in cold weather.

o·ver·come [ō′vər·kum′] *v.* **o·ver·came, o·ver·come, o·ver·com·ing 1** To get the better of; triumph over; conquer; defeat: to *overcome* an enemy; to *overcome* a handicap. **2** To make weak or helpless: to be *overcome* by grief.

o·ver·do [ō′vər·dōō′] *v.* **o·ver·did, o·ver·done, o·ver·do·ing 1** To exaggerate: The actor *overdoes* his part. **2** To cook too long, as meat. **3** To tire or strain oneself by doing too much.

o·ver·dose [ō′vər·dōs′] *n.* Too large or too strong a dose: an *overdose* of sleeping pills.

o·ver·draw [ō′vər·drô′] *v.* **o·ver·drew, o·ver·drawn, o·ver·draw·ing 1** To write checks on (a bank account) for more money than it contains. **2** To exaggerate in writing, speech, or action: His story of the accident is *overdrawn*.

o·ver·dress [ō′vər·dres′] *v.* To dress up too much for the occasion.

o·ver·drive [ō′vər·drīv′] *n.* A gear that causes the driving shaft of a machine to turn faster than the engine, thus saving fuel.

o·ver·due [ō′vər·d(y)o͞o′] *adj.* **1** Remaining unpaid after becoming due. **2** Not on time; late.

o·ver·eat [ō′vər·ēt′] *v.* **o·ver·ate, o·ver·eat·en, o·ver·eat·ing** To eat too much.

o·ver·es·ti·mate [*v.* ō′vər·es′tə·māt, *n.* ō′vər·es′tə·mit] *v.* **o·ver·es·ti·mat·ed, o·ver·es·ti·mat·ing,** *n.* **1** *v.* To estimate at a rate, amount, etc., that is too high. **2** *n.* An estimate that is too high.

o·ver·flow [*v.* ō′vər·flō′, *n.* ō′vər·flō′] **1** *v.* To flow over the banks or brim; flood: The river *overflowed.* **2** *v.* To flow over the boundary of: The river *overflowed* its banks. **3** *n.* The act of overflowing. **4** *v.* To spread over: The running water *overflowed* the bathroom. **5** *v.* To have its contents running over: The tub *overflowed.* **6** *n.* An excess: an *overflow* of population. **7** *v.* To spill over: Guests *overflowed* onto the lawn. **8** *n.* An outlet to drain off liquid that would otherwise spill over, as one near the top of a sink. **9** *v.* To be very full: hearts *overflowing* with love.

Cup overflowing

o·ver·grow [ō′vər·grō′] *v.* **o·ver·grew, o·ver·grown, o·ver·grow·ing 1** To grow over; cover with growth: The wall was *overgrown* with ivy. **2** To grow too large or too rapidly. **3** *adj. use:* an *overgrown* boy.

o·ver·hand [ō′vər·hand′] *adj., adv.* With the hand above the level of the elbow or shoulder: an *overhand* throw; to pass a ball *overhand.*

o·ver·hang [ō′vər·hang′] *v.* **o·ver·hung, o·ver·hang·ing,** *n.* **1** *v.* To hang, project, or jut over. **2** *adj. use: overhanging* cliffs. **3** *n.* A projecting part: the *overhang* of a roof.

Overhanging roof

o·ver·haul [*v.* ō′vər·hôl′, *n.* ō′vər·hôl′] **1** *v.* To inspect thoroughly or take apart so as to make all needed repairs: to *overhaul* an engine. **2** *n.* Complete inspection and repairs: This motorcycle needs an *overhaul.* **3** *v.* To catch up with; gain on: usually said about boats.

o·ver·head [*adv.* ō′vər·hed′, *adj., n.* ō′vər·hed′] **1** *adv.* Above one's head, in the sky, or on the floor above: The couple *overhead* were singing loudly. **2** *adj.* Situated or working above the level of one's head: an *overhead* light. **3** *n.* The general operating expenses of a business, as rent, light, heat, taxes, etc.

o·ver·hear [ō′vər·hir′] *v.* **o·ver·heard, o·ver·hear·ing** To hear when one is not meant to hear; hear by accident: I *overheard* them saying some very nice things about your singing.

o·ver·heat [ō′vər·hēt′] *v.* To make or become too hot: to *overheat* milk so that it curdles.

o·ver·joy [ō′vər·joi′] *v.* **1** To delight or please greatly. **2** *adj. use:* His *overjoyed* parents met him at the train.

o·ver·land [ō′vər·land′] *adj., adv.* Over, across, or by land: an *overland* route; to travel *overland.*

o·ver·lap [*v.* ō′vər·lap′, *n.* ō′vər·lap′] *v.* **o·ver·lapped, o·ver·lap·ping,** *n.* **1** *v.* To lie or extend partly over (another or each other); lap over: The boards on the sides of the house *overlap*; The lives of Washington and Jefferson *overlapped.* **2** *n.* The condition or extent of overlapping. **3** *n.* An overlapping part.

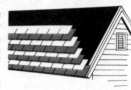
Overlapping shingles

o·ver·lay [*v.* ō′vər·lā′, *n.* ō′vər·lā′] *v.* **o·ver·laid, o·ver·lay·ing,** *n.* **1** *v.* To cover or coat, as with an ornamental pattern or layer: The wood was *overlaid* with mother-of-pearl. **2** *n.* Anything that covers or partly covers something. **3** *n.* An ornamental layer, as veneer.

o·ver·lie [ō′vər·lī′] *v.* **o·ver·lay, o·ver·lain, o·ver·ly·ing** To lie over or upon.

o·ver·load [*v.* ō′vər·lōd′, *n.* ō′vər·lōd′] **1** *v.* To put too large or too heavy a load in or on: to *overload* a boat; to *overload* an electric circuit. **2** *n.* Too heavy or too great a load.

o·ver·look [ō′vər·lo͝ok′] *v.* **1** To afford a view of from above: Our room *overlooked* the valley. **2** To look over or see from a higher place. **3** To fail to see or notice; miss: He checked his work but *overlooked* a small error in arithmetic. **4** To excuse or pretend not to notice; forgive or ignore: to *overlook* a snub.

Overloaded boat

o·ver·lord [ō′vər·lôrd′] *n.* A lord who rules over lesser lords.

o·ver·ly [ō′vər·lē] *adv.* Too much; too: She is *overly* sensitive and easily offended.

o·ver·mas·ter [ō′vər·mas′tər] *v.* To overcome; overpower.

o·ver·much [ō′vər·much′] *adj., adv., n.* Too much.

o·ver·night [ō′vər·nīt′] **1** *adv.* During or through the night: to stay *overnight.* **2** *adj.* Occurring during the night: an *overnight* frost. **3** *adj.* Lasting or staying all night: an *overnight* visit; an *overnight* guest. **4** *adj.* Used for short trips: an *overnight* bag. **5** *adv.* Suddenly or quickly: He became famous *overnight.*

o·ver·pass [ō′vər·pas′] *n.* An elevated section of road or highway passing over and across another travel route.

o·ver·pay [ō′vər·pā′] *v.* **o·ver·paid, o·ver·pay·ing 1** To pay more than (an amount due). **2** To pay (someone) too much. **3** To reward too highly. — **o′ver·pay′ment** *n.*

o·ver·pow·er [ō′vər·pou′ər] *v.* **1** To conquer or subdue by superior force or strength: to *overpower* an opponent. **2** To overcome or master by being strong or intense: Her feelings *overpowered* her. **3** *adj. use:* an *overpowering* odor.

o·ver·pro·duc·tion [ō′vər·prə·duk′shən] *n.* The production of more crops or goods than are needed or of more than can be sold at a profit.

o·ver·rate [ō′vər·rāt′] *v.* **o·ver·rat·ed, o·ver·rat·ing** To rate or value too highly.

o·ver·reach [ō′vər·rēch′] *v.* **1** To reach over or beyond. **2** To miss by reaching too far. **3** To outwit or cheat, as in a deal, by craftiness. — **overreach oneself** To defeat oneself by trying to do or get too much, or by being too crafty.

o·ver·ride [ō′vər·rīd′] *v.* **o·ver·rode, o·ver·rid·den, o·ver·rid·ing 1** To prevail over or set aside; overrule or ignore: The committee *overrode* the objections of its chairman. **2** To take precedence over: This *overrides* all other considerations. **3** To overcome as if by trampling under the feet of one's horse: to *override* all obstacles.

o·ver·rid·ing [ō′vər·rī′ding] *adj.* Chief, primary, or principal: his *overriding* concern.

o·ver·rule [ō′vər·rool′] *v.* **o·ver·ruled, o·ver·rul·ing 1** To set aside or reverse by superior authority: The Supreme Court *overruled* the lower court's decision. **2** To rule against; reject or dismiss: The judge *overruled* the objection. **3** To prevail over: The others *overruled* me.

o·ver·run [ō′vər·run′] *v.* **o·ver·ran, o·ver·run, o·ver·run·ning 1** To spread or swarm over in a harmful way: Barbarians *overran* the empire; Roaches *overran* the kitchen. **2** To spread over and cover: Ivy *overran* the ruins. **3** To run beyond: The TV show *overran* its allotted time.

o·ver·sea [ō′vər·sē′] *adv., adj.* Overseas.

o·ver·seas [ō′vər·sēz′] **1** *adv.* Beyond the sea; abroad: to go *overseas.* **2** *adj.* Beyond or across the sea: an *overseas* telephone call. **3** *adj.* Of, with, for, from, or to countries beyond the sea; foreign: *overseas* trade; *overseas* tourists.

o·ver·see [ō′vər·sē′] *v.* **o·ver·saw, o·ver·seen, o·ver·see·ing** To watch and direct; supervise; superintend: to *oversee* workers.

o·ver·se·er [ō′vər·sē′ər] *n.* A person who supervises laborers at their work.

o·ver·shad·ow [ō′vər·shad′ō] *v.* **1** To be or seem more important than: The leading actor *overshadowed* all the others. **2** To throw a shadow over; darken or obscure: Mystery *overshadowed* his last years.

o·ver·shoe [ō′vər·shoō′] *n.* An outer shoe or boot, as of rubber, plastic, etc., worn over a regular shoe to keep the foot dry or warm.

Overshoes

o·ver·shoot [ō′vər·shoōt′] *v.* **o·ver·shot, o·ver·shoot·ing** To shoot or go over or beyond (the mark, target, etc.): The plane *overshot* the runway.

o·ver·shot [ō′vər·shot′] *adj.* **1** Having the upper part of the jaw sticking out past the lower part, as some dogs' mouths. **2** Driven by water flowing from above: said about a water wheel.

o·ver·sight [ō′vər·sīt′] *n.* **1** An unintentional failure to do, notice, or remember something. **2** Watchful supervision.

o·ver·size [ō′vər·sīz′] *adj.* Of a larger size than necessary or normal: *oversize* feet.

o·ver·sized [ō′vər·sīzd′] *adj.* Oversize.

o·ver·sleep [ō′vər·slēp′] *v.* **o·ver·slept, o·ver·sleep·ing** To sleep too long; sleep past (a certain time, event, etc.).

o·ver·spread [ō′vər·spred′] *v.* **o·ver·spread, o·ver·spread·ing** To spread or extend over: A friendly grin *overspread* his face.

o·ver·state [ō′vər·stāt′] *v.* **o·ver·stat·ed, o·ver·stat·ing** To state in terms that are too strong; exaggerate. — **o′ver·state′ment** *n.*

o·ver·stay [ō′vər·stā′] *v.* To stay beyond the limits or duration of: I *overstayed* my welcome.

o·ver·step [ō′vər·step′] *v.* **o·ver·stepped, o·ver·step·ping** To go beyond; exceed, as a limit or restriction: to *overstep* one's authority.

o·ver·stock [*v.* ō′vər·stok′, *n.* ō′vər·stok′] **1** *v.* To stock with more than is needed, or stock too much. **2** *n.* Too great a stock or supply.

o·ver·sup·ply [*v.* ō′vər·sə·plī′, *n.* ō′vər·sə·plī′] *v.* **o·ver·sup·plied, o·ver·sup·ply·ing,** *n., pl.* **o·ver·sup·plies 1** *v.* To supply with more than is needed. **2** *n.* Too great a supply.

o·vert [ō′vûrt *or* ō·vûrt′] *adj.* Done or shown openly; not concealed: an *overt* act; *overt* dislike. — **o·vert·ly** [ō′vûrt·lē *or* ō·vûrt′lē] *adv.*

o·ver·take [ō′vər·tāk′] *v.* **o·ver·took, o·ver·tak·en, o·ver·tak·ing 1** To catch up with: I *overtook* him at the corner. **2** To come upon suddenly: A thunderstorm *overtook* them.

o·ver·tax [ō′vər·taks′] *v.* **1** To tax too heavily: to *overtax* a commodity. **2** To put too severe a strain on: The steep climb *overtaxed* his heart.

o·ver·throw [*v.* ō′vər·thrō′, *n.* ō′vər·thrō′] *v.* **o·ver·threw, o·ver·thrown, o·ver·throw·ing,** *n.* **1** *v.* To bring down or remove from power by force: to *overthrow* a ruler. **2** *n.* Defeat or ruin: the *overthrow* of a dictator. **3** *v.* To throw over or down; upset. **4** *v.* To throw past or beyond: The outfielder *overthrew* third base.

add, āce, câre, pälm; end, ēqual; it, īce; odd, ōpen, ôrder; toŏk, pool; up, bûrn;
ə = a in *above*, e in *sicken*, i in *possible*, o in *melon*, u in *circus*; yoō = u in *fuse*; oil; pout;
check; **r**ing; **th**in; **th**is; **zh** in *vision*. For ¶ reference, see page 64 · HOW TO

o·ver·time [ō′vər·tīm′] **1** *n.* Time used in working beyond the regular hours. **2** *adv.* Beyond the regular time: to work *overtime.* **3** *n.* Money paid for working beyond the regular time. **4** *adj. use: overtime* pay. **5** *n.* A period of extra playing time to break a tie, as in basketball. **6** *adj. use:* an *overtime* period; *overtime* play.

o·ver·tone [ō′vər·tōn′] *n.* Any of the higher tones that sound along with the main tone produced by a musical instrument or voice and that together create its characteristic quality.

o·ver·top [ō′vər·top′] *v.* **o·ver·topped, o·ver·top·ping 1** To rise above the top of; tower over. **2** To surpass; excel.

o·ver·ture [ō′vər·chər] *n.* **1** A piece of music which an orchestra plays as an introduction to an opera, musical, ballet, etc. **2** An offer or first move, as toward a closer relationship or an agreement: to make friendly *overtures.*

o·ver·turn [*v.* ō′vər·tûrn′, *n.* ō′vər·tûrn′] **1** *v.* To turn over; upset: to *overturn* a table; The car *overturned.* **2** *v.* To destroy the power of; overthrow. **3** *n.* An upset; overthrow.

o·ver·ween·ing [ō′vər·wē′ning] *adj.* **1** Having too high an opinion of oneself; conceited. **2** Excessive; exaggerated: *overweening* ambition.

o·ver·weight [*adj.* ō′vər·wāt′, *n.* ō′vər·wāt′] **1** *adj.* Weighing too much: an *overweight* girl. **2** *n.* Excessive weight or extra weight; weight beyond what is normal, permitted, or required.

o·ver·whelm [ō′vər·(h)welm′] *v.* **1** To bury or submerge completely, as with a wave. **2** To overcome completely; overpower or crush, as with force or feeling: to be *overwhelmed* by sorrow.

o·ver·whelm·ing [ō′vər·(h)wel′ming] *adj.* So great in force or numbers as to overpower: an *overwhelming* response. **—o′ver·whelm′ing·ly** *adv.*

o·ver·work [*v.* ō′vər·wûrk′, *n.* ō′vər·wûrk′] *v.* **o·ver·worked** (or **o·ver·wrought**: seldom used today), **o·ver·work·ing,** *n.* **1** *v.* To work too hard or too much: The farmer *overworks* his horses; My father *overworks* at his job. **2** *n.* Too much work: He is ill from *overwork.*

o·ver·wrought [ō′vər·rôt′] *adj.* **1** Under emotional strain; tense; nervous. **2** Too elaborate: an *overwrought* pattern or design.

o·vi·pos·i·tor [ō′vi·poz′ə·tər] *n.* The organ at the end of the abdomen in many insects by which the eggs are deposited.

o·void [ō′void] **1** *adj.* Egg-shaped; oval. **2** *n.* An egg-shaped object.

o·vule [ō′vyōōl] *n.* **1** A small ovum. **2** A body in a plant that develops into a seed.

o·vum [ō′vəm] *n., pl.* **o·va** [ō′və] A female reproductive cell, produced in the ovary; an egg. When fertilized it develops into a new individual.

owe [ō] *v.* **owed, ow·ing 1** To have to pay or repay; be indebted for: I *owe* him $2.00. **2** To be indebted to: to *owe* the doctor for three visits. **3** To be in debt: to *owe* for a car. **4** To be obligated or feel obligated to pay, give, or offer: I *owe* you an apology.

ow·ing [ō′ing] *adj.* Yet to be paid; due: taxes *owing* on a house. **—owing to** On account of; because of.

owl [oul] *n.* A night bird having large eyes, a large head, a short, hooked bill, and long, powerful claws. Owls hunt small birds, mice, insects, and other small animals.

Barn owl, about 13 in. long

owl·et [ou′lit] *n.* A young or small owl.

owl·ish [ou′lish] *adj.* Like an owl: The shrewd old man had an *owlish* face.

own [ōn] **1** *v.* To have as one's property; possess: They *own* their home. **2** *adj.* Belonging to oneself: my *own* bicycle; my *own* idea. **3** *v.* To admit: I *own* that I made a mistake. **4** *v.* To acknowledge as one's own: His family will not *own* him. **5** *v.* To confess: I *own* to being frightened. **—come into one's own 1** To receive what one rightfully owns. **2** To receive what one deserves, as a reward or success. **—hold one's own** To maintain one's place or position in spite of opposition or difficulty. **—of one's own** Belonging entirely to oneself. **—one's own** Something belonging to oneself. This book is *my own.* **—on one's own** Dependent only on oneself, as for support or success. **—own up** *informal* To confess.

own·er [ō′nər] *n.* The person who rightfully owns a particular thing.

own·er·ship [ō′nər·ship] *n.* Rightful possession of something.

ox [oks] *n., pl.* **ox·en** [ok′sən] **1** An adult castrated bull, used as a draft animal. **2** Any bovine animal, as a buffalo, bison, or yak.

ox·bow [oks′bō′] *n.* **1** A U-shaped wooden collar for an ox. Its ends fit into the yoke above. **2** A U-shaped bend in a river.

ox·cart [oks′kärt′] *n.* A cart pulled by oxen.

ox·en [ok′sən] Plural of ox.

ox·ford [oks′fərd] *n.* *U.S.* **1** A low shoe laced over the instep. **2** A cloth of cotton or rayon used especially for men's shirts.

Ox·ford [oks′fərd] *n.* A city in southern England, the site of **Oxford University.**

oxford gray Very dark gray.

ox·i·da·tion [ok′sə·dā′shən] *n.* The process of combining with oxygen.

ox·ide [ok′sīd] *n.* A compound of oxygen with one other element or with a radical.

ox·i·dize [ok′sə·dīz] *v.* **ox·i·dized, ox·i·diz·ing** To undergo or cause to undergo oxidation. When iron is exposed to air and moisture, it is oxidized and rust results. ¶3

ox·y·a·cet·y·lene [ok′sē·ə·set′ə·lēn] *adj.* Of or having to do with a mixture of oxygen and acetylene: an *oxyacetylene* welding torch.

ox·y·gen [ok′sə·jin] *n.* A colorless, tasteless, odorless gaseous element, making up about a fifth of the earth's atmosphere. It combines with hydrogen to form water and also combines with most other elements. Plants and animals cannot live and fuels cannot burn without it.

ox·y·gen·ate [ok′sə·jən·āt′] *v.* **ox·y·gen·at·ed, ox·y·gen·at·ing** To treat, combine, or supply with oxygen. — **ox′y·gen·a′tion** *n.*

oxygen mask A device worn over the nose and mouth for breathing where oxygen is scarce. It is connected to a container of oxygen.

oxygen tent A tentlike canopy placed over a patient's head and shoulders, within which pure oxygen may be circulated to ease breathing.

o·yez [ō′yes *or* ō′yez] *interj.* Hear! Hear ye! ◆ *Oyez* is a call made, usually three times, by a court crier to ask for silence before a proclamation is made. It comes from an old French word meaning *hear ye.*

oys·ter [ois′tər] *n.* A shellfish having a soft body within a rough, irregularly-shaped shell in two parts hinged together. Some oysters are good to eat and some yield pearls.

oyster bed A place where oysters breed or are grown.

oz. Abbreviation of: **1** OUNCE. **2** (*sometimes written* **ozs.**) Ounces.

O·zark Mountains [ō′zärk] The hilly uplands in SW Missouri, NW Arkansas, and NE Oklahoma. Also **Ozarks.**

o·zone [ō′zōn] *n.* **1** An unstable form of oxygen having a sharp odor, produced by electric sparks in air. **2** *informal* Pure or fresh air.

P

p or **P** [pē] *n., pl.* **p's** or **P's** The 16th letter of the English alphabet. — **mind one's P's and Q's** To be careful of one's behavior.

P The symbol for the element PHOSPHORUS.

p. Abbreviation of: **1** PAGE. **2** PARTICIPLE.

pa [pä] *n. informal* Father.

Pa. Abbreviation of PENNSYLVANIA.

pace [pās] *n., v.* **paced, pac·ing 1** *n.* A step in walking. **2** *v.* To walk back and forth across: to *pace* the floor. **3** *v.* To walk with slow or regular steps. **4** *n.* The length of the average step in walking, about 3 feet. **5** *v.* To measure by paces: to *pace* off a distance. **6** *n.* A rate of speed, as in movement, work, etc. **7** *v.* To set the pace for: to *pace* a runner. **8** *n.* A gait of a horse in which both feet on the same side move forward together. **9** *v.* To move in this way. — **keep pace with** To keep up with. — **put (one) through his paces** To test the abilities, speed, etc., of someone. — **set the pace** To set or be an example for others to follow or keep up with.

pac·er [pā′sər] *n.* **1** A pacing horse. **2** A person who paces or measures by paces.

pach·y·derm [pak′ə·dûrm] *n.* Any of various large, thick-skinned animals, as the elephant, rhinoceros, and hippopotamus. ◆ See EPIDERMIS.

pa·cif·ic [pə·sif′ik] *adj.* **1** Tending to promote peace: a *pacific* policy. **2** Peaceful; calm. — **pa·cif′i·cal·ly** *adv.*

Pa·cif·ic [pə·sif′ik] **1** *n.* The world's largest ocean, extending from the Arctic to the Antarctic between the Americas and Asia and Australia. **2** *adj.* Of, near, in, or having to do with the Pacific Ocean.

pac·i·fism [pas′ə·fiz′əm] *n.* **1** A belief that war and violence are immoral ways of settling disputes. **2** A refusal, for moral or religious reasons, to bear arms during a war. — **pac′i·fist** *n.*

pac·i·fy [pas′ə·fī] *v.* **pac·i·fied, pac·i·fy·ing 1** To bring peace to: to *pacify* a country. **2** To quiet or calm: to *pacify* a noisy dog. — **pac·i·fi·ca·tion** [pas′ə·fə·kā′shən] *n.* — **pac′i·fi·er** *n.*

pack¹ [pak] **1** *n.* A large bundle or package, especially one to be carried on the back of a man or animal. **2** *v.* To carry, as a pack or load. **3** *v.* To make into a pack or bundle. **4** *v.* To put into a suitcase, box, etc.: *Pack* the blankets. **5** *v.* To fill (a suitcase, box, etc.). **6** *n.* A collection, group, or set: a *pack* of lies; a *pack* of cards. **7** *n.* A gang: a *pack* of thieves. **8** *n.* A group of wolves or dogs that hunt together. **9** *v.* To fill completely: The audience *packed* the theatre. **10** *v.* To crowd together: People were *packed* into the train. **11** *n.* A package or the amount it contains. **12** *v.* To fill, cover, or surround so as to prevent damage, leakage, etc.: to *pack* a motor bearing with grease. **13** *v.* To compress: The snow is *packed* solid. **14** *n.* A large mass of floating ice cakes that have frozen together. **15** *v.* To preserve or package, as for sale or shipment: to *pack* meat for export. — **pack off** To send away. — **send packing** To send or chase away quickly.

pack² [pak] *v.* To arrange or select for one's own advantage: to *pack* a jury.

pack·age [pak′ij] *n., v.* **pack·aged, pack·ag·ing 1** *n.* Something packed, wrapped up, or tied together. **2** *n.* A box, case, crate, etc., used for packing. **3** *v.* To arrange or tie into a package. **4** *n.* A combination of items considered as a unit.

---

add, āce, câre, pälm; end, ēqual; it, īce; odd, ōpen, ôrder; tŏŏk, pōōl; up, bûrn; ə = a in *above*, e in *sicken*, i in *possible*, o in *melon*, u in *circus*; yōō = u in *fuse*; oil; pout; check; ring; thin; this; zh in *vision*. For ¶ reference, see page 64 · HOW TO

pack animal An animal, as a horse or mule, used to carry packs or burdens.

Pack animal

pack·er [pak′ər] *n.* A person or thing that packs, especially a person who packs goods for sale.

pack·et [pak′it] *n.* **1** A small package. **2** A packet boat.

packet boat A ship that makes regular trips carrying mail, freight, and passengers, as along a coast.

pack·ing [pak′ing] *n.* **1** The act of a person or thing that packs. **2** The canning or putting up of food. **3** Any material used in packing.

packing house A factory where meats, etc., are packed or canned.

pact [pakt] *n.* An agreement; compact; treaty.

pad¹ [pad] *n., v.* **pad·ded, pad·ding 1** *n.* A cushion or a similar soft object used as protection against jarring, pressure, etc. **2** *v.* To stuff, line, or protect with pads or padding. **3** *n.* A number of sheets of paper gummed together at one edge. **4** *v.* To lengthen by putting in unnecessary material: to *pad* an essay. **5** *n.* The soft, cushionlike part on the bottom of the foot of certain mammals, as cats. **6** *n.* A large, floating leaf of a water plant. **7** *n.* A block of ink-soaked material used to ink a rubber stamp. **8** *n.* A platform for launching a rocket.

pad² [pad] *v.* **pad·ded, pad·ding,** *n.* **1** *v.* To travel by walking. **2** *v.* To walk almost without noise. **3** *n.* A soft, dull sound, as of a footstep.

pad·ding [pad′ing] *n.* **1** Soft material used to pad something. **2** Words added to a speech or to writing just to make it longer.

pad·dle [pad′(ə)l] *n., v.* **pad·dled, pad·dling 1** *n.* An implement like a short oar with a wide, flat blade at one or both ends, used to propel and steer a canoe or other small boat. **2** *v.* To propel (a canoe, etc.) by means of a paddle or paddles. **3** *n.* Something resembling a canoe paddle, used for beating, stirring, etc. **4** *v.* To beat with or as if with a paddle. **5** *v.* To make short movements of the hands and feet in water, often as a way of swimming. **6** *n.* One of the broad, paddlelike boards on the rim of a water wheel or paddle wheel.

Paddle

paddle wheel A wheel with paddles around its rim, that propels a ship as it turns.

pad·dock [pad′ək] *n.* **1** A pasture or lot near a stable, for exercising horses. **2** An enclosed place planted with grass at a race track, where horses are walked and saddled.

pad·dy [pad′ē] *n., pl.* **pad·dies 1** Rice as it grows. **2** The marshy land where rice is grown.

pad·lock [pad′lok′] **1** *n.* A detachable lock having a curved bar that is hinged at one end. The bar is put through a ring, link, etc., and then snapped into a hole in the body of the lock. **2** *v.* To fasten with a padlock.

Padlock

pa·dre [pä′drā] *n.* **1** Father: an Italian, Spanish, and Portuguese title used in addressing or speaking of a priest. **2** A military chaplain.

pae·an [pē′ən] *n.* A song of joy, praise, etc.

pa·gan [pā′gən] **1** *n.* A person who is neither a Christian, a Jew, nor a Moslem; heathen. **2** *adj.* Of or having to do with pagans or paganism. **3** *n.* A person who has no religion.

pa·gan·ism [pā′gən·iz′əm] *n.* The religious beliefs or practices of a pagan.

page¹ [pāj] *n., v.* **paged, pag·ing 1** *n.* One side of a leaf of a book, etc. **2** *n.* The printing or writing on one side of such a leaf. **3** *n.* An entire leaf or sheet of paper in a book, etc.: A *page* is torn out. **4** *v.* To mark the pages of with numbers. **5** *v.* To turn pages: He *paged* through the magazine. **6** *n.* Any event or events worthy of being recorded: a sad *page* in history.

page² [pāj] *n., v.* **paged, pag·ing 1** *n.* A male servant, especially, in the Middle Ages, a boy in training to be a knight. **2** *n.* A boy or man who runs errands, carries messages, etc. **3** *n.* A youth who attends a person of rank. **4** *v.* To try to locate (someone) by calling his name: The doctor was *paged* at the theater.

pag·eant [paj′ənt] *n.* **1** A public entertainment, often performed outdoors, that is based on historical events. **2** A spectacular show or parade.

pag·eant·ry [paj′ən·trē] *n., pl.* **pag·eant·ries 1** Pageants, as a group. **2** Pomp, splendor, or display.

pa·go·da [pə·gō′də] *n.* In China, India, and Japan, a sacred tower or temple.

paid [pād] **1** Past tense and past participle of PAY. **2** *adj.* Getting pay: a *paid* attendant.

pail [pāl] *n.* **1** A deep, round container with a flat bottom and curved handle; bucket. **2** The amount held by a pail. **— pail′ful** *n.*

Pagoda

pain [pān] *n.* **1** An ache or soreness; suffering in either body or mind: a sharp *pain* in his ankle; His mother's long illness made him feel deep *pain*. **2** *v.* To hurt; be painful: My back *pains*. **3** *v.* To cause pain to: It *pained* us to listen. **4** *n.* (*pl.*) Care, trouble, or effort: Don't waste *pains* on that. **— on pain of** Subject to the penalty of. **— take pains** To take care; make an effort.

Paine [pān], **Thomas,** 1737–1809, author and patriot of the American Revolution.

pain·ful [pān′fəl] *adj.* **1** Giving pain; distressing: a *painful* cut. **2** Needing effort or care: a *painful* task. **— pain′ful·ly** *adv.*

pain·less [pān′lis] *adj.* Free from pain; causing no pain. **— pain′less·ly** *adv.*

pains·tak·ing [pānz′tā′king] *adj.* Taking pains; careful. **— pains′tak′ing·ly** *adv.*

paint [pānt] **1** *n.* A color or pigment, either dry or mixed with oil, water, etc., for application to a surface. **2** *n.* A coating of such coloring matter applied to a surface. **3** *v.* To cover or decorate with paint. **4** *v.* To create (pictures) with paint. **5** *v.* To make a representation of with paint: to *paint* a scene. **6** *v.* To describe vividly in words. **7** *v.* To apply medicine to, as with a swab or brush: to *paint* a cut with antiseptic.

paint·brush [pānt′brush′] *n.* A brush for spreading on paint.

paint·er[1] [pān′tər] *n.* **1** A person whose occupation is painting houses, walls, etc. **2** An artist who paints pictures in oils, etc.

paint·er[2] [pān′tər] *n.* A rope used to tie the bow of a boat to a dock, etc.

paint·er[3] [pān′tər] *n.* Another name for COUGAR.

paint·ing [pān′ting] *n.* **1** The act, art, or occupation of a person who paints. **2** A picture made with paint.

pair [pâr] *n., pl.* **pairs** or **pair,** *v.* **1** *n.* A set of two people or things that match, are alike, or belong together: a *pair* of socks. **2** *v.* To arrange in a pair or pairs; match or couple. **3** *n.* A single thing having two similar parts that are used together: a *pair* of pants. **4** *n.* A married or engaged couple. **5** *n.* Two mated animals. **6** *v.* To marry or mate. **7** *n.* Two members of a legislature who are opposed on a particular issue and agree not to vote. **— pair off** To become or make a pair or pairs. ◆ Of the two plural forms for this word, *pair* is the less formal one.

pa·ja·mas [pə·jä′məz] *n.pl.* An outfit for sleeping consisting of loose-fitting pants and a jacket.

Pa·ki·stan [pä′ki·stän′ *or* pak′i·stan] *n.* A country in Asia, a member of the British Commonwealth of Nations.

Pa·ki·sta·ni [pä′ki·stä′nē *or* pak′i·sta′nē] **1** *adj.* Of or from Pakistan. **2** *n.* A person born in or a citizen of Pakistan.

pal [pal] *n., v.* **palled, pal·ling** *informal* **1** *n.* A friend; chum. **2** *v.* To associate as pals.

pal·ace [pal′is] *n.* **1** The official residence of a king or other high dignitary. **2** Any splendid house or grand building.

pal·an·quin or **pal·an·keen** [pal′ən·kēn′] *n.* A covered couch or litter on which a person is carried by two or more bearers.

pal·at·a·ble [pal′it·ə·bəl] *adj.* **1** Pleasant to the taste; savory. **2** Acceptable: a *palatable* suggestion. **— pal′at·a·bly** *adv.*

pal·ate [pal′it] *n.* **1** The roof of the mouth, consisting of a bony part in front, the **hard palate,** and a fleshy part in back, the **soft palate. 2** The sense of taste. **3** Intellectual taste; liking.

pa·la·tial [pə·lā′shəl] *adj.* Of, like, or befitting a palace; grand; magnificent.

pa·lav·er [pə·lav′ər] **1** *n.* Empty talk, especially talk intended to flatter or deceive. **2** *n.* A public discussion or conference. **3** *v.* To talk in an idle or flattering way.

pale[1] [pāl] *adj., v.* **paled, pal·ing 1** *adj.* Of a whitish or ashen color; wan: *pale* skin. **2** *adj.* Faint; weak: a *pale* gleam. **3** *adj.* Of a very light shade: *pale* green. **4** *v.* To make or become pale. **— pale′ly** *adv.* **— pale′ness** *n.*

pale[2] [pāl] *n., v.* **paled, pal·ing 1** *n.* A stake or picket of a fence. **2** *n.* A fence. **3** *n.* Any boundary or limit. **4** *v.* To fence in.

pale·face [pāl′fās′] *n.* A white person: thought to have been used by American Indians.

Pa·le·o·lith·ic [pā′lē·ō·lith′ik] *adj.* Of or having to do with the early Stone Age when men chipped stones roughly to make tools and weapons and painted pictures on cave walls.

pa·le·on·tol·o·gy [pā′lē·on·tol′ə·jē] *n.* The science that studies ancient forms of life, especially as they are known from their fossil remains in the rocks. **— pa′le·on·tol′o·gist** *n.*

Pa·le·o·zo·ic [pā′lē·ō·zō′ik] **1** *adj.* Of or having to do with a very early geological era, from the rise of the first animals to the rise of the reptiles. **2** *n.* The Paleozoic era.

Pal·es·tine [pal′is·tīn] *n.* A territory on the eastern coast of the Mediterranean that was the country of the Jews in Biblical times and was divided in 1947 into Israel and a territory that is now part of Jordan.

pal·ette [pal′it] *n.* **1** A board with a hole for the thumb, used by an artist when mixing paints. **2** The colors used by any one artist.

pal·frey [pôl′frē] *n., pl.* **pal·freys** A saddle horse, especially one gentle enough for a woman: seldom used today.

pal·ing [pā′ling] *n.* **1** A pale. **2** Pales, as a group. **3** A fence made of pales or pickets.

pal·i·sade [pal′ə·sād′] *n., v.* **pal·i·sad·ed, pal·i·sad·ing 1** *n.* A fence of strong stakes set in the ground as a barrier against attack. **2** *n.* One of the stakes forming such a barrier. **3** *v.* To enclose with a palisade. **4** *n.*(*pl.*) A long cliff.

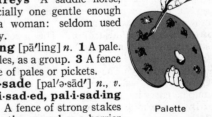

Palette

pall[1] [pôl] *n.* **1** A covering, usually of heavy, black cloth, put over a coffin or tomb. **2** Something that covers, especially something that is dark or gloomy: a *pall* of fog.

---

add, āce, câre, pälm;   end, ēqual;   it, īce;   odd, ōpen, ôrder;   tŏŏk, pōōl;   up, bûrn;

ə = a in *above*, e in *sicken*, i in *possible*, o in *melon*, u in *circus*;   yōō = u in *fuse*;   oil;   pout;

check;   ring;   thin;   this;   zh in *vision*.   For ¶ reference, see page 64 · HOW TO

pall[2] [pôl] *v.* To become uninteresting, dull, etc.: The puzzle *palled* on me.

Pal·las [pal′əs] *n.* In Greek myths, another name for Athena. She was often called Pallas Athena.

pall·bear·er [pôl′bâr′ər] *n.* A person who carries or walks beside the coffin at a funeral.

pal·let [pal′it] *n.* A poor bed or mattress, usually made of or filled with straw.

pal·li·ate [pal′ē·āt] *v.* **pal·li·at·ed, pal·li·at·ing** **1** To cause (a crime, fault, etc.) to appear less serious or terrible. **2** To ease the symptoms or effects of (a disease, illness, etc.) without curing it.

pal·li·a·tive [pal′ē·ə·tiv] **1** *adj.* Tending to palliate. **2** *n.* Something that palliates.

pal·lid [pal′id] *adj.* Pale or wan in appearance; lacking in color or strength; weak: Her long illness had made her face thin and *pallid*.

pal·lor [pal′ər] *n.* Paleness, as of the face.

palm[1] [päm] **1** *n.* The inside surface of the hand between the wrist and the base of the fingers. **2** *v.* To hide (an object) in the palm of the hand. **3** *n.* The width of a hand, about 3 to 4 inches, or the length of a hand, about 8 inches. **4** *n.* Something that covers the palm, as part of a glove. **— palm off** To pass off or dispose of by trickery or fraud.

palm[2] [päm] *n.* **1** Any of a group of tropical evergreen trees or shrubs, usually having a trunk without branches and a crown of broad or feathery leaves. **2** A leaf of the palm, used as a symbol of victory or joy. **3** Triumph; victory. **4** The prize or reward for victory.

palm·er [pä′mər] *n.* In the Middle Ages, a pilgrim who had visited the Holy Land and carried back a palm branch as a sign that he had been there.

pal·met·to [pal·met′ō] *n., pl.* **pal·met·tos** or **pal·met·toes** Any of several kinds of palm trees having crowns of fan-shaped leaves.

Palm tree

palm·is·try [pä′mis·trē] *n.* The practice of supposedly learning a person's past or future from the lines and marks in the palm of his hand.

Palm Sunday The Sunday before Easter, a Christian festival commemorating Jesus' triumphal entry into Jerusalem.

palm·y [pä′mē] *adj.* **palm·i·er, palm·i·est** **1** Prosperous; having success. **2** Having many palms; shaded by palms.

pal·o·mi·no [pal′ə·mē′nō] *n., pl.* **pal·o·mi·nos** A light tan or golden brown horse with a cream-colored mane and tail.

pal·pa·ble [pal′pə·bəl] *adj.* **1** Capable of being touched or felt. **2** Easily known or recognized; clear: a *palpable* insult. **— pal′pa·bly** *adv.*

pal·pi·tate [pal′pə·tāt] *v.* **pal·pi·tat·ed, pal·pi·tat·ing** **1** To shake; tremble. **2** To beat more rapidly than normal; flutter: My heart *palpitated* with fear. **— pal′pi·ta′tion** *n.*

pal·sied [pôl′zēd] *adj.* **1** Having palsy. **2** Trembling.

pal·sy [pôl′zē] *n., v.* **pal·sied, pal·sy·ing** **1** *n.* A form of paralysis resulting in weak, rigid muscles and involuntary trembling of the limbs. **2** *v.* To paralyze. **3** *v.* To cause to tremble or become helpless: Fear *palsied* him.

pal·ter [pôl′tər] *v.* **1** To speak or act in an insincere way. **2** To be fickle or trifling. **3** To haggle or quibble.

pal·try [pôl′trē] *adj.* **pal·tri·er, pal·tri·est** **1** Of small value; trifling: a *paltry* gift. **2** Contemptible; petty. **— pal′tri·ness** *n.*

pam·pas [pam′pəz] *n.pl.* The great treeless plains south of the Amazon River, extending from the Atlantic Ocean to the Andes Mountains.

pam·per [pam′pər] *v.* To treat too kindly; give in to all the wishes of; coddle.

pam·phlet [pam′flit] *n.* A booklet with a paper cover, often on a topic of current interest.

pam·phlet·eer [pam′flə·tir′] **1** *n.* A person who writes pamphlets. **2** *v.* To write and publish pamphlets.

pan [pan] *n., v.* **panned, pan·ning** **1** *n.* A wide, shallow container, usually of metal, used to hold liquids or in cooking. **2** *n.* A container similar to this, as the one used in washing gold out of earth or gravel. **3** *v.* To wash (earth or gravel) in a pan in search of gold. **4** *v.* To separate (gold) from earth or gravel in such a way. **5** *n.* A cup in the lock of an old gun that holds a little powder to set off the charge. **6** *v. informal* To criticize severely. **— pan out** To turn out: How did your plans *pan out*?

Pan [pan] *n.* In Greek myths, a god of forests, flocks, and shepherds, having the horns and hoofs of a goat.

pan·a·ce·a [pan′ə·sē′ə] *n.* A remedy for all diseases or ills; cure-all.

Pan·a·ma [pan′ə·mä] *n.* A country in Central America.

Panama Canal A ship canal across Panama connecting the Atlantic and the Pacific oceans.

panama hat A hat woven from the leaves of a tree that grows in Central and South America.

Pan·a·ma·ni·an [pan′ə·mā′nē·ən] **1** *adj.* Of or from Panama. **2** *n.* A person born in or a citizen of Panama.

Pan-A·mer·i·can [pan′ə·mer′ə·kən] *adj.* Including or having to do with North and South America or all Americans.

pan·cake [pan′kāk′] *n.* A thin, flat cake made of batter fried in a pan or on a griddle.

pan·chro·mat·ic [pan′krō·mat′ik] *adj.* Sensitive to all colors of light: *panchromatic* film.

pan·cre·as [pan′krē·əs] *n.* A large gland behind the lower part of the stomach that discharges digestive juices into the intestine and insulin into the blood.

pan·cre·at·ic [pan′krē·at′ik] *adj.* Of, from, or having to do with the pancreas.

pan·da [pan′də] *n.* **1** A small raccoonlike animal of the Himalayas with reddish brown fur and a long ringed tail. **2** A related bearlike animal of Tibet and China, having a black and white coat and dark rings around the eyes.

Giant panda, about 4 ft. long

pan·de·mo·ni·um (pan′də·mō′nē·əm] *n.* **1** A place of disorder and uproar. **2** Great disorder and uproar.

pan·der [pan′dər] **1** *n.* A person who caters to or aids in the indulgence of the base passions or desires of others. **2** *v.* To act as a pander.

Pan·do·ra [pan·dôr′ə] *n.* In Greek myths, a woman who let all human ills into the world when she opened a box which had been given to her by Zeus and which he had commanded her not to open.

pane [pān] *n.* A single sheet of glass set in the frame of a window, door, etc.

pan·e·gyr·ic [pan′ə·jir′ik] *n.* **1** Formal public praise of someone or something, either spoken or written. **2** Extravagant praise.

pan·el [pan′əl] *n., v.* **pan·eled** or **pan·elled**, **pan·el·ing** or **pan·el·ling 1** *n.* An oblong or square part of a wall, ceiling, door, etc., that is set off from the rest of the surface, as by being raised above the general level or by being of a different material. **2** *v.* To fit or provide with a panel or panels. **3** *n.* A piece of fabric sewn lengthwise into a skirt or the skirt of a dress. **4** *n.* A picture very long for its width. **5** *n.* A group of persons from which a jury is selected. **6** *n.* A jury. **7** *n.* A group of persons chosen to hold a discussion, judge a contest, etc. **8** *n.* A board or mount holding the dials and controls of an automobile, airplane, engine room, etc.

panel discussion A discussion, held in front of an audience, of a special subject by a selected group of people.

pan·el·ist [pan′əl·ist] *n.* A person serving on a panel, especially in a panel discussion.

pang [pang] *n.* A sudden, sharp pain or twinge: *pangs* of conscience; *pangs* of illness.

pan·ic [pan′ik] *n., v.* **pan·icked, pan·ick·ing 1** *n.* Sudden, overwhelming fear, often affecting many people at once: The blast caused great *panic*. **2** *v.* To affect or become affected with panic.

pan·ick·y [pan′ik·ē] *adj.* **1** Like, caused by, or showing panic. **2** Likely or tending to panic; fearful.

pan·nier [pan′yər] *n.* One of a pair of baskets hung across the back of an animal used for carrying burdens.

pan·o·plied [pan′ə·plēd] *adj.* Having or wearing a panoply.

pan·o·ply [pan′ə·plē] *n., pl.* **pan·o·plies 1** A full set of armor and weapons. **2** Any complete covering that protects or is decorative.

pan·o·ram·a [pan′ə·ram′ə] *n.* **1** A clear view in all directions, as from a mountain. **2** A wide picture which, by being unrolled a little at a time, passes slowly before the viewer. **3** A complete view or treatment of a subject or of passing events, sights, etc.: His book gives us an excellent *panorama* of the war.

pan·o·ram·ic [pan′ə·ram′ik] *adj.* Of, like, or having to do with a panorama or panoramas.

pan·sy [pan′zē] *n., pl.* **pan·sies** A common garden flower that grows in a variety of colors. ◆ *Pansy*, known as the flower of thought or remembrance, comes from the French word *pensée*, meaning a *thought*.

pant [pant] **1** *v.* To breathe quickly and jerkily. **2** *n.* A short, gasping breath. **3** *v.* To say while panting: "Hurry," he *panted*. **4** *v.* To make noisy puffs of smoke, steam, etc. **5** *n.* A noisy puff of steam, etc. **6** *v.* To desire strongly; long: to *pant* after power.

pan·ta·lets or **pan·ta·lettes** [pan′tə·lets′] *n.pl.* Long, ruffled or embroidered underpants showing below the skirt, worn by women and girls in the 19th century.

pan·ta·loon [pan′tə·loon′] *n.* **1** (*pl.*) Trousers, especially tight-fitting ones with straps that fit under the instep, worn by men in former times. **2** (*written* **Pantaloon**) In pantomimes, an absurd old man on whom the clown plays tricks.

pan·the·ism [pan′thē·iz′əm] *n.* The belief that everything in the universe is a part of God. **— pan′the·ist** *n.*

Pan·the·on [pan′thē·on] *n.* A circular temple with a dome, dedicated to all the gods, built in Rome in 27 B.C.

pan·ther [pan′thər] *n.* **1** A leopard, especially the black leopard of southern Asia. **2** The cougar or mountain lion. **3** The jaguar.

pant·ies [pan′tēz] *n.pl.* A woman's or child's underpants.

Panther

pan·to·mime [pan′tə·mīm] *n., v.* **pan·to·mimed, pan·to·mim·ing 1** *n.* A play in which the actors express their meaning without speaking. **2** *n.* Gestures without speech. **3** *v.* To express or act out in gestures alone: to *pantomime* rage.

pan·try [pan′trē] *n., pl.* **pan·tries** A place where food, kitchen supplies, etc., are stored.

add, āce, câre, pälm; end, ēqual; it, īce; odd, ōpen, ôrder; to͞ok, po͞ol; up, bûrn;
ə = a in *above*, e in *sicken*, i in *possible*, o in *melon*, u in *circus*; y o͞o = u in *fuse*; oil; pout;
check; ring; thin; this; zh in *vision*. For ¶ reference, see page 64 · HOW TO

pants [pants] *n.pl.* **1** Trousers. **2** Underpants. ◆The word *pants* is short for *pantaloons.*

pap [pap] *n.* Soft food for babies or invalids.

pa·pa [pä′pə *or* pə·pä′] *n.* Father: used especially by or in talking to children.

pa·pa·cy [pā′pə·sē] *n., pl.* **pa·pa·cies 1** The office or power of a Pope. **2** The time of a Pope's reign. **3** The succession of Popes. **4** (*written* **Papacy**) The government of the Roman Catholic Church.

pa·pal [pā′pəl] *adj.* Of or having to do with a Pope, the papacy, or the Roman Catholic Church: a *papal* letter; a *papal* decree.

pa·paw [pə·pô′ *or* pô′pô] *n.* **1** A tree or shrub of North America having fleshy, edible fruit. **2** The fruit of this tree.

pa·pa·ya [pə·pä′yə] *n.* **1** An edible, yellow, melonlike fruit that grows in tropical America. **2** The tree that bears this fruit.

pa·per [pā′pər] **1** *n.* A material made mainly of wood pulp and rags, formed in thin sheets and used for writing, printing, wrapping things, covering walls, etc. **2** *n.* A sheet of this material. **3** *adj. use:* paper money; paper towels. **4** *n.* An essay, report, or other written or printed matter. **5** *n.* (*pl.*) A collection of letters, diaries, etc., usually by one person: the Jefferson *papers.* **6** *n.* A newspaper. **7** *n.* (*pl.*) Important or official documents, as personal identification, contracts, etc. **8** *n.* A written or printed promise to pay money; note. **9** *adj. use:* paper profits. **10** *n.* Wallpaper. **11** *v.* To cover or finish with wallpaper. **12** *n.* A wrapper used to hold small articles for sale: a *paper* of pins. **— on paper 1** In written or printed form. **2** In theory, but not necessarily in fact: The plan looks good *on paper,* but it isn't practical. **— pa′per·er** *n.* ◆ *Paper* comes from the Latin word *papyrus,* which also gives us our word *papyrus.* In old French, Latin *papyrus* became *papier,* which is the basis of our English word *paper.*

pa·per·back [pā′pər·bak′] *n.* A book bound with a paper cover.

pa·per·hang·er [pā′pər·hang′ər] *n.* A person whose business is to cover walls with wallpaper.

pa·per·weight [pā′pər·wāt′] *n.* A small, heavy object placed on loose papers to prevent them from falling or blowing away.

pa·pier-mâ·ché [pā′pər·mə·shā′] **1** *n.* Paper pulp mixed with oil, glue, resin, etc., which can be molded when wet and becomes hard and tough when dry. **2** *adj. use:* a papier-mâché doll.

pa·pil·la [pə·pil′ə] *n., pl.* **pa·pil·lae** [pə·pil′ē] or **pa·pil·las** A small, nipplelike projection, as on the tongue or at the root of a hair.

pa·poose or **pap·poose** [pa·pōōs′] *n.* A North American Indian baby or small child.

pa·pri·ka [pa·prē′kə *or* pap′rə·kə] *n.* A spice made from a mild variety of red pepper.

pa·py·rus [pə·pī′rəs] *n., pl.* **pa·py·ri** [pə·pī′rī] or **pa·py·rus·es 1** A tall rushlike water plant native to Israel, Jordan, Syria, and Ethiopia and once common in Egypt. **2** A kind of paper used by the Egyptians, Greeks, and Romans made

from the pith of the plant. **3** A manuscript written on this. ◆See PAPER.

par [pär] **1** *n.* An accepted standard of comparison: Fred's work is on a *par* with John's. **2** *n.* A normal or average amount, quality, condition, or degree: Production is not up to *par.* **3** *adj.* Normal or average; ordinary. **4** *n.* In golf, a standard number of strokes in which a hole or course should be completed. **5** *n.* The value that is printed on the face of a stock, bond, or other security. **6** *adj. use: par* value.

par·a·ble [par′ə·bəl] *n.* A short tale teaching a moral or religious lesson by comparison with natural or familiar things.

pa·rab·o·la [pə·rab′ə·lə] *n.* The curve formed by the set of all the points that are equally distant from a fixed line and a fixed point; the path of a thrown ball if there is no wind.

Parabola
Distance $AB = AF,$
$EG = GF, CD = DF,$
$JH = HF$

par·a·chute [par′ə·shōōt] *n., v.* **par·a·chut·ed, par·a·chut·ing 1** *n.* A large, expanding, umbrella-shaped device that retards the speed, especially in falling, of an object or person to which it is attached. Parachutes are used in making a descent from an airplane, in dropping supplies from an airplane, or in slowing down an airplane when it lands. **2** *v.* To descend or cause to descend with a parachute. **— par′a·chut·ist** *n.*

Parachute

pa·rade [pə·rād′] *n., v.* **pa·rad·ed, pa·rad·ing 1** *n.* A procession or march for ceremony or display. **2** *v.* To march formally or with display. **3** *n.* A gathering or marching of troops for display or official inspection. **4** *n.* The place where military parades are held. **5** *v.* To cause to march or gather for military display or inspection: to *parade* troops. **6** *n.* A promenade or public walk. **7** *n.* A group of people promenading. **8** *v.* To walk in public in order to show oneself; promenade. **9** *n.* Vain show or display. **10** *v.* To display or show off; flaunt: to *parade* one's accomplishments.

par·a·dise [par′ə·dīs] *n.* **1** Heaven. **2** Any place or condition of great beauty or delight. **3** (*written* **Paradise**) Eden.

par·a·dox [par′ə·doks] *n.* **1** A statement that seems contradictory, but may in fact be true, as "Stone walls do not a prison make, nor iron bars a cage." **2** A statement that contradicts itself, or is false or absurd, as "Everything I say is a lie." **3** A person or thing that seems to act in a contradictory way.

par·a·dox·i·cal [par′ə·doks′i·kəl] *adj.* Of, like, or having to do with a paradox.

par·af·fin [par′ə·fin] **1** *n.* A white, waxy mixture of substances obtained chiefly from petro-leum. It is used for making candles, sealing jelly or preserves, etc. **2** *v.* To treat with paraffin.

par·a·gon [par′ə·gon] *n.* A model or pattern of excellence: a *paragon* of manhood.

par·a·graph [par′ə·graf] **1** *n.* A distinct, sep-arate part or section of something written, gen-erally beginning on a new line and indented from the margin. **2** *v.* To arrange in or into para-graphs. **3** *n.* A short article or item, as in a newspaper. **4** *v.* To write paragraphs about. **5** *n.* A sign (¶) used to indicate a new paragraph or as a reference to a paragraph.

Par·a·guay [par′ə·gwā *or* par′ə·gwī] *n.* A country in central South America.

par·a·keet [par′ə·kēt] *n.* Any of various small parrots with long tails, kept as pets.

par·al·lax [par′ə·laks] *n.* An apparent change in the position of an object caused by a change in the position of the observer. Parallax is used in astronomy for determining distances.

par·al·lel [par′ə·lel] *adj., n., v.* **par·al·leled** or **par·al·lelled, par·al·lel·ing** or **par·al·lel·ling 1** *adj.* Never having a point in common, no matter how far extended, as two lines or two flat surfaces: The floor is *par-allel* to the ceiling. **2** *n.* An object or surface that is al-ways an equal distance from another. **3** *n.* A parallel line or surface. **4** *v.* To be parallel to: The railroad track *parallels* the road. **5** *adj.* Very much alike; closely similar: stories with *parallel* plots. **6** *n.* A comparison: to draw a *parallel* between two things. **7** *v.* To be, find, or provide the equal of: Can you *parallel* that? **8** *n.* Something that is similar to or like some-thing else; match. **9** *v.* To compare; liken. **10** *n.* One of the imaginary circles around the earth parallel to the equator and connecting all the points having a particular latitude. **11** *n.* In an electric circuit, a connection of devices so made that each can be removed without stopping the current to or from any of the others.

Sets of parallels

par·al·lel·ism [par′ə·lel·iz′əm] *n.* **1** The quality or condition of being parallel. **2** Close resem-blance or similarity.

par·al·lel·o·gram [par′ə·lel′ə·gram] *n.* A four-sided plane figure having all of its opposite sides parallel.

pa·ral·y·sis [pə·ral′ə·sis] *n., pl.* **pa·ral·y·ses** [pə·ral′ə·sēz] **1** The loss or lessening of the power of movement or of feeling in any part of the body. **2** A stopping or crippling of normal ac-tivities: Snow caused *paralysis* of travel.

par·a·lyt·ic [par′ə·lit′ik] **1** *adj.* Of, having, or causing paralysis. **2** *n.* A person with paralysis.

par·a·lyze [par′ə·līz] *v.* **par·a·lyzed, par·a·lyz·ing 1** To bring about paralysis in. **2** To

make powerless, helpless, or inactive: The strike *paralyzed* the industry. ¶3

par·a·me·ci·um [par′ə·mē′shē·əm *or* par′ə·mē′·sē·əm] *n., pl.* **par·a·me·ci·a** [par′ə·mē′shē·ə *or* par′ə·mē′·sē·ə] or **par·a·me·ci·ums** A tiny slipper-shaped, one-celled animal covered with fine hairs, or cilia, by which it swims about.

A paramecium

par·a·mount [par′ə·mount] *adj.* Superior to all others; chief in importance or rank.

par·a·noi·a [par′ə·noi′ə] *n.* A mental disorder in which a person often imagines others are perse-cuting him or imagines himself to be a more im-portant person than he actually is.

par·a·noid [par′ə·noid] **1** *adj.* Resembling or suggestive of paranoia. **2** *n.* A person having paranoia or showing some of its symptoms.

par·a·pet [par′ə·pit *or* par′ə·pet] *n.* **1** A low wall around the edge of a roof, terrace, etc. **2** A low wall built by soldiers as a defense.

par·a·pher·na·li·a [par′ə·fər·nāl′yə] *n.pl.* **1** Personal possessions. **2** (*often used with a singu-lar verb*) A group of things, especially as used in some activity; equipment.

par·a·phrase [par′ə·frāz] *n., v.* **par·a·phrased, par·a·phras·ing 1** *n.* A statement expressed in other words of the meaning of a passage, work, etc. **2** *v.* To express in other words the meaning of (a passage, work, etc.).

par·a·site [par′ə·sīt] *n.* **1** A plant or animal that lives in or on another and gets its food and often shelter from the other, as a flea, tapeworm, etc. **2** A person who lives at the expense of an-other without making proper return.

par·a·sit·ic [par′ə·sit′ik] *adj.* Of, like, or caused by a parasite or parasites.

par·a·sol [par′ə·sôl] *n.* A small, light umbrella carried to protect someone from the sun.

par·a·thy·roid gland [par′ə·thī′roid] One of several, usually four, small bean-shaped glands arranged in pairs behind the thyroid gland. They control the amount of calcium in the blood.

par·a·troop·er [par′ə·trōō′pər] *n.* A soldier trained to parachute into battle from an airplane.

par·a·troops [par′ə·trōōps] *n.pl.* Troops trained to parachute into battle.

par·boil [pär′boil′] *v.* To cook partially by boiling, as in preparation for roasting.

par·cel [pär′səl] *n., v.* **par·celed** or **par·celled, par·cel·ing** or **par·cel·ling 1** *n.* Something that is wrapped up; package. **2** *n.* A distinct portion of land: We sold that rocky *parcel* near the river. **3** *v.* To divide or give in parts or shares: to *parcel* out food.

parcel post A mail service for the carrying and delivering of parcels.

parch [pärch] *v.* **1** To make or become dry with heat; shrivel. **2** To make or become thirsty.

parch·ment [pärch′mənt] *n.* **1** The skin of sheep, goats, etc., prepared to be written or painted on. **2** A manuscript written on parchment. **3** Paper that looks like parchment, as that used in stationery and lamp shades.

par·don [pär′dən] **1** *v.* To forgive: *Pardon* me for being late. **2** *n.* The act of forgiving; forgiveness: I beg your *pardon.* **3** *v.* To excuse or free from further punishment: The convict was *pardoned.* **4** *n.* The decision or the legal order that frees a person from punishment.

par·don·a·ble [pär′dən·ə·bəl] *adj.* Capable of being pardoned: a *pardonable* offense.

pare [pâr] *v.* **pared, par·ing 1** To remove the outer layer or skin of (a fruit or vegetable). **2** To make less or smaller, little by little: to *pare* costs.

par·e·gor·ic [par′ə·gôr′ik] *n.* A solution of camphor and a small amount of opium in alcohol, used to relieve pain, coughing, etc.

par·ent [pâr′ənt] *n.* **1** A father or mother. **2** Any plant or animal that produces offspring. **3** A source or cause: Poverty can be the *parent* of crime.

Paring an apple

par·ent·age [pâr′ən·tij] *n.* Descent from parents; lineage; origin.

pa·ren·tal [pə·ren′təl] *adj.* Of, having to do with, or like a parent. **—pa·ren′tal·ly** *adv.*

pa·ren·the·sis [pə·ren′thə·sis] *n., pl.* **pa·ren·the·ses** [pə·ren′thə·sēz] **1** A word, phrase, etc., added to an already complete sentence but set off from it, as *thank heaven* in "He went (thank heaven) home." **2** Either or both of the curved lines () used to enclose such a word or phrase.

par·en·thet·ic [par′ən·thet′ik] *adj.* **1** Put in as a parenthesis: a *parenthetic* remark. **2** Enclosed in a parenthesis. **3** Using many parentheses. **— par′en·thet′i·cal·ly** *adv.*

par·en·thet·i·cal [par′ən·thet′i·kəl] *adj.* Parenthetic.

par·ent·hood [pâr′ənt·hŏŏd] *n.* The condition of being a parent.

par·fait [pär·fā′] *n.* A frozen dessert made with eggs, sugar, whipped cream, flavoring, etc.

pa·ri·ah [pə·rī′ə or par′ē·ə] *n.* A person with whom others do not associate; outcast.

par·ing [pâr′ing] *n.* (*often pl.*) Something that has been pared off, as skin or rind.

Par·is [par′is] *n.* In Greek myths, a Trojan prince who kidnaped Helen, the queen of Sparta, thus causing the Trojan War.

Par·is [par′is] *n.* The capital of France, in the northern part. **— Pa·ri·sian** [pə·rizh′ən or pə·rēzh′ən] *adj., n.*

par·ish [par′ish] *n.* **1** In certain religious groups, a district, usually part of a diocese, having its own church and clergymen. **2** All the people who worship at one church. **3** A district in Louisiana corresponding to a county.

pa·rish·ion·er [pə·rish′ən·ər] *n.* A member of a parish.

par·i·ty [par′ə·tē] *n.* Equality, as of condition, rank, value, etc.

park [pärk] **1** *n.* A piece of land for public use, having trees, grass, benches, walks, playgrounds, etc. **2** *n.* An area set aside for public use by a national or state government because of its beauty, wildlife, etc. **3** *n.* The grounds of a country estate. **4** *v.* To leave (an automobile, etc.) standing somewhere for a time. **5** *v.* To drive (an automobile, etc.) into a place where it may be left.

par·ka [pär′kə] *n.* A fur or cloth jacket or coat with a hood.

park·way [pärk′wā′] *n.* A wide street or road whose edges are planted with grass and trees.

Parka

par·lance [pär′ləns] *n.* Manner of speech; language: legal *parlance.*

par·ley [pär′lē] *n., pl.* **par·leys,** *v.* **1** *n.* A conference, as with an enemy; discussion of terms. **2** *v.* To hold such a conference.

par·lia·ment [pär′lə·mənt] *n.* **1** An assembly whose function is making the laws of a country. **2** (*written* **Parliament**) The legislature of Great Britain, or of any of the self-governing members of the Commonwealth.

par·lia·men·ta·ry [pär′lə·men′tər·ē] *adj.* **1** Of, having to do with, or done by a parliament. **2** According to the rules of a parliament: *parliamentary* procedure. **3** Governed by or having a parliament.

par·lor [pär′lər] *n.* **1** A room for receiving visitors, entertaining guests, etc. **2** A place where a certain kind of business is conducted: a *beauty* parlor. ¶1

par·lous [pär′ləs] *adj.* Dangerous or exciting; perilous: seldom used today.

Par·nas·sus [pär·nas′əs] *n.* A mountain in Greece that was sacred to Apollo and the Muses in ancient times.

pa·ro·chi·al [pə·rō′kē·əl] *adj.* **1** Belonging to, supported by, or limited to a church parish: a *parochial* school. **2** Limited in scope; narrow: *parochial* ideas.

par·o·dy [par′ə·dē] *n., pl.* **par·o·dies,** *v.* **par·o·died, par·o·dy·ing 1** *n.* A humorous imitation of a serious literary or musical work. **2** *v.* To make a parody of.

pa·role [pə·rōl′] *n., v.* **pa·roled, pa·rol·ing 1** *n.* The release of a prisoner from part of his sentence on the conditions that he observe certain rules and behave well. **2** *v.* To release (a prisoner) on these conditions. **3** *n.* A pledge by a prisoner of war to abide by certain conditions in return for his release or for special privileges.

par·ox·ysm [par′ək·siz′əm] *n.* A sudden and violent outburst; fit: a *paroxysm* of tears.

par·quet [pär·kā′] *n.* **1** Flooring of parquetry. **2** The main floor of a theater; orchestra.

par·quet·ry [pär′kit·rē] *n.* Pieces of wood fitted into a pattern, used mainly for floors.

Parquet

par·ra·keet [par′ə·kēt] *n.* Another spelling of PARAKEET.

par·ri·cide [par′ə·sīd] *n.* **1** The killing of a parent. **2** A person who has killed a parent.

par·rot [par′ət] **1** *n.* Any of various brightly colored birds with hooked bills, some of which can imitate human speech. **2** *v.* To imitate or repeat without understanding. **3** *n.* A person who parrots.

par·ry [par′ē] *v.* **par·ried, par·ry·ing,** *n., pl.* **par·ries** **1** *v.* To ward off, as a blow or a thrust from a sword. **2** *v.* To avoid or evade, as a question. **3** *n.* The movement or action of parrying.

Parrot, 30 in. head to tail

parse [pärs] *v.* **parsed, pars·ing** **1** To separate (a sentence) into the parts that make it up, explaining the form, function, and relationship of each of them. **2** To describe (a word) in a sentence, telling its part of speech, its function, and its relationship to the other words.

Par·see or **Par·si** [pär′sē] *n.* A member of a religious sect in India, descended from Persians who fled there in the 8th century.

par·si·mo·ni·ous [pär′sə·mō′nē·əs] *adj.* Too thrifty or miserly; stingy. **— par′si·mo′ni·ous·ly** *adv.*

par·si·mo·ny [pär′sə·mō′nē] *n.* Too much thriftiness; stinginess.

pars·ley [pärs′lē] *n.* A common herb cultivated for its leaves which are used to flavor and decorate foods.

pars·nip [pärs′nip] *n.* An herb with a large, carrotlike root that can be eaten.

par·son [pär′sən] *n.* A clergyman; minister.

par·son·age [pär′sən·ij] *n.* The house that a church provides for its parson.

part [pärt] **1** *n.* A portion or piece of a whole, often one of a group of equal pieces. **2** *v.* To divide or break into parts. **3** *n.* Any of the separate things that make up a working whole, as in a machine: radio *parts.* **4** *n.* An organ, limb, etc., of a plant or animal. **5** *n.* A share, as of work, obligation, etc.: to do one's *part.* **6** *adj.* Being incomplete; not whole: a *part*

owner. **7** *adv.* Partly: The idea is *part* mine. **8** *n.* A side, as in a disagreement or dispute. **9** *n.* The role or lines given to an actor, as in a play. **10** *n.* The music intended for a voice or instrument or a particular group of voices or instruments in a composition: the flute *part.* **11** *n.* A line on the scalp made by combing the hair in opposite directions. **12** *v.* To divide (the hair) by combing in different directions. **13** *v.* To break off, as a relationship: to *part* company. **14** *v.* To separate: to *part* the two fighters; They *parted* at noon. **15** *n.* (*usually pl.*) A gift of mind or character: a man of *parts.* **16** *n.* (*usually pl.*) A region or territory: foreign *parts.* **— for one's part** As far as one is concerned. **— for the most part** To the greatest extent; generally. **— in part** Partly; not wholly. **— part and parcel** An essential or very important part. **— part from** To go away from; leave. **— part with** To give up. **— take part** To join in or share; participate.

par·take [pär·tāk′] *v.* **par·took, par·tak·en, par·tak·ing** **1** To take part or have a share: They *partook* in her good fortune. **2** To receive or take a portion or share: They *partook* of the evening meal. **3** To have something of the quality: answers that *partake* of rudeness. **— par·tak′er** *n.*

Par·the·non [pär′thə·non] *n.* A famous Greek temple on the Acropolis of Athens.

par·tial [pär′shəl] *adj.* **1** Involving or made up of only a part. **2** Favoring one side; prejudiced; biased. **3** Having a special liking: I'm *partial* to ice cream. **— par′tial·ly** *adv.*

The Parthenon

par·ti·al·i·ty [pär′shē·al′ə·tē] *n., pl.* **par·ti·al·i·ties** **1** The condition or quality of being partial. **2** A special fondness.

par·tic·i·pant [pär·tis′ə·pənt] *n.* A person who participates or takes part.

par·tic·i·pate [pär·tis′ə·pāt] *v.* **par·tic·i·pat·ed, par·tic·i·pat·ing** To take part or have a share with others: We all *participated* in the charity bazaar. **— par·tic′i·pa′tion** *n.*

par·ti·cip·i·al [pär′tə·sip′ē·əl] **1** *adj.* Having the form or use of a participle. **2** *adj.* Like or based on a participle. **3** *n.* A participle.

par·ti·ci·ple [pär′tə·sip′əl] *n.* A form of a verb that acts mainly as an adjective, as *thundering* in "the thundering herds," but can also function as a verb where it has tense, voice, and the power to take an object or complement, as *elected* in "He was elected president." See also PAST PARTICIPLE, PRESENT PARTICIPLE.

par·ti·cle [pär′ti·kəl] *n.* **1** A very small part,

piece, or amount; speck. **2** A short word, as an article, preposition, or conjunction. **3** A prefix or suffix.

par·ti-col·ored [pär′tē·kul′ərd] *adj.* Differently colored in different parts.

par·tic·u·lar [pər·tik′yə·lər] **1** *adj.* Having to do with one certain person, thing, time, or place; specific: Building airplane models is my *particular* hobby. **2** *adj.* Apart from others: Each student must choose his own *particular* subject for a term paper. **3** *adj.* Especially noteworthy; special: The lecture you missed was of *particular* importance. **4** *adj.* Giving close attention to details; precise; neat: My mother has always been a *particular* housekeeper. **5** *n.* (*usually pl.*) An item; detail: Give me the *particulars.* — **in particular** Particularly; especially: We did nothing *in particular* last night.

par·tic·u·lar·i·ty [pər·tik′yə·lar′ə·tē] *n., pl.* **par·tic·u·lar·i·ties 1** Exactness in attention to details. **2** A special trait or characteristic. **3** A circumstance or detail; particular.

par·tic·u·lar·ize [pər·tik′yə·lə·rīz′] *v.* **par·tic·u·lar·ized, par·tic·u·lar·iz·ing 1** To speak of or treat in detail. **2** To be specific. — **par·tic′u·lar·i·za′tion** *n.* ¶3

par·tic·u·lar·ly [pər·tik′yə·lər·lē] *adv.* **1** In a particular way: to emphasize one point *particularly*; to study a blueprint *particularly*. **2** More than usually: a *particularly* bad meal.

part·ing [pär′ting] **1** *n.* The act of separating. **2** *n.* The condition of being separated. **3** *adj.* Separating; dividing. **4** *n.* A taking leave; departure. **5** *adj.* Given, done, or said at parting: a *parting* glance. **6** *adj.* Of or having to do with a departure. **7** *adj.* Departing; going.

parting shot A sharp remark or aggressive action made by a person as he is leaving.

par·ti·san [pär′tə·zən] **1** *n.* A person who very strongly supports a party, cause, etc. **2** *adj.* Of or like a partisan: *partisan* politics. **3** *n.* A member of a body of troops not attached to a regular army; guerrilla. — **par′ti·san·ship** *n.*

par·ti·tion [pär·tish′ən] **1** *n.* A division or separation. **2** *v.* To divide into parts or sections. **3** *n.* Something that divides, as a wall, screen, etc. **4** *v.* To separate by a partition: to *partition* off a room.

par·ti·zan [pär′tə·zən] *n., adj.* Partisan.

part·ly [pärt′lē] *adv.* Not wholly; partially.

part·ner [pärt′nər] *n.* **1** A person who is associated with another or others, especially in a business where he shares the profits and losses. **2** A husband or wife. **3** One of two or more people who perform an activity together, as dancing or playing a game.

part·ner·ship [pärt′nər·ship] *n.* **1** The condition or relationship of being a partner. **2** A business that is owned by partners.

part of speech One of the classes of words in English. The parts of speech are usually given as noun, pronoun, verb, adverb, adjective, conjunction, preposition, and interjection.

par·took [pär·took′] Past tense of PARTAKE.

par·tridge [pär′trij] *n.* Any of various small, plump game birds of Europe and America, as the quail and ruffed grouse.

Partridge, about 12 in. long

part song A song for three or more voices, usually without accompaniment.

part-time [pärt′tīm′] *adj.* For only part of the usual time: a *part-time* student.

par·ty [pär′tē] *n., pl.* **par·ties 1** A gathering of people for pleasure and entertainment. **2** A group of people associated together to gain control of a government by electing its candidates to office: a political *party*. **3** A group of people formed to work or act together: a landing *party*; a hunting *party*. **4** A person who takes part in an action, plan, etc.: a *party* to his crime. **5** *informal* A person.

par·ve·nu [pär′və·n(y)oo] *n.* A person who has risen above his social class by gaining wealth or position; upstart.

pass [pas] **1** *v.* To move past or go by: We often *pass* that store; The years *pass* slowly. **2** *v.* To go, move, or make a way: to *pass* through a crowd. **3** *n.* A narrow passage or opening, as one between mountains. **4** *v.* To cause or allow to move, go past or through, advance, etc.: to *pass* a mop over the floor; Miss Hill *passed* Tom into the sixth grade. **5** *n.* A permit giving a person the right to enter, move about, or leave freely: The soldier got a *pass* to go into town. **6** *v.* To succeed in getting through (a test, inspection, etc.): Did you *pass* or fail?; The bill *passed* the Senate. **7** *n.* The passing of a test or course. **8** *v.* To vote in favor of; approve: The Senate *passed* the bill. **9** *v.* To hand down (a judgment, opinion, etc.): to *pass* sentence on a prisoner. **10** *v.* To transfer or go from one person or place to another: *Pass* the salt; to *pass* a ball to a teammate; His fortune *passed* to his children. **11** *n.* The throwing or hitting of a ball, etc., from a player to a teammate. **12** *v.* To change from one condition, form, etc., to another: The sick man *passed* from chills to fever. **13** *v.* To be taken or accepted: They could *pass* for sisters. **14** *v.* To take place; happen: What *passed* in the meeting? **15** *n.* A state of affairs; condition; situation: Events have come to a critical *pass.* **16** *v.* To spend: He *passed* the time in study. **17** *v.* To come to an end: Her fear *passed.* **18** *v.* To die. **19** *v.* To go beyond; exceed: peace that *passes* understanding. **20** *v.* To go by without comment: Let the insult *pass.* **21** *v.* To pull or put: to *pass* a belt about the waist. **22** *v.* To give up a turn to nominate, bet, bid, etc.: I *pass.* **23** *n.* A movement of the hand, a wand, etc., over a person or thing: The magician made a *pass* over the vase and a flower appeared. **24** *v.* In fencing, to thrust or lunge. **25** *n.* Such a thrust or lunge. — **bring to pass** To cause to come about; accomplish. — **come to pass**

To come about; happen. — **pass away 1** To come to an end. **2** To die. — **pass off 1** To come to an end; disappear. **2** To represent falsely: He *passed* himself *off* as a ship's captain. **3** To be given off, as vapor. — **pass out 1** To distribute: *Pass out* the papers. **2** *informal* To faint. — **pass over** To fail to notice, consider, or select. — **pass up** *U.S. informal* To fail or refuse to take advantage of, as a chance or offer. — **pass′er** *n.* ◆ See PAST.

pass·a·ble [pas′ə·bəl] *adj.* **1** Capable of being passed, crossed, or traveled: *passable* roads. **2** Fairly good; acceptable: *passable* entertainment. — **pass′a·bly** *adv.*

pas·sage [pas′ij] *n.* **1** A way through which a person or thing may pass, as a hall, road, water route, etc. **2** The right or freedom to pass: to guarantee him safe *passage*. **3** A voyage or other journey: a stormy *passage*. **4** Room, board, and traveling costs on a ship: He could not pay for his *passage*. **5** The act of passing: the *passage* from winter to summer. **6** The making of a bill into law by a legislature. **7** A portion of a writing, speech, or piece of music: a *passage* from Shakespeare.

pas·sage·way [pas′ij·wā′] *n.* A way through which to pass, as a hall or corridor; passage.

pas·sé [pa·sā′] *adj.* Out-of-date; old-fashioned.

pas·sen·ger [pas′ən·jər] *n.* A person riding in, but not driving, a bus, train, plane, etc.

passenger pigeon The extinct wild pigeon of North America. Flocks were huge up to 1870.

pas·ser-by [pas′ər·bī′] *n., pl.* **pas·sers-by** A person who passes by, often in a casual way.

pass·ing [pas′ing] **1** *adj.* Going by or away: a *passing* parade. **2** *n.* A means or place of passing, as a ford. **3** *adj.* Permitting one to pass an examination, course, etc.: a *passing* grade. **4** *n.* The act of a person or thing that passes. **5** *adj.* Lasting for a brief time only; temporary: a *passing* fad or fancy. **6** *n.* Death. **7** *adj.* Given, made, etc., in a casual manner: a *passing* nod. **8** *adv.* Extremely; exceedingly: no longer used: That story is *passing* strange. — **in passing** By the way; incidentally.

pas·sion [pash′ən] *n.* **1** Any extremely strong emotion or feeling. **2** Great love and longing, as that of a man for a woman. **3** A strong liking or fondness: a *passion* for art. **4** That for which one has a strong liking or fondness: Music is his *passion*. **5** A fit of anger: to fly into a *passion*. **6** (*written* **Passion**) The sufferings of Christ on the Cross or after the Last Supper.

pas·sion·ate [pash′ən·it] *adj.* **1** Filled with or expressing strong feelings: a *passionate* reformer; a *passionate* plea. **2** Easily stirred up or angered. **3** Extremely strong: said about a feeling. — **pas′sion·ate·ly** *adv.*

Passion play A drama dealing with Christ's sufferings and his death on the Cross.

pas·sive [pas′iv] *adj.* **1** Not active or not responding actively; acted upon: The patients were *passive*, did nothing, just waited for nurses to help them. **2** Indicating a verb form which shows that the subject is receiving the action. *Was kicked* in "I was kicked by Mary" is a verb in the passive voice. **3** Not showing resistance; yielding; submissive: *passive* acceptance of a scolding. — **pas′sive·ly** *adv.* — **pas′sive·ness** *n.*

pass·key [pas′kē′] *n.* **1** A key that will unlock two or more locks. **2** Any private key.

Pass·o·ver [pas′ō′vər] *n.* A Jewish feast commemorating the night when God, killing the first-born children of the Egyptians, "passed over" the houses of the Hebrews.

pass·port [pas′pôrt′] *n.* **1** An official document which identifies a citizen and gives him the right to travel abroad under his government's protection. **2** Anything that enables one to gain entrance, acceptance, etc.: Wealth was the businessman's *passport* to high society.

pass·word [pas′wûrd′] *n.* A secret word or phrase which must be spoken to get past a guard or sentry.

past [past] **1** *adj.* Ended or finished; gone by; over: His troubles are *past*. **2** *n.* Time that has passed: memories of the *past*. **3** *adj.* Just passed or gone by: the *past* few days. **4** *adv.* So as to go by: A bus drove *past*. **5** *prep.* Farther than; by: We walked *past* the store. **6** *adj.* Belonging to a former time: a *past* governor. **7** *n.* A former life or career: a woman with a mysterious *past*. **8** *prep.* After: It is *past* noon. **9** *prep.* Older than: a girl *past* ten. **10** *prep.* Beyond the power of: *past* help. ◆ *Passed*, not *past*, is the past tense and past participle of the verb *to pass*: We *passed* the house; The bill was *passed* by Congress. *Past* may be used in many ways, but never as a verb form: a *past* event; It happened in the *past*; The bird flew *past*; We went *past* the house.

paste¹ [pāst] *n., v.* **past·ed, past·ing 1** *n.* A mixture, as of flour and water, used for sticking pieces of paper or lightweight objects together. **2** *v.* To stick with paste, glue, etc.: to *paste* clippings in a scrapbook. **3** *n.* Any of various soft, moist, smooth preparations used as foods, in cleaning teeth, in making pottery, etc. **4** *n.* Dough used for pastry crusts, macaroni, etc. **5** *n.* A hard, brilliant glass used in imitation gems.

paste² [pāst] *v.* **past·ed, past·ing** *slang* To strike, as with the fist; beat.

paste·board [pāst′bôrd′] *n.* A stiff, heavy paper made of sheets of thinner paper pasted together or of pressed and dried paper pulp.

pas·tel [pas·tel′] **1** *n.* Any delicate, soft, pale color. **2** *adj.* Soft and pale: a *pastel* yellow. **3** *n.* A chalklike colored crayon. **4** *n.* A drawing made with such colored crayons.

---

add, āce, câre, pälm;   end, ēqual;   it, īce;   odd, ōpen, ôrder;   took, pool;   up, bûrn;

ə = a in *above*, e in *sicken*, i in *possible*, o in *melon*, u in *circus*;   yoo = u in *fuse*;   oil;   pout;

check;   ring;   thin;   this;   zh in *vision*.   For ¶ reference, see page 64 · HOW TO

pas·tern [pas′tərn] *n.* The part of a horse's foot that is between the fetlock and the hoof.

Pas·teur [päs·tûr′], **Louis,** 1822–1895, French chemist. He discovered that bacteria were carried in the air and found ways to prevent some diseases and to keep milk from fermenting.

Pastern

pas·teur·ize [pas′chə·rīz] *v.* **pas·teur·ized, pas·teur·iz·ing** To heat (beer, milk, wine, etc.) from 140° to about 155° F. in order to destroy bacteria causing fermentation. — **pas′teur·i·za′tion** *n.* ¶3 ◆ The word *pasteurize* was formed after the name of Louis *Pasteur.*

pas·time [pas′tīm′] *n.* Something that makes time pass pleasantly, as a sport or recreation.

pas·tor [pas′tər] *n.* A Christian minister or priest in charge of a church or congregation.

pas·tor·al [pas′tər·əl] **1** *adj.* Of a pastor or his duties. **2** *adj.* Of, like, or dealing with shepherds or simple, peaceful country life. **3** *n.* A poem, picture, etc., dealing with country life or scenes.

pas·tor·ate [pas′tər·it] *n.* **1** A pastor's position or duties. **2** The length of time a pastor serves. **3** Pastors considered as a group.

past participle A form of a verb ending in *-ed* or its equivalent. It is used with the verb *have* to show action that has already taken place, as *cooked* in "I have *cooked,*" or *sunk* in "The boat has *sunk.*" A past participle is also used with the verb *be* to form the passive voice, as *robbed* in "We were *robbed.*" A past participle may also be used as an adjective, as in the *escaped* convict.

pas·try [pās′trē] *n., pl.* **pas·tries 1** Sweet baked foods, such as pies and tarts, having a crust made of dough to which shortening has been added. **2** Any sweet baked foods, as cakes.

past tense A form of a verb used to show that an action or condition occurred at a former time. The past tense of "go" is "went."

pas·tur·age [pas′chər·ij] *n.* Pasture.

pas·ture [pas′chər] *n., v.* **pas·tured, pas·tur·ing 1** *n.* Ground covered with grass and other plants that horses, cattle, or sheep can eat. **2** *n.* Growing grass or other plants that grazing animals eat. **3** *v.* To put (grazing animals) in a pasture. **4** *v.* To graze on grass.

past·y[1] [pās′tē] *adj.* **past·i·er, past·i·est 1** Like paste. **2** Pale and unhealthy, as in appearance: a *pasty* complexion.

past·y[2] [pās′tē *or* pas′tē] *n., pl.* **past·ies** A pie, as of meat, baked in a crust of pastry.

pat [pat] *v.* **pat·ted, pat·ting,** *n., adj.* **pat·ter, pat·test,** *adv.* **1** *v.* To touch or tap lightly with something flat, especially with the hand: to *pat* a cat. **2** *n.* A light stroke or gentle tap, as one given with the hand. **3** *v.* To shape or smooth by patting. **4** *n.* A small, molded mass, as of butter. **5** *v.* To run or walk with light steps: to *pat* across the floor. **6** *n.* The sound of patting or pattering. **7** *adj.* Exactly or too neatly suitable; apt or glib: a *pat* answer. **8** *adv. informal*

Thoroughly or perfectly: He knew his lesson *pat.* — **have down pat** *informal* To know or do perfectly. — **pat on the back 1** To congratulate or praise. **2** A compliment. — **stand pat** *informal* To refuse to change one's position.

patch [pach] **1** *n.* A piece of material used to cover a hole or a torn, worn, or weak spot. **2** *n.* A piece of material worn to cover an injured eye, a defect of the skin, etc. **3** *v.* To repair or cover with a patch or patches: to *patch* torn overalls. **4** *v.* To put together in a hasty way. **5** *n.* A left-over scrap or fragment of something. **6** *n.* A place or spot different from the area around it: a *patch* of fog. **7** *n.* A small piece of ground on which something grows: a briar *patch.* — **patch up** To settle for good or for the time being: to *patch up* differences.

patch·work [pach′wûrk′] *n.* **1** Patches of cloth of different colors, shapes, or patterns sewed together in a design. **2** *adj. use:* a *patchwork* quilt. **3** Anything made up of different materials. **4** Work done hastily.

patch·y [pach′ē] *adj.* **patch·i·er, patch·i·est** Made up of or full of patches; not all alike.

pate [pāt] *n.* A humorous term for the head, the top of the head, or the brains.

Patchwork quilt

pa·tel·la [pə·tel′ə] *n., pl.* **pa·tel·las** or **pa·tel·lae** [pə·tel′ē] The kneecap.

pat·ent [pat′(ə)nt] **1** *n.* A government document giving an inventor the sole right to make and sell a new invention or to use a new process for a certain term of years. **2** *n.* The right granted by such a document. **3** *n.* The invention or process protected by

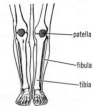

patella

fibula

tibia

such a document. **4** *adj.* Protected or granted by a patent: a *patent* right. **5** *v.* To obtain a patent on: to *patent* an invention. **6** *n.* Any official document granting a right. **7** [pāt′(ə)nt] *adj.* Apparent; obvious: a *patent* falsehood.

pat·en·tee [pat′(ə)n·tē′] *n.* A person who holds a patent on an invention or process.

patent leather Leather finished so that its surface is hard, shiny, and smooth.

pa·tent·ly [pāt′(ə)nt·lē] *adv.* Clearly; obviously: That statement is *patently* absurd.

patent medicine A patented medicine having a trade name and sold without a prescription.

pa·ter·nal [pə·tûr′nəl] *adj.* **1** Of or characteristic of a father; fatherly: *paternal* care. **2** Related to a person through his father: a *paternal* grandmother. — **pa·ter′nal·ly** *adv.*

pa·ter·nal·ism [pə·tûr′nəl·iz′əm] *n.* A method of controlling or taking care of a country, group of employees, etc., in the way that a father looks after his children.

pa·ter·ni·ty [pə·tûr′nə·tē] *n.* **1** The condition of being a father. **2** The identity of one's father: to uncover an orphan's *paternity*.

pa·ter·nos·ter [pät′ər·nos′tər *or* pā′tər·nos′tər] *n.* A Latin name for the Lord's Prayer. ◆ *Paternoster* comes from the Latin words *pater noster*, meaning *our father*, the opening words of the Lord's Prayer in Latin.

path [path] *n.* **1** A way or walk worn or used by persons or animals walking. **2** A road or trail. **3** A track or course along which a thing moves: the *path* of a comet. **4** A course of life or action: the *path* of virtue.

pa·thet·ic [pə·thet′ik] *adj.* Arousing, expressing, or deserving pity or sympathy; pitiful: a *pathetic* wail. **— pa·thet′i·cal·ly** *adv.*

path·find·er [path′fīn′dər] *n.* Someone who finds a way through unexplored regions, whether of land or a field of study; pioneer.

path·o·gen·ic [path′ə·jen′ik] *adj.* Causing a disease: said about bacteria, a virus, etc.

path·o·log·i·cal [path′ə·loj′i·kəl] *adj.* **1** Having to do with pathology. **2** Related to, concerned with, or caused by disease: a *pathological* condition. **— path′o·log′i·cal·ly** *adv.*

pa·thol·o·gy [pə·thol′ə·jē] *n.* **1** The branch of medical science concerned with the origin, nature, causes, and development of disease. **2** The symptoms of or the effects caused by a disease. **— pa·thol′o·gist** *n.*

pa·thos [pā′thos] *n.* The quality, especially in literature or art, that arouses tender feelings of sorrow, pity, or sympathy.

path·way [path′wā′] *n.* A path.

pa·tience [pā′shəns] *n.* **1** The condition or quality of being patient. **2** The ability to be patient. **3** The British name for a card game for one person; solitaire.

pa·tient [pā′shənt] **1** *adj.* Able to wait for someone or something or to endure unpleasant things without complaining: a *patient* sufferer. **2** *adj.* Having or showing patience: a *patient* wait. **3** *adj.* Calm and understanding: Be *patient* with him. **4** *adj.* That continues or goes on in spite of trouble or difficulties: *patient* effort. **5** *n.* A person who is being treated for illness or injury. **— pa′tient·ly** *adv.*

pa·ti·o [pat′ē·ō *or* pä′tē·ō] *n., pl.* **pa·ti·os 1** The open inner courtyard of a Spanish or Spanish-American building. **2** The paved area by the side of some houses, used for parties, barbecues, etc. ◆ *Patio* comes directly from Spanish.

pat·ois [pat′wä] *n., pl.* **pat·ois** [pat′wäz] A local dialect of a language that differs from the standard form and is often considered illiterate. The French of New Orleans is patois.

pa·tri·arch [pā′trē·ärk] *n.* **1** A father who founds, rules, or heads a family, tribe, or race:

Abraham, Isaac, and Jacob were Hebrew *patriarchs*. **2** A title which some churches give to certain bishops of very high rank. **3** A stately old man. **— pa′tri·ar′chal** *adj.* ◆ *Patriarch* comes from a Greek word meaning *the head of a family*.

pa·tri·cian [pə·trish′ən] **1** *n.* A person having a high social position; aristocrat. **2** *adj.* Of, having to do with, or suiting aristocrats; noble: *patrician* tastes. **3** *n.* A member of the upper class in ancient Rome.

Pat·rick [pat′rik] *n.,* 389?–461?, Christian missionary, the patron saint of Ireland.

pat·ri·mo·ny [pat′rə·mō′nē] *n., pl.* **pat·ri·mo·nies** Property inherited from one's father or ancestors. **— pat′ri·mo′ni·al** *adj.*

pa·tri·ot [pā′trē·ət] *n.* A person who loves his country and loyally defends or supports it.

pa·tri·ot·ic [pā′trē·ot′ik] *adj.* Having or showing love, loyalty, and devotion towards one's country. **— pa′tri·ot′i·cal·ly** *adv.*

pa·tri·ot·ism [pā′trē·ə·tiz′əm] *n.* Love for one's country and loyal devotion to it.

pa·trol [pə·trōl′] *v.* **pa·trolled, pa·trol·ling,** *n.* **1** *v.* To go through or around (an area) for the purpose of guarding it: Soldiers *patrolled* the fort. **2** *n.* The act of patrolling. **3** *n.* The guard or group patrolling a district: a police *patrol*. **4** *n.* A group of airplanes, ships, or soldiers sent out to fight or to obtain information about enemy forces. **5** *n.* A division of either a girl scout troop or a boy scout troop, numbering about eight scouts. **6** *n.* A student assigned to direct traffic near a school.

pa·trol·man [pə·trōl′mən] *n., pl.* **pa·trol·men** [pə·trōl′mən] **1** A policeman assigned to patrol a certain section. **2** Any person who patrols.

patrol wagon *U.S.* A small truck used by the police to transport prisoners.

pa·tron [pā′trən] *n.* **1** A person who uses his money or influence to aid or support some person, thing, or enterprise: an artist's *patron*; a *patron* of the opera. **2** A regular customer.

pa·tron·age [pā′trən·ij *or* pat′rən·ij] *n.* **1** The support or protection given by a patron. **2** The power to distribute political offices or to do political favors. **3** A snobbish attitude of being kind to one's inferiors. **4** Business given by regular customers.

pa·tron·ess [pā′trən·is] *n.* A female patron.

pa·tron·ize [pā′trən·īz *or* pat′rən·īz] *v.* **pa·tron·ized, pa·tron·iz·ing 1** To support or encourage as a patron: to *patronize* the opera. **2** To act toward (someone) in a kindly but snobbish or superior way. **3** *adj. use:* a *patronizing* manner. **4** To trade with regularly. ¶3

patron saint A saint regarded as the special protector of a country, city, group, etc.

pa·troon [pə·trōōn′] *n.* A man granted land in the Dutch territory which later became New

York and New Jersey. He was to establish a settlement and was given special rights and powers.

pat·ter[1] [pat′ər] **1** *v.* To make a series of fast, light taps: Little feet *pattered* across the hall. **2** *n.* The act or sound of tapping lightly and quickly: the *patter* of the rain.

pat·ter[2] [pat′ər] **1** *v.* To speak or say in a quick, effortless way. **2** *n.* Quick, easy talk.

pat·tern [pat′ərn] **1** *n.* An arrangement of markings or colors forming a design: a striped *pattern.* **2** *n.* A model or guide used in making or sometimes in test-ing something else: a *pattern* for a coat. **3** *n.* A typical example that may be imitated; model: She was a *pattern* of obedience. **4** *v.* To make cor-respond to a model: He *patterned* himself after his hero. **5** *n.* A method of organization, action, or behavior that is repeated: Do you see a *pattern* in this row of numbers? 246357468

Pattern for making a dress

pat·ty [pat′ē] *n., pl.* **pat·ties 1** A small, flat, molded cake of chopped meat, fish, etc. **2** A small pie.

pau·ci·ty [pô′sə·tē] *n.* Smallness of number or quantity; scarcity: a *paucity* of supplies.

Paul [pôl] *n.,* died A.D. 67?, Christian apostle, missionary, and saint. Many of his letters are books of the New Testament.

Paul VI, born 1897, Pope 1963–.

paunch [pônch] *n.* A big belly that sticks out.

paunch·y [pônch′ē] *adj.* **paunch·i·er, paunch·i·est** Having a big belly that sticks out.

pau·per [pô′pər] *n.* A very poor person, especially one who receives public charity.

pause [pôz] *v.* **paused, paus·ing,** *n.* **1** *v.* To stop temporarily: He *paused* for a drink of water. **2** *n.* A brief stop or short rest. **3** *n.* A sign (⌒ or ⌣) placed over or beneath a musical note or rest to show that it is to be held longer. **4** *v.* To linger: to *pause* on a word.

Paunch

pave [pāv] *v.* **paved, pav·ing** To lay down a surface of asphalt, gravel, concrete, etc., on: to *pave* a road. **— pave the way** To prepare or make ready a way or opportunity: His experiments *paved the way* for the discovery.

pave·ment [pāv′mənt] *n.* **1** A hard, solid sur-face covering a road, walk, etc. **2** A paved road, walk, etc. **3** Material used for paving.

pa·vil·ion [pə·vil′yən] *n.* **1** A building, often having open sides and a pointed roof, used for amusement, shelter, etc., as in a park. **2** Any building set up for temporary use by an exhibitor

at a fair. **3** A building or annex in a group of buildings that form a hospital. **4** A large tent. **5** A canopy.

pav·ing [pā′ving] *n.* **1** A pavement. **2** Paving material. **3** The laying of a pavement.

paw [pô] **1** *n.* The foot of an animal having nails or claws. **2** *v.* To strike or scrape with the feet, paws, or hands: to *paw* the ground or the air. **3** *v. informal* To handle in a rude or clumsy way: to *paw* over things in a trunk.

pawl [pôl] *n.* A mechanical device, as a small hinged bar with a tooth at one end, that lets a notched wheel turn, or turns it, in only one direction.

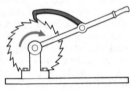
Pawl

pawn[1] [pôn] **1** *v.* To leave (a valuable ob-ject) with a lender in order to get a loan. The object may be redeemed by paying the loan: to *pawn* a ring. **2** *n.* A valuable object pawned for money. **— in pawn** Being held as a pledge for money owed: His violin was *in pawn*.

pawn[2] [pôn] *n.* **1** A chess piece of the least value. **2** A person used to gain another's ends.

pawn·brok·er [pôn′brō′kər] *n.* A person engaged in the business of lending money at interest on valuable objects left in his keeping.

pawn·shop [pôn′shop′] *n.* A pawnbroker's shop.

paw·paw [pô′pô] *n.* Another spelling of PAPAW.

pay [pā] *v.* **paid,** for def. 12 **paid** or **payed, pay·ing,** *n., adj.* **1** *v.* To give something, usually money, to (someone) in exchange for goods or services: to *pay* a repairman. **2** *v.* To give (money, etc.) for goods or services: We *paid* ten dollars for the tennis net. **3** *n.* Money given for work; salary; wages: low *pay.* **4** *v.* To furnish or yield, as in wages: What does the job *pay*? **5** *v.* To furnish the amount of: to *pay* a bill. **6** *adj.* Requiring a payment before use: a *pay* phone. **7** *v.* To bring a benefit: Honesty *pays.* **8** *v.* To suffer or endure: He has *paid* the penalty; They *paid* for their wrongdoing. **9** *n.* A suitable reward or punishment: Their joy was ample *pay* for my efforts. **10** *v.* To give, as a compliment or attention. **11** *v.* To make, as a call or visit. **12** *v.* To loosen and let out, as cable: He *payed* out the rope. **— in the pay of** Employed by for money. **— pay back 1** To replace what one borrowed; repay. **2** To give a suitable reward or punishment to or for. **— pay off** To pay the entire amount of (a debt). **— pay up** To pay in full without delay.

pay·a·ble [pā′ə·bəl] *adj.* **1** Due: accounts *pay-able.* **2** That may be paid: *payable* by the month.

pay·mas·ter [pā′mas′tər] *n.* A person in charge of paying employees their salary.

pay·ment [pā′mənt] *n.* **1** The act of paying. **2** A sum of money paid: monthly *payments* on a house. **3** Pay. **4** Reward or punishment.

pay·roll [pā'rōl'] *n.* **1** A list of workers to be paid, with the amounts owed to each. **2** The total sum of money needed to make the payments.

Pb The symbol for the element LEAD. ◆ The Latin word for lead is *plumbum*.

pd. Abbreviation of PAID.

pea [pē] *n., pl.* **peas** or (*rarely*) **pease** **1** A round seed, often cooked as a vegetable. **2** A climbing plant that has green pods in which these seeds grow. ◆ The English word for *pea*, whether one or many, was once *pease* [pēz], from the Latin word *pisa*. Because *pease* sounded like a plural, *pea* came into being as its singular form, and now *peas* has largely replaced *pease* as the plural.

peace [pēs] *n.* **1** A condition of quiet, calm, or harmony: *peace* of spirit; at *peace*. **2** Freedom from war, violence, or quarreling: *peace* on earth. **3** An ending of fighting or quarreling: to make *peace*. **4** A treaty to end a war. **— hold one's peace** To be silent.

peace·a·ble [pē'sə·bəl] *adj.* **1** Not inclined to quarrel. **2** Peaceful. **— peace'a·bly** *adv.*

peace·ful [pēs'fəl] *adj.* **1** Free from disturbance; quiet; calm: a *peaceful* scene. **2** Not fighting: *peaceful* nations. **3** Inclined to avoid quarrels: a *peaceful* disposition. **4** Not violent or disorderly: by *peaceful* means. **— peace'·ful·ly** *adv.* **— peace'ful·ness** *n.*

peace·mak·er [pēs'mā'kər] *n.* A person who tries to end a quarrel or war between others.

peach [pēch] **1** *n.* A juicy, round fruit having a thin, fuzzy skin and a single large seed. **2** *n.* The tree on which it grows. **3** *n., adj.* Yellowish pink.

pea·cock [pē'kok'] *n.* The male of a large bird, having a long tail that it can spread out like a fan to show brilliantly colored feathers covered with eyelike spots.

Peacock, about 30 in. head to tail

pea·hen [pē'hen'] *n.* The mate of the peacock.

pea jacket A short, warm, outer coat, usually worn by seamen.

peak [pēk] *n.* **1** The pointed top of a steep hill or mountain. **2** A steep or solitary mountain. **3** Any pointed top or projecting part: the *peak* of a roof or of a cap. **4** The highest point or level: at the *peak* of his powers.

peak·ed[1] [pē'kid] *adj.* Looking thin or sickly.

peaked[2] [pēkt] *adj.* Rising to a peak; pointed.

peal [pēl] **1** *n.* A loud, full, echoing sound, as of a bell or thunder. **2** *n.* A set of large, musically tuned bells. **3** *n.* The loud ringing of bells or a set of bells. **4** *v.* To ring out: Bells *peal* for a wedding, toll for a funeral.

pea·nut [pē'nut'] *n.* **1** A vine related to the pea, with pods that ripen underground and hold seeds that are eaten like nuts. **2** The seed or seed pod of this vine.

peanut butter A thick spread for sandwiches, etc., made from ground roasted peanuts.

pear [pâr] *n.* **1** A sweet, juicy fruit, round at the outer end and tapering toward the stem. **2** The tree on which it grows.

pearl [pûrl] **1** *n.* A smooth, rounded, white or variously tinted deposit formed around a grain of sand or the like inside the shell of an oyster or other shellfish. It is valued as a gem. **2** *adj. use:* *pearl* earrings. **3** *n.* Mother-of-pearl. **4** *adj. use:* *pearl* buttons. **5** *n., adj.* Pale bluish gray. **6** *n.* Something resembling a pearl, as in shape, color, luster, or worth. **— pearl'y** *adj.*

Pearl Harbor A harbor in the Hawaiian Islands, not far from Honolulu, where a U.S. naval base was bombed by the Japanese on December 7, 1941.

peas·ant [pez'ənt] *n.* In Europe, a country person of humble birth, as a small farmer.

peas·ant·ry [pez'ən·trē] *n.* The peasant class.

pease [pēz] A plural form of PEA. ◆ See PEA.

peat [pēt] *n.* A substance made up of mosses and plants partly rotted, as in a marsh. When dried, it is burned as fuel. **— peat'y** *adj.*

peat moss Dried, partly rotted moss used to enrich soil, as for growing potted plants.

peb·ble [peb'əl] *n., v.* **peb·bled, peb·bling** **1** *n.* A small, smooth stone, shaped and rounded as by running water. **2** *v.* To cover with pebbles. **3** *v.* To give a rough grain to (leather).

peb·bly [peb'lē] *adj.* **peb·bli·er, peb·bli·est** Having many pebbles: a *pebbly* shore.

pe·can [pi·kän', pi·kan' *or* pē'kan] *n.* **1** An oval nut having a thin shell. **2** The tree on which it grows, common in the southern U.S.

pec·ca·dil·lo [pek'ə·dil'ō] *n., pl.* **pec·ca·dil·loes** or **pec·ca·dil·los** A slight or minor sin; a trifling fault.

pec·ca·ry [pek'ər·ē] *n., pl.* **pec·ca·ries** or **pec·ca·ry** Either of two wild animals of tropical America, like pigs with sharp tusks.

Peccary, about 3 ft. long

peck[1] [pek] *n.* **1** A measure of volume for dry things, as fruit or vegetables, equal to ¼ bushel or 8 quarts. **2** A container holding exactly a peck. **3** *slang* A considerable amount: He was in a *peck* of trouble.

peck[2] [pek] **1** *v.* To strike with the beak, as a bird does. **2** *n.* A stroke with the beak. **3** *n.* A jab, mark, or hole made by pecking. **4** *v.* To make by pecking: The chick *pecked* a hole in its shell. **5** *v.* To pick up with the beak: to *peck*

P

chicken feed. **6** *v.* To eat only a little, in small, fussy bites: Don't *peck* at your food. **7** *n.* *informal* A quick kiss. **8** *v.* *informal* To kiss quickly.

pec·tin [pek'tin] *n.* A carbohydrate substance found in various fruit and vegetable juices. It makes fruit jellies set.

pec·to·ral [pek'tər·əl] *adj.* Of, near, or having to do with the chest: a *pectoral* muscle.

pec·u·late [pek'yə·lāt] *v.* **pec·u·lat·ed, pec·u·lat·ing** To steal (funds, especially public funds, entrusted to one). — **pec'u·la'tion** *n.*

pe·cul·iar [pi·kyōōl'yər] *adj.* **1** Oddly different from the usual; strange: *peculiar* behavior. **2** Found in or belonging to one special place, thing, group, or person. — **pe·cul'iar·ly** *adv.*

pe·cu·li·ar·i·ty [pi·kyōō'lē·ar'ə·tē *or* pi·kyōōl'yar'ə·tē] *n., pl.* **pe·cu·li·ar·i·ties** **1** The quality of being different or peculiar. **2** An odd or unusual trait, style, characteristic, etc.

pe·cu·ni·ar·y [pi·kyōō'nē·er'ē] *adj.* Made up of or having to do with money: *pecuniary* gain.

ped·a·gog·ic [ped'ə·goj'ik *or* ped'ə·gō'jik] *adj.* Of or having to do with teaching.

ped·a·gog·i·cal [ped'ə·goj'i·kəl] *adj.* Pedagogic.

ped·a·gogue or **ped·a·gog** [ped'ə·gog] *n.* A teacher, especially a narrow-minded one who makes learning dull by stressing minor details.

ped·a·go·gy [ped'ə·gō'jē] *n.* The science, study, or profession of teaching.

ped·al [ped'(ə)l] *n., v.* **ped·aled** or **ped·alled, ped·al·ing** or **ped·al·ling,** *adj.* **1** *n.* A lever or mechanical device pushed by the foot to operate or control any of a number of things, as a bicycle, a machine, the tones of a piano, etc. **2** *v.* To move, control, or operate by pushing pedals or a pedal: to *pedal* a bicycle. **3** *adj.* Of or having to do with a pedal. **4** *adj.* Of or having to do with the foot or feet.

ped·ant [ped'ənt] *n.* **1** A person who likes to impress others with his learning. **2** A person who is petty or very fussy about minor details in learning or scholarship.

pe·dan·tic [pi·dan'tik] *adj.* **1** Showing off one's learning or scholarship. **2** Too fussy or narrow about minor details in matters of learning.

ped·ant·ry [ped'ən·trē] *n.* Boring display of learning or too much devotion to petty details.

ped·dle [ped'(ə)l] *v.* **ped·dled, ped·dling** **1** To travel about and sell (small things), as from a cart pushed by hand: to *peddle* fish. **2** To give or deal out in small amounts: to *peddle* advice.

ped·dler [ped'lər] *n.* A person who sells small articles that he carries about with him.

ped·es·tal [ped'is·təl] *n.* **1** The base that supports a column, statue, vase, or the like. **2** Any foundation, base, or support. — **put on a pedestal** To regard as faultless or superior.

Pedestal

pe·des·tri·an [pə·des'trē·ən] **1** *n.* A person who moves about on foot: The car almost hit a *pedestrian*. **2** *adj.* Moving on foot; walking. **3** *adj.* Commonplace or dull: *pedestrian* writing.

pe·di·a·tri·cian [pē'dē·ə·trish'ən] *n.* A doctor specializing in pediatrics.

pe·di·at·rics [pē'dē·at'riks] *n.* The branch of medicine dealing with the care and diseases of babies and children. ◆ See -ICS. ◆ See ORTHO-PEDICS.

ped·i·gree [ped'ə·grē] *n.* **1** A list or record of the ancestors of a thoroughbred animal. **2** A list or record of a person's ancestors. **3** Distinguished ancestry.

ped·i·greed [ped'ə·grēd] *adj.* Having a list of notable or thoroughbred ancestors, as a puppy.

ped·i·ment [ped'ə·mənt] *n.* **1** The low, triangular gable formed by a sloping roof, as found above the columns in a building of the ancient Greek style. **2** Any similar ornament, as over a door.

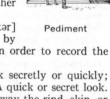
Pediment

ped·lar [ped'lər] *n.* Another spelling of PEDDLER.

pe·dom·e·ter [pi·dom'ə·tər] *n.* An instrument carried by or attached to a person in order to record the distance he walks.

peek [pēk] **1** *v.* To look secretly or quickly; peep: Don't *peek*. **2** *n.* A quick or secret look.

peel [pēl] **1** *v.* To strip away the rind, skin, or bark of: to *peel* fruit. **2** *n.* The skin or rind of certain fruit: lemon *peel*. **3** *v.* To come off in strips or scales: The wallpaper is *peeling*. **4** *v.* To lose skin, bark, paint, etc.: The damp walls are *peeling*. **5** *v.* To strip off; remove: He *peeled* off his sweater.

peel·ing [pē'ling] *n.* Something peeled off, as a strip of rind, skin, or bark.

peep[1] [pēp] **1** *v.* To make the small, sharp cry of a young bird or chick; chirp. **2** *n.* This sound or one like it. **3** *n.* A small sandpiper.

peep[2] [pēp] **1** *v.* To look secretly, as through a small hole or from hiding: to *peep* around a corner. **2** *n.* A brief glance or secret look. **3** *v.* To show just a little: The sun began to *peep* over the hill. **4** *n.* The earliest appearance: the *peep* of day. — **peep'er** *n.*

peep·er [pē'pər] *n.* An animal that chirps or peeps, as a chick or a kind of tree frog.

peer[1] [pir] *v.* **1** To look closely, as in an effort to see clearly: He *peered* at the page by candlelight. **2** To come partly into view: The sun *peers* over the horizon.

peer[2] [pir] *n.* **1** An equal, as in natural gifts, rank, etc.: an artist without *peer*; a jury of one's *peers*. **2** A noble, as a duke, marquis, earl, viscount, or baron in Great Britain.

peer·age [pir'ij] *n.* **1** The rank of a British peer. **2** All peers or nobles as a group. **3** A book listing all the members of noble families.

peer·ess [pir'is] *n.* A woman holding the rank of peer, in her own right or as a peer's wife.

peer·less [pir′lis] *adj.* Without equal in excellence; matchless: a *peerless* playwright.

peeve [pēv] *v.* **peeved, peev·ing,** *n. informal* **1** *v.* To make cross; annoy. **2** *n.* An annoying thing: A pet *peeve* annoys one especially.

pee·vish [pē′vish] *adj.* Easily annoyed or irritated; childishly cross: a *peevish* patient. — **pee′vish·ly** *adv.* — **pee′vish·ness** *n.*

peg [peg] *n., v.* **pegged, peg·ging 1** *n.* A pin, often of wood or metal, used to fasten things together, to hang something on or fasten a rope to, to adjust the tightness of strings on a musical instrument, to stop a hole, to mark a boundary or keep a score, etc. **2** *v.* To fasten, pierce, mark, etc., with pegs: to *peg* timbers together. **3** *n.* A degree or step, as in rank. — **peg away at** To work hard and steadily at. — **take down a peg** To make less conceited.

Pegs

Peg·a·sus [peg′ə·səs] *n.* **1** In Greek myths, a horse with wings. **2** The inspiration that moves poets to write.

Pei·ping [bā′ping′] *n.* The name for Peking from 1928 through 1949.

Pe·kin·ese [pē′kə·nēz′] *n., pl.* **Pe·kin·ese** Another spelling of PEKINGESE.

Pe·king [pē′king′ *or* bā′jing′] *n.* The present capital of China, a large city in the NE part.

Pe·king·ese [pē′kə·nēz′] *n., pl.* **Pe·king·ese** A small dog having long, silky hair, a little pug nose, and short legs.

pe·koe [pē′kō] *n.* A superior black tea of India, Ceylon, and Java. ◆ *Pekoe* comes from two Chinese words meaning *white hair,* referring to the downy tips of the young buds of the tea plant.

pelf [pelf] *n.* Money; wealth, regarded as bad.

pel·i·can [pel′i·kən] *n.* A large web-footed bird with a pouch on the lower jaw in which to carry captured fish.

Pe·li·on [pē′lē·on] *n.* A mountain in NE Greece. In Greek myths, the giant sons of Poseidon tried to reach the home of the gods on Mount Olympus by piling Pelion on Mount Ossa, hence the phrase **to pile Pelion on Ossa,** which means to try to do something that is almost impossible.

Pelican, 5 ft. long

pel·la·gra [pə·lā′grə *or* pə·lag′rə] *n.* A disease resulting from a lack of niacin in the diet. It is marked by skin eruptions, diarrhea, and sometimes nervous disorders.

pel·let [pel′it] *n.* **1** A small round ball, as one rolled from wax, paper, bread, etc. **2** A small bullet or shot. **3** A very small pill.

pell-mell or **pell·mell** [pel′mel′] **1** *adv.* In a confused or disordered way: Papers were thrown down *pell-mell* on his desk. **2** *adj.* Lacking order; headlong; tumultuous: children in a *pell-mell* rush. **3** *adv.* In wild haste: She ran *pell-mell* down the path.

pel·lu·cid [pə·lōō′sid] *adj.* **1** Transparent. **2** Simple and clear: a *pellucid* style of writing.

pelt[1] [pelt] *n.* The skin of an animal, usually with the fur, wool, or hair left on.

pelt[2] [pelt] **1** *v.* To throw, strike, or beat over and over, as with missiles, blows, words, etc.: to *pelt* children with stones; He *pelted* us with abuse; Rain *pelted* the roof. **2** *n.* A blow. **3** *n.* Speed, especially in the expression **at full pelt,** at full speed.

pel·vic [pel′vik] *adj.* Of, having to do with, or near the pelvis.

pel·vis [pel′vis] *n., pl.* **pel·vis·es** or **pel·ves** [pel′vēz] The part of the skeleton in man and other mammals that forms a kind of basinlike structure enclosed by the two hip bones and the lower part of the backbone.

Pelvis

pem·mi·can [pem′ə·kən] *n.* Meat dried and pounded into a paste with fat and pressed into cakes, often used on long journeys by explorers, etc.

pen[1] [pen] *n., v.* **penned, pen·ning 1** *n.* A small fenced area for keeping animals, as pigs. **2** *n.* Any small fenced or enclosed area, as one for babies to play in. **3** *v.* To shut up; confine: to be *penned* up in the house.

pen[2] [pen] *n., v.* **penned, pen·ning 1** *n.* An instrument, usually with a split point, used for writing with liquid ink. **2** *n.* A ball-point pen. **3** *v.* To write: to *pen* a reply. **4** *n.* The art of writing: He makes his living by the *pen.*

pen[3] [pen] *n. slang* A penitentiary; prison.

pe·nal [pē′nəl] *adj.* Of, for, deserving, or having to do with punishment: a *penal* colony; a *penal* offense; a *penal* code.

pe·nal·ize [pē′nəl·īz *or* pen′əl·īz] *v.* **pe·nal·ized, pe·nal·iz·ing 1** To punish by putting on a penalty: to *penalize* a player for breaking rules. **2** To provide a penalty for: Lateness is *penalized* by making offenders stay after school. ¶3

pen·al·ty [pen′əl·tē] *n., pl.* **pen·al·ties 1** The legal punishment for having broken a law: a *penalty* of up to 3 months in jail for drunken driving. **2** In sports, a disadvantage put on one side or player for fouling or breaking the rules. **3** Any unpleasant consequence or result: Lack of privacy is one of the *penalties* of fame.

pen·ance [pen′əns] *n.* A punishment that a person accepts and endures, or an action that he performs, to show that he is sorry for his sins or faults and wants to be forgiven.

add, āce, câre, pälm; end, ēqual; it, īce; odd, ōpen, ôrder; took, pool; up, bûrn; ə = a in *above,* e in *sicken,* i in *possible,* o in *melon,* u in *circus;* yōō = u in *fuse;* oil; pout; check; ring; thin; this; zh in *vision.* For ¶ reference, see page 64 · HOW TO

pence [pens] *n.pl.* A British word for pennies.

pen·chant [pen′chənt] *n.* A strong liking or inclination: He has a *penchant* for modern art.

pen·cil [pen′səl] *n.*, *v.* **pen·ciled** or **pen·cilled, pen·cil·ing** or **pen·cil·ling** 1 *n.* An implement having a stick of graphite, colored chalk, etc., encased in wood or metal, used for writing, drawing, or marking. 2 *v.* To write or mark with a pencil.

pen·dant or **pen·dent** [pen′dənt] *n.* Anything that hangs from something else, especially an ornament, as a jewel on a chain.

pen·dent or **pen·dant** [pen′dənt] *adj.* 1 Hanging downward: *pendent* limbs of trees. 2 Projecting; overhanging: a *pendent* rock. 3 Pending.

pend·ing [pen′ding] 1 *adj.* Not yet decided or settled: a case that is *pending*. 2 *prep.* While awaiting; until: *pending* the verdict. 3 *prep.* During: *Pending* debate we adjourned. 4 *adj.* Ready to happen; threatening: *pending* evils.

pen·du·lous [pen′jōō·ləs] *adj.* 1 Hanging, especially so as to swing: a *pendulous* blossom. 2 Wavering; undecided.

pen·du·lum [pen′jōō·ləm *or* pen′də·ləm] *n.* A weight hung from a support and allowed to swing back and forth. Since the time required for one complete swing is constant, pendulums can be used to regulate clocks.

Pe·nel·o·pe [pə·nel′ə·pē] *n.* In the *Odyssey* by Homer, the faithful wife of Odysseus.

pen·e·tra·ble [pen′ə·trə·bel] *adj.* That can be penetrated: *penetrable* defenses. —

pen·e·tra·bil·i·ty [pen′ə·trə·bil′ə·tē] *n.*

pen·e·trate [pen′ə·trāt] *v.* **pen·e·trat·ed, pen·e·trat·ing** 1 To enter into or through; pierce: The arrow *penetrated* his heart. 2 To see through: We could not *penetrate* the darkness. 3 To come to know or understand: to *penetrate* a theory. 4 To affect or move deeply: Joy *penetrated* his whole being. ◆ *Penetrate* and *permeate* both carry the idea of entering into. Something that *penetrates* moves in a particular direction into or through something else. Whatever *permeates*, however, simply spreads out in all directions, intermixing with another element. A bullet *penetrates* a wall, and the odor of smoke *permeates* the air.

pen·e·trat·ing [pen′ə·trā′ting] *adj.* Able to penetrate, as by being sharp, keen, or piercing: a *penetrating* chill; a *penetrating* mind.

pen·e·tra·tion [pen′ə·trā′shən] *n.* 1 The act

Pendulum

of penetrating. 2 Keen mental ability or insight. 3 The depth to which a thing penetrates.

pen·guin [pen(g)′gwin] *n.* A black and white swimming bird of Antarctic regions with flippers instead of wings, webbed feet, and very short legs on which it stands erect.

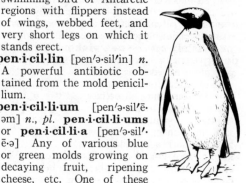

Penguin, 3 ft. high

pen·i·cil·lin [pen′ə·sil′in] *n.* A powerful antibiotic obtained from the mold penicillium.

pen·i·cil·li·um [pen′ə·sil′ē·əm] *n.*, *pl.* **pen·i·cil·li·ums** or **pen·i·cil·li·a** [pen′ə·sil′ē·ə] Any of various blue or green molds growing on decaying fruit, ripening cheese, etc. One of these molds is the source of penicillin.

pen·in·su·la [pə·nin′s(y)ə·lə] *n.* A piece of land nearly surrounded by water, often joined to the mainland by an isthmus. Italy is a peninsula. — **pen·in′su·lar** *adj.*

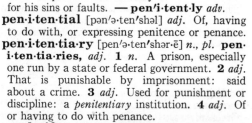

pe·nis [pē′nis] *n.*, *pl.* **pe·nis·es** or **pe·nes** [pē′nēz] A male animal's sex organ.

pen·i·tence [pen′ə·təns] *n.* Sincere sorrow for one's sins or wrongful acts; repentance.

pen·i·tent [pen′ə·tənt] 1 *adj.* Sorry for one's sins or faults. 2 *n.* A person who is sorry for his sins or faults. — **pen′i·tent·ly** *adv.*

pen·i·ten·tial [pen′ə·ten′shəl] *adj.* Of, having to do with, or expressing penitence or penance.

pen·i·ten·tia·ry [pen′ə·ten′shər·ē] *n.*, *pl.* **pen·i·ten·tia·ries,** *adj.* 1 *n.* A prison, especially one run by a state or federal government. 2 *adj.* That is punishable by imprisonment: said about a crime. 3 *adj.* Used for punishment or discipline: a *penitentiary* institution. 4 *adj.* Of or having to do with penance.

pen·knife [pen′nīf′] *n.*, *pl.* **pen·knives** [pen′nīvz′] A small pocketknife.

pen·man [pen′mən] *n.*, *pl.* **pen·men** [pen′mən] 1 A person who has a fine handwriting. 2 A person who writes or copies. 3 An author.

pen·man·ship [pen′mən·ship] *n.* 1 The style or quality of handwriting. 2 The art of writing.

Penn [pen], **William,** 1644–1718, English Quaker, founder of Pennsylvania.

Penn. or **Penna.** Unofficial abbreviations of PENNSYLVANIA.

pen name A made-up name which an author signs to his work instead of his real name: The *pen name* of Samuel Clemens was Mark Twain.

pen·nant [pen′ənt] *n.* 1 A long, narrow, often triangular flag, used as a school emblem, etc. 2 A flag awarded to the winners in some sports contests. 3 A championship in a sport.

pen·ni·less [pen′i·lis] *adj.* Extremely poor.

pen·non [pen′ən] *n.* **1** A small flag ending in a point or points, once carried by knights on their lances. **2** Any banner or flag. **3** A wing.

Penn·syl·va·ni·a [pen·səl·vān′yə *or* pen·səl·vā′nē·ə] *n.* A state in the NE U.S.

Pennsylvania Dutch 1 People of German descent whose ancestors settled in Pennsylvania. **2** The kind of German dialect that they speak. ◆ See DUTCHMAN.

pen·ny [pen′ē] *n., pl.* **pen·nies,** for def. 2 **pence** [pens] **1** A U.S. or Canadian coin worth one cent. **2** A British bronze coin worth $\frac{1}{12}$ of a shilling, being replaced by the new penny. **3** Money in general. **—a pretty penny** *informal* Quite a lot of money.

pen·ny·weight [pen′ē·wāt′] *n.* In troy weight, a unit equal to $\frac{1}{20}$ of an ounce or 24 grains.

pen·ny-wise [pen′ē·wīz′] *adj.* Very careful about saving small sums of money. **— penny-wise and pound-foolish** Careful and thrifty in small matters but wasteful in large ones.

pen·sion [pen′shən] **1** *n.* An allowance regularly paid to a person who has retired from work after long service or because of injury. A pension is sometimes paid to a pensioner's family after his death. **2** *v.* To grant a pension to.

pen·sion·er [pen′shən·ər] *n.* A person who receives a pension.

pen·sive [pen′siv] *adj.* Quietly and seriously thoughtful, often with a touch of sadness: a *pensive* person or mood. **— pen′sive·ly** *adv.*

pent [pent] *adj.* Penned up or in; closely confined: *pent* up in a small room.

pen·ta·gon [pen′tə·gon] *n.* A closed figure having five straight sides and five angles. **— pen·tag·o·nal** [pen·tag′ə·nəl] *adj.* ◆ *Pentagon* comes from Greek words meaning *five angles.*

pen·tam·e·ter [pen·tam′ə·tər] *n.* A line of verse made up of five rhythmic feet, as: "A bōok/ ŏf vēr/sĕs ūn/dĕr·nēath/ thĕ bōugh."

Pentagon

Pen·ta·teuch [pen′tə·t(y)ōōk] *n.* The first five books of the Old Testament.

pen·tath·lon [pen·tath′lən] *n.* An athletic contest made up of five separate events. Each contestant must participate in all events.

Pen·te·cost [pen′tə·kôst] *n.* **1** A Christian festival coming on the seventh Sunday after Easter and commemorating the descent of the Holy Ghost upon the apostles. *Acts* 2. It is also called Whitsunday. **2** A Jewish festival coming 50 days after Passover.

pent·house [pent′hous′] *n.* An apartment, house, or other structure built on the roof of a building.

pent-up [pent′up′] *adj.* Held back; kept in; restrained: *pent-up* emotions.

pe·num·bra [pi·num′brə] *n., pl.* **pe·num·bras** or **pe·num·brae** [pi·num′brē] That part of a shadow which is not completely dark, as the outer, partial shadow in an eclipse.

pe·nu·ri·ous [pə·n(y)ŏŏr′ē·əs] *adj.* Extremely stingy with money. **— pe·nu′ri·ous·ly** *adv.*

pen·u·ry [pen′yə·rē] *n.* Extreme poverty; want.

pe·on [pē′ən *or* pē′on] *n.* In Latin America, an unskilled laborer who gets very low wages. A peon used to be a debtor who was forced to serve until he had worked off his debt.

pe·on·age [pē′ən·ij] *n.* **1** The condition of being a peon. **2** The system by which debtors are forced to serve in order to work off debt.

pe·o·ny [pē′ə·nē] *n., pl.* **pe·o·nies 1** A garden plant with showy, often double flowers ranging from white to red. **2** The flower.

peo·ple [pē′pəl] *n., pl.* **peo·ple,** for def. 2 **peo·ples,** *v.* **peo·pled, peo·pling 1** *n.* Men, women, and children; human beings. **2** *n.* All of the persons making up a nation, race, religion, or cultural group: the Russian *people;* the *peoples* of the earth. **3** *n.* The persons of a given group, place, or class: rich *people;* the *people* of Ohio. **4** *v.* To fill with people or inhabitants; populate: to *people* other planets. **5** *n.* Ordinary persons as distinguished from a class which enjoys special privilege: government by the *people.* **6** *n.* A person's family or relatives: his wife's *people.*

pep [pep] *n., v.* **pepped, pep·ping 1** *n. informal* Energy and high spirits. **2** *v.* To fill with energy or vigor: A nap *pepped* her up.

pep·per [pep′ər] **1** *n.* A seasoning that tastes hot, prepared from the dried immature berries of a tropical plant. Black pepper is ground from the entire berries, white pepper after the outer coats are removed. **2** *n.* The tropical plant itself. **3** *v.* To season with pepper or something like it. **4** *v.* To sprinkle or shower with small objects: to *pepper* a target with bullets. **5** *n.* Red pepper; cayenne. **6** *n.* Any of several garden plants with a large, hollow, sweet or hot fruit. **7** *n.* The green or red fruit of these plants, eaten in salads, relishes, etc.

pep·per·corn [pep′ər·kôrn′] *n.* A berry of the pepper plant to be ground into black pepper.

pep·per·mint [pep′ər·mint′] *n.* **1** A fragrant herb related to the mint, yielding an oil that tastes sweet. **2** The oil itself, used as a flavoring. **3** Candy flavored with the oil.

pep·per·y [pep′ər·ē] *adj.* **1** Like or flavored with pepper; hot: a *peppery* dish. **2** Sharp and stinging: *peppery* language. **3** Quick-tempered.

pep·sin [pep′sin] *n.* **1** An enzyme secreted in the stomach. It acts to break down the proteins in food. **2** A medicine prepared from this substance, used to aid digestion.

per [pûr] *prep.* **1** By means of; by; through: *per* bearer. **2** To or for each: 25 cents *per* yard. **3** By the; every: 70 feet *per* second.

---

add, āce, câre, pälm; end, ēqual; it, īce; odd, ōpen, ôrder; tŏŏk, pŏŏl; up, bûrn;
ə = a in *above,* e in *sicken,* i in *possible,* o in *melon,* u in *circus;* yŏŏ = u in *fuse;* oil; pout;
check; ring; thin; this; zh in *vision.* For ¶ reference, see page 64 · HOW TO

per·ad·ven·ture [pûr′əd·ven′chər] *adv.* It may be; perhaps: seldom used today.

per·am·bu·late [pə·ram′byə·lāt] *v.* **per·am·bu·lat·ed, per·am·bu·lat·ing** **1** To walk through or around, so as to inspect: to *perambulate* the halls. **2** To walk about; stroll. **—per·am′bu·la′tion** *n.*

per·am·bu·la·tor [pə·ram′byə·lā′tər] *n.* *British* A baby carriage.

per an·num [pûr an′əm] By or for the year: a salary of $6,000 *per annum.*

per·cale [pər·kāl′] *n.* A strong, soft cotton cloth, used in making sheets and pillowcases.

per cap·i·ta [pûr kap′ə·tə] For each person: Taxes are based on *per capita* income. ◆ *Per capita* in Latin means literally *by heads.*

per·ceive [pər·sēv′] *v.* **per·ceived, per·ceiv·ing** **1** To become aware of by means of one of the senses; see, hear, feel, smell, or taste. **2** To come to understand. **3** To observe; notice.

per·cent [pər·sent′] *n.* or **per cent** Parts in each hundred; hundredths: 12 *percent* or 12% = 12/100 or .12.

per·cent·age [pər·sen′tij] *n.* **1** Proportion in a hundred parts; rate per hundred. **2** A proportion or part considered in relation to the whole: What *percentage* of the profit will be mine?

per·cen·tile [pər·sen′tīl *or* pər·sen′til] *n.* Any point on a scale of 100 formed by arranging a set of numbers under study in sequence and dividing them into 100 groups of equal size: The ninety-fifth *percentile* is sixth from the top.

per·cep·ti·ble [pər·sep′tə·bəl] *adj.* That can be noticed; observable: a *perceptible* movement of the head. **—per·cep′ti·bly** *adv.*

per·cep·tion [pər·sep′shən] *n.* **1** The act or power of perceiving through a sense or the senses: a keen *perception* of sound. **2** Knowledge obtained by perceiving; understanding.

per·cep·tive [pər·sep′tiv] *adj.* Capable of a quick, ready understanding: a *perceptive* mind.

perch¹ [pûrch] **1** *n.* A pole, branch, bar, etc., used as a roost for birds. **2** *n.* Any place for sitting or standing, especially if high. **3** *v.* To sit or place on or as on a perch: to *perch* oneself on a ladder; The canary *perched* on my finger. **4** *n.* A measure of length equal to 5 1/2 yards.

perch² [pûrch] *n., pl.* **perch** or **perch·es** Any of several fresh-water fishes used as food.

per·chance [pər·chans′] *adv.* Possibly; perhaps: used mostly in poems.

per·co·late [pûr′kə·lāt] *v.* **per·co·lat·ed, per·co·lat·ing** **1** Of a liquid, to pass or cause to pass through many tiny openings; filter. **2** To prepare or be prepared in a percolator.

per·co·la·tor [pûr′kə·lā′tər] *n.* A type of coffee-pot in which boiling water keeps rising in a tube and then filters down through ground coffee to the bottom.

per·cus·sion [pər·kush′ən] *n.* **1** The sharp striking of one body against another. **2** The vibration, sound, or shock produced by the striking of one body against another.

percussion instrument A musical instrument whose tone is produced by striking or hitting, as a cymbal or drum.

per di·em [pər dē′əm] **1** By the day. **2** An allowance for daily expenses. ◆ *Per diem* is a Latin phrase.

per·di·tion [pər·dish′ən] *n.* **1** Everlasting damnation; loss of one's soul. **2** Hell.

per·e·gri·nate [per′ə·gri·nāt′] *v.* **per·e·gri·nat·ed, per·e·gri·nat·ing** **1** To travel from place to place. **2** To travel through or along.

per·e·gri·na·tion [per′ə·grə·nā′shən] *n.* A journey; traveling.

per·e·grine falcon [per′ə·grin] A type of hawk used in falconry.

per·emp·to·ry [pə·remp′tər·ē] *adj.* **1** Not open to argument or refusal: a *peremptory* order. **2** Urgent; final: a *peremptory* writ from a court. **3** Imperious; arrogant: a *peremptory* manner. **—per·emp′tor·i·ly** *adv.*

per·en·ni·al [pə·ren′ē·əl] **1** *adj.* Continuing through the year or through many years. **2** *adj.* Everlasting; perpetual: a *perennial* favorite. **3** *adj.* Lasting and growing for more than two years: a *perennial* plant. **4** *n.* A plant that lives for more than two years. **—per·en′ni·al·ly** *adv.*

per·fect [*adj.* pûr′fikt, *v.* pər·fekt′] **1** *adj.* Without defects or faults; excellent: a *perfect* set of teeth. **2** *adj.* Complete in all its parts: a *perfect* set of dishes. **3** *v.* To finish or improve; make perfect: to *perfect* a new method of teaching reading. **4** *adj.* Accurate; exact: a *perfect* translation. **5** *adj.* Total; utter: a *perfect* fool. **6** *adj.* Completely effective; ideal: a *perfect* answer. **7** *adj.* In grammar, denoting the tense of a verb that expresses an action completed in the past or before a time indicated.

per·fect·i·ble [pər·fek′tə·bəl] *adj.* Capable of being made perfect or arriving at perfection. **—per·fect′i·bil′i·ty** *n.*

per·fec·tion [pər·fek′shən] *n.* **1** The condition of being perfect: the *perfection* of a summer's day. **2** The act of perfecting: the *perfection* of a new invention. **3** A person or thing that is ideal or excellent: As a hostess, she is *perfection.* **—to perfection** Exactly; perfectly: a steak cooked *to perfection.*

per·fec·tion·ist [pər·fek′shən·ist] *n.* A person who demands of himself and others an exceedingly high degree of excellence.

per·fect·ly [pûr′fikt·lē] *adv.* **1** In a perfect manner: The dog did the trick *perfectly.* **2** Completely; altogether: *perfectly* true.

per·fid·i·ous [pər·fid′ē·əs] *adj.* Treacherous; unfaithful: a *perfidious* attack on a friend. **—per·fid′i·ous·ly** *adv.*

per·fi·dy [pûr′fə·dē] *n., pl.* **per·fi·dies** The act of breaking faith; treachery.

per·fo·rate [pûr′fə·rāt] *v.* **per·fo·rat·ed, per·fo·rat·ing** **1** To make a hole or holes through, as by punching or drilling. **2** To pierce with holes in rows, as sheets of postage stamps. **3** *adj. use:* Please tear along the *perforated* line.

per·fo·ra·tion [pûr′fə·rā′shən] *n.* **1** A hole drilled in or punched through something. **2** The act of perforating. **3** The condition of being perforated.

Perforations allow the coupon to be torn out neatly.

per·force [pər·fôrs′] *adv.* By or of necessity.

per·form [pər·fôrm′] *v.* **1** To do; accomplish: to *perform* surgery. **2** To fulfill or discharge, as a duty. **3** To give an exhibition of artistic skill; to act, play an instrument, sing, etc.

per·form·ance [pər·fôr′məns] *n.* **1** The act of performing or doing: A fireman was burned in the *performance* of his duty. **2** A presentation before an audience of a concert, play, opera, etc. **3** An action performed; deed; feat. **4** The manner of operating or functioning: Repairs improved the car's *performance*.

per·form·er [pər·fôr′mər] *n.* A person who performs, especially an actor, musician, etc.

per·fume [*n.* pûr′fyoom; *v.* pər·fyoom′] *n., v.* **per·fumed, per·fum·ing 1** *n.* A fragrant liquid used to scent the body, the clothing, etc. **2** *n.* A pleasant odor, as from flowers. **3** *v.* To fill or scent with a fragrant odor: Flowers *perfumed* the room; to *perfume* a handkerchief.

per·fum·er·y [pər·fyoo′mər·ē] *n., pl.* **per·fum·er·ies 1** The art or business of preparing perfumes. **2** A perfume or perfumes.

per·func·to·ry [pər·fungk′tər·ē] *adj.* **1** Done mechanically and merely for the sake of getting through: a *perfunctory* piece of work. **2** Careless or indifferent: a *perfunctory* student; a *perfunctory* glance. **— per·func′to·ri·ly** *adv.*

per·haps [pər·haps′] *adv.* Maybe; possibly.

Per·i·cles [per′ə·klēz] *n.*, died 429 B.C., Athenian statesman, orator, and general.

per·i·gee [per′ə·jē] *n.* The point in the orbit of a satellite at which it is closest to the earth. ◆ See APHELION.

orbit of satellite

satellite at apogee

earth

satellite at perigee

per·i·he·li·on [per′ə·hē′lē·ən] *n.* The point in the orbit of a planet or comet where it is nearest to the sun. ◆ See APHELION.

per·il [per′əl] *n., v.* **per·iled** or **per·illed, per·il·ing** or **per·il·ling 1** *n.* Exposure to the chance of injury, loss, or destruction; danger; risk. **2** *v.* To expose to danger; imperil: to *peril* one's life for a friend.

per·il·ous [per′əl·əs] *adj.* Full of peril; risky; dangerous. **— per′il·ous·ly** *adv.* **— per′il·ous·ness** *n.*

pe·rim·e·ter [pə·rim′ə·tər] *n.* The outer boundary or the length of the outer boundary of any plane figure.

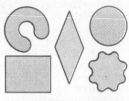

The perimeters of the figures are outlined in red.

pe·ri·od [pir′ē·əd] *n.* **1** A portion of time with a definite beginning and end marked by events that repeat themselves again and again. **2** A time of indefinite length having some specified quality or circumstance. **3** A set portion of time: a lunch *period*. **4** A completion or end. **5** A dot (.) used as a mark of punctuation at the close of a declarative sentence and after abbreviations.

pe·ri·od·ic [pir′ē·od′ik] *adj.* **1** Recurring at regular intervals: *periodic* dental checkups. **2** Happening every now and then; intermittent: *periodic* trips to Europe. **3** Describing a sentence of several clauses, so constructed that its meaning is not completed until the end.

pe·ri·od·i·cal [pir′ē·od′i·kəl] **1** *n.* A publication that appears weekly, monthly, or at larger intervals. Magazines are periodicals. **2** *adj.* Published weekly, monthly, etc. **3** *adj.* Periodic. **— pe′ri·od′i·cal·ly** *adv.*

periodic table A table in which all the chemical elements are arranged in order according to their atomic numbers and in groups according to the similarity of their properties.

per·i·pa·tet·ic [per′i·pə·tet′ik] *adj.* Walking about from place to place; traveling a great deal: a *peripatetic* newspaperman.

pe·riph·er·al [pə·rif′ər·əl] *adj.* Of, having to do with, or forming the outer part or boundary of something. **— pe·riph′er·al·ly** *adv.*

pe·riph·er·y [pə·rif′ər·ē] *n., pl.* **pe·riph·er·ies 1** The outside or outer surface of something. **2** The line bounding a curved figure, especially a circle. **3** A surrounding region or area.

per·i·scope [per′ə·skōp] *n.* A tube with mirrors and lenses so arranged in it that an observer can see over an obstruction. Periscopes allow people in submerged submarines to see objects on the surface.

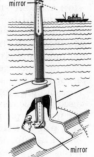

mirror

mirror

A periscope

per·ish [per′ish] *v.* To be completely destroyed; die: The crew *perished* in the plane crash.

per·ish·a·ble [per′ish·ə·bəl] **1** *adj.* Likely to decay or wither quickly: *perishable* crops. **2** *n.* (*usually pl.*) Something likely to spoil, as food: Fruit, milk, and butter are *perishables*.

---

add, āce, câre, pälm;   end, ēqual;   it, īce;   odd, ōpen, ôrder;   took, pool;   up, bûrn;

ə = a in *above*, e in *sicken*, i in *possible*, o in *melon*, u in *circus*;   yoo = u in *fuse*;   oil;   pout;

check; ring; thin; this; zh in *vision*.   For ¶ reference, see page 64 · HOW TO

per·i·wig [per′ə·wig] *n.* A wig or peruke.

per·i·win·kle[1] [per′ə·wing′kəl] *n.* A small sea snail with a coiled shell. It is eaten as a delicacy in Europe.

per·i·win·kle[2] [per′ə·wing′kəl] *n.* A plant having shiny evergreen leaves and white or blue flowers.

per·jure [pûr′jər] *v.* **per·jured, per·jur·ing** To make (oneself) guilty of perjury. — **per′jur·er** *n.*

per·ju·ry [pûr′jə·rē] *n., pl.* **per·ju·ries** **1** A false statement made deliberately while under oath, as in a court of law. **2** The act of making such a false statement.

Periwinkle, up to 1 in. long

perk [pûrk] *v.* **1** To raise quickly and smartly: The donkey *perked* up his long ears. **2** To make trim and smart in appearance: She was *perked* out in a new hat. — **perk up** To become gay and lively; recover one's spirits.

perk·y [pûr′kē] *adj.* **perk·i·er, perk·i·est** Pert and lively: a *perky* kitten.

per·ma·nence [pûr′mə·nəns] *n.* The condition or quality of being permanent or lasting.

per·ma·nen·cy [pûr′mə·nən·sē] *n., pl.* **per·ma·nen·cies** **1** Permanence. **2** Something permanent.

per·ma·nent [pûr′mən·ənt] *adj.* Continuing or intended to continue without change; lasting; enduring; durable: a *permanent* dye. — **per′·ma·nent·ly** *adv.*

permanent wave An artificial wave or curl chemically set in the hair and lasting for several months.

per·me·a·ble [pûr′mē·ə·bəl] *adj.* Capable of being permeated, especially permitting fluids to pass through: Towels are *permeable* by water. — **per′me·a·bil′i·ty** *n.*

per·me·ate [pûr′mē·āt] *v.* **per·me·at·ed, per·me·at·ing** **1** To spread itself or spread through: A spirit of fun *permeated* the group. **2** To pass through the openings or pores of. — **per′me·a′·tion** *n.* ◆ See PENETRATE.

per·mis·si·ble [pər·mis′ə·bəl] *adj.* That can be permitted; allowable. — **per·mis′si·bly** *adv.*

per·mis·sion [pər·mish′ən] *n.* The act of permitting; authorization; leave: He has *permission* to go home early.

per·mis·sive [pər·mis′iv] *adj.* **1** Granting permission; allowing. **2** Permitted. **3** Not strict in discipline; lenient: *permissive* parents.

per·mit [*v.* pər·mit′; *n.* pûr′mit] *v.* **per·mit·ted, per·mit·ting,** *n.* **1** *v.* To allow; let: *Permit* me to help; Smoking is not *permitted*. **2** *v.* To furnish an opportunity: If time *permits*, I'll come to see you. **3** *n.* An official document or card giving permission; license: a hunting *permit*. ◆ See TRANSMIT.

per·ni·cious [pər·nish′əs] *adj.* **1** Highly injurious; very harmful: a climate *pernicious* to health. **2** Killing; deadly. — **per·ni′cious·ly** *adv.*

per·o·ra·tion [per′ə·rā′shən] *n.* The conclusion of a speech, which sums up and urges the points made.

per·ox·ide [pə·rok′sīd] *n.* An oxide in which two atoms of oxygen occupy the place usually taken by one. Hydrogen peroxide is used as a bleach and as a disinfectant.

per·pen·dic·u·lar [pûr′pən·dik′yə·lər] **1** *adj.* Straight up and down; vertical: the canyon's *perpendicular* walls. **2** *adj.* Having a relation to another line like that between two lines which intersect so as to form four equal angles. **3** *n.* A line at right angles to another line.

Perpendicular

per·pe·trate [pûr′pə·trāt] *v.* **per·pe·trat·ed, per·pe·trat·ing** To do, perform, or commit (a crime or other evil). — **per′pe·tra′tion** *n.* — **per′pe·tra′tor** *n.*

per·pet·u·al [pûr·pech′ōō·əl] *adj.* **1** Continuing indefinitely; eternal. **2** Incessant; constant: a *perpetual* bother. — **per·pet′u·al·ly** *adv.*

per·pet·u·ate [pər·pech′ōō·āt] *v.* **per·pet·u·at·ed, per·pet·u·at·ing** To cause to last or to be remembered for a very long time: The Bunker Hill monument *perpetuates* the memory of a battle of the American Revolution. — **per·pet′u·a′tion** *n.*

per·pe·tu·i·ty [pûr′pə·t(y)ōō′ə·tē] *n.* **1** The state of being perpetual. **2** Unlimited time; eternity. — **in perpetuity** Forever.

per·plex [pər·pleks′] *v.* To cause to hesitate or doubt; confuse; bewilder; puzzle: The arithmetic problem *perplexed* the entire class.

per·plex·i·ty [pər·plek′sə·tē] *n., pl.* **per·plex·i·ties** **1** A perplexed condition; doubt; confusion. **2** Something that perplexes.

per·qui·site [pûr′kwə·zit] *n.* Any profit from employment in addition to salary, as a tip.

per·se·cute [pûr′sə·kyōōt] *v.* **per·se·cut·ed, per·se·cut·ing** **1** To keep after so as to attack or injure. **2** To mistreat or oppress because of religion, race, or beliefs. **3** To harass; annoy constantly. — **per′se·cu′tion** *n.* — **per′se·cu′tor** *n.* ◆ *Persecute* and *prosecute* both come from Latin roots meaning *to follow* or *pursue*, but each is combined with a different prefix. *Per-* means *thoroughly*, and one who *persecutes* does pursue relentlessly and cruelly. *Pro-* means *forward*, and one who *prosecutes* does carry forward a legal action to its completion.

Per·seph·o·ne [pər·sef′ə·nē] *n.* The Greek name for PROSERPINE.

Per·seus [pûr′syōōs] *n.* **1** In Greek myths, the slayer of Medusa and rescuer of Andromeda from a sea monster. **2** A northern constellation.

per·se·ver·ance [pûr′sə·vir′əns] *n.* The act or habit of persevering; persistence.

per·se·vere [pûr′sə·vir′] *v.* **per·se·vered, per·se·ver·ing** To continue to try to do something in spite of difficulties: The tortoise *persevered* in the race, even though the hare was swifter.

Per·sia [pûr′zhə] *n.* **1** A former and now un-official name for Iran. **2** An ancient empire in sw Asia, destroyed by Alexander the Great. — **Per·sian** [pûr′zhən] *n., adj.*

Persian Gulf An inlet of the Arabian Sea between Iran and Arabia.

per·si·flage [pûr′sə·fläzh] *n.* A light, playful style of writing or speaking; gentle teasing.

per·sim·mon [pər·sim′ən] *n.* **1** A North American tree that bears reddish, plumlike fruit. **2** This fruit, which puckers the mouth when green but is sweet to eat when ripe.

per·sist [pər·sist′] *v.* **1** To continue firmly or stubbornly in spite of opposition, warning, diffi-culty, etc.: to *persist* in breaking a rule. **2** To be insistent in saying something, asking a ques-tion, etc. **3** To continue to exist; endure: My plants die, but the weeds *persist.*

per·sis·tence [pər·sis′təns] *n.* **1** Stubbornness or determination. **2** A lasting; continuing exis-tence: The *persistence* of fever worried him.

per·sis·ten·cy [pər·sis′tən·sē] *n.* Persistence.

per·sis·tent [pər·sis′tənt] *adj.* **1** Persevering or undaunted: a *persistent* salesman. **2** Enduring; continuing: a *persistent* cough. **— per·sis′-tent·ly** *adv.*

per·son [pûr′sən] *n.* **1** A human being; individ-ual. **2** The body of a human being: The police searched the man and found nothing on his *person.* **3** In grammar, a form of a pronoun or verb distinguishing the speaker (**first person**), the person or thing spoken to (**second person**), and the person or thing spoken of (**third per-son**). **— in person 1** Physically present; live. **2** Acting for oneself.

per·son·a·ble [pûr′sən·ə·bəl] *adj.* Good-look-ing; handsome; attractive: a *personable* man.

per·son·age [pûr′sən·ij] *n.* **1** A man or woman of importance or rank. **2** A person; individual. **3** A character in a book or drama.

per·son·al [pûr′sən·əl] **1** *adj.* Of or having to do with a particular person or persons: a *per-sonal* matter. **2** *adj.* Having to do with the body or physical appearance: *personal* cleanli-ness. **3** *adj.* Private: *personal* mail. **4** *adj.* Referring to a particular person, especially in a critical or offensive way: *personal* remarks. **5** *adj.* Done in person: a *personal* visit. **6** *adj.* Having to do with private property that can be moved and is not part of real estate, as clothing, furniture, etc. **7** *adj.* In grammar, showing person: *personal* pronouns. **8** *n.* A notice in a newspaper containing information intended for a particular person. ◆ *Personal* [pûr′sən·əl] is most often an adjective, and *personnel* [pûr′sə·nel′] is always a noun. A *personal* matter is a private matter that affects only the person or persons involved: a *personal* feeling of guilt. *Personnel* is a rather formal word that refers to a particular group of soldiers or employees.

per·son·al·i·ty [pûr′sən·al′ə·tē] *n., pl.* **per·son·al·i·ties 1** The qualities or characteristics of a person that make him different from every other person. **2** Attractive personal qualities, as charm, friendliness, enthusiasm, etc. **3** The con-dition or fact of being a person and not a thing or idea. **4** A person, especially one of outstanding qualities. **5** (*often pl.*) A personal or slighting remark: Avoid *personalities* in a debate.

per·son·al·ly [pûr′sən·əl·ē] *adv.* **1** In person, not through an agent. **2** As though intended for or directed toward oneself: Don't take his re-marks *personally.* **3** As regards one's own opin-ions, tastes, etc.: *Personally,* I enjoy the movies. **4** With regard to a person as an individual: I like him *personally,* but I disagree with his political statements.

personal pronoun In grammar, a pronoun that varies in form to show person and number, as *I, we, you, he, she, it,* and *they.*

per·son·i·fi·ca·tion [pər·son′ə·fə·kā′shən] *n.* **1** A figure of speech in which inanimate objects or qualities are spoken of as having human characteristics, as in the phrase "joy, that vigor-ous child of goodness." **2** A person or thing thought of as a typical example.

per·son·i·fy [pər·son′ə·fī] *v.* **per·son·i·fied, per·son·i·fy·ing 1** To think of or represent as having life or human qualities. **2** To be a striking example of; typify.

per·son·nel [pûr′sə·nel′] *n.* The persons em-ployed in a business, engaged in military service, etc. ◆ See PERSONAL.

per·spec·tive [pər·spek′tiv] *n.* **1** The art of drawing or painting objects on a flat surface in such a way that they appear to have depth and distance. **2** The effect of distance on space re-lationships and the appearance of objects. **3** A way of seeing and judging things in relation to one another; point of view; outlook.

per·spi·ca·cious [pûr′spə·kā′shəs] *adj.* Having a clear and penetrating mind; mentally alert; wise. **— per′spi·ca′cious·ly** *adv.*

per·spi·cac·i·ty [pûr′spə·kas′ə·tē] *n.* Keenness in judging and understanding; wisdom.

per·spi·cu·i·ty [pûr′spə·kyoo′ə·tē] *n.* Clearness of expression that makes understanding easy.

per·spic·u·ous [pər·spik′yoo·əs] *adj.* Clearly expressed; plain.

per·spi·ra·tion [pûr′spə·rā′shən] *n.* **1** Moisture given off through the pores of the skin; sweat. **2** The act of perspiring; sweating.

per·spire [pər·spīr′] *v.* **per·spired, per·spir·ing** To sweat.

per·suade [pər·swād′] *v.* **per·suad·ed, per·suad·ing** To induce to believe, do, or not do something, by argument, urging, or advice.

per·sua·sion [pər·swā′zhən] *n.* **1** The act of persuading. **2** The ability to persuade. **3** A conviction; belief. **4** A religious belief or sect.

---

add, āce, câre, pälm; end, ēqual; it, īce; odd, ōpen, ôrder; tŏŏk, pōōl; up, bûrn; ə = a in *above*, e in *sicken*, i in *possible*, o in *melon*, u in *circus*; yōō = u in *fuse*; oil; pout; check; ring; thin; this; zh in *vision*. For ¶ reference, see page 64 · HOW TO

per·sua·sive [pər·swā′siv] *adj.* Able or tending to persuade: a *persuasive* manner. **— per·sua′·sive·ly** *adv.* **— per·sua′sive·ness** *n.*

pert [pûrt] *adj.* Saucy or bold; too forward: a *pert* answer. **— pert′ly** *adv.*

per·tain [pər·tān′] *v.* **1** To have reference; relate: The problem *pertains* to health. **2** To belong or be connected: benefits *pertaining* to social security. **3** To be fitting or appropriate.

per·ti·na·cious [pûr′tə·nā′shəs] *adj.* Sticking firmly to a purpose or opinion; obstinate.

per·ti·nac·i·ty [pûr′tə·nas′ə·tē] *n.* A persistent attachment to a belief or purpose; obstinacy.

per·ti·nent [pûr′tə·nənt] *adj.* Related to the matter under discussion; to the point; appropriate: His remarks were not *pertinent* to the discussion. **— per′ti·nence** *n.*

per·turb [pər·tûrb′] *v.* To disturb greatly; alarm; agitate: He was much *perturbed* by the bad news. **— per·tur·ba·tion** [pûr′tər·bā′·shən] *n.*

Pe·ru [pə·rōō′] *n.* A country in western South America.

pe·ruke [pə·rōōk′] *n.* A type of wig worn by men in the 17th and 18th centuries.

pe·rus·al [pə·rōō′zəl] *n.* The act of perusing.

pe·ruse [pə·rōōz′] *v.* **pe·rused, pe·rus·ing** To read carefully and with close attention: to *peruse* a newspaper.

Pe·ru·vi·an [pə·rōō′vē·ən] **1** *adj.* Of or from Peru. **2** *n.* A person born in or a citizen of Peru.

Peruke

per·vade [pər·vād′] *v.* **per·vad·ed, per·vad·ing** To spread through all parts of; extend all over; permeate: The fumes *pervaded* the building.

per·va·sive [pər·vā′siv] *adj.* Thoroughly penetrating or permeating: a *pervasive* odor.

per·verse [pər·vûrs′] *adj.* **1** Stubbornly contrary: Donkeys are *perverse* animals. **2** Peevish; cranky: a *perverse* nature. **3** Morally wrong or erring; wicked. **4** Wrong; incorrect: *perverse* logic. **— per·verse′ly** *adv.* **— per·verse′·ness** *n.*

per·ver·sion [pər·vûr′zhən] *n.* **1** A misuse of or deviation from the proper purpose, meaning, etc.: a *perversion* of power. **2** A wrong or inaccurate form: a *perversion* of art.

per·ver·si·ty [pər·vûr′sə·tē] *n., pl.* **per·ver·si·ties** **1** The condition or quality of being perverse. **2** Perverse nature or behavior.

per·vert [*v.* pər·vûrt′, *n.* pûr′vərt] **1** *v.* To turn from the true end or proper purpose. **2** *v.* To twist or distort the meaning or intent of. **3** *v.* To lead astray; corrupt. **4** *n.* A perverted person.

pes·ky [pes′kē] *adj.* **pes·ki·er, pes·ki·est** *informal* Annoying; troublesome: a *pesky* dog.

pe·so [pā′sō] *n., pl.* **pe·sos** The basic unit of

money in several Spanish-speaking countries, as Mexico and Chile.

pes·si·mism [pes′ə·miz′əm] *n.* **1** The tendency to take a gloomy view of life. **2** The belief that the evil in life outweighs the good. **— pes′si·mist** *n.* **— pes′si·mis′tic** *adj.* **— pes′si·mis′ti·cal·ly** *adv.*

pest [pest] *n.* **1** An irritating or annoying person or thing; nuisance. **2** A destructive or harmful insect, plant, etc. **3** A plague: seldom used today.

pes·ter [pes′tər] *v.* To annoy or bother: The youngster *pestered* everyone with his questions.

pes·tif·er·ous [pes·tif′ər·əs] *adj.* **1** Carrying or spreading infectious disease: *pestiferous* vermin. **2** Having an evil or harmful influence on society. **3** *informal* Annoying; bothersome.

pes·ti·lence [pes′tə·ləns] *n.* Any contagious and often fatal disease, as cholera or plague, that spreads rapidly.

pes·ti·lent [pes′tə·lənt] *adj.* **1** Hurtful or fatal to health or life: a *pestilent* disease. **2** Having a bad influence or effect; harmful to the social or moral welfare of people.

pes·tle [pes′əl] *n., v.* **pes·tled, pes·tling 1** *n.* A tool with a blunt end used for pounding or crushing substances in a mortar. **2** *v.* To pound or crush with or as if with a pestle.

pet¹ [pet] *n., adj., v.* **pet·ted, pet·ting 1** *n.* A tame animal treated lovingly or kept as a companion or playmate. **2** *adj.* Tamed or kept as a pet: a *pet* dog. **3** *n.* A favorite: a teacher's *pet.* **4** *adj.* Regarded as a favorite: a *pet* hobby. **5** *adj.* Showing endearment: a *pet* name. **6** *v.* To pat or stroke gently; fondle.

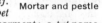

Mortar and pestle

pet² [pet] *n.* A fit of ill temper or sulkiness.

pet·al [pet′əl] *n.* One of the bright-colored leaf-like parts of a flower.

pet·cock [pet′kok′] *n.* A small valve or faucet, as on a steampipe, for draining, releasing pressure, etc.

Pe·ter [pē′tər] *n.,* died A.D. 64?, Christian Apostle and saint. Two letters attributed to him are books of the New Testament. He is also called Simon Peter.

pet·i·ole [pet′ē·ōl] *n.* The stem or slender stalk that supports the broad part of a leaf.

pe·tite [pə·tēt′] *adj.* Small in figure: said of women and girls.

pe·ti·tion [pə·tish′ən] **1** *n.* A formal, written request, often with many signatures, sent to a person or group in authority. **2** *v.* To make a petition or plea to or for: The neighbors *petitioned* the mayor for a park. **3** *n.* An appeal or prayer. **— pe·ti′tion·er** *n.*

pet·it jury [pet′ē] The jury, usually of twelve persons, chosen to hear and decide a civil or criminal case in court.

pet·rel [pet′rəl] *n.* Any of several small, dark, long-winged sea birds, as the storm petrel.

pet·ri·fy [pet′rə·fī] *v.* **pet·ri·fied, pet·ri·fy·ing 1** *v.* To become stone or like stone. **2** *adj.* *use: petrified* wood. **3** *v.* To become rigid or motionless from fear, surprise, etc.

pet·rol [pet′rəl] *n.* *British* Gasoline.

pe·tro·le·um [pə·trō′lē·əm] *n.* An oily liquid mixture of hydrocarbons, found in the earth. It is used as a fuel and as the source of gasoline, benzine, kerosene, paraffin, etc.

pet·ti·coat [pet′ē·kōt] *n.* A skirt, usually hanging from the waist and worn as an undergarment by women and girls.

pet·tish [pet′ish] *adj.* Subject to fits of ill-temper; peevish. — **pet′·tish·ly** *adv.*

pet·ty [pet′ē] *adj.* **pet·ti·er, pet·ti·est 1** Of little worth or importance; minor: *petty* details. **2** Mean; spiteful: a *petty* remark. **3** Low in rank or position. — **pet′ti·ness** *n.*

petty officer In the navy, any of a class of noncommissioned officers.

pet·u·lant [pech′oo·lənt] *adj.* Showing annoyance over trifles; peevish; fretful. — **pet′u·lance** *n.* — **pet′u·lant·ly** *adv.*

pe·tu·ni·a [pə·t(y)oo′nē·ə] *n.* A garden plant with variously colored, funnel-shaped flowers.

Petticoat

pew [pyoo] *n.* **1** Any of the stationary benches with backs for seating people in church. A pew may have a low bench attached, for kneeling. **2** A boxlike enclosure with seats, set aside in a church for a particular family.

pe·wee [pē′wē] *n.* Any of several types of small flycatchers, having a greenish or gray back.

pew·ter [pyoo′tər] **1** *n.* A gray alloy of tin and lead, copper, etc. It is used for pitchers, plates, and other tableware. **2** *n.* Articles made of pewter. **3** *n., adj.* Dull gray.

pha·e·ton [fā′ə·tən] *n.* A light, four-wheeled, open carriage, sometimes having a folding top.

phag·o·cyte [fag′ə·sīt] *n.* A white corpuscle that absorbs and destroys harmful bacteria in the body.

pha·lanx [fā′langks] *n., pl.* **pha·lanx·es** or **pha·lan·ges** [fə·lan′jēz] **1** In ancient Greece, a battle formation of foot soldiers in close order with shields joined and long spears overlapping. **2** Any closely united group that supports or fights for a common cause.

phan·tasm [fan′taz·əm] *n.* Something seen in the imagination, as a ghost; phantom.

phan·ta·sy [fan′tə·sē] *n.* Another spelling of FANTASY.

phan·tom [fan′təm] **1** *n.* Something that exists only in the imagination but seems to be real. **2** *n.* A ghost. **3** *adj.* Ghostlike: a *phantom* ship. **4** *n.* A person or thing of no real substance: only the *phantom* of an army.

Phar·aoh [fâr′ō *or* fā′rō] *n.* Any one of the kings of ancient Egypt.

Phar·i·see [far′ə·sē] *n.* **1** A member of an ancient Jewish sect known for strict observance of traditional laws, rites, and ceremonies. **2** (*often written* **pharisee**) A hypocritical person who thinks he is more moral than others; a self-righteous person.

phar·ma·ceu·tic [fär′mə·soo′tik] *adj.* Pharmaceutical.

phar·ma·ceu·ti·cal [fär′mə·soo′ti·kəl] **1** *adj.* Of, related to, or having to do with drugs or pharmacy. **2** *n.* A pharmaceutical product.

phar·ma·cist [fär′mə·sist] *n.* A person who is licensed to prepare and sell drugs according to doctors' prescriptions.

phar·ma·cy [fär′mə·sē] **1** *n.* The science or business of preparing and selling medicines. **2** *n., pl.* **phar·ma·cies** A drugstore.

phar·ynx [far′ingks] *n., pl.* **pha·ryn·ges** [fə·rin′jēz] or **phar·ynx·es** The cavity at the back of the mouth where passages to the lungs, nose, and stomach originate.

phase [fāz] *n.* **1** A stage in the changing apparent shape of the moon or of a planet. **2** A single stage in any development or cycle. **3** A view or aspect of something: We covered that *phase* of the report today. **4** A step or part of a series: The job will be handled in *phases*.

Ph.D. Abbreviation of DOCTOR OF PHILOSOPHY.

pheas·ant [fez′ənt] *n.* A long-tailed bird noted for the brilliant feathers of the male, often hunted for sport.

phe·nix [fē′niks] *n.* Another spelling of PHOENIX.

phe·nol [fē′nōl] *n.* A poisonous crystalline compound with a sharp odor, obtained from coal tar; carbolic acid. It is used in plastics and resins, and as a disinfectant.

Pheasant, about 33 in. long

phe·nom·e·nal [fi·nom′ə·nəl] *adj.* **1** Having to do with phenomena. **2** Extraordinary or marvelous. — **phe·nom′e·nal·ly** *adv.*

phe·nom·e·non [fi·nom′ə·non] *n., pl.* **phe·nom·e·na** [fi·nom′ə·nə] or **phe·nom·e·nons 1** Any event, occurrence, or condition that can be seen, experienced, and described scientifically: A storm is a natural *phenomenon*. **2** Any rare or unusual person or thing.

phi·al [fī′əl] *n.* Another spelling of VIAL.

Phil·a·del·phi·a [fil′ə·del′fē·ə] *n.* A city in SE Pennsylvania.

phil·an·throp·ic [fil′ən·throp′ik] *adj.* **1** Of, having to do with, or displaying philanthropy. **2** Charitable; benevolent.

add, āce, câre, pälm; end, ēqual; it, īce; odd, ōpen, ôrder; took, pool; up, bûrn;
ə = a in *above*, e in *sicken*, i in *possible*, o in *melon*, u in *circus*; yoo = u in *fuse*; oil; pout;
check; ring; thin; this; zh in *vision*. For ¶ reference, see page 64 · HOW TO

phil·an·throp·i·cal [fil′ən·throp′ə·kəl] *adj.*
Philanthropic. **— phil′an·throp′i·cal·ly** *adv.*

phi·lan·thro·pist [fi·lan′thrə·pist] *n.* A person
who devotes time and money to helping others.

phi·lan·thro·py [fi·lan′thrə·pē] *n., pl.* **phi·lan·thro·pies** 1 Love of mankind, especially as
shown in the desire and effort to lessen the misery
of others and in the giving of money for worthwhile causes. 2 A charitable act or gift.

phi·lat·e·ly [fi·lat′ə·lē] *n.* The hobby of studying and collecting postage stamps, stamped
envelopes, etc. **— phi·lat′e·list** *n.*

phil·har·mon·ic [fil′här·mon′ik] 1 *adj.* Loving
or devoted to music: a *philharmonic* society. 2 *n.*
(*often written* **Philharmonic**) A philharmonic
society or the symphony orchestra it may support.

Phil·ip·pine [fil′ə·pēn] *adj.* Of or having to do
with the Philippines and their inhabitants.

Philippine Islands The Philippines.

Phil·ip·pines [fil′ə·pēnz] *n.pl.* A country in the
Pacific Ocean south-
east of China, made
up of over 7,000 is-
lands.

Phi·lis·tine [fi·lis′-
tin *or* fil′əs·tēn] 1 *n.*
One of an ancient,
warlike people from
coastal Palestine who
were early foes of the

Israelites. 2 *adj.* Of or having to do with the
ancient Philistines. 3 *n.* (*often written* **philis-
tine**) A person with commonplace tastes and
ideas who has no interest in the arts or learning.

phil·o·den·dron [fil′ə·den′drən] *n.* A popular
house plant having glossy, evergreen leaves.

phi·lol·o·gy [fi·lol′ə·jē] *n.* 1 The study of literary texts in order to determine their original form
and meaning. 2 An older word for LINGUISTICS.
— phi·lol′o·gist *n.*

phi·los·o·pher [fi·los′ə·fər] *n.* 1 A student of
philosophy. 2 A person who originates a system
of philosophy. 3 A person who lives and reasons
according to such a system. 4 A wise and patient
person.

phil·o·soph·ic [fil′ə·sof′ik] *adj.* 1 Having to do
with philosophy. 2 Calm and reasonable: a
philosophic point of view.

phil·o·soph·i·cal [fil′ə·sof′ə·kəl] *adj.* Philosophic. **— phil′o·soph′i·cal·ly** *adv.*

phi·los·o·phize [fi·los′ə·fīz] *v.* **phi·los·o·phized, phi·los·o·phiz·ing** To reason like a
philosopher and try to explain things: to *philoso-
phize* about the meaning of life and death. ¶3

phi·los·o·phy [fi·los′ə·fē] *n., pl.* **phi·los·o·phies** 1 A system of thought that concerns itself
with truth and wisdom. Among other things,
philosophy attempts to study and explain the
meanings of life and death, of faith, and of religion, the differences between right and wrong,
the purposes and principles of art, beauty, etc.
2 The basic principles or truths of any system:
the *philosophy* of education. 3 Wisdom, strength,

and calmness of mind in dealing with the experiences and misfortunes of life.

phil·ter or **phil·tre** [fil′tər] *n.* A magic drink
supposed to make one fall in love.

phlegm [flem] *n.* 1 The stringy mucus discharged from the nose and throat, as during a
cold. 2 Indifference; coldness; apathy.

phleg·mat·ic [fleg·mat′ik] *adj.* Not easily
moved or excited; calm; indifferent.

phlo·em [flō′em] *n.* The plant tissue that conducts the sap to all parts of a tree or plant.

phlox [floks] *n.* A plant with clusters of small,
fragrant, variously colored flowers.

pho·bi·a [fō′bē·ə] *n.* 1 An unreasonable and
persistent fear of a particular thing: a *phobia*
about heights. 2 Any strong dislike.

phoe·be [fē′bē] *n.* A grayish brown, American
flycatcher with a crested head.

Phoe·bus [fē′bəs] *n.* 1 In Greek myths, a sun
god; Apollo. 2 The sun: used mostly in poems.

Phoe·ni·cia [fə·nē′shə] *n.* An ancient country
on the eastern end of the Mediterranean Sea.
— Phoe·ni′cian *adj., n.*

phoe·nix [fē′niks] *n.* In Egyptian myths, a
beautiful bird said to live for 500 or 600 years
before burning itself to ashes on an altar, only
to rise again young and beautiful to live through
another cycle.

Phoe·nix [fē′niks] *n.* The capital of Arizona.

phone [fōn] *n., v.* **phoned, phon·ing** *informal*
1 *n.* A telephone. 2 *v.* To telephone. ◆ *Phone*
is the shortened form of *telephone*.

pho·neme [fō′nēm] *n.* A group or cluster of
related sounds that contrasts significantly with
another group of sounds in the same language.
In English, [p] in *pin* contrasts with [t] in *tin*.

pho·net·ic [fə·net′ik] *adj.* 1 Of or having to do
with phonetics. 2 Representing sounds as
actually spoken: A *phonetic* spelling of "love" is
[luv]. **— pho·net′i·cal·ly** *adv.*

pho·net·ics [fə·net′iks] *n.* 1 The study of
speech sounds and the ways in which they are
produced by the organs of speech. 2 The system
of sounds of any language: the *phonetics* of
English. ◆ See -ICS.

phon·ic [fon′ik] *adj.* Having to do with sound,
especially spoken sound.

phon·ics [fon′iks] *n.* 1 Phonetics. 2 The use of
simple phonetic spellings to teach reading and
pronunciation. ◆ See -ICS.

pho·no·graph [fō′nə·graf] *n.* A device that reproduces sound from the ridges and bends in the
grooves of a record.

pho·no·graph·ic [fō′nə·graf′ik] *adj.* Of, related to, like, or produced by a phonograph.

phony [fō′nē] *adj.* **pho·ni·er, pho·ni·est,** *n.,
pl.* **pho·nies** *slang* 1 *adj.* Not genuine; false;
fake: a *phony* doctor; *phony* money. 2 *n.* A
person or thing that is a false imitation of a real
thing: The fireplace was a *phony*.

phos·phate [fos′fāt] *n.* 1 A salt of an acid
containing phosphorus, especially one used as a
fertilizer. 2 A soft drink made from syrup,
carbonated water, and a little phosphoric acid.

phos·phor [fos′fər] *n.* A phosphorescent substance.

phos·phor·es·cent [fos′fə·res′ənt] *adj.* Giving off light without heat: *phosphorescent* insects. — **phos′phor·es′cence** *n.*

phos·phor·ic [fos·fôr′ik] *adj.* Of or containing phosphorus, especially in its higher valence.

phos·phor·ous [fos′fər·əs] *adj.* Of or containing phosphorus, especially in its lower valence.

phos·phor·us [fos′fər·əs] *n.* A soft, nonmetallic element that forms many compounds essential to life, and in its yellow or white form is highly flammable and glows in the dark.

pho·to [fō′tō] *n., pl.* **pho·tos** *informal* A photograph.

pho·to·e·lec·tric cell [fō′tō·ə·lek′trik] A device whose electrical resistance changes in response to the amount of light striking it, used to trigger mechanisms, such as burglar alarms, elevator doors, etc.

pho·to·gen·ic [fō′tō·jen′ik] *adj.* Having qualities that photograph well: a *photogenic* face.

pho·to·graph [fō′tə·graf] **1** *v.* To take a picture or a picture of with a camera. **2** *n.* A picture made with a camera. **3** *v.* To appear in a photograph: She *photographs* beautifully.

pho·tog·ra·pher [fə·tog′rə·fər] *n.* A person who takes pictures or makes a business of photography.

pho·to·graph·ic [fō′tə·graf′ik] *adj.* **1** Of, having to do with, used in, or produced by photography. **2** Like a photograph: a *photographic* painting. — **pho′to·graph′i·cal·ly** *adv.*

pho·tog·ra·phy [fə·tog′rə·fē] *n.* **1** The process or art of forming and preserving an image by using the chemical action of light on a sensitive film in a camera. **2** The art or business of producing and printing photographs.

pho·ton [fō′ton] *n.* The smallest possible unit of light, resembling in some ways a particle; quantum of light.

pho·to·sphere [fō′tə·sfir] *n.* The shining surface of the sun.

pho·to·syn·the·sis [fō′tō·sin′thə·sis] *n.* The process by which plants, in the presence of chlorophyll, and using energy from the sun, form carbohydrates from carbon dioxide and water.

phrase [frāz] *n., v.* **phrased, phras·ing 1** *n.* In grammar, a group of words that has a single thought but no subject and predicate: "In the sky" is a *phrase.* **2** *n.* A brief, catchy expression: to turn a *phrase.* **3** *v.* To express in a particular way: He *phrased* the request badly. **4** *n.* In music, a small unit containing smaller, often rhythmical units within it, which is itself employed in larger structural units. **5** *v.* To group into, or as into, spoken or musical phrases.

phra·se·ol·o·gy [frā′zē·ol′ə·jē] *n., pl.* **phra·se·ol·o·gies** The choice of words and phrases in expressing ideas: medical *phraseology.*

phre·nol·o·gy [fri·nol′ə·jē] *n.* A supposed science of interpreting what the bumps on a person's skull indicate about his intelligence, disposition, etc.

Phryg·i·a [frij′ē·ə] *n.* An ancient country in Asia Minor. — **Phryg′i·an** *adj., n.*

phthi·sis [thī′sis] *n.* Tuberculosis of the lungs: seldom used today.

phy·lum [fī′ləm] *n., pl.* **phy·la** [fī′lə] A large division of animals, and sometimes of plants, ranking just above a class, all the members of which are believed to have a common evolutionary ancestor.

phys·ic [fiz′ik] *n., v.* **phys·icked, phys·ick·ing 1** *n.* A medicine that moves the bowels; laxative. **2** *v.* To treat with a laxative. **3** *n.* The practice of medicine: seldom used today.

phys·i·cal [fiz′i·kəl] *adj.* **1** Of or having to do with the body: *physical* illness. ◆ *Physical* and *bodily* are so close in meaning that one can often be used in place of the other. *Bodily,* however, makes more direct reference to the human body. **2** Of or having to do with matter, material things, or the laws of nature: the *physical* world. **3** Of or having to do with physics. **4** Involving size, shape, density, etc., but not chemical composition or properties: the *physical* change seen in heated metal.

physical education Training in the care, exercise, and development of the body, often including training in athletic sports.

physical geography Geography dealing with the natural features of the earth, as land formations, vegetation, climate, etc.

phys·i·cal·ly [fiz′i·klē] *adv.* **1** In or with regard to the body: He remained *physically* strong. **2** With reference to natural law or to physics: This force can be calculated *physically.*

phy·si·cian [fi·zish′ən] *n.* A doctor of medicine.

phys·i·cist [fiz′ə·sist] *n.* A student of or specialist in physics.

phys·ics [fiz′iks] *n.* The science dealing with matter, energy, motion, and their interrelations, including the study of mechanics, heat, sound, light, electricity, and magnetism. ◆ See -ICS.

phys·i·og·no·my [fiz′ē·og′nə·mē] *n., pl.* **phys·i·og·no·mies 1** The face or features of a person, considered as revealing character or disposition. **2** The outward look of a thing.

phys·i·o·log·i·cal [fiz′ē·ə·loj′i·kəl] *adj.* Of or having to do with physiology. — **phys′i·o·log′i·cal·ly** *adv.*

phys·i·ol·o·gy [fiz′ē·ol′ə·jē] *n.* The study of the activities of a living organism or of the functions of any of its organs, parts, or systems. — **phys′i·ol′o·gist** *n.*

phys·i·o·ther·a·py [fiz′ē·ō·ther′ə·pē] *n.* The treatment of disability, injury, and disease by external physical means, as heat, electricity, massage, exercise, etc.

---

add, āce, câre, pälm; end, ēqual; it, īce; odd, ōpen, ôrder; took, pool; up, bûrn; ə = a in *above,* e in *sicken,* i in *possible,* o in *melon,* u in *circus;* yōō = u in *fuse;* oil; pout; check; ring; thin; this; zh in *vision.* For ¶ reference, see page 64 · HOW TO

phy·sique [fi·zēk′] *n.* The structure, strength, or appearance of the body: a muscular *physique*.

pi [pī] *n.*, *pl.* **pis** [pīz] **1** The sixteenth letter of the Greek alphabet. **2** (*written* π) The ratio of the circumference of a circle to its diameter, equal to approximately 3.1416.

pi·a·nis·si·mo [pē′ə·nis′i·mō] *adj.*, *adv.* In music, very soft or very softly.

pi·an·ist [pē·an′ist *or* pē′ə·nist] *n.* A person who plays the piano.

pi·an·o[1] [pē·an′ō] *n.*, *pl.* **pi·an·os** A large musical instrument played by striking keys on a keyboard with the fingers, each key making a padded hammer strike steel wires to produce a tone.

pi·an·o[2] [pē·ä′nō] *adj.*, *adv.* In music, soft or softly.

pi·an·o·for·te [pē·an′ə·fôr′tā *or* pē·an′ə·fôrt′] *n.* A piano.

pi·az·za [pē·az′ə] *n.* **1** In the U.S., a porch or veranda running along one or more sides of a house. **2** In Italy, a plaza or open square surrounded by buildings. ◆ See PLACE.

pi·broch [pē′brok] *n.* A warlike or, sometimes, sad musical piece played on a bagpipe.

pi·ca [pī′kə] *n.* **1** A size of type. **2** A measure based on this type, equal to about ⅙ inch.

Pic·ar·dy [pik′ər·dē] *n.* A region and former province of northern France.

Pi·cas·so [pē·kä′sō], **Pablo,** born 1881, Spanish painter and sculptor, active in France.

pic·a·yune [pik′i·yōōn′] **1** *adj.* U.S. Too small to be of value or importance; petty. **2** *n.* U.S. Anything of trifling value. **3** *n.* A small, former Spanish-American coin.

pic·ca·lil·li [pik′ə·lil′ē] *n.* A highly seasoned relish of chopped vegetables.

pic·co·lo [pik′ə·lō] *n.*, *pl.* **pic·co·los** A small flute pitched one octave higher than the ordinary flute.

pick[1] [pik] **1** *v.* To choose; select: *Pick* a card. **2** *n.* Right of selection; choice: Take your *pick*. **3** *n.* The act of picking. **4** *n.* Something selected. **5** *n.* The best or choicest one or part: the *pick* of the lot. **6** *v.* To pluck or gather, as with the fingers: to *pick* flowers; to *pick* apples. **7** *n.* The amount of certain crops picked at one time. **8** *v.* To pluck the strings of: to *pick* a guitar. **9** *v.* To scratch, dig at, or pull at lightly: to *pick* a scab. **10** *v.* To stir up on purpose; provoke: to *pick* a fight. **11** *v.* To seek or point out critically: to *pick* flaws. **12** *v.* To remove matter from, as with the fingers or something pointed: to *pick* one's teeth. **13** *v.* To strip or clean by removing something that covers, as feathers or meat: to *pick* a chicken; to *pick* a bone. **14** *v.* To steal from stealthily: to *pick* a pocket. **15** *v.* To open (a lock) by means other than the key, as with a piece of wire. — **pick at** To eat slowly or daintily, in little bits: She wasn't hungry and *picked at* her

Piccolo

food. — **pick off** To hit, as with a bullet, after taking careful aim. — **pick on** *informal* To tease, annoy, or bully. — **pick out 1** To choose. **2** To distinguish (something) from its surroundings. — **pick over** To examine carefully or one by one. — **pick up 1** To take up, as with the hand. **2** U.S. To make (a room, etc.) tidy. **3** To stop for and receive into a vehicle: to *pick up* a passenger. **4** *informal* To become acquainted with informally, without an introduction. **5** To get: *Pick up* some groceries. **6** To find, acquire, or learn easily or by chance: She *picked up* French from her aunt. **7** To gain speed. **8** *informal* To recover health, spirits, etc. — **pick′·er** *n.*

pick[2] [pik] *n.* **1** A pointed metal tool with a double head and a wooden handle, used for breaking ground, rocks, etc. **2** Any pointed implement for piercing, breaking, or picking, as an ice pick. **3** A small, thin piece of metal, plastic, ivory, etc., used to pluck the strings of a mandolin, guitar, etc.; plectrum.

A mandolin pick

pick·a·back [pik′ə·bak′] *adv.*, *adj.* Piggyback.

pick·ax or **pick·axe** [pik′aks′] *n.* A pick with one end of the head edged like a chisel and the other end pointed.

pick·er·el [pik′ər·əl] *n.*, *pl.* **pick·er·el** or **pick·er·els** A fresh-water food fish related to the pike with a narrow snout and sharp teeth.

pick·et [pik′it] **1** *n.* A pointed stick or post, used to make a fence, as a tent peg, etc.; a stake. **2** *v.* To fence or fortify with pickets. **3** *v.* To tie to a picket, as a horse. **4** *n.* A soldier or group of soldiers posted to guard a camp, army, etc., from surprise attack. **5** *n.* A person standing or walking outside a factory, business, government building, etc., in order to protest something. Pickets usually carry signs. **6** *v.* To station or act as a picket or pickets outside (a place of business, etc.): to *picket* a store.

picket fence A fence made of upright pickets.

pick·le [pik′əl] *n.*, *v.* **pick·led, pick·ling** **1** *n.* A cucumber or other piece of food preserved and flavored in a spicy or salty liquid solution usually made of brine or vinegar. **2** *n.* Such a liquid preservative. **3** *v.* To preserve or flavor in pickle: *pickled* beets. **4** *n.* *informal* An embarrassing or difficult situation.

Picket fence

pick·pock·et [pik′pok′it] *n.* A person who steals from pockets or pocketbooks.

pick·up [pik′up′] *n.* **1** The act of picking up. **2** Acceleration, as in the speed of an automobile engine. **3** A small, usually open truck for light loads. **4** A device that changes the vibrations of a phonograph needle into electrical impulses. **5** The reception of sound or images for broadcasting, the apparatus needed, or the location of the apparatus. **6** *informal* An increase of activity: a *pickup* in business.

pic·nic [pik′nik] *n.*, *v.* **pic·nicked, pic·nick·ing 1** *n.* An outing during which a group or family share a meal outdoors. **2** *v.* To have or attend a picnic. **— pic′nick·er** *n.*

pi·cot [pē′kō] *n.* One of the small loops forming an ornamental edging, as on lace or ribbon.

pic·to·graph [pik′tə·graf] *n.* A picture used as a symbol of an idea, such as a hieroglyphic.

pic·to·ri·al [pik·tôr′ē·əl] *adj.* **1** Of or concerned with pictures: *pictorial* art. **2** Using or full of pictures: *pictorial* books; a *pictorial* diagram. **3** Very descriptive; vivid: *pictorial* language. **— pic·to′ri·al·ly** *adv.*

pic·ture [pik′chər] *n.*, *v.* **pic·tured, pic·tur·ing 1** *n.* A painting, drawing, or photograph, or a print of one, showing a scene, person, object, or design. **2** *v.* To make a picture of. **3** *n.* A vivid description in words: That chapter gives a *picture* of pioneer life. **4** *v.* To show or describe: to *picture* life in the West. **5** *v.* To form a mental image of; imagine: *Picture* a desert island. **6** *n.* An idea or impression. **7** *n.* A person or thing that strongly resembles another or is an example of something: He is the *picture* of health. **8** *n.* A lovely person or thing: pretty as a *picture*. **9** *n.* A motion picture. **10** *n.* The image on a television screen. **11** *n.* An overall situation.

pic·tur·esque [pik′chə·resk′] *adj.* **1** Having a very unusual or striking beauty, quaintness, or charm: a *picturesque* town. **2** Calling up a picture in the mind; vivid: *picturesque* writing.

pie [pī] *n.* A baked dish of fruit, custard, meat, etc., in, on, or covered by a pastry crust.

pie·bald [pī′bôld′] **1** *adj.* Having spots or patches of two colors, especially white and black. **2** *n.* A piebald animal, as a horse.

A piebald horse

piece [pēs] *n.*, *v.* **pieced, piec·ing 1** *n.* A portion of something separated from the whole: The mirror broke into *pieces*. **2** *n.* A portion or quantity of something complete in itself: a *piece* of paper. **3** *v.* To join the separate pieces of: to *piece* together a torn letter. **4** *v.* To add a piece or pieces to, in order to mend, enlarge, etc.: to *piece* the torn sleeves of a shirt. **5** *n.* One of a set: a *piece* of luggage; a chess *piece*. **6** *n.* A quantity or length in which an article is manufactured or sold: a *piece* of wallpaper. **7** *n.* An instance, item, or example: a

piece of luck; a *piece* of news. **8** *n.* In music, writing, or art, a single work or composition: to play a *piece*. **9** *n.* A coin: a fifty-cent *piece*. **10** *n.* A firearm, as a cannon or rifle. **— go to pieces 1** To fall apart. **2** *informal* To lose one's self-control; become emotionally upset. **— of a piece** or **of one piece** Of the same kind, sort, or class.

piece goods Fabrics of various widths, cut and sold from bolts in lengths specified by the customer.

piece·meal [pēs′mēl′] **1** *adv.* Piece by piece or bit by bit; gradually. **2** *adj.* Done or made bit by bit. **3** *adv.* In pieces: torn *piecemeal*.

piece of eight The silver dollar used in the Spanish and British colonies in America during the Revolutionary War.

piece·work [pēs′wûrk′] *n.* Work done and paid for by the piece or by the amount done, not by the time spent. **— piece′work′er** *n.*

pied [pīd] *adj.* Having two or more colors in patches; mottled; dappled; piebald.

Pied·mont [pēd′mont] *n.* **1** A plateau just east of the Appalachians extending southward from Virginia. **2** A region in northern Italy.

pier [pir] *n.* **1** A structure built on pillars and extending out over water, used as a landing place, a walk, etc. **2** A massive support, as for the arch of a bridge. **3** A solid portion of a wall between openings, as between windows.

Pier

pierce [pirs] *v.* **pierced, pierc·ing 1** To pass into or through, as something sharp does; penetrate: A spear *pierced* his side; A scream *pierced* the silence. **2** To go through like a knife; affect sharply or deeply: The bitter cold *pierced* us to the bone. **3** *adj. use:* a *piercing* wind. **4** To make a hole in, into, or through. **5** *adj. use:* *pierced* ears. **6** To force a way into or through: to *pierce* the wilderness. **7** To solve or understand: to *pierce* a mystery.

Pierce [pirs], **Franklin,** 1804–1869, 14th president of the U.S., 1853–1857.

Pierre [pir] *n.* The capital of South Dakota.

pi·e·ty [pī′ə·tē] *n.*, *pl.* **pi·e·ties 1** Reverence, strictness, and devotion in practicing one's religion. **2** Honor and obedience due to parents, superiors, etc. **3** A pious act, wish, etc.

pig [pig] *n.* **1** An animal having a short, thick body, cloven hooves, a long snout, and a thick, bristly skin; swine; hog. **2** Its meat; pork. **3** *informal* A person with a hog's bad features; a greedy, selfish, or dirty person. **4** A rough or crude casting of metal, especially iron.

pi·geon [pij′ən] *n.* A bird with short legs, a small head, and a sturdy body; dove.

pi·geon·hole [pij′ən·hōl′] *n.*, *v.* **pi·geon·holed, pi·geon·hol·ing 1** *n.* A hole for pigeons to nest in, especially one of a number of such holes. **2** *n.* A small compartment, as in a desk, for filing papers. **3** *v.* To place in a pigeonhole; file. **4** *v.* To lay aside or file away and ignore: to *pigeonhole* a request. **5** *v.* To arrange in classes or groups; classify.

Pigeonholes

pi·geon-toed [pij′ən·tōd′] *adj.* Having the toes or feet turned inward.

pig·gy·back [pig′ē·bak′] *adv.*, *adj.* **1** On the back or shoulders: to ride *piggyback.* **2** Of or by a method of transportation in which loaded truck trailers are shipped on railway flatcars.

piggy bank A coin bank, often in the shape of a pig, with a slot for inserting coins.

pig·head·ed [pig′hed′id] *adj.* Stubborn.

pig iron Crude iron as it comes from a blast furnace, usually cast in oblong molds.

pig·ment [pig′mənt] *n.* Coloring matter, such as one of the powdered substances mixed with a liquid to give paint its color, or a natural substance that colors living cells or tissues, as the chlorophyll that makes leaves green.

Piggyback ride

pig·men·ta·tion [pig′mən·tā′shən] *n.* The coloring that pigments give to a person or thing.

Pig·my [pig′mē] *n.*, *pl.* **Pig·mies** (*sometimes written* **pigmy**) Another spelling of PYGMY.

pig·pen [pig′pen′] *n.* **1** A pen for pigs. **2** Any filthy place.

pig·skin [pig′skin′] *n.* **1** The skin of a pig or leather made from it. **2** Something made of this skin, as a saddle. **3** *U.S. informal* A football.

pig·sty [pig′stī′] *n.*, *pl.* **pig·sties** A pigpen.

pig·tail [pig′tāl′] *n.* A braid or plait of hair hanging down from the back of the head.

pike¹ [pīk] *n.* A long pole with a metal spearhead, used by foot soldiers in medieval times.

pike² [pīk] *n.* An edible freshwater fish with a slender body, a long snout, and spiny fins.

pike³ [pīk] *n.* A turnpike.

pike·staff [pīk′staf′] *n.*, *pl.* **pike·staves** [pīk′stāvz′] The wooden handle of a pike.

Pilaster

pi·las·ter [pi·las′tər] *n.* A rectangular column that is part of a wall and projects out a bit from it.

Pi·late [pī′lət], **Pontius** The Roman governor of Judea, A.D. 26–36?, who, under pressure, condemned Jesus to be crucified.

pile¹ [pīl] *n.*, *v.* **piled, pil·ing 1** *n.* A number of things stacked up. **2** *n.* A heap; mound: a *pile* of sand. **3** *v.* To make a pile of: to *pile* up papers or hay. **4** *v.* To accumulate in or as if in a pile: The sand *piled* against the side of the cabin; The work *piled* up. **5** *v.* To cover or heap with a large amount: to *pile* a plate with food. **6** *n. informal* A large amount: a *pile* of money. **7** *v.* To move in a confused mass; crowd: They *piled* onto the bus. **8** *n.* A massive building or group of buildings. **9** *n.* A funeral pyre. **10** *n.* In physics, a reactor.

pile² [pīl] *n.* A heavy beam of wood or steel or a concrete pillar driven into the earth to form a foundation for a building, bridge, etc.

pile³ [pīl] *n.* **1** A mass of cut or uncut loops forming the surface of a rug or of a fabric such as velvet or corduroy. **2** Soft, fine hair.

pile driver A machine that is used to drive posts or piles into the ground.

pil·fer [pil′fər] *v.* To steal by taking a little at a time: to *pilfer* candy.

pil·grim [pil′grim] *n.* **1** A person who journeys to some sacred place for religious reasons. **2** Any wanderer or traveler. **3** (*written* **Pilgrim**) One of the English Puritans who established a colony at Plymouth, Massachusetts, in 1620.

pil·grim·age [pil′grə·mij] *n.* **1** A journey to a place that is held in reverence or honor. **2** Any long or difficult journey.

pill [pil] *n.* A small ball or pellet containing medicine, that can be swallowed whole. ◆ *Pill* comes from the Latin word *pilula*, meaning a *little ball* or *globule.*

pil·lage [pil′ij] *v.* **pil·laged, pil·lag·ing,** *n.* **1** *v.* To rob openly and destructively, as in war; plunder. **2** *n.* The act of robbing in this way. **3** *n.* Goods stolen in this way; plunder; loot.

pil·lar [pil′ər] *n.* **1** A slender, firm, upright structure of stone, wood, etc., as one supporting a roof or standing as a monument; column or shaft. **2** Anything resembling a pillar: a *pillar* of dust. **3** A leading member and main support: He is a *pillar* of the church. **— from pillar to post** From one predicament to another.

pil·lion [pil′yən] *n.* A seat behind the saddle of a horse or motorcycle for a second rider.

Pillory

pil·lo·ry [pil′ə·rē] *n.*, *pl.* **pil·lo·ries,** *v.* **pil·lo·ried, pil·lo·ry·ing 1** *n.* A wooden frame having holes cut in it through which a person's head and hands were put and fastened as a form of public punishment. **2** *v.* To put in a pillory. **3** *v.* To hold up to public scorn or ridicule.

P

pil·low [pil′ō] **1** *n.* A bag or case filled with a soft material, as feathers or foam rubber, on which one can rest his head. **2** *v.* To rest on or as if on a pillow. **3** *v.* To act as a pillow for: Her arms *pillowed* the child's head.

pil·low·case [pil′ō-kās′] *n.* A cloth covering which is slipped over a pillow.

pi·lot [pī′lət] **1** *n.* The person who operates or guides an aircraft during flight. **2** *n.* A person licensed to direct ships in and out of ports or through dangerous waters. **3** *n.* A helmsman. **4** *n.* Any guide. **5** *v.* To act or serve as the pilot of; steer; guide. **6** *v.* To guide, conduct, or steer, as past obstacles: Senator Dunn *piloted* the bill through the Senate.

pi·men·to [pi·men′tō] *n.*, *pl.* **pi·men·tos 1** Pimiento. **2** Another word for ALLSPICE.

pi·mien·to [pi·myen′tō] *n.*, *pl.* **pi·mien·tos** A sweet pepper plant or its ripe fruit, used as a relish, a filling for olives, etc.

pim·per·nel [pim′pər·nel] *n.* A plant related to the primrose, usually having red flowers.

pim·ple [pim′pəl] *n.* A small swelling of the skin, usually reddish and sore at the base.

pin [pin] *n.*, *v.* **pinned, pin·ning 1** *n.* A short, stiff piece of wire with a sharp point and a round, usually flattened, head, used for fastening things together. **2** *n.* Anything like a pin in form or use, as a hairpin. **3** *n.* An ornament, as a brooch or badge, mounted on a pin: a sorority *pin.* **4** *n.* A wooden or metal peg or bar used to hang things on, fasten things together, or hold things in place. **5** *v.* To fasten with or as if with a pin or pins. **6** *v.* To hold firmly in one place: The bully *pinned* him to the wall. **7** *n.* In bowling, one of the bottle-shaped pieces to be knocked down. **— on pins and needles** Uneasy or anxious; nervous. **— pin on** *U.S. slang* To accuse of or blame for: They *pinned* the murder *on* him. **— pin (someone) down** To force (someone) to give a definite answer or make a definite decision.

pin·a·fore [pin′ə·fôr] *n.* A sleeveless, apronlike garment, as one worn over a child's dress.

pin·cers [pin′sərz] *n.pl.* (*sometimes used with singular verb*) **1** An instrument having two handles and a pair of jaws working on a pivot, used for holding objects. **2** The claw of a lobster, crab, etc.

pinch [pinch] **1** *v.* To squeeze between two edges or surfaces, as between a finger and thumb. **2** *n.* The act of pinching; squeeze: a *pinch* on the cheek. **3** *n.* As much of a substance as can be taken between the finger and thumb: a *pinch* of salt. **4** *v.* To squeeze or press

Pinafore

upon painfully. **5** *n.* Painful pressure of any kind: the *pinch* of poverty. **6** *v.* To make thin, shriveled, or wrinkled, as from cold or hunger. **7** *adj. use:* his poor, *pinched* face. **8** *n.* An emergency or a time of sudden need. **9** *v.* To be economical or stingy, as with money. **10** *v. slang* To steal. **11** *n. slang* A theft. **12** *v. slang* To arrest or capture. **13** *n. slang* An arrest.

pinch·ers [pin′chərz] *n.pl.* Pincers.

pinch-hit [pinch′hit′] *v.* **pinch-hit, pinch-hit·ting 1** In baseball, to bat for someone else. **2** *U.S. informal* To substitute for someone else in an emergency. **— pinch hitter**

pin·cush·ion [pin′koosh′ən] *n.* A small cushion into which pins are stuck when not being used.

pine¹ [pīn] *n.* **1** Any of a number of trees bearing cones and needle-shaped evergreen leaves in clusters. **2** The wood of any of these trees.

pine² [pīn] *v.* **pined, pin·ing 1** To grow thin or weak with longing, grief, etc.: The imprisoned princess *pined* away. **2** To have great desire or longing: She *pined* for her homeland.

pin·e·al body [pin′ē·əl] A small structure found in the brain and having no known function.

pine·ap·ple [pīn′ap′əl] *n.* **1** A large, juicy, tropical fruit resembling a pine cone. **2** The plant it grows on, having spiny, curved leaves.

pine needle The leaf of a pine.

pin·feath·er [pin′feth′ər] *n.* An undeveloped feather, like a short stub.

pin·hole [pin′hōl′] *n.* A tiny puncture made by or as if by a pin.

pin·ion¹ [pin′yən] **1** *n.* The outer part or segment of a bird's wing. **2** *n.* A wing. **3** *n.* A feather; quill. **4** *v.* To prevent (a bird) from flying by cutting off a pinion or binding the wings. **5** *v.* To cut or bind (the wings). **6** *v.* To bind or hold the arms of (someone) to make him helpless. **7** *v.* To bind or hold (the arms).

pin·ion² [pin′yən] *n.* A small cogwheel driving or driven by a larger cogwheel.

pink¹ [pingk] **1** *n.*, *adj.* Pale red. **2** *n.* Any of several garden plants having fragrant, often pink, flowers. **— in the pink** *informal* In excellent health. **— pink′ish** *adj.*

pink² [pingk] *v.* **1** To cut the edges of (cloth) with a scalloped pattern made by scissors called **pinking shears,** as to prevent raveling. **2** To decorate with a pattern of holes, as leather. **3** To prick or stab with a pointed weapon.

pink·eye [pingk′ī′] *n.* A contagious disease in which the eyeball becomes pinkish or red.

Pinked cloth

pin money A small sum of money, as an allowance, used for minor, personal expenses.

pin·nace [pin′is] *n.* **1** Any small boat on a ship. **2** A small sailing ship.

pin·na·cle [pin′ə·kəl] *n., v.* **pin·na·cled, pin·na·cling** **1** *n.* A tapering turret or spire, as one rising over a roof. **2** *v.* To provide or top with a pinnacle. **3** *n.* A high peak; summit, as of a mountain. **4** *n.* The highest point: the *pinnacle* of success. **5** *v.* To place on or as if on a pinnacle.

pin·nate [pin′āt] *adj.* Like a feather, especially having similar parts arranged on each side of a stem or stalk: a *pinnate* leaf.

pi·noch·le [pē′nuk·əl] *n.* A card game played with a deck of 48 cards having two of every nine, ten, jack, queen, king, and ace.

pin·point [pin′point′] **1** *n.* The point of a pin. **2** *n.* Something that is very small. **3** *v.* To locate or define precisely: to *pinpoint* a target.

pint [pīnt] *n.* **1** A measure of volume for liquids or dry things, equal to half a quart. **2** A container having the capacity of a pint.

pin·to [pin′tō] *adj., n., pl.* **pin·tos 1** *adj.* Having spots, usually of two or more colors. **2** *n.* A pinto horse or pony.

pin·wheel [pin′(h)wēl′] *n.* **1** A toy consisting of a stick to which is attached a small wheel with blades that spin in the wind. **2** A firework that revolves and throws off colored sparks.

Pinwheel

pi·o·neer [pī′ə·nir′] **1** *n.* One of the first explorers, settlers, or colonists of a new country or region. **2** *n.* Someone who leads the way, as in developing a new field, etc. **3** *v.* To lead the way, as into new territory: Copernicus *pioneered* in modern astronomy. **4** *v.* To be a pioneer of: to *pioneer* a new technique of surgery.

pi·ous [pī′əs] *adj.* Religious; devout; reverent.

pip[1] [pip] *n.* **1** A small fruit seed, as of an apple, orange, etc. **2** *slang* A person or thing that is outstanding, admirable, etc.

pip[2] [pip] *n.* A contagious disease of fowls.

pipe [pīp] *n., v.* **piped, pip·ing 1** *n.* A long tube, as of metal, wood, or concrete, for conveying water, oil, gas, steam, etc., from one place to another. **2** *v.* To convey by pipes: to *pipe* oil into a tank. **3** *v.* To provide with pipes. **4** *n.* A hollow stem with a small bowl at one end, as for smoking tobacco. **5** *n.* A tube, as of reed, wood, or metal, that produces musical notes when air is blown through it. **6** *n.* (*pl.*) The bagpipe. **7** *v.* To play on a pipe or bagpipe: to *pipe* a tune. **8** *v.* To speak or sing in a shrill, high-pitched tone. **9** *n.* A bird's note or call. — **pipe down** *slang* To become silent; stop talking or making noise.

pipe·line [pīp′līn′] *n.* A line of pipes for conveying water, oil, gas, etc.

pip·er [pī′pər] *n.* A person who plays on a pipe or pipes, especially on a bagpipe.

pi·pette [pī·pet′] *n.* A small tube for taking up measured quantities of a liquid.

pip·ing [pī′ping] **1** *n.* Music made by playing pipes. **2** *n.* A shrill sound. **3** *adj.* Shrill or high-pitched: *piping* voices. **4** *n.* A system of pipes, as for drainage. **5** *n.* A narrow strip of folded cloth, used for trimming edges or seams. — **piping hot** So hot as to sizzle.

pip·pin [pip′in] *n.* Any of several varieties of apple.

pi·quant [pē′kənt *or* pē·känt′] *adj.* **1** Having an agreeably sharp or spicy taste: a *piquant* relish. **2** Lively and interesting or charming: a *piquant* manner. — **pi·quan·cy** [pē′kən·sē] *n.*

pique [pēk] *n., v.* **piqued, pi·quing 1** *n.* A feeling of anger or resentment coming from wounded pride. **2** *v.* To arouse a hurt and angry or resentful feeling in: The slight *piqued* her. **3** *v.* To stimulate; arouse: to *pique* one's curiosity. — **pique oneself on** To pride oneself on.

Pipette

pi·qué [pē·kā′] *n.* A cloth of cotton, rayon, or silk with raised ribs running lengthwise.

pi·ra·cy [pī′rə·sē] *n., pl.* **pi·ra·cies 1** The robbing of ships on the high seas. **2** The stealing of another's literary work, invention, etc.

pi·ra·nha [pi·rä′nyə] *n.* A small, fierce, freshwater fish of tropical South America, with powerful jaws and sharp teeth, that in schools will attack man or the larger animals.

pi·rate [pī′rit] *n., v.* **pi·rat·ed, pi·rat·ing 1** *n.* A person guilty of piracy, especially a leader or member of a band that sails the high seas robbing ships. **2** *v.* To steal and use or publish (another's invention, literary work, etc.). — **pi·rat·i·cal** [pī·rat′ə·kəl] *adj.*

pi·rogue [pē′rōg′] *n.* A dugout or other canoe.

pir·ou·ette [pir′ōō·et′] *n., v.* **pir·ou·et·ted, pir·ou·et·ting 1** *n.* In dancing, a rapid whirling on the toes or ball of one foot. **2** *v.* To make a pirouette: She *pirouetted* across the stage.

pis·ta·chi·o [pis·tä′shē·ō *or* pis·tash′ē·ō] *n., pl.* **pis·ta·chi·os**, *adj.* **1** *n.* An edible green nut. **2** *n.* The small tree it grows on, native to western Asia and the Levant. **3** *n.* The flavor of the nut, or a food flavored with it, as ice cream. **4** *n., adj.* Light, yellowish green.

pis·til [pis′til] *n.* The seed-bearing organ of flowering plants, composed of the ovary, the stigma, and usually the style.

pis·tol [pis′təl] *n.* A small gun made to be held and fired in one hand.

pis·ton [pis′tən] *n.* A disk or cylinder fitted closely in a tube or hollow cylinder and moved back and forth by pressure of gas or steam, as in an engine, or by a rod, as in a pump.

Pistil

piston ring An adjustable metal ring fitting around the rim of a piston to make a tight fit between the piston and cylinder wall.

pit¹ [pit] *n.*, *v.* **pit·ted, pit·ting 1** *n.* A hole or cavity in the ground, either natural or dug: the *pit* of a mine. **2** *n.* Any cavity, depression, or scar in or on the body: the *pit* of the stomach. **3** *v.* To mark or become marked with pits, dents, scars, etc.: a face *pitted* with pockmarks. **4** *n.* A hole dug in the ground and camouflaged, to trap wild animals. **5** *n.* An enclosed place where animals are made to fight each other. **6** *v.* To put to fight or compete against: to *pit* one's cunning against the cunning of an animal. **7** *n.* A British word for the rear part of the main floor of a theater.

Piston of a gasoline engine

pit² [pit] *n.*, *v.* **pit·ted, pit·ting 1** *n.* The hard stone in certain fruits, as peaches or cherries. **2** *v.* To remove the pit or pits from. ◆ *Pit* comes directly from Dutch and goes back to an older Dutch word meaning *pith* or *kernel*.

pitch¹ [pich] **1** *v.* To throw, toss, or hurl: to *pitch* hay. **2** *v.* In baseball, to throw (the ball) to the batter. **3** *n.* The act or manner of pitching: a wild *pitch*. **4** *n.* Something pitched, as a ball: He swung at the *pitch*. **5** *v.* To erect or set up: to *pitch* a tent; to *pitch* camp. **6** *v.* To set the level, angle, degree, etc., of: to *pitch* a roof at 45 degrees. **7** *v.* To slope downward: The hill *pitched* steeply at the top. **8** *n.* The amount or degree of slope: the *pitch* of a roof. **9** *v.* To fall or plunge forward or headlong. **10** *v.* To rise and fall alternately at the bow and stern: The ship *pitched* and rolled in the gale. **11** *n.* A particular point, degree, or level: The game was played at a high *pitch* of excitement. **12** *n.* The level of a sound's highness or lowness. The pitch of notes depends on their vibration rates. **13** *v.* To set at a certain pitch or in a certain key: *Pitch* the song lower. **14** *adj. use:* a high-*pitched* voice. — **pitch in** *informal* To start working energetically. — **pitch into** To attack.

pitch² [pich] *n.* **1** A thick, sticky, black substance obtained from boiling down tar, etc., and used to pave roads, cover roofs, etc. **2** The sticky sap of certain pines. — **pitch'y** *adj.*

pitch·blende [pich'blend'] *n.* A blackish or brown mineral that is an important ore of radium and uranium.

pitch·er¹ [pich'ər] *n.* **1** A container with a handle and either a lip or spout, used for holding and pouring liquids. **2** As much as a pitcher will hold. — **pitch'er·ful'** *n.*

pitch·er² [pich'ər] *n.* **1** A person who pitches. **2** In baseball, the player who throws the ball that the batter is to hit.

pitch·fork [pich'fôrk'] *n.* A large fork with a long handle, used to lift and throw hay, etc.

pitch pipe A small pipe that sounds a particular tone when blown, used to find a certain pitch for singers or instrumental players.

pit·e·ous [pit'ē·əs] *adj.* Arousing or deserving pity: a *piteous* wail. — **pit'e·ous·ly** *adv.* — **pit'e·ous·ness** *n.*

pit·fall [pit'fôl'] *n.* **1** A camouflaged pit used to trap wild animals. **2** Any hidden danger.

pith [pith] *n.* **1** The mass of soft, spongy tissue that fills the center of the stems and branches of certain plants. **2** Any similar soft substance, as in a feather, hair, etc. **3** The essential part; gist: the *pith* of my argument.

pith·y [pith'ē] *adj.* **pith·i·er, pith·i·est 1** Of, like, or filled with pith. **2** Brief and forceful: a *pithy* remark. — **pith'i·ly** *adv.*

pit·i·a·ble [pit'ē·ə·bəl] *adj.* Arousing or deserving pity or contempt. — **pit'i·a·bly** *adv.*

pit·i·ful [pit'i·fəl] *adj.* **1** Arousing pity or compassion. **2** Arousing a feeling of scorn or contempt. — **pit'i·ful·ly** *adv.*

pit·i·less [pit'i·lis] *adj.* Without pity; cruel; ruthless. — **pit'i·less·ly** *adv.*

pit·tance [pit'əns] *n.* **1** A small allowance of money. **2** Any meager amount or share.

Pitts·burgh [pits'bûrg'] *n.* A city in sw Pennsylvania.

pi·tu·i·tar·y [pi·t(y)ōō'ə·ter'ē] **1** *adj.* Of or having to do with the pituitary gland. **2** *n.* The pituitary gland.

pituitary gland A small, oval endocrine gland at the base of the brain. It secretes hormones that influence growth and most of the basic functions of the body.

pit·y [pit'ē] *n.*, *pl.* **pit·ies**, *v.* **pit·ied, pit·y·ing 1** *n.* A feeling of keen regret or sorrow for the misfortunes or sufferings of others; sympathy. **2** *v.* To feel pity for: *Pity* the poor, lost child. **3** *n.* A reason for regret or sorrow: What a *pity* that he missed the picnic! — **have pity on** or **take pity on** To show pity for.

piv·ot [piv'ət] **1** *n.* Something, as a pin or short shaft, on which a part turns: The needle of a compass rests on a *pivot*. **2** *v.* To place on or provide with a pivot. **3** *v.* To turn on or as if on a pivot: He *pivoted* before throwing the basketball. **4** *n.* A turning or pivoting movement: to make a *pivot*. **5** *n.* A person or thing upon which something hinges or depends: His telegram was the *pivot* of our plan.

The pivot allows the compass needle to revolve freely.

add, āce, câre, pälm; end, ēqual; it, īce; odd, ōpen, ôrder; took, pool; up, bûrn; ə = a in *above*, e in *sicken*, i in *possible*, o in *melon*, u in *circus*; yōō = u in *fuse*; oil; pout; check; ring; thin; this; zh in *vision*. For ¶ reference, see page 64 · HOW TO

piv·ot·al [piv′ət·(ə)l] *adj.* **1** Of, having to do with, or acting as a pivot. **2** Very important; crucial: a *pivotal* decision.

pix·y or **pix·ie** [pik′sē] *n.*, *pl.* **pix·ies** A fairy or elf.

piz·za [pēt′sə] *n.* An Italian food consisting of a crust overlaid with a mixture of cheese, tomatoes, spices, etc., and baked.

piz·ze·ri·a [pēt′sə·rē′ə] *n.* A place where pizzas are prepared, sold, and eaten.

pk. Abbreviation of PECK[1].

pkg. Abbreviation of PACKAGE.

pl. Abbreviation of PLURAL.

pla·ca·ble [plā′kə·bəl] *adj.* Capable of being calmed or pacified; forgiving.

plac·ard [plak′ärd] **1** *n.* A poster publicly displayed. **2** *v.* To post placards on or in.

pla·cate [plā′kāt *or* plak′āt] *v.* **pla·cat·ed, pla·cat·ing** To calm the anger of; pacify.

place [plās] *n.*, *v.* **placed, plac·ing 1** *n.* A space or area occupied by or proper for a certain person or thing: Put each thing in its proper *place*. **2** *n.* A city, town, or other locality. **3** *n.* An open area, short street, or city square. **4** *n.* A house or dwelling: our *place* at the shore. **5** *n.* Any building or area used for a special purpose: a *place* of business; an eating *place*. **6** *n.* A particular point, part, passage, etc.: a soiled *place* on the tablecloth; a card to mark your *place* in a book. **7** *v.* To put in a particular place or position: *Place* your hands in your lap. **8** *v.* To direct or rest with confidence: to *place* trust in a leader. **9** *n.* Order, position, or rank in relation to others: to finish in first *place*. **10** *v.* To finish a race, contest, etc., in a certain position: He *placed* fifth. **11** *n.* In mathematics, the position of a symbol in an Arabic numeral. In 148, 1 is in the hundreds place and is therefore equal to 100. **12** *n.* Social class, rank, or station: The servant forgot his *place*. **13** *n.* A situation, position, or job: In his *place*, I'd have acted differently; No one can take your *place*; a *place* in a firm. **14** *n.* Right or duty: It isn't our *place* to discipline him. **15** *n.* The right or proper position, location, or time: This is no *place* for laughter. **16** *v.* To think of in relation to a place, time, or set of circumstances; identify: I've seen him before, but I can't *place* him. **— give place 1** To make room. **2** To give in or surrender. **— go places** *slang* To advance toward or achieve success. **— in place 1** In its natural or proper place. **2** Right or suitable. **— in place of** Instead of. **— out of place 1** Not in its right or proper place. **2** Not suitable; inappropriate. **— take place** To happen; occur. ◆ *Place, piazza,* and *plaza* all go back to the Latin word *platea,* meaning *a wide street,* but they came into English by way of French, Italian, and Spanish, respectively. *Place* has many other meanings, but it is often used in names to mean an open area, square, or small street: Park *Place*. *Piazza* is usually used of such open areas in Italy, where they abound. Elsewhere, *plaza* is preferred: Rockefeller *Plaza*.

place kick In football, a kick for a goal in which the ball is placed on the ground for kicking.

place·ment [plās′mənt] *n.* **1** The act or an instance of placing. **2** A place kick. **3** The placing of people in jobs, schools, etc.

pla·cen·ta [plə·sen′tə] *n.* In women and most female mammals, a broad, flat, spongy organ by which a fetus in the uterus is nourished and its wastes are removed.

plac·er [plas′ər] *n.* A deposit of sand, gravel, etc., containing gold or other valuable minerals in particles large enough to be washed out.

plac·id [plas′id] *adj.* Calm; peaceful. **— pla·cid·i·ty** [plə·sid′ə·tē] *n.* **— plac′id·ly** *adv.*

plack·et [plak′it] *n.* An opening in a garment, as a skirt, that makes the garment easy to put on. It is usually closed by a zipper.

pla·gia·rism [plā′jə·riz′əm] *n.* The act of plagiarizing. **— pla′gia·rist** *n.*

pla·gia·rize [plā′jə·rīz] *v.* **pla·gia·rized, pla·gia·riz·ing** To steal and pass off as one's own (the writings, ideas, etc., of someone else).

plague [plāg] *n.*, *v.* **plagued, pla·guing 1** *n.* A very contagious, often fatal, disease that spreads rapidly over a large area, as the bubonic plague. **2** *n.* Anything troublesome or distressing. **3** *v.* To trouble, torment, or annoy: to *plague* someone with silly questions.

plaid [plad] **1** *n.* A cloth having horizontal and vertical stripes of various widths and colors crossing each other to form distinctive patterns. **2** *n.* A long, woolen scarf having this pattern, worn in the Scottish Highlands as a cloak over one shoulder. **3** *adj.* Having this pattern. ◆ *Plaid* comes from a Scottish Gaelic word meaning *a blanket.*

Plaid

plain [plān] **1** *adj.* Not obstructed; open; clear: in *plain* sight. **2** *adj.* Easy to understand; clear; obvious: a *plain* statement. **3** *adj.* Not complicated; simple. **4** *adj.* Straightforward; frank: *plain* speaking. **5** *adv.* In a plain manner. **6** *adj.* Not highly educated or sophisticated; ordinary: *plain* folks. **7** *adj.* Not rich, luxurious, or fancy: *plain* food. **8** *adj.* Not decorated or figured: *plain* cloth. **9** *adj.* Not pretty or handsome. **10** *n.* An expanse of almost level, nearly treeless land; prairie. **11** *adj.* Level. **— plain′ly** *adv.* **— plain′ness** *n.*

plain-spo·ken [plān′spō′kən] *adj.* Frank.

plaint [plānt] *n.* A lament or complaint.

plain·tiff [plān′tif] *n.* The person who brings a lawsuit against another called the defendant.

plain·tive [plān′tiv] *adj.* Expressing sadness; mournful; melancholy: **— plain′tive·ly** *adv.*

plait [plat *or* plāt] **1** *n.* A braid, as of hair. **2** *v.* To braid. **3** *n.* A pleat. **4** *v.* To pleat.

plan [plan] *n.*, *v.* **planned, plan·ning 1** *n.* A scheme, method, or design for attaining some object or goal. **2** *v.* To form a scheme or method for doing or achieving (something): to *plan* an

attack. **3** *v.* To intend: I *plan* to leave at noon.
4 *n.* (*pl.*) Intentions or arrangements worked out
in advance: holiday *plans.* **5** *v.* To make plans.
6 *n.* A drawing showing how the parts or sections
of something are arranged: the *plan* of a building.
7 *v.* To make a design or drawing of: to *plan* a
seating arrangement.

plane[1] [plān] **1** *n.* In mathematics, a surface
that includes all the points of a line that connects any two points in it. **2** *adj.* Level; flat.
3 *n.* Any flat surface. **4** *adj.* Dealing only with
flat surfaces: *plane* geometry. **5** *n.* A level or
stage of existence or development: to talk on an
intellectual *plane.* **6** *n.* An airplane.

plane[2] [plān] *n., v.* **planed, plan·ing** **1** *n.* A
tool used for smooth-
ing boards or other
surfaces of wood. **2** *v.*
To make smooth or
even with a plane.
3 *v.* To remove with
or as if with a plane.

plan·et [plan′it] *n.*
Any of the bodies that
move in orbits around
the sun, with the ex-
ception of comets and
meteors. The princi-
pal planets are Mer-

Plane

cury, Venus, Earth, Mars, Jupiter, Saturn, Ura-
nus, Neptune, and Pluto.

plan·e·tar·i·um [plan′ə·târ′ē·əm] *n., pl.* **plan·
e·tar·i·ums** or **plan·e·tar·i·a** [plan′ə·târ′ē·ə]
1 A room or building having an apparatus that
shows on a domed ceiling the stars and other
celestial bodies as they appear or appeared at
any time and from any place on earth. **2** Such
an apparatus.

plan·e·tar·y [plan′ə·ter′ē] *adj.* Of or having to
do with a planet or planets.

plan·et·oid [plan′ə·toid] *n.* An asteroid.

plane tree Any of various large, spreading trees
with broad leaves, as the sycamore.

plank [plangk] **1** *n.* A broad piece of sawed
timber, thicker than a board. **2** *v.* To cover with
planks: to *plank* a floor. **3** *v.* To broil or bake
and serve on a board or plank: to *plank* fish.
4 *n.* One of the principles, ideals, or aims stated
in a political platform. — **plank down** *informal* **1** To put down with force or emphasis. **2** To
pay. — **walk the plank** To walk off a plank
projecting from the side of a ship and die by
drowning: The pirates forced their prisoners to
walk the plank.

plank·ton [plangk′tən] *n.* Marine and fresh-
water plants and animals that cannot swim but
only float or drift in the water. They range in
size from microorganisms to jellyfish.

plan·ner [plan′ər] *n.* A person who plans.

plant [plant] **1** *n.* A living organism that is
not an animal. A plant lacks a nervous system
and cannot move from place to place by itself.
Plants containing chlorophyll are able to make
their own food by photosynthesis. Vegetables,
herbs, trees, fungi, and algae all are plants. **2** *n.*
One of the smaller forms of vegetable life, as
distinguished from shrubs and trees: a potted
plant. **3** *v.* To set in the ground to grow: to
plant seeds. **4** *v.* To furnish with plants or
seed: to *plant* a field. **5** *v.* To deposit (fish or
spawn) in a body of water. **6** *v.* To set or fix
firmly: The climber *planted* his pick in the
ground. **7** *v.* To introduce into the mind; instill:
to *plant* an idea. **8** *v.* To found; establish. **9** *n.*
The machinery, appliances, equipment, and,
often, the buildings and grounds used in operating a business or institution. **10** *n.* A factory.

plan·tain[1] [plan′tin] *n.* A common weed with
large leaves and long spikes of tiny flowers.

plan·tain[2] [plan′tin] *n.* **1** A tropical herb sometimes growing to a height of 30 feet. **2** Its
bananalike fruit, edible when cooked.

plan·ta·tion [plan·tā′shən] *n.* **1** A farm or
estate of many acres having a crop of cotton,
tobacco, rice, etc., planted and tended by laborers who live there. **2** A grove of plants or trees
grown to provide a certain product: a rubber
plantation. **3** A colony, as of new settlers in a
country.

plant·er [plan′tər] *n.* **1** A person or an implement that plants. **2** An owner of a plantation.
3 An early settler. **4** An attractive container in
which plants are grown for decoration.

plaque [plak] *n.* A flat piece of metal, wood,
porcelain, ivory, etc., having designs or lettering
on one side. Plaques may be hung up as ornaments, used as memorial tablets, etc.

plash [plash] **1** *v.* To splash. **2** *n.* A splash.

plas·ma [plaz′mə] *n.* The liquid part of blood,
without the blood corpuscles.

plas·ter [plas′tər] **1** *n.* A mixture of lime, sand,
and water for coating walls, ceilings, and partitions. It hardens as it dries. **2** *v.* To cover with
or as if with plaster: to *plaster* a ceiling; clothes
plastered with mud. **3** *v.* To apply like plaster:
to *plaster* posters on a fence. **4** *n.* A sticky substance spread on cloth and applied to some part
of the body for healing: a mustard *plaster.* **5** *v.*
To lay flat: to *plaster* down a cowlick. **6** *n.*
Plaster of Paris. — **plas′ter·er** *n.*

plaster of Paris Powdered gypsum mixed
with water to form a paste used for making casts,
molds, bandages, and ornamental objects.

plas·tic [plas′tik] **1** *adj.* Capable of being
molded: Clay and wax are *plastic.* **2** *n.* Any of a
class of various materials chemically made and
capable of being molded, cast, woven, etc., into
many products. Cellophane is a plastic. **3** *adj.*
Made of plastic: a *plastic* toy. **4** *adj.* Giving
form or shape to matter: *plastic* art.

add, āce, câre, pälm;   end, ēqual;   it, īce;   odd, ōpen, ôrder;   took, pool;   up, bûrn;
ə = a in *above,* e in *sicken,* i in *possible,* o in *melon,* u in *circus;*   yoo = u in *fuse;*   oil;   pout;
check;   ring;   thin;   this;   zh in *vision.*   For ¶ reference, see page 64 · HOW TO

plas·tic·i·ty [plas·tis′ə·tē] *n.* The quality or condition of being plastic or easily molded.

plas·ti·cize [plas′tə·sīz] *v.* **plas·ti·cized, plas·ti·ciz·ing** To make or become plastic. ¶3

plastic surgery Surgery in which lost, wounded, or deformed parts of the body are restored or repaired, as by grafts of skin or bone.

plate [plāt] *n., v.* **plat·ed, plat·ing 1** *n.* A shallow dish used to hold food at the table. **2** *n.* The food served on a plate. **3** *n.* An individual meal: a benefit dinner at $25 a *plate.* **4** *n.* A dish like a table plate used in taking up collections. **5** *n.* A thin, flat piece or a sheet of metal, glass, etc. **6** *v.* To cover with metal plates for protection: to *plate* the side of a ship. **7** *v.* To coat with a thin layer of gold, silver, etc. **8** *n.* Household articles, as serving dishes, utensils, etc., made of or coated with gold or silver. **9** *n.* A piece of flat metal bearing a design or inscription, especially one that is engraved or embossed. **10** *n.* A reproduction made from a plate of this kind. **11** *n.* A full-page book illustration printed on special paper. **12** *n.* A metal reproduction of a page of type, for printing. **13** *n.* A sheet of glass, metal, etc., that is coated with a material sensitive to light, used for taking photographs. **14** *n.* A set of false teeth. **15** *n.* In baseball, home base. — **plate′ful** *n.*

pla·teau [pla·tō′] *n.* **1** A broad stretch of high, level land; a high plain. **2** A time when change or progress stops temporarily: a *plateau* in the city's growth.

plate glass Glass in clear, thick sheets, suitable for mirrors, display windows, etc.

plate·let [plāt′lit] *n.* One of the tiny circular or oval bodies present in blood and necessary for the clotting of blood.

plat·form [plat′fôrm] *n.* **1** A raised flat surface or floor: a *platform* for a speaker; a *platform* by the track in a station. **2** A set or statement of principles, ideals, or aims put forth by a political party or other group.

plat·ing [plā′ting] *n.* **1** A layer or coating of metal: silver *plating.* **2** A coating of metal plates, as of armor.

plat·i·num [plat′ə·nəm] *n.* A heavy, gray, metallic element that does not tarnish, is very resistant to chemicals, and can be easily worked into many shapes. It is used in industry and science, and in making jewelry.

plat·i·tude [plat′ə·t(y)ood] *n.* A flat, dull, or commonplace statement, such as "You get what you pay for."

Pla·to [plā′tō] *n.,* 427?–347? B.C., Greek philosopher.

Pla·ton·ic [plə·ton′ik] *adj.* **1** Of, having to do with, or like Plato or his philosophy. **2** (*usually written* **platonic**) Friendly but without passion: *platonic* love.

pla·toon [plə·toon′] *n.* **1** A subdivision of a company, troop, or other military unit, commanded by a lieutenant. **2** Any similar group.

plat·ter [plat′ər] *n.* A shallow, oblong dish on which meat or fish is served.

plat·y·pus [plat′ə·pəs] *n., pl.* **plat·y·pus·es** or **plat·y·pi** [plat′ə·pī] A small, egg-laying water mammal of Australia, having a ducklike bill, webbed feet, and a broad, flat tail.

Platypus, about 20 in. long

plau·dit [plô′dit] *n.* (*usually pl.*) An expression of approval or praise, as by cheering, applauding, etc.

plau·si·ble [plô′zə·bəl] *adj.* Seeming reasonable on the surface and appearing worthy to be believed or trusted, yet possibly deceiving: a *plausible* story; a *plausible* liar. — **plau·si·bil·i·ty** [plô′zə·bil′ə·tē] *n.* — **plau′si·bly** *adv.*

play [plā] **1** *v.* To have fun; amuse oneself: to *play* on the beach. **2** *n.* Some act or recreation done for fun and amusement: an hour for *play.* **3** *v.* To pretend: Let's *play* that we're cowboys. **4** *v.* To do or perform for fun: to *play* a trick. **5** *n.* Fun; jest: to say something in *play.* **6** *v.* To engage in (a sport, game, etc.): to *play* tennis. **7** *v.* To oppose in a game or contest: We *played* their best team. **8** *n.* The act of playing: *Play* will continue later. **9** *n.* A move, maneuver, or turn in a game: a winning *play;* It's his *play.* **10** *v.* To bet on: to *play* the horses. **11** *n.* Gambling: to lose at *play.* **12** *v.* To act or behave carelessly, lightly, or insincerely; trifle: to *play* with another's affections. **13** *v.* To act or behave: *Play* fair. **14** *n.* Manner of acting toward or dealing with others: fair *play.* **15** *n.* A story or drama written to be acted on a stage, on television, etc. **16** *v.* To act the part of: to *play* a witch. **17** *v.* To perform or be performed: to *play* a part; What is *playing* at that theater? **18** *v.* In music, to perform or perform on: to *play* a piano sonata; to *play* the piano. **19** *v.* To give forth sound or music: The radio is *playing.* **20** *v.* To move or cause to move quickly, continuously, or irregularly: Shadows were *playing* over the path; They *played* a searchlight over the prison wall. **21** *n.* Light, quick, or easy movement: the *play* of moonbeams. **22** *n.* Freedom or looseness of movement, activity, etc.: The storyteller gave his imagination full *play;* That control stick has too much *play* in it. **23** *n.* Active operation: He brought all his skill into *play.* **24** *v.* To bring about; cause: to *play* havoc. — **a play on words** A pun. — **play down** To treat as being of little importance. — **played out 1** Exhausted. **2** Finished. — **play into someone's hands** To act or respond in a way that gives someone else an advantage over one. — **play off 1** To oppose one against another, as in a rivalry. **2** To decide (a tie) by playing one more game. — **play on** or **play upon** To take unfair advantage of (another's feelings, hopes, etc.) in order to get something: to *play on* one's sympathy. — **play up** *informal* To emphasize. — **play up to** *informal* To try to win the favor of by flattery.

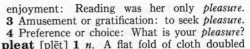

play·bill [plā′bil′] *n.* **1** A bill or poster advertising a play. **2** A program of a play.

play·er [plā′ər] *n.* **1** A person who takes part in a game. **2** A person who plays a musical instrument: a horn *player*. **3** An actor or actress.

play·fel·low [plā′fel′ō] *n.* A playmate.

play·ful [plā′fəl] *adj.* **1** Full of high spirits; fond of playing; frolicsome: a *playful* puppy. **2** Humorous; joking: a *playful* remark. — **play′ful·ly** *adv.* — **play′ful·ness** *n.*

play·ground [plā′ground′] *n.* An area, often next to a school, for children to play in.

play·house [plā′hous′] *n.* **1** A theater. **2** A small house for children to play with or in.

playing card One card of a pack used in playing various games. A pack usually consists of 52 cards divided into four suits (spades, hearts, diamonds, and clubs) of 13 cards each.

Playing cards

play·mate [plā′māt′] *n.* A companion in play.

play·off [plā′ôf′] *n.* An additional game or contest played in order to break a tie.

play·thing [plā′thing′] *n.* A toy.

play·wright [plā′rīt′] *n.* A writer of plays.

pla·za [plä′zə *or* plaz′ə] *n.* An open square or market place in a town or city. ◆See PLACE.

plea [plē] *n.* **1** An appeal or request: a *plea* for aid. **2** An excuse: His *plea* was that he didn't hear the bell. **3** In law, a statement made by or for a defendant concerning a charge against him: He made a *plea* of not guilty.

plead [plēd] *v.* **plead·ed** or **pled, plead·ing** **1** To ask earnestly; beg: to *plead* for help. **2** To argue in a court of law: to *plead* a case. **3** To make a plea of: to *plead* guilty. **4** To give as an excuse or defense: to *plead* insanity.

pleas·ant [plez′ənt] *adj.* **1** Giving pleasure; pleasing. **2** Agreeable or friendly in manner, appearance, etc.: a *pleasant* look. — **pleas′ant·ly** *adv.* — **pleas′ant·ness** *n.*

pleas·an·try [plez′ən·trē] *n., pl.* **pleas·an·tries** A good-natured remark or joke.

please [plēz] *v.* **pleased, pleas·ing** **1** To give pleasure to or satisfy: Your work *pleases* me; A good book always *pleases*. **2** To be so kind as to: usually used when requesting something: *Please* pass the bread. **3** To wish, desire, or prefer: Go where you *please*. **4** To be the will or wish of: May it *please* your Honor.

pleas·ing [plē′zing] *adj.* Pleasant; agreeable.

pleas·ur·a·ble [plezh′ər·ə·bəl] *adj.* Pleasant.

pleas·ure [plezh′ər] *n.* **1** A feeling of enjoyment, delight, or satisfaction: Dancing gives me *pleasure*. **2** A thing that pleases; source of enjoyment: Reading was her only *pleasure*. **3** Amusement or gratification: to seek *pleasure*. **4** Preference or choice: What is your *pleasure*?

pleat [plēt] **1** *n.* A flat fold of cloth doubled on itself and pressed or sewn in place. **2** *v.* To make pleats in. **3** *adj. use: pleated* skirts.

ple·be·ian [pli·bē′ən] **1** *n.* One of the common people, especially of ancient Rome. **2** *n.* A person who is coarse or vulgar. **3** *adj.* Of, like, or having to do with plebeians.

pleb·i·scite [pleb′ə·sīt] *n.* A vote by all the voters of a state or nation concerning some important question, as a change in a constitution.

Pleated skirt

plec·trum [plek′trəm] *n., pl.* **plec·trums** or **plec·tra** [plek′trə] A small object used for plucking the strings of a guitar, mandolin, etc.

pled [pled] Alternative past tense and past participle of PLEAD.

pledge [plej] *n., v.* **pledged, pledg·ing** **1** *n.* A formal or solemn promise: a *pledge* of loyalty. **2** *v.* To bind by a solemn promise. **3** *v.* To promise to give: to *pledge* money for the new tennis courts. **4** *n.* Something that is pledged in this way: a *pledge* of $100.00. **5** *n.* Something given or held as security for a debt. **6** *v.* To give or offer as security for a debt; pawn. **7** *n.* The condition of being held as security for a debt: The guitar is in *pledge*. **8** *n.* The drinking of a toast to one's health, etc. **9** *v.* To drink a toast to: He *pledged* the king's health.

Plei·a·des [plē′ə·dēz] *n.pl.* **1** A cluster of stars, including six which are visible to the naked eye. **2** In Greek myths, the seven daughters of Atlas, set among the stars by Zeus.

ple·na·ry [plē′nə·rē *or* plen′ə·rē] *adj.* **1** Full in all respects; complete; entire. **2** Attended by everyone who has a right to be there.

plen·i·po·ten·ti·a·ry [plen′i·pə·ten′shē·er′ē] *n., pl.* **plen·i·po·ten·ti·ar·ies,** *adj.* **1** *n.* A person having full power to represent a government, as an ambassador, minister, etc. **2** *adj.* Having or giving full power.

plen·i·tude [plen′ə·t(y)ood] *n.* The condition of being full or abundant; fullness.

plen·te·ous [plen′tē·əs] *adj.* Plentiful.

plen·ti·ful [plen′ti·fəl] *adj.* **1** Existing in great quantity; more than enough. **2** Giving or containing plenty. — **plen′ti·ful·ly** *adv.*

plen·ty [plen′tē] *n.* As much as could be needed; an abundance: I have *plenty* of food.

pleth·o·ra [pleth′ər·ə] *n.* Too great an amount; excess; superfluity.

pleu·ri·sy [ploor′ə·sē] *n.* Inflammation of the membrane that covers the lungs and lines the

plexus [plek′səs] *n., pl.* **plex·us·es** or **plex·us** A network of cordlike structures, as blood vessels or nerves.

pli·a·ble [plī′ə·bəl] *adj.* **1** Easily bent, twisted, or molded. **2** Easily persuaded or controlled. **— pli·a·bil·i·ty** [plī′ə·bil′ə·tē] *n.*

pli·an·cy [plī′ən·sē] *n.* The condition or quality of being pliant; pliability.

pli·ant [plī′ənt] *adj.* **1** Easy to bend, twist, or mold. **2** Easy to influence; compliant.

pli·ers [plī′ərz] *n.pl.* Small pincers for bending, holding, or cutting things.

plight[1] [plīt] *n.* A condition or situation, usually bad.

plight[2] [plīt] *v.* To promise solemnly; pledge. **— plight one's troth** To promise to marry.

Pliers

plinth [plinth] *n.* The slab, block, or stone on which a column, pedestal, or statue rests.

plod [plod] *v.* **plod·ded, plod·ding 1** To walk heavily or with great effort; trudge. **2** To work in a dull, laborious way; drudge. **— plod′der** *n.*

plot [plot] *n., v.* **plot·ted, plot·ting 1** *n.* A small piece of ground: a *plot* for vegetables. **2** *n.* A chart, diagram, or map. **3** *v.* To make a map, chart, or plan of, as a ship's course. **4** *n.* A secret plan to do some usually evil or unlawful thing. **5** *v.* To plan in secret; scheme: to *plot* someone's downfall. **6** *n.* The plan of events in a play, novel, etc. **— plot′ter** *n.*

plough [plou] *n., v.* Another spelling of PLOW.

plov·er [pluv′ər *or* plō′vər] *n.* A bird that lives on the shore, having long pointed wings and a short tail.

plow [plou] **1** *n.* A large tool used for breaking up or turning over the soil in preparation for planting. **2** *n.* Something that operates like this, as a machine for moving snow. **3** *v.* To break up and turn over the soil of with a plow; furrow: to *plow* a field. **4** *v.* To use a plow. **5** *v.* To move as a plow; force a passage: The bullet *plowed* through his shoulder.

Plow

plow·man [plou′mən] *n., pl.* **plow·men** [plou′mən] **1** A man who uses a plow. **2** A farmer.

plow·share [plou′shâr′] *n.* The blade or part of a plow that cuts a furrow in the soil.

pluck [pluk] **1** *v.* To pull off or out; pick: to *pluck* a flower. **2** *v.* To pull with force; snatch; drag: to *pluck* a sword from its sheath. **3** *v.* To pull the feathers from: to *pluck* a chicken. **4** *v.* To quickly pull and release (the strings of a musical instrument). **5** *n.* A quick or sudden pull. **6** *n.* Courage or nerve. **— pluck up** To rouse or summon, as one's courage.

pluck·y [pluk′ē] *adj.* **pluck·i·er, pluck·i·est** Brave; courageous. **— pluck′i·ly** *adv.*

plug [plug] *n., v.* **plugged, plug·ging 1** *n.* A piece of rubber, cork, etc., used to stop a hole. **2** *v.* To stop or close; put a plug into. **3** *n.* A device with two prongs, at the end of an electric cord, used to connect a lamp, radio, appliance, etc., to a power line or circuit. **4** *n.* A fireplug. **5** *n.* A flat cake of pressed tobacco for chewing. **6** *n. informal* An old, worn-out horse. **7** *n. slang* A favorable mention or piece of publicity. **8** *v. slang* To mention favorably; publicize. **9** *v. informal* To work doggedly; plod. **10** *v. slang* To shoot a bullet into. **— plug in** To connect (a lamp, radio, etc.) by inserting the plug in an outlet.

plum [plum] **1** *n.* A fruit having a smooth skin, juicy pulp, and a smooth pit. **2** *n.* A tree that bears this fruit. **3** *n.* A raisin, especially as used in cooking. **4** *n., adj.* Dark, reddish purple. **5** *n.* Something desirable or greatly prized: His appointment as college president is a *plum.*

plum·age [ploō′mij] *n.* The feathers of a bird.

plumb [plum] **1** *n.* A weight hung on the end of a cord, used to see if a wall is vertical, test the depth of water, etc. **2** *v.* To test for depth, position, etc., with a plumb. **3** *v.* To investigate fully; get to the bottom of: to *plumb* a mystery. **4** *adj.* Exactly vertical: a *plumb* post. **5** *adv.* Straight down or straight up and down; vertically: The apple fell *plumb* to earth. **6** *adv. informal* Completely; entirely: She's *plumb* stupid. **— out of plumb** or **off plumb** Not truly vertical.

plumb·er [plum′ər] *n.* A person whose business is installing or repairing plumbing.

plumb·ing [plum′ing] *n.* **1** The systems of gas pipes and fixtures and water pipes and fixtures in a building. **2** The work or technique of installing and repairing such systems.

plumb line A cord with a weight attached to one end, used to establish a true vertical line.

plume [ploōm] *n., v.* **plumed, plum·ing 1** *n.* A feather, especially if long and ornamental. **2** *n.* A large feather or group of feathers used as an ornament, as on a helmet or hat. **3** *v.* To decorate, dress, or furnish with plumes. **4** *v.* To smooth (itself or its feathers), as a bird. **5** *v.* To congratulate or take pride in (oneself): He *plumed* himself on his cleverness.

Plumes

plum·met [plum′it] **1** *n.* A plumb. **2** *v.* To fall straight down; plunge.

plump[1] [plump] **1** *adj.* Slightly fat or rounded. **2** *v.* To make or become plump. **— plump′ness** *n.*

plump² [plump] **1** *v.* To fall or let fall suddenly or heavily: The big dog *plumped* before the fire; He *plumped* the box of groceries on the kitchen table. **2** *n.* The action or sound of plumping or falling: He hit the floor with a *plump*. **3** *adv.* Suddenly or heavily: He fell *plump* on the bed. **4** *adj.* Direct; blunt; downright: a *plump* refusal. **— plump for** To give full support to: The newspapers *plumped for* the mayor.

plum pudding A boiled pudding made with flour, suet, raisins, currants, spices, etc.

plun·der [plun′dər] **1** *v.* To rob of goods or property by force; loot: The enemy *plundered* the village. **2** *n.* Goods taken by force. **3** *n.* The act of plundering. **— plun′der·er** *n.*

plunge [plunj] *v.* **plunged, plung·ing,** *n.* **1** *v.* To thrust or force suddenly: He *plunged* his hand into the bag; to *plunge* one's family into poverty. **2** *v.* To jump, dive, or fall, as into water, a chasm, etc. **3** *n.* A jump, dive, or fall, especially into water. **4** *v.* To move suddenly or with a rush: to *plunge* into action. **5** *v.* To toss violently, as a ship or aircraft. **6** *v. informal* To gamble wildly. **7** *n. informal* A gamble or bet. **8** *n.* A short swim.

plung·er [plun′jər] *n.* **1** A person that plunges. **2** A device or machine that works with an up-and-down motion, as a piston.

plunk [plungk] **1** *v.* To fall or let fall heavily: The ball *plunked* into the lake; He *plunked* the money on the table. **2** *v.* To pluck, as the strings of a musical instrument. **3** *v.* To make a sound like a plucked string. **4** *n.* The act of plunking. **5** *n.* The sound made by plunking.

plu·ral [ploor′əl] **1** *adj.* Being or indicating more than one: a *plural* noun. **2** *n.* The form that a word takes when it indicates more than one: "Men" is the *plural* of "man." ◆ The plurals of most nouns are formed by adding *s* to the singular: boy-boy*s*; pocket-pocket*s*; tire-tire*s*. Nouns that end in *y* following a consonant or *qu* become plural by changing the *y* to *i* and adding *es*: cry-cr*ies*; soliloquy-soliloqu*ies*. Nouns ending in *ss, sh, ch, s, x,* and *zz* usually form their plurals by adding *es*: class-class*es*; dish-dish*es*; crutch-crutch*es*; gas-gas*es*; box-box*es*; buzz-buzz*es*. Many plurals, such as *men, moose, crises,* and *data* are formed irregularly.

plu·ral·i·ty [ploo·ral′ə·tē] *n., pl.* **plu·ral·i·ties 1** The number of votes by which the winner of an election defeats his nearest rival. **2** The greater portion or number. **3** A large number, as of persons or things; multitude. **4** The condition of being plural.

plus [plus] **1** *prep.* Added to: Three *plus* two equals five. **2** *prep.* Increased by: salary *plus* commission. **3** *n.* A plus sign. **4** *adj.* Indicating addition. **5** *adj.* Extra; additional: There were many *plus* values. **6** *adj.* Greater than zero, positive. **7** *adj.* And a little more: a grade of B *plus*.

plus sign A symbol (+) indicating addition or a positive quantity.

plush [plush] *n.* A cloth something like velvet but having a deeper pile.

Plu·to [ploo′tō] *n.* **1** In Greek and Roman myths, the god of the dead. **2** A planet of the solar system that is about 3600 miles in diameter and ninth in distance from the sun.

plu·to·crat [ploo′tə·krat] *n.* **1** A member of a class or group that has power and influence because of its wealth. **2** Any wealthy person.

plu·to·ni·um [ploo·tō′nē·əm] *n.* An artificially made radioactive metallic element that is important in the generation of nuclear energy.

ply¹ [plī] *n., pl.* **plies 1** A layer or thickness, as of cloth, wood, etc. **2** A strand of rope, yarn, thread, etc.: three-*ply* yarn.

ply² [plī] *v.* **plied, ply·ing 1** To use, as in working, fighting, etc.: to *ply* an axe. **2** To work at; be engaged in: to *ply* a trade. **3** To supply with or offer repeatedly to: to *ply* a person with food. **4** To address (a person) over and over again with questions, demands, etc. **5** To make regular trips: Delivery trucks *ply* between New York and its suburbs.

Plym·outh [plim′əth] *n.* **1** A town in eastern Massachusetts where the Pilgrims settled in 1620. **2** A seaport in sw England.

Plymouth Rock 1 A rock at Plymouth, Massachusetts, on which the Pilgrims are said to have landed. **2** One of a breed of domestic chickens.

ply·wood [plī′wood′] *n.* A kind of board made of thin layers of wood glued together.

P.M. or **p.m. 1** After noon. **2** The period from noon to midnight. ◆ *P.M.* is an abbreviation of *post meridiem*, a Latin phrase meaning *after noon*.

pneu·mat·ic [n(y)oo·mat′ik] *adj.* **1** Operated by compressed air: a *pneumatic* drill. **2** Filled with compressed air: a *pneumatic* tire. **3** Having to do with air or other gases.

pneu·mo·nia [n(y)oo·mōn′yə] *n.* A disease caused by bacterial or virus infection and marked by inflammation of one or both lungs.

Po [pō] *n.* A river in northern Italy, flowing into the Adriatic Sea.

P.O. Abbreviation of POST OFFICE.

poach¹ [pōch] *v.* To cook in simmering water, milk, or other liquid, as eggs, fish, etc.

poach² [pōch] *v.* **1** To trespass on another's property, especially to hunt or fish. **2** To hunt or fish unlawfully. **— poach′er** *n.*

Po·ca·hon·tas [pō′kə·hon′təs] *n.,* 1595?–1617, American Indian princess. She is said to have saved Captain John Smith from death.

pock [pok] *n.* **1** An eruption of the skin caused by smallpox or a similar disease. **2** A pockmark.

pock·et [pok′it] **1** *n.* A small pouch sewn into a garment, for carrying money or small objects. **2** *v.* To put into a pocket: He *pocketed* his harmonica. **3** *adj.* Having to do with, for, or carried in a pocket: a *pocket* watch. **4** *adj.* Small: a *pocket* book. **5** *n.* A hole or container for something to go into: the *pockets* of a pool table. **6** *v.* To enclose; shut in; hem in. **7** *v.* To take for one's own, especially dishonestly: to *pocket* company funds. **8** *v.* To accept without anger or reply, as an insult. **9** *v.* To conceal or suppress: to *pocket* one's pride. **10** *n.* A sudden downward air current; air pocket.

pock·et·book [pok′it·bŏŏk′] *n.* **1** A small case for carrying money and papers in the pocket; wallet. **2** A woman's purse or handbag.

pock·et·ful [pok′it·fŏŏl′] *n.*, *pl.* **pock·et·fuls** As much as a pocket will hold.

pock·et·knife [pok′it·nīf′] *n.*, *pl.* **pock·et· knives** A small knife having one or more blades that fold into the handle.

pocket veto *U.S.* A method by which the President or a governor can kill without vetoing a bill sent to him late in a legislative session. He keeps it, unsigned, until the session ends.

pock·mark [pok′märk′] *n.* A pit or scar left on the skin by smallpox or a similar disease.

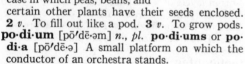

Pocketknife

pod [pod] *n.*, *v.* **pod·ded, pod·ding 1** *n.* The shell or case in which peas, beans, and certain other plants have their seeds enclosed. **2** *v.* To fill out like a pod. **3** *v.* To grow pods.

po·di·um [pō′dē·əm] *n.*, *pl.* **po·di·ums** or **po· di·a** [pō′dē·ə] A small platform on which the conductor of an orchestra stands.

Poe [pō], **Edgar Allan,** 1809–1849, U.S. poet, critic, and short-story writer.

po·em [pō′əm] *n.* A composition in verse and often also in rhyme. The language is used in a very imaginative way to express intense thoughts and feelings and vivid images.

po·e·sy [pō′ə·sē *or* pō′ə·zē] *n.* Poetry.

po·et [pō′it] *n.* A person who writes poetry.

po·et·ess [pō′it·is] *n.* A woman poet. ◆ This word is seldom used. Most women who write poetry prefer to be called poets.

po·et·ic [pō·et′ik] *adj.* **1** Of, like, relating to, or suitable for poetry or poets. **2** Imaginatively beautiful. — **po·et′i·cal·ly** *adv.*

po·et·i·cal [pō·et′i·kəl] *adj.* Poetic.

poetic justice The ideal rewarding of virtue and punishment of evil as often found in plays, stories, and poems.

poet laureate *pl.* **poets laureate** In Great Britain, a poet appointed for life by the king or queen to be official poet of the kingdom.

po·et·ry [pō′it·rē] *n.* **1** The art of writing poems. **2** Poems collectively. **3** The quality or feeling in a poem or in something poetic.

poign·an·cy [poin′(y)ən·sē] *n.* The quality of being poignant.

poign·ant [poin′(y)ənt] *adj.* **1** Keenly felt; painfully affecting: *poignant* grief. **2** Affecting the feelings; touching; moving: a *poignant* scene in a play. **3** Cutting through to the truth; sharp and penetrating: *poignant* criticism; a *poignant* description of life in the slums. — **poign′ant·ly** *adv.*

poin·set·ti·a [poin·set′(ē·)ə] *n.* A tropical American plant having small yellow flowers and red leaves that resemble petals.

point [point] **1** *n.* The sharp or tapered end of something: the *point* of a needle; the *point* of the chin. **2** *v.* To shape or sharpen to a point: to *point* a pencil. **3** *n.* In printing or writing, a dot: a decimal *point*. **4** *n.* A punctuation mark, especially a period. **5** *v.* To mark with punctuation, decimal points, etc.: to *point* a sentence; to *point* off a decimal fraction. **6** *n.* A particular spot or place; location. **7** *n.* In mathematics, an exact location in space, as the place where two lines cross. **8** *n.* One of the 32 equally spaced divisions shown on a compass card. **9** *v.* To direct or aim, as a finger or weapon. **10** *v.* To indicate or direct attention to: to *point* the way; to *point* out errors. **11** *v.* To call attention or indicate direction with or as if with the finger: to *point* at a map; to *point* up the road. **12** *v.* To show the location of game by standing and aiming the body, as a hunting dog. **13** *v.* To be headed or directed: The car *pointed* east; The indicator *points* to 100. **14** *n.* A particular moment or time: At that *point*, we went home. **15** *n.* A particular degree or condition reached: the *point* of exhaustion; the boiling *point*. **16** *n.* A narrow piece of land extending into water; cape. **17** *n.* Purpose or advantage: What is the *point* of that? **18** *n.* A unit of measuring, counting, scoring, etc.: A touchdown equals six *points*. **19** *n.* The main idea; gist: the *point* of a joke. **20** *n.* A prominent feature, quality, or attribute: She has her good *points*. **21** *v.* To give force or emphasis to: to *point* up the logic of an argument. **22** *n.* A single item; detail: to explain something *point* by *point*. — **at the point of** Very near to. — **beside the point** Off the subject; immaterial. — **in point** Related to the matter at hand; pertinent. — **make a point of** To treat as very important. — **on the point of** Almost in the act or condition of. — **point out** To draw attention to; indicate. — **stretch a point** To make an exception. — **to the point** Related to the matter at hand: His answer was short and *to the point*.

point-blank [point′blangk′] **1** *adj.* Aimed directly at a target without allowing for the effect of gravity, as a pistol. **2** *adj.* Close enough to allow this kind of aim: *point-blank* range. **3** *adv.* In a straight line or from close range. **4** *adj.* Direct; plain: a *point-blank* refusal. **5** *adv.* Directly; plainly: to refuse *point-blank*.

point·ed [poin′tid] *adj.* **1** Having a point or points. **2** Sharp and cutting, as a remark. **3** Clearly noticeable; emphatic. **4** Directed or aimed, as at a person. — **point′ed·ly** *adv.*

point·er [poin′tər] *n.* **1** A hand, finger, or other indicator, as on a clock or meter. **2** A slender rod used to point out things on maps, charts, etc. **3** A smooth-haired dog trained to scent and point out game. **4** *informal* A useful bit of information; hint; tip.

Typical pointer

point·less [point′lis] *adj.* **1** Having no point; blunt. **2** Having no meaning or purpose. **3** Having no effect. **— point′·less·ly** *adv.*

point of view *pl.* **points of view 1** The position from which a person looks at or considers an object, situation, etc.: an unusual *point of view*. **2** An attitude or viewpoint.

poise [poiz] *v.* **poised, pois·ing,** *n.* **1** *v.* To balance or hold in balance: The cat *poised* itself on its hind legs; The sword was *poised* in his hand. **2** *n.* Balance or equilibrium. **3** *n.* Ease of manner; self-possession.

poi·son [poi′zən] **1** *n.* A substance whose chemical action is harmful or deadly to a living thing that absorbs or eats it, even in small amounts. **2** *v.* To give or apply poison to; kill or harm with poison. **3** *v.* To put poison into or on: to *poison* a well. **4** *n.* Anything that harms or destroys. **5** *v.* To affect in a bad way; corrupt.

poison ivy A climbing plant having glossy leaves growing in groups of three. It gives most people a severe skin rash if they touch it.

poison oak A plant related to poison ivy.

poi·son·ous [poi′zən·əs] *adj.* Being, containing, or having the effect of a poison.

poke¹ [pōk] *v.* **poked, pok·ing,** *n.* **1** *v.* To push or jab, as with the elbow: to *poke* someone in the ribs. **2** *n.* A push or jab, as with the elbow. **3** *v.* To make by jabbing or thrusting: to *poke* a hole. **4** *v.* To thrust or push in, out, through, etc.: to *poke* one's hand through a hole. **5** *v.* To pry; meddle: to *poke* into someone's business. **6** *v.* To search through: to *poke* around the cellar. **7** *v.* To move about in a slow or sluggish way. **8** *n.* A lazy or slow person. **9** *v. slang* To hit with the fist; punch. **10** *n. slang* A punch. **11** *n.* A bonnet with a brim wide in front. **— poke fun at** To mock; ridicule.

poke² [pōk] *n.* A small bag or sack: now used only in certain regions.

pok·er¹ [pō′kər] *n.* **1** A metal rod for stirring up a fire. **2** A person or thing that pokes.

pok·er² [pō′kər] *n.* Any of several card games in which each player bets that his hand is better than those of the other players.

pok·y or **pok·ey** [pō′kē] *adj.* **pok·i·er, pok·i·est 1** Not brisk; dull; slow. **2** Cramped and stuffy. **3** Shabby or dowdy.

Po·land [pō′lənd] *n.* A country in north central Europe.

po·lar [pō′lər] *adj.* **1** Of or having to do with a pole or poles. **2** Having to do with, coming from, or found near the North or South Pole. **3** Directly opposite in action or character.

polar bear A large bear with white fur, found in the arctic regions.

Polar bear, up to 8 ft. long

Po·lar·is [pō·lar′is] *n.* The North Star.

po·lar·i·ty [pō·lar′ə·tē] *n., pl.* **po·lar·i·ties** The condition of having poles with opposite properties at the ends of an axis, as in a magnet.

po·lar·ize [pō′lə·rīz] *v.* **po·lar·ized, po·lar·iz·ing** To become or make polar; give polarity to. **— po′lar·i·za′·tion** *n.* ¶3

pole¹ [pōl] *n., v.* **poled, pol·ing 1** *n.* A long, thin, wooden or metal rod, usually rounded. **2** *n.* To push along with a pole, as a boat.

pole² [pōl] *n.* **1** Either end of the axis of a sphere. **2** Either end of the earth's axis; the North Pole or the South Pole. **3** A point of maximum strength in a magnetic or electric field.

Pole [pōl] *n.* A person born in or a citizen of Poland.

pole·cat [pōl′kat′] *n.* **1** A European animal related to a weasel, known for its foul odor when annoyed or frightened. **2** *U.S.* A skunk.

po·lem·ic [pō·lem′ik] **1** *adj.* Of or having to do with dispute or argument. **2** *n.* An argument, especially about political or religious beliefs.

pole·star [pōl′stär′] *n.* **1** The North Star; Polaris. **2** Something that guides or governs.

pole vault A jump over a high, horizontal bar, made with the aid of a long pole.

po·lice [pə·lēs′] *n., v.* **po·liced, po·lic·ing 1** *n.* An official force organized to maintain order, prevent and detect crime, and enforce laws. **2** *adj. use:* a *police* car; a *police* station. **3** *n.* (used with *pl. verb*) The members of such a force. **4** *v.* To protect or maintain law and order in, as a city. **5** *n. U.S.* The cleaning of an army camp, or those assigned to clean it. **6** *v. U.S.* To clean, as an army camp.

Pole vault

po·lice·man [pə·lēs′mən] *n., pl.* **po·lice·men** [pə·lēs′mən] A member of a police force.

po·lice·wom·an [pə·lēs′wŏŏm′ən] *n., pl.* **po·lice·wom·en** [pə·lēs′wim′in] A woman member of a police force.

pol·i·cy[1] [pol′ə·sē] *n., pl.* **pol·i·cies** A plan or method of action or conduct: a nation's foreign *policy*; Honesty is the best *policy*.

pol·i·cy[2] [pol′ə·sē] *n., pl.* **pol·i·cies** A written contract by which an insurance company insures someone, as against loss by accident, theft, etc.

po·li·o [pō′lē·ō] *n. informal* Poliomyelitis.

po·li·o·my·e·li·tis [pō′lē·ō·mī′ə·li′tis] *n.* An acute, infectious virus disease most common in children and young adults, marked by inflammation of the spinal cord, and often followed by paralysis; infantile paralysis.

pol·ish [pol′ish] **1** *n.* Smoothness and glossiness of a surface. **2** *n.* Something rubbed on a surface to make it smooth and shiny. **3** *v.* To make or become smooth and shiny, as by rubbing: to *polish* a floor; The car *polishes* well. **4** *v.* To make more nearly perfect: to *polish* a story. **5** *n.* Elegance or refinement of manner, style, etc. — **pol′ish·er** *n.*

Po·lish [pō′lish] **1** *adj.* Of or from Poland. **2** *n.* **(the Polish)** The people of Poland. **3** *n.* The language of Poland.

po·lite [pə·līt′] *adj.* **po·lit·er, po·lit·est** **1** Showing consideration for others; mannerly: It is *polite* to hold doors open for ladies. **2** Refined; cultured: *polite* society. — **po·lite′ly** *adv.* — **po·lite′ness** *n.*

pol·i·tic [pol′ə·tik] *adj.* **1** Skillful, ingenious, or shrewd; crafty: a *politic* statesman. **2** Planned to fit the situation; prudent; expedient: a *politic* remark. **3** Political.

po·lit·i·cal [pə·lit′i·kəl] *adj.* **1** Of, having to do with, or involved in government or politics. **2** Of or about politicians. — **po·lit′i·cal·ly** *adv.*

political science The study of the principles of government.

pol·i·ti·cian [pol′ə·tish′ən] *n.* **1** A person who takes part in or is skillful at politics. **2** A person who takes part in politics for selfish reasons.

pol·i·tics [pol′ə·tiks] *n.* **1** The science or technique of government; political science. **2** The affairs and activities of those who control or seek to control a government. **3** Political principles, as of a party or individual. **4** The occupation or life of a politician: to succeed in *politics.* ◆ See -ICS.

pol·i·ty [pol′ə·tē] *n., pl.* **pol·i·ties** **1** The form or system of a government. **2** A community under some definite government.

Polk [pōk], **James Knox,** 1795–1849, eleventh president of the U.S., 1845–1849.

pol·ka [pō(l)′kə] *n.* **1** A kind of fast, lively dance. **2** Music for this dance, in duple time.

polka dot 1 One of a series of round dots forming a pattern. **2** The pattern so formed.

poll [pōl] **1** *n.* A collection of votes or opinions, as in an election or a public survey. **2** *n.* The total number of votes cast. **3** *n. (often pl.)* The place where votes are cast and counted. **4** *n.* A list of persons. **5** *v.* To register or record the votes or opinions of: to *poll* a jury. **6** *v.* To vote. **7** *v.* To receive (a certain number of votes). **8** *n.* The head. **9** *v.* To cut off or trim the hair, horns, top, etc., of: to *poll* cattle.

pol·len [pol′ən] *n.* A yellow powder containing the male reproductive cells of plants, found on the stamens of flowers. When pollen is transferred to the pistil it fertilizes the flower.

pol·li·nate [pol′ə·nāt] *v.* **pol·li·nat·ed, pol·li·nat·ing** To carry pollen to: Bees and wind *pollinate* flowers. — **pol′li·na′tion** *n.*

pol·li·wog [pol′ē·wog] *n.* Another name for TADPOLE.

Pol·lock [pol′ək], **Jackson,** 1912–1956, U.S. painter.

poll tax A tax on a person, especially as a requirement for voting.

pol·lute [pə·lōōt′] *v.* **pol·lut·ed, pol·lut·ing** To make unclean or impure; dirty; corrupt: Sewage *polluted* the river. — **pol·lu′tion** *n.*

pol·ly·wog [pol′ē·wog] *n.* Another name for TADPOLE.

po·lo [pō′lō] *n.* A game in which players mounted on horses try to drive a wooden ball into the opponents' goal with long-handled mallets.

Po·lo [pō′lō], **Marco,** 1254?–1324?, Venetian traveler who wrote about his travels to Asia.

Polo player

pol·o·naise [pol′ə·nāz′ *or* pō′lə·nāz′] *n.* **1** A stately, marchlike Polish dance. **2** Music for this dance, in three-quarter time.

pol·troon [pol·trōōn′] *n.* A base coward.

po·lyg·a·my [pə·lig′ə·mē] *n.* The condition or practice of having more than one wife or husband at any one time. — **po·lyg′a·mous** *adj.*

pol·y·glot [pol′i·glot] *adj.* **1** Expressed in or written in many languages: a *polyglot* sign. **2** Able to speak or write several languages.

pol·y·gon [pol′i·gon] *n.* A closed plane figure bounded by straight lines. — **po·lyg′on·al** [pə·lig′ə·nəl] *adj.*

pol·y·he·dron [pol′i·hē′drən] *n., pl.* **pol·y·he·dra** [pol′i·hē′drə] *or* **pol·y·he·drons** A solid figure bounded by plane faces, usually more than four.

pol·y·mer [pol′i·mər] *n.* A substance, as some plastics, made by joining similar small molecules to form large ones.

Polygons

Pol·y·ne·sia [pol′i·nē′zhə] *n.* The islands of the central and SE Pacific Ocean, including Hawaii. — **Pol′y·ne′sian** *adj., n.*

pol·y·no·mi·al [pol′i·nō′mē·əl] **1** *adj.* Of or consisting of many names or terms. **2** *n.* A mathematical expression, as 3 a − 2 b + √c, that contains two or more terms. **3** *n.* A scientific name that has more than two parts.

pol·yp [pol′ip] *n.* A water animal shaped like a tube, having a mouth surrounded by tentacles at one end, often found growing in large colonies. Coral and sea anemones are polyps.

pol·y·phon·ic [pol′i·fon′ik] *adj.* Having two or more melodies to be played or sung together.

pol·y·syl·lab·ic [pol′i·si·lab′ik] *adj.* Having more than three syllables, as the words *multifarious* and *plenipotentiary.*

pol·y·tech·nic [pol′i·tek′nik] *adj.* Having to do with or teaching many crafts or sciences.

pol·y·the·ism [pol′i·thē′iz·əm] *n.* The belief in and worship of more than one god.

po·made [pə·mād′] *n.* A perfumed hair dressing or an ointment for the scalp.

pome·gran·ate [pom′gran′it *or* pum′gran′it] *n.* **1** A tropical fruit about the size of an orange, having a pleasantly acid pulp and many seeds. **2** The tree on which this fruit grows.

pom·mel [pum′əl *or* pom′əl] *n., v.* **pom·meled** or **pom·melled, pom·mel·ing** or **pom·mel·ling 1** *n.* A knob, as on the hilt of a sword. **2** *v.* To beat with the fists. **3** *n.* A knob that sticks up at the front of a saddle.

pomp [pomp] *n.* Magnificent, stately display; splendor: the *pomp* of a state funeral.

pom·pa·dour [pom′pə·dôr] *n.* A way of arranging the hair in which it is made to puff straight up from the forehead.

Pom·pe·ii [pom·pā′(ē)] *n.* An ancient city of Italy, buried by an eruption of Mount Vesuvius, A.D. 79. — **Pom·pe′ian** *adj., n.*

pom·pon [pom′pon] *n.* **1** A tuft or ball, as of wool, used to ornament clothing, especially hats. **2** A type of chrysanthemum or dahlia having compact, globe-shaped flowers.

Pompon

pom·pos·i·ty [pom·pos′ə·tē] *n.* The condition or quality of being pompous or pretentious.

pom·pous [pom′pəs] *adj.* **1** Too dignified; self-important: a *pompous* executive. **2** High-flown or ornate: a *pompous* speech. — **pom′pous·ly** *adv.* — **pom′pous·ness** *n.*

Ponce de León [pons′ də lē′ən], **Juan,** 1460?–1521, Spanish explorer; discovered Florida, 1513.

pon·cho [pon′chō] *n., pl.* **pon·chos 1** A South American cloak like a blanket with a hole in the middle for the head. **2** A similar waterproof garment used as a raincoat.

Poncho

pond [pond] *n.* A body of still water smaller than a lake.

pon·der [pon′dər] *v.* To consider carefully; puzzle over: to *ponder* a decision.

pon·der·ous [pon′dər·əs] *adj.* **1** Large, heavy, and often clumsy; lumbering: The elephant is a *ponderous* animal. **2** Dull; boring: a *ponderous* lecture. — **pon′der·ous·ly** *adv.*

pon·gee [pon·jē′] *n.* A thin natural silk having a knotty, rough weave.

pon·iard [pon′yərd] *n.* A dagger.

pon·tiff [pon′tif] *n.* **1** A bishop. **2** The Pope.

pon·tif·i·cal [pon·tif′i·kəl] *adj.* Of or having to do with a Pope or bishop.

pon·tif·i·cate [pon·tif′ə·kāt] *v.* **pon·tif·i·cat·ed, pon·tif·i·cat·ing 1** To perform the duties of a bishop. **2** To write or speak in a pompous or dogmatic way.

pon·toon [pon·tōōn′] *n.* **1** A flat-bottomed boat. **2** A float, often in the form of a flat-bottomed boat or a sealed metal tube, used in building a temporary floating bridge. **3** Either of the floats on the landing gear of a seaplane.

pontoon bridge A temporary bridge supported on pontoons.

po·ny [pō′nē] *n., pl.* **po·nies** One of any of several breeds of very small horses.

pony express An early system for sending mail, etc., between Missouri and California, by relays of horsemen.

poo·dle [pōōd′(ə)l] *n.* One of a breed of intelligent dogs with thick, usually curly hair.

pooh [pōō] *interj.* An exclamation used to show disbelief, annoyance, disapproval, etc.

pooh-pooh [pōō′pōō′] *v.* To dismiss or reject with disdain: to *pooh-pooh* a plan.

pool¹ [pōōl] *n.* **1** A small body of still water. **2** A deep place in a stream. **3** A puddle: a *pool* of blood. **4** A swimming pool.

pool² [pōōl] **1** *n.* A game whose object is to use a cue to make a ball hit others into the pockets of a special table. **2** *n.* A sum of money put together by a group of people for use in a common venture or as the stakes in a contest or race. **3** *n.* A number of persons or things used or available for use by a particular group: a *pool* of typists. **4** *v.* To combine (money, things, efforts, etc.) for common benefit.

poop [pōōp] *n.* **1** The stern or aft end of a ship. **2** A short deck at the stern of a ship, raised above the main deck.

poor [pŏŏr] *adj.* **1** Having too little money and property to live in comfort; needy. **2** *n. use* Poor people: *The poor* are often treated badly. **3** Marked by poverty: a *poor* neighborhood. **4** Lacking in quantity or quality; not good: a *poor* crop; a *poor* job; *poor* soil. **5** Deserving pity; unhappy; wretched: The *poor* cat was in pain. **6** Lacking vigor; feeble; frail: in *poor* health. — **poor′ness** *n.*

poor·house [pŏŏr′hous′] *n.* A home for poor people, maintained by public funds.

poor·ly [pŏŏr′lē] *adv.* In a poor way; badly; unsatisfactorily.

pop[1] [pop] *n., v.* **popped, pop·ping 1** *n.* A sharp, explosive noise. **2** *v.* To make a sharp, explosive sound. **3** *v.* To break open or explode or cause to break open or explode with such a sound: The balloon *popped*; to *pop* corn. **4** *v.* To move or put suddenly: to *pop* into a room; He *popped* his head through the door. **5** *v.* To bulge, as the eyes. **6** *v.* To hit a baseball high but not very far, so that it is easily caught: to *pop* out. **7** *n.* Sweetened and flavored carbonated water; soda.

pop[2] [pop] *n. slang* Father.

pop·corn [pop′kôrn′] *n.* **1** A kind of corn whose kernels pop open and puff up when heated. **2** The kernels after they have popped open.

pope [pōp] *n.* (*usually written* **Pope**) The bishop of Rome, head of the Roman Catholic Church.

pop·gun [pop′gun′] *n.* A toy gun that shoots pellets such as corks with a popping sound.

pop·in·jay [pop′in·jā] *n.* **1** A vain, silly chatterbox. **2** A parrot: seldom used today.

pop·lar [pop′lər] *n.* **1** A tree related to the willow, that grows rapidly and has light, soft wood. **2** The wood of this tree.

pop·lin [pop′lin] *n.* A strong ribbed cloth made of silk, cotton, rayon, etc.

pop·o·ver [pop′ō′vər] *n.* A light muffin that puffs up and is hollow in the center.

pop·pet [pop′it] *n. British* A dainty little person or small child.

pop·py [pop′ē] *n., pl.* **pop·pies 1** Any of various plants having showy red, yellow, or white flowers. One kind of poppy produces opium. **2** The flower of any of these plants.

pop·py·cock [pop′ē·kok] *n.* Nonsense.

pop·u·lace [pop′yə·lis] *n.* The common people of a community or an area.

pop·u·lar [pop′yə·lər] *adj.* **1** Liked by or suited to many people: a *popular* remedy for headaches. **2** Having many friends; well-liked. **3** Of, for, or by the people at large: *popular* government. **4** Suited to the means of most people: *popular* prices. — **pop′u·lar·ly** *adv.* — **pop·u·lar·i·ty** [pop′yə·lar′ə·tē] *n.*

pop·u·lar·ize [pop′yə·lə·rīz′] *v.* **pop·u·lar·ized, pop·u·lar·iz·ing** To make popular: to *popularize* modern art. — **pop′u·lar·i·za′tion** *n.* ¶3

pop·u·late [pop′yə·lāt] *v.* **pop·u·lat·ed, pop·u·lat·ing 1** To provide with inhabitants: England *populated* parts of her colonies. **2** To inhabit: Many strange creatures *populate* the jungle.

pop·u·la·tion [pop′yə·lā′shən] *n.* **1** The total number of people living in a country, city, etc. **2** The total number of people of a particular group, class, etc.: the Irish *population*. **3** The act or process of providing inhabitants.

pop·u·lous [pop′yə·ləs] *adj.* Having many inhabitants; thickly settled.

por·ce·lain [pôrs′lin *or* pôr′sə·lin] *n.* A fine, hard, white earthenware, somewhat translucent, used for plates, dishes, cups, etc.; china.

porch [pôrch] *n.* **1** A covered structure at the entrance to a building. **2** A veranda, either open or closed, along one or more sides of a building.

por·cu·pine [pôr′kyə·pīn] *n.* A large clumsy rodent covered with spines or quills that stand up when it is attacked.

Porcupine, up to 40 in. long

pore[1] [pôr] *v.* **pored, por·ing 1** To gaze steadily or intently. **2** To read or study with great care and attention: to *pore* over one's schoolwork.

pore[2] [pôr] *n.* A tiny opening, as in the skin or a leaf, serving as an outlet or inlet. Perspiration escapes through pores in the skin.

por·gy [pôr′gē] *n., pl.* **por·gy** or **por·gies** Any of various salt-water fishes used for food.

pork [pôrk] *n.* The flesh of a pig used for food. ◆ *Pork* goes back through French to the Latin word *porcus*, meaning a *pig*.

pork·er [pôr′kər] *n.* A pig or hog, especially one fattened for slaughter.

po·ros·i·ty [pô·ros′ə·tē] *n.* The quality of being porous.

por·ous [pôr′əs] *adj.* Full of tiny openings that allow air, water, etc., to pass through.

por·phy·ry [pôr′fə·rē] *n., pl.* **por·phy·ries** A hard rock enclosing white or red crystals.

por·poise [pôr′pəs] *n., pl.* **por·pois·es** or **por·poise 1** A sea mammal like a small whale, mostly blackish, with a blunt snout, often seen in schools. **2** A dolphin.

Porpoise, 4–6 ft. long

por·ridge [pôr′ij] *n. Chiefly British* A soft food made by boiling oatmeal or some other grain in water, milk, etc.

por·rin·ger [pôr′in·jər] *n.* A small shallow bowl used for porridge, soup, etc.

port[1] [pôrt] *n.* A city or place where ships arrive and depart; harbor.

port[2] [pôrt] *n.* A sweet, usually red wine.

port[3] [pôrt] *n.* **1** A small opening in the side of a ship; porthole. **2** A covering for a porthole. **3** An opening, as in an engine, valve, etc., for the passage of air, gas, or a liquid.

port[4] [pôrt] **1** *n.* The left side of a ship or boat, facing the bow. **2** *adj. use:* the *port* side; the *port* guns. **3** *v.* To turn to the left, as a ship.

port[5] [pôrt] *n.* The way a person stands or moves; carriage; bearing: a graceful *port*.

port·a·ble [pôr′tə·bəl] *adj.* That can be easily carried or moved: a *portable* cot.

port·age [pôr′tij] *n.* **1** The carrying of boats and goods overland between two bodies of water.

2 The route over which this is done. **3** The charge for such transportation.

por·tal [pôr′təl] *n.* (*often pl.*) An entrance, door, or gate, especially an impressive one.

port·cul·lis [pôrt·kul′is] *n.* A grating made of strong bars that can be let down to close off the entrance of a fort, castle, etc.

Portcullis

por·tend [pôr·tend′] *v.* To warn or be an omen of: His silence *portends* anger.

por·tent [pôr′tent] *n.* A warning or sign of what is to come; omen.

por·ten·tous [pôr·ten′təs] *adj.* **1** Warning of things to come; ominous: *portentous* thunder. **2** Astonishing; extraordinary: *portentous* strength.

por·ter[1] [pôr′tər] *n.* A keeper of a door or gate; doorman.

por·ter[2] [pôr′tər] *n.* **1** A man hired to carry luggage, etc., as in an airport or station. **2** *U.S.* A male attendant in a Pullman. **3** A man hired to sweep, clean, and do odd jobs.

por·ter[3] [pôr′tər] *n.* A dark, heavy ale.

por·ter·house [pôr′tər·hous′] *n.* A choice cut of beef, including part of the tenderloin.

port·fo·li·o [pôrt·fō′lē·ō] *n., pl.* **port·fo·li·os** **1** A portable case for holding papers, drawings, etc. **2** A list of the holdings, as stocks and bonds, of an investor, bank, etc. **3** The office and duties of a cabinet member or a minister of state.

port·hole [pôrt′hōl′] *n.* **1** A small, windowlike opening in the side of a ship to admit air and light. **2** An opening in the side of a ship, wall, or fort for shooting through.

por·ti·co [pôr′ti·kō] *n., pl.* **por·ti·coes** or **por·ti·cos** An open space or walk covered by a roof held up by columns.

A portico

por·tière [pôr·tyâr′] *n.* A curtain that hangs at a doorway.

por·tion [pôr′shən] **1** *n.* A part or division of a whole. **2** *n.* A part or amount of something given or served to someone; share. **3** *v.* To divide into shares, often for distribution: The farm was *portioned* out between them.

Port·land [pôrt′lənd] *n.* **1** A city in NW Oregon. **2** A city in SW Maine.

port·ly [pôrt′lē] *adj.* **port·li·er**, **port·li·est** **1** Fat; stout. **2** Stately and dignified: a *portly* old general. **— port′li·ness** *n.*

port·man·teau [pôrt·man′tō] *n., pl.* **port·man·teaus** or **port·man·teaux** [pôrt·man′·tōz] *British* A suitcase hinged at the back to form two separate compartments.

Por·to Ri·co [pôr′tō rē′kō] The former name for PUERTO RICO.

por·trait [pôr′trit *or* pôr′trāt] *n.* **1** A drawing, painting, or photograph of a person, showing especially the face. **2** A vivid or imaginative description: Her new novel contains a wonderful *portrait* of a mother.

por·trait·ist [pôr′trā·tist] *n.* A person who makes portraits; a portrait painter or photographer.

por·trai·ture [pôr′tri·chər] *n.* **1** The art or practice of making portraits. **2** A portrait.

por·tray [pôr·trā′] *v.* **1** To make a picture of, as in a drawing or painting. **2** To describe or depict in words. **3** To represent, as in a play: to *portray* Hamlet.

por·tray·al [pôr·trā′əl] *n.* **1** The act or process of portraying. **2** A portrait.

Por·tu·gal [pôr′chə·gəl] *n.* A country in SW Europe.

Por·tu·guese [pôr′chə·gēz′] **1** *adj.* Of or from Portugal. **2** *n.* (**the Portuguese**) The people of Portugal. **3** *n.* The language of Portugal.

pose [pōz] *v.* **posed, pos·ing,** *n.* **1** *v.* To assume or hold a position, as for a portrait. **2** *v.* To cause to assume a position: The artist *posed* his model. **3** *n.* A position of the body, especially one taken for a portrait. **4** *v.* To represent oneself: to *pose* as an expert. **5** *n.* A pretense or sham; affectation: His anger is only a *pose.* **6** *v.* To present or put forward: to *pose* a question.

A model striking a pose

Po·sei·don [pō·sī′dən] *n.* In Greek myths, the god of the sea. His Roman name was Neptune.

po·si·tion [pə·zish′ən] **1** *n.* The way in which a person or thing is placed: a standing *position*; an upside-down *position.* **2** *n.* The place occupied by a person or thing. **3** *n.* The correct or accustomed place: to be in *position.* **4** *v.* To put in a particular or accustomed place: to *position* a chair. **5** *n.* Condition or situation: an embarrassing *position.* **6** *n.* Social standing; rank, especially high rank. **7** *n.* An attitude or point of view; stand: What is your *position* on this question? **8** *n.* A job; post: She has a splendid *position* with an exporting firm.

pos·i·tive [poz′ə·tiv] **1** *adj.* Not allowing doubt, question, or denial: *positive* proof. **2** *adj.* Completely certain; convinced: I'm *positive* he's gone. **3** *adj.* Confident or too confident: a *positive* attitude. **4** *adj.* Complete; unqualified; definite: a *positive* failure. **5** *adj.* Helpful or use-

add, āce, câre, pälm;   end, ēqual;   it, īce;   odd, ōpen, ôrder;   to͝ok, po͞ol;   up, bûrn;
ə = a in *above*, e in *sicken*, i in *possible*, o in *melon*, u in *circus*;   yo͞o = u in *fuse*;   oil;   pout;
check;   ring;   thin;   this;   zh in *vision*.   For ¶ reference, see page 64 · HOW TO

ful: *positive* criticism. **6** *adj.* Being affirmative; saying "yes": a *positive* answer. **7** *adj.* Existing of or by itself; not relative or dependent on other things; real; absolute: a *positive* good. **8** *adj.* Greater than zero, as a number or quantity. **9** *adj.* Being or having the kind of electricity that attracts and is neutralized by electrons. **10** *adj.* Indicating the presence of a certain condition or disease: The result of the test for tuberculosis was *positive.* **11** *n.* Something that is positive or capable of being affirmed. **12** *adj.* Indicating the simple, uncompared degree of an adjective or adverb. **13** *n.* The positive degree of an adjective or adverb. **14** *n.* A photograph having the light and dark areas exactly as they were in the original subject; print. **— pos′i·tive·ly** *adv.*

pos·se [pos′ē] *n.* A force of men summoned by a sheriff to help him in some official duty, as to stop a riot, make an arrest, etc.

pos·sess [pə·zes′] *v.* **1** To have as property; own. **2** To have as a quality, feature, etc.: to *possess* a conscience. **3** To enter and control, sometimes as a demon or evil spirit: The idea *possessed* him.

pos·ses·sion [pə·zesh′ən] *n.* **1** The fact or condition of possessing: to come into *possession* of a relative's fortune. **2** A being possessed, as by an idea, an evil spirit, etc. **3** Something that is possessed. **4** A territory outside of, but controlled by, a country: Guam is a U.S. *possession.* **5** Self-control.

pos·ses·sive [pə·zes′iv] **1** *adj.* Of or related to possession or ownership. **2** *adj.* Having a strong desire for possessions. **3** *adj.* Having a desire or need to dominate or control someone: *possessive* parents. **4** *adj.* Indicating the case of a noun or pronoun that shows possession, origin, etc. **5** *n.* The possessive case, or a word in the possessive case, as *his* and *Mary's* in "His answer is the same as Mary's." **— pos·ses′sive·ly** *adv.* **— pos·ses′sive·ness** *n.*

pos·ses·sor [pə·zes′ər] *n.* A person who possesses; owner.

pos·si·bil·i·ty [pos′ə·bil′ə·tē] *n., pl.* **pos·si·bil·i·ties** **1** The fact or condition of being possible: There is a *possibility* that our plans will be changed. **2** A thing that is possible: A change of plans is always a *possibility.*

pos·si·ble [pos′ə·bəl] *adj.* **1** Having a chance of happening; not contrary to fact or natural law: It is *possible* that you'll grow to over six feet. **2** Having some chance of happening; uncertain but not unlikely: It's *possible* that he'll forgive you. **3** Capable of being done, acquired, made, known, etc.: a *possible* purchase.

pos·si·bly [pos′ə·blē] *adv.* **1** Under any circumstances; for any reason: I can't *possibly* let him go. **2** By any possible means: He can't *possibly* jump fifty feet. **3** Maybe; perhaps: *Possibly* I can do it.

pos·sum [pos′əm] *n.* An informal name for OPOSSUM. **— play possum** To act as if dead, asleep, ill, etc.

post¹ [pōst] **1** *n.* An upright piece of timber or other material, usually used as a support. **2** *v.* To put up (a poster, sign, etc.) in a public place. **3** *v.* To announce by or as if by a poster: to *post* a reward. **4** *v.* To put up signs forbidding trespassing on: to *post* your land during hunting season. **5** *v.* To enter on a list for public notice: to *post* a plane departure. **6** *v.* To fasten a poster or sign on or in.

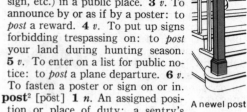
A newel post

post² [pōst] **1** *n.* An assigned position or place of duty: a sentry's *post.* **2** *n.* A job, office, or position: He has a *post* with the new government. **3** *n.* A place where soldiers are stationed. **4** *n.* The soldiers stationed at such a place. **5** *v.* To assign a post to: We *posted* soldiers at each exit. **6** *v.* To give or put up: to *post* bond. **7** *n.* A trading post.

post³ [pōst] **1** *n. chiefly British* Mail or a single delivery of mail: the morning *post.* **2** *v.* To mail: Please *post* these letters. **3** *n.* In former times, any of the stations furnishing relays of men and horses along certain fixed routes. **4** *v.* To inform: He *posted* us on the latest news. **5** *v.* To travel with speed; hurry.

post- A prefix meaning: **1** After or later in time; following, as in *postwar,* after war. **2** After in position; behind, as in *postnasal,* behind the nose.

post·age [pōs′tij] *n.* The charge for sending mail.

postage stamp A small, printed, government label that is put on mail as evidence that postage has been paid.

post·al [pōs′təl] *adj.* Of or having to do with the mails or with post offices.

postal card **1** A card with a stamp printed on it, issued by the government and used to send messages through the mail. **2** A post card.

post card **1** Another name for POSTAL CARD. **2** A card, usually with a picture on the front side, that can be sent through the mails.

post chaise A closed, four-wheeled carriage for hire, formerly used for traveling.

post·er [pōs′tər] *n.* A sign, printed notice, or advertisement posted in some public place.

Poster

pos·te·ri·or [pos·tir′ē·ər] *adj.* **1** Situated behind or toward the back part. **2** Coming after another in a series. **3** Coming after in time; later.

pos·ter·i·ty [pos·ter′ə·tē] *n.* **1** All the people of future times. **2** All of one person's descendants.

pos·tern [pōs′tərn] **1** *n.* A small back gate or door, especially in a fortification or castle. **2** *adj.* Situated at the back or side.

post·grad·u·ate [pōst′graj′oo·it *or* pōst′graj′·

oo·āt] **1** *adj.* Of or having to do with studies pursued after receiving a degree. **2** *n.* A person who goes on with such studies.

post·haste [pōst′hāst′] *adv.* With great speed.

post·hu·mous [pos′chŏŏ·məs] *adj.* **1** Born after the death of its father: a *posthumous* child. **2** Published after the author's death: a *posthumous* novel. **3** Coming after one's death: *posthumous* fame. **— post′hu·mous·ly** *adv.*

pos·til·ion or **pos·til·lion** [pōs·til′yən *or* pos·til′yən] *n.* A man who rides on one of the horses drawing a carriage and drives a pair.

post·man [pōst′mən] *n., pl.* **post·men** [pōst′mən] A man who delivers mail; mailman.

post·mark [pōst′märk′] **1** *n.* A mark put on mail to cancel stamps and to give the date and place of mailing. **2** *v.* To stamp with a postmark.

Postmark

post·mas·ter [pōst′mas′tər] *n.* An official who is in charge of a post office.

postmaster general *pl.* **postmasters general** An official who is in charge of the postal service of an entire country.

post·mis·tress [pōst′mis′tris] *n.* A woman who is in charge of a post office.

post·mor·tem [pōst·môr′təm] **1** *adj.* Happening or performed after death. **2** *n.* A thorough examination of a human body made after death.

post office 1 (*often written* **Post Office**) The branch of a government responsible for carrying and delivering the mail. **2** Any local office that handles mail, sells stamps, etc.

post·paid [pōst′pād′] *adj.* Having the postage paid for by the sender.

post·pone [pōst·pōn′] *v.* **post·poned, post·pon·ing** To put off to a future time; delay: We *postponed* our picnic. **— post·pone′ment** *n.*

post road In former times, a road built for carrying mail, and having stations at regular intervals to furnish fresh horses.

post·script [pōst′skript′] *n.* **1** Any message added to a letter below the writer's signature. **2** A part added to any written or printed work.

It was a lovely visit, and I hope to see you soon.
Best wishes,
Tom
P.S. Don't forget Ann's birthday is next week.

Postscript

pos·tu·late [*v.* pos′chə·lāt, *n.* pos′chə·lit] *v.* **pos·tu·lat·ed, pos·tu·lat·ing,** *n.* **1** *v.* To assume or claim the truth of; take for granted, as in reasoning or arguing: to *postulate* the roundness of the earth. **2** *n.* A fundamental truth or necessary condition claimed or held as a basis for argument or reasoning. **3** *v.* To claim, demand, or require.

pos·ture [pos′chər] *n., v.* **pos·tured, pos·tur·**

ing 1 *n.* The way a person carries his body or a part of his body: an erect *posture*. **2** *n.* A particular way of holding the body, as when a person poses for an artist. **3** *v.* To place in a specific position or pose. **4** *v.* To act or pose in an affected way: She is forever *posturing*. **5** *n.* Situation; state: the present *posture* of the war.

post·war [pōst′wôr′] *adj.* After a war.

po·sy [pō′zē] *n., pl.* **po·sies 1** A single flower or a bouquet. **2** A brief inscription or motto.

pot [pot] *n., v.* **pot·ted, pot·ting 1** *n.* A usually round, deep container made of metal, glass, or earthenware and used for cooking, growing plants, or other household purposes. **2** *n.* Such a container and its contents: a *pot* of stew. **3** *n.* The amount a pot will hold: a *pot* of tea. **4** *v.* To put into a pot or pots: to *pot* plants. **5** *v.* To preserve in a pot. **6** *n.* A trap for lobsters, fish, etc. **7** *n.* In certain card games, the amount of money bet or played for. **8** *n.* A fund of money contributed by a group of people and used by all of them. **9** *n. informal* A large sum of money. **— go to pot** To become bad in character, quality, etc.

pot·ash [pot′ash′] *n.* A white substance made from wood ashes, used as a fertilizer and in making glass, soap, etc.

po·tas·si·um [pə·tas′ē·əm] *n.* A soft, silvery white metallic element forming many compounds used in industry, medicine, etc.

po·ta·to [pə·tā′tō] *n., pl.* **po·ta·toes 1** The thickened, underground stem or tuber of a cultivated plant. It is starchy and widely used as a vegetable. **2** The plant itself. **3** A sweet potato.

potato chip A very thin slice of potato fried crisp and salted.

po·ten·cy [pōt′(ə)n·sē] *n.* The quality of being potent; power; force.

po·tent [pōt′(ə)nt] *adj.* **1** Physically powerful. **2** Having great authority: a *potent* ruler. **3** Able to convince or influence: a *potent* argument. **4** Strong in its physical or chemical effects: a *potent* drug or medicine.

po·ten·tate [pōt′(ə)n·tāt] *n.* A person who has great power or authority; ruler.

po·ten·tial [pə·ten′chəl] **1** *adj.* Possible, but not yet actual: a *potential* danger. **2** *n.* Qualities that make the development of a talent, power, skill, etc., possible or likely: a student with great *potential*. **3** *n.* The difference between two electric charges, or the difference between one charge and zero. **— po·ten′tial·ly** *adv.*

po·ten·ti·al·i·ty [pə·ten′chē·al′ə·tē] *n., pl.* **po·ten·ti·al·i·ties 1** Something capable of being developed. **2** Capacity for development or advancement.

poth·er [poth′ər] **1** *n.* Fuss and commotion. **2** *v.* To worry; bother.

po·tion [pō′shən] *n.* A liquid that is supposed to have medicinal, poisonous, or magical qualities.

add, āce, câre, pälm; end, ēqual; it, īce; odd, ōpen, ôrder; tŏŏk, pōōl; up, bûrn; ə = a in *above*, e in *sicken*, i in *possible*, o in *melon*, u in *circus*; yōō = u in *fuse*; oil; pout; check; ring; thin; this; zh in *vision.* For ¶ reference, see page 64 · HOW TO

pot·luck [pot′luk′] *n.* Whatever food may have been prepared for the family and not especially for guests: Stay with us and take *potluck.*

Po·to·mac [pə·tō′mək] *n.* A river forming the boundaries between Maryland, West Virginia, and Virginia, and flowing into Chesapeake Bay.

pot·pie [pot′pī′] *n.* A dish of meat and vegetables covered with a crust and baked in the oven.

pot·pour·ri [pō·poo·rē′] *n.* **1** A mixture of dried flower petals and spices kept for its fragrance. **2** A medley of tunes or a miscellany of writings: a *potpourri* of opera tunes.

pot shot **1** A sure, easy shot, as one to kill game for food. **2** *informal* A critical remark tossed at an easy, tempting target.

pot·tage [pot′ij] *n.* A thick soup or stew.

pot·ter[1] [pot′ər] *n.* A person who makes pottery.

pot·ter[2] [pot′ər] *v. British* To putter.

potter's field A burial ground for poor or unknown people or, sometimes, for criminals.

potter's wheel A horizontal, rotating disk for holding clay that is being shaped by a potter.

pot·ter·y [pot′ər·ē] *n., pl.* **pot·ter·ies** **1** Vases, pots, etc., molded from clay and hardened by intense heat. **2** The art of making pottery. **3** The place where pottery is made.

Potter's wheel

pouch [pouch] **1** *n.* A small bag or sack. **2** *n.* The pocket of skin on the belly of certain animals, as the kangaroo and opossum, in which the animal's young are carried. **3** *n.* Any similar part, as in the cheeks of a squirrel or in the bill of a pelican. **4** *v.* To put or form into a pouch or into something like a pouch.

poul·tice [pōl′tis] *n.* A moist, usually hot mass of flour, mustard, etc., applied to a sore or inflamed part of the body.

poul·try [pōl′trē] *n.* Fowl kept for meat or eggs, as chickens, ducks, turkeys, etc.

A mailman's pouch

pounce [pouns] *v.* **pounced, pounc·ing,** *n.* **1** *v.* To swoop down or spring, as in seizing prey: The hawk *pounced* on the chicken. **2** *n.* The act of pouncing; a sudden swoop or spring.

pound[1] [pound] *n.* **1** A unit of weight in avoirdupois equal to 16 ounces. **2** A unit of weight in troy equal to 12 ounces. **3** The pound sterling. **4** The basic unit of money in several other countries, including Ireland, Egypt, and Israel.

pound[2] [pound] **1** *v.* To strike heavily and repeatedly; beat: to *pound* a nail into a board; to *pound* a friend on the back; to *pound* on a door; to *pound* on a typewriter. **2** *n.* A heavy blow, or the sound of a heavy blow. **3** *v.* To crush into a pulp or powder: to *pound* grain into meal. **4** *v.* To move with heavy, plodding steps: to *pound*

down the stairs. **5** *v.* To beat or throb heavily: Her heart *pounded.*

pound[3] [pound] *n.* A place for keeping stray animals, especially stray or unlicensed dogs.

pound-foolish [pound′foo′lish] *adj.* See PENNY-WISE.

pound sterling The basic unit of British money, equal to 20 shillings, and now also equal to 100 new pence: symbol. £.

pour [pôr] **1** *v.* To flow or cause to flow in a continuous stream: She *poured* water into a pot; People *poured* out of the theater. **2** *v.* To rain heavily. **3** *v.* To tell or write about freely: to *pour* forth one's sorrows. **4** *v.* To act as a hostess by pouring tea, coffee, etc. **5** *n.* Something poured, as rain.

pout [pout] **1** *v.* To thrust out the lips, especially when one is discontented or annoyed. **2** *n.* A sulky expression made in this way. **3** *v.* To be gloomy or discontented; sulk. **— pout′er** *n.*

pov·er·ty [pov′ər·tē] *n.* **1** The condition of being very poor. **2** A lack or small amount: a *poverty* of talent. **3** Poorness in quality: the *poverty* of the soil.

pov·er·ty-strick·en [pov′ər·tē·strik′ən] *adj.* Suffering from poverty; very poor.

pow·der [pou′dər] **1** *n.* A dry mass of fine particles made by crushing or grinding a solid substance. **2** *n.* Any kind of powder prepared in this way, as talcum powder. **3** *v.* To reduce to powder; grind: *powdered* sugar. **4** *v.* To sprinkle or cover with or as if with powder. **5** *v.* To use powder as a cosmetic, especially on the face.

powder horn The hollow horn of an ox or cow, used in former times for holding gunpowder.

powder puff A soft pad used to apply powder to the skin.

pow·der·y [pou′dər·ē] *adj.* **1** Of or like powder. **2** Covered with or as if with powder; dusty. **3** Capable of being easily crushed into powder.

pow·er [pou′ər] **1** *n.* Ability or capacity to do something or to produce a certain effect: the *power* of speech; the *power* of a novel. **2** *n.* Physical strength or force: to have *power* in one's fists. **3** *n.* Legal authority or capability: the *power* of the Supreme Court. **4** *n.* Any person or thing that has control or influence over others: That country is a *power* in the world. **5** *n.* In physics, the rate at which work is done, measured in watts, horsepower, etc. **6** *n.* Any form of energy available for doing work, as electricity. **7** *adj. use:* a *power* saw. **8** *n.* The result of a number multiplied by itself a given number of times: The third *power* of 2 is 8. **9** *n.* Magnifying capacity, as of a lens. **10** *v.* To provide with power: This saw is *powered* by a gasoline engine.

Powder horn

—in power In control: Hitler was *in power* for 12 years.

pow·er·ful [pou′ər·fəl] *adj.* Having great power: a *powerful* army; a *powerful* country; a *powerful* play. **— pow′er·ful·ly** *adv.*

pow·er·house [pou′ər·hous′] *n.* **1** A station where electricity is generated. **2** *slang* A person or group of great force or energy.

pow·er·less [pou′ər·lis] *adj.* Without power: *powerless* to act. **— pow′er·less·ly** *adv.*

power shovel A large, power-driven machine used for digging.

pow·wow [pou′wou′] **1** *n. informal* Any meeting or conference. **2** *v.* To hold a powwow. **3** *n.* A conference with or of North American Indians. ◆ *Powwow* comes from the Algonquian Indian word *pauwaw*, meaning *he dreams*. A *powwow* was originally an Indian medicine man or priest, who was supposed to have learned his art from his dreams.

pox [poks] *n.* A disease in which the skin breaks out in small blisters, as in chicken pox.

pp. Abbreviation of: **1** Pages. **2** PAST PARTICIPLE.

p.p. Abbreviation of: **1** PARCEL POST. **2** PAST PARTICIPLE. **3** POSTPAID.

prac·ti·ca·ble [prak′ti·kə·bəl] *adj.* **1** That can be put into practice; possible. **2** That can be used; usable. **— prac·ti·ca·bil·i·ty** [prak′ti·kə·bil′ə·tē] *n.* **— prac′ti·ca·bly** *adv.* ◆ See PRACTICAL.

prac·ti·cal [prak′ti·kəl] *adj.* **1** Having to do with actual practice, use, or action rather than ideas or theories: *practical* knowledge. **2** That can be put to use or account; useful: *practical* clothes for hiking. **3** Having or showing common sense; sensible; realistic: a *practical* person; a *practical* plan. **4** Gained from actual practice or experience: a good *practical* knowledge of how to set a bone. **5** Being so in effect though not in name; virtual: Although he is not the principal, he is the *practical* head of our school. **— prac·ti·cal·i·ty** [prak′ti·kal′ə·tē] *n.* **— prac′ti·cal·ly** *adv.* ◆ A particular scheme for making money may be *practicable* (that is, it may be possible) without being *practical* (that is, without being sensible, useful, or realistic). In the same way, a person can be *practical*, but one would never say a person was *practicable*.

practical joke A joke, prank, or trick played on someone.

practical nurse A person who has some training and experience in caring for the sick, but who is not a graduate of a nursing school.

prac·tice [prak′tis] *v.* **prac·ticed, prac·tic·ing,** *n.* **1** *v.* To do over and over to gain greater skill: to *practice* batting. **2** *n.* An action done over and over to gain greater skill: Playing the violin takes *practice*. **3** *n.* The skill gained by such action: I'm out of *practice*. **4** *v.* To do, per-

form, make use of, etc., regularly or habitually: to *practice* kindness. **5** *n.* A person's customary action; habit: It was Ken's *practice* to save a dollar a week. **6** *n.* An established custom: It is the *practice* in our school to have a ten-minute break between classes. **7** *v.* To apply in action: *Practice* what you preach. **8** *v.* To work at (a profession, occupation, etc.): to *practice* law. **9** *n.* The following of a profession: the *practice* of medicine. **10** *n.* The business built up by a lawyer or doctor: Our doctor has a large *practice*. ◆ *Practice, drill,* and *exercise* all refer to some repeated action that is done to gain skill. *Practice* may refer to complicated skills as well as simple ones: acrobats *practicing* on the high trapeze. *Drill* is more routine. It usually has the aim of enabling one to do an action automatically, without thinking: The sergeant *drilled* his men in marching. Physical *exercises* are done to stay healthy or vigorous. But study *exercises* are lessons that give one practice in solving problems.

prac·ticed or **prac·tised** [prak′tist] *adj.* Skilled; experienced; expert.

prac·tise [prak′tis] *v.* **prac·tised, prac·tis·ing** Another spelling of PRACTICE.

prac·ti·tion·er [prak·tish′ən·ər] *n.* A person who practices an art, profession, craft, etc.

prae·tor [prē′tər] *n.* A city magistrate of ancient Rome ranking below a consul.

prae·to·ri·an [pri·tôr′ē·ən] **1** *adj.* Of or having to do with a praetor. **2** *n.* A praetor. **3** *adj.* (*written* **Praetorian**) Of or having to do with the bodyguard of the Roman emperors. **4** *n.* (*written* **Praetorian**) A member of this guard.

Prague [präg] *n.* The capital of Czechoslovakia.

prai·rie [prâr′ē] *n.* A large tract or area of more or less level, grassy land having few or no trees, especially the broad, grassy plain of central North America.

prairie chicken Either of two game birds inhabiting the plains or prairies of North America.

prairie dog A small rodent of the plains of North America that lives in large communities and is very destructive to vegetation.

prairie schooner A covered wagon used for travel by pioneers.

praise [prāz] *n., v.* **praised, prais·ing 1** *n.* An expression of approval or favor. **2** *v.* To express approval or favor of (someone or something): He *praised* her for her singing. **3** *n.* Worship, as of a god, hero, etc. **4** *v.* To express adoration of: Let us *praise* God in song.

Prairie dog, 14–17 in. long

praise·wor·thy [prāz′wûr′thē] *adj.* Worthy of praise.

---

add, āce, câre, pälm;   end, ēqual;   it, īce;   odd, ōpen, ôrder;   took, pool;   up, bûrn;

ə = a in *above*, e in *sicken*, i in *possible*, o in *melon*, u in *circus*;   yoo = u in *fuse*;   oil;   pout;

check;   ring;   thin;   this;   zh in *vision*.   For ¶ reference, see page 64 · HOW TO

pram [pram] *n. British* A baby carriage.

prance [prans] *v.* **pranced, pranc·ing,** *n.* **1** *v.* To bound or spring from the hind legs or move with high steps, as a horse. **2** *v.* To ride a horse that moves in such a way. **3** *v.* To walk or move in a lively, proud way; swagger. **4** *n.* The act of prancing; a lively, high step. **— pranc′er** *n.*

Pram

prank [prangk] *n.* A mischievous, playful act or trick. **— prank′ish** *adj.*

prate [prāt] *v.* **prat·ed, prat·ing** To talk foolishly and at length; chatter. **— prat′er** *n.*

prat·tle [prat′(ə)l] *v.* **prat·tled, prat·tling,** *n.* **1** *v.* To talk foolishly or like a child. **2** *n.* Foolish or childish talk. **3** *n.* The sound of childish speech, or a sound like it. **— prat′tler** *n.*

prawn [prôn] *n.* An edible shellfish related to the shrimp but larger.

pray [prā] *v.* **1** To address words or prayers to God, or to an idol, deity, etc.: They *prayed* for two hours. **2** To ask or beg by prayers or with great earnestness: They *prayed* for rain. **3** To be so good as to; please: *Pray* be still awhile. **4** To get or bring about by praying.

Prawn

prayer [prâr] *n.* **1** The act of praying. **2** An expression of worship, appeal, or thanks to God. **3** A set form of words used in praying. **4** Something prayed for. **5** Any earnest request.

prayer book A book of prayers.

prayer·ful [prâr′fəl] *adj.* **1** Inclined or given to praying. **2** Of or like a prayer. **— prayer′ful·ly** *adv.*

praying mantis See MANTIS.

pre- A prefix meaning: Before in time or order, as in *preschool*, before school.

preach [prēch] *v.* **1** To deliver a sermon. **2** To urge or recommend strongly: to *preach* brotherly love. **3** To give advice, often in a boring or tiresome way.

preach·er [prē′chər] *n.* A person who preaches, especially a clergyman.

pre·am·ble [prē′am·bəl] *n.* An introductory statement, especially an introduction to a formal document explaining its purpose.

pre·ar·ranged [prē·ə·rānjd′] *adj.* Arranged ahead of time: a *prearranged* signal.

Pre-Cam·bri·an [prē·kam′brē·ən] *adj.* Of or having to do with the period in the earth's history extending from the formation of the oldest known rocks to the first appearance of organic life.

pre·car·i·ous [pri·kâr′ē·əs] *adj.* **1** Risky; uncertain: a *precarious* way of earning a living. **2** Dangerous; hazardous: a *precarious* path up the mountain. **— pre·car′i·ous·ly** *adv.*

pre·cau·tion [pri·kô′shən] *n.* **1** Something done in order to avoid a possible danger, evil, etc.: As a *precaution*, we threw water on the campfire.

2 Any care taken ahead of time; caution in advance. **— pre·cau′tion·ar·y** *adj.*

pre·cede [pri·sēd′] *v.* **pre·ced·ed, pre·ced·ing** **1** *v.* To be, go, or come before in order, place, rank, time, etc.: Egypt *preceded* Greece in creating a great civilization. **2** *adj. use:* the *preceding* speaker.

prec·e·dence [pres′ə·dəns *or* pri·sēd′əns] *n.* **1** The act of preceding. **2** The right or condition of being ahead in place, time, rank, etc.: Your business has *precedence* over mine.

prec·e·dent [*n.* pres′ə·dənt, *adj.* pri·sēd′(ə)nt] **1** *n.* An action, decision, usage, etc., that can be used as a guide for a later action, decision, etc. **2** *adj.* Going or coming before, as in time, place, etc.

pre·cept [prē′sept] *n.* A rule or direction to guide conduct or action; maxim. "Haste makes waste" is a precept.

pre·cep·tor [pri·sep′tər] *n.* A teacher.

pre·cinct [prē′singkt] *n.* **1** An area of a city, town, township, etc. marked off as a district for voting or for police supervision. **2** (*often pl.*) A place or enclosure marked off by fixed limits: school *precincts*. **3** A boundary; limit.

pre·cious [presh′əs] **1** *adj.* Highly priced or prized; valuable: a *precious* gem. **2** *adj.* Beloved; cherished; dear: a *precious* child; a *precious* friendship. **3** *adj.* Too refined or delicate, as a style of writing. **4** *adj.* Very great: a *precious* scoundrel. **5** *adv.* Very: *precious* little chance of that. **— pre′cious·ly** *adv.*

prec·i·pice [pres′i·pis] *n.* A face of a cliff that is straight up and down or almost so.

pre·cip·i·tate [*v.* pri·sip′ə·tāt, *adj., n.* pri·sip′ə·tit *or* pri·sip′ə·tāt] *v.* **pre·cip·i·tat·ed, pre·cip·i·tat·ing,** *adj., n.* **1** *v.* To bring about quickly or suddenly: to *precipitate* a quarrel. **2** *v.* To hurl forcefully; throw as from a height. **3** *adj.* Moving or acting with or showing reckless speed; rash. **4** *v.* To separate (a substance) from a solution as a solid. **5** *n.* A substance separated as a solid from a solution. **6** *v.* To cause (vapor, etc.) to condense and fall as dew, rain, etc. **— pre·cip′i·tate·ly** *adv.*

pre·cip·i·ta·tion [pri·sip′ə·tā′shən] *n.* **1** The act or an instance of precipitating: the *precipitation* of a war between nations. **2** Reckless haste or hurry. **3** The depositing of rain, snow, etc., from the atmosphere on the earth; also, the amount of rain, snow, etc. so deposited. **4** The process of separating a substance from a solution as a solid. **5** The substance so separated.

pre·cip·i·tous [pri·sip′ə·təs] *adj.* **1** Like a precipice; very steep. **2** Hasty; rash; reckless. **— pre·cip′i·tous·ly** *adv.*

pre·cise [pri·sīs′] *adj.* **1** Strictly accurate; exact: the *precise* amount of money. **2** Careful or even fussy, as in observing rules, diction, etc. **3** Particular; very: At that *precise* second, he fell. **— pre·cise′ly** *adv.* **— pre·cise′ness** *n.*

pre·ci·sion [pri·sizh′ən] *n.* **1** The condition or quality of being precise; accuracy. **2** *adj. use:* *precision* instruments.

pre·clude [pri·klōōd′] *v.* **pre·clud·ed, pre·clud·ing** To make impossible; prevent: Padded crates *preclude* damage in handling.

pre·co·cious [pri·kō′shəs] *adj.* Unusually mature or advanced for one's age: a *precocious* child. **— pre·co′cious·ly** *adv.* **— pre·coc·i·ty** [pri·kos′ə·tē] *n.*

pre·con·ceived [prē′kən·sēvd′] *adj.* Formed in advance: a *preconceived* plan.

pre·con·cep·tion [prē′kən·sep′shən] *n.* **1** An idea formed in advance. **2** A prejudice; bias.

pre·con·cert·ed [prē′kən·sûr′tid] *adj.* Arranged or agreed upon ahead of time.

pre·cur·sor [pri·kûr′sər] *n.* A person or thing that comes before and indicates what is to follow; forerunner.

pred·a·tor [pred′i·tər] *n.* A predatory person or animal.

pred·a·to·ry [pred′ə·tôr′ē] *adj.* **1** Of, having to do with, or characterized by plundering or robbery. **2** Living by preying upon others: A hawk is a *predatory* bird.

pred·e·ces·sor [pred′ə·ses′ər] *n.* A person who goes or has gone before another in point of time, as a previous holder of a job or position.

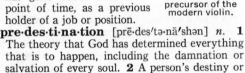

The rebec was a precursor of the modern violin.

pre·des·ti·na·tion [prē·des′tə·nā′shən] *n.* **1** The theory that God has determined everything that is to happen, including the damnation or salvation of every soul. **2** A person's destiny or fate.

pre·des·tine [prē·des′tin] *v.* **pre·des·tined, pre·des·tin·ing** To decide or determine in advance.

pre·de·ter·mine [prē′di·tûr′min] *v.* **pre·de·ter·mined, pre·de·ter·min·ing** To determine beforehand; decide in advance: a *predetermined* orbit.

pre·dic·a·ment [pri·dik′ə·mənt] *n.* A situation that is trying, dangerous, or embarrassing: We had forgotten they were coming to dinner. What a *predicament*!

pred·i·cate [*n., adj.* pred′i·kit, *v.* pred′i·kāt] *n., adj., v.* **pred·i·cat·ed, pred·i·cat·ing 1** *n.* The word or words in a sentence or clause that express something about the subject. A predicate consists of a verb, its object or complement, and any modifiers, as *ate their meal slowly* in "The boys ate their meal slowly." **2** *adj.* Belonging to the predicate. *Red* in "The house is red" is a *predicate* adjective. **3** *v.* To found or base (an action, argument, etc.): His rules in class were *predicated* on reason and fairness. **4** *v.* To prove or state as a quality or attribute: His bravery *predicated* his good character. **5** *v.* To declare; proclaim.

pre·dict [pri·dikt′] *v.* To state beforehand; foretell: to *predict* the outcome of a game.

pre·dict·a·ble [pri·dikt′ə·bəl] *adj.* Capable of being predicted.

pre·dic·tion [pri·dik′shən] *n.* **1** The act of predicting. **2** Something predicted; a prophecy.

pre·di·lec·tion [prē′də·lek′shən *or* pred′ə·lek′·shən] *n.* A preference or liking; partiality.

pre·dis·pose [prē′dis·pōz′] *v.* **pre·dis·posed, pre·dis·pos·ing** To give a tendency; incline: Exhaustion *predisposes* one to sickness. **— pre·dis·po·si·tion** [prē′dis·pə·zish′ən] *n.*

pre·dom·i·nant [pri·dom′ə·nənt] *adj.* Greater or superior in power, effect, number, etc.: The *predominant* color of the rock is dark brown. **— pre·dom′i·nance** *n.* **— pre·dom′i·nant·ly** *adv.*

pre·dom·i·nate [pri·dom′ə·nāt] *v.* **pre·dom·i·nat·ed, pre·dom·i·nat·ing 1** To be greater in power, effect, number, etc.: In this group, the boys *predominate*. **2** To be in control; prevail.

pre·em·i·nent [prē·em′ə·nənt] *adj.* Outstandingly superior; very fine; supreme. **— pre·em′·i·nence** *n.* **— pre·em′i·nent·ly** *adv.*

pre·empt [prē·empt′] *v.* **1** To acquire for oneself before others can: to *preempt* the newest typewriter. **2** To occupy (public land) so as to get the right to purchase it.

preen [prēn] *v.* **1** To clean and arrange (feathers, etc.) with the beak, as a bird. **2** To dress or tidy (oneself) carefully: Sue *preened* herself before the mirror.

pre·ex·ist [prē′ig·zist′] *v.* To exist before.

pre·ex·is·tent [prē′ig·zis′tənt] *adj.* Existing before. **— pre′ex·is′tence** *n.*

pre·fab·ri·cate [prē·fab′rə·kāt] *v.* **pre·fab·ri·cat·ed, pre·fab·ri·cat·ing** To manufacture in standard sections that can be rapidly set up and put together: to *prefabricate* a house.

A girl preening herself

pref·ace [pref′is] *n., v.* **pref·aced, pref·ac·ing 1** *n.* A brief introduction to a book, speech, etc. **2** *v.* To introduce or furnish with a preface.

pref·a·to·ry [pref′ə·tôr′ē] *adj.* Of, like, or serving as a preface; introductory.

pre·fect [prē′fekt] *n.* **1** In ancient Rome, any of various civil and military officials. **2** Any high official or chief officer, as in France.

pre·fec·ture [prē′fek·chər] *n.* The office, jurisdiction, or district of a prefect.

pre·fer [pri·fûr′] *v.* **pre·ferred, pre·fer·ring 1** To like better; value more: I *prefer* history to geography. **2** To bring forward, as charges, before a law court.

pref·er·a·ble [pref′ər·ə·bəl] *adj.* Fit to be preferred; more desirable. **— pref′er·a·bly** *adv.*

---

add, āce, câre, pälm;   end, ēqual;   it, īce;   odd, ōpen, ôrder;   tŏŏk, pōōl;   up, bûrn;

ə = a in *above*, e in *sicken*, i in *possible*, o in *melon*, u in *circus*;   yŏŏ = u in *fuse*;   oil;   pout;

check;   ring;   thin;   this;   zh in *vision*.   For ¶ reference, see page 64 · HOW TO

pref·er·ence [pref′ər·əns] *n.* **1** The act of preferring: Adam sometimes shows bad judgment in his *preferences.* **2** A person or thing preferred: My *preference* is cold weather. **3** The right or power to choose: to give a person his *preference.* **4** A favoring of one person or thing over another or others; partiality: Don't show *preference* when you assign jobs.

pref·er·en·tial [pref′ə·ren′shəl] *adj.* Showing preference or partiality: *preferential* treatment.

pre·fer·ment [pri·fûr′mənt] *n.* Advancement or promotion to a higher rank, office, position, etc.

pre·fig·ure [prē·fig′yər] *v.* **pre·fig·ured, pre·fig·ur·ing 1** To show in advance; be an indication of. **2** To picture to oneself beforehand.

pre·fix [*n.* prē′fiks, *v.* prē·fiks′] **1** *n.* A syllable or syllables put at the beginning of a word or root to modify its meaning or make a new word. *Re* in "renew" is a prefix. **2** *v.* To put or attach before: to *prefix* a title to a person's name.

preg·nan·cy [preg′nən·sē] *n., pl.* **preg·nan·cies** The condition of being pregnant.

preg·nant [preg′nənt] *adj.* **1** Carrying an unborn child or unborn young in the womb; a being with child or with young. **2** Having significance; full of meaning: a *pregnant* pause. **3** Full or filled: *pregnant* with meaning.

pre·his·tor·ic [prē′his·tôr′ik] *adj.* Of or belonging to the period before the start of written history: *prehistoric* reptiles. — **pre′his·tor′i·cal·ly** *adv.*

pre·his·tor·i·cal [prē′his·tôr′i·kəl] *adj.* Prehistoric.

pre·judge [prē·juj′] *v.* **pre·judged, pre·judg·ing** To judge beforehand or without proper knowledge.

prej·u·dice [prej′o͝o·dis] *n., v.* **prej·u·diced, prej·u·dic·ing 1** *n.* An unfair opinion or judgment formed in advance of or without examination of the available facts: a *prejudice* against a new medicine. **2** *n.* Hatred of or dislike for a particular group, race, religion, etc. **3** *v.* To cause to have a prejudice; bias: That breakdown *prejudiced* him against foreign cars. **4** *n.* Injury or damage: His lawyer's oily manner operated to the *prejudice* of a strong case. **5** *v.* To cause harm or disadvantage to: A sliced drive *prejudiced* his chance of winning the match. ♦ *Prejudice* and *bias* both refer to feelings that make a fair judgment impossible. Some forms of *bias* are perfectly understandable. Few people would blame a mother for being *biased* in favor of her own children. But other kinds of *bias,* such as hatred of other people because of their race or religion, are unreasonable and harmful. Such *biases* are forms of *prejudice.*

prej·u·di·cial [prej′o͝o·dish′əl] *adj.* Causing prejudice; damaging.

prel·a·cy [prel′ə·sē] *n., pl.* **prel·a·cies 1** The system of church government by prelates. **2** The position or office of a prelate. **3** Prelates as a group.

prel·ate [prel′it] *n.* A clergyman of high rank, as a bishop or archbishop.

pre·lim·i·nar·y [pri·lim′ə·ner′ē] *adj., n., pl.* **pre·lim·i·nar·ies 1** *adj.* Coming before the main event, proceeding, business, etc.; introductory. **2** *n.* A preliminary act, step, etc.: He cleared his throat as a *preliminary.*

prel·ude [prel′yo͞od *or* prē′lo͞od] *n. v.* **prel·ud·ed, prel·ud·ing 1** *n.* Any introductory action or event. **2** *n.* An opening section or movement of a musical composition. **3** *n.* An instrumental composition of moderate length. **4** *v.* To introduce with a prelude. **5** *v.* To be a prelude to.

pre·ma·ture [prē′mə·cho͝or′ *or* prē′mə·t(y)o͝or′] *adj.* Before the natural or proper time; too early or soon. — **pre′ma·ture′ly** *adv.*

pre·med·i·tat·ed [prē·med′ə·tā·tid] *adj.* Planned or thought about beforehand.

pre·med·i·ta·tion [prē·med′ə·tā′shən] *n.* The act of planning or thinking about beforehand.

pre·mi·er [*adj.* prē′mē·ər, *n.* pri·mir′] **1** *adj.* First in rank or position; principal. **2** *n.* The chief minister and often the chief executive of a government. **3** *adj.* First in occurrence; earliest.

pre·mière [pri·mir′ *or* prə·myâr′] *n.* The first performance of a play, movie, etc.

prem·ise [*n.* prem′is, *v.* prem′is *or* pri·mīz′] *n., v.* **pre·mised, pre·mis·ing 1** *n.* A statement or belief that serves as a basis for an argument, conclusion, theory, etc.: An early false *premise* was the belief that the earth was flat. **2** *v.* To state as a premise. **3** *n.* (*pl.*) An area of land with the buildings that are on it.

pre·mi·um [prē′mē·əm] *n.* **1** A prize or reward offered to help persuade someone to do or buy something. **2** An extra amount or bonus paid in addition to a regular wage, price, etc. **3** The amount paid for insurance, usually in installments. **4** High regard or value: to put a *premium* on truth. — **at a premium 1** Valuable, usually because in great demand. **2** Above the usual price.

pre·mo·ni·tion [prē′mə·nish′ən *or* prem′ə·nish′ən] *n.* A feeling or warning that something is going to happen, usually something bad.

pre·na·tal [prē·nāt′(ə)l] *adj.* Before birth.

pre·oc·cu·py [prē·ok′yə·pī] *v.* **pre·oc·cu·pied, pre·oc·cu·py·ing 1** To interest or occupy fully: The idea *preoccupied* him for hours. **2** *adj. use:* a *preoccupied* student. **3** To take possession of first. — **pre·oc′cu·pa′tion** *n.*

pre·or·dain [prē′ôr·dān′] *v.* To determine or decide in advance what is going to happen.

prep. Abbreviation of PREPOSITION.

pre·paid [prē·pād′] **1** Past tense and past participle of PREPAY. **2** *adj.* Paid for in advance.

prep·a·ra·tion [prep′ə·rā′shən] *n.* **1** The act or process of preparing. **2** A being prepared; readiness. **3** Something done so as to get ready. **4** Something made or prepared, as a medicine.

pre·par·a·to·ry [pri·par′ə·tôr′ē] *adj.* **1** Used or serving as preparation; helping to make ready: *preparatory* work. **2** Occupied in preparation: a *preparatory* scholar.

preparatory school A private school that prepares students for college admission.

pre·pare [pri·pâr′] *v.* **pre·pared, pre·par· ing 1** To make ready, fit, or qualified: to *pre· pare* a class for a test. **2** To get ready: to *prepare* for a trip. **3** To provide with what is needed; outfit; equip: to *prepare* an expedition. **4** To put together; make: to *prepare* a meal.

pre·par·ed·ness [pri·pâr′id·nis *or* pri·pârd′nis] *n.* Readiness, especially readiness for war.

pre·pay [prē·pā′] *v.* **pre·paid, pre·pay·ing** To pay or pay for in advance. **— pre·pay′· ment** *n.*

pre·pon·der·ant [pri·pon′dər·ənt] *adj.* Having greater force, weight, influence, quantity, etc.: Coaches rather than teachers had the *preponderant* effect on him. **— pre·pon′· der·ance** *n.*

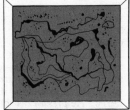

prep·o·si·tion [prep′· ə·zish′ən] *n.* A word that is used to indi- cate the relation of its object, a noun or pronoun, to another

Red is the preponderant color in this painting.

noun or pronoun, as *of* in "The color of the book is brown," to a verb, as *beside* in "Sit beside the fire," or to an adjective, as *at* in "I'm sick at heart." **— prep′o·si′tion·al** *adj.* ◆ It was once said that a sentence should never end with a preposition, but good English sentences some- times do. "What did you laugh at?" is perfectly acceptable English, but "At what did you laugh?" seems awkward and unnatural.

pre·pos·sess·ing [prē′pə·zes′ing] *adj.* Creat- ing a favorable impression; pleasing; attractive.

pre·pos·ter·ous [pri·pos′tər·əs] *adj.* Contrary to nature, reason, or common sense; absurd; ridiculous. **— pre·pos′ter·ous·ly** *adv.*

pre·req·ui·site [prē·rek′wə·zit] **1** *adj.* Neces- sary to something that follows: Chemistry is a *prerequisite* course for medical training. **2** *n.* Something necessary to something else that fol- lows, as a course that a student must pass before taking a more advanced course.

pre·rog·a·tive [pri·rog′ə·tiv] *n.* A right or privilege belonging to a particular person or class: The king had the *prerogative* of exiling anyone he wished.

pres·age [*n.* pres′ij, *v.* pri·sāj′] *n., v.* **pre· saged, pre·sag·ing 1** *n.* An indication or warning of someting to come. **2** *v.* To give an indication or warning of: His words *presaged* trouble. **3** *n.* A feeling that something bad is going to happen. **4** *v.* To have a feeling or pre- sentiment about.

pres·by·ter [prez′bə·tər] *n.* **1** In the early Christian church, an elder. **2** In certain churches, a priest. **3** In the Presbyterian church, a lay person or elder who is a church official.

Pres·by·te·ri·an [prez′bə·tir′ē·ən] **1** *n.* A member of a Protestant church that is governed by elders or presbyters. **2** *adj.* Of or having to do with Presbyterians or their church. **— Pres′by·te′ri·an·ism** *n.*

pres·by·ter·y [prez′bə·ter′ē] *n., pl.* **pres·by· ter·ies 1** A Presbyterian church court made up of the ministers and presbyters of a district. **2** The district so represented. **3** That part of a church set apart for the clergy.

pre·school [prē′skōōl′] *adj.* Of or having to do with a child's life before school, usually between the ages of two and five.

pre·sci·ent [prē′shē·ənt *or* presh′ē·ənt] *adj.* Having knowledge of events before they take place; foreseeing. **— pre′sci·ence** *n.*

pre·scribe [pri·skrīb′] *v.* **pre·scribed, pre· scrib·ing 1** To set down (a rule, direction, etc.) to be followed or obeyed; order. **2** To order the use of (a medicine, treatment, etc.).

pre·scrip·tion [pri·skrip′shən] *n.* **1** A physi- cian's formula for pre- paring and ordering a medicine, usually with directions about its use. **2** The medicine itself. **3** A rule; direc- tion; order.

pres·ence [prez′əns] *n.* **1** The fact or con- dition of being pres- ent: Her *presence* made me happy. **2** The area directly around a person or thing: Do not talk in his *presence.* **3** The bearing or appearance of a person: a digni-

Prescription

fied *presence.* **4** Something invisible that is felt to be near.

presence of mind Full control of one's thoughts and actions, especially in an emergency.

pres·ent¹ [prez′ənt] **1** *adj.* Now existing or going on; not past or future: the *present* time; his *present* work. **2** *n.* The time now going on; the current time: For the *present,* Frank is acting as class secretary. **3** *adj.* Being in view or at hand; not absent: Is the whole class *present?* **4** *adj.* Now being discussed, considered, etc.: the *present* problem. **5** *n.* The present tense or a verb in it. **— at present** Now.

pres·ent² [*v.* pri·zent′, *n.* prez′ənt] **1** *v.* To give as a gift: I *present* this watch to you. **2** *v.* To give a gift to: He *presented* us with the silver box. **3** *n.* A gift. **4** *v.* To cause to be known; introduce: May I *present* Bill Fleming? **5** *v.* To exhibit or show; display: to *present* a good appearance; to *present* a play. **6** *v.* To suggest to the mind: Snow *presents* a problem.

add, āce, câre, pälm;   end, ēqual;   it, īce;   odd, ōpen, ôrder;   tŏŏk, pōōl;   up, bûrn;
ə = a in *above,* e in *sicken,* i in *possible,* o in *melon,* u in *circus;*   yŏŏ = u in *fuse;*   oil;   pout;
check; ring; thin; this; zh in *vision.*   For ¶ reference, see page 64 · HOW TO

pres·ent·a·ble [pri·zen′tə·bəl] *adj.* **1** Fit to be presented, especially in regard to personal appearance. **2** Capable of being presented, expressed, etc.: a story that is *presentable* either as a play or as a motion picture.

pres·en·ta·tion [prez′ən·tā′shən *or* prē′zən·tā′shən] *n.* **1** The act of presenting, giving, or introducing. **2** The thing that is presented, as a play or a gift.

pres·ent-day [prez′ənt·dā′] *adj.* Of the present time; current: *present-day* events.

pre·sen·ti·ment [pri·zen′tə·mənt] *n.* A feeling that something is about to happen; premonition.

pres·ent·ly [prez′ənt·lē] *adv.* **1** Shortly; soon: Sheila will be here *presently.* **2** Now: Where are you working *presently*?

pre·sent·ment [pri·zent′mənt] *n.* **1** The act of presenting or showing. **2** Something presented.

present participle A form of a verb ending in *ing*, used with a form of *be* to show continuing action, as in *He was running.* The form may also be used as an adjective, as *falling* in "a falling star." In "while walking the dog" the present participle *walking* takes an object, whereas in "though being red" the present participle *being* takes a complement.

present tense The form of a verb used to indicate an action or condition in the present time. *Am* in "I am here" is in the present tense.

pres·er·va·tion [prez′ər·vā′shən] *n.* **1** The act of preserving. **2** A being preserved.

pre·ser·va·tive [pri·zûr′və·tiv] **1** *adj.* Having the power or ability to preserve. **2** *n.* Something that preserves, especially a substance added to food to prevent spoiling.

pre·serve [pri·zûrv′] *v.* **pre·served, pre·serv·ing,** *n.* **1** *v.* To keep from danger or harm; watch over; protect: May Heaven *preserve* you. **2** *v.* To keep unchanged; maintain; keep up: to *preserve* appearances. **3** *v.* To prepare (food) for future use by salting, pickling, etc. **4** *n.* (*usually pl.*) Fruit that has been cooked, usually with sugar. **5** *v.* To keep from spoiling or decaying: to *preserve* a specimen in alcohol. **6** *n.* An area set apart for the protection of wildlife, forests, etc. **7** *n.* Such an area kept for limited hunting or fishing. **— pre·serv′er** *n.*

pre·side [pri·zīd′] *v.* **pre·sid·ed, pre·sid·ing 1** To be in authority, as over a meeting; act as chairman or president. **2** To have direction or control: to *preside* over a government.

pres·i·den·cy [prez′ə·dən·sē] *n., pl.* **pres·i·den·cies 1** The office or duties of a president. **2** The time in office of a president.

pres·i·dent [prez′ə·dent] *n.* **1** A person chosen to direct or control an organized body, as a business, college, etc. **2** (*often written* **President**) The chief executive of a republic.

pres·i·den·tial [prez′ə·den′shəl] *adj.* Of, belonging to, or having to do with a president or presidency: a *presidential* veto.

press[1] [pres] **1** *v.* To act upon by weight or pressure: to *press* a button. **2** *v.* To crush or squeeze so as to draw out juice: to *press* grapes.

3 *v.* To draw out by crushing or squeezing: to *press* juice out of grapes. **4** *n.* A machine by which pressure is applied, as for crushing grapes, smoothing clothes, shaping or cutting materials, etc. **5** *v.* To smooth or shape by heat and pressure, as clothes. **6** *n.* The proper creases and folds in clothing: My pants held their *press* in the rain. **7** *v.* To clasp closely; hug. **8** *v.* To ask over and over; keep urging: They *pressed* me to stay for the night. **9** *v.* To place in difficulty; distress; bother:

A tailor pressing clothes

He was *pressed* by a lack of money. **10** *v.* To urge or ask persistently: to *press* for an answer. **11** *n.* The hurry or pressure of affairs: the *press* of business. **12** *v.* To urge onward; hurry: He *pressed* his soldiers onward. **13** *v.* To advance with force or speed: *Press* on! **14** *v.* To crowd; cram: The fans *pressed* into the stadium. **15** *n.* The act of crowding together: the *press* of the mob. **16** *n.* Any medium, as newspapers, magazines, broadcasting, etc., that gathers and distributes news; also, the reporters, editors, broadcasters, etc., who gather, write, or release such news. **17** *n.* The act or business of printing. **18** *n.* A place where printing is done. **19** *n.* A printing press. **20** *n.* A movable closet or case for clothes, books, etc. **— go to press** To begin to be printed.

press[2] [pres] *v.* To force into service, especially military or naval service.

press agent A person employed to further the interests of another person, a business, etc., by means of publicity.

press·ing [pres′ing] *adj.* Needing immediate attention; urgent; important: a *pressing* need.

pres·sure [presh′ər] *n., v.* **pres·sured, pres·sur·ing 1** *n.* The act of pressing or the condition of being pressed: *Pressure* seemed to relieve the pain. **2** *n.* The force pushing against a surface per unit of area: atmospheric *pressure.* **3** *n.* Strong and continued efforts to influence someone: He brought *pressure* to bear on all of us to attend. **4** *v. informal* To urge or influence as if by force: He *pressured* me into buying the book. **5** *n.* Urgent demands on a person's time or strength: the *pressure* of business. **6** *n.* Any heavy load or burden of distress, trouble, etc.: the *pressure* of grief.

pressure cook·er [kook′ər] A strong, airtight pot for cooking food by means of very hot steam under pressure.

pres·sur·ize [presh′ər·īz] *v.* **pres·sur·ized, pres·sur·iz·ing** To maintain in (an aircraft, special suit, etc.) an atmospheric pressure that is normal or almost normal. ¶3

pres·tige [pres·tēzh′ *or* pres·tēj′] *n.* Fame, importance, or respect based on a person's reputation, power, past achievements, etc.

pres·to [pres′tō] **1** *adj.*, *adv.* In music, very quick. **2** *n.* A presto movement or passage.

pre·sum·a·bly [pri·zōo′mə·blē] *adv.* Probably.

pre·sume [pri·zōom′] *v.* **pre·sumed, pre·sum·ing 1** To take for granted; assume; suppose: I *presume* you are right. **2** To take upon oneself without permission; dare: Do you *presume* to give me advice? **3** To rely too heavily: He *presumes* on my good nature.

pre·sump·tion [pri·zump′shən] *n.* **1** Speech or conduct that is too bold or arrogant: What *presumption* he has to speak to his boss like that! **2** The act of presuming. **3** Something presumed: Since he is not here by now, my *presumption* is he's not coming. **4** A reason for presuming something.

pre·sump·tive [pri·zump′tiv] *adj.* **1** Creating or giving grounds for belief: a *presumptive* indication of an infection. **2** Based on probability or likelihood: the *presumptive* outcome of the election. — **pre·sump′tive·ly** *adv.*

pre·sump·tu·ous [pri·zump′chōo·əs] *adj.* Too confident or bold. — **pre·sump′tu·ous·ly** *adv.*

pre·sup·pose [prē′sə·pōz′] *v.* **pre·sup·posed, pre·sup·pos·ing 1** To take for granted; assume to start with: Let's *presuppose* that *x* equals 0. **2** To need or require as a necessary condition: A thunderclap *presupposes* a lightning flash. — **pre·sup·po·si·tion** [prē′sup·ə·zish′· ən] *n.*

pre·tend [pri·tend′] *v.* **1** To give a false appearance of: to *pretend* friendship for an enemy. **2** To claim or say falsely: He *pretended* there was oil on his property. **3** To make believe: Let's *pretend* we're astronauts. **4** To make a claim: to *pretend* to the throne.

pre·tend·er [pri·ten′dər] *n.* **1** A person who puts forward a claim, especially a claim to a throne. **2** A person who pretends.

pre·tense [pri·tens′ *or* prē′tens] *n.* **1** Something pretended; a false act, appearance, excuse, etc.: His friendliness is a *pretense*. **2** The act of pretending; make-believe: *Pretense* is natural to Susan. **3** A claim: He makes no *pretense* of being a good student. **4** A showing off, affectation, or vain display: a man of many *pretenses*.

pre·ten·sion [pri·ten′shən] *n.* **1** A claim put forward, as to an office, privilege, etc. **2** A claim of ability or importance: She has serious *pretensions* as an actress. **3** A showing off; vain display.

pre·ten·tious [pri·ten′shəs] *adj.* **1** Making a flashy, outward show; showy: a *pretentious* gift. **2** Making claims, especially when exaggerated or false. — **pre·ten′tious·ly** *adv.* — **pre·ten′· tious·ness** *n.*

pret·er·it *or* **pret·er·ite** [pret′ər·it] **1** *adj.* Expressing past time or past action. **2** *n.* The tense of a verb that expresses past time; the past tense.

pre·ter·nat·u·ral [prē′tər·nach′ər·əl] *adj.* **1** Different from but not outside nature or what is natural; abnormal. **2** Outside nature or what is natural; supernatural.

pre·text [prē′tekst] *n.* A false reason or motive given to conceal a real one: Being unprepared, I stayed home on the *pretext* of being ill.

pret·ty [prit′ē] *adj.* **pret·ti·er, pret·ti·est,** *n., pl.* **pret·ties,** *adv.* **1** *adj.* Pleasant; attractive; charming: a *pretty* face; a *pretty* melody. **2** *n.* A pretty person or thing. **3** *adj. informal* Terrible; awful: a *pretty* mess. **4** *adv.* To some extent; somewhat; rather: He's doing *pretty* well. — **pret′ti·ly** *adv.* — **pret′·ti·ness** *n.*
◆ *Pretty* has a much more favorable meaning than it once did. In Old English it meant *sly* or *cunning*.

pret·zel [pret′səl] *n.* A crisp biscuit in the shape of a knot with a glazed, salted surface. ◆ *Pretzel* was taken over or "borrowed" directly from German.

pre·vail [pri·vāl′] **1** To gain control; be victorious; win out: The army *prevailed* over the rebels. **2** To be effective, frequent, widespread, or accepted: Some old customs still *prevail*; Joy *prevailed* when we won. — **prevail upon** or **prevail on** To urge or persuade successfully: We *prevailed upon* Marie to sing.

Pretzels

pre·vail·ing [pri·vā′ling] *adj.* **1** In current use; accepted: a *prevailing* opinion. **2** Having power or influence: a *prevailing* motive. **3** Most common or frequent: the *prevailing* winds.

prev·a·lent [prev′ə·lənt] *adj.* Of or having general acceptance or frequent occurrence; common: *prevalent* customs. — **prev′a·lence** *n.*

pre·var·i·cate [pri·var′ə·kāt] *v.* **pre·var·i· cat·ed, pre·var·i·cat·ing** To tell a lie. — **pre·var′i·ca′tion** *n.* — **pre·var′i·ca′tor** *n.*

pre·vent [pri·vent′] *v.* **1** To keep from happening: to *prevent* accidents. **2** To keep or stop; hinder: A flat tire *prevented* us from leaving town.

pre·vent·a·ble or **pre·vent·i·ble** [pri·ven′tə· bəl] *adj.* Capable of being prevented: a *preventable* accident.

pre·ven·tion [pri·ven′shən] *n.* **1** The act of preventing. **2** Something that prevents.

pre·ven·tive [pri·ven′tiv] **1** *adj.* Intended or used to prevent harm, disease, etc.: *preventive* medicine. **2** *n.* Something that prevents disease, harm, etc.

pre·view [prē′vyōo′] **1** *n.* An advance showing of all or parts of a motion picture, fashion show, etc., before it is presented publicly. **2** *v.* To show or view in advance.

pre·vi·ous [prē′vē·əs] *adj.* **1** Existing, happening, coming, etc., before something else in time or order: a *previous* occasion. **2** *informal*

---

add, āce, câre, pälm; end, ēqual; it, īce; odd, ōpen, ôrder; tŏŏk, pōōl; up, bûrn;
ə = a in *above*, e in *sicken*, i in *possible*, o in *melon*, u in *circus*; yōō = u in *fuse*; oil; pout;
check; ring; thin; this; zh in *vision*. For ¶ reference, see page 64 · HOW TO

Impatient; hasty; too quick: Our judgment was a little *previous*. — **previous to** Before. — **pre'vi·ous·ly** *adv.*

pre·war [prē'wôr'] *adj.* Existing or happening before a war: *prewar* prices.

prey [prā] **1** *n.* Any animal seized by another for food. **2** *v.* To seek or take animals to eat: Cats *prey* on birds. **3** *n.* A person or thing made the victim of another person or thing: He was *prey* to all sorts of illnesses. **4** *v.* To have or exert a harmful influence: His failure *preyed* on his mind. **5** *v.* To rob, kill, or commit violence: to *prey* on helpless people. **6** *n.* The habit of killing other animals for food: a bird of *prey*.

Prey

price [prīs] *n., v.* **priced, pric·ing 1** *n.* The amount of money or goods, etc., for which something is bought or sold. **2** *v.* To set a price on: The grocer *prices* milk at 25 cents a quart. **3** *v. informal* To ask the price of: We *priced* bicycles today. **4** *n.* The cost at which something is obtained. **5** *n.* Value; worth: a rug of high *price*. **6** *n.* A reward for the capture or death of someone. — **at any price** No matter how high the price is. — **beyond price** Worth a great deal; priceless.

price·less [prīs'lis] *adj.* **1** Worth more than any price; invaluable. **2** *informal* Very amusing.

prick [prik] **1** *v.* To make a small hole in; puncture: The needle *pricked* her finger. **2** *n.* A sharp, pointed thing. **3** *n.* A mark made by a sharp instrument. **4** *n.* A sharp pain from being pricked. **5** *v.* To affect with a sharp pain or mental anguish: The lie *pricked* his conscience. **6** *n.* A mental sting: the *prick* of conscience. **7** *v.* To mark or outline, as a design, with small holes or dots. — **prick up one's ears 1** To listen carefully. **2** To raise up the ears.

prick·le [prik'əl] *n., v.* **prick·led, prick·ling 1** *n.* A small sharp point, as on the bark of a plant. **2** *n.* A tingling or stinging feeling. **3** *v.* To have or cause a tingling feeling: Woolen clothes sometimes *prickle*. **4** *v.* To prick; pierce.

prick·ly [prik'lē] *adj.* **prick·li·er, prick·li·est 1** Having prickles. **2** Stinging, as if from a prick or sting: a *prickly* feeling.

prickly pear 1 A cactus with a flat stem. **2** Its pear-shaped, often prickly fruit.

pride [prīd] *n., v.* **prid·ed, prid·ing 1** *n.* A too great sense of one's own superiority; vanity; conceit. **2** *n.* A proper sense of one's own dignity and worth; self-respect. **3** *n.* Delight or pleasure: He takes great *pride* in his stamp collection. **4** *n.* Someone or something of which one is proud. **5** *v.* To take pride in (oneself).

Prickly pear

priest [prēst] *n.* **1** A clergyman in the Roman Catholic, Greek Orthodox, or Anglican church. **2** A person who is dedicated to the service of a deity and who performs religious rites.

priest·ess [prēs'tis] *n.* A woman or girl who acts as a priest.

priest·hood [prēst'hŏŏd] *n.* **1** The office or rank of a priest. **2** Priests as a group.

priest·ly [prēst'lē] *adj.* Of, having to do with, or suitable for a priest or the priesthood.

prig [prig] *n.* A person who acts as though he is wiser and more moral than others.

prig·gish [prig'ish] *adj.* Like a prig; smug.

prim [prim] *adj.* **prim·mer, prim·mest** Very precise and formal; stiffly proper and neat.

pri·ma·cy [prī'mə·sē] *n., pl.* **pri·ma·cies 1** The condition of being first in rank or excellence. **2** The duties or office of a primate.

pri·ma don·na [prē'mə don'ə] *pl.* **pri·ma don·nas 1** A leading female opera or concert singer. **2** *informal* A vain, temperamental person.

pri·mal [prī'məl] *adj.* **1** Being at the beginning; first; original. **2** Most important; chief.

pri·ma·ri·ly [prī·mer'ə·lē *or* prī'mer'ə·lē] *adv.* In the first place; originally; essentially.

pri·ma·ry [prī'mer·ē] *adj., n., pl.* **pri·ma·ries 1** *adj.* First in time or order: a *primary* school. **2** *adj.* Basic; from which other things may be made: Red, blue, and yellow are *primary* colors. **3** *adj.* First in degree or importance; chief. **4** *n.* Something that is first in degree or importance. **5** *n.* (*usually pl.*) A primary election.

primary accent A mark (′) used to show where the main accent or stress goes in a word.

primary election A preliminary election in which each political party chooses those candidates it wishes to run for public office.

pri·mate [prī'māt] *n.* **1** The archbishop or bishop ranking above other bishops in a nation or region. **2** Any of an order of mammals, often regarded as the most advanced, including the ape, monkey, lemur, man, etc.

prime [prīm] *adj., n., v.* **primed, prim·ing 1** *adj.* First in rank or importance; chief: the *prime* purpose. **2** *adj.* First in value or excellence; first-rate: a *prime* cut of steak. **3** *n.* The time of greatest activity, beauty, power, etc. **4** *n.* The beginning of anything, as of the year, the day, etc. **5** *n.* Spring. **6** *adj.* Not evenly divisible by any whole number except itself and 1. **3** and 5 are *prime* numbers. **7** *v.* To prepare; make ready for some purpose: A pump is *primed* by pouring water into it.

prime meridian
The meridian passing through Greenwich, England, from which longitude is calculated.

prime minister The chief official of the government in some countries; premier.

prim·er[1] [prim′ər] *n.* **1** A textbook for teaching children to read. **2** Any beginning textbook.

prim·er[2] [prī′mər] *n.* **1** Any device, as a cap, tube, etc., used to set off the main charge of a gun, mine, etc. **2** A person or thing that primes, prepares, or makes ready.

pri·me·val [prī·mē′vəl] *adj.* Belonging to the earliest ages; primitive.

prim·ing [prī′ming] *n.* **1** Something used to set off the charge of a gun, mine, etc. **2** The first layer of paint put on a surface.

prim·i·tive [prim′ə·tiv] **1** *adj.* Coming from or belonging to the earliest times. **2** *adj.* Simple or crude, like that of early ages: *primitive* pottery. **3** *n.* A person or thing that is primitive. **4** *n.* A work of art that comes from a very early period or, because of its simplicity and certain childlike qualities, looks as if it might have. **5** *n.* An artist who creates works that are or look primitive. — **prim′i·tive·ly** *adv.*

pri·mo·gen·i·ture [prī′mə·jen′ə·chər] *n.* **1** The condition of being the first-born child. **2** The right of the eldest son to inherit his father's title, all his property, etc.

pri·mor·di·al [prī·môr′dē·əl] *adj.* First in order or time; original; elemental.

prim·rose [prim′rōz] **1** *n.* A plant with small flowers of various colors. **2** *n., adj.* Pale yellow.

prince [prins] *n.* **1** The son or grandson of a king or queen. **2** A ruler of a small state or principality. **3** A person of the highest rank of any class or occupation: a merchant *prince*.

prince consort The husband of a reigning female sovereign.

Prince Ed·ward Island [ed′wərd] An island province off the coast of Canada, north of Nova Scotia.

prince·ly [prins′lē] *adj.* **prince·li·er, prince·li·est 1** Like a prince; noble; stately. **2** Suitable for a prince; magnificent.

Prince of Wales A title given to the eldest son of the British monarch when he is named heir to the throne.

prin·cess [prin′sis] *n.* **1** A female member of a royal family. **2** The wife of a prince. **3** A female sovereign, especially of a small state.

prin·ci·pal [prin′sə·pəl] **1** *adj.* First in rank or importance; chief; main: the *principal* points of a speech. **2** *n.* A person or thing of first rank or importance. **3** *n.* The head of an elementary school or high school. **4** *n.* Money or capital without interest or income accumulated. ◆ Remember that a *principal* is a person, and a *principle* is an idea. *Principal* is also an adjective meaning *first* or *chief*, whereas *principle* is always a noun: the *principal* actor in the play; the *principal* of our school; Freedom is an American *principle*.

prin·ci·pal·i·ty [prin′sə·pal′ə·tē] *n., pl.* **prin·ci·pal·i·ties 1** A country ruled by a prince. **2** A country that gives a prince his title. **3** The office or power of a prince.

prin·ci·pal·ly [prin′sə·pəl·ē] *adv.* Mainly; chiefly: I will talk *principally* to the girls.

principal parts The infinitive, past tense, past participle, and present participle of a verb. In this dictionary, when they are irregular, the past, past participle, and present participle are shown (*gave, given, giving*). When the principal parts are entirely regular, adding *-ed* and *-ing* to the infinitive with no change in spelling, they are not shown. When the past tense and past participle are the same, only the one is shown (*behaved, behaving*).

prin·ci·ple [prin′sə·pəl] *n.* **1** A general truth or rule on which other truths are based: the *principles* of democracy. **2** A law or rule of personal conduct. **3** Good moral standards; honesty; fairness: The judge is a man of *principle*. **4** A law or way of action by which something works in nature: the *principle* of relativity. — **on principle** Because of a principle or moral standard. ◆ See PRINCIPAL.

print [print] **1** *n.* Letters, words, etc., marked on paper with ink from type, plates, etc. **2** *n.* A picture or design made from an engraved plate or block. **3** *n.* Any fabric stamped with a design. **4** *v.* To stamp or impress (a letter, design, etc.) on or into a surface. **5** *v.* To produce, as a book, with inked type on paper. **6** *v.* To publish, as a newspaper. **7** *n.* A mark made by pressure. **8** *v.* To write in letters like those used in print. **9** *n.* In photography, a positive picture made from a negative. **10** *v.* To make (a positive picture) by light through a negative. — **in print 1** Printed. **2** Available for sale in printed form, as a book.

Floral print blouse

print·er [prin′tər] *n.* A person who sets type or runs a printing press.

print·ing [prin′ting] *n.* **1** The making of reading matter by means of type or plates and a printing press. **2** Something printed. **3** The number of copies of anything printed at one time. **4** Handwriting that looks like print. **5** The act of a person who prints.

printing press A machine used in printing.

pri·or[1] [prī′ər] *adj.* Coming before in time, order, or importance. — **prior to** Before.

pri·or[2] [prī′ər] *n.* A monk who is the head of a priory.

pri·or·ess [prī′ər·is] *n.* A nun who is the head of a priory.

pri·or·i·ty [prī·ôr′ə·tē] *n., pl.* **pri·or·i·ties 1** The condition or fact of being prior. **2** Something that is first in importance or order: High on their

---

add, āce, câre, pälm; end, ēqual; it, īce; odd, ōpen, ôrder; tŏŏk, pōōl; up, bûrn; ə = a in *above*, e in *sicken*, i in *possible*, o in *melon*, u in *circus*; yōō = u in *fuse*; oil; pout; check; ring; thin; this; zh in *vision*. For ¶ reference, see page 64 · HOW TO

priorities was a trip to Europe. **3** The right of being first in importance, order, or rank, as in an emergency: Defense plants have *priorities*.

pri·or·y [prī′ər·ē] *n., pl.* **pri·or·ies** A house or establishment where monks or nuns live and work, headed by a prior or prioress.

prism [priz′əm] *n.* **1** A transparent glass object, triangular in cross section, that can break up white light into rainbow colors. **2** A solid figure whose ends are identical, parallel polygons and whose sides are parallelograms.

Prisms

pris·mat·ic [priz·mat′ik] *adj.* **1** Of or like a prism. **2** Formed by a prism, as the rainbow colors of red, orange, yellow, green, blue, indigo, and violet. — **pris·mat′i·cal·ly** *adv.*

pris·on [priz′(ə)n] **1** *n.* A public building where people are kept while awaiting trial or serving a sentence for breaking the law. **2** *n.* Any place where a person is kept against his will. **3** *v.* To imprison.

pris·on·er [priz′(ə)n·ər] *n.* **1** A person who is held in a prison. **2** A person captured by the enemy during a war.

pris·tine [pris′tēn] *adj.* **1** Of or having to do with the earliest state or time; primitive. **2** Pure or fresh; untouched; unspoiled.

prith·ee [priᵺ′ē] *interj.* I pray thee: used only in poems or old stories.

pri·va·cy [prī′və·sē] *n., pl.* **pri·va·cies** **1** A being private or away from others; seclusion. **2** A being secret; secrecy.

pri·vate [prī′vit] **1** *adj.* Away from public view; secluded. **2** *adj.* Not for public or common use: *private* property. **3** *adj.* Having no official rank or office: a *private* citizen. **4** *adj.* Not generally known; secret. **5** *n.* A military rank. In the U.S. Army, a private is the lowest-ranking soldier, below a corporal. — **in private** In secret. — **pri′vate·ly** *adv.*

pri·va·teer [prī′və·tir′] **1** *n.* An armed ship that is privately owned but is given permission by a government to attack enemy ships in a war. **2** *n.* The commander or one of the crew of such a ship. **3** *v.* To sail in or as a privateer.

pri·va·tion [prī·vā′shən] *n.* The lack of the necessities or common comforts of life: People endure great *privation* during famines.

priv·et [priv′it] *n.* An ornamental, bushy shrub with small leaves, widely used for hedges.

priv·i·lege [priv′ə·lij] *n., v.* **priv·i·leged, priv·i·leg·ing** **1** *n.* A special benefit, favor, or advantage enjoyed only under special conditions. **2** *n.* A basic civil, legal, or political right: the *privilege* of voting. **3** *v.* To grant a privilege to. **4** *adj. use:* a *privileged* person.

priv·i·ly [priv′ə·lē] *adv.* In private; secretly.

priv·y [priv′ē] *adj., n., pl.* **priv·ies** **1** *adj.* Private; confidential: seldom used today. **2** *n.* An outdoor toilet; outhouse. — **privy to** Having private knowledge about.

privy council A group serving as personal advisors to a sovereign.

prize¹ [prīz] *n., adj., v.* **prized, priz·ing 1** *n.* Something that is offered or won as a reward for superiority or success. **2** *n.* Anything to be tried for. **3** *adj.* Awarded as a prize: a *prize* medal. **4** *adj.* Entitled to a prize: a *prize* pig. **5.** *v.* To value highly; treasure.

prize² [prīz] *n., v.* **prized, priz·ing 1** *n.* Plunder, as a captured enemy ship and its cargo. **2** *v.* To seize as plunder, as a ship.

prize fight A fight between professional boxers for which they are paid. — **prize fighter** — **prize fighting**

pro¹ [prō] *n., pl.* **pros,** *adv.* **1** *n.* An argument or vote in favor of something. **2** *n.* (*usually pl.*) A person who votes for or favors something. **3** *adv.* On the side in favor: to discuss a matter *pro* and con.

pro² [prō] *n., pl.* **pros** *informal* **1** A professional athlete. **2** An expert in any field.

prob·a·bil·i·ty [prob′ə·bil′ə·tē] *n., pl.* **prob·a·bil·i·ties** **1** The condition of being probable; likelihood: the *probability* of peace. **2** Something probable, as an event, chance, etc. **3** The likelihood that a particular event or result will occur, often determined as the ratio of its occurrence in a large number of trials to the total number of trials. — **in all probability** Very likely; probably.

prob·a·ble [prob′ə·bəl] *adj.* Likely to be true or to happen: a *probable* outcome.

prob·a·bly [prob′ə·blē] *adv.* In all probability; very likely; presumably.

pro·bate [prō′bāt] *n., adj., v.* **pro·bat·ed, pro·bat·ing 1** *n.* A proving that a will is genuine and lawful. **2** *adj.* Of or having to do with such a proving. **3** *v.* To prove (a will) to be genuine and lawful.

pro·ba·tion [prō·bā′shən] *n.* **1** A method of allowing a person who has been convicted of a minor crime to go free under the supervision of a probation officer and with a suspended sentence. **2** A time of trial designed to test character, qualifications, etc., as of a new employee.

pro·ba·tion·er [prō·bā′shən·ər] *n.* A person on probation.

probation officer A person assigned by a court to supervise persons whose prison sentences have been suspended.

probe [prōb] *v.* **probed, prob·ing,** *n.* **1** *n.* A slender instrument for exploring cavities in the body, wounds, etc. **2** *v.* To explore with a probe. **3** *v.* To investigate or examine thoroughly. **4** *n.* A complete investigation or inquiry, as into crime or wrongdoing.

pro·bi·ty [prō′bə·tē] *n.* Honesty; integrity.

prob·lem [prob′ləm] *n.* **1** A confusing or puzzling question or situation that is difficult to solve. **2** Any puzzling or difficult thing or person. **3** *adj. use:* a *problem* child. **4** In mathematics, something to be done or solved.

prob·lem·at·ic [prob′ləm·at′ik] *adj.* Being or having to do with a problem; questionable.

prob·lem·at·i·cal [prob′ləm·at′i·kəl] *adj.*
Problematic. **— prob′lem·at′i·cal·ly** *adv.*

pro·bos·cis [prō·bos′is] *n., pl.* **pro·bos·cis·es**
or **pro·bos·ci·des** [prō·bos′ə·dēz] **1** An elephant's trunk. **2** A long, flexible snout, as of the
tapir. **3** A tubular structure in some insects used
for sucking: A mosquito has a *proboscis*.

pro·ce·dure [prə·sē′jər] *n.* **1** A way of proceeding; method of doing something. **2** A way of
conducting a meeting, parliament, etc.

pro·ceed [prə·sēd′] *v.* **1** To go on, especially
after a stop. **2** To begin and carry on an activity:
John *proceeded* to read his lesson. **3** To come;
issue: Colds *proceed* from germs.

pro·ceed·ing [prə·sē′ding] *n.* **1** An act or group
of actions. **2** (*pl.*) The records or minutes of the
meetings of a club, business, etc. **3** (*often pl.*) Any
action started in a court; legal action.

pro·ceeds [prō′sēdz] *n.pl.* **1** The money or
profit obtained from the sale of goods, work, etc.
2 The results of an action or procedure.

proc·ess [pros′es] **1** *n.* A series of operations or
a method for producing something: a new *process* for making steel. **2** *v.* To prepare or treat
by a special method: to *process* cloth. **3** *n.* A
series of continuous developments: the *process*
of growth. **4** *n.* A course of action that continues
for a period of time: My mother is in the *process*
of ironing. **5** *n.* A writ or order to a person to
come before a court; summons. **6** *n.* An outgrowth, as from a bone.

pro·ces·sion [prə·sesh′ən] *n.* **1** A group, as of
persons, cars, etc., arranged one behind the other
and moving in a formal way; parade. **2** The act
of proceeding in such a way.

pro·ces·sion·al [prə·sesh′ən·əl] **1** *adj.* Of or
having to do with a procession: a *processional*
anthem. **2** *n.* A book containing the services in
a religious procession. **3** *n.* The music played
or sung in a religious procession.

pro·claim [prō·klām′] *v.* To announce publicly;
make known; declare: to *proclaim* a victory.

proc·la·ma·tion [prok′lə·mā′shən] *n.* **1** A pro-
claiming. **2** An official, public announcement.

pro·con·sul [prō·kon′səl] *n.* In ancient Rome,
the governor or army commander of a province.

pro·cras·ti·nate [prō·kras′tə·nāt] *v.* **pro·cras·
ti·nat·ed, pro·cras·ti·nat·ing** To put off taking action until a future time. **— pro·cras′ti·
na′tion** *n.* **— pro·cras′ti·na′tor** *n.*

proc·tor [prok′tər] **1** *n.* An official in a school
or college in charge of keeping order, supervising
examinations, etc. **2** *v.* To supervise (an examination).

proc·u·ra·tor [prok′yə·rā′tər] *n.* **1** A person
employed to act for and manage the affairs of
another. **2** In ancient Rome, a person in charge
of the finances and revenues of a province.

pro·cure [prō·kyŏŏr′] *v.* **pro·cured, pro·cur·
ing** **1** To get by some effort or means; acquire.

2 To bring about; cause: to *procure* an end of
the fighting. **— pro·cure′ment** *n.*

prod [prod] *v.* **prod·ded, prod·ding** **1** *v.* To
poke with or as if with a
pointed stick. **2** *n.* A thrust
or poke. **3** *n.* Any pointed
stick used for prodding; goad.
4 *v.* To urge; goad: John's
teacher *prodded* him to study.
5 *n.* A reminder.

prod·i·gal [prod′ə·gəl] **1** *adj.*
Wasteful, as of money, time,
etc. **2** *n.* A person who is
wasteful; spendthrift. **3** *adj.*
Bountiful; lavish: a *prodigal*
harvest. **— prod′i·gal·ly**
adv.

Cowboy using prod

prod·i·gal·i·ty [prod′ə·gal′ə·tē] *n., pl.* **prod·i·
gal·i·ties** **1** Wastefulness; extravagance. **2** A
generous supply; abundance.

pro·dig·ious [prə·dij′əs] *adj.* **1** Enormous in
size, quantity, or degree. **2** Marvelous; amazing.

prod·i·gy [prod′ə·jē] *n., pl.* **prod·i·gies** **1** A
child or young person with amazing talent or
brilliance. **2** Something so out of the ordinary
that it produces wonder or amazement.

pro·duce [*v.* prə·d(y)ōōs′, *n.* prod′(y)ōōs *or*
prō′d(y)ōōs] *v.* **pro·duced, pro·duc·ing,** *n.* **1**
v. To bring into being; yield: Orchards *produce*
fruit. **2** *n.* Farm products, as vegetables, fruits,
etc., grown for market. **3** *v.* To bring into being
by mental effort; compose, write, etc.: to *produce*
a book. **4** *v.* To bring about; cause: His words
produced a violent reaction. **5** *v.* To bring into
sight, exhibit; show: to *produce* evidence. **6** *v.*
To manufacture; make: to *produce* automobiles.
7 *v.* To bring to performance, as a play.

pro·duc·er [prə·d(y)ōō′sər] *n.* **1** A person or
thing that produces. **2** A person who puts up
the money for and generally controls the production of a play, concert, movie, etc.

prod·uct [prod′əkt] *n.* **1** Something produced,
as by growth, labor, study, or skill. **2** A result:
Crime is often a *product* of poverty. **3** The result
obtained by multiplication: 12 is the *product* of
4 and 3.

pro·duc·tion [prə·duk′shən] *n.* **1** The act or
process of producing. **2** Something produced: a
new *production* on the Broadway stage.

pro·duc·tive [prə·duk′tiv] *adj.* **1** Producing or
tending to produce; fertile: a *productive* field.
2 Producing profits or value: *productive* labor. **3** Causing; yielding: Our discussions are
productive of many good ideas. **— pro·duc′·
tive·ness** *n.* **— pro′duc·tiv′i·ty** *n.*

prof. Abbreviation of PROFESSOR.

prof·a·na·tion [prof′ə·nā′shən] *n.* The act of
profaning; the dishonoring of sacred things.

pro·fane [prə·fān′] *v.* **pro·faned, pro·fan·
ing,** *adj.* **1** *v.* To treat (something sacred) with

add, āce, câre, pälm;   end, ēqual;   it, īce;   odd, ōpen, ôrder;   tŏŏk, pōōl;   up, bûrn;
ə = a in *above*, e in *sicken*, i in *possible*, o in *melon*, u in *circus*;   yōō = u in *fuse*;   oil;   pout;
check;   ring;   thin;   this;   zh in *vision*.   For ¶ reference, see page 64 · HOW TO

disrespect or abuse. **2** *adj.* Showing disrespect toward the Deity or sacred things; blasphemous. **3** *adj.* Not dealing with sacred things; not religious: *profane* art. **— pro·fane′ly** *adv.* ◆ *Profane* goes back to a Latin word meaning *outside the temple*, and therefore *not sacred*.

pro·fan·i·ty [prə·fan′ə·tē] *n.*, *pl.* **pro·fan·i·ties** **1** A being profane. **2** Profane language; cursing; swearing.

pro·fess [prə·fes′] *v.* **1** To say openly; declare. **2** To make a pretense of; pretend: He *professes* to be very learned. **3** To declare belief in: to *profess* a religion.

pro·fessed [prə·fest′] *adj.* **1** Openly admitted; acknowledged: a *professed* thief. **2** Falsely claimed; pretended: his *professed* innocence.

pro·fes·sion [prə·fesh′ən] *n.* **1** An occupation requiring a good education and mental rather than physical labor. **2** The people as a group who follow such an occupation. **3** A declaration: *professions* of good will. ◆ See TRADE.

pro·fes·sion·al [prə·fesh′ən·əl] **1** *adj.* Of, having to do with, or working in a profession: a lawyer is a *professional* man. **2** *adj.* Doing for money something which others do just for pleasure: a *professional* athlete. **3** *adj.* Performed by or consisting of professional people: *professional* sports. **4** *n.* A person who does professional work. **5** *n.* A person highly skilled in some art, craft, etc. **— pro·fes′sion·al·ly** *adv.*

pro·fes·sor [prə·fes′ər] *n.* **1** A teacher, especially one of the highest rank in a college or university. **2** A person who openly declares his beliefs. **— pro·fes′sor·ship** *n.*

pro·fes·so·ri·al [prō′fə·sôr′ē·əl] *adj.* Of, like, or having to do with a professor.

prof·fer [prof′ər] *v.* To offer: He *proffered* a bouquet of roses.

pro·fi·cient [prə·fish′ənt] *adj.* Very skilled; expert: *proficient* at adding figures. **— pro·fi′·cien·cy** *n.* **— pro·fi′cient·ly** *adv.*

pro·file [prō′fīl] *n.* **1** The outline of a human face as seen from the side. **2** A drawing of this outline. **3** A short biographical sketch.

prof·it [prof′it] **1** *n.* Any advantage or gain; benefit. **2** *v.* To be of advantage or benefit to: Quarrels *profit* no one. **3** *v.* To get an advantage; benefit: We *profited* from the sale of our old car. **4** *n.* (*often pl.*) The amount of money gained in a business transaction after deducting all expenses.

Profile

prof·it·a·ble [prof′it·ə·bəl] *adj.* Bringing profit or gain. **— prof′it·a·bly** *adv.*

prof·i·teer [prof′ə·tir′] **1** *n.* A person who makes an unfair profit by charging high prices for badly needed goods. **2** *v.* To make such profits.

prof·li·ga·cy [prof′lə·gə·sē] *n.* **1** Wild or immoral behavior. **2** Extravagance in spending money.

prof·li·gate [prof′lə·git] **1** *adj.* Without virtue or morals; wicked. **2** *adj.* Spending money wildly. **3** *n.* A person who is profligate.

pro·found [prə·found′] *adj.* **1** Showing deep or penetrating intellect or knowledge. **2** Deep; complete: *profound* sleep. **3** Thorough; sweeping: *profound* changes. **4** Intensely felt: *profound* love. **— pro·found′ly** *adv.*

pro·fun·di·ty [prə·fun′də·tē] *n.*, *pl.* **pro·fun·di·ties** **1** The condition or quality of being profound. **2** Something profound, as a statement, idea, etc.

pro·fuse [prə·fyoōs′] *adj.* **1** Giving lavishly; liberal: *profuse* in his thanks. **2** Overflowing; abundant: *profuse* tears. **— pro·fuse′ly** *adv.*

pro·fu·sion [prə·fyoō′zhən] *n.* A large or abundant supply: a *profusion* of ornaments.

pro·gen·i·tor [prō·jen′ə·tər] *n.* A forefather.

prog·e·ny [proj′ə·nē] *n.* Children; descendants.

prog·nos·tic [prog·nos′tik] **1** *adj.* Predicting or foretelling. **2** *n.* A sign of some future occurrence; an omen.

prog·nos·ti·cate [prog·nos′tə·kāt] *v.* **prog·nos·ti·cat·ed, prog·nos·ti·cat·ing** To foretell or predict. **— prog·nos′ti·ca′tion** *n.*

pro·gram [prō′gram] *n.*, *v.* **pro·gramed** or **pro·grammed, pro·gram·ing** or **pro·gram·ming** **1** *n.* A performance, entertainment, or ceremony, especially a scheduled performance on radio or television. **2** *v.* To include in a program. **3** *n.* A printed announcement or schedule of events, especially one for a theatrical performance. **4** *n.* Any course or plan arranged in advance: I have a good *program* in school. **5** *n.* A series of instructions directing an electronic computer to perform certain operations in a certain order. **6** *v.* To work out or make up a program for: to *program* a computer.

pro·gramme [prō′gram] *n. British* Program.

prog·ress [*n.* prog′res, *v.* prə·gres′] **1** *n.* A moving forward in space. **2** *v.* To move forward. **3** *n.* A gradual development; improvement: the *progress* of civilization. **4** *v.* To advance; develop; improve: to *progress* in one's studies.

pro·gres·sion [prə·gresh′ən] *n.* **1** A progressing; advancement. **2** A series or sequence, as of actions: A *progression* of mistakes cost him his job. **3** A sequence of numbers in which every number is related to the ones after and before it by the same rule, as 3, 8, 13, 18, etc.

pro·gres·sive [prə·gres′iv] **1** *adj.* Moving forward; advancing: *progressive* stages of development. **2** *adj.* Spreading from one part to others; increasing: *progressive* paralysis. **3** *adj.* Working for or desiring progress or reform, especially in politics, education, and religion. **4** *n.* A person who believes in progress or reform. **— pro·gres′sive·ly** *adv.*

pro·hib·it [prō·hib′it] *v.* **1** To forbid, especially by authority or law: to *prohibit* parking. **2** To prevent or hinder: Icy roads *prohibited* us from driving.

pro·hi·bi·tion [prō′ə·bish′ən] *n.* **1** The act of prohibiting. **2** A law forbidding anything, espe-

cially the making and selling of alcoholic liquors.
3 (*written* **Prohibition**) The years from 1920 to
1933, when Federal law prohibited the making
and selling of alcoholic liquors. — **pro'hi·bi'·
tion·ist** *n.*

pro·hib·i·tive [prō·hib'ə·tiv] *adj.* Prohibiting;
tending to prevent: The *prohibitive* cost of mink
coats keeps many people from buying them.

proj·ect [*n.* proj'ekt, *v.* prə·jekt'] **1** *n.* Something thought of in the mind, as a course of action; plan. **2** *v.* To propose or plan. **3** *n.* A
problem, task, or piece of work, as one given to a
student or a group of students. **4** *v.* To extend
forward or out; jut: Bay windows *project* from
houses. **5** *v.* To throw forward, as a missile. **6** *v.*
To cause (an image or shadow) to be visible on a
surface: to *project* a slide on a screen.

pro·jec·tile [prə·jek'təl] **1** *adj.* Projecting or
thrusting forward. **2** *n.* An object thrown or to
be thrown by force, especially one fired from a
cannon, gun, or other weapon.

pro·jec·tion [prə·jek'shən] *n.* **1** A projecting.
2 Something that projects or juts out.

pro·jec·tor [prə·jek'tər] *n.* A device for projecting slides or movies onto a
screen.

Pro·kof·iev [prō·kôf'yəf],
Sergei Sergeyevich,
1891–1953, Russian and Soviet composer.

pro·le·tar·i·an [prō'lə·târ'·
ē·ən] **1** *adj.* Of or having to do
with the proletariat, or working class. **2** *n.* A member of
the proletariat.

pro·le·tar·i·at [prō'lə·târ'·
ē·ət] *n.* The working class, especially those people who do
manual labor or industrial
work.

Motion picture
projector

pro·lif·ic [prō·lif'ik] *adj.* **1** Producing offspring
or fruit abundantly. **2** Producing a great
deal: a *prolific* writer. — **pro·lif'i·cal·ly** *adv.*

pro·lix [prō'liks] *adj.* Too wordy; too long and
boring. — **pro·lix'i·ty** *n.*

pro·logue or **pro·log** [prō'lôg] *n.* **1** An introduction, as a preface to a book or a speech by one
of the actors to an audience before a play begins.
2 Any introductory act or event.

pro·long [prə·lông'] *v.* To make longer in time
or space; continue; lengthen: to *prolong* a meal.

pro·lon·ga·tion [prō'lông·gā'shən] *n.* **1** The
act of prolonging. **2** Something added; extension: a week's *prolongation* of summer school.

prom [prom] *n. U.S. informal* A formal dance
or ball at a school or college.

prom·e·nade [prom'ə·nād' or prom'ə·näd'] *n.,
v.* **prom·e·nad·ed, prom·e·nad·ing 1** *n.* A
walk for amusement or exercise; stroll. **2** *v.* To
take a promenade. **3** *n.* A place for promenading,

as a boardwalk, deck of a ship, etc. **4** *n.* A
march, as at the beginning of a ball.

Pro·me·theus [prə·mē'thyoos *or* prə·mē'thē·əs]
n. In Greek myths, the Titan who stole fire from
heaven and gave it to man. He was chained to a
rock by Zeus as a punishment.

prom·i·nence [prom'ə·nəns] *n.* **1** A being
prominent: His *prominence* in the political world
was very great. **2** Something prominent. **3** One
of the tongues of flame that shoot out from the
sun's surface, seen during a total eclipse.

prom·i·nent [prom'ə·nənt] *adj.* **1** Jutting out;
projecting: *prominent* teeth. **2** Well-known; eminent: *prominent* in the community. **3** Easily
seen; conspicuous: *prominent* signs on the roadside. — **prom'i·nent·ly** *adv.*

pro·mis·cu·ous [prə·mis'kyoo·əs] *adj.* **1** Mixed
together without order: a *promiscuous* pile of
papers. **2** Lacking any thought, purpose, or
plan: a *promiscuous* taste in television programs.
— **pro·mis'cu·ous·ly** *adv.*

prom·ise [prom'is] *n., v.* **prom·ised, prom·is·
ing 1** *n.* A positive statement made by one person to another that he will or will not perform a
certain act. **2** *v.* To make a promise: to *promise*
that goods will be delivered. **3** *v.* To make a
promise of: Tom *promised* his mother flowers.
4 *n.* Something that gives hope or expectation
of future excellence or success: to show *promise*
as an athlete. **5** *v.* To give reason for expecting:
Clouds *promise* rain.

prom·is·ing [prom'is·ing] *adj.* Giving promise
of good results or success: a *promising* student.

Promised Land In the Bible, Canaan, the
land promised to Abraham by God. **2** (*written*
promised land) Any place of expected happiness.

prom·is·so·ry note [prom'ə·sôr'ē] A written
promise to pay a sum of money at a given time or
on demand.

prom·on·to·ry [prom'ən·tôr'ē] *n., pl.* **prom·
on·to·ries** A high point of land sticking out into
the sea; headland.

pro·mote [prə·mōt'] *v.* **pro·mot·ed, pro·mot·
ing 1** To contribute to the progress, development, or growth of; work for: to *promote* good
health. **2** To advance to a higher position,
grade, or honor: Sue was *promoted* from the third
grade to the fourth. **3** To try to make popular,
as by advertising.

pro·mot·er [prə·mō'tər] *n.* **1** A person or thing
that promotes. **2** A person who tries to make a
business successful, as by raising money for it,
selling its products, advertising, etc.

pro·mo·tion [prə·mō'shən] *n.* **1** Advancement
in rank or grade. **2** Encouragement; advancement: *promotion* of a good cause.

prompt [prompt] **1** *adj.* Ready; quick; on
time; punctual: *prompt* to obey. **2** *adj.* Done
quickly: *prompt* service. **3** *v.* To urge; stir up;

add, āce, câre, pälm; end, ēqual; it, īce; odd, ōpen, ôrder; tōŏk, pōōl; up, bûrn;
ə = a in *above*, e in *sicken*, i in *possible*, o in *melon*, u in *circus*; yōō = u in *fuse*; oil; pout;
check; ring; thin; this; zh in *vision*. For ¶ reference, see page 64 · HOW TO

incite: The insult *prompted* them to fight. **4** *v.* To suggest; inspire: Fog *prompts* gloom. **5** *v.* To act as a prompter to: to *prompt* an actor. — **prompt′ly** *adv.* — **prompt′ness** *n.*

prompt·er [promp′tər] *n.* In a theater, a person who reminds the actors of their lines when they forget them.

promp·ti·tude [promp′tə·t(y)ōōd] *n.* Promptness; liveliness; readiness.

pro·mul·gate [prō·mul′gāt *or* prom′əl·gāt] *v.* **pro·mul·gat·ed, pro·mul·gat·ing** To make known officially; put into effect by public announcement: to *promulgate* a new law. — **pro′·mul·ga′tion** *n.*

pron. Abbreviation of PRONOUN.

prone [prōn] *adj.* **1** Lying flat, especially with the face downward. **2** Given or inclined: She is *prone* to gossip. — **prone′ness** *n.*

Prone position

prong [prông] *n.* **1** A pointed end of an instrument, as the tine of a fork. **2** Any pointed part that projects, as on a deer's antler.

pronged [prôngd] *adj.* Having prongs.

prong·horn [prông′hôrn′] *n.*, *pl.* **prong·horns** or **prong·horn** An animal like the antelope, found in western North America.

pro·noun [prō′noun] *n.* A word that is used instead of a noun, as *I* in "I am going," *who* in "Who goes there?" and *whom* in "the man to whom I spoke."

Pronghorn, 30–36 in. high at shoulder

pro·nounce [prə·nouns′] *v.* **pro·nounced, pro·nounc·ing** **1** To make the sound or sounds of: to *pronounce* a word clearly. **2** To declare: to *pronounce* someone guilty. **3** To utter or say officially or solemnly: to *pronounce* judgment.

pro·nounced [prə·nounst′] *adj.* Strongly marked; quite noticeable; decided: She talks with a *pronounced* lisp.

pro·nounce·ment [prə·nouns′mənt] *n.* A formal declaration or announcement.

pro·nun·ci·a·tion [prə·nun′sē·ā′shən] *n.* The act or way of saying words or sounds: A word often has several correct *pronunciations*.

proof [prōōf] **1** *n.* A proving, especially a showing that something is true or accurate by evidence: The test gives *proof* of the fabric's strength. **2** *n.* Anything that is used to show beyond doubt that something is true; evidence. **3** *n.* A trial of strength, truth, excellence, etc.: The *proof* of a boat lies in the sailing. **4** *n.* A trial sheet printed from type, used for making corrections. **5** *n.* A trial print from a negative of a photograph. **6** *adj.* Able to resist: He was *proof* against bribes.

-proof A combining form meaning: **1** Able to stand up to; not damaged by, as in *waterproof*. **2** Protected against, as in *mothproof*.

proof·read [prōōf′rēd′] *v.* **proof·read, proof·read·ing** To read and correct printers' proofs. — **proof′read′er** *n.*

prop [prop] *n., v.* **propped, prop·ping** **1** *n.* A rigid object, as a beam or a pole, used to support or hold something up. **2** *n.* A person who gives support or help. **3** *v.* To support or keep from falling with or as if with a prop: to *prop* up a tree. **4** *v.* To lean or place: He *propped* the oar against the seat of the boat.

prop·a·gan·da [prop′ə·gan′də] *n.* **1** An effort to persuade a group of people to adopt or support certain ideas, attitudes, or actions. **2** A group of facts or ideas used in such an effort. ◆ *Propaganda* is now often thought of as a collection of lies and half-truths calculated to give a false or misleading picture of something.

A plant prop

prop·a·gan·dist [prop′ə·gan′dist] **1** *n.* A person who spreads propaganda. **2** *adj.* Of or like propaganda.

prop·a·gan·dize [prop′ə·gan′dīz] *v.* **prop·a·gan·dized, prop·a·gan·diz·ing** **1** To spread (ideas, etc.) by propaganda. **2** To spread propaganda. ¶3

prop·a·gate [prop′ə·gāt] *v.* **prop·a·gat·ed, prop·a·gat·ing** **1** To cause (animals or plants) to reproduce; breed: to *propagate* oranges. **2** To reproduce or breed. **3** To spread, as an idea or belief: to *propagate* religious faith. **4** To send out (light, heat, sound, etc.) through a medium such as air.

prop·a·ga·tion [prop′ə·gā′shən] *n.* **1** A propagating; reproduction. **2** A sending out or scattering: the *propagation* of news.

pro·pel [prə·pel′] *v.* **pro·pelled, pro·pel·ling** To cause to move forward or ahead; drive or urge forward: Wind *propels* the fallen leaves.

pro·pel·lant [prə·pel′ənt] *n.* **1** A person or thing that propels. **2** The fuel plus the oxygen supply used to propel a rocket.

pro·pel·lent [prə·pel′ənt] **1** *adj.* Able to propel; propelling. **2** *n.* A propellant.

pro·pel·ler [prə·pel′ər] *n.* **1** A person or thing that propels. **2** A device for pulling or pushing an aircraft or vessel through air or water by means of rotating blades set in their hub at a slant so that they bite into the air or water and thrust it back.

Propeller of an outboard motor

pro·pen·si·ty [prə·pen′sə·tē] *n.*, *pl.* **pro·pen·si·ties** A natural tendency or leaning; bent: to have a *propensity* to contradict one's elders.

prop·er [prop′ər] *adj.* **1** Suitable; fitting: Crying is *proper* to babies. **2** Specially suited: the *proper* medicine for a cold. **3** Too formal; prim: a *proper* old lady. **4** Modest; decent. **5** Designating a particular person, place, or thing: *proper* names. **6** Meant in its strict sense: We live in the city *proper*, not in the suburbs.

proper fraction A fraction in which the numerator is less than the denominator, as $\frac{3}{4}$.

prop·er·ly [prop′ər·lē] *adv.* In a proper manner.

proper noun A noun that names a particular person, place, or thing and is always capitalized, as Paul, Venice, Tuesday, etc.

prop·er·ty [prop′ər·tē] *n., pl.* **prop·er·ties 1** Anything that a person may legally own, as land, stocks, etc.; any possession. **2** Legal title; ownership. **3** A piece of land. **4** Any of the special qualities or characteristics that belong to something. **5** Any object used in a play, opera, etc., other than scenery and costumes.

proph·e·cy [prof′ə·sē] *n., pl.* **proph·e·cies 1** A prediction made under divine influence. **2** Any prediction. **3** The ability to prophesy or foretell, or the act of doing it.

proph·e·sy [prof′ə·sī] *v.* **proph·e·sied, proph·e·sy·ing 1** To say or foretell with or as if with divine inspiration. **2** To predict; foretell.

proph·et [prof′it] *n.* **1** A person who speaks or writes with or as if with a divine message. **2** Any person who foretells the future. ◆ *Prophet* goes back to two Greek words meaning *to speak before*.

proph·et·ess [prof′it·is] *n.* A female prophet.

pro·phet·ic [prə·fet′ik] *adj.* Of, having to do with, or like a prophet or a prophecy.

pro·phy·lac·tic [prō′fə·lak′tik] **1** *adj.* Tending to protect against or ward off disease, infection, etc. **2** *n.* A prophylactic medicine, device, or treatment.

pro·pin·qui·ty [prō·ping′kwə·tē] *n.* **1** Nearness in place or time. **2** Nearness in relationship.

pro·pi·ti·ate [prō·pish′ē·āt] *v.* **pro·pi·ti·at·ed, pro·pi·ti·at·ing** To cause to be favorable or friendly; appease. — **pro·pi′ti·a′tion** *n.*

pro·pi·ti·a·to·ry [prō·pish′ē·ə·tôr′ē] *adj.* **1** Of or having to do with propitiation: a *propitiatory* ceremony. **2** That asks for mercy or forgiveness: to send flowers as a *propitiatory* gesture.

pro·pi·tious [prō·pish′əs] *adj.* **1** Favorable; helpful: *propitious* events. **2** Feeling kindly; gracious. — **pro·pi′tious·ly** *adv.*

pro·por·tion [prə·pôr′shən] **1** *n.* Relative size, number, or degree between things; ratio: The *proportion* of students to teachers in our school is twenty to one; that is, there are twenty students for each teacher. **2** *v.* To adjust properly to relative size, amount, or degree: to *proportion* one's expenses to one's income. **3** *n.* Fitting or suitable arrange-

Lack of proportion

ment or balance of parts: His large glasses are not in *proportion* to his small face. **4** *v.* To make with a pleasing or harmonious relation of parts: to *proportion* a piece of sculpture. **5** *n.* A share or part: A large *proportion* of the students were sick last week. **6** *n.* (*pl.*) Size; dimensions: a painting of large *proportions*. **7** *n.* The relation of four numbers when the quotient of the first two equals the quotient of the second two: $8 \div 4 = 6 \div 3$ is a *proportion*.

pro·por·tion·al [prə·pôr′shən·əl] *adj.* Of, having to do with, or being in proportion: Your reward is *proportional* to your effort. — **pro·por′tion·al·ly** *adv.*

pro·por·tion·ate [prə·pôr′shən·it] *adj.* Proportional. — **pro·por′tion·ate·ly** *adv.*

pro·po·sal [prə·pō′zəl] *n.* **1** A proposing. **2** Something proposed, as a scheme or plan. **3** An offer of marriage.

pro·pose [prə·pōz′] *v.* **pro·posed, pro·pos·ing 1** To put forward for acceptance or consideration: to *propose* a budget. **2** To nominate: I *propose* Ann for president. **3** To intend; plan: We *propose* to go home. **4** To offer marriage.

prop·o·si·tion [prop′ə·zish′ən] *n.* **1** A scheme or plan put forth for consideration or approval; proposal. **2** A statement to be discussed or debated. **3** In mathematics, a statement of a truth to be demonstrated or of an operation to be performed.

pro·pound [prə·pound′] *v.* To put forward for consideration, solution, etc.; suggest; submit.

pro·pri·e·tar·y [prə·prī′ə·ter′ē] *adj.* **1** Of, having to do with, or belonging to a proprietor. **2** Indicating a product, as a medicine, owned by a company under a copyright, patent, etc.

pro·pri·e·tor [prə·prī′ə·tər] *n.* The legal owner of something, as a store, business, etc.

pro·pri·e·ty [prə·prī′ə·tē] *n., pl.* **pro·pri·e·ties 1** The quality of being proper; correctness: Mr. Walsh questioned the *propriety* of his daughter's going unescorted to the dance. **2** (*often pl.*) Ways of behaving that are proper according to the standards of good society: to observe the *proprieties*.

pro·pul·sion [prə·pul′shən] *n.* **1** The act or operation of propelling. **2** A propelling force.

pro·sa·ic [prō·zā′ik] *adj.* **1** Not interesting; unimaginative; ordinary; dull. **2** Of or like prose. — **pro·sa′i·cal·ly** *adv.*

pro·scribe [prō·skrīb′] *v.* **pro·scribed, pro·scrib·ing 1** To speak against or condemn; prohibit: The teacher *proscribed* the chewing of gum in class. **2** To outlaw or banish.

pro·scrip·tion [prō·skrip′shən] *n.* **1** A prohibition or condemnation: a *proscription* against the chewing of gum. **2** Banishment.

prose [prōz] *n.* Speech or writing without rhyme or meter; any speech or writing that is not poetry.

---

add, āce, câre, pälm;   end, ēqual;   it, īce;   odd, ōpen, ôrder;   tŏŏk, pōōl;   up, bûrn;
ə = a in *above*, e in *sicken*, i in *possible*, o in *melon*, u in *circus*;   yōō = u in *fuse*;   oil;   pout;
check;   ring;   thin;   this;   zh in *vision*.   For ¶ reference, see page 64 · **HOW TO**

pros·e·cute [pros′ə·kyo͞ot] *v.* **pros·e·cut·ed, pros·e·cut·ing 1** To put on trial for punishment of crime, wrongdoing, etc. **2** To go on with so as to finish: to *prosecute* an unpleasant task. ◆ See PERSECUTE.

pros·e·cu·tion [pros′ə·kyo͞o′shən] *n.* **1** A prosecuting. The starting and carrying out of a legal action to obtain a right or punish a wrong. **3** The side that starts and conducts such an action: evidence for the *prosecution*.

pros·e·cu·tor [pros′ə·kyo͞o′tər] *n.* **1** A lawyer who represents a county, state, or other unit in prosecuting people charged with crime. **2** A person who starts a case against another.

pros·e·lyte [pros′ə·līt] *n., v.* **pros·e·lyt·ed, pros·e·lyt·ing 1** *n.* A person who has been converted to any faith, group, etc., especially from one religion to another. **2** *v.* To proselytize.

pros·e·lyt·ize [pros′ə·lit·īz′] *v.* **pros·e·lyt·ized, pros·e·lyt·iz·ing** To convert a person, as from one religion to another. ¶3

Pro·ser·pi·na [prō·sûr′pə·nə] *n.* Proserpine.

Pros·er·pine [pros′ər·pīn *or* prō·sûr′pə·nē] *n.* In Roman myths, the daughter of Ceres. Her husband, Pluto, carried her off to the underworld. Her Greek name was Persephone.

pros·o·dy [pros′ə·dē] *n.* The study of the forms of verse, including meter, accent, etc.

pros·pect [pros′pekt] **1** *n.* The act of looking ahead; expectation: The *prospect* of a voyage excited him. **2** *n.* (*often pl.*) The chance for future success: That young man has good *prospects*. **3** *n.* A scene spread out before one's eyes; wide view. **4** *n.* A potential buyer or candidate. **5** *v.* To explore or search, as for oil, gold, etc. **— in prospect** Expected; anticipated.

pro·spec·tive [prə·spek′tiv] *adj.* **1** Being still in the future; expected: a *prospective* gift. **2** Looking toward or concerned with the future.

pros·pec·tor [pros′pek·tər] *n.* A person who explores a region for gold, uranium, oil, etc.

pro·spec·tus [prə·spek′təs] *n.* A report on a proposed business, stock issue, etc.

pros·per [pros′pər] *v.* To be successful; thrive; flourish: Crops *prosper* in fertile soil.

pros·per·i·ty [pros·per′ə·tē] *n.* A prosperous condition; material wealth, success, etc.

pros·per·ous [pros′pər·əs] *adj.* Successful; flourishing; thriving. **— pros′per·ous·ly** *adv.*

pros·ti·tute [pros′tə·t(y)o͞ot] *n., v.* **pros·ti·tut·ed, pros·ti·tut·ing 1** *n.* A woman who has sexual relations with men for money. **2** *v.* To be a prostitute. **3** *n.* A person who offers his services purely for money or for unworthy purposes. **4** *v.* To use for immoral or unworthy purposes. **— pros′ti·tu′tion** *n.*

pros·trate [pros′trāt] *adj., v.* **pros·trat·ed, pros·trat·ing 1** *adj.* Lying flat, with the face either upward or downward. **2** *v.* To cast or lay (oneself) down, as in worship or submission. **3** *v.* To throw flat; lay low: One blow *prostrated* him. **4** *adj.* Overcome, as with fear, fatigue, grief, etc. **5** *v.* To exhaust: Overwork *prostrated* her. **— pros·tra′tion** *n.*

pros·y [prō′zē] *adj.* **pros·i·er, pros·i·est 1** Like prose; prosaic. **2** Dull; ordinary.

pro·te·an [prō′tē·ən] *adj.* Easily taking on different forms or looks; changeable.

pro·tect [prə·tekt′] *v.* To shield or defend from attack, harm, or injury; guard; shelter.

The ameba, a protean animal, changes shape as it encircles a food particle.

pro·tec·tion [prə·tek′shən] *n.* **1** A protecting. **2** A being protected. **3** A person or thing that protects: Locks are *protection* against theft.

pro·tec·tive [prə·tek′tiv] *adj.* **1** Giving or suitable for protection; sheltering; defending. **2** Protecting an industry against foreign competition: a *protective* tariff.

protective coloring Coloring some animals have that so closely resembles that of their natural surroundings that they are hard to see and are thus protected from their enemies.

pro·tec·tor [prə·tek′tər] *n.* A person who protects.

pro·tec·tor·ate [prə·tek′tər·it] *n.* **1** A relationship in which a strong nation has control over and protects a weaker nation or territory. **2** A nation or territory so controlled.

pro·té·gé [prō′tə·zhā] *n.* A person whose career is under the protection and guidance of someone older or more powerful.

pro·te·in [prō′tē·in *or* prō′tēn] *n.* Any of a large group of complex organic compounds containing nitrogen. Protein is a necessary part of plant and animal cells and of animal diet.

pro·test [*n.* prō′test, *v.* prə·test′] **1** *n.* A formal objection or declaration. **2** *v.* To make a protest; object: Tom *protested* against going to bed early. **3** *v.* To make a protest against: I *protested* his actions. **4** *v.* To declare formally; assert: to *protest* one's honesty. **— under protest** Unwillingly: I'll go but *under protest*.

Prot·es·tant [prot′is·tənt] **1** *n.* A member of one of the Christian churches split off or derived from the Roman Catholic Church since the Reformation. Baptists, Presbyterians, and Lutherans are Protestants. **2** *adj.* Of or having to do with Protestants or Protestantism.

Protestant Episcopal Church A religious group in the U.S. that is similar in beliefs and practices to the Church of England.

Prot·es·tant·ism [prot′is·tənt·iz′əm] *n.* The principles and beliefs of Protestants.

prot·es·ta·tion [prot′is·tā′shən] *n.* **1** A protesting. **2** A protest, especially a formal declaration or assertion: *protestations* of innocence.

pro·to·col [prō′tə·kôl] *n.* The rules of diplomatic and state etiquette and ceremony.

pro·ton [prō′ton] *n.* A particle in the nucleus of an atom, carrying a single positive electric charge. Each element has a characteristic number of protons in the nucleus of its atom.

pro·to·plasm [prō′tə·plaz′əm] *n.* The basic substance of living matter, a thick grayish substance essential in all plant and animal cells. **— pro′to·plas′mic** *adj.*

pro·to·type [prō′tə·tīp] *n.* The first or original model of anything: *Fulton's steamboat was the* *prototype* *of today's ocean liner.*

pro·to·zo·an [prō′tə·zō′ən] *n.* A microscopic animal having only one cell. Most protozoans live in water or other liquid and reproduce by splitting their one cell into two new animals.

A type of protozoan

pro·tract [prō·trakt′] *v.* **1** To stretch in time; prolong: *to protract a conversation.* **2** To stick out or extend. **— pro·trac′·tion** *n.*

pro·trac·tor [prō·trak′tər] *n.* An instrument for drawing and measuring angles.

pro·trude [prō·trōōd′] *v.* **pro·trud·ed, pro·trud·ing 1** To push out or thrust forth: *to protrude the tongue.* **2** To jut out; project: *The balcony protrudes over the pathway to the garden.*

A protractor

pro·tru·sion [prō·trōō′zhən] *n.* **1** A protruding or thrusting out. **2** Something protruded.

pro·tu·ber·ance [prō·t(y)ōō′bər·əns] *n.* **1** Something that sticks out; bulge. **2** A being protuberant.

pro·tu·ber·ant [prō·t(y)ōō′bər·ənt] *adj.* Sticking out beyond the surrounding surface; bulging. **— pro·tu′ber·ant·ly** *adv.*

proud [proud] *adj.* **1** Having a proper or decent respect for oneself or one's position: *a proud but not conceited girl.* **2** Conceited; haughty; arrogant: *a proud snob.* **3** Having, showing, or causing pleasant feelings of pride: *a proud parent; proud ancestry.* **4** Splendid; glorious: *a proud mansion.* **— proud of** Very pleased or satisfied with. **— proud′ly** *adv.*

prove [prōōv] *v.* **proved, proved** or **prov·en, prov·ing 1** To show to be true, correct, or genuine, as by facts or argument: *I'll prove to you I'm right.* **2** To find out about through testing or experiments: *tests to prove a new rocket fuel.* **3** To turn out to be: *Her love proved false.*

Pro·ven·çal [prō′vən·säl′] *n.* The language of Provence, much used in the literature of the Middle Ages.

Pro·vence [prô·väns′] *n.* A region of SE France. It was once a separate province.

prov·en·der [prov′ən·dər] *n.* **1** Dry food, as hay, for cattle. **2** Any food.

prov·erb [prov′ərb] *n.* An old and often repeated saying of advice or wisdom: *"A rolling stone gathers no moss" is a proverb.*

pro·ver·bi·al [prə·vûr′bē·əl] *adj.* **1** Of, like, or having to do with proverbs. **2** Often spoken of or

about: *the proverbial memory of an elephant.* **— pro·ver′bi·al·ly** *adv.*

Prov·erbs [prov′ərbz] *n.pl.* (*used with singular verb*) A book of the Old Testament, containing a a collection of sayings of wise men of Israel such as Solomon.

pro·vide [prə·vid′] *v.* **pro·vid·ed, pro·vid·ing 1** To make ready beforehand; prepare: *to provide for any emergency.* **2** To supply or furnish: *to provide food.* **3** To set down as a condition. **— pro·vid′er** *n.*

pro·vid·ed [prə·vi′did] *conj.* On condition that; if: *You may eat now, provided you take your pill.*

prov·i·dence [prov′ə·dəns] *n.* **1** The care and protection of God or nature: *Only providence kept us from being drowned.* **2** Care, preparation, or saving for the future. **3** (*written* **Providence**) God.

Prov·i·dence [prov′ə·dəns] *n.* The capital of Rhode Island.

prov·i·dent [prov′ə·dənt] *adj.* Careful about preparing for or looking ahead to the future.

prov·i·den·tial [prov′ə·den′shəl] *adj.* **1** Of or determined by Providence: *providential guidance.* **2** Lucky; fortunate: *a providential escape.* **— prov′i·den′tial·ly** *adv.*

pro·vid·ing [prə·vi′ding] *conj.* On condition that; provided.

prov·ince [prov′ins] *n.* **1** (*often written* **Province**) A main division of a country, similar to a state in the U.S., having its own local government, as any of the Provinces of Canada. **2** (*pl.*) Parts of a country located some distance from the main cities. **3** Particular or special duties, functions, etc.: *Interviewing students was not in her province.* **4** A branch of knowledge: *the province of chemistry.*

pro·vin·cial [prə·vin′shəl] *adj.* **1** Of, having to do with, or originating in a province. **2** Of, like, or coming from rural rather than city areas: *provincial manners; provincial dress.* **3** Having or showing a narrow point of view; narrow-minded: *a provincial attitude.* **— pro·vin′cial·ism** *n.* **— pro·vin′cial·ly** *adv.*

pro·vi·sion [prə·vizh′ən] **1** *n.* The act of providing or supplying. **2** *n.* (*pl.*) Food, or a supply of food. **3** *v.* To provide with food or provisions: *to provision a ship before a voyage.* **4** *n.* Something provided or prepared, as against future needs: *A pension is a provision for one's retirement.* **5** *n.* A requirement or condition: *One provision of the deed was that the building should be maintained by the city as a museum.*

pro·vi·sion·al [prə·vizh′ən·əl] *adj.* Provided or adopted as a temporary thing or until something better can be found: *a provisional schedule for today.* **— pro·vi′sion·al·ly** *adv.*

pro·vi·so [prə·vi′zō] *n., pl.* **pro·vi·sos** or **pro·vi·soes** A requirement or condition: *He made a proviso that if I were to go I must return early.*

---

add, āce, câre, pälm; end, ēqual; it, īce; odd, ōpen, ôrder; tŏŏk, pōōl; up, bûrn;
ə = a in *above*, e in *sicken*, i in *possible*, o in *melon*, u in *circus*; yōō = u in *fuse*; oil; pout;
check; ring; thin; this; zh in *vision*.   For ¶ reference, see page 64 · HOW TO

prov·o·ca·tion [prov′ə·kā′shən] *n.* **1** The act of provoking. **2** Something that provokes, angers, or stirs up: His lateness was the *provocation* for a scolding from the teacher.

pro·voc·a·tive [prə·vok′ə·tiv] *adj.* Serving or tending to make one puzzled, angry, interested, amused, etc.: a *provocative* laugh; a *provocative* reply. **— pro·voc′a·tive·ly** *adv.*

pro·voke [prə·vōk′] *v.* **pro·voked, pro·vok·ing** **1** To make angry or resentful; irritate: His silly remark *provoked* me. **2** *adj. use*: a *provoking* habit. **3** To cause; bring on: The monkey's tricks *provoked* laughter. **4** To stir up: to *provoke* a quarrel.

prov·ost [prov′əst] *n.* A person having charge or authority over others, especially the head of the faculty in some colleges, the head of a cathedral, or the chief magistrate or mayor of a Scottish city.

prow [prou] *n.* The usually pointed forward end or bow of a ship or boat.

prow·ess [prou′is] *n.* **1** Strength and courage, especially in battle. **2** Great skill or ability: He had true *prowess* as a horseman.

prowl [proul] **1** *v.* To roam about quietly and slyly, as in search of food or something to steal: Jungle animals *prowl* at night. **2** *n.* The act of prowling. **— on the prowl** Prowling about.

The prow of a ship

prox·im·i·ty [prok·sim′ə·tē] *n.* Nearness; closeness: The *proximity* of the stores to our home makes shopping easy.

prox·y [prok′sē] *n., pl.* **prox·ies** **1** A person authorized by another to act for him; a substitute. **2** A written statement permitting a person to act as proxy. **3** The right to act as a proxy. **4** The act of a proxy: to vote by *proxy*.

prude [prōōd] *n.* A person who is too prim, modest, or proper.

pru·dence [prōō′dəns] *n.* Careful thought before acting; good judgment.

pru·dent [prōō′dənt] *adj.* **1** Using or showing careful planning and good judgment; cautious: a *prudent* man. **2** Not extravagant; thrifty. **— pru′dent·ly** *adv.*

pru·den·tial [prōō·den′shəl] *adj.* **1** Marked by prudence. **2** Using prudence and wisdom.

prud·er·y [prōō′dər·ē] *n., pl.* **prud·er·ies** **1** The condition of being too modest or too prim. **2** A prudish action or remark.

prud·ish [prōō′dish] *adj.* Of or like a prude; too modest or proper. **— prud′ish·ly** *adv.* **— prud′ish·ness** *n.*

prune[1] [prōōn] *n.* The dried fruit of any of several types of plum.

prune[2] [prōōn] *v.* **pruned, prun·ing** **1** To cut or trim unwanted branches or twigs from (a tree, shrub, etc.). **2** To shorten; reduce the length of: to *prune* a speech.

Prus·sia [prush′ə] *n.* A former state of northern Germany. **— Prus′sian** *n., adj.*

pry[1] [prī] *v.* **pried, pry·ing, n., pl. pries** **1** *v.* To raise, move, or open by means of a lever: to *pry* the lid off a pickle jar. **2** *v.* To get with difficulty: We finally *pried* the real reason out of Tom. **3** *n.* A lever or crowbar.

pry[2] [prī] *v.* **pried, pry·ing, n., pl. pries** **1** *v.* To look carefully and with too much curiosity; snoop. **2** *n.* A person who pries.

P.S. Abbreviation of POSTSCRIPT.

psalm [säm] *n.* A hymn or poem of praise.

psalm·ist [sä′mist] *n.* A person who composes psalms. **— the Psalmist** King David, the traditional author of many psalms in the Book of Psalms.

Psalms [sämz] *n.* A book of the Old Testament containing 150 hymns or psalms.

Psal·ter [sôl′tər] *n.* The Book of Psalms, especially as arranged for church services.

psal·ter·y [sôl′tər·ē] *n., pl.* **psal·ter·ies** An ancient musical instrument played by plucking with the fingers or a plectrum.

pseu·do [sōō′dō] *adj.* Not real or genuine; false; sham; pretended: a *pseudo* precious stone.

Psaltery

pseu·do·nym [sōō′də·nim] *n.* A fictitious name used by a writer or other well-known person in place of his own name: Mark Twain is the *pseudonym* of Samuel Clemens.

pshaw [shô] *interj.* An exclamation of impatience, disgust, or annoyance.

Psy·che [sī′kē] *n.* **1** In Greek and Roman myths, a maiden with butterfly wings who was loved by Cupid. She became a symbol of the soul or mind. **2** (*written* **psyche**) The human soul or mind.

psy·chi·at·ric [sī′kē·at′rik] *adj.* Of or having to do with psychiatry or the treatment of mental illness: *psychiatric* nursing.

psy·chi·a·trist [sī·kī′ə·trist] *n.* A doctor who treats people who are mentally ill.

psy·chi·a·try [sī·kī′ə·trē] *n.* The branch of medicine that deals with the treatment and prevention of mental illness.

psy·chic [sī′kik] *adj.* **1** Of or having to do with the human mind; mental: a *psychic* illness. **2** Sensitive to things that are supernatural or outside normal laws or forces: A *psychic* person often claims to foretell the future. **3** Not to be explained by natural forces or laws.

psy·chi·cal [sī′kik·əl] *adj.* Psychic.

psy·cho·a·nal·y·sis [sī′kō·ə·nal′ə·sis] *n., pl.* **psy·cho·a·nal·y·ses** [sī′kō·ə·nal′ə·sēz] The treatment of emotional disturbances by leading the patient to talk freely about his problems, his childhood, his dreams, etc., so as to uncover and resolve mental conflicts of which he is not aware.

psy·cho·an·a·lyst [sī′kō·an′ə·list] *n.* A person trained to treat patients by psychoanalysis.

psy·cho·an·a·lyze [sī′kō·an′ə·līz] *v.* **psy·cho·**

an·a·lyzed, psy·cho·an·a·lyz·ing To treat by psychoanalysis. ¶3

psy·cho·log·i·cal [sī′kə·loj′i·kəl] *adj.* **1** Of or having to do with the mind; mental. **2** Of or having to do with psychology: *psychological* testing. **3** Most right or most favorable: the *psychological* moment. **— psy′cho·log′i·cal·ly** *adv.*

psy·chol·o·gy [sī·kol′ə·jē] *n.*, *pl.* **psy·chol·o·gies** **1** The study of the mind and the way it works. Psychology tries to explain why people think, feel, and behave as they do and to predict how they will act under certain conditions. **2** The usual ways of thinking, feeling, and acting of a person or group. **— psy·chol′o·gist** *n.*

psy·cho·path·ic [sī′kō·path′ik] *adj.* **1** Of or having to do with mental or emotional disorders. **2** Having or likely to develop a mental disorder: a *psychopathic* personality.

psy·cho·sis [sī·kō′sis] *n.*, *pl.* **psy·cho·ses** [sī·kō′sēz] Any serious mental disturbance or disorder.

psy·chot·ic [sī·kot′ik] **1** *adj.* Having a serious mental disorder or psychosis. **2** *adj.* Of or like a psychosis. **3** *n.* A person suffering from a serious mental disorder or psychosis. **— psy·chot′i·cal·ly** *adv.*

Pt The symbol for the element PLATINUM.

pt. Abbreviation of: **1** PINT (half a quart). **2** (*usually written* **pts.**) Pints. **3** PAST TENSE.

ptar·mi·gan [tär′mə·gən] *n.*, *pl.* **ptar·mi·gan** or **ptar·mi·gans** A grouse of the northern hemisphere. It has feathers on its legs and in winter has white plumage.

pter·o·dac·tyl [ter′ə·dak′til] *n.* An extinct flying reptile that had a birdlike skull and large wing membranes like those of a bat.

Ptol·e·my [tol′ə·mē] *n.* A Greek astronomer and mathematician who lived in Alexandria, Egypt, in the second century A.D.

pto·maine or **pto·main** [tō′mān] *n.* Any of various substances containing nitrogen, produced in spoiled or decaying animal or vegetable matter.

A pterodactyl with wingspread of 25 ft.

ptomaine poisoning Poisoning by bacteria in spoiled food, once blamed on ptomaines.

Pu The symbol for the element PLUTONIUM.

pu·ber·ty [pyōo′bər·tē] *n.*, *pl.* **pu·ber·ties** The beginning of physical maturity in a boy or girl; first manhood or womanhood.

pub·lic [pub′lik] **1** *adj.* Of or by the people as a whole: *public* spirit; a *public* demonstration.
2 *n.* All of the people as a whole: The *public* must be served. **3** *adj.* Open to all; serving everyone: *public* roads; *public* schools. **4** *adj.* Known to most people; not concealed; open: a matter of *public* knowledge; a *public* scandal. **5** *adj.* Acting in behalf of or before a large group of people: a *public* official; a *public* speaker. **6** *n.* People grouped together or thought of as being grouped together for some special purpose: the church-going *public*. **— in public** In a place where all may come, see, or hear: to quarrel *in public*. **— pub′lic·ly** *adv.*

pub·li·can [pub′lə·kən] *n.* **1** In ancient Rome, a collector of taxes. **2** In Britain, the keeper of an inn or tavern.

pub·li·ca·tion [pub′lə·kā′shən] *n.* **1** The act of publishing. **2** Something that is published and offered for sale, as a book, magazine, etc.

public house **1** An inn or hotel. **2** In Great Britain, a bar that sells alcoholic beverages.

pub·li·cist [pub′lə·sist] *n.* **1** An expert on law and public affairs. **2** A reporter or commentator on public affairs. **3** A person hired to bring a person, place, institution, etc., to the notice of the public; press agent.

pub·lic·i·ty [pub·lis′ə·tē] *n.* **1** Any information intended to bring a person or thing to the notice of the public: That story was just *publicity*. **2** The attention or interest of the public: He avoids *publicity*. **3** The means or methods used in bringing a person or thing to the public's attention: Her press agent handles the *publicity*.

pub·li·cize [pub′lə·sīz] *v.* **pub·li·cized, pub·li·ciz·ing** To give publicity to; advertise.

public opinion The ideas, beliefs, and wishes of the people of a country, community, etc.

public school **1** In the U.S., an elementary or secondary school supported by public funds for the free education of the children of a community. **2** In England, a private boarding school for boys to prepare them for the universities.

pub·lic-spir·it·ed [pub′lik·spir′it·id] *adj.* Actively interested in the welfare of a community, nation, etc.: a *public-spirited* man.

public utility A company that supplies water, gas, electricity, etc., to the public and is partly regulated by the government.

pub·lish [pub′lish] *v.* **1** To print and issue (a book, magazine, newspaper, etc.) for sale to the public. **2** To print and issue for sale the work of: We still *publish* Dickens. **3** To have one's work published: He *publishes* regularly. **4** To make known publicly: Don't *publish* your failures.

pub·lish·er [pub′lish·ər] *n.* A person or company that publishes books, magazines, newspapers, etc.

puck [puk] *n.* The black, hard rubber disk used in ice hockey.

Puck [puk] *n.* In English folk tales, a mischievous sprite or hobgoblin.

---

add, āce, câre, pälm; end, ēqual; it, īce; odd, ōpen, ôrder; tŏŏk, pōōl; up, bûrn; ə = a in *above*, e in *sicken*, i in *possible*, o in *melon*, u in *circus*; yōō = u in *fuse*; oil; pout; check; ring; thin; this; zh in *vision*. For ¶ reference, see page 64 · HOW TO

puck·er [puk'ər] **1** *v.* To gather or draw up in small folds or wrinkles: to *pucker* the lips. **2** *n.* A wrinkle or small fold.

pud·ding [pŏŏd'ing] *n.* A sweetened and flavored dessert of soft food, usually made of milk, fruit, eggs, etc.

pud·dle [pud'(ə)l] *n.* A small pool of water, especially dirty or muddy water.

pudg·y [puj'ē] *adj.* **pudg·i·er, pudg·i·est** Short and fat; dumpy; chubby: a *pudgy* man. — **pudg'i·ness** *n.*

pueb·lo [pweb'lō] *n.,* *pl.* **pueb·los** or **pueb·lo** **1** An adobe or stone building or group of buildings of the Indians of the sw U.S. **2** (*written* **Pueblo**) A member of one of the Indian tribes that live in such buildings. ◆ *Pueblo* comes directly from the Spanish word for *village*, which goes back to a Latin word meaning *people*.

Pueblo

pu·er·ile [pyŏŏ'ər·il] *adj.* Childish; immature; silly: a *puerile* remark.

Puer·to Ri·co [pwer'tō rē'kō] An island in the West Indies, self-governing but associated with the U.S. — **Puer'to Ri'can** *adj.,* *n.*

puff [puf] **1** *n.* A sudden, short gust of breath, wind, smoke, or steam. **2** *v.* To breathe heavily; be out of breath: He was *puffing* after the race. **3** *v.* To blow in puffs, as the wind. **4** *v.* To send out puffs of steam, smoke, etc., usually while moving or acting: The locomotive *puffed* across the plains. **5** *v.* To smoke (a cigar, cigarette, etc.) with puffs. **6** *v.* To swell or cause to swell: The wet shirts *puffed* out in the wind; He *puffed* out his chest with pride. **7** *n.* A slight swelling. **8** *n.* A light, hollow piece of pastry, usually filled with custard, whipped cream, etc. **9** *n.* A loose roll of hair, as in a woman's hairdo. **10** *v.* To arrange (hair, etc.) in puffs. **11** *n.* A powder puff. **12** *n.* A quilted bed covering. **13** *n.* A notice or review praising a person or thing. **14** *v.* To praise or advertise highly or too highly.

puff·ball [puf'bôl'] *n.* A rounded fungus which, when ripe, bursts at a touch and sprays out a cloud of spores like brown powder.

puf·fin [puf'in] *n.* A sea bird of the North Atlantic Ocean, having a stubby, ducklike body and a thin, brightly colored, triangular bill.

puff·y [puf'ē] *adj.* **puff·i·er, puff·i·est** **1** Swollen; bloated: *puffy* fingers. **2** Lightly rounded or filled, as with air: *puffy* sleeves. **3** Coming in puffs: *puffy* breathing. **4** Vain; showy: a *puffy* little man. — **puff·i·ly** *adv.* — **puff'i·ness** *n.*

Puffin, about 1 ft. long

pug [pug] *n.* A type of dog having a short, square body, a tightly curled tail, and a flat, upturned nose.

Pu·get Sound [pyŏŏ'jit] An inlet or bay of the Pacific Ocean in NW Washington.

pu·gi·lism [pyŏŏ'jə·liz'əm] *n.* The art or sport of boxing. — **pu'gi·list** *n.* — **pu'·gi·lis'tic** *adj.*

Pug, about 10 in. high at shoulder

pug·na·cious [pug·nā'shəs] *adj.* Fond of fighting; quarrelsome. — **pug·na'cious·ly** *adv.*

pug·nac·i·ty [pug·nas'ə·tē] *n.* Fondness for fighting; inclination to fight.

pug nose A short, blunt nose, tilted upward at the end.

pu·is·sant [pyŏŏ'ə·sənt *or* pwis'ənt] *adj.* Powerful; mighty. — **pu'is·sance** *n.* — **pu'is·sant·ly** *adv.*

pul·chri·tude [pul'krə·t(y)ŏŏd] *n.* Beauty, especially physical beauty; loveliness.

pule [pyŏŏl] *v.* **puled, pul·ing** To whimper as a small child does; whine.

pull [pŏŏl] **1** *v.* To apply force to (a person or thing) so as to bring it closer to or in the direction of the person or thing exerting the force: to *pull* a fish out of water; to *pull* the curtains shut; to *pull* a wagon. **2** *n.* The act or an instance of pulling: The girl gave a *pull* at the dog's leash. **3** *n.* The effort exerted in pulling: a hard *pull.* **4** *n.* Something used in pulling, as the handle on a dresser drawer. **5** *v.* To be capable of moving when pulled: This cart *pulls* easily. **6** *v.* To draw from a fixed place, often with a tool: to *pull* a cork out of a bottle; to *pull* a tooth. **7** *v.* To strain so as to cause injury: to *pull* a tendon. **8** *v.* To draw, rip, or tear apart: The baby *pulled* his sister's doll to pieces. **9** *v.* To move; go: We *pulled* over to the side of the road for our picnic. **10** *v.* To row: to *pull* for shore. **11** *v. slang* To do; carry out: to *pull* a practical joke. **12** *n. slang* Help or influence: He got his job through *pull.* **13** *v. slang* To draw out so as to use: to *pull* a knife. — **pull for** *informal* To hope or work for the success of: to *pull for* the home team. — **pull off** *informal* To succeed in doing. — **pull oneself together** To get back one's self-control, peace of mind, etc. — **pull out** To leave; go away: We *pulled out* for the mountains at dawn. — **pull through** *informal* To manage to get through a dangerous situation, illness, or other difficulty. — **pull up** **1** To come to a halt: The car *pulled up* at our doorstep. **2** To move ahead: *Pull up* to the gas pump. **3** To remove by or as if by the roots: to *pull up* weeds. — **pull up with** To come to a position even with. — **pull'er** *n.*

pul·let [pŏŏl'it] *n.* A young hen, especially in its first year.

P

pul·ley [pŏŏl′ē] *n., pl.* **pul·leys** A small wheel with a grooved rim over which is passed a rope or chain that moves freely with the turning of the wheel.

Pull·man [pŏŏl′mən] *n.* A railroad car having small, private compartments that can be converted into sleeping quarters: a trademark. Also **Pullman car.**

pull·o·ver [pŏŏl′ō′vər] *n.* A garment that is put on by being drawn over the head, as certain sweaters or shirts.

pul·mo·na·ry [pŏŏl′mə·ner′ē *or* pul′mə·ner′ē] *adj.* Of, having to do with, or affecting the lungs: the *pulmonary* artery; *pulmonary* tuberculosis.

pulp [pulp] **1** *n.* The soft, usually edible part of certain fruits or vegetables. **2** *n.* A wet mixture of wood fibers or rags from which paper is manufactured. **3** *v.* To make into or become pulp. **4** *n.* The soft inner part of a tooth containing blood vessels and nerves.

pul·pit [pŏŏl′pit] *n.* **1** A raised platform or desk for a preacher in a church. **2** The work or profession of preaching.

pulp·wood [pulp′wŏŏd′] *n.* The soft wood of certain trees, used in making paper.

pulp·y [pul′pē] *adj.* **pulp·i·er, pulp·i·est 1** Of or like pulp. **2** Soft and juicy.

pul·sate [pul′sāt] *v.* **pul·sat·ed, pul·sat·ing 1** To throb or beat rhythmically, as the pulse or heart. **2** To vibrate; quiver. **— pul·sa′·tion** *n.*

pulse[1] [puls] *n., v.* **pulsed, puls·ing 1** *n.* The rhythmical beating of the arteries resulting from the contractions of the heart, especially as felt in the artery at the wrist. **2** *n.* Any regular throbbing or beat. **3** *n.* A short burst, as of electricity, a radio wave, or light. Pulses are used in communications, radar, computers, etc. **4** *v.* To pulsate; throb.

pulse[2] [puls] *n.* **1** Plants such as peas, beans, etc. **2** Their edible seeds.

pul·ver·ize [pul′və·rīz] *v.* **pul·ver·ized, pul·ver·iz·ing 1** To make into powder or dust, as by crushing. **2** To become dust. **3** To demolish; destroy: The blast *pulverized* the wall. ¶3

pu·ma [pyŏŏ′mə] *n.* Another name for the COUGAR.

pum·ice [pum′is] *n.* Volcanic lava that has hardened on cooling into a spongy, very light rock. It is used, in solid or powdered form, for smoothing, polishing, or cleaning.

A pulley

Pulpit

pum·mel [pum′əl] *v.* **pum·meled** or **pum·melled, pum·mel·ing** or **pum·mel·ling,** *n.* Another spelling of POMMEL.

pump[1] [pump] **1** *n.* A mechanical device for raising, circulating, or compressing liquids or gases by drawing or forcing them through pipes: a gasoline *pump*; a water *pump*. **2** *v.* To raise or move (something) with a pump: to *pump* water. **3** *v.* To inflate with air by means of a pump: to *pump* up an air mattress. **4** *v.* To remove the water, etc., from: to *pump* a flooded ditch dry. **5** *v.* To move or force with a pumping action: The heart *pumps* blood. **6** *v.* To move up and down like a pump or pump handle: He *pumped* my hand. **7** *v.* To get information from by asking many questions: to *pump* a witness. **8** *v.* To get (information, etc.) by such a method: We *pumped* the true story out of him.

pump[2] [pump] *n.* A low-cut shoe without laces or fastenings and having either a high or low heel.

pum·per·nick·el [pum′pər·nik′əl] *n.* A coarse, sour, dark bread made from unsifted rye.

pump·kin [pump′kin *or* pung′kin] *n.* A large, round, yellow-orange fruit that grows on a trailing vine. Its pulp is often used in a pie filling.

pun [pun] *n., v.* **punned, pun·ning 1** *n.* The humorous use of two or more words having the same or similar sounds, but different meanings, as in, "When the bear lost his fur he was all bare." **2** *v.* To make puns.

punch[1] [punch] **1** *v.* To strike sharply, especially with the fists. **2** *n.* A swift blow or poke; jab. **3** *n.* A tool for making holes in leather, paper, etc. **4** *n.* A machine used to stamp and cut a design, especially on a piece of metal. **5** *v.* To cut, perforate, or make with a punch: to *punch* holes in metal; to *punch* a card. **6** *v.* To herd (cattle, etc.).

punch[2] [punch] *n.* A hot or cold drink made of various mixtures of beverages, such as fruit juices, soft drinks, alcoholic liquors, milk, etc.

Punch [punch] *n.* A quarrelsome puppet who is the hero of a comic puppet show, **Punch and Judy.** He always fights with Judy, his wife. **— pleased as Punch** Very pleased; very happy.

pun·cheon [pun′chən] *n.* A large barrel for liquor, holding from 72 to 120 gallons.

Punch and Judy

punc·til·i·ous [pungk·til′ē·əs] *adj.* **1** Very careful or exact in one's social manners and behavior. **2** Careful and painstaking: a *punctilious* housewife.

punc·tu·al [pungk′chŏŏ·əl] *adj.* Acting, finished, or arriving on time: to be *punctual* with homework. **— punc·tu·al·i·ty** [pungk′chŏŏ·al′ə·tē] *n.* **— punc′tu·al·ly** *adv.*

punc·tu·ate [pungk′chŏŏ·āt] *v.* **punc·tu·at·ed, punc·tu·at·ing 1** To divide or mark with

add, āce, câre, pälm; end, ēqual; it, īce; odd, ōpen, ôrder; tŏŏk, pŏŏl; up, bûrn;
ə = a in *above*, e in *sicken*, i in *possible*, o in *melon*, u in *circus*; yŏŏ = u in *fuse*; oil; pout;
check; ring; thin; this; zh in *vision*. For ¶ reference, see page 64 · HOW TO

punctuation marks: *Punctuate* this sentence. **2** To interrupt from time to time: He *punctuated* his speech with many stale jokes.

punc·tu·a·tion [pungk′chōo·ā′shən] *n.* **1** The use of punctuation marks to make clearer the meaning of written or printed matter. **2** Punctuation marks.

punctuation mark Any of the various marks used in printed or written matter to clarify the meaning, as the period, comma, question mark, semicolon, colon, exclamation mark, dash, etc.

punc·ture [pungk′chər] *v.* **punc·tured, punc·tur·ing,** *n.* **1** *v.* To pierce or become pierced with or as if with a sharp point: to *puncture* the skin with a needle; The tire *punctured* a mile from home. **2** *n.* A hole made by piercing with or as if with a sharp point. **3** *v.* To make useless; destroy: to *puncture* a man's self-respect.

pun·gen·cy [pun′jən·sē] *n.* The condition or quality of being pungent.

pun·gent [pun′jənt] *adj.* **1** Sharp or piercing to the taste or smell: *pungent* mustard. **2** Keen and sharp to the mind, often painfully so; biting: He has a *pungent* sense of humor. — **pun′gent·ly** *adv.*

pun·ish [pun′ish] *v.* **1** To cause to undergo pain, discomfort, imprisonment, etc., for a crime or wrongdoing. **2** To inflict a penalty for: to *punish* kidnaping. **3** To inflict punishment: He *punishes* for the least fault. **4** *informal* To cause discomfort or injury to: The hot sun *punished* us.

pun·ish·a·ble [pun′ish·ə·bəl] *adj.* Deserving of or liable to punishment.

pun·ish·ment [pun′ish·mənt] *n.* **1** The act of punishing. **2** The penalty given for a crime or wrongdoing: Jerry's *punishment* was going without dessert. **3** *informal* Rough handling, as in a boxing match.

pu·ni·tive [pyōo′nə·tiv] *adj.* Having to do with or inflicting punishment: *punitive* laws.

punk¹ [pungk] *n.* **1** A dry, often spongy substance that burns slowly, used to light firecrackers, etc. **2** Decayed wood used as tinder to light fires.

punk² [pungk] *slang* **1** *n.* A hoodlum. **2** *n.* A young, inexperienced boy or man. **3** *adj.* Worthless; poor: a *punk* story. **4** *adj.* Not in good health; unwell: I feel *punk.*

punt¹ [punt] **1** *n.* In football, a kick made by dropping the ball from the hands and kicking it before it touches the ground. **2** *v.* In football, to propel (the ball) with a punt. — **punt′er** *n.*

punt² [punt] **1** *n.* A flat-bottomed boat with square ends. **2** *v.* To propel (a boat) by pushing with a pole against the bottom of a lake, stream, etc. — **punt′er** *n.*

Punt

pu·ny [pyōo′nē] *adj.* **pu·ni·er, pu·ni·est** Small and feeble; weak and insignificant: a *puny* kitten. ◆ *Puny* comes from an Old French word *puisne,* meaning *younger* or *junior,* and that is what it originally meant in English. The meanings of *small* and *weak* came later.

pup [pup] *n.* **1** A young dog; puppy. **2** A young seal or shark or any of the young of certain other animals.

pu·pa [pyōo′pə] *n., pl.* **pu·pas** or **pu·pae** [pyōo′pē] **1** The stage in the development of an insect between the larva and the adult. **2** An insect in this stage. — **pu′pal** *adj.*

pu·pate [pyōo′pāt] *v.* **pu·pat·ed, pu·pat·ing** To become or pass through the stage of being a pupa. — **pu·pa′tion** *n.*

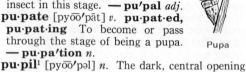

Pupa

pu·pil¹ [pyōo′pəl] *n.* The dark, central opening of the eye through which light is admitted to the retina. The pupil expands and contracts to let in more or less light.

The pupil dilates in the dark.

pu·pil² [pyōo′pəl] *n.* A person of any age who is being instructed by a teacher; student.

pup·pet [pup′it] *n.* **1** A small figure of a person or animal, usually with a cloth body and a solid head, fitting over and moved by the hand. **2** A small figure or doll whose jointed limbs, head, etc., are attached to and moved by wires or strings; marionette. **3** A person without much will power who is told what to do or say by others.

puppet show A play acted with puppets.

pup·py [pup′ē] *n., pl.* **pup·pies** **1** A young dog; pup. **2** A conceited, silly young man.

pur·chase [pûr′chəs] *v.* **pur·chased, pur·chas·ing,** *n.* **1** *v.* To get by paying money; buy: to *purchase* a suit. **2** *n.* Anything that is bought with money: She made many *purchases.* **3** *n..* The act of purchasing: the *purchase* of a boat. **4** *v.* To get as a result of great effort or sacrifice: His success was *purchased* by hard work. **5** *n.* A device, as a tackle or lever, that helps a person to lift or move something. **6** *v.* To use such a device to move or lift (heavy objects). **7** *n.* A firm grasp when moving heavy objects. — **pur′chas·er** *n.*

pure [pyoor] *adj.* **pur·er, pur·est** **1** Not mixed with other substances: *pure* silk. **2** Free from germs or anything unhealthful: *pure* milk; *pure* air. **3** Morally clean; innocent; good: a *pure* life. **4** Nothing but; absolute; sheer: *pure* foolishness. **5** Directed toward or dealing with theory or research more than with practical uses or applications: *pure* science. — **pure′ness** *n.*

pu·rée [pyōo·rā′] *n., v.* **pu·réed, pu·rée·ing** **1** *n.* A thick paste made by forcing food boiled to pulp through a sieve. **2** *n.* A thick soup made with such paste. **3** *v.* To make a purée of.

pure·ly [pyoor′lē] *adv.* **1** Without anything harmful, strange, etc.: to speak a language *purely.* **2** Innocently; virtuously: to live *purely.* **3** Completely; totally: It is *purely* his decision. **4** Merely; simply: It was done *purely* for fun.

pur·ga·tive [pûr′gə·tiv] **1** *adj.* Cleansing; purifying: This medicine has a *purgative* effect. **2** *n.* A medicine that causes the bowels to move.

pur·ga·to·ry [pûr′gə·tôr′ē] *n., pl.* **pur·ga·to·**

ries 1 In Roman Catholic belief, a place where the souls of those who have committed minor sins are made fit for paradise by being punished for a time. **2** Any condition of misery or suffering.

purge [pûrj] *v.* **purged, purg·ing,** *n.* **1** *v.* To remove what is impure or harmful from; make clean: to *purge* a neighborhood of crime. **2** *v.* To cause (the bowels) to move thoroughly by means of a medicine. **3** *n.* A medicine that empties the bowels; a cathartic. **4** *n.* The act of purging.

pu·ri·fy [pyoor′ə·fī] *v.* **pu·ri·fied, pu·ri·fy·ing** To make or become pure or clean: Thunderstorms *purify* the air; The smoky air soon *purified.* — **pu′ri·fi·ca′tion** *n.*

pur·ist [pyoor′ist] *n.* A person who is extremely or even too particular or fussy about correctness of language, matters of style, the following of certain rules, etc.

Pu·ri·tan [pyoor′ə·tən] *n.* **1** One of a group of English Protestants who, in the 16th and 17th centuries, wanted stricter moral laws and simpler services in the Church of England. **2** One of these Puritans who came to settle in New England in the 17th century. **3** (*written* **puritan**) A person who is very strict in his moral or religious life.

pu·ri·tan·ic [pyoor′ə·tan′ik] *adj.* Puritanical.

pu·ri·tan·i·cal [pyoor′ə·tan′i·kəl] *adj.* **1** Strict in religion and morals. **2** (*sometimes written* **Puritanical**) Of or having to do with the Puritans.

Puritans

pu·ri·tan·ism [pyoor′ə·tən·iz′əm] *n.* **1** Strictness in moral and religious life. **2** (*sometimes written* **Puritanism**) The beliefs and practices of the Puritans.

pu·ri·ty [pyoor′ə·tē] *n.* The quality or condition of being pure.

purl[1] [pûrl] *v.* In knitting, to make a stitch backward, usually used to make a rib in the fabric.

purl[2] [pûrl] **1** *v.* To flow with a bubbling, murmuring sound, as a brook. **2** *v.* To flow in a swirling or circling motion. **3** *n.* The sound or movement of bubbling or swirling water.

pur·lieu [pûr′loo] *n.* (*usually pl.*) The outlying parts or outskirts of a place: the *purlieus* of a large town.

pur·loin [pûr·loin′] *v.* To steal; filch.

pur·ple [pûr′pəl] *n., v.* **pur·pled, pur·pling 1** *n.* A color that is a mixture of red and blue. **2** *adj.* Of or having this color. **3** *n.* Deep red robes formerly worn by kings and other persons of high rank. **4** *n.* Royal power or high rank, usually in the phrase **born to the purple.**

Purple Heart A decoration given to members of the U.S. armed services who have been wounded in action against an enemy.

pur·plish [pûr′plish] *adj.* Somewhat purple.

pur·port [*v.* pər·pôrt′, *n.* pûr′pôrt] **1** *v.* To mean or intend: What does his speech *purport*? **2** *v.* To claim: The newspaper *purports* to give all the facts. **3** *n.* The meaning or substance of something: What is the *purport* of that remark?

pur·pose [pûr′pəs] *n., v.* **pur·posed, pur·pos·ing 1** *n.* What one intends or wants to accomplish; plan; aim: What is the *purpose* of your visit? **2** *v.* To intend; aim: seldom used today. **3** *n.* Result or effect: It was all done to no *purpose.* **4** *n.* The reason for which a thing exists; use: What is the *purpose* of the cleats on baseball shoes? **5** *n.* Determination; resolve: He has always been a man of *purpose.* — **on purpose** Intentionally; deliberately: He stepped on my toe *on purpose.* — **to good purpose** With a good result or effect. — **pur′pose·ful** *adj.* — **pur′pose·ful·ly** *adv.* ◆ See REASON.

pur·pose·less [pûr′pəs·lis] *adj.* Having no definite purpose; aimless or meaningless.

pur·pose·ly [pûr′pəs·lē] *adv.* For a purpose; intentionally; on purpose.

purr [pûr] **1** *n.* A murmuring sound, such as a cat makes when pleased. **2** *v.* To make this sound.

purse [pûrs] *n., v.* **pursed, purs·ing 1** *n.* A small bag or pouch for carrying money. **2** *n.* A larger bag carried by women and used to hold money, cosmetics, and other small articles; a handbag. **3** *n.* A sum of money, used as a gift or prize. **4** *v.* To draw into wrinkles; pucker, as the lips.

purs·er [pûr′sər] *n.* An officer on a ship who keeps financial accounts and acts as a cashier.

purs·lane [pûrs′lin *or* pûrs′lān] *n.* A common garden plant with a reddish stem and leaves and small yellow flowers. It is sometimes used in salads.

pur·su·ance [pər·s(y)oo′əns] *n.* The act of pursuing or carrying out, especially in the expression **in pursuance of**: *In pursuance of* the general's orders, the troops retreated.

pur·su·ant [pər·s(y)oo′ənt] *adj.* Done in accordance with; following; carrying out. — **pursuant to** In accordance with; following.

pur·sue [pər·s(y)oo′] *v.* **pur·sued, pur·su·ing 1** To follow in an attempt to overtake or capture; chase: to *pursue* an escaped convict. **2** To proceed with; keep on with: to *pursue* a career; to *pursue* a hobby; to *pursue* an interesting topic of conversation. **3** To try to get; seek to obtain: to *pursue* happiness. **4** To bother; annoy: Poor health *pursued* him all his life. — **pur·su′er** *n.*

pur·suit [pər·s(y)oot′] *n.* **1** The act of pursuing; a chase. **2** Something that is regularly done or followed, as a profession, a hobby, or a sport.

pur·vey [pər·vā′] *v.* To furnish (supplies),

---

add, āce, câre, pälm; end, ēqual; it, īce; odd, ōpen, ôrder; took, pool; up, bûrn;
ə = a in *above*, e in *sicken*, i in *possible*, o in *melon*, u in *circus*; yoo = u in *fuse*; oil; pout;
check; ring; thin; this; zh in *vision*. For ¶ reference, see page 64 · HOW TO

especially food: Dairies *purvey* milk, cheese, and butter. — **pur·vey'or** *n.*

pur·vey·ance [pər·vā'əns] *n.* **1** The act of purveying. **2** Something purveyed, as food supplies.

pus [pus] *n.* A thick, yellowish matter discharged from infected wounds, boils, etc. — **pus·sy** [pus'ē] *adj.*

push [poosh] **1** *v.* To exert force against (an object) in order to move it: to *push* a stalled car. **2** *v.* To carry out the action of pushing: You *push*, and I'll pull. **3** *v.* To make (a passage) by force: The explorers *pushed* their way through the jungle. **4** *v.* To urge or force to do something: He didn't *push* his students to study. **5** *v.* To stick out or project: The point *pushed* far out into the sea. **6** *v.* To exert great effort: We all *pushed* for more pay. **7** *v.* To advocate or promote vigorously: to *push* a new product. **8** *n.* The act of pushing: We gave a *push* against the wall. **9** *n. informal* Great energy and determination; drive: He has no *push*. — **push'er** *n.*

push·o·ver [poosh'ō'vər] *n. slang* **1** Anything that can be done with little or no effort. **2** A person who is easily taken advantage of or beaten.

push·up [poosh'up'] *n.* An exercise in which one lies on his stomach on the floor and pushes up his body with his arms until it is supported only on the hands and toes.

pu·sil·lan·i·mous [pyoo'sə·lan'ə·məs] *adj.* Not courageous; fainthearted; timid.

Man doing push-ups

puss [poos] *n. informal* A cat or kitten.

pus·sy [poos'ē] *n., pl.* **pus·sies 1** A cat or kitten. **2** A silky catkin, as of a willow.

pussy willow A small American willow that has silky catkins in the early spring.

put [poot] *v.* **put, put·ting 1** To set, lay, or place in a given spot or position: to *put* a saddle on a horse; to *put* knives and forks on the table. **2** To bring to a certain condition or action: It *put* him into a rage; He *put* us to work. **3** To express in words; state: Try to *put* your questions more clearly. **4** To assign or impose: to *put* a tax on leather goods; to *put* a high value on one's reputation. **5** To estimate: I *put* the time at about 5 o'clock. **6** To bring to bear; apply: *Put* your mind on your lesson. **7** To give or submit for debate, answering, etc.: to *put* a question to the class. **8** To move or go: The ship *put* out to sea. **9** To throw with a pushing movement of the arm and shoulder: to *put* the shot. — **put about** To change the direction of (a ship or boat). — **put across** *slang* To cause to be understood or received favorably: He is able to *put across* new ideas. — **put by** To save for future use: He *puts by* part of his salary each week. — **put down 1** To write down; record. **2** To repress; put an end to, as an uprising. — **put forth** To grow, as shoots or buds. — **put in 1** To enter a harbor or place of shelter.

2 To spend, as time: to *put in* a Sunday afternoon playing tennis. — **put off 1** To delay; postpone. **2** To get rid of or avoid, often by excuses, etc.: to *put off* a caller. — **put on 1** To pretend. **2** To don, as clothing. **3** To present, as a play or entertainment. **4** To turn on, as a light. — **put out 1** To extinguish, as a fire. **2** To cause to leave; eject. **3** To annoy or inconvenience. — **put over** *informal* To accomplish or perform successfully: to *put over* a song on the radio. — **put through 1** To cause to undergo or do: to *put* a monkey *through* his tricks. **2** To accomplish successfully: to *put through* a long-distance phone call. — **put up 1** To preserve or can (vegetables, fruit, etc.) **2** To build; erect. **3** To supply, as money. **4** To provide with a place to live. **5** To offer: to *put up* a farm for sale. — **put upon** To take unfair advantage of. — **put up to** To urge on to some action: Who *put* you *up to* this silly plan? — **put up with** To endure; bear patiently.

put·out [poot'out'] *n.* In baseball, a play that causes a member of the team at bat to be out.

pu·tre·fy [pyoo'trə·fī] *v.* **pu·tre·fied, pu·tre·fy·ing** To decay or cause to decay; rot; decompose. — **pu·tre·fac·tion** [pyoo'trə·fak'shən] *n.*

pu·trid [pyoo'trid] *adj.* **1** Decaying; rotten: *putrid* meat. **2** Produced by decay: a *putrid* odor.

putt [put] **1** *n.* In golf, a light stroke made to roll the ball into or near the hole. **2** *v.* To strike (the ball) with such a stroke.

put·tee [put'ē *or* pu·tē'] *n.* A protective covering for the lower part of the leg, worn by soldiers, sportsmen, etc. It is either a leather gaiter or a strip of cloth wound spirally from the ankle to the knee.

put·ter[1] [put'ər] *n.* **1** In golf, a person who putts. **2** A golf club used in putting.

put·ter[2] [put'ər] *v.* To work or be busy without really accomplishing much: to *putter* all day.

put·ty [put'ē] *n., pl.* **put·ties**, *v.* **put·tied, put·ty·ing 1** *n.* A soft mixture of powdered chalk and linseed oil, used for filling cracks, holding panes of glass in windows, etc. **2** *v.* To secure or fill with putty.

puz·zle [puz'əl] *n., v.* **puz·zled, puz·zling 1** *v.* To confuse or perplex; mystify: The new instructions *puzzled* him. **2** *v.* To weigh in the mind; ponder: We *puzzled* for a long time on what to say. **3** *n.* Something that puzzles or baffles: It's a *puzzle* how the lion got out. **4** *n.* A toy, word game, etc., that tests one's mental skills or alertness: a picture *puzzle*. — **puzzle out** or **puzzle over** To think about or solve with much effort or study: to *puzzle out* a code; to *puzzle over* a problem. — **puz'zle·ment** *n.* — **puz'zler** *n.*

Pyg·my [pig'mē] *n., pl.* **Pyg·mies**, *adj.* **1** *n.* A member of a small Negroid people of central Africa who are not much more than four feet tall. **2** *adj.* Of or having to do with the Pygmies. **3** *n.* (*written* **pygmy**) A small or insignificant person or thing. **4** *adj.* (*written* **pygmy**) Small or dwarfed: a *pygmy* hippopotamus.

py·ja·mas [pə·jä′məz] *n.pl.* A British spelling of PAJAMAS.

py·lon [pī′lon] *n.* **1** A high tower used to mark a course an airplane should fly, to carry high-tension wires, etc. **2** A large gateway to an Egyptian temple or other large building.

py·or·rhe·a or **py·or·rhoe·a** [pī′ə·rē′ə] *n.* A disease in which the gums become inflamed, discharge pus, and shrink away from the teeth, which become loose.

pyr·a·mid [pir′ə·mid] *n.* **1** A geometrical figure having a flat base of three or more sides. All sides of a pyramid are triangles that slope upward to meet in a point at the top. **2** Any of the huge structures shaped like a pyramid in which ancient Egyptian kings were buried.

Egyptian pyramid

py·ram·i·dal [pi·ram′ə·dəl] *adj.* Of, having to do with, or shaped like a pyramid.

pyre [pīr] *n.* A heap of wood used for burning a dead body, often as a religious ceremony.

Pyr·e·nees [pir′ə·nēz] *n.pl.* A range of mountains between France and Spain.

Py·rex [pī′reks] *n.* A type of glassware that does not break when heated and may be used to cook foods in the oven or on top of the stove: a trademark. Also written **pyrex.**

py·rite [pī′rīt] *n.* **1** A pale yellow mineral consisting of iron and sulfur. It resembles gold and is sometimes called fool's gold. **2** (*pl.*) [pə·rī′tēz or pī·rī′tēz] Any mineral containing sulfur and a metal.

py·ro·ma·ni·a [pī′rə·mā′nē·ə] *n.* A mental disturbance in which a person has strong urges to set things on fire.

py·ro·ma·ni·ac [pī′rə·mā′nē·ak] *n.* A person afflicted with pyromania.

py·ro·tech·nic [pī′rə·tek′nik] *adj.* **1** Of or having to do with fireworks. **2** Brilliant or sensational like fireworks.

py·ro·tech·ni·cal [pī′rə·tek′ni·kəl] *adj.* Pyrotechnic.

py·ro·tech·nics [pī′rə·tek′niks] *n.pl.* **1** (*used with a singular verb*) The art of making or using fireworks. **2** A brilliant display of fireworks. **3** Any showy display, as of public speaking, skill in playing a musical instrument, etc. ◆ See -ICS.

Pyr·rhic victory [pir′ik] A victory won at such a great cost that it is almost a defeat: so called after **Pyr·rhus** [pir′əs], a king of Greece, whose victory over the Romans in 280 B.C. cost the lives of most of his soldiers.

Pyth·i·as [pith′ē·əs] *n.* See DAMON.

py·thon [pī′thon or pī′thən] *n.* A very large, nonpoisonous snake of warm regions, as Africa and Asia, that kills its prey by squeezing.

Python, about 13 ft. long

Q

q or **Q** [kyoo] *n., pl.* **q's** or **Q's** The 17th letter of the English alphabet.

qt. Abbreviation of: **1** QUART. **2** (*usually written* **qts.**) Quarts.

quack[1] [kwak] **1** *v.* To make a harsh, croaking cry, as a duck. **2** *n.* The sound made by a duck, or a similar croaking sound.

quack[2] [kwak] **1** *n.* Someone who pretends to have great knowledge, especially of medicine and healing; charlatan. **2** *adj. use:* a *quack* doctor. **3** *adj.* Of or related to quacks or quackery: a *quack* cure.

quack·er·y [kwak′ər·ē] *n., pl.* **quack·er·ies** The activities and practices of a quack.

quad·ran·gle [kwod′rang·gəl] *n.* **1** A square or oblong courtyard, or the buildings that surround such a courtyard. **2** A closed figure bounded by four straight lines; quadrilateral.

quad·rant [kwod′rənt] *n.* **1** One quarter of a circle; a sector or arc of 90°. **2** An instrument having a 90° scale, used to measure angles.

Quadrants

quad·rat·ic [kwod·rat′ik] *adj.* Indicating a mathematical expression or equation of the second degree: $x^2 + 3x - 2 = 16$ is a *quadratic* equation.

quad·ren·ni·al [kwod·ren′ē·əl] *adj.* **1** Happening every four years. **2** Lasting for four years. **— quad·ren′ni·al·ly** *adv.*

---

add, āce, câre, pälm;   end, ēqual;   it, īce;   odd, ōpen, ôrder;   took, pool;   up, bûrn;
ə = a in *above*, e in *sicken*, i in *possible*, o in *melon*, u in *circus*;   yoo = u in *fuse*;   oil;   pout;
     check;   ring;   thin;   this;   zh in *vision*.   For ¶ reference, see page 64 · HOW TO

quad·ri·lat·er·al [kwod'rə·lat'ər·əl] **1** *n.* A closed figure bounded by four straight lines. **2** *adj.* Four-sided.

Quadrilaterals

qua·drille [kwə·dril'] *n.* **1** A square dance for four couples. **2** Music for this dance.

quad·ru·ped [kwod'rŏo·ped] **1** *n.* A four-footed animal. **2** *adj.* Having four feet.

quad·ru·ple [kwod·rŏo'pəl *or* kwod'rŏo·pəl] *adj.,v.* **quad·ru·pled, quad·ru·pling 1** *adj.* Being four times as large or four times as many. **2** *adj.* Being in four parts or made up of four persons or things: a *quadruple* alliance. **3** *v.* To multiply by four; increase by four times: He *quadrupled* his money; The distance *quadrupled*.

quad·ru·plet [kwod·rŏo'plit *or* kwod'rŏo·plit] *n.* **1** One of four children produced by one mother in a single birth. **2** One of a set or collection of four things.

quaff [kwof *or* kwaf] *v.* To drink in large amounts and with zest: to *quaff* a cool beverage.

quag·mire [kwag'mīr'] *n.* **1** An area of deep, soft mud; bog. **2** A bad or trying situation.

quail[1] [kwāl] *v.* To shrink with fear; lose heart or courage.

quail[2] [kwāl] *n., pl.* **quail** or **quails** Any of several birds related to the partridge, often hunted for food.

quaint [kwānt] *adj.* Pleasantly odd or old-fashioned. **— quaint'ly** *adv.* **— quaint'ness** *n.*

quake [kwāk] *v.* **quaked, quak·ing,** *n.* **1** *v.* To shake or tremble, often with great force: to *quake* with fear; The ground *quaked* from the blast. **2** *n.* A shaking or trembling. **3** *n.* An earthquake.

Quail, 10 in. long

Quak·er [kwā'kər] **1** *n.* A member of the Society of Friends. **2** *adj.* Of or having to do with Quakers or the Society of Friends. ◆ *Quakers* got their name because their founder told them to tremble at the word of the Lord.

qual·i·fi·ca·tion [kwol'ə·fə·kā'shən] *n.* **1** The act of qualifying. **2** The condition of being qualified. **3** (*sometimes pl.*) Abilities, qualities, and training that make a person fit for a particular profession, occupation, etc. **4** Something that limits or restricts: We liked the play, but with certain *qualifications*.

qual·i·fied [kwol'ə·fīd] *adj.* **1** Suitable or competent, as for a particular occupation: a *qualified* engineer. **2** Limited or restricted: an attitude of *qualified* hope.

qual·i·fi·er [kwol'ə·fī'ər] *n.* **1** A person or thing that qualifies. **2** A word, as an adjective or adverb, that modifies another word or words.

qual·i·fy [kwol'ə·fī] *v.* **qual·i·fied, qual·i·fy·ing 1** To be or cause to be suitable or fit, as for a job, office, privilege, etc.: He *qualified* for the job; His knowledge *qualifies* him to speak. **2** To limit, restrict, or soften in some way: to *qualify* a remark; to *qualify* a penalty.

qual·i·ta·tive [kwol'ə·tā'tiv] *adj.* Of or having to do with quality. **— qual'i·ta'tive·ly** *adv.*

qualitative analysis A testing to see what chemical elements or components are present in a substance

qual·i·ty [kwol'ə·tē] *n., pl.* **qual·i·ties 1** That which makes something the way it is; a distinctive feature or characteristic: Wetness is a *quality* of water. **2** The nature or character of something: The poem catches the *quality* of summer. **3** The degree of excellence or worth of something: a poor *quality* of cloth. **4** Excellence: Aim for *quality*, not quantity. **5** A personal characteristic or trait: He has some good and some bad *qualities*. **6** The character of a sound apart from pitch and loudness; timbre. **7** High social rank: seldom used today: a lady of *quality*.

qualm [kwäm] *n.* **1** A twinge of conscience; guilty feeling: to steal with no *qualms*. **2** A touch of fear or anxiety: He has *qualms* about flying. **3** A slight feeling of sickness.

quan·da·ry [kwon'də·rē *or* kwon'drē] *n., pl.* **quan·da·ries** A condition of perplexity; dilemma; puzzle.

quan·ti·ta·tive [kwon'tə·tā'tiv] *adj.* **1** Of or related to quantity. **2** Capable of being measured. **— quan'ti·ta'tive·ly** *adv.*

quantitative analysis A testing to determine the amount or proportion of each of the components that make up a substance or mixture.

quan·ti·ty [kwon'tə·tē] *n., pl.* **quan·ti·ties 1** An amount or number: Buy equal *quantities* of flour and sugar. **2** (*often pl.*) A large amount or number: *quantities* of food; to order in *quantity*. **3** Something having length, size, volume, etc., that can be measured and expressed in suitable units: Pressure is a *quantity*.

quan·tum [kwon'təm] *n., pl.* **quan·ta** [kwon'-tə] A very small, indivisible quantity or unit of energy. For light or any other electromagnetic radiation, one quantum is equal to its frequency multiplied by a particular number that never changes. The energy contained in a moving atomic particle or in a field is also expressed as some multiple of one of its quanta.

quantum theory The theory that energy in its various forms exists as numbers of indivisible units, and that energy and mass are equivalent.

quar·an·tine [kwôr'ən·tēn] *n., v.* **quar·an·tined, quar·an·tin·ing 1** *n.* The isolation for a certain period of time of a ship arriving in port to make sure that there is no infectious disease on board. **2** *n.* The keeping of persons, goods, etc., that have been infected by or exposed to contagious diseases away from other people or things. **3** *n.* The place or length of time of such isolation. **4** *v.* To hold or confine in quarantine: to *quarantine* a child having whooping cough.

quar·rel [kwôr'əl] *n., v.* **quar·reled** or **quar·relled, quar·rel·ing** or **quar·rel·ling 1** *n.* An angry or violent dispute or argument;

a disagreement ending friendly relations. **2** *n.* The cause of a dispute. **3** *v.* To take part in a quarrel: He and his sister sometimes *quarrel.* **4** *v.* To find fault: to *quarrel* with someone's ideas.

quar·rel·some [kwôr'əl·səm] *adj.* Tending or liking to quarrel or find fault.

quar·ry[1] [kwôr'ē] *n., pl.* **quar·ries 1** An animal being hunted by man or another animal. **2** Anything that is hunted or eagerly pursued.

quar·ry[2] [kwôr'ē] *n., pl.* **quar·ries,** *v.* **quar·ried, quar·ry·ing 1** *n.* An excavation from which stone is taken for use in building. **2** *v.* To cut out or take from a quarry: to *quarry* marble.

quart [kwôrt] *n.* **1** A measure of liquid volume equal to 32 ounces, two pints, or 1/4 gallon. **2** A measure of volume for dry things, as grains, berries, etc., equal to 1/8 peck. **3** A container that will hold one quart.

quar·ter [kwôr'tər] **1** *n.* One of four equal parts that make up a whole. **2** *v.* To divide or cut into four equal or almost equal parts: to *quarter* a loaf of bread. **3** *adj.* Being one of four equal or almost equal parts: a *quarter* share of the food. **4** *n.* A U.S. or Canadian coin worth 25 cents. **5** *n.* A period of 15 minutes, especially before or after an hour: It is *quarter* past two. **6** *n.* One of the four periods into which a year is divided, starting on the first day of the first, fourth, seventh, and tenth months. **7** *n.* The time it takes the moon to move one fourth the distance of its path around the earth, about seven days. **8** *n.* One of the four periods of a football game, etc. **9** *n.* Any of the four legs or limbs of an animal, together with the adjacent parts. **10** *n.* One of the four main points of the compass. **11** *n.* A section of a city; district: the French *quarter.* **12** *n.* (*pl.*) A place to live in, or sometimes just to sleep in: They found *quarters* in an inn. **13** *v.* To provide with living or sleeping space: The men were *quartered* in barracks. **14** *n.* Source or place of origin: There's no news from that *quarter.* **15** *n.* Mercy, as shown to a defeated enemy: No *quarter* will be asked or given. **— at close quarters** Close by; at close range.

quar·ter·back [kwôr'tər·bak'] *n.* In football, the player in the backfield who usually calls the signals and receives the ball from the center.

quar·ter·deck or **quar·ter·deck** [kwôr'tər·dek'] *n.* The rear part of a ship's upper deck, reserved for officers.

quar·ter·ly [kwôr'tər·lē] *adj., n., pl.* **quar·ter·lies,** *adv.* **1** *adj.* Happening, done, due, etc., at three-month intervals: *quarterly* payments. **2** *n.* A magazine, etc., issued once every three months. **3** *adv.* Once every three months: to pay taxes *quarterly.*

quar·ter·mas·ter [kwôr'tər·mas'tər] *n.* **1** A military officer in charge of housing, clothing, and supplies for troops. **2** On a ship, a petty officer responsible for steering, signals, etc.

quarter note A musical note that is one-fourth as long as a whole note.

quar·ter·staff [kwôr'tər·staf'] *n., pl.* **quar·ter·staves** [kwôr'tər·stāvz'] A long, stout pole with an iron tip, once used in England as a weapon.

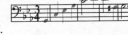

Quarter notes

quar·tet [kwôr·tet'] *n.* **1** A musical composition for four voices or instruments. **2** The people who perform such a composition. **3** A set of four similar things.

quar·to [kwôr'tō] *n., pl.* **quar·tos 1** A page size equal to a quarter of a full sheet. **2** A book whose pages are of this size.

quartz [kwôrts] *n.* A hard, glasslike mineral composed mainly of silica, sometimes found in colored forms as amethyst, onyx, and other gems.

quartz·ite [kwôrt'sīt] *n.* A type of hard rock formed of sandstone and quartz.

quash[1] [kwosh] *v.* In law, to cancel or set aside, as an indictment or writ; annul.

quash[2] [kwosh] *v.* To put down or suppress with force: to *quash* a revolt.

qua·si [kwä'zē *or* kwā'zī] **1** *adj.* Resembling or like but not quite the same as: often used in combination with nouns, as in *quasi-illness,* resembling but not quite the same as an illness. **2** *adv.* Nearly; almost: often used in combination with adjectives, as in *quasi-comic,* almost funny. ◆ *Quasi* comes from a Latin word meaning *as if* or *as if it were.*

qua·ver [kwā'vər] **1** *v.* To tremble or shake in an uncertain way, as a voice. **2** *n.* A trembling, especially of the voice. **3** *v.* To say or sing in a nervous, shaky voice: to *quaver* a plea for mercy.

quay [kē] *n.* A wharf or artificial structure where a ship may dock and load or unload.

quea·sy [kwē'zē] *adj.* **quea·si·er, quea·si·est 1** Sick or causing sickness at the stomach. **2** Having an easily upset stomach. **3** Ill at ease; uncomfortable. **4** Delicate; squeamish. **— quea'si·ly** *adv.* **— quea'si·ness** *n.*

A quay

Que·bec [kwi·bek'] *n.* **1** A province of eastern Canada. **2** Its capital, a port on the St. Lawrence River.

que·bra·cho [kā·brä'chō] *n., pl.* **que·bra·chos** Any of several hardwood trees found in South America, especially in Chile.

queen [kwēn] *n.* **1** The wife of a king, or a woman who rules a country in her own right. **2** A woman who is very important or famous: a movie *queen*. **3** In chess, the most powerful piece, capable of moving any number of squares in any straight or diagonal line. **4** Any of the four playing cards having a picture of a queen. **5** In a colony of ants, bees, etc., a fully developed female, usually the only one, that lays eggs.

Queen Anne's lace [anz] A wild carrot whose white flower resembles a piece of lace.

queen·ly [kwēn′lē] *adj.* **queen·li·er, queen·li·est 1** Of, having to do with, or like a queen. **2** Fit or suitable for a queen.

queen mother A king's widow who is the mother of a reigning king or queen.

Queens·land [kwēnz′lənd] *n.* A state of NE Australia.

queer [kwir] **1** *adj.* Unusual or abnormal; odd; strange: a *queer* notion; a *queer* old woman. **2** *adj.* Suspicious or questionable: *queer* actions. **3** *adj. slang* Counterfeit: *queer* money. **4** *adj.* Not well; queasy: She felt *queer* all day. **5** *v. slang* To spoil or ruin; botch. **— queer′ly** *adv.* **— queer′ness** *n.*

quell [kwel] *v.* **1** To put down or suppress by force: to *quell* a revolt. **2** To quiet or end, as pain or fear: His suspicions were *quelled*.

quench [kwench] *v.* **1** To put out (a fire) by throwing water on it. **2** To end or satisfy with water, as thirst. **3** To cool, as a hot metal, by thrusting into water or other liquid.

quer·u·lous [kwer′(y)ə·ləs] *adj.* **1** Tending to complain or find fault: a *querulous* person. **2** Showing or full of complaints; whining: a *querulous* remark. **— quer′u·lous·ly** *adv.*

que·ry [kwir′ē] *n., pl.* **que·ries, que·ried, que·ry·ing 1** *n.* A question or inquiry. **2** *v.* To ask questions of or about: to *query* a witness; to *query* a loss of money. **3** *n.* A question mark. **4** *v.* To express doubt about: to *query* a statement.

quest [kwest] *n.* **1** A seeking or looking for something; search. **2** An expedition, as by a knight seeking adventure.

ques·tion [kwes′chən] **1** *n.* Something that is asked in order to find out something; something that requires an answer. **2** *n.* The form of a sentence or clause that asks a question. **3** *v.* To ask a question or questions of: The principal *questioned* him thoroughly. **4** *n.* A subject of inquiry or disagreement; a matter of doubt; problem. **5** *v.* To have a doubt about or an objection to; dispute: to *question* a decision. **6** *n.* A matter under discussion: to vote on a *question*. **7** *n.* Doubt or uncertainty: no *question* about it. **— beside the question** Off the subject; not pertinent. **— beyond question** Without any doubt or disagreement. **— call in question** To raise objection to; challenge. **— in question** Under discussion or consideration. **— out of the question** Not to be thought of; impossible. **— ques′tion·er** *n.*

ques·tion·a·ble [kwes′chən·ə·bəl] *adj.* **1** Of or showing doubtful character, honesty, morality, etc.: *questionable* behavior. **2** Likely to be questioned or doubted: a *questionable* conclusion. **— ques′tion·a·bly** *adv.*

question mark A punctuation mark (?) placed at the end of a written question.

ques·tion·naire [kwes′chən·âr′] *n.* A list of questions, usually printed, used to get information from a person or persons.

quet·zal [ket·säl′] *n.* A brightly colored bird, the male of which has very long tail feathers. It is found in Central America.

queue [kyōō] *n., v.* **queued, queu·ing 1** *n.* A single braid of hair hanging from the back of the head; pigtail. **2** *n.* A line of persons, cars, etc., waiting for something. **3** *v. British* To form such a line: to *queue* up for tickets.

quib·ble [kwib′əl] *n., v.* **quib·bled, quib·bling 1** *n.* The use of words in twisted senses or the making of minor objections to avoid the main points in an argument or discussion. **2** *v.* To make quibbles. **— quib′bler** *n.*

Quetzal, to 42 in. long

quick [kwik] **1** *adj.* Done or happening in a short time; swift; fast. **2** *adv.* Rapidly; fast: Please come *quick*. **3** *adj.* Swift to learn, understand, or perceive; alert: a *quick* mind; a *quick* ear. **4** *adj.* Easily excited or aroused: a *quick* temper. **5** *adj.* Able to move rapidly; speedy: *quick* fingers. **6** *n.* All living people, now only in the phrase **the quick and the dead. 7** *n.* The delicate, tender flesh under a fingernail or toenail. **8** *n.* Deep, sensitive feelings: an insult that cuts to the *quick*. **— quick′ly** *adv.* **— quick′ness** *n.*

quick·en [kwik′ən] *v.* **1** To go or cause to go faster: He *quickened* his pace; The flow *quickened*. **2** To make sooner; hasten: Please *quicken* your departure. **3** To return to life or activity; revive: Spring *quickens* the countryside.

quick-freeze [kwik′frēz′] *v.* **quick-froze, quick-fro·zen, quick-freez·ing** To freeze (food) rapidly at low temperatures so as to store without loss of taste or nourishment.

quick·lime [kwik′līm′] *n.* A form of lime used to make mortar. It reacts strongly with water.

quick·sand [kwik′sand′] *n.* A deep bed of sand so filled and soaked with water that it swallows up a person, animal, or object that tries to rest or move upon it.

quick·sil·ver [kwik′sil′vər] *n.* The metal mercury in its liquid form.

quick-tem·pered [kwik′tem′pərd] *adj.* Easily made angry.

quick-wit·ted [kwik′wit′id] *adj.* Having a mind that works quickly; mentally alert.

quid [kwid] *n.* A small piece of tobacco for chewing.

qui·es·cent [kwī·es′ənt] *adj.* In a state of rest; inactive; quiet. **— qui·es′cence** *n.*

qui·et [kwī′ət] **1** *adj.* Having or making little or no noise: a *quiet* room; a *quiet* machine. **2** *adj.* Not moving very much or at all; still; calm: a *quiet* pond. **3** *adj.* Free from stress, strain, or hurried activity: a *quiet* day in the park. **4** *adj.* Calm and restful; gentle; mild: a *quiet* manner. **5** *adj.* Not showy or overdone; modest; restrained: *quiet* decorations. **6** *v.* To make or become quiet: *Quiet* her down! The sea *quieted* after the storm. **7** *n.* A state or condition of calm, repose, silence, etc.: peace and *quiet*. — **qui·et·ly** *adv.* — **qui·et·ness** *n.*

qui·e·tude [kwī'ə·t(y)o͞od] *n.* A state or condition of calm and repose; quiet; rest.

qui·e·tus [kwī·ē'təs] *n.* **1** A silencing or suppressing, as of a rumor. **2** A final settlement or payment, as of a debt. **3** Death, or something that causes death: seldom used today.

quill [kwil] *n.* **1** A large, strong feather from the wing or tail of a bird. **2** Something made from such a feather, especially an old-fashioned pen. **3** A large, sharp spine, as of a porcupine.

quilt [kwilt] **1** *n.* A covering for a bed made by stitching together two layers of cloth in patterns or crossing lines. Between these layers there is another layer of soft, warm material. **2** *v.* To make quilts: The old ladies *quilted* all day. **3** *v.* To make of quilting, or stitch like a quilt. **4** *adj. use:* a *quilted* skirt.

Quill pen

quilt·ing [kwil'ting] *n.* **1** The act of making a quilt. **2** A material for or like a quilt.

quince [kwins] *n.* **1** A hard, acid, yellowish fruit that looks like an apple, used for jelly or preserves. **2** The tree that bears this fruit.

qui·nine [kwī'nīn] *n.* A bitter, crystalline substance contained in the bark of the cinchona tree, used in making drugs to treat malaria. ◆ *Quinine* comes from a South American Indian word.

quin·sy [kwin'zē] *n.* A severe swelling and soreness of the tonsils and throat together with the formation of abscesses.

quin·tes·sence [kwin·tes'əns] *n.* **1** The most essential part of anything, usually in a very pure or concentrated form: The *quintessence* of poetry is rhythm. **2** A perfect or typical example.

quin·tet [kwin·tet'] *n.* **1** A piece of music for five voices or instruments. **2** The five persons who perform such a piece of music. **3** A group of five persons or things.

quin·tu·plet [kwin·tup'lit *or* kwin·t(y)o͞o'plit *or* kwin't(y)o͞o·plit] *n.* **1** One of five children born of the same mother at one birth. **2** One of a set of five things.

quip [kwip] *n., v.* **quipped, quip·ping 1** *n.* A clever or witty, and sometimes sarcastic, remark; gibe. **2** *v.* To make a witty remark; jest.

quire [kwīr] *n.* A group of 24 or 25 sheets of paper of the same size and kind; 1/20 of a ream.

quirk [kwirk] *n.* **1** An odd habit or mannerism;

a peculiarity. **2** A quibble. **3** A sudden curve or twist, as in handwriting. **4** A clever retort.

quirt [kwirt] *n.* A whip with a short handle and a braided rawhide lash, used by horseback riders.

quis·ling [kwiz'ling] *n.* A person who betrays his country to an enemy and is then given political power by the conquerors.

Quirt

quit [kwit] *v.* **quit** or **quit·ted, quit·ting 1** *v.* To cease from; stop: We *quit* work early; to *quit* smoking. **2** *v.* To go away from; leave: to *quit* the country. **3** *v. informal* To give up or leave a job, etc.: John *quit* last Tuesday. **4** *adj.* Relieved or freed from: to be *quit* of a debt. **5** *v.* To conduct (oneself): seldom used today: *Quit* yourselves like men. — **be quits** To be even (with another).

quit·claim [kwit'klām'] *n.* A legal agreement in which one gives up some claim, demand, or right.

quite [kwīt] *adv.* **1** To the full extent; completely; entirely: *quite* ready. **2** Really; truly: I am *quite* able to go. **3** *informal* To a great extent; very much; considerably: *quite* ill. ◆ The phrase *quite a* is used in many expressions to show a large but indefinite number, size, quantity, etc.: *Quite a few* means *many*; *Quite a while* means *a long while*. *Quite a* is also used informally to mean *a great* or *a wonderful*: She's *quite a* girl.

quit·tance [kwit'(ə)ns] *n.* **1** Release, as from a debt or obligation. **2** A document certifying this; receipt. **3** Something given in return or revenge.

quit·ter [kwit'ər] *n.* A person who gives up without making a real effort.

quiv·er[1] [kwiv'ər] **1** *v.* To make a slight trembling motion; vibrate. **2** *n.* A trembling or shaking.

quiv·er[2] [kwiv'ər] *n.* A case or container for carrying arrows.

Quixote, Don. See DON QUIXOTE.

quix·ot·ic [kwik·sot'ik] *adj.* Extremely romantic, chivalrous, or idealistic, but foolish and impractical at the same time. — **quix·ot'i·cal·ly** *adv.*

Quiver

quiz [kwiz] *n., pl.* **quiz·zes,** *v.* **quizzed, quiz·zing 1** *n.* The act of questioning, especially a short or informal test given to a student or students. **2** *v.* To examine by asking questions. **3** *n.* A person who makes fun of others. **4** *v.* To make fun of; ridicule.

---

add, **ā**ce, **câ**re, **pä**lm;   **e**nd, **ē**qual;   **i**t, **ī**ce;   **o**dd, **ō**pen, **ô**rder;   t**oo**k, p**oo**l;   **u**p, b**û**rn;

ə = a in *above*, e in *sicken*, i in *possible*, o in *melon*, u in *circus*;   **y**o͞o = u in *fuse*;   **oi**l;   p**ou**t;

check;   **r**in**g**;   **th**in;   **th**is;   **zh** in *vision*.   For ¶ reference, see page 64 · HOW TO

quiz·zi·cal [kwiz′i·kəl] *adj.* **1** Poking fun; mocking: a *quizzical* smirk. **2** Questioning; puzzled: a *quizzical* frown. **3** Queer; odd.

quoin [koin *or* kwoin] *n.* **1** An external corner or angle of a building. **2** A stone or group of stones forming such a corner.

quoit [kwoit] *n.* **1** A metal or rope ring made so that it may be thrown over a peg set in the ground. **2** (*pl.*) (*used with a singular verb*) A game whose object is the throwing of these rings over a peg.

Quoits

quon·dam [kwon′dəm] *adj.* Having been before; former: a *quondam* companion.

Quon·set hut [kwon′sit] A metal building in the form of half a cylinder resting lengthwise on the ground. It is made up of ready-made sections that may be put together easily.

Quonset hut

quo·rum [kwôr′əm] *n.* The smallest number of a group or assembly that must be present in order to make binding decisions or carry on business.

quo·ta [kwō′tə] *n.* A number or amount that is required from or given to a person, group, etc.: The factory produced its *quota* of cars.

quot·a·ble [kwō′tə·bəl] *adj.* **1** Worth quoting, as a wise or clever saying. **2** Suitable for quoting.

quo·ta·tion [kwō·tā′shən] *n.* **1** Something said or written by one person repeated exactly by another person. **2** The act of quoting. **3** A price, as of stocks, bonds, etc.

quotation mark Either of the marks ('' and '') or (' and ') used at the beginning and end of a quoted passage.

quote [kwōt] *v.* **quot·ed, quot·ing** **1** To use the exact words of: to *quote* a book. **2** To use a quotation or quotations: He *quotes* too often from others. **3** To use (a rule, legal decision, etc.) as an authority or illustration: The lawyer *quoted* an old Supreme Court case. **4** To state (a price): He *quoted* $70 as the lowest price. **5** To give the price of: to *quote* a stock at $70 per share.

quoth [kwōth] *v.* Said; spoke: "Alas," *quoth* he: seldom used today except in poems.

quo·tient [kwō′shənt] *n.* The number that results if one number is divided by another. If 6 is divided by 3, 2 is the quotient. If 7 is divided by 3, 2 is the quotient and the remainder is 1.

R

r or **R** [är] *n., pl.* **r's** or **R's** The 18th letter of the English alphabet. — **the three R's** Reading, writing, and arithmetic.

Ra The symbol for the element RADIUM.

Ra [rä] *n.* The sun god of ancient Egypt.

rab·bi [rab′ī] *n., pl.* **rab·bis** or **rab·bies** A man learned in Jewish religious law who is trained and ordained to be the spiritual head of a Jewish community or a teacher of the religious law.

rab·bit [rab′it] *n.* **1** A small animal with long ears, soft fur, and a short tail. Rabbits are smaller than hares, live in burrows, and move by jumping. **2** The fur of this animal.

rab·ble [rab′əl] *n.* A noisy, disorderly crowd or mob. — **the rabble** The lowest class of people, often thought of as a rude, ignorant mob.

Rabbit, 11–17 in. long

rab·id [rab′id] *adj.* **1** Having rabies; mad: a *rabid* dog. **2** Going to unreasonable extremes in showing or expressing an opinion, feeling, etc.: *rabid* supporters. **3** Furious; raging.

ra·bies [rā′bēz] *n.* A disease that affects the central nervous system of mammals; hydrophobia. It is fatal when not treated. A person may get it if bitten by a rabid animal, as a mad dog.

rac·coon [ra·kōōn′] *n.* **1** A small animal with grayish brown fur and a bushy, striped tail. It lives chiefly in trees and is active at night. **2** Its fur. ◆ *Raccoon* comes from a North American Indian word meaning *he scratches with the hands.*

Raccoon, to 30 in. long

race[1] [rās] *n., v.* **raced, rac·ing** **1** *n.* A contest to decide the comparative speed of the contestants. **2** *v.* To take part in a contest of speed: Runners, swimmers, or sailboats may *race*. **3** *v.* To compete with or cause to compete in a race: John *raced* Harry to the house; to *race* horses. **4** *v.* To run or move swiftly: She *raced* to the phone. **5** *v.* To run at a high speed with no load: to *race* a motor. **6** *n.* A swift current of water or its channel, as a millrace. **7** *n.* Any contest, as for office: a mayoralty *race*.

race[2] [rās] *n.* **1** One of the major divisions of

mankind, whose members are regarded as having a common ancestry or origin and similar physical traits. **2** The condition of belonging to a certain branch of mankind: *to be proud of one's race.* **3** A group or class of plants or animals having common characteristics: *a race of sturdy wheat.* **4** A group or kind of people: *the race of engineers.* **5** A clan, tribe, nation, or people.

ra·ceme [rā·sēm′] *n.* A flower cluster having its flowers, each growing on a short stalk, spaced along a stem, as in a lily of the valley.

rac·er [rā′sər] *n.* **1** A person, animal, or vehicle that races. **2** The blacksnake of the U.S.

race·track [rās′trak′] *n.* A track or course over which a race, such as a horse race, is run.

Ra·chel [rā′chəl] *n.* In the Bible, the second wife of Jacob, mother of Joseph and Benjamin.

ra·cial [rā′shəl] *adj.* Of or having to do with race, origins, or lineage. — **ra′cial·ly** *adv.*

ra·cism [rā′siz·əm] *n.* **1** Exaggeration of the racial differences between individuals. **2** Prejudice in favor of a particular race. — **ra′cist** *n.*

rack[1] [rak] **1** *n.* A frame, stand, etc., that holds things, as for storage or display: a hat *rack;* a book *rack.* **2** *n.* A frame attached to a wagon for carrying hay, straw, etc. **3** *n.* An instrument of torture that stretches the arms and legs of victims. **4** *v.* To torture or torment, by or as if by putting on the rack: *to be racked with pain.* **5** *n.* A bar with teeth on one side that mesh with the teeth of a gearwheel, etc. — **rack one's brains** To think as hard as possible.

rack[2] [rak] *n.* Destruction, especially in the phrase **rack and ruin:** Because of the owner's neglect the business went to *rack and ruin.*

rack·et[1] [rak′it] *n.* **1** Loud noise, clatter, clamor, or commotion. **2** *informal* A dishonest method or scheme for getting money, goods, etc., often by the use of force.

Clothes rack

rack·et[2] [rak′it] *n.* A light bat used in tennis, badminton, etc., consisting of a handle attached to an oval frame strung with a network usually of catgut or nylon. ◆ *Racket* comes from an Arabic word meaning *palm of the hand.*

rack·et·eer [rak′ə·tir′] **1** *n.* A criminal who carries on some illegal business to get money, often by using threats, force, or bribery. **2** *v.* To get money by such methods.

ra·coon [ra·kōōn′] *n.* Another spelling of RACCOON.

rac·quet [rak′it] *n.* Another spelling of RACKET[2].

rac·y [rā′sē] *adj.* **rac·i·er, rac·i·est** **1** Spirited or lively: *a racy style of writing.* **2** Slightly immodest or indecent: *a racy story.*

ra·dar [rā′där] *n.* A device for locating objects and determining their size and speed by sending out radio waves and observing how and from where they are reflected by the objects. ◆ *Radar* comes from *ra(dio) d(etection) a(nd) r(anging).*

ra·di·al [rā′dē·əl] *adj.* **1** Of, being, or like a ray or radius. **2** Extending outward in all directions from one center. — **ra′di·al·ly** *adv.*

ra·di·ance [rā′dē·əns] *n.* Shining brightness.

ra·di·ant [rā′dē·ənt] *adj.* **1** Very bright and shining; brilliant. **2** Beaming with joy, love, energy, etc.: *a radiant smile.* **3** Giving off radiant energy. **4** Coming in rays from a central source: *radiant heat.* — **ra′di·ant·ly** *adv.*

radiant energy Energy that is transmitted in the form of waves, especially electromagnetic waves, as light, X-rays, etc.

ra·di·ate [*v.* rā′dē·āt, *adj.* rā′dē·it] *v.* **ra·di·at·ed, ra·di·at·ing,** *adj.* **1** *v.* To send out rays or radiation. **2** *v.* To send out in rays: *The sun radiates heat.* **3** *v.* To come out in rays: *Light radiates from the sun.* **4** *v.* To spread out from a center, as the spokes of a wheel. **5** *adj.* Having rays or radiating parts: *The sunflower is a radiate flower.* **6** *v.* To show as if shining in rays: *Her eyes radiated joy.*

ra·di·a·tion [rā′dē·ā′shən] *n.* **1** The sending out of radiant energy, as from radioactive substances. **2** The energy sent out.

ra·di·a·tor [rā′dē·ā′tər] *n.* **1** A network of pipes through which is passed steam or hot water to provide heat, as for a room. **2** A set of pipes for cooling circulating water that carries heat away from an engine, as in automobiles.

rad·i·cal [rad′i·kəl] **1** *adj.* Of, coming from, or going to the root; basic: *radical differences.* **2** *adj.* In mathematics, indicating or having to do with a square root or cube root, etc. **3** *adj.* Extreme; thoroughgoing: *radical surgery.* **4** *n.* A person who favors rapid and widespread changes or reforms, especially in politics or government. **5** *adj.* Favoring or having to do with such rapid changes. **6** *n.* A group of atoms that acts as a unit in one or more compounds and that always appears in combination. — **rad′i·cal·ism** *n.* — **rad·i·cal·ly** [rad′ik·lē] *adv.*

radical sign A sign ($\sqrt{\ }$) that indicates a specified root of the number written under it. $\sqrt[3]{8} =$ the cube root of 8, that is, 2.

ra·di·i [rā′dē·ī] Plural of RADIUS.

ra·di·o [rā′dē·ō] *n., pl.* **ra·di·os,** *v.* **ra·di·oed, ra·di·o·ing** **1** *n.* The devices and methods by which sounds or other signals are changed into variations of an electromagnetic wave that travels through space to a receiver where the signals are recovered. **2** *adj. use: a radio* beam; *a radio* broadcast. **3** *n.* A receiver, transmitter, or other radio apparatus. **4** *v.* To send (a message) or communicate with (someone) by radio. **5** *n.* The radio business or industry.

add, āce, câre, pälm;　end, ēqual;　it, īce;　odd, ōpen, ôrder;　tŏŏk, pōōl;　up, bûrn;
ə = a in *above,* e in *sicken,* i in *possible,* o in *melon,* u in *circus;*　yōō = u in *fuse;*　oil;　pout;
check;　ring;　thin;　this;　zh in *vision.*　For ¶ reference, see page 64 · HOW TO

ra·di·o·ac·tive [rā′dē·ō·ak′tiv] *adj.* Giving off energy in the form of atomic particles and gamma rays, as certain elements. Radium is radioactive. **—ra′di·o·ac·tiv′i·ty** *n.*

radio astronomy The study of celestial bodies by observing the radio waves they give off.

ra·di·o·car·bon [rā′dē·ō·kär′bən] *n.* Another name for CARBON 14.

ra·di·o·sonde [rā′dē·ō·sond′] *n.* A device, usually attached to a balloon, that records weather conditions at high altitudes and radios the information back to earth.

radio star A star that emits mostly radio waves.

radio telescope An instrument used to receive radio waves given off by celestial bodies.

radio wave An electromagnetic wave having a frequency between about 10 kilocycles and 30,000 megacycles per second.

rad·ish [rad′ish] *n.* **1** A small, crisp, sharp-tasting plant root, eaten raw. It has a red or white skin. **2** The plant yielding this root.

ra·di·um [rā′dē·əm] *n.* A strongly radioactive metallic element found in ores of uranium. Its salts are sometimes used in medicine.

ra·di·us [rā′dē·əs] *n., pl.* **ra·di·i** or **ra·di·us·es** **1** A straight line from the center of a circle or sphere to the circumference or surface. **2** A circular area or boundary measured by the length of its radius: only two stores within a *radius* of 15 miles. **3** The thicker and shorter bone of the forearm.

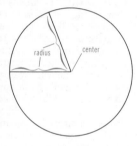
radius   center

raf·fi·a [raf′ē·ə] *n.* Fiber from the leaves of a cultivated palm tree, used for baskets, etc.

raf·fle [raf′əl] *n., v.* **raf·fled, raf·fling** **1** *n.* A lottery in which many people buy tickets, each hoping to win the prize. **2** *v.* To offer as a prize in a raffle: to *raffle* off a turkey.

raft [raft] *n.* A floating platform made of logs, planks, etc., fastened together.

raft·er [raf′tər] *n.* A sloping timber or beam giving form and support to a roof.

rag¹ [rag] *n.* **1** A torn, worn-out, or discarded piece of cloth. **2** A small cloth used for cleaning, etc. **3** (*pl.*) Tattered or shabby clothes.

rag² [rag] *v.* **ragged, ragging** *slang* **1** To tease or bother. **2** To scold.

rag·a·muf·fin [rag′ə·muf′in] *n.* A dirty, ragged person, especially a child.

Rafters

rage [rāj] *n., v.* **raged, raging** **1** *n.* Violent anger; fury; wrath: his face white with *rage*. **2** *n.* A fit of violent anger: He flew into a *rage* at the insult. **3** *v.* To feel or show furious anger. **4**

v. To move or proceed with great violence: The storm *raged*. **5** *n.* Any great violence, as of a storm. **6** *v.* To spread wildly and uncontrolled, as an epidemic. **7** *n.* A fad; fashion: Bulky sweaters were the *rage* last fall.

rag·ged [rag′id] *adj.* **1** Torn or worn into rags; tattered: *ragged* clothes. **2** Wearing tattered or shabby clothes: a *ragged* beggar. **3** Rough, shaggy, or uneven: a *ragged* haircut; *ragged* margins. **4** Jagged; rough: *ragged* rocks. **—rag′ged·ly** *adv.* **—rag′ged·ness** *n.*

rag·lan [rag′lən] **1** *n.* An overcoat or topcoat with sleeves that extend in one piece up to the neckline. **2** *adj. use:* raglan sleeves.

ra·gout [ra·gōō′] *n.* Meat and vegetables stewed with many herbs and spices.

rag·time [rag′tīm′] *n.* An early form of jazz using fast, syncopated rhythms.

rag·weed [rag′wēd′] *n.* A coarse, very common weed. Its pollen gives some people hay fever.

Raglan sleeves

raid [rād] **1** *n.* A sudden attack, as by a band of soldiers. **2** *n.* A sudden entering and seizing of what is found inside: The boys made a *raid* on the refrigerator. **3** *v.* To make a raid on. **4** *v.* To take part in a raid. **—raid′er** *n.*

rail¹ [rāl] *n.* **1** A bar of wood, metal, etc., held up by supports, as in a fence or at the side of a stairway. **2** Either of the parallel steel bars that form a track, as for a train. **3** A railroad: to ship goods by *rail*.

rail² [rāl] *v.* To complain in angry, bitter, or scornful words: to *rail* at one's enemies.

rail³ [rāl] *n., pl.* **rail** or **rails** A bird with short wings and long legs, living in marshes.

rail·ing [rā′ling] *n.* **1** A fence or other barrier made up of one or more rails resting on supports. **2** Rails, or material to make rails.

rail·ler·y [rā′lər·ē] *n.* Good-natured teasing.

rail·road [rāl′rōd′] **1** *n.* A road having parallel steel rails that form a track for the wheels of trains to travel on. **2** *n.* A transportation system consisting of all the tracks and trains under one management, along with the stations, equipment, and employees. **3** *v.* To work on or for a railroad. **4** *v.* *U.S. informal* To rush or force very fast, without enough discussion: to *railroad* a bill through Congress.

rail·way [rāl′wā′] *n.* **1** A railroad. **2** Any tracks similar to those of a railroad.

rai·ment [rā′mənt] *n.* Wearing apparel; clothing: seldom used today.

rain [rān] **1** *n.* Condensed water vapor from the atmosphere, falling to earth in drops. **2** *n.* A fall of such drops; rainstorm or shower. **3** *v.* To fall from the clouds in drops: It is *raining*. **4** *n.* A fast, heavy fall of many similar things: a *rain* of arrows. **5** *v.* To fall like a heavy rain: Tears *rained* down her cheeks. **6** *v.* To send or pour like rain; shower: The old man *rained* gifts on his grandchildren.

rain·bow [rān′bō′] *n.* An arc of light exhibiting many colors: violet, indigo, blue, green, yellow, orange, and red. It appears in the atmosphere when sunlight passes through droplets of water, as mist, spray, or falling rain. ◆ *Rainbow* comes from the Old English word *regnboga*, which was a combination of the words for *rain* and *bow* (the bow of an archer).

rain·coat [rān′kōt′] *n.* A coat, usually waterproof, to be worn in rainy weather.

rain·drop [rān′drop′] *n.* A drop of rain.

rain·fall [rān′fôl′] *n.* **1** A shower. **2** The amount of water that falls as rain, hail, snow, or sleet in a given region within a certain length of time.

rain·storm [rān′stôrm′] *n.* A storm accompanied by rain.

rain·y [rā′nē] *adj.* **rain·i·er, rain·i·est 1** Having much rain. **2** Bringing rain. **3** Made wet by rain: a *rainy* hike.

rainy day Some possible future time of need.

raise [rāz] *v.* **raised, rais·ing,** *n.* **1** *v.* To cause to move upward or to a higher level; lift: He *raised* his hand. **2** *v.* To set up or build; erect: to *raise* a monument. **3** *v.* To make greater in amount, size, value, volume, etc.: to *raise* prices; Don't *raise* your voice. **4** *n.* An increase in amount. **5** *n.* An increase in pay. **6** *v.* To grow or breed: to *raise* corn; to *raise* horses. **7** *v. U.S.* To bring up; rear: to *raise* children. **8** *v.* To bring up for consideration: to *raise* a question. **9** *v.* To bring out; cause: His witty comment *raised* a laugh. **10** *v.* To stir up; make active; arouse. **11** *v.* To gather together; obtain or collect: to *raise* funds. **12** *v.* To end; lift: to *raise* a blockade. ◆ See RISE.

rai·sin [rā′zən] *n.* A sweet grape of a special sort dried in the sun or in an oven.

ra·jah or **ra·ja** [rä′jə] *n.* **1** A Hindu prince or ′tribal chief in India. **2** A Malay ruler.

rake[1] [rāk] *n., v.* **raked, rak·ing 1** *n.* A garden or farm tool consisting of a long handle with evenly spaced long teeth or prongs at the end. **2** *v.* To scrape together with or as if with a rake: to *rake* leaves. **3** *v.* To smooth, clean, or prepare with a rake: to *rake* soil or a lawn. **4** *v.* To search closely or carefully: He *raked* the town for bargains. **5** *v.* To fire along the length of: Enemy guns *raked* the trenches.

rake[2] [rāk] *n.* A man who indulges too much in harmful pleasures, such as drinking, gambling, or loose living.

Rake

rak·ish [rā′kish] *adj.* **1** Dashing; jaunty; smart: a cap worn at a *rakish* angle. **2** Having an appearance that suggests speed, as a boat.

Ra·leigh [rô′lē *or* rä′lē] *n.* The capital of North Carolina.

Ra·leigh [rô′lē *or* rä′lē], **Sir Walter,** 1552?–1618, English colonizer, courtier, and poet.

ral·ly [ral′ē] *n., pl.* **ral·lies,** *v.* **ral·lied, ral·ly·ing 1** *n.* A mass meeting or assembly of persons for some common purpose. **2** *v.* To bring or come together for united or efficient action: to *rally* fleeing troops; The troops *rallied.* **3** *v.* To come to the support of: to *rally* to the cause of peace. **4** *v.* To regain strength; revive: The patient *rallied.* **5** *n.* The act of rallying.

ram [ram] *n., v.* **rammed, ram·ming 1** *n.* A male sheep. **2** *v.* To strike with force: The ship *rammed* into the pier. **3** *v.* To drive or force down or into something. **4** *n.* A machine that strikes powerful blows, as a battering ram.

ram·ble [ram′bəl] *v.* **ram·bled, ram·bling,** *n.* **1** *v.* To walk or stroll freely and aimlessly; roam; wander. **2** *n.* An aimless, unhurried walk or hike. **3** *v.* To speak or write in a disorganized way, wandering from subject to subject. **4** *v.* To twist irregularly, as a vine or path.

ram·bler [ram′blər] *n.* **1** A person or thing that rambles. **2** A type of climbing rose.

ram·bunc·tious [ram·bungk′shəs] *adj. U.S. informal* Wild, unruly, and boisterous in behavior.

ram·i·fi·ca·tion [ram′ə·fə·kā′shən] *n.* **1** The act or process of branching. **2** A branch or branchlike part. **3** Something that develops like a small branch on a big one; outgrowth; result, etc.: the *ramifications* of his plan.

ram·i·fy [ram′ə·fī] *v.* **ram·i·fied, ram·i·fy·ing** To divide or spread out into or as if into branches.

ramp [ramp] *n.* **1** An inclined or sloping passageway or roadway connecting a higher and a lower level. **2** A movable stairway by which passengers enter or leave an airplane.

ram·page [*n.* ram′pāj, *v.* ram·pāj′] *n., v.* **ram·paged, ram·pag·ing 1** *n.* A spree of violent, wild, or angry behavior or dashing about: The dog went on a *rampage.* **2** *v.* To go on a rampage.

ram·pant [ram′pənt] *adj.* **1** Spreading, growing, or acting without check or restraint; wild: Weeds ran *rampant* over the field. **2** Widespread. **3** Standing on one or both hind legs with both forelegs up: a lion *rampant* in a coat of arms.

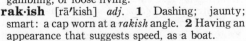

Ramp

ram·part [ram′pärt] *n.* **1** A bank of earth, often with a parapet on top, surrounding a fort as a defense. **2** Any defense or bulwark.

ram·rod [ram′rod′] *n.* **1** A rod used to push

---

down the charge in a gun loaded through the muzzle. **2** A rod for cleaning a rifle, gun, etc.

ram·shack·le [ram'shak'əl] *adj.* Seeming about to fall apart; rickety: a *ramshackle* cabin.

ran [ran] Past tense of RUN.

ranch [ranch] **1** *n.* A large farm devoted to raising or grazing large herds of cattle, horses, etc. **2** *n.* A large farm: a fruit *ranch*. **3** *v.* To manage or work on a ranch. **— ranch'er** *n.*

ran·cid [ran'sid] *adj.* Having the bad taste or smell of spoiled fat or oil: *rancid* butter.

ran·cor [rang'kər] *n.* Bitter resentment, great hatred, or deep spite. **— ran'cor·ous** *adj.* ¶1

ran·dom [ran'dəm] *adj.* Not planned or organized; chance: a *random* selection of candies. **— at random** Without plan, method, or aim; haphazardly.

rang [rang] Past tense of RING[1].

range [rānj] *n., v.* **ranged, rang·ing 1** *n.* The extent or set of limits within which something can move, operate, vary, or be found: the *range* of a missile or a gun; the *range* of a voice; a narrow *range* of choice. **2** *v.* To vary or be found within certain limits: Their ages *ranged* from six to twelve. **3** *n.* A set, selection, or variation within limits: a wide *range* of styles. **4** *n.* A broad tract of land over which cattle, etc., roam and graze. **5** *v.* To roam over: Lions *range* the African plains. **6** *n.* A row, line, or series, as of mountains. **7** *v.* To place or arrange in order, as in a row: to *range* pictures on a wall. **8** *v.* To place (oneself) in line: The Tories *ranged* themselves with the redcoats. **9** *n.* A place where one can practice shooting: a rifle *range*. **10** *n.* A large cooking stove.

rang·er [rān'jər] *n.* **1** An official who patrols and protects a government forest or park. **2** A member of an armed patrol that protects a region. **3** A person or thing that ranges or roves.

rang·y [rān'jē] *adj.* **rang·i·er, rang·i·est** Having long, slender legs and a lean body.

rank[1] [rangk] **1** *n.* A grade in a fixed scale of authority or honor: the *rank* of major. **2** *n.* Relative standing or position: a school of the first *rank*. **3** *v.* To place in a certain order, class, or grade: Would you *rank* him among the great presidents? **4** *v.* To hold a particular place or rank: His plays *rank* high. **5** *n.* High degree or position: a lady of *rank*. **6** *v.* To have a high rank or the highest rank. **7** *adj. use:* a *ranking* member of his profession. **8** *v.* To outrank. **9** *n.* A line, as of soldiers, drawn up side by side. **10** *n.* (*pl.*) All the enlisted men in the armed forces. **11** *n.* (*pl.*) A social or professional class: the *ranks* of authors. **— rank and file 1** The members of an army, union, etc., who are not officers or leaders. **2** The common people.

rank[2] [rangk] *adj.* **1** Growing thickly and abundantly in a coarse way: *rank* weeds. **2** Strong and disagreeable to the taste or smell: a *rank* cigar. **3** Extreme or complete: said about something bad: *rank* injustice. **— rank'ly** *adv.*

ran·kle [rang'kəl] *v.* **ran·kled, ran·kling** To cause pain, anger, or bitterness.

ran·sack [ran'sak] *v.* **1** To search through every part of: to *ransack* a desk for a letter. **2** To search for plunder: Armies *ransacked* the city.

ran·som [ran'səm] **1** *n.* The price demanded or paid for the release of a person held captive. **2** *v.* To cause to be set free by paying ransom for: to *ransom* a kidnaped person. **3** *n.* The freeing of a captive through payment of ransom.

rant [rant] **1** *v.* To speak loudly, wildly, or excitedly; rave. **2** *n.* Wild, extravagant talk.

rap [rap] *v.* **rapped, rap·ping,** *n.* **1** *v.* To knock or strike sharply and quickly: to *rap* on wood. **2** *n.* A light, sharp knock or tap. **3** *v.* To utter in a sharp, forceful way: to *rap* out a command. **4** *n. slang* The blame or punishment for misbehavior, a mistake, or crime.

ra·pa·cious [rə·pā'shəs] *adj.* **1** Ready to take by force whatever one wants: *rapacious* conquerors. **2** Grasping; greedy. **3** Living on prey, as hawks do; predatory. **— ra·pa'cious·ly** *adv.*

ra·pac·i·ty [rə·pas'ə·tē] *n.* The condition of being rapacious.

rape[1] [rāp] *n., v.* **raped, rap·ing 1** *n.* A snatching and carrying off by force. **2** *n.* The crime of having sexual intercourse with a woman or girl against her will and by force. **3** *v.* To commit rape upon (a woman or girl).

rape[2] [rāp] *n.* A European plant whose leaves are used as food for cattle and whose seeds produce an oil.

Raph·a·el [raf'ē·əl *or* rā'fē·əl] *n.,* 1483–1520, Italian painter.

rap·id [rap'id] **1** *adj.* Very quick, swift, or fast. **2** *n.* (*pl.*) A part of a river or stream where the current runs very fast because the bed slopes downhill. **— rap'id·ly** *adv.*

Rapids

rap·id-fire [rap'id·fīr'] *adj.* **1** Firing shots rapidly. **2** Marked by speed, one thing coming rapidly after another: *rapid-fire* questions.

ra·pid·i·ty [rə·pid'ə·tē] *n.* Swiftness; speed.

ra·pi·er [rā'pē·ər] *n.* A long, narrow sword of light weight, used for thrusting.

rap·ine [rap'in] *n.* The taking of property by force, as in war; pillage; plunder.

rap·scal·lion [rap·skal'yən] *n.* A rascal.

rapt [rapt] *adj.* **1** So taken up with one thing as not to know what else is going on: She read with *rapt* attention. **2** Carried away with emotion; enraptured.

rap·ture [rap'chər] *n.* Very great or complete pleasure or delight; ecstasy.

rap·tur·ous [rap'chər·əs] *adj.* Feeling, showing, or full of rapture. **— rap'tur·ous·ly** *adv.*

rare[1] [râr] *adj.* **rar·er, rar·est 1** Seldom seen, found, etc.; unusual; uncommon. **2** Highly valued because scarce or not commonplace: a *rare* book; *rare* beauty. **3** Splendid. **4** Not dense; thin, as air. **— rare'ly** *adv.* **— rare'ness** *n.*

rare[2] [râr] *adj.* **rar·er, rar·est** Not thoroughly cooked: *rare* meat. **—rare′ness** *n.*

rare·bit [râr′bit] *n.* Welsh rabbit.

rar·e·fy [râr′ə·fī] *v.* **rar·e·fied, rar·e·fy·ing** **1** To make or become rare or less dense, as air. **2** To make more refined or delicate.

rar·i·ty [râr′ə·tē] *n., pl.* **rar·i·ties** **1** The condition of being rare, uncommon, or infrequent. **2** Something rare or scarce: A $2 bill is a *rarity*. **3** Thinness, as of the air.

ras·cal [ras′kəl] *n.* **1** A mean, dishonest fellow; rogue; scoundrel. **2** A playfully mischievous child or animal. **—ras′cal·ly** *adv.*

rash[1] [rash] *adj.* Not careful; too hasty; reckless. **—rash′ly** *adv.* **—rash′ness** *n.*

rash[2] [rash] *n.* A breaking out of the skin in reddish blotches: a *rash* from poison ivy.

rash·er [rash′ər] *n.* A thin slice of bacon.

rasp [rasp] **1** *v.* To make a rough, harsh, grating sound. **2** *v.* To say in a harsh, grating voice: He *rasped* out a threat. **3** *n.* A harsh, rough, or grating sound. **4** *v.* To scrape or grate with or as if with a file. **5** *v.* To irritate. **6** *n.* A rough file having sharp points rather than ridges on its cutting surfaces.

rasp·ber·ry [raz′ber′ē] *n., pl.* **rasp·ber·ries** **1** A small, round, red or black fruit full of seeds. **2** The prickly bush on which it grows.

rat [rat] *n., v.* **rat·ted, rat·ting** **1** *n.* A gnawing animal similar to a mouse, but larger. Rats are gray, brown, or black. **2** *v.* To hunt rats. **3** *n. slang* A sneaky, mean, contemptible person, as a traitor. **4** *v. slang* To inform or squeal: The thief *ratted* on his pals. **—smell a rat** To suspect that something is wrong.

Rat, 12–20 in. long

ra·tan [ra·tan′] *n.* Another spelling of RATTAN.

ratch·et [rach′it] *n.* **1** A wheel or bar with slanted notches on its edge that catch on a pawl, preventing reverse motion. **2** The pawl. **3** The entire mechanism.

rate[1] [rāt] *n., v.* **rat·ed, rat·ing** **1** *n.* Amount or degree measured in proportion to something else: a high *rate* of speed. **2** *n.* In mathematics, the ratio of the measures of two quantities. If you go 60 miles in 3 hours, the rate, or speed, is 20 miles an hour. **3** *n.* A price, charge, or payment per unit: a hotel's daily *rates*; a bank's interest *rate*. **4** *v.* To assign a value or grade to: to *rate* someone's work. **5** *n.* A rank or class: first *rate*. **6** *v.* To have a certain worth or rank: Her work *rates* high. **7** *v.* To consider: He is *rated* as a great artist. **8** *v. informal* To deserve: He *rates* a promotion. **—at any rate** In any case; anyhow.

rate[2] [rāt] *v.* **rat·ed, rat·ing** To scold sharply.

rath·er [rath′ər] **1** *adv.* With greater preference; more willingly: I would *rather* walk than

ride. **2** *adv.* Instead of; more properly: He, *rather* than I, should go. **3** *adv.* More accurately: that evening, or, *rather*, late that night. **4** *adv.* On the contrary: The rain didn't hurt him; *rather*, it helped him. **5** *adv.* Somewhat: It's *rather* hot. **6** *interj. British* Yes indeed! **—had rather** Would prefer to or prefer that: I *had rather* not go.

rat·i·fy [rat′ə·fī] *v.* **rat·i·fied, rat·i·fy·ing** To give official approval to; make legal by approving; confirm: to *ratify* a treaty. **—rat·i·fi·ca·tion** [rat′ə·fə·kā′shən] *n.*

rat·ing [rā′ting] *n.* A grade, rank, or standing in relation to other people or things rated: a credit *rating*; a TV show's *rating*.

ra·tio [rā′shō *or* rā′shē·ō] *n., pl.* **ra·tios** The way in which one quantity is related to another; a proportion. It is expressed as the quotient of the first divided by the second: In a group of 10 women and 5 men, the *ratio* of women to men is 2 to 1, or 2/1.

ra·tion [rash′ən *or* rā′shən] **1** *v.* To limit the amount of (something scarce) that a person can have or use: to *ration* meat in wartime. **2** *n.* A portion; share. **3** *n.* Food for one person for one day. **4** *v.* To issue rations to, as an army.

ra·tion·al [rash′ən·əl] *adj.* **1** Able to reason: A porpoise is a *rational* animal. **2** Based on or guided by reason: a *rational* argument. **3** Sane, sensible, or reasonable. **—ra·tion·al·i·ty** [rash′ən·al′ə·tē] *n.* **—ra′tion·al·ly** *adv.*

ra·tion·al·ize [rash′ən·əl·iz′] *v.* **ra·tion·al·ized, ra·tion·al·iz·ing** To explain (behavior, etc.) in a way that is false but seems reasonable, often done unconsciously to protect one's pride: to *rationalize* fear as caution. **—ra·tion·al·i·za·tion** [rash′ən·əl·ə·zā′shən] *n.* ¶3

rational number A number which is an integer or the quotient of two integers.

rat·line or **rat·lin** [rat′lin] *n.* One of the small ropes fastened across the shrouds of a ship, serving as the steps of a rope ladder.

rat·tan [ra·tan′] *n.* **1** The long, tough, flexible stem of various palm trees, used in making wickerwork, light furniture, etc. **2** The tree itself. **3** A cane or switch of rattan.

rat·tle [rat′(ə)l] *v.* **rat·tled, rat·tling,** *n.* **1** *v.* To make or cause to make a rapid series of quick, sharp sounds: The windows *rattled*; to *rattle* keys. **2** *n.* A rapid series of quick, sharp sounds. **3** *n.* A toy or implement made to produce a rattling noise. **4** *n.* Any of the horny rings in the tail of a rattlesnake. **5** *v.* To move with a rattling noise: The

Ratlines

carriage *rattled* along. **6** *v.* To talk rapidly and aimlessly; chatter. **7** *v.* To utter rapidly: to *rattle* off an answer. **8** *v. informal* To confuse or upset: to *rattle* a performer by heckling him.

rat·tler [rat′lər] *n.* A rattlesnake.

rat·tle·snake [rat′(ə)l·snāk′] *n.* A poisonous American snake with a tail ending in a series of horny joints that rattle when shaken.

rau·cous [rô′kəs] *adj.* Rough in sound; hoarse; harsh: a *raucous* voice. — **rau′cous·ly** *adv.*

Rattlesnake, up to 90 in. long

rav·age [rav′ij] *v.* **rav·aged, rav·ag·ing,** *n.* **1** *v.* To hurt or damage severely; destroy. **2** *n.* Destructive action or result: the *ravages* of the hurricane.

rave [rāv] *v.* **raved, rav·ing,** *n.* **1** *v.* To talk in a wild, confused way. **2** *v.* To howl and rage, as the wind does. **3** *v.* To speak with great or too great praise: They *raved* about the play. **4** *n. informal* A highly favorable comment. **5** *adj. use: rave* reviews of the new Italian film. **6** *n.* The act of raving.

rav·el [rav′əl] *v.* **rav·eled** or **rav·elled, rav·el·ing** or **rav·el·ling** **1** To separate into loose threads or fibers: This sweater has begun to *ravel.* **2** To separate the threads of; unravel.

ra·ven [rā′vən] **1** *n.* A large, glossy, black crow with shaggy throat feathers and a powerful beak. **2** *adj.* Black and shining: *raven* hair.

rav·en·ing [rav′ən·ing] *adj.* Greedy; rapacious.

rav·en·ous [rav′ən·əs] *adj.* **1** Wildly hungry. **2** Extremely greedy. — **rav′en·ous·ly** *adv.*

ra·vine [rə·vēn′] *n.* A long, narrow, deep depression in the earth that has steep sides and was usually cut out by a flow of water; gorge.

rav·ish [rav′ish] *v.* **1** To fill with strong emotion, especially delight. **2** To rape.

rav·ish·ing [rav′ish·ing] *adj.* Giving great delight; enchanting: a *ravishing* beauty.

raw [rô] *adj.* **1** Not cooked. **2** In a natural condition; not processed: *raw* sugar. **3** With no experience; untrained: a *raw* recruit. **4** Having the skin rubbed off; sore: Her knees were *raw.* **5** Damp and chilling: *raw* weather. **6** *slang* Harsh or unfair: a *raw* deal. — **raw′ness** *n.*

raw·boned [rô′bōnd′] *adj.* Having little flesh covering the bones; gaunt.

raw·hide [rô′hīd′] *n.* **1** The untanned hide of cattle. **2** A whip made of a strip of this hide.

raw material Material in its natural condition; something that can be processed, treated, or manufactured to make it more useful or valuable: Wood is the *raw material* of most paper.

ray¹ [rā] *n.* **1** A thin beam of light or other radiant energy. **2** A path taken by radiant energy. **3** Any of various forms of radiant energy, as gamma rays, X-rays, etc. **4** One of many lines coming from the same center. **5** A part like this, as an arm of a starfish. **6** A faint gleam; trace: a *ray* of hope.

ray² [rā] *n.* A fish having a flat body, very broad fins, and a long, slender tail.

ray·on [rā′on] *n.* **1** An artificial fiber made of cellulose dissolved in a chemical solution and squeezed into filaments. **2** Cloth, yarn, or thread made of rayon.

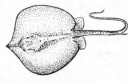

A typical ray

raze [rāz] *v.* **razed, raz·ing** To tear down, as a building; level to the ground; demolish.

ra·zor [rā′zər] *n.* A sharp cutting instrument used for shaving off hair, especially whiskers.

rd. (*often written* **Rd.**) Abbreviation of ROAD.

re [rā] *n.* In music, a syllable used to represent the second tone of a major scale or the fourth tone of a minor scale, or in a fixed system the tone D.

re- A prefix meaning: **1** Again, as in *redo,* to do again. **2** Back, as in *retract,* to take back or draw back. ◆ *Re-* meaning *again* is freely used in forming words. It is followed by a hyphen if the word formed would otherwise be spelled like an existing word with a different meaning. Since *recover* means to get back, the word meaning to cover again is written *re-cover.* Where no confusion would arise, *re-* as a prefix is usually joined to words directly, without a hyphen. However, many writers still prefer to put a hyphen between *re-* and a word beginning with a vowel, especially *e: re-educate.*

reach [rēch] **1** *v.* To stretch one's hand, arm, etc., out or forth: How high can you *reach*?; He *reached* for the candy. **2** *v.* To stretch out or extend: *Reach* out your hand to him. **3** *v.* To touch or get hold of: Can you *reach* that book? **4** *v.* To hand over; pass: *Reach* me the wrench. **5** *n.* The act or power of reaching. **6** *n.* The distance over which a person or thing can reach: The top shelf is out of *reach.* **7** *n.* Range or scope; capacity: Higher mathematics is beyond my *reach.* **8** *v.* To go or extend: The ladder *reached* to the ceiling. **9** *n.* A stretch or expanse: the far *reaches* of Siberia. **10** *v.* To arrive at or come to: to *reach* a destination. **11** *v.* To get in touch with: You can *reach* her at home. **12** *v.* To influence or affect: His speech failed to *reach* his audience.

re·act [rē·akt′] *v.* **1** To act as the result of some happening, stimulus, etc.: The horse *reacted* to the smell of smoke. **2** To act in turn or back and forth: Students and teachers *react* on one another. **3** To act in a contrary way or in opposition: to *react* against too much urging. **4** To take part in or undergo a chemical reaction.

re·ac·tion [rē·ak′shən] *n.* **1** An action in response to a happening, stimulus, etc. **2** Contrary, opposite, or back-and-forth action. **3** A tendency or trend toward an earlier idea or condition. **4** A chemical change. **5** Any change in an atomic nucleus.

re·ac·tion·ar·y [rē·ak′shən·er′ē] *adj., n., pl.* **re·**

ac·tion·ar·ies 1 *adj*. Of, showing, or desiring a return to an earlier idea or condition, especially an out-of-date one. **2** *n*. A person opposed to political or social change.

re·ac·tor [rē·ak′tər] *n*. **1** A person or thing that reacts. **2** An apparatus for the controlled release of atomic energy in which the chain reaction of a radioactive substance is regulated by a moderator, such as layers of graphite.

read[1] [rēd] *v*. **read** [red], **read·ing** [rē′ding] **1** To get the meaning of (a book, chart, piece of music, etc.) by interpreting its printed or written symbols. **2** To say aloud the words of (something written): *Read* the letter to me. **3** To get information from written words: to *read* about the pioneers. **4** To study: to *read* law. **5** To have as its wording: The passage *reads* "principal," not "principle." **6** To use written language: Your speech *reads* well. **7** To guess, find, or tell hidden information in, from, or about: You can *read* my mind; to *read* palms; to *read* the future. **8** To interpret. **9** To register and show: The speedometer *reads* 25 mph. **10** To note the indications of: to *read* a meter. **— read between the lines** To discover a meaning in addition to the open and obvious one. **— read into** To find possible hidden meaning or significance in.

read[2] [red] *adj*. Informed or educated by reading: often used in combination, as in *well-read*.

read·a·ble [rē′də·bəl] *adj*. **1** Clear enough to read; legible. **2** Interesting or fun to read.

read·er [rē′dər] *n*. **1** A person who reads. **2** A schoolbook used to teach reading.

read·i·ly [red′ə·lē] *adv*. **1** Quickly and easily. **2** Without objecting; willingly.

read·ing [rē′ding] *n*. **1** The act of a person who reads. **2** Something that is read or meant to be read. **3** An event at which something written is read aloud. **4** The amount measured and shown by a gauge or instrument: a thermometer *reading* of 88°. **5** An interpretation: a pianist's *reading* of a sonata.

read·y [red′ē] *adj*. **read·i·er, read·i·est,** *v*. **read·ied, read·y·ing 1** *adj*. Prepared for immediate use or action. **2** *v*. To make ready; prepare. **3** *adj*. On hand: *ready* money. **4** *adj*. Willing: *ready* to lend a hand. **5** *adj*. Likely; liable: *ready* to sink. **6** *adj*. Quick; prompt: a *ready* response. **— read′i·ness** *n*.

read·y-made [red′ē-mād′] *adj*. Made up in a standard form in advance of any order; not made for one particular customer.

re·a·gent [rē·ā′jənt] *n*. A substance used as a test of the presence of any of certain chemicals with which it reacts characteristically.

real[1] [rēl *or* rē′əl] *adj*. **1** Existing, actual, or true; not imagined or invented: *real* life; the *real* reason. **2** Genuine: *real* pearls. **3** Made up of land, buildings, or other immovable or permanent property.

re·al[2] [rē′əl *or* rä·äl′] *n., pl*. **re·als** or **re·a·les** [rä·ä′läs] A former Spanish silver coin.

real estate Land, including whatever is on or in it, as trees, houses, minerals, crops, etc.

re·al·ism [rē′əl·iz′əm] *n*. **1** A tendency to face facts and be practical. **2** In literature and art, the picturing of people and things as they are in real life. **— re′al·ist** *n*.

re·al·is·tic [rē′əl·is′tik] *adj*. **1** Having to do with or emphasizing what is real and practical: In *realistic* figures, what would the trip cost? **2** Showing things in a lifelike way: a *realistic* account of life on a Kansas farm. **— re·al·is′ti·cal·ly** *adv*.

re·al·i·ty [rē·al′ə·tē] *n., pl*. **re·al·i·ties 1** A being real; a true condition; actual existence. **2** An actual person, thing, or fact: Our plan became a *reality*. **3** The real world of facts: to face *reality* again after a vacation. **4** Artistic realism. **— in reality** In fact; really.

re·al·ize [rē′əl·īz] *v*. **re·al·ized, re·al·iz·ing 1** To understand or appreciate fully: I *realize* that you're ill. **2** To turn into actual fact or being: to *realize* a hope. **3** To sell (property or assets) for cash. **4** To get as a profit or return: He *realized* $500 on the sale. **— re·al·i·za·tion** [rē′əl·i·zā′shən] *n*. ¶3

re·al·ly [rē′ə·lē *or* rē′lē] *adv*. **1** Actually or truly. **2** Honestly; indeed: *Really*, can't you behave?

realm [relm] *n*. **1** A kingdom. **2** A region or area: the *realm* of imagination.

re·al·ty [rē′əl·tē] *n*. Real estate.

ream[1] [rēm] *n*. **1** An amount of paper consisting of 480, 500, or 516 sheets. **2** (*pl*.) *informal* A great amount or number: *reams* of protests.

ream[2] [rēm] *v*. To enlarge or widen (a hole).

ream·er [rē′mər] *n*. **1** A tool used to enlarge or shape a hole. **2** A device for squeezing juice from fruit.

re·an·i·mate [rē·an′ə·māt] *v*. **re·an·i·mat·ed, re·an·i·mat·ing** To bring back to life; give fresh vigor to.

reap [rēp] *v*. **1** To cut down or gather in (grain); harvest (a crop). **2** To take a grain crop from, as a field. **3** To receive as a return: to *reap* the rewards of hard work. **— reap′er** *n*.

Reamer

rear[1] [rir] **1** *n*. The part or space behind or in the back: the *rear* of the bus. **2** *adj*. At or in the back: *rear* windows. **3** *n*. The part of a military force that is farthest from the front.

rear[2] [rir] *v*. **1** To care for and train; bring up: to *rear* children. **2** To breed or raise: to *rear* animals. **3** To rise upon the hind legs, as a horse does. **4** To set up or build: to *rear* a tower. **5** To lift: Rebellion *reared* its head.

rear admiral A naval rank. In the U.S. Navy, a rear admiral is an officer ranking next above a captain and next below a vice admiral.

---

add, āce, câre, pälm; end, ēqual; it, īce; odd, ōpen, ôrder; tŏŏk, pōōl; up, bûrn;
ə = a in *above*, e in *sicken*, i in *possible*, o in *melon*, u in *circus*; yōō = u in *fuse*; oil; pout;
 check; ring; thin; this; zh in *vision*. For ¶ reference, see page 64 · HOW TO

re·arm [rē·ärm′] *v.* **1** To arm again. **2** To arm with more modern weapons. **—re·ar′ma·ment** *n.*

re·ar·range [rē′ə·rānj′] *v.* **re·ar·ranged, re·ar·rang·ing** To arrange again or differently.

rear·ward [rir′wərd] **1** *adj.* Toward, in, or at the back. **2** *adv.* Toward the rear; backward.

rea·son [rē′zən] **1** *n.* An explanation for an action, belief, etc.: What is your *reason* for being late? **2** *n.* A motive or cause for an action, belief, etc.: Curiosity was my *reason* for asking. **3** *n.* The ability to think things through, have ideas, and reach conclusions: Human beings have *reason*. **4** *v.* To think in a logical, orderly way. **5** *v.* To argue or talk in a logical way meant to persuade: *Reason* with her. **6** *n.* Good judgment; common sense: She won't hear *reason*. **7** *n.* Sanity. **— by reason of** Because of. **— in reason** Within acceptable limits; reasonable. **—it stands to reason** It is logical or reasonable. ◆ *Reason, purpose,* and *motive* explain why people behave in certain ways. When your teacher asks you why you did not do your homework, he wants a *reason,* such as "I was sick" or "I lost the assignment." The *purpose* of homework is to give you practice in learning by yourself, but your *motive* in doing it may simply be to get good grades.

rea·son·a·ble [rē′zən·ə·bəl] *adj.* **1** Having, using, or showing reason, fairness, or common sense; sensible: a *reasonable* man. **2** Moderate; fair: *reasonable* prices. **3** Not expensive.**—rea′son·a·ble·ness** *n.* **— rea′son·a·bly** *adv.*

rea·son·ing [rē′zən·ing] *n.* **1** The process of drawing a conclusion from a set of facts or premises. **2** Reasons; arguments.

re·as·sure [rē′ə·shŏŏr′] *v.* **re·as·sured, re·as·sur·ing** To give confidence back to; free from doubt or fear. **— re′as·sur′ance** *n.*

re·bate [rē′bāt] *n.* A part returned out of a total amount paid, as a discount, refund, etc.

reb·el *n.* or **re·bel** *v.* **re·belled, re·bel·ling** [*n.* reb′əl, *v.* ri·bel′] **1** *n.* A person who refuses to submit to authority and fights against it instead. **2** *adj. use: rebel* troops; a *rebel* army. **3** *v.* To rise up in active resistance, opposing authority: The American colonies *rebelled* against England. **4** *v.* To be filled with dislike or opposition: I *rebel* at the thought of cheating.

re·bel·lion [ri·bel′yən] *n.* **1** An armed uprising or revolt against a government. **2** An active struggle against authority or those in control.

re·bel·lious [ri·bel′yəs] *adj.* **1** Taking part in a rebellion. **2** Full of the disobedient spirit of a rebel. **— re·bel′lious·ly** *adv.*

re·birth [rē·bûrth′ *or* rē′bûrth′] *n.* **1** A new birth. **2** A new feeling or spirit; revival.

re·born [rē·bôrn′] *adj.* Having new vigor or spirit, as though born again.

re·bound [*v.* ri·bound′, *n.* rē′bound′] **1** *v.* To bounce back. **2** *n.* The act of springing or bouncing back: to catch a ball on the *rebound*.

re·buff [ri·buf′] **1** *n.* A sharp, rude rejection or refusal, as of a friendly offer or request. **2** *v.* To reject or refuse sharply or rudely; snub: to *rebuff* someone's unwelcome advice.

re·buke [ri·byŏŏk′] *v.* **re·buked, re·buk·ing,** *n.* **1** *v.* To scold sharply; reprimand. **2** *n.* A strong statement of disapproval; sharp scolding.

re·bus [rē′bəs] *n.* A puzzle representing a word, phrase, or sentence by letters, numbers, pictures, etc.

re·but [ri·but′] *v.* **re·but·ted, re·but·ting** To contradict or disprove (an argument, claim, etc.) by giving contrary evidence or proof.

re·but·tal [ri·but′(ə)l] *n.* The act of rebutting.

re·cal·ci·trant [ri·kal′sə·trənt] *adj.* Stubbornly refusing to obey. **— re·cal′ci·trance** *n.*

A rebus

re·call [*v.* ri·kôl′, *n.* ri·kôl′ *or* rē′kôl] **1** *v.* To bring to mind again; remember: Can you *recall* that day? **2** *n.* A remembering; a bringing back to mind: a *recall* even of the exact words. **3** *v.* To order to return or be returned; call back: The factory *recalled* a shipment of faulty merchandise. **4** *n.* A system by which public officials may be removed from office by vote of the people. **5** *v.* To take back; revoke: to *recall* an order. **6** *n.* The act of calling back or revoking.

re·cant [ri·kant′] *v.* To deny or give up publicly (a belief, opinion, principle, theory, etc., that one has believed before).

re·ca·pit·u·late [rē′kə·pich′ŏŏ·lāt] *v.* **re·ca·pit·u·lat·ed, re·ca·pit·u·lat·ing** To review briefly; summarize; sum up. **— re′ca·pit′u·la′tion** *n.*

re·cap·ture [rē·kap′chər] *v.* **re·cap·tured, re·cap·tur·ing** **1** To capture again. **2** To get back through memory: to *recapture* past joys.

re·cast [rē·kast′] *v.* **re·cast, re·cast·ing** **1** To cast again or mold again. **2** To put in a different or better form: to *recast* a question.

re·cede [ri·sēd′] *v.* **re·ced·ed, re·ced·ing** **1** To move back; withdraw, as flood waters do. **2** To slant backward: His forehead *recedes*.

re·ceipt [ri·sēt′] **1** *n.* A written acknowledgment of money paid, goods delivered, etc. **2** *v.* To mark (a bill, etc.) as having been paid. **3** *n.* The act of receiving or being received: On *receipt* of your note, I came at once. **4** *n.*(*usually pl.*) Money received, or the total amount received. **5** *n.* A recipe.

re·ceive [ri·sēv′] *v.* **re·ceived, re·ceiv·ing** **1** To get or accept (something offered, given, or sent): to *receive* a package. **2** To be given, experience, or suffer: to *receive* a setback. **3** To gain knowledge of; learn: He *received* the news at noon. **4** To admit or welcome: to *receive* callers.

A receipt

5 To welcome callers: She *receives* on Fridays. **6** To carry or hold: These columns *receive* the weight of the house. **7** To convert (a transmitted signal) into a useful form, such as a sound or picture on television.

re·ceiv·er [ri·sē′vər] *n.* **1** A person who receives; recipient. **2** A person appointed by a court to manage the property of another until some official decision is made. **3** A device that converts an electrical signal into some useful form: a radio *receiver*; a telephone *receiver*.

re·ceiv·er·ship [ri·sē′vər·ship] *n.* The condition of being managed by a receiver appointed by a court: a factory in *receivership*.

re·cent [rē′sənt] *adj.* Of a time shortly before the present; not long past. — **re′cent·ly** *adv.*

re·cep·ta·cle [ri·sep′tə·kəl] *n.* A thing made to hold something else; container.

re·cep·tion [ri·sep′shən] *n.* **1** The act or way of receiving or being received: to be given a cool *reception*. **2** A party at which guests are formally greeted. **3** The clearness with which radio or television signals are received.

re·cep·tive [ri·sep′tiv] *adj.* Able or willing to receive ideas, impressions, or suggestions.

re·cess [*n.* ri·ses′ *or* rē′ses, *v.* ri·ses′] **1** *n.* [rē′· ses] A short period of time during which work is stopped. **2** *v.* To take a recess or interrupt for a recess. **3** *n.* A hollow place: a small *recess* in the regular line of a wall. **4** *v.* To place in a recess. **5** *adj. use:* a *recessed* bookcase. **6** *n.* (*usually pl.*) A concealed inner place: the *recesses* of the mind.

re·ces·sion [ri·sesh′ən] *n.* **1** A slight drop in business activity; slight depression. **2** The act of receding or moving back; withdrawal.

re·ces·sion·al [ri·sesh′ən·əl] *n.* A hymn sung as the choir and clergy file out at the end of a church service.

re·ces·sive [ri·ses′iv] *adj.* **1** Tending to go back; receding. **2** Less active and less strong than an opposing hereditary character or trait.

rec·i·pe [res′ə·pē] *n.* **1** A set of directions for cooking or preparing something to eat. **2** A method for getting any desired result.

re·cip·i·ent [ri·sip′ē·ənt] *n.* A person or thing that receives: the *recipient* of an award.

re·cip·ro·cal [ri·sip′rə·kəl] **1** *adj.* Shared or given by both sides; mutual: *reciprocal* friendship. **2** *adj.* Given in exchange: a *reciprocal* baby-sitting arrangement. **3** *adj.* Marked by a mutual, balanced exchange: *reciprocal* motion; a *reciprocal* treaty. **4** *adj.* Expressing mutual relationship or action. *One another* in "They helped one another" is a reciprocal pronoun. **5** *n.* Either of two numbers whose product is 1. 5 is the *recirpocal* of 1/5. — **re·cip′ro·cal·ly** *adv.*

re·cip·ro·cate [ri·sip′rə·kāt] *v.* **re·cip·ro·cat·ed, re·cip·ro·cat·ing** **1** To give and receive in exchange; interchange: We *reciprocated* favors. **2** To return equally: I admire him, and he *reciprocates* my respect. **3** To move backward and forward, as pistons in an engine do.

rec·i·proc·i·ty [res′ə·pros′ə·tē] *n.* **1** Mutual relationship, action, or exchange. **2** A mutual exchange of special trading privileges between two nations.

re·cit·al [ri·sīt′(ə)l] *n.* **1** The act of reciting or telling in great detail: her *recital* of her woes. **2** A detailed statement. **3** A public performance in which musical works or dances are performed, usually by a soloist or pupils.

rec·i·ta·tion [res′ə·tā′shən] *n.* **1** The act of reciting. **2** A school exercise in which pupils are questioned orally on a lesson. **3** The reciting of a memorized piece before an audience. **4** A piece that is or is to be recited.

rec·i·ta·tive [res′ə·tə·tēv′] *n.* Words set to music in a style somewhat like speech, and accompanied by a series of chords.

re·cite [ri·sīt′] *v.* **re·cit·ed, re·cit·ing** **1** To answer questions orally on a lesson in school. **2** To say (something memorized or learned) before an audience. **3** To tell in great detail: to *recite* a tale of woe. — **re·cit′er** *n.*

reck [rek] *v.* **1** To care, heed, or mind. **2** To matter. ◆ This word is seldom used today.

reck·less [rek′lis] *adj.* Taking foolish risks; rash; careless: *reckless* driving. — **reck′less·ly** *adv.* — **reck′less·ness** *n.*

reck·on [rek′ən] *v.* **1** To figure by arithmetic; count; compute: *Reckon* the total amount owed. **2** To look upon as being; consider: I *reckon* him an honest man. **3** *informal* To suppose. **4** To rely or depend: He *reckons* on your aid. — **reckon with** **1** To settle accounts with. **2** To take into account; consider.

reck·on·ing [rek′ən·ing] *n.* **1** The act of figuring; calculation. **2** A settlement of accounts; an answering for conduct: the day of *reckoning*. **3** A bill, as at a hotel. **4** Dead reckoning.

re·claim [ri·klām′] *v.* **1** To bring (a swamp, desert, etc.) into a condition to support cultivation or life, as by draining or irrigating. **2** To get from used things or waste: to *reclaim* rubber. **3** To bring back from a bad state: to *reclaim* bums. — **rec·la·ma·tion** [rek′lə·mā′shən] *n.*

re·cline [ri·klīn′] *v.* **re·clined, re·clin·ing** To lie down, lie back, or lean back.

re·cluse [ri·kloōs′ *or* rek′loōs] *n.* A person who lives by himself, shut away from the world.

rec·og·ni·tion [rek′əg·nish′ən] *n.* **1** The act of recognizing or knowing again. **2** The condition of being recognized: Many famous people wear dark glasses to avoid *recognition*. **3** Fame; great praise: The actor earned *recognition* for his fine performance. **4** A greeting; acknowledgment: a nod of *recognition*.

rec·og·niz·a·ble [rek′əg·nī′zə·bəl] *adj.* Capable of being recognized.

---

add, āce, câre, pälm; end, ēqual; it, īce; odd, ōpen, ôrder; toŏk, poōl; up, bûrn; ə = a in *above*, e in *sicken*, i in *possible*, o in *melon*, u in *circus*; yoō = u in *fuse*; oil; pout; check; ring; thin; this; zh in *vision*. For ¶ reference, see page 64 · HOW TO

re·cog·ni·zance [ri·kog′nə·zəns *or* ri·kon′ə·zəns] *n.* **1** In law, a document that makes a person responsible for carrying out a certain act. **2** A sum of money usually deposited along with such a document. It is returned only after the act is carried out.

rec·og·nize [rek′əg·nīz] *v.* **rec·og·nized, rec·og·niz·ing 1** To be aware of, as someone or something previously known; know again: to *recognize* an apartment one had visited. **2** To know or identify, as if from previous acquaintance: to *recognize* an actor from his photograph. **3** To show appreciation or awareness of: to *recognize* an employee's hard work. **4** To perceive as true; realize: to *recognize* responsibilities. **5** To accept as true and valid and start to deal with: to *recognize* the government of a country. **6** To give formal permission to speak, as at a meeting.

re·coil [*v.* ri·koil′, *n.* ri·koil′ *or* rē′koil] **1** *v.* To react suddenly, as to fear, pain, or danger, by leaping or shrinking back. **2** *n.* A leaping, shrinking, or springing back. **3** *v.* To spring back, as a gun that has just been fired.

rec·ol·lect [rek′ə·lekt′] *v.* To remember or recall to mind: to *recollect* one's childhood.

re·col·lect [rē′kə·lekt′] *v.* **1** To collect again, as things scattered. **2** To regain (one's self-control); pull (oneself) together.

rec·ol·lec·tion [rek′ə·lek′shən] *n.* **1** The act of recollecting or remembering. **2** Something remembered. **3** Remembrance or memory.

rec·om·mend [rek′ə·mend′] *v.* **1** To praise as good, worthy, desirable, etc.: to *recommend* a movie. **2** To be advantageous for or beneficial to: The seclusion of the lake *recommends* it to fishermen. **3** To advise; urge: to *recommend* a vacation. **4** To put in the care of; entrust: His doctor *recommended* him to a specialist.

rec·om·men·da·tion [rek′ə·men·dā′shən] *n.* **1** The act of recommending. **2** A being recommended. **3** Anything that recommends someone or something, as a favorable letter or statement. **4** A suggestion or advice.

rec·om·pense [rek′əm·pens] *v.* **rec·om·pensed, rec·om·pens·ing,** *n.* **1** *v.* To pay or repay; reward: to *recompense* someone for work. **2** *n.* Payment or reward. **3** *v.* To make up for, as a loss.

rec·on·cile [rek′ən·sīl] *v.* **rec·on·ciled, rec·on·cil·ing 1** To bring back to friendship after a quarrel: Could you *reconcile* the two brothers? **2** To settle or adjust, as a quarrel. **3** To make adjusted to; resign: to *reconcile* oneself to living alone. **4** To make or show to be consistent; harmonize: Can he *reconcile* the way he acts with what he tells us to do? **— rec′on·cile′ment** *n.*

rec·on·cil·i·a·tion [rek′ən·sil′ē·ā′shən] *n.* **1** The act of reconciling. **2** A being reconciled.

rec·on·dite [rek′ən·dīt *or* ri·kon′dīt] *adj.* **1** Difficult to understand, as a complex mathematical formula. **2** Having to do with little-known matters: *recondite* learning.

re·con·di·tion [rē′kən·dish′ən] *v.* To overhaul; put back into good condition.

re·con·nais·sance [ri·kon′ə·səns] *n.* An investigation or scouting to get information, especially about an enemy's position, strength, or time of attack.

re·con·noi·ter [rē′kə·noi′tər *or* rek′ə·noi′tər] *v.* To examine or survey (an area, position, etc.), especially to get military information. ¶2

re·con·sid·er [rē′kən·sid′ər] *v.* To consider or think about again, especially with the idea of changing one's mind.

re·con·struct [rē′kən·strukt′] *v.* To put (something) together again, usually as it was originally.

re·con·struc·tion [rē′kən·struk′shən] *n.* **1** The act of reconstructing. **2** Something that has been reconstructed. **3** (*written* **Reconstruction**) The bringing back into the Union of the seceded southern states after the Civil War.

re·cord [*v.* ri·kôrd′, *n. and adj.* rek′ərd] **1** *v.* To note down for future use: to *record* appointments. **2** *v.* To indicate; register, as a thermometer. **3** *n.* An official account, as of a trial. **4** *v.* To change (sounds, images, etc.) into a form that can be stored for later reproduction, usually by electrical means. **5** *n.* A disk whose surface is cut in a long, spiral groove along which sound is stored for later reproduction on a phonograph. **6** *n.* Specific information concerning the action of a person or group: a good high school *record*. **7** *n.* The best listed achievement, as in some sport. **8** *adj.* More, better, etc. than what was formerly the best: a *record* snowfall. **— break a record** To do or be more, better, etc. than the best that has been recorded or achieved. **— off the record** Not meant for publication. **— on record 1** Publicly declared. **2** Preserved in a record. ◆ *Record* comes from Latin roots meaning *back* and *heart* or *mind*, which combined to mean *back to mind* or *remember*.

re·cord·er [ri·kôr′dər] *n.* **1** A person or thing that records. **2** A public official with the power to enforce criminal law. **3** A musical instrument similar to a flute but played in a vertical position.

re·cord·ing [ri·kôr′ding] *n.* **1** The process by which sound is recorded. **2** A phonograph record. **3** A tape recording.

record player A machine on which to play records; phonograph.

re·count [ri·kount′] *v.* To tell in great detail, as a story or event.

re·count [*v.* rē·kount′, *n.* rē′kount′] **1** *v.* To count again. **2** *n.* A second count: a *re-count* of votes.

Recorder

re·coup [ri·koop′] *v.* **1** To win or earn back, as losses. **2** To pay back, as for a loss.

re·course [rē′kôrs *or* ri·kôrs′] *n.* **1** A turning to some person or thing for protection, help, etc.: to have *recourse* to a bank when one must borrow money. **2** The person or thing looked to for help: You are my only *recourse*.

re·cov·er [ri·kuv′ər] *v.* **1** To get back after losing; regain: to *recover* one's balance; to *recover* a lost wallet. **2** To make up for, as a loss. **3** To get well: to *recover* from a cold. **4** To restore (oneself) to balance, health, etc. **5** To make useful again: to *recover* eroded land.

re·cov·er [rē·kuv′ər] *v.* To cover again.

re·cov·er·y [ri·kuv′ər·ē] *n., pl.* **re·cov·er·ies** **1** A coming back to health, a normal condition, etc., as after sickness. **2** The finding of something lost or stolen.

rec·re·ant [rek′rē·ənt] **1** *adj.* Unfaithful to a cause, duty, etc. **2** *adj.* Cowardly. **3** *n.* A person who is recreant.

rec·re·a·tion [rek′rē·ā′shən] *n.* Amusement, relaxation, or play, such as gardening, hiking, music, reading, dancing, sports, etc. **— rec′re·a′tion·al** *adj.*

re·crim·i·na·tion [ri·krim′ə·nā′shən] *n.* An accusation made by a person in return for an accusation made against him: The angry men kept shouting *recriminations* at one another.

re·cru·des·cence [rē′krōō·des′əns] *n.* A breaking out again, as of a disease, epidemic, crime, violence, etc.

re·cruit [ri·krōōt′] **1** *v.* To enlist (men) for the armed services. **2** *n.* A newly enlisted member of the armed forces. **3** *v.* To cause to join a group or organization. **4** *n.* A new member of a group or organization. **5** *v.* To get, increase, or replenish: to *recruit* one's strength; to *recruit* help. **— re·cruit′ment** *n.*

rec·tal [rek′təl] *adj.* Of, for, or having to do with the rectum: a *rectal* thermometer.

rec·tan·gle [rek′tang′gəl] *n.* A parallelogram whose angles are right angles.

rec·tan·gu·lar [rek·tang′-gyə·lər] *adj.* Having the shape of a rectangle: a *rectangular* rug.

rec·ti·fi·er [rek′tə·fī′ər] *n.* **1** A person or thing that rectifies or makes right. **2** A device used to change an alternating electric current into a direct current.

Rectangles

rec·ti·fy [rek′tə·fī] *v.* **rec·ti·fied, rec·ti·fy·ing** **1** To correct or adjust: to *rectify* an error. **2** To change (an alternating electric current) into a direct current. **3** To refine by the process of distillation, as liquids. **— rec·ti·fi·ca·tion** [rek′tə·fə·kā′shən] *n.*

rec·ti·tude [rek′tə·t(y)ōōd] *n.* Honesty and goodness in principles and conduct; righteousness.

rec·tor [rek′tər] *n.* **1** In certain Christian churches, a clergyman who has charge of a parish. **2** A Roman Catholic priest in charge of a seminary or religious house. **3** The head of any of certain schools, colleges, and universities.

rec·to·ry [rek′tər·ē] *n., pl.* **rec·to·ries** A rector's house.

rec·tum [rek′təm] *n.* The lowest portion of the large intestine, connecting with the anus.

re·cum·bent [ri·kum′bənt] *adj.* Lying down, wholly or partly; reclining; leaning.

re·cu·per·ate [ri·k(y)ōō′pə·rāt] *v.* **re·cu·per·a·ted, re·cu·per·a·ting** To regain health or strength, as after being sick or fatigued. **— re·cu′per·a′tion** *n.*

re·cur [ri·kûr′] *v.* **re·curred, re·cur·ring** **1** To happen over and over or at regular intervals: Leap year *recurs* every fourth year. **2** To go back in thought or speech: He *recurred* to his first statement.

re·cur·rent [ri·kûr′ənt] *adj.* Happening or coming over and over or at regular intervals: a *recurrent* thought. **— re·cur′rence** *n.*

red [red] *n., adj.* **red·der, red·dest 1** *n.* The color of fresh blood. **2** *adj.* Having the color of fresh blood. **3** *adj.* (*usually written* **Red**) Of, having to do with, or professing radical or communistic doctrines. **4** *n.* (*written* **Red**) A radical or Communist. **— red′ness** *n.*

red·bird [red′bûrd′] *n.* **1** The cardinal bird. **2** The scarlet tanager.

red·breast [red′brest′] *n.* A bird having a red breast, as the robin.

red·cap [red′kap′] *n. U.S.* A porter at a bus station, railroad station, etc.

red·coat [red′kōt′] *n.* A British soldier during the American Revolution and the War of 1812.

Redcoats

red corpuscle One of the red blood cells that carry oxygen and other nutrients to every part of the body and remove carbon dioxide.

Red Cross An international organization that cares for the sick and wounded in war and gives aid to victims of floods, earthquakes, hurricanes, or other disasters.

red deer **1** The kind of deer commonly found in Europe and Asia. **2** The white-tailed deer of America, when it is wearing its rust-colored summer coat.

red·den [red′(ə)n] *v.* **1** To make red, as by dyeing. **2** To blush; flush.

red·dish [red′ish] *adj.* Somewhat red.

re·deem [ri·dēm′] *v.* **1** To get back by paying a price, as something that has been pawned. **2** To pay off, as a bet or a promissory note. **3** To

---

add, **ā**ce, **c**â**r**e, **p**ä**lm**; **e**nd, **ē**qual; **i**t, **ī**ce; **o**dd, **ō**pen, **ô**rder; t**ōō**k, p**ōō**l; **u**p, b**û**rn;
ə = a in *above*, e in *sicken*, i in *possible*, o in *melon*, u in *circus*; **yōō** = u in *fuse*; **oi**l; p**ou**t;
check; **r**i**ng**; **th**in; **th**is; **zh** in *vision*. For ¶ reference, see page 64 · HOW TO

exchange (coupons, stamps, etc.) for a premium or prize. **4** To fulfill, as an oath or promise. **5** To make amends for: The poor play was *redeemed* by skilled acting. **6** To rescue from sin.

re·deem·a·ble [ri·dē′mə·bəl] *adj.* **1** Capable of being redeemed. **2** That is to be redeemed in the future, as a bond.

re·deem·er [ri·dē′mər] *n.* **1** A person who redeems. **2** (*written* **The Redeemer**) Jesus Christ.

re·demp·tion [ri·demp′shən] *n.* **1** The act of redeeming. **2** The condition of being redeemed. **3** Salvation from sin.

red-hand·ed [red′han′did] *adj.* In the act of committing a crime or before getting rid of evidence of having done it: a burglar caught *red-handed*.

red·head [red′hed′] *n.* A person with red hair.

red·head·ed [red′hed′id] *adj.* Having red hair.

red herring **1** Something brought up to draw attention away from a main issue. **2** Smoked herring.

red-hot [red′hot′] *adj.* **1** Glowing red from heat, as metal in a furnace. **2** Brand-new; fresh: *red-hot* news. **3** Angry or excited: a *red-hot* argument.

red-let·ter [red′let′·ər] *adj.* Memorable; extraordinary: a *red-letter* day.

red man A North American Indian.

Red-hot coals

red·o·lent [red′ə·lənt] *adj.* **1** Giving off a pleasant odor; fragrant. **2** Giving off a strong odor. **3** Suggestive or reminiscent; a story *redolent* of mystery. — **red′o·lence** *n.*

re·doubt [ri·dout′] *n.* A small fort, enclosed all around, often standing alone to defend a hill or pass.

re·doubt·a·ble [ri·dou′tə·bəl] *adj.* Causing fear and dread: a *redoubtable* opponent.

re·dound [ri·dound′] *v.* To have an effect; return; contribute: The success of our graduates *redounds* to the credit of the school.

red pepper A hot, red pepper; cayenne.

re·dress [ri·dres′] **1** *v.* To set right; remedy: Their wrongs were *redressed*. **2** *n.* Correction or satisfaction, as for wrongs and injuries done.

Red Sea A long, narrow sea between NE Africa and Arabia. It is part of the Indian Ocean and is connected to the Mediterranean Sea by the Suez Canal.

red shift A shift toward red of the lines in the spectrum of a star, thought to happen because the star is moving away from the earth at an enormous speed.

red·skin [red′skin′] *n.* A North American Indian.

red·start [red′stärt′] *n.* **1** A small European warbler, with a rust-red breast and tail. **2** A fly-catching North American warbler.

red tape Too much attention to rules and small details, causing a great waste of time.

re·duce [ri·d(y)ōōs′] *v.* **re·duced, re·duc·ing** **1** To make less in size or amount: to *reduce* waste. **2** To express in the smallest possible numbers, as a fraction: $\frac{10}{16}$ can be *reduced* to $\frac{5}{8}$. **3** To lower or degrade: to *reduce* a captain to the rank of a lieutenant. **4** To subdue; conquer: to *reduce* an enemy installation. **5** To bring to a certain form or condition: Fire *reduced* the house to ashes; to *reduce* a person to tears. **6** To remove oxygen from, as a chemical compound. **7** To alter (a compound) so as to lower the valence of the positive element. **8** To decrease one's weight, as by dieting.

re·duc·i·ble [ri·d(y)ōōs′ə·bəl] *adj.* Capable of being reduced.

re·duc·tion [ri·duk′shən] *n.* **1** The act of reducing. **2** The condition of being reduced. **3** Anything that has been reduced: This price is a great *reduction* from the former price. **4** The amount by which something is reduced: a 3% *reduction* in taxes.

re·dun·dance [ri·dun′dəns] *n.* Redundancy.

re·dun·dan·cy [ri·dun′dən·sē] *n., pl.* **re·dun·dan·cies** **1** The condition of being redundant. **2** Something that is redundant. **3** The use of too many or of unnecessary words.

re·dun·dant [ri·dun′dənt] *adj.* **1** More than is needed; too much. **2** Using too many words to express an idea; wordy. "She wore a scarlet red dress" is a redundant sentence.

red·wing [red′wing′] *n.* **1** An American blackbird with bright scarlet patches on the wings of the male. **2** A European thrush with bright, reddish orange patches on the undersides of its wings.

red-winged blackbird [red′wingd′] The redwing of North America.

red·wood [red′wŏŏd′] *n.* **1** A very tall evergreen tree of northern California, often 300 feet high. **2** The durable, reddish wood of this tree.

re·ech·o or **re-ech·o** [rē·ek′ō] *n., pl.* **re·ech·oes** or **re-ech·oes,** *v.* **re·ech·oed** or **re-ech·oed, re·ech·o·ing** or **re-ech·o·ing** **1** *n.* An echo that is echoed or repeated. **2** *v.* To echo again or over and over: Every word they spoke *reechoed* in the tunnel.

Red-winged blackbird, 9–10 in. long

reed [rēd] *n.* **1** Any of certain grasses having hollow stems and growing in wet places. **2** A musical instrument made from the hollow stem of a plant. **3** A thin, flat piece of wood, metal, or plastic in a musical instrument, as the clarinet, oboe, or reed organ. Air blown against a reed causes it to vibrate and produce a musical tone.

reed organ An organ with reeds that are vibrated by air currents to produce the sound.

reed·y [rē′dē] *adj.* **reed·i·er, reed·i·est** **1** Full of reeds: a *reedy* swamp. **2** Like a reed:

a tall, *reedy* boy. **3** Having a sound like a reed instrument.

reef[1] [rēf] *n.* A ridge of sand, rocks, or coral at or near the surface of the water.

reef[2] [rēf] **1** *v.* To reduce or shorten (a sail) by folding or rolling part of it and fastening it down. **2** *n.* The part of the sail that can be taken in or let out.

reef·er [rē′fər] *n.* **1** A person who reefs. **2** A short coat made from a heavy material, worn usually by sailors.

reek [rēk] **1** *v.* To give off a strong, very unpleasant smell: to *reek* of tobacco. **2** *n.* A strong, offensive smell.

reel[1] [rēl] *n.* **1** A lively dance, chiefly Scottish or Irish. **2** The music for this dance.

reel[2] [rēl] *n.*, *v.* **1** *n.* A round, spool-like device that turns or may be turned, and is used for winding rope, wire, thread, film, fishing line, etc. **2** *v.* To wind on a reel, as fishing line, rope, film, etc. **3** *v.* To pull by winding line on a reel: to *reel* in a fish. **4** *n.* The amount wound on one reel, as of film or tape. — **reel off** To say or write quickly and easily: She *reeled off* a long poem.

Reels of a tape recorder

reel[3] [rēl] *v.* **1** To sway from side to side; stagger: The man *reeled* down the street. **2** To be dizzy or giddy: My head is *reeling*. **3** To waver or fall back: The enemy *reeled* under the fierce frontal attack.

re·e·lect or **re-e·lect** [rē′i·lekt′] *v.* To elect again: They *reelected* him governor. — **re′e· lec′tion** or **re′e·lec′tion** *n.*

re·en·force or **re-en·force** [rē′en·fôrs′] *v.* **re· en·forced** or **re-en·forced, re·en·forc·ing** or **re-en·forc·ing** Another spelling of REIN-FORCE. — **re′en·force′ment** or **re′-en· force′ment** *n.*

re·en·ter or **re-en·ter** [rē·en′tər] *v.* To enter again: He *reentered* the room.

re·en·try or **re-en·try** [rē·en′trē] *n.*, *pl.* **re· en·tries** or **re-en·tries** **1** The act of entering again. **2** The return of a rocket or spacecraft to the earth's atmosphere after it has been in orbit or at very high altitudes.

re·es·tab·lish or **re-es·tab·lish** [rē′ə·stab′· lish] *v.* To establish again. — **re′es·tab′lish· ment** or **re′-es·tab′lish·ment** *n.*

re·fec·to·ry [ri·fek′tər·ē] *n.*, *pl.* **re·fec·to·ries** A room or hall for eating, especially in a monastery, convent, or college.

re·fer [ri·fûr′] *v.* **re·ferred, re·fer·ring** **1** To go for information, help, etc.: to *refer* to an encyclopedia. **2** To send for help, information, treatment, etc.: The doctor *referred* her to an eye specialist. **3** To hand over or submit for consideration, settlement, etc.: The problem was

referred to the principal. — **refer to** To make reference to; speak of: She seldom *refers to* her family.

ref·e·ree [ref′ə·rē′] *n.*, *v.* **ref·e·reed, ref·e· ree·ing** **1** *n.* In certain sports, as boxing, basketball, or football, the person whose job is to see that the rules of the game are obeyed. **2** *n.* A person to whom anything is referred for a decision; arbitrator. **3** *v.* To observe and judge as a referee.

ref·er·ence [ref′ər·əns *or* ref′rəns] *n.* **1** The act of calling attention: He made no *reference* to the quarrel. **2** A statement, passage, or book to which attention is called: His *references* offer many examples. **3** Something that provides information or help: An encyclopedia is a book of *reference.* **4** *adj. use:* a *reference* book; a *reference* library. **5** Regard; relation: in *reference* to your second question. **6** A person who can be asked about another's character, qualifications for a job, etc. **7** A statement or letter about a person's character or ability: Take your *references* with you when you go for an interview.

ref·er·en·dum [ref′ə·ren′dəm] *n.*, *pl.* **ref·er· en·dums** or **ref·er·en·da** [ref′ə·ren′də] **1** The presentation to the people of a proposed bill so that they can vote to approve or reject it. **2** The vote in such a procedure.

re·fill [*v.* rē·fil′, *n.* rē′fil] **1** *v.* To fill again. **2** *n.* A product shaped to fit a container that once held the same product: a *refill* for a lipstick case.

re·fine [ri·fīn′] *v.* **re·fined, re·fin·ing** **1** To make or become fine or pure; purify: to *refine* flour. **2** To make or become more polished or cultured: Practice *refined* his piano playing.

re·fined [ri·fīnd′] *adj.* **1** Free from impurities or unwanted substances: *refined* gold. **2** Free from vulgarity or coarseness; cultured: a *refined* taste in books.

re·fine·ment [ri·fīn′mənt] *n.* **1** The act or process of refining; purification. **2** Fineness of thought, taste, language, etc.

re·fin·er·y [ri·fī′nər·ē] *n.*, *pl.* **re·fin·er·ies** A place where some crude material, as sugar or petroleum, is refined.

re·fit [rē·fit′] *v.* **re·fit·ted, re·fit·ting,** *n.* **1** *v.* To make fit or ready again, as by making repairs, replacing equipment, etc. **2** *n.* The repair of damages or wear, as of a ship.

re·flect [ri·flekt′] *v.* **1** To throw or cast back (heat, sound, light, etc.): The white sand *reflects* the sun's rays. **2** To throw back an image of: The sailboat was *reflected* in the quiet lake. **3** To think; ponder: to *reflect* on the past. **4** To show or express: Newspapers *reflect* the opinions of their owners. **5** To cause as a result of one's actions or character: His eagerness to learn *reflects* credit on his parents. **6** To have an unfavorable effect upon: His conduct will *reflect* seriously upon his future career. **7** To bring blame, discredit, etc.: *His lying reflects on his general character.*

re·flec·tion [ri·flek′shən] *n.* **1** The bouncing back or off of light, sound, or other radiant energy when it strikes a surface or something that opposes its passage: *An echo is caused by a reflection of sound.* **2** Something reflected: *The boy stared at his reflection in the mirror.* **3** Meditation; serious thought. **4** A remark or comment made as a result of serious thought. **5** A suggestion of blame or reproach: *His absent-mindedness is no reflection on his intelligence.*

Reflection in a mirror

re·flec·tive [ri·flek′tiv] *adj.* **1** Given to reflection or thought: *a reflective boy.* .**2** Reflecting: *the reflective surface of a polished floor.*

re·flec·tor [ri·flek′tər] *n.* **1** A polished surface for reflecting light, heat, or sound. **2** A telescope that transmits the image to the eyepiece from a mirror.

re·flex [rē′fleks] **1** *n.* An action not controlled by the will, performed in response to the stimulation of a nerve or group of nerves, as a blink of the eye, a yawn, or a sneeze. **2** *adj.* Of or having to do with such an action: *Shivering is a reflex action.*

reflex angle An angle greater than a straight angle.

re·flex·ive [ri·flek′siv] **1** *adj.* Describing a verb having an object that is identical with the subject. In "He dresses himself" *dresses* is a reflexive verb. **2** *adj.* Describing a pronoun that is the object of a reflexive verb. In "She hurt herself" *herself* is a reflexive pronoun. **3** *n.* A reflexive verb or pronoun.

re·for·est [rē·fôr′ist] *v.* To plant trees again in (an area). **— re′for·es·ta′tion** *n.*

re·form [ri·fôrm′] **1** *v.* To make better by correcting wrongs, abuses, etc.: *to reform a city government.* **2** *v.* To become or behave better; improve one's conduct: *The lazy student reformed and began studying.* **3** *n.* A change for the better, as by the correction of wrongs, abuses, etc.

ref·or·ma·tion [ref′ər·mā′shən] *n.* **1** The act of reforming. **2** The condition of being reformed. **3** (*written* **Reformation**) The religious and social movement in the 16th century in Europe that began as an effort to change or reform the Roman Catholic Church and ended with the founding of Protestantism.

re·form·a·to·ry [ri·fôr′mə·tôr′ē] *n., pl.* **re·form·a·to·ries,** *adj.* **1** *n.* An institution for the reformation and teaching of young lawbreakers. **2** *adj.* Tending or aiming to reform.

re·form·er [ri·fôr′mər] *n.* A person who brings about or tries to bring about reforms.

re·fract [ri·frakt′] *v.* To cause refraction of. **— re·frac′tive** *adj.*

re·frac·tion [ri·frak′shən] *n.* A change in direction of a ray of light or other energy as it passes obliquely between media in which it has different wavelengths.

re·frac·tor [ri·frak′tər] *n.* A telescope that uses a second lens, not a mirror, to focus light rays.

re·frac·to·ry [ri·frak′tər·ē] *adj.* **1** Hard to control; obstinate: *a refractory child.* **2** Difficult to melt or work, as some metals or ores.

Light refraction

re·frain¹ [ri·frān′] *v.* To keep oneself back; abstain from action: *to refrain from answering.*

re·frain² [ri·frān′] *n.* A phrase in a poem or song repeated over and over, especially at the end of each stanza.

re·fresh [ri·fresh′] *v.* **1** To make fresh or vigorous again; revive: *The cold drink refreshed him; to refresh one's memory about past events.* **2** To become fresh again; revive.

re·fresh·ing [ri·fresh′ing] *adj.* **1** Tending to refresh or revive: *a refreshing breeze.* **2** Enjoyably unusual or novel: *a refreshing movie.*

re·fresh·ment [ri·fresh′mənt] *n.* **1** The act of refreshing. **2** The condition of being refreshed. **3** Something that refreshes, as food or drink. **4** (*pl.*) Food, drink, or both.

re·frig·er·ant [ri·frij′ər·ənt] *n.* A substance used for obtaining and maintaining a low temperature, as frozen carbon dioxide or ammonia.

re·frig·er·ate [ri·frij′ə·rāt] *v.* **re·frig·er·at·ed, re·frig·er·at·ing** To keep or make cold. **— re·frig′er·a′tion** *n.*

re·frig·er·a·tor [ri·frij′ə·rā′tər] *n.* A cabinet, room, railroad car, etc., for keeping foods fresh by means of ice, mechanical cooling, etc.

re·fu·el [rē·fyōō′əl *or* rē·fyōōl′] *v.* **re·fu·eled, re·fu·el·ing** or **re·fu·elled, re·fu·el·ling** **1** To fill again with fuel. **2** To take on a new supply of fuel.

ref·uge [ref′yōōj] *n.* **1** Shelter or protection from danger or distress. **2** A person or thing that shelters or protects. **3** A safe place.

ref·u·gee [ref′yōō·jē′ *or* ref′yōō·jē′] *n.* A person who flees from persecution or danger.

re·ful·gent [ri·ful′jənt] *adj.* Shining brilliantly; radiant. **— re·ful′gence** *n.*

re·fund [*v.* ri·fund′, *n.* rē′fund] **1** *v.* To pay back (money): *If you are not satisfied with our product, we will refund your money.* **2** *n.* A repayment. **3** *n.* The amount refunded.

re·fus·al [ri·fyōō′zəl] *n.* **1** The act of refusing. **2** A choice of accepting or declining something before it is offered to someone else.

re·fuse¹ [ri·fyōōz′] *v.* **re·fused, re·fus·ing** To say that one will not take, agree to, give, allow, etc. (something); decline: *to refuse a helping of cake; to refuse to leave; to refuse permission.*

ref·use[2] [ref′yōōs] *n.* Worthless things; trash.

re·fute [ri·fyōōt′] *v.* **re·fut·ed, re·fut·ing** **1** To prove the untruth of: to *refute* an argument. **2** To prove (a person) to be in the wrong. — **ref′u·ta′tion** *n.*

re·gain [ri·gān′] *v.* **1** To get possession of again; recover: to *regain* one's health. **2** To reach again; get back to: He had to ask directions twice before he *regained* the street.

re·gal [rē′gəl] *adj.* **1** Of, belonging to, or fit for a king; royal. **2** Stately; splendid.

re·gale [ri·gāl′] *v.* **re·galed, re·gal·ing** To give pleasure or delight to; entertain: He *regaled* us with stories; Our hosts *regaled* us with a fine dinner.

re·ga·li·a [ri·gā′lē·ə *or* ri·gāl′yə] *n.pl.* **1** The symbols and emblems of royalty, as the crown, scepter, etc. **2** The symbols and emblems of any society, order, etc. **3** Fancy clothes; finery.

re·gard [ri·gärd′] **1** *v.* To look at closely or attentively. **2** *n.* A look, especially a steady look. **3** *v.* To look on or think of in a certain way: I *regard* you as a friend. **4** *v.* To show consideration for; respect: to *regard* the opinion of others. **5** *n.* Consideration; respect. **6** *v.* To pay attention to; heed: Nobody *regarded* his warning. **7** *n.* Good opinion; esteem: a high *regard* for his ability. **8** *n.* (*pl.*) Good wishes; affection: My kindest *regards* to your family. — **in regard to** or **with regard to** In reference to; in relation to; about; concerning.

re·gard·ing [ri·gär′ding] *prep.* In reference to; in regard to; about; concerning.

re·gard·less [ri·gärd′lis] **1** *adj.* Having no consideration or concern; heedless: He was *regardless* of other people's feelings. **2** *adv. informal* In spite of everything; anyway.

re·gat·ta [ri·gat′ə *or* ri·gät′ə] *n.* A boat race, or a series of such races.

re·gen·cy [rē′jən·sē] *n., pl.* **re·gen·cies** **1** The government, office, or power of a regent or a group of regents. **2** The period of time during which a regent governs. **3** A group of regents.

re·gen·er·ate [ri·jen′ə·rāt] *v.* **re·gen·er·at·ed, re·gen·er·at·ing** **1** To cause to become better morally or spiritually. **2** To make better by changing thoroughly. **3** To produce, generate, or form again: Worms cut in half easily *regenerate* themselves. — **re·gen′er·a′tion** *n.* — **re·gen·er·a·tive** [ri·jen′ər·ə·tiv] *adj.*

re·gent [rē′jənt] *n.* **1** A person who rules in the name and place of the sovereign: The duke served as *regent* until the king was old enough to rule. **2** A member of a governing board, as of certain universities.

reg·i·cide [rej′ə·sīd] *n.* **1** The act of killing a king. **2** A person who kills a king.

re·gime [ri·zhēm′] *n.* **1** A system or method of government **2** A regimen.

ré·gime [rā·zhēm′] *n.* A regime.

reg·i·men [rej′ə·mən] *n.* A course of treatment as to diet, exercise, etc., to improve health.

reg·i·ment [*n.* rej′ə·mənt, *v.* rej′ə·ment] **1** *n.* An army unit, larger than a battalion and smaller than a division, usually commanded by a colonel. **2** *v.* To require to follow one strict pattern of behavior. — **reg′i·men′tal** *adj.*

reg·i·men·ta·tion [rej′ə·mən·tā′shən] *n.* **1** The act of forming into disciplined, uniform groups. **2** A putting under strict control.

re·gion [rē′jən] *n.* **1** An area of land, usually large; district: a southern *region*; a coal-mining *region*. **2** Any area, place, space, etc.: the abdominal *region*; the *regions* of the sky.

re·gion·al [rē′jən·əl] *adj.* Of, having to do with, or in a region: a *regional* heat wave; a *regional* dialect. — **re′gion·al·ly** *adv.*

reg·is·ter [rej′is·tər] **1** *n.* An official record or list. **2** *n.* A book containing this. **3** *v.* To enter in a register: to *register* a birth. **4** *v.* To enter the name or names of in a register: to *register* students or voters. **5** *v.* To enter one's name in a register, as of voters or students; enroll. **6** *n.* A device for counting or recording: a cash *register*. **7** *v.* To indicate, as on a scale: The thermometer *registered* 70°. **8** *v.* To show; express: His face *registered* surprise. **9** *v.* To cause (mail) to be recorded, by paying a fee, so as to ensure its delivery. **10** *n.* In music, the range, or a certain part of it, of a voice or instrument. **11** *n.* A device that can be opened or closed to admit heated or cooled air to a room.

Cash register

reg·is·trar [rej′is·trär] *n.* A keeper of a register or of records, especially in a college.

reg·is·tra·tion [rej′is·trā′shən] *n.* **1** The act of entering in a register. **2** An entry in a register. **3** The number of people registered.

reg·is·try [rej′is·trē] *n., pl.* **reg·is·tries** **1** A register (*defs. 1 and 2*). **2** A place, such as an office, where a register or registers are kept. **3** The act of registering.

re·gress [ri·gres′] *v.* To go backward; return, as to a former state. — **re·gress′ion** *n.*

re·gret [ri·gret′] *v.* **re·gret·ted, re·gret·ting,** *n.* **1** *v.* To feel sorrow or grief about: to *regret* the loss of a friend; to *regret* having lost one's temper. **2** *n.* Sorrow or grief. **3** *n.* (*pl.*) A polite refusal of an invitation: We send our *regrets*.

re·gret·ful [ri·gret′fəl] *adj.* Feeling or showing regret. — **re·gret′ful·ly** *adv.*

re·gret·ta·ble [ri·gret′ə·bəl] *adj.* Causing regret or distress: a *regrettable* mistake.

reg·u·lar [reg′yə·lər] **1** *adj.* Even or symmetrical: a *regular* design; a *regular* heartbeat. **2** *adj.* Disciplined; orderly: He leads a *regular* life. **3** *adj.* Usual; habitual: my *regular* seat; a store's *regular* customers. **4** *adj.* Always occurring at the same time: a *regular* meeting. **5** *adj.* In grammar, having the normal or most common forms and endings: a *regular* verb. **6** *adj.* Of or belonging to the permanent army, whose men serve during peace as well as war. **7** *n.* A professional soldier; a member of the regular army. **8** *adj.* Qualified to do a certain job: a *regular* nurse. **9** *adj. informal* Thorough; complete: a *regular* crook. **10** *adj. informal* Very pleasant; friendly: a *regular* guy. **— reg′u·lar·ly** *adv.*

reg·u·lar·i·ty [reg′yə·lar′ə·tē] *n., pl.* **reg·u·lar·i·ties** The condition or quality of being regular: A single hill broke the tiresome *regularity* of the plain.

reg·u·late [reg′yə·lāt] *v,* **reg·u·lat·ed, reg·u·lat·ing 1** To control according to certain rules: A policeman *regulates* traffic. **2** To adjust according to a standard: A thermostat *regulates* the heat in a building. **— reg′u·la′tor** *n.*

reg·u·la·tion [reg′yə·lā′shən] **1** *n.* The act of regulating. **2** *n.* The condition of being regulated. **3** *n.* A rule of conduct: army *regulations*. **4** *adj.* Done or made according to a rule or regulation. **5** *adj.* Usual, customary, or required: He is wearing the *regulation* uniform.

re·gur·gi·tate [ri·gûr′jə·tāt] *v.* **re·gur·gi·tat·ed, re·gur·gi·tat·ing 1** To rush or pour back. **2** To bring up partially digested food, as some birds do to feed their young. **3** To vomit. **— re·gur′gi·ta′tion** *n.*

re·ha·bil·i·tate [rē′hə·bil′ə·tāt] *v.* **re·ha·bil·i·tat·ed, re·ha·bil·i·tat·ing 1** To restore to good condition, health, appearance, etc.: to *rehabilitate* a run-down neighborhood. **2** To restore to a former rank, privilege, etc.; reinstate: to *rehabilitate* an army officer who has been stripped of his rank. **— re′ha·bil′i·ta′tion** *n.*

re·hash [*v.* rē·hash′, *n.* rē′hash′] **1** *v.* To work into a new form; go over again: to *rehash* an old quarrel. **2** *n.* Something that has been rehashed: a *rehash* of an old play.

re·hears·al [ri·hûr′səl] *n.* **1** A practice session or performance to prepare for a public performance. **2** The act of rehearsing.

re·hearse [ri·hûrs′] *v.* **re·hearsed, re·hears·ing 1** To practice or cause to practice in preparation for public performance: to *rehearse* a play; The conductor *rehearsed* the orchestra. **2** To tell in detail: She *rehearsed* her complaints to her father.

Reich [rīk] *n.* A former name for Germany or its government. ◆ *Reich* is a German word meaning *empire* or *state*.

reign [rān] **1** *v.* To rule; govern, as a king. **2** *n.* The period during which a sovereign rules: the *reign* of Elizabeth I. **3** *v.* To be everywhere; prevail: Silence *reigned* in the forest. **4** *n.* Controlling influence; power: a *reign* of terror.

re·im·burse [rē′im·bûrs′] *v.* **re·im·bursed, re·im·burs·ing** To pay back an amount that has been spent or lost: You will be *reimbursed* for your expenses. **— re′im·burse′ment** *n.*

rein [rān] **1** *n.* (*usually pl.*) A strap attached to the bit to control a horse or other animal while it is being ridden or driven. **2** *v.* To guide, control, or halt with or as if with reins: to *rein* in a horse; to *rein* in one's temper. **3** *n.* Any means of controlling or restraining. **—**

A horse's reins

draw rein To stop or slow down. **— give rein to** To free, as from control.

re·in·car·nate [rē′in·kär′nāt] *v.* **re·in·car·nat·ed, re·in·car·nat·ing** To provide (a soul) with a new body after death.

re·in·car·na·tion [rē′in·kär·nā′shən] *n.* **1** A belief that the soul may be reborn in a different body. **2** A new embodiment.

rein·deer [rān′dir′] *n., pl.* **rein·deer** A deer found in northern regions, having large, branching antlers. It has been tamed for its milk and meat and is used to carry loads.

Reindeer, 42 in. high at shoulder

re·in·force [rē′in·fôrs′] *v.* **re·in·forced, re·in·forc·ing** To give new force or strength to by adding something: to *reinforce* troops under attack: She *reinforced* her argument with facts.

re·in·force·ment [rē′in·fôrs′mənt] *n.* **1** The act of reinforcing. **2** Anything that strengthens. **3** (*pl.*) Additional troops, aircraft, or ships.

re·in·state [rē′in·stāt′] *v.* **re·in·stat·ed, re·in·stat·ing** To put back into a former condition or situation. **— re′in·state′ment** *n.*

re·it·er·ate [rē·it′ə·rāt] *v.* **re·it·er·at·ed, re·it·er·at·ing** To say or do again and again; repeat: to *reiterate* a request; *reiterated* blows. **— re·it′er·a′tion** *n.*

re·ject [*v.* ri·jekt′, *n.* rē′jekt] **1** *v.* To refuse to take, recognize, believe, grant, etc.: to *reject* help. **2** *v.* To throw away as worthless; discard: to *reject* faulty machine parts. **3** *n.* A person or thing that has been rejected.

re·jec·tion [ri·jek′shən] *n.* **1** The act of rejecting. **2** The condition of being rejected. **3** A thing that is rejected.

re·joice [ri·jois′] *v.* **re·joiced, re·joic·ing** To be or make glad: I *rejoiced* at her good luck; The news *rejoiced* my heart.

re·joic·ing [ri·joi′sing] *n.* The feeling or expressing of joy.

re·join[1] [ri·join′] *v.* To answer; say in reply.

re·join[2] [rē·join′] *v.* **1** To join together again; reunite. **2** To come into company with again: I shall *rejoin* you later.

re·join·der [ri·join′dər] *n.* **1** An answer to a reply. **2** Any answer or reply.

re·ju·ve·nate [ri·jōō′və·nāt] *v.* **re·ju·ve·nat·ed, re·ju·ve·nat·ing** To give new vigor or youthfulness to. — **re·ju′ve·na′tion** *n.*

re·lapse [ri·laps′] *v.* **re·lapsed, re·laps·ing,** *n.* **1** *v.* To fall or lapse back into a former condition or state, as into illness after improving. **2** *n.* A falling back to a former state or condition after improving: Her *relapse* worried the doctor.

re·late [ri·lāt′] *v.* **re·lat·ed, re·lat·ing 1** To tell about; narrate: to *relate* the important events of the Civil War. **2** To bring into connection or relation: to *relate* facts to events. **3** To refer; have to do with: The rumor *relates* to your new neighbors.

re·lat·ed [ri·lā′tid] *adj.* **1** Connected: *related* events. **2** Belonging to the same family or group: He is *related* to me on my mother's side; *related* languages.

re·la·tion [ri·lā′shən] *n.* **1** Connection, as in meaning, significance, or thought. **2** (*pl.*) The connections between people, groups, nations, etc., brought about by business, political, or other contact. **3** Connection by descent or marriage; kinship. **4** A relative; kinsman. **5** An account; narration.

re·la·tion·ship [ri·lā′shən·ship] *n.* The condition of being related; connection.

rel·a·tive [rel′ə·tiv] **1** *adj.* Having to do with; relating: the facts *relative* to a situation. **2** *adj.* Having meaning only as related to something else: "High" is a *relative* term. **3** *adj.* Depending upon relation; comparative: the *relative* values of the dollar and the franc. **4** *n.* A person related to another by blood or marriage. **5** *adj.* In grammar, referring to a person or thing already mentioned. In "The man who spoke was angry" *who* is a relative pronoun and *who spoke* is a relative clause, referring to *man.* **6** *n.* A relative word, as *who* or *that.* — **relative to 1** Concerning; about. **2** In relation or proportion to.

rel·a·tive·ly [rel′ə·tiv·lē] *adv.* As compared with something else or with a standard; comparatively: a *relatively* small town; a *relatively* easy question.

rel·a·tiv·i·ty [rel′ə·tiv′ə·tē] *n.* **1** The quality or condition of being relative. **2** Either of two theories formulated by Albert Einstein explaining the relationship between matter, energy, space, and time. One of them led to the development of atomic energy.

re·lax [ri·laks′] *v.* **1** To avoid work, exercise, etc.; rest: to *relax* on a couch. **2** To make or become less tight or firm: He *relaxed* his grip on the bat; Tired muscles *relax* in a hot bath. **3** To make less severe, acute, etc.: to *relax* one's attention; to *relax* discipline. — **re·lax·a′tion** *n.*

re·lay [*n.* rē′lā, *v.* ri·lā′ *or* rē′lā] **1** *n.* A fresh set, as of men or horses, to replace a tired set. **2** *n.* A relay race, or one of its laps. **3** *v.* To send on-

ward by or as if by relays: to *relay* a message. **4** *n.* An electrical switch that is itself operated by electricity.

relay race A running or swimming race in which each member of a team races a certain distance and is then replaced by a teammate.

Two runners in a relay race

re·lease [ri·lēs′] *v.* **re·leased, re·leas·ing,** *n.* **1** *v.* To set free: *Release* the prisoners. **2** *n.* The act of setting free. **3** *n.* A being set free; liberation: *release* from worry. **4** *v.* To let go; discharge: to *release* a bomb from an airplane. **5** *n.* A spring, catch, or other device that releases or unfastens a part of a machine, etc. **6** *v.* To allow to be presented to the public: to *release* a motion picture. **7** *n.* Anything released to the public, as a motion picture, news story, etc. **8** *n.* The act of giving up a claim. **9** *n.* The legal paper certifying this.

rel·e·gate [rel′ə·gāt] *v.* **rel·e·gat·ed, rel·e·gat·ing 1** To send off or assign, as to a less important position or place: to *relegate* a student to the bottom of the class. **2** To banish; exile. **3** To give over; assign, as a task, piece of business, etc.

re·lent [ri·lent′] *v.* To become gentler or more compassionate: The king *relented* and pardoned the courtier who had offended him.

re·lent·less [ri·lent′lis] *adj.* **1** Without pity; unforgiving; harsh: a *relentless* enemy. **2** Continuing; persistent: a *relentless* noise. — **re·lent′less·ly** *adv.*

rel·e·vance [rel′ə·vəns] *n.* The condition of being relevant; pertinence.

rel·e·van·cy [rel′ə·vən·sē] *n.* Relevance.

rel·e·vant [rel′ə·vənt] *adj.* Connected with or having to do with the point, the matter at hand, etc.; pertinent; related: What he said was not *relevant* to the discussion.

re·li·a·ble [ri·lī′ə·bəl] *adj.* Dependable; trustworthy: a *reliable* friend; a *reliable* report. — **re·li′a·bil′i·ty** *n.* — **re·li′a·bly** *adv.*

re·li·ance [ri·lī′əns] *n.* **1** Confidence; trust. **2** Dependence: a baby's *reliance* on his parents. **3** Something upon which one relies.

re·li·ant [ri·lī′ənt] *adj.* **1** Depending or relying. **2** Confident. **3** Self-reliant.

rel·ic [rel′ik] *n.* **1** Something remaining from what has disappeared or been destroyed: a *relic* of ancient Greece. **2** A memento connected with a saint or his tomb.

re·lief [ri·lēf′] *n.* **1** Lessening of or freeing from pain, a difficulty, etc. **2** Something that relieves: It's a *relief* to be home again. **3** Help in the form of money or food given to the needy. **4** Rest or

freedom from work or duty. **5** A person who relieves another from a duty. **6** In architecture and sculpture, the raising of a figure, ornament, etc., from a surface. **7** A figure, ornament, etc., so raised. —
on relief Receiving money from public funds, as when out of work.

relief map A map on which differences in height above sea level are shown by lines or colors, or by molding surface features, as hills, rivers, valleys, etc., in some solid material.

An Egyptian relief

re·lieve [ri·lēv′] *v.* **re·lieved, re·liev·ing 1** To lessen or ease: to *relieve* a headache. **2** To free (someone) from suffering, pain, fear, etc. **3** To help, as with food or money. **4** To substitute for and free from duty: to *relieve* a guard. **5** To make less dull and monotonous: to *relieve* a gray room with bright curtains.

re·li·gion [ri·lij′ən] *n.* **1** Belief in or worship of God or gods. **2** A particular system of belief or worship: the Jewish *religion*.

re·li·gious [ri·lij′əs] *adj., n., pl.* **re·li·gious 1** *adj.* Of or having to do with religion: a *religious* holiday; *religious* training. **2** *adj.* Devout; pious: My uncle is very *religious* and attends church regularly. **3** *n.* A member of a religious order; a monk or nun. **4** *adj.* Conscientious; strict: He is *religious* about doing his homework. — **re·li′gious·ly** *adv.*

re·lin·quish [ri·ling′kwish] *v.* To give up; let go; surrender: to *relinquish* a claim. — **re·lin′quish·ment** *n.*

rel·ish [rel′ish] **1** *n.* Appetizing flavor or taste. **2** *n.* Something eaten with or put on food to lend it flavor or zest, such as pickles or olives. **3** *n.* Appetite; liking: a *relish* for excitement. **4** *v.* To have an appetite for; like or enjoy.

re·luc·tant [ri·luk′tənt] *adj.* **1** Unwilling; not eager: My little brother is always *reluctant* to go to bed. **2** Expressing unwillingness: a *reluctant* answer. — **re·luc′tance** *n.* — **re·luc′tant·ly** *adv.*

re·ly [ri·lī′] *v.* **re·lied, re·ly·ing** To place trust or confidence: We can *rely* on him.

re·main [ri·mān′] *v.* **1** To stay or continue in a place: He *remained* at the house; Nothing *remained* standing after the explosion. **2** To continue to be: The weather *remained* warm. **3** To be left: It *remains* to be proved.

re·main·der [ri·mān′dər] *n.* **1** A part, group, number, etc., left over; that which remains: We ate the *remainder* of the pie. **2** The part that is left over when a number cannot be evenly divided: $9 \div 4 = 2$ with a *remainder* of 1.

re·mains [ri·mānz′] *n.pl.* **1** That which is left after a part has been destroyed or used up: the *remains* of a picnic lunch. **2** A dead body; corpse.

re·mand [ri·mand′] **1** *v.* To order or send back, especially to jail to await trial. **2** *n.* An act of remanding.

re·mark [ri·märk′] **1** *v.* To mention or comment; say: She *remarked* that the soup was hot. **2** *n.* A brief comment: At the party he made some amusing *remarks*. **3** *v.* To take particular notice of: He *remarked* and pointed out a cut in the wall of the tire.

re·mark·a·ble [ri·mär′kə·bəl] *adj.* Worthy of notice; extraordinary; unusual: She has *remarkable* beauty. — **re·mark′a·bly** *adv.*

Rem·brandt [rem′brant] *n.*, 1606–1669, Dutch painter and etcher.

re·me·di·a·ble [ri·mē′dē·ə·bəl] *adj.* Capable of being remedied or cured.

re·me·di·al [ri·mē′dē·əl] *adj.* Providing a remedy; intended to be used as a remedy.

rem·e·dy [rem′ə·dē] *n., pl.* **rem·e·dies,** *v.* **rem·e·died, rem·e·dy·ing 1** *n.* Something that cures, relieves, or corrects: Aspirin is a *remedy* for headaches. **2** *v.* To heal or make right: to *remedy* poverty.

re·mem·ber [ri·mem′bər] *v.* **1** To bring back to the mind or memory: I never can *remember* telephone numbers. **2** To keep in mind carefully: to *remember* one's manners. **3** To mention as sending greetings: *Remember* me to your mother. **4** To bear in mind as worthy of a gift or reward: to *remember* someone in one's will.

re·mem·brance [ri·mem′brəns] *n.* **1** The act or power of remembering; memory: He had no *remembrance* of the accident. **2** A keepsake; memento. **3** (*pl.*) Greetings; regards.

re·mind [ri·mīnd′] *v.* To cause to remember: I *reminded* her that it was time to go.

re·mind·er [ri·mīn′dər] *n.* Something to help a person remember.

rem·i·nisce [rem′ə·nis′] *v.* **rem·i·nisced, rem·i·nisc·ing** To talk or think about the past, especially in a fond or dreamy way.

rem·i·nis·cence [rem′ə·nis′əns] *n.* **1** The act of remembering. **2** Something remembered from the past. **3** (*pl.*) An account of a person's past experiences: *reminiscences* of childhood.

rem·i·nis·cent [rem′ə·nis′ənt] *adj.* **1** Thinking or talking about the past: The old woman was *reminiscent.* **2** Causing memories; suggestive: a song *reminiscent* of happier days.

re·miss [ri·mis′] *adj.* Careless about things needing attention; negligent; neglectful.

re·mis·sion [ri·mish′ən] *n.* **1** Forgiveness: *remission* of sins. **2** Release from a debt, duty, or the like. **3** Temporary lessening of a pain, fever, etc.

re·mit [ri·mit′] *v.* **re·mit·ted, re·mit·ting 1** To pardon; forgive: to *remit* sins. **2** To release someone from: to *remit* a debt or punishment. **3** To send (money) in payment. **4** To make less; slacken: to *remit* one's vigilance.

re·mit·tance [ri·mit′əns] *n.* **1** The act of sending money. **2** The money sent.

rem·nant [rem′nənt] *n.* **1** A short piece of cloth left over after the rest of a larger piece has been sold or used. **2** A remaining trace: to keep a *remnant* of dignity.

re·mod·el [rē·mod′(ə)l] *v.* **re·mod·eled** or **re·mod·elled, re·mod·el·ing** or **re·mod·el·ling** **1** To model again: to *remodel* a figure. **2** To make over, with changes of design or purpose: to *remodel* a house.

re·mon·strance [ri·mon′strəns] *n.* The act of remonstrating; protest.

re·mon·strate [ri·mon′strāt] *v.* **re·mon·strat·ed, re·mon·strat·ing** To present and urge strong reasons in objecting or protesting: The principal *remonstrated* with the boy about talking in class.

re·morse [ri·môrs′] *n.* Great regret or anguish for something one has done; self-reproach.

re·morse·ful [ri·môrs′fəl] *adj.* Feeling remorse; full of self-reproach or guilt.

re·morse·less [ri·môrs′lis] *adj.* Without pity; cruel; having no compassion.

re·mote [ri·mōt′] *adj.* **re·mot·er, re·mot·est** **1** Distant: Greenland is a *remote* island. **2** From a distance, as by radio waves: *remote* control. **3** Distant in time: the *remote* future. **4** Distant in relationship: a *remote* cousin. **5** Not obvious; slight: a *remote* likeness. **— re·mote′ly** *adv.*

Toy operated by remote control

re·mount [*v.* rē·mount′, *n.* rē′mount′] **1** *v.* To mount again: When his horse was rested, he *remounted* and rode off. **2** *n.* A fresh horse for riding.

re·mov·al [ri·mōō′vəl] *n.* **1** The act of removing. **2** The condition of being removed. **3** Dismissal: *removal* from public office. **4** A changing of location: the *removal* of a corporation to another city.

re·move [ri·mōōv′] *v.* **re·moved, re·mov·ing,** *n.* **1** *v.* To take or move away: George *removed* all his things from the desk. **2** *v.* To take off: to *remove* one's hat. **3** *v.* To get rid of: Using aluminum *removes* any danger of rust. **4** *v.* To dismiss: The mayor was *removed* from office. **5** *v.* To change location; move: to *remove* to another area. **6** *n.* A step or degree: He is one *remove* from a fool. **— re·mov′er** *n.*

re·mu·ner·ate [ri·myōō′nə·rāt] *v.* **re·mu·ner·at·ed, re·mu·ner·at·ing** To pay; reward; compensate: He was *remunerated* for his work.

re·mu·ner·a·tion [ri·myōō′nə·rā′shən] *n.* **1** The act of remunerating. **2** Payment; reward.

re·mu·ner·a·tive [ri·myōō′nə·rā′tiv or ri·myōō′nə·rə·tiv] *adj.* Profitable; paying: a *remunerative* deal.

Re·mus [rē′məs] *n.* In Roman myths, the brother of Romulus. ◆ See ROMULUS.

Ren·ais·sance [ren′ə·säns′] *n.* **1** The great revival of art, literature, and learning that marked the 14th, 15th, and 16th centuries in Europe. **2** The period of this revival. **3** (*written* **renaissance**) Any revival or rebirth.

re·nal [rē′nəl] *adj.* Of, having to do with, or near the kidneys.

Re·nas·cence [ri·nas′əns] *n.* **1** The Renaissance. **2** (*written* **renascence**) A new birth; revival or renewal.

rend [rend] *v.* **rent** or **rend·ed, rend·ing** **1** To tear apart; split; break: to *rend* one's clothing; The silence was *rent* with cries. **2** To distress; grieve: Sorrow *rends* her heart.

ren·der [ren′dər] *v.* **1** To give, present, or submit: to *render* a bill for payment. **2** To provide or furnish: to *render* aid. **3** To give as due: to *render* obedience. **4** To perform; do: to *render* service; to *render* a song. **5** To give in return: to *render* blessings for a curse. **6** To cause to be or become: The blow *rendered* him helpless. **7** To surrender; give up: to *render* a fortress into enemy hands. **8** To translate: to *render* a French ballad into English. **9** To melt down: to *render* fat or lard.

ren·dez·vous [rän′dā·vōō′] *n., pl.* **ren·dez·vous,** *v.* **ren·dez·voused, ren·dez·vous·ing** **1** *n.* A meeting place. **2** *n.* A planned meeting or joining of troops or ships at a certain time and place. **3** *n.* Any meeting or appointment to meet. **4** *v.* To meet or cause to meet at a certain place or time. ◆ *Rendezvous* comes from two French words meaning *present yourself*.

ren·di·tion [ren·dish′ən] *n.* **1** A performance of a musical composition or a part in a play. **2** A translation from one language into another. **3** The act of rendering. **4** Something rendered.

ren·e·gade [ren′ə·gād] *n.* A person who gives up his faith, principles, or party to join the opposite side; traitor.

re·nege [ri·nig′] *v.* **re·neged, re·neg·ing** **1** In card games, to fail to follow suit when able and required by the rules to do so. **2** *informal* To fail to keep a promise.

re·new [ri·n(y)ōō′] *v.* **1** To make new or as if new again; restore: to *renew* one's health. **2** To begin again; resume: to *renew* an argument. **3** To cause to continue in effect; extend: to *renew* a magazine subscription. **4** To replace with something new of the same sort: to *renew* the supply of oil.

re·new·al [ri·n(y)ōō′əl] *n.* **1** The act of renewing. **2** The condition of being renewed.

add, āce, câre, pälm;   end, ēqual;   it, ice;   odd, ōpen, ôrder;   tŏŏk, pōol;   up, bûrn;
ə = a in *above*, e in *sicken*, i in *possible*, o in *melon*, u in *circus*;   yŏŏ = u in *fuse*;   oil;   pout;
check;   ring;   thin;   this;   zh in *vision*.   For ¶ reference, see page 64 · HOW TO

ren·net [ren′it] *n.* The dried extract from the stomach of a young calf. It contains rennin and is used in the manufacture of cheese.

ren·nin [ren′in] *n.* A yellowish substance with a slightly salty taste, obtained from rennet. It is an enzyme used to curdle milk.

Re·noir [rə·nwär′], **Pierre Auguste,** 1840–1919, French painter.

re·nounce [ri·nouns′] *v.* **re·nounced, re·nounc·ing 1** To give up, especially by formal statement: to *renounce* citizenship. **2** To refuse to acknowledge as one's own; disown: to *renounce* one's family. **— re·nounce′ment** *n.*

ren·o·vate [ren′ə·vāt] *v.* **ren·o·vat·ed, ren·o·vat·ing** To make as good as new; repair; freshen: to *renovate* a house. **— ren′o·va′tion** *n.* **— ren′o·va′tor** *n.*

re·nown [ri·noun′] *n.* Fame: He gained *renown* as an athlete.

re·nowned [ri·nound′] *adj.* Famous.

rent[1] [rent] **1** *n.* Money paid to a landlord or owner for the use of land, living quarters, etc. **2** *v.* To use in return for rent: We *rent* our home. **3** *v.* To be used or available for use in exchange for rent: The cabin *rents* for $90 a month. **— for rent** Available for use in return for rent. **— rent′er** *n.*

Renovations

rent[2] [rent] **1** Past tense and past participle of REND. **2** *n.* A rip; tear.

rent·al [ren′təl] *n.* The amount of rent charged or paid: He pays a low *rental.*

re·nun·ci·a·tion [ri·nun′sē·ā′shən] *n.* The act of renouncing or of giving up.

re·or·gan·ize [rē·ôr′gən·īz] *v.* **re·or·gan·ized, re·or·gan·iz·ing** To organize again or in a different way: to *reorganize* a company. **— re′·or·gan·i·za′tion** *n.* ¶3

re·paid [ri·pād′] Past tense and past participle of REPAY.

re·pair[1] [ri·pâr′] **1** *v.* To restore to good or sound condition; mend. **2** *n.* (*often pl.*) A repairing: to make *repairs* about the house. **3** *n.* Condition resulting from proper repairing or from neglect: a car in good *repair*; a fence in poor *repair.* **4** *v.* To make up for, as an injury or wrong.

re·pair[2] [ri·pâr′] *v.* To go: She *repaired* to the garden.

re·pair·man [ri·pâr′man′ *or* ri·pâr′mən] *n., pl.* **re·pair·men** [ri·pâr′men′ *or* ri·pâr′mən] A man whose work is making repairs, as on machines.

rep·a·ra·tion [rep′ə·rā′shən] *n.* **1** The act of making amends for wrong or injury. **2** (*usually pl.*) Something given, as money, by defeated nations as payment for wrongs, damages, or injuries suffered by other nations during a war.

rep·ar·tee [rep′ər·tē′ *or* rep′är·tā′] *n.* **1** A quick, witty reply. **2** Skill or quickness in replying.

re·past [ri·past′] *n.* A meal; food.

re·pa·tri·ate [rē·pā′trē·āt] *v.* **re·pa·tri·at·ed, re·pa·tri·at·ing** To send back to his own country, as a prisoner of war or a refugee. **— re·pa′tri·a′tion** *n.*

re·pay [ri·pā′] *v.* **re·paid, re·pay·ing 1** To pay back: to *repay* a debt; Her kindness *repaid* us for all our work. **2** To pay back someone for: I *repaid* his efforts with thanks. **— re·pay′ment** *n.*

re·peal [ri·pēl′] **1** *v.* To revoke; cancel: to *repeal* a law. **2** *n.* The act of repealing.

re·peat [ri·pēt′] **1** *v.* To say again: to *repeat* a question. **2** *v.* To do, perform, etc., again. **3** *n.* In music, a passage, phrase, section, etc., that is repeated. **4** *v.* To tell to another: to *repeat* gossip. **5** *v.* To recite from memory: to *repeat* a poem. **— repeat oneself** To say again what one has said before.

re·peat·ed [ri·pē′tid] *adj.* Said, done, or occurring again and again; frequent: his *repeated* absences. **— re·peat′ed·ly** *adv.*

re·peat·ing decimal [ri·pē′ting] A decimal in which a pattern is repeated without end. $\frac{7}{11}$ can be expressed as .636363 . . .

re·pel [ri·pel′] *v.* **re·pelled, re·pel·ling 1** To force or drive back; repulse: to *repel* an attack. **2** To push or keep away, especially with invisible force: Like magnetic poles *repel* each other. **3** To resist mixing with, adhering to, or holding: This raincoat *repels* water. **4** To cause to feel distaste or disgust: His manners *repel* me. **5** To reject; refuse: to *repel* a suggestion.

re·pel·lent [ri·pel′ənt] **1** *adj.* That drives or keeps away or back: a *repellent* force. **2** *adj.* Disgusting; distasteful: *repellent* manners. **3** *n.* Something that repels, as a chemical that drives away insects.

re·pent [ri·pent′] *v.* **1** To feel sorrow or remorse about (something one has done, said, etc.): He *repented* his having cheated during the exam. **2** To change one's mind about (something one has done) and come to regret it: He *repented* his generosity.

re·pent·ant [ri·pen′tənt] *adj.* Repenting or showing regret. **— re·pent′ance** *n.*

re·per·cus·sion [rē′pər·kush′ən] *n.* **1** An indirect effect or result of something: A decision of the Supreme Court may have *repercussions* all over the United States. **2** An echo; reverberation. **3** The action of springing back; recoil: the *repercussion* of a gun that has been fired.

rep·er·toire [rep′ər·twär′] *n.* A list of songs, plays, operas, etc., that a person or a group is prepared to perform.

rep·er·to·ry [rep′ər·tôr′ē] *n., pl.* **rep·er·to·ries 1** Another word for REPERTOIRE. **2** A collection: a *repertory* of American folklore.

rep·e·ti·tion [rep′ə·tish′ən] *n.* **1** The act of repeating. **2** Something repeated.

rep·e·ti·tious [rep′ə·tish′əs] *adj.* Full of repetition, especially in a useless or tiresome way. **— rep′e·ti′tious·ly** *adv.*

re·pine [ri·pīn′] *v.* **re·pined, re·pin·ing** To complain; fret; be discontented.

re·place [ri·plās′] *v.* **re·placed, re·plac·ing**
1 To put back in place: to *replace* a card in a file.
2 To take the place of: John *replaced* the class
president. **3** To fill the place of: He *replaced* the
light bulb with a new one.

re·place·ment [ri·plās′mənt] *n.* **1** The act of
replacing. **2** The condition of being replaced.
3 A person or thing that replaces another: I'll
work until you find a *replacement* for me.

re·plen·ish [ri·plen′ish] *v.* To provide with a
new supply; fill up again: to *replenish* the gas
tank. — **re·plen′ish·ment** *n.*

re·plete [ri·plēt′] *adj.* Completely filled; having
a great supply of: a story *replete* with adventures.
— **re·ple′tion** *n.*

rep·li·ca [rep′lə·kə] *n.* A duplicate or copy of a
statue, painting, etc., often made by the artist
himself.

re·ply [ri·plī′] *v.* **re·plied, re·ply·ing,** *n., pl.*
re·plies **1** *v.* To give an answer or response.
2 *n.* An answer or response.

re·port [ri·pôrt′] **1** *v.* To give an account of;
tell of: to *report* the day's happenings. **2** *n.* An
accounting or telling of something, often formal
or in writing: a news *report*; a book *report*. **3** *v.*
To state; announce: The newspaper *reported* his
death. **4** *n.* An announcement or statement: a
report of an accident. **5** *v.* To complain about,
especially to an authority: to *report* a robbery to
the police. **6** *v.* To present oneself: to *report* for
military service. **7** *n.* A rumor: *reports* of flying
saucers. **8** *n.* An explosive sound: a gun's *report*.
9 *n.* Reputation: a man of good *report*.

re·port·er [ri·pôr′tər] *n.* A person who reports,
especially one employed by a newspaper.

re·pose[1] [ri·pōz′] *n., v.* **re·posed, re·pos·ing**
1 *n.* Rest or sleep. **2** *v.* To lie at rest. **3** *v.* To
lay or place in a position of rest: He *reposed* himself on the bed. **4** *n.* Quietness; calmness: His
manner was one of great *repose*.

re·pose[2] [ri·pōz′] *v.* **re·posed, re·pos·ing** To
place, as hope, confidence, etc.: The citizens *reposed* their trust in their leaders.

re·pos·i·to·ry [ri·poz′ə·tôr′ē] *n., pl.* **re·pos·i·
to·ries** A place in which things may be stored
for safekeeping.

re·pos·sess [rē′pə·zes′] *v.* To regain possession
of; get back.

rep·re·hen·si·ble [rep′ri·hen′sə·bəl] *adj.* Deserving blame or rebuke.

rep·re·sent [rep′ri·zent′] *v.* **1** To be the symbol
or expression of; stand for: The letters of the
alphabet *represent* sounds of speech. **2** To be an
example of; typify: She *represents* the ideal
mother. **3** To be an agent of; act and speak for:
Two senators *represent* each state. **4** To depict;
portray: The artist *represented* the woman as
having red hair. **5** To describe: He *represents*
himself as a musician. **6** To act the part of: In
the opera, he *represented* a warrior.

rep·re·sen·ta·tion [rep′ri·zen·tā′shən] *n.*
1 The act of representing. **2** The condition of
being represented. **3** Anything that represents,
as a picture, description, or symbol. **4** Representatives as a group: our *representation* in the state
legislature. **5** (*often pl.*) A statement made
against something or to bring about a change.
— **rep′re·sen·ta′tion·al** *adj.*

rep·re·sen·ta·tive [rep′ri·zen′tə·tiv] **1** *adj.*
Representing: lines *representative* of latitude.
2 *adj.* Serving as an illustration; typical: a
representative sample. **3** *n.* A typical example:
The mouse is a *representative* of the order of rodents. **4** *n.* A person chosen to represent others.
5 *n.* (*often written* **Representative**) In the
U.S., a member of the House of Representatives
or of a state legislature. **6** *adj.* Based on representation, as a government.

re·press [ri·pres′] *v.* **1** To hold back or down;
check: to *repress* a desire to sneeze. **2** To put
down or quell. — **re·pres′sion** *n.*

re·pres·sive [ri·pres′iv] *adj.* Capable of repres-
sing or tending to repress: *repressive* acts. — **re·
pres′sive·ly** *adv.*

re·prieve [ri·prēv′] *n., v.* **re·prieved, re·
priev·ing** **1** *n.* A temporary delay of an order
to execute a person. **2** *n.* The official order for
such a delay. **3** *v.* To give a reprieve to. **4** *n.*
Temporary relief from any danger or trouble.
5 *v.* To give such relief to.

rep·ri·mand [rep′rə·mand] **1** *n.* A severe or
formal reproof. **2** *v.* To reprove sharply or
formally.

re·print [*v.* rē·print′, *n.* rē′print′] **1** *v.* To print
a new edition or copy of. **2** *n.* A reprinted edition
or copy.

re·pri·sal [ri·prī′zəl] *n.* Any act of retaliation,
especially one of force or violence by one nation
against another.

re·proach [ri·prōch′] **1** *v.* To blame for some
wrong: His mother *reproached* him for his bad
manners. **2** *n.* Blame: words of *reproach*. **3** *n.*
Disgrace. **4** *n.* A cause of disgrace.

re·proach·ful [ri·prōch′fəl] *adj.* Filled with or
expressing reproach: a *reproachful* lecture. —
re·proach′ful·ly *adv.*

rep·ro·bate [rep′rə·bāt] **1** *adj.* Wicked; depraved. **2** *n.* A wicked, dishonest person;
scoundrel.

rep·ro·ba·tion [rep′rə·bā′shən] *n.* Disapproval;
condemnation.

re·pro·duce [rē′prə·d(y)o͞os′] *v.* **re·pro·
duced, re·pro·duc·ing** **1** To make a copy of.
2 To produce again: A phonograph *reproduces*
music. **3** To produce offspring: Rabbits *reproduce* in great numbers.

re·pro·duc·tion [rē′prə·duk′shən] *n.* **1** The act
of reproducing. **2** The process by which plants or
animals produce others of their kind. **3** Something that is reproduced, as a copy of a picture.

---

add, āce, câre, pälm;   end, ēqual;   it, īce;   odd, ōpen, ôrder;   to͝ok, po͞ol;   up, bûrn;
ə = a in *above*, e in *sicken*, i in *possible*, o in *melon*, u in *circus*;   yo͞o = u in *fuse*;   oil;   pout;
check;   ring;   thin;   this;   zh in *vision*.   For ¶ reference, see page 64 · HOW TO

re·pro·duc·tive [rē′prə·duk′tiv] *adj.* **1** Reproducing. **2** Having to do with or for reproduction. — **re′pro·duc′tive·ly** *adv.*

re·proof [ri·proof′] *n.* Words of blame; rebuke.

re·prove [ri·proov′] *v.* **re·proved, re·prov·ing** To find fault with; blame; rebuke.

rep·tile [rep′til *or* rep′tīl] *n.* Any of a class of cold-blooded animals that crawl on their bellies or creep on very short legs. Snakes, crocodiles, lizards, and turtles are reptiles.

A reptile

re·pub·lic [ri·pub′lik] *n.* A government in which the power is given to officials elected by and representing the people.

re·pub·li·can [ri·pub′li·kən] **1** *adj.* Of or having to do with a republic: *republican* government. **2** *n.* A person who supports a republic or this form of government. **3** *adj.* (*written* **Republican**) Of or having to do with the Republican Party. **4** *n.* (*written* **Republican**) A member or supporter of the Republican Party.

Republican Party One of the two major political parties of the U.S., founded in 1854.

re·pu·di·ate [ri·pyoo′dē·āt] *v.* **re·pu·di·at·ed, re·pu·di·at·ing** **1** To refuse to accept as true or binding; reject: to *repudiate* an agreement. **2** To refuse to acknowledge or pay: to *repudiate* a debt. **3** To disown: to *repudiate* a son. — **re·pu·di·a′tion** *n.*

re·pug·nant [ri·pug′nənt] *adj.* **1** Disgusting; offensive: Snakes are *repugnant* to many people. **2** Contrary or opposed: deeds *repugnant* to one's conscience. — **re·pug′nance** *n.*

re·pulse [ri·puls′] *v.* **re·pulsed, re·puls·ing,** *n.* **1** *v.* To drive back; repel: to *repulse* an attacker. **2** *n.* The act of repulsing. **3** *n.* The condition of being repulsed. **4** *v.* To repel by coldness, discourtesy, etc.; reject. **5** *n.* Rejection; refusal.

re·pul·sion [ri·pul′shən] *n.* **1** The act of repulsing. **2** Aversion; disgust.

re·pul·sive [ri·pul′siv] *adj.* **1** Disgusting or horrifying. **2** Repelling: a *repulsive* force. — **re·pul′sive·ly** *adv.* — **re·pul′sive·ness** *n.*

rep·u·ta·ble [rep′yə·tə·bəl] *adj.* Well thought of; respected: a *reputable* doctor. — **rep′u·ta·bly** *adv.*

rep·u·ta·tion [rep′yə·tā′shən] *n.* **1** The general estimation in which a person or thing is held by others. **2** A good name: Scandal ruined his *reputation*. **3** Fame or renown.

re·pute [ri·pyoot′] *n.* Reputation: people of good *repute*.

re·put·ed [ri·pyoo′tid] *adj.* Generally thought or supposed: the *reputed* leader of the rebels. — **re·put′ed·ly** *adv.*

re·quest [ri·kwest′] **1** *v.* To ask for: to *request* an appointment. **2** *v.* To ask (a person) to do something. **3** *n.* The act of requesting; petition. **4** *n.* Something asked for: What is your *request*? **5** *n.* Demand: This book is in great *request*.

re·qui·em [rek′wē·əm *or* rē′kwē·əm] *n.* **1** (*often written* **Requiem**) A solemn Mass sung for a person or persons who have died. **2** Music written for parts of this Mass.

re·quire [ri·kwīr′] *v.* **re·quired, re·quir·ing** **1** To have need of: Children *require* plenty of sleep. **2** To order or insist upon: Men are *required* to wear jackets and ties here.

re·quire·ment [ri·kwīr′mənt] *n.* **1** Something needed: Good eyesight is a *requirement* in driving a car. **2** Something demanded: *requirements* for entering college.

req·ui·site [rek′wə·zit] **1** *adj.* Necessary; indispensable. **2** *n.* A necessity; requirement.

req·ui·si·tion [rek′wə·zish′ən] **1** *n.* A formal request or demand, especially in writing: a *requisition* for new typewriters. **2** *v.* To make demands for or upon: to *requisition* supplies; to *requisition* farmers for grain. **3** *n.* The condition of being required or put to use.

re·quit·al [ri·kwīt′(ə)l] *n.* Something done in return for a service or for a wrong.

re·quite [ri·kwīt′] *v.* **re·quit·ed, re·quit·ing** **1** To give or do something in return for: to *requite* a stranger's generosity. **2** To pay back: They never *requited* us for our effort.

re·route [rē·root′ *or* rē·rout′] *v.* **re·rout·ed, re·rout·ing** To send or make go by another route, as mail or traffic.

Traffic being rerouted

re·sale [rē′sāl *or* rē·sāl′] *n.* The act of selling again.

re·scind [ri·sind′] *v.* To make void; repeal: to *rescind* a rule.

res·cue [res′kyoo] *v.* **res·cued, res·cu·ing,** *n.* **1** *v.* To save or free from danger, capture, harm, etc. **2** *n.* A saving from danger, harm, etc.; deliverance: He came to our *rescue*. — **res′cu·er** *n.*

re·search [ri·sûrch′ *or* rē′sûrch] **1** *n.* Careful, patient investigation and study: medical *research*. **2** *v.* To do research or research on. ◆ The verb *research* was derived from the noun, and although the verb form is not new, it was rarely used until recently.

re·sem·blance [ri·zem′bləns] *n.* Similarity; likeness: the *resemblance* between sisters.

re·sem·ble [ri·zem′bəl] *v.* **re·sem·bled, re·sem·bling** To be or look like.

re·sent [ri·zent′] *v.* To feel or show resentment at: to *resent* an insult.

re·sent·ful [ri·zent′fəl] *adj.* Feeling or showing resentment. — **re·sent′ful·ly** *adv.*

re·sent·ment [ri·zent′mənt] *n.* Anger and ill will based on real or imagined wrong or injury.

res·er·va·tion [rez′ər·vā′shən] *n.* **1** The act of reserving. **2** A qualification or condition: The amended bill carried certain *reservations*. **3** A doubt or possible objection: I have one *reservation* about your plan. **4** A tract of government land reserved for a special purpose: an Indian *reservation*. **5** An agreement by which a seat on a plane, a hotel room, etc., is reserved in advance.

re·serve [ri·zûrv′] *v.* **re·served, re·serv·ing,** *n.*, *adj.* **1** *v.* To hold back or set aside for special or future use. **2** *n.* Something reserved: a *reserve* of food. **3** *n.* The condition of being reserved: money kept in *reserve*. **4** *adj.* Kept in reserve: *reserve* troops. **5** *v.* To arrange for ahead of time; have set aside for someone's use: to *reserve* tickets. **6** *n.* Silence as to one's thoughts, feelings, etc. **7** *n.* (*pl.*) Troops who live as civilians and train at certain times in order to be ready to enter the regular armed services in an emergency. **8** *n.* Government land reserved for a special purpose: a forest *reserve*.

re·served [ri·zûrvd′] *adj.* **1** Held in reserve or set apart, as for some person or purpose. **2** Keeping one's feelings, thoughts, and affairs to oneself. — **re·serv·ed·ly** [ri·zûr′vid·lē] *adv.*

re·ser·vist [ri·zûr′vist] *n.* A member of the military reserves.

res·er·voir [rez′ər·vwär *or* rez′ər·vwôr] *n.* **1** A basin, either natural or man-made, for collecting and storing a large supply of water. **2** A container where some material, especially a liquid or gas, may be stored: an ink *reservoir* in a fountain pen. **3** Any large supply: a *reservoir* of information.

re·side [ri·zīd′] *v.* **re·sid·ed, re·sid·ing** **1** To make one's home; live: We *reside* in New York. **2** To be or exist as a quality: It is in such action that real courage *resides*. **3** To be given to or vested in: The power to make laws *resides* in Congress.

res·i·dence [rez′ə·dəns] *n.* **1** The place where a person lives. **2** The act or period of residing: a long *residence* in Denver.

res·i·dent [rez′ə·dənt] **1** *n.* A person who lives in a certain place, not a visitor. **2** *adj.* Living in a place, especially at one's place of work: The hotel has a *resident* physician.

res·i·den·tial [rez′ə·den′shəl] *adj.* **1** Of or suitable for homes: a *residential* area. **2** Of or having to do with residence: *residential* requirements for voting in New York.

re·sid·u·al [ri·zij′oo·əl] *adj.* Left over; remaining: a *residual* amount.

res·i·due [rez′ə·d(y)oo] *n.* The remainder after a part has been removed or treated: When coal is treated, certain tars are left as *residues*.

re·sign [ri·zīn′] *v.* **1** To give up (an office, position, etc.): The judge *resigned* because of poor health. **2** To give up; submit; yield: to *resign* oneself to one's fate.

res·ig·na·tion [rez′ig·nā′shən] *n.* **1** The act of resigning. **2** A written statement that one has

resigned or intends to resign. **3** Patient acceptance: He took his defeat with *resignation*.

re·signed [ri·zīnd′] *adj.* Patient and submissive: to be *resigned* to being ill. — **re·sign·ed·ly** [ri·zī′nid·lē] *adv.*

re·sil·ient [ri·zil′yənt] *adj.* **1** Springing back to a former shape or position: Rubber is *resilient*. **2** Able to bounce back from trouble, sorrow, etc.; buoyant: a *resilient* person. — **re·sil′ience** *n.*

res·in [rez′in] *n.* **1** A gummy, brown or yellowish substance given off by certain plants, especially fir and pine trees, and used in turpentine, glue, and varnishes. **2** Any of a class of synthetic substances with similar properties, used in making plastics. **3** Rosin. — **res′in·ous** *adj.*

re·sist [ri·zist′] *v.* **1** To work or strive against; oppose: He *resisted* the outlaws. **2** To ward off; withstand: This cloth *resists* wrinkles. **3** To keep from: I can't *resist* teasing him.

re·sis·tance [ri·zis′təns] *n.* **1** The act of resisting: Cats offer *resistance* to being bathed. **2** The power of resisting: a metal's *resistance* to rust. **3** Any force tending to hinder motion. **4** The opposition given by a conductor to the passage of an electric current due to a change of electrical energy into heat.

re·sis·tant [ri·zis′tənt] *adj.* Offering resistance; resisting: a fabric *resistant* to wear.

re·sis·tor [ri·zis′tər] *n.* A device used to offer resistance in an electrical circuit.

res·o·lute [rez′ə·loot′] *adj.* Determined or bold: *resolute* courage; *resolute* words. — **res′o·lute′·ly** *adv.* — **res′o·lute′ness** *n.*

res·o·lu·tion [rez′ə·loo′shən] *n.* **1** Something determined or decided upon, as a course of action: a New Year's *resolution* to go on a diet. **2** A formal expression of the feelings or will of an assembly: to adopt a *resolution* thanking the President for his address. **3** Determination; firmness: A successful leader must act with *resolution*. **4** The separation of something into the parts that make it up. **5** A solving, as of a problem; solution.

re·solve [ri·zolv′] *v.* **re·solved, re·solv·ing,** *n.* **1** *v.* To decide or determine: I *resolved* to do better. **2** *n.* A firm determination: a *resolve* to stand up for one's rights. **3** *v.* To solve or make clear: to *resolve* a problem. **4** *v.* To end; remove: to *resolve* doubts. **5** *v.* To decide by vote: The union members *resolved* to strike. **6** *v.* To change; convert: Calm discussion *resolved* itself into angry debate. **7** *v.* To separate or break up into parts: to *resolve* a chemical compound.

res·o·nance [rez′ə·nəns] *n.* **1** A resonant condition or quality. **2** The tendency of some things, as stretched strings, organ pipes, certain electric circuits, etc., to vibrate or allow vibrations most readily at their own natural rate. **3** The reinforcement of sound by vibrations within a room, musical instrument, etc.

---

add, āce, câre, pälm;   end, ēqual;   it, īce;   odd, ōpen, ôrder;   took, pool;   up, bûrn;

ə = a in *above*, e in *sicken*, i in *possible*, o in *melon*, u in *circus*;   yoo = u in *fuse*;   oil;   pout;

check;   ring;   thin;   this;   zh in *vision*.   For ¶ reference, see page 64 · HOW TO

res·o·nant [rez′ə·nənt] *adj.* **1** Deep, rich, and full in tone or sound: a *resonant* voice. **2** Capable of making a sound more full and rich: the *resonant* wood used in a cello. **3** Reflecting or prolonging sound: a *resonant* wall.

re·sort [ri·zôrt′] **1** *v.* To turn for help; have recourse: He *resorted* to shouting so as to be heard. **2** *n.* A person, thing, or act from which one hopes to receive help or aid: Selling their house was their last *resort.* **3** *n.* The act of turning to a person or thing for help: A *resort* to angry words never settles a disagreement. **4** *v.* To go often: to *resort* to the country on weekends. **5** *n.* A place where people go for rest and recreation: a summer *resort.*

re·sound [ri·zound′] *v.* **1** To be filled with sound or echo back: The cave *resounded* with loud cries. **2** To make a loud sound: That night the bells *resounded.* **3** To be much talked about: News of the war's end *resounded.*

re·source [ri·sôrs′ *or* rē′sôrs] *n.* **1** (often *pl.*) A supply of something that can be used or drawn on: natural *resources;* financial *resources; resources* of strength. **2** The ability to act usefully and well in an emergency or difficulty. **3** Something turned to for aid or support: A tired swimmer's *resource* is to float.

re·source·ful [ri·sôrs′fəl] *adj.* Skillful in finding ways of doing things or of resolving difficulties. **— re·source′ful·ness** *n.*

re·spect [ri·spekt′] **1** *v.* To have or show high regard for; esteem; honor. **2** *n.* Honor and esteem. **3** *v.* To treat courteously or with consideration. **4** *n.* Courteous regard: to have *respect* for older people. **5** *n.* (*pl.*) An expression of regard or honor: to pay one's *respects.* **6** *n.* A point or detail; aspect: In what *respect* has he failed? **7** *n.* Reference or relation: Please write us with *respect* to your plans.

re·spect·a·ble [ri·spek′tə·bəl] *adj.* **1** Deserving respect; reputable: *respectable* conduct. **2** Fairly good; average: a *respectable* golf score. **3** Fairly large or great: a *respectable* amount. **— re·spect′a·bil′i·ty** *n.* **— re·spect′a·bly** *adv.*

re·spect·ful [ri·spekt′fəl] *adj.* Showing respect; courteous. **— re·spect′ful·ly** *adv.* **— re·spect′ful·ness** *n.*

re·spect·ing [ri·spek′ting] *prep.* In relation to; regarding: a survey *respecting* population.

re·spec·tive [ri·spek′tiv] *adj.* Of or having to do with each of those mentioned or considered; particular: John and Ken went to their *respective* jobs.

re·spec·tive·ly [ri·spek′tiv·lē] *adv.* Singly in the order given: The first three papers go to John, Jim, and Bill, *respectively.*

res·pi·ra·tion [res′pə·rā′shən] *n.* **1** Breathing. **2** The process by which a plant or animal takes in oxygen from the air and gives off carbon dioxide.

res·pi·ra·tor [res′pə·rā′tər] *n.* **1** A covering, often of gauze, worn over the mouth or nose as protection against breathing harmful substances. **2** A device for artificial respiration.

res·pi·ra·to·ry [res′pə·rə·tôr′ē *or* ri·spīr′ə·tôr′ē] *adj.* Of or having to do with breathing.

re·spire [ri·spīr′] *v.* **re·spired, re·spir·ing** To breathe.

res·pite [res′pit] *n.* **1** A pause for rest: a *respite* from work. **2** A putting off or postponement, as of the carrying out of a sentence of death.

re·splen·dent [ri·splen′dənt] *adj.* Splendid; gorgeous. **— re·splen′dence** *n.*

re·spond [ri·spond′] *v.* **1** To give an answer or reply: Please *respond* to my letter. **2** To react; act as if in reply: His cold *responded* to treatment.

re·sponse [ri·spons′] *n.* **1** A reply or reaction. **2** Words in a service said or sung by a congregation or choir in reply to the clergyman.

re·spon·si·bil·i·ty [ri·spon′sə·bil′ə·tē] *n., pl.* **re·spon·si·bil·i·ties** **1** The condition of being responsible: The age of legal *responsibility* is 21. **2** A person or thing for which one is responsible: His elderly parents are his greatest *responsibility.*

re·spon·si·ble [ri·spon′sə·bəl] *adj.* **1** Obliged to carry out or take care of a duty, trust, debt, etc. **2** Being the cause or reason; accountable: Warm weather is *responsible* for the crowded beaches. **3** Involving trust or important duties: a *responsible* job. **4** Reliable; trustworthy: a *responsible* mechanic. **— re·spon′si·bly** *adv.*

re·spon·sive [ri·spon′siv] *adj.* **1** Responding well; reacting with sympathy, interest, etc.: a *responsive* audience. **2** Expressing a response: a *responsive* wink. **3** Containing responses: a *responsive* prayer.

rest¹ [rest] **1** *v.* To sleep or be still or quiet. **2** *n.* Ease, sleep, or relaxation after work, strain, or effort. **3** *n.* A period of ease, sleep, or relaxation: I need an hour's *rest.* **4** *n.* A temporary stopping of work or activity to get over being tired. **5** *n.* A place for resting, as a shelter for travelers. **6** *v.* To give rest to: to *rest* one's feet. **7** *v.* To support or be supported; lean; lay or lie: *Rest* the ladder against the barn; Her head *rested* on two pillows. **8** *n.* A support for something, as a footrest for the feet. **9** *v.* To be at ease or at peace; be tranquil: I won't *rest* until the test is over. **10** *n.* Freedom from worry, trouble, etc.; peace: Put your mind at *rest.* **11** *v.* To be or become inactive or without change: And there the matter *rests.* **12** *n.* A motionless state: The boulder came to *rest* only a yard away. **13** *v.* To lie in death; be dead. **14** *n.* The grave; death. **15** *n.* A pause or interval of silence, as in music or poetry. **16** *n.* A sign indicating such a pause and its duration. **17** *v.* To rely; depend: Our hope *rests* on you. **18** *v.* To belong or lie: The blame *rests* with me. **19** *v.* To be directed; remain: His eyes *rested* on me.

whole	
half	
quarter	
eighth	
sixteenth	
thirty-second	
sixty-fourth	

Musical rests

rest² [rest] *n.* **1** The part left over; remainder: He threw the *rest* of the apple away. **2** (*used* *with plural verb*) The others: The *rest* are coming soon.

re·state [rē·stāt′] *v.* **re·stat·ed, re·stat·ing** To state again, or in different words. **—re·state′ment** *n.*

res·tau·rant [res′tər·ənt *or* res′tə·ränt] *n.* A place where meals are sold and served to the public; public dining room.

rest·ful [rest′fəl] *adj.* **1** Full of or giving rest: a *restful* trip. **2** Quiet; serene: a *restful* scene.

res·ti·tu·tion [res′tə·t(y)ōō′shən] *n.* **1** The act of paying back or making amends for injury or loss to another. **2** A restoring of something that has been taken away or lost.

res·tive [res′tiv] *adj.* **1** Difficult to manage; unruly: a *restive* crowd. **2** Restless; uneasy.

rest·less [rest′lis] *adj.* **1** Unable to rest or be still; nervous; uneasy. **2** Not restful or relaxing: a *restless* sleep. **3** Never resting or still: *restless* waves. **—rest′less·ly** *adv.* **—rest′less·ness** *n.*

re·stor·a·tive [ri·stôr′ə·tiv] **1** *adj.* Tending or able to restore, especially health, consciousness, etc. **2** *n.* Something that restores, as a medicine.

re·store [ri·stôr′] *v.* **re·stored, re·stor·ing** **1** To bring back to a former or original condition: to *restore* a painting. **2** To bring back; establish once more: Peace and order were *restored*. **3** To give back, as something lost, stolen, etc.; return: The burglar *restored* the silverware. **4** To put back in a former place or position: to *restore* a ruler to power. **—res·to·ra·tion** [res′tə·rā′shən] *n.*

re·strain [ri·strān′] *v.* **1** To hold back; repress. **2** *adj. use:* *restrained* anger.

re·straint [ri·strānt′] *n.* **1** The act of restraining: a *restraint* of trade. **2** A being restrained. **3** A thing that restrains: A leash on a dog is a *restraint*. **4** Self-control.

re·strict [ri·strikt′] *v.* To hold or keep within limits or bounds; confine.

re·strict·ed [ri·strik′tid] *adj.* **1** Limited; confined: A tiger's food is *restricted* to meat. **2** Not available or open to everybody: *restricted* military information.

re·stric·tion [ri·strik′shən] *n.* **1** The act of restricting. **2** The condition of being restricted. **3** A thing that restricts: High taxes place *restrictions* on business.

re·stric·tive [ri·strik′tiv] *adj.* **1** Restricting: a *restrictive* tariff. **2** Describing a word, phrase, or clause, not set off by commas, that is essential to the meaning of a sentence. In "A car that won't run is of little use," *that won't run* is a restrictive clause.

re·sult [ri·zult′] **1** *v.* To be an outcome or consequence; follow: Accidents can *result* from carelessness. **2** *n.* An outcome; consequence. **3** *n.* The outcome of a computation: The *result* of adding 20 and 20 is 40.

re·sul·tant [ri·zul′tənt] **1** *adj.* Resulting: the *resultant* disaster. **2** *n.* A result; consequence. **3** *n.* In physics, a force resulting from two or more forces acting at the same time.

re·sume [ri·zōōm′] *v.* **re·sumed, re·sum·ing** **1** To begin again after stopping: to *resume* work. **2** To take or occupy again: *Resume* your places in line.

ré·su·mé [rez′ōō·mā′ *or* rez′ōō·mā] *n.* A summary, as of a story or of a person's experience and jobs.

re·sump·tion [ri·zump′shən] *n.* A beginning again after stopping: a *resumption* of work after vacation.

re·sur·gence [ri·sûr′jəns] *n.* A surging or rising again.

res·ur·rect [rez′ə·rekt′] *v.* **1** To bring back to life; raise from the dead. **2** To bring back into use or notice: to *resurrect* old rumors.

res·ur·rec·tion [rez′ə·rek′shən] *n.* **1** A rising from the dead. **2** A revival or renewal. **—the Resurrection** The rising of Jesus from the dead.

re·sus·ci·tate [ri·sus′ə·tāt] *v.* **re·sus·ci·tat·ed, re·sus·ci·tat·ing** To bring or come back to life; revive from unconsciousness. **—re·sus′·ci·ta′tion** *n.*

re·tail [rē′tāl] **1** *v.* To sell in small quantities to the actual user. **2** *n.* The selling of goods to consumers in small quantities. **3** *v.* To be sold in small quantities: This dress *retails* at $25. **4** *adj.* Selling or having to do with selling in small quantities: *retail* prices. **5** [ri·tāl′] *v.* To repeat, as gossip. **—at retail** At retail prices. **—re′tail·er** *n.*

re·tain [ri·tān′] *v.* **1** To keep; hold: elastic that *retains* its spring. **2** To keep in mind; remember. **3** To hire by paying a retainer.

re·tain·er[1] [ri·tā′nər] *n.* A fee paid beforehand to obtain services, especially those of a lawyer.

re·tain·er[2] [ri·tā′nər] *n.* A servant, especially to a person of high rank; attendant.

re·take [*v.* rē·tāk′, *n.* rē′tāk] *v.* **re·took, re·tak·en, re·tak·ing,** *n.* **1** *v.* To take back or capture again: to *retake* a fort. **2** *v.* To photograph again. **3** *n.* A motion-picture or television scene, part of a musical recording, etc., done again.

re·tal·i·ate [ri·tal′ē·āt] *v.* **re·tal·i·at·ed, re·tal·i·at·ing** To do something to get even for an injury, wrong, etc.; pay back like for like. **—re·tal′i·a′tion** *n.*

re·tal·i·a·to·ry [ri·tal′ē·ə·tôr′ē] *adj.* Done to pay back an injury, wrong, etc.

re·tard [ri·tärd′] *v.* **1** To slow down; delay; hinder: Illness *retarded* his work. **2** To slow down the tempo of: Please *retard* the end of the song. **—re′tar·da′tion** *n.*

re·tard·ed [ri·tär′did] *adj.* Slow or backward in mental development or in school work.

---

add, āce, câre, pälm; end, ēqual; it, īce; odd, ōpen, ôrder; tŏŏk, pōōl; up, bûrn; ə = a in *above*, e in *sicken*, i in *possible*, o in *melon*, u in *circus*; yōō = u in *fuse*; oil; pout; check; ring; thin; this; zh in *vision*. For ¶ reference, see page 64 · HOW TO

retch [rech] *v.* To make an effort to vomit; go through the motions of vomiting.

re·ten·tion [ri·ten′shən] *n.* **1** The act of retaining. **2** The condition of being retained. **3** The capacity to retain. **4** The ability to remember.

re·ten·tive [ri·ten′tiv] *adj.* **1** Able to retain or keep. **2** Able to remember things easily: a *retentive* mind.

ret·i·cent [ret′ə·sənt] *adj.* Saying little; not inclined to talk about what one thinks or feels; reserved. **— ret′i·cence** *n.*

ret·i·na [ret′ə·nə] *n.* The layer of cells at the back of the eyeball that is sensitive to light and receives images picked up by the lens.

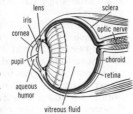

ret·i·nue [ret′ə·n(y)o͞o] *n.* A group of followers serving a person of high rank.

re·tire [ri·tīr′] *v.* **re·tired, re·tir·ing 1** To withdraw or remove from a job, public life, or active service, often because of advancing age: They *retired* the admiral; The man *retired* at 65. **2** *adj. use:* a *retired* officer. **3** To go away for rest, privacy, etc.: to *retire* to a cottage. **4** To go to bed. **5** To fall back; retreat. **6** To pay off and withdraw from circulation: to *retire* bonds. **— re·tire′ment** *n.*

re·tir·ing [ri·tīr′ing] *adj.* Shy; modest.

re·took [rē·to͝ok′] Past tense of RETAKE.

re·tort¹ [ri·tôrt′] **1** *v.* To reply sharply. **2** *n.* A sharp reply.

re·tort² [ri·tôrt′] *n.* A container with a bent tube for distilling or vaporizing chemicals by heat.

re·touch [rē·tuch′] *v.* To improve by adding new touches to: to *retouch* a sketch.

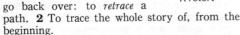

A retort

re·trace [ri·trās′] *v.* **re·traced, re·trac·ing 1** To go back over: to *retrace* a path. **2** To trace the whole story of, from the beginning.

re·tract [ri·trakt′] *v.* **1** To draw back or in: The cat *retracted* her claws. **2** To take back; recant: to *retract* a confession. **— re·trac′tion** *n.*

re·treat [ri·trēt′] **1** *v.* To go back or backward; withdraw. **2** *n.* The act of retreating: the enemy's *retreat.* **3** *n.* A signal for withdrawing. **4** *n.* A signal sounded at sunset when the flag is taken down: The bugle sounded *retreat.* **5** *n.* A quiet refuge: a *retreat* in the hills. **— beat a retreat** To turn back; flee.

re·trench [ri·trench′] *v.* To cut down or reduce (expenses). **— re·trench′ment** *n.*

re·tri·al [rē·trī′əl] *n.* A second or succeeding trial, as of a court case.

ret·ri·bu·tion [ret′rə·byo͞o′shən] *n.* Punishment given in return for wrong a person has done.

re·trieve [ri·trēv′] *v.* **re·trieved, re·triev·ing 1** To get back; regain: to *retrieve* a lost umbrella. **2** To get and bring back: The dog *retrieved* the dead quail. **3** To bring back to an improved condition: to *retrieve* one's good spirits. **4** To make up for; make amends for: to *retrieve* a blunder.

re·triev·er [ri·trē′vər] *n.* A dog bred and trained to retrieve game for hunters.

retro·ac·tive [ret′rō·ak′tiv] *adj.* Having an effect on things that are already past: The new income tax rate is *retroactive* to January 1.

A typical retriever

ret·ro·grade [ret′rə·grād] *v.*

ret·ro·grad·ed, ret·ro·grad·ing, *adj.* **1** *v.* To move backwards; retreat: The glacier is *retrograding.* **2** *adj.* Moving backward. **3** *v.* To go back to a less advanced stage of physical, intellectual, or moral development; deteriorate. **4** *adj.* Declining to or toward a worse condition; deteriorating.

ret·ro·gress [ret′rə·gres] *v.* To go back or revert to an earlier or worse condition. **— ret′ro·gres′sion** *n.*

ret·ro·spect [ret′rə·spekt] *n.* A viewing or consideration of past times, events, etc.: In *retrospect*, his dropping out of school was a bad mistake. **— ret′ro·spec′tion** *n.*

ret·ro·spec·tive [ret′rə·spek′tiv] **1** *adj.* Looking back on the past: a *retrospective* poem. **2** *n.* An exhibit of works done over a period of years by an artist or group. **3** *adj.* Applying to the past. **— ret′ro·spec′tive·ly** *adv.*

re·turn [ri·tûrn′] **1** *v.* To come or go back: to *return* home. **2** *v.* To bring, carry, send, or put back: to *return* a book. **3** *v.* To repay, especially in kind: to *return* a compliment. **4** *n.* The act of returning: a *return* home; the *return* of a pen. **5** *adj.* Of or for a return: a *return* ticket. **6** *n.* Something returned. **7** *adj.* Done, paid, etc., in exchange: a *return* visit. **8** *v.* To answer; respond: "But I'm stronger!" Tom *returned.* **9** *v.* To give or announce: to *return* a verdict. **10** *v.* To yield: to *return* a profit. **11** *n.* A yield; profit: a *return* of $100. **12** *n.* A formal or official report: an income tax *return.* **13** *n.* (*pl.*) A set of statistics that have been tabulated: election *returns.* **— in return** In exchange; as repayment: He did me a favor *in return.*

re·un·ion [rē·yo͞on′yən] *n.* **1** The act of reuniting. **2** A gathering of people who have been apart from each other: a family *reunion.*

re·u·nite [rē′yo͞o·nīt′] *v.* **re·u·nit·ed, re·u·nit·ing** To bring or come together again.

re·vamp [rē·vamp′] *v.* To patch up or make over: to *revamp* an old coat.

re·veal [ri·vēl′] *v.* **1** To make known; disclose: to *reveal* a secret. **2** To make visible; show: The curtain opened to *reveal* a courtroom.

rev·eil·le [rev′i·lē] *n.* A signal by bugle or drum telling soldiers, sailors, etc., to wake up or to form ranks for the first time that day.

rev·el [rev′əl] *v.* **rev·eled** or **rev·elled, rev·el·ing** or **rev·el·ling,** *n.* **1** *v.* To have noisy, boisterous fun. **2** *n.* Boisterous merrymaking. **3** *v.* To take delight: to *revel* in wealth. **— rev'·el·er** or **rev'el·ler** *n.*

rev·e·la·tion [rev′ə·lā′shən] *n.* **1** A making or becoming known. **2** Something made known, especially something surprising: The boy's great knowledge of astronomy was a *revelation* to us. **3** (*written* **Revelation** or **Revelations**) The last book of the New Testament.

rev·el·ry [rev′əl·rē] *n., pl.* **rev·el·ries** Noisy or boisterous merrymaking.

re·venge [ri·venj′] *v.* **re·venged, re·veng·ing,** *n.* **1** *v.* To inflict punishment, injury, etc., in return for a wrong received: to *revenge* oneself for an insult. **2** *n.* The act of revenging. **3** *n.* The desire for or method of vengeance.

re·venge·ful [ri·venj′fəl] *adj.* **1** Desiring revenge. **2** Full of revenge: *revengeful* thoughts.

rev·e·nue [rev′ə·n(y)ōō] *n.* **1** The income that a government receives from taxes, duties, etc. **2** Income from any form of property.

re·ver·ber·ate [ri·vûr′bə·rāt] *v.* **re·ver·ber·at·ed, re·ver·ber·at·ing** **1** To resound or echo back: The shot *reverberated*. **2** To reflect or be reflected, as light or heat.

re·ver·ber·a·tion [ri·vûr′bə·rā′shən] *n.* A reflecting, as of sound waves, light, or heat.

re·vere [ri·vir′] *v.* **re·vered, re·ver·ing** To regard with reverence.

Re·vere [ri·vir′], **Paul,** 1735–1818, American patriot and silversmith, famous for his midnight ride to Lexington, Mass., to warn the colonists that the British troops were coming.

rev·er·ence [rev′ər·əns] *n., v.* **rev·er·enced, rev·er·enc·ing** **1** *n.* A feeling of great respect, often mingled with awe and affection. **2** *v.* To regard with respect and awe.

rev·er·end [rev′ər·ənd] *adj.* **1** Worthy of reverence. **2** (*written* **Reverend**) A title of respect used before the name of a clergyman: the *Reverend* James Henderson.

rev·er·ent [rev′ər·ənt] *adj.* Feeling or showing reverence. **— rev'er·ent·ly** *adv.*

rev·er·ie [rev′ər·ē] *n., pl.,* **rev·er·ies** Distant and pleasant thoughts; daydreaming: lost in *reverie.*

re·ver·sal [ri·vûr′səl] *n.* The act or process of reversing or being reversed.

re·verse [ri·vûrs′] *adj., v.* **re·versed, re·vers·ing,** *n.* **1** *adj.* Turned, facing, or done backward or upside down: the *reverse* side of a rug; to do things in *reverse* order. **2** *v.* To turn upside down or inside out. **3** *n.* The back side: the *reverse* of a coin. **4** *v.* To turn or make go in the opposite direction. **5** *adj.* Causing backward movement: a *reverse* gear. **6** *n* The gear, as in an automobile, that causes backward movement. **7** *n.* (*usually pl.*) A change for the worse; bad fortune: Many people suffer *reverses* during a depression. **8** *v.* To change into something dif-

ferent or opposite: to *reverse* a decision. **9** *n.* Something directly opposite or contrary: The *reverse* of what you say is true.

re·vers·i·ble [ri·vur′sə·bəl] *adj.* **1** Carefully finished on both sides so that either side may be worn on the outside: a *reversible* coat. **2** Capable of going either forward or backward: a *reversible* chemical process.

re·ver·sion [ri·vûr′zhən] *n.* **1** A return to or toward some former condition. **2** In law, the return of an estate to the owner or to his heirs. **3** In law, the right of succession to an estate.

A reversible coat

re·vert [ri·vûrt′] *v.* **1** To go or turn back to a former place, condition, attitude, etc. **2** In law, to return to the former owner or to his heirs: The property *reverted* to Mr. Adams.

re·view [ri·vyōō′] **1** *v.* To go over or examine again: to *review* a lesson. **2** *v.* To think back on: to *review* the events of the past week. **3** *n.* The act of reviewing: a *review* of current events. **4** *v.* To look over carefully or inspect: to *review* a test paper. **5** *n.* A careful inspection or scrutiny. **6** *n.* A formal inspection, as of troops. **7** *n.* An article or essay discussing a book, movie, play, etc. **8** *v.* To write such an article or essay on.

re·view·er [ri·vyōō′ər] *n.* A person who reviews movies, books, plays, etc., as for a newspaper.

re·vile [ri·vīl′] *v.* **re·viled, re·vil·ing** To attack with words of abuse or contempt; call bad names.

re·vise [ri·vīz′] *v.* **re·vised, re·vis·ing** **1** To read carefully so as to correct errors or make improvements and changes: to *revise* a textbook; to *revise* a manuscript. **2** To change: to *revise* a list of prices upward. **— re·vis'er** *n.*

re·vi·sion [ri·vizh′ən] *n.* **1** The act of revising. **2** Something that has been revised: This is a *revision* of an older spelling book.

re·viv·al [ri·vī′vəl] *n.* **1** A restoring or coming back to life, consciousness, or vigor. **2** A renewal of interest in something long neglected or forgotten: a *revival* of learning; a *revival* of an old moving picture. **3** A meeting for stirring up religious faith, usually by means of forceful and dramatic preaching.

re·vive [ri·vīv′] *v.* **re·vived, re·viv·ing** **1** To bring or come back to life or consciousness. **2** To give new strength, vigor, etc., to: The good news *revived* their hopes; Hot coffee *revived* the tired workers. **3** To bring back into notice, use, etc.: to *revive* an old custom.

---

add, āce, câre, pälm; end, ēqual; it, īce; odd, ōpen, ôrder; tŏŏk, pŏŏl; up, bûrn;
ə = a in *above,* e in *sicken,* i in *possible,* o in *melon,* u in *circus;* yŏŏ = u in *fuse;* oil; pout;
check; ring; thin; this; zh in *vision.* For ¶ reference, see page 64 · HOW TO

rev·o·ca·tion [rev′ə·kā′shən] *n.* A revoking, canceling, or repeal.

re·voke [ri·vōk′] *v.* **re·voked, re·vok·ing** To take back, cancel, or repeal, as a license, permit, or a law.

re·volt [ri·vōlt′] **1** *n.* An uprising against authority; rebellion or mutiny. **2** *v.* To rebel against authority. **3** *v.* To fill with disgust: This food *revolts* me. **4** *v.* To turn away in disgust: She *revolted* at the terrible odor.

re·volt·ing [ri·vōl′ting] *adj.* Disgusting.

rev·o·lu·tion [rev′ə·lōō′shən] *n.* **1** The overthrow of an established government by those formerly under its authority. **2** A great change in a condition, method, etc.: Aircraft have caused a *revolution* in travel. **3** Movement in a circle, ellipse, or other closed curve: the moon's *revolution* around the earth. **4** One complete circuit of such a movement. **5** Rotation on an axis.

rev·o·lu·tion·ar·y [rev′ə·lōō′shən·er′ē] *adj., n.* **rev·o·lu·tion·ar·ies** **1** *adj.* Of, having to do with, or causing a revolution or revolt. **2** *n.* A revolutionist. **3** *adj.* Rotating or revolving.

Revolutionary War The war for independence carried on by the 13 American colonies against Great Britain from 1775 to 1783.

rev·o·lu·tion·ist [rev′ə·lōō′shən·ist] *n.* A person who is in favor of or takes part in a revolution.

rev·o·lu·tion·ize [rev′ə·lōō′shən·īz] *v.* **rev·o·lu·tion·ized, rev·o·lu·tion·iz·ing** To make a complete or extreme change in: This new type of train may *revolutionize* the railroads.

re·volve [ri·volv′] *v.* **re·volved, re·volv·ing** **1** To move in a circle or orbit around a center. **2** To spin around on an axis; rotate: The wheel *revolved* slowly. **3** To turn over in one's mind before making a decision, as a problem or plan.

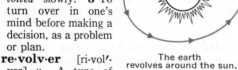
The earth revolves around the sun.

re·volv·er [ri·vol′vər] *n.* A type of pistol having a revolving cylinder with chambers to hold several cartridges that may be fired one after another without loading again.

re·vue [ri·vyōō′] *n.* A type of musical comedy made up of songs, dances, and skits that poke fun at current events and people.

re·vul·sion [ri·vul′shən] *n.* A sudden change of feeling, especially to one of disgust.

re·ward [ri·wôrd′] **1** *n.* Something given or done in return, especially a gift or prize for merit, service, or achievement. **2** *n.* Money offered for capturing a criminal, returning a lost article, etc. **3** *v.* To give a reward to or for: She *rewarded* her dog with a pat; They *rewarded* his kindness with thanks.

re·word [rē·wûrd′] *v.* To put into different words; say again in other words.

re·write [rē·rīt′] *v.* **re·wrote, re·writ·ten** To write over again; revise: to *rewrite* a story.

Reyn·ard [ren′ərd *or* rā′nərd] *n.* A name for the fox in many old tales and poems.

R.F.D. Abbreviation of RURAL FREE DELIVERY.

rhap·so·dy [rap′sə·dē] *n., pl.* **rhap·so·dies** **1** A rapturous utterance, as of delight or excitement: Elsa went into *rhapsodies* over her new fur coat. **2** A piece of instrumental music irregular in form and full of emotion.

rhe·a [rē′ə] *n.* A bird of South America that is like the ostrich, but smaller.

rhe·o·stat [rē′ə·stat] *n.* A device for regulating an electric current by increasing or decreasing the resistance.

rhet·o·ric [ret′ə·rik] *n.* **1** The art of speaking or writing effectively. **2** The study of this art. **3** A book about it. **4** Showy, highflown language.

A rheostat

rhe·tor·i·cal [ri·tôr′i·kəl] *adj.* **1** Of or having to do with rhetoric. **2** Designed for showy oratorical effect: *rhetorical* phrases. **— rhe·tor′i·cal·ly** *adv.*

rhetorical question A question asked only for effect and not requiring an answer.

rheum [rōōm] *n.* A watery discharge from the nose and eyes, as during a cold. **— rheum′y** *adj.*

rheu·mat·ic [rōō·mat′ik] **1** *adj.* Of, having to do with, or caused by rheumatism: *rheumatic* pains. **2** *adj.* Having rheumatism. **3** *n.* A person who has rheumatism.

rheumatic fever A disease, usually affecting young people, marked by pain in the joints, fever, and often serious damage to the heart.

rheu·ma·tism [rōō′mə·tiz′əm] *n.* A painful inflammation and stiffness of the joints.

Rhine [rīn] *n.* A river in west central Europe flowing northward from SE Switzerland through Germany and the Netherlands to the North Sea.

rhine·stone [rīn′stōn′] *n.* An imitation gem made of glass, cut and polished to look like a diamond.

rhi·no [rī′nō] *n., pl.* **rhi·nos** A rhinoceros.

rhi·noc·e·ros [rī·nos′ər·əs] *n., pl.* **rhi·noc·e·ros·es** or **rhi·noc·e·ros** A large, planteating mammal of Africa and Asia having one or two horns on its snout and a very thick hide. ◆ *Rhinoceros* comes from the Greek words for *nose* and *horn*.

Rhinoceros, up to 5 ft. high at shoulder

Rhode Island [rōd] A state in the NE U.S.

Rhode Island Red A breed of domestic chicken.

Rhodes [rōdz] *n.* An island of Greece in the Aegean Sea.

Rhodes [rōdz], **Cecil John,** 1853–1902, British colonial statesman in South Africa.

rho·do·den·dron [rō'də·den'drən] *n.* An evergreen shrub that bears clusters of white, pink, or purple flowers.

rhom·bus [rom'bəs] *n., pl.* **rhom·bus·es** A parallelogram whose sides are all equal, usually having two acute and two obtuse angles.

A rhombus

Rhône [rōn] *n.* A river in Switzerland and SE France, flowing to the Mediterranean Sea.

rhu·barb [rōō'bärb] *n.* **1** A stout, coarse plant having large leaves. Its thick, acid stalks are cooked with sweetening and eaten. **2** *U.S. slang* A violent quarrel or dispute.

rhyme [rīm] *n., v.* **rhymed, rhym·ing 1** *n.* A similarity of the final sounds of words, as *demand* and *unhand*, especially at the ends of lines of poetry. **2** *n.* A word whose sound matches another in this way: "Lake" is a *rhyme* for "rake". **3** *v.* To end in, or have lines ending in, matching sounds: "Hand" *rhymes* with "land"; These verses don't *rhyme*. **4** *v.* To use as a rhyme: Can "plot" be *rhymed* with "out"? **5** *n.* A verse having rhymed lines. **6** *v.* To make rhymes or verses.

rhythm [riŧ H'əm] *n.* **1** The repetition of a beat, sound, accent, motion, etc., usually in a regular way: Dance to the *rhythm* of the music. **2** The relative length and accent of musical sounds, or of the syllables in poetry. **3** A particular arrangement of lengths and stresses in music or poetry: march *rhythm*.

rhyth·mic [riŧ H'mik] *adj.* Rhythmical.

rhyth·mi·cal [riŧ H'mə·kəl] *adj.* Of, having to do with, or having rhythm. **— rhyth'mi·cal·ly** *adv.*

R.I. Abbreviation of RHODE ISLAND.

rib [rib] *n., v.* **ribbed, rib·bing 1** *n.* One of the long, curved bones attached in pairs to the backbone and enclosing the chest in man and in many animals. **2** *n.* Something like a rib in shape or use, as one of the curved timbers in the framework of a boat. **3** *v.* To make or strengthen with ribs: to *rib* a boat. **4** *n.* A cut of meat containing a rib or ribs. **5** *n.* A ridge or raised stripe in cloth, knitting, etc. **6** *v.* To make or mark with ribs: to *rib* a sweater. **7** *n.* A vein of a leaf. **8** *v. slang* To make fun of; tease.

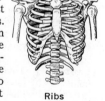

Ribs

rib·ald [rib'əld] *adj.* Using or having to do with crude language or vulgar humor: a *ribald* joke.

rib·ald·ry [rib'əl·drē] *n., pl.* **rib·ald·ries** Crude language or vulgar humor.

rib·bon [rib'ən] **1** *n.* A narrow strip of cloth with finished edges, often used for trimming. **2** *v.* To decorate with or make into ribbons. **3** *n.* Something like a ribbon, as the strip of inked cloth on a typewriter. **4** *n.* (*often pl.*) A narrow strip; shred: torn to *ribbons*.

ri·bo·fla·vin [rī'bō·flā'vin *or* rī'bō·flā'vin] *n.* A member of the vitamin B complex, found in milk, leafy vegetables, egg yolk, and meat.

ri·bo·nu·cle·ic acid [rī'bō·n(y)ōō·klē'ik] A complex substance found in plant and animal cells, having much to do with building up proteins.

rice [rīs] *n., v.* **riced, ric·ing 1** *n.* The starchy seeds of a grasslike plant, forming an important food throughout the world. **2** *n.* The plant itself, grown in warm climates. **3** *v.* To reduce (potatoes or other vegetables) to a form that looks something like rice by pressing them through a kitchen utensil that consists of a container with small holes in it.

rice·bird [rīs'bûrd'] *n.* A bird often found in rice fields, especially the bobolink of the southern U.S.

rich [rich] *adj.* **1** Having a lot of money, goods, or property; wealthy. **2** *n. use* Rich people: *The rich* are sometimes generous. **3** Valuable; costly; precious: *rich* fabrics. **4** Containing much butter, sugar, eggs, etc.: a *rich* dessert. **5** Full and pleasant, as a tone, voice, color, etc. **6** Abundantly supplied: an area *rich* in coal. **7** Giving an abundant return; fruitful: *rich* soil. **8** *informal* Very funny or ridiculous: a *rich* joke. **— rich'ness** *n.*

Rich·ard I [rich'ərd], 1157–1199, king of England, 1189–1199. He was called **Richard the Li·on-Heart·ed** [lī'ən·härt'id].

Ri·che·lieu [rish'ə·lōō] *n.,* 1585–1642, French duke, cardinal, and statesman. He was prime minister of France from 1624 to 1642.

rich·es [rich'iz] *n.pl.* **1** Much money or many valuable possessions; great wealth. **2** Things of great worth: The *riches* of fine recorded music are open to us all.

rich·ly [rich'lē] *adv.* **1** In a rich manner. **2** Fully; justly: a compliment *richly* deserved.

Rich·mond [rich'mənd] *n.* The capital of Virginia.

rick [rik] *n.* A stack of hay, straw, etc., especially one covered for protection against rain.

rick·ets [rik'its] *n.* A disease of young children caused by a lack of vitamin D, resulting in softening and bending of the bones, especially of the legs.

rick·et·y [rik'it·ē] *adj.* **rick·et·i·er, rick·et·i·est 1** Ready to collapse; not sturdy: a *rickety* old bridge. **2** Having or like rickets.

rick·rack [rik'rak'] *n.* Flat braid made in a zigzag form, used as trimming.

rick·shaw *or* **rick·sha** [rik'shô] *n.* Another name for JINRICKSHA.

add, āce, câre, pälm;   end, ēqual;   it, īce;   odd, ōpen, ôrder;   tŏŏk, pōōl;   up, bûrn;
ə = a in *above*, e in *sicken*, i in *possible*, o in *melon*, u in *circus*;   yōō = u in *fuse*;   oil;   pout;
check; ring; thin; this; zh in *vision*.   For ¶ reference, see page 64 · HOW TO

ric·o·chet [rik′ə·shā′] *v.* **ric·o·cheted** [rik′ə·shād′], **ric·o·chet·ing** [rik′ə·shā′ing], *n.* **1** *v.* To bounce or rebound from or off a surface: The bullet *ricocheted* off the wall. **2** *v.* To skip along a surface: The stone *ricocheted* across the water. **3** *n.* The action of ricocheting.

A bullet ricocheting

rid [rid] *v.* **rid** or **rid·ded**, **rid·ding** To free, as from something unwanted: to *rid* a house of termites. **— be rid of** To be free of. **— get rid of 1** To become free of. **2** To dispose of.

rid·dance [rid′(ə)ns] *n.* The clearing out or removal of something unpleasant. **— good riddance** A welcome relief or deliverance from an unwanted person or thing.

rid·den [rid′(ə)n] Past participle of RIDE.

rid·dle[1] [rid′(ə)l] *v.* **rid·dled, rid·dling**, *n.* **1** *v.* To make many holes in, as by shots. **2** *v.* To sift through a coarse sieve. **3** *n.* A coarse sieve. **4** *v.* To corrupt; permeate: The crew was *riddled* with potential mutineers.

rid·dle[2] [rid′(ə)l] *n., v.* **rid·dled, rid·dling 1** *n.* A question or problem having a tricky or puzzling answer, as "What is black and white and red (read) all over?" "A newspaper." **2** *v.* To state or solve riddles. **3** *n.* A puzzling person or thing: His behavior is a *riddle* to us all.

ride [rīd] *v.* **rode, rid·den, rid·ing**, *n.* **1** *v.* To sit on and guide the motion of (a horse, bicycle, etc.). **2** *v.* To be carried along: to *ride* in a car. **3** *n.* A usually short trip made by being carried along, as on a horse, in a car, etc. **4** *v.* To be supported on while moving: Our boat *rode* the waves. **5** *v.* To move or travel, often by mechanical means: This bus *rides* well; We *rode* for three days. **6** *v.* To cause to ride; transport: I'll *ride* you to the corner. **7** *v.* To dominate or control: to be *ridden* by fear. **8** *v. informal* To tease or pester. **9** *v. slang* To go on unchanged: Let the problem *ride* for a while. **10** *n.* A mechanical device, as at an amusement park, in which one rides for fun. **— ride out** To survive or endure successfully: The ship *rode out* a bad storm.

rid·er [rī′dər] *n.* **1** A person who rides. **2** Something added to a document, especially a clause added to a proposed law.

ridge [rij] *n., v.* **ridged, ridg·ing 1** *n.* A long and narrow, raised strip: a cloth with *ridges*. **2** *n.* A long, usually narrow hill or range of hills. **3** *n.* The line where two sloping surfaces meet: the *ridge* of a roof. **4** *v.* To form into or provide with a ridge or ridges.

A ridgepole

ridge·pole [rij′pōl′] *n.* The horizontal timber along the top of a sloping roof.

rid·i·cule [rid′ə·kyōōl] *n., v.* **rid·i·culed, rid·i·cul·ing 1** *n.* Words or actions intended to make another person or thing seem foolish; mockery. **2** *v.* To make fun of; make a laughingstock of; mock.

ri·dic·u·lous [ri·dik′yə·ləs] *adj.* Deserving ridicule or laughter because of its absurdity or silliness. **— ri·dic′u·lous·ly** *adv.*

rife [rīf] *adj.* **1** Great in number or amount; abundant: Rumors were *rife*. **2** Filled; teeming: a city *rife* with crime.

riff·raff [rif′raf′] *n.* **1** Crude or common people; rabble. **2** Trash; rubbish.

ri·fle[1] [rī′fəl] *v.* **ri·fled, ri·fling** To search and rob: to *rifle* a mail sack; to *rifle* a desk.

ri·fle[2] [rī′fəl] *n., v.* **ri·fled, ri·fling 1** *n.* A firearm having grooves that run in a spiral down the barrel giving the bullet a spin as it is shot. **2** *v.* To make spiral grooves in.

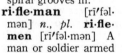

A rifle

ri·fle·man [rī′fəl·mən] *n., pl.* **ri·fle·men** [rī′fəl·mən] A man or soldier armed with or skilled in the use of a rifle.

rift [rift] **1** *n.* A split or crack; cleft. **2** *v.* To break open; split. **3** *n.* A stopping of or a break in a friendship, often only temporary.

rig [rig] *v.* **rigged, rig·ging**, *n.* **1** *v.* To fit (a ship) with sails and related gear. **2** *n.* The arrangement of sails, rigging, etc., on a ship. **3** *v.* To fit out; equip: to *rig* a car with a radio. **4** *v.* To build hurriedly or by makeshifts: to *rig* up a door from old boards. **5** *v. informal* To dress; clothe: He was *rigged* out in his costume. **6** *n. informal* A style of dress or costume. **7** *n. U.S. informal* A buggy or carriage with a horse or horses. **8** *v.* To control by fraud or dishonesty: to *rig* an election. **— rig′ger** *n.*

Ri·gel [rī′jəl *or* rī′gəl] *n.* One of the 20 brightest stars. It is in the constellation Orion.

rig·ging [rig′ing] *n.* **1** The ropes and cables that support a ship's mast, sails, etc. **2** Apparatus; gear; equipment.

Rigging of sailboat

right [rīt] **1** *adj.* In agreement with law or morals; just; good: The thief did the *right* thing when he confessed his crime. **2** *adv.* According to law or morals; justly: The judge acted *right* in sentencing the pickpocket to a fine. **3** *n.* Things that are lawful, moral, and just: Try to do *right*, not wrong. **4** *n.* A just and proper claim: the *right* to vote. **5** *n.* (*often pl.*) Something that may be claimed on just, moral, legal, or customary grounds: I demand my *rights*. **6** *v.* To correct; set right: to *right* a wrong. **7** *adj.* Conforming to truth or fact; correct; accurate: the *right* answer. **8** *adv.* According to truth or fact; correctly: to answer *right*. **9** *adj.* Conforming to standards or prevailing conditions; proper; suitable: *right* clothing for the party. **10** *adv.* Suitably; properly: to dress *right*; to do the job *right*. **11** *adv.* In good condition; orderly: to put things *right*. **12** *v.* To put in order; make neat or proper: to *right* a messy room. **13** *adj.* Of, on, related to, or indicating the side of the body that is toward the south when one faces east: the *right* hand. **14** *adv.* To or toward the right hand or side: Turn *right*. **15** *n.* The right side, direction, or hand. **16** *adj.* Nearer to the right side: Go through the *right* door. **17** *adj.* Holding one direction, as a line; straight; direct. **18** *adv.* In a straight line; directly: Go *right* to school. **19** *adv.* Precisely; exactly: Set it *right* here. **20** *adv.* Immediately: We'll leave *right* after lunch. **21** *adj.* Sound or healthy; well: to be in one's *right* mind. **22** *v.* To return to an upright or proper position: to *right* an overturned glass. **23** *adj.* Made to show or be worn outward: the *right* side of a fabric. **24** *adv.* Completely; all the way: The house burned *right* to the ground. **25** *adv. (written* **Right***)* Exceedingly; very: used in titles: the *Right* Reverend. **26** *adj.* Conservative or reactionary in political views. **27** *n.* A person, group, or party having conservative or reactionary political views. **— by right** or **by rights** According to what is just, right, or proper; rightly. **— in the right** Not wrong. **— right away** or **right off** Without delay; immediately. **— to rights** *informal* In a proper or orderly condition: to put a room *to rights*.

right angle One of the angles formed when two lines intersect so as to form four angles that have the same measure; an angle of 90°.

right·eous [rī′chəs] *adj.* **1** Acting right; virtuous; upright: a *righteous* man. **2** Right according to morals or justice; fair: a *righteous* judgment. **— right′eous·ly** *adv.* **— right′eous·ness** *n.*

right·ful [rīt′fəl] *adj.* **1** Just and fair: a *rightful* claim. **2** According to morals or law: the *rightful* owner of the house. **— right′ful·ly** *adv.*

right-hand [rīt′hand′] *adj.* **1** On or toward the right side. **2** Made for use by or done with the right hand: a *right-hand* glove. **3** Chiefly depended on: the manager's *right-hand* man.

right-hand·ed [rīt′han′did] **1** *adj.* Using the right hand habitually and more easily than the left: a *right-handed* pitcher. **2** *adj.* Done with or made for use by the right hand: a *right-handed* putter. **3** *adj.* Turning or moving from left to right or in a clockwise direction: a *right-handed* thread. **4** *adv.* With the right hand: to pitch *right-handed*.

right·ly [rīt′lē] *adv.* **1** Correctly. **2** Honestly; justly; fairly. **3** Properly; fitly; aptly.

right of way **1** The legal right of a person to pass over the land of another. **2** The right to go or cross ahead of a person, vehicle, etc., as at an intersection.

right triangle A triangle one of whose angles is a right angle.

rig·id [rij′id] *adj.* **1** Not giving or bending; stiff or firm: a *rigid* frame. **2** Fixed; unmoving. **3** Strict; unchanging: *rigid* regulations. **— ri·gid·i·ty** [ri·jid′ə·tē] *n.* **— rig′id·ly** *adv.*

rig·ma·role [rig′mə·rōl] *n.* Confused or senseless talk or writing; nonsense; poppycock.

rig·or [rig′ər] *n.* **1** Strictness, carefulness, or severity: to punish with *rigor*; to think with *rigor*. **2** Harshness or discomfort: the *rigors* of tents and cold showers. ¶1

rig·or·ous [rig′ər·əs] *adj.* **1** Very strict: a *rigorous* teacher. **2** Exact; precise: a *rigorous* science. **3** Harsh; severe: a *rigorous* winter. **— rig′or·ous·ly** *adv.*

rile [rīl] *v.* **riled, ril·ing** *informal* **1** To annoy or irritate. **2** To make (a liquid) muddy or unsettled by stirring up sediment.

rill [ril] *n.* A small stream or brook.

rim [rim] *n., v.* **rimmed, rim·ming 1** *n.* An edge, margin, or border, usually of a round object. **2** *v.* To provide with a rim. **3** *v.* In various sports, to roll around the edge of (the basket, cup, etc.) without falling in.

rime[1] [rīm] *n., v.* **rimed, rim·ing 1** *n.* A white frost formed from frozen fog or mist. **2** *v.* To cover or become covered with rime: The window *rimed* over; Mist and cold *rimed* the trees.

rime[2] [rīm] *n., v.*, **rimed, rim·ing** Another spelling of RHYME.

rind [rīnd] *n.* A skin or outer coating that may be peeled or removed, as of bacon, fruit, etc.

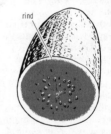

rind

ring[1] [ring] *v.* **rang, rung, ring·ing,** *n.* **1** *v.* To make or cause to make the resonant sound of a bell: The bell *rang*; *Ring* the bell. **2** *n.* The sound made by a bell. **3** *n.* A sound similar to this: the *ring* of coins. **4** *v.* To announce or summon, as by sounding a bell: to *ring* in a New Year. **5** *v.* To be filled with sound; resound: The hall *rang* with music. **6** *v.* To have a sound or quality that suggests truth, falseness, etc.: His story *rings* true. **7** *n.* A sound suggestive of something: the *ring* of truth. **8** *v.* To call by telephone: *Ring* me up. **9** *n.* A telephone call: Give me a *ring*. **10** *v.* To hear noises that are not there: My ears *ring*. **— ring for** To call or summon by a bell: *Ring* for the nurse. **— ring up** To record (a sale) on a cash register. **— ring′er** *n.*

ring[2] [ring] *n., v.* **ringed, ring·ing** **1** *n.* A circle or round loop. **2** *n.* A narrow circle of metal, plastic, etc., worn on a finger as an ornament, used to hang curtains, etc. **3** *v.* To put or make a ring around; enclose: The crowd *ringed* the speaker. **4** *n.* A group of persons or things in a circle: a *ring* of houses. **5** *v.* To form a circle: The children *ringed* about the exhibit. **6** *n.* A group of persons, often organized for some unlawful or evil purpose: a *ring* of smugglers. **7** *n.* A space set apart for a contest or show: a circus *ring*. **8** *n. informal* The sport of prize fighting. **9** *v.* To put a ring in the nose of (a pig, bull, etc.). **10** *v.* In certain games, to throw a ring over (a peg or pin). **— run rings around** *informal* To do or be very much better than. **— ring′er** *n.*

Antique ring

ring·lead·er [ring′lē′dər] *n.* A person who leads a group, especially in some mischief or unlawful activity.

ring·let [ring′lit] *n.* **1** A long, spiral lock of hair; a curl. **2** A small ring.

ring·side [ring′sīd′] *n.* The seats or space very close or next to a ring, as at a boxing match.

ring·worm [ring′wûrm′] *n.* An infectious skin disease caused by a fungus, marked by scaly, discolored patches on the skin.

rink [ringk] *n.* An area or enclosure containing a surface of ice for skating or hockey or having a smooth, wooden floor for roller skating.

rinse [rins] *v.* **rinsed, rins·ing,** *n.* **1** *v.* To remove soap from by putting through clear water. **2** *v.* To wash lightly, as by dipping in water or by running water over or into. **3** *n.* A rinsing. **4** *n.* The water or solution used in rinsing.

Ri·o de Ja·nei·ro [rē′ō də zhə-nâr′ō] A large seaport in SE Brazil, the former capital.

Ri·o Grande [rē′ō grand′] A river in the SW U.S., forming part of the border with Mexico.

ri·ot [rī′ət] **1** *n.* A violent disturbance made by a large group of people behaving in a wild, disorderly way. **2** *v.* To take part in a riot. **3** *n.* A brilliant and sometimes confusing display: a *riot* of colors. **4** *v.* To make merry in a wild, boisterous way. **5** *n. slang* A person or thing that is extremely funny: He's a *riot*. **— read the riot act to** *informal* To scold or warn very bluntly and severely. **— run riot** **1** To act wildly. **2** To grow profusely, as vines. **— ri′ot·er** *n.*

ri·ot·ous [rī′ət·əs] *adj.* **1** Of, like, or having to do with a riot. **2** Causing or taking part in a riot. **3** Loud; uproarious; exuberant: *riotous* laughter. **— ri′ot·ous·ly** *adv.*

rip[1] [rip] *v.* **ripped, rip·ping,** *n.* **1** *v.* To tear or split apart: to *rip* a shirt; Her dress *ripped*. **2** *n.* A place, as in a garment, that is torn open. **3** *v.* To tear, pull, or remove in a rough way: to *rip* down a poster; to *rip* off clothes. **4** *v.* To saw (wood) in the direction of the grain. **5** *n.* A ripsaw.

rip[2] [rip] *n.* **1** The rough water that results when conflicting tides or currents come together. **2** A rapid in a river.

ripe [rīp] *adj.* **rip·er, rip·est** **1** Fully grown and ready to eat, as fruit or grain. **2** Ready to be used, as wine or cheese. **3** Fully developed; mature. **4** In full readiness; prepared: The men are *ripe* for mutiny. **— ripe′ness** *n.*

rip·en [rī′pən] *v.* To make or become ripe.

rip·ple [rip′əl] *v.* **rip·pled, rip·pling,** *n.* **1** *v.* To form into small waves: The water *rippled* as fish jumped; The wind *rippled* the lake. **2** *n.* A small wave or wavelike movement: the *ripple* of a summer breeze. **3** *n.* Any sound like that made by rippling.

rip·saw [rip′sô′] *n.* A saw having large teeth, used to cut wood in the direction of the grain.

Rip Van Win·kle [rip van wing′kəl] In Washington Irving's story *Rip Van Winkle*, the hero, a man who wakes up after sleeping twenty years to find the world changed and himself forgotten.

Ripples

rise [rīz] *v.* **rose, ris·en, ris·ing,** *n.* **1** *v.* To move upward; go to a higher position; ascend: The plane *rose* from the ground. **2** *n.* An upward movement; ascent: The balloon made a quick *rise*. **3** *v.* To incline upward: The ground *rises* here. **4** *n.* An upward incline or a small hill: a *rise* adjoining the plain. **5** *v.* To stand up after sitting or lying down. **6** *v.* To return to life or activity: to *rise* from the grave; to *rise* from sleep. **7** *v.* To become greater in force, strength, amount, value, number, etc.: Prices *rose* alarmingly; The sound *rose* to a roar. **8** *v.* To swell up: Dough *rises*. **9** *n.* Increase: The noise made a sharp *rise*. **10** *v.* To move to a higher rank, status, fortune, etc.: to *rise* to the rank of colonel. **11** *n.* Advance or elevation, as in rank or status: his *rise* to power. **12** *v.* To appear over the horizon, as the sun, moon, etc. **13** *v.* To revolt; rebel: The people *rose* against the tyrant. **14** *v.* To begin, as a river: This river *rises* in the mountains. **15** *n.* A beginning or place of beginning; origin. **16** *v.* To become elated or more cheerful: My spirits *rose*. **— give rise to** To cause to begin; bring about. **— rise to** To handle or deal with successfully: to *rise to* a difficult situation. ◆ *Rise* means to move upward. *Raise* means to cause to move upward. *Rise* does not take an object: The sun *rose*. *Raise* does take an object: Please *raise* your right hand. *Raise* is the word commonly used in the U.S. for an increase in pay. The British call such an increase a *rise*.

ris·en [riz′(ə)n] Past participle of RISE.

ris·er [rīz′ər] *n.* **1** A person who rises, as from bed. **2** The vertical part of a step or stair.

risk [risk] **1** *n.* A chance of meeting with harm or loss; danger; hazard. **2** *v.* To expose to a chance of injury or loss: to *risk* one's life; to *risk* one's money. **3** *v.* To take the risk of; chance: Will you *risk* being shot?

risk·y [ris′kē] *adj.* **risk·i·er, risk·i·est** Full of risk; dangerous; hazardous: a *risky* mountain drive; a *risky* business deal.

rite [rīt] *n.* **1** A formal, solemn, or religious ceremony performed in a set way. **2** The words or acts that make up such a ceremony.

rit·u·al [rich′ōō·əl] **1** *n.* A body or system of rites and ceremonies: to follow a set *ritual* in initiating new members. **2** *n.* A book in which rites or ceremonies are collected. **3** *adj.* Of, related to, or like a rite: a *ritual* act. **— rit′u·al·ly** *adv.*

ri·val [rī′vəl] *n., v.* **ri·valed** or **ri·valled, ri·val·ing** or **ri·val·ling** **1** *n.* A person who tries to equal or outdo another, or who wants the same thing as another; competitor. **2** *adj. use:* a *rival* athlete. **3** *v.* To try to outdo or defeat; compete with: The teams *rivaled* each other for the championship. **4** *v.* To be the equal of: The girls *rival* each other in beauty. ◆ *Rival* comes from a Latin word meaning *those living near the same stream.* They were "rivals" either because they lived on opposite banks or because they both depended on the same stream for water.

ri·val·ry [rī′vəl·rē] *n., pl.* **ri·val·ries** **1** The act of rivaling. **2** The condition of being a rival or rivals; competition: Their *rivalry* had begun the first time they played tennis together.

rive [rīv] *v.* **rived, rived** or **riv·en** [riv′ən], **riv·ing** **1** To split apart by or with force: Lightning had *rived* the old pine in two. **2** *adj. use:* a *riven* tree; a *riven* wall.

riv·er [riv′ər] *n.* **1** A large, natural stream of water, usually fed by smaller streams and flowing to the sea, a lake, etc. **2** Any large flow or stream: a *river* of glacial ice. ◆ *River* comes from a Latin word meaning *bank of a river.* In old French it came to mean the *stream.*

river basin The area of land drained by a river and its branches.

riv·et [riv′it] **1** *n.* A metal pin with a head at one end, used to fasten metal objects together. It is passed through a hole in both pieces and its headless end is hammered down, often while it is red hot. **2** *v.* To fasten with rivets. **3** *v.* To set or fix firmly: He *riveted* his attention on the television set. **— riv′et·er** *n.*

Riv·i·er·a [riv′ē·âr′ə] *n.* A resort area on part of the coast of France and Italy along the Mediterranean.

riv·u·let [riv′yə·lit] *n.* A brook.

rm. Abbreviation of: **1** ROOM. **2** (*usually written* **rms.**) Rooms.

RNA Abbreviation of RIBONUCLEIC ACID.

roach[1] [rōch] *n.* Another name for COCKROACH.

roach[2] [rōch] *n.* A European fresh-water fish related to the carp, having a silvery white body, small mouth and large scales.

Roach,
to 18 in. long

road [rōd] *n.* **1** An open way prepared for vehicles, persons, or animals to travel on from one place to another. **2** A way of reaching some state, condition, reward, etc.: the *road* to fame; the *road* to prison. **3** A railroad. **4** (*usually pl.*) A roadstead.

road·bed [rōd′bed′] *n.* The foundation on which railroad tracks are laid or a road is built.

road·block [rōd′blok′] *n.* **1** An obstruction in a road. **2** Any arrangement of men and materials for blocking passage, as of an enemy's troops.

road hog A driver who keeps his vehicle in or near the middle of a road, making it difficult for other drivers to pass.

road runner A cuckoo of the plains of the western U.S., having a long tail, a shaggy crest, and legs adapted for very swift running.

road·side [rōd′sīd′] **1** *n.* The area along the side of a road. **2** *adj.* Located on the side of a road: a *roadside* restaurant.

road·stead [rōd′sted′] *n.* A sheltered place for ships to anchor offshore.

road·way [rōd′wā′] *n.* A road, especially that part over which vehicles pass.

roam [rōm] *v.* To wander around with no particular purpose: to *roam* freely; to *roam* the plains. ◆ See WANDER.

roan [rōn] **1** *adj., n.* Reddish or yellowish brown heavily speckled with gray or white. **2** *n.* A horse having a color like this.

roar [rôr] **1** *v.* To give a loud, deep cry, as of anger or pain. **2** *n.* A loud, deep cry. **3** *v.* To make a loud noise, as the sea or a cannon. **4** *n.* A loud noise. **5** *v.* To shout or laugh loudly.

roast [rōst] **1** *v.* To cook (meat, etc.) by the action of heat, as in an oven. **2** *n.* A roasted piece of meat or a piece of meat prepared to be roasted. **3** *adj.* Roasted: *roast* chicken. **4** *v.* To treat with heat: to *roast* an ore; to *roast* coffee. **5** *v.* To make or be very hot: We *roasted* in the sun. **6** *v. informal* To make fun of or criticize severely: The critic *roasted* the new novel.

roast·er [rōs′tər] *n.* **1** A pan or pot in which food is roasted. **2** Something to be roasted, as a chicken or young pig.

rob [rob] *v.* **robbed, rob·bing** **1** To seize money or property from, using force or the threat of force: to *rob* a cashier. **2** To take from by trickery or fraud; cheat: The storekeeper *robbed* him by overcharging. **3** To commit robbery. **— rob′ber** *n.*

rob·ber·y [rob′ər·ē] *n., pl.* **rob·ber·ies** The unlawful taking of property or money, as by stealth, force, or the threat of force.

---

add, āce, câre, pälm;   end, ēqual;   it, īce;   odd, ōpen, ôrder;   tŏŏk, pōōl;   up, bûrn;
ə = a in *above*, e in *sicken*, i in *possible*, o in *melon*, u in *circus*;   yōō = u in *fuse*;   oil;   pout;
check;   ring;   thin;   ŧħis;   zh in *vision*.   For ¶ reference, see page 64 · HOW TO

robe [rōb] **1** *n.* A long, loose, flowing garment, usually worn over other clothing on special or ceremonial occasions or to show one's office or rank: a choir *robe*; a judge's *robes*. **2** *n.* Any long, loose, outer garment or gown. **3** *n.* A bathrobe. **4** *v.* To put a robe on; dress. **5** *n.* A blanket or covering for the lap.

rob·in [rob′in] *n.* **1** A large North American thrush having a gray back and rust-red breast. **2** A small European bird, common in England, with yellowish red cheeks and breast.

Robin Hood A legendary outlaw of medieval England, famed for his chivalry and daring, said to have robbed the rich to aid the poor.

Judge's robe

ro·bot [rō′bot *or* rō′bət] *n.* **1** A mechanical man built to do work in the place of human beings. **2** A person who works dully and mechanically. ◆ *Robot* was probably first used of a mechanical creature in the play *R.U.R.* (*Rossum's Universal Robots*) by the Czech playwright Karel Capek, but the word was based on a Czech word meaning *forced labor.*

ro·bust [rō·bust′ *or* rō′bust] *adj.* **1** Strong; sturdy; vigorous: a *robust* athlete; *robust* plants. **2** Strong and rich, as in flavor: a *robust* stew. **3** Crude or rough: *robust* language.

roc [rok] *n.* In Arabian and Persian legend, an enormous and powerful bird of prey.

rock¹ [rok] *n.* **1** A large mass of stone or stony material. **2** A small piece of stone that can be picked up. **3** The hard, dense mass of minerals forming the earth's crust. **4** Something like a rock, as in strength, solidity, etc.

rock² [rok] *v.* **1** To move or cause to move back and forth or from side to side; sway: to *rock* a boat. **2** To disturb; upset: The news *rocked* the town. **3** To stun or daze: The blow *rocked* me.

rock bottom The very bottom; the lowest possible level: Prices hit *rock bottom.*

rock·er [rok′ər] *n.* **1** A person or thing that rocks. **2** One of the curved parts on which a cradle or rocking chair rocks. **3** A rocking chair.

rock·et [rok′it] **1** *n.* A machine that develops power and movement by burning its load of fuel and oxygen and forcing a stream of gases to the rear, used to propel fireworks, missiles, and space vehicles. **2** *v.* To move like or by a rocket.

rock·et·ry [rok′it·rē] *n.* The science and techniques of designing, building, and flying rockets.

rocking chair A chair whose legs are set on curved rails, allowing it to rock back and forth.

Rocking horse

rocking horse A toy horse mounted on rockers, large enough for a child to mount it and rock.

rock salt Common salt in rocklike masses or large crystals.

rock wool A soft, fluffy material made from molten slag and rock, used as a packing and insulating material.

rock·y¹ [rok′ē] *adj.* **rock·i·er, rock·i·est 1** Consisting of, full of, or like rocks. **2** Suggesting rock, as in hardness: a face with *rocky* features.

rock·y² [rok′ē] *adj.* **rock·i·er, rock·i·est 1** Tending to rock or shake; unsteady. **2** *informal* Weak or dizzy; slightly sick.

Rocky Mountains The main mountain system of western North America, extending from the Arctic to Mexico. Also **the Rock·ies** [rok′ēz].

ro·co·co [rə·kō′kō] **1** *n.* The style of European art and architecture in the 18th century, marked by extremely fancy designs and decorations. **2** *n.* The formal, elegant style of European music in the 18th century. **3** *adj.* In or like the rococo style: a *rococo* painting; a *rococo* door.

rod [rod] *n.* **1** A straight, thin piece of wood, metal, etc. **2** A thin stick used in beating someone as punishment. **3** The punishment given this way. **4** A unit of length equal to 5½ yards. **5** A fishing rod. **6** A wand as a sign of power.

rode [rōd] Past tense of RIDE.

ro·dent [rōd′(ə)nt] *n.* Any of a group of mammals found in all parts of the world, including mice, rats, squirrels, and beavers. They have very sharp front teeth that keep growing as they are worn down by gnawing.

ro·de·o [rō′dē·ō *or* rō·dā′ō] *n., pl.* **ro·de·os 1** A public contest in which cowboys compete in riding broncos, roping and throwing cattle, etc. **2** The gathering up and driving together of cattle; roundup.

Ro·din [rō·dan′], **Auguste,** 1840–1917, French sculptor.

roe¹ [rō] *n., pl.* **roe** *or* **roes** A small, graceful deer of Europe and western Asia.

roe² [rō] *n.* The eggs of fishes.

roe·buck [rō′buk′] *n.* A male roe.

roent·gen [rent′gən] *n.* A unit for measuring X-rays, gamma rays, etc., on the basis of their ionizing effect.

Roent·gen ray [rent′gən] Another name for X-RAY.

Roent·gen [rent′gən], **Wilhelm,** 1845–1923, German physicist who discovered X-rays.

rogue [rōg] *n.* **1** A dishonest and sneaky person; trickster; rascal. **2** A person who does innocent or playful mischief. **3** A fierce and dangerous animal, as an elephant, that lives apart from its herd.

ro·guer·y [rō′gər·ē] *n., pl.* **ro·guer·ies 1** Conduct like that of a rogue. **2** A roguish act.

ro·guish [rō′gish] *adj.* **1** Playfully mischievous. **2** Dishonest or sneaky. — **ro′guish·ly** *adv.* — **ro′guish·ness** *n.*

roil [roil] *v.* **1** To make muddy or unclear, as by stirring up material from the bottom: to *roil* a lake. **2** To irritate or make angry; rile.

roist·er [rois′tər] *v.* **1** To carry on loud merry-making; revel. **2** To act in a bullying and boastful way; swagger. **— roist′er·er** *n.*

role or **rôle** [rōl] *n.* **1** A part or character played by an actor. **2** A character or part that a person plays in life: his *role* as a father.

roll [rōl] **1** *v.* To move along a surface by turning over and over: The ball *rolled* five feet; to *roll* a rock off a path. **2** *n.* The act of rolling. **3** *n.* A rolling movement. **4** *v.* To move or be moved on wheels or rollers: The cart *rolled* away. **5** *n.* A roller, especially a cylinder rotating on a fixed axis. **6** *v.* To turn, wrap, or wind so as to make or become a ball or cylinder: *Roll* the yarn up; *Roll* it up in this newspaper; The window shade *rolled* up. **7** *n.* Something rolled into the shape of a ball or cylinder: a *roll* of cloth. **8** *v.* To pass or go: Months *rolled* by; The clouds *rolled* by. **9** *v.* To make a deep, rumbling sound, as thunder. **10** *n.* A deep rumbling sound, as of thunder. **11** *v.* To strike (a drum, etc.) with a series of rapid strokes. **12** *n.* The sound of a series of rapid strokes, as on a drum. **13** *v.* To say or utter with a trilling sound: to *roll* "r's." **14** *v.* To sway, rock, or move up and down or back and forth: The ship *rolled* in the storm; to *roll* one's eyes. **15** *v.* To move or appear to move in swells or billows, as a wave. **16** *n.* A swaying, rocking, or undulating movement: the *roll* of a ship; the *roll* of the sea. **17** *v.* To spread or flatten under a roller: to *roll* tin into sheets; Tar *rolls* easily. **18** *n.* A small, individually shaped piece of bread. **19** *n.* A list of names. **— roll in** *informal* **1** To arrive in large amounts or numbers. **2** To have and take great pleasure in: to *roll in* money. **— roll up** *informal* **1** To collect or accumulate. **2** To arrive, as a car.

roll call The calling out of a list of names so that each person present may reply to his name.

roll·er [rō′lər] *n.* **1** A person or thing that rolls. **2** Any of various cylindrical devices on which something is rolled or which is used to crush, press, smooth, or apply something: a window shade *roller*; a steam*roller*; a paint *roller*. **3** A long, swelling wave that breaks on a beach or shore line. **4** A canary that trills its song.

roller coaster *U.S.* A small railway with open cars that run over a series of sharp dips and curves, found in amusement parks.

roller skate A skate having wheels instead of a runner, used on surfaces other than ice, as pavement.

roll·er-skate [rō′lər-skāt′] *v.* **roll·er-skat·ed, roll·er-skat·ing** To go on roller skates.

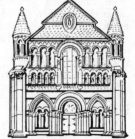

A couple roller-skating

rol·lick·ing [rol′ik·ing] *adj.* Carefree and merry; light-hearted.

rolling mill 1 A factory for rolling metal into sheets or bars. **2** A machine for doing this.

rolling pin A cylinder of wood, plastic, etc., with handles at the ends, used to roll out dough.

rolling stock All of the vehicles, as locomotives, cars, etc., owned and operated by a railroad or bus company.

ro·ly-po·ly [rō′lē·pō′lē] *adj., n., pl.* **ro·ly-po·lies 1** *adj.* Short and fat; pudgy; dumpy. **2** *n.* A roly-poly person or thing.

Ro·man [rō′mən] **1** *adj.* Of, from, or belonging to ancient or modern Rome. **2** *n.* A person born or living in ancient or modern Rome. **3** *adj.* Of or belonging to the Roman Catholic Church. **4** *n.* (*pl. used with singular verb*) A book of the New Testament, written by Paul the Apostle. **5** *n.* (*usually written* **roman**) The common style of type or lettering, in which the letters are upright, not slanting. This sentence is in roman. **6** *adj.* (*usually written* **roman**) Of, having to do with, or printed in roman.

Roman Catholic 1 *adj.* Of, having to do with, or belonging to the Christian church that recognizes the Pope, the bishop of Rome, as its supreme head. **2** *n.* A member of this church.

ro·mance [*n.* rō·mans′ or rō′mans, *v.* rō·mans′] *n., v.* **ro·manced, ro·manc·ing 1** *n.* A love affair. **2** *v.* *informal* To show or tell feelings of love to; woo. **3** *n.* A fascinating, mysterious, or romantic adventure, quality, condition, etc.: the *romance* of faraway places. **4** *n.* A story or poem telling of heroism, adventure, love, etc., often based on medieval legends of knights or other heroes. **5** *n.* A fantastic falsehood. **6** *v.* To write, tell, or make up romances.

Romance language One of the languages that developed from Latin. French, Italian, Spanish, Portuguese, and Rumanian are Romance languages.

Roman Empire The empire of ancient Rome, existing from 27 B.C. to A.D. 395, and including most of the world known at that time.

Ro·man·esque [rō′mən·esk′] **1** *adj.* Of, having to do with, or indicating a style of architecture using rounded arches and vaults. It prevailed in Europe from the 5th to the 12th centuries. **2** *n.* The Romanesque style of art and architecture.

Ro·ma·nia [rō·mān′yə] *n.* Another name for RUMANIA. **— Ro·man′ian** *adj., n.*

Romanesque architecture

Roman numerals The letters of the alphabet,

add, āce, câre, pälm;   end, ēqual;   it, īce;   odd, ōpen, ôrder;   tŏŏk, pōōl;   up, bûrn;
ə = a in *above*, e in *sicken*, i in *possible*, o in *melon*, u in *circus*;   yōō = u in *fuse*;   oil;   pout;
check; ring; thin; this; zh in *vision*.   For ¶ reference, see page 64 · HOW TO

used by the ancient Romans as symbols to represent numbers. In this system I = 1, V = 5, X = 10, L = 50, C = 100, D = 500, M = 1,000.

ro·man·tic [rō·man'tik] **1** *adj.* Of, having to do with, or filled with romance: a *romantic* kind of life; a *romantic* figure in history. **2** *adj.* Having feelings and thoughts of love and romance: a *romantic* girl. **3** *adj.* Suitable for courting or wooing: a *romantic* garden. **4** *adj.* Impractical or unrealistic: *romantic* schemes. **5** *adj.* Of, relating to, or characterized by romanticism. **6** *n.* A romantic person, artist, composer, etc. **— ro·man'ti·cal·ly** *adv.*

ro·man·ti·cism [rō·man'tə·siz'əm] *n.* A movement in art, literature, and music of the late 18th and early 19th centuries. It was characterized by a revolt against rules, forms, and traditions and emphasized strong or lyric feelings, the imagination, and often the supernatural and strange. **— ro·man'ti·cist** *n.*

Rome [rōm] *n.* The capital of Italy, in ancient times the capital of the Roman Empire.

Ro·me·o [rō'mē·ō] *n.* In Shakespeare's play *Romeo and Juliet*, the hero, the lover of Juliet.

romp [romp] **1** *v.* To play in a rough, noisy way. **2** *n.* Rough, noisy play or frolic. **3** *n.* A child who romps, especially a girl.

romp·ers [rom'pərz] *n.pl.* An outer garment combining a shirt and short pants, worn by young children.

Rom·u·lus [rom'yə·ləs] *n.* In Roman myths, the founder and first ruler of Rome, who, along with his twin brother Remus, was nursed and raised by a wolf.

rood [rōōd] *n.* **1** A cross or crucifix. **2** A measure of area equal to ¼ acre.

roof [rōōf] **1** *n.* The top, outer covering of a building. **2** *n.* Something like this in form or use: the *roof* of the mouth. **3** *v.* To cover with or as if with a roof: Trees *roofed* the lane.

roof·ing [rōō'fing] *n.* A material used for building roofs.

roof·tree [rōōf'trē'] *n.* Another name for RIDGEPOLE.

rook¹ [rŏŏk] *n.* In chess, a castle-shaped piece that can move over any number of empty squares parallel to the edges of the board.

rook² [rŏŏk] **1** *n.* A crowlike bird of Europe that likes to nest near buildings. **2** *n.* A cheat or trickster. **3** *v.* To cheat; swindle; defraud.

rook·er·y [rŏŏk'ər·ē] *n., pl.* **rook·er·ies 1** A colony or breeding place of rooks. **2** A place where sea birds, seals, etc., breed. **3** One or more shabby, crowded tenement houses.

rook·ie [rŏŏk'ē] *n. slang* **1** A new recruit in the army, police, etc. **2** A beginner or novice, as in a professional sport.

room [rōōm] **1** *n.* Unoccupied or open space: There is lots of *room*. **2** *n.* A space enclosed by walls, as inside a building: a music *room*. **3** *v.* To occupy a room; lodge: We *roomed* together at college. **4** *n. (pl.)* Lodgings. **5** *n.* Everyone in a room: The *room* was shocked. **6** *n.* A chance, occasion, or opportunity: *room* for doubt.

room·er [rōō'mər] *n.* A person who rents and occupies a room; a lodger.

room·ful [rōōm'fŏŏl'] *n., pl.* **room·fuls** As much or as many as a room will hold: a *roomful* of people.

rooming house *U.S.* A house for roomers.

room·mate [rōōm'māt'] *n.* One of two or more persons who rent and occupy the same lodgings.

room·y [rōō'mē] *adj.* **room·i·er, room·i·est** Having a large amount of room. **— room'i·ness** *n.*

Roo·se·velt [rō'zə·velt], **Eleanor,** 1884–1962, U.S. lecturer, writer, and diplomat, wife of Franklin Delano Roosevelt.

Roo·se·velt [rō'zə·velt], **Franklin Delano,** 1882–1945, U.S. statesman, 32nd president of the U.S., 1933–1945.

Roo·se·velt [rō'zə·velt], **Theodore,** 1858–1919, U.S. army officer and statesman, 26th president of the U.S., 1901–1909.

roost [rōōst] **1** *n.* A perch, ledge, etc., where birds rest at night. **2** *n.* A building, as a hen house or barn, containing a perch or ledge where birds rest at night. **3** *v.* To sit or perch on or in a roost. **4** *v.* To come to rest; settle.

roost·er [rōōs'tər] *n.* A male chicken; cock.

root¹ [rōōt] **1** *n.* The part of a plant that grows into the earth, where it anchors the plant and takes up water and nourishment from the soil. **2** *v.* To put out roots and begin to grow, as a plant. **3** *n.* Any underground plant growth, as a bulb. **4** *n.* A rootlike part of an organ or structure: the *root* of a tooth; the *roots* of hair. **5** *v.* To fix or become fixed firmly: to be *rooted* to the spot. **6** *n.* A source or origin: Money is the *root* of evil. **7** *n.* A number that when multiplied by itself some number of times equals a specified number, or any quantity written under a radical sign: 2 is the fifth *root* of 32; $\sqrt{x-5}$ is a *root*. **8** *n.* A number that satisfies an equation when used in place of one of the unknowns: 2 and −2 are the *roots* of $x^2 - 4 = 0$. **9** *n.* A word or part of a word to which prefixes and suffixes are added to form other words, as *know* in *unknown* and *knowingly*. **— root up** or **root out 1** To pull or tear up by or as if by the roots. **2** To destroy utterly: to *root out* crime.

Rooster, to 30 in. head to tail

root² [rōōt] *v.* **1** To turn up or dig with the snout, as pigs. **2** To search about; rummage: to *root* through a drawer.

root³ [rōōt] *v. U.S. informal* To cheer; shout encouragement: The children *rooted* noisily for our team. **— root'er** *n.*

root beer A carbonated drink made with yeast and the extracts of various roots.

root hair Any of the fine, hairlike growths near the tip of the root of a plant. They help absorb nourishment.

root·let [rŏŏt′lit] *n.* A small root.

rope [rōp] *n.*, *v.* **roped, rop·ing 1** *n.* A thick, strong cord or line made by twisting tightly together several strands of fibers of hemp, cotton, nylon, etc. **2** *v.* To tie or fasten with or as if with rope. **3** *v.* To enclose, mark off, or divide with a rope: to *rope* off an entrance. **4** *n.* A number of things strung together in a line: a *rope* of beads. **5** *n.* A slimy or sticky thread or filament: a *rope* of syrup. **6** *n.* *U.S.* A lasso. **7** *v.* *U.S.* To catch with a lasso. **— know the ropes** To be familiar with a job or situation. **— the end of one's rope** The limit of one's patience, endurance, etc. **— rop′y** *adj.*

Roque·fort [rōk′fərt] *n.* A strong cheese with a blue mold in it, named after a village in France.

ro·sa·ry [rō′zə·rē] *n.*, *pl.* **ro·sa·ries 1** A series of prayers recited by Roman Catholics. **2** A string of beads for keeping count of the prayers recited. **3** A garden or bed of roses.

rose¹ [rōz] **1** *n.* Any of a group of shrubs having thorny stems and fragrant flowers. **2** *n.* The flower of such a shrub, occurring in a wide range of colors, chiefly red, pink, yellow, and white. **3** *n.*, *adj.* Light, pinkish red. **4** *n.* Something that suggests a rose, as in color, form, or odor.

rose² [rōz] Past tense of RISE.

ro·se·ate [rō′zē·it] *adj.* **1** Rose-colored; rosy. **2** Cheerful; optimistic.

rose·bud [rōz′bud′] *n.* The bud of a rose.

rose·bush [rōz′bŏŏsh′] *n.* A rose-bearing shrub or vine.

rose·mar·y [rōz′mâr′ē] *n.*, *pl.* **rose·mar·ies** An evergreen shrub related to the mint, bearing blue flowers and fragrant leaves. It is used in cooking as a seasoning and in perfumes.

ro·sette [rō·zet′] *n.* An ornament or badge resembling a rose and often made of ribbon.

rose water A fragrant preparation made from water and the oil of rose petals, used as a toilet water and in cooking.

rose·wood [rōz′wŏŏd′] *n.* The hard, dark-colored, fragrant wood of certain tropical American trees.

Rosh Ha·sho·nah [rosh *or* rōsh hə·shō′nə] or **Rosh Ha·sha·na** [hə·shä′nə] The Jewish New Year, celebrated in late September or early October.

ros·in [roz′in] **1** *n.* A hard, yellowish substance extracted from crude turpentine, used on violin bows and on athletes' shoes or hands to prevent slipping. **2** *v.* To apply rosin to.

Ross [rôs], **Betsy,** 1752–1836, American patriot, said to have made the first American flag.

ros·ter [ros′tər] *n.* **1** A list of men and of their duties, as of police, soldiers, etc. **2** Any list.

ros·trum [ros′trəm] *n.*, *pl.* **ros·trums** or **ros·tra** [ros′trə] A pulpit or platform from which speeches are given.

ros·y [rō′zē] *adj.* **ros·i·er, ros·i·est 1** Like or having the color of a rose. **2** Bright or optimistic: a *rosy* outlook. **— ros′i·ness** *n.*

rot [rot] *v.* **rot·ted, rot·ting,** *n.* **1** *v.* To decay spoil, or decompose: The dead horse *rotted* in the field. **2** *v.* To fall to pieces; go to ruin: The old mansion *rotted* to the ground. **3** *v.* To cause decay, ruin, or rot in: Too much water *rots* plant roots. **4** *n.* The process of rotting. **5** *n.* A decayed or ruined condition. **6** *n.* Any of several diseases affecting plants or animals and caused by parasites. **7** *n.* *informal* Nonsense; rubbish.

ro·ta·ry [rō′tər·ē] *adj.*, *n.*, *pl.* **ro·ta·ries 1** *adj.* Turning or built to turn around its axis, as a wheel. **2** *adj.* Having some important part that turns on its axis: a *rotary* press. **3** *n.* A traffic circle.

ro·tate [rō′tāt] *v.* **ro·tat·ed, ro·tat·ing 1** To turn or cause to turn on or as if on an axis. **2** To alternate in a definite order: In volleyball the players *rotate*; to *rotate* crops. **— ro′ta·tor** *n.*

ro·ta·tion [rō·tā′shən] *n.* **1** The act or process of rotating. **2** A being rotated. **3** Change or alternation in some particular order; regular variation: *rotation* of crops.

The earth rotates on its axis.

rote [rōt] *n.* A mechanical, unthinking repetition or way of doing something, especially in the phrase **by rote,** by simple memorization, without any interest in what one memorizes.

ro·tis·se·rie [rō·tis′ər·ē] *n.* A device for roasting meat by rotating it slowly over a fire.

ro·to·gra·vure [rō′tə·grə·vyŏŏr′] *n.* **1** A process of printing using engraved copper cylinders on which the pictures, printing, etc., to be reproduced are depressed instead of raised. **2** A section of a newspaper printed in such a way.

ro·tor [rō′tər] *n.* **1** The rotating part of a dynamo, turbine, or other generator of power. **2** The horizontal rotating blades of a helicopter.

rot·ten [rot′(ə)n] *adj.* **1** Spoiled or decayed: *rotten* food. **2** Unpleasant; disagreeable: a *rotten* temper.

Rotor of a helicopter

3 Untrustworthy; corrupt; dishonest: a *rotten* politician. **4** Liable to break, crack, etc.; rotted: *rotten* beams. **5** *informal* Bad or inferior in quality: a *rotten* novel. **— rot′ten·ness** *n.*

Rot·ter·dam [rot′ər·dam] *n.* A seaport in the western part of the Netherlands.

ro·tund [rō·tund′] *adj.* **1** Rounded out; plump: a *rotund* figure. **2** Full and resonant: a *rotund* voice. **— ro·tun′di·ty** *n.*

---

add, āce, câre, pälm;   end, ēqual;   it, īce;   odd, ōpen, ôrder;   tŏŏk, pŏŏl;   up, bûrn;
ə = a in *above*, e in *sicken*, i in *possible*, o in *melon*, u in *circus*;   yŏŏ = u in *fuse*;   oil;   pout;
check;   ring;   thin;   this;   zh in *vision*.   For ¶ reference, see page 64 · HOW TO

ro·tun·da [rō·tun′də] *n.* A circular building, room, or hall, usually having a dome on top.

rou·ble [rōō′bəl] *n.* Another spelling of RUBLE.

Rou·en [rōō·än′] *n.* A city in northern France. Joan of Arc was burned there.

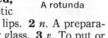
A rotunda

rouge [rōozh] *n., v.* **rouged, roug·ing** **1** *n.* A cosmetic used to color the cheeks or lips. **2** *n.* A preparation used to polish metal or glass. **3** *v.* To put or use rouge on.

rough [ruf] **1** *adj.* Not smooth or even; bumpy; irregular: a *rough* sidewalk. **2** *adj.* Coarse or harsh to the touch: a *rough* cloth. **3** *v.* To make rough; roughen. **4** *adj.* Violent and rugged in action: *rough* sports. **5** *v.* To treat roughly or violently: Their team *roughed* up ours a lot. **6** *adv.* In a rude or violent manner; roughly: He plays *rough*. **7** *adj.* Stormy: *rough* seas. **8** *adj.* Lacking gentleness, courtesy, etc.; crude: a *rough* person. **9** *n.* A rude, loud, or disorderly person. **10** *adj.* Not easy or luxurious; hard; rugged: a *rough* life in the wilderness. **11** *adj.* Done or made quickly without much attention to small details: a *rough* drawing. **12** *adj.* Not polished or finished; crude: These jewels are in a *rough* state. **13** *v.* To make, cut, or sketch roughly: He *roughed* in the details of the drawing. **14** *adj. informal* Difficult; vexing: He gave me a *rough* time. **15** *n.* Any part of a golf course on which tall grass, bushes, etc., grow. **—in the rough** In a crude or unpolished condition. **—rough it** To live, camp out, or travel in a rough manner without any luxuries or comforts. **—rough out** To make a sketchy first version of. **—rough′ness** *n.*

rough·age [ruf′ij] *n.* Any coarse substance, especially coarse, rough foods that help the movement of food through the intestines.

rough·en [ruf′ən] *v.* To make or become rough.

rough·hew [ruf′hyōō′] *v.* **rough·hewed,** or **rough·hewn, rough·hew·ing** To hew or shape roughly or irregularly; make crudely.

rough·ly [ruf′lē] *adv.* **1** In a rough manner. **2** About; approximately: *Roughly* 100 schools were represented at the conference.

rough·neck [ruf′nek′] *n. U.S. slang* A rude or disorderly person; rowdy. ◆ *Roughneck* was formed by combining the words *rough* and *neck.*

rough·shod [ruf′shod′] *adj.* Shod with horseshoes having nails or sharp calks. **—ride roughshod over** To act toward (someone) in a very arrogant way, without any regard for his feelings or wishes.

rou·lette [rōō·let′] *n.* **1** A gambling game in which the players bet on which space of a rotating wheel a small ball will fall into. **2** A small notched disk that makes holes or marks in paper, as the holes between postage stamps.

Rou·ma·ni·a [rōō·mā′nē·ə *or* rōō·män′yə] *n.* Another spelling of RUMANIA. **—Rou·ma′ni·an** *adj., n.*

round [round] **1** *adj.* Having a shape or form that is like a circle, ball, or cylinder: a *round* table. **2** *adj.* Semicircular: a *round* arch. **3** *n.* Something round, as a globe, ring, or rung of a ladder. **4** *v.* To make or become round. **5** *adj.* Formed or moving in a circle: a *round* dance. **6** *n.* A round dance, as the polka. **7** *n.* Movement or motion that is circular or revolving. **8** *adv.* With a circular or rotating motion: The wheels turned *round*. **9** *prep.* So as to make a circle around: a belt *round* his waist. **10** *adj.* Returning to the point of departure: a *round* trip. **11** *v.* To travel or go around; make a circuit of: The ship *rounded* the cape at noon. **12** *adv.* So as to get to the other or opposite side of: to turn *round* the corner. **13** *n. (often pl.)* A route or circuit that ends where it began; beat: the watchman's *rounds*. **14** *adv.* So as to form a complete circuit or cycle of time: The holidays come *round* so slowly each year. **15** *adv.* On all sides: A crowd gathered *round*. **16** *prep.* On every side of: There were mountains *round* us. **17** *prep.* Toward every side of: He peered *round* him. **18** *prep.* To the people or places of: to travel *round* the country. **19** *adv.* From person to person or place to place: We have food enough to go *round*; We walked *round*. **20** *adv.* In a long or roundabout way: We walked *round* by the library on our way to school. **21** *adv.* In the vicinity, neighborhood, etc.: We stayed *round* all day but nothing happened. **22** *prep.* In about, or near: to loaf *round* the drugstore. **23** *adv.* In the opposite direction: to turn *round*. **24** *adv.* In circumference: a log three feet *round*. **25** *n.* A series of actions, events, etc., repeated more or less regularly: the daily *round* of life. **26** *n.* One of a series of actions performed together by many people: a *round* of applause. **27** *adj.* Large; ample: a good *round* fee. **28** *adj.* Plump: a baby's little *round* legs. **29** *adj.* Full; complete: a *round* ton. **30** *adj.* Full and rich; mellow: *round* tones. **31** *adj.* Formed or uttered with the lips rounded, as the vowel *O*. **32** *v.* To utter (a vowel) with the lips in a rounded position. **33** *adj.* Bold; outspoken; frank: a *round* statement. **34** *adj.* Increased or decreased to the nearest ten, hundred, etc.: 400 is a *round* number for 399. **35** *adj.* Quick; brisk: a *round* pace. **36** *n.* One of the divisions or units of a game or contest, as of a boxing match, golf match, etc. **37** *n.* A short song in which each singer or group of singers begins to sing one after the other at a specified word or phrase in the song. **38** *n.* A firing of shots by a military company or squad in which each soldier fires once only; a volley. **39** *n.* A single shot or unit of ammunition. **40** *n.* A cut of beef taken from the thigh. **41** *n.* The condition of being fully carved on all sides and standing apart from any background, etc.: The sculpture was in the *round*. **—round off** or **round out 1** To make or become round or rounded. **2** To bring or come to completeness or perfection: She *rounded out* the class hour with a brief summary. **3** To make into a round number.

— round up 1 To collect (cattle, etc.) in a herd, as for driving to market. **2** *informal* To gather together; assemble: If you can *round up* four people we can play ball. **— round′ness** *n*.

round·a·bout [round′ə·bout′] *adj*. Not direct, straight, or short: to go a *roundabout* way.

round dance 1 A type of folk dance in which the players form and dance in a circle. **2** A ballroom dance, as the waltz or polka, in which the couples whirl and circle around the room.

roun·de·lay [roun′də·lā] *n*. **1** A song having a refrain that is often repeated. **2** A dance in which the dancers form or move in circles.

round·house [round′hous′] *n*. **1** A large, round building for housing locomotives. It is built around a turntable in the center for switching or turning the locomotives around. **2** A cabin on the rear part of a ship's deck.

round·ish [roun′dish] *adj*. Somewhat round.

round·ly [round′lē] *adv*. **1** In a round manner, shape, or form. **2** Severely; vigorously: to be *roundly* whipped. **3** Fully; thoroughly. **4** Frankly; bluntly: He spoke *roundly* to us all.

round number A number that is raised or lowered to the nearest ten, hundred, thousand, etc.: 500 is a *round number* for 496.

round-shoul·dered [round′shōl′dərd] *adj*. Having the upper back stooped or rounded and the shoulders bent forward.

Round Table 1 The table of King Arthur, made exactly circular so that no knight could complain another was nearer the head of the table. **2** King Arthur and his knights. **3** (*written* **round table**) Any group that meets to discuss something.

round trip A trip to a place and back again, usually by the same route.

round·up [round′up′] *n*. *U.S.* **1** A bringing together of cattle scattered over a range, as for branding or inspection. **2** The cowboys, horses, etc., used to do this. **3** *informal* A bringing together of persons or things for any purpose.

round·worm [round′wûrm′] *n*. Any of various threadlike worms, some of which, like the hookworm, are parasitic in the intestines of man.

rouse [rouz] *v*. **roused, rous·ing 1** To wake up from sleep, indifference, etc. **2** To stir up or excite: a crowd *roused* to fury.

Rous·seau [rōō·sō′], **Jean Jacques,** 1712–1778, French philosopher and author.

roust·a·bout [roust′ə·bout′] *n*. A person who does unskilled work on a waterfront, on a ranch, in a circus, etc.

rout[1] [rout] **1** *v*. To defeat thoroughly. **2** *n*. A disastrous defeat. **3** *v*. To make flee or retreat in a disorderly way. **4** *n*. A disorderly retreat.

rout[2] [rout] *v*. **1** To dig or turn up with the snout: a pig *routing* for food. **2** To turn up or bring to view. **3** To hollow out or gouge, as with a scoop. **4** To drive or force out.

route [rōōt *or* rout] *n., v*. **rout·ed, rout·ing 1** *n*. A road or course taken in traveling from one point to another. **2** *v*. To send by a certain way or course: to *route* goods through Chicago. **3** *n*. The territory covered by a newsboy, milkman, etc.

rou·tine [rōō·tēn′] **1** *n*. A fixed, habitual way or method of doing something: His *routine* of exercises was always the same. **2** *adj*. Habitual; customary: a *routine* breakfast. **3** *adj*. Dull; uninspired: a *routine* job; a *routine* speech. **— rou·tine′ly** *adv*.

rove [rōv] *v*. **roved, rov·ing** To roam or move about; wander: to *rove* over the farm; to *rove* the old section of town. ◆ See WANDER.

rov·er [rō′vər] *n*. **1** A person who roves; wanderer. **2** A pirate or pirate ship.

row[1] [rou] *n*. A noisy quarrel or disturbance.

row[2] [rō] **1** *v*. To propel (a boat) by using oars. **2** *v*. To carry or transport in a boat by using oars: We *rowed* our guests across the lake. **3** *n*. A trip in a rowboat. **— row′er** *n*.

row[3] [rō] *n*. An arrangement of things or persons in a line.

row·boat [rō′bōt′] *n*. A boat moved along by oars.

row·dy [rou′dē] *n., pl*. **row·dies,** *adj*. **row·di·er, row·di·est 1** *n*. A rough, disorderly person; hoodlum. **2** *adj*. Rough, loud, and disorderly: a *rowdy* group. **— row′di·ness** or **row′dy·ism** *n*.

A rowing team

row·el [rou′əl] *n*. A small wheel having spikes or teeth around it, as on a spur.

row·lock [rō′lok′] *n*. Another word for OARLOCK.

roy·al [roi′əl] **1** *adj*. Of or for a king or queen: a *royal* hunting lodge. **2** *adj*. From or by a king or queen: a *royal* visit. **3** *adj*. Of or under the command of a king or monarchy: the *royal* guard. **4** *adj*. Like or good enough for a king or queen: a *royal* feast. **5** *n*. A sail next above the topgallant, used in a light breeze. **— roy′al·ly** *adv*.

A rowel

roy·al·ist [roi′əl·ist] **1** *n*. A person who supports a king or queen or a monarchy. **2** *adj*. Of or having to do with royalists.

roy·al·ty [roi′əl·tē] *n., pl*. **roy·al·ties 1** A royal person. **2** Royal persons as a group: the vanishing *royalty* of Europe. **3** Royal rank, birth, authority, etc.: *Royalty* today gives great influence to a king or queen but little power. **4** A royal or regal look, quality, nature, etc.: *Royalty* shows in his bearing. **5** A share of the money earned by a song, play, invention, novel, etc. It is paid to the author or creator for the right to use, sell, or perform his work.

---

add, **ā**ce, câre, pälm;   end, **ē**qual;   **i**t, **ī**ce;   **o**dd, **ō**pen, ôrder;   t**oo**k, p**oo**l;   up, bûrn;
ə = a in *above*, e in *sicken*, i in *possible*, o in *melon*, u in *circus*;   **y**ōō = u in *fuse*;   oil;   pout;
check;   ri**ng**;   **th**in;   **th**is;   **zh** in *vision*.   For ¶ reference, see page 64 · HOW TO

rpm or **r.p.m.** Abbreviation of *revolutions per minute.*

R.R. Abbreviation of RAILROAD.

R.S.V.P. or **r.s.v.p.** Abbreviation of the French phrase *Répondez s'il vous plaît,* which means "Please reply."

rub [rub] *v.* **rubbed, rub·bing,** *n.* **1** *v.* To move over the surface of with pressure or friction: to *rub* a sore muscle; The shoe *rubbed* his heel. **2** *v.* To move with friction; scrape: The cat *rubbed* against his leg. **3** *v.* To cause to move across a surface: to *rub* a towel over one's face. **4** *v.* To cause to become worn or sore from friction: This collar *rubs* my neck. **5** *v.* To apply or spread with pressure and friction: to *rub* polish on a table. **6** *v.* To clean, shine, dry, etc., by mean of rubbing: I *rubbed* the wet dog with a towel. **7** *v.* To remove or be removed by rubbing; erase. **8** *n.* The act of rubbing. **9** *n.* Something that annoys or irritates, as a sarcastic remark. **10** *n.* A difficulty, doubt, or hindrance: There's the *rub.* **— rub down** To massage. **— rub it in** *slang* To remind someone often of his mistakes, faults, etc. **— rub the wrong way** To annoy or irritate.

rub·ber[1] [rub'ər] *n.* **1** An elastic material made from the milky sap of certain tropical plants, or made artificially of chemicals. **2** Something made of rubber, as an elastic band, overshoe, eraser, etc. **3** *adj. use:* a *rubber* raincoat. **4** A person or thing that rubs. **— rub'ber·y** *adj.*

rub·ber[2] [rub'ər] *n.* **1** In certain games, as bridge, a series of contests which ends when one player or team wins either two out of three or three out of five of the contests. **2** The odd contest that breaks a tie in such a series.

rubber band A band made of rubber, that can be stretched, used to hold things together.

rub·ber·ize [rub'ər·īz] *v.* **rub·ber·ized, rub·ber·iz·ing** To coat or cover with rubber. ¶3

rubber plant 1 Any of various plants that yield rubber. **2** A plant having large, shiny, leathery leaves, much used as a decorative plant in the house.

rubber stamp 1 A stamp made of rubber. When coated with ink, it prints dates, names, etc. **2** A person or group that accepts or approves the ideas and plans of others without much thought or without power to refuse.

rub·bish [rub'ish] *n.* **1** Trash, garbage, or refuse. **2** Nonsense: What he said was pure *rubbish.*

rub·ble [rub'əl] *n.* **1** Rough pieces of broken stone. **2** The bricks, stones, etc., of buildings that have been destroyed, as by earthquakes or bombings. **3** Masonry made of rubble.

Ru·bens [rōō'bənz], **Peter Paul,** 1577–1640, Flemish painter.

Ru·bi·con [rōō'bi·kon] *n.* A river in north central Italy, the boundary between Gaul and Italy. By crossing it into Italy in 49 B.C. Caesar deliberately started civil war. **— cross the Rubicon** To be pledged or committed to some course of action.

ru·bi·cund [rōō'bə·kənd] *adj.* Reddish; rosy.

ru·ble [rōō'bəl] *n.* The basic unit of money in the Soviet Union.

ru·bric [rōō'brik] *n.* **1** The part of any early manuscript or book that appears in red or in fancy type, as titles, first letters of a page, etc. **2** A rule or direction for conducting religious ceremonies: the *rubrics* for the Mass.

ru·by [rōō'bē] *n., pl.* **ru·bies,** *adj.* **1** *n.* A rare and valuable jewel, having a clear, deep red color. **2** *n., adj.* Deep red.

ruck·sack [ruk'sak'] *n.* A knapsack, usually made of canvas.

ruck·us [ruk'əs] *n.* *U.S. slang* A noisy uproar.

rud·der [rud'ər] *n.* **1** A broad, flat, movable piece of wood or metal that is hinged to the rear of a boat or ship and is used to steer the vessel. **2** A similar device on an airplane. **3** Anything that guides or directs.

Rudder

rud·dy [rud'ē] *adj.* **rud·di·er, rud·di·est 1** Tinged with red. **2** Having a healthy glow; rosy: a *ruddy* complexion. **— rud'di·ness** *n.*

rude [rōōd] *adj.* **rud·er, rud·est 1** Having no courtesy; impolite: a *rude* remark. **2** Unskillfully made or done; crude; rough: a *rude* little hut. **3** Not refined or educated; rustic; uncouth: the *rude* peasants. **4** Violent; harsh; savage: The storm broke with *rude* fury. **5** Vigorous; strong: *rude* health. **— rude'ly** *adv.* **— rude'ness** *n.*

ru·di·ment [rōō'də·mənt] *n.* **1** A first principle, rule, step, or stage in learning or doing something: the *rudiments* of French. **2** Something which is only partly developed or formed.

ru·di·men·ta·ry [rōō'də·men'tər·ē] *adj.* **1** Of or like a rudiment; beginning; elementary: a *rudimentary* knowledge of art. **2** Imperfectly developed; unformed: a *rudimentary* tail.

rue[1] [rōō] *n.* A small, bushy herb with bitter leaves that were once much used in medicine.

rue[2] [rōō] *v.* **rued, ru·ing** To feel sorrow or regret for: You'll *rue* your nasty temper.

rue·ful [rōō'fəl] *adj.* **1** Feeling or expressing sorrow, regret, or pity: a *rueful* glance. **2** Causing sorrow, regret, or pity: a *rueful* tale.

ruff [ruf] *n.* **1** A wide, pleated, heavily starched collar worn by men and women in the 16th century. **2** A natural collar of feathers or hair found around the necks of certain birds or animals. ◆ *Ruff* is a shortened form of RUFFLE.

A ruff

ruffed grouse [ruft] A grouse of North America, often hunted for sport. It has a ruff of feathers on its neck.

ruf·fi·an [ruf'ē·ən *or* ruf'yən] **1** *n.* A brutal, cruel fellow; hoodlum. **2** *adj.* Recklessly brutal or cruel: to use *ruffian* behavior.

ruf·fle [ruf′əl] *n., v.* **ruf·fled, ruf·fling 1** *n.* A strip of cloth, ribbon, etc., that has been pleated on one edge, used for trimming. **2** *v.* To draw into folds or ruffles; gather: to *ruffle* the edge of cloth. **3** *v.* To put ruffles on: to *ruffle* a dress. **4** *v.* To disturb or irritate; upset. **5** *n.* A feeling of irritation or uneasiness. **6** *n.* The cause of such feelings. **7** *v.* To disturb the smoothness or regularity of: The wind *ruffled* the lake.

Ruffles

8 *n.* A slight disturbance on a surface, as a ripple. **9** *v.* To raise (the feathers) in a ruff, as a bird does.

rug [rug] *n.* **1** A covering for a floor or part of a floor, usually made of a heavy, durable fabric, an animal skin, etc. **2** A robe to put over one's lap.

Rug·by [rug′bē] *n.* **1** A city in central England, site of a famous school for boys founded in 1567. **2** A type of football.

rug·ged [rug′id] *adj.* **1** Having a broken, irregular surface; rough; uneven: a *rugged* strip of land. **2** Strong and robust; sturdy: a *rugged* person. **3** Having strongly marked or wrinkled features; a *rugged*, handsome face. **4** Lacking refinement or culture; coarse: his *rugged* manner. **5** Not easy; harsh; stern: to lead a *rugged* life. **6** Stormy: It was a *rugged* night.

Ruhr [rŏŏr] *n.* **1** A river of western West Germany, flowing west into the Rhine River. **2** An important industrial and coal-mining region north of this river.

ru·in [rŏŏ′in] **1** *n.* (*often pl.*) The remains of something that has decayed or been destroyed: the *ruins* of bombed cities. **2** *n.* The destruction of the value or usefulness of something: the *ruin* of his career. **3** *n.* A condition of destruction or decay: *Ruin* was everywhere. **4** *v.* To destroy, demolish, or damage: The hail *ruined* her garden. **5** *n.* Something that causes destruction, decay, downfall, etc. **6** *v.* To make bankrupt or poor: The fire *ruined* him.

ru·in·a·tion [rŏŏ′in·ā′shən] *n.* **1** The act of ruining. **2** The condition of being ruined. **3** Something that ruins.

ru·in·ous [rŏŏ′in·əs] *adj.* **1** Causing ruin and destruction: a *ruinous* rain. **2** Ruined; decayed; dilapidated: a *ruinous* condition.

rule [rŏŏl] *n., v.* **ruled, rul·ing 1** *n.* A direction, set of instructions, or a law that tells one the correct thing to do or the correct way to do it: the *rules* of a game; the *rules* of a religious order. **2** *v.* To decide or determine: The court *ruled* that his case be tried Tuesday. **3** *v.* To have authority or control over; govern: to *rule* a country; *Rule* your temper. **4** *n.* Government or reign; control: to be under the *rule* of a dictator. **5** *n.* A

common or customary way of acting, thinking, etc.: It was his *rule* to rise early. **6** *n.* The usual or prevailing condition or thing: During this season rain is the *rule* instead of the exception. **7** *v.* To influence greatly; dominate: Greed *ruled* his life. **8** *n.* A straight-edged instrument for measuring, drawing, etc.; ruler. **9** *v.* To mark with straight, usually parallel lines: to *rule* a notebook. **— as a rule:** Ordinarily; usually. **— rule out** To decide to ignore, leave out, or eliminate: We mustn't *rule out* fatigue as a cause of our defeat.

rule of thumb 1 A rule, method, or judgment based on practical experience rather than on scientific knowledge. **2** A rough measurement.

rul·er [rŏŏ′lər] *n.* **1** A person who rules or governs, as a king. **2** A straight-edged instrument for use in measuring or in drawing lines.

rul·ing [rŏŏ′ling] **1** *n.* The act of a person who rules or governs. **2** *adj.* Having power to rule or govern: a *ruling* monarch. **3** *n.* A decision or judgment, as of a court. **4** *adj.* Most important or powerful; predominant: a *ruling* passion.

rum [rum] *n.* **1** An alcoholic liquor made from fermented molasses or sugar cane. **2** Any alcoholic liquor.

Ru·ma·ni·a [rŏŏ·mā′nē·ə *or* rŏŏ·mān′yə] *n.* A country in SE Europe. **— Ru·ma′ni·an** *adj., n.*

rum·ba [rum′bə] *n.* **1** A modern ballroom dance that is based on a dance of Cuban Negroes. **2** The music for this dance.

rum·ble [rum′bəl] *v.* **rum·bled, rum·bling,** *n.* **1** *v.* To make a low, heavy, rolling sound, as thunder. **2** *v.* To move or proceed with such a sound: The trucks *rumbled* off. **3** *n.* A low, heavy, rolling sound. **4** *n.* A seat or baggage compartment in the rear of a carriage. **5** *n.* A folding seat in the back of certain early automobiles, as a coupe. **6** *n. slang* A street fight, usually between gangs of teen-agers.

ru·men [rŏŏ′mən] *n., pl.* **ru·mens** or **ru·mi·na** [rŏŏ′mə·nə] The first of usually four chambers in the stomachs of animals that chew the cud, as sheep or cows. Food goes into the rumen first before being returned to the mouth for chewing.

ru·mi·nant [rŏŏ′mə·nənt] **1** *n.* An animal that eats plants, chews the cud, and has a stomach containing a rumen. Deer, sheep, goats, cows, camels, and giraffes are all ruminants. **2** *adj.* Of, having to do with, or like such animals. **3** *adj.* Liking or given to quiet meditation; thoughtful.

ru·mi·nate [rŏŏ′mə·nāt] *v.* **ru·mi·nat·ed, ru·mi·nat·ing 1** To chew the cud, as a cow. **2** To think or reflect; meditate. **— ru′mi·na′tion** *n.*

rum·mage [rum′ij] *v.* **rum·maged, rum·mag·ing,** *n.* **1** *v.* To search through (a place, box, etc.) by turning things over in a disorderly manner; ransack: The robbers *rummaged* the house but found nothing. **2** *v.* To make a thorough search: We *rummaged* all through the

add, **ā**ce, **c**â**re, p**ä**lm;   **e**nd, **ē**qual;   **i**t, **i**ce;   **o**dd, **ō**pen, **ô**rder;   t**oo**k, p**oo**l;   **u**p, b**û**rn;

ə = a in *above*, e in *sicken*, i in *possible*, o in *melon*, u in *circus*;   **y**oo = u in *fuse*;   **oil**;   pout;

check;   **r**in**g**;   **th**in;   **th**is;   **zh** in *vision*.   For ¶ reference, see page 64 · HOW TO

attic. **3** *n.* A thorough search. **4** *n.* Things sold at a rummage sale.

rummage sale A sale of second-hand objects or other odds and ends, often for a charity.

rum·my [rum′ē] *n.* A card game in which points are scored for three or four of a kind or sequences of three or more of the same suit.

ru·mor [rōō′mər] **1** *n.* A story or report that has not yet been proven true but is being told from person to person. **2** *n.* Common gossip or hearsay. **3** *v.* To tell or spread as a rumor. ¶1

rump [rump] *n.* **1** The round or fleshy upper part of the hind quarters of an animal. **2** A cut of beef from this area. **3** In man, the buttocks.

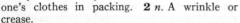

rum·ple [rum′pəl] *v.* **rum·pled, rum·pling,** *n.* **1** *v.* To wrinkle, mess, or crumple: to *rumple* one's clothes in packing. **2** *n.* A wrinkle or crease.

rum·pus [rum′pəs] *n. informal* A row or wrangle; disturbance.

run [run] *v.* **ran, run, run·ning,** *n.* **1** *v.* To move or go along by using steps that are faster than walking steps. **2** *v.* To move, go, or pass rapidly: A whisper *ran* through the crowd. **3** *v.* To take flight; flee: They *ran* for their very lives. **4** *n.* The act of running: He takes a *run* each morning. **5** *n.* The movement or pace of running: He broke into a *run.* **6** *v.* To make a journey or regular trips: We *ran* over to the island; This ship *runs* between New York and London. **7** *n.* A journey, trip, or route: Let's take a *run* up to see her. **8** *v.* To go through or past: The ship *ran* the blockade. **9** *v.* To perform or accomplish by or as if by running: to *run* a race; to *run* an errand. **10** *v.* To flow or cause to flow: The wax *ran* down onto the table; She *ran* water into the pan. **11** *n.* A flowing movement, as of a stream or liquid: the *run* of sap. **12** *n.* A stream or current. **13** *v.* To move (the hand, eye, etc.) quickly or lightly: He *ran* his hand over the table. **14** *v.* To continue or extend in time, space, etc.: Our carnival *ran* only two nights; The wall *runs* to the edge of our property. **15** *v.* To come, bring, pass, etc., into a specified place or condition: We *ran* out of breath; The well *ran* dry. **16** *n.* A continuous series of events, actions, performances, etc.: The play had a long *run;* a *run* of good luck. **17** *n.* An unusually large number of demands, as by bank depositors or store customers. **18** *v.* To enter or take part in a race or contest: He *ran* for president of our class. **19** *n.* A course, direction, or tendency: the *run* of world events; the *run* of the grain in wood. **20** *v.* To climb or grow in long shoots: The ivy *ran* up the wall. **21** *n.* A period of continuous operation, as of a machine, or the amount of work done during this period. **22** *v.* To be or put in operation; work: The car *runs* well now;

He *ran* the machine too long. **23** *v.* To drive or force: He *ran* his car through the fence. **24** *v.* To direct or control; manage: to *run* a shop. **25** *v.* To have a certain price, size, quality, etc.: The corn is *running* small this year. **26** *n.* A type, kind, or class: the ordinary *run* of readers. **27** *v.* To become torn by unraveling: Her stockings *ran.* **28** *n.* A rip or tear running up and down in knitted material: a *run* in her stocking. **29** *n.* A large enclosure for animals or poultry. **30** *n.* A mass migration or movement of animals, especially of fish to their spawning grounds. **31** *v.* To occur or return: An idea *ran* through his mind. **32** *v.* To be told or expressed: The story *runs* that she is sick. **33** *v.* To publish: to *run* an ad in the paper. **34** *v.* To become liable or expose oneself to; incur: to *run* a risk. **35** *v.* To suffer from (a fever, etc.). **36** *v.* To give forth a discharge or flow: My nose is *running.* **37** *v.* To spread or mingle, as colors when wet. **38** *n.* The right to use or move about freely: We had the *run* of the place. **39** *n.* In baseball, a score made by a player's traveling around and touching all of the bases. **40** *n.* In music, a rapid series of notes. **41** *v.* To sew or stitch in a continuous line. **42** *v.* To mold, as from melted metal. **— a run for one's money** **1** Good, strong action or competition. **2** Satisfaction for time, money, or effort spent. **— in the long run** At the final outcome or result; finally. **— on the run** Running away, retreating, or escaping. **— run across** To meet or find by chance. **— run away with** To be far better than all the others in: They *ran away with* all the games. **— run down** **1** To go after and overtake, as a fugitive. **2** To strike down while moving. **3** To stop working or operating, as a clock. **4** To make or become tired or ill, as from overwork. **5** To say bad or evil things about. **— run for it** To run so as to avoid or escape something. **— run foul of** **1** To hit or become tangled in: They *ran foul of* the hidden wires. **2** To get into trouble or conflict with: to *run foul of* the police. **— run in** **1** To include: *Run* in that sentence at the end. **2** *slang* To arrest and put in jail. **— run into** **1** To meet or find by chance. **2** To collide with. **— run off** **1** To make on a typewriter, printing press, etc.: *Run off* 20 copies. **2** To decide (a tied race, game, etc.) by the outcome of an extra race, game, etc. **— run out** To come to an end, as supplies. **— run out of** To come to an end of one's supply of: We *ran out of* gasoline. **— run over** **1** To ride or drive over. **2** To overflow. **3** To rehearse or examine something quickly. **— run riot** **1** To act or behave wildly: The students *ran riot* after the game. **2** To be or grow in abundance: Poppies *ran riot* in the field. **— run through** **1** To spend or use wastefully. **2** To stab or pierce. **3** To read, rehearse, or examine rapidly. **— run up** **1** To produce or make quickly: to *run up* a dress on a sewing machine. **2** To accumulate or grow rapidly: His debts kept *running up.* **3** To raise or rise quickly: *Run up* the flag.

run·a·way [run′ə·wā′] **1** *n.* A person or animal that runs away or flees, especially a horse of which the driver has lost control. **2** *adj.* Running away or escaping: a *runaway* prisoner. **3** *adj.* Easily won: a *runaway* horse race. **4** *adj.* Of or showing a rapid price rise. **5** *adj.* Brought about by running away: a *runaway* marriage.

run·down [run′doun′] *n.* A brief report.

run-down [run′doun′] *adj.* **1** Physically weak, tired, or ill. **2** Falling apart or needing repair; dilapidated: a *run-down* house. **3** Stopped because not wound: a *run-down* clock.

rune [rōōn] *n.* **1** Any of the characters in an ancient alphabet used from about the 3rd to the 13th centuries in certain parts of northern Europe. **2** (*often pl.*) Ancient Norse stories or legends expressed in or as if in runes. **3** A secret or mysterious mark, spell, saying, etc. ◆ *Rune* comes from an Old English and from an old Scandinavian word meaning *mystery* or *secret conversation.*

rung¹ [rung] *n.* **1** A round crosspiece forming one of the steps on a ladder. **2** A crosspiece used in chairs to strengthen or support the legs or back. **3** A spoke of a wheel.

rung² [rung] Past participle of RING¹.

run·ner [run′ər] *n.* **1** A person who runs, as one who runs a race or runs errands. **2** That part of an object on which it runs or slides: the *runner* of a sled. **3** A long, narrow rug, used in hallways, etc. **4** A narrow strip of cloth, used as an ornamental covering for tables, dressers, etc. **5** In certain plants, as the strawberry, the long stem that lies on the ground and puts out roots at various points. **6** A smuggler. **7** A ship used in smuggling.

Rungs

run·ner-up [run′ər·up′] *n.* In a game or contest, a person or team finishing in second place.

run·ning [run′ing] **1** *n.* The act of a person or thing that runs. **2** *n.* A flow, as of a liquid. **3** *adj.* Moving or going rapidly. **4** *adj.* Flowing: *running* water. **5** *adj.* Sending out or discharging pus, saliva, etc.: a *running* sore. **6** *adj.* In operation; going: He had the engine *running.* **7** *adj.* Done or performed with a run: a *running* hop. **8** *adj.* Without a break; continuous: He talked for three hours *running.* **9** *adj.* Of or having to do with a trip or run: a train's *running* time. **— in the running** Still having a chance of winning. **— out of the running** No longer having any chance of winning.

running knot A knot made so that it slips along the rope, forming a noose that tightens when the rope is pulled.

running mate The candidate for the less important of two connected political offices. The candidate for the vice-presidency is the running mate of the candidate for the presidency.

run·off [run′ôf′] *n.* **1** The part of the rainfall that is not absorbed directly by the soil but is drained off in rills or streams. **2** A special game or contest held to break a tie.

runt [runt] *n.* An unusually small animal, person, or plant.

run·way [run′wā′] *n.* **1** A track or path over or through which something runs. **2** A hard, roadlike surface for the take-off and landing of aircraft.

Runway

ru·pee [rōō·pē′] *n.* The basic unit of money in certain countries, as India and Pakistan.

rup·ture [rup′chər] *n., v.* **rup·tured, rup·tur·ing 1** *n.* The act of breaking apart. **2** *n.* The condition of being broken or torn apart: the *rupture* of a muscle. **3** *v.* To break apart; burst: to *rupture* a bodily organ. **4** *n.* The coming out of an organ of the body through a broken part in the surrounding wall of the cavity; hernia. **5** *v.* To cause to have or suffer from a rupture. **6** *n.* An ending of a friendship or of friendly relations.

ru·ral [rōōr′əl] *adj.* Of or having to do with the country or with country people or things.

rural free delivery A government service of delivering mail from house to house in rural districts.

ruse [rōōz] *n.* Some action or trick intended to deceive or mislead: a *ruse* to get out of class.

rush¹ [rush] **1** *v.* To move or go with great speed or haste: They *rushed* from the burning building. **2** *v.* To send, take, push, etc., with great speed or haste: *Rush* the package to us. **3** *v.* To act hastily without thinking or planning: to *rush* into marriage. **4** *v.* To do, perform, etc., with haste or speed: to *rush* one's work; to *rush* through a lesson. **5** *v.* To make a sudden assault upon; attack: The guards *rushed* the rioting prisoners. **6** *n.* The act of rushing. **7** *n.* Great hurry or haste: Why is everyone in such a *rush*? **8** *adj.* Requiring haste or urgency: a *rush* order. **9** *n.* A sudden flocking of people to a new region or area, usually to acquire land, gold, etc. **10** *n.* A sudden or urgent press of traffic or business.

rush² [rush] *n.* Any of various grasslike plants growing in marshy ground and having round, strong, flexible stems that are often used in making baskets, mats, seats of chairs, etc.

rush hour A time when traffic or business is at its height.

rusk [rusk] *n.* **1** A bread or cake that has been made crisp and brown in an oven. **2** A light, sweetened bread or biscuit.

rus·set [rus′it] **1** *n., adj.* Reddish or yellowish brown. **2** *n.* Coarse homemade cloth of this

---

add, āce, câre, pälm;   end, ēqual;   it, īce;   odd, ōpen, ôrder;   tŏŏk, pōōl;   up, bûrn;

ə = a in *above*, e in *sicken*, i in *possible*, o in *melon*, u in *circus*;   yōō = u in *fuse*;   oil;   pout;

check; ring; thin; this; zh in *vision*.   For ¶ reference, see page 64 · HOW TO

color. **3** *n*. A type of apple, greenish with brown spots.

Rus·sia [rush′ə] *n*. **1** The Union of Soviet Socialist Republics; Soviet Union: an unofficial, informal name. **2** The largest republic of the Soviet Union. **3** Before 1917, an empire of eastern Europe and northern Asia. It was ruled by a czar.

Rus·sian [rush′ən] **1** *adj*. Of or from Russia. **2** *n*. A person born in or a citizen of the Soviet Union or of the Russian empire. **3** *n*. The chief language of the Soviet Union.

rust [rust] **1** *n*. The reddish or dark brown coating formed on iron or steel surfaces that have been exposed to moist air. **2** *n., adj*. Reddish brown. **3** *n*. A fungus disease of plants that causes dark blotches on leaves and stems. **4** *v*. To become or cause to become coated with rust. **5** *v*. To make or become weakened or harmed through disuse: to allow one's talents to *rust*.

rus·tic [rus′tik] **1** *adj*. Of or having to do with the country; rural. **2** *n*. A country person of simple manners or character. **3** *adj*. Plain; simple: *rustic* clothes. **4** *adj*. Not polished or refined; awkward: *rustic* manners. **5** *adj*. Roughly and simply made, as of trees or branches: a *rustic* bridge. — **rus′ti·cal·ly** *adv*.

rus·tle [rus′(ə)l] *v*. **rus·tled, rus·tling,** *n*. **1** *v*. To move or cause to move with quick, small, rubbing sounds: The leaves *rustled* in the wind; He *rustled* the papers in his hand. **2** *n*. A rustling sound. **3** *v*. To steal (cattle, etc.).

rus·tler [rus′lər] *n. U.S. informal* **1** A cattle or horse thief. **2** An energetic person.

rust·y [rus′tē] *adj*. **rust·i·er, rust·i·est,** *n*.

1 *adj*. Covered with or affected with rust: a *rusty* hinge. **2** *adj., n*. Reddish brown. **3** *adj*. Without skill, nimbleness, etc., through lack of use or practice: He is *rusty* in algebra. **4** *adj*. Dingy; faded; discolored: a *rusty* old satin dress.

rut [rut] *n., v*. **rut·ted, rut·ting 1** *n*. A sunken track in a road worn by the wheels of an automobile, etc. **2** *v*. To make a rut or ruts in: The trucks *rutted* the road. **3** *n*. A very settled, habitual, and monotonous way of acting or living: He is in a *rut*. ◆ *Rut* may come from the older English word *route*, meaning *track of an animal*.

ru·ta·ba·ga [rōō′tə·bā′gə] *n*. A turnip having a large, yellowish, edible root.

Ruth [rōōth] *n*. **1** In the Bible, a widow who left her own people and went to live with her mother-in-law, Naomi. **2** The book of the Old Testament in which this story is told.

Ruth·er·ford [ruth′ər·fərd], **Sir Ernest,** 1871–1937, British physicist born in New Zealand.

ruth·less [rōōth′lis] *adj*. Without pity, mercy, or compassion; cruel. — **ruth′less·ly** *adv*.

Rwan·da [rōō·än′də] *n*. A country in central Africa.

-ry A suffix that has the same meanings as the suffix -ERY, as in *jewelry*, a collection of jewels, *wizardry*, the actions or attitudes of a wizard, *wintry*, the state or condition of being winter, *treasury*, a place where treasure or money is kept.

Ry. Abbreviation of RAILWAY.

rye [rī] *n*. **1** The grain or seeds of a cereal grass similar to wheat, used in the making of flour and whisky, and as a feed for livestock. **2** The plant from which these seeds or grains come.

S

s or **S** [es] *n., pl*. **s's** or **S's** The 19th letter of the English alphabet.

S The symbol for the element SULFUR.

s. Abbreviation of; **1** SECOND. **2** SHILLING.

Saar [zär] *n*. **1** A river in NE France and West Germany. **2** A state in western West Germany.

Sab·bath [sab′əth] *n*. A day of the week set aside for rest and worship. Saturday is the Sabbath for Jews and some Christians. Sunday is the sabbath for most Christians.

sab·bat·i·cal [sə·bat′i·kəl] **1** *adj* Of, like, or for the Sabbath. **2** *n*. A time of rest, as the year's vacation some teachers get every seven years.

sa·ber [sā′bər] *n*. **1** A heavy cavalry sword with a curved blade. **2** In fencing, a light sword for thrusting or slashing.

sa·ber-toothed tiger [sā′bər·tōōtht′] A large extinct animal with long, curved, upper canine teeth.

sa·ble [sā′bəl] **1** *n*. A slender animal found in northern Europe and Asia, valued for its fur. **2** *n*. The valuable fur of the sable. **3** *adj. use:* a *sable* coat. **4** *n. (usually pl.)* Garments made of sable. **5** *adj., n*. Black.

sa·bot [sab′ō] *n*. **1** A wooden shoe worn by French peasants. **2** A leather shoe with a wooden sole.

sab·o·tage [sab′ə·täzh] *n., v*. **sab·o·taged, sab·o·tag·ing 1** *n*. In time of war, the act of damaging or destroying an enemy's factories, railroads, high-

Sable, about 12 in. long

ways, etc. **2** *n.* Damage to machinery, tools, products, etc., by dissatisfied workers. **3** *v.* To damage or destroy by sabotage.

sab·o·teur [sab′ə·tûr′] *n.* A person who engages in sabotage.

sa·bre [sā′bər] *n.* Another spelling of SABER.

sac [sak] *n.* A pouch or baglike part in an animal or plant, often containing a fluid.

sac·cha·rin [sak′ər·in] *n.* A very sweet substance made from coal tar. It is used as a substitute for sugar.

sac·cha·rine [sak′ər·in] **1** *adj.* Of or like sugar; sweet. **2** *adj.* Sickeningly sweet: a *saccharine* smile. **3** *n.* Saccharin.

sac·er·do·tal [sas′ər·dōt′(ə)l] *adj.* Of or having to do with a priest or the priesthood; priestly.

sa·chem [sā′chəm] *n.* The chief of a North American Indian tribe or of a group of allied tribes.

sa·chet [sa·shā′] *n.* A small, ornamental bag of perfumed powder, used for scenting clothing.

sack[1] [sak] **1** *n.* A bag, especially one of coarse cloth, for holding articles, as food, grain, etc. **2** *v.* To put into a sack. **3** *n.* The amount a sack will hold. **4** *n.* A short, loose jacket, worn by women or babies. **5** *v. slang* To dismiss (someone) from a job.

sack[2] [sak] **1** *v.* To rob or plunder (a city, town, etc.) after capturing it during a war. **2** *n.* The robbing or plundering of a captured city, town, etc.

sack·cloth [sak′klôth′] *n.* **1** Coarse cloth used for making sacks. **2** Coarse cloth worn in penance or mourning.

sack·ful [sak′fool′] *n., pl.* **sack·fuls** As much as a sack will hold: a *sackful* of potatoes.

sack·ing [sak′ing] *n.* Coarse cloth used for making sacks.

sac·ra·ment [sak′rə·mənt] *n.* **1** Any of certain very holy rites in Christian churches, as baptism, communion, etc. **2** (*usually written* Sacrament) Holy Communion. **— sac′ra·men′·tal** *adj.*

Sac·ra·men·to [sak′rə·men′tō] *n.* **1** The capital of California, in the north central part. **2** The river on which this city is located.

sa·cred [sā′krid] *adj.* **1** Of, having to do with, or intended for religion or religious use: a *sacred* book; a *sacred* building. **2** Deserving reverence, honor, or respect: a *sacred* memory; a *sacred* vow. **3** Dedicated to a person or purpose: a church *sacred* to St. Peter. **— sa′cred·ness** *n.*

sac·ri·fice [sak′rə·fīs] *n., v.* **sac·ri·ficed, sac·ri·fic·ing** **1** *n.* The act of offering something, as the life of an animal or human being, to a god in worship or atonement. **2** *n.* The thing so offered. **3** *v.* To make an offering of (an animal, human being, etc.) to a god. **4** *n.* A giving up of something cherished, usually for the sake of something else. **5** *n.* The thing which is given up:

My brothers made a *sacrifice* of their weekends to paint the house. **6** *v.* To give up (something) for someone or something else: She *sacrificed* her own comfort for that of her children. **7** *n.* Loss, as of profit, life, etc.: to sell at a *sacrifice*; The flood caused great *sacrifice* of life. **8** *v.* To sell at a loss. **9** *n.* In baseball, a bunt or fly that allows a runner to reach the next base although the batter is put out.

sac·ri·fi·cial [sak′rə·fish′əl] *adj.* Of, having to do with, or like a sacrifice.

sac·ri·lege [sak′rə·lij] *n.* An act of disrespect for anything sacred. **— sac′ri·le′gious** *adj.*

sac·ris·tan [sak′ris·tən] *n.* A person having charge of the sacristy of a church.

sac·ris·ty [sak′ris·tē] *n., pl.* **sac·ris·ties** A room in a church for the sacred vessels and robes; vestry.

sac·ro·sanct [sak′rō·sangkt] *adj.* Extremely sacred.

sad [sad] *adj.* **sad·der, sad·dest** **1** Unhappy or depressed; sorrowful: to feel *sad*; a *sad* glance. **2** Causing sorrow or pity; distressing: a *sad* sight. **3** *informal* Not good enough: a *sad* effort. **— sad′ly** *adv.*

sad·den [sad′(ə)n] *v.* To make or become sad.

sad·dle [sad′(ə)l] *n., v.* **sad·dled, sad·dling** **1** *n.* A seat or pad for a rider, as on a horse, bicycle, etc. **2** *v.* To put a saddle on: to *saddle* a horse. **3** *n.* A padded cushion for a horse's back, used as part of a harness, to support a pack, etc. **4** *v.* To load, as with a burden, responsibility, etc.: Don't *saddle* me with your troubles. **5** *n.* Something shaped like a saddle. **6** *n.* A cut of meat that includes the undivided hindquarters and both loins. **— in the saddle** In control.

Saddle

sad·dle·bag [sad′(ə)l·bag′] *n.* One of a pair of pouches slung over a horse's back or attached to a saddle.

saddle horse A horse suitable for riding.

sad·dler [sad′lər] *n.* **1** A maker of saddles, harnesses, etc. **2** A saddle horse.

saddle shoes Oxford shoes in a light color with a dark band across the instep.

sad·ist [sā′dist *or* sad′ist] *n.* A person who gets pleasure from being cruel to others. **— sa·dis·tic** [sə·dis′tik] *adj.*

sad·ness [sad′nis] *n.* A being sad.

sa·fa·ri [sə·fä′rē] *n., pl.* **sa·fa·ris** An expedition or journey, as for hunting, especially in eastern Africa.

safe [sāf] *adj.* **saf·er, saf·est, n.** **1** *adj.* Free or freed from danger or evil: *safe* from temptation; *safe* from thieves. **2** *adj.* Not injured; unharmed.

3 *adj.* Not risky; involving no loss: a *safe* invest-ment. **4** *adj.* Trustworthy: a *safe* guide. **5** *adj.* Not likely to cause or do harm; careful: *safe* driving. **6** *n.* A strong metal box for protecting valuables. **7** *adj.* In baseball, having reached base without being put out. — **safe′ly** *adv.*

safe·con·duct [sāf′kon′·dukt] *n.* **1** Protection given to a person passing through a hostile area, as in wartime. **2** A paper authorizing this.

safe·guard [sāf′gärd′] **1** *n.* A person or thing that pro-tects one from danger, in-jury, illness, etc.: a *safeguard* against infection. **2** *v.* To pro-tect or guard.

Safe

safe·keep·ing [sāf′kē′ping] *n.* A keeping or being kept in safety: She gave him her jewels for *safekeeping*.

safe·ty [sāf′tē] *n., pl.* **safe·ties,** *adj.* **1** *n.* Freedom from danger, risk, or injury. **2** *n.* A device or catch designed as a safeguard: the *safety* on a gun. **3** *adj.* Giving or designed to give safety: *safety* glass; a *safety* match; a *safety* valve.

safety belt 1 A belt that goes around the waist and is fastened at both ends to a fixed object, used to prevent falling, worn by window clean-ers, telephone linemen, etc. **2** A seat belt.

safety glass Two sheets of glass having a film of transparent plastic between them that keeps them glued together and prevents shattering.

safety match A match that will light only when struck on a specially treated surface.

safety pin A pin whose point fastens within a protective guard, where it cannot prick.

safety razor A razor that has a metal guard for the blade, in order to prevent accidental cutting of the skin.

safety valve 1 A valve in a steam boiler, etc., that opens automatically to let out steam when the pressure mounts too high. **2** Any outlet for excess energy or emotion.

saf·flow·er [saf′lou′ər] *n.* **1** An Old World herb with spiny heads of orange or red flowers and seeds rich in oil. **2** Its flower heads, used as a dyestuff and to make medicine.

saf·fron [saf′rən] **1** *n.* A variety of crocus. **2** *n.* The dried, yellow-orange center parts of this flower, used in foods for coloring and season-ing. **3** *n., adj.* Bright yellow-orange.

sag [sag] *v.* **sagged, sag·ging,** *n.* **1** *v.* To bend or sink from weight or pressure, especially in the middle. **2** *n.* A place or part that sags: a *sag* in the roof. **3** *v.* To hang unevenly: The hem of her dress *sags*. **4** *v.* To lose strength; weaken, as from being tired, etc.: our spirits *sagged*. **5** *v.* To go down, as in price or value.

sa·ga [sä′gə] *n.* **1** An ancient Scandinavian story of heroes and their deeds. **2** A long story or novel, often telling the history of a family.

sa·ga·cious [sə·gā′shəs] *adj.* Having or show-ing wisdom or shrewdness. — **sa·ga′cious·ly** *adv.*

sa·gac·i·ty [sə·gas′ə·tē] *n.* The quality of being sagacious; ready and accurate judgment; wisdom; shrewdness.

sag·a·more [sag′ə·môr] *n.* A North American Indian chief, usually an Algonquin chief lower in rank than a sachem.

sage[1] [sāj] *adj.* **sag·er, sag·est,** *n.* **1** *adj.* Having or showing great wisdom and good judg-ment: a *sage* remark. **2** *n.* A person of great wisdom. — **sage′ly** *adv.*

sage[2] [sāj] *n.* **1** An herb related to mint, with gray-green leaves, used as a seasoning in food. **2** Sagebrush.

sage·brush [sāj′brush′] *n.* A bitter herb or small shrub with white or yellow flowers, found on the dry plains of the western U.S.

sa·go [sā′gō] *n., pl.* **sa·gos 1** Any of several varieties of palm trees. **2** A starch made from the soft pith of these palms, used to thicken pud-dings, etc.

sa·gua·ro [sə·gwä′rō] *n.* A large desert cactus of the sw U.S.

Sa·har·a [sə·har′ə] *n.* The world's largest desert area, in northern Af-rica.

sa·hib [sä′ib] *n.* Master; sir: a title used in India and Pakistan for men of high rank, especially, for-merly, for Europeans.

said [sed] **1** Past tense and past participle of SAY. **2** *adj.* In legal documents, mentioned before; named before: the *said* party.

sail [sāl] **1** *n.* A piece of strong cloth, as canvas, opened to catch the wind so as to make a ship or boat move on the water. **2** *n.* A boat

Saguaro

or ship having sails. **3** *v.* To manage or steer a boat with sails: Can you *sail*? **4** *adj. use:* a *sailing* ship. **5** *n.* A trip in a sailing ship or in any boat or ship. **6** *v.* To move forward by means of wind and sails: Does it *sail* well? **7** *v.* To travel over water in a ship or boat: to *sail* to Europe. **8** *v.* To begin a voyage over water: We *sail* at dawn. **9** *v.* To move across in a ship or boat: to *sail* the Great Lakes. **10** *n.* Something resem-bling a sail, as one of the broad arms of a wind-mill. **11** *v.* To move, glide, or float in the air: Clouds *sailed* by. **12** *v.* To move in a swift but dignified manner: She *sailed* into the room. — **make sail 1** To open to the wind a sail or sails. **2** To set out on a voyage. — **sail into** *informal* **1** To begin with energy: He *sailed into* his studies. **2** To attack, scold, etc.: She *sailed into* me for not doing the work. — **set sail** To begin a voyage. — **under sail** With sails open to the wind.

sail·boat [sāl′bōt′] *n.* A small boat moved by means of a sail or sails.

sail·cloth [sāl′klôth′] *n.* A closely woven canvas or other material suitable for sails.

sail·fish [sāl′fish′] *n., pl.* **sail·fish** or **sail·fish·es** Any of several ocean fishes having a long body, a spearlike snout, and a large fin on the back that looks like a sail.

Sailfish, to about 11 ft. long

sail·or [sā′lər] *n.* **1** A person who is a member of a ship's crew: a *sailor* in the Navy. **2** A person traveling on water, especially when thought of in terms of whether or not he becomes seasick: Are you a good or a bad *sailor*? **3** A straw hat having a low, flat crown and a brim.

saint [sānt] *n.* **1** A very holy person, especially one who, after his death, has been declared by the Roman Catholic Church to be a saint. **2** Any very good, patient, and unselfish person. ◆ In this dictionary, individual saints are listed under their given names. Place names beginning with **Saint** are listed under **St.**

Saint Ber·nard [bər·närd′] A large dog having a thick, white and brown coat and a massive head, formerly used to rescue travelers lost in the snow in the Swiss Alps.

Saint Bernard, about 27 in. high at shoulder

saint·ed [sān′tid] *adj.* **1** Officially declared a saint; canonized. **2** Very holy; saintly.

saint·hood [sānt′hŏŏd] *n.* The quality or condition of being a saint.

saint·ly [sānt′lē] *adj* **saint·li·er, saint·li·est** Of, like, or fit for a saint. — **saint′li·ness** *n.*

Saint Patrick's Day March 17th, a day celebrated by the Irish in honor of their patron saint.

Saint Valentine's Day February 14th, the anniversary of the beheading of St. Valentine by the Romans, and also a day on which valentines are exchanged.

saith [seth] *v.* An old form of SAYS: used in the Bible, old poetry, etc.

sake [sāk] *n.* **1** Purpose, reason, or aim: Speak slowly for the *sake* of clarity. **2** Welfare; interest; benefit: for your own *sake*.

sa·laam [sə·läm′] **1** *n.* A word that means *peace* and used as a greeting. **2** *n.* A low bow with the palm of the right hand held to the forehead, used in parts of the Orient. **3** *v.* To make a salaam.

sal·a·ble [sā′lə·bəl] *adj.* Fit to be sold; wanted enough to attract buyers: Is the car still *salable*? — **sal′a·bil′i·ty** *n.*

sal·ad [sal′əd] *n.* A mixture of vegetables, usually uncooked and served with a dressing, as of oil, vinegar, etc. A salad can also be made with chopped meat, fish, fruit, etc.

sal·a·man·der [sal′ə·man′dər] *n.* **1** A small lizardlike animal related to the frog, having a smooth, moist skin and living in damp places. **2** In myths, a lizard believed to live in fire.

Salamander, about 3 in. long

sa·la·mi [sə·lä′mē] *n., pl.* **sa·la·mis** A salted, spiced sausage, originally Italian.

sal·a·ried [sal′ər·ēd] *adj.* **1** Getting a salary: a *salaried* worker. **2** Providing a salary: a *salaried* job.

sal·a·ry [sal′ər·ē] *n., pl.* **sal·a·ries** A sum of money paid at regular times to professional and white-collar workers and to executives.

sale [sāl] *n.* **1** The act of selling or exchanging goods or property for money. **2** The selling of goods at bargain prices: a *sale* on shirts. **3** An auction. — **for sale** Offered or ready to be sold: a house *for sale*. — **on sale** Offered at bargain prices: This suit is *on sale*.

sale·a·ble [sā′lə·bəl] *adj* Another spelling of SALABLE.

Sa·lem [sā′ləm] *n.* **1** A city in NE Massachusetts. **2** The capital of Oregon.

sales check [sālz] A piece of paper on which a store records the items purchased by a particular customer, the price of the items, etc.

sales·clerk [sālz′klûrk′] *n. U.S.* A clerk who sells goods in a store.

sales·man [sālz′mən] *n., pl.* **sales·men** [sālz′mən] A man whose job is selling goods, stock, insurance, etc., either in a store or office or by going to prospective customers.

sales·man·ship [sālz′mən·ship] *n.* **1** The work of a salesman. **2** Ability or skill in selling.

sales tax A tax based on the amount paid for goods bought, usually added to the price of the merchandise.

sales·wom·an [sālz′wŏŏm′ən] *n., pl.* **sales·wom·en** [sālz′wim′in] A woman whose job is selling goods, as in a store.

sa·li·ent [sā′lē·ənt] *adj.* Standing out; easily seen or perceived: a *salient* feature in a landscape; the *salient* points of an argument.

sa·line [sā′lēn] **1** *adj.* Of, like, or containing a salt, especially common salt: a *saline* solution. **2** *n.* A salt solution used by biologists and in medicine.

Salis·bur·y steak [sôlz′ber·ē *or* sôlz′brē] Hamburger, usually mixed with seasonings and formed into patties.

sa·li·va [sə·lī′və] *n.* The liquid produced by certain glands in the mouth; spit. It helps to prepare food for digestion.

sal·i·var·y [sal′ə·ver′ē] *adj.* Of or producing saliva: *salivary* glands.

sal·i·vate [sal′ə·vāt] *v.* **sal·i·vat·ed, sal·i·vat·ing** To produce saliva. — **sal′i·va′tion** *n.*

---

add, āce, câre, pälm;   end, ēqual;   it, īce;   odd, ōpen, ôrder;   tŏŏk, pŏŏl;   up, bûrn;   ə = a in *above*, e in *sicken*, i in *possible*, o in *melon*, u in *circus*;   yŏŏ = u in *fuse*;   oil;   pout;   check;   ring;   thin;   this;   zh in *vision*.   For ¶ reference, see page 64 · HOW TO

Salk [sôk], **Jonas Edward,** born 1914, U.S. doctor and bacteriologist who developed a vaccine for polio.

sal·low [sal′ō] *adj.* Of an unhealthy, yellowish color: said chiefly of the human skin.

sal·ly [sal′ē] *v.* **sal·lied, sal·ly·ing,** *n., pl.* **sal·lies 1** *v.* To rush forth or go out suddenly and with energy: We *sallied* forth into the great woods. **2** *n.* A sudden rushing forth: The troops made a *sally* out of the enemy fort. **3** *n.* A little trip or excursion. **4** *n.* A witty remark.

salm·on [sam′ən] **1** *n.* Any of several food fishes having a delicate pink flesh. Salmon live in the Atlantic and Pacific Oceans and swim far up the coastal rivers when it is time to spawn. **2** *n., adj.* Reddish or pinkish orange.

Salmon, to 5 ft. long

sa·lon [sə·lon′] *n.* **1** A rather elaborate and formal room for entertaining guests. **2** A more or less regular meeting of artists, writers, statesmen, etc., in the home of a wealthy or prominent person. **3** A gallery for showing works of art. **4** A business offering some particular service: a beauty *salon.*

sa·loon [sə·lōōn′] *n.* **1** A place where alcoholic drinks are sold; bar. **2** A large, often elaborate room, as the dining room of a ship.

sal·si·fy [sal′sə·fē] *n., pl.* **sal·si·fies** A plant with a white edible root that tastes like oysters.

sal soda [sal] A type of soda used for washing and bleaching.

salt [sôlt] **1** *n.* A white crystalline compound, sodium chloride, found in sea water and as a mineral in the earth. It is used to season and preserve foods, in chemical processes, etc. **2** *adj.* Flavored with salt; salty: *salt* crackers. **3** *v.* To put salt on or in: to *salt* food; to *salt* ice. **4** *v.* To cure or preserve with salt: to *salt* meat. **5** *adj.* Cured or preserved with salt: *salt* pork. **6** *adj.* Containing salt: *salt* water. **7** *adj.* Growing in or overflowed by salt water: *salt* marshes. **8** *n.* In chemistry, a compound consisting of the negative ion of an acid and a metallic or other positive ion except that of hydrogen. **9** *n.* (*pl.*) A medicine used as a laxative. **10** *n.* (*pl.*) Smelling salts. **11** *n. informal* A sailor: an old *salt.* **12** *n.* Anything that gives zest, flavor, or sharpness to something: the *salt* of her wit. **13** *v.* To add zest, fun, or flavor to: to *salt* one's speech with anecdotes. — **salt away 1** To pack or preserve in salt. **2** *informal* To save or hoard, as money. — **salt down** To pack in salt for preserving. — **salt of the earth** The best, kindest, and truest people of the world. — **take with a grain of salt** To have doubts about the truth of. — **worth one's salt** To be worth one's salary, board, etc.

salt·cel·lar [sôlt′sel′ər] *n.* A small container for salt, commonly either an open dish or a shaker, for use at the table. ◆ *Saltcellar* was formed by combining *salt* with *cellar.* The *cellar* part comes from the French word *salière,* which means *saltcellar* and which to English-speaking people sounded like *cellar* [sel′ər], the underground part of a building.

sal·tine [sôl·tēn′] *n.* A crisp, salty cracker.

Salt Lake City The capital of Utah.

salt lick A place, as a dried salt pond, where animals go to lick salt.

salt·pe·ter or **salt·pe·tre** [sôlt′pē′tər] *n.* Any of several minerals that contain nitrates, used in gunpowder, fireworks, fertilizers, etc.

salt·shak·er [sôlt′shā′kər] *n.* A closed container with small holes in its top for sprinkling salt on food.

salt·wa·ter [sôlt′wô′tər] *adj.* Of or living in salt water: *salt-water* plants.

salt·y [sôl′tē] *adj.* **salt·i·er, salt·i·est 1** Tasting of or containing salt. **2** Witty and spicy: a *salty* remark. — **salt′i·ness** *n.*

sa·lu·bri·ous [sə·lōō′brē·əs] *adj.* Good for the health; wholesome: *salubrious* air.

sal·u·tar·y [sal′yə·ter′ē] *adj.* **1** Useful; beneficial: *salutary* advice. **2** Healthful.

sal·u·ta·tion [sal′yə·tā′shən] *n.* **1** A saluting. **2** Any form of greeting. **3** The opening words of a letter, as *Dear Sir.*

sa·lu·ta·to·ri·an [sə·lōō′tə·tôr′ē·ən] *n. U.S.* In schools and colleges, the graduating student who receives the second highest honors and who delivers the salutatory at commencement.

sa·lu·ta·to·ry [sə·lōō′tə·tôr′ē] *n., pl.* **sa·lu·ta·to·ries,** *adj.* **1** *n.* An opening speech, as at a school commencement. **2** *adj.* Giving or expressing a greeting or welcome.

sa·lute [sə·lōōt′] *v.* **sa·lut·ed, sa·lut·ing,** *n.* **1** *v.* To recognize and honor (a superior, leader, flag, etc.) in some special way, as by raising the hand to the forehead, firing guns, etc.: to *salute* an army officer; to *salute* a ship carrying an admiral. **2** *v.* To make a salute: He *saluted* smartly when he saw us. **3** *v.* To greet with a friendly sign of welcome or respect: He *saluted* the ladies with a little bow. **4** *n.* The act of saluting: The young lieutenant's *salute* was perfectly executed.

A salute

sal·vage [sal′vij] *v.* **sal·vaged, sal·vag·ing,** *n.* **1** *v.* To save from being wrecked, ruined, burned, etc.: They *salvaged* the ship and its cargo; He *salvaged* a few clothes from the fire. **2** *n.* The saving of a ship or its cargo from loss or destruction. **3** *n.* The money paid for this. **4** *n.* The act of salvaging anything. **5** *n.* Something salvaged.

sal·va·tion [sal·vā′shən] *n.* **1** The condition of being saved or preserved from danger, evil, etc. **2** Something that saves: The dog's barking was our *salvation* when the house caught fire. **3** In Christian belief, the saving of the soul from sin or from the punishment for sin.

Salvation Army A religious organization engaged in bringing Christianity and help to the poor or to those in trouble.

salve [sav] *n., v.* **salved, salv·ing 1** *n.* A soothing or healing ointment for wounds, burns, sores, etc. **2** *n.* Anything that heals, soothes, calms, etc.: Your kind words were a *salve* to our discouragement. **3** *v.* To soothe or calm.

sal·ver [sal′vər] *n.* A tray, as of silver.

sal·vo [sal′vō] *n., pl.* **sal·vos** or **sal·voes 1** The firing of a number of guns at the same time to hit a target or give a salute. **2** An outburst, as of cheering: a *salvo* of applause.

Sa·mar·i·a [sə·mâr′ē·ə] *n.* **1** In the Bible, a northern part of Palestine. **2** Its main city.

Sa·mar·i·tan [sə·mar′ə·tən] *n.* **1** A person born in or living in ancient Samaria. **2** A person like the Good Samaritan, who helps another in distress.

same [sām] **1** *adj.* Being alike, identical, or equal in every way: Men and women should get the *same* wages for the *same* work. **2** *adj.* Alike or similar in some ways, but not in all: The two boys are of the *same* height. **3** *adj.* Not different; unchanged: My uncle is not the *same* man since his illness. **4** *pron.* The same or identical person or thing. **5** *adv.* In like manner; equally: You must love them the *same* as you do us. — **all the same 1** Nevertheless; however. **2** Equally acceptable or unacceptable; of no importance: It's *all the same* to me. — **just the same 1** Nevertheless; however. **2** Exactly alike or identical. **3** In the same way or manner.

same·ness [sām′nis] *n.* **1** Lack of change or variety: There is a *sameness* in your writing. **2** A being alike or identical: a *sameness* in color.

sam·i·sen [sam′i·sen] *n.* A Japanese guitarlike instrument, having three strings and played with a plectrum.

sa·mite [sā′mīt *or* sam′īt] *n.* A rich fabric of silk often woven with gold or silver threads, used in the Middle Ages.

Sa·mo·a [sə·mō′ə] *n.* An island group in the sw Pacific; divided into **American** or **Eastern Samoa,** a territory of the U.S., and **Western Samoa,** an independent country.

sam·o·var [sam′ə·vär] *n.* A metal urn for heating water, as for making tea, widely used in Russia.

sam·pan [sam′pan] *n.* A small boat sculled with an oar or oars, having a flat bottom and sometimes a sail, used in China and Japan.

sam·ple [sam′pəl] *n., v.* **sam·pled, sam·pling 1** *n.* A part or single piece that shows what the whole is like or is an example of quality: a *sample* of his handwriting. **2** *adj.* use: a *sample* drawing. **3** *v.* To test or examine by samples: to *sample* a mince pie.

Samovar

sam·pler [sam′plər] *n.* **1** A person who samples. **2** A piece of cloth covered with designs, mottoes, etc., done in fancy needlework.

sam·pling [sam′pling] *n.* **1** A small part of something or a number of items from a group chosen for examination in order to estimate the quality or nature of the whole. **2** The act or process of making such a selection.

Sam·son [sam′sən] *n.* **1** In the Bible, a Hebrew judge of great strength. **2** Any very strong man.

Sam·u·el [sam′yoo·əl] *n.* **1** In the Bible, a Hebrew judge and prophet. **2** Either of two books of the Old Testament named for him.

sam·u·rai [sam′oo·rī] *n., pl.* **sam·u·rai 1** In the Japanese feudal system of former times, a soldier who was a member of the lower nobility. **2** A professional Japanese soldier.

San An·to·ni·o [san an·tō′nē·ō] A city in southern Texas, location of the Alamo.

san·a·to·ri·um [san′ə·tôr′ē·əm] *n., pl.* **san·a·to·ri·ums** or **san·a·to·ri·a** [san′ə·tôr′ē·ə] Another spelling of SANITARIUM.

sanc·ti·fy [sangk′tə·fī] *v.* **sanc·ti·fied, sanc·ti·fy·ing 1** To set apart as holy or for holy purposes; consecrate: to *sanctify* a chapel. **2** To free from sin; make holy. **3** To give approval or sanction to: a custom *sanctified* by long use. — **sanc′ti·fi·ca′tion** *n.*

sanc·ti·mo·ni·ous [sangk′tə·mō′nē·əs] *adj.* Pretending to be religious; insincerely righteous or holy. — **sanc′ti·mo′ni·ous·ly** *adv.*

sanc·tion [sangk′shən] **1** *n.* Final and official approval or confirmation of something: Does this rule have the *sanction* of the committee? **2** *v.* To approve officially; confirm; ratify: to *sanction* a new rule. **3** *v.* To permit or allow: How can you *sanction* all this noise? **4** *n.* (*usually pl.*) The steps or measures taken, usually by several nations, to force another nation to obey international law.

sanc·ti·ty [sangk′tə·tē] *n., pl.* **sanc·ti·ties 1** Holiness; saintliness: the *sanctity* of his life. **2** The condition of being very sacred and solemn: the *sanctity* of a religious vow.

sanc·tu·ar·y [sangk′choo·er′ē] *n., pl.* **sanc·tu·ar·ies 1** A holy or sacred place, especially a church or the place in a church where the main altar is located. **2** A place where people or animals can find refuge and safety: a bird *sanctuary*. **3** Safety and peace, as found in a sanctuary: the *sanctuary* of a quiet library.

sanc·tum [sangk′təm] *n., pl.* **sanc·tums** or **sanc·ta** [sangk′tə] **1** A sacred place. **2** A private room where one is not to be disturbed.

sand [sand] **1** *n.* Particles of worn or broken rocks, larger than dust and smaller than gravel, most common in deserts and on beaches. **2** *n.* (*pl.*) Stretches of sandy beach, desert, etc. **3** *v.* To sprinkle, cover, or fill with sand. **4** *v.* To smooth with sand or sandpaper.

add, āce, câre, pälm; end, ēqual; it, īce; odd, ōpen, ôrder; took, pool; up, bûrn;
ə = a in *above*, e in *sicken*, i in *possible*, o in *melon*, u in *circus*; yoo = u in *fuse*; oil; pout;
check; ring; thin; this; zh in *vision*. For ¶ reference, see page 64 · HOW TO

san·dal [san'dəl] *n.* **1** A kind of shoe that usually consists of a sole held to the foot by straps. **2** A light, low-cut shoe with parts of the uppers cut out.

san·dal·wood [san'dəl·wŏŏd'] *n.* The hard, fragrant wood of certain East Indian trees. The wood is used for carvings, boxes, etc., and burned as incense.

Greek sandals

sand·bag [sand'bag'] *n., v.* **sand·bagged, sand·bag·ging 1** *n.* A bag filled with sand, used as ballast in balloons, or to build walls against a flood, enemy fire, etc. **2** *v.* To fill or surround with sandbags. **3** *n.* A small bag filled with sand, used as a weapon. **4** *v.* To hit with a sandbag.

sand·bank [sand'bangk'] *n.* A mound, bar, or shoal made of sand.

sand·bar [sand'bär'] *n.* A ridge of sand in rivers, along beaches, etc., formed by the action of currents or tides.

sand·blast [sand'blast'] **1** *n.* A fine stream of sand, propelled under steam or air pressure and used to clean, grind, or decorate hard surfaces. **2** *v.* To clean or engrave by means of a sandblast: to *sandblast* a building.

Sand·burg [sand'bûrg], **Carl,** born 1878, U.S. poet and biographer.

sand dollar Any small, flat sea urchin having a circular shell.

sand·er [san'dər] *n.* A machine that smooths, polishes, etc., by means of a disk or belt of sandpaper or other rough material.

San Di·e·go [san dē·ā'gō] A city in sw California.

sand·man [sand'man'] *n.* An imaginary person who is supposed to make children sleepy by putting sand in their eyes.

sand·pa·per [sand'pā'pər] **1** *n.* Heavy paper with sand glued on one side, used for smoothing and polishing. **2** *v.* To rub or polish with sandpaper.

sand·pi·per [sand'pī'pər] *n.* Any of certain small wading birds found in flocks on seashores.

sand·stone [sand'stōn'] *n.* A rock composed mainly of sand, held together by silica, clay, lime, etc., used as a building material.

sand·storm [sand'stôrm'] *n.* A strong wind that blows great clouds of sand and dust before it.

Sandpiper, 7–9 in. long

sand·wich [sand'wich *or* san'wich] **1** *n.* Two thin slices of bread with meat, cheese, etc., between them. **2** *v.* To place or squeeze between two objects: Our car was *sandwiched* between two large trucks. ◆ *Sandwich* is named after the fourth Earl of *Sandwich*, 1718–1792, who invented it in order to be able to eat without leaving the gambling table.

Sandwich Islands A former name of the HAWAIIAN ISLANDS.

sand·y [san'dē] *adj.* **sand·i·er, sand·i·est 1** Containing, covered with, or full of sand: a *sandy* beach. **2** Yellowish red: a *sandy* beard.

sane [sān] *adj.* **san·er, san·est 1** Mentally healthy and sound; rational. **2** Reasonable and sensible: a *sane* rule. — **sane'ly** *adv.*

San·for·ized [san'fə·rīzd] *adj.* Treated, as cloth, by a special process that prevents shrinking: a trademark. Also written **sanforized.**

San Fran·cis·co [san'frən·sis'kō] A city in western California, on **San Francisco Bay.**

sang [sang] Past tense of SING.

san·gui·nar·y [sang'gwə·ner'ē] *adj.* **1** Accompanied by bloodshed; bloody: a *sanguinary* murder. **2** Bloodthirsty.

san·guine [sang'gwin] *adj.* **1** Cheerful, confident, or hopeful; optimistic: a *sanguine* disposition. **2** Having a healthy, rosy color, as the skin; ruddy.

san·i·tar·i·um [san'ə·târ'ē·əm] *n., pl.* **san·i·tar·i·ums** or **san·i·tar·i·a** [san'ə·târ'ē·ə] A place where people having or recovering from certain illnesses, as tuberculosis, live and receive treatment.

san·i·tar·y [san'ə·ter'ē] *adj.* **1** Of or having to do with health or the preservation of health: *sanitary* measures. **2** Having or marked by great cleanliness: a *sanitary* container for food.

san·i·ta·tion [san'ə·tā'shən] *n.* **1** The preservation of good health by sanitary methods and measures: Garbage disposal is a method of *sanitation*. **2** The act or result of making something sanitary.

san·i·tize [san'ə·tīz] *v.* **san·i·tized, san·i·tiz·ing** To make sanitary, as by sterilizing.

san·i·ty [san'ə·tē] *n.* **1** The condition of having a sound, healthy mind. **2** Sensible moderation; reasonableness.

San Jo·sé scale [san' hō·zā'] An insect that is destructive to various fruit trees.

San Juan [san hwän'] The capital of Puerto Rico, in the NE part.

sank [sangk] Past tense of SINK.

sans [sanz] *prep.* The French word for *without*: *Sans* beauty, *sans* art, what is life?

San Sal·va·dor [san' sal'və·dôr] **1** The capital of El Salvador. **2** An island in the Bahamas where Columbus first landed in the New World.

San·skrit or **San·scrit** [san'skrit] *n.* The ancient, classical language of India, related to most European languages.

San·ta [san'tə] *n.* Santa Claus.

Santa Claus [klôz] A legendary, fat, jolly, old man with a white beard, supposed to bring presents to children at Christmas. ◆ *Santa Claus* comes from a Dutch dialect pronunciation of *Saint Nicholas.*

San·ta Fe [san'tə fā'] *n.* The capital of New Mexico.

San·ti·a·go [san'tē·ä'gō] *n.* The capital of Chile, in the central part.

San·to Do·min·go [san'tō dō·ming'gō] *n.* The

capital of the Dominican Republic, the first city established by Europeans in the New World.

sap[1] [sap] *n.* **1** The juices that flow through a plant, bringing the materials necessary for growth to its cells. **2** *slang* A foolish person.

sap[2] [sap] *v.* **sapped, sap·ping 1** To weaken by undermining: Termites can *sap* the foundation of a house. **2** To weaken or destroy gradually; impair or exhaust: Overwork *sapped* her strength.

sa·pi·ent [sā′pē·ənt] *adj.* Having great knowledge; wise. **— sa′pi·ence** *n.*

sap·ling [sap′ling] *n.* A young tree.

sa·pon·i·fy [sə·pon′ə·fī] *v.* **sa·pon·i·fied, sa·pon·i·fy·ing** To break up (a fat or oil) with an alkali to form a soap or glycerin. **— sa·pon·i·fi·ca·tion** [sə·pon′ə·fə·kā′shən] *n.*

sap·phire [saf′īr] **1** *n.* A valuable gem having a clear, deep blue color. **2** *adj., n.* Deep blue.

sap·py [sap′ē] *adj.* **sap·pi·er, sap·pi·est 1** Full of sap; juicy. **2** *slang* Childish; silly.

sap·ro·phyte [sap′rə·fīt] *n.* A plant that lives on dead or decaying organic matter, as certain bacteria or fungi.

sap·suck·er [sap′suk′ər] *n.* Any of several small black and white woodpeckers that damage orchard trees by drinking the sap.

sap·wood [sap′wood′] *n.* The moist, usually whitish wood that grows just under the bark of a tree and is the main conductor of sap.

Sapsucker, 8–9 in. long

Sar·a·cen [sar′ə·sən] *n.* **1** A Moslem, especially one during the Crusades. **2** Any Arab.

Sar·ah [sâr′ə] *n.* In the Bible, the mother of Isaac and the wife of Abraham.

sar·casm [sär′kaz·əm] *n.* **1** A cutting, unpleasant remark that mocks or makes fun of something or someone. **2** The use of cutting or mocking language.

sar·cas·tic [sär·kas′tik] *adj.* **1** Mocking; taunting: a *sarcastic* smile. **2** Using sarcasm: a *sarcastic* old man.

sar·coph·a·gus [sär·kof′ə·gəs] *n., pl.* **sar·coph·a·gus·es** or **sar·coph·a·gi** [sär·kof′ə·jī] A decorated stone coffin, usually placed in open view or in a large tomb.

A Greek sarcophagus

sar·dine [sär·dēn′] *n.* A small, edible fish like the herring, commonly canned in oil.

Sar·din·i·a [sär·din′·ē·ə] *n.* An island in the Mediterranean Sea. It is part of Italy.

sar·don·ic [sär·don′ik] *adj.* Bitterly scornful or sneering; cynical. **— sar·don′i·cal·ly** *adv.*

sar·gas·so [sär·gas′ō] *n.* An olive-brown seaweed with small air bladders on the stalks, found floating in great masses in warm seas.

Sargasso Sea A part of the North Atlantic, extending from the West Indies to the Azores. It is known for its relatively still water and the large amount of floating seaweed that collects there.

sa·ri [sä′rē] *n., pl.* **sa·ris** The outer garment of Hindu women. It consists of a long piece of cotton or silk cloth worn wound about the body, one end falling to the feet and the other crossed over the shoulder and sometimes over the head.

sa·rong [sə·rong′] *n.* A skirtlike garment of colored silk or cotton, worn by both sexes in Indonesia, Malaysia, etc.

sar·sa·pa·ril·la [sas′pə·ril′ə or sär′sə·pə·ril′ə] *n.* **1** The dried root of a tropical American plant of the lily family, used to flavor medicine, soft drinks, etc. **2** A soft drink flavored with this root.

sar·to·ri·al [sär·tôr′ē·əl] *adj.* **1** Having to do with a tailor or his work. **2** Having to do with men's clothes: *sartorial* splendor.

Sari

sash[1] [sash] *n., pl.* **sash·es** or **sash** A frame, as of a window, in which glass is set.

sash[2] [sash] *n.* A band, ribbon, or scarf worn around the waist or over the shoulder, often as part of a uniform or as a badge of honor.

Sas·katch·e·wan [sas·kach′ə·won′] *n.* A province of west central Canada.

sas·sa·fras [sas′ə·fras] *n.* **1** A tall North American tree related to the laurel and having yellow flowers. **2** Its dried root, whose bark is used as a flavoring in candy and in medicine.

sas·sy [sas′ē] *adj.* **sas·si·er, sas·si·est** *informal* Saucy and impudent; impertinent: a *sassy* boy.

sat [sat] Past tense and past participle of SIT.

Sat. Abbreviation of SATURDAY.

Sa·tan [sā′tən] *n.* In the Bible, the Devil.

sa·tan·ic [sə·tan′ik] *adj.* Very wicked; evil.

satch·el [sach′əl] *n.* A small bag or case.

sate [sāt] *v.* **sat·ed, sat·ing 1** To satisfy (a desire or appetite) completely. **2** To supply enough to fill too full or disgust; glut.

sa·teen [sa·tēn′] *n.* A cotton cloth woven so that it has a shiny look like satin.

sat·el·lite [sat′ə·līt] *n.* **1** A celestial body that revolves in an orbit around a larger celestial body: The moon is a *satellite* of the earth. **2** An object launched by means of a rocket into an orbit around the earth or other celestial body.

add, āce, câre, pälm; end, èqual; it, īce; odd, ōpen, ôrder; to͝ok, po͞ol; up, bûrn;
ə = a in *above*, e in *sicken*, i in *possible*, o in *melon*, u in *circus*; yo͞o = u in *fuse*; oil; pout;
check; ring; thin; this; zh in *vision*. For ¶ reference, see page 64 · HOW TO

3 A small nation that is controlled by and depends upon a greater, more powerful one. **4** A person who follows or copies someone more important.

sa·ti·ate [sā′shē·āt] *v.* **sa·ti·at·ed, sa·ti·at·ing 1** To satisfy completely the appetite or desire of: The good dinner *satiated* us. **2** To make sick, disgusted, annoyed, etc., by giving or being given too much of something: The hero was *satiated* by all the noise and the cheering crowds.

sa·ti·e·ty [sə·tī′ə·tē] *n.* The condition or feeling of having had too much of something.

sat·in [sat′ən] **1** *n.* A silk, cotton, rayon, or acetate fabric with a smooth glossy finish on one side. **2** *adj.* Of or like satin.

sat·ire [sat′īr] *n.* **1** Sarcasm, irony, wit, or humor used to make known and attack or ridicule evil or foolish people, ideas, customs, or plans. **2** A written composition that attacks foolishness or evil in this way.

sa·tir·ic [sə·tir′ik] *adj.* Satirical.

sa·tir·i·cal [sə·tir′i·kəl] *adj.* **1** Of, like, having, or using satire: a *satirical* writer. **2** Sarcastic: a *satirical* smile. **— sa·tir′i·cal·ly** *adv.*

sat·i·rist [sat′ə·rist] *n.* A person who writes or uses satire.

sat·i·rize [sat′ə·rīz] *v.* **sat·i·rized, sat·i·riz·ing** To attack and make ridiculous by means of satire; criticize by means of mockery: to *satirize* the foolishness of mankind.

sat·is·fac·tion [sat′is·fak′shən] *n.* **1** The act of satisfying. **2** The condition of being satisfied. **3** Something that satisfies: It was a *satisfaction* to him to win. **4** A making up for damage, a hurt, or injury, as by a payment: He says he was slandered and demands $10,000 as *satisfaction*. **— give satisfaction 1** To satisfy. **2** To fight a duel with a person one has insulted.

sat·is·fac·to·ry [sat′is·fak′tər·ē] *adj.* Giving satisfaction; good enough to meet needs or expectations. **— sat′is·fac′to·ri·ly** *adv.*

sat·is·fy [sat′is·fī] *v.* **sat·is·fied, sat·is·fy·ing 1** To supply fully with what is wanted, expected, or needed: The meal *satisfied* them. **2** To free from doubt or worry; convince: The telegram *satisfied* her that he had arrived safely. **3** To give what is due to; pay, as a debt: He *satisfied* his creditors. **4** To fill the conditions or requirements of, as an equation.

sa·trap [sā′trap *or* sat′rap] *n.* **1** In ancient Persia, a governor of a province. **2** Any minor, and often tyrannical, ruler.

sat·u·rate [sach′ə·rāt] *v.* **sat·u·rat·ed, sat·u·rat·ing 1** To soak thoroughly or fill completely: The rain *saturated* the soil. **2** To cause to absorb a substance, influence, etc., to the point where further additions cannot be taken in: to *saturate* a solution with salt; to *saturate* a people with propaganda.

sat·u·rat·ed [sach′ə·rā′tid] *adj.* **1** Incapable of holding or absorbing more of a substance, influence, etc. **2** As pure as possible and containing no white: said about a color. **3** Fully soaked.

sat·u·ra·tion [sach′ə·rā′shən] *n.* **1** The act of saturating. **2** The condition of being saturated. **3** The degree of vividness or purity in a color, the less white in it, the more saturation.

Sat·ur·day [sat′ər·dē *or* sat′ər·dā] *n.* The seventh day of the week.

Sat·urn [sat′ərn] *n.* **1** In Roman myths, the god of agriculture. **2** A planet of the solar system, the second in order of size and the sixth in distance from the sun.

sat·ur·na·li·a [sat′ər·nā′lē·ə] *n.pl.* **1** (*written* **Saturnalia**) In ancient Rome, a feast of Saturn held in December to celebrate the winter solstice. **2** Any season or period for wild parties and riotous revelry.

sat·ur·nine [sat′ər·nīn] *adj.* Having a serious, often gloomy disposition or character.

sat·yr [sat′ər *or* sā′tər] *n.* In Greek myths, a minor woodland god, having a human form but pointed ears, goat's legs, and budding horns.

sauce [sôs] *n., v.* **sauced, sauc·ing 1** *n.* A soft or liquid mixture, as a dressing or relish, served with food to add flavor. **2** *v.* To serve with or cook in a sauce: to *sauce* a fish. **3** *v.* To flavor or season, as with sauce. **4** *n.* A dish of fruit pulp stewed and sweetened: cranberry *sauce*. **5** *n. informal* Impudence. **6** *v. informal* To be saucy to.

Satyr

sauce·pan [sôs′pan′] *n.* A metal or glass pot with a handle, used for cooking food.

sau·cer [sô′sər] *n.* **1** A small, round, shallow dish for holding a cup. **2** Something shaped like a saucer: a flying *saucer*.

sau·cy [sô′sē] *adj.* **sau·ci·er, sau·ci·est 1** Too bold; impudent. **2** Lively with a dash of daring; pert: *saucy* wit. **— sau′ci·ness** *n.*

Sau·di Arabia [sä·ōō′dē] A kingdom in the northern and central part of Arabia.

sauer·bra·ten [sour′brät(ə)n] *n.* Beef that has been marinated in vinegar and spices before being cooked. ◆ *Sauerbraten* comes from two German words meaning *sour* and *to roast*.

sauer·kraut [sour′krout′] *n.* Shredded and salted cabbage fermented in its own juice.

Saul [sôl] *n.* **1** In the Bible, the first king of Israel. **2** St. Paul's Hebrew name.

saun·ter [sôn′tər] **1** *v.* To walk along in a slow, casual way; stroll. **2** *n.* A casual walk.

sau·ri·an [sôr′ē·ən] *n.* Any of a group of reptiles with scaly bodies and usually with four limbs. This group is now restricted mainly to the lizards.

A gecko is a saurian.

sau·sage [sô′sij] *n.* Finely chopped and highly seasoned meat, usually packed into a thin tube or skin, often of prepared animal intestine.

sau·té [sō·tā′] *v.* **sau·téed** [sō·tād′], **sau·té·ing** [sō·tā′ing], *adj.* **1** *v.* To fry quickly in a little fat: to *sauté* onions. **2** *adj.* Fried quickly in this manner.

sav·age [sav′ij] **1** *adj.* Wild, untamed, and often fierce: *savage* beasts. **2** *adj.* Living in a wild condition; not civilized: *savage* tribes. **3** *n.* A person living in a wild or primitive condition. **4** *adj.* Cruel, vicious, and violent: a *savage* attack. **5** *n.* A brutal, fierce, cruel person. — **sav′age·ly** *adv.* — **sav′age·ness** *n.*

sav·age·ry [sav′ij·rē] *n.*, *pl.* **sav·age·ries 1** A savage or cruel quality. **2** A cruel, violent act. **3** A wild or savage condition.

sa·van·na or **sa·van·nah** [sə·van′ə] *n.* A grassy plain with few or no trees.

Sa·van·nah [sə·van′ə] *n.* A seaport in Georgia.

sa·vant [sə·vänt′ *or* sav′ənt] *n.* A learned man.

save¹ [sāv] *v.* **saved, sav·ing 1** To rescue or preserve from danger, harm, or loss: to *save* a man from death; to *save* a life. **2** To free or deliver from sin or evil; redeem. **3** To keep from becoming tired, hurt, damaged, etc.: *Save* your eyes by reading in a good light. **4** To prevent or spare: Your going *saves* him from having to go. **5** To keep from being spent, lost, or wasted: to *save* money, time, or energy. **6** To avoid expense, waste, or loss: She *saves* on clothes by making her own. **7** To set aside or reserve (money, etc.) for future use: to *save* ten dollars a week; *Save* my seat. — **sav′er** *n.*

save² [sāv] *prep.* Except; but: They agree on every issue *save* one.

sav·ing [sā′ving] **1** *n.* Preservation from loss or danger. **2** *adj.* That saves, preserves, or rescues: Truthfulness is her *saving* grace; a labor-*saving* device. **3** *n.* A reduction, as of effort, time, waste, etc.: a *saving* of two hours. **4** *n.* A reduction of money spent: a *saving* of 10%. **5** *adj.* Avoiding needless waste; economical. **6** *n.* (*pl.*) Money saved and set aside for the future. **7** *prep.* Except for: *Saving* one time, he was right. **8** *prep.* With due respect for: *Saving* your presence, I must say what I think.

savings bank A bank that receives and pays interest on money that people want to save.

sav·ior [sāv′yər] *n.* **1** A person who saves, as from danger. **2** (*written* **Savior**) The Saviour.

Sav·iour [sāv′yər] *n.* **1** Jesus Christ. **2** (*written* **saviour**) A savior.

sa·vor [sā′vər] **1** *n.* The taste, smell, or flavor of something: the *savor* of roast beef. **2** *v.* To taste or experience with pleasure; relish. **3** *n.* A quality that is typical or that gives relish: Life lost its *savor* for her. **4** *v.* To have a particular flavor or characteristic: His words *savor* of pride. **5** *v.* To give flavor to; season. ¶1

sa·vor·y¹ [sā′vər·ē] *adj.* **1** Pleasing to the sense of taste or smell: a *savory* steak. **2** Wholesome or respectable: a *savory* character.

sa·vor·y² [sā′vər·ē] *n.* A fragrant herb related to mint, used for seasoning.

saw¹ [sô] *n.*, *v.* **sawed, sawed** or **sawn, saw·ing 1** *n.* A tool used to cut, having a thin, flat blade with pointed teeth along or around its edge. **2** *n.* A machine for operating this tool. **3** *v.* To cut or be cut with a saw: to *saw* logs; This wood *saws* easily. **4** *v.* To fashion with a saw: to *saw* planks. **5** *v.* To cut or slice with the arms as if using a saw: to *saw* the air.

saw² [sô] *n.* A familiar saying; proverb. "All that glitters is not gold" is a saw.

saw³ [sô] Past tense of SEE¹: I *saw* you!

saw·dust [sô′dust′] *n.* Fine, dustlike bits of wood that separate from wood when it is sawed.

saw·horse [sô′hôrs′] *n.* A frame on four legs, often one of a pair, used to hold wood being sawed.

saw·mill [sô′mil′] *n.* A place where logs are sawed up by machines into planks, boards, etc.

sawn [sôn] An alternative past participle of SAW¹.

Sawhorses

saw·yer [sô′yər] *n.* A person who saws wood for a living, as in lumbering or in a sawmill.

sax·i·frage [sak′sə·frij] *n.* Any of various plants found in rocky places and bearing clusters of white, pink, purple, or yellow flowers.

Sax·on [sak′sən] **1** *n.* A member or descendant of an old Germanic tribe. Groups of Saxons invaded England in the fifth and sixth centuries. **2** *adj.* Of or having to do with these people. **3** *n.* An Anglo-Saxon. **4** *adj.* Anglo-Saxon.

Sax·o·ny [sak′sə·nē] *n.* **1** A former kingdom and province of central Germany. **2** A former state of SE East Germany.

sax·o·phone [sak′sə·fōn] *n.* A wind instrument having a single-reed mouthpiece and a body that ends in a flaring curve.

say [sā] *v.* **said** [sed], **say·ing,** *n.* **1** *v.* To pronounce or utter; speak: "Yes," she *said.* **2** *n.* Right or turn to speak: Tom had his *say.* **3** *v.* To express in words; tell; state: This note *says* that Ann is sick. **4** *n.* An opinion or belief: What is your *say* in this matter? **5** *v.* To state positively or as an opinion: *Say* which you prefer. **6** *n.* The right to decide; authority: Our teacher has the final *say.* **7** *v.* To repeat or recite: He is *saying* his prayers. **8** *v.* To suppose or assume: He is six feet tall, I'd *say.* — **go without say-**

Saxophone

ing So well understood that no discussion is needed. **— that is to say** In other words.

say·ing [sā′ing] *n.* **1** A phrase or proverb much repeated: as the *saying* goes. **2** Anything said.

says [sez] *v.* The third person form of SAY, in the present tense, used with *he, she, it,* and singular nouns: She *says* that she will go; The newspaper *says* that it will rain.

Sb The symbol for the element ANTIMONY. ◆ The Latin word for antimony is *stibium*.

S.C. Abbreviation of SOUTH CAROLINA.

scab [skab] *n., v.* **scabbed, scab·bing 1** *n.* A crust that forms over a healing wound or sore. **2** *v.* To become covered with a scab. **3** *n.* A skin disease like mange that affects sheep. **4** *n.* A disease causing crustlike spots on plants. **5** *n. informal* A worker who takes the job of another worker who is on strike. **6** *v. informal* To act as a scab. **— scab′by** *adj.*

scab·bard [skab′ərd] *n.* A case or sheath to protect the blade of a sword, bayonet, etc.

sca·bies [skā′bēz] *n.* A contagious skin ailment caused by tiny mites that get in and

A scimitar and scabbard

live as parasites under the skin. They cause intense itching.

scaf·fold [skaf′əld *or* skaf′ōld] *n.* **1** A temporary structure put up to support workmen and materials above the ground, as in building. **2** A raised platform for the hanging or beheading of criminals. **3** Any raised framework.

scaf·fold·ing [skaf′əl·ding] *n.* **1** A scaffold or system of scaffolds for workmen. **2** Materials for making scaffolds. **3** Any framework.

Scaffold

scal·a·wag [skal′ə·wag] *n.* **1** A native Southern white Republican just after the Civil War: a contemptuous term. **2** *informal* A worthless fellow; scamp.

scald [skôld] **1** *v.* To burn with hot liquid or steam: to *scald* one's arm. **2** *n.* A burn made in this way. **3** *v.* To cleanse or treat with boiling water: to *scald* cups. **4** *v.* To heat (a liquid, as milk) almost to the boiling point.

scale¹ [skāl] *n., v.* **scaled, scal·ing 1** *n.* One of the thin, flat, usually overlapping plates of horny tissue that form a protective cover on the bodies of fishes and reptiles. **2** *n.* A thin part, piece, or layer like this: *scales* of paint. **3** *v.* To strip or clear of scales or a layer of scale: to *scale* fish. **4** *v.* To come off in scales. **5** *n.* A scale insect.

scale² [skāl] *n., v.* **scaled, scal·ing 1** *n.* (*often pl.*) A balance or other device for weighing things: Are your *scales* accurate? **2** *v.* To weigh: He *scaled* 175 pounds. **3** *n.* One of the two shallow pans, scoops, or cups for holding objects to be weighed in a balance. **— tip the scales 1** To

Scales

weigh: He *tips the scales* at 220 lbs. **2** To be a deciding factor: His experience *tips the scales* in his favor. **— turn the scales** To determine or decide.

scale³ [skāl] *n., v.* **scaled, scal·ing 1** *n.* A series of lines and marks placed at regular intervals on an instrument for measuring various quantities, amounts, etc.: the *scale* on a yardstick. **2** *n.* Any system of such graduated lines or marks adapted for a special purpose: the Fahrenheit *scale*; a logarithmic *scale*. **3** *n.* A classification or scheme of different levels, ranks, or grades: a wage *scale*; the social *scale*. **4** *v.* To adjust according to a scale: to *scale* down expenses. **5** *n.* In music, a series of tones going up or down in order through the interval of an octave. **6** *v.* To go up, as by climbing a ladder: to *scale* a high wall. **7** *n.* A fixed proportion between the different parts of a map, model, drawing, etc., and the corresponding parts of what they represent: According to the *scale* of this map, one inch represents one mile. **8** *n.* Relative extent, size, or degree: He is in business on a small *scale*. **9** *n.* A system of writing numbers in terms of a base: the decimal *scale*.

scale insect Any of various small insects that feed on plants. The females are usually covered by a waxy, scalelike shield.

sca·lene [skā′lēn *or* skā·lēn′] *adj.* Having no two sides equal: said about a triangle.

scal·lion [skal′yən] *n.* An onion having a long neck and a narrow bulb, as a young green onion.

scal·lop [skol′əp *or* skal′əp] **1** *n.* A small, soft-bodied sea animal with two shells ribbed in a fan pattern and hinged at the back and a strong muscle that is good to eat. **2** *n.* One of a series of semicircular curves along an edge, as for ornament. **3** *v.* To shape the edge of with scallops. **4** *v.* To bake in a casserole with bread crumbs and a sauce. **5** *adj. use: scalloped* oysters.

scalp [skalp] **1** *n.* The skin of the top and back of the head, usually covered with hair. **2** *n.* A part of this, formerly cut or torn away as a war trophy among certain North American Indians. **3** *v.* To cut or tear the scalp from.

scal·pel [skal′pəl] *n.* A small, pointed knife with a very sharp, thin blade, used in surgery.

scal·y [skā′lē] *adj.* **scal·i·er, scal·i·est 1** Having a covering of scales: a *scaly* fish. **2** Scalelike. **3** Flaky, as stone.

scamp¹ [skamp] *n.* A tricky, mischievous rascal.

scamp² [skamp] *v.* To perform (work) carelessly.

scam·per [skam′pər] **1** *v.* To run quickly or hastily. **2** *n.* A hurried run or departure.

scan [skan] *v.* **scanned, scan·ning 1** To pass the eyes over quickly: He *scanned* the newspaper to find the story. **2** To look at or examine closely and carefully: The detective *scanned* every shred of evidence. **3** To separate (lines of verse) into rhythmic feet, as: "Thĕre wās/ăn ōld wō/măn whŏ līved/ĭn ă shōe." **4** To sweep a beam of light or electrons over (a surface, image, etc.) so as to divide the surface or image into dots that can be transmitted and reproduced electrically.

scan·dal [skan′dəl] *n.* **1** A shameful or shocking act or condition. **2** A person whose conduct is shocking. **3** Disgrace and shame resulting from bad conduct. **4** Gossip or reports which damage a person's reputation.

scan·dal·ize [skan′dəl·īz] *v.* **scan·dal·ized, scan·dal·iz·ing** To shock or offend, as by conduct which is wrong or improper. ¶3

scan·dal·mong·er [skan′dəl·mung′gər] *n.* A person who spreads scandal and gossip.

scan·dal·ous [skan′dəl·əs] *adj.* **1** Causing scandal; disgraceful; shocking: *scandalous* conduct. **2** Spreading harmful gossip or scandal: *scandalous* reports. **— scan′dal·ous·ly** *adv.*

Scan·di·na·vi·a [skan′də·nā′vē·ə] *n.* **1** The region of NW Europe occupied by Sweden, Norway, and Denmark, sometimes including Finland and Iceland. **2** The peninsula containing Norway and Sweden. **-- Scan′di·na′vi·an** *adj., n.*

scan·sion [skan′shən] *n.* The division of lines of verse into feet; the scanning of poetry.

scant [skant] **1** *adj.* Not quite sufficient or enough; meager: *scant* provisions. **2** *v.* To limit or restrict: Don't *scant* the family's food. **3** *adj.* Just short of the measure needed or mentioned: a *scant* two weeks. **— scant of** Without enough: We were *scant of* breath.

scant·ling [skant′ling] *n.* **1** A small beam or piece of lumber. **2** Small pieces of lumber.

scant·y [skan′tē] *adj.* **scant·i·er, scant·i·est** Not quite sufficient or barely enough; meager; scant: a *scanty* supply. **— scant′i·ly** *adv.*

scape·goat [skāp′gōt′] *n.* A person, group, or animal made to bear the blame for the sins or errors of others.

scape·grace [skāp′grās′] *n.* A rascal; scamp.

scap·u·la [skap′yə·lə] *n., pl.* **scap·u·las** or **scap·u·lae** [skap′yə·lē] The shoulder blade.

scar [skär] *n., v.* **scarred, scar·ring 1** *n.* The mark left on the skin after the healing of a wound, burn, or sore. **2** *n.* A mark like this, as a scraped or scuffed place on furniture. **3** *v.* To mark or become marked with a scar. **4** *n.* The mental effect left by a painful experience.

Scapulas

scar·ab [skar′əb] *n.* **1** A large black beetle considered sacred by the ancient Egyptians. **2** A charm or ornament representing this beetle.

scarce [skârs] *adj.* **scarc·er, scarc·est** Hard to find or get; not common; not plentiful: Coins were *scarce* last year. **— make oneself scarce** *informal* To go away or stay away. **— scarce′ness** *n.*

Scarab

scarce·ly [skârs′lē] *adv.* **1** Only just; barely: He *scarcely* felt the blow. **2** Surely not; hardly: He can *scarcely* ask us to accept that. ◆ See HARDLY.

scar·ci·ty [skâr′sə·tē] *n., pl.* **scar·ci·ties** The condition of being scarce; shortage; lack.

scare [skâr] *v.* **scared, scar·ing, n. 1** *v.* To frighten or take fright: Ghost stories *scare* her; He *scares* easily. **2** *n.* A feeling of alarm; a sudden fright: You gave us a *scare*. **3** *v.* To get rid of by frightening: Our dog *scared* the thief away. **— scare up** *informal* To get together in a hurry: to *scare up* a meal.

scare·crow [skâr′krō′] *n.* A crude image of a man, dressed in old clothes and propped up in a field to frighten birds away from crops.

scarf [skärf] *n., pl.* **scarfs** or **scarves** [skärvz] **1** A band or square of cloth worn about the head, neck, or shoulders for warmth or adornment. **2** A long strip of cloth used as a covering for tables, dressers, etc.

scar·let [skär′lit] **1** *n., adj.* Brilliant red with a tinge of orange. **2** *n.* Cloth of this color.

Scarecrow

scarlet fever A contagious disease chiefly affecting young people, marked by a sore throat, fever, and a scarlet rash.

scarlet tanager A North American bird, the male of which has brilliant red plumage with black wings and tail.

scarp [skärp] **1** *n.* A steep slope. **2** *v.* To cut to a steep slope. **3** *n.* The steep inside of a ditch surrounding a fortification.

scar·y [skâr′ē] *adj.* **scar·i·er, scar·i·est** *informal* **1** Easily frightened; timid: a *scary* girl. **2** Causing fright.

scath·ing [skā′t͟hing] *adj.* Painfully severe or bitter: *scathing* criticism. **— scath′ing·ly** *adv.*

Scarlet tanager, about 7 in. long

scat·ter [skat′ər] **1** *v.* To throw about in various places; sprinkle: to *scatter* seed over a garden patch. **2** *n.* A scattering or sprinkling. **3** *v.* To go or drive away in different directions: to *scatter* enemy troops; The audience *scattered* for cover during the thunderstorm.

scat·ter·brained [skat′ər·brānd′] *adj.* Unable to think in an orderly way; flighty; giddy.

scat·ter·ing [skat′ər·ing] **1** *n.* A small number or amount spread out here and there: a *scattering*

add, āce, câre, pälm; end, ēqual; it, īce; odd, ōpen, ôrder; took, pool; up, bûrn;
ə = a in *above*, e in *sicken*, i in *possible*, o in *melon*, u in *circus*; yoo = u in *fuse*; oil; pout;
check; ring; thin; this; zh in *vision*. For ¶ reference, see page 64 · HOW TO

of votes. **2** *adj.* Spread out or coming at intervals: *scattering* drops of rain.

scatter rug A small rug used to cover only part of a floor.

scav·en·ger [skav′in·jər] *n.* **1** An animal that feeds on dead things, as the buzzard. **2** A person who searches through refuse, garbage, etc., for things that he can use or sell. **3** A street cleaner.

sce·nar·i·o [si·när′ē·ō *or* si·nä′rē·ō] *n., pl.* **sce·nar·i·os** Another word for SCREENPLAY.

scene [sēn] *n.* **1** A certain place and everything in it, as presented to view: a charming country *scene.* **2** The place in which an event occurs: the *scene* of the crime. **3** The place and time in which a play, story, motion picture, etc., is set: The *scene* is London in 1944. **4** The scenery used to set the stage to represent a place, room, etc., as in a play or motion picture: The *scene* represents a doctor's office. **5** A section of a play, motion picture, etc., especially a division of an act: Act II, *scene* i. **6** A certain incident or event in a play, story, etc.: the rescue *scene.* **7** A show of anger or other embarrassing behavior: Don't make a *scene* in public. **— behind the scenes 1** Out of sight backstage. **2** In secret. ◆ *Scene,* which comes from a Greek word meaning *tent* or *stage,* has broadened in meaning throughout the years. Now it often refers to actual places and events as well as to stage settings.

scen·er·y [sē′nər·ē] *n.* **1** The visible natural features of an outdoor area: woodland *scenery.* **2** The painted backdrops, hangings, etc., that are used on a stage to represent various places or scenes.

sce·nic [sē′nik *or* sen′ik] *adj.* **1** Of or having to do with outdoor scenery: the *scenic* marvels of the Alps. **2** Having lovely or striking scenery: *scenic* areas. **3** Of stage scenery, lighting, etc.: the *scenic* effects of a play.

scent [sent] **1** *n.* An odor or smell, especially if pleasant: the *scent* of lilacs. **2** *n.* Perfume: to wear *scent.* **3** *v.* To make fragrant; perfume. **4** *n.* The sense of smell. **5** *n.* An odor by which a person or animal can be tracked: Bloodhounds picked up the criminal's *scent.* **6** *v.* To smell: The dogs *scented* a deer. **7** *n.* A trail or track leading to something sought: We are on the right *scent.* **8** *v.* To form a suspicion of: to *scent* a plot.

scep·ter [sep′tər] *n.* A staff or wand carried by a ruler as a sign of his royal power.

scep·tic [skep′tik] *n.* Another spelling of SKEPTIC.

scep·ti·cal [skep′ti·kəl] *adj.* Another spelling of SKEPTICAL.

scep·ti·cism [skep′tə·siz′əm] *n.* Another spelling of SKEPTICISM.

sched·ule [skej′ool] *n., v.* **sched·uled, sched·ul·ing 1** *n.* A plan or program, as of things to be done: He has a full *schedule.* **2** *n.* A list of the times when certain things are to take place; timetable: a TV *schedule.* **3** *n.* The time agreed upon in a plan: to be behind

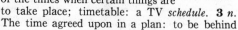

Scepter

schedule. **4** *n.* A written or printed list giving details: a *schedule* of prices. **5** *v.* To place in or on a schedule: to *schedule* a meeting for 2:00 P.M. **6** *v.* To make a schedule of: In order not to waste time, you ought to *schedule* your work.

scheme [skēm] *n., v.* **schemed, schem·ing 1** *n.* A plan or plot, especially if secret and sly or impractical: wicked or mad *schemes.* **2** *v.* To plan or plot, often secretly and slyly: He *schemed* to get the money. **3** *n.* An arrangement of something according to a plan or design: a color *scheme.* **— schem′er** *n.*

scher·zo [sker′tsō] *n., pl.* **scher·zos** or **scher·zi** [sker′tsē] In music, a quick, playful movement, as of a sonata or symphony.

schism [siz′əm] *n.* A division into groups that are opposed to each other, especially a division within a church caused by disagreement in matters of belief.

schis·mat·ic [siz·mat′ik] **1** *adj.* Like, having to do with, or causing schism. **2** *n.* A person who brings about or takes part in a schism.

schist [shist] *n.* A rock, containing mica, that splits easily into flat layers.

schol·ar [skol′ər] *n.* **1** A person who has learned a great deal through serious study. **2** A student who holds a scholarship. **3** A school pupil or student: rarely used.

schol·ar·ly [skol′ər·lē] *adj.* **1** Devoted to serious study: a *scholarly* man. **2** Showing or requiring advanced knowledge: *scholarly* research; a *scholarly* book. **3** Of, like, or suiting a scholar.

schol·ar·ship [skol′ər·ship] *n.* **1** A grant of money awarded to a student to help pay for his education. **2** Advanced learning or devotion to serious study. **3** The methods or quality of a student's study: poor *scholarship.*

scho·las·tic [skə·las′tik] *adj.* Of or having to do with scholars, education, or schools: *scholastic* excellence. **— scho·las′ti·cal·ly** *adv.*

school[1] [skool] **1** *n.* A place set up to teach students: grammar *school*; a cooking *school.* **2** *v.* To educate or teach: She was well *schooled* in the classics. **3** *n.* A schoolhouse or schoolroom. **4** *n.* Pupils and their teachers as a group: Our *school* gave $300 to the fund. **5** *n.* The period during which classes are taught: to keep a pupil in after *school.* **6** *n.* The training or instruction given at a school: *School* was hard for him. **7** *n.* A special division of a university: the medical *school.* **8** *n.* A group of persons whose ideas, beliefs, or methods are alike: an old-fashioned *school* of thought; a *school* of poets. **9** *v.* To train or teach: to *school* a child to obey. **10** *n.* Anything that teaches, as experience, life, etc.: the *school* of hard knocks. ◆ *School* comes from a Greek word that means *spare time, leisure,* and *rest.* It also means *discussion* and *lecture,* because the ancient Greeks thought that serious discussion was a good way to spend one's spare time.

school[2] [skool] *n.* A large number of fish, whales, etc., swimming together; shoal.

school board A group of citizens responsible for directing a local public school system.

school·book [skool′book′] *n.* A book which students study in school; textbook.

school·boy [skool′boi′] *n.* A boy who attends school.

school·fel·low [skool′fel′ō] *n.* A schoolmate.

school·girl [skool′gûrl′] *n.* A girl who attends school.

school·house [skool′hous′] *n.* The building in which the pupils of a school are taught.

school·ing [skool′ing] *n.* Training or education, such as that received in a school.

school·mas·ter [skool′mas′tər] *n.* A man who teaches in a school or acts as its principal.

school·mate [skool′māt′] *n.* A person who is a pupil in the same school as someone else.

school·mis·tress [skool′mis′tris] *n.* A woman who teaches in a school, or is its principal.

school·room [skool′room′] *n.* A room in which pupils are taught their lessons by a teacher.

school·teach·er [skool′tē′chər] *n.* A person whose profession is teaching in a school.

school·yard [skool′yärd′] *n.* The grounds belonging to a school, used to play in, etc.

schoon·er [skoo′nər] *n.* A ship having two or more masts rigged with fore-and-aft sails.

schot·tische [shot′ish] *n.* **1** A round dance similar to the polka, but somewhat slower. **2** Music for such a dance.

Schu·bert [shoo′bərt], **Franz,** 1797–1828, Austrian composer.

schwa [shwä] *n.* A weak vowel sound in a syllable that is not stressed in speech, as the *a* in "alone" or the *e* in "happen." Symbol: ə

Schooner

Schwei·tzer [shvī′tsər], **Albert,** 1875–1965, famous French medical missionary in Africa.

sci·at·i·ca [sī·at′i·kə] *n.* Pain in the lower back, hips, or legs, caused by disturbances along the sciatic nerve.

sci·at·ic nerve [sī·at′ik] A nerve that extends from the hip down the back of the thigh, dividing near the knee into branches.

sci·ence [sī′əns] *n.* **1** Knowledge consisting of a systematic arrangement of facts and principles obtained through observation, experiment, and ordered thinking. **2** A branch of this kind of knowledge. Chemistry is a natural science, and civics is a social science. **3** Skill gained through study or practice: the *science* of swimming. ◆ *Science* comes from the Latin word for *knowing.*

science fiction A made-up, often fantastic adventure story or novel whose plot is built around either real or imaginary scientific developments.

sci·en·tif·ic [sī′ən·tif′ik] *adj.* **1** Of, having to do with, discovered by, or used in science. **2** Following the rules, principles, or methods of science. **— sci′en·tif′i·cal·ly** *adv.*

sci·en·tist [sī′ən·tist] *n.* **1** A person expert in science or devoted to scientific study. **2** (*written* **Scientist**) A Christian Scientist.

scim·i·tar or **scim·i·ter** [sim′ə·tər] *n.* A curved, short Oriental sword.

scin·til·la [sin·til′ə] *n.* The tiniest bit or particle; trace; spark: not a *scintilla* of truth in his entire story.

A scimitar and scabbard

scin·til·late [sin′tə·lāt] *v.* **scin·til·lat·ed, scin·til·lat·ing 1** To give off sparks or sparkle brilliantly. **2** To be sparkling or brilliant: His wit *scintillates* tonight.

scin·til·la·tion [sin′tə·lā′shən] *n.* **1** The act of scintillating. **2** A being scintillating.

sci·on [sī′ən] *n.* **1** A child or descendant, as of an important family. **2** A twig or shoot of a plant, used for grafting; cion.

scis·sors [siz′ərz] *n.pl.* A cutting tool (also called a **pair of scissors**) having a pair of blades pivoted together so that their sharp edges close against each other.

scoff [skof *or* skôf] **1** *v.* To show scorn or mocking disbelief; jeer: to *scoff* at a theory. **2** *n.* A mocking or scornful remark. **— scoff′er** *n.*

scold [skōld] **1** *v.* To criticize (someone) sharply for faults: to *scold* a pupil for misbehaving. **2** *n.* A person who is always scolding, especially a shrewish woman.

scol·lop [skol′əp] *n., v.* Another spelling of SCALLOP.

sconce [skons] *n.* An ornamental wall bracket for holding a candle or other light.

scone [skōn] *n.* A round, flat cake or biscuit, usually eaten with butter.

scoop [skoop] **1** *n.* A tool like a little shovel or a deep, cuplike spoon, used to lift out portions of flour, sugar, ice cream, and the like. **2** *n.* The amount a scoop will hold: a *scoop* of ice cream. **3** *n.* The part of a dredge or power shovel that digs up and lifts mud, dirt, sand, etc. **4** *v.* To lift out or up with or as if with a scoop: to *scoop up* handfuls of sand. **5** *n.* An act of scooping or a scooping movement. **6** *v.* To hollow out, as by scooping: to *scoop* out a hollow. **7** *n.* A bowl-shaped hollow or hole. **8** *n. slang* A bit of information, a news story, etc., heard or published ahead of others. **9** *v. slang* To get and publish a news story before (a rival): One newspaper *scooped* all the others.

Sconce

scoot [skoot] *informal* **1** *v.* To go quickly; dart off. **2** *n.* A hurried darting off.

scoot·er [skoo′tər] *n.* A vehicle consisting of a footboard with a wheel at either end and steered by a handle in front. A child stands on a scooter and pushes with one foot, while a **motor scooter** has a driver's seat and engine.

Motor scooter

scope [skōp] *n.* **1** The area covered; range; extent: the *scope* of a lesson. **2** Extent of understanding; grasp: a mind of limited *scope*. **3** Room or chance for expression, development, etc.: The job gave full *scope* to his talents.

scorch [skôrch] **1** *v.* To burn just a little on the surface; singe: The hot iron *scorched* the dress. **2** *n.* A slight burn on the surface of something. **3** *v.* To wither or shrivel by heat; dry up.

scorch·er [skôr′chər] *n.* **1** A person or thing that scorches. **2** *informal* An extremely hot day.

score [skôr] *n., v.* **scored, scor·ing 1** *n.* The number of points won in a game or competition. **2** *n.* A record of points won: to keep *score*. **3** *v.* To keep such a record for: to *score* a bridge game. **4** *v.* To make (points, runs, etc.), as in a game: Tom *scored* a touchdown. **5** *v.* To win or attain, as a success. **6** *n.* A grade or mark made on a test: Sue got a *score* of 93. **7** *v.* To rate or grade: to *score* test papers. **8** *n.* A debt, wrong, or injury to be repaid or revenged: to settle old *scores*. **9** *n.* Reason, excuse, or account. **10** *v.* To mark with lines, cuts, or notches. **11** *n.* A cut or a similar line or mark. **12** *n.* A copy of a piece of music giving all the parts written for different instruments or voices. **13** *v.* To arrange (music) for an orchestra or instrument. **14** *n.* A set of twenty: a *score* of years. **15** *n.* (*pl.*) An indefinitely large number: *scores* of pigeons. — **scor′·er** *n.* ◆ *Score* comes from an old Scandinavian word meaning *notch*. People once kept track of numbers or *scores* by cutting notches in a stick.

scorn [skôrn] **1** *n.* A feeling of despising someone or something as low, mean, or beneath one's notice; contempt. **2** *n.* An expression of contempt or disdain: His lip curled in *scorn*. **3** *v.* To treat with contempt; despise: to *scorn* a coward. **4** *v.* To refuse as being beneath one; disdain: to *scorn* an offer; She *scorned* to answer. **5** *n.* An object of contempt or disdain. ◆ See CONTEMPT.

scorn·ful [skôrn′fəl] *adj.* Full of or showing scorn: a *scornful* smile. — **scorn′ful·ly** *adv.*

scor·pi·on [skôr′pē·ən] *n.* A small animal related to the spider, having a lobsterlike body and a long, curved tail with a poisonous sting.

Scorpion, 1–8 in. long

Scot [skot] *n.* A person who was born in or comes from Scotland; Scotsman.

scotch [skoch] *v.* **1** To put down or suppress, as by disproving; crush. **2** To wound so as to cripple.

Scotch [skoch] **1** *adj.* Of or from Scotland. **2** *n.* (**the Scotch**) The people of Scotland. **3** *n.* The dialect of English spoken in Scotland. **4** *n.* Whisky made in Scotland. ◆ *Scotch, Scots,* and *Scottish* are all adjectives that refer to Scotland. *Scotch* is used for products of Scotland: *Scotch* tweed; *Scotch* whisky. *Scottish* and *Scots* are used when talking about the people of Scotland or the way they live.

Scotch·man [skoch′mən] *n., pl.* **Scotch·men** [skoch′mən] A Scot; Scotsman.

scot-free [skot′frē′] *adj.* Without punishment or injury: He got off *scot-free*.

Scot·land [skot′lənd] *n.* A political division of Great Britain, to the north of England.

Scotland Yard The headquarters of the London police and of the official detective bureau.

Scots [skots] **1** *adj.* Scottish: *Scots* law. **2** *n.* The dialect of English spoken in Scotland. ◆ See SCOTCH.

Scots·man [skots′mən] *n., pl.* **Scots·men** [skots′mən] A Scot.

Scott [skot], **Sir Walter,** 1771–1832, Scottish novelist and poet.

Scot·tish [skot′ish] **1** *adj.* Of or from Scotland. **2** *n.* (**the Scottish**) The people of Scotland. **3** *n.* The Scotch dialect of English. ◆ See SCOTCH.

Scottish terrier A small terrier with short legs, a large head, and a wiry coat.

Scottish terrier, 9–12 in. high at shoulder

scoun·drel [skoun′drəl] *n.* A mean or dishonest person; rogue; villain.

scour[1] [skour] **1** *v.* To clean or brighten by washing and rubbing hard, as with sand or steel wool: to *scour* a pan. **2** *v.* To clean or clear, as by means of flowing water: to *scour* a drain. **3** *n.* The act of scouring: Give the pot a good *scour*. **4** *v.* To clean (wheat) before milling. — **scour′er** *n.*

scour[2] [skour] *v.* To go over or through every part of, usually with speed, as in making a search: Hunters *scoured* the woods for game.

scourge [skûrj] *n., v.* **scourged, scourg·ing 1** *n.* A whip. **2** *v.* To whip severely; lash. **3** *v.* To punish or cause to suffer severely; afflict: A plague *scourged* the land. **4** *n.* A cause of great suffering or trouble, as war.

scout[1] [skout] **1** *n.* A soldier, plane, or ship sent out to observe and get information about the enemy. **2** *n.* Someone sent to find out about a rival, to locate persons worth hiring, etc.: a talent *scout* for motion pictures. **3** *v.* To observe or explore in order to obtain information: Two soldiers *scouted* the area ahead. **4** *v.* To search or hunt: to *scout* around for a campsite. **5** *n.* A boy scout or girl scout. **6** *n. slang* A fellow or friend: Bill is a good *scout*.

scout[2] [skout] *v.* To scorn and reject as absurd: They *scouted* her odd notions.

scout·mas·ter [skout′mas′tər] *n.* The leader of a troop of Boy Scouts.

scow [skou] *n.* A large boat having a flat bottom and square ends, usually towed, used to carry coal, oil, gravel, garbage, etc. ◆ *Scow* comes from a Dutch word.

scowl [skoul] **1** *v.* To lower the eyebrows and draw them together, as in anger or sullenness; frown. **2** *n.* A frowning look made in this way.

scrag·gly [skrag′lē] *adj.* **scrag·gli·er, scrag·gli·est** Rough, shaggy, or irregular.

scrag·gy [skrag′ē] *adj.* **scrag·gi·er, scrag·gi·est 1** Rough; jagged: the *scraggy* mountain tops. **2** Very thin; scrawny; bony: his *scraggy* little legs.

scram [skram] *v.* **scrammed, scram·ming** *U.S. slang* To go away; get out.

scram·ble [skram′bəl] *v.* **scram·bled, scram·bling,** *n.* **1** *v.* To move or climb hastily, using the hands and feet: to *scramble* down a steep slope. **2** *n.* A hard walk or climb over rough land. **3** *v.* To struggle with others, as in trying to get something: to *scramble* for a place in front. **4** *n.* A struggle, often with pushing and shoving: a mad *scramble* for tickets. **5** *v.* To mix together in a confused way: The nervous boy *scrambled* the messages. **6** *v.* To cook (eggs) by stirring mixed yolks and whites over heat.

scrap¹ [skrap] *n., adj., v.* **scrapped, scrap·ping 1** *n.* A little piece or fragment; bit: *scraps* of food. **2** *n.* Useless material that has been thrown away. **3** *adj.* Made up of scrap: a *scrap* heap. **4** *v.* To throw away or abandon as no good: to *scrap* wrecked autos. **5** *n.* Pieces of old metal used in making new metal. **6** *v.* To break up into scrap. **7** *adj.* In broken pieces of value only as material for making something new: *scrap* iron; *scrap* paper.

scrap² [skrap] *v.* **scrapped, scrap·ping,** *n. slang* **1** *v.* To fight; quarrel. **2** *n.* A noisy fight or disagreement. **— scrap′per** *n.*

scrap·book [skrap′book′] *n.* A blank book for pictures, clippings, and other flat souvenirs.

scrape [skrāp] *v.* **scraped, scrap·ing,** *n.* **1** *v.* To rub (a surface) with or against something edged or rough, so as to take off something stuck on, a layer, etc.: to *scrape* plates before washing them. **2** *v.* To remove from a surface by rubbing with something sharp or rough: to *scrape* ice off a windshield. **3** *n.* A scraped spot. **4** *v.* To rub with a grating noise: to *scrape* fingernails across a blackboard. **5** *n.* A harsh, grating noise. **6** *v.* To draw the foot backward in bowing: to bow and *scrape.* **7** *n.* The act of scraping. **8** *v.* To gather gradually or by effort: They *scraped* up money to pay bills. **9** *v.* To get by barely, with trouble: Those poor people just *scrape* by. **10** *n.* A difficult situation, especially one due to a rash or thoughtless act: He got into one *scrape* after another when he was on his own. **— scrap′er** *n.*

scratch [skrach] **1** *v.* To tear or mark the surface of with something sharp or rough: Briers *scratched* her arms. **2** *n.* A mark or cut made in this way: *scratches* on furniture. **3** *v.* To scrape lightly with the nails, etc., as to relieve itching: *Scratch* my back. **4** *n.* A slight flesh wound: It's only a *scratch.* **5** *v.* To rub with a grating or rasping noise: a dog *scratching* at the door. **6** *n.* A grating or rasping noise: the *scratch* of a match being struck. **7** *v.* To mark out with lines: to *scratch* out a word. **8** *v.* To withdraw (a horse, candidate, etc.) from a competition. **9** *v.* To write awkwardly or hurriedly: to *scratch* off a reply. **10** *adj.* Used for quick notes, etc.: a *scratch* pad. **11** *adj.* Chosen or made by chance: a *scratch* team; a *scratch* shot. **12** *n.* The act of scratching. **— from scratch** From the beginning or from nothing: to begin again *from scratch.* **— up to scratch** *informal* In proper or fit condition: I don't feel *up to scratch.*

scratch·y [skrach′ē] *adj.* **scratch·i·er, scratch·i·est 1** That scratches or irritates: a *scratchy* thicket; a *scratchy* wool dress. **2** Making a scratching noise: a *scratchy* record. **3** Full of scratchlike marks: *scratchy* writing.

scrawl [skrôl] **1** *v.* To write in a hasty, clumsy, or careless way. **2** *n.* Rough or careless handwriting: I could not read his *scrawl.*

scraw·ny [skrô′nē] *adj.* **scraw·ni·er, scraw·ni·est** Lean and bony; skinny; thin.

scream [skrēm] **1** *v.* To utter a long, shrill cry, as in pain, terror, or surprise: to *scream* for help. **2** *v.* To make a loud noise like a scream: The train whistle *screamed.* **3** *n.* A loud, piercing cry or sound. **4** *v.* To shout with a shrill tone: Don't *scream* at me. **5** *n.* *U.S. slang* A person or situation causing shouts of laughter.

scream·ing [skrē′ming] *adj.* **1** Uttering screams. **2** Provoking screams or laughter: a *screaming* farce. **3** Startling: *screaming* colors.

screech [skrēch] **1** *v.* To scream or shriek in a harsh way: That singer is *screeching.* **2** *n.* A shrill, harsh cry or sound; shriek.

screech owl Any of several kinds of small owls that screech weirdly instead of hooting.

screen [skrēn] **1** *n.* A network of woven wires with small open spaces between them, used to cover doors, windows, etc. **2** *n.* A covered frame or other partition used to separate, hide, protect, or ornament: She changed costumes behind a *screen.* **3** *n.* Something that hides, shields, or separates, as a screen: a *screen* of shrubbery. **4** *v.* To hide, shield, or shelter with or as if with a screen: to *screen* a porch; Vines *screen* the window from view. **5** *n.* A smooth surface on which movies, TV shows, etc., are shown. **6** *v.* To exhibit (a

Screech owl,
8–10 in. long

add, āce, câre, pälm; end, ēqual; it, īce; odd, ōpen, ôrder; took, pool; up, bûrn;
ə = a in *above*, e in *sicken*, i in *possible*, o in *melon*, u in *circus*; yoo = u in *fuse*; oil; pout;
check; ring; thin; this; zh in *vision*. For ¶ reference, see page 64 · HOW TO

movie) on a screen. **7** *n.* Motion pictures: a star of stage and *screen.* **8** *n.* A sieve used to separate little pieces of gravel, ashes, etc., from big ones. **9** *v.* To sift through such a sieve: to *screen* coal. **10** *v.* To examine in order to determine qualifications: to *screen* applicants for a scholarship.

screen·play [skrēn′plā′] *n.* The written plot and arrangement of incidents of a motion picture, including cast of characters, dialogue, etc.

screw [skrōō] **1** *n.* A pointed fastener like a nail with a spiral ridge around its length. It is driven in by turning it. **2** *n.* A cylinder with a spiral ridge around it that fits into a socket with a matching spiral groove in its sides. **3** *v.* To attach or be attached with screws: to *screw* a bolt to a door; The towel rack *screws* to the wall. **4** *n.* A turn of or as of a screw: Give the lid a *screw.* **5** *v.* To turn or twist until tight: *Screw* the cap on the tube. **6** *v.* To twist out of the normal shape: He *screwed* up his mouth. **7** *v.* To force, as if by pressure: He *screwed* a promise out of his father that he could go to camp. **8** *v.* To gather for an effort or attempt: He *screwed* up enough courage to ask Mary to dance. **9** *n.* Anything having the form of a screw. **10** *n.* A screw propeller. **— put the screws on** *slang* To use pressure or force on.

screw·driv·er [skrōō′drī′vər] *n.* A tool that fits into the slot in the head of a screw to turn it.

screw propeller A hub having blades attached with their edges at an angle to the direction of rotation, like those of an electric fan, used to drive ships and some aircraft.

scrib·ble [skrib′əl] *v.* **scrib·bled, scrib·bling,** *n.* **1** *v.* To write in a hasty or careless way: to *scribble* a note. **2** *v.* To make marks that mean nothing. **3** *n.* Writing or marks made by scribbling. **— scrib′bler** *n.*

scribe [skrīb] *n., v.* **scribed, scrib·ing 1** *n.* A person who copies manuscripts by hand, as was done before printing was invented. **2** *n.* A clerk or secretary. **3** *n.* A writer. **4** *n.* A teacher of the Jewish law in olden times.

scrim·mage [skrim′ij] *n., v.* **scrim·maged, scrim·mag·ing 1** *n.* A rough, disorderly struggle. **2** *n.* In football, a play after the ball has been placed on the ground and snapped back. **3** *n.* In various sports, a practice session or unofficial game. **4** *v.* To engage in a scrimmage. **— line of scrimmage** In football, the imaginary line running across the field where the ball rests between opposing teams at the start of each play.

scrimp [skrimp] *v.* To limit spending by being very economical or stingy: to *scrimp* and save.

scrip [skrip] *n.* **1** A piece of paper money less than a dollar, formerly issued in the U.S. **2** A document giving the holder the right to receive something else, as shares of stock.

script [skript] *n.* **1** Handwriting. **2** A printing type designed to imitate handwriting. **3** A copy of a play or dramatic role, for the use of actors.

scrip·tur·al [skrip′chər·əl] *adj.* (*usually written* **Scriptural**) Of, having to do with, found in, or according to the Scriptures: Your wording is not *Scriptural,* but the Bible expresses the same idea.

Scrip·ture [skrip′chər] *n.* **1** (*often pl.*) The Bible or a passage from the Bible: The *Scriptures* are often quoted. **2** (*written* **scripture**) Any writing considered sacred or authoritative.

scriv·en·er [skriv′ən·ər *or* skriv′nər] *n.* In olden days, a public clerk or scribe who prepared deeds, contracts, and other writings.

scrod [skrod] *n.* A young codfish split up for cooking.

scrof·u·la [skrof′yə·lə] *n.* Tuberculosis of the lymph glands, chiefly of the neck, marked by abscesses, inflammation, and swelling. **— scrof′u·lous** *adj.*

scroll [skrōl] *n.* **1** A roll of parchment, paper, etc., especially one with writing on it. **2** An ornament like a partly unrolled scroll.

scroll saw A saw with a narrow blade for doing curved or irregular work.

Scrooge [skrōōj] *n.* In Charles Dickens' story *A Christmas Carol,* the mean old miser.

scro·tum [skrō′təm] *n., pl.* **scro·tums** or **scro·ta** [skrō′tə] The pouch of skin that holds the testicles of a male mammal.

scrub¹ [skrub] *v.* **scrubbed, scrub·bing,** *n.* **1** *v.* To wash clean by rubbing hard: to *scrub* clothes. **2** *n.* The act of scrubbing.

scrub² [skrub] **1** *n.* Small, stunted trees or shrubs growing together. **2** *n.* Any small or inferior person or thing. **3** *adj.* Undersized or inferior: *scrub* oak or pine. **4** *n.* A player not on the regular team in sports. **5** *adj.* Of or involving such players: a *scrub* team.

scrub·by [skrub′ē] *adj.* **scrub·bi·er, scrub·bi·est 1** Undersized: a *scrubby* horse. **2** Covered with scrub or underbrush: *scrubby* ground.

scruff [skruf] *n.* The back part, or nape, of the neck or the loose skin that covers it.

scru·ple [skrōō′pəl] *n., v.* **scru·pled, scru·pling 1** *n.* A feeling of doubt that holds someone back from doing what seems to be wrong: He has *scruples* about letting others copy his homework. **2** *v.* To hesitate because of scruples: The pirates did not *scruple* to steal. **3** *n.* A small unit of weight used by druggists, equal to 20 grains.

scru·pu·lous [skrōō′pyə·ləs] *adj.* **1** Giving strict attention to what is right: a *scrupulous* parent. **2** Careful and exact: a *scrupulous* account of money spent. **— scru′pu·lous·ly** *adv.*

A puppy held by the scruff of its neck

scru·ti·nize [skrōō′tə·nīz] *v.* **scru·ti·nized, scru·ti·niz·ing** To look at closely; examine very carefully: to *scrutinize* every clue. ¶3

scru·ti·ny [skrōō′tə·nē] *n., pl.* **scru·ti·nies** A searching look or close, careful examination.

scud [skud] *v.* **scud·ded, scud·ding,** *n.* **1** *v.* To move, run, or fly swiftly: clouds *scudding* before the wind. **2** *n.* Clouds or spray driven before the wind. **3** *n.* The act of scudding.

scuff [skuf] **1** *v.* To roughen or wear down the surface of, as by scraping: Don't *scuff* your shoes. **2** *v.* To drag or scrape the feet, as on the floor. **3** *n.* The act or sound of scuffing.

scuf·fle [skuf'əl] *v.* **scuf·fled, scuf·fling,** *n.* **1** *v.* To struggle roughly or in a confused way: Tempers were short, and twice players *scuffled.* **2** *n.* A confused fight. **3** *v.* To shuffle the feet.

scull [skul] **1** *n.* A long oar worked from side to side over the rear of a boat. **2** *n.* A light, short oar, used in pairs by one person. **3** *v.* To propel (a boat) by a scull or sculls. **4** *n.* A light racing boat rowed with sculls. — **scull'er** *n.*

scul·ler·y [skul'ər·ē] *n., pl.* **scul·ler·ies** A room off a kitchen where vegetables are cleaned, pots and pans washed, etc.

scul·lion [skul'yən] *n.* A servant who washes dishes, pots, and kettles: seldom used today.

sculp·tor [skulp'tər] *n.* An artist who creates sculpture out of stone, metal, wood, clay, etc.

sculp·tress [skulp'tris] *n.* A woman sculptor.

sculp·ture [skulp'chər] *n., v.* **sculp·tured, sculp·tur·ing 1** *n.* The art of making figures or shapes, as by chiseling stone, casting molten metal, or modeling clay. **2** *n.* A work or works of art made in this manner. **3** *v.* To form or represent by carving, shaping, etc.: to *sculpture* a statue. **4** *v.* To beautify or decorate with sculpture. — **sculp'tur·al** *adj.*

scum [skum] *n., v.* **scummed, scum·ming 1** *n.* A film of impure or foreign matter that forms upon the surface of a liquid: *scum* on a stagnant pool. **2** *v.* To become covered with or form scum. **3** *v.* To take scum from; skim. **4** *n.* A vile or worthless person or group.

scum·my [skum'ē] *adj.* **scum·mi·er, scum·mi·est 1** Covered with or like scum. **2** Low; vile.

scup·per [skup'ər] *n.* An opening along the side of a ship's deck, to let water run off.

scup·per·nong [skup'ər·nong] *n.* A delicious yellowish green grape of the southern U.S.

scurf [skûrf] *n.* **1** Tiny scales of skin, shed as in dandruff. **2** Any scaly or flaky covering.

scur·ril·i·ty [skə·ril'ə·tē] *n., pl.* **scur·ril·i·ties 1** Coarseness or vulgarity of language. **2** A coarse or vulgar remark.

scur·ri·lous [skûr'ə·ləs] *adj.* Vulgar and very coarse or abusive: The old lady attacked us with *scurrilous* remarks. ◆ *Scurrilous* goes back to the Latin word for *buffoon* or *clown.*

scur·ry [skûr'ē] *v.* **scur·ried, scur·ry·ing,** *n., pl.* **scur·ries 1** *v.* To run quickly or hastily; scamper. **2** *n.* The act or sound of scurrying.

scur·vy [skûr'vē] *n., adj.* **scur·vi·er, scur·vi·est 1** *n.* A disease caused by a lack of vitamin C

in the diet. It is marked by swollen and bleeding gums and great physical weakness. **2** *adj.* Nasty; mean; low: a *scurvy* trick.

scutch·eon [skuch'ən] *n.* A shield on whose surface there is a coat of arms; escutcheon.

scut·tle¹ [skut'(ə)l] *n.* A bucketlike container in which coal may be kept or carried.

scut·tle² [skut'(ə)l] *v.* **scut·tled, scut·tling** To run quickly; scamper; scurry.

scut·tle³ [skut'(ə)l] *v.* **scut·tled, scut·tling,** *n.* **1** *v.* To sink (a ship) on purpose by making openings in it. **2** *n.* An opening with a lid or cover, as one in the deck or side of a ship.

Scyl·la [sil'ə] *n.* In Greek myths, a sea monster with six heads living in a cave opposite the whirlpool of Charybdis. It represented a dangerous rock in the strait between Italy and Sicily. — **between Scylla and Charybdis** Between two dangers, where avoiding one means taking the risk of running into the other.

scythe [sīth] *n.* A long, curved blade fixed at an angle to a long, bent handle and used to cut down grass or grain.

S.Dak. or **S.D.** Abbreviation of SOUTH DAKOTA.

SE or **S.E.** Abbreviation of: **1** SOUTHEAST. **2** SOUTHEASTERN.

sea [sē] *n.* **1** The large body of salt water that covers most of the earth's surface; the ocean. **2** *adj. use:* a *sea* bird;

Scythe

a *sea* captain **3** A large body of ocean water partly enclosed by land: the Aegean *Sea.* **4** A salt-water or fresh-water lake: the *Sea* of Galilee; the Caspian *Sea.* **5** A wave: The ship floundered in heavy *seas.* **6** The swell or flow of the ocean or of its waves. **7** A very great amount or number: a *sea* of unanswered mail. — **at sea 1** On the ocean. **2** At a loss; confused. — **follow the sea** To make one's living as a sailor. — **go to sea 1** To become a sailor. **2** To take an ocean trip. — **put to sea** To start an ocean trip.

sea anemone A sea animal having a tubelike body with a mouth at one end surrounded by brightly colored tentacles that look like flower petals.

sea·board [sē'bôrd'] *n.* The land or region bordering on the sea; seacoast.

sea·coast [sē'kōst'] *n.* A coast that borders on the sea; seashore.

Sea anemone, to 16 in. high

sea cow A manatee or a related large mammal that lives in the sea.

sea dog An old or experienced sailor.

sea·far·er [sē'fâr'ər] *n.* A seaman; mariner.

sea·far·ing [sē'fâr'ing] **1** *n.* Travel on the sea.

2 *adj.* Traveling by sea. **3** *n.* The occupation of a sailor. **4** *adj.* Working as a sailor.

sea·food [sē'fōod'] *n.* Fish, shellfish, etc., that are good to eat.

sea·girt [sē'gûrt'] *adj.* Surrounded by waters of the sea or ocean.

sea·go·ing [sē'gō'ing] *adj.* **1** Built for use on the ocean: a *seagoing* vessel. **2** Seafaring.

sea gull A gull or large tern.

sea horse **1** A small, salt-water fish having a long slender tail and a head resembling that of a horse. **2** A mythical animal, half horse and half fish. **3** A walrus.

Sea gull, wingspread 54 in.

seal[1] [sēl] **1** *n.* An instrument or device for pressing a mark or design, especially an official one, into a soft material, such as wax or paper. **2** *n.* The mark or design made this way. **3** *v.* To mark with a seal, as to indicate official status, quality, etc. **4** *n.* The paper, wax, etc., that is marked with a seal and attached to something to indicate official status, quality, etc. **5** *n.* A substance or device used to keep something firmly closed: the *seal* of an envelope; a *seal* on a door. **6** *v.* To fasten or close with or as if with a seal: to *seal* a letter; to *seal* a leak. **7** *n.* Something that confirms or makes certain. **8** *v.* To confirm or make certain: to *seal* a bargain with a handshake. **9** *n.* An ornamental stamp, as for Christmas cards, etc. **— seal'er** *n.*

seal[2] [sēl] **1** *n.* Any of various large, fish-eating sea mammals having flippers as limbs. Seals spend part of the time on land. **2** *n.* Fur or leather taken from a seal. **3** *v.* To hunt seals. **— seal'er** *n.*

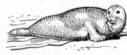

Seal, about 6 ft. long

sea legs The ability to walk steadily on a rolling or pitching ship.

sea level The level of the surface of the ocean, halfway between high and low tide. Elevation of land is measured from sea level.

sealing wax A material that is soft when heated but becomes solid when it cools, used for sealing papers, packages, etc.

sea lion A very large seal of the Pacific coast of North America.

seal·skin [sēl'skin'] *n.* **1** The fur of a seal, especially when treated to remove the longer hairs and dyed brown or black. **2** A coat, etc., made of this fur.

seam [sēm] **1** *n.* A line along which parts have been joined, especially the edges of two pieces of cloth sewn together. **2** *v.* To join by means of a seam. **3** *n.* A mark resembling a seam, as a scar or wrinkle. **4** *v.* To mark with wrinkles, scars,

Sea lion, to 8 ft. long

etc., as the face. **5** *n.* A layer of rock or mineral; stratum.

sea·man [sē'mən] *n.,* *pl.* **sea·men** [sē'mən] **1** A man whose work is to help with the sailing of a ship; sailor. **2** A person expert in managing a ship: John Paul Jones was a fine *seaman.* **3** An enlisted man of low rank in a navy. **— sea'·man·ship** *n.*

sea mew A gull, especially a European variety.

seam·stress [sēm'stris] *n.* A woman skilled at sewing or earning her living by sewing.

seam·y [sē'mē] *adj.* **seam·i·er, seam·i·est** **1** Full of seams, as the wrong side of a garment. **2** Unpleasant or unattractive: Doctors often see the *seamy* side of life.

sé·ance [sā'äns] *n.* **1** A meeting at which people try to communicate with the dead. **2** A session.

sea·plane [sē'plān'] *n.* An airplane designed and built to land on and take off from water.

sea·port [sē'pôrt'] *n.* **1** A harbor or port that ships can reach from the sea. **2** The city or town where it is located.

sea power **1** A nation whose navy is large and strong. **2** The naval strength of a nation.

sear [sir] **1** *v.* To wither; dry up: Sun and drought *seared* the lawn. **2** *adj.* Withered; dried up: used mostly in poems. **3** *v.* To burn the surface of; scorch: The heat *seared* his skin. **4** *v.* To make hard or insensitive: War had *seared* his feelings.

search [sûrch] **1** *v.* To look through or examine thoroughly: to *search* a closet for an overshoe; to *search* a captured prisoner for weapons. **2** *v.* To look very hard: to *search* for a cure. **3** *n.* The act of searching or examining. **— in search of** Looking for.

search·ing [sûr'ching] *adj.* **1** Investigating carefully and in detail: a *searching* inquiry. **2** Penetrating; observant: a *searching* glance.

search·light [sûrch'līt'] *n.* **1** A light with a powerful beam that can be moved about for searching or signaling. **2** The beam of such a light.

search warrant A document issued by a court allowing the police to search a house or building, as for stolen goods, papers, etc.

sea shell The shell of a sea mollusk, as a clam, oyster, etc.

sea·shore [sē'shôr'] *n.* Land that borders on the ocean.

sea·sick [sē'sik'] *adj.* Suffering from nausea, dizziness, weakness, etc., caused by the motion of a ship at sea. **— sea'sick'ness** *n.*

sea·side [sē'sīd'] *n.* **1** The seashore, especially as a place for rest or amusement. **2** *adj. use:* a *seaside* hotel; a *seaside* resort.

sea·son [sē'zən] **1** *n.* One of the four divisions of the year as determined by the earth's position with respect to the sun. The seasons are spring, summer, autumn, and winter. **2** *n.* Some particular part of the year: the planting *season*; the baseball *season.* **3** *v.* To make taste better by adding spices, salt, etc.: to *season* a stew. **4** *v.* To add zest or interest to: to *season* a lecture with jokes. **5** *v.* To make fit for use by aging or drying, as wood. **6** *v.* To harden or make accustomed: to *season* troops for battle. **— in season 1** Naturally ready for use; ripe: Apples are *in season* in the fall. **2** That can be legally caught or hunted, as game. **— in good season** Soon enough. **— out of season** Not in season.

sea·son·a·ble [sē′zən·ə·bəl] *adj.* **1** In keeping with the season; expected at that time of year. **2** Coming or done at the proper time.

sea·son·al [sē′zən·əl] *adj.* Having to do with or happening at a certain season or seasons: *seasonal* storms. **— sea′son·al·ly** *adv.*

sea·son·ing [sē′zən·ing] *n.* **1** Something added to food to improve its flavor. **2** Something added to increase enjoyment, as humor to a speech or lecture.

seat [sēt] **1** *n.* Something on which one sits, as a chair, stool, etc. **2** *n.* The part of a piece of furniture on which one sits: the *seat* of a chair. **3** *v.* To cause to sit: to *seat* guests at the table. **4** *v.* To provide with seats: The theater *seats* 225 people. **5** *n.* The part of the body or of the clothes covering it on which one sits: the *seat* of his pants. **6** *n.* A place where one has a right to sit: a *seat* for the play. **7** *n.* A manner of sitting, as on horseback. **8** *n.* Membership in a legislature, stock exchange, etc.: a *seat* in the Senate. **9** *n.* The place where something is located or established: the *seat* of government; the *seat* of a disease. **10** *n.* A place of residence; estate or mansion. **— be seated 1** To sit. **2** To be sitting. **3** To be located or situated.

seat belt A strap attached to the seat of an airplane, automobile, etc., that buckles about the waist in order to prevent or reduce injury by holding a person firmly in his seat.

seat·ing [sē′ting] *n.* **1** The act of providing with seats. **2** Fabric for upholstering seats. **3** The arrangement of seats, as in a room, auditorium, etc.: The *seating* was carefully planned.

Seat belt

Se·at·tle [sē·at′(ə)l] *n.* A seaport in NW Washington.

sea urchin A small sea animal whose body is enclosed in a round, spiny shell.

sea wall A wall built to keep waves from striking the shore and washing it away, or to serve as a breakwater.

sea·ward [sē′wərd] **1** *adj.* Going toward the sea: a *seaward* trip. **2** *adj.* Coming from the sea, as a wind. **3** *adv.* In the direction of the sea: to fly *seaward.* **4** *n.* The direction toward the sea.

Sea urchin, 1–10 in. across

sea·wards [sē′wərdz] *adv.* Seaward.

sea·way [sē′wā′] *n.* **1** A route over the sea. **2** An inland waterway traveled by seagoing ships.

sea·weed [sē′wēd′] *n.* Any of the plants, especially algae, that grow in the ocean.

sea·wor·thy [sē′wûr′ṯħē] *adj.* In fit condition for a sea voyage, as a ship.

se·ba·ceous [si·bā′shəs] *adj.* **1** Of, like, or having to do with fat. **2** Indicating the glands in the skin that secrete oil.

sec. Abbreviation of: **1** SECOND. **2** Seconds. **3** SECRETARY. **4** SECTION.

se·cant (sē′kant] **1** *adj.* Cutting, especially into two parts. **2** *n.* In geometry, a straight line that cuts a given curve.

se·cede [si·sēd′] *v.* **se·ced·ed, se·ced· ing** To withdraw from a union or association, especially a political or religious one: During the Civil War, certain states *seceded* from the Union.

The red lines are secants.

se·ces·sion [si·sesh′ən] *n.* **1** The act of seceding, especially from a political or religious association. **2** *U.S.* (*written* **Secession**) The withdrawal of the Southern states from the Union in 1860–1861. **— se·ces′sion·ist** *n.*

se·clude [si·klōōd′] *v.* **se·clud·ed, se·clud·ing 1** To remove and keep apart from others: to *seclude* oneself because of shyness. **2** To shut off, as from view; hide. **3** *adj. use:* a *secluded* nook.

se·clu·sion [si·klōō′zhən] *n.* **1** The act of secluding. **2** The condition of being secluded; solitude. **3** A remote or hidden place.

sec·ond[1] [sek′ənd] *n.* **1** A unit of time equal to 1/60 of a minute. **2** A small amount of time: Wait just a *second.* **3** A unit used in measuring angles, equal to 1/60 of a minute or 1/3600 of a degree.

sec·ond[2] [sek′ənd] **1** *adj.* (*sometimes written* **2nd** *or* **2d**) Coming next after the first: the *second* grade in school. **2** *adj.* Ranking next below the first or best: the *second* hitter on a baseball team. **3** *adv.* In the second position, place, rank, etc.: to finish a race *second.* **4** *n.* The one next after the first: She was the *second* to arrive late. **5** *adj.* Being like someone who has gone before; another: a *second* Nero. **6** *adj.* Playing or singing the lower or less important part: *second* soprano; *second* oboe. **7** *n.* (*pl.*) Articles of merchandise that have defects. **8** *n.* A person who supports or assists, as in a duel, boxing match, etc. **9** *v.* To support or help in some way. **10** *v.* To announce support for or agreement with: to *second* a motion. **11** *adv.* As a second point; furthermore; secondly.

sec·on·dar·y [sek′ən·der′ē] *adj., n., pl.* **sec· on·dar·ies 1** *adj.* Coming, used, etc., after that which is first or primary: *secondary* defenses; *secondary* education. **2** *adj.* Depending on or derived from what is primary or original: *secondary* sources; *secondary* colors. **3** *n.* A person or thing that is subordinate or secondary. **4** *n.* A nonmoving coil of wire, as in a transformer, in which an electric current is induced. **5** *adj.* Of, related to, or indicating an induced current, as in a transformer. — **sec·on·dar′i·ly** *adv.*

secondary accent A mark (′) used to show where the secondary or weaker stress is placed in a word. In the word "secondary," the secondary accent is on the third syllable.

sec·ond-class [sek′ənd·klas′] **1** *adj.* Ranking next below the first or best: *second-class* travel accommodations; *second-class* mail. **2** *adj.* Of low quality; inferior: *second-class* goods. **3** *adv.* By or in second-class accommodations, mail, etc.: Magazines are mailed *second-class*.

sec·ond·hand [sek′ənd·hand′] **1** *adj.* Having been owned or used by someone else; not new: a *secondhand* radio. **2** *adj.* Received from another; not direct from the original source: *secondhand* information. **3** *adj.* Buying and selling goods that are not new: a *secondhand* furniture dealer. **4** *adv.* Not directly from the original source: to buy something *secondhand*; to hear news *secondhand*.

second lieutenant A military rank. In the U.S. Army, a second lieutenant is the lowest-ranking commissioned officer, below a first lieutenant.

sec·ond·ly [sek′ənd·lē] *adv.* In the second place.

second nature A habit or quality of behavior that is acquired but becomes so fixed as to seem part of one's nature.

second person The form of a verb or pronoun that refers to the person or persons addressed. *You* and *yours* are in the second person.

sec·ond-rate [sek′ənd·rāt′] *adj.* Second in quality, size, rank, importance, etc.: a *second-rate* song writer.

se·cre·cy [sē′krə·sē] *n.* **1** The condition or quality of being secret or hidden. **2** The habit of keeping secrets or the ability to do so.

se·cret [sē′krit] **1** *adj.* Kept from the view or knowledge of all but the persons concerned; hidden: a *secret* plot; a *secret* passageway. **2** *n.* Something not to be told. **3** *n.* Something that is not known or understood: the *secrets* of nature. **4** *adj.* Acting or having to do with hidden methods or ways: a *secret* agent; a *secret* brotherhood. — **in secret 1** In a private or hidden place. **2** In privacy; without outsiders knowing. — **se′cret·ly** *adv.*

sec·re·tar·i·at [sek′rə·târ′ē·it] *n.* **1** The position of a secretary. **2** The place of business of a secretary. **3** An entire staff of secretaries, especially, a department headed by a governmental secretary.

sec·re·tar·y [sek′rə·ter′ē] *n., pl.* **sec·re·tar·ies 1** A person whose duties involve writing letters, keeping records, etc., for a person, company, club, etc. **2** An official who heads a government

department: the *Secretary* of Defense. **3** A writing desk equipped with drawers, a bookcase, etc. — **sec′re·tar′i·al** *adj.* ◆

Secretary, which comes from a Latin word meaning *secret*, originally meant *someone entrusted with a secret*. Now the word is much broader in meaning and may refer to stenographers as well as to high government officials.

Secretary

se·crete [si·krēt′] *v.* **se·cret·ed, se·cret·ing 1** To keep from sight or knowledge; conceal; hide: to *secrete* a weapon. **2** To produce and give off (a secretion): The pituitary gland *secretes* hormones. — **se·cre′tor** *n.*

se·cre·tion [si·krē′shən] *n.* **1** The process by which a gland produces a substance, as a hormone, that serves some special purpose in the function of the body. **2** The substance produced.

se·cre·tive *adj.* **1** [si·krē′tiv *or* sē′krə·tiv] Inclined to secrecy; tending to keep secrets. **2** [si·krē′tiv] Producing or causing secretion. — **se·cre′tive·ly** *adv.* — **se·cre′tive·ness** *n.*

secret service 1 Secret investigation or spying done by a government. **2** (*written* **Secret Service**) A branch of the U.S. Treasury Department whose most important work is to find and arrest counterfeiters, and to guard the President and members of his immediate family.

sect [sekt] *n.* A group of people who share the same beliefs or who follow the same leader or teacher, especially in religious matters.

sec·tar·i·an [sek·târ′ē·ən] **1** *adj.* Of, like, or devoted to a particular sect. **2** *n.* A member of a sect, especially if narrow-minded and blindly devoted.

sec·tion [sek′shən] **1** *n.* A separate part or division; portion: a *section* of a book; to cut a cake into sections. **2** *v.* To cut into parts or sections: to *section* a chicken. **3** *n.* A part of a city or community; district; area: a *residential* section. **4** *n.* A drawing or diagram of an object as it would look if cut through by a plane; a cross section. **5** *n.* *U.S.* An area of land one mile square, making up 1/36 of a township.

Section of the earth showing rock strata

sec·tion·al [sek′shən·əl] *adj.* **1** Of, related to, or like some particular area or its people; regional. **2** Made up of sections or separate parts: a *sectional* sofa. — **sec′tion·al·ly** *adv.*

sec·tion·al·ism [sek′shən·əl·iz′əm] *n.* An excessive interest or pride in the section or region of a country where one lives or where one was raised.

section gang A crew of workmen who take care of a certain section of railroad track.

sec·tor [sek′tər] *n.* **1** A part of a circle bounded by an arc and two radii. **2** A section of a military area.

sec·u·lar [sek′yə·lər] *adj.* **1** Of or for the world rather than the church; not sacred or concerned with religion: *secular* art; *secular* education. **2** Not bound by monastic vows: *secular* clergy.

se·cure [si·kyŏŏr′] *adj., v.* **se·cured, se·cur·ing 1** *adj.* Not subject or exposed to danger or loss; safe: a *secure* fortress. **2** *v.* To make secure; protect; defend: *Secure* the gates! **3** *adj.* Free from fear or care: a *secure* childhood. **4** *adj.* Fixed or holding firmly in place: a *secure* fastening. **5** *v.* To fasten; make firm: to *secure* a rope. **6** *adj.* Certain; guaranteed: Your future success is *secure.* **7** *v.* To guarantee or ensure: to *secure* a loan. **8** *v.* To come to possess; get: to *secure* lodgings. **— se·cure′ly** *adv.*

se·cur·i·ty [si·kyŏŏr′ə·tē] *n., pl.* **se·cur·i·ties 1** The condition of being secure; freedom from danger, want, or fear. **2** A person or thing that secures or guarantees: A burglar alarm is a *security* against theft. **3** Something given or pledged as a guarantee for payment of money, etc. **4** (*pl.*) Stocks or bonds: My father keeps his *securities* in the bank.

se·dan [si·dan′] *n.* **1** An enclosed automobile having two or four doors and front and back seats. **2** A sedan chair.

sedan chair An enclosed chair carried on two poles extending forward and backward, used in the 17th and 18th centuries.

se·date [si·dāt′] *adj.* Always calm and serious. **— se·date′ly** *adv.* **— se·date′ness** *n.* ◆ *Sedate* comes from a Latin word meaning *to make calm* and goes back to the word meaning *to sit.*

Sedan chair

sed·a·tive [sed′ə·tiv] **1** *adj.* Having a soothing effect or relieving pain. **2** *n.* Something that soothes or relieves pain, as a medicine.

sed·en·tar·y [sed′ən·ter′ē] *adj.* **1** Requiring much sitting: A typist has a *sedentary* job. **2** Accustomed to much sitting: a *sedentary* man.

Se·der [sā′dər] *n., pl.* **Se·ders** or **Se·dar·im** [sə·där′im] In Judaism, the feast in remembrance of the departure of the Israelites from Egypt, celebrated on the eve of the first day of Passover.

sedge [sej] *n.* Any of several coarse, grasslike plants that grow mainly in damp or swampy places.

sed·i·ment [sed′ə·mənt] *n.* **1** Matter that settles to the bottom of a liquid; dregs. **2** Small particles deposited by air or water.

sed·i·men·ta·ry [sed′ə·men′tər·ē] *adj.* **1** Of or like sediment. **2** Formed from sediment, as certain rocks.

sed·i·men·ta·tion [sed′ə·men·tā′shən] *n.* The accumulation or depositing of sediment.

se·di·tion [si·dish′ən] *n.* Speech or conduct that stirs up revolt against a government.

se·di·tious [si·dish′əs] *adj.* **1** Of or having to do with sedition. **2** Taking part in or guilty of sedition. **3** Stirring up revolt.

se·duce [si·d(y)ōōs′] *v.* **se·duced, se·duc·ing** To lead into wrongdoing; tempt: *Seduced* by bribes, he became a spy. **— se·duc′er** *n.*

se·duc·tion [si·duk′shən] *n.* **1** The act of seducing. **2** Something that seduces; a temptation.

se·duc·tive [si·duk′tiv] *adj.* Tempting or enticing; very attractive.

sed·u·lous [sej′ŏŏ·ləs] *adj.* Carefully attentive and hard working; diligent. **— sed′u·lous·ly** *adv.*

see[1] [sē] *v.* **saw, seen, see·ing 1** To be aware of or notice by means of the eyes: to *see* a dog. **2** To get images of things through the eyes: He can't *see* without glasses. **3** To grasp with the mind; understand: Now I *see* what he meant. **4** To find out; determine: Let's *see* how that works. **5** To have experience or knowledge of: The car has *seen* hard use. **6** To chance to meet: I *saw* them today. **7** To have a meeting or interview with: to *see* a dentist. **8** To visit with or receive as a visitor: We went to *see* our cousin; The mayor will *see* you now. **9** To attend as a spectator: to *see* a ball game. **10** To escort or accompany: I will *see* you home. **11** To take care; be sure: *See* that you do it right now! **12** To think hard: Let me *see,* where did I put my glasses? **— see about 1** To find out about; investigate. **2** To take care of; attend to. **— see off** To be at a ship, train, etc., to say good-by. **— see out** To go with as far as an exit. **— see through 1** To help or protect in a period of difficulty or danger. **2** To work or wait until a job, difficulty, etc., is ended. **3** To notice the falseness of; not be fooled by. **— see to** To take care of; attend to.

see[2] [sē] *n.* **1** The office, authority, or rank of a bishop. **2** The district under a bishop's rule. ◆ *See* comes from a Latin word meaning *seat.*

seed [sēd] *n., pl.* **seeds** or **seed,** *v.* **1** *n.* The embryo of a plant and food for its early growth. It is enclosed in a case or covering and is able to grow into a young plant under favorable conditions. **2** *v.* To plant seeds in: to *seed* a garden. **3** *v.* To remove the seeds from: to *seed* grapes. **4** *v.* To mature and produce seeds. **5** *n.* A small beginning from which something grows; source: the *seeds* of revolt. **6** *n.* Children and descendants; offspring: Abraham and his *seed.* **— go to seed 1** To develop and shed seed. **2** To become useless, shabby, etc.; deteriorate. **— seed′er** *n.*

seed·case [sēd′kās′] *n.* The hollow, usually dry fruit containing the seeds of a plant; pod.

add, āce, câre, pälm;   end, ēqual;   it, īce;   odd, ōpen, ôrder;   tŏŏk, pōōl;   up, bûrn;
ə = a in *above,* e in *sicken,* i in *possible,* o in *melon,* u in *circus;*   yōō = u in *fuse;*   oil;   pout;
check;   ring;   thin;   this;   zh in *vision.*   For ¶ reference, see page 64 · HOW TO

seed·ling [sēd′ling] *n.* A young tree or plant, grown from a seed and not from a cutting.

seed pearl A very small, often irregularly shaped pearl, used as trimming on clothes, in jewelry, etc.

seed·y [sē′dē] *adj.* **seed·i·er, seed·i·est 1** Full of seeds: *seedy* oranges. **2** Gone to seed. **3** Poor and ragged; shabby: a *seedy* suit. — **seed′i·ly** *adv.* — **seed′i·ness** *n.*

see·ing [sē′ing] **1** *n.* The ability to see; sight. **2** *conj.* Considering; in view of the fact; because: *Seeing* that it's late, let's hurry. **3** *adj.* Having sight; able to see.

seek [sēk] *v.* **sought, seek·ing 1** To go in search of; look for: to *seek* rare books. **2** To try to get or obtain: to *seek* wealth. **3** To attempt; try: He *seeks* to cheat us. — **seek′er** *n.*

seem [sēm] *v.* **1** To have the appearance of being; look: The bridge *seems* safe. **2** To appear to oneself: I *seem* to smell gas. **3** To appear to be true or clear: It *seems* to be raining.

seem·ing [sē′ming] *adj.* Appearing to be true or real, but possibly false: her *seeming* innocence. — **seem′ing·ly** *adv.*

seem·ly [sēm′lē] *adj.* **seem·li·er, seem·li·est** Decent or proper; fitting; suitable: *seemly* conduct. — **seem′li·ness** *n.*

seen [sēn] Past participle of SEE.

seep [sēp] *v.* To soak through small spaces or openings; ooze: Water *seeped* into the cellar.

seep·age [sē′pij] *n.* **1** The act or process of seeping or oozing. **2** The fluid that seeps.

seer [sē′ər *or* sir] *n.* A person who foretells events; prophet.

seer·suck·er [sir′suk′ər] *n.* A thin fabric of cotton, rayon, etc., with a crinkled surface.

see·saw [sē′sô′] **1** *n.* A long board supported on a pivot at the center so that it can be made to move alternately up and down by persons at opposite ends. **2** *v.* To move up and down on a seesaw. **3** *v.* To move up and down or to and fro. **4** *adj.* Moving up and down or to and fro.

seethe [sēth] *v.* **seethed, seeth·ing 1** To boil, or foam and bubble as if boiling. **2** To be excited or upset: Father will *seethe* with anger when he hears this.

seg·ment [seg′mənt] **1** *n.* A part cut off or divided from the rest of something; section. **2** *v.* To cut or divide into segments. **3** *n.* A part of the interior of a circle bounded by an arc and a straight line. **4** *n.* A line segment. — **seg′men·ta′tion** *n.*

seg·re·gate [seg′rə·gāt] *v.* **seg·re·gat·ed, seg·re·gat·ing 1** To place apart from others; isolate: to *segregate* a sick animal. **2** To set apart and force to use separate schools, housing, parts of parks, buses, etc., because of racial, religious, or social differences. **3** To regulate use of (a school, park, etc.) so as to separate racial, religious, or ethnic groups. **4** To separate, as a small group from a large one or a liquid from a solid.

seg·re·ga·tion [seg′rə·gā′shən] *n.* **1** The act or process of segregating. **2** The practice of sep-arating a racial or religious group from the rest of society, as in schools, housing, parks, etc. — **seg′re·ga′tion·ist** *n.*

sei·gneur [sēn·yûr′] *n.* In the Middle Ages, a feudal lord or noble.

seine [sān] *n., v.* **seined, sein·ing 1** *n.* A long fishnet hanging vertically in the water, having floats at the top and weights at the bottom. **2** *v.* To fish with such a net.

Seine [sān] *n.* A river flowing from NE France to the English Channel.

Seine

seis·mic [sīz′mik] *adj.* Of, having to do with, or caused by earthquakes: a severe *seismic* shock.

seis·mo·graph [sīz′mə·graf] *n.* An instrument that records the duration, direction, and intensity of earthquakes and other shocks in the earth.

seize [sēz] *v.* **seized, seiz·ing 1** To take hold of suddenly and with force; grab; snatch: to *seize* a sword. **2** To take prisoner; capture; arrest. **3** To take possession of by force: to *seize* a city. **4** To take possession of by right or authority. **5** To take quick advantage of: to *seize* a chance. **6** To strike or affect suddenly: to be *seized* with a fit of laughter. — **seize on** or **seize upon** To grab quickly.

sei·zure [sē′zhər] *n.* **1** The act of seizing. **2** A sudden, violent attack, as of a disease.

sel·dom [sel′dəm] *adv.* At widely separated times; rarely; not often.

se·lect [si·lekt′] **1** *v.* To take in preference to another or others; choose: to *select* a hat. **2** *adj.* Chosen for worth or high quality; choice. **3** *adj.* Very particular in choosing; exclusive.

se·lec·tee [si·lek′tē′] *n.* A person who is selected, especially a person drafted for military or naval service.

se·lec·tion [si·lek′shən] *n.* **1** The act of selecting; choice. **2** A group of things from which to choose. **3** A thing chosen.

se·lec·tive [si·lek′tiv] *adj.* **1** Tending to select. **2** Of, related to, or characterized by selection. **3** Responding to a chosen frequency of radio waves and excluding others, as a radio receiver. — **se·lec·tiv·i·ty** [si·lek′tiv′ə·tē] *n.*

selective service A system of choosing young men for required military service; draft.

se·lect·man [si·lekt′mən] *n., pl.* **se·lect·men** [si·lekt′mən] In New England, a member of a board of town officials elected yearly to run public affairs.

se·lec·tor [si·lek′tər] *n.* **1** A person who selects. **2** A switch or control used to choose different actions of a machine.

se·le·ni·um [si·lē′nē·əm] *n.* A gray, crystalline, nonmetallic element related to sulfur. Its electrical resistance changes under the influence of light.

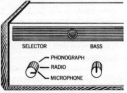
SELECTOR · BASS · PHONOGRAPH · RADIO · MICROPHONE

self [self] *n.*, *pl.* **selves** [selvz], *adj.* **1** *n.* One's own individual personality as distinct from others; one's own person: Today I am not my usual *self*. **2** *n.* One's own benefit or advantage: to put *self* first. **3** *adj.* Made of the same material as that with which it is used: The dress has a *self* belt.

self- A combining form meaning: **1** Of oneself, as in *self-criticism*, criticism of oneself. **2** By oneself, as in *self-educated*, educated by oneself. **3** In or with oneself, as in *self-absorbed*, absorbed in oneself. **4** To oneself, as in *self-injury*, injury to oneself. **5** For oneself, as in *self-love*, love for oneself.

self-ad·dressed [self'ə·drest'] *adj.* Addressed to oneself.

self-ap·point·ed [self'ə·poin'təd] *adj.* Appointed by oneself, with no other authorization and often without the abilities needed: a *self-appointed* critic.

self-as·ser·tion [self'ə·sûr'shən] *n.* The putting forward of oneself or one's ideas, claims, etc.

self-as·sured [self'ə·shŏŏrd'] *adj.* Having confidence in one's own worth and abilities. — **self'-as·sur'ance** *n.*

self-cen·tered [self'sen'tərd] *adj.* Concerned mainly with oneself and often inconsiderate of others. — **self'-cen'tered·ness** *n.* ¶2

self-com·mand [self'kə·mand'] *n.* Full control of oneself and one's powers and feelings.

self-con·fi·dent [self'kon'fə·dənt] *adj.* Confident of oneself; self-assured. — **self'-con'fi·dence** *n.* — **self'-con'fi·dent·ly** *adv.*

self-con·scious [self'kon'shəs] *adj.* **1** So aware of how one appears to others that one is very embarrassed. **2** Showing such awareness or embarrassment: a *self-conscious* grin. — **self'-con'scious·ly** *adv.* — **self'-con'scious·ness** *n.*

self-con·tained [self'kən·tānd'] *adj.* **1** Containing everything it needs to operate or function: a *self-contained* phonograph; a *self-contained* community. **2** Not allowing one's thoughts and feelings to show. **3** Exercising self-control.

self-con·trol [self'kən·trōl'] *n.* Control of one's emotions, actions, etc.

self-de·fense [self'di·fens'] *n.* Defense of oneself or one's property, reputation, etc.

self-de·ni·al [self'di·nī'əl] *n.* The giving up of things that are necessary or wanted.

self-de·ny·ing [self'di·nī'ing] *adj.* Practicing self-denial; unselfish.

self-de·ter·mi·na·tion [self'di·tûr'mə·nā'shən] *n.* **1** The right to make one's own decisions; free will. **2** The right of a people or country to choose its own form of government without outside interference.

self-dis·ci·pline [self'dis'ə·plin] *n.* Control of one's emotions, actions, etc., often in order to improve oneself.

self-ed·u·cat·ed [self'ej'ŏŏ·kā'tid] *adj.* Educated by one's own effort, with little or no instruction in school; self-taught.

self-es·teem [self'ə·stēm'] *n.* **1** A good opinion of oneself. **2** Too good an opinion of oneself.

self-ev·i·dent [self'ev'ə·dənt] *adj.* Needing no evidence, proof, or explanation.

self-ex·plan·a·to·ry [self'ik·splan'ə·tôr'ē] *adj.* Easily understood without explanation; plain.

self-ex·pres·sion [self'ik·spresh'ən] *n.* Expression of one's feelings and thoughts, as in art.

self-gov·ern·ing [self'guv'ər·ning] *adj.* Having control over itself; not subject to an outside authority: a *self-governing* country.

self-gov·ern·ment [self'guv'ərn·mənt] *n.* The governing of an area by its own people.

self-im·por·tant [self'im·pôr'tənt] *adj.* Thinking too well of oneself; pompous or conceited. — **self'-im·por'tance** *n.*

self-in·dul·gent [self'in·dul'jənt] *adj.* Satisfying one's own desires, whims, etc. — **self'-in·dul'gence** *n.*

self-in·ter·est [self'in'tər·ist *or* self'in'trist] *n.* **1** Personal advantage or benefit. **2** Interest in or pursuit of personal advantage; selfishness.

self·ish [sel'fish] *adj.* **1** Caring mainly for oneself and hardly at all about others. **2** Showing or caused by an excessive care for oneself and disregard of others: a *selfish* action. — **self'ish·ly** *adv.* — **self'ish·ness** *n.*

self·less [self'lis] *adj.* Having little or no regard for self; unselfish. — **self'less·ly** *adv.*

self-made [self'mād'] *adj.* **1** Successful, rich, etc., because of one's own hard work. **2** Made by oneself.

self-pit·y [self'pit'ē] *n.* A feeling of pity for oneself.

self-pos·sessed [self'pə·zest'] *adj.* Calm and in full control of one's emotions, actions, etc.

self-pos·ses·sion [self'pə·zesh'ən] *n.* Full control over one's emotions, actions, etc.

self-pres·er·va·tion [self'prez'ər·vā'shən] *n.* The act or instinct of keeping oneself alive or unharmed.

self-pro·pelled [self'prə·peld'] *adj.* Having within itself the means or power by which it moves: An automobile is a *self-propelled* vehicle.

self-re·li·ant [self'ri·lī'ənt] *adj.* Relying on one's own abilities, efforts, judgment, etc. — **self'-re·li'ance** *n.*

self-re·spect [self'ri·spekt'] *n.* A proper sense of pride in or respect for oneself. — **self'-re·spect'ing** *adj.*

self-re·straint [self'ri·strānt'] *n.* Restraint of oneself; self-control.

self-right·eous [self'rī'chəs] *adj.* Believing one's own thoughts and actions to be more righteous than those of other people. — **self'-right'eous·ly** *adv.* — **self'-right'eous·ness** *n.*

self-sac·ri·fice [self'sak'rə·fīs] *n.* The sacrifice

add, āce, câre, pälm;   **end, ēqual;**   **it, īce;**   **odd, ōpen, ôrder;**   **tŏŏk, pōol;**   **up, bûrn;**
ə = a in *above*, e in *sicken*, i in *possible*, o in *melon*, u in *circus*;   **yōō** = u in *fuse*;   **oil;**   **pout,**
check; ring; thin; this; zh in *vision*.   For ¶ reference, see page 64 · HOW TO

of oneself, one's needs or wants, etc., usually because of duty or for the good of others. — **self′-sac′ri·fic′ing** *adj.*

self·same [self′sām′] *adj.* Exactly the same; identical: He did the *selfsame* thing again.

self-sat·is·fac·tion [self′sat′is·fak′shən] *n.* Satisfaction with oneself; conceit.

self-sat·is·fied [self′sat′is·fīd] *adj.* Satisfied with oneself; conceited.

self-seek·ing [self′sē′king] **1** *adj.* Caring only about one's own gain or advancement; selfish. **2** *n.* The attitudes, actions, etc., of a self-seeking person. — **self′-seek′er** *n.*

self-ser·vice [self′sûr′vis] **1** *n.* The practice of having the patrons of a store, restaurant, etc., serve themselves. **2** *adj. use:* a *self-service* market.

self-styled [self′stīld′] *adj.* Called so by oneself: a *self-styled* musician.

self-suf·fi·cient [self′sə·fish′ənt] *adj.* **1** Able to supply everything needed without outside help. **2** Having great or too great confidence in oneself.

self-sup·port·ing [self′sə·pôr′ting] *adj.* Supporting oneself or itself without help.

self-taught [self′tôt′] *adj.* Taught by oneself without formal instruction; self-educated.

self-will [self′wil′] *n.* Stubbornness in having one's own way; disregard for the wishes of others.

self·willed [self′wild′] *adj.* Tending to disregard the wishes of others; stubborn; obstinate.

self-wind·ing [self′wīn′ding] *adj.* Winding itself automatically, as a clock or watch.

sell [sel] *v.* **sold, sell·ing** **1** To give in exchange for money: to *sell* a house. **2** To deal in; offer for sale: Do you *sell* books? **3** To be on sale; be sold: Gold *sells* at a high price. **4** To help or influence the sale of: Advertising *sells* some products. **5** To betray for money or a reward: to *sell* one's honor. **6** *informal* To get approval from or for: They *sold* him on the scheme. — **sell out** **1** To sell one's complete stock of. **2** *slang* To betray (a cause, friend, etc.). — **sell′er** *n.*

sel·vage or **sel·vedge** [sel′vij] *n.* The edge of a woven fabric finished so as to prevent raveling.

se·man·tic [si·man′tik] *adj.* Of or related to the meanings of words.

se·man·tics [si·man′tiks] *n.* The study of the development of and the changes in the meanings of words. ◆ See -ICS.

sem·a·phore [sem′ə·fôr] *n., v.* **sem·a·phored, sem·a·phor·ing** **1** *n.* A system of sending messages by the arms, flags, etc., held in different positions. **2** *v.* To send (a message) by semaphore. **3** *n.* A tower with movable arms used to signal railroad trains.

sem·blance [sem′bləns] *n.* Likeness; outward appearance or show: a *semblance* of cleanliness.

Semaphore

se·men [sē′mən] *n.* The fluid that contains sperm, secreted by male animals.

se·mes·ter [si·mes′tər] *n.* **1** Either of the two parts of a school year, 17–20 weeks long; term. **2** Any term or session of instruction: Our summer school is divided into three *semesters.* ◆ *Semester* comes directly from the German.

semi- A prefix meaning: **1** Not fully; partly, as in *semiautomatic,* partly automatic. **2** Exactly half, as in *semicircle,* exactly half a circle. **3** Happening twice in the period of time mentioned, as in *semiannually,* twice a year. ◆ See BI-.

sem·i·an·nu·al [sem′ē·an′yōō·əl] *adj.* Issued or happening twice a year. — **sem′i·an′nu·al·ly** *adv.*

sem·i·cir·cle [sem′ē·sûr′kəl] *n.* A half circle.

sem·i·cir·cu·lar [sem′ē·sûr′kyə·lər] *adj.* Shaped like a half circle.

sem·i·co·lon [sem′ē·kō′lən] *n.* A mark (;) of punctuation showing a separation that is greater than that shown by a comma but less than that shown by a period.

sem·i·fi·nal [sem′ē·fī′nəl] **1** *n.* A round or match that is next to the last of a contest, competition, etc. **2** *adj.* Of or having to do with such a round or match.

sem·i·month·ly [sem′ē·munth′lē] *adj.* Issued, taking place, etc., twice a month.

sem·i·nar·y [sem′ə·ner′ē] *n., pl.* **sem·i·nar·ies** **1** A high school or school of higher education, especially a boarding school for young women. **2** A school or college that trains clergymen.

Sem·i·nole [sem′ə·nōl] *n.* A member of a tribe of North American Indians living in Florida and now also in Oklahoma.

sem·i·pre·cious [sem′ē·presh′əs] *adj.* Indicating gems, as jade, garnet, opal, etc., that are less valuable or rare than precious stones.

Sem·ite [sem′īt] *n.* A member of a group of peoples that includes the Hebrews, Arabs, and the ancient Assyrians and Babylonians.

Se·mit·ic [sə·mit′ik] *adj.* Of, having to do with, or like the Semites or their languages.

sem·i·tone [sem′ē·tōn′] *n.* The smallest interval of the musical scale, as between a white key and an adjoining black key on a piano.

sem·i·trop·i·cal [sem′ē·trop′i·kəl] *adj.* Partly tropical: Louisiana has a *semitropical* climate.

sem·i·week·ly [sem′ē·wēk′lē] *adj.* Issued, happening, etc., twice weekly.

Sen. Abbreviation of: **1** SENATE. **2** SENATOR.

sen·ate [sen′it] *n.* **1** A governing or law-making body. **2** (*written* **Senate**) The upper house of the Congress of the United States, or of the legislature of a state or other government.

sen·a·tor [sen′ə·tər] *n.* (*sometimes written* **Senator**) A member of a senate or a Senate.

sen·a·to·ri·al [sen′ə·tôr′ē·əl] *adj.* **1** Of, having to do with, or proper for a senator or senate. **2** Made up of senators. **3** Entitled to elect a senator: a *senatorial* district.

send [send] *v.* **sent, send·ing** **1** To cause or direct to go: *Send* him away! **2** To cause to be taken or transferred to another place: to *send* a telegram; The general *sent* more troops. **3** To cause to come, happen, be, etc.: God *send* us peace. **4** To issue; emit: The sun *sends* forth light. **5** To bring into a specific condition: The news *sent* him into a rage. **— send for 1** To ask or order to come; summon. **2** To ask for; request; place an order for. **— send′er** *n.*

Sen·e·ca [sen′ə·kə] *n.* A member of a tribe of North American Indians of western New York. It was the largest tribe of the Iroquois.

Sen·e·gal [sen′ə·gôl] *n.* A country in NW Africa.

sen·e·schal [sen′ə·shəl] *n.* In the residence of a medieval lord, an official in charge of the household, of feasts, etc.; steward.

se·nile [sē′nīl] *adj.* **1** Failing in body and mind because of old age. **2** Related to, caused by, or characteristic of old age: *senile* diseases.

se·nil·i·ty [si·nil′ə·tē] *n.* Mental and physical weakness caused by old age.

sen·ior [sēn′yər] **1** *adj.* Older, higher in rank, or longer in office. **2** *n.* The one who is older, higher in rank, or longer in office. **3** *n.* The older: written after the name of a father whose son has the same name, and usually abbreviated: John Snead, *Sr.* **4** *adj.* Of or during the final year of high school or college. **5** *n.* A student in the final year of high school or college.

senior high school A high school. In the U.S., it usually is made up of grades 10, 11, and 12.

sen·ior·i·ty [sēn·yôr′ə·tē] *n.* **1** Greater age, rank, or length of service. **2** Privileges or preference due to age, rank, or length of service.

sen·na [sen′ə] *n.* **1** The dried leaves of any of several plants related to the pea or bean, used as a laxative. **2** A plant having these leaves.

se·ñor [sā·nyôr′] *n.* The Spanish title of courtesy for a man, equivalent to the English *Mr.*

se·ño·ra [sā·nyō′rä] *n.* The Spanish title of courtesy for a married woman, equivalent to the English *Mrs.*

se·ño·ri·ta [sā·nyō·rē′tä] *n.* The Spanish title of courtesy for an unmarried woman or girl, equivalent to the English *Miss.*

sen·sa·tion [sen·sā′shən] *n.* **1** The awareness of stimulation of any of the senses, as sight, smell, touch, etc.: I have a *sensation* of coldness. **2** A feeling that comes from the mind or the emotions: a *sensation* of hate. **3** Great interest or excitement: The movie caused a *sensation*. **4** Something that causes great interest or excitement.

sen·sa·tion·al [sen·sā′shən·əl] *adj.* **1** Causing great excitement or interest: a *sensational* play. **2** Designed to shock or startle: *sensational* gossip. **3** Of or having to do with the senses. **— sen·sa′tion·al·ly** *adv.*

sense [sens] *n., v.* **sensed, sens·ing 1** *n.* Any of the bodily or mental powers by which one is made aware of the world outside, as sight, hearing, touch, smell, or taste. **2** *n.* A feeling or awareness: a *sense* of fall in the air. **3** *v.* To be-

come aware of: The deer *sensed* danger and ran. **4** *n.* (often *pl.*) Normal ability to think or reason clearly; sound or natural judgment: Chickens have little *sense*; She is coming to her *senses*. **5** *n.* An awareness or understanding: a *sense* of right and wrong. **6** *n.* A meaning, as of a word. **— make sense** To mean something reasonable. **— in a sense** In a way.

sense·less [sens′lis] *adj.* **1** Without feeling or awareness; unconscious. **2** Stupid or without purpose: *senseless* cruelty. **— sense′less·ly** *adv.*

sense organ A part of the body by which one sees, hears, smells, etc., as the eye, ear, or nose.

sen·si·bil·i·ty [sen′sə·bil′ə·tē] *n., pl.* **sen·si·bil·i·ties 1** The capability or power of feeling or being aware: the *sensibility* of the eye to light. **2** (often *pl.*) Sensitive or delicate feelings: Ugliness hurt his *sensibilities*; She has a fine *sensibility* for music.

sen·si·ble [sen′sə·bəl] *adj.* **1** Having or showing wisdom or good judgment. **2** Capable of feeling or reacting; sensitive: *sensible* to heat. **3** Large enough to be noticed: a *sensible* difference of temperature. **4** Emotionally or mentally aware: to be *sensible* of a person's anger. **— sen′si·bly** *adv.*

sen·si·tive [sen′sə·tiv] *adj.* **1** Capable of feeling, reacting, appreciating, etc., quickly or easily: The ear is *sensitive* to sound; a *sensitive* thermometer; a film *sensitive* to light. **2** Easy to upset or make angry; touchy. **3** Extremely or abnormally susceptible: *sensitive* to changes in diet. **4** Tender or painful: a *sensitive* spot on the skin. **— sen′si·tive·ness** *n.*

sen·si·tiv·i·ty [sen′sə·tiv′ə·tē] *n., pl.* **sen·si·tiv·i·ties 1** The condition of being sensitive. **2** The degree to which something is sensitive.

sen·so·ry [sen′sər·ē] *adj.* Of or having to do with sensation: *sensory* nerves.

sen·su·al [sen′shōō·əl] *adj.* **1** Of or having to do with the body or the senses. **2** Indulging too much in bodily pleasures. **— sen·su·al·i·ty** [sen′shōō·al′ə·tē] *n.* **— sen′su·al·ly** *adv.*

sen·su·ous [sen′shōō·əs] *adj.* **1** Coming from, having to do with, or appealing to the senses: a *sensuous* dance; *sensuous* enjoyment of music. **2** Enjoying the pleasures of the senses, especially in a delicate or refined way. **— sen′su·ous·ly** *adv.* **— sen′su·ous·ness** *n.*

sent [sent] Past tense or past participle of SEND.

sen·tence [sen′təns] *n., v.* **sen·tenced, sen·tenc·ing 1** *n.* A word or group of words, grammatically complete, expressing a statement, question, order, etc. "When I came" is not a sentence. "We are hungry" is a sentence. **2** *n.* A final judgment, especially in a criminal case. **3** *n.* The punishment pronounced upon a person convicted of a crime. **4** *v.* To pass sentence upon; condemn.

sen·ten·tious [sen·ten′shəs] *adj.* **1** Using few words but expressing a good deal. **2** Habitually using proverbs or sayings in a dull, pompous, or moralizing way. **— sen·ten′tious·ly** *adv.*

sen·ti·ent [sen′shē·ənt] *adj.* Having awareness, sensations, and feelings: A stone is not a *sentient* thing.

sen·ti·ment [sen′tə·mənt] *n.* **1** A delicate or refined feeling. **2** An expression of such a feeling, especially in words. **3** A mental attitude toward a person, object, or idea, based on feeling instead of reason. **4** (*often pl.*) An attitude, opinion, or feeling: What are your *sentiments* about sports? **5** Feeling or emotion made too important, too obvious, or too much emphasized.

sen·ti·men·tal [sen′tə·men′təl] *adj.* **1** Having, showing, or appealing to very tender feelings: a *sentimental* song. **2** Acting on or influenced by feelings rather than logical thought: Some women are too *sentimental*. **3** Of or having to do with sentiment: to keep an old letter for *sentimental* reasons. **— sen′ti·men′tal·ly** *adv.*

sen·ti·men·tal·i·ty [sen′tə·men·tal′ə·tē] *n., pl.* **sen·ti·men·tal·i·ties** **1** A tendency to indulge in too much sentiment and to be too much influenced by it. **2** An expression of excessive or foolish emotion: This poem is a piece of sheer *sentimentality*.

sen·ti·nel [sen′tə·nəl] *n.* A watcher or guard; sentry. **— stand sentinel** To keep watch; guard.

sen·try [sen′trē] *n., pl.* **sen·tries** A person, especially a soldier, assigned to guard an area against intruders and to look out for danger.

se·pal [sē′pəl] *n.* One of the leaves that form the calyx surrounding the petals of a flower.

sep·a·ra·ble [sep′ər·ə·bəl *or* sep′rə·bəl] *adj.* That can be separated.

sep·a·rate [*v.* sep′ə·rāt, *adj.* sep′ər·it *or* sep′rit] *v.* **sep·a·rat·ed, sep·a·rat·ing,** *adj.* **1** *v.* To move apart; part: to *separate* a couple of boys fighting; *Separate* the curtains. **2** *adj.* Not connected or joined; detached: The swimming pool is in a *separate* building. **3** *v.* To keep apart by being between; divide: The Hudson River *separates* New York City from New Jersey. **4** *v.* To divide into parts, groups, etc.: to *separate* water into oxygen and hydrogen; *Separate* knives from forks. **5** *v.* To take, go, or come apart; make or become disconnected or disunited: The team *separated* after the game. **6** *adj.* Existing or working as a unit distinct from others: the many *separate* parts that make up an engine. **7** *adj.* Not shared or joined; single; individual: to have *separate* rooms; These are two *separate* problems. **— sep′a·rate·ly** *adv.* **— sep′a·ra′tion** *n.*

sep·a·ra·tist [sep′ər·ə·tist] *n.* A person who favors separation, as from a political or religious organization.

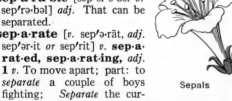

Sepals

sep·a·ra·tor [sep′ə·rā′tər] *n.* **1** Any device that separates things, as chaff from grain, cream from milk, etc. **2** A person who separates.

se·pi·a [sē′pē·ə] **1** *adj., n.* Reddish brown. **2** *n.* A picture or photograph having a sepia color.

Sept. Abbreviation of SEPTEMBER.

Sep·tem·ber [sep·tem′bər] *n.* The ninth month of the year, having 30 days.

sep·tic [sep′tik] *adj.* **1** Of or caused by infection. **2** Causing infection; infectious.

septic tank A tank into which sewage drains to be destroyed by the action of bacteria.

sep·ul·cher or **sep·ul·chre** [sep′əl·kər] *n.* A burial place; grave; tomb.

se·pul·chral [si·pul′krəl] *adj.* **1** Of or having to do with a sepulcher. **2** Gloomy; dismal; sad: a *sepulchral* voice.

se·quel [sē′kwəl] *n.* **1** Something that follows, usually as a development of what went before. **2** A story that, though complete in itself, carries on from where a preceding story ended.

se·quence [sē′kwəns] *n.* **1** The coming of one thing after another in space, time, etc.: the *sequence* of the seasons. **2** The order or arrangement in which one thing comes after another: The correct *sequence* is for the youngest children to enter first. **3** A number of things following each other; series: a *sequence* of events.

se·ques·ter [si·kwes′tər] *v.* **1** To withdraw or hide: to *sequester* oneself in a private hunting lodge. **2** To take over and keep, as enemy property in wartime. **— se′ques·tra′tion** *n.*

se·quin [sē′kwin] *n.* A small, shiny disc used as an ornamental trimming on clothing.

se·quoi·a [si·kwoi′ə] *n.* Either of two gigantic evergreen trees of the western United States. One is the redwood. ◆ *Sequoia* comes from *Sequoyah*, 1770?–1843, a Cherokee Indian who invented the Cherokee alphabet.

se·ra·glio [si·ral′yō] *n.* That part of a Moslem house where the women and girls live; harem.

se·ra·pe [se·rä′pē] *n.* A blanketlike outer garment worn in Latin America, especially in Mexico.

ser·aph [ser′əf] *n., pl.* **ser·aphs** or **ser·a·phim** [ser′ə·fim] An angel of the highest rank, having three pairs of wings.

se·raph·ic [si·raf′ik] *adj.* **1** Of or having to do with a seraph. **2** Like a seraph; angelic.

Serb [sûrb] *n.* A person born in or a citizen of Serbia.

Ser·bi·a [sûr′bē·ə] *n.* A former country, now a region in eastern Yugoslavia. **— Ser′bi·an** *adj., n.*

sere [sir] *adj.* Dried or withered: used mostly in poems.

Serape

ser·e·nade [ser′ə·nād′] *n., v.* **ser·e·nad·ed, ser·e·nad·ing** **1** *n.* A song, usually one sung in the evening by a lover beneath his sweetheart's window. **2** *n.* The music for such a song. **3** *v.* To entertain with a serenade.

se·rene [si·rēn′] *adj.* **1** Clear; fair; calm: a *serene* sky. **2** Peaceful; tranquil; unruffled; calm: a *serene* spirit. **— se·rene′ly** *adv.*

se·ren·i·ty [si·ren′ə·tē] *n.* **1** Peacefulness; repose. **2** Clearness; brightness.

serf [sûrf] *n.* **1** In feudal times, a man who could not leave the land he worked on, and who could be sold along with the land. **2** Any person treated like a slave.

serf·dom [sûrf′dəm] *n.* **1** The condition of being a serf. **2** The practice of having serfs.

serge [sûrj] *n.* A strong, woven fabric, usually of wool, having slanting lines or ridges on its surface, and used for coats, suits, etc.

ser·geant [sär′jənt] *n.* **1** A military rank. In the U.S. Army, a sergeant is a noncommissioned officer ranking above a corporal. **2** A police officer ranking next below a captain or sometimes below a lieutenant. ◆ *Sergeant* comes from an old French word meaning a *servant* or *attendant*, and this was the earliest meaning of the word in English. This meaning is still preserved in *sergeant at arms*.

sergeant at arms An officer whose main duty is to keep order in a legislative body, in certain courts, etc. ◆ See SERGEANT.

se·ri·al [sir′ē·əl] **1** *adj.* Of, having to do with, or arranged in a series: *serial* numbers. **2** *n.* A story whose parts are presented one at a time in the issues of a newspaper or magazine. **3** *n.* A play presented in short, usually daily installments on television or radio. **— se′ri·al·ly** *adv.*

serial number A number given to a person or thing as a means of identification: Every soldier has a *serial number*.

se·ries [sir′ēz] *n., pl.* **se·ries** **1** A number of people or things coming one after another in time, place, etc.: a *series* of visitors; a *series* of buildings; a *series* of battles. **2** A group of batteries, light bulbs, etc., so connected that the same electrical current flows through each of them in turn.

se·ri·ous [sir′ē·əs] *adj.* **1** Grave; solemn; thoughtful: You look *serious* today. **2** Not joking; sincere: Is he *serious* about the trip? **3** Of great importance; weighty: a *serious* problem. **4** Likely to be harmful or dangerous: a *serious* accident; a *serious* illness. **— se′ri·ous·ly** *adv.* **— se′ri·ous·ness** *n.* ◆ *Serious*, *earnest*, and *sober* are all used to describe people. A *serious* person is not playful or silly. He sets about doing his business with real purpose. An *earnest* person is more eager, and his sincerity is obvious. A *sober* person is apt to be more methodical and much less excitable than an *earnest* person, and more detached from what he is doing than a *serious* person.

ser·mon [sûr′mən] *n.* **1** A religious talk, usually delivered by a clergyman as part of a church

service. **2** A serious talk about how a person should act, think, and behave.

se·rous [sir′əs] *adj.* Having to do with, producing, or resembling serum.

ser·pent [sûr′pənt] *n.* **1** A snake, especially a large one. **2** An underhanded, treacherous person. **3** Satan.

ser·pen·tine [sûr′pən·tēn *or* sûr′pən·tīn] **1** *adj.* Of or like a serpent. **2** *adj.* Curving; winding. **3** *adj.* Tricky; sly; subtle: *serpentine* reasoning. **4** *n.* A green, sometimes spotted mineral.

ser·rate [ser′āt] *adj.* **1** Toothed or notched like a saw. **2** Having notched edges, as certain leaves.

ser·rat·ed [ser′ā·tid] *adj.* Serrate.

ser·ried [ser′ēd] *adj.* Crowded or close together: *serried* rows of soldiers.

The knife and the leaf are serrate.

se·rum [sir′əm] *n., pl.* **se·rums** or **se·ra** [sir′ə] **1** The clear, slightly yellow part of an animal fluid that remains when the rest clots, especially this fluid in blood. **2** A liquid obtained from the blood of an animal that has been inoculated with a specific disease. This liquid is then used as an antitoxin against that disease. **3** Any similar fluid.

ser·vant [sûr′vənt] *n.* **1** A person hired to work for another, especially one who assists with work in and around the house, as a maid or gardener. **2** A person who is a government official or holds a public office. **3** A person devoted to some cause: a *servant* of justice.

serve [sûrv] *v.* **served, serv·ing,** *n.* **1** *v.* To work or work for as a servant: He has *served* loyally; She *serves* the Jones family. **2** *v.* To promote the interest of; work for; aid; help: to *serve* one's country. **3** *v.* To obey and worship: to *serve* God. **4** *v.* To satisfy, be enough for, or be satisfactory: One package of food won't *serve* us all; This carton will *serve* as a bookcase. **5** *v.* To perform a duty or function: to *serve* as mayor; to *serve* on a jury. **6** *v.* To go through or put in (a term of punishment, etc.): He *served* four years in prison. **7** *v.* To do military or naval service for: to *serve* a certain country; to *serve* ten years. **8** *v.* To pass time in the armed forces: He *served* loyally. **9** *v.* To furnish or provide: They *serve* the school with heat. **10** *v.* To help or wait on, as at table or in a store: to *serve* at dinner; Have you been *served*? **11** *v.* To bring or distribute: to *serve* dessert. **12** *v.* In tennis, etc., to put (the ball) in play. **13** *v.* In tennis, etc., to put the ball in play as (an ace, etc.). **14** *n.* In tennis, etc., the act or manner of serving. **15** *n.* A person's turn at serving, as in tennis. **16** *v.* To deliver or present: to *serve* a summons. **17** *v.* To be favorable: If the weather *serves*, we'll leave tomorrow. **18** *v.* To reward; deal with: It would *serve* you right if she didn't come to your party.

---

add, āce, câre, pälm; end, ēqual; it, īce; odd, ōpen, ôrder; tŏŏk, pōōl; up, bûrn;
ə = a in *above*, e in *sicken*, i in *possible*, o in *melon*, u in *circus*; yōō = u in *fuse*; oil; pout;
check; **r**ing; **th**in; **th**is; **zh** in *vision*. For ¶ reference, see page 64 · HOW TO

serv·er [sûr′vər] *n.* **1** A person who serves. **2** Something that is used in serving, as a tray.

ser·vice [sûr′vis] *n.*, *v.* **ser·viced, ser·vic·ing** **1** *n.* Any work done or action performed for the benefit of another; assistance; benefit: to render *service* to a friend. **2** *n.* (*often pl.*) A useful work that does not produce a material object: the *services* of a doctor or lawyer. **3** *n.* The act of serving or the manner in which a person is served: The *service* in this store is bad. **4** *n.* Something that benefits or aids the public as a whole: bus *service*; electric *service*. **5** *v.* To supply service to: One bus company *services* the whole city. **6** *n.* Employment in or a particular division of the government: civil *service*; the diplomatic *service*. **7** *n.* Any branch of the armed forces: to enlist in the *service*. **8** *adj.* Of or having to do with military service: *service* stripes. **9** *n.* A religious ceremony: to attend Sunday *service*. **10** *n.* The act, position, or condition of being a servant: to be in *service* with a large family. **11** *n.* A set of tableware for a specific purpose: a tea *service*. **12** *n.* The act of delivering or presenting a summons, writ, etc. **13** *n.* In tennis, etc., the act or manner of serving a ball. **14** *adj.* Of, for, or having to do with service, servants, etc.: a *service* entrance. **15** *v.* To maintain or repair: to *service* a car. **— at one's service** Ready to do what is wanted: I'm *at your service*.

ser·vice·a·ble [sûr′vis·ə·bəl] *adj.* **1** Able to be of service; beneficial; useful. **2** Able to give long service; durable: a *serviceable* coat.

ser·vice·man [sûr′vis·man′] *n.*, *pl.* **ser·vice·men** [sûr′vis·men′] **1** A member of one of the armed forces. **2** A man who repairs or takes care of cars, machines, appliances, etc.

service station **1** A place where drivers bring cars and trucks for gasoline, oil, greasing, repairs, etc. **2** A place for maintaining and repairing machines, etc.

ser·vile [sûr′vīl *or* sûr′vil] *adj.* **1** Without spirit or boldness; like a slave: always *servile* to his boss. **2** Of or appropriate for slaves or servants: a *servile* job. **— ser·vil·i·ty** [sûr·vil′ə·tē] *n.*

serv·ing [sûr′ving] *n.* **1** The act of one who serves. **2** A portion of food: two *servings*.

ser·vi·tor [sûr′və·tər] *n.* A servant or attendant.

ser·vi·tude [sûr′və·t(y)ōod] *n.* **1** Slavery; bondage. **2** Enforced labor as a punishment for crime.

ses·a·me [ses′ə·mē] *n.* **1** A plant of the East Indies. **2** The seeds of this plant, used as food and as a source of a pale yellow oil. **— open sesame** A magic command, used originally by Ali Baba to open a door in a story from the *Arabian Nights*.

ses·sion [sesh′ən] *n.* **1** The meeting of a legislative body, court, class, etc., to conduct its business: a morning *session* in the physics laboratory. **2** A series of such meetings. **3** Any meeting of two or more persons: I had a *session* with the principal this morning. **4** A division of a school year: summer *session*. **— in session** Meeting: Court is *in session*.

set [set] *v.* **set, set·ting,** *n.*, *adj.* **1** *v.* To put in a certain place or position; place: I *set* my cup on a saucer. **2** *v.* To make or become hard, firm, rigid, etc.: The gelatin has *set*; to *set* one's jaw. **3** *n.* The way in which a thing is placed or held: the stubborn *set* of his jaw. **4** *v.* To put in a certain condition: *Set* your mind at ease. **5** *v.* To put back in its proper position: to *set* a bone. **6** *v.* To put into position or condition for proper operation: to *set* a trap; to *set* a clock. **7** *v.* To place knives, forks, etc. on: to *set* a table. **8** *v.* To fix or establish: to *set* a time; to *set* a dance step. **9** *adj.* Fixed or established; deliberate: a *set* time; a *set* speech; a *set* action. **10** *adj.* Stubborn; obstinate: to be *set* in one's ways. **11** *v.* To present or provide so as to be copied: to *set* a bad example. **12** *v.* To direct: He *set* his course for Bermuda. **13** *v.* To place in a setting, as a gem. **14** *v.* To place (a hen) on eggs to hatch them. **15** *v.* To place (eggs) under a hen for hatching. **16** *v.* To sit on eggs, as a hen. **17** *v.* To provide or fit: to *set* words to music or music to words. **18** *v.* In the theater, television, etc., to create or arrange scenery on or for: to *set* the stage for a jungle scene. **19** *n.* The scenery so created or arranged. **20** *v.* To go or pass below the horizon: The sun *set* yesterday at six o'clock. **21** *v.* In printing, to arrange (type) in proper order. **22** *v.* To start: He *set* the machine in motion. **23** *adj.* Ready; prepared: to be all *set*. **24** *adj.* Formed; built: a thick-*set* figure. **25** *n.* A group of persons or things that go or belong together: the jet *set*; a *set* of dishes. **26** *n.* The act of setting. **27** *n.* A being set. **28** *n.* The direction of a current or wind. **29** *n.* A group of six or more games making up part of a tennis match. **30** *n.* A number of different electrical or mechanical parts assembled for use: a radio *set*. **31** *n.* In mathematics, a collection of elements, points, integers, etc., having some characteristic in common: the *set* of all even numbers. **— set about** To start doing; begin. **— set against 1** To balance; compare. **2** To make unfriendly to. **— set apart** To put aside for a special purpose. **— set aside 1** To place apart or to one side. **2** To reject; dismiss. **— set back 1** To check. **2** To hinder or delay. **— set down 1** To place on a surface. **2** To write or print. **3** To consider. **4** To explain as caused by; attribute. **— set forth 1** To state or declare. **2** To start or begin, as a journey. **— set in 1** To begin to occur. **2** To blow or flow toward shore, as wind or tide. **— set off 1** To put apart. **2** To start or start to go. **3** To serve as a contrast for. **4** To cause to explode. **— set on** To urge to attack. **— set out 1** To present to view; display. **2** To plant. **3** To start something, especially a journey. **— set to 1** To start; begin. **2** To start fighting. **— set up 1** To place in an upright position. **2** To place in power, authority, etc. **3** To construct, assemble, or build. **4** To found; establish. **5** To cause; start. **6** To cause to be heard: to *set up* a cry. **7** To claim to be: He *sets* himself *up* as an authority. **8** *informal* To make feel happy or encouraged: Our victory *set* us all *up*. — **set upon** To make an attack upon; assault. ◆ See SIT.

set·back [set′bak′] *n.* A reverse or check, as in progress, success, etc.: a business *setback*.

set·tee [se·tē′] *n.* **1** A long bench with a back. **2** A sofa large enough for two or three people.

set·ter [set′ər] *n.* **1** A person that sets: a *setter* of diamonds. **2** One of a breed of hunting dogs trained to point out game by standing rigid.

set·ting [set′ing] *n.* **1** The act of a person or thing that sets. **2** The mounting that holds a gem. **3** The scene, time, or background of a play,

English setter

motion picture, novel, etc.: This book has a Civil War *setting*. **4** Any background or surroundings. **5** The music written for a poem or for other words. **6** The eggs on which a hen sits for hatching.

set·tle[1] [set′(ə)l] *v.* **set·tled, set·tling** **1** To put in order; set to rights; arrange: to *settle* one's affairs. **2** To put firmly or comfortably in place: to *settle* oneself on a couch. **3** To free of disturbance; calm; quiet: to *settle* one's nerves. **4** To sink or cause to sink: The signpost *settled* in the mud. **5** To make or become clear: *Settle* the coffee; The coffee has *settled*. **6** To decide or determine: to *settle* on a plan. **7** To resolve or reconcile: to *settle* differences. **8** To pay, as a debt; satisfy, as a claim. **9** To establish a home, colony, etc., in: The English *settled* Virginia. **10** To take up residence; make a home: We *settled* in New York when I was ten. **11** To come to rest or as if to rest: A bee *settled* on the rose; Snow *settled* on the roof; A great sadness *settled* over him. — **settle down** **1** To start living a regular, orderly life. **2** To become quiet or orderly. — **settle on** or **settle upon** To give (money, property, etc.) to someone by a legal act.

set·tle[2] [set′(ə)l] *n.* A long wooden seat or bench with a high back.

set·tle·ment [set′(ə)l·mənt] *n.* **1** The act of settling. **2** A being settled. **3** An agreement or arrangement for settling: A *settlement* of the dock strike was reached today. **4** An area newly settled by people; colony. **5** A small community or village. **6** The transfer of money, property, etc., to another, as at marriage or divorce: to arrange for a property *settlement*. **7** The money, property, etc., thus transferred. **8** Payment: the *settlement* of a claim. **9** An institution offering

Settle

advice, entertainment, etc., for the people of a poor neighborhood.

set·tler [set′lər] *n.* **1** A person who settles, especially one who settles in a colony or new country. **2** A person or thing that settles something: a *settler* of labor disputes.

sev·en or **7** [sev′ən] *n., adj.* One more than six.

seven seas All the oceans of the world, by old tradition the north and south Atlantic, the north and south Pacific, the Indian, the Arctic, and the Antarctic oceans.

sev·en·teen or **17** [sev′ən·tēn′] *n., adj.* One more than sixteen.

sev·en·teenth or **17th** [sev′ən·tēnth′] **1** *adj.* Next after the sixteenth. **2** *n.* The seventeenth one. **3** *adj.* Being one of seventeen equal parts. **4** *n.* A seventeenth part.

sev·enth or **7th** [sev′ənth] **1** *adj.* Next after the sixth. **2** *n.* The seventh one. **3** *adj.* Being one of seven equal parts. **4** *n.* A seventh part.

sev·en·ti·eth or **70th** [sev′ən·tē·ith] **1** *adj.* Tenth in order after the sixtieth. **2** *n.* The seventieth one. **3** *adj.* Being one of seventy equal parts. **4** *n.* A seventieth part.

sev·en·ty or **70** [sev′ən·tē] *n., pl.* **sev·en·ties** or **70's,** *adj.* **1** *n., adj.* Ten more than sixty. **2** *n.* (*pl.*) The years between the age of 70 and the age of 80: He's in his *seventies*.

Seven Wonders of the World The seven works of man considered the most remarkable in the ancient world: the Egyptian pyramids, the hanging gardens of Babylon, the temple of Diana at Ephesus, the statue of Zeus by Phidias at Olympia, the mausoleum of King Mausolos at Halicarnassus, the Colossus of Rhodes, and the lighthouse of Alexandria.

sev·er [sev′ər] *v.* **1** To cut or break into two or more parts: to *sever* a rope in half. **2** To separate: The old empire *severed* into two, the Roman and the Byzantine. **3** To break off; end: to *sever* a friendship.

sev·er·al [sev′ər·əl *or* sev′rəl] **1** *adj.* Being more than two, yet not many: I read *several* books last week. **2** *n., pron.* More than two, yet not many: *Several* will come back shortly. **3** *adj.* Single; separate: After class, we all went our *several* ways. ◆ See FEW.

sev·er·ance [sev′ər·əns *or* sev′rəns] *n.* **1** The act of severing. **2** A severed condition; separation; partition.

se·vere [si·vir′] *adj.* **se·ver·er, se·ver·est** **1** Strict; harsh: *severe* discipline; a *severe* criticism. **2** Of grave importance; serious: The *severe* strain broke the hoisting cable. **3** Serious and sober, as in manner or disposition. **4** Plain and simple in style or decoration: *severe* furniture. **5** Causing great pain, anguish, etc.: a *severe* stomach ache. **6** Causing extreme hardship, damage, etc.: a *severe* snowstorm. — **se·vere′ly** *adv.*

add, āce, câre, pälm; end, ēqual; it, īce; odd, ōpen, ôrder; tŏŏk, pōōl; up, bûrn;
ə = a in *above*, e in *sicken*, i in *possible*, o in *melon*, u in *circus*; yōō = u in *fuse*; oil; pout;
check; ring; thin; this; zh in *vision*. For ¶ reference, see page 64 · HOW TO

se·ver·i·ty [si·ver′ə·tē] *n.*, *pl.* **se·ver·i·ties**
1 Sternness; strictness: The *severity* of the punishment was too great. **2** Sharpness; harshness: the *severity* of the blizzard. **3** Simplicity and plainness of design: the *severity* of Puritan dress.

Se·ville [sə·vil′] *n.* A city in sw Spain.

sew [sō] *v.* **sewed, sewed** or **sewn, sew·ing**
1 To make, mend, fasten, etc., by using a needle and thread: to *sew* a dress; to *sew* a ripped place. **2** To work with needle and thread: She *sews* as well as a tailor. **— sew′er** *n.*

sew·age [sōō′ij] *n.* The waste matter which is carried off in sewers.

sew·er [sōō′ər] *n.* A pipe or drain, usually underground, to carry off dirty water, refuse, and other waste matter.

sew·er·age [sōō′ər·ij] *n.* **1** A system of sewers. **2** The removal of waste matter by sewers. **3** Sewage.

sew·ing [sō′ing] *n.* **1** The act, business, or occupation of a person who sews. **2** The thing that is sewed; material on which a person is at work with needle and thread.

sewing machine A machine for sewing, stitching, etc.

sewn [sōn] An alternative past participle of SEW.

An old-fashioned sewing machine

sex [seks] *n.* **1** Either of two groups, male and female, into which people, animals, etc., are divided. **2** The character of being male or female.

sex·tant [seks′tənt] *n.* **1** An instrument for measuring the angular distance between two objects, as between the sun and the horizon, used especially to determine a ship's position at sea. **2** A sixth part of a circle; a sector of 60°.

sex·tet or **sex·tette** [seks·tet′] *n.* **1** A musical composition for six performers. **2** The six singers or players who perform such a composition. **3** Any group of six persons or things.

Sextant

sex·ton [seks′tən] *n.* A janitor of a church, who may also ring the bell, dig graves, etc.

sex·u·al [sek′shōō·əl] *adj.* Of, like, or having to do with sex or the sexes. **— sex′u·al·ly** *adv.*

Sgt. Abbreviation of SERGEANT.

shab·by [shab′ē] *adj.* **shab·bi·er, shab·bi·est 1** Threadbare; ragged, as from hard use or wear: His clothes are *shabby.* **2** Wearing threadbare, ragged clothing. **3** Dilapidated; run-down: a *shabby* neighborhood. **4** Mean or unfair: *shabby* treatment. **— shab′bi·ly** *adv.* **— shab′bi·ness** *n.*

shack [shak] *n.* A small, crudely built, sometimes dilapidated house or cabin; shanty.

shack·le [shak′əl] *n.*, *v.* **shack·led, shack·ling 1** *n.* A metal ring or band, usually one of a pair joined by a chain, put around the wrist or ankle to restrain movement or prevent escape. **2** *n.* Anything that restrains or hinders: the *shackles* of poverty. **3** *v.* To restrain or hinder with or as if with a shackle.

Shackles

shad [shad] *n.*, *pl.* **shad** A fish of the Atlantic coast, related to the herring and highly prized as food.

shade [shād] *n.*, *v.* **shad·ed, shad·ing 1** *n.* The darkness caused by something cutting off part of the light: the *shade* of a tree. **2** *n.* A slightly dark place, where sunshine is cut off: Let's sit in the *shade* where it's cool. **3** *v.* To screen or keep from a source of light; put in shade: A big tree *shades* our garden. **4** *v.* To make dim by cutting down light: to *shade* the light of a lamp. **5** *n.* A device that cuts off or reduces light: a window *shade*; a lamp *shade.* **6** *n.* A small difference, as of lightness or darkness, in a color: There are many *shades* of gray in that picture. **7** *v.* To give the effect of shadows or darkness in: to *shade* a figure in a drawing. **8** *n.* The dark part or parts of a picture, drawing, etc. **9** *v.* To change or vary by degrees: The sunset *shaded* from bright orange to blue. **10** *n.* A slight degree; small amount: There was a *shade* of annoyance in his answer. **11** *n.* A small difference: many *shades* of meaning. **12** *n.* A spirit or ghost. **13** *n.* (*pl.*) The shadows and darkness that come after sunset.

shad·ing [shā′ding] *n.* **1** Protection against light or heat. **2** The lines, dots, dark colors, etc., that show shadows, depth, or darkness in a picture or drawing. **3** A slight difference or variation: *shadings* of meaning.

shad·ow [shad′ō] **1** *n.* Partial darkness where light is cut off: a cat half hidden in *shadow.* **2** *n.* A dark figure or image cast on a surface by a body or object coming between the source of light and the surface: the *shadow* of a man on the wall. **3** *v.* To make or cast a shadow or shadows upon: Trees *shadowed* the garden. **4** *n.* The shaded or dark portion of a picture. **5** *v.* To make shadows in a painting, picture, etc. **6** *n.* Anything unreal or imaginary: Her ambitions were mere *shadows.* **7** *n.* A faint representation or indication: He's just a *shadow* of his former self. **8** *n.* A very small amount; trace: a *shadow* of a doubt. **9** *n.* Gloom or unhappiness: The *shadow* of illness darkened these years. **10** *v.* To

Shadow

make sad or gloomy: Illness *shadowed* her happiness. **11** *v.* To follow closely or secretly; spy on. **12** *n.* A person who spies on or follows someone closely or secretly. **13** *n.* A ghost or spirit. **— in the shadow of** Very close or near to.

shad·ow·y [shad′ō·ē] *adj.* **shad·ow·i·er, shad·ow·i·est 1** Full of shade or shadows; dark; shady: a *shadowy* path in the woods. **2** Like a shadow in being unclear or dim: a *shadowy* recollection.

shad·y [shā′dē] *adj.* **shad·i·er, shad·i·est 1** In the shade; shaded; sheltered: a *shady* spot in the forest. **2** Producing or giving shade: a *shady* beach umbrella. **3** *informal* Questionable as to honesty or legality: a *shady* character; a *shady* business firm. **— shad′i·ness** *n.*

shaft [shaft] *n.* **1** The long, narrow rod of an arrow, spear, etc. **2** An arrow, spear, etc. **3** Anything like an arrow or spear in appearance or effect: a *shaft* of light; *shafts* of ridicule. **4** A long handle, as of an ax or golf club. **5** The part of a column between its top and its base. **6** A slender column. **7** One of the two poles by which a horse is harnessed to a carriage, wagon, etc. **8** In a machine, a rotating rod that transmits power. **9** A deep passage sunk into the earth, as the entrance to a mine. **10** A passage in the earth for light, air, water, etc. **11** An opening through the floors of a building, as for an elevator.

— shaft

shag [shag] *n.* **1** A rough mass of hair, wool, etc. **2** A long nap on cloth. **3** Cloth that has a rough or long nap.

shag·bark [shag′bärk′] *n.* A hickory tree with shaggy gray bark that peels off in long, narrow pieces.

shag·gy [shag′ē] *adj.* **shag·gi·er, shag·gi·est 1** Having rough hair or wool: a *shaggy* animal. **2** Having a rough, fuzzy nap or surface: *shaggy* wool. **3** Rough and untidy: a *shaggy* haircut. **— shag′gi·ness** *n.*

shah [shä] *n.* An Oriental king or ruler, especially of Iran.

shake [shāk] *v.* **shook, shak·en, shak·ing,** *n.* **1** *v.* To move or cause to move back and forth, up and down, or from side to side with short, rapid movements. **2** *v.* To dislodge, force, throw, etc., by a shaking movement: She *shook* salt on her food; to *shake* a cat out of a tree. **3** *v.* To tremble or vibrate, or cause to tremble or vibrate: to *shake* from fear; to *shake* a door with a blow. **4** *v.* To weaken or disturb: to *shake* someone's determination. **5** *v.* *slang* To get rid of or away from: The man tried to *shake* his pursuers. **6** *n.* The act of shaking. **7** *n.* A being shaken. **8** *n.* (*pl.*) A trembling, as from chills or fever. **— no great shakes** *informal* Of no great ability,

excellence, or importance. **— shake down 1** To cause to fall by shaking. **2** To cause to settle; make compact. **3** *slang* To obtain money from in a dishonest way. **— shake hands** To clasp hands as a form of greeting, agreement, etc. **— shake off** To rid oneself of by or as if by shaking. **— shake up 1** To shake, mix, or stir. **2** *informal* To shock or jar.

shak·er [shā′kər] *n.* **1** A person or thing that shakes. **2** A container for shaking something: a cocktail *shaker*. **3** (*written* **Shaker**) A member of a religious sect in the United States, so called because of trembling bodily motions made during their religious meetings.

Shake·speare [shāk′spir], **William,** 1564–1616, English poet and dramatist. **— Shake·spear′e·an** *adj.*

shake·up [shāk′up′] *n.* A sudden, thorough change, as in the running of a company, police department, etc., often with the transfer or dismissal of high officials.

shak·o [shak′ō] *n., pl.* **shak·os** A kind of high, stiff military hat with an upright plume.

shak·y [shā′kē] *adj.* **shak·i·er, shak·i·est 1** Continually shaking or trembling; weak; unsteady. **2** Not trustworthy; unreliable: a *shaky* business firm. **— shak′i·ness** *n.*

shale [shāl] *n.* A rock formed from hardened clay or mud. It splits easily into thin layers.

shall [shal] *v. Present tense for all subjects* **shall,** *past tense* **should** A helping verb used to express: **1** Things happening in the future: I *shall* be there tomorrow. **2** Determination, promise, threat, command, etc.: They *shall* not pass; You *shall* have whatever you need; You *shall* pay for this. ◆ In ordinary usage in the U.S. today, *will* is used with all persons (*I, you, he, she, it, we, you, they*) both to indicate the future and to express determination or command. Traditionally, *shall* in the first person and *will* in the second and third indicate the future, and the reverse indicates determination; but this rule is observed only in very formal writing.

shal·lot [shə·lot′] *n.* A small vegetable resembling an onion, used as a seasoning.

shal·low [shal′ō] **1** *adj.* Having the bottom not far below the surface or top; not deep: a *shallow* pool. **2** *n.* (*usually pl.*) A shallow place in a body of water: We swam in the *shallows* of the river. **3** *adj.* Not wise or profound: a *shallow* thinker. **4** *v.* To make or become shallow. **— shal′low·ly** *adv.* **— shal′low·ness** *n.*

shalt [shalt] A form of the verb SHALL, used with *thou*: seldom used today: Thou *shalt* not kill.

sham [sham] *n., adj., v.* **shammed, shamming 1** *n.* Something not true; pretense; deception: Her good nature is a *sham.* **2** *n.* A person who pretends or deceives. **3** *adj.* Pretended; false: *sham* grief. **4** *v.* To pretend: to *sham* illness.

add, āce, câre, pälm; end, ēqual; it, īce; odd, ōpen, ôrder; took, pool; up, bûrn;
ə = a in *above*, e in *sicken*, i in *possible*, o in *melon*, u in *circus*; yoo = u in *fuse*; oil; pout;
check; ring; thin; this; zh in *vision*. For ¶ reference, see page 64 · HOW TO

sham·ble [shăm′bəl] *v.* **sham·bled, sham·bling,** *n.* **1** *v.* To walk in a shuffling, unsteady manner. **2** *n.* A shuffling, unsteady walk.

sham·bles [shăm′bəlz] *n.pl. (usually used with singular verb)* **1** A slaughterhouse. **2** Any place of execution or bloodshed. **3** A place in which there is great destruction or disorder: The living room was a *shambles* after the party.

shame [shām] *n., v.* **shamed, sham·ing 1** *n.* A painful feeling of guilt caused by one's own or someone else's wrongdoing: He felt *shame* at having made a mistake. **2** *v.* To cause to feel shame; make ashamed. **3** *n.* A person or thing that brings shame or disgrace. **4** *n.* A condition of shame, dishonor, or disgrace: John's actions brought *shame* to his family. **5** *v.* To bring shame upon; disgrace. **6** *n.* Something to bring regret or sorrow: What a *shame* you lost the game. **7** *v.* To force by causing a sense of shame: to *shame* someone into getting a haircut. **—for shame!** You should be ashamed! **—put to shame 1** To disgrace; make ashamed. **2** To do better than; surpass.

shame·faced [shām′fāst′] *adj.* **1** Showing shame in one's face; ashamed. **2** Modest; shy.

shame·ful [shām′fəl] *adj.* **1** Deserving or bringing shame; disgraceful. **2** Indecent. **— shame′ful·ly** *adv.*

shame·less [shām′lis] *adj.* **1** Done without shame. **2** Without modesty; brazen. **— shame′less·ly** *adv.*

sham·poo [shăm·pōō′] *n., v.* **sham·pooed, sham·poo·ing 1** *n.* Any of various preparations, as of soap, oil, etc., used to wash the hair and scalp. **2** *n.* The act or process of washing the hair. **3** *v.* To wash (the hair and scalp) with a shampoo. ◆ *Shampoo* comes from a Hindustani word meaning *to press* in the process of massaging.

sham·rock [shăm′rok] *n.* Any of several three-leaved plants resembling clover, accepted as the national emblem of Ireland. ◆ *Shamrock* comes from an Irish word meaning *small clover.*

shang·hai [shăng′hī] *v.* **shang·haied, shang·hai·ing 1** To drug and make unconscious in order to kidnap for service aboard a ship. **2** To cause to do something by force or trickery.

Shang·hai [shăng′hī′] *n.* A port city in eastern China.

shank [shăngk] *n.* **1** The part of the leg between the knee and the ankle. **2** The whole leg. **3** A cut of meat from the leg of an animal. **4** The part of a tool connecting the handle with the working part, as the stem of a drill.

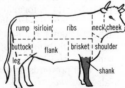

shan't [shănt] Shall not: He *shan't* go to the movies with us.

Shan·tung [shăn′tŭng′] *n.* **1** A province of NE China. **2** (*written* **shantung**) A fabric similar to pongee, originally made in China of silk, now often made of rayon or cotton.

shan·ty [shăn′tē] *n., pl.* **shan·ties** A crude, hastily built shack or cabin.

shape [shāp] *n., v.* **shaped, shap·ing 1** *n.* The outward form or outline of something: the *shape* of a building. **2** *v.* To give a shape to; mold; form. **3** *n.* A definite or developed form: to put an idea into *shape.* **4** *v.* To prepare; develop: to *shape* your ideas into a definite plan. **5** *v.* To become or develop: Fred *shaped* up into a fine student. **6** *n.* Condition: The car's brakes were not in good *shape.* **—take shape** To have or take on a fixed form; become definite.

shape·less [shāp′lis] *adj.* **1** Having no definite shape. **2** Having an unattractive shape.

shape·ly [shāp′lē] *adj.* **shape·li·er, shape·li·est** Having a pleasing shape; well-formed.

shard [shärd] *n.* A broken piece of a brittle substance, as of a clay pot.

share[1] [shâr] *n., v.* **shared, shar·ing 1** *n.* A single portion of something distributed among or contributed by several: my *share* of the ice cream; my *share* of the donation. **2** *v.* To divide and give out, each taking a part: to *share* the ice cream; to *share* the expense. **3** *n.* A part of something enjoyed or suffered in common: our *share* of the blame. **4** *v.* To enjoy or suffer in common: Sue *shared* her sister's joy at her marriage. **5** *v.* To own or use together: We *share* the telephone. **6** *n.* One of the equal parts into which the ownership or total stock of a company is divided. **7** *v.* To have a part or share: to *share* in the profits of a business deal. **—go shares** To take part equally; share in something.

share[2] [shâr] *n.* A plowshare.

share·crop·per [shâr′krop′ər] *n.* A farmer who lives on and farms land not his own and who gives the landowner a share of the crop as rent.

share·hold·er [shâr′hōl′dər] *n.* An owner of a share or shares of a company's stock; stockholder.

shark[1] [shärk] *n.* Any of various long-bodied marine fishes, some very large, that have hard, rough skins and very sharp teeth. Sharks eat other fish, and some kinds will attack man.

Common shark, to 15 ft. long

shark[2] [shärk] *n.* **1** A dishonest person; swindler. **2** *slang* A person who has great skill or ability in some special thing.

sharp [shärp] **1** *adj.* Having a keen edge or a fine point; able to cut or pierce. **2** *adj.* Coming to or having a point: a *sharp* peak. **3** *adj.* Turning or changing abruptly; not gradual: a *sharp* curve. **4** *adj.* Cutting; piercing; stinging: a *sharp* wind; a *sharp* blow. **5** *adj.* Affecting the mind or senses, as if by cutting or piercing: *sharp* pangs of remorse; a *sharp* taste or odor. **6** *adj.* Very keen and sensitive; acute: He has *sharp* vision and hearing. **7** *adj.* Attentive; watchful: Keep a *sharp* lookout. **8** *adj.* Eager; keen: a *sharp* appetite. **9** *adj.* Brisk; quick; active: *sharp* trading. **10** *adj.* Fiery; violent: a *sharp* debate. **11** *adj.* Harsh, irritable, or severe: a *sharp* answer. **12** *adj.* Quick-witted; clever; shrewd: a *sharp* bargainer. **13** *adj.* Not blurred; distinct; clear: a *sharp* outline. **14** *adj. slang* Attractive and excellent: You look *sharp.* **15** *adv.* In a sharp manner; sharply, keenly, quickly, etc.: Look *sharp* now! **16** *adj.* Above the right, true pitch: That note was *sharp.* **17** *adv.* Above the right, true pitch: to sing *sharp.* **18** *n.* A sign (#) placed before a note to show that the note is raised a semitone above the natural pitch. **19** *n.* The note so altered. **20** *v.* To raise in pitch, as by a half tone. **21** *v.* To sing, play, or sound above the right pitch. **22** *adv.* Promptly; exactly: at 12 o'clock *sharp.* — **sharp′ly** *adv.* — **sharp′ness** *n.*

sharp·en [shär′pən] *v.* To make or become sharp. — **sharp′en·er** *n.*

sharp·shoot·er [shärp′shoo′tər] *n.* A skilled marksman, especially with the rifle.

sharp·wit·ted [shärp′wit′id] *adj.* Intelligent; keen; acute; clever.

shat·ter [shat′ər] *v.* **1** To break into pieces. **2** To damage; demolish; ruin.

shave [shāv] *v.* **shaved, shaved** or **shav·en, shav·ing,** *n.* **1** *v.* To cut (hair or beard) close to the skin with a razor: Does he *shave* yet?; He *shaved* off his moustache. **2** *v.* To remove hair or beard from: The barber *shaved* me this morning. **3** *n.* The act or process of cutting off hair with a razor. **4** *v.* To trim closely, as if with a razor: to *shave* a lawn. **5** *v.* To cut thin slices from, as wood. **6** *v.* To touch or scrape in passing. — **close shave** A narrow escape.

shav·er [shā′vər] *n.* **1** A person or a thing that shaves. **2** *informal* A young boy; lad.

shav·ing [shā′ving] *n.* **1** The act of a person or thing that shaves. **2** A very thin piece shaved from anything.

Shaw [shô], **George Bernard,** 1856–1950, British dramatist and critic, born in Ireland.

shawl [shôl] *n.* A wrap, as a square cloth or large scarf, worn over the head or shoulders.

Shaw·nee [shô·nē′] *n.* A member of a tribe of North American Indians now living in Oklahoma.

shay [shā] *n.* A two-wheeled, one-horse carriage for two persons; chaise. ◆ *Shay* comes from the word *chaise* [shāz], which was mistakenly thought to be a plural. The spelling was "Americanized" and *shay* was formed as the singular.

Shay

she [shē] *pron., pl.* **they,** *n., pl.* **shes** **1** *pron.* A female person or animal previously mentioned, or a thing usually spoken of as

feminine, as a ship, machine, etc.: Grace said *she* would come to the party; When you see my sailboat, you'll agree *she's* a beauty. **2** *pron.* Any female: *She* who listens learns. **3** *n.* A female person or animal: Is that dog a he or a *she*?

sheaf [shēf] *n., pl.* **sheaves** [shēvz] **1** A quantity of stalks of cut grain, as rye, wheat, etc., bound together. **2** A collection of things that may be tied or bound together, as papers.

shear [shir] *v.* **sheared, sheared** or **shorn, shear·ing** **1** To cut the hair, fleece, etc., from: to *shear* a sheep. **2** To cut or cut through, with or as if with shears: to *shear* wool. **3** To move or proceed as if by cutting: The arrow *sheared* through the air. **4** To take something away from; deprive: They *sheared* him of all his power.

shears [shirz] *n.pl.* A large cutting tool similar to scissors (also called a **pair of shears**), worked by the crossing of its cutting edges.

sheath [shēth] *n., pl.* **sheaths** [shēthz or shēths] **1** A cover or case for a blade, as of a sword. **2** Any caselike covering, as that on the lower part of a blade of grass. **3** A close-fitting dress having a straight, narrow appearance.

sheathe [shēth] *v.* **sheathed, sheath·ing** **1** To put into a sheath: to *sheathe* a knife. **2** To protect with a covering.

sheave [shēv] *v.* **sheaved, sheav·ing** To gather into sheaves, as grain.

She·ba [shē′bə] *n.* The Old Testament name for a region of sw Arabia. *I Kings,* a book of the Old Testament, tells the story of the Queen of Sheba who visited Solomon to test his wisdom.

shed[1] [shed] *v.* **shed, shed·ding** **1** To pour forth or cause to pour forth: to *shed* tears or blood. **2** To send forth; radiate: The moon *shed* its light. **3** To throw off without allowing to go through: An umbrella *sheds* rain. **4** To cast off (hair, skin, etc.) — **shed blood** To kill. — **shed light on** To furnish information about.

shed[2] [shed] *n.* A small, low building, often with front or sides open.

she'd [shēd] **1** She had. **2** She would.

sheen [shēn] *n.* A glistening brightness; gloss; luster.

sheep [shēp] *n., pl.* **sheep** **1** A domesticated, grazing animal related to the goat. It chews its cud and is bred in many varieties for its wool and meat. **2** The skin of a sheep, or anything made from it, as leather or parchment. **3** A meek, bashful, or timid person.

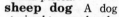

sheep dog A dog trained to guard and control sheep, often a collie.

sheep·fold [shēp′fōld′] *n.* A place where sheep are kept at night; a pen for sheep.

sheep·herd·er [shēp′hûr′dər] *n.* A person who tends a herd of sheep.

sheep·ish [shē′pish] *adj.* **1** Awkwardly shy, embarrassed, or abashed: a *sheepish* expression. **2** Foolish, meek, or timid, as a sheep. — **sheep′ish·ly** *adv.*

sheep's eyes [shēps] Bashful or loving glances.

sheep·skin [shēp′skin′] *n.* **1** The skin of a sheep, or anything made from it, as leather or parchment. **2** A document written on parchment, as a diploma.

sheer¹ [shir] **1** *adj.* Complete; utter; absolute: *sheer* stupidity. **2** *adv.* Completely; utterly; absolutely. **3** *adj.* Very thin and fine: *sheer* fabrics. **4** *adj.* Sloping sharply; very steep; perpendicular: a *sheer* drop. **5** *adv.* Very steeply. — **sheer′ly** *adv.* — **sheer′ness** *n.*

sheer² [shir] **1** *v.* To turn or cause to turn aside from a course; swerve. **2** *n.* A turning aside from a course.

sheet¹ [shēt] **1** *n.* A large, lightweight piece of cloth, often of cotton, used on a bed in sets of two, one beneath the body and one as a cover. **2** *n.* A piece of paper. **3** *n.* A newspaper. **4** *n.* A piece of metal or other substance, hammered, rolled, or cut very thin. **5** *n.* A thin, broad piece: a *sheet* of ice. **6** *v.* To cover or provide with a sheet. **7** *n.* A broad, flat, often moving surface: a *sheet* of water; Rain fell in *sheets*.

sheet² [shēt] *n.* A rope used to control the angle at which a sail is set.

sheet·ing [shē′ting] *n.* Any material in the form of sheets or that can be formed into sheets.

sheet lightning Lightning in sheetlike form, lighting up a broad area of the sky.

sheet metal Metal rolled and pressed into sheets.

sheet music Music printed on unbound sheets of paper, especially music for popular songs.

sheik or **sheikh** [shēk] *n.* The chief or head of an Arab tribe or family.

shek·el [shek′əl] *n.* **1** An ancient Hebrew unit of weight and money. **2** A coin having this weight.

shel·drake [shel′drāk′] *n.* **1** Any of several Old World ducks. **2** Another name for MERGANSER.

shelf [shelf] *n., pl.* **shelves** [shelvz] **1** A thin, flat piece of wood, metal, etc., attached to a wall or supported by a frame and used to hold things. **2** Anything like a shelf, as a ledge or shoal. — **on the shelf** No longer in use.

shell [shel] **1** *n.* Any of various hard outer coverings, as the structure encasing a shellfish, the carapace of a turtle, the fragile outer coat of an egg, or the covering of a nut. **2** *v.* To remove from a shell: to *shell* peas. **3** *v.* To separate from the cob, husk, etc.: to *shell* corn. **4** *n.* Something that resembles a shell in appearance or in being hollow and light: a pie *shell*. **5** *n.* Tortoise shell. **6** *n.* A framework with its interior removed, or one to be filled out or built upon: the *shell* of a house. **7** *n.* A very light, long, and narrow racing rowboat. **8** *n.* A cartridge for a small arm. **9** *n.* A hollow metal projectile full of explosive, fired from cannon, mortars, etc. **10** *v.* To fire shells at with a large gun; bombard: to *shell* a fort. — **shell out** *informal* To hand over, as money.

she'll [shel] A contraction of: **1** She will: *She'll* be here soon. **2** She shall.

Shell

shel·lac [shə·lak′] *n., v.* **shel·lacked, shel·lack·ing** **1** *n.* A resinous material in the form of thin flakes. **2** *n.* A solution of this material in alcohol, used to coat and protect wood. **3** *v.* To cover with shellac: to *shellac* the floors. **4** *v. slang* To defeat badly.

Shel·ley [shel′ē], **Percy Bysshe,** 1792–1822, English poet.

shell·fire [shel′fīr′] *n.* The firing of shells.

shell·fish [shel′fish′] *n., pl.* **shell·fish** or **shell·fish·es** Any animal that lives in the water and has a shell, as an oyster.

shell shock A nervous condition resulting from long exposure to the strain of modern warfare.

shel·ter [shel′tər] **1** *n.* Something that covers or protects, as from danger or exposure to the weather. **2** *n.* The condition of being sheltered, covered, or protected. **3** *v.* To provide shelter or protection for. **4** *v.* To find shelter.

shelve [shelv] *v.* **shelved, shelv·ing** **1** To place on a shelf. **2** To postpone indefinitely; put aside: to *shelve* a project. **3** To provide or fit with shelves. **4** To slope gradually.

shelv·ing [shel′ving] *n.* **1** Shelves. **2** Material for shelves, as wood, metal, etc.

she·nan·i·gans [shi·nan′ə·gənz] *n. pl. informal* Trickery; foolery; nonsense; mischief.

She·ol [shē′ōl] *n.* In the Old Testament, a place under the earth where the dead were believed to go.

shep·herd [shep′ərd] **1** *n.* A man who watches over and herds sheep. **2** *n.* A pastor or religious leader. **3** *v.* To watch over, escort, or guide as a shepherd. — **the Good Shepherd** Jesus.

shep·herd·ess [shep′ərd·is] *n.* A woman or girl who watches over and herds sheep.

sher·bet [shûr′bit] *n.* **1** A frozen dessert made with water, milk, sugar, fruit juice, etc. **2** An Oriental drink made of sweetened fruit juice diluted with water. ◆ *Sherbet* comes from a Turkish word which comes from an Arabic word meaning *drink*.

sher·iff [sher′if] *n.* The leading law-enforcing official of a county.

sher·ry [sher′ē] *n., pl.* **sher·ries** **1** A strong wine of Spanish origin. **2** A wine made in imitation of this, as in California.

Sherwood Forest [shûr′wŏŏd] A forest in England, famous as the home of Robin Hood and his men.

she's [shēz] A contraction of: **1** She is: *She's here now.* **2** She has: *She's gone home.*

Shet·land pony [shet′lənd] A small, hardy, shaggy breed of pony.

shew [shō] *v.* **shewed, shewn, shew·ing** To show: seldom used today.

Shetland pony, to 40 in. at withers

shib·bo·leth [shib′ə·leth] *n.* **1** A custom or use of language by which the members of a particular social class, profession, etc., may be distinguished: *Dinner at eight is a cherished* shibboleth *of the upper class there.* **2** A pet phrase or watchword of a party.

shied [shīd] Past tense and past participle of SHY[1] or SHY[2].

shield [shēld] **1** *n.* A broad piece of armor, once commonly carried on the arm to fend off blows while fighting. **2** *n.* Anything that protects or defends, as a safety device that covers a dangerous machine part. **3** *v.* To protect or guard. **4** *n.* Anything resembling a shield, as a policeman's badge.

Shield

shi·er [shī′ər] Comparative of SHY[1].

shi·est [shī′ist] Superlative of SHY[1].

shift [shift] **1** *v.* To change or move from one position, place, etc., to another: *to* shift *one's weight; to* shift *responsibility; to* shift *gears.* **2** *n.* A change of place, position, direction, etc.: *a* shift *in the wind; a* shift *of responsibility.* **3** *n.* A group of workers: *members of the night* shift. **4** *n.* The working time of such a group: *My* shift *is from 9 to 5.* **5** *n.* A piece of trickery or deceit; dodge; evasion: *Sue used many* shifts *to keep from doing her homework.* **— shift for one-self** To provide for one's own needs; get along on one's own.

shift·less [shift′lis] *adj.* Showing a lack of energy or ambition; lazy.

shift·y [shif′tē] *adj.* **shift·i·er, shift·i·est** Using or expressing tricks, deception, or fraud: *a* shifty *remark;* shifty *eyes.*

shil·ling [shil′ing] *n.* **1** A British unit of money worth $\frac{1}{20}$ pound, once equal to 12 pence, now to five new pence. **2** A coin of this value, gradually being replaced.

shil·ly-shal·ly [shil′ē·shal′ē] *v.* **shil·ly-shal·lied, shil·ly-shal·ly·ing,** *n., adj., adv.* **1** *v.* To keep changing one's mind; be unable to decide. **2** *n.* Weak or foolish indecision; hesitation. **3** *adj.* Undecided; hesitating. **4** *adv.* In an indecisive or hesitating manner.

shim·mer [shim′ər] **1** *v.* To shine with an unsteady, glimmering light. **2** *n.* A faint, unsteady light; glimmer; gleam. **— shim′· mer·y** *adj.*

shim·my [shim′ē] *v.* **shim·mied, shim·my·ing,** *n., pl.* **shim·mies 1** *v.* To vibrate or wobble, as an old automobile. **2** *n.* A shaking; vibration.

shin [shin] *n., v.* **shinned, shin·ning 1** *n.* The front part of the leg, below the knee. **2** *v.* To climb (a pole, rope, etc.) by gripping with the hands and legs: *to* shin *up a mast.*

shin·dig [shin′dig] *n. slang* A dance or noisy party.

shine [shīn] *v.* **shone** or **shined, shin·ing,** *n.* **1** *v.* To give off or reflect light: *The stars are* shining; *The windows* shone *in the sunset.* **2** *n.* The quality of being bright or shining; luster: *the* shine *of her hair.* **3** *v.* To cause to shine: *Shine your flashlight over here.* **4** *v.* To be outstanding; excel: *Ruth* shines *in spelling.* **5** *v.* To brighten by rubbing or polishing: *He* shined *my shoes.* **6** *n.* A polish or gloss. **7** *n.* A polishing. **8** *v.* To be clearly visible: *Happiness* shone *in his eyes.* **9** *n.* Fair weather: *in rain or* shine. **10** *n. informal* A liking or fancy: *to take a* shine *to someone.*

shin·er [shī′nər] *n.* **1** A person or thing that shines. **2** *slang* A black eye from a blow.

shin·gle [shing′gəl] *n., v.* **shin·gled, shin·gling 1** *n.* A thin, tapering piece of wood or other material, used to cover roofs, etc. Shingles are laid in overlapping rows. **2** *v.* To cover (a roof, building, etc.) with or as if with shingles. **3** *n.* A small signboard, as outside a doctor's office. **4** *n.* A short haircut for a woman. **5** *n.* To cut (the hair) in a shingle.

Shingles

shin·gles [shing′gəlz] *n.pl.* (*used with singular or plural verb*) A virus disease characterized by a skin rash along the course of an affected nerve and accompanied by pain.

shin·ing [shī′ning] *adj.* **1** Giving off or reflecting light; gleaming. **2** Distinguished; conspicuous: *The life of Joan of Arc is a* shining *example of courage.*

shin·ny[1] [shin′ē] *v.* **shin·nied, shin·ny·ing** *informal* To climb using one's arms and legs: *to* shinny *up a pole.*

shin·ny[2] [shin′ē] *n.* A game resembling hockey.

Shin·to [shin′tō] *n.* A religion of Japan in which one worships nature, heroes, and one's ancestors.

---

add, āce, câre, pälm;   end, ēqual;   it, īce;   odd, ōpen, ôrder;   to͝ok, po͞ol;   up, bûrn;
ə = a in *above,* e in *sicken,* i in *possible,* o in *melon,* u in *circus;*   yo͞o = u in *fuse;*   oil;   pout;
check; ring; thin; this; zh in *vision.*   For ¶ reference, see page 64 · HOW TO

shin·y [shī′nē] *adj.* **shin·i·er, shin·i·est** Shining in appearance; bright; gleaming; polished; glossy. **— shin′i·ness** *n.*

ship [ship] *n., v.* **shipped, ship·ping 1** *n.* Any large vessel that moves through the water or in the air, driven by sails or engines, as a steamship, tanker, submarine, or airship. **2** *n.* A large sailing vessel with three masts carrying square sails on all three. **3** *v.* To put or go on board a ship. **4** *v.* To travel or go on a ship. **5** *v.* To transport (goods) by ship, railroad, etc. **6** *v.* To take in (water) over the side: *Our sailboat* shipped *water during the squall.* **7** *n.* The crew of a ship. **8** *v.* To take a job on a ship: *to* ship *out as mate.* **9** *v.* To hire and take aboard to work on a ship, as sailors. **10** *v.* To place in its proper position for use on a ship or boat: *to* ship *a rudder.* **11** *v. informal* To get rid of. **— when one's ship comes in** When one's fortune has been made or one's wishes have been granted.

-ship A suffix meaning: **1** The condition or quality of, as in *companionship,* the condition or quality of being companions. **2** The office or rank of, as in *judgeship,* the rank of a judge. **3** The art or skill of, as in *marksmanship,* the skill of a marksman.

ship·board [ship′bôrd′] *n.* A ship, now only in the expression **on shipboard:** In or on a ship; aboard: *Are there enough supplies* on shipboard?

ship·load [ship′lōd′] *n.* The quantity that a ship carries or can carry.

ship·mate [ship′māt′] *n.* A sailor who serves with another on board the same ship.

ship·ment [ship′mənt] *n.* **1** Anything that is shipped. **2** The act of shipping.

ship·per [ship′ər] *n.* A person who ships goods.

ship·ping [ship′ing] *n.* **1** The act of shipping goods. **2** All the ships belonging to a country or port, or their tonnage.

ship·shape [ship′shāp′] *adj.* Orderly and neat, as on a ship; in good order.

ship·wreck [ship′rek′] **1** *n.* The destruction of or damage to a ship at sea. **2** *v.* To wreck, as a vessel. **3** *n.* Scattered remains, as of a wrecked ship; wreckage. **4** *n.* Ruin; destruction: the *shipwreck* of one's hopes. **5** *v.* To ruin; destroy.

ship·yard [ship′yärd′] *n.* A place where ships are built or repaired.

shire [shīr] *n.* In Great Britain, a county: often used in county names, as *Devonshire.*

shirk [shûrk] *v.* To avoid doing (something that should be done): *to* shirk *household chores.* **— shirk′er** *n.*

shirr [shûr] **1** *v.* To draw (cloth) into three or more parallel rows of gathers. **2** *n.* Shirring. **3** *v.* To bake (eggs removed from the shell) in a buttered dish.

shirr·ing [shûr′ing] *n.* A drawing of material into three or more parallel rows of gathers.

shirt [shûrt] *n.* **1** A garment usually worn on the upper part of the body by men and boys. **2** An undershirt. **3** A blouse. ◆ *Shirt* is a native English word, and *skirt* comes from an old Scandinavian word. Both originally meant *shirt*

or *short garment.* The similarity of their older forms shows that they came originally from a common source.

shirt·ing [shûr′ting] *n.* Cloth for shirts.

shirt·waist [shûrt′wāst′] *n.* **1** A woman's tailored blouse that looks something like a man's shirt. **2** A woman's tailored dress having a bodice like a shirtwaist. **3** *adj. use:* a *shirtwaist* dress.

shiv·er¹ [shiv′ər] **1** *v.* To tremble, as with cold or fear; shake; quiver. **2** *n.* The act of shivering; a trembling.

shiv·er² [shiv′ər] **1** *v.* To break suddenly into many pieces; shatter. **2** *n.* A splinter; sliver.

shoal¹ [shōl] **1** *n.* A shallow place in any body of water. **2** *n.* A sandbar or bank under water which makes such a shallow place. **3** *v.* To make or become shallow. **4** *adj.* Shallow: *shoal* water.

shoal² [shōl] *n.* **1** A large group or multitude; throng. **2** A school of fish.

shock¹ [shok] **1** *n.* A violent jolt or blow; sudden impact: the *shock* of an explosion. **2** *v.* To shake by sudden collision; jar. **3** *n.* A sudden and severe upset of the mind or feelings, as in fright or great sorrow. **4** *v.* To disturb the feelings or mind of suddenly and violently; disgust or horrify: *I was* shocked *by his uncouth behavior; The train wreck* shocked *the entire town.* **5** *n.* The physical effects produced by the passing of a strong electric current through the body. **6** *v.* To give or receive an electric shock: *The faulty lamp switch* shocked *him.* **7** *n.* A state of severe or mild bodily collapse, characterized by a sudden failure in blood circulation. It results from injury or major surgical operations.

shock² [shok] **1** *n.* A number of bundles of grain, stalks of corn, etc., stacked upright to dry in a field. **2** *v.* To gather (grain) into a shock or shocks.

shock³ [shok] *n.* A coarse, tangled mass, as of hair.

shock ab·sorb·er [ab·sôr′bər] A device to lessen the shock of sudden bumps or jolts, as on the springs of automobiles.

shock absorbers

shock·ing [shok′ing] *adj.* **1** Causing an unpleasant surprise. **2** Disgusting; objectionable. **3** *informal* Terrible; awful. **— shock′ing·ly** *adv.*

coil springs

shock wave A violent disturbance in a fluid, especially air, that travels outward from a point of impact or explosion, often with destructive effects.

shod [shod] Past tense and past participle of SHOE: *The blacksmith* shod *the horse.*

shod·dy [shod′ē] *n., pl.* **shod·dies,** *adj.* **shod·di·er, shod·di·est 1** *n.* A poor grade of wool made from used or waste wool. **2** *n.* Cloth woven from such wool. **3** *adj.* Made of or containing shoddy. **4** *adj.* Inferior; of poor quality: a *shoddy* piece of furniture. **5** *adj.* Mean; lowdown: a *shoddy* trick.

shoe [shoo] *n., v.* **shod, shoe·ing** **1** *n.* An outer covering, usually of leather, for the human foot. **2** *n.* Something that is like a shoe in position or use, as a horseshoe. **3** *v.* To furnish with shoes. **4** *n.* The part of a brake that presses on a wheel or drum to slow its turning. **— fill one's shoes** To take one's place or position. **— in another's shoes** In another's place or position.

A brake shoe

shoe·horn [shoo′hôrn′] *n.* A smooth, curved implement of horn, metal, etc., used to help slip on a shoe over the heel.

shoe·lace [shoo′lās′] *n.* A cord or lace for fastening a shoe.

shoe·mak·er [shoo′mā′kər] *n.* A person whose trade is making or repairing shoes.

shoe·string [shoo′string′] *n.* A shoelace. **— on a shoestring** With a small sum of money with which to begin: My father began his business *on a shoestring*.

shoe·tree [shoo′trē′] *n.* A form put into a shoe to keep it in shape or to stretch it.

shone [shōn] Past tense and past participle of SHINE: His eyes *shone* with pleasure.

shoo [shoo] *interj., v.* **shooed, shoo·ing** **1** *interj.* Be off! Go away! **2** *v.* To drive away, as by crying "shoo!": to *shoo* chickens away.

shook [shook] Past tense of SHAKE.

shoon [shoon] *n.pl.* Shoes: seldom used today.

shoot [shoot] *v.* **shot, shoot·ing,** *n.* **1** *v.* To hit, wound, or kill with a bullet, arrow, etc.: to *shoot* a deer. **2** *v.* To fire (a weapon): to *shoot* a rifle. **3** *v.* To send out or discharge from a weapon: to *shoot* bullets. **4** *v.* To go off; discharge The pistol jammed and failed to *shoot*. **5** *n.* A shooting match or hunting party. **6** *v.* To send out suddenly and with force: The lawyer *shot* questions at the suspect; to *shoot* out beams of light; to *shoot* a bolt on a door. **7** *v.* To move swiftly; rush: The children *shot* out of the bus; A meteor *shot* across the sky. **8** *v.* To pass over or through swiftly: to *shoot* rapids on a raft; A sharp pain *shot* up his leg. **9** *n.* A slide or passage down which things are slid or dropped; chute. **10** *v.* To film; make a photograph of: to *shoot* a street scene. **11** *v.* To score (a point) in certain games: to *shoot* baskets. **12** *v.* To play, as certain games: to *shoot* pool; to *shoot* nine holes of golf. **13** *v.* To put forth (buds, leaves, etc.): Crocuses *shoot* up in the early spring. **14** *n.* A young bud, leaf, or branch. **15** *v.* To grow quickly: Jimmy *shot* up several inches last year. **16** *v.* To mark with streaks of another color: My mother's red hair is *shot* with gray. **17** *v.* To jut out; project: The pier *shoots* out into the bay. **— shoot′er** *n.*

shooting star Another name for METEOR.

shop [shop] *n., v.* **shopped, shop·ping** **1** *n.* A place for the sale of retail goods; store. **2** *n.* A place for making or repairing things or for doing a certain kind of work: a carpentry *shop*. **3** *v.* To visit shops or stores to purchase or look at goods: We will *shop* for our fall clothes this weekend. **— shop′per** *n.*

shop·keep·er [shop′kē′pər] *n.* A person who runs a shop or store; tradesman.

shop·lift·er [shop′lif′tər] *n.* A person, pretending to be a shopper, who steals goods that are in a store to be sold. **— shop′lift′ing** *n.*

shop·ping [shop′ing] *n.* The act of buying goods at a shop or of looking in one or more shops for the goods one wants.

shop·worn [shop′wôrn′] *adj.* Dingy and soiled from having been on display too long at a shop.

shore[1] [shôr] *n.* The coast or land on the edge of an ocean, sea, lake, or large river.

shore[2] [shôr] *n., v.* **shored, shor·ing** **1** *n.* A beam or timber set as a prop under or against a wall, a boat in drydock, etc. **2** *v.* To prop or support with shores: to *shore* up a rickety porch.

shore·line [shôr′līn′] *n.* The outline of a shore; the line where the shore meets the water.

shore·ward [shôr′wərd] *adv., adj.* Toward the shore.

shorn [shôrn] An alternative past participle of SHEAR.

Shores

short [shôrt] **1** *adj.* Not having great length from end to end or from beginning to end; not long: a *short* piece of rope; a *short* vacation. **2** *adv.* So as to be not long: to have one's hair cut *short*; Cut your visit *short*. **3** *adj.* Below the average height: a *short* woman. **4** *adj.* Rude and curt in manner: a *short* reply. **5** *adv.* In a rude or brief way: to answer *short*. **6** *adj.* Easily broken or crumbled: *short* bread. **7** *adj.* Not reaching a desired or required amount, measure, etc.: My account is *short* five dollars; Our oil supply is *short*. **8** *adv.* So as not to reach or extend to a certain point, condition, etc.: to fall *short*. **9** *n.* Anything that is short, as a brief movie run between showings of a main feature. **10** *n.* (*pl.*) Trousers with legs extending to or part way to the knees. **11** *n.* (*pl.*) Short pants worn by a man as an undergarment. **12** *n.* A short circuit. **13** *adv.* Suddenly: The horse stopped *short* at the fence. **14** *adj.* Relatively brief when sounded in speech, as the "i" in "hit." **— for short** As a short form; for the sake of brevity: Edward is called Ed *for short*. **— in short** Briefly. **— short of 1** Not having a sufficient amount, number, etc., or to be *short of* bread. **2** Less than: She wants nothing *short of* perfection. **3** On the near side of.

short·age [shôr'tij] *n.* A lack in the amount or number needed or desired; deficiency.

short·cake [shôrt'kāk'] *n.* A rich biscuit or layer cake filled or covered with berries or fruit.

short·cir·cuit [shôrt'sûr'kit] *v.* **1** To make a short circuit in. **2** To become a short circuit.

short circuit In an electric circuit, a path of low resistance that allows the current to bypass other circuit elements. Accidental short circuits are caused by faulty wiring or apparatus and can be dangerous: The firemen said that the fire was started by a *short circuit*.

short·com·ing [shôrt'kum'ing] *n.* A failure, weakness, or defect, as in one's character or behavior.

short cut **1** A path or way between two places that is shorter than the regular way. **2** Any way of saving time, distance, or money.

short·en [shôr'tən] *v.* **1** To make or become short or shorter: to *shorten* the sleeves of a coat. **2** To make rich and crumbly, as pastry, by using a large proportion of shortening.

short·en·ing [shôr'tən·ing] *n.* **1** The act of a person who shortens. **2** A fat, such as butter or vegetable oil, used to make pastry rich.

short·hand [shôrt'hand'] *n.* **1** A system of writing rapidly that uses symbols to stand for letters, words, or phrases. **2** Any writing made up of such symbols.

short-hand·ed [shôrt'han'did] *adj.* Not having enough workers, assistants, etc.

short·horn [shôrt'hôrn'] *n.* A breed of cattle with short horns, originally from England.

short-lived [shôrt'līvd' *or* shôrt'livd'] *adj.* Living or lasting only a short time.

short·ly [shôrt'lē] *adv.* **1** In a short time; quickly; soon: Come back *shortly*. **2** In few words; briefly. **3** Rudely; abruptly: He was annoyed and answered *shortly*.

short·sight·ed [shôrt'sī'tid] *adj.* **1** Unable to see clearly at a distance; nearsighted. **2** Not preparing or planning for the future; lacking foresight.

short·stop [shôrt'stop'] *n.* In baseball, an infielder whose position is between second and third base.

short-tem·pered [shôrt'tem'pərd] *adj.* Easily angered; having a quick temper.

short-wave [shôrt'wāv'] *adj.* Indicating, operating by, or carried by short waves: a *short-wave* radio; a *short-wave* broadcast.

short waves Radio waves that are 60 meters or less in length.

short-wind·ed [shôrt'win'did] *adj.* Breathing with difficulty or getting out of breath too quickly.

Shos·ta·ko·vich [shos'tə·kô'vich], **Dimitri,** born 1906, Soviet composer.

shot[1] [shot] *n., pl.* **shots** **1** The act of shooting, especially the discharge of a weapon: We heard *shots* down the street. **2** (*pl.* **shot**) A bullet or pellet of lead to be discharged from a gun. A shotgun usually fires a number of very small lead balls, or shot, at the same time. **3** A person who

shoots; marksman: He's an excellent *shot*. **4** The distance that a bullet or other missile is or can be thrown. **5** A stroke in certain games, as billiards. **6** An attempt to hit, as by shooting: His first *shot* at the ducks missed; a *shot* at the moon. **7** Any attempt or try: I had a *shot* at the trophy. **8** A cruel or unfriendly remark: His parting *shot* was, "You'll be sorry for this!" **9** A heavy metal ball which, in an athletic contest, is thrown overhand as far as possible. **10** A photograph, or a single scene recorded on motion picture film. **11** An injection by means of a hypodermic needle: a *shot* of penicillin. **— a long shot** A contestant, an attempt, etc., that is not likely to succeed. **— not by a long shot** Not at all; not likely.

shot[2] [shot] **1** Past tense and past participle of SHOOT. **2** *adj.* Streaked or mixed with other colors: a sky *shot* with pink. **3** *adj. informal* Exhausted or ruined; worn-out.

shot·gun [shot'gun'] *n.* A gun, with a smooth bore and either a single or double barrel, made to fire cartridges filled with small shot.

shot-put [shot'pŏŏt'] *n.* **1** An athletic contest in which a shot is thrown, or put, for distance. **2** A single throw of the shot.

should [shŏŏd] Past tense of SHALL, used chiefly, however, as a helping verb meaning: **1** Ought to: You *should* do your homework. **2** Were to: If I *should* go, he would go too. **3** Assuming that: *Should* our budget work out, we'll go on vacation next month. **4** Expect to: I *should* be home by noon. ✦ In American usage, either *should* or *would* may be used with the first person in such expressions as "I *should* be glad to come; We *would* be happy to do it." Some people think, however, that *should* with the first person sounds a bit more polite.

shoul·der [shōl'dər] **1** *n.* The part of the body to which the arm in man, an animal's foreleg, or a bird's wing is jointed. **2** *v.* To push with the shoulder: to *shoulder* a person out of the way. **3** *v.* To carry on the shoulder. **4** *v.* To undertake; bear: to *shoulder* one's responsibilities. **5** *n.* The section of a garment that fits over the shoulder. **6** *n.* A cut of meat consisting of the upper part of the foreleg of an animal: a *shoulder* of lamb. **7** *n.* Anything that is shaped like or sticks out like a shoulder: the *shoulder* of a mountain. **8** *n.* Either edge of a road. **— put one's shoulder to the wheel** To set to work with a strong effort. **— shoulder arms** To hold a rifle upright with the butt in one's hand and the barrel resting on the shoulder. **— shoulder to shoulder** **1** Side by side and close together. **2** In cooperation; working together. **— straight from the shoulder** *informal* Straightforwardly; frankly.

shoulder blade Either of two flat, triangular bones in the upper back; scapula.

shoulder strap **1** A strap worn on or over the shoulder to hold up a garment. **2** A strap of cloth marked with insignia of rank, worn by officers in the armed services.

should·n't [shŏŏd′(ə)nt] Should not.

shouldst [shŏŏdst] A form of the verb SHALL, used with *thou*: seldom used today.

shout [shout] **1** *n.* A sudden and loud outcry: a *shout* of anger; a *shout* of laughter. **2** *v.* To say or express with a shout: He *shouted* "Good morning" to me from across the street. **3** *v.* To cry out loudly: The little boy *shouted* with excitement when he saw the elephant. **— shout someone down** To drown out what someone is saying by shouting. **— shout′er** *n.*

shove [shuv] *v.* **shoved, shov·ing,** *n.* **1** *v.* To move by pushing from behind: to *shove* a stalled car. **2** *v.* To push hard against: jostle: to *shove* people in a crowd. **3** *n.* The act of shoving. **— shove off 1** To push along or away, as a boat. **2** *informal* To go; start; leave: Let's *shove off* for home.

shov·el [shuv′əl] *n., v.* **shov·eled** or **shov·elled, shov·el·ing** or **shov·el·ling 1** *n.* A tool with a handle and a somewhat flattened scoop, used for lifting or moving loose soil, coal, etc. **2** *v.* To take up and move or heap up with a shovel. **3** *v.* To dig or clear with a shovel: To *shovel* a path through the snow. **4** *v.* To thrust into the mouth hastily and in large amounts: to *shovel* down one's lunch. **— shov′.el·er** or **shov′el·ler** *n.*

Shovel

show [shō] *v.* **showed, shown** or **showed, show·ing,** *n.* **1** *v.* To cause or allow to see or be seen: He *showed* his ignorance; They *showed* us their new kitten. **2** *v.* To be or become visible; appear: A light *showed* in the window. **3** *n.* The act of showing: a *show* of hands. **4** *n.* Anything shown or made apparent: a *show* of stupidity. **5** *v.* To be seen easily; be obvious: The mended place on my coat *shows*. **6** *v.* To direct; guide: Please *show* us the way home. **7** *v.* To point out: A clock *shows* the time. **8** *v.* To explain; teach: Father *showed* me how to build a bench. **9** *v.* To give; bestow: The judge *showed* mercy to the prisoner. **10** *n.* An entertainment or exhibition: a TV *show*; an art *show*. **11** *n.* An elaborate display: a *show* of wealth. **12** *n.* A false display: She made a great *show* of being sorry. **— for show** For effect; to attract notice. **— show off 1** To try to attract too much attention to oneself or to one's accomplishments. **2** To display proudly: to *show off* one's new car. **— show up 1** To stand out: Red curtains *show up* well on white walls. **2** To expose, as faults. **3** *informal* To arrive.

show·boat [shō′bōt′] *n.* A boat, such as the old steamers on the Mississippi River, on which traveling troupes of actors and musicians give performances.

show·case [shō′kās′] *n.* A glass case for displaying and protecting articles in a store, museum, etc.

show·down [shō′doun′] *n. informal* Any action, argument, discussion, etc., that tries to bring out into the open and settle some conflict or disputed issue: He had a *showdown* with the coach as to why he was not on the regular team.

show·er [shou′ər] **1** *n.* A brief fall of rain, hail, or sleet. **2** *v.* To sprinkle or wet with or as if with a shower. **3** *v.* To fall like a shower. **4** *n.* A large fall, as of tears, sparks, etc. **5** *n.* An abundance; great amount: a *shower* of abuse. **6** *v.* To send or pour out, like a shower; give: His grandmother *showered* affection on the boy. **7** *v.* To give freely: He *showered* gifts on her. **8** *n.* A shower bath. **9** *v.* To take a shower bath. **10** *n.* A party for giving gifts, as to a bride.

shower bath 1 A bath in which water is sprayed on the body from an overhead nozzle. **2** A device that provides such a bath.

show·man [shō′mən] *n., pl.* **show·men** [shō′mən] **1** A person who manages or produces a show. **2** Any person who does things in a showy or dramatic way. **— show′man·ship** *n.*

shown [shōn] An alternative past participle of SHOW.

show-off [shō′ôf′] *n. informal* **1** The act of showing off. **2** A person who shows off.

show·y [shō′ē] *adj.* **show·i·er, show·i·est 1** Making a great or brilliant display: *showy* flowers. **2** So gaudy and flashy as to be in poor taste: Do you think this pin is too *showy* to wear? **— show′i·ly** *adv.* **— show′i·ness** *n.*

shrank [shrangk] Past tense of SHRINK.

shrap·nel [shrap′nəl] *n., pl.* **shrap·nel 1** An artillery shell that explodes in the air and scatters a quantity of small metal balls. **2** Fragments scattered when a shell explodes.

shred [shred] *n., v.* **shred·ded** or **shred, shred·ding 1** *n.* A small, irregular strip torn or cut off: a *shred* of newspaper. **2** *n.* A bit; particle: He hasn't a *shred* of self-respect. **3** *v.* To tear or cut into shreds.

shrew [shrōō] *n.* **1** Any of various small mammals that look like mice. Shrews have long snouts and live mostly on insects. **2** A nagging, scolding woman.

Shrew, 2–4 in. long

shrewd [shrōōd] *adj.* Having sound, practical common sense; sharp; keen: a *shrewd* tradesman. **— shrewd′ly** *adv.* **— shrewd′ness** *n.* ◆ *Shrewd*, based on the Old English word for *shrew*, once meant *evil* or *wicked*. This meaning has softened over the years, and today a *shrewd* person is clever and sharp, and not necessarily evil.

shrew·ish [shrōō′ish] *adj.* Like a shrew; ill-tempered; nagging.

shriek [shrēk] **1** *n.* A sharp, shrill outcry, scream, or sound. **2** *v* To make such a sound: The animal *shrieked* in pain. **3** *v.* To say with a shriek: She *shrieked*, "Help me!"

shrift [shrift] *n.* The act of shriving or giving absolution. **— short shrift** Little or no mercy or delay, as in dealing with a person: The champion gave his opponent *short shrift* and knocked him out early.

shrike [shrīk] *n.* A fierce bird with a hooked bill that feeds on insects and attacks other birds.

shrill [shril] **1** *adj.* Having or making a high-pitched, piercing sound: a *shrill* whistle. **2** *v.* To make a high-pitched, piercing sound. **— shrill′ly** *adj.* **— shrill′ness** *n.*

Shrike, 9–10 in. long

shrimp [shrimp] *n.* **1** Any of several types of edible shellfish with long tails. **2** *slang* A small or unimportant person.

shrine [shrīn] *n.* **1** A place or object, as a tomb, chapel, holy image, etc., sacred to some holy person and often containing relics. **2** A place held in high honor because of the events or ideas connected with it: The Statue of Liberty is a *shrine* of freedom. ◆ In Old English *shrine* meant *a box* or *chest.* The word later came to be associated with sacred objects.

shrink [shringk] *v.* **shrank** or **shrunk, shrunk** or **shrunk·en, shrink·ing** **1** To make or become smaller, as by drawing together, contracting, etc.: to *shrink* dress goods before cutting; Sweaters often *shrink* when washed. **2** To make or become less; diminish: Big bills keep *shrinking* his bank account. **3** To draw back, as in disgust or fear: He *shrank* back from the hissing snake.

shrink·age [shringk′ij] *n.* **1** The act of shrinking; contraction. **2** The amount lost by such shrinking. **3** A decrease in value.

shrive [shrīv] *v.* **shrived** or **shrove, shriv·en** or **shrived, shriv·ing** **1** To receive the confession of and give absolution to. **2** To confess one's sins.

shriv·el [shriv′əl] *v.* **shriv·eled** or **shriv·elled, shriv·el·ing** or **shriv·el·ling** To contract into wrinkles; shrink and dry up: In the hot sun the plants *shriveled* up.

shriv·en [shriv′ən] Alternative past participle of SHRIVE.

Shrouds

shroud [shroud] **1** *n.* A dress or garment for a dead person. **2** *n.* Anything that wraps up or conceals like such a garment: a *shroud* of mist. **3** *v.* To clothe or wrap in or as if in a shroud:

The town is *shrouded* in darkness. **4** *n.* (*usually pl.*) Any of a set of ropes stretched from a masthead to a ship's side to brace the mast.

shrove [shrōv] Alternative past tense of SHRIVE.

shrub [shrub] *n.* A low, woody plant having many stems and branches springing from the base.

shrub·ber·y [shrub′ər·ē] *n., pl.* **shrub·ber·ies** A group of shrubs, as in a garden.

shrub·by [shrub′ē] *adj.* **shrub·bi·er, shrub·bi·est** **1** Covered with or full of shrubs. **2** Like a shrub.

shrug [shrug] *v.,* **shrugged, shrug·ging,** *n.* **1** *v.* To draw up (the shoulders) to show doubt, dislike, indifference, etc. **2** *n.* The action of shrugging.

shrunk [shrungk] Alternative past tense and past participle of SHRINK.

shrunk·en [shrungk′ən] **1** Alternative past participle of SHRINK. **2** *adj.* Grown smaller and thinner; shriveled; withered: a *shrunken* old lady.

shuck [shuk] **1** *n.* A husk, shell, or pod: a corn *shuck.* **2** *v.* To remove the husks or shells from: to *shuck* oysters. **3** *v. informal* To take off, or cast off, as clothes.

shud·der [shud′ər] **1** *v.* To tremble or shake, as from fear or cold; shiver. **2** *n.* The act of shuddering; a shivering.

shuf·fle [shuf′əl] *v.* **shuf·fled, shuf·fling,** *n.* **1** *v.* To drag (the feet) in walking or in a certain type of dancing. **2** *n.* A dragging of the feet in walking or dancing. **3** *v.* To mix the order of playing cards before a deal. **4** *n.* A mixing or changing of the order of playing cards. **5** *n.* A turn to shuffle cards. **6** *v.* To push about or mix together aimlessly: to *shuffle* papers on a desk. **7** *n.* An aimless pushing about or mixing together. **8** *v.* To act or speak in such a way as to deceive or mislead. **9** *n.* A misleading or deceiving action or speech.

shuf·fle·board [shuf′əl·bôrd′] *n.* A game in which large disks are slid, by means of a pronged pole, along a smooth surface toward numbered spaces.

shun [shun] *v.* **shunned, shun·ning** To keep clear of; avoid: Poor health forced him to *shun* active physical sports.

shunt [shunt] **1** *v.* To turn or move to one side or out of the way. **2** *v.* To put off on someone else, as a job. **3** *v.* To switch (a train or railroad car) from one track to another. **4** *n.* The act of shunting. **5** *n.* A railroad switch. **6** *v.* To divert or by-pass, as an electric current or a circuit element. **7** *n.* In electricity, a circuit element, as a resistor, capacitor, etc., connected in parallel with other elements in order to by-pass part of the current.

shut [shut] *v.* **shut, shut·ting,** *adj.* **1** *v.* To bring into such a position as to close an opening: to *shut* a gate; to *shut* the lid of a box. **2** *v.* To be or become closed or in a closed position: This bureau drawer *shuts* easily. **3** *v.* To close the door, windows, lid, etc., of: to *shut* a trunk; to *shut* a beach house for the winter months. **4** *v.*

To close and fasten securely, as with a lock or latch. **5** *v.* To close, fold, or bring together the parts of: to *shut* an umbrella. **6** *adj.* Fastened or closed: Keep the windows *shut* when it rains. **— shut down 1** To keep from or stop operating for a time, as a factory. **2** To come down close: The fog *shut down* over the river. **— shut in** To keep from going outside; enclose. **— shut out 1** To keep from coming in: The new building next door *shut out* the breeze from the ocean. **2** To keep (an opponent) from scoring in a game. **— shut up 1** To close all the entrances to, as a house. **2** *informal* To stop talking or cause to stop talking. **3** To imprison or keep indoors.

shut·down [shut′doun′] *n.* The stopping of work or activity, as in a mine, factory, or place of business.

shut-in [shut′in′] **1** *n.* An invalid who is unable to go out of doors. **2** *adj.* Having to stay at home, as from illness.

shut·out [shut′out′] *n.* In sports, a game in which one side is kept from scoring.

shut·ter [shut′ər] *n.* **1** A hinged panel for covering a window. **2** A device on a camera that opens to admit light through the lens and closes rapidly. **3** A person or thing that shuts.

shut·tle [shut′(ə)l] *n., v.* **shut·tled, shut·tling 1** *n.* A device used in weaving to carry a thread back and forth between the threads that run lengthwise. **2** *n.* The device for carrying the under thread back and forth in a sewing machine. **3** *n.* A plane, train, or bus that operates regularly between two nearby places. **4** *v.* To move back and forth like a shuttle.

shut·tle·cock [shut′(ə)l·kok′] *n.* A rounded piece of cork or other material with a crown of feathers. It is hit back and forth in badminton.

shy[1] [shī] *adj.* **shi·er** or **shy·er, shi·est** or **shy·est,** *v.* **shied, shy·ing 1** *adj.* Bashful or uncomfortable with people; ill at ease. **2** *adj.* Easily frightened or startled; timid: a *shy* wild bird. **3** *v.* To start suddenly aside, as in fear: The horse *shied* at the sound of an automobile's horn. **4** *v.* To draw back, as from fear: to *shy* away from bad influences; He *shied* at going on the carnival ride. **5** *adj. slang* Short; lacking: I am still four dollars *shy* of what I need to buy the camera. **— shy′ly** *adv.* **— shy′ness** *n.*

shy[2] [shī] *v.* **shied, shy·ing** To throw with a swift, sudden motion: to *shy* rocks.

Shy·lock [shī′lok] *n.* In Shakespeare's *The Merchant of Venice,* the man who lent money with the agreement that if it was not paid back on time he was entitled to a pound of the borrower's flesh.

si [sē] *n.* Another name for TI.

Si·am [sī·am′] *n.* The former name for THAILAND. **— Si·a·mese** [sī′ə·mēz′ *or* sī′ə·mēs′] *adj., n.*

Siamese twins Any pair of twins joined together from birth. A famous pair of the 19th century were born in Siam.

Si·be·li·us [si·bā′lē·əs], **Jan,** 1865–1957, Finnish composer.

Si·be·ri·a [sī·bir′ē·ə] *n.* A region of the Soviet Union, east of the Ural Mountains. **— Si·ber′·i·an** *adj., n.*

sib·yl [sib′əl] *n.* In ancient Greece and Rome, any of various women having the power to make prophecies under the inspiration of some god.

Sic·i·ly [sis′ə·lē] *n.* A large island off the sw tip of Italy in the Mediterranean Sea. It is a part of Italy. **— Si·cil′i·an** [si·sil′yən] *adj., n.*

sick [sik] *adj.* **1** Having a disease or illness; ill: a *sick* boy; *sick* with the measles. **2** *n. use:* Sick people: *The sick* need lots of rest and care. **3** Wanting to vomit; nauseated. **4** Of or used by sick people: *sick* leave from work. **5** Feeling disgust: The terrible crime made people *sick.* **6** Tired, bored, or disgusted: I'm *sick* of telling you to be quiet. **7** Filled with longing; sorrowful: *sick* for the open sea. ◆ In Great Britain, when *sick* follows a verb it means *nauseated*: He *feels sick* means He feels like vomiting. But *a sick boy* may mean *a boy who is ill,* just as it does in the U.S.

sick·en [sik′ən] *v.* To make or become sick.

sick·en·ing [sik′ən·ing] *adj.* Causing disgust or making one sick at his stomach.

sick·ish [sik′ish] *adj.* **1** Somewhat sick. **2** Slightly nauseating: a *sickish* perfume.

sick·le [sik′əl] *n.* A tool with a curved blade mounted on a short handle, used to cut tall grass or grain.

sick·ly [sik′lē] *adj.* **sick·li·er, sick·li·est 1** Often sick; unhealthy; frail: a *sickly* old man. **2** Connected with or caused by poor health: a *sickly* complexion. **3** Faint; weak: He gave me a *sickly* smile. **4** Causing sickness or disgust: a *sickly* smell; *sickly* sentimentality. **5** Likely to lead to sickness or ill health: a *sickly* diet. **— sick′li·ness** *n.*

sick·ness [sik′nis] *n.* **1** The condition of being sick. **2** A particular disease or disorder; illness. **3** Vomiting; nausea.

side [sīd] *n., adj., v.,* **sid·ed, sid·ing 1** *n.* Any of the bounding lines or surfaces of something: a rectangle has four *sides.* **2** *n.* Either of the two opposite surfaces of something thin and flat: the right and wrong *sides* of a rug. **3** *n.* One of the two surfaces of anything rectangular that is not the top, bottom, front, or back: the *side* of the church. **4** *n.* A particular surface of something: the rough *side* of a piece of sandpaper; the inner *side* of the arm. **5** *n.* Either the right or left half of the human body, especially the part between the armpit and hip. **6** *adj.* Of, at, or on one side: a *side* exit. **7** *adj.* Directed at some side: a *side* blow. **8** *n.* The space beside or near someone or

---

add, āce, câre, pälm; end, ēqual; it, īce; odd, ōpen, ôrder; to͝ok, po͞ol; up, bûrn; ə = a in *above,* e in *sicken,* i in *possible,* o in *melon,* u in *circus;* yo͞o = u in *fuse;* oil; pout; check; ring; thin; ŧhis; zh in *vision.* For ¶ reference, see page 64 · HOW TO

something: The dog never left his master's *side*.
9 *adj.* Coming from one side: a *side* glance.
10 *n.* The left or right half of an animal slaughtered for food: a *side* of beef. **11** *n.* One of two or more opposite directions or places: the west *side* of town; the other *side* of the street. **12** *n.* A group of people who stand together against another group, as in a contest, a quarrel, a set of beliefs, etc. **13** *n.* A point of view; opinion: Let's hear his *side* of the story. **14** *v.* To support or take the part of: I *sided* with my parents in their difficulties with the neighbors. **15** *n.* A line of descent traced through one's mother or father: an aunt on my mother's *side*. **16** *n.* A particular quality of a person or thing: That story has a humorous *side*. **17** *adj.* Not first in importance: a *side* issue. **18** *n.* A slope, as of a mountain. **— side by side** Beside or next to each other: They walked *side by side*. **— take sides** To support or be in favor of a particular point of view.

side arms Weapons worn at the side, as swords pistols, bayonets, etc.

side·board [sīd′bôrd′] *n.* A piece of dining-room furniture with drawers, shelves, etc., for silverware and table linen.

side·burns [sīd′bûrnz′] *n.pl.* The hair growing on the sides of a man's face below the hairline, in front of his ears.

sid·ed [sī′did] *adj.* Having a certain number or special type of sides: used in combination, as in *four-sided*, having four sides.

side·light [sīd′līt′] *n.* **1** A light coming from the side. **2** An incidental fact or bit of information: The book gave some *sidelights* on his character.

side·line [sīd′līn′] *n.* **1** One of the boundary lines at the sides of a football field, tennis court, etc. **2** (*usually pl.*) The area just outside these lines: The photographers stood on the *sidelines*. **3** A line of goods sold in addition to the main type of goods handled by a business. **4** A type of work carried on in addition to one's regular work.

side·long [sīd′lông′] **1** *adj.* Moving, directed, etc., to one side: a *sidelong* motion. **2** *adv.* Toward the side; sideways: to glance *sidelong*.

si·de·re·al [sī·dir′ē·əl] *adj.* **1** Of or having to do with the stars. **2** Measured by means of the stars: a *sidereal* year.

side·sad·dle [sīd′sad′(ə)l] **1** *n.* A woman's saddle with one stirrup, for riding with both legs on the same side of the horse. **2** *adv.* With both legs on the same side: to ride *sidesaddle*.

side·show [sīd′shō′] *n.* A small show separated from a main show, as in a circus.

side·step [sīd′step′] *v.* **side·stepped, side·step·ping** **1** To step to one side. **2** To avoid or postpone as if by stepping to one side.

side·swipe [sīd′swīp′] *n., v.* **side·swiped, side·swip·ing** **1** *n.* A sweeping blow along the side. **2** *v.* To strike or collide with such a blow.

side·track [sīd′trak′] *v.* **1** To move to a siding, as a railroad train. **2** To turn away or distract from the main subject or line of action.

side·walk [sīd′wôk′] *n. U.S.* A path or pavement for walking along the side of a street.

side·ways [sīd′wāz′] **1** *adv.* From or toward one side: A crab walks *sideways*. **2** *adv.* With one side forward: Hold it *sideways*. **3** *adj.* Moving to or from one side: a *sideways* nod of the head.

side·wise [sīd′wīz′] *adj., adv.* Sideways.

sid·ing [sī′ding] *n.* **1** A railroad track by the side of the main track, onto which cars may be switched. **2** A material, as overlapping boards, used to construct the outside walls of a house or building with a wooden frame.

si·dle [sīd′(ə)l] *v.* **si·dled, si·dling** To move sideways, especially in a cautious or sly manner: He *sidled* away from the growling dog.

siege [sēj] *n.* **1** The surrounding of a fortified place, town, etc., by a military force trying to capture it. **2** A steady and persistent attempt to win something. **3** The time during which one has a prolonged illness or difficulty: a *siege* of measles.

si·er·ra [sē·er′ə] *n.* A mountain range or chain, especially one with a series of jagged peaks.

Si·er·ra Ne·vad·a [sē·er′ə nə·vad′ə *or* nə·vä′də] A mountain range of eastern California, extending 400 miles north and south.

Siding

si·es·ta [sē·es′tə] *n.* In Spain and parts of Latin America, an afternoon nap.

sieve [siv] *n.* A utensil with holes in the bottom, used to separate solids too large to pass through from fine pieces or a liquid.

sift [sift] *v.* **1** To pass through a sieve or strainer in order to separate the fine parts from the coarse: to *sift* flour. **2** To scatter by or as if by passing through a sieve: to *sift* cinnamon and sugar on toast. **3** To use a sieve. **4** To pass or fall through or as if through a sieve: Sand *sifted* into our shoes. **5** To examine carefully or distinguish: to *sift* fact from fiction. **— sift′er** *n.*

sigh [sī] **1** *v.* To draw in and let out a deep, loud breath, as in sadness, weariness, or relief. **2** *v.* To make a sound like a sigh, as the wind does. **3** *n.* The act or sound of or as of sighing: to heave a *sigh* of relief. **4** *v.* To long; yearn: to *sigh* for one's youth. **5** *v.* To say with a sigh: She *sighed* "Good-by."

sight [sīt] **1** *n.* The act of seeing: I remember my first *sight* of them. **2** *n.* The ability to see; vision: Owls have poor *sight* in the daytime. **3** *v.* To see; observe: to *sight* a whale. **4** *n.* That which is seen: The sea is a beautiful *sight*. **5** *n.* (*often pl.*) Things that are worth seeing: the *sights* of Paris. **6** *n.* The distance over or to which the sight reaches: The deer leaped out of *sight*. **7** *n.* (*often pl.*) A device on a gun, surveying instrument, etc., used in aiming. **8** *v.* To look at or aim through sights. **9** *n.* An aim or observation taken with a telescope or other sighting device. **10** *n. informal* Something unusual or ugly to look at: His old, torn cap was a *sight*. **11** *n.* Point of view; estimation: In his *sight* she's a beautiful girl. **— at sight** or **on sight** As soon as seen: to shoot *at sight*; to read music *at sight*. **— know by sight** To be familiar with the appearance of, although not acquainted with. **— not by a long sight** **1** Never; not at all. **2** Not nearly. ◆ See SITE.

sight·less [sīt′lis] *adj.* **1** Lacking sight; blind. **2** Invisible.

sight·see·ing [sīt′sē′ing] *n.* The visiting of places of interest. **— sight′se′er** *n.*

sign [sīn] **1** *n.* A symbol, object, or action that stands for something else: × is the *sign* for multiplication; He waved his hand as a *sign* of greeting. **2** *n.* A board, placard, etc., on which something is written to give information or warning: a street *sign*; a stop *sign*. **3** *n.* An indication, as of a state or condition: Fatigue may be a *sign* of illness. **4** *n.* A gesture or action taking the place of speech: He made *signs* for me to come in. **5** *v.* To communicate by signs or signals: The teacher *signed* to me to go to the board. **6** *v.* To write one's signature or initials on: to *sign* a check. **7** *v.* To hire by getting the signature of on a contract: to *sign* a baseball player. **8** *n.* An indication associated with a number that it is positive or negative, as positive two (+2) or negative three (−3). **— sign off** In radio and television, to announce the close of a day's program and stop broadcasting. **— sign up 1** To enlist, as in the armed services. **2** To hire or be hired for a job. **— sign′er** *n.*

sig·nal [sig′nəl] *n., v.* **sig·naled** or **sig·nalled**, **sig·nal·ing** or **sig·nal·ling**, *adj.* **1** *n.* A sign agreed on as a way of sending a notice, warning, instruction, or other message: a *signal* of distress; a *signal* to announce lunch. **2** *v.* To make a signal or signals to: The driver ahead *signaled* me to pass him. **3** *n.* An electric current or electromagnetic wave that varies in proportion to a sound or picture, as in a radio, etc.

A traffic signal

4 *v.* To make known by a signal: the factory whistle *signals* the end of the day's work. **5** *adj.* Used to signal. **6** *adj.* Outstanding; notable.

sig·nal·ize [sig′nəl·īz] *v.* **sig·nal·ized, sig·nal·iz·ing** To make noteworthy or remarkable: a deed *signalized* by great courage. ¶3

sig·nal·ly [sig′nəl·ē] *adv.* In a remarkable or noteworthy way: to fail *signally*.

sig·na·ture [sig′nə·chər] *n.* **1** The name of a person written by himself. **2** In music, symbols placed at the beginning of a staff to show the key and time.

sign·board [sīn′bôrd′] *n.* A board on which a sign, direction, or advertisement is displayed.

sig·net [sig′nit] *n.* **1** A seal, especially one to make documents official. **2** A mark made by such a seal.

sig·nif·i·cance [sig-nif′ə·kəns] *n.* **1** Meaning; sense: We all understood the *significance* of what he said. **2** Importance; consequence: This is a matter of no *significance*.

sig·nif·i·cant [sig-nif′ə·kənt] *adj.* **1** Important; noteworthy: a *significant* scientific experiment. **2** Having or carrying a hidden meaning: a *significant* glance. **— sig·nif′i·cant·ly** *adv.*

sig·ni·fi·ca·tion [sig′nə·fə·kā′shən] *n.* **1** The act of signifying. **2** Meaning or sense.

sig·ni·fy [sig′nə·fī] *v.* **sig·ni·fied, sig·ni·fy·ing** **1** To make known by signs or words: to *signify* one's disapproval by saying "no." **2** To mean or express: In French, "oui" *signifies* "yes." **3** To be a sign or indication of: The wearing of purple traditionally *signifies* royalty.

sign language A way of communicating by means of signs, such as movements of the hands, instead of by speech. Deaf people often communicate in this way.

si·gno·ra [sē·nyō′rä] *n., pl.* **si·gno·re** [sē·nyō′rā] The Italian title of courtesy for a married woman, equivalent to the English *Mrs.*

si·gno·re [sē·nyō′rā] *n., pl.* **si·gno·ri** [sē·nyō′rē] The Italian title of courtesy for a man, equivalent to the English *Mr.* or *sir*.

si·gno·ri·na [sē′nyō·rē′nä] *n., pl.* **si·gno·ri·ne** [sē′nyō·rē′nā] The Italian title of courtesy for a girl or unmarried woman, equivalent to the English *Miss*.

sign·post [sīn′pōst′] *n.* A post bearing a sign on which directions, notices, etc., are given.

Sikh [sēk] *n.* A member of a Hindu religious sect in India. Sikhs are noted as soldiers.

si·lage [sī′lij] *n.* Another word for ENSILAGE.

si·lence [sī′ləns] *n., v.* **si·lenced, si·lenc·ing** **1** *n.* Absence of sound or noise; stillness: the *silence* of the desert. **2** *n.* A time or condition of keeping still, without noise or talking: After a long *silence*, he began to speak. **3** *v.* To cause to be silent; make quiet: I *silenced* the parrot. **4** *v.* To put down; suppress: to *silence* rumors.

si·lenc·er [sī′lən·sər] *n.* **1** A person or thing which silences. **2** A device attached to the muzzle of a gun to muffle the sound when fired.

si·lent [sī′lənt] *adj.* **1** Not having or making any sound or noise; noiseless; a *silent* motor; the *silent* sea. **2** Not speaking; keeping silence: The talkative woman had a *silent* husband. **3** Not mentioned or spoken: a *silent* vowel; *silent* anger. **4** Taking no active part: a *silent* partner in a business. **— si′lent·ly** *adv.*

Si·le·sia [si·lē′shə] *n.* A region of east central Europe, now divided between Czechoslovakia and Poland.

add, āce, câre, pälm; end, ēqual; it, īce; odd, ōpen, ôrder; took, pool; up, bûrn; ə = a in *above*, e in *sicken*, i in *possible*, o in *melon*, u in *circus*; yoo = u in *fuse*; oil; pout; check; ring; thin; this; zh in *vision*. For ¶ reference, see page 64 · HOW TO

sil·hou·ette [sil'ōō·et'] *n., v.* **sil·hou·et·ted, sil·hou·et·ting** **1** *n.* A portrait in outline, cut out of black paper or drawn and filled in with a dark solid color. **2** *n.* The outline of a person or object seen against a light or a light background. **3** *v.* To cause to appear in silhouette: The moon *silhouetted* the tower against the sky.

Silhouette of Lincoln

sil·i·ca [sil'i·kə] *n.* A white or colorless, very hard silicon dioxide, the main ingredient of sand and quartz.

sil·i·cate [sil'i·kit] *n.* Any of various compounds containing silicon, a metal, and oxygen. Many minerals are silicates.

sil·i·con [sil'ə·kən] *n.* A very common nonmetallic element chemically related to carbon and germanium. Silicon is used in making abrasives, silicones, transistors, etc.

sil·i·cone [sil'ə·kōn] *n.* An organic chemical compound in which one or more carbon atoms have been replaced by silicon. It is used in synthetic waxes and rubbers.

silk [silk] **1** *n.* The very fine fiber spun by silkworms to form their cocoons. **2** *n.* Cloth, thread, or clothing made of this fiber. **3** *adj. use:* a *silk* dress. **4** *n.* Any soft fiber like silk, such as a spider web, or the tassel on an ear of corn.

silk·en [silk'ən] *adj.* **1** Made of silk. **2** Like silk; smooth; glossy: *silken* curls.

silk·worm [silk'wûrm'] *n.* A caterpillar, the larva of any of certain moths, that spins silk to make its cocoon.

silk·y [silk'ē] *adj.* **silk·i·er, silk·i·est** Of or like silk; lustrous; soft; smooth: *silky* hair. **— silk'i·ness** *n.*

sill [sil] *n.* **1** The bottom of a door or window frame. **2** A beam at the base of a wall.

sil·ly [sil'ē] *adj.* **sil·li·er, sil·li·est** **1** Lacking good sense; foolish; stupid: a *silly* girl; *silly* remarks. **2** *informal* Dazed or stunned, as by a blow: to be knocked *silly.* **— sil'li·ness** *n.*

si·lo [sī'lō] *n., pl.* **si·los** A tower in which ensilage or green fodder is stored for cattle.

silt [silt] **1** *n.* Fine particles carried in or deposited by water. **2** *v.* To fill up or be filled with silt, as the mouth of a river. **— silt'y** *adj.*

sil·van [sil'vən] *adj.* Another spelling of SYLVAN.

sil·ver [sil'vər] **1** *n.* A soft, white, metallic element that conducts heat and electricity very well. It is used in medicine, photography, and industry, and in making jewelry and coins. **2** *adj. use:* a *silver* bracelet; *silver* dollars. **3** *n.* Tableware, such as knives, forks, and spoons, usually made of silver. **4** *n.* Coins made of silver. **5** *adj.* Having the color of silver: *silver* moonlight.

sil·ver·smith [sil'vər·smith'] *n.* A person whose work is to make things of silver.

sil·ver·ware [sil'vər·wâr'] *n.* Articles, especially table utensils, made of silver or of metal plated with silver or resembling silver.

sil·ver·y [sil'vər·ē] *adj.* **1** Like silver, as in color or luster: *silvery* moonlight. **2** Soft and clear in sound: *silvery* bells.

sim·i·an [sim'ē·ən] **1** *adj.* Of, related to, or like an ape or monkey. **2** *n.* An ape or monkey.

sim·i·lar [sim'ə·lər] *adj.* **1** Alike, but not completely the same: Bicycles and tricycles are *similar.* **2** Having corresponding angles equal, as two geometric figures. **— sim'i·lar·ly** *adv.*

sim·i·lar·i·ty [sim'ə·lar'ə·tē] *n., pl.* **sim·i·lar·i·ties** **1** The condition or quality of being similar; resemblance; likeness. **2** The point in which objects being compared are similar.

sim·i·le [sim'ə·lē] *n.* A figure of speech in which one thing is compared to another that is different in many ways, by the use of *as* or *like.* "He is as stupid as an ox" is a simile.

sim·mer [sim'ər] **1** *v.* To boil gently with a bubbling, humming sound. **2** *v.* To be or keep just below the boiling point. **3** *n.* The condition or process of simmering. **4** *v.* To be at the point of breaking out, as with rage. **— simmer down** **1** To reduce the liquid content of by boiling gently. **2** *informal* To calm down from a state of anger or excitement.

Si·mon Peter [sī'mən] The full name of the apostle Peter. See PETER.

si·mo·ny [sī'mə·nē] *n.* The buying and selling of sacred things, as valued positions or advancement in the church.

si·moom [si·mōōm'] *n.* A hot, dry wind of the deserts of northern Africa and SW Asia, full of sand and dust.

si·moon [si·mōōn'] *n.* A simoom.

sim·per [sim'pər] **1** *v.* To smile in a silly, self-conscious way; smirk. **2** *v.* To say with a simper. **3** *n.* A silly, self-conscious smile.

sim·ple [sim'pəl] *adj.* **sim·pler, sim·plest** **1** Not complicated or complex; easy to understand or do: a *simple* puzzle. **2** Operating by a basic mechanical principle: The pulley is a *simple* machine. **3** Free from affectation; sincere: a *simple*, frank manner. **4** Feeble-minded; silly. **5** Plain; not decorated: a *simple* wooden chair; This is the *simple* truth. **6** Low in rank; humble: a *simple* laborer. **7** Not divided or subdivided: a *simple* leaf.

sim·ple-heart·ed [sim'pəl·här'·tid] *adj.* Having a warm, sincere heart; honest and open.

The pulley is a simple machine.

sim·ple-mind·ed [sim'pəl·mīn'·did] *adj.* **1** Having low intelligence; feeble-minded. **2** Easily fooled or duped. **3** Stupid; foolish.

simple sentence A sentence made up of one main clause and no subordinate clauses. "The needle always points north" is a simple sentence.

sim·ple·ton [sim'pəl·tən] *n.* A weak-minded or foolish person.

sim·plic·i·ty [sim·plis'ə·tē] *n.* **1** The condition of being simple or free from difficulty. **2** The absence of affectation; sincerity. **3** An absence of decoration; plainness. **4** Lack of intelligence or good sense.

sim·pli·fi·ca·tion [sim′plə·fə·kā′shən] *n.* **1** The act of simplifying: His *simplification* of the physics experiment made it easy to understand. **2** Something that has been simplified.

sim·pli·fy [sim′plə·fī] *v.* **sim·pli·fied, sim·pli·fy·ing** To make more simple, plain, or easy.

sim·ply [sim′plē] *adv.* **1** In a simple or plain manner: a *simply* made dress; Try to explain the problem *simply*. **2** Really; absolutely: *simply* charming. **3** Merely; only; just: I am *simply* trying to save money. **4** Stupidly; unwisely.

sim·u·late [sim′yə·lāt] *v.* **sim·u·lat·ed, sim·u·lat·ing** **1** To take on or have the appearance of; imitate: The stone in her ring *simulated* a ruby. **2** To make a show of; pretend: Actors are able to *simulate* grief. **— sim′u·la′tion** *n.*

si·mul·ta·ne·ous [sī′məl·tā′nē·əs] *adj.* Happening, done, or existing at the same time: The dancers made *simultaneous* movements. **— si′·mul·ta′ne·ous·ly** *adv.*

sin [sin] *n., v.* **sinned, sin·ning** **1** *n.* The breaking of a religious or divine law, especially when it is done deliberately. **2** *n.* A serious fault, wrong, or offense. **3** *v.* To commit a sin.

Si·nai [sī′nī] *n.* **1** A peninsula between the Mediterranean Sea and the Red Sea. **2** In the Bible, the mountain where Moses received the laws from God.

since [sins] **1** *prep.* During or throughout the time after: It has been raining *since* noon. **2** *conj.* Continuously from the time when: She has been ill *since* she arrived. **3** *conj.* During or within the time after which: He has not called us *since* he came home. **4** *conj.* Seeing that; because: You may have the books *since* I no longer need them. **5** *adv.* From a particular past time until now: The dog ran away last week and hasn't been seen *since*. **6** *adv.* At a time between a particular past time and the present: The church was bombed during the war and has *since* been rebuilt. **7** *adv.* Before the present time; ago: Bustles have long *since* been out of style ◆ See BECAUSE.

sin·cere [sin·sir′] *adj.* **sin·cer·er, sin·cer·est** **1** Honest; faithful: He is a *sincere* friend. **2** Real; genuine: *sincere* regret. **— sin·cere′ly** *adv.*

sin·cer·i·ty [sin·ser′ə·tē] *n.* The quality or condition of being sincere, honest, or genuine.

sine [sīn] *n.* In a right triangle, the length of the side opposite an acute angle divided by the length of the hypotenuse. This quotient changes with the size of the angle.

Sine x = b/c

si·ne·cure [sī′nə·kyŏŏr *or* sin′ə·kyŏŏr] *n.* An office or position which requires little or no work, especially one which pays well.

sin·ew [sin′yŏŏ] *n.* **1** A band of tough, fibrous tissue attaching a muscle to some other bodily part, as a bone; tendon. **2** Strength or power. **3** Something that supplies strength or power.

sin·ew·y [sin′yŏŏ·ē] *adj.* **1** Having sinews. **2** Strong, firm, or tough: a *sinewy* man. **3** Forceful; vigorous: a story written in a *sinewy* style.

sin·ful [sin′fəl] *adj.* Wicked; immoral; evil. **— sin′ful·ly** *adv.* **— sin′ful·ness** *n.*

sing [sing] *v.* **sang** or **sung, sung, sing·ing,** *n.* **1** *v.* To produce musical sounds with one's voice. **2** *v.* To utter the music of with the voice: to *sing* a song. **3** *n. informal* A gathering at which people sing songs together. **4** *v.* To bring into some condition by singing: to *sing* a child to sleep. **5** *v.* To tell or tell of in words of song or poetry: The minstrel *sang* of victory. **6** *v.* To speak of enthusiastically: They all *sang* her praises. **7** *v.* To produce sounds like music, as a bird. **8** *v.* To make a sound like singing, as a teakettle or the wind. **9** *v.* To hum or buzz, as a bullet in flight. **— sing out** *informal* To call out loudly; shout.

sing. Abbreviation of SINGULAR.

Sin·ga·pore [sing′(g)ə·pôr] *n.* **1** An island off the southern tip of the Malay Peninsula. It is an independent state. **2** Its capital, a seaport.

singe [sinj] *v.* **singed, singe·ing,** *n.* **1** *v.* To burn slightly; scorch. **2** *n.* A slight burn; scorch. **3** *v.* To remove hair or fuzz from by passing through a flame: to pluck and then *singe* a chicken. **4** *v.* To burn the ends of, as hair.

sing·er [sing′ər] *n.* **1** A person who sings, especially as a profession. **2** A bird that sings.

sin·gle [sing′gəl] *adj., n., v.* **sin·gled, sin·gling** **1** *adj.* One alone; separate; individual: Not a *single* star was visible. **2** *n.* A single person or thing. **3** *v.* To choose or select (one) from others: to *single* a student out. **4** *adj.* Unmarried. **5** *adj.* Designed for use by one person or family: a *single* bed; a *single* room; a *single* house. **6** *adj.* Between two individuals opposing each other: *single* combat. **7** *n.* (*pl.*) In tennis, etc., a game having one player on each side. **8** *adj.* Having only one row of petals: said about flowers. **9** *n.* In baseball, a hit that enables the batter to reach first base safely. **10** *v.* To hit a single. **11** *adj.* Steadfast and not divided; sincere. **— sin′gle·ness** *n.*

Soldiers in single file

single file An arrangement of persons or things one behind another in a single line.

sin·gle-hand·ed [sing′gəl·han′did] *adj.* Without assistance or help; by one's own efforts.

sin·gle-mind·ed [sing′gəl·mīn′did] *adj.* **1** Having only one purpose or aim in mind. **2** Sincere.

sin·gle·tree [sing′gəl·trē′] *n.* A whiffletree.

sin·gly [sing′glē] *adv.* **1** One by one; one at a time. **2** Separately; alone. **3** Without aid.

sing·song [sing′sông′] **1** *adj.* Regular and monotonous in tone and beat, as rhythm or a voice reciting verse. **2** *n.* A way of speaking with a regular, boring rhythm and no expression.

sin·gu·lar [sing′gyə·lər] **1** *adj.* Being or indicating only one: a *singular* noun. **2** *n.* The form that a word takes when it indicates only one: "Mouse" is the *singular* of "mice." **3** *adj.* Being the only one of its type; unique. **4** *adj.* Extraordinary; uncommon: a *singular* determination to win. **5** *adj.* Odd or peculiar: What *singular* behavior! — **sin′gu·lar·ly** *adv.*

sin·gu·lar·i·ty [sing′gyə·lar′ə·tē] *n., pl.* **sin·gu·lar·i·ties 1** Singular nature, quality, or character. **2** An uncommon or remarkable habit, feature, etc.; peculiarity: The stranger's *singularities* of dress made him seem eccentric.

sin·is·ter [sin′is·tər] *adj.* **1** Threatening evil, trouble, or bad luck; ominous: There was something *sinister* about the old house. **2** Wrong, wicked, or evil: a *sinister* conspiracy. ◆ *Sinister* comes from a Latin word meaning *on the left*, which came to mean *unlucky* or *bad* because omens seen on the left were thought to be unfavorable.

sink [singk] *v.* **sank** or **sunk, sunk, sink·ing,** *n.* **1** *v.* To go or cause to go down beneath the surface: to *sink* in quicksand; The storm *sank* our boat. **2** *v.* To make by digging or excavating: to *sink* a mine shaft. **3** *v.* To penetrate; seep: The oil *sank* into the wood. **4** *v.* To go down or seem to go down gradually: The sun *sank.* **5** *v.* To drop, as to a lower level: He *sank* his head into his hands; She *sank* to her knees. **6** *v.* To lessen in force, volume, amount, or value: His voice *sank* to a whisper; Stocks are *sinking.* **7** *v.* To pass gradually into a certain condition: to *sink* into a coma. **8** *v.* To weaken and approach death: He is *sinking* fast. **9** *v.* To become hollow; cave in, as the cheeks. **10** *n.* A hollow where water collects. **11** *n.* A porcelain or metal basin with a drainpipe and faucets. **12** *n.* A place where filth collects or where wicked people gather: a *sink* of iniquity. **13** *n.* A cesspool or sewer. **14** *v.* To invest (money) and lose (it) as a result: I *sank* a million in that deal. **15** *v.* To ruin: If you tell, I'll be *sunk.* — **sink in** To be absorbed, fully understood, or wholly accepted by the mind: His words *sank in.*

sink·er [singk′ər] *n.* **1** A person or thing that sinks. **2** A weight for sinking a fishing line. **3** In baseball, a pitch that curves sharply downward as it approaches home plate.

sin·less [sin′lis] *adj.* Free from sin; innocent.

sin·ner [sin′ər] *n.* A person who has sinned.

sin·u·ous [sin′yōō·əs] *adj.* **1** Full of bends, curves, or turns; winding, as a snake: a *sinuous*

path. **2** Not straightforward; morally crooked or devious. — **sin·u·os·i·ty** [sin′yōō·os′ə·tē] *n.* — **sin′u·ous·ly** *adv.*

si·nus [sī′nəs] *n.* An opening or cavity, especially any of the air-filled cavities in the bones of the skull that open into the nostrils.

-sion A suffix meaning: **1** The act of or the condition of being, as in *permission*, the act of permitting or the condition of being permitted. **2** The result of, as in *explosion*, the result of exploding.

Sioux [sōō] *n., pl.* **Sioux** A member of a group of Indian tribes of the north central U.S.

sip [sip] *v.* **sipped, sip·ping,** *n.* **1** *v.* To drink in small swallows, a little bit at a time: to *sip* hot chocolate. **2** *n.* A very small drink; a taste or swallow. **3** *n.* The act of sipping.

si·phon [sī′fən] **1** *n.* A bent tube used for drawing liquid up and over the edge of a container and carrying it to a lower level by means of air pressure and gravity. **2** *v.* To draw off by or pass through a siphon: to *siphon* off gasoline. **3** *n.* A bottle to hold carbonated water. When a valve is opened, pressure of gas in the bottle forces a stream of the liquid out through a tube.

Siphon

sir [sûr] *n.* **1** A respectful term of address for a man: May I help you, *sir?* **2** (*written* **Sir**) A title used before the given name or the full name of a knight or baronet: *Sir* Winston Churchill was knighted by Elizabeth II.

sire [sīr] *n., v.* **sired, sir·ing 1** *n.* The male parent of a mammal, as a horse. **2** *v.* To father: a filly *sired* by a race horse. **3** *n.* A father or male ancestor: sometimes used in combination, as in *grandsire.* **4** *n.* A respectful form of address used when speaking to a king.

si·ren [sī′rən] *n.* **1** In Greek myths, one of the sea nymphs whose sweet singing lured sailors to destruction on the rocks. **2** A fascinating, dangerous woman. **3** A device that gives out a loud, piercing wail or whistle, used as a warning signal: the *siren* on a police car.

Sir·i·us [sir′ē·əs] *n.* The brightest star in the heavens. It is also called the Dog Star.

sir·loin [sûr′loin] *n.* A cut of beef from the loin, especially the upper portion.

si·roc·co [si·rok′ō] *n., pl.* **si·roc·cos 1** A hot, dry, dusty wind blowing from the African coast to Italy, Sicily, and Spain. **2** Any warm, sultry wind.

sir·rah [sir′ə] *n.* A term of address to a man or boy, once used to show contempt or annoyance.

sir·up [sir′əp] *n.* Another spelling of SYRUP.

sis [sis] *n. informal* Sister.

si·sal [sī′səl] *n.* **1** A strong fiber used to make rope, obtained from the leaves of a West Indian plant. **2** The plant yielding this fiber.

sis·sy [sis′ē] *n., pl.* **sis·sies** *informal* **1** A man or boy who acts too much like a girl to seem manly. **2** A coward or weakling.

sis·ter [sis′tər] *n.* **1** A girl or woman having the same parents as another person of either sex. **2** A girl or woman associated with another or others, as through membership in a group or shared beliefs: sorority *sisters.* **3** A nun.

sis·ter·hood [sis′tər·hŏŏd] *n.* **1** The condition of being sisters. **2** A sisterly relationship. **3** A group of women joined together for some purpose, as work or fellowship.

sis·ter-in-law [sis′tər·in·lô′] *n., pl.* **sis·ters-in-law 1** A sister of one's husband or wife. **2** The wife of one's brother or of one's wife's or husband's brother.

sis·ter·ly [sis′tər·lē] *adj.* **1** Suitable for or like a sister. **2** Affectionate, kindly, or devoted: She has a *sisterly* feeling for me.

sit [sit] *v.* **sat, sit·ting 1** To rest with legs bent and the weight on the lower end of the body: to *sit* on a sofa; A cat *sat* on the sill. **2** To cause to sit; seat: She *sat* the misbehaving boy in the corner. **3** To occupy a seat: to *sit* in front. **4** To have or keep a seat upon: to *sit* a horse well. **5** To have a seat as a member of an assembly: to *sit* in Congress. **6** To hold a meeting or session, as a court. **7** To be or stay in a settled or inactive position: The car *sat* in the driveway overnight. **8** To baby-sit. **9** To pose, as for a portrait. **10** To perch or roost, as a bird. **11** To cover eggs in order to hatch them, as a hen. **12** To lie or press: My sorrows *sit* heavily on me. **13** To be situated or located: The wind *sits* in the east. **14** To fit or suit: That hat *sits* well. **— sit down** To be seated. **— sit in** *U.S.* To join or take part, as in a game or discussion. **— sit on** or **sit upon 1** To belong to (a jury, commission, etc.) as a member. **2** To hold discussions about and look into carefully, as a case. **3** *informal* To suppress or squelch. **— sit out 1** To sit or stay until the end of: to *sit out* a boring lecture. **2** To sit aside during: to *sit out* a dance. **— sit up 1** To draw oneself up to or hold oneself in an upright sitting position. **2** To postpone going to bed. **— sit′ter** *n.* ◆ *Sit* and *set* both mean *to rest. Set* always takes an object, and its most common meaning is *to place*: She *set the dishes* down. *Sit* usually does not take an object: He *sat* down; *Sit* still. However, when *sit* means *to cause to sit*, it does take an object: The teacher *sat him* next to me.

site [sīt] *n.* **1** The place where something is or was situated: Jamestown is the *site* of the first English settlement here. **2** A plot of ground set apart for some special use: a *site* for a housing development. ◆ *Site* is a noun meaning *a place*: the *site* of the Hall of Fame. *Cite* is a verb meaning *to quote or mention*: He *cited* his father as an example of a self-made man. *Sight*, both a noun and verb, refers to one's ability to see or to something seen: the sense of *sight*; He *sighted* a ship in the distance; What a *sight*!

sit-in [sit′in′] *n.* A demonstration in which people sit down in a public place and refuse to move as a protest against a policy or condition they think unjust.

sit·ting [sit′ing] *n.* **1** The act or position of a person who sits. **2** A period during which one remains seated: He did the homework in one *sitting.* **3** A session or term, as of a court.

sitting room A living room or parlor.

sit·u·ate [sich′ŏŏ·āt] *v.* **sit·u·at·ed, sit·u·at·ing 1** To locate: The cottage was *situated* on the hill. **2** To place or settle in certain circumstances. **3** *adj. use:* He is not really wealthy but is well *situated* financially.

sit·u·a·tion [sich′ŏŏ·ā′shən] *n.* **1** A state of affairs brought about by a combination of circumstances: an unpleasant *situation.* **2** Position or location: the convenient *situation* of the hospital. **3** A job: a *situation* as a maid.

six or **6** [siks] *n., adj.* One more than five. **— at sixes and sevens** Confused or disagreeing.

six·pence [siks′pəns] *n.* A British coin worth half a shilling, going out of circulation.

six-shoot·er [siks′shŏŏ′tər] *n. informal* A revolver that may be fired six times before it has to be loaded again.

six·teen or **16** [siks′tēn′] *n., adj.* One more than fifteen.

six·teenth or **16th** [siks′tēnth′] **1** *adj.* Next after the fifteenth. **2** *n.* The sixteenth one. **3** *adj.* Being one of sixteen equal parts. **4** *n.* A sixteenth part.

sixth or **6th** [siksth] **1** *adj.* Next after the fifth. **2** *n.* The sixth one. **3** *adj.* Being one of six equal parts. **4** *n.* A sixth part.

six·ti·eth or **60th** [siks′tē·ith] **1** *adj.* Tenth in order after the fiftieth. **2** *n.* The sixtieth one. **3** *adj.* Being one of sixty equal parts. **4** *n.* A sixtieth part.

six·ty or **60** [siks′tē] *n., pl.* **six·ties** or **60's,** *adj.* **1** *n., adj.* Ten more than fifty. **2** *n. (pl.)* The years between the age of 60 and the age of 70: a man in his *sixties.*

siz·a·ble [sī′zə·bəl] *adj.* Fairly large: a *sizable* estate.

size¹ [sīz] *n., v.* **sized, siz·ing 1** *n.* The amount of space which something occupies; physical proportions: the *size* and weight of a package. **2** *n.* Degree of largeness: Our club increased in *size* when new members joined. **3** *n.* One of a series of measures indicating the degree of largeness of certain goods or products: a *size* 6 shoe; his shirt *size.* **4** *v.* To arrange or classify according to size: to *size* fruit. **5** *n.* Bigness: We caught no fish of any *size.* **— of a size** Of the same size. **— size up** *informal* To form an estimate, judgment, or opinion of.

size² [sīz] *n., v.* **sized, siz·ing 1** *n.* A thin, sticky, jellylike substance used to glaze paper, finish fabrics, etc. **2** *v.* To treat with size.

---

add, āce, câre, pälm;   end, ēqual;   it, īce;   odd, ōpen, ôrder;   tŏŏk, pŏŏl;   up, bûrn;
ə = a in *above*, e in *sicken*, i in *possible*, o in *melon*, u in *circus*;   yŏŏ = u in *fuse*;   oil;   pout;
check;   ring;   thin;   this;   zh in *vision*.   For ¶ reference, see page 64 · HOW TO

size·a·ble [sī′zə·bəl] *adj.* Another spelling of SIZABLE.

siz·zle [siz′(ə)l] *v.* **siz·zled, siz·zling,** *n.* **1** *v.* To give out a hissing sound when very hot, as frying bacon. **2** *n.* A hissing sound.

skate[1] [skāt] *n., v.* **skat·ed, skat·ing 1** *n.* A metal blade, or runner, with a frame over it that is or may be attached to the sole of a boot or shoe, on which a person can glide over ice. It is often called an **ice skate. 2** *n.* The blade alone: to sharpen *skates.* **3** *n.* A roller skate. **4** *v.* To glide or move on or as if on skates. — **skat′er** *n.*

skate[2] [skāt] *n., pl.* **skate** or **skates** A kind of fish with a flat body and broad fins.

ske·dad·dle [ski·dad′(ə)l] *v.* **ske·dad·dled, ske·dad·dling** *informal* To run away or flee in a hurry; scram.

skein [skān] *n.* A quantity of yarn, thread, etc., wound into a long, loose coil.

skel·e·tal [skel′ə·təl] *adj.* Of, having to do with, forming, or resembling a skeleton.

skel·e·ton [skel′ə·tən] *n.* **1** The supporting bony framework of the body of a vertebrate animal, as man. **2** An inner structure like a skeleton, as an outline of a written work or the framework of a house. — **skeleton in the closet** Some shameful fact that is kept hidden.

skeleton key A key filed to a slender shape, used to open a number of different locks.

skep·tic [skep′tik] *n.* **1** A person who doubts or disbelieves things that many people accept as fact or truth. **2** A person who questions the fundamental doctrines of a religion.

skep·ti·cal [skep′ti·kəl] *adj.* **1** Not believing readily; inclined to question or doubt. **2** Showing doubt. — **skep′·ti·cal·ly** *adv.*

skep·ti·cism [skep′tə·siz′əm] *n.* The tendency to question, doubt, disbelieve, or demand proof to support one or more beliefs, theories, or seeming facts that others accept.

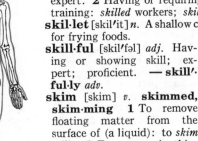

Human skeleton

sketch [skech] **1** *n.* A rough, hasty, or unfinished drawing or description giving a general impression without full details. **2** *n.* A brief outline. **3** *v.* To draw, outline, or describe in a sketch. **4** *v.* To make sketches. **5** *n.* A brief, light story, scene, comic act, etc.

sketch·y [skech′ē] *adj.* **sketch·i·er, sketch·i·est** Like a sketch; lacking detail or made up of a few essentials only; incomplete: a *sketchy* breakfast.

skew [skyoo] **1** *v.* To twist, swerve, or slant. **2** *adj.* Lopsided or distorted. **3** *n.* A slant.

skew·er [skyoo′ər] **1** *n.* A long pin of wood or metal, thrust into meat to hold it while roasting

or broiling. **2** *v.* To run through or fasten with or as if with a skewer.

ski [skē] *n., pl.* **skis,** *v.* **skied** [skēd], **ski·ing 1** *n.* One of a pair of long runners of wood, metal, or plastic that are attached to the soles of boots or shoes for gliding over snow. **2** *v.* To glide or travel on skis. — **ski′er** *n.*

skid [skid] *v.* **skid·ded, skid·ding,** *n.* **1** *v.* To slide sideways, as a car on an icy surface. **2** *n.* The act of skidding. **3** *v.* To slide instead of revolving, as a wheel that does not turn although the vehicle is moving. **4** *n.* A device of metal or wood put under a wheel to keep it from turning. **5** *n.* One of a pair or group of logs, rails, etc., used to support something or as a track on or down which to slide heavy objects. **6** *v.* To put, haul, or slide on skids. — **on the skids** *U.S. slang* Going rapidly down the road to ruin or failure.

skiff [skif] *n.* A light rowboat, sometimes having a small sail and a centerboard.

skill [skil] *n.* **1** Ability developed by training or practice, enabling one to do something with ease or like an expert: She plays the violin with *skill.* **2** A specific art, craft, ability, or technique: Shorthand is an office *skill.*

skilled [skild] *adj.* **1** Having or showing skill; expert. **2** Having or requiring special ability or training: *skilled* workers; *skilled* labor.

skil·let [skil′it] *n.* A shallow cooking utensil used for frying foods.

skill·ful [skil′fəl] *adj.* Having or showing skill; expert; proficient. — **skill′·ful·ly** *adv.*

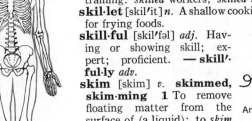

An electric skillet

skim [skim] *v.* **skimmed, skim·ming 1** To remove floating matter from the surface of (a liquid): to *skim* milk. **2** To remove in this way: to *skim* the cream from milk. **3** To move quickly and lightly over or near a surface; glide: skiers *skimming* over the snow. **4** To read hastily in glances, without reading every word. **5** To cover with a thin layer or film: a pond *skimmed* with ice.

skim·mer [skim′ər] *n.* **1** A person or thing that skims, as a shallow ladle for skimming liquids. **2** A sea bird that flies with its beak skimming the surface of the water to catch small fish, etc.

skim milk Milk from which the cream has been removed.

skimp [skimp] *v.* **1** To be very economical or stingy; scrimp: He *skimped* on food to buy books. **2** To put in or supply too little of: Don't *skimp* the sugar. **3** To do carelessly.

skimp·y [skim′pē] *adj.* **skimp·i·er, skimp·i·est** Hardly enough; meager; scanty: a *skimpy* meal.

skin [skin] *n., v.* **skinned, skin·ning 1** *n.* The flexible outer protective tissue that covers the bodies of people and animals. **2** *n.* One's life: to save one's *skin.* **3** *n.* The pelt of a small animal. **4** *n.* A container for liquids made of animal skin. **5** *n.* An outside layer or covering resembling skin, as the rind of a fruit. **6** *v.* To tear or remove the skin of: I *skinned* my knee; to *skin* an onion. **7** *v. slang* To cheat or swindle. **— by the skin of one's teeth** By the narrowest of margins; barely.

skin diving Swimming about under water by a diver wearing a mask attached to a tank of air for breathing. **— skin diver**

Skin diving

skin·flint [skin′flint′] *n.* A stingy person who is hard and mean where money is involved; miser; tightwad.

skin·ny [skin′ē] *adj.* **skin·ni·er, skin·ni·est** Very thin or emaciated; lean.

skip [skip] *v.* **skipped, skip·ping,** *n.* **1** *v.* To move by stepping, hopping, and sliding on each foot in turn. **2** *n.* A light bound, spring, or hop. **3** *v.* To jump lightly over: to *skip* rope. **4** *v.* To bound along, ricochet from, or skim a surface. **5** *v.* To throw so as to cause a bounding, skimming movement: We *skipped* pebbles across the pool. **6** *v.* To pass from one point to another without going through what lies between: *Skip* from the third to the sixth stanza. **7** *v.* To pass over or leave out; omit: He *skipped* the second grade. **8** *n.* The act of passing over; omission. **9** *v. informal* To leave (a place) hurriedly: The crooks *skipped* town.

skip·per [skip′ər] *n.* **1** The master or captain of a ship, especially a small vessel. **2** Any leader.

skir·mish [skûr′mish] **1** *n.* A brief fight between small groups of troops. **2** *n.* Any minor conflict. **3** *v.* To take part in a skirmish.

skirt [skûrt] **1** *n.* The part of a dress, robe, etc., that hangs from the waist downward. **2** *n.* A woman's or girl's separate garment that hangs from the waist. **3** *n.* A thing that hangs or covers like a skirt: the *skirt* of a dressing table. **4** *n.* (*pl.*) The border or edge; outskirts. **5** *v.* To go around, not through; pass along the edge of: The road *skirts* the park. ◆See SHIRT.

skit [skit] *n.* A short sketch, often comic, usually acted out, as for entertainment.

skit·tish [skit′ish] *adj.* **1** Easily frightened; likely to shy, as a horse. **2** Shy or coy. **3** Lively, spirited, or frivolous. **4** Unreliable.

skit·tles [skit′(ə)lz] *n. pl.* A bowling game like ninepins played sometimes with a ball, sometimes with a wooden disk.

skul·dug·ger·y [skul·dug′ər·ē] *n.* Trickery.

skulk [skulk] *v.* To move about, lurk, or hide in a stealthy, sneaky way. **— skulk′er** *n.*

skull [skul] *n.* The bony framework of the head of a vertebrate animal, enclosing the brain.

skull and crossbones A picture of a human skull over two crossed bones, used as a symbol of death, as a warning label on poison, and as an emblem on pirates' flags.

skull·cap [skul′kap′] *n.* A small cap without a brim, fitting snugly over the top of the head.

skunk [skungk] *n.* **1** A small, furry mammal of North America, usually black with white stripes on its back. It shoots out a liquid with a terrible smell when frightened or angry. **2** *informal* A hateful or contemptible person. ◆ *Skunk* comes from an Algonquian Indian word.

Skunk,
11–15 in. long

sky [skī] *n., pl.* **skies 1** The region of the upper air that seems to arch over the earth. **2** (*often pl.*) The condition or appearance of the sky: cloudy *skies*. **3** Heaven. **— out of a clear blue sky** Without any warning. ◆ *Sky* comes from an old Scandinavian word meaning *cloud*.

sky blue A blue like the color of the sky.

sky·lark [skī′lärk′] **1** *n.* A small European songbird that sings as it rises in flight. **2** *v.* To play or frolic in a lighthearted way.

sky·light [skī′līt′] *n.* A window in a roof or ceiling, letting in daylight from above.

sky·line [skī′līn′] *n.* **1** An outline or silhouette, as of city buildings, seen against the sky. **2** The line at which the earth or sea seems to meet the sky; horizon.

sky·rock·et [skī′rok′it] **1** *n.* A rocket, as in a fireworks display, that explodes high in the air with a burst of brilliant sparks. **2** *v.* To rise rapidly or suddenly: Costs *skyrocketed*.

sky·scrap·er [skī′skrā′pər] *n.* A very high building.

sky·ward [skī′wərd] *adj., adv.* Toward the sky.

sky·wards [skī′wərdz] *adv.* Toward the sky.

slab [slab] *n.* **1** A flat, broad, thick piece, as of stone, cheese, etc.: a *slab* of marble. **2** A rough outside piece cut off a log to square it before sawing it into lumber.

slack [slak] **1** *adj.* Not tight, tense, or firm; loose or limp: a *slack* rope; a *slack* grip. **2** *n.* A part of a rope, sail, etc., that is slack or loose: Take up the *slack*. **3** *v.* To slacken: *Slack* the rope. **4** *adj.* Careless or negligent: *slack* service. **5** *adj.* Lacking activity; not busy: a *slack* season. **6** *n.* An inactive period, as in a business. **7** *n.* A halt in the strong flow of the tide or of a current of water. **8** *adj.* Slow, listless, or sluggish: a *slack* pace. **9** *adv.* In a slack manner. **— slack off 1** To slow down or reduce effort. **2** To lessen or loosen. **— slack up** To slow down. **— slack′·ly** *adv.* **— slack′ness** *n.*

slack·en [slak′ən] *v.* **1** To make or become less tight or firm; loosen: to *slacken* a sail. **2** To make or become slower, less active, or less forceful: to *slacken* one's efforts.

slack·er [slak′ər] *n.* A person who shirks his duties or avoids military service in wartime.

slacks [slaks] *n. pl.* Long trousers, especially those worn by men or women for casual or sports wear.

slag [slag] *n.* **1** The cinderlike waste left after metals are separated from their ores by melting. **2** Loose, clinkerlike pieces of lava.

slain [slān] Past participle of SLAY.

slake [slāk] *v.* **slaked, slak·ing 1** To satisfy, quench, or reduce in strength: to *slake* one's thirst by drinking deeply. **2** To cause (lime) to undergo a chemical change by mixing it with water or exposing it to moist air. **3** *adj. use:* *Slaked* lime is mixed with sand to make plaster.

sla·lom [slä′ləm] *n.* In skiing, a race or a descent down a zigzag course laid out between posts and marked with flags.

slam[1] [slam] *v.* **slammed, slam·ming,** *n.* **1** *v.* To close with force and a loud noise; shut loudly: to *slam* a door. **2** *v.* To put, throw, hit, etc., with great force; bang: to *slam* down the phone. **3** *n.* The act or noise of slamming.

Slalom

slam[2] [slam] *n.* In bridge, the bid for and winning of all 13 tricks in a deal (**grand slam**) or of 12 tricks (**little slam** or **small slam**).

slan·der [slan′dər] **1** *n.* A false, spoken statement or report that harms another's reputation or prevents him from carrying on his work. **2** *n.* The act of making such a statement publicly. **3** *v.* To make or spread false and damaging statements about; defame. **— slan′der·er** *n.* **— slan′der·ous** *adj.*

slang [slang] *n.* **1** Words and phrases popular in common speech but not accepted as standard English or used in formal writing. **2** The special vocabulary of a certain group: army *slang.*

slang·y [slang′ē] *adj.* **slang·i·er, slang·i·est** Of, containing, or using a lot of slang.

slant [slant] **1** *v.* To slope, cause to slope, or move at an angle to the horizontal or vertical; incline: Her handwriting *slants* across the page; *Slant* the ladder. **2** *adj.* Sloping; oblique: *slant* eyes. **3** *n.* A slanting direction, surface, or line; slope: the *slant* of the river bank. **4** *n.* A point of view; attitude.

slant·ways [slant′wāz′] *adv.* Slantwise.

slant·wise [slant′wīz′] *adv., adj.* At a slant.

slap [slap] *n., v.* **slapped, slap·ping 1** *n.* A blow delivered with the open hand or with something flat. **2** *v.* To hit or strike with or as if with a slap. **3** *n.* The sound made by or as if by slapping. **4** *v.* To put or throw violently or carelessly: He *slapped* the money down.

slap·stick [slap′stik′] *n.* Comedy full of horseplay in which the actors knock each other around to make people laugh.

slash [slash] **1** *v.* To cut with a long, sharp sweeping stroke or strokes. **2** *v.* To strike with sweeping blows; whip or lash. **3** *n.* A sweeping cut or stroke. **4** *n.* A slit or gash. **5** *v.* To cut slits in, as a garment, so that ornamental material or lining will show. **6** *v.* To reduce sharply: to *slash* prices. **7** *v.* To criticize severely. **8** *n.* The act of slashing.

slat [slat] *n., v.* **slat·ted, slat·ting 1** *n.* A thin, narrow strip of wood or metal. **2** *v.* To provide or make with slats: *Slat* this box to make a cage.

slate [slāt] *n., v.* **slat·ed, slat·ing 1** *n.* A hard, fine-grained rock that splits easily into thin layers. **2** *n.* A thin piece of this rock, as one used as a roofing tile or one to be written on with chalk or a special pencil. **3** *v.* To cover (a roof, etc.) with slate. **4** *n.* The dull, bluish gray color of slate. **5** *n.* A list arranged in advance, as a list of political candidates running for office. **6** *v.* To mark or select in advance: He was *slated* for a promotion. **— a clean slate** A record showing no bad behavior or poor performance in the past.

slat·tern [slat′ərn] *n.* A dirty, sloppy, or untidy woman. **— slat′tern·ly** *adj., adv.*

slaugh·ter [slô′tər] **1** *n.* The act of killing animals for market; butchering. **2** *v.* To butcher: to *slaughter* cattle. **3** *n.* The savage killing of human beings, especially killing on a large scale, as in war. **4** *v.* To kill brutally or savagely, especially in large numbers.

slaugh·ter·house [slô′tər·hous′] *n.* A place where animals are killed and cut up for food.

Slav [släv] *n.* A member of one of the peoples in eastern Europe that speak Slavic languages, including the Russians, Poles, Czechs, Slovaks, Bulgarians, Serbians, etc.

slave [slāv] *n., v.* **slaved, slav·ing 1** *n.* A person owned by another like a piece of property. **2** *v.* To work as hard as a slave may be forced to; drudge; toil. **3** *n.* A person who works as hard as a slave does. **4** *n.* A person mastered or controlled by some habit, vice, influence, or desire: a *slave* to tobacco.

slave·hold·er [slāv′hōl′dər] *n.* An owner of slaves. **— slave′hold′ing** *adj., n.*

slav·er[1] [slav′ər] **1** *v.* To drool. **2** *n.* Saliva dribbling from the mouth.

slav·er[2] [slā′vər] *n.* **1** A ship once used to transport people who were to be sold as slaves. **2** A person whose business is dealing in slaves.

slav·er·y [slā′vər·ē] *n.* **1** The practice of holding human beings as slaves. **2** The condition of being a slave: freed from *slavery.* **3** Hard labor like that of slaves; drudgery.

Slav·ic [slä′vik] **1** *n.* A group of eastern European languages including Russian, Polish, Czech, Slovak, Bulgarian, etc. **2** *adj.* Of or having to do with the Slavs or their languages.

slav·ish [slā′vish] *adj.* **1** Having or showing the humble, submissive spirit of a slave: *slavish* devotion. **2** Lacking independence of mind and originality: a *slavish* copy of a work of art. **— slav′ish·ly** *adv.* **— slav′ish·ness** *n.*

slaw [slô] *n.* Coleslaw.

slay [slā] *v.* **slew, slain, slay·ing** To kill, especially by violence. — **slay′er** *n.*

slea·zy [slē′zē] *adj.* **slea·zi·er, slea·zi·est**
1 Flimsy, shoddy, or shabby: a *sleazy* old chair. **2** Cheap or vulgar in quality, appearance, etc.: a *sleazy* novel. — **slea′zi·ness** *n.*

sled [sled] *n., v.* **sled·ded, sled·ding 1** *n.* A vehicle on runners, used for carrying people or loads over snow and ice. **2** *v.* To carry by sled. **3** *n.* A small vehicle on runners, used for coasting on snow. **4** *v.* To ride on a sled.

sledge [slej] *n., v.* **sledged, sledg·ing 1** *n.* A vehicle mounted on low runners for moving loads, especially over snow and ice. **2** *v.* To travel or carry on a sledge.

sledge hammer A large, heavy hammer, usually held and swung with both hands.

sleek [slēk] **1** *adj.* Smooth and glossy, as the coat of a horse that has been groomed. **2** *adj.* Having smooth, soft, shining hair, fur, skin, etc.: *sleek* dogs. **3** *v.* To make sleek, as by smoothing or brushing; slick. **4** *adj.* Having elegance and style in appearance, design, etc.: the *sleek*, long lines of the boat. **5** *adj.* Insincerely smooth in manner; oily. — **sleek′ly** *adv.*

sleep [slēp] *n., v.* **slept, sleep·ing 1** *n.* A natural condition or period when the eyes close and consciousness is wholly or partly lost so that the body and mind may rest. **2** *v.* To rest in sleep or be asleep; slumber. **3** *v.* To be in an inactive condition resembling sleep, as torpor, hibernation, or death. **4** *n.* A condition resembling sleep: the ground hog's winter *sleep*. — **go to sleep 1** To fall asleep. **2** To become numb and then start to tingle because the blood is not circulating properly: My foot has *gone to sleep*. — **sleep off** To get rid of by sleep: to *sleep off* an irritable mood.

sleep·er [slē′pər] *n.* **1** A person or animal that sleeps. **2** A sleeping car. **3** *British* A tie that supports the rails of a railway track. **4** *U.S. informal* Something, as a play, motion picture, book, etc., that is unexpectedly successful.

sleeping bag A large bag with a warm lining, used for sleeping, especially out of doors.

sleeping car A railroad car with seats that open out into berths for passengers to sleep in.

sleeping sickness A disease marked by fever and abnormal sleepiness, especially a disease common in Africa, caused by the bite of a tsetse fly, and ending in prolonged sleep and death.

sleep·less [slēp′lis] *adj.* **1** Unable to sleep; wakeful. **2** Without sleep: a *sleepless* night.

sleep·walk·er [slēp′wô′kər] *n.* A person who walks while asleep. — **sleep′walk′ing** *n.*

sleep·y [slē′pē] *adj.* **sleep·i·er, sleep·i·est**
1 Ready to or about to go to sleep; drowsy. **2** Quiet, dull, and inactive: a *sleepy* country village. — **sleep′i·ly** *adv.* — **sleep′i·ness** *n.*

sleet [slēt] **1** *n.* A mixture of snow or hail and rain. **2** *n.* A thin coating of ice, as on a road. **3** *n.* A shower of partly frozen rain. **4** *v.* To pour or shower sleet. — **sleet′y** *adj.*

sleeve [slēv] *n.* **1** The part of a garment that fits over the arm. **2** A tube that fits over all or part of a shaft or another tube. — **laugh up one's sleeve** To be secretly amused. — **up one's sleeve** Hidden but readily available.

sleeve·less [slēv′lis] *adj.* Having no sleeves.

sleigh [slā] **1** *n.* A vehicle, usually drawn

A micrometer sleeve

by a horse, with runners for use on snow and ice. **2** *v.* To ride or travel in or drive a sleigh.

sleight [slīt] *n.* **1** Skill; dexterity. **2** Cunning; craft.

sleight of hand 1 Such skill in moving the hands that a spectator either fails to see some movements or is confused by them. **2** A trick or tricks done by a modern magician using this skill.

slen·der [slen′dər] *adj.* **1** Not very wide in proportion to the length or height; slim; thin: The greyhound is tall, *slender*, and fast. **2** Not large or strong; slight, weak, etc.: He won the race by a *slender* margin. **3** Small or inadequate: a *slender* income. — **slen′der·ness** *n.*

slept [slept] Past tense and past participle of SLEEP.

sleuth [slooth] *n.* **1** A bloodhound. **2** *U.S. informal* A detective.

slew[1] [sloo] Past tense of SLAY.

slew[2] [sloo] *n.* *U.S. informal* A large number, crowd, or amount; a lot.

slew[3] [sloo] *v., n.* Another spelling of SLUE[1].

slice [slīs] *n., v.* **sliced, slic·ing 1** *n.* A thin, broad piece cut off from a larger piece: a *slice* of meat. **2** *v.* To cut into slices: to *slice* a tomato. **3** *v.* To cut from a whole or larger piece: to *slice* off a piece of bread. **4** *v.* To cut with or as if with a sharp knife: The boat *sliced* through the waves. **5** *v.* To hit (a golf ball, etc.) with a spin that makes it veer to the right if hit by a right-handed player. — **slic′er** *n.*

slick [slik] **1** *adj.* Smooth, glossy, or oily: *slick* hair. **2** *v.* To make smooth, glossy, or oily: He *slicked* down his hair. **3** *adj.* Slippery, as with oil or ice. **4** *n.* A smooth or slippery place, as a smooth place on a surface of water covered by a film of oil. **5** *adj.* Smart, clever, or tricky: That was a very *slick* answer. **6** *adj.* Smooth in manner but shallow or insincere: *slick* writing.

slick·er [slik′ər] *n.* **1** A waterproof overcoat, as of oilskin or plastic. **2** *informal* A clever, sly person.

slide [slīd] *v.* **slid** [slid], **slid** or **slid·den** [slid′(ə)n], **slid·ing** [slī′ding], *n.* **1** *v.* To pass or send over a surface with a smooth, slipping movement: to *slide* down the banisters. **2** *n.* An act of sliding. **3** *n.* A sliding part. **4** *n.* A smooth, slanting surface down which children, goods, etc., may slide. **5** *v.* To slip: The soap *slid* from my hand. **6** *n.* The slipping of a mass of earth, snow, etc., from a higher to a lower level. **7** *v.* To move easily, smoothly, gradually, or so as not to be noticed: He *slid* stealthily out of the room. **8** *v.* To continue without being acted on: Let the matter *slide.* **9** *n.* A small, transparent plate bearing a picture to be projected on a screen. **10** *n.* A small glass plate for holding an object to be examined under a microscope.

Slide

slide fastener Another name for a ZIPPER.

slide projector A device for projecting magnified images from slides onto a wall or screen.

slide rule A device that looks like a ruler with a strip in the center that slides, both marked with scales of logarithms, used for rapid calculation.

sliding door A door set in long grooves at top and bottom. It opens and closes by sliding sidewise on a track.

sli·er [slī′ər] Comparative of SLY.

sli·est [slī′ist] Superlative of SLY.

slight [slīt] **1** *adj.* Small in amount, degree, intensity, or importance; not great, serious, etc.: a *slight* headache. **2** *adj.* Slender or frail: to have a *slight* build. **3** *v.* To neglect as unimportant or show careless, rude, or scornful disregard for; ignore or snub: to *slight* a friend. **4** *n.* An act or omission showing a lack of courtesy or respect toward another; snub. **— slight′ly** *adv.*

sli·ly [slī′lē] *adv.* Another spelling of SLYLY.

slim [slim] *adj.* **slim·mer, slim·mest,** *v.* **slimmed, slim·ming 1** *adj.* Slender or thin, as the human body. **2** *v.* To make or become thin or thinner: He needs to *slim* down. **3** *adj.* Slight, small, or scant: a *slim* possibility; a *slim* attendance. **— slim′ness** *n.* ◆ *Slim* comes from a Dutch word meaning *bad, crooked,* or *shifty.*

slime [slīm] *n.* Any soft, moist, sticky substance that clings and often soils, as muck.

slim·y [slī′mē] *adj.* **slim·i·er, slim·i·est 1** Covered with or like slime. **2** Foul; filthy.

sling [sling] *n., v.* **slung, sling·ing 1** *n.* A strap, as of leather, usually having a string attached to each end, for hurling a stone or other missile. **2** *n.* A slingshot. **3** *v.* To fling or hurl as if from a sling: to *sling* a pebble. **4** *n.* A rope, strap, chain, etc., used to lift, suspend, or move something, as a heavy object. **5** *v.* To place,

hold, or move in a sling. **6** *v.* To hang loosely by means of strap, ropes, etc.: She *slung* the pocketbook over her shoulder. **7** *n.* A loop of cloth worn around the neck to support an injured arm.

sling·shot [sling′shot′] *n.* A weapon or toy for shooting stones, etc., made of an elastic strap attached to the prongs of a forked stick.

slink [slingk] *v.* **slunk, slink·ing** To move or creep in a sneaky, frightened, or guilty way.

Sling

slip[1] [slip] *v.* **slipped, slip·ping,** *n.* **1** *v.* To shift or fall accidentally out of place or out of the grasp: Don't let the scissors *slip*; The soap *slipped* out of her hand. **2** *v.* To slide accidentally and unexpectedly: I *slipped* and fell. **3** *n.* An act of slipping. **4** *v.* To worsen, fail, err, weaken, or drop: His grades are *slipping*. **5** *v.* To move or put easily and smoothly; slide: to *slip* into a robe; *Slip* the ring on her finger. **6** *n.* A woman's undergarment, usually the length of a dress. **7** *n.* A pillowcase. **8** *n. U.S.* A space for a ship between two wharves. **9** *v.* To come, go, or pass stealthily or unnoticed: He *slipped* into the house; She *slipped* me a note. **10** *v.* To escape from; get away from: It *slipped* my mind. **11** *v.* To escape: That comment simply *slipped* out. **12** *n.* A lapse or error in speech, writing, or conduct: a *slip* of the tongue. **— give one the slip** To get away from someone cleverly. **— let slip** To say without intending to. **— slip up** *informal* To make a mistake.

slip[2] [slip] *n., v.* **slipped, slip·ping 1** *n.* A small piece of paper, as for a note: a deposit *slip.* **2** *n.* A twig or shoot cut from a plant to be separately planted. **3** *v.* To cut a twig or shoot from: to *slip* a plant. **4** *n.* A slender young person: a *slip* of a girl.

slip·cov·er [slip′kuv′ər] *n.* A fitted cloth cover, as for a chair, that is easily removed.

slip·knot [slip′not′] *n.* A knot that slides along a rope and loosens or tightens a loop.

slip·per [slip′ər] *n.* A low, light shoe that is easily slipped on or off the foot.

slip·per·y [slip′ər·ē] *adj.* **slip·per·i·er, slip·per·i·est 1** Hard to hold or stand on because of a slick, greasy, or slimy surface. **2** Not reliable or trustworthy; tricky. **— slip′per·i·ness** *n.*

slip·shod [slip′shod′] *adj.* **1** Careless or slovenly, as work. **2** Shabby, as in appearance.

slit [slit] *n., v.* **slit, slit·ting 1** *n.* A cut that is relatively long and straight. **2** *n.* A long, narrow opening. **3** *v.* To make a long cut in; slash. **4** *v.* To cut lengthwise into strips.

Slipknot

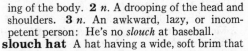
slith·er [slith′ər] *v.* **1** To slide with an unsteady motion down or along a surface. **2** To glide like a snake.

sliv·er [sliv′ər] **1** *n.* A slender piece cut, split, or broken off lengthwise; splinter. **2** *v.* To cut, split, or break into slivers.

slob·ber [slob′ər] **1** *v.* To let liquid flow from the mouth; drool. **2** *n.* Liquid that is drooled. **3** *v.* To be gushy in showing one's feelings.

sloe [slō] *n.* **1** A small, sharp-tasting, plumlike fruit. **2** The shrub on which it grows.

slo·gan [slō′gən] *n.* **1** An often-repeated phrase or motto used in advertising, campaigning, etc., to draw attention. **2** A battle cry.

sloop [slōōp] *n.* A sailing vessel with one mast, a mainsail, and at least one jib.

slop [slop] *v.* **slopped, slop·ping,** *n.* **1** *v.* To splash or spill. **2** *n.* A puddle of splashed or spilled liquid. **3** *n.* Watery mud; slush. **4** *n.* (*often pl.*) Unappetizing, watery food. **5** *n.* (*pl.*) Waste food or swill fed to pigs, etc. **6** *n.* (*often pl.*) Liquid waste to be thrown out. **— slop over** To overflow and splash.

Sloop

slope [slōp] *v.* **sloped, slop·ing,** *n.* **1** *v.* To lie at an angle to the horizontal; slant: The ground *slopes* steeply here. **2** *n.* A piece of ground that slopes, as a snowy hillside down which people ski. **3** *n.* Any slanting surface or line. **4** *n.* The change in elevation of a line or plane per unit of horizontal distance. A hill that rises 10 feet in a horizontal distance of 100 feet has a slope of 10% or 1/10.

slop·py [slop′ē] *adj.* **slop·pi·er, slop·pi·est** **1** Wet and slushy enough to splash: a *sloppy* playing field. **2** *informal* Messy, careless, or untidy. **— slop′pi·ly** *adv.* **— slop′pi·ness** *n.*

slosh [slosh] *v.* To move, wade, or plod with splashes through water, mud, slush, etc.

slot [slot] *n., v.* **slot·ted, slot·ting** **1** *n.* A narrow opening or groove; slit: Put a dime in the *slot.* **2** *v.* To cut a slot in; groove.

sloth [slôth, slôth, *or* sloth] *n.* **1** Laziness. **2** A slow-moving mammal of South America that hangs upside down from tree branches by its claws and sleeps or dozes most of the day.

sloth·ful [slôth′fəl, slôth′fəl *or* sloth′fəl] *adj.* Lazy, sluggish, or indolent.

Sloth, 2 ft. long

slouch [slouch] **1** *v.* To stand, walk, or sit with a drooping of the head and shoulders and a slump-ing of the body. **2** *n.* A drooping of the head and shoulders. **3** *n.* An awkward, lazy, or incompetent person: He's no *slouch* at baseball.

slouch hat A hat having a wide, soft brim that bends easily downward.

slough[1] [slou *or* slōō] *n.* **1** A place of deep mud, mire, or stagnant water, as a bog or swamp. **2** A swampy, stagnant backwater or bayou.

slough[2] [sluf] **1** *n.* The outer skin of a snake, that has been or is about to be shed. **2** *v.* To cast off; shed: The serpent *sloughed* its skin; to *slough* off a bad habit. **3** *v.* To be cast off or shed: dead tissue that *sloughs.* **4** *n.* Something cast off like dead skin. **5** *v.* In certain card games, to discard (an unwanted card).

Slo·vak [slō′vak] **1** *n.* A member of a Slavic people of eastern Czechoslovakia. **2** *n.* The Slavic language of the Slovaks. **3** *adj.* Of or having to do with the Slovaks or their language. **— Slo·va·ki·an** [slō·vä′kē·ən *or* slō·vak′ē·ən] *adj., n.*

Slo·va·ki·a [slō·vä′kē·ə *or* slō·vak′ē·ə] *n.* A region of eastern Czechoslovakia.

slov·en·ly [sluv′ən·lē] *adj.* **slov·en·li·er, slov·en·li·est** **1** Habitually untidy, messy, or dirty, as in personal appearance. **2** Lazily careless, as in work. **— slov′en·li·ness** *n.*

slow [slō] **1** *adj.* Having a low rate of speed; not fast: a *slow* waltz. **2** *v.* To make, go, or become slow or slower: The bus *slowed* down. **3** *adj.* Taking a lot of time or more time than usual: a *slow* trip. **4** *adv.* In a slow or cautious manner or at a slow speed: Go *slow.* **5** *adj.* Behind the true time: The clock is *slow.* **6** *adj.* Hard to move fast on: a *slow* track. **7** *adj.* Not hastily moved: *slow* to anger. **8** *adj.* Not quick to learn: *slow* students. **9** *adj.* Lacking liveliness; dull or sluggish: a *slow* party. **10** *adj.* Inactive: Business is *slow.* **— slow′ly** *adv.* **— slow′ness** *n.*

slow motion A motion-picture technique by means of which filmed action is shown on the screen at a speed much slower than its true speed.

slow·poke [slō′pōk′] *n.* A person who works or moves at a very slow pace.

sludge [sluj] *n.* **1** Slimy mud or icy slush. **2** Any muddy, slimy, or oily refuse or sediment.

slue[1] [slōō] *v.* **slued, slu·ing,** *n.* **1** *v.* To turn, twist, or swing to the side. **2** *n.* The act of sluing, or position after sluing.

slue[2] [slōō] *n.* A swamp, bog, etc.; slough.

slue[3] [slōō] *n.* Another spelling of SLEW[2].

slug[1] [slug] *n.* **1** A bullet or shot, usually round. **2** Any small piece or disk of metal, as one used as a counterfeit coin in machines.

slug[2] [slug] *n.* **1** A snaillike animal without a visible shell, often feeding on garden plants. **2** A smooth, creeping larva or caterpillar.

slug[3] [slug] *v.* **slugged, slug·ging,** *n. informal* **1** *v.* To hit hard, as with a baseball bat or fist. **2** *n.* A heavy blow. **— slug′ger** *n.*

slug·gard [slug′ərd] *n.* A lazy, idle person.

---

add, āce, câre, pälm;   end, ēqual;   it, īce;   odd, ōpen, ôrder;   tŏŏk, pōōl;   up, bûrn;
ə = a in *above*, e in *sicken*, i in *possible*, o in *melon*, u in *circus*;   yōō = u in *fuse*;   oil;   pout;
ch·eck;   ring;   thin;   this;   zh in *vision*.   For ¶ reference, see page 64 · HOW TO

slug·gish [slug′ish] *adj.* **1** Not active or energetic; lazy or dull: The heat made us *sluggish*. **2** Moving very slowly: a *sluggish* brook. — **slug′gish·ly** *adv.* — **slug′gish·ness** *n.*

sluice [slōōs] *n., v.* **sluiced, sluic·ing 1** *n.* An artificial channel for conducting water, equipped with a valve or gate to regulate the flow. **2** The gate that regulates the flow of water; sluice gate. **3** *n.* The water controlled by a sluice gate. **4** *v.* To draw out by or flow out from a sluice. **5** *n.* A trough through which water is run to separate gold, as from sand, or to float logs, etc. **6** *v.* To wash (gold) out of sand, gravel, or dirt with water in a sluice.

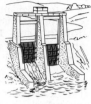

An opened and a closed sluice

sluice gate A gate, as in a dam, to control the flow of water through a sluice.

slum [slum] *n., v.* **slummed, slum·ming 1** *n.* (*often pl.*) A shabby, dirty, run-down section of a city where the poor live crowded together. **2** *v.* To visit slums, as out of curiosity.

slum·ber [slum′bər] **1** *v.* To sleep, especially lightly or quietly. **2** *n.* Sleep. **3** *v.* To be inactive: Rascals held power while reformers *slumbered*. **4** *n.* A condition of inaction.

slum·ber·ous [slum′bər·əs] *adj.* **1** Sleepy; drowsy. **2** Causing or inviting sleep.

slum·brous [slum′brəs] *adj.* Slumberous.

slump [slump] **1** *v.* To stand, walk, or sit with a drooping posture. **2** *v.* To fall suddenly or collapse: He *slumped* to the ground wounded. **3** *n.* A fall or collapse. **4** *n.* A decline or period of decline, as in prices or business.

slung [slung] Past tense and past participle of SLING.

slunk [slungk] Past tense and past participle of SLINK.

slur [slûr] *v.* **slurred, slur·ring,** *n.* **1** *v.* To pronounce in an indistinct way, running together or passing over speech sounds: to *slur* "you all" and say "y'all." **2** *v.* To sing or play (two or more successive musical tones) so that there is no break between them. **3** *n.* A curved line (⌣ or ⌢) used in music to connect notes that are to be slurred. **4** *n.* A slurred pronunciation, sound, or set of notes. **5** *v.* To pass over lightly or hastily: to *slur* over a problem. **6** *v.* To speak of in an insulting way. **7** *n.* An insulting remark or insinuation.

slush [slush] *n.* **1** Soft, sloppy material, as melting snow or soft mud. **2** Foolishly sentimental talk or writing. **3** Grease. — **slush′y** *adj.*

slut [slut] *n.* **1** A dirty, sloppy, or untidy woman. **2** An immoral woman.

sly [slī] *adj.* **sli·er** or **sly·er, sli·est** or **sly·est 1** Clever in a secret, stealthy, or sneaky way; artful in deceiving; cunning; crafty; wily: a *sly* old fox. **2** Hinting secret thoughts: a *sly* wink. **3** Playfully clever: *sly* wit. — **on the sly** Secretly. — **sly′ness** *n.*

sly·ly [slī′lē] *adv.* In a sly manner.

smack[1] [smak] **1** *n.* A quick, sharp noise made by moving the lips apart, as in enjoyment over food. **2** *v.* To make such a noise with: He *smacked* his lips. **3** *n.* A noisy kiss. **4** *n.* A loud slap or blow. **5** *v.* To slap noisily. **6** *adv. informal* Squarely: *smack* on the target.

smack[2] [smak] **1** *v.* To have a taste, flavor, or suggestion: That *smacks* of cowardice. **2** *n.* A faint but distinctive taste or flavor: a *smack* of curry. **3** *n.* A trace.

smack[3] [smak] *n.* A small sailboat used chiefly for fishing, often having a well for live fish.

small [smôl] *adj.* **1** Not large in size, amount, etc.; little: a *small* town; a *small* price. **2** Less large than the average: a *small* elephant. **3** *n. use* The small or slender part: the *small* of the back. **4** Soft and faint: a *small* voice. **5** Not important or significant; minor; trivial: *small* talk. **6** Narrow, mean, or petty: *small* in spirit. — **feel small** To feel humiliated or ashamed: Her scorn made me *feel small*. — **small′ness** *n.*

small arms Weapons, as pistols, rifles, etc., that can be carried and fired by hand.

small change Coins of little value, as nickels, dimes, and quarters.

small fry 1 Small fish. **2** Young children.

small hours The early hours of the morning.

small intestine The longer and narrower portion of the intestine, leading from the stomach to the large intestine.

small letter A letter that is not capitalized.

small·pox [smôl′poks′] *n.* A highly contagious virus disease causing a high fever and skin eruptions that usually leave permanent scars.

smart [smärt] **1** *adj.* Quick in mind; intelligent; bright; clever. **2** *adj.* Keen or shrewd. **3** *adj.* Witty and quick but not deep: *smart* remarks. **4** *adj.* Sharp and stinging: a *smart* cuff on the ear. **5** *n.* A sharp, stinging sensation. **6** *v.* To experience or cause a stinging sensation: eyes *smarting* from smog; The cut *smarts*. **7** *v.* To feel hurt, sorry, irritated, or upset: He still *smarted* over their rude remarks. **8** *adj.* Clean, neat, and trim in appearance. **9** *adj.* Fashionable; stylish: a *smart* outfit. **10** *adj.* Vigorous; brisk; lively: to move at a *smart* pace. — **smart′ly** *adv.* — **smart′ness** *n.*

smart·en [smär′tən] *v.* To make or become more attractive, stylish, brisk, bright, etc.

smash [smash] **1** *v.* To break into many pieces violently and noisily: He *smashed* the glass against the wall; The vase fell and *smashed*. **2** *v.* To crush: to *smash* a rebellion. **3** *v.* To dash or hit violently; crash: The car *smashed* into a post. **4** *n.* The act or sound of smashing. **5** *n.* A wreck or crash resulting from a collision. **6** *v.* To wreck or destroy. **7** *n.* Ruin, failure, or disaster. **8** *n. informal* A great success; hit: The film is a box-office *smash*.

smash·up [smash′up′] *n.* A damaging crash or collision; wreck.

smat·ter·ing [smat′ər·ing] *n.* A slight, surface knowledge: He has a *smattering* of German.

smear [smir] **1** *v.* To spread, rub, or cover with a greasy, sticky, or dirty substance: to *smear* one's hands with paint. **2** *v.* To spread or apply in a thick layer or coating: to *smear* grease on an axle. **3** *v.* To blur or make indistinct: to *smear* the address on a letter. **4** *n.* A soiled spot, streak, etc., caused by smearing. **5** *v.* To say bad or untruthful things about: They *smeared* every politician that ran for office that year. **6** *n.* A slanderous attack or accusation.

smell [smel] *v.* **smelled** or **smelt, smell·ing,** *n.* **1** *v.* To perceive or be aware of by means of the nose and its special nerves: I can *smell* the lilacs. **2** *n.* The special sense by means of which odors are perceived: Bloodhounds track down escaped prisoners by *smell.* **3** *v.* To give off a particular odor or perfume: The field *smells* of clover. **4** *v.* To give off a bad odor: The garbage can *smells.* **5** *n.* The act of smelling: Have a *smell* of this cologne. **6** *n.* An odor or aroma: the *smell* of frying bacon.

smelling salts An ammonia compound having a very strong or burning smell, used to relieve headaches, fainting spells, etc.

smell·y [smel'ē] *adj.* **smell·i·er, smell·i·est** Having a bad odor.

smelt[1] [smelt] *n., pl.* **smelt** or **smelts** Any of various small, silvery fishes of the north Atlantic and Pacific oceans, used as food.

smelt[2] [smelt] *v.* **1** To melt (ore) in a furnace in order to obtain metal. **2** To obtain (metal) by melting away impurities in ore: to *smelt* tin.

smelt[3] [smelt] An alternative past tense and past participle of SMELL.

smelt·er [smel'tər] *n.* **1** A place where ore is smelted. **2** A person whose work is smelting ore.

smile [smīl] *n., v.* **smiled, smil·ing 1** *n.* A pleased, amused, or sometimes bitter or sarcastic expression of the face, made by raising up the corners of the mouth. **2** *v.* To have or give a smile: The baby *smiled.* **3** *v.* To express or show by means of a smile: He *smiled* his consent. **4** *n.* A pleasant look: the *smile* of spring.

smirch [smûrch] **1** *v.* To soil, as by contact with grime or dirt. **2** *n.* A dirty mark or stain. **3** *v.* To bring dishonor or disgrace on: to *smirch* a reputation.

smirk [smûrk] **1** *v.* To smile in a silly, self-satisfied, or affected manner. **2** *n.* Such a smile.

smite [smīt] *v.* **smote, smit·ten, smit·ing 1** To strike or hit very hard: seldom used today. **2** To affect, impress, or attack powerfully and suddenly: Pete was *smitten* with love.

smith [smith] *n.* **1** A person who makes, shapes, or repairs something: often used in combination, as in lock*smith* or tin*smith.* **2** A blacksmith.

Smith [smith], **John,** 1580–1631, English explorer and colonist in Virginia from 1608 to 1609.

Smith [smith], **Joseph,** 1805–1844, American who founded the Mormon Church.

smith·y [smith'ē] *n., pl.* **smith·ies 1** A blacksmith's shop or forge.

2 A blacksmith.

smit·ten [smit'(ə)n] A past participle of SMITE.

smock [smok] **1** *n.* A loose outer garment worn over one's clothes to protect them from being soiled. **2** *v.* To ornament (a garment) with smocking.

smock·ing [smok'ing] *n.* Needlework in which the material is stitched into small pleats or gathers that look like a honeycomb.

Smithy

smog [smog] *n.* A blend of smoke and fog.

smoke [smōk] *n., v.* **smoked, smok·ing 1** *n.* The cloudlike mass of fine carbon particles arising from burning coal, wood, etc. **2** *n.* Any cloud or vapor that looks like smoke. **3** *v.* To give off smoke, especially too much smoke or in an undesired direction: That old stove *smokes.* **4** *v.* To inhale and exhale the smoke of: to *smoke* a pipe. **5** *n. informal* A cigarette, cigar, or pipeful of tobacco. **6** *n.* The act of smoking. **7** *v.* To cure or preserve (meat, fish, etc.) by treating it with smoke. **8** *v.* To force (an animal, criminal, etc.) out of hiding with or as if with smoke.

smoke·house [smōk'hous'] *n.* A building or closed room where meat, fish, hides, etc., are hung and treated with smoke to preserve them.

smoke·jump·er [smōk'jum'pər] *n. informal* A man trained to parachute from an airplane to reach and fight forest fires.

smoke·less [smōk'lis] *adj.* Having or giving off little or no smoke: *smokeless* powder for guns.

smok·er [smō'kər] *n.* **1** A person or thing that smokes. **2** A railroad car where smoking is allowed. **3** A social gathering for men only.

smoke screen A dense cloud of smoke used to keep the enemy from seeing movements of troops, ships, etc.

smoke·stack [smōk'stak'] *n.* A chimney or funnel, as on a factory, ship, or locomotive, for carrying off smoke.

smok·y [smō'kē] *adj.* **smok·i·er, smok·i·est 1** Giving out smoke, especially improperly or unpleasantly: a *smoky* old furnace. **2** Mixed with or containing smoke: *smoky* air. **3** Of or like smoke in color, smell, taste, etc. **4** Made dark or dirty by smoke: *smoky* ceilings. — **smok'i·ly** *adv.* — **smok'i·ness** *n.*

smol·der [smōl'dər] *v.* **1** To burn slowly with smoke but no flame. **2** To exist but in a hidden or controlled state: His anger *smoldered* for days, but he kept it hidden.

add, āce, câre, pälm; end, ēqual; it, īce; odd, ōpen, ôrder; tŏŏk, pōōl; up, bûrn;
ə = a in *above*, e in *sicken*, i in *possible*, o in *melon*, u in *circus*; yōō = u in *fuse*; oil; pout;
check; ring; thin; this; zh in *vision.* For ¶ reference, see page 64 · HOW TO

smooth [smōōth] **1** *adj.* Having a surface without any roughness or unevenness: *smooth* ice. **2** *v.* To make or become smooth on the surface: *Smooth* the ground around the plants; The wet cement *smoothed* easily. **3** *adj.* Without lumps: a *smooth* gravy. **4** *adj.* Free from bumps, shocks, jolts, etc.: The pilot made a *smooth* landing. **5** *adj.* Calm and unruffled; pleasant; mild: a *smooth* disposition. **6** *adj.* Without any difficulties, annoyances, or troubles: the *smooth* course of a journey. **7** *v.* To make easy or less difficult: to *smooth* one's path to success. **8** *adj.* Not harsh or strong in taste, sound, etc.: a *smooth* wine; a *smooth* voice. **9** *v.* To take away crudeness, awkwardness, etc., from; polish: to *smooth* a book report. **10** *adv.* In a smooth manner. — **smooth down** To calm, lull, or soothe. — **smooth over** To make seem less serious, unpleasant, etc.; minimize: She *smoothed over* his mistakes. — **smooth·ly** *adv.* — **smooth·ness** *n.*

smooth·bore [smōōth′bôr′] **1** *adj.* With no spiral grooves cut in the barrel. **2** *n.* A gun whose barrel does not have grooves cut inside it.

smor·gas·bord [smôr′gəs·bôrd] *n.* A Scandinavian meal with a great variety of cheeses, meats, fish, etc., set out as a buffet.

smote [smōt] Past tense of SMITE.

smoth·er [smuth′ər] **1** *v.* To prevent or be prevented from getting air to breathe; suffocate: The old hen *smothered* her chicks; We almost *smothered* in the heat. **2** *v.* To slow down or put out (a fire) with a covering that shuts out air. **3** *n.* A thick, choking cloud of dust or smoke. **4** *v.* To hide or suppress: to *smother* one's feelings. **5** *v.* To cover thickly and cook: to *smother* meat with vegetables.

smudge [smuj] *v.* **smudged, smudg·ing,** *n.* **1** *v.* To smear or soil: I *smudged* the paper. **2** *n.* A soiled spot; smear; stain. **3** *n.* A smoky fire used for driving away insects, preventing damage to crops by frost, etc. — **smudg′y** *adj.*

smug [smug] *adj.* **smug·ger, smug·gest** **1** Very satisfied with oneself to the extent of irritating others. **2** Full of or showing great self-satisfaction: a *smug* look. — **smug′ly** *adv.* — **smug′ness** *n.*

smug·gle [smug′əl] *v.* **smug·gled, smug·gling** **1** To take (merchandise) into or out of a country without payment of lawful duties. **2** To bring in or take out secretly: We *smuggled* our dog into the hotel. **3** To engage in smuggling. — **smug′gler** *n.*

smut [smut] *n.*, *v.* **smut·ted, smut·ting** **1** *n.* A bit of soot or other dirty substance. **2** *n.* A dirty mark made by soot, smoke, etc. **3** *v.* To blacken or stain, as with soot or smoke. **4** *n.* Any of various fungus diseases of plants in which the diseased parts are replaced by a dusty black powder. **5** *n.* Dirty or vulgar language.

smut·ty [smut′ē] *adj.* **smut·ti·er, smut·ti·est** **1** Soiled or blackened with smut. **2** Having the disease smut: *smutty* corn. **3** Vulgar; obscene.

Sn The symbol for the element TIN.

snack [snak] **1** *n.* A light, hurried meal. **2** *n.* Anything eaten between meals. **3** *adj. use:* a *snack* bar. **4** *v.* To eat lightly, especially between meals.

snaf·fle [snaf′əl] *n.* A type of horse's bit that is jointed in the middle.

snag [snag] *n.*, *v.* **snagged, snag·ging** **1** *n.* Anything that is sharp or jagged and on which things may be caught, torn, etc. **2** *n.* The trunk or big branch of a tree caught fast in a river, bayou, etc., by which boats are sometimes pierced. **3** *v.* To injure, destroy, tear, or catch on a snag: She *snagged* her dress on a nail. **4** *n.* A tear or rip made by snagging. **5** *n.* An obstacle that is hidden or not expected: She ran into many *snags* in that job. **6** *v. informal* To block or hinder. **7** *v.* To clear or rid of snags. ◆ *Snag* probably comes from an old Scandinavian word meaning *something sticking out,* as a short branch of a tree.

snail [snāl] *n.* **1** A small, slow-moving animal with a soft body and a spiral shell on its back into which it can pull itself. Some snails live on land, and some in water. **2** A slow or lazy person.

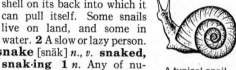
A typical snail

snake [snāk] *n.*, *v.* **snaked, snak·ing** **1** *n.* Any of numerous kinds of scaly, legless reptiles with long, slim bodies and tapering tails. **2** *v.* To move, wind, or crawl like a snake. **3** *n.* An evil or unreliable person. **4** *n.* A long, flexible wire used to clean clogged drains, pipes, etc.

snake·skin [snāk′skin′] *n.* **1** The skin of a snake. **2** Leather made from this.

snak·y [snā′kē] *adj.* **snak·i·er, snak·i·est** **1** Of or like a snake; twisting or winding: a *snaky* path up a mountain. **2** Cunning; treacherous: a *snaky* person. **3** Full of snakes.

snap [snap] *v.* **snapped, snap·ping,** *n.*, *adj.* **1** *v.* To make or cause to make a sharp, quick sound: to *snap* a whip; to *snap* one's fingers. **2** *n.* A sharp, quick sound: The guitar string broke with a *snap*. **3** *v.* To close, fasten, or fit into place with a click or a sharp, quick sound: The door *snapped* shut. **4** *n.* Any catch, fastener, etc., that closes with a snapping sound. **5** *v.* To try to bite or seize with the jaws: The dog *snapped* at me. **6** *n.* The act of snapping. **7** *v.* To seize or snatch quickly: The thief *snapped* up her purse; to *snap* up bargains at a sale. **8** *v.* To break suddenly from strain, stress, etc.: The rubber band *snapped* when I stretched it. **9** *v.* To move or act with quick gestures: The soldier *snapped* to attention. **10** *n.* Brisk vigor and energy; vim. **11** *adj.* Made or done too quickly or without careful thought: a *snap* decision. **12** *v.* To speak sharply or irritably: "Stop that!" she *snapped*. **13** *v.* To sparkle; flash: His eyes *snapped* with anger. **14** *n.* A brief spell, as of cold weather. **15** *n.* A thin, crisp cookie: a chocolate *snap*. **16** *v.* To take a snapshot of: I *snapped* him as he stepped off the plane. **17** *n.*

S

informal Any task or duty that is easy to do: Scrambling eggs is a *snap.* **18** *adj. informal* Requiring little work; easy: a *snap* course. **19** *v.* In football, to put (the ball) in play from its position on the ground. — **snap one's fingers at** To be unimpressed by or unafraid of. — **snap out of it** To recover quickly, as from an illness, fit of anger, etc.

snap·drag·on [snap′drag′ən] *n.* A plant that has showy white, yellow, or purplish red flowers that grow on long spikes.

snap·per [snap′ər] *n.* **1** A person or thing that snaps. **2** A large food fish caught in the Gulf of Mexico, especially the **red snapper. 3** A snapping turtle.

snapping turtle A large American turtle with strong, snapping jaws. It is used as a food.

snap·pish [snap′ish] *adj.* **1** Irritable and cross, especially in one's speech. **2** Apt to bite: a *snappish* dog. — **snap′pish·ly** *adv.* — **snap′- pish·ness** *n.*

snap·py [snap′ē] *adj.* **snap·pi·er, snap·pi· est 1** Snappishly irritable. **2** *informal* Energetic; brisk: a *snappy* salute. **3** *informal* Smart or stylish.

snap·shot [snap′shot′] *n.* A photograph made with a small camera, taken in an instant.

snare[1] [snâr] *n., v.* **snared, snar·ing 1** *n.* A noose that jerks tight, for catching small animals. **2** *n.* Anything that traps or tricks: Some ads are *snares* to catch suckers. **3** *v.* To trap or catch with or as if with a snare.

snare[2] [snâr] *n.* One of the cords or wires stretched across one of the heads of a snare drum.

snare drum A small drum with snares across the bottom head to make a rattling noise.

snarl[1] [snärl] **1** *v.* To growl, showing the teeth, as an angry or frightened dog, wolf, etc. **2** *n.* A harsh, angry growl. **3** *v.* To say or express in an angry, growling tone: "Get out of here," he *snarled.*

snarl[2] [snärl] **1** *n.* A confused, tangled mess or condition, as of hair, yarn, etc. **2** *v.* To put or get into such a condition: Her hair *snarls* easily; The wreck *snarled* traffic for blocks.

snatch [snach] **1** *v.* To grab or take hold of suddenly, hastily, or eagerly. **2** *v.* To take or get when there is a chance: to *snatch* a few hours of sleep. **3** *n.* The act of snatching. **4** *n.* A brief period: a *snatch* of rest. **5** *n.* A small amount: *snatches* of distant music. — **snatch at** To attempt to grab swiftly and suddenly. — **snatch′er** *n.*

sneak [snēk] **1** *v.* To move, act, or go in a quiet, secret, often deceitful manner: He *sneaks* all over the house at night. **2** *v.* To put, give, move, etc., secretly or deceitfully: We *sneaked* the presents out of the closet. **3** *n.* A person who acts in a sly, secret manner. **4** *adj.* Stealthy; sly; secret: a *sneak* attack.

sneak·er [snē′kər] *n.* **1** A person who sneaks. **2** (*pl.*) *informal* Rubber-soled canvas shoes, worn especially for sports.

Sneakers

sneak·ing [snē′king] *adj.* **1** Secretly deceitful; mean; underhand: What a *sneaking* thing to do! **2** Kept hidden or secret; not yet expressed: I had a *sneaking* suspicion she'd go.

sneak·y [snē′kē] *adj.* **sneak·i·er, sneak·i· est** Showing or marked by dishonesty, meanness, secrecy, etc.: a *sneaky* act.

sneer [snir] **1** *n.* A look that shows dislike or contempt, made by slightly raising the upper lip. **2** *v.* To show dislike or contempt in speech, writing, etc. **3** *n.* A mean or contemptuous remark.

sneeze [snēz] *v.* **sneezed, sneez·ing,** *n.* **1** *v.* To drive air out of the mouth and nose by a sudden, involuntary action when the nasal passages are irritated, as by a cold, dust, etc. **2** *n.* The act of sneezing. — **not to be sneezed at** *informal* Not to be treated lightly.

snick·er [snik′ər] **1** *n.* A half-suppressed or smothered laugh, often used in making fun of someone. **2** *v.* To laugh in this way.

sniff [snif] **1** *v.* To breathe in through the nose in short, audible breaths. **2** *v.* To smell or attempt to smell in this way: Our dog kept *sniffing* the ground. **3** *n.* The act or sound of sniffing. **4** *n.* Something smelled or inhaled by sniffing: a *sniff* of snuff. **5** *v.* To show or express dislike or contempt by or as if by sniffing.

snif·fle [snif′əl] *v.* **snif·fled, snif·fling,** *n.* **1** *v.* To breathe noisily through the nose, as when one has a bad head cold. **2** *v.* To sob or whimper. **3** *n.* The act or sound of sniffling. — **the sniffles** *informal* A cold in the head.

snig·ger [snig′ər] *n., v.* Another word for SNICKER.

snip [snip] *v.* **snipped, snip·ping,** *n.* **1** *v.* To cut or clip off with short, light strokes of the scissors. **2** *n.* The act of snipping. **3** *n.* A piece snipped off: a *snip* of cloth. **4** *n.* (*pl.*) Shears for cutting metal. **5** *n. informal* A young, often small or impudent person.

snipe [snīp] *n., pl.* **snipe** or **snipes,** *v.* **sniped, snip·ing 1** *n.* Any of various long-billed birds that live in marshes or along the shore. **2** *v.* To hunt for snipe. **3** *v.* To shoot at enemies one at a time and from some hiding place.

snip·er [snī′pər] *n.* A person who shoots at an enemy from some hiding place.

Snipe, 10–12 in. long

snip·py [snip′ē] *adj.* **snip· pi·er, snip·pi·est** *informal* **1** Impudent; insolent. **2** Brief; rude; curt.

---

add, āce, câre, pälm; end, ēqual; it, īce; odd, ōpen, ôrder; tŏŏk, pōōl; up, bûrn; ə = a in *above,* e in *sicken,* i in *possible,* o in *melon,* u in *circus;* yōō = u in *fuse;* oil; pout; check; ring; thin; this; zh in *vision.* For ¶ reference, see page 64 · HOW TO

sniv·el [sniv′əl] *v.* **sniv·eled** or **sniv·elled,
sniv·el·ing** or **sniv·el·ling 1** To cry in a
sniffling manner. **2** To complain or whine
tearfully.

snob [snob] *n.* A person who looks down on
others because he considers them inferior in
culture, intelligence, or social position.

snob·ber·y [snob′ər·ē] *n., pl.* **snob·ber·ies
1** A snobbish act. **2** The attitude or outlook of a
snob.

snob·bish [snob′ish] *adj.* Of, having to do with,
or like a snob. — **snob′bish·ly** *adj.* — **snob′·
bish·ness** *n.*

snood [snood] *n.* A net worn by women at the
back of the head to keep the hair in place.

snoop [snoop] *informal* **1** *v.* To look or pry into
things which are none of one's business. **2** *n.* A
person who snoops.

snooze [snooz] *v.* **snoozed, snooz·ing,** *n.*
informal **1** *v.* To nap; doze. **2** *n.* A short nap.

snore [snôr] *v.* **snored, snor·ing,** *n.* **1** *v.* To
breathe in sleep through the nose and open
mouth with a hoarse, rough sound. **2** *n.* The
sound of snoring.

snor·kel [snôr′kəl] *n.* **1** A tube extended from a
submerged submarine to the surface in order to
provide ventilation. **2** A similar tube attached
to a skin diver's mask that permits him to
breathe when a little under water.

snort [snôrt] **1** *v.* To force air violently and
noisily through the nostrils. **2** *n.* The act or
sound of snorting. **3** *v.* To express with a snort:
"No!" he *snorted.* **4** *v.* To make a snorting
sound: The engine *snorted* and stalled.

snout [snout] *n.* **1** The forward, projecting part
of the head of many animals,
usually including the nose and
jaws: a hog's *snout.* **2** Something that resembles this.
◆ *Snout* is related to an Old
English word meaning *to blow
the nose.*

Snout

snow [snō] **1** *n.* Frozen water
vapor in the air, usually falling in the form of small white
flakes. **2** *v.* To fall as snow:
It is *snowing.* **3** *v.* To cover, enclose, obstruct,
etc., with snow: The roads are all *snowed* under.
4 *n.* A fall of snow: two *snows* in November. **5** *n.*
Anything resembling snow, especially a type of
interference on a television screen.

snow·ball [snō′bôl′] **1** *n.* A small round mass
of snow packed together for throwing. **2** *v.* To
throw snowballs at. **3** *n.* A bush that has
clusters of white flowers resembling snowballs.
4 *v.* To grow bigger fast, like a rolling snowball:
His endorsement made sales *snowball.*

snow·bank [snō′bangk′] *n.* A large mound or
drift of snow.

snow·bird [snō′bûrd′] *n.* **1** Any of various
small grayish birds of North America commonly
seen in flocks during the winter. **2** A bird of
northern regions, the male of which in breeding
seasons is snow-white with black markings.

snow-blind [snō′blīnd′] *adj.* Blinded temporarily by the glare of sunlight reflected from snow
or ice. — **snow blindness** *n.*

snow·bound [snō′bound′] *adj.* Shut in or
forced to stay in a place because of a heavy snow.

snow·drift [snō′drift′] *n.* A snowbank or heap
of snow drifted or blown together by the wind.

snow·drop [snō′drop′] *n.* A small European
plant that blooms early in the spring and bears a
single, white, drooping flower.

snow·fall [snō′fôl′] *n.* **1** A fall of snow. **2** The
amount of snow that falls in any given period.

snow·flake [snō′flāk′] *n.* A small, feathery
flake made of one or more crystals of snow.

snow line The imaginary line on the sides of
mountains above which there is perpetual snow.

snow·plow [snō′plou′] *n.* Any of various
devices for pushing or throwing snow off of a
road, railroad track, etc.

snow·shoe [snō′shoo′] *n., v.* **snow·shoed,
snow·shoe·ing 1** *n.* A network of leather
thongs or strips set in a wooden frame and
fastened on the foot in order to help a person
walk on soft snow without sinking in. **2** *v.* To
walk on snowshoes.

snow·slide [snō′slīd′] *n.* An avalanche of snow.

snow·storm [snō′stôrm′] *n.* A storm with a
heavy fall of snow.

snow-white [snō′(h)wīt′] *adj.* White as fresh
snow.

snow·y [snō′ē] *adj.* **snow·i·er, snow·i·est
1** Full of snow: *snowy* streets. **2** Having a lot
of snow: a *snowy* winter. **3** Like snow in whiteness, cleanliness, etc.: *snowy* linen.

snub [snub] *v.* **snubbed, snub·bing,** *n., adj.*
1 *v.* To treat with dislike or contempt, especially
by paying no attention to; slight. **2** *n.* An act of
snubbing someone; slight. **3** *v.* To stop or check
(a running rope, etc.) as by winding it around a
post. **4** *n.* The act of snubbing a rope, etc.
5 *adj.* Short and upturned: a *snub* nose.

snuff[1] [snuf] **1** *v.* To draw in or sniff (air, etc.)
through the nose. **2** *v.* To smell or sniff. **3** *n.*
Tobacco ground into a fine powder and inhaled
through the nostrils. — **up to snuff** *informal*
In good condition; as good as usual.

snuff[2] [snuf] *v.* **1** To put out or extinguish, as a
candle. **2** To trim off the burned part of (a
candle wick). — **snuff out 1** To put out;
extinguish. **2** To bring to an end quickly or
violently: The explosion *snuffed out* three lives.

snuff·box [snuf′boks′] *n.* A small box for
carrying snuff.

snuf·fer [snuf′ər] *n.* An instrument something
like a pair of scissors, used to extinguish candles
and to trim their wicks.

snuf·fle [snuf′əl] *v.* **snuf·fled, snuf·fling,** *n.*
1 *v.* To breathe noisily, as when one has a cold.
2 *n.* The act or sound of snuffling. — **the
snuffles** *informal* The sniffles.

snug [snug] *adj.* **snug·ger, snug·gest,** *adv.*
1 *adj.* Closely but comfortably covered, sheltered, etc.; cozy: The bears were *snug* in the
cave all winter. **2** *adj.* Fitting closely; rather

tight: Those pants are *snug*. **3** *adj.* Having room enough but not too much; compact: a *snug* little cabin. **4** *adv.* In a snug way: to fit *snug*. **— snug′ly** *adv.*

snug·gle [snug′əl] *v.* **snug·gled, snug·gling** To lie or hold close, as for comfort, warmth, etc.; cuddle: She *snuggled* the doll in her arms; The puppies *snuggled* near the fire.

so¹ [sō] **1** *adv.* To this or that degree; to such a degree: He has never been *so* quiet. **2** *adv.* In this or that manner: As the twig is bent, so is the tree inclined. **3** *adv.* Just as said or directed: Place your feet *so*. **4** *adv.* According to fact: That is not *so*. **5** *adv. informal* To an extreme degree; very: He is *so* good. **6** *adv. informal* Very much: I admire him *so*. **7** *pron.* About that; more or less: I'll stay a day or *so*. **8** *adv.* Most certainly; absolutely: You can *so* do it. **9** *conj.* Consequently; thus; therefore: He wasn't there, *so* he can't be a witness. **10** *adv.* It seems that; apparently: *So* you don't like it here! **11** *interj.* Ah hah! Indeed!: *So!* that's what you've been up to. **12** *conj.* With the purpose that: They left early *so* they would arrive before dark. **13** *conj. informal* As a result of which: They had an argument, *so* she left early. **— so as** In order to; for the purpose: He runs every day *so as* to keep in condition. ◆ *So, such,* and *such a* are used informally to make an adjective or noun following them stronger: He is *so* handsome; She has *such* intelligence; It was *such a* cold day. This use should be avoided in formal writing.

so² [sō] *n.* In music, another word for SOL.

soak [sōk] **1** *v.* To make completely wet by placing or keeping in a liquid. **2** *v.* To stay in a liquid until completely wet. **3** *v.* To suck up; absorb: Those towels will *soak* up the water. **4** *v.* To take in fully or quickly: to *soak* up knowledge. **5** *v.* To wet thoroughly; drench: The rain *soaked* his shoes. **6** *n.* The act of soaking.

so-and-so [sō′ən·sō′] *n., pl.* **so-and-sos** *informal* A person or thing whose name is not mentioned or can't be recalled.

soap [sōp] **1** *n.* A substance made from vegetable or animal fats mixed with an alkali. It is used with water for washing things clean. **2** *v.* To rub or treat with soap: to *soap* oneself.

soap·stone [sōp′stōn′] *n.* A kind of rock that has a smooth surface with a soapy feel.

soap·suds [sōp′sudz′] *n.pl.* Water mixed with soap until it is foamy and forms suds.

soap·y [sō′pē] *adj.* **soap·i·er, soap·i·est** **1** Of, containing, or like soap or soapsuds. **2** Covered with soap or soapsuds: *soapy* hands.

soar [sôr] *v.* **1** To rise high into the air; fly high: The eagle *soared* effortlessly. **2** To rise sharply above the usual level: Prices *soared*. **3** To reach or approach something grand or lofty: His imagination *soared*.

sob [sob] *v.* **sobbed, sob·bing,** *n.* **1** *v.* To weep with audible catches of the breath. **2** *v.* To utter with sobs: "I'm lost," she *sobbed*. **3** *v.* To bring to a certain state or condition by sobbing: to *sob* oneself to sleep. **4** *v.* To make a sound like a sob, as the wind. **5** *n.* The act or sound of sobbing.

so·ber [sō′bər] **1** *adj.* Not drunk or intoxicated. **2** *adj.* Serious, calm, thoughtful, and well-balanced: a careful, *sober* study of air pollution. **3** *adj.* Solemn; grave: a *sober* look. **4** *adj.* Modest and quiet in color, manner of dress, etc. **5** *v.* To make or become sober. **— so′ber·ly** *adv.* ◆ See SERIOUS.

so·bri·e·ty [sō·brī′ə·tē] *n.* The condition or quality of being sober.

so·bri·quet [sō′bri·kā] *n.* A nickname.

so-called [sō′kôld′] *adj.* Called or stated thus but usually not truthfully or correctly so: Her *so-called* illness was not an illness at all.

soc·cer [sok′ər] *n.* A form of football in which the ball is propelled toward the opponents' goal by kicking or by striking with the body or head.

so·cia·ble [sō′shə·bəl] **1** *adj.* Liking to be with people; agreeable and pleasant in company; social. **2** *adj.* Full of pleasant conversation, companionship, etc.: a very *sociable* party. **3** *n.* A social. **— so′cia·bil′i·ty** *n.* **— so′cia·bly** *adv.*

so·cial [sō′shəl] **1** *adj.* Liking or tending to live together in communities or in a society: Bees as well as men are *social* beings. **2** *adj.* Of or having to do with human beings as they live and act together in society: *social* life; *social* problems. **3** *adj.* Friendly and pleasant toward others; sociable. **4** *adj.* Of, having to do with, or promoting friendliness and companionship: a *social* club. **5** *adj.* Of or having to do with persons prominent in fashionable society: the *social* season. **6** *n.* An informal, friendly gathering, as of church members.

so·cial·ism [sō′shəl·iz′əm] *n.* **1** The idea that the means of production and distribution, such as factories, railroads, and power plants, should be owned by the government or associations of workers and operated without private profit. **2** A political movement favoring putting this idea into practice more completely.

so·cial·ist [sō′shəl·ist] **1** *n.* A person who is in favor of socialism. **2** *n.* (*often written* **Socialist**) A person who is a member of a party that advocates socialism. **3** *adj.* Socialistic.

so·cial·is·tic [sō′shəl·is′tik] *adj.* **1** Of, having to do with, or practicing socialism. **2** Like or tending toward socialism: a *socialistic* belief.

so·cial·ize [sō′shəl·īz] *v.* **so·cial·ized, so·cial·iz·ing** **1** To manage or run according to socialistic principles. **2** To make more friendly, cooperative, or social. **3** To take part in social activities: to *socialize* on weekends. ¶3

add, āce, câre, pälm;   end, ēqual;   it, īce;   odd, ōpen, ôrder;   tŏŏk, pōōl;   up, bûrn;
ə = a in *above*, e in *sicken*, i in *possible*, o in *melon*, u in *circus*;   yōō = u in *fuse*;   oil;   pout;
check;   ring;   thin;   this;   zh in *vision*.   For ¶ reference, see page 64 · HOW TO

so·cial·ly [sō'shə·lē] *adv.* **1** In a social manner: They live very *socially*. **2** With respect to society, a social group, or social activities: He is not at ease *socially*.

social science A body of knowledge that deals with human society and man in his relation to other men, to the state, the family, or any social group or institution to which he belongs. History, anthropology, sociology, economics, and politics are social sciences.

social security In the U.S., a system of payments to the aged, the unemployed, and certain others, supported by fees collected from employers and workers and by government subsidy.

social studies In elementary and secondary schools, a course of study based on the social sciences.

social work Any of various services that attempt to improve the social conditions of a community by providing health clinics, recreational facilities, aid to the poor, the troubled, etc.

so·ci·e·ty [sə·sī'ə·tē] *n., pl.* **so·ci·e·ties** **1** All of the people living: *Society* benefits by these laws. **2** A group or body of persons living together in a particular place or at a particular time and having many things in common: a rural *society*; an ancient *society*. **3** A group of persons who join together for a common purpose or object: a medical *society*. **4** The fashionable or wealthy group of a country or city. **5** Fellowship or companionship: He doesn't care too much for *society*.

Society of Friends A Christian religious group that does not believe in formal religious services and is against violence and war. Its members are also known as Quakers.

so·ci·ol·o·gy [sō'sē·ol'ə·jē *or* sō'shē·ol'ə·jē] *n.* The study of people living in groups or communities, past and present. Often using statistics, sociology deals with the family, marriage, education, religion, crime, slums, etc. — **so·ci·o·log·i·cal** [sō'sē·ə·loj'ə·kəl] *adj.* — **so'ci·ol'o·gist** *n.*

sock[1] [sok] *n.* A short stocking.

sock[2] [sok] *slang* **1** *v.* To strike or hit, especially with the fist. **2** *n.* A hard blow.

sock·et [sok'it] *n.* A hole, cavity, or hollow part that is made to receive and hold something: the *socket* for an electric bulb; the *socket* of the eye.

Soc·ra·tes [sok'rə·tēz] *n.*, 469?–399 B.C., Greek philosopher and teacher, the chief person in the dialogues of Plato.

sod [sod] *n., v.* **sod·ded, sod·ding** **1** *n.* The top layer of the earth, especially when covered with grass. **2** *n.* A piece of this layer held together by matted roots of grass and weeds. **3** *v.* To cover with pieces of sod.

so·da [sō'də] *n.* **1** Any of several compounds containing sodium, as baking soda for cooking. **2** Soda water. **3** A soft drink made of carbonated water and flavoring. **4** A drink made of ice cream, carbonated water, flavoring, etc.

soda fountain A counter at which soft drinks, ice cream, sundaes, etc., are sold.

so·dal·i·ty [sō·dal'ə·tē] *n., pl.* **so·dal·i·ties** In the Roman Catholic Church, a society organized for devotional or charitable purposes.

soda water Water that is made to bubble or fizz by being charged with carbon dioxide gas.

sod·den [sod'(ə)n] *adj.* **1** Soaked with moisture: turf *sodden* with rain. **2** Heavy, doughy, or soggy, as poorly baked bread, biscuits, etc.

so·di·um [sō'dē·əm] *n.* A soft, silver-white, very active metallic element that forms many compounds, the best known of which is common salt.

sodium bicarbonate A white, crystalline compound used in medicine and cooking and commonly known as baking soda.

sodium chloride Common table salt.

sodium hydroxide The hydroxide of sodium, found in lye and used in bleaching, in making soap, paper, etc.

sodium nitrate The sodium salt of nitric acid, often used in fertilizers.

Sod·om [sod'əm] *n.* In the Bible, a city destroyed with the neighboring city, Gomorrah, because of the wickedness of the people.

so·fa [sō'fə] *n.* A long couch, upholstered and with raised arms at both ends and a back. ◆ *Sofa* comes from an Arabic word meaning *long bench* or *part of a floor raised to form a seat.*

Sofa

soft [sôft] **1** *adj.* Not hard or brittle; easily worked, shaped, cut, pressed, etc., usually without breaking: a *soft* dough; *soft* wood; *soft* metal. **2** *adj.* Smooth and delicate to the touch: *soft* skin. **3** *adj.* Not loud or harsh to the ear: *soft* music. **4** *adj.* Mild, gentle, and courteous: *soft* words; a *soft* manner. **5** *adj.* Tender, kind, and sympathetic: a *soft* heart. **6** *adj.* Not able to bear effort, hardship, strain, etc.: *soft* muscles. **7** *adj. informal* Not hard or difficult to do or bear; easy: a *soft* job; a *soft* life. **8** *adj.* Not glaring, bright, or harsh: *soft* colors. **9** *adv.* In a soft manner; softly. **10** *adj.* Containing no alcohol: a *soft* drink. **11** *adj.* Describing the soft, breathy sound of *c* in *cent* and *g* in *gibe*, as opposed to the hard, rough sound of *c* in *cord* or *g* in *good*. **12** *adj.* Free from certain salts, as water: Rain water is *soft* and easy to wash with. — **soft'ly** *adv.* — **soft'ness** *n.*

soft·ball [sôft'bôl'] *n.* **1** A variation of baseball, using a larger, softer ball and a smaller diamond. **2** The ball used in this game.

soft coal Bituminous coal.

soft drink Any drink that does not contain alcohol, especially sweetened soda water, ginger ale, etc.

sof·ten [sôf'ən] *v.* To make or become soft or softer: *Soften* the butter before using it; Her heart *softened* when she saw the poor dog. — **sof'ten·er** *n.*

soft·wood [sôft'wŏŏd'] *n.* **1** Any wood that can be cut or pierced comparatively easily, as pine wood. **2** Any tree, as the pine, that yields such wood.

sog·gy [sog′ē] *adj.* **sog·gi·er, sog·gi·est**
1 Soaked with water or moisture. **2** Heavy and
moist: said of pastry. — **sog′gi·ness** *n.*

soil¹ [soil] *n.* **1** The ground in which plants grow;
dirt; earth. **2** A country or land: one's native
soil. **3** Anything thought of as a place for
growth: Slums are fertile *soil* for disease.

soil² [soil] **1** *v.* To make or become dirty: We
soiled our clothes; This cloth *soils* easily. **2** *v.*
To disgrace: to *soil* one's reputation. **3** *n.* A
soiled spot or stain.

soi·ree or **soi·rée** [swä·rā′] *n.* A party or a
reception given in the evening.

so·journ [*v.* sō′jûrn *or* sō·jûrn′, *n.* sō′jûrn] **1** *v.*
To stay or live for a time: They *sojourned* in
Paris for a month. **2** *n.* A stay or visit in a place.
— **so′journ·er** *n.*

sol [sōl] *n.* In music, a syllable used to represent
the fifth tone of a major scale or the seventh tone
of a minor scale or, in a fixed system, the tone G.

Sol [sol] *n.* **1** The sun. **2** In ancient Roman
myths, the god of the sun.

sol·ace [sol′is] *n., v.* **sol·aced, sol·ac·ing 1** *n.*
Comfort in times of unhappiness or trouble. **2** *n.*
A person or thing that brings such comfort:
Music was her *solace* when she was sad. **3** *v.* To
comfort or cheer in unhappiness or trouble.

so·lar [sō′lər] *adj.* **1** Of, having to do with, or
coming from the sun: the *solar* system; *solar*
energy. **2** Measured by the movement of the
earth around the sun: a *solar* year. **3** Operated
by the action of the sun's rays: a *solar* battery.

solar battery A device that converts energy
from the sun into electricity.

so·lar·i·um [sō·lâr′ē·əm] *n., pl.* **so·lar·i·a** [sō·
lâr′ē·ə] or **so·lar·i·ums** A room or glass-
enclosed porch where people can sun themselves.

solar plexus A large network of nerves just
behind the stomach.

solar system The sun and all the heavenly
bodies that move in
orbit around it.

sold [sōld] Past tense
and past participle of
SELL.

sol·der [sod′ər] **1** *n.*
A metal or alloy that,
when melted, can be
used to join or mend
metal parts or objects.
2 *v.* To join, mend, or
work with solder: We
soldered the pipes to-
gether.

sol·dier [sōl′jər] **1** *n.*
A person serving in
the army, especially an enlisted man rather than
a commissioned officer. **2** *n.* A person who is
experienced or skillful in war. **3** *n.* A person who
works hard for any cause: a *soldier* for equal

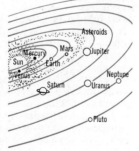
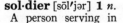

Solar system

rights. **4** *v.* To be a soldier. **5** *v. informal* To
make a show of working, but doing as little as
possible.

sol·dier·ly [sōl′jər·lē] *adj.* Of or like a true
soldier; brave: It was a *soldierly* thing to do.

soldier of fortune An adventurous, restless
person who is willing to serve as a soldier for
whoever will pay him the most.

sol·dier·y [sōl′jər·ē] *n.* **1** Soldiers when thought
of as a group. **2** Military training or skill.

sole¹ [sōl] *n., v.* **soled, sol·ing 1** *n.* The
bottom surface of the foot. **2** *n.* The bottom
surface of a shoe, boot, stocking, etc. **3** *v.* To
furnish with a sole: The shoemaker *soled* our
shoes.

sole² [sōl] *n.* Any of various flatfish related to
the flounder and much used as food.

sole³ [sōl] *adj.* **1** Being the only one: He was the
sole doctor in town. **2** Only: Fishermen were the
sole inhabitants of the island.

sol·e·cism [sol′ə·siz′əm] *n.* **1** A mistake in
grammar or in the correct usage of words: "We
have ate it" is a *solecism.* **2** Any social error or
blunder.

sole·ly [sōl′lē] *adv.* **1** By oneself or itself alone;
singly. **2** Only; exclusively: She lived *solely* for
her children.

sol·emn [sol′əm] *adj.* **1** Majestic, impressive,
and awe-inspiring: a very *solemn* ceremony.
2 Serious, grave, and earnest: a *solemn* expression. **3** Sacred; religious: a *solemn* day of
thanksgiving. **4** Somber; gloomy: *solemn* colors.
— **sol′emn·ly** *adv.*

so·lem·ni·ty [sə·lem′nə·tē] *n., pl.* **so·lem·ni·
ties 1** A serious or religious ceremony or
service: Memorial Day *solemnities.* **2** A solemn
or serious condition, quality, or feeling: the
solemnity of a marriage service.

sol·em·nize [sol′əm·nīz] *v.* **sol·em·nized,
sol·em·niz·ing 1** To perform in a legal,
ceremonious way: to *solemnize* a marriage. **2** To
observe with ceremony, as a religious holiday.
3 To make solemn or dignified. — **sol′em·ni·
za′tion** *n.* ¶3

so·lic·it [sə·lis′it] *v.* To ask or ask for earnestly:
to *solicit* a neighborhood for business; to *solicit*
money for a church. — **so·lic′i·ta′tion** *n.*

so·lic·i·tor [sə·lis′ə·tər] *n.* **1** A person who
solicits, especially one who asks for donations of
money, etc. **2** A lawyer for a city, town, state,
etc. **3** *British* A lawyer who can prepare cases or
advise clients, but may plead cases in the lower
courts only.

so·lic·i·tous [sə·lis′ə·təs] *adj.* **1** Full of concern,
worry, or interest for someone or something:
She was *solicitous* about our health. **2** Eager;
desiring: *solicitous* to get approval. — **so·lic′i·
tous·ly** *adv.*

so·lic·i·tude [sə·lis′ə·t(y)ōōd] *n.* Concern,
anxiety, or care for someone or something.

add, āce, câre, pälm; end, ēqual; it, īce; odd, ōpen, ôrder; tŏŏk, pŏŏl; up, bûrn;
ə = a in *above,* e in *sicken,* i in *possible,* o in *melon,* u in *circus;* yōō = u in *fuse;* oil; pout;
check; ring; thin; this; zh in *vision.* For ¶ reference, see page 64 · HOW TO

sol·id [sol'id] **1** *adj.* Not liquid or gaseous; not easily made to change shape or size; firm: *Lava is* solid *after it cools.* **2** *n.* Something firm and having a more or less definite shape that does not too easily change: *Wood and ice are both* solids. **3** *adj.* Having or dealing with length, width, and thickness: *a* solid *figure;* solid *geometry.* **4** *n.* A body having length, width, and thickness: *A cone, cube, pyramid, and sphere are all* solids. **5** *adj.* Not hollow, but filled with matter: *This piece of wood is* solid *throughout.* **6** *adj.* Containing only one color, metal, etc.: *solid* blue; *solid* gold. **7** *adj.* Strong; sound: *The floor is not too* solid: *solid* opinions. **8** *adj.* Not frivolous, light, or fanciful; deep: *a good,* solid *novel.* **9** *adj.* Continuous; unbroken: *a* solid *hour of study.* **10** *adj.* Showing a united or unanimous spirit: *The mayor had the* solid *support of the townspeople.* — **sol'id·ly** *adv.* — **sol'id·ness** *n.*

sol·i·dar·i·ty [sol'ə·dar'ə·tē] *n.* The condition of being strongly united or in unison: *The* solidarity *of the class was seen in the school election.*

solid geometry The branch of geometry that deals with figures having the three dimensions of length, width, and thickness.

so·lid·i·fy [sə·lid'ə·fī] *v.* **so·lid·i·fied, so·lid·i·fy·ing** **1** To make or become solid, hard, or compact. **2** To make or become strongly united. — **so·lid'i·fi·ca'tion** *n.*

so·lid·i·ty [sə·lid'ə·tē] *n., pl.* **so·lid·i·ties** A solid state; firmness; hardness.

so·lil·o·quize [sə·lil'ə·kwīz] *v.* **so·lil·o·quized, so·lil·o·quiz·ing** To talk to oneself or to deliver a soliloquy. ¶3

so·lil·o·quy [sə·lil'ə·kwē] *n., pl.* **so·lil·o·quies** **1** The act of talking to oneself. **2** In a play, etc., a speech in which an actor reveals his thoughts to the audience, but not to the other actors.

sol·i·taire [sol'ə·târ'] *n.* **1** One of many card games that can be played by one person. **2** A diamond or other gem set alone in a ring.

sol·i·tar·y [sol'ə·ter'ē] *adj.* **1** Living, being, or going alone: *a* solitary *person.* **2** Made, done, or passed alone: *a* solitary *life.* **3** Secluded or lonely: *a* solitary *strip of beach.* **4** Single; sole: *Not a* solitary *soul was there.*

sol·i·tude [sol'ə·t(y)ood] *n.* **1** The condition of being away from others: *At times everyone needs* solitude. **2** A deserted or lonely place.

so·lo [sō'lō] *n., pl.* **so·los,** *adj., v.* **so·loed, so·lo·ing** **1** *n.* A musical composition or passage for a single voice or instrument. **2** *adj.* Played or sung by a single voice or instrument. **3** *n.* A performance given by a single person without a partner or assistant: *a dance* solo. **4** *adj.* Done by a single person: *a* solo *flight.* **5** *adv.* Without another person; alone: *to fly* solo. **6** *v.* To fly an airplane alone, especially for the first time.

so·lo·ist [sō'lō·ist] *n.* A person who performs or sings a solo or solos.

Sol·o·mon [sol'ə·mən] *n.* A very wise king of Israel who lived in the 10th century B.C.

So·lon [sō'lən *or* sō'lon] *n.* **1** An Athenian lawmaker who lived from about 638? to 599? B.C. **2** (*usually written* **solon**) Any wise lawmaker.

sol·stice [sol'stis] *n.* Either of the two times in the year when the sun is at its furthest distance north or south of the equator. In the northern hemisphere, the **summer solstice** is about June 21 and the **winter solstice** is about December 22.

sol·u·bil·i·ty [sol'yə·bil'ə·tē] *n.* The ability of a particular substance to dissolve in another substance, especially in water.

sol·u·ble [sol'yə·bəl] *adj.* **1** Capable of being dissolved, especially in water. **2** Capable of being solved or explained: *a* soluble *mystery.*

so·lu·tion [sə·loo'shən] *n.* **1** The act or method of solving a problem, difficulty, doubt, etc. **2** The answer to a problem, difficulty, doubt, etc.: *Have you found the* solution *yet?* **3** A mixture made by dissolving one substance in another, usually a liquid: *Salt water is a* solution. **4** The act of making such a mixture. **5** The condition of being dissolved: *to hold salt in* solution.

solve [solv] *v.* **solved, solv·ing** To find or work out the answer or solution to: *First we must* solve *the problem of poor study habits.*

sol·ven·cy [sol'vən·sē] *n.* The condition of being solvent.

sol·vent [sol'vənt] **1** *adj.* Capable of paying all debts: *a* solvent *business.* **2** *adj.* Capable of dissolving a substance: *a* solvent *liquid.* **3** *n.* A substance in which some other substance is or can be dissolved: *Alcohol is a* solvent *for shellac.*

So·ma·li·a [sō·mä'lyə *or* sō·mä'lē·ə] *n.* A country in eastern Africa, on the Indian Ocean.

so·mat·ic [sō·mat'ik] *adj.* Of or having to do with the body: *a* somatic *disease.*

som·ber [som'bər] *adj.* **1** Having little light or brightness; dark: *somber* colors; *a* somber *day.* **2** Gloomy and melancholy; sad: *He is in a very* somber *mood today.* — **som'ber·ly** *adv.* — **som'ber·ness** *n.* ¶2

som·bre·ro [som·brâr'ō] *n., pl.* **som·bre·ros** A hat having a very wide brim, much worn in Spain, Latin America, and the sw U.S. ◆ *Sombrero* means *hat* in Spanish. It comes from the Spanish word *sombra*, meaning *shade*, because the wide brim of the hat shades the face from the sun.

some [sum] **1** *adj.* Not definitely known as to quantity, number, or amount: *Some people will not vote; The recipe calls for* some *milk.* **2** *adj.* Not definitely known or recognized: *Some people went by the window.* **3** *pron.* An indefinite number, quantity, or amount: *He spilled* some *of the ink.* **4** *adv.* About: *Some eighty people were present.* **5** *adj. informal* Good, big, or otherwise notable: *That was* some *cake!*

-some[1] A suffix used to form adjectives and meaning: Characterized by or tending to be, as in *frolicsome*, characterized by frolic, or *burdensome*, tending to be a burden.

-some[2] A suffix used to form nouns and meaning: A group consisting of, as in *threesome*, a group consisting of three persons or things.

some·bod·y [sum′bod′ē *or* sum′bəd·ē] *pron., n.,
pl.* **some·bod·ies 1** *pron.* A person unknown
or not named: *Somebody* went out the door.
2 *n.* A person of importance: She's a *somebody*.

some·day [sum′dā′] *adv.* At some future time.

some·how [sum′hou′] *adv.* In some way or in
some manner not known or explained.

some·one [sum′wun′] *pron.* Some person;
somebody.

som·er·sault [sum′ər·sôlt] **1** *n.* An acrobatic
stunt in which a per-
son either jumps or
rolls completely over,
turning heels over
head, forward or back-
ward. **2** *v.* To do a
somersault.

Somersault

some·thing [sum′·
thing] **1** *n.* A thing
not known, named, or understood: *Something*
just flew in the window; Did you have *something*
to say? **2** *n.* A person or thing of importance.
3 *adv.* Somewhat: now only in the phrase
something like: He looks *something like* me.

some·time [sum′tīm′] **1** *adv.* At some future
time: We hope to go there *sometime*. **2** *adv.* At
some time not stated or known: He will arrive
sometime today. **3** *adj.* Former: a *sometime*
student.

some·times [sum′tīmz′] *adv.* Now and then; at
times; occasionally.

some·what [sum′(h)wot′] **1** *adv.* To some degree or extent; rather; slightly: I feel *somewhat*
sick. **2** *n.* A certain amount, degree, or kind of.

some·where [sum′(h)wâr′] *adv.* **1** In, at, or to
some place not known or named: They go *somewhere* every summer. **2** In or at some point in
time: She is *somewhere* in her twenties.

som·nam·bu·list [som·nam′byə·list] *n.* A person who walks in his sleep. **— som·nam′bu·
lism′** *n.*

som·no·lent [som′nə·lənt] *adj.* **1** Inclined to
fall asleep; drowsy. **2** Bringing about sleep or
drowsiness: a *somnolent* tone of voice. **— som′·
no·lence** *n.*

son [sun] *n.* **1** A boy or man, considered in relation to either or both of his parents. **2** A boy or
man regarded as related to a country, cause, etc.,
as a son is to a parent: a *son* of liberty. **— the
Son** Jesus Christ.

so·nar [sō′när] *n.* A device that locates underwater objects by sending out
high-frequency sound waves
and picking up their echoes
with a microphone.

sound
waves

A ship locating an
underwater hazard
by sonar

so·na·ta [sə·nä′tə] *n.* A musical composition for one, two,
or, in older music, three or
more instruments, usually in
several movements.

song [sông] *n.* **1** A musical composition for one
or more voices. **2** The act of singing. **3** A melodious sound: the *song* of a bird. **4** A poem, as a
ballad, that can be sung or spoken. **—for a
song** At a very low price.

song·bird [sông′bûrd′] *n.* Any bird that sings,
as a canary or thrush.

song·ster [sông′stər] *n.* **1** A person who sings.
2 A songbird. **3** A poet.

son·ic [son′ik] *adj.* **1** Of or having to do with
sound. **2** Having a speed approaching that of
sound.

sonic boom A disturbance of the atmosphere,
heard as a loud clap of thunder, made by an airplane flying faster than the speed of sound.

son-in-law [sun′in·lô′] *n., pl.* **sons-in-law**
The husband of one's daughter.

son·net [son′it] *n.* A poem of fourteen lines that
rhyme according to a formal, fixed scheme.

so·no·rous [sə·nôr′əs *or* son′ər·əs] *adj.* **1** Loud
and very full in sound; resonant: That organ
has a *sonorous* tone. **2** Impressive in sound,
effect, style, etc.: a *sonorous* sentence.

soon [sōōn] *adv.* **1** At a time not far off; shortly:
We go *soon* after dark. **2** Without delay; quickly:
Send a doctor as *soon* as possible. **3** Early: We
arrived at the party too *soon*. **4** With willingness
or readiness: He would as *soon* eat four times a
day as not.

soot [sŏŏt *or* sōōt] *n.* A black, powdery substance, mostly carbon, that rises in the air from
the burning of wood, coal, gas, etc.

sooth [sōōth] **1** *n.* Truth: In *sooth*, I saw the
monster. **2** *adj.* True; real. ◆ This word is no
longer used.

soothe [sōōᵺ] *v.* **soothed, sooth·ing 1** To
restore to a quiet or normal state; calm: We
tried to *soothe* the frightened puppy. **2** To soften
or relieve: to *soothe* someone's grief or pain.
3 To have a calming or relieving effect: Soft
colors *soothe*. **4** *adj. use:* a *soothing* sound.

sooth·say·er [sōōth′sā′ər] *n.* A person who
claims to be able to tell what will happen or how
things will turn out. **— sooth′say′ing** *n.*

soot·y [sŏŏt′ē *or* sōō′tē] *adj.* **soot·i·er, soot·i·
est 1** Covered with or blackened by soot.
2 Producing soot: soft, *sooty* coal. **3** Black, like
soot.

sop [sop] *v.* **sopped, sop·ping,** *n.* **1** *v.* To dip
or soak in a liquid: to *sop* bread in milk. **2** *n.* Any
food softened in a liquid, as bread. **3** *v.* To wet
or drench thoroughly; soak: Her dress was *sop-
ping* from the rain. **4** *v.* To take or soak up by
absorption: The old rags *sopped* up the water on
the floor. **5** *n.* Something given to someone to
soothe, satisfy, or please him, as a gift, bribe,
etc.

soph·ist [sof′ist] *n.* **1** A person who argues
cleverly but not always soundly or reasonably.
2 A thinker or philosopher. **— soph′ism** *n.*

add, āce, câre, pälm; end, ēqual; it, īce; odd, ōpen, ôrder; tŏŏk, pōōl; up, bûrn;
ə = a in *above*, e in *sicken*, i in *possible*, o in *melon*, u in *circus*; yōō = u in *fuse*; oil; pout;
check; ring; thin; ᵺhis; zh in *vision*. For ¶ reference, see page 64 · HOW TO

so·phis·ti·cate [sə·fis′tə·kit *or* sə·fis′tə·kāt] *n.*
A sophisticated person.

so·phis·ti·cat·ed [sə·fis′tə·kā′tid] *adj.* **1** Cultured, well-educated, and mature: a *sophisticated* man. **2** Suited to the taste of sophisticated people, as a play or novel. **3** Too wise and experienced in worldly things; lacking a natural simplicity: a *sophisticated* child. **4** Complicated; difficult to operate or maintain: a *sophisticated* machine. **— so·phis′ti·ca′tion** *n.*

soph·is·try [sof′is·trē] *n., pl.* **soph·is·tries**
Argument or reasoning that at first seems correct but actually is false or misleading.

Soph·o·cles [sof′ə·klēz] *n.* 496?–406 B.C., Greek tragic dramatist.

soph·o·more [sof′ə·môr] *n.* In American high schools and colleges, a student in the second year.

sop·py [sop′ē] *adj.* **sop·pi·er, sop·pi·est**
1 Soaked and softened with moisture; very wet: *soppy* shoes. **2** Rainy: *soppy* weather.

so·pran·o [sə·pran′ō] *adj., n., pl.* **so·pran·os**
1 *adj.* Having a high or the highest range, as a voice or instrument. **2** *n.* A soprano voice. **3** *n.* A singer with such a voice. **4** *adj.* Of or for a soprano voice. ◆ *Soprano* comes from an Italian word meaning *above.*

sor·cer·er [sôr′sər·ər] *n.* A wizard, conjurer, or magician.

sor·cer·ess [sôr′sər·is] *n.* A woman sorcerer; witch.

sor·cer·y [sôr′sər·ē] *n., pl.* **sor·cer·ies** The use of magic or witchcraft, usually for some evil purpose.

sor·did [sôr′did] *adj.* **1** Filthy; dirty: a *sordid* area of the city. **2** Mean, selfish, spiteful, etc.: *sordid* desires; a *sordid* argument.

sore [sôr] *adj.* **sor·er, sor·est,** *n.* **1** *adj.* Painful or tender to the touch: a *sore* finger. **2** *adj.* Having or feeling pain: We were *sore* after riding horseback. **3** *n.* A place on the body where the skin is broken, bruised, or inflamed. **4** *adj.* Full of sadness or grief: a *sore* heart. **5** *adj.* Arousing sad or painful feelings: His defeat in the last election is a *sore* point with him. **6** *adj.* Extreme or severe: in *sore* need of money. **7** *adj. informal* Angry: Are you *sore* at me? **— sore′ly** *adv.* **— sore′ness** *n.*

sor·ghum [sôr′gəm] *n.* **1** A tall plant that looks rather like corn, filled with a sweet juice, grown as food for livestock and to make syrup. **2** The sweet syrup made of sorghum.

so·ror·i·ty [sə·rôr′ə·tē] *n., pl.* **so·ror·i·ties** A social club for girls or women, often organized nationally and having local chapters in many schools, colleges, and universities.

sor·rel[1] [sôr′əl] *n.* A plant having sour, edible leaves, used in salads.

sor·rel[2] [sôr′əl] **1** *n., adj.* Reddish brown. **2** *n.* An animal of this color, especially a horse.

sor·row [sor′ō] **1** *n.* Sadness or distress of mind because of some loss or misfortune. **2** *n.* Any event that causes such sadness or distress: The death of a pet animal is a *sorrow.* **3** *v.* To feel or show sorrow; grieve.

sor·row·ful [sor′ə·fəl] *adj.* Feeling, showing, or causing sorrow: a *sorrowful* person; a *sorrowful* event. **— sor′row·ful·ly** *adv.*

sor·ry [sor′ē] *adj.* **sor·ri·er, sor·ri·est**
1 Feeling sorrow or sadness; grieved: We were *sorry* to hear of her accident. **2** Feeling a mild regret: I am *sorry* you have to leave so early. **3** Arousing pity or ridicule: The muddy dog was a *sorry* spectacle.

sort [sôrt] **1** *n.* A kind or type; class: What *sort* of house is that?; a dull *sort* of book. **2** *v.* To divide into groups according to quality, type, etc.: to *sort* eggs by size. **— of sorts** Just passable; not very good: an actor *of sorts.* **— out of sorts** *informal* **1** Mildly ill. **2** Grouchy. **— sort of** *informal* Somewhat; rather: That's *sort of* bad news. ◆ See KIND.

sor·tie [sôr′tē] *n.* **1** An attack of troops from a besieged place on the besiegers. **2** A single military mission against the enemy by one plane.

S O S [es′ō′es′] *n.* **1** The radio signal of distress, used by ships, aircraft, etc. **2** Any call for help.

so-so [sō′sō′] *adj.* Just passable; neither very good nor very bad.

sot [sot] *n.* A habitual drunkard.

sou [sōō] *n., pl.* **sous** A former French coin, worth $\frac{1}{20}$ of a franc.

sou·bri·quet [sōō′bri·kā] *n.* Another spelling of SOBRIQUET.

souf·flé [sōō·flā′] *n.* A light, baked dish made fluffy with beaten egg whites combined with the yolks, often containing cheese, mushrooms, etc.

sough [suf *or* sou] **1** *n.* A rustling sound, as of wind through trees. **2** *v.* To make such a sound.

sought [sôt] Past tense and past participle of SEEK.

soul [sōl] *n.* **1** A part of a person conceived of as being his essential self, within his body but not part of it and not dying with it. **2** Fervor or vitality: His music lacks *soul.* **3** What is essential or vital: Justice is the *soul* of law. **4** A person thought of as being a fine example of a noble quality: the *soul* of generosity. **5** A person: Not a *soul* came.

soul·ful [sōl′fəl] *adj.* Expressing deep feeling: a *soulful* gaze.

soul·less [sōl′lis] *adj.* Without tender feelings; heartless.

sound[1] [sound] **1** *n.* Anything that can be heard. **2** *n.* Energy in the form of pressure waves that travel through air and other elastic materials, being audible when between 20 and 20,000 cycles per second in frequency. **3** *v.* To make a sound. **4** *v.* To cause to sound: *Sound* the bugle. **5** *v.* To pronounce; articulate: *Sound* your *t*'s. **6** *v.* To announce or signal: to *sound* an alarm. **7** *n.* Hearing distance; earshot: within *sound* of the sea. **8** *v.* To seem: The story *sounds* true.

sound[2] [sound] **1** *adj.* Healthy: a *sound* body. **2** *adj.* Without a weakness or defect: *sound* walls. **3** *adj.* True or correct: *sound* reasoning. **4** *adj.* Financially secure; solvent: a *sound* business. **5** *adj.* Not risky: a *sound* venture. **6** *adj.* Deep;

unbroken: a *sound* sleep. **7** *adv*. Completely; deeply: *sound* asleep. **8** *adj*. Thorough: a *sound* beating. — **sound'ly** *adv*. — **sound'ness** *n*.

sound³ [sound] *n*. **1** A long, narrow channel connecting large bodies of water. **2** An inlet of the sea that divides an island from the mainland. **3** A bladder filled with air in the body of a fish by which it controls its equilibrium in the water.

sound⁴ [sound] *v*. **1** To measure the depth of (water) with a weight at the end of a line. **2** To measure (a depth) in such a way. **3** To make a deep, sudden dive, as a whale when harpooned. **4** To examine the views and attitudes of by talking with: to *sound* out a customer.

sound·er [soun'dər] *n*. A device for taking soundings.

sound·ing [soun'ding] *n*. **1** A measurement of depth, as with a weight and line. **2** The depth so measured: a *sounding* of ten fathoms.

Sounding a lake

sound·less [sound'lis] *adj*. Making no sound; silent. — **sound'less·ly** *adv*.

sound·proof [sound'proof'] **1** *adj*. That excludes or confines sound: a *soundproof* room. **2** *v*. To make soundproof.

sound track The part of a motion-picture film on which the sound is recorded.

soup [soop] *n*. Liquid food made by boiling meat, vegetables, fish, or any mixture of them.

sour [sour] **1** *adj*. Having a sharp, acid taste like that of vinegar, lemon juice, or spoiled milk. **2** *v*. To make or become sour. **3** *adj*. Unpleasant or disagreeable. **4** *adj*. Morose, crabbed, or disgusted. **5** *v*. To make bitter or disgusted. **6** *adj*. Too acid to grow crops on, as soil. — **sour'ly** *adv*. — **sour'ness** *n*.

source [sôrs] *n*. **1** The beginning of a stream or river, as a spring, lake, or glacier. **2** A person or thing from which something originates or comes.

souse [sous] *v*. **soused, sous·ing,** *n*. **1** *v*. To dip or steep in a liquid. **2** *v*. To pickle. **3** *n*. The act of sousing. **4** *n*. Something pickled, especially the feet and ears of a pig. **5** *n*. A liquid used in pickling; brine.

south [south] **1** *n*. The direction opposite north; one of the four main points of the compass. If you face the sun at sunrise, south is on your right. **2** *adj*. To, toward, or in the south; southern. **3** *adj*. Coming from the south: the *south* wind. **4** *adv*. In or toward the south; southward. — **south of** Farther south than: Utah is *south of* Idaho. — **the South 1** The southern and

southeastern U.S., especially the part south of the Mason-Dixon line, the Ohio River, and Missouri. **2** The Confederacy.

South Africa, Republic of A country in the extreme southern part of Africa.

South African 1 Of or from South Africa. **2** A person born in or a citizen of South Africa.

South America The southern continent of the Western Hemisphere.

South American 1 Of or from South America. **2** A person born or living in South America.

South Carolina A state in the SE U.S.

South Da·ko·ta [də·kō'tə] A state in the north central U.S.

south·east [south'ēst'] **1** *n*. The direction midway between south and east. **2** *adj*. To, toward, or in the southeast. **3** *adj*. Coming from the southeast: a *southeast* wind. **4** *adv*. In or toward the southeast. — **southeast of** Farther southeast than: Pittsburgh is *southeast of* Detroit. — **the Southeast** The southeastern U.S.

south·east·er [south'ēs'tər] *n*. A gale or storm from the southeast.

south·east·er·ly [south'ēs'tər·lē] *adj., adv.* **1** Toward or in the southeast. **2** From the southeast.

south·east·ern [south'ēs'tərn] *adj*. **1** Of or from the southeast. **2** Toward or in the southeast: the *southeastern* part.

south·er·ly [suth'ər·lē] *adj*. **1** Toward the south. **2** From the south: a *southerly* wind.

south·ern [suth'ərn] *adj*. **1** Of or from the south. **2** Toward or in the south: the *southern* part. **3** (*sometimes written* **Southern**) Of or having to do with the South.

Southern Cross A southern constellation having four bright stars in the form of a cross.

south·ern·er [suth'ərn·ər] *n*. **1** A person born or living in the south. **2** (*often written* **Southerner**) A person born or living in the southern part of the U.S.

Southern Hemisphere The half of the earth south of the equator.

south·ern·most [suth'ərn·mōst'] *adj*. Farthest south.

south·paw [south'pô'] *informal* **1** *n*. In baseball, a left-handed pitcher. **2** *n*. Any left-handed person. **3** *adj*. Left-handed.

South Pole The southern end of the earth's axis; the southernmost point of the earth.

South Sea Islands The islands of the South Pacific Ocean. — **South Sea Islander**

South Vietnam See VIETNAM.

south·ward [south'wərd] **1** *adv., adj.* To or toward the south. **2** *n*. A southward direction or location.

south·wards [south'wərdz] *adv*. Southward.

south·west [south'west'] **1** *n*. The direction midway between south and west. **2** *adj*. To, toward, or in the southwest: the *southwest* part.

north
west ◄———► east
south

3 *adj.* Coming from the southwest: a *southwest* wind. **4** *adv.* In or toward the southwest. **— southwest of** Farther southwest than: Kansas is *southwest of* Iowa. **— the Southwest** The southwestern U.S.

south·west·er [south′wes′tər] *n.* **1** A gale or storm from the southwest. **2** A waterproof hat of oilskin, canvas, etc., with a broad brim behind to protect the neck.

Southwester

south·west·er·ly [south′-wes′tər·lē] *adj., adv.* **1** Toward or in the southwest. **2** From the southwest.

south·west·ern [south′-wes′tərn] *adj.* **1** Of or from the southwest. **2** Toward or in the southwest: the *southwestern* part.

sou·ve·nir [soo′və·nir′] *n.* Something that is kept as a reminder of the past: My mother has many *souvenirs* from her school days.

sov·er·eign [sov′rən] **1** *n.* A monarch; king or queen. **2** *adj.* Having supreme power: a *sovereign* lord. **3** *adj.* Supreme; greatest: the *sovereign* good of the people. **4** *adj.* Free and independent: a *sovereign* nation. **5** *n.* A former British gold coin worth one pound.

sov·er·eign·ty [sov′rən·tē] *n., pl.* **sov·er·eign·ties 1** Supreme authority or power. **2** The rank or status of a sovereign. **3** The condition of being independent and under self-government: the *sovereignty* of a nation.

so·vi·et [sō′vē·et] **1** *adj.* (*written* **Soviet**) Of or having to do with the Soviet Union. **2** *n.* Any of various councils in the Soviet Union formed to govern villages, towns, and larger units. The highest legislative body is called the **Supreme Soviet.**

Soviet Russia The largest republic of the Soviet Union, making up 76% of its total area.

Soviet Union A union of 15 republics occupying most of northern Eurasia. Its official name is the Union of Soviet Socialist Republics.

sow[1] [sō] *v.* **sowed, sown** or **sowed, sow·ing 1** To plant (seed) in the ground so that it will grow. **2** To scatter seed over (land). **3** To spread about; implant: to *sow* suspicion. **— sow′er** *n.*

sow[2] [sou] *n.* A female hog.

soy [soi] *n.* **1** A sauce prepared from soybeans fermented and pickled, used on Chinese and Japanese foods. **2** A soybean.

soy·bean [soi′bēn′] *n.* **1** The edible seed of an Asian plant, widely grown also as a source of oil, flour, and other products. **2** The plant itself.

spa [spä] *n.* **1** A spring of mineral water. **2** A health resort having such a spring or springs.

space [spās] *n., v.* **spaced, spac·ing 1** *n.* The region having an indefinite or boundless height, width, and depth, in parts of which all material things are located. **2** *n.* The region outside the earth's atmosphere; outer space. **3** *adj. use:* a *space* capsule; the *Space* Age. **4** *n.* The area or distance between two or more objects or points,

or the area inside of something: a cupboard with lots of *space*. **5** *n.* A distance or period of time; interval. **6** *v.* To separate by spaces: to *space* chairs. **7** *v.* To put spaces between.

space·craft [spās′kraft′] *n.* A vehicle, such as a rocket or artificial satellite, designed for research or travel in outer space.

space·man [spās′mən] *n., pl.* **space·men** [spās′mən] An astronaut.

space platform A space station.

space·ship [spās′ship′] *n.* A spacecraft.

space station A satellite designed as a base for research or for launching spacecraft.

spac·ing [spā′sing] *n.* **1** The act of separating things so as to leave space between them. **2** The way spaces are arranged. **3** A space or spaces, as between words or lines in print.

spa·cious [spā′shəs] *adj.* Full of open space; roomy; vast: a *spacious* house.

spade[1] [spād] *n., v.* **spad·ed, spad·ing 1** *n.* A tool resembling a shovel, but having a flatter blade. **2** *v.* To dig with a spade. **— call a spade a spade** To speak the plain truth.

spade[2] [spād] *n.* **1** A figure like this: ♠. **2** A playing card of the suit marked with black spades. **3** (*pl.*) The suit of cards so marked.

spa·ghet·ti [spə·get′ē] *n.* Long slender strings of flour paste, boiled as food.

Spain [spān] *n.* A country in SW Europe.

spake [spāk] An alternative past tense of SPEAK: seldom used today: Thus *spake* Moses.

span[1] [span] *n., v.* **spanned, span·ning 1** *n.* The greatest distance that the tips of the thumb and little finger can be spread apart, about 9 inches for a man's hand. **2** *v.* To measure by spans. **3** *v.* To stretch or extend across: The bridge *spans* the river. **4** *n.* The distance between the supports of an arch, bridge, etc. **5** *n.* An interval or distance: a *span* of a week.

span[2] [span] *n.* A team of two oxen or other beasts of burden harnessed together.

span·gle [spang′gəl] *n., v.* **span·gled, span·gling 1** *n.* A small bit of sparkling metal, plastic, etc., used as a decoration on cloth, jewelry, etc. **2** *n.* Any small, sparkling object. **3** *v.* To decorate with or as if with spangles.

Span·iard [span′yərd] *n.* A person born in or a citizen of Spain.

span·iel [span′yəl] *n.* A small or medium-sized dog with large, drooping ears and usually long, silky hair.

Span·ish [span′ish] **1** *adj.* Of or from Spain. **2** *n.* (**the Spanish**) The people of Spain. **3** *n.* The language of Spain and Spanish America.

A typical spaniel

Spanish America The parts of the Western Hemisphere in which Spanish is the main language.

Span·ish-A·mer·i·can [span′ish·ə·mer′ə·kən] **1** *adj.* Of or having to do with Spanish America. **2** *adj.* Of or having to do with Spain and the U.S. **3** *n.* A person born or living in Spanish America.

Spanish-American War A war between Spain and the U.S., fought in 1898.

Spanish Main 1 In former times, South America, especially the northern coast. **2** The Caribbean Sea.

spank [spangk] **1** *v.* To smack with the open hand, a slipper, etc. **2** *n.* A slap with the open hand, a slipper, etc.

spank·ing [spangk′ing] **1** *n.* A series of slaps with the open hand, a slipper, etc. **2** *adj.* Brisk; lively: a *spanking* breeze.

spar[1] [spär] *v.* **sparred, spar·ring 1** To box, especially carefully and skillfully. **2** To argue; wrangle.

spar[2] [spär] *n., v.* **sparred, spar·ring 1** *n.* A mast, yard, boom, etc., that supports or extends a sail. **2** *v.* To furnish (a ship) with spars.

spar[3] [spär] *n.* Any of various shiny, crystalline minerals that cleave easily.

spare [spâr] *adj.* **spar·er, spar·est,** *n., v.* **spared, spar·ing 1** *adj.* Extra or available: *spare* parts. **2** *n.* An extra thing in reserve, as a tire. **3** *v.* To refrain from injuring or destroying: *Spare* his life. **4** *v.* To free or relieve from something unpleasant or harmful: to *spare* a patient pain during an operation. **5** *v.* To part with; give up: to *spare* a dime. **6** *adj.* Scanty or lean: *spare* pickings; a *spare*, wiry man. **7** *v.* To refrain from using, or use in small amounts: to *spare* neither trouble nor expense. **8** *n.* In bowling, the knocking over of all the pins with two rolls of the ball. — **spare′ly** *adv.*

spare·rib [spâr′rib′] *n.* (*usually pl.*) A rib of pork without much meat on it.

spar·ing [spâr′ing] *adj.* Not wasteful or extravagant; frugal. — **spar′ing·ly** *adv.*

spark [spärk] **1** *n.* A small, glowing particle thrown off by a fire, a hot material, etc. **2** *n.* A short flash made by an electric current when it jumps across a gap. **3** *n.* Any bright point of light. **4** *v.* To give off sparks. **5** *v.* To activate or cause: to *spark* a revolt. **6** *n.* A faint trace; glimmer: a *spark* of hope.

spar·kle [spär′kəl] *v.* **spar·kled, spar·kling,** *n.* **1** *v.* To emit sparks or flashes. **2** *adj. use:* *sparkling* diamonds. **3** *n.* A spark or flash. **4** *v.* To bubble, as soda water. **5** *v.* To be witty and lively: The conversation *sparkled.* **6** *adj. use:* *sparkling* wit.

spar·kler [spär′klər] *n.* **1** A thing that sparkles, as a gem. **2** A thin, rodlike type of fireworks that gives off sparks when lighted.

spark plug A device for igniting the fuel mixture in an internal combustion engine by an electric spark.

spar·row [spar′ō] *n.* **1** Any of several small finches. **2** A related bird, a pest in the U.S.

Sparrow, 5–6 in. long

sparse [spärs] *adj.* **spars·er, spars·est** Thinly scattered; not dense: *sparse* woods; a *sparse* crowd. — **sparse′ly** *adv.*

Spar·ta [spär′tə] *n.* A city in ancient Greece.

Spar·tan [spär′tən] **1** *adj.* Of or having to do with Sparta. **2** *n.* A person born or living in ancient Sparta. **3** *adj.* Like the Spartans in character; stern, self-denying, and courageous. **4** *n.* A person of Spartan character.

spasm [spaz′əm] *n.* **1** A sudden, involuntary contraction of a muscle or muscles. **2** Any sudden, brief burst of energy or activity.

spas·mod·ic [spaz·mod′ik] *adj.* Like a spasm; sudden, often intense, and irregular: a *spasmodic* twitch; *spasmodic* bursts of activity. — **spas·mod′i·cal·ly** *adv.*

spas·tic [spas′tik] **1** *adj.* Of, having to do with, or suffering from spasms: a *spastic* muscle. **2** *n.* A person who is afflicted with spasms of the muscles or has cerebral palsy.

spat[1] [spat] *n., v.* **spat·ted, spat·ting 1** *n.* A small quarrel. **2** *v.* To have a small quarrel. **3** *n.* A slight blow; slap. **4** *v.* To slap.

spat[2] [spat] *n.* (*usually pl.*) A cloth covering for the ankle and instep, overlapping the shoe.

spat[3] [spat] Past tense and past participle of SPIT[1].

spa·tial [spā′shəl] *adj.* **1** Of, in, or having to do with space. — **spa′tial·ly** *adv.*

spat·ter [spat′ər] **1** *v.* To fall, scatter, or strike in drops or a shower: Rain *spattered* on the roof; Grease *spattered* her apron. **2** *v.* To stain or mark by or as if by spattering: He *spattered* his shirt with ink. **3** *n.* The act of spattering. **4** *n.* Something that has been spattered; splash: a *spatter* of mud.

spat·u·la [spach′ŏŏ·lə] *n.* A tool with a flat flexible blade, used in mixing, spreading, or lifting foods, mixing paints or drugs, etc.

spav·in [spav′in] *n.* A disease in which the hock of a horse stiffens or swells, causing lameness.

spav·ined [spav′ind] *adj.* Lamed by spavin.

Spatula

spawn [spôn] **1** *n.* The eggs or new offspring of fishes or other water animals. **2** *v.* To deposit great numbers of eggs. **3** *n.* Offspring, especially in huge numbers. **4** *v.* To give rise to: to *spawn* trouble.

speak [spēk] *v.* **spoke** (or **spake:** seldom used today), **speak·ing, spo·ken 1** To say words; talk. **2** To express or tell in this way: to *speak* one's ideas. **3** To make a speech. **4** To use or be able to use (a language) in conversation: to *speak* Spanish. — **so to speak** One might say; to put it this way: He's in a fog, *so to speak.* — **speak for 1** To speak on behalf of. **2** To request. — **speak out** To speak openly or frankly. — **speak up** To make oneself heard. — **speak well for** To show favorably; recommend.

speak·er [spē'kər] *n.* **1** A person who speaks. **2** A person who gives a speech. **3** In certain legislative bodies, the chairman: the *Speaker* of the Assembly. **4** A loudspeaker.

spear [spir] **1** *n.* A long pole with a pointed head at one end, used as a weapon in war, hunting, etc. **2** *v.* To pierce or catch with a spear: to *spear* fish. **3** *n.* A slender leaf or stalk.

spear·head [spir'hed'] **1** *n.* The point of a spear. **2** *n.* The person or group that leads a project, military attack, etc. **3** *v.* To be first in or lead (an attack, etc.).

Spear

spear·mint [spir'mint'] *n.* A plant, a common mint similar to peppermint.

spe·cial [spesh'əl] **1** *adj.* Of a particular kind; distinctive; out of the ordinary: Please do me a *special* favor. **2** *adj.* For a particular purpose or service: a *special* messenger; a *special* train to New York. **3** *n.* A person or thing selected for a special duty, service, etc. **4** *adj.* Intimate; close: a *special* friend.

special delivery Mail delivery at extra cost in advance of the regular delivery.

spe·cial·ist [spesh'əl·ist] *n.* A person who specializes, especially a doctor who concentrates on one branch of medicine.

spe·cial·ize [spesh'əl·īz] *v.* **spe·cial·ized, spe·cial·iz·ing 1** To concentrate on one particular activity or subject. **2** To make or become fit for a particular use, environment, etc. **3** *adj. use:* a *specialized* tool. ¶3

spe·cial·ly [spesh'ə·lē] *adv.* **1** Unusually; distinctively. **2** In a special way.

spe·cial·ty [spesh'əl·tē] *n., pl.* **spe·cial·ties 1** A special study, occupation, etc.: Engineering is his *specialty*. **2** The condition of being special or unusual. **3** A specially featured or outstanding thing: This restaurant makes a *specialty* of Chinese food.

spe·cie [spē'shē] *n.* Coined money; coin.

spe·cies [spē'shēz *or* spē'sēz] *n., pl.* **spe·cies 1** A group of living things that are more or less alike and whose members can interbreed and produce fertile offspring: Leopards and lions are of different *species*. **2** Kind; sort; type.

spe·cif·ic [spi·sif'ik] **1** *adj.* Particular; definite. **2** *n.* Something specific, especially a medicine for a particular disease. **3** *adj.* In biology, of or having to do with a species. — **spe·cif'i·cal·ly** *adv.*

spec·i·fi·ca·tion [spes'ə·fə·kā'shən] *n.* **1** The act of specifying. **2** Something specified, as in a contract, plans, etc. **3** (*usually pl.*) A specific description of types of materials, dimensions, etc.,

to be used in manufacturing or building something.

specific gravity The ratio of the density of a substance to that of water if it is liquid or solid or to that of air or hydrogen if it is a gas.

spec·i·fy [spes'ə·fī] *v.* **spec·i·fied, spec·i·fy·ing 1** To indicate particularly; make definite. **2** To include in a set of specifications.

spec·i·men [spes'ə·mən] *n.* One person or thing of a group, or a small amount taken as a sample of a whole: a fine *specimen* of manhood; a blood *specimen*.

spe·cious [spē'shəs] *adj.* Seeming good, right, or true, but actually not so: a *specious* promise; *specious* reasoning.

speck [spek] **1** *n.* A tiny stain or particle: There is a *speck* of grease on my new tie. **2** *v.* To mark or cover with specks.

speck·le [spek'əl] *v.* **speck·led, speck·ling,** *n.* **1** *v.* To mark with specks: The red dress was *speckled* with gold. **2** *adj. use:* a *speckled* bird. **3** *n.* A speck.

spec·ta·cle [spek'tə·kəl] *n.* **1** Something exhibited to the public, especially something grand and showy. **2** An unusual or painful sight: The beggar on the street was a *spectacle*. **3** (*pl.*) A pair of eyeglasses.

spec·tac·u·lar [spek·tak'yə·lər] **1** *adj.* Amazing to behold: a *spectacular* feat. **2** *adj.* Done on a grand scale: a *spectacular* film. **3** *n.* An imposing spectacle. — **spec·tac'u·lar·ly** *adv.*

spec·ta·tor [spek'tā·tər] *n.* A person who watches an event without taking part in it.

spec·ter [spek'tər] *n.* A ghost. ¶2

spec·tral [spek'trəl] *adj.* **1** Of or like a specter; ghostly. **2** Of or having to do with a spectrum or spectra.

spec·tro·graph [spek'trə·graf] *n.* An instrument for photographing spectra.

spec·tro·scope [spek'trə·skōp] *n.* An instrument that breaks light into spectra for observation.

spec·trum [spek'trəm] *n., pl.* **spec·tra** [spek'trə] **1** The rainbowlike band of color or pattern of lines seen when light from a source is separated according to wavelengths. The visible spectrum of the sun goes from red (long waves) to violet (short waves). **2** A continuous range of wavelengths: the radio *spectrum*.

spec·u·late [spek'yə·lāt] *v.* **spec·u·lat·ed, spec·u·lat·ing 1** To form theories; meditate; ponder; think: People *speculated* about living beings on Mars. **2** To invest money where there is a considerable risk of loss but the possibility of large profits. — **spec·u·la'tor** *n.*

spec·u·la·tion [spek'yə·lā'shən] *n.* **1** The act of speculating. **2** A theory; conjecture. **3** A risky investment of money.

spec·u·la·tive [spek'yə·lā'tiv *or* spek'yə·lə·tiv] *adj.* **1** Based on a guess: a *speculative* reply. **2** Inclined to speculate; reflective: a *speculative* thinker. **3** That is or involves a financial risk: *speculative* buying of stocks.

sped [sped] Past tense of SPEED.

speech [spēch] *n.* **1** The act of speaking; the saying of words. **2** The ability to speak: His *speech* was impaired. **3** A way of speaking that characterizes a person or group: Her *speech* was soft and pleasant; educated *speech*; the *speech* of Mexican farm workers. **4** Something that is spoken, especially a public address or talk: The audience applauded his *speech*.

speech·less [spēch′lis] *adj.* **1** Unable to speak: Dogs are *speechless*. **2** Beyond words, especially because of strong emotion: *speechless* with joy. — **speech′less·ly** *adv.* — **speech′less·ness** *n.*

speed [spēd] *n., v.* **sped, speed·ing** **1** *n.* The distance traveled per unit of time; rate: a *speed* of 4 miles an hour. **2** *n.* Any rate of progress or action: to read at a high *speed*. **3** *v.* To go or cause to go fast or faster: The train *sped* along; Fear *sped* him on. **4** *v.* To drive a motor vehicle faster than the law permits. **5** *n.* A gear of a motor vehicle: a sports car with four forward *speeds*. **6** *n.* Good luck: seldom used today. **7** *v.* To wish (a person) a successful journey. **8** *v.* To promote the success of. — **speed up** To accelerate. — **speed′i·ly** *adv.* ◆ *Speed* comes from the Old English word for *luck* or *prosperity*.

speed·boat [spēd′bōt′] *n.* A fast motorboat.

speed·er [spē′dər] *n.* A person or thing that speeds, especially a person who drives at reckless or illegal speeds.

speed·om·e·ter [spi·dom′ə·tər] *n.* An instrument that shows a driver at what speed his vehicle is traveling.

speed·way [spēd′wā′] *n.* A road for vehicles traveling at high speed.

speed·y [spē′dē] *adj.* **speed·i·er, speed·i·est** Swift; fast; rapid. — **speed′i·ly** *adv.*

spell[1] [spel] *v.* **spelled** or **spelt, spell·ing** **1** To name or write the letters of (a word) in their correct order. **2** To form or be the letters of: C-a-t *spells* cat. **3** To be equivalent to: Timidity *spells* failure. — **spell out** **1** To read with difficulty. **2** To indicate clearly: He *spelled out* his plans.

spell[2] [spel] *n.* **1** A word or words supposedly having magical power; charm. **2** An irresistible fascination or charm.

spell[3] [spel] **1** *n.* An indefinite time. **2** *n.* A time characterized by something: a *spell* of drought. **3** *n.* A fit of unconsciousness, weakness, etc.: a fainting *spell*. **4** *v.* To relieve temporarily of some work or duty: I will *spell* you at painting the woodwork. **5** *n.* Such a turn of duty.

spell·bind·er [spel′bin′dər] *n.* A speaker able to hold his audience spellbound.

spell·bind·ing [spel′bin′ding] *adj.* Fascinating; enchanting.

spell·bound [spel′bound′] *adj.* Fascinated, as if bound by a spell.

spell·er [spel′ər] *n.* **1** A person who spells. **2** An elementary book of exercises in spelling.

spell·ing [spel′ing] *n.* **1** The act of naming or writing down in order the letters which spell a word. **2** The way a person spells.

spelling bee A gathering at which contestants compete in spelling words.

spelt [spelt] An alternative past tense and past participle of SPELL[1].

spend [spend] *v.* **spent, spend·ing** **1** To exchange (money) for goods or services. **2** To use or use up: to *spend* time. **3** To pass or occupy: He *spent* his life helping others.

spend·thrift [spend′thrift′] **1** *n.* Someone who spends money wastefully or foolishly. **2** *adj. use:* a *spendthrift* husband.

Spen·ser [spen′sər], **Edmund,** 1552?–1599, English poet.

spent [spent] **1** Past tense and past participle of SPEND. **2** *adj.* Worn out or used up. **3** *adj.* Having lost its force: a *spent* bullet.

sperm [spûrm] *n.* **1** The fertilizing fluid of a male animal, containing his fully matured reproductive cells. **2** One of these cells.

sper·ma·ce·ti [spûr′mə·set′ē] *n.* A waxy substance obtained from the oil of the sperm whale, used for making candles, ointments, etc.

sperm whale A large, toothed whale of tropical waters, highly valued for its oil.

Sperm whale, 30–60 ft. long

spew [spyōō] **1** *v.* To throw up; vomit: The volcano *spewed* lava. **2** *n.* That which is spewed.

sphere [sfir] *n.* **1** A surface that has all its points the same distance from a particular point called its center; ball. **2** A range or scope: a *sphere* of activity. **3** A level of society; circle.

spher·i·cal [sfer′i·kəl] *adj.* **1** Shaped like a sphere; round; globular. **2** Of or having to do with a sphere or spheres.

sphe·roid [sfir′oid] *n.* An object shaped almost like a sphere.

sphinx [sfingks] *n., pl.* **sphinx·es** or **sphin·ges** [sfin′jēz] **1** In Egyptian myths, a monster with a lion's body and the head of a man, ram, or hawk. **2** A statue of a sphinx. **3** In Greek myths, a monster with wings, a woman's head, and a lion's body, who killed those who failed to guess her riddle. **4** A puzzling or mysterious person. — **the Sphinx** A huge sphinx with a man's head near Cairo, Egypt.

A Greek sphinx

spice [spīs] *n., v.* **spiced, spic·ing** **1** *n.* Any of various vegetable sub-

---

add, āce, câre, pälm; end, ēqual; it, īce; odd, ōpen, ôrder; tŏŏk, pōōl; up, bûrn; ə = a in *above*, e in *sicken*, i in *possible*, o in *melon*, u in *circus*; yōō = u in *fuse*; oil; pout; check; ring; thin; this; zh in *vision*. For ¶ reference, see page 64 · HOW TO

stances, as cloves, nutmeg, etc., used to flavor food. **2** *v.* To season with spice. **3** *n.* Something that adds zest or interest. **4** *v.* To add zest or interest to: to *spice* a talk with jokes.

spick-and-span [spik′ən·span′] *adj.* **1** Neat and clean. **2** Brand new.

spic·y [spī′sē] *adj.* **spic·i·er, spic·i·est 1** Flavored with spices. **2** Having a sharp taste or odor; pungent. **3** Lively or zestful. — **spic′i·ness** *n.*

spi·der [spī′dər] *n.* **1** A small animal with no wings, eight legs, and a body in two segments; a type of arachnid. Many spiders spin webs and catch insects for food. **2** A frying pan with a long handle, sometimes having legs.

Black widow spider, to 1/2 in. long

spi·der·y [spī′dər·ē] *adj.* **1** Like a spider. **2** Thin; fine; delicate, like a spider's legs or web.

spied [spīd] Past tense and past participle of SPY.

spig·ot [spig′ət] *n.* **1** A faucet. **2** A plug or valve to stop up the hole of a cask.

spike¹ [spīk] *n., v.* **spiked, spik·ing 1** *n.* A very large nail. **2** *v.* To fasten, join, or pierce with a spike or spikes. **3** *n.* A sharp or pointed metal projection, as on the top of a fence or on the sole of certain shoes worn in sports. **4** *v.* To provide with spikes. **5** *v.* To pierce with or impale on a spike. **6** *v.* To make useless or unable to function: to *spike* a false rumor.

spike² [spīk] *n.* **1** An ear of grain. **2** A cluster of numerous flowers arranged closely on a long stalk.

spike·nard [spīk′nərd] *n.* A fragrant and costly ointment used in ancient times.

spill¹ [spil] *v.* **spilled** or **spilt, spill·ing,** *n.* **1** *v.* To cause or allow to run out, slop, or fall: The child *spilled* a glass of milk on the table. **2** *v.* To fall, run out, or flow: Milk *spilled* off the table; Water *spilled* over the dam. **3** *n.* The action of spilling. **4** *v.* To shed, as blood. **5** *v.* To cause to fall: The horse *spilled* its rider. **6** *n.* A fall; tumble: I took a bad *spill* on a waxed floor. — **spill the beans** *informal* To give away a secret.

spill² [spil] *n.* A thin strip of wood or rolled paper used for lighting lamps, fires, etc.

spill·way [spil′wā′] *n.* A channel, as in a dam, to let surplus water run off.

spilt [spilt] An alternative past tense and past participle of SPILL¹.

spin [spin] *v.* **spun, spin·ning,** *n.* **1** *v.* To draw out and twist (cotton, flax, etc.) into thread. **2** *v.* To make fibers into (threads, yarn, etc.) by spinning. **3** *v.* To make (a web, cocoon, etc.) from

Spillway

secreted filaments. **4** *v.* To turn or whirl about; revolve; rotate: to *spin* a top. **5** *n.* A turning or whirling about. **6** *v.* To have a feeling of whirling: Excitement made his head *spin.* **7** *v.* To make up or relate (a story or tale). **8** *n.* A ride or drive, often for pleasure. **9** *v.* To go along rapidly. — **spin′ner** *n.*

spin·ach [spin′ich] *n.* **1** A common herb with large, dark green leaves. **2** These leaves, eaten as a vegetable, usually cooked.

spi·nal [spī′nəl] *adj.* Of, in, or having to do with the spine.

spinal column The series of connected bones that form the main support of a vertebrate skeleton; backbone.

spinal cord The cord of nerve tissue inside the spinal column that with the brain forms the central nervous system.

spin·dle [spin′dəl] *n., v.* **spin·dled, spin·dling 1** *n.* A rod on which thread is wound in spinning. **2** *n.* A rod or shaft that turns or on which something turns, as an axle. **3** *v.* To become long and slender, as a plant stalk.

spin·dle-leg·ged [spin′dəl·leg′id *or* spin′dəl·legd′] *adj.* Having long, slender legs.

spin·dling [spind′ling] *adj.* Unusually tall and thin: a *spindling* young tree.

spin·dly [spind′lē] *adj.* **spin·dli·er, spin·dli·est** Spindling.

spin·drift [spin′drift] *n.* Spray blown over the water from the crests of waves.

spine [spīn] *n.* **1** The spinal column; backbone. **2** The main support of something, as the back of a bound book. **3** A hard, pointed growth on a plant or animal, as a thorn on hawthorn or a porcupine's quill.

spine·less [spīn′lis] *adj.* **1** Having no spine or backbone. **2** Without spines. **3** Cowardly.

spin·et [spin′it] *n.* A small harpsichord or low upright piano.

spin·na·ker [spin′ə·kər] *n.* A large, bellying, triangular sail, often set on the other side of the mast from the mainsail of a racing yacht when sailing before the wind.

spin·ner·et [spin′ə·ret] *n.* An organ, as of spiders and silkworms, by which fine thread is spun for webs, cocoons, etc.

spin·ney [spin′ē] *n., pl.* **spin·neys** *British* A small wooded area; thicket.

spinning jenny An early type of spinning machine on which one person could spin several threads at once.

spinning wheel A device for spinning yarn or thread, consisting of a spindle rotated by a large wheel and operated by a treadle.

Spinning wheel

spin·ster [spin′stər] *n.* An unmarried woman, especially one no longer young; old maid.

spin·y [spī′nē] *adj.* **spin·i·er, spin·i·est 1** Like a spine. **2** Having spines; thorny.

spir·a·cle [spir′ə·kəl *or* spī′rə·kəl] *n.* An opening through which various animals breathe, as those on an insect's sides or the one on top of a whale's head.

spi·ral [spī′rəl] *n., adj., v.* **spi·raled** or **spi·ralled, spi·ral·ing** or **spi·ral·ling 1** *n.* A curve traced by a point that moves in a plane and around a fixed center from which its distance continuously increases or decreases. **2** *n.* A curve resembling the thread of a screw; helix. **3** *adj.* Winding or curving like a spiral: a *spiral* staircase; a *spiral* path. **4** *v.* To take or cause to take a spiral path or form. — **spi′ral·ly** *adv.*

spire¹ [spīr] *n.* **1** The pointed top of a tower, steeple, etc. **2** Something that looks like a spire, as a mountain peak.

spire² [spīr] *n.* A spiral or coil.

spi·ril·lum [spī·ril′əm] *n., pl.* **spi·ril·lums** or **spi·ril·la** [spī·ril′ə] Any of a group of active bacteria whose rodlike bodies are twisted into spirals.

spir·it [spir′it] **1** *n.* The life-giving force within a living thing; in man, soul. **2** *n.* A divine being, such as God or an angel. **3** *n.* Any of various supernatural beings, as ghosts, goblins, elves, etc. **4** *adj. use:* the *spirit* world. **5** *n.* Energy; vitality; liveliness: a horse with *spirit.* **6** *n.* A person considered as a vital force: the moving *spirit* of the town. **7** *n.* (*pl.*) State of mind; mood: The news raised his *spirits.* **8** *n.* A widely held feeling or tendency: a *spirit* of rebellion. **9** *n.* Loyalty or devotion: school *spirit.* **10** *n.* Real intent rather than outward form: the *spirit* of the law. **11** *n.* (*pl.*) Strong alcoholic liquor. **12** *n.* (*pl.*) A concentrated substance drawn out or distilled from another: *spirits* of turpentine. **13** *n.* (*pl.*) A solution in alcohol: *spirits* of camphor. **14** *v.* To carry off secretly or mysteriously: The rare book had been *spirited* away.

spir·it·ed [spir′it·id] *adj.* **1** Full of spirit; lively; vigorous: a *spirited* debate; a *spirited* horse. **2** Having a certain kind of spirit or nature: a greedy, *mean-spirited* man. — **spir′it·ed·ly** *adv.* — **spir′it·ed·ness** *n.*

spirit lamp A lamp that burns alcohol or a similar fuel.

spir·it·less [spir′ti·lis] *adj.* Lacking vigor, courage, or enthusiasm; listless.

spir·i·tu·al [spir′i·chōō·əl] **1** *adj.* Of, like, or having to do with the soul or spirit. **2** *adj.* Religious: a *spiritual* life or person; *spiritual* leaders. **3** *n.* A religious folk song originating among the Negroes of the southern U.S. — **spir·i·tu·al·i·ty** [spir′i·chōō·al′ə·tē] *n.* — **spir′·i·tu·al·ly** *adv.*

spir·i·tu·al·ism [spir′i·chōō·əl·iz′əm] *n.* The belief that the spirits of the dead communicate with the living. — **spir′i·tu·al·ist** *n.*

spir·i·tu·ous [spir′i·chōō·əs] *adj.* Containing alcohol, as a distilled liquor.

spi·ro·chete or **spi·ro·chaete** [spī′rə·kēt] *n.* Any of a group of bacteria having flexible, corkscrew-shaped bodies.

spi·ro·gy·ra [spī′rə·jī′rə] *n.* A kind of algae commonly found in ponds.

spirt [spûrt] *n., v.* Another spelling of SPURT.

spit¹ [spit] *v.* **spat** or **spit, spit·ting,** *n.* **1** *v.* To blow or force out saliva, etc., from the mouth. **2** *n.* Spittle; saliva. **3** *n.* An act of spitting. **4** *v.* To throw out or utter violently: to *spit* out a reply. **5** *v.* To hiss or sputter, as does an angry cat. — **spit and image** or **spitting image** *informal* An exact likeness: She is the *spit and image* of her sister.

spit² [spit] *n., v.* **spit·ted, spit·ting 1** *n.* A rod on which meat is speared and roasted. **2** *v.* To pierce with or as if with a spit. **3** *n.* A narrow point of land jutting from a shore.

spite [spīt] *n., v.* **spit·ed, spit·ing 1** *n.* Bitter resentment that leads to mean actions; ill will: She refused out of *spite.* **2** *v.* To show spite toward; try to hurt: He said that just to *spite* you. — **in spite of** Despite; notwithstanding: *In spite of* all his troubles, he was always cheerful.

spite·ful [spīt′fəl] *adj.* **1** Filled with spite. **2** Prompted by spite: a *spiteful* act. — **spite′·ful·ly** *adv.* — **spite′ful·ness** *n.*

spit·fire [spit′fīr′] *n.* A quick-tempered, fiery person, especially a woman or girl.

spit·tle [spit′(ə)l] *n.* The fluid secreted in the mouth; saliva; spit.

spit·toon [spi·tōōn′] *n.* A receptacle to spit into.

splash [splash] **1** *v.* To dash or spatter about: to *splash* mud. **2** *v.* To spatter, wet, or soil in this way: to *splash* a dress with mud. **3** *n.* The act or noise of splashing. **4** *n.* A mark resulting from a splash. **5** *v.* To move, fall, etc., with a splash or splashes: He *splashed* into the pool. **6** *n. informal* A striking impression or success, especially in the phrase **make a splash:** The book *made* quite *a splash.*

splash·y [splash′ē] *adj.* **splash·i·er, splash·i·est 1** Marked by or as if by splashes; blotchy. **2** *informal* Sensational; showy: a *splashy* sports car.

splat·ter [splat′ər] **1** *v.* To spatter or splash. **2** *n.* A spatter or splash.

splay [splā] **1** *adj.* Spread out or broad, especially in an awkward or ungainly way: *splay* feet. **2** *v.* To spread outward; open. **3** *n.* A slanted surface or beveled edge. **4** *v.* To make (a doorway, window opening, etc.) with a splay.

spleen [splēn] *n.* **1** An oval organ near the stomach that has certain effects on the character of the blood. **2** Bad temper; spite; rage: to vent one's *spleen* on a poor dog. ◆ The *spleen* was once thought to be the source of bad temper, low spirits, and spite.

splen·did [splen′did] *adj.* **1** Brilliant or magnificent; glorious: a *splendid* view of the sea.

---

add, āce, câre, pälm; end, ēqual; it, īce; odd, ōpen, ôrder; tŏŏk, pōol; up, bûrn;

ə = a in *above*, e in *sicken*, i in *possible*, o in *melon*, u in *circus*; yōō = u in *fuse*; oil; pout;

check; ring; thin; this; zh in *vision.* For ¶ reference, see page 64 · HOW TO

2 *informal* Very good; excellent: I'm in *splendid* health. — **splen'did·ly** *adv.*

splen·dor [splen'dər] *n.* Brilliance or magnificence. ¶1

sple·net·ic [spli·net'ik] *adj.* **1** Of or having to do with the spleen. **2** Bad-tempered.

splice [splīs] *v.* **spliced, splic·ing,** *n.* **1** *v.* To join by interlacing, twisting together, overlapping, grafting, etc., so that a neat joint results: to *splice* cables; to *splice* two pieces of timber. **2** *n.* A union made by splicing.

splint [splint] *n.* **1** A piece of wood or metal for holding the parts of a fractured bone in position. **2** A thin, flexible strip of wood, used for making baskets, chair bottoms, etc. **3** A splinter.

splin·ter [splin'tər] **1** *n.* A thin, sharp piece of wood, glass, metal, etc., split or torn off. **2** *v.* To split into thin, sharp fragments. — **splin'ter·y** *adj.*

Two stems grafted by splicing

split [split] *v.* **split, split·ting,** *n.* **1** *v.* To cut or break lengthwise or along the grain: to *split* logs; The rock *split.* **2** *adj. use:* a *split* log. **3** *n.* A break or cleft. **4** *v.* To divide into shares: Let's *split* the cost. **5** *n.* The act of splitting. **6** *n.* A break in the unity of an organization. **7** *v.* To become divided or disunited: The club *split* on the proposal of higher dues. **8** *v.* To divide (one's vote or ballot) between political parties. **9** *adj. use:* a *split* ballot. **10** *n.* An acrobatic stunt in which one sits on the floor with the legs stretched in directly opposite directions. — **split hairs** To make overly fine or precise distinctions. — **split the difference** To divide a sum equally.

split·ting [split'ing] *adj.* Intense; piercing: a *splitting* headache.

splotch [sploch] **1** *n.* A spot, soil, or stain. **2** *v.* To spot or soil. — **splotch'y** *adj.*

splurge [splûrj] *n., v.* **splurged, splurg·ing** *informal* **1** *n.* A showing off, especially by spending money lavishly or wastefully. **2** *v.* To show off, as by spending a large amount of money.

splut·ter [splut'ər] **1** *v.* To make explosive sounds, one after the other; hiss; spit. **2** *v.* To speak quickly and incoherently, as from surprise or anger. **3** *n.* The sound of spluttering.

spoil [spoil] *v.* **spoiled** or **spoilt, spoil·ing,** *n.* **1** *v.* To lessen the quality, value, or usefulness of; damage or destroy: to *spoil* supper by overcooking it; to *spoil* film by exposing it to too much light. **2** *v.* To become damaged or rotten, as food: Milk *spoils* if not kept refrigerated. **3** *v.* To weaken or destroy the character of (a child) by giving in to his demands too often. **4** *n.* (*pl.*) Things seized and taken over by force; plunder; loot: the *spoils* of war. **5** *n.* (*pl.*) Public offices that people are appointed to as a reward for services to a victorious political party. — **be spoiling for** To have a great desire for.

spoils system The practice of a victorious political party of making appointment to public office a reward for service to the party.

spoilt [spoilt] An alternative past tense and past participle of SPOIL.

spoke¹ [spōk] **1** *n.* One of the rods or bars that connect the rim of a wheel to the hub. **2** *v.* To provide with spokes.

spoke² [spōk] Past tense of SPEAK.

spo·ken [spō'kən] **1** Past participle of SPEAK. **2** *adj.* Not written; said aloud. **3** *adj.* Speaking or said in a certain way: a *smooth-spoken* man.

spokes·man [spōks'mən] *n., pl.* **spokes·men** [spōks'mən] A person who speaks on behalf of another or others.

sponge [spunj] *n., v.* **sponged, spong·ing 1** *n.* A simple water animal that lives in a colony with others of its kind. **2** *n.* Its dried skeleton or network of light, tough, elastic fibers, used in washing, cleaning, etc., because of its power to absorb water. **3** *n.* Any spongelike substance that is used as an absorbent. **4** *v.* To wipe, wet, or clean with a sponge. **5** *v. informal* To live or get things without cost or at the expense of others. — **spong'er** *n.*

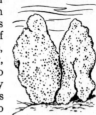

Typical sponges

sponge cake A light cake made of beaten eggs, sugar, and flour, containing no shortening.

spong·y [spun'jē] *adj.* **spong·i·er, spong·i·est** Of or like a sponge; elastic and porous.

spon·sor [spon'sər] **1** *n.* A person who makes himself responsible for a person or thing, as a bill in a legislature. **2** *n.* A godparent. **3** *n.* A business firm that pays for a radio or television program on which it advertises. **4** *v.* To act as a sponsor for. — **spon'sor·ship** *n.*

spon·ta·ne·i·ty [spon'tə·nē'ə·tē] *n.* The quality or condition of being spontaneous.

spon·ta·ne·ous [spon·tā'nē·əs] *adj.* **1** Done naturally from impulse; not planned: a *spontaneous* dance. **2** Arising from or caused by inner forces with no outside cause: *spontaneous* production of gas. — **spon·ta'ne·ous·ly** *adv.*

spontaneous combustion or **spontaneous ignition** The bursting into flame of a substance because of heat produced by rapid oxidation within the substance itself.

spoof [spoof] *informal* **1** *n.* A trick, joke, or humorous exaggeration. **2** *v.* To make mild fun of.

spook [spook] *n. informal* A ghost.

spook·y [spoo'kē] *adj. informal* **spook·i·er, spook·i·est 1** Ghostly. **2** Haunted.

spool [spool] **1** *n.* A cylinder, of wood or metal, with a rim at each end, on which thread, yarn, or wire is wound. **2** *v.* To wind on a spool.

spoon [spoon] **1** *n.* An implement with a small, shallow bowl at the end of a handle, used to lift, stir, or measure food or drink. **2** *v.* To lift up or out with a spoon.

spoon·bill [spoon'bil'] *n.* A long-legged wading bird with a long, flat, spoon-shaped bill.

spoon·ful [spoon'fool'] *n., pl.* **spoon·fuls** As much as a spoon will hold.

spoor [spoor] *n.* A track; trail, especially a footprint or other trace of a wild animal.

spo·rad·ic [spô·rad'ik] *adj.* Occurring here and there or now and then; occasional: *sporadic* bursts of applause. **— spo·rad'i·cal·ly** *adv.*

Spoonbill, 34 in. long

spore [spôr] *n.* A small cell that can grow into a new plant or animal. Ferns, fungi, and algae reproduce by means of spores.

sport [spôrt] **1** *n.* Anything generally amusing; pastime; play: It will be good *sport* to have a picnic. **2** *v.* To amuse oneself; play; frolic: Children like to *sport* in the water. **3** *n.* A game or contest, especially an outdoor or athletic game, as baseball, football, track, etc. **4** *adj.* For informal use: a *sport* coat. **5** *v. informal* To display or wear: to *sport* a new hairdo. **6** *n.* A person thought of in reference to his ability to get along with others or to his sense of fair play: a good *sport*. **7** *n. informal* A person who lives a gay, lively life and is willing to take chances. **8** *n.* An animal or plant that shows a sudden, spontaneous difference from the normal type; mutation. **— in sport** or **for sport** In fun; for a joke. **— make sport of** To make fun of; mock.

sport·ing [spôr'ting] *adj.* **1** Related to, used in, or enjoying sports. **2** Observing the rules of fair play. **3** Interested in or betting on sports: a *sporting* man. **4** Involving the risk of loss or failure: a *sporting* chance.

spor·tive [spôr'tiv] *adj.* Of, having to do with, or fond of sport or play; playful; frolicsome.

sports [spôrts] *adj.* For informal use; casual: a *sports* car; *sports* clothes.

sports·man [spôrts'mən] *n., pl.* **sports·men** [spôrts'mən] **1** A person who is active or interested in sports. **2** A person who believes in fair play.

sports·man·like [spôrts'mən·lik'] *adj.* **1** Having to do with sportsmen. **2** Abiding by the rules of fair play; honorable; generous.

sports·man·ship [spôrts'mən·ship] *n.* Fair play or sportsmanlike conduct, especially in sports. ◆ *Sportsmanship*, like many other English words, was formed by joining a stem, in this case *sports*, with certain suffixes. First *sports* + *man* were joined, then *sportsman* + *ship*.

spot [spot] *n., v.* **spot·ted, spot·ting,** *adj.* **1** *n.* A small part of a surface that is different from the rest, as in color, feeling, etc.: a white dog with black *spots*; a sore *spot* on the cheek. **2** *n.* A soiled place; stain: a *spot* of gravy on a

tablecloth. **3** *v.* To make or become marked or soiled with spots. **4** *n.* A stain or blemish on one's character or reputation. **5** *n.* A particular place or locality: a seaside *spot*. **6** *v.* To place; locate; station: to *spot* a man at each exit. **7** *v. informal* To recognize; see: He *spotted* his sister from the window. **8** *v. informal* To give (an advantage) to someone: We *spotted* them five points. **9** *adj.* Ready; on delivery: to pay *spot* cash. **10** *adj.* Made at random: Police made a *spot* check of cars on the highway. **— hit the spot** *slang* To fill a need or hunger. **— in a spot** *slang* In a difficult or embarrassing situation. **— on the spot 1** At once; immediately. **2** At the very place. **3** *slang* In trouble or difficulty.

spot·less [spot'lis] *adj.* Free from spots; very clean: *spotless* linens. **— spot'less·ly** *adv.*

spot·light [spot'lit'] *n.* **1** A circle of powerful light thrown on a stage to bring a performer into clearer view. **2** The lamp that produces such a light. **3** Public notice; center of attention: to be in the *spotlight*.

spot·ted [spot'id] *adj.* **1** Discolored in spots. **2** Marked with spots, as certain animals.

spot·ty [spot'ē] *adj.* **spot·ti·er, spot·ti·est 1** Having many spots. **2** Uneven; not uniform in quality: *spotty* work.

spouse [spouz *or* spous] *n.* A husband or wife.

spout [spout] **1** *v.* To flow or pour out in large quantities and with force, as a liquid under pressure. **2** *n.* A stream or jet of liquid. **3** *v.* To throw out or discharge (a liquid): The volcano *spouted* lava. **4** *n.* A tube or channel from which liquid can flow. **5** *v. informal* To speak pompously for a long time.

sprain [sprān] **1** *n.* A violent twisting or straining of the ligaments around a joint. **2** *n.* The condition due to such an injury. **3** *v.* To cause a sprain in; wrench; twist: to *sprain* one's ankle.

sprang [sprang] An alternative past tense of SPRING: He *sprang* to his feet.

sprat [sprat] *n.* A small fish like the herring, found off the Atlantic coast of Europe.

sprawl [sprôl] **1** *v.* To sit or lie with the legs and arms stretched out in an ungraceful or relaxed way. **2** *v.* To be stretched out awkwardly or sloppily: His legs *sprawled* over the arm of the sofa. **3** *v.* To spread out awkwardly or unevenly, as handwriting. **4** *n.* The act or position of sprawling: She lay in a *sprawl*.

spray[1] [sprā] **1** *n.* Water or other liquid sent out in fine drops. **2** *n.* A device for sending out such fine drops, as an atomizer. **3** *n.* Anything resembling a spray of liquid: a *spray* of bullets. **4** *v.* To send out (a liquid) in fine drops: Atomizers *spray* perfume. **5** *v.* To apply spray to. **— spray'er** *n.*

spray[2] [sprā] *n.* A small branch of a tree or plant with its leaves, flowers, berries, etc., either growing or cut off.

---

add, āce, câre, pälm;　　end, ēqual;　　it, īce;　　odd, ōpen, ôrder;　　took, pool;　　up, bûrn;
ə = a in *above*, e in *sicken*, i in *possible*, o in *melon*, u in *circus*;　　yoo = u in *fuse*;　　oil;　　pout;
check; ring; thin; this; zh in *vision*.　　For ¶ reference, see page 64 · HOW TO

spray gun A device that resembles a gun and shoots out liquids such as paint or insecticides in a spray by means of air pressure.

spread [spred] *v.* **spread, spread·ing,** *n.* **1** *v.* To open or unfold to full width or extent, as wings, sails, etc. **2** *v.* To extend or stretch out: The city *spread* out before us. **3** *n.* The limit to which something can extend or be spread, as a sail or a bird's wings. **4** *v.* To distribute, as over a surface: to *spread* paint on a wall; to *spread* papers on the floor. **5** *v.* To cover, as with a thin layer: to *spread* toast with marmalade. **6** *n.* Something to spread on bread, crackers, etc.: a cheese *spread*. **7** *v.* To move or force apart or farther apart: to *spread* one's fingers. **8** *v.* To extend over a period of time: to *spread* payments over six months. **9** *v.* To make or become more widely known, active, etc.: to *spread* rumors; The disease *spread* rapidly. **10** *n.* The act of spreading: the *spread* of the gospel. **11** *v.* To set (a table, etc.) for a meal. **12** *v.* To arrange or place on a table, etc.: to *spread* a meal. **13** *n. informal* A meal, especially a lavish one; feast. **14** *n.* A cloth or covering for a bed, etc.

spread·er [spred'ər] *n.* A person or thing that spreads, as a small knife for spreading butter.

spree [sprē] *n.* A lively time of unrestrained activity: a shopping *spree*.

spri·er [sprī'ər] Comparative of SPRY.

spri·est [sprī'ist] Superlative of SPRY.

sprig [sprig] *n.* A shoot or small branch of a tree or plant.

spright·ly [sprīt'lē] *adj.* **spright·li·er, spright·li·est** Brisk; gay; spirited: The young performers danced a *sprightly* jig. — **spright'li·ness** *n.*

spring [spring] *v.* **sprang** or **sprung, sprung, spring·ing,** *n.* **1** *v.* To move or rise suddenly and rapidly; leap; jump: He *sprang* across the creek. **2** *n.* A leaping up or forward suddenly; jump; bound. **3** *v.* To move suddenly, as by elastic reaction: The jaws of the trap *sprang* shut. **4** *n.* The quality of being elastic: the *spring* of a bow. **5** *v.* To cause to act, open, close, snap, etc., suddenly: to *spring* a trap. **6** *n.* A device, as a coiled steel wire, that gives under pressure and returns to its normal shape when the pressure is taken away. **7** *v.* To become warped, bent, etc., as the door of an automobile. **8** *v.* To come up or appear suddenly; begin to grow: New towns have *sprung* up. **9** *v.* To cause to happen, become known, or appear suddenly: to *spring* a surprise. **10** *v.* To originate; proceed, as from a source. **11** *n.* A source or origin. **12** *n.* The season of the year when plants begin to grow again. It comes between winter and summer. **13** *adj. use: spring* weather. **14** *n.* A flow of water out of the ground. — **spring a leak** To develop a leak; begin to leak.

spring·board [spring'bôrd'] *n.* A flexible board that springs back into place, used by athletes and acrobats as an aid in tumbling, leaping, or diving.

spring·bok [spring'bok] *n.* A small South African gazelle that can leap high in the air.

Spring·field [spring'fēld] *n.* The capital of Illinois.

spring·tide [spring'tīd] *n.* Springtime.

spring tide The tide that comes at or shortly after the new or full moon when the rise and fall are greatest. ·

spring·time [spring'tīm'] *n.* The season of spring.

spring·y [spring'ē] *adj.* **spring·i·er, spring·i·est** Able to snap back; elastic.

Springbok, 29–35 in. high at shoulder

sprin·kle [spring'kəl] *v.* **sprin·kled, sprin·kling,** *n.* **1** *v.* To scatter in small drops or particles. **2** *v.* To spray or cover by sprinkling: to *sprinkle* a salad with vinegar. **3** *v.* To fall or rain in scattered drops. **4** *n.* A falling in drops or particles. **5** *n.* A light rain. **6** *n.* A small amount. — **sprin'kler** *n.*

sprin·kling [spring'kling] *n.* A small number or quantity: a *sprinkling* of snow on the ground.

sprint [sprint] **1** *n.* A short race run at top speed. **2** *v.* To run fast, as in a sprint. — **sprint'er** *n.*

sprit [sprit] *n.* On sailboats, a small pole, or spar, that reaches at a slant from a mast to support and spread a fore-and-aft sail.

sprite [sprīt] *n.* A fairy, elf, goblin, etc.

sprit·sail [sprit'səl *or* sprit'sāl'] *n.* A sail held out by a sprit.

sprock·et [sprok'it] *n.* **1** One of a set of teeth, as on the rim of a wheel, for engaging with the links of a chain, as on a bicycle. **2** A wheel with such teeth.

sprout [sprout] **1** *v.* To put out shoots; begin to grow, as a plant. **2** *n.* A new shoot or bud on a plant. **3** *v.* To cause to sprout: This warm rain will *sprout* the seeds you planted.

spruce[1] [sprōōs] *n.* **1** One of various evergreen trees related to the pine, having leaves shaped like needles and bearing cones. **2** The soft wood of such a tree.

spruce[2] [sprōōs] *adj.* **spruc·er, spruc·est,** *v.* **spruced, spruc·ing** **1** *adj.* Neat; trim; smart; dapper. **2** *v.* To make (oneself) spruce: You must *spruce* yourself up for the dance.

sprung [sprung] Past participle and alternative past tense of SPRING.

spry [sprī] *adj.* **spri·er** or **spry·er, spri·est** or **spry·est** Quick and agile. — **spry'ly** *adv.*

spud [spud] *n.* **1** A tool like a spade with a narrow blade or prongs for digging out or cutting the roots of weeds. **2** *informal* A potato.

spume [spyōōm] *n., v.* **spumed, spum·ing** **1** *n.* Froth; foam; scum. **2** *v.* To foam; froth.

spun [spun] Past tense and past participle of SPIN: The top *spun*.

spunk [spungk] *n. informal* Courage; pluck.

spunk·y [spungk'ē] *adj.* **spunk·i·er, spunk·i·est** *informal* Full of courage; spirited.

S

spur [spûr] *n.*, *v.* **spurred, spur·ring 1** *n.* A device worn on a horseman's heel, having a point or a series of sharp points on a wheel. It is used to prick and urge on a horse. **2** *v.* To prick with spurs. **3** *n.* Anything that urges on or goads to action; incentive: The desire for fame was the *spur* that drove him on. **4** *v.* To urge on; goad: Need *spurred* him to work harder. **5** *n.* A ridge sticking out from a mountain, or a line of mountains sticking out from a mountain range. **6** *n.* A sharp, stiff spine, as on the leg of a rooster. **7** *n.* A short branch running out from the main line of a railroad. **— on the spur of the moment** Hastily; on impulse; without planning. **— win one's spurs** To gain honor or distinction.

Spur

spu·ri·ous [spyŏor′ē·əs] *adj.* Not genuine; false; counterfeit: a *spurious* antique.

spurn [spûrn] *v.* **1** To reject with contempt; scorn: We *spurned* their attempts to be friendly. **2** To drive away as by kicking.

spurt [spûrt] **1** *v.* To gush forth in a sudden stream or jet: Water *spurted* from the hose. **2** *n.* A sudden gush of liquid. **3** *v.* To make a sudden and extreme effort: Racers *spurt* near the finish line. **4** *n.* A sudden, brief burst of effort: I do my chores in *spurts*. ◆ *Spurt* was once spelled and pronounced *sprit*. Over the years the [r] and the [i] sounds were reversed, and the word came to be pronounced and spelled *spirt*, which later became *spurt*.

sput·nik [sput′nik *or* spŏot′nik] *n.* Any of several space vehicles launched by the Soviet Union. The first sputnik, 1957, was the first space vehicle put into orbit about the earth.

sput·ter [sput′ər] **1** *v.* To make a series of spitting or hissing sounds. **2** *v.* To spit out particles of saliva, food, etc., from the mouth, as when speaking excitedly. **3** *v.* To speak in a confused, excited, or angry way. **4** *n.* Confused, angry, or excited talk. **5** *n.* The act or sound of sputtering.

spu·tum [spyŏo′təm] *n.* Saliva, often mixed with other matter coughed up from the lungs.

spy [spī] *n.*, *pl.* **spies**, *v.* **spied, spy·ing 1** *n.* A person employed by a government to discover military or other important secrets of an enemy country. **2** *n.* A person who watches others secretly. **3** *v.* To keep watch closely or secretly; act as a spy. **4** *v.* To catch sight of; see: We could *spy* the town from the hill. **5** *v.* To look for or find by careful or secret investigation: to *spy* out a hiding place.

spy·glass [spī′glas′] *n.* A small telescope.

sq. Abbreviation of SQUARE.

squab [skwob] *n.* A young pigeon.

squab·ble [skwob′əl] *v.* **squab·bled, squab· bling 1** *v.* To have a petty quarrel; wrangle.

2 *n.* A petty quarrel; wrangle: The youngsters had their *squabbles* but were really good friends. **— squab′bler** *n.*

squad [skwod] *n.* **1** A small group of people organized to do something. **2** A small unit or group, as of soldiers or policemen. **3** A team.

squad car A car used by police for patrolling, equipped with a special kind of radio for communicating with headquarters.

squad·ron [skwod′rən] *n.* **1** In the U.S. Navy, a group or unit of vessels or aircraft. **2** In the U.S. Air Force, a unit of eight or more aircraft. **3** A unit of cavalry. **4** Any group of people organized to do something.

squal·id [skwol′id] *adj.* **1** Dirty and wretched from poverty or neglect: a *squalid* neighborhood. **2** Sordid; degraded: a *squalid* way of living.

squall¹ [skwôl] **1** *n.* A sudden, violent burst of wind, often accompanied by rain or snow. **2** *v.* To blow a squall; storm. **— squall′y** *adj.*

squall² [skwôl] **1** *v.* To cry loudly, as an angry child. **2** *n.* A loud, harsh, screaming cry.

squal·or [skwol′ər] *n.* A squalid condition; filth, wretched poverty, or degradation.

squan·der [skwon′dər] *v.* To spend (money, time, etc.) wastefully.

square [skwâr] *n.*, *adj.*, *v.* **squared, squar· ing 1** *n.* A flat figure having four equal sides and four right angles. **2** *n.* Any object, part, surface, or arrangement that has this shape. **3** *adj.* Being or resembling a square in shape: a *square* field. **4** *v.* To make square in form: to *square* a block of wood. **5** *v.* To mark off in squares: to *square* off a sheet of paper. **6** *v.* To shape or adjust so as to form or suggest a right angle: *Square* your shoulders. **7** *adj.* Forming a right angle: a *square* corner. **8** *n.* An instrument in the shape of an L or T, having one or more right angles that may be used to lay out or measure other right angles. **9** *adj.* Being the product of two lengths at right angles to one another and so representing area: A *square* mile is the area of a square one mile long and one mile wide. **10** *v.* To multiply (a number) by itself: 7 *squared* is 49. **11** *n.* The product of a number multiplied by itself: The *square* of 6 is 36. **12** *n.* An area in a city or town bounded on four sides by streets and often serving as a park. **13** *n.* An open area in a city or town formed by the intersection of several streets. **14** *adj.* Fair; just; honest: a *square* deal. **15** *adj.* Direct or straight. **16** *v.* To conform; agree: His claim *squares* with the facts. **17** *v.* To make even; settle: to *square* accounts. **18** *adj.* Even; settled: Accounts between us are now *square*. **19** *adj. informal* Good and satisfying: said about a meal. **20** *n. slang* A person considered

T-square

L-square

add, āce, câre, pälm; end, ēqual; it, īce; odd, ōpen, ôrder; tŏŏk, pŏŏl; up, bûrn;
ə = a in *above*, e in *sicken*, i in *possible*, o in *melon*, u in *circus*; yŏŏ = u in *fuse*; oil; pout;
check; ring; thin; this; zh in *vision*. For ¶ reference, see page 64 · HOW TO

as a conformist or as one behind the times.
21 *adj. slang* Conventional or behind the times.
—on the square **1** At right angles.
2 *informal* In a fair and honest manner. **—
square off** To take a position for attack or
defense. **— square oneself** *informal* To make
up for something one did that was wrong: He
tried to *square himself* with the man he had
cheated. **— square peg in a round hole** A
misfit. **— square'ly** *adv.* **— square'ness** *n.*

square dance *U.S* A dance in which four
couples form a square and then do various steps.

square-rigged [skwâr'rigd'] *adj.* Fitted with
four-cornered sails
extended on yards
fastened at the mid-
dle across the mast.

square·rig·ger
[skwâr'rig'ər] *n.* A
square-rigged ship.

square root The
factor of a number
which, multiplied by
itself, gives the origi-
nal number: The
square root of 25 is 5.

A square-rigged ship

squash¹ [skwosh] *n.*
The fleshy, edible fruit of various trailing plants
of the gourd family. ◆ *Squash* comes from an
Algonquian Indian word.

squash² [skwosh] **1** *v.* To crush or become
crushed into a pulp or soft mass. **2** *n.* A crushed
mass. **3** *n.* The sudden fall of a heavy, soft, or
bursting body, or the sound it makes. **4** *n.* The
sound made by walking through ooze or mud.
5 *v.* To press or squeeze: So many people
squashed into the auditorium that it became very
hot and stuffy. **6** *v.* To put down; quell or
suppress: to *squash* a revolt. **7** *n.* A game like
tennis or handball, played on an indoor court
with rackets and a ball.

squash·y [skwosh'ē] *adj.* **squash·i·er,
squash·i·est** **1** Soft, moist, and mushy:
squashy earth. **2** Easily squashed: a soft,
squashy tomato.

squat [skwot] *v.* **squat·ted** or **squat, squat·
ting,** *n., adj.* **1** *v.* To crouch and sit on one's
heels, with the knees bent and the weight usually
on the balls of the feet. **2** *v.* To sit on the ground
with the legs drawn close to the body. **3** *n.* The
act of squatting. **4** *n.* A squatting position. **5**
adj. Crouching. **6** *adj.* Short and thick in shape.
7 *v.* To settle on a piece of land without owning
it, paying for it, or having a right to it. **8** *v.* To
settle on government land in accordance with
laws that will eventually give title to it. **—
squat'ter** *n.*

squaw [skwô] *n.* An American Indian woman
or wife. ◆ *Squaw* comes from an Algonquian
Indian word meaning *woman.*

squawk [skwôk] **1** *v.* To give a shrill, harsh cry,
as a parrot. **2** *n.* Such a shrill, harsh cry. **3** *v.*
slang To complain or protest loudly. **4** *n. slang*
A loud complaint or protest.

squeak [skwēk] **1** *n.* A thin, sharp, shrill
sound. **2** *v.* To make a squeak, as a mouse or
door. **— close squeak** or **narrow squeak**
informal A narrow escape. **— squeak'y** *adj.*

squeal [skwēl] **1** *v.* To give a long, shrill, high-
pitched cry, as a pig. **2** *n.* A cry like this. **3** *v.*
slang To turn informer; tattle.

squeam·ish [skwē'mish] *adj.* **1** Easily made
a little sick at the stomach. **2** Too easily
disgusted or shocked; prudish. **— squeam'·
ish·ness** *n.*

squee·gee [skwē'jē] *n.* A tool with a handle
and a crosspiece edged with
rubber or leather, used to
move a liquid over or off a
surface as in washing windows.

squeeze [skwēz] *v.*
squeezed, squeez·ing, *n.*
1 *v.* To press hard upon or
press together: to *squeeze* an
orange. **2** *n.* A firm press.
3 *v.* To apply pressure:
Don't *squeeze* so hard. **4** *v.* To
yield to pressure: Wet cloth
squeezes easily. **5** *v.* To push
out by pressure: to *squeeze*

A squeegee

juice from fruit; to *squeeze* money from a miser.
6 *v.* To force or push; cram: Try to *squeeze* more
into the suitcase. **7** *v.* To force one's way; push:
to *squeeze* through a tight place. **8** *n.* The act of
squeezing. **9** *v.* To hug; embrace. **10** *n.* A hug.
— squeez'er *n.*

squelch [skwelch] *v. informal* To subdue or
make silent, as with a crushing reply.

squib [skwib] *n.* **1** A small firework that explodes like a rocket after being thrown or rolled.
2 A broken firecracker that burns with a spitting
sound. **3** A short speech or piece of writing that
is witty and critical.

squid [skwid] *n., pl.* **squid** or **squids** A sea
animal like the cuttlefish, but having a longer,
thinner body, tail fins, and two of the ten arms
around its mouth longer than the others.

squint [skwint] **1** *v.* To look with half-closed
eyes, as into bright light. **2** *n.* The act or habit
of squinting. **3** *v.* To look sideways. **4** *n.* A
hasty glance. **5** *v.* To be cross-eyed. **6** *n.* A
cross-eyed condition.

squire [skwīr] *n., v.* **squired, squir·ing 1** *n.*
In England, a country gentleman or a person who
owns much land. **2** *n. U.S.* In small and rural
areas, a title sometimes used for justices of the
peace, etc. **3** *n.* A young man who served as an
attendant to a knight. **4** *n.* A man who escorts
a woman. **5** *v.* To escort (a woman).

squirm [skwûrm] *v.* To bend and twist the body;
wriggle, often from pain, nervousness, etc.

squir·rel [skwûr'əl] *n.* **1** A small, furry animal
that has a long bushy tail, sharp teeth, and lives
in trees. **2** The squirrel's fur.

squirt [skwûrt] **1** *v.* To come out or cause to
come out in a thin stream or jet; spurt. **2** *v.* To
wet by squirting: John *squirted* Tom with his
water pistol. **3** *n.* A squirting or spurting. **4** *n.* A

jet of liquid squirted out. **5** *n. informal* An impudent, usually young, person.

Sr The symbol for the element STRONTIUM.

Sr. Abbreviation of SENIOR.

S.S. Abbreviation of STEAMSHIP

St. Abbreviation, in proper names, of: **1** SAINT. **2** STRAIT. **3** STREET.

stab [stab] *v.* **stabbed, stab·bing,** *n.* **1** *v.* To pierce or wound with a pointed weapon. **2** *v.* To thrust: She *stabbed* the pin into her finger. **3** *v.* To give a wound or inflict pain with or as if with a pointed weapon: The insult *stabbed* through her like a dagger. **4** *n.* A thrust made with a pointed weapon. **5** *n.* A wound made by stabbing. **6** *n.* A sudden, sharp pain or feeling: a *stab* of conscience. **7** *n. informal* A try: to make a *stab* at painting pictures. **— stab in the back** To slander or injure in a treacherous, sly way. **— stab′ber** *n.*

sta·bil·i·ty [stə·bil′ə·tē] *n.* **1** A being stable; steadiness; balance. **2** Firmness of purpose or resolution. **3** Continued existence; permanence; durability.

sta·bi·lize [stā′bə·līz] *v.* **sta·bi·lized, sta·bi·liz·ing 1** To make firm or stable. **2** To keep steady; keep from changing: to *stabilize* prices. **3** To steady the motion of (an aircraft or ship) by means of a stabilizer. **— sta′bil·i·za′tion** *n.* ¶3

sta·bi·liz·er [stā′bə·lī′zər] *n.* **1** A person or thing that stabilizes. **2** A device or special construction to keep the motion of an aircraft or ship steady. ¶3

sta·ble¹ [stā′bəl] *adj.* **sta·bler, sta·blest 1** Not easily moved or shaken; firm; fixed; steadfast. **2** Long lasting or permanent; durable. **3** Able to keep or to return to an original position.

sta·ble² [stā′bəl] *n., v.* **sta·bled, sta·bling 1** *n.* A building set apart for sheltering and feeding horses or cattle. **2** *v.* To put or shelter in a stable: We made sure that the horses were *stabled* for the night. **3** *n.* A group of race horses belonging to a single owner.

stac·ca·to [stə·kä′tō] *adj., adv., n., pl.* **stac·ca·tos 1** *adj.* Sounding for only part of its written value, as a musical note; cut short; disconnected. **2** *adv.* In a staccato manner: to play *staccato.* **3** *adj.* Using staccato notes. **4** *n.* A staccato style or passage.

stack [stak] **1** *n.* A large pile of grain, hay, straw, etc., usually cone-shaped. **2** *n.* Any orderly pile or heap: a *stack* of coins. **3** *v.* To gather or place in a pile; pile up in a stack: to *stack* hay. **4** *n.* A group of rifles set upright and supporting one another. **5** *n.* (*pl.*) The part of a library where most of the books are shelved. **6** *n.* A chimney; smokestack. **7** *v.* To fix in advance in a secret and dishonest way: to *stack* a deck of cards.

sta·di·um [stā′dē·əm] *n., pl.* **sta·di·ums** or **sta·di·a** [stā′dē·ə] A structure with tiers of seats built around an open field, used for sports events, meetings, etc.

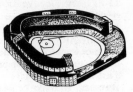

Stadium

staff [staf] *n., pl.* **staffs;** *for def. 1, also* **staves** [stāvz] **1** *n.* A stick or pole carried as an aid in walking or climbing, as a weapon, or as an emblem of authority. **2** *n.* Something that supports or maintains: Bread is the *staff* of life. **3** *n.* A group of people who work together under a manager or chief: the *staff* of a hotel. **4** *v.* To provide or supply with a staff, as of workers. **5** *n.* In music, the five horizontal lines and the spaces between them on which music is written.

stag [stag] **1** *n.* A fully grown male deer. **2** *n.* A man who attends a party, dance, etc., unaccompanied by a woman. **3** *adj.* For men only: a *stag* dinner.

stage [stāj] *n., v.* **staged, stag·ing 1** *n.* A raised platform, as that in a theater for the performance of plays, or that in an auditorium for the delivery of speeches, etc. **2** *n.* Acting as a profession; the occupation of an actor. **3** *n.* The drama. **4** *v.* To put or exhibit on the stage: to *stage* a play. **5** *n.* Any platform, as a dock, scaffold, etc. **6** *n.* The field or plan of action of some notable event: to set the *stage* for war. **7** *v.* To carry on or conduct: to *stage* an invasion. **8** *n.* A stopping point on a journey. **9** *n.* The distance between two stopping points. **10** *n.* A stagecoach. **11** *n.* A step in a development or process: The adult *stage* of this larva is a moth. **12** *n.* Any of the propulsion units of a rocket vehicle, each firing after the one before it burns out and falls away. **— by easy stages** Traveling or acting without hurry and with many stops; slowly.

stage·coach [stāj′kōch′] *n.* A large coach drawn by horses and having a regular route from town to town for carrying passengers, mail, etc.

stage·hand [stāj′-hand′] *n.* A worker in a theater who handles scenery, stage properties, etc.

Stagecoach

stag·ger [stag′ər] **1** *v.* To walk or run unsteadily; sway; reel. **2** *v.* To cause to stagger. **3** *n.* A reeling or swaying motion: He ran with a *stagger.* **4** *v.* To confuse or overwhelm, as by surprise, grief, etc.: The unexpected question *staggered* him. **5** *v.* To place in a zigzag arrangement. **6** *v.* To schedule so as to begin at different

add, āce, câre, pälm; end, ēqual; it, īce; odd, ōpen, ôrder; tŏŏk, pōōl; up, bûrn;
ə = a in *above*, e in *sicken*, i in *possible*, o in *melon*, u in *circus*; yōō = u in *fuse*; oil; pout;
check; ring; thin; this; zh in *vision*. For ¶ reference, see page 64 · HOW TO

times: to *stagger* lunch hours. **— the staggers** (*used with singular verb*) **1** A disease of the nervous system in horses and some cattle, causing them to stagger and fall down. **2** Dizziness.

stag·nant [stag′nənt] *adj.* **1** Stale and dirty because not moving or flowing: said about bodies of water: a *stagnant* pond. **2** Dull; sluggish.

stag·nate [stag′nāt] *v.* **stag·nat·ed, stag·nat·ing** To make or become stagnant. **— stag·na′tion** *n.*

staid [stād] *adj.* Steady and sober; sedate.

stain [stān] **1** *n.* A spot of dirt or discoloration. **2** *v.* To make or become dirty or discolored; soil; spot. **3** *n.* A dye or pigment used to change the color of wood. **4** *v.* To color by the use of a dye or pigment. **5** *n.* A wrong act or disgrace: a *stain* on one's reputation. **6** *v.* To spot by a wrong or dishonorable act; disgrace.

stain·less [stān′lis] *adj.* **1** With no stain; spotless. **2** That will not easily rust, tarnish, etc.: *stainless* steel.

stair [stâr] *n.* **1** A step or one of a series of steps, for going up or down from one level to another. **2** (*usually pl.*) A series of steps.

stair·case [stâr′kās′] *n.* A flight of stairs, including the supports, handrail, etc.

stair·way [stâr′wā′] *n.* One or more flights of stairs.

stake [stāk] *n., v.* **staked, stak·ing 1** *n.* A stick or post sharpened at one end for driving into the ground. **2** *v.* To fasten to or support by means of a stake: to *stake* tomatoes. **3** *v.* To mark the boundaries of with or as with stakes: Where did you *stake* out your claim? **4** *n.* A post to which a person is tied to be executed by being burned alive. **5** *n.* This method of execution: Joan of Arc was sentenced to the *stake*. **6** *n.* (*often pl.*) Something bet or risked, as money on a race. **7** *v.* To bet; wager. **8** *n.* (*often pl.*) A prize in any sort of contest. **9** *n.* An interest or share: a *stake* in a business. **10** *v. informal* To supply with money; finance. **— at stake** To be won or lost; in question. **— pull up stakes** To leave a place; move out.

sta·lac·tite [stə·lak′tīt] *n.* A slender, tapering column of mineral matter, chiefly limestone, hanging like an icicle from the roof of a cave. It is formed by dripping water with lime in it.

sta·lag·mite [stə·lag′mīt] *n.* A limestone column shaped like a cone rising from the floor of a cave.

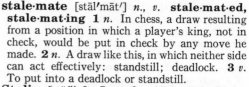
stalactites

stalagmites

stale [stāl] *adj.* **stal·er, stal·est,** *v.* **staled, stal·ing 1** *adj.* Not fresh any longer; slightly changed or gone bad, as air, beer, bread, etc. **2** *adj.* Lacking interest because not new; worn out; trite: a *stale* joke. **3** *adj.* Poor in quality or condition, as from too much or too little activity: A boxer can become *stale* if he breaks training for a long period of time. **4** *v.* To make or become stale. **— stale′ness** *n.*

stale·mate [stāl′māt′] *n., v.* **stale·mat·ed, stale·mat·ing 1** *n.* In chess, a draw resulting from a position in which a player's king, not in check, would be put in check by any move he made. **2** *n.* A draw like this, in which neither side can act effectively; standstill; deadlock. **3** *v.* To put into a deadlock or standstill.

Stalin [stä′lin], **Joseph,** 1879–1953, Soviet statesman; chief of state 1924–1953.

stalk¹ [stôk] *n.* **1** A stem of a plant or any supporting or connecting part. **2** Any support that is like a stem.

stalk² [stôk] **1** *v.* To approach (game, prey, etc.) secretly or stealthily. **2** *v.* To walk in a stiff, dignified, or angry manner: to *stalk* out of a room. **3** *n.* A stiff or angry walk. **4** *n.* The act of stalking. **5** *v.* To spread through: Famine *stalked* the land.

stalk·ing-horse [stô′king-hôrs′] *n.* **1** A horse or a horselike figure behind which a hunter hides in stalking game. **2** Anything that hides what a person thinks, plans to do, etc.

stall¹ [stôl] **1** *n.* A compartment in a stable where a horse or cow is kept. **2** *v.* To place or keep in a stall. **3** *n. mostly British* A small place to show and sell things, as in a market or bazaar. **4** *n. mostly British* A seat, as in the orchestra of a theater or the choir of a church. **5** *v.* To stop or cause to stop, especially unintentionally: to *stall* the engine of a car. **6** *v.* To slow down, as an airplane, to the point where the pilot loses control.

stall² [stôl] *informal* **1** *v.* To delay, usually by not being direct or frank: to *stall* for time. **2** *v.* To put off or divert by not being direct or frank: to *stall* a teacher when she asks a question. **3** *n.* An argument, trick, etc., used to put off or delay an action or decision.

stal·lion [stal′yən] *n.* A male horse that can be used for breeding.

stal·wart [stôl′wərt] **1** *adj.* Strong and muscular; robust. **2** *adj.* Not giving in or yielding; resolute; determined. **3** *adj.* Brave; courageous. **4** *n.* A stalwart person, especially a loyal supporter of a political party, a movement, etc.

sta·men [stā′mən] *n.* The organ of a flower that bears the pollen, consisting of the anther and its stem.

sta·mi·na [stam′ə·nə] *n.* Vitality; vigor; strength; endurance.

stam·mer [stam′ər] **1** *v.* To pause, hesitate, and repeat the same sound without meaning to, in speaking. **2** *n.* The act of stammering. **3** *n.* Stammering speech: to speak with a *stammer*.

Stamens

stamp [stamp] **1** *v.* To strike heavily with the sole of the foot: He *stamped* the floor twice. **2** *v.* To bring down (the foot) heavily and noisily. **3** *v.* To walk with heavy, noisy footsteps. **4** *v.* To affect in some way by or as if by stamping; crush:

to *stamp* a fire out; to *stamp* out all the opposition. **5** *n.* The act of stamping with or as if with the foot. **6** *n.* A die, block, or other device having a pattern, name, or design on it that can, by pressing, be transferred to another surface: a rubber *stamp*. **7** *v.* To print or form by using such a stamp: to *stamp* a design on cloth. **8** *v.* To make marks or figures on by means of a stamp: He *stamped* the paper with his name. **9** *n.* A pattern, official seal, mark, etc., made by stamping. **10** *n.* A device having sharp edges for cutting out articles in its own shape: That *stamp* cuts out squares of cloth. **11** *v.* To form or cut out by using such a stamp. **12** *n.* A small printed piece of paper attached to a letter, article, package, etc., to show that the proper fees or taxes have been paid. **13** *v.* To put a stamp, official seal, etc., on: to *stamp* a package. **14** *n.* A piece of paper similar to a postage stamp, given with certain purchases and later exchanged for various articles or premiums. **15** *v.* To mark or characterize: His stories *stamp* him as a liar. **16** *n.* Character, kind, or quality: I dislike men of his *stamp*.

stam·pede [stam·pēd′] *n.*, *v.* **stam·ped·ed, stam·ped·ing** **1** *n.* A sudden rushing off or flight through panic, as of a herd of cattle, horses, etc. **2** *n.* Any sudden, impulsive rush, as of a crowd: the *stampede* to Alaska for gold. **3** *v.* To be part of or cause a stampede.

stance [stans] *n.* **1** A manner of standing; posture. **2** The position of a golfer's or batter's feet while he makes a swing.

stanch¹ [stanch] **1** *v.* To stop or check the flow of: to *stanch* blood. **2** *v.* To stop or check the flow of blood from: to *stanch* a wound.

stanch² [stanch] *adj.* Another spelling of STAUNCH¹.

stan·chion [stan′shən] *n.* An upright bar that forms the main support of something.

stand [stand] *v.* **stood, stand·ing,** *n.* **1** *v.* To take or keep an upright position on one's feet: *Stand* up! **2** *v.* To be or place in an upright or erect position: The tree used to *stand* here; *Stand* the baby up. **3** *n.* The act of standing. **4** *v.* To have a specified height when standing: He *stands* six feet tall. **5** *v.* To take a certain position: to *stand* aside. **6** *v.* To take on or have a definite opinion, position, or attitude: How do you *stand* on the new tax law? **7** *n.* An opinion, attitude, or position. **8** *v.* To be located; have position; lie: The house *stands* by the side of the road. **9** *n.* The place or position in which someone or something stands: a cab waiting at its *stand*. **10** *v.* To remain unchanged; hold good: My decision *stands*. **11** *v.* To be in a specific state or condition: He *stood* in fear of his life. **12** *v.* To be of a certain rank or class: He *stands* third in his class. **13** *v.* To stop or pause; halt. **14** *n.* A stop or halt, especially one made for putting up a defense. **15** *v.* To take a position for defense or offense: *Stand* and fight. **16** *v.* To put up with; endure; tolerate: I can't *stand* any more. **17** *v.* To withstand; resist, as wear or use. **18** *v.* To be subjected to; endure: to *stand* trial. **19** *n.* A small table on which things may be placed. **20** *n.* A rack or other piece of furniture on which hats, canes, etc., may be put. **21** *n.* A stall, booth, or counter where goods are sold. **22** *n.* A structure on which persons may sit or stand: a witness *stand*. **23** *v. informal* To pay for; bear the expense of: to *stand* a treat. **24** *v.* In sailing, to take or hold a course: The brig *stood* to the west. **25** *n.* A group of growing things, as plants or trees. **— stand a chance** To have a chance, as of success. **— stand by 1** To stay near and be ready to help, operate, or begin. **2** To help; support. **3** To abide by; keep: *Stand by* your promise. **— stand clear** To remain at a safe distance. **— stand for 1** To represent; symbolize. **2** To put up with; tolerate. **— stand off** To keep at a distance. **— stand out 1** To stick out; be conspicuous or prominent. **2** To refuse to agree; remain in opposition. **— stand pat** To resist change. **— stand to reason** To be sensible or logical. **— stand up 1** To stand erect. **2** To withstand wear, criticism, etc. **3** *slang* To fail to keep an appointment with on purpose. **— stand up for** To side with; take the part of.

stan·dard [stan′dərd] **1** *n.* A flag, ensign, or banner used as the special emblem of a nation, body of men, or special cause. **2** *n.* Any established measure of size, quantity, quality, or value: a *standard* of weight. **3** *n.* Any type, model, or example for comparison; measure of excellence: a *standard* of conduct. **4** *adj.* Serving as a gauge or model: a *standard* weight. **5** *adj.* Of recognized excellence or authority: a *standard* author. **6** *adj.* Widely accepted; regularly used: *standard* equipment. **7** *n.* An upright timber, post, etc., used as a support.

stan·dard·ize [stan′dər·dīz] *v.* **stan·dard·ized, stan·dard·iz·ing** To make to or regulate by a standard: Many of the schools *standardized* their requirements for graduation. **— stan′·dard·i·za′tion** *n.* ¶3

standard time (*sometimes written* **Standard Time**) The official time of any place according to its location in one of 24 zones east or west of Greenwich, England. Eight such zones lie in or touch North America.

stand-in [stand′in′] *n.* A person who substitutes in some way for another person, especially a person who takes the place of an actor while lights or cameras are adjusted or put into place.

stand·ing [stan′ding] **1** *adj.* Remaining erect; upright. **2** *adj.* For regular or permanent use: a *standing* rule; a *standing* army. **3** *adj.* Begun while standing: a *standing* high jump. **4** *adj.* Not

add, āce, cãre, pälm;   end, ēqual;   it, īce;   odd, ōpen, ôrder;   tŏŏk, pōōl;   up, bûrn;
ə = a in *above*, e in *sicken*, i in *possible*, o in *melon*, u in *circus*;   yōō = u in *fuse*;   oil;   pout;
check;   ring;   thin;   this;   zh in *vision*.   For ¶ reference, see page 64 · HOW TO

flowing; stagnant, as water. **5** *n.* Relative position or rank; repute: a man of low *standing.* **6** *n.* Time in which something goes on; duration: a custom of long *standing.*

Stan·dish [stan′dish], **Miles,** 1584?–1656, English military leader of the Pilgrims.

stand·point [stand′point′] *n.* A position from which things are seen or judged; point of view: From our *standpoint,* everything looks fine.

stand·still [stand′stil′] *n.* A stop; halt; rest.

stank [stangk] Past tense of STINK.

stan·za [stan′zə] *n.* A certain number of lines of verse grouped together according to a fixed plan to form a section of a poem.

staph·y·lo·coc·cus [staf′ə·lō·kok′əs] *n., pl.* **staph·y·lo·coc·ci** [staf′ə·lō·kok′sī] or **staph·y·lo·coc·cus·es** Any of a group of bacteria, some of which cause boils and infect open wounds.

sta·ple[1] [stā′pəl] *n., v.* **sta·pled, sta·pling** **1** *n.* A U-shaped piece of metal with pointed ends driven into a surface to hold a bolt, hook, wire, etc. in, place. **2** *n.* A thin piece of wire usually shaped like a bracket ([), driven through paper, fabrics, etc., as a fastening. **3** *v.* To fix or fasten by a staple or staples. **— sta′pler** *n.*

sta·ple[2] [stā′pəl] **1** *n.* A basic food or other ordinary item of household use, as flour and sugar. **2** *adj.* Regularly and constantly produced, used, or sold: *staple* foods. **3** *n.* The principal article produced or manufactured in a place or region: Rubber is the *staple* of Akron. **4** *adj.* Main; chief: a *staple* crop. **5** *n.* The carded or combed fiber of cotton, wool, or flax.

star [stär] *n., v.* **starred, star·ring** **1** *n.* Any of the many luminous bodies similar to the sun that are spread through space at vast distances from the earth. At night some are visible as apparently fixed points of light. ◆ Adj. *stellar.* **2** *n.* A planet or other heavenly body, considered in astrology as influencing one's fortune or destiny. **3** *n.* A figure with five or more radiating points (☆), used as an emblem or decoration. **4** *v.* To set or ornament with spangles or stars. **5** *n.* An asterisk (*). **6** *v.* To mark with an asterisk. **7** *n.* An actor or actress who plays a leading part. **8** *v.* To play a leading part; be a star. **9** *n.* Anyone who is very prominent in a field: a sports *star.* **10** *v.* To show outstanding skill; be prominent: He *stars* on the tennis court. **11** *adj.* Prominent; brilliant.

star·board [stär′bərd] *n.* **1** The right-hand side of a ship, as one faces the front or bow. **2** *adj. use:* the *starboard* side. ◆ *Starboard* comes from an Old English word formed by combining *steor,* meaning *steering,* and *bord,* meaning *side of a ship.* Thus *steorbord* was the side of the ship used for steering.

starch [stärch] **1** *n.* A vegetable substance without taste or smell, produced by many plants. Potatoes contain a lot of starch. **2** *n.* A preparation of this substance used to stiffen clothes, to make paste, etc. **3** *v.* To apply starch to; stiffen with or as if with starch. **4** *n.* A stiff, formal manner. **5** *n. informal* Vigor; energy.

starch·y [stär′chē] *adj.* **starch·i·er, starch·i·est** **1** Stiffened with starch. **2** Made of or combined with starch. **3** Stiff; formal: a *starchy* reply to my note.

stare [stâr] *v.* **stared, star·ing,** *n.* **1** *v.* To look steadily for some time, with the eyes wide open, as from surprise, curiosity, wonder, or bad manners. **2** *v.* To look at fixedly. **3** *n.* A fixed, intense gaze. **4** *v.* To stand out; be conspicuous; glare. **— stare down** To stare back at another person until he looks away.

star·fish [stär′fish′] *n., pl.* **star·fish** or **star·fish·es** A small sea animal with a star-shaped body having five or more arms.

stark [stärk] **1** *adj.* Barren; bleak: a *stark* stretch of land. **2** *adj.* Complete; utter; downright: *stark* stupidity. **3** *adv.* Completely; utterly: *stark* naked; *stark* mad. **4** *adj.* Stiff or rigid, as in death. **— stark′ly** *adv.*

star·light [stär′līt′] *n.* The light given by a star or stars.

Common starfish, about 5 in. wide

star·ling [stär′ling] *n.* A bird with an iridescent black body, short tail, and a yellow bill.

star·lit [stär′lit′] *adj.* Lighted by the stars.

star·ry [stär′ē] *adj.* **star·ri·er, star·ri·est** **1** Set with stars; full of stars. **2** Lighted by the stars. **3** Shining like the stars.

Stars and Stripes The flag of the U.S., with thirteen alternately red and white stripes and fifty white stars on a blue square.

star·span·gled [stär′spang′gəld] *adj.* Having many stars; spangled with stars.

Star-Spangled Banner **1** The flag of the U.S. **2** The national anthem of the U.S.

start [stärt] **1** *v.* To make a beginning; set out: We *started* on our trip today. **2** *v.* To begin; commence: The play *starts* at eight o'clock. **3** *v.* To set in motion or circulation; put into action: to *start* an engine; to *start* a rumor. **4** *v.* To set up; establish: to *start* a business. **5** *n.* The act of starting; beginning: to get an early *start.* **6** *n.* The time or place of starting: the *start* of a race. **7** *n.* Advantage or distance in advance at the outset: a *start* of five miles over pursuers. **8** *v.* To move or cause to move suddenly, as from fear or surprise: to make someone *start* by shouting. **9** *n.* A sudden, startled movement or feeling: to give a *start* at a noise. **10** *v.* To move suddenly with a spring, leap, or bound. **11** *v.* To make or become loose, warped, etc. **— start in** To begin; undertake. **— start out 1** To begin a journey. **2** To begin or commence anything: to *start out* on a new career. **— start up 1** To rise or appear suddenly. **2** To begin or cause to begin operations, as an engine. **3** To begin or commence: The pain *started up* again last night.

start·er [stär′tər] *n.* **1** A person or thing that starts. **2** A person who gives the signal for the start of a race. **3** A person who sees that buses, etc., leave on schedule.

star·tle [stär'təl] *v.* **star·tled, star·tling,** *n.*
1 *v.* To frighten, surprise, or excite suddenly:
You *startled* me. **2** *adj. use:* a *startling* story.
3 *v.* To be frightened, surprised, or excited. **4** *n.*
A sudden fright, surprise, or shock.

star·va·tion [stär·vā'shən] *n.* **1** The act of
starving. **2** The condition of being starved.

starve [stärv] *v.* **starved, starv·ing 1** To
grow weak or die from lack of food. **2** To make
suffer or die from lack of food. **3** *informal* To be
very hungry. **4** To bring to a certain condition
by starving: to *starve* an enemy into surrender.
5 To suffer from lack or need: to *starve* for love.
◆ *Starve* once meant simply *to die*, but the
meaning became limited to death caused by
lack of food.

starve·ling [stärv'ling] **1** *n.* A person or
animal that is starving. **2** *adj.* Starving; hungry.

stash [stash] *v. slang* To hide or conceal for
storage and safekeeping.

state [stāt] *n., v.* **stat·ed, stat·ing 1** *n.* The
nature or condition of a person or thing: a *state*
of confusion; mercury in a liquid *state*. **2** *n.* A
frame of mind; mood: a *state* of fear. **3** *n.* A
very grand or formal style of living or doing
something; pomp: to be buried in *state*. **4** *adj.*
use: a *state* dinner. **5** *n.* A nation: the French
state. **6** *n.* (*often written* **State**) A group of
people forming an organized political unit that is
usually part of a larger federal government: the
State of New York. **7** *adj. use:* *state* papers; a
state job. **8** *n.* The territory of a state or nation:
That law does not apply inside this *state*. **9** *v.* To
set forth clearly in speech or writing; declare.
10 *v.* To fix; determine: to *state* a fee.

state·craft [stāt'kraft'] *n.* Skill in conducting
affairs of a state or government.

stat·ed [stā'tid] *adj.* **1** Established; fixed; set:
stated hours. **2** Declared; announced: his
stated reasons.

state·hood [stāt'hŏŏd] *n.* The condition or
status of being a state, especially of being one of
the United States.

state·house [stāt'hous'] *n.* (*often written*
Statehouse) A building in which a state
legislature meets.

state·ly [stāt'lē] *adj.* **state·li·er, state·li·est**
Dignified; imposing: a *stately* home. **— state'·
li·ness** *n.*

state·ment [stāt'mənt] *n.* **1** The act of stating.
2 Something that is stated: He made a *statement*
to the press. **3** A report of an account, showing
the amount of money owed or due: a bank's
monthly *statement*.

state·room [stāt'rŏŏm'] *n.* A private cabin on
a ship or sleeping room on a train.

states·man [stāts'mən] *n., pl.* **states·men**
[stāts'mən] A person who is skilled in the
business of government or diplomacy. **—
states'man·ship** *n.*

state-wide [stāt'wīd'] *adj.* Throughout a
state: a *state-wide* search for the missing couple.

stat·ic [stat'ik] **1** *adj.* Not active, moving, or
changing; at rest: *static* air. **2** *adj.* Of or having
to do with bodies at rest or forces in equilibrium.
3 *adj.* Acting or pressing as weight but without
moving: *static* pressure. **4** *adj.* Of, having to do
with, or producing stationary electric charges:
Static electricity is often produced by friction.
5 *n.* Electrical interference picked up by a radio
or television set, etc.; noise.

stat·ics [stat'iks] *n.* The branch of physics that
deals with bodies at rest and with forces that are
balanced by equal and opposite forces. ◆ See
-ICS.

sta·tion [stā'shən] **1** *n.* A place where a person
or persons are located to perform some duty; an
assigned post: the guard's *station* before the
palace. **2** *n.* A building, headquarters, etc.
occupied and used by a group working together:
a *fire* station. **3** *v.* To assign or place in a certain
spot or position. **4** *n.* A place, and usually a
building, where trains or buses stop regularly and
where passengers get on or off. **5** *n.* Social
standing: a man of noble *station*. **6** *n.* The
offices, studios, and technical equipment of a
radio or television broadcasting unit.

sta·tion·ar·y [stā'shən·er'ē] *adj.* **1** Remaining
in one place; fixed; not movable: *stationary*
equipment. **2** Showing no change of character,
condition, size, etc.: a *stationary* civilization.
◆ *Stationary* (not moving) and *stationery* (writing
materials) should not be confused. *Stationery*
ends in *ery* and is used for *letters*.

sta·tion·er [stā'shən·ər] *n.* A person who sells
paper, envelopes, pens, pencils, ink, etc.

sta·tion·ery [stā'shən·er'ē] *n.* Materials used
in writing, as paper, pens, etc., especially paper
and envelopes for writing letters. ◆ See STA-
TIONARY.

station wagon A closed automobile with rear
seats that fold down or
come out and a door that
opens in the rear for loading.

Station wagon

sta·tis·tic [stə·tis'tik] **1** *adj.*
Statistical. **2** *n.* A fact or
item of information used in a
statistical report or statement.

sta·tis·ti·cal [stə·tis'tə·kəl] *adj.* Of or having
to do with statistics. **— sta·tis'ti·cal·ly** *adv.*

stat·is·ti·cian [stat'is·tish'ən] *n.* A person who
is skilled in statistics.

sta·tis·tics [stə·tis'tiks] *n., pl.* **1** The science of
collecting, arranging, and analyzing numerical
facts so as to arrive at certain conclusions. **2** The
facts collected or the conclusions arrived at:
Statistics show many people have given up
smoking. ◆ See -ICS.

stat·u·ar·y [stach'ŏŏ·er'ē] *n.* **1** Statues, as a
group. **2** The art of making statues.

add, āce, câre, pälm; end, ēqual; it, īce; odd, ōpen, ôrder; tŏŏk, pōōl; up, bûrn;
ə = a in *above*, e in *sicken*, i in *possible*, o in *melon*, u in *circus*; yōō = u in *fuse*; oil; pout;
check; ring; thin; this; zh in *vision*. For ¶ reference, see page 64 · HOW TO

stat·ue [stach′ōō] *n.* A likeness, as of a person or animal, carved, molded, or cast of a substance such as marble, wood, clay, bronze, etc.

stat·u·esque [stach′ōō·esk′] *adj.* Like a statue, as in grace, poise, dignity, form, etc.

stat·u·ette [stach′ōō·et′] *n.* A small statue.

stat·ure [stach′ər] *n.* **1** Natural height, as of a person. **2** Development; growth: moral *stature*.

sta·tus [stā′təs *or* stat′əs] *n.* **1** State; condition: the *status* of a country during wartime. **2** Position or rank: a man of low social *status*.

status quo [kwō] The condition in which a person or thing is at the present time.

stat·ute [stach′ōōt] *n.* A rule or law, especially a law passed by a legislature.

stat·u·to·ry [stach′ə·tôr′ē] *adj.* **1** Having to do with a statute. **2** Created by a statute.

St. Au·gus·tine [sānt ô′gəs·tēn] A city in NE Florida; oldest permanent settlement in the United States.

staunch¹ [stônch *or* stänch] **1** *adj.* Firm and dependable; loyal: a *staunch* friend. **2** *adj.* Strongly and firmly built; substantial. **3** *adj.* Watertight: a *staunch* ship. **— staunch′ly** *adv.* **— staunch′ness** *n.*

staunch² [stônch *or* stänch] *v.* Another spelling of STANCH¹.

stave [stāv] *n.*, *v.* **staved** or **stove, stav·ing** **1** *n.* Any of the curved strips of wood or iron that together form the sides of a barrel, tub, cask, etc. **2** *v.* To furnish with staves. **3** *v.* To break in the staves of: to *stave* a barrel. **4** *v.* To break or make a hole in by crushing or smashing. **5** *n.* A musical staff. **6** *n.* A stanza or verse in a poem or song. **7** *n.* A rod or staff. **— stave off** To ward off; keep away. ◆ *Stave* was formed from the plural of *staff*, which is *staves*.

Staves

staves [stāvz] *n.* **1** A plural of STAFF. **2** The plural of STAVE.

stay¹ [stā] **1** *v.* To continue or remain, as in some certain place or condition: to *stay* indoors; to *stay* healthy. **2** *v.* To remain as a guest, resident, etc.; dwell: to *stay* for a week at the seashore. **3** *v.* To remain for the duration of: to *stay* the night. **4** *n.* The act or time of staying; visit: a week's *stay* at the seashore. **5** *v.* To stop; halt; check: to *stay* sentence pending an appeal. **6** *n.* A delay or putting off of a legal action. **7** *v.* To satisfy temporarily: to *stay* the pangs of hunger. **8** *v.* To be able to keep going and last to the finish, as in a race.

Statue of Liberty

stay² [stā] **1** *v.* To support, prop, or hold up: We *stayed* the weak limb with two poles. **2** *v.* To comfort or strengthen mentally or morally. **3** *n.* Something that gives support or serves as a prop. **4** *n.* A strip of plastic or metal, used to stiffen corsets, girdles, etc.

stay³ [stā] *n.* **1** A strong rope, often of wire, used to support and brace a mast or spar. **2** Any rope, chain, etc., used to steady or support something.

stay·sail [stā′səl *or* stā′sāl′] *n.* A sail, usually triangular, fastened on a stay.

stead [sted] *n.* Place of a person or thing taken by a substitute or, sometimes, by a successor: I could not keep the appointment, so I sent my brother in my *stead*. **— stand in good stead** To be of good use.

stead·fast [sted′fast′] *adj.* Not moving or changing; constant: He was *steadfast* in his devotion to his family. **— stead′fast′ly** *adv.*

stead·y [sted′ē] *adj.* **stead·i·er, stead·i·est,** *v.* **stead·ied, stead·y·ing 1** *adj.* Stable in position; firmly supported; fixed: a *steady* shelf. **2** *adj.* Moving or acting regularly and without changes: a *steady* wind. **3** *adj.* Not easily disturbed or upset: *steady* nerves. **4** *adj.* Industrious; dependable; reliable: *steady* workers. **5** *adj.* Regular: a *steady* customer. **6** *v.* To make or become steady. **— stead′i·ly** *adv.* **— stead′i·ness** *n.*

steak [stāk] *n.* **1** A slice of meat or fish, cooked or to be cooked, usually by broiling or frying. **2** Ground meat formed into a patty for cooking like a steak: hamburger *steak*.

steal [stēl] *v.* **stole, sto·len, steal·ing,** *n.* **1** *v.* To take from another without right or permission, and usually in a secret manner: He *stole* money from a friend. **2** *v.* To take, get, or win over, as by surprise, skill, or trickery: The speaker *stole* our hearts with his charm and wit; The new singer *stole* the show. **3** *v.* To take, get, or do in a secret or concealed way: to *steal* a glance at someone. **4** *v.* To move or go secretly: to *steal* into a room. **5** *v.* In baseball, to reach (second base, etc.) without the aid of a batted ball or an error. **6** *n.* The act of stealing. **7** *n. informal* A bargain.

stealth [stelth] *n.* A manner of acting or doing something that is secret, furtive, or underhand.

stealth·y [stel′thē] *adj.* **stealth·i·er, stealth·i·est** Done in a secret, furtive, or underhand way: The burglar's movements were quick and stealthy. **— stealth′i·ly** *adv.* ◆ *Stealthy, furtive,* and *underhand* all mean *done secretly*. Someone is *stealthy* if he wants to escape notice, but he is *furtive* if he is worried about being discovered: a *stealthy* hunter; a *furtive* thief. *Underhand* is usually applied to methods that are kept quiet because they are shady or dishonest: He won the election by *underhand* means.

steam [stēm] **1** *n.* The gas or vapor into which water is changed by boiling. It is used for heating and, under pressure, as a source of energy. **2** *v.* To give off steam or vapor: The kettle is *steaming*.

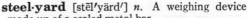

3 *v.* To move or travel by the power of steam: The boat *steamed* up the river. **4** *v.* To treat with steam, as in softening, cooking, cleaning, etc. **5** *n.* The mist into which water vapor is condensed by cooling. **6** *v.* To become covered with condensed water vapor, as a window. **7** *n. informal* Vigor; force; speed: He tired and ran out of *steam*. **— let off steam** *informal* To express pent-up emotions or opinions.

steam·boat [stēm′bōt′] *n.* A boat driven by steam, especially one used on a river.

steam chest The box or chest through which steam is delivered to an engine cylinder.

steam engine An engine driven by steam, especially one in which a piston is moved by the expanding force of steam under pressure.

steam·er [stē′mər] *n.* **1** A vehicle, engine, etc., worked or driven by steam, as a steamship. **2** A container in which something is steamed: a *steamer* for vegetables. **3** A soft-shell clam cooked by steaming.

steam·fit·ter [stēm′fit′ər] *n.* A man who sets up or repairs steam pipes, boilers, etc.

steam·roll·er [stēm′rō′lər] *n.* **1** A machine driven by a steam, gasoline, or diesel engine, with heavy rollers that are used to pack down and level gravel, paving materials, etc. **2** Any power or force that crushes and overcomes whatever is in its way.

steam·ship [stēm′ship′] *n.* A large ship driven by steam.

steam shovel A machine for digging, operated by steam power, or now by a gasoline or diesel engine.

steam·y [stē′mē] *adj.* **steam·i·er, steam·i·est** Consisting of, like, or full of steam; misty.

Steamship

steed [stēd] *n.* A horse, especially a spirited war horse: seldom used today.

steel [stēl] **1** *n.* A tough and widely used metal composed of a mixture of iron, carbon, and sometimes other metals. **2** *n.* Something made of steel, as a sword. **3** *adj. use:* a *steel* hammer. **4** *n.* A quality or nature that is hard, cold, etc., like steel: a heart of *steel*. **5** *v.* To make hard, strong, cold, etc.: to *steel* one's heart against misery.

steel engraving **1** The art and process of engraving on a steel plate. **2** The impression made from such a plate.

steel wool Steel fibers matted together for use in cleaning, polishing, etc.

steel·work·er [stēl′wûr′kər] *n.* A person who works in a steel mill.

steel·y [stē′lē] *adj.* **steel·i·er, steel·i·est** **1** Made of steel. **2** Like steel, as in strength, hardness, or coldness: a *steely* gaze.

steel·yard [stēl′yärd′] *n.* A weighing device made up of a scaled metal bar, a movable counterweight, and hooks. The object to be weighed is hung at the short end of the bar and the counterweight is moved along the long end until the bar is balanced.

Modern and ancient steelyards

steep¹ [stēp] *adj.* **1** Having a sharp incline or slope: a *steep* hill. **2** *informal* High; excessive: a *steep* price. **— steep′ly** *adv.*

steep² [stēp] *v.* To soak in a liquid: *Steep* the tea. **— steeped in** Completely filled, interested, involved, etc.: He is *steeped in* history.

steep·en [stē′pən] *v.* To make or become steep or steeper.

stee·ple [stē′pəl] *n.* **1** A tall, usually tapering structure rising above a church tower; spire. **2** The entire tower of a church.

stee·ple·chase [stē′pəl·chās′] *n.* A horse race over a course prepared with obstacles, as hedges, rails, and water jumps. ◆ *Steeplechase* was formed by combining *steeple* with *chase*. Church steeples were often used as landmarks or goals in races.

Steeplechase

stee·ple·jack [stē′pəl·jak′] *n.* A man whose occupation is to climb steeples and other tall structures to inspect or make repairs.

steer¹ [stir] *v.* **1** To direct the course of (a vessel or vehicle): I *steered* the car; I *steered* with one hand. **2** To be steered or guided: The car *steers* easily. **3** To set and follow; pursue: He *steered* a course for the island. **4** To direct; guide; control: The president *steered* his party to victory. **— steer clear of** To keep away from; avoid.

steer² [stir] *n.* A male of beef cattle, castrated usually before it is fully grown, especially one that is from two to four years old.

steer·age [stir′ij] *n.* The part of a passenger ship open to passengers paying the lowest fares. In former times it offered little or no comfort or privacy.

steering wheel A wheel turned by the driver or pilot of a vehicle, ship, etc., to steer it.

steers·man [stirz′mən] *n., pl.* **steers·men** [stirz′mən] A person who steers a boat; helmsman.

steg·o·sau·rus [steg′ə·sôr′əs] *n.* Any of a genus of large dinosaurs that lived in the western United States.

stein [stīn] *n.* A beer mug.

---

add, āce, câre, pälm;   end, ēqual;   it, īce;   odd, ōpen, ôrder;   tŏŏk, pōōl;   up, bûrn;
ə = a in *above*, e in *sicken*, i in *possible*, o in *melon*, u in *circus*;   yōō = u in *fuse*;   oil;   pout;
check; ring; thin; this; zh in *vision*.   For ¶ reference, see page 64 · HOW TO

stel·lar [stel′ər] *adj.* **1** Of or having to do with the stars. **2** Of, for, or by an important actor, actress, etc.: a *stellar* part in a movie. **3** First-rate; excellent: a *stellar* performance.

St. El·mo's fire [sânt el′mōz] A flamelike light due to electricity produced in the atmosphere, sometimes seen on aircraft wings, the masts of ships, etc.

stem[1] [stem] *n., v.* **stemmed, stem·ming 1** *n.* The main body or stalk of a tree, shrub, or other plant, rising above the ground. **2** *n.* The slender growth that supports the fruit, flower, or leaf of a plant. **3** *v.* To remove the stems of or from. **4** *n.* Something that resembles a stem: a pipe *stem*; a watch *stem*. **5** *n.* The front part of a ship; bow; prow. **6** *n.* A line of descent from a particular ancestor. **7** *v.* To come or originate: His current bad health *stems* from a serious accident. **8** *n.* The part of a word to which inflectional endings are added or which is itself changed by inflection: *Sing* is the *stem* of *sings*, *singing*, and *sung*.

stem[2] [stem] *v.* **stemmed, stem·ming** To stand firm or make progress against: to *stem* the tide.

stem[3] [stem] *v.* **stemmed, stem·ming** To stop, hold back, or dam up, as a current.

stench [stench] *n.* A foul odor; stink.

sten·cil [sten′səl] *n., v.* **sten·ciled** or **sten·cilled, sten·cil·ing** or **sten·cil·ling 1** *n.* A sheet of paper, etc., in which patterns, letters, words, etc., are cut out. When ink or paint is spread over the stencil, which is laid on a surface to be marked, it passes through the holes to the surface. **2** *n.* A decoration or the like produced by means of a stencil. **3** *v.* To mark with a stencil.

ste·nog·ra·pher [stə·nog′rə·fər] *n.* A person whose work is taking dictation, usually in shorthand, and typewriting.

sten·o·graph·ic [sten′ə·graf′ik] *adj.* Of, having to do with, or using stenography.

ste·nog·ra·phy [stə·nog′rə·fē] *n.* The art of writing in shorthand and of reading it.

sten·to·ri·an [sten·tôr′ē·ən] *adj.* Extremely loud.

step [step] *n., v.* **stepped, step·ping 1** *n.* A movement made by lifting one foot and putting it down in a different place; one motion of a leg and foot as in walking or running. **2** *n.* The distance passed over in making such a movement: a short *step*. **3** *v.* To move by changing the position of the leg and foot: *Step* ahead! **4** *v.* To take (a step, pace, etc.): *Step* five paces to the rear. **5** *n.* Any short distance. **6** *v.* To walk a short distance: to *step* across the street. **7** *n.* A place on which to put the foot in going up or down, as a stair or a ladder rung. **8** *n.* A single action regarded as leading to something: the first *step* in our plan for reorganization. **9** *n.* A grade, rank, etc.: A lieutenant colonel is two *steps* above a captain. **10** *n.* The manner of stepping; walk; gait: a heavy *step*. **11** *n.* The sound of a footfall: I hear *steps* on the stairway.

12 *n.* A footprint; track. **13** *n.* A combination or a pattern of foot movements in dancing. **14** *v.* To perform the steps of: to *step* a square dance. **15** *v.* To move or act quickly or briskly: *Step* along, don't dawdle! **16** *v.* To move or pass into a situation or circumstance, as if in a single step: to *step* into a fortune. **17** *v.* To put or press the foot down: to *step* on an ant; to *step* on the brake. **18** *v.* To measure by taking steps: to *step* off five yards. **19** *n.* Something like a step, as a supporting framework, etc.: the *step* of a ship's mast. **20** *v.* To place the lower end of (a mast) in its step. **—in step 1** Walking, dancing, marching, etc., in a way that fits a certain set rhythm, cadence, etc. **2** *informal* In agreement or conformity. **—keep step** To remain in step while walking, marching, etc. **—out of step** Not in step. **—step by step** By gradually advancing; gradually. **—step down 1** To decrease gradually, or by steps or degrees. **2** To resign from an office or position. **—step up** To increase; raise. **—take steps** To do certain things in order to reach a desired end or result. **—watch one's step** To act with care; be careful.

step·broth·er [step′bruth′ər] *n.* The son of a person's stepmother or stepfather by a former marriage.

step·child [step′child′] *n., pl.* **step·chil·dren** [step′chil′drən] The child of a person's husband or wife by a former marriage.

step·daugh·ter [step′dô′tər] *n.* A female stepchild.

step·fa·ther [step′fä′thər] *n.* The husband of a person's mother, but not that person's own father.

step·lad·der [step′lad′ər] *n.* A ladder with flat steps instead of rungs and often with a folding brace at the back.

step·moth·er [step′muth′ər] *n.* The wife of a person's father, but not that person's own mother.

steppe [step] *n.* A vast, treeless plain, especially one of these areas in Soviet Europe and Asia.

step·ping·stone [step′ing·stōn′] *n.* **1** A stone on which a person can step, as when crossing a stream. **2** A step or stage in the fulfillment of a goal: *steppingstones* to fame.

step·sis·ter [step′sis′tər] *n.* The daughter of a person's stepmother or stepfather by a former marriage.

step·son [step′sun′] *n.* A male stepchild.

ster·e·o [ster′ē·ō *or* stir′ē·ō] **1** *n.* A stereophonic system. **2** *adj.* Stereophonic. ◆ *Stereo* is a shortened form of *stereophonic.*

ster·e·o·phon·ic [ster′ē·ə·fon′ik] *adj.* Having to do with a system of recording or broadcasting in which different sounds picked up simultaneously by separated microphones are played back through correspondingly separated loudspeakers.

ster·e·op·ti·con [ster′ē·op′ti·kon *or* stir′ē·op′ti·kon] *n.* A device that projects pictures onto a screen by means of a powerful light; magic lantern.

S

ster·e·o·scope [ster′ē·ə·skōp] *n.* A device through which one looks at two pictures of the same scene or object taken from slightly different angles. The image formed by the combined views no longer appears flat but seems to have depth and solidity.

ster·e·o·scop·ic [ster′ē·ə·skop′ik] *adj.* Of or having to do with a stereoscope.

ster·e·o·type [ster′ē·ə·tīp′ *or* stir′ē·ə·tīp′] *n., v.* **ster·e·o·typed, ster·e·o·typ·ing 1** *n.* A metal plate used in printing. **2** *n.* A mental image or a way of thinking about a person, thing, event, etc., that follows a conventional or fixed pattern and makes no allowances for individual differences. **3** *v.* To make a stereotype of.

ster·e·o·typed [ster′ē·ə·tīpt′ *or* stir′ē·ə·tīpt′] *adj.* **1** Of a conventional, fixed nature; hackneyed; trite; unoriginal: This novel has a *stereotyped* plot. **2** Produced from a stereotype.

ster·ile [ster′əl] *adj.* **1** Unable to produce offspring, plants, etc.; barren: Mules are *sterile*; a *sterile* desert. **2** Free from harmful bacteria or germs. **— ste·ril′i·ty** *n.*

ster·il·ize [ster′əl·īz] *v.* **ster·il·ized, ster·il·iz·ing 1** To free from harmful bacteria or germs: to *sterilize* surgical instruments. **2** To deprive of the power of reproducing. **— ster′il·i·za′tion** *n.* **— ster′il·iz′er** *n.* ¶3

ster·ling [stûr′ling] **1** *n.* English money. **2** *adj.* Of English money: 20 pounds *sterling*. **3** *n.* Sterling silver. **4** *adj.* Of sterling silver: *sterling* candlesticks. **5** *n.* An article or articles made of sterling silver. **6** *adj.* Excellent; genuine: a man of *sterling* qualities.

sterling silver An alloy that is 92.5% pure silver.

stern[1] [stûrn] *adj.* **1** Harsh in nature or manner; strict; severe: a *stern* person; *stern* punishment. **2** Firm; fixed; unyielding: a *stern* resolve. **— stern′ly** *adv.*

stern[2] [stûrn] *n.* The rear part of a ship, boat, etc.

ster·num [stûr′nəm] *n., pl.* **ster·na** [stûr′nə] or **ster·nums** The long, narrow bone in front of the chest to which most of the ribs are attached; the breastbone.

steth·o·scope [steth′ə·skōp] *n.* A small, portable instrument by which doctors can hear sounds produced in the chest, especially in the lungs and heart. ◆ *Stethoscope* comes from two Greek words meaning, translated freely, *chest watcher.*

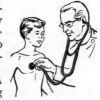
Stethoscope

ste·ve·dore [stē′və·dôr] *n.* A person who works at loading or unloading a ship in port.

Ste·ven·son [stē′vən·sən], **Robert Louis,** 1850–1894, Scottish novelist, essayist, and poet.

stew [st(y)ōō] **1** *v.* To boil slowly and gently, usually for a long time. **2** *n.* Stewed food, especially a preparation of meat or fish and various vegetables, cooked together slowly. **3** *v. informal* To worry. **4** *n. informal* A state of worry or mental agitation.

stew·ard [st(y)ōō′ərd] *n.* **1** A person who manages the property, finances, or other affairs of another person or persons. **2** A person in charge of provisions, servants, etc., for a hotel, club, ship, or the like. **3** A servant on a ship, airplane, etc. ◆ *Steward* comes from an Old English word meaning *sty keeper.* Over the years stewards came to be entrusted with more respectable jobs.

stew·ard·ess [st(y)ōō′ər·dis] *n.* A female steward, especially one who waits on passengers on a ship, airplane, etc.

St. He·le·na [sānt hə·lē′nə] A British island in the South Atlantic, where Napoleon was held in exile, 1815–1821.

stick [stik] *n., v.* **stuck, stick·ing 1** *n.* A twig or branch cut or broken from a tree, bush, etc. **2** *n.* Any long, slender piece of wood, as a cane, baton, wand, etc. **3** *n.* Anything like a stick in form: a *stick* of candy. **4** *n. informal* A stiff or dull person. **5** *v.* To pierce or stab with a pin, knife, or other pointed instrument. **6** *v.* To fasten in place with or as with pins, nails, etc.: to *stick* a ribbon on a dress. **7** *v.* To fasten to a surface by or as if by an adhesive substance: to *stick* on a stamp. **8** *v.* To put or thrust: He *stuck* his hand into his pocket. **9** *v.* To be brought to a stop or halt: Our car was *stuck* in traffic. **10** *v. informal* To puzzle; baffle: The second question in the test really *stuck* me. **11** *v.* To hesitate: Sue *sticks* at nothing when her mind is made up. **12** *v.* To persist; persevere: to *stick* at one's job. **13** *v.* To be loyal or faithful: We must *stick* together. **— stick up** *slang* To hold up or rob.

stick·er [stik′ər] *n.* A gummed label, sign, etc.

stick·le [stik′əl] *v.* **stick·led, stick·ling** To argue about or insist stubbornly.

stick·le·back [stik′əl·bak′] *n.* Any of various small fresh- or salt-water fishes of northern regions, having no scales, but sharp spines on the back. They are noted for the elaborate nests which the male builds for the female's eggs.

stick·ler [stik′lər] *n.* A person who demands that things be done in a certain, very precise way.

stick·pin [stik′pin′] *n.* An ornamental pin for a necktie.

stick·up [stik′up′] *n. slang* A robbery; holdup.

stick·y [stik′ē] *adj.* **stick·i·er, stick·i·est 1** That sticks as glue does: *sticky* syrup. **2** Covered with something that makes things stick: *sticky* hands. **3** Warm and humid: a *sticky* day. **— stick′i·ness** *n.*

stiff [stif] *adj.* **1** Not easy to bend; not flexible; rigid: a *stiff* felt hat. **2** Moved with difficulty or with pain: *stiff* brakes; a *stiff* neck. **3** Not liquid or fluid in consistency; thick: a *stiff* varnish. **4** Not graceful or natural; formal: a *stiff* manner. **5** Strong or powerful: a *stiff* current. **6** Difficult; hard; arduous: a *stiff* test; a *stiff* climb. **7** Harsh; severe: a *stiff* penalty. **8** High; unreasonable: a *stiff* price. **— stiff′ly** *adv.* **— stiff′ness** *n.*

stiff·en [stif′ən] *v.* To make or become stiff or stiffer.

stiff-necked [stif′nekt′] *adj.* Not yielding; stubborn; obstinate.

sti·fle [stī′fəl] *v.* **sti·fled, sti·fling 1** To keep back; suppress; repress: to *stifle* sobs. **2** To die or cause to die by suffocation. **3** To have difficulty in breathing.

stig·ma [stig′mə] *n., pl.* **stig·mas** or **stig·ma·ta** [stig·mä′tə *or* stig′mə·tə] **1** A mark or sign of disgrace or dishonor: He bore the *stigma* of a convicted criminal. **2** The part of a pistil of a flower that receives pollen. **3** (*pl.*) Marks on the hands, feet, and the side, similar to the five wounds received by Jesus at the crucifixion. They are said to appear miraculously on certain persons.

stig·ma·tize [stig′mə·tīz] *v.* **stig·ma·tized, stig·ma·tiz·ing** To describe or name as bad or disgraceful: His conduct *stigmatized* him as a coward. ¶3

stile [stīl] *n.* **1** A step, or series of steps, on each side of a fence or wall to aid in getting over it. **2** Another name for TURNSTILE.

sti·let·to [sti·let′ō] *n., pl.* **sti·let·tos** or **sti·let·toes 1** A small dagger with a slender blade. **2** A small, sharp-pointed instrument for making eyelets in cloth that is to be embroidered.

Stile

still[1] [stil] **1** *adj.* Making no sound; silent. **2** *adj.* Free from disturbance; calm; peaceful. **3** *adj.* Without movement; motionless. **4** *v.* To become or make still: The applause suddenly *stilled*; He *stilled* the anger of the mob. **5** *adv.* All the same; nevertheless: Mary, although shy, is *still* well liked. **6** *adv.* Even; yet: You can get *still* more if you try. **7** *conj.* Nevertheless; and yet: I like her dress; *still* I think the color is unbecoming. **8** *adv.* Up to this or that time; yet: He is *still* here. **— still′ness** *n.*

still[2] [stil] *n.* An apparatus for distilling liquids, especially alcoholic liquors.

still·born [stil′bôrn′] *adj.* Dead at birth.

still life 1 In painting, the representation of inanimate objects, such as vases, fruits, flowers, etc. **2** A picture of such a subject.

stilt [stilt] *n.* **1** One of a pair of long, slender poles made with a projection to support the foot some distance above the ground in walking. **2** A tall post or pillar used as a support for something, as for a dock or building. **3** Any of several long-legged, three-toed, wading birds.

stilt·ed [stil′tid] *adj.* Stiffly formal and dignified in manner; not natural or at ease.

stim·u·lant [stim′yə·lənt] **1** *n.* Something that stimulates or quickens the activity of the body or of a part of the body: Certain drugs are *stimulants*. **2** *n.* An alcoholic beverage. **3** *adj.* Serving or acting as a stimulant.

stim·u·late [stim′yə·lāt] *v.* **stim·u·lat·ed, stim·u·lat·ing 1** To rouse to activity or quickened action; excite; spur: to *stimulate* student interest. **2** To act as a stimulant. **— stim′u·la′tion** *n.*

stim·u·lus [stim′yə·ləs] *n., pl.* **stim·u·li** [stim′yə·lī] **1** Anything that rouses or stirs to action or greater effort. **2** Anything that rouses a part of the body to activity: Light is a *stimulus* to the optic nerve.

sting [sting] *v.* **stung, sting·ing,** *n.* **1** *v.* To pierce or prick painfully: The bee *stung* me. **2** *n.* The act of stinging. **3** *n.* The wound or the pain caused by a sting. **4** *n.* A sharp, pointed organ, as of a bee, able to inflict a painful and sometimes poisonous wound. **5** *v.* To suffer or cause to suffer a sharp pain: His fingers *stung* from the cold; The slap *stung* her face. **6** *v.* To suffer or cause to suffer mentally: She was *stung* with remorse. **7** *n.* Any sharp, painful sensation: the *sting* of remorse. **8** *v. slang* To overcharge; cheat. **— sting′er** *n.*

sting ray Any of several sea fishes having flat bodies, very broad side fins, and long, whiplike tails with sharp stingers that are capable of inflicting severe, often poisonous wounds.

Sting ray, to 7 ft. long

stin·gy [stin′jē] *adj.* **stin·gi·er, stin·gi·est 1** Unwilling to spend or give; miserly. **2** Very small or scanty; meager. **— stin′gi·ly** *adv.* **— stin′gi·ness** *n.*

stink [stingk] *n., v.* **stank** or **stunk, stunk, stink·ing 1** *n.* A strong, foul odor; stench. **2** *v.* To have a strong, foul odor.

stint [stint] **1** *v.* To limit, as in amount or share; be stingy with: Don't *stint* yourself. **2** *v.* To be saving or economical: Don't *stint* when it comes to feeding guests. **3** *n.* A task to be performed; a share of work: Have you finished your *stint* in the office? **4** *n.* A stinting; limit: to give without *stint*.

sti·pend [stī′pend] *n.* An allowance, salary, or pension, paid at regular intervals.

stip·ple [stip′əl] *v.* **stip·pled, stip·pling** To draw, paint, or engrave with dots or short strokes instead of lines.

stip·u·late [stip′yə·lāt] *v.* **stip·u·lat·ed, stip·u·lat·ing** To specify as a condition of an agreement: They *stipulated* that the payments should be made quarterly. **— stip′u·la′tion** *n.*

stip·ule [stip′yool] *n.* One of a pair of small, leaflike growths at the base of the stem of a leaf.

stir [stûr] *v.* **stirred, stir·ring,** *n.* **1** *v.* To move around with a circular motion, as a fluid or group of dry particles, so as to mix thoroughly: *Stir* the soup; This paint *stirs* easily. **2** *n.* The act of stirring: Give the soup a *stir.* **3** *v.* To move or cause to move, especially slightly: The leaves *stirred*; The wind *stirred* the tall grass. **4** *v.* To move or cause to move energetically: Everyone was up and *stirring* around the house; She *stirred* herself to cook dinner. **5** *v.* To bring about; provoke: to *stir* up trouble. **6** *v.* To affect strongly; move with emotion: to *stir* an audience. **7** *n.* Excitement; agitation; interest: The speech provoked quite a *stir.*

stir·ring [stûr′ing] *adj.* **1** Stimulating; inspiring: a *stirring* talk. **2** Lively; brisk: a *stirring* period in history.

stir·rup [stûr′əp *or* stir′əp] *n.* One of a pair of loops with flattened bases suspended by straps on each side of a saddle to support a rider's foot. They are made of wood, metal, or leather. ◆ *Stirrup* comes from an Old English word meaning *mounting rope.*

stirrup bone One of the three small bones of the middle ear. It looks like a stirrup and helps to transmit sound vibrations to the inner ear.

stitch [stich] **1** *n.* A single, complete movement of a threaded needle or other implement through fabric and back again, as in sewing, embroidery, etc. **2** *n.* A single turn of thread or yarn around a needle or other implement, as in knitting or crocheting. **3** *n.* A loop or link made by stitching. **4** *n.* A peculiar or special arrangement of thread or threads in sewing, embroidery, etc.: the chain *stitch.* **5** *v.* To sew or join together with stitches. **6** *n.* A sharp, sudden pain, as in the side. **7** *n. informal* The smallest bit: Not a *stitch* of work was done today.

St. Law·rence River [lôr′əns] A river of SE Canada, flowing from Lake Ontario to the Atlantic Ocean.

St. Lawrence Seaway A system of canals along the St. Lawrence River which, with the river, provides a channel for ships between the Great Lakes and the Atlantic Ocean.

St. Lou·is [lōō′is *or* lōō′ē] A city in Missouri, on the Mississippi River.

stoat [stōt] *n.* The ermine, especially in its brown summer coat.

stock [stok] **1** *n.* A quantity of something got or kept for use or sale; supply: a *stock* of food; a *stock* of dresses. **2** *n.* Livestock. **3** *v.* To furnish with livestock, as a farm, or with merchandise, as a store. **4** *v.* To lay in supplies or goods: to *stock* up on meat. **5** *v.* To keep for sale: This market *stocks* my favorite brand of cereal. **6** *adj.* Kept on hand, as for sale: a *stock* size. **7** *adj.* Commonly used; trite: a *stock* phrase. **8** *adj.* Employed in handling or caring for stocks of goods: a *stock* clerk. **9** *n.* The ownership of a corporation divided into shares. **10** *n.* A share or shares of such ownership. **11** *n.* The trunk or main stem of a tree or other plant. **12** *n.* A line of family descent: He comes from Dutch *stock.* **13** *n.* A related group or family of plants or animals. **14** *n.* The broth from boiled meat or fish used in preparing soups, etc. **15** *n.* (*pl.*) A wooden frame with holes for confining the ankles and often the wrists, formerly used in punishing petty offenders. **16** *n.* A part that serves as a handle or support, as the wooden part of a rifle. **17** *n.* A broad, stiffened band, formerly worn as a necktie. — **take stock 1** To take an inventory. **2** To make a careful estimate or examination: It was time to *take stock* of himself and his achievements.

stock·ade [sto·kād′] *n., v.* **stock·ad·ed, stock·ad·ing 1** *n.* A series of posts, stakes, etc., set upright in the earth to form a fence or barrier. **2** *n.* The area thus enclosed. **3** *v.* To surround or fortify with a stockade.

stock·bro·ker [stok′brō′kər] *n.* A person whose business is the buying and selling of stocks and bonds for others.

stock company 1 An incorporated company that sells shares of stock. **2** A theatrical company that presents a series of plays.

stock exchange 1 A place where stocks and bonds are bought and sold. **2** A group of stockbrokers who deal in stocks, bonds, etc.

stock·hold·er [stok′hōl′dər] *n.* A person who owns stock in a stock company.

Stock·holm [stok′hōm] *n.* The capital of Sweden, a port on the Baltic Sea.

stock·ing [stok′ing] *n.* A close-fitting, knitted or woven covering for the foot and leg.

stocking cap A knitted cap with a cone-shaped end usually decorated with a tassel, etc., worn for skiing, tobogganing, etc.

stock market 1 A stock exchange. **2** The buying and selling of stocks and bonds. **3** The lists of the prices of stocks, bonds, etc.

stock·pile [stok′pīl] *n., v.* **stock·piled, stock·pil·ing 1** *n.* A reserve supply, as of scarce metals. **2** *v.* To accumulate a stockpile of.

stock·room [stok′rōōm′] *n.* A room where stocks of goods are stored.

stock·still [stok′stil′] *adj.* Still as a stock or post; motionless: He stood *stock-still.*

stock·y [stok′ē] *adj.* **stock·i·er, stock·i·est** Solidly built, thickset, and usually short.

stock·yard [stok′yärd′] *n.* A large yard with pens where cattle, sheep, pigs, etc., are kept ready for shipping or slaughter.

stodg·y [stoj′ē] *adj.* **stodg·i·er, stodg·i·est 1** Dull, stuffy, and commonplace: a *stodgy* speech. **2** Indigestible and heavy: a *stodgy* meal.

sto·ic [stō′ik] **1** *n.* A person who is calm and appears to be unaffected by either pleasure or pain. **2** *adj.* Unaffected by pleasure or pain. — **sto′i·cal** *adj.* — **sto′i·cal·ly** *adv.*

sto·i·cism [stō′ə·siz′əm] *n.* A calm indifference to either pleasure or pain.

add, āce, câre, pälm; end, ēqual; it, īce; odd, ōpen, ôrder; tŏŏk, pōōl; up, bûrn;
ə = a in *above*, e in *sicken*, i in *possible*, o in *melon*, u in *circus*; yōō = u in *fuse*; oil; pout;
check; ring; thin; this; zh in *vision*. For ¶ reference, see page 64 · HOW TO

stoke [stōk] *v.* **stoked, stok·ing 1** To supply (a furnace) with fuel. **2** To stir up or tend (a fire or furnace). ◆ The verb *stoke* was formed from *stoker*, which came into English first.

stoke·hold [stōk′hōld′] *n.* The furnace room of a steamship.

stoke·hole [stōk′hōl′] *n.* **1** The opening in a furnace where coal is put in. **2** The space in front of the furnaces of a ship where men stand to shovel in coal.

stok·er [stō′kər] *n.* **1** A person who supplies fuel to a furnace, as a fireman on a locomotive. **2** A device for feeding coal to a furnace.

stole¹ [stōl] *n.* **1** A long, narrow band of silk, linen, etc., worn about the shoulders by clergymen. **2** A long scarf of fur or cloth, worn about the shoulders by women.

stole² [stōl] Past tense of STEAL.

sto·len [stō′lən] Past participle of STEAL.

stol·id [stol′id] *adj.* Having or showing little or no feeling; impassive; dull. **— stol′id·ly** *adv.*

sto·ma [stō′mə] *n.*, *pl.* **sto·ma·ta** [stō′mə·tə] **1** A very small opening or pore, as in the leaves of plants or in the walls of blood vessels. **2** A mouthlike opening in some worms.

Stole

stom·ach [stum′ək] **1** *n.* A pouch or bag in the digestive tract that receives food when it is swallowed, partly digests it, and passes it on to the intestines. **2** *n.* The abdomen or belly. **3** *n.* A desire or inclination: I have no *stomach* for that kind of work. **4** *v.* To put up with; endure: She could not *stomach* mean talk.

stom·ach·er [stum′ək·ər] *n.* A former article of dress, often embroidered or jeweled, worn over the breast and upper abdomen.

stomp [stomp] **1** *v.* To stamp. **2** *n.* A dance involving a heavy and lively step.

stone [stōn] *n.*, *adj.*, *v.* **stoned, ston·ing 1** *n.* The hard mineral substance, not metal, of which rock is composed. **2** *adj.* Of or made of stone: a *stone* ax. **3** *v.* To cover or line with stone, as a well. **4** *n.* A small piece of rock, as a pebble. **5** *v.* To throw stones at or to kill with stones. **6** *n.* A jewel or gem. **7** *n.* A piece of stone shaped for a specific use, as a millstone or a gravestone. **8** *n.* A stony formation in the bladder or kidneys, causing illness and pain. **9** *n.* The hard seed or pit of certain fruits. **10** *v.* To remove the seeds or pits from. **11** *n.*, *pl.* **stone** A unit of weight in Great Britain, equal to 14 pounds. **12** *adj.* Made of earthenware: a *stone* bottle.

Stone Age The earliest known period of human culture, during which stone was used to make tools and weapons.

stone-blind [stōn′blīnd′] *adj.* Totally blind.

stone·cut·ter [stōn′kut′ər] *n.* A person or thing that cuts stone, especially a machine for smoothing, polishing, etc.

stone-deaf [stōn′def′] *adj.* Completely deaf.

stone·work [stōn′wûrk′] *n.* **1** Building or construction with stone as the main material. **2** Something made of stone.

ston·y [stō′nē] *adj.* **ston·i·er, ston·i·est 1** Full of or covered by stones: a *stony* field. **2** Made of stone. **3** Hard as stone. **4** Like stone, as in hardness and coldness; unfeeling: a *stony* glance.

stood [stŏŏd] Past tense and past participle of STAND.

stool [stŏŏl] *n.* **1** A backless and armless seat, high or low, for one person. **2** A low bench or rest for the feet, or for the knees in kneeling.

stool pigeon *slang* An informer or spy, especially for the police.

stoop¹ [stŏŏp] **1** *v.* To bend or lean the body forward and down; crouch. **2** *v.* To stand or walk with the upper part of the body always bent forward; slouch. **3** *n.* The act of stooping; a slouch. **4** *v.* To lower or degrade oneself: to *stoop* to lying.

stoop² [stŏŏp] *n.* A small porch or platform at the entrance of a house.

stop [stop] *v.* **stopped, stop·ping,** *n.* **1** *v.* To come or bring to a halt: The clock *stopped* at noon; to *stop* an automobile. **2** *v.* To come or bring to an end: The performance *stopped* when an actor became sick; to *stop* a fight. **3** *v.* To prevent (someone) from doing something; hold back; restrain: Fred wanted to leave, but I *stopped* him. **4** *v.* To leave off, discontinue, or cease (something): to *stop* trying. **5** *v.* To block; obstruct; clog: The passage was *stopped* up with crates and boxes. **6** *v.* To fill in, cover, or close, as a hole. **7** *v.* To stay; visit; tarry; linger: to *stop* somewhere for a few minutes. **8** *n.* A halt or cessation: It was only a short *stop*. **9** *n.* The place where a stop is made: Where is the bus *stop*? **10** *n.* The act of stopping: Let's put a *stop* to this noise. **11** *n.* Something that stops: A *stop* for a door keeps it from slamming shut. **12** *n. British* A punctuation mark, as a period. **13** *n.* A knob on an organ by which the player can connect or disconnect a whole series of pipes.

stop-gap [stop′gap′] *n.* Something used to fill a need temporarily.

stop·light [stop′līt] *n.* **1** A signal light, usually operated by electricity, that controls movement of traffic. **2** A red light on the rear of a motor vehicle that shines when the brakes are put on.

stop·o·ver [stop′ō′vər] *n.* A stop for a short period, especially one made while traveling and without paying additional fare, continuing the trip with the same ticket on a later train, bus, etc.

stop·page [stop′ij] *n.* **1** The act of stopping. **2** A being stopped. **3** An obstruction: a *stoppage* in a drain.

stop·per [stop′ər] **1** *n.* Something that stops up or closes, as a plug or cork. **2** *v.* To close with a stopper: to *stopper* a bottle.

stop·watch [stop′woch′] *n.* A watch that has a hand that can be started or stopped at will, used for timing races, etc.

stor·age [stôr′ij] *n.* **1** The act of storing. **2** A being stored. **3** A space for storing things. **4** A charge made for storing.

storage battery A battery containing chemicals that can store up energy when an electric current is run through them and give up the energy as electricity when it is needed.

store [stôr] *n., v.* **stored, stor·ing 1** *n.* A place where merchandise of any kind is kept for sale; shop. **2** *n.* Something that is laid up or put away for future need. **3** *v.* To put away for future need. **4** *n.* (*pl.*) Supplies, as of arms or clothing. **5** *v.* To furnish or supply; provide. **6** *n.* A large quantity of something; abundance: a *store* of knowledge. **7** *n.* A place where things are placed for safekeeping; storehouse; warehouse. **8** *v.* To place in a storehouse or warehouse. **— in store** In readiness; about to be used, to happen, etc. **— set store by** To value or esteem; regard highly.

store·house [stôr′hous′] *n.* **1** A building in which goods are stored; warehouse. **2** A large or inexhaustible supply: a *storehouse* of ideas.

store·keep·er [stôr′kē′pər] *n.* A person who keeps a store or shop; shopkeeper.

store·room [stôr′rōōm′] *n.* A room in which things are stored, as supplies.

sto·ried[1] [stôr′ēd] *adj.* Famed in stories or in history; having a notable history: *storied* Greece.

sto·ried[2] [stôr′ēd] *adj.* Having or consisting of stories, as a building: a three-*storied* house.

stork [stôrk] *n.* Any of various large wading birds with long necks and long legs.

storm [stôrm] **1** *n.* A disturbance of the atmosphere, usually a strong wind accompanied by rain, snow, thunder, lightning, etc. **2** *n.* A heavy fall of rain, snow, etc. **3** *v.* To blow with violence; rain, snow, hail, etc., heavily: It *stormed* all day. **4** *n.* A rapid flight or shower of objects, as of bullets or missiles. **5** *n.* A violent outburst: a *storm* of applause. **6** *n.* A violent attack or assault: We took the fort by *storm.* **7** *v.* To attack or assault: to *storm* a fort. **8** *v.* To be very angry; rage. **9** *v.* To move or rush with violence or rage: He *stormed* about the room.

Stork, to 40 in. long

storm cellar An underground shelter for use during violent storms, as cyclones and tornadoes.

storm center The center or area of lowest pressure and comparative calm in a cyclone or hurricane.

storm petrel A small bird having a dusky black body, a forked or square tail, and long narrow wings. It can fly long distances over the ocean, and often stays at sea even in storms.

storm window An extra window outside the ordinary one as a protection against storms or for greater insulation against cold.

storm·y [stôr′mē] *adj.* **storm·i·er, storm·i·est 1** Having or disturbed by a storm: *stormy* weather. **2** Violent; emotional: a *stormy* life.

sto·ry[1] [stôr′ē] *n., pl.* **sto·ries 1** An account or tale of an event or series of events, whether real or made-up. **2** An account or tale, usually made up, intended to entertain a reader or listener. **3** *informal* A lie.

sto·ry[2] [stôr′ē] *n., pl.* **sto·ries** A horizontal division in a building made up of the space between two successive floors.

sto·ry·book [stôr′ē·bŏŏk′] **1** *n.* A book of stories, especially for children. **2** *adj.* Of, having to do with, or occurring in a storybook.

sto·ry·tell·er [stôr′ē·tel′ər] *n.* A person who tells stories, especially to groups of children. **— sto′ry·tell′ing** *n., adj.*

stoup [stōōp] *n.* **1** A basin for holy water at the entrance of a church. **2** A cup or tankard, or its contents: seldom used today.

stout [stout] **1** *adj.* Fat or thickset in body. **2** *adj.* Strong or firm in structure or material: a *stout* fortress. **3** *adj.* Determined; resolute: They put up a *stout* argument. **4** *adj.* Brave; courageous: *stout* warriors. **5** *n.* A strong, very dark, heavy ale or porter. **— stout′ly** *adv.* **— stout′ness** *n.*

stout·heart·ed [stout′här′tid] *adj.* Brave; courageous.

stove[1] [stōv] *n.* An apparatus that uses gas, oil, electricity, coal, etc., to create heat for warmth or cooking.

stove[2] [stōv] An alternative past tense and past participle of STAVE: The rock *stove* a hole in the bottom of the ship.

stove·pipe [stōv′pīp′] *n.* **1** A pipe to carry off smoke and gas from a stove to a chimney flue. **2** *informal* A tall silk hat worn by men.

stow [stō] *v.* **1** To arrange or pack in a neat, close way: to *stow* freight aboard a train. **2** To fill by packing: to *stow* a truck with goods. **— stow away 1** To pack away; store. **2** To be a stowaway.

stow·a·way [stō′ə·wā′] *n.* A person who hides aboard a ship, train, etc., to travel without buying a ticket.

Stowe [stō], **Harriet Beecher,** 1811–1896, U.S. writer. She wrote *Uncle Tom's Cabin.*

St. Paul [sānt pôl] The capital of Minnesota.

strad·dle [strad′(ə)l] *v.* **strad·dled, strad·dling,** *n.* **1** *v.* To stand, sit, or walk with the legs spread apart. **2** *v.* To have or put one leg on each side of: to *straddle* a chair. **3** *n.* The act of straddling. **4** *n.* A straddling position. **5** *v.* To seem to favor both sides of (an issue, question, etc.).

strafe [strāf] *v.* **strafed, straf·ing 1** To fire on (ground troops, etc.) from a low-flying airplane: to *strafe* enemy troops. **2** To bombard heavily. ◆ *Strafe* comes from a German word meaning *to punish.*

strag·gle [strag′əl] *v.* **strag·gled, strag·gling** **1** To lag behind a group that one is traveling with. **2** To wander or stray, as from a road. **3** To be spread unevenly about: Flowers *straggled* all over the garden. — **strag′gler** *n.*

strag·gly [strag′lē] *adj.* **strag·gli·er, strag·gli·est** Scattered or spread out irregularly: *straggly* ivy growing on a wall.

straight [strāt] **1** *adj.* Extending in the same direction without curving; connecting two points in the shortest possible way: a *straight* road; a *straight* line. **2** *adj.* Not curly, as hair. **3** *adj.* In a row: five *straight* misses. **4** *adj.* Level: The picture on the wall isn't *straight.* **5** *adj.* Direct; without detours: a *straight* course. **6** *adj.* True, fair, or honest: a *straight* answer. **7** *adj.* In good condition or order: Is the room *straight?* **8** *adj.* Not smiling; composed: a *straight* face. **9** *adj.* Unmixed: a *straight* drink. **10** *adj.* Strictly following a particular party or policy: to vote a *straight* ticket. **11** *adv.* In a straight manner, line, course, etc.: Stand *straight;* Go *straight* home. — **straight away** or **straight off** Without delay; at once; immediately.

straight angle An angle of 180°.

straight·a·way [strāt′ə·wā′] **1** *adj.* Having no curves or turns. **2** *n.* A straight road, path, or track. **3** *adv.* At once; immediately.

straight·edge [strāt′ej′] *n.* A bar of wood or metal with a straight edge for ruling lines, etc.

straight·en [strāt′(ə)n] *v.* To make or become straight: *Straighten* the picture; When Paul *straightens* up he is as tall as his father.

straight-faced [strāt′fāst′] *adj.* Showing no emotion, as amusement or displeasure.

straight·for·ward [strāt′fôr′wərd] **1** *adj.* Honest; frank. **2** *adj.* Going directly ahead. **3** *adv.* In a straight course. — **straight′·for′ward·ly** *adv.*

straight·way [strāt′wā′] *adv.* At once.

strain¹ [strān] **1** *v.* To use the full power of: to *strain* one's muscles. **2** *v.* To make a great effort: He *strained* to lift the weight. **3** *v.* To injure or damage by twisting, pulling, etc.: to *strain* an arm; to *strain* a hinge. **4** *n.* Damage or injury produced by straining. **5** *v.* To go beyond the proper limits of: to *strain* a rule. **6** *v.* To pour or squeeze (a liquid) through a sieve, strainer, etc., so as to take out solid parts. **7** *v.* To pull or draw tight; stretch: to *strain* a new violin string. **8** *v.* To push or pull with great force: The dog *strained* at his collar. **9** *n.* Force or pressure: The *strain* broke the chain. **10** *n.* The act of straining. **11** *n.* A being strained. **12** *n.* Severe physical, mental, or emotional pressure: She's been under a *strain.* **13** *v.* To hug tightly.

strain² [strān] *n.* **1** Line of heredity or descent; breed; race; stock. **2** An inborn or inherited quality, tendency, or character: a *strain* of in-

sanity in a family. **3** Tone, mood, or style: poetry with a *strain* of sadness. **4** (*often pl.*) A passage of music; melody; tune.

strained [strānd] *adj.* Made with effort; not natural; forced: a *strained* smile.

strain·er [strā′nər] *n.* Any of various devices having many small holes, used to strain things.

strait [strāt] *n.* **1** A narrow body of water connecting two larger bodies of water. **2** (*often pl.*) A condition of trouble or distress: a family in pitiful *straits.*

strait·en [strāt′(ə)n] *v.* To make limited or restricted, now used especially in the phrase **in straitened circumstances,** without money; poor.

Strainer

strait jacket A strong, tight, canvas jacket, used to strap down the arms of a violent person.

strait-laced [strāt′lāst′] *adj.* Very strict about proper conduct, manners, or opinions.

strand¹ [strand] **1** *n.* A shore or beach. **2** *v.* To drive or run aground, as a ship. **3** *v.* To leave behind or in a helpless position: to be *stranded* on a desert island.

strand² [strand] **1** *n.* One of the threads, filaments, wires, etc., twisted together to make a cord, rope, or cable. **2** *n.* Something like a cord, rope, or cable: a *strand* of pearls.

strange [strānj] *adj.* **strang·er, strang·est** **1** Not seen or heard of before; not familiar: A *strange* dog came to the door. **2** Peculiar or odd; not usual; remarkable: *strange* behavior. **3** Not at home or at ease: He felt *strange* when everybody spoke French. **4** Not accustomed or experienced: She is *strange* to her new duties. — **strange′ly** *adv.* — **strange′ness** *n.*

stran·ger [strān′jər] *n.* **1** A person who is unfamiliar or not known. **2** A foreigner. **3** A person who is not acquainted with and knows nothing about something or someone specified: She was a *stranger* to mathematics.

stran·gle [strang′gəl] *v.* **stran·gled, stran·gling** **1** To kill by pressing on the windpipe to prevent breathing. **2** To block the breathing of; choke or suffocate: The gas fumes *strangled* her. **3** To hold back or suppress: to *strangle* a sob. — **stran′gler** *n.*

stran·gu·la·tion [strang′gyə·lā′shən] *n.* **1** The act of strangling. **2** The condition of being strangled.

strap [strap] *n., v.* **strapped, strap·ping** **1** *n.* A long, narrow, flexible strip of leather or other material, usually having a buckle, for fastening about objects. **2** *n.* Any narrow strip that fastens or holds. **3** *v.* To fasten with a strap. **4** *v.* To beat with a strap. **5** *n.* A strop. **6** *v.* To sharpen on a strop.

strap·less [strap′lis] *adj.* Made with or having no shoulder straps, as an evening gown.

strap·ping [strap′ing] *adj. informal* Large and muscular; robust.

stra·ta [strā′tə *or* strat′ə] *n.pl.* Layers, beds, levels, or grades. Its singular form is STRATUM.

strat·a·gem [strat′ə·jəm] *n.* A trick or scheme used to outwit or deceive an enemy or opponent.

Rock strata

stra·te·gic [strə·tē′jik] *adj.* 1 Of or having to do with strategy. 2 Showing, used in, or important to strategy: a *strategic* move for winning the election. — **stra·te′gi·cal·ly** *adv.*

strat·e·gist [strat′ə·jist] *n.* A person who is highly skilled in strategy.

strat·e·gy [strat′ə·jē] *n., pl.* **strat·e·gies** 1 The technique of planning and carrying on a war or a large part of a war. 2 The careful planning and directing of anything in order to gain some end: a boxer's *strategy*.

Strat·ford-on-A·von [strat′fərd-on-ā′vən] *n.* A village in central England where Shakespeare was born and later buried.

strat·i·fi·ca·tion [strat′ə·fə·kā′shən] *n.* Arrangement in or formation into layers or strata.

strat·i·fy [strat′ə·fī] *v.* **strat·i·fied, strat·i·fy·ing** To form into layers or strata; arrange in layers.

strat·o·sphere [strat′ə·sfir] *n.* A layer of the atmosphere beginning about seven miles up, in which temperatures are more or less uniform and clouds are rare.

stra·tum [strā′təm *or* strat′əm] *n., pl.* **stra·ta** or **stra·tums** A layer, bed, or level: a *stratum* of coal; the upper *stratum* of society.

stra·tus [strā′təs *or* strat′əs] *n., pl.* **stra·ti** [strā′tē *or* strat′ē] A low, foglike cloud that lies in a flat layer over a wide area.

Strauss [strous], **Johann,** 1825–1899, Austrian composer.

Strauss [strous], **Richard,** 1864–1949, German composer.

Stra·vin·sky [strə·vin′skē], **Igor,** born 1882, U.S. composer born in Russia.

straw [strô] 1 *n.* The dried stems or stalks of grains or other grasslike plants. 2 *n.* A single such dried stem. 3 *n.* A material woven from straw, used in making hats, etc. 4 *adj.* Of or like straw: a *straw* mat. 5 *n.* A thin tube of paper, glass, etc., used to suck up a drink. 6 *adj.* Yellowish, as the color of straw. 7 *n.* Something almost worthless: He doesn't care a *straw* for music. 8 *adj.* Counting for nothing.

straw·ber·ry [strô′ber·ē] *n., pl.* **straw·ber·ries** 1 A small, red, tasty berry. 2 The stemless plant, related to the rose, on which this berry grows.

straw vote A vote with no official effect, taken to test opinion.

stray [strā] 1 *v.* To wander or turn away from a correct route, group, place, etc. 2 *n.* A person or a domestic animal that is wandering or lost. 3 *adj.* Having strayed; wandering or lost: a *stray* cat. 4 *v.* To turn away; leave off: to *stray* from honesty. 5 *adj.* Scattered about or occasional: a few *stray* trees.

streak [strēk] 1 *n.* A long, thin, and often uneven mark, stripe, etc.: a *streak* of lightning; a *streak* of dirt. 2 *v.* To mark or become marked with streaks: to *streak* a floor with dirt: That wet paint *streaks*. 3 *n.* A small amount; trace: a *streak* of meanness. 4 *n.* A period of time; spell: a losing *streak*. 5 *n.* A layer or strip: a *streak* of coal. 6 *v.* To move, run, or travel at great speed.

streak·y [strē′kē] *adj.* **streak·i·er, streak·i·est** 1 Marked with or occurring in streaks. 2 Variable or uneven: a *streaky* concert, often bad but sometimes brilliant.

stream [strēm] 1 *n.* A small body of flowing water. 2 *n.* A continuous flow of a liquid or gas. 3 *v.* To flow out in a stream: Tears *streamed* from her eyes. 4 *v.* To pour out freely; gush: The wound *streamed* blood. 5 *n.* Any continuous passage or flow, as of people, light, traffic, etc. 6 *v.* To come out or pass by continuously and in large numbers: Hornets *streamed* from their nest. 7 *v.* To float with a waving movement, as a flag in a wind.

stream·er [strē′mər] *n.* 1 A long, ribbonlike flag. 2 Any long, narrow strip of paper, cloth, etc., that flows freely: The ballroom was decorated with *streamers*.

stream·let [strēm′lit] *n.* A small stream.

stream·line [strēm′līn′] *n., v.* **stream·lined, stream·lin·ing** 1 *n.* A path taken by particles of a fluid, as gas, in flowing past an object when there is little or no turbulence. 2 *v.* To provide a shape that will create minimum turbulence when passing through a gas or liquid. 3 *adj. use:* a *streamlined* airplane. 4 *v.* To make more simple or efficient by removing unnecessary parts or stages. 5 *adj. use:* a *streamlined* process.

street [strēt] *n.* 1 A public road in a city or town, usually with sidewalks and buildings on one or both sides. 2 A roadway for vehicles, usually between sidewalks. 3 *informal* The people who live, gather, or work on a particular street: The whole *street* came out to cheer the hero.

street·car [strēt′kär′] *n.* An electric car that runs on rails set into the street; trolley.

Streetcar

strength [streng(k)th] *n.* 1 The quality of being strong; force or power, especially of the muscles. 2 The capacity of resisting a force without bending or breaking; toughness: the *strength* of steel. 3 Effectiveness or potency: the *strength* of a drug. 4 Intensity or concentration: the *strength* of a solution of ammonia. **5** Available numerical force: What is the army's full *strength*? **6** A person or thing that gives or represents strength.

strength·en [streng(k)′thən] *v.* To make or become strong or stronger.

stren·u·ous [stren′yōō·əs] *adj.* **1** Taking much effort or energy: Football is a *strenuous* sport. **2** Vigorously active: a *strenuous* man. — **stren′u·ous·ly** *adv.*

strep·to·coc·cus [strep′tə·kok′əs] *n., pl.* **strep·to·coc·ci** [strep′tə·kok′sī] One of a kind of ball-shaped bacteria grouped together in long chains. Some types cause disease.

strep·to·my·cin [strep′tō·mī′sin] *n.* A strong antibiotic obtained from a soil fungus. It is used to treat certain illnesses, as tuberculosis.

stress [stres] **1** *n.* A pressure or force that tends to change the shape of something; strain. **2** *v.* To apply such a force to: The weight *stressed* the beam. **3** *n.* The resistance of a body to outside forces. **4** *n.* In music or speech, special force or loudness given to a note or syllable; accent. **5** *v.* To give special accent to (a note or syllable). **6** *n.* Special weight or importance. **7** *v.* To give special weight or importance to: to *stress* science and mathematics. **8** *n.* Emotional or mental strain or tension.

stretch [strech] **1** *v.* To extend or be extended to full or normal size or beyond: The heavy weight *stretched* the rope. **2** *v.* To extend or be extended without breaking or losing elasticity: Rubber *stretches* easily. **3** *adj.* Capable of stretching easily so as to fit closely: said of clothing: *stretch* socks. **4** *n.* The ability to be extended in length or width without breaking or losing elasticity: Elastic may lose its *stretch*. **5** *v.* To reach or extend: to *stretch* out a hand in greeting. **6** *v.* To extend the body or a part of it, often to relieve stiffness: The cat *stretched*. **7** *v.* To cause to reach, as between two points: to *stretch* telegraph wires. **8** *n.* The act of stretching. **9** *n.* The condition of being stretched. **10** *v.* To strain or exert to the utmost: to *stretch* every nerve. **11** *v.* To go beyond the proper limits of; abuse: to *stretch* the truth. **12** *v.* To extend, as over an area or between two limits: The desert *stretches* for miles. **13** *n.* An extent or expanse, as of space or time: a *stretch* of forest; a *stretch* of bad luck. **14** *n.* Either of the straight parts of a racetrack, especially the one that includes the finish.

stretch·er [strech′ər] *n.* **1** A person or thing that stretches. **2** A thing used in stretching, as in making shoes larger, drying curtains, etc. **3** A strip of canvas supported on poles, used to carry sick, injured, or dead persons.

Stretcher

strew [strōō] *v.* **strewed**, **strewed** or **strewn**, **strew·ing** **1** To throw about in a disorderly way; scatter: to *strew* bits of paper on the floor. **2** To cover by scattering or sprinkling: The table was *strewn* with magazines.

stri·at·ed [strī′āt·id] *adj.* Having small stripes or parallel grooves.

strick·en [strik′ən] **1** An alternative past participle of STRIKE. **2** *adj.* Strongly affected or overcome, as by a disaster, an illness, etc. **3** *adj.* Wounded or hit, as by an arrow or bullet: a *stricken* hare.

strict [strikt] *adj.* **1** Following or enforcing rules exactly: a *strict* teacher. **2** Exact; precise: a *strict* account of what happened. **3** Rigidly enforced; allowing no exceptions or evasions: *strict* rules. **4** Complete; absolute: Pay *strict* attention. — **strict′ly** *adv.* — **strict′ness** *n.*

stric·ture [strik′chər] *n.* **1** An abnormal narrowing or closing off of a tube or duct in the body. **2** Severe criticism.

stride [strīd] *n., v.* **strode, strid·den** [strid′- (ə)n], **strid·ing** **1** *n.* A long, sweeping step. **2** *n.* The distance covered by such a step. **3** *v.* To walk with long, sweeping steps: to *stride* along the lane. **4** *v.* To walk or cross with a stride or strides: to *stride* the floor; to *stride* over a brook. **5** *n.* (*often pl.*) An advance or achievement: to make great *strides* in science. **6** *v.* To sit or stand with one leg on either side of; straddle.

stri·dent [strīd′(ə)nt] *adj.* Harsh and noisy; grating: a *strident* shout. — **stri′dent·ly** *adv.*

strife [strīf] *n.* Any bitter or angry fight, quarrel, or conflict: *strife* among nations.

strike [strīk] *v.* **struck, struck** or **strick·en** [strik′ən], **strik·ing**, *n.* **1** *v.* To make or cause to make forceful contact with; hit: The car *struck* the wall. **2** *v.* To come into forceful contact; hit: The cars *struck* together. **3** *v.* To hit with a blow: The man *struck* the dog. **4** *v.* To aim or deliver a blow or blows: He *struck* about wildly. **5** *n.* The act of striking or hitting; blow. **6** *n.* In baseball, a pitch that the batter misses, allows to cross home plate between his shoulders and knees, or swings at and hits foul when having less than two strikes. **7** *n.* In bowling, the knocking down of all the pins with the first ball thrown. **8** *v.* To attack or assault: to *strike* the enemy. **9** *n.* An attack or assault, especially one made by air. **10** *v.* To remove: *Strike* it from the record. **11** *v.* To start burning; ignite, as a match. **12** *v.* To form by stamping, printing, etc.: to *strike* coins. **13** *v.* To indicate (the time) by the sound of a bell, etc.: The clock *struck* two. **14** *v.* To be indicated, as by the sound of a bell: Noon has *struck*. **15** *v.* To cause to sound, as by a blow: *Strike* a note on the piano. **16** *v.* To reach, come upon, or discover: The sound *struck* his ear; to *strike* oil. **17** *n.* A new or unexpected discovery, as of oil or ore. **18** *v.* To affect or overcome in a sudden or dramatic way: He was *struck* speechless. **19** *v.* To occur to: An idea *strikes* me. **20** *v.* To give an impression to: He *strikes* me as being honest. **21** *v.* To make an impression on: The dress *struck* her fancy. **22** *v.* To assume; take up: to *strike* an attitude. **23** *v.* To cause to enter suddenly: He *struck* fear into their hearts. **24** *v.* To lower or take down: to *strike* a tent. **25** *v.* To stop work, as a group, until some demands are met: The men *struck* for better pay. **26** *n.* A stopping of work by a group of workers to make an employer meet their demands. **27** *v.* To agree upon: to *strike* a bargain. **28** *v.* To take a course; start: to *strike* for home. **— on strike** Not working because taking part in a strike. **— strike dumb** To astonish; amaze. **— strike home 1** To deal an effective blow. **2** To have a strong effect. **— strike it rich** To suddenly become wealthy. **— strike off** To remove or take off, as from a list. **— strike out 1** To cross out or erase. **2** To aim a blow or blows. **3** To make a start: to *strike out* on one's own. **4** In baseball, to put out or be put out as a result of three strikes. **— strike up** To start up; begin.

strike·break·er [strīk′brā′kər] *n.* A person who helps to make a strike fail by taking a striker's job. **— strike′break′ing** *n.*

strik·er [strī′kər] *n.* **1** A person or thing that strikes. **2** An employee who is on strike.

strik·ing [strī′king] *adj.* Appealing strongly to the eye or to the imagination; impressive: the *striking* colors of the trees in autumn. **— strik′·ing·ly** *adv.*

string [string] *n., v.* **strung, string·ing,** *adj.* **1** *n.* A cord thicker than thread, thinner than rope, used for tying, lacing, etc. **2** *n.* Something else used for tying, as a strip of cloth or leather. **3** *n.* A group of things hung on a string: a *string* of beads. **4** *v.* To hang on or from a string: to *string* pearls. **5** *n.* A stringlike organ or part, as of a plant or animal. **6** *v.* To remove stringlike parts from: to *string* beans. **7** *v.* Cord of gut or wire for musical instruments. **8** *v.* To provide with strings: to *string* a harp. **9** *n.* (*pl.*) Stringed instruments, especially those played with a bow. **10** *adj.* Consisting of or meant to be played by such stringed instruments: a *string* trio. **11** *n.* A succession of things, acts, events, etc.: a *string* of lakes; a *string* of lies. **12** *v.* To extend, stretch, or go, often in a line or series: to *string* a rope from the tree to the house. **13** *n.* (*usually pl.*) *informal* A condition, limitation, or restriction: a gift with no *strings* attached. **— pull strings** To use one's influence to gain an advantage. **— string along** *informal* To trick, deceive, or keep waiting. **— string along with** *informal* To go along or agree with.

string bean 1 A type of bean cultivated for its edible pod. **2** The pod itself. **3** *informal* Any very tall, thin person.

stringed instrument [stringd] An instrument played by plucking or, especially, by bowing its strings.

strin·gen·cy [strin′jən·sē] *n.* The quality or condition of being stringent.

strin·gent [strin′jənt] *adj.* **1** Closely binding; strict; severe: *stringent* rules. **2** Convincing; having force: a *stringent* argument. **3** Having or showing a scarcity of money or a difficulty in giving or receiving credit: a *stringent* economic policy. **— strin′gent·ly** *adv.*

string·er [string′ər] *n.* **1** A person or thing that strings. **2** A horizontal timber used to support or secure other parts of a structure.

string·y [string′ē] *adj.* **string·i·er, string·i·est 1** Suggesting a string or strings: a *stringy* plant; *stringy* hair. **2** Containing tough fibers or sinews: *stringy* meat. **3** Forming strings: *stringy* syrup. **4** Tall and wiry in build.

strip¹ [strip] *v.* **stripped, strip·ping 1** To undress. **2** To remove the covering of: to *strip* a wire. **3** To make bare or empty: to *strip* a theater of seats. **4** To remove; take away: to *strip* the wrapper from a package. **5** To deprive: He was *stripped* of his rank. **6** To break or damage the teeth, thread, etc., of: to *strip* gears; to *strip* a screw. **— strip down** To take apart for repair, as a motor. **— strip′per** *n.*

strip² [strip] *n.* A long, narrow piece of something, as cloth, wood, land, etc.

stripe¹ [strīp] *n., v.* **striped, strip·ing 1** *n.* A line, band, or strip that is of a different color, material, etc., from what is on both sides of it. **2** *v.* To mark with a stripe or stripes. **3** *n.* Kind; sort: a man of his *stripe.* **4** *n.* A strip of material on the sleeve of a uniform, indicating rank, length of service, etc.

stripe² [strīp] *n.* **1** A blow struck with a whip or rod. **2** The welt on the skin caused by this.

striped [strīpt] *adj.* Marked with stripes.

strip·ling [strip′ling] *n.* An adolescent boy; youth.

strive [strīv] *v.* **strove, striv·en** [striv′ən], **striv·ing 1** To make a strong effort: to *strive* for good grades. **2** To contend, struggle, or fight: The two *strove* for the lead.

strode [strōd] Past tense of STRIDE.

stroke [strōk] *n., v.* **stroked, strok·ing 1** *n.* The act of striking; blow or impact: a *stroke* with a whip; a *stroke* of lightning. **2** *n.* A blow or the sound of a blow of a striking mechanism, as of a a clock. **3** *n.* A single movement, as of the hand, arm, or a tool: a tennis *stroke.* **4** *n.* A single mark, as of a pen, brush, etc. **5** *n.* A sudden or dramatic event or action: a *stroke* of good luck. **6** *n.* A brilliant action; feat: a *stroke* of genius. **7** *n. informal* A portion or stint: He hasn't done a *stroke* of work all day. **8** *n.* The bursting of a blood vessel in the brain. **9** *n.* One of a series of repeated motions: a *stroke* of a swimmer; a *stroke* of a machine. **10** *n.* The oarsman who sets the rate of rowing for a crew. **11** *v.* To set the rate or tempo of rowing for: to *stroke* a crew. **12** *v.* To

---

add, āce, câre, pälm;   end, ēqual;   it, īce;   odd, ōpen, ôrder;   tŏŏk, pōōl;   up, bûrn;
ə = a in *above,* e in *sicken,* i in *possible,* o in *melon,* u in *circus;*   yōō = u in *fuse;*   oil;   pout;
check;   ring;   thin;   this;   zh in *vision.*   For ¶ reference, see page 64 · HOW TO

pass the hand over gently; pet. **13** *n.* A gentle rubbing or stroking movement.

stroll [strōl] **1** *v.* To walk in a slow, idle way. **2** *n.* A slow, idle walk. **3** *v.* To travel about; wander.

stroll·er [strō′lər] *n.* **1** A person that strolls. **2** A carriage in which a baby can sit upright.

strong [strông] *adj.* **1** Powerful or forceful: a *strong* wind; a *strong* man; a *strong* voice. **2** Solidly made or constituted; not easily destroyed, injured, or strained: *strong* walls. **3** Very potent or effective: a *strong* drug; a *strong* drink. **4** Having great ability: She is *strong* in mathematics. **5** Absorbing or compelling: a *strong* interest. **6** Resisting temptation and self-indulgence: a *strong* character. **7** Powerful or intense in its effect on the senses or mind: a *strong* odor; a *strong* suggestion. **8** Of a specified number: a force of men 500 *strong*. — **strong′. ly** *adv.*

strong·hold [strông′hōld′] *n.* A fortified place; fortress.

stron·ti·um [stron′shē·əm] *n.* A hard, yellowish, metallic element related to calcium.

strontium 90 A radioactive isotope produced in nuclear explosions and coming to earth in fallout. It is considered a hazard to health.

strop [strop] *n., v.* **stropped, strop·ping 1** *n.* A strip of leather, canvas, etc., on which to sharpen a razor. **2** *v.* To sharpen on a strop.

stro·phe [strō′fē] *n.* A division of a poem; stanza.

strove [strōv] Past tense of STRIVE.

struck [struk] Past tense and past participle of STRIKE.

struc·tur·al [struk′chər·əl] *adj.* **1** Of or having to do with structure: *structural* engineering. **2** Used or needed in construction: *structural* steel. — **struc′tur·al·ly** *adv.*

Strop

structural steel 1 Steel manufactured in the shapes of beams, girders, etc. to be used in building. **2** An alloy of steel suitable for such use.

struc·ture [struk′chər] *n., v.* **struc·tured, struc·tur·ing 1** *n.* Something that is constructed, as a building or machine. **2** *n.* The way in which something is constructed or put together: The *structure* of the cabin was flimsy. **3** *v.* To organize or put together: to *structure* a plan. **4** *n.* A part of an animal or plant: The eye is a delicate *structure*.

strug·gle [strug′əl] *n., v.* **strug·gled, strug·gling 1** *n.* A violent effort or series of efforts. **2** *v.* To make violent efforts; strive. **3** *v.* To make one's way by violent efforts: to *struggle* through mud. **4** *n.* A fight or conflict. **5** *v.* To fight; battle.

strum [strum] *v.* **strummed, strum·ming,** *n.* **1** *v.* To play (a stringed instrument, a tune, etc.) in a careless or unskillful way. **2** *n.* The act of

strumming, or the sound made by such an act.

strung [strung] Past tense of STRING.

strut [strut] *n., v.* **strut·ted, strut·ting 1** *n.* A vain or pompous step or walk. **2** *v.* To walk in a vain or pompous way. **3** *n.* A rod or girder used to support or reinforce a structure. **4** *v.* To brace or support with struts.

strych·nine [strik′nin *or* strik′nēn] *n.* A very poisonous drug, sometimes used in small doses as a stimulant.

stub [stub] *n., v.* **stubbed, stub·bing 1** *n.* A short piece or end that is left after something is used up, torn out, or removed: the *stub* of a pencil; a check *stub*. **2** *n.* A stump of a tree, bush, etc. **3** *n.* Something short or broad, as a pen with a wide point. **4** *v.* To strike (one's toe, etc.) against something.

stub·ble [stub′əl] *n.* **1** The short stalks left in the ground after a crop has been cut. **2** Any short, stubby growth like this, as a short, bristly beard. — **stub′bly** *adj.*

stub·born [stub′ərn] *adj.* **1** Hard to persuade or convince; not giving in easily; obstinate. **2** Hard to handle, cure, etc.: a *stubborn* illness. — **stub′born·ly** *adv.* — **stub′born·ness** *n.* ◆ See OBSTINATE.

stub·by [stub′ē] *adj.* **stub·bi·er, stub·bi·est 1** Short, stiff, and bristly: a *stubby* beard. **2** Short and thick: *stubby* fingers. **3** Full of stubs or stumps: *stubby* fields.

stuc·co [stuk′ō] *n., pl.* **stuc·coes** *or* **stuc·cos,** *v.* **stuc·coed, stuc·co·ing 1** *n.* A strong plaster or cement used to cover outside walls of a house or building. **2** *n.* A fine plaster used to decorate or ornament inside walls. **3** *v.* To apply stucco to.

stuck [stuk] Past tense and past participle of STICK.

stuck-up [stuk′up′] *adj. informal* Conceited, arrogant, or snobbish.

stud¹ [stud] *n., v.* **stud·ded, stud·ding 1** *n.* A small knob, round-headed nail, or other projecting ornament used on a surface. **2** *v.* To set or decorate with studs: to *stud* a belt. **3** *n.* In building a wall, any of the vertical posts to which wallboards or laths are nailed. **4** *n.* A removable button, used to fasten shirts, etc. **5** *v.* To be scattered or strewn over.

stud² [stud] *n.* **1** A collection of horses kept for breeding, riding, hunting, or racing. **2** A male animal kept for breeding purposes.

stu·dent [st(y)ōōd′(ə)nt] *n.* A person who studies, especially in a school or college.

stud·ied [stud′ēd] *adj.* Planned or deliberate; done on purpose: a *studied* insult.

stu·di·o [st(y)ōō′dē·ō] *n., pl.* **stu·di·os 1** The place where an artist, musician, etc., works or teaches. **2** A place in which films, recordings, radio performances, etc., are made.

stu·di·ous [st(y)ōō′dē·əs] *adj.* **1** Devoted to studying: a *studious* boy. **2** Giving or showing serious attention: a *studious* expression; to be *studious* in pleasing others. — **stu′di·ous·ly** *adv.*

stud·y [stud′ē] *v.* **stud·ied, stud·y·ing,** *n., pl.* **stud·ies** **1** *v.* To attempt to learn, know, or understand: to *study* music; to *study* a crime. **2** *n.* The act of studying. **3** *n.* A branch of knowledge: the *study* of physics. **4** *n.* A room set aside for studying, reading, writing, etc. **5** *v.* To take classes in: to *study* dancing. **6** *n.* (*pl.*) Education or training: to do well in one's *studies*. **7** *v.* To examine with care: to *study* a plan to find its flaws. **8** *v.* To devote thought or attention; try: He *studies* to be polite. **9** *n.* Deep concentration or thought. **10** *n.* In art, a preliminary sketch or exercise. **11** *n.* A piece of music designed or played to develop a skill; étude. **12** *n.* A detailed examination or treatment of a subject: to write a *study* on crime.

stuff [stuf] **1** *n.* The basic substance from which something is made: What kind of *stuff* is that doll made of? **2** *n.* Basic character or quality: My brother is made of braver *stuff* than I. **3** *n.* Cloth; material. **4** *v.* To fill, pack, or block: to *stuff* a bag; to *stuff* a crack. **5** *v.* To fill with other food, as bread crumbs, seasoning, etc.: to *stuff* a turkey. **6** *v.* To fill the skin of (a dead bird or animal) in order to produce a lifelike appearance of the original. **7** *v.* To fill or cram with food. **8** *v.* To fill with faked votes: to *stuff* a ballot box. **9** *v.* To cram, jam, or shove: He *stuffed* his handkerchief into his pocket. **10** *n. informal* A collection of objects or possessions. **11** *n.* Worthless things or ideas: *stuff* and nonsense.

stuffed shirt [stuft] *informal* A pompous person.

stuff·ing [stuf′ing] *n.* The material used to stuff something, as the down of a pillow, or the food used to stuff a turkey or roast.

stuff·y [stuf′ē] *adj.* **stuff·i·er, stuff·i·est** **1** Badly ventilated: a *stuffy* room. **2** Stopped up or causing difficult breathing: a *stuffy* nose. **3** *informal* Pompous and dull: a *stuffy* lecture. **4** *informal* Old-fashioned or stodgy. — **stuff′i·ness** *n.*

stum·ble [stum′bəl] *v.* **stum·bled, stum·bling,** *n.* **1** *v.* To miss a step in walking or running; trip. **2** *v.* To move along in an unsteady way: The tired child *stumbled* up the stairs. **3** *v.* To speak, read, etc., in a halting way. **4** *v.* To find by accident: to *stumble* on a bargain. **5** *v.* To fall into wrongdoing or error. **6** *n.* The act of stumbling. **7** *n.* A misstep or blunder.

stumbling block Any obstacle or hindrance: Shyness is a *stumbling block* to making friends.

stump [stump] **1** *n.* The part of something that remains after the larger or principal part has been cut away, removed, used up, etc.; stub: the *stump* of a tree; the *stump* of an arm. **2** *n.* A platform from which political speeches are made. **3** *v.* To go about (an area), making political speeches. **4** *v.* To walk in a stiff, heavy way.

5 *v. informal* To baffle or confuse: Your question certainly *stumps* me. — **stump′y** *adj.*

stun [stun] *v.* **stunned, stun·ning** **1** To make unconscious or unable to act: The blow *stunned* him. **2** To astonish or shock: The play *stunned* us, it was so badly written.

stung [stung] Past tense and past participle of STING.

stunk [stungk] A past tense and past participle of STINK.

stun·ning [stun′ing] *adj.* **1** Causing unconsciousness: a *stunning* blow. **2** *informal* Extremely beautiful, stylish, etc.: a *stunning* hat.

stunt[1] [stunt] *v.* **1** To stop the natural growth or development of: Lack of feed *stunted* the cattle. **2** *adj. use:* a *stunted* tree.

stunt[2] [stunt] *informal* **1** *n.* A trick or show of skill; feat. **2** *v.* To perform a stunt or stunts, especially in an airplane.

stu·pe·fac·tion [st(y)ōō′pə·fak′shən] *n.* **1** A stupefied state. **2** Amazement; astonishment.

stu·pe·fy [st(y)ōō′pə·fī] *v.* **stu·pe·fied, stu·pe·fy·ing** **1** To dull the senses or capabilities of; stun: The enemy was *stupefied* with fear. **2** To amaze; astound.

stu·pen·dous [st(y)ōō·pen′dəs] *adj.* Highly impressive or astonishing, especially because of overwhelming size. — **stu·pen′dous·ly** *adv.*

stu·pid [st(y)ōō′pid] *adj.* **1** Not intelligent or bright; dull. **2** Showing or caused by a lack of intelligence or thought; senseless: a *stupid* mistake. **3** Dull; tedious; boring: a *stupid* play. — **stu′pid·ly** *adv.*

stu·pid·i·ty [st(y)ōō·pid′ə·tē] *n., pl.* **stu·pid·i·ties** **1** Lack of intelligence or understanding; dullness. **2** A foolish action or idea.

stu·por [st(y)ōō′pər] *n.* A dazed state in which the power to feel, think, or act is lost or greatly lessened.

stur·dy [stûr′dē] *adj.* **stur·di·er, stur·di·est** **1** Vigorous; strong: a *sturdy* plant. **2** Not giving in or yielding; firm: a *sturdy* table; *sturdy* defense. — **stur′di·ly** *adv.* — **stur′di·ness** *n.*

stur·geon [stûr′jən] *n.* A large edible fish covered with bony plates, found in northern regions. It is valued as a source of caviar.

stut·ter [stut′ər] **1** *v.* To speak in a jerky, uneven way, often with the same sound repeated many times. **2** *n.* The action or habit of stuttering. — **stut′ter·er** *n.*

sty[1] [stī] *n., pl.* **sties** **1** A pen for hogs. **2** Any very filthy place.

sty[2] [stī] *n., pl.* **sties** An inflamed swelling of an oil gland on the edge of an eyelid.

style [stīl] *n., v.* **styled, styl·ing** **1** *n.* The method or manner in which something is done, written, built, etc.: a medieval *style* of architecture; an Oriental *style* of dress. **2** *n.* A distinctive or individual manner of expression, as in writing or painting: His novel lacks *style*. **3** *n.*

The current or fashionable manner or way of acting, dressing, building, etc.: *That dress is not in style.* **4** *n.* A particular type, kind, or fashion: *a new style of coat; an old style of car.* **5** *v.* To design or fashion: *to style clothes.* **6** *n.* Luxury or elegance: *to live in style.* **7** *v.* To make consistent or correct in spelling, punctuation, etc.: *to style a manuscript.* **8** *n.* A stalk forming part of the pistil of a flower. **9** *n.* A stylus. **10** *v.* To name; call: *Richard I was styled Richard the Lion-Hearted.*

styl·ish [stī′lish] *adj.* In current style or fashion; fashionable. **— styl′ish·ly** *adv.*

sty·lis·tic [stī·lis′tik] *adj.* Of or having to do with style. **— sty·lis′ti·cal·ly** *adv.*

sty·lus [stī′ləs] *n., pl.* **sty·lus·es** or **sty·li** [stī′lī] **1** A pointed tool for engraving, writing on wax, etc. **2** The needle of a phonograph.

styp·tic [stip′tik] **1** *adj.* Causing the tissues to contract, especially so as to check bleeding. **2** *n.* A styptic substance, as alum.

Styx [stiks] *n.* In Greek myths, a river of the lower world. The dead had to pay Charon to ferry them across, to reach Hades.

suave [swäv] *adj.* Smoothly pleasant or polite. **— suave′ly** *adv.* **— suave′ness** or **suav′i·ty** *n.*

sub [sub] *n., v.* **subbed, sub·bing** *informal* **1** *n.* A submarine. **2** *n.* A substitute. **3** *v.* To substitute: *He subbed for the regular shortstop.*

sub- A prefix meaning: **1** Under; beneath; below, as in *subcutaneous*, beneath the skin. **2** Almost; nearly; somewhat, as in *subtropical*, almost tropical. **3** Of a lower rank, grade, or class, as in *subhead*, a secondary head ranking under a main head. **4** Being a division or part of, as in *subdivision*, a division of a division.

sub·al·tern [sə·bôl′tərn] **1** *n.* In the British army, an officer ranking below a captain. **2** *adj.* Having a lower rank or position.

sub·com·mit·tee [sub′kə·mit′ē] *n.* A small committee formed from a larger committee to do some special work.

sub·con·scious [sub·kon′shəs] **1** *n.* The part of one's mind that one is usually not aware of. **2** *adj.* In, of, or having to do with this part of the mind: *a subconscious wish for power.* **— sub·con′scious·ly** *adv.*

sub·cu·ta·ne·ous [sub′kyōō·tā′nē·əs] *adj.* **1** Lying beneath the skin. **2** Applied or put in beneath the skin, as an injection.

sub·di·vide [sub′di·vīd′] *v.* **sub·di·vid·ed, sub·di·vid·ing 1** To divide (a part) into smaller parts. **2** To divide (land) into building lots.

sub·di·vi·sion [sub′di·vizh′ən] *n.* **1** The act or process of subdividing. **2** Something produced by subdividing, especially a piece of land divided into building lots. **3** Any division of a division.

sub·due [sub·d(y)ōō′] *v.* **sub·dued, sub·du·ing 1** To gain power over, as by force; conquer. **2** To overcome or hold back: *to subdue a sneeze; to subdue rage.* **3** To make (a sound, color, etc.) less intense: *I like subdued colors.*

sub·head [sub′hed′] *n.* A secondary heading, as for a subdivision of a chapter, essay, etc.

sub·ject [*adj., n.* sub′jikt, *v.* səb·jekt′] **1** *adj.* Ruled or controlled by another or others: *the subject peoples of the world.* **2** *n.* A person who is under the power or influence of another, as of a monarch: *subjects of the Queen.* **3** *v.* To bring under domination: *The Mongols subjected part of Russia to their rule.* **4** *adj.* Liable to have or be affected by: *subject to disease; subject to criticism.* **5** *v.* To make liable; expose: *Lying will subject you to punishment.* **6** *v.* To force to endure: *They were subjected to long hours of waiting.* **7** *adj.* Dependent or contingent on something or someone: *a plan subject to the approval of the boss.* **8** *n.* The person, thing, act, idea, or field which one writes about, discusses, paints, etc.: *The old mill was the subject of his photograph.* **9** *n.* A person or animal used in an experiment. **10** *n.* The word, phrase, or clause about which something is said in a sentence. In "The boy ate a quart of ice cream," *boy* is the subject. **11** *n.* A musical theme. **12** *n.* A branch of learning or course of study: *History is his best subject in school.* ◆ *Subject* comes from an old French word. It was originally spelled *sujet*, but was later changed to conform with the Latin word *subjectus*, from which the French word comes.

sub·jec·tion [səb·jek′shən] *n.* **1** The act of making subject: *the subjection of a people.* **2** The condition of being subjected.

sub·jec·tive [səb·jek′tiv] *adj.* **1** Of, related to, or coming from a person's emotions, prejudices, interests, etc., rather than from outside facts or evidence: *a subjective opinion.* **2** About or strongly influenced by the feelings and thoughts of the writer, composer, etc.: *a subjective book.* **— sub·jec′tive·ly** *adv.*

subject matter Something that is being considered, discussed, studied, or written about.

sub·ju·gate [sub′jŏō·gāt] *v.* **sub·ju·gat·ed, sub·ju·gat·ing** To bring under domination or control; conquer; subdue. **— sub′ju·ga′tion** *n.*

sub·junc·tive [səb·jungk′tiv] **1** *adj.* Of, in, or indicating the mood of a verb that expresses an act or state not as actual but as wished, doubted, supposed, or depending on an unlikely condition. In "I wish you were here," *were* is subjunctive. **2** *n.* The subjunctive mood, or a verb form in this mood.

sub·lease [*n.* sub′lēs′, *v.* sub·lēs′] *n., v.* **sub·leased, sub·leas·ing 1** *n.* A lease given by a person who rents the property himself. **2** *v.* To give or take a sublease of.

sub·let [sub·let′ *or* sub′let′] *v.* **sub·let, sub·let·ting 1** To rent (property one holds on a lease) to another. **2** To give (part of the work that one has contracted to do) to another contractor.

sub·li·mate [sub′lə·māt] *v.* **sub·li·mat·ed, sub·li·mat·ing 1** To cause (a substance) to change from a solid to a gas and back again without passing through a liquid state. **2** To purify; refine. **3** To change the aim of (a physical drive) to a higher goal. **— sub·li·ma'tion** *n.*

sub·lime [sə·blīm'] *adj., v.* **sub·limed, sub·lim·ing 1** *adj.* Inspiring awe, deep emotion, etc.; grand; noble; supreme: a *sublime* symphony. **2** *v.* To sublimate or be sublimated. **3** *v.* To change directly from a solid state into a vapor, as Dry Ice does. **— sub·lime'ly** *adv.* **— sub·lim·i·ty** [sə·blim'ə·tē] *n.*

sub·ma·chine gun [sub'mə·shēn'] A small machine gun fired from the shoulder or hip.

sub·ma·rine [*adj.* sub'mə·rēn', *n.* sub'mə·rēn] **1** *adj.* Existing, done, or operating beneath the surface of the sea: a *submarine* plant. **2** *n.* A ship designed to operate on or under the surface of the sea. **3** *adj.* Of or having to do with submarines.

sub·merge [səb·mûrj'] *v.* **sub·merged, sub·merg·ing 1** To put or go into or under water or another liquid: to *submerge* a submarine; The walrus *submerged.* **2** To cover with water; inundate.

sub·mer·sion [səb·mûr'shən *or* səb·mûr'zhən] *n.* **1** The act of submerging. **2** A being submerged.

sub·mis·sion [səb·mish'ən] *n.* **1** The act of submitting or giving in. **2** The condition or quality of being submissive or humble. **3** The presenting of something for consideration, approval, etc.

sub·mis·sive [səb·mis'iv] *adj.* Giving in or willing to give in to what is asked or demanded; obedient; docile. **— sub·mis'sive·ly** *adv.*

sub·mit [səb·mit'] *v.* **sub·mit·ted, sub·mit·ting 1** To give up; yield to the authority, power, or will of another: The rebels finally *submitted.* **2** To present for decision, approval, testing, etc.: to *submit* a budget.

sub·nor·mal [sub·nôr'məl] *adj.* **1** Below normal: *subnormal* temperatures. **2** Having less than normal mental ability; dull.

sub·or·di·nate [*adj., n.* sə·bôr'də·nit, *v.* sə·bôr'də·nāt] *adj., n., v.* **sub·or·di·nat·ed, sub·or·di·nat·ing 1** *adj.* Being or belonging in an inferior position or class; secondary; minor. **2** *adj.* Under the authority or control of another: Privates are *subordinate* to sergeants. **3** *n.* A person who is subordinate to someone. **4** *v.* To make subordinate. **5** *adj.* Of, having to do with, or indicating a clause that depends on another clause and acts as a noun, adjective, or adverb. **— sub·or·di·na'tion** *n.*

sub·poe·na or **sub·pe·na** [sə(b)·pē'nə] *n., v.* **sub·poe·naed** or **sub·pe·naed, sub·poe·na·ing** or **sub·pe·na·ing 1** *n.* An official order commanding a person to appear in or submit something to a court. **2** *v.* To summon or call for by a subpoena.

sub·scribe [səb·skrīb'] *v.* **sub·scribed, sub·scrib·ing 1** To support or approve: to *sub-*

scribe to the idea of equal justice for all. **2** To write (one's name) at the bottom of a document, often to show approval or agreement. **3** To agree to pay for and receive a number of issues of a newspaper, magazine, etc. **4** To promise to pay or donate (a sum of money). **— sub·scrib'er** *n.*

sub·script [sub'skript] *n.* A number, letter, letters, etc., written below and to the right or left of a symbol, as $_2$ in H_2O.

sub·scrip·tion [səb·skrip'shən] *n.* **1** The act of subscribing. **2** Approval, support, money, etc., given by subscribing. **3** An agreement to receive a number of issues of a newspaper, magazine, etc.

sub·se·quent [sub'sə·kwənt] *adj.* Following in time, place, or order: *Subsequent* events proved us wrong. **— sub'se·quent·ly** *adv.*

sub·serve [səb·sûrv'] *v.* **sub·served, sub·serv·ing** To help or further (a cause, purpose, action, etc.): to *subserve* justice.

sub·ser·vi·ent [səb·sûr'vē·ənt] *adj.* **1** Annoyingly polite; too eager to please: a *subservient* attendant. **2** Helping to promote or further some purpose or end. **— sub·ser'vi·ence** *n.* **— sub·ser'vi·ent·ly** *adv.*

sub·side [səb·sīd'] *v.* **sub·sid·ed, sub·sid·ing 1** To become less violent or active: The storm *subsided.* **2** To sink to a lower level: The flood waters *subsided.* **— sub·si·dence** [səb·sīd'(ə)ns *or* sub'sə·dəns] *n.*

sub·sid·i·ar·y [səb·sid'ē·er·ē] *adj., n., pl.* **sub·sid·i·ar·ies 1** *adj.* Giving aid or support, especially in a minor way: Even though these plans are *subsidiary*, they are very important. **2** *adj.* Of, like, or having to do with a subsidy. **3** *n.* A company owned and controlled by another company.

sub·si·dize [sub'sə·dīz] *v.* **sub·si·dized, sub·si·diz·ing** To support or assist with a grant of money: States often *subsidize* hospitals. ¶3

sub·si·dy [sub'sə·dē] *n., pl.* **sub·si·dies** Financial aid given to a person or an enterprise by a government, a large corporation, etc.

sub·sist [səb·sist'] *v.* **1** To manage to stay alive: While lost in the woods, we *subsisted* on wild plants. **2** To exist or continue to exist.

sub·sis·tence [səb·sis'təns] *n.* **1** The act of subsisting. **2** Means of support; livelihood: An inheritance from a relative was his only *subsistence.* **3** The minimum amount of food, clothing, etc., necessary to stay alive: They got a bare *subsistence* from farming.

sub·soil [sub'soil'] *n.* The layer of soil that is just below the surface soil.

sub·stance [sub'stəns] *n.* **1** The material of which anything is made or consists. **2** The main or essential idea or part; essence: The *substance* of his novel was lost in its condensation. **3** A solid or substantial quality or character: His ideas have *substance.* **4** Material wealth or property.

sub·stan·dard [sub'stan'dərd] *adj.* Of a quality lower than the established standard or requirement; inferior: *substandard* housing.

sub·stan·tial [səb·stan'shəl] *adj.* **1** Of or having substance; actual; material; real: dangers far from imaginary but quite *substantial*. **2** Solid; strong; firm: a *substantial* foundation. **3** Large in amount, extent, etc.; considerable: *substantial* progress. **4** Wealthy and influential. **5** Having to do with the main points; essential. — **sub·stan'tial·ly** *adv.*

sub·stan·ti·ate [səb·stan'shē·āt] *v.* **sub·stan·ti·at·ed, sub·stan·ti·at·ing** To establish as true by evidence; prove: to *substantiate* a claim. — **sub·stan'ti·a'tion** *n.*

sub·stan·tive [sub'stən·tiv] **1** *n.* A noun or any word or group of words acting as a noun in a sentence. **2** *adj.* Used as a noun. **3** *adj.* Expressing existence: "To be" is called the *substantive* verb. **4** *adj.* Independent in resources; self-supporting: a *substantive* country. **5** *adj.* Considerable in amount; substantial.

sub·sti·tute [sub'stə·t(y)ōōt] *n., v.* **sub·sti·tut·ed, sub·sti·tut·ing** **1** *n.* A person or thing that takes the place of someone or something else. **2** *v.* To be a substitute: He *substituted* for the regular driver. **3** *v.* To use (a person or thing) as a substitute: to *substitute* honey for sugar. — **sub'sti·tu'tion** *n.*

sub·stra·tum [sub·strā'təm *or* sub·strat'əm] *n., pl.* **sub·stra·ta** [sub·strā'tə *or* sub·strat'ə] *or* **sub·stra·tums** An underlying stratum or layer, as of earth or rock.

sub·ter·fuge [sub'tər·fyōōj] *n.* A trick used to avoid something difficult or unpleasant.

sub·ter·ra·ne·an [sub'tə·rā'nē·ən] *adj.* **1** Located or happening under the earth: a *subterranean* pool. **2** Secret or hidden: a *subterranean* plot.

sub·ti·tle [sub'tīt'(ə)l] *n.* **1** A subordinate or explanatory title. **2** In foreign or silent films, a written translation or account of the words spoken, usually at the bottom of the screen.

sub·tle [sut'(ə)l] *adj.* **sub·tler, sub·tlest** **1** Having or showing a keen awareness of small points, differences, etc.: a *subtle* mind in legal matters. **2** Not direct or obvious; hard to see or understand: *subtle* differences in their arguments. **3** Cleverly or skillfully done or made: *subtle* work in gold. **4** Delicate: *subtle* colors. **5** Full of trickery or deceit; cunning; crafty: a *subtle* scheme for gaining power. — **sub'tly** *adv.*

sub·tle·ty [sut'(ə)l·tē] *n., pl.* **sub·tle·ties** **1** The condition or quality of being subtle. **2** Something that is subtle.

sub·tract [səb·trakt'] *v.* **1** To remove or take away, as a part from the whole. **2** To determine what to add to a number to make another number. Since 5 plus 3 equals 8, if 5 is *subtracted* from 8, the difference is 3.

sub·trac·tion [səb·trak'shən] *n.* The act or process of subtracting.

sub·tra·hend [sub'trə·hend] *n.* A number to be subtracted from another number.

sub·trop·i·cal [sub·trop'i·kəl] *adj.* Of, having to do with, or located in the regions near or bordering on the tropical zone.

sub·urb [sub'ûrb] *n.* **1** A town, village, district, etc., that is close to a large city. **2** (*pl.*) The area surrounding a large city.

sub·ur·ban [sə·bûr'bən] *adj.* Of, having to do with, or living in a suburb or the suburbs.

sub·ur·ban·ite [sə·bûr'bən·īt] *n.* A person whose home is in a suburb.

sub·ver·sion [səb·vûr'zhən] *n.* **1** The act of subverting. **2** The condition of being subverted.

sub·ver·sive [səb·vûr'siv] **1** *adj.* Tending to undermine or overthrow a government, law, etc. **2** *n.* A person who uses subversive methods.

sub·vert [səb·vûrt'] *v.* **1** To overthrow completely, as a government, etc. **2** To undermine the character or principles of; corrupt.

sub·way [sub'wā] *n.* **1** An electric railroad that is mainly underground. **2** *adj. use:* a *subway* station. **3** Any underground passage.

suc·ceed [sək·sēd'] *v.* **1** To accomplish what is planned or intended; be successful: The attempt *succeeded*. **2** To follow next in order after: Wilson *succeeded* Taft as President.

suc·cess [sək·ses'] *n.* **1** A favorable or desired outcome; good results. **2** A person or thing that is successful: The party was a *success*. **3** The achievement of wealth, fame, etc.

suc·cess·ful [sək·ses'fəl] *adj.* **1** Reaching a favorable or desired outcome; achieving good results: a *successful* plan. **2** Having become wealthy, famous, etc. — **suc·cess'ful·ly** *adv.*

suc·ces·sion [sək·sesh'ən] *n.* **1** A group of persons or things that follow one after another: a *succession* of victories. **2** The act of following in order after another: the *succession* of the new monarch. **3** The act or right of following another in an office, rank, etc.: The prince's *succession* to the throne was challenged. **4** The order or plan by which an office, rank, etc., changes hands: The vice president is first in *succession* to the presidency. — **in succession** In order, one after another.

suc·ces·sive [sək·ses'iv] *adj.* Following in order without interruption; consecutive: our fifth *successive* defeat. — **suc·ces'sive·ly** *adv.*

suc·ces·sor [sək·ses'ər] *n.* **1** A person or thing that comes after another. **2** A person who succeeds another on a throne, in office, etc.

suc·cinct [sək·singkt'] *adj.* Made or expressed clearly and briefly, with no wasted words: a *succinct* statement. — **suc·cinct'ly** *adv.*

suc·cor [suk'ər] **1** *n.* Help or comfort given in danger or distress. **2** *n.* A person or thing that provides succor. **3** *v.* To comfort or help. ¶1

suc·co·tash [suk'ə·tash] *n.* Kernels of corn and beans, usually lima beans, cooked together.

suc·cu·lent [suk'yə·lənt] *adj.* Full of juice; juicy: *succulent* fruit. — **suc'cu·lence** *n.*

suc·cumb [sə·kum'] *v.* **1** To give in or give way, as to force or persuasion. **2** To die.

such [such] **1** *adj.* Of this kind or that kind; of the same kind: *Such* wit as this is rare. **2** *adj.* Of

the type referred to: There is no *such* place.
3 *pron.* Such a person or thing: He is a writer, or
thinks of himself as *such*. **4** *adj.* So great, good,
bad, extreme, etc.: *Such* a heat wave! **5** *adj.*
Not specified; some: The meeting will be held at
such and *such* a place. **— as such 1** As being
what is indicated: A leader, *as such*, must take
responsibility. **2** In itself: Clothes, *as such*, do
not make the man. **— such as 1** For example.
2 Similar to. ◆ *Such* comes from an Old English
word. See also so.

suck [suk] **1** *v.* To draw into the mouth with the
lips and tongue: A baby *sucks* milk through a
nipple. **2** *v.* To draw fluid from with the mouth:
to *suck* an orange. **3** *v.* To inhale, as air, or
absorb, as liquid: A sponge *sucks* up water. **4** *v.*
To hold in the mouth and lick or draw on with the
mouth: to *suck* hard candy; Don't *suck* your
thumb. **5** *n.* The act of sucking.

suck·er [suk'ər] *n.* **1** A person or thing that
sucks. **2** A fresh-water fish having thick and
fleshy lips adapted for sucking in food. **3** A part
or organ of the body with which certain animals
suck or stick tight to things by suction. **4** A
lollipop. **5** A shoot growing up from a root or
underground stem of a plant. **6** *U.S. slang* A
person who is easy to trick or cheat.

suck·le [suk'əl] *v.* **suck·led, suck·ling 1** To
feed with milk from the breast or udder; nurse.
2 To take milk from the breast by sucking.

suck·ling [suk'ling] *n.* A baby or young animal
that is still feeding on its mother's milk.

su·crose [soo'krōs] *n.* Common sugar, extracted
from sugar cane, sugar beets, etc.

suc·tion [suk'shən] **1** *n.* The lowering of the
pressure in an enclosure below
that of the atmosphere, causing a liquid or gas to be forced
in or a solid to be held fast.
2 *adj.* Working by suction.
3 *n.* The action of sucking.

Su·dan [soo·dan'] *n.* A
country in NE Africa.

sud·den [sud'(ə)n] *adj.* **1**
Happening quickly and without warning: *sudden* death.
2 Quickly made, done, or
occurring: a *sudden* stop. **3**
Causing or likely to cause
surprise: a *sudden* curve in
the highway. **— all of a
sudden** Without warning.
— sud'den·ly *adv.* **— sud'·
den·ness** *n.*

suds [sudz] *n.pl.* Soapy
water, or the bubbles and
froth on its surface. **—
suds'y** *adj.*

sue [soo] *v.* **sued, su·ing**
1 To bring a lawsuit against (a person, company,

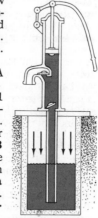

As the piston of
the suction pump is
raised,
atmospheric
pressure raises the
water.

etc.): He *sued* the newspaper for libel. **2** To
ask, plead, or petition: The besieged city *sued*
for peace.

suede [swād] *n.* **1** Leather that has been
rubbed to give it a soft nap like velvet. **2** *adj.
use*: *suede* shoes. **3** A cloth resembling suede.

su·et [soo'it] *n.* The hard fat about the loins and
kidneys of sheep and cattle. It is used in cooking,
to feed birds, and to make tallow.

Su·ez [soo·ez' *or* soo'ez] *n.* **1** A seaport in NE
Egypt, at the southern end of the Suez Canal.
2 The neck of land in NE Egypt, called the
Isthmus of Suez, that connects Asia and
Africa.

Suez Canal A ship canal in NE Egypt that
connects the Mediterranean Sea and the Red Sea.

suf·fer [suf'ər] *v.* **1** To feel or endure (pain or
distress). **2** To undergo, experience, or sustain:
to *suffer* an injury. **3** To be harmed or get worse:
If you don't get enough sleep, your health will
suffer. **4** To allow; permit: Will he *suffer* us to
leave? **— suf'fer·er** *n.*

suf·fer·ance [suf'ər·əns] *n.* Passive permission,
given or implied by failure to forbid.

suf·fer·ing [suf'ər·ing] *n.* Pain, distress,
anguish, misery, etc.

suf·fice [sə·fīs'] *v.* **suf·ficed, suf·fic·ing 1** To
be sufficient: I am wearing a jacket, but a
sweater would *suffice*. **2** To be enough for;
satisfy: Will a dollar *suffice* you for today?

suf·fi·cien·cy [sə·fish'ən·sē] *n.* **1** An amount
large enough to meet needs: a *sufficiency* of
supplies. **2** The condition of being enough.

suf·fi·cient [sə·fish'ənt] *adj.* Equal to what is
needed; enough; adequate: to lack *sufficient*
funds. **— suf·fi'cient·ly** *adv.*

suf·fix [*n.* suf'iks, *v.* suf'iks *or* sə·fiks'] **1** *n.* One
or more syllables added on at the end of a word
to make another word of different meaning or
function, as *-ment, -ness, -ible, -ful, -ous,* or *-ly,* or
to make an inflectional form, as *-ed, -ing,* or *-est.*
2 *v.* To add as a suffix.

suf·fo·cate [suf'ə·kāt] *v.* **suf·fo·cat·ed, suf·
fo·cat·ing 1** To kill by depriving of air;
smother; stifle. **2** To die from lack of air. **3** To
have or cause difficulty in breathing, as because
of stifling heat. **— suf'fo·ca'tion** *n.*

suf·frage [suf'rij] *n.* **1** The right to vote. **2** A
vote on some measure or for some candidate.

suf·fra·gette [suf'rə·jet'] *n.* Formerly, a
woman who fought for women's right to vote.

suf·fuse [sə·fyooz'] *v.* **suf·fused, suf·fus·ing**
To overspread, as with a fluid or color: A deep
blush *suffused* her cheeks. **— suf·fu'sion** *n.*

sug·ar [shoog'ər] **1** *n.* Any of a class of carbohydrates all of which have a more or less sweet
taste. Sucrose, which is extracted from sugar
cane, sugar beets, etc., is the sugar commonly
used for sweetening. **2** *v.* To form or produce
sugar crystals: Fudge *sugars* if it is cooked too

---

add, āce, câre, pälm; end, ēqual; it, īce; odd, ōpen, ôrder; took, pool; up, bûrn;
ə = a in *above*, e in *sicken*, i in *possible*, o in *melon*, u in *circus*; yoo = u in *fuse*; oil; pout;
check; ring; thin; this; zh in *vision*. For ¶ reference, see page 64 · HOW TO

much. **3** *v.* To sweeten, cover, or coat with sugar. **4** *v.* To make agreeable or less distasteful, as by flattery: to *sugar* a refusal. ◆ *Sugar* comes from an Arabic word.

sugar beet A type of beet having a white root from which ordinary sugar is obtained.

sugar cane A tall grass grown in tropical regions, having a solid, jointed stalk which is a major source of ordinary sugar.

sug·ar·plum [shoŏg′ər·plum′] *n.* A small ball or flat oval of candy; bonbon.

sug·ar·y [shoŏg′ər·ē] *adj.* **1** Made of sugar or like sugar; sweet. **2** Too sweet; seeming sweet but not sincerely so: *sugary* compliments.

sug·gest [sə(g)·jest′] *v.* **1** To put forward as a proposal; propose: I *suggest* that we have a party. **2** To offer as a theory or imply as a possibility: Are you *suggesting* that he lied? **3** To bring to mind by association or connection: The bareness of the room *suggested* a monk's cell.

sug·ges·tion [sə(g)·jes′chən] *n.* **1** The act of suggesting: It was changed at my *suggestion*. **2** Something suggested. **3** A touch, trace, or hint: a *suggestion* of annoyance in his tone.

sug·ges·tive [sə(g)·jes′tiv] *adj.* **1** Giving or apt to give a suggestion or hint, often of something indecent. **2** Stimulating to thought.

su·i·cide [soō′ə·sīd] *n.* **1** The act of killing oneself intentionally. **2** A person who kills himself intentionally. **3** Ruin of one's own prospects or interests. — **su′i·ci′dal** *adj.*

suit [soōt] **1** *n.* A matched set of garments, especially a jacket with trousers or a skirt. **2** *n.* An outfit or garment worn for a special purpose: a bathing *suit*. **3** *v.* To fulfill the needs of; be correct or fitting for: Dry soil *suits* some plants. **4** *v.* To make appropriate; adapt: *Suit* the speech to the audience. **5** *v.* To please or satisfy: That *suits* me fine. **6** *n.* One of the four sets of playing cards that make up a pack. Spades, hearts, diamonds, and clubs are suits. **7** *n.* A case brought to a court of law to settle a claim. **8** *n.* An appeal or petition. **9** *n.* The seeking of a woman in marriage. — **follow suit 1** To play a card whose suit matches that of the card led. **2** To do the same: I'll dive and you *follow suit*. — **suit yourself** Do whatever you like.

suit·a·ble [soō′tə·bəl] *adj.* Proper for the purpose or occasion; fitting. — **suit·a·bil·i·ty** [soō′tə·bil′ə·tē] *n.* — **suit′a·bly** *adv.*

suit·case [soōt′kās′] *n.* A boxlike container with a handle, used on trips to carry clothes.

suite *n.* **1** [swēt] A set of connected rooms. **2** [swēt *or* soōt] A set of matching furniture to be used in the same room: a dining room *suite*. **3** [swēt] A set of related musical pieces, in former times always a series of dances. **4** [swēt] A group of attendants or followers; retinue.

suit·or [soō′tər] *n.* **1** A man who courts a woman. **2** A person who pleads or who sues.

sul·fa drug [sul′fə] Any of a group of chemical compounds obtained from coal tar and used to treat various bacterial infections.

sul·fate [sul′fāt] *n.* A salt of sulfuric acid.

sul·fide [sul′fīd] *n.* A compound of sulfur and another element or radical.

sul·fur [sul′fər] *n.* A pale yellow, nonmetallic element found both free and in compounds. It burns with a blue flame and a suffocating odor.

sul·fu·ric [sul·fyoŏr′ik] *adj.* Of, having to do with, derived from, or containing sulfur.

sulfuric acid A colorless, oily, and very corrosive liquid formed of sulfur, hydrogen, and oxygen.

sul·fur·ous [sul′fər·əs *or* sul·fyoŏr′əs] *adj.* **1** Of, like, having to do with, derived from, or containing sulfur. **2** Like hell fire; fiery.

sulk [sulk] **1** *v.* To be sulky or sullen. **2** *n.* (often *pl.*) A sulky mood or humor.

sulk·y[1] [sul′kē] *adj.* **sulk·i·er, sulk·i·est** Sullenly cross or ill-humored. — **sulk′i·ly** *adv.*

sulk·y[2] [sul′kē] *n., pl.* **sulk·ies** A carriage with two wheels and a seat for one person.

Sulkies

sul·len [sul′ən] *adj.* **1** Glumly silent and aloof because ill-humored or resentful. **2** Gloomy; dismal; somber: *sullen* clouds. — **sul′len·ly** *adv.* — **sul′len·ness** *n.*

Sul·li·van [sul′ə·vən], **Sir Arthur,** 1842–1900, English composer and collaborator with Sir William Gilbert on comic operettas.

sul·ly [sul′ē] *v.* **sul·lied, sul·ly·ing** To soil or tarnish: to *sully* one's good name.

sul·phur [sul′fər] *n.* Another spelling of SULFUR.

sul·phu·ric [sul·fyoŏr′ik] *adj.* Another spelling of SULFURIC.

sul·phur·ous [sul′fər·əs *or* sul·fyoŏr′əs] *adj.* Another spelling of SULFUROUS.

sul·tan [sul′tən] *n.* The ruler of a Moslem country.

sul·tan·a [sul·tan′ə *or* sul·tä′nə] *n.* A sultan's wife, daughter, sister, or mother.

sul·tan·ate [sul′tən·āt] *n.* The office, authority, reign, or territory of a sultan.

sul·try [sul′trē] *adj.* **sul·tri·er, sul·tri·est** **1** Uncomfortably hot, humid, and still, as weather. **2** Extremely hot: a *sultry* desert.

sum [sum] *n., v.* **summed, sum·ming 1** *n.* The number or quantity reached by adding two or more other numbers or quantities: The *sum* of 7, 4, and 2 is 13. **2** *v.* To add into one total: to *sum* numbers. **3** *n.* An arithmetic problem. **4** *n.* The full amount; total; whole: the *sum* of human knowledge. **5** *n.* A particular amount, as of money: That's quite a *sum*. — **sum up** To review the main points of; present briefly.

su·mac or **su·mach** [soō′mak *or* shoō′mak] *n.* A shrub or small tree having clusters of small flowers and, later, of berries. Its leaves turn from green to bright red in autumn.

Su·ma·tra [soō·mä′trə] *n.* An island of Indonesia south of the Malay Peninsula.

Su·mer [soō′mər] *n.* An ancient country of Mesopotamia, later a part of Babylonia.

Su·me·ri·an [sōō·mir′ē·ən] **1** *adj.* Of or from Sumer. **2** *n.* A person who was born or lived in Sumer. **3** *n.* The language of Sumer.

sum·ma·ri·ly [sə·mer′ə·lē *or* sum′ər·ə·lē] *adv.* Without ceremony or delay: *summarily* dismissed.

sum·ma·rize [sum′ə·rīz] *v.* **sum·ma·rized, sum·ma·riz·ing** To make a summary of; sum up: to *summarize* a chapter. ¶3

sum·ma·ry [sum′ər·ē] *n., pl.* **sum·ma·ries,** *adj.* **1** *n.* A short statement presenting the main points. **2** *adj.* Presenting the main points in brief form: a *summary* paragraph. **3** *adj.* Done without ceremony or delay: a *summary* dismissal.

sum·mer [sum′ər] **1** *n.* The warmest season of the year, occurring between spring and autumn. **2** *adj.* use: *summer* sports; *summer* clothes. **3** *v.* To spend the summer: to *summer* at the beach.

sum·mer·time [sum′ər·tīm′] *n.* Summer.

sum·mit [sum′it] *n.* **1** The highest point or level; top, as of a mountain. **2** The highest degree or level: the *summit* of human achievement.

summit meeting A meeting at which the heads of two or more governments talk and bargain in an attempt to settle international disputes.

sum·mon [sum′ən] *v.* **1** To send for or order to come. **2** To call together, as a legislature. **3** To order (a person) to appear in court. **4** To call into action; arouse: *Summon* up courage.

sum·mons [sum′ənz] *n., pl.* **sum·mon·ses 1** A request or order to appear at a given place or time. **2** A written order to appear in court.

sump [sump] *n.* A depression or reservoir for receiving water or draining off waste liquids.

sump·tu·ous [sump′chŏŏ·əs] *adj.* Very expensive and luxurious; costly: a *sumptuous* feast.

sun [sun] *n., v.* **sunned, sun·ning 1** *n.* The brilliant star around which the earth and other planets revolve and which provides them with light and heat. ◆ *Adj.*, *solar.* **2** *n.* The light or heat radiated from the sun: This room gets a lot of *sun.* **3** *v.* To expose (oneself) to the light and heat of the sun: Let's *sun* ourselves by the pool. **4** *n.* Any star like our sun that has planets revolving around it. **5** *n.* Anything brilliant and magnificent like the sun.

Sun. Abbreviation of SUNDAY.

sun·beam [sun′bēm′] *n.* A ray of sunlight.

sun·bon·net [sun′bon′it] *n.* A bonnet with a projecting brim and sometimes a ruffle in back, to shade the face and neck from the sun.

sun·burn [sun′bûrn′] *n., v.* **sun·burned** or **sun·burnt, sun·burn·ing 1** *n.* A painful burn that makes the skin red and sore, caused by too much exposure to the sun. **2** *v.* To affect or be affected with sunburn: My back is *sunburned.*

sun·dae [sun′dē] *n.* A dish of ice cream topped with crushed fruit, syrup, nuts, etc.

Sun·day [sun′dē *or* sun′dā] *n.* The first day of the week. It is the Christian day of rest and worship.

Sunday school A school that meets on Sundays, in which religious instruction is given.

sun·der [sun′dər] *v.* To break or split apart; separate or sever: a family *sundered* by war. **—in sunder** Into separate parts; apart.

sun·di·al [sun′dī′əl] *n.* An outdoor device that shows the time of day by means of the shadow cast by a pointer on a numbered dial.

Sundial

sun·down [sun′doun′] *n.* *U.S.* Sunset.

sun·dries [sun′drēz] *n.pl.* Items or things too small or too numerous to be separately named.

sun·dry [sun′drē] *adj.* Various; several; miscellaneous: in *sundry* times and places.

sun·fish [sun′fish′] *n., pl.* **sun·fish** or **sun·fish·es 1** A large ocean fish having a pancake-shaped body, two large fins, and a short tail. **2** A small North American fresh-water fish.

sun·flow·er [sun′flou′ər] *n.* A tall plant with large, circular flowers that have a central dark disk surrounded by bright yellow rays.

sung [sung] Past participle and alternative past tense of SING.

sun·glass·es [sun′glas′iz] *n.pl.* Spectacles to protect the eyes from the glare of the sun, usually made with colored glass.

sunk [sungk] Past participle and alternative past tense of SINK.

sunk·en [sung′kən] *adj.* **1** Located beneath the surface or on the bottom of a body of water. **2** Lower than the surrounding level: *sunken* gardens. **3** Depressed or hollow: *sunken* cheeks.

sun·less [sun′lis] *adj.* Lacking sun or sunlight; overcast or dark: *sunless* skies.

sun·light [sun′līt] *n.* The light of the sun.

sun·lit [sun′lit] *adj.* Lighted by the sun.

sun·ny [sun′ē] *adj.* **sun·ni·er, sun·ni·est 1** Filled with the light and warmth of the sun: a *sunny* afternoon. **2** Open or exposed to sunlight: a *sunny* patio. **3** Bright; cheery: a *sunny* smile.

sun·rise [sun′rīz′] *n.* **1** The appearing of the sun over the horizon. **2** The time when the sun rises. **3** The look of the sky at this time.

sun·set [sun′set′] *n.* **1** The disappearance of the sun below the horizon. **2** The time when the sun sets. **3** The look of the sky at this time.

sun·shade [sun′shād′] *n.* A shield from the sun, as a parasol or awning.

sun·shine [sun′shīn′] *n.* **1** The shining light of the sun. **2** The warmth of the sun's rays. **3** Brightness, cheerfulness, or happiness. **— sun′shin′y** *adj.*

sun·spot [sun′spot′] *n.* One of the dark spots that appear periodically on the surface of the sun,

---

add, āce, câre, pälm;   end, ēqual;   it, īce;   odd, ōpen, ôrder;   tŏŏk, pōōl;   up, bûrn;

ə = a in *above*, e in *sicken*, i in *possible*, o in *melon*, u in *circus*;   y‾o‾o = u in *fuse*;   oil;   pout;

check;   ring;   thin;   this;   zh in *vision.*   For ¶ reference, see page 64 · HOW TO

thought to be connected with magnetic disturbances.

sun·stroke [sun′strōk′] *n.* A sudden illness caused by staying too long in the hot sun.

sun·up [sun′up′] *n. U.S.* Sunrise.

Sun Yat-sen [sŏŏn′yät′sen′] *n.* 1866–1925, Chinese political leader.

sup[1] [sup] *v.* **supped, sup·ping,** *n.* **1** *v.* To take (fluid food) in sips; sip. **2** *n.* A mouthful or taste of liquid or soft food.

sup[2] [sup] *v.* **supped, sup·ping** To eat supper.

super- A prefix meaning: **1** Above in position; over, as in *superstructure,* a structure built above another structure or a base. **2** Above or beyond; more than, as in *superhuman,* beyond the range of normal human powers. **3** Larger than or superior to others of its class, as in *superman,* a man superior to ordinary men. **4** Extremely or excessively, as in *superabundant,* extremely or excessively abundant. **5** Extra, as in *supertax,* an extra tax.

su·per·a·bun·dant [sŏŏ′pər·ə·bun′dənt] *adj.* Much more than enough; extremely plentiful, or excessive. **— su′per·a·bun′dance** *n.*

su·per·an·nu·at·ed [sŏŏ′pər·an′yŏŏ·ā′tid] *adj.* **1** Retired because of age, especially with a pension. **2** Too old to be useful or efficient.

su·perb [sŏŏ·pûrb′] *adj.* **1** Grand; majestic; imposing: a *superb* dignity of manner. **2** Luxurious; elegant: a *superb* mink coat. **3** Excellent; outstandingly good: She has *superb* taste. **— su·perb′ly** *adv.*

su·per·car·go [sŏŏ′pər·kär′gō] *n., pl.* **su·per·car·goes** or **su·per·car·gos** An agent on board ship who is in charge of the cargo and its sale and purchase.

su·per·charg·er [sŏŏ′pər·chär′jər] *n.* A pump or turbine that forces extra air and fuel into an internal-combustion engine.

su·per·cil·i·ous [sŏŏ′pər·sil′ē·əs] *adj.* Full of haughty contempt or indifference; proud and disdainful; arrogant. **— su′per·cil′i·ous·ly** *adv.* ◆ *Supercilious* comes from a Latin word meaning *eyebrow.* A supercilious look often involves a raising of the eyebrows.

su·per·cool [sŏŏ′pər·kŏŏl′] *v.* To cool below the freezing point without changing to a solid.

su·per·fi·cial [sŏŏ′pər·fish′əl] *adj.* **1** Of, on, or affecting only the surface: a *superficial* wound. **2** Not going past the surface or beyond the obvious; not deep or thorough; shallow or hasty: *superficial* understanding; a *superficial* search. **3** Not genuine: a *superficial* likeness. **— su·per·fi·ci·al·i·ty** [sŏŏ′pər·fish′ē·al′ə·tē] *n.* **— su′per·fi′cial·ly** *adv.*

su·per·flu·i·ty [sŏŏ′pər·flŏŏ′ə·tē] *n., pl.* **su·per·flu·i·ties 1** An amount greater than what is needed; excess. **2** An unnecessary thing.

su·per·flu·ous [sŏŏ·pûr′flŏŏ·əs] *adj.* More than is needed or called for; unnecessary: *superfluous* comments. **— su·per′flu·ous·ly** *adv.*

su·per·high·way [sŏŏ′pər·hī′wā′] *n.* A divided highway for traffic moving at high speeds, generally having four or more traffic lanes.

su·per·hu·man [sŏŏ′pər·(h)yŏŏ′mən] *adj.* **1** Above or beyond the human; supernatural or divine. **2** Beyond the range of normal or ordinary human powers: to display *superhuman* strength.

su·per·im·pose [sŏŏ′pər·im·pōz′] *v.* **su·per·im·posed, su·per·im·pos·ing** To place over, above, or on top of something else.

su·per·in·tend [sŏŏ′pər·in·tend′] *v.* To be in charge of and direct; manage; supervise.

su·per·in·ten·dence [sŏŏ′pər·in·ten′dəns] *n.* Direction and management; supervision.

su·per·in·ten·dent [sŏŏ′pər·in·ten′dənt] *n.* **1** A person responsible for directing, managing, or supervising some work, organization, department, etc. **2** In parts of the U.S., a janitor.

su·pe·ri·or [sə·pir′ē·ər] **1** *adj.* Much better than the usual; extremely good; excellent: a *superior* education. **2** *adj.* Conceited or disdainful because of a feeling of being better than others: Don't be so *superior.* **3** *adj.* Higher in rank, grade, authority, etc.: a *superior* officer. **4** *adj.* Greater, as in size, power, ability, etc.: The enemy was *superior* in numbers. **5** *n.* A person of greater authority, ability, etc., than another: He is my *superior* at golf. **6** *n.* The head of a religious order or house, as a convent. **— superior to 1** Better, larger, or more powerful than. **2** Above, as in rank. **3** Beyond the influence of; above giving in to: Try to be *superior to* envy.

Su·pe·ri·or [sə·pir′ē·ər], **Lake** The largest of the Great Lakes, in the U.S. and Canada.

su·pe·ri·or·i·ty [sə·pir′ē·ôr′ə·tē] *n.* The quality or condition of being superior.

su·per·la·tive [sə·pûr′lə·tiv *or* sŏŏ·pûr′lə·tiv] **1** *adj.* Excellent in the highest degree: *superlative* work. **2** *adj.* In the highest degree of comparison of the adjective or adverb. **3** *n.* A form or phrase showing this degree. *Greenest* and *most clearly* are superlatives of *green* and *clearly.* **— su·per′la·tive·ly** *adv.*

su·per·man [sŏŏ′pər·man′] *n., pl.* **su·per·men** [sŏŏ′pər·men′] A man having superhuman powers.

su·per·mar·ket [sŏŏ′pər·mär′kit] *n.* A large grocery store in which the customers select goods from the shelves and pay as they leave.

su·per·nat·u·ral [sŏŏ′pər·nach′ər·əl] *adj.* **1** Outside the known laws or forces of nature: a witch's *supernatural* powers. **2** *n. use:* Supernatural things or events: tales of *the supernatural.*

su·per·nu·mer·ar·y [sŏŏ′pər·n(y)ŏŏ′mə·rer′ē] *adj., n., pl.* **su·per·nu·mer·ar·ies 1** *adj.* Beyond a customary or necessary number; extra. **2** *n.* An extra person or thing. **3** *n.* An actor who plays a member of a crowd and has no lines.

su·per·script [sŏŏ′pər·skript′] *n.* A character written or printed above and often to the side of a larger character, as the [3] in y[3].

su·per·scrip·tion [sŏŏ′pər·skrip′shən] *n.* Something written on the outside or upper part of a thing, especially an address on a letter.

su·per·sede [sŏŏ′pər·sēd′] *v.* **su·per·sed·ed, su·per·sed·ing 1** To cause to be given up or set aside; displace: Buses have largely *superseded* streetcars. **2** To fill the position of; replace: *The new teacher supersedes one who retired.*

su·per·son·ic [soo′pər·son′ik] *adj.* Being or traveling faster than the speed of sound.

su·per·sti·tion [soo′pər·stish′ən] *n.* **1** The unreasoning fear or belief that many helpful and harmful supernatural forces exist and that certain actions will anger or pacify them. **2** A superstitious idea or practice: *the superstition that walking under a ladder is unlucky.*

su·per·sti·tious [soo′pər·stish′əs] *adj.* Of, based on, caused by, influenced by, or showing superstition. **— su′per·sti′tious·ly** *adv.*

su·per·struc·ture [soo′pər·struk′chər] *n.* **1** Any structure built upon another. **2** The part of a building above the foundation. **3** The part of a ship above the main deck.

su·per·tax [soo′pər·taks′] *n.* An extra tax in addition to the normal tax; surtax.

su·per·vise [soo′pər·vīz] *v.* **su·per·vised, su·per·vis·ing** To be in charge of and direct (employees, a process, etc.); superintend; oversee; manage. **— su′per·vi′sor** *n.*

su·per·vi·sion [soo′pər·vizh′ən] *n.* Direction or control; regulation; management.

su·per·vi·so·ry [soo′pər·vī′zər·ē] *adj.* **1** Of or having to do with a supervisor or supervision. **2** Involving or limited to supervision.

su·pine [soo·pīn′] *adj.* **1** Lying on the back with the face upward. **2** Sluggishly inactive.

sup·per [sup′ər] *n.* An evening meal; the last meal of the day.

sup·plant [sə·plant′] *v.* To take the place of, often unfairly: *Jacob supplanted Esau.*

sup·ple [sup′əl] *adj.* **sup·pler** [sup′lər], **sup·plest** [sup′ləst] **1** Bending easily; flexible or limber: *a supple body.* **2** Able to adapt easily to new or different situations: *a supple mind.*

sup·ple·ment [*n.* sup′lə·mənt, *v.* sup′lə·ment] **1** *n.* Something added, often to supply a lack: *a food supplement.* **2** *v.* To add to or provide what is lacking in: *extra reading to supplement the textbook.* **3** *n.* An extra section of a newspaper or book giving additional information: *a yearly supplement to an encyclopedia.*

sup·ple·men·tal [sup′lə·men′təl] *adj.* Supplementary; additional.

sup·ple·men·ta·ry [sup′lə·men′tər·ē] *adj.* **1** Serving as an addition to or to supply a lack. **2** Indicating two angles whose sum is 180°.

Angles *a* and *b* are supplementary.

sup·pli·ant [sup′lē·ənt] **1** *adj.* Asking earnestly and humbly; beseeching. **2** *n.* A person who begs or prays earnestly and humbly.

sup·pli·cant [sup′lə·kənt] **1** *adj.* Asking humbly; beseeching. **2** *n.* A suppliant.

sup·pli·cate [sup′lə·kāt] *v.* **sup·pli·cat·ed, sup·pli·cat·ing** To ask, entreat, or pray earnestly and humbly; beseech; implore.

sup·pli·ca·tion [sup′lə·kā′shən] *n.* An earnest prayer or entreaty.

sup·ply [sə·plī′] *v.* **sup·plied, sup·ply·ing,** *n., pl.* **sup·plies** **1** *v.* To furnish (what is needed); provide: *to supply milk for a city; to supply a class with paper.* **2** *n.* An amount available for use; stock; store: *a supply of fuel.* **3** *n.* (*usually pl.*) Materials, goods, etc., kept on hand to be given out when needed: *office supplies.* **4** *v.* To satisfy, as a want or demand, make up for, as a loss, or fill, as a vacancy. **5** *n.* The act of supplying. **— sup·pli′er** *n.*

sup·port [sə·pôrt′] **1** *v.* To bear the weight of; hold up or hold in place: *Beams support the ceiling.* **2** *v.* To provide the necessities of life for: *He supports five children.* **3** *v.* To keep or tend to keep from failing; maintain: *Oxygen supports burning.* **4** *v.* To help prove the truth or correctness of: *The evidence supports my theory.* **5** *v.* To be for or help; favor or back: *to support a candidate.* **6** *n.* The act of supporting. **7** *n.* The condition of being supported. **8** *n.* A person or thing that supports. **9** *v.* To endure or tolerate: *I cannot support his insolence.* **— sup·port′er** *n.*

sup·pose [sə·pōz′] *v.* **sup·posed, sup·pos·ing** **1** To assume as true, as for the sake of argument: *Suppose he loses the election.* **2** To imagine, think, believe, or guess: *I suppose she is tired.* **3** To expect or require: *He is supposed to be on time.* **4** To require as a necessary condition; imply: *A gift supposes a giver, or donor.*

sup·posed [sə·pōzd′] *adj.* Considered to be true or actual, often by mistake: *his supposed honesty.* **— sup·pos·ed·ly** [sə·pō′zid·lē] *adv.*

sup·po·si·tion [sup′ə·zish′ən] *n.* **1** The act of supposing. **2** Something supposed; assumption.

sup·press [sə·pres′] *v.* **1** To put down or end by force; crush: *to suppress a rebellion.* **2** To keep from getting out or becoming known; hold back: *to suppress a sigh; to suppress news.* **— sup·pres·sion** [sə·presh′ən] *n.*

sup·pu·rate [sup′yə·rāt] *v.* **sup·pu·rat·ed, sup·pu·rat·ing** To fill up with or give out pus; fester.

su·prem·a·cy [sə·prem′ə·sē] *n.* **1** Supreme power or authority. **2** The quality of being supreme.

su·preme [sə·prēm′] *adj.* **1** Highest in power or authority: *supreme headquarters of the allied forces.* **2** Highest in degree, quality, etc.; utmost: *Shakespeare is the supreme English poet.* **— su·preme′ly** *adv.*

Supreme Being God.

Supreme Court 1 The highest and final court of appeal in the U.S., made up of nine justices. **2** The highest court in various States.

Supt. Abbreviation of SUPERINTENDENT.

sur·charge [*n.* sûr′chärj′, *v.* sûr·chärj′] *n., v.* **sur·charged, sur·charg·ing 1** *n.* An extra charge over the regular rate. **2** *n.* An excessive charge or burden. **3** *v.* To charge extra, overcharge, or overload. **4** *n.* Something additional, as a new valuation, printed on a stamp. **5** *v.* To imprint a surcharge on (a stamp).

sur·coat [sûr′kōt′] *n.* An outer coat or garment, as a tunic worn by knights over armor.

sure [shŏŏr] *adj.* **sur·er, sur·est,** *adv.* **1** *adj.* Free from doubt; certain; positive: I'm *sure* you'll succeed. **2** *adv. informal* Certainly; of course: *Sure,* I can go. **3** *adj.* Certain; destined; bound: You're *sure* to win. **4** *adj.* Bound to happen; inevitable: Victory seemed a *sure* thing. **5** *adj.* Not likely to fail: a *sure* shot. **6** *adj.* Dependable; reliable: a *sure* remedy. **7** *adj.* Firm; stable: a *sure* footing. **— to be sure** Certainly. **— sure′ness** *n.*

Surcoat

sure-fire [shŏŏr′fīr′] *adj. informal* Certain to succeed, win, etc.: a *sure-fire* method.

sure-foot·ed [shŏŏr′fŏŏt′id] *adj.* Not liable to slip, stumble, or fall: a *sure-footed* burro.

sure·ly [shŏŏr′lē] *adv.* **1** Without doubt; certainly. **2** Securely; safely.

sure·ty [shŏŏr′(ə·)tē] *n., pl.* **sure·ties 1** A person who takes responsibility for another's debt or action. **2** Security or guarantee against loss, damage, or failure to do something.

surf [sûrf] **1** *n.* The waves of the sea as they break on a beach, reef, or shoal. **2** *n.* The roar or foam of such waves. **3** *v.* To ride on the surf with a surfboard.

sur·face [sûr′fis] *n., v.* **sur·faced, sur·fac·ing 1** *n.* The outer part or face of any solid body, or the upper level of a liquid. **2** *adj. use: surface* activity. **3** *v.* To add a surface to; smooth: to *surface* a drive with asphalt. **4** *v.* To rise to the surface, as a submarine. **5** *n.* The outward part or appearance of a person or thing: He is always pleasant on the *surface.* **6** *adj. use:* a *surface* calm.

surf·board [sûrf′bôrd′] *n.* A long, narrow board, used in the water sport of surfing.

sur·feit [sûr′fit] **1** *n.* Too much or an excess of something, as of food or drink. **2** *n.* The disgust felt by having too much of something. **3** *v.* To feed or supply with too much of something: The public has been *surfeited* with stories of crime.

surge [sûrj] *n., v.* **surged, surg·ing 1** *v.* To move or go with the strong rush of a wave: The crowd *surged* forward. **2** *n.* A surging or rushing movement: the rhythmic *surge* of the waves. **3** *n.* A strong, sudden increase or flow: to feel a *surge* of energy.

sur·geon [sûr′jən] *n.* A doctor whose practice is largely limited to surgery.

sur·ger·y [sûr′jər·ē] *n.* **1** The branch of medical practice dealing with the repair or removal of

diseased or injured organs or parts of the body. **2** An operation in which surgery is used. **3** A place or room where surgery is done.

sur·gi·cal [sûr′ji·kəl] *adj.* Of, having to do with, or used in surgery: a *surgical* mask.

Su·ri·nam [sŏŏr′ə·näm] *n.* A territory of the Netherlands on the NE coast of South America.

sur·ly [sûr′lē] *adj.* **sur·li·er, sur·li·est** Rude and illhumored; cross; gruff. — **sur′li·ness** *n.*

Surgical masks

sur·mise [sər·mīz′] *n., v.* **sur·mised, sur·mis·ing 1** *n.* An opinion based on slight evidence; guess. **2** *v.* To form (such an opinion); guess.

sur·mount [sər·mount′] *v.* **1** To overcome (difficulties, problems, etc.). **2** To reach the top or other side of (an obstacle, mountain, etc.). **3** To be on or at the top of: A steeple *surmounted* the church.

sur·name [sûr′nām′] *n., v.* **sur·named, sur·nam·ing 1** *n.* The name of a person's family; the last name of a person: Some *surnames* are derived from given names, as Johnson from John (John's son). **2** *n.* An added name; nickname: Philip IV was given the *surname* "the Fair." **3** *v.* To give a surname to. **4** *v.* To call or identify by a surname.

sur·pass [sər·pas′] *v.* **1** To be more, greater, or better than: His playing *surpassed* our wildest hopes. **2** To go beyond the reach or powers of: The Acropolis *surpasses* all description.

sur·plice [sûr′plis] *n.* A loose, white garment with full sleeves, worn over a cassock by the clergy, choir, etc., of certain churches.

sur·plus [sûr′plus] **1** *n.* An amount above what is used or needed; something left over; excess. **2** *adj. use: surplus* food; *surplus* production.

Surplices

sur·prise [sə(r)·prīz′] *v.* **sur·prised, sur·pris·ing,** *n.* **1** *v.* To shock confuse, or befuddle by being sudden, unexpected, or unusual; astonish: The gunshot *surprised* us all. **2** *adj. use: surprising* news. **3** *n.* The condition of being surprised; astonishment. **4** *n.* Something that causes surprise: His visit was a happy *surprise.* **5** *adj. use:* a *surprise* party. **6** *v.* To come upon suddenly or unexpectedly; take unawares. **7** *n.* The act of surprising: to take someone by *surprise.*

sur·ren·der [sə·ren′dər] **1** *v.* To give up, as to an enemy; yield. **2** *v.* To abandon or give up possession of: to *surrender* hope; to *surrender* a seat. **3** *n.* The act of surrendering.

sur·rep·ti·tious [sûr′əp·tish′əs] *adj.* **1** Done by secret or improper means: a *surreptitious* removal of the books. **2** Acting secretly or by stealth. — **sur′rep·ti′tious·ly** *adv.*

sur·rey [sûr′ē] *n.* A light carriage having two seats, four wheels, and sometimes a top.

sur·ro·gate [sûr′ə·gāt *or* sûr′ə·git] *n.* **1** A person having the authority to act in place of another; a deputy. **2** A judge of a court having charge of guardianships, settling estates, etc.

Surrey

sur·round [sə·round′] *v.* To enclose on all sides; envelop; encircle.

sur·round·ings [sə·roun′dingz] *n.pl.* The things or the conditions that surround a person or place; environment: pleasant *surroundings.*

sur·tax [sûr′taks′] **1** *n.* An extra or additional tax. **2** *v.* To charge with such a tax.

sur·veil·lance [sər·vā′ləns] *n.* **1** Close watch, as over a prisoner or suspect. **2** The act of watching or supervising closely.

sur·vey [*v.* sər·vā′, *n.* sûr′vā] **1** *v.* To determine the area, boundaries, shape, etc., of (land) by measurement and calculation. **2** *n.* The act or results of surveying. **3** *v.* To get an overall view of; look over as from a height: to *survey* the landscape. **4** *n.* A brief but thorough study or examination: A *survey* put storm damage at two million.

sur·vey·ing [sər·vā′ing] *n.* The methods or profession of measuring and mapping land.

sur·vey·or [sər·vā′ər] *n.* A person whose profession is surveying.

sur·viv·al [sər·vī′vəl] *n.* **1** The act or condition of surviving: Their *survival* depended on the skill of the pilot. **2** Something, as a custom or belief, that persists from a former time.

sur·vive [sər·vīv′] *v.* **sur·vived, sur·viv·ing** **1** To outlive or outlast: to *survive* a relative. **2** To live through: to *survive* a flood. **3** To remain alive or in existence.

sur·vi·vor [sər·vī′vər] *n.* A person or thing that survives.

sus·cep·ti·ble [sə·sep′tə·bəl] *adj.* Easily influenced, moved, affected, etc.: Her *susceptible* sympathies were aroused. — **susceptible of** Capable of receiving, undergoing, or being influenced by: His testimony is *susceptible of* proof. — **susceptible to** Easily affected by; liable to; sensitive to: He was *susceptible to* colds; a child *susceptible to* the least criticism. — **sus·cep′ti·bil′i·ty** *n.*

sus·pect [*v.* sə·spekt′, *n., adj.* sus′pekt] **1** *v.* To believe bad, wrong, guilty, etc., without real proof: to *suspect* a bill to be counterfeit. **2** *n.* A person suspected of a crime or misdeed. **3** *v.* To have doubts about; mistrust: I *suspect* his motives. **4** *v.* To have a suspicion of; think possible: I *suspect* treachery. **5** *adj.* Arousing, open to, or viewed with suspicion: His alibi is *suspect.*

sus·pend [sə·spend′] *v.* **1** To cause to hang down from a support: to *suspend* a bucket. **2** To cause to stop for a time; interrupt: to *suspend* business. **3** To put off for a time; delay action on: to *suspend* sentence on the convicted man. **4** To bar or keep out for a time, as a punishment: He will be *suspended* from the club for a month. **5** To hold in place as though supported: bits of dust *suspended* in the air.

sus·pend·ers [sə·spen′dərz] *n.pl.* A pair of straps worn over the shoulders for holding up the trousers.

sus·pense [sə·spens′] *n.* A condition or situation in which there is a good deal of doubt, worry, fear, uncertainty, etc., about what is going to happen: a mystery play full of *suspense.*

sus·pen·sion [sə·spen′shən] *n.* **1** The act or result of suspending. **2** The condition of being suspended: *Suspension* from school came as a surprise to him. **3** A support from which something is hung. **4** The system of springs, etc., supporting the body of a car on the axles. **5** A mixture in which tiny solid particles stay suspended but not dissolved in a liquid or gas.

suspension bridge A bridge in which the roadway is hung from cables passing over towers and fastened at the ends.

Suspension bridge

sus·pi·cion [sə·spish′ən] *n.* **1** A feeling, thought, or idea, not based on real proof, that something is wrong. **2** The act of suspecting. **3** Consideration as a suspect: to be under *suspicion.* **4** The least bit; hint: a *suspicion* of onion in the soup.

sus·pi·cious [sə·spish′əs] *adj.* **1** Inclined to suspect; distrustful: a *suspicious* person. **2** Apt to arouse suspicion; questionable: a *suspicious* action. **3** Showing suspicion: a *suspicious* glance at the jury. — **sus·pi′cious·ly** *adv.* — **sus·pi′cious·ness** *n.*

Sus·que·han·na [sus′kwə·han′ə] *n.* A river in New York, Pennsylvania, and Maryland, flowing south to Chesapeake Bay.

sus·tain [sə·stān′] *v.* **1** To hold in position; support: Pillars *sustain* the porch roof. **2** To withstand or resist (a force, pressure, effect, etc.). **3** To undergo or suffer: to *sustain* an injury. **4** To keep up the courage or spirits of: His humor *sustained* us all after we lost the game. **5** To keep in effect or in existence: The actor *sustained* the feeling of dread throughout the entire act. **6** To provide nourishment or necessities for: not enough food to *sustain* life. **7** To uphold or establish as correct or fair: The court *sustained* the original verdict of guilty.

sus·te·nance [sus′tə·nəns] *n.* Something that maintains life or strength; nourishment; food.

---

add, **ā**ce, **c**â**r**e, **p**ä**l**m; **e**nd, **ē**qual; **i**t, **ī**ce; **o**dd, **ō**pen, **ô**rder; t**oo**k, p**oo**l; **u**p, b**û**rn; ə = a in *above*, e in *sicken*, i in *possible*, o in *melon*, u in *circus*; **y**oo = u in *fuse*; **oi**l; p**ou**t; **ch**eck; **r**i**ng**; **th**in; **th**is; **zh** in *vision*. For ¶ reference, see page 64 · HOW TO

su·ture [soo′chər] *n., v.* **su·tured, su·tur·ing**
1 *n.* The sewing together of any parts or organs of the body or of the edges of a cut or wound. **2** *v.* To unite or bring together in this way. **3** *n.* The thread, catgut, wire, etc., used in the stitches of this operation. **4** *n.* The line or edge along which two bones join together.

su·ze·rain [soo′zə·rin *or* soo′zə·rān] *n.* **1** Formerly, a feudal lord. **2** A nation that controls the foreign affairs of another nation while giving it full freedom to manage its internal affairs.

SW or **sw, S.W.** or **s.w.** Abbreviation of SOUTHWEST or SOUTHWESTERN.

swab [swob] *n., v.* **swabbed, swab·bing 1** *n.* A wad of absorbent cotton or the like, often wound on the end of a small stick, used for cleaning out wounds, applying medication, etc. **2** *v.* To clean or apply medication to with a swab: to *swab* a wound. **3** *n.* A mop for cleaning decks, floors, etc. **4** *v.* To mop.

swad·dle [swod′(ə)l] *v.* **swad·dled, swad·dling** To wrap (an infant) with a long strip of linen or flannel.

swaddling clothes or **swaddling bands** Strips of cloth wound around an infant.

swag [swag] *n. slang* Property obtained by robbery or theft; plunder.

swag·ger [swag′ər] **1** *v.* To walk with a proud or insolent air; strut. **2** *v.* To boast; bluster. **3** *n.* A swaggering walk or manner.

Swa·hi·li [swä·hē′lē] *n.* A language of East Africa, used widely in African commerce and trade.

swain [swān] *n.* A young country boy, especially one who is courting: seldom used today.

swal·low[1] [swol′ō] *n.* A small bird having a short bill, long pointed wings, and forked tail, noted for its swiftness in flight.

swal·low[2] [swol′ō] **1** *v.* To make the muscular action that causes (food or liquid) to pass from the mouth, through the throat and gullet, and into the stomach. **2** *n.* The act of swallowing. **3** *n.* The amount swallowed at one time. **4** *v.* To take in, as if by swallowing: The night *swallowed* them. **5** *v.* To hold in or conceal: to *swallow* tears; to *swallow* one's pride. **6** *v.* To endure or submit to: to *swallow* insults. **7** *v.* To take back: to *swallow* one's words. **8** *v. informal* To believe without question or criticism: He will *swallow* any old tale.

swal·low·tail [swol′ō·tāl′] *n.* A brightly colored butterfly, having two long tails or points on each hind wing.

swal·low-tailed coat [swol′ō·tāld′] A man's formal dress coat, having two long, tapering tails in the back.

swam [swam] The past tense of SWIM.

swamp [swomp] **1** *n.* An area of low, wet land; bog; marsh. **2** *v.* To drench with water or other liquid. **3** *v.* To overwhelm; flood: *swamped* with invitations. **4** *v.* To fill or be filled with water; sink: The boat *swamped* in the surf. — **swamp′y** *adj.*

swamp·land [swomp′land′] *n.* An area or tract of land covered with swamps.

swan [swon] *n.* A large water bird with a long graceful neck and brilliant white feathers.

swank [swangk] *adj. slang* Fashionable or stylish in a showy way: a *swank* neighborhood.

Mute swan, to 5 ft. long

swan's-down or **swans·down** [swonz′doun′] *n.* **1** The fine, soft feathers of a swan, used to make trimming for dresses, powder puffs, etc. **2** A soft, thick cloth resembling this.

swan song 1 In legend, an exquisite song sung by a swan just before death. **2** The final creative work before death, as of an artist, writer, etc.

swap [swop] *v.* **swapped, swap·ping,** *n. informal* **1** *v.* To exchange (one thing for another); trade. **2** *n.* An exchange or trade; barter.

sward [swôrd] *n.* Land thickly covered with grass.

swarm [swôrm] **1** *n.* A large number of bees, accompanied by a queen, leaving a hive at one time in order to form a new colony. **2** *v.* To leave the hive in a swarm, as bees. **3** *n.* A hive of bees. **4** *n.* A large colony or group of insects or other small creatures: a *swarm* of flies. **5** *n.* A large crowd or throng: a *swarm* of commuters. **6** *v.* To collect, arrive, move, etc., in great numbers: People *swarmed* to the show. **7** *v.* To fill or be filled, as with a large crowd: The platform *swarmed* with arriving passengers.

swarth·y [swôr′thē] *adj.* **swarth·i·er, swarth·i·est** Having a dark complexion.

swash [swosh] **1** *v.* To move, wash, or splash noisily: The wind *swashed* the water against the rocks. **2** *n.* The splash of a liquid.

swash·buck·ler [swosh′buk′lər] *n.* A swaggering, cocky, or boastful soldier or daredevil. — **swash′buck′ling** *adj., n.*

swas·ti·ka [swos′ti·kə] *n.* An ancient symbol, a cross with arms bent at right angles. One form of the swastika was adopted by the Nazis as their emblem.

Swastikas

swat [swot] *v.* **swat·ted, swat·ting,** *n.* **1** *v.* To hit with a sharp blow. **2** *n.* A quick, sharp blow. — **swat′ter** *n.*

swath [swoth] *n.* **1** A row of cut grass, grain, etc. **2** The space or width of one row of grass, grain, etc., cut by any of various mowing devices. **3** Any broad strip: a *swath* of green lawn.

swathe [swäth *or* swāth] *v.* **swathed, swath·ing,** *n.* **1** *v.* To bind or wrap, as in cloth, bandages, etc. **2** *n.* A wrapping or bandage for swathing. **3** *v.* To surround or envelop.

sway [swā] **1** *v.* To move or cause to move from side to side: The wind *swayed* the trees; The street sign *swayed* in the gale. **2** *v.* To lean or bend or cause to lean or bend: The flowers *swayed* to the ground. **3** *v.* To cause (a person, opinion, etc.) to tend in a certain way; influence: What *swayed* him to accept the job? **4** *n.*

Influence, control, or power: Nothing holds any *sway* over his thoughts. **5** *v.* To change from one point of view or opinion to another. **6** *n.* The act of swaying.

sway-backed [swā′bakt′] *adj.* Having an unnatural sagging or curving in the back: a *sway-backed* horse.

swear [swâr] *v.* **swore, sworn, swear·ing** **1** To make a very solemn statement, with an appeal to God or to something held sacred, that something is true. **2** To promise or cause to promise solemnly: He *swore* he would not tell; We *swore* them to secrecy. **3** To use profanity; curse: I hate to hear him *swear.* **— swear by 1** To appeal to (someone or something sacred) in taking an oath: He *swore by* Jupiter that he was innocent. **2** To have complete confidence in: He *swears by* those exercises to keep him fit. **— swear in** To administer a legal oath to: The Chief Justice of the Supreme Court *swears in* the President of the U.S. **— swear off** *informal* To promise to give up: He *swore off* cake.

sweat [swet] *v.* **sweat** or **sweat·ed, sweat·ing,** *n.* **1** *v.* To give off moisture through the pores of the skin; perspire: The team *sweated* during the hot weather. **2** *n.* The salty moisture given off through the pores of the skin. **3** *v.* To gather drops of moisture by condensation: The pitcher of ice water *sweated* in the hot kitchen. **4** *n.* The moisture formed on cold surfaces surrounded by warmer air. **5** *v. informal* To work or cause to work hard: We really *sweated* over that exam; He *sweated* his workers unmercifully. **6** *v.* To get rid of by sweating: to *sweat* away five pounds. **7** *v. informal* To suffer, worry, or be concerned: We *sweated* until we heard she was safe. **8** *n. informal* A condition of worry, hurry, impatience, etc.: Don't get in a *sweat.* **— sweat out** To wait or work through anxiously or tediously.

sweat·er [swet′ər] *n.* A garment for the upper part of the body, made in the form of a pullover or a jacket, with or without sleeves. ◆ *Sweater* comes from the word *sweat. Sweaters* were originally worn by athletes to make themselves sweat.

sweat gland Any of the glands, just below the skin, that secrete sweat.

sweat shirt A heavy cotton pullover, often lined with fleece, worn to soak up sweat.

sweat·shop [swet′shop′] *n.* A place where work is done under poor conditions, for very little pay, and for long hours.

sweat·y [swet′ē] *adj.* **sweat·i·er, sweat·i·est** **1** Covered or wet with sweat. **2** Of or like sweat: a *sweaty* smell. **3** Causing sweat.

Swede [swēd] *n.* A person born in or a citizen of Sweden.

Swe·den [swēd′(ə)n] *n.* A country in NW Europe, east of Norway.

Swed·ish [swē′dish] **1** *adj.* Of or from Sweden. **2** *n.* **(the Swedish)** The people of Sweden. **3** *n.* The language of Sweden.

sweep [swēp] *v.* **swept, sweep·ing,** *n.* **1** *v.* To clean with a broom, brush, etc. **2** *v.* To collect, remove, or clear away with a broom, brush, etc.: Don't *sweep* the dirt under the rug. **3** *n.* The act or an instance of sweeping: He gave the floor a good *sweep.* **4** *n.* A chimney sweep. **5** *v.* To touch or brush: Her dress *swept* the ground. **6** *v.* To walk proudly or swiftly: She *swept* into the room. **7** *v.* To extend with a long line or curve: The road *sweeps* along the shore.

Man sweeping

8 *n.* An open or unbroken area or stretch: a wide *sweep* of beach. **9** *n.* A long, sweeping stroke or movement: a *sweep* of an oar. **10** *v.* To take, remove, or carry along with a long, sweeping movement: The young boy *swept* the pieces of his jigsaw puzzle onto the floor. **11** *v.* To move, put on, etc., with an even, continuous motion: She *swept* the cape over her shoulders. **12** *n.* The range or area covered or reached by something: the great *sweep* of the beacon's light. **13** *n.* A curve or bend: the *sweep* of the scythe blade. **14** *v.* To move, pass, or go swiftly or with force: The train *swept* by; A great wave of joy *swept* through the crowd. **15** *v.* To pass over or through strongly or swiftly: He *swept* the sky with his eyes. **16** *v.* To move, carry, bring, etc., with force or strength: The flood *swept* the bridge away. **17** *n.* A victory or a series of victories. **18** *n.* A long, heavy oar. **19** *n.* A long pole pivoted on a post and having a bucket at one end, used to draw water from a well. **20** *v.* To drag the bottom of (a body of water, etc.). **— sweep′er** *n.* ◆ *Sweep* was originally only a verb. Its use as a noun developed from its verb meanings.

sweep·ing [swē′ping] **1** *adj.* Moving or extending in a long line or curve or over a wide area: a *sweeping* glance. **2** *adj.* Covering or including many things; extensive: He made *sweeping* reforms in the schools. **3** *n.* The act of a person who sweeps. **4** *n.* *(pl.)* Dirt or refuse that has been swept up.

sweep·stakes [swēp′stāks′] *n., pl.* **sweep·stakes** **1** A type of lottery, usually a horse race, in which all the money bet may be won by one or by a few of the betters. **2** Any of various lotteries. **3** Any contest: a political *sweepstakes.*

sweet [swēt] **1** *adj.* Having an agreeable taste, like that of sugar. **2** *adj.* Containing sugar in some form: *sweet* fruit. **3** *n.* Something sweet, as a piece of candy. **4** *adj.* Not salty: *sweet* butter.

---

add, āce, câre, pälm;   end, ēqual;   it, īce;   odd, ōpen, ôrder;   took, pool;   up, bûrn;

ə = a in *above,* e in *sicken,* i in *possible,* o in *melon,* u in *circus;*   yoo = u in *fuse;*   oil;   pout;

check;   ring;   thin;   this;   zh in *vision.*   For ¶ reference, see page 64 · **HOW TO**

5 *adj.* Not spoiled or decaying; fresh: *sweet* cream. **6** *adj.* Agreeable or pleasant to the senses or the mind: *sweet* sounds. **7** *adj.* Having gentle, pleasing qualities: a *sweet* child. **8** *n.* A beloved person; darling. **9** *adv.* In a sweet manner. — **sweet′ly** *adv.* — **sweet′ness** *n.*

sweet·bread [swēt′bred′] *n.* The pancreas or the thymus gland of a calf or other animal, used as food.

sweet·bri·er or **sweet·bri·ar** [swēt′brī′ər] *n.* A rose having very sharp, tough thorns and pink single flowers.

sweet corn A variety of corn having sweet, milky kernels, boiled or roasted as food.

sweet·en [swēt′(ə)n] *v.* To make or become sweet or sweeter. — **sweet′en·er** *n.*

sweet·en·ing [swēt′(ə)n·ing] *n.* **1** The act of making sweet. **2** Something that sweetens.

sweet·heart [swēt′härt′] *n.* A person whom one loves; a lover.

sweet·meat [swēt′mēt′] *n.* (*usually pl.*) Something sweet to eat, as candy, candied fruits, sugar-coated nuts, etc.

sweet pea A climbing plant that has fragrant flowers of many colors.

sweet potato **1** A tropical vine having large, yellowish, sweet roots that are eaten as a vegetable. **2** The edible roots of this plant.

sweet tooth *informal* A fondness for sweets.

sweet william or **sweet William** A garden plant having clusters of showy, many-colored flowers.

swell [swel] *v.* **swelled, swelled** or **swol·len, swell·ing,** *n., adj.* **1** *v.* To increase or cause to increase in size, amount, degree, etc.: A sprain made his wrist *swell* badly. **2** *v.* To increase or cause to increase in loudness: The music *swelled* to a climax. **3** *n.* A gradual increase and then a decrease in the loudness of a sound. **4** *v.* To bulge or cause to bulge: Wind *swelled* the sails. **5** *v.* To rise or cause to rise, as land or water: The streams were *swollen* by rain. **6** *n.* The long, continuous body of a rolling wave. **7** *n.* A rise in the land. **8** *v.* To fill or become filled with some emotion: Her heart *swelled* with sorrow at the sight. **9** *n.* The act of swelling. **10** *n.* A swollen condition. **11** *n. informal* A very fashionably dressed person. **12** *adj. slang* Very fine; excellent: It was a *swell* party.

swell·ing [swel′ing] *n.* **1** An increase in size, amount, etc. **2** An enlargement or swollen part on the body, often due to an injury, etc.

swel·ter [swel′tər] **1** *v.* To become weak, soaked with perspiration, etc., from great heat. **2** *n.* A sweltering condition.

swel·ter·ing [swel′tər·ing] *adj.* **1** Extremely hot: *sweltering* weather. **2** Overcome by or suffering from heat: the *sweltering* crowds.

swept [swept] Past tense and past participle of SWEEP.

swerve [swûrv] *v.* **swerved, swerv·ing,** *n.* **1** *v.* To turn or cause to turn aside from a course: We *swerved* our bicycles out of the car's way. **2** *n.* The act of swerving.

swift [swift] **1** *adj.* Moving or covering space very fast; rapid; quick: a *swift* train. **2** *adj.* Done, happening, acting, etc., quickly: a *swift* change; a *swift* answer; a *swift* worker. **3** *n.* A bird that looks like a swallow and flies extremely fast. — **swift′ly** *adv.* — **swift′ness** *n.*

Swift [swift], **Jonathan,** 1667–1745, English writer and clergyman born in Ireland.

swig [swig] *n., v.* **swigged, swig·ging** *informal* **1** *n.* A big drink or swallow of something. **2** *v.* To drink greedily with big swallows.

swill [swil] **1** *v.* To drink greedily or too much: He *swilled* soda. **2** *n.* Liquid food for animals, especially a mixture of liquid and solid food that is fed to pigs. **3** *n.* Partly liquid garbage.

Chimney swift,
5–6 in. long

swim¹ [swim] *v.* **swam, swum, swim·ming, *n.*** **1** *v.* To move through the water by using the arms, legs, fins, etc. **2** *v.* To cause to swim. **3** *v.* To cross by swimming: to *swim* the English Channel. **4** *v.* To take part in by swimming: to *swim* a race. **5** *n.* The act or distance of swimming: a refreshing *swim*; a long *swim*. **6** *v.* To move with a smooth, flowing motion: The clouds *swam* by. **7** *v.* To be in, covered with, or filled with a liquid: The peas *swam* in butter; Her eyes *swam* with tears. — **in the swim** In the place or places where the important or popular things are happening. — **swim′mer** *n.*

swim² [swim] *v.* **swam, swum, swim·ming, *n.*** **1** *v.* To be dizzy: The lights made her head *swim*. **2** *v.* To seem to whirl or spin: The entire house *swam* before her eyes. **3** *adj. use:* a *swimming* sensation. **4** *n.* A sudden feeling of dizziness.

swim·ming [swim′ing] **1** *n.* The act of a person or thing that swims. **2** *adj.* Of or used for swimming: a *swimming* stroke; a *swimming* pool. **3** *adj.* Able to swim: a *swimming* bird.

swim·ming·ly [swim′ing·lē] *adv.* Easily, rapidly, and successfully: The work went *swimmingly*.

swimming pool An indoor or outdoor tank of water for swimming.

swin·dle [swin′dəl] *v.* **swin·dled, swin·dling,** *n.* **1** *v.* To cheat of money or property: The shopkeeper *swindled* us. **2** *v.* To get by cheating: to *swindle* money out of someone. **3** *n.* An act or instance of swindling. — **swin′dler** *n.*

swine [swin] *n., pl.* **swine 1** A pig, hog, or boar. **2** A mean, greedy, or vicious person.

swine·herd [swin′hûrd′] *n.* A person who takes care of pigs.

swing [swing] *v.* **swung, swung, swing·ing,** *n.* **1** *v.* To move or cause to move backward and forward, as something suspended. **2** *n.* A seat that hangs from ropes or chains and on which a person may move to and fro for recreation. **3** *v.* To move or cause to move in or with a sweeping motion: He *swung* the ax over his head. **4** *n.* The curved or sweeping path of something that swings: the *swing* of an ax. **5** *n.* A sweeping blow or stroke: He took a *swing* at the tree. **6** *v.* To walk with an even, swaying motion: The men *swung* off through the woods. **7** *v.* To move or hoist: They *swung* the mast into place. **8** *v.* To turn or cause to turn or pivot: We *swung* the gate shut. **9** *v.* To hang: *Swing* the lights from the ceiling. **10** *v. informal* To execute or be executed by hanging: He will *swing* for that. **11** *n.* The act, process, or manner of swinging. **12** *n.* Rhythmical movement or quality: Notice the *swing* of his shoulders; Her poems have a great *swing* to them. **13** *n.* A type of jazz music having much improvisation and a strong, lively rhythm. **14** *v. informal* To play or sing (jazz music) in a lively, rhythmical style. **15** *v. informal* To bring to a successful conclusion; manage successfully: to *swing* a business deal. **— in full swing** At the height of activity or movement. ◆ *Swing* was originally a noun. Its use as a verb developed from its noun meanings.

swin·ish [swī'nish] *adj.* Of, like, or fit for swine; beastly; degraded.

swipe [swīp] *v.* **swiped, swip·ing,** *n. informal* **1** *v.* To hit hard with a sweeping or swinging motion. **2** *n.* A hard, sweeping blow. **3** *v.* To steal.

swirl [swûrl] **1** *v.* To move or cause to move with a whirling or twisting motion: The water *swirled* down the drain. **2** *n.* A whirling motion. **3** *v.* To feel dizzy: My head *swirls* in this heat. **4** *n.* A curl or twist; spiral.

swish [swish] **1** *v.* To move or cause to move with a hissing or whistling sound: The arrow *swished* past his ear; to *swish* a stick through the air. **2** *v.* To rustle: Her dress *swished* when she moved. **3** *n.* A hissing or rustling sound. **4** *n.* A movement that produces such a sound. ◆ *Swish* was formed in imitation of the sound [swish] that it describes.

Swiss [swis] **1** *adj.* Of or from Switzerland. **2** *n.* **(the Swiss)** The people of Switzerland. **3** *n.* A person born in or a citizen of Switzerland.

Swiss cheese A pale yellow cheese with many large holes, made in or like that made in Switzerland.

switch [swich] **1** *n.* A small, flexible stick or rod, used for whipping. **2** *v.* To whip or lash with or as if with a switch. **3** *n.* A blow or stroke given with or as if with a switch. **4** *v.* To move or whisk suddenly and sharply: The dog *switched* its tail against my legs. **5** *v.* To change: to *switch* plans. **6** *v.* To exchange: to *switch* hats. **7** *n.* A change or exchange. **8** *n.* A mechanism, usually consisting of a pair of movable rails, for shifting railroad cars, etc., from one track to another. **9** *v.* To shift to another track by means of a switch. **10** *n.* A device for making or breaking a connection in an electrical circuit. **11** *v.* To turn on or off with an electrical switch.

switch·board [swich'bôrd'] *n.* A panel having plugs and switches for connecting or disconnecting electrical circuits: a telephone *switchboard*.

switch·man [swich'mən] *n., pl.* **switch·men** [swich'mən] A person whose job is to switch railroad cars.

Swit·zer·land [swit'sər·lənd] *n.* A country in central Europe.

swiv·el [swiv'əl] *n., v.* **swiv·eled** or **swiv·elled, swiv·el·ing** or **swiv·el·ling 1** *n.* A fastening device that permits anything attached to it, as a chain, to rotate or turn independently. **2** *n.* A support on which a gun may be rested and turned in any direction. **3** *v.* To turn on or as if on a swivel.

swivel chair A chair having a seat that turns on a swivel.

swol·len [swō'lən] Alternative past participle of SWELL.

swoon [swoon] **1** *v.* To faint. **2** *n.* A faint.

swoop [swoop] **1** *v.* To drop or descend suddenly: The bird *swooped* down on its prey. **2** *v.* To take or seize suddenly: Johnny *swooped* up the cake. **3** *n.* A sudden, swift, diving rush or attack, as of a hawk.

Swivel chair

sword [sôrd] *n.* **1** A weapon consisting of a long blade fixed in a handle or hilt. **2** This weapon as the symbol of military force or of war: "The pen is mightier than the *sword*."

sword·fish [sôrd'fish'] *n., pl.* **sword·fish** or **sword·fish·es** A large fish of the open sea, having a very long, pointed upper jawbone.

sword·play [sôrd'plā'] *n.* The act, art, or skill of using the sword, especially in fencing.

Swordfish, to 15 ft. long

swords·man [sôrdz'mən] *n., pl.* **swords·men** [sôrdz'mən] A person skilled in the use of, or armed with a sword.

swore [swôr] Past tense of SWEAR.

sworn [swôrn] Past participle of SWEAR.

swum [swum] Past participle of SWIM.

swung [swung] Past tense and past participle of SWING.

syc·a·more [sik'ə·môr] *n.* **1** A tree of North America having broad leaves and a bark that peels or flakes off easily. **2** A kind of maple tree of Europe and Asia. **3** A variety of fig tree of Egypt and Syria.

syc·o·phant [sik'ə·fənt] *n.* A person who uses flattery in order to gain what he wants.

Syd·ney [sid'nē] *n.* A seaport in SE Australia, the largest city on the continent.

add, āce, câre, pälm; end, ēqual; it, īce; odd, ōpen, ôrder; took, pool; up, bûrn; ə = a in *above*, e in *sicken*, i in *possible*, o in *melon*, u in *circus*; yoo = u in *fuse*; oil; pout; check; ring; thin; this; zh in *vision*. For ¶ reference, see page 64 · HOW TO

syl·lab·ic [si·lab′ik] *adj.* **1** Of, having to do with, or containing a syllable or syllables. **2** Forming a separate syllable.

syl·lab·i·cate [si·lab′ə·kāt] *v.* **syl·lab·i·cat·ed, syl·lab·i·cat·ing** Another word for SYLLABIFY. — **syl·lab′i·ca′tion** *n.*

syl·lab·i·fy [si·lab′ə·fī] *v.* **syl·lab·i·fied, syl·lab·i·fy·ing** To divide into syllables. — **syl·lab·i·fi·ca·tion** [si·lab′ə·fə·kā′shən] *n.*

syl·la·ble [sil′ə·bəl] *n.* **1** A word or part of a word uttered in one single vocal impulse. "Spider" has two syllables; "run" has one syllable. **2** A part of a written word corresponding more or less to the spoken division, used to show how the word is pronounced or how it can best be hyphenated at the end of a line.

syl·la·bus [sil′ə·bəs] *n., pl.* **syl·la·bus·es** or **syl·la·bi** [sil′ə·bī] A brief outline, as that explaining the main points of a course of study.

syl·lo·gism [sil′ə·jiz′əm] *n.* A method of argument or reasoning in which two statements are made, from which a conclusion is drawn in a third statement. Example: All water is wet. Rain is water. Therefore rain is wet.

sylph [silf] *n.* **1** An imaginary being supposed to live in the air. **2** Any slender, graceful young woman or girl.

syl·van [sil′vən] *adj.* **1** Of, having to do with, or living in a forest or wood. **2** Full of trees or forests: a *sylvan* countryside.

sym·bol [sim′bəl] *n.* **1** Something chosen to stand for or represent something else. **2** A mark or sign used to indicate something, as a plus sign, a numeral, a dollar sign, etc.

sym·bol·ic [sim·bol′ik] *adj.* **1** Of, related to, or expressed by a symbol or symbols. **2** Serving as a symbol. — **sym·bol′i·cal·ly** *adv.*

sym·bol·i·cal [sim·bol′ə·kəl] *adj.* Symbolic.

sym·bol·ism [sim′bəl·iz′əm] *n.* **1** The use of symbols to indicate or represent things, as in literature or art. **2** Any group or system of symbols: the *symbolism* of a religion.

sym·bol·ize [sim′bəl·īz] *v.* **sym·bol·ized, sym·bol·iz·ing 1** To be a symbol of; represent; typify. **2** To represent by a symbol or symbols. **3** To use symbols. ¶3

sym·met·ric [si·met′rik] *adj.* Symmetrical.

sym·met·ri·cal [si·met′ri·kəl] *adj.* Having symmetry; well-balanced; regular: a *symmetrical* pattern. — **sym·met′ri·cal·ly** *adv.*

sym·me·try [sim′ə·trē] *n., pl.* **sym·me·tries 1** A condition or arrangement in which each feature on one half of a figure, object, arrangement, etc., has a matching feature in the other half. **2** Beauty or harmony resulting from a symmetrical or nearly symmetrical arrangement of parts. **3** The property that a geometric figure has if each of its

Two examples of symmetry

points has a matching point on the opposite side of and equally distant from a point, line, or plane.

sym·pa·thet·ic [sim′pə·thet′ik] *adj.* **1** Feeling, expressing, or coming from sympathy: a *sympathetic* look. **2** Agreeable to one's tastes, opinions, feelings, etc.; congenial: a *sympathetic* companion. **3** Showing approval; agreeable. — **sym′·pa·thet′i·cal·ly** *adv.*

sym·pa·thize [sim′pə·thīz] *v.* **sym·pa·thized, sym·pa·thiz·ing 1** To share the feelings or ideas of another. **2** To feel or express sympathy or compassion: to *sympathize* with someone's sorrow. — **sym′pa·thiz′er** *n.* ¶3

sym·pa·thy [sim′pə·thē] *n., pl.* **sym·pa·thies 1** The condition of being affected by another's state: to feel *sympathy* for a friend's pain. **2** A condition in which the thoughts, ideas, or feelings of one person are very much the same as those of another. **3** Loyalty, support, or agreement: Our *sympathies* were with the first plan.

sym·phon·ic [sim·fon′ik] *adj.* Having to do with or like a symphony or symphony orchestra.

sym·pho·ny [sim′fə·nē] *n., pl.* **sym·pho·nies 1** A piece of music written to be played by a symphony orchestra and usually consisting of four movements. **2** A symphony orchestra. **3** Harmony or an agreeable blending, as of sounds, color, etc.

symphony orchestra A large orchestra composed usually of strings, brasses, woodwinds, and percussion instruments.

sym·po·si·um [sim·pō′zē·əm] *n., pl.* **sym·po·si·ums** or **sym·po·si·a** [sim·pō′zē·ə] **1** A meeting for the discussion of a particular subject. **2** A collection of comments or opinions by several people on the same subject: A *symposium* on art was published in the magazine.

symp·tom [sim′təm] *n.* A sign or indication of the existence of something, especially an indication of some bodily disease or disorder.

symp·to·mat·ic [simp′tə·mat′ik] *adj.* Being, having to do with, or like a symptom: Fever and vomiting are *symptomatic* of his illness.

syn·a·gogue [sin′ə·gôg] *n.* **1** A place of meeting for Jewish worship and religious instruction. **2** A Jewish congregation.

syn·chro·nize [sing′krə·nīz] *v.* **syn·chro·nized, syn·chro·niz·ing 1** To adjust so as to move together or occur at the same time or speed. In films one must *synchronize* the action with the sound. **2** To cause (timepieces) to agree in keeping time. ¶3

syn·chro·nous [sing′krə·nəs] *adj.* Happening or moving at the same time or speed.

syn·co·pate [sing′kə·pāt] *v.* **syn·co·pat·ed, syn·co·pat·ing 1** To apply syncopation to: to *syncopate* a musical phrase. **2** *adj. use:* synco-*pated* music; a *syncopated* measure.

syn·co·pa·tion [sing′kə·pā′shən] *n.* A condition in which the accented parts of a musical rhythm do not coincide with the normally strong beats.

syn·di·cate [*n.* sin′də·kit, *v.* sin′də·kāt] *n., v.* **syn·di·cat·ed, syn·di·cat·ing 1** *n.* A group of people who have united in order to pursue business or another enterprise requiring a large sum of money. **2** *v.* To combine into or form a syndicate. **3** *n.* An agency that sells articles, stories, etc., to a number of newspapers or magazines. **4** *v.* To sell (an article, story, etc.) for publication in many newspapers or magazines.

syn·drome [sin′drōm] *n.* A group of symptoms that, taken together, indicate the presence and the nature of a disease or disorder.

syn·od [sin′əd] *n.* A regional council of a church, called together to discuss and act on church matters.

syn·o·nym [sin′ə·nim] *n.* A word having the same or almost the same meaning as another word: "Sure" and "certain" are *synonyms.*

syn·on·y·mous [si·non′ə·məs] *adj.* Alike or similar in meaning: "Sad" is *synonymous* with "unhappy."

syn·op·sis [si·nop′sis] *n., pl.* **syn·op·ses** [si·nop′sēz] A brief summary or outline, giving the main points of a story, book, play, etc.

syn·tax [sin′taks] *n.* The arrangement and relationship of words in phrases and sentences.

syn·the·sis [sin′thə·sis] *n., pl.* **syn·the·ses** [sin′thə·sēz] The assembling or combining of separate parts into a whole: The *synthesis* of water is accomplished by chemically combining oxygen and hydrogen.

syn·thet·ic [sin·thet′ik] **1** *adj.* Of, having to do with, or using synthesis. **2** *adj.* In chemistry, produced artificially by synthesis rather than occurring naturally: *synthetic* gems. **3** *adj.* Not true or real: His reasons for not going were *synthetic.* **4** *n.* Something synthetic: Many new fabrics, such as rayon, are *synthetics.* **— syn·thet′i·cal·ly** *adv.*

syph·i·lis [sif′ə·lis] *n.* A contagious venereal disease, which can be long-continued and serious.

sy·phon [sī′fən] *n., v.* Another spelling of SIPHON.

Syr·i·a [sir′ē·ə] *n.* A country in SW Asia. — **Syr′i·an** *n., adj.*

sy·rin·ga [si·ring′gə] *n.* An ornamental shrub having fragrant, cream-colored flowers.

syr·inge [sə·rinj′ *or* sir′inj] *n., v.* **syr·inged, syr·ing·ing 1** *n.* A device consisting of a tube with a rubber bulb or piston at one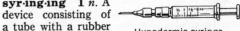

Hypodermic syringe

end for drawing in a liquid and then forcing it out in a fine stream. Syringes are used for injecting fluids into the body, cleaning wounds, etc. **2** *v.* To cleanse or treat with a syringe. **3** *n.* A hypodermic syringe.

syr·up [sir′əp] *n.* A thick, sweet liquid, as that made by boiling sugar with fruit juice or with water. **— syr′up·y** *adj.*

sys·tem [sis′təm] *n.* **1** A group of parts or things that are so related or that act together in such a way that they are considered as a whole: the solar *system;* a railroad *system;* the nervous *system.* **2** Any group of facts, concepts, or beliefs that are organized into an orderly plan: a *system* of teaching languages. **3** An orderly or organized method. **4** The entire body as a whole.

sys·tem·at·ic [sis′tə·mat′ik] *adj.* **1** Done according to, or having, a plan or system: a *systematic* course of study. **2** Orderly, methodical, and thorough: a *systematic* person; a *systematic* investigation. **— sys′tem·at′i·cal·ly** *adv.*

sys·tem·a·tize [sis′tə·mə·tīz′] *v.* **sys·tem·a·tized, sys·tem·a·tiz·ing** To make into a system; arrange in an orderly way. ¶3

sys·to·le [sis′tə·lē] *n.* The regular, periodic contraction of the heart, during which blood is pumped into the arteries. ◆ See DIASTOLE.

T

t or **T** [tē] *n., pl.* **t's** or **T's 1** The 20th letter of the English alphabet. **2** Anything shaped like the letter T: The two pencils formed a *T.* **— to a T** Exactly; precisely: to fit *to a T.*

t. Abbreviation of TEASPOON(S).

T. or **t.** Abbreviation of **1** TON. **2** Tons.

tab [tab] *n.* **1** A small tag, flap, or loop on something, as on a garment or filing card. **2** *informal* A bill or check, as for a meal in a restaurant. — **keep tab on** or **keep tabs on** To pay close attention to; watch carefully: The counselor *kept tabs on* the campers.

tab·ard [tab′ərd] *n.* **1** A knight's cloak with short sleeves worn over his armor and bearing his coat of arms. **2** A herald's short coat which is adorned with his lord's coat of arms.

tab·by [tab′ē] *n., pl.* **tab·bies 1** A brown or gray cat with darker stripes. **2** Any cat which is kept as a pet, especially a female.

tab·er·nac·le [tab′ər·nak′əl] *n.* **1** A large temple or place of worship. **2** A small ornamental receptacle, usually resting on the altar and used to hold the Host or other holy objects. **3** (*written* **Tabernacle**) A curtained wooden

---

add, āce, câre, pälm; end, ēqual; it, īce; odd, ōpen, ôrder; tŏŏk, pōōl; up, bûrn; ə = a in *above*, e in *sicken*, i in *possible*, o in *melon*, u in *circus*; yōō = u in *fuse*; oil; pout; check; ring; thin; **th**is; zh in *vision*. For ¶ reference, see page 64 · HOW TO

table · 756 tactile

framework used by the Jews as a portable place of worship while in the wilderness with Moses. **4** A tent or temporary shelter. **5** The human body as the temporary dwelling place of the soul.

ta·ble [tā′bəl] *n., v.* **ta·bled, ta·bling 1** *n.* A piece of furniture with a flat top that is held up by legs. **2** *v.* To put on a table: She *tabled* the king of spades. **3** *n.* A table prepared for a meal: The *table* was set for six. **4** *n.* The food served on a table. **5** *n.* The people seated at a table: Our *table* finished lunch first. **6** *v.* To put off, usually indefinitely, a discussion of: The committee *tabled* the bill. **7** *n.* A list of related numbers, facts, or items, arranged in some orderly way for reference: a *table* of contents; multiplication *table.* **8** *n.* A tableland; plateau. **9** *n.* A slab of stone, metal, or wood on which writing is carved; tablet: Roman laws were written on *tables.* **— turn the tables** To reverse conditions or relations: The champion had always beaten him, but today Tom *turned the tables.*

tab·leau [tab′lō] *n., pl.* **tab·leaux** [tab′lōz *or* tab′lō] *or* **tab·leaus** [tab′lōz] **1** A picture or scene. **2** A grouping of people dressed in costumes and posed to represent a scene: a *tableau* of Washington crossing the Delaware.

ta·ble·cloth [tā′bəl·klôth′] *n.* A cloth which covers a table, especially at meals.

ta·ble·land [tā′bəl·land′] *n.* A broad, flat, high region; plateau.

ta·ble·spoon [tā′bəl·spoon′] *n.* **1** A fairly large spoon for serving and measuring. **2** As much as a tablespoon will hold, equal to three teaspoons.

ta·ble·spoon·ful [tā′bəl·spoon·fool′] *n., pl.* **ta·ble·spoon·fuls** As much as a tablespoon will hold: Add two *tablespoonfuls* of sugar.

Tableland

tab·let [tab′lit] *n.* **1** A pad of paper made by gluing many sheets together at one edge. **2** A thin sheet of metal, wood, or stone, with words or designs inscribed on it: They put up a *tablet* on the wall listing the names of the soldiers who died in the war. **3** A small, flat disk or square, as of medicine or candy: a sleeping *tablet.*

table tennis A game resembling tennis, played on a table with small paddles and a small hollow ball.

ta·ble·ware [tā′bəl·wâr′] *n.* All the dishes, knives, forks, spoons, etc., used to eat a meal.

Table tennis

tab·loid [tab′loid] *n.* A small-sized newspaper with short articles and many pictures. ◆ *Tabloid* was originally a trademark for a brand of tablets consisting of a number of drugs in condensed form.

ta·boo [tə·boo′ *or* ta′boo] *n., pl.* **ta·boos,** *adj., v.* **ta·booed, ta·boo·ing 1** *n.* A social or religious rule setting certain people or things apart as sacred or untouchable. **2** *n.* A ban or

prohibition. **3** *v.* To forbid by taboo: Some religions *taboo* eating certain kinds of meat. **4** *adj.* Forbidden or protected by taboo.

ta·bor *or* **ta·bour** [tā′bər] *n.* A small drum once used with a pipe or fife.

ta·bu [tə·boo′ *or* ta′boo] *n., pl.* **ta·bus,** *adj., v.* **ta·bued, ta·bu·ing** Another spelling of TABOO.

tab·u·lar [tab′yə·lər] *adj.* **1** Arranged in or having to do with tables or lists: a *tabular* account. **2** Having a flat surface.

tab·u·late [tab′yə·lāt] *v.* **tab·u·lat·ed, tab·u·lat·ing** To arrange in a table or list: to *tabulate* the results. **— tab′u·la′tion** *n.* **— tab′u·la′tor** *n.*

tac·it [tas′it] *adj.* **1** Understood or meant without being said or spoken: a *tacit* agreement. **2** Silent; unspoken. **— tac′it·ly** *adv.*

tac·i·turn [tas′ə·tûrn] *adj.* Not fond of speaking; usually silent or reserved. **— tac′i·tur′ni·ty** *n.*

tack [tak] **1** *n.* A short nail having a sharp point and usually a flat head. **2** *v.* To attach with tacks. **3** *n.* A loose, temporary stitch used in sewing. **4** *v.* To sew with a tack: to *tack* on a sleeve; to *tack* a hem. **5** *v.* To add as something extra: He *tacked* the sales tax onto the bill. **6** *v.* To sail into the wind by means of a zigzag course. **7** *n.* One straight reach of such a course, slanting into the wind. **8** *n.* The direction in which a boat sails in relation to the wind: A boat is on the starboard *tack* when the wind strikes it from the right. **9** *v.* To turn from one tack to the opposite: The sloop *tacked* to round the buoy. **10** *n.* A course of action or behavior: on the wrong *tack.*

tack·le [tak′əl] *n., v.* **tack·led, tack·ling 1** *n.* The equipment used in work or sports; gear: fishing *tackle.* **2** *n.* A set of ropes and pulleys used to hoist or move objects: Men were hoisting a piano to a second-story window by means of a *tackle.* **3** *v.* To grab, grapple with, or attack. **4** *v.* To try to solve or master; deal with: to *tackle* a problem. **5** *v.* To seize and stop, especially by forcing to the ground: In football, the defensive team tries to *tackle* the player with the ball. **6** *n.* The act of tackling. **7** *n.* In football, a player usually stationed between a guard and end. **— tack′ler** *n.*

tact [takt] *n.* The ability to speak and behave so as not to hurt or offend others.

tact·ful [takt′fəl] *adj.* Showing or having tact: a *tactful* remark. **— tact′ful·ly** *adv.*

tac·ti·cal [tak′ti·kəl] *adj.* **1** Of or concerning tactics: a *tactical* error. **2** Showing skill in handling a situation. **— tac′ti·cal·ly** *adv.*

tac·ti·cian [tak·tish′ən] *n.* An expert in tactics.

tac·tics [tak′tiks] *n.* **1** The science or art of moving and handling military, air, or naval forces against an enemy. ◆ See -ICS. **2** The actual operations used. **3** Any means to win an advantage; methods: He changed his *tactics* and stopped shouting.

tac·tile [tak′til] *adj.* **1** Having to do with the sense of touch. **2** Capable of being felt by touch; tangible.

tact·less [takt′lis] *adj.* Having or showing no tact: a *tactless* remark. **— tact′less·ly** *adv.* **— tact′less·ness** *n.*

tad [tad] *n. U.S. informal* A little child, especially a boy.

tad·pole [tad′pōl′] *n.* A young frog or toad when it has a tail and gills and lives in water.

taf·fe·ta [taf′ə·tə] *n.* A fine, stiff, glossy fabric woven from silk, rayon, etc.

taff·rail [taf′rāl′ *or* taf′rəl] *n.* The rail around a ship's stern.

taf·fy [taf′ē] *n.* A candy made from sugar or molasses which is boiled and pulled into strands.

Taft [taft], **William Howard,** 1857–1930, 27th president of the U.S., 1909–1913; also chief justice of the Supreme Court, 1921–1930.

tag¹ [tag] *n., v.* **tagged, tag·ging 1** *n.* A piece of cardboard, paper, leather, etc., tied or fastened to something as a label. **2** *v.* To fasten a tag or tags on: Please *tag* my suitcase. **3** *n.* A small loop or flap, as on a boot or zipper. **4** *n.* A hard tip at the end of a string, as on a shoelace. **5** *n.* The last line or two of a song, poem, or speech. **6** *v.* To follow closely: The boy's sister *tagged* after them.

tag² [tag] *n., v.* **tagged, tag·ging 1** *n.* A children's game in which one who is "it" chases the others trying to touch one, who then becomes "it," and so on. **2** *v.* To touch (someone) with the hand as in tag or baseball.

Ta·hi·ti [tä·hē′tē] *n.* The principal island of a French territory in the South Pacific.

tail [tāl] **1** *n.* The rear part of an animal, especially when it sticks out beyond the body. **2** *n.* Any extension that looks like an animal's tail: the *tail* of a comet. **3** *v.* To provide with a tail. **4** *n.* The rear or end part of something: the *tail* of a rocket. **5** *adj.* At the rear; last: the *tail* end of the year. **6** *n.* (*pl.*) The reverse side of a coin: heads or *tails*. **7** *v. informal* To follow in secret: The police *tailed* him. **8** *adj.* Coming from behind: a *tail* wind. **9** *n.* (*pl.*) The most formal evening dress for men, including a swallow-tailed coat. **— tail off** To diminish or become less: The wind *tailed off.* **— tail′less** *adj.*

tail·gate [tāl′gāt′] *n., v.* **tail·gat·ed, tail·gat·ing 1** *n.* A hinged board or gate at the rear of a truck, wagon, etc. **2** *v. informal* To drive too closely behind for safety: He *tailgated* the truck.

Tailgate

tail·light [tāl′līt′] *n.* A light, usually red, attached to the rear of a car, bicycle, etc.

tai·lor [tā′lər] **1** *n.* A man who makes or repairs outer clothing. **2** *v.* To work as a tailor: Mr. Smith *tailors* for us all. **3** *v.* To make by tailor-ing: He *tailors* only suits and vests. **4** *v.* To make or adjust for a certain purpose: The budget was *tailored* to fit our income.

tail·spin [tāl′spin′] *n.* An uncontrolled plunge of an airplane with its nose pointing down and its tail spinning.

tail wind A wind which blows in the same direction as the course of an airplane, ship, etc.

taint [tānt] **1** *v.* To make or become spoiled, decayed, or infected: Germs *tainted* the food. **2** *v.* To spoil by contact with bad ideas, practices, etc.: The traitor's former patriotism was *tainted* by the persuasions and bribes of enemy agents. **3** *n.* A spot or mark caused by tainting.

Tai·wan [tī′wän′] *n.* An island off the SE coast of China; Formosa.

take [tāk] *v.* **took, tak·en, tak·ing,** *n.* **1** *v.* To grasp: *Take* my hand. **2** *v.* To capture by force, charm, or skill; win: The army *took* the village; She *took* him with her beauty. **3** *v.* To buy or subscribe to: We *take* a daily newspaper. **4** *v.* To steal or remove: A thief *took* Bob's bike. **5** *v. slang* To cheat: He got *taken* at the fair. **6** *v.* To subtract or deduct: Five *taken* from ten is five. **7** *v.* To get from a source: lines *taken* from the Bible. **8** *v.* To occupy or rent: to *take* a seat; to *take* a room. **9** *v.* To hold or let in: The tank *takes* ten gallons. **10** *v.* To learn or find out by study or observation: He *took* French; He *took* my temperature. **11** *v.* To accept or receive: to *take* a bribe; to *take* an offer. **12** *v.* To get for oneself; receive ownership of; assume: to *take* a wife; to *take* office. **13** *v.* To undergo or submit to: to *take* a beating. **14** *v.* To become affected with or by: John *took* cold. **15** *v.* To become: They all *took* ill. **16** *v.* To begin to grow: The seeds *took* in the soil. **17** *v.* To catch hold: The fire *took* at last. **18** *v.* To receive and respond to: He *took* the bad news well. **19** *v.* To feel: She *takes* pride in her son. **20** *v.* To understand: She *took* him to mean that he would not go. **21** *v.* To think of; consider: *Take* an example; He *takes* life so seriously. **22** *v.* To use: *Take* two eggs for this recipe; Please *take* care. **23** *v.* To require or need: It *takes* money to go to college. **24** *v.* To eat, consume, etc.: Can he *take* solid food now? **25** *v.* To perform or make: to *take* a step. **26** *v.* To record, as by photographing or writing down: to *take* a picture; to *take* notes. **27** *v.* To be used with: This verb *takes* an object. **28** *v.* To aim or direct: to *take* a shot; to *take* a look. **29** *v.* To carry: *Take* your book with you. **30** *v.* To lead or escort: The road *takes* you to town; *Take* her to the dance! **31** *v.* To travel by: to *take* a taxi; to *take* the longer route. **32** *n.* The act of taking. **33** *n.* The amount or quantity taken at one time, as of money: The store's daily *take* was small. **— take after** To look or be like; resemble. **— take back** To withdraw (something said). **— take down 1** To write down: *Take down* this address. **2** To reduce the pride of; humble: We *took* him *down* a bit. **— take for** To mistake or think to be: Don't *take* me *for* a fool. **— take in 1** To admit or receive: to *take in* roomers. **2** To include: The homework assignment *takes in* five pages. **3** *informal* To visit: to *take in* a show. **4** To make (clothing) smaller. **5** To notice or understand: to *take in* the situation. **6** *informal* To cheat **— take off 1** To remove: *Take off* your hat. **2** *informal* To imitate or mimic. **3** To leave the ground, as an airplane; depart. **— take on 1** To accept, as a task, duty, or challenge. **2** To hire or employ. **3** *informal* To show violent emotion: Don't *take on* so! **— take over** To take the leadership or control of. **— take place** To happen. **— take to 1** To grow fond of. **2** To go to: They *took to* the ship. **— take up 1** To raise or lift. **2** To absorb (moisture, gas, etc.). **3** To shorten or tighten. **4** To occupy or use, as space or time. **5** To begin to do, use, study, etc.: to *take up* ballet. **— tak'er** *n.*

take-off [tāk'ôf'] *n.* **1** The rising from the ground of an aircraft, a high jumper, etc. **2** *informal* An imitation of someone or something, usually meant to be funny.

Take-off

tak·ing [tā'king] **1** *n.* The act of a person who takes: It's yours for the *taking*. **2** *n.* (*pl.*) Money collected or earned: His *takings* were large. **3** *adj.* Attractive; pleasing: *taking* ways.

talc [talk] *n.* A soft mineral used in powdered form in making talcum powder, soap, paper, etc.

tal·cum powder [tal'kəm] A powder made from talc for the face or body.

tale [tāl] *n.* **1** A story which is either made up or true. **2** A lie or fib. **3** A piece of gossip, usually harmful.

tale·bear·er [tāl'bâr'ər] *n.* A person who tells on another or gives away secrets. **— tale'bear'· ing** *n.*

tal·ent [tal'ənt] *n.* **1** A natural ability to do something well; gift: The lessons developed her *talent* as a singer. **2** People with talent: We must encourage the local *talent*. **3** An ancient unit of weight or money.

tal·ent·ed [tal'ən·tid] *adj.* Having natural aptitude or skill; gifted: a *talented* artist.

tal·is·man [tal'is·mən] *n.*, *pl.* **tal·is·mans 1** A ring, stone, etc., bearing symbols believed to bring good luck. **2** Any magic charm.

talk [tôk] **1** *v.* To use spoken words; speak. **2** *n.* Speech; conversation: Can you hear the *talk* in the hall? **3** *v.* To communicate without spoken words: to *talk* by signs. **4** *v.* To use in speaking: Many Indians *talk* English. **5** *n.* A special set of words or way of talking: baby *talk*; baseball *talk*. **6** *v.* To speak about; discuss: to *talk* politics. **7** *v.* To consult or confer: The teacher *talked* with

the parents. **8** *n.* A conference: The world leaders held peace *talks*. **9** *v.* To make a speech; lecture. **10** *n.* A speech; lecture. **11** *n.* The person or thing spoken about: Her dress was the *talk* of the party. **12** *v.* To influence, persuade, affect, etc., by speaking: They *talked* him around to their way of thinking. **13** *v.* To gossip or spread rumors. **14** *n.* A rumor, report, or gossip: There is *talk* of war. **— talk back** To answer in a rude way: to *talk back* to a teacher. **— talk down to** To talk too simply to, thus showing no respect for the listener's ability to understand. **— talk'er** *n.*

talk·a·tive [tôk'ə·tiv] *adj.* Liking to talk a lot or characterized by much talk: a *talkative* person.

tall [tôl] *adj.* **1** Of more than average height; high: a *tall* mountain. **2** Having a certain height: six feet *tall*. **3** *informal* Not easy to believe; exaggerated: a *tall* story.

Tal·la·has·see [tal'ə·has'ē] *n.* The capital of Florida.

tal·low [tal'ō] *n.* The fat of certain animals, as of cows or sheep, used in making candles, soap, etc.

tal·ly [tal'ē] *n.*, *pl.* **tal·lies**, *v.* **tal·lied, tal·ly· ing 1** *n.* A count, record, or score: The *tally* showed 500 steers. **2** *n.* Anything on which scores or counts are kept. **3** *v.* To score, as on a tally: He *tallied* three runs. **4** *v.* To add: He *tallied* up the results. **5** *v.* To match, correspond, or agree.

tal·ly·ho [tal'ē·hō'] *interj.*, *n.*, *pl.* **tal·ly·hos 1** *interj.* A hunter's cry when a fox being chased is sighted. **2** *n.* A coach drawn by a team of four horses.

Tal·mud [tal'mud] *n.* A book containing and discussing certain early Jewish civil and religious laws.

tal·on [tal'ən] *n.* The claw of a bird or animal, especially of a bird that feeds on other animals.

tam [tam] *n.* A tam-o'-shanter.

ta·ma·le [tə·mä'lē] *n.* A spicy Mexican food made from chopped meat, red peppers, and cornmeal, wrapped in corn husks, and steamed.

tam·a·rack [tam'ə·rak] *n.* A larch tree of North America or its wood.

tam·a·rind [tam'ə·rind] *n.* **1** A tropical tree with hard yellow wood, yellow flowers, and brown pods. **2** The pods of the tamarind tree, used in cooking, medicine, etc.

tam·bou·rine [tam'bə·rēn'] *n.* A shallow drum with jingling metal disks in the sides, played by shaking or striking with the hand.

tame [tām] *adj.* **tam·er, tam·est,** *v.* **tamed, tam· ing 1** *adj.* Naturally wild but made gentle, obedient, and not afraid of man: a *tame* lion. **2** *adj.* Used to being managed and cared for by people, as dogs, cats, and farm animals. **3** *v.* To make or become gentle, obedient, and not afraid of man:

Tambourine

Talisman

He *tamed* the lion; Some birds do not *tame* easily. **4** *v.* To bring under control; subdue: to *tame* a river; They tried to *tame* the boy. **5** *adj.* Not having much spirit or force: a *tame* fight. — **tame′ly** *adv.* — **tam′er** *n.*

tame·less [tām′lis] *adj.* Untamed or untamable. — **tame′less·ness** *n.*

tam-o′-shan·ter [tam′ə·shan′tər] *n.* A soft, round Scottish cap with a baggy top and often a pompon.

tamp [tamp] *v.* **1** To ram or pack down: The dentist *tamped* the filling in. **2** To fill (a hole containing explosives) with clay or sand, as in blasting.

Tam-o′-shanter

tam·per¹ [tam′pər] *v.* **1** To meddle so as to damage, put out of adjustment, etc.: Don't *tamper* with my camera. **2** To interfere in a dishonest way, as by bribery or threats: A witness had been *tampered* with.

tamp·er² [tam′pər] *n.* **1** A person who tamps. **2** An instrument for tamping.

tan [tan] *n., adj.* **tan·ner, tan·nest,** *v.* **tanned, tan·ning 1** *n., adj.* Yellowish brown. **2** *n.* A darkening of the skin caused by the sun. **3** *v.* To make or become tan, as by the sun: The sun *tanned* John; He *tans* quickly. **4** *n.* Tanbark. **5** *v.* To make (hides) into leather by treating with tannin. **6** *v. informal* To whip; thrash.

tan·a·ger [tan′ə·jər] *n.* Any of several small American birds related to the finch, as the scarlet tanager. The males are usually brightly colored.

tan·bark [tan′bärk′] *n.* The bark of certain trees, especially oak or hemlock, containing tannin. After the tannin is removed or used up, the bark is used to cover circus rings, racecourses, etc.

tan·dem [tan′dəm] **1** *adv.* One in front of the other. **2** *n.* A team of two or more horses harnessed in single file. **3** *n.* A carriage with two wheels, pulled by a tandem of horses. **4** *n.* A bicycle with two or more seats, one in front of the other. It is also called a **tandem bicycle.**

Tandem

tang [tang] *n.* **1** A sharp, strong taste or flavor: Lemon has a *tang*. **2** A trace; hint. **3** A shank or prong, as on a tool or sword, that fits into a handle. **4** A tonguelike part, as of a belt buckle.

Tang [täng] A Chinese dynasty, 618–906, one of China's greatest periods of literature and art.

Tan·gan·yi·ka [tan′gən·yē′kə] *n.* A region of eastern Africa, forming part of Tanzania.

tan·gent [tan′jənt] **1** *adj.* Touching a curve at a particular point but not crossing it there. **2** *n.* A line that is tangent to a curve. **3** *n.* In a right triangle, the length of the short side opposite an acute angle divided by the length of the short side next to the acute angle. This quotient depends on the size of the angle. — **fly off on a tangent** or **go off on a tangent** To go suddenly from one course of action or line of thought to another.

Illustration at top shows tangents in red. In illustration below, tangent of $x = \frac{b}{a}$.

tan·ger·ine [tan′jə·rēn′] *n.* **1** A small, juicy orange with a skin that is loose and easily removed. **2** A reddish orange color.

tan·gi·ble [tan′jə·bəl] *adj.* **1** Capable of being felt by the sense of touch: Still air is not *tangible.* **2** Real; concrete; definite: no *tangible* cause for alarm.

tan·gle [tang′gəl] *v.* **tan·gled, tan·gling,** *n.* **1** *v.* To twist or become twisted together into a confused mass: Don't *tangle* the wool; The ropes *tangled.* **2** *n.* A confused mass; snarl: She combed the *tangles* out of her hair. **3** *v.* To trap or hold as in a snare: Brambles *tangled* his feet and tripped him. **4** *n.* A state of confusion; disorder: His mind was in a *tangle* and he could not think.

tank [tangk] *n.* **1** A large container used to store fluids: a gasoline *tank.* **2** An armored military vehicle which carries guns and moves on two endless metal tracks. **3** A swimming pool. — **tank′ful** *n.*

tank·ard [tangk′ərd] *n.* A large drinking cup, usually having a handle and a hinged lid.

Tank

tank·er [tangk′ər] *n.* A cargo ship built to carry liquids, especially oil.

tan·ner [tan′ər] *n.* A person who makes leather out of hides by tanning.

tan·ner·y [tan′ər·ē] *n., pl.* **tan·ner·ies** A place where hides are tanned to make leather.

tan·nic acid [tan′ik] Tannin.

tan·nin [tan′in] *n.* An acid obtained from oak bark and from parts of other plants, used in tanning, dyeing, and making ink, and in medicine.

tan·sy [tan′zē] *n., pl.* **tan·sies** An herb with small yellow flowers, a strong smell, and a bitter taste, once much used in medicine.

tan·ta·lize [tan′tə·līz] *v.* **tan·ta·lized, tan·ta·liz·ing** To torment by making something that one desires almost but never quite available: The thought of water *tantalized* him in the desert. ¶3

tan·ta·mount [tan′tə·mount] *adj.* Having the same value or effect; equivalent: Not to help an injured man is *tantamount* to injuring him yourself.

tan·trum [tan′trəm] *n.* A fit of rage or anger.

Tan·za·ni·a [tan′zə·nē′ə] *n.* A country in eastern Africa, consisting of Tanganyika and Zanzibar, a member of the British Commonwealth.

tap[1] [tap] *n., v.* **tapped, tap·ping 1** *n.* A light blow. **2** *v.* To touch or strike gently: He *tapped* the desk with his pen. **3** *v.* To give a light blow with: He *tapped* his hand against the door. **4** *v.* To make or produce by tapping: The telegraph *tapped* out the message.

tap[2] [tap] *n., v.* **tapped, tap·ping 1** *n.* A faucet or spigot which regulates the flow of liquids: He took water from the *tap*. **2** *n.* A plug or cork which stops up a hole in a cask. **3** *v.* To release the flow of liquid from, as by drilling or unstopping a hole: to *tap* a barrel. **4** *v.* To allow to pour out: to *tap* cider. **5** *v.* To open up to use: to *tap* resources. **6** *v.* To make a connection with, as by wires or pipes: to *tap* a gas line. **7** *n.* A connection in an electrical circuit or pipe. **— on tap 1** Ready to be drawn from a cask: beer *on tap*. **2** *informal* Available; ready.

tap dance A dance accented by sharp taps on the floor with the dancer's heel or toe.

tape [tāp] *n., v.* **taped, tap·ing 1** *n.* A narrow strip of cloth, paper, etc., sometimes with one sticky side, used to bind, bandage, etc.: adhesive *tape*. **2** *v.* To fasten or bind with tape: He *taped* his ankle. **3** *n.* A plastic strip coated with a magnetic material on which sound, television programs, etc., can be recorded. **4** *v.* To record on tape. **5** *n.* A tape measure. **6** *v.* To measure with a tape. **7** *n.* The ribbon or string stretched above the finish line at a race.

tape measure A cloth or metal tape marked off like a ruler and used to measure areas and distances.

ta·per [tā′pər] **1** *v.* To make or become smaller or thinner toward one end: The trousers *tapered* toward the cuffs; John *tapered* the stick. **2** *n.* A gradually tapering shape: the *taper* of the church's steeple. **3** *v.* To lessen gradually; diminish: The fire *tapered* off. **4** *n.* A long, slender candle.

tape recorder A machine that changes sound, video signals, etc., into magnetic patterns on a length of tape that can be played back later.

tape recording A recording made on magnetic tape.

tap·es·try [tap′is·trē] *n., pl.* **tap·es·tries** A heavy ornamental cloth with designs or pictures woven into it, usually hung on a wall or used to cover furniture.

Tape recorder

tape·worm [tāp′wûrm′] *n.* A long, ribbonlike worm that in its adult stage lives in the intestines of man or animals.

tap·i·o·ca [tap′ē·ō′kə] *n.* A starchy substance obtained from the dried root of the cassava plant, used in puddings and to thicken liquids.

ta·pir [tā′pər] *n.* A large piglike animal with a long, flexible snout, living in tropical America.

tap·room [tap′rōōm′] *n.* A bar or tavern.

tap·root [tap′rōōt′] *n.* A plant's main root growing downward.

taps [taps] *n.pl. (often used with a singular verb)* A military call sounded on a bugle or on a drum to signal the time to turn off the lights at night. It is often sounded at a military funeral or at memorial services.

tar[1] [tär] *n., v.* **tarred, tar·ring 1** *n.* A dark, thick, gummy mixture of substances obtained from distilling wood or coal. **2** *v.* To cover with or as with tar. **— tar and feather** To cover (someone) with tar and feathers as a punishment.

tar[2] [tär] *n. informal* A sailor.

ta·ran·tu·la [tə·ran′chə·lə] *n.* A large, hairy spider of southern Europe and the sw U.S. The bite of the U.S. variety is painful but not dangerous.

tar·dy [tär′dē] *adj.* **tar·di·er, tar·di·est 1** Late; delayed: a *tardy* boy. **2** Moving slowly. **— tar′di·ly** *adv.* **— tar′di·ness** *n.*

tare[1] [târ] *n.* **1** A weed mentioned in the Bible as growing among the wheat. **2** A kind of vetch grown to feed cattle, sometimes eaten by man.

tare[2] [târ] *n.* The weight of the container or wrappings which is deducted from the total weight of something to determine the net weight.

tar·get [tär′git] *n.* **1** The object that one aims or shoots at, as with arrows, guns, darts, etc. **2** The object of criticism, attack, attention, etc.: the *target* of all eyes.

tar·iff [tar′if] *n.* **1** A list of duties or taxes to be charged on imported or exported goods. **2** A duty or tax found on such a list: a *tariff* on perfume. **3** Any list of rates, prices, etc.

Target

tarn [tärn] *n.* A small mountain lake or pool.

tar·nish [tär′nish] **1** *v.* To dull the brightness of: Egg *tarnishes* silver. **2** *v.* To lose its brightness. **3** *n.* A loss of brightness. **4** *n.* A dull, discolored coating. **5** *v.* To stain or disgrace: to *tarnish* one's honor.

ta·ro [tä′rō *or* tar′ō] *n., pl.* **ta·ros** A tropical plant having an edible, starchy root.

tar·pau·lin [tär·pô′lin *or* tär′pə·lin] *n.* A piece of canvas or other material that has been made waterproof, used to cover exposed objects.

tar·pon [tär′pon *or* tär′pən] *n., pl.* **tar·pon** or **tar·pons** A large, silvery game fish found off the West Indies and Florida.

tar·ry[1] [tar′ē] *v.* **tar·ried, tar·ry·ing 1** To stay for a while; linger. **2** To delay, wait, or be late: Don't *tarry*; you will miss the bus.

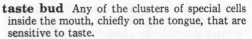
tar·ry[2] [tär′ē] *adj.* **tar·ri·er, tar·ri·est**
1 Covered with tar: a *tarry* surface. **2** Of or like tar.

tart[1] [tärt] *adj.* **1** Having a sharp, sour taste. **2** Sharp and biting: a *tart* answer. **— tart′ly** *adv.* **— tart′ness** *n.*

tart[2] [tärt] *n.* A small pastry shell filled with fruit or jam.

tar·tan [tär′tən] *n.* **1** A plaid woolen cloth worn by Scottish Highlanders. Each clan has its own plaid. **2** Any plaid cloth.

tar·tar [tär′tər] *n.* **1** A hard mineral substance that forms on teeth. **2** A pinkish acid substance that is deposited in casks or barrels of wine. When purified, it is called cream of tartar.

Tar·tar [tär′tər] *n.* **1** A Tatar. **2** (*sometimes written* **tartar**) A person with a wild temper.

task [task] **1** *n.* A piece of work to be done; duty: Your *task* is to water the plants. **2** *n.* A strain or exhausting burden: It is a *task* to climb to the top. **3** *v.* To put a strain on; burden: Practicing *tasked* his patience. **— take to task** To scold or lecture.

task force A temporary group of soldiers, sailors, etc., under one leader and assigned to carry out some special mission.

task·mas·ter [task′mas′tər] *n.* A person who gives out tasks for others to do.

Tas·ma·ni·a [taz·mā′nē·ə] *n.* An island south of Australia. It is an Australian state.

tas·sel [tas′əl] *n., v.* **tas·seled** or **tas·selled, tas·sel·ing** or **tas·sel·ling 1** *n.* A hanging tuft of threads, cords, etc., fastened together at the top. **2** *n.* Any similar object: There are *tassels* on corn. **3** *v.* To form into or provide with tassels. **4** *v.* To grow tassels: Corn *tassels* in summer. **5** *v.* To remove tassels from.

taste [tāst] *v.* **tast·ed, tast·ing,** *n.* **1** *v.* To experience or perceive the flavor of, by taking into the mouth or touching with the tongue. **2** *n.* The sense that perceives flavor: the sense of *taste*. **3** *n.* The sensation or flavor felt, as sweet, sour, salt, or bitter. **4** *v.* To have a certain flavor or quality: Sugar *tastes* sweet. **5** *v.* To sample, so as to test the quality or flavor: Mother *tasted* the stew. **6** *v.* To eat or drink very little of: He only *tasted* his lunch. **7** *v.* To experience: We all *taste* sorrow at one time or another. **8** *n.* A small quantity, experience, or sample of something: a *taste* of your cake; a *taste* of success. **9** *n.* A fondness; liking: a *taste* for music. **10** *n.* The ability to know and value what is good, beautiful, or appropriate: His *taste* in books was good. **11** *n.* A manner of acting or a personal quality that shows this ability: to dress in good *taste*. **— tast′er** *n.*

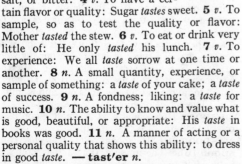

Tassel

taste bud Any of the clusters of special cells inside the mouth, chiefly on the tongue, that are sensitive to taste.

taste·ful [tāst′fəl] *adj.* Having, showing, or conforming to good taste. **— taste′ful·ly** *adv.*

taste·less [tāst′lis] *adj.* **1** Having no flavor. **2** Lacking, or showing a lack of, good taste: *tasteless* behavior. **— taste′less·ly** *adv.*

tast·y [tās′tē] *adj.* **tast·i·er, tast·i·est** Having a good flavor; savory. **— tast′i·ness** *n.*

tat [tat] *v.* **tat·ted, tat·ting** To make lace by tatting.

Ta·tar [tä′tər] *n.* Any of several Turkish or Mongolian peoples of central and western Asia and eastern Europe.

tat·ter [tat′ər] **1** *n.* A torn shred, as of cloth or paper; rag. **2** *n.* (*pl.*) Ragged clothing. **3** *v.* To tear into shreds. **4** *adj. use:* a *tattered* shirt.

tat·ting [tat′ing] *n.* **1** The act or process of making lace by hand, by looping and knotting threads with a small shuttle. **2** The lace made in this way.

tat·tle [tat′(ə)l] *v.* **tat·tled, tat·tling,** *n.* **1** *v.* To tell tales or secrets; gossip. **2** *v.* To talk for the sake of talking; chatter. **3** *n.* Chatter or gossip. **— tat′tler** *n.*

tat·tle·tale [tat′(ə)l·tāl′] *n.* A person who reveals secrets or who gossips; talebearer.

tat·too[1] [ta·tōō′] *v.* **tat·tooed, tat·too·ing,** *n.*, *pl.* **tat·toos 1** *v.* To mark (the skin) with colors, by pricking with needles: to *tattoo* an arm. **2** *v.* To draw on the skin in this way: A flag was *tattooed* on his chest. **3** *n.* A design or picture produced by tattooing.

tat·too[2] [ta·tōō′] *n.*, *pl.* **tat·toos 1** A steady rapping or drumming sound: He beat out a *tattoo* with his foot. **2** A drum or bugle call used to signal the time at night for sailors and soldiers to return to their quarters.

taught [tôt] Past tense and past participle of TEACH.

taunt [tônt] **1** *n.* A scornful or sarcastic remark. **2** *v.* To insult or make fun of, as by taunts.

taupe [tōp] *n., adj.* Deep, brownish gray.

Tau·rus [tôr′əs] *n.* A constellation in the northern sky, thought of as shaped like a bull.

taut [tôt] *adj.* **1** Stretched tight; not loose or slack. **2** Tense; strained. **3** Trim and neat.

tav·ern [tav′ərn] *n.* **1** A place where people buy and drink whisky, beer, etc.; bar. **2** An inn.

taw [tô] *n.* **1** A fancy marble to shoot marbles with. **2** A game of marbles. **3** The line from which players shoot when playing marbles.

taw·dry [tô′drē] *adj.* **taw·dri·er, taw·dri·est** Cheap and gaudy; showy. **— taw′dri·ness** *n.* ◆ *Tawdry* comes from *tawdry lace*, a ribbonlike ornament once worn by women around their necks. During the Middle Ages these ornaments were sold at *St. Audrey*'s fair in England. At some point [sānt·ô′drē] became

add, āce, câre, pälm;   end, ēqual;   it, īce;   odd, ōpen, ôrder;   tŏŏk, pŏŏl;   up, bûrn;
ə = a in *above*, e in *sicken*, i in *possible*, o in *melon*, u in *circus*;   y ŏŏ = u in *fuse*;   oil;   pout;
check; ring; thin; this; zh in *vision*.   For ¶ reference, see page 64 · HOW TO

[sān·tô′drē]. This was shortened to [tô′drē], which came to be spelled *tawdry*.

taw·ny [tô′nē] *adj.* **taw·ni·er, taw·ni·est** Tan-colored; brownish yellow.

tax [taks] **1** *n.* A charge paid by people, businesses, etc., for support of government in a city, county, state, or nation. **2** *n.* A heavy strain or burden: A mile run puts a *tax* on one's endurance. **3** *v.* To put a tax on: to *tax* real estate; Running *taxed* him. **4** *v.* To accuse or blame: They *taxed* him with being reckless.

tax·a·ble [tak′sə·bəl] *adj.* That may be taxed; subject to taxation: *taxable* property.

tax·a·tion [tak·sā′shən] *n.* **1** The act of taxing. **2** The amount charged or paid in taxes.

tax·i [tak′sē] *n., pl.* **tax·is,** *v.* **tax·ied, tax·i·ing** or **tax·y·ing 1** *n.* A taxicab. **2** *v.* To ride in a taxi. **3** *v.* To move or cause to move slowly along the ground or water before a take-off or after a landing: said about an airplane.

tax·i·cab [tak′sē·kab′] *n.* An automobile hired to carry passengers. It usually has a meter that measures and shows the fare to be paid.

tax·i·der·my [tak′sə·dûr′mē] *n.* The art of stuffing and mounting the skins of dead animals, making them look alive. **— tax′i·der′mist** *n.*

tax·on·o·my [tak·son′ə·mē] *n.* The science of classifying animals, plants, etc., in related groups and subdivisions.

tax·pay·er [taks′pā′ər] *n.* A person who pays taxes or is subject to taxation.

Tay·lor [tā′lər], **Zachary,** 1784–1850, U.S. general and 12th president of the U.S., 1849–1850.

TB or **T.B.** Abbreviation of TUBERCULOSIS.

tbs. or **tbsp.** Abbreviation of **1** TABLESPOON. **2** Tablespoons.

Tchai·kov·sky [chī·kof′skē], **Peter Ilych,** 1840–1893, Russian composer.

tea [tē] *n.* **1** A drink made by soaking dried leaves of an Asian shrub in hot water. **2** The dried leaves. **3** The shrub. **4** A light, afternoon meal at which tea is served. **5** An afternoon party at which tea is served. **6** A tealike drink made from some other herb or from meat: beef *tea*. ◆ *Tea* comes from a Chinese word.

teach [tēch] *v.* **taught, teach·ing 1** To help to learn; explain or explain to: to *teach* art; to *teach* a class. **2** To show how; train: He *taught* us to swim. **3** To give lessons as a teacher: He started to *teach* last year. **4** To make understand through experience: Sickness *taught* him to value health. ◆ *Learn* as a synonym for *teach*, as in *I'll learn you*, is not acceptable.

teach·a·ble [tē′chə·bəl] *adj.* Capable of being taught: a highly *teachable* pupil.

teach·er [tē′chər] *n.* A person who teaches, especially in a school.

teach·ing [tē′ching] *n.* **1** The act or occupation of a teacher. **2** (*often pl.*) That which is taught.

tea·cup [tē′kup′] *n.* A cup for drinking tea.

teak [tēk] *n.* **1** A large East Indian tree that has hard, heavy, durable wood. **2** The wood of this tree, used for furniture, ships, etc.

tea·ket·tle [tē′ket′(ə)l] *n.* A kettle with a spout, used to boil water.

teal [tēl] *n., pl.* **teal** or **teals 1** Any of several small, fresh-water wild ducks with short necks. **2** A dark greenish blue.

Teakettle

team [tēm] **1** *n.* A set of two or more horses, mules, etc., harnessed together. **2** *v.* To harness together in a team. **3** *n.* A set of people who work or play together as a unit: a baseball *team*. **4** *v.* To work or join together as a team: Tom *teamed* up with with Bill, Dick, Joe, and Jimmy.

team·mate [tēm′māt′] *n.* Another member of the same team.

team·ster [tēm′stər] *n.* A person who drives a team or truck as an occupation.

team·work [tēm′wûrk′] *n.* The effective working together of members of a team or group; united effort: *Teamwork* is needed to win.

tea·pot [tē′pot′] *n.* A pot with a handle and spout, used to brew and serve tea.

tear[1] [târ] *v.* **tore, torn, tear·ing,** *n.* **1** *v.* To pull apart or rip by force: to *tear* a letter open. **2** *n.* A rip or hole: There's a *tear* in the mattress. **3** *v.* To make by tearing: He *tore* a hole in his shirt. **4** *v.* To become torn: cloth that *tears* easily. **5** *v.* To make one or more ragged wounds or deep scratches in: Briers *tore* his flesh. **6** *v.* To divide by fighting, disagreement, etc.: The committee was *torn* over the issue. **7** *v.* To distress greatly: a heart *torn* by grief. **8** *v.* To rush or move with great speed or force: He *tore* around the corner. **9** *n.* The act of tearing. **— tear down 1** To take apart; destroy, uproot, etc. **2** To discredit, as a reputation. **— tear into** To attack fiercely.

tear[2] [tir] *n.* A drop of salty liquid in or shed from the eye, as in crying. **— in tears** Weeping.

tear·drop [tir′drop′] *n.* A tear.

tear·ful [tir′fəl] *adj.* **1** In tears; weeping: She was *tearful*. •**2** Causing tears; woeful: a *tearful* tale. **— tear′ful·ly** *adv.*

tear gas [tir] A gas that irritates the eyes and temporarily blinds them with tears.

tease [tēz] *v.* **teased, teas·ing,** *n.* **1** *v.* To pick on or fool with (another) for fun, in order to annoy or provoke: It is dangerous to *tease* an unfriendly dog; I was only *teasing*. **2** *v.* To pester with demands or questions: He *teased* his father for a new toy. **3** *n.* A person who teases. **4** *v.* To comb or straighten out, as wool or flax. **5** *v.* To scratch (cloth, etc.) on the surface in order to raise a nap. **6** *v.* To comb (hair) in layers so that it stands out and is fluffy. **7** *n.* The act of teasing.

tea·spoon [tē′spoon′] *n.* **1** A small spoon used to stir tea, etc. **2** A teaspoonful.

tea·spoon·ful [tē′spoon·fool′] *n., pl.* **tea·spoon·fuls** The amount that a teaspoon will hold, equal to $\frac{1}{3}$ of a tablespoon or $1\frac{1}{3}$ fluid drams.

teat [tēt] *n.* The nipple on a breast or udder.

tech·nic [tek′nik] **1** *n.* A technique. **2** *adj.* Technical.

tech·ni·cal [tek′ni·kəl] *adj.* **1** Of or having to do with mechanical or industrial skills or applied science: a *technical* school. **2** Of or having to do with special facts, ideas, or words of a particular art or science: "Patella" is a *technical* term for the kneecap. **3** Having to do with, according to, or strictly following the rules or special techniques of a game, art, science, etc.: the *technical* classification of a plant. — **tech′ni·cal·ly** *adv.*

tech·ni·cal·i·ty [tek′ni·kal′ə·tē] *n., pl.* **tech·ni·cal·i·ties 1** The state or quality of being technical. **2** A small, formal point or detail: *Technicalities* kept many from voting. **3** A technical detail, idea, or word known to a specialist in an art, science, etc.: He did not understand all the *technicalities* in the book.

tech·ni·cian [tek·nish′ən] *n.* A person skilled in the use of the instruments, machinery, or details of an art or science: a radio *technician*.

tech·nique [tek·nēk′] *n.* **1** A way of or skill in handling tools, instruments, materials, one's body, etc., in an art, science, sport, craft, or the like: Both boxers and violinists need lots of *technique*. **2** A special method of doing something: a new *technique* of brain surgery.

tech·no·log·i·cal [tek′nə·loj′i·kəl] *adj.* Having to do with or resulting from technology.

tech·nol·o·gy [tek·nol′ə·jē] *n.* The application of scientific and industrial skills to practical uses.

Te De·um [tē dē′əm *or* tā dā′əm] An ancient Christian hymn of praise to God, or its music.

te·di·ous [tē′dē·əs] *adj.* Long, dull, and tiresome: a *tedious* job. — **te′di·ous·ly** *adv.*

te·di·um [tē′dē·əm] *n.* The condition of being boring or monotonous.

tee [tē] *n., v.* **teed, tee·ing 1** *n.* A small peg on which a golf ball may be placed for the first stroke in playing a hole. **2** *v.* To place (a golf ball) on a tee. **3** *n.* The area where a player must start to play a hole. **4** *n.* A mark aimed at in certain sports, as in curling. — **tee off** To strike a golf ball from a tee.

teem [tēm] *v.* To be full and almost overflowing; abound: The ship *teems* with rats.

teen-age [tēn′āj′] *adj.* **1** Being in one's teens. **2** Of or for teen-age people.

teen-aged [tēn′ājd′] *adj.* In one's teens.

teen-ag·er [tēn′ā′jər] *n.* A person in his teens.

teens [tēnz] *n.pl.* The years of one's age from 13 to 19.

tee·pee [tē′pē] *n.* Another spelling of TEPEE.

tee·ter [tē′tər] **1** *v.* To rock from side to side as if about to fall. **2** *n.* A teetering movement. **3** *n.* A seesaw. **4** *v.* To seesaw.

tee·ter-tot·ter [tē′tər·tot′ər] *n.* A seesaw.

teeth [tēth] Plural of TOOTH. — **in the teeth of** Directly against; in defiance of.

teethe [tēth] *v.* **teethed, teeth·ing** To cut or develop teeth, as babies do.

tee·to·tal·er [tē·tōt′(ə)l·ər] *n.* A person who does not drink alcoholic beverages. ◆ *Teetotaler* relies as much on what has been left out as on what remains. It started with *total* (abstaining from alcoholic liquor). The initial *t* of *total* was duplicated by *tee*, and *-er* was added, meaning *a person who totally* (abstains).

Te·he·ran or **Te·hran** [te′ə·rän′] *n.* The capital of Iran, in the north central part.

Tel A·viv [tel′ä·vēv′] A city in western Israel.

tel·e·cast [tel′ə·kast] *n., v.* **tel·e·cast** or **tel·e·cast·ed, tel·e·cast·ing 1** *n.* A program broadcast by television. **2** *v.* To broadcast by television. See TELEVISION.

tel·e·gram [tel′ə·gram] *n.* A message sent by telegraph.

tel·e·graph [tel′ə·graf] **1** *n.* A device for sending and receiving messages by means of a series of electrical or electromagnetic pulses. **2** *v.* To send (a message) by telegraph. **3** *v.* To send a message to, by telegraph.

tel·e·graph·ic [tel′ə·graf′ik] *adj.* Having to do with or sent by telegraph.

te·leg·ra·phy [tə·leg′rə·fē] *n.* The use or operation of a telegraphic system.

tel·e·me·ter [tel′ə·mē′tər] **1** *n.* Any of various electronic devices for measuring and recording various quantities, as temperature, speed, radiation, etc., and then transmitting the data to distant points. **2** *v.* To measure and transmit (various quantities, etc.) by telemeter.

te·lem·e·try [tə·lem′ə·trē] *n.* The theory and practice of using telemeters.

tel·e·path·ic [tel′ə·path′ik] *adj.* Having to do with or sent by telepathy: a *telepathic* message.

te·lep·a·thy [tə·lep′ə·thē] *n.* Communication from one mind to another, apparently received without use of hearing, sight, touch, etc.

tel·e·phone [tel′ə·fōn] *n., v.* **tel·e·phoned, tel·e·phon·ing 1** *n.* A system for sending and receiving speech by electricity. **2** *n.* A device in this system that changes sounds to pulses in electric current and converts incoming pulses into sounds. **3** *v.* To call by telephone. **4** *v.* To send by telephone: I *telephoned* my order.

tel·e·phon·ic [tel′ə·fon′ik] *adj.* Having to do with, or sent by the telephone.

tel·e·pho·to lens [tel′ə·fō′tō] A camera lens used to make distant objects look nearer or larger.

tel·e·scope [tel′ə·skōp] *n., v.* **tel·e·scoped, tel·e·scop·ing 1** *n.* An instrument that uses lenses, and sometimes mirrors, to make far-off objects look nearer or larger. **2** *v.* To force or be forced into one another, like the sliding tubes of a folding telescope: The collision *telescoped* three cars. **3** *v.* To shorten, squeeze, or compress: The play *telescoped* the events of years into a single day. ◆ See TELEVISION.

tel·e·scop·ic [tel′ə·skop′ik] *adj.* **1** Of or having to do with a telescope. **2** Visible only through a

---

add, āce, câre, pälm; end, ēqual; it, īce; odd, ōpen, ôrder; tŏŏk, pōōl; up, bûrn; ə = a in *above*, e in *sicken*, i in *possible*, o in *melon*, u in *circus*; yōō = u in *fuse*; oil; pout; check; ring; thin; this; zh in *vision*. For ¶ reference, see page 64 · HOW TO

telescope: a *telescopic* star. **3** Seen by, or as if by, telescope. **4** Having parts that slide inside each other, like the sections of a telescope.

Tel·e·type [tel′ə·tīp] *n.* **1** A teletypewriter: a trademark. **2** The message sent on a teletypewriter. Also written **teletype.**

tel·e·type·writ·er [tel′ə·tīp′rī′tər] *n.* A telegraph on which a message is sent from a typewriterlike keyboard and then is typed out automatically at its destination.

tel·e·vise [tel′ə·vīz] *v.* **tel·e·vised, tel·e·vis· ing** To transmit or receive by television. ◆ See TELEVISION.

tel·e·vi·sion [tel′ə·vizh′ən] *n.* **1** The devices and methods by which moving images, usually with sound, are changed into variations of an electromagnetic wave that travels through space or over cables to a receiver where the signals are recovered. **2** *adj. use:* a *television* program; a *television* set. **3** A television receiver. **4** The television industry. ◆ The combining form *tele-* comes from a Greek word meaning *far.* Thus *television* literally means *far or distant vision,* and *telescope* means *watcher from afar.* When there was a need for a verb with the meaning *to transmit by television, televise,* modeled after *television,* was created, filling a similar need, was formed from *tele-* + *(broad)cast.*

tell [tel] *v.* **told, tell·ing** **1** To say in words; utter: to *tell* a lie. **2** To give facts to; inform: *Tell* me about the book. **3** To give information or description: The book *tells* about Japan. **4** To make known: to *tell* secrets. **5** To give away a secret or inform on someone: Please don't *tell.* **6** To show; indicate: Her face *told* how amused she was. **7** To distinguish or decide: I can't *tell* which dog is older. **8** To give an order to: *Tell* him to go. **9** *informal* To say to with force or emphasis: It's dangerous, I *tell* you! **10** To have a marked effect: TV debates *told* in his favor. **11** To count: All *told,* 19 chemicals were tested; to *tell* one's rosary beads while praying. **— tell off 1** To count and set apart. **2** *informal* To scold severely. **— tell on 1** To tire: The heat began to *tell on* them. **2** To inform on; bear tales about: A tattletale *tells on* others. **— tell time** To read the time shown on a clock or watch.

tell·er [tel′ər] *n.* **1** A person who tells: a *teller* of tales. **2** A person who counts and gives out or takes in money in a bank.

tell·ing [tel′ing] *adj.* Having a marked effect; effective: a *telling* speech.

tell·tale [tel′tāl′] **1** *n.* A person who informs on others or gives out secret or private information. **2** *adj.* Showing or revealing what is meant to be hidden: a *telltale* blush.

te·mer·i·ty [tə·mer′ə·tē] *n.* Rash boldness.

tem·per [tem′pər] **1** *n.* A frame of mind; mood: in a good *temper.* **2** *n.* A tendency to become angry: to have a *temper.* **3** *n.* A rage: to fly into a *temper.* **4** *n.* Self-command; calmness: to lose one's *temper.* **5** *v.* To make less harsh, strong, etc., as by adding something; moderate:

to *temper* very hot coffee with ice. **6** *n.* The condition of a metal, clay, etc., regarding its hardness or elasticity. **7** *v.* To bring to the condition or temper desired by treating, as by heating and suddenly cooling (metal) or by moistening (clay).

tem·per·a·ment [tem′pər·ə·mənt] *n.* **1** The nature or emotional make-up of a person; disposition. **2** A sensitive, easily excited nature.

tem·per·a·men·tal [tem′prə·men′təl *or* tem′· pər·ə·men′təl] *adj.* **1** Of or having to do with temperament. **2** Easily excited, irritated, or upset; sensitive. **— tem′per·a·men′tal·ly** *adv.*

tem·per·ance [tem′pər·əns] *n.* **1** The quality of being temperate; moderation. **2** The rule or practice of taking no alcoholic drinks.

tem·per·ate [tem′pər·it] *adj.* **1** Practicing or showing moderation or self-control in one's actions, in eating, in drinking alcoholic beverages, etc. **2** Moderate in temperature; mild: a *temperate* zone. **— tem′per·ate·ly** *adv.*

tem·per·a·ture [tem′pər·ə·chər *or* tem′prə· chər] *n.* **1** The degree of heat or cold in a body or thing, as measured on some definite scale. **2** Excessive body heat; fever, especially in a human being. Normal heat for the human body is 98.6° F.

tem·pered [tem′pərd] *adj.* **1** Having a certain disposition: usually used in combination, as in ill-*tempered.* **2** Having the right degree of hardness and elasticity: *tempered* steel.

tem·pest [tem′pist] *n.* **1** A violent wind or storm. **2** A violent outburst or disturbance.

tem·pes·tu·ous [tem·pes′chōō·əs] *adj.* Stormy; violent; turbulent.

Tem·plar [tem′plər] *n.* A member of a medieval military and religious order, the **Knights Templars,** founded by the Crusaders for the defense of Jerusalem and the protection of pilgrims.

tem·ple[1] [tem′pəl] *n.* **1** A stately building dedicated to the worship of a god or gods. **2** A church or synagogue. **3** (*written* **Temple**) Any of the three temples built one after the other by the Jews in ancient Jerusalem. **4** A building, usually of great beauty or size, that is devoted to some special purpose: a *temple* of the arts.

An ancient Greek temple

tem·ple[2] [tem′pəl] *n.* The flattened area extending back from the forehead on either side about as far as the ear.

tem·po [tem′pō] *n., pl.* **tem·pos** or **tem·pi** [tem′pē] **1** The relative speed at which a piece of music is played. **2** The pace or rate of activity: the fast *tempo* of city life.

tem·po·ral[1] [tem′pər·əl] *adj.* **1** Of or having to do with life on earth. **2** Of or having to do with time. **3** Temporary or passing. **4** Not sacred, religious, or ecclesiastic; secular; worldly.

tem·po·ral[2] [tem′pər·əl] *adj.* Of or near the temple or temples of the head: the *temporal* bones.

tem·po·rar·y [tem′pə·rer′ē] *adj.* Lasting or meant to be used for a short time only; not permanent. — **tem′po·rar′i·ly** *adv.*

tem·po·rize [tem′pə·rīz] *v.* **tem·po·rized, tem·po·riz·ing 1** To talk or act in an evasive or noncommittal way so as to gain time or postpone making a decision. **2** To talk or act in a way that suits the time or circumstances. ¶3

tempt [tempt] *v.* **1** To try to persuade (a person) to do something wrong or foolish. **2** To attract or invite: The aroma *tempts* me. **3** *adj. use:* a *tempting* idea. **4** To provoke or risk provoking: It is unwise to *tempt* fate. — **tempt′er** *n.*

temp·ta·tion [temp·tā′shən] *n.* **1** The act of tempting. **2** The condition of being tempted. **3** A tempting thing.

ten or **10** [ten] *n., adj.* One more than nine.

ten·a·ble [ten′ə·bəl] *adj.* Capable of being believed, maintained, or defended: The theory that the earth is flat is no longer *tenable.*

te·na·cious [ti·nā′shəs] *adj.* **1** Holding or grasping firmly: a *tenacious* grip. **2** Having parts that hold together well; cohesive, as a metal. **3** Clinging or sticky: a *tenacious* climbing plant. **4** Apt to retain, as memory. — **te·na′cious·ly** *adv.*

te·nac·i·ty [ti·nas′ə·tē] *n.* The condition or quality of being tenacious.

ten·an·cy [ten′ən·sē] *n., pl.* **ten·an·cies 1** The condition of being a tenant. **2** The time during which one is a tenant.

ten·ant [ten′ənt] **1** *n.* A person who rents land, a house, apartment, etc., from another. **2** *n.* A dweller in any place; occupant. **3** *v.* To occupy or inhabit as a tenant.

Ten Commandments In the Bible, the set of laws given by God to Moses on Mount Sinai.

tend¹ [tend] *v.* To attend to; take care of; watch over: to *tend* a herd.

tend² [tend] *v.* **1** To be apt; have an inclination: He *tends* to bore me. **2** To move or go in a certain direction: The road *tends* south.

ten·den·cy [ten′dən·sē] *n., pl.* **ten·den·cies** A leaning or inclination toward some condition, action, etc.: Iron has a *tendency* to rust; He has a *tendency* to argue.

ten·der¹ [ten′dər] *adj.* **1** Easily injured or damaged; delicate; sensitive: a *tender* plant. **2** Easily chewed or cut, as meat. **3** Young; immature: a *tender* age. **4** Kind and gentle; loving: *tender* care. **5** Easily moved; sympathetic; compassionate: a *tender* heart. **6** Painful if touched: a *tender* sore. **7** Likely to provoke strong feelings; touchy: a *tender* subject. — **ten′der·ly** *adv.* — **ten′der·ness** *n.*

ten·der² [ten′dər] **1** *v.* To offer, especially formally, or to present in payment: to *tender* a resignation. **2** *n.* An offer, especially a formal one. **3** *n.* Something offered as payment.

ten·der³ [ten′dər] *n.* **1** A boat used to carry passengers, supplies, etc., to and from a larger vessel. **2** A car that carries coal and water for a steam locomotive. **3** A person who tends.

ten·der·foot [ten′dər·fŏŏt′] *n., pl.* **ten·der·foots** or **ten·der·feet** [ten′dər·fēt′] **1** A person who is not used to a rugged, outdoor life. **2** Any inexperienced person. **3** A beginning boy scout. ♦ *Tenderfoot* comes from combining *tender* and *foot,* and first meant someone who got sore feet from hiking in the pioneer West.

Tender

ten·der·heart·ed [ten′dər·här′tid] *adj.* Easily moved to sympathy or compassion.

ten·der·loin [ten′dər·loin′] *n.* The tender part of the loin of beef, pork, etc.

ten·don [ten′dən] *n.* A tough band of tissue that connects a muscle to a bone, etc.

ten·dril [ten′dril] *n.* **1** A thin, curling stem or growth by which a climbing plant attaches itself to something. **2** Anything that looks like this.

ten·e·ment [ten′ə·mənt] *n.* **1** An apartment house that is poorly built or maintained, usually overcrowded, and often in a slum. **2** A room or set of rooms for a single tenant or family.

ten·et [ten′it] *n.* An opinion, doctrine, or principle held to be true by a person or group.

Ten·nes·see [ten′ə·sē′] *n.* A state in the SE U.S.

ten·nis [ten′is] *n.* A game played by striking a ball back and forth with rackets over a net stretched between two equal areas.

Ten·ny·son [ten′ə·sən], **Alfred,** 1809–1892, English poet, known as Alfred, Lord Tennyson.

ten·on [ten′ən] *n.* A projection on the end of a piece of wood, etc., for fitting into a mortise to form a joint.

ten·or [ten′ər] *n.* **1** An adult male singing voice next higher than a baritone. **2** A man with such a voice. **3** The range of or a part for such a voice. **4** An instrument with such a range. **5** *adj. use:* a *tenor* saxophone. **6** The general course: the *tenor* of city life. **7** The main meaning or drift: the *tenor* of an essay.

tenon

mortise

ten·pins [ten′pinz′] *n.pl.* (*used with singular verb*) A game played in a

add, āce, câre, pälm; end, ēqual; it, īce; odd, ōpen, ôrder; tŏŏk, pōōl; up, bûrn;
ə = a in *above,* e in *sicken,* i in *possible,* o in *melon,* u in *circus;* yōō = u in *fuse;* oil; pout;
check; ring; thin; this; zh in *vision.*   For ¶ reference, see page 64 · HOW TO

bowling alley in which the players use a ball to try to knock down ten pins set up at one end of the alley.

tense[1] [tens] *adj.* **tens·er, tens·est,** *v.* **tensed, tens·ing 1** *adj.* Stretched tight; taut. **2** *adj.* Marked by, feeling, or causing nervous strain. **3** *v.* To make or become tense. — **tense′ly** *adv.*

tense[2] [tens] *n.* A feature of verbs relating to expression of meanings of time. Most English verbs have two tenses, present and past, for example, *walk* and *walked.* Past tenses generally show something occurring in past time.

ten·sile [ten′sil] *adj.* **1** Of or having to do with tension: *tensile* strength. **2** Capable of being drawn out without breaking.

ten·sion [ten′shən] *n.* **1** The act of stretching. **2** The condition of being stretched. **3** Mental strain; nervous anxiety. **4** Electrical potential; voltage.

tent [tent] **1** *n.* A shelter of canvas, skins, etc., supported by poles and ropes. **2** *v.* To camp out or live in a tent.

ten·ta·cle [ten′tə·kəl] *n.* **1** A long, flexible outgrowth from the main body of an animal, as an octopus, squid, etc., used for moving, seizing prey, etc. **2** A sensitive plant hair.

ten·ta·tive [ten′tə·tiv] *adj.* Done or made as an experiment or for a short trial period; subject to change or revision; not final: a *tentative* agreement. — **ten′ta·tive·ly** *adv.*

ten·ter·hook [ten′tər·hŏŏk′] *n.* A sharp hook for holding cloth on a stretching frame. — **be on tenterhooks** To be in suspense; nervous.

tenth or **10th** [tenth] **1** *adj.* Next after the ninth. **2** *n.* The tenth one. **3** *adj.* Being one of ten equal parts. **4** *n.* A tenth part.

ten·u·ous [ten′yŏŏ·əs] *adj.* **1** Thin; slim; delicate: a *tenuous* web. **2** Weak; flimsy; unsubstantial: a *tenuous* idea. **3** Having slight density; rarefied, as a gas. — **ten′u·ous·ly** *adv.*

ten·ure [ten′yər] *n.* **1** The act or right of holding land, a position, etc. **2** The conditions or manner of holding. **3** The time during which land, a position, etc., is held.

te·pee [tē′pē] *n.* A cone-shaped tent used by some North American Indians. ◆ *Tepee* goes back to two North American Indian words meaning *used for dwelling.*

tep·id [tep′id] *adj.* Slightly warm; lukewarm.

term [tûrm] **1** *n.* A word or phrase having a certain meaning, especially in some particular field: a scientific *term*; to speak in vague *terms.* **2** *v.* To apply a term to; name or call: I *term* him a fool. **3** *n.* An established

Tepee

period of time, as one of the divisions of the school year. **4** *n.* (*pl.*) Mutual relations: to be on friendly *terms.* **5** *n.* (*pl.*) Agreement: to come to *terms.* **6** *n.* (*pl.*) Conditions or stipulations, as of a sale, contract, etc. **7** *n.* The numerator or denominator of a fraction. **8** *n.* The parts of a mathematical expression that are added or subtracted, as ax^2, bx, and c in $ax^2 + bx - c$.

ter·ma·gant [tûr′mə·gənt] *n.* A harsh, scolding woman; shrew.

ter·mi·na·ble [tûr′mə·nə·bəl] *adj.* Capable of being ended, as a contract.

ter·mi·nal [tûr′mə·nəl] **1** *adj.* Of, at, having to do with, or forming a limit or end. **2** *n.* An end or limit. **3** *n.* The station at the end of a railway, bus route, etc. **4** *n.* Any of the points where electricity may enter or leave a device.

ter·mi·nate [tûr′mə·nāt] *v.* **ter·mi·nat·ed, ter·mi·nat·ing 1** To end; stop; finish: The road *terminates* there; to *terminate* a discussion. **2** To form the end of; bound: The field was *terminated* by a forest. — **ter′mi·na′tion** *n.*

ter·mi·nol·o·gy [tûr′mə·nol′ə·jē] *n.* The technical words and phrases of a trade, science, etc.

ter·mi·nus [tûr′mə·nəs] *n., pl.* **ter·mi·nus·es** or **ter·mi·ni** [tûr′mə·nī] **1** The final point or goal; end. **2** Either end of a railroad, bus, or air line.

ter·mite [tûr′mīt] *n.* A small, pale insect that looks like a white ant. Termites are very destructive to things made of wood.

tern [tûrn] *n.* A small, gull-like bird with a slender body, pointed wings, and forked tail.

ter·race [ter′is] *n., v.* **ter·raced, ter·rac·ing 1** *n.* A raised, level space, as of lawn, with one or more sloping sides. **2** *n.* One of a series of such spaces, as on a hill. **3** *v.* To form into or provide with a terrace or terraces. **4** *n.* A row of houses built on ground raised above a street, or the street on which such houses face. **5** *n.* A paved area adjoining a house; patio. **6** *n.* The flat roof of a house. **7** *n.* An open gallery or balcony.

Terrace

ter·ra cot·ta [ter′ə kot′ə] **1** A hard, reddish brown clay, used in sculpture, making pottery, and in building. **2** Brownish orange.

ter·ra fir·ma [ter′ə fûr′mə] Firm, solid ground.

ter·rain [tə·rān′] *n.* An area of land, especially as considered with respect to its use for military operations or some other purpose.

Ter·ra·my·cin [ter′ə·mī′sin] *n.* A trademark for an antibiotic made from a soil mold. Also written **terramycin.**

ter·ra·pin [ter′ə·pin] *n.* Any of various edible North American turtles that live in fresh or partly salt water.

ter·rar·i·um [te·râr′ē·əm] *n., pl.* **ter·rar·i·ums** or **ter·rar·i·a** [te·râr′ē·ə] A transparent box in which small land animals or plants are grown and kept.

ter·res·tri·al [tə·res′trē·əl] *adj.* **1** Of, having to do with, or made up of earth or land. **2** Living on or growing in the ground, not in the air, trees, etc. **3** Worldly; mundane.

ter·ri·ble [ter′ə·bəl] *adj.* **1** Causing terror or awe: a *terrible* storm. **2** *informal* Unpleasant or inferior: a *terrible* book.

ter·ri·bly [ter′ə·blē] *adv.* **1** In a terrible way or manner. **2** *informal* Very: He's *terribly* nice.

ter·ri·er [ter′ē·ər] *n.* Any of various small, active dogs, formerly used to hunt burrowing animals.

ter·rif·ic [tə·rif′ik] *adj.* **1** *informal* Wonderful; splendid: a *terrific* book. **2** *informal* Extreme or very great: under *terrific* pressure. **3** Causing great terror or fear. **— ter·rif′i·cal·ly** *adv.*

ter·ri·fy [ter′ə·fī] *v.* **ter·ri·fied, ter·ri·fy·ing** To fill with extreme fear; frighten greatly.

ter·ri·to·ri·al [ter′ə·tôr′ē·əl] **1** Of or having to do with a territory or territories. **2** Limited to or governed by a particular territory or region: *territorial* waters.

ter·ri·to·ry [ter′ə·tôr′ē] *n., pl.* **ter·ri·to·ries** **1** The geographical area ruled by a nation, state, etc. **2** A large division of a nation or country, having a limited amount of self-government. **3** Any large area of land; region. **4** An area assigned for a special purpose: a salesman's *territory.*

ter·ror [ter′ər] *n.* **1** Great fear; extreme fright or dread. **2** A person or thing that causes such fear: Indians were once the *terror* of the frontier. **3** *informal* A person or thing that is annoying; nuisance.

ter·ror·ism [ter′ə·riz′əm] *n.* The use of violence and threats to frighten a people or a government into submission. **— ter′ror·ist** *n.*

ter·ror·ize [ter′ə·rīz] *v.* **ter·ror·ized, ter·ror·iz·ing** **1** To make very frightened; terrify. **2** To control or rule by threats and violence. ¶3

ter·ry cloth [ter′ē] A thick, absorbent cotton cloth covered with small loops, used in making towels, bathrobes, etc.

terse [tûrs] *adj.* **ters·er, ters·est** Short and to the point; concise. **— terse′ly** *adv.*

ter·ti·ar·y [tûr′shē·er′ē *or* tûr′shə·rē] *adj.* Of the third degree, rank, class, etc.; third.

test [test] **1** *n.* A trial, examination, or experiment to determine the nature, worth, extent, etc., of something: a *test* of ore. **2** *n.* A series of questions or problems intended to measure knowledge, skills, etc. **3** *n.* A set of difficult conditions likened to a test; ordeal: Army life was a severe *test* for him. **4** *v.* To subject (a person or thing) to a test. **5** *n.* A means of testing or judging; criterion. **6** *v.* To show certain properties or qualities when tested: The solution *tested* acid. **— test′er** *n.*

tes·ta·ment [tes′tə·mənt] *n.* **1** In law, one's will, used chiefly in the phrase **last will and**

testament. 2 (*written* **Testament**) Either the Old Testament or the New Testament, but especially the New Testament.

tes·ta·men·ta·ry [tes′tə·men′tə·rē] *adj.* Of, having to do with, stated in, or given by a will.

tes·ta·tor [tes′tā·tər] *n.* Someone who makes a will or dies leaving a valid will.

tes·ti·cle [tes′ti·kəl] *n.* One of the two male sex glands in which the sperm is formed.

tes·ti·fy [tes′tə·fī] *v.* **tes·ti·fied, tes·ti·fy·ing** **1** To declare, especially under oath in a court. **2** To give evidence; bear witness: Her eyes *testified* to her joy. **3** To give evidence of; indicate: The dog *testified* his distrust by a growl.

tes·ti·mo·ni·al [tes′tə·mō′nē·əl] *n.* **1** A letter, statement, etc., praising or recommending a person or thing. **2** A token, statement, etc., of praise or thanks.

tes·ti·mo·ny [tes′tə·mō′nē] *n., pl.* **tes·ti·mo·nies** **1** A declaration, especially before a court and under oath. **2** Evidence or proof. **3** An open statement of one's faith.

test tube A glass tube open at one end, and usually with a rounded bottom, used in making chemical tests, etc.

tes·ty [tes′tē] *adj.* **tes·ti·er, tes·ti·est** Easily made angry; touchy. **— tes′ti·ly** *adv.*

tet·a·nus [tet′ə·nəs] *n.* A disease marked by stiffening and spasms of the muscles, especially of the neck and jaw, caused by a bacterium that enters the body through a wound.

Test tubes

tête-à-tête [tāt′ə·tāt′] **1** *n.* A private chat between two people. **2** *adj.* Private and confidential. **3** *adv.* Two together privately.

teth·er [teth′ər] **1** *n.* A rope or chain used to tie an animal so that it can range only so far. **2** *v.* To fasten or confine by a tether. **— at the end of one's tether** At the end of one's strength, resources, etc.

tet·ra·he·dron [tet′rə·hē′drən] *n., pl.* **tet·ra·he·drons** or **tet·ra·he·dra** [tet′rə·hē′drə] *n.* A solid bounded by four triangular faces.

Teu·ton [t(y)oo′t(ə)n] *n.* **1** A member of an ancient German tribe. **2** A member of a group of northern European peoples, including the Dutch, the Scandinavians, and, especially, the Germans.

Teu·ton·ic [t(y)oo·ton′ik] *adj.* Of or having to do with the Germanic peoples of northern Europe, as the Germans, Dutch, Swedes, etc.

Tex·as [tek′səs] *n.* A state in the sw U.S.

text [tekst] *n.* **1** The main written or printed matter in a book or on a page, but not any notes, illustrations, etc. **2** The original words of an author. **3** A quotation from the Bible, especially when used as the basis of a sermon. **4** A subject; topic. **5** A textbook.

text·book [tekst′book′] *n.* A book used in the teaching of a subject, especially in a school.

tex·tile [teks′til *or* teks′tīl] **1** *n.* A woven fabric. **2** *adj.* Of or having to do with weaving or woven fabrics. **3** *adj.* Made by weaving.

tex·tu·al [teks′chōō·əl] *adj.* Having to do with, found in, or based on the text of a book.

tex·ture [teks′chər] *n.* **1** The arrangement of the threads of a woven fabric: Satin has a smooth *texture*. **2** The look or feel of the surface of any substance: the grainy *texture* of cement.

Th The symbol for the element THORIUM.

-th A suffix used to form ordinal numbers: *tenth*. It is written *-eth* after vowels: *fortieth*.

Thack·er·ay [thak′ər·ē], **William Make-peace,** 1811–1863, British author of novels.

Thai [tī] **1** *adj.* Of or from Thailand. **2** *n.* A person born in or a citizen of Thailand. **3** *n.* The language of Thailand.

Thai·land [tī′land] *n.* A country in SE Asia.

thal·lo·phyte [thal′ə·fīt] *n.* Any of a group of primitive plants that do not have true roots, stems, or leaves, as fungi and algae.

Thames [temz] *n.* A river in England, flowing through London into the North Sea.

than [ŧħan *or* ŧħən] **1** *conj.* In comparison with: I am wiser *than* he. **2** *conj.* Except; but: no colors other *than* black and white. **3** *prep.* Compared to: a boy *than* whom none was smarter.

thane [thān] *n.* **1** In early England, a man who ranked above an ordinary freeman but below a nobleman. He held land of and performed military service for a lord or the king. **2** In early Scotland, a nobleman.

thank [thangk] *v.* **1** To express gratitude to; give thanks to. **2** To hold at fault; blame: You can *thank* yourself for this mess. **— thank you** I thank you; I am grateful to you.

thank·ful [thangk′fəl] *adj.* Feeling or expressing thanks; grateful. **— thank′ful·ly** *adv.* **— thank′ful·ness** *n.*

thank·less [thangk′lis] *adj.* **1** Not thankful; ungrateful. **2** Not likely to be appreciated: a *thankless* job. **— thank′less·ly** *adv.*

thanks [thangks] **1** *n.pl.* An expression or acknowledgment of obligation in return for a gift, favor, etc. **2** *interj.* Thank you. **— thanks to** Because of.

thanks·giv·ing [thangks′giv′ing] *n.* **1** Expression of thanks, especially to God. **2** (*written* **Thanksgiving**) A holiday of thanksgiving in the U.S., usually held the fourth Thursday in November. It is more often called **Thanksgiving Day.**

that [ŧħat *or* ŧħət] *pron. & adj., pl.* **those** [ŧħōz], *adv., conj.* **1** *pron.* The person or thing mentioned or indicated: *That* is the one. **2** *adj.* Being the person or thing mentioned or indicated: *That* house is for sale. **3** *pron.* The person or thing indicated as different, farther away, etc.: Keep this, not *that*. **4** *adj.* Indicated as different,

farther away, etc.: Do it this way, not *that* way. **5** *pron.* Who, whom, or which: We need a man *that* can run. **6** *adv.* To that extent; so: He can't run *that* fast. **7** *conj.* *That* may be used to join a subordinate clause to its main clause. It can mean **a** As a fact: I say *that* it is so. **b** As a result: He ate so much *that* he became ill. **c** At which time; when: It was only yesterday *that* I saw him. **d** So that; in order that: I tell you *that* you may know. **e** Because: She is angry *that* we are late. **f** I wish: O *that* we were there! **— in that** Because. ◆ See also THIS.

thatch [thach] **1** *n.* A covering of reeds, straw, etc., used on a roof. **2** *v.* To cover with or as with thatch. **3** *n.* Anything that resembles such a covering: a *thatch* of hair.

thaw [thô] **1** *v.* To melt, as something frozen: Will the ice *thaw*?; The heat *thawed* the snow. **2** *v.* To get warm enough so that ice and snow will melt: It should *thaw* soon. **3** *n.* Weather that melts the snow of winter: a spring *thaw*. **4** *v.* To make or become less coldly formal or unfriendly. **5** *n.* The act of thawing. **6** *n.* A being thawed.

Thatched roof

the [ŧħē, ŧħə, *or* ŧħi] **1** *adj.* The definite article used to modify nouns or noun phrases. It can mean **a** That particular one or those particular ones here, mentioned, understood, etc.: *the* house; *the* players. **b** That which is or those which are: *The* just will overcome *the* wicked. **c** Any one, and therefore all, of a kind, group, species, etc.: *The* tiger is a fierce beast. **d** That well-known person, place, or thing: *the* Pope; *the* Statue of Liberty. **e** That particular one which is most outstanding: *the* game to see. **f** My, your, his, her, our, their: He gave me a pat on *the* back; How is *the* family? **2** *adv.* By that much; by so much; to this extent: *the* more, *the* merrier.

the·a·ter or **the·a·tre** [thē′ə·tər] *n.* **1** A place built for the presentation of plays, films, etc. **2** The arts, crafts, etc., involved in presenting plays. **3** A room arranged with rising rows of seats. **4** A place or area where something happens or is carried on: a *theater* of war.

the·at·ri·cal [thē·at′ri·kəl] **1** *adj.* Having to do with the theater or with dramatic performances. **2** *n.* (*pl.*) Dramatic performances, especially by amateurs. **3** *adj.* Suited to being presented on a stage: a *theatrical* novel. **4** *adj.* Artificial and dramatic: He shouted in a *theatrical* manner. **— the·at′ri·cal·ly** *adv.*

Thebes [thēbz] *n.* **1** A city in ancient Egypt, famous for its temples and tombs. **2** A city in ancient Greece.

thee [thē] *pron.* An old singular form of *you*, used as the object of a verb or preposition: seldom used today.

theft [theft] *n.* The act or crime of stealing.

their [ŧħâr] *pron.* A possessive form of *they*; belonging to them: *their* toys.

theirs [thârz] *pron.* The one or ones belonging to or having to do with them: That house is *theirs.*

them [them *or* thəm] *pron.* The form of *they* used as the object of a verb or preposition: It belongs to *them;* Don't hurt *them.*

theme [thēm] *n.* **1** A topic to be discussed in speech or writing. **2** A short composition, especially one written as a school assignment. **3** The subject in a piece of fiction, work of art, etc. **4** The main melody of a piece of music. **5** A melody that identifies a radio or television program.

them·selves [them'selvz' *or* thəm·selvz'] *pron.* **1** The ones that they really are; their very own selves. *Themselves* in this sense is used to refer back to the subject *they* or to make the *they* more emphatic: They helped *themselves;* They *themselves* did the work. **2** Their normal, healthy, usual, or proper condition: They weren't *themselves* then.

then [then] **1** *adv.* At that time: It was cold *then.* **2** *adj.* In or of that time: the *then* president. **3** *adv.* Soon or just afterward; next in space or time: You speak first, and *then* it will be my turn. **4** *n.* The time mentioned or understood: I will be there by *then.* **5** *adv.* For that reason or by that means: If you succeed, *then* you'll be famous. **6** *adv.* In that case: If you won't do it, *then* I will. **7** *adv.* Also; besides: I like fruit, and *then* it's good for me. **8** *adv.* At another time: Now she's happy, *then* she's sad.

thence [thens] *adv.* **1** From that place. **2** From that time; after that time.

thence·forth [thens'fôrth'] *adv.* From that time on; thereafter.

thence·for·ward [thens'fôr'wərd] *adv.* **1** Thenceforth. **2** From that time or place forward.

the·oc·ra·cy [thē·ok'rə·sē] *n., pl.* **the·oc·ra·cies 1** Government of a country by a group of people that claims a god as its ruler or by a church. **2** A country that is ruled in such a way.

the·o·lo·gi·an [thē'ə·lō'jē·ən *or* thē'ə·lō'jən] *n.* A person who is learned in theology.

the·o·log·i·cal [thē'ə·loj'i·kəl] *adj.* Of or having to do with theology.

the·ol·o·gy [thē·ol'ə·jē] *n., pl.* **the·ol·o·gies 1** The study of God and religion. **2** A group of doctrines or beliefs set forth by a particular church or religious group.

the·o·rem [thē'ər·əm *or* thir'əm] *n.* **1** A proposition that can be proved or is taken to be true. **2** In mathematics, a proposition to be proved or one that has been proved or is taken to be true.

the·o·ret·ic [thē'ə·ret'ik] *adj.* Theoretical.

the·o·ret·i·cal [thē'ə·ret'i·kəl] *adj.* **1** Of, having to do with, or existing in theory. **2** Dealing best or easily with theory: a *theoretical* thinker. — **the'o·ret'i·cal·ly** *adv.*

the·o·rist [thē'ər·ist] *n.* A person who theorizes.

the·o·rize [thē'ə·rīz] *v.* **the·o·rized, the·o·riz·ing** To form or express a theory. ¶3

the·o·ry [thē'ə·rē *or* thir'ē] *n., pl.* **the·o·ries 1** A set of principles suggested as an explanation of observed events, often supported or proved by its usefulness in making predictions: the *theory* of relativity. **2** The basic principles of a branch of science, mathematics, or the arts: the *theory* of numbers; the *theory* of music. **3** Knowledge, as distinguished from its practical use: In *theory,* you are correct. **4** An unsupported opinion.

ther·a·peu·tic [ther'ə·pyōō'tik] *adj.* **1** Having healing powers; curative. **2** Having to do with or used in the treatment of disease.

ther·a·pist [ther'ə·pist] *n.* A person whose work is treating diseases, disabilities, etc.

ther·a·py [ther'ə·pē] *n., pl.* **ther·a·pies** Treatment, as medication, exercise, etc., meant to cure or correct diseases or disabilities.

there [thâr] **1** *adv.* In, at, or about that place: Put it *there.* **2** *adv.* To, toward, or into that place: I'm going *there* now. **3** *adv.* At that stage or point of action or time: Begin *there,* please. **4** *n.* That place, or stage, or point. **5** *adv.* In that matter: *There* I can't agree with you. **6** *interj.* An exclamation of relief, triumph, sympathy, etc.: *There!* It's over. ◆ *There* is used to introduce a verb, usually a form of the verb *be,* whose subject follows it: Once *there* were three bears; *There* ought to be a law. When used in this way, *there* is not stressed. However, when it is used to indicate place or time it receives a noticeable stress: Put the book *there.* The adverb *there* should never come before a noun, as in *that there girl. That girl there* is the proper order. *There* is also used before a verb to point out a thing or call attention to it: *There's* a good boy.

there·a·bout [thâr'ə·bout'] *adv.* Thereabouts.

there·a·bouts [thâr'ə·bouts'] *adv.* Near that number, quantity, degree, place, or time.

there·af·ter [thâr'af'tər] *adv.* After that time.

there·at [thâr'at'] *adv.* **1** At that place; there. **2** At that time. ◆ This word is seldom used today.

there·by [thâr·bī' *or* thâr'bī'] *adv.* **1** By means of that. **2** In connection with that. **3** Near there: seldom used today.

there·for [thâr·fôr'] *adv.* For this, that, it, or them: used mostly in legal documents.

there·fore [thâr'fôr'] *adv., conj.* For this or that reason or cause: A bus ran into her taxi; *therefore* she was late for work.

there·from [thâr·frum'] *adv.* From that place; from there: used mostly in legal documents.

there·in [thâr·in'] *adv.* **1** In that place or time. **2** In that matter or respect.

there·of [thâr·uv'] *adv.* **1** Of it, them, or that. **2** From that source: seldom used today.

there's [thârz] There is.

there·to [thâr′tōō′] *adv.* **1** To this, that, it, or them. **2** In addition; also. ◆ This word is seldom used today.

there·un·to [thâr′un·tōō′] *adv.* Thereto.

there·up·on [thâr′ə·pon′] *adv.* **1** Upon this, that, etc. **2** Just after, as a result of, or in response to that: He insulted me; *thereupon* I departed angrily.

there·with [thâr′with′ *or* thâr′with′] *adv.* **1** With this, that, etc. **2** Immediately afterward. ◆ This word is seldom used today.

there·with·al [thâr′with·ôl′] *adv.* **1** With all this or that. **2** Besides. ◆ This word is seldom used today.

ther·mal [thûr′məl] **1** *adj.* Of, having to do with, using, or caused by heat. **2** *adj.* Hot or warm. **3** *n.* A rising current of warm air.

ther·mo·dy·nam·ics [thûr′mō·dī·nam′iks] *n.* The branch of physics dealing with heat and its relations to other forms of energy. ◆ See -ICS.

ther·mom·e·ter [thər·mom′ə·tər] *n.* An instrument for measuring temperature, often consisting of a sealed glass tube containing a liquid that rises or falls with changes of temperature. ◆ *Thermometer* comes from the Greek *thermo-*, meaning *heat* or *warmth*, and *meter*, a *measuring instrument.*

ther·mo·nu·cle·ar [thûr′mō·n(y)ōō′klē·ər] *adj.* Of, related to, or using the fusion of atomic nuclei at high temperatures, as in stars or in a hydrogen bomb.

Ther·mop·y·lae [thər·mop′ə·lē] *n.* A mountain pass in Greece where, in 480 B.C., a small force of Spartans resisted the Persian army for three days and finally died rather than yield.

Ther·mos bottle [thûr′məs] A bottle, jug, etc., for keeping liquids hot or cold by means of a vacuum surrounding an inner container: a trademark. Also written **thermos bottle.**

ther·mo·stat [thûr′mə·stat] *n.* A device that automatically regulates temperature, as by turning a furnace on or off as required. ◆ *Thermostat* comes from *thermo-*, meaning *heat* or *warmth*, and another Greek word meaning *standing still.*

the·sau·rus [thə·sôr′əs] *n., pl.* **the·sau·ri** [thə·sôr′ī] *or* **the·sau·rus·es** A book that contains synonyms and antonyms arranged in categories.

these [thēz] *adj., pron.* Plural of THIS.

The·seus [thē′sōōs *or* thē′sē·əs] *n.* In Greek myths, a hero who killed the Minotaur.

the·sis [thē′sis] *n., pl.* **the·ses** [thē′sēz] **1** A proposition to be defended by argument. **2** A long, formal essay, as written by a candidate for a university degree.

thes·pi·an [thes′pē·ən] (*often written* **Thespian**) **1** *adj.* Of or having to do with the theater. **2** *n.* An actor or actress.

Thes·sa·ly [thes′ə·lē] *n.* A region of north central Greece.

thews [thyōōz] *n.pl.* **1** Muscles or sinews, especially strong ones. **2** Bodily strength; power.

they [thā] *pron.* **1** The plural of HE, SHE, or IT; the persons, things, etc., understood or being talked about: The animals knew where *they* could find water; Our team knew what *they* had to do to win. **2** People in general: *They* say the climate here is nice.

they'd [thād] **1** They had. **2** They would.

they'll [thāl] They will.

they're [thâr] They are.

they've [thāv] They have.

thi·a·mine [thī′ə·mēn *or* thī′ə·min] *n.* A part of the vitamin B complex. It is necessary to human nutrition.

thick [thik] **1** *adj.* Having opposite surfaces rather far apart: a *thick* post. **2** *adj.* Measuring a certain amount between opposite surfaces: an inch *thick.* **3** *adj.* Built heavily: *thick* legs. **4** *adj.* Close together or having parts that are close together in space or time; dense: a *thick* forest; *thick* grass; a *thick* fog; a *thick* rain of blows. **5** *adv.* So as to be thick: Slice the bread *thick.* **6** *n.* The most crowded or thickest part: the *thick* of the battle. **7** *adj.* Dense and difficult to pour: *thick* oil. **8** *adj.* Hard to hear or understand; not distinct: a *thick* accent; a *thick* voice. **9** *adj.* Dull; stupid. **10** *adj. informal* Very friendly. **— through thick and thin** Through both good times and difficult times. **— thick′ly** *adv.*

thick·en [thik′ən] *v.* **1** To make or become thick or thicker. **2** To make or become more complicated: The plot *thickens.*

thick·et [thik′it] *n.* A thick, dense growth, as of trees and bushes.

thick·head·ed [thik′hed′id] *adj.* Stupid.

thick·ness [thik′nis] *n.* **1** The condition or quality of being thick. **2** The measurement of a solid, other than its length or width. **3** A layer.

thick·set [thik′set′] *adj.* **1** Having a short, thick body; stout. **2** Set close together.

thick·skinned [thik′skind′] *adj.* **1** Having a thick skin. **2** Not bothered by insults, criticism, etc.

thief [thēf] *n., pl.* **thieves** [thēvz] A person who steals, especially secretly and without using violence.

thieve [thēv] *v.* **thieved, thiev·ing** To steal.

thiev·er·y [thē′vər·ē] *n., pl.* **thiev·er·ies** The practice or act of thieving; theft.

thiev·ish [thē′vish] *adj.* **1** Of or like a thief. **2** Tending to steal.

thigh [thī] *n.* The part of the leg between the hip and the knee.

thim·ble [thim′bəl] *n.* A cap of metal, plastic, etc., worn to protect the end of the finger that pushes the needle in sewing.

thin [thin] *adj.* **thin·ner, thin·nest,** *adv., v.* **thinned, thin·ning** **1** *adj.* Having opposite surfaces rather close together: *thin* walls. **2** *adj.* Few and scattered or having parts or members that are few and scattered; not dense; sparse: a *thin* hedge; *thin* grass; a *thin* drizzle. **3** *adj.* Lacking in body, substance, richness, force, etc.: a *thin* voice; *thin* blood; a *thin* excuse. **4** *adv.* So as to be thin: butter spread *thin*. **5** *adj*. Not fat or plump; lean; slender. **6** *adj*. Having a light texture and easy to pour; watery. **7** *v*. To make or become thin or thinner. **— thin′ly** *adv*.

thine [t͟hīn] *pron*. **1** The possessive case of THOU; an old singular form of YOURS. **2** A form of THY used before a word beginning with a vowel sound or, sometimes, before *h*.

thing [thing] *n*. **1** An object, event, creature, act, idea, etc., thought of as separate from all others: *A rose is a beautiful* thing; *What a nasty* thing *to do*; *What kind of* thing *is that?* **2** A person or animal: used to show pity, affection, contempt, etc.: "O, you poor *thing*!" "You stupid *thing*!" **3** (*pl*.) A matter or circumstance: *Things* have changed. **4** (*pl*.) Clothing or belongings: "Get your *things*." **5** A proper or fashionable act, manner of dress, etc.: used with *the*: Wearing big hats was *the thing* when she was young.

think [thingk] *v*. **thought** [thôt], **think·ing** **1** To use the mind; have thoughts or ideas; reason: I want to *think* before I make a decision. **2** To have in the mind: *Think* happy thoughts. **3** To examine or solve in the mind: *Think* the problem over for a day or two. **4** To decide: *Think* what you ought to say to him. **5** To have a particular opinion or idea; believe; imagine: I *think* that you are right. **6** To regard or consider as being: I *think* him guilty. **7** To plan or intend: I had *thought* to go today. **8** To expect: We had *thought* to see them here. **9** To remember: I never *thought* to tell him. **— think about** To consider; ponder. **— think better of 1** To decide against; reconsider: We *thought better of* that plan. **2** To form a better opinion of. **— think nothing of** To consider unimportant, easy to do, etc. **— think of 1** To bring to mind; recall. **2** To invent in the mind; imagine. **3** To have an opinion or attitude toward; regard. **4** To be considerate of: *Think of* our feelings. **5** To have concern: He *thinks* only of himself. **— think out** To work out, devise, or invent by thinking. **— think over** To ponder; consider. **— think twice** To consider carefully: I would *think twice* before leaving a steady job. **— think up** To arrive at or invent by thinking. **— think′er** *n*.

thin-skinned [thin′skind′] *adj*. **1** Having a thin skin. **2** Easily hurt or insulted; touchy.

third or **3rd** [thûrd] **1** *adj*. Next after the second. **2** *n*. The third one. **3** *adj*. Being one of three equal parts. **4** *n*. A third part. **5** *adv*. In the third order, rank, or place.

third degree Harsh or brutal questioning by the police to make a prisoner confess.

third·ly [thûrd′lē] *adv*. In the third place.

third person That form of a pronoun or verb used in referring to the person or thing spoken of: *He, she, it, they*, etc., are third person pronouns.

thirst [thûrst] **1** *n*. An uneasy feeling of dryness in the mouth and throat caused by a need to drink. **2** *n*. A bodily need for water. **3** *v*. To feel thirst. **4** *n*. A great longing or desire: a *thirst* for excitement. **5** *v*. To desire; long; yearn.

thirst·y [thûrs′tē] *adj*. **thirst·i·er, thirst·i·est 1** Having or feeling thirst. **2** Very dry; parched: a *thirsty* garden. **— thirst′i·ly** *adv*.

thir·teen or **13** [thûr′tēn′] *n., adj*. One more than twelve.

thir·teenth or **13th** [thûr′tēnth] **1** *adj*. Next after the twelfth. **2** *n*. The thirteenth one. **3** *adj*. Being one of thirteen equal parts. **4** *n*. A thirteenth part.

thir·ti·eth or **30th** [thûr′tē·ith] **1** *adj*. Tenth in order after the twentieth. **2** *n*. The thirtieth one. **3** *adj*. Being one of thirty equal parts. **4** *n*. A thirtieth part.

thir·ty or **30** [thûr′tē] *n., pl*. **thir·ties** or **30's 1** *n., adj*. Ten more than twenty. **2** *n*. (*pl*.) The years between the age of 30 and the age of 40.

this [t͟his] *pron. & adj., pl*. **these** [t͟hēz], *adv*. **1** *pron*. The person or thing mentioned, indicated, or understood: *This* is the place I told you about. **2** *adj*. Being the person or thing mentioned, indicated, or understood: *This* house is for sale. **3** *pron*. The person or thing indicated as nearer than or in contrast with someone or something else: Keep *this*, not that. **4** *adj*. Being the one that is nearer or in contrast: Do it *this* way, not that way. **5** *pron*. The fact, idea, statement, etc., about to be made clear: Listen to *this*! **6** *pron*. The present time: We should have returned before *this*. **7** *adv*. To this extent or degree: I didn't know things were *this* bad. ◆ *This* and *that* are often very similar in meaning. For instance, one could as well point something out by saying "Look at *this*," as by saying "Look at *that*." When they are used together, however, *this* refers to the thing closer in time or space, and *that* refers to the thing farther away.

this·tle [this′əl] *n*. A plant with prickly leaves, having flowers of purple, white, etc.

this·tle·down [this′əl·doun′] *n*. The silky fluff from the dry, ripe flower of a thistle.

thith·er [thit͟h′ər *or* t͟hit͟h′ər] *adv*. To or toward that place; in that direction.

tho [t͟hō] *conj., adv*. Another spelling of THOUGH.

thole [thōl] *n*. A peg, usually one of four set closely together in pairs on each side of a boat, used to hold an oar in rowing. It is often called a **thole pin.**

Thom·as [tom′əs] *n*. In the Bible, an Apostle who at first doubted the resurrection of Jesus.

Thom·as [tom′əs], **Dylan,** 1914–1953, British poet.

thong [thông] *n*. A narrow strip of leather, used as a whiplash or more often for tying or fastening.

Thor [thôr] *n*. In Norse myths, the god of war, thunder, and strength.

---

add, āce, câre, pälm;   end, ēqual;   it, īce;   odd, ōpen, ôrder;   took, pool;   up, bûrn;
ə = a in *above*, e in *sicken*, i in *possible*, o in *melon*, u in *circus*;   yoo = u in *fuse*;   oil;   pout;
check; ring; thin; t͟his; zh in *vision*.   For ¶ reference, see page 64 · HOW TO

tho·rac·ic [thô·ras′ik] *adj.* Of, having to do with, or near the thorax.

tho·rax [thôr′aks] *n.* **1** The part of the body between the neck and the abdomen, enclosed by the ribs; chest. **2** The middle region of the body of an insect.

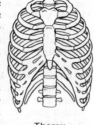

Thorax

Tho·reau [thôr′ō *or* thə·rō′], **Henry David**, 1817–1862, U.S. author and philosopher.

tho·ri·um [thôr′ē·əm] *n.* A gray, radioactive, metallic element that is sometimes used in the generation of atomic energy.

thorn [thôrn] *n.* **1** A sharp, leafless spine growing from a plant. **2** A plant that bears thorns. **3** A person or thing that is painful or annoying.

thorn·y [thôr′nē] *adj.* **thorn·i·er, thorn·i·est** **1** Full of thorns. **2** Sharp, as a thorn. **3** Causing trouble or annoyance.

thor·ough [thûr′ō] *adj.* **1** Complete and detailed in every respect: a *thorough* investigation. **2** Painstaking and careful: a *thorough* worker. **3** Utter; absolute; outright: a *thorough* idiot. **— thor′ough·ly** *adv.*

thor·ough·bred [thûr′ō·bred′] **1** *adj.* Bred from pure stock, as an animal. **2** *n.* (*written* **Thoroughbred**) A distinct breed of racing or jumping horse, originally bred in England from three famous sires. **3** *n.* A thoroughbred animal. **4** *n.* A person of culture and breeding.

thor·ough·fare [thûr′ō·fâr′] *n.* **1** A roadway open to the public. **2** A highway.

thor·ough·go·ing [thûr′ə·gō′ing] *adj.* Thorough: a *thoroughgoing* search.

those [ᵺōz] *adj., pron.* Plural of THAT: Whose are *those* books? *Those* are mine.

thou [ᵺou] *pron.* An old singular form of YOU, used as the subject of a verb: seldom used today.

though [ᵺō] **1** *conj.* Despite the fact that: *Though* it's hot, it's nice here; *Though* it's hard, we'll try anyhow. **2** *conj.* And yet; still; however: I'm well, *though* not strong. **3** *conj.* Even if: *Though* I were starving, I would never beg. **4** *adv.* Nevertheless; however: The rain was falling; we continued on our way, *though*. **— as though** As if.

thought[1] [thôt] *n.* **1** The act or process of using the mind; thinking. **2** The result of thinking; an idea, judgment, etc. **3** A way of thinking, as of a particular people or period: modern *thought*. **4** Consideration or attention: Give it some *thought*. **5** Intention or expectation: We gave up all *thought* of going. **6** A bit; a small amount: Go a *thought* slower.

thought[2] [thôt] Past tense and past participle of THINK.

thought·ful [thôt′fəl] *adj.* **1** Full of or occupied with thought. **2** Showing or causing thought: a *thoughtful* book. **3** Considerate; attentive: a *thoughtful* gift. **— thought′ful·ly** *adv.* **— thought′ful·ness** *n.*

thought·less [thôt′lis] *adj.* **1** Without thought; careless. **2** Inconsiderate of others. **— thought′·less·ly** *adv.* **— thought′less·ness** *n.*

thou·sand or **1000** [thou′zənd] *n., adj.* Ten times one hundred.

thou·sandth or **1000th** [thou′zəndth] **1** *adj.* Hundredth in order after the nine hundredth. **2** *n.* The thousandth one. **3** *adj.* Being one of a thousand equal parts. **4** *n.* A thousandth equal part.

Thrace [thrās] *n.* A region and province of ancient Rome in the eastern Balkan Peninsula.

thral·dom [thrôl′dəm] *n.* Another spelling of THRALLDOM.

thrall [thrôl] *n.* **1** Slavery or subjection; bondage. **2** Someone in this condition; slave.

thrall·dom [thrôl′dəm] *n.* Slavery; bondage.

thrash [thrash] *v.* **1** To beat with or as with something that is swung violently; whip. **2** To defeat soundly: The team *thrashed* its opponents. **3** To make or cause to make violent swinging or twisting movements: The fish *thrashed* about in the net. **4** To thresh (grain). **— thrash out** To settle by thorough discussion, as a problem. **— thrash′er** *n.*

thrash·er [thrash′ər] *n.* An American songbird resembling a thrush and having a long tail.

thread [thred] **1** *n.* A thin cord made of several strands of cotton, nylon, etc., twisted together. **2** *v.* To pass a thread through the eye of (a needle). **3** *v.* To arrange or string on a thread: to *thread* beads. **4** *n.* Anything resembling a thread, as a fine strand or a thin beam of light. **5** *n.* The spiral groove cut into a screw, nut, etc. **6** *v.* To cut such a thread on or in: to *thread* a hole. **7** *v.* To make (one's way) with care, as through a crowd. **8** *v.* To make one's way through: to *thread* a maze. **9** *n.* Something, like a series of events, a train of thought, etc., that continues or runs through something else: the many *threads* of violence in his novel.

thread·bare [thred′bâr′] *adj.* **1** So badly worn that the threads show, as a rug or garment. **2** Wearing threadbare clothing: a clean but *threadbare* old man. **3** Commonplace or worn out; stale: *threadbare* humor.

threat [thret] *n.* **1** A warning or a promise that one intends to hurt or punish another person or thing. **2** A sign or indication of something bad or unfavorable to come: a *threat* of rain.

threat·en [thret′(ə)n] *v.* **1** To make or utter a threat: The judge *threatened* to put us in jail if we didn't pay the fine. **2** To make a threat against: to *threaten* one's life. **3** To put in danger; menace: Fire *threatened* the hut. **4** To give a warning or sign of: The smoking volcano *threatened* another eruption.

three or **3** [thrē] *n., adj.* One more than two.

three·fold [thrē′fōld′] **1** *adj.* Three times as great or as many: a *threefold* amount. **2** *adv.* So as to be three times as great or as many: to increase *threefold*. **3** *adj.* Made up of or having three parts: a *threefold* accusation.

three·score [thrē′skôr′] *n., adj.* Sixty.

three·some [thrē′səm] *n.* A group of three persons.

thren·o·dy [thren′ə·dē] *n., pl.* **thren·o·dies** An ode or song of sorrow for the dead; dirge.

thresh [thresh] *v.* **1** To beat, shake, etc. (ripened grain) to separate the seeds from the straw and husks. **2** To move or thrash about. — **thresh out** To thrash out.

thresh·er [thresh′ər] *n.* **1** A person or thing that threshes, especially a large machine for threshing. **2** A large shark of warm seas.

thresh·old [thresh′(h)ōld] *n.* **1** The bar of wood, stone, etc., placed under a door. **2** The entrance or beginning of anything.

threw [thrōō] Past tense of THROW.

thrice [thrīs] *adv.* Three times.

thrift [thrift] *n.* Care and economy in handling expenses; the habit of saving.

thrift·y [thrif′tē] *adj.* **thrift·i·er, thrift·i·est** **1** Careful about expenses; economical: a *thrifty* wife. **2** Growing vigorously, as a plant.

thrill [thril] **1** *v.* To feel or cause to feel great or tingling emotion or excitement. **2** *n.* A feeling of great excitement. **3** *n.* Something that causes such a feeling. **4** *v.* To vibrate or tremble: Her voice *thrilled* with emotion.

thrill·er [thril′ər] *n.* A person or thing that thrills, especially a story, movie, play, etc., that is full of suspense and excitement.

thrive [thrīv] *v.* **thrived** or **throve, thrived** or **thriv·en** [thriv′ən], **thriv·ing** **1** To prosper or be successful. **2** To grow vigorously; flourish.

thro′ or **thro** [thrōō] *prep., adv., adj.* Other spellings of THROUGH.

throat [thrōt] *n.* **1** The upper part of the passage leading from the back of the mouth to the stomach and lungs. **2** The front part of the neck under the chin. **3** The voice. **4** Any narrow part or entrance: the *throat* of a vase. **— a lump in the throat** A difficulty in swallowing, usually due to a feeling, as when one tries not to cry.

Human throat

(labels: pharynx, uvula, nasal cavity, palate, tongue, tonsils, larynx, vocal chords, esophagus, epiglottis, trachea)

throat·y [thrō′tē] *adj.* **throat·i·er, throat·i·est** Having or producing a deep, husky sound; guttural: She has a *throaty* voice.

throb [throb] *v.* **throbbed, throb·bing,** *n.* **1** *v.* To beat or pulsate, especially rapidly or violently, as the heart from excitement, etc. **2** *n.* A quick or strong beat or pulsation.

throe [thrō] *n.* (*often pl.*) **1** A violent pang or pain. **2** (*pl.*) A difficult struggle or ordeal: a country in the *throes* of civil war.

throm·bo·sis [throm·bō′sis] *n.* The formation or presence of a clot that blocks a blood vessel.

throne [thrōn] *n.* **1** The raised, often ornamented seat used by a monarch or high church official on important occasions. **2** The office or power of a monarch: to renounce a *throne*.

throng [throng] **1** *n.* A great crowd; multitude. **2** *v.* To move in or form a crowd. **3** *v.* To crowd into or around: The students *thronged* the street.

throt·tle [throt′(ə)l] *n., v.* **throt·tled, throt·tling** **1** *n.* A valve controlling the supply of steam to a steam engine or of fuel and air to an internal-combustion engine. **2** *n.* The lever or pedal that operates this valve. **3** *v.* To reduce or stop the flow of steam or fuel to (an engine). **4** *v.* To slow (an engine) in this way. **5** *v.* To strangle or choke. **6** *v.* To suppress; stop: to *throttle* objections.

through [thrōō] **1** *prep., adv.* Into one side, end, point, etc., and out the other: The ball went *through* the window; The bullet went right *through*. **2** *prep.* From one place to another or to all parts of: to ride *through* the streets; Odors spread *through* the house. **3** *adj.* Making few or no stops along its route: a *through* bus. **4** *adj.* Open; clear: a *through* route. **5** *prep.* During the whole time of: He worked *through* the summer. **6** *adv.* To success or conclusion: to see something *through*. **7** *adj.* Finished; done: We're *through* for the day. **8** *prep.* To or at the end of: I'm *through* that ordeal. **9** *prep.* By way of: He left *through* the window. **10** *prep.* By means of, with the help of, or on account of: He succeeded *through* effort; He got the job *through* a friend. **11** *adv.* Completely; thoroughly: to be soaked *through*. ◆ *Through* goes back to the Old English word *thurh*. Eventually the [r] came to be pronounced before the vowel rather than after it.

through·out [thrōō·out′] *adv., prep.* All through; all about: to search a house *throughout*; to travel *throughout* the nation.

throve [thrōv] A past tense of THRIVE.

throw [thrō] *v.* **threw, thrown, throw·ing,** *n.* **1** *v.* To cause to fly through the air by or as by a rapid motion of the arm; fling; hurl; toss. **2** *v.* To make or do by throwing: to *throw* a pitch. **3** *n.* An act of throwing. **4** *n.* The distance a thing is thrown. **5** *v.* To direct or cast: to *throw* a beam of light. **6** *v.* To cause to fall: The horse *threw* its rider. **7** *v.* To defeat in wrestling. **8** *v.* To put on or off carelessly: to *throw* on a coat. **9** *v.* To bring or put into a place or condition, often suddenly or violently: It *threw* us into panic; *Throw* him into the street. **10** *v.* To connect or disconnect (a switch, clutch, motor, etc.) by moving a lever or other control. **11** *v. informal* To lose deliberately, as a game, contest, etc. **— throw away 1** To cast off; discard. **2** To waste; squander. **— throw in** To add at no cost, often as an inducement to buy. — **throw off 1** To rid oneself of; cast away. **2** To give off; emit. **— throw out 1** To throw away; discard. **2** To offer casually: to *throw out* suggestions. **3** In baseball, to assist in putting

---

add, āce, câre, pälm;   end, ēqual;   it, īce;   odd, ōpen, ôrder;   tŏŏk, pōōl;   up, bûrn;
ə = a in *above*, e in *sicken*, i in *possible*, o in *melon*, u in *circus*;   yōō = u in *fuse*;   oil;   pout;
    check; ring; thin; this; zh in *vision*.   For ¶ reference, see page 64 · HOW TO

out (a runner) by throwing the ball to a teammate who makes the play. — **throw over** 1 To overturn. 2 To discard. 3 To abandon or jilt. — **throw up** 1 To vomit. 2 To give up; release. 3 To build hurriedly. — **throw′er** n.

throw·back [thrō′bak′] n. 1 A return or reversion to some ancestral type or character. 2 An example of such reversion: a *throwback* to some Viking ancestor.

thrown [thrōn] Past participle of THROW.

thru [thrōō] prep., adv., adj. Another spelling of THROUGH.

thrum [thrum] v. **thrummed, thrum·ming,** n. 1 v. To pluck on, as a guitar, etc., especially idly. 2 v. To drum or tap idly with the fingers. 3 n. A monotonous drumming sound.

thrush [thrush] n. Any of a large group of songbirds, as the robin, bluebird, etc.

thrust [thrust] v. **thrust, thrust·ing,** n. 1 v. To push or shove with force or on sudden impulse: She *thrust* the child into my arms; He *thrust* her aside roughly. 2 n. A sudden, forceful push or shove. 3 v. To stab or run through. 4 v. To force one's way, as into a crowd. 5 n. A propelling force, as produced by an airplane propeller, jet engine, rocket, etc.

thru·way [thrōō′wā′] n. A large superhighway.

thud [thud] n., v. **thud·ded, thud·ding** 1 n. A deep, dull sound, as of a heavy weight striking the floor. 2 v. To hit or fall on something with a thud: The sack of flour *thudded* to the floor.

thug [thug] n. A violent or brutal gangster or hoodlum.

thumb [thum] 1 n. The short, thick finger nearest the wrist. 2 n. The part of a glove or mitten that covers the thumb. 3 v. To handle, press, rub, soil, etc., with the thumb: to *thumb* the pages of a book. 4 v. *informal* To ask for (a ride) by signaling with the thumb. — **thumbs down** *informal* No: a phrase or sign indicating disapproval or rejection. — **under the thumb of** Under the control or influence of.

thumb·nail [thum′nāl′] 1 n. The nail of the thumb. 2 adj. Brief but giving important details: Write a *thumbnail* sketch of your life.

thumb·screw [thum′skrōō′] n. 1 A screw made to be turned by the thumb and forefinger. 2 An instrument of torture for compressing thumbs.

thumb·tack [thum′tak′] n. A tack with a flat, broad head, easily pushed in by the thumb.

thump [thump] 1 n. A blow made with a blunt or heavy object. 2 n. The dull, heavy sound of a thump. 3 v. To beat with or as with thumps; pound: The dog *thumped* his tail on the floor.

thun·der [thun′dər] 1 n. The sound that accompanies lightning, caused by the sudden heating and expansion of the air along the path of the electrical discharge. 2 n. Any loud, rumbling noise. 3 v. To make or give forth thunder or a sound like it. 4 v. To speak or express with a thundering sound: to *thunder* a warning.

thun·der·bolt [thun′dər·bōlt′] n. 1 A flash of lightning together with a clap of thunder. 2 Something very shocking and sudden.

thun·der·clap [thun′dər·klap′] n. 1 A loud crash of thunder. 2 Something sudden or violent.

thun·der·cloud [thun′dər·kloud′] n. A dark, heavy cloud highly charged with electricity.

thun·der·head [thun′dər·hed′] n. A rounded mass of cumulus cloud that often develops into a thundercloud.

thun·der·ing [thun′dər·ing] adj. 1 Of, related to, like, or accompanied by thunder. 2 *informal* Unusually great, large, or extreme.

thun·der·ous [thun′dər·əs] adj. Of or like thunder. — **thun′der·ous·ly** adv.

thun·der·show·er [thun′dər·shou′ər] n. A rain shower with thunder and lightning.

thun·der·storm [thun′dər·stôrm′] n. A storm with thunder and lightning.

thun·der·struck [thun′dər·struk′] adj. Amazed, astonished, shocked, or puzzled, as with fear, surprise, etc.: We were *thunderstruck* when the team lost.

Thurs·day [thûrz′dē or thûrz′dā] n. The fifth day of the week.

thus [thus] adv. 1 In this, that, or the following way: Do it *thus*. 2 To such a degree; so: *Thus* far he seems to be improving. 3 Therefore; hence: *Thus* we knew he was wrong.

thwack [thwak] 1 v. To strike with something flat; whack. 2 n. A blow with something flat.

thwart [thwôrt] 1 v. To keep from doing or succeeding; foil; balk: to *thwart* an attempt by the prisoners to escape. 2 adj. Lying, moving, or extending across; transverse. 3 n. A seat extending across a boat for an oarsman. 4 n. A crosswise brace in a canoe.

thy [thī] adj. An old singular form of YOUR: seldom used today.

thyme [tīm] n. A small thing related to mint, with fragrant leaves used as a seasoning.

thy·mus [thī′məs] n. A small glandular organ in the upper part of the chest, thought to help in immunizing the body against certain diseases.

thy·roid [thī′roid] 1 n. A large gland situated in front of and on each side of the windpipe. It secretes hormones that regulate body growth and metabolism. 2 adj. Of or from the thyroid: a *thyroid* hormone.

thyroid gland The thyroid.

thy·rox·in [thī·rok′sin] n. A thyroid hormone containing iodine.

thy·self [thī·self′] pron. An old singular form of YOURSELF: seldom used today.

ti [tē] n. In music, a syllable used to represent the seventh tone of a major scale or the second tone of a minor scale, or in a fixed system the tone B.

Ti The symbol for the element TITANIUM.

ti·ar·a [tē·âr′ə or tē·är′ə] n. 1 A semicircular band of jewels or flowers worn on a woman's head on formal occasions. 2 The Pope's triple crown, worn on certain special occasions.

Ti·ber [tī′bər] n. A river in Italy flowing through Rome.

Ti·bet [ti·bet′] n. A region in sw China in very high country north of India. — **Ti·bet′an** n., adj.

tib·i·a [tib′ē·ə] *n.*, *pl.* **tib·i·ae** [tib′i·ē] or **tib·i· as** The larger of the two bones that extend from the knee to the ankle; shin bone.

tic [tik] *n.* An involuntary twitch of a muscle, especially in the face.

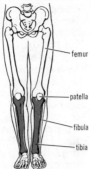

tick[1] [tik] **1** *n.* A light sound, as that made by a watch, clock, or other mechanism. **2** *v.* To make a tick. **3** *v.* To indicate by ticking: to *tick* off seconds. **4** *n.* A mark, as a check or dash, used to check off items. **5** *v. British* To mark with ticks: to *tick* off items.

tick[2] [tik] *n.* Any of several small, flat animals related to spiders. Ticks suck blood from men and animals.

tick[3] [tik] *n.* The outer covering of a mattress or pillow, usually made of strong cloth.

tick·er [tik′ər] *n.* An instrument that receives and prints stock prices, news, etc., on a tape.

ticker tape The paper tape on which a ticker records stock prices.

tick·et [tik′it] **1** *n.* A card or slip which entitles the holder to ride on a bus or train, enter a theater, etc. **2** *n.* A label or tag: This *ticket* on the dress gives its price, color, and size. **3** *v.* To put a ticket on; label. **4** *n.* A legal summons to appear in court, as for a traffic violation. **5** *n.* A list of candidates for nomination or election, supported by a party or group; slate.

tick·ing [tik′ing] *n.* A strong cotton or linen fabric used for ticks, awnings, etc.

tick·le [tik′əl] *v.* **tick·led, tick·ling,** *n.* **1** *v.* To touch or scratch so as to cause a laugh or twitch: He *tickled* me. **2** *v.* To have such a sensation: My foot *tickles.* **3** *n.* The act of tickling. **4** *n.* The feeling produced by tickling. **5** *v. informal* To delight: I'm *tickled* to be going.

tick·lish [tik′lish] *adj.* **1** Sensitive to tickling. **2** Liable to be upset or easily offended: John is *ticklish* about his large ears. **3** Difficult; delicate: a *ticklish* situation.

tid·al [tīd′(ə)l] *adj.* Of, having to do with, or caused by the tides: a *tidal* wave.

tidal wave A huge, destructive wave caused by an undersea earthquake, hurricane, etc.

tid·bit [tid′bit′] *n.* A choice bit, as of food or gossip.

tide [tīd] *n.*, *v.* **tid·ed, tid·ing 1** *n.* The periodic rise and fall of the surface of an ocean or of waters connected with an ocean, caused by the attraction of the sun and moon. The tide rises and falls twice daily, or about every 12 hours. **2** *n.* Anything that rises and falls like the tide: the *tide* of men's fortunes. **3** *n.* A tendency, current, or drift: the *tide* of events. **4** *v.* To give

necessary help to: This money will *tide* you over until tomorrow. **— turn the tide** To change the course or outcome: One battle can *turn the tide* of a war.

tide·land [tīd′land′] *n.* Land covered and uncovered by the rise and fall of the tide.

tide·wa·ter [tīd′wô′tər] *n.* **1** Water influenced by the tide. **2** Any area, such as a seacoast, having such water. **3** *adj. use: tidewater* country.

ti·dings [tī′dingz] *n.pl.* Information; news.

ti·dy [tī′dē] *adj.* **ti·di·er, ti·di·est,** *v.* **ti·died, ti·dy·ing 1** *adj.* Neat and orderly: a *tidy* desk. **2** *v.* To make tidy or straighten: to *tidy* a room. **3** *adj. informal* Fairly large: a *tidy* sum. **— ti′· di·ly** *adv.* **— ti′di·ness** *n.*

tie [tī] *v.* **tied, ty·ing,** *n.* **1** *v.* To fasten, as by knotting cord, rope, etc.: to *tie* a bundle. **2** *v.* To lace up or tie a knot or bow in: to *tie* shoes; to *tie* a necktie. **3** *v.* To make or form, as a knot or bow. **4** *n.* A string, cord, lace, etc., with which something is tied. **5** *n.* A necktie. **6** *n.* Any bond or obligation: *ties* of affection. **7** *v.* To attach or bind: He's *tied* to his family. **8** *n.* In music, a curved sign that indicates that two notes of the same pitch are to be played as one continuous tone. **9** *n.* A crossbar or beam to hold rails in place. **10** *v.* To make or become equal: Both of them *tied* for first place. **11** *n.* A contest in which neither side wins; draw: The game was a *tie.* **12** *n.* The score of such a contest. **— tie down** To hinder, restrict, or confine. **— tie up 1** To fasten or tie tightly. **2** To block or hinder: to *tie up* traffic. **3** To keep or be busy or unavailable: We're *tied up* Monday.

Tien·tsin [tin′(t)sin′] *n.* A large seaport in NE China.

tier [tir] *n.* A row of things, as seats, placed one above another.

Two tiers of seats in a theater

Tier·ra del Fue·go [tyer′ä del fwā′gō] A group of islands at the southern end of South America, some belonging to Chile and some to Argentina.

tie-up [tī′up′] *n.* **1** A situation in which action or progress has been blocked. **2** *informal* A connection or relation.

tiff [tif] *n.* A minor quarrel.

ti·ger [tī′gər] *n.* A large, powerful, flesh-eating animal of the cat family. It has a tawny body with wavy black stripes and is found in the jungles of Asia.

tiger lily A tall lily with orange flowers spotted with black.

tiger moth A striped or spotted moth.

tight [tīt] **1** *adj.* Firmly fixed or fastened in place; secure: a *tight* screw. **2** *adj.* Not letting air, water, etc., in: a *tight* container. **3** *adj.* Taut: a *tight* wire. **4** *adv.* In a tight manner: to hold

---

add, āce, câre, pälm;   end, ēqual;   it, īce;   odd, ōpen, ôrder;   tŏŏk, pool;   up, bûrn;
ə = a in *above*, e in *sicken*, i in *possible*, o in *melon*, u in *circus*;   yōō = u in *fuse*;   oil;   pout;
check;   ring;   thin;   this;   zh in *vision*.   For ¶ reference, see page 64 · HOW TO

tight; to stop a bottle *tight*. **5** *adj*. Fitting closely or too closely: *tight* shoes. **6** *adj. informal* Difficult; troublesome: to be in a *tight* spot. **7** *adj*. Hard to get; scarce: *tight* money. **8** *adj. informal* Stingy. **9** *adj*. Very close; even: a *tight* contest. **— sit tight** To keep one's position without moving or acting. **— tight′ly** *adv*. **— tight′ness** *n*.

tight·en [tīt′(ə)n] *v*. To make or become tight or tighter: to *tighten* a knot.

tight·fist·ed [tīt′fis′tid] *adj*. Stingy.

tight-lipped [tīt′lipt′] *adj*. Unwilling to talk much or give away secrets.

tight·rope [tīt′rōp′] *n*. A rope or cable stretched tight above the ground, on which acrobats do balancing acts, etc.

tights [tīts] *n.pl*. A tight garment usually covering the legs and body below the waist.

tight·wad [tīt′wod′] *n. U.S. informal* A person who hates to spend money; miser.

ti·gress [tī′gris] *n*. A female tiger.

Ti·gris [tī′gris] *n*. A river in sw Asia flowing from Turkey through Iraq to the Euphrates.

tike [tīk] *n*. Another spelling of TYKE.

til·de [til′də] *n*. A pronunciation mark (~) showing certain special pronunciations. In Spanish it is placed over an "ñ" to show that the "n" is pronounced [ny], as in señor.

tile [tīl] *n., v*. **tiled, til·ing 1** *n*. A thin, hard plate, often of baked clay, used to cover roofs, floors, etc., or as an ornament. **2** *v*. To cover or provide with tiles. **3** *n*. A thin block, usually marked, and used in games. **4** *n*. A short pipe used as a drain.

til·ing [tī′ling] *n*. Tiles or a tile covering.

till¹ [til] **1** *prep., conj*. Until. **2** *prep*. Before: used with *not*: I can't go *till* noon.

till² [til] *v*. To work or cultivate (soil) by plowing, hoeing, etc. **— till′er** *n*.

till³ [til] *n*. A drawer, tray, etc., in which money or valuables are kept.

till·age [til′ij] *n*. The cultivation of land.

till·er [til′ər] *n*. A bar or handle for turning the rudder in steering a boat.

tilt [tilt] **1** *v*. To incline at an angle; lean; tip: *Tilt* your head; The boat *tilted*. **2** *n*. Any inclination, slant, or slope. **3** *n*. A medieval sport in which two mounted knights, charging with lances, attempt to unseat each other; joust. **4** *v*. To practice this sport; joust. **5** *n*. A quarrel or dispute. **— full tilt** Full speed or force.

A tilt

tim·ber [tim′bər] **1** *n*. Wood or a piece of wood suitable for use in building. **2** *v*. To provide with timber. **3** *n*. Trees or woodland.

tim·bered [tim′bərd] *adj*. **1** Made of timber. **2** Covered with growing trees.

tim·ber·land [tim′bər·land′] *n*. Land covered with forests.

timber line The line or height, as on a mountain or in arctic regions, above or beyond which trees do not grow.

timber wolf A large gray or brownish gray wolf of the forests of Canada and the northern U.S.

tim·bre [tim′bər *or* tam′bər] *n*. The quality of a sound, aside from its pitch or loudness, that distinguishes it from another sound.

tim·brel [tim′brəl] *n*. An ancient tambourine.

time [tim] *n., adj., v*. **timed, tim·ing 1** *n*. All of the moments that have been, are, or ever will be: *time* everlasting. **2** *n*. The moment, interval, or period in or during which something exists, happens, continues, or is done: the *time* of youth. **3** *n*. A definite or appointed moment, hour, day, period, etc.: The *time* is 6:30; to serve *time* in prison. **4** *n*. A system of reckoning or measuring passage of time: standard *time*. **5** *v*. To measure or record the speed or duration of: to *time* a race. **6** *n*. An occurrence or reoccurrence of some action, happening, etc.: the first *time*; three *times* at bat. **7** *adj*. Of or having to do with time: a *time* study. **8** *n*. (*often pl*.) A period of time having certain characteristics: modern *times*; the *time* of Christ. **9** *n*. (*often pl*.) The conditions existing at any specific period of time: *Times* are hard today. **10** *v*. To choose or arrange the time or occasion for: He *timed* his arrival for noon. **11** *adj*. Set to operate at a certain time: a *time* bomb. **12** *n*. A fitting moment: *time* to go. **13** *n*. Leisure: no *time* to read. **14** *n*. A person's experience or reaction: to have a good *time*. **15** *n*. In music or poetry, the tempo or rate of movement: waltz *time*. **16** *v*. To cause to match or correspond in tempo, rhythm, etc.: They *timed* their steps to the music. **17** *n*. The period during which a worker works or the pay given for this: to receive *time* and a half for overtime. **— against time** As quickly as possible, so as to finish at a certain time: to work *against time*. **— at the same time** However: *At the same time*, I don't think it'll work. **— at times** Sometimes; occasionally: *At times* he barks. **— behind the times** Old-fashioned. **— for the time being** For now; temporarily. **— from time to time** Now and then; occasionally. **— in no time** Right away; immediately. **— in time 1** Before it is too late. **2** Eventually. **3** In the proper meter, tempo, etc. **— make time** To go, work, make, etc., rapidly. **— on time 1** Not late; prompt. **2** Paid for or to be paid for in installments. **— time after time** or **time and again** Repeatedly. **— times 1** To multiply by. **2** Multiplied by: Five *times* five is 25.

time exposure 1 Exposure of photographic film for a relatively long time. **2** A photograph made by such an exposure.

time-honored [tīm′on′ərd] *adj.* Followed or honored because of long use or existence: *time-honored* ways. ¶1

time·keep·er [tīm′kē′pər] *n.* **1** A person or thing that keeps time. **2** A person who times a race or other sports event. **3** A person who records the hours worked by employees.

time·less [tīm′lis] *adj.* **1** Having no ending; eternal. **2** Not limited to a certain time or era: the *timeless* arguments as to the nature of God. **3** Not changed or affected by time: the *timeless* beauty of a Greek temple.

time·ly [tīm′lē] *adj.* **time·li·er, time·li·est** Happening or coming at a good or suitable time: a *timely* letter. **— time′li·ness** *n.*

time-out [tīm′out′] *n.* In sports, a short recess not counted in the playing time of a game.

time·piece [tīm′pēs′] *n.* A watch or clock.

tim·er [tī′mər] *n.* **1** A timekeeper. **2** A stopwatch.

time·ta·ble [tīm′tā′bəl] *n.* A schedule showing the time at which something happens, as the time of arrivals and departures for trains, buses, etc.

time zone One of the 24 zones on the earth, within each of which a single standard time is used or followed. The time in any zone is an hour earlier or later than that in the next one.

tim·id [tim′id] *adj.* Fearful or shy. **— ti·mid·i·ty** [ti·mid′ə·tē] *n.* **— tim′id·ly** *adv.*

tim·ing [tī′ming] *n.* The act or art of finding and then using the rhythm, tempo, or speed that will give the most effective result: A swimmer needs good *timing* in his strokes.

tim·or·ous [tim′ər·əs] *adj.* Fearful; timid.

tim·o·thy [tim′ə·thē] *n.* A perennial grass with long leaves and spikes, grown as fodder.

Tim·o·thy [tim′ə·thē] *n.* A companion and disciple of St. Paul. Two New Testament epistles of St. Paul are addressed to him.

tim·pa·ni [tim′pə·nē] *n.pl.* A set of large, bowl-shaped, metal drums with parchment heads that can be tuned to various pitches; kettledrums.

tin [tin] *n., v.* **tinned, tin·ning 1** *n.* A soft, white metallic element used in many alloys. **2** *adj. use:* tin alloys. **3** *n.* Tin plate. **4** *adj. use:* a *tin* can. **5** *v.* To coat or cover with tin or solder. **6** *n.* A tin container or box.

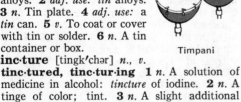

Timpani

tinc·ture [tingk′chər] *n., v.* **tinc·tured, tinc·tur·ing 1** *n.* A solution of medicine in alcohol: *tincture* of iodine. **2** *n.* A tinge of color; tint. **3** *n.* A slight additional flavor, quality, etc.: a *tincture* of sadness in his smile. **4** *v.* To give a slight tint, flavor, etc., to.

tin·der [tin′dər] *n.* Anything dry that will catch fire easily on contact with a spark.

tin·der·box [tin′dər·boks′] *n.* **1** A metal box for holding tinder and usually flint and steel. **2** Anything very flammable, explosive, touchy, etc.

tine [tīn] *n.* A spike or prong, as of a fork or antler.

tin·foil [tin′foil′] *n.* A thin sheet of tin or a tin alloy, used as a wrapping material, etc.

tinge [tinj] *v.* **tinged, tinge·ing** or **ting·ing,** *n.* **1** *v.* To give a trace of color to: The cold *tinged* his face with red. **2** *n.* A trace of color. **3** *v.* To change or modify in some slight way: laughter *tinged* with tears. **4** *n.* A slight trace of something: a *tinge* of sadness.

tin·gle [ting′gəl] *v.* **tin·gled, tin·gling,** *n.* **1** *v.* To give or have a prickly or slightly stinging feeling: Winter *tingles* the skin; to *tingle* with excitement. **2** *n.* Such a feeling.

tink·er [tingk′ər] **1** *n.* A person who travels about and mends pots, pans, and other utensils. **2** *v.* To mend or work as a tinker. **3** *v.* To work or repair in a clumsy way. **4** *v.* To putter; fuss: to *tinker* around the house.

tin·kle [ting′kəl] *n., v.* **tin·kled, tin·kling 1** *n.* A slight, clear, metallic sound, as of a small bell. **2** *v.* To make or cause to make this sound.

tin·ny [tin′ē] *adj.* **tin·ni·er, tin·ni·est 1** Made of or containing tin. **2** Like tin in appearance. **3** Cheap or poor in quality: a *tinny* old car. **4** Having a thin sound, like that of tin being struck. **5** Tasting of tin, as food from a can.

tin plate Sheet iron or steel plated with tin.

tin·sel [tin′səl] *n., v.* **tin·seled** or **tin·selled, tin·sel·ing** or **tin·sel·ling,** *adj.* **1** *n.* Very thin, glittering bits or strips of metal or foil, used as a decoration. **2** *v.* To decorate with tinsel. **3** *adj.* Made of or decorated with tinsel. **4** *n.* Anything cheap but showy in appearance. **5** *adj.* Cheap; showy: *tinsel* emotions. **6** *v.* To give a showy appearance to: to *tinsel* one's true feelings.

tin·smith [tin′smith′] *n.* A person who works with tin or tin plate.

tint [tint] **1** *n.* A slightly different shade of any one color. **2** *n.* Any pale or delicate color. **3** *n.* A slight trace or quality: a *tint* of fear in her voice. **4** *v.* To give a tint to.

tin·ware [tin′wâr′] *n.* Articles made of tin.

ti·ny [tī′nē] *adj.* **ti·ni·er, ti·ni·est** Very small: *tiny* wrists.

-tion A suffix meaning: **1** The act or process of, as in *rejection*, the act or process of rejecting. **2** The condition or state of being, as in *completion*, the condition or state of being completed. **3** The result of, as in *connection*, the result of connecting.

tip¹ [tip] *n., v.* **tipped, tip·ping 1** *n.* The point or end of anything tapering: the *tip* of his finger. **2** *n.* A piece or part made to form the end of anything: the gold *tip* of the pen. **3** *v.* To furnish or cover with a tip: to *tip* a cane with rubber. **4** *v.* To form the tip of.

---

add, āce, câre, pälm; end, ēqual; it, īce; odd, ōpen, ôrder; tŏŏk, pōōl; up, bûrn; ə = a in *above*, e in *sicken*, i in *possible*, o in *melon*, u in *circus*; yōō = u in *fuse*; oil; pout; check; ring; thin; this; zh in *vision*. For ¶ reference, see page 64 · HOW TO

tip² [tip] *n., v.* **tipped, tip·ping 1** *n.* A small gift of money for service rendered. **2** *v.* To give a tip to: to *tip* a waiter. **3** *n.* A piece of helpful, expert, or secret information or advice: He gave me a *tip* on how to win. **4** *v.* To inform with a tip: to *tip* off the newspapers. **5** *v.* To hit very lightly: He *tipped* the pitch. **6** *n.* A light tap.

tip³ [tip] *v.* **tipped, tip·ping,** *n.* **1** *v.* To lean or cause to lean; tilt: The table is *tipping* slightly. **2** *v.* To raise slightly: to *tip* one's hat. **3** *n.* A slanting or inclined position; tilt. **4** *v.* To overturn or upset: to *tip* over a chair.

tip·pet [tip′it] *n.* **1** A scarf for the neck and shoulders, with ends hanging down in front. **2** Formerly, the long, narrow, hanging part of a hood, sleeve, cape, etc.

tip·ple [tip′əl] *v.* **tip·pled, tip·pling,** *n.* **1** *v.* To drink alcoholic liquor frequently. **2** *n.* Alcoholic liquor. — **tip′pler** *n.*

tip·sy [tip′sē] *adj.* **tip·si·er, tip·si·est** Somewhat drunk; high. — **tip′si·ly** *adv.*

tip·toe [tip′tō] *n., v.* **tip·toed, tip·toe·ing 1** *n.* The tip of a toe. **2** *v.* To walk softly on or as on one's toes. — **on tiptoe 1** On the tips of the toes. **2** Eagerly: waiting *on tiptoe.* **3** Secretly or quietly.

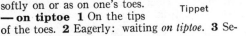

Tippet

tip·top [tip′top′] **1** *n.* The highest point. **2** *adj.* At the tiptop. **3** *adj. informal* Excellent; first-rate: in *tiptop* condition for the race.

ti·rade [tī′rād *or* tə·rād′] *n.* A long angry speech.

tire¹ [tīr] *v.* **tired, tir·ing 1** To make or become weary or exhausted: The hike *tired* her. **2** To make or become bored or impatient: The lecture *tired* us all.

tire² [tīr] *n.* A circular tube of rubber and cords, filled with air, used on a wheel of a car, bus, etc. A tire absorbs shock and provides traction.

tired [tīrd] *adj.* Weary; exhausted.

tire·less [tīr′lis] *adj.* Never tiring: a *tireless* worker. — **tire′less·ly** *adv.*

tire·some [tīr′səm] *adj.* Tedious; boring.

'tis [tiz] It is: used mostly in poems.

tis·sue [tish′oo] *n.* **1** In a plant or animal, a group of cells that are somewhat alike and perform a particular function: bone *tissue.* **2** A light, absorbent paper. **3** Tissue paper. **4** Any gauzelike fabric. **5** A group of things woven together; network: a *tissue* of myths.

tissue paper A very thin, soft paper for wrapping and protecting delicate articles.

tit [tit] *n.* A titmouse, titlark, or any of certain other small birds.

Ti·tan [tīt′(ə)n] *n.* **1** In Greek myths, one of a race of giant gods. **2** (*written* **titan**) A person of great size, strength, skill, etc.

Ti·ta·ni·a [ti·tā′nē·ə] *n.* Queen of the fairies, as in Shakespeare's play *A Midsummer Night's Dream.*

ti·tan·ic [tī·tan′ik] *adj.* Very great; huge.

ti·ta·ni·um [tī·tā′nē·əm] *n.* A dark gray, metallic element, often added to steel to toughen it.

tit·bit [tit′bit′] *n.* A British word for TIDBIT.

tithe [tīth] *n., v.* **tithed, tith·ing 1** *n.* A tax or offering of ten per cent of one's income to support a church. **2** *n.* A small or tenth part of anything. **3** *v.* To tax with a tithe: to *tithe* the entire parish. **4** *v.* To give or pay a tithe or a tenth part of: to *tithe* one's income.

Ti·tian [tish′ən], 1477?–1576, Venetian painter.

tit·il·late [tit′ə·lāt] *v.* **tit·il·lat·ed, tit·il·lat·ing** To tickle or excite pleasantly. — **tit′il·la′·tion** *n.*

tit·lark [tit′lärk′] *n.* A pipit.

ti·tle [tīt′(ə)l] *n., v.* **ti·tled, ti·tling 1** *n.* The name of a book, play, poem, etc. **2** *v.* To give a title to; name: to *title* a new book. **3** *n.* A word or name showing one's rank, office, profession, etc.: "Doctor" and "professor" are *titles,* as are the words "Mister," "Miss," "lord," etc. **4** *n.* The right to own or possess a piece of property, as a house or car. **5** *n.* The deed or other document that is evidence of such a right. **6** *n.* In some sports, a championship: to play for the *title.*

ti·tled [tīt′(ə)ld] *adj.* Having a title, especially one of nobility.

title page The page of a book on which the title appears and usually the name of the author, the publisher, and the place of publication.

tit·mouse [tit′mous′] *n., pl.* **tit·mice** [tit′mīs′] A chickadee.

tit·ter [tit′ər] **1** *v.* To laugh in a suppressed way, as from nervousness or in making fun; giggle; snicker. **2** *n.* Such a laugh.

tit·tle [tit′(ə)l] *n.* **1** A very small bit. **2** A small mark in writing, as the dot over an *i.*

tit·tle-tat·tle [tit′(ə)l·tat′(ə)l] *n., v.* **tit·tle-tat·tled, tit·tle-tat·tling 1** *n.* Foolish talk or gossip. **2** *v.* To gossip. **3** *n.* A tattletale.

tit·u·lar [tich′oo·lər *or* tit′yə·lər] *adj.* **1** In name or title only. **2** Of or having to do with a title. **3** Having a title.

TNT *or* **T.N.T.** [tē′en′tē′] *n.* An explosive containing nitrogen, used in blasting and warfare.

to [too, *unstressed* tə] **1** *prep.* In the direction of: *to* the right. **2** *adv.* Toward something else; forward: The flat side is wrong side *to.* **3** *prep.* As far as or until: Go *to* the end of the line; from Christmas *to* New Year's. **4** *prep.* In contact with; against; on: pinned *to* the wall. **5** *adv.* Shut; closed: Pull the door *to.* **6** *prep.* For the purpose of: He came *to* the rescue. **7** *prep.* In relation to; concerning: His affairs are nothing *to* me. **8** *adv.* Into action or work: They fell *to* and ate. **9** *prep.* Resulting in: blown *to* bits; *to* my surprise. **10** *prep.* Along with or accompanying: salt added *to* gravy. **11** *prep.* Agreeable with; for: not *to* my liking. **12** *prep.* Compared with: a score of 15 *to* 14. **13** *prep.* In each: three feet *to* a yard. **14** *prep.* Belonging or used in connection with: the key *to* the door. **15** *adv.* Into consciousness: to come *to.* **16** *prep.* *To* is also used with an indirect object after a verb, as in "Give the ring *to* me," or *to* can be used after a noun or adjective to indicate a particular viewpoint or condition, as in "He was always a hero *to* me; They were not known *to* us," or to point out the receiver of an action, as in "She gave a talk *to* the children." ◆ *To* is also used to indicate the infinitive or is often used in place of it: I don't know whether *to* go or *to* stay; He knows a lot more than he seems *to*. — **to and fro** Back and forth.

toad [tōd] *n*. A small, tailless, froglike animal that lives chiefly on land.

toad·stool [tōd′stool′] *n*. Any mushroom with an umbrella-shaped top, especially a poisonous one.

toad·y [tō′dē] *n*., *pl*. **toad·ies**, *v*. **toad·ied**, **toad·y·ing** 1 *n*. A person who fawns on or flatters others to gain favors from them. 2 *v*. To act as a toady to (someone).

A typical toad

toast[1] [tōst] 1 *v*. To brown by heating, as bread, etc. 2 *n*. Toasted bread. 3 *v*. To make or become warm before a fire.

toast[2] [tōst] 1 *v*. To drink in honor of (a person, event, etc.). 2 *n*. The act of or a proposal for toasting. 3 *n*. A person, event, sentiment, etc., that is toasted: the *toast* of the town.

toast·er [tōs′tər] *n*. A device for making toast.

toast·mas·ter [tōst′mas′tər] *n*. A person who gives toasts and introduces speakers at banquets.

to·bac·co [tə·bak′ō] *n*., *pl*. **to·bac·cos** or **to·bac·coes** 1 A plant with fragrant flowers and numerous large leaves. 2 The dried leaves of this plant used for smoking, chewing, etc.

to·bog·gan [tə·bog′ən] 1 *n*. A long, narrow sled without runners, used for coasting. 2 *v*. To coast on a toboggan. 3 *v*. To move downward swiftly: Prices *tobogganed* yesterday. ◆ *Toboggan* comes from a French-Canadian word for *sleigh*, which in turn is from an Algonquian Indian word.

toc·sin [tok′sin] *n*. 1 An alarm signal given on a bell. 2 A bell used to give an alarm.

to·day [tə·dā′] 1 *n*. The present day, time, or age: *Today* is Monday. 2 *adv*. On or during the present day: We'll go *today*. 3 *adv*. Nowadays: *Today* traveling is convenient.

tod·dle [tod′(ə)l] *v*. **tod·dled**, **tod·dling** To walk unsteadily and with short steps, as a little child. — **tod′dler** *n*.

tod·dy [tod′ē] *n*., *pl*. **tod·dies** A drink made with liquor, hot water, sugar, and lemon.

to·do [tə·doo′] *n*., *pl*. **to·dos** *informal* A fuss.

toe [tō] *n*., *v*. **toed**, **toe·ing** 1 *n*. One of the five parts at the end of a foot. 2 *n*. The portion of a shoe, sock, skate, etc., that covers the toes. 3 *v*. To touch with the toes: to *toe* the starting line. 4 *n*. Something like or suggesting a toe. — **on one's toes** Alert. — **toe the line** or **toe the mark** To follow strictly the rules or orders.

toe·nail [tō′nāl′] *n*. The nail on a human toe.

tof·fee or **tof·fy** [tôf′ē] *n*. A kind of brittle taffy.

to·ga [tō′gə] *n*. The loose outer garment worn in public by a citizen of ancient Rome.

to·geth·er [tə·geth′ər] *adv*. 1 With each other: to sing *together*. 2 Into union or contact with each other: Fasten the two sections *together*. 3 In the same place or at the same spot: Bring all the old books *together*. 4 At the same time; simultaneously: to sound the horns *together*. 5 In or into harmony, agreement, etc.: These colors go well *together*.

togs [togz] *n.pl*. Clothes; outfit: tennis *togs*.

Toga

toil [toil] 1 *n*. Hard work; tiring labor. 2 *v*. To work hard. 3 *v*. To walk, go, etc., with difficulty: to *toil* up the steps. — **toil′er** *n*.

toi·let [toi′lit] 1 *n*. A fixture with a seat atop a bowl in which bodily wastes may be flushed away. 2 *n*. A room with a toilet; bathroom. 3 *n*. The act or process of grooming oneself. 4 *adj*. Used in grooming: *toilet* articles.

toi·let·ry [toi′lit·rē] *n*., *pl*. **toi·let·ries** Any toilet article, as a comb, soap, etc.

toi·lette [toi·let′] *n*. 1 The act of grooming oneself. 2 A person's dress or style of dress.

toilet water A scented liquid containing some alcohol, used after bathing, shaving, etc.

toils [toilz] *n.pl*. Anything that traps or ensnares.

toil·some [toil′səm] *adj*. Demanding hard work; laborious: a *toilsome* duty.

to·ken [tō′kən] 1 *n*. A visible sign or symbol: a *token* of love. 2 *adj*. Done or given merely to fulfill an obligation, and often in as small a way as possible: *token* payments; *token* integration. 3 *n*. A metal piece used in place of money, as for a fare. 4 *n*. Something given as a sign of friendship; memento; keepsake.

To·ky·o [tō′kē·ō] *n*. The capital of Japan.

told [tōld] Past tense and past participle of TELL.

tol·er·a·ble [tol′ər·ə·bəl] *adj*. 1 Capable of being borne or put up with; bearable: a *tolerable* grief. 2 Neither good nor bad; fair: a *tolerable* play. — **tol′er·a·bly** *adv*.

tol·er·ance [tol′ər·əns] *n*. 1 An attitude toward others which is fair and free from emotional bias regardless of differences in beliefs, customs, race, etc. 2 A similar attitude toward ideas and beliefs contrary to one's own. 3 The ability to withstand the action of a drug or poison without ill effects.

tol·er·ant [tol′ər·ənt] *adj*. Having or showing tolerance: a *tolerant* person; a *tolerant* attitude. — **tol′er·ant·ly** *adv*.

---

add, āce, câre, pälm; end, ēqual; it, īce; odd, ōpen, ôrder; took, pool; up, bûrn; ə = a in *above*, e in *sicken*, i in *possible*, o in *melon*, u in *circus*; yoo = u in *fuse*; oil; pout; check; ring; thin; this; zh in *vision*. For ¶ reference, see page 64 · HOW TO

tol·er·ate [tol′ər·āt] v. **tol·er·at·ed, tol·er·at· ing** **1** To allow to be or permit without opposition: to *tolerate* other beliefs. **2** To bear or endure: He couldn't *tolerate* spicy foods. **3** To be immune to, as to a poison or drug.

tol·er·a·tion [tol′ə·rā′shən] n. Tolerance, especially in matters of religion.

toll[1] [tōl] n. **1** A charge, tax, or service fee, as on a bridge, turnpike, etc. **2** An amount of suffering endured, lives lost, etc.: The famine took a heavy *toll* in deaths.

toll[2] [tōl] **1** v. To sound or cause to sound slowly and at regular intervals: The bell *tolled* all day. **2** n. The act or sound of tolling. **3** v. To announce by tolling, as the hour, a funeral, etc.

toll·gate [tōl′gāt′] n. A gate on a bridge or road where tolls are paid.

Tol·stoy [tol′stoi or tōl′stoi], **Leo,** 1828–1910, Russian novelist.

Tol·tec [tol′tek] **1** n. A member of a nation of ancient Mexican Indians. **2** adj. Of or having to do with the Toltecs.

tom·a·hawk [tom′ə·hôk] **1** n. An axlike weapon used by North American Indians. **2** v. To strike or kill with a tomahawk. ◆ *Tomahawk* goes back to an Algonquian Indian word meaning *he cuts.*

Tomahawks

to·ma·to [tə·mā′tō or tə·mä′· tō] n., pl. **to·ma·toes** **1** The large, round, pulpy fruit of a perennial plant, yellow or red when ripe and widely used as a vegetable. **2** This plant.

tomb [tōōm] n. A place for the burial of the dead, as a vault or grave.

tom·boy [tom′boi] n. A girl who prefers boys' games, dress, etc. ◆ *Tomboy* was formed by combining *Tom*, a boy's name, with *boy*.

tomb·stone [tōōm′stōn′] n. A stone marking a person's burial place, usually inscribed with the person's name and the dates of his birth and death.

tom·cat [tom′kat′] n. A male cat.

tome [tōm] n. A large book; volume.

tom·fool·er·y [tom′fōō′lər·ē] n., pl. **tom·fool· er·ies** Foolish behavior.

to·mor·row [tə·mor′ō or tə·môr′ō] **1** n. The next day after today. **2** n. Some time in the future. **3** adv. On or for tomorrow: We'll go *tomorrow*.

tom·tit [tom′tit′] n. Any of various small birds, as a titmouse or wren.

tom-tom [tom′tom′] n. A drum, originally of India and Africa, usually beaten with the hands.

ton [tun] n. A measure of weight, as the **short ton** of 2,000 pounds, used in the U.S. and Canada, the **long ton** of 2,240 pounds, used in England, and the **metric ton** of 1,000 kilograms.

to·nal [tō′nəl] adj. Of or having to do with a tone or tones, or with tonality.

to·nal·i·ty [tō·nal′ə·tē] n., pl. **to·nal·i·ties** **1** The tendency, in most music, for one tone to

dominate and become central to all the others. **2** A key, scale, etc., in which this happens. **3** The general color scheme or tone of a painting.

tone [tōn] n., v. **toned, ton·ing** **1** n. A sound having a definite pitch. **2** n. A sound, especially in relation to its quality, volume, duration, or pitch: a harsh *tone*; a loud *tone*; a short *tone*; a high *tone*. **3** n. Any musical interval equal to the interval between do and re in a major scale: A is one *tone* above G. **4** n. A shade, hue, or tint: *tones* of red. **5** n. A manner of speech or writing that expresses a certain mood, style, or feeling: to answer in a happy *tone*. **6** n. A certain style or character: the subdued *tone* of the room; the moral *tone* of a country. **7** v. To give a certain tone to. **8** v. To blend or harmonize. **9** n. Health or firmness of a muscle, organ, etc.: to lose muscle *tone* through lack of exercise. — **tone down** To soften the tone of. — **tone up** To make brighter, livelier, or stronger.

tongs [tôngz] n.pl. An implement for grasping or lifting objects, usually consisting of a pair of arms hinged or pivoted together.

tongue [tung] n., v. **tongued, tongu·ing** **1** n. The movable muscular organ in the mouth that is used in eating, tasting, and, in man, in speaking. **2** n. An animal's tongue, as of beef, prepared as food. **3** n. The power or manner of speech: to lose one's *tongue*; a smooth *tongue*. **4** n. A language or dialect: the Greek *tongue*. **5** n. Anything resembling a tongue, as a slender projection of land or water, a strip of leather under the laces of a shoe, a jet of flame, etc. **6** v. To begin (a note or notes) by moving the tongue, as in certain wind instruments. — **hold one's tongue** To keep quiet. — **on the tip of one's tongue** **1** Ready to be said. **2** Almost said.

tongue-tied [tung′tīd′] adj. **1** Unable to speak or move the tongue properly because the membrane connecting the bottom of the tongue to the mouth is too short. **2** Speechless or nearly so from shyness, embarrassment, etc.

ton·ic [ton′ik] **1** adj. Giving, increasing, or restoring strength or energy; stimulating: A cold shower can have a *tonic* effect on the body. **2** n. Anything, as certain medicines, supposed to make a person feel better or more energetic. **3** n. In music, the keynote of a scale or key. **4** adj. Of or having to do with a keynote: a *tonic* chord.

to·night [tə·nīt′] **1** n. This night; the night of today. **2** adv. In or during tonight.

ton·nage [tun′ij] n. **1** The capacity of a ship expressed in terms of one ton per 100 cubic feet. A tonnage of 800 tons means 80,000 cubic feet of cargo space. **2** The total amount of shipping, as of a country or port, expressed in tons. **3** The total weight of any load in tons. **4** A shipping tax given at a rate per ton.

ton·sil [ton′səl] n. One of two oval masses of soft glandular tissue, one on each side of the throat back of the mouth.

ton·sil·lec·to·my [ton′sə·lek′tə·mē] n., pl. **ton· sil·lec·to·mies** A surgical operation in which the tonsils are removed.

ton·sil·li·tis [ton′sə·lī′tis] *n.* An inflammation and swelling of the tonsils.

ton·so·ri·al [ton·sôr′ē·əl] *adj.* Of or having to do with barbers: often used humorously.

ton·sure [ton′shər] *n.* **1** The shaving of all or part of the head, as of a priest or monk. **2** The part of the head left bare by tonsure.

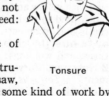

Tonsure

too [to͞o] *adv.* **1** In addition; also: I'm going *too.* **2** More than is necessary; excessively: *too* large. **3** Very: That's not *too* likely. **4** *informal* Indeed: You are *too* coming!

took [to͝ok] Past tense of TAKE.

tool [to͞ol] **1** *n.* An instrument, as a hammer, saw, chisel, etc., used for doing some kind of work by hand. **2** *n.* A similar instrument driven by a motor. **3** *v.* To make, shape, or ornament with a tool: to *tool* book covers. **4** *v.* To provide with tools. **5** *n.* A person or thing used to accomplish something: Words are a writer's *tools.*

toot [to͞ot] **1** *n.* A short note or blast on a horn, whistle, etc. **2** *v.* To sound with short blasts: to *toot* a horn. **— toot′er** *n.*

tooth [to͞oth] *n., pl.* **teeth** [tēth] **1** One of the hard, white, bony parts in the mouth, used to bite and chew food, and in animals, often used as a weapon. **2** Something resembling a tooth in form or use, as one of the projecting points on a comb, fork, saw, or gearwheel. **3** Appetite; liking: used chiefly in the expression **sweet tooth,** a liking for sweet foods. **— tooth and nail** With all possible strength; fiercely.

tooth·ache [to͞oth′āk′] *n.* A pain in a tooth.

tooth·brush [to͞oth′brush′] *n.* A small brush for cleaning the teeth.

toothed [to͞otht *or* to͞othd] *adj.* **1** Having teeth or teeth of a certain kind: sharp-*toothed.* **2** Notched or indented: a *toothed* leaf.

tooth·less [to͞oth′lis] *ad!.* Without teeth.

tooth·paste [to͞oth′pāst′] *n.* A paste used in cleaning the teeth.

tooth·pick [to͞oth′pik′] *n.* A small sliver of wood, plastic, etc., used for removing particles of food from between the teeth.

tooth·some [to͞oth′səm] *adj.* Pleasant or tasty.

top¹ [top] *n., v.* **topped, top·ping,** *adj.* **1** *n.* The highest or uppermost part, side, surface, etc., of anything: the *top* of the mountain; the *top* of the bookcase. **2** *n.* A lid or cover: a bottle *top.* **3** *v.* To form the top of: Snow *topped* the highest mountains. **4** *v.* To provide with a top, lid, etc.: to *top* a bottle. **5** *v.* To reach or pass over the top of: to *top* a horse in gym. **6** *n.* The crown of the head. **7** *n.* The part of a plant that grows above the ground: carrot or beet *tops.* **8** *v.* To cut, trim, or remove the top of, as a plant or tree.

9 *adj.* Of, having to do with, or forming the top or upper part: the *top* layer of soil. **10** *n.* The highest degree, range, rank, etc.: the *top* of one's ambition; the *top* of one's profession. **11** *adj.* Highest or greatest in amount, degree, rank, etc.: *top* authors; *top* speed. **12** *v.* To be or do more, greater, better, etc., than: to *top* someone at tennis. **13** *v.* To be at or reach the top of: She *topped* the graduating class. **14** *n.* The highest pitch or volume: at the *top* of his voice. **15** *n.* The best or choicest part: the *top* of the crop. **16** *n.* A platform at the head of the lower section of a ship's mast. **— on top 1** Very successful. **2** In a position of power or dominance. **— on top of 1** Resting or pressing on from above. **2** In addition to. **— top off** To complete or finish with a final touch.

top² [top] *n.* A cone-shaped toy with a point on which it is made to spin.

to·paz [tō′paz] *n.* A mineral found in the form of transparent or translucent crystals, yellow to brownish, that are valued as gems.

top·coat [top′kōt′] *n.* A lightweight overcoat.

To·pe·ka [tə·pē′kə] *n.* The capital of Kansas.

top·gal·lant [tə·gal′ənt *or* top′gal′ənt] **1** *n.* The third section above the deck of a ship's mast, above the topmast. **2** *n.* The sail that belongs to this section. **3** *adj.* Having to do with this section.

top hat A man's hat for formal wear, having a tall, cylindrical crown and a narrow brim.

top-heav·y [top′hev′ē] *adj.* **top-heav·i·er, top-heav·i·est** Having the top part heavier than the base; inclined to topple over.

top·ic [top′ik] *n.* A subject discussed in speech or in writing.

top·i·cal [top′i·kəl] *adj.* **1** Of or having to do with topics. **2** Having to do with a subject of current or local interest.

top·knot [top′not′] *n.* A crest of feathers or a knot of hair on top of the head.

top·mast [top′məst *or* top′mast′] *n.* The mast next above the lowest mast of a ship.

top·most [top′mōst′] *n.* Being at the very top: the *topmost* shelf of a bookcase.

top·o·graph·i·cal [top′ə·graf′i·kəl] *adj.* Of or having to do with topography; descriptive of an area or place.

to·pog·ra·phy [tə·pog′rə·fē] *n., pl.* **to·pog·ra·phies 1** The physical features of a region or place, as mountains, rivers, roads, parks, etc. **2** The art of showing these on a map or chart. **— to·pog′ra·pher** *n.*

top·ple [top′əl] *v.* **top·pled, top·pling 1** To push and cause to fall by its own weight: She *toppled* over the stack of plates. **2** To fall over, as if from its own weight: The baby took a few steps and *toppled.*

top·sail [top′səl *or* top′sāl′] *n.* A sail set next above the lowest sail on a mast.

add, āce, câre, pälm; end, ēqual; it, īce; odd, ōpen, ôrder; to͝ok, po͞ol; up, bûrn;
ə = a in *above,* e in *sicken,* i in *possible,* o in *melon,* u in *circus;* yo͞o = u in *fuse;* oil; pout;
check; ring; thin; this; zh in *vision.* For ¶ reference, see page 64 · HOW TO

top·soil [top′soil′] *n.* The surface or top layer of soil, usually more fertile than the soil beneath.

top·sy·tur·vy [top′sē·tûr′vē] **1** *adv.* Upside-down. **2** *adv.* In great disorder. **3** *adj.* Being upside-down or in great disorder.

toque [tōk] *n.* A close-fitting, brimless hat worn by women.

Tor·ah [tôr′ə *or* tō′rə] *n.* In Judaism, the Pentateuch, or first five books of the Old Testament.

torch [tôrch] *n.* **1** A source of light, as a burning stick of wood that can be carried in the hand. **2** Anything that guides or sheds light. **3** A device that gives off a very hot flame, as a blowtorch. **4** *British* A flashlight.

torch·light [tôrch′līt′] *n.* The light of a torch or torches.

tore [tôr] Past tense of TEAR[1].

to·re·a·dor [tôr′ē·ə·dôr′] *n.* A bullfighter.

tor·ment [*n.* tôr′ment, *v.* tôr·ment′] **1** *n.* Great bodily pain or mental agony. **2** *v.* To cause to suffer physically or mentally: My mother's tight shoes *tormented* her. **3** *n.* A person or thing that torments. **4** *v.* To make miserable or annoyed: The patient *tormented* his nurse with complaints. — **tor·men′tor** *or* **tor·men′ter** *n.*

torn [tôrn] Past participle of TEAR[1].

tor·na·do [tôr·nā′dō] *n., pl.* **tor·na·does** *or* **tor·na·dos** A violent, destructive, whirling wind, forming a funnel-shaped cloud that extends downward from a mass of cloud and moves along in a narrow path.

To·ron·to [tə·ron′tō] *n.* The capital of Ontario, Canada, on Lake Ontario.

tor·pe·do [tôr·pē′dō] *n., pl.* **tor·pe·dos** *or* **tor·pe·does**, *v.* **tor·pe·doed**, **tor·pe·do·ing 1** *n.* A large, underwater projectile that moves under its own power. It is shaped like a cigar and is filled with high explosives that blow up when it strikes a ship. **2** *v.* To damage or sink (a ship) with a torpedo.

torpedo boat A small, swift warship equipped with tubes for discharging torpedos.

tor·pid [tôr′pid] *adj.* **1** Not able to feel or move much, if at all, as a hibernating animal; dormant. **2** Sluggish; dull: The big meal made us all *torpid.*

tor·por [tôr′pər] *n.* The condition of being torpid or sluggish; stupor.

torque [tôrk] *n.* **1** A force acting in a way that tends to produce rotation. **2** The degree to which a force can make something rotate.

tor·rent [tôr′ənt] *n.* **1** A stream of water flowing with great speed and violence. **2** Any great or rapid flow: a *torrent* of tears; a *torrent* of words.

tor·ren·tial [tô·ren′shəl] *adj.* Of, like, or resulting from a torrent.

tor·rid [tôr′id] *adj.* Very hot; scorching; burning: a *torrid* climate.

tor·sion [tôr′shən] *n.* **1** The act of twisting. **2** A twisted condition. **3** The twisting of a body along the direction of its greatest length.

tor·so [tôr′sō] *n.* **1** The human body, apart from the head, arms, and legs; the trunk. **2** A sculpture of a human trunk.

tor·til·la [tôr·tē′yä] *n.* In Mexico, a flat cake made of coarse cornmeal baked on a sheet of iron or a slab of stone.

tortoise [tôr′təs] *n., pl.* **tor·tois·es** *or* **tortoise 1** A turtle, especially one of the species that live entirely on land. **2** A slow-moving person or thing.

tortoise shell The shell of certain turtles. It is brown and mottled with yellow and is much used in making combs and ornaments.

Tortoise, to 18 in. long

tor·tu·ous [tôr′chōō·əs] *adj.* **1** Full of twists, turns, and windings: a *tortuous* mountain road. **2** Not straightforward; devious: a *tortuous* argument. ◆ *Tortuous* and *torturous* both go back to the Latin word *tortus*, meaning *twisted*. Something *tortuous* has many twists or turns: a *tortuous* path. Something *torturous* often involves twisting part of the body to cause pain: a *torturous* punishment.

tor·ture [tôr′chər] *n., v.* **tor·tured, tor·tur·ing 1** *n.* The infliction of great physical pain. **2** *n.* Great mental or physical suffering: the *torture* of an abscessed tooth; the *torture* of embarrassment. **3** *v.* To cause to suffer great pain. **4** *v.* To twist or turn the form, meaning, etc., of. — **tor′tur·er** *n.*

tor·tur·ous [tôr′chər·əs] *adj.* Extremely painful; causing torture. ◆ See TORTUOUS.

To·ry [tôr′ē] *n., pl.* **To·ries 1** During the American Revolution, a colonist who was on the British side. **2** A member of an old British political party, officially named the **Conservative Party** since about 1832. **3** (*often written* **tory**) A person who is very conservative, especially in politics.

toss [tôs] **1** *v.* To throw or fling or be thrown or flung about: The wind *tossed* the treetops; The ships *tossed* in the stormy sea. **2** *v.* To throw lightly and easily with the hand: Please *toss* me an apple. **3** *v.* To lift with a quick motion, as the head. **4** *v.* To throw (a coin) into the air to decide something, the outcome depending on the side on which the coin falls. **5** *v.* To throw oneself from side to side; move about restlessly, as in sleep. **6** *n.* The act of tossing. — **toss off 1** To drink all at once in one draft. **2** To do, write, etc., quickly and in an offhand manner.

toss·up *or* **toss-up** [tôs′up′] *n. informal* **1** The throwing up of a coin to decide something. **2** An even chance: It's a *tossup* whether he wins or not.

tot [tot] *n.* **1** A little child; toddler. **2** A small drink or portion of liquor.

to·tal [tōt′(ə)l] *n., adj., v.* **to·taled** *or* **to·talled, to·tal·ing** *or* **to·tal·ling 1** *n.* The whole sum or amount; whole. **2** *adj. use:* the *total* amount. **3** *v.* To find the total of; add: to *total* a column of figures. **4** *v.* To come to or reach as a total: The bill *totaled* $26. **5** *adj.* Complete; absolute: The storm caused *total* destruction of the town. — **to′tal·ly** *adv.*

to·tal·i·tar·i·an [tō·tal′ə·târ′ē·ən] *adj.* Of or having to do with a type of government controlled exclusively by one political party and forbidding all other parties.

to·tal·i·ty [tō·tal′ə·tē] *n.*, *pl.* **to·tal·i·ties** The whole sum or quantity.

tote [tōt] *v.*, **tot·ed, tot·ing** *informal* **1** To carry about on one's person, as a gun. **2** To haul; carry, as supplies.

to·tem [tō′təm] *n.* **1** An animal, plant, or other natural object thought by certain primitive tribes to be the ancestor or guardian spirit of the clan. **2** A carved or painted image of such an animal, plant, or object.

totem pole A tall pole carved or painted with symbols of totems by North American Indians, especially on the NW coast.

tot·ter [tot′ər] *v.* **1** To walk feebly and unsteadily: The old lady *tottered* across the room. **2** To shake or sway as if about to fall: People *totter* when they are dizzy.

tou·can [tōō′kan] *n.* A large bird of tropical America with brightly colored plumage and a huge, thin-walled bill.

touch [tuch] **1** *v.* To bring a bodily part, especially a finger, fingers, or the hand, into contact with; feel: to *touch* a statue. **2** *v.* To come into contact by hitting or striking lightly; tap: Whoever *touches* the tree trunk first wins the race. **3** *v.* To be in contact or in contact with: His nose and chin almost *touch*; The car behind us is *touching* ours. **4** *n.* The act of touching: Some seed pods burst at a *touch*. **5** *n.* A being touched. **6** *n.* The sense by which the size, shape, and texture of outside objects are felt by any part of the body, especially the fingers. **7** *n.* The sensation one gets from touching something: Sandpaper has a rough *touch*. **8** *n.* Communication; connection: The two old friends had kept in *touch* since their school days. **9** *v.* To reach to; come up to: His head *touched* the ceiling. **10** *v.* To handle or disturb: One shouldn't *touch* an injured person before the doctor comes. **11** *v.* To handle, use, eat, or drink: I could never *touch* oysters or clams. **12** *v.* To damage slightly: The tomato plants were *touched* by an early frost. **13** *v.* To stir the emotions of, especially to sympathy or gratitude: Your kind letter *touched* us

Totem pole

Toucan, about 20 in. long

all. **14** *v.* To talk briefly: The statesmen *touched* on many topics. **15** *v.* To have to do with; concern: Our decisions *touch* your future plans. **16** *v.* To come up to; equal: My athletic abilities will never *touch* those of my brother. **17** *v.* To occupy or concern oneself with; set about: He hasn't *touched* his homework. **18** *n.* A small quantity; dash: a *touch* of garlic. **19** *n.* A slight attack or twinge: a *touch* of arthritis. **20** *n.* A slight detail or change given to a story, picture, etc. **21** *n.* A stroke, as with a pencil or brush. **22** *n.* The manner in which a musician presses the keys of a piano, etc. **23** *n.* The manner or style in which an artist, workman, author, etc., works. **— touch off 1** To cause to explode. **2** To cause to happen or begin. **— touch up** To make small changes so as to improve.

touch·down [tuch′doun′] *n.* In football, a play worth six points, ending with the ball in the possession of an attacking player over the opponent's goal line.

touch·ing [tuch′ing] **1** *adj.* Appealing to the emotions; moving. **2** *prep.* Concerning.

touch·stone [tuch′stōn] *n.* **1** A dark, fine-grained stone once used to test the purity of gold or silver by the color of the streak left on the stone after rubbing it with the metal. **2** Anything by which the qualities of something are tested.

touch·y [tuch′ē] *adj.* **touch·i·er, touch·i·est 1** Easily offended or hurt; irritable. **2** Risky; delicate: a *touchy* subject of conversation.

tough [tuf] **1** *adj.* Capable of being bent without tearing or cracking: *tough* leather. **2** *adj.* Healthy and rugged; robust. **3** *adj.* Difficult to cut or chew: *tough* steak. **4** *adj.* Hard to do, play, beat, etc.; difficult: Digging ditches is *tough* work; a *tough* team. **5** *adj.* Stern, severe, or demanding: a *tough* teacher; a *tough* law. **6** *adj.* Rough, rowdy, or dangerous: a *tough* neighborhood. **7** *n.* A rough, dangerous, or lawless person. **8** *adj.* Stubborn or difficult to deal with. **9** *adj.* Bitterly fought, played, etc.: a *tough* game. **— tough′ness** *n.*

tough·en [tuf′ən] *v.* To make or become tough.

tou·pee [tōō·pā′] *n.* A small wig to cover a bald spot on the head.

tour [tōōr] **1** *n.* A trip during which one visits a number of places for pleasure or to perform, as a theatrical company, musician, athlete, etc. **2** *n.* A walk or ramble through: a *tour* of a museum. **3** *v.* To make a tour of: to *tour* Ireland. **4** *v.* To make a tour: We *toured* for three months. **5** *v.* To take (a play, etc.) on a tour.

tour·ist [tōōr′ist] **1** *n.* A person who makes a tour for pleasure. **2** *adj. use: tourist* class.

tour·ma·line [tōōr′mə·lēn *or* tōōr′mə·lin] *n.* A mineral that occurs in various varieties and colors, of which transparent blues, pinks, reds, and greens are used as gems.

tour·na·ment [tŏŏr′nə·mənt *or* tûr′nə·mənt] *n.*
1 In medieval times, a contest in which mounted knights armed with lances tried to knock their opponents off their horses. **2** A series of matches in a sport or game involving many players: a *chess* tournament.

tour·ney [tŏŏr′nē *or* tûr′nē] *n., pl.* **tour·neys,** *v.* **tour·neyed, tour·ney·ing 1** *n.* A tournament. **2** *v.* To take part in a tournament.

tour·ni·quet [tŏŏr′nə·ket] *n.* A device for stopping bleeding by closing a blood vessel, such as a bandage twisted tightly with a stick.

Tourniquet

tou·sle *or* **tou·zle** [tou′zəl] *v.* **tou·sled** *or* **tou·zled, tou·sling** *or* **tou·zling** To make untidy or disheveled; muss up: to *tousle* hair.

tow[1] [tō] **1** *v.* To pull or drag by a rope or chain: to *tow* a wrecked car. **2** *n.* The act of towing. **3** *n.* A being towed. **4** *n.* Something that is towed, as barges by a tugboat. **5** *n.* A rope or cable used in towing. — **take in tow 1** To attach a line to, for towing. **2** To take under one's care; take charge of.

tow[2] [tō] *n.* Coarse, short fibers of flax or hemp ready for spinning.

to·ward [tôrd *or* tə·wôrd′] *prep.* **1** In the direction of; facing: to turn *toward* the door. **2** Near: *Toward* evening we went home. **3** In anticipation of; for: to save *toward* one's old age. **4** With respect to; regarding: to feel kindly *toward* animals. **5** Designed to result in.

to·wards [tôrdz *or* tə·wôrdz′] *prep.* Toward.

tow·el [toul *or* tou′əl] *n., v.* **tow·eled** *or* **tow·elled, tow·el·ing** *or* **tow·el·ling 1** *n.* A cloth or paper for drying anything by wiping. **2** *v.* To wipe or dry with a towel.

tow·er [tou′ər] **1** *n.* A tall but rather narrow structure, either standing alone or built as part of another building: a church *tower*; an observation *tower*. **2** *n.* A person, place, or thing that seems to give safety or security: During our trouble, he was a *tower* of strength. **3** *v.* To rise or stand high, like a tower: A giraffe *towers* over most other animals.

tow·er·ing [tou′ər·ing] *adj.* **1** Like a tower; lofty. **2** Great; outstanding: a *towering* genius. **3** Violent; furious: a *towering* rage.

tow·head [tō′hed′] *n.* **1** A head of very blond or flaxen hair. **2** A person having such hair.

town [toun] *n.* **1** A large collection of homes and other buildings, usually larger than a village but smaller than a city. **2** The people who live in such a place: The whole *town* came to the fair. **3** A city: New York is a noisy *town.* **4** The business district of a city: Let's go to *town* and do some shopping.

town crier In former times, an official who went about the streets calling out news or public announcements.

town hall A building containing the offices of the officials of a town, used for meetings and other town business.

town meeting A meeting of the qualified voters of a town, as in New England, to transact town business.

towns·folk [tounz′fōk] *n.pl.* Townspeople.

town·ship [toun′ship] *n.* **1** A division of a county that has certain powers of municipal government. **2** A unit or area in surveys of U.S. public lands, usually six miles square.

towns·man [tounz′mən] *n., pl.* **towns·men** [tounz′mən] **1** A resident of a town. **2** A person who lives in one's town; a fellow citizen.

towns·peo·ple [tounz′pē·pəl] *n.pl.* People who live in towns or in a particular town.

tow·path [tō′path′] *n.* A path along a river or canal, used by draft animals for towing boats.

tox·ic [tok′sik] *adj.* **1** Having to do with or caused by poison. **2** Poisonous.

tox·in [tok′sin] *n.* **1** Any of various poisons produced by certain bacteria and viruses and causing diseases. **2** A poison produced by a plant or animal, as snake venom.

tox·oid [tok′soid] *n.* A toxin treated with chemicals so that it is nonpoisonous. It is often used in immunization.

toy [toi] **1** *n.* An article made to amuse a child; plaything. **2** *adj. use:* a *toy* tractor. **3** *n.* Any object of little importance or value. **4** *v.* To amuse oneself; fiddle; play: to *toy* with a rubber band. **5** *adj.* Of miniature size: a *toy* poodle.

trace[1] [trās] *n., v.* **traced, trac·ing 1** *n.* A mark, sign, or indication left by some person, animal, or past action or event: The Vikings left few *traces* of their voyage to North America; the *traces* left by an earthquake. **2** *v.* To follow the tracks or trail of: to *trace* an animal to its den. **3** *v.* To follow the course or development of: to *trace* the origin of a word. **4** *v.* To copy (a drawing, etc.) by placing a transparent sheet of paper over it and following the lines exactly. **5** *v.* To draw or mark out carefully with lines: to *trace* the plan of a building. **6** *n.* A small amount or indication: just a *trace* of onion in the salad.

trace[2] [trās] *n.* Either of two straps or chains that fasten a horse to the vehicle he pulls.

trac·er·y [trā′sər·ē] *n., pl.* **trac·er·ies 1** A group of interlacing and branching lines forming an ornamental pattern, as in stonework, wood carving, etc. **2** Any design resembling this: a *tracery* of frost on a window.

tra·che·a [trā′kē·ə] *n., pl.* **tra·che·ae** [trā′kē·ē] *or* **tra·che·as** The windpipe.

trac·ing [trā′sing] *n.* A copy made by following exactly the lines of the original on transparent paper placed over it.

track [trak] **1** *n.* A mark, trail, or series of footprints left by the passing of something: tire *tracks*; bear *tracks.* **2** *v.* To follow the tracks or trail of: to *track* a criminal; to *track* down information. **3** *v.* To make footprints on: to *track* up the kitchen floor. **4** *v.* To make tracks with: to *track* mud on the carpet. **5** *n.* Any regular path or course. **6** *n.* Any kind of race-course, as for people, horses, or automobiles. **7** *n.* Sports performed on such a course. **8** *adj. use:* a *track* meet. **9** *n.* A rail or pair of rails on which something may travel, especially the steel rails for railroads. **10** *n.* A course of action or thought followed to reach a goal: on the *track* of a new discovery. **11** *n.* Either of the endless metal belts on which a tank or bulldozer moves. **— in one's tracks** Right where one is; on the spot. **— keep track of** To keep in touch with, informed about, or aware of. **— lose track of** To fail to keep in touch with, informed about, or aware of: I *lost track of* the time. **— make tracks** *informal* To get away in a hurry.

track·less [trak′lis] *adj.* **1** Unmarked by trails or paths: a *trackless* desert. **2** Not running on tracks: a *trackless* trolley.

tract[1] [trakt] *n.* **1** A large area, as of land or water. **2** An extensive region of the body made up of a system of parts or organs that perform some special function: the digestive *tract.*

tract[2] [trakt] *n.* A short treatise, especially a pamphlet on a religious topic.

tract·a·ble [trak′tə·bəl] *adj.* **1** Easily led or controlled; not stubborn; docile: a *tractable* animal. **2** Easily worked or shaped: Silver is a *tractable* metal.

trac·tion [trak′shən] *n.* **1** The act of pulling or drawing over a surface. **2** A being drawn or pulled. **3** The power used for such pulling or drawing. **4** The power to grip a surface and not slip while in motion: In the mud the tires lost *traction.* **5** Contraction, as of a muscle.

trac·tor [trak′tər] *n.* **1** A powerful, motor-driven vehicle used, as on farms, for pulling a plow, reaper, etc. **2** A vehicle with a driver's cab and a powerful truck engine, used to pull large trailers.

Tractor

trade [trād] *n., v.* **trad·ed, trad·ing 1** *n.* A business or occupation, especially a spe-cialized kind of work with the hands that requires training: His *trade* is bricklaying. **2** *n.* Commerce; buying and selling: domestic and foreign *trade.* **3** *v.* To engage in or carry on buying and selling: to *trade* in furs. **4** *n.* The people engaged in a particular kind of work: the clothing *trade.* **5** *n.* Regular customers. **6** *v.* To buy or shop: to *trade* at a store. **7** *n.* An exchange of one thing for another; barter. **8** *v.* To exchange (one thing for another): He *traded* me his ice skates for my sled. **9** *n.* (*usually pl.*) A trade wind. **— trade in** To give in exchange or as part payment: to *trade in* an old car on a new one. **— trade on** or **trade upon** To get advantage from; exploit: He *trades on* his father's fame. ◆ A *trade* usually

involves skill with the hands, whereas a *pro-fession* depends more on knowledge and judg-ment, and therefore requires a longer period of educational training. One speaks of a carpenter, barber, or plumber as having a *trade,* but of a doctor, lawyer, or teacher as belonging to a *profession.* See also OCCUPATION.

trade·mark [trād′märk′] *n.* A name or symbol used by a merchant to distinguish his goods from those made or sold by others. Registered trade-marks are the legal property of their owners.

trade name 1 The name given to a product, process, service, etc., by the company that deals in it. **2** The name of a business firm.

trad·er [trā′dər] *n.* **1** A person who engages in trade. **2** A ship used in trade.

trade school A school in which students learn trades, as carpentry, plumbing, etc.

trade union Another name for LABOR UNION.

trade wind Either of two winds that blow con-tinuously toward the equator, one from the northeast and the other from the southeast.

trading post A store in wild or unsettled country where trading and bartering are done.

tra·di·tion [trə·dish′ən] *n.* **1** The passing down of customs, beliefs, tales, etc., from one genera-tion to the next. **2** A custom, belief, set of practices, etc., passed down in this way.

tra·di·tion·al [trə·dish′ən·əl] *adj.* Of, handed down by, or following tradition: the *traditional* wedding march. **— tra·di′·tion·al·ly** *adv.*

tra·duce [trə·d(y)oos′] *v.* **tra·duced, tra·duc·ing** To say untrue things that damage the reputation of; slander. **— tra·duc′er** *n.*

traf·fic [traf′ik] *n., adj., v.* **traf·ficked, traf·fick·ing 1** *n.* The number or movement of vehicles, people, ships, etc., passing along a route: heavy *traffic;* slow *traffic.* **2** *adj.* Having to do with or directing traffic: a *traffic* jam; a *traffic* cop. **3** *n.* The business of buying and sell-ing, especially when wrongful or illegal: *traffic* in stolen goods. **4** *v.* To engage in buying, selling, or trade, especially illegally. **5** *n.* The amount of freight or number of passengers carried by a transportation system. **6** *n.* Dealings: I have no *traffic* with traitors.

traffic circle *U.S.* An intersection where vehicles move around a central circle, counter-clockwise, to get from one road to another.

tra·ge·di·an [trə·jē′dē·ən] *n.* **1** An actor in tragedy. **2** A writer of tragedies.

trag·e·dy [traj′ə·dē] *n., pl.* **trag·e·dies 1** A serious play which ends unhappily. "Julius Caesar" is a tragedy. **2** A sad or disastrous event. ◆ *Tragedy* once referred only to plays, but now it commonly refers to actual disasters as well: The destruction of the town by an earth-quake was a terrible *tragedy.*

trag·ic [traj′ik] *adj.* **1** Of, like, or having to do with dramatic tragedy. **2** Causing or involving

add, āce, câre, pälm; end, ēqual; it, īce; odd, ōpen, ôrder; tŏŏk, pōōl; up, bûrn;
ə = a in *above,* e in *sicken,* i in *possible,* o in *melon,* u in *circus;* yōō = u in *fuse;* oil; pout;
check; ring; thin; this; zh in *vision.* For ¶ reference, see page 64 · HOW TO

great suffering, injury, or unhappiness: a *tragic* accident. — **trag′i·cal·ly** *adv.*

trail [trāl] **1** *v.* To drag or draw along behind: The cat's tail *trailed* in the grass. **2** *v.* To float or stream behind, as smoke or dust. **3** *n.* Anything that trails behind: a *trail* of bubbles. **4** *v.* To follow the track or scent of: to *trail* a deer. **5** *n.* A track or scent left by something that has passed: a *bear's* trail. **6** *n.* A path, as through a wood or wilderness. **7** *v.* To follow or lag behind, as in a race. **8** *v.* To grow along the ground in a creeping way, as ivy. **9** *v.* To become fainter: The thunder *trailed* off into a rumble.

trail·blaz·er [trāl′blā·zər] *n.* **1** A person who marks a trail by cutting blazes. **2** A person who leads the way in any field or project; pioneer.

trail·er [trā′lər] *n.* **1** A person, animal, or thing that trails. **2** A vehicle pulled by a car, truck, or tractor and equipped to carry goods or to serve as a home.

train [trān] **1** *n.* A line of railway cars coupled together and operated as a unit. **2** *n.* A group of attendants or servants, as those that follow a king in a procession. **3** *n.* An extension of a dress skirt, trailing behind the wearer. **4** *n.* A line of vehicles, pack animals, persons, etc., traveling together: a wagon *train*. **5** *n.* A series or sequence of connected things: the valve *train* in an automobile engine; a *train* of thought. **6** *v.* To instruct, discipline, or drill for a special purpose: to *train* a girl to be a nurse; to *train* a dog to obey. **7** *v.* To bring up; rear: to *train* children properly. **8** *v.* To bring oneself to good physical condition by exercise and proper diet: to *train* for a boxing match. **9** *v.* To cause (a plant) to grow in a desired direction by bending or tying: to *train* ivy on a trellis. **10** *v.* To point or aim: to *train* the telescope on the moon.

train·ee [trā·nē′] *n.* A person who is being trained, as for a job; learner; apprentice.

train·er [trā′nər] *n.* **1** A person who trains. **2** A person who directs a course of physical training or who coaches athletes. **3** A person who trains animals for shows, animal acts, etc.

train·ing [trā′ning] *n.* **1** Practical instruction needed to do or be something: driver *training*. **2** The process of being trained. **3** Good physical condition, or a program or regimen to keep one in condition: an athlete in *training*.

train·man [trān′mən] *n., pl.* **train·men** [trān′mən] A man who is employed on a railroad train, especially a brakeman.

traipse [trāps] *v.* **traipsed, traips·ing** *informal* To walk about in an idle or aimless manner.

trait [trāt] *n.* A special feature or quality of one's character: Patience is a good *trait*.

trai·tor [trā′tər] *n.* A person who betrays his friends, a cause, an obligation, etc., especially one who betrays his country. ◆ *Traitor* comes from the Latin word *traditor*, meaning *a betrayer*, which in turn comes from *tradere*, meaning *to deliver* (into the hands of the enemy).

trai·tor·ous [trā′tər·əs] *adj.* Of or like a traitor or treason.

tra·jec·to·ry [trə·jek′tər·ē] *n., pl.* **tra·jec·to·ries** The curved path followed by a projectile, a comet, etc., in its flight.

tram [tram] *n.* **1** A four-wheeled vehicle for carrying coal in coal mines. **2** *British* A streetcar.

tram·mel [tram′əl] *n., v.* **tram·meled** or **tram·melled, tram·mel·ing** or **tram·mel·ling** **1** *n.* (*usually pl.*) Anything that hinders freedom or activity: the *trammels* of poverty. **2** *v.* To hinder or restrict. **3** *n.* A shackle used in training horses. **4** *n.* A net for catching birds, fish, etc. **5** *n.* A hook on which to hang pots over a fire in a fireplace.

tramp [tramp] **1** *n.* A homeless person who wanders around and begs for a living; vagrant. **2** *v.* To walk or wander, especially as a vagrant. **3** *n.* A long stroll or hike: a *tramp* along the beach. **4** *n.* A heavy tread; stamping. **5** *n.* The sound made by heavy walking or stamping. **6** *v.* To step or walk heavily: to *tramp* on someone's toes; to *tramp* up the steps. **7** *n.* A steamer that goes from port to port picking up freight wherever it may be found.

tram·ple [tram′pəl] *v.* **tram·pled, tram·pling 1** To walk heavily. **2** To walk or stamp on heavily, especially so as to crush or hurt: The runaway horse *trampled* the flower garden; to *trample* on someone's feeling of self-respect.

tram·po·line [tram′pə·lēn′] *n.* A piece of strong net or canvas stretched on a frame, which a person may use as a springboard in tumbling.

Trampoline

tram·way [tram′wā′] *n. British* The tracks for a streetcar.

trance [trans] *n.* **1** A condition between sleep and wakefulness brought on by illness, hypnosis, etc., in which a person cannot act or move by his own free choice. **2** A dreamlike state in which a person is completely absorbed in thought.

tran·quil [trang′kwil *or* tran′kwil] *adj.* Calm; serene: a *tranquil* evening; a *tranquil* mind. — **tran·quil′li·ty** or **tran·quil′i·ty** *n.* — **tran′quil·ly** *adv.*

tran·quil·iz·er or **tran·quil·liz·er** [trang′-kwəl·ī′zər *or* tran′kwəl·ī′zər] *n.* A kind of drug used to reduce tension or anxiety. ¶3

trans- A prefix meaning: Across, through, beyond, or on the other side of, as in *transcontinental*, across or through a continent from end to end.

trans·act [trans·akt′ *or* tranz·akt′] *v.* To carry through; do: to *transact* business.

trans·ac·tion [trans·ak′shən *or* tranz·ak′shən] *n.* **1** The act of transacting. **2** Something transacted, as a business deal. **3** (*pl.*) The reports or minutes of a formal meeting, often published.

trans·at·lan·tic [trans′ət·lan′tik] *adj.* **1** On the other side of the Atlantic Ocean. **2** Across or crossing the Atlantic Ocean: a *transatlantic* voyage.

tran·scend [tran·send′] *v.* **1** To go beyond; overstep the limits of: His politeness *transcends* ordinary good manners. **2** To be superior to; excel: His ability *transcends* that of his brother.

tran·scen·dent [tran·sen′dənt] *adj.* Going beyond what is usual; remarkable in every way; extraordinary: a *transcendent* experience.

tran·scen·den·tal [tran′sən·den′təl] *adj.* **1** Transcendent. **2** Supernatural.

trans·con·ti·nen·tal [trans′kon′tə·nen′təl] *adj.* Going from one side of the continent to the other: a *transcontinental* trip.

tran·scribe [tran·skrīb′] *v.* **tran·scribed, tran·scrib·ing 1** To copy or recopy in handwriting or typewriting from an original or from shorthand notes. **2** To record (a radio or television program) for later use.

tran·script [tran′skript] *n.* A written or typewritten copy: a *transcript* of a school record.

tran·scrip·tion [tran·skrip′shən] *n.* **1** The act of transcribing. **2** A copy; transcript. **3** A radio or television performance that has been recorded for later use.

tran·sept [tran′sept] *n.* Either of the arms at the sides of the nave of a church that is built in the form of a cross.

trans·fer [*v.* trans′fər *or* trans·fûr′, *n.* trans′fər] *v.* **trans·ferred, trans·fer·ring,** *n.* **1** *v.* To move or send from one place or person to another: to *transfer* a book from a table to a shelf; He was *transferred* to another city to work. **2** *v.* To convey (a design or drawing) from one surface to another, as by specially prepared paper. **3** *v.* To make over the possession of to another or others: He *transferred* his car to his younger son. **4** *n.* The act of transferring. **5** *n.* A being transferred. **6** *n.* A person or thing that is transferred, as a design. **7** *n.* A ticket permitting a passenger to change from one public vehicle to another without paying the full fare again. **8** *v.* To change from one public vehicle to another with such a ticket.

trans·fer·a·ble [trans·fûr′ə·bəl] *adj.* Capable of being transferred.

trans·fer·ence [trans·fûr′əns] *n.* **1** The act of transferring. **2** A being transferred.

trans·fig·ur·a·tion [trans′fig·yə·rā′shən] *n.* A change in appearance or form.

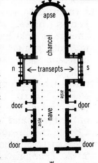

Trans·fig·ur·a·tion [trans′fig·yə·rā′shən] *n.* In the New Testament, the supernatural change in Christ's appearance on the mountain.

trans·fig·ure [trans·fig′yər] *v.* **trans·fig·ured, trans·fig·ur·ing 1** To change the form or appearance of. **2** To make exalted or glorious: Love *transfigured* her face.

trans·fix [trans·fiks′] *v.* **1** To pierce through; impale: His hand was *transfixed* by an arrow. **2** To make motionless, as with horror or fear.

trans·form [trans·fôrm′] *v.* **1** To change the form or appearance of: High heels *transformed* her from a little girl to a young lady. **2** To change the character or condition of: The basement has been *transformed* into a play room. **3** In electricity, to change the ratio of current to voltage, as of an alternating currrent. **— trans·for·ma′tion** *n.*

trans·form·er [trans·fôr′mər] *n.* **1** A person or thing that transforms. **2** An electromagnetic device used in alternating current circuits to alter the ratio of current to voltage with very small loss of power.

trans·fuse [trans·fyo͞oz′] *v.* **trans·fused, trans·fus·ing 1** To transfer (blood) from one person or animal to another. **2** To cause to pass from one person or thing to another; instill: Her scream *transfused* her fear into all of us. **— trans·fu′sion** *n.*

trans·gress [trans·gres′] *v.* **1** To break or violate, as a law, oath, etc. **2** To sin. **3** To pass beyond or over: Her dress *transgressed* the limits of good taste. **— trans·gres′sor** *n.*

trans·gres·sion [trans·gresh′ən] *n.* The act of transgressing, especially a sin or violation of a law.

tran·sient [tran′shənt] **1** *adj.* Passing away quickly; staying only a short time: *transient* pain. **2** *n.* A person who remains in one place for only a short time.

tran·sis·tor [tran·zis′tər] *n.* An electronic device made of specially prepared germanium or silicon, that allows the current in one circuit to control the current in another. It is used to replace electron tubes in many applications, as in radios, television sets, computers, etc. ◆ *Transistor* is a blend of *trans(fer)* + *(res)istor.*

tran·sit [tran′sit] *n.* **1** The act of passing over or through; passage. **2** The act of carrying across or through; conveyance: Our new furniture was damaged in *transit.* **3** An instrument for measuring angles, used in surveying.

tran·si·tion [tran·zish′ən] *n.* The act or condition of changing from one form, place, type of existence, etc., to another: a *transition* from country to city life. **— tran·si′tion·al** *adj.*

tran·si·tive [tran′sə·tiv] *adj.* Referring to a verb that takes a direct object as *stubbed* in "I stubbed my toe on the rock." **— tran′si·tive·ly** *adv.*

---

add, āce, câre, pälm;   end, ēqual;   it, īce;   odd, ōpen, ôrder;   to͝ok, po͞ol;   up, bûrn;
ə = a in *above,* e in *sicken,* i in *possible,* o in *melon,* u in *circus;*   yo͞o = u in *fuse;*   oil;   pout;
   check;   **r**ing;   **th**in;   **th**is;   **zh** in *vision.*   For ¶ reference, see page 64 · HOW TO

tran·si·to·ry [tran′sə·tôr′ē] *adj.* Existing for a short time only: *transitory* grief.

trans·late [trans·lāt′] *v.* **trans·lat·ed, trans·lat·ing** 1 To change (something spoken or written) into another language. 2 To explain in other words: Medical terms sometimes have to be *translated* to a patient. 3 To move or change to another place or condition: to *translate* promises into deeds.

trans·la·tion [trans·lā′shən] *n.* 1 The act of translating. 2 Something that has been translated, especially a work translated into another language.

trans·la·tor [trans·lā′tər] *n.* A person who translates or interprets from one language to another.

trans·lu·cent [trans·lōō′sənt] *adj.* Allowing light to pass through, but blocking a view of objects on the other side: a *translucent* window.

trans·mi·gra·tion [trans′mī·grā′shən] *n.* 1 A moving from one place or country to another to live. 2 The passing of the soul after death to a new body or a new form of life, as is believed in certain religions.

trans·mis·sion [trans·mish′ən] *n.* 1 The act of transmitting or passing on. 2 Something that is transmitted. 3 The transfer of power, electricity, etc., from one point to another. 4 A device for this purpose, as the mechanism in an automobile that connects the engine and the driving wheels. 5 The passage through space of radio waves.

trans·mit [trans·mit′] *v.* **trans·mit·ted, trans·mit·ting** 1 To send or pass on from one person or place to another; transfer: to *transmit* a package by messenger; Dirty hands *transmit* disease. 2 To pass on by means of heredity. 3 To send out (messages, radio programs, etc.) by means of electricity or electromagnetic waves. 4 To cause (light, sound, etc.) to pass through a medium. ◆ The *-mit* in *transmit, emit,* and *permit* comes from the Latin word meaning *to send.* Thus *transmit* literally means *to send across,* or, more exactly, *from one place or person to another*: A walkie-talkie *transmits* messages. *Emit* means *to send out,* or *to give off* or *discharge*: Automobile exhausts *emit* fumes. *Permit* means *to send through* in the sense of letting go through or allowing.

trans·mit·ter [trans·mit′ər] *n.* 1 A person or thing that transmits. 2 In a radio, telegraph, or other communication system, a device that sends out electrical or electromagnetic energy in a way that corresponds to the message, picture, etc., to be transmitted.

trans·mute [trans·myōōt′] *v.* **trans·mut·ed, trans·mut·ing** 1 To change in nature, form, quality, etc. 2 In physics and formerly in alchemy, to change (an element) into another element. — **trans′mu·ta′tion** *n.*

tran·som [tran′səm] *n.* 1 A small window above a door or window, usually hinged to a horizontal crosspiece. 2 This crosspiece.

trans·par·en·cy [trans·pâr′ən·sē] *n., pl.* **trans·par·en·cies** 1 The quality of being

transparent. 2 A picture on a transparent substance, as glass, intended to be viewed by shining a light through it.

trans·par·ent [trans·pâr′ənt] *adj.* 1 So clear or sheer as to be easily seen through: *transparent* paper. 2 Easy to see or understand; obvious.

tran·spire [tran·spīr′] *v.* **tran·spired, tran·spir·ing** 1 To give off (waste products) in the form of moisture from the surface, as the human body does or as leaves do. 2 To become known. 3 *informal* To happen; occur.

trans·plant [trans·plant′] *v.* 1 To dig up (a plant, etc.) from where it is growing and plant it again in another place. 2 To transfer (a piece of tissue or an organ) from one part of the body to another or from one person to another. — **trans′plan·ta′tion** *n.*

trans·port [*v.* trans·pôrt′, *n.* trans′pôrt] 1 *v.* To carry or convey from one place to another. 2 *n.* The act of conveying from one place to another: Freight trains are used for the *transport* of many goods. 3 *n.* A ship used to carry troops and military supplies. 4 *n.* An aircraft for carrying passengers, mail, etc. 5 *v.* To carry away with strong emotion. 6 *n.* A strong emotion or feeling. 7 *v.* To send (criminals) to a penal colony, especially across the sea.

trans·por·ta·tion [trans′pər·tā′shən] *n.* 1 The act of transporting. 2 A being transported. 3 A means or system of transporting: air *transportation.* 4 A charge for transport; a ticket or fare.

trans·pose [trans·pōz′] *v.* **trans·posed, trans·pos·ing** 1 To reverse the order or change the place of: If you *transpose* the letters in "but" you get "tub." 2 In music, to put in a different key. — **trans·po·si·tion** [trans′pə·zish′ən] *n.*

tran·sub·stan·ti·a·tion [tran′səb·stan′shē·ā′·shən] 1 In the Communion ceremony of some Christian churches, the change of the substance of the bread and wine into the body and blood of Christ, the bread and wine keeping unchanged their material qualities of taste and appearance. 2 A changing of anything into something different.

trans·ver·sal [trans·vûr′səl] 1 *adj.* Transverse. 2 *n.* In geometry, a line intersecting a system of lines.

trans·verse [trans·vûrs′] *adj.* Lying or being across or from side to side: *transverse* braces.

trap [trap] *n., v.* **trapped, trap·ping** 1 *n.* A device for catching or snaring animals. 2 *n.* Any trick by which a person may be put off guard or deceived: The sale was a *trap* to attract customers. 3 *v.* To catch in a trap; ensnare: to *trap* beavers. 4 *v.* To set traps to catch game animals. 5 *n.* A device for hurling clay targets into the air for sportsmen to shoot at. 6 *n.* A U-shaped bend in a drainpipe to keep sewer gas from coming up. 7 *n.* A light, two-wheeled carriage suspended by springs. 8 *n.* A trap door. 9 *n.* (*pl.*) Percussion instruments, as drums and cymbals.

trap door A hinged or sliding door to cover an opening in a floor or roof.

tra·peze [trə·pēz′] *n.* A short swinging bar, suspended by two ropes, used by gymnasts, etc.

trap·e·zoid [trap′ə·zoid] *n.* A four-sided geometric figure having two sides parallel and the other two not parallel.

a and b are parallel, c and d are not.

trap·per [trap′ər] *n.* A person whose work is the trapping of fur-bearing animals.

trap·pings [trap′ingz] *n.pl.* 1 An ornamental covering or harness for a horse. 2 Very elaborate ornaments, garments, etc.

trap·shoot·ing [trap′shoo′ting] *n.* The sport of shooting clay targets sent up from traps.

trash [trash] *n.* 1 Worthless things to be thrown out; rubbish. 2 Worthless ideas, writing, etc.; nonsense. 3 Worthless, disreputable people. — **trash′y** *adj.*

trav·ail [trav′āl *or* trə·vāl′] 1 *n.* Strenuous physical or mental labor; toil. 2 *v.* To work very hard. 3 *n.* The pains of childbirth. 4 *v.* To undergo the pains of childbirth. ◆See TRAVEL.

trav·el [trav′əl] *v.* **trav·eled** *or* **trav·elled**, **trav·el·ing** *or* **trav·el·ling**, *n.* 1 *v.* To go from one place to another; make a journey or tour: to *travel* through France; to *travel* as a salesman. 2 *n.* The act of traveling. 3 *n.* (*pl.*) Journeys or trips. 4 *v.* To move or journey over, across, or through: to *travel* the open highway. 5 *v.* To be transmitted, as light, sound, etc. 6 *v.* To move in a fixed path, as a piston. — **trav′el·er** *or* **trav′el·ler** *n.* ◆The word *travel* developed as another form of *travail*, one of whose meanings was *journey.*

trav·eled *or* **trav·elled** [trav′əld] *adj.* 1 Having made many journeys or travels. 2 Used constantly by travelers: a *traveled* highway.

trav·e·logue *or* **trav·e·log** [trav′ə·lôg] *n.* A lecture or film describing travels.

trav·erse [trav′ərs *or* trə·vûrs′] *v.* **trav·ersed**, **trav·ers·ing**, *n.*, *adj.* 1 *v.* To pass or travel over, across, or through: They *traversed* the glacier safely. 2 *n.* A part, as of a structure, placed across another part. 3 *adj.* Lying or being across; transverse. 4 *v.* To swing or turn (a gun, telescope, etc.) to the right or left.

trav·es·ty [trav′is·tē] *n.*, *pl.* **trav·es·ties**, *v.* **trav·es·tied**, **trav·es·ty·ing** 1 *n.* An imitation or burlesque of a serious book, play, speech, etc., that makes it sound ridiculous. 2 *n.* Any careless or absurd treatment of something important: In countries having only one political party, elections are *travesties.* 3 *v.* To make (something serious) ridiculous by a comic imitation.

trawl [trôl] 1 *n.* A great fishing net shaped like a flattened bag and towed along the bottom of the

ocean by a ship. 2 *n.* A long line having many short fishing lines fastened along it at intervals. It is held up by buoys. 3 *v.* To catch (fish) with a trawl.

trawl·er [trô′lər] *n.* A boat used in trawling.

tray [trā] *n.* A flat receptacle with a low rim, made of wood, metal, etc., and used to carry or hold food or small articles.

treach·er·ous [trech′ər·əs] *adj.* 1 Likely to betray; disloyal; unreliable: a *treacherous* gossip. 2 Not as good or safe as it appears: a *treacherous* path. — **treach′er·ous·ly** *adv.*

treach·er·y [trech′ər·ē] *n.*, *pl.* **treach·er·ies** 1 Disloyal action; betrayal. 2 Treason.

trea·cle [trē′kəl] *n. British* Molasses.

tread [tred] *v.* **trod**, **trod·den** *or* **trod**, **tread·ing**, *n.* 1 *v.* To step or walk on, over, or along: We *trod* the boardwalk all morning. 2 *v.* To press with the feet; trample: The clumsy boy always *treads* on people's feet. 3 *v.* To make or form by trampling: to *tread* a path through the snow. 4 *v.* To do or accomplish in walking or in dancing: to *tread* a measure. 5 *n.* The act, manner, or sound of walking: A cat's *tread* is very soft. 6 *n.* The flat part of a step in a staircase. 7 *n.* The part of an automobile tire that touches the ground. —

Tread

tread water (*past tense* **treaded**) In swimming, to keep the body erect and the head above water by moving the feet up and down as if walking.

tread·le [tred′(ə)l] *n.*, *v.* **tread·led**, **tread·ling** 1 *n.* A lever operated by the foot, usually to make the wheel of a machine rotate. 2 *v.* To work a treadle.

tread·mill [tred′mil′] *n.* 1 A device turned by the walking motion of persons on steps around the rim of a large wheel. It was once used as a form of punishment for prisoners. 2 A somewhat similar device turned by the walking motion of persons or animals on a sloping, endless belt. 3 Any monotonous work or routine.

Treadle

treas. Abbreviation of: 1 Treasurer. 2 Treasury.

trea·son [trē′zən] *n.* An act of betrayal, treachery, or breach of allegiance to one's country or sovereign.

trea·son·a·ble [trē′zən·ə·bəl] *adj.* Of or having to do with treason.

trea·son·ous [trē′zən·əs] *adj.* Treasonable.

treas·ure [trezh′ər] *n.*, *v.* **treas·ured**, **treas·ur·ing** 1 *n.* Valuables stored up and carefully kept, especially money and jewels. **2** *n.* A person or thing that is regarded as valuable, rare, or very dear. **3** *v.* To set a high value upon; prize: He *treasures* a letter from the President. **4** *v.* To store or hoard up as treasure.

treas·ur·er [trezh′ər·ər] *n.* An officer of a state, city, company, club, etc., who is in charge of its money.

treas·ur·y [trezh′ər·ē] *n., pl.* **treas·ur·ies 1** The place where the funds of a government, firm, club, etc., are kept and paid out. **2** Funds; money: Can we pay for the party out of the club *treasury?* **3** (*written* **Treasury**) The department of the U.S. government that is in charge of the country's money. **4** Any collection of valuable or rare things, as in art, literature, etc.

treat [trēt] **1** *v.* To act toward or deal with in a certain way: to *treat* one's parents with respect. **2** *v.* To look upon; consider: to *treat* a joke as an insult. **3** *v.* To try to cure or make better: The doctor *treated* my poison ivy. **4** *v.* To subject to some chemical or physical action in order to improve: wool *treated* against moths. **5** *v.* To discuss in writing or speaking: This books *treats* mountain climbing. **6** *v.* To pay for the entertainment, food, or drink of: to *treat* a friend to dinner. **7** *n.* The act of treating in such a way, or one's turn to treat. **8** *n.* Entertainment or refreshments paid for by another. **9** *n.* Anything that gives pleasure or satisfaction. **10** *v.* To arrange terms; negotiate.

trea·tise [trē′tis] *n.* A generally long and detailed discussion of a subject in writing.

treat·ment [trēt′mənt] *n.* **1** The act, process, or way of treating a person or thing: The prisoners received good *treatment.* **2** The action taken or the materials used in treating something, as a disease.

treat·y [trēt′ē] *n., pl.* **treat·ies** A formal agreement between two or more nations in reference to peace, commerce, etc.

treb·le [treb′əl] *v.* **treb·led, treb·ling,** *n., adj.* **1** *v.* To multiply by three; triple: This year he *trebled* his income. **2** *adj.* Threefold; triple. **3** *adj.* Very high; soprano: the *treble* voices of children. **4** *n.* In music, the highest part; soprano. **5** *n.* A singer, instrument, or player taking this part. **— treb′ly** *adv.*

treble clef The clef usually used to write the notes for high-pitched instruments and voices.

tree [trē] *n., v.* **treed, tree·ing 1** *n.* A tall, woody plant, usually with a single trunk, having branches and leaves growing out at some distance above the ground. **2** *v.* To chase or drive up a tree: to *tree* a squirrel. **3** *n.* A pole or other piece of wood used for a special purpose: a hat *tree*; a shoe *tree.* **4** *n.* A diagram that looks like a tree, showing family descent. **— up a tree** *informal* In a situation that is embarrassing or hard to get out of; cornered.

tre·foil [trē′foil] *n.* **1** A plant, such as the clover, whose leaves are divided into three leaflets. **2** An ornament, especially in architecture, shaped like such a leaf.

trek [trek] *v.* **trekked, trek·king,** *n.* **1** *v.* To travel, especially slowly or laboriously. **2** *n.* A journey, especially a slow one. **3** *v.* In South Africa, to travel by ox wagon.

trel·lis [trel′is] *n.* A structure made of crossed strips, as of wood, metal, etc., used as a screen or support for climbing plants.

trem·ble [trem′bəl] *v.* **trem·bled, trem·bling,** *n.* **1** *v.* To shake with agitation, fear, weakness, cold, etc. **2** *n.* The act of trembling. **3** *v.* To shake or move gently: Sunlight *trembled* on the dancing ripples. **4** *v.* To feel anxious or afraid.

tre·men·dous [tri·men′dəs] *adj.* **1** Dreadful; awful; overwhelming: a *tremendous* disaster. **2** *informal* Unusually large; enormous: a *tremendous* elephant. **3** *informal* Unusually great; wonderful: The actor was *tremendous* in *Hamlet.* **— tre·men′dous·ly** *adv.*

trem·or [trem′ər] *n.* **1** A quick, vibrating movement; a shaking. **2** A quivering feeling of excitement, nervousness, insecurity, etc.

trem·u·lous [trem′yə·ləs] *adj.* **1** Affected by trembling; shaking: *tremulous* speech. **2** Showing fear; timid: a *tremulous* mouse.

trench [trench] **1** *n.* A long, narrow opening that has been dug in the earth; ditch. **2** *n.* A long ditch with earth piled up in front, used by soldiers in battle to protect themselves from enemy fire. **3** *v.* To dig a trench in.

trench·ant [tren′chənt] *adj.* **1** Sharp and to the point; cutting; keen: a *trenchant* remark. **2** Forceful; effective: a *trenchant* argument.

trench coat A belted raincoat styled like those worn by military officers.

trend [trend] **1** *n.* A general course or direction: new *trends* in men's sportswear. **2** *v.* To have or take a particular trend; tend.

Tren·ton [tren′tən] *n.* The capital of New Jersey, in the western part on the Delaware River.

trep·i·da·tion [trep′ə·dā′shən] *n.* **1** Fear; anxiety; dread. **2** A trembling.

tres·pass [tres′pəs *or* tres′pas′] **1** *v.* To enter or go without right on another's property. **2** *v.* To thrust oneself rudely in; intrude: to *trespass* on another's privacy. **3** *n.* The act of trespassing. **4** *v.* To sin. **5** *n.* A sin or wrongdoing. **— tres′pas·ser** *n.*

tress [tres] (*usually pl.*) A lock of hair, especially the long, loose hair of a woman or girl.

tres·tle [tres′əl] *n.* **1** A frame like a sawhorse used to hold up part of a table top, platform, etc. **2** An open, braced framework used to support a road, railroad tracks, etc.

tri- A prefix meaning: **1** Having or containing three parts, groups, atoms, etc., as in *tricycle*, a vehicle with three wheels. **2** Into three, as in *trilobite*, an extinct animal having its body divided lengthwise into three sections. **3** Occurring every three (times, etc.), as in *triennial*, every three years. **4** Occurring three times within a (period, interval, etc.).

tri·ad [trī′ad] *n.* A group of three, usually closely related persons or things.

tri·al [trī'əl *or* trīl] **1** *n*. The examination before a court of the charges made in a case in order to prove such charges either true or false. **2** *n*. The act of testing or proving by experience or use: the *trial* of a new vaccine. **3** *n*. An attempt or effort to do something; try: He had three *trials* at hitting the mark. **4** *adj. use:* a *trial* shot at the moon. **5** *n*. A being tried or tested by difficulties, suffering, etc.: his hour of *trial*. **6** *n*. A cause of suffering, annoyance, or vexation: His laziness was a *trial* to his family. **— on trial** In the process of being tried or tested.

trial and error A method of attacking a problem by trying different approaches and discarding those that do not work.

tri·an·gle [trī'ang'gəl] *n*. **1** A plane figure having three sides and three angles. **2** Something shaped like this. **3** A musical instrument consisting of a metal bar bent into a triangle and sounded by being struck with a metal rod.

tri·an·gu·lar [trī-ang'gyə-lər] *adj*. Of, having to do with, or shaped like a triangle.

trib·al [trī'bəl] *adj*. Of or having to do with a tribe or tribes.

tribe [trīb] *n*. **1** A group of people, often a primitive people, having a leader and usually sharing the same customs, religious beliefs, etc. **2** A number of persons of any class or profession, taken together: the theatrical *tribe*. **3** A group of related plants or animals.

tribes·man [trībz'mən] *n., pl.* **tribes·men** [trībz'mən] A member of a tribe.

trib·u·la·tion [trib'yə·lā'shən] *n*. **1** Misery; distress; suffering: the *tribulation* caused by poverty. **2** An instance of such misery or suffering: The pioneers of America suffered many *tribulations*.

tri·bu·nal [tri-byoo'nəl *or* trī-byoo'nəl] *n*. **1** A court or place of justice. **2** The seat set apart for judges, magistrates, etc.

trib·une[1] [trib'yoon] *n*. **1** In ancient Rome, an official chosen by the common people to protect them against oppression. **2** Any person who defends the rights of the people.

trib·une[2] [trib'yoon] *n*. A raised platform for a speaker.

trib·u·tar·y [trib'yə·ter'ē] **1** *n*. A stream flowing into a larger stream or body of water. **2** *adj*. Bringing supplies, etc., to something larger: a *tributary* stream. **3** *n*. A person or state that pays tribute (def. 2). **4** *adj*. Paying tribute: a *tributary* nation.

trib·ute [trib'yoot] *n*. **1** A speech, compliment, gift, etc., given to show admiration, gratitude, or respect. **2** Money or other payment given by one ruler or state to another as an act of submission or as the price of peace and protection. **3** Any enforced payment.

trice [trīs] *n*. An instant, used only in the phrase **in a trice.**

tri·ceps [trī'seps] *n*. A large muscle at the back of the upper arm that extends from the shoulder blade to the elbow joint and has to do with extending the forearm.

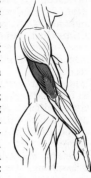

Triceps

trick [trik] **1** *n*. Something done to fool, deceive, or outwit: The little girl cried as a *trick* to avoid punishment. **2** *v*. To deceive or cheat; fool: He *tricked* us by coming in the back door. **3** *n*. A malicious, injurious, or annoying act: a dirty *trick*. **4** *n*. A practical joke; prank. **5** *n*. A particular habit or manner: the *trick* of cracking one's knuckles. **6** *n*. A peculiar skill or knack: the *trick* of playing rapid scales on the piano. **7** *n*. An act of magic. **8** *adj*. Of, having to do with, or using tricks or trickery: a *trick* photograph. **9** *v*. To dress, usually in a fancy manner: The girls were *tricked* out in old gowns. **10** *n*. In card games, the whole number of cards played in one round. **11** *n*. A period of work, especially steering a ship. **— do the trick** *slang* To bring about the desired result.

trick·er·y [trik'ər·ē] *n., pl.* **trick·er·ies** The act of using tricks to cheat or deceive.

trick·le [trik'əl] *v*. **trick·led, trick·ling,** *n*. **1** *v*. To flow or cause to flow in a thin stream or drop by drop: Water *trickled* out of the spout. **2** *v*. To move slowly or bit by bit. **3** *n*. A thin stream or drip.

trick·ster [trik'stər] *n*. Someone who plays tricks; a mischievous or dishonest person.

trick·y [trik'ē] *adj*. **trick·i·er, trick·i·est 1** Likely to use or involve tricks; deceptive. **2** Not working as expected; difficult.

tri·col·or [trī'kul'ər] **1** *adj*. Having three colors. **2** *n*. A flag having three colors. **3** *n*. (*sometimes written* **Tricolor**) The French flag.

tri·cy·cle [trī'sik·əl] *n*. A three-wheeled vehicle, especially such a vehicle with pedals, used by children.

Trident

tri·dent [trīd'(ə)nt] **1** *n*. A three-pronged spear, as the one carried by the god of the sea in classical mythology. **2** *adj*. Having three teeth or prongs.

tried [trīd] **1** Past tense and past participle of TRY. **2** *adj.* Tested; trustworthy: a *tried* friendship. **— tried and true** Tested by experience and found to be good.

tri·en·ni·al [trī·en′ē·el] **1** *adj.* Taking place every third year. **2** *n.* Something that takes place every third year. **3** *adj.* Lasting three years.

Tri·este [trē·est′] *n.* A port city in NE Italy, on an inlet of the Adriatic Sea.

tri·fle [trī′fəl] *n., v.* **tri·fled, tri·fling 1** *n.* Anything of very little value or importance: It did not do a *trifle* of harm. **2** *n.* A small amount of money. **3** *v.* To act or deal with someone or something in a light, frivolous way: to *trifle* with a friendship. **4** *v.* To play; toy: to *trifle* with one's dinner. **5** *v.* To spend or waste in a worthless way, as time or money. **— tri′fler** *n.*

tri·fling [trī′fling] *adj.* **1** Lacking seriousness or importance; frivolous: a *trifling* conversation. **2** Lacking size, quantity, or value; trivial: a *trifling* sum.

trig·ger [trig′ər] **1** *n.* The lever or other device pressed by the finger to fire a gun. **2** Something that acts like a trigger in that it serves to begin some action or operation. **3** *v.* To begin; set off: An insult *triggered* the fight.

trig·o·no·met·ric [trig′ə·nə·met′rik] *adj.* Of, having to do with, or occurring in trigonometry.

trig·o·nom·e·try [trig′ə·nom′ə·trē] *n.* The branch of mathematics that deals with the relations of the sides and angles of triangles.
◆ *Trigonometry* comes from two Greek words meaning *triangle measure.*

trill [tril] **1** *n.* In music, a rapid alternation of two tones either a tone or a semitone apart. **2** *n.* A sound like this, as that made by certain insects or birds. **3** *n.* A rapid vibration made by a speech organ, as in making the sound of *r* in some varieties of German. **4** *n.* The sound so made. **5** *v.* To sing, say, or play with a trill.

tril·lion [tril′yən] *n., adj.* **1** In the U.S., a thousand billion, written as 1,000,000,000,000. **2** In Great Britain, a million British billions, written as 1,000,000,000,000,000,000.

tril·li·um [tril′ē·əm] *n.* Any of various plants related to the lily, having a stout stem bearing three leaves and a single flower with three petals.

tri·lo·bite [trī′lə·bīt] *n.* One of a group of extinct animals having long, flattened bodies divided lengthwise into three sections and enclosed in horny shells.

tril·o·gy [tril′ə·jē] *n., pl.* **tril·o·gies** A group of three plays or sometimes three novels or musical compositions, each complete in itself but making with the others a related series.

trim [trim] *v.* **trimmed, trim·ming,** *n., adj.,* **trim·mer, trim·mest 1** *v.* To put in or restore to order or good condition, as by clipping, pruning, etc.: to *trim* hair; to *trim* a rose bush. **2** *n.* A condition of fitness, order, etc.: The boxer had to get in *trim* before his fight. **3** *adj.* Being in good condition or order; neat, smart, tidy, etc.: a *trim* uniform. **4** *v.* To remove by cutting: to

trim away the lower branches of a tree. **5** *n.* The act of trimming, cutting, or clipping: The rose bush is in need of a *trim.* **6** *v.* To decorate; ornament: to *trim* a Christmas tree. **7** *n.* Decoration; ornament: the *trim* of a car. **8** *n.* Something used to ornament the inside of a building, as the moldings around doors or windows. **9** *adj.* Well built or designed: a *trim* figure; the *trim* lines of a car. **10** *v.* To adjust (sails) for sailing. **11** *v.* To balance (a ship, boat, or aircraft) by adjusting cargo, ballast, etc. **12** *n.* The balancing of a boat, ship, or aircraft by such adjustment. **13** *n.* The fitness of a ship for sailing. **14** *v.* To act so as to appear to favor both sides in a quarrel or dispute. **15** *v. informal* To defeat: Joe *trimmed* me in tennis. **— trim′ly** *adv.*

trim·ming [trim′ing] *n.* **1** Something used to decorate or ornament. **2** (*pl.*) The usual things that accompany a particular food or dish: turkey and all the *trimmings.* **3** (*pl.*) Something that is removed by trimming, cutting, etc. **4** The act of a person who trims.

Trin·i·dad and To·ba·go [trin′ə·dad; tō·bā′·gō] An independent member of the British Commonwealth of Nations, consisting of two islands off the northern coast of Venezuela.

trin·i·ty [trin′ə·tē] *n., pl.* **trin·i·ties 1** Any union of three parts in one; trio. **2** (*written* **Trinity**) In Christian theology, the union in one God of three separate, divine persons, the Father, Son, and Holy Ghost.

trin·ket [tring′kit] *n.* **1** Any small ornament, as of jewelry. **2** Any small toy or object of little value.

tri·o [trē′ō] *n., pl.* **tri·os 1** A group of three. **2** A musical composition for three voices or three instruments. **3** A group of three persons who perform such a composition.

trip [trip] *n., v.* **tripped, trip·ping 1** *n.* A journey or voyage. **2** *n.* A misstep or stumble. **3** *v.* To stumble or cause to stumble: He *tripped* on the doorstep. **4** *n.* The act of making a person stumble and fall. **5** *n.* A blunder; mistake. **6** *v.* To make or cause to make a blunder or mistake: I *tripped* on the first question. **7** *n.* A light, nimble step. **8** *v.* To move with light, nimble steps: She *tripped* gracefully into the room.

tripe [trīp] *n.* **1** A part of the stomach of an animal such as a deer, sheep, cow, etc., used for food. **2** *informal* Anything worthless; nonsense.

trip hammer A very heavy hammer that is raised or tilted by power and then allowed to drop.

trip·le [trip′əl] *adj., n., v.* **trip·led, trip·ling 1** *adj.* Consisting of three things or parts: a *triple* mirror. **2** *n.* A set or group of three. **3** *adj.* Three times as great or as many: We're carrying a *triple* load today. **4** *n.* A number, amount, etc., three times as great or as many. **5** *v.* To make or become three times as great or as many: We've *tripled* the load. **6** *n.* In baseball, a hit that enables the batter to reach third base. **7** *v.* In baseball, to hit a triple.

trip·let [trip′lit] *n.* **1** A group of three of a kind. **2** One of three children born at one birth. **3** In music, a group of three equal notes played in the time usually given to two notes of the same type.

Triplet

trip·li·cate [trip′lə·kit] **1** *adj.* Consisting of three parts, copies, etc.: a *triplicate* form. **2** *n.* A set of or one of three identical things: Prepare this letter in *triplicate*.

tri·pod [trī′pod] *n.* **1** A three-legged stand for a camera, transit, etc. **2** Anything that stands on three legs, as a stool, table, or pot.

trip·ping [trip′ing] *adj.* Light, nimble, and easy, as in action or movement. — **trip′ping·ly** *adv.*

tri·reme [trī′rēm] *n.* An ancient Greek or Roman warship with three rows of oars on each side.

trite [trīt] *adj.* **trit·er, trit·est** Used so often as to be stale and dull; commonplace: "It never rains but it pours" is a *trite* saying.

Tri·ton [trīt′(ə)n] *n.* In Greek myths, a sea god with a man's head and upper body and a dolphin's tail.

tri·umph [trī′əmf] **1** *n.* A victory or success of any kind: a *triumph* over poverty. **2** *v.* To win a victory; be successful: the home team *triumphed* over their visitors. **3** *n.* Joy over victory or success: His *triumph* at winning the race was long and loud. **4** *v.* To be joyous over a victory.

tri·um·phal [trī·um′fəl] *adj.* **1** Of or having to do with a triumph. **2** Celebrating a triumph.

tri·um·phant [trī·um′fənt] *adj.* **1** Joyful over victory or success. **2** Victorious: The *triumphant* army marched by. — **tri·um′phant·ly** *adv.*

tri·um·vir [trī·um′vər] *n., pl.* **tri·um·virs** or **tri·um·vi·ri** [trī·um′və·rī] In ancient Rome, one of three officials who shared authority in certain public offices.

tri·um·vi·rate [trī·um′vər·it] *n.* **1** A group of three men who, together, are the heads of a government. **2** Government by such a group or the period during which they are in power. **3** Any group of three men; trio.

triv·et [triv′it] *n.* A three-legged stand for holding cooking pans in a fireplace, a hot dish on a table, etc.

triv·i·a [triv′ē·ə] *n.pl.* Insignificant or unimportant matters: They talk of nothing but *trivia*.

triv·i·al [triv′ē·əl] *adj.* **1** Of little value or importance; insignificant: a *trivial* argument. **2** Ordinary; commonplace: a *trivial* mind.

triv·i·al·i·ty [triv′ē·al′ə·tē] *n., pl.* **triv·i·al·i·ties** **1** The quality of being trivial. **2** A trivial matter.

trod [trod] Past tense and alternative past participle of TREAD: We *trod* country roads for hours.

Tro·jan [trō′jən] **1** *n.* A native of ancient Troy. **2** *adj.* Of or having to do with ancient Troy or its

people. **3** *n.* A person who works hard or is courageous: We worked like *Trojans*.

Trojan War In Greek legend, the ten years' war waged by the Greeks against the Trojans to recover Helen, wife of the king of Sparta, who had been kidnaped by Paris, a prince of Troy.

troll[1] [trōl] **1** *v.* To fish or fish for with a moving line and hook, as from a slowly moving boat: to *troll* in a quiet stream. **2** *v.* To sing in succession, as in a round. **3** *n.* In music, a round; catch. **4** *v.* To sing loudly.

troll[2] [trōl] *n.* In folklore, a mischievous dwarf or a giant that lived underground or in caves.

trol·ley [trol′ē] *n., pl.* **trol·leys** **1** A streetcar. **2** A grooved metal wheel that conveys electric current from a wire to an electric vehicle, as to a trolley bus. **3** A basket, case, etc., hung from wheels that run along an overhead cable or rail.

trolley bus A bus run by electric current conveyed from two overhead wires by trolleys.

trom·bone [trom·bōn′ *or* trom′bōn′] *n.* A brass instrument related to the trumpet, but larger and lower in pitch than the trumpet. A slide trombone changes notes by means of a sliding U-shaped tube.

Trombone

troop [troop] **1** *n.* A group or gathering of persons or animals: a *troop* of students. **2** *v.* To move along or gather as a troop or as a crowd: Our class *trooped* into the auditorium. **3** *n.* (*usually pl.*) A body of soldiers or soldiers as a group: The *troops* retreated. **4** *n.* A unit of Boy or Girl Scouts.

troop·er [troo′pər] *n.* **1** A cavalryman. **2** A mounted policeman. **3** A state policeman.

troop·ship [troop′ship′] *n.* A ship for carrying troops; a transport.

tro·phy [trō′fē] *n., pl.* **tro·phies** Something representing victory or success, as a cup awarded for an athletic achievement, a weapon captured from an enemy, etc.

trop·ic [trop′ik] **1** *n.* (*pl.*) The hot, often humid region of the earth between the tropic of Cancer and the tropic of Capricorn. **2** *adj.* Of, having to do with, or located in the tropics; tropical.

trop·i·cal [trop′i·kəl] *adj.* Of, having to do with, or located in the tropics: a *tropical* climate.

tropical fish Any of various small, brightly colored fishes native to warm waters, often kept in aquariums.

tropic of Cancer An imaginary circle on the earth's surface about $23\frac{1}{2}°$ north of the equator, the northern limit of the area on which the sun shines straight down a part of each year.

tropic of Capricorn An imaginary circle on the earth's surface about $23\frac{1}{2}°$ south of the equator, the southern limit of the area on which the sun shines straight down a part of each year.

tro·pism [trō′piz·əm] *n.* An involuntary turning or movement of a plant or animal toward or away from a stimulus.

trop·o·sphere [trop′ə·sfir] *n.* The region of the atmosphere extending from the earth's surface to the stratosphere. In this region there are marked changes of weather.

trot [trot] *n., v.* **trot·ted, trot·ting 1** *n.* The gait of a horse, mule, etc. in which one front leg and the opposite hind leg are moved forward almost at the same time, then the other two, and so on. **2** *v.* To move or cause to move at a trot: to *trot* a horse. **3** *n.* A rapid but not too fast run: an easy *trot* across the field. **4** *v.* To move at such a pace.

troth [trôth] *n.* **1** A promise, especially a promise to marry. **2** Loyalty; fidelity. **3** Truth. ◆ This word is seldom used today.

trou·ba·dour [trōō′bə·dôr] *n.* One of a class of poets and musicians, usually of the noble class, who lived in southern France, northern Italy, and eastern Spain during the 12th and 13th centuries.

troub·le [trub′əl] *n., v.* **troub·led, troub·ling 1** *n.* Distress, difficulty, worry, suffering, etc.: She is always in *trouble*. **2** *v.* To make or become distressed, annoyed, worried, ill, etc.: Did the noise *trouble* you? **3** *n.* Any difficulty, problem, or disturbance: Riots and *troubles* there kept the police busy. **4** *n.* Effort; inconvenience; pains: She went to lots of *trouble* to entertain us. **5** *v.* To put to extra work or inconvenience: Don't *trouble* yourself; I'll answer the phone myself. **6** *n.* A sick or diseased condition: lung *trouble*. **7** *v.* To stir up or disturb, as water.

troub·le·mak·er [trub′əl·mā′kər] *n.* A person who causes trouble, disturbances, or problems.

troub·le·some [trub′əl·səm] *adj.* Causing trouble; trying; disturbing: a *troublesome* illness.

trough [trôf] *n.* **1** A long, narrow, open container for holding food or water for animals. **2** A long, narrow depression or hollow, as between ridges on land or waves at sea. **3** A gutter along or below the eaves of a house, for carrying off rain water from the roof.

trounce [trouns] *v.* **trounced, trounc·ing 1** To beat or thrash severely. **2** *informal* To defeat badly: They *trounced* us in that game!

troupe [trōōp] *n.* A company of actors or other performers.

trou·sers [trou′zərz] *n.pl.* An outer garment, especially for men and boys, covering the body from the waist to the ankles or knees, and divided so as to make a separate covering for each leg.

trous·seau [trōō′sō *or* trōō·sō′] *n., pl.* **trous·seaux** [trōō′sōz *or* trōō·sōz′] *or* **trous·seaus** A bride's outfit, including her clothing, household linens, etc.

trout [trout] *n., pl.* **trout** or **trouts** Any of various chiefly fresh-water fish of Europe and North America related to the salmon but smaller, valued as game and food fishes.

trow [trō] *v.* To suppose; think; believe: seldom used today.

trow·el [trou′əl *or* troul] *n.* **1** A flat-bladed, sometimes pointed implement, used to smooth plaster, mortar, etc. **2** A small, usually scoop-shaped implement, used in digging around small plants, planting or potting them, etc.

troy [troi] *n.* A system of weights used by jewelers to weigh jewels, gold, etc. Compare AVOIRDUPOIS.

Troy [troi] *n.* An ancient city in NW Asia Minor, famed in Greek myth and legend.

Trowels

tru·an·cy [trōō′ən·sē] *n., pl.* **tru·an·cies 1** A truant condition. **2** An act of being truant.

tru·ant [trōō′ənt] **1** *n.* A person who is absent without permission from a duty or task, especially from school. **2** *adj.* Being absent in this manner: a *truant* student. **3** *adj.* Of or having to do with a truant or truancy: a *truant* officer. **4** *adj.* Idle; lazy.

truce [trōōs] *n.* **1** A temporary stop in warfare or fighting by agreement of both sides. **2** A temporary relief or rest, as from pain, etc.

truck[1] [truk] *n.* **1** Any of various motor vehicles for carrying heavy loads, freight, etc. **2** *n.* A low frame or vehicle having two wheels at one end and handles at the other end, used for moving trunks, boxes, etc. **3** *n.* A small, low, flat-topped vehicle on four wheels for moving heavy objects. **4** *v.* To carry (goods) on a truck. **5** *v.* To drive a truck. **6** *n.* A frame with usually two or more pairs of wheels, supporting an end of a railroad car or the like. **7** *n.* A small wheel. — **truck′er** *n.*

truck[2] [truk] *n.* **1** Vegetables grown for sale at market. **2** *informal* Worthless articles; rubbish; trash. **3** *informal* Dealings: I'll have no *truck* with them.

truck farm A farm on which vegetables are grown for sale at market.

truck·le [truk′əl] *v.* **truck·led, truck·ling** To yield or give in weakly or too easily: He *truckled* to his rich uncle's every wish.

truckle bed Another name for TRUNDLE BED.

truc·u·lent [truk′yə·lənt] *adj.* **1** Ferocious; savage; fierce. **2** Angry and aggressive; hostile; belligerent: He was in a *truculent* mood. — **truc′u·lence** *n.*

trudge [truj] *v.* **trudged, trudg·ing,** *n.* **1** *v.* To walk wearily or with great effort; plod: to *trudge* five miles. **2** *n.* A tiresome walk.

true [trōō] *adj.* **tru·er, tru·est,** *adv.* **1** *adj.* Faithful to fact or reality; not false: a *true* story. **2** *adj.* Real or natural; genuine, not counterfeit: *true* gold. **3** *adj.* Faithful, as to promises, principles, etc.; loyal; steadfast: a *true* friend. **4** *adj.* Conforming to a standard type or pattern; accurate; exact: a *true* copy. **5** *adj.* Properly belonging to a class: not a *true* antelope. **6** *adj.*

Placed, shaped, fitted, etc., accurately: The door that sticks is not *true*. **7** *adv*. In a true and accurate manner: The wheel runs *true*. **8** *adj*. Lawful; legitimate: the *true* king. **— come true** To happen as desired, expected, or predicted.

truf·fle [truf′əl] *n*. Any of various fleshy underground fungi, highly valued as food.

tru·ism [troo′iz·əm] *n*. A statement that is so widely known to be true that it does not need to be mentioned, such as: Ice is frozen water.

tru·ly [troo′lē] *adv*. **1** In agreement with truth and fact; really: Are those *truly* your clothes? **2** With loyalty or faithfulness: I *truly* like her.

Tru·man [troo′mən], **Harry S**, born 1884, 33rd president of the United States, 1945–1953.

trump[1] [trump] **1** *n*. In various card games, a card of a suit which temporarily ranks above all other suits. **2** *n*. (*usually pl*.) This suit itself. **3** *v*. To play a trump. **4** *v*. To take with a trump: to *trump* your opponent's trick. **— trump up** To invent or concoct in order to deceive: He *trumped up* an excuse.

trump·er·y [trump′pər·ē] *n*., *pl*. **trump·er·ies**, *adj*. **1** *n*. Something showy but worthless. **2** *n*. Nonsense. **3** *adj*. Showy but worthless.

trum·pet [trum′pit] **1** *n*. A brass instrument of high range with a flaring bell and a long, curved metal tube, whose pitch is varied by means of valves. **2** *v*. To blow a trumpet. **3** *n*. Something like a trumpet in shape. **4** *n*. A sound like that made by a trumpet. **5** *v*. To make a sound like that of a trumpet. **6** *v*. To proclaim by or as by a trumpet: to *trumpet* the good news. **— trum′pet·er** *n*.

trun·cheon [trun′chən] *n*. **1** A policeman's club; billy. **2** A short staff carried as an emblem of authority or privilege.

trun·dle [trun′dəl] *n*., *v*. **trun·dled, trun·dling 1** *n*. A small wheel, as a caster. **2** *v*. To roll or propel as if by rolling. **3** *n*. A trundle bed.

trundle bed A bed with a very low frame resting on casters, so that it may be rolled under another bed.

trunk [trungk] *n*.
1 The main stem or stock of a tree, not including the limbs or roots. **2** The human body, apart from the head, neck, and limbs.

Trundle bed

3 A main or central section of anything, as the main section of a nerve or blood vessel. **4** A long, flexible snout, as that of the elephant. **5** A large piece of luggage used for packing and carrying clothes, etc., as for a journey. **6** A compartment of an automobile for storing luggage, etc. **7** (*pl*.) Very short pants or trousers, worn by swimmers, athletes, etc.

trunk line The main line of a transportation, supply, or communication system: the *trunk line* of a railroad.

truss [trus] **1** *n*. A bandage or support for a hernia. **2** *n*. A braced framework or support, as for a roof, etc. **3** *v*. To tie or bind; fasten.

trust [trust] **1** *n*. A confidence or belief in the ability, honesty, justice, truth, etc., of a person or thing. **2** *n*. The person or thing in which confidence is placed: Money was his *trust*. **3** *v*. To have trust in; rely upon: Jim *trusts* his lawyer. **4** *v*. To place trust: I *trust* in the experience of our mayor. **5** *adj*. *use*: a *trusting* soul. **6** *n*. Something given to a person's care for use or safekeeping; a charge: Her patient's health is a nurse's *trust*. **7** *n*. Custody; care: to give something to another's *trust*. **8** *v*. To commit something to the care of: She *trusted* her sister with her best evening gown. **9** *v*. To believe: I *trust* everything he said. **10** *v*. To expect with confidence and hope: I *trust* the weather will improve tomorrow. **11** *n*. Confidence in the honesty or ability of a person, firm, etc., to pay at a later date; credit: to sell something on *trust*. **12** *v*. To allow credit to: to *trust* someone for groceries. **13** *n*. Property held and managed by a person, firm, etc., for the benefit of another. **14** *adj*. Held in trust: *trust* money. **15** *n*. A group of several or more firms or businesses that have united for the purpose of controlling production, prices, etc. **16** *adj*. Managing the property of others: a *trust* company. **— in trust** Given to another for care, safekeeping, or management but not to own: His estate was *in trust* until he reached 21. **— trust to** To depend upon. ◆ *Trust, confidence,* and *faith* all describe a belief that someone or something is good, honest, or true. You have *trust* in someone if you believe in the truth of what he says or in the honesty and goodness of his actions. *Confidence* is very similar to this and both rely heavily on evidence of things seen or heard. *Faith,* however, is more a feeling or emotion than either of the other two and as such it does not depend on proof or evidence. One can have *faith* in a person or thing without really being able to explain why.

trus·tee [trus·tē′] *n*. **1** A person who holds property in trust. **2** One of a group of persons who hold in trust the property and manage the affairs of a college, church, foundation, etc.

trus·tee·ship [trus·tē′ship] *n*. The office or duties of a trustee.

trust·ful [trust′fəl] *adj*. Inclined to trust or believe; trusting. **— trust′ful·ly** *adv*.

trust fund Money, securities, etc., held in trust.

trust·wor·thy [trust′wûr′thē] *adj*. Worthy of confidence; reliable: He proved to be my most *trustworthy* and devoted friend. **— trust′wor′thi·ness** *n*.

add, āce, câre, pälm;   end, ēqual;   it, īce;   odd, ōpen, ôrder;   took, pool;   up, bûrn;
ə = a in *above*, e in *sicken*, i in *possible*, o in *melon*, u in *circus*;   yoo = u in *fuse*;   oil;   pout;
check; ring; thin; this; zh in *vision*.   For ¶ reference, see page 64 · HOW TO

trust·y [trus′tē] *adj.* **trust·i·er, trust·i·est,**
n., pl. **trust·ies 1** *adj.* Dependable; faithful;
reliable. **2** *n.* A trustworthy person, especially a
convict who has been found reliable and who is
granted special privileges.

truth [trōōth] *n., pl.* **truths** [trōō*th*z *or* trōōths]
1 The condition or quality of being true: That
man is a liar; there is no *truth* in him. **2** Something, as a statement, belief, etc., that is true: In
his testimony, it is hard to separate the *truths*
from the lies. **3** A theory, proposition, principle,
etc., that is accepted as fact: a group of scientific
truths. — **in truth** In fact; really.

truth·ful [trōōth′fəl] *adj.* **1** Habitually telling
the truth: a *truthful* person. **2** Faithful to truth
or to the facts: a *truthful* story. — **truth′ful·ly**
adv. — **truth′ful·ness** *n.*

try [trī] *v.* **tried, try·ing,** *n., pl.* **tries 1** *v.* To
make an attempt or an attempt at: *Try* the high
dive now; You can do it if you *try.* **2** *v.* To test
by using or doing: to *try* a new method; to *try* a
new pen. **3** *v.* To put or subject to a hard test:
to *try* one's patience. **4** *n.* The act of trying;
effort; attempt: Let's have a *try* at our homework. **5** *v.* To determine the guilt or innocence
of by judicial trial: to *try* a man for murder. **6** *v.*
To examine or determine judicially: to *try* a case.
7 *v.* To put severe strain upon: This light *tries*
my eyes. — **try and** *informal* To try to: *Try*
and make the dance. — **try on** To put on (a
garment, etc.) to test its fit and appearance. —
try out 1 To attempt to qualify. **2** To test, as
by use. ◆ *Try and* for *try to* is acceptable in
informal English: *Try and* catch me! In formal
speaking and writing it should be avoided.

try·ing [trī′ing] *adj.* Hard to endure; difficult:
a *trying* person; a *trying* experience.

try·out [trī′out′] *n.* **1** A test of ability, as of an
actor or an athlete. **2** A trial performance, as of
a play, to discover its strengths and weaknesses.

tryst [trist] *n.* **1** An appointment, as between
sweethearts, to meet at a certain time and place.
2 The meeting place agreed upon. ◆ *Tryst* comes
from an old French word for a *hunting station.*

tsar [tsär] *n.* Another spelling of CZAR.

tsa·ri·na [tsä·rē′nə] *n.* Another spelling of
CZARINA.

tset·se [tset′sē] *n.* A small, biting African fly
that sucks the blood of cattle, horses, other animals, and man. One kind transmits the parasite
that causes sleeping sickness.

T-shirt [tē′shûrt′] *n.* **1** A collarless undershirt
with short sleeves. **2** A similar shirt for outer
wear.

tsp. Abbreviation of TEASPOON.

T-square [tē′skwâr′] *n.* A T-shaped instrument
for measuring or laying out right angles or parallel lines.

tub [tub] *n., v.* **tubbed, tub·bing 1** *n.* A
broad, open container made of wood or metal,
used for various purposes, as for washing, etc.
2 *n.* A bathtub. **3** *n. British* A bath taken in a
tub. **4** *v.* To wash, bathe, or place in a tub.
5 *n.* The amount that a tub contains.

tu·ba [t(y)ōō′bə] *n.* Any of several large brass
instruments with a
deep tone. Pitch is
controlled by three,
four, or sometimes five
valves.

tube [t(y)ōōb] *n.* **1** A
long, hollow pipe,
as of metal or rubber,
usually used to carry
gas or liquids. **2** A
cylinder of soft metal
used to hold paints,
toothpaste, etc. **3** Any
long, tubelike part
or organ: a bronchial
tube. **4** A flexible, in-
flatable tube, usually
of rubber, used inside
an automobile tire.

Tuba

5 An electron tube. **6** A tunnel or subway for
cars, trains, etc.

tu·ber [t(y)ōō′bər] *n.* A short, thickened portion
of an underground stem, as in the potato.

tu·ber·cle [t(y)ōō′bər·kəl] *n.* **1** A small,
rounded, humplike swelling, as on the roots of
certain plants, on a bone, or on the surface of
the skin. **2** One of the firm, rounded swellings,
or knobs, caused in the body by tuberculosis and
characteristic of it.

tu·ber·cu·lar [t(y)ōō·bûr′kyə·lər] **1** *adj.* Of,
having to do with, or affected with tuberculosis.
2 *n.* A person who has tuberculosis. **3** *adj.* Of,
having, or like tubercles.

tu·ber·cu·lo·sis [t(y)ōō·bûr′kyə·lō′sis] *n.* A
disease caused by certain bacteria and marked by
the formation of tubercles in various parts of
the body. It chiefly affects the lungs, and is accompanied by a slow wasting away of strength
and vitality. Tuberculosis is often called *TB.*

tu·ber·ous [t(y)ōō′bər·əs] *adj.* **1** Of, like, or
having tubers. **2** Having small, rounded knobs
or swellings.

tub·ing [t(y)ōō′bing] *n.* **1** A series of tubes, as
in a heating system. **2** A piece of tube.
3 Material for tubes.

tu·bu·lar [t(y)ōō′byə·lər] *adj.* **1** Having the
shape of a tube. **2** Of or having to do with one
or more tubes.

tuck [tuk] **1** *v.* To fold or gather into folds so
as to shorten. **2** *v.* To fold or push the loose
edges or ends of (something) into place firmly: to *tuck* sheets under a mattress. **3** *v.* To wrap
or cover snugly: to *tuck* in a baby. **4** *v.* To put
or press into a close or hidden place: to *tuck*
a handkerchief into a pocket. **5** *v.* To draw in,
contract, or bring close to something else. **6** *n.* A
fold stitched into a garment for a better fit or
decoration. **7** *v.* To make tucks or folds in.

tuck·er [tuk′ər] *n.* A covering of linen, lace, etc.,
formerly worn over the neck and shoulders by
women.

Tuc·son [tōō·son′ *or* tōō′son] *n.* A city in SE
Arizona.

Tu·dor [t(y)o͞o′dər] **1** *n*. A royal family of England that reigned from 1485 to 1603. **2** *adj*. Of or like the architecture, poetry, etc., developed during the reigns of the Tudors.

Tues. Abbreviation of TUESDAY.

Tues·day [t(y)o͞oz′dē *or* t(y)o͞oz′dā] *n*. The third day of the week.

tuft [tuft] **1** *n*. A collection or bunch of small, flexible parts, as hair, grass, or feathers, growing or held together at the base and free at the opposite ends. **2** *v*. To cover or adorn with tufts. **3** *n*. A clump or knot, as a cluster of threads drawn tightly through a quilt, mattress, or upholstery to keep the stuffing in place. **4** *v*. To form tufts in (a mattress, quilt, etc.).

tug [tug] *v*. **tugged, tug·ging,** *n*. **1** *v*. To pull at with effort: to *tug* an oar; to *tug* at a chain. **2** *v*. To move by pulling with strength: The horse *tugged* the plow. **3** *n*. An act of tugging; a violent pull. **4** *v*. To tow with a tugboat. **5** *n*. A tugboat. **6** *n*. A trace, part of a harness.

tug·boat [tug′bōt′] *n*. A small, strongly built boat used to tow ships, barges, etc.; tug.

tug of war A contest in which a number of persons at one end of a rope pull against a like number at the other end, each side trying to drag the other across a line marked between.

tu·i·tion [t(y)o͞o·ish′ən] *n*. **1** The charge or payment for instruction in a school. **2** The act or business of teaching; instruction.

tu·lip [t(y)o͞o′lip] *n*. A hardy plant related to the lily, grown from bulbs, and bearing large cup-shaped flowers in many colors.

tulle [to͞ol] *n*. A fine, open-meshed, often stiffened material of silk, rayon, etc., used for veiling, ballet costumes, etc.

Tul·sa [tul′sə] *n*. A city in NE Oklahoma.

tum·ble [tum′bəl] *v*. **tum·bled, tum·bling,** *n*. **1** *v*. To roll, toss, or whirl about: The children *tumbled* on the lawn; to *tumble* clothes in a dryer. **2** *v*. To fall or cause to fall: to *tumble* down a staircase. **3** *v*. To perform acrobatics, as somersaults, etc. **4** *n*. A fall, somersault, etc. **5** *v*. To move quickly and awkwardly; stumble: The crowd *tumbled* out of the auditorium. **6** *v*. To throw into disorder or confusion. **7** *n*. A condition of disorder and confusion.

tum·ble·down [tum′bəl·doun′] *adj*. Rickety, as if about to fall down or into pieces; dilapidated.

tum·bler [tum′blər] *n*. **1** A drinking glass without a stem. **2** An acrobat or gymnast. **3** A part of a lock that must be moved to a certain position, as by a key, before the lock can be opened.

tum·ble·weed [tum′bəl·wēd′] *n*. A plant that, when withered, breaks from its roots and is blown about by the wind, scattering its seed.

tum·brel or **tum·bril** [tum′bril] *n*. **1** A farmer's cart. **2** A cart which took prisoners to the guillotine during the French Revolution.

tu·mor [t(y)o͞o′mər] *n*. **1** A swelling. **2** An abnormal growth of tissue in some part of the body, which may or may not become harmful. ¶1

tu·mult [t(y)o͞o′mult] *n*. **1** Commotion or noise, as that made by a loud, disorderly crowd. **2** Any violent agitation or disturbance.

tu·mul·tu·ous [t(y)o͞o·mul′cho͞o·əs] *adj*. **1** Full of tumult; noisy and disorderly: a *tumultuous* reception for the astronaut. **2** Deeply disturbed; stormy: *tumultuous* feelings.

tun [tun] *n*. **1** A large cask, especially for wine, beer, etc. **2** A varying measure of capacity, usually equal to 252 gallons.

tu·na [to͞o′nə] *n*., *pl*. **tu·na** or **tu·nas** A large ocean food fish related to the mackerel.

tun·dra [tun′drə *or* to͞on′drə] *n*. A large, almost flat plain of the arctic regions, with no trees.

tune [t(y)o͞on] *n*., *v*. **tuned, tun·ing 1** *n*. A melody or air, usually simple and easy to remember. **2** *n*. The condition of being at the proper musical pitch: out of *tune*. **3** *v*. To adjust the pitch of to a standard or correct pitch: to *tune* a violin. **4** *n*. Agreement; accord; harmony: These colors are not in *tune* with each other. **— change one's tune** To change one's manner, attitude, or approach. **— to the tune of** To the price of: *to the tune of* fifty dollars. **— tune in** or **tune in on** To adjust a radio or television receiver so as to hear or see (a station, broadcast, etc.). **— tune up 1** To bring (musical instruments) to a standard pitch. **2** To put in proper working order, as an engine.

tune·ful [t(y)o͞on′fəl] *adj*. Melodious; musical.

tun·er [t(y)o͞o′nər] *n*. A person who tunes keyboard musical instruments.

tung·sten [tung′stən] *n*. A steel-gray, heavy metallic chemical element, used in making electric light filaments and very hard steel alloys.

tu·nic [t(y)o͞o′nik] *n*. **1** In ancient Greece and Rome, a knee-length garment with or without sleeves, worn by men and women, usually without a belt. **2** A modern outer garment, usually of hip length and gathered at the waist: a soldier's *tunic*.

tun·ing fork [t(y)o͞o′ning] A two-pronged, metal instrument that sounds a fixed tone when struck.

Tu·nis [t(y)o͞o′nis] *n*. The capital of Tunisia, on the Mediterranean Sea.

Tu·ni·sia [t(y)o͞o·nish′ē·ə *or* t(y)o͞o·nē′zhə] *n*. A country in northern Africa.

tun·nel [tun′əl] *n*., *v*. **tun·neled** or **tun·nelled, tun·nel·ing** or **tun·nel·ling 1** *n*. A man-made underground passage, as for a railway. **2** *n*. Any passage under or through something, as the burrow of an animal. **3** *v*. To make a tunnel.

Tuning fork

add, āce, câre, pälm; end, ēqual; it, īce; odd, ōpen, ôrder; to͞ok, po͞ol; up, bûrn; ə = a in *above*, e in *sicken*, i in *possible*, o in *melon*, u in *circus*; yo͞o = u in *fuse*; oil; pout; check; ring; thin; this; zh in *vision*. For ¶ reference, see page 64 · HOW TO

tun·ny [tun′ē] *n., pl.* **tun·ny** or **tun·nies** The tuna.

tu·pe·lo [t(y)ōō′pə·lō] *n., pl.* **tu·pe·los** **1** A tree of Asia and North America, bearing small, greenish-white flowers and dark blue or purple fruit. **2** Its tough wood.

tup·pence [tup′əns] *n.* Another spelling of TWOPENCE.

tur·ban [tûr′bən] *n.* **1** An oriental headdress consisting of a sash or shawl, twisted around the head or around a cap. **2** Any similar headdress.

tur·bid [tûr′bid] *adj.* **1** Cloudy or opaque; muddy: a *turbid* lake. **2** Mixed up; confused: *turbid* thinking.

tur·bine [tûr′bin *or* tûr′bīn] *n.* A machine that changes the motion of a fluid, as steam, water, or gas, into rotary mechanical power by allowing the fluid to exert pressure on a series of vanes mounted on a rotating shaft.

tur·bo·jet [tûr′bō·jet′] *n.* An airplane propelled by a turbojet engine.

turbojet engine A jet engine in which a turbine supplies the power to compress the air that is taken in.

tur·bot [tûr′bət] *n., pl.* **tur·bot** or **tur·bots** A large, flat-bodied European fish resembling the flounder and valued as food.

tur·bu·lent [tûr′byə·lənt] *adj.* **1** Being in violent agitation or commotion; disturbed; a *turbulent* sea. **2** Restless; disorderly; rebellious: a *turbulent* mob. **— tur′bu·lence** *n.*

tu·reen [t(y)ōō·rēn′] *n.* A deep, covered dish, as for holding soup to be served at the table.

turf [tûrf] *n., pl.* **turfs** **1** The top level of the soil together with grass and other fine plants and their matted roots; sod. **2** A piece of this. **3** A piece of peat. **— the turf** **1** A racetrack for horses. **2** Horse racing.

tur·gid [tûr′jid] *adj.* **1** Unnaturally puffed out; swollen. **2** Too fancy and pompous, as in choice of words, literary style, etc.: a *turgid* speech. **— tur·gid·i·ty** [tûr·jid′ə·tē] *n.*

Turk [tûrk] *n.* A person born in or a citizen of Turkey.

tur·key [tûr′kē] *n., pl.* **tur·keys** **1** A large American bird related to the pheasant, having a head without feathers and a spreading tail. **2** The turkey's flesh, used as food.

Tur·key [tûr′kē] *n.* A country stretching from SE Europe to western Asia, south of the Black Sea.

Turkey, to 48 in. long

turkey buzzard or **turkey vulture** A sooty black vulture with no feathers on its red head and neck, of North and South America.

Turk·ish [tûr′kish] **1** *adj.* Of or from Turkey. **2** *n.* (**the Turkish**) The people of Turkey. **3** *n.* The language of Turkey.

Turkish towel A heavy, rough towel with loose, uncut pile.

tur·moil [tûr′moil] *n.* A condition of great confusion or agitation; disturbance; tumult.

turn [tûrn] **1** *v.* To move or cause to move around or as around an axis; rotate: The key *turned* in the lock; to *turn* a wheel. **2** *n.* A rotation or revolution: the *turn* of a key. **3** *v.* To shift or swing part way around: He *turned* and ran. **4** *v.* To change or cause to change direction or position: The tide is *turning*; to *turn* a glass upside down. **5** *n.* A change of direction or position: a *turn* to the left. **6** *n.* The point where a change in direction occurs: a *turn* in a path. **7** *v.* To move so that the under part becomes the upper; reverse: to *turn* a page; to *turn* the soil. **8** *v.* To sprain or strain: to *turn* an ankle. **9** *v.* To shape in rounded form by turning in a lathe, etc.: to *turn* a chair leg. **10** *v.* To give graceful or finished form to: to *turn* a phrase. **11** *n.* A particular form or style: the *turn* of a phrase. **12** *v.* To perform by revolving: to *turn* cartwheels. **13** *v.* To change to a different form, condition, color, etc.: to *turn* stocks into cash; The water *turned* into ice; Her hair *turned* gray. **14** *v.* To change color: The leaves *turn* in autumn. **15** *n.* A change in condition, form, etc.: a *turn* for the better. **16** *v.* To make or become sour or rancid, as milk. **17** *v.* To make or become upset or nauseated; sicken: The odor *turned* my stomach. **18** *v.* To make or become disturbed, unsettled, giddy, etc.: Compliments *turned* her head. **19** *v.* To change the direction or focus of (thought, attention, etc.): Let's *turn* our attention to the next problem. **20** *v.* To change one's interest, attention, etc.: In later life, he *turned* to politics. **21** *n.* Direction; course: The talk took a serious *turn*. **22** *v.* To go around or to the other side of: to *turn* a corner. **23** *v.* To reach or pass beyond: He *turned* 21 yesterday. **24** *v.* To depend; hinge: His decision *turns* on this afternoon's meeting. **25** *n.* The act of turning or changing. **26** *n.* The time of turning or changing: *turn* of the century. **27** *n.* A regular time or chance: It's my *turn* to play. **28** *n.* A deed performed: a good *turn*; a bad *turn*. **29** *n.* A short walk, drive, etc.: a *turn* in the park. **30** *n. informal* A shock or startling surprise: He gave us quite a *turn*. **— by turns** One after another; in succession. **— in turn** In the proper order or sequence. **— out of turn** Not in the proper order or sequence. **— take turns** To talk, act, play, etc., one after another in proper order. **— to a turn** Just right; perfectly or exactly: The steak's done *to a turn*. **— turn against** To become or cause to become opposed or hostile to: All her friends *turned against* her. **— turn down** **1** To diminish the flow, volume, intensity, etc., of: to *turn down* the gas. **2** To reject or refuse. **— turn in** **1** To turn and enter: *Turn in* that side road. **2** To bend or incline inward: Her toes *turn in*. **3** To hand over; deliver: *Turn in* your test papers. **4** *informal* To go to bed. **— turn loose** *informal* To set free; release. **— turn off** **1** To cause to stop operating, flowing, etc. **2** To make a turn and leave, as a road. — **turn on 1** To cause to operate, flow, burn, etc., as a radio, a faucet, water, or an electric light. **2** To become hostile to or attack: to *turn on* one's friend. — **turn out 1** To put out, as an electric light. **2** To put outside: They *turned* him *out* of the house. **3** To bend or incline outward. **4** To produce; make: The factory *turns out* a thousand cases an hour. **5** To come or go out: A large crowd *turned out* for the election. **6** To prove in the final result: He *turned out* to be a good student. **7** To dress or equip, especially in an elaborate way. — **turn over 1** To hand over; transfer or give. **2** To ponder or consider; think about. — **turn tail** To run away; flee. — **turn to 1** To set to work. **2** To go to for help. — **turn up 1** To find or be found. **2** To arrive. **3** To happen or occur. **4** To increase the flow, volume, intensity, etc., of. — **turn′er** *n.*

turn·coat [tûrn′kōt′] *n.* A person who goes over to the opposing side or party; traitor.

tur·nip [tûr′nip] *n.* **1** The round, white or yellow, fleshy root of a plant related to the cabbage. It is cooked and eaten as a vegetable. **2** The plant yielding this root.

turn·key [tûrn′kē] *n., pl.* **turn·keys** A person who has charge of the keys of a prison; jailer.

turn·out [tûrn′out′] *n.* **1** A group of people; gathering. **2** A quantity produced; output. **3** Equipment; outfit. **4** A manner or style of dress, especially an elaborate style. **5** A wide place in a narrow road where vehicles can pass one another.

turn·o·ver [tûrn′ō′vər] **1** *n.* The act of turning over; an upset, as of a vehicle. **2** *n.* The rate at which employees, hospital patients, etc., move on and are replaced. **3** *n.* A small pie made by filling half of a crust and turning the other half over on top. **4** *n.* The amount of business done during a given period. **5** *adj.* Capable of being turned over, folded down, or reversed.

turn·pike [tûrn′pīk′] *n.* **1** A highway on which there are tollgates. **2** A tollgate. ◆ *Turnpike* comes from an older English word *turnpyke*, meaning a *spiked road barrier*, from the verb *turn* + *pike*, a medieval spear.

turn·stile [tûrn′stīl′] *n.* A gate-like device, having revolving, horizontal arms, set in an entrance or exit, used to control the passage or count the number of people passing through it.

turn·ta·ble [tûrn′tā′bəl] *n.* **1** A disk that rotates to turn a phonograph record. **2** A track on a revolving platform used to turn a locomotive around.

Turntable

tur·pen·tine [tûr′pən·tīn] *n.* An oily liquid obtained from various cone-bearing trees, especially pines. It is used chiefly to thin paints and varnishes.

tur·pi·tude [tûr′pə·t(y)ōod] *n.* **1** Wickedness or baseness; depravity. **2** A base or wicked act.

tur·quoise [tûr′k(w)oiz] **1** *n.* A sky-blue to greenish-blue mineral, some varieties of which, when highly polished, are used as gems. **2** *n., adj.* Light greenish blue.

tur·ret [tûr′it] *n.* **1** A rotating armed tower, large enough to contain powerful guns, forming a part of a warship, fort, tank, airplane, etc. **2** A small tower, often at the corner of a large building or castle. **3** A part of a lathe fitted with a device for holding various tools.

tur·ret·ed [tûr′it·id] *adj.* Having one or more turrets.

tur·tle [tûr′təl] *n.* A type of reptile that lives both on land and in the water and has a flat, oval body covered with a hard shell into which it can draw its four limbs, head, and tail. Certain turtles are valued as food.

tur·tle·dove [tûr′təl·duv′] *n.* A small wild dove having a black tail edged with white, and noted for its soft, mournful cooing.

turtle neck A high collar, as on sweaters, that fits snugly about the neck, usually turned over double.

tusk [tusk] *n.* A long, pointed, projecting tooth, generally one of a pair, as in the boar, walrus, or elephant.

tus·sle [tus′əl] *v.* **tus·sled, tus·sling,** *n.* **1** *v.* To fight or struggle roughly. **2** *n.* A rough struggle.

tus·sock [tus′ək] *n.* A clump of growing grass or the like.

tut [tut] *interj.* An exclamation of impatience, annoyance, disapproval, disbelief, etc.

Tusks

tu·te·lage [t(y)ōo′tə·lij] *n.* **1** Protection, care, or patronage, as of a guardian. **2** Instruction.

tu·te·lar·y [t(y)ōo′tə·ler′ē] *adj.* **1** Protecting or guarding: the *tutelary* goddess of Athens. **2** Having to do with a guardian.

tu·tor [t(y)ōo′tər] **1** *n.* A person who teaches another, usually privately. **2** *v.* To give or receive private instruction. — **tu·to·ri·al** [t(y)ōo·tôr′ē·əl] *adj.*

tux·e·do [tuk·sē′dō] *n., pl.* **tux·e·dos 1** A man's formal jacket, usually black or in dark colors but without tails, worn at dances, formal dinners, etc. **2** The suit of which such a jacket is part. ◆ *Tuxedo* was named after *Tuxedo* Park, New York, because the garment was first worn at a country club there.

TV [tē′vē′] **1** Television. **2** *adj. use:* a *TV* program.

---

add, āce, câre, pälm; end, ēqual; it, īce; odd, ōpen, ôrder; tŏŏk, pōōl; up, bûrn; ə = a in *above*, e in *sicken*, i in *possible*, o in *melon*, u in *circus*; yōō = u in *fuse*; oil; pout; check; ring; thin; this; zh in *vision*. For ¶ reference, see page 64 · **HOW TO**

twad·dle [twod′(ə)l] *v.* **twad·dled, twad·dling,** *n.* **1** *v.* To talk foolishly. **2** *n.* Foolish, silly talk.

twain [twān] *n., adj.* Two: used mostly in poems.

Twain [twān], **Mark,** 1835–1910, American humorist and novelist. His real name was Samuel L. Clemens.

twang [twang] *n., v.* **twanged, twang·ing 1** *n.* A sharp, vibrating sound, as of an instrument's string that has been plucked. **2** *v.* To make or cause to make such a sound. **3** *n.* Nasal speech or sound. **4** *v.* To speak or utter with a nasal sound.

'twas [twuz *or* twoz] It was.

tweak [twēk] **1** *v.* To pinch and twist sharply. **2** *n.* A twisting pinch: He gave her nose a *tweak*.

tweed [twēd] *n.* **1** A woolen cloth with a rough texture, usually woven of yarns in two or more colors. **2** (*pl.*) Clothing made of tweed.

tweet [twēt] **1** *n.* A thin, chirping note, as that of a young bird. **2** *v.* To make such a sound.

tweez·ers [twē′zərz] *n. pl.* Small pincers for grasping and holding small objects.

twelfth *or* **12th** [twelfth] **1** *adj.* Next after the eleventh. **2** *n.* The twelfth one. **3** *adj.* Being one of twelve equal parts. **4** *n.* A twelfth part.

twelve *or* **12** [twelv] *n., adj.* One more than eleven.

twen·ti·eth *or* **20th** [twen′tē·ith] **1** *adj.* Tenth in order after the tenth. **2** *n.* The twentieth one. **3** *adj.* Being one of twenty equal parts. **4** *n.* A twentieth part.

twen·ty *or* **20** [twen′tē] *n., pl.* **twen·ties,** *adj.* **1** *n., adj.* One more than nineteen. **2** *n.* (*pl.*) The years between the age of 20 and the age of 30.

twice [twīs] *adv.* **1** Two times: He ran *twice* in one day. **2** Two times as much; doubly.

twid·dle [twid′(ə)l] *v.* **twid·dled, twid·dling,** *n.* **1** *v.* To twirl or play with idly. **2** *n.* A gentle twirling, as of the fingers. **— twiddle one's thumbs 1** To rotate one's thumbs idly around one another. **2** To pass time in doing nothing.

twig [twig] *n.* A shoot or small branch of a tree.

twi·light [twī′līt′] *n.* **1** The light in the sky just after sunset or just before sunrise. **2** *adj. use:* a *twilight* glow. **3** A period of decline: The *twilight* of ancient Rome.

twill [twil] **1** *n.* A weave which produces diagonal ribs or lines in cloth. **2** *n.* A cloth woven with such a weave. **3** *v.* To weave (cloth) in this way. **4** *adj. use:* a *twilled* fabric.

'twill [twil] It will.

twin [twin] **1** *n.* One of two offspring born at the same time to the same mother. **2** *adj. use:* *twin* brothers. **3** *n.* One of two persons or things that are very much alike. **4** *adj. use:* *twin* chairs.

twine [twīn] *v.* **twined, twin·ing,** *n.* **1** *v.* To twist together: to *twine* threads. **2** *v.* To form by such twisting: to *twine* a wreath.

An airplane with twin engines

3 *n.* A string made up of two or more strands twisted together. **4** *v.* To coil or wind: Vines *twine* around the trunk. **5** *v.* To wind or meander, as a stream.

twinge [twinj] **1** *n.* A sharp, local, darting pain. **2** *n.* A mental, moral, or emotional pang: a *twinge* of grief. **3** *v.* To give or feel a twinge.

twin·kle [twing′kəl] *v.* **twin·kled, twin·kling,** *n.* **1** *v.* To shine with a sparkling light. **2** *n.* A flashing gleam of light; sparkle. **3** *v.* To be bright, as with amusement or happiness: The little girl's eyes *twinkled.* **4** *n.* A sparkle of the eyes. **5** *v.* To move rapidly to and fro.

twin·kling [twing′kling] *n.* **1** A sparkle or gleam; twinkle. **2** A moment; instant.

twirl [twûrl] **1** *v.* To turn around rapidly; rotate; whirl. **2** *n.* A twirling motion; whirl. **3** *n.* A curl; twist; coil. **— twirl′er** *n.*

twist [twist] **1** *v.* To wind (strands, etc.) around each other. **2** *v.* To form by such winding: to *twist* thread. **3** *v.* To force out of shape or place; wrench or sprain: to *twist* a wrist. **4** *v.* To turn or revolve: to *twist* a bracelet on an arm. **5** *v.* To curve or bend: The river *twisted* through the valley. **6** *n.* The act of twisting: a *twist* of the arm. **7** *n.* The condition of being twisted. **8** *n.* Something made by twisting: a bread *twist.* **9** *v.* To change the meaning of so as to mislead: She *twisted* my story around. **10** *n.* A change, as in meaning or sense. **11** *n.* A strange or unexpected happening or development: a plot with many *twists.* **12** *n. informal* A new approach or way of doing something; gimmick.

twist·er [twis′tər] *n.* **1** A person or thing that twists. **2** *informal* A tornado.

twit [twit] *v.* **twit·ted, twit·ting,** *n.* **1** *v.* To taunt, tease, or annoy, as by reminding of a mistake, fault, etc. **2** *n.* A taunt or reproach.

twitch [twich] **1** *v.* To move or pull with a sharp, quick jerk: He *twitched* off the cloth. **2** *n.* A sudden jerk or pull. **3** *n.* A sudden movement, not intended, of a part of the body.

twit·ter [twit′ər] **1** *v.* To utter light chirping notes, as a bird. **2** *n.* A series of light chirping notes. **3** *v.* To be excited; tremble. **4** *n.* An excited state.

twixt *or* **'twixt** [twikst] *prep.* Betwixt; between: used mostly in poems.

two *or* **2** [tōō] *n., adj.* One more than one. **— in two** So as to be in two parts or pieces.

two-by-four [tōō′bī·fôr′] *n.* A piece of lumber actually measuring $1\frac{5}{8}$ inches by $3\frac{3}{8}$ inches.

two-edged [tōō′ejd′] *adj.* **1** Having two edges, as a sword. **2** Having two meanings, effects, etc., as an argument.

two-faced [tōō′fāst′] *adj.* **1** Having two faces. **2** Dishonest; false; deceitful.

two·fold [tōō′fōld′] **1** *adj.* Made up of two parts. **2** *adj.* Two times as many or as great. **3** *adv.* So as to be two times as many or as great.

two·pence [tup′əns] *n.* A sum equal to two British pennies.

two-pen·ny [tup′ən·ē] *adj.* **1** Of the price or value of twopence. **2** Cheap; worthless.

two-ply [tōō'plī'] *adj.* Made of two strands, layers, or thicknesses of material.

two-some [tōō'səm] *n.* Two persons together; couple.

two-step [tōō'step'] *n.* **1** A ballroom dance. **2** Music for such a dance, in march time.

two-way [tōō'wā'] *adj.* **1** Having or permitting movement in two directions: a *two-way* street. **2** Designed so as to send or receive messages: a *two-way* radio. **3** Having or allowing exchange or communication between two persons, groups, etc.: a *two-way* telephone conversation.

-ty[1] A suffix meaning: the condition of being, as in *sanity*, the condition of being sane.

-ty[2] A suffix meaning: Tens or times ten, as in *seventy*, seven times ten.

ty-coon [tī-kōōn'] *n.* *informal* A wealthy and powerful industrial or business leader.

ty-ing [tī'ing] Present participle of TIE.

tyke [tīk] *n.* **1** *informal* A small child. **2** A mongrel dog; cur.

Ty-ler [tī'lər], **John,** 1790–1862, tenth president of the U.S., 1841–1845.

tym-pan-ic membrane [tim-pan'ik] The eardrum.

tym-pa-num [tim'pə-nəm] *n., pl.* **tym-pa-na** [tim'pə-nə] or **tym-pa-nums 1** The middle ear. **2** The eardrum.

type [tīp] *n., v.* **typed, typ-ing 1** *n.* A class, kind, or group of persons or things that have one or more characteristics in common: an outboard *type* of engine. **2** *n.* A person or thing displaying the characteristics common to a class or group; example: This church is a fine *type* of Byzantine architecture. **3** *v.* To be a model for; typify: Peter Pan *types* all the people who refuse to grow up. **4** *v.* To place in a class or group: He was usually *typed* to play a butler. **5** *v.* To find the type of; identify: to *type* a blood sample. **6** *n.* A piece of metal topped by a reversed letter, figure, or mark for use in printing. **7** *n.* A group of such pieces. **8** *n.* Printed or typewritten letters, figures, or marks. **9** *v.* To typewrite (something). ◆ In business English and informal speech, *type* is often used alone for *type of*, as in This *type* car is very popular. In formal writing *type of* is preferred.

type-set-ter [tīp'set'ər] *n.* **1** A person who sets type. **2** A machine that sets type.

type-write [tīp'rīt'] *v.* **type-wrote, type-writ-ten, type-writ-ing 1** *v.* To write with a typewriter. **2** *adj. use:* a *typewritten* letter.

type-writ-er [tīp'rī'tər] *n.* A machine with a keyboard that produces printed characters by impressing type upon paper through an inked ribbon.

ty-phoid [tī'foid] *n.* A disease caused by bacteria found in infected food, milk, or water. It is marked by fever, exhaustion, intestinal disorders, and skin blotches.

ty-phoon [tī-fōōn'] *n.* A violent hurricane originating over tropical waters in the western Pacific and the China Seas.

ty-phus [tī'fəs] *n.* An acute, contagious disease caused by a germ carried by certain body lice or fleas. It is marked by high fever, skin eruptions, and extreme physical weakness.

typ-i-cal [tip'i-kəl] *adj.* **1** Having qualities or features common to the whole group, class, etc.: a *typical* American. **2** Being or having the essential features of a species, group, class, etc.; characteristic: symptoms *typical* of measles. — **typ'i-cal-ly** *adv.*

typ-i-fy [tip'ə-fī] *v.* **typ-i-fied, typ-i-fy-ing** To be or serve as a type or example of: She *typifies* the students of our school.

typ-ist [tī'pist] *n.* A person who typewrites, especially one whose work is using a typewriter.

ty-po [tī'pō] *n.* *informal* A typographical error.

ty-pog-ra-phy [tī-pog'rə-fē] *n.* **1** The art or process of setting type and printing from it. **2** The style and appearance of printed matter. — **ty-pog'ra-pher** *n.* — **ty-po-graph-i-cal** [tī'pə-graf'i-kəl] *adj.*

Tyr [tir] *n.* In Norse myths, the god of war and son of Odin.

ty-ran-nic [ti-ran'ik] *adj.* Tyrannical.

ty-ran-ni-cal [ti-ran'i-kəl] *adj.* Of or like a tyrant; harsh; cruel: a *tyrannical* manager. — **ty-ran'ni-cal-ly** *adv.*

tyr-an-nize [tir'ə-nīz] *v.* **tyr-an-nized, tyr-an-niz-ing 1** To rule as a tyrant. **2** To be cruel and harsh in treatment or rule: Pharaoh *tyrannized* over the Hebrews. ¶3

ty-ran-no-sau-rus [ti-ran'ə-sôr'əs] *n., pl.* **ty-ran-no-sau-rus-es** or **ty-ran-no-sau-ri** [ti-ran'ə-sôr'ī] A huge, flesh-eating dinosaur that walked on its hind legs, common in western North America about 100 million years ago.

tyr-an-nous [tir'ə-nəs] *adj.* Harsh; cruel; tyrannical.

tyr-an-ny [tir'ə-nē] *n., pl.* **tyr-an-nies 1** Government in which a single ruler has absolute power. **2** Absolute power unfairly or cruelly used. **3** A cruel or tyrannical act.

ty-rant [tī'rənt] *n.* **1** A ruler having absolute power. **2** A ruler who exercises power cruelly or unfairly. **3** Any person who exerts power in such a way.

Tyre [tir] *n.* A port and capital of ancient Phoenicia. — **Tyr-i-an** [tir'ē-ən] *adj., n.*

ty-ro [tī'rō] *n., pl.* **ty-ros** A beginner; novice: In photography he was only a *tyro*.

Ty-rol [ti-rōl' or tī'rōl] *n.* A region of western Austria and northern Italy, in the Alps. — **Ty-rol-e-an** [ti-rō'lē-ən or tī-rō'lē-ən] *adj., n.*

tzar [tsär] *n.* Another spelling of CZAR.

tza-ri-na [tsä-rē'nə] *n.* Another spelling of CZARINA.

tzet-ze [tset'sē] Another spelling of TSETSE.

---

add, āce, câre, pälm; end, ēqual; it, īce; odd, ōpen, ôrder; tŏŏk, pōōl; up, bûrn; ə = a in *above*, e in *sicken*, i in *possible*, o in *melon*, u in *circus*; yōō = u in *fuse*; oil; pout; check; ring; thin; this; zh in *vision*. For ¶ reference, see page 64 · HOW TO

U

u or **U** [yoo] *n., pl.* **u's** or **U's** The 21st letter of the English alphabet.

U The symbol for the element URANIUM.

U.A.R. Abbreviation of UNITED ARAB REPUBLIC.

u·biq·ui·tous [yoo·bik′wə·təs] *adj.* Existing, or seeming to exist, everywhere at once.

u·biq·ui·ty [yoo·bik′wə·tē] *n.* The condition of being everywhere or in many places at once.

U-boat [yoo′bōt′] *n.* A German submarine.

ud·der [ud′ər] *n.* A large, hanging bag, as of a cow, where milk is made and given down.

ugh [ug, u, *or* ŏŏ] *interj.* Any of various sounds expressing disgust, horror, etc.

ug·ly [ug′lē] *adj.* **ug·li·er, ug·li·est** **1** Very disagreeable in appearance: *an ugly old witch.* **2** *informal* Ill-tempered; quarrelsome; cross: She was *ugly* about sharing the candy. **3** Bad in nature or effect: *an ugly* cut; *ugly* rumors. **4** Horrible or disgusting: *ugly* sins. **5** Threatening: *ugly* weather. **— ug′li·ness** *n.* ◆ *Ugly* goes back to an old Scandinavian word meaning *fear.*

UHF Abbreviation of ULTRAHIGH FREQUENCY.

U.K. Abbreviation of UNITED KINGDOM.

u·kase [yoo′kās *or* yoo·kāz′] *n.* An official decree, as one handed down by a czar of Russia.

U·kraine [yoo·krān′ *or* yoo′krān] *n.* A republic which is part of the Soviet Union, in the sw part. **— U·krain·i·an** [yoo·krā′nē·ən] *adj., n.*

u·ku·le·le [(y)oo′kə·lā′lē] *n.* A small guitarlike musical instrument having four strings. ◆ *Ukulele* is also the Hawaiian word for *flea.* The link may be that guitars and fleas first reached Hawaii together, by the same ship.

ul·cer [ul′sər] *n.* **1** An open sore on an external or internal surface of the body. It usually contains pus, and is sometimes very painful. **2** A rotten or corrupting condition; evil: the *ulcer* of envy.

Ukulele

ul·cer·ate [ul′sə·rāt] *v.* **ul·cer·at·ed, ul·cer·at·ing** **1** To cause, form, or develop an ulcer or ulcers. **2** *adj. use:* an *ulcerated* gum.

ul·cer·ous [ul′sər·əs] *adj.* **1** Like an ulcer. **2** Affected with an ulcer or ulcers.

ul·na [ul′nə] *n., pl.* **ul·nae** [ul′nē] or **ul·nas** **1** The thinner of the two bones of the forearm, on the same side as the little finger. **2** A corresponding bone in the foreleg of an animal.

ul·ster [ul′stər] *n.* A very long, loose, heavy overcoat, sometimes belted at the waist.

Ul·ster [ul′stər] *n.* A former province in northern Ireland, now divided between Northern Ireland and the Republic of Ireland.

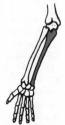

Ulna of the right arm

ul·te·ri·or [ul·tir′ē·ər] *adj.* **1** Beneath what is shown or expressed; hidden: *ulterior* motives. **2** Lying beyond or on the farther side of some boundary: *ulterior* regions. **3** Following; future; further: *ulterior* measures.

ul·ti·ma [ul′tə·mə] *n.* The final syllable of a word.

ul·ti·mate [ul′tə·mit] **1** *adj.* Last, final, or eventual: his *ultimate* goal. **2** *adj.* Most distant in time or space; farthest or earliest: man's *ultimate* origins. **3** *adj.* Greatest or highest possible; maximum: the *ultimate* stress that a structure can bear. **4** *n.* Something ultimate: the *ultimate* in fashion. **5** *adj.* Basic, underlying, or fundamental: the *ultimate* facts of existence. **6** *n.* A fundamental or basic fact.

ul·ti·mate·ly [ul′tə·mit·lē] *adv.* In the end; at last; finally: *Ultimately,* we will win.

ul·ti·ma·tum [ul′tə·mā′təm] *n., pl.* **ul·ti·ma·tums** or **ul·ti·ma·ta** [ul′tə·mā′tə] A final proposal, offer, or demand, to be refused only at the risk of force or punishment.

ul·tra [ul′trə] *adj.* Going beyond regular limits; immoderate; extreme: an *ultra* conservative.

ultra- A prefix meaning: **1** Beyond or above, as in *ultrasonic,* above the range of human hearing. **2** Highly or extremely, as in *ultramodern,* highly or extremely modern.

ul·tra·high frequency [ul′trə·hī′] Any radio wave frequency between 300 and 3000 megacycles per second.

ul·tra·ma·rine [ul′trə·mə·rēn′] **1** *n.* A deep blue pigment. **2** *n., adj.* Deep blue. **3** *adj.* Beyond or across the sea, as provinces.

ul·tra·son·ic [ul′trə·son′ik] *adj.* Indicating, operating by, or having to do with sound waves that are above the range of human hearing.

ul·tra·vi·o·let [ul′trə·vī′ə·lit] **1** *adj.* Describing electromagnetic waves that are shorter than those of visible violet light and longer than X-rays. **2** *n.* Ultraviolet radiation.

U·lys·ses [yōō·lis′ēz] *n.* The Latin name for ODYSSEUS.

um·bel [um′bəl] *n.* A flower cluster in which a number of flower stalks of almost equal length grow from the top of the main stem.

um·ber [um′bər] **1** *n.* A brown earth used as a pigment, either in its raw state or burnt. **2** *n., adj.* Yellowish brown or reddish brown.

um·bil·i·cal cord [um·bil′i·kəl] The tough, ropelike tissue that connects an unborn child with the placenta of its mother.

um·bra [um′brə] *n., pl.* **um·bras** or **um·brae** [um′brē] **1** A shadow or dark area. **2** The part of the moon's or the earth's shadow that completely hides the sun or moon in an eclipse.

um·brage [um′brij] *n.* A feeling of resentment or offense, especially in the phrase **take umbrage:** She *took umbrage* at his remarks.

um·brel·la [um·brel′ə] *n.* A folding, ribbed frame covered with light cloth or plastic, used as a protection against rain or sun. ◆ *Umbrella* comes from an Italian word which literally means *a little shade*, because it gives protection from the sun.

u·mi·ak [ōō′mē·ak] *n.* A large, open, Eskimo boat, made of skins drawn over a wooden frame.

Umiak

um·pire [um′pīr] *n., v.* **um·pired, um·pir·ing 1** *n.* An official who rules on the plays in a sports contest, as baseball. **2** *n.* A person called upon to settle a disagreement. **3** *v.* To act as umpire of: He *umpired* the game. **4** *v.* To act as umpire.

un-[1] A prefix meaning: Not; the opposite of, as in *unfair*, not fair, the opposite of fair. ◆ *Un-*[1] is used to express the opposite or lack of something. It can be prefixed to many adjectives and adverbs, and sometimes to nouns: *unhappy, unready, unbecomingly, uncertainty.* ◆ More words with *un-*[1] are listed below and on the next few pages. The meaning of each is: not + the meaning of the part after *un-*[1], as *unharmed*, not hurt or damaged.

un-[2] A prefix meaning: To do the opposite of, as in *unchain*, to do the opposite of chain by removing a chain or chains. ◆ *Un-*[2] is used chiefly to reverse the action of verbs, as in *uncover, undo, unseat.*

UN or **U.N.** Abbreviation of UNITED NATIONS.

un·a·ble [un·ā′bəl] *adj.* Lacking the necessary power or conditions; not able: *unable* to hear.

un·ac·count·a·ble [un′ə·koun′tə·bəl] *adj.* **1** Impossible to explain: *unaccountable* rudeness. **2** Not responsible or liable to be called to account. — **un′ac·count′a·bly** *adv.*

un·ac·cus·tomed [un′ə·kus′təmd] *adj.* **1** Not accustomed; not used: *unaccustomed* to hardship. **2** Not familiar; strange: an *unaccustomed* sight.

un·ad·vis·ed·ly [un′əd·vī′zid·lē] *adv.* In a rash or unwise way: He acted *unadvisedly.*

un·af·fect·ed[1] [un′ə·fek′tid] *adj.* Not changed or influenced: He was *unaffected* by her tears.

un·af·fect·ed[2] [un′ə·fek′tid] *adj.* Natural, simple, and sincere. — **un′af·fect′ed·ly** *adv.*

un-A·mer·i·can [un′ə·mer′ə·kən] *adj.* Contrary to the character, customs, ideals, interests, etc., of the U.S.: *un-American* activities.

u·na·nim·i·ty [yōō′nə·nim′ə·tē] *n.* Total agreement: the *unanimity* of the jurors.

u·nan·i·mous [yōō·nan′ə·məs] *adj.* **1** In total agreement: We are *unanimous* in our approval of the plan. **2** Showing total agreement: a *unanimous* opinion or vote. — **u·nan′i·mous·ly** *adv.*

un·ap·proach·a·ble [un′ə·prō′chə·bəl] *adj.* **1** Not easy to know or speak to; aloof: The judge seemed *unapproachable.* **2** Not capable of being reached: an *unapproachable* cliff. **3** Having no rival: *unapproachable* excellence.

un·armed [un·ärmd′] *adj.* **1** Not armed; without arms or weapons, especially a gun. **2** Without sharp prickles or points, as the spines, plates, etc., of some animals or plants.

un·as·sail·a·ble [un′ə·sāl′ə·bəl] *adj.* Too strong to be attacked or challenged: an *unassailable* fortress; an *unassailable* argument.

un·as·sum·ing [un′ə·sōō′ming] *adj.* Not vain or conceited; modest. — **un′as·sum′ing·ly** *adv.*

un·at·tached [un′ə·tacht′] *adj.* **1** Not fastened or attached. **2** Not married or engaged.

un·a·vail·ing [un′ə·vā′ling] *adj.* Without success; useless: His efforts were *unavailing.*

un·a·void·a·ble [un′ə·voi′də·bəl] *adj.* Not capable of being avoided or prevented: an *unavoidable* delay. — **un′a·void′a·bly** *adv.*

In the words below *un-* means *not.*

unabashed	unadorned	unannounced	unasked
unabated	unadulterated	unanswered	unassigned
unabridged	unafraid	unappetizing	unattainable
unaccented	unaided	unappreciated	unattempted
unacceptable	unaltered	unappreciative	unattractive
unacquainted	unambitious	unapproved	unauthorized
unadapted	unamusing	unashamed	unavailable

---

add, āce, câre, pälm; end, ēqual; it, īce; odd, ōpen, ôrder; tŏŏk, pōōl; up, bûrn; ə = a in *above*, e in *sicken*, i in *possible*, o in *melon*, u in *circus*; yōō = u in *fuse*; oil; pout; check; ring; thin; this; zh in *vision*. For ¶ reference, see page 64 · HOW TO

un·a·ware [un′ə·wâr′] **1** *adj.* Not aware; ignorant; unconscious: I was *unaware* of what was going on. **2** *adv.* Unawares: seldom used today.

un·a·wares [un′ə·wârz′] *adv.* In an unexpected way; by surprise; without warning: He came upon us *unawares*.

un·bal·anced [un·bal′ənst] *adj.* **1** Not balanced: *unbalanced* weights; an *unbalanced* checkbook. **2** Mentally disturbed; not wholly sane.

un·bar [un·bär′] *v.* **un·barred, un·bar·ring** To remove the bar from; open: *Unbar* the door.

un·beat·en [un′bēt′(ə)n] *adj.* **1** Not defeated. **2** Not traveled; not worn by footsteps, as a path. **3** Not shaped or mixed by beating.

un·be·com·ing [un′bi·kum′ing] *adj.* Not suitable, attractive, or proper; not becoming: *unbecoming* clothes; *unbecoming* conduct.

un·be·knownst [un′bi·nōnst′] *adj.* Unknown: *Unbeknownst* to her, he was a king in disguise.

un·be·lief [un′bi·lēf′] *n.* Lack of belief or faith, especially a lack of religious belief.

un·be·liev·er [un′bi·lēv′ər] *n.* **1** A person who does not believe; skeptic. **2** A person who does not believe in a particular religion.

un·be·liev·ing [un′bi·lēv′ing] *adj.* Not believing; doubting; questioning.

un·bend [un·bend′] *v.* **un·bent, un·bend·ing** **1** To straighten: to *unbend* a wire hanger. **2** To relax, as after strain or formality: Once the party started, I *unbent* and had a good time.

un·bend·ing [un·ben′ding] *adj.* **1** Not bending easily. **2** Not yielding or compromising; firm.

un·bent [un·bent′] Past tense and past participle of UNBEND.

un·bi·ased or **un·bi·assed** [un·bī′əst] *adj.* Not prejudiced or partial; fair: an *unbiased* jury.

un·bid·den [un·bid′(ə)n] *adj.* Without having been asked, called, or invited: an *unbidden* guest.

un·bind [un·bīnd′] *v.* **un·bound, un·bind·ing** To release, as by untying; let loose.

un·blessed or **un·blest** [un·blest′] *adj.* **1** Not blessed. **2** Unholy; evil. **3** Unhappy; wretched.

un·blush·ing [un·blush′ing] *adj.* **1** Not blushing. **2** Shameless. — **un·blush′ing·ly** *adv.*

un·bolt [un·bōlt′] *v.* To unlock or open, as a door, by drawing back a bolt; unfasten.

un·bolt·ed [un·bōl′tid] *adj.* Not fastened by bolts: an *unbolted* door.

un·born [un·bôrn′] *adj.* Not born, or yet to be born; to come; to be: *unborn* generations.

un·bos·om [un·bo͞oz′əm] *v.* To reveal, as one's thoughts or secrets. — **unbosom oneself** To tell one's thoughts, feelings, troubles, etc.

un·bound [un·bound′] **1** Past tense and past participle of UNBIND. **2** *adj.* Not bound in covers: an *unbound* book. **3** *adj.* Freed from bonds or fastenings: long, *unbound* hair.

un·bound·ed [un·boun′did] *adj.* **1** Without bounds or limits; very great: *unbounded* optimism. **2** Not restrained: *unbounded* freedom.

un·bowed [un·boud′] *adj.* Not bent or bowed down, as in defeat: a head bloody but *unbowed*.

un·bri·dled [un·brid′(ə)ld] *adj.* **1** Wearing no bridle: an *unbridled* horse. **2** Not held in or controlled: *unbridled* anger.

un·bro·ken [un·brō′kən] *adj.* **1** Not broken; whole; entire: an *unbroken* seal. **2** Not violated: an *unbroken* promise. **3** Going on without interruption: an *unbroken* series; *unbroken* sleep. **4** Not tamed or trained, as a horse.

un·buck·le [un·buk′əl] *v.* **un·buck·led, un·buck·ling** To undo the buckle or buckles of: to *unbuckle* the straps of a suitcase.

un·bur·den [un·bûr′dən] *v.* To free from a burden, fear, worry, etc.

un·but·ton [un·but′(ə)n] *v.* To unfasten the button or buttons of (a coat, shirt, etc.).

un·called-for [un·kôld′fôr′] *adj.* Not necessary or asked for: an *uncalled-for* outburst.

un·can·ny [un·kan′ē] *adj.* **1** Weird and mysterious; eerie: *uncanny* noises in the night. **2** So good as to seem beyond human powers: *uncanny* accuracy. — **un·can′ni·ly** *adv.*

un·cap [un·kap′] *v.* **un·capped, un·cap·ping** To take the cap off: to *uncap* a tube of toothpaste; to *uncap* a bottle.

un·ceas·ing [un·sē′sing] *adj.* Never stopping or ending: *unceasing* noise; *unceasing* devotion.

un·cer·e·mo·ni·ous [un′ser·ə·mō′nē·əs] *adj.* **1** Not very courteous; abrupt or rude. **2** Informal. — **un′cer·e·mo′ni·ous·ly** *adv.*

un·cer·tain [un·sûr′tən] *adj.* **1** Not certain; unsure; doubtful: He was *uncertain* of the answer. **2** Not capable of being known or predicted: The outcome is *uncertain*. **3** Not to be counted on; apt to change quickly: *uncertain* sunshine. **4** Capable of being misunderstood: in no *uncertain* terms. — **un·cer′tain·ly** *adv.*

un·cer·tain·ty [un·sûr′tən·tē] *n., pl.* **un·cer·tain·ties** **1** The condition of being uncertain; doubt. **2** Something uncertain.

un·chain [un·chān′] *v.* To release from a chain or chains; set free.

un·char·i·ta·ble [un·char′ə·tə·bəl] *adj.* Not kind or understanding; harsh in judging others.

un·chris·tian [un·kris′chən] *adj.* **1** Not Christian. **2** Contrary to Christian principles or teachings; not good, kind, etc.

un·civ·il [un·siv′əl] *adj.* Not polite; rude.

un·civ·i·lized [un·siv′ə·līzd] *adj.* **1** Not civilized; savage. **2** Not refined, as behavior. ¶3

un·clasp [un·klasp′] *v.* **1** To undo the clasp of: to *unclasp* a necklace. **2** To free or be freed from a clasp or grasp.

In the words below *un-* means *not*.

unbearable	unburnt	unchallenged	unchecked
unblemished	uncanceled	unchangeable	unchewed
unbreakable	uncaught	unchanging	unclad
unburied	uncensored	uncharted	unclaimed

un·cle [ung′kəl] *n.* **1** The brother of one's father or mother. **2** The husband of one's aunt.

un·clean [un·klēn′] *adj.* **1** Dirty; foul. **2** Not pure in a spiritual or religious sense.

un·clean·ly [un·klen′lē] *adj.* Dirty or impure.

Uncle Sam [sam] The personification of the U.S. government or people, a tall, lean man with chin whiskers. ◆ *Uncle Sam* is an expansion of U.S. based on the nickname of *Samuel* Wilson, 1766–1854, a New York State businessman.

un·cloak [un·klōk′] *v.* **1** To take off the coat or cloak of. **2** To expose; reveal.

un·clothed [un·klōᵗʜd′] *adj.* Without clothes.

un·coil [un·koil′] *v.* To unwind: to *uncoil* a rope; The snake *uncoiled.*

un·com·fort·a·ble [un·kum′fər·tə·bəl *or* un·kumf′tə·bəl] *adj.* **1** Not comfortable in body or mind. **2** Not allowing comfort or ease: an *uncomfortable* seat. — **un·com′fort·a·bly** *adv.*

un·com·mon [un·kom′ən] *adj.* **1** Not common or usual; rare. **2** Remarkable; outstanding. — **un·com′mon·ly** *adv.*

un·com·mu·ni·ca·tive [un′kə·myōō′nə·kə·tiv *or* un′kə·myōō′nə·kā′tiv] *adj.* Not willing to say much or to give much information; reserved.

un·com·pro·mis·ing [un·kom′prə·mī′zing] *adj.* Not yielding on any point; firm.

un·con·cern [un′kən·sûrn′] *n.* Lack of interest or freedom from anxiety.

un·con·cerned [un′kən·sûrnd′] *adj.* Not interested, involved, or anxious.

un·con·di·tion·al [un′kən·dish′ən·əl] *adj.* Not limited by conditions; absolute: *unconditional* surrender. — **un′con·di′tion·al·ly** *adv.*

un·con·quer·a·ble [un·kong′kər·ə·bəl] *adj.* Not capable of being conquered or defeated.

un·con·scion·a·ble [un·kon′shən·ə·bəl] *adj.* **1** Exceeding what is reasonable; excessive: an *unconscionable* delay. **2** Not restrained by conscience: an *unconscionable* liar.

un·con·scious [un·kon′shəs] *adj.* **1** Not able to feel and think; not conscious: He was *unconscious* during the operation. **2** Not aware; ignorant: *unconscious* of his charm. **3** Done or made without meaning to or realizing it: an *unconscious* imitation. — **the unconscious** The part of our mental life of which we are seldom or only briefly aware. — **un·con′scious·ly** *adv.* — **un·con′scious·ness** *n.*

un·con·sti·tu·tion·al [un′kon·sti·t(y)ōō′shən·əl] *adj.* Contrary to the constitution of a nation, etc. — **un·con·sti·tu·tion·al·i·ty** [un′kon·stə·t(y)ōō′shən·al′ə·tē] *n.*

un·con·trol·la·ble [un′kən·trō′lə·bəl] *adj.* That cannot be controlled.

un·con·ven·tion·al [un′kən·ven′shən·əl] *adj.* Not conforming to accepted custom or established practice; out of the ordinary.

un·cork [un·kôrk′] *v.* To draw the cork from.

un·count·ed [un·koun′tid] *adj.* **1** Not counted. **2** Too many to count; countless; innumerable.

un·coup·le [un·kup′əl] *v.* **un·coup·led, un·coup·ling** To unfasten or disconnect: to *uncouple* the cars of a train.

un·couth [un·kōōth′] *adj.* Crude, rude, awkward or clumsy: *uncouth* behavior; *uncouth* men.

un·cov·er [un·kuv′ər] *v.* **1** To take the cover or covering off of: to *uncover* a pot. **2** To make known; reveal: to *uncover* a scheme. **3** To raise or remove one's hat, as to show respect.

unc·tion [ungk′shən] *n.* **1** The act of applying oil or ointment to someone, often as part of a religious ceremony, as the rite of anointing the sick or the dying. **2** A substance used in anointing; oil or ointment. **3** Something that comforts or soothes, as flattery. **4** A deep feeling; earnestness; fervor. **5** A false or exaggerated earnestness of speech or manner, often used to arouse the fervor of others.

unc·tu·ous [ungk′chōō·əs] *adj.* **1** Like an ointment; oily, greasy, soft, etc. **2** Too smooth or too obviously persuasive, as in manner or speech.

un·curl [un·kûrl′] *v.* To straighten from a curled condition; unroll, untwist, or unwind.

un·daunt·ed [un·dôn′tid] *adj.* Not discouraged or fearful: *undaunted* in the face of defeat.

un·de·ceive [un′di·sēv′] *v.* **un·de·ceived, un·de·ceiv·ing** To free from error or illusion, as by informing of the truth.

un·de·cid·ed [un′di·sī′did] *adj.* **1** Not having the mind made up: *undecided* about what to do. **2** Not yet settled or decided: Details are still *undecided.* — **un′de·cid′ed·ly** *adv.*

un·de·mon·stra·tive [un′di·mon′strə·tiv] *adj.* Not showing one's feelings, as of affection.

un·de·ni·a·ble [un′di·nī′ə·bəl] *adj.* Too true, good, etc., to be denied or questioned: *undeniable* excellence. — **un′de·ni′a·bly** *adv.*

In the words below *un-* means *not.*

unclouded	unconfined	uncooperative	undeclared
uncolored	unconfirmed	uncoordinated	undecorated
uncombed	unconquered	uncritical	undefeated
uncomplaining	unconstrained	uncrowded	undefended
uncomplicated	uncontaminated	uncultivated	undefined
uncomplimentary	uncontrolled	undamaged	undelivered
uncomprehending	unconvincing	undated	undemocratic
unconcealed	uncooked	undebatable	undependable

---

add, āce, câre, pälm;   end, ēqual;   it, īce;   odd, ōpen, ôrder;   tŏŏk, pōŏl;   up, bûrn;
ə = a in *above*, e in *sicken*, i in *possible*, o in *melon*, u in *circus*;   yōō = u in *fuse*;   oil;   pout;
check; ring; thin; ᴛʜis; zh in *vision*. For ¶ reference, see page 64 · HOW TO

un·der [un′dər] **1** *prep*. Beneath, so as to have something directly above: *under* the bed; *under* an umbrella. **2** *adv*. In or into a position below something: The wave knocked him *under*. **3** *prep*. Lower than the surface of: *under* the ground. **4** *adj*. Lower, as in position: the *under* parts. **5** *prep*. Beneath the cover of: to wear a shirt *under* a sweater; He writes *under* a pen name. **6** *adv*. So as to be covered or concealed: a desk snowed *under* with papers. **7** *prep*. Within the group or class of: That book is listed *under* adventure. **8** *prep*. Lower than or less than; below: a number *under* 100. **9** *adv*. Less: three pounds or *under*. **10** *prep*. Subject to the action, force, influence, or authority of: *under* control; to serve *under* an officer. **11** *prep*. During the period or reign of: Rome *under* Caesar. **12** *prep*. Bound, controlled, or driven by: *under* oath; *under* orders; *under* sail. **13** *prep*. Because of: *under* the circumstances. **— go under 1** To fail or collapse, as a business. **2** To give in or yield.

under- A prefix meaning: **1** Below in position; situated below or beneath, as in *underbrush*, small trees and shrubs situated beneath large trees in a forest, etc. **2** Below a surface or covering, as in *undershirt*, a garment worn below a covering. **3** Inferior in rank or importance, as in *undersecretary*, an official inferior in rank to the secretary. **4** Less than is usual or proper, as in *undervalue*, to value less than is proper.

un·der·age [un′dər·āj′] *adj*. Not old enough, as to have certain legal rights and duties.

un·der·arm [un′dər·ärm′] **1** *adj*. Found or put under the arm or in the armpit: an *underarm* deodorant. **2** *n*. The armpit.

un·der·bid [un′dər·bid′] *v*. **un·der·bid, un·der·bid·ding** To offer to accept a lower payment than (a rival bidder), as for doing work.

un·der·brush [un′dər·brush′] *n*. Small trees and shrubs growing under trees in the woods.

un·der·clothes [un′dər·klōz′ or un′dər·klōt͟hz′] *n.pl.* Garments worn next to the skin and covered by one's outer clothing; underwear.

un·der·cloth·ing [un′dər·klōt͟h′ing] *n*. Underclothes; underwear.

un·der·cov·er [un′dər·kuv′ər] *adj*. Acting or done in secret: an *undercover* investigator.

un·der·cur·rent [un′dər·kûr′ənt] *n*. **1** A current, as of water or air, below the surface or below another current. **2** An underlying or hidden feeling, attitude, etc.: He sensed an *undercurrent* of fear beneath their boasts.

un·der·cut [*v*. un′dər·kut′, *n*. un′dər·kut′] *v*. **un·der·cut, un·der·cut·ting,** *n*. **1** *v*. To cut under: to *undercut* a mass of coal to remove it. **2** *v*. To cut away a lower portion of: to *undercut* a carved design to make the upper part stand out. **3** *n*. The act or result of cutting under. **4** *v*. To work or sell for lower payment than (a rival).

un·der·dog [un′dər·dôg′] *n*. **1** A person or side expected to lose in a contest, fight, etc. **2** A person who is oppressed by society or by those in power.

un·der·done [un′dər·dun′] *adj*. Not fully cooked; not cooked enough: *underdone* beef.

un·der·es·ti·mate [*v*. un′dər·es′tə·māt, *n*. un′dər·es′tə·mit] *v*. **un·der·es·ti·mat·ed, un·der·es·ti·mat·ing,** *n*. **1** *v*. To judge to be less or lower than actually is the case: We *underestimated* the cost of the trip. **2** *n*. An estimate that is too low.

un·der·ex·pose [un′dər·ik·spōz′] *v*. **un·der·ex·posed, un·der·ex·pos·ing** To expose (a photographic film) to too weak a light or to enough light for too short a time.

un·der·feed [un′dər·fēd′] *v*. **un·der·fed, un·der·feed·ing** To provide with too little food.

un·der·foot [un′dər·foot′] *adv*. **1** Beneath the feet: The ground is very wet *underfoot*. **2** In the way: a little brother always *underfoot*.

un·der·gar·ment [un′dər·gär′mənt] *n*. Any piece of underwear.

un·der·go [un′dər·gō′] *v*. **un·der·went, un·der·gone, un·der·go·ing 1** To go through; experience: A person *undergoes* many changes as he gets older. **2** To be subjected to; endure or suffer: He *underwent* having his ankle taped.

un·der·grad·u·ate [un′dər·graj′oo·it] *n*. **1** A college student who has not yet received a degree. **2** *adj. use:* an *undergraduate* course.

un·der·ground [*adv*. un′dər·ground′, *adj., n.* un′dər·ground′] **1** *adv*. Beneath the surface of the ground: A subway runs *underground*. **2** *adj*. Situated, done, or operating beneath the surface of the ground: an *underground* passage. **3** *n*. A space or passage beneath the surface of the ground. **4** *adj*. Done in secret: *underground* revolutionary activity. **5** *adv*. In or into hiding or concealment: The patriots were forced to go *underground*. **6** *n*. A group secretly organized to work against the government or conquerors of their country.

un·der·growth [un′dər·grōth′] *n*. Underbrush.

un·der·hand [un′dər·hand′] **1** *adj*. Made with the hand lower than the elbow: an *underhand* throw. **2** *adv*. With an underhand motion: to throw a ball *underhand*. **3** *adj*. Sly and unfair or dishonest: to win an election by *underhand* methods. **4** *adv*. In a secret and sly manner. ◆ See STEALTHY.

un·der·hand·ed [un′dər·han′did] *adj*. Sly and unfair or dishonest; underhand. **— un′der·hand′ed·ly** *adv*.

un·der·lie [un′dər·lī′] *v*. **un·der·lay, un·der·lain, un·der·ly·ing 1** To lie below or under: A layer of rock *underlies* the coal. **2** To be the basis or support of: What causes *underlie* his action?

un·der·line [un′dər·līn′] *v*. **un·der·lined, un·der·lin·ing 1** To draw a line beneath: to *underline* written words. **2** To emphasize: to *underline* spoken words by stressing them.

un·der·ling [un′dər·ling] *n*. A person inferior in rank and under the authority of others.

un·der·ly·ing [un′dər·lī′ing] *adj*. **1** Lying under: an *underlying* layer. **2** Basic; fundamental; primary: *underlying* principles.

un·der·mine [un′dər·mīn *or* un′dər·mīn′] *v.* **un·der·mined, un·der·min·ing** **1** To dig a hole or passage under: to *undermine* a fortress. **2** To weaken by wearing away at the base: The river was *undermining* its high banks. **3** To weaken slowly or by sly means: The lies told to them *undermined* their faith in their leader.

un·der·most [un′dər·mōst′] **1** *adj.* Lowest. **2** *adv.* In the lowest place or position.

un·der·neath [un′dər·nēth′] **1** *prep.* Beneath; under; below: *underneath* the table. **2** *adv.* Beneath or on the underside: They picked it up to see what was *underneath.* **3** *n.* The lower part or underside.

un·der·nour·ished [un′dər·nûr′isht] *adj.* Not getting enough food to stay healthy or to grow.

un·der·pants [un′dər·pants′] *n.pl.* An undergarment having either long or short legs.

un·der·pass [un′dər·pas′] *n.* *U.S.* A passage under a highway, railway, etc., as for a road.

un·der·pin·ning [un′dər·pin′ing] *n.* Supports or the foundation under a wall or building.

un·der·priv·i·leged [un′dər·priv′ə·lijd] *adj.* Lacking advantages and rights that everyone should have, usually because of being poor.

un·der·rate [un′dər·rāt′] *v.* **un·der·rat·ed, un·der·rat·ing** To rate too low; underestimate: Don't *underrate* our ability.

un·der·score [un′dər·skôr′] *v.* **un·der·scored, un·der·scor·ing** To underline.

un·der·sea [un′dər·sē′] **1** *adj.* Existing, carried on, or used below the surface of the sea. **2** *adv.* Beneath the surface of the sea.

un·der·seas [un′dər·sēz′] *adv.* Undersea.

un·der·sec·re·tar·y [un′dər·sek′rə·ter′ē] *n., pl.* **un·der·sec·re·tar·ies** In a government department, the official who ranks next below the secretary.

un·der·sell [un′dər·sel′] *v.* **un·der·sold, un·der·sell·ing** To sell at a lower price than.

un·der·shirt [un′dər·shûrt′] *n.* A garment, generally of cotton, worn beneath the shirt.

un·der·shot [un′dər·shot′] *adj.* **1** Moved by water flowing underneath: said about a water wheel. **2** Having the lower jaw or teeth sticking out past the upper when the mouth is shut.

un·der·side [un′dər·sīd′] *n.* The lower or bottom side or surface.

Undershot water wheel

un·der·signed [un′dər·sīnd′] *adj.* **1** Signed at or having one's signature at the bottom of a document. **2** *n. use* The signer or signers of a document: The *undersigned* were witnesses.

un·der·sized [un′dər·sīzd′] *adj.* Of less than the normal or average size: an *undersized* fish.

un·der·sold [un′dər·sōld′] Past tense and past participle of UNDERSELL.

un·der·stand [un′dər·stand′] *v.* **un·der·stood, un·der·stand·ing** **1** To take in the meaning or purpose of; grasp with the mind: Do you *understand* the instructions? **2** To have been told or have the impression: We *understand* that she is ill. **3** To think, take, or interpret: He *understood* the light to be a signal. **4** To accept as being agreed upon: It was *understood* that we would take turns. **5** To supply in thought when not expressed. In "My dog is bigger than yours," the word *is* is understood after *yours.* **6** To know well or appreciate: He *understands* modern art. **7** To know or be aware of the nature of, or be in sympathy with: They *understand* each other. **8** To have understanding or sympathy: Mother always *understands.*

un·der·stand·a·ble [un′dər·stan′də·bəl] *adj.* Capable of being understood.

un·der·stand·ing [un′dər·stan′ding] **1** *n.* A grasping of the essentials or meaning; knowledge: his *understanding* of mathematics. **2** *n.* The ability to take in meaning, to interpret, reason, and judge; intelligence. **3** *n.* Opinion or interpretation. **4** *n.* Insight or sympathy. **5** *adj.* Full of insight or sympathy: an *understanding* smile. **6** *n.* An informal agreement, as to marry. **7** *n.* A settlement of differences: The opposing sides came to an *understanding.*

un·der·state [un′dər·stāt′] *v.* **un·der·stat·ed, un·der·stat·ing** To describe or talk about as less than, or less important or colorful than, the actuality: He always *understated* his success, calling it luck. — **un′der·state′ment** *n.*

un·der·stood [un′dər·stŏŏd′] Past tense and past participle of UNDERSTAND.

un·der·stud·y [un′dər·stud′ē] *n., pl.* **un·der·stud·ies,** *v.* **un·der·stud·ied, un·der·stud·y·ing** **1** *n.* An actor who can take the place of another in a given role when necessary. **2** *v.* To study (a part) as an understudy. **3** *v.* To act as an understudy to (another actor).

un·der·take [un′dər·tāk′] *v.* **un·der·took, un·der·tak·en, un·der·tak·ing** **1** To take upon oneself; agree or promise to do: to *undertake* a task. **2** To engage in; start upon; begin: to *undertake* a journey.

un·der·tak·er [un′dər·tā′kər] *n.* A person whose business is to prepare dead people for burial and to manage and conduct funerals; mortician.

un·der·tak·ing [un′dər·tā′king *for defs.* 1, 3, un′dər·tā′king *for def.* 2] *n.* **1** Something that a person promises or attempts to do, usually an important or difficult task. **2** The work or profession of an undertaker. **3** A pledge or promise.

un·der·tone [un′dər·tōn′] *n.* **1** A low sound, vocal tone, or whisper. **2** A soft or subdued shade of a color. **3** A color that is in back of and is seen through other colors: an *undertone* of red in this orange. **4** An emotional quality that is behind what a person says or does: an *undertone* of fear in his voice.

un·der·took [un′dər·to͝ok′] Past tense of UNDERTAKE.

un·der·tow [un′dər·tō′] *n.* A strong current under the surface of the water, as one flowing back out to sea or sideways along the beach while the surface current flows in to shore.

un·der·val·ue [un′dər·val′yo͞o] *v.* **un·der·val·ued, un·der·val·u·ing** To set too low a value upon: He *undervalues* his own talents.

un·der·wa·ter [un′dər·wô′tər] *adj.* Found, done, or used beneath the surface of the water.

un·der·wear [un′dər·wâr′] *n.* Garments worn under one's outer clothes.

un·der·weight [un′dər·wāt′] **1** *adj.* Below the normal or proper weight. **2** *n.* Weight that does not come up to a standard or requirement.

un·der·went [un′dər·went′] Past tense of UNDERGO.

un·der·world [un′dər·wûrld′] *n.* **1** The part of society engaged in crime, especially organized criminals. **2** Hades, the kingdom of the dead.

un·der·write [un′dər·rīt′] *v.* **un·der·wrote, un·der·writ·ten, un·der·writ·ing 1** To assume responsibility for or support, as with money: Business firms *underwrote* the opera's losses. **2** To issue (an insurance policy), assuming the risk for the property insured. **3** To agree to buy all or part of (an issue of stocks, bonds, etc.) that remains unsold. **— un′der·writ′er** *n.*

un·de·sir·a·ble [un′di·zīr′ə·bəl] **1** *adj.* Not desirable or pleasing; unwanted or objectionable. **2** *n.* An undesirable person.

un·did [un·did′] Past tense of UNDO.

un·dis·tin·guished [un′dis·ting′gwisht] *adj.* Not distinguished or outstanding; commonplace.

un·do [un·do͞o′] *v.* **un·did, un·done, un·do·ing 1** To loosen, untie, unfasten, or unwrap: to *undo* a clasp. **2** To cause to be as if never done; reverse or cancel: to try to *undo* a wrong that has been done. **3** To bring to ruin; destroy: He was *undone* by his own greed.

un·do·ing [un·do͞o′ing] *n.* **1** Ruin or cause of ruin: Pride was her *undoing*. **2** The act of reversing or canceling what has been done. **3** The act of opening, untying, unfastening, etc.

un·done [un·dun′] **1** Past participle of UNDO. **2** *adj.* Not completed. **3** *adj.* Ruined. **4** *adj.* Untied; unfastened.

un·doubt·ed [un·dou′tid] *adj.* Not open to question; not doubted: *undoubted* superiority.

un·doubt·ed·ly [un·dou′tid·lē] *adv.* Without doubt; surely: You are *undoubtedly* right.

un·dreamed-of [un·drēmd′uv′] *adj.* Never even imagined or dreamed of: *undreamed-of* happiness.

un·dress [un·dres′] **1** *v.* To take off the clothes of: She *undressed* the baby. **2** *v.* To take one's clothes off. **3** *n.* Casual, informal clothes.

un·due [un·d(y)o͞o′] *adj.* **1** Not suitable; not proper. **2** Too much; excessive: *undue* severity.

un·du·lant [un′d(y)ə·lənt] *adj.* Moving or shaped in waves; wavy or rolling.

un·du·late [un′d(y)ə·lāt] *v.* **un·du·lat·ed, un·du·lat·ing 1** To move or cause to move like a wave or in waves: The wheat *undulates* in the wind. **2** To have a wavy shape or appearance, as land full of hills. **— un′du·la′tion** *n.*

un·du·ly [un·d(y)o͞o′lē] *adv.* **1** More than is fitting or proper: *unduly* confident. **2** Unjustly or illegally: *unduly* influenced.

un·dy·ing [un·dī′ing] *adj.* Never dying or ending; everlasting: my *undying* gratitude.

un·earth [un·ûrth′] *v.* **1** To dig up from the ground: to *unearth* bones. **2** To discover by or as if by searching: to *unearth* the true facts.

un·earth·ly [un·ûrth′lē] *adj.* **1** Not of this earth; supernatural. **2** Weird and frightening.

un·eas·y [un·ē′zē] *adj.* **un·eas·i·er, un·eas·i·est 1** Troubled; worried: *uneasy* about their safety. **2** Restless or nervous. **3** Not relaxed or natural; embarrassed; awkward: an *uneasy* laugh. **4** Not secure; unstable: an *uneasy* truce. **— un·eas′i·ly** *adv.* **— un·eas′i·ness** *n.*

un·em·ployed [un′im·ploid′] *adj.* **1** Without a job; out of work. **2** *n. use* People who have no jobs: to find work for *the unemployed*. **3** Not put to use: *unemployed* resources.

un·em·ploy·ment [un′im·ploi′mənt] *n.* The condition of being unemployed.

un·e·qual [un·ē′kwəl] *adj.* **1** Not equal or balanced, as in size, strength, amount, ability, worth, etc. **2** Unfair: an *unequal* contest. **3** Not the same throughout; uneven: an *unequal* performance. **— unequal to** Lacking the ability, power, etc., needed for: She was *unequal to* the demands of the job. **— un·e′qual·ly** *adv.*

un·e·qualed or **un·e·qualled** [un·ē′kwəld] *adj.* Having no equal; going beyond any other.

un·e·quiv·o·cal [un′i·kwiv′ə·kəl] *adj.* Plain, not ambiguous or open to misunderstanding: an *unequivocal* refusal. **— un′e·quiv′o·cal·ly** *adv.*

un·err·ing [un·ûr′ing *or* un·er′ing] *adj.* Making no mistakes; free from error; exact; perfect: *unerring* accuracy. **— un·err′ing·ly** *adv.*

UNESCO or **U·nes·co** [yo͞o·nes′kō] *n.* The United Nations Educational, Scientific, and Cultural Organization.

un·e·ven [un·ē′vən] *adj.* **1** Not even, smooth, level, or equal: *uneven* floors; *uneven* margins. **2** Not equal or well matched: an *uneven* battle. **3** Changeable or varying, as in quality: *uneven* work. **4** Not capable of being divided by 2 with

---

In the words below *un-* means *not*.

undeserved	undiminished	undivided	unemotional
undetected	undisciplined	undramatic	unending
undeveloped	undiscovered	uneaten	unendurable
undignified	undisturbed	unembarrassed	unenthusiastic

out leaving a remainder. *7 is an uneven number.*
— **un·e'ven·ly** *adv.* — **un·e'ven·ness** *n.*

un·e·vent·ful [un'i·vent'fəl] *adj.* Without any interesting or important happenings: *an uneventful day.* — **un'e·vent'ful·ly** *adv.*

un·ex·am·pled [un'ig·zam'pəld] *adj.* Not like anything seen before or to be found elsewhere; unique: *unexampled courtesy.*

un·ex·cep·tion·a·ble [un'ik·sep'shən·ə·bəl] *adj.* Not open to any criticism; beyond reproach; completely correct: *unexceptionable conduct.*

un·ex·pect·ed [un'ik·spek'tid] *adj.* Coming or happening without warning; not expected: *an unexpected shower.* — **un'ex·pect'ed·ly** *adv.*

un·ex·plain·a·ble [un'ik·splān'ə·bəl] *adj.* Impossible to explain; inexplicable.

un·fail·ing [un·fā'ling] *adj.* **1** Never lessening, running out, or stopping. **2** Certain; sure: *an unfailing remedy.* — **un·fail'ing·ly** *adv.*

un·fair [un·fâr'] *adj.* **1** Not fair, right, or just. **2** Dishonest. — **un·fair'ly** *adv.*

un·faith·ful [un·fāth'fəl] *adj.* **1** Breaking promises or ignoring duty; disloyal; faithless. **2** Not accurate, true, or exact: *an unfaithful portrait.* — **un·faith'ful·ness** *n.*

un·fal·ter·ing [un·fôl'tər·ing] *adj.* Not hesitating or wavering; firm; steadfast.

un·fa·mil·iar [un'fə·mil'yər] *adj.* **1** Not recognized or known; strange: *an unfamiliar neighborhood.* **2** Not acquainted or familiar: *a stranger unfamiliar with local laws.* — **un·fa·mil·i·ar·i·ty** [un'fə·mil'ē·ar'ə·tē] *n.*

un·fast·en [un·fas'ən] *v.* To undo the fastenings of; unlatch; detach.

un·fath·om·a·ble [un·fath'əm·ə·bəl] *adj.* **1** Too deep to be measured, as seas. **2** Impossible to understand: *an unfathomable mystery.*

un·fa·vor·a·ble [un·fā'vər·ə·bəl] *adj.* Not favorable, helpful, encouraging, or approving. — **un·fa'vor·a·bly** *adv.* ¶1

un·feel·ing [un·fē'ling] *adj.* **1** Not sympathetic; hardhearted; cruel. **2** Not able to feel; numb. — **un·feel'ing·ly** *adv.*

un·feigned [un·fānd'] *adj.* Not pretended; sincere; genuine: *unfeigned admiration.*

un·fin·ished [un·fin'isht] *adj.* **1** Not completed. **2** Lacking a particular finish, as not painted or not polished: *unfinished furniture.*

un·fit [un·fit'] *adj., v.* **un·fit·ted, un·fit·ting** **1** *adj.* Not fit, suitable, qualified, or in proper condition: *supplies unfit for use.* **2** *v.* To make unfit or not qualified: *His injury unfits him for military service.* — **un·fit'ness** *n.*

un·fledged [un·flejd'] *adj.* **1** Not yet feathered, as a young bird. **2** Not mature; inexperienced.

un·flinch·ing [un·flin'ching] *adj.* Not shrinking from danger, pain, etc.; steadfast.

un·fold [un·fōld'] *v.* **1** To open from a folded state; spread out: *Unfold this sheet.* **2** To open out, as a bud; develop. **3** To extend or be revealed: *The valley unfolded before them.* **4** To reveal or explain: *He unfolded his plan.*

un·for·get·ta·ble [un'fər·get'ə·bəl] *adj.* Impossible to forget; memorable.

un·for·tu·nate [un·fôr'chə·nit] **1** *adj.* Not fortunate or lucky: *to be unfortunate in business.* **2** *n.* An unlucky, poor, or outcast person. **3** *adj.* Not suitable or fitting: *an unfortunate choice of words.* — **un·for'tu·nate·ly** *adv.*

un·found·ed [un·foun'did] *adj.* Having no basis in fact; groundless: *unfounded suspicions.*

un·friend·ly [un·frend'lē] *adj.* **1** Showing ill will; not friendly or kind. **2** Not favorable.

un·fruit·ful [un·frōot'fəl] *adj.* Not producing fruit, offspring, or good results; barren.

un·furl [un·fûrl'] *v.* To spread out or open; unroll or unfold, as a sail or flag.

un·gain·ly [un·gān'lē] *adj.* Awkward; clumsy.

un·god·ly [un·god'lē] *adj.* **1** Having no reverence for God. **2** Wicked; sinful. **3** *informal* Outrageous: *at an ungodly hour.*

un·gov·ern·a·ble [un·guv'ər·nə·bəl] *adj.* Hard or impossible to govern, control, or restrain: *ungovernable anger.* — **un·gov'ern·a·bly** *adv.*

un·grate·ful [un·grāt'fəl] *adj.* **1** Lacking gratitude; not thankful. **2** Not pleasant; disagreeable, as a task. — **un·grate'ful·ly** *adv.*

un·ground·ed [un·groun'did] *adj.* Having no basis in fact; without foundation: *ungrounded complaints.*

un·guent [ung'gwənt] *n.* An ointment or salve.

un·gu·late [ung'gyə·lit] **1** *adj.* Having hoofs, as the horse, cow, etc. **2** *n.* A hoofed mammal.

un·hand [un·hand'] *v.* To stop holding with the hands; let go.

un·hap·py [un·hap'ē] *adj.* **un·hap·pi·er, un·hap·pi·est** **1** Not happy or content; sad, miserable, or dissatisfied. **2** Not lucky; unfortunate: *Unhappy day!* **3** Not suitable or appropriate: *an unhappy remark.* — **un·hap'pi·ly** *adv.* — **un·hap'pi·ness** *n.*

un·health·y [un·hel'thē] *adj.* **un·health·i·er, un·health·i·est** **1** Not in good health; not well; sickly. **2** Harmful to the health or morals; not wholesome: *an unhealthy climate; unhealthy influences.*

In the words below *un-* means *not.*

unexaggerated	**unexposed**	**unfettered**	**unfulfilled**
unexcelled	**unfashionable**	**unflattering**	**unfurnished**
unexcited	**unfastened**	**unforced**	**ungraceful**
unexplored	**unfed**	**unforeseen**	**unharmed**

---

add, āce, câre, pälm;   end, ēqual;   it, īce;   odd, ōpen, ôrder;   tŏŏk, pōōl;   up, bûrn;
ə = a in *above*, e in *sicken*, i in *possible*, o in *melon*, u in *circus*;   yōō = u in *fuse*;   oil;   pout;
check;   ring;   thin;   this;   zh in *vision.*   For ¶ reference, see page 64 · HOW TO

un·heard [un·hûrd′] *adj.* **1** Not heard. **2** Not listened to or heeded. **3** Not given a hearing.

un·heard-of [un·hûrd′uv′] *adj.* Not ever heard of, done, or known before: *unheard-of* inventions.

un·hinge [un·hinj′] *v.* **un·hinged, un·hing·ing 1** To take from the hinges or remove the hinges of: to *unhinge* a door. **2** To detach, separate, or remove. **3** To throw into disorder; unsettle: The shock *unhinged* her mind.

un·hitch [un·hich′] *v.* To free from being attached or fastened; unfasten: to *unhitch* a tractor from a trailer.

un·ho·ly [un·hō′lē] *adj.* **un·ho·li·er, un·ho·li·est 1** Not sacred or holy. **2** Wicked.

un·hook [un·hŏŏk′] *v.* **1** To unfasten by undoing a hook or hooks: to *unhook* a gate. **2** To become undone or loose from a hook. **3** To remove from a hook: to *unhook* a trout.

un·horse [un·hôrs′] *v.* **un·horsed, un·hors·ing** To knock or throw from a horse, as a knight.

uni- A prefix meaning: Having or consisting of one only, as *unicellular*, having one cell only.

u·ni·cam·er·al [yōō′nə·kam′ər·əl] *adj.* Made up of only one legislative house or chamber.

UNICEF or **U·ni·cef** [yōō′nə·sef] United Nations International Children's Emergency Fund.

u·ni·cel·lu·lar [yōō′nə·sel′yə·lər] *adj.* Consisting of a single cell, as a protozoan.

u·ni·corn [yōō′nə·kôrn] *n.* An imaginary animal said to look like a horse with one long horn projecting from its forehead.

u·ni·fi·ca·tion [yōō′nə·fə·kā′shən] *n.* **1** The act of unifying. **2** A unified condition.

u·ni·form [yōō′nə·fôrm] **1** *adj.* Always the same; not varying or changing: a canal

Unicorn

of *uniform* depth. **2** *adj.* The same as one another; all alike: boxes *uniform* in shape. **3** *n.* A special kind of outfit worn by all members of a certain group. **4** *v.* To put into a uniform: to *uniform* a soldier. **— u′ni·form·ly** *adv.*

u·ni·form·i·ty [yōō′nə·fôr′mə·tē] *n.* The condition or quality of being uniform; sameness.

u·ni·fy [yōō′nə·fī] *v.* **u·ni·fied, u·ni·fy·ing** To bring or come together into one; unite.

u·ni·lat·er·al [yōō′nə·lat′ər·əl] *adj.* On or by one side only: *unilateral* disarmament.

un·im·ag·i·na·ble [un′i·maj′ə·nə·bəl] *adj.* Impossible to imagine: *unimaginable* hardships.

un·im·peach·a·ble [un′im·pē′chə·bəl] *adj.* Not to be questioned or doubted; faultless: I got the information from an *unimpeachable* source.

un·im·por·tant [un′im·pôr′tənt] *adj.* **1** Not important or significant. **2** Trivial; petty.

un·in·ter·est·ed [un·in′tər·is·tid *or* un·in′tris·tid] *adj.* Not interested: A blind person is *uninterested* in TV. ◆ See DISINTERESTED.

un·ion [yōōn′yən] *n.* **1** The act of joining together or uniting: Great Britain was formed by the *union* of Scotland with England and Wales. **2** The condition of being joined or united; combination. **3** An association of persons, nations, states, etc., united for a common purpose: the *Union* of Soviet Socialist Republics. **4** The joining of two persons in marriage. **5** Another name for LABOR UNION. **6** A device for connecting parts of machinery, as a coupling for pipes. **— the Union 1** The United States. **2** The Federal government during the Civil War. ◆ *Union* goes back to the Latin word *unus*, meaning *one*.

un·ion·ist [yōōn′yən·ist] *n.* **1** A person who favors or supports union or labor unions. **2** (*written* **Unionist**) A supporter of the Federal government during the Civil War. **3** A member of a labor union. **— un′ion·ism** *n.*

un·ion·ize [yōōn′yən·īz] *v.* **un·ion·ized, un·ion·iz·ing 1** To cause to join or organize into a labor union: to *unionize* workers. **2** To put under union rules: to *unionize* a craft. **— un·ion·i·za·tion** [yōōn′yən·ə·zā′shən] *n.* ¶3

union jack 1 A flag consisting of the symbol of union from a national flag, as an American flag with 50 white stars on a blue field. **2** (*written* **Union Jack**) The flag of the United Kingdom.

Union of Soviet Socialist Republics A union of 15 republics under the rule of the Soviet Communist government. It extends over most of northern Eurasia.

u·nique [yōō·nēk′] *adj.* **1** Being the only one of its type; without an equal or like; singular: a *unique* gem. **2** Unusual, rare, or notable: a *unique* opportunity. **— u·nique′ly** *adv.*

u·ni·son [yōō′nə·sən] *n.* **1** Agreement in pitch, as among two or more voices or instruments. **2** Agreement. **— in unison** Sounding the same notes, speaking the same words, or making the same movements at the same time.

u·nit [yōō′nit] *n.* **1** A single person or thing, complete in itself but considered as part of a larger whole: The cell is the structural *unit* of animals and plants. **2** A group of persons or things thought of as being complete in itself: a military *unit.* **3** A part serving a special purpose: the cooling *unit* of a freezer. **4** A standard quantity used as a measure: An hour is a *unit* of time. **5** Unity (*def.* 2).

In the words below *un-* means *not.*

unheeding	unidentified	uninformed	unintentional
unhelpful	unimaginative	uninhabited	uninteresting
unhesitating	unimpressed	uninhibited	uninterrupted
unhistorical	unimpressive	uninspired	uninvited
unhurt	unincorporated	unintelligible	uninviting

U·ni·tar·i·an [yōō′nə·târ′ē·ən] *n.* A member of a religious denomination that does not believe in the divinity of Jesus or in the Trinity and which emphasizes complete freedom of religious opinion.

u·nite [yōō·nīt′] *v.* **u·nit·ed, u·nit·ing 1** To join together so as to form a unit; combine: to *unite* two ingredients; The states *united* to form a nation. **2** To join together in action, interest, etc.: to *unite* in song.

u·nit·ed [yōō·nī′tid] *adj.* **1** Joined into one; combined: *united* voices. **2** Made or done by joint action of more than one. **3** In harmony and closely knit: a *united* family.

United Arab Republic The official name for EGYPT.

United Kingdom A kingdom made up of Great Britain, Northern Ireland, and nearby islands.

United Nations An organization made up of most of the world's nations, founded in 1945 to maintain international peace and security and work for economic and social betterment.

United States Another name for the UNITED STATES OF AMERICA.

United States of America A federal republic of 50 states, the District of Columbia, and Puerto Rico. All of the states are in North America except Hawaii, and 48 of them lie between Canada and Mexico.

u·ni·ty [yōō′nə·tē] *n., pl.* **u·ni·ties 1** The quality of being one or the power of acting as one; oneness: A regular team has greater *unity* than a group of new players. **2** A number that when multiplied with any other number gives that other number as their product. **3** Singleness, as of purpose. **4** In art and literature, the fitting together of parts so as to create a single effect. **5** Harmony; agreement.

u·ni·ver·sal [yōō′nə·vûr′səl] *adj.* **1** Of, for, common to, or involving all: a *universal* practice. **2** Occurring everywhere: the *universal* desire for security. **—u·ni·ver·sal·i·ty** [yōō′nə·vər·sal′ə·tē] *n.*

U·ni·ver·sal·ist [yōō′nə·vûr′səl·ist] *n.* A member of a Christian church that believes that all souls will finally be saved.

universal joint A joint for coupling the end of a rotating shaft to the end of another that is at a slight angle to it.

u·ni·ver·sal·ly [yōō′nə·vûr′sə·lē] *adv.* **1** In all cases: *universally* valid. **2** Everywhere or by everyone: He was *universally* admired as a fine statesman.

A universal joint

u·ni·verse [yōō′nə·vûrs] *n.* The whole that is made up of everything that exists, including earth, sun, stars, planets, and outer space.

u·ni·ver·si·ty [yōō′nə·vûr′sə·tē] *n., pl.* **u·ni·ver·si·ties** An institution of higher learning, usually including a regular college or colleges as well as one or more schools for graduate or professional study, as in law, medicine, etc.

un·just [un·just′] *adj.* Not fair or just. **—un·just′ly** *adv.*

un·kempt [un·kempt′] *adj.* **1** Not combed. **2** Not clean, neat, or tidy: His clothing is usually *unkempt.*

un·kind [un·kīnd′] *adj.* Not kind, thoughtful, or sympathetic; mean, harsh, or cruel. **—un·kind′ly** *adv.* **—un·kind′ness** *n.*

un·known [un·nōn′] *adj.* **1** Not known or not recognized: an *unknown* person. **2** Not yet discovered: an *unknown* quantity. **3** *n. use* Unknown persons, things, etc.: fear of the *unknown.*

un·lace [un·lās′] *v.* **un·laced, un·lac·ing** To loosen or undo the laces of: to *unlace* boots.

un·latch [un·lach′] *v.* To open or unlock by lifting or releasing a latch: *Unlatch* the door.

un·law·ful [un·lô′fəl] *adj.* Not allowed by law; illegal. **—un·law′ful·ly** *adv.*

un·learn [un·lûrn′] *v.* **un·learned** or **un·learnt, un·learn·ing** To forget or get rid of (something learned), as because it is wrong: to *unlearn* prejudices; to *unlearn* bad manners.

un·learn·ed *adj.* **1** [un·lûr′nid] Not educated; ignorant. **2** [un·lûrnd′] Not known by study or learning, as something known naturally: A baby's crying is an *unlearned* reaction.

un·leash [un·lēsh′] *v.* To let loose from or as if from a leash: to *unleash* a pet; The challenge *unleashed* all their energies.

un·leav·ened [un·lev′ənd] *adj.* Made without yeast or other leaven: *unleavened* bread.

un·less [un·les′] *conj.* In any event other than; except if: I'll come *unless* I'm sick.

un·let·tered [un·let′ərd] *adj.* **1** Not educated. **2** Unable to read or write; illiterate.

un·like [un·līk′] **1** *adj.* Different from one another: I never saw two sisters more *unlike.* **2** *prep.* Not like or different from: It was *unlike* him to go; His watch is *unlike* mine.

un·like·ly [un·līk′lē] *adj.* **1** Not probable or likely. **2** Not likely to be successful.

un·lim·it·ed [un·lim′it·id] *adj.* Having no set limits: *unlimited* time; *unlimited* power.

un·load [un·lōd′] *v.* **1** To remove the load or cargo from: to *unload* a truck. **2** To remove (cargo, passengers, etc.): to *unload* boxes. **3** To

---

In the words below *un-* means *not.*

unjustifiable	unlabeled	unlicensed	unlikable
unknowing	unlabelled	unlighted	unlined

---

discharge a cargo. **4** To pour out onto another: *Unload* your grief. **5** To remove the cartridges or other charge from (a gun, etc.).

un·lock [un·lok′] *v.* **1** To unfasten or undo the lock of. **2** To lay open; reveal: Scientists *unlock* the secrets of life.

un·looked-for [un·lo͝okt′fôr′] *adj.* Unexpected.

un·loose [un·lo͞os′] *v.* **un·loosed, un·loos·ing** To set loose or set free; loosen or release.

un·loos·en [un·lo͞o′sən] *v.* To loose; unloose.

un·luck·y [un·luk′ē] *adj.* **un·luck·i·er, un·luck·i·est** Marked by, having, or bringing bad luck; not lucky. **— un·luck′i·ly** *adv.*

un·man [un·man′] *v.* **un·manned, un·man·ning** **1** To cause to lose courage, strength, or other manly qualities: The shock completely *unmanned* him. **2** To remove the men from: to *unman* a ship.

un·man·ly [un·man′lē] *adj.* **1** Lacking masculine qualities, as strength and courage; effeminate. **2** Weak or cowardly: Boys are often taught that it is *unmanly* to cry.

un·man·ner·ly [un·man′ər·lē] *adj.* Lacking manners; rude.

un·mask [un·mask′] *v.* **1** To remove a mask or disguise from: He *unmasked* himself at midnight. **2** To remove one's mask or disguise: Everyone *unmasked* when the clock struck. **3** To reveal or disclose the truth about: The police *unmasked* the entire spy ring.

un·mean·ing [un·mē′ning] *adj.* **1** Having no meaning; senseless. **2** Showing no expression of intelligence or interest: an *unmeaning* stare.

un·men·tion·a·ble [un·men′shən·ə·bəl] *adj.* Not suitable or proper for mention or discussion in polite conversation.

un·mer·ci·ful [un·mûr′sə·fəl] *adj.* Showing no mercy; cruel.

un·mind·ful [un·mīnd′fəl] *adj.* Not keeping in mind; inattentive; careless.

un·mis·tak·a·ble [un′mis·tā′kə·bəl] *adj.* That cannot be mistaken or misunderstood; clear; plain. **— un′mis·tak′a·bly** *adv.*

un·mit·i·gat·ed [un·mit′ə·gā′tid] *adj.* **1** Not lessened or lightened: *unmitigated* sorrow. **2** Absolute; total: He is an *unmitigated* bore.

un·mor·al [un·môr′əl] *adj.* Not aware of or not involving right and wrong; neither moral nor immoral.

un·moved [un·mo͞ovd′] *adj.* **1** Not affected by feelings such as sympathy: Their sufferings left him *unmoved*. **2** Not changed in purpose, policy, or opinion: He was *unmoved* by all our arguments. **3** Not changed in position or place.

un·nat·u·ral [un·nach′ər·əl] *adj.* **1** Not natural or normal; strange; abnormal. **2** Artificial; affected: an *unnatural* manner. **3** Very evil or shocking; inhuman: *unnatural* cruelty. **— un·nat′u·ral·ly** *adv.*

un·nec·es·sar·y [un·nes′ə·ser′ē] *adj.* Not required or necessary; needless. **— un·nec′es·sar′i·ly** *adv.*

un·nerve [un·nûrv′] *v.* **un·nerved, un·nerv·ing** To cause to lose strength, firmness, self-control, or courage: The pistol shots *unnerved* us.

un·num·bered [un·num′bərd] *adj.* **1** Not given or marked with a number. **2** Too many to count; innumerable: the *unnumbered* stars of the Milky Way.

un·ob·tru·sive [un′əb·tro͞o′siv] *adj.* Not demanding notice; inconspicuous.

un·of·fi·cial [un′ə·fish′əl] *adj.* Not official. **— un′of·fi′cial·ly** *adv.*

un·or·tho·dox [un·ôr′thə·doks] *adj.* Not orthodox, conventional, or approved.

un·pack [un·pak′] *v.* **1** To open and take out the contents of: to *unpack* a trunk. **2** To take out from a box or other container: to *unpack* china. **3** To remove things from their containers: We *unpacked* all day long.

un·par·al·leled [un·par′ə·ləld] *adj.* Without parallel, equal, or match: He was *unparalleled* in his lifetime as a tenor.

un·pin [un·pin′] *v.* **un·pinned, un·pin·ning** To unfasten or loosen by removing a pin or pins from: She *unpinned* her long hair.

un·pleas·ant [un·plez′ənt] *adj.* Not pleasing; disagreeable; objectionable. **— un·pleas′ant·ly** *adv.* **— un·pleas′ant·ness** *n.*

un·pop·u·lar [un·pop′yə·lər] *adj.* Not liked or approved of by a rather large number of people: an *unpopular* actress; an *unpopular* idea. **— un·pop·u·lar·i·ty** [un·pop′yə·lar′ə·tē] *n.*

un·prac·ticed [un·prak′tist] *adj.* **1** Without practice or skill; not expert. **2** Not used often: an *unpracticed* skill. ¶3

un·prec·e·dent·ed [un·pres′ə·den′tid] *adj.* Having no precedent or earlier example; unheard-of: an *unprecedented* victory.

un·prej·u·diced [un·prej′o͝o·dist] *adj.* Free from prejudice; fair; impartial.

un·pre·ten·tious [un′pri·ten′shəs] *adj.* Not showy; simple; modest: a very *unpretentious* little cottage.

un·prin·ci·pled [un·prin′sə·pəld] *adj.* Lacking moral principles; unscrupulous.

un·print·a·ble [un·prin′tə·bəl] *adj.* Not fit to be printed; too indecent or profane to be printed.

In the words below *un-* means *not.*

unlovable	unnoticeable	unpardonable	unplanted
unloved	unnoticed	unpatriotic	unplayed
unmanageable	unobliging	unperceived	unplowed
unmarried	unobservable	unperfected	unpoetical
unmerited	unobtainable	unpicked	unpolished
unnamed	unopened	unpitying	unpopulated
unneeded	unopposed	unplanned	unpreventable

un·pro·fes·sion·al [un′prə·fesh′ən·əl] *adj.* Not according to professional standards, conduct, etc.: It is *unprofessional* for a doctor to advertise for patients.

un·pro·nounce·a·ble [un′prə·noun′sə·bəl] *adj.* Not easy to pronounce or pronounce properly.

un·qual·i·fied [un·kwol′ə·fīd] *adj.* **1** Not having the proper qualifications; unfit. **2** Without any limitation or restriction; absolute; entire: His ideas have my *unqualified* approval.

un·quench·a·ble [un·kwench′ə·bəl] *adj.* That cannot be quenched or extinguished: an *unquenchable* thirst; *unquenchable* enthusiasm.

un·ques·tion·a·ble [un·kwes′chən·ə·bəl] *adj.* Not to be doubted; absolutely certain: It was an *unquestionable* victory for us. **— un·ques′tion·a·bly** *adv.*

un·ques·tioned [un·kwes′chənd] *adj.* Not doubted or disputed.

un·qui·et [un·kwī′ət] *adj.* **1** Not still or quiet; agitated: the *unquiet* sea. **2** Uneasy or restless: *unquiet* times; an *unquiet* mind.

un·quote [un·kwōt′] *v.* **un·quot·ed, un·quot·ing** To close or end a quotation.

un·rav·el [un·rav′əl] *v.* **un·rav·eled** or **un·rav·elled, un·rav·el·ing** or **un·rav·el·ling** **1** To separate or pull apart the threads of (something knitted, woven, or tangled): She *unraveled* the sleeve of her sweater. **2** To solve, make clear, or explain: to *unravel* the plot of a mystery story. **3** To become unraveled.

un·read [un·red′] *adj.* **1** Having read very little: He was *unread* in history. **2** Not yet read: an *unread* book.

un·real [un·rēl′ *or* un·rē′əl] *adj.* Not real or actual; imaginary: Dreams are *unreal* things. **— un·re·al·i·ty** [un′rē·al′ə·tē] *n.*

un·rea·son·a·ble [un·rē′zən·ə·bəl] *adj.* **1** Not reasonable or sensible: Your objection to him is *unreasonable.* **2** Greater than what is reasonable; excessive; exorbitant: He is asking for an *unreasonable* salary. **— un·rea′son·a·bly** *adv.*

un·re·gen·er·ate [un′ri·jen′ər·it] *adj.* **1** Wicked; sinful. **2** Not spiritually reborn; not reformed.

un·re·lent·ing [un′ri·len′ting] *adj.* **1** Not softened by kindness or pity; merciless: He was an *unrelenting* taskmaster in class. **2** Not relaxing or growing less: *unrelenting* efforts.

un·re·mit·ting [un′ri·mit′ing] *adj.* Not letting up or stopping; constant: *unremitting* noise.

un·re·served [un′ri·zûrvd′] *adj.* **1** Not limited; full; unqualified: *unreserved* approval. **2** Open, frank, and informal in manner, speech, etc.: He is very *unreserved*, even with strangers. **— un·re·serv·ed·ly** [un′ri·zûr′vid·lē] *adv.*

un·rest [un·rest′] *n.* **1** Restlessness, especially of the mind. **2** Angry discontent or turmoil sometimes not far from rebellion.

un·right·eous [un·rī′chəs] *adj.* Not righteous; wicked; sinful. **— un·right′eous·ness** *n.*

un·ri·valed or **un·ri·valled** [un·rī′vəld] *adj.* Having no rival or competitor; unequaled; matchless: the *unrivaled* beauty of the sea.

un·roll [un·rōl′] *v.* **1** To spread out or open (something rolled up). **2** To become opened or rolled out flat. **3** To show or reveal: He *unrolled* before us the whole history of the family.

un·ruf·fled [un·ruf′əld] *adj.* **1** Not nervous, disturbed, or upset; calm. **2** Not disturbed; smooth: The lake was *unruffled.*

un·ru·ly [un·rōō′lē] *adj.* **un·ru·li·er, un·ru·li·est** Difficult to control or discipline; disobedient: an *unruly* child; an *unruly* class.

un·sad·dle [un·sad′(ə)l] *v.* **un·sad·dled, un·sad·dling** **1** To remove a saddle, as from a horse. **2** To throw from a saddle.

un·said [un·sed′] **1** Past tense and past participle of UNSAY. **2** *adj.* Not said; not spoken.

un·sat·u·rat·ed [un·sach′ə·rā′tid] *adj.* **1** Able to absorb more of a substance, as a solution. **2** Able to join with additional elements or radicals without the loss of any of those already present, as certain chemical compounds.

un·sa·vor·y [un·sā′vər·ē] *adj.* **1** Having a disagreeable taste or odor. **2** Morally bad or offensive: an *unsavory* reputation.

un·say [un·sā′] *v.* **un·said, un·say·ing** To take back or retract (something said).

un·scathed [un·skāt̸hd′] *adj.* Not hurt or injured.

un·scram·ble [un·skram′bəl] *v.* **un·scram·bled, un·scram·bling** To make orderly, clear, or intelligible: Can you *unscramble* his answer?

un·screw [un·skrōō′] *v.* **1** To remove the screw or screws from: *Unscrew* the hinge. **2** To loosen or take off or out by turning, as a nut, a jar lid, a light bulb, etc.

In the words below *un-* means *not.*

unpromising	unrecognized	unreturned	unsatisfactory
unprotected	unrecorded	unrevealed	unsatisfied
unproved	unrefined	unrewarded	unsatisfying
unprovoked	unregistered	unripe	unscarred
unpunished	unrehearsed	unromantic	unscheduled
unreachable	unrepentant	unsafe	unscholarly
unreceptive	unreported	unsalaried	unscientific
unrecognizable	unretentive	unsanitary	unscratched

---

add, āce, câre, pälm; end, ēqual; it, īce; odd, ōpen, ôrder; tŏŏk, pōōl; up, bûrn; ə = a in *above*, e in *sicken*, i in *possible*, o in *melon*, u in *circus*; yōō = u in *fuse*; oil; pout; check; ring; thin; ŧhis; zh in *vision.* For ¶ reference, see page 64 · HOW TO

un·scru·pu·lous [un·skroo′pyə·ləs] *adj.* Having no scruples, principles, or conscience; dishonest: an *unscrupulous* dealer in stolen goods. **— un·scru′pu·lous·ly** *adv.*

un·seal [un·sēl′] *v.* **1** To break or take off the seal of; open: *Unseal* the letter, please. **2** To open (something tightly closed): Not even torture could *unseal* his lips.

un·sea·son·a·ble [un·sē′zən·ə·bəl] *adj.* **1** Not normal for nor suited to the season: This cold weather is *unseasonable* for summer. **2** Not coming at the right time: July is an *unseasonable* time to sell skis.

un·seat [un·sēt′] *v.* **1** To throw (a rider) from his seat on horseback. **2** To remove from office: to *unseat* a public official.

un·seem·ly [un·sēm′lē] *adj.* **un·seem·li·er, un·seem·li·est 1** *adj.* Not proper or decent; unbecoming: *unseemly* behavior. **2** *adv.* In an improper or unseemly manner.

un·self·ish [un·sel′fish] *adj.* Not selfish; generous in helping, giving to, or caring for others. **— un·self′ish·ly** *adv.* **— un·self′ish·ness** *n.*

un·set·tle [un·set′(ə)l] *v.* **un·set·tled, un·set·tling 1** To make or become confused, disturbed, upset, etc.: The breakdown of the electric plants *unsettled* every activity in the city. **2** To make or become unsteady or unfixed.

un·set·tled [un·set′(ə)ld] *adj.* **1** Not orderly or calm; disturbed; confused. **2** Uncertain; changeable: *unsettled* weather. **3** Not yet decided or determined: The answer to that question is still *unsettled.* **4** Not lived in; unpopulated: an *unsettled* county in the West. **5** Not paid or disposed of, as a debt or estate.

un·sheathe [un·shēth] *v.* **un·sheathed, un·sheath·ing** To take from or as if from a scabbard or sheath: The cat *unsheathed* its claws.

un·shod [un·shod′] *adj.* Not wearing shoes.

un·sight·ly [un·sīt′lē] *adj.* **un·sight·li·er, un·sight·li·est** Not pleasing to look at; ugly.

un·skilled [un·skild′] *adj.* **1** Having no special skill or training: an *unskilled* worker. **2** Requiring no special skills: *unskilled* work.

un·skill·ful or **un·skil·ful** [un·skil′fəl] *adj.* Not expert; bungling; clumsy.

un·snap [un·snap′] *v.* **un·snapped, un·snapping** To undo the snap or snaps of; unfasten.

un·snarl [un·snärl′] *v.* To take the snarls out of; untangle.

un·so·phis·ti·cat·ed [un′sə·fis′tə·kā′tid] *adj.* Not sophisticated; simple, natural, or innocent; inexperienced in worldly things.

un·sound [un·sound′] *adj.* **1** Not solid or strong; weak: an *unsound* floor. **2** Not healthy: an *unsound* mind. **3** Not true or logical: an *unsound* argument. **4** Not deep or restful: an *unsound* sleep.

un·spar·ing [un·spâr′ing] *adj.* **1** Not sparing or stingy; generous; liberal: to be *unsparing* in one's efforts to help. **2** Showing no mercy; severe; harsh. **— un·spar′ing·ly** *adv.*

un·speak·a·ble [un·spē′kə·bəl] *adj.* **1** That cannot be expressed because it is so great; unutterable: *unspeakable* joy. **2** Extremely bad or objectionable: an *unspeakable* crime. **— un·speak′a·bly** *adv.*

un·sta·ble [un·stā′bəl] *adj.* **1** Not stable, firm, or fixed; liable to shake, move, etc.: an *unstable* building. **2** Not emotionally steady; variable: an *unstable* person. **3** Easily decomposed, as a chemical compound.

un·stead·y [un·sted′ē] *adj.* **1** Not steady or firm; shaky. **2** Not regular or constant; changeable: the old machine's *unsteady* speed.

un·strung [un·strung′] *adj.* **1** Having the strings removed or loosened. **2** Nervous and upset; distressed.

un·sub·stan·tial [un′səb·stan′shəl] *adj.* **1** Not substantial; lacking strength or solidity: an *unsubstantial* little shack. **2** Not true or valid: *unsubstantial* claims. **3** Not real: Ghosts are *unsubstantial* beings.

un·sung [un·sung′] *adj.* **1** Not yet sung. **2** Not honored or celebrated; obscure: *unsung* heroes.

un·tan·gle [un·tang′gəl] *v.* **un·tan·gled, un·tan·gling 1** To free from snarls or tangles: to *untangle* a fishing line. **2** To clear up or solve: to *untangle* a problem.

un·taught [un·tôt′] *adj.* **1** Not having been taught or educated; ignorant. **2** Known or learned without being taught; natural.

un·ten·a·ble [un·ten′ə·bəl] *adj.* That cannot be proved or defended: *untenable* theories.

un·think·a·ble [un·thingk′ə·bəl] *adj.* Impossible to imagine or consider; inconceivable: It is *unthinkable* that she could be so rude.

un·think·ing [un·thingk′ing] *adj.* **1** Not thinking; thoughtless. **2** Showing no thoughtfulness or consideration for others: That was an *unthinking* remark. **— un·think′ing·ly** *adv.*

un·ti·dy [un·tī′dē] *adj.* **un·ti·di·er, un·ti·di·est** Not orderly or neat; messy. **— un·ti′di·ly** *adv.* **— un·ti′di·ness** *n.*

un·tie [un·tī′] *v.* **un·tied, un·ty·ing 1** To loosen or undo, as a knot. **2** To let loose; free: He *untied* the dog and let him run.

In the words below *un-* means *not.*

unsealed	unsought	unsupported	untactful
unshaken	unspecified	unsure	untalented
unshaven	unspent	unsurpassed	untamed
unsmiling	unspoiled	unsuspicious	untaxable
unsoiled	unspoken	unsweetened	untested
unsold	unsportsmanlike	unsympathetic	unthoughtful
unsolved	unstated	unsystematic	unthrifty

un·til [un·til′] **1** *prep.* Up to the time of; till: We will wait *until* midnight. **2** *conj.* To the time when: I'll remember that *until* I die. **3** *prep.* Before: The music doesn't begin *until* nine. **4** *conj.* Before: He couldn't leave *until* the car came for him. **5** *conj.* To the place or degree that: Walk east *until* you reach the river; We shouted *until* we were hoarse.

un·time·ly [un·tīm′lē] **1** *adj.* Coming or happening at a wrong or unsuitable time, as too early: his *untimely* death. **2** *adv.* Too soon or at any wrong time.

un·to [un′tōō] *prep.* To: seldom used today.

un·told [un·tōld′] *adj.* **1** Not told: a tale *untold*. **2** Not counted or measured: *Untold* millions were affected by the flood. **3** Too many or too much to be counted or measured: *untold* misery.

un·touch·a·ble [un·tuch′ə·bəl] **1** *adj.* Located or lying beyond a person's reach. **2** *adj.* Not to be touched; protected from being touched by rules. **3** *adj.* Protected or exempt from criticism or control. **4** *adj.* Unpleasant or dangerous to the touch. **5** *n.* In India, a member of the lowest caste, whose touch was formerly thought to defile anyone of a higher caste.

un·to·ward [un·tôrd′] *adj.* **1** Unlucky; unfavorable; adverse: an *untoward* delay. **2** Stubborn; unruly; hard to manage: an *untoward* pupil.

un·true [un·trōō′] *adj.* **1** Not true or correct; false. **2** Not loyal, constant, or faithful: an *untrue* servant. **3** Not level, upright, etc.: The walls slanted and the windows were *untrue*. — **un·tru′ly** *adv.*

un·truth [un·trōōth′] *n.* **1** Something that is not true, as a lie. **2** The fact, quality, or condition of not being true.

un·truth·ful [un·trōōth′fəl] *adj.* **1** Not truthful; untrue. **2** Apt to tell lies: an *untruthful* person. — **un·truth′ful·ly** *adv.*

un·tu·tored [un·tōō′tərd] *adj.* **1** Untaught. **2** Simple; not sophisticated.

un·twist [un·twist′] *v.* To separate, unravel, or undo (something twisted): to *untwist* a rope.

un·used *adj.* **1** [un·yōōzd′] Not made use of or never having been used: Here is a lot of *unused* machinery. **2** [un·yōōst′] Not accustomed: He is *unused* to working very hard.

un·u·su·al [un·yōō′zhōō·əl] *adj.* Not usual or ordinary; uncommon. — **un·u′su·al·ly** *adv.*

un·ut·ter·a·ble [un·ut′ər·ə·bəl] *adj.* Too great to be expressed by words: *unutterable* bliss. — **un·ut′ter·a·bly** *adv.*

un·veil [un·vāl′] *v.* **1** To remove the veil or covering from so as to disclose to view; reveal: He *unveiled* his new picture. **2** To remove a veil from one's face or person.

un·war·y [un·wâr′ē] *adj.* Not careful or cautious; careless: an *unwary* shopper.

un·well [un·wel′] *adj.* Not well; ailing; sick.

un·wield·y [un·wēl′dē] *adj.* Hard to handle or manage, usually because of size, weight, shape, etc.; awkward: an *unwieldy* box.

un·will·ing [un·wil′ing] *adj.* **1** Not willing; reluctant: He is *unwilling* to go. **2** Done, said, given, etc., against one's will: an *unwilling* consent. — **un·will′ing·ly** *adv.* — **un·will′ing·ness** *n.*

un·wind [un·wīnd′] *v.* **un·wound, un·wind·ing** **1** To loosen or undo (something wound up) by twisting or turning in the opposite direction. **2** To become unwound.

un·wise [un·wīz′] *adj.* Showing a lack of wisdom, good sense, or sound judgment; foolish: It was a very *unwise* thing to do. — **un·wise′·ly** *adv.*

un·wit·ting [un·wit′ing] *adj.* **1** Not aware or knowing: The camera caught the *unwitting* lions behaving naturally. **2** Not intentional or done on purpose: an *unwitting* benefit. — **un·wit′ting·ly** *adv.*

un·wont·ed [un·wun′tid] *adj.* Not usual, customary, or habitual: an *unwonted* severity of manner.

un·wor·thy [un·wûr′thē] *adj.* **un·wor·thi·er, un·wor·thi·est** **1** Not worthy or deserving: I feel *unworthy* of this honor. **2** Not proper or fit: a poor book, *unworthy* of its distinguished author. — **un·wor′thi·ness** *n.*

un·wound [un·wound′] Past tense and past participle of UNWIND.

un·wrap [un·rap′] *v.* **un·wrapped, un·wrap·ping** **1** To take the wrapping from; open; undo: to *unwrap* a present. **2** To become unwrapped.

un·writ·ten [un·rit′(ə)n] *adj.* **1** Not written or in writing: an *unwritten* understanding between the two companies. **2** Traditional and customary, although not written or recorded: an *unwritten* law.

un·yoke [un·yōk′] *v.* **un·yoked, un·yok·ing** **1** To set free from a yoke: to *unyoke* oxen. **2** To separate or disconnect. **3** To become unyoked.

up [up] *adv., prep., adj., v.* **upped, up·ping** **1** *adv.* In, on, or to a higher place, level, position, etc.: The flag went *up*; Come on *up*. **2** *adv.* To or at a higher price: The bus fares went *up*.

In the words below *un-* means *not.*

untiring	**untranslatable**	**unverified**	**unwed**
untouched	**untroubled**	**unwashed**	**unwelcome**
untraceable	**unuttered**	**unwasted**	**unworkable**
untrained	**unvanquished**	**unwavering**	**unyielding**

---

add, āce, câre, pälm; end, ēqual; it, īce; odd, ōpen, ôrder; tŏŏk, pōōl; up, bûrn;
ə = a in *above*, e in *sicken*, i in *possible*, o in *melon*, u in *circus*; yōō = u in *fuse*; oil; pout;
check; ring; thin; this; zh in *vision*. For ¶ reference, see page 64 · HOW TO

3 *prep.* From a lower to a higher point or place of, on, or along: We ran *up* the side of the hill. **4** *adj.* Moving or directed upward or in a direction, position, or condition thought of as upward: The window blinds are *up*; The moon is *up*; The cost of living is *up*; an *up* grade. **5** *v. informal* To go, put, or lift up: We *upped* the end of the box. **6** *v. informal* To increase: The theater *upped* its prices. **7** *adv.* To or at a higher rank or station: to come *up* in the world. **8** *prep.* To a higher condition or rank on or in: He went *up* the social ladder. **9** *adv.* To or at a greater size or amount: to swell *up*. **10** *adv.* To or at a place that is regarded as higher: The sun came *up*; to go *up* north. **11** *prep.* To or at a point farther above, along, or toward the source of: The farm is *up* the road; We sailed *up* the river. **12** *adv.* To a later time or period: from the Middle Ages *up*. **13** *adv.* To a conclusion, source, etc.: Follow *up* this lead. **14** *adj.* At an end or close: The hour is *up*. **15** *adv.* In or to a vertical position: Get *up*. **16** *adj.* Out of bed: Are you *up* yet? **17** *adv.* So as to be compact, safe, or secure: Tie *up* the boxes. **18** *adv.* In or into a place of safekeeping: to lay *up* gold and riches. **19** *adv.* So as to be even or level with in time, space, amount, etc.: Keep the records *up* to date. **20** *adv.* In or into view, discussion, or existence: Don't bring *up* that subject again. **21** *adv.* Completely; totally; wholly: The house burned *up*; to eat *up* the food. **22** *adj.* In baseball, at bat: He was *up* three times. **23** *adv.* Apiece; alike: The score is 40 *up*. **24** *adj.* Running as a candidate: He is *up* for mayor. **25** *adj.* On trial: He is *up* for murder. **26** *adj. informal* Going on; taking place: What's *up*? **27** *adj. informal* In an active or excited state: His temper is *up*. **28** *adv.* To a greater or higher degree, volume, intensity, tension, etc.: Turn *up* the sound on the TV; Turn *up* the oven to 400°; Her blood pressure went *up*. **— up against** *informal* Face to face with: They will be *up against* many dangers. **— ups and downs** Periods of happiness, good luck, etc., followed by periods of unhappiness, bad luck, etc.: to have one's *ups and downs*. **— up to 1** *informal* Doing or plotting: What is he *up to*? **2** Equal to or capable of: I'm not *up to* cleaning the house today. **3** Put before or left to for decision or action: It's *up to* her where we go; It's *up to* him to tell us. ◆ In informal speaking or writing, *up*, as an adverb, is often added to a verb without changing the meaning of the sentence, as in: The fire lit *up* the room; Please write *up* the report; She tore his letter *up*.

up·braid [up·brād'] *v.* To scold, criticize, or rebuke: She *upbraided* him for his rudeness.

up·bring·ing [up'bring'ing] *n.* The care and training received by a person during childhood.

up·date [up·dāt'] *v.* **up·dat·ed, up·dat·ing** To bring up to date by adding the latest facts, figures, corrections, etc.: to *update* a textbook.

up·end [up'end'] *v.* To set or stand on end.

up·grade [*n.* up'grād', *v.* up·grād'] *n., v.* **up·grad·ed, up·grad·ing 1** *n.* An upward in-cline or slope. **2** *v.* To raise to a higher grade, rank, quality, etc.: to *upgrade* a person's job. **— on the upgrade 1** Improving: His test scores are *on the upgrade*. **2** Rising: The number of automobile accidents is *on the upgrade*.

up·heav·al [up·hē'vəl] *n.* **1** A sudden or violent heaving or raising up, as of a portion of the earth's crust by an earthquake or volcanic action. **2** A violent disturbance or change: the terrible social *upheavals* caused by war.

up·held [up·held'] Past tense and past participle of UPHOLD.

up·hill [up'hil'] **1** *adv.* Up a hill: to walk *uphill*. **2** *adj.* Going up a hill; ascending: an *uphill* walk. **3** *adj.* Filled with difficulties: an *uphill* fight against crime.

up·hold [up·hōld'] *v.* **up·held, up·hold·ing 1** To keep from falling or sinking; hold up: These few columns *uphold* the entire roof. **2** To give aid or support to; agree with: He *upheld* the students in their desire for a better cafeteria. **— up·hold'er** *n.*

up·hol·ster [up·hōl'stər] *v.* To fit (a sofa, chair, etc.) with springs, padding, cushions, etc., and then cover with fabric. **— up·hol'ster·er** *n.*

up·hol·ster·y [up·hōl'stər·ē *or* up·hōl'strē] *n., pl.* **up·hol·ster·ies** The springs, padding, cushions, fabric, etc., with which furniture is upholstered.

up·keep [up'kēp'] *n.* **1** The maintaining of something in good condition. **2** The cost of this: the high *upkeep* of a house.

up·land [up'lənd *or* up'land'] *n.* **1** The higher parts or sections of a region, district, farm, etc. **2** *adj. use:* an *upland* town.

up·lift [*v.* up·lift', *n.* up'lift'] **1** *v.* To raise or lift up. **2** *n.* The act of lifting or raising. **3** *v.* To raise or improve socially or morally. **4** *n.* Social or moral betterment, or the effort to secure it.

up·most [up'mōst'] *adj.* Uppermost.

up·on [ə·pon'] **1** *prep.* On. **2** *adv.* On: This paper has been written *upon*. ◆ *Upon* now differs little in use from *on*. However, when rest or support is indicated *on* is preferred: He stood *on* the platform. When movement into position is involved *upon* is preferred: The piano was lifted *upon* the stage.

up·per [up'ər] **1** *adj.* Higher than something else; being above: an *upper* story. **2** *adj.* Higher or farther inland in location, place, etc.: the *upper* valley. **3** *adj.* Higher in station, rank, dignity, etc.: *upper* classmen. **4** *n.* The part of a boot or shoe above the sole.

up·per·most [up'ər·mōst'] **1** *adj.* Highest; top: the *uppermost* tip of the mast. **2** *adj.* Most important: Something to eat was his *uppermost* concern. **3** *adv.* To or in the highest or most important place: She placed new shoes *uppermost* among her needs.

Upper Vol·ta [vol'tə] A country in western Africa.

up·raise [up·rāz'] *v.* **up·raised, up·rais·ing** To lift up; elevate: with swords *upraised*.

up·right [up′rīt′] **1** *adj.* Straight up; erect; in a vertical position: an *upright* post. **2** *n.* Something in a vertical position, as a mast or flagpole. **3** *n.* An upright piano. **4** *adv.* In an upright position; vertically: Gorillas sometimes stand *upright.* **5** *adj.* Just and honest: an *upright* man.

upright piano A piano smaller than a grand piano, having the strings arranged vertically in a rectangular case placed at right angles to the keyboard.

up·ris·ing [up·rī′zing *or* up′rī′zing] *n.* **1** The act of rising up. **2** A revolt; rebellion.

up·roar [up′rôr′] *n.* **1** A condition of violent agitation, disturbance, or noisy confusion: The outbreak of fire threw the audience into an *uproar.* **2** A loud and confused noise.

up·roar·i·ous [up·rôr′ē·əs] *adj.* **1** Making an uproar. **2** Loud and noisy. **3** Very funny: an *uproarious* play. **— up·roar′i·ous·ly** *adv.*

up·root [up·rōōt′] *v.* **1** To tear up by the roots. **2** To destroy completely: to *uproot* bad habits.

up·set [*v.* up·set′, *n.* up′set′, *adj.* up·set′ *or* up′set′] *v.* **up·set, up·set·ting,** *n., adj.* **1** *v.* To overturn or become overturned: to *upset* a vase of flowers; a table that *upsets* easily. **2** *n.* The act of upsetting. **3** *adj.* Tipped or turned over: an *upset* cup of coffee. **4** *v.* To disturb (something ordered or arranged): He *upset* our plans. **5** *v.* To make ill: Rich food *upsets* her. **6** *v.* To disturb mentally: The bad news *upset* us all. **7** *adj.* Mentally or physically disturbed or ill: She is *upset* about it; an *upset* stomach. **8** *n.* A disturbed condition: a stomach *upset.* **9** *v.* To defeat (an opponent favored to win): The amateur team *upset* the professionals. **10** *n.* A defeat of an opponent favored to win.

up·shot [up′shot′] *n.* The final outcome or result.

up·side down [up′sīd′] **1** With the upper part or side down: We turned the table *upside down* to fix it. **2** In or into disorder: He turned the whole house *upside down* in order to find the ring.

up·stairs [up′stârz′] **1** *n.pl.* (*used with singular verb*) An upper story or stories, especially the part of a house above the ground floor. **2** *adj.* Of, having to do with, or located in an upper story: an *upstairs* bedroom. **3** *adv.* In, to, or toward an upper story: We ran *upstairs.*

up·stand·ing [up·stan′ding] *adj.* Honest and upright: a fine, *upstanding* citizen.

up·start [up′stärt′] *n.* **1** A person who has suddenly become wealthy or important, especially one who is conceited or arrogant. **2** Any forward, arrogant person impressed with his own importance: You young *upstart!*

up·stream [up′strēm′] *adv.* Toward or at the upper part or source of a stream; against the current.

up-to-date [up′tə·dāt′] *adj.* **1** Having the latest information, improvements, etc.: an *up-to-date* textbook. **2** Modern in manner, fashion, or style: an *up-to-date* coat.

up·town [up′toun′] *adv., adj.* To, toward, or in the upper section of a town or city: to move *uptown*; an *uptown* restaurant.

up·turn [*n.* up′tûrn′, *v.* up·tûrn′] **1** *n.* A change toward a better or improved condition: There was a slow *upturn* in the country's economy. **2** *v.* To turn up.

up·ward [up′wərd] **1** *adv.* In, to, or toward a higher point or place: to look *upward.* **2** *adj.* Going toward a higher place: an *upward* slope. **3** *adv.* To or toward the source, origin, etc.: to trace a stream *upward.* **4** *adv.* To or toward a higher rank, amount, age, etc.: He fought his way *upward* from poverty; prices from $3.00 *upward*; He had played the violin from the age of ten *upward.* **5** *adv.* More; over: boys 18 years old and *upward.* **— upward of** *or* **upwards of** More than: It cost *upwards of* $200.00.

up·wards [up′wərdz] *adv.* Upward.

Ur [ûr] *n.* An ancient city located on the Euphrates River in southern Babylonia.

U·ral [yōōr′əl] *n.* A river in the Soviet Union, flowing south to the Caspian Sea.

Ural Mountains A mountain system in the Soviet Union, the traditional boundary between Europe and Asia.

u·ra·ni·um [yōō·rā′nē·əm] *n.* A heavy, white, radioactive metallic element, used in the production of atomic energy.

U·ra·nus [yə·rā′nəs] *n.* **1** In Greek myths, the father of the Titans, Furies, and Cyclopes. **2** A planet of the solar system, the third in size and seventh in distance from the sun.

ur·ban [ûr′bən] *adj.* **1** Of, having to do with, or characteristic of a city: *urban* problems. **2** Living or located in a city: *urban* voters.

ur·bane [ûr·bān′] *adj.* Very refined and polite in behavior or manner; suave. **— ur·bane′ly** *adv.* **— ur·ban·i·ty** [ûr·ban′ə·tē] *n.*

ur·chin [ûr′chin] *n.* **1** A young, mischievous boy. **2** A poor, usually ragged child.

-ure A suffix meaning: **1** The act, process, or result of, as in *pressure*, the act, process, or result of pressing. **2** The condition of being, as in *pleasure*, the condition of being pleased. **3** A group that, as in *legislature*, a group that legislates. **4** The rank or office of, as in *prefecture*, the office of a prefect.

u·re·a [yōō·rē′ə] *n.* A substance found in urine and also made artificially. It is used in making plastics, fertilizers, etc.

u·re·ter [yōō·rē′tər] *n.* The duct in the body by which urine passes from a kidney to the bladder.

u·re·thra [yōō·rē′thrə] *n., pl.* **u·re·thras** *or* **u·re·thrae** [yōō·rē′thrē] The canal by which urine is discharged from the bladder.

urge [ûrj] *v.* **urged, urg·ing,** *n.* **1** *v.* To drive or force forward: to *urge* the horses on. **2** *v.* To plead with or try to persuade (someone) to do something: We *urged* them to try our plan. **3** *v.* To recommend or advocate strongly: He *urged* more practice for the tennis team. **4** *n.* A strong impulse or desire to do something: a sudden *urge* to take a walk.

ur·gen·cy [ûr′jən·sē] *n.*, *pl.* **ur·gen·cies** **1** Urgent or pressing nature or character; need or demand for prompt action or attention: a matter of great *urgency*. **2** An insistent tone or manner: There was great *urgency* in his voice.

ur·gent [ûr′jənt] *adj.* **1** Needing or demanding prompt action or attention; pressing: an *urgent* need. **2** Pressing; insistent: an *urgent* appeal for funds. **— ur′gent·ly** *adv.*

u·ri·nal [yŏŏr′ə·nəl] *n.* An upright wall fixture in which to urinate, or a room with such a fixture.

u·ri·nal·y·sis [yŏŏr′ə·nal′ə·sis] *n.*, *pl.* **u·ri·nal·y·ses** [yŏŏr′ə·nal′ə·sēz] A chemical analysis of urine in order to detect various diseases, etc.

u·ri·nar·y [yŏŏr′ə·ner′ē] *adj.* Of or having to do with urine or the organs that produce or excrete it.

u·ri·nate [yŏŏr′ə·nāt] *v.* **u·ri·nat·ed, u·ri·nat·ing** To pass or get rid of urine from the body.

u·rine [yŏŏr′in] *n.* A liquid containing body wastes, secreted by the kidneys, stored in the bladder, and then discharged from the body.

urn [ûrn] *n.* **1** A large vase, usually supported on a pedestal. It is used for flowers or plants and often for holding the ashes of a cremated body. **2** A receptacle having a faucet, used for the making and pouring of coffee or tea.

A coffee urn and an ornamental urn

Ur·sa Major [ûr′sə] A constellation of northern skies, containing the stars forming the Big Dipper. ◆ *Ursa* is the Latin word for she-bear. *Ursa Major* means the Greater Bear, and *Ursa Minor* the Lesser (or Little) Bear.

Ursa Minor A constellation located near Ursa Major and containing the star Polaris. ◆ See URSA MAJOR.

U·ru·guay [yŏŏr′ə·gwī] *n.* A country in SE South America, located on the Atlantic Ocean.

us [us] *pron.* The form of *we* that serves as the object of a verb or of a preposition: He told *us* what to do; Please talk to *us* again.

U.S. Abbreviation of UNITED STATES.

U.S.A. Abbreviation of UNITED STATES OF AMERICA.

us·a·ble [yŏŏ′zə·bəl] *adj.* **1** That can be used. **2** Ready or convenient to use.

us·age [yŏŏ′sij or yŏŏ′zij] *n.* **1** The manner of using or treating a person or thing; use; treatment: He gives his work clothes a lot of hard *usage*. **2** The act of using. **3** A customary or habitual practice or way of doing something. **4** The customary way of using words or phrases.

usage note A note that tells how, where, when, or how often certain words are used or should be used. In this dictionary, usage notes are introduced by a colon or a red diamond.

use [*v.* yŏŏz, *n.* yŏŏs] *v.* **used, us·ing,** *n.* **1** *v.* To employ or operate; put into action, service, or practice: to *use* a can opener; to *use* caution in hunting. **2** *v.* To consume or spend: to *use* all one's energy; to *use* up one's allowance. **3** *v.* To partake of: Does he *use* tobacco? **4** *n.* The act of using: the *use* of one's talents; Skills improve through *use*. **5** *n.* The condition of being used: Is that car still in *use*? **6** *n.* The right to use something: I'll never give you the *use* of my pen again. **7** *n.* Occasion, reason, or need to use something: I may have *use* for that later. **8** *n.* The ability to use something: to lose the *use* of one's leg. **9** *n.* The way or manner of using something: That is not the correct *use* of that word. **10** *n.* Advantage, profit, or usefulness: There is no *use* in being angry. **11** *v.* To behave toward; treat: He *used* us badly. **— have no use for** **1** To have no need of: I *have no use for* that rope now. **2** *informal* To want nothing to do with; dislike: I *have no use for* that person. **— used to** [yŏŏs tŏŏ] **1** Familiar with or accustomed to by habit or practice: He is *used to* the cold by now. **2** Did at one time, did often, or did habitually in the past: We *used to* go there every summer. **— us′er** *n.*

use·a·ble [yŏŏ′zə·bəl] *adj.* Another spelling of USABLE.

used [yŏŏzd] *adj.* That has had use or has belonged to another; secondhand: a *used* car.

use·ful [yŏŏs′fəl] *adj.* Having a use; giving service; helpful; beneficial: a *useful* suggestion. **— use′ful·ly** *adv.* **— use′ful·ness** *n.*

use·less [yŏŏs′lis] *adj.* Having no use; not helpful or beneficial; worthless: a *useless* old lawn mower. **— use′less·ly** *adv.* **— use′less·ness** *n.*

ush·er [ush′ər] **1** *n.* A person who conducts people to their seats, as in a theater or church. **2** *v.* To lead, escort, or conduct, as to a seat. **— usher in** To lead in or announce the coming of: The rooster's crowing *ushered in* the morning.

U.S.S.R. Abbreviation of UNION OF SOVIET SOCIALIST REPUBLICS.

u·su·al [yŏŏ′zhŏŏ·əl] *adj.* Common or expected in the ordinary course of events; regular or normal: the *usual* childhood illnesses. **— as usual** In the regular or normal way. **— u′su·al·ly** *adv.*

u·su·rer [yŏŏ′zhər·ər] *n.* A person who lends money at a very high or illegal rate of interest.

u·su·ri·ous [yŏŏ·zhŏŏr′ē·əs] *adj.* Practicing or having to do with usury.

u·surp [yŏŏ·zûrp′ or yŏŏ·sûrp′] *v.* To seize and hold without legal right or by force: The duke *usurped* the throne. **— u·sur·pa·tion** [yŏŏ′zər·pā′shən or yŏŏ′sər·pā′shən] *n.* **— u·surp′er** *n.*

u·su·ry [yŏŏ′zhər·ē] *n.*, *pl.* **u·su·ries** **1** The act or practice of lending money and charging a very high or illegal rate of interest. **2** A very high or illegal interest charged on a loan.

U·tah [yōō′tô *or* yōō′tä] *n.* A state in the western U.S.

u·ten·sil [yōō·ten′səl] *n.* A tool, implement, container, etc., used to do or make something: Spades, rakes, and hoes are garden *utensils*.

u·ter·us [yōō′tər·əs] *n., pl.* **u·ter·us·es** or **u·ter·i** [yōō′tər·ī] The organ of female mammals in which the young develop before birth; womb.

u·til·i·tar·i·an [yōō·til′ə·târ′ē·ən] *adj.* 1 Having to do with utility. 2 Aiming for or possessing usefulness rather than beauty. 3 Concerned only with what is useful and practical.

u·til·i·ty [yōō·til′ə·tē] *n., pl.* **u·til·i·ties** 1 The quality or condition of being useful. 2 Something useful to the public, as gas, water, electricity, etc. 3 A company that provides services, as transportation, gas, water, etc., for the public.

u·til·ize [yōō′təl·īz] *v.* **u·til·ized, u·til·iz·ing** To make good or profitable use of: He has *utilized* every resource of the library. — **u·til·i·za·tion** [yōō′təl·ə·zā′shən] *n.* ¶3

ut·most [ut′mōst′] 1 *adj.* Greatest, highest, or largest in amount, degree, number, etc.: Use the *utmost* caution. 2 *adj.* Being at the farthest limit or point: the *utmost* reaches of the universe. 3 *n.* The greatest possible degree or the fullest extent: to play to the *utmost* of one's ability.

u·to·pi·a [yōō·tō′pē·ə] *n.* 1 (*sometimes written* **Utopia**) An imaginary place having a perfect social and political life where complete happiness is enjoyed by all. 2 Any impractical plan for bringing perfect happiness and peace to all people. — **u·to′pi·an** or **U·to′pi·an** *adj., n.*

ut·ter[1] [ut′ər] *adj.* Complete; total: *utter* misery; *utter* darkness. — **ut′ter·ly** *adv.*

ut·ter[2] [ut′ər] *v.* To express, say, or give out in words or sounds: They *uttered* a cry of joy.

ut·ter·ance [ut′ər·əns] *n.* 1 The act of uttering or expressing in words or sounds; vocal expression: to give *utterance* to one's feelings. 2 Something uttered, spoken, or said. 3 The manner of speaking: a loud *utterance*.

ut·ter·most [ut′ər·mōst′] *adj., n.* Utmost: He did his *uttermost* to encourage his students.

u·vu·la [yōō′vyə·lə] *n., pl.* **u·vu·las** or **u·vu·lae** [yōō′vyə·lē] The small, fleshy portion of the soft palate that hangs down in the back of the mouth.

V

v or **V** [vē] *n., pl.* **v's** or **V's** The 22nd letter of the English alphabet.

v. Abbreviation of VERB.

Va. Abbreviation of VIRGINIA.

va·can·cy [vā′kən·sē] *n., pl.* **va·can·cies** 1 The condition of being vacant or empty; emptiness. 2 A vacant job or position that is to be filled. 3 A vacant house, office, room, etc., especially one that is for rent. 4 Emptiness of mind; lack of intelligence or interest.

va·cant [vā′kənt] *adj.* 1 Empty, unfilled, or unused: a *vacant* house; a *vacant* job; a *vacant* lot. 2 Being or appearing to be without thought, intelligence, or interest: a *vacant* look; a *vacant* mind. 3 Free from cares, work, duties, etc.: a *vacant* moment. — **va′cant·ly** *adv.*

va·cate [vā′kāt] *v.* **va·cat·ed, va·cat·ing** 1 To make vacant by leaving: They *vacated* the house. 2 To give up or quit: to *vacate* a position.

va·ca·tion [vā·kā′shən] 1 *n.* A period of time for rest or recreation, away from regular work, study, etc. 2 *v.* To take a vacation.

vac·ci·nate [vak′sə·nāt] *v.* **vac·ci·nat·ed, vac·ci·nat·ing** To inoculate (a person or animal) with a vaccine to protect against certain diseases, especially smallpox.

vac·ci·na·tion [vak′sə·nā′shən] *n.* 1 The act of vaccinating. 2 The scar left by vaccinating.

vac·cine [vak′sēn] *n.* 1 A substance made from the mild virus of cowpox and used for vaccination against the more dangerous disease of smallpox. 2 Any similar preparation of weakened or dead viruses or bacteria used in vaccinations.

vac·il·late [vas′ə·lāt] *v.* **vac·il·lat·ed, vac·il·lat·ing** 1 To change one's mind often; waver. 2 To sway back and forth. — **vac′il·la′tion** *n.*

va·cu·i·ty [va·kyōō′ə·tē] *n., pl.* **va·cu·i·ties** 1 Emptiness. 2 An empty space; vacuum; void. 3 Idleness or emptiness of mind.

vac·u·ole [vak′yōō·ōl] *n.* A small cavity in a cell containing air or fluid or solid matter.

vac·u·ous [vak′yōō·əs] *adj.* 1 Having nothing inside; empty. 2 Without intelligence; stupid. 3 Without occupation or purpose; idle.

vac·u·um [vak′yōō(ə)m] *n., pl.* **vac·u·ums** or **vac·u·a** [vak′yōō·ə], *v.* 1 *n.* A space completely empty of matter. 2 *n.* A portion of space, as in a thermos bottle, from which nearly all the air has been removed. 3 *v. informal* To use a vacuum cleaner on (a rug, etc.).

vacuum bottle Another name for THERMOS BOTTLE.

---

add, āce, câre, pälm;   end, ēqual;   it, īce;   odd, ōpen, ôrder;   tŏŏk, pōol;   up, bûrn;
ə = a in *above*, e in *sicken*, i in *possible*, o in *melon*, u in *circus*;   yōō = u in *fuse*;   oil;   pout;
check; ring; thin; this; zh in *vision*.   For ¶ reference, see page 64 · HOW TO

vacuum cleaner A machine that cleans carpets, furnishings, etc., by sucking up the dirt.

vacuum tube An electron tube in which the electrodes are separated by a vacuum.

vag·a·bond [vag′ə·bond] **1** *n.* A wandering tramp. **2** *n.* A person without a settled home; wanderer. **3** *adj.* Wandering: The old prospector lived a *vagabond* life. **4** *n.* A rascal.

va·gar·y [vā′gər·ē *or* və·gâr′ē] *n., pl.* **va·gar·ies** An odd or unexpected notion or act: the *vagaries* of a spoiled child.

va·gi·na [və·jī′nə] *n.* The canal leading to the uterus through which the fetus passes at birth.

va·gran·cy [vā′grən·sē] *n., pl.* **va·gran·cies** The condition of being a vagrant.

va·grant [vā′grənt] **1** *n.* A person without a settled home or regular job; vagabond; tramp. **2** *adj.* Wandering about as a vagrant. **3** *adj.* Having a wandering course: a *vagrant* breeze.

vague [vāg] *adj.* **va·guer, va·guest 1** Not definite, clear, precise, or distinct: *vague* ideas; a *vague* outline. **2** Not thinking clearly or stating thoughts precisely: a *vague* person. **3** Of uncertain authority or source: a *vague* rumor. — **vague′ly** *adv.* — **vague′ness** *n.*

vain [vān] *adj.* **1** Taking or showing too much pride in oneself, one's looks, abilities, etc. **2** Unsuccessful; useless: a *vain* attempt. **3** Having no worth or purpose; empty: *vain* chatter. — **in vain 1** Without success or results: Our work was *in vain.* **2** In a manner that is not reverent or respectful: to pronounce the Lord's name *in vain.* ◆ *Vain* comes from a French word derived from the Latin word for *empty.*

vain·glo·ri·ous [vān′glôr′ē·əs] *adj.* Showing too much vanity or pride; boasting.

vain·glo·ry [vān′glôr′ē] *n.* Too much pride, boasting, or display.

val·ance [val′əns] *n.* **1** A drapery hanging from the edge of a bed, shelf, etc. **2** A short curtain, board, etc., placed across the top of a window to hide the curtain rods or other fixtures.

vale [vāl] *n.* A valley: used mainly in poems.

val·e·dic·to·ri·an [val′ə·dik·tôr′ē·ən] *n.* The graduate, usually the one having the highest grades, who makes the farewell speech at graduation.

val·e·dic·to·ry [val′ə·dik′tər·ē] *adj., n., pl.* **val·e·dic·to·ries 1** *adj.* Having to do with saying farewell. **2** *n.* A farewell speech.

va·lence [vā′ləns] *n.* A number indicating how many electrons per atom of an element can be or have been added or moved closer (negative valence) or subtracted or moved away (positive valence) in forming a compound.

Val·en·tine [val′ən·tīn] *n.* **1** A third-century Christian martyr and saint. **2** (*written* **valentine**) A card or gift sent on Saint Valentine's Day, February 14. **3** (*written* **valentine**) A sweetheart.

va·le·ri·an [və·lir′ē·ən] *n.* **1** Any of several herbs, as the heliotrope, whose roots are used in medicine as sedatives. **2** A drug made from such a root.

val·et [val′ā *or* val′it] *n.* A servant whose work is to look after his employer's clothing, help him dress, etc.

Val·hal·la [val·hal′ə] *n.* In Norse myths, the hall where the souls of heroes who were killed in battle were feasted by Odin.

val·iant [val′yənt] *adj.* Having or showing courage; brave. — **val′iant·ly** *adv.*

val·id [val′id] *adj.* **1** Truthful, acceptable, or reasonable: a *valid* excuse. **2** Legally binding: a *valid* will. **3** Based on proper logic; sound: a *valid* conclusion.

val·i·date [val′ə·dāt] *v.* **val·i·dat·ed, val·i·dat·ing 1** To make valid; prove correct; verify: to *validate* an excuse. **2** To make legal: to *validate* a will. — **val′i·da′tion** *n.*

va·lid·i·ty [və·lid′ə·tē] *n.* The condition or quality of being valid.

va·lise [və·lēs′] *n.* A suitcase.

Val·kyr·ie [val·kir′ē] *n.* In Norse myths, one of the maidens who carry the souls of the heroes killed in battle to Valhalla.

val·ley [val′ē] *n., pl.* **val·leys 1** A low area on the earth's surface, as between hills or mountains. **2** An area drained or watered by a river and its tributaries: the *valley* of the Hudson.

val·or [val′ər] *n.* Great courage or bravery, especially in war. ¶1

val·or·ous [val′ər·əs] *adj.* Having or showing valor; courageous; valiant. — **val′or·ous·ly** *adv.*

val·u·a·ble [val′y(ōō·)ə·bəl] **1** *adj.* Being worth money, effort, etc.; having value. **2** *adj.* Being worth a great deal: a *valuable* painting. **3** *n.* (*usually pl.*) Something worth much money, as jewelry. **4** *adj.* Worthy of respect or esteem: a *valuable* friend.

val·u·ate [val′yōō·āt] *v.* **val·u·at·ed, val·u·at·ing** To give a value to; evaluate.

val·u·a·tion [val′yōō·ā′shən] *n.* **1** The act of determining what something is worth: Would you make a *valuation* of my aunt's jewels? **2** The set or estimated value of something: The *valuation* of her jewels was very high.

val·ue [val′yōō] *n., v.* **val·ued, val·u·ing 1** *n.* The relative worth, importance, or usefulness of a person or thing: Do you think education has more *value* than experience? **2** *v.* To place or rate as to worth, importance, or usefulness: He *valued* fair play above winning. **3** *v.* To regard highly; prize: to *value* one's friends. **4** *adj. use:* a *valued* book. **5** *n.* The worth of something in money or other exchangeable goods: What *value* would you place on your camera? **6** *v.* To determine or estimate the value of: They *valued* his car at $800. **7** *adj. use:* a car *valued* at $800. **8** *n.* A fair return or exchange in service, goods, or money: This store gives excellent *value* for its prices. **9** *n.* (*pl.*) The beliefs, standards, principles, or ideals of a person or persons. **10** *n.* The meaning, quality, effect, etc., as of a word: the emotional *value* of certain phrases. **11** *n.* In mathematics, a particular number or quantity represented by a variable.

valve [valv] *n.* **1** Any device that regulates or controls the flow of a fluid, as through a pipe, etc. **2** One of the folds of tissue that control the flow of body fluids, as those which control the flow of blood to and from the heart. **3** In certain brass instruments, a device that allows the player to change the pitch by connecting additional lengths of tubing. **4** One of the two halves of the shell of an oyster, clam, etc.

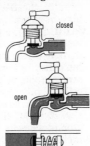

closed

open

closed

open

Valves

va·moose [va·moos′] *v.* **va·moosed, va·moos·ing** *U.S. slang* To leave in a hurry.

vamp [vamp] **1** *n.* The piece of leather forming the upper front part of a boot or shoe. **2** *v.* To repair or patch, as with a new vamp.

vam·pire [vam′pīr] *n.* **1** In folk tales, a corpse that rises from its grave at night to suck the blood of sleeping people. **2** A bat of tropical America that sucks the blood of livestock, and sometimes of men. It is often called the **vampire bat.**

van[1] [van] *n.* A vanguard.

van[2] [van] *n.* A large, covered truck for moving furniture, livestock, etc.

va·na·di·um [və·nā′dē·əm] *n.* A rare, silver-white metallic element, used in steel alloys.

Van Al·len radiation [van al′ən] Rapidly moving atomic particles held by the earth's magnetic field at the fringes of the atmosphere in two belts often called the **Van Allen belts.**

Van Bu·ren [van byoor′ən], **Martin,** 1782–1862, eighth president of the U.S., 1837–1841.

Van·cou·ver [van·koo′vər] *n.* **1** A seaport in sw British Columbia, Canada. **2** A large island off the sw coast of Canada, near this city.

van·dal [van′dəl] **1** *n.* A person who commits vandalism. **2** *adj.* Willfully destructive. **3** *n.* (*written* **Vandal**) One of a Germanic people who invaded the western Roman Empire early in the fifth century and pillaged the city of Rome in 455.

van·dal·ism [van′dəl·iz′əm] *n.* Willful or ignorant destruction of art, beautiful things, etc.

vane [vān] *n.* **1** A flat blade pivoted at the top of a spire, roof, or high place so that it will turn and point to the direction of the wind. **2** A blade on a waterwheel, electric fan, etc.

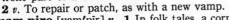

Vanes on waterwheel

van Eyck [van īk′], **Jan,** 1385?–1440, Flemish painter, a pioneer of oil painting.

van Gogh [van gō′], **Vincent,** 1853–1890, Dutch painter who worked mainly in France.

van·guard [van′gärd] *n.* **1** The advance troops of an army. **2** The leaders of any movement, as in art, culture, etc.

va·nil·la [və·nil′ə] *n.* **1** A flavoring made from the seed pods of a climbing tropical orchid. **2** The seed pod or bean of this plant.

van·ish [van′ish] *v.* **1** To disappear suddenly from sight. **2** To pass out of existence: Certain customs have *vanished.*

van·i·ty [van′ə·tē] *n., pl.* **van·i·ties 1** Too much pride in oneself or in one's appearance; conceit. **2** Uselessness, emptiness, or worthlessness. **3** Something that is useless, empty, or worthless. **4** A dressing table.

van·quish [vang′kwish] *v.* To defeat or overcome: to *vanquish* an enemy; to *vanquish* fear.

van·tage [van′tij] *n.* Superiority or advantage, as over an opponent.

vap·id [vap′id *or* vā′pid] *adj.* Lacking life or flavor; flat; dull: a *vapid* pudding; a *vapid* conversation.

va·por [vā′pər] *n.* **1** Moisture in the form of water droplets floating in the air as mist, fog, or steam. **2** The gas formed when a solid or liquid has been heated to a certain temperature: sodium *vapor.* — **va′por·ous** *adj.* ¶1

va·por·ize [vā′pə·rīz] *v.* **va·por·ized, va·por·iz·ing** To change into or become vapor: A spray gun *vaporizes* insecticide; Water *vaporizes* when heated. — **va′por·iz′er** *n.* ¶3

va·que·ro [vä·kā′rō] *n., pl.* **va·que·ros** A cowboy: a Spanish word used in the sw U.S.

var·i·a·ble [vâr′ē·ə·bəl] **1** *adj.* Likely or able to vary; changeable: *variable* weather. **2** *n.* Something that varies or is liable to change. **3** *n.* In algebra, etc., a number or quantity to which any of a set of values may be given. — **var·i·a·bil·i·ty** [vâr′ē·ə·bil′ə·tē] *n.*

var·i·ance [vâr′ē·əns] *n.* The condition of being variant or different; difference: Some *variance* between thermometers is to be expected. — **at variance 1** Disagreeing; conflicting, as facts. **2** Arguing; quarreling.

var·i·ant [vâr′ē·ənt] **1** *adj.* Having or showing certain differences: "Grey" is a *variant* spelling of "gray." **2** *n.* A different or variant form, spelling, etc.: "Grey" is a *variant* of "gray."

var·i·a·tion [vâr′ē·ā′shən] *n.* **1** A varying or changing in degree, condition, etc. **2** A changed or altered form. **3** The amount or range of change: a *variation* of 15 degrees. **4** A change in the rhythm, harmony, melodic pattern, etc., of a musical theme.

var·i·col·ored [vâr′i·kul′ərd] *adj.* Of various colors; marked with different colors. ¶1

var·i·cose [var′ə·kōs] *adj.* Extremely swollen or enlarged: *varicose* veins.

var·ied [vâr′ēd] *adj.* **1** Changed; altered: On Fridays his usual lunch is *varied.* **2** Having or made up of different things or parts: a *varied* menu. **3** Varicolored.

var·i·e·gat·ed [vâr′ē·ə·gā′tid] *adj.* **1** Spotted or streaked with different colors. **2** Having or showing different forms, styles, varieties, etc.: a *variegated* collection of flowers.

va·ri·e·ty [və·rī′ə·tē] *n.* **1** An absence of sameness; change: We all enjoy *variety* in our work. **2** A collection of different things; assortment: a *variety* of candies. **3** A class of things; sort; kind: a rose of a red *variety*.

var·i·ous [vâr′ē·əs] *adj.* **1** Different from one another; of different kinds: *various* kinds of fruit. **2** More than one; several: *various* wars. — **var′i·ous·ly** *adv.* ◆ See FEW.

var·let [vär′lit] *n.* **1** A servant or page. **2** A knave; scoundrel. ◆ This word is seldom used today.

var·mint [vär′mənt] *n.* Any person or animal considered as a pest. ◆ *Varmint*, often used in rural parts of the U.S. and England, is a variation of the word *vermin*. Both words come from the Latin word meaning *worm*.

var·nish [vär′nish] **1** *n.* A solution of certain gums or resins in alcohol, linseed oil, etc., used to give a shiny coat to a surface. **2** *v.* To cover with varnish: to *varnish* floors. **3** *n.* The hard covering or surface made by varnish when it dries. **4** *n.* An outward show or appearance: a *varnish* of politeness. **5** *v.* To hide under a false appearance: to *varnish* the actual facts.

var·si·ty [vär′sə·tē] *n., pl.* **var·si·ties** The highest ranking team representing a school in an activity, as in football, debating, etc.

var·y [vâr′ē] *v.* **var·ied, var·y·ing** **1** To make or become different in some way; change: The time of sunrise *varies* almost daily; She *varies* her programs each week. **2** To be unlike; differ: These furs *vary* in quality. **3** To differ or deviate, as from the usual or normal: A six-toed cat *varies* from the common type.

vas·cu·lar [vas′kyə·lər] *adj.* Of, having to do with, or containing vessels or ducts to carry blood, lymph, etc.

vase [vās, vāz, *or* väz] *n.* An ornamental container often used for holding flowers.

Vas·e·line [vas′ə·lēn] *n.* A white or yellow jelly made from highly refined petroleum, used as a salve: a trademark. Also written **vaseline.**

vas·sal [vas′əl] **1** *n.* In feudalism, a man who held land and received protection from a lord to whom he owed, in return, military or other service. **2** *n.* Any person or country in the dependent position of a vassal. **3** *adj.* Of or like a vassal.

vas·sal·age [vas′əl·ij] *n.* **1** The condition of being a vassal. **2** The duties and obligations owed to a lord by a vassal. **3** Servitude.

vast [vast] *adj.* **1** Of very large size; enormous; huge: the *vast* ocean. **2** Very great: *vast* significance. — **vast′ly** *adv.* — **vast′ness** *n.*

vat [vat] *n.* A large tank or tub for liquids.

Vat·i·can [vat′ə·kən] *n.* **1** The palace of the Pope in Vatican City. **2** The government, authority, or office of the Pope.

Vatican City An independent state within the city of Rome. It is governed by the Pope.

vau·de·ville [vôd′(ə·)vil *or* vōd′(ə·)vil] *n.* A type of theatrical show made up of unrelated acts, as songs, dances, skits, trained animals, etc.

vault¹ [vôlt] **1** *n.* An arched structure, as a ceiling or roof. **2** *v.* To cover with or as if with a vault. **3** *v.* To build in the form of a vault. **4** *n.* A room with an arched ceiling or roof. **5** *n.* Any vaultlike covering, as the sky. **6** *n.* A cellar or underground room. **7** *n.* A strongly protected place for keeping valuables, as in a bank. **8** *n.* A burial chamber.

Vaults in a ceiling

vault² [vôlt] **1** *v.* To leap or leap over with the help of a pole or the hands. **2** *n.* A springing leap, as one made with the aid of a pole.

vaunt [vônt *or* vänt] **1** *v.* To speak boastfully. **2** *v.* To boast of. **3** *adj. use:* their *vaunted* hospitality to strangers. **4** *n.* A boast; bragging.

veal [vēl] *n.* The flesh of a calf, used as food. ◆ *Veal* is from an old French word for *calf*.

vec·tor [vek′tər] *n.* A line segment that begins at one specified point and ends at another. All vectors of the same length and direction are considered equivalent.

veer [vir] **1** *v.* To shift or change direction. **2** *v.* To change the course of: to *veer* a boat. **3** *n.* A change in direction; turn.

Ve·ga [vē′gə *or* vā′gə] *n.* A very bright star in the constellation Lyra.

veg·e·ta·ble [vej′(ə)tə·bəl] *n.* **1** A plant or part of a plant used as food, as corn, carrots, lettuce, etc. **2** Any plant. **3** *adj. use:* *vegetable* oil; the *vegetable* kingdom.

veg·e·tar·i·an [vej′ə·târ′ē·ən] **1** *n.* A person who eats mostly fruits and vegetables and no meat. **2** *adj.* Of, for, or having to do with vegetarians. **3** *adj.* Consisting only of fruits and vegetables: a *vegetarian* diet.

veg·e·tate [vej′ə·tāt] *v.* **veg·e·tat·ed veg·e·tat·ing** **1** To grow, as a plant. **2** To live sluggishly with little feeling, action, or thought.

veg·e·ta·tion [vej′ə·tā′shən] *n.* **1** Plant life: lush *vegetation*. **2** The act of vegetating.

veg·e·ta·tive [vej′ə·tā′tiv] *adj.* **1** Growing or capable of growing, as a plant. **2** Without much action, feeling, or thought: a *vegetative* existence.

ve·he·ment [vē′ə·mənt] *adj.* **1** Marked by strong feeling or passion; intense: a *vehement* outcry. **2** Acting with great force or energy; violent. — **ve′he·mence** *n.* — **ve′he·ment·ly** *adv.*

ve·hi·cle [vē′ə·kəl] *n.* **1** Any device with wheels or runners used to carry something, as a car, bus, bicycle, or sled. **2** A means of expressing, making known, etc.: a *vehicle* for new ideas. **3** Oil or any other substance in which coloring matter is mixed to form paint.

veil [vāl] **1** *n.* A piece of thin fabric, as net, worn to cover or adorn the face or head. **2** *v.* To cover with a veil. **3** *n.* Anything that hides or covers: a *veil* of smoke. **4** *v.* To hide or disguise. — **take the veil** To become a nun.

vein [vān] **1** *n.* One of the muscular, tubelike vessels that carry blood back to the heart. **2** *n.* One of the radiating ribs forming the framework of a leaf or of an insect's wings. **3** *n.* A deposit of ore or of a mineral substance, as found in the earth or rocks: a *vein* of iron; a *vein* of coal. **4** *n.* A colored strip or streak, as in marble. **5** *v.* To mark or ornament, as with veins. **6** *n.* A trait, mood, quality, etc.: A *vein* of sadness filled his speech.

Veins

veldt or **veld** [velt *or* felt] *n.* In South Africa, open grassland with few shrubs or trees.

vel·lum [vel′əm] *n.* **1** Fine parchment used for expensive binding, printing, etc. **2** Paper made to look like parchment.

ve·loc·i·pede [və·los′ə·pēd] *n.* **1** An early type of bicycle or tricycle. **2** A child's tricycle.

ve·loc·i·ty [və·los′ə·tē] *n., pl.* **ve·loc·i·ties** **1** Speed or swiftness. **2** Rate of motion in a certain direction: a *velocity* of 50 mph.

ve·lours or **ve·lour** [və·lŏŏr′] *n., pl.* **ve·lours** [və·lŏŏrz] A closely woven fabric of cotton, wool, etc., having a smooth, velvetlike surface.

vel·vet [vel′vit] **1** *n.* A cloth of silk, rayon, cotton, etc., with a thick, smooth pile on one side. **2** *adj. use:* a *velvet* dress. **3** *adj.* Soft and smooth to the touch. — **vel′vet·y** *adj.* ◆ *Velvet* goes back to a Latin word meaning *shaggy hair.*

vel·vet·een [vel′və·tēn′] *n.* A cotton fabric with a short, thick velvetlike pile.

ve·na ca·va [vē′nə kā′və] *pl.* **ve·nae ca·vae** [vē′nē kā′vē] One of two large veins by which blood is returned to the right chamber of the heart.

ve·nal [vē′nəl] *adj.* **1** Willing to give up honor or principles for money; capable of being bought or bribed. **2** Controlled or influenced by hope of gain or reward. — **ve·nal′i·ty** *n.*

vend [vend] *v.* **1** To sell. **2** To be a vender.

vend·er [ven′dər] *n.* A person who sells something, often out-of-doors or from door to door.

ven·det·ta [ven·det′ə] *n.* A feud or private warfare, often waged in revenge for murder.

ven·dor [ven′dər] *n.* Another spelling of VENDER.

ven·due [ven·d(y)ōō′] *n.* A public auction.

ve·neer [və·nir′] **1** *n.* A thin layer, as of a valuable wood on a cheaper surface or ivory on piano keys. **2** *v.* To cover with a veneer. **3** *n.* An outward show; gloss: a *veneer* of politeness.

ven·er·a·ble [ven′ər·ə·bəl] *adj.* Worthy of respect because of age, good qualities, etc.: a *venerable* doctor.

ven·er·ate [ven′ə·rāt] *v.* **ven·er·at·ed, ven·er·at·ing** To look upon with respect or reverence; revere. — **ven′er·a′tion** *n.*

ve·ne·re·al [və·nir′ē·əl] *adj.* Resulting from or communicated by sexual intercourse with an infected person: a *venereal* disease.

Ve·ne·tian [və·nē′shən] **1** *adj.* Of or from Venice. **2** *n.* A person born or living in Venice. **3** *n.* In former times, a citizen of Venice.

Venetian blind A flexible screen commonly hung over the interior of a window and consisting of overlapping horizontal slats that can be tilted. It may be raised or lowered by means of attached cords.

Venetian blind

Ven·e·zue·la [ven′ə·zwā′lə *or* ven′ə·zwē′lə] *n.* A country in northern South America. — **Ven′e·zue′lan** *adj., n.*

ven·geance [ven′jəns] *n.* Punishment inflicted in return for a wrong done; revenge. — **with a vengeance** **1** With great force or violence: The storm broke *with a vengeance.* **2** To an unusual extent; extremely.

venge·ful [venj′fəl] *adj.* Seeking or showing vengeance; vindictive: a *vengeful* nature; a *vengeful* action. — **venge′ful·ly** *adv.*

ve·ni·al [vē′nē·əl *or* vēn′yəl] *adj.* Easily pardonable or forgiven; minor: a *venial* sin.

Ven·ice [ven′is] *n.* A city in NE Italy. It is built on over 100 small islands and many of its streets are canals.

ven·i·son [ven′ə·sən *or* ven′ə·zən] *n.* The flesh of the deer, used as food. ◆ *Venison,* derived from the French, ultimately goes back to the Latin word *venatus,* meaning *hunted.*

ven·om [ven′əm] *n.* **1** The poison secreted by certain snakes, spiders, etc. **2** Bitterness of feeling; malice; spite: to write with *venom.*

ven·om·ous [ven′əm·əs] *adj.* **1** Poisonous; able to secrete venom. **2** Full of spite; malicious: a *venomous* letter. — **ven′om·ous·ly** *adv.* — **ven′om·ous·ness** *n.*

ve·nous [vē′nəs] *adj.* Of, having to do with, or carried by the veins of the body: *venous* blood.

vent [vent] **1** *n.* An opening, usually small, for gases or liquids to pass through. **2** *v.* To permit to escape from an opening. **3** *n.* A means of escape; outlet: a *vent* for one's energies. **4** *v.* To relieve or express freely: to *vent* one's rage by shouting. — **give vent to** To relieve or express freely: She *gave vent to* her feelings by hitting him.

ven·ti·late [ven′tə·lāt] *v.* **ven·ti·lat·ed, ven·ti·lat·ing** **1** To fill with fresh air or change the air in: to *ventilate* a room. **2** To make fresh or cool, as by a current of air: The sea breezes *ventilated* the entire house. **3** To examine and discuss openly and freely: to *ventilate* all one's complaints. — **ven′ti·la′tion** *n.*

ven·ti·la·tor [ven′tə·lā′tər] *n.* A device or opening for changing the air, as in a room.

ven·tral [ven′trəl] *adj.* Of, near, on, or having to do with the belly or abdomen.

ven·tri·cle [ven′trə·kəl] *n.* One of the two lower chambers of the heart from which blood is pumped into the arteries.

ventral fins

ven·tril·o·quism [ven·tril′ə·kwiz′əm] *n.* The art of speaking in such a way that the sounds seem to come from some source other than the person speaking. **— ven·tril′o·quist** *n.*

ven·ture [ven′chər] *v.* **ven·tured, ven·tur·ing,** *n.* **1** *v.* To expose to chance or risk; place in danger; hazard: to *venture* one's life. **2** *v.* To run the risk of; brave: to *venture* the unknown. **3** *n.* A risky or dangerous undertaking; risk, especially a business investment. **4** *v.* To dare: Nobody *ventured* to answer. **5** *v.* To say or put forward at the risk of being contradicted or denied: to *venture* a suggestion.

ven·ture·some [ven′chər·səm] *adj.* **1** Bold; daring. **2** Full of danger; risky.

ven·tur·ous [ven′chər·əs] *adj.* **1** Willing to take risks; adventurous. **2** Risky; dangerous.

Ve·nus [vē′nəs] *n.* **1** A planet of the solar system, sixth is size and second in distance from the sun. **2** In Roman myths, the goddess of love and beauty. Her Greek name was Aphrodite.

Venus's fly·trap [flī′trap′] A plant having leaves edged with spikes that close instantly when touched by insects on which it feeds.

ve·ra·cious [və·rā′shəs] *adj.* **1** Truthful; honest: a *veracious* witness. **2** True; accurate.

ve·rac·i·ty [və·ras′ə·tē] *n., pl.* **ve·rac·i·ties 1** Truthfulness; honesty. **2** Truth.

ve·ran·da or **ve·ran·dah** [və·ran′də] *n.* A long, open, outdoor porch, usually roofed, along the outside of a building.

verb [vûrb] *n.* A word used to express action or a condition of being. Verbs change in form to express tense, person, and number. In "She was a teacher" and "We ran home," *was* and *ran* are verbs. A **helping verb** helps to express the tense, mood, voice, etc., of another verb. *Will* in "He will go tomorrow" is a helping verb.

ver·bal [vûr′bəl] **1** *adj.* In or of words: a *verbal* picture of the falls. **2** *adj.* Concerned with words only rather than with the ideas they convey: *Verbal* changes in a manuscript. **3** *adj.* Not written; spoken; oral: a *verbal* contract. **4** *adj.* Word for word; literal: a *verbal* translation. **5** *adj.* Formed from a verb: a *verbal* noun. **6** *adj.* Of or having to do with a verb. **7** *n.* A noun or modifier formed from a verb. **— ver′bal·ly** *adv.*

ver·ba·tim [vər·bā′tim] *adj., adv.* Word for word; in exactly the same words: a *verbatim* account; She repeated his remarks *verbatim.*

ver·be·na [vər·bē′nə] *n.* A plant grown for its clusters of showy red, pink, or white flowers.

ver·bi·age [vûr′bē·ij] *n.* The use of more words than are necessary for clearness.

ver·bose [vər·bōs′] *adj.* Using or containing an unnecessary number of words; wordy.

ver·bos·i·ty [vər·bos′ə·tē] *n., pl.* **ver·bos·i·ties** The use of too many words; wordiness.

ver·dant [vûr′dənt] *adj.* **1** Green: *verdant* plants. **2** Green with vegetation: *verdant* forests.

Verde [vûrd], **Cape** The westernmost point in Africa. It is in Senegal.

Ver·di [ver′dē], **Giuseppe,** 1813–1901, Italian composer of operas.

ver·dict [vûr′dikt] *n.* **1** The decision of a jury after a trial. **2** Any judgment or decision.

ver·di·gris [vûr′də·grēs *or* vûr′də·gris] *n.* A greenish coating that forms on the surface of copper, bronze, or brass after long exposure to air.

ver·dure [vûr′jər] *n.* The fresh greenness of growing plants, or the plants themselves.

verge [vûrj] *n., v.* **verged, verg·ing 1** *n.* The edge of something; margin: at the garden's *verge.* **2** *n.* The point at which some action or condition is likely to occur: on the *verge* of failure. **3** *v.* To come near; border: Her story *verged* on foolishness.

Ver·gil [vûr′jil] *n.,* 70–19 B.C., Roman poet who wrote the *Aeneid.*

ver·i·fi·a·ble [ver′ə·fī′ə·bəl] *adj.* Capable of being verified or shown to be true or accurate.

ver·i·fi·ca·tion [ver′ə·fə·kā′shən] *n.* **1** The act of verifying. **2** The condition of being verified.

ver·i·fy [ver′ə·fī] *v.* **ver·i·fied, ver·i·fy·ing 1** To prove to be true or accurate; confirm: to *verify* a report. **2** To test or check the accuracy or truth of: to *verify* a list of prices.

ver·i·ly [ver′ə·lē] *adv.* In truth; certainly; really: seldom used today.

ver·i·ta·ble [ver′ə·tə·bəl] *adj.* Authentic; true: a *veritable* monster. **— ver′i·ta·bly** *adv.*

ver·i·ty [ver′ə·tē] *n., pl.* **ver·i·ties 1** Correctness; truth. **2** A true statement; fact.

ver·mi·cel·li [vûr′mə·sel′ē *or* vûr′mə·chel′ē] *n.* A very thin spaghetti.

ver·mi·form [vûr′mə·fôrm] *adj.* Shaped like a worm.

ver·mil·ion [vər·mil′yən] **1** *n.* A brilliant red pigment. **2** *n., adj.* Bright orange-red.

ver·min [vûr′min] *n., pl.* **ver·min 1** Insects and small animals harmful or troublesome to man, as flies, grasshoppers, mice, rats, lice, etc. **2** A harmful or unpleasant person. ◆ See VARMINT.

Ver·mont [vər·mont′] *n.* A state in the NE U.S.

ver·nac·u·lar [vər·nak′yə·lər] **1** *n.* The language that is common to or most often heard in a particular place or locality. **2** *adj.* In, belonging to, or using language that is common to a particular place or region. **3** *n.* The common, everyday speech of the people. **4** *adj.* In or using common, everyday speech or language: a *vernacular* writer. **5** *n.* The vocabulary or jargon that is used by a certain group, profession, etc.

ver·nal [vûr′nəl] *adj.* **1** Of, belonging to, or appearing in the spring: The *vernal* equinox is the time near March 21 when the days and nights are of equal length. **2** Fresh or youthful.

Ver·sailles [vər·sī′] *n.* A city in France, near Paris. It is the site of the great palace of Louis XVI, the place where the treaty ending World War I was signed in 1919.

ver·sa·tile [vûr′sə·til] *adj.* **1** Able to do many things well: a *versatile* person. **2** Having many uses: a *versatile* machine. — **ver′sa·til′i·ty** *n.*

verse [vûrs] *n.* **1** The type of writing that uses regular meter and often rhyme; poetry. **2** A particular kind of poetry or poem: iambic *verse*. **3** A poem. **4** A stanza or a single line of a poem. **5** A short, numbered division of a chapter of the Bible.

versed [vûrst] *adj.* Educated, experienced, or skilled: He is well *versed* in science.

ver·si·fi·ca·tion [vûr′sə·fə·kā′shən] *n.* **1** The writing of poetry. **2** The structure of a poem with regard to rhyme, meter, stress, etc.

ver·si·fy [vûr′sə·fī] *v.* **ver·si·fied, ver·si·fy·ing** **1** To compose verses. **2** To tell about in verse. — **ver′si·fi′er** *n.*

ver·sion [vûr′zhən] *n.* **1** A description or account, usually from one person's point of view: the driver's *version* of the accident. **2** A translation from one language into another, especially such a translation of the Bible. **3** A particular form or adaptation of something: a movie *version* of a play.

ver·sus [vûr′səs] *prep.* **1** Against: the home team *versus* the visitors. **2** Rather than; in contrast to: theory *versus* practice.

ver·te·bra [vûr′tə·brə] *n., pl.* **ver·te·brae** [vûr′tə·brē] or **ver·te·bras** One of the bones forming the spinal column. — **ver′te·bral** *adj.*

ver·te·brate [vûr′tə·brāt *or* vûr′tə·brit] **1** *adj.* Having a spinal column or backbone. **2** *n.* Any of a group of animals with backbones, as fish, reptiles, amphibians, birds, and mammals.

The second vertebra of the neck, shown in place and from above.

ver·tex [vûr′teks] *n., pl.* **ver·tex·es** or **ver·ti·ces** [vûr′tə·sēz] **1** The highest point; point farthest from the base; apex: the *vertex* of a pyramid. **2** The intersection of any two sides of a polygon or the point where several lines meet.

ver·ti·cal [vûr′ti·kəl] **1** *adj.* Straight up and down; making right angles with horizontal lines: a *vertical* column of figures. **2** *n.* A vertical line, plane, etc. — **ver′ti·cal·ly** *adv.*

horizontal

diagonal

vertical

ver·ti·go [vûr′tə·gō] *n.* A feeling of dizziness.

verve [vûrv] *n.* High spirits; enthusiasm; energy.

ver·y [ver′ē] *adv., adj.* **ver·i·er, ver·i·est** **1** *adv.* To or in a high degree; extremely; exceedingly: *very* weak; *very* generous. **2** *adv.* In fact; truly: the *very* same color. **3** *adj.* Actual or true: the *very* truth. **4** *adj.* Same; identical: my *very* words. **5** *adj.* Bare; mere: The *very* idea of going made him happy. **6** *adj.* Exact; absolute: the *very* middle of the night. **7** *adj.* Exactly suitable or right: the *very* hammer we needed. **8** *adj.* Total; unqualified: the *very* horror of it. — **the very** Even the: *The very* stones cry out. ◆ *Very* comes from the Latin word meaning *true*, and originally this is what the word meant in English: A *very* woman, she could not make up her mind. *Very* is now a much more general term used to intensify or strengthen the word that follows it: *very* lazy; *very* excited; the *very* truth.

very high frequency Any radio wave frequency between 30 and 300 megacycles per second.

ves·i·cle [ves′i·kəl] *n.* **1** A small bladderlike sac or cavity in the body, containing liquid. **2** A blister on the skin.

ves·pers [ves′pərz] *n., pl.* (*used with a singular or plural verb*) **1** (*sometimes written* **Vespers**) In certain churches, a service of worship held in the late afternoon or evening. **2** (*sometimes written* **Vespers**) The prayers said or sung at this service.

Ves·puc·ci [ves·p(y)ōō′chē], **Amerigo,** 1451–1512, Italian explorer for whom America was named.

ves·sel [ves′(ə)l] *n.* **1** A hollow container, as a bowl, pitcher, vat, etc. **2** A ship or boat larger than a rowboat. **3** A tube, duct, or canal for carrying a body fluid: a blood *vessel*.

vest [vest] **1** *n.* A sleeveless garment worn by men over a shirt and under a suit coat, or a garment for women with a similar cut. **2** *v.* To dress (oneself), especially in church vestments. **3** *v.* To give (authority, rights, ownership, etc.) to some person or persons: The right to build roads is *vested* in local government. **4** *v.* To give authority, ownership, etc., to: The court *vested* him with the right to sell the property.

Ves·ta [ves′tə] *n.* The ancient Roman goddess of the hearth and the hearth fire.

ves·tal [ves′təl] *n.* **1** A priestess who kept the sacred fire burning in the temple of Vesta; often called a **vestal virgin**. **2** A virgin.

vest·ed [ves′tid] *adj.* **1** Put absolutely in the possession of a person or persons; not contingent on anything; settled: *vested* powers. **2** Dressed or robed, especially in church vestments.

ves·ti·bule [ves′tə·byōol] *n.* **1** An entrance hall or lobby. **2** The enclosed passageway between the connected cars of a passenger train.

ves·tige [ves′tij] *n.* **1** A trace or mark left by something absent, lost, or gone: In the caves we saw *vestiges* of prehistoric men. **2** A part or

add, āce, câre, pälm; end, ēqual; it, īce; odd, ōpen, ôrder; tŏŏk, pōōl; up, bûrn;
ə = a in *above*, e in *sicken*, i in *possible*, o in *melon*, u in *circus*; yōō = u in *fuse*; oil; pout;
check; ring; thin; this; zh in *vision*. For ¶ reference, see page 64 · HOW TO

organ that is small or useless but which once had a use or function in ancestors of the organism: Man's appendix is a *vestige*.

ves·tig·i·al [ves·tij′ē·əl] *adj.* Of, like, or being a vestige: a *vestigial* part.

vest·ment [vest′mənt] *n.* A garment, especially any of various garments worn by the clergy in religious services.

ves·try [ves′trē] *n., pl.* **ves·tries** **1** A room in a church where vestments, altar linens, etc., are kept. **2** A room in a church used for Sunday school, meetings, etc. **3** In certain churches, a group of people who take care of the business affairs of a parish.

ves·try·man [ves′trē·mən] *n., pl.* **ves·try·men** [ves′trē·mən] A member of a vestry.

ves·ture [ves′chər] *n.* Garments; clothing.

Ve·su·vi·us [və·sōō′vē·əs] *n.* An active volcano near Naples, Italy.

vet [vet] *n. informal* **1** A veteran. **2** A veterinarian.

vetch [vech] *n.* A climbing vine related to the pea, grown as food for cattle, sheep, etc.

vet·er·an [vet′ər·ən *or* vet′rən] *n.* **1** A former member of the armed forces. **2** A person who has had much experience in doing something: a *veteran* at shortstop. **3** *adj. use:* a *veteran* actor.

Veterans Day November 11th, a U.S. national holiday honoring veterans of the armed forces: formerly called Armistice Day.

vet·er·i·nar·i·an [vet′ər·ə·nâr′ē·ən] *n.* A doctor who gives medical treatment to animals.

vet·er·i·nar·y [vet′ər·ə·ner′ē] *n., pl.* **vet·er·i·nar·ies,** *adj.* **1** *n.* A veterinarian. **2** *adj.* Having to do with the diseases of animals and their treatment: *veterinary* medicine.

ve·to [vē′tō] *n., pl.* **ve·toes,** *v.* **ve·toed, ve·to·ing** **1** *n.* The right of a chief executive, as a president or governor, to reject a bill already passed by a legislature. **2** *v.* To use the veto on: to *veto* a new bill. **3** *n.* The official document containing and giving reasons for a veto. **4** *v.* To forbid or prohibit with authority: Our teacher *vetoed* the picnic. **5** *n.* The act of vetoing.

veto power A power possessed by the chief executive, as of a state or nation, to prevent a bill passed by the legislature from becoming law. Usually it can, however, be overridden.

vex [veks] *v.* **1** To irritate or annoy: The delay *vexed* us. **2** To trouble or afflict.

vex·a·tion [vek·sā′shən] *n.* **1** The act of vexing. **2** The condition of being vexed: His *vexation* at us was brief. **3** A person or thing that vexes: The puppy was a *vexation* to us all.

vex·a·tious [vek·sā′shəs] *adj.* Troublesome; annoying.

VHF Abbreviation of VERY HIGH FREQUENCY.

vi·a [vī′ə *or* vē′ə] *prep.* By way of: He went to Asia *via* Europe. ◆ In informal usage *via* can refer to the means of travel as well as to the route: We went *via* train. *Via* means *way* in Latin.

vi·a·ble [vī′ə·bəl] *adj.* **1** Capable of living and growing, as a newborn infant, seed, etc. **2** Practical; workable: It is a good, *viable* plan.

vi·a·duct [vī′ə·dukt] *n.* A bridgelike structure, especially one that carries a roadway, railroad, etc., over a ravine, railroad, etc.

Viaduct

vi·al [vī′əl] *n.* A small bottle for liquids.

vi·and [vī′ənd] *n.* **1** An article of food. **2** (*pl.*) Food, especially choice or expensive food.

vi·brant [vī′brənt] *adj.* **1** Having vibrations; vibrating; pulsing. **2** Full of energy; vigorous: a *vibrant* personality. **3** Full, deep, and resonant: *vibrant* tones.

vi·brate [vī′brāt] *v.* **vi·brat·ed, vi·brat·ing** **1** To move back and forth rapidly; quiver: The drum *vibrates* when it is struck. **2** To sound or echo: the note *vibrated* on the ear. **3** To be moved; thrill: to *vibrate* with emotion.

vi·bra·tion [vī·brā′shən] *n.* **1** A rapid or quivering motion from side to side. **2** A motion from side to side of a position of equilibrium; oscillation.

vi·bra·to [vi·brä′tō] *n., pl.* **vi·bra·tos** In music, a trembling effect given to a tone by rapid but very small changes in pitch.

vi·bra·tor [vī′brā·tər] *n.* Something that vibrates, especially an electrically operated device used to massage parts of the body.

vi·bur·num [vī·bûr′nəm] *n.* Any of various shrubs related to honeysuckle, having small flowers.

vic·ar [vik′ər] *n.* **1** In the Church of England, a parish priest who receives only a salary and not tithes. **2** In the Episcopal Church, a cleric in charge of a chapel or mission. **3** In the Roman Catholic Church, a representative of a bishop or the Pope. **4** Any substitute or deputy.

vic·ar·age [vik′ər·ij] *n.* **1** The residence of a vicar. **2** The salary and the duties of a vicar.

vi·car·i·ous [vī·kâr′ē·əs] *adj.* **1** Experienced or felt as if one person were doing or feeling what is actually being done or felt by another: While watching Helen's wedding, Janet felt a *vicarious* joy. **2** Done or suffered by one person acting as a substitute for another: a *vicarious* sacrifice. **3** Acting or substituting for another. — **vi·car′i·ous·ly** *adv.*

vice¹ [vīs] *n.* Another spelling of VISE.

vice² [vīs] *n.* **1** An evil or immoral habit: Cheating is a *vice*. **2** Bad or wicked behavior.

vice- A prefix meaning: Acting in the place of; substitute, as in *vice-president*, a man acting in the place of a president.

vice admiral In the U.S. Navy, an officer ranking next below an admiral.

vice-pres·i·den·cy [vīs′prez′ə·dən·sē] *n.* The office or term of a vice-president.

vice-pres·i·dent [vīs′prez′i·dənt] *n.* An officer ranking next below a president and acting, on occasion, in his place.

vice·roy [vīs′roi] *n.* A person who rules a country, colony, or province as the deputy of a king or other sovereign.

vi·ce ver·sa [vī′sə vûr′sə *or* vīs′ vûr′sə] The same action or idea reversed; the other way around: We visit them and *vice versa.*

vi·cin·i·ty [vi·sin′ə·tē] *n., pl.* **vi·cin·i·ties 1** A region nearby; neighborhood: He lives in the *vicinity* of the school. **2** Nearness in space; closeness; proximity.

vi·cious [vish′əs] *adj.* **1** Spiteful or mean: *vicious* lies. **2** Violent or fierce: a *vicious* blow. **3** Having many vices; wicked. **4** Dangerous or likely to attack, as an animal. **5** *informal* Severe; intense: a *vicious* storm. **— vi′cious·ly** *adv.* **— vi′cious·ness** *n.*

vicious circle A situation in which solving a problem raises a new problem, and each successive solution raises another, until one comes back to the original problem.

vi·cis·si·tude [vi·sis′ə·t(y)ōōd] *n.* (often *pl.*) Any of the sudden, unexpected changes, whether good or bad, that occur during a person's life, career, etc.

vic·tim [vik′tim] *n.* **1** A person or animal that is killed, injured, or made to suffer: a war *victim*; a sacrificial *victim*. **2** A person who is swindled or tricked.

vic·tim·ize [vik′tim·īz] *v.* **vic·tim·ized, vic·tim·iz·ing 1** To make a victim of. **2** To cheat or take advantage of. ¶3

vic·tor [vik′tər] *n.* The winner of a battle, war, struggle, contest, etc.

vic·to·ri·a [vik·tôr′ē·ə] *n.* A low, four-wheeled carriage with a folding top, a raised driver's seat in front, and a rear seat for two people.

Victoria

Vic·to·ri·a [vik·tôr′ē·ə] *n.,* 1819–1901, queen of England, 1837–1901.

Vic·to·ri·a [vik·tôr′ē·ə] *n.* **1** A state in SE Australia. **2** The capital of British Columbia, Canada.

Victoria, Lake A large lake in eastern Africa.

Victoria Falls A large waterfall on the Zambesi river in Africa.

Vic·to·ri·an [vik·tôr′ē·ən] **1** *adj.* Of or having to do with the time during which Queen Victoria reigned. **2** *adj.* Outwardly proper, stuffy, and conventional, as conduct during those years seems to us to have been. **3** *n.* A person, especially a writer, who lived during Queen Victoria's reign.

vic·to·ri·ous [vik·tôr′ē·əs] *adj.* **1** Having gained a victory; winning. **2** Of or related to victory.

vic·to·ry [vik′tər·ē] *n., pl.* **vic·to·ries** The overcoming of an enemy, opponent, or difficulty; triumph; success.

vict·uals [vit′(ə)lz] *n.pl.* Food. ♦ *Victual,* the singular form, goes back to the Latin word *victualis,* meaning *of food.* In older English it was spelled *vittle,* but more recent writers changed its spelling to conform with the original Latin. However, people kept on pronouncing it [vit′(ə)l].

vi·cu·ña [vi·kōōn′yə *or* vi·kyōō′nə] *n.* **1** An animal from the high Andes, related to the llama and alpaca, with soft, valuable wool. **2** Cloth made from this wool.

vid·e·o [vid′ē·ō] *adj.* Having to do with television, especially the picture part of a broadcast.

video tape A special magnetic tape on which both the sound and image of television programs are recorded.

Vicuña, about 3 ft. high at shoulder

vie [vī] *v.* **vied, vy·ing** To compete or strive: They *vied* for the prize; to *vie* with a rival.

Vi·en·na [vē·en′ə] *n.* The capital of Austria, in the NE part.

Vi·en·nese [vē′ə·nēz′] **1** *adj.* Of or from Vienna. **2** *n.* A person born or living in Vienna.

Vi·et·nam or **Vi·et-Nam** [vē′et·näm′ *or* vyet′·näm′] *n.* A country in SE Asia divided into **North Vietnam** and **South Vietnam.**

view [vyōō] **1** *n.* The act of seeing or inspecting; examination: a close *view.* **2** *v.* To look at carefully; examine; inspect: He *viewed* the ancient jug for a long time. **3** *v.* To look at; see: Come and *view* the sunset. **4** *n.* The distance or range of one's vision; sight: Have the mountains come into *view*? **5** *n.* That which is seen: a beautiful *view.* **6** *n.* A picture, drawing, etc., of something seen: She painted a *view* of the bay. **7** *v.* To think of or consider: He *viewed* the situation with alarm. **8** *n.* An opinion, or judgment: Are these your *views* on the subject? **9** *n.* A mental impression or idea: I have not yet formed a clear *view* of the situation. **— in view 1** In range of vision. **2** Under consideration. **3** As a goal or end. **— in view of** On account of; considering. **— on view** Set up for public inspection. **— with a view to** With the aim or hope of. **— view′er** *n.*

view·point [vyōō′point′] *n.* **1** A position from which one looks at or considers an object, situation, etc. **2** A mental attitude or conviction.

vig·il [vij′əl] *n.* **1** The act of staying awake in order to observe, protect, etc.; watch: a *vigil* at the bedside of a sick person. **2** The day or eve before a holy day. **3** (*pl.*) Religious services on such a day or eve.

vig·i·lant [vij′ə·lənt] *adj.* Alert; watchful; wary. **— vig′i·lance** *n.* **— vig′i·lant·ly** *adv.*

vig·i·lan·te [vij′ə·lan′tē] *n.* A member of a group who, without authority, take upon them-

add, āce, câre, pälm;   end, ēqual;   it, īce;   odd, ōpen, ôrder;   tŏŏk, pōōl;   up, bûrn;
ə = a in *above*, e in *sicken*, i in *possible*, o in *melon*, u in *circus*;   yōō = u in *fuse*;   oil;   pout;
check;   ring;   thin;   this;   zh in *vision*.   For ¶ reference, see page 64 · HOW TO

selves the punishment of crime and the keeping of order.

vi·gnette [vin·yet′] *n.* **1** A short description or picture in words written with charm and style. **2** A photograph or drawing with a background that shades off gradually at the edges.

vig·or [vig′ər] *n.* Active strength or force of mind or body; healthy energy. ¶1

vig·or·ous [vig′ər·əs] *adj.* **1** Full of vigor; robust; energetic. **2** Performed with vigor: a *vigorous* job of cleaning. — **vig′or·ous·ly** *adv.*

vi·king [vī′king] *n.* (*often written* **Viking**) One of the Scandinavian warriors who raided the coasts of Europe from the eighth to the tenth centuries.

vile [vīl] *adj.* **vil·er, vil·est** **1** Very unpleasant; bad: *vile* weather. **2** Disgusting; horrible: a *vile* stink. **3** Evil; low; depraved: *vile* abuse; *vile* language. **4** Degrading; humiliating; lowly: to serve in a *vile* position.

vil·i·fy [vil′ə·fī] *v.* **vil·i·fied, vil·i·fy·ing** To speak or write to or about with slander or abuse; revile.

vil·la [vil′ə] *n.* A large, luxurious house in the country, at the seashore, etc.

vil·lage [vil′ij] *n.* **1** A collection of houses in the country, smaller than a town but larger than a hamlet. **2** The people of a village.

vil·lag·er [vil′ij·ər] *n.* A person who lives in a village.

vil·lain [vil′ən] *n.* **1** A wicked or evil person, especially a wicked character in a novel, play, etc. **2** A villein. ◆ *Villain* comes from an old French word for farm servant. In those days farm workers had the reputation of being rude, coarse people, and the word *villain* finally came to mean *a scoundrel* or *evil person.*

vil·lain·ous [vil′ən·əs] *adj.* Very bad; wicked.

vil·lain·y [vil′ən·ē] *n., pl.* **vil·lain·ies** **1** The quality of being wicked. **2** Wicked behavior or a wicked act: his many *villainies*.

vil·lein [vil′ən] *n.* In the Middle Ages, a peasant who was regarded legally as a freeman to all but his lord, to whom he was bound as a slave.

vil·lus [vil′əs] *n., pl.* **vil·li** [vil′ī] One of the hairlike processes on certain membranes, as of the small intestine, where they aid in digestion.

vim [vim] *n.* Force or vigor; energy; spirit.

Vin·ci [vin′chē], **Leonardo da** See DA VINCI.

vin·di·cate [vin′də·kāt] *v.* **vin·di·cat·ed, vin·di·cat·ing** **1** To clear of accusation, blame, suspicion of wrongdoing, etc.: The trial *vindicated* the defendant. **2** To defend successfully against challenge or attack; justify: Historians have *vindicated* the statesman's actions.

vin·di·ca·tion [vin′də·kā′shən] *n.* **1** The act of vindicating. **2** A being vindicated. **3** Justification; defense.

vin·dic·tive [vin·dik′tiv] *adj.* Moved by or showing a mean desire for revenge. — **vin·dic′tive·ly** *adv.* — **vin·dic′tive·ness** *n.*

vine [vīn] *n.* **1** A plant with a weak stem that grows along the ground or climbs by twining around or clasping a support. **2** A grapevine.

vin·e·gar [vin′ə·gər] *n.* An acid liquid obtained by fermenting cider, wine, etc., used to preserve or flavor foods. ◆ *Vinegar* comes from two old French words meaning *sour wine.*

vine·yard [vin′yərd] *n.* An area where grapevines are planted.

vin·tage [vin′tij] **1** *n.* A season's crop of grapes in a certain district. **2** *n.* The wine made from it. **3** *adj.* Of the highest quality: *vintage* wine. **4** *n.* The harvesting of a vineyard. **5** *n. informal* A type popular in the past: a joke of ancient *vintage.*

vint·ner [vint′nər] *n. British* A wine merchant.

vi·nyl [vī′nəl] *n.* A plastic used in making phonograph records, combs, floor coverings, etc.

vi·ol [vī′əl] *n.* Any of a group of old musical instruments usually having six strings and played with a bow. Viols were the forerunners of the violin family.

vi·o·la [vē·ō′lə] *n.* An instrument similar to the violin, but larger and lower in pitch.

vi·o·late [vī′ə·lāt] *v.* **vi·o·lat·ed, vi·o·lat·ing** **1** To break or fail to follow, as a law, rule, or agreement: to *violate* a city ordinance. **2** To treat in a disrespectful or sacrilegious way: Vandals *violated* the cemetary by overturning gravestones. **3** To break in upon; disturb: to *violate* a hermit's solitude. — **vi·o·la·tor** *n.*

vi·o·la·tion [vī′ə·lā′shən] *n.* **1** The act of violating. **2** The condition of being violated. **3** An instance of breaking a law, rule, regulation, etc.: fined for a traffic *violation.*

vi·o·lence [vī′ə·ləns] *n.* **1** Unrestrained and often destructive force; intensity; fury: the *violence* of the hurricane; the *violence* of his rage. **2** Rough, harmful, or destructive use of force: crimes of *violence.* **3** Injury or damage caused by a failure to respect: Denying his beliefs would do *violence* to his conscience.

vi·o·lent [vī′ə·lənt] *adj.* **1** Acting with or showing rough, harmful, or destructive force: a *violent* eruption; a *violent* attack. **2** Resulting from unusual force: a *violent* death. **3** Showing or resulting from extremely strong feelings: *violent* words. **4** Intense, extreme, or severe: a *violent* headache. — **vi·o·lent·ly** *adv.*

vi·o·let [vī′ə·lit] **1** *n.* A small plant bearing flowers that are usually bluish purple but sometimes yellow or white. **2** *n.* The flower of this plant. **3** *n., adj.* Bluish purple.

vi·o·lin [vī′ə·lin′] *n.* A musical instrument with a wooden body and four strings, played with a bow. The **violin family** of instruments includes the violin, viola, and cello.

vi·o·lin·ist [vī′ə·lin′ist] *n.* A violin player.

vi·o·lon·cel·lo [vē′ə·lən·chel′ō] *n., pl.* **vi·o·lon·cel·los** Another name for a CELLO.

Violin

vi·per [vī′pər] *n.* **1** Any of various poisonous snakes. **2** A treacherous or spiteful person.

vi·ra·go [vi·rä′gō] *n., pl.* **vi·ra·goes** or **vi·ra·gos** A quarrelsome, ill-tempered woman.

vir·e·o [vir′ē·ō] *n., pl.* **vir·e·os** A small, grayish green songbird that eats insects.

Vir·gil [vûr′jəl] *n.* Another spelling of VERGIL.

vir·gin [vûr′jin] **1** *n.* A woman who has never had sexual intercourse; maiden. **2** *adj.* Of, being, or suiting a virgin. **3** *adj.* Chaste; modest. **4** *adj.* Not yet or not previously touched, used, etc.: a *virgin* forest. **5** *adj.* Not dirtied; pure: *virgin* snow. — **the Virgin** The Virgin Mary. — **vir′gin·al** *adj.*

vir·gin·al [vûr′jin·əl] *n.* (*often pl.*) A small, rectangular harpsichord having no legs.

Vir·gin·ia [vər·jin′yə] *n.* A state in the SE U.S., on the Atlantic Ocean.

Virginia reel A lively American folk dance performed by two facing lines of dancers.

Virgin Islands A group of islands in the West Indies. Three islands belong to the U.S. The rest make up a British colony.

vir·gin·i·ty [vər·jin′ə·tē] *n.* The condition of being a virgin or of being virgin.

Virgin Mary Mary, the mother of Jesus.

vir·ile [vir′əl] *adj.* **1** Having the characteristics of adult manhood; masculine. **2** Having a man's vigor and strength; manly. **3** Forceful.

vi·ril·i·ty [və·ril′ə·tē] *n.* **1** Manhood or masculinity. **2** Manly vigor, strength, or force.

vi·rol·o·gy [və·rol′ə·jē] *n.* The study of viruses. — **vi·rol′o·gist** *n.*

vir·tu·al [vûr′chōō·əl] *adj.* Being (the thing specified) in effect, though not in name or in fact: a *virtual* certainty. — **vir′tu·al·ly** *adv.*

vir·tue [vûr′chōō] *n.* **1** Moral excellence; right living; morality; goodness. **2** A particular type of moral excellence. **3** A good quality or feature: He explained the *virtues* of his policy. **4** Purity; chastity. **5** Effectiveness: a medicine of great *virtue*. — **by virtue of** or **in virtue of** Because of or by means of. ◆ *Virtue* comes from the Latin word *virtus*, meaning *manliness, strength,* or *bravery,* from *vir,* meaning *man.*

vir·tu·os·i·ty [vûr′chōō·os′ə·tē] *n.* The skill or technical mastery of a virtuoso, as in music.

vir·tu·o·so [vûr′chōō·ō′sō] *n,. pl.* **vir·tu·o·sos** or **vir·tu·o·si** [vûr′chōō·ō′sē] An artist who displays dazzling skill or technique in performance, especially in performing music.

vir·tu·ous [vûr′chōō·əs] *adj.* Having or showing virtue; good or pure. — **vir′tu·ous·ly** *adv.*

vir·u·lent [vir′(y)ə·lənt] *adj.* **1** Extremely harmful, infectious, or poisonous: a *virulent* ulcer. **2** Full of bitter hate or spite. — **vir′u·lence** *n.* — **vir′u·lent·ly** *adv.*

vi·rus [vī′rəs] *n.* Any of a class of tiny particles smaller than bacteria, capable of multiplying only in certain living cells and causing various diseases in man, animals, and plants. Influenza, colds, measles, etc., are caused by viruses.

vi·sa [vē′zə] *n.* A mark of approval made on a passport by an official of a foreign country, giving the bearer of the passport special permission to visit that country.

vis·age [viz′ij] *n.* The face or expression of the face of a person: a frowning *visage.*

vis·cer·a [vis′ər·ə] *n.pl.* The internal organs of the body, as the intestines, stomach, heart, lungs, etc. — **vis′cer·al** *adj.*

vis·cid [vis′id] *adj.* **1** Sticky, thick, and hard to pour. **2** Having a sticky surface.

vis·cose [vis′kōs] *n.* A thick, honeylike substance chemically prepared from cellulose and used in the making of rayon, cellophane, etc.

vis·cos·i·ty [vis·kos′ə·tē] *n., pl.* **vis·cos·i·ties** The condition, quality, or degree of being viscous: oils of differing *viscosities.*

vis·count [vī′kount] *n.* A nobleman who ranks below an earl or count and above a baron.

vis·count·ess [vī′koun·tis] *n.* **1** The wife or widow of a viscount. **2** A woman holding a rank equal to that of a viscount.

vis·cous [vis′kəs] *adj.* **1** Sticky; adhesive. **2** Thick and hard to pour, as certain oils.

vise [vīs] *n.* A clamp having two jaws that can be closed together with a screw, used to grasp and hold objects as they are worked on.

vis·i·bil·i·ty [viz′ə·bil′ə·tē] *n.* **1** The condition of being visible. **2** The distance to which objects can be clearly seen under given weather conditions: *visibility,* one mile.

Vise

vis·i·ble [viz′ə·bəl] *adj.* **1** Capable of being seen: No star was *visible.* **2** Apparent; evident: He had no *visible* motive for doing it.

vis·i·bly [viz′ə·blē] *adv.* In a noticeable way; evidently; plainly: He was *visibly* uneasy.

Vis·i·goth [viz′ə·goth] *n.* One of the western Goths that sacked Rome in 410.

vi·sion [vizh′ən] *n.* **1** The ability to see; sense of sight: Glasses sharpen his *vision.* **2** A sight of something imagined or spiritually revealed, seen in the mind, in a dream, in a trancelike state, etc.: He had a *vision* of an ideal world. **3** Insight; imagination. **4** The ability to look ahead into the future; foresight: Leaders should be men of *vision.* **5** A very beautiful or pleasing sight.

vi·sion·ar·y [vizh′ən·er′ē] *adj., n., pl.* **vi·sion·ar·ies** **1** *adj.* Being, like, or in a vision; not real; imaginary. **2** *adj.* Likely to daydream or have visions. **3** *n.* A person who has visions. **4** *adj.* Idealistic but not practical: *visionary* schemes. **5** *n.* A person full of impractical ideas, ideals, or schemes; dreamer.

vis·it [viz′it] **1** *v.* To go or come to see (a person, persons, or a place). **2** *v.* To stay with (a person) or in (a place) as a temporary guest.

3 *n.* The act or time of visiting: long *visits*. **4** *v.* To send or come upon; inflict or afflict: He *visited* his anger on the disobedient; They were *visited* by an epidemic of yellow fever.

vis·i·tant [viz′ə·tənt] *n.* A visitor.

vis·i·ta·tion [viz′ə·tā′shən] *n.* **1** The act of visiting; visit. **2** An official inspection. **3** A punishment or reward thought to come from God or from a god: a *visitation* of famine.

vis·i·tor [viz′ə·tər] *n.* A person who visits.

vi·sor [vī′zər] *n.* **1** Something that shades the eyes, as the projecting part of a cap. **2** The movable part of a helmet that shields the face.

Visors

vis·ta [vis′tə] *n.* **1** A view, especially one shut in at the sides and reaching into a distance: A walk lined with high hedges provided a *vista* of the sea. **2** A long mental view of past events or events to come: The discovery opened up new *vistas* to the scientist.

vis·u·al [vizh′oo·əl] *adj.* **1** Of, having to do with, or serving the sense of sight. **2** Capable of being seen; visible. **— vis′u·al·ly** *adv.*

visual aid Any map, diagram, picture, film strip, etc., that helps one to learn, as in school.

vis·u·al·ize [vizh′oo·əl·īz′] *v.* **vis·u·al·ized, vis·u·al·iz·ing** To form a mental image of; see in the mind: *Visualize* your kitchen. ¶3

vi·tal [vīt′(ə)l] *adj.* **1** Of or having to do with life or human lives: *vital* energy; *vital* statistics. **2** Necessary or essential to life: The lungs are *vital* organs. **3** Lively and energetic: She has a *vital* personality. **4** Having great or essential importance: a *vital* question. **5** Dangerous, fatal, or ruinous: a *vital* error. **— vi′tal·ly** *adv.*

vi·tal·i·ty [vī·tal′ə·tē] *n.* **1** Energy, as that which sustains life; vigor. **2** The power to go on living or enduring. **3** Liveliness.

vi·tal·ize [vīt′(ə)l·īz] *v.* **vi·tal·ized, vi·tal·iz·ing** To give life, energy, or vigor to. ¶3

vi·tals [vīt′(ə)lz] *n.pl.* **1** The parts or organs necessary to life, as the lungs, heart, brain, etc. **2** The essential parts of anything.

vi·ta·min [vī′tə·min] *n.* Any of a group of organic substances found in most natural foodstuffs and required, usually in very small amounts, for the proper health of the body.

vitamin A A vitamin needed for growth and good vision, found in carrots, cod-liver oil, etc.

vitamin B complex A group of vitamins which includes thiamine, riboflavin, and others.

vitamin C A vitamin found in citrus fruits, tomatoes, green leafy vegetables, etc.; ascorbic acid. A lack of it causes scurvy.

vitamin D A vitamin that helps the growth of bones and teeth, found in cod-liver oil, milk, egg yolks, etc. A lack of it causes rickets.

vi·ti·ate [vish′ē·āt] *v.* **vi·ti·at·ed, vi·ti·at·ing** **1** To spoil or weaken the goodness, purity, or

effectiveness of: Fermentation *vitiates* the freshness of milk. **2** To make void; cancel: Fraud *vitiates* a contract.

vit·re·ous [vit′rē·əs] *adj.* Of, having to do with, made from, or like glass: *vitreous* china.

vitreous humor The transparent, jellylike substance between the lens and retina of the eye.

vit·ri·fy [vit′rə·fī] *v.* **vit·ri·fied, vit·ri·fy·ing** To change into glass or a glassy substance through the action of heat.

vit·ri·ol [vit′rē·ōl *or* vit′rē·əl] *n.* **1** Sulfuric acid. **2** A sulfate of a heavy metal, as **green vitriol,** iron sulfate, **blue vitriol,** copper sulfate, and **white vitriol,** zinc sulfate.

vit·ri·ol·ic [vit′rē·ol′ik] *adj.* **1** Of, derived from, or like vitriol. **2** Painfully sharp, cutting, or sarcastic: a *vitriolic* letter.

vi·tu·per·ate [vī·t(y)oo′pə·rāt] *v.* **vi·tu·per·at·ed, vi·tu·per·at·ing** To attack with harsh words; scold severely. **— vi·tu′per·a′tion** *n.* **— vi·tu·per·a·tive** [vī·t(y)oo′pər·ə·tiv] *adj.*

vi·va·cious [vi·vā′shəs *or* vī·vā′shəs] *adj.* Full of life and spirit; lively; sprightly. **— vi·va′cious·ly** *adv.* **— vi·va′cious·ness** *n.*

vi·vac·i·ty [vi·vas′ə·tē *or* vī·vas′ə·tē] *n.* Liveliness; animation.

viv·id [viv′id] *adj.* **1** Very bright or strong; intense: *vivid* orange. **2** Creating clear, lifelike, or original images in the mind: a *vivid* account of an adventure; a *vivid* imagination. **3** Full of life or seeming very much alive: a *vivid* character in a book. **— viv′id·ly** *adv.*

viv·i·fy [viv′ə·fī] *v.* **viv·i·fied, viv·i·fy·ing** **1** To give life to. **2** To make vivid.

vi·vip·a·rous [vī·vip′ər·əs] *adj.* Bringing forth live young and not eggs, as most mammals do.

viv·i·sec·tion [viv′ə·sek′shən] *n.* Biological or medical experimentation that involves surgery, etc., on living animals.

vix·en [vik′sən] *n.* **1** A female fox. **2** An ill-tempered, quarrelsome woman; shrew.

viz. Namely: A sentence typically consists of two parts, *viz.*, subject and predicate. ◆ *Viz.* is an abbreviation of the Latin word *videlicet.*

vi·zier *or* **vi·zir** [vi·zir′] *n.* A high official of a Moslem country, as a minister of state.

vi·zor [vī′zər] *n.* Another spelling of VISOR.

Vla·di·vos·tok [vlad′ə·vos·tok′] *n.* A seaport in the SE Soviet Union.

vo·cab·u·lar·y [vō·kab′yə·ler′ē] *n., pl.* **vo·cab·u·lar·ies** **1** The total number of words that a person knows and can use. **2** The set of words used by a certain group or in a special field or activity: the *vocabulary* of jazz. **3** All the words of a language. **4** A list of words, usually arranged in alphabetical order, together with their meanings.

vo·cal [vō′kəl] *adj.* **1** Of, having to do with, or made by the voice: *vocal* sounds. **2** Capable of speaking or uttering sounds; having a voice. **3** Open in expressing one's opinions; outspoken: a highly *vocal* critic. **— vo′cal·ly** *adv.*

vocal cords Either of two pairs of folds of membrane that stick out into the throat. The lower pair can be made to vibrate and produce voice sounds when air from the lungs passes between them.

vo·cal·ist [vō′kəl·ist] *n.* A singer.

vo·cal·ize [vō′kəl·īz] *v.* **vo·cal·ized, vo·cal·iz·ing** To sing, speak, or make vocal sounds. ¶3

vo·ca·tion [vō·kā′shən] *n.* **1** A profession, career, or trade, especially the one a person chooses or for which he is best suited; calling. **2** A call to or fitness for a certain career, especially the religious life. ◆ See OCCUPATION.

vo·ca·tion·al [vō·kā′shən·əl] *adj.* Having to do with an occupation or trade, or the choice of one: *vocational* guidance; a *vocational* school.

vo·cif·er·ous [vō·sif′ər·əs] *adj.* Making or marked by a loud outcry; clamorous; noisy: a *vociferous* baseball fan; *vociferous* protests.

vod·ka [vod′kə] *n.* An alcoholic liquor, originally from Russia, made from grain or potatoes.

vogue [vōg] *n.* **1** Style; fashion: Vests are back in *vogue.* **2** Popular acceptance; popularity: Science fiction enjoyed a great *vogue* then.

voice [vois] *n., v.* **voiced, voic·ing 1** *n.* The sound made through the mouth of a person or animal, especially the sound made by human beings in speaking, singing, etc. **2** *v.* To utter or produce with a sound made by vibration of the vocal cords. **3** *adj. use: B, d,* and *z* are *voiced* consonants. **4** *n.* The ability to make vocal sounds: to lose one's *voice.* **5** *n.* The quality or character of one's vocal sound: a melodious *voice.* **6** *n.* The ability to sing. **7** *n.* The condition of the vocal organs as it affects one's singing ability: to be in poor *voice.* **8** *n.* Something thought of as like the human voice or speech: the *voice* of the wind; the *voice* of experience. **9** *n.* In music, a part, as for a single singer or instrument. **10** *v.* To express in words; utter: He *voiced* an objection. **11** *n.* Expression, as in words: to give *voice* to one's ideas. **12** *n.* The right to express an opinion, preference, or judgment; vote or say: We had no *voice* in the selection of the winner. **13** *n.* Expressed opinion, preference, or judgment: One juror's *voice* was for acquittal. **14** *n.* A form of a verb which shows that the subject of the sentence is either performing the action (**active voice**) or being acted upon (**passive voice**). *Wrote* in "He wrote the letter" is in the active voice. *Was written* in "The letter was written by him" is in the passive voice.

voice·less [vois′lis] *adj.* **1** Having no voice, speech, or vote. **2** Produced or uttered without vibration of the vocal cords. *P, t,* and *s* are voiceless consonants.

void [void] **1** *adj.* Without legal force or effect; invalid: The permit had expired and was *void.* **2** *v.* To take away the legal force or effect of; cancel; annul: to *void* a contract. **3** *adj.* Not occupied; empty; vacant: a *void* space. **4** *n.* An empty space or gap: to fill a *void.* **5** *n.* An empty condition or feeling: The loss of his friend left a *void* in his life. **6** *v.* To send out; discharge: to *void* urine. **7** *v.* To empty out; make vacant. **8** *adj.* Entirely lacking; destitute; free: an action *void* of reason.

voile [voil] *n.* A type of fine, sheer cloth.

vol. Abbreviation of VOLUME.

vol·a·tile [vol′ə·təl] *adj.* **1** Evaporating quickly at ordinary temperatures, as gasoline or ether. **2** Fickle; changeable: a *volatile* girl.

vol·can·ic [vol·kan′ik] *adj.* **1** Of, produced by, or thrown up from a volcano: a *volcanic* eruption; *volcanic* ash. **2** Like a volcano; apt to erupt violently; explosive: *volcanic* anger.

vol·ca·no [vol·kā′nō] *n., pl.* **vol·ca·noes** or **vol·ca·nos 1** An opening in the earth's crust from which hot gases, lava, ashes, etc., are thrown up, forming a cone-shaped hill or mountain with a central crater. **2** The hill or mountain itself.

vole [vōl] *n.* A small rodent resembling a mouse or rat, having a stocky body and a short tail.

Vol·ga [vol′gə] *n.* A long river in the western Soviet Union, flowing down to the Caspian Sea.

vo·li·tion [vō·lish′ən] *n.* The act or power of exercising one's own will in choosing or deciding; will: He left of his own *volition.*

cone of volcanic ash

escaped gases

crater

lava flow

molten rock

Volcano

vol·ley [vol′ē] *n., pl.* **vol·leys,** *v.* **vol·leyed, vol·ley·ing 1** *n.* The shooting or firing of a number of weapons at the same moment. **2** *v.* To shoot or fire or be shot or fired in a volley. **3** *n.* A shower of things shot off at the same time, as bullets, questions, etc. **4** *v.* To hit or return (a tennis ball) before it bounces. **5** *n.* The hitting of a tennis ball before it touches the ground.

vol·ley·ball [vol′ē·bôl′] *n.* **1** A game in which two teams on either side of a high net strike a large ball with the hands in an attempt to send the ball over the net without letting it touch the ground. **2** The large ball itself.

volt [vōlt] *n.* A unit for measuring the difference of potential between two points in a circuit. If a resistance of one ohm carries a current of one ampere, one volt is developed across its terminals.

volt·age [vōl′tij] *n.* Electromotive force expressed in volts: high *voltage.*

---

add, āce, câre, pälm;   end, ēqual;   it, īce;   odd, ōpen, ôrder;   tŏŏk, pōōl;   up, bûrn;

ə = a in *above,* e in *sicken,* i in *possible,* o in *melon,* u in *circus;*   yōō = u in *fuse;*   oil;   pout;

check;   ring;   thin;   this;   zh in *vision.*   For ¶ reference, see page 64 · HOW TO

vol·ta·ic cell [vōl·tā′ik] A cell that produces electricity by chemical action.

Vol·taire [vol·târ′] *n.* 1694–1778, French author and philosopher. His real name was François Marie Arouet.

volt·me·ter [vōlt′mē′tər] *n.* An instrument used to measure voltage.

vol·u·ble [vol′yə·bəl] *adj.* Talking a great deal or with great ease; talkative. — **vol·u·bil·i·ty** [vol′yə·bil′ə·tē] *n.* — **vol′u·bly** *adv.*

vol·ume [vol′yəm *or* vol′yōōm] *n.* **1** A book. **2** A book that is part of a set of two or more books. **3** The measure of the space inside a closed figure of three dimensions: A box 3 feet by 3 feet by 3 feet has a *volume* of 27 cubic feet. **4** A quantity or amount: to do a larger *volume* of business. **5** Fullness of sound or tone; loudness: Turn down the *volume* of the TV.

vo·lu·mi·nous [və·lōō′mə·nəs] *adj.* **1** Being enough or writing enough to fill whole books: *voluminous* letters; a *voluminous* writer. **2** Of great bulk or size: a *voluminous* cape.

vol·un·tar·y [vol′ən·ter′ē] *adj.* **1** Given, made, or done by one's own will or choice; not compelled: a *voluntary* donation. **2** Acting by one's own choice: an unpaid, *voluntary* group. **3** Done on purpose; not accidental. **4** Supported by free gifts: a *voluntary* hospital. **5** Under the control of the will: The action of the heart is not *voluntary*. — **vol′un·tar′i·ly** *adv.*

vol·un·teer [vol′ən·tir′] **1** *n.* A person who offers of his own free will to do some service, as military service. **2** *adj. use: volunteer* firemen. **3** *v.* To offer without being asked or compelled to do so: to *volunteer* advice; He *volunteered* to go. **4** *v.* To offer oneself or one's services: to *volunteer* for extra duty.

vo·lup·tu·ar·y [və·lup′chōō·er′ē] *n., pl.* **vo·lup·tu·ar·ies** A person who devotes himself to luxury and the pleasures of the senses.

vo·lup·tu·ous [və·lup′chōō·əs] *adj.* **1** Delighting the senses: *voluptuous* music. **2** Devoted to the pleasures of the senses: a *voluptuous* life. — **vo·lup′tu·ous·ness** *n.*

vom·it [vom′it] **1** *v.* To throw up (matter that has been eaten or swallowed), as when sick at the stomach. **2** *n.* Matter that is thrown up from the stomach in this way. **3** *v.* To send or come forth in a way that suggests vomiting: The volcano *vomited* smoke.

voo·doo [vōō′dōō] *n., pl.* **voo·doos 1** A religion of African origin, characterized by belief in magic and the use of charms, witchcraft, etc. **2** A person who practices this religion. ◆ *Voodoo* comes from an African word. See also MAGIC.

voo·doo·ism [vōō′dōō·iz′əm] *n.* **1** The religion of voodoo. **2** Belief in or practice of voodoo.

vo·ra·cious [vô·rā′shəs] *adj.* **1** Eating with great appetite; greedy; ravenous. **2** Taking a great deal of anything without getting enough: a *voracious* reader. — **vo·ra′cious·ly** *adv.* — **vo·rac·i·ty** [vô·ras′ə·tē] *n.*

vor·tex [vôr′teks] *n., pl.* **vor·tex·es** *or* **vor·ti·ces** [vôr′tə·sēz] A whirling current, as in water or air, usually spiraling in toward a center and tending to drag things with it; a whirlpool or whirlwind.

vo·ta·ry [vō′tər·ē] *n., pl.* **vo·ta·ries 1** A person bound by a vow or promise, as a nun. **2** A person devoted to some particular worship, pursuit, study, etc.: a *votary* of art.

vote [vōt] *n., v.* **vot·ed, vot·ing 1** *n.* A formal expression of opinion, preference, or choice, made by those individuals who have a say in a group decision or election. **2** *n.* The ballot, spoken "aye" or "no," raised hand, etc., on or by which a voter expresses his choice: to tally *votes.* **3** *v.* To cast a vote: to *vote* against a proposal; to *vote* for a candidate. **4** *n.* The right to vote: to be granted the *vote.* **5** *n.* The number of votes cast: a light *vote.* **6** *n.* Votes thought of as a group or bloc: the farm *vote.* **7** *n.* The result of an election: He won by a *vote* of 20 to 12 **8** *v.* To decide, elect, defeat, grant, or bring into effect by a vote: Let's *vote* on it; Congress *voted* a tax cut. **9** *v. informal* To declare by general agreement: The critics *voted* the show a success.

vot·er [vōt′ər] *n.* A person who votes or who has the right to vote.

vo·tive [vō′tiv] *adj* Done, given, made, lit, etc., to fulfill a vow or as an act of worship or devotion: a *votive* light.

vouch [vouch] *v.* To give a guarantee; give assurance: I'll *vouch* for my cousin's honesty.

vouch·er [vou′chər] *n.* **1** A paper or other piece of evidence that serves to prove something, as a receipt showing that a bill was paid. **2** A person who vouches for someone or something.

vouch·safe [vouch′sāf′] *v.* **vouch·safed, vouch·saf·ing** To grant or give, often as though doing a kindness to an inferior.

vow [vou] **1** *n.* A solemn promise to God. **2** *n.* Any solemn promise or pledge: *marriage* vows. **3** *v.* To make a vow to give, do, get, etc.: to *vow* one's loyalty. **4** *v.* To promise or declare earnestly; swear: He *vowed* never to return.

vow·el [vou′əl] *n.* **1** A speech sound made when the breath is not blocked by the teeth, tongue, or lips in the way that it is when a consonant is pronounced. **2** *adj. use: Cat* has one *vowel* sound. **3** A letter representing such a sound, as *a, e, i, o, u,* and sometimes *y,* as in *sky.*

voy·age [voi′ij] *n., v.* **voy·aged, voy·ag·ing 1** *n.* A journey by water, especially by sea. **2** *n.* Any journey, as one through air or space: a *voyage* in a spaceship. **3** *v.* To travel on a voyage or voyages. — **voy′a·ger** *n.*

V.P. Abbreviation of VICE PRESIDENT.

vs. Abbreviation of VERSUS.

Vt. Abbreviation of VERMONT.

Vul·can [vul′kən] *n.* In Roman myths, the god of fire and the forge.

vul·can·ize [vul′kən·iz] *v.* **vul·can·ized, vul·can·iz·ing** To treat (rubber) with chemicals, usually combining it with sulfur and heating it, to increase its strength and elasticity and improve other physical properties. — **vul·can·i·za·tion** [vul′kən·ə·zā′shən] *n.* ¶3

vul·gar [vul′gər] *adj.* **1** Lacking refinement or good taste; low, crude, or coarse: *vulgar* language; *vulgar* clothes. **2** Of, like, or having to do with the common people: Dante wrote poetry in the *vulgar* tongue, Italian, instead of in the literary language, Latin. ◆*Vulgar* comes from a Latin word meaning *the common people.*

vul·gar·ism [vul′gə·riz′əm] *n.* A word, phrase, or expression that is not used by educated people. *That ain't no good* is a vulgarism.

vul·gar·i·ty [vul·gar′ə·tē] *n., pl.* **vul·gar·i·ties** **1** The quality of being vulgar or crude. **2** Something vulgar, as an action or remark.

vul·gar·ize [vul′gə·rīz] *v.* **vul·gar·ized, vul·gar·iz·ing** **1** To make vulgar. **2** To simplify and popularize. ¶3

Vul·gate [vul′gāt] *n.* A Latin version of the Bible, translated in the fourth century by St. Jerome, now revised and used as the authorized version by the Roman Catholic Church.

vul·ner·a·ble [vul′nər·ə·bəl] *adj.* **1** Capable of being hurt, injured, or wounded: the *vulnerable* human body; a person who is *vulnerable* to criticism. **2** Open to attack; without sufficient defenses: The fort was located in a *vulnerable* position. **— vul·ner·a·bil·i·ty** [vul′-nər·ə·bil′ə·tē] *n.*

vul·ture [vul′chər] *n.* **1** A large bird, usually with a naked head, that feeds mostly on decaying flesh. It is related to eagles and hawks. **2** A savagely greedy person.

vy·ing [vī′ing] Present participle of VIE.

W

w or **W** [dub′əl·yoo] *n., pl.* **w's** or **W's** The 23rd letter of the English alphabet.

W or **w** Abbreviation of: **1** WEST. **2** WESTERN.

wab·ble [wob′əl] *v.* **wab·bled, wab·bling,** *n.* Another spelling of WOBBLE.

wad [wod] *n., v.* **wad·ded, wad·ding** **1** *n.* A small, compact mass: a *wad* of gum. **2** *v.* To press into a wad: to *wad* paper. **3** *n.* A thin plug to hold the charge in place in a gun or cartridge. **4** *v.* To pack with wadded material for protection, as valuables. **5** *n.* A tight bundle, as of paper money. **6** *n. informal* Great wealth.

wad·dle [wod′(ə)l] *v.* **wad·dled, wad·dling,** *n.* **1** *v.* To sway from side to side in walking. **2** *n.* A clumsy, swaying walk, like that of a duck.

wade [wād] *v.* **wad·ed, wad·ing** **1** To walk through water, mud, or anything that hinders one's progress. **2** To cross (a stream, pond, etc.) by wading. **3** To proceed with much labor and difficulty: to *wade* through a textbook. **— wade in** or **wade into** *informal* To attack or begin energetically or vigorously.

wad·er [wā′dər] *n.* **1** A person who wades. **2** Any bird with long legs that wades in water in search of food. **3** (*pl.*) High, waterproof boots for wading.

wa·fer [wā′fər] *n.* **1** A thin, crisp biscuit. **2** A small, flat piece of candy. **3** A small, flat disk of unleavened bread used in the Holy Communion service of some churches. **4** A small, adhesive disk used for sealing letters, documents, etc.

waf·fle [wof′əl *or* wô′fəl] *n.* A batter cake, crisper than a pancake, baked between two metal plates that have rows of knobs on them.

waffle iron Hinged plates for baking waffles.

waft [waft *or* wäft] **1** *v.* To carry or move gently through air or over water: The scent of flowers *wafted* in. **2** *n.* A sound, smell, puff of smoke, etc., borne by the air. **3** *n.* A puff of breeze.

Waffle iron

wag[1] [wag] *v.* **wagged, wag·ging,** *n.* **1** *v.* To swing back and forth or up and down: The dog *wags* its tail. **2** *v.* To move busily in producing speech: Tongues will *wag.* **3** *n.* The act or motion of wagging.

wag[2] [wag] *n.* A person who likes to make jokes.

wage [wāj] *v.* **waged, wag·ing,** *n.* **1** *v.* To engage in; carry on: to *wage* war. **2** *n.* (*often pl.*) Money paid for the services of an employee. **3** *n.* (*often pl. and used with a singular verb*) Payment; reward: The *wages* of sin is death.

wa·ger [wā′jər] **1** *n.* A bet. **2** *v.* To bet.

wag·ish [wag′ish] *adj.* **1** Inclined to make jokes; playful. **2** Comical; droll: a *waggish* grin.

Wag·ner [väg′nər], **Richard,** 1813–1883, German composer, famous for his operas.

wag·on [wag′ən] *n.* **1** Any of various large vehicles, drawn by animals and used mainly to carry freight. **2** Any small vehicle with wheels that is pulled by hand.

Wagon

wag·on·er [wag′ən·ər] *n.* A person whose work is driving wagons.

---

add, āce, câre, pälm;   end, ēqual;   it, īce;   odd, ōpen, ôrder;   toŏk, poōl;   up, bûrn; ə = a in *above*, e in *sicken*, i in *possible*, o in *melon*, u in *circus*;   yoō = u in *fuse*;   oil;   pout; check;   ring;   thin;   this;   zh in *vision*.   For ¶ reference, see page 64 · HOW TO

waif [wāf] *n.* A homeless, lost, or abandoned creature, especially a child or a pet.

wail [wāl] **1** *n.* A long, high cry, as of pain or grief. **2** *n.* A sound that is like this, as that of the wind. **3** *v.* To make or utter a wail.

wain·scot [wān′skət *or* wān′skot] *n.*, *v.* **wain·scot·ed** *or* **wain·scot·ted**, **wain·scot·ing** *or* **wain·scot·ting** **1** *n.* A facing for the walls inside a room, usually of wooden panels. **2** *n.* The lower part of an inside wall when finished differently from the rest of the wall. **3** *v.* To cover with wainscot.

wain·scot·ing *or* **wain·scot·ting** [wān′·skōt·ing *or* wān′skot·ing] *n.* Material for a wainscot, especially wooden panels.

waist [wāst] *n.* **1** The part of the body below the ribs and above the hips. **2** The part of a garment that covers the body from the neck or shoulders to the waist. **3** A blouse. **4** A waistband. **5** The middle of something, especially if narrower than the rest of it.

waist·band [wāst′band] *n.* A band circling the waist as of a skirt or pair of trousers.

waist·coat [wāst′kōt *or* wes′kit] *n. British* A man's vest.

waist·line [wāst′līn′] *n.* **1** The line thought of as being around the waist. **2** The line at which the skirt of a dress meets the waist.

wait [wāt] **1** *v.* To remain or stay until something happens: to *wait* for the bus to come; The car is *waiting*; *Wait* five minutes, then attack. **2** *n.* Time spent in waiting. **3** *n.* The act of waiting. **4** *v.* To remain temporarily neglected or undone: That will have to *wait* until tomorrow. **5** *v.* To act as a waiter or waitress. **6** *v. informal* To put off; postpone: Don't *wait* breakfast for me. **— in waiting** In attendance, as upon a monarch. **— wait on** or **wait upon** **1** To act as a servant, waiter, etc., to. **2** To pay a respectful visit to.

Waistcoat

wait·er [wā′tər] *n.* A man or boy who serves food and drink at tables in restaurants, etc.

waiting room A room for persons who are waiting, as for a train, a doctor, dentist, etc.

wait·ress [wā′tris] *n.* A woman or girl who waits on guests at tables, as in a restaurant.

waive [wāv] *v.* **waived**, **waiv·ing** **1** To give up voluntarily, as a claim, right, or privilege. **2** To put aside; postpone; delay.

waiv·er [wā′vər] *n.* **1** The voluntary giving up of a right, claim, etc. **2** A written declaration of this.

wake¹ [wāk] *v.* **woke** *or* **waked, waked, wak·ing,** *n.* **1** *v.* To stop or cause to stop sleeping; awake. **2** *v.* To become alert or aware: He *woke* to the demands of the situation. **3** *v.* To make or become active or aroused: to *wake* memories of the past. **4** *n.* A watch kept over a dead person through the night before burial.

wake² [wāk] *n.* **1** The trail of turbulent water left by a moving vessel. **2** The path or course over which any person or thing has passed: The fire left chaos in its *wake*. **— in the wake of** Following closely or resulting from.

wake·ful [wāk′fəl] *adj.* **1** Unable to sleep. **2** Without sleep. **3** Alert; watchful.

Wake Island [wāk] A small island in the northern Pacific Ocean, belonging to the U.S.

wak·en [wā′kən] *v.* To wake.

wale [wāl] *n.*, *v.* **waled, wal·ing** **1** *n.* A stripe raised on the skin by a blow; welt. **2** *v.* To raise wales on, as with a whip. **3** *n.* A ridge on the surface of cloth. **4** *v.* To weave (cloth) with ridges or ribs.

Wales [wālz] *n.* A division of Great Britain, west of England.

walk [wôk] **1** *v.* To move on foot at a normal rate. When a person walks, one of his feet is always touching the ground. **2** *v.* To pass through, over, along, etc., by walking: to *walk* the plank. **3** *n.* The act of walking: a morning *walk*. **4** *n.* The distance walked, or the time taken by one who walks: a five-mile *walk*; a three-hour *walk*. **5** *n.* A manner of walking; gait. **6** *n.* A pathway, usually paved, intended for walking. **7** *v.* To cause or allow (a horse, dog, etc.) to walk. **8** *v.* To go with on a walk: I'll *walk* her home. **9** *v.* In baseball, to reach or allow to reach first base as a result of the pitching of four balls. **10** *n.* In baseball, an instance of walking. **11** *n.* Manner or station: various *walks* of life. **— walk′er** *n.*

walk·ie-talk·ie [wô′kē-tô′kē] *n.* A radio transmitter and receiver that one person can carry.

walk·ing stick [wô′king] **1** A staff or cane carried in the hand. **2** An insect having long, slender legs and body. It resembles a twig.

walk·out [wôk′out′] *n. informal* A workmen's strike.

wall [wôl] **1** *n.* An upright structure built to enclose or divide a space, especially one side of a room or building. **2** *v.* To provide, surround, protect, etc., with or as if with a wall. **3** *v.* To divide, fill, or block with a wall: to *wall* up a door; to *wall* off an area. **4** *n.* Something that suggests a wall: a *wall* of flame. **5** *n.* The side of any cavity, vessel, or receptacle: the *wall* of a furnace. **— go to the wall 1** To be beaten; give way. **2** To fail in business.

wal·la·by [wol′ə·bē] *n., pl.* **wal·la·by** *or* **wal·la·bies** Any of various small kangaroos.

wall·board [wôl′bôrd] *n.* Any of various materials manufactured in large panels for use instead of plaster or wood for walls and ceilings.

wal·let [wol′it] *n.* A small folding case, usually of leather, for holding paper money, personal papers, etc.

wall·eyed [wôl′īd] *adj.* **1** Having the pupils of the eyes turned out to the sides so that a great amount of the white shows. **2** Having eyes with white or light-colored irises. **3** Having large, staring eyes, as certain fishes.

wall·flow·er [wôl′flou′ər] *n.* **1** A garden plant having fragrant yellow, orange, or red flowers. **2** *informal* A person, especially a woman, who at a party sits by the wall because she cannot attract partners for dancing.

wal·lop [wol′əp] *informal* **1** *n.* A hard blow. **2** *v.* To strike with a wallop. **3** *v.* To beat soundly.

wal·low [wol′ō] **1** *v.* To roll or tumble about; flounder, as in mud, water, etc.: Pigs *wallow* in mud. **2** *n.* A muddy place where animals like to wallow. **3** *v.* To indulge or debase oneself: to *wallow* in filth; to *wallow* in luxury.

wall·pa·per [wôl′pā′pər] *n.* Paper specially prepared and printed in colors and designs, for covering walls and ceilings of rooms.

wal·nut [wôl′nut] **1** *n.* A large, edible nut with its seed divided in halves. **2** *n.* The tree it grows on. **3** *n.* The wood of this tree, used to make furniture. **4** *adj.*, *n.* Dark brown.

wal·rus [wôl′rəs *or* wol′rəs] *n.*, *pl.* **wal·rus·es** or **wal·rus** A large, seallike animal of the arctic, having two long tusks in the upper jaw.

Walrus, 9–12 ft. long

waltz [wôlts] **1** *n.* A smooth, flowing dance for couples, done to music in triple time. **2** *v.* To dance a waltz. **3** *n.* Music for a waltz.

wam·pum [wom′pəm] *n.* Beads made of shells, often worked into belts, bracelets, etc., once used as money by North American Indians. ◆ *Wampum* comes from an Algonquian Indian word meaning *white string (of beads).*

wan [won] *adj.* **wan·ner, wan·nest** Pale or faint, as from being ill or very tired.

wand [wond] *n.* A thin stick or rod, as one used to do magic tricks.

wan·der [won′dər] *v.* **1** To move or travel about in an aimless or leisurely way; roam. **2** To stray: to *wander* off course. **3** To take an irregular, twisting route: The stream *wanders* by. **4** To become confused or irrational: His mind often *wanders.* **— wan′der·er** *n.* ◆ *Wander, rove,* and *roam* all mean to move about with no fixed destination. To *wander* is to move about aimlessly, as if lost, but *roam* and *rove* suggest movement over a large area, with a purpose, although it may be indefinite.

wan·der·lust [won′dər·lust′] *n.* A strong impulse or desire to travel about or wander.

wane [wān] *v.* **waned, wan·ing,** *n.* **1** *v.* To grow progressively less or smaller in size, brightness, etc.: The moon *waned.* **2** *v.* To decline or decrease gradually; draw to an end. **3** *n.* The action of waning. **— on the wane** Decreasing; fading out.

wan·gle [wang′gəl] *v.* **wan·gled, wan·gling,** *n. informal* **1** *v.* To get or accomplish by sly or irregular means: to *wangle* an invitation to a party. **2** *n.* An act of wangling.

want [wont *or* wônt] **1** *v.* To feel a desire or wish for: We *want* to go home; Do you *want* a glass of milk? **2** *n.* Something required or desired: to have few *wants.* **3** *v.* To need or lack: This food *wants* salt. **4** *n.* A lack or scarcity; need: They failed for *want* of planning. **5** *n.* Poverty; need: to be in *want.* **6** *v.* To be very poor or needy. **7** *v.* To wish to see or speak to: Did you *want* me? **8** *v.* To seek in order to arrest: The police *want* him for armed robbery.

want·ing [won′ting *or* wôn′ting] *adj.* **1** Not at hand; missing; lacking: There is one volume *wanting* in our encyclopedia. **2** Not up to standard: His work was found *wanting.*

wan·ton [won′tən] *adj.* **1** Brutal or destructive without reason or purpose: *wanton* murder; *wanton* mischief. **2** Playful in an unrestrained manner: a *wanton* boy. **3** Immoral; lewd. **— wan′ton·ly** *adv.* **— wan′ton·ness** *n.*

wap·i·ti [wop′ə·tē] *n.*, *pl.* **wap·i·tis** or **wap·i·ti** The elk of North America.

war [wôr] *n.*, *v.* **warred, war·ring 1** *n.* Conflict between the armed forces of nations or states, especially on a large scale. **2** *n.* Any condition of conflict or enmity: a *war* on poverty. **3** *v.* To make war, or carry on a war.

War between the States The American Civil War.

war·ble [wôr′bəl] *v.* **war·bled, war·bling,** *n.* **1** *v.* To sing with trills or runs, as some birds. **2** *v.* To make a liquid, murmuring sound, as a stream. **3** *n.* A bird's song, or a sound like it.

war·bler [wôr′blər] *n.* **1** A person or thing that warbles. **2** Any of several songbirds.

ward [wôrd] *n.* **1** A large room in a hospital, usually equipped to care for six or more patients. **2** A political division of a city. **3** A young person who is in the charge of a guardian or of a court of law. **— ward off** To repel; turn aside: to *ward off* a thrust; to *ward off* an illness.

-ward A suffix meaning: Toward; in the direction of, as in *homeward,* toward home.

war·den [wôr′dən] *n.* **1** The chief officer of a prison. **2** Someone who guards an area, enforces regulations, etc.: a fire *warden.* ◆ *Warden* and *guardian* come from an old French word meaning *to guard.*

war·der [wôr′dər] *n.* A keeper; guard; watchman.

ward·robe [wôrd′rōb′] *n.* **1** A personal supply of clothing. **2** A collection of costumes, as in a theater. **3** A cabinet or other storage place for clothing or costumes.

-wards Another form of -WARD.

ware [wâr] *n.* **1** Manufactured goods of a stated kind: often used in combination: *kitchenware; glassware.* **2** (*pl.*) Items for sale; goods. **3** Pottery; earthenware.

ware·house [wâr′hous′] *n.* A storehouse for goods or merchandise.

war·fare [wôr′fâr′] *n.* Fighting; war; conflict.

war·head [wôr′hed′] *n.* The front end of a torpedo, missile, etc., which carries the explosive.

war·i·ly [wâr′ə·lē] *adv.* With care; cautiously.

war·i·ness [wâr′ə·nis] *n.* Caution; care.

war·like [wôr′līk′] *adj.* **1** Fit and ready for war; liking war: *warlike* Indians. **2** Threatening war. **3** Of or having to do with war.

warm [wôrm] **1** *adj.* Moderately or comfortably hot. **2** *v.* To make or become warm. **3** *adj.* Giving or keeping in warmth: *warm* gloves. **4** *adj.* Suggestive of warmth: *warm* colors. **5** *adj.* Affectionate, kind, enthusiastic, etc.: a *warm* greeting; a *warm* smile. **6** *v.* To fill with good feeling: It *warms* my heart. **7** *adj.* Excited; passionate: a *warm* discussion. **8** *v.* To make or become passionate or enthusiastic: to *warm* to a subject. — **warm up 1** To warm. **2** To exercise, operate, etc., in preparation for activity or use: The pitcher *warmed up* before the game. — **warm′ly** *adv.*

warm-blood·ed [wôrm′blud′id] *adj.* **1** Having a constant warm body temperature regardless of surroundings. Mammals are warm-blooded animals; reptiles are not. **2** Enthusiastic.

warm front The boundary between a moving mass of warm air and the cold air it displaces.

warm·heart·ed [wôrm′här′tid] *adj.* Kind; affectionate.

warm·ing pan [wôr′ming] A closed metal pan with a long handle, containing hot coals or water, used in former times to warm a bed.

warmth [wôrmth] *n.* The condition or feeling of being warm.

Warming pan

warn [wôrn] *v.* **1** To make aware of possible harm or danger; put on guard; caution: to *warn* children to be careful in crossing streets. **2** To inform; give notice in advance: The bell *warned* of the train's approach.

warn·ing [wôr′ning] *n.* **1** A notice of danger: a storm *warning.* **2** Something that warns or reproves: a *warning* from the principal.

War of 1812 The war between the U.S. and Great Britain, lasting from 1812 to 1815.

War of Independence The American Revolution.

warp [wôrp] **1** *v.* To turn or twist out of shape. **2** *n.* A bend or twist, as in a plank. **3** *v.* To make evil, immoral, etc.; corrupt. **4** *v.* To move (a vessel) by hauling on a rope fastened to a pier or anchor. **5** *n.* The threads that run along the length of a fabric, crossed by the woof.

war·path [wôr′path′] *n.* The road to battle taken by American Indians, especially in the phrase **on the warpath,** meaning: **1** Making war, or eager to make war. **2** Ready for a fight; furious.

war·rant [wôr′ənt] **1** *n.* A legal paper giving authority to arrest, search, seize, etc. **2** *n.* Something that is a guarantee, proof, or confirmation of something else: Wanting a victory is no *warrant* of having one. **3** *n.* A reason or justification for an action, belief, etc.: He has no *warrant* to think that I failed the test deliberately. **4** *v.* To be sufficient grounds for; justify: The situation *warrants* bold action.

warrant officer An officer in the armed forces who ranks below commissioned officers and above enlisted men.

war·ran·ty [wôr′ən·tē] *n., pl.* **war·ran·ties** **1** Something that guarantees, authorizes, or justifies something else; warrant. **2** A usually written guarantee that the product being sold belongs to the person selling it and that it is as described to the buyer.

war·ren [wôr′ən] *n.* **1** A place where rabbits live and breed. **2** An enclosure for small game. **3** Any crowded place where people live.

war·ri·or [wôr′ē·ər] *n.* A man engaged in or experienced in war; soldier: used mostly in poems.

War·saw [wôr′sô] *n.* The capital of Poland.

war·ship [wôr′ship′] *n.* Any ship used in naval combat.

wart [wôrt] *n.* **1** A small, hard lump growing on the skin. **2** A similar growth on a plant.

wart hog An African wild hog having wartlike knobs on the face and large tusks in both jaws.

war·time [wôr′tīm′] *n.* A time of war.

war·y [wâr′ē] *adj.* **war·i·er, war·i·est** Watchful and suspicious; very careful; cautious.

was [wuz *or* woz] A form of the verb BE. It shows past time, and is used with *I, he, she, it,* or singular nouns: I *was* on time.

wash [wäsh *or* wôsh] **1** *v.* To free of dirt or other unwanted material by the action of a liquid, as water, and usually a soap. **2** *v.* To wash clothes. **3** *n.* An amount, as of clothing, washed at one time. **4** *v.* To wash oneself: *Wash* before you eat. **5** *v.* To pass water over or through (gravel, earth, ore, etc.) in order to obtain something: to *wash* sand for gold. **6** *v.* To carry away, move, or remove by the action of water: *Wash* that dirt off; The sea *washed* the boat ashore. **7** *v.* To be carried or worn away, moved, or removed by the action of water: All the color *washed* out. **8** *v.* To withstand washing without damage: Will this shirt *wash*? **9** *n.* The act, process, or an instance of washing: the weekly *wash.* **10** *v.* To flow over or against: Waves *washed* the shore. **11** *n.* The breaking or the sound of the breaking of waves against a shore. **12** *v.* To apply a thin layer of paint, color, or metal to: to *wash* a copper pan with tin. **13** *n.* Something used in coating or washing: a *wash* of color; a *wash* of tin. **14** *n.* Liquid or semiliquid garbage; swill. **15** *n.* The eddies or currents produced in the air or water by an airplane, rocket, boat, etc. **16** *n.* A shallow part of a river, bay, etc. **17** *n.* Material such as mud, silt, etc., collected and deposited by flowing water. — **wash one's hands of** To end all connection with; have nothing more to do with. —

wash up 1 To wash oneself. 2 To wash the dishes, etc., after a meal.

Wash. Abbreviation of WASHINGTON.

wash·a·ble [wäsh′ə·bəl *or* wôsh′ə·bəl] *adj.* Capable of being washed without damage.

wash·board [wäsh′bôrd′ *or* wôsh′bôrd′] *n.* A board or frame having a ridged surface on which to rub clothes while washing them.

wash·cloth [wäsh′klôth′ *or* wôsh′klôth′] *n.* A small cloth used for washing the body.

wash·er [wäsh′ər *or* wôsh′ər] *n.* 1 A person or thing that washes. 2 A washing machine. 3 A flat ring of metal, rubber, etc. It takes pressure, stops leaking, etc.

wash·er·wom·an [wäsh′ər·wŏŏm′·ən *or* wô′shər·wŏŏm′ən] *n., pl.*

wash·er·wom·en [wäsh′ər·wim′·in *or* wô′shər·wim′in] A laundress.

wash·ing [wäsh′ing *or* wôsh′ing] *n.* 1 The act of a person or thing that washes. 2 A group of things washed or to be washed at a certain time. 3 Something obtained by washing: a *washing* of ore. 4 A thin coat of metal.

Washer

washing machine A machine, now usually automatic, for washing laundry.

Wash·ing·ton [wäsh′ing·tən *or* wôsh′ing·tən] *n.* 1 A state in the NW U.S. 2 The capital of the U.S., in the District of Columbia.

Wash·ing·ton [wäsh′ing·tən *or* wôsh′ing·tən], **George,** 1732–1799, first president of the U.S., 1789–1797; commander in chief of the American troops in the Revolutionary War.

wash·out [wäsh′out′ *or* wôsh′out′] *n.* 1 The washing away of earth, a road, path, etc., by flowing water. 2 The break or gap made by it. 3 *slang* A complete failure.

wash·room [wäsh′rŏŏm′ *or* wôsh′rŏŏm′] *n.* A room equipped with sinks and toilets.

wash·stand [wäsh′stand′ *or* wôsh′stand′] *n.* 1 A bowl with pipes and faucets for washing the hands and face. 2 A stand to hold a basin, pitcher, etc., for washing the hands and face.

was·n't [wuz′ənt *or* woz′ənt] Was not.

wasp [wäsp *or* wôsp] *n.* Any of various stinging insects related to bees and ants.

wasp·ish [wäs′pish *or* wôs′pish] *adj.* 1 Like a wasp. 2 Easily made angry; irritable.

was·sail [wos′əl *or* wo·sâl′] 1 *n.* An ancient party at which toasts were drunk. 2 *n.* The liquor prepared for such a festivity. 3 *v.* To take part in a wassail. 4 *v.* To drink the health of; toast. — **was′sail·er** *n.*

wast [wost] An old form of WAS used with *thou.*

wast·age [wās′tij] *n.* Something that is lost by wear, waste, etc.

waste [wāst] *v.* **wast·ed, wast·ing,** *n.* 1 *v.* To use, spend, or let pass to no good purpose or advantage: to *waste* fuel; to *waste* a chance. 2 *v.* To destroy or consume utterly: Insects *wasted*

the crops. 3 *v.* To make or become less vigorous, strong, etc.: She *wasted* away from arthritis. 4 *n.* An act or instance of wasting. 5 *n.* The condition of being wasted. 6 *n.* A barren or desolate region; wilderness. 7 *adj. use:* a *waste* plain. 8 *n.* Something to be thrown away as not usable or wanted, etc. 9 *adj. use: waste* gases; *waste* scrap. 10 *n.* Cotton threads used in bunches to wipe machinery, soak up oil, etc. — **lay waste** To destroy utterly.

waste·bas·ket [wāst′bas′kit] *n.* A container for paper scraps and other waste.

waste·ful [wāst′fəl] *adj.* Tending to waste food, money, materials, etc.; extravagant.

waste·pa·per [wāst′pā′pər] *n.* Paper thrown away as useless.

watch [woch] 1 *v.* To look or look at; observe: to *watch* a play; Just sit and *watch.* 2 *v.* To wait or look expectantly or alertly: *Watch* for the signal. 3 *v.* To keep in one's care; guard. 4 *v.* To pay attention or keep informed about: to *watch* an actor's rise to fame. 5 *v.* To remain awake, as in tending a sick person through the night. 6 *n.* The act of watching: The shepherd keeps *watch* over his sheep. 7 *n.* One or more persons set to watch; guard. 8 *n.* A guard's or a watchman's period of duty. 9 *n.* One of the two sections of a ship's officers and crew that take alternating duty. 10 *n.* A period of duty for a ship's watch. 11 *n.* A small timepiece that can be worn on the person. — **watch out** To be on guard; take care. — **watch′er** *n.*

watch·dog [woch′dôg′] *n.* A dog kept to guard a building or other property.

watch·ful [woch′fəl] *adj.* Watching carefully; alert; vigilant. — **watch′ful·ly** *adv.*

watch·man [woch′mən] *n., pl.* **watch·men** [woch′mən] *n.* A man who keeps watch, as one hired to guard a building, etc., at night.

watch·tow·er [woch′tou′ər] *n.* A tower from which a person may keep watch.

watch·word [woch′wûrd′] *n.* 1 A password. 2 A rallying cry or slogan.

wa·ter [wô′tər *or* wot′ər] 1 *n.* A liquid compound of hydrogen and oxygen that freezes at 32° F. and boils at 212° F. It falls as rain from the clouds, and, as rivers, lakes, seas, etc., it covers nearly 75 percent of the earth. It is essential to living things. 2 *v.* To provide with water; give water to: to *water* livestock. 3 *v.* To make moist or wet by water, as by sprinkling or soaking. 4 *v.* To drink or take in water. 5 *v.* To weaken or dilute with water: to *water* wine. 6 *n.* Any body of water, as a lake, river, ocean, etc. 7 *n.* (*usually pl.*) Still, flowing, or moving water, as of a lake, river, or ocean: the *waters* of the Hudson. 8 *n.* A liquid like or containing water: soda *water*; toilet *water.* 9 *n.* Any of the body fluids that resemble water, as saliva, tears, etc. 10 *v.* To secrete or discharge one of these fluids:

The eyes *water* when irritated; The steak made my mouth *water*. **11** *n*. The clarity or luster of a gem: a pearl of the first *water*. **12** *n*. A wavy sheen put on some fabrics or metals. **13** *v*. To put a wavy sheen on. — **hold water** To be acceptable or effective: That story doesn't *hold water*.

water bird A wading or swimming bird, or one usually found near water.

wa·ter·buck [wôt′ər·buk′ or wo′tər·buk′] *n*. A large African antelope with long horns, generally found close to water.

water buffalo A powerful buffalo of India, Africa, and the Philippines, having very wide curving horns. It is used to pull heavy loads.

Water buffalo,
5–6 ft. high at shoulder

water clock An ancient instrument for measuring time by a regulated flow of water.

water closet A toilet.

water color **1** A color for painting made ready for use by mixing with water. **2** A painting done in such colors.

wa·ter·course [wô′tər·kôrs′ or wot′ər·kôrs′] *n*. **1** A stream of water; river; brook. **2** A channel for, or made by, water.

wa·ter·cress [wô′tər·kres or wot′ər·kres] *n*. A creeping plant that grows in water, having leaves that are used in salads.

wa·ter·fall [wô′tər·fôl′ or wot′ər·fôl′] *n*. A stream falling from a high place, as from a cliff.

wa·ter·fowl [wô′tər·foul′ or wot′ər·foul′] *n.*, *pl.* **wa·ter·fowls** or **wa·ter·fowl** A water bird, especially a bird that swims.

wa·ter·front [wô′tər·frunt′ or wot′ər·frunt′] *n*. An area next to a body of water, especially a part of a city that contains docks, etc.

water hole A small pond or pool of water, especially one from which animals drink.

wa·ter·ing place [wô′tər·ing or wot′ər·ing] **1** A source of drinking water. **2** A resort that is near water or mineral springs.

water lily A water plant having large floating leaves and bright, showy flowers.

water line **1** The line where the surface of the water meets the side of a ship or boat. **2** One of the lines marked on a ship's hull to measure how far its load lowers it in the water.

wa·ter·logged [wô′tər·lôgd′ or wot′ər·logd′] *adj*. Flooded or soaked with water: a *waterlogged* boat; a *waterlogged* sponge.

Wa·ter·loo [wô′tər·loo] *n*. **1** A village in central Belgium where Napoleon met his final defeat in 1815. **2** A final and utter defeat, as in the phrase **to meet one's Waterloo.**

water main A large pipe for carrying water, especially underground.

wa·ter·mark [wô′tər·märk′ or wot′ər·märk′] *n*. **1** A mark showing the height to which water has risen. **2** A faint mark or design formed in paper as it is being made.

wa·ter·mel·on [wô′tər·mel′ən or wot′ər·mel′ən] *n*. A large melon with a thick rind, many seeds, and a very juicy pink pulp.

water moccasin A large, heavy, dark-colored, poisonous snake of the southern U.S.

water polo A water game in which two teams of swimmers try to pass or carry a large ball across opposite goal lines.

water power Power obtained from flowing or falling water and used to drive machinery.

wa·ter·proof [wô′tər·proof′ or wot′ər·proof′] **1** *adj*. Allowing no water to penetrate or enter. **2** *v*. To make waterproof.

water rat **1** A rat or ratlike animal that makes its home on the banks of streams or ponds. **2** A muskrat.

wa·ter·shed [wô′tər·shed′ or wot′ər·shed′] *n*. **1** The region from which a river drains its water. **2** A ridge separating two such regions.

wa·ter·ski [wô′tər·skē or wot′ər·skē′] *n.*, *v*. **wa·ter·skied, wa·ter·ski·ing** **1** *n*. One of a pair of skilike runners on which one glides over water while being towed by a motorboat. **2** *v*. To travel on water-skis. — **wa′ter·ski′er** *n*.

wa·ter·spout [wô′tər·spout′ or wot′ər·spout′] *n*. **1** A whirling storm, often similar to a tornado, occurring over a large body of water and carrying a good deal of water vapor and spray, mostly in its lower part. **2** A pipe that carries off water, as from a roof.

Water-skiing

water strid·er [strī′dər] A type of insect having long middle and hind legs adapted for darting over the surface of water.

water table The upper limit of the underground zone that is saturated with water.

wa·ter·tight [wô′tər·tīt′ or wot′ər·tīt′] *adj*. **1** Closing so tightly that no water can leak in or out. **2** Having no weak point; foolproof.

water vapor Water in gaseous form.

wa·ter·way [wô′tər·wā′ or wot′ər·wā′] *n*. A river, channel, canal, etc., used as a means of travel.

water wheel A wheel turned by moving water, used to provide power.

wa·ter·works [wô′tər·wûrks′ or wot′ər·wûrks′] *n.pl.* (*often used with a singular verb*) **1** The system that supplies water to a community. **2** A pumping station in such a system.

wa·ter·y [wô′tər·ē or wot′ər·ē] *adj*. **1** Of water. **2** Like water; thin or liquid. **3** Brimming with water: *watery* eyes. **4** Diluted with too much water: *watery* tea.

watt [wot] *n*. A unit of power equal to about 0.7377 foot-pounds per second, or the electrical equivalent of this, the power developed in one ohm by a current of one ampere. ◆ The unit *watt* is named after James *Watt*.

Watt [wot], **James,** 1736–1819, Scottish inventor and engineer.

wat·tage [wot′ij] *n.* Electric power as measured in watts.

wat·tle [wot′(ə)l] *n., v.* **wat·tled, wat·tling 1** *n.* A frame of rods or twigs woven together to make fences, roofs, etc. **2** *v.* To weave or twist, as twigs, into a network. **3** *v.* To form by intertwining twigs. **4** *n.* A fold of flesh, often brightly colored, hanging from the throat or neck of a chicken, turkey, etc., and of some reptiles.

wave [wāv] *v.* **waved, wav·ing,** *n.* **1** *v.* To move or cause to move back and forth or with a fluttering motion. **2** *v.* To wave something, especially the hand, as in giving a signal. **3** *n.* The act of waving. **4** *n.* A disturbance consisting of a peak followed by a dip that travels across the surface of a liquid. **5** *n.* Any energy, as light or sound, that exists in the form of pulses or alternations of one kind or another. **6** *n.* A single such pulse or alternation. **7** *n.* Something that seems to travel or pass like a wave: a *wave* of protest; a tropical heat *wave.* **8** *v.* To form into a series of ridges and dips: to *wave* one's hair. **9** *n.* One of a series of wide curves or ridges in the hair.

wave·length [wāv′leng(k)th′] *n.* The distance between corresponding parts of successive waves.

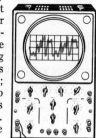

Sound wave from an oboe shown on an oscilloscope

wa·ver [wā′vər] *v.* **1** To move one way and the other; sway; flutter. **2** To be uncertain or undecided. **3** To show signs of falling back or giving way; falter.

wav·y [wā′vē] *adj.* **wav·i·er, wav·i·est** Full of, or like, waves: *wavy* hair; a *wavy* pattern.

wax[1] [waks] **1** *n.* Any of various dense, fatty substances occurring in plants and animals and also made artificially. **2** *n.* Beeswax. **3** *n.* A substance like wax, as paraffin, which is used in making candles, polishes, etc. **4** *v.* To coat or treat with a wax or polish: to *wax* a floor.

wax[2] [waks] *v.* **1** To increase gradually, as in size, brightness, effect, etc.: The moon is *waxing.* **2** To become: to *wax* poetic.

wax·en [wak′sən] *adj.* **1** Made of wax: *waxen* flowers. **2** Having the whitish or yellowish color of wax: a *waxen* complexion.

wax·wing [waks′wing′] *n.* A bird having soft, brown feathers except for the wings, which are tipped with red or yellow.

wax·y [wak′sē] *adj.* **wax·i·er, wax·i·est 1** Like wax, as in color. **2** Of, containing, or covered with wax.

way [wā] *n.* **1** A manner or method: He greeted me in a polite *way*; He has an unusual *way* of doing things. **2** A specific point; a particular: This is wrong in two *ways*. **3** A path, track, or course: He knew the *way* through the swamp. **4** Room for passage: Make *way* for the ambulance. **5** Direction or vicinity: It's over that *way*. **6** Distance or expanse: a long *way* between towns. **7** Route from one place to another: Show me the *way* to your house. **8** Behavior, habits, or practices: the *ways* of Indians. **9** Desire or will: to have one's own *way*. **10** *informal* Condition, as of health: You're in a bad *way*. **— by the way** In connection with that; incidentally. **— by way of 1** For the purpose of: to pack a tent *by way of* shelter. **2** On a route through or past: *by way of* the North Pole. **— out of the way 1** Removed or settled, as an obstacle or problem. **2** Odd or unusual. **3** Wrong; improper. **4** Remote or secluded. **— under way** Moving; making progress: Let's get *under way*.

way·far·er [wā′fâr′ər] *n.* A person who journeys; traveler. **— way′far·ing** *adj., n.*

way·lay [wā′lā′ *or* wā′lā′] *v.* **way·laid, way·lay·ing 1** To attack from ambush, as in order to rob. **2** To stop to question or speak to.

-ways A suffix meaning: In a (specified) manner, direction, or position, as in *noways*, in no manner or degree.

way·side [wā′sīd′] *n.* **1** The side or edge of a road or highway. **2** *adj. use*: a *wayside* inn.

way·ward [wā′wərd] *adj.* **1** Insisting on what one wishes; willful; disobedient. **2** Irregular and unsteady; capricious. **— way′ward·ness** *n.*

we [wē] *pron.* The persons speaking or writing; I and one or more others. ◆ A monarch speaking formally or a person writing formally will often use *we* instead of *I* in order to sound more solemn or impersonal: *We* are not pleased with our royal advisers; *We* say this is not true.

weak [wēk] *adj.* **1** Lacking in strength or effectiveness: to be *weak* after a long illness; a *weak* character; a *weak* protest. **2** Lacking the ability to withstand strain, wear, etc.: The bridge collapsed because of *weak* construction. **3** Without the usual strength or force: *weak* coffee; a *weak* heart. **4** Lacking or not strong in something specified: to be *weak* in reading.

weak·en [wē′kən] *v.* To make or become weak or weaker.

weak·fish [wēk′fish′] *n., pl.* **weak·fish** or **weak·fish·es** A food fish found along the Atlantic coastal waters of the U.S.

weak·ling [wēk′ling] *n.* A feeble person or animal.

weak·ly [wēk′lē] *adj.* **weak·li·er, weak·li·est,** *adv.* **1** *adj.* Sickly; feeble; weak. **2** *adv.* In a weak or feeble way.

weak·ness [wēk′nis] *n.* **1** The condition or quality of being weak. **2** A fault or flaw: a *weakness* in a foundation. **3** A liking that is hard to resist: a *weakness* for cakes or pies.

weal¹ [wēl] *n.* Welfare or sound condition: the *weal* of the community: seldom used today.

weal² [wēl] *n.* A mark on the skin, as from a blow; welt.

wealth [welth] *n.* **1** An abundance of personal property; riches. **2** Anything of value, as products or natural resources: the *wealth* of a nation. **3** An abundance: a *wealth* of golden hair.

wealth·y [wel′thē] *adj.* **wealth·i·er, wealth·i·est** Having wealth; rich.

wean [wēn] *v.* **1** To accustom (a young mammal) to food other than its mother's milk. **2** To cause (someone) gradually to give up a habit, dependence, etc.: to *wean* oneself from candy.

weap·on [wep′ən] *n.* **1** Any tool, device, or part of the body used in fighting or killing, as a pistol, the claws of a cat, etc. **2** Anything used for attack or defense: the *weapon* of wit.

wear [wâr] *v.* **wore, worn, wear·ing,** *n.* **1** *v.* To have or carry (a garment, ornament, etc.) on the person. **2** *n.* Clothing; apparel: men's *wear*: often used in combination: foot*wear.* **3** *n.* The act of wearing: clothing for formal *wear.* **4** *n.* The condition of being worn: clothing in constant *wear.* **5** *n.* Capability for being used, worn, etc.: the *wear* left in a car. **6** *v.* To withstand use, friction, etc.: a rug that *wears* well. **7** *v.* To weaken, tire out, or deteriorate by much use: She was *worn* by years of hard work; to *wear* a coat threadbare. **8** *n.* The destructive effect of work, use, time, etc. **9** *v.* To make (a hole, groove, etc.) by or as if by rubbing. **10** *v.* To remove material from by friction: to *wear* away rock. **11** *v.* To pass in a dull way: The hours *wore* on. **12** *v.* To exhibit; display: to *wear* a smile. **— wear down** To break down or overcome by repeated effort. **— wear off** To lessen gradually: His headache *wore off.* **— wear out 1** To wear until no longer suitable for use: to *wear out* one's shoes. **2** To tire out; exhaust: The heat *wore* him *out.* **— wear′er** *n.*

wea·ri·some [wir′i·səm] *adj.* Causing fatigue; tiresome; tedious.

wea·ry [wir′ē] *adj.* **wea·ri·er, wea·ri·est,** *v.* **wea·ried, wea·ry·ing 1** *adj.* Tired; fatigued: to be *weary* after work. **2** *adj.* Discontented or bored: *weary* of this job. **3** *adj.* Causing weariness or boredom: a *weary* task; a dull, *weary* lecture. **4** *v.* To make or become weary. **— wea′ri·ly** *adv.* **— wea′ri·ness** *n.*

wea·sel [wē′zəl] *n.* A small, slender animal with brownish fur that preys on smaller animals and birds.

weath·er [weth′ər] **1** *n.* The condition of the atmosphere with respect to temperature, moisture, winds, etc.: rainy *weather.* **2** *v.* To expose to the action of the weather. **3** *v.* To undergo changes from exposure

Weasel,
5–10 in. long

to the weather: lumber that has *weathered.* **4** *v.* To pass through successfully: to *weather* a crisis. **5** *adj.* That is toward the wind; windward. **6** *v.* To pass to the windward of. **— under the weather** *informal* Somewhat ill; out of sorts.

weath·er-beat·en [weth′ər-bēt′(ə)n] *adj.* Toughened or worn by exposure to the weather.

weath·er·cock [weth′ər-kok′] *n.* A weather vane shaped like a cock.

weath·er·glass [weth′ər-glas′] *n.* **1** A simple device to show changes in atmospheric pressure. **2** Any barometer.

weather vane A vane that turns with the wind and shows in which direction it is blowing.

weave [wēv] *v.* **wove** or for def. 10 **weaved, wov·en** or **wove** or for def. 10 **weaved, weav·ing,** *n.* **1** *v.* To form or produce by interlacing threads, strands, strips, etc.: to *weave* a fabric; to *weave* a basket. **2** *v.* To interlace (threads, strips, grass, etc.) in weaving something. **3** *v.* To work at weaving, as at a loom. **4** *n.* A particular method or pattern of weaving. **5** *v.* To become woven or interlaced. **6** *v.* To make by combining details or elements: to *weave* a tale. **7** *v.* To combine so as to make a whole: to *weave* ideas together. **8** *v.* To twist into, about, or through something else. **9** *v.* To make (a web), as a spider. **10** *v.* To move in a twisting or zigzag path. **— weav′er** *n.*

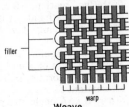
filler
warp
Weave

web [web] *n., v.* **webbed, web·bing 1** *n.* Something woven from threads, strips, etc., especially a whole piece of cloth woven or being woven. **2** *n.* A mesh or network, as that woven by a spider: a *web* of cables; a *web* of falsehoods. **3** *n.* A fold of skin connecting the toes of various water birds, frogs, otters, etc. **4** *v.* To connect, cover, or surround with a web.

webbed [webd] *adj.* **1** Formed like or having a web. **2** Having the toes united by folds of skin.

web·bing [web′ing] *n.* **1** A woven strip of strong fiber, used in upholstery, etc. **2** Any structure or material forming a web.

web·foot·ed [web′foot′id] *adj.* Having the toes connected by a fold of skin: a *webfooted* bird.

Web·ster [web′stər], **Dan·iel,** 1782–1852, U.S. statesman and orator.

Webster, Noah, 1758–1843, U.S. writer and compiler of dictionaries.

wed [wed] *v.* **wed·ded, wed·ding 1** To marry. **2** To unite; combine.

we'd [wēd] **1** We had. **2** We would. **3** We should.

Wed. Abbreviation of WEDNESDAY.

wed·ded [wed′id] *adj.* **1** Married. **2** Joined. **3** United by devotion: He is *wedded* to his music.

Webfooted birds

wed·ding [wed′ing] *n.* **1** The ceremony or celebration of a marriage. **2** A special anniversary of a marriage: a golden *wedding*.

wedge [wej] *n., v.* **wedged, wedg·ing 1** *n.* A tapering piece of wood, metal, etc., that can be forced into a narrow opening to split something apart, secure movable parts, etc. **2** *v.* To split or secure with or as if with a wedge. **3** *n.* Anything shaped like a wedge: a *wedge* of cake. **4** *n.* A small beginning or opening for changes, new plans, etc. **5** *v.* To crowd or squeeze (people or things) into a small or confined space.

wed·lock [wed′lok] *n.* The condition or relation of being married; matrimony.

Wednes·day [wenz′dē *or* wenz′dā] *n.* The fourth day of the week. ✦ See WODEN.

wee [wē] *adj.* **we·er, we·est** Very small; tiny.

weed [wēd] **1** *n.* Any useless or unsightly plant, especially one that grows abundantly and tends to crowd out cultivated plants. **2** *v.* To remove weeds from (a garden, lawn, etc.). **3** *v.* To eliminate what is useless, inadequate, or harmful: to *weed* out failing students. — **weed′y** *adv.*

weeds [wēdz] *n.pl.* The black mourning clothes worn by a widow.

week [wēk] *n.* **1** A period of seven days, especially such a period beginning with Sunday. **2** The days or time within a week devoted to work: The office has a 35-hour *week*.

week·day [wēk′dā′] *n.* Any day of the week except Sunday, or except Saturday and Sunday.

week·end [wēk′end′] *n.* Saturday and Sunday, or the time from Friday evening to the following Monday morning.

week·ly [wēk′lē] *adv., adj., n., pl.* **week·lies 1** *adv.* Once a week. **2** *adj.* Done, occurring, computed, etc., once a week or by the week: a *weekly* wash; a *weekly* wage. **3** *n.* A publication issued once a week.

ween [wēn] *v.* To suppose; guess; fancy: seldom used today.

weep [wēp] *v.* **wept, weep·ing 1** To show grief or other strong emotion by shedding tears. **2** To shed: to *weep* hot tears. **3** To mourn: She *wept* for her lost child. **4** To release (a liquid, as sap) slowly; ooze.

weep·ing [wē′ping] *adj.* **1** That weeps. **2** Having slim, drooping branches, as a willow.

wee·vil [wē′vəl] *n.* Any of various small beetles whose larvae destroy cotton, grain, nuts, etc.

weft [weft] *n.* Another name for WOOF.

weigh [wā] *v.* **1** To determine the weight of, as by using a scale. **2** To have as weight: That rock *weighs* a ton. **3** To measure (a substance or an amount) by weight: to *weigh* out five pounds of potatoes. **4** To consider carefully: to *weigh* an offer; to *weigh* one's words. **5** To bend or press down by weight; burden: The load *weighed* down the car. **6** To bear down; be a burden: Cares *weighed* upon her mind. **7** To have influence or be of importance: A good education will *weigh* in your favor. **8** To raise (an anchor) in preparation for sailing: to *weigh* anchor.

weight [wāt] **1** *n.* The heaviness of a thing; the amount a thing weighs: The *weight* of the roast is six pounds. **2** *n.* The force with which a thing presses downward, equal to its mass multiplied by the acceleration of gravity. **3** *n.* A piece of metal of known heaviness used as a standard in weighing on a balance. **4** *v.* To add weight to; make heavier. **5** *n.* A unit or system for measuring weight: troy *weight*; avoirdupois *weight*. **6** *n.* A load or burden. **7** *n.* Something like a load; burden: the *weight* of responsibility. **8** *v.* To put a load or burden on. **9** *n.* Influence or significance: His ideas carry *weight*.

weight·less [wāt′lis] *adj.* Having or seeming to have no weight: Objects inside a space capsule in orbit are *weightless*. — **weight′less·ness** *n.*

weight·y [wā′tē] *adj.* **weight·i·er, weight·i·est 1** Of great importance, influence, or significance: *weighty* discussions; *weighty* problems. **2** Difficult to bear; burdensome. **3** Heavy.

weir [wir] *n.* **1** A small dam placed in a stream. **2** A fence of stakes, etc., set in a stream in order to trap fishes.

weird [wird] *adj.* **1** Strange in an unearthly or supernatural way; eerie. **2** *informal* Peculiar; odd: a *weird* necktie. — **weird′ly** *adv.*

wel·come [wel′kəm] *adj., v.* **wel·comed, wel·com·ing,** *n., interj.* **1** *adj.* Received with joy or gladness: a *welcome* visitor; a *welcome* relief. **2** *v.* To greet gladly or receive with pleasure. **3** *n.* The act of welcoming; a warm *welcome*. **4** *adj.* Under no obligation for kindness, gifts, etc.: You are *welcome*. **5** *adj.* Freely given the possession, use, etc., of something: You're *welcome* to the book. **6** *interj.* An exclamation expressing greeting: *Welcome*, friend. **7** *v.* To accept with calmness, pleasure, or courage: to *welcome* criticism. — **wear out one's welcome** To impose upon a person so much that one is no longer welcome.

weld [weld] **1** *v.* To unite (pieces of metal) by softening with heat and pressing together. **2** *v.* To be welded or capable of being welded. **3** *n.* A joint or seam formed by welding pieces of metal. **4** *v.* To join closely; unite: The coach *welded* them into a unit. — **weld′er** *n.*

wel·fare [wel′fâr] *n.* **1** The condition of being healthy, prosperous, happy, etc.; well-being. **2** Organized efforts by a community or group of people to give money and aid to those who are poor and in need. **3** *adj. use: welfare* work.

welfare state A state or community in which the government assumes responsibility for the health and prosperity of its citizens.

well[1] [wel] **1** *n.* A hole or shaft dug or drilled into the earth to reach a deposit of water, petroleum, gas, etc. **2** *n.* A natural spring of water. **3** *v.* To rise or pour forth, as water from a spring: Blood *welled* up from the wound. **4** *n.* A container holding a supply of a liquid: an ink*well*. **5** *n.* A source of continuing supply: a *well* of information. **6** *n.* A vertical opening through the floors of a building: a stair*well*; an elevator *well*.

well² [wel] *adv.* **bet·ter, best,** *adj., interj.* **1** *adv.* In a good, proper, favorable, or satisfying way: He plays *well*; to eat *well*. **2** *adj.* In good health: Are you *well*? **3** *adv.* To a considerable or large extent or degree: *well* over six feet: I knew him *well*. **4** *adv.* Thoroughly; completely: Wash your hands *well*. **5** *adv.* Properly; rightly; fairly: We can't *well* refuse him. **6** *adj.* Satisfactory, fortunate, or wise: All is *well*; It is *well* he called early. **7** *interj.* An expression of mild surprise, doubt, relief, etc. **8** *interj.* A word used just to introduce the next remark: *Well*, I'm tired. **— as well 1** Also; in addition. **2** With equal effect: You might *as well* go. **— as well as** In addition to being: He was strong *as well as* fast. ◆ See GOOD.

we'll [wēl] **1** We will. **2** We shall.

well-bal·anced [wel'bal'ənst] *adj.* **1** Having the right amount or proportion of everything: a *well-balanced* diet. **2** Sensible; sane.

well-be·ing [wel'bē'ing] *n.* A condition of good health, happiness, prosperity, etc.

well-born [wel'bôrn'] *adj.* Of good birth or ancestry; coming from a distinguished family.

well-bred [wel'bred'] *adj.* Polite and refined; having good maners.

well-done [wel'dun'] *adj.* **1** Done well; properly executed. **2** Thoroughly cooked.

well-fed [wel'fed'] *adj.* **1** Plump. **2** Properly fed.

well-found·ed [wel'foun'did] *adj.* Based on fact, sound evidence, etc.: a *well-founded* theory.

well-groomed [wel'grōōmd'] *adj.* Neat in appearance: a *well-groomed* man.

Wel·ling·ton [wel'ing·tən], **Duke of,** 1769–1852, British general and statesman who defeated Napoleon at Waterloo.

well-known [wel'nōn'] *adj.* **1** Widely known: a *well-known* fact. **2** Famous: a *well-known* author.

well-mean·ing [wel'mē'ning] *adj.* **1** Having good intentions. **2** Done with good intentions.

well-nigh [wel'nī'] *adv.* Very nearly; almost.

well-off [wel'ôf'] *adj.* **1** Being in a good or favorable condition; fortunate. **2** Wealthy.

well-read [wel'red'] *adj.* Having a wide knowledge of books and literature; having read much.

Wells [welz], **Herbert George,** 1866–1946, English author.

well·spring [wel'spring'] *n.* **1** The source of a stream or spring; fountainhead. **2** A source of continual supply: a *wellspring* of inspiration.

well-to-do [wel'tə·dōō'] *adj.* Well supplied with material comforts; prosperous; rich.

Welsh [welsh] **1** *adj.* Of or from Wales. **2** *n.* **(the Welsh)** The people of Wales. **3** *n.* The Celtic language of Wales.

Welsh·man [welsh'mən] *n., pl.* **Welsh·men** [welsh'mən] A person born or living in Wales.

Welsh rabbit Melted cheese cooked in cream or milk, often with ale or beer added, and served hot on toast or crackers.

Welsh rarebit Welsh rabbit.

welt [welt] **1** *n.* A strip of leather or other material that reinforces the seam between the upper part of a shoe and the sole. **2** *v.* To supply with a welt or welts. **3** *n.* A stripe raised on the skin by a blow. **4** *v. informal* To whip so as to raise welts.

wel·ter [wel'tər] **1** *v.* To roll about; wallow. **2** *n.* A rolling movement, as of waves. **3** *v.* To lie or be soaked in some fluid. **4** *n.* A commotion; turmoil.

wel·ter·weight [wel'tər·wāt'] *n.* A boxer or wrestler whose fighting weight is between 136 and 147 pounds.

wen [wen] *n.* A harmless tumor on the skin, often on the face or scalp.

wench [wench] *n.* **1** A young woman or girl: used humorously. **2** A female servant; maid: seldom used today.

wend [wend] *v.* To go or proceed on (one's course or way): seldom used today.

went [went] Past tense of GO.

wept [wept] Past tense of WEEP.

were [wûr] A form of the verb *be*, in the past tense, used with *you, we, they* and plural nouns. *Were* is also used as the subjunctive with all persons to express wishing, supposing, etc.: If I *were* you, I wouldn't do that.

we're [wir] We are.

weren't [wûrnt *or* wûr'ənt] Were not.

were·wolf [wir'woolf'] *n., pl.* **were·wolves** [wir'woolvz'] In folk tales, a man who has been changed, or who can change himself, into a wolf.

wert [wûrt] An old form of WERE, used with *thou.*

Wes·ley [wes'lē *or* wez'lē] The name of two English clergymen, **John,** 1703–1791, the founder of Methodism, and his brother **Charles,** 1708–1788, a writer of hymns.

west [west] **1** *n.* The direction opposite east; one of the four main points of the compass. If you face the sun at sunset, you are facing west. **2** *adj.* To, toward, or in the west; western. **3** *adj.* Coming from the west: the *west* wind. **4** *adv.* In or toward the west; westward. **5** *n.* Any place or region in the western part of a specified area or lying west of a specified point. **— the West 1** The countries west of Asia and Turkey, especially the countries of North America, South America, and Europe; Occident. **2** The Western Hemisphere. **3** The western part of the U.S., especially the part west of the Mississippi River. **— west of** Farther west than: Chicago is *west* of New York.

west·er·ly [wes'tər·lē] **1** *adj.* In or of the west. **2** *adj., adv.* Toward or from the west.

west·ern [wes′tərn] **1** *adj.* Of, to, or in the west. **2** *adj.* From the west: *a western* breeze. **3** *adj.* (*often written* **Western**) Of, referring to, or like the West. **4** *n.* A movie, story, radio show, or TV program about cowboy life or pioneer days in the western U.S.

west·ern·er [wes′tər·nər] *n.* **1** A person born or living in the west. **2** (*usually written* **Westerner**) A person born or living in the West, especially in the western U.S.

Western Hemisphere The half of the earth that lies west of the Atlantic Ocean, including North America and South America.

west·ern·most [wes′tərn·mōst′] *adj.* Farthest west.

West Germany The western part of Germany, now a separate state called the **Federal Republic of Germany,** whose capital is Bonn.

West Indies A series of island groups in the Atlantic Ocean and Caribbean Sea between North and South America, divided into the Bahamas and the Antilles. **— West Indian** *adj., n.*

West·min·ster Abbey [west′min·stər] A large church in London where English kings and queens are crowned and many notable people are buried.

West Point A U.S. military reservation in New York State on the Hudson River. The U.S. Military Academy is situated there.

West Virginia A state in the east central U.S.

west·ward [west′wərd] **1** *adj. adv.* Toward the west. **2** *n.* A westward direction or location.

west·wards [west′wərdz] *adv.* Westward.

wet [wet] *adj.* **wet·ter, wet·test,** *v.* **wet** or **wet·ted, wet·ting,** *n.* **1** *adj.* Covered, soaked, or moist with water or another liquid: *wet* laundry. **2** *v.* To make or become wet: to *wet* a washcloth; Her doll *wets*. **3** *adj.* Not yet dry: *wet* paint. **4** *n.* Water or moisture. **5** *adj.* Rainy: the *wet* season. **6** *n.* Rainy weather; rain: He caught cold out in the *wet*. **7** *adj. informal* Permitting the sale of alcoholic beverages: a *wet* county. **— wet′ness** *n.*

wet blanket *informal* A person or thing that spoils people's fun or enthusiasm.

we've [wēv] We have.

whack [(h)wak] *informal* **1** *v.* To hit with a sharp, loud blow. **2** *n.* A sharp blow that makes a loud noise, or the noise itself. **3** *n.* A try.

whale[1] [(h)wāl] *n., v.* **whaled, whal·ing 1** *n.* A mammal that lives in the ocean and resembles a gigantic fish. Whales have a thick layer of blubber under a smooth skin, and this blubber is a source of oil. **2** *v.* To hunt for whales.

Whale, 60–70 ft. long

whale[2] [(h)wāl] *v.* **whaled, whal·ing** *informal* To strike or beat; thrash.

whale·boat [(h)wāl′bōt′] *n.* A long, deep rowboat, sharp at both ends, first used in whaling but now used as a coast-guard boat for rescue.

whale·bone [(h)wāl′bōn′] *n.* **1** The horny, elastic substance hanging from the upper jaw of toothless whales in long, narrow plates with frayed, bristly inner edges. These bristly plates strain out of the water the tiny sea animals that such whales eat. **2** A strip of whalebone, once used to stiffen corsets, etc.

whal·er [(h)wā′lər] *n.* A person employed or a ship used in whaling.

whal·ing [(h)wā′ling] *n.* The industry of hunting, catching, and killing whales.

wharf [(h)wôrf] *n., pl.* **wharves** [(h)wôrvz] or **wharfs** A structure, usually a platform, built along or out from a shore, alongside which ships or boats may lie to load or unload.

what [(h)wot *or* (h)wut] **1** *pron.* Which thing, things, action, condition, type, class, etc.: I don't know *what* to do; *What* is he holding in his hand? **2** *adj.* Which or which type of: *What* refreshments shall we bring? **3** *pron.* That or those which: I know *what* I want to buy. **4** *pron.* Anything that; whatever: Wear *what* you choose. **5** *adj.* Whatever or whichever; any that: Choose *what* story you would like to hear. **6** *conj. informal* That: I do not doubt but *what* he will come. **7** *interj.* An exclamation of surprise, annoyance, disbelief, etc.: *What!* He didn't come? **8** *adv.* In which specific way: *What* does it matter if we take a later train? **9** *pron., adj.* How much: *What* did it cost?; *What* difference does it make? **10** *adj.* How great, surprising, etc.: *What* a shame! *What* talent! **11** *adv.* In part; partly: *What* with the heat and *what* with the noise, he couldn't sleep. **— and what not** And other things that need not be mentioned. **— what for** For what reason; why: *What* did you do that *for*? **— what if** What would happen if; suppose that. —

what's what *informal* The real situation or state of affairs.

what·e'er [(h)wot′âr′ *or* (h)wut′âr′] *pron., adj.* Whatever: used mostly in poems.

what·ev·er [(h)wot′ev′ər *or* (h)wut′ev′ər] **1** *pron.* Anything that or all that: Do *whatever* you can. **2** *adj.* Any that or all that: *Whatever* games I play, I lose. **3** *pron.* No matter what: *Whatever* happens, don't be afraid. **4** *pron. informal* What: used in questions for added emphasis: *Whatever* is the matter? **5** *adj.* Of any type, character, or kind.

what·not [(h)wot′not′ *or* (h)wut′not′] *n.* A set of shelves to hold ornaments, figurines, etc.

what's [(h)wots *or* (h)wuts] What is.

what·so·ev·er [(h)wot′sō·ev′ər *or* (h)wut′sō·əv′ər] *pron., adj.* Whatever.

---

add, āce, câre, pälm;   end, ēqual;   it, īce;   odd, ōpen, ôrder;   tŏŏk, pōōl;   up, bûrn;

ə = a in *above*, e in *sicken*, i in *possible*, o in *melon*, u in *circus*;   **yōō** = u in *fuse*;   oil;   pout;

check;   ring;   thin;   this;   zh in *vision*.   For ¶ reference, see page 64 · HOW TO

wheat [(h)wēt] *n.* **1** The grain of a cereal plant, out of which flour is made. **2** The plant bearing this grain on dense spikes at the top.

wheat·en [(h)wēt′(ə)n] *adj.* Of, having to do with, or made of wheat.

whee·dle [(h)wēd′(ə)l] *v.* **whee·dled, whee·dling** **1** To coax or persuade by flattering in a sweet and gentle way: We *wheedled* them into staying. **2** To obtain by wheedling: She managed to *wheedle* the information out of me.

wheel [(h)wēl] **1** *n.* A circular framework or disk that is attached to a central axle, on which it turns. **2** *v.* To turn on or as if on an axis; rotate, revolve, or pivot: He *wheeled* around and went back. **3** *n.* Anything round or going around like a wheel. **4** *v.* To move on wheels or in a wheeled vehicle: to *wheel* a baby in a carriage. **5** *n.* Something having a wheel as its distinctive feature, as a steering wheel or spinning wheel. **6** *n. informal* A bicycle. **7** *n.* (*pl.*) The forces that direct motion or control activity: the *wheels* of industry. **— at the wheel 1** Driving or steering a car, boat, etc. **2** In control; in charge.

wheel·bar·row [(h)wēl′bar′ō] *n.* A boxlike vehicle ordinarily having one wheel and two handles, used for moving small loads.

wheel·base [(h)wēl′bās′] *n.* The distance in inches between the central points of the front and rear axles of an automobile, truck, etc.

wheel chair A chair mounted on large wheels, for the use of sick or injured people.

wheel·house [(h)wēl′hous′] *n.* An enclosure on a ship containing the steering wheel.

wheel·wright [(h)wēl′rīt′] *n.* A man who makes or repairs wheels, carriages, wagons, etc.

wheeze [(h)wēz] *v.* **wheezed, wheez·ing,** *n.* **1** *v.* To breathe hard with a husky, whistling sound, as with a chest cold. **2** *n.* A wheezing sound. **3** *v.* To make such a sound: The old car *wheezed* up the hill. **4** *n. informal* A joke, especially one that is old or widely known.

wheez·y [(h)wē′zē] *adj.* **wheez·i·er, wheez·i·est** Wheezing or making a wheezing sound: a *wheezy* old horse; a *wheezy* laugh.

whelk [(h)welk] *n.* A large sea mollusk with a spiral shell. One kind of whelk is eaten.

whelm [(h)welm] *v.* To overwhelm.

whelp [(h)welp] **1** *n.* One of the young of a dog, wolf, lion, or other beast; puppy or cub. **2** *v.* To give birth to (young).

when [(h)wen] **1** *adv., conj.* At what or which time: *When* did you arrive?; I know *when* he left; They waited for midnight, *when* they all shouted, "Happy New Year!" **2** *pron.* What or which time: Until *when* will the meeting last?; It happened Monday, since *when* we have heard nothing. **3** *conj.* At which: the time *when* dinner is served. **4** *conj.* After which; and then: We had just eaten *when* you called. **5** *conj.* As soon as: He laughed *when* he heard it. **6** *conj.* Whenever: We play inside *when* it rains.

Whelk, to 9 in. long

7 *conj.* During or at the time that; while: *when* you were a baby. **8** *conj.* Although: He walks *when* he might ride. **9** *conj.* Considering that; if: How can I go *when* I have no money?

whence [(h)wens] **1** *adv., conj.* From what or which place, source, or cause: *Whence* does this stranger come?; He holds to his faith, *whence* comes his courage. **2** *conj.* From which: Find the place *whence* these sounds arise. **3** *conj.* To the place from which: Return *whence* you came. ◆ This word is seldom used today.

when·e'er [(h)wen′âr′] *adv., conj.* Whenever: used mostly in poems.

when·ev·er [(h)wen′ev′ər] *adv., conj.* At whatever time.

when·so·ev·er [(h)wen′sō·ev′ər] *adv., conj.* At whatever time; whenever: seldom used today.

where [(h)wâr] **1** *adv.* At or in what place: *Where* is my book? **2** *conj.* At which place: Let's go home *where* we can relax. **3** *adv., conj.* To what place: *Where* are you going?; Let him go *where* he likes. **4** *adv.* From what place, source, or cause: *Where* did you get that idea? **5** *pron.* What place: *Where* did you come from? **6** *conj.* The place in which: The bear passed three yards from *where* we stood. **7** *adv.* At, in, or to which: The place *where* it happened is the place *where* we are going. **8** *conj.* To, at, or in the place to which or in which: Let's go *where* they went; Put it *where* I told you to. **9** *adv.* In what way or respect; how: *Where* does it concern us? **10** *conj.* With the condition that: $V = \frac{D}{T}$ where V is velocity, D is distance, and T is time.

where·a·bouts [(h)wâr′ə·bouts′] **1** *n.pl.* (*often used with singular verb*) The place where a person or thing is: His present *whereabouts* is unknown. **2** *adv.* Near or at what place; about where: *Whereabouts* did you put my coat?

where·as [(h)wâr′az′] *conj.* **1** Because of the fact that; since: *Whereas* he died heroically, serving his country, be it resolved that a monument be erected in his honor. **2** And on the other hand; while: Heat causes metals to expand, *whereas* cold causes them to contract.

where·at [(h)wâr′at′] **1** *conj.* At which or for which reason. **2** *adv.* At what: *Whereat* are you angry? ◆ This word is seldom used today.

where·by [(h)wâr′bī′] *adv., conj.* By means of which; through which: a treaty *whereby* both nations agreed to a common defense.

where·fore [(h)wâr′fôr′] **1** *adv.* For what reason; why: seldom used today: *Wherefore* do you doubt me? **2** *conj.* For which reason; therefore: seldom used today. **3** *n.* A cause or reason: all the whys and *wherefores* of the verdict.

where·in [(h)wâr′in′] *adv., conj.* **1** In what particular or regard: *Wherein* is the error? **2** In which: a home *wherein* joy dwells.

where·of [(h)wâr′uv′ *or* (h)wâr′ov′] *adv., conj.* Of or about what, which, or whom: He seems to know *whereof* he speaks.

where·on [(h)wâr′on′] *adv., conj.* On what or on which: seldom used today: the spot *whereon* I stand.

where·so·ev·er [(h)wâr′sō·ev′ər] *adv., conj.* In or to whatever place; wherever: seldom used today: *Wheresoever* you go, I will follow.

where·to [(h)wâr′tōō′] **1** *adv.* To what place or end: *Whereto* is this leading? **2** *conj.* To which or to whom: the place *whereto* he hastens. ◆ This word is seldom used today.

where·up·on [(h)wâr′ə·pon′] **1** *conj.* At which; after which: He refused, *whereupon* the plaintiff sued. **2** *adv.* Upon what or which; whereon: seldom used today.

wher·ev·er [(h)wâr′ev′ər] **1** *conj.* In, at, or to whatever place: Sit *wherever* you like. **2** *adv. informal* Where: used in questions for added emphasis: *Wherever* did you find that book?

where·with [(h)wâr′with′ *or* (h)wâr′with′] *conj., adv.* With which or with what: seldom used today.

where·with·al [*n.* (h)wâr′with·ôl′, *adv.* (h)wâr′with·ôl′] **1** *n.* Whatever is needed to do a certain thing, especially the necessary money: Do they have the *wherewithal* to go to Europe? **2** *adv.* With which or with what: no longer used.

wher·ry [(h)wer′ē] *n., pl.* **wher·ries** A light, fast rowboat.

whet [(h)wet] *v.* **whet·ted, whet·ting** *n.* **1** *v.* To sharpen, as a knife or tool, by rubbing. **2** *n.* The act of whetting. **3** *v.* To make more keen or eager: to *whet* one's appetite.

wheth·er [(h)weth′ər] *conj.* **1** If it is true or probable that: Tell me *whether* or not you are going. **2** Either: *Whether* by luck or hard work, he will succeed. **3** In either case if: *Whether* it rains or snows, the roads become slippery.

whet·stone [(h)wet′stōn′] *n.* A stone on which to sharpen knives, axes, and other edged tools.

whew [(h)wōō *or* (h)wyōō] *interj.* A word that expresses amazement, relief, discomfort, etc.

whey [(h)wā] *n.* The clear, watery liquid left when the curd is separated from milk, as in making cheese.

which [(h)wich] **1** *adj., pron.* What one or ones out of a number of things or people: *Which* song is your favorite?; *Which* of these boys can swim? **2** *pron.* The one or those ones that: You may have several, so choose *which* you prefer. **3** *pron.* That: the song *which* we sang. **4** *pron.* The thing or things just mentioned: a story with *which* I am familiar; The party, *which* was held outdoors, was fun.

which·ev·er [(h)wich′ev′ər] **1** *pron.* Any one or ones that: Select three colors, *whichever* you prefer. **2** *adj.* Any: Wear *whichever* dress you choose. **3** *adj.* No matter which: *Whichever* route you take, you'll have to cross the river.

which·so·ev·er [(h)wich′sō·ev′ər] *pron., adj.* Whichever: seldom used today.

whiff [(h)wif] **1** *n.* A slight puff, as of air or smoke. **2** *n.* A slight smell borne on a puff of air. **3** *v.* To blow, move, or sniff in whiffs.

whif·fle·tree [(h)wif′əl·trē′] *n.* A crossbar in front of a wagon, to which the ends of the traces of a harness are fastened.

Whig [(h)wig] *n.* **1** A member of an old British political party, opposed to the Tories and later known as the **Liberal Party. 2** An American colonist who supported the Revolutionary War against England. **3** A member of a political party in the U.S. during the middle 1800's that was formed to oppose the Democratic Party.

while [(h)wīl] *n., v.* **whiled, whil·ing,** *conj.* **1** *n.* Any period of time, especially a short period: Rest a *while.* **2** *v.* To cause (time) to pass lightly and pleasantly: to *while* away a summer's afternoon. **3** *conj.* During the time that; as long as: *While* he was in school he wore glasses. **4** *conj.* Although: *While* he is a big, strong boy, he dislikes sports. **5** *conj.* Whereas: This man is short, *while* that one is tall. ◆ *While* is widely used with this meaning, although in traditional usage *whereas* is preferred. **— the while** At the same time. **— worth one's while** Worth time, effort, trouble, or expense.

whi·lom [(h)wī′ləm] **1** *adj.* Former: Her *whilom* friends turned against her. **2** *adv.* Formerly. ◆ This word is seldom used today.

whilst [(h)wilst] *conj. British* While.

whim [(h)wim] *n.* A sudden notion, desire, or fancy having no special cause.

whim·per [(h)wim′pər] **1** *v.* To cry with low, mournful, broken sounds: The puppy *whimpered* all night. **2** *n.* A low, broken, whining cry.

whim·sey [(h)wim′zē] *n., pl.* **whim·seys** Another spelling of WHIMSY.

whim·si·cal [(h)wim′zi·kəl] *adj.* **1** Full of whims, caprices, curious ideas, or fanciful notions. **2** Odd, quaint, or fanciful, often in an amusing way. **— whim′si·cal·ly** *adv,*

whim·sy [(h)wim′zē] *n., pl.* **whim·sies 1** A sudden, fanciful or curious notion or desire. **2** Quaint, fanciful humor, as in a story.

whine [(h)wīn] *v.* **whined, whin·ing,** *n.* **1** *v.* To make a low, wailing sound or cry. **2** *v.* To complain, beg, or plead in a tiresome or childish way. **3** *n.* The act or sound of whining.

whin·ny [(h)win′ē] *n., pl.* **whin·nies,** *v.* **whin·nied, whin·ny·ing 1** *n.* A gentle neigh made by a horse. **2** *v.* To neigh in a low or gentle way.

whip [(h)wip] *n., v.* **whipped** *or* **whipt, whip·ping 1** *n.* An instrument for striking or beating, consisting of a lash attached to a handle. **2** *v.* To strike with or as if with a whip; beat. **3** *v. U.S. informal* To defeat. **4** *n.* A stroke, blow, or lashing motion made with or as if with a whip. **5** *n.* A leader in a legislature who directs other members of his party. **6** *v.* To move or pull quickly and suddenly: The sheriff *whipped* out his revolver. **7** *v.* To thrash about: pennants *whipping* in the wind. **8** *v.* To beat to a froth: to *whip* egg whites. **9** *adj. use: whipped* cream.

---

add, āce, câre, pälm; end, ēqual; it, īce; odd, ōpen, ôrder; tŏŏk, pōōl; up, bûrn; ə = a in *above*, e in *sicken*, i in *possible*, o in *melon*, u in *circus*; yōō = u in *fuse*; oil; pout; check; ring; thin; ᵺis; zh in *vision*. For ¶ reference, see page 64 · HOW TO

10 *n.* A dessert containing cream or egg whites beaten to a froth: apricot *whip.*

whip·lash [(h)wip′lash′] *n.* The lash of a whip.

whip·per·snap·per [(h)wip′ər·snap′ər] *n.* A person, especially a young one, who thinks highly of himself and shows disrespect for older or more important people.

whip·pet [(h)wip′it] *n.* A swift breed of dog very much like a small grey-hound, used in racing.

whip·ping [(h)wip′ing] *n.* The act of a person or thing that whips, especially a beating.

whip·ple·tree [(h)wip′əl·trē′] *n.* Another spelling of WHIFFLETREE.

whip·poor·will [(h)wip′ər·wil] *n.* A small bird of North America that is active at night and gives a call which sounds like its name.

Whippet, 19–22 in. high at shoulder

whir [(h)wûr] *v.* **whirred, whir·ring,** *n.* **1** *v.* To fly, move, or whirl with a hum or buzz: The engine, idling, *whirred* softly. **2** *n.* Such a sound: the *whir* of a bird's wings.

whirl [(h)wûrl] **1** *v.* To turn very fast with a circular motion; spin rapidly: The cowboy *whirled* his lasso. **2** *v.* To carry along with a revolving motion: The wind *whirled* the dust into the air. **3** *n.* A turning motion: the *whirl* of propellers. **4** *n.* Something whirling, as a cloud of dust. **5** *v.* To move or go swiftly: The bicycles *whirled* past. **6** *v.* To have the feeling of spinning: My mind *whirls* when I think of outer space. **7** *n.* A short drive or run; spin. **8** *n.* A giddy or confused condition: Her head was in a *whirl.* **9** *n.* A rapid series of events, parties, etc. **10** *n. informal* A try.

whirl·i·gig [(h)wûr′lə·gig′] *n.* **1** A toy that spins, as a top. **2** A merry-go-round. **3** Something that is always whirling or changing. **4** A whirling motion.

whirl·pool [(h)wûrl′pool′] *n.* A rapidly whirl-ing current of water, usually spiraling in toward a depressed center and tending to drag things down with it.

whirl·wind [(h)wûrl′wind′] *n.* A funnel-shaped column of air whirling rapidly, with an upward spiral motion.

whisk [(h)wisk] **1** *v.* To sweep or brush with light motions: to *whisk* away flies. **2** *v.* To move quickly and softly: The snake *whisked* into the grass. **3** *n.* A light, sweeping motion: a *whisk* of a horse's tail. **4** *n.* A whisk broom. **5** *n.* A small wire instrument used in cooking for whipping cream, eggs, etc., to a froth.

whisk broom A small, short-handled broom for brushing clothing, upholstered furniture, etc.

whisk·er [(h)wis′kər] *n.* **1** (*pl.*) The hair that grows on the sides of a man's face. **2** A single hair in a man's beard. **3** One of the long, stiff hairs on the sides of the mouth of cats, rats, etc. — **whisk′ered** *adj.*

whis·ky or **whis·key** [(h)wis′kē] *n., pl.* **whis·kies** or **whis·keys** An alcoholic liquor made by distilling certain fermented grains, as rye, barley, corn, etc.

whis·per [(h)wis′pər] **1** *v.* To speak, say, or tell in a soft, low tone. **2** *n.* The act of whisper-ing. **3** *n.* A soft, low voice, tone, sound, or utterance. **4** *v.* To tell privately, as a secret or rumor. **5** *n.* A hint, rumor, or suggestion: not a *whisper* of scandal. **6** *v.* To murmur or rustle: The waves *whispered* on the sand. **7** *n.* A low, rustling sound.

whist [(h)wist] *n.* A card game for two pairs of partners. It was the forerunner of bridge.

whis·tle [(h)wis′(ə)l] *v.* **whis·tled, whis·tling,** *n.* **1** *v.* To make a shrill, piping sound by forcing the breath through the teeth or through pursed lips. **2** *n.* The act of whistling. **3** *v.* To produce (a tune or melody) by whistling. **4** *n.* A device for producing a shrill tone by forcing air or steam through a pipe or tube with a narrow opening. **5** *v.* To blow or sound a whistle. **6** *v.* To move with a whistling sound: A bullet *whistled* over our heads. **7** *n.* Any whistling sound. — **whis′tler** *n.*

whit [(h)wit] *n.* The least or slightest bit: He was not one *whit* ashamed.

white [(h)wīt] *n., adj.* **whit·er, whit·est,** *v.* **whit·ed, whit·ing 1** *n.* The opposite of black; the lightest of all colors. White is the color of the margins on this page. **2** *adj.* Having the color white. **3** *v.* To make white; whiten or bleach. **4** *n.* A white paint or pigment. **5** *n.* (*sometimes pl.*) White clothes: Nurses wear *white*; a sailor's summer *whites.* **6** *n.* The white or light-colored part of an egg, the eye, etc. **7** *adj.* Light in color: the *white* meat of a turkey. **8** *adj.* Having a light-colored skin, as a Caucasian. **9** *n.* A person having light-colored skin; a Caucasian. **10** *adj.* Pale; bloodless: to turn *white* with terror. **11** *adj.* Silvery, as with age: *white* hair. **12** *adj.* Snowy: *white* slopes. **13** *adj.* Innocent or pure. — **white′ness** *n.*

white ant Another name for TERMITE.

white·cap [(h)wīt′kap′] *n.* A wave with a crest of foam.

white-col·lar [(h)wīt′kol′ər] *adj.* Having to do with workers expected to be well-groomed, as in offices, or having to do with their positions.

white corpuscle One of the white or colorless cells forming part of the blood; leucocyte.

white elephant A possession that is of little use and is expensive or bothersome to keep, store, or take care of.

white feather A mark of cowardice.

white·fish [(h)wīt′fish′] *n., pl.* **white·fish** or **white·fish·es** A fish with whitish or silvery sides, found in lakes, and eaten as food.

white flag A white flag or cloth shown as a sign of truce or surrender.

white gold An alloy of gold and a white metal. White gold looks like platinum.

white-hot [(h)wīt′hot′] *adj.* So hot that it gives off a bright, white light: *white-hot* metal.

White House, The 1 The official residence of the President of the United States, in Washington, D.C. 2 The executive branch of the United States government.

The White House

white lie An unimportant lie, often told in order to be polite or kind.

white matter The portion of the brain and spinal cord made up chiefly of nerve fibers.

White Mountains A range of the Appalachian Mountains in north central New Hampshire.

whit·en [(h)wīt′(ə)n] v. To make or become white; bleach.

White Russia Another name for BYELORUSSIA.

white·wash [(h)wīt′wäsh′ or (h)wīt′wôsh′] 1 n. A mixture of lime and water used for whitening walls, fences, etc. 2 v. To coat with whitewash. 3 v. To cover up, hide, or gloss over the bad things about: to whitewash an official. 4 n. A covering up of mistakes or faults. 5 n. Something that covers up mistakes or faults. 6 v. informal In sports, to defeat (an opponent) without allowing him to score.

whith·er [(h)with′ər] adv., conj. To what or which place; where: used mostly in poems.

whit·ing¹ [(h)wīt′ing] n. Any of various fishes found in the ocean and used for food.

whit·ing² [(h)wīt′ing] n. A pure white, powdered chalk, used in making whitewash, putty, and silver polish.

whit·ish [(h)wīt′ish] adj. Somewhat white.

Whit·man [(h)wit′mən], **Walt,** 1819–1892, U.S. poet.

Whit·ney [(h)wit′nē], **Eli,** 1765–1825, U.S. inventor who invented the cotton gin.

Whit·ney [(h)wit′nē], **Mount** A peak in eastern California.

Whit·sun·day [(h)wit′sun′dē or (h)wit′sən·dā′] n. The seventh Sunday after Easter; Pentecost.

Whit·sun·tide [(h)wit′sən·tīd′] n. The week that begins with Whitsunday, especially the first three days.

whit·tle [(h)wit′(ə)l] v. **whit·tled, whit·tling** 1 To cut or shave bits from (wood, a stick, etc.). 2 To make by whittling: to whittle a toy horse. 3 To reduce gradually: to whittle down taxes.

whiz or **whizz** [(h)wiz] v. **whizzed, whiz·zing,** n., pl. **whiz·zes** 1 v. To make a hissing or humming sound while passing through the air. 2 n. A whizzing sound. 3 v. To move or pass with such a sound: The bullet whizzed by. 4 n. slang A skillful person; expert.

who [hōō] pron. 1 Which or what person or persons: Who is coming to the party?; I don't know who she is. 2 That: The man who has the big dog is nice. 3 Whoever: Who delays, pays.

whoa [(h)wō] interj. Stop! Stand still! ◆ This word is used as a command to a horse.

who·ev·er [hōō·ev′ər] pron. 1 Any person who:

Whoever wants a cookie may have one. 2 No matter who: Whoever comes, don't let anyone in. 3 Who: used in questions for added emphasis: Whoever is making all that noise?

whole [hōl] 1 adj. Having all parts or components; complete: I have a whole set of Shakespeare's plays. 2 n. All of the parts making up a thing: The whole of his salary was spent on hospital bills. 3 adj. With no part left out or left over; entire: He spent the whole night pacing the floor. 4 n. An organization of parts that make a complete thing; system: The players in a string quartet make up a whole. 5 adj. Not broken; intact: not a whole cup and saucer in the house. 6 adj. Not divided or cut into pieces. 7 adj. Not injured or hurt; sound of body. 8 adj. Being an integer, not a fraction. **— on the whole** Taking everything into consideration.

whole·heart·ed [hōl′här′tid] adj. Earnest; hearty: wholehearted support.

whole note A note in music having a time value equal to twice that of a half note.

whole number An integer.

whole·sale [hōl′sāl′] n., adj., adv., v. **whole·saled, whole·sal·ing** 1 n. The selling of goods in large quantities, especially to retail stores for resale to the public. 2 adj. Of, having to do with, or engaged in this method of selling goods: wholesale prices; a wholesale druggist. 3 adv. In bulk or quantity and at lower prices: to buy goods wholesale. 4 v. To sell or be sold wholesale. 5 adj. Made or done on a large scale: wholesale killing. **— whole′sal·er** n.

Whole notes

whole·some [hōl′səm] adj. 1 Beneficial to the health; healthful: wholesome air and food. 2 Favorable to the development of the mind or character: wholesome entertainment. 3 Having or showing health: wholesome red cheeks.

whole-wheat [hōl′(h)wēt′] adj. Made of the entire grain of the wheat, including the bran: whole-wheat bread.

who'll [hōōl] 1 Who will. 2 Who shall

whol·ly [hō′lē] adv. Completely; totally: He was wholly deaf; I don't wholly agree.

whom [hōōm] pron. The form of WHO used as the object of a verb or preposition: Whom did you visit?; To whom am I speaking?

whom·ev·er [hōōm′ev′ər] pron. The form of WHOEVER used as object of a verb or preposition.

whom·so·ev·er [hōōm′sō·ev′ər] pron. The form of WHOSOEVER used as object of a verb or preposition.

whoop [h(w)ōōp or h(w)ōop] 1 n. A loud cry, as of excitement, surprise, etc. 2 v. To make loud cries. 3 n. The loud drawing in of the breath as after a series of coughs in whooping cough. 4 v. To make such a sound. **— whoop it up**

add, āce, câre, pälm;   end, ēqual;   it, īce;   odd, ōpen, ôrder;   tŏŏk, pōōl;   up, bûrn;
ə = a in above, e in sicken, i in possible, o in melon, u in circus;   yŏŏ = u in fuse;   oil;   pout;
check;   ring;   thin;   this;   zh in vision.   For ¶ reference, see page 64 · HOW TO

1 To have a noisy good time. **2** To arouse enthusiasm.

whooping cough A contagious disease of childhood in which there are violent fits of coughing ending in whoops.

whooping crane A large, long-legged North American crane that has a whooplike call.

whop·per [(h)wop′ər] *n. informal* Something large or remarkable, especially a big lie.

whore [hôr] *n.* A prostitute.

whorl [(h)wûrl *or* (h)wôrl] *n.* An arrangement of things in the form of a circle, as leaves coming from the same point on a stem, a turn of a spiral shell, or curves in the pattern of a fingerprint.

who's [hōōz] **1** Who is. **2** Who has.

whose [hōōz] *pron.* The possessive form of WHO or WHICH: *Whose* coat is this?; a cat *whose* whiskers are white.

who·so·ev·er [hōō′sō·ev′ər] *pron.* Any person whatever; who; whoever.

why [(h)wī] *adv., n., pl.* **whys 1** *adv.* For what cause, purpose, or reason: *Why* are you wearing dark glasses? **2** *adv.* The reason or cause for which: I don't know *why* he went. **3** *adv.* Because of which; for which: I know no reason *why* he went. **4** *n.* A reason or cause: the *whys* and wherefores of the case. **5** *interj.* A word used to express surprise, hesitation, etc., or to gain time: *Why*, there's the key I lost yesterday.

wick [wik] *n.* A band of loosely woven or twisted fibers in a lamp, candle, etc. that draws up fuel, which burns on it when lighted.

wick·ed [wik′id] *adj.* **1** Evil; sinful; depraved: a *wicked* act. **2** Playfully mischievous; naughty: a *wicked* prank. **3** *informal* Severe or painful: a *wicked* wind; a *wicked* toothache. **— wick′ed·ly** *adv.* **— wick′ed·ness** *n.*

wick·er [wik′ər] **1** *n.* A pliant young branch or twig, as of osier. **2** *n.* Such branches or twigs woven into a kind of fabric used in making baskets, light furniture, etc. **3** *adj. use:* a *wicker* chair. **4** *n.* Objects made of wicker.

wick·er·work [wik′ər·wûrk′] *n.* **1** Branches or twigs woven into a kind of fabric; wicker. **2** Objects made of wicker.

wick·et [wik′it] *n.* **1** A small door or gate near or within a larger one. **2** A small window, often partly covered by a grating, as one where tickets are sold. **3** In croquet, any of the wire arches through which the ball must be hit. **4** In cricket, either of two groups of sticks which one side tries to hit with the ball.

wide [wīd] **wid·er, wid·est,** *adj., adv.* **1** *adj.* Extending far from side to side; broad: a *wide* river. **2** *adj.* Extending far in every direction; vast: a *wide* area. **3** *adj.* Having a certain width: a table 36 inches *wide*. **4** *adj.* Large in range or content; including many or much: a *wide* selection of ties. **5** *adj., adv.* Far distant from the target, goal, etc.: to fall *wide* of the mark. **6** *adj.* Very far or fully open: *wide* eyes. **7** *adv.* Fully or almost fully: Open the window *wide*. **8** *adv.* To a great distance: to wander far and *wide*. **— wide′ly** *adv.*

wide-a·wake [wīd′ə·wāk′] *adj.* **1** Fully awake. **2** Alert, attentive, and watchful.

wide-eyed [wīd′īd′] *adj.* With the eyes wide open, as in wonder or surprise.

wid·en [wīd′(ə)n] *v.* To make or become wide or wider.

wide·spread [wīd′spread′] *adj.* **1** Spread wide, as wings. **2** Spreading over, happening in, or affecting a wide area: a *widespread* rumor.

wid·ow [wid′ō] **1** *n.* A woman who has lost her husband by death and has not married again. **2** *v.* To make a widow of.

wid·ow·er [wid′ō·ər] *n.* A man whose wife is dead, and who has not married again.

width [width] *n.* **1** The size of something, as measured from one side to the other; wideness; breadth. **2** A piece of something, as cloth, having a certain width.

wield [wēld] *v.* **1** To hold and use (a weapon, tool, etc.); handle: to *wield* a knife. **2** To hold and use (authority, power, etc.).

wie·ner [wē′nər] *n. U.S.* A sausage made of beef and pork; a frankfurter or a shorter sausage.

wife [wīf] *n., pl.* **wives** [wīvz] A woman to whom a man is married; a married woman.

wife·ly [wīf′lē] *adj.* **wife·li·er, wife·li·est** Of, like, or fitting for a wife.

wig [wig] *n.* A covering of hair for the head, used to hide one's own hair, cover baldness, complete a costume, etc.

wig·gle [wig′əl] *v.* **wig·gled, wig·gling,** *n.* **1** *v.* To move or twist from side to side: The dog *wiggled* his nose; He *wiggled* under the fence. **2** *n.* A wiggling motion.

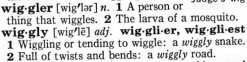

Judge's wig

wig·gler [wig′lər] *n.* **1** A person or thing that wiggles. **2** The larva of a mosquito.

wig·gly [wig′lē] *adj.* **wig·gli·er, wig·gli·est 1** Wiggling or tending to wiggle: a *wiggly* snake. **2** Full of twists and bends: a *wiggly* road.

wight [wīt] *n.* A person; creature: seldom used today.

wig·wag [wig′wag′] *v.* **wig·wagged, wig·wag·ging,** *n.* **1** *v.* To send (a message) by moving small flags, lights, etc., according to a code. **2** *n.* The action or method of sending messages in this way.

wig·wam [wig′wom] *n.* A hut in the shape of a cone or dome built by North American Indians, and consisting of a framework of poles covered by bark, hides, etc.

wild [wīld] **1** *adj.* Living in the fields, plains, or forests; not tamed or domesticated: *wild* dogs. **2** *adj.* Growing in a natural state; not cultivated: *wild* flowers. **3** *adj.* Not lived in or used by civilized people: *wild* country. **4** *n.* (*usually pl.*) Uninhabited or uncultivated country: the Arctic *wilds*. **5** *adj.* Savage or primitive; uncivilized: *wild* tribesmen in the jungle. **6** *adj.*

Not controlled or restrained, and often unruly or disorderly: a *wild* crowd; a *wild* dance; *wild* with delight. **7** *adj*. Fantastic or odd: a *wild* story. **8** *adj*. Violent or turbulent: a *wild* sea. **9** *adj*. Missing the intended target by a large amount: a *wild* throw. **10** *adv*. In a wild way: to run *wild*. **— wild′ly** *adv*. **— wild′ness** *n*.

wild·cat [wĭld′kat′] *n., v.* **wild·cat·ted, wild·cat·ting,** *adj*. **1** *n*. A wild animal related to the domestic cat, but somewhat larger. It is also called a lynx. **2** *n*. A person who is always ready to quarrel or fight, especially a woman. **3** *n*. A successful oil well drilled in an area thought not to contain oil. **4** *v*. To drill for oil in an area not known to contain it. **5** *n*. A risky business venture. **6** *adj*. Likely to fail; risky: a *wildcat* investment. **7** *adj*. Made, done, or carried on without official permission; unauthorized: a *wildcat* strike. **— wild′cat′ter** *n*.

wil·der·ness [wĭl′dər·nĭs] *n*. A region that is not cultivated or lived in.

wild·flow·er [wĭld′flou′ər] *n*. or **wild flower** An uncultivated flowering plant or its flower.

wild·fowl [wĭld′foul′] *n*. or **wild fowl,** *pl*. **wild·fowl** or **wild·fowls** or **wild fowl** or **wild fowls** A wild duck, pheasant, or other game bird.

wild·life [wĭld′lïf′] *n*. Animals and plants in their natural or wild state.

Wild West The western U.S. during the early pioneer period.

wile [wïl] *n., v.* **wiled, wil·ing 1** *n*. A trick or scheme to deceive or entice: *wiles* that hook a fish. **2** *v*. To coax or lure by wiles.

wi·li·ness [wï′lē·nĭs] *n*. The condition or quality of being wily.

will¹ [wĭl] *v. Present tense for all subjects* **will,** *past tense* **would** A helping verb used to express: **1** Things happening in the future: I *will* ride there; He said he *would* come. **2** Capability: *Will* the plan work?; It certainly *will*. **3** Willingness: Why *will* you not tell the truth? **4** Custom or habit: She *will* get upset over trifles. **5** A command: You *will* come when I call you. ◆ See SHALL.

will² [wĭl] *n., v.* **willed, will·ing 1** *n*. The power that the mind has to make choices and decisions and acts to carry them out: a person of strong *will*. **2** *n*. Something chosen or decided upon; a desire, wish, etc.: What is her majesty's *will*? **3** *v*. To choose or decide: Elections show what the people *will*; Do as you *will*. **4** *n*. Strong determination or self-control: With her *will*, she'll succeed. **5** *v*. To control or bring about by the exercise of the will. **6** *n*. The way a person feels toward another: to show good *will*. **7** *n*. A legal document telling how a person wishes his wealth and property to be disposed of after his death. **8** *v*. To give by means of a will: to *will* money to a son. **— at will** As one wishes.

will·full or **wil·ful** [wĭl′fəl] *adj*. **1** Insisting on having one's own way: a *willful* child. **2** Done on purpose; deliberate: *willful* damage; a *willful* action. **— will′ful·ness** or **wil′ful·ness** *n*.

will·ful·ly or **wil·ful·ly** [wĭl′fəl·ē] *adv*. **1** On purpose. **2** In a stubborn or obstinate way.

Wil·liam I [wĭl′yəm], 1027?–1087, Duke of Normandy who invaded England in 1066 and was King of England 1066–1087. He was called **William the Conquerer.**

Wil·liams [wĭl′yəmz], **Roger,** 1603?–1683, English clergyman in New England. He founded Rhode Island.

Wil·liams·burg [wĭl′yəmz·bûrg] *n*. A town in eastern Virginia, capital of Virginia 1699–1779.

will·ing [wĭl′ĭng] *adj*. **1** Ready or disposed; prepared: He is *willing* to do it. **2** Cheerfully meeting demands and requirements: a *willing* worker. **3** Gladly given or done: *willing* service. **— will′ing·ly** *adv*. **— will′ing·ness** *n*.

will-o'-the-wisp [wĭl′ə·thə·wĭsp′] *n*. **1** A flickering light seen over marshes and swamps at night. **2** Anything that misleads by luring one on but staying out of reach.

wil·low [wĭl′ō] *n*. **1** One of a group of trees and shrubs having smooth branches, thin flexible twigs which hang down, and long narrow leaves. **2** The wood of one of these trees.

wil·low·y [wĭl′ō·ē] *adj*. **1** Full of willows: a *willowy* shore. **2** Slender or supple; graceful in form or movement: a *willowy* young girl.

wil·ly-nil·ly [wĭl′ē·nĭl′ē] *adv*. Whether one wants to or not: He will pay the bill *willy-nilly*.

Wil·son [wĭl′sən], **Woodrow,** 1856–1924, U.S. statesman, 28th president of the U.S. 1913–1921.

wilt¹ [wĭlt] *v*. To lose or cause to lose freshness, energy, vitality, etc.; make or become limp: Dryness *wilted* the grass; He *wilted* in the heat.

wilt² [wĭlt] A form of the verb WILL used with *thou*: seldom used today.

wi·ly [wï′lē] *adj*. **wi·li·er, wi·li·est** Full of or using wiles; sly; cunning. **— wi′li·ness** *n*.

wim·ple [wĭm′pəl] *n*. A cloth wrapped around the head and neck, exposing only the face, formerly worn by women. It is now worn only by nuns.

win [wĭn] *v*. **won, win·ning,** *n*. **1** *v*. To be victorious in (a game, contest, war, struggle, etc.): to *win* a game; The home team *won*. **2** *n*. An instance of winning; victory. **3** *v*. To get by effort or hard work: to *win* fame and fortune. **4** *v*. To get the good will or favor of: He *won* the opposition over. **5** *v*. To suceed in reaching after some effort: The ship *won* a safe harbor.

Nun wearing a wimple

wince [wĭns] *v*. **winced, winc·ing,** *n*. **1** *v*. To shrink or draw back, as from a blow or a pain; flinch. **2** *n*. The act of wincing.

add, āce, câre, pälm; end, ēqual; it, īce; odd, ōpen, ôrder; tŏŏk, pōōl; up, bûrn; ə = a in *above*, e in *sicken*, i in *possible*, o in *melon*, u in *circus*; yōō = u in *fuse*; oil; pout; check; ring; thin; **th**is; zh in *vision*. For ¶ reference, see page 64 · HOW TO

winch [winch] *n.* A machine for lifting or pulling, consisting of a drum onto which a rope or cable is wound by a hand crank or by a motor.

wind[1] [wind] **1** *n.* A movement or current of air of any speed. **2** *n.* Air that carries some scent: The dogs got *wind* of the fox. **3** *n.* The power of breathing; breath. **4** *v.* To make short of breath: The long run *winded* him. **5** *n.* Idle or useless talk: That's a lot of *wind*. **6** *n.* (*pl.*) Wind instruments, as in an orchestra. **— get wind of** Find out about; discover. **— in the wind** In progress or about to happen.

wind[2] [wīnd] *v.* **wound, wind·ing,** *n.* **1** *v.* To coil or pass (thread, rope, etc.) around itself or around something else: to *wind* thread. **2** *v.* To coil or twine, as around some central object: The rope *winds* on this drum. **3** *v.* To cover with something by coiling: to *wind* a spool with thread. **4** *v.* To make (a machine, as a clock) go by coiling a spring or raising a weight. **5** *v.* To run or move in a turning, twisting course; meander: The road *winds* through town. **6** *n.* A winding; turn or twist. **— wind up 1** To coil onto a reel, drum, etc. **2** To bring to an end. **3** To put in readiness for action; excite or arouse. **4** To move the arm and body in preparation for pitching a ball.

wind·break [wind'brāk'] *n.* Something, as a line of trees, a hedge, or a fence, used to break the force of the wind.

wind·fall [wind'fôl'] *n.* **1** An unexpected lucky event, profit, etc. **2** Something blown down by the wind, especially ripe fruit.

wind·flow·er [wind'flou'ər] *n.* Another name for ANEMONE.

wind·ing [wīn'ding] **1** *n.* The act of a person or thing that winds. **2** *n.* A bend, turn, etc., or a series of them. **3** *adj.* Having or making bends or turns. **4** *n.* Something that is wound or coiled about an object.

wind·ing sheet [wīn'ding] A sheet that in former times was wrapped around a corpse.

wind instrument [wind] An instrument whose sound is produced by a stream of air, especially air from the player's breath.

wind·jam·mer [wind'jam'ər] *n.* A ship with sails.

wind·lass [wind'ləs] *n.* A device for hauling or lifting; a kind of winch.

wind·mill [wind'mil'] *n.* A machine that gets its power from a set of vanes turned by the wind. It is used especially to pump water.

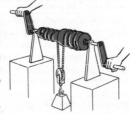

Windlass

win·dow [win'dō] *n.* **1** An opening in the side of a building to let in light and air. **2** The frame and panes of glass used to close such an opening. ◆ *Window* comes from two old Scandinavian words meaning *wind* and *eye*.

win·dow·pane [win'dō·pān'] *n.* A sheet of glass used in a window.

win·dow-shop [win'dō·shop'] *v.* **win·dow-shopped, win·dow-shop·ping** To look at the goods shown in store windows without buying them.

wind·pipe [wind'pīp'] *n.* The passage that connects the throat to the lungs; trachea.

wind·row [wind'rō'] *n.* A long ridge of hay raked together to be piled into haystacks.

wind·shield [wind'shēld'] *n.* A sheet of glass or plastic in front of the driver and riders in a vehicle, plane, or boat to block off wind, rain, etc.

wind sock A conical sleeve open at both ends, mounted on a pivot so that the big end points to the direction of the wind.

Wind·sor [win'zər] *n.* The name of the royal family of Great Britain since 1917.

Windsor Castle A castle in southern England, a residence of the British sovereign.

wind·storm [wind'stôrm'] *n.* A strong wind with little or no rain.

wind tunnel A large cylindrical structure in which models of aircraft, rockets, boats, etc., are tested with measured, artificially made winds.

wind-up [wīnd'up'] *n.* **1** An ending or closing; conclusion. **2** The movements of the arm and body made in preparation for pitching a ball.

wind vane Another name for WEATHER VANE.

wind·ward [wind'wərd] **1** *n.* The side the wind strikes. **2** *adj.* On the side the wind strikes. **3** *n.* The direction from which the wind comes. **4** *adj.* In the direction from which the wind comes. **5** *adv.* Toward the wind.

wind·y [win'dē] *adj.* **wind·i·er, wind·i·est 1** Having or exposed to much wind: a *windy* plain. **2** Making dull, pompous talk.

wine [wīn] **1** *n.* Grape juice fermented so that it contains alcohol. **2** *n.* A similar drink made from the juice of any fruit or plant. **3** *n.*, *adj.* Deep, purplish red. **— wine and dine** To entertain or treat with food and drink.

wing [wing] **1** *n.* One of a pair of parts, or set of two pairs, that a bird, bat, or insect extends and moves in order to fly. **2** *n.* Something like a wing in shape, position, or use: an airplane *wing*. **3** *v.* To cause to be rapid or go quickly: Hope *winged* his steps. **4** *v.* To damage the wing or arm of with a bullet, arrow, etc. **5** *n.* Something sticking out to the side from the main part: a *wing* of a house; the *wings* of a stage. **6** *n.* A group holding extreme views, as in a political organization: the left *wing*. **7** *n.* Either the right or left section of an army or fleet. **— on the wing 1** In flight. **2** In motion; hardly stopping. **— take wing** To fly away. **— under one's wing** Under one's protection.

winged [wingd *or* wing'id] *adj.* **1** Having wings. **2** Passing swiftly; fast; rapid.

wing·less [wing'lis] *adj.* Having no wings, or having incompletely developed wings.

wing·spread [wing'spred'] *n.* The distance between the tips of a pair of fully extended wings.

wink [wingk] **1** *v.* To close and open (the eyes,

or especially one eye) rapidly, often as a sign or hint. **2** *n.* The act of winking. **3** *n.* A hint or sign given by winking. **4** *v.* To give off light in short flashes; twinkle. **5** *n.* A short time; instant: He'll be here in a *wink.* — **wink at** To pretend not to see: to *wink at* a prank.

win·ner [win′ər] *n.* A person or thing that wins.

win·ning [win′ing] **1** *adj.* Successful, especially in competition. **2** *n.* The act of a person or thing that wins. **3** *n.* (*pl.*) Something won, especially money won, as by gambling. **4** *adj.* Charming; attractive; winsome: a *winning* manner.

Win·ni·peg [win′ə·peg] *n.* The capital of Manitoba, Canada.

win·now [win′ō] *v.* **1** To blow the chaff from (grain). **2** To blow off (chaff) from grain. **3** To sift out; separate: to *winnow* facts from myths.

win·some [win′səm] *adj.* Having a charming, attractive appearance or manner.

win·ter [win′tər] **1** *n.* The coldest season of the year, occurring between autumn and spring. **2** *adj. use:* *winter* sports; a *winter* coat. **3** *v.* To pass the winter: to *winter* in the tropics. **4** *v.* To feed or care for during the winter: to *winter* animals.

win·ter·green [win′tər·grēn] *n.* **1** A small evergreen plant whose oval leaves yield an aromatic oil. **2** The oil from this plant, used as a flavoring.

win·ter·ize [win′tə·rīz] *v.* **win·ter·ized, win·ter·iz·ing** To equip or prepare (an engine, automobile, etc.) for winter. ¶3

winter solstice In the Northern Hemisphere, the time when the sun is farthest south of the equator, about December 22.

win·ter·time [win′tər·tīm′] *n.* The winter season.

win·try [win′trē] *adj.* **win·tri·er, win·tri·est** Of or like winter; cold; frosty.

wipe [wīp] *v.* **wiped, wip·ing,** *n.* **1** *v.* To rub, usually with a soft or absorbent material: to *wipe* a table dry. **2** *v.* To apply or remove by rubbing lightly: to *wipe* on polish; to *wipe* off grease. **3** *v.* To clean or dry by or as if by rubbing: to *wipe* one's shoes on a doormat; to *wipe* the dishes. **4** *v.* To move along or across; cause to rub: to *wipe* your hand across your brow. **5** *n.* The act of wiping. — **wipe out** To destroy completely, as by killing. — **wip′er** *n.*

wire [wīr] *n., v.* **wired, wir·ing 1** *n.* Metal that has been drawn into a slender rod, strand, or thread. **2** *n.* Such metal covered with insulation, used to carry electricity. **3** *v.* To fasten with wire: to *wire* a box shut. **4** *v.* To equip with wires for carrying electricity: to *wire* a radio. **5** *n.* A telegraph system: to signal by *wire.* **6** *v. informal* To telegraph or telegraph to: to *wire* a message; to *wire* a senator. **7** *n. informal* A telegram. — **pull wires** To use hidden influence.

wire-haired [wīr′hârd′] *adj.* Having thick, stiff hairs: a *wire-haired* terrier.

wire·less [wīr′lis] **1** *adj.* Having no wires; operating without a connection by wire. **2** *n. British* Radio. **3** *n. British* A telegram sent by radio. **4** *v. British* To send a telegram by radio.

wire·worm [wīr′wûrm] *n.* The stiff, wiry larva of certain beetles, some of which destroy plant roots.

wir·ing [wīr′ing] *n.* A system of wires used to carry an electric current.

wir·y [wīr′ē] *adj.* **wir·i·er, wir·i·est 1** Like wire; thin and stiff. **2** Slender, but tough and strong: a *wiry* prize fighter.

Wis. or **Wisc.** Abbreviation of WISCONSIN.

Wis·con·sin [wis·kon′sən] *n.* A state in the north central U.S.

wis·dom [wiz′dəm] *n.* **1** Good judgment and knowledge of what is true or right, based on experience. **2** Accumulated knowledge or learning: the *wisdom* of the ancients.

wisdom tooth The last tooth on either side of the upper or lower jaw in man; usually appearing between the 17th and 22nd year.

wise¹ [wīz] *adj.* **wis·er, wis·est 1** Having or showing wisdom: to act in a *wise* manner; to be *wiser* as a result of study. **2** *U.S. slang* Offensively bold and arrogant: a *wise* guy. — **wise to** *informal* Aware of: I'm *wise to* his tricks. — **wise′ly** *adv.*

wise² [wīz] *n.* Way, manner, or method: He is in no *wise* clever.

-wise A combining form meaning: **1** In a certain manner, as in *likewise,* in like manner. **2** In a certain direction or position, as in *clockwise,* in the direction traveled by the hands of a clock. **3** In regard to or with reference to, as in *moneywise,* in regard to money.

wise·a·cre [wiz′ā′kər] *n.* A person who thinks he is or who pretends to be very wise.

wise·crack [wīz′krak′] *slang* **1** *n.* A short, witty remark, often disrespectful or mocking. **2** *v.* To make a wisecrack or wisecracks.

wish [wish] **1** *v.* To want, desire, or be glad to have: We *wish* to make sure; Do you *wish* lunch? **2** *n.* A desire or hope to do, get, have, be, or experience something: a *wish* to travel. **3** *v.* To have or express a desire or craving: She *wished* for a new dress. **4** *n.* Something hoped or wished for: Cinderella got her *wish.* **5** *v.* To want or desire (something) for someone: I *wish* you luck. **6** *n.* The expression of a wish: Bob sends his best *wishes.* **7** *v.* To request or command: I *wish* you to be quiet.

wish·bone [wish′bōn′] *n.* In many birds, a forked bone located in front of the breastbone.

wish·ful [wish′fəl] *adj.* Having or showing a wish or desire: *wishful* thinking.

wish·y-wash·y [wish′ē·wosh′ē] *adj.* **1** Weak, thin, or diluted, as watered wine. **2** Without strength, character, or decisiveness: a *wishy-washy* man who is never able to make up his mind.

wisp [wisp] *n.* **1** A small bunch, as of hay, hair, etc. **2** A small bit: a *wisp* of vapor. **3** A frail or slight person or thing: a *wisp* of a child. — **wisp′y** *adj.*

wist [wist] Past tense and past participle of WIT².

wis·tar·i·a [wis·târ′ē·ə] *n.* Another spelling of WISTERIA.

wis·ter·i·a [wis·tir′ē·ə] *n.* Any of various climbing shrubs related to the bean and having clusters of blue, purple, or white flowers.

wist·ful [wist′fəl] *adj.* **1** Wishful; longing. **2** Thoughtful; pensive. — **wist′ful·ly** *adv.* — **wist′ful·ness** *n.*

wit¹ [wit] *n.* **1** The ability to say or write clever, intelligent, and amusing things: The critic's *wit* was sharp but constructive. **2** A person who has this ability: He was a true *wit.* **3** (*pl.*) The ability to perceive and understand: a person of quick *wits.* **4** (*pl.*) Mental balance: to be frightened out of one's *wits.* — **at one's wit's end** Not able to know what to do, say, or think.

wit² [wit] *v.* **wist, wit·ting** To learn or know: seldom used today. — **to wit** That is to say; namely: I told two people; *to wit,* my father and mother.

witch [wich] *n.* **1** A woman supposed to have magical powers, especially the power to work evil. **2** Any mean or ugly old woman; hag.

witch·craft [wich′kraft′] *n.* **1** The supernatural power of a witch. **2** The use of this power. ◆ See MAGIC.

witch doctor Among certain primitive people, a person thought to be able to work magic or to keep witchcraft from working; medicine man.

witch·er·y [wich′ər·ē] *n., pl.* **witch·er·ies** **1** The power to charm; fascination. **2** Witchcraft.

witch hazel **1** A shrub of the U.S. and Canada, having crooked trunks and small, yellow flowers. **2** A liquid preparation made from the bark and leaves of this shrub, used as a soothing, cooling lotion for the skin.

witch·ing [wich′ing] *adj.* **1** Charming; fascinating. **2** Of or suitable for witchery.

with [with *or* with] *prep.* **1** In the company of: She went *with* Bob and me. **2** Having or exhibiting: a hat *with* a feather. **3** By adding, having, or containing: a dress trimmed *with* lace. **4** As a member or associate of: He has been *with* the school for years. **5** Among: to be counted *with* the others. **6** In the course of; during: One forgets *with* time. **7** So as to be separated from: to do away *with* luxuries. **8** Against: to fight *with* someone. **9** In the opinion of: That is all right *with* me. **10** Because of: to be faint *with* hunger. **11** In charge or in possession of: Leave the key *with* the janitor. **12** By means or aid of: to write *with* a pencil. **13** In spite of: *With* all his money, he can't buy health. **14** At the same time as: to go to bed *with* the chickens. **15** In the same direction as: to drift *with* the crowd. **16** In regard to; in the case of: I am angry *with* them.

17 Onto; to: Join this tube *with* that one. **18** Into: Mix the water *with* the flour. **19** In proportion to: His fame grew *with* his deeds. **20** In support of: He voted *with* the other party. **21** Of the same opinion as: I'm *with* you there! **22** Compared or contrasted to: Consider this book *with* that one. **23** Immediately after; following: *With* that, he slammed the door. **24** Having received or been granted: *With* his consent, I left. **25** As well as: She can cook *with* the best of them.

with·al [with·ôl′ *or* with·ôl′] *adv.* In addition; besides: seldom used today.

with·draw [with·drô′ *or* with·drô′] *v.* **with·drew, with·drawn, with·draw·ing** **1** To take away or remove: She *withdrew* her hand from mine. **2** To take back: to *withdraw* a statement. **3** To move or go back or away: She *withdrew* from the room. **4** To resign or retire; leave: to *withdraw* from the committee.

with·draw·al [with·drô′əl *or* with·drô′əl] *n.* The act or process of withdrawing.

with·drawn [with·drôn′ *or* with·drôn′] **1** Past participle of WITHDRAW. **2** *adj.* Very quiet and reserved, as if in deep thought: He seems *withdrawn* today.

with·drew [with·drōō′ *or* with·drōō′] Past tense of WITHDRAW.

withe [with *or* with] *n.* A long twig, usually of willow, that bends easily and can be used to tie things together.

with·er [with′ər] *v.* **1** To become or cause to become limp, dry, or lifeless: Drought *withered* the crop. **2** To lose force or vitality; weaken: Once halted, the rebellion soon *withered.* **3** To make incapable of speech or action; stun: a *withering* glance.

with·ers [with′ərz] *n.pl.* The highest part of the back of a horse, deer, ox, etc., located between the shoulder blades.

with·hold [with·hōld′ *or* with·hōld′] *v.* **with·held, with·hold·ing** **1** To hold back; restrain: Please *withhold* your impatience. **2** To refuse to grant or give: She *withheld* her permission.

withholding tax A portion of an employee's wages deducted and given to the government as part payment of his income tax.

with·in [with·in′ *or* with·in′] **1** *adv.* In, on, or to the inner part: Paths lead *within.* **2** *adv.* Indoors: Go *within* at once. **3** *n.* An inner part or place: trouble from *within.* **4** *prep.* In the inner part or parts of; inside: *within* the house. **5** *prep.* In the limits or range of; not farther than: *within* a mile of here. **6** *prep.* In the reach, limit, or scope of; not beyond: *within* my power.

with·out [with·out′ *or* with·out′] **1** *prep.* Not having, doing, or making; lacking; with no:

coffee *without* sugar; to get in *without* paying. **2** *prep.* Free from: *without* fear. **3** *adv.* In, on, or to the outer part: Smoke passed *without*. **4** *prep.* In, on, at, or to the outside of: *Without* the harbor, the storm raged. **5** *adv.* Outdoors; outside a building: It was cold *without*. **6** *n.* An outer part or place: to get help from *without*. **7** *prep.* Outside the range, scope, or limits of: traffic both within and *without* the city.

with·stand [with·stand′ or with·stand′] *v.* **with·stood, with·stand·ing** To stand up against; oppose; resist: to *withstand* hard use.

wit·less [wit′lis] *adj.* Lacking in wit or intelligence; stupid; foolish.

wit·ness [wit′nis] **1** *n.* A person who has seen or knows something and can give evidence concerning it: a *witness* to the murder. **2** *v.* To see or know by personal experience: to *witness* an accident. **3** *n.* A person who, under oath, gives evidence in a court of law. **4** *n.* A person who is present at a transaction, ceremony, etc., and who then signs a document stating or proving that the event actually took place: a *witness* to a marriage. **5** *v.* To act as a witness of: He *witnessed* the signing of my contract. **6** *n.* Evidence; proof; testimony: false *witness*. **7** *v.* To give evidence of; show: His grin *witnessed* his satisfaction. — **bear witness** To be or serve as evidence or proof of something: Our happy faces *bore witness* to our victory.

wit·ted [wit′id] *adj.* Having a certain kind of wit: often used in combination, as in *quick-witted*, having a quick, sharp wit.

wit·ti·cism [wit′ə·siz′əm] *n.* A witty saying.

wit·ty [wit′ē] *adj.* **wit·ti·er, wit·ti·est** Full of or having wit; clever or amusing: a *witty* person. — **wit′ti·ly** *adv.* — **wit′ti·ness** *n.*

wiz·ard [wiz′ərd] *n.* **1** A man thought to have magical powers; sorcerer. **2** *informal* Any very clever or skillful person.

wiz·ard·ry [wiz′ərd·rē] *n.* **1** Magic. **2** Skill so great that it seems magical.

wiz·ened [wiz′ənd] *adj.* Shrunken and dried up; withered: the old lady's *wizened* cheeks.

wk. Abbreviation of WEEK.

wo [wō] *n., pl.* **wos** Woe: seldom used today.

wob·ble [wob′əl] *v.* **wob·bled, wob·bling,** *n.* **1** *v.* To move or sway or cause to move or sway unsteadily: The top *wobbled* as it slowed down. **2** *n.* An unsteady, wobbling motion. **3** *v.* To be uncertain or undecided. — **wob′bly** *adj.*

Wo·den [wōd′(ə)n] *n.* The Old English name for Odin, the chief Norse god. Wednesday is named for Woden.

woe [wō] *n.* **1** Great sorrow; grief. **2** Terrible trouble; calamity; disaster.

woe·be·gone or **wo·be·gone** [wō′bi·gôn′] *adj.* Overcome with or showing woe or sadness.

woe·ful or **wo·ful** [wō′fəl] *adj.* **1** Full of woe; sad; mournful. **2** Causing woe; pitiful: a *woeful* lack of food. **3** Of very poor quality. — **woe′ful·ly** or **wo′ful·ly** *adv.*

woke [wōk] Past tense of WAKE¹: I *woke* early.

wold [wōld] *n.* A tract of open upland, often hilly or rolling.

wolf [wŏŏlf] *n., pl.* **wolves** [wŏŏlvz] *v.* **1** *n.* Any of a group of wild animals related to the dog. Wolves usually hunt in packs and prey on other animals. **2** *n.* Any cruel, ravenous, or greedy person or thing. **3** *v.* To eat in a greedy manner; gulp down.

Wolf, to 30 in. high at shoulder

— **cry wolf** To give a false alarm. — **keep the wolf from the door** To keep from being hungry or needy. — **wolf′ish** *adj.*

wolf·hound [wŏŏlf′hound′] *n.* A large dog of any of several breeds originally trained to catch and kill wolves.

wol·ver·ine or **wol·ver·ene** [wŏŏl′və·rēn′] *n.* A strong, heavily built, carnivorous animal of North American forests, related to the weasel.

wolves [wŏŏlvz] The plural of WOLF.

wom·an [wŏŏm′ən] *n., pl.* **wom·en** [wim′in] **1** An adult human female. **2** *adj. use:* a *woman* doctor. **3** Women as a group. **4** A female attendant or servant. ◆See LADY.

wom·an·hood [wŏŏm′ən·hŏŏd] *n.* **1** The condition of being a woman. **2** Women as a group. **3** The traits or qualities of women.

wom·an·ish [wŏŏm′ən·ish] *adj.* **1** Like or for a woman. **2** Unmanly; effeminate.

wom·an·kind [wŏŏm′ən·kīnd′] *n.* Women as a group.

wom·an·ly [wŏŏm′ən·lē] *adj.* **1** Becoming to or fit for a woman: a *womanly* voice. **2** Having qualities becoming to or fit for a woman: a *womanly* person. — **wom′an·li·ness** *n.*

womb [wŏŏm] *n.* The organ of female mammals in which the young develop before birth; uterus.

wom·bat [wom′bat] *n.* An Australian animal that looks like a small bear. The female carries her young in a pouch outside her body.

wom·en [wim′in] Plural of WOMAN.

won [wun] Past tense and past participle of WIN.

won·der [wun′dər] **1** *n.* A feeling of curiosity and surprise; astonishment: We looked with *wonder* at the falling star. **2** *n.* Something strange or unusual that makes one have such a feeling. **3** *v.* To be filled with wonder or awe; marvel: We *wondered* at the sight of the huge falls. **4** *v.* To be doubtful or curious about something; want to know: I *wonder* what the painting was sold for. **5** *v.* To feel surprise.

won·der·ful [wun′dər·fəl] *adj.* **1** Causing wonder or awe. **2** Unusually good; excellent: a *wonderful* concert. — **won′der·ful·ly** *adv.*

---

add, āce, câre, pälm; end, ēqual; it, īce; odd, ōpen, ôrder; tŏŏk, pōōl; up, bûrn; ə = a in *above*, e in *sicken*, i in *possible*, o in *melon*, u in *circus*; yŏŏ = u in *fuse*; oil; pout; check; ring; thin; this; zh in *vision*. For ¶ reference, see page 64 · HOW TO

won·der·land [wun′dər·land′] *n.* A place, usually imaginary, filled with wonders.

won·der·ment [wun′dər·mənt] *n.* **1** Wonder; awe. **2** Great surprise; astonishment.

won·drous [wun′drəs] **1** *adj.* Wonderful; marvelous. **2** *adv.* Surprisingly; unusually: seldom used today.

wont [wunt *or* wônt] **1** *adj.* Accustomed; used: He is *wont* to smoke after dinner. **2** *n.* Ordinary or accustomed practice or habit: It is his *wont* to walk five miles every day.

won't [wōnt] Will not: He simply *won't* go.

wont·ed [wun′tid *or* wôn′tid] *adj.* Habitual; accustomed: to leave at one's *wonted* hour.

woo [wōō] *v.* **1** To seek the love or affection of, especially in order to marry; court: to *woo* a young lady. **2** To try to obtain; seek: to *woo* fortune. **3** To seek the favor or influence of: Politicians *woo* the public. — **woo′er** *n.*

wood [wŏŏd] **1** *n.* The hard substance found beneath the bark of a tree or shrub. **2** *n.* This hard substance cut for use in building, as fuel, etc. **3** *adj. use:* a *wood* pail. **4** *n.* (*pl.*) Woodwinds in an orchestra. **5** *n.* (*often pl.*) A large group of growing trees; forest. **6** *adj.* Living or growing in woods: a *wood* flower. — **out of the woods** Clear of doubts, difficulties, or danger.

wood alcohol A poisonous alcohol distilled from wood or made artificially, used as a fuel, solvent, antifreeze, etc.

wood·bine [wŏŏd′bīn′] *n.* Any of several climbing plants, as the common honeysuckle of Europe or the Virginia creeper.

wood·chuck [wŏŏd′chuk′] *n.* A chunky animal, a marmot of North America, having coarse brown fur and a short tail. It can climb and swim and sleeps in its burrow all winter; ground hog. ◆ *Woodchuck* comes from the word *wejack*, of a North American Indian language. The Indian word sounded strange to English-speaking settlers, and they substituted the more familiar sounds of *wood* and *chuck*.

Woodchuck, 2 ft. long

wood·cock [wŏŏd′kok′] *n.* A small American bird with long bill and short legs.

wood·craft [wŏŏd′kraft′] *n.* **1** Skill in things having to do with life in the woods, as hunting or camping. **2** Skill in woodworking.

wood·cut [wŏŏd′kut′] *n.* **1** A block of wood on which a picture, design, etc., has been cut. **2** A print made from such a block.

wood·ed [wŏŏd′id] *adj.* Covered with trees or woods: *wooded* hills.

wood·en [wŏŏd′(ə)n] *adj.* **1** Made of wood. **2** Awkward and stiff: a *wooden* pose. **3** Dull; stupid: a *wooden* look. — **wood′en·ly** *adv.*

wood·land [wŏŏd′lənd *or* wŏŏd′land′] **1** *n.* Land covered with woods. **2** *adj.* Belonging to, growing in, or living in the woods.

wood louse *pl.* **wood lice** Any of numerous very small animals with flat oval bodies, usually found under old logs and decaying wood.

wood·man [wŏŏd′mən] *n., pl.* **wood·men** [wŏŏd′mən] Another spelling of WOODSMAN.

wood·peck·er [wŏŏd′pek′ər] *n.* Any of a group of birds having strong claws, stiff tail feathers, and a sharp bill for drilling holes in trees, etc., in search of insects.

wood·pile [wŏŏd′pīl′] *n.* A pile of wood, especially of wood cut or split in sizes for burning in a fireplace, stove, or campfire.

wood·shed [wŏŏd′shed′] *n.* A shed for storing firewood.

woods·man [wŏŏdz′mən] *n., pl.* **woods·men** [wŏŏdz′mən] **1** A man who lives or works in the woods. **2** A man skilled in woodcraft.

wood thrush A large thrush of North American woods, noted for its clear, sweet song.

wood·wind [wŏŏd′wind′] **1** *n.* Any of a group of wind instruments made mainly of wood and sounded by a player's breath passing through a reed or striking a sharp edge, as oboes, bassoons, clarinets, flutes, etc. **2** *adj.* Of or for these instruments: a *woodwind* player or part. **3** *n.* (*pl.*) The woodwind section of an orchestra.

wood·work [wŏŏd′wûrk′] *n.* Something made of wood, especially the doors, moldings, stairways, etc., of a house or room.

wood·work·ing [wŏŏd′wûr′king] *n.* The act, art, or work of forming things of wood.

wood·y [wŏŏd′ē] *adj.* **wood·i·er, wood·i·est** **1** Of, like, or containing wood. **2** Covered with trees: a *woody* tract of land. — **wood′i·ness** *n.*

woof [wŏŏf] *n.* **1** In weaving, the threads that are carried from side to side across the fixed threads of the warp in a loom; weft. **2** A fabric, or the texture of a fabric.

wool [wŏŏl] *n.* **1** The soft, curly hair obtained from the fleece of sheep and some related animals. **2** Yarn, cloth, or clothes made of wool. **3** *adj. use:* a *wool* suit. **4** Something like wool, as curly or kinky human hair. — **pull the wool over one's eyes** To trick or deceive one.

wool·en [wŏŏl′ən] **1** *adj.* Made of wool. **2** *n.* (*pl.*) Cloth or garments made of wool. **3** *adj.* Having to do with wool, its manufacture, or its sale: the *woolen* industry.

wool·gath·er·ing [wŏŏl′gath′ər·ing] *n.* Daydreaming, idle reverie, or absentmindedness.

wool·len [wŏŏl′ən] *adj., n.* Another spelling of WOOLEN.

wool·ly [wŏŏl′ē] *adj.* **wool·li·er, wool·li·est** *n., pl.* **wool·lies** **1** *adj.* Made of, covered with, or like wool. **2** *n.* (*often pl.*) A woolen garment, especially heavy or woolen underwear. **3** *adj.* Not clear, definite, or precise; fuzzy: *woolly* thinking. **4** *adj.* Rough and exciting: The old West was wild and *woolly*.

woolly bear The caterpillar of certain moths, having a body covered with long, soft hairs.

wool·y [wŏŏl′ē] *adj.* **wool·i·er, wool·i·est**, *n., pl.* **wool·ies** Another spelling of WOOLLY.

word [wûrd] **1** *n.* A spoken sound or group of sounds having a definite meaning. **2** *n.* The letters or characters used in writing or printing such a sound or sounds. **3** *adj. use:* a *word* game.

4 *v.* To write or express in words: How did you *word* the telegram? **5** *n.* (*usually pl.*) Conversation; talk: a man of few *words*. **6** *n.* A brief remark or statement: a *word* of warning. **7** *n.* A piece of news or information: Send him *word* when you arrive. **8** *n.* A command, signal, or direction: Give the *word* to start. **9** *n.* (*pl.*) An angry quarrel: They had *words*. **10** *n.* A promise: to keep one's *word*. **— be as good as one's word** To keep one's promises. **— by word of mouth** By means of speech rather than writing; orally. **— eat one's words** To take back something one has said. **— have a word with** To have a brief conversation with. **— man of his word** A man who keeps his promises. **— mince words** To avoid coming to the point, be evasive. **— take one at his word** To take seriously what a person says and to act accordingly. **— take the words out of one's mouth** To say what another person was just about to say. **— the Word** The Bible. **— word for word** Using exactly the same words.

word·book [wûrd′bŏŏk′] *n.* A collection of words, as a vocabulary or dictionary.

word·ing [wûr′ding] *n.* The way in which something is said, especially in writing; choice and arrangement of words: awkward *wording*.

Words·worth [wûrdz′wûrth′], **William,** 1770–1850, English poet.

word·y [wûr′dē] *adj.* **word·i·er, word·i·est** Using or having more words than is necessary. **— word′i·ness** *n.*

wore [wôr] Past tense of WEAR.

work [wûrk] *n., v.* **worked** (or **wrought:** used in metalwork), **work·ing,** *adj.* **1** *n.* Any labor or effort, whether physical or mental, that is intended to accomplish something. **2** *v.* To exert oneself either physically or mentally in order to accomplish something; labor; toil. **3** *v.* To cause or bring about: to *work* a miracle. **4** *n.* What one does to earn a living; occupation, profession, or trade. **5** *v.* To be employed; have a position or job. **6** *adj.* Of, having to do with, or used for work: *work* clothes. **7** *n.* A place of employment: He is at *work*. **8** *n.* (*pl., usually used with a singular verb*) A factory: The gas *works* is on fire. **9** *v.* To cause to do work: He *works* us too hard. **10** *n.* Something written, painted, composed, etc.; a creation of the imagination: the *works* of Beethoven. **11** *n.* A job, chore, or task. **12** *n.* A person's manner of working or the quality of his work: slow, careful *work*. **13** *v.* To cause to function or be productive; operate: to *work* a machine; to *work* a mine. **14** *v.* To perform properly; operate: This machine *works*. **15** *n.* (*pl.*) The machinery or inner moving parts of something: the *works* of a watch. **16** *n.* A righteous deed: His good *works* live on. **17** *v.* To come or cause to come to some

specified condition: The bolts *worked* loose; He *worked* himself into a passion. **18** *v.* To make or achieve by effort: He *worked* his way through college. **19** *v.* To make, shape, or prepare by toil, skill, or manipulation: He *worked* the copper into a bowl. **20** *v.* To solve: to *work* a puzzle. **21** *v.* To be effective; succeed: His plan *worked* well. **22** *v.* To ferment or cause to ferment: The heat caused the juice to *work*. **23** *v.* To carry on some activity in: to *work* a stream for trout. **24** *n.* In physics, the transfer of energy from one body or system to another. **25** *n.* (*pl.*) *slang* The whole of anything; everything: I sold the *works*. **— shoot the works** *slang* To risk everything in one try or attempt. **— work in** To insert or be inserted. **— work off** To get rid of. **— work on** Try to influence or persuade. **— work out 1** To make its way out or through. **2** To accomplish, solve, or develop. **3** To come to some outcome or result. **4** *informal* To have a workout. **— work up 1** To excite; arouse. **2** To form, shape, or develop. **3** To go or move up; advance.

work·a·ble [wûr′kə·bəl] *adj.* Capable of being worked, put into operation, carried out, etc.: a *workable* plan; in *workable* condition.

work·a·day [wûrk′ə·dā′] *adj.* **1** Of, related to, or fit for working days. **2** Commonplace; ordinary: a *workaday* type of story.

work·bench [wûrk′bench′] *n.* A heavy, strong table on which work is done, as by a carpenter or machinist.

work·book [wûrk′bŏŏk′] *n.* **1** A book based on a course of study, with problems and exercises that a student works out directly on the pages. **2** A book of instructions for running a machine.

work·day [wûrk′dā′] *n.* **1** A day on which work is done, usually not a holiday or Sunday. **2** The part of a day, or the number of hours, spent in work.

work·er [wûr′kər] *n.* **1** A person who works. **2** Any of a class of bees, ants, wasps, or termites unable to produce offspring but performing the work of a hive or colony.

work·horse [wûrk′hôrs′] *n.* **1** A horse used for pulling loads rather than for riding or racing. **2** A person who works very hard.

work·house [wûrk′hous′] *n.* **1** A prison where criminals who commit minor crimes are kept and made to work. **2** *British* A poorhouse where the inmates are made to work.

work·ing [wûr′king] **1** *adj.* Engaged in work or some employment. **2** *adj.* Of, having to do with, or used in work: Monday is a *working* day; *working* shoes. **3** *n.* The act or operation of a person or thing that works: the *working* of nature. **4** *adj.* Enough for use or action: a *working* knowledge of French; a *working* majority. **5** *n.* (*usually pl.*) The part of a mine or quarry where excavation is going on or has gone on.

---

add, āce, câre, pälm; end, ēqual; it, īce; odd, ōpen, ôrder; tŏŏk, pŏŏl; up, bûrn; ə = a in *above*, e in *sicken*, i in *possible*, o in *melon*, u in *circus*; yŏŏ = u in *fuse*; oil; pout; check; ring; thin; this; zh in *vision*. For ¶ reference, see page 64 · HOW TO

work·ing·man [wûr′king·man′] *n., pl.* **work·ing·men** [wûr′king·men′] A man who works, especially a man who does hard, manual labor.

work·man [wûrk′mən] *n., pl.* **work·men** [wûrk′mən] A workingman.

work·man·like [wûrk′mən·līk] *adj.* Done with care and skill.

work·man·ship [wûrk′mən·ship] *n.* **1** The art or skill of a craftsman. **2** The quality of work done: This table shows excellent *workmanship.* **3** Something produced by work.

work·out [wûrk′out′] *n. informal* **1** A session of athletic activity for exercise, practice, or training. **2** Any vigorous activity.

work·room [wûrk′rōōm′] *n.* A room where work is done, especially manual work.

work·shop [wûrk′shop′] *n.* **1** A building or room where work is carried on. **2** A group of people who work on or study together some special project or subject: a drama *workshop.*

world [wûrld] *n.* **1** The earth. **2** A division or part of the earth: the Old *World.* **3** The universe; cosmos. **4** A division or section of things on or of the earth: the animal and plant *worlds.* **5** A definite group of people having common interests, characteristics, etc.: the *world* of sports; the music *world.* **6** The people of the earth; mankind: The *world* knew little of him. **7** The people, places, and things of public or social life: He fled from the *world* and became a monk. **8** A division of time or history: the modern *world.* **9** A great deal or quantity; very much: Your help made a *world* of difference. **— for all the world** In every respect; exactly.

world·ly [wûrld′lē] *adj.* **world·li·er, world·li·est** **1** Of or having to do with the world or earthly existence rather than with religious or spiritual things. **2** Caring a great deal for and knowing a lot about the things of this world: a *worldly* person. **— world′li·ness** *n.*

World War I A war between France, Great Britain, Russia, the United States, etc., on one side and Germany, Austria-Hungary, etc., on the other side. It lasted from 1914 to 1918.

World War II A war between France, England, the Soviet Union, the United States, etc., on one side and Germany, Italy, Japan, etc., on the other side. It lasted from 1939 to 1945.

world·wide [wûrld′wīd′] *adj.* Extended throughout the world: a *worldwide* conflict.

worm [wûrm] **1** *n.* A small, creeping animal having a long, soft, slender body and no legs. **2** *n.* Any creeping animal like a worm. **3** *n.* (*pl.*) A disease due to the presence of parasitic worms in the body. **4** *v.* To get the worms out of: to *worm* a puppy. **5** *n.* Something like a worm in appearance or movement, as the spiral thread of a screw. **6** *n.* A mean, groveling, contemptible person. **7** *v.* To get by stealthy or indirect ways or methods: to *worm* a secret out of someone. **— worm one's way** **1** To move or progress slowly and stealthily, often by crawling or creeping: to *worm one's way* through underbrush. **2** To put oneself in a certain condition or place

by clever, stealthy, or persistent methods: to *worm one's way* into society.

worm gear A toothed wheel turned by a revolving screw.

worm·wood [wûrm′wŏŏd′] *n.* **1** Any of several European herbs or shrubs having a strong smell and bitter taste. **2** Something that causes feelings of bitterness or unpleasantness.

worm·y [wûr′mē] *adj.* **worm·i·er, worm·i·est** **1** Having worms. **2** Spoiled by worms.

worn [wôrn] **1** Past participle of WEAR. **2** *adj.* Damaged or affected by much use or wear: a *worn* suit. **3** *adj.* Tired, as from worry, anxiety, illness, etc.: Her face looked *worn.*

worn-out [wôrn′out′] *adj.* **1** Used until it has no usefulness. **2** Very tired; exhausted.

wor·ri·some [wûr′i·səm] *adj.* **1** Causing worry or anxiety. **2** Often worrying; given to worry.

wor·ry [wûr′ē] *v.* **wor·ried, wor·ry·ing, *n., pl.* wor·ries** **1** *v.* To be or cause to be uneasy in the mind; feel or make anxious: She must not *worry* any longer; You *worry* me. **2** *n.* A feeling of anxiety, vexation, or uneasiness: to be filled with *worry.* **3** *n.* Something that causes such a feeling: Debts were *worries.* **4** *v.* To bother; pester. **5** *v.* To pull, tear, or shake with the teeth, as a dog does. ◆ *Worry* comes from an Old English word meaning *to choke* or *strangle.*

worse [wûrs] **1** Comparative of BAD, BADLY, and ILL. **2** *adj.* More harmful, evil, unpleasant, faulty, etc.: A *worse* deed I can't imagine. **3** *adj.* More ill; less well: The patient is *worse* today. **4** *adv.* In a worse way or degree: He played *worse* than usual. **5** *n.* Something more unsatisfactory or evil: There is even *worse* to come.

wors·en [wûr′sən] *v.* To make or become worse.

wor·ship [wûr′ship] *n., v.* **wor·shiped** or **wor·shipped, wor·ship·ing** or **wor·ship·ping** **1** *n.* Respect, honor, or love given to God or something held sacred. **2** *n.* A prayer or rite showing such feeling. **3** *v.* To express such feeling to, by a prayer or rite. **4** *v.* To participate in a church service: They *worship* every Sunday. **5** *n.* Great love or admiration for someone or something. **6** *v.* To love or admire a great deal: to *worship* one's father. **7** *n. British* A title of honor used in addressing persons of rank or station: your *worship;* his *worship.* **— wor′ship·er** or **wor′ship·per** *n.*

wor·ship·ful [wûr′ship·fəl] *adj.* **1** Giving or feeling worship. **2** *British* Worthy of respect: the *worshipful* master.

worst [wûrst] **1** Superlative of BAD, BADLY, and ILL. **2** *adj.* Most harmful, evil, unpleasant, faulty, etc.: the *worst* performance of all. **3** *adv.* In the worst way or degree: He sang *worst* of all. **4** *n.* That which is worst: The *worst* that can happen is a scolding. **5** *v.* To defeat; vanquish: They *worsted* us badly. **— at worst** Under the most unfavorable circumstances. **— if worst comes to worst** If the worst or most awful thing actually happens. **— in the worst way** *slang* Very much.

wors·ted [wŏŏs′tid *or* wûr′stid] *n.* **1** A yarn

spun from long strands of wool. **2** Cloth woven with this yarn, having a firm surface and no nap. **3** *adj. use:* a *worsted* suit.

worth [wûrth] **1** *n.* Any quality or qualities that can make a person or thing valuable, desirable, useful, etc.: a teacher of great *worth*. **2** *prep.* Deserving of: a place *worth* a visit. **3** *n.* The value of anything in money or other exchangeable goods: a car of little *worth*. **4** *prep.* Equal in value to; exchangeable for: a house *worth* $20,000. **5** *n.* The amount of something to be had for a specific sum: three cents' *worth* of candy. **6** *n.* Wealth: What is his *worth*? **7** *prep.* Having money or possessions amounting to.

worth·less [wûrth′lis] *adj.* Having no worth, value, goodness, or usefulness. **— worth′less·ness** *n.*

worth·while [wûrth′(h)wīl′] *adj.* Having enough value or importance to be worth the effort, time, money, etc., involved: a *worthwhile* trip.

wor·thy [wûr′thē] *adj.* **wor·thi·er, wor·thi·est,** *n., pl.* **wor·thies 1** *adj.* Having worth, value, or merit: a *worthy* charity. **2** *adj.* Fit or suitable for; deserving: courage *worthy* of a better cause. **3** *n.* A person of great worth. **— wor′thi·ly** *adv.* **— wor′thi·ness** *n.*

wot [wot] Present tense of WIT²: formerly used with nouns or with *I, he, she,* or *it,* as in "God *wot*" which means "God knows."

would [wŏŏd] Past tense of WILL, used chiefly, however, as a helping verb to express: **1** Desire or inclination: those who *would* ban noisy scooters. **2** Something depending on a condition contrary to the actual one: He *would* give if he were able. **3** Determination: He *would* not speak. **4** Preference: We *would* have you succeed rather than fail. **5** Request: *Would* you give us a call? **6** Custom or habit: We *would* ride together every day. **7** Doubt or uncertainty: It *would* seem to be wrong. ◆ See SHOULD.

would-be [wŏŏd′bē′] *adj.* **1** Desiring or pretending to be: a *would-be* poet. **2** Intended to be: His *would-be* jokes annoyed us all.

would·n't [wŏŏd′(ə)nt] Would not.

wouldst [wŏŏdst] *v.* A form of the verb WOULD, used with *thou:* seldom used today.

wound¹ [wŏŏnd] **1** *n.* A hurt or injury caused by something piercing, cutting, or tearing through the skin. **2** *v.* To injure by penetrating through the skin. **3** *n.* Any hurt to the feelings, pride, etc. **4** *v.* To injure in the feelings, pride, etc.

wound² [wound] Past tense and past participle of WIND²: He *wound* the clock last night.

wove [wōv] Past tense and alternative past participle of WEAVE.

wo·ven [wō′vən] Past participle of WEAVE.

wrack [rak] *n.* **1** Ruin and destruction, especially in the phrase **wrack and ruin. 2** Seaweed or other vegetation washed ashore by the sea.

wraith [rāth] *n.* **1** A ghostlike image of a person, seen shortly before or shortly after his death. **2** Any ghost or specter.

wran·gle [rang′gəl] *v.* **wran·gled, wran·gling,** *n.* **1** *v.* To argue or quarrel noisily or angrily. **2** *n.* An angry or noisy quarrel. **3** *v. U.S.* To herd or round up (horses).

wrap [rap] *v.* **wrapped** or **wrapt** [rapt], **wrap·ping,** *n.* **1** *v.* To surround and cover by something folded or wound about: She *wrapped* the rolls in a napkin. **2** *v.* To wind or fold about something: We *wrapped* a towel around his head. **3** *v.* To cover with paper or the like and tie or fasten: to *wrap* a box. **4** *n.* An outer cloak or garment. **5** *v.* To blot out or conceal; envelop: The city was *wrapped* in smoke. **— wrapped up in 1** To be clothed or enveloped by. **2** To be exclusively interested or involved in.

wrap·per [rap′ər] *n.* **1** Something used to cover or protect, as a paper wrapped around a magazine before mailing. **2** A woman's dressing gown. **3** A person or thing that wraps.

wrap·ping [rap′ing] *n.* (*often pl.*) A covering in which something is wrapped.

wrapt [rapt] An alternative past tense and past participle of WRAP.

wrath [rath] *n.* Great or violent anger; rage.

wrath·ful [rath′fəl] *adj.* Extremely angry; feeling or showing wrath. **— wrath′ful·ly** *adv.*

wreak [rēk] *v.* **1** To give free expression to (anger, hatred, etc.). **2** To inflict (vengeance, punishment, etc.): He *wreaked* vengeance on us.

wreath [rēth] *n., pl.* **wreaths** [rēthz] **1** A ring of flowers or leaves woven together. **2** Any curled or spiral shape, as of smoke.

wreathe [rēth] *v.* **wreathed, wreath·ing 1** To form into a wreath: to *wreathe* flowers. **2** To decorate or encircle with or as if with wreaths: to *wreathe* a window at Christmas. **3** To cover or envelop: His face was *wreathed* in smiles.

wreck [rek] **1** *v.* To undergo or cause to undergo ruin, damage, or destruction: The storm *wrecked* the ship. **2** *v.* To tear down: to *wreck* a building. **3** *n.* Something that has been ruined, damaged, or destroyed: We saw a *wreck* on the side of the road. **4** *n.* Destruction, ruin, or loss: The depression led to the *wreck* of many banks. **5** *v.* To change, frustrate, or put an end to: The rain *wrecked* our plans. **6** *n.* A person who is physically, mentally, or morally in a very bad condition.

wreck·age [rek′ij] *n.* **1** The act of wrecking. **2** A wrecked condition. **3** The remains or fragments of a wreck.

wreck·er [rek′ər] *n.* **1** A person or thing that causes destruction, damage, frustration, etc. **2** A person whose occupation is tearing down old buildings, bridges, etc. **3** A person, train, car, or machine that clears away wrecks.

---

add, āce, câre, pälm; end, ēqual; it, īce; odd, ōpen, ôrder; tŏŏk, pōōl; up, bûrn;
ə = a in *above,* e in *sicken,* i in *possible,* o in *melon,* u in *circus;* yōō = u in *fuse;* oil; pout;
check; ring; thin; this; zh in *vision.* For ¶ reference, see page 64 · HOW TO

wren [ren] *n.* Any of numerous small songbirds, having a short, sometimes upturned tail.

wrench [rench] **1** *v.* To twist or pull violently or with force: He *wrenched* the knife from her hand. **2** *n.* A violent twist: Give the lid a *wrench* and it will come off. **3** *v.* To twist, so as to cause a sprain or injury: I *wrenched* my shoulder. **4** *n.* A sprain or injury caused by a sharp or violent twist or pull. **5** *n.* Any of various tools for holding or turning bolts, nuts, pipe, etc. **6** *n.* Any sudden grief or pain: It gave us a *wrench* to say goodbye. **7** *v.* To distort (what another says) so as to change the intended meaning.

Wrenches

wrest [rest] *v.* **1** To pull or force away by violent twisting or wringing: to *wrest* a weapon from one's grasp. **2** To seize by violence: to *wrest* power from a king. **3** To twist (words) into meanings not intended. **4** To gain or get by toil and effort: to *wrest* a living from barren soil.

wres·tle [res′(ə)l] *v.* **wres·tled, wres·tling,** *n.* **1** *v.* To engage in wrestling. **2** *v.* To engage in a wrestling contest with. **3** *n.* The act of wrestling. **4** *v.* To struggle for mastery, a solution, etc.: to *wrestle* with a problem. **5** *n.* Any hard struggle. **— wres′tler** *n.*

wres·tling [res′ling] *n.* A sport or exercise in which each of two unarmed contestants tries to throw or force the other to the ground or into a certain position on the ground.

wretch [rech] *n.* **1** A vile or wicked person. **2** An unfortunate or miserable person.

wretch·ed [rech′id] *adj.* **1** Very unhappy, miserable, or dejected. **2** Causing discomfort, misery, or grief: *wretched* surroundings. **3** Mean, wicked, or bad: a *wretched* criminal. **4** Poor, worthless, or unsatisfactory: a *wretched* movie. **— wretch′ed·ly** *adv.* **— wretch′ed·ness** *n.*

wri·er [rī′ər] The comparative of WRY.

wri·est [rī′əst] The superlative of WRY.

wrig·gle [rig′əl] *v.* **wrig·gled, wrig·gling,** *n.* **1** *v.* To twist or squirm: After an hour all the children were *wriggling* in their chairs. **2** *v.* To move or proceed by twisting or crawling: The worm *wriggled* across my hand. **3** *n.* A wriggling motion. **4** *v.* To escape or get out of something in a sneaky, sly manner: He *wriggles* out of every unpleasant situation. **— wrig′gler** *n.*

wright [rīt] *n.* A person who builds, writes, or creates: used chiefly in combination, as in *shipwright*, a builder of ships.

Wright [rīt], **Frank Lloyd,** 1869–1959, U.S. architect.

Wright [rīt], **Orville,** 1871–1948, and his brother **Wilbur,** 1867–1912, U.S. pioneers in aviation who built and flew an airplane in 1903, the first successful flight.

wri·ly [rī′lē] *adv.* Another spelling of WRYLY.

wring [ring] *v.* **wrung** [rung], **wring·ing,** *n.* **1** *v.* To squeeze or twist, usually to get water out of something: to *wring* wet clothes. **2** *v.* To

squeeze or press out, usually by twisting: to *wring* water out of a bathing suit. **3** *v.* To get or acquire by force, violence, or threats: to *wring* an answer out of someone. **4** *v.* To press and twist (the hands) together: She *wrung* her hands. **5** *v.* To make sad; torment: The family's poverty *wrung* our hearts. **6** *n.* The act of wringing. **— wring′er** *n.*

wrin·kle [ring′kəl] *n., v.* **wrin·kled, wrin·kling** **1** *n.* A small ridge, crease, or fold on a surface: *wrinkles* on one's skin. **2** *v.* To make a wrinkle or wrinkles in: to *wrinkle* a dress. **3** *v.* To become wrinkled: His face *wrinkled* with laughter.

wrist [rist] *n.* The joint that connects the hand and the forearm.

wrist·band [rist′band′] *n.* **1** The part of a sleeve that covers the wrist; cuff. **2** A strap for a wrist watch.

wrist watch A watch on a band or bracelet worn on the wrist.

writ [rit] **1** A past tense and past participle of WRITE: seldom used today. **2** *n.* An order written and issued by a court of law commanding the person to whom it is issued to do or not to do something. **3** *n.* Something written, now chiefly used in **Holy Writ,** meaning the Bible.

write [rīt] *v.* **wrote, writ·ten, writ·ing** **1** To make or form (letters, words, numbers, etc.) on a surface, usually with a pen or pencil. **2** To make or put down the letters, words, numbers, etc., of: *Write* your phone number in this space. **3** To cover or fill with writing: to *write* ten pages every day. **4** To tell or tell something to by writing, usually by writing a letter: He *wrote* that he would be home soon; They *wrote* us every day. **5** To be the author or composer of: to *write* a song. **6** To be a writer: He *writes* for a living. **7** To produce a specified quality of writing: She *writes* very well. **8** To draw up or draft by writing: to *write* a check or a will. **9** To show or make visible: Fear was *written* on his face. **— write down** To put into writing. **— write off** To cancel (debts, etc.). **— write out 1** To put into writing. **2** To write in full or complete form. **— write up** To describe in writing.

writ·er [rī′tər] *n.* A person who writes, especially a person who writes for a living.

write-up [rīt′up′] *n. informal* A written description, record, or account of something.

writhe [rīth] *v.* **writhed, writh·ing** **1** To twist or distort the body, face, etc., as in pain. **2** To suffer mentally from embarrassment, shame, sorrow, etc.

writ·ing [rī′ting] *n.* **1** The act of a person who writes. **2** Anything written or expressed in letters, especially a literary composition. **3** Handwriting: I can't read her *writing*. **4** Written form: Your order must be in *writing*. **5** The art or profession of a writer.

writ·ten [rit′(ə)n] Past participle of WRITE.

wrong [rông] **1** *adj.* Not right, moral, just, lawful, etc.: It is *wrong* to cheat. **2** *adj.* Not correct or true: a *wrong* estimate. **3** *adj.* Not suitable, fit, or proper: the *wrong* clothes. **4** *n.* Something that is wrong, especially an evil or unjust act: I did him a *wrong*. **5** *v.* To do something that is wrong, evil, or unjust to: You *wrong* him by saying that. **6** *adj.* Not working or acting properly: Something is *wrong* with the lock. **7** *adj.* Not desired or intended: to take a *wrong* road. **8** *adv.* In a wrong direction or place: You turned *wrong*. **9** *adv.* In a wrong, incorrect, or unsatisfactory manner: to answer *wrong*. **10** *n.* The condition of being wrong: to be in the *wrong*. **11** *adj.* Intended or made to be turned under, inward, or so as not to be seen: the *wrong* side of the cloth. **— go wrong 1** To turn out badly or unsatisfactorily. **2** To do things that are not right, good, or just. **— wrong'ly** *adv.*

wrong·do·ing [rông'dōō'ing] *n.* The doing of something evil or wicked. **— wrong'do'er** *n.*

wrong·ful [rông'fəl] *adj.* Not right, just, lawful, etc.; wrong. **— wrong'ful·ly** *adv.*

wrong·head·ed [rông'hed'id] *adj.* Stubbornly wrong in one's ideas, judgments, opinions, etc.

wrote [rōt] Past tense of WRITE.

wroth [rôth] *adj.* Angry; furious: seldom used today.

wrought [rôt] **1** A past tense and past participle of WORK. **2** *adj.* Beaten or hammered into shape by tools: *wrought* gold. **3** *adj.* Formed or fashioned: a delicately *wrought* clock. **— wrought up** Excited; agitated: She gets *wrought up* over trifles.

wrought iron Iron with little carbon in it, that can be easily forged or hammered into various shapes but is very strong and hard to break or crack.

wrung [rung] Past tense and past participle of WRING: Have you *wrung* the clothes dry?

wry [rī] *adj.* **wri·er, wri·est 1** Bent, twisted, or turned to one side: a *wry* smile. **2** Grim, bitter, or ironic: His comments are full of *wry* humor. **— wry'ly** *adv.*

wt. Abbreviation of WEIGHT.

W. Va. Abbreviation of WEST VIRGINIA.

Wyo. Abbreviation of WYOMING.

Wy·o·ming [wī-ō'ming] *n.* A state in the NW U.S.

X

x or **X** [eks] *n., pl.* **x's** or **X's** [ek'siz] **1** The 24th letter of the English alphabet. **2** An unknown quantity, factor, result, etc. **3** (*usually written* **X**) The Roman numeral for ten. **4** A mark shaped like an X, representing the signature of a person who cannot write. **5** A mark used in maps, diagrams, etc., to direct attention to a place, a figure, etc.

Xa·vi·er [zā'vē·ər *or* zav'ē·ər], **Saint Francis,** 1506–1552, Spanish missionary in the Orient.

X-ax·is [eks'ak'sis] *n., pl.* **X-ax·es** [eks'ak'·sēz] On a graph, the axis that extends most usually from the left of the figure to the right; the axis of abscissas.

X-chro·mo·some [eks'krō'·mə·sōm] *n.* One of the paired chromosomes that determine sex in animals and plants.

xe·bec [zē'bek] *n.* A small, three-masted vessel, formerly used by Algerian pirates in the Mediterranean Sea.

X-axis and Y-axis

xe·non [zē'non] *n.* A heavy gaseous element found in small quantities in the air.

Xen·o·phon [zen'ə·fən], 435?–355? B.C., Greek historian and soldier.

Xerx·es I [zûrk'sēz], 519?–465? B.C., king of Persia, 486?–465? B.C.

Xmas Christmas. ◆ The *X* in *Xmas* stands for the Greek letter *chi*, which is the first letter of *Christ* when written in Greek. *X* has been used as a symbol for *Christ* for hundreds of years, but *Xmas* should be avoided in formal writing.

X-ray [eks'rā'] **1** *n.* (*usually pl.*) Electromagnetic waves that have very short wavelengths and great penetrating power. Their ability to penetrate solids makes them useful in medical diagnosis and in inspecting machine parts. **2** *adj. use:* an *X-ray* machine. **3** *n.* A picture made with X-rays. **4** *v.* To examine, photograph, or treat with X-rays. ◆ The word *X-rays* is a translation from the German. They were so named because their nature was unknown.

Xylophone

xy·lem [zī'ləm] *n.* The woody tissue of a plant, found in the stems or trunk.

xy·lo·phone [zī'lə·fōn] *n.* A musical instrument having wooden bars of different sizes that are sounded by being struck with mallets.

---

add, **ā**ce, c**â**re, p**ä**lm;　**e**nd, **ē**qual;　**i**t, **ī**ce;　**o**dd, **ō**pen, **ô**rder;　t**oŏ**k, p**oō**l;　**u**p, b**û**rn;

ə = a in *above*, e in *sicken*, i in *possible*, o in *melon*, u in *circus*;　**yoō** = u in *fuse*;　**oi**l;　p**ou**t;

check;　ri**ng**;　**th**in;　**th**is;　**zh** in *vision*.　For ¶ reference, see page 64 · HOW TO

Y

y or **Y** [wī] *n.*, *pl.* **y's** or **Y's** [wīz] **1** The 25th letter of the English alphabet. **2** Anything shaped like Y: a *Y* in the road.

y. Abbreviation of: **1** YARD(S). **2** YEAR(S).

-y¹ A suffix meaning: **1** Having the quality of or full of, as in *snowy*, having the quality or full of snow. **2** Resembling or like, as in *summery*, like summer. **3** Somewhat; rather, as in *chilly*, somewhat chill. **4** Inclined to; apt to, as in *sleepy*, inclined to sleep.

-y² A suffix meaning: **1** The quality or state of being, as in *victory*, the state of being victorious. **2** The act, action, or activity of, as in *entreaty*, the act of entreating.

-y³ A suffix meaning: **1** Little; small, as in *kitty*, little kitten. **2** Dear, as in *aunty* or *Billy*.

yacht [yot] **1** *n.* A vessel for racing or for private cruising for pleasure. **2** *v.* To cruise, race, or sail in a yacht. — **yacht'ing** *n.*

yachts·man [yots'mən] *n.*, *pl.* **yachts·men** [yots'mən] A person who owns or sails a yacht.

yak [yak] *n.* A large ox with long hair, found in Tibet and central Asia, often used as a beast of burden.

yam [yam] *n.* **1** The fleshy, edible root of any of several vines growing mostly in warm regions. **2** The vine having such a root. **3** A variety of sweet potato.

Yak, to 6 ft. high at shoulder

Yang·tze [yang'(t)sē'] *n.* The longest river of Asia, flowing from the Tibetan highlands to the China Sea.

yank [yangk] *informal* **1** *v.* To jerk or pull suddenly. **2** *n.* A sudden, sharp pull; jerk.

Yan·kee [yang'kē] **1** *n.* A person born or living in New England. **2** *n.* A person born or living in the northern United States. **3** *n.* A person born in or a citizen of the United States; an American: chiefly a foreign usage. **4** *adj.* Of or having to do with a Yankee or Yankees.

yap [yap] *n.*, *v.* **yapped**, **yap·ping 1** *n.* A bark or yelp. **2** *v.* To bark or yelp.

yard¹ [yärd] *n.* **1** A measure of length equal to 3 feet, or 36 inches, or 0.914 meter. **2** A long, slender pole set crosswise on a mast and used to support sails.

yard² [yärd] *n.* **1** A piece of ground next to or around a residence, church, school, etc. **2** An enclosed area used for some specific work: often used in combination, as in *shipyard*. **3** An area

with tracks where cars are stored, trains made up, etc.

yard·age [yär'dij] *n.* The amount or length of something, expressed in yards.

yard·arm [yärd'ärm'] *n.* Either end of a yard that supports a sail.

yard·stick [yärd'stik'] *n.* **1** A measuring stick a yard in length. **2** Any standard of comparison.

yarn [yärn] *n.* **1** Any spun strand, natural or synthetic, prepared for use in weaving, knitting, etc. **2** An adventure story, especially one that is made up.

yar·row [yar'ō] *n.* Any of several hardy perennial plants having narrow, fernlike leaves, clusters of small flowers, and a sharp smell.

yaw [yô] **1** *v.* To turn or move out of its course, as a ship when struck by a heavy sea. **2** *n.* A movement away from a straight course.

yawl [yôl] **1** *n.* A sailboat with a mainmast near the bow and a shorter mast very near the stern. **2** A ship's boat, rowed by oars.

yawn [yôn] **1** *v.* To open the mouth wide, usually in a way that cannot be controlled, with a long intake of breath, as when one is sleepy or bored. **2** *n.* The act of yawning: He tried to stifle a *yawn*. **3** *v.* To be or stand wide open, as a cave.

Yawl

yaws [yôz] *n.pl.* A contagious disease of the tropics, marked by skin eruptions.

Y-ax·is [wī'ak'sis] *n.*, *pl.* **Y-ax·es** [wī'ak'sēz] On a graph, the axis that is most usually vertical; the axis of ordinates. See picture at X-AXIS.

Y-chro·mo·some [wī'krō'mə·sōm] *n.* One of the paired chromosomes that determine sex in animals and plants.

y·clept or **y·cleped** [i·klept'] *adj.* Called; named: seldom used today.

yd. Abbreviation of: **1** YARD. **2** (*usually written* **yds.**) Yards.

ye¹ [yē] *pron.* You: seldom used today.

ye² [ᵺē] *adj.* The: a mistaken form resulting from the substitution of the character *y* for the character that represented the sound *th* in the Old English alphabet: seldom used today.

yea [yā] **1** *adv.* Yes: seldom used today. **2** *adv.* In reality; indeed. **3** *n.* An affirmative vote or voter.

year [yir] *n.* **1** The period of time in which the earth completes one revolution around the sun, consisting of 365 or, in leap year, 366 days, divided into 12 months, beginning January 1 and ending December 31. **2** A period of 12 months starting at any time: *a year* from now. **3** A period of time, usually less than a year, given over to some special work, activity, etc.: the school *year*. **4** (*pl.*) Age: He is active for his *years*. **— year after year** Every year.

year·book [yir′b͝ook′] *n.* A book published annually presenting information about the previous year.

year·ling [yir′ling *or* yûr′ling] **1** *n.* An animal between one and two years old. **2** *adj.* A year old: *a yearling* filly.

year·ly [yir′lē] **1** *adj.* Happening, done, seen, etc., once a year: *a yearly* visit. **2** *adv.* Once a year; annually: He pays us a visit *yearly*. **3** *adj.* Of, for, or lasting for a year: *a yearly* income.

yearn [yûrn] *v.* **1** To have an earnest desire; feel a longing: to *yearn* for security. **2** To be deeply moved; feel sympathy. **— yearn′ing** *n.*

yeast [yēst] *n.* **1** A substance formed by the clumping together of certain tiny fungi in a thick, frothy, yellow mass. It is used to make bread rise and in the brewing of beer. **2** A cake of this substance mixed with flour or meal.

yell [yel] **1** *v.* To shout; scream; roar. **2** *n.* A sharp, loud cry or scream. **3** *v.* To cheer. **4** *n.* A rhythmic cheer, made up of a series of words or nonsense syllables and shouted by a group, as at a football game.

yel·low [yel′ō] **1** *n.* The color of ripe lemons or of sunflowers. **2** *adj.* Of or having this color. **3** *v.* To make or become yellow. **4** *n.* Any paint or dye having such a color. **5** *adj.* Having a yellowish complexion. **6** *n.* The yolk of an egg. **7** *adj. informal* Cowardly. **— yel′low·ish** *adj.* **— yel′low·ness** *n.*

yellow fever An infectious disease of warm countries caused by a virus transmitted to man by the bite of certain mosquitoes. It is marked by fever, vomiting, and a yellowing of the skin.

yel·low·ham·mer [yel′ō·ham′ər] *n.* A bird like the bunting, the male of which has bright yellow plumage.

yellow jack 1 The yellow flag raised on a ship in quarantine. **2** Yellow fever.

yellow jacket Any of various wasps having bright yellow markings on the body.

Yellow River Another name for Hwang Ho.

Yellow Sea An inlet of the Pacific Ocean between Korea and China.

Yel·low·stone National Park [yel′ō·stōn] The largest and oldest U.S. national park, largely in NW Wyoming, famous for geysers, hot springs, etc.

yelp [yelp] **1** *n.* A sharp, shrill cry or bark. **2** *v.* To utter or express by a yelp.

Yem·en [yem′ən *or* yä′mən] *n.* A country in SW Arabia.

yen[1] [yen] *n., pl.* **yen** The basic unit of money in Japan.

yen[2] [yen] *informal* An intense longing or desire.

yeo·man [yō′mən] *n., pl.* **yeo·men** [yō′mən] **1** In the U.S. Navy or Coast Guard, a petty officer who performs clerical duties. **2** *British* A person who cultivates his own farm.

yes [yes] *adv., n., pl.* **yes·es** *or* **yes·ses 1** *adv.* As you say; truly; just so. **2** *adv.* And in addition; moreover: He will lie to you, *yes*, and cheat you as well. **3** *n.* An affirmative reply: My answer to your question is "*yes*." **4** *n.* A vote in favor of something.

yes·ter·day [yes′tər·dē *or* yes′tər·dā′] **1** *n.* The day before today. **2** *adv.* On the day before today. **3** *n.* The near past. **4** *adv.* In the near past.

yes·ter·night [yes′tər·nīt′] **1** *n.* The night last past. **2** *adv.* In or during the night last past. ◆ This word is used mostly in poems.

yes·ter·year [yes′tər·yir′] **1** *n.* Last year. **2** *adv.* In or during the last year. ◆ This word is used mostly in poems.

yet [yet] **1** *adv.* Up to the present time; so far: He hasn't lied to me *yet*. **2** *adv.* At the present time; now: Don't go *yet*. **3** *adv.* Now as previously; still: I can hear him *yet*. **4** *adv.* Sometime; eventually: He'll succeed *yet*. **5** *adv.* After all the time passed away: Aren't you ready *yet*? **6** *adv.* In addition; still: We have to go a mile *yet*. **7** *adv.* Even; still: a *yet* higher price. **8** *adv.* Nevertheless; however: It was hot, *yet* not unpleasant. **9** *conj.* Nevertheless; but: I ask as a friend, *yet* you will not help. **— as yet** Up to now.

yew [y͞oo] *n.* **1** Any of various evergreen trees having flat, slender needles, a berrylike fruit, and a hard, fine-grained wood. **2** The wood of the yew.

Yid·dish [yid′ish] **1** *n.* A Germanic language written in Hebrew letters and spoken by many Jews in central and eastern Europe and by Jewish immigrants in other places. **2** *adj.* Of or having to do with Yiddish; written or spoken in Yiddish.

yield [yēld] **1** *v.* To give forth; produce: The field will *yield* a good crop. **2** *n.* The amount yielded; product; result. **3** *v.* To give up, as to superior power; surrender: to *yield* a fortress. **4** *v.* To grant or concede: to *yield* consent. **5** *v.* To give way, as to pressure or force. **6** *v.* To assent; consent: to *yield* to persuasion. **7** *v.* To give place: I *yield* to no man.

yield·ing [yēl′ding] *adj.* Willing or likely to yield; submissive.

Y.M.C.A. Abbreviation of Young Men's Christian Association.

yo·del [yōd′(ə)l] *v.* **yo·deled** *or* **yo·delled, yo·del·ing** *or* **yo·del·ling,** *n.* **1** *v.* To sing in the form of a warble, by changing one's voice rapidly back and forth from its natural tone to a shrill falsetto, as is done in the Swiss mountains. **2** *n.*

---

add, āce, câre, pälm;   end, ēqual;   it, īce;   odd, ōpen, ôrder;   t͝ook, p͞ool;   up, bûrn; ə = a in *above*, e in *sicken*, i in *possible*, o in *melon*, u in *circus*;   y͞oo = u in *fuse*;   oil;   pout; check; ring; thin; this; zh in *vision*.   For ¶ reference, see page 64 · HOW TO

The act or sound of yodeling. **3** *n.* A melody sung by yodeling. — **yo′del·er** or **yo′del·ler** *n.*

yo·ga [yō′gə] *n.* **1** A Hindu system of mystical philosophy and meditation in which the individual human spirit seeks union with that of the universe. **2** A related system of exercises which help to attain physical and mental well-being. ◆ *Yoga* comes from a Hindustani word derived from a Sanskrit word meaning *union.*

yo·gurt or **yo·ghurt** [yō′gŏŏrt] *n.* A thick milk food made by the addition of bacteria to curdled milk. ◆ *Yogurt* comes from a Turkish word.

yoke [yōk] *n., v.* **yoked, yok·ing 1** *n.* A curved, wooden frame with attachments used to join together two animals, as oxen. **2** *v.* To attach (an animal): to *yoke* an ox to a plow. **3** *n., pl.* **yoke** A pair of animals, as oxen, joined by a yoke. **4** *n.* Any of various yokelike de-

Yoke

vices, as a frame fitted to a person's shoulders for carrying a bucket hung at each end. **5** *v.* To put a yoke upon. **6** *v.* To join or unite: to be *yoked* in marriage. **7** *n.* Something that binds or connects; bond: the *yoke* of love. **8** *n.* A force or influence that holds people in submission or bondage: under the *yoke* of tyranny. **9** *n.* A fitted part of a garment, usually over the shoulders or hips.

yo·kel [yō′kəl] *n.* A simple or naive country fellow.

Yo·ko·ha·ma [yō′kə·hä′mə] *n.* A port city of Japan.

yolk [yōk] *n.* The yellow portion of an egg.

Yom Kip·pur [yom kip′ər] A Jewish holiday marked by prayer and fasting for 24 hours; the Day of Atonement.

yon [yon] *adj., adv.* Yonder: seldom used today.

yon·der [yon′dər] **1** *adj.* Being at a distance, but in sight. **2** *adv.* In or to that place; there.

yore [yôr] *n.* Time long past. — **of yore** Of long ago: in days *of yore.*

York·shire [yôrk′shir] *n.* A county of NE England.

Yorkshire pudding A batter cake baked under roasting meat so as to catch the drippings.

York·town [yôrk′toun] *n.* A town in SE Virginia where a large British force surrendered in the Revolutionary War.

Yo·sem·i·te National Park [yō·sem′ə·tē] A national park in east central California. A section of the park, **Yosemite Valley,** is noted for its famous waterfalls.

you [yōō] *pron., pl.* **you 1** The person or persons addressed: *You* are right; I'll see *you* tomorrow. **2** Any person; one: *You* learn by trying. ◆ The expression *you all,* sometimes pronounced [yôl], is especially common in the American South. It has the meaning of the

plural *you.* "How are *you* all?" means "How are you and your family?"

you'd [yōōd] **1** You had. **2** You would.

you'll [yōōl] **1** You will. **2** You shall.

young [yung] *adj.* **young·er** [yung′gər], **young·est** [yung′gist], *n.* **1** *adj.* Being in the early period of life, growth, or development; not old: a *young* boy; The night is still *young.* **2** *n. use* Young people: *The young* are often foolhardy. **3** *n.* Offspring, especially of animals: The lioness played with her *young.* **4** *adj.* Of or having to do with youth or early life; fresh; vigorous: My grandmother has *young* ideas. **5** *adj.* Inexperienced; immature: He is a little *young* to read that book. **6** *adj.* Younger than another person having the same name or title; junior: I came to see *young* Fred, not Fred, senior. — **with young** With child; pregnant.

Young [yung], **Brigham,** 1801–1877, U.S. Mormon leader.

young·ish [yung′ish] *adj.* Rather young.

young·ling [yung′ling] **1** *n.* A young person, animal, or plant. **2** *adj.* Young. ◆ This word is seldom used today.

young·ster [yung′stər] *n.* A child or young person.

your [yôr *or* yŏŏr] *pron.* A possessive form of YOU used before the person or thing possessed: *your* hat.

you're [yŏŏr *or* yôr] You are.

yours [yôrz *or* yŏŏrz] *pron.* A possessive form of YOU used standing alone: My bike is lighter than *yours.* ◆ *Yours* is often used with another word at the end of a letter to form a polite closing, as in "Sincerely *yours.*"

your·self [yôr·self′ *or* yŏŏr·self′] *pron., pl.* **your·selves** [yôr·selvz′ *or* yŏŏr·selvz′] **1** The one that you really are; your very own self. *Yourself* in this sense is used to refer back to the subject *you* or to make *you* more emphatic: You help *yourself;* You *yourselves* must do it. **2** Your normal, usual, or proper self: Why can't you be *yourself* instead of putting on airs?

youth [yōōth] *n., pl.* **youths** [yōōths *or* yōŏthz] **1** The period of time when one is young; the part of life between childhood and manhood. **2** The condition or quality of being young: The old man is full of *youth.* **3** The early period of being or development: during the *youth* of a nation. **4** A young man. **5** (*often used with a plural verb*) Young people as a group: The *youth* of that community are very well educated.

youth·ful [yōōth′fəl] *adj.* **1** Having youth; being still young. **2** Having the quality of youth; fresh; vigorous: a *youthful* outlook on life. **3** Of, having to do with, or proper for youth: a *youthful* wardrobe.

you've [yōōv] You have.

yowl [youl] **1** *n.* A loud, prolonged, wailing cry; a howl. **2** *v.* To make such a sound; howl; yell.

yo-yo [yō′yō′] *n., pl.* **yo-yos** A wheellike toy with a string about it in a deep groove. The yo-yo spins up and down the string which is held and manipulated by the operator's hand.

yr. Abbreviation of: **1** YEAR. **2** (*usually written* **yrs.**) Years.

Yu·ca·tán [yōō′kə·tan′] *n.* A peninsula of SE Mexico and NE Central America.

yuc·ca [yuk′ə] *n.* Any of various plants of the southern U.S. and Mexico having long pointed leaves and clusters of white bell-shaped flowers growing on a tall stalk.

Yu·go·slav [yōō′gō·släv] **1** *n.* A person born in or a citizen of Yugoslavia. **2** *adj.* Of or having to do with Yugoslavia or its people.

Yu·go·sla·vi·a [yōō′gō·slä′vē·ə] *n.* A country in SE Europe, on the Adriatic Sea. — **Yu′go· sla′vi·an** *adj., n.*

Yu·kon [yōō′kon] *n.* **1** A territory of NW Canada. **2** A river in NW Canada and central Alaska.

yule [yōōl] *n.* (*often written* **Yule**) Christmas time, or the feast of Christmas.

yule log A large log burned on Christmas eve.

yule·tide [yōōl′tīd′] *n.* (*often written* **Yuletide**) Christmas time.

Y.W.C.A. Abbreviation of YOUNG WOMEN'S CHRISTIAN ASSOCIATION.

Z

z or **Z** [zē] *n., pl.* **z's** or **Z's** The 26th letter of the English alphabet.

Zam·be·zi [zam·bē′zē] *n.* A river in southern Africa flowing to the Indian Ocean.

za·ny [zā′nē] *adj.* **za·ni·er, za·ni·est,** *n., pl.* **za·nies 1** *adj.* Odd and comical; funny; ridiculous: a *zany* movie. **2** *n.* An odd, funny person. **3** *n.* A fool.

Zan·zi·bar [zan′zə·bär] *n.* An island off the coast of eastern Africa, forming part of Tanzania.

zeal [zēl] *n.* Great interest and devotion, as when working for a cause; enthusiasm.

zeal·ot [zel′ət] *n.* A person who displays too much zeal or enthusiasm; fanatic.

zeal·ous [zel′əs] *adj.* Filled with or caused by zeal. — **zeal′· ous·ly** *adv.*

ze·bra [zē′brə] *n.* Any

Zebra, about 4 ft. high at shoulder

of several wild animals of Africa related to the horse, having white or tan bodies striped with dark bands.

ze·bu [zē′byōō] *n.* A domesticated ox of Asia and Africa, having a hump on the shoulders, a large dewlap, and short, curved horns.

Zech·a·ri·ah [zek′ə· rī′ə] *n.* **1** In the Bible, a Hebrew prophet of the 6th century B.C. **2** A book of the Old Testament named after him.

Zebu, about 4 ft. high at shoulder

ze·nith [zē′nith] *n.* **1** The point in the sky directly overhead. **2** The highest or most important point; peak: at the *zenith* of his career.

zeph·yr [zef′ər] *n.* **1** The west wind. **2** Any soft, gentle wind. **3** A soft, lightweight yarn.

zep·pe·lin [zep′ə·lin] *n.* A large dirigible having a rigid, cigar-shaped body. ◆ The *zeppelin* was named after Count von Zeppelin, 1838–1917, who designed it.

ze·ro [zir′ō *or* zē′rō] *n., pl.* **ze·ros** or **ze·roes,** *adj.* **1** *n.* The numeral or symbol 0; cipher; naught. **2** *n.* The number which, when added to any other number, gives that other number as their sum. **3** *n.* Nothing. **4** *n.* The point on a scale, as of a thermometer, from which something is measured. **5** *n.* The lowest point: The bad news made my hopes hit *zero.* **6** *adj.* Of or at zero. ◆ *Zero* and *cipher* go back to the same Arabic word.

zest [zest] *n.* **1** A quality of excitement or enjoyment: A surprise gift added *zest* to my birthday party. **2** Keen enjoyment; great pleasure: to read with *zest.* — **zest′ful** *adj.*

Zeus [zōōs] *n.* In Greek myths, the supreme god, ruling all other gods. He was called Jupiter by the Romans.

zig·zag [zig′zag] *n., adj., adv., v.* **zig·zagged, zig·zag·ging 1** *n.* A series of short, sharp turns or angles. **2** *n.* Something having such angles or turns, as a path or pattern. **3** *adj.* Of or having short sharp turns or angles. **4** *adv.* In a zigzag manner. **5** *v.* To move in or form a zigzag.

zinc [zingk] *n., v.* **zincked** or **zinced, zinck· ing** or **zinc·ing 1** *n.* A bluish white, metallic chemical element, used in making alloys, for coating metals, in medicine, and as an electrode in electric batteries. **2** *v.* To coat or cover with zinc; galvanize.

add, āce, câre, pälm;   end, ēqual;   it, īce;   odd, ōpen, ôrder;   tŏŏk, pōōl;   up, bûrn;
ə = a in *above,* e in *sicken,* i in *possible,* o in *melon,* u in *circus;*   yōō = u in *fuse;*   oil;   pout;
check; ring; thin; this; zh in *vision.*   For ¶ reference, see page 64 · HOW TO

zin·ni·a [zin′ē·ə] *n.* Any of several North American plants having brightly colored, showy flowers with many petals like rays.

Zi·on [zī·ən] *n.* **1** A hill in Jerusalem, site of the royal palace of David and his successors and of the Temple. Also **Mount Zion. 2** The Jewish people. **3** Heaven.

Zi·on·ism [zī′ən·iz′əm] *n.* A movement for the reestablishment of a Jewish nation in Palestine. — **Zi′on·ist** *adj., n.*

zip [zip] *n., v.* **zipped, zip·ping 1** *n.* A sharp, hissing sound, as of a bullet passing through the air. **2** *v.* To travel with such a sound. **3** *n. informal* Energy; vitality; vim. **4** *v. informal* To move or act with energy and speed. **5** *v.* To fasten with a zipper. ◆ The word *zip* was formed in imitation of the kind of sound made by something moving very fast.

ZIP Code or **Zip Code** [zip] A numerical code made up by the U.S. Post Office to aid in the distribution of domestic mail. ◆ *Zip* code comes from Z(ONE) I(MPROVEMENT) P(LAN).

zip·per [zip′ər] *n.* A fastener having two rows of interlocking teeth that may be joined or separated by a sliding device.

zir·con [zûr′kon] *n.* A crystalline mineral, some clear varieties of which are used as jewels.

zith·er [zith′ər] *n.* A musical instrument having 30 to 40 strings stretched across a flat resonant board. It is played by plucking the strings.

Zither

Zn The symbol for the element ZINC.

zo·di·ac [zō′dē·ak] *n.* **1** An imaginary belt in the sky along which the sun appears to travel. It is divided into twelve sections, each of which is named after a different constellation. **2** A diagram or chart representing this belt and its signs, used in astrology.

zom·bi or **zom·bie** [zom′bē] *n., pl.* **zom·bis** or **zom·bies 1** The supernatural power believed by some West Indian natives to enter a dead body and make it move and act. **2** A dead body brought back to physical life in this way.

zone [zōn] *n., v.* **zoned, zon·ing 1** *n.* Any of the five divisions of the earth's surface, each bounded by parallels of latitude and named for the climate most frequently found in the division. **2** *n.* An area set apart from nearby areas for some special reason or purpose: a war *zone*; a no-parking *zone*. **3** *n.* Any of the areas around a particular mailing point, set up by the post office to determine parcel post rates for packages mailed from that particular point. **4** *n.* A section of a city set apart by law for a certain use: a residential *zone*; a business *zone*. **5** *n.* A section of a city to which a number is assigned to aid in the distribution of mail. **6** *v.* To divide into zones. **7** *n.* A belt or girdle: seldom used today. **8** *v.* To surround or encircle with a zone, belt, etc. ◆ *Zone* goes back to a Greek word meaning *belt* or *girdle*, which is what the word once meant in English.

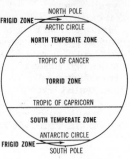

zoo [zoo] *n., pl.* **zoos** A park or garden in which wild animals are kept and shown to the public.

zo·o·log·i·cal [zō′ə·loj′i·kəl] *adj.* **1** Of or having to do with zoology. **2** Of or having to do with animals.

zoological garden Another name for ZOO.

zo·ol·o·gy [zō·ol′ə·jē] *n.* The science that has to do with animals, their classification, structure, development, etc. — **zo·ol′o·gist** *n.*

zoom [zoom] **1** *v.* To make a low-pitched but loud humming sound. **2** *v.* To move with such a sound. **3** *v.* To climb sharply in an airplane. **4** *v.* In TV and motion pictures, to move the camera rapidly toward or away from the subject pictured. **5** *n.* The act of zooming.

Zo·ro·as·ter [zō′rō·as′tər] *n.* Sixth- or seventh-century B.C. Persian religious leader, founder of Zoroastrianism.

Zo·ro·as·tri·an·ism [zō′rō·as′trē·ən·iz′əm] *n.* The religious system of the ancient Persians, founded by Zoroaster.

zounds [zoundz] *interj.* A mild oath used to express surprise or anger: seldom used today.

Zui·der Zee [zī′dər zē] A former shallow inlet of the North Sea in the NW Netherlands, now shut off by a dike.

Zu·lu [zoo′loo] *n., pl.* **Zu·lus** or **Zu·lu,** *adj.* **1** *n.* A member of a people in SE Africa. **2** *n.* The Bantu language of this people. **3** *adj.* Of or having to do with the Zulus or their language.

Zuy·der Zee [zī′dər zē] Another spelling of ZUIDER ZEE.

zwie·back [zwī′bak *or* zwē′bäk *or* swī′bäk] *n.* A kind of biscuit or bread baked in a loaf and later sliced and toasted in an oven.

zy·gote [zī′gōt] *n.* An egg cell after its fertilization by the male germ cell.